The Complete
Libertarian
Forum
1969–1984

Volume 1: 1969–1975

The Complete

Libertarian Forum

1969–1984

Volume 1: 1969–1975

Edited by Murray N. Rothbard

Ludwig von Mises Institute

AUBURN, ALABAMA

The Ludwig von Mises Institute dedicates these two volumes to all of its generous donors, and in particular wishes to thank these Patrons.

Steven R. Berger
Walter Block
John Hamilton Bolstad
John Brätland
Carl Creager
George and Joele Eddy
José M. Farré
Douglas E. French and Deanna Forbush
In honor of Ruby Campbell Hays
Mr. and Mrs. William Lowndes
Nelson and Mary Nash
Don Printz, M.D.
James M. Rodney
Ed and Pat Schoppe
Norman K. Singleton
Joan Thompson

The Mises Institute also thanks Walter Block for suggesting
and making possible the publication of *Libertarian Forum* on the web,
and Laurence Vance for the idea for this reprint, and his
gathering of the issues and scanning them for publication.

ISBN 13: 978-1-933550-02-2
ISBN 10: 1-933550-02-3

Contents

1969

1970

1971

1973

1975

A Semi-Monthly Newsletter

The Libertarian

Joseph R. Peden, Publisher   Washington Editor, Karl Hess   Murray N. Rothbard, Editor

PREVIEW ISSUE   MARCH 1, 1969   35¢

Why *The Libertarian?*

The libertarian movement is growing at a remarkable pace throughout the country. Yet the organizational forms, the means of communication, among libertarians are not only miniscule, but actually suffered a considerable blow during 1968. Last year saw the collapse of the Freedom School-Ramparts College of Palmer Lake, Colorado, with its attendant *Ramparts Journal*, Pine Tree Press, and Pine Tree Features. *New Individualist Review*, the theoretical quarterly published by graduate students at the University of Chicago, is all but defunct, and had been moribund for a long time. The need is acute for far more cohesion and inter-communication in the libertarian movement; in fact, it must become a movement and cease being merely an inchoate collection of diffuse and haphazard personal contacts.

The launching of *The Libertarian* , a twice-monthly newsletter, was announced at the first meeting of The Libertarian Forum, founded by Gerald Woloz and Joseph Peden in New York City for periodic dinners, lectures and discussions among libertarians. The fact that over sixty persons attended this initial dinner-meeting, some coming from as far away as Buffalo, Delaware, and South Carolina for the affair, demonstrates both the rapid growth of the movement and the widespread eagerness for increased activity and organization.

We believe that one of the greatest needs of the movement at this time is for a frequently appearing magazine that could act as a nucleus and communications center for libertarians across the country. We also believe that while many libertarians have thought long and hard about their ideal system, few of them have been able to rise above the merely sectarian exposition of the pure system to engage in a critique of the present state of affairs armed with the libertarian world-view. This kind of critique is not merely "negative", as many libertarian sectarians believe. For it is the kind of work that is indispensable if we are ever to achieve *victory* , if we are ever to get our ideal system off the drawing board and applied to the real world. In order to change the present system we must be able to analyze and explore it, and to see in the concrete how our libertarian view can be applied to such an analysis and to the prospects for social change.

One would think that such a need would be obvious. No movement that has been successful has ever been *without* organs carrying out this kind of analysis and critique. The key word here is "successful"; for a magazine like *The Libertarian* is desperately needed only if we wish to unite theory and action, if we wish not only to elaborate an ideal system but to see how the current system may be transformed into the ideal. In short, it is needed *only if* our aim is victory; those who conceive of liberty as only an intellectual parlor game, or as a method for generating investment tips, will, alas, find little here to interest them. But let us hope that *The Libertarian* will be able to play a part in inspiring a truly dedicated movement on behalf of liberty.

The Nixon Administration: Creeping Cornuellism

Changeovers in Administration are always a disheartening time for any thoughtful observer of the political scene. The volume of treacle and pap rises to the heavens, as the wit and wisdom and the high statesmanship of both the outgoing and incoming rascals are trumpeted across the land. But this year things are even worse than ever. First we had to suffer the apotheosis of Lyndon Baines Johnson, before last November the most universally reviled President of modern times; but *after* November, suddenly lovable and wise. And now Richard Nixon has had his sharp edges dissolved and his whole Person made diffuse and mellow; he too has become uniquely lovable to all. How much longer must we suffer this tripe? It is bad enough that we have to live under a despotic government; must we also have our intelligence systematically defiled? Already, Ted Lewis of the New York *Daily News*, a dedicated Nixonian, tells us gleefully that the new charm and grace and folksy friendliness of Dick and his

aides are so pronounced that maybe this time the Presidential "honeymoon" will last the full four years.

Amidst the cloud of goo surrounding the new Administration, it has been difficult for anyone to penetrate the fog and figure out what the new President is all about. Of the thousands of top jobs at the immediate disposal of the new Administration, only 90 have been filled. We have been getting inured to both parties and both sets of rulers having the same policies; but now it looks as if the very same *people* continue in power, regardless of who happens to be chosen by the public. How much clearer can it be that the much vaunted free elections in the United States are a sham and a fraud, designed to lull the public into believing that their votes really count? It had long become physically impossible for any of us to cast a vote *against* such ageless and lifetime oligarchs as J. Edgar Hoover; now the same

(Continued on page 2)

(Continued from page 1)

applies to almost everyone in government. In the few cases where the same people do not remain, there is a game of musical chairs with a few people shuffling in and out of the usual Establishment institutions: General Dynamics, Cal Tech, Litton Industries, the Chase Bank, etc. Certainly nothing startling can be expected on Vietnam, where Ellsworth Bunker remains as Ambassador, William Bundy, a longtime hawk, remains in the State Department post on Southeast Asia, and Henry Sabotage returns to head the negotiations in Paris.

Add to all this the fact that the Nixon Administration has been remarkably quiet and torpid--to the hosannahs of the press who proclaim that a return to Babbitt is just what the country needs--and one begins to wonder if there will be any change at all. To the *cognoscenti* , a little-heralded article in the *Washington Post* (Jan. 26) makes clear that a new note will indeed be added. It is a note that will mark the peculiar essence of the Nixon content and style; we might call it "Creeping Cornuellism".

The rise to fame and fortune of Richard C. Cornuelle is a peculiarly 20th-century variant of the Alger success story. Twenty years ago, Dick, a bright young libertarian, was a student of the eminent *laissez-faire* economist Ludwig von Mises at New York University; and with a few other libertarians of that era he soon saw that the consistent libertarian and *laissez-faire* position is really "right-wing anarchism".

As the years went on, Dick decided to abandon the world of scholarship for direct action, which he originally saw as bringing us closer to anarchism in practical, realistic terms. On reading De Tocqueville, he claims to have been the first person in over a century to realize that there exists, in addition to government and private business, a third set of institutions--non-profit organizations. Anyone who had ever heard of a church bazaar also realized this, but Dick brushed such considerations aside; he had found his gimmick, his *shtick*. He dubbed these non-profit institutions the "independent sector", and he was off to the races.

After several years of promoting such startlingly new activities as private welfare to the aged, and loans to college students, Dick found a disciple: T. George Harris, an editor of *Look*. Taking advantage of the Goldwater debacle, Harris published an article in *Look* at the year's end of 1964, hailing Dick Cornuelle as the New Messiah, of the Republican party and of the nation, and heralding as the new Gospel a book which Cornuelle was working on--with the substantial assistance of Harris himself. On the strength of the article, Dick's book was published by Random House, he became Executive Vice-President of the National Association of Manufacturers, and revered advisor to Nixon, Romney, *and* Reagan, thus pulling off one of the neatest tricks of the decade.

Cornuelle's stress was on the glory of private charitable institutions, and on the importance of businessmen contributing to more private welfare programs. In another worshipful article following up the *Look* piece, the *San Francisco Examiner* (March 28, 1965) asked Dick the $64 question: In essence, if the voluntary welfare sector is so great, where do *you* fit in? In short, what's your program? Here entered the virus of Cornuellism. For it seems that, as superb as it is, the "Independent Sector didn't keep pace while the rest of the country was developing." The Independent Sector, it seems, has "never learned to organize human activity efficiently." The *Examiner* adds: "To show the Independents how, Cornuelle thinks it may be necessary to add another department to the Federal government, of all things . . . It would be an agency that would find out what public problems are coming up and decide how to meet them effectively." Proclaiming enthusiastic support from all wings of the Republican Party, as well as--big surprise!--a "number

of liberal Democrats", Cornuelle wistfully admitted that the one exception to the Cornuelle bandwagon was Governor Rockefeller, *because* "He's committed to state action as opposed to Federal action." So much for right-wing anarchism!

There is no need to keep belaboring the Cornuelle Saga. After all we are not so much interested in the triumph of one man's career over "dogmatism" as we are in what this portends for the Nixon Administration. For here is what the Washington Post now reports: a "central theme" of the new Administration will be a nationwide drive to stimulate "voluntary action" against social ills. It adds that Secretary George Romney is "in charge of planning the voluntary action effort." This concept needs to be savored: government, the quintessence of coercion, is going to *plan* a nationwide "voluntary" effort. George Orwell, where art thou now? War is Peace, Freedom is Slavery, Voluntary Action is Government Planning.

The *Post* goes on to say that Romney, Secretary Finch, and the President "are devotees of the idea that vast and untapped energies of volunteers in an 'independent sector' can transform the Nation." Nixon endorsed the idea in 1965, and recently declared that "the President should be the chief patron of citizen efforts." And it turns out that last year, Secretary Finch was co-author of a book on the independent sector, with--you guessed it--Richard C. Cornuelle, the "godfather of independent action" and head of the Nixon task-force on independent voluntary action. Two major programs are emerging: a mixed public-private organization chartered by the Federal government to stimulate voluntary action drives, and a series of Presidental awards, like the World War II Navy "E" for Efficiency, to be bestowed by the President in person for outstanding voluntary efforts.

Oh right-wing anarchy, where art thou now? So now we are to have "voluntary" actors bedecked with honors by their Chief, the nation's top coercive actor; and we will have Dick's long-standing dream of a Federal agency to stimulate and coordinate these efforts. *The Libertarian*, for one, would not bet a substantial sum against the prospect of our old friend Dick being appointed to head the new bureau. Who, after all, is better qualified?

But we must not look at this sordid story as merely the saga of a former anarchist who coined a "new" political philosophy which might well result in his climbing to a high post in government. The situation is far more sinister than that. For this "voluntary" hogwash has a familiar smell: the smell of the Presidency of Herbert Hoover, whose political life-style was one of frenetically promoting "voluntary" programs, with the mailed fist of governmental coercion always resting inside the velvet glove. Hoover's pseudo-"voluntary" New Deal was the complete forerunner of Franklin Roosevelt's candidly coercive New Deal. It has another smell: the smell of Mussolini's fascism, in which coercive government multiplied its power by mobilizing the support of masses of misguided "volunteers" from among the citizenry. And finally, Nixon-Cornuellism has the smell of the burgeoning corporate state--the political economy of fascism--which has increasingly marked the American system. It is the "enlightened" corporate state where nothing is any longer distinctively "private" or "public"; everything is cozily mixed, in an ever-intensifying "partnership" of Big Government and Big Business (with Big Unionism as the happy junior partner). This is the sort of polity and economy that we have in the United States, and Creeping Cornuellism embodies still more of it.

Not only more of it; for Nixon-Cornuellism is, to the libertarian, a peculiarly repulsive variant of American corporatism. For it cloaks and camouflages the viper of statism in the soothing raiment of voluntaristic and pseudolibertarian rhetoric. What political style can be more disgusting than that?

State Of Palestine Launched

During February, the state of Palestine is being launched at Cairo. For the first time in many centuries, Palestine is being proclaimed as an independent nation, free, at least in aspiration, from foreign imperial domination. The delegates are a mixed team of guerrilla fighters from Al Fatah, the largest of the Palestinian guerrilla organizations, as well as members of the Popular Liberation Front.

A highly significant preliminary meeting took place in January in Cairo, at a conference called by the Communist Party, and shepherded by delegates from the Soviet Union. The Communist line has been to force the Arabs to accept the Soviet peace plan and the UN resolution of November, 1967, which is to guarantee the borders of Israel once it surrenders its gains acquired during the Israel-Arab war of 1967: In short, to ratify all the previous aggressive gains of Israel if she withdraws from her latest conquests. Despite the fact that the conference was loaded in favor of the Communist line, the conference was swung from Communist control in favor of a militant position by the leadership and the oratory of Dr. Nabeel Shaath, 30-year-old American-educated professor, formerly teaching at the University of Pennsylvania and now head of the proposed Palestinian state residing in unoccupied Jordan.

Dr. Shaath, a Christian like most of the Palestinian delegation to the conference, declared that "We will not accept any substitute for a war of national liberation. We will not accept any settlement that denies our rights, be it the Security Council or any other proposal or political settlement." Shaath proclaimed the goal of the Palestinians to be the return of the forcibly exiled Arab refugees to their homes and properties in Palestine, and declared: "We are fighting today to create the new Palestine of tomorrow, a progressive and democratic nonsectarian Palestine in which Christian, Moslem and Jew worship, live peacefully and enjoy equal rights."

Previous to this meeting, Al Fatah affirmed its emphasis on the independence of its "armed Palestine revolution" from all governments everywhere, obviously implying the reactionary machinations of the Arab governments of the Middle East as well as of the long-standing cynical maneuvers and manipulations by the Soviet Union.

"Private" Enterprise At Work

The way "private" enterprise works in our era of the neo-fascist corporate state is well shown in an article in the *Wall St. Journal* (Feb. 5) on the National Corporation for Housing Partnerships. The NCHP, created by President Johnson, but supposedly run along the Nixonian lines of revving up the "engine of private enterprise", wants to raise $50 million from private industry to invest in low-rent housing projects which would eventually mount up to $2 billion of capital.

Praiseworthy? But wait. In order for the corporation to get started, there must be a substantial flow of Federal funds to subsidize rentals in the new projects. The NCHP wants $150 million from the Federal government for this year and next before it sets up business as a corporation. With this huge subsidy, "private enterprise" in the form of the NCHP would be willing to build 10,000 low-rent units in the first year, and hopefully move up to 60,000 units annually.

A particularly desired form of federal subsidy would be to pay a subsidy that would keep mortgage interest costs down

> "Whenever the ends of government are perverted, and public liberty manifestly endangered, and all other means of redress are ineffectual, the people may, and of a right ought to reform the old, or establish a new government; the doctrine of non-resistance against arbitrary power and oppression is absurd, slavish and destructive of the good and happiness of mankind."
>
> ---Declaration of Rights of Maryland, 1867

to a near-zero sum of 1% per year. With this kind of subsidy, a whole roster of the nation's largest corporations stand eager to do their great humanitarian work. This includes Kaiser Industries Corp, whose head, Edgar Kaiser, is the president of the NCHP, Westinghouse, Metropolitan Life, Deere and Co., and Ling-Temco-Vought. Many of the biggest banks, such as Chase Manhattan, First National City, Bank of America, Mellon National, would be willing to lend the corporation money to launch its operations. Also, not surprisingly, a host of local realty firms would be happy to join in the bonanza.

The big attraction, apart from humanitarianism, is a huge, guaranteed profit, or, as the *Journal* puts it, "a guaranteed, Government-supported market to attract profit-motivated private industry and investors." The estimated annual rate of profit for these investors would begin at over 24% and end at 17%. Pretty good returns for "helping the poor"!

A People's Court?

In the January 1969 issue of *The Center Magazine* Gerald Gottlieb, a consultant to the Center For Democratic Institutions in Santa Barbara, Calif., has made a proposal of great interest to libertarians. Reviewing the failure of the World Court and other international judicial bodies to preserve the peace and ensure justice to individuals, he proposes the creation by private citizens of a universal court of man "independent of nations and able to render judgment upon those who misuse sovereign power". Its jurisdiction: crimes against human rights and peace; its legitimacy: arising from the sovereign rights of the people retained by them and not granted to governments. How would such a body enforce its jurisdiction and decisions against sovereign states? By arousing world public opinion through any and all media, through appeals from professional and business associations, churches, social institutions, etc. Recalcitrant States would be faced with boycott and public degradation by an aroused world public. While Gottlieb eventually would depend upon the coercive influence of other states, this is not crucial to his argument. The recent success of the Bertrand Russell War Crimes Tribunal in arousing European sentiment against American actions in Vietnam, and the propaganda success of the American Commission of Inquiry on Conditions in Ireland in 1920-22 in forcing the British government to moderate its policy in the Irish rebellion, suggests that privately-constituted international courts may serve to mitigate the criminality of sovereign states, or at least focus world attention on their grosser violations of human liberties.

Perhaps libertarian foundations and scholars could sponsor further study of this proposal--so libertarian in principle and so feasible in practice.

                                                                                          J.R.P.

Sitting On Sidewalk Outlawed

The city of San Francisco has adopted a law giving the police the right to arrest anyone found sitting, lying, or sleeping on the sidewalk. The criminal sitter is subject to punishment of six months in jail and a $500 fine. The law, passed to the great glee of the citizens of the town, is commonly known as the "anti-hippie" law, and everyone is looking forward with enthusiasm to cracking down on hippies who are notorious users of the streets.

While we hold no particular brief for hippies, we must note one more step on the road to a totalitarian America. So now we can't sit on the street! The police are assuring everyone that the law will be used reasonably, and only against large groups of sitters who obstruct the sidewalks. But liberty requires not that despotic laws be passed and then only moderately enforced, but that the law not be passed at all.

This new incident points up a vital problem in political philosophy: who gets to own and therefore to control the streets. For so long as the urban governments are allowed to continue to own the streets, we are at any time liable to be oppressed by all sorts of regulations and controls made over those of us who use the streets--which means everyone. Thus, during the riots of the summer of 1967, all the cities decreed compulsory curfews for everyone, thus making criminals out of anyone having the effrontery to walk out of his home after, say, 10:00 P. M. How much more despotism over our daily lives is needed before we question whether we are, indeed, a free country?

The only ultimate solution to this problem is to abolish all government ownership and control of the streets, and to turn the nation's streets over to private ownership, which might assume all sorts of individual, cooperative, or corporate forms. But until that golden day, we must at least see to it that government exercise its ownership powers as little as possible. We must proclaim that the streets belong not to the government, but to the people, for the people to use as they see fit. Community no-ownership is far better than government ownership; for a little obstruction of the streets is better than frozen tyranny.

In the meanwhile, the citizens of San Francisco can count their small blessings, for their streets were saved from a graver fate. One of the eager beavers on the board of supervisors urged a law prohibiting anyone from "standing aimlessly" on the pavement. The law failed to pass, not of course because the supervisors were taken with a sudden fit of concern for the liberty of the individual who might, sometime, wish to stroll or even stand, rather than stride purposefully down the street. No, as so often in the past, vested self-interest came to the unwitting rescue of liberty. For the anti-sitting law was passed under pressure of the local merchants, and the merchants became uneasy at the thought of throngs of aimlessly strolling tourists, with money in their pockets, getting hauled off unceremoniously in the paddy wagon. Like politics, liberty sometimes makes strange bedfellows.

RECOMMENDED READING

Irving Louis Horowitz, "Young Radicals and Professorial Critics", Commonweal (January 31, 1969). A thoughtful defense of young student radicals and a critique of their conservative Social Democratic opposition among the faculty.

Paul M. Sweezy, "Thoughts on the American System", Monthly Review (February, 1969). Keen insight into the nature of the American system by one of America's most intelligent Marxists. Sweezy sees the Nixon appointments as demonstrating an interchangeable ruling class shuttling back and forth between industry and government, and he also examines the differences and "contradictions" between national and local ruling elites. He is also refreshing on the Left for not dismissing the Vietnam War as already ended.

TWO NEW LIBERTARIAN PERIODICALS!

Factotum Bulletin, a bulletin for news of the libertarian movement. Can be obtained from the Center for Libertarian Studies, 1507 W. Hildebrand, San Antonio, Texas 78201. Irregularly published, as supplement to the Center's Libertarian American.

The Libertarian Connection: a unique bi-monthly. For the subscription price of $2.50, every subscriber has the right to send in stencils which the editors guarantee to mimeograph and staple. It is truly the readers' magazine. Available at 5610 Smiley, Los Angeles, Calif. 90016.

Also—Regular Washington Column By Karl Hess

The Libertarian
BOX 341 —Dept B
MADISON SQUARE STATION
NEW YORK, NEW YORK 10010

A Semi-Monthly Newsletter

The Libertarian

Joseph R. Peden, Publisher   Washington Editor, Karl Hess   Murray N. Rothbard, Editor

VOL. I, NO. I   APRIL 1, 1969   35¢

The Scientific Imperial Counsellor: "To Restore Faith In Government"

America now has, whether we know it or not, an imperial Counsellor. He is a new kind of appointee of the Nixon Administration, a White House aide but with Cabinet rank, empowered to range all over the sphere of domestic policy. The astute *Business Week* calls him "The adviser who may be closest to Nixon": Dr. Arthur F. Burns. (*Business Week*, March 1).

Arthur Burns, a professor of economics at Columbia University, was the first Chairman of the Council of Economic Advisers of the Eisenhower Administration. In that Administration Burns took his stand against the old-fashioned conservatives who wanted to roll back some of the New Deal aggrandizement of the federal apparatus. Though he had his technical quarrels with the Keynesians, Arthur Burns was instrumental in saving the day for the permanent Keynesian policy of expanding during recessions and cutting back during booms, and in saving the very existence of the Keynesian-interventionist Council of Economic Advisers itself. Now that old-fashioned conservatives have disappeared from the Republican party, no one talks in terms of abolishing the CEA or its mandate toward perpetual statism.

One of the curious aspects of Arthur Burns's rise to the pinnacle of power is that, among all economists, he was preeminent as the supposedly value-free "scientist", the technician, the man who eschews politics and ideology. And yet here he is, at the peak of his career, in the most political, the most ideological job of them all. But, oddly, Burns himself does not acknowledge this fact. He *still* thinks of himself as a simple scientific technician, at the service of society; he now says of his own role: "I'm not interested in power and influence, I'm interested in doing a job."

Thus, Burns has become almost the caricature of modern American social science: a group of disciplines swarming with supposedly value-free technicians, self-proclaimed non-ideological workmen simply "doing a job" in service to their masters of the State apparatus: that is, to their military-political-industrial overlords. For their "scientific" and "value-free" outlook turns out to be simply marginal wheeling and maneuvering within the broad frames of reference set by the American *status quo* and by their masters who enforce that *status quo*. Lack of ideology simply means lack of any ideology that *differs* at all fundamentally from the ruling system.

But it seems that these are days of crisis, and in times like these, even the most narrow of statistical craftsmen must become "philosophers", i. e., must give the show away. So Arthur Frank Burns. Burns himself allows to *Business Week* that economic problems nowadays are "trivial", in comparison to the larger domestic concerns over which he now assumes his suzerainty. For, Burns opines, the really important problem is that "a great many of our citizens have lost faith in our basic institutions . . . They have lost faith in the processes of the government itself." "The President keeps scratching his head," Burns goes on, "and I as his adviser keep scratching my head--trying to know how to build new institutions . . . to restore faith in government."

So *that* is what our new imperial Counsellor is up to. The aggressively "scientific" statistician has become our purported faith-healer, our evangelical Witch Doctor, who has come to restore our faith in that monster Idol; the State. Let us hereby resolve, everyone, one and all, that Arthur is not going to get away with it.

But soft, we must guard our flank, for there is a host of so-called "libertarians" and free-market advocates who swear up and down that Arthur Burns is God's gift to a free-market economy. Which says a great deal about the quality of *their* devotion to liberty, as compared to their evident devotion to Power.

Letter From Washington

By Karl Hess

FBI And CIA

Washington power struggles are off and squirming. We note that H. E. W. and Agriculture are vying for control of the programs with which to feed, and also co-opt, the hottest current item among political constituencies, hungry Americans. We hear that the Army, sensing a danger that the endless ground war in Vietnam might not be endless after all and certainly can't be victorious anyway, is looking for new frontiers on which to place its guidons and that chemical-bacteriological warfare may be just the ticket. (A ticket which, incidentally, may also gain it a better seat than ever at the game of riot control.) All the other services, of course, want their own bug battalions.

We sense, also, that the jet setters of the aero-space conglomerates are pitted in some sort of dinosaurian battle against the graying herd-elders of the industrial establishment for control of not only the available soul of the Administration itself but for the control of the more wordly goodies to be found in taking over government programs (at cost-plus) as we move from the vilified practice of a welfare state run from the White House to the now panegyrized practice of a welfare state, run for fun and profit, from corporate board rooms with the White House just signing the checks and setting the goals. There is little change in who pays the bills, of course.

Libertarians have every reason to view all of these matters with knowledgeable horror. They could predict any enormity of the state simply because they know that enormities are the nature of the state, enormities and crimes against liberty.

There is one area of struggle in Washington, however, that may be viewed with special horror. It is the struggle between the CIA and the FBI for covert control of the government, the world, the galaxy or whatever else comes along.

Talk of the rivalry between these two agencies, or baronies, is a Washington commonplace. Most comments on the struggle, however, reflect mainly from the exotic persons and bureaucratic principalities involved, with endless speculation, for instance, upon whether there were more FBI or CIA informers and paid provocateurs involved in our recent spate of political assassinations. Actually these arguments are rather like parsing scaldic verse, almost entirely academic, in that they concentrate on bureaucratic commas and semi-colons without attending much at all to content.

The content of the struggle mainly involves the weapons with which it is being fought, and the styles of the wielders of the weapons. There is no basic difference beyond that inasmuch as both factions are merely symptoms of an inevitable sickness of the State itself.

The CIA has far and away the greater edge in economic power and in freedom of violent movement. Assassination has been its business overseas all along. There are obvious restraints on its use at home. There also are obvious opportunities for its selective and discreet employment; particularly against the more obscure obstructionists in any situation, persons who mightn't be widely missed but who might be the crucial difference between one policy or another in its early, intimate stages. The political murder of private citizens has never really caught on here but that is not to say that an imaginative man might not have a go at it anyway--particularly with the vast conspiratorial depths of the CIA upon which to draw.

When it comes to money the CIA has no equal. Although the FBI does have some special and very confidential funds to spend on informers and other covert employees, and even though some cynics might suspect that it could even keep for its own uses some of the vast criminal funds which it regularly, and pridefully, "recovers" when busting bandits, the Bureau has got to come in second. The Agency is not audited at all. There is a Congressional group that is supposed to supervise it but no one really imagines that they can do anything like a thorough job. For one thing, the personnel of the CIA is carried on the payrolls of other agencies and its continual involvement with "national security" means that official secrecy cloaks its daggers and its doings quite effectively.

It is from the CIA's money-power that much of its realpolitik powers derive. Its subsidy of everything from publishing houses to labor organizations is now well known. No newsman to whom I have recently spoken doubts for a moment that this subsidized estate within a subsidized state is not still thriving. Even if the excuse for the subsidy is, as it always is claimed, exclusively for activities of the person or group outside of the country, these CIA subsidies provide a selective means of encouraging persons or groups who, despite international activities, almost invariably must have some domestic clout as well. This clout, do not misunderstand, is not used on direct behalf of the CIA. But it can be used on behalf of those policies of which the CIA approves and which *ultimately* will enhance its power.

Where the CIA uses dough, the FBI uses data. Its chief influence, as opposed to outright pressure, derives from the selective use of its files. It is not imaginable, for instance, that even a President could get an item from the FBI's files if the Director specifically did not want him to have it. After all, it is employees of the Director, not of the President, who tend those files and everyone knows how easy it is for a piece of paper to either appear or disappear in a bureaucracy.

Thus, from President to legislator to syndicated columnist, the FBI can offer data not as something that may be demanded but as a boon which may be conferred--upon the helpful. President Johnson's notorious use of FBI data to persecute political foes is another Washington press corps conversational commonplace as is the mock dismay at the fact that J. Edgar Hoover should have found in or made of Lyndon Johnson one of his most eloquent supporters despite the fact that, at the outset of The Great Society, it was assumed that the President and the Director followed somewhat different muses.

Thus, in this modern Machiavellian melodrama, we see directly pitted against one another the old-fashioned money and muscle. Florentine intrigue, cloak-and-daggerism of the CIA and the more American, corporate-organizational, file-case, computer-card snoop-and-snitchism of the FBI.

Libertarians, for what small comfort it may bring to a group which probably occupies a special place in files of both the Agency and the Bureau, happen to have the only sure solution to the disease of secret-policism which is what both CIA and FBI represent in a germicidal sense: cure the disease by curing the cause, the State. Every State, sooner or later, has had an urge to defend itself against foes real or imagined, foreign or domestic. This has always resulted in some form of secret or political police

organization. There are no exceptions to this iron law of the dungeon.

So long as nation states exist, so long will political police prowl amongst us.

All of which brings us to the remarkable story, recently revealed in the press, of how, according to Nikita Krushchev, the top cop of the Soviet Union, Lavrenti Beria, was done in.

Director Beria, it is now said, made the mistake of entering a Kremlin meeting without his bodyguard whereupon Krushchev, a genuine genius at getting to the nitty gritty of any situation, shot him.

It is predictable that conservatives, particularly, are still clucking and tushing about this latest revelation of the brutality of politics in a totalitarian state. It could not happen, they may exult, in a safe and civilized land such as ours.

And that is precisely the point.

In democratic America there has appeared no way to relieve the head of the political or secret police of his command. In short, what this great Republic lacks in vivid personnel relations, it more than makes up for in tenure.

"Dear Ted": Prelude To Repression?

There is nothing quite so ominous as the emergence of Richard Milhous Nixon as educational theorist. In his tenure in office so far, Mr. Nixon has been the Man Who Isn't There, a zero wrapped in a vacuum. *Except* in the case of our kids; there the President has made a stand, in his "Dear Ted" letter to Father Theodore M. Hesburgh, president of Notre Dame University, and a man who has rivalled the clownish S. I. Hayakawa in vowing to get tough with our students.

So eager was the President to get his views known on this subject that he released the letter to the press (New York *Times*, Feb. 24) even before Ted had received it. As might be expected, our new educational philosopher came out foursquare against "violence", "intimidation", and "threats", and called for the "rule of reason" to prevail. "Whoever rejects that principle," intoned Nixon, "forfeits his right to be a member of the academic community."

Mr. and Mrs. America, how long are we going to suffer this solemn farce? Here is the President of the United States, in command of the mightiest engine of terror and intimidation the world has ever known, a man who every day murders American soldiers and Vietnamese peasants in the hills and rice paddies of Vietnam, a man whose entire machinery of State lives off systematic theft, a man who heads the machinery of slavery known as the draft. And he has the gall to express his horror at the violence of some kids who have broken a few windows, or who

have stepped on some campus grass. He has the sheer bravado to call for the substitution of reason for force! In this he shows himself an apt pupil of his beloved predecessor, who had the brass to say, during the July, 1967 urban riots: "We will not endure violence. It matters not by whom it is done, or under what slogan or banner. It will not be tolerated." Someone should instruct these worthies about the mote and the beam.

But apart from the farcical elements of the situation, Nixon's entry into educational theory poses an ominous question: Is this the prelude to general repression on our campuses? For Nixon, in the Dear Ted letter, openly hinted about possible action "at the state and Federal levels" to crack down on the college campuses. This was supposed to be the prelude to a call for Federal investigation of the campuses at the National Governors' Conference a few days later. Despite the dubious constitutionality of this proposal, Governor Reagan ardently pushed for the idea, but happily the governors turned it down. Perhaps this has stopped any political groundswell for a Federal crackdown on the campuses; at any rate, the governors have at least given a setback to the Reagan theory of education by bayonet. Let us hope the setback isn't just temporary.

_____

LIBERTARIAN ASSOCIATES

The following people were generous, and even heroic enough to subscribe to The Libertarian as Libertarian Associates, paying $15 or more:

Mr. James Altes   New York, N.Y.
Mr. and Mrs. Walter Block   New York, N.Y.
Mr. J. M. Foley   Burlingame, California
Mr. Walter Grinder   Bogota, New Jersey
Dr. Harold H. Saxton   Mayville, N.Y.
Mr. and Mrs. Harry Stern   Wilmington, Del.

> "There are but three ways for the populace to escape its wretched lot. The first two are by the routes of the wineshop or the church; the third is by that of the social revolution."
> — Mikhail Bakunin, 1871

RECOMMENDED READING

Donald Barnett, "Angola: Report from Hanoi II". *Ramparts* (April, 1969). Happy Day! *Ramparts* lives! The reports of its death were greatly exaggerated. In this article, the anthropologist Dr. Barnett presents an exciting and heartwarming story of his stay with the guerrilla forces of the national liberation movement in Portuguese-run Angola. One thing is made clear: what with the Portuguese government taxing all the peasants' surplus above subsistence and burning peasant villages and herding them into concentration hamlets, and the guerrillas scrupulously buying everything they use from the peasants, *whom* do you think the overwhelming mass of peasants supports?

P. T. Bauer and B. S. Yamey, *Markets, Market Control and Marketing Reform* (London: Weidenfeld and Nicolson, 1968). 421 pp. 90s. Not really about marketing, but a collection of articles about the free market and government interference, particularly in underdeveloped countries. Professor Bauer is the world's preeminent economist specializing in underdeveloped countries.

Daniel and Gabriel Cohn-Bendit, *Obsolete Communism: The Left-Wing Alternative* (New York: McGraw-Hill). 256 pp. $5.95. The story of the almost-victorious French revolution of May, 1968 by its heroic young anarchist leader. The case for an anarchist rather than a Bolshevik revolution.

John Duffett, ed., *Against the Crime of Silence* (New York: Bertrand Russell Peace Foundation, 1968. Available from O'Hare Books, Flanders, N.J. 07836). 662 pp. $8.50 hardbound, $5.75 Flexicloth. The War Crimes Tribunal, sponsored by Bertrand Russell, held its sessions on genocidal American aggression and atrocities in Vietnam at Stockholm and at Copenhagen during 1967. The Tribunal was outrageously smeared in the American press. Here is the detailed record of its hearings and reports. Indispensable for any serious student of the Vietnam War.

Karl Hess, "The Death of Politics", *Playboy* (March, 1969). This article marks the appearance of a shining new star in the libertarian firmament. An excellent article, and the first time that the libertarian position has hit the mass market. Lingering traces of statism are due to the fact that the article was written while Mr. Hess was in a period of transition toward the full and complete libertarian credo.

————, *The Lawless State*. (Lansing, Mich.: Constitutional Alliance, Feb. 5, 1969. Available from Constitutional Alliance, P.O. Box 836, Lansing, Mich. 48904). 30pp. 40¢. Rousing libertarian attack on the State. One of the first of a series of handy and inexpensive "minibooks" from this publisher.

David Horowitz with David Kolodney, "The Foundations", *Ramparts* (April, 1969). David Horowitz is becoming the best and most intelligent of a new and much-needed breed: muckrakers of the present State Monopoly system. Here he exposes the work of the big foundations, their tie-ins with the government, corporations, universities, and the black movement. First of two parts.

James Ridgeway, *The Closed Corporation: American Universities in Crisis* (New York: Ballantine Books, 1968). Paper. 241 pp. 95¢. Excellent muckraking book on the universities and their tie-in with the military and governmental-industrial complex. Should silence those naive souls who still think of our universities as private institutions and dedicated communities of scholars.

Madeleine B. Stern, *The Pantarch: A Biography of Stephen Pearl Andrews* (Austin, Tex.: University of Texas Press, 1968). 208 pp. $6.00. A scholarly, though often sneering, biography of a brilliant if eccentric founder of American individualist anarchism.

The Libertarian
BOX 341
MADISON SQUARE STATION
NEW YORK, NEW YORK 10010

PUBLISHED ON THE FIRST AND FIFTEENTH OF EVERY MONTH   SUBSCRIPTION RATE. $7.00 PER YEAR

A Semi-Monthly Newsletter

The Libertarian

| Joseph R. Peden, Publisher | Washington Editor, Karl Hess | Murray N. Rothbard, Editor |

VOL. I, NO. II   APRIL 15, 1969   35¢

Tax Day

April 15, that dread Income Tax day, is around again, and gives us a chance to ruminate on the nature of taxes and of the government itself.

The first great lesson to learn about taxation is that taxation is simply robbery. No more and no less. For what is "robbery"? Robbery is the taking of a man's property by the use of violence or the threat thereof, and therefore without the victim's consent. And yet what else is taxation?

Those who claim that taxation is, in some mystical sense, really "voluntary" should then have no qualms about getting rid of that vital feature of the law which says that failure to pay one's taxes is criminal and subject to appropriate penalty. But does anyone seriously believe that if the payment of taxation were *really* made voluntary, say in the sense of contributing to the American Cancer Society, that any appreciable revenue would find itself into the coffers of government? Then why don't we try it as an experi-ment for a few years, or a few decades, and find out?

But if taxation is robbery, then it follows as the night the day that those people who engage in, and live off, robbery are a gang of thieves. Hence the government is a group of thieves, and deserves, morally, aesthetically, and philosophically, to be treated exactly as a group of less socially respectable ruffians would be treated.

This issue of *The Libertarian* is dedicated to that growing legion of Americans who are engaging in various forms of that one weapon, that one act of the public which our rulers fear the most: tax rebellion, the cutting off the funds by which the host public is sapped to maintain the parasitic ruling classes. Here is a burning issue which could appeal to everyone, young and old, poor and wealthy, "working class" and middle class, regardless of race, color, or creed. Here is an issue which everyone understands, only too well. Taxation.

TAX REVOLT IN WISCONSIN

On Tuesday, April 1, the most significant American election since last November occurred in northern Wisconsin. Mel Laird had been elevated from his long-time post as Congressman from this district to his present berth as mighty, hawkish Secretary of Defense. A special election was held on April 1 to fill the Congressional spot.

The Republicans had won this post with great ease for decades, usually amassing about two-thirds of the vote. This year, State Senator Walter Chilsen, Laird's hand-picked successor, was seemingly safe, and he made his safety even more secure by wrapping himself in the mantle of the Nixon-Laird Administration, and making the election a referendum of the supposedly popular new regime.

Yet, this April, young David Obey, the Democratic choice, defeated Chilsen handily in a stunning upset; the vote was approximately 63,000 to 59,000. Everyone is agreed on the major reason for the upset: the great issue which Obey hammered at again and again--high and crushing taxation. Wisconsin's Republican Governor Warren Knowles had run for re-election on a platform of pride on not raising taxes; true to political form, as soon as he was safely back in, his political greed came to the fore, and the Republicans of Wisconsin swung behind a program of higher taxes. The outraged public rallied around Obey's attacks on high taxes, and taxes proved to be a hotter and more important public issue than the Nixon Administration, the Party of Our Fathers, and even love for Mel Laird. An explosion over taxes is at hand, if leaders should arise to articulate the people's deepest wishes.

> "To force a man to pay for the violation of his own liberty is indeed an addition of insult to injury. But that is exactly what the State is doing."
> ---Benjamin R. Tucker, 1893

Letter From Washington

By Karl Hess

TAX REVOLT

For those who retain a residual, if not romantic attachment to the notion of peaceful change there is at least one Springlike sign of encouragement along the Potomac. A substantial tax rebellion is underway.

Far and away the largest share of mail to Capitol Hill as well as to the White House concerns taxes-- not comments on them, but angry statements of refusals to pay either some or all of the State's lootish tribute. The same thing is happening at local levels in the 50 states where, as a matter of fact, taxation has been growing overall at a more rapid pace than even at the Federal level. Farmers in Pennsylvania, householders in Brooklyn, housewives in the southwest, all have mounted direct assaults against organized theft by the State. At the local level the success of tax rebellions is astonishing. Any group that can gather a hundred or so members seems assured of, at least, protection against flagrant suppression and has, obviously, a good chance of success. The picture is neither so clear nor so rosy at the Federal level. The number of resistors is surely growing but, because there is no organized or united force in the field, the Federals have open to them such means of suppression as the selective persecution of 'leaders' to set Spockian examples. Attorney General Mitchell's selection of just that device to deal with campus disorders could be a hint of direction but should it fail to suppress the campuses--as hopefully seems to be the case--then it may not be tried against tax resistors.

Another approach could be in the broadest social pressure, with impassioned campaigns to vilify those who resist, as near or actual traitors, and to extol for the "quiet majority" the patriotic, humble, and holy virtues of submitting to taxation without so much as a whimper and certainly not a groan. The Stakhanovites of the Nixon Administration, we may anticipate, will be quiet and eager taxpayers (let's hear it for Quiet Quentin, he didn't even claim a deduction for *himself*!) and their children, equally docile on the campus.

The tax rebellion, also, has evolutionary stages. It will pass from rebellion into revolution at approximately the moment it coalesces, either around a conscious organizing effort or spontaneously around a particular incident.

In either case there seems little that the State could do about it--as a broadly based movement rather than one in which individuals may, as at present, be picked off and/or terrorized without support or succor.

At any rate it is the nightmare of the State today.

*   *   *

Washington, a far cry from most cities, is provided with three competing daily newspapers, not to mention several in the nearby suburbs of Maryland and Virginia. Freedom of the press, you might think, would be enhanced by this fortuitous situation. The truth is drearily different.

Washington also has an 'underground' newspaper, the Free Press. It is, as are so many of the type, a generally lighthearted mixture of psychedelic coming and ahhing and radical politics. It has perhaps as great as, but surely no greater, a range of explicitly sexual or scatalogical slang as any current best-seller.

The Free Press is regularly harassed by the police. It now must print hundreds of miles away. Persons selling it have been arrested for the possession of pornography while, in full admission of the essentially *political* nature of the paper, a judicial refugee from the Flintstones in nearby Maryland has arranged to have some of the editors charged with, believe it or not, sedition against the Free State. (Yea, Free.)

Meantime, how have the watchdogs of liberty responded? The 'open Administration' of Richard Nixon apparently couldn't care less if the paper were closed down. The journalism clubs, associations, and guilds are as silent as the grave. The Washington Post says the fuzz might as well leave the Freep alone because it isn't influential anyway, thus reducing freedom of the press to a solely utilitarian level and adding a new sub-basement to the structure of The Post's morality. But the Freep, bless it, still appears.

*   *   *

Daily there is new evidence that probing and defending the military-industrial complex is to become a major matter in Congress this session--perhaps *the* hottest issue of all if the war can be cooled down or, as at present, virtually ignored. In the continuing drama of disputes without difference, opponents of the welfare state now will rise mightily to man the battlements of the warfare state--and, of course, vice versa. As as American President once remarked, in another regard, one hopes neither side runs out of ammunition.

> "The schoolboy whips his taxed top, the beardless youth manages his taxed horse with a taxed bridle, on a taxed road; and the dying Englishmen, pouring his medicine, which has paid seven per cent, flings himself back on his chintz bed, which has paid twenty-two per cent, and expires in the arms of an apothecary who has paid a license of a hundred pounds for the privilege of putting him to death."
> ---Sydney Smith, 1830

LIBERTARIAN ASSOCIATES

The deepest thanks of The Libertarian go to the newest group of those generous enough to become Libertarian Associates by subscribing at $15 or more:

Mr. R. Dale Grinder   Columbia, Mo.
Mr. Milton M. Shapiro   Claremont, Calif.
Mr. James Evans, Jr.   Los Angeles, Calif.
A. R. Pruitt, M.D.   Halstead. Kan.

TRANSFORMATION OF A NEWSPAPER

Since the early nineteen-fifties, the *National Guardian* was considered by many to be a firebrand radical newspaper on the furthermost fringes of the left. It had been so branded for its heroic stand against the onslaught of McCarthyism. In many ways it is true that the *National Guardian* was the spokesman for "far-left" opinion. But it is equally true that beyond its outspoken anti-McCarthyism, the *National Guardian* surely was not a radical newspaper.

In a subheading under the *National Guardian's* banner was the accompanying motto which expressed both the content and the purpose of its existence. It read: "An Independent Progressive Newsweekly." Reformism, *not* radicalism, was indeed its intent and its history, ever since its origins in the reformist Wallace campaign of 1948.

A couple of years ago, after the New Left had begun to stir, the management and direction of the *National Guardian* began to change. As 1967 became 1968, the "*coup*" was all but complete. What remained was to alert the public to the newspaper's new intentions. In February 1968, the statist-patriotic term *National* was dropped from the paper's masthead; and, more importantly, the accompanying motto was changed to read: "Independent Radical Newsweekly."

Although it was from the beginning true to its announced intentions of being a genuinely radical newspaper, i. e., attacking the United States monopoly capitalist-imperialist system rather than simply trying to reform a depraved system that was beyond repair, the new *Guardian* did have its share of problems. It was indeed radical, but it could no longer truly be called a newspaper.

The new management and staff were inexperienced. The call to radicalism stepped on the ideological toes of many of the *National Guardian's* former readers. Subscriptions expired, unrenewed. Impassioned letters of disbelief and abhorrence stormed in with cries of anti-Semitism because of the new leadership's stand on Black Power and the Arab-Israeli conflict in the Middle East.

Confronted with the major task of rebuilding a large part of its circulation and saddled with an inexperienced, underpaid (often unpaid), and sometimes incompetent staff, the *Guardian* hobbled along, leaving much to be desired in the area of reportorial journalism.

Most of the pages of the *Guardian* were given to editorializing. Series after series of eight and ten-part "think pieces" filled its pages for six or seven months. The only really redeeming feature of the Guardian during this period was the weekly report of Wilfred Burchett from Cambodia on the Vietnam War. Burchett's articles were always poignant, perceptive and uncannily correct in their predictions of unfolding events in southeast Asia.

During the last two months, and particularly in the last several issues, a happy change has been taking place. The pages of the *Guardian* have been filled with what a newspaper should contain--news. Gone are the misplaced and often incompetent "think pieces". Editorials are at a minimum. The news stories are most often relevant, and many of them are well-written. The *Guardian* seems on its way to becoming a first-rate newspaper.

> "Of all debts, men are least willing to pay taxes. What a satire is this on government!"
> ---Ralph Waldo Emerson, 1841

There appears to be a battle going on under the surface for ideological control of the *Guardian* between the New Left anarchists and ddcentralized socialists and some remaining remnants of Old Left Marxism, but it seems certain that it is a battle which the Old Left is doomed to lose. Most of the young radicals see the old Marxists for what they really are--conservative authoritarians.

In many of the news stories and some of the editorials there is a disquieting, almost inexplicable, sentimental disposition toward a working class movement. This tends to produce some news stories and editorials which are irrelevant to libertarian concerns; but, fortunately, this does not interfere with the fine reporting done in other areas.

Apart from Burchett's reports, now coming from Paris, there are many on-the-spot reports on American Imperialist activities from such places as Latin America, North Korea, and Africa. There is also excellent coverage of the accelerating student movement across the country.

The coverage of the United States military-industrial-university complex and its inner machinations has become increasingly pointed and revealing. Especially fine in this area has been the research and reporting done by the staff of the North American Congress of Latin America. NACLA is a young research group which has expanded far beyond its original intent to study the origins and effects of American Imperialism in Latin America. The NACLA people are doing the laudatory and very necessary work of finding out just which corporations and which universities are receiving government contracts and funds. They are reporting this information along with the discoverable facts on exactly which perverted project each of these corporations and universities is pursuing!

One other weekly attraction is well worth mentioning. The "Wanted" feature picks out one of the members of the state-industrial-university system and gives a brief sketch of his personal criminal activity; thereby giving us a more meaningful concrete and personal understanding of the Power Elite.

The *Guardian* is, of course, not a libertarian newspaper; but as it improves as a newspaper, it has become increasingly a better source of pertinent information which can be quite helpful to libertarians. In fact, it is the only place where one can find detailed and comprehensive reporting on all aspects of what is generally known as The Movement. As such, it now, more than ever, deserves to be read by libertarians.
                                                    ---Walter E. Grinder

RECOMMENDED READING

LEFT AND RIGHT. The latest, special 1968 issue of this journal of libertarian thought features a substantial, definitive article by the late historian Harry Elmer Barnes on "The Final Story of Pearl Harbor". This was Dr. Barnes' last work, and synthesizes the "revisionist" insights over the past two decades on the *real* story of Pearl. $1.25, available from Left and Right, Box 395, Cathedral Station, New York, N. Y. 10025.

Leviathan, Vol. 1, No. 1 (March, 1969). New monthly magazine, 56 pp. in tabloid form. New Left periodical, with high-level muckraking and insights into the current American scene. Particularly recommended is the article by Jim Jacobs and Larry Laskowski, "The New Rebels in Industrial America", a sympathetic insight into the Wallaceite trends among many industrial workers. Also Peter Wiley and Beverly Leman, "Crisis in the Cities: Part One", on government-corporate "partnership" in the ghettoes, James O'Connor's overview of the linkage of State and university, and Steve Weissman's critique of the government-corporate world at Stanford.

Economic Age, Vol. 1, No. 1 (November-December, 1968). A new semi-popular, semi-scholarly English bi-monthly, published by the Economic Research Council, and specializing in free-marketish articles. Recommended in the first issue is G. Warren Nutter, "Trends in Eastern Europe". In contrast to many free-market economists whose fanatical anti-Communism blinds them to the enormous and heartening changes in Eastern Europe, Professor Nutter hails the accelerating shift from socialism to the free market in the Communist countries. He even concludes that "In a profound sense, the hope of the West lies today in the East." 2 pounds sterling per year; available from *Economic Age,* 10 Upper Berkeley St., London W1, England.

Yale Brozen, "Is Government The Source of Monopoly?", *Intercollegiate Review* (Winter, 1968-69). A good article in this ISI periodical is something

to savor. Professor Brozen shows how government is the source of monopoly in many ways, direct and indirect. Major concentration of the article is the ICC.

Gabriel Kolko. *The Politics of War: The World and United States Foreign Policy, 1943-1945* (New York: Random House, 1968), 685 pp. $12.95. Monumental and definitive. This is *it*; the first of a multi-volume study of the origins of the Cold War. Kolko is far superior to such previous leading Cold War revisionists as D. F. Fleming, because Fleming worshipped FDR and thought of Roosevelt's foreign policy as noble, only to be sabotaged after his death. Kolko is revisionist on U.S. imperialism *during* as well as after World War II, and shows that America launched the Cold War while World War II was still going on. Kolko exposes the economic interests amidst U.S. imperialism during these years, and also is the first leading historian to develop the Trotskyist insight that the "sellout" at Yalta and other World War II conferences came from Stalin selling out the Communist revolution throughout Europe and Asia on behalf of his Great Power imperial agreement with the U.S. Indispensable for understanding the history of the Cold War and of U.S. foreign policy in our time.

Marion Mainwaring, "Brittany: Revolution in a Cemetery", *The Nation* (February 24, 1969). A charming article from Brittany on a grievously neglected national liberation movement--this one from the oppressed Breton people, a Celtic people with their own language and culture, who have been ruled for over 400 years by an illegal occupation by the French. Like other national liberation movements throughout the world, the Breton movement has been growing rapidly. Eventual goal is a Celtic Federation including independent nations in: Ireland, Scotland, Cornwall, the Isle of Man, and Wales. Normans and Occitans (the southern French speaking the *langue d'oc* and akin to the Catalans oppressed by Spain) are also beginning to yearn for their freedom.

The Libertarian
BOX 341 · *DEPT β*
MADISON SQUARE STATION
NEW YORK, NEW YORK 10010

A Semi-Monthly Newsletter

The Libertarian

Joseph R. Peden, Publisher   Washington Editor, Karl Hess   Murray N. Rothbard, Editor

VOL. I, NO. III   MAY 1, 1969   35¢

The Student Revolution

All through the land, this wondrous month of April, the student revolution has spread to campus after campus, even to the most conservative and the most apathetic. Last year confined to Columbia and a few other campuses, this spring's revolutionary wave has hit all types of campuses, from mighty elite Harvard to working-class San Francisco State, from poor-boy Queensborough Community to formerly conservative Catholic Fordham. This is a wave that must be considered, that must be understood, for it clearly heralds a mighty and accelerating phenomenon in American life.

Many of us, including this writer, thought that the dearth of student revolutionary activity last fall, after the high point at Columbia the previous spring, meant that the campus revolution was fizzling, and was in serious trouble. But, beginning in the late fall with San Francisco State and then Berkeley, the student rebellion has reached a crescendo this spring which few of us have ever dreamed could be possible in America. Of course, the pattern of student activity--of all types--is to start slowly in the fall and reach a peak in the spring. But this year's peak is so far above last year's that the permanence of the student revolution seems evident. And all reports state that each succeeding class is more revolutionary than its elders, that freshmen are more radical than seniors; finally, the sudden emergence of radical high-school movements throughout the country again ensures the deepening of the campus rebellion in the years to come.

How, then, should we respond to this remarkable new phenomenon? There are two typical responses to *any* revolution against State power anywhere, whether it be campus, Negro, or national liberation front. These are the Conservative and the Liberal. The Conservative "answer" is to shoot them down, to use maximum coercion, to bring in courts, police, armies, missiles, you name it, anything to crush and kill. This response accords with the conservative view of the State generally, which is to preserve and cherish the State's rule at all costs. The Liberal "answer" is to cozen and sweeten, to co-opt with petty and trivial reforms fueled by great gobs of Federal tax-money. In the end, if the revolutionaries persist and refuse to be either beaten or bribed into submission, the liberal, too, turns to State coercion, but with more hand-wringing and more do-gooding pieties. In the end, he will use almost as much force as the conservative, but his "humanitarian" patina often makes him even more repellent to the true libertarian.

In our judgment, neither of these tactics--apart from their morality or immorality--is going to work. The conservative tactic, in fact, is precisely the one that has led to the greatest victories for the revolution. The model proceeds somewhat as follows: a small group of radicals presents their demands; the demands are brushed off by the Administration; the radicals seize a building and/or strike; the Administration calls in the cops, who wade in and beat and club and arrest; this naked manifestation of State brutality polarizes and radicalizes the campuses, pushes almost all the moderate students to the side of the radicals, and the revolution is on. This was the pattern, for example, at Columbia, at San Francisco State, at Harvard. The liberal tactic is by far the most dangerous for the revolution--most clearly successful at this year's sit-in at formerly sedate Sarah Lawrence--but this too is increasingly failing, witness Cornell and the City College of New York. What, then, would be the successful tactic in dealing with the student revolution? It is beginning to look as if the only successful tactic, ultimately, will be what the press calls "capitulation". It is interesting that the press and the politicians are beginning to refer to the student body of our nation as one of those "aggressor enemies" that we have become all too familiar with in the past: the "Huns", the Nazis, the Commies; and now it is our kids, virtually the entire generation of them. What are we supposed to do with them, Mr. Conservative? A little napalm? Or maybe the H-bomb, a "clean" one perhaps, so it won't fall on too many of us adults? How far are you prepared to go in using brutality and suppression as your answer to all the problems of this century?

For make no mistake; a generation is speaking. Anyone who is the slightest bit familiar with the campus situation knows the total absurdity of the typical conservative belief that the whole thing is being manipulated by a few "Commies" and "outside agitators" who nip from campus to campus exerting their supposedly Svengali-like effect on the nation's youth. These rebellions are spontaneous and spur-of-the-moment; they take inspiration and heart from rebellions on their fellow campuses, but they are in no sense manipulated by any arcane forces from outside. They stem from the deepest yearnings and values of the kids on campus.

Whether or not capitulation is the only tactic that will work, it is our contention that it is the only moral response we can make. Let us approach this question by considering the usual baffled cry: What do these kids want? Capitulate to *what*?

The goals of the revolution can be broken down into two different categories: the immediate and the ultimate demands. The immediate goals are the concrete, day-to-day

(Continued on next page)

demands that emerge from the everyday crises and irritants of each campus, and each campus and each group of kids will have different variations on a very similar national theme. The ultimate demands deal with the kids' perception of the fundamental evils inherent in our present educational system, as well as a vision of what that system could and should be like in the future.

The immediate demands deal with concrete cases of the particular university either being repressive or tying in with the military-industrial complex and the war activities of the government. The prime goal is to sever the universities' all-pervading tie-ins and linkages with the government and its war machine. This year's major protest demanded the abolition of ROTC on campus. ROTC has become intolerable to our youth; the spectacle of military training insinuating itself as a legitimate part of academic life and of the educational process, the realization that ROTC is training officers to enslave their fellow soldiers and to murder *en masse* in Vietnam, has become too obscene for any of our articulate and self-respecting kids to tolerate. And these kids never forget that the ROTC is training an elite officer corps who will be employed to enslave and command that hapless mass of youngsters--among whom will be many from our campuses--who will become enmeshed in the toils of the draft. One of the events that radicalized the ordinarily cool Harvard student body was an arrogant speech by President Pusey defending ROTC on campus as supplying a much-needed Harvard elite to our officer corps. This sort of pretension of the right of Harvard men to rule was much too blatantly despotic for the libertarian instincts of the present student generation.

This year ROTC; last year the protests were against the university's intimate connections with the Institute of Defense Analysis (Columbia), and against the university allowing its facilities to be used for recruiting purposes by the armed forces and its mass of murderers, and by corporations such as Dow Chemical heavily involved in the production of napalm, an instrument of this mass murder.

Everyone gets excited over student disruptions, sit-ins, a few bread crumbs left in rooms, a few blades of grass trampled on; all this leads the general public to a frenzy of denunciation of the "violence" committed by the students. But where oh where is anything like the equivalent frenzy directed at the monstrous engines of violence, slavery, and mass murder against which the kids are directing their protests: the army, the draft, the war, the police? Why not try to tote up the balance sheet of violence committed by both sides and see what comes out?

We are particularly puzzled by that legion of "libertarian conservatives" who condemn the kids unreservedly for "initiating violence". But *who* has initiated violence? The kids, or the universities that collaborate in the draft and the war machine, who eagerly obtain funds from the taxpayers for all manner of research and grants, including research for germ warfare? The tie-ins between government and the universities link them inexorably, as witness the acts set forth in James Ridgeway's recent *The Closed Corporation*. Particularly grotesque was the Randian argument, put forward by Robert Hessen in a widely distributed article, that Columbia was private property and that therefore the students were and are everywhere violating the sacred rights of private property; in addition, there is a definite sense in the Randian approach that our university system is really pretty good and that the rebel students are in the process of busting up a sound and virtuous institution. Apart from the various specific tie-ins with the State which the Columbia rebels were pinpointing (such as the IDA), nearly two-thirds of Columbia's income comes from governmental rather than *private* sources. How in the world can we continue to call it a *private* institution? Where does private property come in?

In fact, Columbia, as most of our universities--and of course *all* of our frankly state-owned universities such as San Francisco State or Berkeley--is governmental property, paid for by government though run by corporate leaders tied in with government. And *government* property is always and everywhere fair game for the libertarian; for the libertarian must rejoice every time any piece of governmental, and therefore *stolen*, property is returned by any means necessary to the private sector. (In libertarian theory, it is not possible to *steal* from someone who is already a thief and who is only losing property that he has stolen. On the contrary, the person who takes stolen property from a thief is virtuously returning it to innocent private hands.)

Therefore, the libertarian must cheer any attempt to return stolen, governmental property to the private sector: whether it be in the cry, "The streets belong to the people", or "the parks belong to the people", or the schools belong to those who use them, i.e. the students and faculty. The libertarian believes that things not properly owned revert to the first person who uses and possesses them, e.g. the homesteader who first clears and uses virgin land; similarly, the libertarian must support any attempt by campus "homesteaders", the students and faculty, to seize power in the universities from the governmental or quasi-governmental bureaucracy.

Randians retort that public universities, too, are under the rule of legitimate authority because these authorities are elected by the taxpayers, who therefore "own" these campuses. Apart from the fact that university trustees are scarcely elected by anyone, this is a particularly grotesque argument for alleged libertarians to use. For it brings them squarely back to the virus of Social Democracy against which they began to rebel decades ago. The government "represents" the taxpayers indeed! If this were true, then any kind of libertarian viewpoint goes by the board, and we may as well all become Social Democrats, applauding any conceivable activity of government so long as an elected government performs the deed. Surely the basic libertarian insight is that the taxpayers do *not* rule, that, on the contrary, they are mulcted and robbed for the benefit of the State and its cohorts, and therefore the idea that the "public" or the "taxpayers" really *own* anything is a fundamental lie palmed off on us by the apologists for the State. It is not we but the *government* rulers that own "public" property, and hence the vital importance of getting all this property from the "public" to the private or "people's" sector as rapidly as possible. "Homesteading" is often the easiest and most rapid way of accomplishing this goal.

It is particularly amusing that the one act of students which upset the most people, and especially called upon their heads the charge of "initiating violence", was the act of the Cornell black students in bringing rifles and ammunition on campus. Laws were immediately and hysterically passed imposing the severest penalties on such action. But what's wrong with carrying guns? Does not every American have a constitutional right to bear arms? And these weren't even *concealed* arms, so why the fuss? Surely the *crime* comes not in carrying weapons but in using them aggressively. Libertarians and conservatives know this full well when they quite properly call for the repeal of gun laws, restricting the right of everyone to bear arms. Why does everyone forget all this when Negro students bear arms? Could it be that for many "libertarian conservatives" racism runs far deeper than devotion to liberty?

Another broad type of immediate demand is the ending of the university's use of the property-killing power of eminent domain to oust ghetto poor from their homes (major charges at Columbia and Harvard). Surely the libertarian, opposed to urban renewal and eminent domain, can only applaud this goal. A third type of widespread demand is an insistence on simple academic freedom--an insistence that the university is a place for freedom to express radical political views without harassment. The

San Francsico State rebellion was touched off by the university's firing of instructor George Mason Murray, a Black Panther, and this year's Berkeley strike by the attempted firing of Panther Eldridge Cleaver. The current Queensborough Community College rebellion was touched off by the firing of a Progressive Labor member of the faculty, Don Silberman. In all these cases the rebels are fighting for an elemental feature of what makes a genuine university.

Again, conservatives might protest that the trustees have the right to fire anyone they please. But, as we have pointed out, this is not so in the vast bulk of our universities that are openly or covertly governmental. The trustees of those colleges that are genuinely private have the legal *right* to fire anyone, it is true; but so then do the faculty and the students have the right to quit, to demonstrate, or to strike--in protest against the kind of a university where the trustees would do such a thing. And here again, any person concerned with education and freedom of inquiry must agree with that vision of a university where academic freedom rather than trustee dictation prevails.

Another crucially important demand concerns the ways in which the university reacts to the other demands of the rebels: that the State *must not* be called in to decide the issue. Again, everyone gripes at the disruption of the educational process caused by canceled classes or a barricaded door. But the really violent destruction consists in calling in the police, the brutal cops with their mace and their clubs and their tear gas. It is no wonder that police brutality has been the major and almost instant catalyst of radicalization on campus. There can be no education, no dialogue, no community of scholars, where there are helmets and clubs and bayonets. "Cops Out!" is an elemental and crucial cry that erupts from the embattled rebels, and it is one that any person of elemental good will, let alone a libertarian, must commend. Even more despotic is the new and sinister instrument of Statism first employed this year by Columbia University: the court injunction. The labor unions knew precisely what they were doing when they lobbied to pass the Norris-LaGuardia law outlawing the use of injunctions in labor disputes; libertarian theory requires the extension of this principle to abolishing injunctions everywhere!

For the injunction has two profoundly tyrannical features: (a) it moves to prohibit someone in advance from specific actions that, for libertarians, are totally legitimate. Thus, Mr. X. is enjoined by the courts from demonstrating at College Y because the courts have concluded that X might engage in an illegal action. But to move thus in advance of action is totally illegitimate; a libertarian legal order moves only against people *after* they have proceeded to commit a crime, and not before. And (b) the alleged violator of an injunction gets thrown into jail by the judge at the latter's discretion, without a jury trial, without a proper defense, the right to cross-examine, etc. Furthermore, the judge can keep jailing anyone whom he adjudges in "contempt of court"--whether for violating injunctions or for any other reason--as long as he feels like it. The whole area of "contempt of court" is one where judges can reign by their whim unchecked by law or rights. The entire field must be swept aside in the system of libertarian law.

Along with the demand for keeping the State and its minions out of campus disputes comes one for general amnesty, both civil and criminal, in the courts and in the university. Again a perfectly legitimate demand, especially since in the

---

"There are but three ways for the populace to escape its wretched lot. The first two are by the routes of the wineshop or the church; the third is by that of the social revolution."

---Mikhail Bakunin, 1871

Letter From Washington

By Karl Hess

My Taxes

On April 15, I sent the following letter, accompanying my filled-out 1040 Form, to the Tax Collector:

The Declaration of Independence of the United States of America establishes a bill of particulars in regard to intolerable infringements, abuses, and denials of political power which belongs to the people.

The Federal government of the United States of America today is guilty of exactly every sort of infringement, abuse, and denial stated as intolerable by the Declaration of Independence.

I cannot, in conscience, sanction that government by the payment of taxes.

Further, the Federal government of the United States of America has established as a principle, and ruthlessly by the power of its officials enforces as a practice, that it can demand the primary loyalty of the people, that it can exercise all political power on their behalf, that it can wage war without their approval, and that it can and should establish the standards of their behavior and the goals of their lives.

I could not in conscience sanction such a government by the payment of taxes.

Finally, the Declaration of Independence, in the clearest possible language, tells Americans that when a government becomes destructive of the ends of life, liberty, and the pursuit of happiness that it is the right and the duty of the people to abolish such government, to "throw off such government."

It is in the spirit of that Declaration, and in comradeship with men everywhere who seek freedom and to throw off such governments, that I now refuse to pay the taxes demanded by the government in the attached form.

---

vast majority of cases the kids have done nothing wrong according to libertarian doctrine. Somehow, the curious theory prevails that "it's okay to disobey a law or a rule, provided you're willing to take your punishment", and therefore amnesty very often meets widespread resentment. But the whole point is that the kids, and libertarians too, don't recognize the justice of the particular rule or law, and that is precisely why they violate it. So therefore they should not, at least according to their lights, be punished. Besides, Mr. Christian Conservative, what's wrong with mercy?

If the bulk of the immediate demands of the student rebels is proper and praiseworthy from the libertarian point of view, what of the ultimate demands? What do "they" want, down deep? Mainly it is what we touched on earlier: (1) the demand to transfer power from the trustees to students and faculty; and (2) the severing of the university from the government-military-industrial complex. Both demands are interconnected; for the students perceive as few others do, that the American university is a critical and vital part of the ruling system, the instrument by which the Establishment

(Continued on page 4)

trains the rising generation to become cogs in the military-industrial machine. The new rebels want no part of being such cogs; and all libertarians must bless them for their revulsion against the educational *status quo*. The students see that the only way to remove the universities from their "brainwashing" and apologetic role on behalf of the State and its allies is to transform the very nature of the university into student-faculty rule. And why not? As we have seen, for governmental universities this is an eminently libertarian demand, a necessary means for transforming governmental into private property. But, in addition, it is a worthy objective for genuine education, and there is no libertarian reason why even legitimate trustees cannot transfer power voluntarily. Such eminent universities as Oxford and Cambridge are essentially "producers' co-ops", owned and directed by the faculty. Student-faculty power means a shift back to the university, not as servitor of the military-industrial complex, not as apologist for the State, but as a genuine community of scholars searching for and discovering the truth. This is the vision that animates the student revolutionaries, and it is a noble vision indeed. Considering what our universities have become, it is also a vision radically different from the *status quo*: hence it is revolutionary.

It is particularly ironic that conservatives and libertarians should be so distressed at the prospect of students having a say in the universities. After all, a free-market proponent is supposed to favor "consumer sovereignty", and what are students but the consumers of the educational product? Why react with hatred to any attempt by the consumers to influence their education?

Furthermore, conservatives have for decades inveighed, and properly so, against the American educational system. They have seen how that system imprisons and indoctrinates the youth of America into the statist system, how it functions as intellectual apologists for the State apparatus. For decades, no one did anything about this insight. Now, at long last, that the students are reacting precisely against this system, now that they see the evil and are trying to change it, why, Mr. Conservative, why in hell are you on the other side?

The students see even more than the traditional Conservatives did. They see that, apart from other tie-ins, corporations have been using the government schools and colleges as institutions that train their future workers and executives at the expense of *others*, i.e. the taxpayers. This is but one way that our corporate state uses the coercive taxing power either to accumulate corporate capital or to lower corporate costs. Whatever that process may be called, it is *not* "free

enterprise", except in the most ironic sense.

And so, libertarians must hail the student revolution, their _means_ and their ends, their demands both immediate and ultimate. These kids, the first generation in a century to really see and understand the evils of the State, deserve encouragement and support and not our condemnation or our petty complaints. Libertarian students and adults alike have begun to realize this truth. One heartening event has been *libertarian* participation in *some* of the recent rebellions. One prominent young libertarian not only participated whole-heartedly in the Cornell rebellion, but he was the only person among the rebels to vote *against* thanking President Perkins for his liberal concessions to student demands.

The most striking adherence came at Fordham University, where the Fordham Libertarian Alliance constitutes our best-organized chapter on the college campuses--hopefully, a harbinger of the future. FLA was the first group on the Fordham campus to raise the libertarian demand of "Abolish ROTC"; SDS, dominated by Progressive Labor on that campus, hung back for weeks because of fear that the "working class" would not go along with such a demand. But finally, SDS swung into line, and the Fordham sit-in on April 23-24, which lasted over 24 hours, included members of SDS, FLA, and mainly, unaffiliated individuals. The sit-in was unpremeditated, spontaneous; there was no manipulation by a few sinister persons, let along outsiders. Instead, everything was spontaneous, joyous, done by discussion and genuine *consensus*. FLA members conveyed their exhiliration at the true spirit of community animating all of the students, and their joy at the liberating act of taking control of their own lives, at acting dramatically and even heroically for a moral cause. They experienced, for that unforgettable day in their lives, the shared joy of liberation, one that, perhaps some day, all of us may share. God bless them and their generation.

Perhaps the whole thing can be summed up by a sign carried by some of the kids at an anti-war march in New York City on April 5. The sign read simply: "Death to the State. Power to the People." How can you fault a movement having *that* as a slogan?

Also—Regular Washington Column By Karl Hess

The Libertarian
BOX 341
MADISON SQUARE STATION
NEW YORK, NEW YORK 10010

PUBLISHED ON THE FIRST AND FIFTEENTH OF EVERY MONTH   SUBSCRIPTION RATE. $7.00 PER YEAR

A Semi-Monthly Newsletter

The Libertarian

Joseph R. Peden, Publisher   Washington Editor, Karl Hess   Murray N. Rothbard, Editor

VOL. I, NO. IV   MAY 15, 1969   35¢

MAILER FOR MAYOR

Norman Mailer's surprise entry into the Democratic primary for Mayor of New York City, to be held on June 17, provides the most refreshming libertarian political campaign in decades. Mailer has taken everyone by surprise by his platform as well as his sudden entry into the political ranks. The Mailer platform stems from one brilliantly penetrating overriding plank: the absolute decentralization of the swollen New York City bureaucracy into dozens of constituent neighborhood villages. This is the logic of the recent proposals for "decentralization" and "community control" brought to its consistent and ultimate conclusion: the turmoil and plight of our overblown and shattered urban government structures, most especially New York, are to be solved by smashing the urban governmental apparatus, and fragmenting it into a myriad of constituent fragments. Each neighborhood will then be running its own affairs, on all matters, taxation, education, police, welfare, etc. Do conservative whites object to compulsory bussing of black kids into their neighborhood schools? Well, says Mailer, with each neighborhood in absolute control of its own schools this problem could not arise. Do the blacks object to white dictation over the education of black children? This problem too would be solved if Harlem were wholly independent, running its own affairs. In the Mailer plan, black and white could at long last live peacefully side-by-side, with each group and each self-constituted neighborhood running its own affairs.

Mailer and his running mate for City Council President, the writer Jimmy Breslin, realize full well that this striking new idea cuts totally across old-fashioned "left"-"right" lines, that it could logically have an appeal to both groups, or rather to those in both groups that are truly attracted by an essentially libertarian vision. Those who want compulsory integration or those who want the blacks to continue under white rule will not be satisfied with this vision; but those who yearn for liberty, who want whites and blacks to treat each other as independent equals rather than as rulers of one over the other, should flock to the Mailer standard.

Mailer's other positions flow from his basic libertarian insight. He is opposed to compulsory fluoridation of the water supply, *and* he favors the freeing of Huey Newton-- both libertarian positions in the freeing of the individual and the community from the boot of the State. One of Mailer's key proposals is that New York City secede from New York State and form a separate 51st State: a position not only consistent with breaking up large governmental bodies but also with the crucial libertarian principle of *secession*. Secession is a crucial part of the libertarian philosophy: that every state be allowed to secede from the nation, every sub-state from the state, every neighborhood from the city, and, logically, every individual or group from the neighborhood. Mailer's vision actively promotes this position. He is the first political campaigner since the Civil War to raise the banner of secession, a mighty call which unfortunately became discredited in the eyes of Americans because (a) the South lost the Civil War, and (b) because it was associated in their minds with slavery.

Another superb part of Mailer's libertarian vision is his reply about where the New York City government would raise funds; he points out that citizens of New York City pay approximately $22 billion in income taxes to the federal government, and that New Yorkers only receive back about $6 billion from federal coffers. Hence, if New Yorkers *kept* that $22 billion in their own hands ... That way lies secession indeed!'

While Mailer's all-out decentralization should appeal to left and right alike, in actual fact so far the great bulk of his support is coming from the kids of the New Left. On the West Side of Manhattan, there is in the New Left-oriented Community Free Democratic club at least a strong bloc of ardent Mailer-Breslin adherents. As far as I know, there is nothing like this support on the Right-wing. Again I put the question to Mrs. Conservative: how come? You've been griping, and properly so, about swollen governmental bureaucracy for thirty years. For all that time you've been calling for decentralization, for fragmenting the government. Now, at long last, a candidate comes along that takes this position (Mailer calls himself a "left conservative", by the way). Why aren't you supporting him?

And so *The Libertarian* makes its first political endorsement: Mailer for Mayor of New York City and Breslin for President of the City Council. But this of course runs us squarely into the very widespread sentiment among libertarians against any support, vote or endorsement whatever for any political candidate. The contention is that any such support constitutes support of, and joining in with, the State apparatus and is therefore immoral for the libertarian.

While I respect this position, I consider it unduly sectarian. The point is that whether we vote or endorse or not, the offices of President, Senator, Mayor or whatever will *not* become vacant; *someone* will continue to fill these offices during the coming years. Since there is no way for us to opt for keeping these offices vacant, since we will be stuck with someone in these positions come what may, why shouldn't we at least express a hope that someone rather than someone else will fill such positions? If we know that either X or Y will fill a given political post, why can't we express our hope that X will win, or, more likely, that Y will lose? Since we are not yet able to reach that blessed state when *both* can lose, why not do the best we can with the material at hand for the time being? Or, to put it another way, the State apparatus allows us our biennial or quadrennial

(Continued on next page)

17

electoral choice. It is, to be sure, a piddling choice, a marginal choice, a choice which means little and which of and by itself cannot radically change the existing system. But it is at least *something*, it is at least some kind of a choice that we are allowed between different groups of would-be masters, and often such a choice may be important --as in the Mailer ideas and candidacy for this year. Why shouldn't we take advantage of the choices, however piddling, that our State rulers permit us to exercise?

I take as my text Lysander Spooner, one of the great Founding Fathers of individualist anarchism. Spooner wrote:

"in the case of individuals, their actual voting is not to be taken as proof of consent [to the U. S. government] . . . On the contrary, it is to be considered that, without his consent having even been asked a man finds himself environed by a government that he cannot resist; a government that forces him to pay money, render service, and forego the exercise of many of his natural rights, under peril of weighty punishments . . .

Doubtless the most miserable of men, under the most oppressive government in the world, if allowed the ballot, would use it, if they could see any chance of thereby ameliorating their condition. But it would not, therefore, be a legitimate inference that the government itself, that crushes them, was one which they had voluntarily set up, or even consented to." (Spooner, *No Treason*: Larkspur, Colorado, 1966, p. 13.)

There is another important reason for not necessarily scorning the endorsement of political parties or candidates. And that is the seeming fact that it is almost impossible to organize ordinary middle-class citizens into action except through political parties. Blacks are organized in the ghettoes, students on campuses, workers--for good or ill--in labor unions, but where are the permanent *issue*-oriented organizations that successfully attract the great bulk of the country in the middle-class? It seems that the middle-class is only organizationally attracted by political parties, party clubs, etc. If this is so, then political parties become a necessary instrument of the libertarian movement, because if we are to achieve victory we must eventually obtain at the very least the passive support, and hopefully a more active support, of the majority of the middle-class of the country. No organizing among the middle-class has been done by the New Left, although there have been perennial futile attempts to organize the industrial workers by the Marxist elements. The issues, I am convinced, are there: high taxes, inflation, inter-racial clashes arising from failure to achieve community control, a losing or stale-mated war, all this can be brought home to the majority of the population. The rhetoric, of course, will have to differ from the rhetoric that appeals to students; but the underlying ideas and philosophy can be the same: individual liberty. But it seems clear the the organizational form for organizing the middle class will have to be a political party or something very much like it.

Libertarian sectarians should ask themselves seriously: do we want victory? If we really want victory for liberty, then we must employ the means necessary for its attainment, and it looks as if political action will be one--though by no means all--of those necessary means. And so Mailer for Mayor.

Letter From Washington

By Karl Hess

REPRESSION, DOMESTIC AND FOREIGN

Latest horrifying report in town is that the Department of Justice, perhaps making use of the barbaric special-arrest-and-detention-camp provisions of the McCarran Act, is planning to escalate its war against dissenters from sniper attacks against leaders to mass arrests of activists generally.

Whether the rumor is true or not, the very existence of the McCarran Act's provisions for broad round-ups of 'dangerous' persons during a time of 'emergency' plus the actual maintenance of prison camps on a stand-by basis (as graphically portrayed in *Look* magazine some time back) is bound to make one wonder.

Should any Senator or Congressman seriously be looking for a libertarian cause to pursue, the abolition of the McCarran Act's repressive provisions would be an interesting one to consider. For one thing, even proposing it should polarize the legislators, very usefully and very visibly. The lip-service liberty lovers who reach for state power whenever their special notion of order is disordered would, of course, recoil in horror, pompously shouting that the nation *must* thus defend itself. Liberals would be in their usual dilemma, trying to figure out whether they would lose any patronage or power if the prison camps were closed.

****

Not a rumor, but just as horrifying, are plans for the new Civil Disorders War Room at the Pentagon. Fed by FBI data channeled through the White House, the new war room will seek completely to computerize all the factors involved in civil disorder such as the location at all times of known activists, militants, dissenters, critics--in short, everyone who attacks the state--as well as the availability and location of all repressive forces from U.S. marshals to paratroopers, state troopers and just plain old storm troopers such as the new Federally-trained phalanxes of paramilitary 'riot' police from most of the major cities.

Perhaps the most innovative feature of the war room will be the computer's reported ability to deal with pictures as input data. It is said that police routinely will photograph all public (and as many private as possible) meetings of dissenters. The photos will then be scanned and, if they show sufficient visual identity points for a face, persons pictured can instantly be identified and their presence at the particular meeting added to the disorder data bank for use in future analyses. Onward and upward with science in the service of the state.

****

Behind the farce of Vietnam there is tragedy, of course. Its main outline is the number of men, women, children, and soldiers who will die while the politicians in Saigon continue to use the politicians in Washington to bolster their bureaucratic barony. The bureaucrats in Washington, meanwhile, will be concerned solely by the electoral implications of what they do and not by the murder in which they are involved. The tragedy involves all those who must pay for this role-playing with their lives or sanity.

That the tragic sense has reached many in Washington is becoming more and more obvious, although there is no indication that it has penetrated the high, black-iron fence of the White House. At other levels of government, and particularly in the Pentagon itself, there is a growing recognition of the fact that the war is being and will be won by the NLF. Bitterest of all is the recognition that in justice they should win. In the months just ahead this should result

(Continued on page 4)

S. D. S. And Black Self-Determination

Passing a resolution shining throughout with pure libertarianism and marred by only a few traces of Marxism, the recent Students for a Democratic Society convention in Austin, Texas committed themselves wholeheartedly to the support of the radical Black Panther Party and other black revolutionary groups who have as their purpose the abolition of the American State.

The text of the resolution began: "The sharpest struggles in the world today are those of the oppressed nations against imperialism and for national liberation. Within this country the sharpest struggle is that of the black colony for its liberation . . ." It might have added, of course, that as long as the American Leviathan exists most of us, even the Caucasians, will be enslaved; but it is true that, due to such brutes as the racist white police, far more oppression is executed upon the Negro community.

The Panthers were looked upon by the resolution as the most promising liberators of the blacks. Certainly, now that Negroes everywhere are rejecting the Statist fallacies of the NAACP and other conservative groups and embracing the demands for total freedom advocated by harbingers like Rap Brown, the Panthers offer much potential as an organizing body. in the struggle to unshackle the chains that Big White Brother has imposed. As long as it confines itself to freeing the people from political power while not imposing its own rule, the Black People's (Panther) Army, which is "to be used not only in the defense of the black community but also for its liberation," may be most important.

Though one or two socialist fallacies blemish the logic of the document, it is made clear that the abolition of the State is the primary and ultimate goal. "The demand for self-determination becomes the most basic demand of the oppressed colony." Self-determination, taken to its logical conclusion, means the right of every single individual to be free of all political power, i. e., anarchism. Thus it is quite ironic that the U.S. Government, which holds millions in bondage everywhere, pays lip service to the right of self-determination (remember LBJ's sophisms wherein he pleaded for the self-determination of the South Vietnamese).

Reactionary nationalism, the type of nationalism best exemplified by Hitler and encompassing the Führers of all nation-states in history, is totally rejected, while the completely different revolutionary nationalism, which means simply the uniting of individuals to throw off colonial tyranny, is applauded. As Panther leader G. M. Murray made clear, "We must destroy all cultural nationalism, because it is reactionary and has become a tool of Richard Milhous Nixon and all the U.S. power structure which divides the poor and oppressed, and is used by the greasy-slick black bourgeoisie to exploit black people in the ghetto."

Everyone professing libertarianism must go hand-in-hand with SDS in "its commitment to join with the Black Panther Party and other black revolutionary groups in the fight against white national chauvinism and white supremacy." The right of every individual to be free of any nation-state in general, and the U.S. despotism in particular, must be actively supported.

(Note: for the full text of the SDS resolution, see *New Left Notes*, April 4, 1969, p. 3.)

--Stephen Halbrook

EDITOR'S COMMENT:

The Panthers And Black Liberation

While I do not want to detract from Mr. Halbrook's excellent article, and while I realize that the great majority of revolutionary anarcho-capitalists are highly enthusiastic about the Black Panthers and their potential for leading a black liberation movement, I must record my serious reservations about the value of the Panthers.

The Panthers have three great virtues: (1) their enormous ability to upset and aggravate the white society, simply by going around armed and in uniform--the supposed Constitutional privilege of every free American but apparently to be denied to radical militant blacks; (2) their considerable capacity for organizing black youth; and (3) excellent black nationalist ideas--particularly in emphasizing a black nation with their own land in such areas as the Black Belt of the South--as expressed in some writings of Eldridge Cleaver.

But there are growing offsetting tendencies so serious as to call the overall merit of the Panthers into grave question. In the first place, there are increasing tendencies for the Panthers to abandon black nationalism almost completely for the Old Left virus of black-white Marxist working-class action. The problem is not only increasing infusions of Marxist rhetoric into the Panther material, but an unfortunate eagerness to reach out and make alliances with white radicals, thereby contradicting the whole point of black power, which is to develop separate black movements resulting in black national self-determination. Even tactically, the original idea was to have alliances between strong, independent black and white radical movements; neither the Panthers nor the white radical movements have grown sufficiently to validate any sort of alliance now, even as a tactic. The most absurd example of this was the decision of the Peace and Freedom Party last year to nominate Eldridge Cleaver for President--a ridiculous decision for both the white and black movements since it involved a supposed black nationalist running for President of a white Republic--the U.S.A. It makes black nationalist sense to run candidates from Harlem or Watts; but not for Senators or Presidents from predominantly white constituencies. The question then arises: are the Panthers *really* black nationalists?

The second big reservation comes from the increasingly thuggish and Stalinoid tendencies in the Panther movement: viz. (1) the inexcusable pulling of a gun by the Panthers on SNCC leader James Forman, a fellow revolutionary black-nationalist, at a presumed peace meeting between the two groups. Pulling a gun on the State enemy is one thing; pulling a gun on fellow revolutionaries is quite another, and cannot be condoned in any way. Eldridge Cleaver's reported statement that Forman should have been shot because his strategic views make him "objectively counter-revolutionary" puts the whole affair in an even more grisly light. (2) The equally inexcusable pulling of a gun by the Panthers on the Peace and Freedom party leaders in New York to force those veteran bootlickers of the Panthers to withdraw their duly nominated candidate for the Senate, the pacifist David McReynolds, in order to leave the line blank and allow the Panthers to secretly support the black nationalist Herman Ferguson, who ran a predictably poor race for the Senate on the competing Freedom and Peace party ticket. (3) The outrageous and vicious attack on black revolutionary columnist Julius Lester by Kathleen Cleaver in the *Guardian* of May 3 for his tactical disagreement with the SDS resolution on the Panthers. This article, devoid of analysis and long on snarling invective, was in the worst tradition of Stalinist billingsgate, in those days often preparatory to a Stalinist purge.

All this means that we should, at the very least, withdraw our enthusiasm from the Panthers. In any event, it is the responsibility of whites to build the white movement, and to concentrate our time and energies therefore on white rather than black affairs.

RECOMMENDED READING

COUNTERPOINT. The nation's finest student libertarian periodical. Free, and published irregularly in mimeographed form by the Fordham Libertarian Alliance. Solidly anarcho-capitalist, *Counterpoint* has become increasingly trenchant and radical over the past year. Vol. 2, No. 7 has an excellent article expounding free-market anarchism by Mario J. Rizzo, an exposure of the relations between big business and government in founding the ICC by Joseph Castrovinci, and a refutation of the familiar "if you don't like it here, why don't you leave?" argument by David Hagner. FLA led the Fordham sit-in for the ouster of ROTC and every libertarian will enjoy FLA's handbill "ROTC OUT", published at the height of the agitation. All available from Fordham Libertarian Alliance, Box 763, Fordham University, The Bronx, N. Y. 10458.

Leviathan. In our April 15 issue, we neglected to give the address of this New Left monthly. It can be obtained from Subscription Department, Leviathan, 2700 Broadway, New York, N.Y. 10025. Price is $5 a year, single copy 50 cents.

NACLA Newsletter. Published 10 times a year by the North American Congress on Latin America. NACLA is the country's best muckraking organization, no longer confining itself to Latin America as the title might suggest. Latest NACLA publication is the booklet Michael Klare, ed., *The University-Military Complex* , price $1.00, an indispensable reference handbook of the detailed tie-ins between university professors and the military. Available from North American Congress on Latin America,

LETTER FROM WASHINGTON —

(Continued from page 2)

in some interesting psychiatric, if not political studies and introspections. No matter what, militarists will continue to justify the war. It should sink them deeper and deeper into a brooding paranoia in which, although all of the facts are against them, they continue to think that it's all simply an assault on their honest patriotism. But for men of some residual conscience, every day that the war continues will create more of a crisis. Some may even be forced to make decisions--to renounce their role in the tragedy and to seek the redress of immediate withdrawal from Vietnam and long-range withdrawal from imperialism altogether.

P. O. Box 57, Cathedral Park Sta., New York, N. Y. 10025.

Barton Bernstein, ed., *Towards A New Past:Dissenting Essays in American History* (Random House, 1968: Random House-Vintage Paperbacks, 1969). A collection of representative essays, some excellent, by younger New Left American historians. Particularly recommended are Jesse Lemisch on the "mobs" during the American Revolution, and the Revisionist foreign policy articles of Lloyd Gardner and Robert F. Smith. Both are Revisionist on World War II *and* the Cold War, and Smith is the first historian to footnote Jim Martin's *American Liberalism and World Politics* , the mammoth 2-volume dissection of the shift of American Liberals from "isolationism" to war during World War II.

James Weinstein, *The Corporate Ideal in the Liberal State* 1900-18 (Beacon Press, 1968; Beacon Paperback, 1969). Indispensable complement to Gabriel Kolko's work on the origin of government regulation of business in the Progressive Era from the desire of Big Business to achieve monopolistic privilege through government. Weinstein concentrates on the pro-government intervention ideology of Big Businessmen. The "enlightened" Big Business leaders scornfully referred to the NAM (in those days controlled by free-market small businessmen) as "anarchists".

The Libertarian
BOX 341
MADISON SQUARE STATION
NEW YORK, NEW YORK 10010

PUBLISHED ON THE FIRST AND FIFTEENTH OF EVERY MONTH   SUBSCRIPTION RATE. $7.00 PER YEAR

A Semi-Monthly Newsletter

The Libertarian

Joseph R. Peden, Publisher	Washington Editor, Karl Hess	Murray N. Rothbard, Editor
VOL. 1, NO. V	JUNE 1, 1969	35¢

THE MOVEMENT GROWS

The libertarian movement, bless it, is on the march. For the first time in memory, there is now a nationwide libertarian organization in existence, the Radical Libertarian Alliance. It was born on May 17, on the occasion of the third meeting of the Libertarian Forum in New York City.

Until this year, the libertarian movement was pitifully small and beleaguered, and any talk of any sort of libertarian organization or even occasional meetings was hopelessly Utopian. But now the movement has been escalating with extraordinary rapidity. In the old days, there would be one new convert a year, and he would be worked on with painful slowness before his conversion could be complete. But now we keep running into kids, some college freshmen, who are not only libertarians, but full-fledged and self-converted, with the "correct line" on everything, from competing private defense agencies to private property rights to war revisionism to alliance with the New Left. It has all been very gratifying.

Compare the state of the movement now, say, to that of a year ago. One year ago the New York movement contained about half a dozen people; now, for the first time in living memory it has escalated to far beyond the capacity of one person's living room. It was for that reason that Joseph Peden and Jerry Woloz decided to found the Libertarian Forum, basically conceived as a way for the whole New York movement to meet periodically in the confines of one room. We met for the first time on January 31 at the Great Shanghai restaurant in New York City. We expected about 20 people to appear; we got over seventy. It was a glorious moment. People came from as far away as South Carolina and Buffalo for the occasion. The editor spoke about the necessity for thinking in revolutionary terms.

The next meeting was on April 11, when Karl Hess, our most recent and our best-known convert, spoke on the need to avoid letting a sectarian emphasis on economics block our alliance with other, New Left, groups which are overall libertarian in thrust without being sophisticated in economics. The attendance at this meeting was again over seventy. The atmosphere at both meetings was highly enthusiastic, and several on-the-spot conversions were made to the cause. The "Devil" was represented in both cases by his advocates in the form of assorted Randians and red-baiters, who served as useful foils for spirited argument.

The spirit and the attendance at the Forums gave rise to much agitation to progress beyond these simple meetings, and to advance toward a wider and better-organized movement. Our best organized group had been the Fordham Libertarian Alliance, which led the sit-in at the once conservative Fordham campus demanding the ouster of the military cadre known as ROTC from the campus. The FLA

had begun only in this academic year, with Gerald P. O'Driscoll, Jr., who graduates this spring with honors in economics, as its dynamic leader. Two years ago, Jerry was a bright young right-winger and ROTC leader, who favored the war in Vietnam. Now he stands as one of the leading spirits of anarcho-capitalist youth. Jerry will proceed next year to graduate work in economics at UCLA, leaving FLA in the capable hands of Frank X. Richter, Dave Hagner, and a host of others.

An important anarcho-capitalist group has also rapidly emerged at Wesleyan College, phenomenal in that it consists almost exclusively of freshmen, led by John Hagel III. Hagel and his remarkable colleagues have already seized control of the Free University at Wesleyan, at which John is already teaching a course in anarchism, and have done extensive organizing work in colleges and prep schools throughout the New England and even Middle Atlantic states. The Wesleyan group also helped lead an anti-ROTC sit-in at the Administration Building there. Adopting the principle of alliance with the New Left, the entire Wesleyan group formed the Earl Francis Memorial Chapter of SDS, and will battle within SDS against the Marxist forces. (Earl Francis was a heroic individualist martyr to the U.S. government; the government refused to recognize his homesteading claim to a gold mine on U.S. land on the grounds that the mine was too small, and ordered him off the land and his house blown up; Francis complied, blowing himself up along with it.)

At State University of New York at Buffalo, Roy A. Childs, Jr. has made the paradigmatic progressive transition from Randianism to Lefevrian pacifism to revolutionary anarcho-capitalism, and has been writing a column in one of the college newspapers and been heard on Buffalo radio.

In the meanwhile, at Stanford University Professor Ronald Hamowy of the history and contemporary civilization departments has been carrying on radical libertarian activities of his own. To old friends, the emergence of the former moderate Ronald as revolutionary is one of the joyous surprises of this age of polarization. Last year, Ronald Hamowy was one of the two or three Stanford professors to support the sit-in for university reform. In the course of his radical activities there, he gave a notable speech, carried in the Stanford paper, which sharply criticized the rigidly non-violent tendency of the draft resistance movement of that era. This year, it was Ronald who suggested the sit-in tactic employed by the student rebels against military research at the Stanford Research Institute, and he sat in for the week-long demonstration. Then, when a court injunction threatened to be employed against a second group of sit-ins, Ronald organized an open letter to the Admin-

(Continued on page 2)

THE MOVEMENT GROWS— *(Continued from page 1)*

istration threatening a faculty strike--i. e. refusal to hand
in grades--should any student be jailed for violating the
injunction against them from even attending their own
classes. Not only has Stanford been threatening to fire the
signers of this letter, but there have been mutterings that
Ronald by his action is trying to "intimidate" the court and
is therefore in a state of contempt of court and could be
immediately jailed. Such is just one aspect of the repression
that is growing and accelerating against the dissenters in
this "free" country. (In the old days, libertarians always
used to be asked the question: "Well, after all, what liberties
have we lost?" No one has asked this question for a long
while; the repression is too obvious.)

Speaking of repression, a little whiff of it was felt at the
third meeting of the Libertarian Forum at the Jager House
in New York, when the libertarian scholar and activist
Leonard P. Liggio spoke on the libertarian nature of the
New Left. Less than twenty-four hours after the end of this
harmless meeting, we heard from unimpeachable sources
of someone who had read the report in sextuplicate of a cop
spy at the meeting, the other carbons going to other cop
organizations. And yet, countless libertarian-conservatives
still revere and identify with the *polizei*! It seems that there
were SDS members--horrors!--at the Forum meeting, and
that many SDS people are tailed wherever they go by some
form of undercover cop.

At any rate, out of that Forum meeting emerged the
Radical Libertarian Alliance. In keeping with its libertarian
nature, it is envisioned that RLA will be organized in the
form of strictly autonomous chapters. At the beginning,
most of the chapters will be in various colleges, but there
are also several non-campus chapters. There are regional
organizers, and there will be meetings in the various
regions. The national functions are ones of service: education and coordination. There will be a national Speakers'
Bureau, which will send speakers around to the various
chapters for purposes of education and inspiration and a
national Publications Bureau to print leaflets and other
material. The first material to be issued by the Publications
Bureau will be a founding statement of aims and principles,
a statement which defines the goals, the strategy, and the
principles of the Radical Libertarian Alliance. All who agree
with this statement will be admitted to the individual
chapters.

Officers of RLA are as follows: Regional Coordinators:
John Hagel III for New England and for Prep Schools, Wilson
A. Clark, Jr. of the University of North Carolina for the
South, and Gerald O'Driscoll as the "missionary" coordinator for California. Overall North American Coordinator
is Karl Hess, 1085 National Press Building, N. W., Washington, D. C. Treasurer is Walter Block, 380 Riverdale-side
Drive, New York, N. Y. Anyone who wants to send funds to
RLA should send them to Walter. The key post of corresponding secretary has gone to Roy A. Childs, Jr., 109
Wende, Buffalo, New York 14211. Anyone who wants information or advice on joining the organization, forming
chapters, getting speakers, etc. or who wishes to send news
to other members, should contact Roy Childs.

It is estimated that already, when RLA has hardly been
formed, there are at least 26 college chapters alone. The
potential for rapid growth is enormous, beginning this fall,
especially on those campuses where SDS has come under
the control of Marxist elements and where RLA could fill
an immediate libertarian vacuum.

Onward and upward!

> "An oppressed people are authorized whenever they can to
> rise and break their fetters."
>
> ---Henry Clay, 1818

Letter From Washington

By Karl Hess

The Coming White Terror

There is going to be a time of repression in this
country. It may be quite harsh. For many, including
libertarians, it may be frightening and discouraging.
For the only vaguely committed it will be too much to
bear and they will move back to safe positions in liberal-
land or conservative-country, those establishment enclaves whose philosophically peripatetic borders seem
now to overlap lovingly and lastingly on the American
political landscape.

The facts of the repression are clear, even if not overt.
The Deputy Attorney General, Richard Kleindienst, an
old friend who, I can assure you, is more than capable
of matching rhetoric to action, has been quoted in The
Atlantic as saying that student dissenters would be
"rounded up" and placed in "detention camps". His subsequent denial of the quotation was not categorial but
only complained that he had been, as politicians apparently always are, misquoted and that, ah hah, even if he
had said something like that he hadn't meant anything like
that.

Mr. Kleindienst, as with every one of his political
associates with whom I have worked, is sensitive first
and foremost to national mood. Although they may sometimes seem to buck its ordinary ebb and flow, they all
turn and run in the face of its occasional floods. Such a
flood is now evident, with more than 80 percent of persons
answering recent polls saying that they approve of
stringent crack-downs on student dissent. It is my notion
that buried in these responses, and not by too much
racist dirt at that, is an implicit desire also for a crackdown on black militants.

The Administration, with some of the most attentive
political antennae we have ever seen--look at the power
wielded in it by publicists!--is surely going to play the
repressive mood for all it is worth. And how much it is
worth is, in turn, clearly evident in the fact that Super
Semanticist S. I. Hayakawa has become Puissant Politician merely and solely because he has bumbled himself,
like the British at Balaclava, into a bloody, dumb,
eventually disastrous position of pig-headed glory. The
fact that merely cracking a few student skulls has been
enough to propel this second-rate social democrat into a
first rank of right-wing respect, equal to and possibly
even in advance of that other pillar of West Coast educa-
tionism, Max Rafferty, must be lesson enough to Richard
Nixon and his court that there are political riches in the
blood of repression.

There is, however, a growing interpretation, even
among some who call themselves libertarians but who
probably would be more comfortable as conservatives,
that the New Left has brought it all on themselves and,
consequently, upon the rest of us and that, in a convenient
application of what the Christians might call the Agnus
Dei shift, it is the New Left into whom all the daggers of
recrimination may be thrust.

No.

It is the libertarian instinct and interpretation that tells us that it is the state, and not those who attack or resist it, that is the guilty or most guilty party in the development of any repression and that to call repression merely reaction is to overlook or even deny the dynamics of state development.

In that dynamic development, the state, any state, always becomes more repressive over the long run rather than less. There are no exceptions to this in the development of any state where the power has been delegated by the people to the politicians, no matter how benign those politicians may seem at any particular point of the development.

Thus, the actions by the New Left, or even the Crazies, that have goaded the state into its current quiet frenzy, are hastened by but not created by those actions. The state must, sooner or later, become more rather than less coercive and repressive. That movement may be accelerated by people's resistance but it is not created by that resistance. Has not, in fact, the structure of government, state, local, and national, actually become more repressive year by year in this country whether in times of peace, war, languor or riot? The answer is that it has and the very political party which now occupies (and occupies is just the word) the positions of power today is also the very political party which in past campaigns has documented and dealt with that onward course of repression in greatest detail. They are silent now, of course, because what it once called oppressive under Democrats becomes orderliness under Republicans.

Libertarians, who, throughout modern political history, have presented the only clear and consistent analysis of state power, know that the difference between the natural or spontaneous order of a free society, and the enforced order of a state system, is the very difference between the day of human liberation and the night of state coerciveness.

(Some details of that night as it now unfolds in Washington, appear to include the systematic arrest, on a wide variety of unrelated charges and as often as possible by local police, of student leaders and, subsequently, and perhaps depending upon the reaction to that, of nonstudent militants and radicals. The Black Panthers, of course, face a repression far more harsh and the key to its success very liekly is simply to what extent local police forces, now frothing with a really rabid zeal, can execute Panthers without publicity. They will be helped, probably, by all of those liberal and conservative editors who feel that Panther revolutionary rhetoric is a threat to the orderly development of their own political programs.)

Libertarians have a rather clear-cut choice in facing the repression. They tacitly or otherwise support the state or they can remain with the *Resistance*. There is no convenient middle course such as simply opting out of the struggle. There may be an appearance of such an option but it is illusory. For instance, even if one is able to retreat to a position in which one has no contact with either the state or the Resistance, a reaction in regard to the state-resistance question is inevitable. For one thing there will be many times when a friend who has not retreated could use your help. By not helping him, and if he is resisting, the state itself has been helped. This is not to call for selfless heroics, but only for principled recognition of the fact that there are two sides in this struggle and libertarians, whose analysis is the most pertinent of all, should not contemplate being able to avoid taking one of those sides. Nor should they avoid the possibility--and I say it is inevitability--that a choice which does not support the Resistance, even if with grave reservations regarding some of its character or characters, actually opposes it and that any choice which does not oppose the state, actually supports it.

Not every libertarian should or could be found at the

DON'T TREAD ON ME

If the Rubber Manufacturers Association can buy enough bureaucrats, the old Fisk slogan "Time to Re-tire" will cease to be a mere advertising slogan and become a gunpoint command.

The April newsletter of the National Highway Users Conference notes that the RMA has "suggested" to the Federal Highway Administration a three-part "tire safety program". It calls for state laws that would require tire inspection 1) on a periodic basis, preferably semi-annually at a state inspection station; 2) by law enforcement authorities on a spot-check or random basis, and 3) as a pre-condition to the sale of all used vehicles.

The RMA inspection program would make it mandatory to remove passenger car tires from service when tread depth is less than 1/16th of an inch. The association pointed out to the Government that this depth has already been recognized by the National Highway Safety Bureau, which requires all new tires to have molded tread wear indicators at the 1/16-inch mark.

The RMA said that only a few states already have compulsory tire inspection programs and expressed dismay that two-thirds of all cars on the road can still be driven without periodic checks for worn-out tires (i. e. by people other than the owner).

All states should enact statutes which would permit "policing authorities" to require removal from a vehicle of any unsafe tire whenever and wherever it may be found, the RMA stated.

The inspection program, the newsletter said, was "submitted in response to proposed Federal motor vehicle safety standards for vehicles in use." It's a classic example of how business uses the Government for its own benefit, and helps explain why, after a short bleat of protest for the record, the auto industry crawled in bed with Ralph Nader when he made his propositions.

The propagandists would have you believe the consumer is being protected by the "auto safety" program, but what consumer has the time or the know-how to "respond" to "proposed motor vehicle safety standards"? Car-buying, after all, takes up a very small part of his day.

RMA lobbyists, on the other hand, have absolutely nothing better to do all day than badger and bribe bureaucrats into passing laws that will force more tires on an unwilling public. Once again it is being demonstrated that regulatory agencies work to the benefit of the producer instead of the consumer.

How sweet it is for the country club set in Akron. They can cut loose some of that high-price marketing help that tries to tempt drivers into buying new tires and rely instead on tax-supported state police to do the "selling".

Some day soon you may be flagged down by a cop with a .38 caliber pistol in one and .38 caliber calipers in the other. He's authorized to poke around in your tire tread, then force you into the tire store that happens to be nearby. It promises to be the best fee-splitting scheme since justices of the peace started going out of style.

Traditionally the tire industry has been relatively unregulated and consequently highly competitive. But now it is trying to blow out the little Fisk boy's candle and climb on the wide-tread bandwagon of the Federal Highway Administration.

--Peter Blake

barricades resisting or in the tunnels undermining state power. *None, of course, want to end up in jail.* And now they will see the power of the state, awesome and even frightening, and they will see the jails eagerly eating the revolution.

Tactics may have to change. That is only wisdom. But direction? Never! The course is to liberty. The state is the enemy.

FOR REVOLUTIONARY ANARCHO-CAPITALISM

A fully consistent concern with human liberty such as that which *The Libertarian* espouses, necessarily involves the acceptance of what may be called Revolutionary Anarcho-Capitalism. Let us see why.

Liberty can only exist when no one's rights are violated. Since man rightfully owns his own body and the produce of any unclaimed natural resources he mixes his labor with, he has a right to trade this produce with other individuals or groups of individuals. Any threat or initiation of violence against a man or his property is in violation of man's rights and hence inimical to liberty. So far, Capitalism. (Note, however, the difference

RECOMMENDED READING

Karl Hess, "In Defense of Hess," *The New Guard* (April, 1969). It is rare indeed for us to be recommending any article in this YAF publication, but Hess' article is a stirring defense of anarchism. Interestingly enough, reports are that Jerome Tuccille, who argues the archist point of view in the same issue, has since been virtually converted to the libertarian position.

Ferdinand Lundberg, *The Rich and the Super-Rich* (Bantam, paper). A huge, sprawling, badly organized best-seller, which yet contains indispensable information on the rich families and their relationship with government.

Lewis Mumford, *The City in History* (Harcourt, Brace, and World, paper). A fascinating, monumental history of the city. Includes analysis of the original city as being a parasitic, military arm of the State, living off society.

Albert Jay Nock, *Memoirs of a Superfluous Man* (Regnery, paper). It is great to have this modern classic back in print, and in paperback. Nock was an excellent stylist and a profound libertarian, and his book is must reading, despite its suffering from a profound historical pessimism that isolated Nock and robbed him of most of the impact he could have had.

Jacobus ten Broek, Edward Barnhart, and Floyd Matson, *Prejudice, War and the Constitution* (University of California Press, paper). A reprint of a thorough, scholarly account of America's most vicious invasion of civil liberties: the mass evacuation into concentration camps of America's Japanese-American citizens in World War II.

Gordon Zahn, *German Catholics and Hitler's Wars* (Dutton, paper). An impressive indictment of the favorable attitude of the German Catholic hierarchy toward the German State and therefore toward Hitler's wars.

between this free-market philosophy and that of our present liberal corporate "capitalism".)

The "Anarcho" part comes in when it is realized that government by its very nature is coercive. Even a "pure" democracy, one not ruled by a power-elite, such as ours is, is coercive. People who have not consented to the democratic process in the first place will be coerced if they are outvoted. The Anarchistic strain is strengthened by the understanding that the free market provides a better product at a lower price for *all* goods. For defense, courts, police, roads, information, a money medium, as well as for goods where even classical liberals would restrict government intervention. So far, Anarcho-Capitalism.

Anarcho-Capitalism is not enough, however. Unless we realize that *defensive* violence in response to aggression is fully consistent with libertarianism, Anarcho-Capitalism can lead to a sterile pacifism. ("Government depredations are immoral, but opposition is also immoral; we can therefore only educate."). Education *alone* cannot achieve liberty as can be seen by assuming the most favorable case for "educationalism". Let's suppose, for example, that all the people in the world who presently reject Anarcho-Capitalism through lack of knowledge learn the error of their ways. While this would be a great boon, what of the people who defend statism not through error, but through immorality? No ruling class in history has ever given up its power through sweet reasonableness and rational argument. For this, a Revolutionary Anarcho-Capitalist *movement* is needed.

--Walter Block

The Libertarian
BOX 341
MADISON SQUARE STATION
NEW YORK, NEW YORK 10010

Published on the first and fifteenth of every month

Subscription rate: $7.00 per year

A Semi-Monthly Newsletter

THE
Libertarian Forum

Joseph R. Peden, Publisher   Washington Editor, Karl Hess   Murray N. Rothbard, Editor

VOL. I, NO. VI   JUNE 15, 1969   20¢ 35¢

MASSACRE AT PEOPLE'S PARK

Sometimes it is difficult to escape the conviction that there is a sickness so deep in the soul of the American people that they are beyond redemption. On May 15 and in ensuing days the massed armed might of the State, local police, state police, National Guardsmen, zeroed in on a few thousand unarmed citizens of Berkeley, California, who were doing what? Who had taken a muddy lot and transformed it lovingly into a "people's park". For this crime, and for the crime of refusing to move from this park which they had created with their own hands, the brutal forces of the State, led by Governor Reagan, moved in with fixed bayonets; shot into the unarmed crowd, wounding over 70 people and murdering the innocent bystander James Rector; flew a helicopter over the crowd and sprayed a super-form of mace over everyone in the area, including children and hospital patients; rounded up hundreds of people and humiliated and tortured them in the infamous Santa Rita concentration camp--one of the major camps for Japanese-Americans during World War II. All this has happened in our America of 1969, and where oh where is the nationwide cry of outrage? Where is the demand for the impeachment of the murderer Reagan and all of the lesser governmental cohorts implicated in this monstrosity?

Sure, there are a few protests from liberals who feel that the use of force was a bit excessive, but one gets the distinct impressive that for the great American masses the massacre was a pretty good show. There is our pervasive sickness. Why this range of reaction from indifference to enthusiasm for this terrible deed? Because the Berkeley park-creators were apparently longhairs and "hippies", and *therefore* subhuman with no rights or liberties that need to be respected. There are apparently tens of millions of God-fearing Americans who favor the genocidal destruction of hundreds of thousands or even millions of young people whose only crime is to persist in esthetic differentiation from the mass of the populace.

The American soul-sickness is also manifest in the pervasive reaction to the problem of "violence" in America. Mention "violence" and the average person begins to fulminate against isolated muggers, against Negroes who burn down stores, and against students who blacken a few ash-trays in university buildings. Never does this average American, when he contemplates violence in our epoch, consider the American army and its genocidal destruction of the people of Vietnam, or the American police in their clubbing at Chicago, or their murdering and gassing at People's Park. Because apparently when the State, the monopolizer of violence, the great bestial Moloch of mass destruction, when the *State* uses violence it apparently is not violence at all. Only virtually unarmed citizens using force against the State, or even simply refusing to obey State orders, only these citizens are considered to be "violent". It is this kind of insane blindness that permitted President Johnson to trumpet that "we shall not tolerate

violence, no matter the slogan", and President Nixon to denounce student violence while lauding the military-industrial complex, and not be laughed out of office.

The cry has gone up that all this was necessary to defend the "private property" of the University of California. In the first place, even if this little lot *was* private property, the bayoneting, gassing, torturing, and shooting of these unarmed park-developers would have been "overkill" so excessive and grotesque as to be mass murder and torture and therefore far more criminal than the original trespass on the lot. You do not machine-run someone for stealing an apple; this is punishment so far beyond the proportion that "fits the crime" as to be itself far more criminal than the original infraction. So that even if this property were legitimately private the massacre is still to be condemned.

Secondly, it is surely grotesquerie to call the muddy lot "private property". The University of California is a governmental institution which acquires its funds and its property from mulcting the taxpayers. It is *not* in any sense private property then, but stolen property, and as such is morally unowned, and subject to the libertarian homesteading principle which we discuss below. The people of Berkeley were homesteaders in the best American--and libertarian--tradition, taking an unused, morally unowned, muddy lot, and transforming it by their homesteading labor into a pleasant and useful people's park. For this they were massacred.

This is it; this is an acid test of whether any person can in reason and in conscience call himself a "libertarian". Here the issues are clear and simple; here there are no complicating factors. There is no alleged "national security" involved; there is no "international Communist conspiracy" at work; there are no stores being burned; there are no solipsistic students bellyaching about classes being suspended. The issues are crystal-clear: the armed, brutal, oppressive forces of the State stomping upon peaceful, unarmed, homesteading citizens. Anyone who fails to raise his voice in absolute condemnation of this reign of terror, anyone who equivocates or excuses or condones, can no longer call himself a libertarian. On the contrary, he thereby ranges himself with the forces of despotism; he becomes part of the Enemy.

TO OUR READERS:
Change Of Name

After we had launched *The Libertarian*, we discovered that a monthly mimeographed periodical with the same name emanating from New Jersey had been publishing for several years. To avoid confusion with this publication, we are hereby changing our name to *The Libertarian Forum*; no change is involved in policy or format.

Letter From
Washington

By Karl Hess

Where Are The Specifics?

Libertarianism is clearly the most, perhaps the only truly radical movement in America. It grasps the problems of society by the roots. It is not reformist in any sense. It is revolutionary in every sense.

Because so many of its people, however, have come from the right there remains about it at least an aura or, perhaps, miasma of defensiveness, as though its interests really center in, for instance, defending private property. The truth, of course, is that libertarianism wants to advance *principles* of property but that it in no way wishes to *defend*, willy nilly, all property which now is called private.

Much of that property is stolen. Much is of dubious title. All of it is deeply intertwined with an immoral, coercive state system which has condoned, built on, and profited from slavery; has expanded through and exploited a brutal and aggressive imperial and colonial foreign policy, and continues to hold the people in a roughly serf-master relationship to political-economic power concentrations.

Libertarians are concerned, first and foremost, with that most valuable of properties, the life of each individual. That is the property most brutally and constantly abused by state systems whether they are of the right or left. Property rights pertaining to material objects are seen by libertarians as stemming from and as importantly secondary to the right to own, direct, and enjoy one's own life and those appurtenances thereto which may be acquired *without coercion.*

Libertarians, in short, simply do not believe that theft is proper whether it is committed in the name of a state, a class, a crises, a credo, or a cliche.

This is a far cry from sharing common ground with those who want to create a society in which super capitalists are free to amass vast holdings and who say that that is ultimately the most important purpose of freedom. This is proto-heroic nonsense.

Libertarianism is a people's movement and a liberation movement. It seeks the sort of open, non-coercive society in which the people, the living, free, distinct people may voluntarily associate, dis-associate, and, as they see fit, participate in the decisions affecting their lives. This means a truly free market in everything from ideas to idiosyncrasies. It means people free *collectively* to organize the resources of their immediate community or individualistically to organize them; it means the freedom to have a community-based and supported judiciary where wanted, none where not, or private arbitration services where that is seen as most desirable. The same with police. The same with schools, hospitals, factories, farms, laboratories, parks, and pensions. Liberty means the right to shape your own institutions. It opposes the right of those institutions to shape you simply because of accreted power or gerontological status.

For many, however, these root principles of radical libertarianism will remain mere abstractions, and even suspect, until they are developed into aggressive, specific proposals.

There is scarcely anything radical about, for instance,

those who say that the poor should have a larger share of the Federal budget. That is reactionary, asking that the institution of state theft be made merely more palatable by distributing its loot to more sympathetic persons. Perhaps no one of sound mind could object more to giving Federal funds to poor people than to spending the money on the slaughter of Vietnamese peasant fighters. But to argue such relative merits must end being simply reformist and not revolutionary.

Libertarians could and should propose specific revolutionary tactics and goals which would have specific meaning to poor people and to all people; to analyze in depth and to demonstrate in example the meaning of liberty, revolutionary liberty to them.

I, for one, earnestly beseech such thinking from my comrades.

The proposals should take into account the revolutionary treatment of stolen 'private' and 'public' property in libertarian, radical, and revolutionary terms; the factors which have oppressed people so far, and so forth. Murray Rothbard and others have done much theoretical work along these lines but it can never be enough for just a few to shoulder so much of the burden.

Let me propose just a few examples of the sort of specific, revolutionary and radical questions to which members of our Movement might well address themselves.

--Land ownership and/or usage in a situation of declining state power. The Tijerina situation suggests one approach. There must be many others. And what about (realistically, not romantically) water and air pollution liability and prevention?

--Worker, share-owner, community roles or rights in productive facilities in terms of libertarian analysis and as specific proposals in a radical and revolutionary context. What, for instance, might or should happen to General Motors in a liberated society?

Of particular interest, to me at any rate, is focusing libertarian analysis and ingenuity on finishing the great unfinished business of the abolition of slavery. Simply setting slaves free, in a world still owned by their masters, obviously was an historic inequity. (Libertarians hold that the South should have been permitted to secede so that the slaves themselves, along with their Northern friends, could have built a revolutionary liberation movement, overthrown the masters, and thus shaped the reparations of revolution.) Thoughts of reparations today are clouded by concern that it would be taken out against innocent persons who in no way could be connected to former oppression. There is an area where that could be avoided: in the use of government-'owned' lands and facilities as items of exchange in compensating the descendants of slaves and making it possible for them to participate in the communities of the land, finally, as equals and not wards.

Somewhere, I must assume, there is a libertarian who, sharing the idea, might work out a good and consistent proposal for justice in that area.

Obviously the list is endless. But the point is finite and finely focused.

With libertarianism now developing as a Movement, it earnestly and urgently requires innovative proposals, radical and specific goals, and a revolutionary agenda which can translate its great and enduring principles into timely and commanding courses of possible and even practical action.

"What country can preserve its liberties if their rulers are not warned from time to time that their people preserve the spirit of resistance? Let them take arms."

--Thomas Jefferson, 1787

CONFISCATION AND THE HOMESTEAD PRINCIPLE

Karl Hess's brilliant and challenging article in this issue raises a problem of specifics that ranges further than the libertarian movement. For example, there must be hundreds of thousands of "professional" anti-Communists in this country. Yet not one of these gentry, in the course of their fulminations, has come up with a specific plan for de-Communization. Suppose, for example, that Messers. Brezhnev and Co. become converted to the principles of a free society; they than ask our anti-Communists, all right, *how* do we go about de-socializing? What could our anti-Communists offer them?

This question has been essentially answered by the exciting developments of Tito's Yugoslavia. Beginning in 1952, Yugoslavia has been de-socializing at a remarkable rate. The principle the Yugoslavs have used is the libertarian "homesteading" one: the state-owned factories to the workers that work in them! The nationalized plants in the "public" sector have all been transferred in virtual ownership to the specific workers who work in the particular plants, thus making them producers' coops, and moving rapidly in the direction of individual shares of virtual ownership to the individual worker. What other practicable route toward destatization could there be? The principle in the Communist countries should be: land to the peasants and the factories to the workers, thereby getting the property out of the hands of the State and into private, homesteading hands.

The homesteading principle means that the way that unowned property gets into private ownership is by the principle that this property justly belongs to the person who finds, occupies, and transforms it by his labor. This is clear in the case of the pioneer and virgin land. But what of the case of stolen property?

Suppose, for example, that A steals B's horse. Then C comes along and takes the horse from A. Can C be called a thief? Certainly not, for we cannot call a man a criminal for stealing goods from a thief. On the contrary, C is performing a *virtuous* act of confiscation, for he is depriving thief A of the fruits of his crime of aggression, and he is at least returning the horse to the innocent "private" sector and out of the "criminal" sector. C has done a noble act and should be applauded. Of course, it would be still better if he returned the horse to B, the original victim. But even if he does not, the horse is far more justly in C's hands than it is in the hands of A, the thief and criminal.

Let us now apply our libertarian theory of property to the case of property in the har¹s of, or derived from, the State apparatus. The libertarian sees the State as a giant gang of organized criminals, who live off the theft called "taxation" and use the proceeds to kill, enslave, and generally push people around. Therefore, any property in the hands of the State is in the hands of thieves, and should be liberated as quickly as possible. *Any* person or group who liberates such property, who confiscates or appropriates it from the State, is performing a virtuous act and a signal service to the cause of liberty. In the case of the State, furthermore, the victim is not readily identifiable as B, the horse-owner. All taxpayers, all draftees, all victims of the State have been mulcted. How to go about returning all this property to the taxpayers? What proportions should be used in this terrific tangle of robbery and injustice that we have all suffered at the hands of the State? Often, the most practical method of de-statizing is simply to grant the moral right of ownership on the person or group who seizes the property from the State. Of this group, the most morally deserving are the ones who are already using the property but who have no moral complicity in the State's act of aggression. These people then become the "homesteaders" of the stolen property and hence the rightful owners.

Take, for example, the State universities. This is property built on funds stolen from the taxpayers. Since the State has not found or put into effect a way of returning ownership of this property to the taxpaying public, the proper owners of this university are the "homesteaders", those who have already been using and therefore "mixing their labor" with the facilities. The prime consideration is to deprive the thief, in this case the State, as quickly as possible of the ownership and control of its ill-gotten gains, to return the property to the innocent, private sector. This means student and/or faculty ownership of the universities.

As between the two groups, the students have a prior claim, for the students have been paying at least some amount to support the university whereas the faculty suffer from the moral taint of living off State funds and thereby becoming to some extent a part of the State apparatus.

The same principle applies to nominally "private" property which really comes from the State as a result of zealous lobbying on behalf of the recipient. Columbia University, for example, which receives nearly two-thirds of its income from government, is only a "private" college in the most ironic sense. It deserves a similar fate of virtuous homesteading confiscation.

But if Columbia University, what of General Dynamics? What of the myriad of corporations which are integral parts of the military-industrial complex, which not only get over half or sometimes virtually all their revenue from the government but also participate in mass murder? What are *their* credentials to "private" property? Surely less than zero. As eager lobbyists for these contracts and subsidies, as co-founders of the garrison state, they deserve confiscation and reversion of their property to the *genuine* private sector as rapidly as possible. To say that their "private" property must be respected is to say that the property stolen by the horsethief and the murdered must be "respected".

But how then do we go about destatizing the entire mass of government property, as well as the "private property" of General Dynamics? All this needs detailed thought and inquiry on the part of libertarians. One method would be to turn over ownership to the homesteading workers in the particular plants; another to turn over pro-rata ownership to the individual taxpayers. But we must face the fact that it *might* prove the most practical route to first nationalize the property as a prelude to redistribution. Thus, how could the ownership of General Dynamics be transferred to the deserving taxpayers without first being nationalized enroute? And, further more, *even if* the government should decide to nationalize General Dynamics--without compensation, of course-- *per se* and *not* as a prelude to redistribution to the taxpayers, this is not immoral or something to be combatted. For it would only mean that one gang of thieves--the government--would be confiscating property from another previously cooperating gang, the corporation that has lived off the government. I do not often agree with John Kenneth Galbraith, but his recent suggestion to nationalize businesses which get more than 75% of their revenue from government, or from the military, has considerable merit. Certainly it does not mean aggression against *private* property, and, furthermore, we could expect a considerable diminution of zeal from the military-industrial complex if much of the profits were taken out of war and plunder. And besides, it would make the American military machine less efficient, being governmental, and that is surely all to the good. But why stop at 75%? Fifty per cent seems to be a reasonable

(Continued on page 4)

CONFISCATION — *(Continued from page 3)*

cutoff point on whether an organizati.. is largely public or largely private.

And there is another consideration. Dow Chemical, for example, has been heavily criticized for making napalm for the U.S. military machine. The percentage of its sales coming from napalm is undoubtedly small, so that on a percentage basis the company may not seem very guilty; but napalm is and can only be an instrument of mass murder, and therefore Dow Chemical is heavily up to its neck in being an accessory and hence a co-partner in the mass murder in Vietnam. No percentage of sales, however small, can absolve its guilt.

This brings us to Karl's point about slaves. One of the tragic aspects of the emancipation of the serfs in Russia in 1861 was that while the serfs gained their personal freedom, the land--their means of production and of life, their land was retained under the ownership of their feudal masters. The land *should* have gone to the serfs themselves, for under the homestead principle they had tilled the land and deserved its title. Furthermore, the serfs were entitled to a host of *reparations* from their masters for the centuries of oppression and exploitation. The fact that the land remained in the hands of the lords paved the way inexorably for the Bolshevik Revolution, since the revolution that had freed the serfs remained unfinished.

The same is true of the abolition of slavery in the United States. The slaves gained their freedom, it is true, but the land, the plantations that they had tilled and therefore deserved to own under the homestead principle, remained in the hands of their former masters. Furthermore, no reparations were granted the slaves for their oppression out of the hides of their masters. Hence the abolition of slavery remained unfinished, and the seeds of a new revolt have remained to intensify to the present day. Hence, the great importance of the shift in Negro demands from greater welfare handouts to "reparations", reparations for the years of slavery and exploitation and for the failure to grant the Negroes their land, the failure to heed the Radical abolitionist's call for "40 acres and a mule" to the former slaves. In many cases, moreover, the old plantations and the heirs and descendants of the former slaves can be identified, and the reparations can become highly specific indeed.

Alan Milchman, in the days when he was a brilliant young libertarian activist, first pointed out that libertarians had misled themselves by making their main dichotomy "government" vs. "private" with the former bad and the latter good. Government, he pointed out, is after all not a mystical entity but a group of individuals, "private" individuals if you will, acting in the manner of an organized criminal gang. But this means that there may also be "private" criminals

as well as people directly affiliated with the government. What we libertarians object to, then, is not *government* per se but crime, what we object to is unjust or criminal property titles; what we are for is not "private" property *per se* but just, innocent, non-criminal private property. It is justice vs. injustice, innocence vs. criminality that must be our major libertarian focus.

A Semi-Monthly Newsletter

THE
Libertarian Forum

Joseph R. Peden, Publisher	Washington Editor, Karl Hess	Murray N. Rothbard, Editor

VOL. I, NO. VII   JULY 1, 1969   35¢

The Meaning Of Revolution

In his vitally important article in this issue, Karl Hess properly refers to the genuine libertarian movement as a "revolutionary" movement. This raises the point that very few Americans understand the true meaning of the word "revolution".

Most people, when they hear the word "revolution", think immediately and only of direct acts of physical confrontation with the State: raising barricades in the streets, battling a cop, storming the Bastille or other government buildings. But this is only one small part of revolution. Revolution is a mighty, complex, long-run process, a complicated movement with many vital parts and functions. It is the pamphleteer writing in his study, it is the journalist, the political club, the agitator, the organizer, the campus activist, the theoretician, the philanthropist. It is all this and much more. Each person and group has its part to play in this great complex movement.

Let us take, for example, the major model for libertarians in our time: the great classical liberal, or better, "classical radical", revolutionary movement of the seventeenth, eighteenth, and nineteenth centuries. These our ancestors created a vast, sprawling, and brilliant revolutionary movement, not only in the United States but throughout the Western world, that lasted for several centuries. This was the movement largely responsible for radically changing history, for almost destroying history as it was previously known to man. For before these centuries, the history of man, with one or two luminous exceptions, was a dark and gory record of tyranny and despotism, a record of various absolute States and monarchs crushing and exploiting their underlying populations, largely peasants, who lived a brief and brutish life at bare subsistence, devoid of hope or promise. It was a classical liberalism and radicalism that brought to the mass of people that hope and that promise, and which launched the great process of fulfillment. All that man has achieved today, in progress, in hope, in living standards, we can attribute to that revolutionary movement, to that "revolution". This great revolution was our father; it is now our task to complete its unfinished promise.

This classical revolutionary movement was made up of many parts. It was the libertarian theorists and ideologists, the men who created and wove the strands of libertarian theory and principle: the La Boeties, the Levellers in seventeenth-century England, the eighteenth-century radicals-- the *philosophes*, the physiocrats, the English radicals, the Patrick Henrys and Tom Paines of the American Revolution, the James Mills and Cobdens of nineteenth-century England,

the Jacksonians and abolitionists and Thoreaus in America, the Bastiats and Molinaris in France. The vital scholarly work of Caroline Robbins and Bernard Bailyn, for example, has demonstrated the continuity of libertarian classical radical ideas and movements, from the seventeenth-century English revolutionaries down through the American Revolution a century and a half later.

Theories blended into activist movements, rising movements calling for individual liberty, a free-market economy, the overthrow of feudalism and mercantilist statism, an end to theocracy and war and their replacement by freedom and international peace. Once in a while, these movements erupted into violent "revolutions" that brought giant steps in the direction of liberty: the English Civil War, the American Revolution, the French Revolution. (Barrington Moore, Jr. has shown the intimate connection between these violent revolutions and the freedoms that the Western world has been able to take from the State.) The result was enormous strides for freedom and the prosperity unleashed by the consequent Industrial Revolution. The barricades, while important, were just one small part of this great process.

Socialism is neither genuinely radical nor truly revolutionary. Socialism is a reactionary reversion, a self-contradictory attempt to achieve classical radical ends liberty, progress, the withering away or abolition of the State, by using old-fashioned statist and Tory means: collectivism and State control. Socialism is a New Toryism doomed to rapid failure whenever it is tried, a failure demonstrated by the collapse of central planning in the Communist countries of Eastern Europe. Only libertarianism is truly radical. Only we can complete the unfinished revolution of our great forebears, the bringing of the world from the realm of despotism into the realm of freedom. Only we can replace the governance of men by the administration of things.

"The right of revolution is an inherent one. When people are oppressed by their government, it is a natural right they enjoy to relieve themselves of the oppression, if they are strong enough, either by a withdrawal from it, or by overthrowing it and substituting a government more acceptable."
--Ulysses S. Grant, 1885

Letter From Washington

By Karl Hess

What The Movement Needs

This may well be a long, cool summer of consolidation. The political establishment will be seeking to consolidate its power behind an advancing wave of law-and-order blue-nose, Constitutional 'constructionism'. (Constructionism is a new code word for reading the Constitution as instrument of state power rather than individual freedom.)

Radical opponents of the state also will be consolidating. The picture with SDS is now one of building new structures on either side of a schism. YAF is said to be facing a similar task with pro-state "trads" under lively assault from those with at least anti-statist tendencies if not fully fledged libertarian positions. The Resistance, after Staughton Lynd's moving plea for a "new beginning", will be attempting to broaden its base far beyond that of fighting the draft. And, of course, the Panthers will simply be trying to stay alive.

For libertarianism, burgeoning now as a movement rather than merely a mood, it will be a crucial time, testing the difference between the dedicated and the dilettante.

The young people in the movement are irrepressible and, in the long term, so is the movement. In the short term, however, much of its velocity will depend upon whether it attracts, along with its great and growing ranks of young militants, those few men of substance who, in the early stages of most movements, can make a difference of years in the movement's development. Engels' financial support of Marx is an example. The few who supported the early spokesmen of the New Left are a latter-day example. There are few similar examples on the right, interestingly enough, inasmuch as right-wing support almost exclusively has been toward the institutionalization of a currently vested interest (i. e. anti-Communism, corporate protectionism, class or race privilege, religion) rather than in the development of a new movement.

Because, therefore, there may be a man of substance, and libertarian values, somewhere, who, watching the movement develop, may want to participate in it rather than just talk about it, some words of friendly (dare we say comradely?) advice may be in order.

First there is the simple responsibility to be serious. Taking a pioneering interest without following through could be more destructive of morale than silence. For young people, particularly, the idea of faintheartedness may be the hardest of all to take. There always is hope that heroes will come along and it would be better to have that hope remain unrequited than to have it dashed.

Then there is resistance to a familiar syndrome, the notion of "one thing for sure, we can't do the whole job alone." There are two points to make about this to anyone who may appear as a serious supporter of the libertarian movement.
1. You may have to.
2. If so, you can.

The first point, of course, is that it shouldn't make any difference how many are similarly interested. For an individualist and a libertarian, surely, his own interest should be sufficient to the action. If only one such person appears, that is 100% more than we have now anyway!

The second point is simply a citation of the need of the most effective use of what resources are available rather than any despair that they are limited. If they are all that there is, then prudence says only "use them well." And courage says, only, "use them!"

One consideration arising from that is the need to use available resources to produce a well-rounded *base*, if nothing else, hoping that on the base, subsequently, new support will arise. At the same time, securing a base also helps secure the on-going momentum of the movement itself, by recognizing that it *is* a movement and that it does require not just casual advancement but hard, full-time organizing, propagandizing, crusading and so forth.

If, on the other hand, there already was a more general sort of support available, the movement could afford what is now a luxury: the support of very specific researches or programs. As it stands, the urge to build various super-structures before the movement is firmly based *as* a movement is to tactically do just what such imprudence would do tectonically: create a top-heavy structure which would topple in any stiff wind.

One course, in forming the base, would be to inventory needs and evaluate priority versus cost and so forth. Practical as well as visionary men should examine this agenda carefully lest the caution of the one extinguish the beacons of the other or the passions of the latter ignore the prudence of the former.

Some of the items which should, in my view, earnestly be considered are these:

—Full-time movement organizers and co-ordinators, at least on a regional basis.

—Creation of even the most modest East Coast 'center' for libertarian studies to fill an incredible geographic vaccuum. Although the West Coast has seen the development of such centers, the East remains barren.

—Support of our own movement activists, the spearhead people whose speaking on campus, pamphleteering, even arrests and trials, provide the sort of excitement centers which, to cite a compelling example, turned the New Left from a phrase by C. Wright Mills into the wedge which has now opened wide the entire range of radical, revolutionary developments in America.

—Entry into new media, such as films, for libertarian ideas as well as on-going encouragement for those who can break into the regular media. How many good libertarian books or articles go down the drain each year simply because potentially productive people cannot take the time, or afford to do the work on a speculative basis? The number, no matter how small, is too large if the libertarian mood is to turn into the libertarian movement.

—A campus organization. Plans for the Radical Libertarian Alliance already are well advanced *as plans*. But practical organizational work, production of recruiting materials and so forth requires some practical support which the non-existent means of the founding members simply cannot provide. This does not mean that R. L. A. will not move at all, without added support. It will move, indeed, no matter what. Its founding chapters and members are not to be stopped. But its people know full well that they will not move with the summer-lightning speed of, say, SDS or YAF because, as in the one case, it does not have (thankfully) the relatively well-heeled zeal of a Progressive Labor Party to send travelers across the country and keep the literature coming or, as in the other case, it does not offer eccentric millionaires a chance to advance their own quirky causes by buying the energies of the young. R. L. A., to be precise about this point, would rather poop along on pennies than take *anybody's* money if it came marked with any word other than LIBERTY.

--Travel support for permitting libertarians with something to say to say it where the action is. The fact that the several outstanding libertarian-SDSers couldn't even afford the train fare to the Chicago convention is just another evidence of wasting major opportunities for want of minor investments.

Not one of those suggestions is made in a spirit of exclusion or primacy. They cover areas which seem common-sensical but they are intended to convey, first and foremost, a sense of base-building as opposed to panacea-pathing. The libertarian who says that this action or that action is all that should be taken or that this or that will 'solve' everything is avoiding action, not taking it.

Fixated, narrowly focused approaches may build egos but they can scarcely build movements. The purpose of a revolutionary, in one of the truisms of our time, is to make the revolution. To a libertarian that should mean that the advancement of liberty and the opposition to coercion by all means possible and necessary. It means each person making his part of the revolution as he can best do it, recognizing always that each part is subsumed under the vision of a movement. Many of us may be always restricted to just doing one job or another in the movement. None of us, happily, if we retain faith with liberty itself, will waste our time seeking to be leaders or wanting to be.

We do not want to lead or be led. We want to be free.

We now sense in a way that gives us ties with men in many lands and in many postures of political development, that being free always will be a chancy, iffy, and very conditional transitory condition until the institutions of coercive power have been brought down.

We have advanced through the stage when many thought that freedom could be found simply by retiring to a hilltop somewhere far distant. We know that such a hilltop may be by next Tuesday the site of another government radar station, just as the valley below it may be a detention camp.

We now know that men who want to be free cannot run forever. Sometime, somewhere they must stand firm--and fight, not as the state's agents fight, with bloody hands and blazing eyes, but as free men fight, in a movement of resistance, with respect for life, each man as he can and each man as he will.

My overall point is that a movement demands many elements. It requires public heroes and private genius; it must work out in the streets as though it were the confident spearhead of a triumphant cause, it must work in garrets and offices as though there would be no tomorrow, it must sometimes bite its tongue at tactical errors, loving the sinner even while deploring the sin.

It must seek its friends in other lands, creating a new citizenry of un-bordered liberty. It must create and recreate its literature. It must teach its young and, equally important, it must *find* its young.

It must sustain its weary, heal its wounded, and protect its cadre. And, above all, it must know its own heart and mind and be aware of itself *as* a Movement. Finally, it must have a sense of time and place, knowing where the world is and

not nostalgically looking back at where it was. And if it errs it should err on the side of dedication and vision, not on the side of inaction.

Libertarians are not determinists who feel that unseen, mystic forces move men and history in inexorable patterns, up and down fated graphs. Libertarians, being radicals, know that men can move history, that Man *is* history, and that men can grasp their own fate, at the root, and advance it.

Interestingly and compellingly, libertarians have been through much of this before in this lovely but looted land. The first American revolution, just as with the Russian, was almost a libertarian and not a statist victory. The victory, instead, of the Federalists, with their glib talk of "legal systems" and of measuring liberty in terms of special favors to those who would best "serve" society, was not a foregone conclusion any more than Stalin's victory was the end in Russia. Contrary forces now seethe in both lands.

Also, in the days before the first American revolution, men heard the same arguments we hear today--that we could never beat the system, so why try; why risk oppression by being uppity; why not keep on trying to go through channels and why not chuck it all because the majority of people don't want any trouble anyway.

In those days it was erring on the side of militancy and civil disobedience that gave libertarians the opportunity even to speak and to speculate. Caution then would have meant an even deeper gloom today (just look at the Mother Country!).

We are again at such a time and place.

You--whoever you are!--now have it in your power to some extent or another move history and advance libertarianism as a Movement and not a mere moral mutter.

This summer, then, should be the time when you decide just how seriously you actually do take the times--and yourself.

DEFENSE FUNDS

As the oppressive reign of the White Terror begins to roll over the land, defense of the elementary civil liberties of dissenters becomes ever more acutely necessary. Two new defense funds merit our interest and our contribution.

One is for bail money and legal and medical expenses for the arrested and wounded in the People's Park massacre. Contributions should be sent to: The People's Park Defense Fund, c/o Free Church, 2200 Parker St., Berkeley, Calif.

The other is for the defense of the eight political dissenters at Chicago last year who have been shamefully indicted by the federal authorities for "conspiracy to promote disorder and riot" under the infamous "anti-riot" Title XVIII of the Civil Rights Act of 1968. The entire spectrum of laws against "conspiracy", along with "incitement", are methods of suppressing, not concrete action but political defense and freedom of speech. Laws against "conspiracy" have no part in libertarian law, which is only concerned with defending persons and their rights against acts of invasion. Contributions toward the costly defense against this mass indictment may be made out to "Chicago Defense Fund", and mailed to the Capital Committee to Defend the Conspiracy, 28 E. Jackson Blvd., Chicago, Ill. 60604.

Recommended Reading

Faustino Ballve,*Essentials of Economics* (Irvington-on-Hudson, New York; Foundation for Economic Education, $3.00 cloth, $1.50 paper). The best single brief introduction to economics. Written from an Austrian rather than Chicagoite viewpoint. Fills an extremely important need.

Andrew Kopkind and James Ridgeway, "Law and Power in Washington", *Hard Times* (June 16-23, 1969). A brilliant muckraking dissection of the politics not only of Abe Fortas but of Fortas' important Washington law firm. Its editors are New Left radicals; this impressive weekly newsletter has improved considerably since the departure of Old Left liberal R. Sherrill. *Hard Times* is available for $7.50 per year, $6 for

students, at 80 Irving Place, New York, N. Y. 10003.

Frederic Bastiat, *Economic Sophisms* (Foundation for Economic Education, $2.00 paper), and *Selected Essays in Political Economy* (Foundation for Economic Education, $2.00 paper). The most significant writings of the great 19th-century libertarian *laissez-faire* economist. Both highly recommended, but the latter more important as containing more systematic articles.

Benjamin Page, "Signals from North Korea", *The Nation* (May 19, 1969). Indispensable if you want to find out what's going on at the next hot spot which the U. S. might be cooking up in Asia.

Libertarian Forum Associates

The deepest thanks of The Libertarian Forum go to the newest group of those generous enough to become Libertarian Forum Associates by subscribing at $15 or more:

William L. Brown	Glen Ellyn, Ill.
Kenneth Berger	Palos Verdes, Calif.
Ronald Hamowy	Stanford, Calif.
Leonard P. Liggio	Bronx, N. Y.
Felix Morley	Gibson Island, Md.
John V. Peters	Canal Zone, Panama
Richard Riemann	Berkeley, Calif.
Robert J. Smith	Red Bank, N. J.

SUBSCRIBE NOW
Please enter a subscription for:

Name _____

Street _____

City _____ State _____ Zip _____

Subscription is $7.00 per year.
Libertarian Forum Associate subscription is $15.00 or more.
Wholesale Bulk rates are 20¢ per copy with a discount of
10% for over 50 copies.
THE LIBERTARIAN FORUM
Box 341   Madison Square Station
New York, New York 10010

The Libertarian Forum
BOX 341
MADISON SQUARE STATION
NEW YORK, NEW YORK 10010

Published on the first and fifteenth of every month   Subscription rate: $7.00 per year; Student subscription rate: $5.00 per year

A Semi-Monthly Newsletter

THE
Libertarian Forum

Joseph R. Peden, Publisher   Washington Editor, Karl Hess   Murray N. Rothbard, Editor

VOL. I, NO. VIII   JULY 15, 1969   35¢

Nixon's Decisions

After half a year of painful agonizing, of backing and filling, of puttering delays, the pattern of decisions of the Nixon Administration is finally becoming clear. It is not a pretty picture. In every single case, the Nixon Administration has managed to come down on the wrong side, on the side of burgeoning statism.

In Vietnam, *the war goes on* . A simple statement, which the American public hasn't seemed to understand ever since the negotiations began in Paris last May. The United States has been using the negotiations as a smoke-screen cover behind which to step up the war in South Vietnam, where of course the war began. But first the initial euphoria led Americans, even most of the young anti-war activists, to proclaim that the war was over. And then everyone waited to "give Nixon a chance" to end the war. How long must we wait for this "chance"? How long must we wait to proclaim that the Emperor has no clothes, and that the war goes on? The peace forces in Congress are beginning at last to wake up, and indications are that the anti-war movement will rouse itself from its year-long sleep by this fall. Disgusted by Nixon's deliberate delays, the National Liberation Front has finally formed the Provisional Revolutionary Government of South Vietnam which has already been recognized by many countries. The final step in the NLF plan will be to form a provisional coalition government of all anti-imperialist and neutralist forces, which will deliver the final hammer-blows that will shatter the Saigon puppet regime.

In the vital area of the draft, Nixon put on a typically Nixonian performance. After muttering about replacing the draft with a volunteer army and appointing a committee to study the subject, Nixon finally came out in favor of a lottery-draft, the old Kennedy scheme which would replace the current selective slavery system with slavery-by-chance. Hardly an improvement. But, once again, the smokescreen of reform befuddles the public into thinking that a significant improvement is being made.

The military-industrial state has proceeded apace, and the arms race stepped up with the Nixon decision to go ahead with the ABM and MIRV missile boondoggles. Chemical and bacteriological research and experiments continue despite some public exposure. In the field of civil liberties, we shudder in expectation of Burger Court reversals of the excellent landmark libertarian decisions of the Warren Court. The Administration continues to speak about crackdowns on student dissidents, and Deputy Attorney-General Kleindienst spoke of rounding up student dissenters and placing them in "detention camps". And now the Depart-

ment of Justice, in a memorandum submitted in the infamous trial of the Chicago 8, brazenly asserts the right of the President or his aides to invade illegally the privacy and property of Americans through electronic snooping if the President in his wisdom and majesty should decide that the people spied upon might be acting against some form of "national security", foreign or domestic.

In the sphere of economics the Nixon Administration had been highly touted among conservatives. It was supposed to herald a return to the free-market and a check upon galloping inflation through monetary restriction. Again, nothing has happened. The much publicized monetary tightening has been half-hearted at best, and provides no real test of the effectiveness of monetary policy. For the Administration has been doing precisely what its spokesmen had been deriding the Democrats for doing: trying to "fine-tune" the economy, trying to cut back ever so gently on inflation so as not to precipitate any recession. But it can't be done. If restrictionist measures were ever sharp enough to check the inflationary boom, they would also be strong enough to generate a temporary recession. Furthermore, the basic Nixon Administration commitment to inflation is revealed by its devotion to the world inflationary Special Drawing Rights, and its refusal to consider any rise in the gold price, much less any return to the gold standard.

Instead of cutting back on its *own* monetary inflation (generated by Federal Reserve purchases of government securities), the Administration has perpetuated the tyranny and the red herring of the 10% income surcharge, another statist heritage of the Johnson Administration. What happens is that the federal government pumps new money into the economy through Federal Reserve expansion, and *then*, when the people begin to spend their new money and prices begin to rise, the government proceeds to denounce the public for "spending too much" and levies higher income taxes to "sop up their excess purchasing power"--thus levying both a swindle and a double burden upon the long-suffering public. Spending and government fiscal policy, furthermore, are irrelevant to price inflation, which is determined by the supply and demand of money. And even if it were *not* irrelevant, it is surely unmitigated gall to assume that a *tax*, a payment for which the consumer receives no service in return, is somehow worse than a *price* , for which the consumer at least receives a product in exchange. To advocate higher taxes in order to check higher prices is like advocating a person's murder in order to cure him of disease.

(Continued on page 4)

SDS — Two Views

I: Liberated Zone

The chickens came home to roost for SDS. The SDS national convention was in the process of being taken over by the Progressive Labor Party when SDS split in two in June. By its ability to move its members to key national meetings PL was in a position to take control of the national convention which most SDS members avoid as irrelevant to the real political work which occurs on the local level. SDS chapters are independent of the national convention and disregard its decisions.

PL as a Communist organization was welcomed by the trade union wing of the SDS old guard who wished in 1966 to counterbalance the overwhelming flood of students who had joined SDS to oppose the Vietnam war. Committed to clearly radical anti-imperialism rather than Marxist reformism, the mass infusion of youth had already brought about the election of newcomer Carl Oglesby as SDS president in 1965.

PL had made original contributions to the black liberation struggle, student freedom and support of freedom of travel to Cuba. When the May 2nd Movement was founded in the spring of 1964 to oppose the dangerously escalating American intervention in Vietnam by sending medical aid to the NLF, PL members participated in its work. In 1965 when M2M played a leading role in developing a consciousness of opposition to the draft while SDS leaders fumbled the issue, PL members tried to restrain this radicalism and replace anti-imperialist struggle by a trade union fight for socialism. While M2M members viewed Lin Piao's "Long live the victory of people's war" as the crucial analysis for anti-imperialist struggle, PL adopted the sectarian and trade unionist socialism associated with the anti-Mao Communists in China. PL forced the dissolution of M2M in order to work in the wider recruiting ground of SDS, but many PL members in M2M, viewing this action as Stalinist, resigned from PL to continue the struggle against the draft and imperialism.

PL had come to oppose the NLF and Ho Chi Minh as capitalist, black liberation as nationalist rather than socialist, Fidel Castro and the Cuban revolution because of the 26th of July Movement was no socialist, Castro was not a Communist and Cuba not a Marxist State. Clearly PL was a crippling counterweight to the revolutionary mass of students in SDS. But, the trade unionist SDS old guard was ousted at the 1966 Clear Lake, Iowa convention by "Prairie Power", an anarchist trend that swept in from the trans-Mississippi Great Plains region. Although increasingly militant against the draft and university complicity in the war, SDS was held back by PL's conservatism which fears alienating trade union workers by 'adventurous' anti-war action.

The 1968 East Lansing, Mich. SDS convention met in a crisis situation. PL paralyzed the convention, and sought to deflect SDS from anti-war action to a Worker-Student Alliance. SDS national leadership found itself unable to challenge PL effectively. Strong opposition to PL was presented by the SDS anarchist groups whose many black banners of libertarianism were rallying standards against PL. Finally, a lengthy criticism of PL was launched in which former M2M members took a leading role. As a result PL's attempt to elect members to the SDS national committee was defeated by a narrow margin.

The warning of these events did not effectively penetrate the SDS national leadership. The three national officers ultimately split into three different directions. One became allied with PL, which gained supporters because it empha-

(Continued on page 3)

II: Continue The Struggle

There is no question about the fact that the PL cancer had to be excised. In structure, PL was imposing upon a previously open and warm-hearted movement the rigid party discipline and the manipulative maneuverings of a typical Marxist-Stalinist cadre. In content, PL had become systematically counter-revolutionary; every struggle, whether it be for black national self-determination, national liberation against U. S. imperialism, against ROTC and the draft and the war in Vietnam, for student power or the People's Park, every one of these struggles was hampered or seriously crippled by PL's opposition, in the name of the sainted Marxian "working class" and because the "working class wouldn't like it." In the end it became clear that PL and its WSA satellites would have to go.

The problem is that in the course of this injection of PL and the reactive battle against it, SDS might have been poisoned permanently. For in too many quarters, especially in the vocal national leadership, the old 1966-67 libertarian spirit had been replaced by the virus of Marxism-Stalinism. The mere excising of PL is not nearly enough to insure healthy survival; continuing struggle is necessary to save the "old" SDS.

For while the virtue of the old SDS is that it had an open libertarian spirit rather than a dogmatic Marxian ideology, this very absence of positive theory left a vacuum which, inevitably, Marxism came to fill. For in the course of struggling against PL's invasion, too many of the "New Left" opponents of PL began to adopt their enemy's ideology, to call themselves "communists" (even if with a "small c"), and to take on more and more of the trappings of Marxism and socialism. The most infected group within the newly purged SDS is the "Factory Faction" or the "RYM-2" group, headed by Mike Klonsky and Bob Avakian. The Klonsky clique, while being worshippers of the Panthers, place major emphasis on student permeation and conversion of the industrial working class--probably the most reactionary group in the country today. The Klonsky clique also wants to convert SDS into a Marxist-Stalinist cadre organization--a fate which would be equally as bad as becoming a Progressive Labor front. While it is true that the Factory Faction was defeated in the election of officers of the purged SDS, it still remains a menace, especially for its working-class ideology.

Another irritant within the new SDS is the Trotskyite-Draperite Independent Socialist Club, which, like PL, hurled nearly all of its members into SDS and into voting at the national convention. Dogmatically Marxist and so "third camp" as to oppose national liberation struggles, the ISC remains a danger in the wings; its power to manipulate and destroy was well seen last year when it showed itself able, despite being a tiny minority, to control completely and thereby in effect to wreck the fledgling Peace and Freedom Party.

Leonard Liggio has mentioned uncritical "Panthermania" as another large continuing problem for SDS. A further problem, inherently absurd but growing as a menace because nearly everyone in the movement has been too chicken to fight it, is the hokum of the "women's liberation struggle". The women's liberation movement is *not* a rational and sensible battle against discrimination against women in employment, or against the "feminine mystique". These positions are scorned by the women's liberationists as akin to "white liberalism" and "integrationism". Insisting on a total analogy with black liberation, the women's liberationists claim that women, too, are systematically oppressed

(Continued on page 3)

CONTINUE THE STRUGGLE — *(Continued from page 2)*

by men and that therefore a separate women's power struggle is needed against this oppression. This idea seems to me absurd, and probably at least as good a case could be made for the view that *men* are oppressed and exploited by parasitic women (e.g. through divorce and alimony laws). But, at any rate, the insistence on analogy with the black movement is even more absurd, for the logical conclusion of the women's liberation struggle would then be . . . women's nationalism or separatism. Are we supposed to grant women an Amazonian state somewhere? Men-and-women, happily, are inherently "integrationist" and one may hope that they will remain that way.

In practice, women's liberation seems to boil down to (a) girls allowing themselves to be as ugly as possible; (b) conning the husband into taking care of the baby; and/or (c) a neo-Puritan ideology of crypto-Lesbianism. At any rate, in allowing women's liberationism to grow in influence unchallenged, SDS is in danger of making a mockery of its own principles.

But the major problem in SDS is that in order to expel PL, SDS found it necessary, for the first time, to lay down ideological requirements for membership. Until now, there have been no such requirements; now SDS has adopted two principles which every SDSer must support. These are the principles which Leonard Liggio cites in his article. There is nothing wrong with them; on the contrary, they set down an excellent line of support for national liberation struggles, both foreign and domestic, external and internal, against U. S. imperialism. But the problem is that if *good* principles can be adopted as conditions for membership, then so can bad principles, and it behooves us to be on guard against them.

In fact, waiting in the wings is an expanded set of "unity principles", which were introduced by the Klonsky clique, but happily rejected by the rank-and-file of "old" SDSers at the convention. But these five principles now get referred to the membership and the chapters for discussion, and it is imperative that at least "point 5" be rejected. Points 1 and 3 are essentially a reaffirmation of the already adopted two points: support for national liberation struggles, internal and external, against U. S. imperialism. Point 4 is an innocuous repudiation of red-baiting. So far so good. But Point 3 fully endorses the women's liberation hogwash, e.g.: "The struggle for women's liberation is a powerful force against U. S. imperialism. We are dedicated to fighting male supremacy, to destroying the physical and spiritual oppression of women by men . . . We encourage the formation of 'women's militias' to ensure the fulfillment of the program of total equality for women."

But if Point 3 should simply be defeated in the interests of sanity, Point 5 is intolerable for any libertarian. Point 5 is a flat-out commitment for socialism: "Recognizing that only through socialism, the public ownership and control of the means of producing wealth, can the people be freed from misery, we declare ourselves a socialist movement . . . Further; . . . socialism can only come through the leading role of the proletariat." Here is the sticking-point; no libertarian can be a member of an explicitly socialist organization, and one, furthermore, that would make socialism a condition of membership.

But in the meantime there is no cause for despair. The five points failed of adoption at the SDS convention. Furthermore, at Chicago a group of "anarchists, libertarians, and independent revolutionaries" met, symbolically at IWW hall, to form a separate third-force caucus. This group is still in SDS, and remains to continue struggle. That struggle now begins for the minds and the hearts of the local campus chapters, where the membership resides, and where Marxist-Stalinist sectarian factionalism is at a minimum. A particularly shining opportunity appears in those areas (such as New England, and parts of New York City and the

LIBERATED ZONE — *(Continued from page 2)*

sized the necessity of winning over the major part of the American people and opposed excesses of Panther-mania, which not only supports the Black Panthers against police repression but uncritically accepts the excessive posturing and the Stalinism that had developed since the jailing of their founder, Huey Newton.

This Panther-mania was created by Mike Klonsky, a second national officer acting as a self-appointed white nominator of the vanguard of the Black liberation movement. Emerging at the 1969 convention as the Revolutionary Youth Movement II, this position views the proletariat as the main force of revolution. The third national officer, Bernardine Dohrn, identified with the Action Faction which denies the leading role in revolutionary struggle to the industrial working class. Recognizing the validity of the revolutionary nationalism and right to self-determination of the Black and Spanish nations in America, they consider the international context--United States involvement in imperialist adventures--as central to undermining the monopoly system and creating the basis for revolutionary action. At the 1969 convention its position paper was called "Weatherman" after its slogan taken from an anti-authoritarian folk song-- "You don't need a weatherman to know which way the wind blows." The paper declared:

As imperialism struggles to hold together this decaying social fabric, it inevitably resorts to brute force and authoritarian ideology. People, especially young people, more and more find themselves in the iron grip of authoritarian institutions. Reaction against the pigs or teachers in the schools, welfare pigs or the army is generalizable and extends beyond the particular repressive institution to the society and the State as a whole. The legitimacy of the State is called into question for the first time in at least 30 years, and the anti-authoritarianism which characterizes the youth rebellion turns into rejection of the State, a refusal to be socialized into American society.

SDS split into two conventions at Chicago. One is dominated by PL's Worker-Student Alliance and includes the SDS Labor Committee. The New Left SDS includes about a dozen tendencies including the Action Faction, RYM II, Praxis Axis, ISC, Marxist humanists, old guard SDS populists, Prairie Power activists, anarchists and libertarians. (One SDSer's reaction to the convention was, "Us anarchists have got to get organized.")

The New Left SDS has adopted two basic principles at its convention: "One: We support the struggle of the Black and Latin colonies within the U. S. for national liberation and we recognize those nations' rights to self-determination (including the right to political secession if they desire it).

"Two: We support the struggle for national liberation of the people of South Vietnam, led by the National Liberation Front and Provisional Revolutionary Government of South Vietnam, led by President Ho Chi Minh . . . We support the right of all people to pick up the gun to free themselves from the brutal rule of U. S. imperialism."

Having been on the defensive for some time because of PL's dogmatic hegemony, the original movement spirit has re-emerged in SDS. The ultimate result of the 1969 New Left convention was the reaffirmation of native American radicalism as part of the international anti-imperialist revolution.

— Leonard P. Liggio

San Francisco Bay Area) where SDS chapters have been dominated by PL. Here, an opportunity arises to form new, libertarian-oriented "true" SDS chapters in competition to Progressive Labor.

Even more does the crisis in SDS provide a striking opportunity for the growing student libertarian movement to organize itself as a radical, militant movement free at last

(Continued on page 4)

NIXON'S DECISIONS — *(Continued from page 1)*

And waiting in the shadows, for the time when the income tax surcharge clearly will have failed--as it already has--lies the spectre of price and wage controls. Secretary of Treasury Kennedy has already threatened us with this spectre, this program for economic dictatorship which is at the opposite pole from anyone's definition of the free market. Not only is it dictatorship, *but it doesn't work,* only serving to add massive economic dislocations to the inflation that proceeds on its merry way. Why, one might ask, does powerful multi-millionaire businessman David Kennedy ponder price and wage controls? *Not* because he has been somehow brain-washed by "leftists" or because he suffers from capitalist guilt feelings, as conservatives like to

---

Recommended Reading

NEW AMERICAN REVIEW, NO. 6. (New American Library: Signet paperback, $1.25. $4.00 for four issues.) Editor T. Solataroff, of this paperback periodical, writes that the word that best expresses recent trends of thought is "libertarian". Particularly recommended in this issue are:

Jane Jacobs, "Why Cities Stagnate", an excellent and perceptive libertarian analysis of the vital importance of the free play of small, innovative entrepreneurs in a city's healthy growth. A keen attack on government planning and public housing while the same government prevents blacks and other urban dwellers from launching their own activities.

Emile Capouya, "The Red Flag and the Black": how anarchism has been reviving, particularly during the French revolution last year.

Paul Sweezy and Harry Magdoff, "The Merger Movement: A Study in Power", *Monthly Review* (June, 1969). A highly perceptive study of how the Established corporations have used the political arm to cripple and harass conglomerate mergers and their "new men" entrepreneurs. Why don't free-market economists have as keen a sense of political realities?

Tiziano Terzani, "Storming the Institutions", *The Nation* (June 16, 1969). Important article on the revolutionary situation that is rapidly developing in Italy--provides a good background to the current Italian political crisis.

---

believe. But because the business community is beginning to turn more and more to price and wage controls, as a means of using the power of government to clamp down on wage increases. For in the later stages of an inflationary boom, wages begin to catch up to price increases, and this has been happening in recent months. One more example of the present-day "partnership" between government and business!

In addition to this pattern of statism, the Nixon Administration, led by leading conservative-liberal Daniel Moynihan, is seriously considering proposing a nation-wide guaranteed annual income through a "negative income tax". Both conservatives and liberals have become enamoured of this scheme in recent years--a scheme that would inevitably cripple the incentives to work and earn and thereby wreck the American economy.

So what do you say about all this, Mr. "Libertarian-Conservative"--you who looked forward to a "Fabian" rollback of the State during the Nixon Administration, you who put your trust in all those Chicagoite and Randian advisers? When are you going to abandon your reformist illusions? When are you going to face up to the necessity for *real* opposition to government?

In the meanwhile, it has now become evident that everywhere, down the line, foreign and domestic, there is no difference whatsoever between the Johnson and the Nixon Administrations (even unto the repeated attacks on the "neo-isolationism" of the critics). The only difference is in style and personnel, the replacement of vulgar Texas cornpone by bland uptight hypocritical Northern WASP. And even in esthetic repulsiveness, it is very difficult to choose between them.

CONTINUE THE STRUGGLE — *(Continued from page 3)*

from any possibility of socialist subjugation. Radical libertarians are becoming strong enough to organize themselves into a separate movement for the first time. Already, there are two militantly radical libertarian organizations in the field: the Radical Libertarian Alliance, and the Student Libertarian Action Movement, centered in Arizona and with chapters in Georgia and Colorado. There is also a strong possibility that anarcho-libertarians increasingly persecuted in the Young Americans for Freedom will split off after the YAF national convention on Labor Day and form their own organization, freed at last from YAFite fascism. A merger of these three organizations could form a powerful force on the nation's campuses next year.

— M. N. R.

Also — Regular Washington Column By Karl Hess

Published on the first and fifteenth of every month   Subscription rate: $7.00 per year; Student subscription rate: $5.00 per year

A Semi-Monthly Newsletter

THE
Libertarian Forum

Joseph R. Peden, Publisher   Washington Editor, Karl Hess   Murray N. Rothbard, Editor

VOL. I, NO. IX   AUGUST 1, 1969   35¢

PEOPLE'S MONEY:

Revolt In Minnesota

The idea prevails that to favor gold or silver money is to be a mossback reactionary; nothing could be further from the truth. For gold (as well as silver) is the People's Money; it is a valuable commodity that has developed, on the free market, as the monetary means of exchange. Gold has been replaced, at the dictate of the State, by fiat paper—by pieces of paper issued and imprinted by the government. Gold cannot be produced very easily; it must be dug laboriously out of the ground. But if paper tickets are to be money, and the State is to have the sole power to issue these virtually costless tickets, then we are all at the mercy of this gang of legalized, sovereign counterfeiters. Yet this is the accepted monetary system of today.

Not only is this system of the State's having absolute control of our money been accepted by Establishment economists; it has been just as warmly endorsed by the powerful "Chicago" branch of free-market economists. Twenty years ago, almost all conservative, or free-market oriented, economists, favored a return to the gold standard and the elimination of fiat paper. But now the gold standard economists have almost all died out and been replaced by the glib, technically expert Chicagoites, to a man scoffers at gold and simple-minded endorsers of fiat paper. The gold standard has died from desertion of its cause by the right-wing and its economists. Numerous right-wingers who should know better yet continue to fawn upon Milton Friedman and his Chicagoites. Why? Presumably, because they have power and influence, and one never finds conservatives lacking these days when it comes to toadying the power.

In the midst of this monetary miasma, there has now come a voice from out of the past, from the Old Right, and it is one of the most heartwarming events of the year.

Two years ago, Jerome Daly, a citizen of Savage, Minnesota, a suburban town just south of Minneapolis, refused to make any further payments on the mortgage which he had owed to his bank. At his jury trial (First National Bank of Montgomery vs. Jerome Daly) in December, 1968 before Justice of the Peace Martin V. Mahoney, a farmer and carpenter by trade, at which the bank tried to repossess the property, Mr. Daly argued that he owed the bank nothing. Why? Because, the bank, in lending him money, had loaned him not *real* money but bank credit which the bank had created out of thin air. Not being genuine money, the credit was not a valid consideration, and therefore the contract was null and void. Daly argued that he did not owe the bank anything.

In making this seemingly preposterous argument, Jerome Daly was being a far better economist—and libertarian—

than anyone knew. For fractional reserve banking—now a system at the behest and direction of the Federal Reserve Banks—is, like fiat paper, legalized counterfeiting, the creation of claims which are invalid and impossible to redeem. Furthermore, Daly contended that this kind of creation of money by banks is illegal and unconstitutional.

Even more remarkable than Mr. Daly's thesis is that the jury unanimously held for him, and declared the mortgage null and void; and Justice Mahoney's supporting decision, delivered last Dec. 9, is a gem of radical assertion of the rights of the people and a thoroughgoing assault on the unwisdom and fraudulence and unconstitutionality of fractional reserve banking.

Bewildered, the First National Bank of Montgomery, Minnesota proceeded in routine fashion to file an appeal with Justice Mahoney for a higher court. But the catch is that in order to file an appeal, the plaintiff has to pay a fee of two dollars. Justice Mahoney, O happy day, refused to accept the appeal on January 22 because Federal Reserve Notes, which of course constituted the fee, are not lawful money. Only gold and silver coin, affirmed the judge, can be made legal tender, and therefore the fee for appeal had not been paid. Justice Mahoney followed this up with supporting memoranda on January 30 and February 5, which are heartwarming blends of sound economics and strict legal constructionism, and which also declared the unconstitutionality of the Federal Reserve Act and the National Banking Act, the capstones of our current interventionist and statist monetary system.

There the matter rests at the moment; but *where* does it rest? We have it on the authority of Justice Mahoney that debts to fractional reserve banks (i.e. the current banking system) are null and void, that their very nature is fraudulent and illegal (in short, that the banks belong to the people!), that Federal Reserve Notes and fiat paper are unlawful and unconstitutional.

Never has there been a more radical attack upon the whole nature of our fraudulent and statist banking system.

Furthermore, with these embattled Minnesotans, their radicalism is not only rhetoric; they are prepared to back it up with still further concrete acts. Jerome Daly has already announced that if any higher court of the United States, "perpetrates a fraud upon the People by defying the Constitutional Law of the United States (Justice) Mahoney has resolved that he will convene another Jury in Credit River Township (where Savage is located) to try the issue of the Fraud on the part of any State or Federal Judge". Daly

(Continued on page 4)

LISTEN YAF — *(Continued from page 1)*

berating these Rightists as tools of the Kremlin. But now your Right-wing leaders embrace every socialist, every leftist with a 100% ADA voting record, every Sidney Hook and Paul Douglas and Thomas Dodd, just so long as they stand ready to incinerate the world rather than suffer one Communist to live. What kind of a libertarian policy, what kind even of "fusionist" policy is that justifies the slaughter of tens of thousands of American soldiers, of hundreds of thousands of Vietnamese peasants, for the sake of bringing Christianity to the heathen by sword and brimstone? I can understand why the authoritarians applaud all this, they who would like nothing more than the return of Cotton Mather or Torquemada. But what are *you* doing supporting them?

Surely every libertarian supports civil liberties, the corollary and complement of private property rights and the free-market economy. Where does the Right-wing stand on civil liberties? You know all too well. Communists, of course, have to be slaughtered or rounded up in detention camps. Being "agents of the Devil", they are no longer human and therefore have no rights. Is that it? But it is not only on the Communist question where the conservatives are despots; don't think this is just one flaw in their armor. For in recent years, American politics has instructively begun to focus on very crucial issues--on the nature of the State and on State coercion itself. Thus, the cops. The cops, with their monopoly of coercion and their overwhelming superiority of arms, tend to brutalize, club, and torture confessions from people who are either innocent or have not been proven guilty. What has been the attitude of the Right-wing, and your fusionist leaders, toward this systematic brutality, or toward the libertarian decisions of the Warren Court that have put up protections for the individual rights of the accused? You know very well. They hate the Warren Court almost as much as they do Reds, for "coddling criminals", and the cry goes up everywhere for all power to the police. What can be more profoundly statist, despotic, and anti-libertarian than that?

When Mayor Daley's cops clubbed and gassed their way through Chicago last year against unarmed demonstrators, the only libertarian reaction was to revile Daley and the cops and to support the rights of the demonstrators. But your fusionist leaders loved and applauded Daley, with his "manly will to govern", and the brutality unleashed by his cop goons. And take the massacre at People's Park at Berkeley this year, when one unarmed bystander was killed, and hundreds wounded, and thousands gassed by the armed constabulary for the crime of trying to remain in a park which they had built with their own hands on a state-owned muddy lot. Yet your "fusionists" denounced People's Park and hailed Reagan and the cops.

And then there is the draft--that obnoxious system of slavery and forced murder. There is nothing anyone even remotely calling himself a libertarian can say about the draft except that it is slavery and that it must be combatted. And yet how namby-pamby YAF has been on the draft, how ambiguous and tangled the fusionist leaders become when they approach the subject? Even those who reject the draft do so only apologetically, and only on the grounds that we could have a more efficient army if it were volunteer. But the real issue is moral. The issue is not to build up a more efficient group of hired killers for the U. S. government; the issue is to oppose slavery as an absolute moral evil. And this no fusionist or Rightist has even considered doing. And even those who reject the draft as inefficient love the army itself, with its hierarchical despotism, its aggressive violence, its unthinking obedience. What sort of "libertarians" are these?

And what of the nation's educational system in which so many of you have been enmeshed? For years, I heard your fusionist leaders condemn *in toto*, the American educational system as coercive and statist, and, when in their cups and heedless of their political status, even call for abolition of the public school system. Fine! So what happens when, in the last few years, we have seen a dedicated and determined movement to smash this system--to return control to the parents, as in Ocean Hill-Brownsville in Brooklyn, and take it from the entrenched educationists--or, as with SDS and the colleges, to overthrow the educational rule of the government and the military-industrial complex? Shouldn't the fusionists have hailed and come to the support of these educational opposition movements? But instead, they have called on the cops to suppress them.

Here is surely an acid test of the fusionists' alleged love of liberty. Liberty goes by the board as soon as their precious "gder" is threatened, and "order" means, simply, State dictation and State-controlled property. Is that what libertarians are to end up doing--fronting for despots and apologists for "lawnorder"? Our stand should be on the other side--with the people, with the citizenry, and against the State and its hired goon squads. And yet YAF's central theme this year is its boasting about inventing tactics to call in the judges, call in the cops, to suppress SDS opposition--opposition to *what*? To the State's gigantic factory for brainwashing! What are *you* doing on the barricades defending the State's indoctrination centers?

It's pretty clear, or should be by now, what *they're* doing there, the fusionists. They're right where they belong, doing their job--the job of apologists for the State using libertarian rhetoric as their cloak. And since, in recent years, they have snuggled close to Power, these apologetics have become more and more blatant. Fifteen, twenty years ago, the "libertarian-conservatives" used to hail Thoreau and the idea of civil disobedience against unjust laws. But now, now that civil disobedience has become an actual living movement, Thoreau is only heard on the New Left, while the Right, even the "libertarian" or fusionist Right, talk only of lawn-n-order, suppression and the bayonet, defense of State power by any and all means necessary.

You don't belong with these deceivers on the political make. I plead with you to leave YAF now, for you should know by now that there is no hope of your ever capturing it. It is as dictatorial, as oligarchic, as close to fascism in structure as is so much of the content of YAF's program. There is no way that you can overthrow the Jones-Teague clique, for this clique is entrenched in power. And behind this clique lie the fusionist gurus: the Buckleys, and Rushers, and Meyers. And behind them lie the real power in YAF-- the moneybags, the wealthy business men who finance and therefore run the organization, the same moneybags who reacted hard a few years ago when some of your leaders decided to take a strong stand against the draft.

When YAF was founded, on the Buckley estate at Sharon, Connecticut, there was heavy sentiment among the founders against the title, because, they said, "freedom is a left-wing word." But the "fusionists" won out, and freedom was included in the title. In retrospect, it is clear that this was a shame, because all that happened was that the precious word "freedom" came to be used as an Orwellian cloak for its very opposite. Why don't you leave now, and let the "F" in YAF stand then for what it has secretly stood for all along--"fascism"?

Why don't you get out, form your own organization, breathe the clean air of freedom, and then take your stand, proudly and squarely, not with the despotism of the power elite and the government of the United States, but with the rising movement in opposition to that government? Then you will be libertarians indeed, in act as well as in theory. What hangover, what remnant of devotion to the monster State, is holding you back? Come join us, come realize that to break once and for all with statism is to break once and for all with the Right-wing. We stand ready to welcome you.

Yours in liberty,
Murray N. Rothbard

How then neutrality here on earth?

The timeless revolutionary question is timely again: which side *are* you on? Are you an enemy or friend of liberty? Are you an enemy or friend of the state? Will you be content to act as an agent of the state, or hide as a refugee from it? Or will you resist it where you can, as you can, when you can?

It is liberty that is the idea most threatening to the state. And all men who hold it as an ideal are enemies of the state. Welcome!

Nelson's Waterloo

President Nixon's sending of none other than Nelson Rockefeller on an extensive tour of Latin America demonstrates Nixon's moral obtuseness to the hilt. Sending Nelson on a fact-finding tour of Latin America is like sending a fox on a fact-finding tour of the chicken coops. And while Americans are conveniently blind to the facts of U. S. imperialism, the people of Latin America--the cooped chickens--are all too well aware of them. They know that Rockefeller is their Emperor, that the Rockefeller Empire, with its intimate blend of political and economic rule, is far more their dictator than any of the petty generals ruling over them can ever hope to be.

And so the people of Latin America, at every stop, gave their hated Emperor the reception which he so richly deserved. Three countries barred his entry, and in virtually every stop, riots, demonstrations, anger were the order of the day. Even Rockefeller's military satraps in charge of the various countries could not keep their subjects in check. All this is prelude to the Latin American Revolution to come, a revolution which will make Vietnam look like a tea party.

The New Deal And Fascism

Interesting new evidence has emerged on the close ties of Roosevelt's New Deal and fascism. George Rawick reports that some ten years ago he spent a considerable amount of time with Frances Perkins, then professor of labor economics at Cornell University and Secretary of Labor under FDR. Madame Perkins related that at the first meeting of the Roosevelt Cabinet in March 1933, Bernard Baruch, financier and key adviser to almost every President of modern times, walked in with his disciple General Hugh Johnson, soon to become head of the NRA, bringing to each member of the Cabinet a copy of a book by Giovanni Gentile, the Italian Fascist theoretician. La Perkins adds that "we all read it with great care." (Additional query: what was Baruch doing at a Cabinet meeting?) To be found in George Rawick, "Working Class Self-Activity", *Radical America* (March-April, 1969), p. 25.

Radical America is an excellent bi-monthly journal of U. S. radicalism, and is the closest thing to a theoretical journal that is associated with SDS. Available at 50¢ per issue or $3 per year at 1237 Spaight St., Madison, Wisconsin 53703.

> "The art of revolutionizing and overturning states is to undermine established customs, by going back to their origin, in order to mark their want of justice."
> ---Pascal, 1670

HEINLEIN AND LIBERTY: A Warning

One of the more distressing tendencies among American right-wing "libertarians" is a symptomatic willingness to identify popular authors as freedom-loving if they so much as use the term liberty in their works. The undisputed guru of this coterie is Robert A. Heinlein, writer of scores of science fiction short stories and novels; his book, "The Moon is a Harsh Mistress", is often singled out as representative of "anarchist" or "libertarian" science fiction. It is an enthralling novelette describing a futuristic moon colony which rebels against planet Earth under the aegis of a small group of classical liberals who have come into power via revolution. The rhetoric of these bourgeois revolutionaries is unabashedly Randian, although a signal character is identified as a "rational anarchist".

"Moon" is the latest production of the prolific Mr. Heinlein, noted also for "Stranger in a Strange Land", which supposedly captivated the attention of hip people several years ago. One would expect Heinlein to be somewhat sympathetic to the Movement, having read his utopian creations which hint at the possibilities of an open society; to the contrary, a bitter awakening is in store for Heinlein fans who are more than armchair devotees of liberty.

According to a February issue of *National Review* magazine, Robert Heinlein is one of 270 signers of a jingoist petition circulated in the U. S. Author's Guild by the facile William Buckley and his spiritual cohort Frank S. Meyer. The petition, a belated retort to an earlier anti-Vietnam war roster of authors (which was eminently successful), calls for "the vigorous prosecution of the Vietnam war to an honorable conclusion." Deep contemplation is not necessary to comprehend the statist, authoritarian implications of such New Right weasel words and the concomitant beliefs of men who would endorse it.

Only one other science fiction writer joins Heinlein in the missive, Poul Anderson; the other signatories are well known in the rightist arsenal (Stefan Possony, Eugene Lyons, Brent Bozell, John Dos Passos, Francis Russell . . . *ad nauseam*). The case of Robert Heinlein is useful in evaluating both the politics of his followers and the commitments of entrenched and established American writers: It is clear that a writer cannot serve two masters, both justice and the mighty dollar--one must give way, if not on the written page, then in one's personal life. While Heinlein has never been so explicitly libertarian as to be judged hypocritical, the lesson remains an open and obvious one.

An interesting footnote to this question comes from our British comrades: Several years ago, in *Anarchy* magazine, the monthly publication of Freedom Press in London, an article appeared on science fiction in the English language, in which Heinlein was singled out as "the only fascist science fiction writer in America." This prophetic note comes from a libertarian community that has no need for propertied quislings.

— Wilson A. Clark, Jr.

REVOLT IN MINNESOTA —

(Continued from page 1)

adds, moreover, that the Constable and the Citizens' Militia of Credit River Township are prepared to use their power to back up the jury's decision and keep Mr. Daly in possession of his land. The people of Savage, Minnesota, in short, are prepared to fight, to resist the decrees of the state and federal governments, to use their power on the local level to resist the State.

Many dimwits in the libertarian movement--and they are, unfortunately, legion--have charged that in recent years, I have simply become a "leftist". From the literature of Mr. Daly and his supporters, it is quite clear that this is a heroic band of Old Rightists, of people who have *not* been nurtured on *National Review* or the lesser organs of current Right-wing opinion. I am equally and eagerly as willing to hail their libertarian action for the people and against the State, as I am such "leftist" actions as People's Park.

The test, as Karl Hess indicates in this issue of *The Libertarian Forum*, is action; action now *vis à vis* the State. Those who side with the liberties of the people against the government are our friends and allies; those who side with the State against the people are our enemies. It is as simple as all that. The problem, as far as the Right goes, is that in recent years there have been zero actions by the Right against the State; on the contrary, the Right has almost invariably been on the side of the State: *against* the demonstrators at Chicago, *against* People's Park, *against* the Student Revolution, *against* the Black Panthers, etc. If the test is, as I hold it to be, action, and "which side are you on, the people or the State", and *not* the closeness of agreement on the fifth Lemma of the third Syllogism deduced from whether or not A A, then the Right-wing in recent years--and this means the entire right, from Buckleyites and Randians straight through to phony "anarchists" (or "anarcho-rightists")--has been a dismal failure. Indeed, it has ranged itself on the side of the Enemy. Thus, in the matter of tax resistance, ten or fifteen years ago the banner of tax refusal was carried by such "rightists" as Vivien Kellems; now the self-same flag is carried by such "leftists" as Joan Baez.

If the "libertarians" of the Right-wing are at all interested in my approbation, there is a simple way to attain it: to acquire one-hundredth of the fortitude and the revolutionary spirit of the New Left resisters against the State; to return to the tradition of Sam Adams and Tom Paine, of Garrison and John Brown, and, in recent years, of Frank Chodorov and Vivien Kellems. Let them return to that great tradition or let them, as rapidly as possible, sink into the well-deserved dustbin of history.

In the meanwhile, all hail to the heroic rebels of Savage, Minnesota, to the perceptive and courageous Jerome Daly and Justice Martin Mahoney. Anyone who wishes to read the full documentation of this case can write to Jerome Daly, 28 East Minnesota St., Savage, Minn. 55378. Anyone who wants to contribute funds (in donations of $1 or more) to carry this case to the Supreme Court is urged to send his checks to the Minnesota Action Fund, 628 Stryker Ave., St. Paul, Minn. 55107.

Recommended Reading

RAMPARTS. August 1969 issue. An all-star issue, featuring the best and fullest report to date on the battle of People's Park. Also: a perceptive article on Mel Laird by Karl Hess, a stress on the central importance of Vietnam by Franz Schurmann, and a superior piece of Rocky-baiting by David Horowitz.

Michael Gamarnikow, *Economic Reforms in Eastern Europe* (Wayne State University Press). The best single book on the remarkable rush of the Communist countries of Eastern Europe to shift from central planning to a free market. Unfortunately omits Yugoslavia.

Harry Magdoff, *The Age of Imperialism* (Monthly Review Press, paper). Useful material on current U.S. imperialism, particularly on banking connections and foreign aid.

Scott Nearing and Joseph Freeman, *Dollar Diplomacy* (Monthly Review Press, paper). Reprint of the first great dissection of early twentieth-century American imperialism.

Jack Newfield, "T. H. White: Groupie of the Power Elite", *The Village Voice* (July 17, 1969). Brilliant and acidulous dissection of the best-selling political reporter "Teddy" White.

Peter Temin, *The Jacksonian Economy* (W. W. Norton, paper). Refutes the standard historians' myth that Jackson, by his war against the Second Bank of the U.S., engendered bank inflation and then collapse.

The Libertarian Forum
BOX 341
MADISON SQUARE STATION
NEW YORK, NEW YORK 10010

Published on the first and fifteenth of every month   Subscription rate: $7.00 per year; Student subscription rate: $5.00 per year

40

A Semi-Monthly Newsletter

THE
Libertarian Forum

Joseph R. Peden, Publisher   Washington Editor, Karl Hess   Murray N. Rothbard, Editor

VOL. I, NO. X   August 15, 1969   35¢

LISTEN, YAF

This open letter is addressed to the libertarians attending the YAF national convention in St. Louis this Labor Day weekend. Notice I said the *libertarians* in YAF; I have nothing to say to the so-called "traditionalists" (a misnomer, by the way, for we libertarians have *our* traditions too, and they are glorious ones. It all depends on *which* traditions: the libertarian ones of Paine and Price, of Cobden and Thoreau, or the authoritarian ones of Torquemada and Burke and Metternich.) Let us leave the authoritarians to their Edmund Burkes and their Crowns of St. Something-or-other. We have more serious matters to discuss.

In the famous words of Jimmy Durante: "Have ya ever had the feelin' that ya wanted to go, and yet ya had the feelin' that ya wanted to stay?" This letter is a plea that you use the occasion of the public forum of the YAF convention to go, to split, to leave the conservative movement where it belongs: in the hands of the St. Something-or-others, and where it is going to stay regardless of what action you take. Leave the house of your false friends, for they are your enemies.

For years you have taken your political advice and much of your line from assorted "exes": ex-Communists, ex-Trots, ex-Maoists, ex-fellow-travellers. I have never been any of these. I grew up a right-winger, and became more intensely a libertarian rightist as I grew older. How come I am an exile from the Right-wing, while the conservative movement is being run by a gaggle of ex-Communists and monarchists? What kind of a conservative movement is this? This kind: one that you have no business being in. I got out of the Right-wing not because I ceased believing in liberty, but because being a libertarian above all, I came to see that the Right-wing specialized in cloaking its authoritarian and neo-fascist policies in the honeyed words of libertarian rhetoric. They need you for their libertarian cover; stop providing it for them!

You can see for yourselves that you have nothing in common with the frank theocrats, the worshippers of monarchy, the hawkers after a New Inquisition, the Bozells and the Wilhelmsens. Yet you continue in harness with them. Why? Because of the siren songs of the so-called "fusionists"--the Meyers and Buckleys and Evanses--who claim to be integrating and synthesizing the best of "tradition" and liberty. And even if you don't quite believe in the synthesis, the existence of these "centrists" as the leaders of the Right gives you the false sense of security that you can join a united front under their aegis. It is for that very reason that the fusionists, those misleaders, are the most dangerous of all--much more so than the frank and open worshippers of the Crown of St. Wenceslas.

For note what the fusionists are saying behind their seemingly libertarian rhetoric. The only liberty they are willing to grant is a liberty *within* "tradition", within "order", in others words a weak and puny false imitation of liberty within a framework dictated by the State apparatus. Let us consider the typically YAFite-fusionist position on various critical issues. Surely, you might say, the fusionists are in favor of a free-market economy. But are they indeed? The fusionists, for example, favor the outlawry of marijuana and other drugs--after some hemming and hawing, of course, and much hogwash about "community responsibility", values and the ontological order--but outlawry just the same. Every time some kid is busted for pot smoking you can pin much of the responsibility on the Conservative Movement and its fusionist-Buckleyite misleaders. So what kind of a free market position is one that favors the outlawry of marijuana? Where is the private property right to grow, purchase, exchange, and use?

Alright, so you know the Right-wing is very bad on questions of compulsory morality. But what about the hundreds of billions of dollars siphoned off from the producers and taxpayers to build up the power of the State's overkill military machine? And what of the state-monopoly military-industrial complex that the system has spawned? What kind of a free market is *that*? Recently, *National Review* emitted its typical patrician scorn against leftist carpers who dared to criticize the space moon-doggle. $24 billion of taxpayers' money of precious resources that could have been used on earth, have been poured into the purely and totally collectivistic moon-doggle program. And now our Conservative Hero, Vice-President Agnew, wants us to proceed on to Mars, at Lord knows what multiple of the cost. This is a free-market!? Poor Bastiat and Cobden must be turning over in their graves!

What has YAF, in its *action programs*, ever done on behalf of the free market? Its only action related to the free market has been to *oppose* it, to call for embargoes on Polish hams and other products from Eastern Europe. What kind of a free-market program is *that*?

YAF, the fusionists, and the Right-wing generally, have led the parade, in happy tandem with their supposed enemies the liberals, in supporting the Cold War and various hot wars against Communist movements abroad. This global crusading against the heathen is a total reversal of the Old "isolationist" Right-wing of my youth, the Right-wing that scorned foreign intervention and "globaloney", and attacked these adventures as statist imperialism while the *Nation* and the *New Republic* and other liberals were

(Continued on page 2)

LISTEN YAF — *(Continued from page 1)*

berating these Rightists as tools of the Kremlin. But now your Right-wing leaders embrace every socialist, every leftist with a 100% ADA voting record, every Sidney Hook and Paul Douglas and Thomas Dodd, just so long as they stand ready to incinerate the world rather than suffer one Communist to live. What kind of a libertarian policy, what kind even of "fusionist" policy is that justifies the slaughter of tens of thousands of American soldiers, of hundreds of thousands of Vietnamese peasants, for the sake of bringing Christianity to the heathen by sword and brimstone? I can understand why the authoritarians applaud all this, they who would like nothing more than the return of Cotton Mather or Torquemada. But what are *you* doing supporting them?

Surely every libertarian supports civil liberties, the corollary and complement of private property rights and the free-market economy. Where does the Right-wing stand on civil liberties? You know all too well. Communists, of course, have to be slaughtered or rounded up in detention camps. Being "agents of the Devil", they are no longer human and therefore have no rights. Is that it? But it is not only on the Communist question where the conservatives are despots; don't think this is just one flaw in their armor. For in recent years, American politics has instructively begun to focus on very crucial issues--on the nature of the State and on State coercion itself. Thus, the cops. The cops, with their monopoly of coercion and their overwhelming superiority of arms, tend to brutalize, club, and torture confessions from people who are either innocent or have not been proven guilty. What has been the attitude of the Right-wing, and your fusionist leaders, toward this systematic brutality, or toward the libertarian decisions of the Warren Court that have put up protections for the individual rights of the accused? You know very well. They hate the Warren Court almost as much as they do Reds, for "coddling criminals", and the cry goes up everywhere for all power to the police. What can be more profoundly statist, despotic, and anti-libertarian than that?

When Mayor Daley's cops clubbed and gassed their way through Chicago last year against unarmed demonstrators, the only libertarian reaction was to revile Daley and the cops and to support the rights of the demonstrators. But your fusionist leaders loved and applauded Daley, with his "manly will to govern", and the brutality unleashed by his cop goons. And take the massacre at People's Park at Berkeley this year, when one unarmed bystander was killed, and hundreds wounded, and thousands gassed by the armed constabulary for the crime of trying to remain in a park which they had built with their own hands on a state-owned muddy lot. Yet your "fusionists" denounced People's Park and hailed Reagan and the cops.

And then there is the draft--that obnoxious system of slavery and forced murder. There is nothing anyone even remotely calling himself a libertarian can say about the draft except that it is slavery and that it must be combatted. And yet how namby-pamby YAF has been on the draft, how ambiguous and tangled the fusionist leaders become when they approach the subject? Even those who reject the draft do so only apologetically, and only on the grounds that we could have a more efficient army if it were volunteer. But the real issue is moral. The issue is not to build up a more efficient group of hired killers for the U. S. government; the issue is to oppose slavery as an absolute moral evil. And this no fusionist or Rightist has even considered doing. And even those who reject the draft as inefficient love the army itself, with its hierarchical despotism, its aggressive violence, its unthinking obedience. What sort of "libertarians" are these?

And what of the nation's educational system in which so many of you have been enmeshed? For years, I heard your fusionist leaders condemn *in toto*, the American educational system as coercive and statist, and, when in their cups and heedless of their political status, even call for abolition of the public school system. Fine! So what happens when, in the last few years, we have seen a dedicated and determined movement to smash this system--to return control to the parents, as in Ocean Hill-Brownsville in Brooklyn, and take it from the entrenched educationists--or, as with SDS and the colleges, to overthrow the educational rule of the government and the military-industrial complex? Shouldn't the fusionists have hailed and come to the support of these educational opposition movements? But instead, they have called on the cops to suppress them.

Here is surely an acid test of the fusionists' alleged love of liberty. Liberty goes by the board as soon as their precious "gder" is threatened, and "order" means, simply, State dictation and State-controlled property. Is that what libertarians are to end up doing--fronting for despots and apologists for "lawnorder"? Our stand should be on the other side--with the people, with the citizenry, and against the State and its hired goon squads. And yet YAF's central theme this year is its boasting about inventing tactics to call in the judges, call in the cops, to suppress SDS opposition--opposition to *what*? To the State's gigantic factory for brainwashing! What are *you* doing on the barricades defending the State's indoctrination centers?

It's pretty clear, or should be by now, what *they're* doing there, the fusionists. They're right where they belong, doing their job--the job of apologists for the State using libertarian rhetoric as their cloak. And since, in recent years, they have snuggled close to Power, these apologetics have become more and more blatant. Fifteen, twenty years ago, the "libertarian-conservatives" used to hail Thoreau and the idea of civil disobedience against unjust laws. But now, now that civil disobedience has become an actual living movement, Thoreau is only heard on the New Left, while the Right, even the "libertarian" or fusionist Right, talk only of lawn-n-order, suppression and the bayonet, defense of State power by any and all means necessary.

You don't belong with these deceivers on the political make. I plead with you to leave YAF now, for you should know by now that there is no hope of your ever capturing it. It is as dictatorial, as oligarchic, as close to fascism in structure as is so much of the content of YAF's program. There is no way that you can overthrow the Jones-Teague clique, for this clique is entrenched in power. And behind this clique lie the fusionist gurus: the Buckleys, and Rushers, and Meyers. And behind them lie the real power in YAF--the moneybags, the wealthy business men who finance and therefore run the organization, the same moneybags who reacted hard a few years ago when some of your leaders decided to take a strong stand against the draft.

When YAF was founded, on the Buckley estate at Sharon, Connecticut, there was heavy sentiment among the founders against the title, because, they said, "freedom is a left-wing word." But the "fusionists" won out, and freedom was included in the title. In retrospect, it is clear that this was a shame, because all that happened was that the precious word "freedom" came to be used as an Orwellian cloak for its very opposite. Why don't you leave now, and let the "F" in YAF stand then for what it has secretly stood for all along--"fascism"?

Why don't you get out, form your own organization, breathe the clean air of freedom, and then take your stand, proudly and squarely, not with the despotism of the power elite and the government of the United States, but with the rising movement in opposition to that government? Then you will be libertarians indeed, in act as well as in theory. What hangover, what remnant of devotion to the monster State, is holding you back? Come join us, come realize that to break once and for all with statism is to break once and for all with the Right-wing. We stand ready to welcome you.

Yours in liberty,
Murray N. Rothbard

Letter From Washington

By Karl Hess

Leaders And Heroes

We had a chance to learn a lot about leaders lately. Also heroes.

There was, for example, the moonshot. The three Federal employees who went on the trip were passengers in fact, passengers in life-style, passengers in character, the great culminating passengers of the great bureaucratic trip. But by going along for the ride they have become heroes, instand, officially certified heroes who, in all probability, will be featured, like meat loaf, in the menus of the state's school system until some other Federal employee makes it to Mars.

Politically there was another great passenger hanging on for all he was worth (and that *is* all he's worth, come to think of it). Richard Nixon, whose only discernible qualification for any office has been that he wants it (oh, does he want it!) treated the affair in proper perspective. He said, gosh, that it was man's greatest moment. He meant his greatest moment, of course--a fact he gave away by both dropping his name on the moon and dropping his cool with the astronauts, telling the entire world that the neatest thing about being President was actually getting to take free rides to historic events rather than staying home to watch them like all the kids who didn't want to be leaders quite bad enough. (One recalled, as this marionette figure spoke, that he also had remaked, while helicoptering over Washington's rush hour traffic, that he was glad he didn't have to drive to work. His attitude toward the moon thing seemed just about on the same level: he was *really* glad to get to see the doings close up instead of at home like the working stiffs.)

There was also that leader of the downtrodden, Ralph Abernathy. He said that the whole thing was so awe inspiring that it even made him forget poverty for a moment. And why not? He had an entire special section of seats reserved for him at the launching, thus becoming the first extraterrestrial Tom, you might say. The awesome demonstration probably also made him forget, if he ever had bothered to think about it in the first place, that a lot of his brothers and sisters are being killed these days because they happen to want to solve their problems here on earth.

There also was Billy Graham, gently chiding his old buddy Dick about the moon thing being the greatest moment in man's history. Fourth greatest, he corrected, right after Christmas, the Crucifixion, and the Resurrection. (Or maybe fifth, right after the invention of the padded collection plate and the 100% religion depletion tax allowance.)

For the best performance by an American leader, however, the prize really had to go to Teddy Kennedy, starring in a re-run of Dickie Nixon's little-dog-Checkers speech,

as produced in actual tragedy by the inmates of the state of Massachusetts under the direction of dynastic destiny out of sheer chutzpah. Since nobody else seems to give a damn that somebody got killed in the process why should we, eh folks?

To savor the play we must first appreciate the scenery. Here is the Senator from Massachusetts, one of the nation's richest, most pampered young men. Unlike the temporary President of the United States, who got the job by holding his breath and threatening to turn blue unless we let him have it, Teddy Kennedy is widely felt to have some dibs on the job by sheer hereditary right, having not made much ado about any more profound qualification. And here, of course, is this tragedy; indeed, one dead girl in a world full of dead and dying can be called tragic. The point is how it is all perceived. And it is perceived as a problem in practical politics, nothing more. Even the surviving partner in the tragedy perceives it as nothing more and goes on TV to make the point as publicly as possible.

Teddy, it is said, just as it was said of Nixon in *his* time of crisis, is fighting for his life. It's a stirring thought. It would be the only thing *in* that life he ever did have to fight for.

But what manner of warped and hollow men could be said to be fighting for their lives--even forgiving journalistic hyperbole--when all that is involved is whether or not the man will hold a public office? And what manner of people can take seriously the posturings of such public men or translate such public puling into private agony?

The incident, indeed all of the incidents, tell us perhaps more about our society, our 'system' than even about the cardboard cutouts, the political Barbies and Kens who strut on the particular stage at the particular moment.

This supposedly noble land had been bred and fed on this obviously ignoble fare. It seems now impossible to say that all of this horseshit is just some aberration of an otherwise perfect civil comity and economic dynamism. It rather seems that all of this sort of loathsome leadership is the inevitable result of a system which, along with its vast capacity for producing goods, has an exactly equal capacity for producing evils.

Teddy Kennedy, telling *his* people (*his* forelock-pulling people down there in the Kennedy village that is the laughably sovereign state of Massachusetts) telling *his* people that he must be loved if he is to lead them, suggestively warning that if he had to step down they would lose more than a great man, they would lose a great name, asking the ever-loving folk in his ever-loving village to make the great decision for him (oh, my god; decisions, decisions, why not ask the little people to share this great burden with me); Teddy Kennedy who must actually think that whether he stays in the Senate or not is somewhere near as important as whether some man in Roxbury can pay his rent this month, or whether any man will live the night through in Vietnam, that Teddy Kennedy *is* your Teddy Kennedy America! Just as Richard Nixon is. Just as are Bobby Baker, Litton Industries, Dow Chemical, Nelson Rockefeller and all the other great practitioners of state capitalism and the profiteers of state imperialism.

What I kept thinking as I watched the *national* leaders disport themselves, and thought of their origins, was that to really love this land you must first learn to loathe this nation and the system for which it stands.

Against The Volunteer Military

Many libertarians have been misled into supporting the volunteer military proposal. The argument typically goes something like this: the draft is a clear violation of the principle that each man is a complete self-owner; that to take away the free use of a man's life for two years is to nationalize his most important piece of private property-- his own person.

The argument continues: the lottery merely bases the slavery inherent in a draft system on mathematical chance instead of on the chance of getting a deferment and is therefore equally servile. Universal service merely seeks to hide the slavery inherent in the draft system under the cloak of egalitarianism-slavery for all.

The volunteer military idea is seemingly strengthened by analogy to the free market: coercive systems are always inefficient and this applies to coercive systems of acquiring military personnel. A market wage for soldiers will attract the most highly motivated soldiers, the soldiers most likely to re-enlist. Below market-wage soldiers will be poorly motivated, inefficient and will not re-enlist in high percentages--necessitating high training costs due to the high turnover in personnel.

In order to see why the above argument is fallacious, mischievous, and anti-libertarian let us consider the following: A concentration camp is set up whose purpose it is to tortue innocent victims. Those unfortunates are dragged in kicking and screaming, are then subdued, tortured, maimed and finally killed. There is only one fact disturbing this otherwise idyllic picture--the concentration camp torturers are not hired at the going market rate as "free enterprise" demands; rather, they are, horrors! draftees. A group of "libertarians" is worried about the poor motivation and inefficiency of the torturers who were drafted against their will and "who just cannot seem to put their hearts into it." In addition, the sad fact is that the re-enlistment rate is low--necessitating high training costs due to the high turnover in personnel.

What does this "libertarian" group then recommend? It recommends that future torturers be hired at market wage rates--a "volunteer torturary" as it were.

It is not hard for the true libertarian to see the error in volunteer military sentiment when viewed through this analogy. The point is that we must *first* determine whether the proposed job of the hirelings is consistent with libertarian principles. If it is, only *then* do we look into the method of hiring which must, of course, be voluntary.

If we mistakenly support voluntary methods of hiring people *before* we consider precisely what they are being hired to do, we may well become unwitting supporters of the *efficient* violation of liberties.

In the present political context the consistent libertarian must oppose the draft, but he must *also* oppose all imperialistic armies, be they drafted or hired.

What the proponents of the volunteer military forget is that there is a fifth alternative to manning imperialistic armies by the draft, lottery, universal service, or the volunteer military--opposition to imperialism under any guise even under the guise of the free market.

Is the libertarian, then, a pacifist, opposed to all armies? Far from it. The libertarian supports *defensive* armies whose soldiers are hired voluntarily. But this is not enough! Such armies must be paid for only by people who desire defense services and who voluntarily pay for them. Such armies would be more efficient than many presently known, but this efficiency the libertarian could whole-heartedly applaud since it would be used to protect, not violate, liberties. Moreover, such armies would be fully just since they would also be support without violating liberties.

— Walter Block

Published on the first and fifteenth of every month   Subscription rate: $7.00 per year; Student subscription rate: $5.00 per year

A Semi-Monthly Newsletter

THE
Libertarian Forum

Joseph R. Peden, Publisher   Washington Editor, Karl Hess   Murray N. Rothbard, Editor

VOL. I, NO. XI   September 1, 1969   35¢

National Liberation

The recent rioting and virtual civil war in Northern Ireland points up, both for libertarians and for the world at large, the vital importance of pushing for and attaining the goal of national liberation for all oppressed peoples. Aside from being a necessary condition to the achievement of justice, national liberation is the only solution to the great world problems of territorial disputes and oppressive national rule. Yet all too many anarchists and libertarians mistakenly scorn the idea of national liberation and independence as simply setting up more nation-states; they tragically do not realize that, taking this stand, they become in the concrete, objective supporters of the bloated, imperialistic nation-states of today.

Sometimes this mistake has had tragic consequences. Thus, it is clear from Paul Avrich's fascinating and definitive book (*The Russian Anarchists*, Princeton University Press, 1967), that the anarchists in Russia had at least a fighting chance to take control of the October Revolution rather than the Bolsheviks, but that they lost out for two major reasons: (1) their sectarian view that any kind of definite organization of their own movement violated anarchist principles; and (2) their opposition to the national independence movements for the Ukraine and White Russia on the ground that this would simply be setting up other states. In this way, they became the objective defenders of Great Russian imperialism, and this led them to the disastrous course of opposing Lenin's statesmanlike "appeasement peace" of Brest-Litovsk in 1918, where Lenin, for the sake of ending the war with Germany, surrendered Ukrainian and White Russian territory from the Greater Russian imperium. Disastrously, both for their own principles and for their standing in the eyes of the war-weary Russian people, the Russian anarchists called for continuing the war against "German imperialism", thereby somehow identifying with anarchy the centuries-old land grabs of Russian imperialism.

Let us first examine the whole question of national liberation from the point of view of libertarian principle. Suppose that there are two hypothetical countries, "Ruritania" and "Walldavia". Ruritania invades Walldavia and seizes the northern part of the country. This situation continues over decades or even centuries. But the underlying condition remains: The Ruritanian State has invaded and continues to occupy and exploit, very often trying to eradicate the language and culture of, the North Walldavian subject people. There now arises, both in northern and southern Walldavia, a "North Walldavian Liberation Movement". Where should we stand on the matter?

It seems clear to me that libertarians are bound to give this liberation movement their ardent support. For their object, while it might not be to achieve an ultimate Stateless society, is to liberate the oppressed North Walldavians from their Ruritanian State rulers. The fact that we may not agree with the Walldavian rebels on all philosophical or political points is irrelevant. The whole point of their existence--to free the northern Walldavians from their imperial oppressors--deserves our whole-hearted support.

Thus is solved the dilemma of how libertarians and anarchists should react toward the whole phenomenon of "nationalism". Nationalism is not a unitary, monolithic phenomenon. If it is aggressive, we should oppose it, if liberatory we should favor it. Thus, in the Ruritanian-Walldavian case, those Ruritanians who defend the aggression or occupation on the grounds of "Greater Ruritania" or "Ruritanian national honor" or whatever are being aggressive nationalists, or "imperialists". Those of either country who favor North Walldavian liberation from the imperial Ruritanian yoke are being liberators, and therefore deserve our support.

One of the great swindles behind the idea of "collective security against aggression", as spread by the "internationalist"-interventionists of the 1920's and ever since, is that this requires us to regard as sacred all of the national boundaries which have been often imposed by aggression in the first place. Such a concept requires us to put our stamp of approval upon the countries and territories created by previous imperial aggression.

Let us now apply our analysis to the problem of Northern Ireland. The Northern Irish rulers--the Protestants--insist on their present borders and institutions; the Southern Irish or Catholics demand a unitary state in Ireland. Of the two, the Southern Irish have the better case, for all of the Protestants were "planted" centuries ago into Ireland by English imperialism, at the expense of murdering the Catholic Irish and robbing their lands. But unless documentation exists to enable restoration of the land and property to the heirs of the victims--and it is highly dubious that such exists--the proper libertarian solution has been advanced by neither side and, as far as we can tell, by no one in the public press. For the present partition line does *not*, as most people believe, divide the Catholic South from the Protestant North. The partition, as imposed by Britain after World War I and accepted by the craven Irish rebel leadership, arbitrarily handed a great deal of Catholic territory to the North. Specifically, over half of the territory of Northern Ireland has a majority of Catholics, and should revert immediately to the South: this includes

(Continued on page 2)

45

NATIONAL LIBERTARIAN—*(Continued from page 1)*

Western Derry (including Derry City), all of Tyrone and Fermanagh, southern Armagh, and southern Down. Essentially, this would leave as Northern Ireland only the city of Belfast and the rural areas directly to the north.

While this solution would leave the Catholics of Belfast oppressed by outrageous Protestant discrimination and exploitation, at least the problem of the substantial Catholic minority in Northern Ireland—the *majority* in the areas enumerated above—would be solved, and the whole question of Northern Ireland would be reduced to tolerable dimensions. In this way, the libertarian solution—of applying national self-determination and removing imperial oppression—would at the same time bring about justice and solve the immediate utilitarian question.

Letter From Washington

By Karl Hess

REFORM

Liberal reformers, among their many mystical rites, particularly are devoted to the rational use of the state's taxing power. The most rational use, they seem to feel, is in the redistribution of income.

Thus, when Richard the Reformer Nixon recently announced that he too had seen the light and now was ready to smite the rich and relieve the poor, the pitty-patting of the vested ventricles could be heard loud in the land.

Alas, it is all nonsense.

Taxes can never seriously affect the incomes of the rich. Nor are there any known instances of the government actually transferring substantial sums of money to the poor regardless of its source.

Begin, if you will, with the corporations, those artificial, state-coddled economic monstrosities from whose especially privileged endeavors flow the major wealth of the very rich. Corporations cannot pay taxes. Customers pay taxes. Corporations merely collect them. The point is that corporations are not taxed like thee and me. They are taxed only on what they have left over after deducting *all* of the costs of making it in the first place. They do not pay taxes out of savings, the way individuals must. It is, therefore, apparent that tax increases, for corporations, are paid simply out of price rises or, to repeat, by the customers.

The liberal zeal simply to increase taxes on the corporations is witless at best. It just shifts more of the heavy spending of the state into a relatively "painless" area where the dumb taxpayer, not realizing how the state happily encourages such fictions, growls about rising costs rather than about rising taxes which may, in fact, be what the price rise is about anyway.

But what about just taxing away all of the profits, wouldn't that discourage price rises? Liberals just don't know their corporations, apparently. The corporation is perfectly capable of declaring a zero profit at the end of any given year just by raising the bonuses, dividends or even salaries of its owning fat cats.

Conservatives, of course, hav long since understood the invulnerability of the preferred position in which laws place corporations. They wouldn't dream of blowing the whistle on them, however, because (1) conservative ideologues and muckrakers usually get their support from corporations, (2) they tend to be the relatives of corporate owners, or (3) they actually feel that the corporations represent some sort of countervailing power to the state.

That, on the conservative side, is as dumb a posture as the reform zeal is on the liberal side. Corporations in no way present a countervailing force to the state. They are, in effect, licensed by the state, they are treated in special ways (i.e. as though no one in them had any individual responsibility) by the state, taxed in special ways by the state, and so forth. They are either simply economic arms of the state or, to put it another way, the state is simply the police arm of the corporations. Under the American system of state capitalism, as under the similar system in the Soviet Union, that's just the way it is.

The liberal reformists, however, at least feel that they have been given a great lift by Richard the Righteous in that he has closed up a lot of loopholes through which the very rich have crawled without paying any taxes on huge incomes. They miss, in their mean little zeal for revenge, the big point about such people. The closing of one set of loopholes or, indeed, all loopholes, just means that the rich guy must shift his method of income. It is one of the concomitant strengths of being rich in a state-capitalist system in the first place that it supposes an ability to collect income in whatever form, whenever, and however desired. Only the poor must live pinned tightly to urgent weekly demands of wages and withheld taxes.

There are some loopholes, of course, that would cause pain if obliterated, such as the still scarcely scratched oil depletion allowance. On the other hand, it actually would be more productive of benefit to the poor if, instead of simply clobbering the oily ones, the notion of depletion simply was extended. Manual laborers, for instance, obviously are depleted faster than any damn oil well but the state obdurately refuses to acknowledge it.

Something similar may be observed in another liberal attitude toward the poor. The Nixon Administration's decision to relieve the very poor of any tax payment at all is liberally viewed as government's reasonable attempt to get more money into the hands of the poor.

The money belonged to the people in the first place! The government now is just refraining itself from stealing so much of it. But are the poor relieved of the war tax on telephones when they use them? Are they relieved of war taxes on other items? Are they relieved of the taxes and the tolls of the predatory local governments who prey on them? Of course not. In short, for every dollar that government boasts that it is getting into the hands of the poor, it is still likely—and there are no real studies on the subject—that the poor continue to pay more out in tribute to the state at all its wretched levels.

For instance, when government liberally boasts that the poor 'get' something from government they include in their bookkeeping the poor's share of the monstrous defense budget or the lunatic lunar boondoggles. Those are programs the poor would probably would be quite happy to forego if only the government would get altogether off their backs.

The point of all this is that among the grandest mistakes reformers ever make is summed up in the attitude toward taxes and corporations and poor people. The state is simply a gigantic corporation, just like G.M, just as predatory, just as bureaucratic, just as 'profit' (power) crazed, but with the added horror of having at its disposal the entire machinery of actual physical coercion.

To regard the taxes (profits) of the state as somehow more pleasant than the profits of the state-sheltered corporation, to think that the bureaucrats of the state have any more concern for the poor than the bureaucrats of the corporation, is one of the most fatal flaws in the reformist character.

THE CZECH CRISIS:

PART I:
The Eastern European Roots
By Leonard P. Liggio

Czechoslovakia, the most industrially advanced East European country when the Communist party assumed power at the end of World War II, had in two decades become economically stagnant. Serious slowing of economic growth was evident by 1962 when the aggregate product grew only 1.4 percent and industrial output declined 0.7 percent. In 1963 aggregate product declined 2.2 percent and national income declined 3.7 percent. Heavy subsidies were expanded for two decades to construct and operate industries without regard for their ultimate productivity. The annual subsidies to maintain these 'white elephant' factories has been a phenomenal fifteen percent of the total net national income. Further, twenty percent of the claimed national income consists of unsold finished products which are unsalable due to poor quality or high prices because of inefficient production.

In 1962 there was a deep agricultural failure when production fell 6 percent. This catastrophe was the final result of Communist leader Antonin Novotny's reversal in 1955 of the party policy of full support for private farmers. Systematic pressure was placed on the small and medium private farmers to enter collective farms. Novotny in 1963 appointed a new premier to try to deflect public opinion toward the political superstructure and away from the real causes in the basic economic system. However, Czech economists began an overall study of the economy. A commission of the economic institute headed by Prof. Ota Sik was strongly influenced by the Yugoslav system of market socialism based upon free price mechanism and profitability as the test of value.

Yugoslavia made the earliest major innovations when it was read out of the Soviet bloc in 1948. The Yugoslav League of Communist leadership, headed by Josef Tito, survived Soviet denunciation because it had gained public support by recognizing that the solution of the problems of the peasant farmers and of agricultural productivity was crucial for an underdeveloped country. Experience indicated that collectivization of agriculture was not the solution for agricultural productivity; this deviation from the Soviet model was a major accusation against Tito.

Brutal purges were conducted in East Europe between 1948-53 against national communists who advocated the principle of autonomy from the Soviet party and its practical application in abandoning agricultural collectivization. Wladislaw Gomulka, Polish party leader until purged as a 'Titoist' in 1948, explained (after his rehabilitation in 1956) the root of Stalin's 'cult of the personality' in the Soviet Union as primarily based in Stalin's policy of collectivization of agriculture after 1929. Gomulka indicated that the introduction of mass violence for the first time in Soviet society led to the elimination of Leninist principles in the communist party and the complete domination of police-state methods in the Soviet Union. (In 1956 Gomulka reversed the collectivization of agriculture in Poland.)

Having challenged the Soviet model in agriculture, the Yugoslavs adopted new techniques in industry. Tito called for the initiation of the gradual withering away of the state apparatus beginning with workers' ownership of state enterprises. "In the Soviet Union after thirty-one years," Tito said in 1948, "the factories belong to the state, not to the people . . . they are run by civil servants."

The Yugoslav party aimed to replace the role of the state bureaucracy in firms by substitution of workers' self-management. The firm's workers would control the management of the firm and share in its profits. The test of efficiency is directed to the firm's competition in the supply and demand market. The goal of eliminating compulsion was introduced. According to vice-president Edward Kardelj: "The maximum effort and initiative of the individual does not depend so much upon directives and controls as it does upon the personal, economic, social, cultural and material interest of the worker who is working and creating in freedom."

The influence of the Yugoslav experience was very important during the 1956 Thaw. In East Germany, the faculty of the German Academy of Economic Science had engaged in extended discussions of the problems of the withering away of the state. The Academy's director, Prof. Fritz Behrens, had prepared detailed programs for major decentralization of the economy. It was held that rationality and productivity required autonomy for industrial enterprises. These programs were severely criticized as "anarchism" by the East German government.

Nevertheless, these economic policies received partial application in the New Economic System of the 1960's. Despite East Germany's rise to the sixth largest industrial producer in Europe, and three-fold increase in workers' real income, its investment costs in 1965 had risen phenomenally and it was paying six times what it did fifteen years earlier. The unfinished investments were valued at one year's gross fixed investment. Planning in building and housing construction had created a disaster. The compulsory collectivization of agriculture in 1960 severely crippled that sector with slaughter of livestock, neglect of fields, and flight of farmers to the cities. The regime was forced to increase investment in agriculture by thirty percent to maintain a stagnant rate of production. Additionally, food comprised twenty-five percent of East Germany's imports in place of further investment in agriculture. Much of the food imports came from Poland's private agricultural system.

East Germany's New Economic System was introduced to gain reliable cost accounting, reduction of production costs, and managerial autonomy. But, the emphasis has been upon achieving this through the panacea of the electronic computer, leaving the central planners in ultimate control. Thus far, the results have not been a major transformation of East German economic production.

In Hungary during the mid-1950's the popularity of workers' councils and self-management of firms developed in newspaper discussion of Yugoslav policies following exchange visits of Hungarian and Yugoslav workers. In 1954 the Institute of Economics was established and it presented detailed criticisms of the centralized planned economy, the development of heavy industry at the expense of agriculture, the lack of a role for industrial profitability, the unreal price system. The untenability of planning was examined by Janos Konrai, *The Excessive Centralization of Economic Management*, Budapest, 1957. Thus, in 1957 the Committee of Economic Experts was formed to propose reform of the economy. Its program called for decentralization, price reform, material incentives, independence for individual firms, abolition of the state control of foreign trade and encouragement of private farms. The government never responded to the proposal, but it contained the ideas which appeared in the New Economic Mechanism, prepared in 1965-66 and implemented in 1968 because of the growing economic crisis. The Hungarian program is the most far-reaching with the exception of Yugoslavia.

In Poland during the 1956 Thaw decentralization and workers' self-management were introduced. As described in a Polish student weekly, "Workers' self-government was initiated in Yugoslavia essentially as an initiative from above, in the form of a decree, prepared for the most part by comrade Kardelj on a theoretical basis. In our

(Continued on page 4)

THE CZECH CRISIS — *(Continued from page 3)*
country, as we all know, it was wrested from the ministers by the workers themselves." But Gomulka rebuked the idea of far-reaching administrative decentralization in May 1957. "If every factory became a kind of cooperative enterprise," Gomulka said, "all the laws governing capitalist enterprise would immediately come into effect and produce all the usual results. Central planning and administration . . . would have to disappear."

As a result, Poland's cooperation was limited to pioneering in the advocacy of radical economic theory. Oskar Lange's writings were especially important. Lange has emphasized that Austrian economics, especially the work of Ludwig von Mises, is the sole rational alternative to Marxist theory. The Misesian critique of planning and of calculation under socialism is the major problem for Marxist economists. But even in theoretical discussions, the Polish economists can only go so far. Thus, Stefan Kurowski, the leading Polish exponent of the free market, has, with a few exceptions, not been allowed to publish his studies.

Thus, in the 1960's, advocacy has been limited to regulated markets and free price formation within central planning. Warsaw Professor Wlodzimierz Brus (*General Problems of the Functioning of a Socialist Economy*, 1961) was attacked in 1967 ("The Antinomies of the Market Theories under Socialism") for arguing that planning and the free market are mutually exclusive and that not only a free market in labor but also in capital goods is necessary.

The failure in Poland to proceed with market economy reforms delayed economic development. Late in 1967 three Communist Party plenums were devoted to the economic crisis which was causing unrest in major industrial cities. Food and clothing were in short supply; state warehouses were bursting with unsalable goods due to high prices or inferior quality. In November there was a thirty percent increase in the price of meat. The government explained the meat shortage: managers of minimally controlled enterprises had such good consumer response that they hired more employees to meet the demand but this "excessive increase in employment" was not called for in the central plan and their wages drove up the price of meat. General agricultural problems have developed since Gomulka reversed his private-oriented farm policy; the production of small tractors necessary for Polish farms was halted and only large tractors, for state farms, were available. The private farmers' fear of collectivization has caused declines in production growth.

With economic crisis threatening to generate popular protest, free market-oriented economists became the scapegoats to hide the real causes rooted in central planning. In March 1968 protests against the existing system had been spearheaded by university students. To the slogan "Long Live Czechoslovakia" they marched through the streets and occupied university buildings and the Ministry of Education with predictable results: a police riot. The student demand for an investigation of the police was met with expulsion of students and dismissal of liberal faculty, such as Adam Schaff for his *Marxism and the Individual* Leszek Kolakowski, the principal theorist of anti-authoritarian Marxism. Brus and Kurowski were charged with encouraging the students by their programs to undermine central control of the economy ("Socialist Democracy and Market Socialism" in the party newspaper). Brus, Tadeusz Kowalik and Ignacy Sachs were expelled from the party for holding that only the "market can guarantee the basic economic structure during the process of development."

The intellectual as well as material impact of the economic collapse of orthodox Marxist economics in East Europe has been compared with the 1929 Depression for the West. While the politicians in both cases resisted change, there is a marked difference between the response of economists and intellectuals in the West during the 1930's and those in the East in the 1960's. The former, refusing to challenge the Establishment seriously, opted for more elaborately theorized forms of the *status quo* in the form of Keynesian and Marxist economic theory. In the East the Establishment was really challenged by the intellectuals and economists, who embraced free market economic theory.

Their adoption of market economics was both a response to real conditions and the result of intellectual willingness of some economists East and West to seek dialogue and exchange of conflicting ideas. It is a credit to the East European economists, often members of Communist parties, that they were open to non-Marxist ideas. As Marxists they came to recognize that there were no differences between Marxist economics and the mercantilist, monopoly economics dominant in Western universities; the only clear alternative to the catastrophic planned economics in the East was the free market. Equally important was the openness of European market economists in originating discussions with Marxists. Year after year, they attended joint East-West conference, travelled to the East to initiate dialogue, and invited East Europeans to discuss their Marxism in the West. Unlike Americans they were not inhibited by adherence to the official Anti-communist line, although identification with U. S. policy hardly appears deducible from free market economics. Their healthy, self-confident activism in overcoming the obstacles to dialogue with Marxists has had important historical effects.

(The concluding part will appear in the next issue.)

The Libertarian Forum
BOX 341
MADISON SQUARE STATION
NEW YORK, NEW YORK 10010

A Semi-Monthly Newsletter

THE
Libertarian Forum

| Joseph R. Peden, Publisher | Washington Editor, Karl Hess | Murray N. Rothbard, Editor |

| VOL. I, NO. XII | September 15, 1969 | 35¢ |

REPORT FROM ST. LOUIS:

The Revolution Comes To YAF

BY JEROME TUCCILLE

The *place* was Stouffer's Riverfront Inn, St. Louis, Missouri.

The *time*, August 38-31, 1969.

The *occasion*, the annual National Convention of the "conservative" student organization, Young Americans for Freedom.

It had been apparent for six months and longer that the leadership of YAF, a traditionally conservative youth organization since the days of its inception in 1961, was being challenged from within by a persistent group of disaffected intellectuals. Just how strong they were, how many they numbered, was impossible to say. Their presence within YAF was revealed every now and then through the publication in *The New Guard*, the official YAF magazine, of an occasional article dealing with anarchist philosophy or the organization and operation of an anarchist society. But, by and large, *The New Guard* reflected the conservative thinking of the majority of its readership.

On the surface, there was no indication whatsoever of any major confrontation arising at the convention. Key speakers for the occasion, secured by the conservative YAF leadership, included the usual right-wing luminaries: William F. Buckley, William Rusher, Al Capp (Yes, Al Capp!), Fulton Lewis III, Barry Goldwater, Jr., Phyllis Schafly, Phillip Abbott Luce; major emphasis in the various seminars was placed on formulating an effective strategy for combatting the New Left on campus. All in all, if one merely read the proposed agenda circulated several weeks before the convention, it promised to be a routine excoriation of everyone to the left of Richard Nixon and Billy Graham, with maybe a few wrist-slapping comments for George Wallace and the fire-breathing ultra right.

However, several hours before opening session a group of New York rebels distributed the August 15th issue of *The Libertarian Forum* which contained an open letter to the convention from Dr. Murray N. Rothbard, urging the libertarians to split completely from the conservative movement.

At the same time, rumors were circulated to the effect that Karl Hess was arriving in St. Louis to address the convention on opening night. Since he was not a scheduled speaker, the implication here was that a demonstration would have to be staged by the radicals to demand that Hess be given a chance to express the opposition point of view.

The conservatives, applying their overkill mentality to this potential crisis, were visibly dismayed by the fact that the rebels had come up with a "name" speaker of their own. The fact that the YAF leadership had loaded the convention with some sixteen hard-line conservatives of impeccable *anti-communist* credentials was, apparently, not enough. The enemy had come up with Hess as a gesture of defiance, and the only thing to do, of course, was "escalate" their side of the conflict.

To make matters worse for the conservative point of view, Barry Goldwater, Jr. sent word prior to the convention—evidently upon hearing that there might be some 'trouble' in St. Louis—that he could not attend. He suddenly felt a need to be with his constituents over the Labor Day weekend.

At approximately 4:30 P.M., just three and a half hours before William Buckley was scheduled to deliver the opening address, Karl Hess' son, Karl Hess IV, received word that his father would not be permitted to speak on the floor of the convention. Also, many of the anarchist and radical libertarian delegates discovered that they were having difficulty receiving the proper credentials which would admit them for the voting session on Saturday. Young Hess announced to the press that a 'mini-convention' would be held under the arch, the symbolic gateway to the west, at 11:00 P.M. following Buckley's speech. His father was arriving later that evening and would speak to any dissident YAFers who wished to hear his remarks.

Realizing that a major split was underway—made all the more apparent by the heavy television and press attention the anarchists were receiving as they arrived in St. Louis with their black flags unfurled—William F. Buckley called a press conference at 5:30 P.M. Buckley was questioned mainly as to the nature and seriousness of the imminent split which now threatened to disrupt the entire convention. He denied that the confrontation was serious, claiming that the dissident element was too miniscule to be of any real importance. At this point, Karl Hess IV, leader of YAF's Anarcho-Libertarian Alliance, Walter Block and myself acting as spokesmen for the Radical Libertarian Alliance, broke into the conference and invited Buckley publicly to debate with Hess under the arch later that night, since the YAF leadership would not provide for such an encounter as

(Continued on page 2)

49

REPORT FROM ST. LOUIS — *(Continued from page 1)*

part of the official proceedings. Buckley declined, stating that he had an article to write that evening and, in any event, he did not think the issue was important enough that it could not wait until a later date.

Now the breach was visible, having been made an issue in Buckley's own press conference, and the only question that now remained was *how many* dissident YAFers would split off to the open-air meeting in support of the opposition. The matter remained in abeyance until 8:00 P.M., at which time the convention was officially declared open. But before Mr. Buckley could be introduced to the crowd, a delegation of California anarchists staged a demonstration, demanding that their chapter chairman, Pat Dowd, who had earlier been dismissed for his radical views, be given a seat with the delegates on the stage. The demonstration would have remained a procedural one, rotating around the seating of the ousted chairman, had the conservatives not sent up a ringing chant in support of Buckley. Cries of, "We want Buckley! We want Buckley!" now dinned throughout the ballroom, only to be met with the opposition call, "We want Hess! We want Hess!"

It was only now that the press and the conventioners themselves had a chance to estimate the size of the dissident faction. The ferocity of the cries in opposition to the conservatives clearly startled the traditionalist contingent which now stated chanting the official slogan of the convention:

"Sock it to the Left! Sock it to the Left!"

"Sock it to the State! Sock it to the State!" was the answer to this new attempt to drown them out.

Finally, after a half-hour delay during which the ousted California chairman succeeded in claiming his seat upon the stage, William F. Buckley rose to deliver the official opening remarks of the convention.

The fact that he was, indeed, more than just a little concerned over the size of the opposition forces present in the hall was immediately apparent by the direction of his speech. The first fifteen minutes was devoted to a ringing denunciation of Rothbard's open letter to the convention, and criticism of some remarks made by Karl Hess in the same issue of their *Libertarian Forum*. As usual for Buckley, his excoriation dealt with the style rather than the content of the letter, as if the main crime committed was their bad manners in confronting the issues head on rather than fondling them like gentlemen. He continued his speech with the usual conservative tirade about the perils of international communism and our need to arm ourselves at all costs and defend our nation even "unto the consummation of the world."

Presumably, then, we would all go to heaven with the Pope for blowing up the earth in the name of God.

Another interesting fact worth mentioning here is Mr. Buckley's attitude on the question of freedom. In his speech he mentioned that freedom is for those who agree to live within the framework of our traditions. Those who deny these traditions become "*excommunicants*" who then lose their right to the freedom guaranteed by our constitutional republic. Here, precisely, is the mystical element in the conservative mentality which has pushed them so far apart from their former allies: the notion that freedom is a gift to be dispensed among our worthy citizens by a moralistic government. The anarchists claim that freedom is a natural right, and if the state denies it to its citizens, they have a right to seize it themselves.

At 11:00 P.M., following the opening ceremonies, a slow trickle of students began heading for the silver arch dazzling in the moonlight. Gradually their numbers grew, swelling to a crowd of some three hundred sprawled along the hillside beneath the arch facing the Mississippi. Hess, surrounded by his son and other leaders of the radical faction, then delivered his now familiar message. The

YAF Power Play

In an article written on the St. Louis convention, "Young Authoritarians for 'Freedom'", our anarcho-libertarian comrade, Joseph M. Cobb, former editor of the *New Individualist Review*, contributes an important insight about the racket inherent in the YAF organization. Speaking with one of the founders and long-time leaders of YAF at the convention, Cobb was surprised to find this leader admitting the following:

The anarchists, he charged, were "ruining everything". Why? Because, Cobb reports, the "National Office of YAF is playing a double game with the older generation of businessmen and politicians, and making it pay"--pay in the form of plush offices, high salaries, and expense accounts. From these right-wing moneybags YAF raises a great deal of money for such theocratic programs, beloved of the right-wing, as the "Campaign for Voluntary Prayer" in public schools. But few students would be attracted by such programs, so programs such as the prayer campaign "generated money which was used to cover money-losing projects, but ones which the kids dig --such as abolishing the draft." Thus, the YAF leadership obtain money for right-wing causes, but then must use part of the money to attract a mass base of kids, without whom the money would disappear in the long run--thus making YAF a kind of two-way racket. Cobb adds that "YAF is upset because these crazy kids, with their principled opposition to the state, are going to overturn the National Office's carefully balanced financial-ideological system."

Cobb concludes with the important insight that "the only way the National Office people can get away with their programs for fund-raising and semi-reformist free-market-ism is to promote the philosophy of "fusionism"! . . . Fusionism is a pseudo-philosophy which attempts to reconcile the libertarian anti-statist position with the traditional conservative authoritarianism. The fusionists are almost perfect examples of the Marxist sociology-of-ideas theory: each social class will invent ideas which further its own class interests."

Right had abandoned its stated principles championing the individual. Power to the People was formerly an old Republican concept, and was now a policy of the New Left. The conservatives, heretofore critical of our expanding federal bureaucracy, were now aggrandizing more power unto the state in order to fight 'the communist menace'. The chief threat to liberty in the United States was not the splintered radical left, but the efficient, and near-omnipotent United States government. Decentralization and neighborhood control was the only answer for the growing urban crisis, and the Right must join forces with the New Left in a united attempt to realize these goals.

The Hess message was a popular one for those assembled on the hillside--an estimated 20-25% of the total 1200 attending the convention--but his endorsement of a Libertarian Right and New Left coalition clearly polarized the group into two broad camps. The more radical element was enthusiastic about joining forces with at least some libertarian (voluntary commune) factions of the New Left; the more conservative were visibly disturbed and registered some doubts about the "inherent totalitarian tendencies" of collectivism, whether voluntary or otherwise. After Hess' speech, the crowd broke up into discussion groups, and that's how the night ended at approximately 3:00 A.M., with a dozen units of concerned students debating issues under the stars.

The main hope of the conservatives the following morning was to divide their opposition into two weak and ineffectual camps. These would be the more "conservative" liber-

(Continued on page 3)

REPORT FROM ST. LOUIS — *(Continued from page 2)*

tarians who were interested in working within YAF to elect their own directors to the National Board which was completely controlled by hard-line Buckleyites, and to adopt a few libertarian planks into the official platform, calling for: active resistance against the draft; a denunciation of domestic fascism as a twin evil to international communism; legalization of marijuana; immediate pull-out from Vietnam; several changes in YAF's official Sharon Statement; and an assortment of other pertinent resolutions. These libertarians, led by Don Ernsberger and Dana Rohrabacher, were by far the larger of the two dissident groups, claiming over three hundred members for their Libertarian Caucus.

The second faction of rebels consisted of radical libertarians of anarchists, most of them belonging to Karl Hess IV's Anarcho-Libertarian Alliance. This contingent was more interested in splitting off from YAF entirely and forming a new alliance with New Left anarchists and anti-statists. They numbered no more than fifty hard-core radicals, but had high hopes of siphoning off as many of the libertarian group as possible by the end of the convention.

The second day proceeded pretty well along the lines that the conservatives had planned. Except for Dr. Harold Demsetz' speech in the morning enumerating various benefits of the free market, the general tone of the speeches of the day was a hammering away at the negative theme of anti-communism.

But if Friday was a field day for the conservatives, Saturday would be remembered as the day on which all those of even quasi-libertarian sentiment consolidated their forces in general disgust against the whole tone of the convention. The session opened at 11:30 A. M., an hour and a half later than scheduled. The first ninety minutes were occupied by challenges from the floor on the seating of delegates, with the libertarians charging that many of their people were being purged by the conservative leadership in order to minimize their strength during the voting for directors to the National Board and platform resolutions.

Finally the rollcall of states began. The Libertarian Caucus was basing its hope on a slate of nine candidates ranging ideologically from moderate libertarian to anarchist. If two or three of their candidates were elected, and perhaps one or two of their minority plank resolutions passed, the Ernsberger group would have considered it a victory and divorced themselves entirely from the radical Anarcho-Libertarian Alliance. However, this was not to be the case. Before half the roll was called, it was evident that every one of the libertarian candidates was being thoroughly routed and the conservatives eventually succeeded in electing all their candidates to the nine available positions. It was at this point that talk of a walk-out began.

Note On Libertarians

It is dramatic and heartwarming that the Revolution has come to YAF. But the euphoria engendered by St. Louis must not be allowed to obscure the fact that this Revolution has not yet succeeded, for the moderate "Libertarian Caucus" has largely decided to stay within this authoritarian organization, to work from within for change. As long as they continue to do so, they will continue to provide a libertarian cover for fascism. They may have been radicalized by the confrontation at St. Louis, but they clearly have not been radicalized enough. To discover why this is so, the curious phenomenon of "conservative" libertarians or even anarchists must be analyzed at length, and this will be done in the next issue of the *Libertarian Forum*.

to spread, for the first time, into the ranks of the moderate libertarians.

Next came the voting on the minority platform resolutions. Disaffection spread rapidly among the entire opposition as, one by one, they saw their resolutions hammered down by the conservatives: immediate withdrawal from Vietnam--defeated; legalization of marijuama--tabled; denunciation of domestic fascism--hooted down and defeated. Then came the issue which was finally to polarize the convention into two hostile, openly-warring camps. The libertarians offered their resolution advocating active resistance to the military draft, and saw it trammeled by a solid majority. It was after the reading of the majority plank on the draft which limited anti-draft agitation to legal channels, that the event took place which was to force everyone present to make an instant decision: either in support of the conservative majority, or against them with the radical libertarians. There could no longer be any room for fence-straddling.

A young man, who shall remain nameless for obvious reasons, stepped forward and grabbed a microphone in the center of the floor. Clearly announcing that it was the right of every individual to defend himself from violence, including state violence, he lifted a card, touched it with a flame from a cigarette lighter, and lifted it over his head while it burned freely into a curling black ash. For fifteen or twenty seconds the hall was locked in numb silence, finally to be shattered by an enraged war cry:
"Kill the commies!"

The next second can best be described as the instant radicalization of the moderate libertarians. While the first onrushers were knocked back by five or six radicals surrounding the "criminal commie", the ranks of the Libertarian Caucus solidified into a barrier separating the radicals from the howling conservative majority. In the swinging and pushing which followed, the young student who had triggered the melee escaped outside the convention hall. The libertarians, stepping on chairs and raising their fists against the conservatives, sent up a chant:
"Laissez faire! Laissez faire!"

There was no question where they stood now: in clear opposition to the conservative majority.

The majority found their own voices, and howled back in reply:
"Sock it to the Left! Sock it to the Left!"
This was countered with:
"Sock it to the State! Sock it to the State!"

The issues were clearly drawn, and three hundred and fifty libertarians suddenly found themselves in violent opposition to their former conservative allies numbering some eight or nine hundred strong. It took the best part of the next half hour to calm everyone down and get them outside the convention hall. In the early evening hours that followed, the conservatives met privately and passed a resolution condemning the card-burning act as "illegal", and denouncing the radicals as being "outside the mainstream of Young Americans for Freedom" (echoes of 1964).

This was not to be the end of the visible conflict separating the two groups. Later that night, while the libertarians were conducting their own meeting to discuss future strategy, a swarm of conservatives went stomping throughout the floors of the inn shouting: "Kill the libertarians! Kill the libertarians!" Suddenly it dawned on the minority opposition exactly who their main enemy really was. The New Left? New Leftists had never demanded the blood of the anti-statist Right. The situation was so shocking to some of the instantly-radicalized that there was even talk of traveling only in groups, and locking themselves into their rooms.

However, this defensive attitude was not to last for any considerable length of time. The smell of success had been

(Continued on page 4)

51

REPORT FROM ST. LOUIS — *(Continued from page 3)*

too exhilarating. In the corridor outside the main convention hall, Dana Rohrabacher, Don Ernsberger, and several of the "moderate" libertarian group were actually setting the pace for the radical anarchists. The former moderates were now painting placards with anarchist slogans--"Smash the State!" "I am an enemy of the State!"--and posting them up on the walls. While a chorus of boos greeted them from conservative onlookers, Rohrabacher mounted a chair and started the now-familiar cry:

"Laissez faire! Laissez faire!"

This was picked up instantly by about a hundred fifty of the former moderates, and now it was their turn to go tromping through the corridors of the hotel, forcing the conservatives to scurry into locked rooms. When the

---

Recommended Reading

The *Tranquil* Statement. A brilliant, rip-roaring statement, adopted aboard the S. S. *Tranquil*, by the Anarchist Caucus of the Young Americans for Freedom. 15 pp. Available for 35¢ from Elizabeth Crain, 1085 National Press Building, 14th and F Sts., N. W., Washington, D. C. 20004.

Noam Chomsky, *American Power and the New Mandarins* (Pantheon). A great and unusual book. Not only the best scholarly but angry dissection of the intellectuals in the ruling class, centering on their role in Vietnam. But also excellent for World War II Revisionism in the Pacific, and Spanish War revisionism (pro-anarchist). Professor Chomsky has a clear fondness for the anarchist position.

David Horowitz, ed., *Containment and Revolution* (Beacon Press, paper). Good essays on the origins of the Cold War; includes a fine paper by Todd Gitlin on the origins of the Cold War in Greece during World War II, and an appreciation of Senator Taft by a young New Left historian.

F. J. P. Veale, *Advance to Barbarism* (Devin-Adair). It is good to have this outstanding early work of World War II Revisionism, hitherto only published in Britain, at last available in the U. S. The first work that showed that it was Britain, not Germany, that began deliberate mass strategic bombing of civilians.

---

counter-demonstration finally exhausted itself, the conservatives managed to muster a small counter-counter-offensive, chanting the cry, "Lazy fairies!" as they passed the radicals, thereby putting themselves in the unique position of repudiating their own economic philosophy and openly embracing our current system of state-corporate fascism.

The climax of the convention for the radicals came in the form of a meeting of all the libertarian and anarchist groups, including two SDS anarchist chapters. The meeting decided to form a communications network to keep all the organizations, including any New Left organizations that care to participate, in continuous contact with one another. This new loosely-knit organization will be called the Libertarian Confederation, and will be managed and operated by the Maryland-based Society for Rational Individualism.

Some of the radicals will split off entirely from YAF; others will remain on an individual basis and continue to proselytize among the conservative ranks. The most important thing to emerge from this convention is that, for the first time, the most influential forces on the Libertarian Right will be working to establish an open and working coalition with the New Left in their common struggle to resist the abuses of the United States government.

Also: Regular Washington Column By Karl Hess

Published on the first and fifteenth of every month   Subscription rate: $7.00 per year; Student subscription rate: $5.00 per year

A Semi-Monthly Newsletter

THE
Libertarian Forum

Joseph R. Peden, Publisher   Washington Editor, Karl Hess   Murray N. Rothbard, Editor

VOL. I, NO. XIII   October 1, 1969   35¢

Anarcho-Rightism

Karl Hess's brilliant article in this issue turns the spotlight on a new and curious phenomenon of "libertarians" and even "anarchists" who yet are strongly opposed to revolutionary change, and who therefore at least objectively stamp themselves as defenders of the existing state and the *status quo*. But this opposition to revolution is no accident; it is part and parcel of the entire world-view of these people --whom we may call "anarcho-rightists". For the anarcho-rightist, beneath the veneer of his professed anarchism, still remains what he generally was before his anarchistic conversion: a benighted right-winger.

In a sense, it is heartwarming that the overwhelming logic and consistency of the anarcho-capitalist position has won over a large number of former laissez-fairists and Randians. But every rapidly developing movement has growing pains; anarchism's growing pain is that this conversion has, in all too many cases, been skin deep. The curious conservatism and moderation of the Libertarian Caucus of YAF is but one glaring example of this defect.

Let us analyze the anarcho-rightist. In effect, he says: "O. K., I'm convinced that it is immoral for a government to impose a monopoly of coercion by the use of force, and it possible or even probable that the free market could supply all services now considered governmental, including judicial and police protection. Since this is anarchism, I am an anarchist."

But his anarchism is only an anarchism for the far distant future, to be achieved solely by patient education, the issuing of leaflets and pronouncements, etc. *In the meanwhile*, in his concrete, day-to-day attitudes, the anarcho-rightist remains fully as right-wing as he was before. His anarchism is only a thin veneer laid on top of a moral of profoundly "anarchist" and statist views, views that he has not bothered to root out of his social philosophy.

Thus, the anarcho-rightist remains an American patriot. He reveres the American government as the "freest in the world", he worships the Founding Fathers (failing to realize that the Constitution was a profoundly statist *coup d'etat* imposed upon the far more libertarian Articles of Confederation), he loves and admires the two major enforcement-good squad arms of the State: the army and the police. *Defining* the police *a priori* as defenders of person and property, he supports their clubbing, beating, and torturing of dissenters and opposition movements to the State. Totally ignorant of the American guilt for the Cold War and of the long-time expansionist nature of U.S. imperialism, he supports that Cold War in the belief that the "international Communist conspiracy" is a direct military threat to American liberties. Critical of Establishment propaganda in domestic affairs, he yet has allowed himself to be totally sucked in by the Establishment propaganda about the Communist bogey. Hence, he supports the American military. Even if he opposes the Vietnam War, he does so only as a tactical error that is not in American "national interests". Although a self-proclaimed libertarian, he shows no concern whatever for the genocidal American murder of millions of innocent Vietnamese peasants. And, beset by a narrow, solipsistic desire to keep his university classes open, he actually takes the lead in defending the State's brainwashing apparatus--the American schools and colleges (either State-owned or State-subvened)--against the rising opposition to that educational system.

In short, the fact that, in philosophic theory, the anarcho-rightist is indeed an anarchist should cut very little ice with those anarchists who are truly opponents of the American State, and who are therefore revolutionaries. For when it comes to concrete *actions*, actions in which he must line up either for the State or for the opposition to that State, he has generally lined up on the wrong side of the barricades-- defending the American State against its enemies. So long as he does so, he remains an opponent rather than an ally.

A strategic argument has been raging for some time among revolutionaries whether or to what extent the anarcho-rightist offers prime material for conversion to the revolutionary position. Basically, how much time one spends working on any given rightist is a matter of personal temperament and patience. But one gloomy note must be sounded: there is a grave tendency among many rightists to be solipsistic: in short, to not give a damn about principle, about justice, or, in the last analysis, about liberty. There is a tendency for rightists to be concerned only with their own narrow monetary profits and immediate creature comforts, and therefore to scorn those of us who are dedicated to liberty and justice as a cause. For these ignoble solipsists, any form of dedication to principle smacks of "collectivism" or "altruism". I had wondered for years why so many Randians, for example, place such great emphasis on combatting "altruism" (which has always struck me as an absurd social philosophy of little importance.) Now I am beginning to realize that for many of these people, "altruism" means any form of devotion to principle, to liberty and justice for all men, to any principle, indeed, which may disturb their own cozy accommodations to the statist evils which they recognize in the abstract.

Thus, when, many years ago, I raised a call for a *revolutionary* libertarian movement, I was dismissed by these people as crackpotty and unrealistic. There could never be a revolution here, and that was that. Then, in the mid-1960's, when, almost miraculously, the New Left revolutionary

(Continued on page 4)

Letter From Washington

By Karl Hess

Conservative Libertarianism

Libertarianism has managed to develop its own form of counter-revolutionary conservatism. Its future as a movement, much less as an influence on future social change, could be crushed by it if unopposed and unanalyzed.

Underlying this conservatism are an undying and undeniable respect for institutionalized, *traditional* injustice, as opposed to possible future injustice, and the unbeatable contradictions of reformism.

No person even on the fringes of a libertarian discussion can have escaped the explicit wording of the former or the overtones of the latter.

Libertarians, this conservative position holds, cannot take part in revolutionary action because, as it now stands, such action always is dominated by persons with a healthy disrespect for private property and a feverish fondness for communist rhetoric.

The argument is made, time and time again, that "if *they* get power, *they* will be worse than what we have." The notion that *they* might include libertarians if only libertarians were up there on the barricades working *with* them either eludes these conservatives or they reject it because of their spotless, yea immaculate conceptions of theoretical purity. But most pernicious is the possibility that such persons truly mean what they say: that they prefer the certainty of the injustices we have to any risk of injustices that we *might* have. There is a trap here deep enough to engulf freedom itself. Theories do not produce revolutionary action. Rather, revolutionary actions *enable* theories to become practices. It is from the ferment of the action that the ferment of the idea brews its future impact. Long before Mao or machineguns it was apparent that political thought, without political act, equalled zero and that political ideas born in the minds of men have a chance to grow only after actions by the hands of men. Not even Christianity or Ghandian resistance grew solely as an idea. All great ideas have grown as the result of great actions.

No example comes to mind of a great teacher who was not also a great exemplar, a personification of and not merely a mouthpiece of his ideas. Take Christ and the money-lenders. He unquestionably had the benefit of sound advice in regard to economic analysis and pedagogy. He could have held classes to expose usury to a few who would go out and expose it to more and so on and on until the entire world was revulsed by the practice and ceased doing business with the usurers. The story, of course, is different. It tells of a decision to teach by acting.

In the more real, or at least contemporary world we can think of the many political and economic theorists--some of them libertarians!--who did not have the act of revolution to spread their thoughts, as did Karl Marx.

If Bakunin or Warren had had a Lenin we might live in a free and anarchistic world today.

The consequence of conservative libertarianism's concentration on ideas to the exclusion of action is to turn a prudent sense of priority on its head. The priorities, as I see them, are to first participate in social change so that, second, there will be a chance of influencing its direction later on. Unless one can reject flatly the possibility that there is even going to be a change, the priority should not be to fret about what it might be like, the priority is to maintain a position

from which or in which you can do something about it.

The impossibility of simple neutrality in this situation should be apparent. You cannot just say "a pox on both of your houses" because, unfortunately, you happen actually to live in one of the houses. By that act alone neutrality is made impossible--except for those very rare few who actually can withdraw totally, to dream out their isolation so long as, and only so long as, the unleashed dogs of the system, against which they have refused to struggle, are not set upon them.

From the conservative position comes the position of libertarian reformism. It holds that, since there is a good base to build upon--the at least lip-service traditions of liberty in this country, for instance--that the way to avoid the dangers that might lurk on the other side of revolutionary change is to opt for evolutionary change. The repeal of certain laws is, in this position, held as crucial and, of course, it probably is true that if the withholding tax were repealed that the government would be bankrupted as millions of taxpayers simply found themselves unable to pay up.

That is, this situation might be true if it were not for the amazing ingenuity of American state-monopoly-capitalism. Few if any corporation heads would stand idly by and see the source of their prosperity--a partnership with the state --seriously jeopardized. One can imagine a "voluntary" tax withholding system going into effect which, if anything, might be more effective than the state system which, after all, *is* operated by businessmen anyway even though with a lot of wasteful bureaucratic interference. Same with the voluntary or even 'corporate' military concepts. A libertarian should be the first to recognize that such systems would, if anything, make imperialism more effective by making its military machine more efficient. Such reforms, in short, would not necessarily end injustices but might merely streamline them.

More pertinent is the central error of reformism as a possible instrument of change. To reform a system you must, first of all, preserve it against attacks more precipitous than those called for in the reformist timetable. This position not only makes neutrality impossible, it makes siding with the system (the state) unavoidable in the long run.

I sum up my concern over these matters in this way: Libertarians are faced with a real, not merely theoretical world in which revolutionary change is at the very least a real possibility everywhere. If libertarians will not participate in that change they cannot influence that change now *or* later. It is the important characteristic of this journal that it does not intend to relegate the black flag of the most revolutionary of positions, libertarianism, to the sidelines of any revolution, no matter the color of the other banners unfurling.

The New Boston Tea Party

While thousands of libertarians sit on the sidelines, griping about any *action* that might ruffle the feathers of the State, two hundred and fifty rebellious and admirable taxpayers staged a new Boston Tea Party, on September 14, at the small community of Boston, Pennsylvania, about 20 miles southeast of Pittsburgh. These citizens, many of them conservative businessmen and women, were vigorously portesting the proposal of Governor Raymond P. Shafer to impose that iniquitous instrument, a state income tax.

The protestors, dressed like their illustrious forebears as Indians, paddled a canoe onto the waters of the Youghiogheny River, and dumped into the river cardboard containers labelled "tea".

The tax rebels also revived another institution with a glorious and long-lived tradition in America--hanging politicians in effigy. Governor Shafer was hung in effigy, and any politicians who arrived at the demonstration in person were given a hostile, though non-violent, reception.

National Review Rides Again

National Review, the intellectual Field Marshal of the New Right, is getting worried. After several attacks on myself during the course of this year, N. R. has begun to make clear that the rapid growth of the libertarian movement is getting to be a burr under its "fusionist" saddle. In our last issue, Jerry Tuccille detailed Bill Buckley's devotion of the first half-hour of his keynote address at the YAF convention at St. Louis to a bitter attack upon mine and Karl Hess's articles in the "Listen, YAF" issue of the *Libertarian Forum* . Now, Jared C. Lobdell, in the official report on St. Louis (NR, Sept. 23) tries to pooh-pooh the dramatic confrontation at the convention, repeats the same tired old line that "traditionalists" and libertarians are in perfect agreement (on liberty "within the framework of the Western tradition"), except, of course, for a few "extremists" who are for liberty *outside* Western tradition (whatever that is supposed to mean). That's us folks, us who *really* believe, as Buckley correctly charged at St. Louis, that extremism in the defense of liberty is no vice and that moderation in the pursuit of justice is no virtue.

But now NR has wheeled out its heaviest gun, Frank S. Meyer, to do battle with libertarianism ("Libertarianism or Libertinism?", NR, Sept. 9)--a sure sign that we are really hurting the Right-wing, for Meyer, a shrewd political strategist, never wastes his words on purely intellectual controversy. All of his columns are calculated for their political impact. Seven years ago, Meyer felt called upon (in his "Twisted Tree of Liberty", now reprinted in his collection, *The Conservative Mainstream*) to print an attack upon what was then a very tiny group because we split with the Right-wing on the presumptuous grounds of being opposed to nuclear annihilation. Now that our polarization from the Right-wing is complete and our ranks growing every day, Meyer attempts a more comprehensive critique of libertarianism.

Meyer begins with the complaint that libertarians are really "libertines" (hedonists? sex-fiends?) because we "reject" the "reality" of five thousand years of Western civilization, and propose to substitute an abstract construction. Very true; in other words, we, like Lord Acton, propose to weight the growth of encrusted tradition and institutions in the light of man's natural reason, and of course we find these often despotic institutions wanting. To Meyer, we propose to "replace God's creation of this multifarious, complex world . . . and substitute for it their own creation". Very neat. The world as it is, in short the *status quo* of statism and tyranny, is, in the oldest theocratic trick in history, stamped with the approval of being "God's creation", while any radical change from that tyranny is sneered at as "man's creation". Meyer, the self-proclaimed fusionist and "conservative libertarian", thus stamps himself as simply another incarnation of Sir Robert Fillmer and Bishop Bossuet, another intellectual apologist for the divine right of kings.

Meyer then proceeds to set up a straw man: we libertines, he thunders, believe in liberty as man's highest end, whereas conservatives uphold liberty as man's highest political end, i.e. to free man so that he can pursue his own ends. But no libertarian I have ever heard of considers liberty as anything but the highest *political* end; the whole idea of liberty is to free man so that every individual can pursue whatever personal ends he wishes.

Having knocked down this straw man, Meyer leaps to his real complaint: that we libertines wish to free man so that each person can pursue whatever goals he desires. *This*, not the phony political end vs. absolute end, is Meyer's real grievance. No, he declares, men should only be free to pursue their ends within the framework of tradition and "civilizational order". I have wondered for years what Meyer and his cohorts have really meant by their constant talismanic incantations to "Western civilization". What, after all, *is* "Western civilization" or "civilizational order"? In attacking us for our sympahty with the "rampaging mobs of campus and ghetto" and our opposition to the war machine against Communism, the answer becomes fairly clear; what Meyer means by the "bulwarks of civilizational order" is, plainly and bluntly, the State apparatus. It is the State that Meyer is anxious to preserve and protect; it is the State that he holds to be synonymous with, or at the very least, essential to, his beloved but highly vague "Western civilization". If one reads the *National Review* theocrats long enough, one almost begins to sympathize with the Russian "Anarcho-Futurists" of Kharkov who, in 1918, raised the cry, "Death to world civilization!"

If Meyer's poorly reasoned piece is the best that can be hurled against us, and I suppose it is, then we libertarians have nothing to fear on the intellectual front. Libertines of the world, unite! You have nothing to lose but your chains-- and the privilege of endless subjection to theocratic cant.

Abolition: An Acid Test

It has come to our attention increasingly of late that many self-proclaimed libertarians balk at the idea of abolishing slavery. It is almost incredible to contemplate, for one would think that at least the minimal definition of a libertarian is someone who favors the immediate abolition of slavery. Surely, slavery is the polar opposite of liberty?

But it appears that many libertarians argue as follows: the slave-masters bought their slaves on the market in good faith. They have the bill of sale. Therefore, respect for their property rights requires that slavery be left intact, or at the very least that the slave-master be compensated for any loss of his slave at the market value.

I used to believe, and have written articles to that effect, that the idea that right-wingers uphold "property rights over human rights" is only a left-wing smear. But evidently it is not a smear. For these libertarians indeed go to the grotesque length of upholding property rights at the expense of the human right of self-ownership of every person. Not only that: by taking this fetishistic position these pro-slavery libertarians negate the very concept, the very basis, of property right itself. For where does property right come from? It can only come from one basic and ultimate source --and that is *not* the pronouncement of the State that Mr. A belongs to Mr. B. That source is the property right of every man in his own body, his right of self-ownership. From this right of self-ownership is derived his right to whatever previously unowned and unused resources a man can find and transform by the use of his labor energy. But if every man has a property right in his own person, this immediately negates any grotesquely proclaimed "property right" in other people.

There are five possible positions on the abolition of slavery question. (1) That slavery must be protected as a part of the right of property; and (2) that abolition may only be accompanied by full compensation to the masters, seem to me to fall on the basis of our above discussion. But the third route--simple abolition--the one that was adopted, was also unsatisfactory, since it meant that the means of production, the plantations on which the slaves worked, remained in the hands, in the property, of their masters. On the libertarian homesteading principle, the plantations should have reverted to the ownership of the slaves, those who were forced to work them, and not have remained in the hands of their criminal masters. That is the fourth alternative. But there is a fifth alternative that is even more just: the punishment of the criminal masters for the benefit of their former slaves--in short, the imposition of reparations or damages upon the former criminal class, for the benefit of their victims. All this recalls the excellent statement of the Manchester Liberal, Benjamin Pearson,

(Continued on page 4)

ABOLITION: AN ACID TEST — *(Continued from page 3)*

who, when he heard the argument that the masters should be compensated replied that "he had thought it was the slaves who should have been compensated."

It should be clear that this discussion is of far more than antiquarian interest. For there are a great many analogues to slavery today, an enormous number of cases where property has been acquired not through legitimate effort but through State theft, and where, therefore, similar alternatives will have to be faced once more.

ANARCHO-RIGHTISM — *(Continued from page 1)*

movement began to take hold in America, these libertarians shifted to a new position: that a revolution in this country would never be libertarian, it would only be Marxist and dictatorial. But *now*, now when libertarian revolutionism has begun to spread like wildfire among the youth, now the anarcho-rightists have begun to display their cloven hooves: they have begun to reveal that they oppose even a *libertarian* movement. Several of such people have recently declared that I, or rather the revolutionary libertarian movement of

which I am a part, am "more of a threat to them" than the State. Why? There appear to be two reasons. First, that *any* revolution will disturb their cozy accommodations, their petty profits, their lousy classes. In short, their dedication to liberty is so weak, so feeble, that they oppose bitterly any rocking of the boat, any disturbance to their cozy little lives. They don't really oppose the State, certainly not in practice. They can "live with" the State quite contentedly. The second reason is that many of these people cringe from revolutionary justice, because they know that much of their income and wealth have derived from unjust State robbery.

And so these anarcho-rightists sit basely on the sidelines, hugging their petty comforts, griping and carping about the revolution while the New Left and other revolutionaries put their lives on the line in opposition to the very State which they *claim* to oppose but do so much to defend. And yet, should the revolution ever succeed, these people expect that the fruits of liberty will drop into their laps, that they will reap benefits which they have done not one whit to earn through struggle. And O the recriminations that they will heap upon us if liberty is not then handed to them, unearned, upon a silver platter. For their own opportunist sakes, anarcho-rightists might ponder the fact that successful revolutionaries, no matter how libertarian, tend to be very impatient with those who have opposed them every step of the way. As Karl Hess has eloquently written, the position of any revolutionary tends to be: "No voice, no choice; no tickee no shirtee; no commitment now, no commitments later."

Published on the first and fifteenth of every month   Subscription rate: $7.00 per year; Student subscription rate: $5.00 per year

A Semi-Monthly Newsletter

THE
Libertarian Forum

Joseph R. Peden, Publisher   Washington Editor, Karl Hess   Murray N. Rothbard, Editor

VOL. I, NO. XIV   October 15, 1969   35¢

We Make The Media

The dynamic, cascading, coruscating upsurge of the revolutionary libertarian movement has finally broken into the nation's mass media--a sure sign, in those unsympathetic quarters, that we are becoming a force to be reckoned with. In the last few weeks, our movement has garnered important publicity in the nation's press.

Item: The New York *Times*, for Sunday, September 28, has a long, objective article on Karl Hess, entitled "Goldwater Aide Now a Radical; Adopts Anarchism Philosophy", along with a fine picture of Karl. After reporting on the influence of the war in Vietnam and the suppression of the student revolt in turning Karl into a pure libertarian, the *Times* quotes him on Vietnam: " 'We should not have intervened in Vietnam,' he said. 'If we had to intervene, we should have been on the other side.' In comparison to Ngo Dinh Diem, the N. L. F. sounds like a bunch of constitutionalists." On his shift from anti-Communism to anarchism: "I concluded that my enemy is not a particular state--not Cuba or North Vietnam, for example--but the state itself."

Item: *Newsweek*, September 29, has another article on Karl, "Ideologues: You Know He's Right". In contrast to the objective tone of the *Times*, the *Newsweek* article is snide and supercilious. Typically, in the course of sneering at Karl's "zigzag" career, *Newsweek* conveniently forgets to mention that Karl Hess was once one of its own editors. But, in the annals of public relations, "every knock is a boost", so long as the name gets spelled right, and not only is Karl mentioned, but so too is our own little, no-budget *Libertarian Forum* --our first breakthrough into the mass media!

Item: the sober, well-edited journal of corporate liberalism, *Business Week*, has a lengthy article in its September 27 issue, "Economics: Radicals try to rewrite the book". This is an objective portrayal of new trends in New Left economics, particularly as embodied in the Union for Radical Political Economics (URPE). In addition to the inevitable socialist and Marxist trends in the New Left, *Business Week* notes, in some surprise, a new element: "free-market anarchism". The feature in this section is our friend Mike Zweig, a leader of URPE and assistant professor of economics at SUNY at Stony Brook. There is a very good picture of Zweig, with the caption, "calls himself a free-market anarchist", and then Zweig's views are discussed as follows:

"There is, in fact, a decided strain of anarchism among the New Left that persists even when the radicalism takes more systematic form. Zweig argues for a society that begins with a revolution to redistribute property ('the existing distribution of property is the result of theft') and ends with freedom from any governmental interference.

According to his analysis, modern capitalism has failed because so many of the 'real costs' of economic activity are borne by the public at large. Air pollution is an obvious example. A free market that forced everyone to pay the real social costs of production would probably maximize welfare with a minimum of constraints, he contends."

To *Business Week*, all this is a "powerful challenge" but "to economists over thirty, such utopian thinking is a sign of intellectual confusion." But far from being confusion, what Mike is clearly advocating is the extension of private property rights so as to prevent such invasion of private property as has been permitted to occur in the case of air pollution--a pollutant invasion of the person and property of much of the population. What Mike, in short, is advocating is the very "free market" which so many Establishment economists are *supposed* to be advocating but, alas, in rhetoric only.

And so we're on the march. Onward and upward.

Class Analysis

Many right-wing libertarians appear to be uneasy in the face of class analysis when it is used to interpret and explicate the nature of political reality. Indeed, one gentlemen at the first Libertarian Forum took the position that there is no such thing as a class. Now obviously the word "exists" is used equivocally; no collective entities exist apart from the individuals which constitute these entities. Yet to say, for instance, that "society" does not exist as some strange entity over and above the individuals who live together in certain relationships and constitute society is not to say that these individuals do not in fact relate to each other in a certain way. Likewise people who share common interests and/or characteristics are said to belong to a class, or sub-division of the society which they help to constitute. Thus, all redheaded females belong to a class, as do all Roman Catholics, and so forth. All who have an interest in a particular piece of legislation also belong to a class. And, all those who share a common commitment to a wide variety of measures, the net result of which is to protect, secure and enhance their power and wealth--to preserve the *status quo*--belong to an *economic* class (to characterize the class relevantly). The class above described would in fact be a *ruling* class, assuming of course that their ends are actually effected. The key distinction here is

(Continued on page 4)

The Czech Crisis

Conclusion

The Prague Spring . . . And After

By Leonard P. Liggio

The New Economic Model prepared in 1963 by the Czech economic institute commission headed by Ota Sik contained more advanced concepts than other East European proposals. This was due to the fact that the Czechs had begun their free inquiry later and thus were able to begin at the point where the economists of the other countries had ended. Also, there were a few Czech economists who were willing to espouse entirely radical positions which gave their colleagues the opportunity to present far-reaching changes as a moderate program. Eugen Loebl, director of the Bank of Slovakia, courageously led the criticism of orthodox Marxist economic theory. Although he had just been rehabilitated after years as a political prisoner, Loebl declared that the country needed a mixed economy with 200,000 (30%) of small privately-owned enterprises. (According to Stanford Research Institute-International, entrepreneurs in Czechoslovakia are "already quite free to start small industries" under the 1968 reforms.) Prof. Radoslav Selucky was dismissed from his professorship for the radical market program that he proposed.

Sik's New Economic Model required that enterprises earn their own way, that investments be financed by the enterprises from their own resources or by borrowing at interest, that prices by determined in the competitive free market based upon the law of supply and demand, and that profits be the criterion of economic efficiency. After strong attacks on it by orthodox theorists, the party adopted it in 1965 and it was scheduled for implementation in January 1967 with the withdrawal of subsidies and central planning and the freeing of enterprises to decide what to produce and at what price to sell it.

Not only was the New Economic Model diluted from the beginning, but ultimately it was made ineffective by the party leadership. Nevertheless, the cumulative effect of the partial implementation as well as earlier removal of controls in selected sectors was reflected in major reductions in material costs of production (the first decline in fifteen years). About 40 percent of the 9 percent rise in the gross income of industrial enterprises during 1967 resulted from savings on material costs. There was a 7 percent growth in industry and 8 percent in national income. The opposition of the right-wing, dogmatic party leadership headed by President Novotny was increasingly resented by the younger party leaders. This was given expression by Alexander Dubcek in his October 1967 criticism of the regime for its hostility to radical economics and its suppression of freedom. This attack on authoritarianism projected Dubcek to prominence and led to his election as first party secretary in January.

The immediate issue in the Communist party's October plenary meeting was the assault by clubs and tear gas by the Prague police against the thousands of Czech students marching in protest against conditions at the university. Orthodox communist establishments are as fearful of the anti-authoritarian spirit of youth as are the liberal bureaucratic establishments in the West. The students demanded (and eventually were granted) the dismissal of the police officials responsible for the assault on the student protesters. Thereafter, during the 'Prague Spring' Czech students were at the center of the radicalization process in their country. "There was an incredible spirit of Liberation. Especially among students--young people generally--there was a spirit of defying anything laid down by authority--the Government, the Party, schools, parents. The atmosphere of questioning was everywhere." ("Spirit of defiance", *New Left Notes*, Sept. 16, 1968).

The student struggle was initiated by an ideologically developed cadre of university dissenters called the Prague Radicals; many of them had been expelled or drafted into the army for their organized protests in the universities. But after January 1968 the Prague Radicals were free to organize openly; bypassing the established Czech student association, they formed new youth organizations. The final removal of Novotny by his resignation as president in March was the result of Prague student demonstrations welcoming a national student cavalcade to protest U. S. genocide in Vietnam.

The Soviet invasion forced radical political activism upon the vast majority of Czech students. On November 17 Prague Radicals announced a student strike and occupied the university buildings. They were inspired by the example of the Columbia SDS; SDS activists had been in contact with the Czech students. On the following day all the universities in Czechoslovakia were closed by student strikes and two-thirds of Prague university students joined the occupation of the buildings were SDS-style teach-ins were held. In the succeeding months Prague Radicals demonstrated against censorship and limitations on freedoms until the regime ordered the dissolution of the new student organizations in June 1969.

The sabotage of the New Economic Model by the party right-wing during 1967 had led to the critical central committee plenary session on December 19 which was characterized by violent debates between conservative supporters of central planning and the liberals favoring market economics. Sik led the attack, insisting that to achieve economic reforms and combat bureaucracy the party and government structure would have to be blasted apart by popular action. The centrists were won over to reform and Dubcek was elected party first secretary on Jan. 5, 1968.

Although Ota Sik was appointed deputy premier in charge of the committee of economic advisers, a much more conservative deputy premier was entrusted with actual control over economic departments. Czech radicals proposed market determination of prices, competition among enterprises, incentives for worker productivity, and the end of bureaucratic planning and controls. Centrists preferred cautious change ideologically, politically and economically, and denounced "excessive" freedom. They placed emphasis upon half-way measures such as managerial efficiency, and on maintaining economic planning by technicians and computers with some price freedom but limitations upon the independence of enterprises. Centrists resisted complete decentralization of industrial management, worker self-management of firms, and competition among enterprises for credits and markets. Centrist attitudes parallel those formulated in the Soviet Union under the inspiration of the pioneering but limited contributions of Prof. Liberman of Kharkov University. But Ota Sik has criticized Libermanism as inadequate and simplistic despite its great impact on Soviet economics. Such reforms merely substitute improved goals or indicators, or are "an endeavor merely to limit the number of directive tasks and indicators set by the central planning and managing body." (Ota Sik, Plan and Market under Socialism, White Plains, 1968).

Thus, the centrists desired a convergence with the humane, manipulative bureaucracy of Western Europe and America behind whose facade of political democracy the bureaucracy's control expands. Czech radicals continued to publicize their demand for dismantling the bureaucracy, restoration of self-ownership to individual firms and implementation of the free market. Dubcek condemned the "ingrained evil of excessive levelling of incomes and egalitarianism which has rewarded unskilled work more highly than skilled work." Sik emphasized protection of the consumer: from high prices due to inefficient workers or enterprises and from inferior products caused by "the monopoly position" of state enterprises. "All the lagging enterprises," Sik noted, "are

(Continued on page 3)

THE CZECH CRISIS — *(Continued from page 2)*

being protected to the detriment of good enterprises which show initiative and also to the detriment of the consumer."

To achieve these objectives the Czech radicals sought the reorganization of the Communist Party in order to create a popular movement for reform: the 14th Communist Party Congress was announced for early September 1968. Preparations had been made during preceding months through district elections of Congress delegates; these were almost completely younger members dedicated to reform. The obvious result of the Congress would be the election of a party central committee devoid of conservatives and overwhelmingly radical in commitment. To forestall the party Congress which would have been a qualitative transformation in the nature of a Communist party, the Soviet invasion was launched on August 21. The day before the Soviet invastion Pravda blasted Czech radicals as subverters of socialism for refusing to follow orthodox Marxist economic planning and centralization.

Within days of the invasion an extraordinary party Congress was held secretly in a Prague industrial plant protected by a volunteer workers' guard. While the Soviet army 'controlled' Prague a new party leadership was appointed by the Congress. The support of the reformers by the students is understandable given the revolutionary spirit of modern youth against authoritarianism. What is the explanation of the widespread, ideologically developed support of the general public and of the workers in particular? For about a year economists had conducted "evening schools of economic policy" for workers in the major industrial centers in order to provide a clear understanding of the New Economic Model and its benefits to the workers as producers and consumers. Thus, during the 'Prague Spring' new elections were held for local and general trade union leaders, and younger activists committed to the reforms were elected. After the invasion the trade unions assumed important roles in resisting restrictions on freedoms and organizing mass support for the economic and political reforms which had been introduced. Trade union newspapers and educational departments have become the sanctuaries for reform writers and economists removed after the invasion.

The strong support of the general public for the reform program is the result of the heavy involvement of intellectuals and writers in the reform movement. The year previous, in June 1967 during the Congress of the Writers' Union, several leading writers and editors were expelled from the party for attacks on the conservative cultural functionaries. The Writers' Union journal was suspended. The writers and intellectuals realized that their freedom was at the sufferance of the bureaucracy so long as the government controlled the budget for books and periodicals as well as all jobs and salaries. The need of writers to control the media through which they express themselves caused them to join the advocates of free market economics. Economic independence from the government for quality intellectual production was recognized as analogous to economic independence for quality material production. Similarly, it was clear that intellectuals had suffered from pay equalization standards as much as managers, and that the introduction of salary differentiation in the New Economic Model would mean equivalent increases for managers and intellectuals.

The strong intellectual commitment of the Czech public to political and economic reforms will have positive effects in the long-run despite the immediate obstacles. Similarly, the material conditions which impelled consciousness of the need for reforms will not be solved by half-way measures. The Soviet Union has slowed but it has not erminated the reduction of its advantageous trading position in East Europe. West European business has sought East European markets to escape U. S. financial domination; the six East European countries are "the fastest growing regional

market in the world" and West European business earned about $3 billion in exports there during 1967. East Europe offers the advantages of large reservoirs of engineers and technicians educated at the tax expense of East Europeans and a low wage labor force disciplined by twenty years of Communist trade unionism. The U. S. share of that trade is minimal since U. S. products tend to be non-competitive with West Europe to whom the East Europeans have turned to escape Soviet economic hegemony. The U. S. would prefer to establish semi-political bilateral trade agreements with the Soviet Union, thus avoiding the embarrassment of the non-competitiveness of U. S. products. Thus, the coolness if not hostility of the U. S. toward the "Prague Spring", since economic liberalization would not benefit the U. S.; and the refusal of the U. S. to aid Czechoslovakia by returning the gold deposited in here during World War II. The U. S. by its official statements virtually invited the Soviet invasion, and despite a few muted protests, insisted that there would be no interruption in bilateral U. S.-Soviet negotiations.

In comparison, it was several years after the 1956 Hungarian crisis before U. S. disappointment at the failure of its Hungarian supporters wore off sufficiently for bilateral negotiations. Hungarian events were extremely complex with positive as well as negative aspects, and the heartfelt speeches by Czech delegates (since purged) at the U. N. protesting the Soviet invasion clearly differentiated between the two in the face of the U. S. delegate's self-interested joining of the two events. There was no assumption as in Hungary of army commands by officers previously retired because of their connections with the CIA and NATO (instead a leading conservative general fled to the U. S. when Dubcek was elected). There was no withdrawal of Czechoslovakia from the Warsaw Pact. There was no Czech appeal for intervention of U. S. forces. On the other hand, radical reforms based upon free market economics were not an issue in Hungary. The Czech delegates noted the U. S. disinterest if not hostility to the Czech free market reforms, and denounced the U. S. as equally responsible for the Soviet invasion because the U. S. had initiated the Cold War which had created the atmosphere for internal repression in Czechoslovakia. The concepts of freedom in the "Prague Spring" did not find their inspiration in America; therefore the Czechs could not be disappointed in the lack of American interest in their liberation.

Compared to the situation in Hungary after November 1956 the current situation in Czechoslovakia is far worse. The replacement of Alexander Dubcek by Gustav Husak after more than fifteen months of the January reforms is a major step backwards, while the accessions of Janos Kadar in Hungary and Wladyslaw Gomulka in Poland in the fall of 1956 were forward steps compared to the Stalinist regimes they replaced. Hungary and Poland are agricultural countries (60%) compared to Czechoslovakia (30%), with the heaviest concentration in Slovakia. The Hungarian and Polish farmers benefited from the liberalization of the Kadar and Gomulka leaderships and have played an important role as stabilizing forces since 1956. Similarly, the Catholic Church plays a significant moderating role in rural Hungary and Poland, which is of great assistance to the Communist parties. Only in Slovakia does the Catholic Church have great influence, and that is the most moderate region, causing the least problems for the post-Dubcek leadership.

Having exhausted other means of resistance the Czechs have undertaken a passive resistance campaign in the arena of production. A producers' strike has been in progress in Czechoslovakia for many months, and the economy has become the central point of struggle. Inflation, shortages, poor quality goods have been the result of the passive resistance responding to central planning, abandonment of workers' councils, and rejection of free market principles. In Prague, for example, during the first half of 1969 only 276 apartments were completed; fifteen per cent of last

(Continued on page 4)

THE CZECH CRISIS — *(Continued from page 3)*

year's rate. An official economic report declared that production continues to fall, imbalance grows, increased wages representing the largest part of income growth. The Soviet interruption of the Czech Radicals' development of freedom has resulted economically in a great leap backwards. The current general strike of the producers has created a grave economic crisis in Czechoslovakia, and the Novotny regime fell precisely because it could not solve the economic crisis.

CLASS ANALYSIS — *(Continued from page 1)*

not that the ruling class wishes to preserve the avenues by which people can competitively attain positions of wealth, but rather the ruling class is one which seeks to prevent the above, and to use *political* means (i.e., the coercive power of the state) to secure and expand further the class's economic gains.

A ruling class, or power elite if you will, can be semi-liquid in composition, admitting new members selectively. Also, other classes may be allowed to share in specific spoils so that people victimized by those in power can be occasionally placated, and made to feel that they also have a stake in the system. It is necessary to the maintenance of any ruling class that it convince other groups that what it is doing is in their interest as well--that is, what in fact is intended to benefit the few must be peddled as being in the "general interest". For instance, historian Gabriel Kolko has done a magnificent job of showing how federal regulation of business, long heralded as government control of business for the commonweal, is in fact business control of government, in order to limit competition and cartellize the various industries affected. Moreover, in each instance such regulation was conceived and supported by business to do just this. Yet, the masses have been sufficiently propagandized to believe the opposite of the reality of the situation (cf. *The Triumph of Conservatism* and *Railroads and Regulation*). Today, as a result, there exists a welter of enactments which have effectively cartellized the economy to a large extent (something not possible on a real free market as Kolko and others have demonstrated). In other words, there exists a system of monopoly capitalism in which the business elite have, by gaining effective control of the state apparatus, isolated themselves from the full effects of competition. Backing this system up is the whole defense complex which through massive contracts, and, in the last analysis, war, insures that the system keeps operating. Labor is but a junior partner in all this, with small business getting enough to keep this segment relatively

content. The poor--those excluded from sharing in the power and wealth of the state capitalism system--are given sops of poverty programs.

The intellectual's role in all this is crucial. He must effectively propagandize the mass of people by extolling the virtues of the system, and by helping the ruling class come up with suitable reform measures to patch up the more glaring problems, And, in the final analysis, the intellectual, as has been seen at the Stanford Research Institute, stands ready to assist in subduing the natives if they become restless. The intellectual also has a share in the system.

The task of the libertarian is two-fold. He must work as a scholar to destroy the myths which serve to justify and perpetuate the *status quo*. It is a sad commentary on the right-wing that whereas they were once in the forefront of this endeavor, with men such as Albert Jay Nock and Frank Chodorov, they are now the backbone of the intellectual apologists for the state apparatus. Today the debunking task has fallen to the New Left.

Secondly, and crucially, the libertarian as activist must be ready to step in to help in an overt way to aid in the destruction of the system. No ruling class has ever voluntarily given up power. Education must never stop, but there comes a time when action is also called for (as the Marxists have perceived, there is also education-through-struggle). Those so-called libertarians who, while espousing high sounding principles in support of liberty, in the concrete support state power against any active resistance have clearly failed in both tasks. And those who seek to avoid the problem by trying to "escape" have not only failed as libertarians, but also failed as human beings. Whereas the former group have consigned themselves to the dustbin of history, the latter have a "class" all to themselves: human ostriches.

— Gerald O'Driscoll, Jr.

Also — A Regular Washington Column By Karl Hess

The Libertarian Forum
BOX 341
MADISON SQUARE STATION
NEW YORK, NEW YORK 10010

A Semi-Monthly Newsletter

THE
Libertarian Forum

Joseph R. Peden, Publisher   Washington Editor, Karl Hess   Murray N. Rothbard, Editor

VOL. I, NO. XV   November 1, 1969   35¢

Two Steps Forward, Two Steps Back

THE CONFERENCE

The first New York Libertarian Conference is over. It was a wild and woolly time, both exciting and dull, wonderful and a shambles. It was great that we held it, but it is highly doubtful that another conference will ever be held in the same form. To quote Dickens: "It was the best of times, it was the worst of times; it was the age of wisdom, it was the age of foolishness . . . it was the season of Light, it was the season of Darkness . . ."

In contrast to the P.R. snow jobs handed out by other conference organizers, attesting to the joy and grandeur abounding at their meetings, this will be a candid, unvarnished report and appraisal of the Conference. Our readers deserve no less. It is only fair to add that the appraisal of most of the other organizers of the Conference is far more favorable than my own.

PHASE I: The Triumph

Looking backward, the Conference may be divided into two phases, which differed as Day and Night. Phase I, from Friday night through Saturday afternoon, was indeed a triumphant occasion. In the first place, the attendance. By forgetting to put in our ads that anyone could attend a single session for only $2.50, we unwittingly discouraged a lot of our New York people; perhaps thirty or forty more would have appeared if not for this oversight. But even so, over 200 people attended the Conference, perhaps as high as 220, almost all of whom came from out of town. And what out of town it was incredible. People came, just for this Conference, all the way from California, Florida, Texas, Iowa, Kansas, Wisconsin, Illinois, Ohio, Missouri, New Hampshire, Massachusetts, a large contingent from Michigan, and one heroic young man, John H. C. Pierce, who gave up his summer vacation in order to hitch-hike to the Conference from northern Manitoba! We, the organizers of the Conference, looked out across this sea of faces and hardly recognized a soul. It was a great and historic moment.

As amateur organizers of conferences, it is true that we packed far too much material in the Saturday afternoon panels. There was virtually no break between noon and six P.M. But what material! The papers were of a uniformly high and even scintillating level, and made real contributions to libertarian knowledge. We hope to publish the papers and speeches at the conference in paperback form, to make them available to libertarians across the country and as a permanent part of the libertarian literature.

In the meanwhile, a brief summary of the Phase I papers: On Friday night, I gave a lengthy overview of the libertarian system, beginning with the natural right of self-ownership, developing the structure of property rights in libertarian theory, and ending with a call for the abolition of the State as quickly as possible. On Saturday, in the Economics panel, Professor Laurence Moss of Columbia and Queens Universities, gave a spirited and witty talk on the "Economics of Sin", pointing out that the State is continually redefining the "sin" that it outlaws in order to extend its power over the mass of the people, especially the poorest sectors of the populace. Jerry Tuccille, our most recent important convert from the idea of limited government, gave a rousing talk pointing out that *laissez-faire*, considered logically, must lead one to free-market anarchism. We are honored to be the first publication to announce that Jerry's book, *Radical Libertarianism*, will soon be published by Bobbs-Merrill. Mario J. Rizzo, an honors senior in economics at Fordham University, proved to be one of the stars of the Conference, giving a brilliant paper standing Marx on his head, and arguing that, in the kind of interventionist, corporate state economy that we have today, business profits indeed tend to be an index of exploitation of the rest of society, since they are usually derived from the use of State privilege. In short, much of Marx, while totally fallacious for competitive, free-market capitalism, turns out to be unwittingly applicable to the state-monopoly system that we suffer under today. Professor Walter Block, of Rutgers and New York Universities, delivered a sharp critique of the statism and deviations from liberty of Milton Friedman and the Chicago School.

In the "Politics and Liberty" panel, Roy A. Childs, Jr., a student in history and philosophy at SUNY, Buffalo, summarized his recent article which brilliantly used Randian terminology to demolish the inner contributions of the Randian concept of "limited government". (Roy's article is "Objectivism and the State: An Open Letter to Ayn Rand", *The Rational Individualist*, August, 1969). I gave a talk on how competing police forces and courts could work, and work well, in an anarchist society, and Professor Joseph R. Peden of Baruch College, CUNY, gave a learned and fascinating paper on the thousand years of successful, anarchistic "law and order" in medieval Ireland, an eminently workable society that only fell to the brutal English conquest in the seventeenth century.

(Continued on page 2)

THE CONVENTION — *(Continued from page 1)*

The Foreign Policy panel was another highlight of the meeting. R. Dale Grinder, of the history department of the University of Missouri, delivered a learned, witty, and illuminating paper on United States imperialism in China and the Far East, from 1880-1920. Walter Grinder, graduate student at New York University, traced the origins of the Cold War to the counter-revolutionary, expansionist drive of the United States, back from World War II through the aftermath of the first World War. Professor Leonard Liggio, of City College, CUNY, recalled for us the great founder of modern isolationism and anti-imperialism, the *laissez-faire* economist (and abolitionist) Edward Atkinson, who founded the Anti-Imperialist League during the Spanish-American War, and even sent "subversive" anti-war pamphlets to our soldiers waging an imperialist conquest of the Philippines. *This* is the isolationist heritage which the New Left has now taken up and the Right-wing has unfortunately abandoned.

So far, so great; but during the Saturday session, an undercurrent of rebellion rumbled from various "Young Turks" who, apparently restive at having to follow trains of thought for more than one paragraph, began to gripe about the "over-structuring" of the conference and to call for general "rapping" (open discussion). The time was to come, all too soon, when general rapping would unfortunately take over. And with this rapping came the disintegration of the conference.

PHASE II: Disintegration

Phase II covers Saturday night through the end of the conference the following night. The disintegration began after Karl Hess' rousing speech Saturday night, calling for action against the State. Karl threw the meeting open to questions and general rapping, and that's when trouble arose. The first thing that happened was an intensifying polarization of left and right-wings, each pushing the other into harder, more extreme, and more disparate stands. The point is that within the New York movement, agreement is intense and widespread, and the divergence between "right" and "left" is only a matter of tactics and nuance rather than fundamental principle. But hold a conference like this one, advertised widely and open to one and all, and massive extremes of left and right are bound to appear. It was inevitable that, once widespread rapping began, the almost total lack of communication between extreme left and extreme right, between ultra-left anarchists and anarcho-rightists, would lead to an aggravating polarization between them. Each extreme reacted on the other with cutting dialectical force, each pushing the other farther away from its position. Instead of the conference bringing both extremes, both "deviations" from the main line, together, the rap sessions only served to drive them further apart.

Take, for example, the late Sunday afternoon session, supposed to be devoted to Campus Organizing. The polarization process had continued through Sunday (the demoralization being aggravated by another one of our tactical miscalculations, since half of the people left for home around that time. We did not realize that, outside of New York, no school or business observed Columbus Day). The Campus Organizing session was to be a vital part of the conference, when our campus chapters were to discuss student organizing, development of RLA (the Radical Libertarian Alliance), relations with other fraternal libertarian campus groups, etc. Instead, everyone was so caught up with the intensifying left vs. right struggle that no one bothered to deal with campus organizing, and every speaker plunged further into an orgy of hatred, with left and right winding up literally screaming at each other.

In my view, the major source of intellectual aggression at the conference came from the ultra-left. The problem is

that the Sober Center, the intelligent main-line forces, had been geared all along to withstand assault from the extreme right, from those forces that still revere the U. S. government, still favor the Cold War, and still want to "protect" the government-run campuses from student rebellions. The extreme right was there, sure enough, but a larger menace came from the ultra-left, and the center, being geared psychologically only to oppose the right-wing, never really realized the extent of the ultra-left problem that was becoming a major force at the conference.

Thus, the major assault on the center (that is on the Conference itself, which was largely centrist-run), came from ultra-leftist Wilson A. Clark, Jr., formerly a student at the University of North Carolina, and now residing in Washington, D. C. Denouncing the New York group and the "power structure" of RLA (what a laugh *that* is!), Wilson proceeded to identify two groups as the major Enemy on which the libertarian movement is supposed to concentrate its ire: (a) *all* academic economists, without exception, that is economics *per se*; and (b) all people who wear neckties. As a special bonus, Wilson went on to attack people who favor proper English, in contrast to such cultural goodies as soul rapping, street argot, and whatever. Wilson's inchoate tirade was certainly one of the low points of the conference.

Various other speakers, carried along on a tidal wave of ultra-leftism, *even those who knew better*, called for an abandonment of the "capitalist" part of anarcho-capitalism, and presumed to claim that a viable anarchist society could be composed of "psychic" exchanges and "tribal sharing" carried on by hippie communes.

By far the best reply to the Clark forces came from Mario Rizzo who, nattily dressed in jacket and tie, announced that one could see from his attire which side of the cultural struggle he was on. Rizzo pointed out that the ultra-left was really abandoning the proper emphasis on *political* revolution, on abolition of the State, to stress "cultural revolution", a "revolution" whose implications range from misleading and irrelevant to totally wrong-headed and divisive. Addressing the cultural revolutionaries, Mario concluded by saying that *if*, as he suspected, they proposed to use coercion to impose their anti-necktieism, then "to hell with you."

If polarization and "cultural" hogwash was one measure of the disintegration during Phase II, another was the sudden emergency of a typically ultra-left call for immediate action, virtually *any* action, against the State. The cry was first raised on Saturday night when one ultra-leftist in the audience raised the call, "On to Fort Dix!" This referred to a New Left action against Ft. Dix, New Jersey that had been planned for Sunday. Theoretically, it was supposed to involve merely a demonstration at the fort on behalf of various military prisoners and in opposition to the war. But it was also rumored that an attempt would be made to march onto the fort itself. While there is nothing morally wrong, of course, with the idea of people invading an army fort--quite the contrary--there is a vast gulf between moral correctness and strategic and tactical wisdom. It was that wisdom that was so conspicuously lacking. Nothing could be achieved by such an "invasion"--certainly not a successful capture--and the only thing that could possible be accomplished would be to be gassed and/or bayoneted, and/or clubbed, and/or shot, plus a possible ten years in jail for (literally!) stepping on the grass of army property.

What is more, the wisdom was particularly lacking from the people at our conference, few of whom had heard of the Ft. Dix action until that moment. But the process of polarization had done its ugly work. Goaded beyond endurance by the right-wing's attack on the very concept and morality of revolution, not only the ultra-left but even the bulk of the center responded swiftly and emotionally to the cry of "On to Ft. Dix!" It was as if, after defending the very concept of action against the State, the center and left felt that they

(Continued on page 3)

Letter From Washington

By Karl Hess

Robin Hood Revisionism

When I was a wee conservative, counting bond revenues at my mother's knee, it was the dear lady's practice to frighten me to death with tales of that arch-bandit, Robin Hood. The conservative wisdom was and is that no more dastardly crime lurks in the heart of man than the infamy of taking from the rich to give to the poor. Entire sweeps of political philosophy, in fact, seem to have been motivated by little else than antagonism to poor Robin and his hoods. On the other hand, an entire sweep of political reality, in this nation, was and is motivated by the reverse proposition,

that it is okay to rob from the poor and give to the rich.

The Democrats have done it through a welfare system in which the poor are "client" victims who get the crumbs from the bureaucratic table which is the system's principal purpose. They also characteristically steal the poor blind through construction projects, licenses and franchises, and such other thefts as are most appropriate to men who have risen from precinct politics.

The Republicans have done it through, most lately, the warfare state of corporate liberalism, in which the lives of the poor are daily robbed of meaning or hope so that they may be used solely as cogs in the industrial machine which is the system's principal purpose. They also steal through the total use of the state and its power, its credit, its regulations, to the end of special advantage for the corporate elite, a form of theft most appropriate to men who have gone to the best schools.

So much for the reverse. What about Robinhoodism, straight and unalloyed? Should we frighten tots with his image? Was his the worst of crimes?

Robin, after sober reflection, wasn't a half-bad sort. He had one wretched notion that we shall discuss later, but his work, by and large, was healthy, useful, and quite impec-

(Continued on page 4)

THE CONVENTION — *(Continued from page 2)*

had to rush out and seize the opportunity for any action whatever. It reached the monstrous point that the entire center was willing to call off the whole Sunday daytime proceedings of the convention, a convention for which they had lovingly prepared for many months, in order to rush off in a delirium to embrace the receiving end of the tear-gas canister and the bayonet. Anarcho-martyrism rearing its ugly head!

This sudden onrush at the conference was a superb example of one of the major reasons that anarchist revolutions have never been effective. It demonstrates, for example, why the anarchists lost out to their allies the Bolsheviks after the October 1917 Revolution in Russia. The anarchists were strong in Russia; but anarchists have, tragically, always been what the Randians very effectively call "whim-worshippers", creatures of the emotional moment, worshippers of the immediate spontaneous emotion of the hour, people who scorn rational forethought and purposeful, long-range planning. One of the main reasons that the Russian anarchists lost out to Lenin is because Lenin, above all, was no whim-worshipper, but a master of patient organization, strategic insight, rational forethought, long-range planning and tactical timing. It is always the kooky anarchists who suddenly raise the cry, "Seize the street!", "Storm that government building!", "Charge the cops!", and of course it is always the kooky anarchists who are first to get their heads beaten in—and to no avail. Note that it is not the *morality* of these anarchist actions that is in question (as it is in the case of anarcho-rightists who *defend* the government or government schools) but the sanity of the actions.

My own role, all of late Saturday night and early Sunday afternoon, was a hasty but in many ways effective one-man crusade to stem the ultra-left tide, and to save the conference by opposing the Ft. Dix mania. I managed to persuade the great bulk of the center to remain at the conference on Sunday, thus permitting the sessions to continue, so that only a small ultra-left contingent went on the Dix escapade. Most of the speeches on early Sunday afternoon were an implicit or explicit attack on ultra-leftism: Jerry Tuccille effectively reminding the meeting that our main reservoir of potential mass support was the vast middle class (the same middle class so scornfully written off as The Enemy by Clark and others); Leonard Liggio gently but firmly reminding worshippers of the Black Panthers of the Panthers' abandonment of black nationalism; and myself directly attacking ultra-leftism, Panther-mania, and the Ft. Dix adventure.

As the warriors began returning from Ft. Dix, ultra-left emotionalism started to reach another peak. One left youth leader lamented that he had not been gassed at Dix. And undoubtedly the all-time low arrived when an ultra-left woman from the Phoenix Coalition of Michigan (so ultra-left as to make Wilson Clark appear like a corporation executive) rushed to the podium, fresh from her gassing, to curse obscenely and hysterically at the entire audience for being in New York rather than at the barricades.

The conference ended ingloriously Sunday night on a note of (unfortunately rational) paranoia. For it became evident that the hotel room, the lobby of the hotel, and the street outside were suddenly crawling with plainclothes cops, their badges and their guns bulging prominently from their supposedly civilian attire. One Wobbly leader, familiar with the New York fuzz, spotted a Bureau of Special Services plainclothesman (the division specializing in political dissent). Why were they there? Were they going to bust the convention? Were they going to apprehend the Ft. Dix marchers? Were some or all of us going to be charged with Conspiracy to cross state lines to incite a riot, *à la* the infamous Chicago case? Nobody knew, and we still don't know, but prudence at last won over *machismo*, and most of us beat it the hell out of there. The convention petered out on a grotesquely ironic note, with the remaining rappers still griping that the main trouble with the conference was that there had not been enough rapping!

Lessons Of The Conference

One obvious lesson of the Conference is the emergence of ultra-left adventurism as a major threat to the movement. And so just as we have devoted several issues of the *Libertarian Forum* to an attack on anarcho-rightism, we must now devote some energy to a critique of ultra-leftism (which will be appearing soon).

A second lesson is that this sort of large, totally open convention--gathering all manner of leftists, rightists, and cops--has become counter-productive. The need now is for smaller, far more selective, and more homogeneous meetings, in which there will be far more room for much-needed internal education of cadre, and for genuine discussion and dialogue. Leftists and rightists can only be moved toward the center separately, where they cannot reinforce each other's errors through mutual denunciation. Only when and if left and right have effectively blended into the center will there be need for a second open convention.

ROBIN HOOD REVISIONISM — *(Continued from page 3)*

cable politically--so far as it went.

Who did he rob? He robbed a bunch of rich churchmen, for one thing. Now what in the world is wrong with that? To hear the conservative diatribes against Robin Hood you would think that the mere fact of *having* riches is the only standard against which to judge the theft of those riches. In short, the conservative notion is that to steal anything from anybody is a crime--regardless of the source of the thing being ripped off or the nature of the owner's position in regard to the society in general.

The churchmen, whom Robin robbed, represented one of the great ruling classes of all time and, like every ruling class, their power and their pelf was the result of the sort of theft that becomes legitimized by longevity. Although much of the income being derived by churches today is from voluntary contributions, much of the capital upon which churches base their economies was extracted in times when the churches had real clout and could force contributions. The Roman Catholic church, of course, is the main user of such capital and is coming under increasing pressure from its priests to divest itself of what even a rudimentary ethical sense should be able to identify as ill-gotten gains. Robin didn't wait for divestiture. He helped out. So, on the count of robbing rich churchmen, Robin seems quite acceptable to a libertarian.

Robin was most noted, as a matter of fact, for stealing from government officials. Rich government officials. Now how do government officials become rich? How did the Sheriff of Nottingham make his? Or Lyndon Johnson? Or you name him. Politicians make their money by using their office; by, in an ethical sense, stealing advantages which lead to gains. I would say that such gains also are stolen. So, apparently, did Robin Hood.

It seems to me, as a matter of fact, that Robin Hood's attacks against the militant arm of the state have been purposefully overlooked by conservatives in their attacks against Robin Hood. There has been a preoccupation, instead, with the technicalities of whose forest it was, whether the Sheriff represented a mere aberration in the divinely inspired order of Western civilization, and whether Robin wouldn't have been better advised to press his case in a duly constituted court (presided over by the Sheriff of Nottingham!).

The reason for this oversight on the part of conservatives may not be innocent or merely myopic. Robin Hood's main crime, you see, was against an established order, one duly established in accord with the laws, customs, etc., of the time. Robin, on the other hand, thought it was illegitimate. He was, it should be recalled, a very political cat. His gripe

was--ah hah--against THE STATE. Those upon whom he preyed were lackeys or running dogs of THE STATE. It is possible that the specter of Robin Hood today haunts so many conservative dreams not because of their pure thoughts on property rights so much as because of the possibly impure origins of the property dearest to their own hearts. Otherwise, why get so excited about Robin Hood?

There is one reason. It is the only thing that I hold against the old boy and his gassy greenclad gang. They were hung up on King Richard. Now, being hung up on any king is a mistake, I feel. But, until Dick showed up, big as life and raring to get back in the king business, Robin was a beautiful guy. As often happens in life, he was the sort you could go along with wholeheartedly so long as he didn't have the power he eventually wanted. When the king came back, of course, libertarians in the gang should have just gone back to the woods and started all over again and, by then, they should have had enough local support to stand a better chance than ever of success.

In short, while Robin was robbing, he was doing nothing that should offend libertarian sensibilities and the fact that so much of what he was doing was aimed specifically against state authority should actually draw libertarian cheers. The subsequent fact that he took some of the loot from his anti-state forays and returned it to the people most sorely victimized by the state should draw not only libertarian cheers but humanist ones as well.

There is one other thing about Robin Hood. He apparently is alive and well in Latin America today. The inter-urban guerrillas in Uruguay seem to operate in his spirit but without that hang-up about kings. Good.

I bet you a monk's bag of silver that conservatives line up with the Sheriff of Nottingham. But don't worry, Robin, libertarians are on your side.

The Libertarian Forum
BOX 341
MADISON SQUARE STATION
NEW YORK, NEW YORK 10010

Published on the first and fifteenth of every month.   Subscription rate: $7.00 per year; Student subscription rate: $5.00 per year.

A Semi-Monthly Newsletter

THE
Libertarian Forum

Joseph R. Peden, Publisher   Washington Editor, Karl Hess   Murray N. Rothbard, Editor

VOL. I, NO. XVI   November 15, 1969   35¢

ULTRA-LEFTISM

The Marxians, who have thought longer and harder about revolutionary change than anyone else, have very perceptively discovered two major contrasting errors, two major deviations from the proper revolutionary "line": "right-wing opportunism" or "liquidationism", and "ultra-left adventurism". Right-wing opportunism is above all a moral failure, a willingness to abandon principle for the sake of a "practical" working within the system, a course which invariably leads to becoming a part of the system itself and to opposing the very cause to which the rightist is supposedly devoted. "Ultra-left adventurism" is by no means a moral failure; in fact, the ultra-leftist acts in the world to attempt to achieve the common goal as rapidly as he can. The problem is the ultra-leftist's total lack of strategic sense; in rushing at the Enemy blindly, emotionally, and with insufficient preparation for allies, he not only inevitably gets clobbered, but he also sinks his own cause at the same time. While the ultra-leftist is morally lovable, his emotional lashing-out at the system can be equally as disastrous to the cause he espouses as the cynical opportunism of the right-liquidationist. Both deviations from the main revolutionary line of rational, protracted struggle must be combatted.

In recent months, ultra-leftism has emerged as a serious problem both in the New Left and in the libertarian movement. On the New Left, ultra-leftism has been chiefly responsible for the galloping disintegration of SDS. The ouster of the Progressive Labor wing of SDS provided an opportunity and a challenge to the remainder of this leading New Left group to return to the libertarian, non-Stalinist, revolutionary path which had marked SDS for a year or two after its 1966 convention. Within the non-PL wing of SDS, the triumph of the "Weatherman" faction over RYM-II was also a hopeful sign, since RYM-II's Marxism, Stalinism, and worship of the "working class" was almost as aggravated as that of PL. But now the Weathermen are wrecking SDS through their total immersion in ultra-left adventurism.

The Weatherman strategy consists largely of kamikaze charges against the police. Calling for a massive "invasion" of Chicago ("pig city") on October 8-11, only a couple of hundred frenzied Weathermen and Weatherwomen showed up, to charge the police and get clobbered and arrested for their pains. The latest issue of the Weathermen's *New Left Notes*, which used to be the most important theoretical and strategic journal for the New Left, consists solely of pictures of Weathermen and cops slugging it out, interspersed with a few incoherent paragraphs cursing at American society. The curses are understandable; but this whole hysteria has about as much in common with genuine revolution as a barroom brawl has with truly mass action.

The hysteria, and the pitiful failure, of the Weathermen stem not so much from personal psychosis as from incorrect strategic theory. The Weathermen are superb in realizing *who* the enemy is; the enemy is the State, the State's goon-squad police, and the public school system, which the Weathermen correctly identify as a vast prison-house for the nation's youth. (In contrast, PL and RYM-II *oppose* the Weathermen's goal of destroying the public school system, because the "working class" likes the schools.) Furthermore, in contrast to all other Marxian sects, the Weathermen have come to realize that they cannot rely on the industrial "working class" as their potential reservoir of allies. Everyone recognizes that the working class is precisely the most reactionary, the most social-fascist, the most racist element of American society, and the Weathermen realize that American Marxists have boxed themselves into a complete dead end in pinning their hopes on the workers.

But if not the working class, who? Who is to be the "agency of social change", the main reservoir of recruits for the revolution? The most sensible answer would be the "middle class" (or as former SDS theorist Greg Calvert called them, the "new working class"), which is after all the vast bulk of the population. But the Weathermen are blocked from trying to appeal to the middle class, (a) because this would end the chronic Marxian-New Left emphasis on the most evidently downtrodden groups, for even though the middle-classes *are* exploited by the ruling class, it is hard for ultra-left romantics to get stirred up over injustice to those who are not super-poverty-stricken; and (b) because the New Left is so filled with hatred of the middle-class "bourgeois" life-style that it refuses to consider the middle-class as anything but part of the Enemy. If not the working class, or the middle-class, then who? In desperation, the Weathermen reached toward another group: working-class *youth*--motorcycle hoods, outlaws, high-school dropouts, etc. They fail to realize that even if they *could* organize the young hoods, they couldn't accomplish anything, because the hoods have even less social leverage, less potential to mobilize masses of people (almost all of whom hate the hoods, and with good reason) than the students of SDS.

Having disastrously decided to concentrate on organizing the youth-*lumpen*, the Weathermen had to decide how to go about it. How to reach the *lumpen*? It was obvious that campus groups were not the way, and neither could the young *lumpen* be reached by journals or theoretical discussions. The only way seemed to be to "gain the respect" of the

(Continued on page 2)

ULTRA-LEFTISM — *(Continued from page 1)*

machismo --instincts of the young hoods by engaging in street-combat with the cops. These street fights were supposed to serve as "exemplary actions" (a current in-phrase) which would mobilize and inspire the young hoods and lead them toward the Weathermen. Well, of course, this nonsensical tactic has not worked and will not work. The only "example", the only lesson, that any sensible young hood can draw from Weathermanship is that here are a bunch of loonies who go charging the cops and only get clobbered and busted for their pains. What even remotely national young hood would be other than repulsed by the Weatherman "example"?

As far as the Weathermen go, the interesting problem for speculation is what they will do in a year or so, when it will have become obvious, even to them, that they have failed and that they have not raised the standard to which the hoods and dropouts have repaired. If any of the Weathermen are alive and out of jail by that time, perhaps they will then come to their senses, and rethink their strategy and tactics.

Contrast to the futile desperation of the Weathermen the brilliantly successful strategy and tactics of the Vietnam Moratorium. Returning to the successful grass-roots tactics of the Vietnam 1965 teach-ins, the Moratorium of October 15 mobilized literally millions of the "silent majority", the middle-class, in every village and community in the country, in dramatic opposition to the endless war in Vietnam. While all the factions of SDS stood aloof, scornful of the insufficient radicalism of the Moratorium people, millions of Americans poured out in the largest demonstration in America's history, and in support of a demand that was phenomenally radical for a middle-class movement: immediate and unconditional withdrawal from Vietnam. If we realize that only a year ago, the middle-class would not support any demand more radical than "please, Mr. President, stop the bombing", the achievement of the Moratorium is seen to be dazzling indeed. For the future, the idea of escalating the pressure one day per month of the war, is another superb tactical method for mobilizing millions for a continuing increase of pressure on the U. S. government. (But let us hope that the anti-war movement will not be diverted, as it was in 1965, away from local grass-roots actions to spectacular but scarcely productive mass demonstrations confined to Washington.)

The success of the Moratorium stems from its focusing on winning the support of and radicalizing the middle-class --the great bulk of the American population. And here, in particular, lies a crucial lesson for the libertarian movement. The prime center of our movement, as well as the New Left, is now and will continue to be the college campus. Here is the recruitment ground for our cadre and the immediate theatre of our activity. But insofar as we wish to move out into the adult community--and we can never hope to win unless we ultimately do so--we libertarians have a particularly ripe potential in the vast middle class. Here is where we have our "comparative advantage" as compared to the Marxian New Left, and so here is where we should move from our campus *focos.*

Let me put it this way: at our Libertarian Conference on the Columbus Day weekend, it became evident that both our right-wing and our ultra-leftists were focusing on the wrong problem. The right-wing began the error by charging that, comes the revolution, we libertarians would inevitably lose out to the Marxists, and another State would replace the current monstrosity. *In response to* this charge, our ultra-lefts proclaimed that what we must do is march out on the barricades with the New Left, earn their respect, and then use this respect to convert the New Left from Marxism to libertarianism. This, I submit, misconceives the problem and the nature of the revolutionary process. The revolutionary process is a huge, complex pattern of activity, with each person and each group concentrating on what it does

best--the division of labor is just as important and as valid in revolution in any other sphere of activity. Our objective should not be to convert the Weathermen or the Panthers-- probably a hopeless task, and less than crucial in any case. Our objective should be to act where we have a comparative advantage--with the middle class. Put it this way: suppose that it came to a revolutionary crunch, and somehow the mass of the middle-class found themselves forced to choose between us and the Marxists, us and the Weathermen. Which of us would they choose? I don't think there is any question about the answer. They would choose us, because we stand for freedom and for the rights of private property.

So we don't have to have an inferiority complex relative to the Marxian New Left. In the long run, our attraction for the middle-class masses is infinitely greater than theirs. So let us pursue the division of labor within the revolutionary process. Let the Weathermen or the Panthers charge the police or try to storm the Department of Justice building. Let us cheer them on as they do battle with the U. S. State Leviathan. But let us not confuse cheering for them with our own strategic and tactical needs. Let us do what we can do best, which is to spread the message and the actions of freedom, and of radical defense of property rights, to the middle-class masses who are potentially our allies and supporters. If we do so, then we won't have to worry about who will win out in the final result.

For years I have advocated an alliance between libertarians and SDS, but many people have misinterpreted the meaning of such an alliance. I meant, first of all, that when SDS battles the State, it is morally incumbent upon us to support and cheer SDS on, but this does not mean that we should be participating in these actions. Again--the division of labor. (In the same way, we should cheer on the Biafrans as they battle for their freedom against the massed might of the Nigerian State--but that doesn't mean that it somehow our duty to rush out there and participate in the war.) Secondly, SDS was, in those days, the only revolutionary movement going, it was itself instinctively libertarian, and the only way that our tiny handful of pure libertarians could act to change the world was to orient ourselves to SDS. But now all that is changed: SDS, in the past year, has become largely Stalinoid and is rapidly disintegrating, and the pure libertarian movement has been growing by great leaps and bounds. In this situation, our best strategy is not to join SDS but to develop our own libertarian organizations, on campus and in the adult world, to recruit new pure cadre and to attract the scores of thousands of radical and instinctively libertarian kids who are properly disgusted with the disintegrating SDS and are looking for a place to go. We can provide that ideological and activist home. This is our historic opportunity, and we would be derelict in not taking advantage of this ripe potential for rapid growth.

But if we must orient to the middle-class as our long-range strategy, then this means that many of us must give up much of the petty and irrelevant nonsense that is wrapped up in today's "cultural revolution"--a "revolution" that can never do anything but totally alienate the middle-class. It is too bad that the middle-class is silly enough to place any importance whatever on the fripperies of hair, life-style, etc. But as long as they do, it is criminal negligence to toss away opportunities to influence them in order to cling to the dubious benefits of the drug-rock culture. If millions of kids could go "Clean for Gene" in 1968, isn't it infinitely more important to go "Clean for Anarchy"?

> "Everything I see about me is sowing the seeds of a revolution that is inevitable, though I shall not have the pleasure of seeing it. The lightning is so close at hand that it will strike at the first chance, and then there will be a pretty uproar. The young are fortunate, for they will see fine things."
>
> —Voltaire, 1764

FDP:
NEOLIBERALS IN GERMAN POLITICS

West German President Gustav Heinemann, following this fall's election, called on Social Democratic Party leader Willy Brandt to become chancellor and Free Democratic Party leader Walter Scheel to become foreign minister in a new cabinet. This coalition's domestic program is centered upon the reduction of taxes for the white collar and blue collar middle classes, civilian control over the military, and increased individual freedoms. In foreign affairs, they propose permanent good relations with the Soviet Union based upon West Germany's recognition of the "inviolability of the borders and demarcation lines." in Europe, including the border between East and West Germany, de facto recognition of the East German government through a general treaty, and diplomatic recognition to Poland, Czechoslovakia, Hungary and Bulgaria. This would mean a renunciation of the Hallstein Doctrine whereby West Germany withdrew diplomatic relations from any country recognizing East Germany; now many countries of Asia, Africa and Latin America will be likely to recognize East Germany. Meanwhile, West Germany will be able to improve its trading position in East European countries which have long had relations with the U. S., England and France. The Free Democratic Party (FDP) controlling the foreign ministry will give the impetus to this East Bloc diplomatic policy.

The FDP's policies have been characterized as the "traditions of libertarianism and economic neoliberalism". It is the heir of the radical individualism of Locke and the rationalism of the French Revolution. Rooted in the values of education and indpenedent property, FDP has been the party of creativity and rebellion. It came into existence after World War II when there was a widespread belief that radical liberalism was outmoded and must disappear before the conservatives' militarism, clericalism, and authoritarianism or the socialists' manipulation, repressive tolerance, and exploitation. But, FDP challenged the post-war world with the radical economics of the Austrian School of Mises and Hayek against the Christian Democratic (CDU) and Social Democratic (SPD) parties. When Konrad Adenauer organized the CDU his 1947 program called for nationalization of industry. But, the early necessity for CDU to form a coalition with FDP forced the laissez-faire economist Ludwig Erhard up on the U. S. and Adenauer in 1948 as post-war economic coordinator. Since Erhard belonged to the CDU it was that party and not FDP which gained popular credit for Erhard's rigorous monetary policies. When the West German government was formed, FDP leader Prof. Theodor Heuss became president, and FDP assumed the justice and interior (police) ministries to keep watch that civil liberties were not violated by the state.

FDP's disenchantment with CDU came from Adenauer's pro-U. S. foreign policy. Germans were not enamoured of the U. S. after the brutality they had suffered during the war (cf. Veale, *Advance to Barbarism*) and during occupation (cf. Salomon, *Fragebogen*, which was the most widely read post-war German book). Adenauer was viewed as betraying Germany's historic role of balancing East and West, both during the nineteenth century and the inter-war period. FDP challenged the re-militarization of Germany by the U. S. and led the battle alongside the SPD for reunion of the Saarland Germans when Adenauer sought to sacrifice them to France to gain approval for German re-militarization.

By the mid-1950's FDP's demands for diplomatic relations with the Soviet Union, trade with East Europe and a neutralist foreign policy pointed to an end to the coalition with the CDU. Extra-parliamentary protest in the streets against U. S.-

dominated foreign policy influenced the FDP and SPD in parliament into opposition. This street protest was led by now president Heinemann who had resigned from Adenauer's cabinet and party in 1950 over CDU militarism. As a leading Protestant and anti-collectivist, Heinemann led a campaign for neutralism, and later joined the SPD to agitate for his principles.

In 1957 Adenauer split the FDP, absorbing its cabinet members into CDU while the majority of FDP went into parliamentary opposition. From that date CDU leaders have sought to abolish the proportional representation electoral law in order to destroy the FDP. Dr. Thomas Dehler became FDP chairman and opened party posts to the "Young Rebels" who sought coalition with SPD, who were FDP partners in several state governments. These angry young men rejected the "end of idology" concept of the 1950's and replaced "practical" objectives with a totally ideological commitment summarized as "Repeal laws, bureaucracy, and taxation." They represented the same intellectual ferment which produced the New Left in England and America. The "Young Rebels" established the magazine *Liberal* and the Friedrich Naumann Foundation for radical education. The "Young Rebels"-FDP alliances with SPD in state governments obviously required a broader agreement than opposition to NATO and U. S. foreign policy, or support for civil liberties. Along with the FDP, SPD reacted to the feudal, corporatist, Christian socialism of CDU; SPD denounced economic planning in its new program: "Competition and the freedom of initiative of the entrepreneur are important elements of the SPD economic policy." It further declared: "We Social Democrats demand a free economic development, free competition and private property conscious of its responsiblities to the general good." Thereafter, SPD often supported Erhard when the statists of the CDU deserted his laissez-faire programs.

Opposition to Erhard in CDU was centered among the Christian trade unionists and major business interests. In 1959 when President Heuss' term ended, Adenauer was persuaded to accept the presidency until he realized that Erhard was the popular choice to succeed him as chancellor. Adenauer then tried unsuccessfully to force Erhard to become president. Thereafter, FDP campaigned for the retirement of Adenauer and the appointment of Erhard as chancellor. In 1961 that issue gave FDP its highest vote depriving CDU of a majority in Parliament. A CDU-FDP coalition was based on Adenauer's retirement.

The coalition temporarily split in October 1962 in the *Spiegel* affair. That magazine, which had the closest ties to FDP, was closed by government police and its editors imprisoned on charges that they had earlier printed information critical of NATO military policy. This suppression

(Continued on page 4)

ATTENTION, LIBERTARIANS

Many readers of the *Libertarian Forum* have expressed interest in finding other libertarians near them. Therefore, early next year, the *Forum* will begin to publish the names and addresses of people who would like to be contacted by other readers of the *Libertarian Forum*. If you'd like your name to be included, please fill out the coupon on the back of this notice.

A YAF Conversion

Many of us have known Ralph Fucetola III, until recently state chairman of New Jersey YAF and member of the Libertarian Caucus, as an extreme right-winger, and a warmongering and red-baiting "libertarian". From a recent letter of Fucetola's to the New Left newsletter *Hard Times* (Oct. 20-27), it appears that Ralph has seen the light. He writes that he was the one who originally introduced Don Meinshausen (HUAC agent in SDS who later recanted publicly) to Herb Romerstein, long-time HUAC operative and anti-Communist "expert" on youth movements. Ralph adds: "In return, Don introduced me and the rest of the almost–libertarian right to what was happening to our generation. Now it's three months later, the right is splitting, "anarchy" is the wave of the future. With Don's—and Karl Hess's—help we learned the quasi-fascist nature of much of the conservative movement; we learned that we have a role in *the* Movement, that the state can be stopped, that freedom can be won." Great, Ralph. May your example be followed by many others. There is more joy in Heaven . . .

GERMAN POLITICS— *(Continued from page 3)*
occurred in the same week that followed Kennedy's launching of the Cuban crisis about the editors were known to be critical. Amidst student demonstrations against a police state, FDP ministers resigned and returned only on the dismissal of the guilty party, defense minuster Franz Josef Strauss. Adenauer was forced to set his own resignation for mid-1963 when SPD threatened to join FDP in a coalition headed by Erhard. Erhard became chancellor in 1963 in a coalition with FDP. This coalition was successful in the 1965 national elections. But, when Erhard was pressured by the U. S. in 1966 to impose tax increases to pay U. S. occupation army costs to offset the expenses of the Vietnam war, FDP voted against the taxes and Erhard resigned. The new CDU chancellor, Kurt Georg Kiesinger, restored Strauss (a supporter of U. S. war in Vietnam) to the cabinet. To FDP, coalition was impossible with anyone like Kiesinger who had declared: "the question these days is not one of the freedom of the individual *vis-à-vis* the state, but vice versa, a question of how to defend the authority of the state against an unbridled, anarchic freedom."

Thereafter, FDP, under the chairmanship of Walter Scheel, used its opposition role to champion the right of protest of German youth and citizens' rights against the state. In the spring of 1969 FDP joined with SPD to elect Heinemann as West German president in preparation for a joint campaign against Kiesinger in the fall elections. The authoritarianism of Kiesinger, Strauss and the CDU were repudiated by the voters.
— Leonard P. Liggio

Recommended Reading

RAMPARTS, November 1969. With former editors Scheer and Hinckle out, Ramparts is better than ever. Particularly good are: J. Goulden and M. Singer, "Dial-A-Bomb: AT&T and ABM", an excellent dissection of the giant monopoly AT&T's political clout in American's government-industrial complex (and note the revelations about the exploitative super-proci exploitative super-profits made from defense sub-contracting); Sol Stern's "Canyon: A Troubled Paradise", about the persecution of the private property of hippieish Canyon, California by all conceivable agencies of local government; and Earl Shorris' dissection of the new Social-Democrat idol of the right-wing, "Hayakawa in Thought and Action".

Peter Brock, *Pacifism in the United States* (Princeton University Press). This huge, sprawling (1,005 pages) and expensive book is a thorough, definitive history of religious and consistent pacifism before the Civil War. Much material on such great people and individualist anarchists as William Lloyd Garrison and Henry Clarke Wright.

Michael A. Heilperin, *Aspects of the Pathology of Money* (London: Michael Joseph), $9.50. Professor Heilperin, a student of Ludwig von Mises, is one of the very few economists who still favor a return to the gold standard. This is a collection of his valuable monetary essays ranging over four decades.

Wilhelm von Humboldt, *The Limits of State Action* (Cambridge University Press), $7.50. A new translation of this little classic, one of the best defenses of laissez-faire in political philosophy. This book influenced Mill's On Liberty, and is considerably better than Mill's compromising work.

Corinne Jacker, *The Black Flag of Anarchy: Anti-statism in the United States* (Charles Scribner's Sons), $4.50. A pleasant, though superficial, little book which, however, serves as a useful introduction to the history of American anarchism. For one thing, it is the only history of American anarchism now in print.

The Libertarian Forum
BOX 341
MADISON SQUARE STATION
NEW YORK, NEW YORK 10010

Published on the first and fifteenth of every month.   Subscription rate: $7.00 per year; Student subscription rate: $5.00 per year.

A Semi-Monthly Newsletter

THE
Libertarian Forum

Joseph R. Peden, Publisher   Washington Editor, Karl Hess   Murray N. Rothbard, Editor

VOL. I, NO. XVII   November 15, 1969   35¢

The Anti-War Movement

October and November saw the outpouring of the most massive opposition movement in the long, black history of the government of the United States. In the October Moratorium literally millions of Americans demonstrated in every village and hamlet in the land. In November, nearly a million took the trouble to travel to Washington and San Francisco for a weekend of demonstration. In a country long inured to "backing the President" in any foreign crisis, this determined and ever growing mass movement against the war is a truly remarkable phenomenon. Who among us, ten, five years ago, could have predicted that millions of Americans would raise their voices and bring their persons to the point of total opposition to an American war effort?

Too many libertarians make various "domestic" questions: the census, taxation, neighborhood control, the central cutting edge of their anti-state concerns. As vitally important as these issues are, they pale into insignificance beside the vital importance of the war and its creator, American imperialism. It is war, losing, perpetual, stalemated war, that will ultimately bring down the American Leviathan. If we look at all the successful revolutions of this century, all of them (with the exception of the Cuban in a very small country) were made possible by a losing or a stalemated war into which the State had brought the country. The stage for the Russian Revolution was set by a disastrous and losing war fomented by the Russian Empire. The Chinese Revolution was made possible by Chiang's lengthy war against the Japanese. Even the French Revolution of 1789 was the consequence of heavy war debts incurred by the French State. Nothing brings about a revolutionary crisis situation--and no revolutions can occur without such crises--so completely as a "no-win" war; nothing so starkly reveals the inadequacy of the existing State to its citizenry. A losing war is more powerful than decades of patient education in the vital task of demystifying and desanctifying the State apparatus in the eyes of its subject population.

America truly has a bear by the tail in Vietnam. Vietnam is not simply an unfortunate blunder, a mistake that can be promptly rectified. Vietnam is part and parcel of the entire concept of U. S. foreign policy since World War II (in many ways since Woodrow Wilson). For the whole thrust of that policy is to create and preserve American politico-economic domination of the world, or at the very least to preserve that degree of world domination which she already has. This means an American policy of world-wide counter-revolution: the suppression of revolutionary and national liberation movements throughout the "Third World". Until Vietnam, America was able to exercise its control through

puppet and client states, and therefore suffered only a minimal drain on its manpower and financial resources. But in Vietnam this policy was shattered forever on the rock of people's guerrilla war, a war backed to the hilt by virtually the entire population of Vietnam, North and South. Contrary to much liberal opinion, the Vietnamese war is not a civil war--either between North and South or between different factions within the South. It is a war fought by imperial America and a few of its puppets in Saigon against the liberation movement of the Vietnamese people. It is therefore a war which America cannot win.

The massacre at Song My is not a question of a few battle-crazed soldiers becoming trigger-happy. Such massacres are inherent in the American war effort, and must needs occur time and time again. They have to be a systematic part of the American effort because that effort consists of attempting to use our superior firepower to suppress the independence and the liberation of an entire people. In that sense, the entire population is "VC", and therefore our war inevitably consists of deliberate slaughter of that huge "enemy". There is only one way to stop the American massacre policy: to get America the hell out of Vietnam.

Despite the common mythology, President Nixon doesn't "want peace"--except, of course, the peace of death to the instincts for freedom of the people of Vietnam. For in a way not mentioned by the Establishment, the "domino theory" is correct. It is correct not in the sense that mythical Chinese will "aggress" against more countries in Asia; but in the sense that a clear-cut victory of the Vietnamese people against the American oppressors will give great heart to similar victims of American imperialism throughout the Third World. More liberation struggles will then erupt in Asia and Latin America, and we will have "many Vietnams". American imperialism will result in a series of permanent stalemate wars, and thereby Death to Leviathan.

The conflict between the dove-moderates and the hawks is but one consequence of the losing Vietnam war. What the Marxists call "the sober circles of American imperialism"--the Harrimans, the Cliffords, etc., seeing the disastrous mess in Vietnam, are now willing to "cut and run", to take their stand for American imperialism elsewhere--in what would hopefully be more favorable terrain. The right-wingers, as ever motivated by their frenzied and "principled" desire to crush all opposition everywhere without quarter, are determined to save every single domino, come what may.

It is increasingly clear that the Nixon Administration is a

(Continued on page 2)

THE ANTI-WAR MOVEMENT— *(Continued from page 1)*

right-wing administration. Richard Nixon is an unprincipled and pragmatic opportunist on all conceivable questions but one: "anti-Communism", that is world counter-
revolution. Hence the negotiations at Paris, never very
advanced, are moving rapidly backward, and hence the
phoniness of the troop withdrawals. I am willing to make the
flat prediction that the war in Vietnam will continue for the
duration of the Nixon Administration, because the President, cast in the mold of 1940's anti-Communism, is
incapable of liberal co-optation, is incapable of a graceful
"cut and run" pullout.

Therefore, the war will go on and on. And therefore, "the
movement" is, and will continue to be for many years,
primarily an anti-war movement. From May 1968 until the
end of that year, virtually the entire Left was duped by the
Paris negotiations into thinking that the war was over; then
for many months, the Left was paralyzed by the view that
Nixon would keep his promises and end the war shortly. Now
all that is over. The growth of the anti-war movement is all
the more remarkable because it has only been alive for a
few months, after a lapse of a year and a half.

And so the renascent anti-war movement builds and builds,
surge after mighty surge, month after month. The "silent
majority", a concept based on a few thousand hack Republican
telegrams to the White House, pales beside the many
vociferous millions, whose number and whose radicalism
escalates every week that the war drags on. Every month's
Moratorium will build the pressure, will escalate slowly
but surely in its massive pressure on the government, and
will continue to radicalize countless millions of middle-
class liberals. Yesterday it was "stop the bombing"; today
it is "immediate withdrawal"; tomorrow it will be support
for the NLF and/or mass civil disobedience, and/or a tax
strike or a general strike. The endless war will be the open
sluice-gate for massive radicalization.

In the face of this great upsurge, the Nixon Administration
has made clear its bursting desire to move over into open
fascism--to all-out repression of anti-war dissent. The
evidence has been clear for several weeks: Spiro Agnew's
shift from unconscious fascist clown to conscious fascist threatener
of the press and the media; Attorney-General Mitchell's
incredible assertion that Agnew was too soft on the traitorous dissenters; Deputy Attorney-General Kleindienst's move
to attempt to indict the life-long pacifist David Dellinger for
"incitement to violence"; White House aide Kevin Phillips'
call for the "willingness to go out and crack skulls". The
right-wing Administration is obviously straining at the
leash, bursting to give vent to the typical rightist desire to
crush and stomp on all opposition.

Only one thing is restraining the Administration from
moving into open fascism: the knowledge that the cardinal
point of the liberal credo is at least the facade of civil
liberties. This facade of freedom to dissent is vital to the
whole system and ideology of corporate liberalism; this is
its central distinction from open dictatorship. And both
conservatives and liberals know that if all-out repression
comes, it will have to be far worse than in the old McCarthy-
HUAC era of the 1940's and 1950's. For the reason why the
corporate liberals went along with this repression, or did
not fight it too strongly, is that the repression was carefully
confined to Communist party members and "Communist
fronts". The witch-hunters of those days always claimed to
be perfectly content with "heretics" and dissenters; it was
not their ideas or their active opposition that concerned
them, went the line, but the fact that these were "transmission belts" for the "international Communist conspiracy"
through "Communist fronts" certified by the Attorney-
General or other sources. Liberals could then step aside
and be unconcerned with a narrowly pin-pointed repression.
But as even the Department of Justice knows by now, there
are no Communist fronts any longer; no one can point to

A Letter To Moloch

For some time past I have been telling others that the best
way to kill a beast is to starve him to death, to withhold
from him that particular type of nourishment which keeps
him alive, well and powerful. Moloch thrives on human
sacrifice; he demands a sizable portion of human productivity in the form of tax dollars which he converts into
weapons of murder and other tools of coercion to oppress
the very people from whom he exacts his nourishment.
Since it is hypocritical to incite others to action while
doing nothing oneself, I have decided to take a few small
actions designed to give Moloch a hunger pang or two.

The first is membership in the War Resisters League
by which one agrees to withhold the tax portion of his
monthly phone bill, which is largely used to finance the war
in Vietnam. Those desiring more information about this
project can contact WRL at Room 1025, 5 Beekman Street,
N.Y., N.Y. 10038.

The second step is of a "religious" nature. After careful
consideration I have decided to become an ordained minister
of the Universal Life Church, an honor which carries with
it broad benefits in the form of tax reductions. Anyone
discovering a sudden yen for that old-time religion can
write the Universal Life Church, 1766 Poland Rd., Modesto,
California 95351, and be ordained just for the asking.

Other measures will include refusal to pay my surtax,
sales tax on COD purchases, and any other steps anyone
can suggest as a means of bumping Moloch from his
pedestal. All suggestions are welcomed and will be held in
confidence.

To the list of rallying cries now being raised across the
nation by our fellow revolutionaries, I would like to add yet
another:
STARVE THE BEAST!

—— Jerome Tuccille

Mr. X's membership in so-and-so many front groups. Any
repression will *have* to be directed against any and all
members of the opposition, which *could* include liberals
as well as anyone else.

Therefore, if Nixon-Agnew attempt open fascism, the
result will be a fantastic shift leftward of all liberals
everywhere. Even the austere New York Times will be
ready to man the barricades. Open fascism could well
generate a real revolutionary crisis in the United States.

Our present situation, then, is fraught with enormous
opportunities. The prognosis is that, since the war will go
on, the anti-war movement will spread and intensify; and
if Nixon unleashes his right-wing instincts for all-out
repression, he could generate a successful revolution.
Only one thing could spoil this picture: if the Administration succeeds in maneuvering the anti-war movement into
precipitate violence, and then making that violence an
excuse for moving into open fascism. If the movement
gives Nixon that excuse, then it would tragically polarize
the mass of middle-class liberals rightward instead of
leftward, and thus so isolate itself that Nixon could stomp
on the radicals without generating liberal resistance. In the
coming period, then, it becomes especially important for
radicals in the anti-war movement to avoid as the plague
any stigma of violence, which would reverse the process of
radicalizing the liberal masses, and give Nixon the opportunity to move unopposed into open fascism. Great success
is in the air for the anti-war movement; let us not kick it
away in futile ultra-left adventures.

The Airline Cartel

As Adam Smith so wisely noted: "People of the same trade seldom meet together but the conversation ends in a conspiracy against the public, or in some diversion to raise prices." For many decades the world's international airlines have met seasonally to act out Smith's scenario under the auspices of their cartel--the International Air Transport Association. At these meetings the airline representatives would seek to eliminate competition in the vital area of international fare rates. Fixing prices for air travel meant that competition was limited to auxiliary services--the quality of food, the beauty of stewardesses, the supply of magazines and sweets.

But three factors have recently converged to destroy, at least for the moment, the smooth working of the cartel. Within the next year, 27 airlines will be receiving the first of some 183 Boeing 747 jumbo jets now on order. These carriers are designed to accommodate 350 to 500 passengers and demand a very rapid rise in the number of overseas passengers if they are to be economically profitable. But the whole thrust of the IATA rate policy has been to prefer high fares to an expanded market. Now the market must be expanded as the jumbo jet enters the scene.

Secondly, a number of airline executives have been urging drastic fare reductions, coupled with redirecting merchandising efforts toward creating a mass market for off-season overseas travel. But others have preferred to base their off-season rates on the small but steady stream of businessmen customers who must travel during the off-season whatever the fare. And so the regular fares have remained high and the passenger traffic low, the summer traffic paying for the underutilized winter flights. This dispute over merchandising has been heightened by the desire of certain European countries to expand their tourist season to increase regular year-round employment and develop their winter resort facilities. Advertising has begun to push ski holidays in the Alps, theatre holidays in London, winter music and art festivals in Paris, Amsterdam and Rome.

Lastly, the various governmental bodies which supervise the airlines have, under the pressures of conflicting national interest groups, been less able to coordinate their policies to maintain the cartel and its rate schedules. The dam finally broke when on Sept. 19, Alitalia announced that, since the American CAB had failed to approve, except on a temporary basis, the rate schedule agreed upon at the IATA conference in Dallas, Alitalia was breaking the cartel agreement and cutting its economy fare for New York-Rome round trip off-season flights from $573 to $299 for a minimum of 22 days' stay abroad. Pan American and the other lines soon announced that they would meet the Alitalia rates. Fares to all points in Europe dropped proportionately, and some lines like Iberian offered free additional flights to Stockholm, Paris and other cities for passengers buying an Iberian flight to Madrid. The immediate effect of the fare reduction was a dramatic jump in sales and passenger loads. The stimulation of the free market has brought new interest in off-season travel and good bargains for vacation seekers. But the big question remains whether the IATA will be able to put the lid on again. A meeting is due to be held in Caracas to establish the fares for the summer of 1970. If the proponents of competition have their way, no such agreement will be made, and the international cartel will be smashed. As Paul Friedlander put it in the N.Y. Times (11/16/69), "if the lesson holds, and the industry can sweep away its 50 year old IATA-dominated tradition of restrictive pricing, selling and treatment of the customer, it might give the spirit of competition an opportunity to build new

markets for the airlines, expanding the present limited market to a genuine mass market able to pay the prevailing air fares and willing to fill all the new seats in the brave new airplanes about to come competitively into aviation's marketplace." Or as Adam Smith put it, they must recognize that "consumption is the sole end and purpose of production".

Note: The N.Y. Times (11/26/69) reports that the IATA meeting in Caracas has tentatively agreed upon a new uniform trans-Atlantic rate schedule which, while reducing fares somewhat from the old IATA rates, would eliminate competition among the airlines in the area of individual and group ticket prices. How long the monopoly can maintain itself is still open to question, since the factors contributing to its breakdown still exist.

— J.R.P.

A Leftist Looks At YAF

The circus came to town in St. Louis over Labor Day weekend, and the freaks on display were truly an entertaining bunch. John MacKay and Randy Teague were co-ringmasters, making sure that everything came off just as they had planned. Main attractions included William F. Buckley, Jr., doing his famous word game act. He can cut another notch in his pencil for having won over yet another audience without having used one iota of logic in his entire speech. Also on hand were Fulton Lewis III and Buz Lukens, with Buz stealing the show with some of the most hate-filled, nonsensical demagoguery we have heard in a long time. Keep it up, Buz, we war lovers are behind you all the way! Among the most touching scenes of the show was provided by Officer McClintock of the Pueblo. Most of the audience pitied him because of what he had been through and because the United States government refused to annihilate his captors. A small clique of true libertarians also pitied him, because they couldn't believe that anyone could be so stupid as to go through what he went through and still come out of it with the same narrow-minded Weltanschauung that he had been fed originally by U. S. propagandists. And what circus would be complete without a clown? On hand to keep everyone in high spirits was that old stand-by, Al Capp. Al was in his usual form, regaling all with such insightful witticisms as the one about how it's better to be in a rice paddy with the enemy in your cross-hair than to be in

(Continued on page 4)

A LEFTIST LOOKS AT YAF— *(Continued from page 3)*

college. With rib-ticklers like that, it is no wonder he is the darling of the right.

So if one went to St. Louis for entertainment, one was sure to find satisfaction. The trouble is, is that the above named performers and the bulk of their audience were not simply making idle jests about the desirability of stamping out freedom and self-determination around the world, but were actually serious in their threats and fulminations. The leaders of this venomous gang call themselves "traditionalists", or "trads". But with a program like theirs, one wonders what tradition they referring to. Certainly no organization which espouses collective massacre can claim any attachment to a tradition of individual liberty. No organization so adoring of the destructive powers of government can say the philosophy of laissez-faire is part of their tradition. What tradition can there be for an organization which descries the growth of state power one minute, and calls for a greater "defense" budget the next? What philosophy of yesteryear hailed the freedom of the individual to determine his own life as a paramount good, and still insisted that he could not break a law even if obeying meant he became a slave to the government's will? Even Thomas Hobbes had the generosity to allow for the individual's self-defense in the face of government aggression. Who, then, can these trads call their intellectual ancestors? Looking back over the history of man, there is only one theory which can be found that is consistent with the ideas of these trads: the theory of the fascist, totalitarian state.

YAF is a morass of contradictions. It wants to be radical but it doesn't want to break the law. It claims to be fighting for democracy, yet its own internal policy is dictated by a dogma which allows for democratic process only when the majority decision of the voters agrees with the policy of the National Board. YAF board members seem to think that democracy consists of purging all dissenting voices within the organization. The most glaring contradiction in YAF is, of course, the name itself. If "young" means having a senile, illogical, hate-filled mind encased in a young body, then the "Y" in YAF makes sense. If "American" means love of aggressive imperialism abroad and violent repression at home, then the "A" in YAF fits. And if "freedom" means enslavement to arbitrary rule, then the "F" in YAF is comprehensible. I, however, do not share their definition of these terms. Nor will the bulk of American youth be able to make much sense of them. As a youth movement, YAF is hopelessly out of step. YAFers march more with Metternich than Marcuse. Intelligent American youths will be found joining SDS, the RLA, SLAM, the Panthers, or some other such militant anti-government force. Even militant right-wingers with essentially the same viewpoint as YAF will shun it because of YAF's aversion to action. YAF will continue to exist, though, as a showplace where conservative American businessmen can go to reaffirm their faith in a fascist future for America. That is all that YAF ever really was--or will be.

— John Hogen

Recommended Reading

Milton Kotler, *Neighborhood Government* (Bobbs-Merrill, hard cover and paper). Brief work on neighborhoods vs. the expanding central city. Particularly valuable is the historical discussion of the "imperialist" way in which the central cities in the U. S. have seized control over the outlying neighborhoods, very often through the state legislatures and without the neighborhoods' consent. (Also see Karl Hess's review of the Kotler book in the December *Ramparts*.)

Murray N. Rothbard, "Review of J. Weinstein's The Corporate Ideal in the Liberal State, 1900-1918", *Ramparts*, December 1969. Review of a book that ranks with Gabriel Kolko's in revealing how our present interventionist, Mixed Economy, was put in by Big Business for purposes of monopolization.

I. F. Stone, *The Hidden Theory of the Korean War* (Monthly Review Press), $7.50. It is good to have this great Revisionist work on the Korean War back in print (originally published in 1952). Stone shows conclusively that the U. S. was responsible for the war. For you anarcho-rightists still bamboozled by Cold War myths, read it!

Alfred F. Young, *The Democratic Republicans of New York: The Origins 1763-1797* (University of North Carolina Press). Brilliant, definitive, neo-Beardian work on the political struggles over the Constitution and in the 1790's in New York. One of the best books on the whole period.

Famous Last Words

"Ultra-left adventurism is fun."

— A libertarian militant

The Libertarian Forum
BOX 341
MADISON SQUARE STATION
NEW YORK, NEW YORK 10010

You may publish my name and address as a reader of the *Libertarian Forum* who would like to meet other *Forum* readers:

NAME ....

ADDRESS ....

CITY, STATE and ZIP ....

Published on the first and fifteenth of every month.   Subscription rate: $7.00 per year; Student subscription rate: $5.00 per year.

A Semi-Monthly Newsletter

THE
Libertarian Forum

Joseph R. Peden, Publisher   Washington Editor, Karl Hess   Murray N. Rothbard, Editor

VOL. I, NO. XVIII   December 15, 1969   35¢

Notes On Repression

I – JUDICIAL FASCISM

As the Nixon Administration bursts at the seams in its eagerness to move into all-out repression of dissent, some crucial implications of its current actions have gone largely unnoticed. Take, for example, the notorious "Conspiracy" trial of the Chicago 8. Many people have remarked that the law itself, which appropriately was passed by Congress as a "civil rights" measure, is unconstitutional, since it outlaws the crossing of state lines with "intent" to "incite" to riot, all of which vagueness clearly violates the First Amendment guarantee of freedom of speech.

Many more people have noted the unbelievable actions of Judge Julius Hoffman, who has made a continuing mockery of any meaningful principles of justice. Thus, Hoffman sent marshals across the continent in order to arrest two lawyers and drag them to Chicago as prisoners, for the sole "crime" of withdrawing from the case by telegram instead of in person. The judge proceeded to force Panther leader, Bobby Seale, to be represented by William Kunstler, even though Seale refused Kunstler's aid and in lieu of his ailing lawyer Charles Garry, preferred to defend his own case. Not only did Judge Hoffman force Seale to be defended by a lawyer not of his own choice, but Kunstler himself didn't want to defend Seale against the latter's wishes. What kind of a "free country" is it when a man is forced to accept an unwanted lawyer? Then, when Bobby Seale proceeded to defend his own case anyway, Judge Hoffman had Seale gagged and shackled in court, to form a sight strongly reminiscent of Nazi or Soviet "justice". Finally, when Seale tried to escape his bondage and protest his treatment, Judge Hoffman quickly sentenced the prisoner to an unprecedented four years in jail for "contempt of court".

The point for libertarians to focus on is not the particular despotism of Judge Hoffman, but the evil of the system itself, the American legal and judicial system, that establishes federal judges as petty despots, free to dictate to people at will and virtually unchallenged. The judge is absolute ruler in his court, in practice really not subject to higher judicial review. Furthermore, the power to declare guilty and sentence someone for contempt of court totally violates the basic legal rule of separation between prosecutor and judge. The judge makes the charge of contempt against the defendant. The judge then "hears" his own case as he sees fit, and then the judge, without benefit of jury trial, declares the defendant guilty and pronounces sentence. There is no excuse for this kind of judicial proceedings, and it is high time that libertarians, always alive to the evils of tyranny in the moral and economic spheres, turn their attention to the legal field as well. Libertarian law must be a law shorn of all elements of tyranny and aggression against those not yet proven to be criminal invaders

of the person and just property of another man. Judicial despotism is a good place to begin.

II – RADIO-TV

Vice President Agnew's ugly attacks against the news media, with their clear threats of censorship and their danger to the freedom of the press, have obscured the fact that the news media, and especially radio and television, *are* closely tied in with the Establishment, with the powers-that-be. Any one of independent mind has long discovered that fact about the American media. Agnew's seemingly radical attack on the media is a phony, a mere reflection of the deep split, especially over Vietnam, between the two major factions of the ruling class: the sophisticated corporate liberals and the relatively Neanderthal conservatives. Agnew did not care to attack the vast majority of the nation's newspapers, which are fiercely conservative; instead, he centered his ire on the two bastions of Eastern corporate liberalism: the New York *Times* and the Washington *Post* . The networks, which are solidly corporate liberal, came in for a far more roundhouse treatment.

Agnew's proto-fascist assault should not be allowed to obscure the fact that the networks *are* monopolistic, and also that virtually no one, certainly not Agnew, has zeroed in on the roots and essence of this monopoly. The original sin came in 1927, when Secretary of Commerce Herbert Hoover put through the Radio Act of 1927 which nationalized the ownership of air waves (and television channels); from then on, radio frequencies and TV channels continued to be owned by the federal government, which granted licenses to use these frequencies and channels, and set up a Federal Communications Commission to regulate their use. The result could scarcely have been other than censorship and monopoly. As Professor Coase writes: "The situation in the American broadcasting industry is not essentially different in character from that which could be found if a commission appointed by the federal government had the task of selecting those who were to be allowed to publish newspapers and periodicals in each city, town, and village of the United States." (Ronald H. Coase, "The Federal Communications Commission," *The Journal of Law and Economics*, October, 1959, p. 7). In particular, the networks have been able to use the FCC as their tool in outlawing the use of pay-TV, a potentially powerful competitor to the present system of advertiser-paid television.

Radio and television frequencies were, when first discovered, analogous to the opening up of a new Continent. They should have been allocated just as the land of the American Continent was in the main allocated: on the

(Continued on page 4)

Letter From Washington

By Karl Hess

Cults And Criticisms

One of the most recondite of Christian heresies is that of stercoranism in which proponents argue to the death over whether the sacred elements of the communion wafer are retained forever in the body or whether they are expelled excretally. This and all other such heresies gained headway, and popularity, rather long after Christianity had emerged as a revolutionary doctrine. In its revolutionary phase, Christianity had emerged as a revolutionary doctrine. In its revolutionary phase, Christianity split no such hairs. It was a thunderous on-my-side-or-against-me sort of thing and, in the houses on either side of that single division there were, as one well known Christian put it, "many rooms".

In the existential struggle between liberty and authority there also are many rooms, indeed, a thousand flowers bloom on either side of the dividing line.

My own summary of the matter is known as The Oink Principle. It states that if it oinks it is your enemy. If it does not oink it may not be your best friend but it is, at least, not your enemy.

I have consulted lately with my very dear friend, Murray Rothbard, on this matter and he tells me that although he will continue to criticize my, and others', left wing adventurism, that he has not detected a single oink from my room. I have not, in turn, heard any such sound from his.

There are others, however, who may take Murray's criticisms as some sort of anathema being pronounced upon them. They may mistake simple criticism for lethal exclusionism. This strikes me as a needless reaction. There are many anarchists who hold, for instance, that not even God is god. Why should they make the mistake of thinking that Rothbard is? He is a comrade, not a deity; a brilliant economist, not a burning bush; a revolutionary theorist, not an executioner.

It is clear by my actions, I am sure, that I do not agree with a substantial portion of Murray's recent criticism. I even disagree with the emphasis upon criticism itself which seems to have overtaken him. I would prefer, and hopefully expect, that his talents would be turned more to analysis of the political situation generally rather than to the personalities of our part of it in particular. Having even said that, however, I must admit that his latest criticisms of left wing adventurism, which did contain pointed comments about many of us, also contained a thoughtful commentary upon the possibilities of politicizing liberals. I am, as a matter of fact, in close and regular contact with several of the other adventurists criticized in Murray's commentary. Neither they nor I feel personally offended at all by what he had to say.

We simply disagree.

We say, in effect, "Well, that's Murray." We expect that, when all is said and done, Murray, similarly, will sigh and say, "Well, that's them."

In struggle there must be room for diversity or else what's a revolution for? But diversity need not mean bitter divisiveness. Let us divide, indeed, from those who do not stand with us against the common enemies—authority, reaction, counter-revolutionism, elitism, the state. Let us divide, indeed, from the pure theory pettifoggers who seek sanctuary from the state in their solipsism, who support

imperialism if it is profitable, genocide if it is by Westerners, and injustice if it is legal.

Of course, divide from them. They are on the other side anyway. But Murray, Clean for Anarchy, is not the enemy of those of us who are Dirty for Dope, Hirsute for Hedonism, Rowdy for Revolution, Randy for Rutting, or Pouring Down for the Weather Bureau. He is the critic of those things. Not the enemy of those things.

Parse not every subordinate clause for an offense. Don't look under every verb for a worm. Look at the heart of the man and not the varicose veins of his occasional prose. Maybe even then there will be those offended or discontented. So be it. Look then away from the single man there and to the single movement everywhere, the movement toward liberty. If we permit any one of us to so dominate our emotions as to defeat our purposes, then we offer to our enemy a nasty little victory on the platter of personality.

I do not believe in the organic reality of the state or of the movement. I do not believe in things of Man that exist apart from Man. Man's works are done by men's hands and heads. But I believe in cooperation. I believe in movements *of* men. I believe in orders of priority in those movements and in that cooperation. And I believe that not one of us is so important, influential, charismatic, or anointed as to form in and of ourselves a movement or even a focus for a movement.

Therefore, to take the criticism of one person, or the resentment of another, as somehow of an order of importance comparable to the movement itself strikes me as crucially bad judgment.

Let those with grievances discuss them, by all means, aggrieved with griper. Let a thousand memos blossom, a hundred thousand affinity groups flower, and let them carp and cavil--and grow.

But let us not mistake any such part for the whole of the movement. One man's criticism is one man's suggestions. But let two men's reactions overcome their other concerns and what should have been a suggestion may well become a psychosis. This is not to say that the persons criticized are most at fault. It is not to say that anyone is at fault. It is to say that when Rothbard rumbles all need not quake and similarly it is to say that Rothbard, rumbling, should realize that for many who feel him as their mentor, it is difficult to resist an over-reaction. Above all it is not to say that the tactics of the movement must not be debated, even if the debate inevitably involves personalities, life styles, etc. Of course there needs to be such debate.

What we need to do is to debate, disagree, decide, go ahead, often following different courses, sometimes with new comrades but not wasting our time just on making points. We want to make a movement, instead; we want to make our history, not feather our nests or feed our egos.

Murray is not the movement. I am not. You are not. We are. Anarchists are not the movement. Communists are not the movement. Utopian socialists or Utopian laissez-faire-ists are not the movement. Revolutionary nationalists are not the movement. Pacificists are not the movement. Retreatists are not the movement. Weathermen are not the movement. Fidel is not. Ho is not. Eldridge is not. Spock is not. Liggio is not. Abbie is not. They are. We are.

Take the Weathermen for just an instance. Some hate what they did. But how could you in all good conscience hate what they are? *They are your brothers.*

Murray may dislike what many of us do. He may dwell overlong on it and over loud. Is that an exorbitant price to pay, for instance, for his "Anatomy of the State"? I say it's a bargain.

Similarly, there are many who dislike what he does. But surely they must recognize that Murray cannot put them in jail, steal them blind, censor them, kill them—as can

(Continued on page 3)

CRITICISMS — *(Continued from page 2)*
agents of the state.

Finally, if there must be an ongoing debate about decorum among our little band then at least let it be open and even in the pages of this journal. Murray has raised points to which some, obviously, are dying to answer. Let them do it and let them do it promptly and precisely. Inter-personal notes or memos, as I suggested earlier, might be best of

all, but mutterings and rumors will not do at all.

Why don't I write such answers? Because, as Murray knows, I have heard his criticism, respectfully, and I have rejected it for myself alone. My heart truly does belong to the left. And it is an adventure. An adventure in liberty. And not even Clean Murray, I know, really considers that leprosy.

To my comrades: I love you all!

The Military-Industrial-University Complex

As good as it is, there is more to the October *Ramparts* than Karl Hess' masterful "Open Letter to Barry Goldwater". David Horowitz (author, among other works, of *The Free World Colossus*) has a hardhitting piece on the universities and those controlling influences, the foundations; or, as Horowitz terms the two, "The Sinews of Empire". The esteemed editor of this newsletter has pointed out time and again how the rôle of the intellectual in the statist society is to act as apologist for the ruling class. Horowitz graphically demonstrates specifically how the kept intellectual of today's United States has in fact apologized for, influenced, and helped shape U. S. foreign policy.

At the end of the Second World War, a new discipline, that of International Studies, with its numerous subdivisions of specific area studies, was inaugurated. Horowitz views this new discipline as a major weapon forged by the foundations in order to gain a great deal of control over major universities in support of ruling class interests. It is, after all, necessary for any ruling class to insure the perpetuation of views salutary to its interests, as well as the recruiting of new personnel to carry out these interests in policy rôles. Specifically, a rationale for the new U. S. global imperium was needed, and the foundations, mainly through the various new Institutes of International Studies, determined that the universities would come up with same (or at least those key universities which provide "leadership" to the academic community). The institutes soon became devices for insuring that those academicians who held the "correct line" were rewarded, and that those who did not died on the vine. Power in the affected universities shifted to a marked degree from the relevant departments to the new institutes. Advancement was fastest and most lucrative in these new fields. As anyone who understands the market process could have guessed, resources, talent and research went into the newly subsidized areas. But of course only "productive" (productive to the interests of the foundations, i.e., the ruling class) research would be rewarded. Small wonder that dissent is so lacking in the academic world--it literally was starved while establishment intellectuals prospered. Where would a young man in Harvard or Stanford go but where the money, power and prestige lay?

Who were the men who controlled the foundation money which went to universities after the war? To cite an example, the Russian Institute of Columbia, the first of this new breed of academic subdivisions, was first headed by Geroid T. Robinson, who had been head of the OSS Research and Analysis Branch, USSR Division. In 1945 the Rockefeller Foundation had made a five-year grant of $1,250,000 for the purpose of setting up the institute. The man who was responsible for the disbursing of this money was one Joseph Willits who, like Robinson, was a member of the prestigious Council on Foreign Relations (as were, of course, David, Nelson and John D. Rockefeller). The man who succeeded Robinson in 1951, Philip E. Mosley, was also a member of the CFR, and a former state department officer. Indeed, of the five who headed the institute, only one--Robinson--had had any prior connection with Columbia. Four had been with the OSS or State Department, and three were in the CFR. The new academic discipline

had a membership with strange and curious credentials.

In 1948 Columbia received an East Asian Institute from the Rockefeller Foundation. In 1949 it was the Carnegie Foundation's turn to set up a Columbia institute--the European. The cast here was especially interesting. The European Institute was initially headed by Grayson Kirk--Columbia professor, Carnegie Corp. trustee, CFR member, and Mobil Oil Director. Next year Kirk resigned to become Columbia provost, and was succeeded by Schuyler Wallace, CFR member in good standing. The present head is . . . Philip Mosley, the second head of the Russian Institute. This basic pattern was repeated at Yale, Harvard, Princeton, Stanford, etc. As Horowitz puts it, "Like the Hapsburg Royalty, they like to keep the family small and intimate."

Anyone who thinks that academic freedom, or its offspring, intellectual honesty, can survive long in an atmosphere as described above is either terribly naive or rather stupid. Pressure for intellectual conformity can be as subtle as the lure of handsome grants. Or it can be as explicit as the guiding directive of the Hoover Institution on War, Revolution and Peace, wherein the purpose of the Institution is described as ". . . to demonstrate the evils of the doctrines of Karl Marx--whether Communism, Socialism, economic materialism, or atheism--thus to protect the American way of life from such ideologies, their conspiracies and to reaffirm the validity of the American system." If in fact communism, socialism and atheism (Does this make the non-theist, Henry Hazlitt, a conspirator in the promulgation of the evil teachings of Karl Marx?) are evil, such an institute is a very poor device for either discovering the evils, or producing effective counter-arguments (as can readily be seen from the Institution's output). *A priori* assumptions do not make for objective analysis. A university's function is not to produce propaganda but the truth. To do anything else is to cease to function as a center of learning. To function consciously as a "protector" is to become a tool of whomever one is protecting. To become a "protector" of, and to "reaffirm the validity of the American system", is to become a tool of the U. S. corporate state and its global imperium. This

(Continued on page 4)

REPRESSION — *(Continued from page 1)*

libertarian, homesteading principle of total private ownership to the first user. Radio and TV frequencies should be private just as land is private; only thus can the airwaves escape the blight of corporate-governmental monopoly. The homesteading principle applies equally to both cases.

There are two common arguments against private property in airwaves. One is that different radio and TV stations would be able to interfere and drown out each other's signals, thus causing "chaos". This ignores the crucial

COMPLEX — *(Continued from page 3)*

is what Stanford has done. This is what most universities have done.

It is especially tragic that conservatives, who have talked so much in the past about the "liberal establishment", should be so cold towards the findings of such scholars as Horowitz. For what is the "military-industrial-university" -complex but the "liberal establishment" writ large? The only difference is that the rather ridiculous assumption of conservatives that men like Roosevelt and Rockefeller were (are) crypto-socialists has been replaced by the reality of their being proto-fascists. Of course the reason for this shift in the thinking of conservatives is quite obvious, as can be seen strikingly in the case of their chief spokesman, Bill Buckley, the man whom Gore Vidal has so charmingly referred to as a "pro-crypto Nazi". Buckley, the "liberals' conservative", has, like so many of his followers, become part of this establishment. Now that conservatives are in power (even if they have to share it with their partners in the welfare/warfare system, the liberals), and have their man, Strom Nixon, in the White House, they want no more anti-establishment talk. Also explained is why conservatives have reacted so strongly against all recent attempts to carry out one of their former lofty ideals—smashing the statist educational power, be it Columbia, Ocean Hill-Brownsville, or whatever.

No, if the New Right has joined the Old Left, and if the Old Right is literally almost dead, then it is clear that libertarians can turn only to the New Left in their opposition to statism. It is not a question of whether they will make good or bad allies, but that the New Left are the only possible allies. Not to ally with them would be to ratify the existing statist oppression, together with its infrastructure (e. g., the universities). Besides, as can be seen from a little study, the New Left has been correct all along on most major issues (e. g., the universities). The New Left is essentially correct in both theory and practice. They are for "Power to the People". Damn it, Mr. Conservative, *whom* are you for power to?

— Gerald O'Driscoll, Jr.

historical fact that the American common-law courts were, in the 1920's, working out the perfectly sound doctrine that one station's interference with a previous station's signal is an invasion of property rights, and can be prevented on that basis. Thus, as Coase says, "In the case of Tribune Co. v. Oak Leaves Broadcasting Station [Circuit Court, Cook County, Illinois, 1926]. . . it was held that the operator of an existing station had a sufficient property right, acquired by priority, to enjoin a newcomer from using a frequency so as to cause any material interference." (Coase, p. 31*n*.) Hoover and other statist-monopolists, knowing this full well, rushed through the Radio Act of 1927 so as to prevent the development of competition and private property rights in the airwaves. As Professor Milton Friedman writes in an excellent and lucid article on the subject, "The owners of these rights [in the airwaves] would have private property in them, which they would protect from trespass as you and I protect our land from trespass, through the courts. They could buy and sell the rights, subdivide them, recombine them, as you and I do with our land. They would have the full protection of the Bill of Rights just as the press now does." (Milton Friedman, "How to Free TV", *Newsweek*, Dec. 1, 1969, p. 82).

The second popular argument against private property in the airwaves is that air frequencies are "limited" in supply. Such an argument can only stem from profound economic ignorance. All resources, all goods are "limited": that is why they are owned in the first place, and that is why they command a price on the market. If a good were unlimited-- as, say, clean air in the days before pollution--there would be no question of owning it or pricing it, since the good would be superabundant in relation to human desires. It is precisely goods that are limited in supply that must be owned by someone--whether by private persons or government--and thereby allocated to their most productive uses through the price system. Iron mines are limited; land is limited; labor is limited; raw materials are limited; capital goods are limited; Rembrandts are limited. Must all these be nationalized therefore?

Now that government has preempted and retained its "domain" over the airwaves, the precise path of getting from nationalized to private airwaves is far less important than getting rid of the present abomination. There are two cogent alternatives: one is the Coase-Friedman plan of the FCC's selling the existing frequencies to the highest bidders. The trouble with this is that the money for the sale goes to an illegitimate recipient: the federal government. The other path is more in accord with homesteading principles: simply granting private property in fee simple to the existing stations. In either case, the FCC would then go promptly go out of existence. Governmental monopolizing of the airwaves would at last be at an end.

The Libertarian Forum
BOX 341
MADISON SQUARE STATION
NEW YORK, NEW YORK 10010

Published on the first and fifteenth of every month.   Subscription rate: $7.00 per year; Student subscription rate: $5.00 per year.

A Semi-Monthly Newsletter

THE
Libertarian Forum

Joseph R. Peden, Publisher   Washington Editor, Karl Hess   Murray N. Rothbard, Editor

VOL. II, NO. 1   January 1, 1970   35¢

Anarcho-Communism

Now that the New Left has abandoned its earlier loose, flexible non-ideological stance, two ideologies have been adopted as guiding theoretical positions by New Leftists: Marxism-Stalinism, and anarcho-communism. Marxism-Stalinism has unfortunately conquered SDS, but anarcho-communism has attracted many leftists who are looking for a way out of the bureaucratic and statist tyranny that has marked the Stalinist road. And many libertarians, who are looking for forms of action and for allies in such actions, have become attracted by an anarchist creed which seemingly exalts the voluntary way and calls for the abolition of the coercive State. It is fatal, however, to abandon and lose sight of one's own principles in the quest for allies in specific tactical actions. Anarcho-communism, both in its original Bakunin-Kropotkin form and its current irrationalist and "post-scarcity" variety, is poles apart from genuine libertarian principle.

If there is one thing, for example, that anarcho-communism hates and reviles *more* than the State it is the rights of private property; as a matter of fact, the major reason that anarcho-communists oppose the State is because they wrongly believe that it is the creator and protector of private property, and therefore that the only route toward abolition of property is by destruction of the State apparatus. They totally fail to realize that the State has always been the great enemy and invader of the rights of private property. Furthermore, scorning and detesting the free-market, the profit-and-loss economy, private property, and material affluence--all of which are corollaries of each other-- anarcho-communists wrongly identify anarchism with communal living, with tribal sharing, and with other aspects of our emerging drug-rock "youth culture".

The only good thing that one might say about anarcho-communism is that, in contrast to Stalinism, its form of communism would, supposedly, be voluntary. Presumably, no one would be forced to join the communes, and those who would continue to live individually, and to engage in market activities, would remain unmolested.   Or would they? Anarcho-communists have always been extremely vague and cloudy about the lineaments of their proposed anarchist society of the future. Many of them have been propounding the profoundly *anti*-libertarian doctrine that the anarcho-communist revolution will have to confiscate and abolish all private property, so as to wean everyone from their psychological attachment to the property they own. Furthermore, it is hard to forget the fact that when the Spanish Anarchists (anarcho-communists of the Bakunin-Kropotkin type) took over large sections of Spain during the Civil War of the 1930's, they confiscated and destroyed all the money

in their areas and promptly decreed the death penalty for the use of money. None of this can give one confidence in the good, voluntarist intentions of anarcho-communism.

On all other grounds, anarcho-communism ranges from mischievous to absurd. Philosophically, this creed is an all-out assault on individuality and on reason. The individual's desire for private property, his drive to better himself, to specialize, to accumulate profits and income, are reviled by all branches of communism. Instead, every one is supposed to live in communes, sharing all his meager possessions with his fellows, and each being careful not to advance beyond his communal brothers. At the root of all forms of communism, compulsory or voluntary, lies a profound hatred of individual excellence, a denial of the natural or intellectual superiority of some men over others, and a desire to tear down every individual to the level of a communal ant-heap. In the name of a phony "humanism", an irrational and profoundly anti-human egalitarianism is to rob every individual of his specific and precious humanity.

Furthermore, anarcho-communism scorns reason, and its corollaries long-range purpose, forethought, hard work, and individual achievement; instead, it exalts irrational feelings, whim, and caprice--all this in the name of "freedom". The "freedom" of the anarcho-communist has nothing to do with the genuine libertarian absence of interpersonal invasion or molestation; it is, instead, a "freedom" that means enslavement to unreason, to unexamined whim, and to childish caprice. Socially and philosophically, anarcho-communism is a misfortune.

Economically, anarcho-communism is an absurdity. The anarcho-communist seeks to abolish money, prices, and employment, and proposes to conduct a modern economy purely by the automatic registry of "needs" in some central data bank. No one who has the slightest understanding of economics can trifle with this theory for a single second. Fifty years ago, Ludwig von Mises exposed the total inability of a planned, moneyless economy to operate above the most primitive level. For he showed that money-prices are indispensable for the rational allocation of all of our scarce resources--labor, land, and capital goods--to the fields and the areas where they are most desired by the consumers and where they could operate with greatest efficiency. The socialists conceded the correctness of Mises' challenge, and set about--in vain--to find a way to have a rational, market price system within the context of a socialist planned economy.

The Russians, after trying an approach to the communist moneyless economy in their "War Communism" shortly
(Continued on page 4)

A Comment

The Working Class

The recent *Libertarian Forum* articles on "The Conference" and "Ultra-Leftism" are among the most thought-provoking I have read in a long time. Since I find myself in total and sometimes violent disagreement with about ninety-five per cent of the statements made, I shall confine this rebuttal to a few major points. This does not mean that I concur with any other points made.

Since it is a term that has validity only in retrospect, "ultra-leftism" provides an excellent whipping boy for radical historians. The "ultra-leftist" is the guy that failed; had he succeeded, he would have been a "daring tactician" or a "charismatic figure". While in some cases "ultra-leftism", whatever it really is, may have been the revolution's downfall, in other cases (most notably Spain) it could have saved the day.

At any rate, Murray is wrong to regard "ultra-leftism" as a cause of the decline of SDS; the true lesson for us here is that it was a symptom of the true cause, a far greater danger. Murray states that, "The hysteria, and the pitiful failure, of the Weathermen stem not so much from personal psychosis as from incorrect strategic theory." Exactly the reverse is true since Weatherman's "ultra-left" errors have psychological origins. Upper middle-class and upper-class kids, instead of sticking to their own valid, campus-related issues, feel so hung-up about their soft easy upbringing that they try desperately to attach themselves to someone else's more urgent, "down-to-earth" struggles (e.g. Blacks, rank-and-file unionists, etc.). Furthermore, no longer being "down-to-earth" at all themselves once they leave their own sphere, the campus, they adopt a revolutionary ideology totally alien to the American situation. Finally, rejected by Blacks and workers and community people for being pushy, elitist, scrawny idiots, they set out to prove their manhood after a crash course in karate and get their asses whipped, setting back serious radical organization everywhere they go.

Few people will join a revolution unless it is in their own self-interest. All too much of the Movement consists of people who have arrived at a purely intellectual commitment to a revolution that will bring about the society they visualize. When their appeals in the name of humanity, social justice, freedom, equality, or other vague concepts fail to create a mass movement, they withdraw into their own little self-righteous circles, and put out increasingly sectarian and increasingly unread manifestoes.

Murray, as with so many other radicals, declares that the working class is hopelessly reactionary, racist, etc. OK, make your revolution without them--if you can. And if you can, what will you do with this large, restive, powerful, and hopeless group afterwards--the final solution to the labor problem? Equally valid sweeping criticisms can be directed against the middle class (or any other class)--smugness, reformism, even racism of a more sophisticated and less easily eradicable form. At any rate, if "American Marxists have boxed themselves into a complete dead end in pinning their hopes on the workers," couldn't this be because most American Marxists are declasse middle class with absolutely nothing to offer the working class?

If anyone thinks the role of the working class is irrelevant, he should ask himself a few questions: Who could shut the country down faster, ten million intellectuals or one million dockers and truckers? If labor is hopelessly co-opted, why is the country being swept with wildcat strikes and even with sanctioned strikes for that matter; why are the fat-ass unions plagued with black caucuses, rank-and-file caucuses, etc.? If the workers were not a potential danger, why does the whole system, especially the schools, the press, and

Lurking In The Wings

In the days of the First World War, when governments were wildly stomping out the lives and futures of their people in the name of nationalism and national destiny, one American radical described the process: War is the health of the State. In time of war, the subjects of rulers enthusiastically rally to them--hate the Enemy, volunteer to kill whomever the government wants eliminated, and cheerfully contribute higher taxes. The power and wealth at the command of the state positively swells beyond the peacetime bureaucrat's wildest dreams. But the issuing of commands always requires willing ears to hear and obey them.

Let it never be said that Uncle Sam doesn't plan ahead. In 1961 the Office of Emergency Preparedness sprang up meiotically from the four Civil Defense agencies which have functioned for twenty years. The star program of the O.E.P. is the National Defense Executive Reserve: when the war comes, and the government gets its chance to expand overnight, the personnel problem will be solved--in advance. Just as the army maintains officers in reserve status to fight the Enemy, the bureaucracy has the N.D.E.R. standing like 4,000 minutemen ready to fight on the home front--fighting the people (as it were).

Any agency or department head can establish an N.D.E.R. unit. Units currently exist for the Secretary of Commerce, Business and Defense Services Administration, Office of Oil and Gas, Office of Minerals and Solid Fuels, Bureau of Public Roads, Office of Emergency Transportation, Economic Stabilization Agency, Office of Defense Resources, and others.

In times of national emergency, isn't it curious how the conventional wisdom holds that the spontaneous powers of citizens to organize and bring resources to bear on problems should and must be *constrained* by bureaucratic control? This is the philosophy of the state, of state-socialism and state-capitalism; the philosophy behind the National Defense Executive Reserve. At the very moment when red-tape and bureaucracy should step aside and let people solve the emergency problems, the government plans to step in, reinforced, to strangle the nation! Who can estimate the added cost in wealth and human life which the growth of bureaucracy and bureaucratic inefficiency has imposed in the past, and will impose tenfold in any future war or national emergency? At a time when the mechanisms of trade and decentralized decision-making--the ability to take instant action, at one's own economic risk on the basis of localized, specific information--are more than ever needed, the government has habitually aggrandized its own power and authority by *prohibiting* any activity not first initiated or sanctioned by some bureaucrat's authority.

In cases where a man supplies an urgent demand and makes
(Continued on page 4)

the church, try so determinedly to keep them from thinking for themselves? History shows that workers can act when they see the necessity. And they do ACT. Murray has a distaste for action, but seriously, how else will the Revolution come about?

Aside from the accuracy or error of the articles in question, the articles are a tactical error. *Ad hominem* attacks, and indiscriminate blasts at important segments of the libertarian movement can only serve the purpose of turning the *Libertarian Forum* into a minor sectarian sheet constantly congratulating itself on its own correctness. In its short lifetime the *Forum* has done two difficult jobs: it has demonstrated, in the language of the "rightist" libertarian and to the "rightist" libertarian, the necessity of revolution; and it has called together a lot of people who otherwise would be struggling alone. Is it now to drive them apart?

—— Bill Goring

My Loyalty Oath

"GAINESVILLE, FLA. — Three University of Florida professors and one librarian were fired Nov. 26 because they refused to sign the state's loyalty oath. Dismissed were law professor Leroy L. Lamborn, psychology instructor Evan Suits, architecture instructor Jerome Miller, and library clerk Ann Bardsley . . ."

The whole thing is pretty ludicrous, really, and I suppose I should be laughing. But being fired has had an unfortunate effect upon my sense of humor. Last week I was an unoffensive librarian, laboring among my catalog cards and dusty bookshelves. Now I am unemployed and publically branded as an enemy of the state. And all because of a little green IBM card with a seven-line loyalty oath printed on it.

The State of Florida has required a loyalty oath of all recipients of its funds since the early Cold War days back in 1949. When I went to work for the University of Florida a year ago, the oath appeared under my pen between fingerprinting and a form detailing my life history. I signed it with distaste, but I needed the job very badly, and had no choice. The law requires that the oath be notarized. Early this year the university administration decided it had been a bit lax about having the oath notarized--a matter that the Board of Regents and other reactionary politicians consider of utmost importance. So the University's 3,000 fulltime employees and several thousand more part-time student employees, graduate assistants, and others on the state payroll, were ordered to take a little green IBM card with the oath printed on it and sign it before a notary. All, of course, at the taxpayer's expense.

The oath originally had a provision in it stipulating that the signer was not a member of the Communist party. A suit by Stella Connell, an Orlando, Fla., schoolteacher, won a court decision knocking out the clause about being a Communist as unconstitutional, so the signing stopped while the University ran around printing up new oaths without the offending clause. Then they began collecting signatures all over again. We were told that those who refused to sign would not be paid until they did. Most of the employees were irritated from having to chase around notarizing the oath, and several hundred--including two entire departments of the University--were so offended by the principle of the thing that they threatened to refuse to sign. But by the November 26 deadline, almost all had surrendered to economic necessity and signed the oath. The three professors and I who still maintained our refusal to sign, were fired. Since I am not a professional educator, I shall probably be able to find a new job. But the three professors, whose jobs are inextricably tied to the government-dominated field of education, face financial and professional ruin.

Because of the events of the past few weeks I now have a great deal of time to consider not only my own reasons for not signing the oath, but the whole purpose and consequence of this oath.

The oath we refused to sign says:

"I the above-named, a citizen of the State of Florida and the United States of America, and being employed by or an officer of the University of Florida and recipient of public funds as such employee or officer, do hereby swear or affirm that I will support the Constitution of the United States and of the State of Florida; that I do not believe in the overthrow of the United States or of the State of Florida by force or violence."

I refused to sign this oath because it is a piece of pernicious nonsense and an unwarranted invasion by the state into the privacy of the individual. It is nonsense because even if it were desirable to root subversives out of the University, whether they were floor cleaners or professors, no dedicated subversive would blow his cover by signing it. It is per-

nicious for a number of reasons.

On a practical level, it is a waste of the taxpayer's money. On a legal level, the many citizens of other states and countries who had to sign it perjured themselves by doing so. Most of my foreign friends were amused--in a contemptuous sort of way--by having to sign the oath, but several were bitterly resentful. If they had refused to sign, they could have lost their visas and been deported. "If I am forced to sign this," a Persian friend told me, "then the constitution to which I am affirming my support really is not worth the paper it is written on, is it?"

But to me, the worst aspect of being coerced into signing this oath is its effect on individual liberty. What business is it of anyone's what I support or do not support, believe in or do not believe in? As long as I am an efficient and reliable librarian, who cares what I think about the Constitution of the State of Florida? The answer is, of course, that the state is so unsure of the loyalty of its citizens, particularly the more intelligent people that work in universities, that it cannot rest until it has extracted a pledge of fealty from them.

One of the dangers in making people sign these silly things is, of course, that it reminds the individual that the only way to stay safe and secure is by unquestioning obedience to the state. Unquestioning obedience leads to Buchenwald and Song My, and the destruction of all individual initiative and responsibility. In a University, any kind of loyalty requirement strangles the atmosphere of intellectual freedom which is necessary for scholarly inquiry.

Looking back on this, I wonder: was it better to keep quiet, sign, and stay, or get fired, leaving the university to those more reactionary or subservient than I? Either way, it seems to me, we would have a mighty quiet university. If we had backed down on this, Evan Suits, Lee Lamborn, Jerome Miller, and I would be working for the University of Florida today. And perhaps our sensitivity to individual freedom might have served as some kind of good influence. But it also seems that one can surrender a little here, and a little there--always hoping to fight back next time--until the will to resist is gone.

Since I wasn't planning the violent overthrow of the government, etc., I could honestly have signed the oath. But the government that demands loyalty to some constitution or belief today, will tomorrow demand our allegiance to some party, or governor, or religion, or . . . *Fuehrer.* The time to stop the state is now, not when it has become so oppressive that you no longer have the strength or the means to fight.

The American Civil Liberties Union, which is taking our suit for reinstatement through the courts, has a motto: "Eternal Vigilance is the Price of Liberty".

I agree.

— Ann C. Bardsley

ATTENTION, LIBERTARIANS

Many readers of the *Libertarian Forum* have expressed interest in finding other libertarians near them. Therefore, early this year, the *Forum* will begin to publish the names and addresses of people who would like to be contacted by other readers of the *Libertarian Forum.* If you'd like your name to be included, please fill out the coupon on the back of this notice.

ANARCHO-COMMUNISM— *(Continued from page 1)*

after the Bolshevik Revolution, reacted in horror as they saw the Russian economy heading to disaster. Even Stalin never tried to revive it, and since World War II the East European countries have seen a total abandonment of this communist ideal and a rapid move toward free markets, a free price system, proft-and-loss tests, and a promotion of consumer affluence. It is no accident that it was precisely the *economists* in the Communist countries who led the rush away from communism, socialism, and central planning, and toward free markets. It is no crime to be ignorant of economics, which is, after all, a specialized discipline and one that most people consider to be a "dismal science". But it *is* totally irresponsible to have a loud and vociferous *opinion* on economic subjects while remaining in this state of ignorance. Yet this sort of aggressive ignorance is inherent in the creed of anarcho-communism.

The same comment can be made on the widespread belief, held by many New Leftists and by all anarcho-communists, that there is no longer need to worry about economics or production because we are supposedly living in a "post-scarcity" world, where such problems do not arise. But while our condition of scarcity is clearly superior to that of the cave-man, we are still living in a world of pervasive economic scarcity. How will we know when the world has achieved "post-scarcity"? Simply, when all the goods and services that we may want have become so superabundant that their prices have fallen to zero; in short, when we can acquire all goods and services as in a Garden of Eden-- without effort, without work, without using any scarce resources.

The anti-rational spirit of anarcho-communism was expressed by Norman O. Brown, one of the *gurus* of the new "counter-culture": "The great economist von Mises tried to refute socialism by demonstrating that, in abolishing exchange, socialism made economic calculation, and hence economic rationality, impossible . . . But if von Mises is right, then what he discovered is not a refutation but a psychoanalytical justification of socialism . . . It is one of the sad ironies of contemporary intellectual life that the reply of socialist economists to von Mises' arguments was to attempt to show that socialism was not incompatible with 'rational economic calculation'--that is to say, that it could retain the inhuman principle of economizing." (*Life Against Death*, Random House, paperback, 1959, pp. 238-39.)

The fact that the abandonment of rationality and economics in behalf of "freedom" and whim will lead to the scrapping of modern production and civilization and return us to barbarism does not feaze our anarcho-communists and other exponents of the new "counter-culture". But what they

LURKING IN THE WINGS—*(Continued from page 2)*

a good profit (which should encourage others to watch for similar urgent demands in the future, and supply them in advance), the government makes sure that the is castigated as a "war profiteer", and certainly taxed if not imprisoned or killed! Such activities will be the duty of the expanded bureaucracy, staffed by the National Defense Executive Reserve force. War is the health of the state.

The state is the pathology of modern society. The expanding substitution of Authority for Trade as the proper form of interaction among people is the full-time job of the millions of little statesmen who labor "in the public interest". It is the symbiotic relationship between the Authority-merchants of the state and profit-seeking entrepreneurs which causes the perversion of honest economic activity into the exploitative system of state-capitalism. Amazing is the magic of Authority, so legitimate in the public's mind in contrast to raw, coercive Power; and nothing legitimates the use of Power as well as an Enemy danger. Just like far-sighted land speculators, the bureaucrat Authority-merchants are prepared: the National Defense Executive Reserve awaits their country's call.

—— J. M. Cobb

do not seem to realize is that the result of this return to primitivism would be starvation and death for nearly all of mankind and a grinding subsistence for the ones remaining. If they have their way, they will find that it is difficult indeed to be jolly and "unrepressed" while starving to death.

All this brings us back to the wisdom of the great Spanish philosopher Ortega y Gasset: "In the disturbances caused by scarcity of food, the mob goes in search of bread, and the means it employs is generally to wreck the bakeries. This may serve as a symbol of the attitude adopted, on a greater and more complicated scale, by the masses of today towards the civilization by which they are supported . . . Civilization is not 'just here', it is not self-supporting. It is artificial . . . If you want to make use of the advantages of civilization, but are not prepared to concern yourself with the upholding of civilization--you are done. In a trice you find yourself left without civilization. Just a slip, and when you look everything has vanished into air. The primitive forest appears in its native state, just as if curtains covering pure Nature had been drawn back. *The jungle is always primitive and, vice versa, everything primitive is mere jungle.*" (José Ortega y Gasset, The *Revolt of the Masses*, New York: W. W. Norton, 1932, p. 97).

You may publish my name and address as a reader of the *Libertarian Forum* who would like to meet other *Forum* readers:

NAME . . . .

ADDRESS . . . .

CITY, STATE and ZIP . . . .

. . . .

Published on the first and fifteenth of every month.   Subscription rate: $7.00 per year; Student subscription rate: $5.00 per year.

80

A Semi-Monthly Newsletter

THE
Libertarian Forum

Joseph R. Peden, Publisher   Washington Editor, Karl Hess   Murray N. Rothbard, Editor

VOL. II, NO. 2   January 15, 1970   35¢

AHA CONVENTION

By Leonard P. Liggio

I. Anarchism on the Agenda

Libertarianism has become academically respectable. Just as the respectability of isolationism emerged five years ago, here is another debt that we probably owe to the New Left. Within a month, a symposium on anarchism was held at a major university with Murray Rothbard and Karl Hess as the principal speakers, and a session of the American Historical Association was devoted to Anarchism. The historical significance of a filled-to-capacity AHA session on anarchism was noted in his introductory remarks by Richard Drinnon of Bucknell University, the chairman. Paul Avrich, Queens College, who gave the first paper, is the author of a recently published book on Russian anarchists; his book was the subject some months ago of an intensive oral commentary by Murray Rothbard. As in almost everything concerned with the growth of libertarian perspectives, Murray Rothbard has been the preeminent pioneer; his open and world-ranging inquiry into libertarian thought and action is the exemplary standard toward which all others' achievements in libertarian analysis has been directed.

Avrich's discussion indicated that the monumental conflict between the respective world-views of Marx and Bakunin remain as significant today as a century ago; yet, despite Avrich's depth of scholarship, a resolution of Bakunin's own contradictory positions appears as distant as ever. Marx's call for regimented industrial and agricultural armies had no appeal for the peasant who might be already oppressed by just such a feudal organization of agriculture. Anarchists historically have had a strong interest in peasant farmers and agricultural land as anarchism has flourished in opposition to the feudal landholding systems.

Gabriel Jackson, U. of California-San Diego, discussed the very controversial question of the institutions of Spanish Civil War Anarchism. The participation of an expert such as James J. Martin would have been invaluable. In the anarchist regions of civil war Spain, the free peasants' land ownership was recognized and tenants turned their lands into freeholds. But, serfs in completely feudal situations were generally transformed into workers on a collective, with occasional liberation into cooperatives. Anarchist ideologists in Spain, after a year, called for a reexamination of the collectivist organization, as it was not productive and was simply living off earlier capital accumulation. Similarly, they had intense criticism of the anarchist military columns for their sectarianism. When their campaigns took them into a district they sought to impose their

rationalism by church burnings; peasants were forced to transfer their private farms into collectives; money was outlawed on pain of execution. This anarchist sectarianism of the military columns contributed to the famous popularity of the Spanish Communist Party--as the defender of private property and money, the peasants and townsmen sought protection in C. P. membership. (Noam Chomsky's "Objectivity and Liberal Scholarship", in his *American Power and the New Mandarins*, presents a libertarian critique of Jackson's liberal treatment of the Spanish Civil War.)

Paul Goodman, the concluding speaker at the session, began with a critical examination of the radical proposals presented at the convention (see Part II). He said that the radical appeal to the historians should have been on the basis of their competence and professional independence, which are being oppressed by political and academic authorities. Anarchists historically found their support among the skilled workers whose competence excluded external management or control, as well as among workers in potentially dangerous work where success was based not on authority but on mutual trust and self-control. The migrants from rural areas who were the main source of unskilled labor were not familiar with self-managing modes in industry and sought solutions in the collectivism of the Marxist unions.

Goodman explained the Marxist rhetoric among student protestors as originating in a similar distinction. The majority of American students are not interested in attending school; they are inmates of school-jails because of the compulsory attendance laws, conscription, etc. They should be permitted to gain their education in appealing work situations; collectivism appears as a reasonable solution only to those in an unnatural situation. Those students who benefit from liberal arts education have sought an improvement in the educational method by transforming the authoritarian classroom situation necessitated by the school-jail institutions into situations permitting more and better study. Five years of intensive investigation have shown that the main student dissatisfaction and support for transformation of universities comes from the upper half of the student body' the lower half is satisfied since the educational system is aimed at their level.

Adam Smith's free market economics was noted by Goodman as the epitome of anarchism. The attempt to establish private property against its negation in the state made laissez-faire a revolutionary ideology before its adherents came to compromise with, rather than destroy, feudalism and accepted state monopoly economies. The independence of the competent, the innovator, the entrepreneur, the

(Continued on page 3)

From Libertine To Libertarian

When left-wing critics of the 1930's attacked him for not embracing doctrinaire Marxism, Ernest Hemingway replied:

". . . I cannot be a communist now because I believe in only one thing: liberty. First I would look after myself and do my work. Then I would care for my family. Then I would help my neighbor. But the state I care nothing for. All the state has ever meant to me is unjust taxation . . . I believe in the absolute minimum of government.

"A writer is an outlyer like a gypsy . . . If he is a good writer he will never like the government he lives under. His hand should be against it . . ." (*Ernest Hemingway: A Life Story* by Carlos Baker, Charles Scribner's Sons, 1969).

In the foreword to his own book, Baker writes:

"[Hemingway] was the fierce individualist who resisted fad and fashion like the plague . . . who believed that that government is best which governs least, who hated tyranny, bureaucracy, taxation, propaganda . . ."

It is clear to anyone who has read Hemingway's work that the novelist, while never an advanced political thinker--and never pretending to be one--, was writing from the viewpoint of a man obsessed with the raw concept of individual freedom. He was the ultimate artist, the essential loner, the recalcitrant individualist who gave substance to William Hazlitt's theory of "living unto oneself", of being "a part of the world and yet apart from it at the same time." Hemingway was the libertarian in embryo, the undeveloped philosopher with a mania for personal liberty, with a hunger for life and the pleasures of life, who gave full reign to his drives and desires without regard for those who would squeeze him into a neat ideological compartment. His only cause was his art, his writing, the perfection of his language, and a search for truth as reflected through his novels.

Hemingway operated within the framework of a basic *libertinism*, a kind of humanized but non-intellectualized hedonism. The tragedy of his life is that he never advanced beyond this embryonic stage philosophically. While he pursued liberty and spent his life learning how to "live free", he neglected to construct an ethic to discipline his actions. Consequently, the "spiritual" aspect of his life-- the part that is concerned with basic questions of morality, with right and wrong, with good and evil--suffered beyond repair. Peace of mind eluded him; an elemental happiness was denied him to the end. He took his life with his own hand less than a month before his sixty-second birthday.

Frank Meyer notwithstanding, the *philosophy of libertarianism* and the *attitude of libertinism* are not to be confused by any except the ignorant. If the libertine is the libertarian in embryo, the true libertarian is the libertine developed to the highest level of ideational morality. He is the libertine strung out to the limits of his potentiality. While the libertine is concerned solely with liberty, the libertarian turns his attention to *liberty and justice* as an inseparable concept. The libertine operates from the basic premise: I have a right to be free; the libertarian from the premise: I have a right to be free--and so does everyone else.

We can only speculate as to what Hemingway might have become psychologically and emotionally had he been exposed to the writings of Mises, Bastiat, Spooner, Hayek, Rothbard, etc. Perhaps he would have dismissed philosophical libertarianism in the same manner he dismissed doctrinaire Marxism, without realizing that an artist's morality is evident in his product and affects its final quality. Then again, having rejected Marxism as incompatible with his own notion of freedom, he might have rejoiced at the discovery of a philosophy more attuned to his own native urges.

Today it is possible to look back on Hemingway's life with some degree of objectivity. The art he produced, if it is good, will long outlive the memory of the man. In reviewing his career nine years after his death, it is possible to appreciate an individual who was a lifelong friend of liberty, though sadly enough, never its master-- a libertarian in embryo who failed to idealize his basic attitude toward life.

— Jerome Tuccille

What's Your Excuse Now?

Last spring, the big revolutionary event in America was the Columbia Revolution. Most "libertarians" condemned this particularly successful New Left venture on the grounds of injury to "private property rights", putting forth the quaint theory that Columbia University is private property.

This winter, the big revolutionary event is the strike at San Francisco State, a strike which, even more successfully than at Columbia, managed to induce black and white students and the nearby black community to join forces against the administration, and also to enlist essentially conservative and guild-minded faculty. Surely no one could possibly call San Francisco State College a wholly government-owned institution, any kind of "private property". It is government property, and therefore an institution which all self-proclaimed libertarians are supposed to be against. And yet, despite this most successful disruptive strike against SF State, rumblings and gripings are emerging from the California libertarian movement, including petty peevishness about classes being obstructed. So what's your excuse now, comrades, for being counter-revolutionary?

Against Taxation

One of the most hopeful recent developments has been the rise of opposition to taxation. Taxation is the vital fuel on which the State runs and has its being. Cut off its funds, its supply, and the State Leviathan will wither and die. Furthermore, a movement in opposition to taxation is bound to strike a responsive chord with the entire tax-exploited middle class. There has recently been formed a National Taxpayers Union, which is dedicated to lancing the State at its vital core: its swollen and unchallenged power of taxation. The energetic libertarian James D. Davidson is the executive director, and Murray Rothbard is one of the four members of the executive committee. For information, write to the National Taxpayers Union, Suite 100, 415 Second Street, N. E., Washington, D. C. 20002.

USIA Network

One of the most repellent aspects of statism is that we the taxpayers are forced to pay for our own brainwashing-- for the propaganda which the government beams in our direction. One of our ministries of propaganda, the United States Information Agency, is beamed at hapless people overseas. It was to be expected that when our right-wing Administration took over, the thrust of conservatives in power would not be to dismantle the USIA, but rather to boot out subsidies for liberal books and replace them with well-stocked libraries filled with the works of deserving conservatives.

This, indeed, is exactly what has happened. Frank Shakespeare, new head of USIA, is an ultra-conservative, and a friend of conservatism's pre-eminent TV personality, William F. Buckley, Jr. Buckley was promptly appointed as a member of the USIA's Advisory Commission. Buckley began to push for more conservative books in USIA libraries, and induced Shakespeare to hire Jim Burnham, Buckley's co-editor on *National Review*, to compile a list of deserving books. For nearly $1000, Burnham came up with a five-page list, which--surprise of surprises!--included prominently the works of both Burnham and Buckley, to which

(Continued on page 3)

AHA CONVENTION — *(Continued from page 1)*

creator, said Goodman, is at the root of anarchism. Technological progress, Goodman pointed out, has been achieved by the independent innovator and entrepreneur outside of the authoritarian universities and monopoly institutions. The struggle to affirm private property, the absolute ownership of the fruit of one's free innovation or competence, and to abolish the present negation of private property ownership, is central to anarchist action. Since modern society prepares people more completely for competent independence, the flowering of anarchist thought and action is a reasonable expectation.

II. Long March Made Longer

A major aspect of the AHA convention was the business meetings. In the last couple of years the major scholarly associations in America have been placed on record by their members as opposed to United States aggression against the Vietnamese people. Last year, at the AHA convention which was moved to New York from Chicago to protest the police riot by Mayor Daley's 'finest' during the Democratic National Convention, the major debate concerned the boycott of Chicago. The right-wing liberals proposed that the convention should have been held in Chicago to bring the benefits of the liberals' "superior enlightenment" to Chicago. The caucus of younger members was totally ineffectual last year. The main speeches were a series of Marxist circumlocutions which drove the majority from the hall in search of freedom from boredom. A minor theme was the attack on the movement of student protests at universities by the leading academic Marxist, Eugene D. Genovese, who since has been appointed chairman of the history department at the University of Rochester.

After almost a year of inaction, a revived committee of younger historians popped-up under the ubiquitous Arthur Waskow. Waskow had acted during the early years of the Anti-Vietnam war movement as a retarding influence seeking dialogue rather than confrontation with Rusk, Bundy, Rostow et al., and as late as last spring spoke at a major conference at the New York Hilton against political organization around anti-militarist issues, proposing instead the liberal issues of environment and ecology. Now he appeared at the convention in the colors of a militant. In the early years of this decade a Conference on Peace Research in History (in which several of the contributors to the Libertarian Forum participated) was organized in the AHA by William L. Neumann--revisionist historian, anti-imperialist spokesman and a leading student of Harry Elmer Barnes. This Conference's December 1965 meeting in San Francisco occurred after almost a year of U. S. bombardment and invasion of Vietnam. But the program of which Waskow was chairman avoided historical analysis of U. S. policy in the Pacific upon which the Vietnam intervention was premised. On the eve of the 1965 convention the press had announced that the leading radical historian, Staughton Lynd, then at Yale, had arrived in Hanoi to study the effects of U. S. bombing as a representative of *Viet-Report*. Waskow criticized Lynd for his efforts opposing the Vietnam war by confronting the U. S. government.

The proposals at the 1969 convention which issued forth from Waskow could only have been composed in Bedlam. In essence, they were an attack on the concept of competence. Instead of appealing to historians on the basis of their alienation due to the authoritarian denial of their professionalism in the universities and the AHA, their expertise was equally attacked by the Waskow group. This explicit denial of the historian's role could not seriously have been proposed, as a means of radically educating historians-- and, needless to say, it did not. In contrast, at the Modern Languages Association convention, the radicals led by the

USIA NETWORK — *(Continued from page 2)*

Burnham gave high praise. Buckley, wrote Burnham, is "one of the best-known writers of his generation", and, what is more, "James Burnham's books have been translated and debated in every major country." Pretty neat all around. As lagniappe, Burnham also recommended the works of several other editors and contributors of *National Review*: M. Stanton Evans, John Chamberlain, Russell Kirk, Henry Hazlitt, Stefan T. Possony, and the late Whittaker Chambers.

And so, the result of the Buckley-Burnham shuffle is that *National Review* has reaped its reward for loyalty to the Nixon campaign and to the Administration. The loser, as usual, is the American taxpayer.

New University Conference were able to organize their colleagues on the basis of the general denial of their professionalism, to reform the association and to elect as president for the following year, Louis Kampf, MIT humanities chairman. Despite this problematic AHA situation, Staughton Lynd received about thirty per cent of the votes cast for the AHA presidency.

The final business meeting was devoted to a discussion of resolutions, especially concerning Vietnam. A lengthy resolution emanated from the Waskow group; it began with an opposition to the Vietnam war but mainly dealt with a number of domestic issues such as the police murders of the Black Panthers. Perhaps it was believed that the wider opposition to the Vietnam war would carry a resolution containing issues for which there would be less support. Such a scheme has about it much of the odor of the Old Left rather than the honesty of the New Left which faces issues directly no matter how unpleasant the answers. Additionally, the resolution was burdened with having Waskow as floor leader; as he appeared to be speaking half the time through a dozen interventions, many neutral participants drew negative conclusions about the anti-Vietnam positions.

A substitute motion was offered by William L. Neumann as chairman of the Conference on Peace Research in History. It stated: "We, historians and citizens in this meeting of the American Historical Association, deplore and condemn the war in Vietnam as ill-advised and immoral; we urge immediate withdrawal of all military involvement; and we further pledge ourselves to a fundamental reevaluation of the assumptions of American foreign policy." Staughton Lynd called on the meeting to support this resolution. Neumann's anti-war resolution was narrowly defeated by a vote of 610 to 645 in a meeting attended by ten times the number of members who had attended any previous business meeting.

The most outspoken critic was Eugene Genovese, who during the convention was described as having become the Sidney Hook of the younger generation of scholars. For several years Genovese has conducted a personal vendetta against Staughton Lynd because Lynd is not a Marxist and thus bases his politics upon universal moral concepts. Although one might wish Lynd were more rigorous in some historical analyses, he has made the greatest contribution during the 1960's to post-American Revolution historical scholarship. Genovese's Marxism causes him to adopt positions of traditionalist, official historians against revisionist radicalism. The logic of Marxism led Genovese to become the leading contemporary spokesman for southern slaveholding, and Karl Marx's humane opposition to the crime of slaveholding is condemned because this was inconsistent with Marxism. During the past year Genovese opened a wide-front attack on the student movement because he views the New Left as the major impediment to Marxism. At the AHA convention Genovese demanded that the executive council "put down the New Left, put it down now, and put it down *hard*." Genovese is becoming the heir-presumptive to the repression propounded by the ex-communists of *National Review* and the *New Leader*.

ORGANIZED CRIME

It is a commonplace of history that laws drafted to harass or suppress one socially deviant group will at some future time be used to attack groups or individuals other than those originally persecuted. Thus the emergency powers granted the German Chancellor by the Weimar Republic were used by Hitler to destroy the Weimar regime and plunge Germany into the horrors of the Nazi dictatorship. It is with this in mind that libertarians should examine more closely the Nixon administration's new legislative war against "organized crime".

In the President's message to Congress last April, "organized crime" was identified as the *Cosa Nostra*-- or the *Mafia*--an "alien" organization said to number some 5,000 individuals working regionally in 24 "families". (New York Congressman Mario Biaggi, a much-decorated police hero, considers this a gratuitous insult to the Italian-American community.) In the eyes of the Feds, the *Mafia's* most heinous crime seems to be that it successfully serves a profitable and expanding market with goods and services which the State has either outlawed or monopolized for itself.

According to Nixon, the *Cosa Nostra* has a virtual monopoly on illegal gambling--by which he means that the government's licensed gambling operations are its only real competition; they also are responsbile for supplying the American public with illegal drugs like heroin--which is needed by those who become addicted in much the same way a diabetic needs insulin, or like marijuana, whose effects have been described by responsible physicians as less harmful than alcohol or tobacco. (That alcohol and tobacco remain legal may be due to their being a major source of State revenue.) To complete the picture, "organized crime" is accused of underwriting the loan-shark business and actively participating in fraudulent bankruptcies. In other words, the *Mafia* lends money to high-risk debtors at interest rates commensurate with the probability of default, rates forbidden by law despite the obvious needs of the market; and as for fraudulent bankruptcy, the whole concept of bankruptcy is *itself* a fraud and a theft by which the State cancels the legitimate indebtedness of the debtor at the expense of the creditor. Indeed the principal criminal actions of the *Mafia* used to justify the Nixon war on crime are crimes only because they are defined as such by the tyrannical statists who rule America. The *Cosa Nostra*--serving well its vast American market with profits estimated at $50 billion from gambling alone--is no more sinister than Dow Chemical Company--probably less so.

What then is the real purpose of this new Crusade? Let us look at the weapons which the Feds are demanding from the Congress. Already authorized to use wiretapping, Nixon wants Congress to legalize the granting of personal immunity from prosecution for witnesses called before federal juries; the result will be to compel witnesses to testify against their will--to become informers or rot in prison. In New York where such a law is already in effect, a professor from the State University has twice been sent to jail for a term of 30 days for refusing to tell a grand jury which of his students is smoking pot.

A second weapon will be to make it a federal crime for a local policeman or public official to accept a bribe from gamblers; also, any gambling operation which involves 5 or more persons or lasts for 30 days or whose daily take exceeds $2,000 will be a federal crime. The clear effect of these laws is to create the skeleton of a national police force reaching into every city and hamlet, every home, factory and shop in America. The ubiquitous football pool will now become a potential federal criminal conspiracy!

But even more ominous is the proposal to create a panoply of weapons to attack the property of "organized crime" through the injunctive powers of contempt and seizure (shades of Truman and the steel mills!), through "monetary fines and treble damage suits" and "the powers of a forfeiture of property". Let it be noted that none of these extraordinary powers can be limited to the *Cosa Nostra*--since no such entity exists in law. These "weapons" will apply to the persons and properties of individual citizens who will be convicted of crimes against the State. Or will anyone be safe from sudden disruption or seizure of his wealth on the ground that it is tainted as having been derived from some Mafioso? The President specifically cites his desire to strike "a critical blow at the organized crime conspiracy" by levying fines on their real estate corporations, treble damages against their trucking firms and banks, and seizing the liquor in their warehouses.

In case you still doubt the broader implications of the Nixon war, the President promises that if the Federal Racket Squads successfully enforce the new laws--squads composed of agents of the FBI, SEC, IRS, Post Office, Narcotics and Customs Bureaus and the Secret Service among others--"building on this experience" the Attorney General "will determine" whether "this concept of governmental partnership should be expanded (to other major problem areas) through the formation of additional squads."

We wonder who will succeed the *Mafia* as public enemy Number One? Mr. Kleindienst's "ideological criminals"?

— J.R.P.

Published on the first and fifteenth of every month.   Subscription rate: $7.00 per year; Student subscription rate: $5.00 per year.

A Semi-Monthly Newsletter

THE
Libertarian Forum

Joseph R. Peden, Publisher   Washington Editor, Karl Hess   Murray N. Rothbard, Editor

VOL. II, NO. 3   February 1, 1970   35¢

BIAFRA, RIP

After more than two years of heroic struggle against overwhelming odds, little Biafra lies murdered--murdered by the centralizing State forces of Nigeria, forces that were backed, of course, by those two great centralizing powers of our time, the United States and the Soviet Union. Over two million Ibo tribesmen--the bulk of the citizens of Biafra--lie dead, two million more lives racked up on the permanently bloody altar of central State power.

The American public is totally unfamiliar with the real situation in Africa. They tend to think of "countries" like Nigeria, the Congo, Gabon, etc. as genuine countries, as people bound together by common ties of culture, language, fellowship, and other attributes of nationhood. Nothing could be further from the truth. None of these African countries are countries in any legitimate sense of the term; they are geographical figments, grotesque parodies of nationhood.

How did they get that way? These nations, though now independent or quasi-independent, are all legacies of Western imperialism. In the latter half of the nineteenth century, Britain, France, and Portugal engaged in a mad scramble to conquer and carve up the numerous tribes and the vast land area of the African continent. The carving was purely the result of scramble and agreement, and had nothing to do with the ethnic, cultural, or tribal boundaries in the continent. Regions and districts were based purely on the administrative convenience of the imperial power, not on the needs or realities of the tribes involved. Many tribes were split down the middle by the boundaries of these "countries".

One would think that when the British and French finally left Africa, this unholy mess would be straightened out and the needed realignment and splitting-up of countries finally take place. But this was not to be. For the British and French could only rule the immensely greater populations in Africa by finding local rulers, satraps and collaborators, to govern the native population on behalf of the imperial power. The first step of an imperial power is to find or create channels of rule by creating native satraps and "quislings" who can serve as transmission belts for imperial dictation. The Western powers found those satraps in two ways. One was by working through existing tribal chieftains, helping these chieftains cement their rule over their own tribes and over other tribes in the region. Another was by creating an educated urban elite who would staff the offices of government and rule the scattered but silent rural majority of the country. When the British and French made their orderly withdrawal from their official empire, they

took care to leave their bureaucratic and feudal satraps in charge of the various countries. Britain and France then remain as *de facto*, though no longer *de jure*, imperialists, and the new native elites remain close economic and political collaborators with their old masters. The last thing that the new elites want is self-determination and national justice for the numerous African tribes; their own parasitic and exploitative power rests on retaining the old imperial boundaries and strong central governments derived from imperial rule.

Nigeria, for the libertarian, is a particularly poignant example of the African middle. By favoritism and gerry-mandering, the British made sure that the newly independent Nigeria would be governed by the feudal chieftains and emirs of the backward Moslem North. Not only suppressed but also systematically slaughtered were the Ibos of Eastern Nigeria. Everyone knows that the Ibos are generally hated in West Africa for being the embodiment of the "Protestant" virtues: intelligence, hard work, thrift, entrepreneurial ability. Give a few Ibos half a chance and they will create jobs, commerce, and wealth wherever they go. Even more fascinating for the libertarian is that the Ibos, of all the tribes in the region, have always been libertarian and quasi-anarchistic. Their tribe never suffered from central-ized rule, and their methods of government were so loose and so local as to be virtually tantamount to no aggressive government--no State--at all. Hence they gave the British conquerors of the nineteenth century by far the most trouble of all the tribes, because the British could find no tribal rulers, no satraps, to act as transmission belts for their rule. Because of the anarchism of the Ibos, the British found them almost unconquerable and found that they could not be ruled. Hence the British, too, hated the Ibos.

When the government of Nigeria began to subject the Ibos to persecution and slaughter, they declared their inde-pendence and established the nation of Biafra. Of course Britain supported the Nigerian State. Of course Soviet Russia, with its horror of decentralization, secession, or national independence from central rule, backed the Nigerian State. And of course the United States did the same, piously inveighing against the "Balkanization" of the African con-tinent. All of these Empires want the Third World to have unitary and "efficient" rulers who can follow their own orders, and dictate easily to their subjects below. All of these monster States are implicated in the shame of the murder of little Biafra.

We can only hope that someday Biafra will rise again, and that ethnic justice, come that resurrection morn, will redraw the map of Africa.

85

LEFT AND RIGHT

The Psychology Of Opposites

What is Left? What is Right?

On the rapidly changing American scene the distinction between Left and Right is becoming more and more a question of personal psychology. The scramble of ideologies is undergoing such an upheaval at present it is virtually impossible to label a political candidate on the basis of his position papers. When Norman Mailer ran in the Democratic Mayoralty primary in New York City last year he identified his political position as "to the left and to the right of everybody else." And he was right. His radical decentralist program defied all standards of liberal/conservative traditionalism. He scornfully referred to this tradition as "the soft center of American politics" and offered a program closest to the quasi-anarchist position of Paul Goodman.

Anarchists, and those calling themselves anarchists, abound on both sides of the political spectrum, from the grabbag collection of SDS to the split-off faction of YAF. Timothy Leary, running for Governor of California, adopts a platform of pure free-market libertarianism and is called a "Radical Leftist". Ronnie Reagan, long-time favorite of conservative free enterprisers, promises to Preserve and Protect the corporate-liberal status quo even if he has to break some skulls doing it.

(Curious, isn't it, what superb bulldogs the conservatives make for the liberal superstructure?).

As Bulldog Nixon swings the Right more accurately into a position of total repression, and Spiro the Righteous roams the earth impugning the courage of those who would rather live than die in Vietnam, everyone of even the slightest libertarian sympathies is polarized more sharply to the Left. So Left is Right and Right is Left. Free market is Left and Socialism is Right. Voluntary communes are Left and State Capitalism is Right.

It's enough to give you a headache.

But the long-term test of whether an individual will identify with the Left or with the Right is one--as I mentioned earlier--of personal psychology. The Left, it seems to me, has the capacity of bleeding for flesh-and-blood human beings. Even the horrible liberals, lately scorned by both radical capitalists and pot-happy flower children, were originally motivated by the desire to "help the oppressed". The fact that they chose the worst means possible of doing it--coercion rather than freedom--is another question entirely. The concern for fellow human beings which originally motivated them was genuine. Now they are fat and powerful and they use the Reagans and Agnews to protect them when all attempts at co-optation end in failure. They are the New Conservatives while those who call themselves conservatives are nothing more than bully boys for their corporate-liberal mentors.

The Left bleeds for flesh-and-blood people.

The New Left--the radicals, the revolutionaries, the students who are turning against their social democratic parents--are driven by outrage; they are obsessed with a mania for justice because other human beings are victimized by racism, because fellow humans are imprisoned in rotting tenements riddled with filth and rats. They see the injustice that exists around them and they are incensed because they have the capacity to identify with the victims of an unyielding and thoroughly unresponsive superstructure, a system controlled and operated by insatiable racketeers and their political puppets who will never give up power until they are smashed out of existence.

The Left bleeds for people.

While the Right--even our anarchist friends recently separated from YAF--concern themselves with abstractions. They are more upset over the fact that their free

market principles are not given a chance to operate than they are because fellow humans are trapped in overcrowded schools and ghettos. They seem to be incapable of emphasizing with suffering individuals and dismiss all such concern as misguided *altruism*. Their notion of justice is one which involves only themselves, and they fail to see that they will never enjoy personal freedom until *all men* are free of injustice. The Objectivist drive for liberty is *not* so much to create a world in which all men are free to live their lives in peace, but *rather* to conjure a society in which Galt-like superheroes with wavy hair and "ice-blue eyes" can demonstrate their economic superiority over "parasitic illiterates who litter the welfare rolls."

Thus it is possible for our anarcho-Objectivist friends in Philadelphia to hold demonstrations calling for the "Release of John Galt"--while Bobby Seale is fighting for his existence in Chicago.

Thus it is possible for our Objectivist friends in Maryland to ask me to prove that Fred Hampton and Mark Clark "had not committed or threatened to commit violations of the rights of others . . ."--after they had been shot in their beds at four in the morning by Chicago police (this article is my answer to them).

Thus it is possible for these same right-wing anarchists to speak of the Vietcong as "communists" and "morally evil" despite the fact that ninety-five percent of them have probably never read Karl Marx and are concerned mainly with the swollen bellies of peasant children.

How does one begin to understand such a mentality? How does one begin to understand an individual who can bleed for an unlikely, dehumanized character out of fiction but not for the young victims of an early-morning police raid on the apartment? How does one understand the special arrogance of fellow "anarchists" who are content to establish a personal sphere of economic freedom and let the rest of society go to hell with itself? How does one understand a "libertarian" organization which wears on its masthead the American dollar sign (hardly the symbol of free market currency), or fellow "anarchists" who cavort in public in stretch suits and gigantic dollar signs plastered over their torsos?

It would be too easy to blame it all on Ayn Rand. This gentle lady did not create this special psycho-mentality out of nothing; she merely tapped an attitude that was already there simmering under the surface and brought it into the open. The fact that so many people responded so enthusiastically to her Cult of Total Self-Absorption (as distinct from genuinely rational self-interest) provides a good deal of insight into the makeup of the right-wing mentality.

The Objectivists, despite all their talk of individual liberty and limited government, are inveterate Right Wingers. Anarcho-Objectivists are no exception for they still adhere to the psychology of fiction-worship and are incapable of bleeding for the flesh-and-blood world surrounding them.

The philosophical division between free market anarchists and voluntary communists is growing less important in light of the current struggle to free the neighborhoods from outside control. The purist ideals of total communal sharing and a totally free market of individual traders are important in themselves *as ideals*, as logical ends of different though consistent processes of reasoning. But the most important factor in the rough-and-tumble struggle for survival, the war to secure the right of flesh-and-blood people to control their own affairs, is the *psychology of*

(Continued on page 4)

Massacres In Vietnam

The Old Right's great responsibility over the last quarter century has been that of bearer of the most profound truth about the American state. As Harry Elmer Barnes expressed it after the U. S. had unleashed its massive bombings of Vietnam--"*we always knew that the business of the U. S. government is mass murder.*" The Old Right at the end of the second great imperialist war in 1945 recognized the special repugnance of the U. S. government. The burden of that fact was so great that many sought to evade the responsibility by adopting the historical amnesia of the New Right which paralleled the historical blackout about that war imposed by the Old Left (that this parallel is more than accidental may be suggested by the fact that many of the philosophers of the New Right had been the creators of the historical blackout when they were part of the Old Left).

The massive bombings of civilians by the U.S. air force was a natural development of American imperialism. The fire bombings of German cities such as Hamburg and Dresden, of Japanese cities such as Tokyo, and finally the atomic bombing of two Japanese cities, was the result of the unquestioned assumption which formed the foundation of U. S. policy. The development and application of strategic airpower to civilian populations is the unique contribution of the U. S. to that whimsical facade labeled Christian Civilization.

The Old Right found a uniting element in its condemnation of the U. S. technological implementation of its program which declared a whole people to be The Enemy. On October 5, 1946, in his famous Kenyon College speech "Equal Justice under Law", (in Arthur Ekirch, *Voices in Dissent, An Anthology of Individualist Thought in the United States* Citadel Press), which attacked the launching of the Cold War by the untried war criminals of the second world war, Churchill, Truman et al., Senator Robert A. Taft analyzed this American advance to barbarism. Taft described the Cold War policy as an abandonment of international law and the substitution of naked U. S. police power. This was a continuation of the American foreign policy which had lost sight of the truth that the police are incidental to the law, and that any deviation by the police from absolute adherence to law makes the police the creators of complete disorder in society. The U. S. failure to respect the law of humanity by its war against civilians had created the postwar disorder in world society. "Our whole attitude in the world, for a year after V-E Day," Taft declared, "including the use of the atomic bomb at Hiroshima and Nagasaki, seems to me a departure from the principle of fair and equal treatment which has made America respected throughout the world before the second World War."

The continued application of total war against civilians was carried out against the Korean people by the U. S. air force, 1950-53. Although some of the facts of U. S. genocide against the Korean people were reported at the time in European papers, little was known about it in America due to the blackout by the government-inspired press (the tentative moves recently by a few elements of the media toward independence brought forth the massive bellows from the offices of the chief magistrate as well as of the president of the senate).

Thus, when the U. S. unleashed its massive fire power against the Vietnamese people, it was remnants of the Old Right who understood immediately the absolute barbarism being applied in Vietnam while the Old Left and most of the amorphous New Left spent months in utter confusion about the realities of U. S. policy due to an almost incurable patriotism. The pacifist movement had shared the Old Right's analysis and burden regarding American barbarism during and since the second world war. As a result they were equally in the forefront in understanding the geno-

cidal nature of the war against the Vietnamese people (A. J. Muste, Dave Dellinger and Staughton Lynd were most active in this regard).

Old Right elements in the current anti-imperialist movement emphasized what others had not the memory or the experience with U. S. barbarism to know. Thus, they were in a position to perform a vanguard function by initially raising the issue of genocide and presenting the earlier history of U. S. barbarism to convince those anti-imperialists who had not yet shed their love affair with the U. S. government. Finally, after the U. S. intervention in Vietnam had become understood, the anti-imperialist movement adopted the radical critique presented by the Old Right. The Old Right transmitted to the Movement as a whole the realization that the U. S. government and its agents are war criminals. The recognition of the criminal nature of the U. S. state and its servants was the major intellectual advance which permitted the Movement to grow from protest to resistance.

The Vietnamese in the northern and southern parts of their country have been subjected to the war crimes committed by the U. S. war criminals for more than five years. They have been poisoned with chemicals and anti-personnel gases, bombed by anti-personnel bombs, cluster bombs and the many other devices developed by U. S. know-how. B-52 saturation bombings, 'free fire zones' air strikes, search and destroy missions, torture, atrocities and massacres by the U. S. have become the everyday life of the Vietnamese people. Having suffered this genocide the Vietnamese may wonder if it was not irony when the incumbent chief U. S. war criminal insisted that the atrocities and barbarism must continue in order to save them from . . . massacres. As recent revelations have verified, the Vietnamese are being subjected daily to massacres by the U. S. The victims include men, women and children. The most famous crime attributed to the Germans during World War II was the 1942 massacre in the Czech town of Lidice where every male was shot, but not the women and children. The U. S., unlike the Germans, has universalized the atrocity to make a Lidice out of the whole of Vietnam.

The chief manager of genocide touched all our hearts by his sincerity when he declared recently: "We saw the prelude of what would happen in South Vietnam when the Communists entered the city of Hué last year. During their brief rule there, there was a bloody reign of terror in which 3,000 civilians were clubbed, shot to death and buried in mass graves." The case of Hué was discussed in an article in *The Christian Century* (Nov. 5, 1969) by Len Ackland who had lived in Hué and speaks Vietnamese. Writing about the seizure of Hué by the National Liberation Front, he said: "When on the first day of the attack, about 20 Vietcong entered Gia Hoi (a precinct of 25,000 residents in Hué) in order to secure the area, they carried with them a list of those who were to be killed immediately as 'enemies of the people.' According to Le Ngan, director of Hué's special police, the list consisted of five names, all those of officers of special police." The Catholic priest of the district explained that "none of his clergy or parishioners were harmed by the NLF." The Saigon rulers refused to make Hué an open city to save the lives of the citizens. Instead, the Saigon army and U. S. marines undertook the systematic destruction of Hué by bombing and artillery in order to dislodge the NLF who had gained control of the city without resistance. No Saigon officials have sought to estimate the number of people killed by the American bombings and artillery attacks on Hué. Tran Van Dinh, a former Vietnamese envoy to Washington who broke with the Thieu-Ky regime, is a resident of Hué and described how members of his own family had been reported by the Saigon government as killed by the NLF while the family knew they had been victims of the U. S. bombing and had been buried in

(Continued on page 4)

87

MASSACRES IN VIETNAM — *(Continued from page 3)*

temporary graves since a regular burial was impossible during the U. S. bombardments. As George McT. Kahin, Cornell professor and America's most prestigious Southeast Asian scholar, has noted, the three thousand people who died in Hué were mainly the victims of U. S. bombs, bullets, shells and napalm--an additional aspect of the overall genocide committed by the U. S. against the Viet-

---

Recommended Reading

ANTIOCH REVIEW. The Fall, 1969 issue ($1.50) is a special issue devoted to a critique of the professional scholarly associations. Particularly recommended are Alan Wolfe on the political science association and Martin Nicolaus on the sociologists.

Frederick Forsyth, *The Biafra Story* (Baltimore: Penguin Books, paper, $1.45). A sympathetic account of the Biafran struggle by a British journalist.

H. D. Graham and T. R. Gurr, *The History of Violence in America* (New York Times: Bantam Books, paper, $1.25, 822 pp.) Fascinating report on the history of American violence, as delivered to the national commission on violence. Particularly recommended are the two deeply and thoroughly researched articles by Prof. Richard M. Brown: "Historical Patterns of Violence in America", and "The American Vigilante Tradition", on the numerous American movements for private, non-governmental justice.

George Kateb, "The Political Thought of Herbert Marcuse", *Commentary* (January, 1970), 15 pp. A quietly effective refutation of much of the nonsense perpetrated by the leading New Left philosopher.

Mickey and John Rowntree, "More on the Political Economy of Women's Liberation", *Monthly Review* (January, 1970), 6 pp. The first sensible article on the women's liberation hokum, pointing out that capitalism emphatically does *not* insist that women remain in the home (certainly a precapitalist hangover), and rational economic reasons why wage rates for women tend to be lower and unemployment rates higher than for men.

---

namese people. So much for the fabricated "Vietcong massacres".

Having observed the complete lack of accuracy in the presidential statement, it is necessary to ask why it was possible for the NLF to take Hué in a few hours without many shots while it required 26 days for the U. S. marine corps to recapture Hué at the price of thousands killed by American bombardments. The northern half of South Vietnam (part of the province of Annam which is divided by the 17th parallel) had been the center of the struggle of Vietnam's Buddhist majority for freedom from the Diem dictatorship which they caused to be overthrown in 1963. When the Thieu-Ky government imposed similar restrictions on their freedom, the Buddhist students in cooperation with the civil authorities and army commanders in this region in this region established an autonomous government in early 1966. Accepting the good faith of U. S. pro-consul, Henry Cabot Lodge, these civil, military and religious leaders of the Vietnamese of the region were betrayed and the Saigon troops were flown into Hué and other cities in U. S. transports to seize control and arrest the local leaders. Those who escaped became members of the National Liberation Front. Thus, leading the forces which entered Hue two years later were the former Buddhist leaders of Hue. These were welcomed by their compatriots, the citizens of Hué, while the Saigon officers and troops fled. Given the purges and executions committed by the Saigon police in Hué for two years, that only five special police in the district, according to the non-NLF source, were to be punished suggests the validity of the frequent accusation against the NLF that they are too mild and insufficiently rigorous in carrying out popular justice against the major criminals of the state apparatus. But, then it has always been beyond the conception of our European minds how Asians have such reverence for human life, even of an enemy. The race against time is whether the Vietnamese will have taught this to Americans before they are exterminated.

—— Leonard P. Liggio

LEFT AND RIGHT — *(Continued from page 2)*

comradeship. It is the ability to identify with the actual victims of injustice that cements the bond uniting revolutionaries on the Left, whether they call themselves anarcho-communists, free market anarchists, or just plain radicals.

Terminology has ceased to be important. As we enter a period of overt repression it is this crucial psychological attitude toward our fellow human beings that will determine on which side of the political fence each one of us will stand.

—— Jerome Tuccille

Published on the first and fifteenth of every month.   Subscription rate: $7.00 per year; Student subscription rate: $5.00 per year

A Semi-Monthly Newsletter

THE
Libertarian Forum

Joseph R. Peden, Publisher   Washington Editor, Karl Hess   Murray N. Rothbard, Editor

VOL. II, NO. 4   February 15, 1970   35¢

THE TASK AHEAD

The libertarian movement stands on the threshhold of a notable future. In the past year, the movement was launched into the "take-off" stage of its hoped-for future growth. In the past year, libertarianism has changed from a congeries of local small "circles" into an emergent mass movement, largely among the nation's youth. The strong and militant libertarian minority broke off, or was broken off, from the conservative-statist Young Americans for Freedom, including virtually the entire YAF body from California, Pennsylvania, New Jersey, and Virginia. The large and growing California movement is moving toward its own organization, and is organizing its own Left/Right conference in Los Angeles at the end of February. The Pennsylvania and other ex-YAF elements have merged with the Society for Rational Individualism to form the new, many-thousand strong Society for Individual Liberty. The Student Libertarian Action Movement, several "Libertarian Alliances" and numerous organs and journals of opinion have emerged during the past year. Articles expressing or commenting on this new and vibrant trend have appeared in such mass-circulation magazines as *Playboy, Ramparts, Newsweek,* and--the latest-- *Cavalier* (March, 1970), and the accession of Karl Hess to the pure libertarian cause has had an enormous impact.

The burning question before us is: where do we go from here? How do we accelerate our growth and build upon, rather than lose, our momentum? This is a problem which all of us must think about and discuss, especially since strategy and tactics are an art rather than anything like an exact science.

It seems to me that the prime consideration is to develop the libertarian movement--the "cadre"--as such. Many libertarians spend too much of their time and energy worrying about alliances: should they ally themselves with Right or Left or whatever? A far more important task is to build our own movement, especially now that we are strong enough to do so. Only by building our own movement, after all, can we spread and develop our own notably important and striking body of ideas. Strategic and tactical alliances with other groups are all very well, but they should flow from our own strength, with the idea always uppermost that we are "using" our allies as leverage to make our own ideas more effective.

Unfortunately what has happened all too often is that libertarians have forged alliances out of weakness, and then have begun to abase themselves before those allies, whether of Right or Left, so that soon the means becomes an end in itself, and preserving the alliance, or keeping our allies happy, comes to take on more importance than the spread of our own doctrines. Let us always remember that we

should be using our allies, rather than the other way round. This means that it is fatal to stop criticizing our allies from our own principled point of view; for once we stop doing that, we begin to abase outselves before tactical allies, and to lose sight of the point of the whole proceeding: the advancement of libertarianism. We should stop worrying about alienating our allies, and let them worry more about alienating *us*.

Furthermore, we have reached a point in history where there is little room for fruitful alliances with other *organizations*. YAF is of course impossible; but so now is SDS, which has become either orthodox Stalinist, or, as in the case of the Weathermen, politically psychotic. What has happened is that the Weathermen, finding no mass base of support anywhere, has decided that the entire American population, that is those who are not Weathermen members, are The Enemy, and therefore must be wiped out--in a despairing and crazed attempt thereby to help the liberation movements overseas. Therefore, the Weatherman leadership now exalts indiscriminate violence against any Americans, including even the abominable and psychotic murder of Sharon Tate. As a result, the Weathermen chanted "Charlie Manson power", and hailed the murder of "the pig" Sharon Tate, since in their lexicon, everyone, not simply the police, have become "pigs" who are to be "offed" (gotten rid of). There is little or nothing to be gained, at this point, from organizational alliances; what we must do, then, is to attract the myriad of unorganized individuals, on the Left or the Right, who are instinctively libertarian, and who are groping for libertarian guidance and fellowship. This, as I understand it, is part of what the February California conference is designed to do.

But if we are to concentrate on developing our own organization, then we must be able to deal with divisions among ourselves, for right now we encompass a very wide spectrum from "extreme right" to "extreme left". Unless we can find a way to "peacefully coexist" among ourselves, there is little we can do to advance our cause in the "outside" world. But this means that the width of our spectrum has to be reduced, for if our differences are too wide, we become inherently more antagonistic than harmonious, and any attempts at unity will be a phony papering-over of differences that will fail just as readily as an alliance with YAF or SDS.

What I would like to see, then, is for both the extreme right and the extreme left of our movement to move sharply toward the center--to use an odious term, toward our "mainstream". For our "anarcho-rightists": for our ex-YAFers, ex-Randians, etc. this means largely abandoning

(Continued on page 4)

Phony Libertarianism

Shortly after the YAF convention last August that organization was stripped of its libertarian veneer when several hundred libertarian radicals and anarchists split away to form their own society. Now it is apparent, judging by the YAF magazine *The New Guard*, that subtle attempts at co-optation are being made to seduce the dissidents back to YAF.

Co-optation is a rare practice for the Right Wing. The Right has always preferred to bludgeon its opponents out of existence than to corrupt them with favors. After all, it is ungentlemanly for any self-righteous protector of Christian civilization to sully his reputation by flirting with the Devil.

But the latest editor of *The New Guard*, Ken Grubbs, is a decent fellow in many ways. He really thinks of himself as a libertarian and he would rather sit down and reason with the occupiers of People's Park before unleashing Ronnie Reagan to chew them up. I suspect that if it comes to a final showdown Ken Grubbs will turn his head sadly rather than stay and enjoy the massacre. And that is more than one can say about your run-of-the-mill Buckleyite.

Understanding this, we can now flip through the January, 1970 issue of *The New Guard* until we come to an editorial entitle, "YAF: a Philosophical and Political Profile". The editorial deals with the results of a "survey" designed to ascertain the philosophical/political makeup of the YAF membership. For the first time to my knowledge Objectivism has now been admitted into the "mainstream" of YAF thought. According to this mythical "survey" ten percent of the YAF membership subscribe to the Objectivism of Ayn Rand while another twelve percent adhere to the libertarianism of Ludwig von Mises. How does the rest of YAF break down? Nine percent apparently like Frank Meyer's "fusionism"; forty-eight percent thrill to the tune of Bill Buckley's "conservatism"; another fifteen percent dance to the beat of Russell Kirk's "traditionalism"; and the final six percent march in goose-like step to L. Brent Bozell's "radical traditionalism".

Even if we were to accept these figures as the results of a genuine survey it would still mean that seventy-eight percent of the YAF membership subscribe to a pro-administration, pro-status quo position ranging the Right Wing gamut from Frank Meyer to Brent Bozell (Bozell, by the way, recommends a church-state reverence for a Christian past with Roman Catholicism offered as the "path to our salvation" while Russell Kirk relies upon "moral prescriptions from our ancestors" and an "aristocracy based upon vocational, artistic and intellectual excellence.").

But even Objectivism these days is no guarantee of libertarian principles. Jeffrey St. John is an Objectivist and he continually makes the rounds tooting his horn for the destruction of "international communism" and the suppression of dissidents at home. In short he is a conservative, as Ayn Rand herself has become a *selfish* conservative, adding a dash of atheism to the Right Wing brew which is only now becoming fully assimilated into it.

All this is nothing more than a prelude to the *piece de resistance* of the January issue, an article entitled "The Theatre of the 'Conspiracy'", authored by the Hippie Hatchet Man of the New Right, Phillip Abbott Luce.

What is one to make of Luce?

What is one to make of anyone who exchanges one brand of fascism for another and, hypocritically enough, tries to label his new position *libertarianism*? The very word, *libertarian*, is shortened to four letters in the mouth of someone like Luce. It is easier to respect the raw, open, undisguised hatred of Strom Thurmond than the same Right Wing line when it is deliberately concealed by long hair, aromatic weed, and New Left cultural jargon.

Luce begins his article by describing the Conspiracy Trial in Chicago as a "legal happening". He then goes on to excoriate the defendants for their "overt refusal . . . to cater to the generally accepted etiquette of courtroom procedure."

He continues:

"The defendants have made it abundantly clear from the time of their indictments that they consider the trial a crock. One of the defendants, Tom Hayden of SDS infamy, has written, 'Since the trial has sparked widespread international concern, the Conspiracy hopes to turn it into a political showdown.' "

"From the outset, the eight defendants have attempted to make a mockery of the trial."

". . . Judge Hoffman is in a most unenviable position of having to attempt to act as a responsible and reasonable judge over a group of incorrigible media-oriented indictees. What indeed is a judge, conditioned to sane trials, to do when a defendant keeps shouting 'You fascist dog! You fascist pig!'?"

". . . to the Conspiracy the whole thing is a revolutionary game to be played on their terms or not at all."

"The defendants have done everything possible to turn their trial into a stage show."

"Bobby Seale had the dubious distinction of being the most outrageous of the defendants . . . He was aiming for publicity and possible martyrdom. His outbursts gained him both when the judge was forced to bind and gag him lest he continue to disrupt the trial."

"Judge Hoffman was ultimately forced to sentence Seale to four years in prison for contempt of court."

In the course of his despicable diatribe Luce refers to himself as a "civil libertarian" and even hints that he is a "radical".

He is, of course, nothing of the sort. It would be too easy to dissect his analysis of the trial (part of which was originally published in *National Review*) and show him up for what he really is, but his own words condemn him more effectively than anyone else's possible could.

Can any libertarian doubt that the Chicago trial is a political act staged by the federal government to make an example of some of the leading dissidents in the country?

How can any libertarian condemn the defendants for refusing to play according to the rules established by their executioners?

If the trial is not a mockery of justice, then what is it? And if it is a mockery, how can a libertarian fault the victims for treating it as such?

How can any judge be forced to sentence anyone to four years for contempt of court--unless by the political authorities?

How can any libertarian criticize Seale for demanding his moral right to defend himself? And how can any libertarian regard such a demand as contempt of court deserving of punishment?

How can anyone of even the slightest libertarian persuasion portray Judge Hoffman in the role of a reluctant victim of circumstances--a man who has shown nothing but contempt for the defendants and their attorneys from the start, mispronouncing their names and upholding every objection raised to every point they have tried to make in their own behalf?

No, Phillip Abbott Luce is not a libertarian. Nor is he a radical. With his long hair and hippie demeanor he is an effective weapon for the New Right in its attempts to co-opt the libertarian Right and in its desire to cloak its authoritarian nature with a facade of superficial libertarianism.

Whatever the reasons, he has allowed himself to be used as bait by the Buckley establishment. When they tire of his services they will cut him off. Perhaps, then, he can head up the Libertarian Wing of the American Nazi Party or go

(Continued on page 4)

MEET LIBERTARIANS

EAST

Massachusetts

William Baumgarth
114 A Richards Hall
Harvard University
Cambridge, Mass. 02138

Scott Borowsky
62 Overbrook Drive
Wellesley, Mass. 02181

Cathy Longinotti
Dawes House
Smith College
Northampton, Mass. 01060

Connecticut

Sign of the Dollar
219 Hamilton St.
Hartford, Conn. 06106

New York

Edward Smith
627 Second Ave.
New York, N. Y. 10016

New Jersey

Ralph Fucetola III
65 Mount Prospect Ave.
Verona, N. J. 07044

Pennsylvania

R. Lawrence Conley
923 4th Ave.
E. McKeesport, Pa. 15035

Delaware

Sally Stern
533 Country Club Drive
Woodbrook,
Wilmington, Del. 19803

SOUTH

Virginia

Teddy G. Caudell
4043 Tennessee Ave., N. W.
Roanoke, Va. 24017

Tennessee

Karen and Garrett Vaughan
Apt. 2201
5709 Lyons View Pike
Knoxville, Tenn. 37919

Georgia

John L. Snare
Box 33
Mercer University
Macon, Ga. 31207

Florida

Stephen Halbrook
514 Leisure Lane
Tallahassee, Fla. 32304

Randy Sides
Box 14481
Gainesville, Fla. 32601

Alabama

E. E. Culver
3405 Atlanta Ave.
Montgomery, Ala. 36109

Louisiana

Richard C. Johnson
Box 20882
Louisiana State Univ.
Baton Rouge, La. 70803

Texas

Mike Holmes
113 Baker College
Rice University
Houston, Tex. 77001

MID—WEST

Wisconsin

Donald McKowen
9343 West Lincoln
Milwaukee, Wisc. 53227

Ted Sanstadt
Box G
Waushara Argus
Wautoma, Wisc. 54982

Illinois

William J. Haga
Box 2068, Sta. A
Urbana, Ill. 61820

Missouri

David Zubatsky
323 Clara
Apt. 202
St. Louis, Mo. 63112

Mike Medvic
9018 Tudor
Overland, Mo. 63114

FAR WEST

Nevada

Arene Hackett
2150 Pinon Hill Dr.
Carson City, Nev. 89701

California

Northern California

Chris Gould
40 Tappan Lane
Orinda, Calif. 94563

Hal Jindrich
555 Middlefield # 5201
Mountain View, Cal. 94040

Rod Manis
Hoover Institution
Stanford, Calif. 94305

Sharon Presley
1154 Hanover
Daly City, Calif. 94014

Rosalie Nichols
2861 37th Ave.
Sacramento, Calif. 95824

Southern California

Kenneth Berger
2125 Via Rivera
Palos Verdes Estates,
Calif. 90274

Lowell Ponte
511 Terracina Boulevard
Redlands, Calif. 92373

Milton Shapiro
451 Converse Ave.
Claremont, Calif. 91711

Armed Forces

Jerry Whitworth
CR Division
USS Ranger CUAGI
FPO San Francisco, Calif. 96601

Hawaii

William Danks
1645 Dole St.
Apt. 402
Honolulu, Hawaii 96822

Canada

John Egolf
Box 523
Souris, Manitoba, Canada

Byron Fraser
5487 Buckingham Ave.
Burnaby 2, British Columbia,
Canada

OUR TASK — *(Continued from page 1)*

totally their vestigial devotion to the American State: toward our Constitution, our foreign policy, our army, and our police. We must hold as our foremost objective the abolition of that State. For our anarcho-leftists this means abandoning the capricious urge for immediate "action" against that State, regardless of its certain failure, and the tendency to abandon free-market and individualist principles for the sake of unity with a powerless and trivial handful of communist-anarchists. Both extreme groups should prepare themselves to settle down, calmly and soberly but with cool and passionate dedication, to a thoughtful and protracted lifelong struggle for liberty and against the State. But this means that we must try to build a permanent movement, *and* that we try to develop lifetime careers that would enable each one of us to maximize our influence on behalf of liberty. And this means abandoning the "now generation's" heedless and hedonic emphasis on the immediate present moment, and instead returning to the old-fashioned "Protestant ethic" emphasis on building steadily and rationally toward the longer future. We must try our best to become, as much as possible, "professional libertarians", that is, people with lifelong careers in the service of libertarianism.

One important form of struggle which tends to be scorned by both of our extremes is simple, orthodox political action. This kind of working for political candidates is surely unglamorous, but it is often important for itself-- in keeping a far "greater evil" out of office on behalf of a decidedly "lesser evil"--and also in reaching vast numbers of middle-class citizens who cannot be reached in any other way. We would *like* to abolish these various political offices, but so long as these offices exist, and the State offers us a choice, however puny, we often can influence our fate in an important way by deciding between them. And while, in the ultimate sense, we oppose both candidates, there are often times when one is far worse than the other; if, for example, we were faced with a choice between Richard Cobden or Genghis Khan for President, we would surely plunge into the Cobdenite movement with enthusiasm, despite Cobden's falling a bit short of the pure anarchist position. But what we should then do would not be to bury our own identify within that movement, but rather continually propagandize within it for a more pure and consistent libertarian viewpoint. Such is the proper role of an ideological alliance.

What the movement needs more of, in short, is what the country as a whole needs more of nowadays: the tempering of the immediate, hot-headed, irrational passions of the moment into a sober, rational, farseeing, dedicated, protracted struggle toward a libertarian future.

PHONY LIBERTARIANISM — *(Continued from page 2)*

scuttling back to Progressive Labor.

What genuine libertarianism has to offer is *consistent* and *persistent* opposition to the policies of the U. S. government. Anything less gives libertarianism a bad name.

— Jerome Tuccille

Recommended Reading

James M. Buchanan, *Cost and Choice* (Chicago: Markham Pub. Co., 1969). A prominent Chicago School economist goes a long way toward adopting the Austrian theory of individualist, subjective value economics. Brief and non-mathematical, the book adopts the Mise-Hayek theory of costs.

Jane Jacobs, *The Economy of Cities* (New York: Random House, $5.95). Brilliant, scintillating work celebrating the primacy for economic development, past and present, of free-market cities. Also see the appreciative review by Richard Sennett, "The Anarchism of Jane Jacobs", *New York Review of Books* (January 1, 1970).

James O'Connor, "The Fiscal Crisis of the State: Part I", *Socialist Revolution* (January-February, 1970), 42 pp. (Available for $1.50 from Agenda Publishing Co., 1445 Stockton St., San Francisco, Calif. 94133). Analysis of current statism by a young Marxist economist who understands that the struggle to control and use the State is the current form of the "class struggle".

Joseph Pechman, "The Rich, the Poor, and the Taxes They Pay", *The Public Interest* (Fall, 1969), 22 pp. (Available for $1.50 at 404 Park Ave. So., New York, N. Y. 10016.) How the poor, rather than the rich, pay the taxes for the modern American welfare state.

John M. Peterson and Charles T. Stewart, Jr., *Employment Effects of Minimum Wage Rates* (Washington, D. C.: American Enterprise Institute, August, 1969), 165 pp. (Available for $2.00 from the American Enterprise Institute, 1200 17th St. N. W., Washington, D. C. 20036.) The most thorough, up-to-date study on the extent to which minimum wage rates have caused unemployment.

SUBSCRIBE NOW

Please enter a subscription for:

Name _____

Street _____

City _____ State _____ Zip _____

Subscription is $7.00 per year.
Student subscription $5.00 per year.

Bulk Rates. 20 or more. 10¢ each. 50 or more, 5¢ each.
Libertarian Forum Associate subscription is $15.00 or more.

THE LIBERTARIAN FORUM

Box 341   Madison Square Station
New York, New York 10010

Published on the first and fifteenth of every month.   Subscription rate: $7.00 per year; Student subscription rate: $5.00 per year

A Semi-Monthly Newsletter

THE Libertarian Forum

Joseph R. Peden, Publisher   Washington Editor, Karl Hess   Murray N. Rothbard, Editor

VOL. II, NO. 5   March 1, 1970   35¢

Free Bill Kunstler!

The infamous Conspiracy trial in Chicago has piled repressive horror upon horror: conviction under a patently unconstitutional law that sends people to jail not for any criminal actions but solely for "intent"; the dragging of defense lawyers across the continent under arrest because they withdrew from the case by telegram; the refusal to permit Bobby Seale to defend himself; the subsequent shackling of Seale and then his summary conviction by Judge Hoffman for contempt and being sent to jail for four years; the convictions and sentencing of the defendants by Hoffman for contempt; the willingness of the minority jurors to override their belief in innocence in order to get home; and finally and most infamously, the summary conviction of the defense lawyers for contempt, with the chief lawyer, William Kunstler, being sentenced for more than four years in jail, for the crime of zealous and militant defense of his clients.

The actions of Judge Hoffman have, as nothing else, exposed for all to see the despotic nature of the federal judicial system in America. The judge is a tinpot tyrant, and very little that he says and does has, in actual fact, been subject to the review even of other judges, let alone the public at large. Contempt convictions enable the judge, the allegedly aggrieved party, to "try" the case himself, without benefit of jury or defense counsel or the usual safeguards of the legal system, and then to declare guilt himself and to carry out the sentence.

All this is bad enough, and the contempt convictions of the defendants are bad enough, but the conviction of Bill Kunstler strikes at the heart of *any* chance that defendants, especially political defendants who are charged with the crime of dissent, will be able to get any sort of fair trial in America. For if Bill Kunstler is sent to jail, what lawyer is going to put his neck in a noose for any future defendants? Who is going to be active and zealous and try his very best on behalf of his clients? And that, of course, is the purpose of Judge Hoffman: to strike a mortal blow at militant legal defense, and thereby to deprive any further dissenters of the right to the best defense they can possibly get.

As in everything else, Judge Hoffman was brutally frank about his purpose. In the course of sentencing Kunstler, Hoffman said: "If crime is, in fact, on the increase today, it is due in large part to the fact that waiting in the wings are lawyers who are willing to go beyond professional responsibilities, professional obligations, professional duty in their defense." He added that the knowledge that such lawyers were available had a "stimulating effect" on potential criminals. Sure; if we eliminated defense lawyers altogether, it is still more sure that the conviction rate in

this country would skyrocket; and we would also be hip-deep into a totalitarian society. One of the glories of the Anglo-Saxon legal structure is that everyone is innocent until proven guilty after the best possible case has been put up in his defense; if we are going to scrap this elementary legal safeguard, then this country is really lost, and none of us are safe.

(Continued on page 4)

Renew! Subscribe!

The *Libertarian Forum* is coming close to its glorious first anniversary, and the time for renewals is fast approaching. We are already the longest-lived, and the most important, libertarian organ in the country. Where else do you know that regularly, twice a month, you will receive news of the libertarian movement, analysis of events of the day from a libertarian perspective, discussion and critique of libertarian theory and practice? Furthermore, we have a nationwide circulation, and this means that each one of us, who tend to be isolated in his or her own community, can keep contact regularly with the broader, nationwide movement. The *Libertarian Forum* provides to each of us a sense of broader community which, at least so far, is the only one that we have.

So we urge each one of you to renew your subscriptions as they fall due. Furthermore, we are operating on a shoestring, and so any more subscriptions that you can get for us would be deeply appreciated. If each one of you found just one more subscriber for us we would be on a handsome footing.

We have only done as well as we have out of the generosity of our Libertarian Associates, who have earned our lasting gratitude by donating $15 or more during this first year of our existence. Renewals, and expansion, of our Associates is vital to our continued existence and growth. Associates and potential Associates should realize that it is only their generosity that allows us to make the *Forum* available to students at a reduced rate, and s t u d e n t s, of course, are by far the largest source of new libertarians.

We welcome the following to the ranks of the Libertarian Associates:

Roy Halliday, Saugerties, N. Y.
H. G. Jinrich, Mountain View, Calif.
Jack Montgomery, State University, Arkansas.

PEOPLE JUSTICE

A significant control element in the preservation of law and peace within a society is the potential criminal's fear of public exposure--not the imprisonment or fines he may suffer, but the humiliation and personal shame that results from the discovery and the publication of his delinquency. All criminals avoid, if they can, exposure to the censorious judgment of public opinion. By the same token, if a particular act is not judged criminal by public opinion, the State has great difficulty in capturing, prosecuting and convicting the alleged criminal successfully. Ultimately, in any society, a crime is any act that is not socially acceptable to the community as a whole, and the criminal is an isolated social deviant from the mores which the community by the widest social consensus determines to be "the law". This would be just as true in an anarchic society as it is in a society which has developed the instrumentality we call the State.

This suggests that libertarians might do well to turn their attention to the task of exposing the manifest criminality of the State and its lackeys--not only by decrying taxation as theft or in the generalized terms so common in libertarian literature--but in specific and concrete terms with names, dates, places, victims and the specific crimes committed.

In the early history of the Celtic and Germanic tribes from whom so many of us are descended, free men met regularly with their neighbors to denounce alleged criminal acts committed by members of the community and to demand justice in the form of compensation to the victim for his injury. The community as a whole heard the case and in various ways aided the injured party to achieve his rights. Henry II of England is given credit for "creating" the grand jury as a means by which crimes could be detected and criminals brought to justice. Actually his jury system was part of a successful attempt to transfer the prosecution and punishment of crimes from the hands of free men acting within the traditions and with the consent of their neighbors to the hands of the royal justices and the royal courts imposing royal law for royal profit. The primitive but effective people's courts were coopted and transformed into State courts, imposing legal rules and penalties unknown previously, and creating a State monopoly over the means of securing justice. As is well attested, this monopoly became the chief instrument by which the medieval state was strengthened and the profits of the courts were a most valued source of its income. In our own times, the grand jury has become an instrument of State oppression, controlled by judges and district attorneys, and selected from a narrow, unrepresentative panel of citizens. It is notorious that prospective jurors are selected from lists of property holders, chambers of commerce, and other highly select groups. This selectivity is used to ensure that the grand jurors reflect and protect the interests of the local ruling elites--racial, social and economic. In some areas, the grand jurors have openly acknowledged their group role by forming permanent "grand jurors' associations" which perpetuate their collective self-identity and enhance their social solidarity. Thus the grand jury system is an important agency for the ruling elite who wield the power of the State, and monopolize the processes of justice. It seems to me that libertarians must find a way to reverse this process. We must take the law into our own hands once again like our ancient forefathers. We do so already in many ways--for example, we usually punish those who fail to pay their debts by publicizing the fact, thus alerting the community at large and greatly limiting the debtor's future opportunities for delinquency. Newspapers publish the names of persons arrested, convicted or even suspected of crimes, thus open-

ing them to public shame and ostracism. We regularly ask prospective employees, tenants, borrowers for letters of recommendation as to their character, and general reputation. A good reputation is still among a man's most valued possessions.

Since we no longer possess the power to attain justice by threat or use of violent force upon those who have aggressed against us, deprived us of rights or property, (the State having seized and monopolized this power)-- we must seek justice by the only means still readily available to us--the mobilization of public opinion. The criminals must be identified, their crimes exposed to the public eye, their reputations in society blackened until they are overtaken by remorse and offer to submit to justice and make compensation to the victims of their crimes.

Is this just another Utopian libertarian scheme? Another moral tract on what might be if we can "smash the State" in an apocalyptic moment? I believe it is not. Let us look for a moment at the Song My massacre and the Vietnam war as a whole. It is very likely that the immediate perpetrators of this atrocious crime will never be tried and punished by the courts of the United States, military or civil. The technicalities of the law, the pre-trial publicity, the lack of jurisdiction of military courts over ex-soldiers, and of civil courts over acts perpetrated outside their jurisdiction, the general political nature of the whole episode make it unlikely that much will come of the case. What would be valuable, however, is for some means to be found to determine the actual scope of the massacre, the names of those responsible and the degree of their guilt. If the men involved were so ruined in reputation that they were driven to retire from the army, or even forced into exile--the cause of justice would be served and the next time an officer led his troops into another Song My he would think more than once about murdering its population. If the government cannot perform this service, it could and should be done by *private* citizens who could constitute themselves as a Commission of Inquiry and set about the task of publicizing the nature of the crimes and the identification of the criminals.

In fact, on a broader scale, this job has already been done. In 1967 Bertrand Lord Russell, the distinguished British mathematician and philosopher, convoked an international panel of famed writers, historians, lawyers and scientists to sit as a tribunal to inquire into charges that the United States government had perpetrated a series of war crimes in violation of specific international treaties on the rules of war and a host of common crimes against the Vietnamese people. Two sessions were held, in Stockholm and then in Copenhagen, in which expert witnesses gave testimony in vivid detail as to the enormity of U. S. criminal acts in the Vietnam war. Though invited to testify, American officials refused to answer the charges and confined themselves to harassing the members of the tribunal and its staff, and demanding that their NATO allies cooperate in the task. The testimony was completed *four months before* the Song My massacre--but the American people were kept unaware of its findings. It documented in the most damning detail a record of human bestiality that places the United States among the all-time greats as a criminal State. (The full record of the testimony before the tribunal is available in paperback from O'Hare Books, 10 Bartley Road, Flanders, New Jersey, Price $5.75, appropriately titled *Against the Crime of Silence*.)

Indeed, the same technique is being used by former Justice Arthur Goldberg and Roy Wilkins of the NAACP to investigate the nationwide crackdown on the militant Black Panther Party. Since J. Edgar Hoohaw described the Panthers as the greatest single threat to the internal security of America (whatever happened to the Communist Party?), local police across the country have slain 28 Panthers, wounded, arrested and harassed hundreds of others, and
(Continued on page 3)

Doctors And Drugs

Two recent medical reports on drugs make an important contribution to the raging controversy over the endemic use of drugs among the "now" generation.

I. The Canadian Report

Canada has appointed a commission of inquiry into the spreading use of drugs, headed by Dr. Keith Yonge, president of the Canadian Psychiatric Association. A memorandum by Dr. Yonge, summing up what will be concluded in the report, has been published in the Toronto *Globe and Mail*. Dr. Yonge's findings lend scientific confirmation to the empirical impressions of many of us who have observed friends and acquaintances becoming absorbed into the "drug culture". Dr. Yonge writes:

". . . the use of these drugs [from marijuana on up] does indeed induce lasting changes in personality functioning, changes which are pathological in so much as they impair the 'mental and social well-being' . . . . The harmful effects are of the same order as the pathology of serious mental illness (psychosis), namely in distorting the perceptual and thinking processes and in diverting awareness from reality, impairing the individual's capacity to deal with the realities of life.

"The argument that marijuana is no more harmful than alcohol is specious . . . The primary action of alcohol is that of a relaxant. Impairment of mental functioning occurs when intoxicating quantities are taken. Marijuana, as with all the psychotropic drugs, on the other hand, acts solely as an intoxicant, its effects being primarily the distortion of perception and reasoning.

"In psycho-social development man grows from the prevalence of self-gratification and dependency, with little regard for reality, to the prevalence of self-determination and . . . involvement in his society. Against this progression, the trend toward 'instant' self-gratification and artificial self-exploration (by the use of psychotropic drugs) is distinctly regressive--a reversion to the immature, the primitive. The regression is further evidenced in the other trends in group behavior with which the non-medical use of drugs tends to be associated--reversion to the crude or primitive . . . however much these may be rationalized as emancipation from socio-cultural oppression."

Right on, Doctor!

II. The Berger Report

A remarkably keen insight into one of the major causes of the spreading drug abuse was contained in an article in the December issue of *Medical Times* , by Dr. Herbert Berger, chairman of the Committee on Drug Abuse of the Coordinating Council of the City of New York, and associate professor of clinical medicine at New York Medical College. Reporting on a study of 343 teenage drug addicts and their families over a seven-year period, Dr. Berger found one striking factor common to all these youths: "an absolute hatred of 'Compulsory Education' ", a hatred that came upon them early in primary school and had become fully

developed by the age of 12. As Dr. Berger writes: "These are often uneducatable individuals. They believe that we arbitrarily deny them their freedom and insist on their attendance in school. Like all who are jailed they resent both the jailer and the jail. Society has incarcerated them in school--against their will. This is, in their eyes, an unjust punishment, therefore they feel within their rights to retaliate by breaking school windows, by criminal activity and by disrupting classes."

Dr. Berger concludes that if education were made voluntary, some students would go eagerly to school, while "others would embrace apprenticeship in trades where they are sorely needed . . . Left to their own devices these adolescents may develop at their own pace: some quicker, some slower than that which an arbitrary society has chosen for them. Their goals may be vastly different from those which we have established. They are not necessarily wrong. Who would dare argue that a good carpenter is not a greater asset than a poor lawyer!"

Dr. Berger's findings independently confirm the writings of Paul Goodman and others on the crippling effects of compulsory attendance laws on the nation's youth. The youth are now indeed being imprisoned in the vast jailhouse of our public schools merely for the "crime" of being under 16 or 18 years of age. To liberate them the compulsory attendance laws must be repealed.

PEOPLE'S JUSTICE — *(Continued from page 2)*

subjected them to such violence that their white attorney has described it as "genocidal". While the Goldberg-Wilkins Commission is clearly not sympathetic to the Panthers' political views, its own prestige as part of the American Establishment, its very existence as an independent focus of public scrutiny of the police and their repressive tactics, ought to make the State and its lackeys more cautious in their continuing repression, and awaken those many Americans who still believe "It can't happen here!". The Russell Tribunal and the Goldberg-Wilkins Commission of Inquiry offer libertarians excellent models for future action. Serious thought should be given to the possible creation of private commissions of inquiry, local or national in scope, to expose the criminality of the State and its minions, to arouse the public against the vile and dastardly invasions of personal privacy by the FBI and other wiretappers, to inform them of the political and economic links between various special interests and the officials of the State, and of the rampant criminality of the police themselves. There is already a widespread suspicion that the cause of justice is deflected for reasons of State. When a respected member of the Warren Commission, Sen. Russell of Georgia, publicly admits that he thinks Lee Oswald was part of a conspiracy whose other members are still at large, how can the public believe in the integrity of justice under our State? When the admitted assassin of Martin Luther King publicly disputed the judge who sentenced him, insisting that he was not the sole murderer, the court silenced him and the case was closed. As Tom Wicker pointed out in the *New York Times*, (Dec. 16, 1969):

By now it is almost established practice for the Government to look outside existing institutions for a remedy or an explanation when serious crimes or shocking situations become too apparent to ignore. (This) derives from a developing mistrust of the official institutions and agencies of American justice --a mistrust, most seriously, of their motives, their very willingness to be fair and impartial, and a growing skepticism about their ability to function.

If Wicker is correct, the American people may be waiting for us to act!

— J. R. P.

Postal Note

We have been hearing from several subscribers that they have not received some issues of the *Forum* , or that an issue has been severely delayed. The fault, dear reader, lies not in us but in our beloved Post Service. So if any of you should fail to get any issue, let us know, and we will try to send you the missing copy.

FREE BILL KUNSTLER! — *(Continued from page 1)*

If we are going to prevent total fascism in this country, if we are going to save the vestiges of American freedom, then all of us must make the freeing of Bill Kunstler a central concern. Here is a cause which surely our entire libertarian spectrum, regardless of other differences, should be able to back without stint or qualification. As Jerry Tuccille has urged, let us worry less about the oppression meted out to a non-existent fictional character, and more about the *real* oppression going on around us. One leading young writer, who calls himself a "philosophical anarchist", has complacently and smugly declared: "After all, America is 95% free." Well, Bill Kunstler is soon going to be zero free, and if his conviction for defending dissenters is allowed to stand, if he is going to be incarcerated for that sort of "crime", then make no mistake, none of us is free.

The Great Society

"What, then, is the productive contribution of government?"
——Murray N. Rothbard

———

The distant, leveled ground is stubbled with the stumps of
   trees.
The masons holler to teams of workmen on the slope
Pushing boulders by twos and threes.
The masters, waiting on the raised catwalk,
Shrug their stooping shoulders.
The stonecutters lay their chalk and chisels down.

Nimrod has come today.
To put an old crone to work.
Sweeping up.

——James D. Davidson

Recommended Reading

Benjamin Quarles, *Black Abolitionists* (Oxford Univ. Press, paper, $1.95). The neglected story of the role played by Negroes in the abolitionist movement.

Ronald Radosh, "The Bare-Knuckled Historians", *The Nation* (February 2, 1970). Excellent report on the fracas at the December historians' convention.

Peter Dale Scott, "Tonkin Bay: Was There a Conspiracy?", *New York Review of Books* (Jan. 29, 1970), 11 pp. (Available for 50¢, annual sub. for $10, at 250 West 57th St., New York, N. Y. 10019.) The best work yet on Tonkin Gulf revisionism, showing not only that there was *no* North Vietnamese attack even after severe U. S. provocation, but also that lower echelon intelligence officials undoubtedly fabricated the attack to induce the President to attack the North.

A. J. P. Taylor, *The Origins of the Second World War* (Fawcett, paper, 95¢). The great revisionist work on 1939, now out in a second edition, in which Taylor effectively answers his critics.

Stanley Diamond, "Who Killed Biafra?", *New York Review of Books* (Feb. 26, 1970). Excellent pro-Biafra article by a distinguished anthropologist.

Edmundo Flores, "Land Reform in Peru", *The Nation* (Feb. 16, 1970). The story of the only relatively thoroughgoing land reform not put into effect by Communist-led governments.

Peter Michelson, "Fictive Babble: Review of Ayn Rand's *The Romantic Manifesto*", *New Republic* (Feb. 21, 1970). Slashing critique of Rand's latest book, including the point that the Rand of 1969 has begun to write like the villains of her own novels.

Murray N. Rothbard, "The Guaranteed Annual Income", *The Rational Individualist* (September, 1969). (Available for 50¢, annual sub. $4.00, at 800 Hillsboro Drive, Silver Spring, Md. 20902.) A critique of the Nixon welfare program.

Robert Z. Aliber, "Gresham's Law and the Demand for NRU's and SDR's: A Reply", *Quarterly Journal of Economics* (November, 1969), pp. 704-05. Points out that the SDR "paper gold" will not necessarily cure the U. S. balance of payments. Gresham's Law will induce foreign countries to prefer SDR's to dollars, not just to gold.

(In general, the *New York Review of Books* is a brilliantly edited, scholarly bi-weekly tabloid eminently worth reading.)

First Class

Published on the first and fifteenth of every month.   **Subscription rate: $7.00 per year; Student subscription rate: $5.00 per year**

A Semi-Monthly Newsletter

THE
Libertarian Forum

Joseph R. Peden, Publisher   Washington Editor, Karl Hess   Murray N. Rothbard, Editor

VOL. II, NO. 6   March 15, 1970   35¢

The New Left, RIP

We have to face it; we must face it: The New Left is dead. Dead as a doornail. *Kaput.* For those of us who hailed the New Left when it appeared, and urged libertarians to ally with it, this is a painful realization. But reality must be faced. That glorious, heady, revolutionary period of the life of the New Left (1964-1969) has come to an end.

First, the evidences of death. The evidence is everywhere. Perhaps the patient is not totally dead, but surely it is "medically dead"; the brain is long gone, the heart and spirit are failing fast, and what we are left with are the final reflexive convulsions of the corpse: the mindless and febrile twitchings of such pathetic and decaying groups as the Weathermen and the Patriot Party, the feeble high-camp of Yippie guerrilla theatre, the arrant nonsense of Women's Liberation. The heart and body of the New Left are gone.

Almost from its inception, SDS was the heart and soul of the New Left, the bearer and carrier of its best libertarian and revolutionary instincts. SDS is dead, in an aggravated state of rapid disintegration, its onetime open libertarianism replaced by a handful of fanatic Stalinoid sects. The broader anti-war movement, which had SDS at its core, has folded completely in a few short months. At the brink of a crucial take-off after the October and November 1969 demonstrations, the left-liberal Moratorium, possibly scared of its own potential, possibly intimidated by Mitchell and Agnew, simply tucked tail and ran, folding at the horrifying prospect of its own rapid growth. And the New Mobe, organizer of the successful November demonstration, has sundered apart, taken over by feeble ultra-Left groups who want to graft on to the anti-war issue every cause but the kitchen sink. While America's genocidal war in Vietnam goes on, virtually the entire Left has suddenly gotten bored with the whole issue and hived off to worry about the Environment—an eminently safe and co-optable issue where even Richard Nixon has become a militant. (Will the fellow who *advocates* air pollution please stand up?) Sure, Nixon's cunning and demagogic Nov. 3 speech won over the "silent majority" temporarily. But what kind of a movement is it, how viable is it, that folds up and disappears at the first sign of a setback? Even the Democratic politicians, who had rediscovered the war issue at the time of the October moratorium, have slipped back into innocuous silence.

The student movement, which again had SDS at its heart, has also faded away. Columbia, Berkeley, San Francisco State, City College, Cornell, all the great centers of past struggle, are quiet and likely to remain so. It's true that it's been a cold winter, and that come spring, the students may well start up again. But even if they do, their *demands*

are no longer in any sense revolutionary or even meaningful. Let's face it: does one more "black studies institute" really matter? Are we supposed to go to the barricades for a demand that is innocuous at best, ludicrous at worst? The revolutionary student movement is dead also.

And black nationalism, the only sometime revolutionary force outside the students, has also shot its bolt. SNCC, the great and imaginative co-founder of the New Left and of the black liberation struggle, is dead. The Muslim groups and the Republic of New Africa have faded away. The cultural nationalists have disappeared. What we are left with are the Black Panthers who have (a) abandoned black nationalism for Marxism, and (b) are being systematically chopped down by the police, who are overreacting to a threat that never really existed, since the Panthers have far more support among adoring white radicals than they do in the black community. In retrospect, black nationalism has been finished since the murder of that superb leader, one of the great men of our epoch, Malcolm X. Those who murdered Malcolm knew that the black community would not be able to come up with anyone remotely approaching his stature and his potential. Those who came after Malcolm have been pygmies, excrescences upon a dying though only emerging cause. Instead of black national liberation, we now have only . . . what? Demands of black studies institutes, and, of course, the *dashiki* and the Afro haircut. The black liberation movement is dead.

II

If, then, the New Left is dead, this does not mean that its short life was not a glorious one. Its accomplishments were many and remarkable. It created the most intense, the most notable, and the most far-flung anti-war movement in the history of protest against American imperial wars. The New Left anti-war movement was begun by SDS in early 1965, and spread to almost an entire generation, and beyond. It succeeded in toppling an American President, and in forcing a halt to the bombing of North Vietnam. It managed to use that war, furthermore, to bring a consciousness of the imperialist nature of American foreign policy to millions of people. And it also managed to use the war to radicalize countless numbers of Americans, to reveal the imperial corporate state nature of the American system.

In the process; and here is perhaps the New Left's biggest achievement, it destroyed Liberalism. Liberalism, with its muddled thinking, its hypocrisies, its almost universally accepted cover for corporate state tyranny and imperial

(Continued on page 2)

THE NEW LEFT, RIP — *(Continued from page 1)*

aggression, has been forever exposed, in its total intellectual bankruptcy, by the young New Left movement. No one will hereafter take Arthur Schlesinger, Jr. or Max Lerner, or Walt Rostow seriously. To accomplish this destruction of Liberalism with no support in the Establishment, with virtually no financial resources, and in complete opposition to a State-subvened culture, was a remarkable feat. And it took the New Left, with its passionate dedication and its ability to expose the consequences in reality of Liberalism's rhetoric, to do the job.

The New Left began in late 1964, with the Berkeley Free Speech Movement, and while it hardly succeeded in overturning the American university system, it has made an indelible mark. Before the New Left, corporate liberalism had succeeded in establishing a monstrous educational Leviathan that treated the growing mass of students as passive cogs in the machinery, as raw material to be processed to take their place in the state-monopoly system. The New Left has changed all that; the students and the youth are no longer the passive instruments of the "Age of Apathy" of the 1950's, no longer the "Organization Men" of that epoch choosing jobs upon graduation with careful calculation of their pension rights. The youth are now almost universally active, independent, critical, even militant. Moreover, the universities will never again be able to treat the students as simple cogs; at least partial reforms have taken place, so that the wishes and views of the students will be at least consulted and to some extent heeded. The Liberal educationists will never again sit so pretty and comfortable upon their educational thrones.

Thus, the New Left made an indelible imprint upon an entire generation, a whole age-group becoming adults in fundamental opposition to bureaucracy and authoritarianism, refusing totally to be the Organization Men of their predecessors. This legacy of the New Left will remain, as will, of course, continuing notable contributions from particular individuals and scholars: the inspiring insights of Paul Goodman, the blend of moral passion and historical scholarship of Noam Chomsky, the fundamental revision of the study of the domestic and foreign American Leviathan by William Appleman Williams and his numerous and able young students in the historical profession.

III

But the New Left leaves also an unfortunate and negative tendency in American Life, and one that shows every sign of spreading through the country even as the *political* revolution goes to its grave. I refer to the so-called "cultural revolution", or "counter-culture", that blight of blatant irrationality that has hit the younger generation and the intellectual world like a veritable plague. There are strong signs, in fact, that the spread of the cultural "revolution" even as the political revolution fades is no accident; for, as Aldous Huxley foresaw in his remarkable *Brave New World* three decades ago, it is relatively easy for the Establishment to co-opt the cultural rebels by simply adopting the new "counter-culture", and keeping the erstwhile rebels content on the ancient formula of despots: "bread and circuses", except that now it's dope and circuses. What better way to pull the teeth of knowledgeable dissent than to spread the ethic of indiscriminate "love", the substitution of the hallucinatory exploration of a mythical "inner space" for a rational and purposeful acting upon reality in order to change it, the conscious abolition of reason and clarity of thought on behalf of vague, inarticulate stumblings and primitive "non-verbal communication"?

There are growing signs that the Establishment has indeed decided to embrace the "counter-culture". *Time*, in

its review of the 1960's, called for precisely this kind of co-optation. And *Time*, *Life*, and the New York *Times* all celebrated the passive puerilities of the "Woodstock Nation", while carefully and completely ignoring the murders and the systematic violence at the West Coast rock festival last December at Altamont. A particularly horrifying straw in the wind is the fact that the New York *Times* devoted the coveted front page of its Sunday Book Review of February 22 to a laudatory blurb for the works of the English psychiatrist R. D. Laing. Laing, the logical culmination of the militant irrationality of the counter-culture, goes so far as to proclaim the superior virtues of insanity in our "sick society".

Thirty years ago, Ludwig von Mises wrote of a "revolt against reason" which he saw around him. But that revolt was tiddly-winks compared to the current open, all-out drive to liquidate reason and to substitute the ethic and the epistemology and the life-style of insanity.

How did the counter-culture take hold of the New Left? It began with an admirable desire to avoid the mistakes of the Old Left, especially the Old Left's emphasis on government action and reform through government. Instead, the New Left wished to emphasize individual or personal liberation. But instead of arriving at a philosophy of individualism and rationality, the form of personal "liberation" which it came to adopt was the counter-cultural "liberation" from reason and the consequent enslavement to unexamined whim.

Let us look more closely at this spreading counter-culture: the contempt for reason, logic, clarity, systematic thought, or *knowledge* of history; the hostility to science, technology, and human material progress; the hatred of hard work, planning, and long-range forethought; the hostility to "bourgeois comfort". In education, the cultural rebels are opposed to reading, to course content, to gaining knowledge, as "structured" and "repressive"; in place of which they would put free-form, gradeless, "rapping" about their own unexamined and puerile "feelings". And, the counter-culture exalts: immediate, momentary sensory awareness, aggravated by hallucinatory drugs; a corollary Rousseauan worship of the primitive, the "noble savage", the poverty-stricken, of "back-to-nature"; dropoutism and living from moment to moment on pure subsistence. In religion, the strong rational elements of our Western Greco-Judeo-Christian tradition have been thrown overboard for a banal Oriental mysticism and devotion to magic, astrology and Tarot cards. All in all, we are being hit with an extreme, mystical, anti-intellectual degenerate form of what Sorokin called "sensate culture". What it amounts to is a systematic, multi-faceted attack on human reason.

Noam Chomsky has written, on the counter-culture: "One bad effect is the revival of fanaticism. A lot of youthful dissidents think in terms of an unrealistic time-scale when they think of social change. When Marx wrote about capitalism, he was highly indignant, but he didn't go out and have tantrums in the streets. Youth, like other marginal groups, will fail to make a distinction between what's emotional and what's rational. Rationality is not a gift you should concede to the enemy if you want to succeed."

For those who are eager to discover a different culture, what a blessed relief it is to turn from the sewage of the counter-culture to the genuine, rational culture of the Enlightenment! The recently published second volume of Peter Gay's superb history of the Enlightenment, *The Science of Freedom* (New York: Alfred A. Knopf, 1969, $10.00, 705 pp.) carries one into a glorious world, of Condorcet, of Hume, the Physiocrats, the *philosophes*; they were not, most of them, anything like consistent libertarians; but their entire cultural framework was one of devotion to: reason, science, technology, human progress, individual liberty, free trade, and the free-market economy. We find the great Condorcet and his paean to rational liberty: "The moment will come,

(Continued on page 3)

THE NEW LEFT, RIP — *(Continued from page 2)*

then, when the sun will shine only on free men on this earth, on men who will recognize no master but their reason." One Condorcet, one *philosophe*, is worth the whole contemporary pig-pen.

The time has come for us to make a stand for reason. The time has come for us to realize that liberty, no matter how glorious, is not enough; for what good would liberty be, what good *any* social system, if entire generations go crazy, following Leary into a drug-besotted retreat from the world, following Marcuse into a "liberated" and "unrepressed" ignorance and whim-worship, following Laing into open insanity? We must raise the banner of Liberty and Reason, Now and Forever, One and Inseparable! We must eradicate the counter-culture before it destroys the world.

IV

If the genuine, the political New Left is dead, and what we are left with, overshadowing its positive legacy, is the spreading plague of the counter-culture being embraced by the Establishment, then what of the future? What is now the prognosis for the Movement? In the first place, there is no necessity for long-run despair. All revolutionary movements proceed in zigs and zags, with revolutionary periods succeeded by periods of counter-revolution and falling-back. We are now at the beginning of a period of counter-revolution.

As the Marxists discovered long ago, there is a proper strategy and tactic for periods of recession and counter-revolution. This strategy amounts to a sobering up, a cool abstinence from provoking State repression, a quiet concentration on patient, long-range educational work, on what the Marxists call "base-building". The heady wine of r-r-r-revolutionary posturing and phrasemongering must be replaced by the cool draught of rational analysis.

Furthermore, there may well be great positive benefits from this coming period of recession. Leonard Liggio has offered a brilliant analogy between the zig-zag fortunes of the Movement and the Austrian (Mises-Hayek) theory of the business cycle. In Austrian theory, the recession is the healthy and necessary response of the economy to the excesses and malinvestments of the preceding inflationary boom. Perhaps there are similar cycles in the fortunes of revolutionary movements. For just as the late stages of an economic boom throw up excesses and malinvestments which must be cleansed by recession, so the later years of the New Left had increasingly buried its sound elements and thrown up unsound and degenerate forms which are now all that survive. Perhaps the function of the coming recession is to serve as a healthy purgative: to cleanse the Movement of these excrescences, of this diseased tissue, so that, come the opportunity, the Movement will be a sound and healthy organism ready for the next advance.

For A New America

The now unfortunately defunct journal *Studies on the Left* was by far the outstanding theoretical and scholarly product of the New Left. It began in 1959, when the New Left was only a gleam upon the horizon, founded by a bright young group of graduate history students at the University of Wisconsin, who were under the inspiration of Professor William Appleman Williams. The first, or Wisconsin, phase of *Studies* was, in my view, its finest; there, it brought to the intellectual world the insights and researches of Williams and his students, insights that were destined to change the course of American historiography and even the way in which young scholars began to look at current America. The Williams contribution was to destroy the generally accepted

(Continued on page 4)

FOR A NEW AMERICA — *(Continued from page 3)*

image of the New Deal and of the Wilsonian and Progressive periods of twentieth-century America. The Williams school has shown that, rather than the Progressive-Wilson-New Deal being "progressive" movements by the mass of the people to curb and regulate Big Business and establish an anti-business form of welfare state, they were really generated by Big Business leaders themselves in order to cartellize and monopolize the economy through the instrument of Big Government. And rather than the foreign wars and interventions by Wilson and FDR being "enlightened" moves to spread democracy and "collective security" throughout the world, they turn out to have been aggressive acts to establish the world-wide hegemony of an American Empire, at the service of this same Big Business ruling class. The function of the Liberal intellectuals was to serve as ideological apologists for this neo-mercantilist corporate state. Hence, Williams' brilliant term, "corporate liberals".

After the movement of *Studies* to New York in 1963, the journal lost much of its emphasis on scholarship and revisionist American history, and plunged actively into New Left "movement" activity, with lengthy reports and commentaries, for example, on the short-lived "community action projects" among the urban poor. In its later years, *Studies* was increasingly torn apart between those of its editors who wanted to continue to stress movement activism as well as the emerging "cultural revolution", and the more theoretical who wished to turn the journal into a center for building a frankly socialist theory on behalf of a supposedly imminent socialist party. But the problem was that both tendencies were no longer interested in continuing the real genius of *Studies*, its historical scholarship. The deadlock among the editors caused *Studies* to fold in 1967.

In a profound sense, the opening and closing of *Studies* performed similar historic roles: for just as the emergence of *Studies* foreshadowed the later birth of the New Left, so its death also foreshadowed the New Left's demise. The same tendencies which tore *Studies* apart (mindless activism and the counter-culture on the one hand, sectarian Marxian socialism on the other) were two of the major reasons for the later dissolution of the New Left as a whole.

An important book has now been published which contains the best of the articles from *Studies on the Left*. It is a pleasure to see that the best articles from *Studies* have been resurrected, enshrined, and available in book form. The book is *For a New America* (New York: Random House, $10.00), edited by James Weinstein and David W. Eakins, two of the editors of *Studies* (Weinstein being undoubtedly the single most important editor over its life-span.)

The star of the collection is undoubtedly Part I, "American

Corporate Liberalism, 1900-1948", which presents a Williamsite revision of modern American history. Every article in this section is important and to be recommended. They include William A. Williams' review-article of Ernest May's whitewash of American Imperialism at the turn of the century; Martin J. Sklar's lengthy and devastating critique of Wilsonian "liberalism"; James Weinstein's discussion and explanation of the pro-union attitudes of the Big Business Establishment during the Progressive period and Ronald Radosh's exposition of the pro-corporate state views of American union leaders; Murray N. Rothbard's critique of the widespread myth that Herbert Hoover believed in *laissez-faire*, showing instead that Hoover was the founder of Roosevelt's New Deal and corporate state; and John Steinke and James Weinstein's delightful little revelation that Joe McCarthy learned his red-baiting from none other than the liberal Norman Thomas.

Parts III and IV, which deal with ethnic questions, are also excellent, featuring one of the earliest statements of the black power position (1962) by Harold Cruse, and a scintillating defense of Hannah Arendt against her Zionist detractors by Norman Fruchter. Part II, "An American Socialism", is the least valuable part of the book, representing a tortured attempt of the "theoretical" wing of the later Studies board to develop a new prolegomena to the theory for a new socialist party. But even here, Weinstein's review-article of the scholarly literature on the Socialist Party is very useful, as is especially Gabriel Kolko's realistic pessimism on the viability of both the Old and New Lefts.

There are, inevitably for such a collection, a few articles from the old *Studies* which I miss, and which could easily have been included if the tendentious socialist articles had been dumped: the conflict which raged around the Fruchter article, between Fruchter and Old Left Judeophile Marxists Louis Harap and Morris U. Schappes (Fall, 1965); Michael A. Lebowitz' brilliant review-article of Lee Benson's *Concept of Jacksonian Democracy* (Winter, 1963); Joseph R. Conlin's review of Old Left Marxist Philip Foner's history of the IWW (Mar.-Apr., 1966); and Todd Gitlin's and Shin'ya Ono's searching critiques of the dominant "pluralist" theorists of American political science (Summer, 1965).

All in all, one of the most important books of the year.

The Libertarian Forum

BOX 341
MADISON SQUARE STATION
NEW YORK, NEW YORK 10010

First Class

Published on the first and fifteenth of every month.   Subscription rate: $7.00 per year; Student subscription rate: $5.00 per year

-First Anniversary Issue-

A Semi-Monthly Newsletter

THE
Libertarian Forum

Joseph R. Peden, Publisher   Washington Editor, Karl Hess   Murray N. Rothbard, Editor

VOL. II, No. 7   April 1, 1970   35¢

THE MAD BOMBERS

Over fifteen years ago, a nutty, oddly likeable little man named George Metesky started placing bombs around mid-town New York City, fortunately setting them in such a way that no one was injured. After several bombings, Metesky, dubbed the "Mad Bomber" by the press, was finally picked up and put away. Nowadays, not only would he be a hero of the Left, but he is almost a model of its current incarnation. Like the Newest Left, he had a genuine political grievance, in fact much the same political grievance; in his case, it was injustice at the hands of Con Edison, a State-created and privileged monopoly. And like the present Left, he despaired of or was uninterested in carrying out a protracted ideological and political struggle against Con Ed and the State which created it. Instead, like the newest Looney Left, though devoid of mass popular support (to put it mildly) he decided to go over into armed struggle. His decision was certainly less conscious and less ideological than that of the Newest Left; but it was also considerably less dangerous.

There have been mutterings on the Left for months about going over into armed struggle, or into urban guerrilla warfare against the System. Now it looks as if they have done so. The insanity of their decision can be easily gleaned by reading the works and studying the examples of the *successful* revolutionaries and guerrilla warriors. Over and over, the vital point is that before launching armed struggle, the guerrillas *must* have the support of the bulk of the population of the area (whether peasants or urban residents). They must, in the metaphor of Mao and Che, "swim as a fish in the water" of the surrounding population. Fidel, for example, did not begin his revolution by landing with a handful of armed men in Oriente Province. He began it with years of previous political education and preparation which built up enthusiastic support in the Cuban population, especially among the peasantry. He arrived at the proper "water" first before putting in the "fish". And it was precisely Che's complete failure to heed his own advice that led to his own murder and to the rapid extinction of his guerrilla band in Bolivia.

If guerrillas launch their struggle without public support, they are doomed to total failure, to ending just like Metesky and Che. But not only that: the reason why American counter-insurgency quickly evolved into genocidal slaughter in Vietnam is precisely because the Vietnamese guerrillas had the support of virtually the entire population, and therefore the American effort necessarily meant war conducted against the entire population. In short, armed struggle

against popular support means genocidal war. It is hard to see how the new Mad Bombers of the Left can help but deteriorate in a similar way. The Mad Bombers, of course, have nothing like the power of the U. S. war machine in Vietnam. But they face an urban population in America who are totally and violently opposed to their aims and their tactics. They are operating in a water in which they cannot hope to swim. Therefore, the logic of the situation demands that they begin to bomb everyone and everything. So far, they have been scrupulous in setting their bombs at night, and in giving advance warning to clear the buildings. But how long will it go on before the Bombers begin to escalate their struggle against the entire American population?

The Looney Left has apparently fallen for the old turn-of-the-century Left-wing anarchist and nihilist nonsense of the "propaganda of the deed", the notion that daring and violent deeds will attract the support of the masses to one's cause. All that these deeds can attract will be the undying hatred of the vast bulk of the American population, which will call down upon the head of the Looney Left the full force of the State apparatus. The only question now is how many innocents will be dragged off to the pokey from the provocations of the unhinged. And so, in a striking illustration of the "cleansing" process that we mentioned in our last editorial ("The New Left, RIP", Mar. 15), the Looney Left, frenzied, unhinged, its judgment hopelessly addled by drugs, proceeds to bomb its way to self-destruction.

The Knudson Revolt

Four years ago, Ken Knudson, a member of the pacifist Peacemaker Movement, pioneered in a new form of tax resistance: the idea of claiming enough exemptions on the Form W-4 Employee's Withholding Exemption Certificate so that no tax can be withheld from one's wages. Last fall, on October 5, at Lincoln Park in Chicago, a dozen people gathered to form the first tax resistance group based on the Knudson method. All the members adopt the Knudson approach and claim the exemptions; then they take the money which would have been paid into the U. S. treasury and pool it into a cooperative association, the Chicago Area Alternative Fund, which uses the funds for constructive, as well as voluntary, purposes. Anyone interested can write the Fund at 1209 W. Farwell, Chicago, Ill. 60626.

Liberty And The University

I recently received from a colleague a little packet of literature publicizing the activities of the University Centers for Rational Alternatives, Inc., a loose organization of scholars and educators formed for the purpose of defending academic freedom, "the freedom to speak, to teach, to learn, to inquire, to criticize, and to challenge" within the university community. Perceiving these to be principles which I strongly support myself, my first reaction was a cautious Bravo! and I read further. Soon I found the UCRA taking a position against arson, assault and battery, deliberate destruction of academic hardware, looting of files, forcible occupation of buildings, and intimidation of students. Right on! I said to myself, and read right through the little packet of literature.

Strangely, however, my enthusiasm began to cool by the time I had finished. Although I did not encounter a single statement which, in isolation, could be construed to violate sound libertarian principles, going back to read between the lines, to study what was left unsaid as well as what was said, to consider the context in which high-sounding principles were presented, I began to find grounds for suspecting that the UCRA was not such a staunchly libertarian organization as its rhetoric implied.

The big tip-off was that in all the pages devoted to elaboration of the ways in which SDS goonsquads posed a threat to freedom in the university community, there was barely a mention of the frequent failures of the university itself to promote liberty within and without its institutional perimeters. And one need not appeal to some specious, new-leftish distortion of the meaning of the term "freedom" to show that the university's record is not spotless. Let us examine three ways in which the university falls short of the ideal:

First, if a free society means one in which the threat to the individual of coercion by arbitrary authority is minimized by strict observance of the principle of the rule of law, the academic community should form itself as a model, a miniature replica, of such a society. Yet within the university, the range of arbitrary authority which the student is expected to accept in exchange for access to the knowledge he seeks is often unnecessarily broad. It must not be forgotten that what the students are protesting is often the meddlesome paternalism of an administration which, far from promoting the development of the student as a free individual, seems aimed instead at inculcating the pseudo-value of "respect for authority" as an end in itself. How can the UCRA insist that the rule of law (a system, we are taught, based on the impartial application of explicitly formulated general rules to decisions for specific cases) must extend to the university campus when the procedures for disciplining students, selecting administrators, and dismissing faculty members are a model of the rule not of law, but of caprice, favoritism, prejudice, and vacillating submission to transient pressure groups? Sidney Hook, the founding father of the UCRA, gives away too much of his true position when he fondly recalls his golden undergraduate days at Columbia when "Nicolas Murray Butler was both the reigning and ruling monarch." (NYU Alumni News, May 1968).

The second way in which the university too often violates libertarian principles occurs when it itself strays across the line, so insistently drawn by the UCRA, between mere advocacy of a cause, defensible no matter how repugnant the cause itself, and the actual use of physical force or threat of force to advance that cause. We don't need to be so abstract as to point out that every time the university accepts a dollar in tax money, extorted from citizens by the Internal Revenue Service, it is cooperating in the perpetration of initiated violence. There are more direct instances

available. When the university cooperates with the Selective Service System, it is contributing to the biggest sell-out of the American tradition in the history of the nation. (One constructive accomplishment of the campus left has been to bring about a limitation of university complicity in this form of legalized slavery.) Again, when it allows its relations with the military to drift beyond the point of allowing the military to state its own case against the pacifists (recruiting and probably even most ROTC activities are defensible on grounds of academic freedom) to the point of donating the time of its salaried staff or permitting unpaid use of its facilities and real estate to pursue military objectives, the university is coming dangerously close to putting its corporate finger on the trigger.

Finally, one of the oldest principles of libertarianism holds that although the use of defensive violence is legitimate to counter force initiated by others, defensive force must never be excessive. You don't hang a pickpocket; and you don't flog a peeping Tom. So why should the UCRA cheer university administrations on when the police whom they call in to quell campus disturbances throw restraint to the wind and, instead of exacting an eye for an eye, take ten for one?

If the UCRA were truly a libertarian group, they would be as concerned with those threats to freedom that originate from within the academic establishment as they are with those posed by the campus rebels. The fact that its members are silent on these points is sufficient reason to suspect that it is something quite different. But what? Not simply another stuffy voice protesting youthful affronts to decorum and good grooming (although Hook lets his guard slip again to expose a good measure of this attitude as well: "during a talk I was giving, one of these bearded fellows stood up and tried to break up the meeting. He had a big black beard. It probably hid a weak chin." (NYT, Jan. 26, 1969).

No, no such petty principle could have united Abba Lerner, A. A. Berle, Zbigniew Brzezinski, Lewis Feuer, Edward Teller, Henry Walich, and Bertram Wolfe! What does this motley collection of corporate liberals, old socialists, and unreconstructed conservatives have in common that could have brought them together, if that common principle is not a true concern for academic freedom? One doesn't have to exercise much imagination to see that what they all have in common is a position of privilege within the academic establishment. The UCRA is a united front action of the academic elite to defend themselves against a perceived threat to their status!

But still, shouldn't the campus libertarian welcome the voice of the UCRA speaking out on behalf of academic freedom, even though their perception of the problem is

(Continued on page 3)

LIBERTY AND THE UNIVERSITY — *(Continued from page 2)*

one-sided and their motives are suspect? No, because an organization of this type actually poses a threat to the advancement of academic freedom. It addresses itself to those scholars and teachers with natural libertarian inclination, who are alarmed by campus disruptions, and attempts to persuade them that to defend academic freedom they must uphold the state quo (or even the status quo ante, in some cases). Intentional or unintentional, this is a splitting tactic by which the UCRA forestalls what would be the only genuine hope for establishing academic freedom (and the only genuine threat to the privileged position of the academic establishment), which lies in the potential of *an alliance between the libertarian right and the radical left.*

Libertarians in the academic community must learn to keep a cool head in the campus crisis, and not be panicked into thinking that the only alternatives are to support the UCRA elite, who benefit from their position of power within the old repressive institutions, or to sell out to the new left, which aims at replacing these old with new but equally repressive revolutionary institutions. Instead, they must pursue the goal, no matter how difficult it may seem, of promoting a libertarian alternative with an appeal to the best elements of both the left and the right. Academic freedom, yes; academic privilege, no!

—Edwin G. Dolan
Ass't. Prof. of Economics
Dartmouth College

Articles Welcome

We have neglected to inform our readers that we welcome articles for the *Libertarian Forum*. Be assured that we do. If any of you feel that the representation of authors in the *Forum* is too narrow, there is one excellent way that you can help to widen that representation: submit an article. If, however, you want any article which we decide not to print to be returned, please enclose a stamped, self-addressed envelope.

Also welcome are clippings and news items that would be of interest to libertarian readers. This would greatly increase the flow of news into our offices and therefore out to the body of our readers. And we also welcome letters, criticisms, comments on our articles, etc. If we are too dilatory to answer your letters personally, rest assured that they are all read carefully--even if we are too stubborn to heed them!

Tax Resistance

With the income tax deadline looming steadily on the horizon, those who have been flirting with the idea of not filing might pick up a small paperback entitled, *How to Refuse Income Taxes,* authored and published by Lucille E. Moran. The book can be obtained by sending a dollar to Miss Moran at P. O. Box 641, Tavernier, Florida 33070. I have not yet read the book, but Miss Moran says she has been refusing to file for eight years at this point (legally) and has gotten away with it. The key point is *not to file at all,* claims the authoress. Her book will fill you in on what to do from there.

Free market libertarians are not the only ones concerned with tax resistance. The *Manhattan Tribune,* a radical left weekly published in New York City, has recently offered two articles on tax refusal by Bob Wolf who is also a regular contributor to *The Realist.* One of his pieces dealt with the ten percent surcharge added to the phone bill four years ago to help finance the war in Vietnam. Bob states that about six thousand people including himself have so far refused to pay the tax. When the federal government tried to collect $2.97 from him last April, he wrote to his tax collector and advised him that since the war was illegal he (the revenue agent) might want to re-examine his own position to avoid being tried at a war crimes trial in the future. He also offered to help find the taxman a job in some legitimate field of work.

Finally, the government managed to collect $6.00 in back taxes from Bob by sending a couple of agents to his employer's office and putting a garnishee on his salary. The cost in time and labor to the government certainly far exceeded the amount collected. As Bob still refuses to pay the tax voluntarily he again owes some $16.00 in outstanding taxes. He is patiently waiting for some well-salaried government agents to drop around at his employer's office once again and personally demand Uncle Sam's "protection" money.

The second article dealt with the War Tax Resistance, 330 Lafayette St., New York City, an organization that distributes anti-war tax literature and offers the services of tax-resistance counselors. Among the sponsors are Dr. Benjamin Spock, Joan Baez, Pete Seeger and Allen Ginsberg.

This group is mainly concerned with the deduction of that portion of our total taxes used to finance the war and to manufacture war machinery. In the original statement issued by this organization the point was made that the "right of conscientious objection to war belongs to all people, not just to those of draft age." Bob Wolfe in his own letter to the tax assessor warns that those seeking to enforce the collection of war taxes may be guilty of complicity in the commission of war crimes.

The main drawback in using the Vietnam war as the basis for one's refusal to pay taxes is that this position is invalidated the minute the war ends. For this reason free market radicals who *conscientiously object* to all taxes might be more interested in Miss Moran's proposal for its long-range possibility. In any case tax resistance is an area where radicals of every persuasion can make common cause, using whatever arguments they will to serve their own libertarian ideals.

— Jerome Tuccille

(Ed. Note: The February 13 issue of *Tax Talk,* published by War Tax Resistance, lists the names and addresses of the War Tax Resistance centers throughout the country, as well as news of other WTR activities.)

Recommended Reading

A. S. DeVany *et al.*, "A Property System for Market Allocation of the Electromagnetic Spectrum: A Legal-Economic-Engineering Study", *Stanford Law Review* (June, 1969), pp. 1499-1561. Comprehensive article on how private property rights could be allocated in radio-TV frequencies.

F. A. Hayek, "Three Elucidations of the Ricardo Effect", *Journal of Political Economy* (March-April, 1969), pp. 274-85. It's great to have Hayek back writing economics, this time a welcome addition to Austrian business cycle theory, in rebuttal to the criticisms of Sir John Hicks.

Henry Hazlitt, "Compounding the Welfare Mess", *National Review* (Feb. 24, 1970). Brief critique of the Nixon welfare program.

Robert A. Mundell, "Real Gold, Dollars, and Paper Gold", *American Economic Review* (May, 1969), pp. 324-31. An anti-gold Chicago economist concedes that the root cause of the balance of payments problem has been the American artificial undervaluation of gold.

Robert R. Palmer, *The Age of the Democratic Revolution* (2 vols., Princeton University Press, paperback). Professor Palmer's epochal work now in paperback. An integrated study of the French and other European--as well as the American--Revolutions, showing the connections. Definitive. American Revolution is shown to be a truly radical one. Sympathetic to the revolutionary cause.

Warren C. Robinson, "A Critical Note on the New Conservationism", *Land Economics* (November, 1969), pp. 453-56. When the ignorant blather of conservationists was at last refuted by economists a decade or so ago, the conservationists fell back to a more limited position, of preserving a few natural amenities. Refuted here by Prof. Robinson, who also points out that the average taxpayer earns hardly more than half the average income of the wilderness camper whom that taxpayer is forced, by the conservation program, to subsidize.

SUBSCRIBE NOW

Please enter a subscription for:

Name _____

Street _____

City _____ State _____ Zip _____

Subscription is $7.00 per year.
Student subscription $5.00 per year.

Bulk Rates. 20 or more, 10¢ each; 50 or more, 8¢ each.
Libertarian Forum Associate subscription is $15.00 or more.

THE LIBERTARIAN FORUM
Box 341   Madison Square Station
New York, New York 10010

Census Resistance

This is the year of the decennial Federal snoop, the compulsory invasion of the privacy of each one of us by our Big Brother in Washington. In addition to the usual head count, the Census Bureau will mail every person a questionnaire, forcing us to answer a minimum of 23 questions, under penalty of a $100 fine. Furthermore, twenty percent of us will be compelled to fill out an additional questionnaire containing over 66 questions.

One way of combatting the compulsory Census is to support those bills in Congress to make the non-head count questions strictly voluntary. Another way is Resistance. If you decide to resist (the maximum penalty for this step being a $100 fine after legal prosecution) or even to answer the questions under protest, CENSUS RESISTANCE '70 provides a form for you to send to them, informing them whether you are answering under protest or are refusing to answer the questions; they also have a form for you to attach to your census questionnaire telling the Census Bureau of your protest or refusal. In this way, CENSUS RESISTANCE '70 is organizing a mass protest movement. Furthermore, this organization plans to take to the federal courts and on up to the Supreme Court to fight the first case in which the government tries to fine someone for census refusal (Only two such fines were levied in the 1960 census). For information, write to: CENSUS RESISTANCE '70, 304 Empire Building, 13th and Walnut Sts., Philadelphia, Pennsylvania 19107.

Capsule Wisdom

"Is it reason that produces everything: virtue, genius, wit, talent and taste. What is Virtue? Reason in practice. Talent? Reason enveloped in glory. Wit? Reason which is chastely expressed. Taste is nothing else than reason delicately put in force, and genius is reason in its most sublime form."

M. J. DeChenier — 1806

NEW!

Book Service, selling pamphlets by Murray Rothbard, Karl Hess, Lysander Spooner, and others. Also, laissez-faire and anarchist buttons. For information, write to:

LIBERTARIAN—ANARCHIST BOOKSERVICE
GPO Box 2487, New York, N. Y. 10001

The Libertarian Forum
BOX 341
MADISON SQUARE STATION
NEW YORK, NEW YORK 10010

First Class

Published on the first and fifteenth of every month.   Subscription rate: $7.00 per year; Student subscription rate: $5.00 per year

A Semi-Monthly Newsletter

THE
Libertarian Forum

Joseph R. Peden, Publisher   Washington Editor, Karl Hess   Murray N. Rothbard, Editor

VOL. II, NO. 8   APRIL 15, 1970   35¢

The Cure For Air Pollution

The new glamor issue in American politics is pollution. It is common to hear predictions that human life has only a few more decades left on this planet. And it is common to hear increasingly strident demands for massive governmental action to stop pollution NOW. Only the government can save us, so the chorus goes, from the evil industrialists who pollute in order to make a profit.

This "emergency" is exactly what the Monster in Washington wants. Just as war and depression are used as excuses for stampeding the people into turning their lives over to an all-too-eager government, so pollution promises to be the issue that will keep the Monster fed now that the people are taking its war away from it. Before we feed the Monster, let us look at its role in causing the pollution crisis.

We will not look at the multitude of ways government itself pollutes (Atomic Energy Commission, Army Engineers, Supersonic Transport, etc.) or encourages others to pollute (farm program, oil import restrictions, highway construction program, etc.). Instead we will do what must seem rather strange for a libertarian, by focusing on an area where government should have acted but didn't (which is rather strange for a government). Government has defaulted in the little-known corner of the law known as the law of nuisance.

The right to property necessarily implies the right to use one's property free from the interference of others, as well as the obligation not to use it in any way which interferes with the rights of others. One who dumps garbage on your lawn is violating your right to property. More subtly, one who allows particulate matter to escape from his factory smokestack five miles away so that it leaves a layer of soot on your house is also violating your right to property. Because he is violating your rights, he has no right to operate in such a manner. His only moral alternatives are to find a way of running the factory so that it doesn't pollute your property, to pay you to put up with the pollution, or to close the factory.

Unfortunately, the law of nuisance has applied this principle only partially. The reason is the peculiar division of the law of nuisance into two parts—private and public—which have little in common with each other. Private nuisance is a field of tort liability in which an individual can maintain an action to collect damages for or to enjoin any unreasonable intereference with his use or enjoyment of his land. Public nuisance is a field of criminal law in which the state can prosecute anyone whose act or omission causes incon-venience or damage to the public at large. Almost all public nuisances are defined by statutes. The only time an individual is allowed to bring an action for public nuisance is when he has suffered a special damage which the public at large has not suffered.

Air and water pollution caused by industry obviously fall into the category of public, rather than private, nuisance because it often affects thousands of people. And since it affects the people in a given area relatively uniformly, no private individual is allowed to sue. The only thing left is government prosecution, but government has typically been the "partner" of industrial polluters until now.

Why does government prohibit private suits for public nuisances? The official reason is to prevent a "multiplicity of suits", but the reason underlying that is to prevent the hindrance of industrial expansion by making industry pay for its pollution or stop polluting.

Even if private suits for public nuisances were allowed, the slowness and costliness of the statist adjudication system would be an effective bar to the maintenance of property rights in most cases. A major reason why people have not put more pressure on the courts to allow private suits for public nuisances is probably that most people realize that the courts are simply too inefficient to help them.

What is the result of all this? Pollution has reached its present destructive level largely because people whose rights have been violated have not been provided a legal remedy, and because the monopolistic nature of government prevents them from turning elsewhere for a remedy. It is as if the government were to tell you that it will (attempt to) protect you from a thief who steals only from you, but that it will not protect you if the thief also steals from everyone else in the neighborhood, and further, that it will prevent you from protecting yourself.

Now that the pollution problem has literally thrust itself into people's faces, they attack the profit system and demand that government "go after" industry. To continue the above analogy, it is as if people were to respond to a rash of thefts by attacking the character of everyone who enters the neighborhood and by demanding that the government lock up all such strangers.

The solution is not to protect businessmen from paying for their own pollution, nor is it to penalize businessmen for being businessmen. The solution is to recognize the right of individual people to protect their property rights.

—— Frank Bubb

U.S. IMPERIALISM

Spurred on the experience in Vietnam, a whole new generation is demanding to know the truth about American foreign policy. They no longer believe the continual flow of lies coming from the State Department and Pentagon. They want to know why U. S. soldiers, bombs and napalm are massacring a whole people in southeast Asia. Why are American boys being sent to kill and die in the hills and jungles of a peasant country ten thousand miles away? Whose interests are these soldiers defending? Since it is the peasants who are being slaughtered (perhaps by the millions), it is obvious that it is not the peasants' interests that are being defended. The questioning generation in the U. S. knows that it is not *their* interests that are being "defended". Just *whose* interests are being defended?

Fortunately, each year brings an increasing number of profound Cold War myth-debunking or "revisionist" articles and books into publication. During the past decade an important reawakening to place among academics, and among radicals in general, concerning the nature and history of U. S. imperialism which have helped to shed light on whose interests America's foreign policy has been defending in southeast Asia and elsewhere. 1969 was a vintage year for such works. Apologizing for passing over other important contributions, it seems fair to limit the field to the following three works mainly because of their brevity, pointedness and clarity: *Corporations and the Cold War* , ed. by David Horowitz (Monthly Review Press, 249 pp.); *The Roots of American Foreign Policy* by Gabriel Kolko (Beacon Press, 166 pp.); and *The Age of Imperialism* by Harry Magdorff Monthly Review Press, 208 pp.). Each of these books is an important contribution in its own right; taken together, they combine to become a superb introduction to a clearer understanding of U. S. imperialism.

The Horowitz collection contains a seminal essay by William A. Williams, "The Large Corporation and American Foreign Policy", in which this master revisionist sets forth his grand thesis: In the 1890's after the manifest destiny of continental empire had been fulfilled, the businessmen and governmental leaders continued on with the "frontier thesis" mentality. That is, they believed that the option of continental expansion had acted as a safety valve which served to ease the social and economic dislocations among the more populous and established business, industrial and agricultural communities. There was some truth to this thesis, and since the depressed economic conditions of the 1890's coincided with the end of the continental frontier, the "frontier thesis" was further confirmed in the minds of the ruling elite. This confirmation was fashioned into an institutionalized ideological faith.

Rather than busying themselves with the necessary task of restructuring (decentralizing and liberating, my solution, not Williams') the domestic economy (an economy which was seriously distorted by both the Civil War and postwar intervention), the U. S. ruling class began on a well planned course of extra-national political-economic expansion within the categories of the "frontier thesis" in order both to "solve" the domestic ills and to maintain and extend their own position of economic control within the domestic sphere. The ideology which accompanied this expansion was that the extension of the free market was an extension of freedom. However they, of course, never tried to reconcile the inherent contradiction of free trade rhetoric and the central role that the state played in bringing about that "free trade". Freedom, self-determination and international peace came to be defined in terms of conditions which did not interfere with the new engine of international peace and freedom— "America's" expanding commercial relationships otherwise known as the Open Door Policy.

The American foreign policy over the past seven decades has been a continuous implementation of this basic policy. "Economic expansion abroad equals prosperity at home" has been the constant theme.

Lloyd C. Gardner's "The New Deal, New Frontiers, and the Cold War: A Re-examination of American Expansion 1933-1944" in the Horowitz collection is a brilliant reinterpretation of the "Good Neighbor" Roosevelt Era. The New Deal, far from being a period of "socializing" the economy, was, in its first phase, a period when the corporate-liberal leaders of U. S. state capitalism regrouped themselves for reentry into the shattered international economy, this time better prepared at home (more centralized control) to gain absolute global domination. Foreign political-economic expansion once again became the key to pulling the domestic economy out of depression. Armed with the Reciprocal Trade Act, the Import-Export Band, Lend-Lease, and finally with massive military might, the U. S. leaders had, by 1946, gained what they sought—control of the "free world" empire including the IMF and World Bank abroad and the Full Employment Act at home.

The Open Door Policy had but one more nut to crack, Bolshivism, and so the Americans began and heated up the Cold War. Not only was entry into the Russian markets important, but perhaps even more importantly, the Cold War was needed (along with export and investment outlets) to maintain Keynesian "defense" spending which would ensure the smooth operation of the whole vast system, as well as keeping the "free world" from throwing off its imperialist yoke through leftist insurgency.

Gabriel Kolko begins his book with a very important chapter, "The Men of Power", in which he convincingly identifies Big Business leaders as the ruling class in America. He shows that this ruling class dominates all of the important command posts through which limits are placed on the American System, both economic and political. There is a definite appearance of pluralism throughout the system; however, although certain competition and dissent is tolerated with the limiting parameters laid down by the ruling class, no competition or dissent is tolerated which would change the fundamental character the system's limits.

Big Business needs have become the singularly important "fount" for determining both domestic and especially foreign policy. Two excellent essays in the Horowitz collection complement Kolko's findings perfectly: "Business Planners and American Postwar Expansion" by David W. Eakins is, in a word, a gem, and one looks forward with anticipation to reading his forthcoming book along similar lines. The corporate liberal research associations were very busy and very influential throughout the New Deal, WW II, and in the postwar period. These business "think tanks" served as the key link between Big Business and government both as a repository of policy plans and as a willing source of supply for key personnel to implement those policies.

The intricate interrelationships between the National Planning Association, the Committee for Economic Development and the plans and implementation of the Marshall Plan are studied in detail. The NPA had what was later to become the Marshall Plan ready in 1944 and they were only waiting for a politically propitious moment to make it operative. The plan had no humanitarian intent whatsoever and was based solely on American domestic needs to keep corporate liberalism from retreating back into depression, to bring all of Europe under the American hegemony, and to increase corporate profits. The Truman, Acheson, Harriman "Red Menace" campaign came to their aid, and the business community increased the velocity of that scare campaign to the

(Continued on page 3)

106

U. S. IMPERIALISM — *(Continued from page 2)*

point where the politically propitious moment did arrive.

The second of these essays is G. William Domhoff's "Who Made American Foreign Policy, 1945-1963?" The answer is that Wall Street made and implemented the policy during these years. Domhoff explores the vital importance of the Council on Foreign Relations as the key link between Big Business and the various executive departments which carry out U. S. foreign policy. In addition to the CFR, the importance of the CED, the RAND Corporation, the National Security Council and other organizations as additional links are discussed.

Kolko's chapter, "The U. S. and World Economic Power", is an important overview of the international economy and the U. S. role in it. Fortunately Harry Magdoff's more detailed work fits in with Kolko's essay to give a more complete picture of the international web of U. S. imperialism.

Together they show how important the Third World's raw materials are to the U. S. domestic economy and that it is imperative for the U. S. ruling class to maintain access to and control over these materials.

Foreign aid is used in various ways to serve U. S. corporate interests (it serves no-one else's). It is used as a subsidy to the export sector. It is used to build infrastructure for the import sector. It is used to buy and maintain friendly *comprador* governments and oligarchies. It is used as a carrot to woo while military and CIA presence is used as the stick to convince. A careful mixture of grants and loans are used to make the various "free world" economies mere political-economic appendages to the U. S. economy. Both Kolko and Magdoff stress the "oneness" of U. S. economic, political and military foreign policy aspects. Magdoff's chapter "Aid and Trade" is an absolutely devastating exposure of foreign aid.

In his chapter "The Financial Network", Magdoff displays a keen depth of understanding concerning the nature of central banking and its role in the U. S. as an agency of imperialism. Central banking (the Fed), credit expansion, the major banks and their overseas branches, the IMF, and the dollar as the international reserve currency; all of these are discussed along with their interrelationships with one another and their relation to foreign aid and the spread of U. S. economic-military presence throughout the world.

Magdoff also destroys the "GNP myth" which states that since the annual foreign trade is less than 10% of the GNP, it is not very important to the economy, and therefore any talk of economic imperialism is just so much Marxist-Leninist propaganda. To say that, say, 5% of GNP is somehow unimportant in the first place would be ridiculous because 5% is a big chunk in absolute terms. But more importantly, what kinds of goods are included in that 5%? GNP figures tell us little. The imports are materials which are absolutely necessary for the survival of the system as it now functions. The exports are vital to those corporations which do the exporting. And, then, who generally controls these exporting and importing businesses? Members of the ruling class, of course. But even more important than the import-export trade is the overseas investment. Only the yearly capital exports are included in the GNP figures, the accumulated totals are not. Total revenues flowing from overseas investments have now reached the point where, by themselves, they are higher than the GNP of any other western nation. The relation between overseas investment, government aid in making those investments, and the profits thereby generated to the ruling class cannot be over-estimated. U. S. imperialism is a fact, GNP or not.

The two final chapters of the Horowitz collection strike the final death knell to any lingering illusions concerning the relation between free enterprise and the U. S. economy. The U. S. economy may be a market economy, but it is a

The Individualist

An excellent new libertarian magazine has just been launched! This is *The Individualist*, the new monthly journal of the Society for Individual Liberty, and an outgrowth of *The Rational Individualist*, the magazine of the predecessor Society for Rational Individualism. *The Individualist* is a fully professional magazine, with numerous ads, and excellent layout and art work; the new publisher is the young libertarian, James Dale Davidson, who is also executive director of the new and rapidly growing National Taxpayers Union. Featured in the initial, February, 1970 issue (recently off the press) is an article on "The Great Ecology Issue: Conservation and the Free Market", by Murray N. Rothbard, who will contribute a monthly economic column for the magazine. The article is a libertarian critique of all aspects of the latest Ecology, or Environment, craze.

The forthcoming March issue will focus on a critique of the Pentagon and military spending, featuring an informative inside look at military spending by former Assistant Secretary of Defense A. Ernest Fitzgerald.

The Individualist is a bargain, available for 75¢ a copy, or $5.00 per year, at 415 Second St., N. E., Washington, D. C. 20002.

---

ruling class encapsulated, increasingly fascistic market economy. Joseph D. Phillips' "Economic Effects of the Cold War" and Charles E. Nathanson's "The Militarization of the American Economy" are frightening essays which show just how intimately interrelated business and government have become. It is increasingly difficult (often impossible) to tell where the one sphere ends and the other begins.

Kolko's final chapter "The U. S. in Vietnam, 1944-1966: Origins and Objectives" is probably the best short (52 pp.) overviews yet to appear on the history of the Vietnam War and on Vietnam's strategic importance to the U. S. world empire. The Vietnamese War was *not* an inexplicable mistake into which the U. S. just happened to slip. *Neither* is the war a civil war. It is an imperialist war between the people of Vietnam and the American imperialist aggressors aided by their *compradors* in Saigon.

Kolko goes through the history of U. S. involvement in Vietnam from Yalta and Potsdam, to the victory of the people's revolution in China, to the complete economic support of the French via Marshall Plan funds, to the Geneva Conference of 1954, to American "advisors", and finally through the massive buildup of ground troops and the introduction of advanced mass murder techniques—good old "Yankee knowhow".

One point is brought out with particular clarity. The U. S. ruling class is indeed rightly worried about the "fall" of Vietnam leading to a series of similar "falls" throughout southeast Asia and elsewhere; for the domino theory *is correct*, though not in the crude sense that it is usually presented. As the Vietnamese win their self-determination by throwing off the American aggressors and their *comprador* Saigon regime, other peasants will see that it can be done, and together, the peoples of southeast Asia will ultimately push the American beast from their lands. As this happens the U. S. world hegemony will begin to crumble everywhere, and consequently the domestic system which depends for its stable existence on the world empire will enter a period of internal convulsions.

If libertarians are ever to forge a movement, they must be knowledgeable social critics, thoughtful strategists and relevant activists. To do this, they must know and understand the enemy (they must know whose interests are being defended in Vietnam), i. e., they must know and understand U. S. imperialism. An investment of several hours in reading these three books will take one a long way towards such an understanding.

— Vincent Ninell

The Tuccille Book

Sound the trumpet! Ring dem bells! I have recently had the privilege of reading the manuscript of Jerome Tuccille's forthcoming new book, *Radical Libertarianism: A Right-Wing Alternative*, which Bobbs-Merrill will be publishing in May. It is an extremely important book, and one which I can recommend wholeheartedly.

The vital importance of Jerry Tuccille's book lies in its filling a critical gap that has long existed in the libertarian literature. In the past year especially, numerous college students and other new people have shown increasing interest in libertarianism and in our libertarian activities. But, when they come to us and ask for a single book that will clearly, simply, yet comprehensively show them what libertarianism is all about, what have we been able to offer them? Only a scattering of mighty tomes, leaflets, and journal articles, all important, but none of which can provide to the newcomer a clear and comprehensive survey of the field. The loss of adherents to our cause because of this defect has undoubtedly been great.

But now Jerry Tuccille arrives to remedy this crucial defect. The Tuccille book provides, with great lucidity and clarity, inexpensively and in remarkably short space, a thorough survey of not only the basic principles, political, economic, and strategic, of libertarianism, but also an exciting recent history of the libertarian movement, and its relationship to the various strands of "Left" and "Right". Now we have a book to give to the budding libertarian—and one which all of us can enjoy as an overview of the field. After the neophyte reads *Radical Libertarianism* we can then supply him with more specialized readings as he so desires.

Another great boon for the cause is the fact that Jerry's book is being published by a prominent, major publisher. This means that the book can and hopefully will be widely available, and also that each one of us can push the book in our local book, library, college, radio, and TV outlets. The Tuccille book gives us a focus for education, and for agitation, a central focal point for our activity. Many youthful libertarians have been understandably restive at the lack of clear-cut forms of activity which they may usefully undertake. Well, here is a center for their activity of which they can be truly proud.

A particularly welcome feature of the book, from my point of view, is the remarkable soundness of Jerry Tuccille's positions on virtually every one of the problems with which he deals. It is not very often that a critic as notoriously finicky as myself, as ready as I am to do battle with "heresies" of the right or the left, can find so little to disagree with as in Tuccille's *Radical Libertarianism*.

You owe it to yourself: read this book, then recommend or buy it for your friends. And then *push it*—everywhere!

Details on the price, etc., will be printed here as soon as the book is available.

Note: The book has already received a good advance notice in Virginia Kirkus' newsletter for librarians, an excellent one in *Publishers' Weekly*, and a grudging acknowledgment in *National Review*. Onward and upward!

Recommended Reading

Now in paperback:
Two excellent new books, reviewed earlier in the *Forum* :
James Weinstein and David W. Eakins, eds., *For a New America* (Random House, paper, $2.95), reviewed Mar. 15.
Jane Jacobs, *The Economy of Cities* (Random House, paper, $1.95), reviewed Feb. 15.

Two *economics* textbooks: new and improved editions have recently appeared of the following excellent economic texts:
Morris Bornstein, ed., *Comparative Economic Systems* (Revised edition, Homewood, Ill.: Richard D. Irwin). By far the best reader on this topic. Contains crucial articles by Mises and Hayek on the impossibility of economic calculation under socialism, Hayek's famous article on the price system as a transmitter of knowledge, Eucken on central planning in Germany, and the best single article on free-market developments in Yugoslavia by Rudolf Bicanic.
W. E. Kuhn, *The Evolution of Economic Thought* (2nd edition, Cincinnati, Ohio: Southwestern Pub. Co.). A completely neglected volume, this is the best text on the history of economic thought. Contains a full and fair account of Menger, Bohm-Bawerk and the Austrian School, the Mises-Hayek theory of the business cycle, and the Mises-Hayek refutation of economic calculation under socialism.

SUBSCRIBE NOW
Please enter a subscription for:
Name ___
Street ___
City ___ State ___ Zip ___
Subscription is $7.00 per year.
Student subscription $5.00 per year.
Bulk Rates. 20 or more. 10¢ each; 50 or more. 8¢ each.
Libertarian Forum Associate subscription is $15.00 or more.
THE LIBERTARIAN FORUM
Box 341   Madison Square Station
New York, New York 10010

The Libertarian Forum
BOX 341
MADISON SQUARE STATION
NEW YORK, NEW YORK 10010

First Class

Published on the first and fifteenth of every month.   Subscription rate: $7.00 per year; Student subscription rate: $5.00 per year

A Semi-Monthly Newsletter

THE
Libertarian Forum

Joseph R. Peden, Publisher

Murray N. Rothbard, Editor

VOL. II, NO. 9   MAY 1, 1970   35¢

Farewell To The Left

Now that Spring has arrived, the Left is on the move again, but where is it going, and how is it trying to get there? After five months of torpor, the anti-war demonstrations on April 15 were a feeble shadow of last November, and the fragmented crowds seemed more interested in the irrelevant problem of the Black Panthers than in opposing the expanding war in Southeast Asia. Concentrating on the Panthers not only deflects support and attention from the anti-war cause; it also focuses efforts on purely legal defense instead of opposition to the government's war policies.

And there is another consideration. Too many in our movement are willing to sacrifice truth and the making of vital distinctions on the altar of political "unity" with our supposed allies. It is true that the police murder of Panthers Hampton and Clark in Chicago last December was unconscionable. It is also true that a systematic campaign to destroy the Panthers by all levels of government seems to be underway. But we must also distinguish the New York trial of the Panthers from the Hampton-Clark murder and the Chicago trial of the Conspiracy 7. For the Panthers in New York are charged, not with dissenting speech as was the Conspiracy, but with a conspiracy to bomb department stores—an undoubted criminal offense. The fact that their excruciating high bail discriminates against the poor and serves to imprison the Panthers before conviction is true and deplorable. But it is also true that these particular Panthers *might well* be a group of criminals and therefore deserving of no support whatever from anyone claiming to be a libertarian.

In recent months, in fact, there has been an increasingly dominant tendency on the Left—apart from the nefarious bombings—to engage in wanton violence against property that is indisputably private. The latest tactic of the Left is "trashing"—the indiscriminate breaking of windows on houses, buildings, cars. Trashing may be psychologically satisfying to those who enjoy acts of destruction; but what else can it accomplish? Strategically, trashing is an excellent means of "turning off" almost everyone, working class and middle class alike, all of whom react in horror to such wanton nihilism, and who know full well that their own properties might be next. And even apart from strategy, what is the meaning and purpose of trashing? What but an indiscriminate assault on private property, and therefore on the concept of private property itself?

In the days of the New Left, of for example the Berkeley, Columbia, San Francisco State and Peoples' Park struggles, their assault was against property that was either clearly governmental, or was governmental down-deep (such as Columbia). It was then possible for libertarians to support such people's campaigns against State and State-created property. But the current, or Newest Left, shows no interest in any such distinctions; it seems to be against all property period, and especially property that is private. Take, for example, last year's seizure of a small, undeniably private, and non-governmental Spanish church in East Harlem by a Puerto Rican gang called the Young Lords. The Young Lords seized the church by force and violence, and demanded the "right" to use the church premises to feed and indoctrinate the public, all in the name of calling themselves "the community" and "the people". As if the congregation that owns the Church is not just as much a part of "the people" as this youth gang! Being anti-Christian, furthermore, the Young Lords could only see the Church space as remaining "unused", since religious services cannot qualify as legitimate "use".

The shocking point about this hooligan action was not so much the act itself, but the response on the part of New Yorkers. The entire Liberal community reacted by lavishing praise upon the Young Lords, and it chastised the church for not being responsive to the "needs of the people". Not one word was devoted to attacking this deed as aggression against private property. Even the libertarian movement in New York was strangely silent.

Recently, hooliganesses of the Women's Liberation Movement seized the offices of Grove Press, and issued numerous "demands". One particularly revealing demand was the call upon Grove Press to stop printing "dirty books" which "degrade women". Once again, Women's Lib shows itself to be a twisted 20th-century reincarnation of Puritanism, of the old harridan Carrie Nation destroying bars and saloons with her ax. But the point is that once again the Left, almost automatically, employed violence—not against government property, or quasi-government property, or against the police—but against property that is indisputably private. Fortunately, Grove Press did not answer in the spineless Liberal manner of John Mack Carter, editor of the *Ladies' Home Journal*, to a similar recent invasion. Instead of defending his office, Carter spoke to these intruders for 11 hours, and wound up paying them to put out a women's lib supplement of the *Journal*. Grove Press called in the police to carry those female invaders out, and proceeded to charge them with criminal trespass. Crime is crime, and it must be put down with due and proper firmness; otherwise, appeasement of the criminal aggressor will only encourage his (or her) voraciousness for further aggression. As libertarians, and as people, we want a non-aggressive world; and to achieve this we must reinforce the general reluctance to commit crime by apprehending and punishing the criminal.

But, it might be asked, isn't it a terrible thing to call in the State police for self-defense? Certainly not. While no

(Continued on page 2)

109

FAREWELL TO THE LEFT — *(Continued from page 1)*

libertarian enjoys calling upon the State for defense, the fact remains that the State has arrogated to itself a compulsory monopoly of the function of police protection. In such a situation, the State police are the only ones we *can* call upon for defense. Who among us, set upon by a gang of muggers, would fail to call for the police if we could? But the defense of property against Left hooligans differs not one iota from its defense against non-political muggers. To say that calling in the police for defense against crime is immoral is also to say that walking on the streets is immoral or flying on planes is immoral, or sending a letter is immoral, because these are all, unfortunately, monopolized or subsidized by government. If it is moral to use the monopoly Post Office, it is equally moral to use the services of the State police to aid in one's defense against crime. For while the State is the *major* criminal organization in our society, it is by no means the *only* one.

And it is not only the current *means* employed by the Left that I am attacking; it is their new-found *ends* as well. Of what relevance to libertarianism, for example, are the demands of the Women's Liberationists? In what way is it "libertarian" to foist their perverted values upon the general culture and upon society? In what way is it libertarian to agitate for black studies institutes, or for a 5% raise for cafeteria workers? In what way is it libertarian in any sense to call for umpteen billion dollars of tax money to "beautify" the environment? Let us take, for example, the current demands of the student rebels and contrast them to the student rebellions of 1968 and 1969. The major 1968 demand at Columbia, the main purpose in view, was eminently libertarian: the divesting of Columbia from support of the American war machine. The 1968-69 student demand at Fordham was similar: to divest Fordham of the mercenaries of ROTC. But what are the current demands of the student rebels? At Columbia, the demand is so absurd as to be understandable only to the psychotic participants in our "counter-culture": that Columbia put up the bail money for the Black Panthers. What in the world has Columbia to *do* with the Panthers? The absurdity and irrationality of this "December 4" movement at Columbia should be evident. This is apart from the important point that the Panthers may well be guilty of the serious charges against them.

The current Fordham rebellion is demanding . . . what? Equal student participation with the faculty in determining curriculum and policy, and, in particular, the retention of an English professor who was denied tenure. Is this what the student "revolution" has come to? Once anti-militarist, are we now going to the barricades to enforce the principle that any teacher, no matter how incompetent, must be continued for life once he is hired? But who is better able to determine his competence, or who should be more in a position to pass such judgment, than his own colleagues in a department? Furthermore, to call for a voice for students in decision-making is scarcely the same as calling for equal or total student power. Students, after all, *do* know far less than their teachers; otherwise, why do they agree in such large numbers to pay considerable sums in tuition to supply salaries to those same teachers? The educational theory of the counter-culture: that students and teachers are all "equal", that no one knows more than anyone else, that courses should consist not of content and knowledge but of "rapping" about students' feelings; all this makes nonsense of going to school or college in the first place. For this kind of rapping can far better take place at the local candy store.

We can go further than this. If both the ends and the means of the current Left have become either irrelevant or antithetical to liberty, we must then ask ourselves: do we *want* the current Left revolutionary movement to succeed? Let us put it this way: if we could push a magic button, and replace Nixon and his Administration by, say, Mark Rudd

or Robin Morgan of Women's Lib, would we push that button? In my view, no rational libertarian could answer Yes to this crucial question. To contemplate America in the grip of the Weathermen or Women's Lib is to envision a truly nightmare world. Not only does Dick Nixon shine in comparison; I would venture to predict that a Rudd or a Morgan reign would make even Joe Stalin seem like Albert Schweitzer. For make no mistake: the Left is now in the grip, not just of Marxists-Stalinists, but also, for the first time in the history of Marxism, it is a movement that is Marxist in ideology but totally nihilist in attitude, worldview, and lifestyle. There have been few more repellent blends in the history of social thought than the current one of the goals of Stalin blended with the attitude and tactics of the nihilist Nechayev. For at least the Marxism of Stalin's day tried its best to be rational, to pursue the goals of science and reason; they did not pursue insanity almost for its own sake, or as a "liberating" force.

If, then, we have nothing in common with either the means *or* the purposes of the current Left, then we must cease thinking of ourselves, in the current political and ideological context, as "Leftists". We must bid farewell to the Left.

One tragedy in this whole affair is that many of the libertarians of New York, New England, and Washington, D. C. have completely forgotten the crucial strategic principle of Lenin: that, in associating with other groups, one must remain firm and steadfast in one's principles, while remaining open and flexible in one's tactics, in response to everchanging institutional conditions. The original idea in allying ourselves with the New Left was to work with a new generation permeated with strong libertarian elements. Now that the New Left has died, and its genuine libertarian elements have disappeared, objective conditions require that we make a tactical shift away from the current Left. Instead, too many of our young East Coast libertarians have done just the opposite of Lenin's strategic advice: they cling as a vital principle to the mere tactic of alliance with the Left; and they abandon their original principles (free-market, private property rights) that led them to becoming libertarians, and therefore into making tactical alliances in the first place. They have placed their very libertarian principles in the category of a disposable tactic, while they raise to the status of a mighty principle a mere tactical alliance. They have tragically allowed the means to become an end, and the end to become a mere means.

It was several years ago, I believe, that the brilliant young Marxist historian, Eugene D. Genovese, began denouncing the New Left as "nihilistic gangsters". At the time, I thought he was unfairly traducing a great and hopeful young movement. Now I think he might well have been more prescient, more far-seeing, than the rest of us. Perhaps Gene saw more deeply into the processes of change as they had begun their work. At any rate, "nihilistic gangsters" is certainly

(Continued on page 4)

NOTICE

Karl Hess is no longer associated with the Libertarian Forum and has had no responsibility for the material published in the Libertarian Forum other than that which appeared under his own name. For mechanical reasons his name failed to be removed from the masthead of this issue.

The shaky all was originally predicated on the assumption that, despite their obvious differences, they were really "natural allies" beneath the surface. Now that the breach on the Right has become a permanent fissure it might be worthwhile to re-examine this premise more closely to see just how valid it was to begin with.

Surely the rhetoric delivered by both camps was similar if not identical. Rand and Reagan, von Mises and Buckley have all spoken in terms of "individualism", "self-reliance", "free enterprise", "private initiative"; without exception libertarians and conservatives alike have denounced "collectivism" as the prime evil afflicting modern society. Theoretically, they appeared to be cut of the same cloth and when they disagreed on specific issues it was regarded more as a family squabble than as a serious falling-out over fundamentals.

The main bond cementing the libertarian-conservative alliance was an economic one; both schools identified themselves primarily with free-market economic principles. When conservatives became repressive on questions of civil liberties, censorship, sex and abortion laws, military conscription, libertarians took them to task but still continued to fall back on the "natural allies" argument. After all, conservatives were still champions of the free market. If they got a bit touchy on other issues it was because their basic premises were mangled. So what if they were a little inconsistent? Everybody knew that most conservatives were anti-intellectual and none too clever. All they needed was a little education. Stick with them and pretty soon they would all be libertarian radicals, quoting Aristotle instead of Jesus and Pope Paul, starting their own post offices and hiding draft dodgers in their finished basements.

Slowly it became apparent that the *only* common ground uniting libertarians and conservatives was their theoretical adherence to the free market. On virtually every single issue that came to prominence in the '60's—anti-abortion legislation; censorship of "offensive" literature; civil disobedience and dissent; repressive sex laws; the war; draft resistance; decentralization and neighborhood control; pollution; ad infinitum—libertarians and conservatives found themselves on opposite sides of the fence. It was at this point that libertarians began to ask themselves a key question: just what is the free market anyway? Is the free market merely the elimination of public welfare? Is it an end to income and corporate taxes? Is it freedom for company A and company B to produce war machinery for an overseas military escapade?

Or is the free market something else? Is the free market primarily the right of people, individually or cooperatively, to trade voluntarily without interference? If the free market is another name for voluntarism, voluntary trade and voluntary association, then does it not include *all* the issues enumerated above? Is not abortion a free-market decision between doctor and patient; "offensive" literature a free-market decision between seller and buyer; civil disobedience a free-market decision by individuals not to put up with legalized violence; sex a free-market decision between or among consenting adults; decentralization a free-market attempt to take power away from centralized bureaucracies? If the answer to all these questions was *yes*, then could it be said that conservatives really believed in the free market?

So it has come to pass that the free-market rhetoric of conservatives is just that: flimsy sloganeering. Neither Nixon in Washington nor Reagan in California is any more a free enterpriser in practice than were the liberals who

istration with a conservative one and you have merely come up with a change in priorities. The conservatives would rather fill the bellies of cops than those of welfare recipients, and perhaps they would prefer to raise public funds through a different set of taxing procedures—but these are the only real differences. It's difficult to see how any one administration is more *laissez-faire* in the economic sense than another.

If this is the case, it follows that the only bond left uniting libertarians and conservatives—dedication to the free market—is actually nonexistent. In fact, on an issue-to-issue basis, a better case can be made for the claim that there are more points of agreement between libertarians and liberals. At least liberals are more frequently libertarian on noneconomic questions and, as we are witnessing, *not much worse* than conservatives on the economic issues.

One practicing liberal who has grasped this fact lately is Tom Wicker of the New York *Times*. His article in the January, 1970 issue of *Playboy*, "Forging a Left-Right Coalition", was a perceptive look at the startling similarities between libertarians of the Left and Right. His column in the New York *Times*, March 29, 1970, "Will the Real Conservatives Please Stand Up?", describes how Senator Sam Ervin's bitter attack on No Knock and Preventive Detention laws is not inconsistent with his opposition to civil rights legislation. "Ervin's kind of conservatism . . . is not the kind . . . that holds cheap the rights themselves. It is not affected with the myopia that prevents fearful men from seeing that if individual rights are taken away from any man or class of men they are taken away from all; and that once suspended or destroyed they are most unlikely to be recognized again by a state power that will have been loosed from the restraints of the ages." We hear little talk of this kind from conservatives these days who talk instead of suspending certain liberties until the world is safe from communism.

Murray Rothbard has frequently spoken of the importance of both revolutionary and reformist tactics in the struggle for liberty. While we are organizing our tax rebellions and anti-war protests we might also consider the possibility of turning libertarianism into a major political force in the United States. The Free Democrats of West Germany have served a useful purpose, aligning themselves with whatever party comes closest at the time to their own ideals. The election of civil libertarians to office is useful for the very practical reason that they are less likely than conservatives to use repressive measures in order to crush anti-state activities. If we can stop thinking of libertarianism primarily in economic terms, and consider it instead in its broader aspects involving civil, social, moral, and intellectual freedoms as well, we will finally stop regarding ourselves as a "rational" subdivision of the Republican Party.

Libertarians and conservatives are no more "natural allies" than were Lysander Spooner and Edmund Burke. As free enterprise becomes less and less a part of Right Wing economic policy in American, the bond that tied libertarians to the Right grows more and more threadbare. So we find ourselves once again assuming the traditional libertarian position: intellectuals in opposition to authoritarian government—the disloyal opposition. As radicals in opposition to the status quo we are, by definition, members of the Radical Left as far as political posture is concerned.

As the '70's roll on it will, I think, be on the Left among the Paul Goodmans, Carl Oglesbys, and Norman Mailers that we find our future allies for freedom.

— Jermone Tuccille

FAREWELL TO THE LEFT — *(Continued from page 2)*

what the Left has become. Let us therefore bid them farewell.

I agree with all of Jerry Tuccille's strictures against conservatives in this issue; but the Left provides us no solace either. The distinguished Leftists he mentions are only a few of the honorable exceptions to the bleak Left-wing landscape.

We must face the hard facts: in the current world, we should think of ourselves as neither Leftists nor Rightists. We are libertarians period, with precious little hope of allies among the organizations of either wing. Since there is therefore no hope whatsoever for a libertarian revolution in the foreseeable future, our only viable strategy is to abandon the current thirst for mindless activism, and to build a long-run libertarian movement. In short, to leave the streets for the study, to place our emphasis on education, not just

for other people but also for ourselves, to build up and add to the noble structure of libertarian theory and scholarship that already exists. There is much work to be done, in developing libertarian theory as well as in spreading the gospel of that theory to those who have not yet heard of it. For those who are looking so desperately for something "to do", here is an enormous task waiting to be done:

We must abandon the range-of-the-moment view so typical of our counter-culture, and we must return to the long-range view of such of our founders as Albert Jay Nock. Nock, writing in an age (the 1930's and 1940's) of rock-bottom hope for libertarians, said that he did not despair, because in every age, no matter how benighted, there are always a few, a Remnant, that understands. At the very least, that Remnant will pass the torch of rational libertarianism to future generations. *There* is a goal which, while limited, has the virtue of being eminently attainable, if we but have the will.

Recommended Reading

Anarcho-capitalism, the idea that the free market can supply police and judicial protection by means of privately competitive agencies, was once only a gleam in the eye of the editor of the *Libertarian Forum* . In the past, the libertarian French economist Gustave de Monlinari championed the idea in 1848, shocking his mentor Frederic Bastiat with his "extremism"; but Molinari didn't elaborate the concept, and in later years he partially retreated from it. The American individualist anarchists of the late 19th century, Benjamin R. Tucker and Lysander Spooner, also championed the idea, but again rather sketchily. The major flaw in their proposal was that each jury was supposed to make an *ad hoc* , on-the-spot decision, without any guidance from a rational, objective Law Code requiring adherence to the rights of person and property.

In the last year or so, however, anarcho-capitalism has come into its own, and there are now available three expositions on how Stateless, privately competitive courts and police forces could work.

One, published last year, is a booklet by Jarret B. Wollstein, *Society Without Coercion* , available for $1.50 from the Society for Individual Liberty, 800 Hillsboro Drive, Silver Spring, Md. 20902. Another is the booklet by Morris and Linda Tannehill, *The Market for Liberty*, available for $3.95 from M. G. Tannehill, Box 1383, Lansing, Mich. 48904. And finally, there is an article by David Friedman, one of the most recent converts to anarcho-capitalism,

"The Prescriptions of 2001", in his column. "The Radical", published in the YAF magazine, *The New Guard* (March, 1970), available at 60¢ a copy or $4 a year, at 1221 Massachusetts Ave., N. W., Washington, D. C. 20005. Bets are now open on how long Friedman will be able to put up with YAF, and/or vice versa.

A fourth exposition will soon be available in the midst of a new, full-sized book by Murray N. Rothbard, called *Power and Market*. More news later.

Jerry Tuccille's scintillating new book, *Radical Libertarianism: A Right-Wing Alternative* (Bobbs-Merrill), will be available in early May. The price is $5.00, a veritable bargain!

Three excellent articles have appeared recently which, from different perspectives, strongly and trenchantly attack the irrational counter-culture of today's youth, while at the same time attacking the "rational" statism of the Establishment against which the youth are reacting. These are:

Robert Brustein, "Revolution as Theatre", *The New Republic* (March 14). The young left as irrational "guerrilla theatre".

Michael Novak, "Do Students Want Education?", *Commonweal* (March 13). No, answers Novak, sadly but strongly.

Robert Nisbet, "Subjective Si! Objective No!", *New York Times Book Review* (April 5). Assailing the anti-objectivity of recent radical "social science".

Published on the first and fifteenth of every month.   Subscription rate: $7.00 per year; Student subscription rate: $5.00 per year

A Semi-Monthly Newsletter

THE Libertarian Forum

Joseph R. Peden, Publisher   Murray N. Rothbard, Editor

VOL. II, NO. 10   MAY 15, 1970   35¢

THE STATE OF THE MOVEMENT

(Editorial Note: We are proud to reserve this issue for an article on the state of the Left by Professor Leonard P. Liggio. Of all the libertarians in this country, Leonard Liggio has had the closest long-time association with the New Left and with its most important publications. In the light of this special knowledge, Professor Liggio's analysis of the current state of the Left takes on particular importance. Leonard Liggio teaches history at the City College of the City University of New York.)

BY LEONARD P. LIGGIO

I

The Movement has been facing the disintegration of the primary centers of the New Left, especially SDS, with confusion and dismay. What is really necessary is rational, cool-headed and realistic analysis. First, the general reaction of confusion and dismay reflects both emotionalism and conservatism (the same thing ultimately)—sadness at the loss of something familiar. Second, it reflects a refusal to face reality, to understand the current state of the Movement on the basis of analysis of the past and allocation of responsibility.

The Movement is defined by the central issue of American politics—foreign affairs. American imperialism, abroad and imposed on the Black nation on this continent, establishes the American political spectrum. The Movement is the opposition to that imperialism. While the issues were not presented as clearly in the first half of the 1960's, in 1965 it became unquestioned. Vietnam has been world historically significant on a multitude of levels. The Movement's progenitors were the remnants whose commitment to anti-U.S. imperialism survived the New Deal's intervention in 1941: the Old Right, pacifists, and independent socialists. What had not been united by common ideology before, was fused by the common fate of sedition trials, FBI harassment, draft resistance convictions, etc. during the Second World War. A decade later this decimated group provided the chief opposition to U. S. intervention in Korea.

Draft resistance is the major focus of anti-imperialist activity. As a result those imprisoned for draft resistance have historically been the moral leadership of the Movement —after what they have suffered there is little more that the State can do. Dave Dellinger served his prison term for heroic opposition in the Second World War just as Larry Gara and Staughton Lynd did during the Korean War. Of that period, Michael Harrington wrote:

Thus the leading figures in the pacifist peace movement in the early '50's—among them A. J. Muste, Dorothy Day and David Dellinger—were from an earlier political generation. By and large they were isolated from the mainstream of American liberalism which supported the containment policies of the Truman Administration, backed the Korean War and

had not yet reacted to the H-Bomb. And being without any great political influence, they found themselves having to devote most of their efforts to defending their own political ideas: raising funds to aid conscientious objectors and draft resisters and fighting the government, particularly the FBI, which tended to confuse all opposition with support of the Soviet Union. ("The New Peace Movement", The New Leader, August 20, 1962.)

Opposing corporate liberalism, aiding draft resisters and fighting the government—the essentials remain constant!

When the Johnson-Humphrey administration escalated the U. S. intervention in Vietnam in early 1965, a unique grass-roots response developed on college campuses—the teach-ins. Spontaneous individual opposition to the government was offered the dual opportunity of immediate protest and of information for continuing protest. The teach-ins were organized by faculty and student groups, frequently including the local SDS chapter. The government's reaction was swift: to try to discourage them and where that was not possible to send out government speakers to repeat Dean Rusk's brilliant analysis of world affairs. On each campus the teach-ins became the starting point for long-term organizing against the war among the students and among their neighbors. But, their non-continuation relieved the government of the daily indications of grass-roots opposition represented in every college teach-in.

SDS played a central role in these events, since its radical opposition attracted thousands of students who were awakened politically by the war. SDS itself became temporarily paralyzed after the summer of 1965. Its opposition to the government had lost it its last friends among defenders of the American welfare state, starting with Irving Howe. It was in that milieu that some of the old guard SDS leadership had received its inspiration; and yet the popularly elected president, Carl Oglesby, and vice president, Jeff Shero, represented the large number of new members drawn from all over the country (bad-mouthed as "Texas anarchists" by the Old Guard). This newer group was described at the time by Staughton Lynd:

In SDS as in SNCC workers seek to apply the participatory philosophy to their own organizations, ask that central offices be abolished, leaders rotated, and executive committees be curbed by general staff meetings . . . For the moment participatory democracy cherishes the practice of parallelism as a way of saying No to organized American, and of initiating the unorganized into the experience of self-government. The SNCC or SDS worker does not build a parallel institution to impose an ideology on it. He views himself as a catalyst, helping to create an environment which will help the local people to decide what they want . . . In the meantime the very existence of the parallel institutions is felt to be a healthier and more genuine experience than any available alternative. It seems better to sit in the back of the room in silent protest against the bureaucrats up front than to seek to elect a man to join the executive committee. ("The New Radicals and 'Participatory Democracy'" *Dissent*, Summer 1965.)

With native American genius the SDS mass membership opted for direct opposition to U. S. imperialism—by confrontation with the draft. Coming from within the American people, they did not fear the Justice Department, Federal Courts or the rest of the U. S. apparatus of repression. The SDS Old Guard, however, faced by the FBI, sought the familiar cover of the government's apron strings, and using its vast liberal contacts in the Johnson-Humphrey administration, it managed to blunt SDS opposition during the fall of 1965. In this situation, others began to fish in troubled waters.

II

A coalition of groups was formed in Berkeley in the fall of 1965 to hold a mass demonstration against the war. Instead of the long-term organizing and hard ideological work that characterized the New Left, the Berkeley march was based upon the idea that U. S. aggression in Vietnam could be stopped quickly by the impression made upon the government by a mass demonstration. While one-shot mass action appealed to the traditions of the Old Left, the underlying conception was something different—the politics of theatre. Emphasis was placed upon publicity, *any* kind of publicity, for its own sake. The march was supposed to shake the foundations of imperial America by the "energy" that theatrical politics represented. This introduction of the theatre of politics alongside serious political work has had profound consequences, for it occurred simultaneously with the widespread introduction of the drug culture and was viewed as the politicized aspect of that culture.

That this occurred at Berkeley was not accidental. The Berkeley Free Speech Movement in the fall of 1964 against the educational factory system was one of the most revealing events of the 1960's. Its target, Clark Kerr, was the monarch of the academic establishment. One of his foremost contributions to contemporary civilization was the recommendation that to prevent rebellion against the "new slavery" (Clark Kerr's own term) that current American bureaucracy represents, the general use of drugs among the population should be introduced during leisure hours. Is it accidental that as the opposition and resistance to the Vietnam aggression became widespared among educated American youth, vast infusions of drugs occurred throughout the United States? Principals of high schools in major metropolitan areas permit the known selling of "foreign mud", as the Chinese call drugs, since it maintains their primary objective—order, which would otherwise be disturbed by the students' rage against the compulsory education system. As Henry Anderson has noted:

> What is needed is not more people blasted out of their minds. There are more than enough people out of their minds already, including almost all the world's statesmen. What is needed is more people in their minds—their right minds. It is not really humanizing to hallucinate that everything is lovable, loving and lovely. For everything is not. What is needed is more people who can see what is really there . . . Nothing pleases the keepers of our political-economic zoo more than contented, amiable, unambitious inmates. Nothing displeases them more than critics who voice their discontents and do something affirmative about them. Aldous Huxley perceived this clearly in *Brave New World*, and it is one of the ironies in this vale of ironies that Huxley himself became enthralled by what he had earlier perceived as one of the techniques of Anti-Man.

That irony is all the more significant for libertarians since

Huxley's example contributed mightily to getting libertarianism of its promising organizational and literary potential (in southern California typically); mescaline cultism in the late 1950's made libertarianism the weak reed it is today.

The Berkeley Free Speech Movement raised very significant issues about American society and its domination by corporate liberals. The role of libertarians in its leadership was heartening. However, it may be meaningful that once the Vietnam intervention had escalated and raised the level of consciousness, local libertarians tended to abandon their leadership roles and refused to participate in the development of the anti-war protest that led to the massive Vietnam Day rally at Berkeley in late May. Local libertarians were indeed denouncing the anti-war activists and leading the "filthy speech movement" instead. Why? Libertarians must examine their attitudes to explain their continuous failure to participate in meaningful opposition to the government, and their attraction to irrelevent actions. Libertarians must be credited with positive stands opposing the draft and contributing to the New Left's attack on conscription. But once that was achieved there was a tendency to reject long-term commitment to the practice of that policy and the inspiration of other policies consistent with it. Except for the rare individual libertarians, young and mature, who wrote, spoke or acted publicly against the war, the libertarians' silence on such real issues have been deafening. And then they wonder why they are not taken seriously.

III

During 1966 the Movement regained its momentum and its media-centered politics was balanced by serious organizing programs. This new impetus in SDS was the result of the emergence of "Prairie Power"; a real takeoff in the Movement had occurred. (Those interested in Movement thinking during this transition period should read the essays of SDS and SNCC organizers, and comments including Ronald Hamowy's "Left and Right Meet" in Andrew Kopkind (ed), *Thoughts of Young Radicals*.) SDS engaged in quiet, efficient and successfal organizing. It boycotted all mass demonstrations.

Among the reasons they were successful was the loose organizational and ideological nature of SDS. With almost no real national bureaucracy, each organizer and each autonomous chapter established its own forms, its own place, its own image. Since there was little official SDS ideology, and what there was was populist and libertarian, it was attractive to the large numbers of American students who were growing conscious of their opposition to the educational factory system, the bureaucracy, the draft and the war. They could develop politically in a Movement which could desire victory of the National Liberation Front in South Vietnam while wishing their own victory in America on a different set of priorities and philosophy. SDS's decentralization permitted the articulation of people's natural instincts for freedom.

If numbers of libertarians had participated in this development there was every reason to expect that libertarian inclinations could have been clarified into a consistent libertarian philosophy. At the time Movement people hoped very much that libertarians would participate actively. But libertarians generally attacked the New Left and criticized the few libertarians who understood the importance of the Movement to the future growth of libertarianism and the importance of libertarianism to the future growth of the Movement. No libertarian can honestly criticize the Movement who has participated in it. To those who bemoan the current situation of the New Left, one must legitimately ask: where were the libertarians when their participation would have made a difference?

Thus, in the absence of any number of consistent libertarians in the Movement, the natural instincts in SDS became confused. This confusion was aided by the entry into SDS of members of traditional socialist groups. Although traditional socialist groups hated SDS for its anarchism, *their* response was not criticism but participation. Just as libertarians assumed important roles in the Berkeley Free Speech Movement and anti-draft resistance because they had a consistent ideological analysis of affairs, so with the refusal of libertarians to participate, others with a consistent ideological analysis, in this case socialists, naturally assumed leading roles. In the reaction of SDS activists to this process, many became psychologically exhausted and retired, while others sought to fight the socialists organizationally without opposing their philosophy. In the end these activists rationalized their complete alienation from the rank and file of SDS and, in the last year, abandoned the rank-and-file SDS (after pestering them with their socialistic harangues), and sought a new rank-and-file among the street corner youth and the drug culture.

The roots of that turn in direction had two sources. One was the recognition after these elements in SDS had adopted socialism that the American blue- and white-collar worker as well as the SDS-oriented college student all rejected socialism as the means of liberation from total slavery in America. Second was the widespread growth of the hippie culture with its adoption of conservative, i. e., communitarian, ideas. The hippies with their biblical coats of many colors, modes of life, etc. became a ready attraction for the picture-oriented newsmedia. Their publicity attraction to the media was a magnet to those who, in contrast to the serious SDS organizers for whom anonymity was a primary premise, felt that publicity and politics were the same things. Some of the publicity-minded organizers of the Berkeley mass march, such as Jerry Rubin, had made the claim that the hippies were the revolutionaries. Along with Abbie Hoffman, a protest at the Pentagon in the fall of 1967 was turned into a hippie "happening" to levitate the Pentagon. (While politicized hippies were charging the ranks of the airborne division—once they had broken through they did not know why they had done it and withdrew—a last-minute SDS decision to send experienced organizers resulted in their convincing several dozen troops to defect and led to the new development of GI organizing.) From that "happening" the sky was the limit for media-oriented politics and the Yippie party was established to run a pig in the 1968 presidential election. Membership in the Yippie party never exceeded three but the media treated it as though it had fifty million. Why?

Perhaps some explanation is to be found in the following comment by Irving Howe, prince of the right-wing socialist gang who form the intellectual vanguard defending the existing academic system and who represent everything that libertarians are against. After abstracting the political New Left from his comments, he discussed the cultural New Left:

The "new leftist" appears, at times, as a figure embodying a style of speech, dress, work and culture. Often, especially if white, the son of the middle class . . . he asserts his rebellion against the deceit and hollowness of American society. Very good; there is plenty to rebel against . . . He tends to think of style as the very substance of his revolt, and while he may, on one side of himself, engage in valuable activities in behalf of civil rights, student freedom, etc., he nevertheless tacitly accepts the "givenness" of American society, has little hope or expectation of changing it, and thereby, in effect, settles for a mode of personal differentiation.

Primarily that means the wish to shock, the wish to assault the sensibilities of a world he cannot overcome. If he cannot change it, then at least he can outrage it . . . But "the new leftist" is frequently trapped in a symbiotic relationship with the very middle class he rejects, dependent upon it for his self-definition quite as the professional anti-Com-

munist of a few years ago was caught up with the Communist party which, had it not existed, he would have had to invent—as indeed at times he did invent. So that for all its humor and charm, the style of the "new leftist" tends to become a rigid anti-style, dependent for its survival on the enemy it is supposed to panic. To *épater le bourgeois*—in this case, perhaps, to *épater le père*—is to acquiesce in a basic assumption of at least the more sophisticated segments of the middle class: that values can be inferred from, or are resident in, the externals of dress, appearance, furnishings and hair-dos . . .

Victimized by a lack of the historical sense, the "new leftist" does not realize that the desire to shock and create sensations has itself a long and largely disastrous history. The notion, as Meyer Schapiro has remarked, that opium is the revolution of the people has been luring powerless intellectuals and semi-intellectuals for a long time. But the damnable thing is that for an almost equally long time the more sophisticated and urban sectors of the middle class have refused to be shocked. They know the repertoire of sensationalism quite as well as the "new leftist"; and if he is to succeed in shocking them or even himself, he must keep raising the ante. ("New Styles in 'Leftism'", *Dissent*, Summer 1965.)

The shared commitment of adult and youth to physical externals explains the media's insatiable hunger for new sensations and avoidance of serious political values. Among the media's creations has been the Black Panthers.

IV

Huey Newton had a brilliant approach to resistance to oppression: by tailing the Oakland police in the ghetto and insisting on police observance of ordinary civil liberties; Newton's insistence on the vindication of every person's right to carry arms was another positive contribution. However, the media found this a new sensation, and instead of encouraging Black people in other cities to develop similar neighborhood self-defense programs the Panthers launched a national party that imposed local units in other cities. The media trap has been literally fatal to the Panthers. The ever-thoughtful Julius Lester has offered an excellent analysis:

I see around me almost an entire generation of black youth being martyred needlessly and because I have been a part of the movement, because I have contributed my thinking to this revolution of ours, I must bear some of the responsibility for the needless deaths. It takes more than guts to make a revolution. It takes more than courage to risk one's life for an ideal. It takes more than a willingness to die. It takes sense enought to know when to say "Advance" and when to say "Retreat". It takes sense enough to know what your organization can do and what it can't do. Because one has a gun and some bullets doesn't mean to go out and shoot a cop. Cops, guns and bullets are not in short supply. They'll be there whenever one is ready. Prior to that, however, one needs to build himself a base, so that when he proceeds to shoot that copy, he has minimized as much as possible the dangers of losing his own life . . .

The deaths of Hampton and Clark were needless because they were totally without protection against what eventually happened. If they had a base in the black community, the police would not have dared come in and shoot them in cold blood. The Black Panther Party has support within the black community, but it has no real base. Its base is among the white radicals. Black America has related to the Panthers as involved spectators at a football game. They have not been involved as active participants. And because they have not, it is a simple matter for the police to come into the community and take off whomever it wants to . . . Just as it hurts the parent of a soldier killed in Vietnam that his child died for no reason, it hurts to say the same about Hampton and Clark. But it must be said in the hope that some lives will be saved . . . The young are the revolution's most valuable resource. The Panthers have used that resource irresponsibly, endangering lives when it was not necessary, and most of all, by adhering to a politics of romanticism, not revolution, a politics which enshrines the dead and does little for the living . . . And tactically, the Panthers should be supported . . . Though I find the politics of the Panthers to be, in great part, but not wholly, destructive, it is impossible to forget that the Black Panther Party is composed of individuals . . . I must oppose the organization and support the individuals in it whom 'the man' is trying to take off. (*Liberation*, February 1970.)

White radicals have been committed to media showmanship and not to serious politics. When SNCC in 1966 emphasized the concept of Black Power among Black people, the white former organizers of SNCC were asked to organize their fellow white people. For white America's liberation was the best thing possible for Black America's liberation. But this path was not pursued, since it was realized that organizing white Americans was not possible when grounded on the socialist concepts being espoused in SDS. Instead, SDS's leadership attacked those in the Movement who did begin such work. Thus, in April, 1969, at the Austin national council meeting, SDS condemned SSOC (Southern Student Organizing Committee centered in Nashville), which along with SNCC was SDS's fraternal associate. SSOC had been founded by the southern whites who had worked in SNCC. With the Confederate flag as its symbol it sought to develop political consciousness of their oppression among southern whites on the basis of their equally separate culture. The assault on SSOC was the clearest signal to the Movement of the New Left's organizational disintegration. Carl Oglesby has commented:

At the last SDS Thing I was at, the Austin NC, the handwriting was already on the wall . . . For a long time I was baffled. Last fall the word began to reach me: It was being said that I had "bad politics". How could that be, I wondered, since I thought I had no politics at all. But by winter I conceded the point: no politics is the same as bad politics. So there followed a time in which I experimented with only the "mass line". It didn't come to much. My mind and my instincts only became adversaries. By spring I had to deactivate, couldn't function, had to float. What I know now is that this did not happen to me alone. On every quarter of the white Left, high and low, the attempt to reduce the New Left's inchoate vision to the Old Left's perfected remembrance has produced a layer of bewilderment and demoralization which no cop with his club or senator with his committee could ever have induced . . . SDS will have to take its share of the blame for this. Much more interested in shining with the borrowed light of Panther charisma than in asking all the hard practical questions, much more interested in laying out the metaphysical maxims that identify the "vanguard" than in assuming real political responsibility, this SDS, which so often chews its own tongue for being "petty bourgeois", must shamefully confess its origins precisely when it tries to vainly transcend them in worship of "solidarity" which really amounts to so much hero-worship . . . it is not lost causes, however heroic, or martyrs, however fine, that our movement needs. It needs shrewd politicians and concrete social programs. Not theoretical (really theological) proofs that The People Will Win in the End, but tangible social achievements now. Not the defiance of a small, isolated band of supercharged

cadre who, knowing they stand shoulder to shoulder with mankind itself, will face repression with the inner peace of early Christians, but a mounting fugue of attacks on political crime of all sorts, on all fronts, at all levels of aspiration, from all sectors and classes of the population, so that repression can never rest, never find a fixed or predictable target. (*Liberation*, August-September 1969; this special issue has not been as widely read as it deserves.)

V

The restoration of good politics is required for the Movement's future. The disappearance of organizational efforts which practiced bad politics is a very favorable development and is a reflection of the basic health of the Movement. Furthermore, the conditions from which the Movement sprang have intensified. The factory educational system has not been restructured; the military system has not been abolished. Yet those who are subject to those systems, who are in schools and have to arrange their future choices facing taxes on their bodies and on their incomes to maintain militarism, are increasing daily. The overwhelming significance of this was presented in a special issue of *Fortune*, "American Youth: Its Outlook is Changing the World" (January 1969), which is must reading for anyone interested in the Movement; particularly important are the articles "A Special Kind of Rebellion" by Daniel Seligman, and "Student Activists: Free-Form Revolutionaries" by Charles Burck. The latter concludes: "Philosophically, what seems likely to be most durable is the Movement's strong individualism and its quest for personal freedom."

Seligman emphasizes that youth would be important today if only by their sheer numbers; additionally, "there is undeniably something special in the educational level of today's youth. Educated youth have to be taken seriously in any society; even when they condemn it bitterly, they are presumed to be its future leaders. Almost eight million members of the young generation today are or have been in college (versus about two million for that 1938 group). No other society in history has ever had to deal with *mass* educated youth." But *Fortune* is concerned not merely with college youth but with what it calls the "forerunners" among college students. "Forerunners", now almost 45% of college students, are those whose attitudes differ from others in college, but whose attitudes will become increasingly prevalent in society. Thus, *Fortune* emphasizes that it is not a question of a generation gap, which has the agreeable implication that this younger generation will accommodate eventually to the State. It is the attitudes of the 'forerunners' that will become dominant in America; "this particular young generation is by all odds the most interesting to come along in all of U.S. history," *Fortune* editorialized, "it will shortly preside over the revolutionary changes that await us."

The Libertarian Forum

BOX 341
MADISON SQUARE STATION
NEW YORK, NEW YORK 10010

A Semi-Monthly Newsletter

THE
Libertarian Forum

Joseph R. Peden, Publisher   Murray N. Rothbard, Editor

VOL. II, NO. 11   JUNE 1, 1970   35¢

The New Movement: Peace Politics

There is no doubt about it: Richard Milhous Nixon is the most effective organizer that the anti-war movement has ever had. Before Cambodia, and its ancillary Kent State, the anti-war movement was dead as a dodo. Confused and lulled by the Johnson Paris negotiations followed by Nixon's promises of withdrawal, the anti-war movement had all but disappeared into ecology and into the febrile nonsense of guerrilla theatre, Women's Lib, Weathermania, Panther worship, Yippies and Crazies, etc. The only organization with a potential for heading a mass movement, the Vietnam Moratorium, had dissolved in despair. Now, at the one stroke of the aggression into Cambodia and the consequent massacre at Kent State, Dick Nixon has revived the anti-war movement at a pitch, an intensity, a breadth and a sanity many times what it ever was before. A veritable Phoenix, a giant, has arisen from the ashes, and it's all a brand new ballgame.

None of this glorious flowering renders obsolete our recent pessimistic editorials ("The New Left, RIP", Mar. 15; "Farewell to the Left", May 1). On the contrary, one of the happiest facts about the recent upsurge is that, at long last, it consists of "real people", and this great influx of real people has totally dwarfed and rendered insignificant the whole gaggle of Crazies-Panthers-Weathermen, etc. of the extreme Left. The interesting point is that the shocking events of Cambodia and Kent State impelled millions of people to think at long last: "Alright, *now* this is serious. *Now* we *must* stop this monstrous war." And with this welcome turn to seriousness, the movement suddenly realized that all the hogwash and puerility, the guerrilla theatrics and the indiscriminate "trashings", the pointless demonstrations and the rock-throwings, had to go. Seriousness had to replace self-indulgence. And it was clear that seriousness could mean only one thing: concerted, non-violent purposive political action, that is, action upon our political "representatives".

To those libertrians who reject violent revolutionary action, either out of moral or strategic principle, I would say this: If you oppose violent action, then you have the profound moral obligation to favor and to press all effective forms of *non*-violent action. Non-violence must not mean passivity. In the present context, non-violent political action can take numerous effective forms, all of them amounting to irresistible political pressure upon the politicians in Congress and even the executive branch. The new anti-war movement has swiftly moved into these forms of action. There is the lobbying and the petition campaigns in Congress; one of the most effective and "consciousness-raising" is the petitions for the McGovern-Hatfield bill to cut off all appropriations for our Southeast Asia adventure after July of next year. Another is the mass campaign for the impeachment of Richard Nixon for his barbaric aggression in Southeast Asia, an aggression that is unconstitutional for its violation of the sole power of Congress to declare war, and flagrantly anti-libertarian for its high crimes against peace and against humanity, its mass murder and mass destruction. The fact that the impeachment campaign will undoubtedly not succeed is totally beside the point; its effectiveness lies in getting the previously unthinkable *idea* of impeachment of our rulers into the public consciousness; the result will be a massive desanctification and delegitimation of our rulers among the populace. So that maybe the "fifth" impeachment campaign from now *will* succeed.

Vigorous peace lobbying and political petitions mean finally, peace politics. It means favoring or punishing political candidates, particularly in the national arena, on the single crucial political theme of our epoch: war or peace. It means the same sort of ruthless concentration on this overriding issue that brought the Anti-Saloon League its victory in the Prohibition Amendment. It means, in short, that if two people are running for office, of whom A favors immediate withdrawal from Southeast Asia, while B is better on lower taxes or on price control but fudges on the war, we must choose A, and regardless of his party affiliation.

It has taken the Left-liberals, i. e. those who make up the bulk of the anti-war movement, a very long time to arrive at this sensible and cogent idea of Peace Politics. Indeed, this was precisely the overriding issue, the issue of war, peace and America's imperial foreign policy, that led me and a tiny handful of friends to "leave" the Right-wing over a decade ago. It was the Right-wing's inexorable shift from pro-peace "isolationism" in the thirties, forties and early fifties, to its current position of all-out war that made our break with the Right-wing inevitable.

It is long forgotten now, but the unsung originator of Peace Politics was Mark Lane, then an Assemblyman in New York. Many months before tragic events were to thrust him into the role of pioneer in Kennedy Assassination Revisionism, and at a time when the peace movement was Old Left and embodied in the SANE Nuclear Policy Committee, Mark conceived the simple but cogent idea that the Left should concentrate its political action on the one overriding issue of war or peace, and, for example, that it be prepared to endorse otherwise conservative candidates who might be better on the peace question than their liberal opponents.

I well remember the small meeting in New York called by Mark Lane to propagate his idea among the Left and among the peace groups. Aside from Leonard Liggio and myself, I don't think there was one person in that room who had anything but scorn for Mark's proposal. Pacifist after pacifist,

(Continued on page 2)

117

THE NEW MOVEMENT — *(Continued from page 1)*

leftist after leftist, liberal after liberal, arose to denounce
the idea: it would neglect and disparage civil rights for
Negroes, it would neglect the crucial goal of socialism, it
would subordinate personal "witness" and street demonstration for the more comfortable indoor activity of old-fashioned
political action. And so the opportunity was lost, the Left
and the anti-war movement drifted impotently for several
more years—until our bombing campaign against North
Vietnam, and the Lane idea of peace politics was lost and
forgotten, seemingly beyond repair.

But now the idea of peace politics has been almost
miraculously revived. The *student* movement has been
transformed into a *university-wide* movement of students,
faculty, and even college presidents. Young people who
became Clean for Gene are now, in far greater numbers,
becoming Clean for McGovern and Hatfield. Anti-war sentiment has expanded in the ranks of businessmen, particularly
those who do not subsist on the handouts of war contracts,
and even unto the President's Cabinet. The anti-war movement has, for the first time, become a truly *mass* movement,
made up in the greatest part, as we said above, of "real
people". These real people will be nothing if not repelled by
trashing, guerrilla politics, Panthermania, and all the rest
of the nonsense of the ultra-Left. Real people understand
lobbying and petitions, and they understand political action
at the polls. They can readily understand Peace Politics.
Here is the only direction that the anti-war movement can
go if it is to succeed. Already, the movement had succeeded
in toppling Lyndon Johnson, and now it has certainly caused
the Nixon Administration to be at least more cautious in its
evident aim of expanding the war.

You can't fool all of the people all of the time. The *Libertarian Forum* takes no pleasure in being consistent and
almost along, left, right or center, in predicting that Richard
Nixon's aim was not to withdraw from Vietnam but to get
further into the war under the guise of a rhetorical withdrawal. Nixon's lies and hypocrisies will no longer work.
The supposedly absolute June 30 deadline for withdrawal
from Cambodia is already seen at the time of writing (May
23) to be a sham and a hoax; for we will continue at the very
least to supply a i r and artillery support to t h e Saigon
invaders of Cambodia, and we will continue to use our fleet
to blockade the Cambodian coast. And what will happen when
the forces of Prince Sihanouk of Cambodia (recently deposed
by a CIA-led military clique) and his National United Front
(misleadingly smeared in the American press as "North Vietnamese") capture the Cambodian capital of Pnom Penh? At
the very least, a strong, militant and growing Peace Politics
movement might be able to prevent Nixon from following
his instinct to move into Cambodia *en masse* to make "free
Cambodia" safe for its current military dictatorship. At

the most, Peace Politics might be able to force America
to get out of Southeast Asia.

Jerry Tuccille's article in this issue, written before the
Cambodian invasion, turns out to be remarkably prescient.
For now its call for a form of tactical rapprochement with
Left-liberalism h a s suddenly become of t h e highest
relevance. And Peace Politics is the path.

The New Libertarianism

With the official disbanding of the Vietnam Moratorium
Committee and the disintegration of New Left activism in
general, a vacuum has been created within the radical movement. As the productive elements of New Leftism fade away,
the void is quickly being filled by a familiar two-headed
beast: the old scarred and ugly face of doctrinaire Marxism
and the more hideous visage of self-righteous nihilism. The
absence of a well-formulated philosophical base to support
the activist programs of the New Left has given birth to a
new generation of crusading irrationalists, frustrated bomb-
throwers, and penis-hating feminists.

What this means to libertarians is that the fundamental
anti-authoritarianism and anarchism of the radical movement is in serious danger of being eroded. The great
challenge that is presented to libertarians at the beginning
of the 1970's is to salvage this splintering movement and
transform it into a healthy and creative radicalism over
the next ten years.

It is to make the *New Libertarianism* the movement of the
1970's; to make our brand of radicalism as influential in the
next decade as the New Left was in the middle and late
1960's.

How do we go about it?

The first thing we ought to learn is how to avoid the
mistakes of our predecessors. The *last best* chance for
free market radicalism in the United States came in the
late 1950's following the publication of *Atlas Shrugged*
and the establishment of Objectivism as an organized
intellectual movement. Some twelve or thirteen years later
we now see that Objectivism has failed in its long-range
goals; it has failed to strike a responsive chord in the
general population. While Objectivist literature has sold into
the millions, the basic tenets of Objectivist philosophy have
not, and I think we can safely say, will not take root in
society at large. The high sale of books is no guarantee that
the public is also buying the *ideas* presented. A quick scan
of the best-seller lists is ample proof that people prefer a
"good read" more than anything else.

Objectivism has failed to become a mass movement
primarily because it failed to grapple, except in an arrogant
and highly superficial manner, with the key issues of the
past ten years. While Objectivists engaged in the exclusive
luxury of abstractions and ideology, a war was going on,
housing and education among other vital institutions were
coming apart, the cities were exploding with violence, the
American middle class was falling into a daze, and government grew increasingly more repressive.

What was the Objectivist cure for this? *Selfishness.*

What was the cause of all our ills? *Altruism.*

What should we do about exploited minorities? *Leave them
alone.*

This is hardly the stuff to fire the imagination of a populace literally begging for solutions and definitive answers
to their questions. *Why?* The Objectivists failed to respond.
Champions of the marketplace, they remained aloof from
the disordered marketplace of American society and the
public has rewarded them accordingly with silence.

If the New Libertarianism is to succeed it will have to
do so by responding to the issues, by applying theory to
the marketplace. The way things are shaping up, the primary

(Continued on page 3)

118

THE NEW LIBERTARIANISM —*(Continued from page 2)*

concerns of the next few years are going to be: the continuing war in Asia and its progenitor, an imperious U. S. foreign policy; ecology and pollution control; housing and education; women's rights (as distinct from the loony women's separatist fringe); day care centers for working mothers; the development of expanded abortion facilities; cheaper and better medical assistance for the poor. To these we can add our own *bête noir*—taxation and the regulated economy.

Instead of replying, "rational self-interest", when people want to know how to meet these concerns, we will have to demonstrate how a strict enforcement of property rights will protect them from environmental contaminants; why the free market will provide them with abortion clinics and day care centers (perhaps as a fringe benefit of private employment); how expanded health care can be made available to all without the AMA to lobby against competition and restrain the flow of medics into society. After all, is it not the purpose of the free market to supply demand in the most efficient m a n n e r? Why should suggestions to meet t h e demands of low-income groups be simplistically dismissed as altruism if these suggestions are in accord with libertarian principles? Is it not in our own interest to offer solutions to the issues before the authoritarians co-opt them for their own ends?

Another tactic we will have to develop if we are to build a mass libertarian movement is obtaining *favorable exposure* in the major media. The major organs of communication are largely controlled by liberals. It was the liberal news-media which actually brought the New Left into prominence through constant and favorable exposure. A blackout in the mass media will lead to the certain death of any incipient movement. If the ideas are not favorably analyzed by the opinion-makers (And let's face it. Public opinion is a manufactured product. If most people were rational enough to formulate their own opinions we would now be living in at least a *reasonably libertarian* society), their chances of taking root are reduced to nil.

To do this will require severing any lingering ties with the brand of "conservatism" currently practiced by the Nixon-Agnew-Reagan-Buckley Club and staking out a more independent course. The liberals are completely down on the New Left these days. They have finally realized that the current crop of New Leftists actually wants to kill them. "Kill a Parent a Day" was the theme of a recent SDS gathering. The liberals in their usual muddled and soft-headed manner are capable of sitting down over martinis and debating the pros and cons of whether they should be wiped out or not. By merely *not* advocating the wholesale slaughter of liberals we offer a Modest Proposal (If only Jonathan Swift were alive today) agreeable to at least the less-masochistic liberals. I have no doubt that some of them crave Death by Flagellation. But most are ready to lionize anybody who is not in favor of exterminating them and I see no reason why we should not capitalize on this situation while it lasts.

There is an area on the Left, ranging from Mailer and Goodman among the radicals to Hamill and Wicker among the quasi-libertarian liberals, that is becoming more receptive to the New Libertarian position. It strikes me that this is the best strategic position for us at the beginning of the 1970's, with the more outspoken critics of government repression who have access to the major communications media. The alternative is to remain in an ideological Ivory Tower, vilifying everyone not in full agreement with ourselves as "irrational" and "immoral", where we are certain to die the slow inevitable death of the Objectivists. If the New Libertarianism follows a similar fate, any hope for free marketism in the foreseeable future will vanish with it. It will certainly be a long time before an opportunity such as this is made available again.

It is for us now to succeed where the Rand and her mimics failed before us.

—— Jerome Tuccille

The Judges

Americans used to have an enormous, almost religious, reverence for the federal judiciary, and especially for the members of the Supreme Court. They were as gods. As a result, this group of life-appointed oligarchs, with the absolute power to make the final, ultimate decisions on interpretation of the laws and of the Constitution, had unquestioned power to rule our lives. Calhoun, one hundred and forty years ago, forecast the pernicious, statizing role of the Supreme Court, deducing his prediction from the very nature of government. If you have a Constitution, he pointed out, however rigorous the limits it places on government, these limits will dissolve if you leave the power to interpret that Constitution in the hands of a monopoly Supreme Court, appointed by the government itself. This means that one organ of government is able to decide on the limits of its own power, and over the years, the party in power will inevitably decide to keep expanding that power, and weakening its limits. The results, Calhoun saw early on in the process, will necessarily be to dissolve the constitutional checks on federal power. And that is precisely what has happened. The idea of a strictly limited, *laissez-faire* government turns out to be a Utopian, unrealistic one. It can never work, which is one of the main reasons why anarchists see the necessity for eliminating the State altogether, rather than try to limit and confine it once it is there.

In recent years, however, we have had the growth of a healthy skepticism and irreverence toward the Supreme Court, and the more this spirit of doubt and hostility spreads, the better. This means that libertarians should welcome all the campaigns to question or impeach the Supreme Court, regardless of the specific merits or demerits of the people involved. The seemingly foolish Birch Society campaign to impeach Earl Warren had the liberating effect of desanctifying, or de-legitimating, the Chief Justice in the eyes of much of the public. Ditto the roar of disapproval that ousted Abe Fortas, ditto the lengthy and caustic going-over accorded Clement Haynsworth and Harrold Carswell, ditto the impassioned drive to impeach Justice Douglas. All of these have their very useful cumulative impact. The Supreme Court will never be the same.

Movers, Write!

We have a highly mobile readership. Fine; but if you're going to be mobile, please send us a notice of your new address. Otherwise, the copy comes back to us unread, while you pine away for your missing copies of the *Lib. Forum*, railing at the Fates or at the inefficiencies of the magazine or the Post Office. In this case, the inefficiency is your own. So, especially now that colleges are out for the summer months, remember: send us your new address!

The Lenin Centennial

April 22 marks the 100th anniversary of the birth of
Vladimir Ilich Lenin, and is a date which should not pass
unnoticed by libertarians. And not alone because of our
gratitude to him for providing a colossal practical confirmation of Benjamin Tucker's 1897 prediction that "whatever
the State Socialists may claim or disclaim, their system, if
adopted, is doomed to end in a State religion, to the expense
of which all must contribute and at the altar of which all
must kneel!"

Quite aside from their socialist content, he who takes
advantage of this centennial year to review a few of Lenin's
writings will discover many sound principles of importance
to any movement opposing the *status quo.* The following
examples are drawn from the famous pamphlet "*What is to
be Done?*"

On theory: "Without a revolutionary theory, there can be
no revolutionary movement." The importance of theory is
still greater, because "our party is only in the process of
formation, its features are only just becoming outlined, and
it has not yet completely settled its reckoning with other
tendencies in revolutionary thought which threaten to divert
the movement from the proper path."

On alliances: "Only those who have no reliance in themselves can fear to enter into temporary alliances with
unreliable people." But, [now quoting Marx], "If you must
combine, then enter into agreements to satisfy the practical
aims of the movement, but do not haggle over principles, do
not make 'concessions' in theory."

On spontaneity vs. consciousness: Lenin mocks the view
that "in the same way as men and women will multiply in the
old-fashioned way notwithstanding all the discoveries of
natural science, so the new social order will come about in
the future *mainly* as a result of elemental outbursts, notwithstanding all the discoveries of social science and the
increase in the number of conscious fighters." He warns

that following the spontaneous movement, the line of least
resistance, leads to "the domination of bourgeois [read
"statist"] ideology for the simple reason that bourgeois
ideology is far older in origin than Social-Democratic
[read "libertarian"] ideology; because it is more fully
developed and because it possesses *immeasurably* more
opportunities for becoming widespread."

On terrorism: The terrorists argued that their methods
were necessary to "excite" the movement, and give it a
"strong impetus". Lenin replied, "It is difficult to imagine
an argument that disproves itself more than does this one!
Are there not enough outrages committed in Russian life
that a special 'stimulant' has to be invented? On the other
hand, is it not obvious that those who are not, and cannot be,
roused to excitement even by Russian tyranny will stand by
'twiddling their thumbs' even while a handful of terrorists
are engaged in single combat with the government?"

On organization: "Our primary and most imperative
practical task [is], namely, to establish an *organization of
revolutionists* capable of maintaining the energy, the stability, and continuity of the political struggle."

These and many other passages deserve the attention of
libertarians as the 1970's begin, for our movement today
has much in common with the bolshevism of the *Iskra*
period. As Lenin wrote in 1902,

> We are marching in a compact group along a pre-
> cipitous and difficult path, firmly holding each other
> by the hand. We are surrounded on all sides by ene-
> mies, and are under their almost constant fire. We
> have combined voluntarily, especially for the purpose
> of fighting the enemy and not to retreat into the adja-
> cent marsh, the inhabitants of which, right from the
> outset, have reproached us with having separated our-
> selves into an exclusive group, and with having chosen
> the path of struggle instead of the path of conciliation.
> And now several in our crowd begin to cry out: Let
> us go into this marsh! . . .
> Oh yes, gentlemen! You are free, not only to invite
> us, but to go yourselves wherever you will, even into
> the marsh. In fact, we think that the marsh is your
> proper place, and will render you every assistance
> to get there. Only let go of our hands, don't clutch at
> us, and don't besmirch the grand word "freedom". . . .

Within fifteen years of writing these words, Lenin's
"compact group" had become the dominant political force
in Russia. What can we learn from him to help us do as
well? What will 1984 bring if we fail?

—— Edwin G. Dolan

The Libertarian Forum
BOX 341
MADISON SQUARE STATION
NEW YORK, NEW YORK 10010

First Class

Published on the first and fifteenth of every month.   Subscription rate: $7.00 per year; Student subscription rate: $5.00 per year

A Semi-Monthly Newsletter

THE
Libertarian Forum

Joseph R. Peden, Publisher   Murray N. Rothbard, Editor

VOL. II, NO. 12   JUNE 15, 1970   35¢

THE NIXON MESS

It is increasingly apparent that the major qualities necessary to a man's becoming President (demagogy, slick political opportunism) are unsuited to resolving what the Marxists call the "inner contradictions" of his program and of the system for which he has become responsible. A President invariably begins his term with the enormous advantage of a lengthy "honeymoon" and the best of support from press and country; he continues with the enormous advantage of the power and prestige of his monarchial office. But his usual eclectic, vacillating, and *ad hoc* policies cannot, by their nature, resolve any major crises into which he and his predecessors' programs may have embroiled the country. It took "master politician" Lyndon Johnson four years to lose his "credibility" among the public; it has taken master politician Richard Nixon only a year to get into the equivalent mess.

The central feature of Nixon's Administration is the absolute contradiction between the rhetoric of his promises and the reality of his program. He has promised peace, prosperity, withdrawal from Vietnam, and a turn toward freedom of enterprise; he has brought us precisely the opposite. The contradictions have been so glaring that even the long-patient American public has begun to awaken to the true situation.

Take, for example, the draft. Nixon begins on a cloud of voluntarist rhetoric, hints about a volunteer army, and the appointment of the Gates Commission which recommends immediate repeal of the draft. Anarcho-Nixonite friends assured me at the start of his reign that, if he brought us no other goodies, *at least* he would end conscription-slavery. What has he wrought, in reality? A phony lottery scheme, phony because the high numbers are being drafted in addition to the low. And phony also because along with the supposed relief of the lottery came the increased slavery of removal of collegiate and graduate school deferments. So that the draft has gotten worse rather than better. Never before have so many of our youth contemplated flight to Canada.

Promising early withdrawal from Vietnam, Nixon has brought us only a widening and deepening of the war into all of Southeast Asia. The CIA-engineered overthrow of the popular neutralist Prince Sihanouk of Cambodia by a military clique meant that the tiny Cambodian Communist guerrilla forces (the Khmer Rouge) were joined by a mighty mass movement headed by Prince Sihanouk himself; now we and our puppets face the forces of the new National United Front, overwhelmingly backed by the Cambodian population. We have gotten ourselves into a much deeper tangle than before, even if our forces really leave eastern Cambodia by the end of June.

On the economic front, Richard Nixon's "free enterprise"

government has proposed a catastrophically statist guaranteed annual income program, which destroys the incentives to work among the mass of the population, a program which has only been temporarily halted by Senator John Williams' (R., Del.) embarrassing discovery that, in Massachusetts, for example, a family on the "negative income tax" dole can make over $7,000 a year, considerably more than the annual income of the average working family of the area.

Particularly embarrassing for Nixon and his "free market" economic advisers is Nixon's inflationary recession. Since approximately last November, the American economy has been in a decided recession, with industrial production and "real" GNP falling, other indicators of economic activity declining, unemployment rising, the stock market in dire trouble; *and yet*, price inflation continues galloping away at a rate of about 7% a year, while interest rates, already the highest for over a century, continue their inexorable march upward. All that Nixon's economic advisers can do is to continue to assure us that prosperity is just around the corner. As Gore Vidal acidly put it, historically Democrats have gotten us into wars, and Republicans into recessions; Richard Nixon has performed the notable feat of getting us into both, and at the same time!

The phenomenon of inflationary recession *cannot* be understood by Establishment economists, whether of the Keynesian or the Milton Friedman variety. Neither of these prominent groups has any tools to understand what is going on. Both Keynesians and Friedmanites see business cycles in a very simple-minded way; business fluctuations are basically considered inexplicable, causeless, due to arcane changes within the economy, although Friedman believes that these cycles can be aggravated by unwise monetary policies of government.

I remember vividly a prophetic incident during the 1958 recession, when the phenomenon of inflation-during-recession hit the country for the first time. I attended a series of lectures by Dr. Arthur F. Burns, former head of the Council of Economic Advisers, now head of the Federal Reserve Board, and someone curiously beloved by many free-market adherents. I asked him what policies he would advocate if the inflationary recession continued. He assured me that it wouldn't, that prices were soon levelling off, and the recession soon approaching and end; I conceded this, but pressed him to say what he would do in a future recession of this kind. "Then," he said, "we would all have to resign." It is high time that we all took Burns and his colleagues up on that promise.

For both Keynesians and Friedmanites have essentially one set of recommended policies for business fluctuations. In an inflationary boom, taxes are supposed to rise, monetary

(Continued on page 2)

THE NIXON MESS — *(Continued from page 1)*

policy to be more stringent; in various ways, and with different emphases among the two groups, money is taken out of, or not fed into, the economy. Conversely, during a recession, money is fed into the economy, deficits are incurred, and the economy stimulated. But, during recessions, activity and employment are supposed to be falling off, and prices falling; what happens if prices are still rising? Our economic managers are then caught on the horns of an escapable dilemma; if they pump money into the economy, they may turn around the recession, but then prices will gallop away at an alarming rate; and if they tighten the monetary screws in order to stop the inflation, then recession and unemployment will deepen alarmingly. The Nixon response, predictably, has been to take neither clear-cut line, but to fudge, hesitate, vacillate, do both and neither. And the result, predictably, is that Nixon has prolonged the dilemma, has prolonged the mess of inflation-*cum*-recession. With no clear-cut program, Nixon has impaled himself more and more upon the dilemma's horns.

When Nixon first came to office, he continued the rapid rate of monetary inflation of the Johnson Administration. Finally, his conservative advisers won out and Nixon stopped expanding the money supply, which remained constant from about June, 1969 to February, 1970. He was prepared to accept the recession which inevitably arrives when monetary inflation stops, or at least a mild form of recession; but he was also assured by his Friedmanite advisers that price inflation would end by the end of the year. The recession arrived, all right, on Friedmanite schedule, but lo and behold! prices have continued on their rapid advance. Having no theoretical tools to explain this, the Friedmanites could only come up desperately with wider and wider statistical "time lags", to the extent that Friedman has now begun to talk, almost absurdly, of two-year time lags between cessation of monetary inflation and a fall in prices. Frightened by the failure of Friedmanite policy, the Federal Reserve Board, under the supposedly free-marked and anti-inflationary Arthur Burns, has resumed, since February, the old disastrous 9-10% annual rate of monetary inflation.

The fact is that only "Austrian School" economics, virtually unknown today, can explain the phenomenon of price inflation of consumer goods during recession. It is not at all a question of mechanical statistical "lags", lags which seem always to change as the desired economic result disappears over the horizon. The Austrians point to two reasons for continuing price increases. One is unknown to the mechanistic Friedmanites, but acknowledged by other, more sensible economists: that prices depend not only on the quantity of money but also on the subjective demand to hold money on the part of the populace. As an inflationary boom proceeds and prices continually rise, *expectations* of future increases become built-in to the psychology of the public. Hence, their demand to hold money begins to fall, as people decide to make their purchases now rather than later when they know that prices will be higher. The mere cessation of monetary inflation cannot, all at once, reverse these inflationary expectations. Hence, prices will keep rising until the determination of the government *not* to inflate the money supply further becomes credible among the public. The Nixon Administration's anti-inflationary sincerity has never become credible, partly due to the hysterical attacks by Friedman and his followers on the hard-money, non-inflationary Nixon policy from June, 1969 on. With the money supply constant at long last, Friedman and his influential followers began a continuing drum-fire of attack, calling for resumption of Friedman's talismanic proposal of a continuing expansion of the money supply by 3-4% per year. When Burns and Nixon finally resumed monetary inflation in February, of course, Friedman now felt that they had gone too far, but the point is that Friedman's moderate inflationism had a disastrous effect upon the short-lived

non-inflationism of the Administration and upon its credibility among the public.

The second basic reason for inflation of consumer goods' prices in a recession is a uniquely Austrian explanation. For the heart of the Austrian theory of the business cycle is that the inflationary boom leads to over-investment of the "higher orders of production", an over-expansion in capital goods' industries. What is needed during a recession, and what the recession accomplishes, is a shift of resources from the swollen capital goods, to the underinvested consumers' goods industries. What impels this necessary readjustment is a fall of prices in the capital goods industries relative to consumer goods, or, to look at it another way, a rise in consumer goods' prices relative to other prices. The beginning of a recession is marked by wage and cost pressure upon profits in the capital goods industries, with selling prices in these industries relatively falling, and the relative rise in prices and therefore in profits in consumer goods inducing resources to move into these latter industries. The process ends with the end of, and therefore recovery from, the recession.

As a result, every recession in the past has been marked by this shift of resources, and a rise in consumer goods prices *relative to* capital goods prices (and also to other "producers' goods" prices, such as wages in capital goods industries.) But the point is that nobody worried about this, because in past recessions monetary deflation, contraction of the money supply, meant that prices in general were falling. Nobody cared, for example, if consumer goods' prices fell by 10% while producers' goods prices were falling by 20%. But now, absolute federal control of the banking system means that we never can enjoy an outright contraction of the money supply, and hence prices *in general* can never fall. Therefore, the relative rise in consumer goods prices that occurs in every recession now takes the most unpleasant form of an absolute rise in the cost of living.

The absence of monetary deflation and hence of a general fall in prices has unpleasantly removed the veil over the usual rise of relative consumer prices. The absence of the old-fashioned monetary deflation means that the consumers have to suffer both recession and unemployment *and* ever-higher prices of the goods they must buy. The supposedly "humanitarian" manipulation of the monetary and credit system to end old-fashioned deflation during recessions (a manipulation agreed to by Keynesians, Friedmanites, and even many Austrians), has brought us only the worst of both worlds: the worst features of both inflation and recession.

As for those annoyingly high interest rates, they must continue to climb ever upward; the only thing that can bring them down is a really stiff recession, a recession which *includes* the levelling off of prices. But since the Nixon Administration is not willing to contemplate a stiff recession and a truly anti-inflationary program, interest rates can only continue their march into the stratosphere. (And since the high interest rates were probably the major factor in the stock collapse, it is hard to see the stock market engaging in any brisk recovery.)

In the short run, the only sound way out for the Nixon Administration is to be willing to engage in a truly rigorous anti-monetary inflation program, to stop inflating the monetary supply and, indeed, to engage in some old-fashioned monetary contraction. The recession would then be sharp but short-lived, and recovery would be brisk and healthy. The anti-inflationary monetary contraction must be sharp and determined enough to offset the inevitable rise in relative consumer prices and to change the inflationary expectations of the public; it must be rigorously "hard money". Only then will prices level off and even (gloryosky!) decline, and only then will interest rates fall. The Administration must cease pursuing the Friedmanite pipe dream of a levelling off of

(Continued on page 3)

THE NIXON MESS — *(Continued from page 2)*

prices along with recovery but without abandoning monetary inflation. In the long run, of course, we need a total overhaul of our inherently statist and inflationary monetary system, with a liquidation of the Federal Reserve System and a return to a genuine gold standard.

But the Nixon Administration is likely to turn, if turn decisively it does, in precisely the opposite direction. Unwilling to bring monetary inflation to a halt, unwilling to go into a truly "hard money" program, it might very well add onto its vacillation and drift a turn toward the totalitarian method of wage-and-price controls. Already there are ominous signs of wage-price controls on the horizon. Arthur F. Burns, the man our anarcho-Nixonites assured us was soundly free-enterprise, now talks of "voluntary" or even coercive price controls. Such business economists as Pierre Rinfret and Lionel Edie and Co., have already frankly called for wage-price controls. There are two things wrong with such controls: one, they are the totalitarian antithesis of freedom or the free economy, and two, they don't work, leading instead to the "suppressed" inflation of black markets and eternal shortages and misallocation of resources. Why, then, are so many of our "conservative" business economists reaching for such controls? Precisely because profit margins are being squeezed by the pressure of wage-costs, as they always are in recessions; and therefore, these business economists hope to stop wage increases by the use of compulsion and the State bayonet.

Guaranteed income schemes; continuing budget deficits; monetary inflation; and now wage-price controls; under the cover of traditional free-enterprise rhetoric, the Nixon Administration continues us ever further down the path toward the economy of fascism. But none of this will solve the crises brought on by his and his predecessors' policies. He cannot end the war in Southeast Asia by expanding it, and he cannot end price inflation by continuing to inflate the money supply, or by coercive attempts to overrule the forces of supply and demand. Richard Nixon is sinking deeper into his own quagmire. He cannot bring us peace, he cannot bring us inflation-less prosperity. Nixon's goose is cooked.

ANARCHISM AND GOVERNMENT

Ludwig von Mises, the greatest modern advocate of democracy and representative government, has never raised any objection against the modern anarchist position; every critique of anarchism made by Professor Mises has been aimed at the older authors of the movement, those who believed that the members of society would all voluntarily submit to the moral code. The older anarchists who held this view were utopians, i.e., they believed that a perfect society was attainable, where no one would break the moral code. Modern anarchists do not hold this view, however. Rather, they recognize that no social system could conceivably *guarantee* that no one would break the moral code. Modern anarchists are fully aware that the search is not for a *perfect* social system, but for the best (most moral) system among those conceivable. Because anarchists seek the best, they naturally choose that system which in no way institutes the breaking of the moral code. This means a system in which no government, i.e., taxing authority or legalized coercive agent, exists. Anarchism, like any other projected social system, is based upon fundamental moral principles. In dealing with social systems, the primary question we must ask is the moral one. Only secondarily is it necessary to inquire into the utilitarian aspects of the system we have chosen. Thus, the demonstration that in a perfectly moral, anarchist, society—perfectly moral in the sense that no criminal actions are legalized—everyone would be better off materially and psychically is secondary to our major concern. The question whether anarchist society is "workable" betrays an immaturity of mind and lack of knowledge and vision. One thing is outstandingly clear to the student of history: Free men are capable of devising methods of coping with all their problems, moral and utilitarian, without invading the freedom and property rights of others. Historical examples are innumerable. In short, anarchism does not expect that everyone will obey the moral code requiring that no one invade the property rights of another; but, anarchism does hold that, in our efforts to prevent and punish such invasions as do occur, we may not invade these same rights (as is done when government is established). Thus, anarchism simply requires that human rights not be invaded by any*one* or any *group* for any *reason*, supposedly beneficial or otherwise. The State is by nature an invader of men's rights, just like any "private" criminal; and government must be subject to the same moral sanctions as are imposed already upon such "private" criminals. Anarchists hold that morality must be upheld in all cases, and not abandoned whenever State actions are involved. Men have long since rejected the Divine Right of Kings; surely it is now past time to do the same with all claims that the State is Extra-Human or Extra-Moral. The State must be judged on the same level and by the same principles as all other human actions and institutions; one rule applies to all. If, upon examination, the State is found to be committing immoral or criminal acts (as anarchists hold it *is*), then the State must be treated in the same way that we treat a "private" criminal. Anarchists ask no more than this. It is often objected to the anarchist analysis that, while morally it is correct, it ignores the fact that government is a *necessary* part of any society, that no society could exist without it. This argument would, indeed, carry much weight if it were valid. But it is, in fact, a perfect example of the logical fallacy of begging the question. The necessity of government is just *assumed*. The Statist, if he wishes to use this argument, must first explain *why* the State is a necessary part of any social system. In fact, the requirement of explanation lies doubly heavy upon the Statist's shoulders because he is arguing that he be allowed to institute criminalism. He is, in effect, arguing that there must be an *outlaw* in every society in order for that society to remain intact. This doctrine is not only paradoxical; it is obviously absurd as well. For the whole purpose of morality is that outlaws should be eliminated from society. Yet the Statist has the temerity to assert that in every geographical area one outlaw (and his legions) are required if the moral code is to be upheld. Reason demands that this criminal assertion be rejected.

— John V. Peters

Abortion Repeal

On one point, at least, the Women's Liberation forces are libertarian and correct: and that is the basic libertarian concept that every person and therefore every woman has the absolute right to govern and control her own body (or, as we might put it, everyone has the fundamental property right in his own body, or the "right of self-ownership"). This fundamental property right immediately rules out slavery, and the draft. And it also rules out any and all laws restricting any woman's right to perform an abortion.

Too many libertarians tend to dismiss the traditional Catholic counter-argument as unworthy of discussion. That argument is important and cogent, but, I believe, wrong: that abortion constitutes the killing of a living human being, and is therefore tantamount to murder. *If* the Catholic position were correct, then all abortion would have to be outlawed as murder. The proper answer, I believe, has nothing to do with turgid and slippery arguments as to when life really begins, when the fetus becomes human, when the soul arrives, etc. The vital consideration, from my point of view, is not whether or to what extent the fetus lives or is human, but precisely the fundamental libertarian axiom that each individual has the absolute right of property in his or her own body.

The crucial point is that the fetus is contained within the body of its mother; it is, in fact, a parasite upon that body. The mother has the absolute right to get rid of this parasitic growth, this internatl part of her body. Period. Therefore, abortions should be legal.

From The "Old Curmudgeon"

A German politician of a few decades ago once said: "When I hear the word 'culture' I reach for my revolver." I'm sure we can all think of a lot of words we'd like to substitute for "culture" in that remark. For example: "counter-culture"; "youth culture"; "alienation"; "sense of belonging"; "the Environment"; "the community"; "relevant"; "Women's Liberation"; "where his head's at"; "groovy"; "rapping"; and "Right On!"

RECOMMENDED READING

Individualist Anarchism. Until recently, there have been virtually no books in print on the fertile field of the American tradition of individualist anarchism. Now, two important books fill some of this need.

Henry J. Silverman, ed., *American Radical Thought: The Libertarian Tradition* (Lexington, Mass.: D. C. Heath Co., 1970, paper), immediately replaces Krimerman and Perry's *Patterns of Anarchy* as the best collection of readings in individualist anarchism. Professor Silverman has collected significant readings on American libertarianism, beginning with Jefferson and Paine, and then moving quickly to the anarchists, most of whom, fortunately, were individualists. Included in this handsome volume are contributions, among others, from Warren, Tucker, Spooner, Thoreau, Garrison, Ballou, as well as contemporary contributions from American anarchists. The latter include Carl Oglesby's call for a left-right alliance, Karl Hess's classic "Death of Politics" from *Playboy*, the scintillating "Tranquil Statement" of the Anarchist Caucus of YAF in the summer of 1969, co-authored by Karl Hess's son, and two contributions from Murray N. Rothbard: "Confessions of a Right-Wing Liberal" from *Ramparts*, as well as the "Student Revolution" from the May 1, 1969 issue of your own *Lib. Forum* . The collection is nothing if not up-to-date. Price is not listed on the cover; this paperback must be ordered either from Heath or from a college bookstore.

The pioneering history of American individualist anarchism has just been reprinted: the 1932 study by Eunice Minette Schuster, *Native American Anarchism: A Study of Left-wing American Individualism* (available at $12.50 from the Da Capo Press, 227 West 17th St., New York, N. Y. 10011). Schuster's study is much less satisfactory than James J. Martin's *Men Against the State* for Warren, Spooner and Tucker, but Martin's book is out of print, and also does not cover such important Christian anarchists as Ann Hutchinson, and the Garrison movement. So Schuster is indispensable for students of American anarchism.

First Class

Published on the first and fifteenth of every month.   Subscription rate: $7.00 per year; Student subscription rate: $5.00 per year

124

~~~~ DOUBLE ISSUE ~~~~
A Semi-Monthly Newsletter

THE
Libertarian Forum

Joseph R. Peden, Publisher   Murray N. Rothbard, Editor

VOL. II, NO. 13-14   JULY, 1970   35¢

On Civil Obedience

Mr. Leonard E. Read, President of the Foundation for Economic Education, the oldest established organization for *laissez-faire*, has now given us all an Independence Day present: a frank repudiation of the American Revolution and of that great libertarian document, the Declaration of Independence, on which that Revolution was grounded. ("Civil ▇obedience", *Notes from FEE*, July.) How have Mr. Read and FEE, who proclaim themselves to be libertarian and have many times hailed that same Declaration, gotten themselves into this odd position? FEE was the organization where, over twenty years ago, I first met the late Frank Chodorov, a great libertarian who introduced our generation of young libertarians to Thoreau and his Essay on Civil Disobedience. How is it that now Leonard E. Read writes an essay sternly calling upon everyone to obey the law at all times, regardless of how immoral or unjust any law may be? For twenty-five years, Leonard Read has labored to bring us liberty, and, behold, he has brought us the profoundly anti-libertarian stone of Civil ▇obedience.

Apparently, Mr. Read was provoked into writing this essay by running into trouble with his youth cadre. He tells us that after he and his colleagues had finished instructing their Undergraduate Seminar on the immorality and injustice of the bulk of our laws, the main question raised by the students was: "Am I not warranted in breaking an immoral law?" An excellent question, indeed, but one that apparently distrubed Mr. Read. For even a believer in *laissez-faire*, let along an anarchist, must concede that the great bulk of our laws is despotic, exploitative, immoral and unjust. Why, then, should these criminal and unjust edicts be obeyed? Why indeed?

Mr. Read is very firm on his answer to the students: no law, no matter how immoral, may be disobeyed. No one must knowingly disobey *any* law, regardless of its content. He is not nearly as clear, however, on the *reasons* for his stand, which quickly become cloudy, self-contradictory, and irrelevant.

Mr. Read's first reason for commanding obedience to all law is a curious one, considering his past record as an

ardent defender of each individual's following his own moral principles, of being true to himself, whatever these principles may be. After preaching the immorality of invading the natural rights and the property of any individual for nearly twenty-five years, Mr. Read has apparently and suddenly become a moral relativist. If the individual is to disobey an immoral law, he wonders, "how is an immoral law to be defined?" Even if *he* is sure that regulation or special privilege is immoral, he says, his is "quite a minority view these days". And then he adds, rather sadly for someone who had once been so firm on each individual's following his own moral judgment: "contemporary ethical standards vary so that no law will pass everyone's test of morality", and so no person may use his conviction of a law's immorality to break that law.

Let us be quite clear what Mr. Read's current position implies. The government, let us say, passes a law, ordering every citizen to turn everyone known by him to be a Jew (or Negro, or redhead, or whatever) over to the authorities to be shipped to a concentration camp. Mr. Read would surely consider such a law criminally unjust; but he would feel morally obligated to obey, because who is he to set his own ethical views against "contemporary ethical standards?" Mr. Read considers conscription a monstrous slave law; and yet, he would presumably condemn any young person evading the draft for disobeying the law, and presumably would also turn this young draft evader in to the authorities if the law so decreed.

Mr. Read's argument evidently suffers from a grave inner contradiction. He raises the variability of definitions of morality and of ethical standards as an argument for *not* acting on one's own perception of the injustice of any law. And yet he turns around and enjoins upon us all the absolute ethical commandment of obeying all laws, no matter their content, even though he admits in his article that many people dispute the justice of these laws. In short, Mr. Read uses ethical variability as the reason for ethical relativism, for preventing people from acting on their own moral judgments, and yet from that selfsame ethical variability he somehow comes up with a universal ethical absolute: obedience to every law, regardless of one's moral judgment. If, indeed, ethical standards are variable and therefore we should not presume to act on our own moral principles, then neither can there be an absolute ethical imperative for everyone to obey the law. Mr. Read can't have it both ways.

Let us contrast Mr. Read's ethical relativism and plea for civil obedience to some of his own earlier writings,

(Continued on page 2)

DOUBLE ISSUE

NOTICE: During July and August, we will publish special Double Issues: one covering July 1-July 15, and another August 1-August 15. We will return to our regular publishing schedule in September.

125

ON CIVIL OBEDIENCE — *(Continued from page 1)*

writings in those golden days when FEE was at the center of libertarian thought and activity in this country. Thus, in his "The Penalty of Surrender" (*Essays on Liberty, Vol. I*, FEE, 1952, pp. 253-63), Read wrote eloquently that one must not compromise one's moral principles, because, in the field of morality, the slightest compromise can only mean surrender. Read recognized then, of course, that no person is infallible, and that therefore one's moral principles might be in error, but that he must follow them nevertheless. "A principle . . . is a matter of personal moral judgment . . . I am convinced that no person is capable of rising above his best judgment. To live in strict accordance with one's best judgment is to live as perfectly as one can . . . A rule of conduct emerges with crystal clarity: *reflect in word and in deed, always and accurately, that which one's best judgment dictates.* (Italics Read's.) . . . To do less, to deviate one iota, is to sin against yourself, that is, against your Maker as He has manifested Himself in you. To do less is not to compromise. To do less is to surrender!" (*Ibid.*, pp. 258-60.) Hear, hear! But how does the eloquent and uncompromisingly principled Leonard Read of the early 1950's square with the Leonard Read of 1970, who claims that since "comtemporary ethical standards vary, and the majority may not agree, no individual is justified in breaking a law that he may consider deeply immoral? Isn't his later position "surrender" and "sin"? And, furthermore, the early Read said: "Principle does not lend itself to bending or to compromising. It stands impregnable. I must either abide by it, or in all fairness I must on this point regard myself, not as a rational, reasonable person, but rather as an unprincipled person." (*Ibid.*, p. 256.)

Another eloquent product of the early Read was "On That Day Began Lies." (*Ibid.*, pp. 231-252.) Read took his essay from a text by the frankly anarchist Leo Tolstoy: "From the day when the first members of councils placed exterior authority higher than interior, that is to say, recognized the decisions of men united in councils as more important and more sacred than reason and conscience; on that day began lies that caused the loss of millions of human beings and which continue their work to the present day." Read built his article on this superb passage. Again Read wrote: "the nearest that any person can get to right principles— truth—is that which his highest personal judgment dictates as right. Beyond that one cannot go or achieve. *Truth, then, as nearly as any individual can express it, is in strict accordance with his inner, personal dictate of rightness.* (Italics Read's.) The accurate representation of this inner, personal dictate is intellectual integrity. It is the expressing, living, acting of such truth as any given person is in possession of. Inaccurate representation of what one believes to be right is untruth. It is a lie . . . Thus, the best we can do with ourselves is to represent ourselves at our best. To do otherwise is to tell a lie. To tell lies is to destroy such truth as is known. To deny truth is to destroy ourselves." (*Ibid.*, p. 233.)

Read went on to attack the idea of subordinating one's own perception of truth to the opinions of other men in "councils", organizations or governments, and particularly to attack the idea that a group of men labelling themselves "government" can morally perform acts (murder, theft, etc.) that individual men would not perform. He concludes: "How to stop lies? It is simply a matter of personal resolve to act and speak in strict accordance with one's inner, personal dictate of what is right. And for each of us to see to it that no other man or set of men is given permission to represent us otherwise." (*Ibid.*, p. 252.) And let us underline here that, in both of these early essays, Mr. Read writes of "acting" and of "deeds" as well as merely *speaking* in accordance with one's inner convictions.

And finally, Leonard Read's noble *Conscience on the Battlefield* (FEE, 1951), a pamphlet which seems to have been long out of print at the Foundation. Here Read candidly

condemned war as "liberty's greatest enemy" and as, simply, "evil". The essay is written in the form of a dialogue between Read's current self—or his Conscience—and with what would have been his self if he had then been dying on a battlefield in Korea. Read admonishes the dying soldier that, simply because the government had sent him there to fight, the soldier cannot escape moral guilt for killing his fellow human beings. The government's calling it moral or legal or calling it war cannot alter the fact that killing in that war was unjustified murder of his fellow men.

Read wrote of the "failure to grasp the idea that when the right to act on behalf of one's self is delegated to another, this cannot reasonably be done without an acceptance of personal responsibility for the results of the delegated authority . . . Let authority for your actions be transferred to government, a collective, without an exact accompaniment of your personal responsibility for that authority . . . and . . . you will act without personal discipline as a result of the mistaken belief that there can be authority without responsibility . . . And this, I submit, is the illogical process—call it foreign policy or whatever—which leads you to kill another person without remorse or a feeling of guilt." (*Ibid.*, pp. 30-31.) And the fact of government action is no moral aid to one's conscience, for government "is but a name given to an arrangement which consists only of individuals. They—and they alone—are responsible for what they do collectively as government. They—and they alone— are subject to Judgment." (*Ibid.*, p. 29.)

And the early Read went even further in his moral condemnation of the American war-machine; in the guilt for "there can be no distinction between those who do the shooting and those who aid the act—whether they aid it behind the lines by making the ammunition (the "merchants of death"?) or by submitting to the payment of taxes for war." (*Ibid.*, p. 11.)

Now I am not saying that the Leonard Read of 1951 would have counselled the soldier or the taxpayer for the war machine to break the law—to refuse to involve himself in the guilt of mass murder. But surely it is inconceivable that the Read of 1951 would have *condemned* the man of conscience who broke the law by refusing to participate in mass murder, especially by referring to minority positions and to differing "contemporary ethical standards".

So much for Read's argument against an individual refusing to obey a law he considers immoral. Read's second argument against law-breaking is scarcely an argument at all: it is the raising of the old spectre, the old bogety, of "anarchy". He seems to place himself squarely in the middle-of-the-road, in the middle between socialism on the one hand and the "enormous anarchistic reaction" to socialism on the other. But from his tone, and from his curious injunction that State laws must be obeyed regardless of their content, it is abundantly clear that Mr. Read regards anarchism—the maximum of individual liberty—as somehow a far *greater* threat to his version of liberty than socialism itself. He must, else he would not opt for obedience to all state laws, no matter how despotic, as compared to the outside chance of anarchism! A curious position indeed, especially since the ranks of anarchism are enormously weaker than the might and power of the State. That Mr. Read has gone far down the statist road is evident also from the fact that his legendary politeness and courtesy in polemic has begun to slip: "I see an enormous anarchistic reaction . . . And back of it all—giving the movement a false dignity—are an increasing number of persuasive writers and speakers flaunting the labels of scholarship." (*Notes from FEE*, p. 1.) Never has Mr. Read written in such angry personal tones of writers and speakers on behalf of statism or socialism. Curious once more!

"Anarchy," writes the current Mr. Read, is "approaching epidemic proportions." (Would that it were so!) Anarchy, Read warns, is "unplanned chaos", which is no better than

(Continued on page 3)

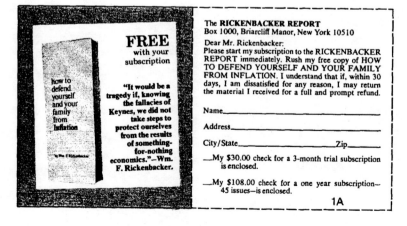

ON CIVIL OBEDIENCE — *(Continued from page 2)*

the "planned chaos" of socialism. "Unplanned chaos"—an interesting term. Does Mr. Read mean by this term the free market, for that is precisely what we free-market anarchists advocate? But if freedom and the free market is "chaos", how then does Leonard Read's view of the market differ from that of Karl Marx, who scornfully referred to the market as "anarchy of production"? Is freedom, at last, to be called "chaos"?

The term "planned chaos" is taken from a booklet of the same title by the distinguished *laissez-faire* economist, Ludwig von Mises. But Mises does not, as does Read, contrast government planning to planlessness as the available polar alternatives. To Mises, the desideratum is that *each individual* plans *for himself*: "The alternative is not plan or no plan. The question is: whose planning? Should each member of society plan for himself or should the paternal government alone plan for all? The issue . . . is spontaneous action of each individual versus the exclusive action of the government. It is freedom versus governmental omnipotence." (Ludwig von Mises, *Planning for Freedom*, South Holland, Ill.: Libertarian Press, 1952, p. 45.) And Mises adds: "There is no other planning for freedom and general welfare than to let the market system work." (*Ibid.*, p. 17.) The aim of free-market anarchists is precisely to end governmental omnipotence and planning, and to substitute for this each man's planning for himself. Or does Mr. Read, in contrast to Mises, consider each man's planning for himself to be "planless chaos"? (This is not to say that Mises is an anarchist, but that Mises would not make the egregious error of referring to the market as "planless chaos".)

We should add that the early Read had a far different view of "chaos"; to him, "chaos" signified the individual's abandonment of principle: "If principle is abandoned, even compromise will not be possible. Nothing but chaos!" (*Essays on Liberty, Vol. I*, p. 263.)

Mr. Read admits that almost everyone breaks laws every day, but only, he hastens to add, because they *don't know* what the laws may be. Thus, he cites a business firm which might or might not be breaking the antitrust laws for almost any action it may perform. So far, so good (although this contradicts the position taken in *Conscience on the Battlefield*, pp. 14-15.) But Mr. Read has not looked deeply enough at reality. Surely, he must be familiar with the fact that every citizen breaks laws, *knowingly* and intentionally, every day. Does he not know that millions, every day, discard gum wrappers on streets, fudge a bit on their income taxes, cross the street on the red light, commit fornication out of wedlock, etc.—and without the world falling apart? Has not even Leonard Read himself, even he, once in a while driven 62 miles per hour in a 60-mile per hour zone?

Read professes joining the revolutionaries in his "distaste for the plethora of oppressive laws presently on the statute books". But the remedy, he insists, must only be repeal of the laws rather than breaking them. But how in the world does he think that laws *get* repealed? The best way of forcing our politicians to repeal a law is to render that law absolutely non-enforceable, in short, by mass breakage of that law. How does Mr. Read believe that perhaps the single greatest tyrannical law in American history—Prohibition—got repealed? Prohibition got repealed because it had become totally unenforceable in that greater part of the country where people decided that the act—even as a Constitutional amendment—was absurd and despotic, and they simply and knowingly ignored the law. The mass drinking during Prohibition was one of the greatest—and most successful—movements of mass civil disobedience in history. It won, and surely every lbertarian must consider this victory a great triumph for liberty—a triumph brought about by nothing else than mass breakage of The Law. Leonard Read

writes that "lawbreaking merely adds to the existing confusion", and that "if any idea or action does not lead to enlightenment, it is worthless, if not downright destructive." Contrary to Mr. Read, the lawbreaking during Prohibition was very clear, and extremely enlightening, both to the government and to the general public. What it told the government was that Prohibition was an act so despotic and so invasive of the personal freedom of the public that that law could not be enforced, regardless of the sums of taxpayers' money spent on government snoopers and prohibition enforcement agents. The lawbreaking enlightened the public and the government that there are *some* limits beyond which the government *may* not go in its dictatorship over society. The government will never attempt Prohibition again, thanks to that lawbreaking and that enlightenment. This is a process of enlightenment which the Marxists have aptly called "education through struggle".

Mr. Read, in contrast, apparently believes that laws are repealed by one individual genius rising up and sounding the trump, and then, presto, the unjust law is dissolved. This Great Man view of history is all too popular among the public ignorant of historical processes, and Mr. Read picks a peculiarly absurd example by singling out the alleged influence toward libertarian repeal of oppressive laws by one Father Paolo Sarpi. Sarpi, according to Read, was a sixteenth-century Venetian priest, "whose analysus, reasoning and expositions crumpled the mighty power combination of Church and State . . ." He then quotes the historian Andrew Dickson White as hailing Sarpi, who had "fought the most bitter fight for humanity ever known in any Latin nation, and won a victory by which the whole world has profited ever since." (*Notes from FEE*, p. 2.)

Leonard Read accuses some of us of giving the anarchist movement a "false dignity" by "flaunting the labels of scholarship". Well, that is *one* sin which Mr. Read can never be accused of committing. No scholarship—or historical knowledge whatsoever—is being flaunted here. In the first place, it is historiographical nonsense to think that a law, let alone a structure of laws, can be "crumpled" by one person writing a book, no matter how persuasive that book. *Other things* have to happen, too, but these are things which Mr. Read does not choose to face, for they involve pressure, social forces, politics, and even violence. They involve, in short, a struggle against Power. But setting this point aside, one boggles at the ignorance of history flaunted by Mr. Read: no one with the slightest knowledge of sixteenth or seventeenth-century European history can treat Mr. Read's account of Father Sarpi with anything but a round horselaugh. Not only didn't Father Sarpi "crumple" a darn thing, either directly or indirectly; Sarpi's role was, to the contrary, to *defend* the laws of the Venetian State against the Church. Rather than the prophet of "repeal of oppressive laws", Father Sarpi was the apologist for existing State law against its Churchly critics. Furthermore, and to put the cap on Mr. Read's historical balderdash, these Venetian laws were decidedly oppressive and anti-libertarian. They included the refusal of the Venetian State to allow the Church the right to establish orders or erect religious buildings without state permission, and the expulsion of the Jesuit order from Venetian territory. Leonard Read's heroic prophet of liberty who supposedly "crumpled" an entire structure of oppressive laws by writing a book, turns out to be merely an apologist for existing oppressive laws! Leonard Read the historian makes Leonard Read the social philosopher tower like Aristotle.

Perhaps Mr. Read's problem is that he took as his historical authority one Andrew Dickson White, a man who was not even a very good historian when he wrote his works in the late nineteenth century. History is a cumulative discipline, and historical scholarship seventy-five odd years ago was in its infancy. And even in that age of flagrant bias and feeble scholarship among all too many historians,

(Continued on page 4)

ON CIVIL OBEDIENCE — *(Continued from page 3)*

Andrew Dickson White was particularly blinded in his historical outlook by his almost fanatical anti-Catholic bias. Father Sarpi was against the Papacy, and for Andrew Dickson White that was credentials enough.

Is Mr. Read, then, counselling obedience to *all* law? Is there *no* edict, no oppression, no injustice, no matter how flagrant or how gruesome, that Leonard Read will not swallow? No, he is willing to draw the line *somewhere*: where freedom of speech is infringed. I shall obey the law, Mr. Read states, "so long as I am free to speak my piece and write about it." He adds with self-satisfaction: *"That's my criterion!"* for "turning revolutionary".

I have heard this criterion from Ayn Rand and now from Leonard Read, but I must confess that I simply cannot understand how this criterion is arrived at. How is it grounded in libertarian principle? Neither Read nor Rand has offered any derivation for their criterion. In fact, the criterion seems to me an absurd one for a libertarian to promulgate. Suppose that a man burgles my home, assaults me and my family, and kidnaps me; have I no moral right to defend myself *provided* that he allows me to register my protest and even send a letter to the *Times*? What sort of libertarian principle is *this*? For that is what Mr. Read is saying: no matter how much the government criminally robs us, kidnaps us, enslaves us, brutalizes us, we must not defy or disobey the edicts of this criminal gang provided they allow us to raise our voices in protest. But why? *Why*?

I can understand such an argument from Social Democrats like Sidney Hook. For people like Hook, property rights are unimportant; indeed the *only* right worth defending is freedom of speech (and to press the lever at the ballot-box). Given the preservation of such freedom of speech, such "human right", every act of government is morally legitimate and therefore must morally be obeyed. But Leonard Read and Ayn Rand are *supposed* to be upholders of property right; they are supposed to believe that property right is a human right just as sacred as freedom of speech. How come this abandonment, this surrender of the rights of property, including the property right in one's own person as is violated in conscription? How can libertarians and defenders of property rights suddenly abandon such rights as unimportant, and claim that the right of self-defense, or even the moral right to disobey unjust laws, arises only when freedom of speech is violated? Do not Read and Rand know that freedom is indivisible, that the willingness to sanction the loss of freedom in one area means that other areas inevitably are abandoned? Surely they have written this many times, as did Mr. Read in "The Penalty of Surrender". On *what* day began lies?

Furthermore, aside from his abandonment of libertarian principle, Mr. Read, as in his acceptance of the Sarpi fable, betrays a curiously naive view of strategy in the real world. Does he *really* believe that he can accept an increasingly totalitarian framework of laws and of State power, keep counselling total civil obedience, and *then*, when the State puts the final nail in our coffin by suppressing our freedom os speech, suddenly say: "OK, that's it. I now become a revolutionary." Does he really believe that one can meekly accept 99% of one's enslavement and then suddenly stand up, a defiant revolutionary, at the last nail in the coffin? Read the revolutionary would last about ten seconds before finding his way to the nearest hoosegow. But perhaps Mr. Read believes that, like Father Sarpi, he need then only rise and proclaim: "I become a revolutionary", for the State's oppressive regime to "crumple" once more.

I agree with Herbert Marcuse on virtually nothing, but his analysis of freedom of speech in the United States as the keystone in a system of "repressive tolerance" is close to the mark. It is as if the Establishment can oppress us by all manner of laws, privileges, and regulations, but then ostentatiously allow dissenters like Ayn Rand or Leonard Read to speak and publish, and then tell everyone here and abroad: "See, we *do* have a free country. What are you all complaining about?" Freedom of speech, *especially* when, as in the case of Leonard E. Read, it conspicuously does *not* lead to action against the State, serves the State well as its showcase, its "Potemkin village", to bamboozle the public into believing that we in fact live in a "free society". By embracing freedom of speech as the *only* freedom worth defending or clinging to, Leonard Read and Ayn Rand fall beautifully into the co-opting trap of repressive tolerance.

One wonders, too, whether Mr. Read realizes that even freedom of speech, especially that of the more annoying dissenters, is being interfered with, harassed, and crippled, *right now* in the United States. Such repression has taken myriad forms: for example, the Chicago Trial of the Conspiracy 8, the Chicago police riot of 1968, FCC regulation of radio and TV stations, the outlawing of the Washington *Free Press*, the persistent governmental harassment of the San Diego underground press, the endemic wiretapping indulged in by government, and numerous other examples. What was the massacre at Kent State but the murder of students who were exercising their freedom of speech and assembly by peaceful demonstrations? Even if our puny little libertarian movement has been harassed and intimidated in our exercise of freedom of speech and assembly by the force of government. Every one of our dinners and conferences in New York was infiltrated and reported on in detail by police spies, plainclothesmen virtually surrounded our major New York conference, and FBI agents have intimidated people who had attended the conference (obviously getting their names from police spies.) Do you, Leonard, consider this an invasion of our freedom of speech and communication? What of your criterion now?

Senator Sam Ervin (D., N. C.), one of the few conservatives in Congress genuinely concerned about liberty of the person, has been conducting a lone, one-man campaign in the Senate attacking the existence of computerized files in the Federal government containing a dossier on hundreds of thousands of American "malcontents" who have committed no crimes. Senator Ervin says that the existence of these files brings us close to being a "police state". The Senator charges that "the very existence of government files on how people exercise First Amendment rights, how they think, speak, assemble and act in lawful pursuits, is a form of official psychological coercion to keep silent and to refrain from acting." (*New York. Times*, June 28.) Are you, Leonard Read, going to be *less* critical of our burgeoning police-state than Senator Ervin, a man who has never claimed to be a consistent libertarian? I know, too, that I and many other peaceful libertarians are on that infamous list.

Of course, it is very possible that Mr. Read simply does not care about this repression of freedom of speech, even of the speech of libertarians. For he *does* say that his criterion rests on whether "*I* am free to speak my piece and write about it." I have no doubt whatever that, long after the freedom of speech and communication of others, of active anti-Statists, has been suppressed, Leonard E. Read will be allowed to speak and publish unhampered. *His* freedom of speech is not likely to be in danger, not so long as any tolerance remains in our system of repressive tolerance. Perhaps, after all, Mr. Read is only concerned about *his* freedom of speech, and the devil take anyone else's. But at least he should ask himself: why? Why is it that *my* freedom of speech remains unsullied while others are suppressed? Is it because the State considers me a boon rather than a bane, especially as I continue to preach ardently in favor of civil obedience?

Having proclaimed, but not defended, the criterion of free speech for disobeying any law, Mr. Read goes on to a third argument for civil obedience: an argument from strategy. Mr. Read asserts that anarchists, "who flout law and order

(Continued on page 5)

ON CIVIL OBEDIENCE — *(Continued from page 4)*

as a matter of principle, cannot logically or convincingly present the case for freedom," whereas himself and FEE can do so, because "our respect for law and order may well engender a corresponding respect for our commitments to freedom." Perhaps, but I don't see it; it seems to me rather that anarchists who declare that unjust laws may morally be disobeyed, will engender respect for their consistency in upholding the principle of freedom, for their consistency in principle and in deed. On the other hand, FEE's respect for a system of law which surely observes, at the hands of any libertarian, only condemnation, can only seem to most people, and to most budding libertarians, as craven surrender of principle. To quote the early Read, FEE's course will seem to most thinking people as "sin" and "surrender". Why in blazes does a system of laws and decrees which even Leonard Read acknowledges to be unjust and oppressive deserve "respect"? Does the burglar, the kidnapper, the mugger, deserve "respect" for his decrees? On that day began lies!

Finally, Mr. Read gives us our Independence Day present: his repudiation of the Declaration of Independence. Quoting the Declaration, "whenever any form of government becomes destructive of these ends, it is the right of the people to alter it or abolish it", Read makes an enormous concession: that, on the grounds of the Declaration, we should all long ago have become revolutionaries! He admits: "the grievances listed (in the Declaration) are hardly distinguishable from the oppressive laws imposed on us by our own government. According to the Declaration, I should have turned revolutionary several decades ago." Hear, hear! However, he says, he rejects the criterion of the Declaration—which amounts to the right of self-defense against long-continued abuses of liberty—for his own "criterion" of invasion of freedom of speech.

His argument against the Declaration, however, is not in his own realm of libertarian social philosophy but in the rôle of Leonard Read as Historian. "The more I study the history of revolutions," Read intones, "the more evident" it is that "the replacement (is) worse than the government overthrown!" The American Revolution is, apparently, a miraculous exception to this historical rule. So much for revolution!

In contrast to his *gaffe* on Father Sarpi, Leonard Read is joined in this historical error by many historians and by the great mass of the American public, who have thereby been lulled into repudiating revolutions and denying their own revolutionary past. This old bromide is, however, dead wrong; we might almost say, in reverse, that *most* revolutionary governments have been far better, on balance, than the ones overthrown. Even the French Revolution, much abused by Tories and Conservatives then and since, and surrounded by armed invaders from counter-revolutionary crowned heads, was on net balance a great blessing for liberty and free enterprise. The French Revolution swept aside crippling feudal and mercantilist restrictions and oppressions, and set the stage for agricultural liberty and for the Industrial Revolution in France. I will here simply refer Mr. Read—and other counter-revolutionaries—to a monumental work of comparative history, Barrington Moore's *Social Origins of Dictatorship and Democracy*. Moore conclusively demonstrates that, in contrast to Tory mythology, it was precisely through violent revolution that America, Britain, and France were able to achieve as much liberty and democracy as they did; in contrast, it was those countries which industrialized *without* internal violence: e. g. Germany and Japan, which landed in modern totalitarianism. (Indeed, poring through Moore, now available in paperback, is one of the best single antidotes to the ignorance of history that unfortunately goes beyond Mr. Read to the entire libertarian movement.)

Mr. Read and FEE have not always been so down on the Declaration of Independence. Quite the contrary. Thus, in an article for FEE lionizing the Declaration, Ralph Bradford hurled this challenge to his contemporaries: "Would *You* Have Signed It?" (Ralph Bradford, "Would *You* Have Signed It?", *Essays on Liberty, Vol. VI*, FEE, 1959, pp. 9-18.) Obviously the Leonard Read of 1970 would *not* have. Stoutly defending the Declaration and its signers, Bradford denounced the modern critics who dismiss the Declaration "because the principles asserted in those documents come between them and their plans for collectivization by force." (*Ibid.*, p. 11.) Bradford concluded his article: "The thing to remember is that when the chips were down, they (the signers) were men! The piece of paper they had signed was not a thing a signer could squirm out of or explain away later. *It was not a vague statement of political and social principles.* (Italics mine.) . . . In bold phrases it recited the political and economic sins of the King of England, and it declared that the Colonies were free from the rule of the British government. In the eyes of that government, such statements were treasonable; and treason was punishable by death . . . Would *you* have signed it?" No, most assuredly, the Leonard Read of today would not, in a million years, have signed such a document.

To conclude: Leonard E. Read, sternly and with unusual asperity, has told us in no uncertain terms that we must respect and obey all laws whatsoever, regardless of how unjust, unless and until Leonard Read's freedom of speech shall be impaired. He has offered no intelligible argument whatsoever, let alone an argument grounded in libertarian principle, for this commandment to civil obedience. The conservative theorist James Burnham was far clearer and more candid in *his* ultimate argument for government: irrational mystery, Burnham wrote: "there is no adequate rational explanation for the existence and effective working of government . . . Neither the source nor the justification of government can be put in wholly rational terms . . . Consider the problem of government from the point of view of the reflective individual. I, as an individual, do in fact submit myself . . . to the rule of another—to government. But suppose that I ask myself: *why* should I do so? why should I submit myself to the rule of another? *what* justifies his rule? To these questions there are no objectively convincing answers in rational terms alone . . . why should I accept the hereditary or democratic or any other principle of legitimacy? Why should a principle justify the rule of that man over me? . . . I accept the principle, well . . . because I do, because that is the way it is and has been." So enamoured is Burnham of this mystical "argument" for civil obedience that he actually lauds the mythology that States were founded by gods, and thereby have divine sanction: "In ancient times, before the illusions of science had corrupted traditional wisdom, the founders of Cities were known to be gods or demigods." (James Burnham, *Congress and the American Tradition*, Chicago: Henry Regnery, 1959, pp. 3, 6-8.) But suppose, we may counter to Jim Burnham, we now begin *not* to accept the principle of the legitimacy of rule. What then? Obviously, Burnham's mystical decrees can scarcely be persuasive argument to anyone but Burnham himself, if that. We must be guided by reason and by libertarian principle, and in that realm, Mr. Read's case has not even begun to be made—perhaps, because he dimly sees that he can make no case for civil disobedience in reason and in liberty.

As we look over this sorry record, a persistent question confronts us: where are the *laissez-faire* revolutionaries? You don't *have* to be an anarchist, after all, to be a revolutionary (although it helps). Tom Paine, Thomas Jefferson, Sam Adams, the signers of the Declaration, the patriots of the Boston Tea Party, none of these men were anarchists. no, they were, somewhat like Leonard E. Read, *laissez-faire* libertarians. And yet what splendid revolutionaries they were! There is a world of difference, however,

(Continued on page 6)

ON CIVIL OBEDIENCE – *(Continued from page 5)*

between them and Leonard E. Read—and what a difference,
O my countrymen! Somewhere in the explanation of that
difference lies the key to the tragic decline of the American
Republic. Frank Chodorov and Ralph Bradford and the
Leonard E. Read of twenty years ago understood that differ-
ence full well.

Meanwhile, while Mr. Read stands up and orders our youth
to respect and obey all laws whatsoever while their (or his!)
freedom of speech remains, I for one am willing to stand
behind our *earlier* group of *laissez-faire* libertarians, they
who were "men", they who never surrendered principle,
they for whom on *no* day began lies, they who magnificently
wrote:

> We hold these Truths to be self-evident, that all
> Men are created equal, that they are endowed by
> their Creator with certain unalienable Rights, that
> among these are Life, Liberty, and the Pursuit of
> Happiness—That to secure these Rights, Governments
> are instituted among Men, deriving their just Powers
> from the Consent of the Governed, that whenever any
> Form of Government becomes destructive of these
> Ends, it is the Right of the People to alter or to abolish
> it, and to institute new Government, laying its Founda-
> tion on such Principles, and organizing its Powers in
> such Form, as to them shall seem most likely to effect
> their Safety and Happiness . . . when a long Train of
> Abuses and Usurpations, pursuing invariably the same
> Object, evinces a Design to reduce them under absolute
> Despotism, it is their Right, it is their Duty, to throw
> off such Government, and to provide new Guards for
> their future Security.

From The "Old Curmudgeon"

Penn Central may be in a veritable mess, but one recent
managerial tactic at that railroad was truly a stroke of
genius. Six female employees, beguiled by the propaganda of
Women's Lib, had protested vigorously that they were being
shunted into the "stereotyped roles" of secretaries and
typists. They demanded absolutely equal treatment with men.
The management responded by giving them the equal treatment they so richly deserved: shifting them to the dangerous
and backbreaking job of checking freight cars, a job that had
previously been confined to the male "oppressors". Liberated
females, however, somehow are never satisfied. When they
complained about the shift, the management retorted: "They
wanted equal rights, didn't they?"

It's about time the Women's Libbers realized that not all
male jobs are the glamourous ones of advertising executives,
publishers, lawyers, etc. The Women's Libbers deserve the
"liberation" they want; first step: freight-car checking.

SUBSCRIBE NOW

Please enter a subscription for:

Name _____

Street _____

City _____ State _____ Zip _____

Subscription is $7.00 per year.
Student subscription $5.00 per year.

Bulk Rates. 20 or more, 10¢ each; 50 or more, 8¢ each.
Libertarian Forum Associate subscription is $15.00 or more.

THE LIBERTARIAN FORUM

Box 341   Madison Square Station
New York, New York 10010

RECOMMENDED READING

Panther Revisionism.

Robert Brustein, "When the Panther Came to Yale",
New York Times Magazine (June 21). Panther
disruption at Yale.
Tom Wolfe, "Radical Chic: That Party at Lenny's",
New York (June 8, 40¢). A brilliant, scintillating
article that is the Talk of the Town. Witty, insightful dissection of Panther-worship among New
York's Beautiful People. Lenny Bernstein and his
cohorts will never be the same.

Drug Culture.

Milton Travers, "Each Other's Victims," *McCall's*
(June). A moving true story of a father's struggle
to save his son from the drug culture.

Anarchism.

Benjamin R. Tucker, *Instead of a Book* (New York:
Haskell Reprints, $15.00). At last, back in print,
the great classic of individualist anarchism; it's
a pleasure to read Tucker's logical, "plumb-line"
dissection of numerous deviationists.

*American History: Big Business, Big Labor, Big
Government*

Melvin I. Urofsky, *Big Steel and the Wilson Adminis-
tration* (Columbus, Ohio: Ohio State University
Press, $8100). Excellent Kolko-esque study of the
role of Big Business in the statism and collect-
ivism of the Wilson era, concentrating on the steel
industry.
Robert H. Zieger, *Republicans and Labor, 1919-1929*
(Lexington, Ky., University of Kentucky Press,
$8.25). Excellent work on the pro-union views of
Herbert Hoover and his wing of the Republican
Party.
Ronald Radosh, *American Labor and United States
Foreign Policy* (New York: Random House,
$10.00). The best book so far on U.S. labor lead-
ers as willing servants of American imperialism
abroad. Concentrates on U.S. labor in World War
I, also in the Cold War.

The Libertarian Forum
BOX 341
MADISON SQUARE STATION
NEW YORK, NEW YORK 10010

First Class

Published on the first and fifteenth of every month.   Subscription rate: $7.00 per year; Student subscription rate: $5.00 per year

~~~ DOUBLE ISSUE ~~~

A Semi-Monthly Newsletter

THE
Libertarian Forum

Joseph R. Peden, Publisher   Murray N. Rothbard, Editor

VOL. II, NO. 15-16   AUGUST, 1970   35¢

Hatfield For President?

Senator Mark Hatfield (R., Oregon) has become famous in recent years for his courageous independence from the Nixon Administration, and for his intrepid battle against the draft and the Vietnam War. Year after year Senator Hatfield has introduced bills for the abolition of conscription, and he is now co-author of the McGovern-Hatfield amendment designed to cut off all funds for the war in Southeast Asia by 1971. At the end of June, Senator Hatfield amazed Washington by breaking party protocol and sharply suggesting that Richard Nixon and Spiro Agnew might not be nominated in 1972, especially if the war and the economy continue in the mess that they're in now. Columnist Mary McGrory reports that "some of Hatfield's like-minded colleagues in the Senate whispered 'Right On' to him the morning after". (New York *Post*, June 30.)

A friendly Senate colleague of Hatfield's explained to Miss McGrory, concerning Hatfield's statement that the party might turn to Ronald Reagan in 1972, that "Mark did not want to seem to be pushing himself forward as a candidate." And the knowledgeable Miss McGrory adds: "The disillusioned Senator's name might turn up in the New Hampshire primary ballot in 1972. He might even be running as an independent with John V. Lindsay. . ."

There has been rising interest within the peace movement in a third political party, a party that would mobilize all the forces against conscription and war in a broad coalition that would, once and for all, smash the old frozen party structures, especially the Democratic Party, run by the bosses and hacks, and bring vital issues and choices concerning them back into American politics. As the extreme Right said six years ago (but not lately): we need a choice not an echo, and we have been getting only echoes for far too long. The Republican Party was born in the 1850's, when the Whig party structure refused to take a clear-cut stand on the extension of slavery, and so they were shunted aside for a new party designed to focus upon that neglected issue. The Democratic Party has refused to take a clear-cut stand against the war and against conscription, it has been virtually indistinguishable from the Republicans in the great blob of the Center, and it deserves therefore to disappear in the wake of a new party which will mobilize the public on these vital issues.

When most people think of a possible new party, they think of a candidate something like John Lindsay, and, indeed, most people think of Senator Hatfield as being ideologically similar to the liberal New York mayor. But this is not the case, and libertarians especially should be alerted to the crucial differences. Mark Hatfield thinks of himself, not as a modern-day liberal but as a "classical liberal", a nineteenth-century liberal devoted to the creed of a strictly limited government: limited at home and abroad. Hatfield thinks of himself as a disciple of Senator Robert Taft, and his courageously anti-war policy is of a piece with Taft's "isolationism", the foreign-policy of the Old Right before the "World Anti-Communist Crusade"-mentality infected and took over the conservative movement in this country. In domestic affairs, too, Mark Hatfield believes in reducing the power of government to its classical liberal dimension of defending the free-market economy.

Above all, Mark Hatfield has had the acute perceptiveness to be virtually the only one of the small band of classical liberals in Congress to see that the old rhetoric, the old political labels, have lost their usefulness. He has been the only one to see that the classical liberal is more happy with many aspects of the New Left than he is with his old-time allies in the conservative movement. In short, Mark Hatfield is the only classical-liberal politician I know of who understands and agrees with the Left/Right concept--with the idea that the libertarian has more in common with the New Left than with the contemporary Right. More important, Mark Hatfield sees that the only hope for liberty on the political front is to forge a new coalition, a coalition combining the libertarian ideas of both Left and Right, and consisting of the constituencies to whom these ideas would appeal: students, anti-war people, blacks, *and* middle-class whites opposed to statism and war. A Hatfield-forged coalition would base itself squarely on slashing the powers of government at home and abroad: in getting out of Southeast Asia and re-establishing a pro-peace, "isolationist", foreign policy; in repeal of the draft; and, domestically, in reducing the powers of Big Government in favor of a free, decentralized society.

Senator Hatfield is intelligent enough to see that, in contrast to a generation ago, a libertarian program of today, in today's political climate, cannot be couched in rhetoric

(Continued on page 4)

DOUBLE ISSUE

NOTICE: During July and August, we will publish special Double Issues: one covering July 1-July 15, and another August 1-August 15. We will return to our regular publishing schedule in September.

Black Flag For A New Decade

Radical Libertarianism: A Right Wing Alternative. By
Jerome Tuccille. Indianapolis: Bobbs-Merrill, 1970.
109 pp. $5.00.

Here is a book which goes on the must read list for
radicals interested in sorting out the politics of the sixties
with an eye to identifying some blind alleys and finding some
new directions. Tuccille speaks for the rapidly growing
numbers of radical libertarians, people who know where they
are going, and speaks to the broadest possible spectrum of
people who want to get to the same place but just haven't
gotten things quite straight in their heads yet. He has written,
quite simply, the best, most up-to-date, statement of radical
libertarian principles there is around, and, since a major
publisher has had the good business sense to see its enormous sales potential, everybody can get a copy without
writing to some obscure P. O. Box in New York.

Unless you are a very recent subscriber to this magazine,
and have thus missed articles here by radical libertarians
Murray Rothbard (June 15, 1969) and Karl Hess (October,
1969) you don't have to ask what *is* radical libertarianism.
But in case you do want an answer to that question, Tuccille's
book is where to find it. That's what he wrote it for. When
you read it, you will find that radical libertarianism (or
anarcho-libertarianism, a label some prefer) is a movement
right-wing in origin and ecumenical in appeal. Taking one
thing at a time, let's look at the right-wing origin first.

You don't have to get very far into the book before you
find out that radical libertarianism is *not* a "new right"
being set up to complement the new left. The *new* right
are the finks—William Buckley deserves and gets more
abuse than anyone else—who sold out on the last shreds of
the American Revolution along about the time of the Korean
War. They are the ones who, in Rothbard's words, dedicated
themselves to "the preservation of tradition, order, Christianity and good manners against the modern sins of reason,
license, atheism and boorishness". The new right are the
Greek Colonels and John Mitchells.

The old right used to have a pretty strong libertarian
element in it, although anyone who can't remember back that
far himself will probably not have heard of three-
quarters of the names Tuccille cites. If you go way back,
you get to Benjamin Tucker and Lysander Spooner—
Lysander who?? These were men who didn't like American
imperialism and militarism, state monopoly capitalism,
high taxes, and parasitic bureaucrats, cops climbing your
fire escape to peek and see if you are violating the laws
which regulate sexual conduct among consenting adults, or
customs agents who snoop to see what sort of imports you
are bringing back from Acapulco. They *did* like isolationism
and volunteer armies (if any), community control, doing
your own thing, and, if anyone had thought it up yet, they
would have liked Black Power (as Tuccille does).

Well, it is nice to know that radical libertarians are for
all those good things, you may be saying to yourself, and
maybe all the quotes from Thomas Jefferson will be useful
for winning over a few YAFers (in fact, Tuccille has a
very interesting appendix on the subject of the libertarian
breakaway faction of the YAF), but of what interest is all
this *right-wing* stuff to *me*, a card-carrying member of the
Woodstock generation? Answer is simple: radical libertarians know how to bridge the phony "gap" between left and
right. That means that you can get enough people on your
side to make things happen *now*, in the seventies, before
1984 catches your fraction of a faction with its pants down.

The simple libertarian lesson is that left and right are
only irreconcilable opposites so long as they are fighting it
out for who gets to run the state. As long as it is class
against class, state capitalism vs. state socialism, then
politics of revolution is just a matter of *kto-kovo* (trans-

lation: who screws whom) as Lenin would have put it. The
irreconcilability of the *statist* left and the *statist* right
derives from two simple axioms. (1) There can only be one
state in a given country at a given time, and (2) all states
are alike regardless of who runs them. That last is important. If there were any *substantive* difference between state
capitalism and state socialism, the historical process might
someday bring about a resolution of the conflict. But as it
is, it's just scorpions in a bottle.

So, now we are all convinced that statism is a hopelessly
bad trip, but does that help? Won't we just have another
round of *kto-kovo* with the anarcho-socialists fighting it out
with anarcho-capitalists? Tuccille makes a big point of
raising this question and answers a decisive *no*. It is worth
quoting him at some length on this.

> This is the beauty of anarcho-libertarianism: utter
> and complete toleration for any and all styles of life
> so long as they are voluntary and nonaggressive in
> nature. Only under such a system can the capitalist
> and socialist mentalities coexist peacefully, without
> infringing on the rights of other individuals and com-
> munities.

> The capitalist and socialist schools of anarchy . . .
> are united on the most crucial question of all: the
> absolute necessity for people to take control over their
> own lives, and the dismantling and final elimination of
> state authority over the life of man. Their major dis-
> agreement is one of personal attitudes concerning the
> makeup of human nature itself. Will man, left to his
> own devices, elect to live privately, trade his wits and
> talents on the open market, accept the fruits of his own
> labor and provide for his own happiness, and agree to
> relieve the misfortunes of those less talented than
> himself by voluntary means—or would he prefer to
> organize himself in voluntary communes, share the
> tools of production and the fruits of labor without
> angling for a larger proportionate share than his
> fellows, and live in a condition of spontaneous social
> communism?

Tuccille thinks the former. Tom Hayden thinks the latter.
The two could cheerfully coexist in separate enclaves in an
anarchist society. But far more important than the *possibility* that they could cheerfully coexist is the *fact* that even
if their contrasting life styles generated the utmost antipathy
and personal hatred, as long as the *state* had been dismantled and finally eliminated, and as long as both recognized and acted on the fundamental libertarian principle that
"every individual has the right to defend himself against any
person or organization . . . that initiates the use of force
against him", then the prejudice of the one could never mean
the enslavement of the other.

— Edwin G. Dolan

The State: ENEMY OF LATIN AMERICA

Unfortunately it seems that all too often libertarians, when debunking the great "U. S. Government is the international good guy" myth by pointing to the revisionist histories which are so unmarred by jingoism and great power chauvinism, concentrate on the topics which Leviathan's apologists choose to emphasize--namely the world wars, the Cold War, and Vietnam--and ignore the other manifestations of U. S. imperialist aggression which the press of the U. S. ruling class fails to mention. Why always be on the defensive and explode only the lies Amerika chooses to discuss, why not attack every oppression the world's greatest oppressor executes? The broad revisionist must be broad indeed.

The subject of U. S. imperialism in Latin America is undoubtedly one of such ignored topics. Moreover, the study of Latin America is doubly the responsibility of the libertarian, for the domestic situation there, besides being inseparable from U. S. imperialism, is highly significant on its own account as a problem which demands consistent explanation from the viewpoint of free market economics. Can any school ignore Third World development and still hope to win adherents in this day and age?

Many on both Left and Right have attempted to explain the political and economic problems of Latin America--the poverty and misery, the lack of freedom, and so forth--and have contributed highly significant but questionable analyses. These pitfalls are recognizable in two well-known representatives of the Left and Right, men who are highly libertarian in many areas--namely, Che Guevara and Ludwig Von Mises.

Che presented the Left analysis clearly in his speech "On Sacrifice and Dedication" delivered on June 18, 1960. The U. S. imperialists had been kicked out because "the first thing we want is to be masters of our own destiny, to be an independent country, a country free from foreign interference, a country that seeks out its own system of development without interference and that can trade freely anywhere in the world." In a word, the libertarian imperative of national self-determination was finally a reality. But what next? "Basically, there are two ways. . .One of them is called the free enterprise way. It used to be expressed by a French phrase, which in Spanish means 'let be.'" All economic forces, supposedly on an equal footing, would freely compete with each other and bring about the country's development." So far, so good. "That is what we had in Cuba, and what did it get us?" Wait a minute, Che, did not the U. S. and Cuban States consistently sabotage the free market in Cuba before the Revolution? Indeed, every example of "free enterprise" Che enumerates may be traced to dislocations caused by, in his own words, the tendency of Cuba's businessmen "to make deals with the soldiers of the moment, with the politicians in power, and to gain more advantages." In such a system "wealth is concentrated in the hands of a fortunate few, the friends of the government, the best wheeler-dealers." Naturally Che also pointed out how the U. S. Government prevented Cuban development. Hence, if anything, his critique of the old system should have led him to advocate its opposite--the free market--instead of rejecting economic freedom just because the old ruling class misleadingly called their system free enterprise. Yet, on the contrary, after tracing all evils to the State, Che exclaimed that "we, the government, should carry the weight and the direction of industrialization, so that there will not be any anarchy." But the Cuban people abhorred this (no doubt Batista had used the same excuse!): "And today, in the process of industrialization which gives such great importance to the state, the workers consider the state as just one more boss, and they treat it as a boss." The workers acted so for good reason: in spite of the laudable--but fruitless--fight of certain elements within the Cuban government against bureaucracy and

commandism through the 60s, the inherent nature of the all glorious Plan, the antithesis of the free market, reveals itself today in the increasing authoritarianism and bureaucraticism of the new Cuban State. According to the latest reports--e.g., Adam Hochschild in *Liberation*, Dec. 1969 and Maurice Zeitlin in *Ramparts*, March 1970--all decisions are made by the top elite and shoved down the throats of the masses below.

Enough of the Left analysis at this point; it has a good critique but very bad proposals. The Right analysis does not even offer a decent critique. Take Mises; to be sure, in the purest economic theory he is the age's greatest economist, but his views on world affairs, particularily his naive beliefs on U. S. history, are totally unrealistic. According to Mises, the wealth of the West, especially Amerika, and the poverty of the East and the Third World stem from the fact that the former have been peaceful "free" enterprisers while the latter, due to several factors such as statism, suffer from a shortage of capital. (cf. *Human Action*, 3rd ed., pp. 496-8). Mises' solution for Latin America would no doubt be more capital investments from their kindly Northern Neighbor.

Paul Baran knew much more about Latin America and the rest of the Third World than does Mises. He states categorically that "the principle obstacle to their development is *not* shortage of capital." Baran, a Marxist, could just as well have been a free market economist on this question: he clearly traced the present gross *misallocation*(not *scarcity*) of most Third World capital to State intervention in the market (cf. Baran, *Political Economy of Growth*, Ch. 7). Andre Gunder Frank, James Petras, and other Marxists have written a wealth of literature documenting--sometimes consciously, sometimes unconsciously--the essential role played by the State in keeping the masses of Latin America in poverty. Actually, any competent writer on Latin America, including everyone from UN (and hence U. S. imperialist) propagandists like Raul Prebisch to neo-fascists such as Helio Jaguaribe, cannot fail to mention that which is inseparable from Latin American under-development and poverty: the Imperial Northamerican State and the various Latin American semi-feudal States. To be sure, virtually everyone, like Che, discounts the inherent oppressiveness of the State when it comes time to propose a solution; yet if they offered a solution consonent with their critiques, they could propose nothing other than revolutionary free market anarchism.

One of the best comprehensive documentaries on the subject, which would serve as an excellent introduction to interested libertarians, is *Latin American Radicalism*, ed. by Horowitz, Castro, and Gerassi (Vintage, $2.45). There is obviously no space here to discuss all the many State interventions which have sabotaged the economies of the various Latin American countries; a short summary of the general position of the articles in this volume indicates the astounding role of the State in insuring utter poverty for the masses.

O. M. Carpeaux traces U. S. imperialism in Latin America from the time of the Monroe Doctrine, promulgated to give the U. S. privileges in world commerce and as a cover for Western expansion, and from the aggressions against Mexico, Cuba, Puerto Rico, etc., TR's Big Stick imperialism, the

(Continued on page 4)

ENEMY OF LATIN AMERICA — *(Continued from page 3)*

various Marine invasions in this and the last century, and so forth *ad nauseam*. Ample evidence is given to prove how the U. S. over and over has invaded Latin American countries and killed its people, monopolized its resources and seized its means of production in order to insure Amerikan hegemony primarily so that big business could secure--through privileges denied competitors--high yielding investments, rich deposits of raw materials, and restricted markets. The U. S. has never been content to abide by the rules of fair play in the market place of the world; no, Amerikan business has always demanded State-enforced privileges to suppress competition in "her" markets, to monopolize the sources of raw materials, and to insure a higher return on investments than the market would have set.

The story of U. S. intervention in the Dominican Republic in 1965 is told by Goff and Locker, who document the sugar interests of LBJ's advisors. This of course is part of a more general study concerning the alliance between the U. S. imperialists and the feudal Latin American oligarchies by which both use each other to oppress the masses but ultimately the latter play marionette to the former or face a coup sponsored by the CIA. John Saxe-Fernandez documents the military aid by which the U. S. keeps the Central American dictators in power. What is to be done? is answered by Debray, Che, Torres and other revolutionaries in the last section. The volume clearly demonstrates the truth of the prediction by the great liberator Bolívar in 1829: "The United States appear to be destined by Providence to plague America with misery in the name of liberty."

And Mises says the road to development is paved with more Western capital! Naturally, the libertarian would never want to see free trade restricted; but the U. S. Government has forever insisted on sabotaging the free market and bringing the rest of the world to its knees by bribes in the form of "grants" from the Alliance for "Progress" and other such organs, or force in the form of CIA assassinations or Marine Massacres. Truly, liberation from U. S. domination would do much to unshackle the chains on the Latin American economies.

An added effect of the death of U. S. imperialism would be that the various dictators could be overthrown and the means of production seized by the masses, who would have owned them in the first place had a free market existed all along rather than feudalism/state capitalism. Few if any of the Latin American oligarchies could stay in power a week if there were no U. S. imperialism to back them up.

One has only to study the economic history of almost any country in Latin America to understand how governments, kept in power by foreign governments (first Spain and other European colonialists, later the U. S.) have never allowed a free market so as to hold the masses in serfdom and guarantee the small ruling elite all the wealth. Every government intervention in the economy has as its purpose to grab more wealth for the ruling class; it is no accident that wherever a State exists wealth coincides with--not the ability to serve consumers in the market--but ruling power, i.e., the ability to plunder the poorer members of society.

Aldo Ferrer, by no means a radical, shows how the process works in his important book *The Argentine Economy*. While he does not say so in those words, Ferrer traces stagnation to the State and offers economic analyses and empirical data to substantiate how the Argentine State intervenes in the economy to increase the wealth of the rich, the ruling class. Virtually every single upset in the economy or reason for under-development in Argentine history was directly caused by the State; the inference which Ferrer fails to draw, the other side of the same coin, is that none of this could have occurred without a State. It takes a State to plunder the masses, it takes a State to make the poor poorer so the rich can get richer, it takes a State to make the free market an

HATFIELD FOR PRESIDENT? — *(Continued from page 1)*

pleasing only to an extreme right-wing that is now hopelessly anti-libertarian. His rhetoric will be modern, in keeping with the perceptions of today, and in keeping with his knowledge of how a broad libertarian coalition could be forged. And make no mistake: the Senator does refer to himself, consciously, as a libertarian, and this in itself is almost unheard of in American politics.

I know, I know; I know all about the cries of protest that will now be welling up in scores of libertarian hearts, those hearts which, like mine, are steeped in innate and instinctive distrust for any and every politician. The remarkable thing is that Mark Hatfield himself understands such distrust just as well, and probably shares it. A while ago he told a group of us, spontaneously bringing up the point himself: "I have not, like Faust, sold my soul to politics." I believe him. And if the time should ever come when Mark Hatfield runs for the Presidency, I shall enlist without hesitation behind his banner.

impossibility. The present State was exported from the State of Spain. Its purpose was an imperialist one, namely, to extract wealth from the colony so that, through mercantilist manipulation of the economy, the ruling class would become richer. Together with the new requirement of plunder by a new ruling class--the one residing in the colony, this necessitated the extermination of the Indians (Argentina rapidly learned "free enterprise" à la Northamerica!) and monopolization of the land. All of this presupposed a State. Unused land reserved for monopolists by the State, Ferrer points out, had as its purpose exploitation of the poor by their rich oppressors by perpetuating a monopoly of the valuable land resource in the hands of a small elite. Wages were forced down well below their marginal productivity, since the masses were not allowed to homestead and so had to work for wages in order to survive, and since the big landowners could get by with gross inefficiency and hence high agricultural prices since they owned all the natural resources.

The masses were (and are) also exploited by the wealthy elite through the State's policy of never-ending inflation. As Ferrer clearly shows, inflation is based on a governmental desire to spend money it has "created" on those holding the puppet strings, but even more on the fact that prices rise faster than wages, i.e., real wages decrease while profits zoom upwards. This profit inflation is all the better for the rich in control of the State to make plundering returns and capital accumulation through theft; furthermore, import costs rise which means a bounty on exports, all of which amounts to price increases for the masses and State privileges for domestic producers on the home and foreign markets. Finally, as if the above were not enough to fulfill the parasitic urges of the criminal class controlling the State to concentrate all the wealth in their hands, all sorts of blatantly regressive taxes--especially tariffs and excise taxes--are imposed upon the masses. Tariffs, which are high as heaven in Argentina, of course allow domestic business to be grossly inefficient and charge exorbitant prices to the poor. Insult is added to injury when the plunder extracted by regressive taxation is spent progressively--that is, all the subsidies and spending of the State are for the benefit of the ruling oligarchy.

Ferrer hesitates to employ such strong language, but his data certainly back it up. They back up the class nature of the Argentine State, the principle that the purpose of the State is to make the rich richer by making the poor poorer, and the inference that the State must be abolished, the expropriators expropriated, and a completely free market substituted for the present system of monopoly State feudalism/capitalism if real economic development is ever to occur.

——Stephen P. Halbrook

Bits And Pieces

By Jerome Tuccille

The Black Declaration of Independence printed in the New York *Times*, July 3, 1970, is one of the most refreshing documents to emerge from the Black Power movement since the speeches of Malcolm X. With incisive clarity the authors of this statement have brilliantly paraphrased the language of the original Declaration of Independence and catalogued a long list of grievances with a notable absence of emotionalism and simplistic rhetoric. The document was prepared by the National Committee of Black Churchmen, 110 East 125th St., New York City, and signed by forty black clergymen of various faiths.

Starting with the opening words of the Declaration of Independence—"When in the course of Human Events, it becomes necessary for a people . . ."—the Black Declaration goes on to enumerate a multitude of abuses inflicted on the black community by government. These include: the "desecration" of "Dwelling Places, under the Pretense of Urban Renewal"; swarms of "Social Workers, Officers and Investigators" sent into the black communities to "harass our People"; the stationing of "Armies of Police, State Troopers and National Guardsmen" in ghetto neighborhoods "without the consent of our People"; "the dissolution of school districts controlled by Blacks" whenever they oppose outside domination; and racist attitudes in general which have isolated blacks in dilapidated areas and denied them adequate housing, schooling and employment as well as their ordinary Constitutional Rights.

The value of this Declaration rests in the fact that its creators have confined themselves to a careful historical analysis of calculated injustice, and they have stayed clear of generalized polemics about "fascism", "capitalist exploitation", and the usual sloganeering that has replaced reasonable discussion at a time it is needed most.

The document ends with the statement that blacks have continually petitioned government for an end to "Repressive Control" and that government has "been deaf to the voice of Justice and of Humanity." The final tone is ominous: ". . . unless we receive full Redress and Relief from these Inhumanities we shall move to renounce all Allegiance to this Nation, and will refuse, in every way, to cooperate with the Evil which is Perpetrated upon ourselves and our Communities."

This breath of fresh air is a welcome change at a time when the American nation is being inundated on all levels by torrents of fiery prose. Unless there is a sharp reversal of our government's foreign and domestic policies at once, the Second American Revolution may pre-date the two-hundredth anniversary of the first.

* * * * * *

From the New York *Times*, July 5, 1970, comes word that Governor William G. Milliken of Michigan will sign a bill allowing citizens the right to file suit against public agencies and private industries which pollute the environment. Michigan will become the first state to *specifically* insure citizens of this fundamental right to protect their own property against unwanted invasion by contaminating elements. Other states planning similar legislation are New York, Massachusetts, Pennsylvania, Tennessee, Colorado, California and Texas, and a federal bill is now before the U. S. Senate.

All the authorities are doing here is putting on the books a right which has always belonged by Natural Law to the people: the right of self-defense. The injection of harmful ingredients into our air supply is automatically a violation of property rights since they will eventually find their way into someone else's lungs. Likewise, water, sound and soil

Nixon And The Economy

The editor has commented recently (June 15 issue) on "The Nixon Mess." In some respects Professor Rothbard has understated the case against Nixon. Consider what is euphemistically being referred to as "the liquidity crisis." What this crisis amounts to is a profit squeeze on firms in the capital goods industries--Professor Hayek's "higher orders of production." Rothbard has explained in the June 15 article that liquidation in the capital goods industries is a necessary condition for the end of a boom, and a return to economic "normalcy." Much investment specialized to these industries must become worthless in the process; it would have been better, of course, if the investments had never been made. However, bygones are bygones, and no policy could be more wistful and ill-conceived than one which would attempt to "save" investments which have been demonstrated (on the market) to have been unwisely pursued. As much capital as is possible must be salvaged, and re-invested in the production of consumers' goods, so that resources can be applied to the production of goods that are most highly desired. It is this latter process which eventually slows the price-inflation in the consumers' goods industries (by increasing the supply of consumers' goods), and eventually results in the proper ratio of investment in capital goods relative to consumers' goods--the correct "structure of production."

In effect, the Nixon Administration has announced that it will not permit this process to be carried out. Arthur Burns

(Continued on page 6)

pollution invariably results in physical harm to other persons.

So we can thank the politicians for stating a principle which should have been obvious to everyone years ago. One beneficial aspect of this legislation is that, for a rare change, legality coincides with Natural Law. The Law 'n' Order Neanderthals don't have to worry anymore about breaking a law when they sue the Atomic Energy Commission for poisoning their children.

* * * * * * * *

Lately, a few libertarians have grown fond of supporting the Mafia as a legitimate black market organization operating outside the entrepreneurial restraints of government. They reason that many Mafia activities such as gambling, melting silver coins, loansharking, prostitution, even peddling narcotics are voluntaristic in nature and ought not to be considered illegal.

Much of this is true. But what is overlooked is the fact that the Mafia no more welcomes competition in its various enterprises than does the federal government, and has gone to even greater lengths to suppress it. The racketeers have supplied their competitors with cement boots before taking them swimming, firebombed their places of business, and run competing ice cream and garbage trucks from the highways. They have utilized torture, mutilation and murder to keep their "free market" businesses from enduring the hardships of competitive enterprise.

In addition, Mafia-controlled unions are responsible for the grand-scale pilfering that has gone on for years on the docks and at our airports. The Cosa Nostra families are no strangers to the less-than-subtle art of extortion— shaking down neighborhood storekeepers for the right to stay in business. So, while there is a hilarious side to the spectacle of exotic characters with names like Tony "Big Walnuts" Perrotta or Mario "Apricots" Terrazzo eluding the clutches of Big Government, it is dangerous to romanticize their peculiar brand of Black Market Monopoly. The Mafia is every bit as Law 'n' Order-happy as Spiro Agnew. It is its own law and its own order. And Mafiosi have never been too strong on due process.

NIXON AND THE ECONOMY — *(Continued from page 5)*

recently stated (*The Wall Street Journal*, July 3, 1970) that the Federal Reserve System "is fully aware of its responsibility to prevent . . . a scramble for liquidity" (i.e., disinvestment)." An unnamed official of the Fed (WSJ, 7/3/70) has stated that that organization finds even Friedman's suggestion for steady growth in the money supply too extreme (calling Friedman's idea "sheer fanaticism").

Consider also the implications of the Penn Central fiasco. The Nixon Administration, by its actions, is all but saying that it will not permit any large corporation to go under. The railroads are a clear case of an industry which needs disinvestment. Conservative estimates see 35 percent of the nation's trackage as not being economically justifiable. Probably at least that much of Penn Central's trackage should be pared. Yet the government wants to step in, to lend the corporation money, in order to try to prevent the inevitable. For years the railroad has been covertly disinvesting in the only way it could--given the tight regulation of the industry--, by allowing the quality of its service to deteriorate. This is no longer enough. Unfortunately, the Nixon Administration will undoubtedly duplicate the policies of the Eisenhower Administration as regards the railroads: grant loans to the weakest lines in order to tide them over a recession. Professor George Hilton, in his *The Transportation Act of 1958*, has amply demonstrated the folly of the previous loan guarantees given the railroads. Railroads are even more susceptible to economic fluctuations (especially the Eastern lines) than a capital goods industry like steel. A given percentage downturn in steel or auto production often results in a greater percentage downturn in rail profits. If the railroads had been permitted to disinvest earlier, they would not be in the trouble they are in now. If not permitted to disinvest now, they will be in even worse shape when the next recession hits.

Nixon, however, is not satisfied to emulate past follies. He is apparently determined to extend government aid to any major firm in any industry that wants it. A lot of ignorant people have written a lot of arrant nonsense about inflation's being caused by a "wage-price spiral." But the kernel of truth hidden in all this talk must not be overlooked. Ever since the Hoover New Deal, the policy of the federal government has been moving toward one of assuring the profitability of American big business (thus guaranteeing for itself an important source of support for its policies--foreign and domestic). With the government more and more willing to underwrite losses, there is less and less incentive for corporate heads to heed the warnings of the market, and curtail

operations where indicated. If he should continue to invest when he should be disinvesting, the businessman can now go to the federal government should crisis strike. All of this, we are told (WSJ, 7/3/70), has led some of Nixon's top aides to an "anti-business feeling"; these aides point out that business executives preach free enterprise, but "come running to us" when they get into trouble. One can be sure that these aides will soon "shape up," or be "shipped out!"

The point here is that the business executive now need not cut prices in the face of falling demand; or resist wage demands of unions. Union leaders need worry less about whether they are asking for more than a market wage. The federal government has announced its willingness to supply cash--virtually to print money up if necessary--to major corporations that find themselves in a "liquidity crisis" (i.e., find themselves over-extended). Keynesian Walter Heller has spoken of an "inflationary bias" in our economy. In doing so, he is perhaps being more prescient than Milton Friedman (for some reason inexplicable to this author, Professor Friedman considers Nixon to be a brilliant man bent on bringing libertarianism to America). Up with free enterprise!

What is happening now is what Ludwig von Mises predicted nearly sixty years ago would happen to those countries which adopted the economics of inflationism. Inflation up until very recently in this country has been largely unanticipated; it has in effect been a tax on money holdings. The public is now beginning to expect further inflation, and, as with any tax, are finding ways to avoid the tax. In economic terms, they are decreasing their demand for money. Rather than go through the painful process of contradicting these inflationary expectations, the government has apparently chosen to meet them. To do this, the government must continue to inflate at something like the present 9 to 10 percent rate. But this will lead to expectations of inflation, and a further decrease in the demand for money; and to a "need" for further inflation . . . Mises has been largely dismissed by modern economists. His analysis is not supposed to be "applicable" to a modern economy (wasn't Germany a modern economy in the 1920's?). Yet seldom has an analysis been so applicable as is Mises' now. Unless the present course is reversed, we are on the long, slow (but inevitable) road to the destruction of our monetary system. And, as Mises has so often and so ably pointed out, if there is any one institution whose evolution is necessary for modern civilization as we know it, it is that of money. If this administration does not blow us up, it may have the dubious distinction of having brought us to the economic ruin that so many others have failed in accomplishing.

—Gerald O'Driscoll, Jr.

The Libertarian Forum
BOX 341
MADISON SQUARE STATION
NEW YORK, NEW YORK 10010

Published on the first and fifteenth of every month.   Subscription rate: $7.00 per year; Student subscription rate: $5.00 per year

A Semi-Monthly Newsletter

THE
Libertarian Forum

Joseph R. Peden, Publisher

Murray N. Rothbard, Editor

VOLUME II, NO. 17   SEPTEMBER 1, 1970   35¢

THE SOCIALIST SCHOLARS CAPER

Once again, dear reader, your own *Lib. Forum* has made the mass media. The fact that the reference, though prominent, was also malicious, distorted, and absurd, should not make us despair. However distorted, "as long as the name is spelled right" and it was, *some* of the tens of thousands out there who read about us might have the urge to look into us more closely, to see the Devil plain as it were, and then their conversion is always possible.

The story begins with the Socialist Scholars Conference, which, confusedly, is the name both for an organization of socialist scholars *and* for the conferences that they have held in New York every year since 1965. Not being a socialist, I am not a member of the SSC organization, but I have attended many of their conferences, for many of their papers and panels have been lively, interesting, and informative. Never having much influence on the Left, the SSC conferences have been declining in recent years, since they have suffered, along with the rest of the Left, from a growing group of young militants who hold scholarship and intellect to be worthless and "irrelevant", and who therefore long to purge the word "Scholars" from the title. (If we ask the logical question: If they don't want scholarship, *why* do they join an organization of scholars and then try to wreck it? Why do they bother?—then we are in deep waters indeed, for then we would be trying to explain much of the destructiveness and unreason that has overcome the Left in recent years.)

From the beginning, into these pleasant if not earth-shaking sessions strode one Mrs. Alice Widener, wealthy owner and editor of an unimportant, Red-baiting newsletter called *USA*. A self-styled "authority" on the Left, La Widener arrived every year at the SSC sessions, and reported on them with unwavering mininterpretation and ignorance of what the whole thing was all about. La Widener trying to make sense of all the nuances of social philosophy was truly a bull let loose in a china shop. One famous *gaffe* of hers was the time she attended a session on slavery featuring Eugene D. Genovese and Herbert Aptheker. Trying desperately to link the then famously radical Genovese with the admitted Communist Aptheker, Widener had them in solid agreement, when the entire scholarly world knows that, in their views on slavery, Genovese and Aptheker could not be further apart in every possible way. But apart from the mininterpretations of Widener was her strange notion that the SSC was in some way the Politburo of the Left, so that its papers and panels set down the annual line for all the Left underlings everywhere. Widener's annual reports from the conferences, ever agog with new crisis and horror, have always provided welcome horselaughs for the SSC members, who were particularly amused by the fact that, of all the people in the country, in or out of the SSC, only Mrs. Widener seemed

to think of these sessions as having any earth-shaking importance.

Mrs. Widener's annual blatherings only took on importance from the fact that they have been solemnly reprinted, year after year, as lead articles in *Barron's*, a pro-*laissez-faire* Wall St. weekly of large circulation, blessed with an editor of neo-Randian persuasion; from *Barron's*, they percolated to a readership of conservatives who imbibed her annual nonsense as Gospel, and took from it their world-view as to what was going on in the world of Left scholarship.

Well, comes 1970 and the June 13-14 meeting, and Professor Leonard Liggio and myself were invited to speak at a panel to be organized by Professor Liggio, and devoted to "Left/Rightism"—specifically, to a reassessment of the Old Right and how it prefigured much of the New Left criticisms of welfare-warfare America. We devoted considerable care to preparation of the papers, and I must say that much enjoyment was had by all, although how much influence we had on the assembled Left is dubious, since the overwhelming majority of our audience were our own libertarians, with an occasional leftist wandering in who didn't seem to know the difference between Franklin and Teddy Roosevelt. At any rate, our entire panel was devoted to an appreciative portrayal of the hard-hitting views of the Old Right and their libertarian approach to war, foreign policy and militarism, as well as to education, state-monopoly-capitalism, decentralization, the judiciary, and civil liberties. Especially lauded by us were such "Old Rightists" as: Senator Taft, John T. Flynn, Frank Chodorov, Albert Jay Nock, Garet Garrett, Felix Morley, Senator borah, H. L. Mencken, Rep. Howard Beffett, etc.

Enter La Widener. (USA, June 19-July 3; *Barron's*, July 13.) Or rather, enter La Widener by remote control, since it is all too clear that she did not attend any of the Conference. Her entire report is taken up with lengthy quotes from unimportant position papers issued ahead of the Conference by the SSC organizers; there is not a word on any of the panels, that is, on the content of the Conference itself, *except, mirabile dictu*, on *ours*! To our panel came her assistant, one Falzone, accompanied by a certain Miss Poor from the Orlando *Sentinel*. (In thus ignoring all the other panels, Widener-Poor-Falzon completely missed the *real* story of the Conference, which was its total domination by the crazed forces of Women's Liberation, whose well-attended and almost continuous panels barred The Enemy—men—from daring to attend. Seconded, I might add, by singularly truculent and unscholarly youths from the Free Joan Bird Committee.)

So there we are, Leonard Liggio and myself, with our names spelled correctly, on the front page of the mighty

(Continued on page 2)

SOCIALIST SCHOLARS CAPER — *(Continued from page 1)*

Barron's! There, Poor-Falzon-Widener report that in introducing me, Professor Ronald Radosh, moderator of the panel, made "snide remarks" about the American flag (Oh no! Good God! Not that!), and added that I had once, somewhere, described the flag as a "rag", and they noted that I did not immediately leap up and protest this attribution. So much for what I *didn't* say at the panel. Next, in a truly cunning piece of research that must leave us all agog, our intrepid authority on social movements finds repeated links between Professor Liggio and myself (Oh, wow!). From there, our indefatigable scholar goes on to find what she believes to be the *key*, the key evil article which set the line for the entire Socialist Scholars Conference, and since we already know that the SSC in turn functions as the Politburo of the Left, for the entire Left-wing in America. And that article, dear reader, is none other than Leonard Liggio's "State of the Movement", which comprised the *Lib. Forum* of May 15. So there we are, emblazoned on the front page of *Barron's* as kingpin of the entire Left in America! There follows two quotes from the Liggio article: one in which Leonard dared to quote favorably from Julius Lester (in a highly intelligent attack that he had levelled on the ultra-adventurism of the Panthers), and another in which she scoffs at an example of Liggio's "so-called Libertarian thinking, the example being praise for early SDS opposition to the draft!

I suppose we must reconcile ourselves to the fact that there *are* people in this world so divorced from reality that they really believe that Leonard Liggio and the *Lib. Forum* are the high panjandrums of the American Left—just as there are people who believe that the world is being run by twelve secret Jewish Illuminati. And I suppose we must accept the fact that there are "authorities" on political philosophy so lame-brained as to believe that a libertarian is someone who approves of the draft. But what is this nonsense doing on the front page of *Barron's*?

But, and here we rise from the merely stupid to the slightly sinister, isn't it odd that in all the concentration by Mrs. Widener on our panel, there is not a single word of what we actually *said* at the panel, at the content of our rather lengthy remarks? On this, the actual substance of what we said at the Conference, the team of Poor-Falzon-Widener falls strangely silent. The reason for this odd silence should be clear; if she had written one word of what we actually said at the Conference, it would have blown her entire thesis of us as leading Marxists and socialists sky-high. For even a gullible conservative readership that has virtually forgotten its past might think twice at talks exclusively devoted to praising Taft, Nock, Flynn, etc.

The *Barron's* article predictably sent many conservative readers into a tizzy. Instead of rejoicing at the fact that some socialists, at least, are coming to see a great deal of merit in libertarian, Old Right perspectives, their reaction was just the opposite. "What! Murray Rothbard, a free-market economist, is now a socialist! What happened?" Obviously, what these people need badly is to stop reading La Widener and to start reading the *Lib. Forum* and its ancillary and recommended readings. Like all prospective readers, they are welcome. Why did we put on this panel at the Socialist Scholars Conference? Because we were asked. I am sure that we would do the same at a conference of conservative intellectuals; but the important point is that we have *not* been asked by any such conference, which says a great deal about the current ideological scene.

At any rate, I have written a letter of protest to *Barron's* setting the record straight, which has of this writing not been printed (perhaps following the Randian line of denouncing but not "giving sanction to" The Enemy?). If it is printed, then the Great Socialist Scholars Caper will have one more installment.

More On Ardrey

Some further notes on Jerry Tuccille's critique of the Ardrey-Lorenz fad among libertarians:

1. The "territorial imperative" thesis can be, and has been, used far more easily to defend *not* individual private property but collective-herd property, as well as interstate wars. Thus, dogs prefer to use lampposts which other dogs have also used, thereby displaying a collective tribal "property" "instinct"?

2. The "instinct" concept is generally tacked on when we lack a genuine explanation for a phenomenon. Thus, even Adam Smith explained the universal phenomenon of exchange and market, not in terms of mutually rational advantage, but of an innate "instinct", or "propensity to truck and barter". Man, in particular, must use his mind to learn, to formulate his goals and the means to attain them. He has no inborn instinct to guide him automatically to the correct
(Continued on page 4)

Bits And Pieces
By Jerome Tuccille

A subject getting much attention lately is the studies on evolution and human behavior performed by a new breed of ethnologists whose chief pioneers are Konrad Lorenz, Robert Ardrey, and Desmond Morris. *Playboy* covered the new ethnologists in an article by Morton Hunt appearing in the July, 1970 issue, and the *New York Times Magazine* recently published an interview with Konrad Lorenz. Basically, what the ethnologists are saying, is that man has survived and become dominant over all other earthly creatures because he was the most murderous and most savage of all the primates. The primordial ancestors of man were the first to develop the use of weapons, and in the struggle for survival through evolutionary time, man emerged triumphant because he learned the art of murder and violence better than his competitors. Man, according to the ethnologists, is still largely driven by violent genetic instincts which set him off from time to time on an orgy of war and mass destruction.

The part of this theory which is of primary concern to propertarians is the claim that man's hunger for real estate, for a private plot of earth over which he can reign supreme, is an integral part of his nature as a violent being. According to Ardrey, it is useless for the social engineers to try to "socialize" man, to take away his property and make him share his possessions with the multitudes, because to do so is to tamper with the basic nature of man as a private, acquisitive animal. What the socialists are doing is forcing man to act in variance with his own nature, and thus they are setting the stage for revolutionary uprisings against their governments. The "territorial imperative", man's drive for private chunks of real estate, say the ethnologists, is stronger than his sexual urge. Ardrey argues that since this instinct is inborn in man it will be part of his genetic makeup as long as he exists. It is better to leave man alone, to let him have his land and possessions, since to tinker with his instincts will only increase his penchant for violence.

The controversy involved here is that most free-market libertarians base their arguments for private property and free trade on reason: the private-property, free-trade system is better because it is the most rational way for man to exist. What Ardrey is saying, at least implicitly, is that a socialist society is somehow more rational and would be a less violent way for man to live. But since man is more instinct-driven, more apt to act on irrational instincts than he will on rational considerations, and since this is part of his basic, unchanging nature, it is better to leave him alone with his selfishness, his greed, his drive for land and gadgets.

Both Ardrey and Lorenz seem to be contradicting themselves later when they state that man does have the capacity, because of his evolving brain, to overcome his violent nature. Both Ardrey and Lorenz declare explicitly that man's emerging capacity for reason may enable him to chain down his murderous instincts and live in harmony with his fellows. They have put themselves in the precarious position of saying, on the one hand, that man can never overcome his violent nature because it is permanent in his genes and, on the other, that man's reason does give him a chance for peace after all. They are attempting to have it both ways and therefore their arguments in favor of man the competitive property owner are tenuous at best.

The great weakness in this position, it seems to me, rests in the fact that the ethnologists attribute man's survival over the millenia to his "violence-prone" nature.

If it is true that the ancestors of man (and here a layman has to defer to the knowledge obtained through years of scientific studies) survived by developing weapons and slaughtering their fellow primates, does this necessarily mean that they did so because they were instinctively murderous? If original man created tools and weapons half a million years ago it is indicative that, even then, he was beginning to develop his capacity for reason. Ardrey admits that it was a time of fantastic hardship for all living creatures on the continent of Africa, where he claims our species first emerged. If this is the case and the various primate species were forced down from the trees onto the land in their quest for a dwindling food supply, it follows that the creatures who survived would be those who were best able to *defend* their food and land from marauding bands. In the age of pre-civilization there simply was not enough to go around. Many had to die and only a limited few were able to stay alive and procreate their species. Does this mean that the few, those who developed the means of survival were "murderous" and "savage"?

For one to reason this way he would also have to believe that, in a present crisis, if the earth were savaged by a massive famine with not enough food to feed the world, only the most violent and murderous would survive. This is simply not the case. It is the most rational, the most capable and productive of our species who would outlast the rest. Murder would be primarily an act of self-defense committed against those who were also capable of murdering for a crust of bread.

If the originals of our species were able to survive the perils of the ice age, as well as the designs of less-acquisitive, less-inventive creatures, they are to be commended instead of denigrated as "savages" and "murderers". We surely have a great inheritance to live up to. They have shown us that our drive for property, food and comfort is ours because it is good and rational, and not because we are genetically-driven killers. It is here, in their *basic premise*, that Ardrey and his colleagues have gone astray.

*   *   *   *   *

One of the best statements to date on the question of abortion *reform* appears in the August, 1970 issue of *Ramparts*. In an article entitled, "Abortion Reform: The New Tokenism", Lucinda Cisler, president of New Yorkers for Abortion Law Repeal, warns against the enthusiasm engendered by the sudden rush to liberalize abortion laws in many of our states. Cisler's message is directed primarily at feminists, but her reasoning has ecumenical appeal because of its basic libertarian foundation.

She begins by listing the usual arguments given by legislators for their endorsement of abortion law reform: "they are concerned with important issues like the public health problem presented by illegal abortions, the doctor's right to offer patients good medical care, the suffering of unwanted children and unhappy families, and the burgeoning of our population at a rate too high for *any* economic system to handle."

(Continued on page 4)

141

BITS AND PIECES — *(Continued from page 3)*

All these reasons are good in themselves, she continues, but in the final analysis they are peripheral to the key principle involved: justice for women. The liberalizers of existing abortion laws are operating under the premise that a woman's body belongs to the state, and because of this underlying logic the mere *reform* of abortion laws is insulting and patronizing to women. Cisler sets her sights on the total *repeal* of all regulatory codes governing abortions on the grounds that a woman "belongs to herself and not to the state", and the decision to have or not to have an abortion is hers alone to make.

While many advocates of abortion law *repeal* have welcomed *reform* of abortion laws as a "step in the right direction", the author warns that in the long run it may be a dangerous seduction since "it can buy off most middle-class women and make them believe things have really changed, while it leaves poor women to suffer and keeps us all saddled with abortion laws for many years to come." The four major restrictions imposed on even the most liberal of the new reform bills are as follows:

1. *Abortions may only be performed in licensed hospitals.* Cisler argues that this not only drives up the cost of abortions, but it subjects women unnecessarily to a new host of "guidelines" established by generally conservative hospital administrations. It also limits the number of abortions that can be performed by making it illegal to obtain an abortion at a clinic or in a doctor's office;

2. *Abortions may only be performed by licensed physicians.* This again serves the purpose of driving the cost over $300, and it protects the doctors' monopoly from paramedics who can "be trained to do a great many things that physicians do not";

3. *Abortions may not be performed beyond a certain time in pregnancy, unless the woman's life is at stake.* This restriction is insidious since, in effect, it says to women that "(a) at a certain stage your body suddenly belongs to the state . . . and (b) because late abortion entails more risk than early abortion, the state must 'protect' you, even if your considered decision is that you want to run that risk . . ." This regulation requires "that we must be in a state of tutelage and cannot assume responsibility for our own acts";

4. *Abortions may only be performed when the married woman's husband or the young single woman's parents give their consent.* According to the author, the "objection to vesting a veto power in anyone other than the pregnant women is too obvious to need any elaboration."

All in all, this is one of the most eloquent and cogent declarations yet from a prominent leader in the struggle for individual rights for women.

"With reasonable men, I will reason; with humane men, I will plead; but to tyrants, I will give no quarter . . ."
                                                          William Lloyd Garrison

MORE ON ARDREY — *(Continued from page 2)*

choices, as the bird or the salmon are *supposed* to be guided.

3. The whole basis for the "territorial imperative" among animals rests on the fact that animals are bound *within* the environment in which they find themselves. If a group of animals are adapted only to the environment of a certain area, X, and they are forced to leave X they will die. They must then defend this environment to the death. Man, on the contrary, is unique among living beings for his capacity to *change* his environment, to leave, transform, and alter his circumstances on behalf of his own survival and progress. Man is not bound to a fixed plot of earth and all the environmental conditions upon it; he can move, he can build shelter against the elements, he can transform the earth, etc. And so the animal-derived argument for territory cannot apply to man.

4. As for scholarly authority, a friend of mine tried to organize a scholarly conference of biologists, ethnologists, etc. to discuss the Lorenz thesis; try as he might, he could not find *one* scholar to take the Lorenz side. All the others had flatly rejected it.

The Libertarian Forum
BOX 341
MADISON SQUARE STATION
NEW YORK, NEW YORK 10010

First Class

Published on the first and fifteenth of every month.   Subscription rate: $7.00 per year; Student subscription rate: $5.00 per year

A Semi-Monthly Newsletter

THE
Libertarian Forum

Joseph R. Peden, Publisher

Murray N. Rothbard, Editor

VOLUME II, NO. 18   SEPTEMBER 15, 1970   35¢

FALL READING

Anarchism.

Great News! The outstanding history of individualist anarchism in America, the superb and scholarly James J. Martin, *Men Against the State: The Expositors of Individualist Anarchism in America, 1827-1908*, is back in print! (paperback, Ralph Myles, Publisher, Colorado Springs, Colo., 315 pp., $2.50). This edition is remarkably inexpensive, yet excellently printed—in contrast to the 1953 original. The footnotes are actually at the bottom of the page! Also photographs are added of the leading individualist anarchists: Josiah Warren, Benjamin R. Tucker, Lysander Spooner, and Ezra Heywood. A *must* book.

Minor correction: the updated Martin bibliography omits to mention the recent reprints by Burt Franklin, New York, of Stephen Pearl Andrews, *The Basic Outline of Universology* (1967), Andrews, *The Primary Synopsis of Universology* (1967), Josiah Warren, *Equitable Commerce* (1965), and Warren, *True Civilisation* . . . (1965).

Daniel Guérin, *Anarchism: From Theory to Practice* (New York: Monthly Review Press, $6.00, 166 pp.), is a concise, highly lucid work that deals with the history of anarchist theory (European, there is no mention or seeming knowledge of the American individualists) topically rather chronologically, and with a history of the outstanding examples of anarcho-syndicalism. This French anarchist is clearly influenced primarily by the quasi-individualist Frenchman, Proudhon, and so his exposition of anarchist theory gives little offense to the individualist or even the believer in the free-market. However, Guérin's version of the collectivist-communist anarchists Kropotkin and Bakunin, as well as of the amoral might-makes-rightist Max Stirner, considerably prettifies and distorts their views, to make them appear to be almost reasonable men. The unfortunate introduction by Noam Chomsky goes far beyond Guérin to assert that an anarchist must be a socialist (!) Professor Chomsky would be well-advised to steep himself in the Martin book, and then see if he will maintain this view. An appreciative review of Guérin can be found in the *Liberated Guardian* (July 14) by Leonard P. Liggio. There is, alas, no index.

Spencer H. MacCallum, *The Art of Community* (Institute for Humane Studies, 1134 Crane St., Menlo Park, Calif. 94025, paperback, $2.00; hardcover, $4.00; 118 pp.), is also well calculated to disquiet Professor Chomsky. This is the first systematic presentation in print of what might be called the "Heathian" sub-variant of anarchism, after its creator, Mr. MacCallum's grandfather, Spencer Heath. The Heathian goal is to have cities and large land areas owned by single private corporations, which would own and rent out the land and housing over the area, and provide all conceivable "public services": police, fire, roads, courts, etc., out of the voluntarily-paid rent. Heathianism is Henry Georgism stood on its head; like George, Heath and MacCallum would provide for all public services out of rent; but unlike George, the rent would be collected, and the land owned, by private corporate landlords rather than by the government, and the payment therefore voluntary rather than coercive. The Heathian "proprietary community" is, of course, in stark contrast to the scruffy egalitarian commune dreamed of by anarchists of the Left.

William O. Reichert, "Anarchism, Freedom, and Power", *Anarchy* (London, May, 1970. Available for 40¢, or $5.00 per year from Freedom Press, 84B Whitechapel High St., London, E. 1, England.) A pleasant article on anarchism, reprinted from the American philosophical journal, *Ethics*.

Libertarianism and Libertarians.

Carl Bode, *Mencken* (Carbondale, Ill.: Southern Illinois University Press). While Bode does not give much space to Mencken's deep and pervasive libertarian views, this is a thorough and sympathetic biography of the great wit and individualist. The best biography of Mencken in English, it will probably not be surpassed until the French biography by Guy Forgue is translated.

Hugh Gardner, "The New Gypsies" (*Esquire*, September, 1970, $1 per copy, $7.50 per year, pp. 109-10). A scathingly satirical report on the libertarian retreatists, the "nomads" and "troglodytes", a group that richly deserves satire.

Middle-aged libertarians who enjoy wallowing in nostalgia, as well as the young who are eager to read of the history of their movement in the 1950's, will find indispensable Eckard Vance Toy, Jr., *Ideology and Conflict in American Ultra-conservatism, 1945-1960* (Unpublished doctoral dissertation in history, University of Oregon, 1965; available in Xeroxed paper-bound copy from University Microfilms, Ann Arbor, Michigan.). Based solely on the extensive correspondence of the conservative Seattle industrialist James Clise, this study focusses on the activities and problems of the Foundation for Economic Education and Spiritual Mobilization. Anyone who had anything to do with either organization in those days will find himself prominently in these pages, usually fairly portrayed. One interesting point is a reminder of how Spiritual Mobilization was wrecked by a peculiar, right-wing variant of the drug culture (usually mescaline in those days) and mystical personality-cult centered around the English-born *guru* Gerald Heard.

Milton Mayer, *Man v. The State* (paperback, Santa Barbara,

(Continued on page 2)

FALL READING— *(Continued from page 1)*

Calif.: Center for the Study of Democratic Institutions, $2.25, 191 pp.) is a beautifully written essay on behalf of liberty and in opposition to the State by a veteran and consistent opponent of war. Discussion of law, dissent, and civil disobedience, with praise for such seemingly disparate libertarians as Thoreau and the "right-wing anarchist" publisher R. C. Hoiles. It is obvious that his discussants at the Center, in the Epilogue of the book, have completely missed the point, and these include the New Left communitarians.

Herbert Spencer, *The Man Versus The State* (paperback, Baltimore: Penguin Books, $1.95, 350 pp.) First reprint in eighty years of this classic by one of the outstanding libertarian theorists of the nineteenth century. Also includes four other essays by Spencer.

Women's "Liberation".

Murray N. Rothbard, "The Great Women's Liberation Issue: Setting It Straight", *The Individualist* (May, 1970. 75¢ the issue, $7.50 per year, from 415 Second St., N. E., Washington, D. C. 20002). Ironically for the argument that women are "oppressed", this is the *only* systematic, hard-hitting critique of women's "liberation" that has ever been published. This article has already brought forth a stream of hysterical abuse and vituperation from various (male) libertarian youth leaders, who seem particularly offended by favorable references to heterosexuality.

William Davis, "Let's Have Equality for Men", *Punch* (England, November 12, 1969). Delightful article, taking the position that it is the men, not the women, of the world who are the "niggers". Davis writers: "Man is the nigger of the world, condemned to slavery so that the privileged sex can have its baubles, bangles, and beads." This is the speech that turned the tide against the Women's Lib resolution before the Oxford Union.

Nancy R. McWilliams, "Feminism and Femininity", *Commonweal* (May 15, 1970), pp. 219-221. A highly sensible, most welcome article on Women's Lib by a young psychologist.

Youth and Youth-Culture.

John W. Aldridge, *In the Country of the Young* (Harper Magazine Press, $5.00). Highly perceptive critique of the herd, or tribal, mentality of the current generation of youth.

Richard Hofstadter, "The Age of Rubbish", *Newsweek* (July 6). The eminent historian perceptively pin-points the crucial problem of the current youth-culture: the sudden loss of a sense of "vocation", of craftsmanship and purposeful work. Hofstadter points out that: "Young people don't have anything they want to do . . . I think this is one of the roots of the dissatisfaction in college. Students keep saying that they don't know why they are there. They are less disposed than they used to be to keep order partly because the sense that they are leading a purposeful life is gone. They have the feeling that . . . they don't have any say about their lives. The truth is that all too often they haven't decided what they want their lives to say."

Education.

James D. Koerner, "The Case of Marjorie Webster", *The Public Interest* (Summer, 1970, $1.50 the copy, $5.00 per year.), pp. 40-64. An excellent report and discussion on the case of Marjorie Webster Junior College for girls in Washington, a proprietary, profit-making college victimized by regional accrediting associations, nominally private but tied in to the federal government bureaucracy, and which refuse to accredit profit-making colleges as a matter of "principle".

James M. Buchanan and Nicos E. Devletoglou, *Academia in Anarchy* (New York: Basic Books, $5.95, 187 pp.). A hard-hitting critique, from a Chicago School, free-market economic point of view, of our peculiar higher educational system in which the consumers do not buy the product, the producers do not sell it, and the "owners" do not control the process. A well-balanced review of the book can be found in the Dartmouth *Conservative Idea* for June, 1970, by Professor Edwin G. Dolan.

Anti-Egalitarianism.

One of the most important books in years is Helmut Schoeck, *Envy: A Theory of Social Behaviour* (New York: Harcourt, Brace, and World, $7.50, 408 pp.). This lengthy, erudite work by a conservative-libertarian German sociologist focusses on the overriding problem of the envy of one's betters (in any way—achievement, intelligence, good fortune, etc.). He demonstrates that the heart of socialism and communism is an overwhelming desire to eliminate envy by appeasing its aggressive appetites: by rendering everyone uniform and equal. Schoeck demonstrates that this is a vain dream, that envy cannot be appeased out of existence. He uses anthropological findings to show that egalitarian tribal and peasant communities, happy, loving and sharing in the fantasy world of Left-intellectuals, are actually worlds driven by hate, suspicion, envy, and the fear of the envy of one's neighbors. Much of the current drive for egalitarianism, Schoeck indicates, comes from affluent intellectuals driven by guilt and therefore shame over the supposed envy of others. The supposedly idyllic Israeli *kibbutz* is also cut down to size. This book will give a firmer and more rigorous perspective to opponents of socialism, communism, and communalism.

George P. Elliott, "Revolution Instead—Notes on Passions and Politics", *The Public Interest* (Summer, 1970), pp. 65-89, is a discursive but fascinating series of notes on the political scene. Professor Elliott calls himself a "libertarian", is highly critical of hippies, youth culture, and child-centeredness, and has an original critique of "getting stoned". Elliott, too, zeroes in on egalitarianism as a vain and destructive attempt to appease envy, only to aggravate it.

Gustave Le Bon, *The Crowd* (paperback, New York: The Viking Press, $1.45). Reprint of the classic turn-of-the-century critique by a French sociologist of crowd behavior, and of the herd-mentality.

Ethnic Politics.

It was only as recently as the 1950's that Samuel Lubell became the first political analyst with the courage to break the iron taboo against the acknowledgment of the great importance of the ethnic in politics: of the Jewish vote, the Irish vote, etc.—something, of course, that every working politico knew full well. Now, Nathan Glazer and Daniel P. Moynihan, in their sparkling 95-page introduction to the second edition of their classic *Beyond the Melting Pot* (2nd ed., Cambridge, Mass.: The M. I. T. Press, $1.95, 458 pp.), achieve another breakthrough: the zeroing in on the new alliance of Jews, upper-class WASPs, and lower-class Negroes, that has achieved power in New York City, at the expense of everyone else, particularly the mass of working-class and lower-middle-class Irish and Italian Catholics.

Murray Schumach, "Neighborhoods: 69 Homes in Corona at Stake", *New York Times* (August 11, 1970), p. 35. The touching story of how the New York City government is preparing to bulldoze the homes of several blocks of

(Continued on page 4)

A Not So Radical Guide

A Radical's Guide to Economic Reality. By Angus Black.
Holt, Rinehart and Winston, Inc., 1970. 87 pages.

Angus Black is a pseudonym, but the word is out that the
book was written by a Ph.D. candidate in economics at the
University of Chicago. The Chicago influence is strong. In
fact, in many ways, *A Radical's Guide to Economic Reality*
is a "hip" version of Milton Friedman's *Capitalism and
Freedom*. Black is apparently trying to appeal to participants
in the drug culture, and other such "dropouts." He seems to
be making an honest effort to educate his audience to economic reality by speaking about subjects that they're likely
to have special interest in, and in terms that they will understand. However, Black has adopted an exceedingly patronizing attitude toward his readers. One doubts that any of
the people to whom he is ostensibly appealing will either
appreciate his style, or accept his arguments (indeed, some
of his readers may be impervious to any form of argument,
but that is another matter).

A more fundamental weakness is the intellectual tradition
within which the book is written. The Chicago School is not
generally characterized by any insight in the basic problems which beset the United States today. Milton Friedman,
titular head of the school, thinks Richard Nixon is a profoundly intelligent man who is leading this country back to
laissez-faire. The real meaning of the Vietnam War (the war
was not a mistake) is lost on the Chicagoites. Analyzing the
American economy through the rosy glasses of a model of
"perfect competition," they are unable to see the brute reality
of the military-industrial complex. Moreover, their economic analysis is faulty in certain other respects, so that
on key questions (e.g., inflation), they fail to come up with the
fundamental objections to current policy. *A Radical's Guide*
suffers from all of these deficiencies, and some of its own.

Still, the book is a beginning—an attempt to communicate
free market solutions to specific problems, to classes of
people usually inimical to this approach. Would that Black
had written less flippantly, though. Len Liggio has an article
on Anarchism in the July 14 *Liberated Guardian*, written in
plain English, and devoid of a patronizing attitude, which is
far more likely to bridge the gap with the Left.

The book is short. A glimpse at the chapter titles gives an
indication of what is in order for the reader: "Big Business
or Screw the Customer and Full Speed Ahead"; "Our Tax
System—A Field Day for the Rich"; and so on. Black is
particularly good on some points. On the California grape
boycott:

> I want to help the grape pickers, so I eat grapes
> for breakfast, grapes for midmorning snack, grapes
> for dinner, and grapes for that midnight raid on the
> ice box. In this way, besides the makers of Keo-
> pectate, I help grape pickers. How? Simply by
> raising the value of grapes and therefore in-
> creasing the demand for grape pickers.

Besides taking up the grape boycott, Black examines the
problem of unions in general, pointing out the necessarily
discriminatory nature of unions. But he pulls his punches
on major issues, and often comes up with "compromise"
solutions which perpetuate the very problem he concerns
himself with. In taking on the tax system, Black makes a
telling point as to who really pays the taxes, and then
lamely suggests a flat 20% income tax (plus a negative income tax for the poor). No analysis is attempted of why the
tax system is set up the way it is presently. Surely Black
doesn't believe that the electorate, given fresh insight by
a reading of Black's book, could go off to Washington, and

change the tax system. This is to overlook the vested interests who are responsible for the system as it is now; it is
also to assume naively that power is wielded by the general
populace in the country. It is to fail to analyze the situation
realistically.

More importantly, one must ask why there is no critique
of the federal income tax *per se* (à la Frank Chodorov's
classic essay, "Taxation is Robbery"). One would think that
anyone with pretentions to being a libertarian would at least
take up the issue of the morality of taxation. Black does not.

Like most Chicagoites, Black is reasonably good in his
critique of economic fallacies, but has a penchant for discovering "problem" areas where the market is alleged not
to work. Thus, to solve the problem of poverty, we need a
negative income tax. There is "underinvestment" in education, so we need educational vouchers. No analysis of why
the market sometimes "fails" is offered (on the alleged
problem of market failure, see Murray Rothbard's new work,
Power and Market).

Alas, one suspects that there may be a problem of class
interest in all this. The idea of educational subsidies is
generally a favorite of Chicagoites. This despite their
critiques of so many other subsidy ideas. One feels that
their position on this matter may be colored by a beneficial interest in the subject of education.

The last chapter is perhaps the most curious, as it is
titled: "A Plea for Anarchy." Certainly if one had bought
Black's basic critique (even though it is not flawless), he
might be on his way to a position of anarchy. But, "No,"
says Black, we can't have anarchy because:

> There would be open season on wops, wetbacks,
> kikes, niggers, hippies, redheads, and cripples if
> the constitution didn't exist . . . Anarchy is not the
> answer. We would therefore keep government, but
> reduce its power over our economic, moral and
> social lives.

For anarchy to work, according to Black, "all members of society must be fairly homogeneous." Now, the
arguments in this book are, at times, deficient, but nowhere
else are they as bad as the above.

The argument as stated by Black is an old canard. Only,
in fact, if the population were (absolutely) homogeneous
could government be justified (Why one would be desired
is a separate question). Only in a heterogeneous world (such
as we have) is there a problem of individual liberty. If we
all thought alike, and desired exactly the same ends, then
living under an absolute "dictatorship" would not involve an
infringement on individual liberty; *ex hypothesi*, the dictator would merely be telling us to do what we wanted to
do. In a heterogeneous world, on the other hand, people do
not think alike. Therefore, any authority which would coerce man is a violation of individual liberty. John Stuart
Mill put it perceptively:

> If all mankind minus one were of one opinion,
> and only one person were of contrary opinion,
> mankind would be no more justified in silencing
> that one person, than he, if he had the power,
> would be justified in silencing mankind.
>
> (From *On Liberty*)

It took thinkers more perceptive than Mill to see that
the existence of any government, however limited, is inconsistent with individual liberty.

In sum, *A Radical's Guide to Economic Reality* is worthy
of the attention of libertarians; it could and should have been
a better book. For a better book, see Jerry Tuccille's
Radical Libertarianism.

—Gerald P. O'Driscoll, Jr.

FALL READING—
(Continued from page 2)

independent but politically powerless Italian homeowners in Corona, Queens, while an upper-class Jewish country club, using city-owned land, thumbs its nose nearby.

Father Andrew Greeley, "The Intellectuals as an Ethnic Group", *New York Sunday Times Magazine* (June 15). Father Greeley, a sociologist with a uniquely witty, intelligent, and orthodox role in Catholic journalism, here wields the rapier against the snobbishness and cultism, the ethnic "in-group"-ism, of the fashionable liberal intellectuals.

Revolutions.

John Womack, Jr., *Zapata and the Mexican Revolution* (New York: Afred A. Knopf, $10.00, 456 pp.). A model of an historical work: thorough, definitive, scholarly, and beautifully written. The saga of the libertarian, peasant *Zapatista* revolution, centered in the Mexican state of Morelos.

K. S. Karol, "The Two Honeymoons of Fidel Castro", *Scanlan's Monthly* (September, 1970, $1.00 a copy, $12.00 per year). Critical overview of the peregrinations of Castro's Cuba.

Thomas L. Blair, *The Land To Those Who Work It* (Garden City, L. I.: Doubleday Anchor paperbacks, $1.95). The history of the quasi-syndicalist "self-management" experiment in Algeria during the Ben Bella regime, and before Colonel Boumedienne imposed the current Stalinist system.

Military-Industrial Complex.

Seymour Melman, *Pentagon Capitalism* (New York: McGraw-Hill, $8.50). Critical study of the increasingly "state-managed" military-industrial complex.

Murray L. Weidenbaum, *The Modern Public Sector* (New York: Basic Books, $5.95). Sophisticated but clearly written. On the new ways by which government has penetrated and permeated the "private" sector, especially in military and space areas.

U. S. Foreign Policy.

Peter Dale Scott, "Laos: The Story Nixon Won't Tell", *New York Review of Books* (April 9); Scott, "Cambodia: Why the Generals Won", *New York Review of Books* (June 18). Excellent, scholarly information on our newest plague-spots; shows the duplicity of the CIA toward even our own government leaders.

I. F. Stone, "A Century of Futility", *New York Review of*

Books (April 9); "Theatre of Delusion", *ibid.* (April 23); "The Test Ban Comedy", *ibid.* (May 7). Excellent and thorough review of America's disarmament duplicities over the past generation. Particularly important is the April 23 article, which highlights the crucial but generally unknown decision of the United States to rescind completely its own offer of general disarmament *with* inspection, *after* Khrushchev had accepted it on May 10, 1955.

Murray N. Rothbard, "Review of David Horowitz, ed., *Corporations and the Cold War*", *Ramparts* (September). Review of new book of essays which presents studies of the responsibility of U. S. corporations for American imperialism and the Cold War, as well as the growth of the military-industrial complex. Particularly interesting are the articles by Professors Domhoff and Eakins on the foreign policy roles of such "corporate liberal" organizations as the Council on Foreign Relations and the Committee for Economic Development.

Big Business and Politics.

Warren Hinckle, "The Law Firm That Runs California", *Scanlan's Monthly* (September). The story of the sinister and pervasive role of the Los Angeles law firm of O'Melveny and Myers in running California politics.

European History.

A. J. P. Taylor, "Scarred Monuments", *New York Review of Books* (April 9). The witty, iconoclastic English historian comes out squarely against Tories, and in favor of revolutionary 18th-century liberalism.

Crime Revisionism.

For generations, it was an article of emotional faith among Left-liberals that Sacco and Vanzetti, in the famous murder-and-robbery case of the 1920's, were innocent martyrs. Then, only a decade ago, Sacco-Vanzetti Revisionism was launched by R. H. Montgomery and by Francis X. Busch, and then by David Felix and especially Francis Russell in his *Tragedy at Dedham*. Now, Francis Russell, in "Sacco-Vanzetti: The End of the Chapter", *National Review* (May 5), finds new evidence which confirms his thesis that Sacco was definitely guilty, while Vanzetti was not—but knowingly shielded the guilty party.

A Correction

Sorry: in Jerome Tuccille's article in the September 1 issue, the word "ethology" was misspelled "ethnology" in a typographical error.

The Libertarian Forum

BOX 341
MADISON SQUARE STATION
NEW YORK, NEW YORK 10010

First Class

Published on the first and fifteenth of every month.   Subscription rate: $7.00 per year; Student subscription rate: $5.00 per year

A Semi-Monthly Newsletter

THE
Libertarian Forum

Joseph R. Peden, Publisher   Murray N. Rothbard, Editor

VOLUME II, NO. 19   OCTOBER 1, 1970   35¢

WHEN REVOLUTION?

To the anarcho-rightist, to say nothing of rightists generally, I am a veritable Mephisto, inciting my young and unformed charges to bloody riot, violence, and rapine. To the anarcho-leftist, on the other hand, I am a reactionary cop-out, weakening the revolutionary will and doing the State's work by calling for study, scholarship, and passivity. To others, it seems that I career wildly from month to month, calling for bloody revolution in one issue and denouncing it in the next. In the meanwhile, the fixed principles which I attempt to apply to the changing flux of events, tend to disappear amidst the hubbub.

Let us then hammer out the libertarian principles step by step. First, it is axiom of libertarian thought that the State is a criminal gang, living off the robbery of tax-coercion and using these funds to murder, pillage, enslave, and endow favored groups with special privilege. The State is founded and has its very being in the use of aggressive violence. Therefore, any violence used against the State is *moral*, for it is the moral equivalent of using violence to protect one's person and property from armed marauders. The act of revolution is, therefore, always moral. For similar reasons, any revolutionary act against any State is aesthetically pleasing, for at least some State is being weakened, or some State official is getting his deserved comeuppance.

Having said this, however, we must bring other vectors of principle into our final judgment: into our final decision on whether to "support" (which means at least to *cheer for*) any given concrete revolution. Let us detach principle from emotion for the moment, and postulate the hypothetical government of Ruritania. We read that a revolutionary movement has been formed in Ruritania and has just blown up a government post office. Since revolution *per se* is both moral and aesthetically pleasing, our initial judgment is to cheer: Hooray, a monopoly post office has been destroyed, part of the criminal Ruritanian apparatus has been whittled away.

But having made this judgment, we must inquire further into the specific context. What, for example, are the principles of this revolutionary movement? What political ends does it have in mind? Suppose we find that the Ruritanian Revolution has one guiding principle: the destruction of all redheads, under the theory that all redheads are agents of the Devil. We must now weigh two principles in making our judgment on the Revolution: one, the joy in seeing a criminal State weakened and overthrown; and two, the consideration of what might replace this State. We must then consider: how bad is the existing State (perhaps it is dedicated to murdering all blondes for the same reason), and then weigh this against the probable badness of the new Anti-

Redhead State once it achieves power. The point here is that our final judgment is complex, and that different libertarians, no matter how similar and pure in their libertarian principle, can and will make different judgments on whether or not to support the Revolution. Thus, Libertarian A may say: The existing Ruritanian State is bad, of course, but at least it doesn't wantonly murder redheads; holding my nose, I denounce the Revolution and support the existing State as the lesser evil. But Libertarian B may say: Of course, I deplore the prospective murder of redheads. But the Revolutionary regime will probably impose far lower taxes, and will be less harsh on brunettes than the current regime; so *I* will hold my nose and support the Revolution. And Libertarian C can have an entirely different kind of judgment. *He* may say: I agree with A that if the Revolution actually ever seized and held power, their murdering of redheads would make them *more* evil than the existing State. *However* my judgment of the situation tells me that the Revolution can never hope to achieve power. They might well, however, be able so to weaken the existing State that *neither* will be able to rule, and Ruritania will be transformed, despite the desires of both parties, into a decentralized, almost Stateless society, with small pockets of local rulers, and even local anarchies. Therefore, *I* support the Revolution.

The point is that, once we pass the first step: the first vector of cheering for any armed self-defense against the State, we can no longer be guided by pure theory alone. We must then use our strategic and tactical judgment; we then have to employ libertarian principle as a complex "art" rather than as strict application of pure science. And, on these judgments, equally good libertarians will necessarily differ. Or, to put it this way: we live, to use the Randian terminology, in a mixed-premise world. In a sense different from the way they mean it, the villains in Randian novels are right: governments, political parties, and most people, are neither "black" nor "white"; they are bundles of varying shades of mixed-premise "gray." And therefore, libertarian judgments on varying States, political leaders, revolutions or whatnot are always difficult and never carry the guarantee of absolute truth. To crib from one of my own examples, if Richard Cobden were leading a political or a revolutionary movement against Genghis Khan, our moral choice between them would be easy indeed; but in the real world, we are usually not confronted with such clear-cut polar choices, and hence we must make our difficult judgments between mixed-premise people, institutions and movements; we must always make complex choices of "lesser evils."

(Continued on page 4)

147

Bits And Pieces
By Jerome Tuccille

ON SEXISM

The effort this time around is an unpleasant one for I find myself obliged to comment on Murray Rothbard's women's liberation article in the Spring-Summer issue of *The Individualist*, a former monthly publication which now seems to be coming out semi-annually.

A topic as controversial and as much in the news as women's lib is these days requires a strong, uncompromising stand on one side of the issue or the other. Clearly, Dr. Rothbard's moderate, middle-of-the-road approach to the subject is not a fair one for either side. People have a right to know the facts. They expect to read an article and come away with a clear understanding of the ethical and psycho-epistomer . . . mer . . . mer, the abstract questions around which the whole issue revolves. Dr. Rothbard, eager as always to please both factions, the pros and cons, the Lefts and Rights, has written a vacillating, bleeding-heart type article which can only please whim-worshipping concrete-bound second-handers and muscle-mystics.

As anyone who has been following the current struggle for women's liberation knows, there is a tight bond uniting the rational fringes of Left and Right in their common sisterhood. One is quick to detect a touching parallel between Dolly Tanner decked out in her superman shirt, Lucy Komisar in her purple jumpsuit, and Rand's Galt-like heroine, Dagny Taggart, dashing off in a billowing evening gown to save the railroads. Only the cynical would see this as a shrill undertone, an element of just-barely-controlled hysteria uniting the fringes in their sisterhood. The gentle Rand would no more welcome Ti-Grace Atkinson into her living room than Ti-Grace would send Miss Rand a Mother's Day card, and yet their jaws are clenched, though separately, in a common struggle to liberate their species.

One of Rand's earliest ideals was the image of the liberated female who never cooked her own meals (or anyone else's), who did little or no housework, who rose to the top of the business world through competitive efforts and won the admiration of men who previously resented her presence among them. The parallels between the ideals listed above and the current cry of "No more diapers, no more dishes, no more housework!" are obvious enough.

On the question of sex, the Randian heroine is invariably a free agent, judging her partners according to a merit system, selecting the highest ranking in her own hierarchy of values, discarding a present lover as soon as she meets another who is more rational. Sexism, although it goes by a different name, has no place in the Objectivist Ethic. It is the height of immorality for a man and woman to hop in bed simply because they like the shape of each other's buttocks. There is no toleration of *sex object-ism* in Objectivism. Disciples are permitted carnal bliss only if they are intellectually compatible and share the same values, the same sense-of-life, the same moral code.

But Rand puts a curious twist on her analysis of how people are supposed to know when and if they are intellectually compatible. Obviously, lengthy philosophical discussions are time-consuming and extremely distracting, especially if one has an itch to satisfy his sexual needs. Upcoming students of Objectivism will be happy to know that Rand has provided them with a shortcut. It is not necessary for would-be bedmates to probe each other's psyches at length to determine whether they can make it together or not. Truly rational people have the capacity of recognizing each other *on sight*. This is not the same as regarding each other as sex objects. Of course not.

Intellectual compatibility can be seen in the set of someone's jaw and the direct, confident glare of his or her eyes. Rational men and women are invariably tall, beauteous and lean, with thick wavy hair, drilling eyes and strong jutting jaws something like Barry Goldwater's. This poses a problem for short dumpy individualists who can practice eye exercises *ad infinitum*, but can never alter their stature and bone structure no matter how hard they try.

So, when rational human beings recognize each other on sight they are permitted to ravish each other at once in a violent, all-consuming act of love. The crowning height of ecstasy, of course, is to be raped on the steps of the New York Stock Exchange by a philosophical heir of William Graham Sumner.

Another infectious group on the fringes is the "Stick-It-In-The-Wall-Mother-****** Collective" of Boston, Massachusetts. According to a leading commissar for this outfit, all talk about oppressed blacks, chicanos, Indians, etc. . . is nothing but "irrelevant crap" promoted by "the mainstream pig media." (She and Spiro Agnew are apparently intellectually *simpatico*). Women are the most oppressed of all, of course, and "lesbianism is a new way of relating now that women have rejected bullshit traditional heterosexuality."

(By the way. Has anyone ever noticed what a great set of knockers Gloria Steinem has?)

                          ****

Just for the record, it might be worthwhile to comment on this business of "sex objects." One can sympathize with the cry against the "thingification" of women--the psychological phenomenon of regarding them as brainless mannequins and receptacles for consumer goods (the "you've come a long way, baby" syndrome)--but this ought to be separated from the issue of sex objectification. This is largely an involuntary reaction to begin with. Most strongly-sexed heterosexual men automatically begin to melt a little at the sight of a shapely, partially exposed leg, a soft heaving bosom, a glimpse of flesh along the midriff. This is purely a physiological reaction based on one's personal aesthetics.

Women also view men as sex objects and, fortunately, they have been doing it from time immemorial. Those little eye games you see played by strangers on subways and buses are proof enough of that. Certainly, the sexes are not responding to one another's sense-of-life, Ayn Rand notwithstanding.

And since it is impossible to recognize a philosophical bedfellow on sight, people are initially attracted to one another's physical attributes. This is what draws them together first. Later on, after they have had a chance to know each other better, they can make a more balanced assessment of the other's overall qualities and decide if there is any basis for a lasting relationship.

(Steinem's legs aren't bad either).

The Case For Elites

In an attempt to sidle up to the Left, many libertarians have been given to denouncing "elitism". The cornerstone of the individualist-libertarian insight, however, is that all people are different. Every individual is unique. Every man differs in his character, personality, intelligence, and range of interests. Given a free society, then, every individual will find his own level of ability and interest. Libertarians, then, are the reverse of egalitarians; we do not subscribe to the impossible Left-ideal of compulsory egalitarianism, of an antheap world in which every person will be identical, uniform, and equal. As individualists, we know and glory in the fact that a free society will release the energies of every individual to develop his capacity and his interests to their full extent.

In that free society, then, "natural" or voluntary elites will arise in every form of human endeavor. There will be a division of labor, and therefore voluntarily accepted leaders, or elites, in every activity, whether in scholarship, corporations, lodge meetings, or the local bridge club. As Jefferson pointed out, we oppose not "aristocracies" or elites *per se* but "artificial", coercive elites, men who achieve and wield power by means of aggressive violence and exploitation. We are "egalitarian" only to the extent that we oppose a ruling class that extracts its revenue by violence and uses violence to push people around; we are opposed to such a ruling class or to the special privileges which such rulers inevitably dispense. But we do not believe that a free society will result in equality of income or condition; instead, people will then be free to rise to whatever natural elite status their abilities can bring them, and which they will earn as leaders or producers in various fields of endeavor. We recognize, and delight in the fact, that Edison was a better inventor than the tinkerer next door, or that Ludwig von Mises is a greater economist than the instructor around the corner. We simply do not believe (as neither did they) that this natural superiority gives them the right to rule coercively over the local instructor or tinkerer.

In our proper indignation against the ruling class, let us not throw out the elitist baby with the statist bathwater.

From The "Old Curmudgeon"

Highly recommended Movie: "Joe". Setting aside the rather melodramatic plot, the film brilliantly and fairly contrasts three distinctive New York cultures: Upper Class-WASP, hippie-youth, and working-class Queens Irish (Joe himself). See it and find out which of the three cultures *you* identify with, an identification which is no problem at all for Old Curmudgeons everywhere.

****

Note that the Women's Libbers are now "demanding" *not* abortion-freedom, but "free" (that is costless) abortions, a notable example of the absurdity of the movement and of the Left generally these days. *Who* do they think are going to supply these free abortions?

****

Perceptive recent cartoon by the brilliant Left-cartoonist Jules Feiffer:
He: Have you ever been in love?
She: Yes, I love the people.
He: I mean something smaller than the people.
She: I love the kids. I think they're great.
He: But a person--have you ever been in love with a person?
She: *One* person?
He: Like a man.
She: I've loved men . . . Dylan. Che. Mao.
He: Can you ever love *me*?
She: (eyes narrowing). Sexist!

ANARCHY

Ever reviled, accursed, ne'er understood
    Thou art the grisly terror of our age.
"Wreck of all order," cry the multitude,
    "Art thou, and war and murder's endless rage."
O, let them cry. To them that ne'er have striven
    The truth that lies behind a word to find,
To them the word's right meaning was not given.
    They shall continue blind among the blind.
But thou, O word, so clear, so strong, so pure,
    Thou sayest all which I for goal have taken.
I give thee to the future! Thine secure
    When each at least unto himself shall waken.
Comes it in sunshine? In the tempest's thrill?
    I cannot tell--but it the earth shall see!
I am an Anarchist! Wherefore I will
    Not rule, and also ruled I will not be!

--John Henry Mackay

149

WHEN REVOLUTION? — *(Continued from page 1)*

And here we have a vital clue into the inner totalitarian nature of the Randian Cult. For Randians firmly believe, not only that their group must agree on the same basic principles, but that they also must agree on every single specific application: down to such remote cases as who to vote for in the New York mayoralty election. But since even those who agree completely on the science of liberty will inevitably differ on its application to our mixed-premise world, the Randian movement had to face the choice between allowing its members to take many different positions on concrete applications, *or* enforcing a total "line" on its membership; and unfortunately it chose the latter.

At this point, many libertarians will cry out: but why must we choose at all? Why can't we take a neutral position on all these choices, and support no one except pure libertarians wherever they emerge? The answer is that we can't because we live in a real world, a world of different grades of mixed-premises, a world where not everyone is equally bad. And in this world, events continue to happen whether we approve or not; elections take place, wars are fought, revolutions are waged. If we are to be aware people in a real world, we *must* take sides in these events, if only to favor one or the other outcome. Richard Cobden *was* not only better than Genghis Khan but also better than the Tories of his day; Robert A. Taft was better than Franklin Roosevelt; Mark Hatfield *is* better than Hubert Humphrey or Richard Nixon. How can we live in the world and not choose between outcomes of events whenever there are *any* gradations of value that we can place upon such outcome? We live, to be sure, in a mixed-premise world, but some mixes are better, and some worse, than others. Furthermore, to "choose", or to "support", does not necessarily mean voting or active participation; it can mean simply: whom do we cheer for on election night? Or, whom do we cheer *against*? Not to make even *this* kind of choice is to surrender hopelessly to ignorance and obscurantism.

Suppose now that we do not face mixed-premise choices; suppose that we have a flourishing revolutionary movement consisting only of certified 100% pure libertarians. Given such a pure libertarian movement, we then know that the world ushered in by such a revolution will be far superior to the present. Do we *then* call for immediate armed insurrection against the State? Not necessarily, for now we must exercise the highly difficult--and again unscientific--art of strategic and tactical judgment. For while we have the absolute moral *right* to use force to repel armed marauders, we do not have the moral *duty* to do so. We may often find ourselves in situations where we are hopelessly outnumbered by the armed burglars, and therefore our strategically wise course is to give in. Man has no moral duty to seek martyrdom. Therefore, even where a revolution would be unimpeachably and unequivocally moral, it would not necessarily be strategically or tactically correct; *when* to launch a moral revolution, if at all, depends on one's concrete judgment of the relative strength of forces, of the probabilities of success, etc. And, again, in this necessary but difficult judgment, opinions among pure libertarians will differ, and differ markedly.

As for the current situation in the United States, it seems to me that we can be as close to scientific as any strategic judgment can ever get: there is no hope whatever, now or in the foreseeable future, for a successful libertarian revolution in America. Such a revolution must then remain in the realm of moral theory for any foreseeable time to come; and surely no sober person, acquainted at all with American reality, can disagree with this judgment. In that case, the libertarian movement, whatever its tactical alliance with right or left on this or that concrete issue, must concentrate its energies, now and in the future, on the indispensable educational work of expanding its theory and spreading it to as many "converts" as possible. Our major areas of concentration must be the study, the library, the press, the living-room, the seminar, the lecture-hall. We are primarily an educational movement or we are nothing.

Gems Of Statism

1. From William F. Buckley's column of September 10: "Mr. Lindbergh's journals will revive a debate which almost tore America apart, from the ultimate business of which we were saved by the Japanese attack on Pearl Harbor, which annealed the whole nation. What experience could do such a thing for America today?" Hoping for another Pearl Harbor to "anneal" the nation, Chairman Bill?

2. Monsignor John Sheridan, asked in his column for *Our Sunday Visitor* (August 30), why there is an absence of priests and monsignori in peace marches, replied: "We must remember that we have delegated certain community responsibilities to our elected government and we must cooperate with that government in its broad strategy; otherwise, we shall have chaos."

3. Humanist Quote of the Month: "Senator Long (D-La.) told his colleagues that Mideast terrorists should be 'killed and strung up by their heels until the flies eat their flesh'." *Los Angeles Times* (September 21).

Published on the first and fifteenth of every month.   Subscription rate: $7.00 per year; Student subscription rate: $5.00 per year

A Semi-Monthly Newsletter

THE
Libertarian Forum

Joseph R. Peden, Publisher

Murray N. Rothbard, Editor

VOLUME II, NO. 20   OCTOBER 15, 1970   35¢

POLARIZATION

The "radicLeft" (to coin a phrase) is getting what it wants: polarization. And so Bernardine Dohrn, the Voice from Underground, sounds the trumpet call for the Mad Bombers and their supposed legion of supporters; while, on the other side, Vice-President Agnew tours the country having great success in mobilizing Middle America to smash the Left. I will give you one very swift guess which side the vast majority of the American people are going to join, ever more vociferously out for blood.

Let's look at the matter for a moment from the point of view of the "average American", now known as the "Middle American", the average, sober, industrious Forgotten Man of William Graham Sumner who pays but pays uncomplainingly in taxes and inflation for all the mixed-economy, welfarist, and subsidy programs of government. He is the Forgotten Man who works hard, improves his lot but finds much of the improvement taken from him by taxes and rising prices, goes to Church with fair regularity, and puts his overwhelming trust and devotion in the American flag and the Constitution. Beset by problems but correctly convinced that his lot is the best on earth, our Forgotten Man finds his greatest joy in what Left-intellectuals savagely deride as "bourgeois culture": in Lawrence Welk, in drinking beer in front of televised football on Sunday afternoons. Now, in the last several years, the Forgotten Man looks around him and finds all of his most cherished values, his devotion to thrift, cleanliness, hard work, improvement of his material standard of living, and "bourgeois" enjoyment in his leisure standard of living, and "bourgeois" hours, derided with great savagery by what looks like the whole mass of the younger generation. And he finds his most cherished moral precepts derided also. The Forgotten American has always been, in theory, in favor of the virtues of chastity, decency, and fidelity. He had never completely cleaved to them in practice, but his missteps were always furtive, shamefaced, and therefore kept hidden, so that while he had sometimes deviated from the rules in practice, their theoretical purity remained unsullied. Now he finds the Youth Culture openly proclaiming and flaunting the rupture of all the rules, for the youth now proclaim that what he had thought were vices are now really the New Virtues: promiscuity, pornography, drug addition, obscenity, bisexuality, total disrespect for private property.

And he finds his own cleaving to the rules derided by the young as "hypocrisy"; the fact that few people, no matter how high-minded, can be 100% perfect in cleaving to moral rules is now used by the young to damn him self-righteously while they proclaim the old hated vices to be the True Morality. He finds cleanliness replaced by filth, virtue by vice, movies with an enjoyable plot and identifiable heroes replaced by pornography and morbid irrationality.

And then, to top it off, the Forgotten American finds this generation of youth trampling on property, destroying colleges, and burning and defiling the symbol he has been taught to revere most highly--the American flag, as well as calling for defeat in wars in which his country has engaged. And when he looks to find the focus for this monstrosity, he finds it in the nation's colleges. He had always vaguely distrusted the intellectuality and the seeming bent toward some sort of subversion of existing values and institutions among academics. During the "consensus" world of the 1950's and early 1960's, when intellectuals had rediscovered America and found power positions in the system, this suspicion was overlayed; but now it was back in full fury. It particularly hurt that the sons and daughters of upper and upper-middle classes, the ones who had enjoyed the advantages of affluence and education which the Forgotten American had always vainly desired for his own children, that these were the heart and soul of the new horror. And furthermore, the Youth Culture is clearly in league with the accelerating drive toward ever greater welfare handouts, with what he sees as the pampering of the blacks and their ever-increasing commission of crime, and which are far more visible to him than the equally increasing handouts to the military-industrial complex.

Amidst this continuing and increasing assault on everything which he holds dear, the Forgotten American has been almost remarkably patient. Part of this patience has undoubtedly been bewilderment, bewilderment at the fantastic rapidity of social change in the last few years, and because he is far less articulate than the youth and their host of "radiclib" supporters among the *intelligentsia*. Alone, the Forgotten American cannot rouse himself to action; he needs a leader, a man who can articulate his anguish, who can mount a vociferous counter-attack upon his enemies. In Vice-President Agnew he has at last found such a leader; hence the great success with which Agnew, a man hardly possessed of magnetism or inner charisma, has been mobilizing Middle America. Middle America has at last found a champion, and God help the Left if ever the Nixon Administration should abandon its shilly-shallying stance Of 90% rhetoric and 10% action and actually devise a comprehensive program of action. For the Young Left has spat in the face of Middle America for a long time now, with surprisingly little retaliation. What will happen when that sleeping giant awakens, and gets in some blows of his own, especially now that Mr. Agnew has articulated his resentment?

The Middle American backlash against the left youth has already begun. The famous books by Kevin Phillips, and more

(Continued on page 3)

O CANADA

Recently Americans have become more aware than usual that something exists to the north of us besides Alaska and the North Pole. To some it is a happy refuge from the long arm of the draft board; to others a last frontier where rugged individualism can express itself creatively and successfully; some wish to enjoy life at a pace thirty years behind that of the Pepsi generation; others look to exploit a cornucopia of natural riches for the benefit of God's chosen ones--the Americans. Yes, Canada is, at last, penetrating the consciousness of the American public--and to the Canadians nothing should be more frightening than that!

Canada, compared with the U. S., is an underdeveloped country; larger in area, it has but a tenth the population of its aggressive neighbor. In the nature of things, the two nations have been linked economically, and to a great extent culturally. Only within French Quebec does an American feel himself a foreigner--and the English-speaking Canadian has felt the same. Canadian national culture may have deep roots but the leaves of the plant are rather fragile, and the flowers are often cut and shipped to market in New York, Boston and California.

Apart from the perennial questions of bilingualism and Quebec separatism, the most ubiquitous concern of Canadians is the quest for economic development. Acutely conscious of their lower standard of living, rural poverty, and dependency upon American capital and markets, Canadians see industrialization as the magic formula for catching up with America in terms of modernity and prosperity. In their desire for speedy progress, they have, unfortunately, been persuaded to rely on the use of governmental coercion to accumulate capital and direct its allocation. The chief instrumentality of this policy is the so-called development plan and the development corporation. While the plan establishes how and in what areas capital is to be allocated, the development corporation gives or lends capital taken from the taxpayers to corporate capitalists unwilling or unable to risk their own funds on the government's plans. While the transfer of capital from one group--the taxpayers--to another--subsidized private corporation--is well known in the United States (the World Bank, AID and Small Business Administration to mention but a few examples), the practice has recently accelerated rapidly in Canada at the federal, provincial and even municipal levels, and in the last few years the inevitable results are beginning to appear.

Let us confine our attention to the Maritime Provinces-- Nova Scotia, New Brunswick, and Prince Edward Island, a region which suffers endemic unemployment (10.8% against the national average of 6.7%) and a per capita income of $1712 compared to the national average of $2317 (1967). Between 1961-1966 the region lost through migration 103,000 persons--leaving behind less than two million inhabitants. (We will exclude Newfoundland which entered the Canadian confederation in 1949 and suffers the same ailments as the older maritime provinces). The outmigration includes people of all social classes and educational levels, including university graduates who find that the newly attracted industries tend to draw their managerial and technical personnel from their home bases in the United States, Europe or Toronto. Even local governmental bodies hire outsiders to an inexplicable extent. The Halifax city council recently planned to hire as city manager an American from Oklahoma! Only the protests of the city's small black population who learned of the American's reputation as a racist ended the negotiations.

Yet despite these economic conditions, the region is blessed with great natural riches: fine harbors, good fishing grounds, bountiful forests, a good mixture of fine pasture and croplands, an energetic and intelligent people,

and a nearness to both European and American markets. Why then the lack of material prosperity?

Part of the answer lies in events which occurred a century ago but still dominate the economic condition of the Maritime provinces. There were very grave reasons why the Maritime provinces should never have joined Canada in the first place. The trade of the provinces was almost wholly directed to the United States and Europe; its products were not needed in upper Canada, and the manufactured goods made there could be purchased more cheaply in the U. S. The only economic reason for joining the Canadian confederation was that the Maritime provinces, particularly Prince Edward, had developed a mania for building railroads--the costs of which far exceeded the potential revenues of the governments. The Canadians offered to absorb the large public debts of the provinces and link the Maritime provinces by rail with upper Canada. Anti-confederation feeling was so strong that for years after Confederation (1967-73) the Maritime governments were controlled by anti-confederate political parties--but they had so few members in the Ottawa parliament that they could safely be ignored. However, the region's trade was now subordinated to the economic interests of upper Canada which used Confederation to raise tariffs on manufactured goods coming from the U. S., thus increasing the cost of living of the Maritimers without any noticeable advantages to its inhabitants.

This unfavorable trade situation persists and is well illustrated by the recent announcement that railroad rates in the Maritime region are to be raised 25% and in Sept. 1970 a further rate increase is planned. But, the increases do *not* apply to shipments of grain and flour, meat, zinc fertilizer, potash, sulfur, phosphates, nickel concentrate, or butter; some iron and steel products, trailers on flatcars and all freight carried between the U. S. and Canadian depots are also excluded. Manufactured goods shipped from West (Ontario) to East (Maritimes) also enjoy special discounts, which do not apply to such goods moving from the Maritimes westward. As can be clearly seen, the railroad rates reflect the economic needs of upper Canada, and discriminate against the local products and manufactures of the Maritime provinces, which serve simply as a bridge for goods being imported and exported by upper Canadian interests. The building of the St. Lawrence Seaway was but another blow to local Maritime interests, which have continually been sacrificed by federal laws favoring upper Canadian capitalists.

Since the mid-sixties, the Maritime provincial governments have sought economic prosperity through provincially-financed industrial development corporations. As in the U. S., all the political parties espouse this approach and differ only in their claims to be more efficient, farseeing and honest servents of corporate capitalism. The New Democratic party, which is routinely described as Canada's socialist party, has at least one leader, Premier Schreyer of Manitoba, who boasts that the New Deal is his model. Apparently there is no vocal libertarian criticism or analysis of the Canadian scene, although three new publications in the Maritime area have recently begun to zero in on the development corporation boondoggle (*The Mysterious East*, Fredericton, N. B.; the *Fourth Estate*, a newspaper published in Halifax, N. S., and *The Square Deal*, a monthly paper concerned with affairs on P. B. I.) But the tone of these is reformist and muckraking rather than analytic and ideological.

What has the development corporation achieved so far?

Without any appreciable increase in population, the Maritime Provinces have greatly increased their public debt: between 1962 and 1969 the debt of Prince Edward has risen from $36m to $78.3m; New Brunswick's from $195m to $323m and Nova Scotia's from $220 to $329.5m. New

(Continued on page 3)

O CANADA — *(Continued from page 2)*

Brunswick is having considerable difficulty in finding new tax sources due to concessions given to industry and a retail sales tax already at the prohibitive rate of 8%. If this indebtedness continues to rise it may well end in the termination of all provincial autonomy. How did this come about? And is this the end of it?

In 1963, despite a decision by federal authorities not to invest in it, the Nova Scotian development corporation at government bidding agreed to finance the construction of a "heavy water" plant in cooperation with an American inventor-entrepreneur Jerome Spivack. It invested $12m in 51% of Spivack's Deuterium Corp. of New York on the understanding that Spivack would raise the remaining $18m needed to construct the $30m project. The American firm of Brown and Root were to do the construction. By 1966 the costs had risen to $40m due to labor disputes with B&R, Spivack had failed to raise the $18m and the development corporation decided to buy him out for $2m and become sole owners of the uncompleted plant. Two years later, still incomplete, it was decided to double the plant's capacity, raising the estimated costs now to $83m without producing an ounce of heavy water. Shortly after, it was discovered that someone had left salt water stagnating in miles of tubes and cylinders which had ruined them through corrosion. The Nova Scotian government now came to the rescue of its own development corporation by buying 51% of its shares in Deuterium; it then hired consultants who reported that it would take at least two more years and another $30m to complete the work. The cost to the Nova Scotian taxpayers now has reached the staggering sum of $110m with $700,000 interest paid annually. The population of the province is about 756,000. At the present time the plant is still not in production and the Premier, Mr. Smith, admits it will probably operate at an annual deficit of $5-6m. This is but one example, albeit the most spectacular, of progress via development corporations.

Puny by comparison is the Nova Scotian loan of $18m to two Toronto businessmen to build a plant for their Clairtone Sound Corp. at Stellarton, N. S. The new plant was to bring work to at least 640 local people. Three years after construction, the owners suddenly sold out to the development corporation for $2m. A few weeks later it was revealed that Clairtone had lost $800,000 during the first half of that year. The plant is still producing with a work force of less than 100, its deficit has now risen to $18m, and the value of its stock-wholly owned by the development corporation--is now one-tenth the price paid to the carpetbaggers from Toronto.

In New Brunswick the development corporation has achieved comparable successes. It planned to make the town of Dorchester an industrial center by financing the building of a fertilizer plant, and eventually subsidiary facilities, in the Westmoreland Chemical Park; electric lines, roads and railways were built to link the park with the floating dock to which ships would bring the raw chemicals through the Bay of Fundy, noted for its herculean tides. Today the $6m park lies idle; the Fundy tides make it impossible to dock the ships that carry the vital raw materials.

When in 1966 an election brought to power the Liberal party led by young Alex Campbell, Prince Edward Island's 108,000 people were still without the benefit of an industrial development plan. The new premier soon created the Economic Improvement Corp., which hired experts who took three years to tell the islanders what they already knew--that their economy was based solely on agriculture and fishing, that their real income was declining, and that they needed an industrial development corporation. It was suggested that the government invest $750m over 15 years

POLARIZATION — *(Continued from page 1)*

recently by Scammon and Wattenberg, have enraged the liberals, but none has successfully refuted their observations: that the wave of the political future lies with the Middle American who is fed to the gills with students, youth, bombings, crime, and the blacks.

The Democratic National Committee, adopting Scammon-Wattenberg as their text, and alive to these "social issues", is moving to purge the liberals of their influence in party councils.

Why, we might ask, is Agnew having more success in his campaign than did Joe McCarthy in his attempt in the 1950's to rouse the masses in populist fashion against the liberals? The main difference is that in the 1950's the Establishment *was* liberal, and McCarthy therefore found himself trying to lead a populist assault against the Establishment, including such a mighty symbol as the American Army itself. Now Mr. Agnew is using all the resources of the Executive branch, and therefore of the Establishment , against the liberals and the Left. As a result, the press and media, which while centrist is far less liberal than in the 1950's, have been effectively neutralized by the pressures inherent in a Vice-President, whereas they were able to gut McCarthy (and Goldwater, for that matter) savagely with blessings from the federal government.

As for the radicLeft, they have only just begun to pay the price of their years of arrogant self-isolation from Middle America, of their total failure even to try to convince the man whose values they so utterly despise. Their increasing radicalization has only served to demoralize and confuse their own supporters, while mobilizing the mass of the American people against them with accelerating intensity. In their insulated and hopped-up frenzy, the Weathermen have totally forgotten the stragetic advice of their own supposed mentors: Mao, Fidel, and Che--the warning that

(Continued on page 5)

to encourage the establishment of new industries, consolidated farms (clear the land of people) and processing plants, and encourage tourism. The key to industrialization must remain better communication with the mainland, but proposals for a bridge across the channel to New Brunswick were laid aside. In summer, motorists wait four and five hours to cross on the ferries and until something can be done to make access of people, cars, and freight easier, it is difficult to believe that the $750m will be well spent. But the plan has been accepted by the electorate and we may await the almost certain recurrence of the Nova Scotia-New Brunswick experience.

About 5% of our subscribers are residents of Canada, and it encourages us to hope that we might hear from them in future regarding developments in their own provinces. With so much to offer its people, Canada should become one of the most prosperous societies in the world, if it can avoid wars, and the waste and theft of its people's capital and talents. This can only be assured by the operations of the free market; we see them, in Canada, a magnificent opportunity for libertarians to alert their countrymen to the real character of corporate capitalism, its alliance with the state to rob and pillage the people through taxation to enrich the few who can make the right political connections; its inevitable destruction of local economic interests in favor of national or international elites. We would hope that our readers across the border would enter into dialogue with the dissenting voices that are appearing in the pages of the *Last Post, The Mysterious East* and *Canadian Dimension* so that libertarian ideas may enter the consciousness of the thinking Canadian public.

--J. R. P.

Gun Laws

The indifference which seems to pervade many libertarian circles regarding recent gun control laws—laws which are likely to forge the final links on the chains shackled to the average American citizen—is dangerously surprising. Apparently no one perceives the importance of what has occurred.

Few realize the extreme shackles placed on actual or potential gun owners by the acts snowballing into the Gun Control Act of 1968 (Public Law 90-618). To purchase a gun one must make a sworn statement of identity, which is sent to the local police chief—who decides whether the applicant may own a gun on the basis of whether he is a "law-abiding" citizen (i.e., if he obeys every order of the power elite). Firearm ownership is denied to convicted felons, dishonorably discharged veterans, aliens illegally in the U. S., and former citizens who have renounced their citizenship, viz., *all potential opposers of the Establishment* . Users of "dangerous drugs" like pot, anyone under 21, as well as many others are also denied the right of ownership. Ownership of fully automatic, large caliber, or other firearms is absolutely prohibited to everyone but the State.

Even those qualified to own an arm are hampered by total registration, a fact unknown to the general public. Besides direct registration of newly purchased guns, "backdoor registration" of all other guns occurs due to the requirement that merchants record the name, address, etc., of all buyers of ammunition. These records are subject to police and Federal snooping. All producers and retailers are also fettered by high license fees and other outrages.

Some state and local governments have gone even more berserk. In many areas, anyone possessing a firearm is under constant harassment by the police. Complete regis-

tration, as well as the charging of atrociously high license fees, have left many with the necessity of surrendering their guns. The states of New York, New Jersey, and Illinois are particularly oppressive in this regard.

On the local level, the situation in Miami reads like a chapter from *1984.* To apply for gun ownership, one must submit to the police extensive personal information. While at this point they have not gone quite as far as Rhodesia, where 32 blacks were recently sentenced to death for the "crime" of possessing firearms, anyone who is caught carrying a "dangerous weapon" without police approval gets a minimum of 6 months or $1,000 in fines. To help enforce these repressions, a $100 bounty is paid to anyone who is willing to squeal on his neighbor for firearms violations. Other cities are on the same road.

The ultimate goal of the power structure is the total abolition of private (non-ruling class) gun ownership. In mid-January 1969 the Illinois Academy of Criminology spoke favorably of this goal, and hundreds of other groups and individuals openly admit similar ambitions. The minimum they will settle for is complete police control of all firearms as is the case in Soviet Russia.

The masses are taught to believe the lie that such laws will reduce crime. Nothing could be further from the truth, because gun ownership by the general population simply does not cause crime. In 1966, twice as many guns per home were owned in Canada as compared with the U. S., yet the gun homicide rate of the former was only one-fifth that of the latter (*American Rifleman*, Aug., 1968, p. 46). And surely, if one wants to kill another, the absence of a gun will act as no safeguard; in Japan, where civilian guns are outlawed, the murder rate without guns is almost twice as high as the U. S. rate without guns (*American Rifleman.*, Nov., 1968, p. 17).

(Continued on page 5)

154

GUN LAWS — *(Continued from page 4)*

On the contrary, gun ownership by the immense majority serves to prevent crime. Criminals have second thoughts regarding killing and plundering peaceful individuals who may be armed. But they have no hesitations when they are confident that their victims are helpless. Since criminals will always have guns (no criminals would register their guns, and besides, zip guns are easy to make), it is necessary that potential victims be able to arm themselves to prevent crime. Each month the *American Rifleman*, under the column "The Armed Citizen", cites numerous instances in which private guns have prevented crimes.

Thus the avowed goal of State gun control is false. What,

POLARIZATION — *(Continued from page 3)*

one does not go over into guerrilla action until one is supported by the mass of the population. In their fanaticism, Bernardine and her comrades believe that a few "exemplary" bombings will arouse the masses to their call; the masses will be aroused alright, but in the opposite direction. Every new outrage by the Left brings us a giant step closer to fascism, a fascism which will inevitably fall not only upon those who have been continually trying to provoke it but upon many innocents as well.

If President Nixon were only smart--which he gives no signs of being--he would get us pronto out of Vietnam and abolish the draft. This would totally defuse the major political issue of the Left, neutralize the liberals, and allow the Administration to smash the then totally isolated radicals with a minimum of fuss or "spillover." In their blindness, the conservatives fail to see that Vietnam is the one issue on which the Left can hope to mobilize any sort of mass support, and that deprived of that issue, the Left Revolution would crumble completely.

In the meanwhile, however, the exuberant hopes of the new Peace Politics of last spring have been dashed on the rocks of the accelerating polarization between the bombers of the campus and the bombers of Vietnam. President Nixon's meretricious gestures in the direction of peace have temporarily defused the Vietnam issue. Still, the only sane political course is to try to preserve and strengthen the peace bloc in Congress. This means to support in particular the races of Duffey (D.) in Connecticut, Metzenbaum (D.) in Ohio, Grossman (D.) in Arizona, Hoff (D.) in Vermont, Sesler (D.) in Pennsylvania; and the re-election attempts of Hartke (D.) in Indiana, Hart (D.) in Michigan, Burdick (D.) in North Dakota, Williams (D.) in New Jersey, Moss (D.) in Utah, Proxmire (D.) in Wisconsin, and Goodell (R.), in New York. All of these men voted correctly, from the libertarian viewpoint, on the three most important votes of the current Congress: No on the ABM, Yes on the Hatfield-Goldwater bill to move rapidly toward raising the pay of GI's so as to abolish the draft, and Yes on the McGovern-Hatfield resolution to pull totally out of Vietnam by mid-1971. Particularly important (though not very likely) would be the re-election of Senator Goodell, as a reward for his courage and independence in bucking a Republican President on the Vietnam War, and thereby earning the bitter attacks of the Vice-President; in Charles Goodell lies the lingering hope for Peace Republicanism, and that is precisely why the Administration and the Conservative Party want him retired.

At this point, however, support for Peace Politics seems as dim a hope within the libertarian movement as it is in the nation at large. To some this would be an interruption in their task of "making revolution" in a couple of weeks; to others it would sully their sectarian purity; to still others it would interfere with their personal careers. And so confrontation and repression loom around the corner, with few caring about any last-minute attempt to steer our nation onto a saner course.

then, is the real reason why the power elite wants to leave the people defenseless?

It has already been observed that guns are necessary for peaceful individuals to protect themselves from criminals. But who has been the most ferocious criminal in history? It is obvious: *the State*!

The U. S. Government, though they trust themselves with the largest arsenal the world has ever known, including everything from napalm and M-16's to tanks and H-bombs, will not trust its thralls with .22-cal. revolvers. Why does this trust not exist? The people want to be free, a great number of blacks as well as many non-ruling class whites desire self-determination, and the Establishment must frustrate these movements. *Laissez-faire* gun ownership is feared for the same reason that Hitler would have been afraid of a gun-owning Jewish population or Stalin a bunch of pistol-packing Ukrainians. Well does the State know Mao's dictum: "political power grows out of the barrel of a gun." The rulers realize that the only way to retain their control

(Continued on page 6)

155

Recommended Reading

Out in Paperback:

John Womack, Jr., *Zapata and the Mexican Revolution* (Random House, Vintage, $2.95). See *Lib. Forum*, Sept. 15.

H. L. Nieburg, *In the Name of Science* (Quadrangle). Incursions of the U. S. Government into science.

Arno J. Mayer, *The Political Origins of the New Diplomacy, 1917-18* (Random House, Vintage, $2.95), and *Politics and Diplomacy of Peacemaking, 1918-19* (Random House, Vintage, $3.95). Brilliant two volumes on the development of Wilsonian imperialism after World War I. A truly trans-national history that deals with the American and various European internal political struggles as well as with conventional diplomatic history. A work of historical tapestry that ranks with Robert R. Palmer on the age of the French Revolution.

Conservation.

E. F. Roberts, "Plead the Ninth Amendment!", *Natural History* (August). A law professor at Cornell urges the use of the highly libertarian Ninth Amendment by citizens who sue polluters in the courts.

The Middle East.

Uri Avnery, *Israel Without Zionists* (Macmillan, $6.95). An anti-Zionist work by the leader of the Israeli "New Left."

Women's Lib.

Perhaps the backlash against Women's Lib has at last begun. Midge Decter's "The Liberated Women", *Commentary* (October, $1.00), is a devastating portrait of the typical woman's libber, who scorns her true freedom of choice in order to agitate for a "freedom demanded by children and enjoyed by no one: the freedom from all difficulty."

Left/Right.

It is a measure of the parlous state we are in that some of the sanest comments on social and ideological matters can now be found in such (formerly despised) Social Democratic organs as *Comentary, Encounter, Public Interest,* and *Dissent.* Thus, Nathan Glazer, in "On Being Deradicalized," *Commentary* (October), affectingly relates his hegira from "mild radical" in the late 1950's to "mild conservative today. Glazer's "radicalism" was his attraction to the libertarian, anti-war, and decentralization positions of such as Paul Goodman and Dwight MacDonald; his shift "rightward" came not so much from a basic change of view as from his realization that the radical Left has become bent on destroying the university, and from his growing awareness that no society can survive without the inner self-disciplines of hard work and without modern technology and the industrial system, all of which our Youth Culture Rousseauists are out to destroy.

GUN LAWS — *(Continued from page 5)*

over the people is to monopolize the firearms. The powers-that-be perceive that the people can never exercise their *right* to be free if they have no *might* to be free. Thus it is in part by gun control that Big Brother perpetuates his hegemony.

Besides those already mentioned, one of the most important steps taken by the U. S. Leviathan has been to forbid the importation into the U. S. of surplus military rifles. American gun manufacturers, including Winchester-Western, Remington, and Savage gave tremendous support to the passage of this act to prevent competition from old and low-priced but reliable foreign arms. The State's motive is evident too: these inexpensive guns were within the buying power of everyone, and outlawing further importation prevents the many who cannot afford expensive American guns from acquiring a means of self-defense.

Understanding the political (or rather, the *anti-political*)

utility of guns for the people, it is deplorable that the police can know who owns which firearms. But unless present trends are reversed, these quasi-private guns will not be around to worry about—they will be confiscated, leaving the people with no protection whatever.

There are few methods available to prevent this. The National Rifle Association has been a somewhat effective lobbyist in Congress to preserve the Second Amendment freedom to keep and bear arms, but it is likely that such efforts will only delay confiscation. The best mode available seems to be that employed by the people of Chicago last fall: only one-third of the city's 1,200,000 firearms were registered in accordance with the ordinance requiring total registration, and of the two million gun owners in Illinois, less than one-fourth obtained the required license (*American Rifleman.*, Dec., 1968, p. 6). Only mass civil disobedience can prevent Big Brother from totally disarming his serfs.

—— Stephen Halbrook

Published on the first and fifteenth of every month.   Subscription rate: $7.00 per year; Student subscription rate: $5.00 per year

A Semi-Monthly Newsletter

THE
Libertarian Forum

Joseph R. Peden, Publisher

Murray N. Rothbard, Editor

VOLUME II, NO. 21   NOVEMBER 1, 1970   35¢

White Terror In Quebec

The press, as usual, has it all backward; as usual, it strains at a gnat while cheerfully swallowing a camel. The wave of horror at the kidnapping of two government officials by the *Front de Liberation du Quebec* has hardly been matched by any indignation at the wave of White Terror that Prime Minister Trudeau has imposed on that long-suffering province. Quite the contrary. Thus, the good grey *New York Times* (October 19) denounces the "atrocity" of the "cold-blooded murder" of Quebec's Labor Minister, but hails the "vigorous and necessary" measures of despotic repression that Mr. Trudeau has brought to the province. These measures include the decree outlawing all members of the FLQ, and the rounding up, without search warrant or indictment, of hundreds of separatist leaders and placing them in jail without trial. One man's "atrocity" is another man's "vigor".

Even more ominous is the reaction of U. S. officials to this shining example north of the border. While Attorney-General Mitchell made the headlines in assuring us that this can never happen here, the *Times* reports that unnamed State Department officials take great comfort in Mr. Trudeau's "gutsy" actions, and see them as a model for dealing with our own dissidents and revolutionaries. Total fascism may well come to America in the name of "guts."

The deeper problem in Canada is also studiously ignored. For Canada is really not a nation at all, but rather a geographical expression. In our October 15 issue, Professor Peden showed that this is true even for Canada's beleaguered Maritime Provinces; how much more is this true of the French nation of Quebec, which has groaned under the Anglo heel for over two centuries! In the mid-eighteenth century, Canada was French; it was then conquered, in a naked act of aggression by Great Britain, and the French of Quebec have lived under Anglo tyranny, discrimination, and exploitation ever since. Now that Quebec is becoming increasingly urban and educated, its people are increasingly anxious to end this carefully fostered myth of a Canadian "nation", and to achieve independence for their own French nation once more.

Here, again, our purely educationist Libertarians are caught in an impossible bind. What is *their* prescription for freeing Quebec, with it s French language, culture, and nationality, from the Canadian yoke? Education will not do the job here, because no amount of "education" will persuade Canada simply to give up the prestige and perquisites of its imperial rule over Quebec. Any attempt by Quebec to secede peacefully would be met in the same brutal and violent way that the "free" United States met the attempt by the South to secede a century ago. A peaceful solution, therefore, will unfortunately not work, simply because Anglo Canada will not permit it. Hence, the going over by the FLQ into guerrilla warfare and armed insurrection. The FLQ are not the northern equivalent of our crazed Weathermen, simply because the mass of the Quebeckers endorse its goals, though not yet its current tactics. The only chance of a peaceful secession lies in the separtist political party, the *Parti Quebecois*, which, while newly formed, had great successes in the last provincial elections. But then again, I don't see any great huzzahs among our libertarians for the PQ either, presumably because it indulges in the impurity of running for electoral office. But again we must put the question to our educationists: what advice would *you* give the Quebec people?

Gems Of Statism

1. *Chairman Moa and the Church*.

National Review-niks had better take a second look at the "martyred" Bishop James Walsh, recently released from twelve years in a Chinese Communist prison. For the 79-year-old bishop, now safe in Rome, praised the Chinese regime for three great advances it is supposed to have made: equality of women, equality of races, and, in particular, "an absolute ban and prohibition on all manifestations of immorality and indecency in regard to theatrical displays, or publicity, or action." (*New York Times*, August 27). And, come to think of it, this item might also give pause to those libertarians who have embraced Chairman Mao as the "greatest libertarian of the twentieth. century."

2. *Most Persecuted Minority-Department*

Contrary to Ayn Rand, big businessmen scarcely consider themselves as "America's most persecuted minority." Thus, in mid-October a group of the nation's leading and most powerful corporation executives, assembled as the Business Council advising the Nixon Administration, hinted strongly in the direction of new government policies that would hold down wage increases. The businessmen claimed that they certainly were not thinking of wage or price controls, but this danger looms increasingly large as the Administration loses its timid and fitful battle against inflation. Austrian theory shows that in the later stages of a boom wages tend to catch up with prices, squeezing profits, and it is then that businessmen are tempted to turn to the totalitarian (and ineffective) coercion of price-wage controls. (New York Times, October 18).

Free Enterprise And Free Education

Higher education in the United States, as everyone knows, is a field in which private institutions are engaged in a desperate struggle to hold their own against the competition of the heavily subsidized state run multiversities. In this business, just keeping your head above water is a tough assignment. After all, how long do you think a private barber shop or restaurant could stay in business faced with state financed competitors, where the customers did not have to pay for their purchases, the producers did not have to sell their products, and the owners (taxpayers) exercised only nominal and sporadic control?

The system under which higher education is organized and financed in this country has had widespread and deleterious effects on the quality of the services rendered. The first effect is the most widely publicized. The low cost of matriculation has meant that our colleges and universities have been filled with a flood of "students" who value the education relatively little by comparison with alternative pursuits, but are willing to drop in and see the show given a sufficient subsidy. If they take it into their heads that they don't like what they see, they lose next to nothing by shutting the school down or tearing it up. Faculty members, whose paychecks keep rolling in strike or no strike (and think of all that extra time to devote to publications! hardly have an interest in standing up to the students, and the result is chaos.

The second effect is perhaps less widely known, but even though less spectacular is equally disturbing. According to a study reported in the *New York Times* of July 19, our institutions of higher education are year by year becoming more uniform, more like one another. Anyone in academic life is familiar with the pressures in any college which tend to work against diversity of political views, teaching methods, life styles, etc. within a given institution. The chief redeeming feature of the system heretofore has been the great range and diversity existing among institutions. Now, it seems, this diversity is gradually being nibbled away by the pressures of the system.

The third effect of the organizational and financial peculiarities of American higher education is, however, the most serious of all. It has, in fact, contributed substantially to the other problems just mentioned. Faced with the overwhelming financial pressures generated by the competition of state subsidized institutions, almost all of what we nominally call "private" institutions have swallowed hard once or twice, and then put their hands out too. Building grants, research grants, development planning grants, matching grants, travel grants, and above all, the half-hidden grants implicit in the tax deductibility of alumni contributions have flooded in, each with its attached earmark, restriction, provision, loyalty oath, reporting procedure or other string by some other name. A lucky few have become rich, powerful clients of the state and are able to throw their weight around a bit in Washington, but most, like the welfare poor, have been given just enough to stay alive in a state of abject, impoverished dependence.

Against this bleak background, Royalton College of South Royalton, Vermont stands out in startling contrast. Incorporated in 1965 as a proprietary, stock corporation, with its President and Director the principal stock holder by virtue of ownership of all but two of 2000 shares, Royalton College has never accepted aid from the state in any form (although it has from time to time accepted students who in turn have, as individuals, accepted government assistance in the form of veterans' benefits and the like). Royalton College has not even accepted the indirect subsidy of tax-deductible contributions since, although it has never in fact made a profit (for reasons which will become clear below, not by intention) and has amended its articles of association so that any potential profits would

automatically be plowed back into improvement in its educational facilities, it has refused to reorganized as a non profit institution.

In 1967, the College received a visiting committee from the board of higher education. On the basis of the enthusiastic report that committee concerning the high academic achievements of the infant institution, the board voted to give the college the power to grant four year degrees. This privilege was accomplished by a list of 17 conditions to which the college must adhere, but since these conditions related only to the type of academic qualifications which would be the concern of any certifying agency public or private, the college agreed to them.

It was too much to hope, however, that the state would permit a wholly free and independent institution to exist peacefully and grant degrees within the realm of its authority. In 1968, less than a year later, some reports appeared in the local yellow press questioning the advisability of permitting education to be conducted by an institution with Royalton's unique (unique in the educational world, that is) financial organization. The board of education panicked, sent another visiting team, and, on the basis of the college's financial structure, suspended its degree granting powers.

At this point, the school filed suit to nullify the suspension. The argument was made that the degree granting powers were essential to continued operation of the college, and especially that suspension of the powers once granted was much more damaging than would have been a delay or refusal of the original grant of certification. It was contended that the action of the board was unreasonable, arbitrary and capricious, constituted a breach of contract, and violated the college's rights to equal protection and due process as guaranteed by the federal and state constitutions. The petition of the college was sustained by the Vermont Supreme Court, and the order of the board was vacated. The grounds of the decision, however, were relatively narrow. The court based its action on the fact that nothing had been said about the school's finances that in the future, the board might decide to refuse certification of some other institution solely on the basis of its proprietary status.

Meanwhile, in the District of Columbia, another case was making its way through the courts that was to provide a direct test of this important principle. The school involved in this case was Marjorie Webster Junior College. This institution had asked the Middle States Association of Colleges and Secondary Schools to accept an application for accreditation, and had been refused on the grounds that in order to be considered for evaluation, an institution must be a non-profit organization with a governing board representing the "public interest." The Marjorie Webster case was brought under the Sherman Anti-Trust Act, on the grounds that the Middle States Association exercised a monopoly in the field of granting accreditation. Middle States argued, on the other hand, that education was not a "trade," and that a combining to restrain the conduct of education thus did not constitute a restraint of trade. The U. S. District Court for the District of Columbia found in favor of Marjorie Webster, writing that "Higher education in America today possesses many of the attributes of business. To hold otherwise would ignore the obvious and challenge reality."

Thus the important principle appeared to be established that an accrediting association could look only at the genuine academic credentials of an institution, and could not arbitrarily refuse even to consider a proprietary institution. The way seemed open for Royalton to make an application to the New England Association of Colleges for the full

(Continued on page 4)

Bits And Pieces
By Jerome Tuccille

Congratulations to Dana Rohrabacher for having been chosen Libertarian Pinup Boy of the Month by the editors of Rap, the apparent successor to *Pine Tree* magazine. *Rap* is real groovy, man, with all sorts of penetrating insights into contemporary hippie jargon. The next issue will feature a pullout centerfold in living color of Robert LeFerve being transmogrified to a mountaintop while he contemplates whether or not to slash the chains that bind him. Private property you know.

* * * *

Which brings us to the subject of *anarcho-land grabbism* and *anarcho-shopping centerism*.

Free market anarchists base their theories of private property rights on the homestead principle: a person has the right to a private piece of real estate provided he mixes his labor with it and alters it in some way. Anarcho-land grabbers recognize no such restrictions. Simply climb to the highest mountain peak and claim all you can see. It then becomes morally and sacredly your own and no one else can so much as step on it.

But, you might contend. Suppose fifty people claimed all the land in the United States? In an age of rocket ships it is even possible for one rather self-centered propertarian to go into orbit around the earth and claim the entire globe as his personal backyard. What would the other unfortunate three billion do if our space-age propertarian ordered them all off the planet?

Have no fear, counter the land-grabbers. Such a state of affairs would be so inconvenient, not only to the three billion trespassers, but to the landlord (earthlord?) as well that reason would induce him to sell off large chunks of land to the highest bidders, and rent out the rest. So you see, nobody would actually have to leave the earth, although the least Galt-like among us would no doubt find themselves confined to the cheapest plots on Antarctica.

Anarcho-shopping centerism is better known by its official name, the proprietary community idea. Its chief proponent is Spencer H. MacCallum, grandson of Spencer Heath, who outlines his philosophy in a recently published book, *The Art of Community*. On one level the book is a very interesting history of the development of real estate interests and the organization of commercial properties. MacCallum describes the trend leading away from the neighborhood structure of small village shops and community meeting-places toward large shopping centers and industrial parks servicing the needs of larger and larger segments of the community. He records this development over the last two centuries and shows how, today, shopping and industrial centers offer, not only supermarkets and other shopping services to the public, but movie houses and theaters, restaurants, health and recreational facilities, nightclubs and taverns, and even centers of employment.

No one who has grown up in the United States in the years following World War II will argue with MacCallum over this point. Social chroniclers from John Updike to Norman Mailer have been satirizing the suburban sprawl in fiction and in articles since the early 1950's. The ugliness of plasticized suburbia complete with its manicured lawns, jack-in-the-box houses, cocktail-shaker morality and creeping-horror shopping centers is a well-documented fact by now. It is only when MacCallum the Historian becomes MacCallum the Advocate that one turns back to his book with a kind of fascinated horror.

As the story unfolds one becomes aware of the fact that the "proprietary community people" are *actually in love* with shopping centers. They are mad about those enormous parking lots with their giant-sized Korvette's and Grant's knick-knack stores and Hills supermarkets and Cinema Artsy I and II and penny bubble gum machines and psychedelic pizza parlors and Tony-the-lover barbershops and *bouffant* beauty salons and Fred Astaire dance emporiums and Jerome Mackey judo schools. The Heathians are so crazy about them, in fact, that they want to make them bigger and more complex and *move people into them*. Yes, they want to erect high-rise apartment buildings on the premises, the ones with orange and lavender walls and spotted goldfish swimming in imitation-marble fountains in the lobbies. They see no point in making people drive on public roads to get to this real-life Disneyland; they want them to move in and be a real part of this mind-blowing phantasmagoria.

They want America to become one big shopping center, one great big Lefrak City.

This way, you see, with Heath-MacCallum Real Estate Enterprises providing all the essential services one can hope for in life—housing, schools, police and fire protection, garbage removal, judo lessons, roads and parking areas, pizza parlors, bubble gum machines, art theaters featuring the latest Rock Hudson movie—there won't be any need for Uncle Sam anymore.

The government will just wither and die away.

Now you know why Right Wing businessmen are so partial to this brand of "libertarianism." Why they like to keep the idea up on a "flagpole" where more people can see it. Why they like to slap it against the wall and see if it will stick.

* * * *

There is nothing radical or even political about the schemes of "retreatist" or "escapist" libertarians. Their pipedreams are only entrepreneurial fantasies—rather hideous ones at that—designed to "maximize profits." They have nothing whatsoever to do with the world of conscription, military imperialism, federal curtailment of civil liberties and institutionalized racism. Libertarianism is meaningless unless it tells us what we can do in terms of political reality to liberate our society.

As long as the apparatus of power remains in the hands of the power-elite, it is still for the present authorities to use and misuse that power in any manner they choose. It is for them to snuff out the "alternatives" any time they decide to do so. While one is creating his voluntary institutions it is mandatory that he encourage tax and draft resistance, and engage in radical politics at the same time to keep the pressure on the authorities while the new society is being built. Or else he may find it smashed before the foundation has begun to set.

(If shopping centers are the alternative, that may not be such a bad idea.)

The Shaffer Dictionary
By Butler Shaffer

The following definitions comprise a part of my view of reality, in all its humorous—and often frustrating—manner.

GOVERNMENT: an institution of war, theft, murder, rape and predation, . . . the absence of which, it is said, would lead to disorder.

TAXATION: a practice employed by governments in looting all of its citizens in order to obtain the necessary funds to chase down and punish looters.

WAR: the price men are forced to pay in order to keep peace among the politicians.

FREE ENTERPRISE — *(Continued from page 2)*

accreditation which, unlike the not nationally recognized certification of the Vermont State Board, would enable the college to be a full-fledged member of the educational community.

Once again, however, it proved too much to hope that all would be smooth sailing for proprietary education, for recently the Court of Appeals for the District of Columbia reversed the lower court's ruling in Marjorie Webster vs. Middle States. This court, in addition to ruling that education was not part of the business world and hence outside the scope of the Sherman Act, wrote that "it is not unreasonable for Middle States to conclude that the desire for personal profit might influence educational goals in subtle ways difficult to detect but destructive, in the long run, of that atmosphere of academic inquiry which, perhaps even more than any quantitative measure of educational quality, appellant's standards for accreditation seek to foster."

Did it never occur to Middle States or to the Learned Judges that financial dependence on the civilian and military agencies of the state might also influence educational goals "in subtle ways" (!) and destroy academic freedom? Did they never learn in their principles of economics courses that it is not upon the charity of the butcher and the baker that we depend for our meat and bread, but upon their profit-seeking self interest? The decision of the court represents the kind of thinking that is turning all of American higher education into one giant academic soup line--the meat and bread is free, yes, but the quality???

The Middle States and New England Associations are, of course, private, voluntary, non-profit organizations, and the courts were wise in recognizing this as a factor in the case which should make them reluctant to intervene hastily or casually in their affairs. However, two aspects of the nature and activities of these associations are objectionable, I think, on strict libertarian grounds. First, the associations in question seem to exercise an effective monopoly in the area of certification. Whether or not this is a benign, "natural" monopoly, or one aided and abetted by the state is, at least, open to question. Second, and much more important, various governmental agencies concerned with education base certain actions of their own on the decisions of the associations to accredit or not to accredit. For Royalton, the most directly harmful of these decisions have not been any refusals to hand out unwanted grants or aid, but actions which have made it virtually impossible, in certain area, for the college to help itself! For example, it turns out that foreign students cannot get permission

from the State Department to study at schools which are not on the list, a matter of critical importance to a school like Royalton which specializes in international affairs.

In short, the future of free, independent, proprietary higher education in the United States looks to be trouble. The ultimate answer may be to establish a competing accreditation agency which will not suffer from the delusion that quality education must be socialized education, but this will, to say the least, take time. Meanwhile, *you* can do something now to help proprietary education by *patronizing* it. We do not need handouts; we need just a few, serious, qualified, paying students. For a catalog and a bonus copy of the details of the court cases described above, write to the Director of Admissions, Royalton College, South Royalton, Vermont 05068.

--Edwin G. Dolan

RECOMMENDED READING

Education

Jacques Barzun, "The Conflict of Action and Liberty", *The Humanist* (September-October, 75¢), pp. 14-18. For years there has been no wiser critic of our educational system than Barzun, who now in a brilliant and bitterly pessimistic article declares that the American university is dead. Murdered by two groups: first by the scientist behaviorists and vocationalists, and finally by barbarian youth. The only hope is to form new small "lay monasteries" to ride out the dark ages ahead.

Statism in America

I never thought that I would agree with J. K. Galbraith on anything, but his witty "Richard Nixon and the Great Socialist Revival", *New York* (September 21, 40¢) correctly zeros in on the acceleration of pro-Big Business "socialism" under the Nixon regime. Galbraith particularly discusses the Lockheed affair and the business drive (seconded, incidentally, by *National Review*) for the nationalization of the bankrupt Penn Central railroad.

The Libertarian Forum

BOX 341
MADISON SQUARE STATION
NEW YORK, NEW YORK 10010

First Class

Published on the first and fifteenth of every month.   **Subscription rate: $7.00 per year; Student subscription rate: $5.00 per year**

A Semi-Monthly Newsletter

THE
Libertarian Forum

Joseph R. Peden, Publisher   Murray N. Rothbard, Editor

VOLUME II, NOS. 22-23   NOVEMBER 15 - DECEMBER 1, 1970   35¢

THE ELECTIONS

We live in a time of increasingly intense and unpredictable changes in attitudes and values, a time when a valid analysis of existing social and ideological trends may be completely outmoded a few months later. Who, for example, could have predicted last spring that the flourishing antiwar movement would now be dead as a dodo? Dead. . .or dormant? Any analysis of the November elections has to keep this humbling fact in mind.

Be that as it may, the press has underestimated the crushing defeat suffered by the Nixon Administration. Despite an ardent nation-wide galvanizing effort by Nixon and Agnew, despite their continual hammering at the seemingly popular issue of polarization against the Left, despite enormously greater financing and a demoralized Democratic opposition, the Democratic Party has emerged from the 1970 elections as the secure majority of the country. The Democrats gained nine Congressmen and no less than eleven governors, and their victories were scored throughout the country, South, West and Middle West. The famous Nixonian "Southern strategy" totally collapsed, and governorship races were lost throughout the South; only in Tennessee did the strategy succeed. In fact, only in Tennessee, New York, and Connecticut did the Republicans do very well at all. The common argument that the Republicans lost far fewer House races than the Administration usually loses in off-year elections overlooks a crucially important fact: that President Nixon, in contrast to all previous Presidents, did *not* bring a Republican House into office with him.

Furthermore, the fact that the Democrats lost a few seats in the Senate takes on proper perspective only when we realize that an unusually large number of Democratic senators were up for re-election this year–the products of the Democratic sweeps in the 1958 recession year and in the 1964 Goldwater debacle. It is all too easily forgotten that the Republicans began 1970 with the expectation of capturing the Senate.

It is about time that political commentators face the fact that the Republicans have not organized either house of Congress since 1954, and that, apart from the Presidency, we are drifting close to a one-party Democratic nation. Furthermore, there is no hope for Republican control of Congress in the foreseeable future.

The Nixon-Agnew failure seems to be due to several factors. One is the offsetting of the anti-Left "social issue" by the mess that the Nixon Administration has made of the economy; a second is the fact that the peace issue, despite its dormancy, still remains (the peace candidates in Congress did fairly well). Another reason is the fact that Nixon-Agnew overplayed their hand. While Middle Americans revile the Left, hippies, students, bom-

bers, etc., they also have a great need to *revere* their President, to consider him as a wise authority figure a bit above the battle. And so the brawling nature of the Nixon-Agnew campaign put the Middle American voters off, discomfited them, made their wise authority images seem too much like local wardheelers for comfort. Furthermore, the Democrats were able to draw the teeth of Agnewism by shifting notably rightward, by stressing their own devotion to "law and order". Thus, the clumsy attempt by the Republicans to turn such a generally revered and moderate figure as Adlai Stevenson into a crypto-Weatherman backfired badly by making the Republicans rather ridiculous, a backfiring that also beset Agnew's attempts at rhetorical alliteration.

The failure to polarize the country against the Left was also considerably helped by the fact that the Left seems to have suddenly disappeared. The campuses are always quieter in the fall than in the spring, but even so the extent of campus relapse into apolitical passivity this fall has been truly remarkable. The Yale students have turned dramatically from the Panthers to football and Boola-Boola, and on campus after campus the story is the same.

The larger meaning of the election, then, is that the prospect of civil war that seemed to be looming on the horizon, a war in which fascist repression would have crushed a vociferous Left, seems now but a ghost of the past. The Center still holds, and more strongly than it has for several years.

Retreat From Freedom

Leonard E. Read seems to be worried; apparently he is having considerable difficulty in defending the thesis that everyone must obey all laws, no matter how noxious they may be. And so in the current *Notes from FEE* ("Defiance of Law", November), Mr. Read returns to the dialogue (see "On Civil Obedience," *Lib. Forum*, July). Except that it is a curious form of dialogue indeed, for Mr. Read cleaves to his lofty principle that no critic or emitter of fallacy may be mentioned in his work. At first glance, this principle seems to have a monkish, almost saintly air, an air of discussing only ideas and never people; until we realize that this attitude stifles any sort of intellectual dialogue whatever, for it means that one need never comes to grips with anyone else's views. If philosophers or scholars upheld this view, any sort of intellectual advance would be stifled; there would be no book reviews, no critique of the unsound or advance of the sound in anyone's work. If, for example, Henry

(Continued on page 8)

STIRRINGS, RIGHT AND LEFT

In these changing times, it becomes increasingly difficult to tell "left", "right" or in between without a detailed scorecard. There are new stirrings throughout the left-right spectrum, and all through that spectrum authoritarian and libertarian elements appear and vie for support. The November Festival of Liberation in Los Angeles, for example, was addressed not only by such veteran anarcho-capitalists as Robert LeFevre and the editor of the *Lib. Forum*, but also by the confused and inconsistent but definitely anarchistic "leftist" Paul Goodman, and also by the great one-man crusader for liberty in the psychiatric profession, Dr. Thomas Szasz, who while now embraced by the New Left, himself looks upon Hayek and Mises as his philosophical mentors. And over at the bastion of Conservatism, *National Review*, a recent reviewer, while hailing Soviet Democrat Irving Howe's recent edited work attacking the New Left, *also* praised the New Leftist journalist Nicholas von Hoffman for *his* critiques of Liberal Social Democracy.

On the Left, increasing support for the libertarian and anarchist positions has appeared recently in several forms. The liberal weekly *The Nation* has recently acquired the veteran left-anarchoid Emile Capouya as its literary editor, a move which is perhaps reflected in the recent favorable lead review of several recent anarchist books. (Kingsley Widmer, "Anarchism Revived: Left, Right, and All Around," *The Nation*, November 16). Professor Widmer, himself an anarchist (probably of the anarcho-syndicalist variety), reviews the Tuccille book, *Radical Libertarianism*, Daniel Guerin's *Anarchism* (both recently reviewed in the *Lib. Forum*), and Professor Robert Paul Wolff's (a recent convert to anarchism) *In Defense of Anarchism*. (Harper & Row, 86 pp. $4.50, Paper $1.00). Even though he disagrees with Tuccille's *laissez-faire* capitalism, Widmer's treatment of Jerry's book is the most favorable of the three. Widmer sees that our kind of anarchism is the expression of a native American libertarianism which "may be one of our finest and most redeeming heritages." Widmer calls our position "anarcho-rightism", which "takes *laissez-faire* economics and open competition seriously—not just as a rhetorical cover for corporate merger with the state-and rigorously holds to liberal notions of the absolute autonomy of the individual." Again , accurately, Widmer adds that "Anarcho-rightism can be related to many avowed 19th-century anarchists, such as Lysander Spooner and Benjamin Tucker, and . . . to a long line of right-wing iconoclasts, such as H. L. Mencken, and to elements in the thought of our contradictory agrarians and Populists." He then mentions the role of myself and Karl Hess, and gives an accurate account of Tuccille's positions on police, neighborhood and voluntary associations, removal or drastic limitation on the State, etc. While friendly to Tuccille, Widmer shows lack of understanding of the free market in speaking of Tuccille's "mad faith in the harmonious morality of the market place". It is, of course, not at all a matter of "faith" but of rational understanding of economic law, an understanding of which most anarchists, past and present, have been lamentably ignorant. There is also the usual left contention that even free-market corporations are somehow private "states", which Widmer wishes to see replaced by "workers' control". However, Widmer concedes the sincerity of the anarcho-capitalist position, and declares that "it's a pleasure to hear from a rightism which is not merely a cover for snobbery and greed." He ends the review of Tuccille by noting Carl Oglesby's call of a few years ago for "the fusion of libertarian Right and Left in America", and he brands Tuccille superior to Noam Chomsky's introduction to the Guerin book in recognizing the need of the American movement to "break out of leftist cliches", and not, like Chomsky, identifying anarchism with socialism.

In his review of Guerin, Widmer criticizes the French follower of Proudhon and Bakunin for still being tied to the mystique of the "working class" and ignoring the individualist aspects of anarchism, while Chomsky is criticized for "his narrow insistence on following somewhat doctrinaire European historians and seeing anarchism as purely integral to socialism. . . . He does not recognize that much of what can, and has been, reasonably called anarchism, from William Godwin through Paul Goodman, has been non-Socialist in any usual leftist sense. The anarcho-Marxism of the New Left, now often subordinated to neo-Leninism, linguistically misleads him."

Widmer concludes his review-article on a hopeful and ecumenical note. "Whether by way of traditional European Left-libertarianism, native American individualistic rightism, or philosophical anarchism, we arrive at the necessity for transforming our institutions. Why are we anarchists now almost in fashion in America? Because, in fact, the state's illegitimacy is becoming widely, if fragmentarily, manifest to many."

In the meanwhile, left-liberal Margot Hentoff has a perceptive review of Bill Buckley's *The Governor Listeth* in the *New York Review of Books* (December 3). (Worth the price of admission is the cartoon of Chairman Bill by the marvelous political caricaturist David Levine, making Buckley look something like an evil chipmunk). Essentially, Mrs. Hentoff is nostalgic about Buckley's former libertarianism and attacks him for abandoning his previous quasi-libertarianism principles to sit at the feet of Power and the Establishment. Mrs. Hentoff observes the fact that in his recent essays, "we come upon him in the middle of a journey toward a rather awful kind of moderation," a moderation that has come upon Bill as he "moves away from the absence of power, that condition which was his abiding charm." Hear, hear! Buckley, she notes, "is beginning to take on the weight of middle-aged responsibility, sounding more often like a resilient prince of the Church than like a purifying spirit."

For example, Mrs. Hentoff notes that Buckley comes out in favor of the government having the "responsibility to declare hopelessly irresponsible parents unqualified to bring up children, who could then be turned over to charitable organizations to bring up"; at this point, she adds, "one realizes that Mr. Buckley is very far from either the radical right or the conservative libertarians." She then notes that Bill Buckley has read the free-market economist Milton Friedman out of his movement (on much the same grounds as he read me out years ago-for the supposed intellectual frivolity of advocating denationalization of lighthouses). Arguing about legalization of narcotics. Buckley reports that Friedman came out against the licensing and compulsory inspection of prostitutes, noting that "after all, if the customer contracts a venereal disease, the prostitute having warranted that she was clean, he has available a tort action against her."

What Professor Friedman was adumbrating here was simply the libertarian common law, and the availability of tort actions at that law for fraud, a method for more moral than, and superior to, any government inspection. And what, Mrs. Hentoff asks, is Buckley's comment on this? "The articulation of libertarian theory to such lengths as Mr. Friedman is able to take it ought to be understood as a form of intellectual sport. . . . But it is terribly important not to take this kind of thing seriously."

As Bill Buckley moves toward the seats of Power, confers with the President in the Bahamas, and becomes a kind of intellectual Clown Prince of the Administration, any kind of serious devotion to liberty can seem only like

(Continued on page 3)

STIRRINGS — *(Continued from page 2)*

sport and frivolity in his eyes. It seems that "seriousness" is only warranted by the imprimatur of the State. From the master of the arch and recondite quip, from a man who once claimed to be a libertarian, all this is high irony indeed.

Mrs. Hentoff perceptively sees that "what happened to Mr. Buckley, along with the rest of us, was the breaking down of traditional ideological compartments, the blurring of traditional alliances and enmities. Not only did the old New Deal and New Frontier politics lose credence with the left, but the left then walked off with the conservative banners of nonintervention, freedom from government coercion, rugged individualism, decentralization, and, in some cases, radial separatism." At the same time, Bill Buckley was abandoning these very causes and becoming an effete and impudent servitor of Power.

While Bill Buckley is attacked for abandoning libertarianism by a left-liberal, an olive branch has been held out to libertarians from a most unexpected quarter. Young ultra-traditionalist Brad Evans, in a fascinating article, "The Young Conservatives: Coming Unglued", *Triumph* (November), virtually calls for an alliance with the libertarians at the opposite pole, as against the Power-loving statist Buckleyites in the "fusionist" Center. Coming from a leading follower of Brent Bozell and his pro-Carlist Spanish Catholics, men who revile Generalissimo Franco as a liberal sellout, this is wondrous news indeed. But it makes a considerable amount of sense. For Mr. Evans sees that, unlike the fusionists and their steady march toward apologetics for the American State and the *status quo*, the libertarians, like his own Triumphantists, totally reject the American Leviathan. Both groups cleave to principle and both eschew the opportunism of Power.

But, furthermore, Mr. Evans displays a genuine admiration for the libertarian position, for he understands that like the Catholic libertarian Lord Acton , the clinging to an absolute moral position provides a solid groundwork for a radical attack on the *status quo*. In contrast, Brad Evans has nothing but scorn for Buckleyite fusionists, at whose hands fusionism "provides a haven for those who theoretically espouse maximum individual freedom, but recognize that cause to be outside the conventional American political configuration, and so quake at the consequences of carrying through the logic of their position." Furthermore, fusionism is "a convenient tool for those who see the currents and would make their damnedest for political paydirt." Similarly, the yen for power leads the fusionists to take a Burkean stand for the American Constitution; as Evans perceptively sees, the trouble with this Burkean mentality "is its compatibility to *any* regime, whatever its virtues or lack of them, so long as it is the established regime. For opportunistic fusionists it thus affords a rational for conformity to, even apologetics for, a going order that is the object of the critique of both of the constituent theses, libertarian or traditionalist, of the fusionist synthesis. Because of the Burkean reverence for *what is*, that is to say, the aspiring fusionist politician can identify himself with the order while at the same time maintaining fundamental *theoretical* opposition to its characteristics."

Turning from the despised fusionists to the libertarians, particularly the ex-YAF libertarians, Mr. Evans describes their various schools of thought, and tries, gently but firmly, to point us on the "road to Rome." Recognition of an objective moral order, such as is provided in Roman Catholic thought, would provide the libertarian, as in the case of Acton, with a firm and comprehensive philosophical groundwork from which to oppose State power. Mr. Evans declares that "the good life is the life lived in accordance with the natural order of man's being-the life that flows from a well-ordered soul"; and a

society possessing a state "which cuts itself off from moral authority has at its command only naked power, without the justification of any authority."

Mr. Evans concludes his interesting article by stating that "The fact that libertarians and traditionalists have chosen to eschew the pursuit of pluralistic contentment and have cast off the shackles of political power-mongering is perhaps a sign of the inauguration of a higher, fuller commitment. It raises the encouraging prospect that the two may soon rise from their seats at the Piraeus and make their way, together, back to the city-and then to The City."

I am willing to engage in a philosophical dialogue with Mr. Evans; it may surprise him that I, at least, believe firmly in the existence of an objective moral order, one discoverable by man's reason. Furthermore, I see nothing at all wrong with any religious tradition, among which Roman Catholicism is out-standing, which endorses this rational moral order and attempts to encase it in a theistic framework. Some of the best libertarians I know are devoted Roman Catholics. Even Carlist Catholic-Triumphantists had their Carlist State, one which they believed to have sufficient moral and theological "authority", their alliance with libertarianism might come to an abrupt end. Thus, Mr. Evans does disquietingly say that "the laws of the American state which they (the libertarians) properly recognize as evil are not evil because they issue from a *state*, but rather because they lack any grounding in legitimate authority." Perhaps if Mr. Evans delved more deeply into the rational (and even theological) moral order, he might find that the State, *any* state *per se*, is morally evil because it is founded and has its very being in permanent aggression against the life and property of its subjects. Then Mr. Evans and the libertarians could indeed return together to the city, and some of us even to The City.

Among all the fusionists, I have always had a particular fondness for Frank S. Meyer, the founder of fusionism, and despite his numerous ideological sins: his fondness for Voegelinian traditionalism, for the American Constitution, for war and militarism, and for a global crusade for the slaughter of Communists, at home and abroad. For despite these sins, Frank Meyer has always been the one Buckleyite who has been visibly uneasy at the toadying to Nixonism that the Conservative Movement has become; he has been by far the most libertarian, as well as the most rationalistic, of the *National Review* crew, as his numerous debates within that movement--e.g. with Bozell, Burnham, and Donald Zoll--can well attest. Of all the Buckleyites, he has been virtually the only writer willing to make waves, willing to stand up for principle even when it becomes embarrassing. Thus, only Meyer had the courage to oppose the disastrous and statist Nixon-Friedman g u a r a n t e e d income program from the very start. Take, also several of Meyer's recent writings. There is his slashing review of Garry Wills' new book, *Nixon Agonistes* (*National Review*, October 20). Now it is true that one would expect Meyer to read Wills out of the conservative movement for having become a New Leftist. But the brunt of Meyer's hard-hitting critique is that Garry Wills, now as before when he was a conservative, has been throughout largely animated by a deep-seated hatred of nineteenth-century liberalism. The step from a pro-Ruskin anti-free-market Catholic Conservative to an anti-free market New Left communalist is not so very great, after all.

Another fine reaffirmation of his libertarianish position is Meyer's recent "Richard M. Weaver: An Appreciation", *Modern Age* (Summer-Fall, 1970), in which Meyer pays tribute to the late Professor Weaver's blend of the traditionalist and libertarian (though of course still archist) position. And then, Frank Meyer has become the only *National Review*-fusionist with the guts to take out completely after the "counter-culture"; for the rest of the

(Continued on page 4)

STIRRINGS — *(Continued from page 3)*

fusionists, with their fine eye to the main chance, have clearly been reluctant to alienate their youth constituency. Meyer's recent "Counterculture or Anticulture?", (*National Review*, Novermber 3) is a slashing rationalistic attack on the new nihilism. Meyer calls the counterculture, "that amalgam of dope, rock, scruff, amorality and superstition which thrives on the campuses and in the pseude-intellectual enclaves of our great cities." But it is not a counterculture, but an "anticulture", "for culture is and always has been dependent for its very existence on civility, on a widespread acceptance of standards which make civilized order possible."

In contrast, charges Meyer, "the hallmark of the counter-culture . . . is precisely its principled hatred of civility, its violent opposition at all levels to ordered freedom, to the tradition of rational discourse, to the very structure of civilized life. Above all, it hates the prime characteristic of the civilized man, that internalized discipline which looks with suscipicion upon these spontaneous, unexamined emotional reactions we have inherited from our barbarian and animal past. The unexamined life which Socrates found unworthy of civilized man is to the devotees of the counter-culture their be-all and end-all . . . The constant target of their attack is "middle-class values", a phrase that inquiring analysis reveals to denote the entire gamut of the values upon which Western civilization is founded . . . Whatever one may think of the specific components of the counterculture, considered severally each of them has an anticivilizational aspect; taken together. . .these aspects reinforce each other to make of the counterculture as a whole a formidable attack on civilized values."

Specifically: "The styles in hair and dress are the least dangerous of these phenomena, except insofar as they are consciously directed toward antagonizing the rest of society and insofar as the predilection for dirt and scruff breaks down self-discipline. Rock, with its incessant and insisting sensual destruction of an ordered universe, with the nihilistic impact of so much of its verbal content, 'provides the kids', as John Coyne writes in his new book *The Kumquat Statement*, 'with their phraseology, their philosophy, their life-style, the ideas and attitudes that motivate them. . .' Marijuana. . .is celebrated as a mode of escape from conceptual thinking, from the pressures of self-discipline without which civilization is impossible. Add to this stew the sort of beliefs and myths that pervade the counter-culture—the hatred of 'the ethic of achievement', the attack upon the nuclear family and heterosexual monogamy in the name of "polymorphous sexuality"; stir in the superstitions that proliferate within it—astrology, phony Eastern mysticism, Satanism. Corrosive of reason and tradition alike, this devil's brew", concludes Meyer, constitutes a great danger to civilization.

To turn from the libertarian and rationalistic stirrings of Evans and Meyer to the recent work of Leonard Read's youth leader, Dr. George C. Roche III, is a dizzying plunge into banality. Roche's article "On Anarcho-Libertarianism: What's In a Name?", (*New Guard*, November) is only interesting as an indication that Mr. Read has been hurting from our exposure of his retreat from freedom, and young Roche has apparently been assigned to make the rebuttal. Mr. Roche does not *quite* violate the Readian tenet of never mentioning the name of an opponent, but he *does* quote the editor of the *Lib. Forum* at some length without mentioning my name. (Under its new management, the *New Guard* has obviously jettisoned any and all pretense at libertarianism, as can be seen from its recent gutter-review of the book by its former valued contributor, Jerry Tuccille, by one Jared Lobdell). Mr. Roche, who Jerry Tuccille, by one Jared Lobdell). Mr. Roche, whom FEE has absurdly billed as having completed Lord Acton's history of freedom, repeats the discredited Widener smear

about my appearance at a Socialist Scholars Conference, and points with horror to Kent State having been described by me as the murder of peacefully demonstrating students, and the Chicago Conspiracy trial as having also been described as a repression of free speech. (What *else* were they?) After Roche somehow tries to mesh me with Russian Nihilists, Herbert Marcuse, and Mark Rudd, we can mercifully leave this great "historian of freedom" to his invicible ignorance; except that I am also attacked for daring to praise the French Revolution as being fought for property rights; our historian avers that "the French Revolution was totally unconcerned with property rights or personal rights for anyone." Apparently this eminent historian of freedom has never heard of Sieyes, or Condorcet, or the Declaration of the Rights of Man or the enormous influence that the American Revolution had upon the French. But it suffices here to inform Mr. Roche that there is on the staff of the Foundation for Economic Education one Ludwig von Mises, and Mr. Roche might find it illuminating and disturbing to ask Professor Mises sometimes about the French Revolution. Perhaps that will shake him out of the Burkean quagmire into which he has sunk.

POWER AND MARKET

Power and Market: Government and the Economy, by Murray N. Rothbard. Menlo Park, Calif.: Institute for Humane Studies. Hard Cover, $6.00; paperback, $3.00. 225 pp. Also available from Society for Individual Liberty, 400 Bonifant Road, Silver Spring, Maryland 20904.

by R. A. Childs, Jr.

Nearly nineteen years ago, a young man in his mid-twenties, not yet having received his Ph.D., set out on the task of boiling down the *magnum opus* of Ludwig von Mises–Human Action–into a concise volume suitable for use as a college text in economics. Over the years, the plan was changed; the task snowballed until it was finished in 1959. No longer a "boiled down" version of HUMAN ACTION, the work had become a master-piece in its own right, more comprehensive in purely *economic* issues than HUMAN ACTION itself, more carefully systematic, encompassing more issues in the subject than any work before or since. The work, however, was pronounced "too long" and "too anarchistic" by its financier-publisher; most of the last third was thrown out altogether; the rest was severely condensed into the last chapter of the published work.

The book was poorly promoted. Instead of being advanced as *the* work to supplement or even replace Mises, as a purely *economic* treatise (and as being much easier to read and understand), it was publicized by the Foundation for Economic Education as merely "a graduate-level comprehensive development of the economic principles of the free market by one of the outstanding young students of von Mises". It has since gone out of print.

The work was MAN, ECONOMY, AND STATE: A Treatise on Economic Principles (2 vols., Van Nostrand, 1962). The author is Murray N. Rothbard.

Now, at last, what was to have been the third volume of that work, the literal culmination of an entire school of economic thought (Austrianism), has been published, revised and updated, by the Institute for Humane Studies. It is entitled POWER AND MARKET: Government and the Economy. In 225 closely-packed pages, it presents a comprehensive critique of the role of the state in the economic system. It now can be said of POWER AND MARKET, when taken together with MAN, ECONOMY AND STATE, which is still independent of it. What Henry Hazlitt correctly said of *HUMAN ACTION* when it appeared in 1949: it extends the logical unity and precision of economics beyond any other work. As Mises went beyond

(Continued on page 5)

POWER AND MARKET — *(Continued from page 4)*

his teacher, Eugen von Bohm-Bawerk, so Murray Rothbard has gone beyond Mises.

It is important at the outset to point out precisely how and where Rothbard has gone beyond Mises, with the publication of this work. It is undeniable that Mises' contributions to the science of economics have been immense, but his philosophical framework is unfortunately Kantian. Rothbard is, on the other hand, an unblemished Aristotelian, taking note of many of the contributions to philosophy made by the Thomists.

Mises believes in the subjectivity of values, that all ethical standards are arbitrary, that concerns with justice are idle; he is a frank ethical nihilist. Rothbard, on the other hand, believes in the necessity of establishing principles to guide men's choices and actions–in a rational ethic. With such differences in philosophical frameworks, it is to be expected that Rothbard and Mises will have some differences.

In particular, Mises' value-subjectivism and anti-justice positions lead him to simply dismiss ethical questions out of hand. It also leads him to adopt many starkly anti-libertarian positions. In *HUMAN ACTION,* he states that "he who in our age opposes armaments and conscription is. . .an abbettor of those aiming at the enslavement of all. The maintenance of a government apparatus of courts, police officers, prisons and of armed forces requires considerable expenditure. To levy taxes for these purposes is fully compatible with the freedom the individual enjoys in a free market economy." Thus, Mises does not even consider taxation and the draft to be violations of freedom! How, with positions like these, can Mises objectively analyze these and other statist measures? The answer is that he only skims over them.

Murray N. Rothbard thus becomes the first major economist to be a ruthlessly consistent adherent to free-market principles. Mises' statist positions blinded him to many things which Rothbard treats as interventions–simply because Mises thought them "necessary." The position which Rothbard takes in *POWER AND MARKET* is a position which Mises *should have taken* more than twenty years ago. If he had, he would have saved all of us a lot of trouble arriving where we have at last arrived without him.

POWER AND MARKET is Rothbard's departure from the mistaken path Mises has taken. It consists of seven tightly integrated chapters taking up government intervention in the dealings of men, and refuting the rationalizations so often used to justify the initiation of force by the state against individuals.

In chapter one, and in the last part of his chapter on taxation (the section on "Voluntary Contributions to Government"), Rothbard takes up a great many arguments against a purely free,*stateless,* market, and gives summary answers to the questions of how a free market can enforce the rights of person and property against aggressors without a government. Unfortunately, he doesn't go into this practical problem enough, but his work here can easily be supplemented by such works as Morris & Linda Tannehill's *THE MARKET FOR LIBERTY,* and Jarret Wollstein's SOCIETY WITHOUT COERCION (especially the 2nd edition, now in preparation). He shows brilliantly, however, why a government cannot conform to the libertarian rule of non-initiation of force; in this respect, Rothbard takes a radical turn away from even traditional laissez-faire economists, by repudiating the state in its entirety. Answering the charge that a government is a necessary *precondition* for the free market, Rothbard says that "It was the fallacy of the classical economists to consider goods and services in terms of large *classes;* instead, modern economics demonstrated that services must be considered in terms of *marginal units.*. . .If we begin to treat whole classes instead of marginal units, we can discover a

great myriad of necessary, indispensable goods and services, all of which might be considered as 'preconditions' of market activity. Is not land room vital, or food, . . . or clothing, or shelter? Can a market long exist without them?. . .Must all these goods and services therefore be supplied by the State and the State only?" Especially interesting is his integration of ethical and economic arguments. Discussing the hotly debated question of whether or not a State can exist without initiating force, Rothbard rebuts the "limited governmentalists" in a crucial ethical-economic argument which no archist has yet succeeded in refuting.

Chapter two is a presentation of the fundamentals of intervention into peaceful social relations. Unlike Mises, who treats only a relatively small class of coercive actions as "interventions" into the free market, Rothbard takes up the issue systematically, classifying as "intervention" *any* initiation of force in social relations. Thus it is important to note that this is not merely a work on economics; in a much wider and important sense, it is an analysis of the indirect effects of the initiation of force in society. It fills in the skeleton, so to speak, of the fundamental libertarian principle of non-initiation of force, with complex theoretical analysis–showing both its *direct* consequences, and its complex *indirect* consequences.

Three broad categories are treated: auistic, binary and triangular intervention. "Autistic intervention" is when the intervener commands "an individual subject to do or not to do certain things when these actions directly involve the individual's person or property *alone.*" It occurs when the aggressor coerces a person (or many persons) but does not receive any good or service in exchange. "Binary intervention" occurs when the aggressor enforces "a exchange between the individual subject and himself, or a coerced 'gift' to himself from the subject," such as highway robbery, taxes, enslavement, and conscription. Thirdly, there is "triangular intervention," in which the aggressor compels or prohibits an exchange between a *pair* of subjects. Rothbard analyses the relations between intervention and conflict, the nature of democracy and voluntary actions, the relationship between individual "utility" and resistance to invasion, and several other issues.

Chapter three treats a host of interventions under the general heading of "triangular intervention". Price control, product control, licenses, standards of quality & safety, immigration laws, child labor laws, conscription, antitrust laws, conservation laws, eminent domain, and a host of other things fall before Rothbard's logic. Rothbard is here, as elsewhere, a master of the "reductio ad absurdum". Thus, for example, he reduces the principle behind tariffs to smithereens, just by extending it to its logical outcome– to show that it is an attack on trade *itself* and thus leads inevitably to economic solipsism. If we cannot legitimately trade freely with people outside the *state?* or *city?* or, finally and absurdly, Jones' farm? Where does it suddenly become absurd to keep on extending the principle and halting trade for the benefit of incompetents? His arguments are clean, concise and ruthless.

Chapter four and five are a back-to-back treatment of two major forms of "binary interventionism": Taxation and government expenditures. He shows the distortions wrought on the free market by all forms of both. In the Chapter on government expenditures, he offers an analysis of subsidies and government ownership, showing how they distort the market, and undertakes very incisive critiques of both public ownership and democracy. He lays bare the fallacies of ever trying to conduct government on a so-called "business basis."

Murray Rothbard's chapter on taxation is the most incisive analysis in existence. While Mises, in HUMAN ACTION, devoted only six pages to the intervention of

(Continued on page 6)

POWER AND MARKET — *(Continued from page 5)*

taxation, and even claims that there can be such a thing as a "neutral tax," Rothbard devotes over 65 pages to ruthlessly dissecting all economic and moral arguments for taxation. Rothbard considers the market effects of virtually every form of taxation, and virtually demolishes the notion of neutral taxation, a mythical beast which, Mises says, "would not divert the operation of the market from the lines in which it would develop in the absence of any taxation." Especially interesting is his section on the so-called "canons of justice in taxation," offering a criticism of all the traditional notions of this absurd concept. As in the rest of POWER AND MARKET, Rothbard is not content merely to refute the trivial arguments usually brought forth in all sorts of economic issues, and turns his guns on the fundamentals, such as stopping to consider why the economists consider the canons of "justice" in taxation in the first place. In this case, the quest arose from the earlier philosophical quest for the "just price" of goods in general. Eventually, in economic thought, the "just price" was simply dropped, or considered coextensive with the free market price. But why then do economists still harp on a "just tax"? Obviously because while the just price would be equated with the market price, there is simply no "market tax" for taxation to be linked with, since it cannot be voluntary. The quest for a "just tax," then, has its roots in statist apologetics–in the minds of those economists who will simply not carefully and objectively consider the nature of the state itself. As for the commonly considered notions of the "just tax," says Rothbard, all merely smuggle a fundamental presupposition in through the back door–the notion that taxation *itself* is somehow "just". The "justice" of a particular *form* of a treatment, after all, is derived from the justice of the fundamental treatment *itself*. And nobody has ever succeeded in justifying taxation itself. Rothbard, in point after point, succeeds in reducing taxation on economic and ethical grounds to oblivion.

Chapter six is perhaps the most innovative in the book. It is the introduction of a new task for praxeology in philosophy: the title is "Antimarket Ethics: A Praxeological Critique." It consists of a critique of over 16 different ethical positions in their objections to a free market –everything from the position of altruism to the position of the Aristotelian-Thomistic school of philosophical thought, ranging over such diverse issues as the morality of human nature, the impossibility of equality, the problem of security, the problem of "luck", charity, poverty, human rights and property rights, over-and under-development and the natures of power and coercion. This last is especially exciting. Rothbard takes up the difference between power over nature and power over man; he reduces the bogey of "economic power" to dust, showing that it is simply "the right under freedom to refuse to make an exchange." Every case of "economic power," he shows, rests solely on someone's right to refuse to make, or to continue to make, a certain exchange on the market. And more: he shows that there are only two options open to us, and that we *must* choose between them. This is a marvelous dissection of what he calls the "middle of the road statist." Suppose, says Rothbard, that "A refuses to make an exchange with B. What are we to say, or what is the government to do, if B brandishes a gun and orders A to make the exchange? This is the crucial question. There are only two positions we may take on the matter: *either* that B is committing violence and should be stopped at once, *or* that B is perfectly justified in taking this step because he is simply 'counteracting the subtle coercion' of economic power wielded by A." Whether we like it or not, in other words, we must *either* defend, in moral principle, A's person & property against invasion by B, or we defend B's alleged "right" to enforce an exchange. "If we choose the 'economic power' concept," says Rothbard, "we must employ violence to combat any refusal of exchange; if we reject it we employ violence to prevent any violent imposition of exchange. There is no way to escape this either-or choirce." And: "What would be the consequence of adopting the 'economic-power' premise? It would be a society of slavery: for what else is prohibiting the refusal to work?"

The final chapter treats crucial questions of the nature of economics and its uses, the nature of the *implicit* moralizing of most economists, economics and social ethics, and the differences between the market principle and the principle of coercion. His notion of the relation between economics and ethics is especially vital: economics, he says, cannot *by itself* establish ethical positions, "but it does furnish existential laws which cannot be ignored by anyone framing ethical conclusions--just as no one can rationally decide whether product X is a good or bad food until its

(Continued on page 7)

Bits And Pieces

By Jerome Tuccille

Optimism One

Libertarians who have not yet discovered the writings of F. M. Esfandiary are in for an electrifying experience as they come across this author for the first time. Esfandiary is an Iranian-born novelist, essayist and social critic, now living in this country, who has recently published his fourth book. I have had the pleasure of reading two of his novels—*Identity Card* and *Day of Sacrifice* — both of them dealing with the incredible stagnation of governmental bureaucracy and cultural reactionism in the middle east. Now this author has come out with his first book of nonfiction, *Optimism One*, published by W. W. Norton & Co., New York City.

Optimism One is the product of one of the most original and revolutionary thinkers of our time. In a crystal-clear prose style, carefully trimmed of all verbal fat, Esfandiary sets forth a philosophy that runs counter, on every level, to the prevailing intellectual pessimism espoused by most current writers. Esfandiary is in love with life, in love with being on earth and the prospect of reaching across the universe, in love with the modern technology that has brought the human race the highest standard of living it has ever known. There are times when he sounds a bit like an open-ended Ayn Rand might sound today had she developed her vision and expanded it, instead of choking it off with personal biases.

Esfandiary sees a day, not too far off, when man will have shucked off all his old gods: religion; cultural stagnation; fear of his own potential; guilt reactions to feats of accomplishment; the myth that "things are worse now than they have ever been" (according to the author, there is more freedom and less violence in the world today than ever before and the trend is continuing); the notion that the ego and the self is somehow evil; the idea that man needs the institution of government to survive; and ultimately, the myth that death is inevitable. As the author puts it: "If it is natural to die then the hell with nature. Why submit to its tyranny? We must rise above nature. We must refuse to die."

Esfandiary is not the first to talk about suspended animation (cryonics), the implantation of the human brain in more durable synthetic bodies (cyborgs), controlled mutation and anti-gravity centers as a means of creating physical immortality. But he is the first non-science fiction writer, to my knowledge, to speak of these developments as inevitable and as beneficial for the human race. The reaction of most people to the concept of cryonics (freezing a dying body until a day when science can reverse the process) has been: "But there are too many people on earth already! What will we do if nobody dies anymore?"

Space travel and the distribution of the human race on other planets is usually the first solution offered by advocates of cryonics. But Esfandiary's vision is more far-ranging than that. He regards the act of in-body conception as primitive and reactionary. Civilized people of the near-future will refuse to procreate in the old way but will, instead, generate life outside the body (this has already been accomplished in Italy and elsewhere although, as far as I know, the foetuses were destroyed within a week or two after conception). Women's liberationists will be happy to know that they may soon be liberated from the "tyranny of childbirth." With more and more people living indefinitely, the need for procreation will diminish. The quality of life will come under the direct control of science; more durable life-forms will be generated outside the human body and the birthrate will fall to a level now undreamed of.

Current concepts of education, housing, entertainment and commercial enterprise will also be radically altered in the rapidly-approaching age of communications satellites, lasers, magnetic tapes, telepsychic communication, individual cartridges for television, transportable dwelling units (Buckminster Fuller, Safdi and others already have working plans for apartment units that can be detached from apartment complexes and navigated over land and water).

Esfandiary also considers government to be an archaic institution, and he is optimistic that more people will come to realize this and do away with it just as they are doing away with their immature psychological dependence on religion and other forms of superstition. At the same time he recognizes the need for political action to reduce the misery and enslavement many people are suffering at the hands of government today.

Esfandiary is a radical in the purest sense of the word. He accepts nothing on faith, nothing as an absolute merely because most others happen to accept it as a given truth. His vision transcends the present and speaks of the future in its historical perspective, as a logical development to what has already taken place. He does have idiosyncrasies which sometimes get in the way of his logic (he is moralistic about not eating meat and fish for example), but most of his ideas are solid. Buy *Optimism One* · and read it. Then go back and read his fiction. He is a writer whose voice, I am reasonably sure, will rise high above the usual babble that passes for serious thought today.

*The subject of cryonics and life extension in general is one that will become more important as time goes on. Readers with any information on the subject are invited to write me % P.O. Box 41, East White Plains, N.Y. 10604. No hate mail please.

POWER AND MARKET — *(Continued from page 6)*.
consequences on the human body are ascertained and taken into account."

POWER AND MARKET is replete with intellectual ammunition for the libertarian. In fact, no other book provides so much information which can be readily digested and used in debating crucial issues of our day, when they involve the free market. It is original and comprehensive in scope: its systematic critiques of statism are devastating on every level. This is not merely a book on economics–it is a book on the nature and forms of coercion on every level. It shows the fallacies of everything from taxation, to democracy, to government spending, and devastates such arguments as those of "economic power" and the bogey of "production vs. distribution"–merely by pointing out, in this last case, that it is the existence of *taxation* and government itself which creates for the first time a separation of "distribution" from production, bringing the whole pseudo-problem into being. In case after case, Rothbard squashes the arguments of statists of every breed, by reducing them to absurdities, by pointing out their unadmitted premises, smuggled-in ethical positions, and plain logical fallacies.

With POWER AND MARKET, libertarianism and Austrian economics move into the intellectual vanguard of economic thought. It is the best work in economics since Rothbard's own MAN, ECONOMY AND STATE, which was in turn the best work since Mises' HUMAN ACTION.

Saying that reading POWER AND MARKET is a must for any libertarian interested in presenting an intellectual case for liberty is an understatement. With works of this caliber in every field of intellectual endeavor, the foundations for a comprehensive and fully integrated libertarian ideology would be firmly established.

POWER AND MARKET does not, as some might think, belong on a shelf besides MAN, ECONOMY AND STATE, nor next to HUMAN ACTION. In more than one way, it belongs on a shelf by itself.

RETREAT FROM FREEDOM — *(Continued from page 1)*

Hazlitt, a valued contributor to Fee, had cleaved to this principle, he would never have been able to come to grips with and refute the views of Lord Keynes, for Keynes cannot be refuted without his name being mentioned enroute.

At any rate: Mr. Read seems to be worried about the anarchist critique of his worship of unjust law, and so he now returns to a further defense, a defense in which he can only sink into a quagmire of ever deeper statism. In the first place, taking up our example of Prohibition, Mr. Read advances the curious argument that if one persisted in drinking in violation of the law, no one would be interested in repealing it, since the liquor would then be readily obtained. Here, Read ignores the fact that liquor was indeed obtained during the 1920's, but only at the high cost of decline in quality, rise in price, deprivation of access, and occasional arrest. Historically, Prohibition was repealed precisely because law enforcement broke down in the face of massive civil disobedience, *not* because the law was piously heeded and then people turned to legal channels of repeal. But perhaps it is also a lofty principle of Mr. Read's to ignore inconvenient historical fact as well as the names of his Opposition.

There is no point in going over Mr. Read's latest lucubrations in fine detail, except to indicate that in his desperate attempt to salvage his apotheosis of The Law he falls into two statist fallacies so grievous as to cause the late Frank Chodorov, great individualist and former staff member of FEE, to revolve in anguish in his grave. First, Read asserts that man in *not only* an individual, he is also, in addition, a "social being", and that therefore he must adopt not only self-responsibility but *also*, "social responsibility". In declaring that "society" exists as a sort of super-entity more than, and clearly higher than, each individual member, Read is flying against the great principle of methodological individualism held by FEE staffer Ludwig von Mises and against the truth noted by Chodorov that "society are people." Second, and still worse for a presumed libertarian, Mr. Read makes a second mighty leap to imply that "society" is somehow embodied in whatever structure of positive law happens to exist, and that therefore the very fact of being human and living in society requires that one obey all the laws, because one is necessarily stuck in the existing society; "Law breaking," declares Read, is therefore "no more rational than resigning from the human race." In thus presuming to identify the individual with society and then society with the State, Mr. Read completes his steady path away from liberty and toward despotism, for he has thereby repeated the essence of every statist apologia in modern history. Even though

one of his FEE staff members is head of the Nockian Society, Mr. Read has tragically forgotten Albert Jay Nock's great demonstration of the inherent disparity and conflict between society and the State.

Nock; Chodorov; Mises; Tolstoy; Thoreau; wherever we look, we find that in recent years Leonard E. Read has beat a steady and increasingly rapid retreat from freedom. It is a sad tale, but one not uncommon in the history of thought.

The Shaffer Dictionary

By Butler Shaffer

The following definitions comprise a part of my view of reality, in all its humorous—and often frustrating—manner.

EDUCATION: the method I use to promote my ideas.

PROPAGANDA: the method you use to promote your ideas.

DO-GOODER: one who has demonstrated total incompetence at handling his own affairs, and who seeks to make this talent available to others.

PUBLIC EDUCATION: the recognition that, in an egalitarian society even the ignorance should be shared.

DICTATORSHIP: the kind of government under which other men live.

CIVIC-MINDED: that quality exemplified by those who work unselfishly for the realization of government projects which will provide them with government contracts.

POLITICIAN: one who, recognizing the value of truth and reason, seeks to preserve the same by economizing their use.

STATEMANSHIP: the distinction between "statesmanship" and "tyranny" is the distinction between "seduction" and "rape": a brief sales pitch.

CONSPIRACY: anything done by two or more persons of which I disapprove or do not understand.

The Libertarian Forum
BOX 341
MADISON SQUARE STATION
NEW YORK, NEW YORK 10010

First Class

Published on the first and fifteenth of every month.   Subscription rate: $7.00 per year; Student subscription rate: $5.00 per year

A Semi-Monthly Newsletter

THE
Libertarian Forum

Joseph R. Peden, Publisher   Murray N. Rothbard, Editor

VOLUME II, NO. 24   December 15, 1970   35¢

DEATH OF THE LEFT

Signs of the death of the Left are everywhere. When we proclaimed last spring that the New Left was dead, at least in heart and brain ("The New Left, RIP", March 15) we shocked many of our readers; but now it is clear to all that the Left is in a state of total collapse. For example, the campus. Last spring, the eminent conservative sociologist R.A. Nisbet wrote an article asserting that the student revolution was finished; Cambodia and Kent State seemed to make a mockery of Professor Nisbet's claim, but now he has had the last laugh. It is true that the student movement is always least active in the fall, and then picks up momentum in the spring; but not since the glorious days of the apathy of the 1950's has the student movement, on campus after campus across the country, been so totally *kaput*. Reports from all over the country confirm this observation.

Thus, take Columbia and Yale, two hotbeds of insurrection only a short while ago. Only last spring, Panthermania had seized the Yale campus like a frenetic disease; agitation for the Panthermania had seized the disease; agitation for the Panthers was everywhere, even unto afflicting Yale's liberal President Kingman Brewster. But now numerous unbelieving obeservers report that politics is totally dead at Yale; that the students have returned to the supposedly long gone Old Cultural pursuits of football, frat parties, and boola boola; students have resumed their pre-1965 concerns with studies, note-taking, and personal careers. The same story holds at Columbia, once a seedbed of the student revolution. At the Polytechnic Institute of Brooklyn, which struck for about a week after Cambodia, students have reverted to their ancient conservatism; the only political activity this fall on campus was for Jim the student preferential poll by a large majority. But not only at Brooklyn Poly; the Left and the liberals had engineered a week or two-week pre-election recess on the campuses in the expectation of student antiwar activity; but the only really conspicuous student activity in New York this fall was for Buckley. The absence of all but conservative political activity on the campuses is for example, noted in "The New Right", *Newsweek,* December 7).

In our rapidly changing society it is perhaps perilous to analyze *any* phenomenon as permanent, but this seemingly strange happening can be easily explained. Our revolutionaries have long analyzed the escalating march of revolution as seemingly inevitable: beginning with leaflets and petitions for civil rights or for an end to bombing North Vietnam, the students, frustrated at the lack of success, escalated to mass demonstrations; then to sit-ins and non-violent resistance; then finally to violent revolution. Pursuing every route, every alternative, without success, the students finally turned to violent uprising. The litany of excalation proclaimed by

the revolutionaries proved to be correct; but what they forgot to ask was what would happen once the turn to violence came. What then? There were two possibilities; one was a successful, spreading insurrection–a possibility which had no chance at all, given the hatred for the students by the vast bulk of the American population. And the other was that once the violent route had begun, once the students had taken their climatic peek into the abyss, that the entire movement would then fizzle and die. The orgiastic climax came this year–with the mad bombings of the Weathermen and the murders at Kent State. The students had their climactic look at violence and its consequences; *that* was obviously not working; the other paths hadn't worked; and so everyone went home, forgot about politics, and sunk back into the peace and quiet of the 1950's. What the revolutionaries forgot was that, with all routes exhausted, the more probable conclusion was not all-out violent revolution but abandonment of the whole losing business. It was a Long March through six years of trouble and excitement and turbulence; but it looks very much as if Baby has Come Home at last. It was precisely the fact that the student revolution had gone blooey that accounts for the lack of success of Agnew in trying to polarize the masses against the kids this fall; for it was clear to many voters that our Vice-President was engaged in thumping a very dead horse.

What was accomplished by the six years of turmoil? On the campuses, not very much. The larger anti-war movement, I believe, accomplished a great deal in creating a climate of opposition to the war, in preventing any further escalation, and in ousting Lyndon Johnson from office. But, on the campuses, the center of the troubles, very little was changed except for the worse. The large, impersonal bureaucracracies of our universities remain just as large and even more impersonal than before; our State-ridden colleges are even more State-ridden than they were when the whole business began. What has been added is negative: a crumbling still further of educational standards on behalf of aimless "rapping" and the absurd myth that everyone, regardless of ability or fitness, is entitled to a bachelor's degree by divine right. And as a corollary: idiotic "black studies" institutes, "women's studies" institutes and similar boondoggles. Six years is surely sufficient to evaluate the results of any movement; and on that basis, any sensible person should greet the death of the student revolution not with mourning and lamentations but with a sense of profound relief. "Social Darwinism" has once again been vindicated, a movement with bad premises (febrile, egalitarian, anti-intellectual and anti-rational) has burned itself out. The

(Continued on page 2)

DEATH OF THE LEFT — *(Continued from page 1)*

road is now cleared for a new and better beginning.

In the larger culture the Left is also in its death throes. We have been living in an increasingly sick culture; over the last year, that sickness has been embodied in intense and febrile faddism; the media, almost as if someone had pushed a button, have taken one absurd ideological fad after another, pushed it to an intensity unheard of before, and then dropped it as suddenly as it had begun in order to run after some new glamorous craze. Thus, from sometime after the end of October 1969, all of a sudden the media had discovered The Environment; and it was impossible for anyone to pick up a book or a magazine, to listen to the radio or to watch a TV show, without The Environment being beamed at you from all directions. Environment clubs were everywhere; paperbacks were poured out, each repeating the data of every other in a frantic quest for the quick buck; and then, Boom!, the orgiastic climax of Earth Day last spring, and Bingo! The Environment was forgotten, finished. Now whatever merit the Environment or pollution has as an issue, of one thing we can be damned sure: we did *not* have a pollution-free environment up till October 1969, suffer grievously from it until Earth Day, and then have pollution magically disappear ever since.

After Earth Day, we were happily spared hearing any further about The Environment, but then Women's Lib took its place. Once again, it was impossible to pick up a magazine or watch a TV show without being subjected to the endless repetitions of the Women's Lib cacaphony; and once again, dozens of paperbacks were rushed to press to take advantage of the new hoopla. But, praise the Lord, there is only just so much that the human mind can take, and once again there are sweet signs that Women's Lib has begun to have its day. The one good thing about sick faddism is that it *must* burn itself out; after the 2000th harangue about Women's Lib or The Environment, the audience finally calls a halt, and sanity, at least on this particular fad, must return.

The sickness of our culture is also embodied in the total, the complete absence of a sense of humor, particularly among our youth. If we had any sense of humor at all, any sense of perspective on the absurd and the idiotic, then the faddism and cultism of our time would never get under way. What we need today is not the magnificent rationality and wit of *one* H.L. Mencken, but a platoon, an army of Menckens to clean the Augean stables and to save us from the next onslaught of faddism, to prick the balloons before they get under way to plague us with month after month of solemn and raucous hooey.

In the meanwhile we happily have Tom Wolfe, and Wolfe has, almost singlehanded, destroyed the phenomenon that he himself named "radical chic." In the June 8 issue of *New York*, Wolfe, in a brilliant, witty article, "Radical Chic: That Party at Lenny's" (see the *Lib. Forum,* July), devastatingly reported on and lampooned the "radical chic" of Panthermania among affluent New York liberals. Neither the Panthers nor Panthermania nor "Lenny" Bernstein has been the same since. Now Stewart Alsop reports that, partly because of the self-destructive inner nature of faddism, partly from the Wolfe article, "Radical Chic is Dead." (*Newsweek*, December 14.) As Alsop notes: "Watch the faces at some more-or-less politically sophisticated gathering the next time the 'rage and alienation' of 'the kids' is mentioned. Is there not a certain glazing of the eyeballs? Or when Eldridge Cleaver, say, or the Black Panthers, or Dr. Timothy Leary, or the youth culture, or Ti-Grace Atkinson, or women's lib, or the Gay Liberation Front, or some other icon of radical chic is introduced . . . The fact is that radical chic . . . was essentially a fad, and all fads die . . . The promoters of the fads go from excess to greater excess, to hold the attention of the faddists, until appetite

sickens on the surfeit, and so dies. When this crossover point is reached, the fad suddenly comes to seem a bit silly, or a little sickening, or very boring, or all three together."

Now, Tom Wolfe has hammered a few more nails in the coffin, with the reprint of his article in book form, along with another hilarious article, "Mau-Mauing the Flak-Catchers", showing how radical leaders of minority groups in San Francisco organize confrontations in order to frighten and intimidate liberal anti-poverty bureaucrats ("Mau-Mauing"), so that these bureaucrats (who "catch the flak") will put these leaders onto the state gravy train. (Tom Wolfe, *Radical Chic and Mau-Mauing the Flak-Catchers,* Farrar, Straus & Giroux, $5.95.) The Left is hollering like stuck pigs, but none of their clamor can put radical chic back together again. Tom Wolfe has never been known as a conservative, but a long-time association with left-liberals will do the trick; and now Wolfe reports to the New York Sunday *Times Book Review* that Helmut Schoeck's important conservative-libertarian work *Envy* (*Lib. Forum*, Sept. 15) is one of his three favorite books of 1970.

And now women's lib, too, is beginning to fade—partly under the hammer blows of writers who have begun to mount a counter-attack. In *Commentary*, Midge Decter and others have slashed away at women's lib; also John Corry in *Harper's*, Martha Lawrenson in *Esquire*. And now the weightiest dissection of all: a long review-article of Kate Millett's *Sexual Politics* by the brilliant Social-Democrat polemicist Irving Howe. (Irving Howe, "The Middle-Class Mind of Kate Millett", *Harper's*, December, $1.00.) Howe eviscerates Millett as theorist, as historian, and as literary critic; and when he is done, there is nothing left, either of Miss Millett or of the rationalizations for women's "liberation." Furthermore, Howe asserts that, in all probability, there are important biological differences between men and women, derived from (1) "the distinctive female experience of maternity"; (2) "the hormonic components of our bodies"; (3) "the varying possibilities for work created by varying amounts of musculature and physical controls"; and (4) "the psychological consequences of different sexual postures and possibilities", namely, the "fundamental distinction between the active and passive sexual roles" as biologically determined in men and women respectively. Howe also notes that Miss Millett cites with approval Dr. Eleanor Maccoby's study of female intelligence, but neglects to mention Dr. Maccoby's admission that "it is quite possible that there are genetic factors that differentiate the two sexes and bear upon their intellectual performance . . . For example, there is good reason to believe that boys are innately more aggressive than girls—and I mean aggressive in the broader sense, not just as it implies fighting, but as it implies dominance and initiative as well—and if this quality is one which underlies the later growth of analytic thinking, then boys have an advantage which girls . . . will find difficult to overcome." Maccoby adds that "if you try to divide child training among males and females, we might find out that females need to do it and males don't."

Irving Howe sees that underlying Miss Millett's attitude is a rage against the very existence of women. "Miss Millett dislikes the psycho-biological distinctiveness of women, and she will go no further than to recognize—what choice is there, alas?—the inescapable differences of anatomy. She hates the perverse refusal of most women to recognize the magnitude of their humiliation, the shameful dependence they show in regard to . . . men, the maddening pleasures they even take in cooking dinners for 'the master group' and wiping the noses of their snotty brats. Raging against the notion that such roles and attitudes are biologically determined, since the very thought of the biological seems to her a way of forever reducing women to subordinate

(Continued on page 3)

DEATH OF THE LEFT — *(Continued from page 2)*

status, she nevertheless attributes to 'culture' so staggering a range of customs, outrages, and evils that this 'culture' comes to seem a force more immovable and ominous than biology itself."

Howe also perceptively points out that, in a wider sense, underlying the revolutionaries of the Left is a hatred for "the usual", a raging contempt for the ordinary life of men and women, a life which is sneered at as "one-dimensional": "this scorn for the inherited pleasures, ruses, and modes of survival by which most of us live; this nagging insistence that life be forever heroic and dramatic, even if ordinary humanity must be herded by authoritarian party bosses and ideologues to x make it so." Howe sums this up as the left intellectuals' "contempt for ordinary life, contempt for ordinary people, contempt for the unwashed and unenlightened, contempt for the unschooled, contempt for blue-collar workers, contempt for those who find some gratification in family life, contempt for 'the usual.'"

Howe concludes that "you would never know from Miss Millett's book that there are families where men and women work together in a reasonable approximation of humanness, fraternity, and even equality." Movingly, he declares that he has known two worlds; one, the world of his current intellectual friends, is a world where the women, along with their men, "have it hard", but, "are struggling and fulfilled human beings creating the terms of their freedom even as they recognize the bounds of limitation that circumstance, gender, history and fortune impose upon them." The other world he has known was the world of his parents, poor struggling immigrant Jewish workers on the Lower East Side.

I recall my mother and father sharing their years in trouble and affection, meeting together the bitterness of sudden poverty during the Depression, both of them working for wretched wages in the stinking garment center, helping one another, in the shop, on the subways, at home, through dreadful years. And I ... know that ... there were thousands of other such families in the neighborhoods in which we lived. Was my mother a drudge in subordination to the "master group"? No more a drudge than my father who used to come home with hands and feet blistered from his job as presser. Was she a "sexual object"? I would never have thought to ask, but now, in the shadow of decades, I should like to think that at least sometimes she was."

Three cheers, Irving. Right On!

And yet women's lib has taken its toll. I personally know half a dozen couples whose lives have been wrecked by the canker of women's lib. Previously happily married, in each case the wife absorbed the sweet poison of the supposed existence of "male oppression", stormed against her husband as living embodiment of this oppression, and then broke up their home. Worst of all, in each of these cases the stunned male continues to assert that his wife was somehow right, as he wallows in the masochistic guilt of the "male liberal." One New Left leader in this situation, writing to us in objection to our stand against women's lib, tells us that we do not understand that women, suffering from "male colonial oppression", have to separate themselves from men for years to "get their sisterhood together." O judgment, thou hast fled to brutish beasts, and men have lost their reason!

HAWAII—GROWTH AND REPRESSION

One of the most important and fastest growing libertarian movements in the country is in the state of Hawaii. Led by the intrepid Bill Danks, a graduate student in American Studies at the University of Hawaii, the Hawaiian movement is organizing a giant libertarian conference in January. The theme of the conference will be "Freedom in our Time", and there will be panels on Ecology, Poverty, War and Peace, Students Versus the System, the Free Market and Monopoly, and Strategy for Change. Speakers from the mainland will include Paul Goodman, Robert LeFevre, David Friedman, Roy A. Childs, Jr., and Tibor Machan; Hawaiian speakers will include Danks and Dr. Arthur Carol, professor of economics at the University of Hawaii, and a distinguished new addition to libertarian ranks.

Even more remarkable is the fact that the libertarian movement was able to take control of a major radio station in Honolulu, KTRG, which for two years was beaming libertarianism at the listeners for many hours per day. Or at least was until recently, when the naked arm of fascist repression descended upon the station-and none so bold or so interested as to make any protest. It was a two-pronged assault; for one thing, the FCC, which has life and death control over the nationalized radio-TV airwaves, closed the station down. The second prong was the indictment of several of the leading personnel of the station on the heinous grounds of . . . refusal to answer questions in the 1970 census!

On the mainland, there have been little or no attempts to crack down on either the massive number of census violators, or even on the intrepid libertarians who agitated for census resistance. But in Honolulu, in a case where an important radio station had come under libertarian control, the State clearly used this absurd "crime"

in order to crack down on libertarian dissent from the existing system. (How about it, Leonard Read? Is civil disobedience moral *now?*)

Specifically, on November 19, penal summonses charging refusal to answer census questions were served on: David Watamull, president and general manager of station KTRG, Donald P. Dickinson, manager and moderator of the station, and Bill Danks, leader of Census Resistance '70 in Hawaii. Conviction carries a maximum penalty of $100 fine and 60 days in jail. The government wanted to try these men at the hands of the U.S. Commissioner, since this is classified as a "petty offense", but the three defendants successfully insisted on moving the trial to Federal Court, where they can demand a trial by jury. Our three libertarians are being defended by the American Civil Liberties Union, and are expected to challenge the constitutionality of the compulsory census laws. A warrant was also made out for Bill Steele, former head of Hawaii YAF, but Steele has apparently skipped the country. Even our little movement now has its martyrs and exiles!

And now we have *our* slogans of liberation: Free Dave Watamull! Free Don Dickinson! Free Bill Danks! Amnesty for Bill Steele! Let the cry resound throughout the land.

Anarchism—A New Convert

In Defense of Anarchism
   by Robert Paul Wolff. Harper & Row, 1970. 86 pp. $4.50; paperback $1. Reviewed by Jerome Tuccille.

Professor Wolff has presented us with a valuable contribution to the expanding anarchist library. In his preface the author admits that he has failed to analyze the "material, social, or psychological conditions under which anarchism might be a feasible mode of social organization." This defect he hopes to correct in a larger work on the subject in the foreseeable future. What is important about the book is that Professor Wolff, after a long period of careful research and exploration during which he tried to find a satisfactory justification for political authority, has reached the conclusion that "anarchism would seem to be the only reasonable political belief for an enlightened man." In the course of this brief and lucid account of the subject he proceeds to explain why this is so.

The author opens his book with a three-part section dealing with: the concept of political authority; the concept of individual autonomy; and the inevitable conflict that must arise between the two. The largest drawback in this section rests in the fact that Wolff assumes the morality of individual autonomy as a given absolute, and is therefore rather sketchy in his philosophical justification for individual self-determination.

In Part Two he analyzes the several forms of democratic government that have been suggested in the attempt to bridge the gap between political authority and individual autonomy. He discusses unanimous direct democracy, representative democracy, and majoritarian democracy in turn, spending a bit too much time attacking Rousseau's shaky defense of majoritarianism in the *Social Contract*. Wolff concludes that unanimous democracy is totally unworkable and that *direct* majoritarian democracy, with each citizen voting on every issue that comes up (possible now through technological development), is still a long way from guaranteeing the autonomy of each individual in society. Every form of political rule depends on the abridgment, to one degree or another, of the right of the individual to determine the course of his own life. To agree to abide by the will of the majority, or the will of parliament, of that of a dictator, requires the surrender of one's personal autonomy, and no matter how "democratic" or "benevolent" the rule it is still "no more than voluntary slavery . . ."

The final section offers "utopian glimpses of a world without states." By the author's admission it is the weakest part of his presentation, speaking in general terms about "far-reaching decentralization" and "voluntary compliance." For practical alternatives readers are advised to turn elsewhere (Jane Jacobs, some of Goodman, some of Jefferson, Rothbard, others). Individualist libertarians will also find Wolff's comments on the free market a bit naive and unsophisticated.

All in all, however, this is a good, tightly-written, basic text to recommend to friends who are interested in a justification for *philosophical* anarchism.

Recommended Reading

Sunday December 6 was "Karl Hess Day" in the nation's media. On that same day, two major articles on Karl, both substantial, well-written, and sympathetic, appeared in the nation's press. These were Tony Lang, "Karl Hess Is Aflame With the Idea that Every Man Can Run His Own Life", *Washington Post* magazine section, with a picture of Karl on the front cover; and James Boyd, "From Far Right to Far Left—and Farther", *New York Sunday Times Magazine*. The Boyd article is particularly good, as Jim is sympathetic to the libertarian cause and knowledgeable about the movement. The Boyd article also twice mentions the *Libertarian Forum* as the leading libertarian publication! Both articles play up Karl's quintessential (and lifelong) instinctive libertarianism, and both gloss over his current flirtations with communalist, syndicalist, and anti-capitalist heresies.

The libertarian movement is also discussed in "The New Right", *Newsweek*, Dec. 7. Noting that Jim Buckley had most of the student activists in his camp this fall, *Newsweek* goes on to speak of the division among rightist youth between "libertarians" and "traditionalists". Also, the word "libertarianism" has been mentioned in several previous issues of the *New York Times*, with articles on its new "Op-Ed" page by libertarian rightist journalist Jeffrey St. John.

Hey, could it be that libertarianism is going to be the new fad to replace Women's Lib, as the latter nears the inevitable end of its run in the media?

The Libertarian Forum
BOX 341
MADISON SQUARE STATION
NEW YORK, NEW YORK 10010

First Class

Published on the first and fifteenth of every month.   **Subscription rate: $7.00 per year; Student subscription rate: $5.00 per year**

A Monthly Newsletter

THE
Libertarian Forum

Joseph R. Peden, Publisher　　　　　　　　　　　　　　　　Murray N. Rothbard, Editor

VOLUME III, NO. 1　　　　　　　　　　January, 1971　　　　　　　　　　35¢

Nixonite Socialism

It is traditional at the turn of the year to survey the state of the economy and to try to forecast what lies ahead. Despite the Pollyanna chorus with which we have been deluged for the last year by "conservative" and "free-market" economist-whores for the Nixon Administration, we can state flatly that the state of the economy is rotten, and destined to get worse.

In the 1960 campaign there first appeared the curious phenomenon of "anarcho-Nixonites", several friends of mine who had become aides to Dick Nixon, and who assured me that Tricky Dick had assured *them* that he was "really an anarchist at heart"; once campaign pressures were over, and Nixon as President was allowed his head, we would see an onrush toward the free market and the libertarian society. In the 1968 campaign, anarcho-Nixonism redoubled in intensity, and we were assured that Nixon was surrounded by assorted Randians, libertarians, and free-market folk straining at the leash to put their principles into action.

Well, we have had two years of Nixonism, and what we are undergoing is a super-Great Society--in fact, what we are seeing is the greatest single thrust toward socialism since the days of Franklin Roosevelt. It is not Marxian socialism, to be sure, but neither was FDR's; it is, as J. K. Galbraith wittily pointed out in New York (Sept. 21). a big-business socialism, or state corporatism, but that is cold comfort indeed. There are only two major differences in *content* between Nixon and Kennedy-Johnson (setting aside purely stylistic differences between uptight WASP, earthy Texan, and glittering upper-class Bostonian): (1) that the march into socialism is faster because the teeth of conservative Republican opposition have been drawn; and (2) that the erstwhile "free-market" conservatives, basking in the seats of Power, have betrayed whatever principles they may have had for the service of the State. Thus, we have Paul McCracken and Arthur F. Burns, dedicated opponents of wage-price "guideline" dictation and wage-price controls when *out* of power, now moving rapidly in the very direction they had previously deplored. And *National Review*, acidulous opponent of the march toward statism under the Democrats, happily goes along with an even more rapid forced march under their friends the Republicans.

Let us list some of the more prominent features of the Nixonite drive--features which have met no opposition whatever in the conservative press. There took place during 1970 the nationalization of all railroad passenger service in this country. Where was the conservative outcry? It was a nationalization, of course, that the railroads welcomed, for it meant saddling upon the taxpayer

responsibility for a losing enterprise--thus reminding us of one perceptive definition of the economy of fascism: an economy in which big business reaps the profits while the taxpayer underwrites the losses. There took place also the Nixonite fight for the SST boondoggle, in which $300 million are going to follow a previous $700 million of taxpayers' money down the rathole of gigantic subsidy to an uneconomic mess. Bill and Jim Buckley can find

(Continued on page 2)

TO OUR READERS

With this issue, the *Libertarian Forum* completes almost two years of successful, unbroken semi-monthly publication, and we have accomplished this task without sending out letters pleading for funds. The time has come, however, when financial pressures have forced a change in our publishing policy. We have suffered, first, from the inexorable inflation of costs that has hit all enterprises, and which we, at least, know is fundamentally due to the expansion of money and credit generated by the federal government. We have suffered, also, from a loss of revenue stemming from two sources: (a) a shift of many subscribers from regular to the student category--a sign that we are reaching more young people but also a financial loss to the magazine; and (b) a falling off of Libertarian Associates who subscribed at $15 and above, a falling off that is inevitable after a new publishing venture has become self-sustaining and established.

Since the Libertarian Associates had, in effect, been subsidizing our student subscribers, we can therefore no longer afford to carry the latter at a financial loss. We are therefore hereby eliminating the student category, and raising all of our subscription rates to $7.00 per year.

We are also cutting costs substantially by going over to a *monthly*, 8-page, publication. This is our first monthly issue. By becoming a monthly we will save a considerable amount on costs of mailing, handling, and shipping, as well as personal wear and tear on our miniscule staff. And while we will no longer be able to comment as rapidly on the news, we will benefit our readers by having more space available per month (saving on space for mastheads and addresses), and more room for longer articles.

And so, from the new monthly *Libertarian Forum*, Happy New Year to all!

NIXON SOCIALISM – *(Continued from page 1)*

only ecological pollution as an argument against the SST--
an outright looting raid upon the taxpayer without even
a flimsy cover of "national security" as a pretext. The
only argument seems to be that if we do not subsidize
the SST, our airlines will have to purchase the plane
from–horrors!--France; on this sort of argument, of
course, we might as well prohibit imports altogether,
and go over to an attempted self-sufficiency within our
borders. How many SST's might be purchased on an
unsubsidized market is, of course, problematic; since
the airlines are losing money as it is, it is doubtful how
much revenue they will obtain from an airfare estimated
at 40% higher than current first-class rates.

And then there is the outright $700 million gift from
the U. S. government to Lockheed, to keep that flagrantly
submarginal and uneconomic company in business indefinitely. And then there is agitation for the friendly
nationalization of Penn Central Railroad. Senator Javits is
already muttering about legislation for the federal bailing
out of all businesses suffering losses, which is the logical
conclusion of the current trend.

Neither has any note been taken of the Nixon Administration's plan for tidying up the construction industry. Many
people have scoffed at the revisionist view (held by such
New Left historians as Ronald Radosh) that the pro-
union legislation of the twentieth century has been put in
at the behest of big business itself, which seeks a large,
unified , if tamed labor union junior partnership in corporate state rule over the nation's economy. And yet the
Railway Labor Act of 1926, which in effect compulsorily
unionized the railroad industry in exchange for compulsory arbitration and a no-strike policy, was put in at
the behest of the rail industry, anticipating the later
labor policy of the New Deal. And now the construction
industry has gotten the Nixon Administration behind a
similar plan; all the members of the present small but
pesky and powerful construction unions are to be dragooned
into one big, area-wide industrial union, and then to be
subject to massive compulsory arbitration. The fascization
of America proceeds apace.

To top it off, the Administration is readying two socialistic "welfare" measures of great importance: one further
socializes medicine through nationwide major medical
"insurance" to be paid by the long-suffering poor and lower-
middle class Social Security taxpayer. And surely it is only
a matter of time until the disastrous Friedman-Theobald-
Nixon scheme of a guaranteed annual income for everyone
is forced through Congress, a scheme that would give
everyone an automatic and facile claim upon production,
and thereby disastrously cripple the incentives to work
of the mass of the population.

In the area of the business cycle, it should be evident
to everyone by this time that the Administration, trying
subtly and carefully to "fine-tune" us out of inflation without
causing a recession, has done just the opposite; bringing
us a sharp nationwide recession without having any appreciable impact upon the price inflation. A continuing
inflationary recession--combining the worst of both worlds
of depression and inflation--is the great contribution of
Nixon-Burns-Friedman to the American scene. While it is
true that a recession was inevitable if inflation was to be
stopped, the continuing inflation was *not* inevitable if
the Administration had had the guts to institute a truly
"hard" money policy. Instead, after only a few months of
refraining from monetary inflation, the Administration
has been increasingly opening the monetary floodgates
in a highly problematic attempt to cure the recession--while
at the same time failing to recognize that one sure result
will be to redouble the chronic rise in prices. But now

Social Darwinism Reconsidered

My esteemed libertarian colleague, Professor Leonard
Liggio, who has always been out on the frontier of libertarian
thought and practice, has of late been ruminating on Social
Darwinism. There is no creed over the past century, in fact,
with the possible exception of the Nazi movement, that
has received as bad an intellectual "press" as Social
Darwinism. It is high time that we subject this much reviled
Social Darwinism to a re-evaluation.

The Liberal stereotype of the Social Darwinist is of a
sadistic monster, calling for the "extermination of the
unfit." But in reality the true Social Darwinist is a benign
and cheerful optimist, and he arrives at his optimism from
a scientific inquiry into the processes of natural law
and of cause and effect. For the Social Darwinist is above
all a scientist, and as a scientist he sees that the natural
law of what is best for man may be violated but never
avoided. The natural law of cause and effect works its
inexorable way, and what this means is that bad premises,
bad goals and ineffective means, are dysfunctional for
man and inevitably wreak their toll. On the other hand,
rational premises, values and techniques, lead with equal
inexorability to benign results. This means, that *over the
long run,* the dysfunctional must come to a bad end, must
cleanse itself and wipe itself out, while only the truly
functional and proper can remain and prosper. Any artificial interference in these beneficent natural processes
can only delay and distort the results; hence, we have a

(Continued on page 3)

the Administration has swung around to the Liberal thesis
of monetary and fiscal expansion to cure the recession,
while yelling and griping at labor and employers not to
raise wages and prices--a "guidelines" or "incomes"
policy that is only one step away from wage and price
controls. This direct intervention is supposed to slow
down the wage-price spiral. In actual fact, the direct
intervention cannot slow down price increases, which
are caused by monetary factors; it can only create dis-
location and shortages. Pumping in more money while
imposing direct price controls and hoping thereby to
stem inflation is very much like trying to cure a fever
by holding down the mercury column in the thermometer.

Not only is it impossible for direct controls to work;
their imposition adds the final link in the forging of a
totalitarian economy, of an American fascism. What is it
but totalitarian to outlaw any sort of voluntary exchange,
any voluntary sale of a product, or hiring of a laborer?
But once again Richard Nixon is responsive to his credo
of big business liberalism, for direct controls satisfy
the ideological creed of liberals while at the same time
they are urged by big business in order to try to hold
down the pressure of wages on selling prices which
always appears in the late stages of a boom.

While we can firmly predict accelerating inflation,
and dislocations stemming from direct controls, we cannot
so readily predict whether the Nixonite expansionism will
lead to a prompt business recovery. That is problematic;
surely, in any case we cannot expect any sort of rampant
boom in the stock market, which will inevitably be held
back by interest rates which, despite the Administration
propaganda, must remain high so long as inflation continues.

All in all, how much more of Nixonite "anarchism"
can freedom stand?

SOCIAL DARWINISM RECONSIDERED –

(Continued from page 2)

powerful argument for non-interference in these natural workings.

Take, for example, hippie culture and hippie values, with its hatred of reason, its emphasis on instant whim and mystical irrationality, its communalism and repudiation of the division of labor, its scorn of science, technology, work, private property, long-range thinking, and the production of material goods and services. There have been few creeds in human history that have been more dysfunctional than this. Now since men possess free will, since they are therefore free to adopt and act upon any creed they wish, it is possible for masses of men to become hippies; but it is *not* possible for them to remain long in this condition, because of the built-in "self-destruct" mechanism that the law of cause and effect imposes upon those who pursue this philosophy. Thus, when some time ago I began to despair at the spreading of hippie communes throughout society, Leonard Liggio commented cheerfully: "Don't worry about it; one hard winter will dispose of the problem."

There is a great deal of wisdom in this "Social Darwinian" attitude. Unfortunately, this dysfunctionality has not been as vivid as it could be, because foolish parents and taxpayers mulcted for welfare payments have been around to subsidize this anti-life credo and to maintain it indefinitely. Remove these subsidies, take away the indulgent check filled out by parent or welfare board, and the hippie phenomenon would have died a much deserved natural death long before now. Social cleansing brought about by the workings of natural law would have steered these misguided folk onto the proper and functional path long ago.

Let us consider two troubled parents of my acquaintance and the contrasting ways in which they have dealt with the phenomenon of hippie children. One parent said to his daughter who was yearning to drop out of college and to try the hippie path: "O. K. I'm not going to try and stop you. But I'm not going to subsidize this decision. If you want to drop out and become a hippie, you get no further financial support from me." The daughter dropped out, tried romantic hippie poverty, and in six months concluded that this was not for her; next year, she was back in college and enjoying it. The other parent, in contrast, himself steeped in foolish permissivism, said, after considerable wailing and anguish: "I don't agree with what you're doing, but I will always stand behind you and send you money if you need it." This course virtually insured that his children would continue on the hippie path indefinitely. Cause and effect were prevented from teaching their salutary lessons.

At a recent libertarian conference I ran across a man who put his libertarian position on drugs in starkly Social Darwinian terms. He said, in effect: "Let's legalize all drugs. Then these drug-taking kids will kill themselves off, and the problem will be eliminated." Harshly and crudely put, perhaps, and of course there are other libertarian grounds for legalization. But again our friend had a keen point: take away the artificial props, allow premises and nature their head, and the law of cause and effect will correct the situation with dispatch. If, as I firmly believe, psychedelic drugs destroy mind and body, then the removal of artificial restrictions will reveal this fact starkly and clearly, and the drug-takers will either fall by the wayside or correct their disastrous path.

The great libertarian Social Darwinist William Graham Sumner put the matter very clearly: "Almost all legislative effort to prevent vice is really protective of vice, because all such legislation saves the vicious man from the penalty of his vice. Nature's remedies against vice are terrible . . . A drunkard in the gutter is just where

he ought to be, according to the fitness and tendency of things. Nature has set upon him the process of decline and dissolution by which she removes things which have survived their usefulness . . . Now, we can never annihilate a penalty. We can only divert it from the head of the man who has incurred it to the heads of others who have not incurred it. A vast amount of 'social reform' consists in just this operation. The consequence is that those who have gone astray, being relieved from Nature's fierce discipline, go on to worse, and that there is a constantly heavier burden for the others to bear. Who are the others? When we see a drunkard in the gutter we pity him. If a policeman picks him up, we say that society has interfered to save him from perishing. 'Society' is a fine word, and it saves us the trouble of thinking. The industrious and sober workman, who is mulcted of a percentage of his day's wages to pay the policeman, is the one who bears the penalty. But he is the Forgotten Man. He passes by and is never noticed, because he has behaved himself, fulfilled his contracts. and asked for nothing." (Sumner, *What Social Classes Owe to Each Other*, Caxton Printers, 1966, pp. 113-115.)

Or, as that other great libertarian Social Darwinist Herbert Spencer pointed out, both the state welfare system and unthinking private charity "not only stop the purifying process, but even increases the vitiation--absolutely encourages the multiplication of the reckless and incompetent by offering them an unfailing provision, and *dis*courages the multiplication of the competent and provident by heightening the prospective difficulty of maintaining a family. And thus, in their eagerness to prevent the really salutary sufferings that surround us, these sigh-wise and groan-foolish people bequeath to posterity a continually increasing curse." (Herbert Spencer, *Social Statics*, London, 1851, p. 324). But both Sumner and Spencer strongly endorsed that great maxim of nineteenth-century private charity: helping men to help themselves, so that they can set themselves on the proper, functional, and rational path.

Libertarians have never given proper weight to the immense significance of the demonstration by Ludwig von Mises, fifty years ago, that socialism cannot calculate, and therefore that socialism and communism simply cannot function in a modern industrial society. And since the immense population of the modern world requires an industrial society to survive, this means that socialism, being totally dysfunctional, cannot endure and must inevitably collapse. Already we have seen crucial illustrations of this great truth: notably in Lenin's total backtracking from the attempt to leap into the Communist goal of a moneyless "War Communism" shortly after the Bolshevik Revolution and his shift back to the quasi-market economy of the NEP; and in the rapid shift, since the 1950's, of Eastern Europe (notably Yugoslavia) away from socialist planning and toward a free-market economy. All this indicates that socialism cannot endure, and that the long-run victory of liberty and the free market is virtually inevitable.

All this does not mean that libertarians should remain passive and quiescent, or that we should refrain from speeding up Nature's timetable as much as we possibly can. But the point is that, quintessentially and metaphysically, we should remain of good cheer. The eventual victory of liberty is inevitable, because only liberty is functional for modern man. There is no need, therefore, for libertarians to thirst manically for Instant Action and Instant Victory, and then to fall into bleak despair when that Instant Victory is not forthcoming. Reality, and therefore history, *is* on our side. Social Darwinism--that seemingly bleak and bitter creed--provides us, through the instrument of science and reason, with the unquenchable long-run optimism that liberty one day shall triumph.

Native Americans And Property Rights

By Leonard P. Liggio

PART I

Libertarians owe a debt of gratitude to *The Individualist* for publishing "The Property Rights of American Indians," by Rosalie Nichols (February, 1970). I do not agree with some of the points made by Miss Nichols, but I think that the topic is one of fundamental importance to libertarians. The matter of precise understanding of property rights in actual practice is basic to libertarianism; yet it is an area of the most profound ignorance and plain sloppiness among many libertarian-oriented people. If such people are not reliable on the matter of property rights, one wonders whether they have been drawn to libertarianism not by its rigorous theory and practice but by heaven knows what accidental cultural attractions. Central to the libertarian is which claims and titles are and which are not property; flowing from this theoretical discovery must be action to defend property in the hands of its rightful owners and to place it in the hands of these rightful owners wherever non-owners have occupied or used it. Justice is the ultimate objective of libertarians.

Obviously, any libertarian who concerns himself or herself with such matters is engaged in the preeminent libertarian activity. Rosalie Nichols clearly is such a person. Any differences which I may have with her are secondary to the fact that she has embarked upon preeminent libertarian activity. It is an honor to engage in a dialogue with her.

The history of the European immigrants' relations with the native Americans is one of unrelieved violence. In that shameful history the English immigrants were conspicuous by their violence. Other European peoples have been less violent, and the French were reknowned for the almost good relations which they maintained with all Indians, gaining friends even among former enemies, as Rosalie Nichols notes. For almost four hundred years the English immigrants have maintained a permanent system of violence against the native Americans.

The original sovereignty claimed by Europeans over the American Indians and over the land of North America was based upon the European claim of religious superiority. Since Christianity was viewed by the Europeans as giving Christian governments and Christian individuals a superior claim compared with others, including the inhabitants, the European claim to dominance is based on their Christian religion. This was the basis by which the native Americans were denoted as 'savages' while the barbaric Europeans were denoted as 'civilized.' As Rosalie Nichols indicates, it was the designation as 'savage' or pagan upon which the rights of the American Indians to life, liberty or property were violated. One recalls the famous description of the landing of the English in North America: "First, they fell on their knees to pray; then, they fell on the Indians."

Fall on the Indians they did. In New England the Indians first encountered by the English immigrants had the misfortune to occupy and cultivate the better farm lands as well as to prefer to sell their furs to the highest bidder. Clearly savages par excellence; extermination was their fate. The other New England Indian tribes inhabiting the valuable river valleys flowing into Long Island Sound—Pequots, Narragansetts, Mohegans, etc.—were later massacred or sold into slavery in the West Indies by methods too gruesome to describe . . . but sanctioned, when not led, by ministers of religion and civilized officials. In Virginia several campaigns were fought against the Indians who had originally welcomed the settlers in the James River region; the institutionalization of Black slavery (the Indians were too

'savage' to accept enslavement which was the original hope of the labor-short, land-rich European officials) led directly to the desire for huge plantation tracts and the wars to oust the Indians from the other river valleys.

Whatever the roots of European violence, even the argument that the profound differences between Europeans and native Americans could mitigate some of the violence—irrational as that argument is—is unsupportable; the model of the methods, attitudes and practice of violence carried on by the English upon the native Americans was established in the violence of the English 'plantations' imposed on the Christian, European, and neighboring Irish (of which the current civil war in Ulster is one product). Late nineteenth century English and American social theorists (mainly socialists), creating the intellectual foundation for the New Imperialism of this last century, singled out their English forebears' violence against the Irish, native Americans, *et al.* as proof of their racial superiority—aggressors and conquerors are defined as superior to the exploited and oppressed in superman theories—and as the justification for the wars of extermination and conquest launched by England and America, and which have culminated in the American aggression in Vietnam.

However rationalized, the Europeans' claim to sovereignty over North America is logically unsupportable. However, Rosalie Nichols claims that the North American continent could be legitimately claimed by the native Americans. She says: "The American continents were not ownerless." Yes, if it is meant that certain lands were owned. Certain lands were owned and the major part was unowned. I doubt if she means that the native Americans claimed sovereignty over North America (although, of course, if such a thing as sovereignty could be legitimate the native Americans would have possessed it and not the Europeans). But, the property rights of the Indians to the land they owned must be recognized; as well as the fact that that right was totally violated by the English immigrants.

When the English immigrants landed in the Chesapeake Bay and the Massachusetts Bay they were welcomed by the Indians. The English settlers brought manufactured products not yet developed by the Indians and the Indians taught the English immigrants agricultural methods not yet developed by the English. The Indians did not view the establishment of private property in land by the immigrants as anything wrong, immoral or in violation of their rights. The Indians along the Atlantic coast recognized that there was more than enough land there to satisfy many hundreds of times the tens of thousands of immigrants who poured out of England to find a freer and better life in America. The difficulty was that the English immigrants were not satisfied to live alongside the Indians in mutual recognition of rights. The English insisted upon the power of government over the lives and the lands of the Indians. According to the English, there could be no free exchange between individuals and groups living their own lives on the wide land. The English had to have the monopoly over people and land. The people and the land had to be obedient to English immigrant officials.

The problem then was not the matter of settlement and private property, but the matter of government. Where government exists, private property rights are negated. When the English immigrants came, they were divided into two groups, or classes, the farmers who settled and worked their private property and the rulers who had

(Continued on page 5)

NATIVE AMERICANS — *(Continued from page 4)*

assumed government positions. The English immigrant farmers and the Indians tended to live in peace and mutual respect. It was the claim of government over the Indians by the English immigrant officials which was the cause of aggression and genocide against the Indians. The government officials in all the colonies used their offices as the means of their personal enrichment; since there was little in the form of liquid capital to be seized, they seized lands in the hopes that future immigrants would have to purchase lands from them if there were none available for free settlement. The governors did not attempt to develop the land to turn it into private property; rather they assigned each other large tracts of lands which they left unimproved and undeveloped--there was no mixing of labor with the lands. It was pure feudalism or land monopoly, the negation of private property. Most of the lands in the colonies not occupied by settlers were distributed among the government officials as land grants (there were also large land grants given to the courtiers by the English kings).

Of course, these tracts included the areas on which the Indians were settled and had carried out their industries of farming, fishing and hunting. So the Indians suffered the double violence of being placed under the government of English immigrant officials and of English land grantees--often the same people. If the Indians did not accept English immigrant government, war would be made upon them; if they did not accept English feudal landholders, war would be made upon them--by governments. In addition, if the Indians continued to live and to work these lands it would be difficult to get new immigrants, who now had to go to one of the land monopolists to get land, to pay much or any money for land which the Indians already lived upon and worked. The ordinary settler had enough common sense and respect for rights not to want to claim land which the Indians already lived upon and worked.

If the immigrants merely went in and worked unused land the Indians would have no objections, or if they came to an understanding with the Indians who might be using the land--the Indians valued very low economically their marginal uses of the land for hunting and fishing,--the Indians would have no objections. But, this disturbed the feudal landlords who wished to assign lands and collect 'prices' or taxes. The existence of Indian settlement and farming undermined the feudal land monopolies, so the land had to be cleared by the extermination of the native Americans.

During the colonial period, the Middle Colonies witnessed less violence against the Indians. In part, this was due to the fact that most of the settlers there were not English. Like the French in the St. Lawrence and Ohio-Mississippi valleys, the Dutch, Swedes and Germans were more interested in the profits of commerce and good farming in peaceful accord with the Indians than in the destruction of lives and money in the plundering of the Indians. This situation was institutionalized with the founding of Pennsylvania by the Quakers; as in so many other matters, the Quakers are worthy of close analysis by libertarians.

The relations of the Quakers with the Indians were a model of justice which was constantly commended by the Indians themselves. The last of a series of mutually agreeable treaties between the Indians and the Quakers, the Treaty of Easton of 1758, placed the final limitation on European settlement. Pennsylvania released all claim to the soil west of the Alleghenies and of a large section east of the Alleghenies and north of the present Sunbury, as long as the Indians did not sell the territory to any other government.

This treaty of the Quakers was used by English government officials at a conference with northern Indian chiefs at Canajoharie on the Mohawk River west of Albany as an example of English intentions (April, 1759): "I hope this surrender will convince you and all other Indians how ready your brethren the English are to remove from your hearts all jealousies and uneasiness of their desiring to encroach upon your hunting lands, and be a convincing proof to you how false the accusations of the French are that we are at war with them, in order to get your country from you." Of course, the French accusation was accurate; the English had gone to war against the French to gain the trans-Appalachian Indians' land which was protected by the French.

The officials in England in league with the American officials and the heirs of officials, who inherited the huge feudal domains that were the fruits of office-holding in America, hoped for even larger rewards by gaining land monopolies across the Appalachian Mts. Having monopolized the lands along the Atlantic coast, the planters by control of the government apparatus excluded the newer immigrants from homesteading the wide lands along the Atlantic coast. Since the Atlantic coast region is able to support many times its present population there was no economic need for Europeans to settle beyond the mountains. The only attractive resources--minerals--were either in the Appalachian Mts. or bordered major waterways such as the Great Lakes, and could have been extracted by miners whose settlements would be approved by the Indians without any difficulties.

But, as a result of the feudal land system along the Atlantic coast, the new immigrants could not pay the high 'prices' demanded by the government officials and their heirs; they hoped to be able to homestead across the mountains. Crossing out of the control of the seaboard officials, into the lands of the western Indian tribes, these settlers could and did homestead farms and gained the recognition of the local Indians. An ideal situation would have been the acceptance by the European settlers of the essentially stateless society of the Indians. The Europeans could have developed among themselves and with the Indians a social system based on free exchange which was the basis of much of the economic life of the Indians. The Quakers' excellent relations with the Indians were based on the fact that they were the only Europeans dedicated to social relations based upon equal and free exchange--which explains why Quakers have always been out of step with other Europeans.

An imperfect but acceptable system was proposed by some of the wise organizers who carried forward the American Revolutionary struggle against English officialdom and their associated American feudal landholders. The revolutionary impetus for the abolition of feudal holdings and their replacement with the institution of private property would have meant that there would be plenty of land for homesteading along the Atlantic seaboard. But, retaining elements of Christian messianism, the United States government claimed the trans-Appalachian territories inhabited by the Indian tribes. However, the trans-Appalachian areas were projected as states in the American Confederation: states composed of and controlled by the Indians themselves.

During the period of the American Revolution the control of the trans-Appalachian territory by the Indians was recognized in treaties with the American Congress such as that between the Delawares and the Continental Congress (September, 1778). In return for a trade dependency in which the Americans had the monopoly right of supplying goods for purchase by the Indians, the United States proposed that the Indians could form state governments in the trans-Appalachian area which would be equal to the states of the European settlers on the Atlantic coast. " . . . the United States do engage to guarantee to the aforesaid nation of Delawares, and their heirs, all their territorial

(Continued on page 6)

NATIVE AMERICANS — *(Continued from page 5)*

rights in the fullest and most ample manner as it hath been bound by former treaties, as long as the said Delaware nation shall abide by and hold fast the chain of friendship now entered into. And it is further agreed on between the contracting parties should it for the future be found conducive for the mutual interest of both parties to invite any other tribes who have been friends in the interest of the United States, to join the present confederation, and to form a state whereof the Delaware nation shall be the head, and have a representation in Congress." A similar project was promised to the Southwest Indians in the Hopewell Treaty of November, 1785 with the Cherokee Nation: "That the Indians may have full confidence in the justice of the United States, respecting their interest, they shall have the right to send a deputy of their choice, whenever they think fit, to Congress."

The Northwest Ordinance passed by the Continental Congress in 1787 declared: "The utmost good faith shall always be observed towards the Indians; their land and property shall never be taken from them without their consent; and in their property, rights, and liberty, they never shall be invaded or disturbed, unless in just and lawful wars authorized by Congress." In conforming with that a treaty was drawn up with the Indian tribes north of the Ohio River and west of the Allegheny mountains. Signed in January, 1789, the United States did "confirm the said boundary line; to the end that the same may remain as a division line between the lands of the United States of America, and the lands of said nations forever," and did "relinquish and quit claim to the said nations respectively, all the lands lying between the limits above described, for them the said Indians to live and hunt upon, and otherwise to occupy as they shall see fit."

This reasonable arrangement was quickly overthrown by the new government which took control in April, 1789 as a result of the overthrow of the Continental Congress and the Articles of Confederation by the *coup d'etat* in Philadelphia in 1787. The control and exploitation of the lands west of the mountains was a major cause for the calling of the secret conclave in Philadelphia and for the Constitution it produced. Just as the impetus for the abolition of feudal holdings and the institution of private property following the revolution was blunted, so the impetus for the abolition of slavery had been blunted. Part of the drive for the new, more powerful central government was in defense of slavery. The limitation against slavery in the whole west as originally intended was restricted to the Northwest territory, opening the Southwest territory to slavery. The plantation areas of the coast had become depleted and the slave-holders required new territories extending through Georgia, Florida, Tennessee, Alabama, and Mississippi for plantation cultivation. Land clearing by the extermination of the Indians was necessary to make room for the slave quarters.

The early aggressions by the new United States government were defeated by the Northwest Indians in November 1791; but the United States army reversed this defeat and "the big push westward over the prostrate bodies of slaughtered Indians was begun." A thorough and detailed description of the process of genocide carried out by the United States government against the American Indians would be required for a final view of the subject. A study of the "Five Civilized Nations" of the Old Southwest would be a good beginning. The Cherokee, Chocktaw, Chickasaw, Creek and Seminole had some of the most developed and productive villages among the American Indians. Their skill in agricultural industry made them especially subject to elimination. By 1838 the "Five Civilized Nations" had been driven over the "Trail of Tears" from their rich lands to the barren territory across the Mississippi River.

Bits And Pieces
By Jerome Tuccille

A few months back I mentioned in this column that a short booklet, HOW TO REFUSE INCOME TAXES - LEGALLY, written by Lucille E. Moran, might be a good investment for libertarians interested in beating the revenue authorities. My good friend and "legal advisor," Lucille Moran, has now come up with another booklet called WHAT LICENSE?, available for one fiat dollar through the Independent Bar Association of Massachusetts, P.O. Box 187, Islamorada, Florida 33036. I have read the piece in manuscript form and can testify that it is a truly radical attack on the judicial system in the best libertarian tradition and well worth the price. Miss Moran is a muckraker and radical of the Old Right variety (an anarchist although she doesn't like the word), an individualist activist well versed in natural law and early-American history centering around the revolution. She analyzes the stranglehold that privileged groups have on our judicial system and advocates the creation of independent bar associations such as her own (of which I am a board member). Lucille is now opening shop as a legal advisor at an initial fee of $100 for those who need counsel in avoiding the income tax.

What are her credentials? The fact that she has not filed and gotten away with it for over eight years. What establishment lawyer can make that claim?

* * * * * *

The libertarian movement has grown at a refreshing pace during the past year. It has received favorable coverage in such diverse publications as *Playboy, Penthouse, Cavalier, The Wall Street Journal* and *Nation's Business,* and was deemed worthy of a lampooning in the September, 1970 issue of *Esquire*. Any idea that catches on and becomes fashionable runs the risk of being exploited by unsavory characters with a firm grasp on the "pulsebeat" of the nation. So it was predictable that such a one as Jeffrey St. John, a fanatical Buckley conservative four years ago, a slavishly devout Objectivist two years ago, and a fanatically slavish Buckleyite Objectivist today, would publish an article in the *New York Times* identifying himself as a libertarian. They are stumbling out of the woodwork, tripping over one another's ambitions in a mad race to latch onto an accelerating bandwagon. Others of that stripe are sure to follow.

* * * * * *

Realistically speaking, libertarianism is still a minor fringe movement virtually unknown among the general population which can barely pronounce it let alone understand what it's all about. For this reason libertarians must seek out alliances with larger groups in order to achieve even limited political goals. There simply are not enough libertarians around to constitute a single movement independent of all others. Murray Rothbard touched on this in his October 1st editorial, "When Revolution?" The question that poses the biggest problem for us today is: alliances with whom?

The Right Wing is, of course, hopeless all the way down the list of issues important on today's political scene: foreign policy; economics; civil liberties; a broad range of domestic policies including the draft, abortion laws and censorship (if only libertarians had known three years ago what the traditionalist half of the conservative alliance would be like once it ascended to power)! Our old friend, "Chairman Bill," has now established himself as a self-

(Continued on page 7)

BITS AND PIECES – *(Continued from page 6)*

appointed censor of the publishing world. Recent issues of *National Review* have singled out Bobbs-Merrill and Pantheon as prime vehicles for radical left literature. These latest broadsides, along with Agnew's open threats against the major media, have not been without some effect on at least one of these publishing houses that I know of firsthand. "Private" censorship, like private anything, may prove far more efficient than the heavy-fisted state variety.

So we turn leftward in our search for potential allies and what do we find? On the farthest Left a rather rancid bunch of murderers, bombers, self-righteous faggots, dykish loudmouths, and crusading nihilists (that's nihilists, *not* anarchists). Murdering, bombing and bank-robbing in the present political context may be called a lot of things, but none of them revolutionary. The situation is different in Uruguay where the Tupamaros have turned bank-robbing into a highly effective revolutionary tactic. Ninety-five per cent of the population can barely feed itself let alone put its money away in a savings account. When a bank is hit down there it is the wealth of the ruling class that is being stolen and a loud cheer goes up from the exploited peasantry. In the United States eighty percent of the population has the sweat of its brow tied up in the banking system; an attack on the banks is an attack on the vast majority of the "people" in the country and can hardly be considered a "revolutionary act against the state."

The brainless adventurists of the far Left have been too dim-witted to see the distinction, and have virtually destroyed the radical movement by the employment of tactics totally unsuited to the current American situation. This mania for copying examples set by rebels in foreign societies, and inability to analyze what needs to be done in our uniquely "American" situation, is responsible for much of the failure of the activist Left. Knee-jerk radicalism has become as much - or more - of a problem as knee-jerk liberalism.

Closer to the center on the liberal Left we find the same sorry bunch of welfare statists and New Deal bureaucrats that libertarians had criticized (along with their traditionalist allies) when they were conservatives. These think-tank experts and central planners have have always been consistently inconsistent and will remain so; they are remarkably "pragmatic" on all issues including the war and the military draft, formulating their positions a la John Lindsay according to the results of the most recent polls. It is clear that libertarians have nothing to gain by an alliance with this claque.

Broadly speaking, this leaves us with one remaining option for alliances on the Left: the radical Left as distinguished from the nihilists on the far Left and the liberals on the center Left. This group is comprised of all constructive rebels with a positive commitment to immediate peace abroad, radical decentralization and community organizing domestically, repeal of abortion laws, elimination of all censorship regulations, true social and economic equality for women (as opposed to the absurd smokescreen issue revolving around "sex objects"), and an end to racial discrimination. In my view, at least, the most effective tactics are political education and civil disobedience--a boycott of government institutions if you will and the construction of neighborhood alternatives. More activist measures such as the seizure of abandoned housing and public property in poverty areas has also proven effective in certain instances.

Indiscriminate violence against the innocent as well as against the political authorities can never have any place in a libertarian strategy. The "offing of pigs" is a blind tactic which, as Dave Dellinger has frequently pointed out, fails to consider that cops and firemen, to name just two groups, are merely small pawns carrying out the

Knee-Jerk Radicalism
I – Free Whom?

We are all familiar with, and properly scornful of, "knee-jerk liberalism", the kind of attitude which for every problem calls for the passing of a law or the vast expenditure of Federal funds. But many of us have been less attuned to the equally egregious "knee-jerk radicalism", and it is about time that we call this attitude to account.

For example, there is our perfectly proper hostility toward repression, toward any sort of crippling of free speech or inquiry by the State apparatus. But for radicals this is generally an unthinking reflex; and so the cry goes up: Free X! Free Jim! Free Joe! Free Horace! Free the Oshkosh Eleven and the Kalamazoo Twelve! The libertarian, of course, has at the center of his being the call for freedom for *everyone*, with, however, one vital exception: the criminal. In the libertarian creed, the criminal deserves not freedom but punishment, a punishment, to be sure, that does not go beyond the extent to which he has deprived some innocent victim of the latter's liberty. It follows, then, that it is not permissible to raise the cry of freedom automatically and unthinkingly; if the State claims that Joe Blow is an axe murderer, it is not *a priori* impossible that the State is right; and that Mr. Blow deserves the gallows rather than mass hysteria and demonstrations on his behalf. It all depends then, (a) on the nature of the crime with which Mr. Blow is charged; and (b) *if* the "crime" is truly a crime for the libertarian, on the facts of whether Mr. Blow is guilty as charged. Each case must be considered and judged on its own merits; discrimination between cases is a libertarian necessity.

In some of its recent campaigns, then, the Left has been evidently correct: these are the cases where the "crime" itself is simply a legitimate exercise of freedom of speech or assembly. Thus, the Chicago Conspiracy trial was clearly an invasion of free speech in its very charge (of "conspiring to cross state lines with intent to incite riot"); so too were the old Smith Act trials ("conspiracy to advocate overthrow of the government"), and so too is the recent conviction of Juan Farinas for distributing anti-draft leaflets at an induction center (and thereby allegedly

(Continued on page 8)

orders of a superior power. The destruction of a police station or the murder of a cop does not make a revolution; a large-scale tax rebellion, a proliferation of "strikes" in the ranks of the military, a boycott of centrally-controlled schools and of elections when no real alternatives are offered, might add up in the long run to a genuine revolutionary movement with mass support.

Violence, even morally-justified violence like the destruction of draft board files, has only succeeded in chasing large groups of potential allies further to the Right. Many in the middle class who would like to see an end to the war and who believe that government has gotten "too big" have been frightened into a repressive political attitude. More bombings, more bank robberies and "offing of pigs" will usher in 1984 ten years ahead of schedule.

179

KNEE-JERK RADICALISM – *(Continued from page 7)*

"disrupting the Selective Service System"). The Left is also correct in its defense of the Fathers Berrigan, who, while passing over from speech to action, destroyed draft records, records of a criminal organization engaged in enslaving our youth--and so hardly a "crime" by libertarian standards. Other Left agitations *may* be justified on the grounds of unclarity of the facts: for example, in the cases of Huey Newton or the Rosenbergs or Alger Hiss.

But in their most recent agitations the Left has been engaging in unjustifiable knee-jerk activity. "Free Angela?" But Angela might well be a murderess as charged, and surely murder comes under the rubric of high crime for a libertarian. "Free Bobby?" But Bobby too might well have murdered Alex Rackley, and it is to the eternal shame of the Left that the torture and murder of the Negro Rackley has received nothing but shrugs and even approbation by our radical "civil libertarians". And there does not seem to be, either in the Seale or the Davis cases, any of the fuzziness of the facts that legitimately called the Hiss and Rosenberg cases into question. Indeed, the Left seems to come dangerously close to saying that it does not *care* about the facts, and that Angela and Bobby must be freed simply because they are leftists and radicals-- a position for which no genuine libertarian can have anything but contempt. If they are murderers then they should pay the price. And neither is it obvious that we should "free Eldridge"--a convicted rapist who violated the terms of his parole.

Let us keep our "repression" straight.

II – The New York Review

The New York Review of Books is a brilliant and extremely well-edited radical bi-weekly; but despite its important contributions, particularly in foreign policy, it has sometimes suffered from knee-jerk radicalism. But the January 7 issue contains welcome signs of a shift toward a more independent and rational view. Thus, the literary critic Elizabeth Hardwick has a blistering attack on the counter-culture ("Militant Nudes"), in a review of several movies (*Ice, The Groupies, Trash,* and *Gimme Shelter*) as well as a novel by Marge Piercy. And Murray Kempton has a sardonic review of Tom Hayden's *Trial* ("Three Who Didn't Make a Revolution").

But particularly important is an article by the prominent Harvard economist Wassily W. Leontief, "The Trouble With Cuban Socialism". As a highly sympathetic observer of the Castro regime, Leontief sadly engages in a critique of Cuban socialism which could hardly be exceeded by a laissez-faire capitalist. Leontief is forced to record the Cuban system as an economic disaster, and cites the basic causes as the elimination of a rational market price system

destroying economic calculation of benefits and costs, and the low morale and productivity brought about by the Cuban attempt to replace economic incentives by "moral" (altruistic) ones. The successes of the early days of Castroism are perceptively attributed to the Cubans living off the accumulated capital of the previous regime. That the Cuban economy has not collapsed totally is attributed to the fact that Cuba is a small island which exports and imports heavily from the world market, and therefore can take many of its accounting prices from that market.

All in all, the article is a triumph of rationality over sentiment, and should be required reading for all leftists-- including those libertarians who have become enamoured of the communist and anti-market path.

Recommended Reading

Youth Culture. A former leading beatnik warns that the younger generation is repeating the major reason for the failure of the beats: the ignoring of intellect and reality. James Lincoln Collier writes: "Our hearts were all in the right place . . . The ingredient that was missing was thought . . . the intellectual center was all mush . . . The failure of Kerouac and his friends was . . . that they did not recognize that nature has its rules. They thought that by an act of sheer will they could change the world. In fact they could not. You cannot do anything out of sheer will. To change anything you have first to study and read and most of all think like hell until you begin to grasp where you are, what the world is like, and what the problem is."

"And this is what troubles me", Collier continues, "about the young people who are today the focus of the attempt to change things. They have not bothered to think anything through. I listen to 20-year old political activists who have never read "The Republic" or "Das Kapital" or for God's sake even the American Constitution . . . Arguing with people who don't know what they're talking about is pretty hopeless. They keep telling you . . . 'all that rationalist stuff never worked, we're going to do it by intuition.' This, precisely, is what the leaders of the Beat generation were saying, and it is why they all came to nothing in the end: they never did find out what it is really like out there. It is not reason which has failed: it is man's failure to use it which has caused all the trouble . . .

Reality is iron: it can only be managed by people who understand what iron is like. Nixon and Agnew and Lyndon Johnson and J. Edgar Hoover have bad hearts . . . but by Jesus they have done their homework . . . A good heart is not enough." James Lincoln Collier, "No Satori in Iron", *the Village Voice* (Dec. 24).

The Libertarian Forum
BOX 341
MADISON SQUARE STATION
NEW YORK, NEW YORK 10010

First Class

Published Every Month. Subscription Rate: $7.00 Per Year.

A Monthly Newsletter

THE
Libertarian Forum

Joseph R. Peden, Publisher

Murray N. Rothbard, Editor

VOLUME III, NO. 2   February, 1971

TAKE OFF

After two years of rapid growth and accumulating publicity, the libertarian movement has at last taken off into the empyrean. How long this will last no one can foretell, but at least for the moment we have become well-known, and, even, who could have predicted? respectable!

The critical turning-point has come with the article by Stan Lehr and Louis Rossetto, Jr., "The New Right Credo – Libertarianism", in the New York *Sunday Times Magazine* of January 10. Not only that – but this audience of over a million influential readers was also treated to the article as a front cover picture: with Lehr and Rossetto looking at the reader flanking an enormous red fist, under which was the caption "laissez-faire". It is surely well over a century since *laissez-faire* has been widely represented as the radical and even pugnacious creed that it really is, and it was a pleasure to see the article if for this reason alone. The *Times* and other media had previously given considerable publicity to Karl Hess, but rather as a lone curio than as a member of an ever-widening movement. Here was the first major piece on the movement itself, and written by two of its young leaders. The article is festooned with pictures of some members of the libertarian pantheon, the relevant ones being Hess, Rand, Tuccille, and myself, a juxtaposition well calculated to send Ayn Rand, at least, up the wall.

Lehr and Rossetto are the leaders of the "Freedom Conspiracy" – the libertarian club at Columbia University, affiliated with SIL. It is ironic, and also indicative of the divergence among libertarians in applying their creed, that Lehr and Rossetto first came to the attention of the *Times* and the media for their work for Buckley for Senate, – a political stance with which at least three, and possibly all, of the pantheon were in profound disagreement.

The rewards of fame are heady indeed; in my case, consisting of several college friends whom I had not seen in over a decade calling to ask "hey, what is this libertarianism?" and the hardware man on the corner slapping me on the back: "So you're an ulta-liberal, eh?" More tangibly, Chairman Bill himself was goaded into devoting an entire column (Jan. 14) to the libertarians. So long as the libertarian split in YAF remained unpublicized, Bill Buckley could ignore the movement from his lofty papal perch and print blather in *National Review* about the harmonious convention at St. Louis. But now that the split on the right was in the open, and the *Times* had devoted two lengthy articles in two months to this new creed, Buckley clearly felt that he owed it to the conservative legions to protect their flank from this new threat – especially when the threat was particularly annoying in taking seriously the conservative rhetoric about individual liberty.

Buckley's column was characteristic: a blend of cheap debating points (e.g. smirking at the kids for "co-opting"

Spinoza as a libertarian, when the co-optation was clearly a feat performed by the *Times'* picture editor); pseudo-scholarship ("absolutization of freedom . . . is the oldest and most tempting heresy". Where, Bill? *Who* are this legion of ancient libertarian heretics? Tell us so we can add them to the pantheon); and petty bitchery (e.g. referring to Jerry Tuccille only as a "semi-literate gentleman"). As for myself, I am apparently back in Buckley's good graces as a lovable (or perhaps not quite so lovable) nut, endlessly intoning my well-known passion for de-nationalizing lighthouses. (The changes are rung on the well-worn lighthouse theme in a particularly cretinous review of my Power and Market by a spiritual whelp of Buckley's in *National Review* Jan. 26). The only new feature of the review is the charge that the purely free market society would be tantamount to feudalism – this from a magazine that has endlessly extolled the virtues of feudalism as compared to the modern despotic state! Karl Hess is found to be "nauseating" rather than lovable for his pointing out that the Soviet Union is at least one up on us for having executed Beria, while we still have J. Edgar Hoover; apparently Chairman Bill's appreciation of political wit suddenly disappears when it is, for once, directed against his own totems.

The most interesting aspect of the Buckley column is the fact that in the last paragraph, Buckley apparently felt driven to concede grudgingly that perhaps his friend Nixon "has not sufficiently indulged the presumptions in favor of individual liberty". The fact that Buckley has been driven by the libertarian publicity to criticize the Nixon Administration for the first time since it assumed office is itself testimony to the anxiety of Chairman Bill to protect the libertarian flank of his conservative coalition. Thus, the libertarian movement has already made a significant impact on the American political scene.

(Continued on page 8)

Come One! Come All!

Hear ye! Hear ye! The rapidly growing Libertarian movement in New York City is holding a libertarian conference, the first conference since the October, 1969 gala at the Hotel Diplomat. This conference will be held on the weekend of March 13-14, at Columbia University Law School. Speakers include Murray Rothbard on Strategy for Liberty, and Austrianism vs. Friedmanism; Jerry Tuccille on Psychology of Left and Right; and a debate between Roy A. Childs, Jr. and Jeffrey St. John on Anarcho-Capitalism vs. Limited Government. The conference is being organized by the New York Libertarian Alliance, an affiliate of the Society for Individual Liberty. For details on the conference, write to Gary Greenberg, 460-5D Old Town Road, Port Jefferson Sta., N. Y. 11776.

Libertarianism: A Warning

Libertarianism is experiencing, paradoxically, both a fantastic upsurge in numbers and popularity and a serious blow to its continued effectiveness. In order to make this clear, it will be necessary to take a serious look at what effectiveness within the context of libertarianism would have to be (and is, on many occasions). Before I do that, let me adduce some facts which I think will serve to demonstrate my claim.

Today America is experiencing what might properly be considered a very important choice in its political directions. This choice has existed, of course, throughout America's history — which is to say, individual citizens in this country have always had the choice between pursuing wise or unwise political ends (as well as, and logically tied to, wise or unwise personal ends). The culmination of past errors has, however, flowered only in the last few years. To put it bluntly, the curtain may be falling on the close of the few decades of individualism in the world.

There is no inevitability to this, of course, but, free will notwithstanding, the implications of past misbehavior cannot be avoided; at best, they may be coped with rationally. Which is just what our problem is. Unless libertarians attend carefully to coping with the implications of the misbehavior of past members of this society — including, of course, at times their own past misbehavior — there is not very likely going to be *a way* to cope with it and thus no successful, rational *actions will be taken* to cope with it.

From the realms of industry, education, military defense, criminal court procedures, farming, ecology, to those of unionism, poverty, and art (yes!), the implications of corruption and bankruptcy in values are surrounding us. What are libertarians, on the whole, doing these days? Well, here we are getting into some delicate matters, so let me point out that I am dealing in generalizations, statistical ones, based not on a precise count but on the general but oft reliable knowledge I gain by keeping tabs on both the world in general and libertarianism in particular. As such, my answer to the above question must be seen for the generalization that it can only be. As regards, then, the great majority of young libertarians, writing in the various journals, active on the various campuses, present at the numerous meetings — scholarly and other — the bulk of them is concerned with dealing with utopianism. Too many have lifted their eyes from reality to the never-to-be-reached future. Even those who are non-utopians in their theoretical explorations in libertarian political philosophy are engaged predominatly in scholastical debates about the most minute details of — of all things — the structure of a libertarian society. This concern with Platonic perfection, this attitude of producing a final, absolute, static, non-contextually perfect societal structure is now a part of the libertarian intellectual movement — but not practiced by intellectuals, individuals who have become specialists at for example political theory, ethics, epistemology, economics, sociology, psychology, or other intellectual fields. Everyone in the libertarian movement included in this special category of utopian involvement has become an "expert" at everything relating to society and man. There simply is no division of labor, on the whole, within this new class of people. Without the slightest awareness of the difficulties of ethics and meta-ethics, young libertarians are writing books on the subject of how men ought to act in all kinds of specialized circumstances, of what should men in voluntary cooperation or out of it do for themselves in all kinds of specialized circumstances, etc. There is very little respect for education among the libertarians; there is, in fact, an anti-intellectualism in the sense that matters of intellectual concern are treated frivolously, in two page essays and in hundred page dissertations alike. Intellectual rigor which gave birth to the movement in men's minds, which produced the discoveries of Locke, Spencer, Mill, Hayek, Mises, Rothbard, Rand, *et al.* through hard work, has fallen by the wayside. Respect for the human mind, resulting in respect for reality, is slowly leaving libertarianism, at least in many circles.

Many, of course, are doing hard work — which is where man's salvation lies. Hopefully these reap beneficial results in their own personal lives. It would be so much more productive in behalf of our central aims to do the hard work we can do *well* within our respective fields of competence. If we haven't got such a field, we ought to find one. For, to get back to a point I promised I would return to, our effectiveness lies centrally in our own individual abilities to lead the best lives we can within the context — needs, abilities, requirements, obstacles, problems, realities - of our own lives. It does not appear that many libertarians are taking their own philosophical position seriously enough to live it within their own lives consistently (or at least to try to do so to the best of their abilities). The evidence for this lies in what I have laid before the reader. It is clearly bad for one to do something badly — and so many libertarians are doing bad thinking these days, thinking which produces no knowledge because it is thinking about things that are very difficult to think about without very thorough preparation. We would not trust a man totally untrained in medicine to be our doctor. And so forth. Nor should we trust people totally untrained in the specialized thinking required to cope with very complicated and refined philosophical, political, psychological, sociological, economic, etc. problems to do this thinking for us well. Others who are not libertarians catch on to this, of course, and there is just one important place where effectiveness is suffering. We aspire to be doctors of these fields, but few go through the difficulty of earning their doctorates — not necessarily in universities (they are not always the right places these days to earn a meaningful doctorate, although they ought to be). Too many of us do not earn doctorates simply by failing to educate ourselves thoroughly within the fields in which we make pronouncements. Too many of us have lost respect for man's mind and, therefore, our own absolute need to become mentally equipped to cope with reality. That, in part, explains why so many of us turn to problems of future societies — the context within those realms is as open as is the context within speculations about dancing angels on the head of a pin. Tomorrow is not around to fly in the face of our speculations, so tomorrow is an easy target for those willing to speculate wildly.

I say all this with utter sincerity; partly I say it as a result of some self-investigations, partly because I know the substance of the libertarian intellectual movement, and mostly because of my love of liberty for myself and all human beings. I hope, therefore, that, instead of hostile reactions, we may embark upon some serious considerations as we come across the ideas expressed above.
— Tibor R. Machan

CORRECTION

The full title of the booklet by Lucille Moran being published by the Independent Bar Association of Massachusetts, P. O. Box 187, Islamorada, Florida 33036 is — WHAT LICENSE? sub-titled WHY YOU CAN SUE YOUR DOCTOR, BUT *NOT* YOUR 'LAWYER'. The price of this booklet is $2 and not the price previously quoted.

ON WOMEN'S LIBERATION

The benefit which the libertarian right can derive from alliance with the radical left, as well as the strictly defined limits of this alliance, arise from the nature of socialism as an inherently incompatible mix of polar-opposite political philosophies – libertarianism and mercantilistic statism. From the former, the left draws its sensitivity to the abuse of power, and from the latter, the readiness to wield state power to advance its chosen ends. Those who imbibe this strange mixture develop an uncanny ability to sniff out with great accuracy the large and the petty pathologies of our social system, and an equally uncanny ability to propose solutions which surpass the disease in destructiveness.

The latest fad of the left is Women's Liberation, and in pursuit of this cause, its combined forces have surely reached new heights of muddled thinking and misdirected rhetoric. Nonetheless, libertarians would be well advised to consider the old maxim, that fifty million freaks can't be all wrong all of the time, before writing off Women's Lib all together. History tells us time and again that when the left says something's wrong here, something is indeed wrong. To find out just what is wrong and what to do about it, the libertarian need only rotate the analysis and recommendations of the left by 180 degrees or so and extrapolate according to the tables in the back of *The Wealth of Nations*.

In the case of Women's Lib, for example, the left wing analysis has it that the feminine half of humanity is being brutally exploited by the capitalistic, male-chauvinist sexist "system", and that the State in shining armor must come riding to the rescue on a bundle of tax money. The libertarian, decoding this message, concludes correctly that the male-dominated state is riding roughshod over the fairer sex, and that only a quick injection of laissez-faire can save the day.

Now, let's be more specific. The exploitee dearest to the hearts of the braless set is Mrs. American Housewife, inexorably trapped by the system in the triple role of sex object, nursemaid, and cleaning woman. Trapped by the system, yes, but by just what part of the system. By the brainwashing of the socialization process? By the prejudice of the male-chauvinist captains of industry? The leftists gloss over this delicate issue with a little sloganeering, but the libertarian, with his usual incisive insight, quickly identifies the true mechanism of oppression – the TAX SYSTEM. *Here* is the chain which binds the housewife to her stereotyped role – a multi-billion dollar subsidy from Washington for her husband-oppressor!

How does it work? Well, to begin with, we must note a fact which is somehow passed over by the leftist Women's Libbers, namely, that the housewife is a highly productive and in many respects highly skilled worker, producing an extremely valuable service. Corresponding to the massive aggregate service output of American housewives is an income stream of equal magnitude – but an income stream which remains wholly implicit, never makes it into the national income accounts, and is never tapped by the Internal Revenue Service. Compared to this most gargantuan of tax loopholes, the oil depletion allowance and municipal bonds are mere pinpricks!

Now, as any student of Economics 1 knows, when differential rates of taxation are applied to different lines of production, a misallocation of resources develops. If oil production is taxed and coal mining is tax exempt, we may be sure that the use of coal will increase, and that coal will be used unproductively in areas where oil would in fact be a more efficient fuel. Likewise, then, if housewife services are untaxed, while commercial janitorial services, child care centers, laundries, restaurants, and houses of prostitution are taxed, then housewives will have a competitive edge, and every male wanting any of these services will be encouraged to contract for them via *marriage* rather than contracting for them via the *market*.

Suppose a woman, before marriage, has been trained in the skill, let us say, of computer programming. Suppose her marginal product as a computer programmer is $3.00 an hour, while her marginal product as a domestic servant is only $2.25. Clearly, it would be good economics for her to find employment as a programmer and hire various specialists to fulfill the bulk of her cleaning, cooking, and child care functions, pocketing a clear premium of 75 cents an hour. Yet what if her husband is already earning $10,000 a year, putting her in the 30 percent tax bracket? That leaves her with $2.10 takehome from her programming job, less than enough to pay the cooking, cleaning, and child care contractors. This poor woman is indeed trapped in the home in an employment which does not exploit her full training and productivity, just as the Women's Liberationists claim. Oddly enough, however, the conventional order of villain and hero (tax supported state sector vs. profit supported capitalist sector) is reversed – who now appears to set the trap, and who would offer her a way out if left free to do so?

What is to be done to end this massive misallocation of human resources? Short of the ideal, but long-range, solution of abolishing the income tax altogether, it would appear that there are two ways to end the distortion. On the one hand, an attempt could be made to measure the income generated by domestically employed housewives, and subject it to taxation at the rates applicable to all other forms of income. Alternatively, a tax deduction could be allowed for the purchase of commercially produced "domestic" services.

From the point of view of equity and pure theory, I think that the first approach has superior merit, if one must choose between the two inequitable and theoretically objectionable alternatives. The weight of practical arguments, however, I think, favors the latter. The key issue in choosing between the options is that of information gathering. If domestic income were taxed, the incentive for the household would be to hide it, and for the IRS to build up a huge snooping and prying apparatus to combat this tendency. People are already objecting, after all, to a census form which once every ten years asks how many toilets you have in the house. What if in addition you had to fill out a monthly report detailing the number of times you mopped the kitchen floor or washed your underwear? In contrast, if domestic service substitutes were tax exempt, the information required would be happily volunteered by the tax payer. In addition to keeping track of the number of gallons-worth of gas tax paid, and of expense-account dinners, he would also keep receipts and records of payments to janatorial contractors, day care centers, appliance sales and rental outlets, etc.

For a dramatic example that clinches the relative superiority of the deduction scheme, consider the important household service of sex. The extended taxation method would not only require records to be kept of the frequency of intercourse, but would have to tackle the forbidding problem of deciding which partner was the "producer" and which the "consumer"! In contrast, under the deduction system, it would only be necessary for the taxpayer to keep receipts from the services of (male or female) prostitutes. Here, consumer and producer would be clearly identified, and, if the taxpayer preferred to keep his sex-life private rather than to claim his deduction, he could do so at his own discretion.

Removal of the tax incentive for household production would have immediate beneficial repercussions of both an

(Continued on page 8)

183

Living Free

For some time now I have seen enunciated in the libertarian press the view that the *important* thing about liberty is not the "negative" and rather petty goal of getting rid of statism, but the "positive" act by each libertarian of 'liberating himself", of "living a truly free life", of "living anarchy", etc. Now I must confess that I simply do not understand what these people are talking about, or, more concretely, that *either* they are writing pure rhetorical gibberish, *or* they are slipping into grave and even dangerous error.

Since their inception, libertarians have always been accused of being "negative". "Why do you always attack the government? Why can't you advocate positive programs?" has always been a popular charge against us. Happily the "living free" advocates do not wish to achieve their "positive" goals through government, but the fundamental error still remains. The point is that the fundamental definition of liberty *is* "negative": it consists in the *absence* of molestation, the absence of invasion of anyone's property rights in his person or material goods by other people. And the first philosophical error of every statist or socialist, left or right, is always to denounce the "superficiality" of "negative" freedom, and to set forth their views of "positive" freedom, which can include a grab-bag of goodies from full employment and three-square-meals a day to the present fad for "personal liberation." One of F. A. Hayek's great contributions in his *Road To Serfdom* was, once and for all, to eviscerate the call for "positive" freedom, to reveal the fatal admixture of the concepts of freedom and positive power or wealth in the same context. This is not to deny the value of wealth or other positive goods, but simply to *distinguish* between freedom and other good things in life.

It follows then that libertarianism *per se* is indeed "negative", and that liberty is, to be sure, *not* the be-all and end-all of anyone's personal philosophy. The libertarian does not believe that liberty *per se* provides the magic panacea for all ills or the magic guide for all actions; he simply advocates the liberty for every man to work out his own goals and his own personal philosophy. Once liberty is achieved, there can be all sorts of moral philosophies which different libertarians can pursue; the *rationalist* libertarians, for example, among whom I include myself, would hope that the free man would use his liberty in accordance with a rational ethic, an ethic derived from a rational study of the objective nature of man. But this plea for rationalism is on a different plane than the wider plea for liberty.

Talk about "living a free life" or "living anarchy" then becomes, at best, meaningless pap. As long as the State exists and has its being, none of us can be totally free; on the other hand, we all enjoy varying degrees of partial freedom, of partial non-molestation. Obviously, the enslaved draftee, for example, enjoys little or no freedom. If we zero in on coercive violence as being the sole obstacle to freedom, then, the hokum about "personal freedom" allows us to bask complacently in our present highly imperfect state. It is dangerously close to the old reactionary view that "the slave is completely free so long as he *knows* he's a slave" – a bromide that has always struck me as being almost obscene in its smugness. The concept of "living free" comes close to being the age-old opium of the intellectual. Over the centuries this is a bromide that has taken many forms: from the Hegelian "freedom is the opportunity to obey the perfect orders of the perfect State" to the present-day "true freedom is exploring your inner feelings." In none of these forms should this cop-out concept be at all palatable to the libertarian.

Take for example the latest Winter 1970 issue of the quarterly RAP, the organ of Rampart College of Los Angeles.

This issue has the advantage over the previous one of featuring a profile of Kathy Forte, who is a lot prettier than the previously featured Dana Rohrabacher (and if this be "sexism", then make the most of it!) But Kathy's "philosophy", as described in the article, seems to consist largely of defining freedom as dancing barefoot on the beach. An estimable activity perhaps - though what do you do with those of us who don't like sand? – but surely having nothing in the world to do with freedom. If Kathy wishes to *define* freedom as dancing on the beach, then us anti-sanders are going to rise up angry in protest; if, on the other hand, she merely wants to use her freedom in this way, well that's fine, but then the whole discussion has been shifted from "freedom" to moral or esthetic philosophy. And the danger is that the freedom-dancing group will come to regard the whole problem of statism and violence as irrelevant and unimportant; for as long as they let you dance on the beach, why worry?

Thus, Kathy states: "There are many external ways to achieve liberation . . . but all of them mean looking very deeply inside yourself. That's where you must find your own spiritual high – without politics, without institutions, without the games designed to keep people cut off from experiencing life." Without politics, fine. But "without institutions"? How can any civilized life be conducted without institutions? And suppose many people don't *want* to "look very deeply inside themselves"? What's wrong with that? Why is it supposed to be our function to pester and harangue them into doing so? Why can't one be a libertarian without "looking deeply"? And what "games" is she talking about? It is easy to sneer at other people's values and life-styles as "games"; if we wished to be nasty, we might even apply such derogatory terms to spending one's life dancing on the sand.

Elsewhere in the article, Kathy indicates that she means such "games" as "power games" and "ego trips" such as are allegedly prevalent in YAF, trips which block one off from "a higher trip called life." But why is Kathy's "life trip" any more moral, any more rational, than the "ego trips" in YAF? I am the last person to leap to the defense of YAF as an institution or as a group of people, but it is not self-evident to me that the desire of YAFers' both to advance their ideals in the world and to advance their personal careers is "anti-life". On the contrary, and setting aside the unfortunate YAF involvement with Republican politics, it strikes me that the YAFers' desire to advance both personal careers and ideals in the world is a lot more moral, a lot more rational, and a lot more attuned to the life of man as a purposive, goal-seeking being, than pirouetting on the seashore.

After all, libertarians, if they have any personal philosophy beyond freedom from coercion, are supposed to be at the very least *individualists*, and if they are individualists they should be heartily in favor of each individual's advancing of his own "ego". What's wrong with ego? and why are libertarians falling into the cultural-New Left trap of denigrating ego and purpose in favor of some sort of cloudy ego-less whim?

There is a basic and important problem here for the libertarian movement. And that is that most libertarians are ex-Randians, and that, after having liberated themselves from the totalitarian and bizarre aspects of the Rand cult, all too many libertarians have tossed over the important core of Aristotelian doctrine: the emphasis on reason and purpose, the cleaving of one's actions to an objective and purpose, the cleaving of one's actions to an objective, rational ethic. Too many libertarians have thrown out the rational baby with the Randian bathwater. And since no man can live with no personal ethic at all, the unfortunate drift has been in the direction of "cultural New Leftism", and all the aimlessness, irrationality, and whim-worship which this doctrine implies.

Thus, for example, in the same issue of RAP, the editors answer a question from a reader about prostitution, and

(Continued on page 5)

Bits And Pieces
By Jerome Tuccille

THE PSYCHOLOGICAL-POLITICAL DICHOTOMY

Much of the confusion concerning the question of whether libertarianism is now a phenomenon of the Left or of the Right can be resolved if we think in terms of Left and Right politics and Left and Right psychology. It is my contention that an individual can be a *psychological* Right Winger and a *political* Leftist, a psychological Leftist with Right Wing politics, or that he can belong psychologically and politically to the same side of the division.

In the broadest sense, Left Wing psychology operates in terms of concretes. Left Wingers are more apt to see the world in its specific reality; they relate directly to sensual experience; they identify with the victims of injustice and therefore have a more naturalistic understanding of what injustice means. Psychological Leftists are more feeling-oriented in the sense that they are more willing to break a philosophical principle to rectify an unjust situation. Even if they *do not believe* in robbing the rich to feed the poor they may be willing to do so if they see someone going hungry. They are also philosophical in that they intellectualize their own attitudes, but they are usually not so bound by philosophical absolutes that they will not break one for the sake of relieving someone else's misery.

The psychological Right Winger, on the other hand, deals more with abstractions. He is also against injustice and on the side of liberty, but he is more likely to become incensed because his theories are not being put into operation than he is because somebody's baby was bitten by a rat. He knows that there is discrimination in the world, that some people are denied decent housing and adequate employment, but he is more annoyed at the "irrationality" of this condition than he is by its real-life effect on human beings. Not only is the psychological Right Winger unconcerned about the specifics of injustice, he may even denounce all sympathy for the misery of others as misguided "altruism."

Both psychological Left Wingers and psychological Rightists can be violently anti-state, but their different psychological attitudes will flavor the nature of their anti-statist motivation. The psychological Leftists will fight the authorities, even to the point of sacrificing their own lives, as long as there is one little pocket of injustice remaining in the world; the efforts of the psychological Rightist will be directed toward securing his own personal freedom and putting his theories into practice if only on a limited scale. The psychology of the Left is primarily *altruistic* and *world-oriented;* that of the Right *selfish* and *ego-oriented.* From this we can see that the psychology of Left and Right can co-exist within the framework of a *Left Wing political* perspective (in the case of anti-establishment radicals), and also within the framework of a *Right Wing political* perspective (in the case of pro-establishment liberals and conservatives).

The great danger inherent in this condition is that the psychological *Right Winger* may abandon his Left Wing political position and align with the political Right *if the going gets too rough.* His doctrinaire selfishness renders his mania for self-preservation paramount over all other considerations, and he may temporarily renew his alliance with his Right Wing political counterpart in a crisis situation. The psychological *Left Winger* runs the risk of being so self-*less* and other-oriented that he will be driven to Left Wing adventurism if his goals are not achieved tomorrow. In other words, the radical movement can be

betrayed on both counts – by the psychological Rightist who will compromise his political principles to save his own neck; by the psychological Left Winger who will adopt suicidal tactics in the cause of his service to humanity.

At its worst, the psychology of the Left rejects reason altogether. It can be so selfless, so other-oriented, so concerned about the happiness of the "general community" that it exhibits little if any understanding of personal interests, the value of self-esteem or even self-regard, or the importance of rational considerations as a guideline for human action. To die rather than to live for one's beliefs takes on heroic proportions. To go to jail is regarded as morally superior to remaining free and struggling for an ideal. So is born the adventurism of the psychological far Left which is every bit as defeatist and destined to failure as the retreatism of the extreme psychological Right.

So it would seem that a mixed psychology is the ideal condition: a mentality that is committed to reason but not to the extent that it begins to regard itself as infallible; a mentality concerned with personal happiness, but not to the extent that it is willing to sacrifice the happiness of others to attain its own ends; a mentality that recognizes good and evil in the world, but not to the point where all others not in agreement with itself are viewed as reincarnations of Beelzebub; a mentality vitally concerned about abstract questions of morality but, again, not to the extent that it is unwilling to re-evaluate the abstract when concrete evidence calls it into question; in brief, a balanced mixture of the ego and the other, the abstract and the concrete.

As for politics? If Left is broadly defined as opposition to an inequitable status quo, and Right as an attempt to preserve and protect an inequitable condition in society, then it is mandatory by any standard of morality to throw one's lot in with the political Left. But the Right sees itself as safeguarding, not inequity, but a just and moral religious and cultural tradition. To my way of thinking, Right Wing politics is justified only in a libertarian or reasonably libertarian society providing a great degree of liberty and justice for all its citizens. The Right Wing sees this condition as already having been largely achieved. It is for each individual to make up his own mind on this subject, to weigh the evidence pro and con and reach his own conclusions.

When the war is over, when all American troops are home, when the institutions of this country are in the hands of the people in the neighborhoods, when there is a semblance of economic and social justice for the myriad groups which constitute this society, it will be time enough to talk about preserving and protecting the status quo. When that day arrives the onus of being a political Right Winger, a custodian of the status quo, will have become, happily enough, a thing of the past.

LIVING FREE – *(Continued from page 4)*

they write that "prostitution is the outgrowth of psychological and political repression, not of freedom", and "we think that free choice would be a liberating force and that most people would seek beauty rather than ugliness." Without discussing the morality of prostitution, we are here on very dangerous waters indeed. What, for example, is "psychological repression"? "Repression" of *what?* Methinks there is underlying these words the cloven hoof of Herbert Marcuse and "left-Freudianism", a doctrine highly fashionable on the Left today but I believe highly pernicious. We have seen in the last couple of years the danger of libertarians catering to anti-libertarian ideologies on the New Left; the same holds true for the catering to the pervasive anti-rationalism of the New Left "counter-culture."

185

Recommended Reading

The Right. There have been several annotated guides to the right-wing, but none so thorough, perceptive, and fair-minded as the new booklet by Ferdinand V. Solara, *58 Key Influences in the American Right* (available for $1.95 from Polifax Press, P. O. Box 20067, Denver, Colo. 80220). Ignore the soggy title; Mr. Solara has done his homework; he has done thorough independent research, as well as eliciting information from the groups and publications involved. Admittedly, he has unavoidable difficulties in defining "right-wing", as well as difficulties with his numerical scale: O for total "1984" government; 10 for zero government and total individual freedom. (Where, for example, would Mr. Solara place anarcho-syndicalists or anarcho-communists?) However, I can have no objections to a scale which, delightfully, places myself and the *Lib. Forum* as the only publication or organization with a 10 rating. We at the *Forum* are proud to accept the accolade. Solara's comments on us are amusing and perceptive, e. g.: "The *Libertarian Forum* . . . is the end-point of the American political spectrum; beyond this, there lies only the static of random noise. Its editor . . . is . . . consistent in his thinking to the point that he frightens 99% of his compatriots on the American Right." Characteristically, *not one* of the other "rightist" outfits mentioned the *Forum* admiringly; however, we may not be loved, but we're feared!

In his questionnaire, Mr. Solara asked each group or publication to list other right-wing groups which it admired or disliked; it is typical of the namby-pamby attitude of most of the groups that very few – excluding, of course, ourselves – could bring themselves to express public antipathy toward any other group.

Mr. Solara divides the American Right into five separate nuclei or sectors, each of which have their separate groupings, central and satellite organizations: the *National Review* group, the Birch Society group, the Liberty Lobby sector, the racist-paramilitary sector, and the admittedly far looser "independent" sector, which is very roughly free-market or libertarian, and among whom we are included. Certainly *Human Events* and probably "Our Peoples Underworld" are better included in the *National Review* than in the Independent sector, but apart from this there are remarkably few errors in the volume. There are important omissions, (e.g. *Modern Age*, Intercollegiate Studies Institute) but but these are probably accounted for by Mr. Solara's policy not to include organizations that did not care to reply to his questionnaire (typically, *The Objectivist* specifically requested that it not be included in the book.) Highly recommended.

Pollution and the Law.

All those interested in the legal defense of property rights against pollution will find indispensable the summary of recent developments in tort liability law by Harvard professor Milton Katz, *The Function of Tort Liability in Technology Assessment* (pamphlet available free from the Harvard University Program on Technology and Society, 61 Kirkland St., Cambridge, Mass. 02138). It becomes clear to the libertarian in the article that the stopping of an invasive nuisance requires more than simple compensation for damages (the Chicagoite solution); it requires also a permanent injunction against continuing invasion. The injunctive proceeding is one of the great legal defenses against invasion of property, and it must be used to the hilt.

Privatizing the Public Sector.

Some of the ways in which "public" activities are being turned over to the infinitely more efficient private sector are summarized in "Creeping Capitalism", *Forbes*

(Sept. 1, 1970). *Forbes* points out that even liberals, fed up with the ever-growing urban mess, are beginning to look with favor on private, market solutions to our problems.

Thus, on police: two-thirds of all the nation's law enforcement officers are now private. And, to those who think it's impossible: "on a typical block of big corporate headquarters buildings in Manhattan . . . it's possible that perhaps 20 different private police forces are working at any one time." Private fire-fighting companies are discussed, including the Rural/Metropolitan Fire Department, a private corporation which has been fighting fire for over two decades in a wide area of Arizona, ranging from large cities to small towns and rural regions.

Education.

Richard F. Schier, "The Problem of the Lumpenprofessoriat", *AAUP Bulletin* (Winter, 1970, $1.50). A blistering critique of the educational Left, especially of the discontented younger faculty, who lead in the debasement of educational standards. Thus, Professor Schier: "it is not surprising that people are drawn to reform who cannot, in their own careers, meet the traditional expectations. For such people the seemingly modest insistence that they have little, if anything, to teach students aside from a narrow and technical specialty. . . has more than a germ of truth. Professionalism *does* require specialization and cerebration and is not well adapted to the heightening of sensory awareness nor sympathetic to what is called, in the modish jargon, nonrational ways of knowing. Hence the drive away from traditional education, with its emphasis on the intellect, to affective education designed to educate the whole man . . . . Nor is the popularity of such innovations with students difficult to understand . . . . The competitiveness of the grading system is unpleasantly demanding, and it is pleasurable to be told that one's emotions are an adequate or perhaps a surer guide to Truth. Scholarship is painful in a way that the eroticization of experience is not." Schier goes on to add that the especial popularity of the new reforms at the "best" colleges is a way of trying to keep down a competitiveness in getting ahead which has always been annoying to Establishments already in power. And the working-class students at the lower-ranking colleges resist these "humanitarian" reforms for the same reason.

Isolationism.

The Wartime Journals of Charles A. Lindbergh (Harcourt, Brace, Jovanovich, $12.95, 1038 pp.) The massive, fascinating pre-war and wartime diaries of a fearless opponent of America's entry into World War II. Particularly interesting is the courage of a moral leader who could not think in terms of the political jungle; hence Lindy's spurning of the opportunity to become the mobilizer of the isolationist forces even after Pearl Harbor. (Note particularly his confrontations with John T. Flynn (541) and Herbert Hoover (546)). The friendly reviews in some liberal journals (e. g. the *New Republic*) of the man for long most hated by liberals indicates a growing willingness to re-evaluate *all* of America's wars.

Economics.

F. A. Hayek, "Three Elucidations of the Ricardo Effect," *Journal of Political Economy* (Mar.-Apr. 1969), pp. 274-85. An important article in which Hayek, returning for the first time in decades to economics, explains how, in Austrian theory, injections of increased money can lead to continuing distortions in relative prices.

John K. Gifford, "Critical Remarks on the Phillips

(Continued on page 7)

RECOMMENDED READING — *(Continued from page 6)*

Curve and the Phillips Hypothesis", *Weltwirschaftliches Archiv* (1969-I), pp. 79-94. A much-welcomed critique of the highly overrated "Phillips curve", which allegedly sets off against each other price changes and unemployment, in inverse ratio.

Journal of Law and Economics (April, 1970). Steven Cheung, "The Structure of a Contract and the Theory of a Non-Exclusive Resource", on property and externalities, particularly as applied to weaknesses of absence of private property rights in the fisheries.

Kenneth G. Elzinga, "Predatory Pricing: the Case of the Gunpowder Trust". A decade ago in the same journal, John S. McGee exploded once and for all the common myth that Rockefeller built his Standard Oil complex on 'predatory price cutting': on deliberately cutting prices below cost, driving out competitors, and finally raising prices. Now, Elzinga does a similar demolition job on the same myth as applied to the Gunpowder Trust at the turn of the twentieth century.

Bernard H. Siegan, "Non-Zoning in Houston". A lengthy, excellent article demonstrating in detail how the absence of all zoning works well in Houston, indeed better than in zoned cities. The aims of zoning are accomplished better through private covenants in real estate contracts, restricting development in the area to certain activities.

Journal of Law and Economics (October, 1970). Yale Brozen's "The Antitrust Task Force Deconcentration Recommendation", taken together with the paper by Eugene M. Singer, "Industrial Organization: Price Models and Public Policy", *American Economic Review, Papers and Proceedings* (May, 1970), provide the most up-to-the minute refutation of the common left-liberal contention that "highly concentrated" industries have higher rates of profit; Brozen and Singer refute the major studies proposing this view.

Negroes and Education. Thomas Sowell, "Colleges are Skipping Over Competent Blacks to Admit 'Authentic' Ghetto Types," *New York Sunday Times Magazine* (Dec. 20). A black free-market economist points to the scandal of university discrimination against competent Negro students, in order to give scholarships to incompetent but politically "in" blacks.

Women's Lib. The counter-revolution against women's lib noted by TIME ("Women's Lib: A Second Look", Dec. 14).

Reprints.

Greenwood Press, Westport Conn., has reprinted the full run of a large number of radical American journals, from 1890 on, and is engaged in the task of doing the same for right-wing magazines. Of particular interest to libertarians is Greenwood's reprint of the entire run of Benjamin R. Tucker's magnificent *Liberty*, all 17 volumes, bound, 1881-1908, with an introduction by Prof. Herbert Gutman. The price, unfortunately, is a prohibitive $545.00, but we understand that *Liberty* will soon be available for something like one-tenth the cost on microfiche.

Greenwood Press has also reprinted the following books: George L. Anderson, ed., *Issues and Conflicts* (1959). A forgotten but important book of revisionist essays, brought together by the William Volker Fund. Particularly good are the essays by William Neumann on China, Alfred M. Lilienthal on the Middle East, Louis Martin Sears on Revisionism, Roland Stromberg on "collective security", and Richard N. Current on the Kellogg Pact. Price: $15.25.

Harry Elmer Barnes, ed., *Perpetual War for Perpetual Peace* (1953). Long out of print, this is a classic, the last great work of World War II revisionism, especially on Pearl Harbor, and including Harry Barnes' blast against the "historical blackout." Also includes excellent articles on early Cold War Revisionism by George Lundberg, William L. Neumann. Includes articles by Tansill, Sanborn, Morgenstern, Greaves. Price: $19.50.

Charles A. Beard, *The Devil Theory of War* (1936). An important between-the-wars work of revisionism. Price: $8.25.

Charles Vevier, *The United States and China, 1906-1913* (1955). A Williamsite revisionist view of U. S. imperialism and the quest for investments in China. Ranks with McCormick in applying the Williams view to Asia. Price: $10.75.

187

ON WOMEN'S LIBERATION – (Continued from page 3)

economic and sociological nature. Those women who did not have a natural comparative advantage for the performance of housework would flow into the labor force, creating an immediate spur to production. At the same time, millions of new jobs would be opened up in the rapidly expanding fields of commercial child care, janitorial contracting, production of ready-to-wear clothing and ready-to-eat foods, manufacture of labor-saving appliances, and so forth. As soon as these services became widely available (many of them at reduced cost because of the opportunity to exploit economies of scale) women would no longer have to duck in and out of the labor force every time a child arrived, or of necessity hold only part-time jobs. Employers would immediately recognize this, and drop their reluctance to put female employees through expensive managerial and on-the-job training programs. The next generation, fully accustomed to female bus drivers and bank presidents, and to male secretaries and school teachers, would grow up without the occupational stereotypes of our present society which the Women's Liberationists find so unnecessary and artificial.

Of course, the full liberation of women would require a few other changes in addition to tax reform. Needless to say, all of the misguidedly paternalistic laws designed to "protect" the "weaker sex" by barring females from certain lines of employment, or limiting their hours of work, would have to be written off the books. The cultural adjustment of the younger generation would be facilitated by replacing public with private education, so that women would not be forced to send their children to schools where the curriculum, dictated by male-chauvinist boards of education, shunted little girls into home-ec classes, and little boys into wood working and machine shop. The institution of marriage would have to be put on a truly contractual basis, that is to say, restrictions on the scope, nature, and duration of marriage contracts would have to be abolished. This would open the way for experimentation with fixed-term marriages, various forms of alimony and child support clauses or none at all, homosexual marriages for both sexes, and assorted communal, multi-lateral, interlocking, or even Heinleinian chain marriages.

So you see, beneath the phantasmagoria of RAT and SCUM, there is something to the idea of Women's Liberation after all, for the plight of women in our society is but a specific manifestation of the *general* lack of liberation. As in the case of blacks, migrant workers, soldiers, and hippies, the left has once again pointed out to us one of the multiple projecting tips of the huge iceberg of statist repression. The leftists, not knowing that all of these visible sore points of society are connected underneath to a common mass, think that the iceberg can be done away with by cutting off the tips, but we libertarians know that this would have the effect only of making another, probably larger part of the iceberg rise to the surface at another point!

How easy it is to expose the Women's Lib radicals for what they are, a group of pudding-headed, slogan-chanting neo-amazons, but this is only half the task which libertarians must undertake. We must go beyond this to include a Women's Liberation plank in our general program, to use the Women's Lib issue as an opening for libertarian agitation and propaganda, and to hammer, hammer, hammer in the point that no single oppressed group will be free until all men are free, living in a society where repression is abolished and the free market is triumphant!

--Edwin G. Dolan

TAKE OFF – (Continued from page 1)

An important consequence of the Buckley column is the keen interest promptly taken in the whole affair by the highly influential "Op-Ed" page of the New York *Times* – the new forum for opinion and controversy opposite the *Times*' daily editorial page. On January 28, the *Times* published a blistering reply to Buckley by Jerry Tuccille, "A Split in the Right Wing". At this writing, it is scheduled to publish a follow-up column by myself, further attacking Buckley and expounding the libertarian philosophy in the issue of Feb. 9, to be followed perhaps by further comments from Buckley and Karl Hess.

Libertarianism is the new rage, and it is incumbent upon all of us to strike while the iron is hot; in this receptive atmosphere to push the creed in book, article, lecture, radio and TV. Let us seize the opportunity to expand the cause. One of the revelations of this new atmosphere is the friendly interest in us by liberals of all persuasions, in and out of the media. Fifteen, twenty years ago, the liberals, if they heard of us at all, considered us as more extreme, more evil, than the conservatives. Now, however, seeing our devotion to peace, freedom from conscription, decentralization, and civil liberties, the liberals realize that, from their point of view, we are much better than conservatives, and, indeed, almost allies. There are two factors at work here: the "tactical" political insight that we can be useful allies to the liberals in whacking the conservatives; and, more deeply, the realization by very many liberals that there is something profoundly wrong with the Leviathan State they have wrought upon us since the New Deal, and that maybe these libertarians are in some way on the correct path out of our contemporary troubles. In any case, now that libertarianism is having its day in the sun, may we prove as adept at taking advantage of the opportunities for success as we have been in years of slogging through the ideological wilderness.

The Libertarian Forum
BOX 341
MADISON SQUARE STATION
NEW YORK, NEW YORK 10010

Published Every Month. Subscription Rate: $7.00 Per Year.

A Monthly Newsletter

THE
Libertarian Forum

Joseph R. Peden, Publisher   *March*   Murray N. Rothbard, Editor

VOLUME III, NO. 2   ~~February~~ 1971   75¢

TAKEOFF II

The past month has seen a ballooning, an expanding, a veritable wonderment of publicity for the libertarian movement. For the first time in my life, I meet average intellectuals: in colleges, in TV studies, in the press, who are extremely sympathetic toward and interested in the libertarian doctrine. Libertarians are literally popping up everywhere, and the chances are large that the next intellectual or opinion-moulder you meet will either consider himself a libertarian or at least be interested in the idea. The basic reason seems to be the failure of Liberalism, a failure evident to all but the most obtuse liberals. After all, Liberals have been in power for nearly forty years, and what they have wrought has been the Frankenstein's Monster of Presidential war and dictatorship, the war in Vietnam, and the Leviathan government, the military-industrial complex, and big bureaucracy at home. And so many Liberals are ripe for a way out. The New Left, to the extent that it still exists, has become Stalinist and crazed; the conservatives, with their devotion to Throne, Altar, and the Big Bomb are out of the question. So who does that leave as the new road to salvation? Us!

The current tidal wave of publicity was touched off by Chairman Bill's overreaction to the Lehr-Rossetto piece in the New York Sunday Times magazine section, as noted in our last month's editorial. The momentum might have died with Buckley's snide and bitchy column of Jan. 14; but Jerry Tuccille, having been sneered at by Buckley as a "semi-literate gentleman", was provoked into belting out an attack on The Chairman, which he simply sent in to the New York *Times* remarkably influential Op-Ed section (the new page of the daily *Times* opposite the editorial page which is devoted to lively controversy and challenging ideas.) The editors liked the Tuccille piece, and printed it on Jan. 28: "A Split in the Right Wing." Jerry pointed out that Buckley's anti-libertarian hysteria was prompted by the fact that, with the Times article by Lehr-Rossetto, the libertarian-conservative split on the Right has at last received nationwide publicity, thereby eroding Chairman Bill's much-coveted power base.

The Op-Ed editors then asked me to follow up Tuccille's piece with a philosophic statement of what this new libertarianism is all about; and this was printed as "The New Libertarian Creed" in the *Times* of Feb. 9. I pointed out the evil influence of *National Review* in converting the old Taft-era right-wing from a roughly libertarian, individualist, and isolationist creed to the present crusade for extirpating Communists at home and abroad, and apologia for Big Government at home, both of which we have come to know so well. I also briefly outlined the libertarian philosophy as resting on two basic axioms: the absolute right of every individual to "self-ownership", to the ownership of his own body; and the right to own all virgin resources that the individual finds and transforms by his personal energy. From these two axioms can be derived the entire system of property rights, freedom of contract and bequest, and free-market economy. I also pointed out that the conservative's revered "law and order" really means the coercive dictation of the State, the historic harbinger of disorder and aggression, an aggression against person and property which it habitually commits through the robbery of taxation, the enslavement of conscription, and the mass murder of war. I ended by pointing out that libertarians are in the historic American tradition of Jefferson, Paine, Jackson, and Garrison; and that in contrast, James Burnham, in a recent *National Review* (Dec. 1) called for a new Bismarck for America and for a re-evaluation of fascism. Accompanying the article were pictures of Mencken, Jefferson, and Robert Taft.

The "New Libertarian Creed" was then placed into the *Congressional Record* (Feb. 24, pp. S1888-S1889) by Senator Mark Hatfield (R., Ore.) Senator Hatfield declared: "One of the unique and well articulated new philosophies on the political scene is libertarianism. Although it claims a long history, it has not received much public attention until rather recently. Its proponents vary in their intellectual histories, coming to this point of view via the right wing of the Republican Party on one extreme and from the New Left on the other." Hatfield then proceeded to read my article into the Record as a "most comprehensive and concise presentation of this perspective."

Buckley wound up the exchange with his "The Conservative Reply", *New York Times* (Feb. 16). The article was a typical Buckley performance: a series of catty *ad hominem* smears and misrepresentations, carefully avoiding the substantive issues. One gets the impression, indeed, that Buckley has ceased to think at least a decade ago, so caught up is he in his career as the rich man's insult-comic (although somehow less lovable than Jack E. Leonard).

As usual Buckley rings the changes: first, on the Karl Hess comparison of Beria and J. Edgar Hoover. As usual, Chairman Bill misses the point. It was not that Karl claimed

(Continued on page 2)

Notice To Subscribers

Because of the imminent rate increase in postage the subscription price of the Libertarian Forum will be $8.00 per year.

The Libertarian Forum will soon resume its former twice-monthly publication schedule in response to reader reaction.

TAKEOFF II — *(Continued from page 1)*

that Hoover is as bad a character as Beria; the point Karl was making was that *in one sense* at least, Soviet Russia is more democratic than the United States: that they managed to depose the head of their secret police, whereas we are apparently unable to do so. An astute and witty point. And then, once more, for the 858th time, there is me and lighthouses. It should be clear to the most superficial reader of mine and Buckley's writings, that he and his cohorts have devoted at least twenty times as much space to the lighthouse question as I ever have. Bill Buckley may consider socialized lighthouses to be one of the burning questions of our time, but I certainly do not.

In his article, in fact, Buckley affirms that the State does good as well as bad things, but the only positive example he can point to are those lighthouses again. One begins to wonder what accounts for Chairman Bill's strange obsession with lighthouses? Setting aside with reluctance the possible Freudian interpretation, we are left with the thought that Mr. Buckley is very anxious to keep coercing landlubbing taxpayers into donating free light to his beloved sailboat – a true example of the "welfare state" in action, and surely a worthy reason for abandoning the free market.

Bill, I'm willing to make a trade: if you'll give up the Cold War and the war in Southeast Asia, I'll let you have your beloved socialized lighthouses, and may Social Darwinism work its way on your boat!

Buckley tries to defend himself against my charge of statism by wheeling into position four distinguished free-market economists, "whose intellectual fortress continues to be National Review." The problem is that of those he mentions, one (Wilhelm Ropke) has been dead for years, another (Ludwig von Mises) has never written for his magazine, and a third (F. A. Hayek) broke with the magazine many years ago, vigorously denouncing Bill Buckley for his tasteless implication after the death of Dag Hammerskjold in an airplane crash that the latter had been cheating at cards. Buckley's reply to Hayek was typical of his aristocratic taste and refinement: tossing off his remark as a *jeu d'idee* and implying that Hayek was not familiar enough with the English language to appreciate the Buckleyite wit. That leaves only Henry Hazlitt, who writes but seldom for *National Review* in any case.

Again for the umpteenth time, Buckley repeats Hazlitt's charge that I am an "extreme a priorist", a charge coming with ill grace from Henry, since the methodology of his own and his mentor Mises' economics is precisely "extreme a priorism." In the only piece of reasoning in his article, Buckley again gets matters completely mixed up: presuming to link me with the "extreme a priorist" view that every landowner owns the heavens up till infinity, Buckley conveniently ignores the fact that this is diametrically contrary to my own "homesteading" theory of property. On the contrary, it is his and Hazlitt's presumably sensible and non-extremist common law that takes this admittedly absurd position. And so it goes, a farrago of smear, error, and clouding of substantive issues.

It might have struck some of Buckley's readers that there was one curious omission in his pantheon of free-market economists: Professor Milton Friedman. Undoubtedly because even such a sober, conservative and Establishment economist as Friedman has been read out of the movement by Buckley for *his* kooky, "frivolous", and extremist defense of free trade, legalized narcotics, and freedom for prostitution. In fact, it becomes ever clearer that *any* theorist who does not fit in cozily and completely as a champion of the *status quo* will be denounced by Chairman Bill for frivolity and absolutism.

It is clear that the conservatives are hurting from the libertarian upsurge, otherwise Buckley would not be devoting so much valuable space to our continuing excommunication.

Sure enough, on Feb. 23, *National Review* returned to the attack with a malicious editorial, "Serving Their Times". Stooping to the very conspiracy view of history for which Buckley once read the Birchers out of the movement, *N. R.* asserts that the evil liberal New York *Times* has entered into a conspiracy with me and other libertarians to do the *Times'* "dirty work" in attacking conservatism. Well, well! And, terrible thing, we were *paid* for this work by the *Times*, "with its offer of the check and the space to frolic in." Buckley's fulmination that we are all paid agents of the *Times* runs up against a few cold facts: (1) that the *Times* slipped badly enough in its conspiratorial work to give Buckley rather than myself or any other libertarian the last word in the dispute, thereby allowing his smears and innuendos to remain unanswered. (2) that the *Times* magazine recently did a laudatory story on the Buckley family without visible protest from the chairman. (3) that the amount of money all of us received from the Times is as nothing compared to the money which Chairman Bill receives, day in and day out, for his regular column in the ultra-Liberal *New York Post*. Who's selling out to whom, Mr. Chairman? To cap the irony, Buckley conveniently forgets how Lehr and Rossetto came to write their article in the *Times*, which touched off the entire furor. They came to the *Times'* attention for their ardent work for Buckley for Senate in last fall's campaign!

Here we must record a refreshing interlude in the Buckleyite snake pit. William F. Rickenbacker, former editor of *National Review* and libertarian economist, has a letter in the March 9 issue of *N. R.*, gently but firmly reproving one Witonski for his Buckleyite review of my *Power and Market*. This break in the N. R. monolith of hostility to liberty must be chalked up to the fact that the magazine could hardly refuse to print a letter from one of its former editors.

Turning to more pleasant matters, the next piece of scintillating publicity for our cause came in an organ which hardly fits the pattern of liberal conspiracy. The widely-read weekly, the *National Observer*, published a lengthy, amusing, sprightly, and perceptive article on the libertarian movement in its issue of March 1. The article by James R. Dickenson, "Abolish Government", takes up the entire coveted upper half of the front page of the issue, and spills over to a large part of an inside page. Other subtitles in the Dickenson article are: "Down with all Governments!", and "Own Your Own Road, Hire Your Own Police". Dickenson did a great deal of work on the article, as is evident from the contents, and he is perceptive enough to base his summaries of the libertarian position on lengthy interviews and quotes from myself, Leonard Liggio, Jerome Tuccille, and Karl Hess – and is also astute enough to perceive the differences between Karl and the rest of the movement. Generally a delightful article, highlighted by an amusing front-page cartoon on the movement, depicting a group of Breughel-like libertarians with swords aloft, blindfolded, carrying flags upside-down, and dancing around an eagle tied to the stake.

Another important contribution to the recent publicity on libertarianism is the March 1 issue of WIN, the semi-monthly journal of the pacifist War Resisters' League (30¢ per copy, $5.00 per year, available from 339 Lafayette St., New York, N. Y. 10012.) Virtually the entire issue is devoted to "right-wing libertarianism." The lead is an article by myself, "Know Your Rights", the most comprehensive survey to date of the libertarian movement – who we are, and what are the different positions in the libertarian spectrum. The article first outlines the central core of the libertarian creed, and then goes on to a description and critique of the positions of FEE, the Randian movement, the neo-Randians, Robert LeFevre, the California and Hawaii movements, the development of SIL and RLA, the split within RLA, and the emergence of the
(Continued on page 8)

190

Facing Bureaucracy

BY NORMAN H. CROWHURST

But when a long train of abuses and usurpations, pursuing invariably the same Object, evinces a design to reduce them under absolute Despotism, it is their right, it is their duty, to throw off such government, and to provide new Guards for their future security.

--Declaration of Independence.

To me, for whom the "long train" has extended over nearly 20 years, that particular sentence of the Declaration of Independence, as well as the mechanism by which "mankind are more disposed to suffer, while the evils are sufferable, than to right themselves by abolishing the forms to which they are accustomed," has come to have very real meaning.

Only when I was faced with a choice of what crime I should elect to commit at the instigation of a government agent, for which I, not he, would be punishable, did I finally realize that something is very, very wrong in America.

But let me start at the beginning, for my story will show how almost imperceptibly freedom can be encroached upon – just as others may have experienced it, with the difference that encroachment on mine was pushed further than the average citizen's, for reasons that will emerge from my story.

My career, a highly successful one, started in England before World War 2. I was chief engineer of a leading electronics company, not long after 'electronics' was prevalently explained as 'an outgrowth of radio, which is an outgrowth of electricity'! At the same time I was senior lecturer at two of London's colleges, with responsibility for curriculum coordination between districts.

World War 2 resulted in concentrating my attention on the electronic communications equipment needed to win the war. After the war, bureaucracy raised its ugly head very quickly in Britain, making life quite difficult. After countless frustrations with the socialist government, the Land of Opportunity attracted my attention, and my wife and I emigrated in 1953.

Because my reputation preceded me I found work easily – in fact I had a choice. The first selection was a job with Fairchild Recording, developing multi-track sound to go with the then-new wide-screen movies. Fairchild also had government contracts to develop systems for the armed services, which had been "my bag' in my native England.

This was where I should have been alerted that trouble was brewing, but perhaps America was too new for me to see the trend. I was precluded from this development work, because (a) I was not yet an American citizen, and (b) I did not possess security clearance. However, with my reputation, I encountered no difficulty finding other work.

After a little more than a year with Fairchild, I left full-time employ with that company, continued as a consultant to do work permitted to me, and extended my consulting clientele elsewhere. Being precluded from government-connected projects created "no sweat" for the time being.

From 1958 to 1961, one of my major clients was CBS Laboratories in Stamford, Connecticut. The Labs had a similar mix of work to that at Fairchild, part for consumer or industrial application, part for government contracts. However, several times engineers working on a particular government contract intimated that they would like to consult me about what they were doing, but were not permitted to do so.

In 1961, the CBS executive made a decision that affected me seriously: the Labs were to do no work except that 'covered' by government contracts. However, a coincidence gave me one more job before our association terminated. The classified job about which the engineers had wanted to consult me became declassified by being authorized as operational. It was called "NetAlert."

So my final job was writing the operating manual for NetAlert. As an engineer, I could not resist asking why they adopted somewhat inefficient ways of designing certain parts of the system. Then I learned that these places were precisely where they could have used my services. I found it a little frustrating to describe a system that I could easily have improved upon, when it was 'frozen' – all I could do was describe it.

During the late 50s and early 60s, I received several work offers for which I was highly qualified – both the people offering and I knew that – but when they learned that I had no clearance record, they sought other means of getting the work done – or else forgot about the contract opportunity altogether.

The reason for this reaction was simple. Obtaining clearance for a person of foreign birth (even if he eventually gets it) takes about 18 months. Such contracts are open for competitive bid between different companies. So a company cannot make a bid contingent on perhaps securing the services of a man necessary to its fulfilment, when that "perhaps" cannot be resolved for 18 months hence.

So I continued to work in areas that avoided this problem. However, I began to realize that my work opportunities were dwindling, as the government extended its activities into more and more fields, under one pretext or another. I have received dozens of letters from newly-formed government agencies, asking for personnel recommendations, to fill vacancies for which I was qualified, but "need not apply" for this reason.

In 1960 my wife and I became citizens. We liked what we learned, in studying about our new country. The Declaration of Independence and the Constitution of the United States made a lot of sense to us, and we identified very readily with the principles there enunciated. Citizenship should be a step toward solving what was obviously looming as a problem.

In 1962, I started renewing my interest in education, and to further this, I wrote to England to obtain written confirmation about my career there. That was when I discovered that the Department Head under whom I did most of my work could not obtain written verification, because all records of my schooling and teaching work before World War 2 were destroyed by enemy action during the war.

Complicating my problem was the Englishman's typical attitude, "Don't those stupid Americans know we had a war here? Why should they insist on us producing documents that no longer exist?" I had letters explaining the situation from people who knew me – wouldn't that be enough for anyone?

In 1962, something else began, that promised to help. I received a letter typed on plain paper, with a Virginia address, and signed 'Earl Holliman.' He wrote to ask me some technical questions, which I answered, as I did all letters from readers of my books and articles. Next came a letter on the stationery of the U. S. Joint Chiefs of Staff, identifying Earl Holliman as a Colonel in that service, thanking me for my information and asking more questions.

To cut a long story short, in 1964, Colonel Holliman asked if I would be prepared for retention by the U. S. Army Security Agency as a consultant, for which a relatively low order of security clearance was needed. As a possible door to resolve my growing problem, I readily agreed.

As a precaution, I mentioned the difficulty in verifying certain parts of my record in England, but was told to submit this application, that this need not prevent my

(Continued on page 4)

FACING BUREAUCRACY — *(Continued from page 3)*

securing clearance. So I filed some forms in quintuplicate and recieved notification they had been received: I should know the result in about 6 months.

But about 3 months later, I received a letter with another, much larger bunch of forms, saying the requirements for clearance had changed, would I please complete these? It did not occur to me at the time that the reason for a change in requirements might be because they had changed the clearance being sought for me – nothing was said about that. I just assumed this was still the same application.

I did not receive a response until over 2 years from my original application: clearance denied. No reason given, and a letter asking for explanation received the answer that reasons could not be given as a matter of "national security."

During this time, while my reputation continued to expand, my work opportunities continued to contract: more people would ask me to undertake something, then withdraw the offer when the security problem was mentioned. They apparently assumed that anyone with my background would have "picked up" security clearance somewhere along the way. When they found I had not, they dropped me like the proverbial hot potato: to even discuss anything with me could be "dangerous" for them.

So when I got this freeze-out letter, I wrote to Senator Wayne Morse, who tried to elicit some information from the U. S. Army Security Agency, as unsuccessfully as I had myself. After Senator Hatfield was elected to office, I wrote to him; he tried again, with more success.

The answer he obtained was that there were 3 reasons why I had been refused clearance: (1) my wife's parents were not American citizens, being British by birth, and having lived, worked and now retired, in their native England; (2) my records could not be verified satisfactorily; and (3) they could trace no details of my pre-World-War-2 associations, either those I mentioned in my application, or any others. They made it quite clear that there was no suspicion that I might have had 'undesirable' associations. On the other hand, there was no evidence that I had not.

About this time, Bob Packwood defeated Wayne Morse as Senator from Oregon, and Bob became interested in my case. He took up the matter, and as a result of his representations in my behalf, the first and third reasons were withdrawn, but on the second the agency remained adamant: they must have access to original written documents; no affidavits and no copies of information that I had in my possession would be acceptable as evidence of my career back there.

Now, the reason given for this rigid requirement was the relatively high order of security clearance being sought. For lesser levels, the requirement might not be so stringent.

What had happened? Where did my clearance application get "upped" in level? What was that change in forms, about 3 months after my initial application? A piece of news about a year later gave me a clue as to a possible, but I hoped improbable, reason, but I tried to pursue the possibility anyway.

This was when the dispute about deployment of ABMs first came up. I read one small news item suggesting that there was doubt about the effectiveness of the weapon, and that it had never been tested, even on a simulated interception. So I wrote to ask about this and the only responses I could get were assertions that all kinds of "experts" had "testified."

Some time later a conservative group solicited my support for lobbying for the ABM. So I wrote to this group to question its validity as a weapon, saying that I believe we vitally need such a weapon, if we could be sure it works. In reply this group sent me a booklet, issued by the American Security Council, prepared by a committee of 31 experts.

The names of the 31 experts are listed. They include not a single person competent to judge the question I have persistently asked, and concerning which I certainly could answer, IF I had the facts. In the book's 72 pages, less than one page is devoted to the objection, "It Won't Work," in which my question is not even mentioned.

The main argument of the book is that deploying ABMs is a matter of military strategy. No argument about that. But I suggest that if the enemy should obtain reliable information that the weapon does not work, the strategy is not very strong! Which brings me to my question, and its relation to my security clearance application.

For an ABM to successfully intercept an incoming enemy ICBM, it needs four essential parts:

1. A warhead capable of destroying the incoming ICBM when it meets it.

2. A propulsion system (rocket) capable of thrusting it up into space fast enough to effect the interception at a safe distance before the ICBM's intended arrival here.

3. A steering mechanism capable of ensuring that the ABM does actually intercept the ICBM.

4. An electronic guidance system, capable of receiving data about the course of the ICBM, and correcting its own course to ensure that the steering mechanism does its job of intercepting properly.

The panel of experts address themselves to the first three requirements, but not to the fourth, and no expert on the panel is competent to judge this. Nor has the ABM been tested.

The layman has no way of knowing what is involved, so he tends to trust the experts. Congressmen are laymen, in this sense. But the communists have people who are not laymen in this field. Of that you can be sure!

Let me explain the problem this way: can you fire a gun to "shoot down" a bullet coming toward you? The best gunman alive (or dead) has never attempted this. Bullets travel faster than sound, at about 1000 mph. ICBMs travel through space at from 3 to 10 times the speed of a bullet, and any ABM that can intercept them must travel at least at an equal speed.

Presumably this possibility has been verified under item 2 above. And presumably item 3, the capability of steering precisely enough to hit head-on at a cumulative speed of approaching 20,000 mph has been verified too. What has not been verified is the electronic system that can direct the steering so it actually DOES that.

Electronic systems can be designed to function in millionths of a second. But in a millionth of a second, these two objects, the ICBM and the ABM, will be approaching one another by a distance of more than 100 feet. And if their courses miss one another by 100 feet, they miss one another, period!

If the electronic system reacts only a millionth of a second slow, or over-reacts in a way equivalent to a millionth of a second fast, no hit! And if the system is designed that way – which has not been checked, either way – the possibilities of an "accidental hit" are not even as good as the possibility of your shooting down a bullet speeding toward you.

The notion that a sheer quantity of such defense will prevent some of the mass of enemy ICBMs getting through – the pepper-pot theory – is sheer nonsense, in this context. How many bullets would you have to fire off to stop the other man's bullet hitting you, "by accident"?

That is the key question, now how do I connect this with my security clearance application? One of the jobs about which I gave information was with a technical school where I wrote the very first textbook published about Electronic Navigational Aids and Guidance Systems, right after World War 2.

I did not name the book in my application, because I have more than 40 books and close to 1000 magazine and journal articles published, so it seemed pointless to attempt to

(Continued on page 5)

FACING BUREAUCRACY — *(Continued from page 4)*

list them. But one of the first things the investigators would learn, on checking my work at that job, would be that I wrote that book, which is still used as a text.

Realizing this I began to see why my clearance application was apparently uprated. Somebody saw that I could be useful to check the ABM guidance system, unaware that somebody else in the bureaucracy had reasons for not wanting it checked!

This was affirmed later, when I met another electronic engineer, a native-born American, with capabilities similar to my own, who had also been invited to apply for clearance, and been refused in a similar way, although he had no basis for determining why he was refused.

Now put these items together: the only thing not checked about the ABM is that item 4, which is vital – and nobody competent to do that has been retained as an expert. Two people with that competence (to my knowledge – there may be more) have been invited to apply for clearance, and both have been inexplicably refused.

Had I been asked to check the design, even if I could find no fault in the theoretical design, I would want to see it tested on an actual simulated intercept mission: it is too easy to be a microsecond "off" here or there. Such a test has never been conducted either. Some experts with no knowledge of this kind of system have declared it will work, and that no test is necessary!

In my own case, the reason finally given for refusing clearance, and stated with adamance as an unbendable "rule," is the one that I was told at the beginning did not matter – loss of prewar records. Had there truly been such a rule, I should have been so informed, to save unnecessary application and processing at taxpayer expense. Obviously, this "reason" was invented after the event. What other explanation is possible? And why the "need" to invent such a "rule"?

While uncovering this basis for the peculiar action – and this issue seems too hot for anyone to tackle – portends ill for our country's future, the problems that the action itself has created for me personally are no small ones either.

During that same period, in an endeavor to break the growing impasse, at my own expense I developed a new circuit principle which became the subject of a U. S. patent in 1967. This cost me a great deal of my own resources, and I produced a convincing demonstration of its effectiveness. Its first major application would be in high power sound projection, for which any company wanting to develop it would seek government support, for application by army, navy or airforce.

As soon as the patent was issued, several companies contacted me about it, hoping I would work with them as consultant on its development with some arrangement to our mutual benefit. As such a possibility was based on an enquiry from a government agency, one question inevitably asked was, did I have security clearance? Upon learning my status, the matter was promptly dropped. So I have invested thousands of dollars, plus a few years of my time, in something that government bureaucracy is effectively prohibiting from further development, because of their other decision.

In 1967 I encountered yet another severe setback. Much of my income, as other sources receded, had been from my books and articles. But that year proved a bad one, for several distributors went bankrupt, returning their stocks of books to the publishers for refund or credit. This resulted in reverse royalties that wiped out my income that year. Actually, this was a cancellation of a large part of my 1966 income, and should be treatable as such.

But the Internal Revenue Service refused to accept this

explanation, and insisted that I pay tax based on my cancelled earnings, even when I had no actual income. I was living on loans from the bank to support future work, and by advances from publishers, also against future work. The IRS agent was not satisfied: I must negotiate more contracts with advances, for work I could not possibly do, and then declare bankruptcy, when I had "found" that I could not fulfil the contracts.

He made some other suggestions, each of which was equally dishonest, if not outright illegal. He also told me that it was fruitless to appeal his decision, since I had already written to the Commissioner of Internal Revenue in Washington, as a result of which letter (and a few more) he was visiting me.

I managed, at the time, to get a further loan to pay the immediate tax he demanded, partly because he threatened that if I did not, and if I did not sign a completely false statement of my financial position that he wrote for me to sign, he could seize all my property, including my technical library, thus preventing me from even fulfilling the contracts I had already signed.

The following year, I retained a tax accountant to prepare my return. Then I found that, not only do I not get any refund for income extracted as return against previous years, but when I repay the loans I obtained to carry on living, these are also taxable as further income! I am being taxed several times over. The only offset to make it possible for me to live is to have the accountant fill in all kinds of deductions I could not possibly have paid to anyone, to which I put my signature on the 1040 form.

This was when I reread the Declaration of Independence and the Constitution of the United States and saw the light. Twice already I had been coerced into perjury: this must stop. The only way was to refuse to cooperate at all. Putting anything on that form committed me, and there was no legal way I could make a true return.

Somewhere around this time I learned about Leonard Read and the Foundation for Economic Education, and about Willis Stone's Liberty Amendment. When I made the decision to quit allowing myself to be forced into perjury, and to stand upon the Constitution, as we had undertaken to do when we took the oath as citizens, I wrote to Leonard Read. His response was that he would not refuse to pay taxes in any way whatever, unless he was ready to start a revolution, which he was not! Did I have any choice?

I also attended a "tax revolt" meeting organized by the Liberty Amendment people. They urged me to support their cause – at a time when I could not afford a penny to support anything! Willis Stone himself told me, when I tried to explain my position, that I must pay my taxes first, and then support his movement to get taxes repealed: that was the democratic way, he told me. When I asked him what I could use for money, first to pay impossible taxes on fictional income that I did not even have, then to support his program, he did not understand and said I must obey the law. He could not seem to understand that I had been given no possible way of obeying the law: my choice was only how I must choose to disobey it!

That was about the time when I realized the full import of those words in the Declaration of Independence that I put at the head of this article. I wrote a 10-page statement, setting this forth, sent a copy with my blank, but signed 1040 form, to the IRS, with copies to President Nixon, our two Senators and the District congressman.

It is high time that we did just what the words that head this article say. It is our right and our duty. But we sure have to be pushed, before we realize it!

∎

"War is the statesman's game, the priest's delight, The lawyer's jest, the hired assassin's trade." --- Percy Bysshe Shelley.

IN DEFENSE OF NON-ROMANTIC LITERATURE

BY JEROME TUCCILLE

It should be self-evident that there is something seriously amiss with the literary views of someone who regards Mickey Spillane as one of the great writers of our time, but this apparently is not the case. A growing number of libertarians are now entering society with erroneous ideas about the great body of literature that pre-dates the publication of *The Fountainhead*. It is almost ironic that these New Intellectuals, who are so far advanced in the fields of economics and philosophy, are almost passionately illiterate when it comes to the subject of literature. They have accepted the literary pronouncements of Ayn Rand at face value without bothering to explore them as deeply as they have her more abstract theories, and they are willing to champion publicly the literary tradition of Victor Hugo — Ayn Rand — Mickey Spillane even as they challenge Randian political concepts.

This article is an attempt to add more balance to the *Objectivist Inheritance*. In the last year or two many Objectivists have abandoned the trappings of classical liberalism for the more consistent doctrine of political anarchism (thanks in large part to the hortatory talents of Roy Childs). Now these same Objectivists who have had the independence of mind to break officially from the papal aspects of Randianism ought to look more closely at her views regarding literature.

In her article, "What is Romanticism? (Part 1)," appearing in the May, 1969 issue of *The Objectivist*, Rand cites the following "Romantic" novelists as belonging to the "top rank" in the literary hierarchy: Victor Hugo, Dostoevsky, Henryk Sienkiewicz in *Quo Vadis*, Nathaniel Hawthorne in *The Scarlet Letter*; and among "Romantic" Playwrights, Schiller and Rostand. Later in the same article she blames "Naturalistic" tendencies for the "breakup of Romanticism." She lists H. G. Wells, Jules Verne and Sinclair Lewis as being among the "better-known" Naturalists (as far as characterization is concerned) and the best that Naturalism has to offer, which is of course many notches below that of even the mediocre Romantics. For contemporary examples of the best authors in the "simplified, more obvious" Romantic School she names: Mickey Spillane, Ian Fleming and Donald Hamilton, all mystery-pulp writers (Part 2 of the same article, *The Objectivist*, June, 1969).

The "destroyer of Romanticism was", predictably enough, "the altruist morality." Again in the same article she compares Naturalism with journalism, the mere recording of "real life" events and characters, and she vilifies Balzac, Tolstoy and Zola as the archetypical practitioners of this accursed art. They dealt with "stolen concepts", "social determinism", and their values are "concrete-bound." Apparently there are wide gaps in the Rand's reading background for she makes no mention at all of English and American literary giants of the late-nineteenth and early-twentieth centuries: Hardy, Galsworthy, Maugham, Sherwood Anderson, Fitzgerald, Hemingway, Steinbeck, Waugh, and others. This is a serious omission and necessarily belongs in any valid discussion of the nature of literature.

In rebutting her thesis, it has unfortunately become necessary to state the obvious: Ayn Rand to the contrary, Naturalism and journalism are not to be confused. There is a world of difference between a realistic accounting of last night's riot in a daily newspaper and a Naturalistic portrayal of the quality of life in a given society at a given time by an accomplished novelist. The novelist brings a depth of insight to his subject matter which a journalist may not possess. Those journalists who do have this incisiveness of mind   usually graduate into novelists, a la Hemingway.

The best literature usually combines good Naturalism with good Romantic values — that is, a superb rendering of what it was like to live in a certain place at a certain time, along with a moral message which will aid the reader in his own quest for values to live by. The element that makes *We The Living* a better novel than *Atlas Shrugged* is Miss Rand's gripping and Naturalistic account of what it was like to be in Leningrad, circa 1920s, when the revolution had already been betrayed by power-lusting bureaucrats, combined with the Romantic struggle of a young woman and her lover for the right to live their own lives. It portrays believable people in a believable situation while expressing positive moral values. On the other hand, the dialogue in *Atlas Shrugged* belongs in a comic strip and the characters in a James Bond fantasy.

The quality that separates *good* Naturalistic rendering of events from *bad* Naturalism is the artist's capacity for selectivity — knowing what to put in and knowing what to leave out. This is what makes Hemingway and Maugham *good* Naturalists (economy of style; saying more with fewer words), and Thomas Wolfe a *bad* Naturalist (including every extraneous detail with a floodtide of words). If it weren't for good Naturalists such as Hardy, Galsworthy, Anderson, Fitzgerald, we would all be harder pressed to understand the true quality of life that existed in nineteenth and twentieth century England and America. A single novel of Hardy's is worth far more than a thousand newspaper clippings from his era. Journalists relay surface events to the public; a good Naturalist drives beneath the surface to the spiritual, intellectual, and psychological currents of his time.

Didn't Victor Hugo employ Naturalism in his Romantic story of the life of Jean Valjean? What else would you call his artistic rendering of the conditions of French society that Valjean found himself enmeshed in? Or Dostoevsky in *Crime and Punishment* or *The Brothers Karamazov* or *The Possessed*? What else would you call the vivid imagery he used to describe the street scenes of Moscow and the Siberian countryside? It is apparent that Rand excoriates the Naturalist Emile Zola because she views his intriguing descriptions of working conditions in eighteenth-century France as an attack on capitalism. It is — an attack on *state* capitalism, but Rand has not troubled to see the distinction and berates Zola for his "moral depravity."

Rand has little to say about comedy and satire. On the two occasions on which I heard her speak about the subject she denounced both as "negative" values, and satire as particularly evil because it negates viciously. It would be too easy to attribute these views to the fact that Miss Rand is incapable of writing comedy and has absolutely no understanding of the nature or purpose of satire.

Satire is the highest form of comedy and the best satire is an extremely *positive* value because it negates that which *deserves to be negated*. It's purpose is to destroy that which is evil by holding it on a skewer for public ridicule. Even a "sense of humor" and "laughing at oneself" (condemned, of course, by the Rand as a chipping away of self-esteem) is an attempt to eliminate the worst in man (and in ourselves) by focusing on human imperfections with the hope of doing something about them. But if one is perfect to begin with . . . Evelyn Waugh was probably the greatest satirist writing in English this century, and his son Auberon is following closely in his steps. Kurt Vonnegut is the closest approximation we have in this country of a first-rate satirist using the novel as an effective vehicle for social criticism. Art Buchwald and Jules Feiffer are now attempting to use satire in the theater, but whether they will stake out

(Continued on page 7)

194

IN DEFENSE OF NON-ROMANTIC LITERATURE —

(Continued from page 6)

lasting reputations in this direction remains to be seen. So what if satire doesn't offer positive values for the reader to identify with? Isn't the stripping away of hypocrisy and immorality value enough? Does one have to produce a philosophical treatise every time he writes a story?

A contemporary "serious writer" whom Ayn Rand admires very much is Allen Drury. Drury has produced some of the dreariest prose since Theodore Dreiser, and his novels are little more than *apologias* for the type of gunboat diplomacy advanced by Teddy Roosevelt. He calls himself a Robert Taft Republican but he is really a hard-line conservative, which is why he is so popular with the Buckleyites – and now the Randians. Mickey Spillane, presenting Mike Hammer as his protagonist in the struggle between "good guys" and "bad guys", permits his hero to break the arms of innocent people in order to extract information from them and he is praised by Miss Rand as a valuable Romantic writer. The fantasy world of James Bond is surely not "concrete-bound" (entertaining fantasy, yes; concrete-bound realism, definitely not) so it is promoted as the best of contemporary Romantic literature. This is the type of absurdity that the literary views of Ayn Rand inevitably lead to. I would suggest that she has fallen into the pitfalls of her own "mind-body dichotomy" regarding the subject of literature. More concrete-bound Naturalism in the field of Romantic fantasy might help to elevate it to the level of serious literature.

Despite all the trash that is offered in the pages of the *New York Times Book Review* as "good modern fiction," one does not have to turn to Mickey Spillane or Allen Drury as an alternative. There are many good writers publishing fiction today whom Ayn Rand has apparently never even heard about. She might pick up the novels of Friedrich Duerrenmatt and discover concise Naturalistic description as a background for Romantic moral themes. She might read *An Operational Necessity* by Gwyn Griffin or *King Rat* or *Tai-Pan* by James Clavell for valuable Naturalistic Romanticism of the type she employed in *The Fountainhead*. *The Godfather* by Mario Puzo reveals more insight into the psychology of mobsters than can be found in a hundred news reports.

She might read *Mother Night* or *Slaughterhouse 5* by Kurt Vonnegut for good social and political satire; Arthur C. Clarke and Isaac Asimov for Romantic themes in the realm of science fiction.

Anyone who thinks Naturalism is *unplotted* should study *An Operational Necessity* for tense and exciting plot structure. Those who think Naturalistic description is *journalism* ought to re-read Hemingway and Fitzgerald for economy of style and precise selection of detail. Miss Rand, herself, could use a jolt of imagination to liven her own predictable phraseology. Those who see only *real-life characters* in Naturalism fail to understand the subtleties of interpersonal relationships depicted by first-rate Naturalists such as Mary McCarthy. Any who think that Naturalism is devoid of *moral themes* should read *The Quarry* by Duerrenmatt. Or they can read any one of the above books for all four of these basic ingredients in a single work. *Plot, theme, characterization* and *style* are not copyrighted products of Romantic fantasists.

Literature is an exciting and multifaceted subject. It ought to be explored in great detail by those who want to enlarge their capacity for knowledge and enjoyment. Anyone who pretends to compartmentalize it with trite sloganeering does an injustice to himself. And rational men are capable of better things than parrotting the simplistic, school-girl rhetoric of others.

◘

Recommended Reading

Libertarianism.

The Individualist, monthly organ of SIL (415 2nd St., N. E., Washington, D. C., 50¢ per copy) has a particularly stellar product in its February issue. Featured are Murray N. Rothbard's "Milton Friedman Unraveled", an evisceration of Friedman's "libertarian" pretensions; a laudatory review of Rothbard's *Power and Market* by U. S. Senator Mark Hatfield (R., Ore.); an excellent critique of the Friedmanite scheme for school vouchers to parents by George H. Pearson, "How Tuition Vouchers Socialize Private Education"; a defense of free will by Jarret B. Wollstein, "Free Will and the Natural Order"; and James D. Davidson's attack on psychiatric tyranny, "The Dangers of Psychiatry". The issue also features an ad for pro-private school leaflets available from the Center for Independent Education, at which George Pearson is associate director. (Address of the Center for Independent Education is 9115 East Thirteenth, Wichita, Kansas 67206).

In his review of *Power and Market*, Senator Hatfield writes that it "argue(s) persuasively against the economic functions of government", and "suggests alternative method of dealing with problems normally assumed by government." Hatfield concludes that "I look forward . . . to the further application of this praxeological method to the practical problems of today . . . " and ends with the famous quote from Thoreau that "That government is best which governs not at all."

Also to be commended is the February issue of *Reason* (75¢ per month, $6.00 per year, P. O. Box 6151, Santa Barbara, Calif. 93105). There is a very good article by Robert Poole, Jr., "The Power Crisis", on the ways in which government has been creating crises through its various interventions in different parts of the fuel industry. And an excellent article by Roy Childs, Jr., "Big Business and the Rise of American Statism: A Revisionist History", the first of a two-part article in which Roy sets forth a revisionist analysis of the intimate connection between big business and the emergence of statism in twentieth-century America. The article also features an analysis by Roy of the philosophy of history and historical inquiry.

One thing which the libertarian movement has been in desperate need of is a quarterly scholarly journal. We now have a libertarian quarterly, *Libertarian Analysis*, whose first Winter, 1970 issue has recently been published ($1.25 per copy, $5.00 per year; P. O. Box 210, Village Station, New York, N. Y. 10014.) Its basic stance emerges out of the RLA (Radical Libertarian Alliance) background of its editorial board: a quest for unity between "left" and "right"-wing anarchists. Aside from reprinted articles from Paul Avrich, Paul Buhle, and Noam Chomsky, the first issue contains three original articles: Murray N. Rothbard's "Individualist Anarchism in the United States: the Origins", a history of little-known anarchist thought and practice in 17th century America; Joseph R. Peden's "Courts against the State", a case study of three notable twentieth-century private commissions of inquiry against governmental atrocities; and a letter by Karl Hess calling for a revolutionary strategy.

195

From The 'Old Curmudgeon'

Have you noticed how many leftists *at one and the same time* hold (a) that we have entered a "post-scarcity world" making obsolete any concern with private property, a free price system, or with work and the Protestant ethic; *and* (b) that capitalist greed is destroying our natural resources, and therefore that government must step in and plan for their conservation? To the observer, this may seem irrational and inconsistent; but there is a "higher" consistency here: use *any* stick, self-contradictory or not, with which to clobber the free market and the rights of private property.

In every cloud there is a silver lining, and so there is *one* good fall-out from Women's Liberation: the savage attack that the women's libbers have been mounting against Freudianism. Until a year or so ago, the Left-liberal intellectual held Freudianism, an irrationalist creed which all Old Curmudgeons have been opposing for many years, as virtually their prime article of faith. But now the Women's Lib assault has seriously weakened the devotion of the guilt-ridden male liberals to their Freudian faith. In a war between Freudians and Libbers, we are reminded of the old joke about the wife who hated her husband and found her husband attacked by a bear. Torn in her sympathies, she alternately shouted: "Go Husband! Go Bear!" in the hopes that these two antagonists would kill each other off. In the same spirit, we raise the cry: "Go Libbers! Go Freudians!"

One of the more amusing items in the grim news of the day was the recent report that Mrs. Patricia Buckley Bozell, managing editor of the Ultra-Catholic *Triumph,* had taken a swing at Ti-Grace Atkinson, leading Women's Libber, for charging at a speech at Catholic University that, even assuming the Virgin Birth to be correct, that this makes God's "male chauvinism" even worse, for this means that God had impregnated Mary without even sex as a compensation. While of course all libertarians deplore any physical assault upon the exercise of free speech, I confess to a sneaking sympathy for Mrs. Bozell. To have this creature spawned by the dregs of our culture heap obscene abuse upon the Catholic faith on the campus of a Catholic university would seem almost too much provocation for a dedicated Catholic to bear.

Apart from this: by what right did the federal judge force Catholic University to permit Atkinson to speak on its campus? Here was a clear invasion of Catholic University's property right in its own campus, and the clear implication that anyone has the right to speak on anyone *else's* property, even unto abusing the property owner himself. This is the kind of "free speech" which every genuine libertarian should steadfastly oppose.

TAKEOFF II — *(Continued from page 2)*

National Taxpayers' Union. Then there is an excellent article by Leonard Liggio, "Your Right to be Against War", in which Leonard sets forth and analyzes the history of the anti-militarist and anti-imperialist movement in the twentieth century, the filiation from Old Right to New Left, the roles of Albert Jay Nock and Senator Taft, etc.

Another article in the WIN issue is an interesting contribution by a left-wing Friedmanite, Henry Bass, "Libertarian Economics." Bass instructs his fellow syndicalists that they must incorporate the insights and truths of free-market economics in any vision of a utopian syndicalist society. Finally, Karl Hess contributes "What's Left?", a critique of the extreme right-wing of the libertarian movement, in particular Stanford's Harvey Hukari, Jr. and the striking gap between Ayn Rand's novels and her current political views. While Karl's strictures are well-taken against the extreme right-wing of the movement, he does not come to grips with the sober center-mainstream of anarcho-capitalism. To top off the issue, one Bob Calese has compiled a useful bibliography of right-wing libertarian literature which includes the individualist anarchists: Andrews, Warren, Tucker, Spooner, Greene, Mackay, Swartz; libertarian classics such as Spencer and Nock; modern contributions such as Mises, Rand, Rothbard, Tannehill, Wollstein, Tuccille; and historical accounts and collections such as Martin, Silverman, Krimerman and Perry.

All in all, the issue is must reading for libertarians.

Newspapers and magazines: can other media be far behind? Numerous radio appearances by various libertarians were capped by my appearance on the NBC-TV Today show on March 8. Furthermore, books galore by major publishers on libertarianism are scheduled for next winter's season; there will be libertarian manifestoes, readers, personal statements, reprints, and non-fiction novels. If *National Review* is livid now, it had better brace itself for the flood of books next season. Onward and upward!

Published on the first and fifteenth of every month.   **Subscription rate:** $8.00 per year;

A Monthly Newsletter

THE
Libertarian Forum

Joseph R. Peden, Publisher

Murray N. Rothbard, Editor

VOLUME III, NO. 4   April, 1971   75¢

The Conning Of America

Never let it be said that the *Lib. Forum* is a grim, relentless monolith. Indeed, even within the Sober Center of the anarcho-capitalist movement, we have a range of views stretching all the way from Jerry Tuccille to myself. Everyone *else*, from Bill Buckley to Ed Muskie to Abbie Hoffman, is a damned extremist, outside of our mainstream dialogue.

Thus, I disagree totally with Jerry's overall estimate of Charles Reich and his "greening". To the contrary, I regard Reich's Con Game as largely a P. R. shuck, and to the extent that the phenomenon is real, as a symptom of a diseased society and a degenerate culture rather than any sort of ally in the fight for liberty.

To raise the least important point first, the aesthetics of the title is itself enough to render to Reich the back of our hand. Who can fail to reach for his figurative musket at anyone who uses a word like "greening" in the title of a book — or anywhere else for that matter? Have we lost all respect for the English language? Indeed, if we wished to skirt the edges of obscenity, the "browning" of America would be a far more accurate title.

But the concept of "greening" has more important implications. For Professor Reich is in his book a naive and adoring celebrant of every repellent aspect of our youth anti-culture. The "greening" is Reich's symbol of his hoped-for massive rejection of technology and civilization *per se* and the return to the tribe, the commune, the soil, and primitivism generally. The fact that Reich is opposed to Con II I find less than impressive, since he is hardly the first to take up the cudgels against the ideology of state corporatism. More important is Reich's equally scornful rejection of Con I: i.e., the ethic of work, purpose, reason, the free market, technology, civilization, and private property — which, I insist, is intimately wrapped up with libertarianism and certainly with any libertarianism that is rational and workable in a country of two hundred million population. Above all, and like so much of the Left, Reich and the anti-culture totally reject the division of labor — a system absolutely crucial to the survival of man in the age of mass population as well as to the full development of the faculties and abilities of every man. But the Left hates and reviles the division of labor because such division leads straight to variety and diversity — to the individuation of every man — and there by negates the Left-socialist-communalist ideal of equality and uniformity of all men. Equality and uniformity can only be achieved in a world of small primitive communes, in which every man and woman does everything at once. The least one can say about such a world is that the vast bulk of the current population would quickly starve and die out; the most one can say is

that, in addition, the true humanity — the individuation of every person and his full creative development — would be stifled in the bud, would be destroyed on the altar of the crippling and profoundly anti-human ideal of equality and uniformity.

Reich's hatred of work and the division of labor erupts in all sorts of ways: for example, his glorification of hippie youth because they wear all-purpose uniforms, where one set of clothes suffices every person for all his activities: playing, sleeping, etc. Those of us who wear suits for working, dressier clothes for parties, shorts for athletics, pajamas for sleeping, etc. are reviled for "alienating" themselves by splitting themselves up into different roles. The uni-clothed man or woman, on the contrary, is ready at any moment to roll in the grass or mud, to sleep, walk around, etc., thus preserving his perpetual state of *ad hoc* spontaneity (read: irresponsibility and caprice, or "whim-worship"). Let us set aside the correct but too easy point that one great attraction for the hippies is that the uni-clothes don't have to be washed. More important, this example at one and the same time reveals the hippie-Reich hatred for work, and for the division of labor.

On work: it is clear that no one, even in our permissive age, is going to hold a job for long wearing uni-clothes, especially if he has just rolled in the mud. Secondly, the adoration of caprice and whim-worship means that no one will be able to launch a career, to do a concentrated job of productive work, to advance his mind and intellect, or indeed to do any amount of passable work at all. And as for the division of labor, the old left-wing assault on "alienation" is very precisely the product of the absurd leftist myth that specialization, concentration on a particular line of endeavor, "alienates" one from the "whole man", from the product of one's labor, etc. In recent years, it has been fashionable on the Left to exalt the "early Marx", who concentrated his hostility upon "alienation" and the division of labor, as contrasted to the "later Marx" beloved of the Old Left. But the later Marx, as baneful as he was, at least tried to arrive at a rational system, and tried to understand the workings of society in a systematic way. In our proper reaction against the Old Left, let us not leap from the frying pan of Old Left state despotism to the fire of New Left nihilism and barbarism.

In short, I say to hell with both Con II and Con III. The only hope for America, and for the rest of the world for that matter, is a return to Con I.

To quote again from Frank S. Meyer's devastating

(Continued on page 2)

197

THE CONNING OF AMERICA —
(Continued from page 1)

blast at the youth culture ("Counterculture or Anti-culture?", *National Review*, Nov. 3):

"It is not a counterculture, it is an anti-culture, for culture is and always has been dependent for its very existence on civility . . . The hallmark of the counterculture, however, is precisely its principled hatred of civility, its violent opposition at all levels to ordered freedom, to the tradition of rational discourse, to the very structure of civilized life. Above all, it hates the prime characteristic of the civilized man, that internalized discipline which looks with suspicion upon those spontaneous, unexamined emotional reactions we have inherited from our barbarian and animal past. The unexamined life which Socrates found unworthy of civilized man is to the devotees of the counterculture their be-all and end-all . . . The constant target of their attack is 'middle-class values', a phrase that inquiring analysis reveals to denote the entire gamut of the values upon which Western civilization is founded . . . Marijuana, addictive or not, physically harmful or not, is celebrated as a mode of escape from conceptual thinking, from the pressures of self-discipline without which civilization is impossible".

"Add to this stew the sort of beliefs and myths that pervade the counterculture — the hatred of the 'ethic of achievement', the attack upon the nuclear family and heterosexual monogamy in the name of 'polymorphous sexuality': stir in the superstitions that proliferate within it — astrology, phony Eastern mysticism, Satanism. Corrosive of reason and tradition alike . . . "

One point that the youth culture makes is a perpetual gripe at the alleged "hypocrisy" of their elders. Yet what is more grossly hypocritical than the spectre of this Charles Reich, very comfortably ensconced in his professorship at Yale, wearing love beads, celebrating the hip, and calling upon *everyone else* to drop out, to take to the tribal and the communal hills? What is more repulsive than this man, living high on the hog from the royalties of a runaway best seller, sneering at "capitalist greed", scoffing at the materialism of our culture, etc.? I think it perfectly legitimate to call upon Professor Reich to put up or shut up: to drop out himself, to leave Con II Yale, to abandon his materialistic royalties, and to hie him to a hippie commune, or forever hold his peace. Are there any takers on a bet that the good professor will do no such thing? How much longer are we going to reward these parasites, waxing fat by exploiting a "materialism" which they themselves proclaim to be the quintessence of evil? How much longer are we to take such Con Men seriously?

Unquestionably the best article I have seen on the Reichian greening was by the sociologists Peter and Brigitte Berger in the New York *Times* Op-Ed page of Feb. 15, "On the Eve of the Blueing of America". The Bergers brilliantly and incisively make the crucial point: that despite Reich's arrogant claim to be the prophet of a coming America composed exclusively of primitive tribal communes, that this counter-cultural dropping out will only affect the sons and daughters of the upper classes. Perhaps there will be mass dropouts from work, from reason, from responsibility and purpose, but these dropouts will come only from upper-class Jews and WASPS, dropping out from affluence, Harvard, and Berkeley. But the working-class kids, the students at Fordham and Wichita State, are *not* about to drop out, not by a long shot. They have not been raised in a luxury which they can afford to scorn in order to seek out a "romantic" life of egalitarian poverty. They have been raised close enough to poverty to hate it and to devote themselves to escaping from its spectre. In short, the working class kids, and especially such "ethnics" as Poles, Irish, and Italians, are not going to drop out; on the contrary, *they* will rise up rapidly to fill the needed

technological and business jobs to keep our society and our economy going and progressing. In short, the sons of the blue-collar workers will rise rapidly to fill the jobs abandoned by the effete and permissively raised children of the affluent. In this way, the "working class" will triumph in a manner which will be as gall and wormwood to the Marxists who have called for a proletarian uprising. Surely this is an excellent and hopeful prognosis for America — an America where Horatio Alger will be more relevant than he has been for many decades.

In short, Con III is profoundly dysfunctional — a tragic dead end for America. Whoever follows that route will end up as the flotsam and jetsam of our society; far from allying ourselves with the "greens", we should give them nothing but our contempt. We should ally ourselves with the healthy rather than the diseased forces in America — with the decent citizens of the working and middle classes — and upper as well — who cleave to the Con I virtues of hard work, purpose, and rational individualism. The real struggle of the future is Con I vs. Con II, and our task is to "raise the consciousness" of the Con I's, to show them that so long as the corporate statists of Con II are on their backs, they will never be allowed to achieve their own values and life-goals. Let the Con III dropouts sink into the cesspools of their own making. Our lot is with William Graham Sumner's Forgotten Man, the "honest, sober, industrious citizen, unknown outside his little circle, paying his debts and taxes, "the man "who has no political influence, and who has known no way in which to secure the chances of life except to deserve them", the man "hard at work tilling the soil to get out of it the fund for all the jobbery, the object of all the plunder, the cost of all the economic quackery, and the pay of all the politicians and statesmen who have sacrificed his interests to his enemies." Our lot is with Middle America.

◘

First Midwest Libertarian Festival

Come one, come all! The Middle West, which has been lagging behind the two Coasts in holding libertarian festivals, announce its first libertarian conference!

The Midwest Libertarian Festival will be held on Saturday, May 1, at Northern Illinois University, DeKalb, Illinois, at 10:00 A. M. Host: Paul Varnell.

Exact location of the conference will be available at the Information Desk, Student Center.

Guest Speakers: Tibor Machan, David Friedman, Joseph DeJan.

◘

"Feudalism, serfdom, slavery, all tyrannical institutions, are merely the most vigorous kind of rule, springing out of, and necessary to, a bad state of man. The progress from these is in all cases the same—less government." --- Herbert Spencer.

Stateless Societies: Ancient Ireland

By Joseph R. Peden

Libertarians have often dreamed of escaping the tyranny of the State; some have sought to do so by seeking refuge in distant and uninhabited lands where they could live in solitary hermitage or in small communities held together by the principle of voluntary association and mutual aid. But historians know that such experiments seldom survive in peace for long; sooner or later the State finds and confronts them with its instinctive will to violence, its mania for coercion rather than persuasion, for compulsion rather than voluntarism. Such has been the fate of the Mormons and Mennonites, the Jehovah's Witnesses and the Amish people, among others.

As exploited peoples all over the world are beginning to realize, their true enemy is always within their midst – the coercive violence of the State – and it must be fought constantly in the very heart of its dominions. Every libertarian must fight the State from where he is: in his home, his place of business, in the schools, community and the world at large. His task is to resist the State and to dismantle it by whatever means are at hand.

Historically, States do not dismantle willingly or easily. While they can disintegrate with startling speed, as in Russia in 1917 or France in 1968, almost always new States arise to take their place. The reason for this, I believe, is that men cannot bring themselves to believe in the practical feasibility of a society in which perfect liberty, security of life and property, and law and justice can be attained without the coercive violence of the State. Men have for so long been enslaved by the State that they cannot rid themselves of a Statist mentality. The myth of the State as a necessary part of social reality constitutes the greatest single obstacle to the achievement of a libertarian voluntarist society.

Yet the historian, if he but chooses to look and report his findings, knows that many societies have functioned successfully without the existence of the State, its coercive apparatus and monopoly of organized violence. It is my purpose here to present one example of such a society, one that existed for more than a thousand years of recorded history, terminated only by the massive military efforts of a more populous, wealthy and aggressive neighboring State. I will describe for you the millenial – long anarchic society of Celtic Ireland – destroyed after a six-century struggle against the English State in the wake of the military victories, confiscations and genocidal policies of successive English governments in the 17th century.

English historians have usually justified Ireland's fate by characterizing its people as uncivilized and barbaric, its society as being anarchic. Christopher Dawson is quite clear on this point: "The essence of barbaric society is that it rests upon the principle of kinship rather than on that of citizenship, or that of the absolute authority of the State". Ireland certainly relied upon kinship relationships in its social cohesion and it never by any stretch of imagination enjoyed the dubious benefit of a citizenship conferred by the absolute authority of the State.

The distinguished Anglo-Irish historian of the Norman invasion and colonization of Ireland, G. H. Orpen, said quite frankly that Celtic Irish society was "anarchic" in that it had scarcely any of the political institutions or officials customary in a "civilized society". Nationalist historians like Eoin MacNeill, who actively participated in the overthrow of English rule in the period 1916-1922, considered these opinions just another smear by the English conquerors and insisted that the ancient Irish had as much of a State as they needed.

A younger generation of Irish historians, less caught up in the great struggle for national liberation than Mac-Neill, have candidly admitted the embarrassing fact: Irish society was indeed anarchic. As D. A. Binchy, the leading contemporary Irish expert on ancient Irish law, has written: "there was no legislature, no bailiffs, no police, no public enforcement of justice" and "the State existed only in embryo". "There was no trace of State-administered justice".

But if Ireland was essentially an anarchistic (or libertarian) society, how was law and order maintained? How was justice secured? Was there not incessant warfare and rampant criminality?

To answer the last of these questions first – of course there were wars and crime. Has there ever been a society-statist or otherwise – without war and crime? But Irish wars were almost never on the scale known among other "civilized" European peoples. Without the coercive apparatus of the State which can through taxation and conscription mobilize large amounts of arms and manpower, the Irish were unable to sustain any large scale military force in the field for any length of time. Irish wars, until the last phase of the English conquest in the 16th and 17th centuries, were pitiful brawls and cattle raids by European standards. The contemporary Irish historian, Kathleen Hughes, has remarked that one reason why the English conquest, begun in the 12th century under Henry II and completed only under William III in the late 17th century, was so long in being achieved was the lack of a well-organized State in Celtic Ireland. A people not habituated to a Statist conception of authority are incapable of considering a defeat in war as anything more than a temporary limitation upon their liberty. Submission to the enemy is viewed as no more than a necessary and temporary expedient to preserve one's life until opportunity for revolt and recovery of liberty presents itself. The English, of course, considered the Irish notorious in their faithlessness (they repeatedly repudiated oaths of submission and allegiance to their English conquerors); they were repeatedly characterized by English commentators as natural-born, incorrigible rebels, barbarians, savages who refused to submit to the kind of law and order offered by the English State. The Irish, unfettered by the slave mentality of people accustomed to the tyranny of the State, simply refused to surrender their liberty and libertarian ways.

Let us now examine more closely Irish society and Irish social institutions.

The basic polity of the ancient Irish was the *Tuath*. Membership was restricted to Free men who owned land, or were members of recognized learned professions, – poets, seers, physicians, jurists or clergymen, or who were skilled craftsmen, millers, metal workers, architects, wood carvers, shipwrights, fishermen, musicians, chariot-makers, etc. Excluded were propertyless men, slaves, foreigners, outlaws and minor artisans. Political actions were undertaken within the annual assembly of all the Free men; kings were elected or deposed, wars declared and peace treaties agreed upon, questions of common interest discussed and policies decided. The assembly was the sovereign people acting.

The members of the *tuath* were not necessarily bound by ties of kinship, except incidentally. It was not a tribe or clan in the sense of being based upon a common kinship – real or imaginary. Kinsmen often lived and acted within different *Tuatha* and individual members could and often did secede, and join another *tuath*. Also two or more *tuatha* could and did coalesce into one body. The *tuath* is

(Continued on page 4)

199

STATELESS SOCIETIES: ANCIENT IRELAND

(Continued from page 4)

thus a body of persons voluntarily united for socially beneficial purposes and the sum total of the landed properties of its members constituted its territorial dimension. Historically there were from 80 to 100 or so *tuatha* at different periods in Irish history, and few were larger than perhaps a quarter to a third of the modern Irish county. The population is unlikely to have exceeded 25,000 souls, and was usually smaller.

The chief personage within the *tuath* was the king. The nature of kingship in ancient Ireland must be sought in pre-Christian times. As is commonly the case among ancient peoples, the basic social unit — here the *tuath* — was essentially a cultic association. The cult is the basis for social, political and military cooperation among the body of worshippers. The king is first and foremost the high priest of the cult; he likewise presides over the assembly of worshippers and acts in their behalf in secular as well as sacred functions. The Irish kings were clearly the chief priests of the *tuath;* their inauguration ceremonies, the sites of the assemblies, the traditions of the people confirm this fact. The conversion to Christianity modified the religious functions of the kings to fit the requirements of Christian practices, but did not entirely eliminate them.

As was common, the kingship was hereditary, like pagan priesthoods. The king was elected by the *tuath* from within a royal kin-group (the *derbfine*) consisting of all males in three generations descending from a common ancestor who was a king. The royal kin-group usually nominated one of its members, or if a dispute arose and could not be settled otherwise, joint kings were elected. Kings who displeased the *tuath* were often deposed, and those who were mutilated in any way had to abdicate — the result of a religious taboo, one of many that were attached to the office of king.

To what extent was the king the representative of a State? The Irish kings had only two functions of a State-like character: they were required to preside over the assembly of the *tuath* and represent it in negotiations with other *tuatha;* and they were expected to lead the *tuath* into battle when it went to war. He clearly was not a Sovereign himself and exercised no rights of administering justice over the members of the *tuath*. When he himself was party to a suit, he submitted his case to an independent judicial arbiter. And he did not legislate.

How then was law and order maintained?

First of all, the law itself was based upon immemorial custom passed down orally through a class of professional jurists known as the *filid*. These jurists added glosses to the basic law from time to time to make it fit the needs of the times; several schools of jurisprudence existed, and the professional jurists were consulted by parties to disputes for advice as to what the law was in particular cases, and these same men often acted as arbitrators between suitors. They remained at all times private persons, not public officials; their functioning depended upon their knowledge of the law and the integrity of their judicial reputations. They are the only "judges" Celtic Ireland knew; their jurisprudence was her only law, national in scope, and completely detached from the *tuath*, the kings and their respective wishes.

How was this law of the *filid* enforced? The law was enforced by the action of private individuals allied with the plaintiff and defendant through a system of sureties. Men were linked together by a number of individual relationships by which they were obligated to stand surety for one another guaranteeing that wrongs would be righted, debts paid, judgements honored, and the law enforced.

The system of sureties was so well developed in Irish law that there was no need for a Statist system of justice. There were three different kinds of surety: in one the surety guaranteed with his own property the payment of a debt which the debtor did not or could not pay; another kind saw the surety pledge his person that the debtor would not default; if the debtor did default, the surety had to surrender himself as a hostage to the creditor; he then had to negotiate a settlement with his captor. In a third instance, a man might pledge to join the creditor in enforcing the judgement against the debtor if he failed to pay the full amount of the judgement; in this case the debtor was liable to double damages since he must pay the original creditor and also pay a compensation to the surety for compromising his honor.

Almost every conceivable legal transaction was worked out through the taking and giving of sureties. As the Irish law made no distinction between torts and criminal offences, all criminals were considered as debtors — owing restitution and compensation to their victims — who thereby became their creditors. The victim gathered his sureties and proceeded to apprehend the criminal or to publicly proclaim his suit and demand that the criminal submit to adjudication of their differences. At this point the criminal might send his sureties to negotiate a settlement on the the spot or agree to submit the case to one of the *filid*.

The Irish law recognized the all too likely fact that a poor man may have difficulty in getting a rich, powerful man to submit a dispute to negotiation or arbitration by the *filid*. It therefore provided for a special kind of distraint. According to this procedure, the plaintiff was obliged to appear at the gate of the defendant's house and sit there from sunset until sunrise fasting the whole while; the defendant was likewise bound either to keep a similar fast, or submit to adjudication of the dispute. If he broke his fast, or refused to submit to adjudication for three days, he was said to have lost his honor within the community, and could not enforce any claim of his own. As the law code put it: "He who does not give a pledge to fasting is an evader of all. He who disregards all things is paid by neither God nor man". Thus the ultimate sanction was to be considered an outlaw by the community — to lose one's own legal status. This custom, which invokes the moral feelings of the community to insure justice, was used during the Anglo-Irish war of 1916-22 when Irish prisoners in English custody used the hunger strike to win public sympathy for their cause. (Those reminded of the tactic of Gandhi in his struggle against British imperialism should not be surprised to learn that ancient Hindu law has a fasting procedure just like that in ancient Irish law).

The essentially libertarian nature of Irish society can also be seen in the fact that the native Irish never issued coinage. Historians have generally interpreted this phenomenon as another sign of the barbaric nature of the Irish society and its economic and technological backwardness. Indeed, although in contact with the Celtic states of ancient Britain and Gaul, and later with the Roman and Anglo-Saxon peoples of Britain, and with the Viking princes who established trading colonies all around the coasts of Ireland, all of whom issued silver coinage within their realms, it is strange that the Irish never followed suit. They certainly had access to both gold and silver from native sources; they travelled abroad and knew the monetary usages of their neighbors; and the metalworkers capable of creating such masterpieces as the Tara brooch or the Ardagh chalice were certainly capable of striking coins.

Why then did they not do so? Libertarians can see one possible reason immediately. Coinage is usually the product of the State monopolists, who, through legal tender laws, compel sellers to accept state coinage which is always overvalued in comparison to its bullion value. Only the coercive power of the State can sustain the use of a debased coinage in the free market which prefers bullion which

(Continued on page 8)

Bits And Pieces
By Jerome Tuccille

(This article will appear in a paperback anthology, dealing with Charles A. Reich's The Greening of America, to be published later this year.)

The division between libertarians and conservatives in Right Wing circles has received a good deal of publicity in the past few years, and especially since the early fall of 1970. Libertarians have accused the Buckleyites of sacrificing their stated principles in favor of individual liberties in order to carry on an increasingly hawkish foreign policy against Communist China and the Soviet Union; the conservatives have derided libertarians for failing to understand the ominous nature of the communist threat which they regard as the single greatest evil afflicting mankind today. For those on the Left who have been confused by all this ideological squabbling off their starboard, it is worth taking a look at some of these distinctions more closely.

The libertarian-conservative rift does not merely involve differences over foreign policy, as some have claimed. While the conservatives have included a large dose of libertarian rhetoric in the presentation of their philosophy, especially as regards economic freedom in the marketplace, their main concern has always been the maintenance of traditional order in society. They speak of individual liberty, but by no means in absolutist terms. According to William F. Buckley, Jr., the freedom of the individual is to be contained within the structure of an orderly society based on the preservation of traditional western religious and cultural values. Order has always taken dominance over liberty in the conservative hierachy, and this accounts for their championship of censorship laws and other legislation governing the sexual and moral practices of the population.

Libertarians, on the other hand, are absolutists on the question of individual liberties. While free market libertarians are committed to an Ethic of private property and economic freedom, their main emphasis is on *voluntarism;* that is, they are not concerned about the habits and lifestyles of other people so long as they remain non-aggresive. The individualist libertarian is willing to permit others to group together in communes, to share their wealth and property and means of production, if such a system is organized on a voluntary basis. He is not interested in regulating the non-violent activities of the general citizenry in any way, even when he considers their moral and cultural values to be at total variance with his own. The libertarian believes in defensive violence when his own freedom is threatened, but he will never try to violate the rights of others or force them to adopt a certain pattern of life because he thinks it is morally superior.

So we see how David Brudnoy, writing in the December 15, 1970 issue of *National Review,* can denigrate *The Greening of America* by Charles A. Reich as an "Epistle to the Unwashed." The conservative is morally outraged by Reich's infatuation with the youth subculture, and not impressed at all by the fact that Reich's message is profoundly libertarian in most of its major aspects. The sensibilities of the conservative, his disdain for all cultural innovations outside the mainstream of the American tradition, take priority over his rhetorical devotion to the principles of voluntarism and individual freedom.

There is much one can say against the Reich book. He is too eager to embrace every aspect of the youth subculture

as positive and beneficial. He is too tolerant of the wide-Suit epitomized the American Corporate immage, and prospread use of drugs and their so-called "mind-expanding" faculties, even as drugs – especially hard drugs – are becoming less and less important on the campus social scene. Most damaging of all is Reich's condemnation of reason and logical thought in favor of "less rigid" forms of communication: mind expansion, mysticism, rapping, etc. . . . It was precisely this lack of commitment to logical and constructive thinking which was responsible for the gradual degeneration of the New Left between 1965 and 1970. Starting out with a healthy, though basically instinctive penchant for decentralized political power at home and anti-militarism in foreign affairs, the New Left, largely because of its failure to develop a positive and rational program of its own, turned to philosophical nihilism and terroristic acts of "propaganda by the deed" as a means of bringing down the Corporate State. Without a sound philosophical base, and the ability to translate abstract principle into concrete political terms, no movement can hope to survive over the long run. It would be a sad development if this basic flaw in Reich's conception of Consciousness III was to become responsible for its demise over the next few years.

Less crucial than this is the fact that Reich doesn't seem to fully understand the cause of the transition between Consciousness I and Consciousness II. He defines Consciousness I as the "American dream . . . that success is determined by character, morality, hard work and self-denial." Consciousness I believes in self-interest, competitiveness and suspicion of one's neighbors. Consciousness II is defined as the belief in the supremacy of organizations and institutions over the Ethic of individual freedom. Consciousness II is the "assumption of corporate power to plan the economy, allocate resources, divide areas of business activity, fix prices, limit entry of new businesses, and . . . control the buyers themselves." But Reich refers to the growth of monopolies and corporate power, and the consequent destruction of the free market, as the aggrandizement of "private power" which later gave way to the creation of the "Corporate State." He fails to understand that the emergence of Corporate Power and the development of the Corporate State are one and the same thing. He still clings to the erroneous view that the free market brought about its own destruction and resulted in "monopolistic private power," and that the Corporate State was established during the Roosevelt era as a means of regulating the inequities of the marketplace.

This is simply not the case. As we have learned from a variety of sources – free market economists Murray Rothbard, Ludwig von Mises and Henry Hazlitt on the Right; revisionist historians Gabriel Kolko, William A. Williams and G. William Domhoff on the Left – the consolidation of monopoly power in the late-nineteenth century was brought about with the vital assistance of an already-emerging Corporate State sixty years before Franklin D. Roosevelt came along. Reich correctly identifies the great "Robber Barons" of the 1900's – Vanderbilt, Carnegie, Harriman and Ford among others – as the real "socialists" and "collectivizers" of American society, the "uprooters" and "killers" of the "American dream." But he does not recognize the fact that these "subversives" did not destroy the freedom of Consciousness I by "market exploitation," but, rather, they used State Power as a means of destroying the competitiveness and decentralization of the market to further their own interests. Consciousness I and the freedom of the marketplace was not subverted by a "Calvinistic" uptightness and suspicion of one's fellow man, as negative and unhealthy as these attitudes are. The Ethic of individualism and free trade was ultimately brought down by the only power capable of doing the job – the power of political authority acting to further the interests of a few

(Continued on page 6)

BITS AND PIECES — *(Continued from page 5)*

corporate lobbyists at the expense of the powerless multitudes.

Against these defects in the Reich presentation, we can counterbalance his masterful dissection of Consciousness II and his description of Consciousness III and the prospects it offers for the "Greening" of the American society of the future. No one has succeeded as Reich has in driving to the core of the Corporate State mentality. In the 1950's the Organization Man and the Man in the Gray Flannel Suit epitomized the American Corporate image, and provided us with a good deal of insight into the dehumanizing aspects of a society in which the individual had lost almost complete control over the direction of his own life. We lived with this new awareness for a while and lamented the fact that Big Government, Big Business, Big Labor, Big Bombs and Big Politics seemed to dominate our entire way of life. But before we could do anything to rectify the situation, we suddenly passed from the bland and faceless Eisenhower era into the grinding crush of John F. Kennedy's Ivy League imperialism. From Dwight D. Eisenhower, father of all the people – he *was* the American people for Christ's sake! – we placed our fate in the hands of J.F.K.'s think-tank intellectuals and his legions of pragmatic social engineers. And then, of course, in the aftermath – the aftermath of L.B.J. and Vietnam and the inevitable erosion of civil liberties at home – the problems of the Man in the Gray Flannel Suit were suddenly trivial by comparison. We now look back to the "Ike" days with a certain fondness, as if everything was really okay back in the '50's, those halcyon years of "free enterprise," rock 'n roll and Thursday night bowling games.

This is the great power of the Reich analysis. He opens our eyes wide and clear to the fact that we have been living a dream for fifty years and longer. On one hand there is the Consciousness II mentality reassuring us that things will be all right again with the proper planning, proper organization, proper reordering of priorities; the Consciousness II mentality with the sheer arrogance to assert that Vietnam would never have been if only J.F.K. were still around – the same J.F.K. of the Bay of Pigs and Cuban Missile showdown, the same J.F.K. who was responsible for unleashing Robert MacNamara on the world. And on the other hand we have Consciousness I still adhering to the brainless assumption that the Organization Man was a free enterpriser, that the Man in the Gray Flannel Suit was a heroic individualist who would find his true level through integrity and hard work in the open marketplace.

Both Consciousness I and II are living the lie. I is more lovable, perhaps, in that he is the one who has had his ideals shot down and his dreams destroyed. But II has also become victimized by his own system to such an extent that he believes – he actually *believes* after all that has happened – that another forty billion dollars or a new busing law is going to cure the ills of mankind.

In one of Reich's most incisive chapters, "The Machine Begins to Self-Destruct," he describes how this gigantic bureaucratic Monolith is already collapsing of its own inefficiency. The Corporate State is falling apart because of its inability to function any longer. We see it happening every day, all around us, particularly in our urban centers. We are undergoing nothing less than a complete institutional breakdown. Our educational facilities for elementary and high school grades are virtually inoperative, and in many cases they have become a physical as well as a mental hazard to the young. Police protection – theoretically a necessary evil designed for the protection of life and property – has long been an agency of domestic imperialism. Sanitation, fire prevention, housing, libraries, museums, parks, transportation, nearly every civic service one can think of is either in a state of disrepair, or else it is operat-

ing on a level far below that which we have a right to expect. On top of it all the tax schedule is higher now than it has ever been – many claim we have reached the saturation point – and our local governments are all claiming bankruptcy. So we have empty public coffers, a near collapse in all our vital institutions *and* an excruciating tax rate which, if it is raised much higher, will most likely foster a state of active resistance in the law-abiding middle class. No one but the most adamant Consciousness II will deny that the machine is, indeed, self-destructing.

Now we come to Consciousness III. According to Reich, Consciousness III "starts with self. In contrast to Consciousness II, which accepts society, the public interest, and institutions as the primary reality, III declares that the individual self is the only true reality." III "postulates the absolute worth of every human being – every self." "But III's do not compete in 'real life." They do not measure others, they do not see others as something to struggle against. People are brothers, the world is ample for all." "Consciousness III rejects . . . manipulation of others, for one's own purpose. . . ." This emphasis on individual self-esteem and corresponding respect for the individuality of all others, with the accent on non-violence, non-coercion and non-aggression, is the basis for the *libertarian* philosophy. Consciousness III, shorn of the negative aspects outlined earlier – reliance on drugs and denigration of rational thought – is profoundly libertarian in all its elements.

If Reich is guilty of anything in his discussion of the Consciousness III mentality, his guilt rests in a naive faith that a change in consciousness will revolutionize the entire face of American society. It is true, certainly, that a fundamental change in everyone's basic attitudes toward life will eventually result in a complete restructuring of a society's political, social and cultural institutions. But this is rather like saying: if everyone refuses to aggress against his neighbors, we will have eliminated the need for police protection; or, if everyone stopped drinking to excess we will have done away with alcoholism. The Reich prescription for a Revolution by Consciousness is actually a tautology. The Revolution and the adoption of Consciousness III are identical. We *will* have a libertarian society if everyone becomes a libertarian. We *will* have an end to military imperialism and an expansion of domestic civil liberties if Richard Nixon, J. Edgar Hoover, Melvin Laird, John Mitchell and every other power-merchant in the country becomes a III, a libertarian. Until that happens, unfortunately, we must continue to resist, to disobey, to fight against the Corporate machine in the most intelligent manner we know how. It is necessary, as long as the military draft remains in force, to fight it openly and support those who refuse to have their lives nationalized in the name of national defense; to engage in tax resistance as a means of weakening the power of centralized government; to boycott elections when no real alternatives are offered; to agitate for local control of schools, police, sanitation and other civic institutions; to keep the pressure continually on the political structure in order to break it down and make it more responsive; to work for reform within the system to achieve desired changes in our judicial, social and economic policies, and to implement revolutionary tactics such as massive civil disobedience whenever reform becomes impossible.

This is not to minimize the impact of the Reich message, however. He has given us a valuable document in this time of violence and militaristic nation-states. Charles Reich is a true revolutionary, a brother in the struggle against power and political tyranny. It is for libertarians, and anyone else who believes in the future of mankind, to join in the expansion of Consciousness III, to improve upon it and intellectualize it in the areas it is weakest, and to get on with the struggle to "Green" and libertarianize the earth.

202

A Libertarian Rebuttal: Conservatism Examined

By James Dale Davidson

Those who have followed the growing split in the right wing movement realize that many old-fashioned, red-blooded Americans would be perfectly happy to see the collapse of the U. S. Government. This – you may say – is not an ordinary opinion. Obviously not. But it is hardly so harebrained as it might seem. Advocates of libertarianism have made a compelling case for a totally free market, a case which most people have never heard and much of which has only recently been set forth for the first time. Dr. Murray Rothbard, the outstanding economist, has published POWER AND MARKET, a devastating critique of all functions of government. It would be hard to over-estimate the force of Dr. Rothbard's ideas. Writing in the February issue of the INDIVIDUALIST, Senator Mark Hatfield comments as follows: "(N)ot only does he argue persuasively against the economic functions of government, but also suggests alternative methods of dealing with problems normally assumed by government. In other words, one cannot off-handedly reject the thesis of this book as a flight of fancy."

When a U. S. Senator says that a proposal to abolish his job cannot be dismissed as a flight of fancy, you may properly infer he is telling the truth. Libertarianism makes sense. Those who have never been attracted to conventional "right wing" thought find libertarianism appealing. This is not lost on Mr. William Buckley and his conservative cohorts at NATIONAL REVIEW. Ever since libertarian ideas came to public attention, the Buckley crowd has tried desperately to obviate their appeal. Having no arguments to answer libertarianism, the conservatives have turned to ad hominem attack. At first, Buckley suggested that all libertarians were, in his words, "irresponsible libertines." The contention was that anyone who takes liberty seriously invites being debauched. The conservatives abandoned this approach only when the appeal of debauchery proved irresistible. After one speech delivered by Mr. Buckley to a Young Americans for Freedom group, hundreds of listeners responded to warnings of "libertinism" by seeking out a libertarian meeting in order to join in the fun.

It is now obvious, even to conservatives, that in a country where "X"-rated movies are sold out the charge of debauchery does little to discourage converts. The latest conservative tactic, one presently employed, is to suggest that all libertarians are crude, naive fanatics. The conservatives' version of a libertarian, if he could be brought to life, would be a sort of humorless, philosophic bird-watcher who falls out of bed every morning at four to sneak out in the woods in search of a previously unsighted solipsism. Consider the notion, popularized by Buckley, that libertarianism arises from a desire to de-nationalize lighthouses. In a flood of articles in various publications in recent months conservatives have harped continuously about lighthouses, so much so that one wonders about the source of their fascination. In all of libertarian literature there is scarcely one sentence about lighthouses.

So why – you wonder – is there such a big fuss? The answer is that as always it is the conservative tactic to portray any departure from the status quo as something ridiculous. In all the conservative attacks upon libertarians one would be hard pressed to find one argument which does not rest upon the contention that an idea is silly if its implications extend beyond the bounds of consensus politics. But surely, you may tell yourself, there must be more to conservatism than that. No, hardly. Conservatism is just what Russell Kirk has always insisted it should be – the belief that whatever exists is good.

Mr. Buckley says that libertarians are naive, but one could hardly imagine a more naive, mindless doctrine than conservatism. Conservatives do not believe anything in particular. They have no specific philosophy. In practice, they are always a generation or so behind the times. Whatever the liberals advocated 25 years ago, conservatives are defending today. If you doubt it, employ an empirical test. Read today's Mr. Buckley and try to distinguish his pitch from that of yesterday's Harry Truman. The difference is not worth yawning over.

It does not take much of a philosopher to realize that with the conservative position constantly (if slowly) changing, those who advocate it are caught up in a plexus of absurdities. For example, Buckley is deeply offended by unflattering comparisons between heroes of the American state and their counterparts abroad. His attitude is inevitable, for by the very nature of conservatism, conservatives cannot see all societies in the same light. Conservatives favor stability and preservation of the status quo. But they can favor only one status quo at a time. If they were logical, they could hardly help but admire such noble personages as Premier Kosygin, who has probably done more to maintain the status quo than any government leader in this century. Kosygin is one of history's great conservatives.

Buckley and his crowd cleave to contradictions which would make modest men blush. They claim to be a force against statism. Yet their most notable libertarian gesture of the past decade was when James Burnham came out in favor of legalizing firecrackers. They say they favor liberty. But their prime occupation is apologizing for Richard Nixon, a man who has about as much respect for human liberty as Mao Tse Tung. Buckley says that he and his chums understand what the free market really is. Yet who among them (I do not count Henry Hazlitt as part of the Buckley crowd) was ever concerned or knowledgable about economics? Look at the backgrounds of the NATIONAL REVIEW contributors. They are a coterie of ex-commies and religious mystics and theocrats.

As the American state becomes more totalitarian (and who could deny that it is?), Mr. Buckley will be impelled by the dynamics of his own illogic to apologize for whatever happens. He has gone along with the gag this far. Why stop now? Unless he admits to the libertarian contention that political positions need not be defined by what is admissible in the status quo, Buckley will turn out to be no better than the tired old men of another time who shrugged over Auschwitz and Buchenwald.

◘

INTELLECTUAL AMMUNITION. The *Sil Services Bulletin*, the largest periodic listing and review of new and classic, libertarian and Objectivist works is now available FREE to all interested persons. Every *Bulletin* includes reviews of over 20 different libertarian books and publications, in objective philosophy, free market economics, revisionist history, romantic fiction and anti-politics. Magazines offered include the *Individualist, Reason, The Libertarian Forum, the Libertarian Connection, Efficacy, the Personalist and Invictus*. Authors of books offered include Rand, Rothbard, LeFevre, Hazlitt, Branden, Kolko, Spooner, Tucker and many others. If you have been looking for intellectual ammunition, you will find it in the *Sil Services Bulletin*. For your free subscription write: SIL, Dept. LF, 40C Bonifant Road, Silver Spring, Md. 20904.

STATELESS SOCIETIES: *(Continued from page 4)*

exchanges at its free market value rather than at a state imposed exchange rate.

Thus the peculiar absence of coinage among the Irish a thousand years after its introduction in Britain is further testimony to the absence of the State in Irish society.

Under the impact of the Norman invasion of Ireland in the twelfth century, Irish institutions and customs underwent considerable strain as they tried to cope with so alien a social and political system as that represented by the statism of the English imperialists. But in the end the two systems were incompatible. Under the Tudor monarchy with its strong absolutist tendencies, a systematic, intense and ultimately successful policy of conquest and cultural genocide was directed against the native Irish. The rebellions, conquests, and confiscations of the 17th century finished the destruction of the old anarchic society. Yet surely the spirit of liberty lived on in the hearts of the Irish peasantry to emerge again and again down to the present day whenever the oppression of the foreigners became too great. The shadow of the past is always very real and present in Ireland, and the memory of liberty has never faded from the minds of the people.

Note: Historians writing about stateless societies have a tendency to use "statist" terminology and conceptions in describing essentially stateless ideas and institutions. Irish historians have been particularly guilty in this respect. Least affected are the works of Myles Dillion, *The Celtic Realms* (London, 1967), and *Early Irish Society* (Dublin, 1954); also D. A. Binchy, *Anglo-Saxon and Irish Kingship* (London, 1970); and Kathleen Hughes, in her introduction to *A History of Medieval Ireland* (London, 1968), by A. J. Otway-Ruthven.

◘

Libertarian Conference

The libertarian conference held at Columbia University Law School, New York City, on March 13-14, was a resounding success. Three hundred people attended the conference, and everyone was struck by the seriousness and eagerness to learn of virtually everyone in the audience. Gary Greenberg, the New York Libertarian Association, and Society for Individual Liberty (SIL), are to be commended for an excellent and expert organizing job. In contrast to the RLA conference in New York a year and a half ago, there was no hysteria, no uproar, no screaming at each other by Left, Center, and Right factions of the movement.

There was no lunging for the microphone by rowdies of any of the factions. More and more it becomes clear that SIL and its affiliates – and regardless of minor differences within its ranks – are going to be the major conduits for libertarian organizing in this country.

Highlight of the conference was the debate between Roy Childs, Jr. and the sinister Jeffrey St. John, veteran Randian-Buckleyite radio and TV commentator, on "anarcho-capitalism vs. limited government". Making his debut as a debater, Roy gladdened the hearts of all libertarians by clobbering and turning-inside-out the suave rhetorician, trapping St. John repeatedly in ignorance, logical contradictions, and outright evasions. More important, the largely neo-Randian audience realized this full well, and was deeply impressed by Roy's superior logic. Now that the Randian monolith has been shattered forevermore, there are a great many Randians around the country who are interested in and susceptible to the rational arguments for anarcho-capitalism.

All this illustrates a growing truth about our movement: that the most susceptible to extensive and long-lasting conversion to Liberty are far more the sober, sensible middle classes of our country, rather than the drug-besotted ranters against work, individualism, and private property, that handful calling for destruction of "Amerika" and all its works.

Army Intelligence Reads The Forum

Recent revelations of the snooping activities of Army Counterintelligence showed that the Army was engaged in massive spying and reportage on virtually every group – left or right-wing – in some way outside the Establishment consensus in American life. One of the activities of the Army's Counterintelligence Analysis Branch (CIAB) was to subscribe to "underground" publications, and the cover address it used was "R. Allan Lee Associates" of Alexandria, Va. When the revelation broke recently, we realized that, sure enough, R. Allan Lee Associates had been until recently subscribers to the *Lib Forum*, only failing to renew just before the publicity hit the fan.

Who knows what secret name and address the CIAB is using now, somewhere among our vast array of subscribers? But at any rate, welcome CIAB, even if you *are* using stolen taxpayers' money to report on taxpayers; maybe you'll learn something from reading us. And more important, to you, Mr. and Mrs. Libertarian out there, if the CIAB is reading us avidly and with care, can *you* afford to lag behind?

The Libertarian Forum
BOX 341
MADISON SQUARE STATION
NEW YORK, NEW YORK 10010

Published Every Month. Subscription Rate: $8.00 Per Year

A Monthly Newsletter

THE
Libertarian Forum

Joseph R. Peden, Publisher

Murray N. Rothbard, Editor

VOLUME III, NO. 5
MAY, 1971
75¢

ORWELL LIVES

Do you ever get the feeling that the *rest* of the world is crazy and that you are one of the few sane people in it? I suppose that psychologists would consider such a feeling a sign of deep neurosis – *except* of course if you happened, empirically, to be correct. And reading the daily press is enough to induce such a feeling in even the sanest amongst us. In particular the stream of pronouncements emanating from the Nixon Administration. Every President, every Administration, has lied, lied grossly and systematically, to the public; but surely none before Nixon has elevated the Lie, big and small, to the constant and the universal. There used to be the charge against Hitler that he used the technique of the Big Lie; yet Nixon lies continually and habitually, on virtually every issue, and the horrendous problem that arises is: how can he get away with it? Why don't the American people laugh him off every public forum?

Take for example the unemployment statistics. Every month a new statistic emerges, and the Nixonian experts anxiously examine its entrails for signs and omens. Always, and invariably, and *whatever happens*, the omens are pronounced to be superb. Thus, in one month, the unemployment falls by one-tenth of one per cent. So small as to be meaningless, right? Wrong, for Nixon's crew will pronounce this to be the beginning of recovery from our recession. And then, the next month, the unemployment rate rises again by one tenth of one per cent. What does the Nixon team do? Do they admit that by their own logic things are looking gloomy? Do they at least have the good taste to keep their mouths shut? Not on your tintype. For there they are again, saying: Yes, this is a very good thing, for it shows that "unemployment is bottoming out."

Better is good; worse is good; whatever happens is terrific. On this Orwellian logic rests the rock of our Republic. There is first the Nixonian expansion of the war into Cambodia and Laos, each time proclaiming that, of course you ninny, this is how you "wind down" the war; any dolt knows that the way to phase out a war is to expand it. In Orwell's world, the Ministry of War has become the Ministry of Peace, and so in the world of Tricky Dick. And the Laos invasion: we were going to nip into Laos, "cut the Ho Cho Minh trail" – as if this "trail" were some sort of superhighway which we tear up (It is, in fact, an enormous, thirty-fifty mile wide network of jungle trails) – capture the base of Schepone, and maybe even stay there permanently to keep the trail "cut". So then we get bogged down, and the military genius of Gen. Vo Nguyen Giap, the hero of Dienbienphu – turns the American-Saigon invasion into another Dienbienphu, a veritable disaster, in which the cream of the Saigon puppet troops get chopped up, from which the remainder barely escaped with their lives, and in which we lost many hun-

dreds of helicopters. And our reaction? It was a great victory, we did just as we meant to do, we never, er, never meant to capture Schepone, or even to cut the trail – but by George we delayed their "timetable"! And since no one is privy to this mystic timetable, or even whether it exists at all, *any* thing can be said about it without fear of contradiction. So it doesn't matter whether we win, lose, or whatnot – whatever happens, it was a glorious victory. How can we put up for another minute with this systemic fabrication and falsehood?

Or take Mr. Nixon solemnly proclaiming that all his life he has been "a deeply committed pacifist"! How can he *say* this, how can he dare, this mass murderer, this supporter of all of America's wars and chief murderer of the current war? Whether one is a pacifist or not, this is surely a new height of affront.

Or Nixon's gall in coming out against abortion because he is deeply committed to the "sanctity of human life". Again from a mass murderer, a man who can order the systematic bombing of thousands upon thousands of innocent peasant women and babies, this killer and bomber and napalmer has the unmitigated gall to pout because women are ejecting fetusus from their bodies! For shame!

And then Nixon, the self-proclaimed champion of law and order, rushes in to interfere with the judicial process because of his "compassion" for the convicted little mass murderer Calley. Mr. Nixon was indignant enough about the mass murderer Manson to interfere *against* him in the judicial process. But Calley killed far more people than Manson, and yet here Nixon intervenes in the murderer's favor.

Here it must be conceded that large numbers of Americans participated too in the mass outpouring of "compassion" for this convicted butcher. Orwell lives here again, for this was

(Continued on page 8)

From An Old Curmudgeon

Beauty is Youth, Youth Beauty . . . From Harriet Van Horne's column (New York *Post*, April 16): "When we tune in a Late Late Show and see young players named Ingrid Bergman, Henry Fonda, Joan Bennett and such we feel we are looking upon a lost super-race. They had shining hair and fine bones and the whites of their eyes were always clear. Their diction was crisp, they moved through terrible plots with innocent goodwill. They stood straight and they laughed beautifully. By comparison, today's young people look messy, dull and terribly uninteresting." ◻

Ireland: Neutralist And State Capitalist

by John P. McCarthy

Although virtually unnoticed until quite recently, the Northern Irish Government's record of maltreatment of its Catholic minority is now obvious to any well-informed person, particularly to anyone of libertarian sentiments. At the same time many libertarians might be unaware of the situation in the rest of Ireland. There things are much more pleasant, especially in the matters of minority treatment and social harmony, although certain criticisms are in order. Possibly the following analysis by a non-libertarian, or at least a non-anarchist who has, however, certain libertarian instincts, might be of interest.

Back in the ideologically uncomplicated days of the late 1950's and early 1960's Robert Welch was able to give mathematical percentages indicating the degree to which nations were under the "operational control" of International Communism. One of the nations, along with the Union of South Africa, Portugal, Spain, South Korea, and Nationalist China, that he found all but completely free from Communist influence was the Republic of Ireland. Admittedly, the dozen or so members of the Irish Communist Party of that time did not swing much political clout, and in that sense Welch's ratings can be considered legitimate. However, one cannot avoid the suspicion that Welch rated Ireland, which was put in most inappropriate company, by a most second-hand evaluation that drew very little from actual knowledge of the conditions in the nation. Probably Welch gave Ireland a good rating for the simple reason that his enemies - the "Comsymps" and the "Globaliberals" - disliked Ireland. But their views were as unfounded, and were based not so much on the situation in Ireland as on both Establishment Liberalism's inherent Anglophilism and the decided anti-Establishmentarianism of pre-Kennedy Irish-America with its reputation of isolationism, McCarthyism, and pre-Vatican II Catholicism.

In point of fact, the Irish socio-political situation, then and now, does not fit the simplistic black and white categories of either the Birchers or the Liberals. For instance, the Irish were among the pioneers in the revolutionary nationalist tactic of guerilla warfare, yet the Republic of Ireland almost uniquely has permitted the old ascendant class - the Anglo-Irish Protestants - to maintain their predominant status in the economic and social structure of the nation, as well as preserve an inordinate degree of political influence. Furthermore, while the Irish Government has had a record of imposing certain moral regulations on the population, such as literary censorship (greatly relaxed of late) and prohibition of the sale of contraceptives, it has scarcely penalized or inhibited Protestants as such from the free exercise or propagation of their religious beliefs. (One might argue that Protestants are more desirous of the prohibited literature and the contraceptives, yet the prohibitions apply to everyone and are not specifically designed to discomfort Protestants.)

The Irish Government did not join the Soviet Union, the Republic of China, Great Britain, and the United States in the democratic anti-Axis crusade of the 1940's. Yet her record as a functioning, multi-party, proportionally-represented, functioning parliamentary democracy has few rivals in the twentieth century, and she is rather dissimilar to the authoritarian regimes that had similar strongly non-Communist ratings in the Birch score card. Her neutrality has been consistent throughout the Second World War and the Cold War, as she envisions herself - only recently a European colony - as having a special relationship with the recently independent Afro-Asian nations. Indeed, Ireland even takes the United Nations seriously - so seriously that her representatives, to the disappointment of most Irishmen, have hesitated to mount the U. N. soap-box over the Northern issue even though most members use the General Assembly for such purposes. The record of Conor Cruise O'Brien, the scholar, academician, and former Irish diplomat (probably most famous for his Congo adventurism, but more deserving of fame for permanently deflating Arthur Schlesinger, Jr., in a television debate concerning the C.I.A.), was not really a departure from an Irish diplomatic tradition that places primary emphasis on questions like the inviolability of neutral and small nation rights against big power pressure. Irish compassion for Biafra is a more recent manifestation of this tradition.

Cruise O'Brien has now become the most celebrated member of the Irish Labour Party, a group that was red-baited by the governing Fianna Fail Party in the last general election because of its espousal of an "alien" ideology - socialism. Paradoxically, one of the seventeen Labour representatives in the 144 seat Dail (the Irish National Assembly) in addition to Cruise O'Brien is Stephen Coughlan, the former Mayor of Limerick, whose political views and manner are somewhere between those of Father Coughlin and Joe McCarthy. Actually, very few in Ireland find anything wrong with socialism, and public corporations occupy a greater role in the economy there than in almost any nation this side of the Iron Curtain. It is only the name, which suggests atheism and materialism, that offends. But even that is changing, as in the last few years the Catholic Church in Ireland has become taken up with an interest in socialism. Church-sponsored seminars have started to emphasize the compatibility of Christianity and Marxism.

Irish students, emerging from a period of political indifference and careermindedness, like students everywhere have been taken up with the charm of socialism. As might be expected they identify the Irish state-capitalism with capitalism, and when pressed for an example of socialism suggest various voluntary cooperatives like that organized by Father James McDyer at Glencolumbkille, Co. Donegal, where local peasants, combining their capital with donations from exiles in America, have had relative success in setting up a weaving factory and a vegetable processing plant. But many of the leaders of these highly decentralized cooperative movements, like Father Patrick Campbell, who is connected with the Achill, Co. Mayo cooperative, prefer to avoid association with the state and, possibly unconsciously, are much closer to the free economy ideal than the state-capitalism condemned by the students.

There have been two major phases in the state-capitalist record of the Irish Government (which has been controlled by the Fianna Fail Party since 1932, with the brief exceptions of 1948-1951 and 1954-1957). The first phase was the attempt between 1932 and 1959 to implement the revolutionary ideal of national economic self-sufficiency with the usual weapons of protective tariffs, subsidized industries, and state corporations. Much of this, of course, grew out of Prime Minister (the Taioseach) Eamon DeValera's aim to complete the severance of any ties with Great Britain. DeValera's opposition, the Old Free State Party (now known as the Fine Gael Party) that he had ousted from power, naturally was hostile to this unrealistic effort of Ireland to end her economic relationship with England. Appropriately, larger Irish businesses with international outlets sympathized with that party. However, aside from this historic opposition to the economic self-sufficiency dreams, Fine Gael is scarcely opposed to state-capitalism on general principle.

The second phase of Fianna Fail's state-capitalist policy began in 1959 when DeValera moved upstairs to the honorific Presidency of Ireland, being succeeded as Taoiseach by

(Continued on page 3)

IRELAND —*(Continued from page 2)*

Sean Lemass who was not taken up with any of DeValera's enthusiasm for preserving traditional rural Ireland and maintaining economic and cultural isolation. However, his policies were no less state-capitalist. It is true that he did take steps towards customs reductions, freer trade with England, and eventual Irish membership in the Common Market. He also reversed an earlier policy inhibiting foreign ownership of businesses in Ireland, as he sought to encourage foreign investors in Ireland with long-term tax exemptions and government-built plants, only insisting that most of their production be for export. Relatively soon thereafter improved balance of trade and export figures drew great acclaim for Lemass. In 1966 he retired, leaving his successor, Jack Lynch, to handle a skyrocketing inflation and strongly revived trade imbalance among other problems.

In the midst of all this, the Irish Government is proceeding with its plans for preparing Ireland for the expected admission to the Common Market. The planning consists of deciding the economically appropriate areas for industrial, commercial, and agricultural development, and directing government funds, subsidies, and tax exemptions to these areas. Other places, particularly in the West in large sections of Donegal, Mayo, and Kerry, are consigned by the planners to further depopulation and economic decline. To ease the economic death agony, the government will continue its palliatives such as munificent welfare assistance and home improvement grants. But only in tourism, which is highly subsidized, is any possibility seen for development and expansion.

Many in Ireland, from Churchmen through cooperative organizations to the I.R.A., are critical of the Government's plans and suspicious of E.E.C. membership because of the Government's acceptance of and commitment to the merciful elimination of the Western peasant communities. Possibly the West's demise is an inevitable economic development paralleling tendencies in other lands, but now it must also be seen as being positively promoted by state action, even if only in the directing of subsidies to other areas. Admittedly most of the critics would only want to redirect the subsidies to the peasant areas and apply other protective devices. But such would fail to get at the root of much of the rapid depopulation of the Western Irish countryside.

The psychological and numerical erosion of the traditional Western Irish peasant life can be attributed to historical and contemporary circumstances. Centuries of imperialist landlordism with arbitrary evictions and higher rents for self-improved holdings induced a reluctance to innovate and advance. Even in the twentieth century, when the peasants obtained title to their holdings, government paternalism has prevented the natural self-improvement and development that ought to coincide with private property ownership. A passive waiting on outside direction and assistance has combined with cynicism about the success of the ostensibly benevolent assistance programs of the government. For instance, improvements in either living quarters or agricultural methods usually await government grants before being undertaken, even when such could easily be afforded by the recipient. The natural sources of potential wealth in the West of Ireland such as vegetable cultivation and fishing are scarcely developed, while local leaders pressure the authorities for prestige projects like subsidized factories in areas completely inappropriate in terms of skilled labor, raw materials, or transportation. The people, who are more realistic, encourage their youth to disdain the miserable pay in the subsidized factories in favor of better wages in London and elsewhere.

The extraordinary work ethic and entrepreneurial energy of immigrants to the United States from the West of Ireland

is adequate proof of the wonders that could ensue from the shedding of paternalism. This suggests that similar energies among their kinfolk at home could disprove the government planners and make a relative success of the West of Ireland if allowed to be unwrapped.

Another recent enthusiasm of the Irish Government is for the centralization of various public services and quasi-public industries. For instance, in education, in the name of improvement and expansion, small one-room country school houses are being closed to allow amalgamation into larger schools covering greater districts. Similarly, there is a drive underway for centralization of the three colleges of the National University and the unification of the Dublin college with Trinity College. Enlightened opinion is overwhelmingly sympathetic to these rationalizing and modernizing steps. Yet, here is an instance in which a lesson might be taken from the misery of the overcentralized educational systems, on both elementary and university levels, of the United States. However, statist planners are certain to remain unaware of the merits of decentralization in such matters as personal responsibility, creativity, and human contact. ◻

Contempt For The Usual

In his scintillating dissection of Women's Lib in the December *Harper's* (see the *Lib. Forum*, Dec. 15), Irving Howe set forth an insight which deserves elaboration: the "contempt for the usual" endemic on the Left, New and Old. For apart from the tendency on the Left to employ coercion, the Left seems to be constitutionally incapable of leaving people alone in the most fundamental sense; it seems incapable of refraining from a continual pestering, haranguing and harassment of everyone in sight or earshot. (And here the Randian movement falls into much the same error.) The Left is incapable of recognizing the legitimacy of the average person's peaceful pursuit of his own goals and his own values in his quietly sensible life. Many libertarians who are enamoured of the principles of Maoism point out that, in *theory* at least, the decentralized communes and eternal self-and-mutual-criticism sessions are supposed to be voluntary and not imposed by violence. Even granting this point, Maoism at its best, forswearing violence, would be well-nigh intolerable to most of us, and certainly to anyone wishing to pursue a truly individualist life. For Maoism depends on a continual badgering, harassing, and pestering of every person in one's purview to bring him into the full scale of values, attitudes, and convictions held by the rest of his neighbors. I am reminded of several ardent American Maoists who, a few years ago, were taking a Chinese plane out of Hanoi. On the plane they were politely but persistently subjected to a continuing high dosage of Maoist propaganda: not only were pictures and booklets of the Chairman virtually everywhere, but the Chinese anthem "East is Red" was played over and over on the loudspeaker and the hostess sweetly but urgently demanded to know why these Americans were not joining in the community sing. By the time the plane ride was thankfully over, the young Americans had permanently lost their enthusiasm for the Maoist ideal. The point is that in the Maoist world, even at its most civilized, the propaganda barrage is everywhere.

To put it another way: one crucial and permanent difference between libertarians and the Left is in their vision of a future society. Libertarians want the *end* of politics; they wish to abolish politics forever, so that each individual may live his life unmolested and as he sees fit. But the Left, in contrast, wants to politicize *everything*; for the Left, every individual action, no matter how trivial or

(Continued on page 4)

CONTEMPT FOR THE USUAL —

(*Continued from page 3*)

picayune, becomes a "political" act, to be examined, criticized, denounced, and rehabilitated in accordance with the Left's standards. No person can pick up a spoon, go for a walk to his favorite pub, or turn on TV, without being carefully watched and denounced for taking a wrong political line, or for not moulding all of his values and his life in accordance with "genuine revolutionary" standards. (In the Randian movement, a badgering of almost equivalent intensity is beamed at all movement members to mould them into models of Randian "rationality".) On the Left, this politicizing of life has accelerated in intensity in recent years.

The Women's Lib movement, of course, has been in the forefront of this elevating of hectoring and pestering into a universal moral obligation. No one can pick up a dish rag without his or her action being weighed and judged in the light of its "politics". Mutual aid and cooperation between loved ones, hitherto spontaneous and unforced, becomes a matter of endless debate, rigorous weighing and computing, and the grim toting of ledgers and accounts.

The "ordinary man", the average person, is a particular target of the Left demons of politics. Recently, for example, football has come under the heavy guns of the Left intellecutals. There is nothing the "middle American" enjoys more than sitting in front of a TV set on a weekend afternoon, beer can in hand, watching a pro football game. Now this innocent and delightful pastime, this surcease from the cares of the day, comes under the scorn and gunfire of our contemporary Medusas and Savonorolas. Football, they claim, is evil because it is rugged and competitive; scoring should be abolished so that there are no winners and no losers (and hence no excellence and no mediocrity). Every player is dragged down to the same level, and all the fun goes out of the sport. Furthermore, watching pro football is also deemed an evil because it is the acme of the division of labor, of the general specialization in the economy and society which is the one thing hated above all by the Left-wing. What a sin to have football played by those who are best at the game while others delight in the spectacle and pay for the privilege! And so the Left moves in, hell-bent for the stamping out of joy, of excellence, of the market, of specialization. Away with pro football! Let everyone go out there on the greensward, and let everyone participate in eurythmic exercises! And as in the old joke about the revolution and "strawberries and cream" ("Comes the revolution, everyone will have strawberries and cream . . . and like it!"), the New Communist Man is expected to be a man or woman who finds his highest delight in non-competitive eurythmics. And if he or she is so benighted, so mired in "bourgeois hangups" as to resist the move from the TV set to the eurythmic field, then a little coercion will be applied to guide him to the proper path.

The crucial point here is that those libertarians whose *only* philosophy is to oppose coercive violence are missing a great deal of the essence of the ideological struggles of our time. The trouble with the Left is *not* simply its propensity for coercion; it is *also*, and in some sense more fundamentally, its hatred of excellence and individuality, its hostility to the division of labor, its itch for total uniformity, and its dedication to the Universal and Permanent Pester. And as it looks around the world, it finds that the main object of its hatred is the Middle American, the man who quietly holds all of the values which it cannot tolerate. And since most Americans are now Middle Americans, the Left's chances for success are predictably close to zero.

The great libertarian William Graham Sumner once wrote that *the* moral law of the free society can be summed up in the phrase: "mind your own business!" At first sight, this

seems a rather narrow ethic for mankind. But Sumner, if one looks more deeply, has hold of an extremely important point: the great reluctance of the Reformer to leave people alone, to allow them to run their lives as they see fit, without subjecting them to the chronic nagging and badgering of the Universal Social Worker. One would hope that the free society of the future would be free, not only of aggressive violence, but also of self-righteous and arrogant nagging and harassment. "Mind your own business" implies that each person attend well to his own affairs, and allow every other man the same privilege. It is a morality of basic civility, of courtesy, of civilized life, of respect for the dignity of every individual. It does not encompass all of morality, but by God it is a necessary ingredient to a truly rational and civilized social ethic.

To examine whence comes this attitude of the intellectual would require a mighty treatise. (Such treatises are all too rare; intellectuals write extensive and caustic studies of social classes, businessmen, politicians, middle classes, etc., but almost never of intellectuals themselves). But a bit of speculation is in order. One reason might be that every intellectual, as he grows up, acquires a sense of the superiority of himself and his confreres to the ordinary folk around him. Sometimes this sense of superiority may be justified; often it is not. But for many intellectuals this leads to a life-long attempt to *demonstrate*, to flaunt their superiority to the average man. Instead of peacefully and cheerfully going about his own affairs and his own productive work without worrying about his social ranking in relation to others, the intellectual begins to express his cosmic contempt by mocking the insights and values of those around him. It is not merely that football and beer are derided on behalf of pot and eurythmics. It is far more serious than that. The rot begins to permeate the entire culture. Thus, the average man is an unself-conscious philosophical realist; he believes that the world and consciousness both exist; he believes in purpose, rationality, advancement of his career and his standards of living. So the intellectual throws over realism in supreme contempt as trivial and "superficial"; instead he substitutes one form or other of philosophical subjectivism and mocking paradox. The average man also possesses and unself-conscious rational esthetics: he enjoys fiction with a plot and with a dramatization of moral struggle; he enjoys art that depicts real things in a beautiful form; he enjoys music with melody, harmony, and rhythm. And so all of these must also be thrown over as naive and superficial, and we are subjected to the triumph of the *avant-garde:* of "art" that is meaningless design, of fiction that is morbid and absurd, of "music" that is stripped of melody or balance, of movies that substitute lunatic montage and grainy photography for truly artistic blends of narrative, plot, and rational continuity — virtues that are, again, derided as "slick" and bourgeois. In one area of culture after another, and in one discipline of knowledge after another, the morbid, the absurd, the irrational, systematically replace the "bourgeois" virtues of reason, advancement and harmonious blend of form and content. And whoever refuses to like the new culture is mocked and scorned as a naive and hopeless clod, brainwashed by old-fashioned bourgeois standards. And all this to exalt the phony superiority of the intelligentsia and to degrade the instinctive rationality of the average man.

What I am saying then is that in this unequal war between the intellectual and the bourgeois, a war in which the clever and facile intellectual has all the aces in his hand, that the average man, beset and bewildered though he may be, is really right. The average man may not see deeply, but he sees clearly and correctly. And this means that one of the great and unfilled tasks of the rationalist intellectual, the true intellectual if you will, is to come to the aid of the

(*Continued on page 5*)

CONTEMPT FOR THE USUAL —
(Continued from page 4)

bourgeoisie, to rescue the Middle American from his triumphant tormentors. Our task is to provide for the bourgeois the intellectual tools, the philosophical groundwork and framework for his correct but half-formed instincts. In the name of truth and reason, we must rise up as the shield and the hammer of the average American. In the present state of our corrupt and decadent culture, there is no nobler task. And in the course of our doing so, there will come about a re-integration of theory and practice, of the intellectual and the bourgeois, which will provide a far more harmonious base for genuine fraternity and solidarity than all the *avant-garde* communes, than all the nagging and pestering, on the face of the globe. ◘

Chamberlain And Hess

By Robert LeFevre

John Chamberlain, appearing in the New Haven (Connecticut) *Register*, recently unsheathed his pen and took a stab at the growing libertarian movement. He chose as his *bete noir* Karl Hess, of Goldwater fame and misfortune. According to Chamberlain, Hess may be a general of a libertarian cause, but this general lacks an army. In the course of putting down the libertarian movement he linked Hess with "his brother-in-merry-anarchism" Murray Rothbard and then stated: "Here and there a shy libertarian bloom pokes its head above the snows. But it is a delusion to think that an army is following Karl Hess."

Now I am among those who did not approve of Karl's boisterous insistence that the way to attain freedom is to "man the barricades" in the streets and to use any type of violence necessary to destroy political office holders. As a matter of fact, at USC a year ago, when Karl had made just such an appeal, I followed him to the platform and in large measure "turned off" the libertarians present. Since then, so far as I am able to learn, Karl has moved toward the position of Progressive Labor or even the Trotskyite camp, and apparently has disclaimed the libertarian position. If Karl is calling himself an anarchist, it is certainly not the anarchism of Murray Rothbard, who proclaims unceasingly the validity of private property and a market without intervention.

But the real purpose of Chamberlain was not to attack Karl Hess. Rather, it was to link the libertarian movement to Hess, who may be a falling star, and by this process to sweep the deck clean of any riff-raff who don't buy the Conservative position of "I hate and fear Russia"; "I hate and fear China"; "I hate and fear Cuba"; etc., ad nauseam.

Now, it is no wonder that John Chamberlain has not been able to sniff many new libertarian blooms lately. He hasn't been in the garden where they grow. So I want to encourage John to go out of his office so he can learn just what is happening. Apparently he is hoping for a resurgence of a love of liberty on campus. At least it is possible to glean this bit of grain from the bushel of chaff that accompanied his article. The steam behind the "New Left," so called, may very well be subsiding.

After all, the sop thrown to many campus lefties by the Nixon administration by legalizing the ballot for eighteen-year-olds may very well have brought a substantial number of New Left people into the arms of the Establishment. But you don't look for libertarians among those who slavishly manipulate the ballots and hope the monster will spew a few crumbs from its table. You'll find libertarians among the rapidly growing number of campus people who don't want to play political darts and in consequence aren't going to vote at all.

Now in THIS area, if John cares to look, he may find the

Is Pot Harmless?

A recent dispatch from Berkeley (Doug Shuit, "Expert Switches, Sees Harm in Pot," New York *Post*, Mar. 29) reports that the distinguished psychiatrist Dr. D. Harvey Powelson, director of the Student Psychiatric Clinic at Berkeley, has changed his mind about the "harmlessness" of marijuana. His previous Polyanna view, he reports, was based on a limited sampling of students; but now, after observing 500 students in the last five years, Dr. Powelson has changed his mind.

What Powelson reports is what most of us, observing kids on drugs, have also seen with our own eyes: for example, that pot has a "cumulative effect, and that prolonged use . . . could result in chronic changes similar to those seen in organic brain diseases — islands of lucidity intermixed with areas of loss of function." Furthermore, use of marijuana often results in a "disorder of thinking characterized by a general lack of coherence and an exacerbation of pathological thinking processes." Regular pot-users often become "will-less – anomic", "to do anything requires a gigantic effort". As to the contention of the drug-enthusiasts that marijuana "heightens perception", Powelson retorts: "It affects you in the same way any kind of delirium does. It focuses your attention. But it's pathological in a sense because it results in cutting out all the peripheral things a person looks at. When an ordinary person looks at something, he sees everything, all the peripheral things. But when you're in a delirium and you see, for example, a shadow, you have a heightened sense of the shadow because all your attention is focused on the shadow and you see nothing else."

Powelson adds that one reason that drug users claim that there are no harmful effects from pot "is that often a person high on marijuana cannot determine the changes that occur in his thinking. One of the first things that's impaired is your judgement of your own system."

No doubt out drug-enthusiasts can come up with some psychiatric swinger or other to deny this point. But this overlooks a vital point. And that is the curious and brusque dismissal of the judgement of the overwhelming majority of the medical profession. The usual rebuttal by our drug fans is that the doctors are engaged in some sort of Calvinistic conspiracy against enjoyment, as embodied in pot and other psychedelic drugs. Now I am the first one to concede that there are many political conspiracies around, and that there are monopolistic collusions in the medical profession. But what earthly *reason* would there be for such a "conspiracy"? What would doctors have to gain? And as for Calvinism, we have not been living in a Calvinist culture for a long, long time. The entire emphasis of our culture is hedonic, sensate, pleasure-loving. To postulate some sort of mass Calvinistic throwback among conspiring physicians is too grotesque to warrant the slightest consideration.

And moreover: suppose we concede for a moment that all the returns are not yet in, that there are two points of view, that there is a great need for further study in this area. So what? Surely the sensible and rational person, confronted with a new, powerful, and unstudied drug which a large body of physicians claim is harmful, surely such a person will abstain from this needless danger until all the returns are in? What is the masochism that leads our youth to rush pell-mell into the grave risk of destruction of their mind and consciousness? From whatever angle we look at the problem, once again the instincts of Middle America are right, and the anti-culture is tragically wrong. ◘

---

beginning of an army. It wears many cloaks and it marshals under a number of banners. And it isn't following Hess or anyone else to the barricades. It is insisting on reason and logic and a revolution of the mind that impels individual rejection of the coercion of government per se. ◘

Recommended Reading

Nixon and Co.

Witty, sardonic, emphatically "in", unerring in zeroing in on the defects of those persons and groups (a vast number) whom he hates, and unique in being absolutely unafraid to use ethnic humor, Noel E. Parmentel, Jr. is back! This time he eviscerates a pet hate, Henry Kissinger, and along the way spears his boss Nixon. See Noel's two-part piece in the *Village Voice,* "Portnoy in Tall Cotton: Or Making It on the Potomac" (March 11, March 18). Thus, Noel says of Kissinger, author of an adoring study of Metternich, that "the man is more Sammy Glick than Metternich." On Betty Friedan: "Mrs. Betty Friedan takes on Norman Mailer and any and all other comers whose male chauvinism and sexism seek to exploit her obvious and manifest visual appeal." On White House aide Martin Anderson: "'Dr.' Anderson is, or was, roughly equivalent to Cardinal, played off against Miss Ayn Rand's Popess, in the Objectivist church or synagogue . . . In any case, 'Dr.' Anderson bears more resemblance to Elisha Cooke, Jr. in the 'Maltese Falcon' than to Gary Cooper in 'The Fountainhead' ('Dr.' Anderson has since foresworn the epistemology of John Galt for that of Spiro Agnew.)" For his pains, *National Review* accused Noel of being anti-Semitic, while one irate *Voice* reader called him a "closet Nazi". Well, aren't these the days when *all* oppressed minority groups are being called on "to come out of the closet?"

The Left.

I have been meaning to recommend in the highest terms a brilliant article that appeared in the Dec. 1, 15th Anniversary issue of *National Review* by Eugene D. Genovese (!), "The Fortunes of the Left." One of this generation's outstanding Marxist scholars, Genovese, who has spent his entire life on the Left, has for it nothing but almost total contempt. Genovese begins by pointing out that the Left is in total ruin; that its chances of seizing power "are slightly inferior to the chances of a seizure of power by a coaliton of the Campfire Girls and the Gay Liberation Front under the leadership of Ti-Grace Atkinson." Whereas the New Left of the early and mid-60's had considerable promise, it has descended into suicidal "madness", into a "cult of violence generally manifested in blustering and sporadic and self-defeating acts of nihilism, which are no more than the acting out of adolescent fantasies of revolution . . ."

The Weathermen, Genovese points out, are largely an invention of the media, who found them "cute"; while the "cultural revolutionaries" of the youth culture are the "problem children of the solid bourgeoisie", a phenomenon that terrifies the solid citizens of the Right and Center, "who interpret their own inability to discipline their children as the beginning of the end of civilization. (I suspect that it is, in fact, only the beginning of the end of the quaint notion that children can be raised without occasional spankings.)" So long as the cultural revolutionaries persist, supported by the media "that hail everything young as intrinsically good and misunderstood", so long will working class and middle-class Americans be totally

repulsed, and so long will it be impossible to build a sober and decent Left in this country. The idealogy of the current youth-Left is "liberal-nihilist", and therefore associates the entire Left in the public mind with a "repudiation of those values which are necessary to any civilized existence."

The original New Left, Genovese adds, contributed many positive virtues: its libertarian instincts, its "critical spirit, an assertion of humane values, a hatred for regimentation and, on a more direct political level, a strong suspicion of centralization in general and Big Daddy government in particular." But now, these early strivings, which intersected at many points with the best of conservatism, have been reversed: partly because of the "inability of the Now Generation to bear setbacks, defeats and other irritants to the compulsion for instant gratification."

What Genovese is calling for is a sort of socialist, or decentralized-socialist, counterpart of what I have been calling for in the libertarian movement with equal lack of success: taking one's place in a sober, protracted commitment to a libertarian (or, in his case, socialist) caucus within a broader anti-war political coalition, amid the anti-war politicians of the McCarthy-Lindsay-McGovern-Hatfield variety. But this sort of program fails to fulfill the lust for instant gratification so endemic in the present-day. Genovese calls also for a dialogue between the Left and Right opposition to the current *status quo,* and hails such socialist intellectuals as William Appleman Williams for striving to incorporate decentralist-conservative insights into a socialist program.

In his analysis of the current political scene, Genovese presents to the *N. R.* readers for the first time in their lives the great truth that there is not very much difference between Old Left and New Right: "President Nixon's right-wing liberalism is the counterpart of the Communist Party's left-wing liberalism – that is, each advances solutions within the established consensus of liberal social policy."

The only hope for a sane Left opposition, Genovese concludes, is the disappearance of the youthful nihilists; it is only the "certain defeat of the carriers of apocalyptic fantasies" that can "clear the way for the long, slow work of finding new ground on which to stand . . ."

****

Conservation.

It hurts to recommend anything in *National Review,* but truth must always triumph in our hearts over prejudice. The April 6 issue has an excellent article by the *Lib. Forum*'s own discovery, Edwin G. Dolan, "Why Not Sell the National Parks?" Dolan, far more of an outdoorsman than many of us effetes in the New York movement, makes the point: if the conservationists want to preserve the parks, wilderness, etc., why don't they *buy* these areas? Shouldn't they trust *themselves* to preserve these areas rather than some government bureaucrat?

We Beat The SST

The glorious triumph over the SST was not only an important victory for liberty over the Leviathan State and the military-industrial complex; it was also an instructive lesson for libertarians on who our natural political allies may be in the present historical period. Who favored this billion-dollar boondoggle? The Nixon Administration, the war-mongers, the Conservative Movement, the entire uneconomic and sub-marginal aircraft industry, Big Unionism – tied in with that industry: in short, the entire Establishment force of the Unholy Triad: Big Business – Big Government – Big Unionism, working together in that unholy "partnership" that characterizes the current American political system. Who opposed the SST? First and foremost, every single economist, regardless of political persuasion, left, right, and center; and then, Left-liberals of the anti-war and anti-militarist movement; Old Right conservatives opposed to the waste of taxpayers' money; and libertarians.

One of the most amusing and enlightening aspects of this new-found unity among economists: from Friedman to Heller and Galbraith, was the Congressional testimony of the high panjandrum of Orthodox Keynesian economics, Professor Paul Samuelson. Samuelson declared that we must stop the orgy of "pyramid-building" in which we have engaged for many years. This was an "in-joke" reference to one of the most famous remarks of Samuelson's Master, Lord Keynes, to the effect that the building of pyramids is just as economically sound as any more productive expenditure, for both will increase that revered figure, the Gross National Product, by the same extent. In fact, pyramid-building is *better!* Samuelson's repudiation of pyramid-building, his justifiable concern for *what* is being done with our productive resources, signals The End of Keynes. For the Liberals have had their Keynesian Economics rule us for over thirty years; and now they are beginning to realize that what they have reaped is vast governmental waste in behalf of the GNP, the growth of a State Leviathan, and the proliferation of endless imperial wars. Yearning for pyramids, the Liberals have reaped missiles and napalm and H-bombs and germ warfare. And they don't like the results.

If we analyze the vote in the Senate, we find that the leading Conservatives voted *en masse* for this statist boondoggle: Brock, Buckley, Curtis, Dole, Fannin, Goldwater (ponder that, ex-Goldwaterite libertarians!), Gurney, Hruska, Thurmond, Tower, *et al.* They were joined by the war-liberals among the Democrats: Inouye, Jackson, McGee, Symington. But the interesting – and crucially significant – votes were those cast *against* the SST by a minority of conservatives: Bentsen, Byrd (Va.), Chiles, Ervin, Gambrell, Griffin, Hansen, Jordan (Id.), Miller, Prouty, Roth. (And for nostalgic Old Rightists, there was the glorious spectacle of veteran isolationist-libertarian H. R. Gross (R.,Io.), that veteran guardian of the taxpayer, voting against as well.) We have it on good authority that at least two of the Senate conservative votes were shifted by the testimony before the Senate Appropriations Committee of the intrepid libertarian, James Davidson of the National Taxpayers Union. And so the libertarian movement, for the first time, exercises its political muscle – not through violence or hysteria but through the use of reason and persuasion. And if we remember that a shift of three votes in the Senate would have put the SST over, we can see the importance of the libertarian "intervention" into the political scene. Onward and upward! ◻

Libertarian Book News

The fall and winter season will be a surging, glorious time for the publication of important new libertarian books from *major* publishers. Watch this space for developments as they occur.

One of the most important books – and one which will get major publicity – is by our own Jerome Tuccille. Stein and Day will be publishing a book by Jerry on the current right-wing and libertarian movements, and it is shaping up as a veritable blockbuster. Present plans are for the book to be a "non-fiction novelized non-fiction, the closest parallel being the witty and insightful novels of the French writer, Roger Peyrefitte. There will be a fictional hero, a Yossarian – Everyman, in search of the truth, who goes from one right-wing movement to another, and finally from one branch of the libertarian movement to another; in each group the Everyman encounters real people with real names, and they engage in fictionalized dialogue in which they present their real views, and Jerry's hero responds with the author's real reactions.

And it's going to be a blockbuster: witty, hilarious, iconoclastic, as St. Jerome rides out to slay the Dragons of Deviationism, to expose the crazies, to prick the balloons of posturing pomposity, to employ the sword-pen of satire on behalf of reason and common sense. And so: deviationists of all stripes, beware! Humorless fanatics, en garde! Jerry is out to get you! And you will probably find yourself, named and revealed, in the pages of his sparkling book. And the *title* – oh boy, the title – the title, my friends, is calculated to send three-quarters of the libertarian movement into an instant conniption fit. The title is: IT USUALLY STARTS WITH AYN RAND. And so libertarians, gird your loins; brace yourselves for the Tuccille blitz.

****

Also this fall, Jerry Tuccille's *Radical Libertarianism*, so far the only book on our movement, is coming out in paperback. The hard-cover edition, which came out early last year, encountered two misfortunes: the fact that the book predated by a year the sudden publicity storm for the libertarian movement, and the early death of the book's brilliant young editor, a man highly sympathetic to the cause. But now the major publishing house of Harper and Row will be putting out the book in paper this fall, and so we can expect a major publicity push for this book as well – as well as the tapping of the vital mass paperback market.

****

Coming also in the fall season is a new libertarian book by Harry Browne, author of the current runaway best seller for Arlington House, *How You Can Profit From the Coming Devaluation* ($5.95). (The book has sold a phenomenal 90,000 copies to date, largely on the strength of personal radio and TV appearances by the author.) The new book, tentatively titled *How I Found Freedom In An Unfree World*, will be published by Macmillian, and will get top publicity – (it will have to, to recoup the amazing advance paid by the publisher.) Judging from Harry's general position, the book will probably stress how the individual (either Harry or the reader) can escape the crippling hand of the State in his own life.

****

Also, Harper and Row is scheduled or rumored to be producing other paperbacks of interest in the fall: a collection of essays by David Friedman, and a reader on capitalism edited by Professor Dorothy James, which will consist of original articles from all ends of the spectrum, left and right, critical of the existing *status quo*. Especially featured will be libertarian authors, since Professor James (and we hope she's right!) expects libertarianism to be the wave of the future on college campuses. Included in the James collection will be essays by Rod Manis, Tibor Machan, and Murray N. Rothbard. ◻

211

ORWELL LIVES — *(Continued from page 1)*

an American public that showed no compassion whatever when millions, yes millions, of Vietnamese and Cambodian and Laotian peasants were brutally and genocidally massacred by American weaponry. They showed precious little compassion for the women and babies whom Calley slaughtered at My Lai. No, it was only to Calley that their warmth and goodness reached, these same Americans who sternly oppose the "coddling of criminals", who yearn for law and order. Let us indeed cease coddling criminals, especially those who have been duly convicted. Indeed, not being liberals, libertarians do not shrink from capital punishment when capital crimes are involved. "Let the punishment fit the crime!" is the old motto, and it remains good today.

Meanwhile, one good thing has emerged from this mess – the arrival of an authentic hero, Capt. Aubrey M. Daniel, III, of Orange, Va., the fearless and tireless prosecutor of the murderer Calley. Not only did he resist pressures within the Army; but Capt. Daniel sat down and wrote a tart and trenchant letter to Mr. Nixon attacking the President's gross interference with the judicial process. There are precious few heroes in American life for us to ignore or fail to salute one when he finally comes along. ◻

For Bengal

Considering the traditional apathy and ignorance of most libertarians in foreign affairs, I don't suppose that many have taken a stand on what the press misleadingly terms a "civil war" in East Pakistan. In fact, the situation there is scarcely a "civil war"; it is a mass movement by the people of East Pakistan – the Bengalis – to rid themselves, once and for all, of the tyranny and despotism of the Punjabi-run central government of the West.

One of the major problems blocking most libertarians from supporting national independence movements is their pettifogging semantic hangup on the phrase "national self-determination", a concept, by the way, that loomed large in that very nineteenth-century liberalism to which libertarians consider themselves the heir. "National self-determination", most libertarians patiently explain, is an erroneous concept, an equivocation on the world "self"; since the self can only be each individual, libertarians should only support "individual self-determination" rather than national. But this analysis, while philosophically correct, misses the whole essential point: the point that these national movements are primarily concerned with

getting other imperial states and nations off their backs. "National self-determination" is only a harmless metaphor for a movement against imperial dictation. The point, for example, about the nascent but growing Scottish National movement is that it is concerned with ending the domination of Scotland by English imperialism, a domination which is cultural, economic, and throughout political.

The same is true for the crisis in Pakistan. For Pakistan is in no sense a genuine nation, but a geographical abortion, created by the British as they were forced to leave the Indian subcontinent shortly after World War II. The Bengalis of the East have nothing whatsoever in common, except for their religion, with the Punjabis of the West; culturally, linguistically, ethnically and by every other criteria, they are separate nations. Furthermore, the political structure of Pakistan establishes a despotism by the Punjabis over the numerically superior, and far more productive, Bengalis. The Bengalis are the merchants and the traders of India; and a large chunk of their productive earnings are taxed away by the central Punjabi government to build up a vast Punjabi-staffed army and central bureaucracy, as well as to subsidize the Punjabi large-landlord class. The Punjab government has always been a thinly-veiled military dictatorship; and it was the decision of that government to suspend Parliament in the wake of its loss in the recent Pakistani elections that touched off the current crisis. It was that suspension that finally convinced the long-suffering Bengalis that there was no hope for them to attain autonomy within the Pakistan framework, and that decided them for national Bengali independence.

The fighting in Bengal is not a civil war, but a counter-revolutionary struggle by a Punjabi army to crush the independence forces, in other words the people of Bengal. Hence the use by that army of familiar genocidal tactics, for it realizes that the entire population of Bengal *is* its "enemy." Hence its systematic massacre of civilians, hence its imposition of curfew and censorship, and its expulsion of all foreign correspondents from the country. The similarity with the American use of mass terrorism in Southeast Asia should be striking and expectable, for in Southeast Asia we, too, are trying to impose an external rule on an entire population, all of which therefore *becomes* "the enemy", to be slaughtered wherever found. Genocidal slaughter is the logical conclusion of imperial war.

Another instructive point: the Great Powers, including the United States and Communist China, are all supporting the Pakistan government, since they all have deals with that government and they all value "stability" everywhere. Which shows where Great Powers, whoever they may be, will stand when it comes to justice and statism. ◻

The Libertarian Forum
BOX 341
MADISON SQUARE STATION
NEW YORK, NEW YORK 10010

First Class

Published Every Month. Subscription Rate: $8.00 Per Year

A Monthly Newsletter

THE
Libertarian Forum

Joseph R. Peden, Publisher   Murray N. Rothbard, Editor

VOLUME III, NO. 5   JUNE, 1971   75c

How To Destatize

The libertarian movement has long been far stronger on ultimate principle than it has in strategic thinking. While we cannot overrate the importance of providing a theoretical picture of the society toward which we are striving, we have done much more of this needed theorizing than we have considered how in the world to get from our current "here" to the ideal "there." This deficiency of strategy and tactics is highlighted by our general failure to consider two dramatic recent victories for liberty, for destatizing, and to ponder what lessons they may offer for future strategy. These recent victories are the generally rapid movement for the repeal of abortion laws, and the successful movement to rollback and eventually abolish rent controls in New York State.

To use those much-abused terms once more, the "right-wing" of the libertarian movement tends to be pure "educationists", while the "left-wing" tends to call for immediate destruction of existing society. Both strategies are self-defeating, and both in effect insure that the success of liberty can never be achieved. The educationists call for increased devotion to education, to spreading the ideas and the scholarship of libertarianism throughout society, for a new form of "cultural revolution" in behalf of reason and liberty. Now while I wholeheartedly endorse the proposal for ever-wider education, the problem is that this strategy is necessary but scarcely *sufficient* for victory, i.e. for translating these libertarian concepts into the real world. The educationist view tends to hold that as more people are converted, the State will somehow automatically wither away. But how? And by what mechanism? Often the educationists explicitly rule out all possible mechanisms for pressuring the State to roll itself back or dismantle itself: violence is dismissed as evil, mass demonstrations as coercive, voting or influencing politicians as injuring libertarian purity, civil disobedience as violating the principle that while the laws are on the books they must be obeyed. But how then is the State to be rolled back? The educationists have thereby systematically ruled out all ways but one: convincing the men in power to resign.

In short, Richard Nixon or Lyndon Johnson or Henry Kissinger or whoever is supposed to read *Atlas Shrugged* or *Power and Market* or *Human Action* or *This Bread is Mine* or whatever and say: "Eureka! This is it! They're right, and I've been wrong. I resign and look for honest employment." Now certainly such instant conversions by our sinners are conceptually *possible*, and once in a while, in isolated cases, they indeed happen, and should be saluted and cheered. But surely history shows that such large-scale conversions are highly unlikely, to say the least; no ruling elite in history has voluntarily surrendered its power on any grounds, much less on massive recognition

of its own sins. And surely for libertarians to rest their strategic perspective on such conversion of sinners would be folly indeed. And yet that is the strategic dead-end to which our educationists would consign us.

It is true that our left-wing R-r-revolutionaries confront the problem of Power, which the educationists do not; but their strategic prescription of instant and indiscriminate destruction is not only self-defeating but suicidal as well. The moral legitmacy of self-defense against the State is beside the strategic point: the point being that the use of violence only serves to alienate the very American public whom we are trying to convince. And "alienate" is of course a very tame word here: "polarize", "enrage", would be far more accurate. Another point which the violent revolutionaries forget is that there has never been a successful armed revolution against a democratic government; all toppled governments have been seen by the public to be *outside* themselves, either as dictatorships or monarchies (Cuba, China, Russia, 18th Century France, 17th Century England) or as imperial powers (the American Revolution, the Algerian Revolution). The Left is fond of pointing to the Tupamaros of Uruguay as a successful urban guerrilla movement, but the evident point here is that the Tupamaros have *not* at this writing succeeded, or shown any signs of doing so. So long as free elections exist, then, the use of violence by American rebels will only prove suicidal and counter-productive.

We must reject then both strategies: the defeatist torpor of the educationists, and the frenzied nihilism of the Revolutionaries. What then should be our positive strategy? This is a difficult problem, especially since the art of strategy and tactics depends on the forces at work at the particular time. But here is a prime strategic lesson: that while we must be pure and consistent in principle, we must be flexible in tactics. We must be willing to adopt any tactic that seems likely to bring about the goal of liberty, any tactic, that is, that is not in itself immoral and itself violates the libertarian creed. Take, for example, the MayDay Tribe demonstrations this spring in Washington. In contrast to the effective and moving demonstrations that preceded MayDay, the goal of the Tribe seemed to be to blockade and "trash" private automobiles, thus typically expressing the Left's hatred against the private car. For the libertarian, however, not only was the MayDay tactic counterproductive in alienating the great bulk of Americans, it also violated libertarian principle by directing its ire against private property — the very thing that the libertarian is concerned to defend and expand. No genuine libertarian could consider such trashing in any way except with abhorrence.

For a more positive model, let us consider the two most

(Continued on page 2)

213

HOW TO DESTATIZE — *(Continued from page 1)*

prominent victories for destatizing in recent years: the repeal of abortion laws and the substantial removal of rent control in New York. How did these victories come about? Let us consider the rent decontrol case first, as a simpler model. Rent control has been imposed in New York since World War II, and a few years ago it was even imposed anew on post-war buildings. Seemingly, it was a system destined to last forever. All these years, the aggrieved landlords of New York had protested, but in vain. The new recent ingredient was clearly the patent failure and collapse of housing in New York City in the last few years. For few new apartment houses have been built in recent years, due to rent controls and zoning restrictions; existing housing has deteriorated, and abandonments of houses by landlords unable to pay taxes have increased, adding to the plight of the homeless. Furthermore, the Liberal claim that rent controls are merely a temporary device until the apartment shortage disappeared was given the lie by the fact that the shortage of apartments in New York has gotten visibly worse rather than better. In short, as a result of rent controls and high property taxes, the housing situation in New York has reached a *crisis* stage, and it was this crisis situation that impelled the state authorities to turn to new solutions – to turn, indeed, onto the firm path of decontrol. But the lesson here is that the government cannot be induced to change its ways by theory alone; it was the *crisis situation* brought about by controls that led Governor Rockefeller and the state legislators to turn to the free-market theorists who were there with the decontrol solution at hand. Theory, however correct, will *not* be put into effect unless a crisis situation arrives to force the government out of its habitual bureaucratic inertia and onto a search for new solutions.

Abortion reform also had the ingredients of sound libertarian theory at work plus a crisis situation. The theory had been propounded for years by pro-abortion groups, but was accelerated recently by the fact that the Women's Lib groups, in their raucous and annoying manner, had stumbled across a purely libertarian theory which they propounded with force and effect: that every woman has the absolute right to own and control her own body. The attention devoted to Women's Lib by the media assured that the politicians finally were able to hear, not a wishy-washy liberal plea for moderate abortion reform, but the "extreme" – and consistent – view that the State had no right to pass any abortion restrictions whatever.

While libertarian theory had been firmed up and spread more aggressively, a crisis situation was becoming ever more blatant: and this was the massive, non-violent civil disobedience of women and doctors who obtained their abortions illegally. And not only were increasing numbers of women and doctors willing to ignore the law; but others were increasingly willing to broaden the fuzzy zone that often exists between legality and illegality: for example, doctors willing to stretch the definition of "endangering the health of the mother", which made abortion permissible. Furthermore, it was also becoming evident that, taking place as they did under conditions of illegality, the abortions were both unnecessarily expensive and unnecessarily dangerous. In the case of abortions, then, it was mass civil disobedience that brought about the crisis situation, while the spread of libertarian theory made the government more willing to turn to the de-statizing solution. But not only theory: also the *use* of the theory to pressure the politicians, by petition, by noise, by threat of votes, etc.

As the Marxists would say, there is needed for victory both the "objective conditions" and the "subjective conditions." The objective conditions refer to crisis situations in the real world; for libertarians, finding crisis situations is easy, especially since these crises (e.g. the abortion

Syndical Syndrome

New Yorkers have recently had to suffer yet another irresponsible blackjacking at the hands of power-drunk labor unions. This time it was the bridge tenders and garbage incinerator workers who, angered at the state legislature's balking at their receiving pensions which no private industry could afford, took their frustrations out on an innocent public by not only striking but sabotaging traffic facilities. Admittedly, there was no way that they could *win* their strike, since upstate legislators could hardly be brought to their knees by traffic tieups and sabotage in New York City, but it was a nice way to have a couple of days off while sticking a knife into the ribs of John Q. Public. Libertarians must always concede the right to strike, since otherwise labor would be compulsory rather than voluntary; but if employers had the fortitude and they were allowed to do so by law, they would automatically fire any and all strikers, and thereby take the strikers' quitting their jobs with the serious response that they deserve. In the case of outright sabotage and destruction, along with threats of violence against those who continue to work or are hired to replace the strikers, the unions who commit such aggression should be treated as the criminals that they are. And since such coercion is the general rule in strikes, these criminal penalties would, in a libertarian society, be widespread rather than non-existent as they are now. For it should never be forgotten that a libertarian society does *not* mean the total absence

(Continued on page 3)

mills, housing decay) have invariably been created by the government itself. The subjective conditions refer to the need for groups of libertarians to propound the libertarian solutions to these crises and to pressure the politicians when the objective conditions are ripe. Both methods were applied in the successes of housing and abortion – and both successes were won without a self-conscious group of pure libertarians bringing their wider and more systematic doctrines to bear on the struggle. How much greater will the success be when libertarians will have made their mark as an active, expanding, self-conscious movement, stepping into crises as they appear and providing the benefit of their far more systematic insight, or, to paraphrase the Marxists, "raising the level of libertarian consciousness" among all parties concerned! Times, moreover, are going to be increasingly ripe for this sort of action, because crises are piling up as the failure of the Welfare-Warfare State becomes increasingly manifest in field after field: education, foreign policy, conscription, welfare, transportation, etc. As crisis situations multiply, libertarians will find their own opportunities multiplying as well, provided we are not stultified by the educationists or discredited by the nihilists. And we must remember that if we do not pursue these opportunities, more sinister forces – socialists or more likely fascists – will be standing in the wings to offer *their* alternatives to the failure of the Liberal-Conservative Consensus. Considering the numerous failures and tyrannies of socialism and fascism it will be easy to discredit these alternatives – *provided* that we are there to offer liberty as the only rational – and reasonable – alternative to the existing order. But a reasonable alternative emphatically does *not* include insane blatherings about "ripping off Amerika". Liberty is profoundly American; we come to fulfill the best of the American tradition, from Ann Hutchinson and Roger Williams to the Declaration of Independence, the Bill of Rights, and the Jeffersonian movement, and beyond. As Benjamin R. Tucker put it, we are "unterrified Jeffersonian democrats", and we come not to destroy the American dream but to fulfill it.

SYNDICAL SYNDROME — *(Continued from page 2)*

of coercion but only the absence of coercion against *non-criminals*. Those who invade the rights of others by violence deserve their proper check and punishment by the force of law.

In the light of the black record of union violence and intimidation over the years – a violence inherent in their assumed power to keep non-strikers off "their" jobs – it is difficult to understand why so many libertarians have lately become enamoured of anarcho-syndicalism and the "working class". For the arrogant and coercive labor unions *are* indeed "syndicalism" in embryo, and the harbinger of any future fully syndicalist society.

Of the three major proposals for running an advanced industrial society – socialism, syndicalism, and free-market capitalism – syndicalism is the most blatantly unworkable and most rapidly disastrous. For in such a society, there must be *some* rational mechanism for allocating resources efficiently, for seeing to it that the proper amounts of labor, land, and capital equipment are employed in those areas and in those ways most efficient for satisfying the wants and desires of the mass of consumers. Free-market capitalism not only provides the most smoothly efficient way, it is also the only method that relies solely on voluntary inducements. Thus, suppose that a great number of new workers are needed in a new and expanding industry, say, plastics or electronics. How are these workers to be supplied? The market way is to offer new jobs at higher wages in these new areas and fields, while firing people or cutting wages in those industries that are in decline (say the horse-and-buggy industry). The *pure* socialist way is to direct the labor out of one industry and into another purely by coercive violence, i.e. by forced labor direction. The socialist method is both despotic and highly inefficient, and so even the socialist countries have been turning more and more to free-market methods in the allocation of labor. But at least socialism is an *attempt* at a rational allocation of labor in a modern, industrial society.

Syndicalism, on the other hand, i.e. full worker "ownership" of "their" industries, does not even attempt to achieve a rational allocation of resources. Both the free method of market allocation and the coercive method of central dictation are eliminated. And what is to take their place? In effect, nothing but chaos. Instead of a coordinating mechanism there is now only the chaotic will of groups of brawling monopoloid syndics, each demanding parity and control regardless of economic law. Does anyone think for one moment that the horse and buggy workers would have permitted higher wages in the budding automobile industry? Or have permitted the dismissal of workers? All one need do is to observe the arrogant behavior of unions with monopoly power to know the answer. But the problem lies deeper than bad will on the part of union syndics. The problem is that, even in a community of "saints", even in an improbable world of meek and altruistic union monopolists, there would be *no way* for the syndics to make their decisions on wages, employment, or allocation of production. Only a system of market pricing and wage rates, guided by profit and loss considerations for market firms, can provide a mechanism for such decisions.

Furthermore, the myriad jurisdictional disputes that already plague our system of unionism would be far more intense and out of control in a syndicalist society. Take for example carpenters working in the steel industry. Would the carpenter syndic "own" the product of their carpentry, or would they be merged unheralded and unsung into the general syndic of steel workers? Professor von Mises has scoffed at the syndicalist cry of "steel to the steel workers, aluminum to the aluminum workers,

and . . . garbage to the garbage collectors?" And in a syndical society, who indeed would own the garbage, the garbage collecting syndic or the street maintenance and repair syndic?

Syndicalism would therefore be totally incapable of organizing an industrial economy, and this total failure is, indeed, the economic embodiment of the dysfunctionality of the anti-technological youth culture which has given rise to the new syndicalism. In a recent *Firing Line* interview, Bill Buckley asked Karl Hess the elementally silly question: in an anarchist society, if one group of workers wanted to work from 8 to 4, and another set in the same plant wished to work from 9 to 5, who would decide? Karl, trapped in an anarcho-syndicalist framework, could only lamely reply that the workers would come to some sort of agreement. The proper and swift answer would have been that the stockholder-*owners* would decide, just as they are doing now. Anarcho-*capitalism* is an easily explainable system, precisely because its configuration would be very similar in most ways to the society that we have now.

Like the New Left generally, the proponents of syndicalism suffer most from a total ignorance of economics, and therefore of the ways in which an industrial society can function. If the syndicalists can be persuaded to get "into" reading, especially of a subject which they usually define as being inherently "repressive", they might learn something from the critiques of syndicalism in Mises' *Socialism* and *Human Action*, and in Henry Simons', *Economic Policy for a Free Society*.

It is true that the Yugoslav economy is working well, but the remarkable Yugoslav shift from socialist central planning to a relatively free market economy has never been clasped to the New Left bosom. For while the workers in each plant indeed own their plants, the relations between plants are strictly governed by a free price system, and by profit and loss tests. It is precisely the adoption of the free market, of money, prices, competition, self-reliance, etc. by the Yugoslavs which prevents the anarcho-syndicalists and the other egalitarians and anti-marketeers of the New Left from treating Yugoslavia with anything but pained silence. Furthermore, the Yugoslavs are rapidly moving in the direction of individual shares of ownership for each worker, and the subsequent trading of such shares in some sort of "people's stock market", which will culminate their shift to a free-market economy.

The Yugoslav system, therefore, is indeed *not* syndicalist, but a market economy of producers' cooperatives. If this is really *all* that the anarcho-syndicalists demand, then they can easily bring the new society into being, by simply forming producers' coops owned by the workers themselves. In free-market capitalism, there have never been any restrictions on workers banding together in producers' coops to own their own capital equipment. And yet, in the free economy, producers' coops have been notorious by their non-existence, or rapid failure in competition with "capitalist" firms. The reason is that, unknown to the economically ignorant syndicalists, the capitalists perform an extremely important service to the workers, as a result of which most people prefer to be hired by capitalists rather than be self or cooperatively employed. The two basic functions are those of the "capitalist" *per se* and those of the "entrepreneur". As a capitalist, the employer saves money from his possible consumption, and invests the money in paying workers their income *in advance* of sale of product. In an automobile factory, the capitalist pays workers their weekly wages *now*; in a producers' cooperative factory, the workers would have to go without income for months or years, until their product is finally sold to the consumers. The capitalist earning of "interest" for this advance payment is precisely equivalent to the creditor who earns interest by lending someone

(Continued on page 4)

SYNDICAL SYNDROME — *(Continued from page 3)*

money *now* while being repaid at some point in the future. In both cases, "interest" is earned as payment for savings and time preference for income *now* rather than waiting for the future.

The second service performed by the employer is to assume the significant risks of entrepreneurship. A producers' cooperative firm invests resources in a product, and then hopes to sell that product to the consumers at a net profit. But suppose that the efficiency and the foresight of the workers is minimal; suppose, in short, that they produce an Edsel that fails to sell? If they do, their income is negative rather than positive, and they lose capital assets which they can scarcely afford. In the capitalist economy, the employer assumes these capital risks, and only he therefore is subject to monetary losses if his product is inefficiently produced or if he cannot achieve satisfactory sales.

Most workers are unwilling or unable to assume these risks of entrepreneurship, and therefore they greet the employer's willingness to do so, as well as to pay them in advance of sales, with sighs of relief. Or *would* if they understood the process. We can confidently predict that if Yugoslavia ever allows full-scale capitalist employment (as it does now for small-scale enterprise) that its producers' coops will rapidly give way to orthodox "capitalist" modes of production – to the benefit of all concerned.

The question of whether a future free society will be "coop" or communal or capitalist brings up the most disturbing problem about the anarcho-syndicalists and communalists. This is the famous "question of Auban" – the question that "Auban", the individualist anarchist hero of John Henry Mackay's novel *The Anarchists*, put to the left-wing anarchists. In essence: would *you*, in your proposed anarchist society, permit those who so wished to have private property, to engage in free market transactions, to hire workers in "capitalist" relations, etc.? The communist anarchists in Mackay's book never answered the question clearly and lucidly, and neither do any left-wing anarchists that one may encounter today. (For the Auban speech from Mackay, see Krimerman and Perry, eds., *Patterns of Anarchy* (Doubleday, 1966), pp. 16-33.) Generally, the left-anarchists reply that, in their Utopian society, no one will be so base as to *want* to indulge in private property or in capitalist social relations. But suppose they do? one persists. The answer is generally either a repeat of the Utopian answer or an evasive silence.

And when the left-anarchists can be pressed for an answer, the response is disturbing indeed. Take for example one of our most distinguished socialist-anarchists, Professor Noam Chomsky. Professor Chomsky has recently expressed a great deal of worry about the recent rise of our "right-wing" libertarian movement; apparently he is – I am afraid unrealistically – concerned that *we* might succeed in abolishing the State before the State has succeeded in abolishing private property! Secondly, Chomsky has written that the anarcho-capitalist society would constitute "the greatest tyranny the world has ever known". (What, Noam? Greater than Hitler? than Ghengis Khan?) Whether or not anarcho-capitalism would be tyrannical is here irrelevant; the problem is that, in so expressing his horror at the possible results of complete freedom, Professor Chomsky reveals that he is not *really* an "anarchist" at all, indeed that he prefers statism to an anarcho-capitalist world. That of course is his prerogative, and scarcely unusual, but what *is* illegitimate is for this distinguished linguist to call himself an "anarchist". And I very much fear that the same can be said for the other varieties of left-anarchists: communal, syndical, or whatever. Beneath a thin veneer of libertarian rhetoric there lies the same compulsory and coercive collectivist that we have en-

Jerome Daly Once More

Readers of the *Forum* may remember that we had pointed to the struggle of the intrepid libertarian activist, attorney Jerome Daly of Savage, Minnesota, against fractional reserve fiat banking (*Lib. Forum*, Aug. 1, 1969). In 1967, Mr. Daly refused to make any further mortgage payments to his bank; at his jury trial (First National Bank of Montgomery v. Jerome Daly) in December, 1968, Daly argued that the bank had loaned him, not *real* specie money but only bank credit which it had created out of thin air, and which was therefore valueless. Since it was valueless, the credit was not a valid consideration, and the contract was, according to Daly, null and void. Remarkably, the jury and Justice of the Peace Martin Mahoney ruled in Daly's favor, and, furthermore, Mahoney refused to accept the required fee from the Bank for a judicial appeal, on the ground that only gold and silver can be used to pay such fees.

The unfortunate death of Judge Mahoney ended the Daly case; but now Mr. Daly is back in action. In 1966, Mr. Daly had deposited $71 in silver coin in a savings account at the Savage State Bank. Now he is suing the bank for return of the silver coin which he had deposited; he refuses to accept the fiat paper of the government. At the end of April, the Justice of the Peace of Credit River Township decreed that the bank must pay gold and silver coin to a depositor upon demand! In a companion decision, the same court held that the State Treasurer of Minnesota must pay an income tax refund check of $61 in nothing but gold or silver coin. This decision is being appealed to the U. S. Supreme Court, not on the correctness of the decision but on whether the Justice of the Peace had jurisdiction in the case.

In the meanwhile, Mr. Daly has also been active on the tax resistance front. He hasn't paid income taxes since 1965, claiming that the income tax is unconstitutional and also that the IRS returns violate the Fifth Amendment. Daly also ties the claim in with the Minnesota court decision on the unconstitutionality of banks' issue of fiat money. What Daly does is to submit an income tax return, consisting of over 40 pages of his legal claims, and suggesting that the IRS sue him for the tax in U. S. District Court. So far IRS has not sued Mr. Daly, who is now holding seminars around the country instructing people how to fill out similar income tax forms. (For further information, Mr. Daly can be reached at 28 East Minnesota St., Savage, Minn. 55378).

◻

---

countered all too often in the last two centuries. Scratch a left-wing "anarchist" and you will find a coercive egalitarian despot who makes the true lover of freedom yearn even for Richard Nixon (Arghh!) in contrast.

If this analysis is correct, as I believe it is, then it makes all the more absurd the hankering by so many of our "left-wing" for an intimate comradely alliance with the anarcho-left. Beneath superficial agreement in rhetoric, there is nothing in common between genuine libertarians and collectivist "anarchists". Superficially, we both oppose the existing system – but so too do monarchists, Nazis, and those who hanker for a return to the Inquisition – scarcely enough for a warm and comradely dialogue. It is indeed fortunate for Liberty that the left-anarchists have about as much chance of victory as some of our Conservatives have to restore the Bourbon dynasty. For if they did, we would soon find that the embrace of left-anarchy is the embrace of Death.

◻

Recommended Reading

The Individualist. The April issue, just out, features an article by Murray N. Rothbard, "Education: Free and Compulsory", a philosophical discussion of the nature of the education of children and a critique of compulsory education by the State. Also featured are two excellent review-articles: Professor Edwin G. Dolan's review of Robert P. Wolff's *In Defense of Anarchism;* and Roy Childs' review of G. William Domhoff's *The Higher Circles.*

Revisionism. In the March issue of *Reason,* Roy Childs continues his great educational work in instructing SIL members in the nature of empirical reality in twentieth-century America. This is the conclusion of his two-part article on "Big Business and the Rise of American Statism: A Revisionist History".

Education. A valuable stream of inexpensive leaflets ~rally priced at 10¢), has been pouring forth from the Center of Independent Education, 9115 East Thirteenth, Wichita, Kansas 67206. These include leaflets on education by Armen Alchian, Robert L. Cunningham, David Friedman, Benjamin A. Rogge, E. G. West, and James M. Buchanan. Particularly important is a critique of the dangerous Friedmanite scheme for educational vouchers by George Pearson, *Another Look at Education Vouchers,* which can also be found as "The Case Against Education Vouchers" in the April-May issue of *Reason.*

Libertarian Growth. The burgeoning importance of libertarianism is reflected in the Spring issue of *Modern Age,* the leading conservative quarterly. (743 North Wabash Ave., Chicago, Ill. 60611, $4.00 per year, $1.25 per issue.) Rothbard and libertarianism are discussed in no less than four places in the Spring issue, ranging from the highly favorable review of *Power and Market* by H. George Resch, to an objective and respectful account in M. Stanton Evans' "Varieties of Conservative Experience", to a harsh account by Gary North, to a silly smear by Donald Zoll, who accuses us of being secret agents of Herbert Spencer. (I for one am happy, now and formerly, to hail Spencer's *Social Statics* as the greatest single work of libertarian political philosophy ever written.)

Meanwhile, our favorable recognition in the media continues to expand. David Deitch wrote a series of three articles on our movement in the *Boston Globe,* April 10, 11, and 12. The first deals with the National Taxpayers Union, the second is a general interview with Murray Rothbard, and the third deals with Senator Hatfield's proposals for tax reform. The Philadelphia *Sunday Bulletin* or January 24 has a lengthy article on SIL's Philadelphia offices, including pictures of David Walter and Don Ernsberger. And the *Stanford Daily* of May 27 has a long article proclaiming the death of YAF and its replacement by the new libertarians.

Garland Reprints. In these days of massive reprinting, the libertarian should be alert to reprints of classics in his areas of interest (unfortunately they are usually very expensive.) Now Garland Publishing, Inc., 24 West 45th St., New York, N. Y. 10036, has announced the publication of a Garland Library of War and Peace, a mighty series of 328 volumes, largely anti-war and isolationist, and focussing most heavily on World War I and environs. The books are available individually, or in a complete collection for $4500, and are *supposed* to be available now (though this is doubtful). Many of these works are indispensable for any libertarian interested

in foreign policy, and at the very least, everyone should send away for the handsomely produced catalog. Some of the important titles follow.

John Foster Dulles, *War, Peace and Change* (1939). $11.00. Dulles' isolationist work about Europe in the 1930's.

Charles H. Hamlin, *Propaganda and Myth in Time of War.* $9.00. Includes Hamlin's excellent 1927 booklet on U. S. aggressive wars throughout its history, as well as his critique of U. S. war propaganda by educators during World War I.

Harold Lasswell, *Propaganda Technique in the World War.* $13.00. A classic on war propaganda.

Harold Lavine and James Wechsler, *Propaganda and the War* (1940) $18.00. An excellent and detailed study of war propaganda in the late 1930's.

Edmund D. Morel, *Truth and War* (1916) $17.00. The leader of English revisionism on secret diplomacy and World War I.

Albert Jay Nock, *The Myth of a Guilty Nation* (1922). $7.50. The first American revisionist work on World War I. By the great libertarian writer and theorist.

Caroline Playne, *The Neuroses of the Nations* (1925), $21.00. Comprehensive work on English revisionism of World War I.

Arthur Ponsonby, *Falsehood in War Time* (1928), $11.00. The classic work on British atrocity stories fabricated about Germany in World War I.

Sidney Rogerson, *Propaganda in the Next War* (1938) $11.00. A chilling forecast of British propaganda to be used to draw the U. S. into World War II.

Irene Cooper Willis, *England's Holy War* (1928), $19.50. Critique of English press propaganda in World War I.

John Bakeless, *The Economic Causes of Modern War* (1921), $14.50. On the economic causes and colonial rivalries leading to World War I.

Frederic Bastiat, *Paix et Liberte* 1849), on classical liberalism, free trade, and peace, and their opposition by socialism and nationalism; includes within it the later classical liberal work by Emile Laveleye, On the *Causes of War* (1872). Both for $10.

Richard Cobden, *The Political Writings of R. Cobden,* 2 vols. $34.00. A treasure chest — the collected works of the great libertarian and "isolationist".

John A. Hobson, *The War in South Africa* 1900). $18.00. The book also includes G. P. Gooch's pamphlet *The War and its Causes* (1900); the classic volume on Boer War Revisionism.

Carl Marzani, *We Can Be Friends* (1952). $18.00. The first work of Cold War Revisionism, which stood alone for a decade until Fleming.

Gustave de Molinari, *The Society of Tomorrow* (1904). $11.00. A great libertarian work, and of all the Garland collection, a *must* for every libertarian. Deals not so much with war and peace as with the free market economy, in which Molinari, the Belgian libertarian economist and successor to Bastiat, goes beyond the master to the brink of free-market anarchism.

Parker T. Moon, *Imperialism and World Politics* (1926). $24.00. A classic, this remains the best single work ever written on imperialism. A country by country history of the development of imperialism, it is objective and unmarred by Marxian fallacies.

Charles A. Beard, *The Devil Theory of War* (1936), $7.50. A brief analysis of the U. S. entry into World War I based on the revelations of the Nye Committee. By the Dean of revisionist history.

(Continued on page 6)

RECOMMENDED READING — *(Continued from page 5)*

Henry N. Brailsford, *The War of Steel and Gold* (1914), $16.00. A blistering critique of competing European imperialisms, written on the brink of world war.

H. C. Engelbrecht and Frank C. Hanighen, *Merchants of Death* (1934), $16.00. The classic muckraking work on the tie-in between war and the munitions industry, or what would now be termed the "military-industrial complex."

Seymour Waldsman, *Death and Profits* (1932), $10.00. The first critique of the armaments industry and World War I.

Edwin M. Borchard and William P. Lage, *Neutrality for the United States* (1940), $21.00. The great work of "international law revisionism", by the leader of "isolationist" international lawyers. Mostly on World War I, with a supplement on World War II. Shows that the U. S. consistently violated international law, and that we had far more international-law grievances against Britain than we had against Germany.

Clarence M. Case, *Non-Violent Coercion* (1923), $19.75. A classic sociological espousal of non-violent action.

Barthelemy de Ligt, *The Conquest of Violence* (1938), $15.00. A classic work by a Dutch non-violent revolutionary left-anarchist.

Cook, Chatfield, and Cooper, eds., *Three Generals on War* $22.00. Three pamphlets from the 1920's and 1930's by generals who turned against war. Includes the revulsion against the killing that he had done by General Frank Crozier, a blistering attack on World War I by General Christopher Thomson, and the famous repudiation of his own service to the U. S. military-industrial complex by General Smedley D. Butler, *War is a Racket*.

Cook, Chatfield, and Cooper, eds., *Sermons on War by Theodore Parker*. $6.00. Three sermons attacking the Mexican War by the great minister, abolitionist, and classical liberal.

Franziskus Stratmann, *The Church and War, a Catholic Study* (1928), $12.00. The classic repudiation of the Thomist doctrine of the "just war" in the light of modern conditions of warfare, by an eminent Catholic theologian.

Blanche Cook, ed., *American Anti-Imperialism, 1895-1901*, $15.00. A collection of essays and previously unpublished correspondence by the great *laissez-faire* anti-imperialists of the turn of the century, including Edward T. Atkinson, and William Graham Sumner.

Blanche Cook, ed., *Max and Crystal Eastman on Peace, Revolution and War*. $15.00. Selected essays and correspondence by the great libertarian-inclined journalist Max Eastman, including his early days as a left anti-militarist and his later views of the cold war. Also includes essays by Eastman's sister Crystal, a leading anti-militarist in the feminist movement.

Blanche Cook, ed., *Oswald Garrison Villard: The Dilemmas of the Absolute Pacifist in Two World Wars*. $15.00. Until now the only biography of the great pacifist and *laissez-faire* liberal journalist has been the Old Left hatchet job by Michael Wreszin. Now Professor Cook collects writings and unpublished correspondence to show the consistency of Villard's pacifism and anti-militarism in World Wars I *and* II. A very important work.

The Senate And The Draft

It is one thing to be against the draft *pro forma*, even to vote against it in Congress; it is quite another to really fight against it *in the crunch*, on a crucial vote that might have some possiblilty of success. This year, the crunch came on the Senate vote, on June 23, to impose cloture to shut off a planned filibuster on the two-year extension of the draft. Since two-thirds of those voting are needed to shut off debate, and since many Southerners have been supposedly committed to the filibuster as preserving the right of the minority to talk an objectionable measure to death, here was a *real* chance, and the only one on the horizon, to smash the draft. Here then, on the cloture vote, is a real test of the dedication of a Senator, either to abolition of the draft or to retention of the filibuster principle.

Most Southerners, lifelong devotees of the filibuster, hung their heads and voted for cloture, since "national security" (i.e. military slavery) was at stake, and the latter came first. On the other hand, many liberals, supposedly against the draft, voted for cloture because they are *more* devoted to majority tyranny than to the abolition of slavery. Most shameful are those supposedly anti-draft conservatives, headed by Barry Goldwater, who voted for the anti-draft Hatfield-Goldwater amendment last session, but who voted *for* cloture this June. These include Goldwater, Fannin (R., Ariz.), Boggs (R., Del.), Gurney (R., Fla.), Fong (R., Haw.), Jordan (R., Id.), Dole (R., Kan.), Pearson (R. Kan.), Cook (R., Ky.), and Prouty (R., Vt.). Since a shift of only three votes in the Senate was needed to preserve the anti-draft filibuster, a special cry of shame should be directed against these ten renegades.

In fact, only five Republican senators withstood Administration pressure enough to stand fast against cloture. These five men deserve a special vote of thanks from all Americans dedicated to liberty: Case (N. J.), Hatfield (Ore.), Javits (N. Y.), Mathias (Md.), and Schweiker (Pa.).

As for the Democrats, we should record that handful of Southerners who favor the draft but who love the filibuster principle better: Allen (Ala.), Byrd (Va.), Ellender (La.), Fulbright (Ark.), McClellan (Ark.), and Spong (Va.). Among the liberals, the egregious Hubert Humphrey, Mike Mansfield (Mont.), and Edmund Muskie, all voted for cloture, although Muskie's vote was perfectly in keeping with his vote against Hatfield-Goldwater last year. The most pleasant surprise was the anti-cloture vote of Teddy Kennedy, notorious champion of the lottery system and opponent of the Hatfield-Goldwater amendment. Good Lord! Does this mean we might be getting Camelot again?

Special commendation should be meted out to the major organizers of the draft filibuster, Senators Mike Gravel (D., Alaska) and Alan Cranston (D., Calif.) This is Gravel's first leadership role in the Senate, and bears a happy augury of the future.

◘

"Many politicians of our time are in the habit of laying it down as a self-evident proposition, that no people ought to be free till they are fit to use their freedom. The maxim is worthy of the fool in the old story, who resolved not to go into the water till he had learned to swim. If men are to wait for liberty till they become wise and good in slavery, they may indeed wait forever." --- Thomas Babington Macauley.

◘

Bits And Pieces

By Jerome Tuccille

VANDENBERG by Oliver Lange. Stein and Day, New York. 1971. DELIVERANCE by James Dickey. Houghton Mifflin Company, Boston. 1970.

Good fiction is a product that has always been difficult to find. There are many elements which go into the making of a novel, and a weakness in any one of them can either destroy the final product completely or provide it with a structural flaw that seriously reduces its total impact. The author's style, his use of dialogue, his narrative skill, his depth of insight into his own characters, his plot structure and the organization of his material, his discipline and architectural control over the building of his book, his selection of detail — knowing what to put in and what to leave out — his ability to maintain a firm grasp on his basic theme and thread it into his story so the reader is drawn into the fiction progressively as it unfolds — all these are essential pillars upon which the final product will rest. If any one is seriously flawed, the novel will fail. If all are good and sound and carefully developed by the author, the novel will stand firm and endure.

It is because of all these fickle variables that go into the creation of a novel, because of the overwhelming difficulty an author faces in getting all these pieces to fit together and work as a whole that the writing of good fiction is the most difficult job a writer can attempt. It is nerve-racking work and exhausting work. There are only a handful of people in any generation who can do it well. More novels are closed and left unread after fifty pages than are given a thorough and enthusiastic reading. There simply isn't enough good fiction, in the avalanche of books that is published every year, to satisfy the appetites of people like myself who literally hunger after a good piece of serious fictional writing.

For this reason it is an exciting experience to come across two new novels in the span of a couple of weeks which not only qualify as top-quality fiction, but fiction which is also of interest to the libertarian reader. *Vandenberg,* the more recent of the two books, a current bestseller published this past Spring by Stein and Day, is explicitly libertarian in theme. In perhaps the only serious flaw in the story the pseudonymous author, Oliver Lange, has invented a Russian dictatorship in the United States sometime in the near future. The means of takeover is never adequately explained. We only know that it was bloodless and mysterious and somehow not completely credible in terms of contemporary political reality. Lange would have been much better off had he stuck with our present regime in Washington and shown how it might have evolved into a full-scale dictatorship, a much more likely possibility than the one he presents. The story he tells would have been equally valid and a bit more credible.

Overlooking this point, the bulk of the novel is rich with exciting narrative and vivid description, crisp dialogue and a tense momentum which carries the reader right on through to the final pages. The story deals with the attempts of an individual, a fifty-year-old painter named Vandenberg, to avoid the reaches of dictatorial government and live his life as a self-owned human being. He escapes from a "rehabilitation" center in the southwest where the authorities, through the use of drugs and political indoctrination, attempt to break down the resistance of recalcitrant individualists and fit them into a state-controlled socio-economic system. Vandenberg escapes and is driven into the mountains with nothing more than the clothes on his back. With a powerful driving style and descriptive detail, Lange shows us how Vandenberg is able to obtain food and the materials essential to his own survival, and elude the various efforts to re-capture him over an extended period of time. Later on, after he has established a mountain hideaway and the search is virtually abandoned by the political authorities, Vandenberg is joined by several cronies who are as anxious as he is — for various reasons — to assert their own individuality. The final section of the book deals with Vandenberg's plan to dynamite the "rehabilitation" center from which he escaped and free the political prisoners, to set an example for others who feel as he does and eventually launch an underground movement to actively resist the rule of total government. The ending is about as up-beat as it could be in the time-span Lange is covering, and the reader is left with the understanding that Vandenberg's efforts will bear fruit over a period of time.

Several reviewers have referred to the "Hemingway-esque" tone of Lange's style, dialogue and characterizations, and the comparison is not without substance. Vandenberg himself is a hard-drinking, hard-talking, hard-living individualist — not unlike a Hemingway hero. The dialogue is terse, clipped and to-the-point, another Hemingway trademark. The survival scenes in the mountains are reminiscent of Hemingway's Nick Adams stories in that they deal with the individual and his ability to dominate his natural environment. Finally, Lange's description of the raid on the "rehabilitation" camp is as exciting as some of the war scenes in *For Whom the Bell Tolls*. But comparisons are always dangerous. Hemingway was a master novelist who produced a great body of work over a period of more than thirty years. Lange (as far as I can tell, not knowing his true identity) has given us a single novel, a fine piece of art which deserves to be judged on its own merits. And there is much in it to make it a more-than-worthwhile experience for the libertarian, and for the general reader.

Deliverance by James Dickey is one of those landmark novels which comes along every twenty years or so, a novel which towers in every respect so high above everything else written in its time that it belongs to its own category. James Dickey turned form advertising to full-time poetry in 1961 when he was thirty-eight-years-old, and through the decade of the '60s he has staked out a reputation as one of our leading poets. In 1970 he published his first novel, *Deliverance,* which has just come out as a $1.25 paperback.

Reading *Deliverance* is, simultaneously, one of the most terrifying and ennobling experiences one is apt to find anywhere — short of actually living the adventure Dickey unfolds in his book. Dickey's status as a major poet is evident in virtually every sentence for a solid 278 pages. The sensuous floodtide of his language has a narcotic effect on the reader as the author pulls you deeper and deeper into the flow of his narrative. The story itself is about three generally average men — one a salesman, another a supervisor in a soft-drink company, the other an art director in an advertising firm — and a fourth man, an expert archer and outdoorsman, who decide to break from routine and take a canoe trip down a remote river in a southern mountain range. Their adventure starts off quietly enough, with each man making plans to be away from job and family for a three-day period. But before they are actually in the water and launched on their way downriver, the reader is aware that there are dark times looming ahead and all will not come off according to plan.

On the second day of the trip, two of the party are ambushed and attacked by a couple of mountaineers who are totally hostile to any visitors from the world beyond their mountain range. From this point onward the story becomes a flooding, cascading exercise in terror and human

(Continued on page 8)

BITS AND PIECES — *(Continued from page 7)*

endurance. What we are faced with is this: four men from an established world of laws, order, organization and social structure have entered a place in which there is none of these. Suddenly our four adventurers find themselves in a direct confrontation with nature and human aggression. There is no court of appeals out here, no law or police they can turn to for protection, no source of authority higher than themselves. They are in a place where every citizen is a deputy sheriff, where their attackers represent the forces of law and order. Our four adventurers are devoid of any peaceful means of protecting their rights of survival. Their choices are now, either to "take the law into their own hands" and provide for their own defense, or to submit to the tyranny that is forced upon them.

Their predicament is complicated by the fact that the leader of the expedition, the archer-outdoorsman, suffers a crippling injury which puts him out of action. One of the three "average" men, the advertising art director who has no prior experience in a survival situation, is forced to take command and lead his party to safety. Dickey's description of what this average individual is capable of doing, of the heights he is capable of reaching, of the mental and physical gymnastics he is able to perform when it literally becomes a matter of life-or-death, is without equal in recent fiction. The powerful driving force of the author's narrative is all-of-a-piece with the violent cascading rush of the river. And the river with its many rapids and treacherous falls, representing as it does their only means of exit from this lawless place, seems to be symbolic of life itself. Here are four individuals who are suddenly and unexpectedly forced to combat the tyranny of nature and human depravity, forced to rise above it all in their struggle for survival.

Vandenberg and *Deliverance* are similar in that they both deal with individual men locked in a life-and-death struggle with other men and with their natural environment. But each book is a unique and separate reading experience unto itself. They are different from each other in more ways than they are similar. Each book is a fine example of good first-class fiction. If at all possible, they should be read together, one right after the other. One can only hope that Lange and Dickey will give us more like this in the future.

◻

"Whatever fosters militarism makes for barbarism; whatever fosters peace makes for civilization." --- Herbert Spencer.

Nixonite Socialism
(Continued)

1. *The Lockheed Boondoggle.* The Lockheed scandal was first broken by a Pentagon official, the libertarian-oriented A. Ernest Fitzgerald, who was fired by the Pentagon for his pains, and now heads the Businessmen's Educational Fund, dedicated to the reduction of wasteful military spending. Now, the Nixon Administration proposes a $250 million guaranteed loan to bail out this flagrantly inefficient corporation. Secretary of Treasury Connally, defending the Lockheed subsidy on behalf of a "conservative" Administration, declared that we don't have a free enterprise economy anyway, so why not bail out our largest defense contractor. In contrast, "liberal" Senator Proxmire (D., Wisconsin), who is close to Fitzgerald and who has the highest rating of the National Taxpayers Union of anyone in the Senate on tax-and-spending bills, charged that a loan guarantee to Lockheed and other such firms would wreck the entire "vitality and discipline" of the free enterprise system.

So who's the "liberal" and who the "conservative"? Senator Proxmire, by the way, is running for the Democratic nomination for President, although one would never know it from the studied lack of publicity he has been receiving from the press.

2. *The Deficit.* The astute Establishment columnists Evans and Novak report that the Nixon Administration, which had actually forecast a budget *surplus* for fiscal 1971, is now expecting a $23 billion deficit. The estimate has been getting ever larger for months. Added to a currently estimated $23 billion deficit for fiscal 1972, this amounts to the largest two-year deficit in American history, barring the all-out war of World War II. Evans and Novak report that many economists are beginning to worry about perpepual inflation (Well, well!). They are *also* beginning to realize that the perpetual deficits and inflation are raising interest rates, and thereby possibly keeping the economy in a state of simultaneous recession. It is indeed *possible* that the astute "free enterprise" economists of the Nixon Administration will have ushered in the lovable era of perpetual inflation-recession.

◻

"A man's liberties are none the less aggressed upon because those who coerce him do so in the belief that he will be benefitted." --- Herbert Spencer.

The Libertarian Forum

BOX 341
MADISON SQUARE STATION
NEW YORK, NEW YORK 10010

First Class

Published Every Month. Subscription Rate: $8.00 Per Year

A Monthly Newsletter

THE
Libertarian Forum

Joseph R. Peden, Publisher   Murray N. Rothbard, Editor

VOLUME III, NOS. 6-7   July-August, 1971   75c

DUMPING NIXON

We are now entering a daffy, exciting, exuberant season of Presidential politics. Perhaps come the fall of '72, with all the hoopla over, we shall be faced with the grim, cold, sobering choice of Nixon vs. Muskie, and the fix is probably in already. But at this stage of the game, we can exult in the seemingly limitless possibilities, as dozens of Democratic candidates jostle each other, black, female, Third Sex, and Lord knows how many other caucuses abound, and third and fourth parties make noises in the wings. At this point, the great quadrennial American extravaganza looms as the most exciting in decades.

Let us begin with a few clear guidelines. For the libertarian, other things being equal, the first desideratum is to punish the incumbent. If we cannot yet abolish the office of President, we can at least make a start toward redressing our grievances by ousting the existing tenant for his numerous high and low crimes and misdemeanors. If we cannot punish the President to the full extent of the natural law, we can at least retire him to the private life he so richly deserves. We can extablish a new and glorious tradition of the one-term President.

That's if other things are equal, and that at least provides us with our first guideline. But other things, of course, are never equal. When we come further to consider the record in office of Richard Milhous Nixon, it is hard to find one redeeming feature, one splotch of white in the black record of the Nixon regime.

Let us summarize:

The shameful genocidal war in Vietnam and Southeast Asia continues, and Nixon has fiercely resisted every attempt by the Congress, no matter how feeble, to put an end to the war. The latest Hanoi-NLF offer totally exposes the Nixon mendacity on the phony prisoner-of-war issue, but still the Administration refuses to accept the offer, and the genocide continues.

The draft continues in full force, despite anarcho-Nixonite assurance that *at least* Nixon would remove conscription-slavery. Instead, Nixon simply adopted the old Kennedy lottery scheme, which conservatives and libertarians had scorned for years.

"Conservative", neo-Friedmanite economic manipulation by the Nixon Administration has brought us the new and glorious phenomenon of the inflationary recession. The recession is still with us, while inflation proceeds merrily on its way.

"Conservative" Nixon economics has brought us the largest peacetime federal deficit in our history, which now looms as something like $27 billion, with another $30 billion promised for next year.

"Conservative" Nixon economics is eagerly attempting to foist on us probably the single most disastrous plan ever proposed in America: the neo-Friedmanite Family Assistance Program, which will lock an increasing number of Americans into a parasitic automatic dole.

Nixon has accelerated the system of what has aptly been called "Big Business socialism" or "corporate communism", in which the government comes ever more nakedly to the support and rescue of inefficient large corporations: e.g. the SST, Lockheed, passenger railroad service boondoggles.

The Nixon administration has moved ever closer to wage and price controls, which have been advocated by high Administration economists. In the meanwhile, it has exercised such controls in the construction industry, and for the rest of industry has adopted the old Democratic "jawboning" policy of verbal threats and intimidation which it had previously spurned.

The Nixon administration has savagely moved to suppress freedom of the press in the famous Pentagon Papers affair, including the criminal indictment of Daniel Ellsberg and an unprecedented attempt to impose prior censorship before publication. The despotic and reprehensible dissents of Nixonite judges Blackmun and Burger, coupled with the narrow and flimsy arguments of most of the other members of the bench, show that we are scarcely out of the woods even on prior censorship. (O.K., Read and Rand: is *this* enough to make you revolutionaries?) One of the major reasons for dumping Nixon is the looming menace to the structure of civil liberties built up by the Warren Court. With Justice Douglas and the magnificent Hugo Black nearing retirement, our personal and civil liberties are truly in peril unless Richard Nixon is removed from office.

When we add the unrelieved horror of the Nixon record to the original guideline against incumbents, we conclude with one great injunction that every libertarian should be able to support with enthusiasm for 1972: DUMP NIXON!

Here is a goal which all shades of the varied libertarian spectrum should find exhilirating, and indeed the signs are that a broad coalition of left, right, and center libertarians are banding together to work with other anti-Nixon forces in this crusade of cleansing and retribution. It is particularly significant that many of the current anti-Nixon libertarians were high in the Nixon-youth forces in the 1968 campaign.

Clearly, the first place to try to dump Nixon is the Republican primaries. Unfortunately, Senator Mark Hatfield (R., Ore.) has resisted all efforts urging him to run for President, and Nixon's only Republican opponent is Rep. Paul McCloskey (Calif.), whose only libertarian asset, aside from a dogged and sincere manner, is his staunch opposition to the war in Vietnam. But still this is the major single issue,

(Continued on page 2)

DUMPING NIXON — *(Continued from page 1)*

and the more votes racked up for McCloskey the more the embarrassment and discomfiture for King Richard. At best, there is always the possibility that McCloskey might be able to emulate Gene McCarthy in being so successful as to force the President to withdraw; and at worst, the embarrassing support for the relatively unknown Congressman will clearly be a vote of non-confidence in the President, and will soften him up for the election in November.

Some YAFers and other honest conservatives, in despair at the Family Assistance Plan and especially at Nixon's grandstand visit to China. which is a deep affront to their most cherished rhetoric if not really significant in itself, are turning in despair to a Draft Reagan movement. But honesty ha never been a strong conservative suit, and indications are that the Buckleyite *realpolitik* will triumph, and that Republican conservatives, including of course Mr. Reagan, will dutifully if painfully keep their counsel and support the President. Is there no indignity which conservatives are not prepared to swallow?

Let us assume then that, after as much trouble as can be made for him, Mr. Nixon will sweep into the renomination. What then? The Democratic field is a crowded and ebullient one. In order to make some sense of the large lineup, let us first divide the hopefuls into a rough left-center-right grouping, depending on the intensity of their opposition to the abomination in Southeast Asia.

On the Right, we have those Democrats who are roughly Johnson-Nixon hawks on Vietnam. There is, first, that egregious gasbag and onetime darling of New Deal liberalism, Hubert Horatio Humphrey. Humphrey's record of toadying to LBJ marked a new low even for American politics, and the thought of a Nixon-Humphrey replay is almost too much for the human soul to contemplate. No, no, not that! Then there is the man who represents the antithesis of libertarianism in American politics, the man who is wrong on every conceivable question, the "Senator from Boeing", Henry "Scoop" Jackson (Wash.) Bad on the war, bad on the military-industrial complex, bad on the draft, bad on economics, bad, bad, bad. Mr. Statism. Another right-wing hopeful is Rep. Wilbur Mills (D., Ark.), bad on the war and draft, "conservative" fiscal expert and advocate of wage-price controls. Never. And finally, Mayor Sam Yorty of Los Angeles, rightist, clown, crusher of civil liberties, and happily with no chance whatsoever of the nomination.

In the center, demarkations between center and left become rather fuzzy. The epitome of the Center is Ed Muskie (Me.), cool, grey, colorless, fairly good on the war at this point, fairly bad on the draft. Probably the eventual candidate when the party hacks have had their day, Ed Muskie is the futherest right candidate who could be acceptable as an alternative to Nixon, and then of course only barely and without enthusiasm. Teddy Kennedy, possessed of lots of family charisma, is under the twin clouds of Chappaquiddick and Camelot, but has been moving leftward in an interesting fashion – especially his recent vote in support of the Gravel filibuster against extending the draft. Ramsay Clark is a shadowy dark horse with mysterious backing, whose only claim to our attention seems to be his revulsion against even his own tyrannies as Attorney-General. Senator Birch Bayh (Ind.) is a colorless middle-of-the reader with some labor union support, which makes him suspect, and whose only leadership came in electoral reform and the Haynesworth-Carrswell cases, estimable perhaps but hardly making him Presidential timber.

On the Left, the man with by far the best libertarian credentials in the Democratic Party has been so badly treated by the press that scarcely anyone knows that he is in the race. This is Senator William Proxmire (D., Wisc.), a man with an impeccable record on the war and the draft, and heroic leader in the Senate on behalf of economy in

government and in opposition to the SST and Lockheed boondoggles. Highly knowledgeable and of proven leadership ability, William Proxmire has the highest rating in the entire Senate from the National Taxpayers Union on spending-and-tax votes in the last Congress, far higher than any other Senator. Proxmire is close to libertarian financial expert A. Ernest Fitzgerald, who broke the Lockheed scandal, and is sympathetic to the broad libertarian cause. PROXMIRE FOR PRESIDENT!

Of the remainder of the Left, Senator George McGovern (S. D.) is the respected leader of the anti-war constituency, especially now that Senator Hughes's (Io.) propensity for the occult has apparently led him to withdraw from the race. McGovern is also solid on the draft. However, he (1) lacks charisma, and (2) suffers from domestic statism, especially the guaranteed annual income scheme.

It now appears that we are not to be spared a resurgence of Eugene McCarthy. Symbolically important on the war three years ago, McCarthy is poor on the draft, and is an odd sort of anti-hero in style and performance: erratic, off-handed, lazy, he has a generally poor sense of timing in manner as well as substance.

It is hard to take the loudly proclaimed entry of Senator Fred Harris (Okla.) very seriously. A Johnny-come-lately on the war and the draft, Harris just seems to be a statist with an affected "populist" style. Having done a poor job in the national committee, and facing certain defeat in primary and re-election races next year, Fred Harris apparently concluded that he had no place to go, after failing on a smaller scale, than failing as presidential candidate. Neither can we take seriously the candidacy of Rep. Anderson (Tenn.) whose one political issue seems to be support for the Berrigan brothers.

Of course, the big dramatic race is now expected to be made by one candidate possessing authentic charisma: Mayor John Lindsay of New York, expected to make a melodramatic switch of parties and then run for the Presidency. Lindsay has charisma, that is, everywhere except in New York City, and it would be hard to find *any* New Yorker, regardless of political persuasion, who will not predictably spit fire and curses at the very mention of Lindsay's name. And with good reason. If it is unfair to blame the entire visible deterioration of New York City in recent years on Lindsay's stewardship, it is also evidently true that he has hardly succeeded in stemming the tide. In fact, Lindsay is a spectacularly bad administrator; he manages to alienate all concerned groups in every area without helping the situation, and he approaches every problem with a scout-masterish air of moral superiority that is far more annoying for being totally unjustified. I concede Lindsay's good record on Vietnam and the draft, but no New Yorker can contemplate Lindsay's accession to the administration of the entire country without a grimace of horror. Only one good thing has John Lindsay done as Mayor: he has evinced a genuine concern for civil liberties. He has kept the cops more or less under leash; and his concern for civil liberties has led him to place New York City in the forefront of freedom for pornography and prostitution. Until recently, that is; for in recent weeks, the onset of Presidential fever has apparently led Lindsay to a drastic shift rightward on the matter, and he has instituted a continuing crackdown on "vice" – thus cancelling the only good deed of the Lindsay regime.

The Democrats' chances in 1972 are excellent; predictably, therefore, in view of their long-standing genius for self-destruction, we can count on them trying desperately to kick those chances away. The latest manifestation is the new Women's Caucus, almost completely left-Democratic, which might well bolt the ticket if a woman is not nominated. Already, Rep. Shirley Chisholm (N. Y.) has decided to run for President, her major qualification being that she is *both* black *and* female, and thereby can run as

(Continued on page 3)

222

LIBERTY: FROM RAND TO CHRIST

by Joseph R. Peden

In the midst of what appears to be a renaissance of libertarian thought, and a period of rapid increase in the numbers of its adherents – especially among the young college activists – it might be well for us to devote some attention to a remarkable personal testament entitled "Road to Freedom – Or to Nowhere?" published in *Rough Beast* #4 (1522 Connecticut Ave. NW, Washington, D. C. 20036). The author, Warren Carroll, formerly publisher of *Freedom's Way*, a pioneer libertarian publication, has produced a rare document – an analytic repudiation of libertarianism by a onetime true believer.

Although Carroll is familiar with several schools of libertarian thought – that of the individualist anarchists such as Albert Jay Nock, Frank Chodorov and the Rampart College group, and the limited-government classical liberals of The Foundation for Economic Education, he tends to identify libertarianism with Objectivism. As a former Randian Carroll knows the strengths and weaknesses of Objectivism intimately and his detailed and often perceptive critical analysis and disillusionment is colored by this personal experience.

Carroll begins his analysis by pinpointing a basic dilemma

DUMPING NIXON — *(Continued from page 2)*

representative of two "oppressed" caucuses. If only Mrs. Chisholm had been *also* a Chicana, a student, a Youth, an Old Person and a Welfare Mother, she could be the living embodiment of every "oppressed" and un-liberated group in the country. But even as it is, we are unfortunately living in a world where the candidacy of Mrs. Chisholm is *not* automatically laughed into the oblivion it so richly deserves.

A third and even a fourth party also loom as possibilities in 1972. About George Corley Wallace one can only have mixed feelings. In contrast to Fred Harris an authentic populist, Wallace makes many sound and trenchant criticisms of the existing system: of its corporate statism, its unholy alliance between Establishment rich and welfare recipients to exploit the bulk of the working and middle classes, of its compulsory integration and school bussing. But, alas!, the Wallace *policies* hardly sustain the promise of his sound critiques; a superhawk on Vietnam and the Cold War, Wallace is also scarcely known for devotion to civil liberties; on the contrary, we can expect the ultimate unleashing of the police and of repression under a Wallace as President.

There remains the possibility of a New Left fourth party, as yet unnamed. In *theory*, a fourth party could do an effective job in pushing the Democrats to the Left and in a pro-peace direction, by using the time-honored device of the carrot-and-the-stick, promising (a) that if the Democrats nominate a Proxmire or a McGovern, the New Party would run him on its line as well; *but* (b) that if the Democrats nominate a Hubert Humphrey, the New Party would run its own man in opposition. This *seems* to be a simple and effective strategy, but for some reason few third parties – among whom New York's Liberal and Conservative Parties are notable exceptions – have the wisdom and maturity to pursue such a course. Going on past record, we can predict that *either* the New Party will collapse and not be heard from again, *or* that it will stubbornly insist on running its own candidate no matter what the Democrats do, and thereby threaten a dangerous split in the anti-war forces. If the black and female caucuses do not succeed in wrecking the Democrats' chances, then perhaps the New Party will finish the job. ◘

which besets Objectivists: how can they most effectively create an objectivist social order? If they plunge into the political cauldron they are bound to compromise or sacrifice intellectual consistency – the hallmark of Objectivist morality. If they refrain from political action, they remain intellectually chaste, but doom their movement to "perpetual ineffectiveness". To Carroll this dilemma is a "fatal short-coming" of libertarianism. Moreover, faced with this inner conflict, the libertarian is likely to be assaulted by a sense of despair that mankind in general will ever have the same passion for intellectual consistency that he has.

"By definition, the existing pattern of government every-where prevents the realization of the libertarian dream, and the trend of current history sets steadily toward more and more concentration of power in government. Participation on any significant scale in either the political or economic system now existing entails compromises of principle that most libertarians find unacceptable. Increasingly they find themselves hemmed in and blocked on every side by their own philosophy. What was to have been a road to freedom becomes, in the real world, a cage."

"As the realization grows . . . that he is caught in a trap, . . . increasingly his thought turns either to violence or to flight." Those who succumb to violence "are quickly absorbed by the New Left and cease to be libertarians"; those who turn to flight – to desert isles or nomadism or her-mitage – thereby affirm the utopian character of libertarian philosophy. "In these two swamps of failure the libertarian movement in all its forms is being swallowed up."

Clearly Carroll knows whereof he speaks. He seems to have undergone the great intellectual crisis he so accurately describes. The sordid public dispute between Ayn Rand and Nathaniel Branden seems to have precipitated a decision by Carroll to flee to the uninhabited waste of Tasmania. There he was further traumatized by finding the few isolated inhabitants gathered around a TV set watching the Ed Sullivan Show and the Australian government firmly in control of all uninhabited lands. His faith in libertarianism as a workable moral philosophy was finally shattered.

From this disillusionment, Carroll now sees three funda-mental errors and a "still more fundamental failure of vision which taken together are fatal to the libertarian dream".

First of all, says Carroll, there is a "drastic misap-prehension of the nature of man". Libertarians view man as naturally good and rational but corrupted by institutions i.e. the State, the schools, the family, etc. But equally, libertarians know that institutions are merely individuals acting in concert in accordance with their interests, instincts or traditional ways. Therefore, the responsibility for the evils in society cannot be placed upon institutions but upon the individuals acting within the collective behavioral frame-work we call an institution. "But if men got themselves into their present state through their own corruption, how then do libertarians expect to bring them out of it? The failure of all their specific programs gives the answer to that question: they cannot".

Here one should note that Carroll raises the very crucial question of the nature of evil in man – a subject of the greatest philosophical and practical importance which de-serves serious analysis by libertarians. But he also asserts that because of their inadequate theory as to the true nature of man, the specific programs of libertarians have, histori-cally, failed and in fact cannot succeed. Since he does not give further detail or example to illustrate what he has in

(Continued on page 4)

LIBERTY: FROM CHRIST TO RAND

(Continued from page 3)

mind, one hesitates to comment further than to say that as no fully libertarian society has existed in European civilization since libertarian philosophy first emerged in the age of the Enlightenment, one can hardly prove or disprove Carroll's sweeping judgement as to its pragmatic effectiveness. One can only point empirically and historically to the fact that since the 18th century there has been a continual expansion of individual liberty as an ideal and social reality in a host of areas of human thought and action. I would give Carroll's indictment a Scottish verdict of "Not Proven".

A second error, according to Carroll, is the libertarian's "optimistic misreading of history", his assumption that "his system has never failed because it never has been tried, while in fact it has never been tried because it would certainly fail! The failure of the approaches to a libertarian society which were made in the past, particularly in the 19th century, is the proof we have that a fully libertarian society would be even shorter-lived and less successful." I have already stated my belief that Carroll's historical verdict on libertarian efforts in previous centuries is not proven. But his accusation of misplaced optimism is central to the condition of despair which permeates his entire attitude towards libertarianism. As a professional historian Carroll shows a surprisingly crude appreciation of the complexity of human society and of the process by which societies undergo change. Libertarian philosophy is largely the product of the 19th century drawing inspiration from the intellectual legacy of the enlightenment. Does he really think that scarcely two centuries would see the triumph of so radical a moral, social and economic philosophy? Christianity as a wholly integrated moral and practical philosophy has been with us for two thousand years and its failures are at least as glaring as those of libertarianism. Does the failure of Christians and their society to conform to the ideals of the philosophy of Christ mean that their "system" would totally fail if ever tried? Are both Christians and libertarians hopeless Utopians? I think not. They may well be the only true realists. Only a person of the narrowest historical perception could dismiss libertarians as guilty of "optimistic misjudgement of history". They are simply not historical determinists and they recognize that a century is but a minute in the history of the human race. They do have faith in the ultimate value of and vindication of their philosophical insights – as do believing Christians.

I think that Carroll is so frustrated by the collapse of his own utopian libertarianism that he has lost historical perspective. As Paul Goodman has pointed out, the libertarian revolution is not the work of a day – or a decade – or a lifetime. It is a continuous process through the ages. The focus of the struggle changes from time to time and place to place. Once it involved the abolition of slavery; now it may be women's liberation; here it may be a struggle for national independence; there it may center on civil liberties; at one moment it may require electioneering and party politics; at another armed self-defense and revolution. Carroll expected too much too soon. There is a tendency among many libertarians to look for an apocalyptic moment when the State will be smashed forever and anarchy prevail. When they realize that the great moment isn't about to come in their time, if ever, they lose faith in the integrity and plausibility of the libertarian philosophy. Like a Christian awaiting the Second Coming of Christ when the reign of Justice shall be established and evil men receive their just punishment, the libertarian awaits the coming of the rational and anarchic age. But to lose one's faith in the validity of Christianity because evil continues to thrive in the world makes as much sense as losing one's faith in libertarianism because the New Order has not yet triumphed over the Old. Such attitudes are naive and not be be expected from mature, sophisticated men of learning. Carroll's experience should

warn us that libertarianism can quite easily become merely an adolescent fantasy in minds that are immature and unseasoned by a broad humanistic understanding. It should not be an *idee fixe* or magic formula, but a moral imperative with which one approaches the complexities of social reality.

In his discussion of what he considers to be a third fatal error, Carroll gives further clue to what ultimately repelled him in libertarianism – the "fundamental inadequacy of the materialistic value system which, in essence, they all accept". Crediting Ayn Rand with at least attempting to transcend the obvious limitation of materialism by setting up life itself as the source of value, Carroll accurately perceives that "objectivism in practice measures the value of life in material terms, by the financial profit or the personal satisfaction that can be realized from it". It is one of the great ironies that Leftists who philosophically are materialists are psychologically quite ready to sacrifice life, liberty and personal comfort for the Cause; yet Objectivists who are rhetorically preoccupied with morals, concepts, dialectic and reason are notoriously adverse to anything that smacks of idealistic altruism. Wealth and the bitch goddess success are the household dieties of the Randian cult. Who else but a Randian would sport a dollar sign as a personal fetish or totem? If they were not so narrowly chauvinistic the Randians might have chosen the more universal symbol of their cult – the golden calf. Worshippers of wealth and success, and hedonists, are seldom very attractive people. They are incapable of either love or true friendship for both are founded upon disinterested loyalty and self-sacrifice to the needs of another. It is not surprising that an audience at a West coast convention should wildly applaud a young man who openly bragged that he had betrayed his fellow students to the police and his only regret was that he had not done it for money! Or as an ex-Randian once put it, the only poetry that will ever come from the Randians will be an Ode to Greed.

Under the circumstances, it is not surprising that Mr. Carroll has abandoned libertarianism (which he tends to identify with Objectivism) and sought elsewhere for a new certitude and a new basis for his moral values. Indeed, it is to his credit that he did so. He has found a new faith; he has become a Christian. The great tragedy here is that he fails to perceive that libertarianism is not incompatible with a Christian world view. Libertarianism is not the atheism, materialism and unrestrained egoism of Objectivism or of Stirnerism or other variant schools. It is essentially the belief that voluntarism is the only just basis for human social relationships; that man is a creature whose inherent worth and dignity is beyond price; that man should live in conformity to his nature as perceived through the light of reason; that you should do unto others as you would have them do unto you. Is this at all incompatible with Christianity? The Christian is, I would argue, a natural anarchist by faith. He has a profound respect for life and human dignity; he governs himself by the inner law of conscience illumined by the teachings of Christ; he denies the State as a source of good or truth – at best it is a punishment placed upon men for their evil deeds; and he accepts moral responsibility for the consequences of his acts. The Christian finds true liberty by living his life in conformity to the will of God as manifest in the law of nature and the revealed wisdom of the great poets, prophets and sages of all ages. If Tolstoy, Dorothy Day, the Anabaptists, and Jehovah's Witnesses are not libertarians and Christians, the words are meaningless.

Carroll has done us a great service in underscoring the ultimate inadequacy of Objectivism as a social and personal philosophy, and the danger of equating libertarianism as a social philosophy with objectivism's often perverse and anti-human values. The Randian value system is a potential millstone around the neck of the libertarian movement. Many observers have noted that Objectivist rhetoric is re-

(Continued on page 5)

LIBERTY: FROM CHRIST TO RAND

(Continued from page 4)

pellent to many people otherwise attracted to libertarian voluntarism, decentralization, and even the market economy. Carroll's experience should alert us to the spiritual bankruptcy of that particular school of libertarian thought, and direct us to introduce young libertarians to alternative ethical value systems – such as Christianity – which are rationally and historically compatible with essential libertarian principles. ◻

Comment

by M. N. R.

Dr. Warren Carroll's Leap Over the Wall from Randianism to Triumphantist Christianity highlights two important problems that deserve far more attention than they have received from libertarians: the growing problem of defection, and the status of Christianity and the Christian ethic within the *movement*.

As Professor Peden points out, a major reason for Carroll's defection was his thirst for Instant Victory – a flaw that he shared with all too many libertarians. When that Instant Victory was not forthcoming, Carroll took flight for a retreatist Utopia in Tasmania, and when that proved abortive, abandoned the cause altogether. Why can't libertarians settle down cheerfully to a lifelong struggle for liberty? Carroll says repeatedly that libertarianism offers "no reward along the way", no "reward in the road itself" except for the eventual attainment of liberty. But why not? Why is there not joy in dedication to the advancement of truth, justice, and liberty? The businessman, after all, finds joy in the ceaseless pursuit of profit and growth, the scientist in the endless quest for ever-expanding truth; why may not the libertarian obtain the same from the "long march" toward liberty? Every *other* "career" offers joys and satisfactions in the functioning of the career itself, and apart from specific achievements emanating from it. Why should the "career" of liberty hold any less excitement and reward for the libertarian?

Carroll does have a small point here, however. In that all too many libertarians have, in their commendable "purism", systematically ruled out *any* conceivable strategy for even ultimate or eventual victory. By ruling out virtually all tactics except pure education, libertarians have almost doomed themselves to perpetual defeat, which might be enough to discourage even the stoutest of heart. On the contrary, it is precisely in the area of strategy and tactics where the libertarian should be flexible and pragmatic – in contrast to the realm of principle where he should be "doctrinaire" and consistent.

On the whole issue that Carroll raises about the nature of man and his institutions, Carroll is about the one millionth person to totally misinterpret the libertarian view in this area. He states that "all libertarian schools view man as naturally good and naturally rational"; in contrast, I don't know of *one* that holds such an absurdly naive doctrine. And yet this has been the major charge hurled at us by archists for generations. To set the record straight hopefully for good and all, the libertarian believes, along with everyone else, that man is a mixture of good and evil. What we are trying to do is to eliminate institutions which are inherently evil and thereby provide a legalized, legitimated channel for evil to proceed unchecked in society. There should be nothing very mysterious about *that*.

This brings me to the whole question of Christianity and the Christian ethic. Not a Christian myself, I have seen for years how Christian libertarians have been abused, badgered, and hectored by militant atheists and presump-

tuous Randians, and their libertarian *bona fides* sharply questioned. Being on the whole – perhaps as a result of their Christian training – far nicer people than their tormentors, these Christian libertarians have put up with this shabby treatment with calm and good humor. But it should be crystal clear that a libertarian movement which imperiously insists upon atheism as a necessary condition for membership is going to needlessly alienate countless numbers of potential supporters. Atheists, to be sure, believe that Christianity, like other theism, is an error; but there are millions of errors in the world, and it passeth understanding why this particular one should bar Christians from the libertarian community. There is certainly no substantial reason why Christians and atheists cannot peacefully co-exist within the libertarian movement. It is high time, therefore, for all libertarians, Christian and atheist alike, to blow the whistle on the anti-Christian abuse that has infected the movement for so long a time.

But there is more to the tale than that. For while every rationalist libertarian must hold reason higher than tradition, there is *one* sense in which the traditionalist conservatives have gotten hold of a very important point, and one that has been unfortunately overlooked by the rationalists. And that is wrapped up in the great truth of the division of labor: the fact that the vast majority of people have neither the ability nor the skill to carve out a rational ethic on their own. Ethics is a science, a discipline like other disciplines; and as in any other branch of knowledge it is vain folly to begin exploration of the science afresh and on one's own while disregarding all the other explorers and thinkers who have gone before. I once knew a Randian who tried to deduce astronomy *a priori* and out of his own head without bothering to consult any of the other literature in the field. While this was a caricature and a half-jest on his part, it exemplified all too well the rationalist – and particularly the Randian – disposition to attempt to carve out a body of thought without bothering to read one's predecessors. In the field of ethics and philosophy in general, it is simply an empirical fact that the greatest thinkers, for two thousand years, have been Christian; and to ignore these Christian philosophers and to attempt to carve out an ethical system purely on one's own is to court folly and disaster.

Apart from their respective merits, then, it is no accident that, in practical application – from sex to music – Christian ethicists should have a far more rational batting average than the Randian. After all, Randian thought has only been in existence for a decade or two, while Christianity has had two thousand years to develop. We stand on the shoulders of the thinkers of the past, even though of course we must use our reason to correct them.

But there are further, and grimmer, implications here for rationalists. For if few people have the ability or inclination to carve out an ethical system on their own, this means that they must – if their actions are to be guided by any coherent set of values – take them passively, almost on trust. But who then are the masses of men to trust for their system of values? Surely *that system* with the longest and most successful tradition, with the largest quota of great minds – in short, the Christian ethic. This is a bitter pill for many of us non-Christians to swallow, but I am afraid it is inescapable nevertheless.

This conclusion is reinforced when we look around at what has happened to much of today's libertarian movement. The peculiar aspects of the Randian ethic are as nothing to the *bizarreries*, to the outright lunacies, into which so many ex-Randians (who constitute the bulk of the libertarian movement) have sunk, in their vain attempts to carve out a system of objective ethics on their own. (The latest craze, so we have heard, is "rational bestiality.") The Christian ethic is, in the words of the old hymn, a Rock of Ages, and it is at least incumbent upon the individual to think long and hard before he abandons that Rock lest he sink into the quagmire of the capricious and the bizarre.

225

Bits And Pieces
By Jerome Tuccille

PRESIDENTIAL POLITICS

At this writing libertarians are about to enter a working coalition with Allard Lowenstein's Dump Nixon movement for the Presidential campaign of 1972. The New York Times is scheduled to publish a letter, authored by myself and signed by representatives of the leading libertarian groups in the country, announcing our support for the Lowenstein organization and our reasons for supporting it. Toward the end of July a press conference will be held to further publicize these efforts.

A libertarian-left liberal alliance? The prospect shouldn't be any more surprising than the libertarian-conservative alliance that existed in this country until the middle of 1969. Less so. In today's political atmosphere the bonds of agreement between ourselves and the liberal left are more numerous than they ever were between libertarians and William Buckley conservatives, with whom we shared only a *rhetorical* commitment to a free market economy. Liberals of the George McGovern-Allard Lowenstein-Eugene McCarthy school are closer to our views on (1) the war in southeast Asia where they favor an immediate end to *all* American hostilities, (2) the military draft which they consistently oppose, (3) civil liberties at home, a vital area in which conservatives have traditionally made their weakest showing (the Nixonite assault on freedom of the press, along with Nixon's infatuation with no-knock legislation, are two of the most dangerous threats to basic freedoms we have faced in recent years), and (4) international economic, cultural and social cooperation where left liberals are more consistently in line with libertarian principles while conservatives, despite Nixon's recent overtures to Red China, maintain a primarily protectionist attitude.

Only in the area of domestic economic policy do left liberals differ sharply with free market libertarians, but even here we see that a conservative administration has not come any closer to our own ideal (if anything, it has been more disastrous since it promotes the same centralist schemes with *laissez faire* sloganeering).

So why should we bother entering coalitions with anyone? Why not remain aloof from the manswarm of American politicking and continue to push our own brand of philosophical purism?

First of all, we must remember that any alliance is undertaken strictly for tactical reasons. Basic principles are never compromised. The idea is to convert those with whom we come in contact.

Second, libertarianism *per se* is not large enough to operate effectively as an independent movement. We have to broaden our base of operation and become directly involved in the give-and-take of *realpolitik* if we are to be taken seriously by the general public. We have to offer solutions that make sense, and to do this we have to get out into the arena where the battles are being waged. Articles and books are not enough.

Third, in order that we may make life a bit more bearable for ourselves, it is in our own best interests to see that the "best" candidates get into office. Liberalized draft laws, abortion laws, tax laws, trade laws, sex laws, ad infinitum, are better than oppressive laws in all these areas. While reforms tend to co-opt and defuse the radical thrust toward an ideal condition, co-optation is never more than temporary at best.

Fourth. As we fight for the right kind of reforms we must simultaneously maintain our revolutionary posture.

That is, while we are fighting to *libertarianize* society through the vote, we must also refuse to be drafted, to pay taxes, to obey the myriad restrictions on peaceful activities.

If we are going to work with non-libertarians, it follows that we must seek out a viable group somewhere along the political spectrum with whom we find ourselves most compatible. By "a viable group" I mean one that is politically alive and active and operating with a good measure of support. Reform liberals fit that bill for us at the present moment. If we are far apart on economic principle, it is the one area where we are miles apart from every other major faction in the country. At the very least, left liberals are sympathetic to the politics of radical decentralization, and it is through this avenue that we must channel our efforts to achieve the libertarian ideal of individual liberty (Every time I bring up the subject of "decentralization," I am hounded by morons who want to know why we should fool around with a system which might lead to neighborhood tyranny. If the reasons aren't apparent by now, then to hell with it. Suffice it to say that neighborhood dictators are easier to deal with than the immensely more powerful ones in federal, state and city governments).

As far as actual candidates are concerned, again we are talking about the "lesser of evils," about the "best of a bad lot." Politicians, by definition, are a "bad lot" according to libertarian theory. But as long as we are saddled with a system based on patronage, graft, corruption and the apportioning of power — with no real hope of eliminating that system in the near future — we are forced to think in terms of "degrees of evil" whenever we step beyond the confines of ivory-tower purism. It is only by working with other groups, such as reform liberals, that we can hope to influence them in their own choice of political candidates — perhaps guide them toward one or two more acceptable to us out of a stable of half a dozen or so.

The way the political sweepstakes are shaping up for 1972, this is how the various entries look from this observer's vantage point:

MARK HATFIELD is perhaps the most acceptable of all. He is serious about getting out of southeast Asia, about eliminating the military draft, about liberalizing trade and diplomatic relations with all other nations, and he has taken a uniquely libertarian position on the middle east — that is, he is the only major politician to speak out publicly for the displaced Palestinians, the real victims of the Arab-Israeli conflict. On the negative side, he continues to vote for centralist welfare schemes, although he has lately spoken favorably of Rothbardian economic principles. Most damaging of all, he voted *for* Nixon's no-knock legislation, an inexcusable violation of libertarian principle which requires a very cautious attitude toward his general position on civil liberties.

GEORGE McGOVERN. Good on the war. Good on the draft. Speaks favorably about political decentralization. His stand on the middle east is typically liberal establishment: unabashedly and unqualifiedly pro-Israel. Economically, he is liberal-welfarist, though he seems open to decentralist alternatives.

EUGENE McCARTHY. The remarks on McGovern apply generally here with one major exception: he appears to be a bit more flexible on the middle east. However, his credibility as a serious contender has been considerably weakened by his own inertia following the 1968 campaign.

PAUL McCLOSKY continues to be a one-issue candidate; he is against further U. S. participation in the war. His position on other issues has remained vague until this writing. Most damaging: he is on record as being *in favor* of the military draft. Still, he might be worth supporting

(*Continued on page 7*)

226

BITS AND PIECES — *(Continued from page 6)*

as an anti-Nixon candidate in the primaries if there is no-one else, since he will be an embarrassment to the administration if nothing else. Another important consideration here is the fact that McClosky is backed by Norton Simon, reported to be a strong economic libertarian who will influence McClosky considerably. This possibility is worth watching closely.

JOHN LINDSAY. Bad in so many different ways. He is an unprincipled wheeler-dealer who bends with the political winds. One thing he does have going for him is the fact that he is highly susceptible to pressure. He is good on civil liberties and not likely to come down hard against radical activism (draft and tax resistance, general civil disobedience) if it has any degree of public support at all. This could be a valuable asset to the radical movement.

EDMUND MUSKIE still looks like the front-runner among Democratic hopefuls. Muskie has a history of vagueness and vacillation on virtually every issue one can think of: the war in Asia; the draft; civil liberties; international trade; domestic social and economic policies; even on the question of environmental pollution in which he is supposed to have a strong interest. Not much here to offer the libertarian cause.

HUBERT HUMPHREY. Equally bad. He operates with the New Deal mentality of thirty years ago and his role as Vice President during the early and middle war years borders on the criminal, despite his recent babblings about "withdrawal from Vietnam." The worst of the traditional political hacks either party has to offer.

HENRY JACKSON. Totally unacceptable from a libertarian point-of-view. He is a New Deal-Great Society welfarist on domestic issues, and his past and present position on Vietnam makes Barry Goldwater sound dovish by comparison. He would also deal severely with domestic dissenters. A disaster for the libertarian cause.

TED KENNEDY. The dimmest of the Kennedy brothers, and completely unacceptable to libertarians. He is adamantly pro-draft, militantly pro-Israel, and as deeply committed to a centralized, quasi-socialistic economy as any other candidate. He is unintelligent and dominated by advisers – the wrong advisers for libertarian purposes.

Right now these are the only men who can be considered serious presidential hopefuls by any stretch of the imagination. Another dark horse possibility rests with the New Party, a left-liberal reformist group, founded by Gore Vidal among others. Vidal is a thorough-going cultural and civil libertarian with a Menckenesque view of the American scene in all its aspects. He is highly individualistic on social, cultural, spiritual and moral questions and, while exhibiting some New Dealist tendencies in his economic philosophy, he is highly sympathetic to the concept of local control of institutions. The New Party is touting Ralph Nader, muckraking critic of the Corporate State, as a presidential hopeful. Nader's great contribution to date has been as an effective gadfly on the governmental hide. He is most assuredly *not* an economic libertarian, but he is a disruptive force in opposition to the American status quo, and the reforms that will be generated by his movement will likely serve to benefit the individual – especially in the area of economic consumption.

Beginning in the fall of 1971, libertarian groups in the northeast will be making concrete plans for the new Hampshire primary to be held the following spring. Bill Baumgarth and others in the area have founded Citizens for a Restructured Republic, a libertarian front group, to work actively with other anti-Nixon forces. We should all dig in and lend these efforts our support, in any way possible. The candidate (or candidates) who will receive our support in the primaries depends largely on what happens over the next six months or so.

All in all, it is shaping up to be one hell of a time.

Traditional China And Anarchism

By Murray Rubinstein

(Professor Rubinstein's fine summary of traditional Chinese political concepts suggests an important lesson for libertarians. In Chinese thought the anarchist ideas were applied within a statist structure; there had been no attempt to overthrow the state but merely to introduce anarchist practices to modify and improve the situation. The result was oppressive; anarchist ideas cannot be applied while the state system continues in existence. In fact, it may be that the application of anarchist ideas within a statist structure can only lead to worse oppression. The state is the central issue; its abolition is the central objective. The introduction of anarchist practices or operations while the state continues to exist may not only be irrelevant but if widespread in application may result in worse oppression. This is an important warning for libertarians. What was the reason for the failure in China to move to an anarchist society? Elitism. There was a disdain for the common people and their institutions. The clan and self-help organizations provided a suitable basis for a libertarian legal system. But their powers were curtailed and limited because they were viewed as a threat to the state structure from which the ruling class drew its wealth. Although they might be committed to the anarchistic philosophy of the Chinese sages, the local rulers recognized that they drew their wealth from the statist structure. Thus, they viewed all activities against the standard of the preservation of the statist structure and acted in their official capacities not as anarchist philosophers but as statist oppressors. --Leonard P. Liggio).

The Chinese Civil Service System with it complicated

examination path and its structured pattern of rule and control from above seems far distant from an anarchistic model of society based on free association or voluntarism, and a laissez-faire economy. Yet at the heart of this system are basic concepts very close to those libertarians adopt as their own.

The ideological basis of the System was a combination of Taoism and Confucianism which represented a functional application of these seemingly contradictory thought systems. It is my purpose to examine some of these basic tenets and see how they were modified in the process of application.

Taoism, in its philosophical form, is represented by two major works, the Tao Te Ching (Book of the Way) and the Chuang Tzu. Each of these books is a product of the Warring States period, an age in which much of Chinese philosophy was developed. Taoism on this level is a pantheistic thought system which holds that the universe is a continuum in which all matter is in the process of becoming differentiated and then non-differentiated. The Taoist believes that there is a single source to the "ten thousand things" and that he must reestablish his unity with the universe. The inner harmony of nature should be related to the outer harmony of man's actions. To achieve this external harmony is to leave things alone. The best government is the least government; the best ruler is he who is content to leave his subjects alone.

Confucianism on the surface seems the opposite of this WuWei (non-action) form of rule (or non-rule). It is a

(Continued on page 8)

227

TRADITIONAL CHINA AND ANARCHISM
Continued from page 7)

philosophy that seems to stress precedent and strict adherence to rites and ceremonies. Li (ritual) is only one aspect of the Confucian ideology, for there is also deep faith in Jen (benevolence-good) and chih (wisdom). The operation of government and thus of society should be in the hands of the Chun-tzu - the gentleman who advises the ruler and leads by moral virtue. The Confucians viewed formal punitive law as negative and only to be used as last resort. There was no formal concept of civil law, for in a society based on virtue such would be unnecessary. In the *Analects*, this belief in government by virtue is expounded at length:

95. Confucius said, "If a ruler himself is upright, all will go well without orders. But if he himself is not upright, even though he gives orders, they will not be obeyed."

97. Confucius said, "Lead the people by laws and regulate them by penalties and the people will try to keep out of jail, but will have no sense of shame. Lead the people by virtue and restrain them by rules of decorum and the people will have a sense of shame and moreover will become good." Theoretically, therefore government means good men, living properly, rather than good laws, strictly enforced.

How did these ideas, Taoist and Confucian, work out in application? Taoist political thought was never put into practice, but the ethics became formalized and a concrete set of rituals and church structure were developed. This religious Taoism can still be seen in operation today on Taiwan.

Confucianism, on the other hand, did become the state orthodoxy. In the reign of the Han emperor Wu Ti the philosophy of Confucius, as it had been passed down and thus modified since 500 B. C., became the theoretical basis for government. During the T'ang Dynasty a method of examination was developed and a complicated government structure developed to make use of the talents of the trained scholars. The means of choosing and utilizing the potential Chuntzu was thus devised. Once the student had passed through the three stages of exams, the district level, the province level and the central administration level and had achieved the degree of Chin Shih, he was ready to put into practice the lessons he had learned (lessons learned by memorizing and analyzing the works of Confucius and the other "Classics"). He became on the district level the embodiment of the concept of 'rule by good men'. But instead of letting society run itself, he found himself forced to rule as a despot, acting as tax collector, judge, jury and prosecuting attorney, defense chief, police chief, flood control expert, and moral instructor to the local gentry. He was constantly under the scrutiny of his superiors and had to move to a new post every three years in accordance with custom. The magistrate was thus an overburdened local bureaucrat.

very far from the ideal of a man leading by the force of moral virtue alone.

The lesson of Traditional China for those who believe in freedom and the creation of a totally free society is this: that ideas are not enough, that even concepts conceived of by men such as Confucius and Lao Tzu can become stale, rigid, even despotic in application. China in the formative centuries developed proto-anarchistic ideas. The total, unsystematic application of those ideas created a system as rigid, as formalistic, as tyrannical as any we have today.

◻

From The Old Curmudgeon

(Once again, the need for him arises. Tall and lean, he dons his mask, leaps on his trusty white horse, and rides off into the West. Champion of Truth, Defender of Justice, scourge of deviationists, heretics, sinners, and evildoers, the bane of Young Whippersnappers, he rides again. In a storm of thundering hooves, with a hearty "Hi-yo Silver", here he is, back by popular demand . . . the Old Curmudgeon.)

Excess Curmudgeonry.

I never though I'd have to say this, but as a long-time champion of both Old Curmudgeonry and the Golden Mean, I have to admit that there *can* be such a thing as being too much of a curmudgeon. For example: under the guidance of Jerome Tuccille and Murray Rothbard as Advisory Editors, Arno Press, a respected reprint publisher and subsidiary of the New York *Times*, is putting out a series, hopefully by this Christmas, of reprints on "The Right-Wing Individualist Tradition in America." One would think that libertarians and individualists would jump at the chance of wide distribution in hard cover. But no! Several Old Right-wing Curmudgeons, sequestered away on their literal or figurative mountaintops for decades, have sniffed some sort of Establishment Plot in all this and have refused to sell their copyrights to Arno — preferring to clasp their privately printed and almost unknown editions to their hermitic bosoms.

Come on, fellas; we respect and admire you for your lonely battles over the decades. But new times have arrived; it is at last "in" to be an individualist. Come on, relax and enjoy the New Dispensation; after all, we wouldn't want to vindicate the old left-wing smear that we became individualists in order to justify our anti-social psyches, would we? ◻

The Libertarian Forum
BOX 341
MADISON SQUARE STATION
NEW YORK, NEW YORK 10010.

Published Every Month. Subscription Rate: $8.00 Per Year

Special Issue On The Freeze

THE Libertarian Forum

Joseph R. Peden, Publisher

Murray N. Rothbard, Editor

VOLUME III, NO. 8　　　　　September, 1971　　　　　75c

The End Of Economic Freedom

On August 15, 1971, economic freedom died in America. And the terrible thing is that everybody cheered. Where was the opposition? Where are the people who, for four decades now, have been denouncing wage and price controls?

Where are the businessmen? For decades, the business community has been proclaiming its devotion to free enterprise, to the free price system. For decades, they have been attacking direct controls on prices and wages. Where are they now? They are the loudest and most delighted of the cheering squad for Mr. Nixon's New Totalitarian Economic Policy. On the day after Nixon's sudden and dramatic price freeze, the Washington *Post* reported that the mood of the business and banking community was "almost euphoric." William P. Gullander, head of the National Association of Manufacturers, expressed his delight at the wage-price freeze; and George G. Hagedorn, chief economist of the NAM, and who has many times proclaimed his devotion to the free market, joined in the hosannahs. The Chamber of Commerce of the United States, which in 1951 had issued a report on *The Price of Price Control* demonstrating that price and wage controls do not work and impose a terrible burden on the economy, was scarcely less enthusiastic in hailing the program.

On August 24, furthermore, Secretary of Commerce Maurice Stans met with eleven of the heads of the nation's biggest corporations; Stans reported delightedly that all of our biggest businessmen not only hailed the controls, but "want to be sure the program does not terminate on Nov. 12". In fact, not a single businessman of any stature, not one, has been reported to be anything but enthusiastic about the wage-price freeze. And so where is all the talk about the free enterprise system? Where are the men to rise and defend our lost economic freedom?

The conservatives of this country have scarcely done any better. For decades, they too have opposed "creeping socialism" and have been particularly vehement in attacking direct controls over wages and prices and their dictation to the individual on what price or wage he may charge or pay on the market. Where are the conservatives now? For the most part, we have heard only a resounding silence. In fact, many conservatives have simply joined in the cheering, have hailed the dramatic move by our "strong" President, and have curiously forgotten their supposed devotion to "strict" construction of the Constitution as a protection for our liberties. The slight amount of conservative criticism that

has appeared has been timid and wistful, with a nary a mention of the dictatorship that has suddenly buried our economic freedom, and scarcely a fraction of the righteous indignation with which they greeted Mr. Nixon's grandstand announcement of his trip to Communist China. *Human Events* expressed the hope that the controls would not be permanent; and the nation's most prominent conservative, William F. Buckley, in a dithering column of August 19, stated that the controls were not necessary but that, on the other hand, Mr. Nixon saw that controls could work for an "intermediate length" of time, even though they cannot work either in the "short" or the "long" run. By what principles or what precise length of time we can enjoy "intermediate" success with price and wage controls, neither Mr. Nixon nor Mr. Buckley has bothered to let us know.

And where are the nation's economists? For at least two decades, virtually all the nation's economists, let alone Arthur Burns, Paul McCracken and the other Administration economists who have led us to the destruction of the free economy, have told us, with all the certainty of which they are capable, that price and wage controls do not work, that they tackle only the symptoms and not the causes of inflation, that controls do not halt inflation but only bring about shortages, distortions, disruptions, and black markets. Yet, virtually all of them have jumped on the control bandwagon, with no hesitation whatever – even Professor Samuelson, whose own best-selling textbook reveals the unworkability of direct price controls on the market. It is no wonder that virtually the only economist to champion controls all along – J. K. Galbraith – has hailed Mr. Nixon as a "repentant sinner"; he could have included the nation's economists in the gibe. There have been only a few honorable exceptions to the stampede: Milton Friedman mildly criticized the controls as unworkable – but without denouncing the invasion of freedom involved. And 16 Chicago School economists headed by Allen Meltzer of Carnegie-Mellon University, did issue a statement denouncing wage and price controls as "inequitable, wasteful, inefficient and destructive of personal freedom". But that is literally all. How ironic that the only large-scale and determined attack on the wage-price freeze was launched by the very Democrats and labor unions that had been calling for controls for many months! Some of the union rhetoric was impassioned and even denounced the controls as dictatorial and unconstitutional – thus reminiscent of the conservatives and businessmen of days gone by.

Leonard Woodcock, head of the United Automobile Workers, even charged that "Nixon's is the hand that held the dagger" but that the Democrats, in passing the authorization for controls in the first place, had put the dagger into his hand.

But it is highly unlikely that the nation's unions, despite their passion and their early talk of non-compliance and a general strike, will be the instrument to save American freedom. For the unions, after all, have long championed such controls, and merely resent the fact that profits weren't frozen as well. Furthermore, they are already showing indications that if unions are given their share as partners in a tripartite control arrangement, such as ruled the country during the days of NRA and World War II – a tripartite rule of big business, big unions, and big government – they will end their outcry. In short, labor unions hardly oppose the controls in principle; they just want a bigger share of the pie.

The Cause of Inflation

The controls won't work. The prime reason why they won't work is that they do not tackle the *cause* of inflation, but only lash out at the symptoms. Let us see why. Every *price* is simply the terms of an exchange on the market, an exchange with money on one side and some good or service on the other. When I buy a newspaper for a dime, ten cents in money is being exchanged for one newspaper; when I buy a hat for $5, five dollars in money is being exchanged for one hat. And so the key to what makes prices high or low is the relationship between the supply of goods available and the supply of money which can be used to purchase them. Suppose, for example, that by some magic process, the quantity of money available in the country doubles overnight. The supply of goods remains the same, for nothing has really happened to lower or raise them. But then we will all enter the market with twice as many dollars burning a hole in our pocket as compared to yesterday. And if consumer tastes remain about the same, this means that twice as much money will be bidding for the same amount of goods, and all their prices will approximately double; we will all have to pay twenty cents for the same newspaper and $10 for the same hat.

In the unhampered free market economy, the supply of goods and services usually increases, as investment and productivity rise. This means that the tendency of the free market will be for prices to *fall,* some prices of course more than others, depending on where productivity increases the most. It is rare that production actually *decreases* in a free economy, and certainly in the last decade as inflation has continued and accelerated, production has generally continued to go up rather than down. So we cannot account for the continuing inflation from the production side. Where then is the culprit? It is the *money* side, for the supply of dollars has continued to go up, and even to accelerate, especially during the Johnson and Nixon Administrations. And as the supply of dollars has risen and risen ever faster, prices have gone up as well – all prices: including rents, wages, and interest rates. This year, for example, the supply of money has been increasing at a rate of 12-16%; is it any wonder that prices have kept increasing as well? Furthermore, in all the hullaballoo about everything being "frozen", one of the vital factors conspicuous for *not* being frozen is the money supply, which keeps on rocketing upward.

Who, then, is responsible for the continual and growing increases in the supply of money? It is *not* big business or little business or labor unions or consumer "greed" or international speculators or any of the other economic forces that government has focussed on to pin the blame for inflation. *The culprit is none other than the federal government itself.* It is the federal government and no other organization that has absolute and effective control of the supply of money, and regulates it to its own content. It is the federal government that has been merrily increasing the supply of money, to "stimulate" the economy, to finance its own now enormous budget deficits, to help out favored borrowers, to lower interest rates, or for any other reason.

Note then the stance of the government, whether it is the Nixon or Johnson or any other administration in the history of inflation. First it pumps more money into the economy, and continues to do so. *Then,* as the new money inevitably spreads throughout the society, and as prices and wages and rents inevitably increase in response, the government itself becomes increasingly possessed with righteous indignation. It issues edicts, bellows about social responsibility, and denounces various groups in turn for supposedly causing the price inflation. Business is denounced for raising prices, labor unions for asking and obtaining wage increases, landlords for raising rents, and sometimes consumers for spending too much. But never, never does the government bother to point to its own responsibility for the whole problem. Instead, it continues to pour more money into the system, and then to wax indignant when prices and wages rise in inevitable response. The White Knight of government, with its myriad of experts and advisers, marching out to man the ramparts of the "fight against inflation", turns out to be the very culprit who is the source and origin of the whole problem.

How does the government increase the money supply? The old candid days of simply printing more greenbacks, such as caused inflation during the Revolutionary War and the Civil War, is now hopelessly out of date. For one thing, the process was too clear, and when the "Continental dollar" printed in massive lots during the American Revolution became virtually worthless, it was clear to almost everyone that the unlimited printing press of government was the responsible agent. It was from that experience, by the way, that the old American phrase, "Not Worth a Continental", originated. The current inflationary process is much more subtle, though no less effective, and hence understood by very few non-economists. It works something as follows:

The controller and virtual dictator of the money and banking system is the Federal Reserve Board, appointed by the President. The Federal Reserve Act gives to the Federal Reserve Banks, run by the Board, the monopoly of the issuance of paper money, and forces the nation's commercial banks – *not,* by the way, against their will – to keep their reserves at the Fed. The commercial banks are then allowed to *create* money – in the form of demand deposits, or checking accounts – to a multiple of approximately 1:6 on top of their total reserves. In short, if total bank reserves at the Fed are $10 billion, the banks are allowed to create and lend out up to $50 billion more, until their checking accounts total $60 billion. Almost always, the banks are eager to do so. If, then, bank reserves increase by another $1 billion, they will create $6 billion in new money in the economy.

The key lever in the creation of new money and the expansion of the money supply, then, is the total of bank reserves. These are under the complete control of the Federal Reserve Board itself, which keeps seeing to it that bank reserves increase, and at a rapid rate. How does the Fed do this? Basically, by going into the "open market" and buying assets. Actually, it doesn't matter *what kind* of assets the Federal Reserve Banks decide to buy. Suppose, for some reason, the Fed takes it into its head to buy one of my old typewriters. It purchases a typewriter from me for $30. The Fed now has another typewriter in its offices, valued at $30. I – and this is the crucial step here – have a check for $30 on the Federal Reserve Bank of New York. I can't do anything with the check; the Fed does not have personal accounts with the public. I have to take my $30 check and *deposit* it with my commercial bank, say Chase Manhattan. I now have an increase in $30 in my bank account; the total money supply in the economy has already increased by $30, since checking accounts function as money.

But this is by no means all; the Chase Bank delightedly takes the $30 check on the Fed and deposits it in its own account at the Federal Reserve Bank of New York. This increases the Chase's reserves by $30, and it – or more precisely, the banks as a whole – can now increase the nation's money supply by a multiple of 6:1, by $180 altogether, $150 of which go into new loans to business.

Therefore, if the Fed buys any asset from a member of the public, total bank reserves increase by the same amount, and the total money supply increases by *six times* that amount.

In actual practice, the Fed doesn't bother seeking out my old typewriters. Neither does it incur the charge of favoritism involved in buying corporate stocks. In practice, it confines its purchases to existing U. S. government bonds and other securities. If the Fed buys $1 million worth of U. S.

You Read It Here

"In the short run, the only sound way out for the Nixon Administration is to be willing to engage in a truly rigorous anti-monetary inflation program, to stop inflating the monetary supply and, indeed, to engage in some old-fashioned monetary contraction. The recession would then be sharp but short-lived, and recovery would be brisk and healthy. The anti-inflationary monetary contraction must be sharp and determined enough to offset the inevitable rise in relative consumer prices and to change the inflationary expectations of the public; it must be rigorously 'hard money'. Only then will prices level off and even (gloryosky!) decline, and only then will interest rates fall. The Administration must cease pursuing the Friedmanite pipe dream of a levelling off of prices along with recovery but without abandoning monetary inflation. In the long run, of course, we need a total overhaul of our inherently statist and inflationary monetary system, with a liquidation of the Federal Reserve System and a return to a genuine gold standard."

"But the Nixon Administration is likely to turn . . . in precisely the opposite direction. Unwilling to bring monetary inflation to a halt, unwilling to go into a truly 'hard money' program, it might very well add onto its vacillation and drift a turn toward the totalitarian method of wage-and-price controls. Already there are ominous signs of wage-price controls on the horizon. Arthur F. Burns, the man our anarcho-Nixonites assured us was soundly free-enterprise, now talks of 'voluntary' or even coercive price controls. Such business economists as Pierre Rinfret and Linel Edie and Co. have already frankly called for wage-price controls. There are two things wrong with such controls: one, they are the totalitarian antithesis of freedom or the free economy, and two, they don't work, leading instead to the 'suppressed' inflation of black markets and eternal shortages and misallocation of resources. Why, then are so many of our 'conservative' business economists reaching for such controls? Precisely because profit margins are being squeezed by the pressure of wage-costs, as they always are in recessions; and therefore, these business economists hope to stop wage increases by the use of compulsion and the State bayonet.

Guaranteed income schemes; continuing budget deficits; monetary inflation; and now wage-price controls; under the cover of traditional free-enterprise rhetoric, the Nixon Administration continues us ever further down the path toward the economy of fascism."

– "The Nixon Mess", *The Libertarian Forum*, June 15, 1970.

government bonds from private bond dealers, total bank reserves will increase by $1 million, and the money supply as a whole by $6 million.

And so the major culprit of the inflation has been the Federal Reserve Board, which has been merrily buying government securities on the open market and thereby levering the money supply ever upward. The chairman of the Fed for the last year and a half, and therefore the biggest single culprit, the bearer of the major share of the guilt, for our inflation, has been none other than Arthur F. Burns – the same Arthur Burns who has been hailed so fulsomely by the press for his great work in pressuring President Nixon to freeze wages and prices. Arthur F. Burns, the man most responsible for inflation, thereby becomes in the eyes of the public the greatest battler against it.

The Function of the Price System

The free price system, the free fluctuation of all prices, wages, and rents, which has been so blithely destroyed by the President, is the heart and soul of the functioning of the market economy. The Freeze, or any direct control, of prices strikes at the heart of the effective working of our economy, and will act to reduce the economic system to chaos. For each and every price, of the innumerable prices of all varieties of goods and services in the economy, reflect the individual forces of supply and demand. If the demand for frisbees rises and the demand for hula hoops falls, the price of the former will increase and the price of the latter will fall, and this will give the signal to the toy manufacturers, through the increased profits in frisbees and the decline in hula hoops, to shift from producing the latter to the former. Similarly, if copper becomes more scarce, its price will rise, and the scarce product will be allocated to those uses and firms which can most profitably and productively employ copper. The more marginal uses will be sacrificed for the more important. And if a new invention occurs, say, in frisbee machinery, the lowered costs will lead to a greater production and hence a fall in frisbee prices. In this way, prices - all prices, including wages and rents - are a sensitive and ever responding indicator to the changes in the underlying forces of supply and demand. A free price system leads businessmen in pursuit of profit and in avoidance of loss, to produce most efficiently those products most desired by the mass of consumers. Cripple that system and the intricate price mechanism for conveying signals and information to producers is destroyed. The economy is then at sea without a rudder, with nothing to tell the producers what they should produce and what means of producing are most efficient.

The Freeze Won't Work

At the very beginning of a freeze, not much appears to be different - understandably, since prices and wages as of August 14 reflected the supply and demand forces on August 14. At first, then, the frozen prices approximate the free market results. But as time goes on, the freeze becomes more and more artificial, more and more out of tune with the ever-changing forces of consumer taste and demand, and producer supply and efficiency. The longer the freeze continues, the more distortions, inefficiencies, and misallocations of resources appear in the economy. That is why in the history of controls, such as OPA in World War II, they begin in euphoria and increasingly become ineffective, diastrous, and unworkable.

Indeed, as of the writing of this article in the first week of September, intractable problems have already appeared in the freeze. Teachers are hired continuously but they only are hired officially at the beginning of the fall term; shall they receive a previously-agreed upon wage increase? The September 6 issue of the New York *Times* reports a series of totally contradictory answers to tough questions posed about the freeze in Internal Revenue offices throughout the country. For example: can a landlord raise rent if he puts in a new incinerator? No, say some IRS offices, that's a violation of the freeze; yes, say others, because the incinerator improves the dwelling which is therefore a different, and superior, housing product deserving of more rents. But if we adopt the latter, highly sensible, position, *what standard* does the government at in setting the new fixed rent? On wages, the government at first tried to freeze wages even if the person is promoted - an absurd position which then freezes a man's salary for more productive work, and which cuts his real wages and ends the incentive to accept promotions. It then reversed itself, allowing higher pay for promotions. But then again: how high can the increase be? If the standard is the prevailing job, suppose "new" jobs, both real and phony, are created; what is the standard then? Another good question that the *Times* posed to the IRS: suppose that an employer wants to reward an employee. He can't give him a wage rise or a bonus during the freeze, but is he permitted to grant an extra week's vacation? This is of course an increase in the employee's pay per unit of work. The befuddled reaction of the government officials is just the beginning of the headaches they will confront, and the evasions they will, step by step, inevitably concede:

"The question about whether an employee could be given an extra week's vacation as a reward for good work produced slightly more no's than yes's. But one official, who said that the extra vacation was prohibited by the freeze, volunteered the suggestion that the company go ahead and do it anyway. 'It would be considered a bonus,' the official said. 'But who will know. Just don't say anything about it.' "

Problems are endemic. The professional athletes justly complain that their brief working life means that they suffer a greater injustice from the freeze than the rest of the labor force. An owner of a laundromat in New York State had just been about to raise his prices, after a considerable rise in costs; but now that he cannot, he is losing money and announces that he will have to go out of business.

The freezing of all unit prices, indeed, does not necessarily insure the continuing profits of each business. Take, for example, the case of a businessman who must replace worn-out machinery or a landlord who must install a new boiler. His rents, and his profits, were calculated on the basis of his old costs; but the boiler or machinery price, while no higher than on August 15, is likely to be considerably higher than it was in, say, 1960, when it was originally installed. And so the higher capital prices will cut severely into his profits.

There is another point here that must be emphasized. There are other elements that enter into a firm's costs besides the prices it must pay for specific units of labor or raw materials or equipment. For a firm might have to shift its purchases from a less expensive to a more expensive material, or from less to more highly skilled labor. And, if it does so, its costs will increase, and its profits possibly turn into losses, even though the price of each particular thing has remained the same. (On these and other problems of price controls and freezes, see Jules Backman, ed., *Price Practices and Price Policies*, New York, Ronald Press, 1953, Part V.)

Any price control will, of necessity, fix the price higher, lower, or precisely the same as the free market would have set. The freeze begins with the latter and rapidly deviates as time goes on. If the price is set too high, then unsold surpluses will pile up; if the price is set too low, then - provided that the controls are carried

---

You Read It Here

"Consider also the implications of the Penn Central fiasco. The Nixon Administration, by its actions, is all but saying that it will not permit any large corporation to go under . . . Nixon is apparently determined to extend government aid to any major firm in any industry that wants it . . . Ever since the Hoover New Deal, the policy of the federal government has been moving toward one of assuring the profitability of American big business . . . With the government more and more willing to underwrite losses, there is less and less incentive for corporate heads to heed the warnings of the market, and curtail operations where indicated . . .

The point here is that the business executive now need not cut prices in the face of falling demand; or resist wage demands of unions. Union leaders need worry less about whether they are asking for more than a market wage. The federal government has announced its willingness to supply cash - virtually to print money up if necessary - to major corporations that find themselves in a 'liquidity' crisis (i.e. find themselves overextended)."

- Gerald P. O'Driscoll, Jr., "Nixon and the Economy", *The Libertarian Forum* (August, 1970).

---

out - shortages will develop. Since the purpose of the freeze and further controls is to set maxima rather than minima, and since they are being imposed to deal with an inflationary problem, then we can expect that shortages will grow and intensify as the controls continue.

In short, prices rise in the first place because the federal government has been pumping too much money into the economy, and increasing money leads to higher prices. If, then, the government tries to cure the price rise by issuing freeze or control orders, this is equivalent to a physician trying to cure his patients fever by breaking open the thermometer and holding down the mercury column. More to the point, the analogy would be complete if the physician has been injecting fever germs into the patient all along.

As controls continue, then, either or both of the following will happen: (1) to the extent the controls are effective, shortages will emerge and intensify - and we will once again all enjoy the wartime phenomena of shortages of meat, cigarettes, gasoline, and whatnot. During World War II, people were more willing to bear these conditions because they thought — wrongly —that the shortages were the inevitable result of the war effort and not of the OPA price ceilings. But now there is no all-out war to mask the grim economic realities. (2) The controls can and will be increasingly avoided and evaded. One form will be outright "black" markets, with all the scarcity, corruption, and disallocations that they imply. Actually, the "black market" is simply *the* market, the free market, trying desperately to emerge in the midst of the crippling network of controls. Another form will be all manner of indirect avoidance and outwitting of the controls. We have already mentioned in wage controls such devices as phony promotions and extra vacations. There are numerous others, including getting around price ceilings by subtle reduction in the quality or size of the product. Soon we will find, for example, our candy bar packages containing even more air than they already do, or the quality of the chocolate declining still more. Even with a vast network of controls, even with a million-man enforcement arm, it would be impossible to police all of these end-runs around controls.

A well-known method of getting around a price freeze

is simply to shift to a new product. Since the product wasn't being produced at all at the date of the freeze, there are no price guidelines for the government to impose. In Allied-occupied Germany after World War II, where the Allies imposed severe price ceilings specifically to punish Germany and to cripple its industrial recovery, the result of the controls was truly grave shortages in the necessities of life, food, clothing, etc., which had been produced in the pre-World War II base year. Instead, the energies of the German industrial machine poured into all sorts of trivial new products – toys, gimcracks, etc. Germans went starving and poorly clothed while surfeited in toys. It was only with the "Currency Reform" of 1948 which lifted the price controls that Germany was able to eliminate the shortages rapidly, to shift from toys to useful products again, and to move on to the famous "economic miracle" of the postwar years. (For the instructive story of price control in occupied Germany, see Nicholas Balabkins, *Germany Under Direct Controls*, New Brunswick, N. J.: Rutgers University Press, 1964).

And so, the attempt to hold down the symptons – price inflation – while pouring in new money only leads to what has aptly been called "repressed inflation", in which the repression bursts forth in the form of evasions and black markets.

Or else the government itself will reluctantly and increasingly grant exceptions and exemptions to the undoubted

You Read It Here

"Well, we have had two years of Nixonism, and what we are undergoing is a super-Great Society – in fact, what we are seeing is the greatest single thrust toward socialism since the days of Franklin Roosevlet. It is not Marxian socialism, to be sure but neither was FDR's; it is . . . a big-business socialism, or state corporatism, but that is cold comfort indeed. There are only two major differences in *content* between Nixon and Kennedy-Johnson . . . (1) that the march into socialism is faster because the teeth of conservative Republican opposition have been drawn; and (2) that the erstwhile 'free-market' conservatives, basking in the seats of Power, have betrayed whatever principles they may have had for the service of the State. Thus, we have Paul McCracken and Arthur F. Burns, dedicated opponents of wage-price 'guideline' dictation and wage-price controls when *out* of power, now moving rapidly in the very direction they had previously deplored . . .

But now the Administration has swung around to the Liberal thesis of monetary fiscal expansion to cure the recession, while yelling and griping at labor and employers not to raise wages and prices – a 'guidelines' or 'incomes' policy that is only one step away from wage and price controls . . .

Not only is it impossible for direct controls to work; their imposition adds the final link in the forging of a totalitarian economy, of an American fascism. What is it but totalitarian to outlaw any sort of voluntary exchange, any voluntary sale of a product, or hiring of a laborer? But once again Richard Nixon is responsive to his credo of big business liberalism, for direct controls satisfy the ideological creed of liberals while at the same time they are urged by big business in order to try to hold down the pressure of wages on selling prices which always appears in the late stages of a boom."
     – "Nixonite Socialism", *The Libertarian Forum*, January, 1971.

"inequities" of the price and wage freeze. We have seen that these insoluble inequities have already emerged. Suppose that we have Mr. Jones, who is making $2000 below the prevailing wage in his occupation, and was just about to receive an increase. Or take the laundromat owner going on the rocks. It is obvious – and openly acknowledged in Washington – that the absolute price-wage freeze cannot be extended forever. *Something* will have to be done about the inequity cases, the businesses losing money, the athletes with special problems, etc., and these problems of a changing economy will develop increasingly as time goes on. But if the economy can't be *frozen* indefinitely, then neither – in the eyes of the Administration – can the freeze be simply lifted at the end of 90 days. For then the repressed inflation will burst into the open, and prices and wages will soar to compensate for the enforced freeze. The only other option for the Administration will have to be *permanent* price and wage controls – with a vast army of bureaucrats making decisions about every individual inequity. In short, a recrudescence of the already failed OPA of World War II.

In recent years, Europe has seen a dismal record of failure of wage-price controls. From 1965 to 1970, for example the Labor government of Great Britain imposed a wage-price freeze to combat inflation, "voluntary" for the first year and compulsory thereafter. By 1970, it was clear that wages and prices had been advancing *faster* during the freeze than it ever had before. By June, 1970, when the British government abandoned the controls as hopeless, wages were rising at an annual rate of 10% and prices by 7%.

Price-controls have also played a vital but little-known part in the political history of Asia. One of the major reasons for the downfall of Chiang-kai-Shek, for example, was the fact that, due to national deficits and paper money inflation, China had been suffering, before and during World War II, from a runaway inflation, and Chiang had met the problem by imposing severe price and wage controls. The inevitable result of the controls was grave shortages throughout the country, and, as in so many cases in the past since the Edict of Diocletian in ancient Rome, the government met the problem by escalating the penalties for evading controls. Chiang, in fact, ended by making an example of black marketeers by executing them publicly in the streets. In this way, he lost his merchant and middle-class support; in contrast, the Communists, whenever they occupied an area of China, ended the monetary expansion and thereby cured the inflation. Is it any wonder that Chiang lost China?

As shortages pile up from the price controls, we can expect the next totalitarian advance: rationing. With demand permanently greater than supply at the frozen price, the government will try, in one area after the other, to impose compulsory quotas for everyone's purchases, as it did during World War II. The result will be further dictation and bureaucracy, a vast network of ration points and ration coupons, favoritism, inequities, corruption, and further black markets. For in the free economy, it is *price* that performs the rationing function, smoothly and easily. But it does more; for if there is a shortage of, say, tires, a higher price will not only "ration" the tires to those demanding them the most, it will also call more tires into production. Compulsory rationing will perpetuate the shortage.

Americans should never forget our last tragic experience with peacetime controls. After World War II, the Truman Administration tried to cling to vestiges of price controls; in particular, the ceilings on prices of meat. The result, during 1946, was a severe meat shortage, and a diversion of meat into the black markets. Finally, President Truman reluctantly lifted the controls on meat on October 14, 1946, after which the meat shortage quickly disappeared. At that time, Truman said:

> "I recognize the hardships that many of you have undergone because of the lack of meat. I sympathize with millions of housewives hard-pressed to provide nourishing meals for their families . . . thousands of veterans and other patients in hospitals throughout the country . . . Many workers have been thrown out of work by the meat shortage. The by-products from lawful slaughter of livestock are sorely needed . . . for insulin and other necessary medicines . . . and for hides; and already some of our shoe factories are closing and workers are being laid off for lack of leather . . . There are reports of widespread disregard and violations of the price-control law. Experience shows that this leads to a tendency to disregard the sanctity of other laws of the country."

But while President Truman was forced to throw in the towel on controls, the disquieting point for all of us and for the future is that he had given long and serious consideration to mobilizing the army and seizing meat in the packing-houses. Recognizing, however, that the meat was not in the packing-houses but in the farms, Truman added:

> "Some have even suggested that the government go out on the farms and ranges and seize the cattle for slaughter . . . We gave it long and serious consideration . . . We decided . . . it would be wholly impracticable because the cattle are spread throughout all parts of the country."

And so, the President concluded wistfully, "there is only one remedy left - that is, to lift controls on meat."

And so, President Truman recognized that he had two basic alternatives to remedy the mess that controls had created: either return to a free economy or go on to a totalitarian state. His decision for freedom was reluctant and hairline - and influenced undoubtedly by the farm vote that was being lost for the coming 1946 elections. Is President Nixon going to bring us the totalitarian society that we barely escaped under Harry Truman?

The Phony Freeze

Apart from all other considerations, the freeze is a phony one. Democrats and unions have centered on the failure to freeze profits, without realizing that profits are not a regular price but a residual, which may and do shift wildly from being large, small, zero, or negative. But other prices have not been frozen.

For example: cunningly, the government exempted from the freeze fresh foods. This means that the scandalous farm price support program, in which the taxpayer is forced to pay farmers for growing less or even no food, will continue merrily on its way, contributing to price inflation. The government gave as its argument that if price ceilings are imposed on seasonal foods, say cantaloupes, this would create grave shortages of cantaloupes as their supply becomes scarce in the autumn. Very true; but doesn't this mean that the supply of *all other* goods will also become short, though not as quickly and evidently? Freezing prices of *processed* foods while allowing the price of *raw* foods to rise, furthermore, will aid the farmers, but will also mean that the wholesalers and retailers of these foods will be suffering losses and will either stop operating altogether or go into black markets. Isn't it insane to allow plentiful supplies and free prices in, say, fresh strawberries, while imposing ceilings and therefore shortages in the frozen variety?

Secondly, interest rates are free, the government again giving as its argument that a ceiling on interest rates will dry up the supply of credit. Very true - but again, why not

apply the logic elsewhere? Furthermore, if the government did go on, as the Democrats have urged, to freeze interest rates, they could never freeze interest yields on bonds, which will rise as bond prices fall.

Thirdly, consider this grave inconsistency: on August 16, Secretary Connally exulted that the price freeze had caused stockmarket prices to rise by 30 points. What kind of thinking is this — to force prices down while chortling because stock prices are going up? Aren't stock prices also prices? Why cheer when they go up while forcing others to stay down?

Fourthly, state and local taxes are specifically exempt from the freeze. The Oregon cigarette tax, for example, is going up as scheduled. Aren't taxes prices? Doesn't a higher tax also contribute to price inflation? Or do our rulers think that it is a hardship to pay more for goods that we want and use while it is *not* a hardship to pay more - taxes - for services that are nonexistent or negative (the activities of government)? What is the logic here?

Fifthly, as everyone knows, President Nixon accompanied the freeze by announcing a 10% across-the-board surcharge on imports. This is going to raise the price of imported products by approximately 10%. So Mr. Nixon is combatting inflation by deliberately raising a whole host of prices! For the consumer this makes no sense; it makes sense only as a giant subsidy to inefficient domestic firms and industries that have been hit by efficient competition from foreign firms.

Sixthly, the government announced that *welfare payments* are not included in the freeze. And here we have probably the most horrendous single piece of logic in the entire program. For the announcement read that only prices and wages in payment *for productive services* are being frozen. Since welfare payments are not made for productive services, they call rise willy-nilly. In short, it is *evil* for someone to pay a worker more for his productive services; it is perfectly OK to pay a welfare client more for not producing at all! What sort of insane logic is this?

Big Business and Unions

One of the main reasons that the American public as a whole, and many conservatives and businessmen, favor the wage-price freeze is because they believe that unions and their demands are responsible for inflation. They are flatly wrong. The unions are responsible for a host of economic ills, feather-bedding, restrictionism, misallocation of resources and wages, but inflation of prices is not one of them. Consider this: a union makes a demand for a large wage increase. *Why* does the employer agree to pay it? This is the crucial question. *Demands* mean nothing; I, for example, could demand a tripling of my salary and be thrown out of the office as a result. The point is that employers are *able* to pay the demands, and the question to ask is: how come? Why are they able to pay? The idea that businessmen simply pay higher wages and then "pass it on" in higher prices is economic nonsense. For surely businessmen are *always* trying to sell their products at as high a price as possible. If they can get a higher price, why in the world should they wait for unions to ask more before they raise their prices?

Or look at it this way: suppose all unions in the country should demand an immediate quadrupling of their wages and salaries. Does anyone think that the employers would agree? Why not, if all they have to do is to pass the raise on in higher prices? Furthermore, consider real estate prices, which have risen rapidly in recent years. How come, since there are no unions, no collective bargaining, involved here?

Obviously, something else is involved – and that something else is the aforesaid increase in the money supply. If the money supply increases at 10% per year, then all prices and wages will tend to rise by approximately 10%, and the employers will be able to pay the 10% increase. Once again, it is the hidden force of the money supply that is at work in determining the inflation.

Furthermore, empirically, union wage rates do not rise, overall, faster than non-union wages; in fact, in an inflation, the slowness of collective bargaining tends to make union wages lag behind non-union. Consider, for example, how very much the wages of domestic servants have gone up since World War II. Everyone knows this, and everyone also knows that there is no union in the domestic service field. So, again, unions cannot be the culprit.

One of the characteristics of the late stages of an inflation is that wage rates begin to press on prices, and profits are squeezed. It is clear that many big businessmen favor the freeze because they are trying to coerce wage rates from rising. Furthermore, they know that while both are in the long run unenforceable, price controls are easier to evade than wage controls. The worker is a visible, and indivisible, entity, and so his wage rate is more controllable; but the candy bar can easily be shaved a bit or its quality lowered without attracting attention. Furthermore, the reason for the enthusiasm of General Motors and Ford for the whole Nixon package is evident: for in addition to wage control, the auto manufacturers reap the benefits of the 7% excise tax cut on autos, and of the burden of the import tax surcharge on their burgeoning European competitors – to say nothing of the further burden that the dollar devaluation places on foreign imports.

Furthermore, the "voluntary" freeze on dividends clearly hurts the small investor, while leaving the large stockholders, who are more interested in a rise of stock prices than in dividends, completely unscathed. Here is another reason for big business to look kindly on the program.

Permanent Controls Equal Fascism

It is now clear that price and wage controls of some sort will succeed the 90-day freeze – in short, that we have now entered a political economy of permanent direct controls. There is only one word for this New Economic Policy, a word that is at first glance harsh and exaggerated, but is in fact precisely appropriate. That word is "fascism." A system of permanent price and wage controls, administered by a central government bureaucracy, probably headed by some form of tripartite board including Big Business, Big Labor, and Big Government – this is precisely what fascism is, precisely the economic system of Mussolini's Italy and Hitler's Germany. This is the economy of the "corporate state", administered by dictation from the top, controlled and monopolized by Big Business and Big Union interests, with the individual, and the consumer, the person who

NOTES ON THE NEW ECONOMIC POLICY

Nixon's grasp of affairs economic
Is so sparse as to be almost comic.
But it's not so amusing
That our rights he's abusing
As his deficits grow astronomic.
     - David F. Nolan

suffers. In short, the mass of the American public will suffer from this system of corporate statism, from the death of the free price system, from the invasion of individual rights, from the hampering of growth, efficiency, and productivity, that the system will entail.

For now for the first time we have permanent peace-time controls. At least the World War II and Korean War controls, as bad as they were, were recognized as purely a wartime emergency expedient; they were not supposed to herald a new totalitarian economic system. But now we have such a system. And no organized group, left, right, or center, Democrat or Republican, liberal or conservative, has come out in principled opposition to the New Economic Fascism. The unions have already made it clear that they will accept the new system if they achieve their due share of power as junior partners in the tripartite control system. Presumably they will get their wish.

Far more important than the grave economic consequences of the new system are the political and moral implications. For where are our inalienable rights? By what conceivable right does the federal government dare to step in and tell free individuals how much they can agree to pay for goods and services? By what right does it step in to say that I cannot pay X-amount for a product or a service, or that someone cannot sell it to me for the agreed price. If two kids are swapping, for example, a penknife for two frisbees, how dare the government step in and threaten penalties or even jail if the kids do not exchange one penknife for one or for three frisbees – for this is what price control in essence means.

Even the price controls of World War II, moreover, exempted newspapers from the controls, because the government realized that price controls on newspapers implies a grave infringement on freedom of the press. But even the press is not exempt from the controls; does freedom of the press mean so much less nowadays?

There is also the Caesarism involved in the freeze by Presidential edict. If the President can simply go on TV and unilaterally declare an immediate freeze, then all of our liberties, moral, political, and Constitutional, are truly gone. If the President can do this, then he is truly another Caesar, another Mussolini, another Hitler; his power is then absolute. Is our Constitution completely forgotten? Are we going to put up passively with a slide into absolute Presidential dictatorship? And by what stretch of Constitutional finagling can the President freeze local rents? What gives him the power to freeze rents in a Peoria boardinghouse? Where is the "interstate commerce" here? Are there to be no restraints on the President's absolute power?

Already, a few law professors have spoken out against the new despotism. Four law professors at Catholic University Law School are bringing suit against the government to outlaw the freeze. And, in a trenchant letter to the New York *Times* of September 6, Professor Arthur S. Miller of George Washington University Law School warns that "Congress has abdicated its legislative function." He adds that "no such sweeping delegation has ever been upheld (by the courts) outside of wartime . . . The war powers, furthermore, are not usable to uphold the delegation or the President's actions", or even the Economic Stabilization Act of 1970 itself. Miller also points out that the President acted secretly and in great haste, while Congress was out of session: "That is government by *fait accompli* – hardly in consonance with the spirit of the Constitution." Miller also points out that the government's abrogation of contractual wage increases after Aug. 14 "varies the obligation of contracts. It takes contract rights (property rights under the law) without paying just compensation required by the Constitution." Miller adds that "World War II and Korean War precedents, if that they are, are not controlling. The war powers are not a source of power here. Even if they were, Chief Justice Warren said in 1967 that they do not 'remove constitutional limitations sageguarding essential liberties.'"

Professor Miller concludes his welcome letter by warning that "President Nixon's declaration of national emergency can hardly add to his constitutional powers. It is part of a growing package of government by executive decree or fiat. The American people should be very sure that they want to travel much further down the perilous path of economic controls and executive domination."

Selective Controls

There are hints that the Nixon Administration, in a vain attempt to impose permanent price and wage controls without constructing a huge bureaucratic apparatus to run our lives, may try to impose "selective" controls on a few industries. One prediction is that controls may be imposed only on industries composed of large businesses. It is true that big business, being highly visible and in the public eye, are superficially easier to control than smaller firms. But "selective" controls, however selected, can never work for long. If, for example, the prices of automobiles are frozen, and the prices of the numerous parts that the auto companies buy from small manufacturers are allowed to rise, then clearly the auto firms will begin to suffer heavy losses. The pressure will then be great to extend the controls to the parts industries, and so on to the various raw material industries. Capital, furthermore, will begin to leave the frozen industries for the unfrozen. And if wages in big firms are frozen while those in small firms are allowed to rise, then obviously workers will begin to leave the former for the latter. Selective controls, in short, are soon found to be unworkable; they set up inexorable pressures either to remove the controls altogether and return to a free economy, or else extend the controls to the entire economy.

Wake Up America

And so fascism is here – and it doesn't even work. We have sold our birthright of freedom for a mess of inedible pottage. Our economic dictators should at least heed the warning of their predecessor, Field Marshal Hermann Goering. After his capture by the Allies, Goering stated: Your America is doing many things in the economic field which we found out caused us so much trouble. You are trying to control people's wages and prices – people's work. If you do that, you must control people's lives. And no country can do that part way. I tried it and failed. Nor can any country do it all the way either. I tried that too and it failed. You are no better planners than we. I should think your economists would read what happened here." (Quoted in F. A. Harper, "A Just Price and Emergency Price Fixing," *Essays on Liberty, Volume II*, Irvington on Hudson, N. Y.: Foundation for Economic Education, 1954, pp. 198-99.)

With both political parties silent or enthusiastic about the new statism, and all the organized groups scrambling aboard to increase their share of the pie, there is only one way that we can be freed from this monstrous incubus of permanent price-wage controls. And that is if the American public itself takes a hand. Only the American public can break the new chains which our Caesar has forged. Only the American public can render the wage-price controls unenforceable, by "voting with their feet" in their everyday lives. But to do this, the public must be able to hear voices of opposition, voices who will raise the cry: "This shall not pass!"

◻

"An autocrat's a ruler that does what th' people wants, an' takes th' blame f'r it. A constitootional ixicutive, Hinnissy, is a ruler that does as he dam pleases, an' blames th' people." --- Mr. Dooley.

The Libertarian Forum

BOX 341
MADISON SQUARE STATION
NEW YORK, NEW YORK 10010.

First Class

Published Every Month. Subscription Rate: $8.00 Per Year

THE
Libertarian Forum

Joseph R. Peden, Publisher   Murray N. Rothbard, Editor

VOLUME III, NO. 9   October, 1971   75c

ATTICA

Some political issues are crystal-clear for the libertarian, issues on which he can come to firm conclusions very quickly – such as wage-price controls or the draft. Others, however, are morally more complex, and require the fine scalpel of rigorous analysis before the libertarian may take his stand on one side or another. Such an issue is Attica and the entire prison problem in which it is wrapped.

Unless I miss my guess, the left-wing of the libertarian movement has already taken its stand, in the following kind of simplistic syllogism: (a) prisons are State-run; (b) prisons are coercive; (c) Attica was a rebellion by political "revolutionaries" against the State. Ergo, we should take our stand with the prisoners and denounce the resolution of the Attica question as a "massacre."

I contend that the conclusion is dead wrong. But before analyzing the core of the problem – the libertarian attitude towards prisons and criminals – let us clear up some tangential but dramatically important issues.

(1) *The Fuss.* In the first place, one wonders what the great fuss – the sense of surprise, shock, of a felling among many people that somehow Attica marks a significant milestone – is all about. For those of us who were raised on the prison movies of the 1930's, there is nothing surprising or shocking about the course of events. There were countless scenes the prisoners in the mess banging their spoons against their cups, and led by young Jimmy Cagney or Dane Clark; then finally some guards are grabbed as hostages, the prisoners capture the inside cells, a young prison psychiatrist tries in vain to mediate, and then comes the great climactic scene when the state reestablished its authority, and Jimmy Cagney dies in agony. It's all there, and the conclusion of the scenario is inevitable. It should be clear to everyone that (a) the government runs the prisons; (b) that by the nature of the prisoner situation, prisoners are ruled severely by their jailers; and (c) that any mutiny by the prisoners is going to be put down and put down hard.

In fact, the entire fuss, and the whole spate of fascinated publicity, was generated by a grave strategic and tactical error on the part of the prison authorities. By "negotiating" with these hoodlums and criminals, by treating them as if they were a legitimate political pressure group, the authorities fed the absurd fantasies of the prisoners of being "revolutionaries" engaged in a profound revolutionary act. By negotiating day after day, furthermore, the authorities fed similar fantasies on the part of the liberals and leftists on the outside – and the whole farce was intensified by the institution of the negotiating committee, and the host of free publicity granted to such agitators as William Kunstler and Bobby Seale, who accomplished nothing except a publicity build-up for themselves. And they "accomplished" something else: consciously or unconsciously feeding the absurd hopes

of the prisoners that somehow they might "win", and thereby hardening the prisoners' stand. Of course, when the crunch came, agitators like Kunstler, Seale, and Tom Soto of YAWF were safely outside the gates.

It is clear that the major error of the authorities was the shilly-shallying, the endless negotiating that built up the prisoners' fantasies and morale. What the authorities should have done was to move in fast and hard, immediately, say a half hour after the mutiny. At worst, the killing would certainly not have been more extensive than it turned out to be.

The tragedy of the hostages does not negate this position. For one of the points that prison guards have made clear all during this crisis: that the authorities must move quickly and not be swayed by the hostage problem. For if they are, then this will serve as an open invitation to all prisoners everywhere to grab a few guards, and the guards would be helpless as a result. And as for the moral guilt of the killings, it should be clear that this lies upon the head of the kidnappers themselves, and not upon the guardsmen who were trying to end the crisis and rescue the hostages.

There are other points that came out during the crisis. The time-honored prison method of dealing with troublemakers is to break them up – if there are, say, 50 troublemakers, they are broken into five or so groups, with each being shipped out to different prisons in the system. But, under the influence of debilitating liberalism, the state of New York had previously prohibited this sort of treatment – thus allowing the buildup of a cohesive mutinous group within Attica prison.

And then, under an excess of sentimental liberalism, New York State had, a few years ago, abolished capital punishment for murderers. This meant that a hard core of murderers existed within Attica, ready to stir up trouble and take maximum measures for mutiny.

Thus, at least within the immediate context of the prison system, the conservatives are right: the crisis was allowed to develop and intensify because of the debilitating influence of liberalism – in abolishing capital punishment, in disallowing the breaking up of criminal cadres in the prisons, and in allowing endless "negotiations" which were bound anyway to end in failure.

(2) *The "Revolutionaries."*
The old-fashioned criminal has always tended to be a "right-winger", for he has generally acknowledged that his actions were morally wrong, that he had broken the moral law. Hence, while personally trying to keep out of prison as much as possible, the old-fashioned criminal does not challenge the correctness or propriety of the prison system

(Continued on page 7)

REPRINT BONANZA

A vertiable reprint bonanza for libertarians will be issued this winter by Arno Press, 330 Madison Ave., New York, N. Y. 10017. Arno, a subdivision of the New York Times, specializes in reprint series devoted to some phase of American history. The forthcoming series, "The Right Wing Individualist Tradition in America", all bound similarly in hard-cover, will be available either as an entire set or in individual volumes. Advisory Editors for the series were Murray N. Rothbard and Jerome Tuccille; the series will be advertised in an annotated brochure written by the advisory editors. The series is not perfection: for one thing it was limited to 38 volumes, for another, many books we would have loved to reprint have already been reprinted by other publishers or are scheduled for reprinting. And furthermore, various curmudgeons refused to sell reprint rights to their books to Arno. Still and all, the series should be a great boon for libertarians to catch up on great books which have long been unavailable. Furthermore, the advisory editors went to special pains to balance the list, so that the 38 books are roughly equally divided into five categories: libertarian, anarchist, free-market economics, isolationist, and conservative.

The entire set of "The Right Wing Individualist Tradition in America" will be available for $492.00. Urge every library you know to obtain one! Show the publisher the large size of the libertarian market! Furthermore, if you order the set before December, you will get a 15% discount - $418 for the set!

The individual books and their estimated prices follow:

William Bailie, *Josiah Warren: The First American Anarchist* (1906), 182pp. $8.00. The only biography of any of the great giants of American individualist anarchism - by a follower.

Thomas H. Barber, *Where We Are At* (1950). 268pp. $11.00. A charming book, lashing out at American bureaucracy, and employing "economic determinism", by a lovable old curmudgeon. Witty, hard-hitting.

Harry Elmer Barnes, *Pearl Harbor After A Quarter Of A Century* (1968). 138 pp. $7.00 The final story of Pearl, by the dean of American Revisionists. Reprinted from the final issue of Left and Right.

Harry Elmer Barnes, *In Quest of Truth and Justice: De-Bunking the War Guilt Myth* (1928). 438 pp. $19.00. A delightful book, with Harry lashing out at all his enemies on World War I Revisionism. A treasure-trove, including the evisceration of war propaganda by America's eminent historians during the War, by C. Hartley Grattan.

Harry Elmer Barnes, *Selected Revisionist Pamphlets*. 332 pp. $14.00. Harry Barnes was a great pamphleteer, and this collection includes all of Harry's post-World War II Revisionist pamphlets, all of which were privately printed and were known only to a tiny "under-ground" of right-wing isolationists. The collection includes Barnes *Blasting the Historical Blackout*, a review-essay on A. J. P. Taylor's Origins of the Second World War; *The Chickens of the Interventionist Liberals Have Come Home to Roost: The Bitter Fruits of Globaloney; The Court Historians Versus Revisionism* - a critique of Langer and Gleason, and of Feis, on the road to World War II; *Rauch on Roosevelt*, a critique of Basil Rauch; *Revisionism and Brainwashing: A Survey of the War-Guilt Question in Germany After Two World Wars*, which includes a discussion of the monumental revisionist work on 1939 by David L. Hoggan; *Select Bibliography of Revisionist Books*, an annotated bibliography dealing with World Wars I, II,

and Cold; *The Struggle Against the Historical Black-out* (9th, final edition), an exciting blast, detailing the discrimination against revisionist literature by "objective" historians and reviewers; and *Was Roosevelt Pushed Into War By Popular Demand in 1941?* Must reading.

Louis Bromfield, *A New Pattern for a Tired World* (1954), 344pp. $15.00. The last product of the "Old Right" - a plea for domestic liberty and foreign "isolationism" by the famous novelist. Attacks the Cold War from "the right".

John W. Burgess, *Recent Changes in American Constitutional Theory* (1923). 130 pp. $7.00. Read this, if you want to know what *real* "strict constructionism" looks like. The eminent political scientist and constitutional lawyer claimed that both the draft and the income tax were unconstitutional.

Charles H. Carroll, *Organization of Debt Into Currency: And Other Papers*. (1964). 468 pp. $20.00 Reprint of the collected essays of an ultra-hard money, 100% gold economist of the mid nineteenth century. From the old Volker Fund, Van Nostrand series.

Harold M. Fleming, *Ten Thousand Commandments: A Story of the Antitrust Laws*. (1951). 228pp. $10.00. Excellent critique of the antitrust system, and the way it promotes rather than combats "monopoly", and *restricts* competition.

John T. Flynn, *As We Go Marching* (1944). 284pp. $12.00. A brilliant work, analyzing the similarities between the political economies of fascist Italy, Germany, and the New Deal, and prophesying that the New Deal and its World War II would bring to the United States the permanent rule of the military, the garrison state, and the political economy of fascism. Flynn's concluding sentence: "My only purpose is to sound a warning against the dark road upon which we have set our feet as we go marching to the salvation of the world and along which every step we now take leads us farther and farther from the things we want and the things that we cherish."

George Harris, *Inequality and Progress*. (1897). 174pp. $7.00. An excellent and neglected work that stresses the importance and necessity for *inequality*. Particularly needed now in an age when fatuous egalitarianism has infected even the libertarian movement. Stresses the variety and individuality of man.

Individualist Anarchist Pamphlets. 140pp. $7.00. A collection of excellent, rare individualist anarchist pamphlets of late nineteenth century America. A great bargain. Includes: Henry Bool's *Apology for his* Jeffersonian Anarchism, Lysander Spooner's *No Treason, Nos. 1 and 2* - from the great master of individualist anarchism and antistatism, the great critic of the Constitution; and Edwin C. Walker's *Communism and Conscience*. A must.

Bruce W. Knight, *How to Run a War* (1936), 258pp. $11.00. A slashing, sardonic critique of war, especially America in World War I. With a new preface by Professor Knight.

Rose Wilder Lane, *The Discovery of Freedom: Man's Struggle Against Authority* (1943). 282pp. $12.00. A great individualist and rationalist, Rose Lane was the unsung heroine and inspiration for libertarians in the 1940's and 50's. A beautifully written, lilting prose-poem to freedom in human history. Rose Lane stopped writting for many years in protest against the self-

(Continued on page 3)

REPRINT BONANZA — *(Continued from page 2)*
employed social security tax, and she deserves the widest distribution. With a new introduction by Roger MacBride and a new forward by Robert LeFevre.

Flash! Because of the great interest in Mrs. Lane's book, Arno Press will also print simultaneously an inexpensive paperback of the book. Available from Rampart College as well as Arno Press.

Left and Right: Selected Essays. 124pp. $7.00. A great bargain; this includes two rare pamphlets. One is the all-isolationist, all anti-Cold War issue of the right-wing individualist monthly *Faith and Freedom*, April, 1954 issue. This issue includes essays by Garet Garrett, Ernest T. Weir, and "Aubrey Herbert" (Murray N. Rothbard). The other selection is the now classic, and long out-of-print, first issue of the libertarian journal *Left and Right* 1965), containing articles by Murray N. Rothbard and Leonard P. Liggio.

James McGurrin, *Bourke Cockran: A Free Lance in American Politics.* (1948). 388pp. $17.00. Sympathetic biography of a leader of the Bourbon Democracy of the late nineteenth century: an aggressive champion of free trade, individual liberty, anti-imperialism, and opponent of the income tax.

H. L. Mencken and Robert R. La Monte, *Men Versus the Man* (1910). 260pp. $11.00. The only important work by Mencken as yet out of print, this features the scintillating debate between Mencken, individualist, libertarian, and sparkling wit, and a leading socialist of the period.

Zacariah Montgomery, comp. *Poison Drops in the Federal Senate* (1889). 146pp. $7.00. A blistering attack on the growth of compulsory attendance laws in the American school system.

Albert Jay Nock, *Our Enemy the State* (1935). 220pp. $9.00. A great libertarian classic. No libertarian should be without this, one of the great works in libertarian political philosophy. Also anticipates Kolko's views of big business with a hard-hitting Beardian analysis of the development of the American Constitution and government.

Marshall Olds, *Analysis of the Interchurch World Move-*
(Continued on page 4)

The Collected Works of Lysander Spooner

The only collection available . . . 34 rare and provocative works (1834-1886) in six volumes . . . With an extensive critical biography and individual introductions by Charles Shively . . . Bound in durable library cloth and printed on acid-free paper.

> Send for free brochure listing other research editions, including *The Collected Works of John Jay Chapman* in 12 volumes, introductions by Melvin H. Bernstein.   Write to M & S Press, Box 311, Weston, Mass. 02193.

Lysander Spooner (1808-1887) was an intellectual activist — for 50 years not only probing; but vigorously prodding his government and society. Prolific, producing more than 30 separately published books, pamphlets, and broadsides (the existence of many not even known to the Library of Congress), Spooner is one of 19th century America's most profound and coherent minds. While producing some of the finest constitutional arguments ever devised against slavery, Spooner concerned himself equally with the subtle subjugation of supposedly free citizens by a governmental system which he saw become increasingly restrictive of personal rights.

"There is no difference, in principle — but only in degree — between political and chattel slavery," he declared in 1867. A nation which fought to free slaves should be prepared to fight to free the rest of its people — even if (as he suspected) this required the overthrow of the Constitution.

Lysander Spooner had an absolute genius for opposing the government; and his protests against governmental restraint were not limited to brilliant writings on slavery, the Constitution, the jury system, copyright practices, and the economics of our rapidly industrializing country. Spooner actually forced a reduction in postal rates — by setting up his own private mail company in competition with the U.S. Post Office — and at the same time scored important points for freedom of the press. Charles Shively's biography, using hitherto unexamined Spooner papers and letters only recently deposited in the New York Historical Society, brings to light much in Spooner's life that is important to 19th century American history including, for example, Spooner's little known plan to force the release of John Brown after Harper's Ferry — by kidnapping Governor Wise of Virginia — and Spooner's own personal relations with such men as Brown and Gerrit Smith.

Lysander Spooner is remarkably prophetic of governmental interventions into personal and community life, and in his understanding of the psychological as well as the economic problems of industrialization and the dangerous pressures of conformity. These M & S Press volumes provide a rich and vital historical dimension for much of our own contemporary social and political protest.

CONTENTS

Volume I: Biography and Miscellaneous Writings
A. DEIST
Deist's Immortality (1834)
Deist's Reply (1836)
B. MAIL COMPANY
The Unconstitutionality of the Laws . . . Prohibiting Private Mails (1844)
Who caused the Reduction? (1850)
C. RADICALISM & ANARCHISM
No Treason, No. 1 (1867)
No Treason, No. 2 (1867)
No Treason, No. 6 (1870)
Revolution (1880)
Letter to Bayard (1882)
Natural Law (1882)
Letter to Cleveland (1886)

Volume II: Legal Writings (I)
"To the Members of the Legis. of Mass." (1835)
Spooner vs. M'Connell (1839)
Illegality of the Trial of Webster (1850)
Trial by Jury (1852)
Drew vs. Clark (1869)

Volume III: Legal Writings (II)
Law of Intellectual Property (1855)
Articles of Association of the Spooner Copyright Co. (1863)
Letter to Scientists and Inventors (1884)

Volume IV: Anti-Slavery Writings
Unconstitutionality of Slavery (1845-60)
Defence for Fugitive Slaves (1850)
Plan for the Abolition of Slavery (1858)
Address of the Free Constitutionalists (1860)
Letter to Sumner (1864)

Volume V: Economic Writings (I)
Constitutional Law Relative to Credit (1843)
Poverty (1846)
New System of Paper Currency (1861)
Our Mechanical Industry (1862)

Volume VI: Economic Writings (II)
Considerations for Bankers (1864)
A New Banking System (1873)
Our Financiers (1877)
Law of Prices (1877)
Gold and Silver (1878)
Universal Wealth (1879)

6 hardcover volumes • 2400 pages • ISBN 087730-006-2 • $140.00 per set

REPRINT BONANZA — *(Continued from page 3)*

ment Report on the Steel Strike (1922). 504pp. $21.00. One of the great and undeserved victories of organized liberalism was the Interchurch report on the steel strike of 1919, which won great sympathy, and paved the way for federal government pressure to force the steel industry into an 8-hour day. Here is the totally neglected other side of the picture, the comprehensive critique of the report from the point of view of the steel industry.

Franz Oppenheimer, *The State: Its History and Development Viewed Sociologically* (1926). 324pp. $14.00. The great work on the State, its history and its nature Indispensable for libertarians. Oppenheimer punctures completely the mystical "social contract" view of the State, and shows that it was born in violence and conquest, and continued on this course thereafter.

Isabel Paterson, *The God of the Machine* (1943). 302pp. $13.00. Another indispensable work for libertarians, a great and challenging work on political philosophy. Particularly important are Mrs. Paterson's critique of the anti-trust laws, her defense of the gold standard, her superb dissection of progressive education ("Our Japanized Educational System"), and her devastating blast at the politics of liberal altruism ("The Humanitarian with the Guillotine").

C. A. Phillips, T. F. McManus, and R. W. Nelson, *Banking and the Business Cycle: A Study of the Great Depression in the United States*. (1937). 292pp. $12.00. One of the best books on the 1929 depression, applying Mises-Hayek business cycle theory to the facts of the depression. Unfortunately has been totally neglected by economists and others.

Helmut Schoeck and James W. Wiggins, eds., *Scientism and Values* (1960). 290pp. $12.00. One of the best of the out-of-print Volker Fund series of books, embodying conservative and libertarian scholarship. This is a critique of dictatorial scientism in the social sciences. Includes articles by Richard M. Weaver, Pieter Geyl, Eliseo Vivas, Helmut Schoeck, Murray N. Rothbard, and others.

John W. Scoville, *Labor Monopolies — Or Freedom* (1946). 196pp. $8.00. One of the best, and most hard-hitting, books ever written on labor unionism. Includes an economic critique and a dissection of the habitual violence of unions. By a former economist for Chrysler Corporation.

John W. Scoville and Noel Sargent, comps., *Fact and Fancy in the TNEC Monographs* (1942). 830pp. $35.00. A massive, thorough, monograph-by-monograph critique of the TNEC monographs, the greatest single force for trust-busting during the New Deal. Totally neglected.

Carl Snyder, *Capitalism the Creator: the Economic Foundations of Modern Industrial Society* (1940). 492pp. $21.00. An excellent economic — and moral — defense of capitalism and its beneficial creative force in civilization. By the former economist for the Federal Reserve Bank of New York. Poor on money, however.

Society Without Government (1969-70). $10.00. The first hard-cover compilation of two works indispensable for libertarians: Morris and Linda Tannehill, *The Market for Liberty*, and Jarret B. Wollsteing, *Society Without Coercion*. Both answer the vital question: how could a libertarian society, without a State, provide police and judicial defense activities purely through the free market?

Lysander Spooner, *Let's Abolish Government*. 418pp. $18.00. Absolutely indispensable. Here is a collection of the major works of the greatest individualist anarchist theorist of all time. Contains: *An Essay on the Trial by Jury* (1852), *A Letter to Thomas F. Bayard* (1882), the magnificent *No Treason: The Constitution of No Authority* #6 (1870), and the brilliantly hard-hitting *Letter to Grover Cleveland* (1886).

Charles T. Sprading, ed., *Liberty and the Great Libertarians: An Anthology on Liberty; A Hand-Book of Freedom*. (1913). 546pp. $23.00. Another indispensable book for libertarians. The best libertarian anthology ever compiled, by an individualist anarchist follower of Spooner and Tucker. Contains articles by: Edmund Burke (his repudiated, anarchist book), Thomas Paine, Thomas Jefferson, William Godwin, Wilhelm von Humboldt, Emerson, William Lloyd Garrison, Wendell Phillips, Josiah Warren, Max Stirner, Thoreau, Herbert Spencer, Stephen Pearl Andrews, Josiah Warren, Robert Ingersoll, Spooner, Tolstoy, Benjamin R. Tucker, William B. Greene, Auberon Herbert, and many, many others. Also an excellent introduction by Sprading. Don't miss it!

William Graham Sumner, *What Social Classes Owe to Each Other* (1883). 172pp. $7.00. A superb work, a great classic of political philosophy by this leading libertarian, individualist, and "Social Darwinist." Great critique of liberal reformers and "uplifters."

Frederick B. Tolles, *George Logan of Philadelphia*. (1953). 388pp. $17.00. Sympathetic biography of this leading individualist, pacifist, and Jeffersonian. Broke with Jefferson on Logan's opposition to the war of 1812 against Britain. The "Logan Act" was designed to suppress his peacemaking activities.

Benjamin R. Tucker, *Instead of a Book: By a Man Too Busy to Write One: A Fragmentary Exposition of Philosophical Anarchism*. (1893). 528pp. $22.00. The greatest single classic of individualist anarchism. A collection from Tucker's magazine *Liberty*, featuring Tucker's brilliant, lucid, logical, and withering critiques of any and all deviations from Tucker's "plumb line". Particularly good on the State and on land, weak on money and economic theory.

Hamilton Vreeland, Jr., *Twilight of Individual Liberty* (1944). 188pp. $8.00. Excellent work, detailing the areas in which the courts have weakened the constitutional defenses of individual liberty and have aggrandized government power.

What is Money? 106pp. $7.00. A compilation of two books, one modern, the other of the late nineteenth century, setting forth a libertarian analysis and prescription for money — in short, favoring the separation of money from the State. They are: Murray N. Rothbard's *What Has Government Done to Our Money?* (1963), and the totally neglected Isaiah W. Sylvester, *Bullion Certificates: The Safest and Best Money Possible: The People's National Currency* (1884). Both available for the first time in hard cover.

Harold F. Williamson, *Edward Atkinson: The Biography of an American Liberal*, 1827-1905. (1934). 326pp. $14.00. Sympathetic biography by one of our leading economic historians of one of the great leaders of nineteenth-century *laissez-faire* liberals in America. A Boston businessman, Atkinson was also a distinguished journalist, economist, champion of free trade and hard money, and vigorous battler against late-nineteenth century American imperialism.

Ambrose Pare Winston, *Judicial Economics: The Doctrine of Monopoly as Set Forth by Judges of the U.S. Federal Courts in Suits under the Anit-Trust Laws*. (1957). 194pp. $8.00. A devastating and totally neglected little book, in which economist Winston rigorously dissects the classic anti-trust cases, the ones in which the government supposedly had the best case against business, the cases "in restraint of trade." Using the detailed court hearings for the first time, Winston shows the utter fallacy — legal, economic, and philosophical — behind the trust-busting in every instance. ◻

240

Disestablish Public Education

by Leonard P. Liggio

One had to be struck by the vehemence with which Ivan Illich's *Deschooling Society* (New York, Harper & Row, 1971) has been attacked. The review in the New York *Times Book Review* (July 11, 1971) by one of the educational establishment is an example. Why this violent reaction, one wondered, reading through the review? And then, the answer came. Illich's advocacy of the free market in education is the bone in the throat that is choking the public educators. The reviewer says: "If the consumer approach has misled and cheated people in supermarkets (and particularly poor and uneducated people), why would any of the free market mechanisms so popular in radical circles work better in education?"

One cannot allow to pass un-noted the reviewer's remark that "free market mechanisms" are "so popular in radical circles." The historic conjunction of free market and radical when free market concepts were in their prime and really challenged the monopoly system, has been restored. After being long lost in the baggage of stand-pattism, the free market has been liberated as the result of the hard work of recent libertarian economists, philosophers, and historians, and has moved to the forefront as the only solution to the chaos of the monopoly system.

Illich begins by saying that "I had never questioned the value of extending obligatory schooling to all people. Together we have come to realize that for most men the right to learn is curtailed by the obligation to attend school." He feels that the public school system is the paradigm of all the "bureaucratic agencies of the corporate state," and that his basic approach to de-monopolizing education (ending its compulsory nature in all its aspects) is the answer for the rest of the corporate state's bureaucracy. Illich's solution is to de-finance these institutions – remove their tax support. Illich notes: "Justice William O. Douglas observed that 'the only way to establish an institution is to finance it.' The corollary is also true." Illich wants to eliminate the tax support for the schools as well as health, welfare and one supposes American business in general. Illich contrasts right-wing (monopoly) institutions with left-wing (free market) institutions, showing the advantages of the un-tax supported, competitive approach to serving consumer wants:

"Right-wing institutions, as we can see clearly in the case of schools, both invite compulsively repetitive use and frustrate alternative ways of achieving similar results.

Toward, but not at, the left on the institutional spectrum, we can locate enterprises which compete with others in their own field, but have not begun notably to engage in advertising. Here we find hand laundries, small bakeries, hairdressers, and – to speak of professionals – some lawyers and music teachers. Characteristically left of center, then, are self-employed persons who have institutionalized their services but not their publicity. They acquire clients through their personal touch and the comparative quality of their services."

Illich places public education near the extreme right of the spectrum: "they belong near the extreme of the institutional spectrum occupied by total asylums." Illich presents an interesting contrast between science in a free market and science in the monopoly system:

"An even more valuable body of scientific objects and data may be withheld from general access – and even from qualified scientists – under the guise of national security. Until recently science was the one forum which functioned like an anarchist's dream. Each man capable of doing research had more or less the same opportunity

of access to its tools and to a hearing by the community of peers. Now bureaucratization and organization have placed much of science beyond public reach. Indeed, what used to be an international network of scientific information has been splintered into an arena of competing teams."

Just as the role of the state has transformed science and deformed it, the role of the state has been to deform education and learning. Compulsion and public tax support are the common destructive elements. The right-wing or tax-supported approach – the current matter of government aid to Lockheed which developed from government contracts is instructive – with its twin of compulsion must be confronted.

"School has become the world religion of a modernized proletariat, and makes futile promises of salvation to the poor of the technological age. The nation-state has adopted it, drafting all citizens into a graded curriculum leading to sequential diplomas not unlike the initiation rituals and hieratic promotions of former times. The modern state has assumed the duty of enforcing the judgment of its educators through well-meant truant officers and job requirements, much as did the Spanish kings who enforced the judgments of their theologians through the conquistadors and the Inquisition. Two centuries ago the United States led the world in a movement to disestablish the monopoly of a single church. Now we need the constitutional disestablishment of the monopoly of the school, and thereby of a system which legally combines prejudice with discrimination. The first article of a bill of rights for a modern, humanist society would correspond to the First Amendment to the U. S. Constitution: "The State shall make no law with respect to the establishment of education."

Until that happy day when education is disestablished Illich is searching for methods of moving strongly away from the public education system. He has been influenced by the conversations and papers of members of the Chicago school of economists who advocate a program of tuition grants.

"Taxpayers are not yet accustomed to permitting three billion dollars to vanish from HEW as if it were the Pentagon. The present administration may believe that it can afford the wrath of educators. Middle-class Americans have nothing to lose if the program is cut. Poor parents think they do, but, even more, they are demanding control of the funds meant for their children. A logical way of cutting the budget and, one hopes, of increasing benefits is a system of tuition grants such as that proposed by Milton Friedman and others. Funds would be channeled to the beneficiary, enabling him to buy his share of the schooling of his choice."

The approach of the Chicago school of economists, in this as in so much else, requires two comments: first, they more than any other group address themselves to real issues and not imaginary constructs; and second, as they are not libertarians, their solutions fall far short of the answers which the free market offers. A tax credit approach, for instance, would be preferable. But, however much they may be holders of the truth, libertarians do not bring that truth to those such as Illich who are seeking it. While Chicagoans are here, there and everywhere, giving or attending seminars, libertarians retreat. How many libertarian scholars will be contributing to the seminar on "Alternatives in Education" next year at Illich's Center for International Documentation in Cuernavaca, Mexico?

A Note On Revolution

BY R. A. CHILDS, JR.

"Revolution" has been defined, by all too many libertarians as well as by most other people, as simply massive acts of direct violence. But "revolution" is really the application of Aristotelian final casualty to the process of social and political change, and should not be confused with throwing bricks or any other random acts of violence. But what does this mean?

It means that revolution, in contradistinction to evolution as an approach to social and political change, is truly *goal-directed*, having as its end the ending of any current political-statist system, and the replacement of statism with a libertarian society. Final casualty is really not anything complex: it is the process of choosing and acting which results when the *end* one has established determines the *means* required to attain it. These means must be truly worthy of the end, or capable of attaining it, which means that they must be determined by *reason*, by thinking about the context in which one finds oneself and one's political system, and deciding what would be the best possible way of attaining the end.

Does revolution involve violence? Not necessarily, but probably most likely it will, at least in its final stages. What the libertarian must focus on is that such violence must always be *defensive* or *retaliatory* violence, not invasive, aggressive violence. It may be necessary in the final stages of any revolution because there always tend to be those in the "ruling class" who will not simply quit using aggression and intimidation voluntarily, and whom people must defend themselves against, peacefully if possible, violently if not.

What I want to call special attention to here is the fact that revolution is not merely any concrete violence against the state apparatus, the set of institutions and men who systematically use aggression to accomplish their ends. Indeed, in many *not* itexts such violence will be truly *counter-revolutionary* and unproductive of the end of liberty. But violence should not therefore on that account alone be ruled out *a priori* as a means of dealing with the systematic coercion of the State.

To quote Murray N. Rothbard, in July of 1969 ("The Meaning of Revolution," LIBERTARIAN FORUM): "Revolution is a mighty, complex, long-run process, a complicated movement with many vital parts and functions. It is the pamphleteer writing in his study, it is the journalist, the political club, the agitator, the organizer, the campus activist, the theoretician, the philanthropist. It is all this and much more. Each person and group has its part to play in this great complex movement."

What integrates all of these actions and functions? Very simply, the *end* of getting rid of the coercive apparatus of the State. If one believes in a "limited government," then he must *still* admit that by his own standards what we have today is light-years from any such thing, and that therefore he too is in favor of getting rid of the coercive apparatus of the present State.

The point that I want to make, then, is a simple one. In answer to the oft-asked question of "when is it time for a revolution?" the real answer becomes, in view of the above: it is *always* time for revolution, *whenever* there is a State ruling over any people anywhere. Because, remember, revolution is not merely the acts of violence near the end of the road, when victory is almost won – *it is each and every action which is taken to attain the final end of the abolition of the State*. The tactics and strategy will change from time to time and place to place, depending upon the concrete nature of the State which a movement is concerned with. And, finally, we should also be aware

that there are such things as *roundabout means of production,* i.e. establishing certain pre-conditions for the final victory. If we ignore these points, then we run the risk of becoming irrelevant to the time and place we live in. If we remember them, then at least we have a *chance* for victory, for we shall understand the true meaning of what it is to advocate setting a revolution into motion. ◻

ATTICA — *(Continued from page 1)*

per se. Hence, when sent to prison, he tries not to be a trouble-maker, tires to win privileges and early parole by good behavior, etc.

But, in the last few decades, liberals and leftists have turned their mischievous attentions to the prison system, and to the concept of crime and punishment. They have promulgated the absurd theory, for example, that "society" (i.e. everyone *except* the criminal, including his *victim*) is responsible for crime, and not the criminal himself. Criminals have of course become adept at using their increasing literacy to wrap themselves in left-wing justifications for their misdeeds. In the thirties and onward, it was sentimental liberalism that they clasped to their bosoms, whining that *they* were not responsible, but only the fact that not enough playgrounds had been provided for their childhood, or because their mother and father hated each other. In recent years, this liberal cop-out has been succeeded by revolutionary leftism. Now the murderer, the rapist, the mugger, can preen himself as a member of the vanguard of the "revolution"; every time he knifes an old lady he can proudly label it a "revolutionary act" against the Establishment."

This phony "revolutionism" was rife at Attica, expecially among the hard core of the mutineers, and it will continue to be rife so long as softheaded liberals in the media continue to disseminate this hogwash.

Once begins at last to sympathize with the exasperated Conservative Party leader in Queens, who, after the umteenth justification by Black Panthers and others of themselves as "political prisoners" or "prisoners of war," finally said: "O. K., if these people are prisoners of war, let them be treated as such. In other words, let them be locked up until the 'war' is over." For another curious aspect of this whole line of argument is this: why do criminals expect, and often *get,* preferential treatment when they proclaim that they are "revolutionaries" dedicated to overthrowing society and the existing system? If you knife a candy store owner and then trumpet this as an "act of the revolution", why shouldn't you expect to be treated even *worse* than otherwise by authorities whose very task it is to protect existing society? Why expect "acts of violent overthrow" to be treated especially gently by the very people who are being "overthrown"? On the contrary, they should expect even harsher treatment as a result, for what kind of boobs are they who take threats of violence against themselves as passports for that violence? And yet, such boobs have obviously abounded in recent years. Once again, only firm and swift action against criminals, regardless of alibi, will restore proper perspective and end this latest form of "revolutionary" cop-out for crime.

(3) *Liberal "Humanitarianism".*

Another interesting point in the whole prison question is the pernicious role of liberal "humanitarianism" in dealing with crime. The classical argument for punishment of crime is that the purpose is (a) retribution for the criminal's invasion of the victim's rights; and (b) deterrence of future crime by isolating the criminal from other potential victims. And yet, liberals have for decades denounced retribution and the very concept of "punishment" itself as barbaric; instead, they would substitute the idea of "rehabilitating" the criminal so that he would re-enter society as a better person. Superfically more humane, the objective consequence of this liberal humanitarianism, as libertarian psychiatrist Dr. Thomas Szasz has pointed out in the case of psychiatric methods of dealing with crime, has been a monstrous and unjustified tyranny over the prisoner.

For example: suppose that a certain crime calls for a punishment of five years in the pokey. The liberal comes along and says: No, this is barbaric punishment; let us not simply give this man five years, let us let him loose when he

becomes "rehabilitated", when he becomes a better person. A better person, that is, according to the prison authority, who now is supposed to become a healer, teacher, and ethical guide as well – or, in the case of the psychiatrist, when the prisoner is pronounced psychiatrically "cured." This may mean, of course, that, of the original five year prisoners, Prisoner A may get turned loose after a few months. But it *also* means that Prisoner B may receive a life sentence, because he has not yet been "rehabilitated." In short, objective law and therefore objective punishment which "fits the crime" and is somehow proportionate to it, gets tossed away, and is replaced by the subjective decisions and whims of the "humanitarian" overlords of the prison system. As a result, some prisoners receive "indeterminate sentences" of inordinate length; and also as a result, the jailers *have* to become the censors of the prisoners' reading, associations, and writing in jail; for how else will they become "rehabilitated"?

In short, the "humanitarian" program of liberalism becomes a far worse – and a far less justified – tyranny over the prisoners, who no longer enjoy the certainty of objective punishment, who must work to please their Big Brother rulers, and whose lives are now permanently at the mercy of their brain-washing authorities. Once again, Dr. Szasz has almost singlehandedly begun to force a re-examination of the tyranny of psychiatric liberalism in ruling over the prisoners.

We conclude, therefore, that in every aspect the liberals and the left have failed or are dead wrong, and that the response of hard-headed conservatism on the prison question and on the Attica crisis has been the correct one.

But wait, the libertarian left, might cry, what of the context? You might be correct *within* the context of the prison system, but what of that system itself? Shouldn't a libertarian be totally opposed to it? Here, there are three questions to distinguish: (A) are the prisoners really criminals? (B) Aren't prisons themselves tyrannical rule over the prisoners? And (C) Aren't the prisons government institutions and therefore to be combatted?

On the first point, it is true that the prison population contains not only people whom libertarians would agree are

(Continued on page 8)

243

ATTICA — *(Continued from page 7)*

criminals (murderers, muggers, thieves, rapists, etc.) but also non-criminals who have engaged in what are now called "victimless" actions: pornographers, drug possessors, pimps, income tax evaders, draft resisters. But the point is that in the question of Attica this point is irrelevant. For Attica is a "maximum security prison", a prison specifically designed for people whom libertarians acknowledge to be criminals: murders, rapists, etc.

The second point brings up the whole problem of crime and punishment in a libertarian society. Would prisons exist in such a society? In my view, libertarianism does not bar *defensive* violence, which is perfectly legitimate as a defense or punishment against violent aggression. In my view, the libertarian creed states that an aggressor loses his rights *to the extent* that he has deprived victims of theirs. Hence, it is perfectly proper to exact capital punishment on murderers, who have deprived victims of their right to life, or to exact a lesser punishment which is in some way proportionate to other crimes. It is true that the focus of punishment in a libertarian world would be different than it is now, for the *focus* would be on forcing the criminal to recompense the *victim* rather than on exacting such recompense to a meaningless "society" as a whole. But force against the criminal, isolating him from potential victims, forcing him to work to repay the victim, etc. would still remain, and therefore a prison system might remain as well. Certainly there is nothing in the libertarian creed to rule out the existence of prisons, and much to imply that they will still be here. And, again, since criminals lose their rights proportionally to their crimes, they will be subject to rule by prison authorities as they are now.

Thirdly, it is true that prisons are now government owned and that this would change in the purely libertarian society. But we must always distinguish carefully between *legitimate services* that the State has now monopolized and arrogated to itself, and illegitimate activities that no one, including the State, should be permitted to perform. An example of the latter is the *draft*, which is the illegitimate enslavement of innocent people to serve the purposes of others. The draft could therefore never exist in a purely libertarian world. But other services are legitimate but now coercively monopolized by the government: e.g., postal service, roads, police, . . . and prisons. In opposing the Post Office, libertarians do *not* oppose postal service *per se;* on the contrary, we wish to make that service more efficient and of higher quality by allowing competing private postal businesses. The case of the prisons is similar; a libertarian world would not be devoid of prisons, but would have more efficient ones run on a competitive private basis. *Until* the day when the government divests itself of the compulsory monopoly of the post, roads, and police, therefore, we must continue to make use

Recommended Reading

Psychology, Culture, and Standards.

There is never much to recommend in the New York *Sunday Times Book Review*, but the July 4 issue has a superb, slashing attack on the Esalen hokum and, by extension, modern culture generally. This is Donald Kaplan's review of the new book, *Here Comes Everybody*, by William Schutz, founder of Esalen and the Encounter group "therapy." In the course of his demolition of Schutz and the Encounter cult, Dr. Kaplan also makes a fine, wistful defense of intellectual standards and points up the evident decline of standards in our present culture. Kaplan concludes: In psychology, "the learned community that ultimately maintained intellectual standards is becoming less learned by leaps and bounds . . . By all that has ever been worth believing, a book like "Here Comes Everybody" should be the beginning of the end for the movement it mirrors. But at this moment I am persuaded by Professor Chargaff's observation: 'That in our days such pygmies throw such giant shadows only shows how late in the day it has become.'"

Contra Women's Lib.

The counter-attack on the Women's Lib pathology continues. James Lincoln Collier has a valuable anthropological critique, "Millett-Mailer Nuptials: The Anthropology of Sexism", *Village Voice*, July 1. And Mary McCarthy, certainly a fiercely independent writer for three decades, scoffs at Women's Lib as well. Miss McCarthy states that "I have more sympathy for American men than women". She reports that French Women's Lib is particularly exercised by wife-beating, but comments that "The dominance of American husbands by their wives is worse than a Saturday night beating. The Craig's-wife type still exists. Even thought control of a husband is common in the United States. The whole business of the man in the office and the wife as the culture bearer gives an ineffable superiority to women." And, on the current rejection of men by the Libbers: "To have a fatherless child is a terrible mistake and hard on the child. To bring up a child in a community of women is like a Greek satire." Miss McCarthy might have added that large parts of our culture are becoming unconscious satire.

of their services, and the same applies to prisons as well.

We conclude therefore that, even when taking the widest context into account, the libertarian must support the tough conservative line on the question of Attica and other prison mutinies. ◘

The Libertarian Forum

BOX 341
MADISON SQUARE STATION
NEW YORK, NEW YORK 10010

Published Every Month. Subscription Rate: $8.00 Per Year

THE
Libertarian Forum

Joseph R. Peden, Publisher

Murray N. Rothbard, Editor

VOLUME III, NO. 10   November, 1971   75c

NIXON'S NEP

In our special September issue on the wage-price freeze (which received considerable attention throughout the country), we did not have a chance to examine the other, vitally important aspects of President Nixon's New Economic Policy. To us, it is unaccountable that many conservatives and even libertarians reacted in this way to the Nixon economic package: "Well, of course we don't like wage-price controls, but . . . the rest of the package is so good that the overall effect might be favorable." For the rest of the package is almost as bad as the price controls, and is likely to have even more disastrous long-range effects.

I don't speak of the piddling proposals for an investment tax credit, which would only return us to the Democratic policy, or the even more piddling proposals to reduce a deficit which will still constitute the largest two-year deficit in peacetime American history. For the critical remainder of the package is its international economic and monetary policy. In the international part of the NEP, President Nixon announced, single-handedly and dramatically, perhaps the most savage program of nationalistic economic warfare in our history. After decades of lauding our allies of the "free world", Mr. Nixon turned suddenly and dealt them a vicious economic blow, a blow which changed the world economic picture overnight, and returned the world to the disastrous economic warfare of the 1930's. The brutal assault on exports from efficient foreign competitors, particularly from the amazingly productive and thrifty Japanese, will shatter the structure of international trade and the international division of labor, and lead to pernicious political consequences. It is true that the proclaimed American "free trade" policy, from Cordell Hull onward, has always been far more solicitous for freedom for *our* exports than for freedom for exports *from abroad*. But the unilateral imposition of the 10% surcharge, coupled with going off gold and bludgeoning the Japanese into accepting stringent quotas on their exports of textiles, is a blatant reversion to economic nationalism, warfare, and autarchy. It is true that, for many years, American industry has been losing the competitive race in many areas, partly because so much capital and technological research have been diverted to unproductive military channels, partly because the increasingly inflated dollar has been overvalued. But attempting to cure this inefficiency by a reversion to blatant protectionism will not only injure the American and the foreign consumer in countless ways: in the long run it will not even aid American industry, *or* the deficit in the balance of payments.

Protectionism not only injures the American consumer directly, by using coercion to prevent him from buying the cheaper textiles or cameras or automobiles that he would like to buy. It also injures the consumer indirectly and even more intensively, by freezing labor, land, and capital resources in

the increasingly inefficient industries, and thereby preventing them from moving into those industries that are more efficient and have a competitive advantage in selling at home and abroad. By this freeze, the efficient export industries are prevented from expanding, and thus these industries are hurt, along with the consumers who would benefit from the more efficient allocation of resources. But, as the 19th century libertarian economist Frederic Bastiat put it, the latter effect, however crucial, is "unseen", whereas the direct aid to the inefficient and floundering textile, steel, and camera industries is visible and "seen." And furthermore, of course, the foreign countries cannot be expected to take this brutal affront lying down forever. Already, Denmark has placed its own 10% surcharge on American exports, and we can expect American exports, and consumers everywhere, to suffer grievously from the general and accumulating breakdown in international trade. As Western Europe moves toward economic unity, we can expect ever stronger measures of retaliation from the disillusioned and understandably embittered nations of Europe. The tough, "hard-nosed" negotiating attitude of Secretary Connally, who seems to think that he is dealing with Mexican field hands on a Texas ranch, will of course only accelerate the disintegration of the world market.

Particularly disquieting politically is the attitude pervading the Administration toward Japan, which it is hardly an exaggeration to say verges on the war hysteria that developed in the 1930's. We have to go back to George Orwell's *1984*, or to some of the imaginative writings of the Old Right revisionists, to catch the flavor of the anti-Japanese hysteria that has been sweeping the American government. For Orwell and the revisionist writers postulated that it is almost as if, every twenty years or so, the ruling insiders in the Establishment push a few buttons, and suddenly national "friends" become national "enemies" and *vice versa*, not only in the government but throughout the nation's press and media. Thus, in the late 19th century, Germany was "good" and Russia "bad"; in the first decades of the 20th, however, Russia was "good" and Germany "bad". After World War I, Germany was "good" again and Russia "bad"; in the mid-1930's, Germany shifted to "bad" and Russia became "good"; and since World War II, Germany has been "good" again and Russia "bad." Who knows when the next switch will occur? On the Asian front, in the early years of the twentieth century, Japan was "good" and China "bad"; and then, by the mid-1930's, Japan became "bad" and China "good"; and, finally, after World War II, Japan became "good" again and China was "bad". But now, another dramatic Asian reversal appears to be underway. At the same time that the Establishment is beginning to move toward a "China good" policy once

(Continued on Page 2)

245

NIXON'S NEP — *(Continued from Page 1)*

again, Japan is swiftly becoming "bad". We seem to be back in the atmosphere of 1937 once more. Japan, so recently a progressive and staunch bastion of the "free world", is being referred to in the press once more as "aggressive", expansionist, troublesome. A friend of ours who was until recently on the senior staff of the Council of Economic Advisors reports that, throughout the Administration, every time Japan sells another yard of textiles or another camera in the U. S., the anti-Japanese hysteria pervading our government rises another notch. As one cynical wag put it, it's a good thing that Japan is unarmed, otherwise we would be provoking it into another Pearl Harbor.

So what was there about the Nixon package that could tempt some libertarians into partial approval? Ironically, it was Nixon's going off gold, a step that did even more than the 10% surcharge in driving the world into a competitive policy of national economic warfare. The irony is particularly acute because for over twenty-five years, the small, unsung – and still unsung – band of "Austrian" economists: headed by Mises, Rueff, Heilperin, Hazlitt, and including your editor, warned day in and day out that the Bretton Woods system was headed for certain collapse. The irony is that for twenty-five years the Establishment economists, now so righteous in ditching Bretton Woods, pooh-poohed the Austrian warnings, and asserted that the system was graven in stone, that the dollar was an eternal rock, and could not be shattered. And now, though some libertarians have been slow to realize it, Bretton Woods has been ditched in the *reverse* of an Austrian direction, and toward even worse and more pernicious systems.

Some historical background: for generations before 1914, the world monetary system was roughly one of free trade, allied to and intertwined with a "classical" international gold standard. Every national currency was defined as a certain weight of gold, and therefore *was*, in effect, that weight. All paper currencies were convertible into gold, and, therefore, into each other, freely and without governmental restraint. Not only did this mean the monetary and therefore the virtual economic unification of the international economy. It also meant that the redeemability of paper currency into gold provided a vital check upon the inflation of paper currency by governments, and hence kept inflation and the business cycle within moderate bounds. (The fact that the gold standard was partly vitiated by central banking and fractional reserve banking only weakened but did not destroy the effectiveness of the world monetary order.)

World War I wrecked the international gold standard and the pieces were never put back together again. Every country financed the war effort by large-scale currency inflation, and every major country but the U. S. abandoned the gold standard, to go over into paper currencies governed by the fiat of the nation-State. During the 1920's, the world moved, *not* back to a classical gold standard, but to currencies tied only nominally to gold, and actually to the British pound, which in turn was tied to the dollar, which remained the only currency clinging to the older gold standard. Britain, furthermore, insisted on returning to nominal gold at a highly overvalued par, overvalued in relation to the severe inflation of the pound during and after the War. The result was a chronic British deficit in the balance of payments, and inflation in the U. S. to alleviate that deficit. The overinflated currencies collapsed in the Great Depression, and every country, including the United States, went over to a world of fiat paper currencies, inflation, exchange control and blocked currencies, competing devaluations to stimulate one country's exports and block the other fellow's exports, competing protective tariffs, and a general breakdown of international trade which helped perpetuate and intensify the depression on a world scale. And no less an authority than Secretary of State Cordell Hull repeatedly testified that the economic warfare of the 1930's was directly responsible for the outbreak of World War II.

One of the major American war aims was to reconstruct a new international monetary order from the shambles of the 1930's. But, once again, it was not to be a classical gold standard, with its concomitant of free trade, *laissez-faire*, and avoidance of inflation. The new order, established by severe American pressure at Bretton Woods in 1944-45, was a recrudescence of the shaky and unsound system of the 1920's, with two important differences: (a) the new order rested on the dollar, and not at all on the pound; and (b) no country, including the U. S., returned to a full gold standard, in which each currency was redeemable in gold. Instead, gold was re-established as redeemable only for dollar balances held by foreign central banks; American citizens were no longer to enjoy the gold hedge against inflation. American citizens were still prohibited from owning gold, as they had been since 1933, ostensibly for the duration of the bank crisis "emergency." The dollar price of gold was fixed at $35 an ounce, which had been the official price since 1934, and all other currencies were fixed in terms of dollars. Moreover, the other countries were allowed to fix their currencies in terms of their pre-war exchange rates, rates which did not reflect their considerable inflation. Hence, most foreign currencies were overvalued in terms of dollars, while dollars in turn were undervalued.

The world returned to an international monetary order, with roughly fixed exchange rates and a fair amount of interconvertibility of currencies. But foreign countries now held their reserves in dollars more than in gold, and the supply of dollars was in the hands of an ever-inflating American government. Thus, in the early post-war period overvalued foreign currencies suffered from a predictable "dollar shortage", and the propaganda then arose that the U. S. had a "world responsibility" to supply dollars to these countries in foreign aid to "cure" their continuing and ever-present shortage. But around 1950, international economic conditions began inexorably to change. European – and Japanese – economies and currencies became sounder and relatively less inflated, helped by the advice of highly-placed Austrian and semi-Austrian economists: Wilhelm Ropke and Alfred Muller-Armack in Germany, Jacques Rueff in France, President Luigi Einaudi in Italy. Gradually, as Keynesianism took hold in the U. S. and lost credit abroad, the dollar became increasingly inflated, both absolutely and relatively to the continent of Europe. The dollar became increasingly *over*valued, (a) in relation to such "hard" currencies as the West German mark, the French franc, the Swiss franc, and the Japanese yen, and (b) and equally important, overvalued in relation to gold at the frozen price of $35 an ounce. The continuing dollar inflation brought about an increasing overvaluation and a perpetual deficit in the U. S. balance of payments, made up by the piling up of dollar balances abroad, *along with* a continuing outflow of gold, bringing down American gold holdings from $22 billion to less than $10 billion.

The Austrian economists continually warned against the coming collapse of the system, and urged the end of dollar inflation as a cure to the deficits, along with the return to an international gold standard as a permanent check on inflation. The Austrians differed on the best path to return to gold; the soundest plan was that of Rueff and Heilperin for a drastic increase in the price of gold as part of the return; such an increase would cure the overvaluation of *every* inflated currency with respect to gold, and, by putting more gold behind every currency, facilitate a general return to the gold standard. The Mises-Hazlitt proposal for an initial floating of currencies to find the "free-market price" of gold ignored the basic fact that, on a *truly* free-market, there would *be* no independent national currencies, and that every currency, being only a different weight of gold, would automatically find its "exchange rates" fixed in relation to one another. In the

(Continued on Page 3)

NIXON'S NEP — *(Continued from Page 2)*

deepest sense, to talk about a "free market" of dollars and francs is as absurd as calling for a "free market" between ounces and pounds: both are eternally fixed at a weight ratio of 16:1.

The Establishment met the challenge by moving in the opposite direction. Anxious in the long-run to destroy gold altogether as a monetary commodity so as to allow unlimited inflation and dictation of the money supply by governments, the world central banks first abandoned the vain attempt to keep gold at its undervalued $35 an ounce on the free market. Instead, the authorities, in the late 1960's, destroyed the single gold price, and established a "two tier" gold price system, attempting to insulate the central bank price at $35 from the higher market price. Next, as gold flowed out and dollar balances piled up, even distinguished American economists — some of them "renegade" Austrians — devised the absurd theory of "benign neglect." Let the Europeans sizzle, the theory went, they can do nothing else than pile up dollars. Dollars are anyway more important than gold; gold is an obsolete relic, and dollars are backed by the most productive economy in the world. Therefore, why worry about deficits? To reinforce the trend away from gold and toward inflatable paper, the world authorities then established an SDR system of paper units to supplement gold in American currency reserves.

But none of these expedients helped for long. By August, 1971, over $40 billion of dollar claims to gold had piled up in European hands, and Europeans expressed their unwillingness to continue subsidizing American dollar inflation by holding off on their right to redeem in gold. President Nixon was faced with a crisis run on the dollar, and met it by plunging the world back into the monetary and economic chaos of the 1930's. "Benign neglect" was clearly no longer enough.

By cutting all ties with gold, furthermore, Nixon has gone over into totally fiat money; he has cut the last link with an independent, market, commodity check upon inflation. Austrian economists like Rueff realized that, while the dollar may have been overvalued in relation to foreign currencies, going over to a floating rate is a cure worse than the disease: for it abandons the last, balance-of-payments, check upon American inflation. Before August 15, the American authorities at least had to keep a wary eye on the balance of payments deficit and the gold outflow, and therefore were at least partially restrained in their inflation of the money supply. Now, only falling exchange rates remain as a check, and this is a flimsy reed, especially since American export interests are whooping it up for devalued dollars which would bring them competitive advantages abroad.

What else could President Nixon have done? He could have adopted the Rueff plan: of a drastic increase in the price of gold, and a concomitant move toward restoration of the full international gold standard. But this of course is the last thing the Administration — and the entire economic Establishment — wants. Note, for example, how stubbornly Secretary Connally has resisted even the most feeble West European efforts to induce us to raise the price of gold by only a negligible amount. The reason is that the Establishment knows full well that a rise in the price of gold would bring gold back more strongly into the international scene. It would hinder the long-run aim of the Establishment to abandon gold altogether. Hence, no libertarian can look upon the abandonment of Bretton Woods for a *far worse* system as anything but an economic disaster.

Libertarian perception of the international monetary scene has been grievously distorted by the pernicious role of the Friedmanites of the Chicago School. For the Friedmanites have long advocated their pet solution for world money: the total abandonment of gold, *and* freely-fluctuating exchange rates between the various national fiat paper moneys. Hence, he Friedmanites have helped divert libertarian and con-

servative opinion away from gold and toward the absolute control of the monetary system by the nation-State, a State which invariably leans toward inflation. Hence, the misguided cheers of many libertarians for at least the international side of the NEP package. But, apart from the evils of abandoning commodity money and relying on absolute state control of money, the Friedmanites are unrealistic Utopians whistling in the dark. *Even if* freely fluctuating exchange rates were desirable (which I would not concede for a moment) it is absurd of the Friedmanites *first* to grant absolute monetary power to the State and *then* to call upon the State to leave exchange rates free to fluctuate. No government, possessed of the monetary power granted to it by the Friedmanites, will consent to leave exchange rates alone. Hence, the naivete of the cry of many Friedmanites and quasi-Friedmanites since August 15: "Hey, the governments are not allowing floating rates; instead they are instituting a 'dirty float', with exchange controls, interferences in convertibility, etc." What did the Friedmanites expect? Will they ever *stop* putting their trust in Power?

Equally ludicrous was the expectation of the Friedmanites — and even some Austrians who should have known better — that now that the dollar has been severed from gold, the U. S. government will allow American citizens to own and sell gold. Again, the Friedmanites miss the point — that the Establishment is interested, not in maximizing economic freedom, even in distorted Friedmanite terms — but in abolishing gold altogether to pave the way for unchallenged fiat paper. If the government should allow gold, which they have so long proclaimed to be a "worthless", Neanderthal "relic", to be owned by American citizens, then the ever-present threat will be there for Americans to turn from increasingly worthless paper dollars to their own use of gold as a stable and sound currency. This is what many Americans, especially in gold-plentiful California, did during the disastrous greenback inflation of the Civil War. The outlawry of gold is a vital step on the road to unchecked government control of money and toward unchecked paper inflation.

And so President Nixon, in the international part of his NEP package, has plunged the world into a system far worse than the unfortunate Bretton Woods system that is now dead as a doornail. Our Caesar has plunged us back into the destructive world of the 1930's, into a world of unchecked paper inflation, of exchange controls, economic warfare, accelerating protectionism, and breakup of the world market. He has plunged us, in short, into the precise *international* counterpart of the economic fascism at home. The package is, we must admit, consistent and of a piece: in both domestic and foreign economic policy, the aggrandizement of the nation-state, the crushing of the market economy, the perpetuation of inflation, the substitution of statism and conflict for the harmony and voluntarism of the free market. We are faced, in the economic sphere, with fascism in domestic policy and foreign, at home and abroad. And all this, mind you, in the name of "freedom".

Meanwhile, on the domestic front, those libertarians still bemused by the "good old Dick Nixon" syndrome, and who foolishly predicted that all controls would disappear after the 90 days, have one hopes, learned an instructive lesson. Phase II is almost here, and we are promised the first permanent peacetime controls since the unlamented, and still unconstitutional, NRA. Of course, not "permanent", only for two, three . . . how many? years. Pervading the whole show is the stream of private and even quasi-public utterances assuring us that the President doesn't "really" believe in the controls, and that he and his economic planners know that they won't work. Rather than reassuring, all this tells us is the certain knowledge that the Administration has transcended mere economic ignorance and error, and is actively and cynically guilty of moral turpitude. In the meanwhile, the President's rhetoric, as for example in his

(Continued on Page 4)

NIXON'S NEP — *(Continued from Page 3)*

Phase II address of October 7, becomes increasingly Orwellian and collectivist.

Thus, the architect of international monetary chaos calls his program a "campaign to create a new monetary stability"; the creator of a new protectionism says that "this nation welcomes foreign competition." The speech was studded with altruist-collectivist rhetoric, ominously reminiscent of the famous Nazi slogan: "Gemeinnutz geht vor Eigennutz." ("The common good comes before the individual good" – the "common good", of course, as interpreted by the rulers of the State apparatus.) Thus, the President spoke of his "call to put the public interest ahead of the special interest," and to "put their country's interest above their interest in fighting this battle." Even more blatantly collectivist was the President's egregious "What is best for all of us is best for each of us." Whenever the government speaks of "sacrifices", furthermore, it is time for the citizen to guard his pocket and to run for the hills; sure enough, the President called for willingness to "sacrifice for a long-term goal". It is characteristic of such pleas, of course, that it is always "you and him sacrifice"; I have not seen any dramatic evidence lately of any great sacrifices incurred by President Nixon, Secretary Connally, or the rest of their coterie.

"Confident", moreover, that the wage-price controls can be sustained "on a voluntary basis", the President sternly warned that if any Americans should fail to cooperate with this system of "voluntary restraint", the "Government must be and will be prepared to act against them", and will "be backed by authority of law" to make its "decisions stick." Thus, the President has given us a new and creative definition of the "voluntary" – that is, the "voluntary" backed by a hefty measure of coercion. Challenged by libertarian questioners in a debate on the NEP with your editor in Washington on October 19, Dr. Herbert Stein, quasi-Friedmanite member of the Council of Economic Advisers and principal architect of Phase II, seriously replied – after a spell of being befuddled by the question – that the program is indeed voluntary, "just as voluntary as taxes." A wave of sardonic libertarian laughter greeted Stein's remark, at which point I could not refrain from pointing out that for the first time that night I whole-heartedly agreed with a statement by Dr. Stein.

In fact, Stein's open cynicism is indicative of all too much

(Continued on Page 5)

The Collected Works of Lysander Spooner

The only collection available . . . 34 rare and provocative works (1834-1886) in six volumes . . . With an extensive critical biography and individual introductions by Charles Shively . . . Bound in durable library cloth and printed on acid-free paper.

Send for free brochure listing other research editions, including *The Collected Works of John Jay Chapman* in 12 volumes, introductions by Melvin H. Bernstein. Write to M & S Press, Box 311, Weston, Mass. 02193.

Lysander Spooner (1808-1887) was an intellectual activist — for 50 years not only probing; but vigorously prodding his government and society. Prolific, producing more than 30 separately published books, pamphlets, and broadsides (the existence of many not even known to the Library of Congress), Spooner is one of 19th century America's most profound and coherent minds. While producing some of the finest constitutional arguments ever devised against slavery, Spooner concerned himself equally with the subtle subjugation of supposedly free citizens by a governmental system which he saw become increasingly restrictive of personal rights.

"There is no difference, in principle — but only in degree — between political and chattel slavery," he declared in 1867. A nation which fought to free slaves should be prepared to fight to free the rest of its people — even if (as he suspected) this required the overthrow of the Constitution.

Lysander Spooner had an absolute genius for opposing the government; and his protests against governmental restraint were not limited to brilliant writings on slavery, the Constitution, the jury system, copyright practices, and the economics of our rapidly industrializing country. Spooner actually forced a reduction in postal rates — by setting up his own private mail company in competition with the U.S. Post Office — and at the same time scored important points for freedom of the press. Charles Shively's biography, using hitherto unexamined Spooner papers and letters only recently deposited in the New York Historical Society, brings to light much in Spooner's life that is important to 19th century American history including, for example, Spooner's little known plan to force the release of John Brown after Harper's Ferry — by kidnapping Governor Wise of Virginia — and Spooner's own personal relations with such men as Brown and Gerrit Smith.

Lysander Spooner is remarkably prophetic of governmental interventions into personal and community life, and in his understanding of the psychological as well as the economic problems of industrialization and the dangerous pressures of conformity. These M & S Press volumes provide a rich and vital historical dimension for much of our own contemporary social and political protest.

CONTENTS

Volume I: Biography and Miscellaneous Writings

A. DEIST
Deist's Immortality (1834)
Deist's Reply (1836)

B. MAIL COMPANY
The Unconstitutionality of the Laws
. . . Prohibiting Private Mails (1844)
Who caused the Reduction ? (1850)

C. RADICALISM & ANARCHISM
No Treason, No. 1 (1867)
No Treason, No. 2 (1867)
No Treason, No. 6 (1870)
Revolution (1880)
Letter to Bayard (1882)
Natural Law (1882)
Letter to Cleveland (1886)

Volume II: Legal Writings (I)
"To the Members of the Legis. of Mass." (1835)
Spooner vs. M'Connell (1839)
Illegality of the Trial of Webster (1850)
Trial by Jury (1852)
Drew vs. Clark (1869)

Volume III: Legal Writings (II)
Law of Intellectual Property (1855)
Articles of Association of the Spooner Copyright Co. (1863)
Letter to Scientists and Inventors (1884)

Volume IV: Anti-Slavery Writings
Unconstitutionality of Slavery (1845-60)
Defence for Fugitive Slaves (1850)
Plan for the Abolition of Slavery (1858)
Address of the Free Constitutionalists (1860)
Letter to Sumner (1864)

Volume V: Economic Writings (I)
Constitutional Law Relative to Credit (1843)
Poverty (1846)
New System of Paper Currency (1861)
Our Mechanical Industry (1862)

Volume VI: Economic Writings (II)
Considerations for Bankers (1864)
A New Banking System (1873)
Our Financiers (1877)
Law of Prices (1877)
Gold and Silver (1878)
Universal Wealth (1879)

6 hardcover volumes ●● 2400 pages ●● ISBN 087730-006-2 ●● $140.00 per set

NIXON'S NEP — *(Continued from Page 4)*

the criticism of Friedman himself and many of his disciples has been strangely muted. Thus, Stein, commenting on my charge that the controls won't work in checking inflation, really agreed, and added, in effect, "so why worry about them?" In short, since the controls won't work, they are simply icing on the cake, or "cosmetic" in Friedman's words, and will therefore eventually be repealed. There is no recognition here of the economic harm that will be wrought, the distortions, black markets, declines in quality, as well as the political harm in foisting a system of fascistic controls on the public — not to speak of the immorality of a demagogic appeal to the public in the razzle-dazzle showmanship of the NEP. Furthermore, the smug view that simply because a policy won't work means that it will shortly disappear ignores the political dynamics. The President, for example, is trying to carry water on both shoulders by imposing controls, and yet by keeping a minimal bureaucracy for enforcement and for making the almost infinite number of price and wage decisions that make up the economy from day to day. After the controls fail, then, the Democrats will inevitably call for a wider bureaucracy and for more stringent enforcement, and the economic disaster can be prolonged for many years.

All this is reminiscent of the time when he, and numerous other economists, ranging from the Austrians through the Chicagoites to the Democrats and New Dealers, participated in a conference on inflation and price controls during the last control period, in the Korean War. After Austrian Henry Hazlitt had attacked price controls for causing a meat famine, Friedman made a comment which frankly put him "in between" Hazlitt and the defenders of controls. Friedman

of the Friedmanite response to the wage-price controls, for said: "I think the real argument against price control is precisely that it produces this illusion of famine when there is none." (A. Director, ed., *Defense, Controls, and Inflation,* University of Chicago Press, 1952, p. 243.) In short, while price controls do not work, they have no harmful effects either — an ironic twist to those who suffered from the meat famine of 1946 under the OPA.

Just as this issue was about to go to press, Milton Friedman has to some extent redeemed himself by writing a two-part critique of the controls in the New York *Times Op-Ed* page of October 28 and 29, "Morality and Controls." Particularly in the latter article, Friedman at last took a strong stand on the *immorality* and on the dictatorial nature of the government's presuming to outlaw voluntary price and wage agreements between buyer and seller, employer and worker. It was a bit late in the day, but we are glad that Friedman finally saw the light.

There is a sense, of course, in which Phase II rests, even for short-term success, not on the "voluntary" consent, but on the support of the great majority of the public. For lacking a large bureaucracy, enforcement will have to be placed largely in the hands of the public. And that is why libertarians have a unique opportunity to help wreck the controls earlier than otherwise: for it is up to us to raise the banner of opposition, to educate the public on the unworkability and the evils of the New Economic Policy. We have an historic responsibility; we can strike a blow for freedom far beyond what seems likely from our small numbers. By merely pricking the bubble of the bemused national consensus, we can help restore sanity and liberty to the nation. ◘

We Fight The Freeze

Unfortunately — since it reflects a massive default by conservatives, businessmen, and economists — the task of openly and resolutely battling the wage-price freeze has fallen to the libertarian movement. We have, however, risen to the occasion.

In this struggle, the lead has been taken by your editor. In addition to the widely noted special issue of the *Lib. Forum* in September, which generated a need for a massive reprinting, Murray Rothbard denounced the freeze as "fascism" in the New York *Times Op-Ed* page of September 4, in a lead article called "The President's Economic Betrayal." There was the aforementioned debate in Washington with Herbert Stein on October 19, parts of which were carried on CBS-TV and which was noted for strong audience opposition to the freeze in the *Wall Street Journal* of Oct. 22. In addition, Rothbard opposed the freeze on the Lee Leonard TV Show (Channel 5), and on radio stations WNYC, and WBAI-FM, there inaugurating a monthly libertarian series on that station. Furthermore, a lengthy interview with Rothbard on the freeze appeared in the (Denver) *Rocky Mountain News Global* of Aug. 22, entitled *Is This the Death of the Free Market?* The sympathetic interview appeared on the initiative of libertarian reporter Peter Blake. The Times Op-Ed article stimulated the New York *Sunday News* (Brooklyn) to do an interview with Rothbard on October 17, neatly titled *Laissez Faire Called Fairest System of All.*

The most massive organized libertarian effort against the controls was a full-page ad that appeared in the Sunday *Washington Post* of Oct. 10. Drawn up largely by Rothbard and James Davidson, executive director of the National Taxpayers Union, the ad was submitted by the newly-formed Committee to Restore Freedom, organized by the NTU. Denouncing the controls as tyranny as well as being unworkable, the ad pointed out that the price inflation is caused by monetary expansion by the Federal Reserve System, and called on everyone to "do his part

to see to it that wage-price controls are made unenforceable." All libertarians are urged to send their names and their contributions for further ads and television appearances to the Committee to Restore Freedom, which can be reached at 319 5th St., S. E. Washington, D. C. 20003.

The list of signers of the CRF ad constitute a veritable roll-call of honor in these dark days. Among economists they include: Henry Hazlitt; Dr. Hans Sennholz, Chairman of the Economics Dept., Grove City College; Dr. D. T. Armentano, Economics Dept., Hartford University; Dr. John Snare; Dr. H. E. French, III; Dr. Laurence Moss, Economics Dept., University of Virginia; Colonel E. C. Harwood, head of the American Institute for Economic Research; and in a sense our prize catch, Dr. Sam Peltzman, Economics Dept., UCLA and until recently a senior staff economist of the Council of Economic Advisers.

Businessmen who signed the ad should be particularly honored, defying as they did not only the general run of business opinion but also risking possible retaliation against their businesses by the federal control bureaucracy. Businessmen signers included: Charles Koch, head of Koch Industries; Robert D. Love, head of the Love Box Co.; and John L. D. Frazier; all of Wichita, Kansas; William L. Law, head of Cudahy Tanning Co. of Cudahy, Wisc.; William Grede, head of Grede Foundries, Milwaukee, Wisc.; Frank Bond, head of Holiday Universal of Baltimore; Charles A. Pillsbury, of the Pillsbury family of Minneapolis; Henry J. Hohenstein of Creative Equity Corp.; Mrs. Fabiola C. Moorman and Leonard P. Cassidy, of Quincy, Ill.; George E. Judd, head of Judd & Detweiler; Alvin M. Benesch, of AIM Enterprises, Washington, D. C.; and John Zeigler, head of John Zeigler, Inc. of New York City.

Other libertarian leaders who signed the ad included: Robert D. Kephart, publisher of *Human Events;* Stephen
(Continued on Page 6)

249

WE FIGHT THE FREEZE — *(Continued from Page 5)*
J. Ganslen, of *Human Events;* Edward Nash, head of Nash Publishing Co., Los Angeles; George Pearson, of Wichita, Kan.; Jarret B. Wollstein of SIL, and editor of the *Individualist*; Roy A. Childs, Jr. and James A. Webb of the *Individualist* and SIL; Phillip Abbott Luce; Gary Greenberg, head of the New York Libertarian Association; A. Ernest Fitzgerald, formerly of the Dept. of Defense and now head of the National Taxpayers Union; Leonard P. Liggio of the History Dept. of City College, CUNY; C. Merton Tyrrell; and attorney David J. Mandel of New York City.

One constructive thing that libertarians can do is to place this ad in local newspapers around the country. Already, Charles Koch is in the process of placing the ad in the Wichita, Kansas press, and young libertarian lawyer Butler Shaffer is placing it in the Omaha, Nebraska papers.

We have had strong differences in the past with objectivist commentator Jeffrey St. John, but St. John rose nobly to the occasion: delivering a moving tribute to Professor Ludwig von Mises on his 90th birthday, September 29, over CBS-Radio *Spectrum*. In the course of his tribute,

St. John mentioned that a group of disciples of Professor Mises has single-handedly rallied to battle the wage-price controls, and to place the ad in the Washington *Post*. St. John referred to the wage-price freeze as Nixon's *Mein Kampf*.

Other trenchant attacks on the controls have now begun to appear: Henry Hazlitt in *Human Events* (Sept. 4); Davis Keeler in his *Research Review* (Sept. 20) (The review is published monthly by the Economic Research Corp., P. O. Box 365, Barrington, Ill. 60010); and Frank S. Meyer in a critique of Phase II in *National Review* (Nov. 5). Also doing good work against the freeze have been the *Research Reports* of the American Institute for Economic Research of Great Barrington, Mass., and the magazine *Cointact* in Dennison, Ohio. I am also informed that the Birch Society has been attacking the wage-price controls as fascism.

In sum, libertarians have acquitted themselves well in quickly and strongly reacting to the New Economic Policy. As the bloom falls off the rose – and there are increasing signs of disenchantment among business and the public as the freeze is beginning to fall apart – hopefully the public will begin to turn to libertarians for politico-economic leadership.   ▫

Confession—Pavlovian Style

BY Lucille E. Moran

Before quizzing individual witnesses or suspects, every police officer from village constable to FBI agent, including those of intermediate jurisdiction, such as city cops and county sheriffs, utters the assurances of the Miranda warning.

Even Revenue agents piously intone the Miranda options in face-to-face interviews with witnesses or suspects. But, in their instance, the recitation is MEANINGLESS, when they say:

"Under the Constitution of the United States you have the right to refuse to answer any questions or make any statements that may tend to incriminate you under the laws of the United States. However, anything you say or any evidence which you produce may be used against you in any proceeding which may hereafter be undertaken by the United States. Do you fully understand this?"

While other statist investigators seeking leads, information and evidence on which prosecutors can build cases, arrange to immunize those who agree to perform as State Witnesses, revenuers usually start off with such a whopping advantage over their marks that they tend to believe no need for similar amnesties exists for the kind of people they pursue.

Their activities begin where most other detective work leaves off. They start with a confession signed and submitted by their prey and work backwards. The confession they hold is known as a Tax Return Form.

This wondrous state of affairs arises from an easy device so simple and obvious it is overlooked by the guileless and unwary it aims to entrap: *The MIRANDA options are slyly omitted from where they rightfully belong— ON TAX RETURN FORMS.*

The whole income tax strategem has survived to date by wilfully mistiming the announcement that what you confess on Tax Return Forms may be used against you. By the time revenuers get around to notifying the gullible of this fact, they are already attempting to shake them down on the basis of their signed confessions.

Revenue attorneys and Justice Department prosecutors (who do their pinch-hitting) promote the mendacity that

in tax suits the accused and their star witness should be one and the same person.

Unfortunately, this falsity is similarly entertained by people who think of themselves as "tax-payers".

But, of the two opposing parties perpetuating this fraud, the act of consent by members of the body politic is the more grievous. For it has encouraged the opposition to practice the misconception that in cases concerning tax collections the immunities from prosecution, penalties and punishment, routinely afforded State witnesses, may be suspended and the law of this land still observed.

The error committed by timid souls who file returns and accept the label "tax-payers" (as if it indicated a fixed status or political class) might have the mortal effect of a complete forfeiture of their rights to the Enemy consistent with the legal maxim *"volenti non fit injuria"* (if you consent to a wrong, you can't claim to be injured by it) – except for certain inadvertencies that gained emphasis during the past decade.

The most significant took form as a suddenly fastidious concern by members of the entrenched bench-bar to protect persons accused of offenses against Natural Law from self-incrimination – which, of course, is itself a far more serious breach of Natural Law. What we know as Fifth Amendment securities are restraints on the eternal temptation of Inquisitors to coerce people into acting as witnesses against themselves, under threat of prosecution, penalty or punishment. The 'Fifth' consistent with Natural Law politics, thereby prohibits under any legalistic pretext, circumstances by which people could be called to an accounting by accusing them of that old favorite of tyrants: CRIMES AGAINST THE STATE.

Reciting the Miranda options to punks and hoods suspected of pulling jobs or being material witnesses thereto, amounts to carrying coals to Newcastle. They've been around enough to know they aren't obliged to trade their secrets for NOTHING.

They demand and get something in return. Before consenting to supply information expected of State witnesses and informants, experienced hoods exact their price in

(Continued on Page 7)

CONFESSION – PAVLOVIAN STYLE –

(Continued from Page 6)

the immunities they are due. Having pegged the opposition's modus operandi, they jolly well know their adversary can't proceed into prosecution without the information and evidence they have to barter.

No one need grandstand advisements to cons and felons to avoid the mistake of relinquishing their right to claim injury by going along with statist treacheries. They already know who needs whom most. And, that self-confession is violative of Natural Law unless it has a return, at least in absolutions, if not always in money, from those who rely on receiving their statements.

Can you imagine the hue and cry from "sharing" Liberals were legislation enacted making it a crime for punks and felons to refuse, on the one hand, to supply statists the information needed to prosecute them; or for making confessions on the other, that statists don't believe are quite up to snuff? The opposition might have to set up a separate court system along the lines of Star Chamber devoted exclusively to handling such Crimes against the State.

Yet, the adversary has done JUST THAT and successfully hooked reputable persons of irresolute character into going along with the tax strategem. Revenuers dispose of most cases of resistance through the dummy 'Tax Court of the United States', which isn't a court at all, but a deliberately misnamed executive chamber. It is operated by Treasury Department employees for quietly disposing of matters involving revenue collection from their view – and property rights and entitlements from yours – without jury-trial. A handful are tried by Justice Department prosecutors in United States District Courts in hopes of busting people as "criminals" as object lessons to others that don't think of themselves as fixed in some class called "tax-payers".

Although the first line of the CODE OF ETHICS subscribed to by Internal Revenue employees admits that the act of informing against one's self, or anyone else for that matter, *can't be made compulsory*, by the following language, "The Federal system of taxation is based on *voluntary* compliance by the people of the United States", (emphasis mine) revenuers and Justice Department dudes depend heavily on making the tax scheme *seem* involuntary and mandatory to trusting souls, who being unwise to the ways of the world are susceptible to programs for conditioning their responses so they will react predictably.

These worthies rush to file an annual confession of their activities, as if it were their Easter duty, with a display of signal responses comparable to Pavlov's dogs failing to obey their instinct to bite when their food is withdrawn.

Evading publication of the Miranda options on Tax Return Forms is the first deception used to sensitize the unwary in order to enlist their help and consent for a scuttling of Natural Law processes and safeguards.

The quarry is further conditioned by the statists' covert withholding (oops) of the fact that the Federal system of taxation has always rested on the volition of individual members of the body politic. This operates to suppress the principle that – those who don't care to contribute to their own undoing, DON'T HAVE TO – and, conversely, those who want to tell on themselves and/or make free will donations, CAN.

By thus joining these two failures to supply timely information, a majority is led into the misapprehension that within a Natural Law political system, they are

still duty-bound to fling themselves into the role of victims of any ruse devised by the minds of cunning men.

Heartened by their ability to induce otherwise honorable members of the body politic into reacting with attitudes

reflecting the misguided notions of Old World politics, the opposition has availed itself of the other side of this fantasy and enacted legislative frivolities on this basis.

Section 7203 of United States Code Chapter 26, the Internal Revenue Title, dramatizes the extent of delusions belabored by servants, acting solely on delegated authority, in presuming to exchange roles with their natural lords and masters in this land from "sea to shining sea."

By the oddest coincidence, Section 7203 of Chapter 26, just happens to be entitled, "WILFUL FAILURE TO FILE RETURNS, SUPPLY INFORMATION OR PAY TAX". And, its provisions attest to the objective of neutralizing Natural Law politics under pretensions of "law" and process in order to regiment people into classes and destroy the body politic:

"Any person required under this title to pay an estimated tax or tax, or required by this title or by regulations made under authority thereof to make a return, keep any records, or supply information, who wilfully fails to pay such estimated tax or tax; make such return, keep records, or supply such information at the time or times required by law (sic) or regulations, shall in addition to other penalties provided by law, be guilty of a misdemeanor and upon conviction thereof, shall be fined not more than $10,000.00 or imprisoned not more than 1 year, or both, together with the costs of prosecution."

Consider the handsome reduction in salaries for FBI agents and money for paying off their informants, if similar accommodations could be written for FBI convenience. The savings in informants' fees alone would be substantial, if the value attached to such necessary services by one Bureau spokesman is an index. He acknowledges that – "one good informant is worth 50 agents."

If crooks and hoods would only cooperate enough to give a yearly accounting of themselves to their friendly, neighborhood FBI office, on or before a designated day of holy obligation, Federal agents could enjoy the fun of busting them for Crimes against the State. This would be a much easier task than trying to nail them for crimes against natural law without demolishing it, in the doing.

Then, shady characters could be prosecuted for wilful failure to file annual confessions, supply information, etc., and tried by jury in a United States District Court on charges of such disobedient deportment. With any luck at all, Justice Department prosecutors could show that the defendant lacked the proper demeanor of docility and refused to cooperate by failing to comply voluntarily with the rule of men. Then the culprit would be convicted, locked up and federal coffers would ring just as merrily. He'd have to ante up the costs of his own prosecution, as

(Continued on Page 8)

CONFESSION - PAVLOVIAN STYLE —

(Continued from Page 7)

well as a disobedience tax of not more than $10,000.

In light of the foregoing, the Independent Bar Association uses, and advocates the use by Tax Rebels, of three techniques for check-mating the opposition with their own implements:

It places the burden on the other side by citing the first line of the CODE OF ETHICS subscribed to by Internal Revenue employees, about "voluntary compliance"; it reminds the adversary of its plan to hoodwink respectable members of the body politic into walking into Federalist traps by a wilful and calculated omission of the Miranda options from Tax Return Forms; and, at the first sign of revenuers' interest in an individual's business, it slaps them with a piece of certified mail containing an Independent Bar Association DEMAND FOR IMMUNITY FORM, which states in part, "Please further take notice, that this is only what every run-of-the-mill punk and hoodlum knows he can demand and get for providing Federalists with the information they need to proceed."

LIBERTARIAN WIT

Review of Jerome Tuccille, *It Usually Begins With Ayn Rand* New York: Stein & Day. 192pp. $6.95

by The Old Curmudgeon

Humor is the key. The dividing line on the new Tuccille book is whether or not you have a sense of humor. And by humor I do not mean the ability to enjoy one-liners by a stand-up comic. I mean socio-political wit and satire. In any age, this sort of a sense of humor is in all too short supply. In the present age, this high sense of wit and satire has disappeared almost to a vanishing point. We are surrounded by belligerent and humorless fanatics, blighted souls who believe that in order to be "serious about your values", wit and humor must be tossed into the discard. And, sad to say, the libertarian movement is scarcely a conspicuous exception to this miasma, to say the least. It is not just that wit and satire are great joys in themselves, a part of the happy and joyous affirmation of life and its values that should be enjoyed by everyone. It is also that a sense of humor lends one a rational perspective, keeps one in tune with reality and what is generally known as "common sense." It is impossible to conceive of people blessed with a sense of humor, for example, howling that the titles "Mrs." and "Miss" must be purged from the language, or coming to the view that the practice of bestiality is a rational moral obligation.

What the libertarian movement needs most is a bracing dose of wit and satire, and this is precisely what Tuccille offers in his new book. If you have a sense of humor, you'll find it consistently hilarious; if you don't, you'll hate it. If you don't, then take a few Miltowns first, but read it anyway. It will do you good.

Already the carping has begun. "There are a whole host of factual errors in the book." This criticism misses the whole point of the book. Tuccille is not and does not claim to be a scholarly historian; he is a novelist, and his portrayal of the persons and events in the libertarian movement is a novelist's satiric and hilarious reconstruction; it is not the literal truth but the novelist's truth, the keen perception of the essence of the movement by reconstructing events through Tuccille's vivid and satiric imagination. It is novelized non-fiction, somewhere in between the witty and more novelistic political novels of Roger Peyrefitte and the personal journalism of Jimmy Breslin. By presenting poetic truth it captures the spirit of our often kooky movement far better than a sobersided and scholarly history could do. The book is already a best-seller, so . . . relax and enjoy it.

The Libertarian Forum

BOX 341
MADISON SQUARE STATION
NEW YORK, NEW YORK 10010

First Class

Published Every Month. Subscription Rate: $8.00 Per Year

252

THE
Libertarian Forum

Joseph R. Peden, Publisher

Murray N. Rothbard, Editor

VOLUME III, NO. 11   December, 1971   75c

The UN And The War

As we write, the UN has sat down to thrash over the new war between India and Pakistan, and anguished cries are being raised about the unfortunate "ineffectuality" of the United Nations. The anguish is sadly misplaced. For the real points about the UN is that it is only tolerable *so long as it remains ineffectual.*

For the whole concept of the United Nations is mischievous. First, because underneath the UN lurks the possible danger of a genuine world government, that world government that used to be the rallying cry for all manner of well-meaning liberals. Give us a world government, give us "One World", and there will be nowhere on the planet to escape its tyranny. At least nowadays, we can shop around from one government to the next, and excape from a site of greater tyranny to a lesser – and our retreatists can at least dream of setting up their own private and stateless islands. But come a world government, and these options will be rudely taken from us.

Happily, the dream of world government remains a misty and far-off ideal, smashed on the rock of Great Power hostility. But a grave danger remains, the highly dangerous principle that lies at the heart of the UN philosophy. This principle is the New Deal-Wilsonian concept of "collective security against aggression," the siren song under which two World Wars and a Cold War have been fought in our century. The "collective security" principle postulates that in every war there is a clear-cut, easily discernible, "aggressor." Usually the "aggressor" is simple-mindedly branded as the first State that crosses another State's borders with troops. The "collective security" principle holds that all the nations of the world are then duty-bound to get together to use *force majeure* against the "aggressor", and to defeat his evil designs. In practice, in our century, the United States has taken upon itself the "collective security" role, the White Knight in shining armor that sets out to defend the entire world against the Bad Dragon of aggression.

The fallacies and dangers in this doctrine abound at every hand. The first problem is the simplistic definition of "aggression." The analogy, usually implicit but sometimes expressly held, is always taken from aggression by one *individual* upon another. If Smith is seen to be jumping on and stealing a watch from Jones, then Smith can easily be labelled the "aggressor", and police may be called upon to defend Jones and apprehend the criminal for return of the loot. But while we might be able to say easily that Jones deserved to have the watch and that therefore Smith was an aggressor, the same can scarcely be said for State X which has been invaded by State Y. For to call State Y an "aggressor" *per se* must mean that the present territorial boundaries of State X are somehow morally and rightfully

its own, in the same way that Jones' watch is rightfully *his* own. But since national territories have invariably been acquired by *previous* aggression rather than by voluntary social contract, to leap automatically to the defense of the invaded State is an absurdity. On what moral grounds are we to cry "Halt" and thereby ratify every aggression *previous* to, say, December 1971 as legitimate and moral?

To turn the analogy around, suppose that on deeper investigation we find that Smith was *not* stealing Jones' watch, but simply catching Jones who had previously stolen Smith's watch, and that therefore Smith's seeming act of "aggression" was really an act of self-defense? This is certainly possible among individuals, and indeed often happens. But how then can we justify an automatic ganging up on State Y which might be retrieving territory previously grabbed by State X? Furthermore, since *all* States are aggressors anyway against their own population, even the most aggrieved State can never, for libertarians, aspire to the simple status of innocent victim, as say Jones may have been when set upon by Smith. No State, in fact, is worth the extra State aggression upon their subjects that will be involved in every State's ganging up on the "aggressor" in the collective-security *mystique*.

In the collective security myth, then, all States are supposed to join against the aggressor in the same spirit as a policeman against an individual criminal. Hence, the absurd American use of the term "police action" rather than "war" to characterize our imbroglio in Korea in the early 1950's.

Furthermore, there is no way to prevent the ganging up of collective security from being a league of States dedicated to defending the *status quo*, no matter how pernicious, by coercion. The League of Nations or United Nations then necessarily becomes a gang of States trying to preserve their territories and privileges by force against the newer nations that are trying to win their place in the sun, or against aggrieved States trying to recover some of their national territory. Moreover, the ganging up insures that any war, anywhere in the globe, no matter how trivial, will be maximized into a world-wide conflict. Collective security then becomes a method for the global aggrandizement of dispute and conflict, so that all peoples everywhere get drawn into the net of warfare and killing. In these days of brutal weapons of mass destruction, in our age when warfare rests on the mass murder of innocent civilians, the globalizing of conflict *via* collective security is a monstrous death trap for the peoples of the world. The sooner the United Nations, or any other scheme of collective security, disappears, the safer shall all of us be.

As for the United States government, ever since the beknighted Woodrow Wilson (the self-righteous prig whom H. L.

(Continued on page 2)

253

THE UN AND THE WAR — *(Continued from page 1)*

Mencken dubbed "The Archangel Woodrow"), we have been the world's number one champion of the *status quo*. Therefore, in the complex world of foreign affairs, there is a good rule of thumb for the libertarian: find out the stand of the Untied States, and it will be the wrong one. The American genius for taking the wrong side is unfailing.

Such has been the case in the current war on the Indian subcontinent. To speak of the "territorial integrity" of Pakistan — or India, too, for that matter — is a grisly joke. Neither country is a "nation" in any sense; both are disparate congeries of clashing ethnic, cultural, racial, and linguistic groups. Both "nations" are creatures carved out by British imperialism, Britain's last bitter legacy to the conquered nations of the subcontinent. But of these injustices, the worst and most glaring is the situation in East Pakistan (East Bengal). As we pointed out in our May, 1971 issue ("For Bengal"), the Punjabis of West Pakistan have, since the inception of this absurdly divided State, been exploiting and ruling over the far more productive Bengalis of the East. Last Spring, the Bengali crisis came to a head when the ruling oligarchy of Punjab, defeated in an election, suspended Parliament and arrested the Bengali leadership. This was the final straw that provoked the Bengali drive for autonomy and home rule into a determined movement for independence, for "Bangla Desh" (Bengal Nation). The Punjabis of the West responded by wielding the Pakistani army (totally Western) as an instrument of repression, mass torture, and literal genocide against the Bengali population, especially against the hated Hindu minority. As in all forms of counter-revolution, and counter-guerrilla warfare, genocide against the mass of the population was made necessary by the fact that the *entire* population of Bengal are opposed to the Punjabi oppressors.

Here, in Bengal, there is no clique of generals, no Communist question, to cloud the issue, as there is in Indochina; here is simply a nation of Bengalis trying to throw off an imperial Punjabi yoke. And yet, once more, the United States takes the Pakistani side; the U. S.'s deep yearnings for stability and order — for the *status quo* — and its military alliances with Pakistan, clearly come before any considerations of justice for the Bengali people.

India could have continued to serve as a base for Bengali guerrilla war and as a haven for the mass of Bengali refugees — already the staggering total of over 9 million. But India was forced to move quickly — not only from overwhelming sympathy for its Bengali brethren (West Bengal is part of India), but also because the flood of refugees has created an enormous economic problem in West Bengal, a state already impoverished and over-populated. For the inflow of refugees has already greatly lowered the West Bengali wage rate and driven up the price of food and other necessities; to return the refugees to their homes without delay, India felt forced to strike quickly. Naturally, the United States, defending the *status quo* and true to the fetish of collective security and "aggression", leaped in to try to use the UN as a club for forcing India to suspend hostilities. (With China and Russia bitterly on opposing sides, our knee-jerk anti-Communists must feel puzzled about what side to take.) Fortunately, it looks as if the Russian veto will bar UN coercion; but if not for this happenstance, the nations of the world would have been mobilized to fasten the chains upon the people of Bengal. But this was a fortuitous accident. It is high time that we cease to rely on some Great Power veto, and that we ditch the collective security myth altogether; it is high time to revive the grand old "isolationist" slogan: that we withdraw from the United Nations. ◘

"Those who expect to reap the blessings of freedom, must, like men, undergo the fatigue of supporting it." --- Thomas Paine.

Mises Festschrift

The Institute for Humane Studies (1134 Crane St., Menlo Park, Calif. 94025) is to be commended for its noble work in organizing and publishing a handsome two-volume *festschrift* in honor of the 90th birthday of the beloved Grand Old Man of economics, social philosophy, and *laissez-faire*, Ludwig von Mises. The book, *Toward Liberty*, is beautifully bound, contains the imprint of Mises' signature, and includes contributions from 67 members of the Mont Pelerin Society, an international association of free-market oriented economists and intellectuals. The contributions are photographed from the typescripts. A recent photograph of our Nestor graces the front of the book.

The most important contribution of this volume is the fact that it exists, embodying as it does a small portion of the debt and the honor that all of us owe to Professor von Mises; the book will endure as a living testament to the esteem in which all of us hold our *lieber meister*.

The contents themselves are, as is inevitable in this kind of volume, a mixed bag. Some articles hastily rephrase the author's well-known themes; many others set forth in a kind of primer fashion the functions of the market economy. Other articles are unfortunately written as if Mises' great body of work never existed: their content is either non or even implicitly anti-Misesian. There are, however, when all this said, an unusually large number of articles that contribute important and original material, and within the Misesian framework.

Let us review the outstanding articles, taking them in order of their appearance in *Toward Liberty*. (Here I must note my lack of competence in assessing the twelve articles written in a foreign language.) *Professor George A. Duncan* of the University of Dublin contributes an excellent, hard-hitting critique of modern "growth economics", "Growth Delusions." In the course of the article, Professor Duncan provides a trenchant critique of modern mathematical economics. *Professor Sven Rydenfelt* of the University of Lund, in his "Rent Control in Sweden", outlines the unfortunate consequences of rent control in creating a shortage of housing; the article is particularly welcome because historical and illustrative studies of the effects of rent control are almost non-existent.

Professor William Hutt of the University of Dallas provides us with the latest chapter in the unique and continuing saga of his one-man crusade against Keynesian economics ("Reflections on the Keynesian Episode.") *Professor Ludwig M. Lachmann* of the University of Witwatersrand, South Africa, one of the world's most subtle and high-powered members of the "Austrian School" of economics, provides a superb essay which one might wish were typical of all the contributions: an "Austrian" essay in subtle and sophisticated critique of currently orthodox "equilibrium theory." I myself think that Lachmann puts a little too much emphasis on the attack on equilibrium, which after all does provide a useful tool in explaining the *direction* in which the market economy is always moving. In going further to assert that the market does not even move in a consistent equilibrating *direction*, Professor Lachmann is following in the Hayekian rather than in the straight Misesian path. But Lachmann's "Ludwig von Mises and the Market Process" remains an outstanding contribution, and should send readers back to his totally-neglected book, *Capital and Its Structure*, an excellent contribution to the Austrian theory of capital and its intricate interrelations.

An article of comparable importance by another leading Austrian School economist is *Professor Israel M. Kirzner's* "Entrepreneurship and the Market Approach to Development." Professor Kirzner, of New York University, here develops his important battle on behalf of the Misesian, and

(Continued on page 3)

MISES FESTSCHRIFT — *(Continued from page 2)*

in criticism of the dominant Schumpeterian approach to the role of the entrepreneur. Kirzner points out that the entrepreneur is not the *disrupter* of equilibrium, the disturber of the peace as it were, but rather the person who leaps *toward* equilibrium by spotting maladjustments in the economy and taking steps to correct them. Kirzner also cogently points out the important political implications of this distinction for the underdeveloped countries.

In a rather hastily organized but fascinating article, *Professor Simon Rottenberg* of the University of Massa-chusetts provides a pro-market critique of the fashionable new book by the British socialist R. M. Titmuss, attacking the idea of the sale and purchase, rather than the free gift, of human blood. ("The Production and Exchange of Used Body Parts.") And finally, *Professor Hans F. Sennholz*, of Grove City College, in one of his best articles in years, provides an excellent and devastating critique of the now-popular Friedmanite views on money. Sennholz's "Chicago Monetary Tradition in the Light of Austrian Theory" is the best extant Austrian critique of Chicagoite monetarism. ◘

Recommended Reading

Jerome Tuccille, *Radical Libertarianism: A New Political Alternative* (Harper & Row, paper, $1.25). Jerry Tuccille's first book, still the best introduction to libertarianism and the libertarian movement, had the misfortune of coming out (1970) just too early for the boom in libertarian publicity in the spring of this year. Now it is out in inexpensive paperback, and suitable for being spread throughout the land by every "missionary" for libertarianism. Buy it! Push it!

Branden Talks! The monthly magazine *Reason* (Box 6151, Santa Barbara, Calif. 93111) has an excellent special October issue ($1.25), containing a reprint of the important Sennholz-Austrian critique of Friedmanite monetarism. It also features a lengthy, fascinating interview with Nathaniel Branden, in which Branden for the first time in print reveals much of the true inner nature of the upper strata of the Ayn Rand cult. Those of us who have been personally familiar with the Randian cult can endorse all of Branden's sharp criticisms, and welcome the putting into print of what has until now been only an oral tradition of exposure of the true nature of Randianism in action. The Rand-Branden split has had a happy effect on the development of the Objectivist movement, for it has meant that Objectivism has become "polycentric", and hence the breakup of the old Randian monolith has encouraged individual Objectivists to do something which they were never able to do under orthodox Randianism: to think for themselves. (It is typical that when a friend of ours showed a leading Orthodox Randian this issue of *Reason*, the latter expostulated: "Of course you're going to cancel your subscription!" Protect yourself from creeping heresy by never reading it!)

Paul Lepanto, *Return to Reason: An Introduction to Objectivism* (New York: Exposition Press, 154 pp. $6.00). A comprehensive introduction to objectivist philosophy, undoubtedly the best available. It is written – *mirabile dictu* – without the traditional Randian rancor against all heretics and unbelievers, actual or potential. One suspects that a major reason for Mr. Lepanto's sane approach is his statement, "I am not personally acquainted with Miss Rand or her associates, past or present; I know them only through their works." Would that other Randians had taken the same course!

Libertarian Analysis. We have a libertarian quarterly (Box 210, Village Station, New York, N. Y. 10014, $1.00 per issue, $4.00 per year), of which two issues have appeared since the first, Winter 1970 issue. Its potential excellence has been marred by its dubious fundamental premise: a close working alliance between "right-wing" and left-wing anarchism. But the result is that each issue has at least one article to be recommended. In the first issue, Murray N. Rothbard, "Individualist Anarchism in the United States: the Origins", explores the unknown history of anarchist theorists and institutions in several colonies in 17th century America. Joseph R. Peden's "Courts Against the State" is a welcome exploration of three cases in the twentieth century when private commissions of inquiry into criminal actions of States played an important role. The first such commission, the 1920-21 American Commission of Inquiry on Conditions in Ireland has been the most neglected, and is now the most timely.

In the second, Spring 1971 issue, Professor Justus Doenecke's "Lawrence Dennis: the Continuity of American Isolationism" is an excellent article by America's foremost scholar of isolationism on one of its foremost – and most consistent – leaders and theorists. And in the current, September, 1971 issue, the brilliant young libertarian historian R. Dale Grinder, in "H. L. Mencken: Notes on a Libertarian", provides a fine introduction to the work of one of the great, and certainly the wittiest, libertarians of this century.

Sacco-Vanzetti Revisionism. Francis Russell's definitive history of the Sacco-Vanzetti case, *Tragedy in Dedham* (New York: McGraw-Hill, paper, 503 pp., $3.95), is now out in paper, with a new introduction on the latest aspects of the case. Russell shows that, contrary to left-wing mythology, Sacco was guilty of murder while Vanzetti was probably an accessory. Other revisionist works are the books by Busch (1952), Montgomery (1960), and Felix (1965).

Ludwig von Mises. In celebration of Mises' 90th birthday, Murray N. Rothbard, "Ludwig von Mises and the Paradigm for Our Age," *Modern Age*, Fall 1971 (743 North Wabash Ave., Chicago, Ill. 60611), not only sets forth Mises' notable accomplishments, but provides a philosophic-sociological explanation of the general contemporary neglect of Mises and the Austrian School. Based on the seminal sociological work in the history of science by Thomas S. Kuhn.

Genetics and the IQ. There is nothing better calculated to send egalitarian leftists up the wall than any acknowledgment of the genetic, hereditary basis of intelligence. And yet, it is true – *eppur si muove*. In a critically important article, Professor Richard Herrnstein of Harvard, in "I. Q.", *Atlantic Monthly*, September, 1971, summarizes the best evidence on this controversial subject. Must reading. Herrnstein also points out that economic egalitarian measures will only leave *more* room for inequalities based on intelligence.

The Myth of the Welfare State. Several recent articles have done much to destroy the myth that the current welfare state really aids the poor and redistributes income and wealth on their behalf. Leonard Ross, "The Myth that Things are Getting Better," *New York Review of Books* (August 12), summarizes recent studies, in taxes and in higher education particularly, showing that the welfare state, in the U. S. *and* in England, does *not*, on net, take from the richer and give to the poor. Irving Kristol, "Welfare", *Atlantic Monthly*, August 1971, indicts left-wing social workers as being largely responsible for the disgraceful acceleration of the welfare rolls in recent years. Roger A. Freeman, "The Wayward Welfare State", *Modern Age* (Fall, 1971), focusses on the federal budget, the level of welfare payments as the cause of increasing welfare, and education, urban renewal and crime in the welfare state. ◘

THE POPULATION HYSTERIA

By Jerome Tuccille
(an excerpt from a forthcoming book)

The problem of overpopulation is usually the first objection raised against the prospect of extended life.

If the human race keeps procreating at its present rate, there will be only one square yard for every person by the year 2500. How can we think about permitting people to stay alive another twenty or thirty years when there are so many of us going hungry today? When we are increasing our numbers by one million a week? When there will be six or seven billion humans on this planet by the year 2000?

With the possible exception of environmental pollution, no subject has incited the ire of the Doomsday Prophets as much as the population problem. One can remember the day, back in the early 1960's, when the Machine Age Scare was the cause of apoplexy and near-hysteria in Think Tanks around the country. Apparently, we were entering an age of Creeping Mechanization which was destined to drive battalions of American blue-collar workers to the welfare rolls. By 1966, it seemed, the unemployment rate would be pushing 40 or 50 percent, and computerized robots would be prancing about the countryside doing everything from repairing faulty carburetors to boiling three-minute eggs in roadside diners. When 1966 passed into history, human automobile mechanics were still fleecing the public as though they had been tutored by John Dillinger; flesh-and-blood plumbers and electricians were moving into neighborhoods inhabited primarily by doctors, politicians and other racketeers; hash slingers across the nation had been unionized and commanded wages that turned insurance executives green with envy. The machines, far from putting the American workforce on relief, had created entire new industries and thousands of jobs that *never existed before.*

A few years later the American public was treated to the next in a never-ending series of globe-shattering crises: the Famine Scare of 1967. In this year the brothers Paddock, Paul and William, warned us in their highly-acclaimed book, *Famine — 1975,* that India was doomed to be ravaged by large-scale famines. The famines would occur possibly as early as 1970 or 1971, definitely by 1972 or 1973, and most of its population would be decimated by 1975. The Paddocks promoted a "triage" system to save the world, a system used in military hospitals during wartime in which only those patients with some chance of survival are given medical treatment. They advocated that the United States, as the most productive country on earth, initiate massive foreign aid programs to those starving nations with a small chance of survival, and cut out foreign aid altogether to undeveloped nations, like India. for whom starvation was inevitable. Fortunately for India several private foundations ignored the advice of the Paddocks, and as a result India was able to develop a hardier wheat strain leading to a bumper crop in 1970. Now we anticipate that — barring some unforeseen cataclysm such as earthquakes or major war — India will be self-sufficient in food production early in this decade. The Paddocks made some other ominous predictions — among them: experimentation with rice and wheat strains would end in failure, and Pakistan would be wasted by famine before 1972. Statistics show that the development of hybrid rice and wheat strains enabled Pakistan to talk about exporting wheat in 1971, prior to the resurgence of its political disputes with East Pakistan and India. 1971 United Nations figures indicate that food production in the Far East — another area condemned to annihilation by the Paddocks — was "rising at a rate comfortably ahead of the population growth" because of the development of high-yield rice and wheat strains.

Another Doomsday Prophet, Dr. Paul R. Ehrlich, Professor of Biology at Stanford University, informed us in

(Continued on page 5)

Libertarian Conference

The libertarian conference held in New York City on the weekend of November 13-14 was by far the most successful libertarian conference ever held, at least on the East Coast. It was a striking success not simply because it drew the largest audience yet for East Coast libertarians — over 400 persons. And not just because it was capably and smoothly organized by the New York Libertarian Association and the Society for Individual Liberty. For here was a deeper success story that struck everyone attending the conference. This was the harmony of views and attitudes that pervaded all factions gathered there. For in striking and dramatic contrast to the fiasco at the Hotel Diplomat on Columbus Day 1969, and even in visible contrast to the successful conference held last March, there was no brawling and clashing of factions, no marked hostility or mutual excommunications. While of course there are still marked differences between the various groups and tendencies in the movement, the various extremes have clearly drawn closer together. This drawing together enables all the factions to work harmoniously, not in an artificial "unity" that tries to paper over severe disagreement, but in a genuine harmony of common interest and enthusiasm. To borrow the Marxian phrasing, what were previously "antagonistic contradictions" within the libertarian movement have happily given way to "non-antagonistic contradictions." The libertarian movement is now united as never before.

What has happened is that a new maturity, a new sense of responsibility, has now permeated all factions of the movement, at least on the East Coast. The wild-eyed extremes, both on the left and on the right, have both moved sharply toward the sober and responsible Center. Specifically, the febrile *militantes* of the ultra-left have abandoned their shrill cries to "rip off Amerika", their yen for street warfare, and their enthusiasm for anarcho-communism and anarcho-syndicalism. The left-wing has come to a new and sober appreciation of the virtues of Middle America and the middle class, and seems to have found once more at least some of its old devotion to private property and the free market. For their part, the right-wing "deviationists" have learned a great deal about the Establishment and about foreign policy; they seem to have lost most of their old enthusiasm for the Cold War, for red-baiting, and for the Founding Fathers. At the November conference, when Professors Leonard Liggio and Walter Grinder set forth their pro-isolationist, anti-imperialist, and anti-ruling elite analysis, the former hostility of th ght-wing was replaced by a kind of resigned accepta . The Sober Center, firmly pro-private property *and* anti-imperialist, which for a long time seemed to its despairing members. to consist of twelve people trying to cope with ten thousand "deviationists" on their far left and right, has apparently triumphed at last.

And so there is reason to be more optimistic about the future of the movement than ever before. Our growing pains seem to be over. The quantitative leap forward in the last two years has at last been matched by a new accession of maturity and responsibility. We advance into the future with high hope.

THE POPULATION HYSTERIA — *(Continued from page 4)*

1969 that it was utopian to expect underwater agriculture to lead to increased food production in the near future. Farming of the sea is "another myth promoted by the ignorant or the irresponsible," according to Dr. Ehrlich. Yet, the facts show that advances in marine agriculture have played a decisive role in the increase in food production throughout Asia in 1970 – a year after Ehrlich's dire prediction.

Next we arrived at a point in time when we might normally expect a new crisis of monumental proportions to erupt on the American scene, and the experts have not disappointed us; not many take global famine seriously any longer, but overpopulation and environmental pollution are the twin juggernauts destined to destroy life on earth forevermore. Dr. Ehrlich is back again with *The Population Bomb*, predictably predicting that, not only are "hundreds of millions of people going to starve to death in spite of any crash foreign aid programs," but also that nothing now can "prevent a substantial increase in the world deathrate . . ." From this he goes on to tell us that seven billion people will inhabit our little ball by 2000 AD, and by 2800 AD the population of earth will be housed in a *two-thousand storey apartment house* *that covers the entire planet* no less. The author, having already determined that the battle against famine was lost and that world-wide famines would grip the earth by the early 1970's does not tell us how we will manage to survive until 2800 AD in sufficient numbers to fill a high-rise dwelling of such mammoth dimensions.

In the late 1960's, when Madan G. Kaul, Minister of the Indian Embassy, predicted that his country would be self-sufficient in food production by 1971, Dr. Ehrlich dismissed him as a utopian dreamer, claiming that he had yet to meet anyone as optimistic as Kaul. But, as mentioned earlier, India is on the brink of self-sufficiency. When India launched a vasectomy program in 1964 to control population growth, Ehrlich stated that this was also doomed to failure due to the reluctance of the citizenry and the technical problems involved in performing so many. Yet, a New York Times article in October, 1971, informs us that the turnout for voluntary vasectomies has far exceeded expectations, and new vasectomy camps are planned for all of India's 320 districts. The Indian government had originally distributed condoms to the male population, but later discovered that they weren't being used properly. Accordingly, vasectomies are now regarded as a safer alternative.

Dr. Ehrlich presents us with several scenarios for the years ahead guaranteed to titallate the fancies of necrophilec the world over. They range in scope from the destruction of the entire population of earth, with cockroaches as the planet's only survivors, to his most "optimistic" outlook in which only 500 million people will have starved to death by 1980. Even the United States, the world's only remaining hope, is doing next to nothing to reduce its own birthrate – merely "bailing out a sinking ship with a small and leaky thimble" is the way he puts it. This last is somewhat at variance with most recent statistics on the subject, showing that U.S. fertility rate in summer of 1971 had dropped to its lowest level since the late 1930's, and the trend is ever-downward. The present figure is just slightly above the "optimum" level set by the advocates of Z. P. G. (Zero Population Growth). Moreover, the results of a study released in October, 1971, reveal that half the American population now favors liberalized abortion laws, an incredible jump from the 15 percent of 1968. Ehrlich concludes by criticizing our growing concern for *organ transplants* and *life extension* techniques at a time when the human race is tottering over the abyss, and he recommends governmental remedies that border on totalitarianism: prohibitive taxes on cribs, diapers, toys and other baby items; reverse progressive taxation rising for each

birth; government-authorized vasectomies; nationalized adoption agencies; and, *piece de resistance*, a powerful federal agency authorized to take *whatever steps are necessary* to establish a "reasonable population level" in the United States. The only thing he leaves out is Jonathan Swift's Modest Proposal that we eat unwanted children. He suggests that we lower the population of earth to one or two billion from the current level of 3.5 or 3.6 billions of human beings.

Compared with Dr. Ehrlich, Philip Appleman, another population alarmist who authorized *The Silent Explosion*, is a veritable Pollyanna. While he claims that his projected world population of six billion for the year 2000 is more than we can properly feed, he at least refrains from predicting the certain demise of civilization by that time. He makes some incisive attacks on both the Catholic Church and the Communist Party for shaping the attitudes of their respective constituencies against the entire concept of planned parenthood. Marxist ideology, says Appleman, defines socialism as an economic system capable of providing abundance for everyone on earth. By *definition* there is no such thing as overpopulation in a communist society. Numbers are irrelevant.

The Catholic Church, of course, has not only opposed birth control for its own adherents, but it has traditionally fought to impose its own morality on the general population through the legislative process. It has taken the attitude that it is the duty of every Catholic mother to bear as many children as nature will allow, and the moral obligation of the "have" nations of the world to feed them all. "The Roman Catholic Church," according to Appleman, "is the only Western institution of any importance that is consciously and actively obstructing population limitation."

In both cases, however, Appleman concedes that there is ground for optimism. Despite ideology, there is good evidence that Communist China is concerned about burgeoning population and is taking measures to control it behind the scenes. Author Edgar Snow reports that Party functionaries receive no extra compensation for more than two children; contraceptives are widely available and extremely inexpensive; practice, both in Red China and in the Soviet Union, is in *dialectical opposition* to Marxist propaganda. As far as the Catholic Church is concerned, the clergy as well as the "faithful" are in open revolt. Progressive Catholic journals such as *Commonweal* have been leading much of the fight, exhorting their readers to re-evaluate traditional Church teachings on papal infallibility, celibacy for the priesthood, and the birth control issue. *America*, another Catholic publication which used to editorialize against "unilateral depopulation in the West" lest we all "find ourselves eating with chopsticks," has grown less belligerent of late. Ironically enough, Roman Catholics are declining in proportion to the overall population, partly because of defections from their own ranks, partly because of their opposition to birth control for non-Catholics as well as themselves. The Catholic Church at various times throughout its history has violently opposed surgery, inoculation, lending money on interest, eating meat on Fridays, belief in a heliocentric solar system, reading certain books and watching certain films, and, of course, family planning. This last prohibition, one can safely predict, is destined to go the way of the others.

Another cause for carefully guarded optimism, according to Appleman, is the decline of militarism among the young. For centuries our generals have been yelling for larger and larger populations, presumably to supply them with fodder for their armies. Presently, the "More People, More Power" mentality has been all but discredited in the more advanced countries at least. Latin American machismo which measures a man's masculinity by the size of his progeny is

(Continued on page 6)

THE POPULATION HYSTERIA — *(Continued from page 5)*

also in a state of rising disrepute. Religious traditions at work in other parts of the world (India, for example, has approximately one-fourth of the world's cattle supply, but refuses to slaughter it for meat because most of the population holds the cow to be a sacred animal) will be challenged with increasing literacy and education of the masses.

On the other end of the spectrum we have the Utopian Futurists who dismiss all concern over rising population with the same casual optimism they exhibit on the Clonal Hitler Scare. "Don't worry about it. We'll work it out somehow." Arthur McCormack, a Catholic priest who takes a "middle-of-the-road" position on the population issue, has little patience with extreme optimists who claim that "as long as man possesses the capacity for thought, he has no reason to fear the future."

R. Buckminster Fuller, one of the great visionaries of the twentieth century, has earned the everlasting enmity of Z. P. G. enthusiasts by claiming that he could take the entire population of earth today and provide everyone with decent housing and adequate privacy on the islands of Japan. His plan calls for the erection of a gigantic, mile-high apartment complex, with each unit self-contained for power and sewage and a recycled water supply, and capable of being separated from the complex and used as a vehicle for transportation. In one fell swoop he solves the housing shortage and the parking problem, as well as pollution of the environment. Those who are inclined to shrug off this proposal with a laugh might do well to recall that Fuller's dymaxion houses and geodesic domes were once roundly denounced as "impractical" and hopelessly "utopian," and his theories on the tetrahedronal structure of matter have made a profound impact in the field of sub-atomic physics. Fuller started to talk about building homes with self-contained electricity and recycled water supplies in 1928, thirty years before this concept became a reality in American and Russian space capsules. According to Fuller, there is virtually no limit to the amount of people that can be comfortably supported on earth with proper architectural and recycling techniques. Whether or not one looks forward to sharing the planet with a trillion human beings tiered on top of one another, however privately, in cities reaching to the stars, we cannot help but admire a man with the courage to propose such daring schemes at a time when technology and procreation have become synonomous with racistsexistfascistkapitalistexploitation.

Another unbridled Utopian is Iranian-born novelist and essayist, F. M. Esfandiary, who teaches a course on futurism at the New School for Social Research in New York City. The highlights of Esfandiary's course are his lectures on physical immortality and the New Technology. He has been called a "radical optimist" by *Publisher's Weekly*, and his theories have been simultaneously endorsed by Dr. Glenn Seaborg, former Chairman of the U.S. Atomic Energy Commission, and a reviewer for the *Village Voice*. Esfandiary casually discusses such concepts as universal solar and nuclear power and colonization of the planets as though they have virtually been accomplished, and Doomsday predictions are rejected impatiently. He maintains that the human race advanced a half step through-out history until the beginning of the twentieth century, and fifty miles during the past seventy years or so. He charts our present rate of development on a hyperbolic curve quickly accelerating upward toward infinity, and says that no one can fully anticipate the changes that will occur in the next twenty years let alone the next one hundred. Esfandiary considers pessimism to be a result of a lack of historical perspective, an inability to comprehend the fact that forty years ago people spent most of their waking hours scrubbing out a bare existence while, today, technology has freed a large portion of western civilization from the drudgery of menial labor. Having spent his earliest years growing up in Iran, Esfandiary makes the statement — "I have seen the past, and it doesn't work" — as he awaits the future with optimism.

Other visionaries have taken the position that there is

(Continued on page 7)

THE POPULATION HYSTERIA — *(Continued from page 6)*

no need to worry about overpopulation because, with proper technology, the state of Kansas can produce enough food to feed the entire world; there are more open spaces on earth today than a hundred years ago (latest census figures in the U.S. show that both the countryside and the central cities have lost population to the suburbs, resulting in a pattern of more abundant natural land and more even distribution of people around our urban areas); the earth can easily support upwards of 500 billion people; if we gave every family alive today a decent housing plot, they would all fit inside Texas with room to spare; ground fish and other marine products offer a revolutionary breakthrough in the struggle to create a high-protein, low-cost food supply; there is more than enough timber in the Amazon jungle to build a house for every family on earth; when India decides to slaughter its cattle, it will become a major exporter of beef to the developing nations; arid and frozen lands can now be brought under cultivation for the first time. These statements are denounced in the most excoriating language by Messers. Paddock, Appleman, Ehrlich and other Doomsday Prophets, and they are given a fair hearing by middle-of-the-road population alarmists like the priest and author, Arthur McCormack.

Behind most of the hysteria surrounding the rising population of earth is the spectre of the Rev. Thomas Robert Malthus who, back in 1798, presented the world with his now-famous dictum. The Malthusian Absolute holds that population growth increases geometrically, while growth in food production increases arithmetically. If this is true, it follows that any increase in population anywhere on earth is bound to result in dwindling food supplies, hunger and starvation.

It is somewhat incredible that this formula is still taken seriously when it was at least partially discredited in Malthus' own lifetime. Neo-Malthusians invariably fail to tell us that the good reverend qualified his own "Absolute" in 1817 when he admitted that some population growth can be beneficial until the time when a "proper or natural limit" is reached. While Malthus lived out his final years, England, his native land, increased its own population fivefold through immigration, rising birthrate and declining infant mortality while *at the same time* enjoying a period of economic growth and prosperity during the Industrial Revolution. The United States, again experiencing rising affluence and economic prosperity, increased its population tenfold during the nineteenth century. Both England and the United States became major exporters of food while simultaneously importing labor and assimilating more and more people. In modern times, the island-city of Hong Kong had the fastest population growth on earth during the 1960's - primarily due to mass emigration from mainland China - and it has become a bustling focal point of market activities in the Orient. Conversely, Ireland and Sicily have been losing people steadily from the beginning of the century until the present, and they are among the poorest countries in the West.

Doomsday Prophets usually cite China as an example of what can happen economically to a nation with too many mouths to feed. What they leave out is the fact that China, with its 800 millions or so, has a population density of only 200 per square mile - roughly a *third* that of England and a *fifth* that of Holland which is importing labor from southern Europe to keep pace with a constantly rising living standard. Breakthroughs in marine agriculture and hardier wheat and rice strains have enabled much of the Far East to keep food production roughly 3 percent ahead of population growth in recent years. In addition, freer trade policies with countries like China are bound to result in an expansion of their sluggish

economies, and a concomitant liberalization of domestic political rule as they open their borders to other countries of the world.

Another favorite bogeyman theory of the population alarmists is the Spreading Desert Scare. Poor cultivation methods of the past have turned much of the earth into desert, with 17 percent of it now arid and another sizable chunk too frost-covered to farm. The theory holds that poor farming techniques still being used will increase the amount of land unusable by man in the future. But here again we learn from U. N. statistics that most increases in food production during the past thirty years have been accomplished on land already under cultivation; in the United States, for instance, 75 percent *more* corn is being grown on 27 percent *less* land than was used in 1938. A new variety of rice developed in Taiwan has six or seven times the yield of the old kind, and is more resistant to adverse weather conditions. Arthur McCormack tells us that the arable land of the world can be doubled easily with present methods, and with heavy expenditures of capital and new techniques it can be increased eightfold if it should ever become necessary.

As new machinery is brought onto the farms, children are less in demand as extra hands and, instead, become a drain on parents whose rising affluence is independent of manual labor. As we study the history of the industrialized nations, we learn that a general pattern has developed: rising industrialization and affluence results in a leveling off and then a decline in the birthrate. It makes far better sense, then, for proponents of Z. P. G. and other population alarmists to support industrialization rather than oppose it, as many of them have done with their call for a "return to nature."

A case in point is the hullabaloo over the use of insecticides that gripped the nation in the middle 1960's, and is still with us today. While concern that pesticides eventually find their way into human bodies is justified, pesticide abolitionists have overlooked the fact that some 33 million tons of food a year - enough to feed more than 500 million people - are destroyed by rats and insects. It is a bit irresponsible for people who are worried about food production to take such an extremist position before thay investigate alternatives to the indiscriminate use of DDT. Many of these same individuals have also opposed the development of processed marine products, a low-cost protein source, with the argument that ground fish heads and organs are "unpalatable". Yet they rail against the fact that the starch content in the American diet is only 25 percent while it climbs over 50 percent in Africa, Asia and South America.

Turning again to the United Nations - an organization which no one has ever accused of trying to whitewash the existing poverty in the world - we learn that the problem is largely one of "undernourishment" rather than mass starvation. 14 percent of earth's population is said to be undernourished - that is, subsisting on unbalanced diets usually heavy with starch - a different thing entirely from "starvation in the streets." Yet, when an enterprising American firm tried to export a low-cost protein supplement made from marine products, the federal government banned it from the market on the grounds that it was "unsuitable for human consumption." Presumably, the authorities with their boundless humanitarianism preferred that everyone on earth should have a pound of steak each week instead, but, unfortunately for the "Third World" people, there is precious little protein content in the good intentions of "humane" politicians.

In 1950 Julian Huxley warned the world that there would be three billion people on earth by 2000 AD, more than this tiny globe could possibly support. His crystal ball must have been slightly cracked the day he wrote that article, for

(Continued on page 8)

259

THE POPULATION HYSTERIA — *(Continued from page 7)*

the figure was reached in the 1960's — almost forty years ahead of schedule — and the general living standard of man on earth has continued to rise with each passing year. U.N. estimates for the year 2000 are for somewhere between 5.4 and 7.5 billion people to be romping about the earth. Dr. Ehrlich states that, unless we reduce our numbers to one or two billion, we will all be starving in the streets; R. Buckminster Fuller maintains there is no limit to what man, with his incredible ingenuity, can achieve.

Who is right?

Arthur McCormack, taking his stand with the moderates, says that 50 billion people seems to be the limit considering the habitable land now available, and the possibility that some desert and frost regions will be cultivated in the future. This figure, at the current rate of population growth, will be reached in 2110 AD. Others, a bit less optimistic, put the limit at 30 billion which would be attained in a hundred years at out present rate of growth.

The key questions it seems to me are, first of all, is there any such thing as a "natural limit" to human population on earth and, second, is it realistic to base projections on the current rate of growth? If it is true, as precedent has shown it to be, that industrialization leads to declining birthrate, and that virtually the entire planet will be industrialized within the next twenty-five years, then we can expect a sharply reduced birthrate for the whole world before the year 2000. Z.P.G. advocates have been quick to inform us that the rate of growth is a relative factor — that is, it is based on the ratio between the birthrate *and* the deathrate — and that, if man should finally succeed in conquering death, it will mean that the human race would have to stop reproducing altogether merely to maintain a steady level. But if the day arrives when the human race does attain mastery over natural death, we will still be exposed to the dangers of the unforeseen: the speeding vehicle; a falling rock; environmental disasters. Some of us will elect, for religious, philosophical or psychological reasons, to pass away normally rather than prolong physical life. People will continue to die even if we have the means of preserving life indefinitely, so it does not follow that any procreation at all will necessarily mean a rise in population.

Another item the Doomsday Prophets never consider is the fact that two-thirds of this planet is covered by water, and the "square yard for every human" projections are invariably based on figures for land mass. We are now talking about building jetports at sea, and once this is done the construction of hotels, shops and permanent communities around the jetports will follow inevitably. Donald H El-

liott, director of the New York City Planning Commission, talks about the development of a gigantic offshore complex that will include a jetport, nuclear power plant, waste-disposal center and deep-water seaport. He maintains that the technical problems have already been solved. In Holland a variation of this concept has been realized in the form of "Polders" — area reclaimed from the sea housing more than seven million Hollanders. Cleveland and Chicago are studying proposals for floating jetports and facilities supported on caissons in Lake Erie and Lake Michigan. Cost studies indicate that the sale of land-based airports to private developers could raise much of the money required for the projects. Eventually, the notion of floating cities further out to sea will become a reality. Environmentalists like to howl about the "desecration of the oceans" when these alternatives are suggested, yet they are the first ones to decry the lack of beachfront areas for the masses. Seaborne cities will solve the problem of *lebensraum* for future populations, and they will also create thousands of miles of man-made "coastline" for surfers and sunbathers throughout the world. International communities for those tired of life in belligerent nation-states should be a more-than-welcome change.

Surely by the time we have the technology to eliminate natural death as a threat to man, the problems of interplanetary travel and the "homesteading" of space will be small in comparison. No one today can seriously doubt that there will be some form of human settlements on the moon before the end of this century; villages on other planets will be established shortly afterward. Until that day arrives, the human birthrate will continue to decline through education further industrialization and technological advances.

The prospect of overpopulation should not be taken seriously as an argument against our efforts to make man immortal. Chances are good that the timber of the Amazon is not going to be merchandised to house the entire world, and Kansas is not going to be called upon to feed it. Even if Buckminster Fuller's schemes for supporting a limitless population should turn out to be practicable, most likely it will never be necessary for the human race to cluster together in mile-high file cabinets. We all have a vested interest in keeping the place we live from becoming as crowded as an anthill. Present trends continuing, the birthrate will continue to decline in the advanced nations, and this decline will spread to other areas as they become industrialized. Through cloning and modernized farming techniques we will be able to lay the Malthusian Absolute forever to rest. And the technology that enables us to minimize the risks of death will also provide us with the means to live our lives in comfort and prosperity. ◻

A Monthly Newsletter

THE
Libertarian Forum

Joseph R. Peden, Publisher

Murray N. Rothbard, Editor

VOLUME IV, NO. 1   January, 1972   75c

POLITICS '72

1972 — the year of the great quadrennial circus and extravaganza, the one year out of every four when the American public is most attentive to politics, if not to political issues. Where should libertarians stand on the 1972 election?

Already, it is evident that libertarians will be roughly divided into two camps on their attitudes toward the 1972 campaign. One camp, perhaps the majority, takes the purist *non-voting* position: the view that all politicians and parties are evil, the State is evil, and that for any libertarian to vote is to lend his moral sanction to the electoral process and therefore to the State apparatus which rides to power on the strength of that process. The only moral course for the libertarian, this position holds, is therefore not to vote and to promulgate non-voting among the population. The latest manifestation of the non-voting camp is the newly formed League of Non-Voters (Box 1406, Santa Ana, Calif. 92702), organized by Sy Leon and other libertarians in Southern California.

Non-voting — or "voting for oneself" — is the classic anarchist position, and no libertarian can be unsympathetic to an organized drive for non-participation in elections. This is especially true if we consider that all politicians of whatever party are constantly exhorting the electorate: "We don't care *how* you vote, but vote!", which obviously means that they care deeply about being able to claim a "mandate" from a large turnout of voters. A small turnout would deflate any such claim.

Yet there are flaws and dangers in this simplistic non-voting stance. The chief danger is that the moral sanction argument is the *other side of the coin* of the statist argument for the legitimacy of democratic government: that *since* X millions have voted for President or Senator so-and-so, *this means* that these rulers have broad popular support, or even that their rule is "voluntary", and sanctioned by the public. It is precisely this argument that has formed the chief stumbling-block for libertarians in arguing against government action under a democracy.

In arguing against voting as a moral sanction we need only turn to the Founding Father of pure libertarianism, Lysander Spooner. Spooner built a large part of his individualist anarchist position on refuting the notion that voting necessarily means support. Thus Spooner:

"In truth, in the case of individuals, their actual voting is not to be taken as proof of consent, even for the time being. On the contrary, it is to be considered that, without his consent having ever been asked, a man finds himself environed by a government that he cannot resist; a government that forces him to pay money,

render service, and forego the exercise of many of his natural rights, under peril of weighty punishments. He sees, too, that other men practice this tyranny over him by the use of the ballot. He sees further that, if he will but use the ballot himself, he has some chance of relieving himself from this tyranny of others, by subjecting them to his own. In short, he finds himself, without his consent, so situated that, if he use the ballot, he may become a master; if he does not use it, he must become a slave. And he has no other alternative than these two. In self-defense, he attempts the former. His case is analogous to that of a man who has been forced into battle, where he must either kill others, or be killed himself. Because, to save his own life in battle, a man attempts to take the lives of his opponents, it is not to be inferred that the battle is one of his own choosing. Neither in contests with the ballot — which is a mere substitute for a bullet — because, as his only chance of self-preservation, a man uses a ballot, is it to be inferred that the contest is one into which he voluntarily entered; that he voluntarily set up all his own natural rights, as a stake against those of others, to be lost or won by the mere power of numbers. On the contrary, it is to be considered that, in an exigency, into which he had been forced by others, and in which no other means of self-defense offered, he, as a matter of necessity, used the only one that was left to him."

Doubtless the most miserable of men, under the most oppressive government in the world, if allowed the ballot, would use it, if they could see any chance of thereby ameliorating their condition. But it would not therefore be a legitimate inference that the government itself, that crushes them, was one which they had voluntarily set up, or ever consented to."

(Lysander Spooner, "No Treason, No. II", pp. 5-6, in *The Collected Works of Lysander Spooner* (Weston, Mass.: M & S Press, 1971, Volume I).

In short, if the rulers allow us to make this *one* choice, as petty and miserable as it may be, this one say over our political lives, it is not immoral to make use of this opportunity. As I wrote somewhere else, if Richard Cobden and Ghenghis Khan were running against each other for President, the libertarian would surely have no hesitation supporting and voting for Cobden, despite his falling short of full purity. But if that is so, then the fact that we have no Cobdens, alas!, running now is only a matter of degree; it is still not immoral to use the electoral process when a significant choice presents itself. The use of the electoral

(Continued on page 2)

POLITICS '72 — *(Continued from page 1)*

process is not, then, immoral *per se,* as the non-voting camp would have us believe.

A second error is that the non-voters misconstrue the nature of our problem. The major problem is not whether or not we should vote; the major problem is that, regardless of what we do, the office of the Presidency and other political offices will not, unfortunately, be declared vacant. Regardless of what we do, there will be a President, 100 Senators, etc., come 1973. In that case, what attitude do we take on the question of who occupies these offices? Even if we do not vote ourselves this November, whom do we hope that *others* will vote for? When the ballots begin to trickle in, whom do we cheer for, or whom do we cheer *against,* on Election Night? To argue against voting is not the same thing as arguing that, in public or even in our hearts, we must be completely and totally indifferent to the outcome of the election. Why? What possible moral position holds that we must be neutral in word and deed? Come Election Night, perhaps even Mr. Leon and his colleagues will, in the quiet of their living-rooms, be silently cheering for one rather than the other candidate. If *not,* then they must hold that both candidates are, and must forever be, completely identical, so that there will be literally no difference in the outcome. But since we know from the nature of man that no two people or parties can ever be *totally* identical, that there is always *some* diversity however marginal, it then follows that the idea that there is literally *no* difference between the candidates is a fallacious construction of the nature of man. There is, then, always a difference of sorts; Cobden we would clearly choose over Ghenghis Khan; what then of 1972? We must therefore discard the *a priori* indifferentist position, and begin to examine the parties and candidates to see if the differences are sufficient to merit our taking a stand. And, again, the important question here is not whom we vote for, but whom we support or oppose.

This brings us to the real world of 1972, and it brings us also to the other major libertarian camp for this year: the camp that says – DUMP NIXON! The *Lib. Forum* has repeatedly called for the dumping of Mr. Nixon, most recently in the July-August 1971 issue ("Dumping Nixon"), and Mr. Nixon's record is even more monstrous now than it was last summer.

In the first place, other things being equal (which, granted, they rarely are), the libertarian always favors the dumping of an incumbent President and party. If Mr. Nixon and his opponent were simply Mr. X and Y, alike as two peas in a pod, then the libertarian would favor the dumping of the incumbent X. For two reasons: one, because it is always best to overthrow any entrenched machine or President, lest their entrenchment sink ever deeper into society. And two, to punish – to punish the incumbent for the inevitable transgressions and invasions of rights during his term of office.

For the libertarian, then, any incumbent begins his campaign with one strike against him, even if he were simply Mr. X. But Richard Nixon is not simply Mr. X, not just another holder of the Presidential chair; he has compiled a record of malignity on every front, foreign and domestic, that has not been matched since the days of Franklin Rossevelt. Since our last catalog of Nixonite horrors last summer, the President has enormously accelerated the gravity of his sins. The wage-price freeze, suddenly brought to us over television on the night of August 15, catapulted America into the full-fledged economy of fascism, with its panoply of tripartite economic controls under the direction of an all-powerful Executive. The first establishment of peacetime price-wage controls since the unconstitutional NRA of the New Deal, Mr. Nixon's New Economic Policy was by far the biggest single leap into statism since the days of Franklin D. Roosevelt. The displacement of the mar-

ket by central controls through Presidential fiat was accompanied by an equally drastic, and even more savage, repudiation of the dollar's backing in gold, thereby threatening a world-wide depression as a result of international monetary and economic warfare. The re-establishment of fixed exchange rates and the slight devaluation of the dollar in December, has restored some health to the international money market, but the resolution is clearly temporary, since neither the fixity nor the devaluation make any sense while the currencies remain in no way redeemable in gold. Again, President Nixon has aped FDR in his plunge into totally fiat money; the difference being that, after 1934, FDR at least continued to redeem foreign-held dollars in gold; this last shred of soundness in the world's monetary system has not been torn away.

On the crucially important foreign policy front, the *Libertarian Forum* and its editors have been virtually alone, year in and year out, in proclaiming that the Vietnam and Indochina war has *not* been about to "wind down." Even the most ardently anti-imperialist forces on the Left have been completely fooled twice: once, after Lyndon Johnson's retirement and the opening of the Paris peace talks; and next, after the inauguration of Mr. Nixon's "Vietnamization" policy, aided and abetted by Nixon's grandstand announcement of his trip to China. The recent resumption of large-scale bombing of North Vietnam should at last make it crystal-clear that the war in Indochina is *not* over – and that Mr. Nixon has simply been returning to Johnson's discredited policy of pre-1965: that is, providing financial and air support, plus "residual" artillery and other support, while our Indochinese puppet troops absorb the brunt of the fighting on the ground. In short, "Vietnamization", or rather, "Indochinization".

Nixon's seemingly cunning policy was to draw the teeth of American protest by eliminating American ground casualties, and foisting them on the Indochinese, while confining our military action to increasingly devastating bombing of the NLF forces in South Vietnam – thereby avoiding the more spectacular and less politically palatable bombing of the North. That crafty policy – to continue the war while quieting American interest in the proceedings – has now been smashed on the rock that Nixon and his predecessors have always overlooked: the total lack of support for our puppets among the Indochinese population. In particular, the American puppet forces in Cambodia and Laos are on the brink of total defeat. In Cambodia, they virtually hold only Phnom Penh, the capital, and their hold on *that* is increasingly shaky; the rest of the country belongs to the Communist-led National United Front. Nixon's unpopular and disastrous invasion of Cambodia in 1969 has led only to the total defeat of the American puppet forces in that country. Similarly, the even more disastrous American invasion of Laos, an invasion which was ambushed and routed by the North Vietnamese-Pathet Lao forces, has led only to the recent resounding successes for the Pathet Lao in the most strategic areas of Laos: the total conquest of the Plain of Jars and the Boloven plateau. Particularly important here was the conquest of the Plain of Jars in late December, including the wiping out of no less than seven battalions of American-sponsored Thai troops and the severe crippling of three more; and the wiping out of four battalions of CIA-trained Vang Pao mercenaries and the crippling of six more. The American skein has about run out in Laos and Cambodia – and this at only the beginning of the Communist-led offensive of the 1971-72 dry season. In desperation, Richard Nixon turned to the only tactic he knows: punishing the innocent civilians of North Vietnam by mass terror bombing. Nixon hopes that such massive bombings will somehow induce the Communist forces to suspend their operations throughout Indochina, but he will fail just as surely as

(Continued on page 3)

POLITICS '72 — *(Continued from page 2)*

as the similarly aimed Johnson-McNamara bombings failed before.

Richard Nixon came to the White House after making crucial promises to the American people: he promised us an end to the war in Vietnam, an end to the draft, prosperity without inflation, a sound fiscal policy, and the preservation of the free market economy. He promised us bread, and he has given us a stone. The war in Indochina goes on, indeed was further expanded into Laos and Cambodia; the draft goes on, with the Kennedy-style lottery put in to allay protest; and we have a long-drawn-out Nixon recession wedded to a continuing high rate of inflation. We have the greatest peace-time deficits in American history and instead of preserving the free economy President Nixon has buried it in an avalanche of wage-price controls. Looming ahead of us we have two cherished plans of the Nixon Administration: a disastrous guaranteed annual income scheme (the Family Assistance Program), and socialized medicine through national health insurance. All this, and also a large increase in executive power and dictation, and Supreme Court appointments who can be counted on to erode and reverse the hard-won civil liberties gains of the Warren Court. All in all, the greatest single leap into collectivism since FDR.

There can be only one reaction of libertarians to the grisly Nixon record: punish, punish, punish. Get him out of office! Retire him to the private life which he so richly deserves.

There is only arrow left to the bow of the libertarian opponent of the Dump-Nixon strategy: might not the Democrat be even worse? He would have to be considerably worse to have us abandon the joy of defeating Richard Nixon, though I concede that that would be logically possible. But in fact any likely Democrat on the horizon is bound to be considerably better. Let us take the vital areas. On the Indochina War, we can expect that any Democrat (except for Jackson and possibly Humphrey) will end the war in short order. On the draft, we have a far better chance for abolition, and certainly for amnesty to draft resisters, with any Democrat (except Jackson) than with our supposedly anti-draft President. On civil liberties, any of the Democrats (except Jackson) will be far superior to Nixon. But what about the economy, it may be asked? What indeed? Considering Nixon's fascist record, it is hardly possible for any of the Democrats to do worse. *Particularly* when we consider the vital strategic fact that no Democratic President would have been able to drum so many statist measures through a rather conservative Congress. If Muskie or McGovern had been President this year, any price controls would have faced a chorus of opposition and would have been rendered unworkable very quickly; and neither man would have as much chance as Nixon to push through FAP or national health insurance. The one area that conservative Republicans have been fairly good on over the years has been government interference in the economy; but their opposition has been totally neutralized by the fact that their "conservative" President, using their own rhetoric and from their own party, has been driving through the collectivist legislation. Only removal of Nixon from office will enable the conservative Republicans to rouse themselves, and once again provide some opposition to socialistic measures by the Executive. Thus, even in the area of the seemingly strongest case for Nixon over a Democrat, we find that absolutely indispensable to the rebirth of a conservative opposition to galloping socialism is the defeat of Richard M. Nixon. Only the nomination of Scoop Jackson by the Democrats would seriously vitiate this argument of "anyone but Nixon."

One of the most heartening political developments of recent months is the recognition by many conservative militants of the strategic necessity of defeating Richard Nixon. Rep. John Ashbrook (R., Ohio) has courageously

decided to enter several early primaries against the President, backed by most of the conservative theorists and organizers, including YAF and the American Conservative Union, *National Review* and *Human Events*. The more votes that Ashbrook rolls up in the primaries, the more embarrassing for the President, and the greater the possibility of a really significant conservative rebellion against Nixon: the running of Ashbrook for President on a "fifth party" ticket. The hurting of Nixon in the primaries will be only symbolic and psychological; it is the running of an independent Ashbrook in selected key states with a large conservative constituency (e.g. Ohio, Illinois, California, Pennsylvania) that could wreck the President's bid for another term. Many of these states are usually so close that a candidate hiving off 10-15% of the conservative vote from Nixon could submarine the President.

The danger is that Ashbrook and the fifth party might be bought off with a few militaristic concessions — since unfortunately the agitation of the conservatives is not so much over price-wage controls or FAP as it is over the China trip and the conservative call for even more expenditure on overkill missiles. But if the conservatives are mad enough and can stay mad, and if Ashbrook builds up considerable support in the primaries, then an independent conservative candidacy could perform the much reviled but generally necessary role of the "spoiler".

All this means that what happens in the Democratic convention becomes of primary political importance to the libertarian. His major goal here is to see to it that the Democrats do not nominate someone totally unacceptable (Jackson, Wilbur Mills, Mayor Sam Yorty of Los Angeles), and that the Democrats are not riven by irresponsible and kooky caucuses (Chisholm) or fifth parties (Spock, McCarthy), though the *threat* of a Spock or McCarthy ticket is a useful means of combatting a Jackson or Humphrey candidacy.

Of the viable candidates, we do not face a spectacularly worthy lot. The *Lib. Forum's* endorsed candidate, Senator William Proxmire (D., Wis.) — one of only *four* Senators to vote against extension of wage-price control authority (the others being Goldwater, Fulbright, and Harris) — bowed out of the race with an eloquent and charming statement to the effect that he had managed to alienate both Big Labor and Big Business and was therefore bereft of campaign funds. Harris' absurd candidacy was over almost as soon as it began, and Birch Bayh (D., Ind.) has been replaced by his Indiana colleague and factional enemy, the even more obscure Vance Hartke. Eugene McCarthy is too erratic to take seriously. This leaves us three candidates: Lindsay, McGovern, and Muskie. The fascination of much of the nation for Lindsay is one of any New Yorker's abiding puzzles; for it is very difficult to mention the name "Lindsay" to *any* New Yorker, be he left, right, or center, and whatever his occupation or income, without unleashing a geyser of abuse. Everyone in New York reviles Lindsay, and with good reason: for he has succeeded in blending an arrogant High Moral Tone with an almost spectacularly inept and bungling administration. We favor peace, amnesty and civil liberties — issues on which Lindsay's record is a good one, but does America deserve Lindsay the Administrator? The danger of a Lindsay candidacy, however, is remote; for he will surely manage to alienate most of the party cadre before he finishes his run. George McGovern, in contrast to Lindsay, has a deadly lack of charisma; worse from the libertarian point of view is McGovern's unrelenting socialist thrust on domestic issues.

This leaves us with Ed Muskie, the leading contender. We have written that Muskie is grey, colorless, and the favorite of the party hacks. All this is true. But relative to his *confreres,* Muskie is beginning to look pretty good.

(Continued on page 5)

Purist Deviationism: A Strategic Fallacy

By William Danks

A growing problem exists among many newly radicalized libertarians. In coming to realize the vicious immorality and blatant evil of statism, they often attempt to "purify" themselves from their social and cultural context. They try to cleanse themselves from what is felt to be the all-pervading sickness of their surroundings. This is a mistake. Logically, the idea of stepping out of one's environment is confused. Psychologically, it's an acceptance of collective guilt-by-association. Strategically, in terms of building an effective, relevant libertarian movement, it's the worst sort of fallacy.

The "purification" process has several aspects: 1) removal of oneself from any source of income that comes directly *or indirectly* from the government, 2) refusal to make use of government services, 3) refusal to become involved in politics, 4) total refusal to co-operate with (i.e. supposedly "sanction") the government in any way, and 5) armed resistance against the state.

Clearly, any of these actions *are* moral, and *can be* tactically useful in specific circumstances. The point is, however, that such efforts *can not* achieve their own ultimate purposes and are positively harmful to both the individuals involved and to the libertarian movement that they ostensibly support.

In the sense that the "purist" desires, it is simply impossible to have an absolutely "non-governmental" income. No matter how "private" one's occupation appears to be, there will always be a certain percentage of one's customers that either work for the state or for a company that does state business. To be consistent the "purist" must view all revenue so derived as "tainted."

Given the nature of our statist economy, there is simply no place to go for someone who "wants nothing to do with the whole rotten mess." The sector of the economy known as "private" is only relatively so, and is degenerating rapidly. Even the so-called "parallel economy" of the libertarian market is infected with some money coming from state sources.

But so what? The only way out of this supposed dilemma is either suicide or total retreatism — two unreasonable options that are in no way morally required of man. A much better alternative, both logically and strategically, is to realize the revolutionary context in which one lives and then act accordingly. The "purists" are correct in feeling that no sanction should be given to the state. Yet, that's exactly what they are doing when they accept the coercive conditions imposed by the state and then try to act "morally" as if they were in a moral context (i.e. volitional freedom). Rand called this the "sanction of the victim." It's what the rulers are counting on.

The same applies to the use of government services. LeFevre and others have pointed out the practical advantages of self-reliance in the face of increasing governmental inefficiency. But the refusal to call the police or fire department, or to ride on public transportation, or to use a library, or attend a state university, is oftentimes just plain foolish. It's a misidentification of government to view it as some kind of organism with a life of its own. Government is nothing more than a parasite living off the people. When the people make use of a government service they are only reclaiming a little of their own life's blood. Again the moral question is inapplicable. You can't steal from a thief. You can't be a parasite *of* a parasite — you can only be either a parasite or a host.

In this regard the strategic fallacy of "purism" leads to tremendous alienation of libertarians from the lower and middle classes. By attacking government workers, welfare-recipients, public-housing residents, food-stamp users, etc. libertarians appear to be attacking the victims of the state (for a brief reminder see Rod Manis' "Government vs. the Poor" — Rampart College pamphlet) and thereby (implicitly) defending the real villain, the state itself. The crucial polarization should always be between the people and the government, not between different groups of people.

Refusal to become involved in politics is impossible. Everyone living in a nation-state is "involved" in politics to the very extent that their life is not theirs to live as they please. When the time comes when a person has a *real* option to not be involved in politics, then the revolution will be over and we will have won.

Of course, what the "purist" means is refusal to vote, run for office, or support any candidates. Again these are moral choices that anyone is free to make, but also again they are far more harmful than good. Although there will be crisis situations when a non-vote drive can be tactically worthwhile (in terms of publicity and education), the nature of today's social/political context indicates little general value in political celibacy. Libertarians and libertarianism will simply be passed by.

The proper libertarian political activity is abolitionism. A ballot can work two ways. Libertarians should never allow a proposal to pass by that they don't vote against. This will also be the role of libertarian candidates, when and if they are developed — to veto bills. In the meantime selective support should be given to those traditional politicians that are most opposed to the worst aspects of the present system (e.g. Vietnam, the draft, censorship, etc.).

Points 4 and 5 of the "purification" process run together and are the most dangerous to everyone concerned. A case with which I am personally acquainted serves as a good example. A young man recently converted to libertarianism drives a car daily but refuses to get a license. He can't bring himself down to the level of asking the state for permission to drive. The possible penalties if he is caught (which is only a matter of time) — $1,000 fine and a year in jail.

Of course the young man's position is morally correct. Of course the state is ripping-off the fee it charges for driver's licenses. Of course such license requirements are infringements of liberty. And the young man is quite willing to resist if they try to take him in. Fine. But this is not the place to fight. The price of victory on this issue is too high, the results of the victory would be nearly inconsequential anyway, and most importantly — the issue presents an easy way to put libertarians away without attracting much sympathy for their cause.

If a distinction must be made between "statist" and "Anti-statist" actions, let the distinction be a rational and sophisticated one, arrived at through careful "in-context" analysis. A basic division to be considered is whether an action (be it voting, working, etc.) is performed *in* the system in order to bring it down and abolish it, or whether it's performed *for* the system in order to perpetuate and expand it. Therefore it's at least conceivable that virtually any government job (short of something like state executioner) could serve an anti-statist purpose. In extreme circumstances a libertarian could even take such abhorrent jobs as tax-collector or FBI agent and still be actively furthering the anti-statist cause (by internal sabotage, inefficiency, purposely following false leads, etc.). In today's more normal times there is certainly

(Continued on page 5)

POLITICS '72 — *(Continued from page 3)*

There is in his very coolness, his very lack of color and his extreme caution, a happy augury of a President who, like Calvin Coolidge, might just snooze his way through the White House. In short, Muskie looks to have the makings of an inactive President, which, short of a Libertarian Hero who will roll back the New Deal, is about the best that a libertarian can hope for these days. It is difficult to conjure up an image of Muskie girding us all for a further leap into collectivism, or of Muskie pushing the buttons for another war somewhere in the world.

Two minor serendipities with Muskie. One was his refreshingly honest statement that a Negro could not be elected Vice-President, a welcome bit of candor on an issue mired in hypocrisy and cant; another is the marvellous information that Muskie is disliked by his flinty old mother. What other Presidential candidate in decades can make such a statement? ◙

Libertarians Versus Controls

The fight of the libertarian movement against the Nixon wage-price controls continues to receive recognition by the media. Increasingly, for example, your editor and John Kenneth Galbraith have been juxtaposed as the major protagonists in the battle over direct controls. Thus, in his review of the second edition of Galbraith's *New Industrial State*, economist Professor Robert Eisner of Northwestern (*Saturday Review*, October 2, 1971, pp. 45-46) found himself torn between the two points of view. After praising Galbraith, Eisner added: "But in an eloquent recent contribution to the Op Ed page of *The New York Times*, Murray Rothbard declared that on August 15 fascism came to America. I winced a bit at the rhetoric, but winced more when President Nixon, in his Labor Day address to the nation, defended his wage-price freeze with an appeal to each American for 'personal sacrifice' and 'faith in his country.' This does have a rather totalitarian ring about it . . . Galbraith, along with many of us, complains at the clear big-business bias in Nixon's new economic policy . . . But what should Galbraith have expected in view of his own compelling artuments on the inextricable interweaving of the mature corporation and the State? Is the moral of all this that we should turn over more power to the government? And will democracy and justice really be served if George Meany's belated protests are heeded and tripartite boards of government, business, *and* labor set the terms of the transactions by which we work and live? I seem to recall that tripartite boards of this type were indeed the hallmark of Benito Mussolini's overhaul of the Italian economy a few decades ago."

The Galbraith-Rothbard polarization has just appeared in the January, 1972 issue of the *Intellectual Digest*, a well-edited monthly of several hundred thousand circulation. Under the headings: "Economics: left & right", several pages are excerpted from Galbraith's recent book, under the caption of "The Inevitability of Controls". Immediately following Galbraith, there is a condensation of your editor's *Lib. Forum* piece on the freeze of last September, under the caption "Controls Won't Work."

Choose, America: Rothbard or Galbraith!

We are happy to see increasing signs of disaffection from the controls by conservatives, economists, and businessmen. *Human Events, National Review, the Freeman*, YAF, The American Conservative Union, have all, if sometimes belatedly, taken a stand against the price-wage controls. Without attempting to slight anyone, we might mention: Frank Chodorov, "The Tale of Two Students", *The Freeman*, December, 1971 (it is a pleasure to see this reprint from the eloquent and hard-hitting writings of the great individualist, and to have Chodorov introduced to the current generation); Allan C. Brownfeld, "Phase II: Challenge to Economic Freedom," *Roll Call*, October 28, 1971 (a conservative Washington publication); W. Allen Wallis, "Wage-Price Controls Won't Work," *Wall St. Journal*, December 22, 1971(from a leading Friedmanite economist); and Hendrik S. Houthakker, "No Use for Controls",

Barrons, November 8, 1971 (particularly important as emanating from a former member of Nixon's Council of Economic Advisers. Prof. Houthakker concentrates on the price-*raising* policies of the federal government in construction and oil.)

Meanwhile, Rothbard's use of the term "fascism" to describe the leap into controls has drawn an anguished outcry from the social-democratic author Theodore Draper, "The Specter of Weimar," *Commentary* (December), Mr. Draper lumps this charge with various left-wing uses of the term for contemporary America. In his easy pointing to the fact that we do not have concentration camps or brownshirts, Draper totally overlooks the fact that I was pointing to the fascist *economy* — though of course it is legitimate to conjecture that a fascist economy may well breed the rest of the fascist trappings. The *Wall St. Journal* (Dec. 20, 1971), while editorially commending the Draper article, is clearly worried about the totalitarian implications of the wage-price freeze, as well as the "evident willingness on the part of many to give up on the individual and on all the enormous potentialities of individual liberty." The *Journal* concludes that "the public's current docility toward the aggrandizement of the state" might well portend "socialism or some Orwellian type of totalitarian horror." ◙

PURIST DEVIATIONISM — *(Continued from page 4)*

a place, uncompromised and as *rationally* pure as possible, for libertarians in *all* parts of their society.

We have only one world to live in, and that's the world we have to win. Libertarianism is the philosophy of reason, justice, peace and freedom. It can not be betrayed by recognizing the facts of reality and acting accordingly. It can only be betrayed by not doing so; by accepting such spuriously self-righteous positions as that of utopian "purism." ◙

The Shaffer Dictionary

By Butler Shaffer

The following definitions comprise a part of my view of reality, in all its humorous—and often frustrating—manner.

GREEDY: one who puts his selfish interests ahead of mine.

HONOR: the last refuge of a man whose prejudices have come into conflict with his judgment.

LOYALTY: continuing to lend one's support to an institution when no good reason exists for doing so.

SOCIALISM: meatless cannibalism.
      Also, the idea that we should divide up the wealth of all those who have more than I do.

On Punishment: Two Comments And A Reply

I

Dear Editor:

I wish to take issue with certain assertions which you made in your October article on "Attica" with regard to capital punishment.

In your view, and I quote, "the libertarian creed states that an aggressor loses his rights to the extent that he has deprived victims of theirs. Hence, it is perfectly proper to exact capital punishment on murderers, who have deprived victims of their right to life, or to exact a lesser punishment which is in some way proportionate to other crimes."

My question is; in your view, is the libertarian "creed" based on the moral concept of justice, or not? If it is based on justice, then by what stretch of the imagination could "a life for a life", or "an eye for an eye", or "a leg for a leg", etc., fill the criteria for justice? In *my* view, justice is concerned with the *repayment of*, or *compensation for*, values which have been taken away. If an aggressor breaks my leg, or causes me to lose the use of an eye, how will my breaking *his* leg, or depriving him of the use of *his* eye, compensate me for the loss of the use of mine!

You talk about "punishment" as though it is a necessary and valid part of justice; it is not – in fact punishment is a biblical concept which is quite irrelevant to the concept "justice". My own view, based on the moral concept of justice is that anyone who deprives another of his rightful values, owes a *debt* to the deprived person, which is proportionate to the val loss, and the deprived person has the right to use defe ..ve force in order to obtain compensation (as much as humanly possible). This does not imply "an eye for an eye". You may ask the question, "what then would you have done with a murderer?" Let us assume a rational anarchistic society based on the moral principles of non-sacrifice, non-aggression, and justice, and someone commits a murder. Of course, there is *no way* by which the dead person can ever be recompensed; how then would we apply the principle of justice?

Let us not forget that the victim of the murder is not the *only* person to whom a debt is owed by the murderer. True, the victim is dead, but what of others who may have been deprived of their rightful values as a result of the untimely death of the victim! What of a wife's loss of values, or children, or persons for whom the victim had assumed responsibility? Here at least *some* measure of compensation (albeit insignificant by contrast to the value loss) can be made by the murderer by having him productively employed (in strict security premises), and for the rest of *his* life he pays not only for his own upkeep, but the balance of his earnings he pays to his victim's estate. We can assume that the victim would have lived and accumulated values, for as long as the murderer lives. Of course if the murderer refuses to work, he does not eat, and by so doing he would be depriving himself of his own values. No one has any moral obligation whatsoever to sustain the murderer's life, but *he*, by his dastardly act of aggression, owes a life-long debt. To send him to his own death, is to deny the other persons whom he deprived, of their right to as much compensation *as is humanly possible*.

—Ernestine Perkins

II

Dear Editor:

In the October, 1971 issue of the *Libertarian Forum*, Murray Rothbard endorsed the tough conservative line on the Attica prison riot. Some of Rothbard's factual statements conflict with other accounts I have seen, but rather than dispute his "facts" I would like to question his theory of punishment.

It is important to understand what punishment is. It is a hardship imposed on someone, (usually someone judged to be an offender) above and beyond mere correction of physical damage or return of stolen property. Punishment is *not* self-defense, it is *not* restitution of property; it is an additional hardship imposed against the will of the recipient.

The recipient of punishment is the victim of coercion imposed on him, usually with the *intention* of harming him and, perhaps, deterring others from breaking the rules of the punishers. The prisoners at Attica were not there for restitution of property, or self-defense, but for punishment.

The form of punishment advocated by liberals is aimed at rehabilitation. As Rothbard rightly observed, the terms of this kind of punishment are determined by the "subjective decisions and whims of the 'humanitarian' overlords of the prison system."

The inmates at rehabilitation centers are not volunteers and they do not know beforehand the length of their imprisonment. Rothbard contends that punishment through rehabilitation is bad because the prisoners "no longer enjoy the certainty of objective punishment" and that, a libertarian world would not be devoid of prisons, but would have more efficient ones run on a competitive private basis.

In order to decide whether punishment through rehabilitation is worse than "objective" punishment, we must know what "objective" punishment means. If it means penal laws written down in books and enforced uniformly, then either 1) there must be unanimity of opinion in society about what the laws should be or 2) there must be a State monopoly to impose one set of laws. Anyone who knows Murray Rothbard knows that he does not advocate State monopoly of anything, so he must think there is unanimity of opinion about penal laws. He must think there is an objective standard which each of us can use to decide the correct amount of punishment appropriate for each particular crime. The fact that there is neither unanimity of opinion nor uniformity of punishment practices (even among libertarians) seems to contradict the notion of a natural criterion for punishment. If such a criterion exists I would like to know what it is.

The only clues Rothbard gives are that the punishment should be proportional to the crime and should somehow fit the crime. This implies a measurement of crime and a measurement of punishment. Such measurements require units to objectively calibrate the subjective experiences of pain and suffering associated with crime or punishment. This assumes not only that pain and suffering can be measured, but that everyone experiences the same degree of pain and suffering from the same punishment.

Many of the arguments that Rothbard so brilliantly expressed against the quest for a just tax in *Power and Market* seem to be equally valid when used against his theory of just punishment. An objective theory of punishment seems to require interpersonal measurement of utility.

Such measurement is impossible. All codes of punishment are arbitrary, whether they be based on the principle of

(Continued on page 7)

"Government is actually the worst failure of civilized man. There has never been a really good one, and even those that are most tolerable are arbitrary, cruel, grasping and unintelligent. Indeed, it would not be far wrong to describe the best as the common enemy of all decent citizens." --- H. L. Mencken.

ON PUNISHMENT — *(Continued from page 6)*

"an eye for an eye" or "two eyes for an eye" or any other sadistic scheme. The only way to have a uniform "objective" system of punishment is to impose one of the arbitrary punishment codes by force on the whole society.

This can only be done by a government. It is the realization of this fact, I think, which caused Ayn Rand to reject the doctrine of anarchism. This knowledge is implicit in her definition of government in her essay "The Nature of Government."

> "A government is the means of placing the retaliatory use of physical force under objective control – i.e., under objectively defined laws."

This is a correct statement of fact and it gives a clue to the mystery of what it is about government which appeals to Ayn Rand. If you believe in retaliation, the only alternative to a government, which (ideally) retaliates against people in accordance with laws that are written down and enforced equally on everyone, is a system with competing retaliation agencies. These agencies would retaliate against criminals in different ways and in different amounts, which would obviously be inequitable and unfair. If retaliation were permitted in the absence of government, criminals would suffer unequal amounts of punishment for similar crimes and some would suffer more for small crimes than others would for big ones – depending upon the state of mind and whims of the ones determining the punishment. This is unacceptable to Ayn Rand – it isn't objective enough.

Only a government, which enjoys a monopoly on the "right" of retaliation in a geographic area, can lend a sense of impartiality, and uniformity to the administration of punishment and, by so doing, make retaliation seem like justice. It is because Ayn Rand believes in reataliation more than she believes in the right to not be aggressed against, that she is willing to condone the coercive monopoly of government.

Ayn Rand was forced to choose between two mutually exclusive concepts of justice: vindictive vengeance objectively and uniformly administered *or* the inalienable right of everyone to freedon from aggression. The former requires a coercive government, the latter requires anarchy. Ayn Rand, being basically a hater, chose the former.

I hope that Murray Rothbard will prove to be more devoted to the principle of nonaggression than to the lust for revenge.

--Roy Halliday

III

Editor's Reply:

The comments of Ernestine Perkins and Roy Halliday provide a welcome opportunity to expound a bit on one of the most grievously neglected areas of libertarian theory: the theory of punishment. I hasten to add that the burden of formulating a theory of objective punishment (i.e. punishment that is not simply a whim of the legal code) falls not only upon us, but on *all* legal systems anywhere: be they democratic, socialist, or monarchical. All except the absolute pacifists, who would allow all criminals to go scot free, have to search for a rational principle for punishment of crime.

In the first place, most libertarians, exempting again the absolute pacifists, would certainly agree that the prime focus of punishment must certainly be *restitution* to the victim, forcing the criminal to restore his ill-gotten loot to the person he injured. This, indeed, *was* the prime focus of punishment in ancient times, and it is only with the rise of the modern State that the focus of punishment became payment of a so-called "debt" to "society", while the hapless victim is forced to pay taxes for the support of his persecutor in jail. (on the history of the legal concept of restitution and its decline, see the excellent work by

Stephen Schafer, *Restitution to Victims of Crime*, Chicago: Quadrangle Books, 1960).

My contention, however, is that simple restitution is not enough. In the first place it would grant to the thief a virtual license to steal; if A steals $5,000 from B, A would rest secure in the knowledge that the worst that could happen to him is that he would have to pay back the $5,000 (the including of interest and the cost of apprehension doesn't change the magnitudes very much.) Secondly, the restitution concept cannot handle satisfactorily what happens to the criminal who assaults or maims or murders his victim; an attempt to assess a scale of monetary equivalents which he would be forced to pay the victim (or, in the case of murder, his heirs) is grotesque, and was one of the great failings of the ancient law. A beaten man does not simply have to pay medical costs; he loses his dignity, he suffers pain, and he suffers the invasion of his most precious possession: himself.

I hold, instead, that any criminal loses his own rights *to the extent* that he has aggressed against another; in other words, that the victim (or his heirs) can exact a punishment up to whatever may be considered equivalent or proportionate to the extent of the original crime. The attempt to do this is summed up in the famous legal maxim: "let the punishment fit the crime." There is no doubt about the fact that such measurement is often difficult; but it must be attempted nevertheless. The great turn-of-the-century English libertarian Auberon Herbert put the case very well: "...a man has forfeited his own rights (to the extent of the aggression he has committed in attacking the rights of others . . . It may be very difficult to translate into concrete terms the amount of aggression, and of resulting restraint; but all just law seems to be the effort to do this. We punish a man in a certain way if he has inflicted an injury which lays me up for a day; in another way if he takes my life. No doubt the law of every country is most imperfect . . . but there is generally underlying it the view (which is, I think, true) that the punishment or redress – both in civil and criminal matters – should be measured by the amount of aggression; in other words that the aggressor – after a rough fashion – loses as much liberty as that of which he has deprived others." (Auberon Herbert and J. H. Levy, *Taxation and Anarchism*, London: The Personal Rights Association, 1912, p. 38.)

How do we begin to approximate proportionality? A few guidelines present themselves. First, in the question of theft, the above criminal A who stole $5,000 should *also* have $5,000 taken *from him*. In short, he should have to pay back the victim, B, *not only* the original $5,000 (plus interest and costs) but also another $5,000 which is the amount that he forfeits as punishment for the act of aggression. This principle of double payment has been accurately termed by a libertarian wag "two teeth for a tooth." In the case of personal assault, it seems clear that the most precise proportionality is to inflict the exact same beating or assault upon the criminal as he had inflicted on the victim – although, here, too, more must be added to compensate the victim for the terror of uncertainty and sudden invasion of rights that accompanied the original act, and that a simple equivalent beating cannot really equal. In the case of murder, of course, the only equivalent is capital punishment, and it is precisely this fitting of the punishment to the crime that is the rational groundwork for this maximum penalty. The case for prisons is not the prison *per se* but the probable necessity of isolating the criminal from his future victims: the idea that the prisoner should labor in prison until his victim is fully compensated was, again, prevalent in older law, and was Herbert Spencer's suggestion to be restored as the guiding principle of prison punishment. Of course, it should also be noted that in the future libertarian society where *all* land, in-

(Continued on page 8)

ON PUNISHMENT — *(Continued from page 7)*

cluding streets, is privately owned, much of the need for segregating criminals will be taken care of by not allowing criminals or risky types into various private areas: the rules for admission being of course determined by the land and street owners themselves.

The concept of *vengeance* has received a very bad press in recent decades, but I have never seen a satisfactory refutation of it; invariably the modern punishment theorist quickly dismisses it as "barbaric" before he races on to treat the deterrence (utilitarian) or "reform" (liberal-humanitarian) concepts of punishment. The pseudo-humanitarian concept of "reform" I have already discussed in the "Attica" editorial; and to rely primarily on deterrence leads one into the *genuine* barbarism of – say – advocating capital punishment for stealing an apple and a much *lesser* punishment for murder, since most people have an innate reluctance to commit murder while many people are not loath to steal apples, so that more intensive deterrence is then required. In my view, proportionate vengeance is not only the most just, but also the most *genuinely* humanitarian, of these three alternative theories of punishment. In any case, I see nothing wrong with the desire for vengeance; if a man's infant daughter is cruelly butchered, why should he not desire the butchery of the criminal in return, and why should he not have this desire executed? Professor Schafer well calls this exaction of vengeance "spiritual restitution" to the victim; most libertarians would agree to material restitution of a theft – why not spiritual restitution as well? Schafer writes: "The evil visited on the wrongdoer in punishment is intended . . . to endeavour to compensate the victim for his encroached or destroyed right by offering him some spiritual satisfaction... it is generally accepted that one of the tasks of punishment is what might be called 'idealistic damages' or 'spiritual restitution.'" (Schafer, p. 120). (See also the defense of capital punishment by Donald Atwell Zoll, in "A Wistful Goodbye to Capital Punishment," *National Review*, December 3, 1971).

In the libertarian society of the future, however, there would still be a way out for pacifists and quasi-pacifists like Mr. Halliday. For all prosecution would be exercised by the victim or his agents, and not by any sort of "district attorney" presuming to speak for "society" as a whole. If, then, Mr. Halliday were victimized by criminals, he could choose not to exercise his right to punish at all, or may choose to exercise it to any extent less than is his due. (Or, if he were murdered, he could instruct his heirs in advance, by notice, not to do so.) Alternatively, he could make a voluntary contract with the criminal, allowing the wrongdoer to buy his way out of any exacted punishment. If, for example, someone beats up Mr. Halliday,

he could allow the criminal to buy his way out of a retaliatory beating. The situation, then, would by truly libertarian. Pacifists, or others who desire money over precise vengeance, could relieve the criminal of his punishment; those of us who prefer vengeance would of course allow such victims to do so. Why will *they* not allow *us* to exact due punishment? And if they don't, what sort of libertarianism is this? In the libertarian society of the future, moreover, Mr. Halliday could continue to try to convince future victims to become pacifists or quasi-pacifists; while I could continue to persuade them otherwise. No one could compel those victims who are opposed to punishment to exact such punishment; and, similarly, *they* should not be able to prohibit vengeance-bound victims from doing so.

I need only comment on a few observations by Mr. Halliday. First, there is no attempt here to measure subjective pain or utility, but to "measure" objective deeds of aggression and retaliate in kind. Second, Mr. Halliday is really saying that it is impossible to have *any* sort of objective law, or objective law code (not just for punishment) without a coercive monopoly government. Here he is simply falling into Miss Rand's trap. Objective law existed long before government (e.g. in the common law, the law merchant, admiralty law) and was worked out by privately competitive judges long before the State imposed its monopoly. Since law *is* objective, it is discoverable by reason and doesn't need government to formulate it – on the contrary, government, subject as it is to the caprice and whims of legislators, is most unlikely to respect objective law, as history has amply demonstrated. The objective Law Code would be the libertarian law of outlawing aggression against person and property, defining what that property is, setting up rules for trials to determine who the criminals are (e.g. permitting cross-examination of witnesses, etc.), and, in the libertarian society that I envision, all the privately competing courts and defense agencies would be pledged to abide by this objective Code. Any court which flouted this libertarian Code and imposed its own rules would be deemed to be itself guilty of aggression (e.g. courts which decided that all redheads are *ipso facto* criminals.)

Third, Mr. Halliday liberally sprinkles his comment with smear terms: "sadistic", "vindictive", "hater", etc. These are simply that – smear terms – and prove nothing. Not only do I see nothing wrong with "hating" crime and injustice, I hold that genuine love of justice *requires* such hatred. As Professor Zoll writes, "A humane society is a compassionate society, but compassion is only significant in terms of justice, of a sensitivity to the valid claims of men which rest upon the restraints on usurpation, aggression and terror." (Zoll, p. 1354).

First Class

Published Every Month. Subscription Rate: $8.00 Per Year

A Monthly Newsletter

THE
Libertarian Forum

Joseph R. Peden, Publisher   Murray N. Rothbard, Editor

VOLUME IV, NO. 2   February, 1972   75c

PHASE II CRACKING

Richard Milhous Nixon has achieved another "first": generally it takes a year or two of price-wage controls before they visibly begin to collapse, and the heady euphoria of the public turns to sour recrimination. But in his wisdom, Richard Nixon has managed to have Phase II visibly cracking before it has hardly begun. The bloom is off the rose, for the public, for unions, and even for the staunchest supporters of the controls, the nation's businessmen. As the ardently pro-control *Business Week* put it (Jan. 29) "The Phase II honeymoon is over." Prices skyrocket in the stores, coal miners gain a 17% wage increase, while other people's wages are frozen and rent controls are firmly imposed. Some businesses are allowed price increases; others are brought sharply to book. Throughout the land, there is a crazy patchwork pattern of discrimination, enforcement, and exemptions, and the early euphoria of the public has turned to disgust and anger. The controls were expected by the Administration to put an end to the "inflationary expectations" of the public; and of course they have not succeeded.

The Administration has, predictably, met this problem with a blend of ever more Byzantine evasions and rationalizations, combined with a Connally-led exercise in hard-nosed "toughness" directed against the controls' staunchest supporters: the businessmen. Herbert Stein meets rapid price increases with the declaration that this is great because he expected the post Phase I price "bulge" to be even greater than it is. Robert F. Lanzilotti, economist and member of the Price Commission, complains that consumers do not realize that raw agricultural products are exempt from controls, and therefore should not complain about their rapid rise. "I wish," he added wistfully, "we could get this message across to the housewives." (Lotsa luck.) *(Business Week)*. In the meanwhile, the Administration has helped the food-price raising process along by boosting price supports for milk. Utility rates and postal rates – and of course – taxes go up, and, as we predicted, the quality and size of many products have declined, thus constituting a hidden price increase. Jergens Lotion in Denver, for example, now costs the same 59¢ for a bottle that has oddly diminished from 4 3/4 to 4 oz.

But the Administration is nothing if not "tough". While prices have been decontrolled for small business, the Justice Dept. suddenly lashed out at Time Saver Food Stores of New Orleans, suing the store for over $100,000 in price control violations. Secretary of the Treasury Connally, too, has been addressing meetings of businessmen and denouncing them for not bringing about economic recovery. He attacked them for complaining about the vast uncertainty brought about by the patchwork price-wage controls, and for not being stimulated by the investment tax credit to increase capital spending (this in a time of large amounts of excess capacity!) The problem, as acknowledged by Argus investment research, is that Phase I and Phase II "evidently had a more depressing effect on business spending for inventories and other requirements of economic recovery than anyone had expected" (not us!). Connally will find out that no amount of Texas toughness is going to induce businessmen to suffer losses voluntarily in order to pull the Nixonite chestnuts out of the fire. Finally, the Administration sternly insists that they will keep wage and price controls indefinitely; or as Connally told businessmen in a burst of madcap illogic that will make old pragmatist John Dewey turn over in his grave, they will keep the control program "until it works." In an age of socio-economic lunacy, this is probably the most lunatic statement of them all.

Finally, C. Jackson Grayson, head of the Price Commission, threatened that if the price-wage controls do not work, we will have to go over into "socialism"; there we have it – the final wormy promise in the Nixonite apple-barrel.

America, America! How much more of the Monster Milhous will we have to take before he is dumped?

But never fear; the nation's economic big-wigs, conspicuously including "free market" economist Milton Friedman, have declared their contentment with Nixon's economics. In a recent issue, *Newsweek* (Jan. 31) coyly asked their three-man panel of economists to give President Nixon "marks" for his economic performance for 1971. Right-centrist Nixonite Henry Wallich predictably checked in with the fawning: "President Nixon has clearly earned the top grade of honors." Liberal Paul Samuelson recorded a "69" or "C+" for Nixon, since the President's "new economic policy pulled up his average for the year." But what of Milton Friedman, who allegedly provides the "right-wing" balance to the other two? Curiously enough, his mark for Tricky Dick was almost the same as Samuelson's: "75." Why such a high grade, since Friedman added that Nixon's monetary policy was "terrible" (though he blamed this on the Federal Reserve Board), the deficit too high, and the wage-price controls a "major mistake". (Remember when the Communist fellow-travellers used to mildly deplore the "mistakes" of Stalin – like slave labor camps?) So why a mark as high as 75? Nixon's "bold", "highly desirable and long overdue" action in "closing the gold window" – that means plunging the country and the world into a totally fiat currency, divorced from the sound commodity money: gold. Apparently, in the eyes of Friedman, the boldness and beauty of Nixon's fiat declaration of bankruptcy was good enough to offset the other "mistakes".

If you had asked *me, Newsweek,* for my "grade" for Richard Milhous Nixon, I would have loudly and unhesitatingly given the correct libertarian answer: "F", *and expulsion.*

269

The Political Circus

I *New Left Redux?*

The tattered remnants of whatever debris remains from the defunct New Left have gathered themselves together in a "People's Party": their major mass base is the old Peace and Freedom Party of California (the other state PFP's have long since folded); the leading theoreticians and organizers are the intellectuals from the Institute of Policy Studies, in Washington; and their current national candidates are Dr. Spock for President and Negro civil rights leader Julius Hobson for V. P. Their "big names" are Spock and the acidulous Gore Vidal.

For many years now, the intellectuals of the New Left have been promising us some "new" form of socialism, a decentralized, quasi-libertarian, anti-statist system that would discard the bad old Leviathan State. Until now, the New Left intellectuals have contented themselves with cloudy rhetoric, some of it promising, while presumably hard at work cogitating and hammering out the concrete shape of their new concept. What, exactly, would any sort of "libertarian" socialism look like? And how could the free-market be suppressed without establishing a Leviathan State? And if the free market were allowed, how would this be "socialism"?

Well, after many years, we now have our answer: the platform of the new People's Party, a platform designed as a "transitional program to decentralized, democratic socialism." (Charles Briody, national chairman of the People's Party, in *The Guardian*, Feb. 2, 1972). There are one or two obeisances to decentralization: community control of the police, and "guaranteeing the rights of minorities (how about majorities?) to control their own communities." Launching his campaign in Washington, Dr. Spock added local control of schools, including opposition to compulsory bussing. (New York *Times*, Jan. 28, 1972). But there we have it. For the rest we are offered:

A Federal Jobs Administration to provide "meaningful" work for the unemployed;

An end to the wage freeze, *but* a "real freeze on prices and corporate profits";

A vigorous campaign of federal trust-busting;

A guaranteed annual income of $6500 a year for a family of four, *plus* a national pension adjusted yearly for cost of living increases for every American over 60;

A sharply progressive tax structure which would soak the very rich and the corporations, "along with legislation prohibiting the passing on of such taxation to consumers";

Prohibition of all discrimination against women, blacks, and homosexuals (but not against WASPS?);

Free medical care for everyone, "of the highest possible quality" (Wanna bet?);

Courts and prisons designed to "rehabilitate, rather than punish, criminals";

Governmental child care centers everywhere (the parents, however, to decide their policies);

Government provision of educational opportunities for all, "including the guarantee of free tuition and living expenses through the college, technical or professional school of one's choice."

What does all this amount to? Something unfortunately all too familiar to all of us. There is nothing libertarian, voluntary, or even decentralized about any of it; it is, purely and simply, our old friend Socialism, our old tyrant the Leviathan State. After years of flim-flammery, of soul-searching, of lofty talk about alliances with the middle class and with Goldwaterites and Wallaceites, the New Left magician has finally whisked off the cloak from his new product, and what we have is . . . just the Old Left. *Plus ça change, plus c'est la même chose.*

II *Chisholm*

When the great H. L. Mencken, libertarian and political satirist, lanced the pomposities and imbecilities of the America of his day, he – and the other great satirists of the past – had the advantage of being able to take existing reality and exaggerate and parody its less attractive features. In short, they had a healthy base in reality from which to work, from which to lampoon the absurd parts of society. But sometimes it seems that life *itself* has become a parody, defying in its buffoonery any attempt of the satirist.

What would Mencken have done, for example, with the entry into the Presidential race of Rep. Shirley Chisholm (D., Brooklyn?) Mrs. Chisholm, in the kickoff speech of her campaign, announced that not only did she "represent" all the women and all the blacks and Chicanos in America, but even "all the people of the United States." (Loud applause.) In the immortal words of Samuel Goldwyn, "Kindly include me out" of this "representation." Standard political hyperbole? Perhaps. But let us ponder Mrs. Chisholm's interview in the New York *Post* (Jan. 26). Striking what some objectivists might applaud as the right note of megalomaniacal "self-esteem" tinged with paranoia, Mrs. Chisholm asserted: "I am self-confident. Enormously self-confident. Otherwise I never would have survived those people who are looking to destroy me politically." Who, Shirley? Name names; how many billions, how much psychic energy is being poured into this nationwide plot? But the reporter adds that "she brushes aside the question of who they are." Yes indeed.

Mrs. Chisholm then pressed on to explain why she is more qualified than virtually all past Presidents to hold down the office. "Thirty-six or more persons have been President of these United States. Experientially (?) and educationally I am better than all, excepting six or seven (come, come, no false humility now.) I have four college degrees, I am 10 points away from a doctorate (Oh, wow!) and I have a near-genius IQ. Close to 160." (Mohammed Ali may be the "greatest", but Shirley is the "smartest.")

And still more: "I am a very brilliant-minded woman. I can *feel* political questions. And I am quick on the draw." (The fastest mouth in the East?) Of the other Presidential candidates Mrs. Chisholm likes best none other than that Lochinvar of urban problems, Mayor Lindsay. Why? Replied the near-genius. "We're both Sagitarians, with strong leadership traits."

H. L. Mencken, Where Are You Now, When We Need You Most?

Of Interest To Libertarians

Those who are seriously interested in the prospect of income tax evasion can now buy, for $15.00, a packet called THE COMPLETE GUIDE FOR INCOME TAX RE-FUSERS. The packet has been put together by Lucille Moran who states: "If you are a serious tax rebel, this packet is your answer. This is a simple, tough assault *that works* because it strikes directly at the heart of the income tax strategy." The kit contains a step-by-step approach for those who no longer want to cooperate with IRS. The packet can be obtained by sending a check for the above amount to Lucille E. Moran, P.O. Box 641, Tavernier, Fla. 33070, and mentioning that you saw this information in the *Libertarian Forum*.

Another tax rebel, Gordon L. Cruikshank, has founded a new religion, akin to the Universal Life Church, for those seeking the political benefits of spiritual ordination. The church is the LIFE SCIENCE CHURCH, and you can be ordained by writing to the Rev. Cruikshank at 2207 Cardinal Drive., Rolling Meadows, Ill. 60008.

—Jerome Tuccille

For Croatia

The turbulent history of Yugoslavia, since World War II and indeed since World War I, can only be fully understood in terms of age-old ethnic and national struggles within the Balkans. The latest rioting and purges in Croatia are only the most recent chapter in a story that is just beginning. The major problem is that "Yugoslavia" is not really a nation; it was a typical misbegotten product of Woodrow Wilson's imperialism after the first World War. In the good name of "national self-determination", the U. S., the British, and the French created a group of ill-conceived client states. "Yugoslavia" was such an artificial creation, a geographical entity rather than a nation in which the Serbs constituting about half the total population were established as imperial dictators over the other ethnic and national entities in the new country. Backward and dedicated to statism within and without their own land, the Serbs tyrannized over the other national groups: the Croats, Slovenes, Hungarians, Albanians, Montenegrins, Macedonians, and Bosnian Muslims — each one of which constituted national, cultural, territorial and linguistic entities of their own. Of these oppressed minority nations, the most important were the Slovenes and the far more numerous Croats — progressive, Western-oriented, enterprising, and productive far beyond the other "Yugoslavian" nations. To add to their differences, the Croats and Slovenes were Catholics, while the others were Orthodox or Muslims.

During World War II, under German tutelage, the Croats, after centuries of struggle, achieved a truncated form of independent state under their leading independence and guerrilla organization, the Ustashi. But their independence was severely limited by German and Italian occupation, and especially by Italian annexation of large chunks of Croatia and the imposition of an Italian King. Furthermore, while the Ustashi slaughtered the Serb minority in Croatia and in the mixed region of Bosnia-Hercegovina, the Italians looked favorably on the activities of the Serbian terrorist organization, the Chetniks, who massacred Croats in the Italian zone. With the pacifist Croatian peasant leader Vladko Matchek (representing the bulk of the Croats) refusing either to collaborate with the Germans and replace the fanatical Ustashis *or* to lead a guerrilla resistance movement against the occupation, the anti-German guerrilla movement in Yugoslavia soon divided into two groups: the exclusively Serb Chetniks, under Draja Mihajlovitch, and a multi-ethnic Partisan movement under the Croat Marshal Tito (Josip Broz). Tito's thundering success over Mihajlovitch was due not so much to his Communism, as to the fact that he had forged a movement of ethnic equals, while Mihajlovitch largely confined his activities to the age-old Serb occupation of slaughtering Croats.

Since World War II, and especially since Tito's courageous break with Stalin and the international Communist movement, Tito has led Yugoslavia into a remarkably rapid shift away from socialist planning and a strong central state into an amazing degree of decentralization and autonomy for the various nations, as well as toward an explicitly individualist social philosophy and a free-market economy of extensive private ownership, worker ownership of factories replacing state ownership, a free price system based on profit-and-loss, private control of investment and credit, the welcoming of private foreign investment, and freedom to emigrate abroad. So autonomous are the various Yugoslav nations, for example, that Slovenia is allowed to have its own consular treaties with Austria, treaties that do not apply to the rest of the country.

Leading the struggle both for political decentralization and for a purely free-market economy have been the Communists of Croatia and Slovenia, the most industrialized, productive, and thrifty areas, and particularly in the forefront have been the Croatian and Slovenian economists, whose writings sound very much like Goldwater, Reagan, or Ludwig von Mises. The Croats, for example, have bitterly attacked the establishment of "political factories" by the Yugoslav central government, in which the productive Croats have been taxed to subsidize lazy and unproductive people in the Albanian region and Montenegro. And throughout this exciting period of rapid shift from socialism to freedom (a shift which soon envisions a free stock-market and ownership by *individual* instead of collective workers), it has been the Serbs — the "conservatives" — who have clung to the Old Order and been most resistant to this libertarian advance. It is almost exclusively the Serbs, for example, who staff the organs of the central government. To the extent that in 1967, Tito was forced to fire his Number 2 man and picked successor, Aleksandr Rankovitch, who had been in control of the hated secret police, after which that sinister agency of every totalitarian state was dismantled. And throughout the argument among economists it was always the Croats, centered in Zagreb, battling against the conservative crypto-Stalinists in Serb Belgrade.

The rapid and inexorable change in Yugoslavia pursued the logic of freedom; and it is characteristic of such an era of great change that the expectations of the people, especially in Crotia, rose to demand the pursuing of that logic to its conclusion. The Croats, led by the Croatian Communist League and more militantly by striking university students, came to demand: a wider free market, and abolishing the practice of the central government taxing Croatian earnings of foreign exchange in order to subsidize the rest of Yugoslavia. And looming behind these demands was the ultimate logic: Croatian independence at long last, after a thousand years of oppression.

Tragically, the aging Tito refused to pursue this logic the final step. Last December, Tito partially reverted to his Stalinist past. Over a thousand Croat students were arrested, and a ruthless purge has hit the Croatian Communist and intellectual leadership, many of whom are now awaiting trial for such high crimes as "counter-revolution" and "denigration of the state." The Croatian Communist leadership, headed by Miko Tripalo and Mrs. Savka Dabeevic-Kucar, have all been ousted and may themselves be brought to trial, perhaps for "high treason." As one Croat woman lamented, "We used to feel that we were so different from the Poles and the Czechs, now we don't feel different at all." (James Feron, in the New York *Times*, Jan. 25).

Meanwhile, the old Ustashi movement lives on in exile, in West Germany, home of over half a million Yugoslavs, mainly Croats, working temporarily abroad. From there, the Ustashi conduct some guerrilla activities against Yugoslavia. The poor befuddled New York *Times*, failing as always to comprehend national liberation movements, can't make up its mind whether the Ustashi, and its current leader, Dr. Branko Jelic, are "Nazis" or "Communists." On the one hand, they ruled under the tutelage of the Nazis in World War II; on the other hand, they recently organized the "League of Croatian Communists Abroad", and are rumored to have accepted funds from Soviet intelligence. The solution to the puzzle should be plain, however; the Ustashi are simply Croat nationalists, and as Dr. Jelic candidly admitted, he would "sleep with the devil" is necessary to achieve an independent Croatia. (James Feron, and David Binder, in the New York *Times*, Jan. 28).

Last year, the *Lib. Forum* called for and predicted the rise of an independent Bangladesh. Our predictions were fulfilled. We cannot predict an independent Croatia so readily, but the logic of events is clearly in that direction. Marshal Tito cannot live forever, and the centrifugal forces which he himself set in motion make almost inevitable the collapse of the "collective presidency" representing each nation which is to succeed him, and the division of the misbegotten country of Yugoslavia into its constituent parts. Croatia will rise again.

◘

271

Will The Real
(Howard Hughes, Clifford Erving,
Helga Hughes, George Holmes,
Hannah Rosencrantz . . .)
Please Stand Up.?

What a lot of glorious fun the Howard Hughes caper is! It has all the necessary ingredients: an unfolding, ever more labyrinthine tale of mystery, chicanery, high finance and high level intrigue, subject to numerous interpretations and endless specualtion — and all of no importance whatsoever. For surcease from worldly care, it is just what we all needed to tide us over between the Super Bowl and the New Hampshire primary. ◘

The Shaffer Dictionary

By Butler Shaffer

The following definitions comprise a part of my view of reality, in all its humorous—and often frustrating—manner.

ANARCHY: a chaotic system devoid of political government; hence, the absence of wars, depressions, and other manifestations of law and order.

CANNIBALISM: pre-capitalistic socialism.

MARXISM: a New Deal program for atheists.
A philosophy which would have won the overwhelming support of the Catholic and Protestant churches, and the Democratic and Republican parties, but for the strategic blunder of having endorsed atheism.

GENERAL WELFARE: that which serves my personal interests.

BOONDOGGLE: that which serves yours.

BANDIT: one who believes that even a little man can aspire to a political career.

WAR-HERO: a man who commits atrocities for our side.

INFIDEL: one whose judgment has been distorted by fact, reason, and logic. ◘

The Movement
Marches On

The distinguished English weekly, *The Manchester Guardian*, has published an article that will cheer the heart of every libertarian. (John Windsor, "A Right State of Affairs," *The Manchester Guardian Weekly*, December 25, 1971, p. 15.) The *Guardian* reports that the British libertarian movement, which it calls "guerrilla capitalism," "threatens to become the New Year's trendy political curiosity." While acknowledging that the British movement still has only about thirty members, it takes its future quite seriously. There are quotes and descriptions of the new movement, which centers around an American-style hamburger restaurant in Kingston-upon-Thames run by the American-

Recommended Reading

Rothbard pamphlets. Murray Rothbard has recently had two pamphlets published. One is *Freedom, Inequality, Primitivism and the Division of Labor* (50¢, from the Institute for Humane Studies, 1134 Crane St., Menlo Park, Calif. 94025.) This is a reprint of the article in *Modern Age* (Summer, 1971), attacking left-wing egalitarianism and the yen to crush the division of labor and therefore individual freedom and development. The other is *Education, Free and Compulsory* (available from the Center for Independent Education, 9115 E. Thirteenth, Wichita, Kan. 67206); the first part of this pamphlet appeared in the April, 1971 *Individualist*. The pamphlet is a history and critique of compulsory attendance laws, and outlines an individualistic philosophy of education.

Rule of Law. One of the most dangerous notions, which caught on in some libertarian circles in the early 1960's, was F. A. Hayek's grounding of political philosophy on the "rule of law." Now Professor Ronald Hamowy, a former student of Hayek's, has published a brilliant, thorough, and scholarly evisceration of the rule of law, and demonstrates that it provides no groundwork whatsoever for a libertarian political philosophy. See Ronald Hamowy, "Freedom and the Rule of Law in F. A. Hayek", *Il Politico* (Pavia), (1971, No. 2), pp. 349-77.

Cold War Revisionism. *Cold War Critics* is a book containing an excellent series of articles on early critics of the Cold War. Of particular interest to libertarians is: Ronald Radosh and Leonard P. Liggio, "Henry A. Wallace and the Open Door", pp. 76-113; and Henry W. Berger, "Senator Robert A. Taft Dissents from Military Escalation." (Leonard Liggio is the historian, long-time libertarian, and valued *Lib. Forum* contributor). The brunt of the two articles is that Robert Taft was a far more trenchant and consistent critic of the Cold War and American imperialism than Henry Wallace, who was himself an imperialist of a slightly more pacific and sophisticated breed. See Thomas G. Paterson, ed., *Cold War Critics* (Chicago: Quadrangle Books, 1971, paper $2.95).

Wage-Price Controls. Now that direct controls are once again upon us, the American Enterprise Institute (1150 17th St., N. W., Washington, D. C. 20036) has performed an important service by publishing a pamphlet, Colin Campbell, ed., *Wage-Price Controls in World War II, United States and Germany*, 73 pp., $3.00, collecting and reprinting notable contemporary articles critical of the workings of American and German controls. Included are articles by Mansfield, Cherne, Keezer, Mendershausen, and Eucken.

born Pauline Russell, a graduate of UCLA. The restaurant, the Transatlantic Success, publishes the magazine *The Guerrilla Capitalist*, selling for ten pence, and the group is called the Radical Libertarian Alliance. Also mentioned in the article is Richard King, former Australian bee remover who ran a "guerrilla capitalist" postal service during the British postal strike, delivering magazines profitably at one-third the charge levied by the British Post Office. Other libertarians cited in the group are Chris Tame and the Indian Mansur Nathoo, editor of the *Guerrilla Capitalist*, who is studying for a Ph. D. at the University of London.

One happy note: the article declares that in the USA there are "an estimated 200,000 practicing libertarians." Well, well, well! We hadn't thought it was nearly that many, but who are we to correct such a distinguished journal?? ◘

Immortality And The Law

By Jerome Tuccille
(an excerpt from a forthcoming book)

The legal problems created by extended life – not to mention immortality – would be overwhelming say the critics. We would have to rewrite the law books, probably redefine the entire question of death. Such items as suicide and murder would assume radically new meanings for all of us. Morality would be more throughly intertwined with politics, involving spokesmen from the various religious denominations and further eroding the wall dividing church and state. As government has gotten itself progressively entangled in moral issues – abortion; birth control; sexual customs; pornography; prostitution – it has penetrated more and more deeply into a province considered to be the exclusive domain of the religious authorities. One can imagine a life-death freeze in 1984 modeled after Richard Nixon's wage-price freeze of 1971, with a tripartite board of rabbis, priests and ministers advising the president. To be sure, Holy Rollers, fakirs, theosophists and whirling dervishes will all be clamoring for equal representation, charging the government with oppression for not adopting a "quota system" for religious minorities.

Insurance companies, too, are bound to suffer a dramatic upheaval. Do they pay off life insurance policies on people suspended in liquid nitrogen? Are they "dead" or not? What about inheritance? Does the estate of a suspended human being pass on to his family, or is it held in abeyance until he is reanimated? How about pension plans? It's one thing to retire an individual at sixty-five and pay him a salary until he expires five, ten or fifteen years later. But for sixty or seventy years? The whole question of "mandatory retirement age" will have to be re-evaluated.

Government has also gotten itself firmly entwined in the insurance business through social security, medicare and similar welfare measures. When our average life expectancy is increased to a hundred and twenty-five, social security payments will continue for sixty years instead of five or ten. Government pension plans are the most outrageous in existence anywhere. In New York City it is possible for a man to join the police force or fire department at twenty-one and retire at forty-one with three-quarters pay until he dies. Presently, he can expect to live another thirty years and already the money paid out annually in pensions to retired New York City employees *is equal to the amount paid in salaries to contemporary civil servants,* and it is rising proportionately every year. With a major breakthrough in the anti-aging field the pension fund could double or triple in a matter of years, and the private wage earner in New York City will find most of his taxes winding up in the pockets of ex-cops and firemen.

No private industry in the world could survive for long with such corrupt and shortsighted policies. The government, with its stranglehold on the earnings of honest citizens, is not subject to market competition and can keep the fantasy going a bit longer. But sooner or later the bubble has to explode.

The error made by opponents of immortality from the viewpoint of legality is the old familiar one of putting the cart before the horse; they fail to comprehend that legal forms do not determine reality, that the case is quite the opposite. Any legal structure which does not conform to the reality of the world we live in is at best archaic and obsolete, at worst immoral and dictatorial. Since the reality of the world around us is fluid, dynamic, constantly changing because of experimentation and new discoveries, it is incumbent upon the legal system to adapt itself to the evolving reality of life.

Historically, legality has never been able to keep up with the rapid pace of human achievement. It has always lagged two and three generations behind the times, and at any given moment there are laws on the books which reflect the thinking and social attitudes of fifty years before. In New York State today it is illegal to call a tavern a "saloon" – a hangover from the pre-Prohibition era when the word *saloon* identified a place where intoxicating beverages were sold without meals and was later outlawed. Today it is legal to operate such an establishment, but illegal to use the word which describes it. A well-known bar in New York City, O'Neal's Baloon, originally opened with the name O'Neal's Saloon in the late 1960's. The state liquor authorities stepped in shortly afterward and demanded that the name be changed. Rather than spending a lot of money having a new sign put up, the owner – actor Patrick O'Neal – merely took a can of paint and changed the S to an awkward B. Patrons still refer to the pub as O'Neal's Saloon even though the official name over the door conforms to the requirements of legislators in Albany.

There are many reasons why the legal code remains resistant to change while the reality of life progresses as a result of human ingenuity. The most obvious is the nature of the men who invariably control the structure of government. Those attracted to government seem to be, with few exceptions, the most cautious, shortsighted, conformist and authoritarian among us. Our journalists, media spokesmen and university intellectuals are constantly crying out for "new, young, progressive and charismatic" leaders to enter the breach and launch a New Great Frontier to save the world. Yesterday's hero was John F. Kennedy; today's is John Lindsay; tomorrow's will surely be the anti-war veteran John Kerry of Massachusetts (with his initials J. F. K., his tousled hair and New England accent, how can he miss?). But aspiring politicians, however intelligent, charismatic or redolent of Camelot, must make deals along the way with czars of labor, business and the military who tend to be somewhat less than inspired. The drive to power breeds its own corruption, hence conformity and devotion to the status quo and the the balance of political power.

Another, more subtle reason why legality always lags behind reality is that a large portion of the general population despises individual greatness and always acts to whittle it down to a less threatening level – a level it can readily understand and cope with. Any innovation is seen as a threat to tradition, the general standard of living and vested interests. Witness the hue and cry in recent years over the "tracking" of New York City public school students according to their level of development. The idea that someone else's child may be more advanced in a given area than one's own is unacceptable to many people. The fact that we are not all equal in capability and intelligence, that some people are more talented or able to make money than we are, is a subject guaranteed to turn any relaxed social gathering into an emotional free-for-all. Paradoxically, it is usually the Law and Order custodian of our so-called "free enterprise" system who is the first to yell for the gestapo at the first sign of Social Darwinism arising in his own neighborhood.

The fundamental question behind all this is whether the legal structure should concern itself with matters of morality in the first place, or whether it should limit its concerns strictly to aggressive social behavior. Early in 1971, when crime figures for the preceding year were released, a sharp distinction was drawn between "victimless crimes" and "crimes involving one or more victims." The overwhelming majority of legislation on the books deals with the victimless

(Continued on page 6)

Immortality and the Law — *(Continued from page 5)*

variety – things people do to themselves or do voluntarily with other adults: whom they sleep with; how they sleep with them; the books they read; the plays and movies they watch; the stuff they pump into their own arms or suck into their own lungs; the list is endless. Obviously, the subject of legality becomes extremely complicated as the law presumes to dictate more and more standards of behavior to the public.

But if one believes that the law should have nothing to say about non-aggressive behavior, as libertarians have long argued and many others now appear to be discovering, then the issue is seen from a different viewpoint entirely. If one maintains that abortion, birth control, reading matter, public entertainment, sexual practices, gambling, drug addiction, self-abuse in general, ad infinitum, ought to be left to the discretion of each individual, the issue of legality is separated from morality and confined to its only legitimate function: protecting the innocent from aggression.

Does this mean that there should be no way of determining the answers to the questions raised at the beginning of this chapter? That far-reaching issues like inheritance and pension payments should be left up in the air with each individual making up his own rules? Not at all. Over the years, for whatever reasons, we have become increasingly dependent on government to write our contracts for us. It's difficult to think of one major contractual agreement that is not regulated by government to one extent or another: marriage; divorce; alimony; wage-price contracts; buying and selling of businesses; domestic and international trade agreements; insurance policies; etc. Not only has government entered the moral sphere and regulated non-aggressive behavior, it has also become the major author or arbiter of virtually every contract signed in the United States; this is another activity that should be left to the exclusive province of the people concerned.

If an individual wants to have himself stored in a cryo-capsule rather than planted in the earth, he has a right to sign a contract with some "freezer plan" company stipulating that he be reanimated as soon as possible. What happens if the cryonics outfit pulls out the plug and has him chopped up for icecubes? The would-be *reincarnee* can minimize his risks by dealing with a reputable firm (just as he does with any product he buys) and avoiding the fly-by-night charlatan who operates out of his icebox, or he can appoint a third party – family or attorney – to protect his interests while he is suspended. A bank account of five hundred dollars, with compounded interest over a period of forty or fifty years, can buy a hell of a lot of protection, as the banks are quick to inform us. A willful violation of contract is an aggressive act, and it is at this point that the legal authorities should step in to safeguard the rights of the innocent. In this case it would be murder as well, since the suspended party would be deprived of all hope of biological life.

The question of whether an individual can have himself frozen *any time he wants to* also comes up. Should suicide be illegal? (If so, what is the proper penalty for a suicide – twenty years standing in the corner?) In any case, suspension with the possibility of reincarnation could not really be considered self-destruction. It may be that a depressed forty-year-old who wants to have himself frozen even though he is in good health needs a psychiatrist rather than a cryonics engineer, but no one has yet found a way of legislating sanity. Some governments have managed to legislate *in*sanity by declaring radicals mentally ill, but that's another story.

If our frozen hero also happens to be well-heeled, we still don't need the law to tell us what to do with his estate. It's up to him to decide beforehand whether he wants to pass it on to his family, in which case he could leave a will, or keep it in his own name, earning interest to pay expenses

while he is suspended, which could be written into the contract with the cryonics company. There are any number of variations on these two options, all of which could be accounted for in a contract, with a law firm appointed as trustee. He might want to stipulate that, if he cannot be resuscitated after a hundred years, everything he owns passes on to his living descendants. Lawyers are very good at drawing up long, complicated, and extremely boring documents. The point is, we don't need politicians to tell us how to handle these affairs. What happens if he hops into the freezer without leaving any will or contract behind? This would probably be handled the same way it is today – the family takes the case to court and agrees to live with its decision.

A more delicate question is what to do with somebody who really does want to commit suicide. He decides he hates life completely and doesn't want to live another minute let alone three hundred years. So he turns on the gas jets and asphyxiates himself. But his family decides that he was nuts at the time and didn't know what he was doing, and they have him resuscitated. The poor guy wakes up in a hospital room and wonders, "what the hell am I doing here? I seem to be alive again." Every time he knocks himself off, somebody has him reanimated. Maybe his estranged wife wants him alive to keep making alimony payments. There's no way out for him. He can't even kill himself. If we really want to do ourselves in permanently, we may find it necessary to literally blow ourselves to bits.

The state of death will have to be redefined in legal terms to protect the interests of the living. If we can bring people back from what is considered clinical death today, then, obviously, the word "death" in its present context ceases to have any meaning. To keep abreast of evolving reality, the concept of death can only be applied to those beyond all hope of biological reanimation. We cannot force reality to conform to obsolete concepts. The concepts themselves have to change, and the body of law which "legalizes" them must harmonize with reality if the law is to be considered just. Death, simply, is the absence of life. At present, life ceases with clinical death. In the foreseeable future, it will continue

(Continued on page 7)

Immortality and the Law — *(Continued from page 6)*

to exist until all traces of biological life have been destroyed.

When should life insurance policies be paid off? Every insurance policy has a list of insuring agreements, definitions, exclusions and conditions. Moreover, these various categories are in a constant state of change; almost every time we renew an automobile or a homeowner's policy, definitions have changed slightly, exclusions have been added or eliminated, agreements have been expanded or restricted to keep pace with changing social conditions. These contracts between insurer and insured are rewritten every year, and the question of death and payments can be redefined just like any other provisions in the contract. It is hardly a cataclysmic concern requiring action from the federal government. In fact, the easiest way to confuse the issue is for government and its legions of Think Tank "intellectuals" to "study the situation." Perhaps there will be a provision that partial payments are made to the family while a policy holder is suspended; perhaps the policy will cover the costs of his suspension; perhaps interest from his estate will be used toward premium payments until he is biologically dead; most likely there will be variations on all these alternatives, and a proliferation of different types of insuring agreements. If an individual merely wants to protect his wife and children from starvation when he is no longer earning a living for them, the old policy, payable on clinical death, will serve the purpose.

The most serious obstacles will probably lie in the field of pensions and retirement. The original pension plans were devised as a form of old age insurance, a means of providing people with an income when they could no longer support themselves. Inducing companies to take care of ex-employees

who had devoted most of their lives to industry was a major breakthrough for the trade union movement. Over the years, however, the concept of pensions, like that of "relief" programs for the hungry, has been perverted completely from its original meaning. When you reach a situation like we have with civil employees in New York City, described earlier, pension plans are really welfare programs for workers still in the prime of life. The idea of the overburdened taxpayer supplying a man in his forties with eight or nine thousand dollars a year, while he is earning a full salary on a new job, is nothing less than criminal.

(If you want to have a little fun sometime, walk into any bar in the Inwood section of Manhattan on a Friday night, and strike up a conversation with the nearest patron. Mention casually that you think the New York City pension system should be scrapped tomorrow, then sit back and watch the reaction. Don't get too comfortable, though. Chances are you won't be conscious long enough to finish your drink.)

Supporters of federal welfare measures talk about social security as though it were the greatest invention since the frozen daiquiri. In reality, any private insurer that operated an insurance program the way Uncle Sam does the social security system would be hauled before a Senate Subcommittee on Un-American Activities, then flogged on the steps of the Lincoln Memorial by Ralph Nader. Can you imagine Aetna Insurance Company, for example, *forcing* the public to buy an old age policy under the pain of arrest, and then *refusing* to pay on it if the policy holder had the audacity to earn more than X dollars a year past the age of sixty-two? It simply wouldn't be tolerated. Yet, when the government treats people in such cavalier fashion, it is heralded as a

(Continued on page 8)

From The Old Curmudgeon

I. *From the Personal to the Cosmic.*

It is becoming increasingly evident that one of the most important aspects of the sickness of twentieth century American culture is the tendency to "cosmicize" the personal. By investing grand cosmic significance to every random personal *qvetch* and petty complaint, the would-be intellectual easily acquires a swollen *efflatus* of unearned importance. Reality is short-circuited, and the desire of non-achievers for instant weight and moment without the need for brains or effort is thereby fulfilled. It is surely no coincidence that the cult of psychoanalysis achieved by far its greatest popular success in the United States. Every random emotion, every trivial dream, became pregnant with great moment and significance, and every analysand and fellow-traveller of analysis found himself possessed of an inexhaustible treasure-trove for meditation and discussion.

The Women's Lib movement has now gone psychoanalysis one better in the rush to pander to the *hubris* of every member and devotee. For now every random *qvetch* and complaint becomes not only of great personal moment, but of world-historical significance; every petty squabble becomes another cosmic battle in the ten-thousand year struggle against the conspiracy of "male oppression." Psychoanalysis is now left far behind, as, in the words of one Women's Lib leader, "more and more women were learning that what was once considered personal and private was in fact part of a larger system of political oppression." (Gail Pellet, "The Dialectic of Sex: the Case for Feminist Revolution," *Socialist Revolution*, March-April 1972, p. 138.) Thus, one of the most vicious tendencies of the Left, the politicalization of life, marches on to a higher plane. Libertarians must realize with full clarity that their goal

is precisely the opposite — the total depoliticalization of life, including politics. Politicalization crushes the individual; depoliticalization frees him. Between these conflicting tendencies no quarter is possible.

II. *A Hostage to Censorship.*

It is time to blow the whistle on an argument against censorship of pornography that has been commonly adopted by liberals: that it is absurd to censor manifestations of sex (which is "clean and healthy"), while depictions of violence (John Wayne movies, etc.) remain uncensored. Instead of taking a stand on the absolute right of person and property to sell, buy, or possess any sort of literature, pictures, films, etc. that anyone may wish, the liberals shift the argument to maintaining that the depiction of sex is healthy and violence "unhealthy".

Clearly, the liberal argument is a two-edged sword that can result in more censorship rather than less. For the reaction of the authorities may well be to impose a new censorship on depictions of violence, either instead of or in addition to the traditional censorship of pornography. We would be no better off than before. The public has just as much of a right to see or purchase portrayals of violence as of sex, free of invasive interference by governmental censors. Arguments over "health" are necessarily inconclusive, ephemeral, and can differ from one expert to the next, from one year to another. Only the argument from the natural rights of the individual is absolute, apodictic, and eternal, cutting through differences of time, place, or expert opinion. Here is yet another lesson on why the libertarian must take his stand on natural rights rather than on the shifting sands of alleged "social utility."

◾

ON PUNISHMENT — *(Continued from page 7)*

cluding streets, is privately owned, much of the need for segregating criminals will be taken care of by not allowing criminals or risky types into various private areas: the rules for admission being of course determined by the land and street owners themselves.

The concept of *vengeance* has received a very bad press in recent decades, but I have never seen a satisfactory refutation of it; invariably the modern punishment theorist quickly dismisses it as "barbaric" before he races on to treat the deterrence (utilitarian) or "reform" (liberal-humanitarian) concepts of punishment. The pseudo-humanitarian concept of "reform" I have already discussed in the "Attica" editorial, and to rely primarily on deterrence leads one into the *genuine* barbarism of — say — advocating capital punishment for stealing an apple and a much *lesser* punishment for murder, since most people have an innate reluctance to commit murder while many people are not loath to steal apples, so that more intensive deterrence is then required. In my view, proportionate vengeance is not only the most just, but also the most *genuinely* humanitarian, of these three alternative theories of punishment. In any case, I see nothing wrong with the desire for vengeance; if a man's infant daughter is cruelly butchered, why should he not desire the butchery of the criminal in return, and why should he not have this desire executed? Professor Schafer well calls this exaction of vengeance "spiritual restitution" to the victim; most libertarians would agree to material restitution of a theft — why not spiritual restitution as well? Schafer writes: "The evil visited on the wrongdoer in punishment is intended . . . to endeavour to compensate the victim for his encroached or destroyed right by offering him some spiritual satisfaction . . . it is generally accepted that one of the tasks of punishment is what might be called 'idealistic damages' or 'spiritual restitution.'" (Schafer, p. 120). (See also the defense of capital punishment by Donald Atwell Zoll in "A Wistful Goodbye to Capital Punishment," *National Review*, December 3, 1971).

In the libertarian society of the future, however, there would still be a way out for pacifists and quasi-pacifists like Mr. Halliday. For all prosecution would be exercised by the victim or his agents, and not by any sort of "district attorney" presuming to speak for "society" as a whole. If, then, Mr. Halliday were victimized by criminals, he could choose not to exercise his right to punish at all, or may choose to exercise it to any extent less than is his due. (Or, if he were murdered, he could instruct his heirs in advance, by notice, not to do so.) Alternatively, he could make a voluntary contract with the criminal, allowing the wrongdoer to buy his way out of any exacted punishment. If, for example, someone beats up Mr. Halliday,

he could allow the criminal to buy his way out of a retaliatory beating. The situation, then, would by truly libertarian. Pacifists, or others who desire money over precise vengeance, could relieve the criminal of his punishment; those of us who prefer vengeance would of course allow such victims to do so. Why will *they* not allow *us* to exact due punishment? And if they don't, what sort of libertarianism is this? In the libertarian society of the future, moreover, Mr. Halliday could continue to try to convince future victims to become pacifists or quasi-pacifists; while I could continue to persuade them otherwise. No one could compel those victims who are opposed to punishment to exact such punishment; and, similarly, *they* should not be able to prohibit vengeance-bound victims from doing so.

I need only comment on a few observations by Mr. Halliday. First, there is no attempt here to measure subjective pain or utility, but to "measure" objective deeds of aggression and retaliate in kind. Second, Mr. Halliday is really saying that it is impossible to have *any* sort of objective law, or objective law code (not just for punishment) without a coercive monopoly government. Here he is simply falling into Miss Rand's trap. Objective law existed long before government (e.g. in the common law, the law merchant, admiralty law) and was worked out by privately competitive judges long before the State imposed its monopoly. Since law *is* objective, it is discoverable by reason and doesn't need government to formulate it — on the contrary, government, subject as it is to the caprice and whims of legislators, is most unlikely to respect objective law, as history has amply demonstrated. The objective Law Code would be the libertarian law of outlawing aggression against person and property, defining what that property is, setting up rules for trials to determine who the criminals are (e.g. permitting cross-examination of witnesses, etc.), and, in the libertarian society that I envision, all the privately competing courts and defense agencies would be pledged to abide by this objective Code. Any court which flouted this libertarian Code and imposed its own rules would be deemed to be itself guilty of aggression (e.g. courts which decided that all redheads are *ipso facto* criminals.)

Third, Mr. Halliday liberally sprinkles his comment with smear terms: "sadistic", "vindictive", "hater", etc. These are simply that — smear terms — and prove nothing. Not only do I see nothing wrong with "hating" crime and injustice, I hold that genuine love of justice *requires* such hatred. As Professor Zoll writes, "A humane society is a compassionate society, but compassion is only significant in terms of justice, of a sensitivity to the valid claims of men which rest upon the restraints on usurpation, aggression and terror." (Zoll, p. 1354).

A Monthly Newsletter

THE
Libertarian Forum

Joseph R. Peden, Publisher

Murray N. Rothbard, Editor

VOLUME IV, NO. 2   February, 1972   75c

PHASE II CRACKING

Richard Milhous Nixon has achieved another "first": generally it takes a year or two of price-wage controls before they visibly begin to collapse, and the heady euphoria of the public turns to sour recrimination. But in his wisdom, Richard Nixon has managed to have Phase II visibly cracking before it has hardly begun. The bloom is off the rose, for the public, for unions, and even for the staunchest supporters of the controls, the nation's businessmen. As the ardently pro-control *Business Week* put it (Jan. 29) "The Phase II honeymoon is over." Prices skyrocket in the stores, coal miners gain a 17% wage increase, while other people's wages are frozen and rent controls are firmly imposed. Some businesses are allowed price increases; others are brought sharply to book. Throughout the land, there is a crazy patchwork pattern of discrimination, enforcement, and exemptions, and the early euphoria of the public has turned to disgust and anger. The controls were expected by the Administration to put an end to the "inflationary expectations" of the public; and of course they have not succeeded.

The Administration has, predictably, met this problem with a blend of ever more Byzantine evasions and rationalizations, combined with a Connally-led exercise in hard-nosed "toughness" directed against the controls' staunchest supporters: the businessmen. Herbert Stein meets rapid price increases with the declaration that this is great because he expected the post Phase I price "bulge" to be even greater than it is. Robert F. Lanzilotti, economist and member of the Price Commission, complains that consumers do not realize that raw agricultural products are exempt from controls, and therefore should not complain about their rapid rise. "I wish," he added wistfully, "we could get this message across to the housewives." (Lotsa luck.) *(Business Week).* In the meanwhile, the Administration has helped the food-price raising process along by boosting price supports for milk. Utility rates and postal rates – and of course – taxes go up, and, as we predicted, the quality and size of many products have declined, thus constituting a hidden price increase. Jergens Lotion in Denver, for example, now costs the same 59¢ for a bottle that has oddly diminished from 4 3/4 to 4 oz.

But the Administration is nothing if not "tough". While prices have been decontrolled for small business, the Justice Dept. suddenly lashed out at Time Saver Food Stores of New Orleans, suing the store for over $100,000 in price control violations. Secretary of the Treasury Connally, too, has been addressing meetings of businessmen and denouncing them for not bringing about economic recovery. He attacked them for complaining about the vast uncertainty brought about by the patchwork price-wage controls, and for not being stimulated by the investment tax credit to increase capital spending (this in a time of large amounts of excess capacity!) The problem, as acknowledged by Argus investment research, is that Phase I and Phase II "evidently had a more depressing effect on business spending for inventories and other requirements of economic recovery than anyone had expected" (not us!). Connally will find out that no amount of Texas toughness is going to induce businessmen to suffer losses voluntarily in order to pull the Nixonite chestnuts out of the fire. Finally, the Administration sternly insists that they will keep wage and price controls indefinitely; or as Connally told businessmen in a burst of madcap illogic that will make old pragmatist John Dewey turn over in his grave, they will keep the control program "until it works." In an age of socio-economic lunacy, this is probably the most lunatic statement of them all.

Finally, C. Jackson Grayson, head of the Price Commission, threatened that if the price-wage controls do not work, we will have to go over into "socialism"; there we have it – the final wormy promise in the Nixonite apple-barrel.

America, America! How much more of the Monster Milhous will we have to take before he is dumped?

But never fear; the nation's economic big-wigs, conspicuously including "free market" economist Milton Friedman, have declared their contentment with Nixon's economics. In a recent issue, *Newsweek* (Jan. 31) coyly asked their three-man panel of economists to give President Nixon "marks" for his economic performance for 1971. Right-centrist Nixonite Henry Wallich predictably checked in with the fawning: "President Nixon has clearly earned the top grade of honors." Liberal Paul Samuelson recorded a "69" or "C+" for Nixon, since the President's "new economic policy pulled up his average for the year." But what of Milton Friedman, who allegedly provides the "right-wing" balance to the other two? Curiously enough, his mark for Tricky Dick was almost the same as Samuelson's: "75." Why such a high grade, since Friedman added that Nixon's monetary policy was "terrible" (though he blamed this on the Federal Reserve Board), the deficit too high, and the wage-price controls a "major mistake". (Remember when the Communist fellow-travellers used to mildly deplore the "mistakes" of Stalin – like slave labor camps?) So why a mark as high as 75? Nixon's "bold", "highly desirable and long overdue" action in "closing the gold window" – that means plunging the country and the world into a totally fiat currency, divorced from the sound commodity money: gold. Apparently, in the eyes of Friedman, the boldness and beauty of Nixon's fiat declaration of bankruptcy was good enough to offset the other "mistakes".

If you had asked *me, Newsweek,* for my "grade" for Richard Milhous Nixon, I would have loudly and unhesitatingly given the correct libertarian answer: "F", *and expulsion.*

277

The Political Circus

I *New Left Redux?*

The tattered remnants of whatever debris remains from the defunct New Left have gathered themselves together in a "People's Party": their major mass base is the old Peace and Freedom Party of California (the other state PFP's have long since folded); the leading theoreticians and organizers are the intellectuals from the Institute of Policy Studies, in Washington; and their current national candidates are Dr. Spock for President and Negro civil rights leader Julius Hobson for V. P. Their "big names" are Spock and the acidulous Gore Vidal.

For many years now, the intellectuals of the New Left have been promising us some "new" form of socialism, a decentralized, quasi-libertarian, anti-statist system that would discard the bad old Leviathan State. Until now, the New Left intellectuals have contented themselves with cloudy rhetoric, some of it promising, while presumably hard at work cogitating and hammering out the concrete shape of their new concept. What, exactly, would any sort of "libertarian" socialism look like? And how could the free-market be suppressed without establishing a Leviathan State? And if the free market were allowed, how would this be "socialism"?

Well, after many years, we now have our answer: the platform of the new People's Party, a platform designed as a "transitional program to decentralized, democratic socialism." (Charles Briody, national chairman of the People's Party, in *The Guardian*, Feb. 2, 1972). There are one or two obeisances to decentralization: community control of the police, and "guaranteeing the rights of minorities (how about majorities?) to control their own communities." Launching his campaign in Washington, Dr. Spock added local control of schools, including opposition to compulsory bussing. (New York *Times*, Jan. 28, 1972). But there we have it. For the rest we are offered:

A Federal Jobs Administration to provide "meaningful" work for the unemployed;

An end to the wage freeze, *but* a "real freeze on prices and corporate profits";

A vigorous campaign of federal trust-busting;

A guaranteed annual income of $6500 a year for a family of four, *plus* a national pension adjusted yearly for cost of living increases for every American over 60;

A sharply progressive tax structure which would soak the very rich and the corporations, "along with legislation prohibiting the passing on of such taxation to consumers";

Prohibition of all discrimination against women, blacks, and homosexuals (but not against WASPS?);

Free medical care for everyone, "of the highest possible quality" (Wanna bet?);

Courts and prisons designed to "rehabilitate, rather than punish, criminals";

Govermental child care centers everywhere (the parents, however, to decide their policies);

Government provision of educational opportunities for all, "including the guarantee of free tuition and living expenses through the college, technical or professional school of one's choice."

What does all this amount to? Something unfortunately all too familiar to all of us. There is nothing libertarian, voluntary, or even decentralized about any of it; it is, purely and simply, our old friend Socialism, our old tyrant the Leviathan State. After years of flim-flammery, of soul-searching, of lofty talk about alliances with the middle class and with Goldwaterites and Wallaceites, the New Left magician has finally whisked off the cloak from his new product, and what we have is . . . just the Old Left. *Plus ça change, plus c'est la même chose.*

II *Chisholm*

When the great H. L. Mencken, libertarian and political satirist, lanced the pomposities and imbecilities of the America of his day, he – and the other great satirists of the past – had the advantage of being able to take existing reality and exaggerate and parody its less attractive features. In short, they had a healthy base in reality from which to work, from which to lampoon the absurd parts of society. But sometimes it seems that life *itself* has become a parody, defying in its buffoonery any attempt of the satirist.

What would Mencken have done, for example, with the entry into the Presidential race of Rep. Shirley Chisholm (D., Brooklyn?) Mrs. Chisholm, in the kickoff speech of her campaign, announced that not only did she "represent" all the women and all the blacks and Chicanos in America, but even "all the people of the United States." (Loud applause.) In the immortal words of Samuel Goldwyn, "Kindly include me out" of this "representation." Standard political hyperbole? Perhaps. But let us ponder Mrs. Chisholm's interview in the New York *Post* (Jan. 26). Striking what some objectivists might applaud as the right note of megalomaniacal "self-esteem" tinged with paranoia, Mrs. Chisholm asserted: "I am self-confident. Enormously self-confident. Otherwise I never would have survived those people who are looking to destroy me politically." Who, Shirley? Name names; how many billions, how much psychic energy is being poured into this nationwide plot? But the reporter adds that "she brushes aside the question of who they are." Yes indeed.

Mrs. Chisholm then pressed on to explain why she is more qualified than virtually all past Presidents to hold down the office. "Thirty-six or more persons have been President of these United States. Experientially (?) and educationally I am better than all, excepting six or seven (come, come, no false humility now.) I have four college degrees, I am 10 points away from a doctorate (Oh, wow!) and I have a near-genius IQ. Close to 160." (Mohammed Ali may be the "greatest", but Shirley is the "smartest.")

And still more: "I am a very brilliant-minded woman. I can *feel* political questions. And I am quick on the draw." (The fastest mouth in the East?) Of the other Presidential candidates Mrs. Chisholm likes best none other than that Lochinvar of urban problems, Mayor Lindsay. Why? Replied the near-genius. "We're *both* Sagitarians, with strong leadership traits."

H. L. Mencken, Where Are You Now, When We Need You Most? ◘

Of Interest To Libertarians

Those who are seriously interested in the prospect of income tax evasion can now buy, for $15.00, a packet called THE COMPLETE GUIDE FOR INCOME TAX RE-FUSERS. The packet has been put together by Lucille Moran who states: "If you are a serious tax rebel, this packet is your answer. This is a simple, tough assault *that works* because it strikes directly at the heart of the income tax strategy." The kit contains a step-by-step approach for those who no longer want to cooperate with IRS. The packet can be obtained by sending a check for the above amount to Lucille E. Moran, P.O. Box 641, Tavernier, Fla. 33070, and mentioning that you saw this information in the *Libertarian Forum.*

Another tax rebel, Gordon L. Cruikshank, has founded a new religion, akin to the Universal Life Church, for those seeking the political benefits of spiritual ordination. The church is the LIFE SCIENCE CHURCH, and you can be ordained by writing to the Rev. Cruikshank at 2207 Cardinal Drive., Rolling Meadows, Ill. 60008.
◘

–Jerome Tuccille

For Croatia

The turbulent history of Yugoslavia, since World War II and indeed since World War I, can only be fully understood in terms of age-old ethnic and national struggles within the Balkans. The latest rioting and purges in Croatia are only the most recent chapter in a story that is just beginning. The major problem is that "Yugoslavia" is not really a nation; it was a typical misbegotten product of Woodrow Wilson's imperialism after the first World War. In the good name of "national self-determination", the U. S., the British, and the French created a group of ill-conceived client states. "Yugoslavia" was such an artificial creation, a geographical entity rather than a nation in which the Serbs constituting about half the total population were established as imperial dictators over the other ethnic and national entities in the new country. Backward and dedicated to statism within and without their own land, the Serbs tyrannized over the other national groups: the Croats, Slovenes, Hungarians, Albanians, Montenegrins, Macedonians, and Bosnian Muslims – each one of which constituted national, cultural, territorial and linguistic entities of their own. Of these oppressed minority nations, the most important were the Slovenes and the far more numerous Croats – progressive, Western-oriented, enterprising, and productive far beyond the other "Yugoslavian" nations. To add to their differences, the Croats and Slovenes were Catholics, while the others were Orthodox or Muslims.

During World War II, under German tutelage, the Croats, after centuries of struggle, achieved a truncated form of independent state under their leading independence and guerrilla organization, the Ustashi. But their independence was severely limited by German and Italian occupation, and especially by Italian annexation of large chunks of Croatia and the imposition of an Italian King. Furthermore, while the Ustashi slaughtered the Serb minority in Croatia and in the mixed region of Bosnia-Hercegovina, the Italians looked favorably on the activities of the Serbian terrorist organization, the Chetniks, who massacred Croats in the Italian zone. With the pacifist Croatian peasant leader Vladko Matchek (representing the bulk of the Croats) refusing either to collaborate with the Germans and replace the fanatical Ustashis *or* to lead a guerrilla resistance movement against the occupation, the anti-German guerrilla movement in Yugoslavia soon divided into two groups: the exclusively Serb Chetniks, under Draja Mihajlovitch, and a multi-ethnic Partisan movement under the Croat Marshal Tito (Josip Broz). Tito's thundering success over Mihajlovitch was due not so much to his Communism, as to the fact that he had forged a movement of ethnic equals, while Mihajlovitch largely confined his activities to the age-old Serb occupation of slaughtering Croats.

Since World War II, and especially since Tito's courageous break with Stalin and the international Communist movement, Tito has led Yugoslavia into a remarkably rapid shift away from socialist planning and a strong central state into an amazing degree of decentralization and autonomy for the various nations, as well as toward an explicitly individualist social philosophy and a free-market economy of extensive private ownership, worker ownership of factories replacing state ownership, a free price system based on profit-and-loss, private control of investment and credit, the welcoming of private foreign investment, and freedom to emigrate abroad. So autonomous are the various Yugoslav nations, for example, that Slovenia is allowed to have its own consular treaties with Austria, treaties that do not apply to the rest of the country.

Leading the struggle both for political decentralization and for a purely free-market economy have been the Communists of Croatia and Slovenia, the most industrialized, productive, and thrifty areas, and particularly in the fore front have been the Croatian and Slovenian economists, whose writings sound very much like Goldwater, Reagan, or Ludwig von Mises. The Croats, for example, have bitterly attacked the establishment of "political factories" by the Yugoslav central government, in which the productive Croats have been taxed to subsidize lazy and unproductive people in the Albanian region and Montenegro. And throughout this exciting period of rapid shift from socialism to freedom (a shift which soon envisions a free stock-market and ownership by *individual* instead of collective workers), it has been the Serbs – the "conservatives" – who have clung to the Old Order and been most resistant to this libertarian advance. It is almost exclusively the Serbs, for example, who staff the organs of the central government. To the extent that in 1967, Tito was forced to fire his Number 2 man and picked successor, Aleksandr Rankovitch, who had been in control of the hated secret police, after which that sinister agency of every totalitarian state was dismantled. And throughout the argument among economists it was always the Croats, centered in Zagreb, battling against the conservative crypto-Stalinists in Serb Belgrade.

The rapid and inexorable change in Yugoslavia pursued the logic of freedom; and it is characteristic of such an era of great change that the expectations of the people, especially in Crotia, rose to demand the pursuing of that logic to its conclusion. The Croats, led by the Croatian Communist League and more militantly by striking university students, came to demand: a wider free market, and abolishing the practice of the central government taxing Croatian earnings of foreign exchange in order to subsidize the rest of Yugoslavia. And looming behind these demands was the ultimate logic: Croatian independence at long last, after a thousand years of oppression.

Tragically, the aging Tito refused to pursue this logic the final step. Last December, Tito partially reverted to his Stalinist past. Over a thousand Croat students were arrested, and a ruthless purge has hit the Croatian Communist and intellectual leadership, many of whom are now awaiting trial for such high crimes as "counter-revolution" and "denigration of the state." The Croatian Communist leadership, headed by Miko Tripalo and Mrs. Savka Dabeevic-Kucar, have all been ousted and may themselves be brought to trial, perhaps for "high treason." As one Croat woman lamented, "We used to feel that we were so different from the Poles and the Czechs, now we don't feel different at all." (James Feron, in the New York *Times*, Jan. 25).

Meanwhile, the old Ustashi movement lives on in exile, in West Germany, home of over half a million Yugoslavs, mainly Croats, working temporarily abroad. From there, the Ustashi conduct some guerrilla activities against Yugoslavia. The poor befuddled New York *Times*, failing as always to comprehend national liberation movements, can't make up its mind whether the Ustashi, and its current leader, Dr. Branko Jelic, are "Nazis" or "Communists." On the one hand, they ruled under the tutelage of the Nazis in World War II; on the other hand, they recently organized the "League of Croatian Communists Abroad", and are rumored to have accepted funds from Soviet intelligence. The solution to the puzzle should be plain, however; the Ustashi are simply Croat nationalists, and as Dr. Jelic candidly admitted, he would "sleep with the devil" is necessary to achieve an independent Croatia. (James Feron, and David Binder, in the New York *Times*, Jan. 28).

Last year, the *Lib. Forum* called for and predicted the rise of an independent Bangladesh. Our predictions were fulfilled. We cannot predict an independent Croatia so readily, but the logic of events is clearly in that direction. Marshal Tito cannot live forever, and the centrifugal forces which he himself set in motion make almost inevitable the collapse of the "collective presidency" representing each nation which is to succeed him, and the division of the misbegotten country of Yugoslavia into its constituent parts. Croatia will rise again.

◻

Will The Real
(Howard Hughes, Clifford Erving, Helga Hughes, George Holmes, Hannah Rosencrantz . . .) Please Stand Up.?

What a lot of glorious fun the Howard Hughes caper is! It has all the necessary ingredients: an unfolding, ever more labyrinthine tale of mystery, chicanery, high finance and high level intrigue, subject to numerous interpretations and endless specualtion — and all of no importance whatsoever. For surcease from worldly care, it is just what we all needed to tide us over between the Super Bowl and the New Hampshire primary. ◘

The Shaffer Dictionary

By Butler Shaffer

The following definitions comprise a part of my view of reality, in all its humorous—and often frustrating—manner.

ANARCHY: a chaotic system devoid of political government; hence, the absence of wars, depressions, and other manifestations of law and order.

CANNIBALISM: pre-capitalistic socialism.

MARXISM: a New Deal program for atheists.
A philosophy which would have won the overwhelming support of the Catholic and Protestant churches, and the Democratic and Republican parties, but for the strategic blunder of having endorsed atheism.

GENERAL WELFARE: that which serves my personal interests.

BOONDOGGLE: that which serves yours.

BANDIT: one who believes that even a little man can aspire to a political career.

WAR-HERO: a man who commits atrocities for our side.

INFIDEL: one whose judgment has been distorted by fact, reason, and logic. ◘

The Movement Marches On

The distinguished English weekly, *The Manchester Guardian*, has published an article that will cheer the heart of every libertarian. (John Windsor, "A Right State of Affairs," *The Manchester Guardian Weekly*, December 25, 1971, p. 15.) The *Guardian* reports that the British libertarian movement, which it calls "guerrilla capitalism," "threatens to become the New Year's trendy political curiosity." While acknowledging that the British movement still has only about thirty members, it takes its future quite seriously. There are quotes and descriptions of the new movement, which centers around an American-style hamburger restaurant in Kingston-upon-Thames run by the American-

Recommended Reading

Rothbard pamphlets. Murray Rothbard has recently had two pamphlets published. One is *Freedom, Inequality, Primitivism and the Division of Labor* (50¢, from the Institute for Humane Studies, 1134 Crane St., Menlo Park, Calif. 94025.) This is a reprint of the article in *Modern Age* (Summer, 1971), attacking left-wing egalitarianism and the yen to crush the division of labor and therefore individual freedom and development. The other is *Education, Free and Compulsory* (available from the Center for Independent Education, 9115 E. Thirteenth, Wichita, Kan. 67206); the first part of this pamphlet appeared in the April, 1971 *Individualist*. The pamphlet is a history and critique of compulsory attendance laws, and outlines an individualistic philosophy of education.

Rule of Law. One of the most dangerous notions, which caught on in some libertarian circles in the early 1960's, was F. A. Hayek's grounding of political philosophy on the "rule of law." Now Professor Ronald Hamowy, a former student of Hayek's, has published a brilliant, thorough, and scholarly evisceration of the rule of law, and demonstrates that it provides no groundwork whatsoever for a libertarian political philosophy. See Ronald Hamowy, "Freedom and the Rule of Law in F. A. Hayek", *Il Politico* (Pavia), (1971, No. 2), pp. 349-77.

Cold War Revisionism. *Cold War Critics* is a book containing an excellent series of articles on early critics of the Cold War. Of particular interest to libertarians is: Ronald Radosh and Leonard P. Liggio, "Henry A. Wallace and the Open Door", pp. 76-113; and Henry W. Berger, "Senator Robert A. Taft Dissents from Military Escalation." (Leonard Liggio is the historian, long-time libertarian, and valued *Lib. Forum* contributor). The brunt of the two articles is that Robert Taft was a far more trenchant and consistent critic of the Cold War and American imperialism than Henry Wallace, who was himself an imperialist of a slightly more pacific and sophisticated breed. See Thomas G. Paterson, ed., *Cold War Critics* (Chicago: Quadrangle Books, 1971, paper $2.95).

Wage-Price Controls. Now that direct controls are once again upon us, the American Enterprise Institute (1150 17th St., N. W., Washington, D. C. 20036) has performed an important service by publishing a pamphlet, Colin Campbell, ed., *Wage-Price Controls in World War II, United States and Germany*, 73 pp., $3.00, collecting and reprinting notable contemporary articles critical of the workings of American and German controls. Included are articles by Mansfield, Cherne, Keezer, Mendershausen, and Eucken.

born Pauline Russell, a graduate of UCLA. The restaurant, the Transatlantic Success, publishes the magazine *The Guerrilla Capitalist*, selling for ten pence, and the group is called the Radical Libertarian Alliance. Also mentioned in the article is Richard King, former Australian bee remover who ran a "guerrilla capitalist" postal service during the British postal strike, delivering magazines profitably at one-third the charge levied by the British Post Office. Other libertarians cited in the group are Chris Tame and the Indian Mansur Nathoo, editor of the *Guerrilla Capitalist*, who is studying for a Ph. D. at the University of London.

One happy note: the article declares that in the USA there are "an estimated 200,000 practicing libertarians." Well, well, well! We hadn't thought it was nearly that many, but who are we to correct such a distinguished journal?? ◘

Immortality And The Law

By Jerome Tuccille
(an excerpt from a forthcoming book)

The legal problems created by extended life – not to mention immortality – would be overwhelming say the critics. We would have to rewrite the law books, probably redefine the entire question of death. Such items as suicide and murder would assume radically new meanings for all of us. Morality would be more throughly intertwined with politics, involving spokesmen from the various religious denominations and further eroding the wall dividing church and state. As government has gotten itself progressively entangled in moral issues – abortion; birth control; sexual customs; pornography; prostitution – it has penetrated more and more deeply into a province considered to be the exclusive domain of the religious authorities. One can imagine a life-death freeze in 1984 modeled after Richard Nixon's wage-price freeze of 1971, with a tripartite board of rabbis, priests and ministers advising the president. To be sure, Holy Rollers, fakirs, theosophists and whirling dervishes will all be clamoring for equal representation, charging the government with oppression for not adopting a "quota system" for religious minorities.

Insurance companies, too, are bound to suffer a dramatic upheaval. Do they pay off life insurance policies on people suspended in liquid nitrogen? Are they "dead" or not? What about inheritance? Does the estate of a suspended human being pass on to his family, or is it held in abeyance until he is reanimated? How about pension plans? It's one thing to retire an individual at sixty-five and pay him a salary until he expires five, ten or fifteen years later. But for sixty or seventy years? The whole question of "mandatory retirement age" will have to be re-evaluated.

Government has also gotten itself firmly entwined in the insurance business through social security, medicare and similar welfare measures. When our average life expectancy is increased to a hundred and twenty-five, social security payments will continue for sixty years instead of five or ten. Government pension plans are the most outrageous in existence anywhere. In New York City it is possible for a man to join the police force or fire department at twenty-one and retire at forty-one with three-quarters pay until he dies. Presently, he can expect to live another thirty years and already the money paid out annually in pensions to retired New York City employees *is equal to the amount paid in salaries to contemporary civil servants,* and it is rising proportionately every year. With a major breakthrough in the anti-aging field the pension fund could double or triple in a matter of years, and the private wage earner in New York City will find most of his taxes winding up in the pockets of ex-cops and firemen.

No private industry in the world could survive for long with such corrupt and shortsighted policies. The government, with its stranglehold on the earnings of honest citizens, is not subject to market competition and can keep the fantasy going a bit longer. But sooner or later the bubble has to explode.

The error made by opponents of immortality from the viewpoint of legality is the old familiar one of putting the cart before the horse; they fail to comprehend that legal forms do not determine reality, that the case is quite the opposite. Any legal structure which does not conform to the reality of the world we live in is at best archaic and obsolete, at worst immoral and dictatorial. Since the reality of the world around us is fluid, dynamic, constantly changing because of experimentation and new discoveries, it is incumbent upon the legal system to adapt itself to the evolving reality of life.

Historically, legality has never been able to keep up with the rapid pace of human achievement. It has always lagged two and three generations behind the times, and at any given moment there are laws on the books which reflect the thinking and social attitudes of fifty years before. In New York State today it is illegal to call a tavern a "saloon" – a hangover from the pre-Prohibition era when the word *saloon* identified a place where intoxicating beverages were sold without meals and was later outlawed. Today it is legal to operate such an establishment, but illegal to use the word which describes it. A well-known bar in New York City, O'Neal's Baloon, originally opened with the name O'Neal's Saloon in the late 1960's. The state liquor authorities stepped in shortly afterward and demanded that the name be changed. Rather than spending a lot of money having a new sign put up, the owner – actor Patrick O'Neal – merely took a can of paint and changed the S to an awkward B. Patrons still refer to the pub as O'Neal's Saloon even though the official name over the door conforms to the requirements of legislators in Albany.

There are many reasons why the legal code remains resistant to change while the reality of life progresses as a result of human ingenuity. The most obvious is the nature of the men who invariably control the structure of government. Those attracted to government seem to be, with few exceptions, the most cautious, shortsighted, conformist and authoritarian among us. Our journalists, media spokesmen and university intellectuals are constantly crying out for "new, young, progressive and charismatic" leaders to enter the breach and launch a New Great Frontier Deal to save the world. Yesterday's hero was John F. Kennedy; today's is John Lindsay; tomorrow's will surely be the anti-war veteran John Kerry of Massachusetts (with his initials J. F. K., his tousled hair and New England accent, how can he miss?). But aspiring politicians, however intelligent, charismatic or redolent of Camelot, must make deals along the way with czars of labor, business and the military who tend to be somewhat less than inspired. The drive to power breeds its own corruption, hence conformity and devotion to the status quo and the the balance of political power.

Another, more subtle reason why legality always lags behind reality is that a large portion of the general population despises individual greatness and always acts to whittle it down to a less threatening level – a level it can readily understand and cope with. Any innovation is seen as a threat to tradition, the general standard of living and vested interests. Witness the hue and cry in recent years over the "tracking" of New York City public school students according to their level of development. The idea that someone else's child may be more advanced in a given area than one's own is unacceptable to many people. The fact that we are not all equal in capability and intelligence, that some people are more talented or able to make money than we are, is a subject guaranteed to turn any relaxed social gathering into an emotional free-for-all. Paradoxically, it is usually the Law and Order custodian of our so-called "free enterprise" system who is the first to yell for the gestapo at the first sign of Social Darwinism arising in his own neighborhood.

The fundamental question behind all this is whether the legal structure should concern itself with matters of morality in the first place, or whether it should limit its concerns strictly to aggressive social behavior. Early in 1971, when crime figures for the preceding year were released, a sharp distinction was drawn between "victimless crimes" and "crimes involving one or more victims." The overwhelming majority of legislation on the books deals with the victimless

(Continued on page 6)

Immortality and the Law — *(Continued from page 5)*

variety — things people do to themselves or do voluntarily with other adults: whom they sleep with; how they sleep with them; the books they read; the plays and movies they watch; the stuff they pump into their own arms or suck into their own lungs; the list is endless. Obviously, the subject of legality becomes extremely complicated as the law presumes to dictate more and more standards of behavior to the public.

But if one believes that the law should have nothing to say about non-aggressive behavior, as libertarians have long argued and many others now appear to be discovering, then the issue is seen from a different viewpoint entirely. If one maintains that abortion, birth control, reading matter, public entertainment, sexual practices, gambling, drug addiction, self-abuse in general, ad infinitum, ought to be left to the discretion of each individual, the issue of legality is separated from morality and confined to its only legitimate function: protecting the innocent from aggression.

Does this mean that there should be no way of determining the answers to the questions raised at the beginning of this chapter? That far-reaching issues like inheritance and pension payments should be left up in the air with each individual making up his own rules? Not at all. Over the years, for whatever reasons, we have become increasingly dependent on government to write our contracts for us. It's difficult to think of one major contractual agreement that is not regulated by government to one extent or another: marriage; divorce; alimony; wage-price contracts; buying and selling of businesses; domestic and international trade agreements; insurance policies; etc. Not only has government entered the moral sphere and regulated non-aggressive behavior, it has also become the major author or arbiter of virtually every contract signed in the United States; this is another activity that should be left to the exclusive province of the people concerned.

If an individual wants to have himself stored in a cryo-capsule rather than planted in the earth, he has a right to sign a contract with some "freezer plan" company stipulating that he be reanimated as soon as possible. What happens if the cryonics outfit pulls out the plug and has him chopped up for icecubes? The would-be *reincarnee* can minimize his risks by dealing with a reputable firm (just as he does with any product he buys) and avoiding the fly-by-night charlatan who operates out of his icebox, or he can appoint a third party — family or attorney — to protect his interests while he is suspended. A bank account of five hundred dollars, with compounded interest over a period of forty or fifty years, can buy a hell of a lot of protection, as the banks are quick to inform us. A willful violation of contract is an aggressive act, and it is at this point that the legal authorities should step in to safeguard the rights of the innocent. In this case it would be murder as well, since the suspended party would be deprived of all hope of biological life.

The question of whether an individual can have himself frozen *any time he wants to* also comes up. Should suicide be illegal? (If so, what is the proper penalty for a suicide — twenty years standing in the corner?) In any case, suspension with the possibility of reincarnation could not really be considered self-destruction. It may be that a depressed forty-year-old who wants to have himself frozen even though he is in good health needs a psychiatrist rather than a cryonics engineer, but no one has yet found a way of legislating sanity. Some governments have managed to legislate *insanity* by declaring radicals mentally ill, but that's another story.

If our frozen hero also happens to be well-heeled, we still don't need the law to tell us what to do with his estate. It's up to him to decide beforehand whether he wants to pass it on to his family, in which case he could leave a will, or keep it in his own name, earning interest to pay expenses

while he is suspended, which could be written into the contract with the cryonics company. There are any number of variations on these two options, all of which could be accounted for in a contract, with a law firm appointed as trustee. He might want to stipulate that, if he cannot be resuscitated after a hundred years, everything he owns passes on to his living descendants. Lawyers are very good at drawing up long, complicated, and extremely boring documents. The point is, we don't need politicians to tell us how to handle these affairs. What happens if he hops into the freezer without leaving any will or contract behind? This would probably be handled the same way it is today — the family takes the case to court and agrees to live with its decision.

A more delicate question is what to do with somebody who really does want to commit suicide. He decides he hates life completely and doesn't want to live another minute let alone three hundred years. So he turns on the gas jets and asphyxiates himself. But his family decides that he was nuts at the time and didn't know what he was doing, and they have him resuscitated. The poor guy wakes up in a hospital room and wonders, "what the hell am I doing here? I seem to be alive again." Every time he knocks himself off, somebody has him reanimated. Maybe his estranged wife wants him alive to keep making alimony payments. There's no way out for him. He can't even kill himself. If we really want to do ourselves in permanently, we may find it necessary to literally blow ourselves to bits.

The state of death will have to be redefined in legal terms to protect the interests of the living. If we can bring people back from what is considered clinical death today, then, obviously, the word "death" in its present context ceases to have any meaning. To keep abreast of evolving reality, the concept of death can only be applied to those beyond all hope of biological reanimation. We cannot force reality to conform to obsolete concepts. The concepts themselves have to change, and the body of law which "legalizes" them must harmonize with reality if the law is to be considered just. Death, simply, is the absence of life. At present, life ceases with clinical death. In the foreseeable future, it will continue

(Continued on page 7)

Immortality and the Law — *(Continued from page 6)*

to exist until all traces of biological life have been destroyed.

When should life insurance policies be paid off? Every insurance policy has a list of insuring agreements, definitions, exclusions and conditions. Moreover, these various categories are in a constant state of change; almost every time we renew an automobile or a homeowner's policy, definitions have changed slightly, exclusions have been added or eliminated, agreements have been expanded or restricted to keep pace with changing social conditions. These contracts between insurer and insured are rewritten every year, and the question of death and payments can be redefined just like any other provisions in the contract. It is hardly a cataclysmic concern requiring action from the federal government. In fact, the easiest way to confuse the issue is for government and its legions of Think Tank "intellectuals" to "study the situation." Perhaps there will be a provision that partial payments are made to the family while a policy holder is suspended; perhaps the policy will cover the costs of his suspension; perhaps interest from his estate will be used toward premium payments until he is biologically dead; most likely there will be variations on all these alternatives, and a proliferation of different types of insuring agreements. If an individual merely wants to protect his wife and children from starvation when he is no longer earning a living for them, the old policy, payable on clinical death, will serve the purpose.

The most serious obstacles will probably lie in the field of pensions and retirement. The original pension plans were devised as a form of old age insurance, a means of providing people with an income when they could no longer support themselves. Inducing companies to take care of ex-employees who had devoted most of their lives to industry was a major breakthrough for the trade union movement. Over the years, however, the concept of pensions, like that of "relief" programs for the hungry, has been perverted completely from its original meaning. When you reach a situation like we have with civil employees in New York City, described earlier, pension plans are really welfare programs for workers still in the prime of life. The idea of the overburdened taxpayer supplying a man in his forties with eight or nine thousand dollars a year, while he is earning a full salary on a new job, is nothing less than criminal.

(If you want to have a little fun sometime, walk into any bar in the Inwood section of Manhattan on a Friday night, and strike up a conversation with the nearest patron. Mention casually that you think the New York City pension system should be scrapped tomorrow, then sit back and watch the reaction. Don't get too comfortable, though. Chances are you won't be conscious long enough to finish your drink.)

Supporters of federal welfare measures talk about social security as though it were the greatest invention since the frozen daiquiri. In reality, any private insurer that operated an insurance program the way Uncle Sam does the social security system would be hauled before a Senate Subcommittee on Un-American Activities, then flogged on the steps of the Lincoln Memorial by Ralph Nader. Can you imagine Aetna Insurance Company, for example, *forcing* the public to buy an old age policy under the pain of arrest, and then *refusing* to pay on it if the policy holder had the audacity to earn more than X dollars a year past the age of sixty-two? It simply wouldn't be tolerated. Yet, when the government treats people in such cavalier fashion, it is heralded as a

(Continued on page 8)

From The Old Curmudgeon

I. *From the Personal to the Cosmic.*

It is becoming increasingly evident that one of the most important aspects of the sickness of twentieth century American culture is the tendency to "cosmicize" the personal. By investing grand cosmic significance to every random personal *qvetch* and petty complaint, the would-be intellectual easily acquires a swollen *efflatus* of unearned importance. Reality is short-circuited, and the desire of non-achievers for instant weight and moment without the need for brains or effort is thereby fulfilled. It is surely no coincidence that the cult of psychoanalysis achieved by far its greatest popular success in the United States. Every random emotion, every trivial dream, became pregnant with great moment and significance, and every analysand and fellow-traveller of analysis found himself possessed of an inexhaustible treasure-trove for meditation and discussion.

The Women's Lib movement has now gone psychoanalysis one better in the rush to pander to the *hubris* of every member and devotee. For now every random *qvetch* and complaint becomes not only of great personal moment, but of world-historical significance; every petty squabble becomes another cosmic battle in the ten-thousand year struggle against the conspiracy of "male oppression." Psychoanalysis is now left far behind, as, in the words of one Women's Lib leader, "more and more women were learning that what was once considered personal and private was in fact part of a larger system of political oppression." (Gail Pellet, "The Dialectic of Sex: the Case for Feminist Revolution," *Socialist Revolution*, March-April 1972, p. 138.) Thus, one of the most vicious tendencies of the Left, the politicalization of life, marches on to a higher plane. Libertarians must realize with full clarity that their goal is precisely the opposite – the total depoliticalization of life, including politics. Politicalization crushes the individual; depoliticalization frees him. Between these conflicting tendencies no quarter is possible.

II. *A Hostage to Censorship.*

It is time to blow the whistle on an argument against censorship of pornography that has been commonly adopted by liberals: that it is absurd to censor manifestations of sex (which is "clean and healthy"), while depictions of violence (John Wayne movies, etc.) remain uncensored. Instead of taking a stand on the absolute right of person and property to sell, buy, or possess any sort of literature, pictures, films, etc. that anyone may wish, the liberals shift the argument to maintaining that the depiction of sex is healthy and violence "unhealthy".

Clearly, the liberal argument is a two-edged sword that can result in more censorship rather than less. For the reaction of the authorities may well be to impose a new censorship on depictions of violence, either instead of or in addition to the traditional censorship of pornography. We would be no better off than before. The public has just as much of a right to see or purchase portrayals of violence as of sex, free of invasive interference by governmental censors. Arguments over "health" are necessarily inconclusive, ephemeral, and can differ from one expert to the next, from one year to another. Only the argument from the natural rights of the individual is absolute, apodictic, and eternal, cutting through differences of time, place, or expert opinion. Here is yet another lesson on why the libertarian must take his stand on natural rights rather than on the shifting sands of alleged "social utility."

THE LONE EAGLE — *(Continued from page 7)*

Eagle kept emphasizing that the United States was safe from armed attack, one wonders whether or not he was envisioning a world policed by America in one sphere Germany in another – a world which might perhaps see the end of "Asiatic" power?

Lindbergh fails to make clear why he did not return his Order of the German Eagle, or why he did not clarify his Des Moines speech in which he accused "Jewish groups" of fomenting war and asserted that only a peaceful America could remain racially tolerant. One biographer, more friendly to Lindbergh than most, declared that these words could either be interpreted as a threat or a prophetic insight, based upon first-hand observation of Nazi life.[3] At any rate criticism came not only from such liberal non-interventionists as Chester Bowles, Philip Jessup and John T. Flynn, but from Herbert Hoover (who called it "an anti-Jewish speech"),[4] the *Chicago Tribune*, and the Hearst papers. Bowles in particular wanted clarification, as he had urged Lindbergh to run for the Senate. In the eyes of the New York advertising executive, Lindbergh would be the "technological expert who can talk objectively and convincingly about the millions of Americans who lack the proper food, the numbers who lack the proper housing, the proper hospital care . . ."[5]

Other points need confirmation. If Senator Harry F. Byrd of Virginia was sympathetic to isolation, why did he not rally other southern conservatives? (pp. 261, 263) Did FDR really toy with offering Lindbergh a new cabinet post, Secretary for Air, in order to retain his silence? Did Lindbergh, as John Chamberlain claims, really go on a mission to Germany to rescue the Jews of Europe?[6] In light of the superior maneuverability of the British Hurricanes and Spitfires to the Messerschmitt 109s, and in light of the shortage of fighters during the Battle of Britain, was not Lindbergh's stress on the superiority of the German airforce overdone?

The last section of the book is in many ways the most revealing. Though believing that war would invariably result in the loss of freedom at home, the Colonel felt duty-bound to participate in the conflict, (pp. 566-7). Rejected by the Roosevelt Administration for military service, and receiving personal insults from Secretary of War Stimson concerning his "political views" and "lack of aggressiveness," Lindbergh flew over fifty combat missions as a civilian test pilot. Here one of the world's leading proponents of airpower becomes outraged over the impersonality of bombing. Not only does he equate the bombing of Cologne with Canterbury, but his own firsthand experience sobers him. "You press the trigger and death leaps forth," he writes after one mission. "—4,200 projectiles a minute.

Tracers bury themselves in wall and roof . . . Inside may be death or writhing agony. You never know" (p. 822). At one point he refuses to kill a possible enemy he sees from the air, noting the quiet courage in the man's deliberate pace. "His bearing, his stride, his dignity – there is something in them that has formed a bond between us . . . I shall always remember his figure striding over the sand, the fearless dignity of his steps" (p. 821).

The air ace is continually shocked by the callousness of American troops who would, according to Lindbergh, often shoot on sight Japanese prisoners desiring to surrender (pp. 880-1). American forces, he confessed, "have no respect for death, the courage of an enemy soldier, or many of the ordinary decencies of life" (p. 859). After witnessing the American conquest of Biak Island, he noted, "We hold his (the Japanese) examples of atrocity screamingly to the heavens while we cover up our own and condone them as just retribution for his acts . . . for our people to kill by torture and to descend to throwing the bodies into a bomb crater and dumping garbage on them nauseates me" (pp. 880, 883). These aspects of the volume were ignored by reviewers of all political persuasions: as far as either the *New York Review of Books*, the *New Republic* or *National Review* is concerned, World War II must still be seen through Star-Spangled glasses.

Little wonder that when the Lone Eagle visited the German Concentration Dora, he was reminded of the atrocities of the coral caves of Biak (p. 996).[7] "It is not the Germans alone," he wrote, "or the Japs, but the men of all nations to whom this war has brought shame and degradation" (p. 998). For some, such comparisons might be a grievous crime; for others, let us hope, it is the beginning of wisdom.

---

[3]Walter S. Ross, *The Last Hero: Charles A. Lindbergh* (New York: Harper and Row, 1968), p. 317 Wayne S. Cole notes that many anti-Semites were encouraged by his comments. *America. First* (Madison: University of Wisconsin Press, 1953), p. 144.

[4]H. Hoover to J. Scott, September 14, 1941, the Papers of Herbert Hoover, Herbert Hoover Presidential Library, West Branch, Iowa.

[5]C. Bowles to R. D. Stuart, Jr., July 15, 1941, the Papers of the America First Committee, Hoover Library of War, Peace, and Revolution, Palo Alto, California.

[6]"Adventure in Honesty," *National Review*, November 17, 1970, p. 1213.

[7]Though Lindbergh has never regretted his militant non-interventionism, he did claim in May, 1945, that it was Hitler who "threw the human world into the greatest convulsion it has ever known" and whose plans had "brought such disaster to the world" (p. 949).

The Libertarian Forum
BOX 341
MADISON SQUARE STATION
NEW YORK, NEW YORK 10010

First Class

Published Every Month. Subscription Rate: $8.00 Per Year

A Monthly Newsletter

THE
Libertarian Forum

Joseph R. Peden, Publisher

Murray N. Rothbard, Editor

VOLUME IV, NO. 4　　　　　　　　APRIL, 1972　　　　　　　　75c

A BUNCH OF LOSERS

Perhaps we are being what the Marxists call "impressionistic" (or what the Randians call "journalistic" rather than "metaphysical"), but it is very hard to escape the impression from the early Democratic primaries that the contenders are all a bunch of losers, every one. Let us ponder our gaggle of aspirants in turn.

Lindsay. Certainly the most heartwarming result of the Florida primary was the evisceration of John V. Lindsay. Striding arrogantly through the state as he does through New York City, assuming the mantle of God's gift to the American public, Big John was the recipient of almost universal adoration by the media, and of spectacularly lavish financing. Coming out of a record of administrative disaster coupled with corruption and centralized statism, Lindsay was able to pre-empt the Left with a frankly despotic position on compulsory busing. The upshot of the charisma, the media acclaim, and the billboards plastering the state of Florida was a measly 7% of the Democratic vote, at a phenomenal cost of $6 per vote. (Generally, $1 per vote is considered the outsize figure in politics; John Ashbrook emerged from the Republican primary at about 25 cents a vote.) Surely we have now heard the last of John Vliet, and it couldn't have happened to a more deserving guy.

Muskie. After a disappointing victory in New Hampshire, Muskie's 9% in Florida should, by rights and by logic, put the quietus to his chances for the nomination. After all, his appeal was that of a Lincolnesque frontrunner, but what kind of a frontrunner amasses 9%? Unfortunately – unfortunately because he has clearly been repudiated by the American public – the Democrats might still turn to Muskie in the end. Muskie has all the qualities that commend themselves to centrist Democrats anxious to unify the party: a Lincolnesque air, a colorless, "sincere" personality, and very tepidly liberal on the issues. The only trouble with that strategy is that he can't seem to get any *votes* – but given the factionalism and the genius for self-destruction of the Democracy, they might still wind up with Muskie. Note, for example, the desperate clinging to Muskie in the New York *Times* editorial of March 16, as the good grey *Times* surveyed the Florida debacle. But Muskie is a loser, and he would surely go down to a craggy, Lincolnesque defeat in November.

The Muskie defeat has been attributed by his own aides to an interesting factor: he spoke too much. They now claim that he should have kept his mouth shut, and victory would have been his. An ironic commentary on the quality of our leaders! Then there was Muskie's sobbing on coast-to-coast television. Liberal columnist Harriet van Horne (for whom the term "bleeding heart" would have to be invented if it didn't exist) gushed that Muskie's breakdown showed him to

be a gentle man, and not hung up on "masculine role playing". Fine and dandy, but this was clearly not the reaction of the American voter, who wondered, not without some justice, how Muskie would react to really important emotional stress in a national crisis.

McGovern. It is true that McGovern did not campaign in Florida, but still he was on the ballot, and a whopping 6% hardly brands McGovern as the emerging choice of the American people. McGovern and Lindsay both claim to be the new "populists", but there were precious few of "the people" to cheer them on. McGovern's good showing in New Hampshire could have been largely due to a negative interest in Muskie, as well as the intense concentration of left-wing college youth, which will not be duplicated elsewhere.

Finally, McGovern is just too far left for the American people, and he would be clobbered handily should he gain the nomination. There is one aspect of the Florida returns that has not been noted: the right-of-center candidates in the Democratic primary got a huge 75% of the votes, leaving only 25% for the left. Say what you will about the conservatism of Florida, but the figures remain eloquent on the repudiation of the left by the mass of the voters.

Wallace. The real winner in Florida, of course, was George Wallace, and this was not an unwelcome sight. Let us ponder the issues on which Wallace pounded hard in the campaign: opposition to compulsory busing, opposition to high taxes, to bureaucracy, and to foreign aid. There has a lot of loose talk about the importance of a "new populism", of a populist campaign against the ruling classes. But George Wallace was the only true populist in the race, the only true champion of the average American against the ruling elite. It is not a coincidence that each one of these populist issues were libertarian issues as well. The New Left, for all its obeisances to "populism", for all its talk about someday appealing to the Goldwater and Wallace voters, has never been able to make the grade: largely because it has never been able to bring itself to call for a lowering of taxes (they merely want to shift the "priorities" of government spending). And secondly, because the New Left, for all its bowing to black nationalism, has never been able to abandon the civil rights ideal of compulsory integration, which, in busing, involves the transporting of children to outlying areas for alleged "social gains." George Wallace has been able to denounce high taxes and busing without flinching, and so he captured the votes. A further irony is that the National Black Political Convention, meeting in Gary, Indiana, itself denounced compulsory

(Continued on page 4)

Ashlosky For President

By Edwin G. Dolan

With the field already so crowded a rumor – not even confirmed – of another congressman about to enter the race for president runs the danger of being greeted by a yawn. But to ignore congressman John Paul Ashlosky, representative from an obscure district in one of our midwestern states, would be a serious mistake – he is definitely a candidate with a difference.

His possible entry into the Republican primaries is especially significant in view of the two opposition candidates who had been running in New Hampshire.

On the one hand, we have John Ashbrook of Ohio, who offers voters an opportunity to express their outrage at Richard Nixon's sellout of everything he personally and the Republican Party generally have ever stood for in the area of economic policy. But many who would like a chance to register their dismay at Phase I and Phase II and inflationary recession are held back by the fear that a vote for Ashbrook would be interpreted as an endorsement of that candidate's stance on foreign policy, which sustains a degree of militarism, interventionism, and crusading anti-Communism which they would just as soon see left behind as we head into the fourth quarter of the century.

On the other hand, there is the late candidacy of Paul McCloskey of California, who gave the voter a chance to tell the Administration that he hasn't been fooled by the troop withdrawals and other cosmetics of Vietnamization – that Nixon's stance during the Bangla Desh crisis shows him as willing as ever to prop up sagging military dictatorships everywhere, and to stand four-square for reaction in the four corners of the earth. Yet a vote for Mc-Closkey might have been taken as a vote for Republican me-too-ism on that whole range of policies, domestic as well as foreign, on which the left-wing of the Democratic party is basing its presidential drive.

So in this situation, the hoped-for candidacy of Ash-losky will combine the best elements of both opposition candidates (Nixon himself already combines the worst) and give the voters a chance to express themselves unambiguously on the issues. A few remarks from a recent speech by the congressman will show the form his platform is taking:

"What we have witnessed in recent decades is a convergence of Conservatives and Liberals, Republicans and Democrats, on one fundamental tenet of ideology – that whatever the problems we face, the solution is to be sought through ever more high-handed use of the power of the federal government.

"When political realignments seem imminent in any part of the world, the response is the power of bombs, fleets, and military aid. When the bankrupt economic policies of three administrations face us with runaway inflation and history's largest budget deficits, the answer is more power – the power to abrogate contracts, stifle the market, and impose a totalitarian-style system of comprehensive controls. And when our public school system reveals its failure either to educate our sons and daughters, or to do anything but exacerbate tensions between races and economic classes, the answer is still more power – power which can't lift us up but can force us down to a uniform level of mediocrity.

"In my view, the runaway growth of government power is not the solution to our problems – it *is* the problem. To this policy based on *power*, I oppose a policy based on *freedom*. Freedon for the people of the world to struggle with their own problems and if need be, to fight their own wars with their own weapons. Freedom for the individual to enter the market place to buy and sell, to bargain and negotiate without the crushing burden of economic controls, confiscatory taxation, and inflationary spending and monetary policy. And freedom for people to seek local solutions to local problems, solutions based on decentralization and community control, on diversity and individual initiative.

"I believe that American politics in coming years will witness the rise of a united opposition, based on the principles of anti-imperialism abroad and individual sovereignty at home, which will defy the outmoded labels of left and right. If you feel that my candidacy for president would hasten the emergence of this movement, I will be your candidate."

John Paul, where are you? America needs you! We have not yet begun to fight! ◼

Philosophy And Immortality

By Jerome Tuccille
(an excerpt from a forthcoming book)

Are philosophical principles absolute? Or will philosophy and political ideology, like our legal codes, have to evolve with new developments in technology and social structure in order to keep from growing obsolete?

Several writers of science fact and fiction have claimed that present struggles between "capitalism" and "socialism," "fascism" and "communism," "individualism" and "collectivism" will have no place in the world of the near future. Novelist F. M. Esfandiary talks not only about the coming New Technology, but about New Economic principles as well in his first non-fiction book, *Optimism One*. In *Future Shock*, Alvin Toffler states that present-day economic and political ideologies are already obsolete, and the notion of total individual freedom is a romantic pipedream. B. F. Skinner, in his 1971 best-seller, *Beyond Freedom and Dignity*, claims that man is so totally conditioned by his environment that the concepts of personal liberty and free will are nothing more than utopian myths. He argues that people must be conditioned from birth to live in peace with their neighbors if the human race is to survive – although, exactly who will do the conditioning is never fully explained. Arthur C. Clarke and Buckminster Fuller take the position that property, both communal and private, will be an archaic concept in an age of transience and universal mobility. Toffler also thinks that ownership and property are losing their meaning with built-in obsolescence, mass-produced throw-away items, rental rather than purchase of automobiles and housing, and the corresponding decline in materialistic permanence.

These are intriguing assertions, especially since they come from writers who have been imaginative visionaries in the field of technology and science. Fuller and Clarke, particularly, have been remarkably prescient in writing about such varied concepts as weather prediction, space travel, global communication satellites, fusion power, moving sidewalks, recycling, domed cities, etc. . . ., years before anyone else decided they were practical. At this writing, New Jersey is looking into the feasibility of building a domed city according to Fuller's specifications – approximately thirty-five years after Fuller discussed this possibility in connection with New York City. When a few strong-willed individuals have been right so many times while virtually everyone else was dismissing them as incorrigible utopians, there is a tendency to take everything they say on faith once their ideas have been vindicated. In reality, however, their individualism and tenacity in the face of criticism puts the lie to their own statements concerning the obsolescence of choice, free will and individual determination.

It seems to me that we do someone, as well as ourselves, a disservice whenever we institutionalize him as an omniscient seer, oracle or harbinger of the future. Every new proposal, regardless of who is presenting it, deserves to be scrutinized on its own merits. The fully infallible man has not been invented yet, and chances are good that infallibility will continue to elude us long after immortality has become routine. The problem, when it comes to analyzing predictions, is to strike a happy balance between our natural tendency to demolish everyone who sounds original and creative, and to deify those who turn out to be right more frequently than not. We have to develop the ability to distinguish between the Jeanne Dixons and the Buckminster Fullers of the world – even the element of Jeanne Dixon residing within a Buckminster Fuller.

Although the various circumstances of life already mentioned – law, technology, social structure, political institutions – continue to change with increasing momentum, there are certain universal truths which remain constant through the ages. Our visionaries, for the most part, have developed an expertise at speculating on the variables of life while at the same time ignoring completely the abstract principles which *ought to* govern human affairs. There are few exceptions – Heinlein and Robert Silverberg come immediately to mind – who have tackled moral and social problems while fictionalizing the concrete world of tomorrow, but they remain a small minority. Some futurists have even been known to bend their avowed philosophical precepts when it comes to securing funds for a pet scientific project of their own. While the human race can save itself some time and agony by listening more carefully to technological projections which may seem quixotic for the moment, we should also understand that philosophy is a separate discipline with little or no connection to the hard sciences.

Certain principles are so fundamental to the entire human condition that no serious person, regardless of his politics, will take exception to them. For example, it is hard to visualize anyone in his right mind maintaining that non-aggressive people do not have a right to basic human freedoms: freedom of speech, of assembly, of picketing and dissent, of association, of economic trade. Anyone who openly advocated that some men have the moral right to enslave others would be roundly denounced as a "fascist," a "communist," a "racist," a "sexist," and a no good SOB. Anyone maintaining that some individuals have a right to dictate reading matter, sexual habits and general lifestyle to others invariably means that he would be among those doing the dictating. Many of us may harbor these ambitions secretly, but hardly anyone stands up at a public podium expressing these secret desires in abstract terms.

As we look at the world around us, we see that most political regimes are based on singularly non-libertarian principles, though whenever political leaders are interviewed they always claim that their prime interests are the "freedom and prosperity" of their constituents. The Greek colonels, Generalissimo Franco, Mao, Brezhnev, and Spiro Agnew are all in power to further the principles of human liberty, even as they do everything in their power to suppress the civil liberties mentioned above.

So, it seems, the human race does not practice what it preaches. We have a unique way of translating universal truisms – always based on the axiom that man has a right to his freedom – into the most grotesque political forms imaginable. There appears to be a bit of the dictator in too many of us – the urge to be in a position to tell others how to live, what books to read, what flags to salute, ad nauseam. Otherwise we would not tolerate the authoritarian regimes now governing most of the world. If man truly desired his freedom, he would rise up *en masse* and seize it from those who withhold it from him. Revolution would be a spontaneous outcry heard around the globe. Instead, sadly enough, our rulers rule with the tacit approval of the masses while the human race continues to delude itself with verbal devotion to the abstract principles of liberty. We get, apparently, the kind of society that the majority secretly desires.

Yet all this does not alter the fact that the principles themselves are still valid. Man *does* have a natural right to conduct his affairs without interference from others so

(Continued on page 5)

A BUNCH OF LOSERS — *(Continued from page 1)*

busing, and called for black control of black education. This is not only a stand that harmonizes with the anti-busing whites (one faction at the Balck Convention actually called for a Presidential ticket of Wallace-Chisholm!) but approaches the libertarian position as well.

This is not to say that the libertarian could endorse Wallace for the presidency; there are two major stumbling-blocks – his ultra-hawkish attitude on Vietnam, and his questionable devotion to civil liberties. But Wallace, as many of the liberal Democrats have acknowledged, has raised the issues that touch the hearts of the American voter, and he has raised them correctly; and no Democrat who ignores this challenge and continues to talk in terms of the tired, old, statist and centralizing liberalism can hope to win the Presidency.

But Wallace, in his own way, is a loser too, for he could scarcely hope to be nominated by the national Democratic party. We are back to Square One.

Mills. No observer has mentioned the fact, but the Florida primary has also put the boots to the candidacy of Wilbur Mills. In New Hampshire, he was a write-in candidate, but in Florida he was on the ballot in a sympathetic, fellow-Southern state. Mills amassed close to zero votes. Let us hear no more of Wilbur Mills, and let us be thankful.

Humphrey. The egregious gasbag, the old retread of the Fair Deal – undoubtedly he is the second winner in Florida, coming in after Wallace with 18% of the vote. The really dismal feature of the voting is the recrudescence of Hubert. No, no, not that! To top everything, Humphrey has lately shucked off his dovish clothing and returned to the Vietnam hawk he truly is. It is too much; another choice between Humphrey and Nixon is too much for the human soul to stomach. Furthermore, even if Hubert should win the nomination, which he might well do, the Democrat Left would, and properly so, react in horror and mobilize a vengeance-fourth party – and all the more power to them. And so Hubert, in November, would be a hopeless loser too.

Jackson. Scoop also did fairly well in Florida, although 13% of the vote hardly reflects a public clamor. Ideologically, though, Scoop is even worse than Humphrey; he would be the "McBrook" Mr. Hyde to Professor Dolan's "Ashlosky". Scoop, furthermore, would be even more likely to face an angry fourth party uprising – and so he too would lose in November.

Chisholm. Shirley Chisholm, after campaigning long and in Florida, and after claiming to be the living embodiment of every black, Chicano, and female, got 4% of the vote. Enough said.

McCarthy. It is true, again, that McCarthy did not campaign in Florida. But he *was* on the ballot, after all, and his nearly zero vote should be enough to end any possibility of a McCarthy boomlet.

Yorty. Sam Yorty, with close to a zero vote dropped out.

Hartke. Vance Hartke supplied the comic relief of the campaign. He had one billboard up in the state of Florida, a billboard that will go down in the history of American politics. It read "WALLACE SUPPORTS HARTKE"; it was only in tiny letters that the reader was informed that this was *not* George, but Milton Wallace, Hartke's campaign director in Florida. Milton brought Hartke, however, close to a zero vote. If anyone in the country exists who happened to be worried about a "Hartke threat", he need worry no longer.

And so there we have it, as sorry a lot as it has been our misfortune to see in many a day. Where is our shining knight to lead us to the dethronement of the Monster Milhous? Where, indeed, for he is surely not on our list. It begins to look as if there is one man, and one only, who has the charisma, the magnetism, and the broad support in all wings of the party and in all classes and ethnic groups

Recommended Reading

Rothbardiana.

Murray Rothbard has a dissection of the Value-Added Tax in the conservative weekly *Human Events* ("The Value-Added Tax is Not the Answer", March 11.) He also has a review of the *Festschrift* for F. A. Hayek, *Roads to Freedom*, sketching the Austrian philosophical position, and praising the contributions of Lachmann, Bauer, and Popper. (In the *Political Science Quarterly*, March 1972). There is also a free-swinging and lengthy interview with Rothbard in the Feb. 25 issue of the new anarcho-objectivist fortnightly tabloid, The New Banner (available in a special reprint for 10¢, and for a year for $7.00, from *The New Banner*, Box 1972, Columbia, S. C. 29202). Here Rothbard comments on Ayn Rand, anarchism, political parties, the New Left, strategy for libertarians, the movement, the Friedmans – father-and-son, price controls, and many other topics.

Banfield. One of the most brilliant books of the last couple of years is Edward C. Banfields's *The Unheavenly City*, now out in paperback (Little, Brown.) Banfield details the destructive influence of government on urban economics and urban society, and turns the Marxists neatly on their head by pointing out that the major problem with the poor is their "lower class" values and "lower class" culture that most of them have adopted. The book is a fine, ringing defense of the importance of what have been much derided as "bourgeois values": thrift, hard work, low time preference, foresight, rational purpose, etc. No book in years has infuriated the Left as has Banfield.

Ecology and all That. The libertarian answer has now been provided for us on the ecology question, and by our own Edwin G. Dolan, in his paperback: *TANSTAAFL: Economic Strategy for the Environmental Crisis* (Holt, Rinehart, and Winston). Here is a handy and brief reply to the ecological Left – and written by someone who is obviously personally fond of conservation and the great outdoors! As a special lagniappe, also, this is the first book to mention the *Lib. Forum* – specifically, Frank Bubb's fine article on property rights and pollution.

Retreatism. Before our perfervid retreatists rush off to a coral reef or an ocean platform, they might well stop and consider a less quixotic solution – to live in one of the *Safe Places* outlined by David and Holly Franke in their best-selling book (Arlington House, 932 pp., $13.95). The Frankes unearthed 46 towns in the U. S. which enjoy low crime rates, low pollution, and low taxes – and they describe them all in detail. Moreover, the book is very handsomely produced, with hundreds of charts, maps, and photographs.

"The freest form of government is only the least objectionable form." --- Herbert Spencer.

in the country to do the job. And he isn't running . . . or is he?

An ironic sidelight to the affair is the spectacular counter-productivity of *Lib. Forum* endorsements. First we endorsed Senator Hatfield, and he didn't run. Then, we endorsed Senator Proxmire (who, incidentally, was the only "liberal" Democrat to vote strongly against busing), and he promptly dropped out. Then we began to sidle up a bit to Ed Muskie, and we see what has happened to *him*. Is there Somebody Out There Who Doesn't Like Us? ◘

PHILOSOPHY AND IMMORTALITY —
(Continued from page 3)
long as he does so in a non-aggressive fashion. We may differ on what exactly constitutes an act of aggression. Some maintain that private ownership of a parcel of real estate is a "rip-off" which ought to be suppressed; others think pornography is an attack on the "moral climate" of the nation and ought not be available to the public. Between these extremes, however, most people can agree on a long host of issues which clearly fall into one category or another. Murder, assault, robbery, fraud, destruction of property, pollution are all obviously aggressive activities; gambling, the voluntary exchange of goods, the various forms of self-abuse and victimless acts are just as clearly non-aggressive. Even though honorable people may disagree over concrete issues, the abstract principles behind them remain constant nonetheless.

Consequently, when Alvin Toffler states that individual freedom is a pipedream — when B. F. Skinner claims that free will and liberty is nonexistent because of environmental conditioning — what they are doing is speculating subjectively about certain conditions of contemporary life. It may well be (although neither author has succeeded in proving his theory) that man's actions and decisions are predetermined by his conditioning and he is unable to exercise individual freedom in any real sense. It may also be true that built-in obsolescence and rental of commodities will change our ideas about property and ownership. But these are all descriptions of real or imagined social conditions, and have nothing whatsoever to do with the abstract principles of natural human rights. The axiom that man has a right to his freedom has not been called into question; whether or not he is capable of exercising that freedom is another story.

Both Toffler and Skinner go a step further, however, when they turn from speculation to advocacy journalism. Toffler talks about the obsolescence of present-day economic principles and political ideology. Since economics and politics are nothing more or less than the result of philosophical principles applied to concrete issues, Toffler is saying in effect that we need to develop a new metaphysics to help us deal with the world of the future. Where Toffler is somewhat circumspect, Skinner goes all the way and calls for the politicization of his behavioristic psychological theories. Not only does he speculate about man's inability to function freely, he evidently wants a board of behavioristic bureaucrats appointed to plan the kind of conditioning man will be subjected to. (With Ehrlich's panel of experts determining the size of our population, a board of rabbis, priests and ministers telling us who will be frozen and who will die, and now Skinner's corps of behavior determinists, the New Great Fair Society of today will look like a *laissez faire* paradise in comparison.)

While new scientific discoveries add to the body of knowledge available to man, it is difficult to foresee any developments requiring that we re-evaluate our natural rights as human beings. More specifically, no matter how many people we freeze and bring back to life, how many clones and ectogenes we create in the laboratory, how many cyborgs we manufacture, how many space ships we send toward the stars, how many diseases we learn to cure through biofeedback, and how many immortalists are walking the earth five hundred years from today, it will not alter the philosophical fact that aggression is immoral and people have the right (even if not the ability) to go to heaven or hell in their own way. This principle is unchanging and will remain so until all intelligent life, whether it is flesh and blood or mostly machine, becomes extinct.

It may be that struggles between "capitalism" and "socialism," "individualism" and "collectivism" will die out as the years roll by; but this will be due to a change in terminology more than anything else. The distinctions between totalitarianism and freedom, between coercion and voluntarism, between repression and spontaneity will be with us for as long as some people try to exercise power over others. It makes little difference whether we *call* a free society socialist or capitalist, collectivist or individualist. Language is flexible while reality is not. Lables are unimportant, but concrete conditions are vital to everyone.

Looking at *Future Shock* merely as a speculative work, we find that Toffler's predictions concerning free choice and liberty are refuted by some of his own technological projections. While he is telling us that freedom of choice is a "meaningless concept," romantic rhetoric to the contrary, he goes on to state there will be more diversity in the near future through a proliferation of consumer goods and lifestyles and, consequently, more flexibility and options for everyone. He is telling us, simultaneously, that there will be more choices available in all areas of life, and that our ability to choose will be increasingly limited. Does he mean that Madison Avenue will become more adroit at molding public opinion and controlling consumer demands? Or that we will be paralyzed with indecision when faced with more than a small variety of alternatives? He does not tell us, unfortunately.

Logically, it would seem that man's ability to use his power of choice assumes an added dimension with every increase in available alternatives. "Freedom," "free will," and "self-determination" had a strictly limited meaning when most people labored twelve and fourteen hours a day merely to feed and house themselves. A "free" man was still a slave to economic hardship. Even today, many people are required to spend half their waking hours at boring, dissatisfying jobs just to buy necessities. In this respect we are more "free" than we were forty years ago, but it is a relative factor. In the kind of world Toffler is speaking of, however, where machines do all man's drudgery for him, where today's luxuries are mass-produced inexpensively for everyone, where moral codes, family structure and lifestyles are flexible and dynamic, *total freedom* becomes possible for the first time in history. Yet this is the world in which Toffler says individual freedom and choice will be a meaningless concept. If there is one way to free man from his present "conditioning" by hardship, drudgery and puritanical traditions it is through the technological advances and mobility which Toffler anticipates.

It is also difficult to understand how contemporary economic principles can ever become obsolete.

An advanced economy depends upon the availability and exchange of goods. Since no society however affluent is totally self-sufficient, worldwide prosperity depends upon the mobility and transfer of goods as they are required from one society to the next. This will always be so unless we reach a day when each individual is capable of manufacturing all goods and services for himself, an unlikely if not impossible situation.

The economic options available in the future will be basically the same as they are today. Societies can either own goods in common, produce them collectively and closely manage their distribution and exchange, or ownership, production and trade can be carried out privately in a free and fluid marketplace. There are, of course, many variations on these alternatives: nationalization; management without nationalization; domestic management with international *laissez faire;* national *laissez faire* and international management; one-world nationalization or management; one-world *laissez faire;* etc. . . Even the colonization of other planets will not alter these conditions, for the same principles will apply to extraterrestrial societies as they develop. While honorable men can (and probably will) disagree among themselves as to what type of arrangement will produce the

(Continued on page 6)

289

PHILOSOPHY AND IMMORTALITY —
(Continued from page 5)

best results (the same as with political institutions), the abstract principles underlying these issues remain constant: should man be free or controlled? should economic trade be free or managed?

Even concepts like ownership and property, which will grow obsolete according to Fuller and Clarke, will be subject to the same analysis. It seems to be true that we rent many goods today that were purchased yesterday, and the life-expectancy of most consumer items is far less than it used to be, but this doesn't change the nature of property and ownership *per se* It only means there are fewer owners and more renters today than existed thirty years ago, and there are likely to be even fewer owners and more renters by the year 2000, present trends continuing. This may be what Clarke and Fuller mean to say, but in their enthusiasm for forecasting scientific developments they seem to be advocating a change in economic principles as well.

As for the kind of economic order we are heading toward? Latest indications are that, on the international level at least, we are evolving toward a freer market in trade and co-operation. It is becoming more and more difficult for a single nation to place restrictions on the free movement of goods across national boundaries. When that avowed "free trader," Richard Nixon, imposed a 10 percent surcharge on U. S. imports in 1971, it was the first serious attempt by a major country in a decade to derail the movement toward freer global trade that has been building since World War II. And it met with failure. The age when a superpower, however super it may be, can dictate self-protective economic policies to the rest of the world is now over. The new age is characterized by a more even balance of economic power distributed among the United States, the European Common Market, the Communist bloc, Japan, and the developing African and "Third World" nations.

In the closing days of 1971, twelve leading economists from various countries met in Washington, D. C. and unanimously recommended major changes in world economic policies. While each proposal was not pure *laissez faire*, the general tone was certainly in favor of freer trade among nations. Among the list of recommendations to avoid "further economic and political crises" were: elimination of all remaining tariffs on industrial goods over a ten-year period; negotiations to limit high-price domestic policies which create food surpluses and lead to import barriers (ironically enough, while the United States was allegedly fighting inflation in 1971, Nixon was promising the farmers that the government would do all it could to keep food prices from falling too low); a gradual phasing out of agreements limiting free trade in steel, textiles and similar products; a reduced role for the U. S. dollar as a world reserve currency, and adoption of some form of fixed standard — possibly gold — to determine exchange rates. These proposals, coming as they did from the Brookings Institute and other liberal organizations rather than from *laissez faire* economic associations, indicate a broader acceptance of free market systems. Even more pertinent is the fact that these economists acknowledged the relationship between restrictive trade policies and political turmoil, including war.

"What is involved," said a spokesman for the group, "is the wider question of how the international community should order relationships. If economic differences drive countries apart, world order will be notably prejudiced."

The relationship between economic warfare and nationalistic militarism has been well catalogued by both revisionist historians and libertarian scholars during the past twenty years. Now this kinship is more generally accepted, and with this new awareness will come a broad-based movement toward a free global marketplace. What we are witnessing in the world today is *n ot* the adoption of

The Conservation Question

By Gerald P. O'Driscoll, Jr.

During a fight over "saving" a cluster of redwoods, Ronald Reagan is reported to have remarked that "If you've seen one, you've seen them all." Needless to say, the good governor was roundly berated for his callousness. Yet there was some truth in what the governor had to say. One wonders whether the more extreme (consistent?) members of the conservation lobby would have us save every last tree, plant, and repulsive reptile from extinction, no matter what the cost. There is some question whether the early American colonists would have ever gotten off the boats if there had been an incipient Sierra Club in the 17th century. After all, to have felled a tree, or killed a turkey would have been to upset the ecology of the continent. All the other species and creatures of the earth are supposed to be permitted to run loose, preying on their natural enemies, consuming natural resources, etc., but man is supposed to recriminate about what he does in order to survive, and sometimes, advance his standard of living. Nature, too, destroys, but this is often overlooked in all the blather from conservationists. In fact, man is, in one important respect, at a disadvantage *vis à vis* other animals; he does not possess instincts to insure his survival. Man must rely on his reason, and his ability to conquer natural forces in order to survive. There is no question that in the process man destroys forests, fouls streams, and, yes, exterminates whole species of other animals. So what? Species have disappeared quite independently of any action by man, as have forests. We are constantly reminded by ecologists that man is part of nature, yet when he does what every other species does — grow and expand at the expense of other species — his actions are condemned as unharmonic with, and destructive of nature. In fact, the truth is precisely the opposite. It is in man's nature to control and subdue what are termed "natural forces," to build "artificial" dwelling places, precisely because, if he does not, man will not survive. Like it or not, there is a struggle in nature for the world's scarce resources, and if men do not use their unique talents, these resources will go to the ants and elephants. Then, surely, there will be a return to pristine nature; no man, however, will be there to appreciate it. Lest we forget, the business of man is man, and this does not necessarily imply that either the number or the comfort of seals and alligators should be maximized.

Of course, my quip about the early colonists was silly. There were no conservationists among the colonists for a very good reason. People who have to confront nature on a day to day basis are not given to waxing eloquent about the joys of same. The sunrise on a desert may be beautiful to the middle class urban dweller, but it spells frost and ruin to the citrus grower. A winter scene in the Rockies makes for a beautiful Christmas card, but it means starving cattle for the rancher. Nature is beautiful to those who can choose the conditions in which they wish to confront it, and who have a place to retreat to after they have dabbled in pioneer life.

It should also be noted that the original motive of conservation was to preserve natural resources for future growth of the economy. It was feared that too fast a depletion of the nation's resources would lead to economic stagnation and decline, and that for a variety of reasons, it was doubted

(Continued on page 7)

a new metaphysics and new economic principles but, instead, the vindication of basic libertarian principles as they apply to all areas of human intercourse. These principles are emerging by default as authoritarian institutions decay and fall along the wayside on our march toward a civilized world community. ∎

THE CONSERVATION QUESTION —
(Continued from page 6)

that the market could effectively allocate these resources over time. Most conservationists would agree that this is not the problem anymore. The demonstrated ability of technology to advance faster than resources are depleted has obviated any need for guardianship over the earth's resources in order to prevent economic stagnation. Indeed, today's conservationists seem to desire economic stagnation! And there in lies the difference between the "old" and "new" conservationism. Today, conservation is seen as providing for the present and future amenities associated with unspoiled natural environments, for which the market (again) is alleged to fail to make adequate provision.[1]

But "amenities" associated with contact with the natural environment are hardly to be compared with the need to conserve natural resources in order to insure the continued growth of a complex economy. Nor does what is known as the "irreproducibility" argument stand up to scrutiny. There are some wonders, such as the Grand Canyon, which must be kept, or be lost forever (though, again, this fact does not, of and by itself, prove that they should be preserved). But such is the exception. For most, contact with nature means a visit to a state park, a drive through the country, or a picnic on a scenic overlook. But such assets are reproducible, and, in fact, have been growing steadily as state parks *and* other public and private facilities have grown to meet increasing demand.[2]

Some economists have argued that such amenities are so-called "collective consumption goods", and must, therefore, be provided by the government. Besides the fact that the conclusion doesn't even follow given the collective good assumption, the assumption is wrong. We do not see much private investment in the saving of threatened scenic wonders (though the fact we see any should at least give pause to the conservationists), because as long as there is a reasonable hope of governmental action to supply desired services, the consumer-conservationist will be well-advised to put his money into lobbying aimed at obtaining the desired services "free," or at well below cost, rather than into purchasing a private supply. To take Professor Robinson's example, suppose a group of wealthy individuals started a "Cadillac for the people" organization, and contributed $1,000 each to lobby to get the government to supply Cadillacs at $2,000 each. If the lobbying were successful, it would have proved a bargain. If the supply of Cadillacs dried up as a result, it would not prove that Cadillacs are a common consumption good which cannot be supplied by the market. It would only serve to prove anew that when something is sold at a price below the market-clearing price, demand will exceed supply.[3]

The old conservationism did not stand on solid grounds, either. The allocation of natural resources over time is one with any other capital problem. To conserve means to postpone use of a resource – to consume less today in order to consume more tomorrow. It is a matter of less now, more later. To follow the famous dictum of Gifford Pinchot that "conservation means the greatest good of the greatest number, and that for the longest time," would be to never use resources at all. What we can do, however, is to maximize the *value* of our natural resources. But, this the free market does as it does in maximizing the value of any asset over time.[4]

Moreover, it must be emphasized that to conserve or postpone the use of one resource usually involves depleting or accelerating the use of another resource. Resources are substitutes for one another. If coal, for instance, is conserved for heating purposes, more oil will have to be used. Conserving *all* resources would be literally impossible, without a drastic lowering of the standard of living, if not the extinction, of the human race. Again, we get back to what seems to be the logical end of conservationism, old or new.

the impoverishment or destruction of the human species.

To say that the market doesn't save enough resources for the future is to express an unsupported value judgment about how well people should be off now relative to those who live in the future. Why should people in the future have a special claim on the people who live now? Either the conservationist is saying that the future does have a claim on the present, or that the market does not allocate properly over time. Neither has ever been successfully argued.

All This is not to say that there is no truth in what "ecologists" have to say. However, the observed "pollution" problem stems from the government's laxity in enforcing the ordinary law of torts against industrial polluters. By lowering the cost of "pollution-intensive" production, the government has, in effect, encouraged pollution, and the growth of pollution producing industries at the expense of non-polluting industries. Air and water pollutio involve poisoning people. There is an elementary property rights problem involved – the right of people to their lives and property. As usual, the government isn't doing what a policing agency should be doing, and is doing what is shouldn't. There are hopeful signs that pollution law will take a new turn, recognizing a principle that would be the cornerstone of any libertarian legal code: that people shall not be deprived of their persons or property without due process. ◼

[1]On the differences between the old and new conservationism, see Warren C. Robinson, "A Critical Note on the New Conservationism," *Land Economics*, XLV, No. 4 (November, 1969), 45-56.

[2]For a statistical mathematical argument that at least one state government (California) has actually supplied *fewer* parks and campgrounds than would be supplied on the free market, see Gordon Brown, Jr., "Pricing Seasonal Recreation Services," *Western Economic Journal*, IX, No. 2 (June, 1971), 218-25.

[3]It is often assumed that the federally operated recreation network is redistributive. Lower income groups by and large receive no benefit from such services. The 1959 study of Wilderness Areas in California found that the average income of wilderness campers was over $10,000 compared to a U. S. average annual income of about $6,000 (think of all the expensive, specific capital required for camping). To the extent that taxes from lower income groups support the National Parks and Forests, it is these groups who are subsidizing upper middle class consumers of "amenities."

[4]For an excellent article on this problem, see Scott Gordon, "Economics and the Conservation Question,"*Journal of Law and Economics,* I (October, 1958), 110-21.

THE STATE

The harpies attack
Snitching from blind masses' plates,
Screeching platitudes.
        --Jack Wright

"This was the American Dream: a sanctuary on earth for individual man: a condition in which he could be free not only of the old established closed-corporation hierarchies of arbitrary power which had oppressed him as a mass, but free of that mass into which the hierarchies of church and state had compressed him and held him individually thralled and individually impotent." --- William Faulkner.

Short People, Arise!

Surely, one of the most imbecilic movements of our time is the drive to secure *pro rata* quotas everywhere for various "minority groups." Academic departments in universities are being assaulted, by the government as well by propaganda, for not assuring their quotal "rights" to "minorities", now illogically defined as: women, blacks, Chicanos, and youth. And every state delegation to the Democratic convention is supposed to have its assigned women-black-Chicano-youth quota, or the gods will descend in their wrath. The full absurdity of this hoopla has gone undetected because not fully and totally applied. Why aren't Irish, Italians, Albanians, Poles, Mormons, etc., assured *their* quotas in the Pantheon? Are we to have endless legal challenges, for example, because the Alabama delegation doesn't have enough one-legged Swedes, or because Harvard University doesn't employ enough Polish Catholics? And, of course, no one seems to mention which ethnic or whatever groups will have to be dumped and lose their jobs to accommodate the rising minorities. Which groups are *over* their assigned quotas?

All this was highlighted some months ago when J. K. Galbraith called on all corporations to hire blacks as top executives, in proportion to their number in the total population, and, to go further, to hire them in proportion to the surrounding population in their immediate geographic area. Father Andrew Greeley, the highly intelligent conservative sociologist, countered to ask whether Galbraith is prepared to give up his post at Harvard, and to call upon Harvard to hire Irish Catholic academics in proportion to their share of the population in the Boston area. *Touché!*

As long as all the various "oppressed minority" groups are getting into the act, I would like to put in a plea for another, unsung, oppressed minority: short people. We "shorts", I have long believed, are the first to be fired and the last to be hired; our median income is far below the income of the "talls"; and where in blazes are the short people in the top management posts? Where are the short corporation leaders, the short bankers, the short Senators and Presidents? There is surely no genetic evidence to prove that short people are inferior to talls (look at Napoleon!) Short people: end oppression by the talls! Develop short pride! Call for short institutes, short history courses, stop internalizing the age-old propaganda by the talls that you must be consigned to inferior roles in our society! Demand short quotas everywhere!

It is good to see that scholarship is now bolstering our perceptive instincts about short oppression. Professor Saul D. Feldman, a sociologist at Case-Western Reserve, and himself a distinguished short, has now brought science to bear on our problem (Arthur J. Snider, "Society Favors Tall Men: Prof." New York *Post*, Feb. 19). Feldman reports that of recent University of Pittsburgh graduating seniors, those 6-2 and taller received an average starting salary 12.4% higher than graduates under 6 feet. Aha! Furthermore, a marketing professor at Eastern Michigan University quizzed 140 business recruiters about their preferences between two hypothetical, equally qualified applicants for the job of salesman. One of the hypothetical salesmen was to be 6-1, the other 5-5. The recruiters answered as follows: 27% expressed no preference (Hooray!), 1% would hire the short man, but 72% said that they would hire the tall man!! For shame!

Professor Feldman went on to point out that scorn of the short pervades our entire American culture (a "sick" culture, surely.) Women discriminate notoriously in favor of the talls over the shorts, and in movies how many shorts have played romantic leads? (Some, like Alan Ladd, *were* short, but his shortness was always cunningly disguised by the bigoted movie moguls, e.g. Ladd stood on a box in the love scenes.) Feldman also pointed out the subtle corruption of our language (presumably as engineered by the tall-conspiracy) Look how "shorts" are treated: people are "short-sighted, short-changed, short-circuited, and short in cash". Feldman also declared that when two people run for President, the taller is almost invariably elected.

OK, short people: we now have the ineluctable findings of statictical science to bolster out qualitative folk-wisdom. Short people of the world, arise! Demand your rights! You have nothing to lose but you elevator shoes!

Oh, one final note: short liberation, we must all realize, does not in *any* way mean an anti-tall movement. Despite the age-old tyranny of the talls, we are out to liberate all people, short and tall alike. Consciousness-raising groups for guilt-ridden tall sympathizers with our movement are now in order. ◼

"The word state is identical with the word war. Each state tries to weaken and ruin another in order to force upon that other its laws, its policies and its commerce, and to enrich itself thereby."

                        --P. A. Kropotkin

The Libertarian Forum

BOX 341
MADISON SQUARE STATION
NEW YORK, NEW YORK 10010

Published Every Month. Subscription Rate: $8.00 Per Year

A Monthly Newsletter

THE
Libertarian Forum

Joseph R. Peden, Publisher   Murray N. Rothbard, Editor

VOLUME IV, NO. 5   MAY, 1972   75c

NIXON'S WORLD

Richard Milhous Nixon has long thought of himself as a world statesman. His genius, he has felt, really lies in foreign affairs: not in domestic policy, but in the impact he would have as President on the world scene. Let us assess the Nixonian record.

1. *Vietnam*.

In 1968 Richard Nixon had a plan for ending the war in Vietnam; it was a plan which he clasped to his bosom; it was a secret plan, the fruits of which we would all be contemplating should he attain the Presidential office. We have a lot to contemplate. Milhous has become the greatest bomber in the history of mankind; he had rained more tonnage of bombs than anyone else in history. The latest offensive of the NLF-DRV in Vietnam shows quite clearly how successful Milhous has been in "winding down the war."

At the *Lib. Forum* we take no pride in our Cassandra-like warnings, day in and day out, that the war in Vietnam was *not* over, was not "winding down", was and would continue to be the prime and central issue. Sometimes we stood alone: during the Paris negotiations, and before Cambodia when almost the entire anti-war movement was convinced that Vietnam was over. Nixon *could* have ended the war as soon as he took office; he could have blamed the whole thing on the Democrats, packed up his marbles, and gone home. But we knew, given the Nixonian mindset, that he wouldn't. "Vietnamization" was the palpably absurd but typically Nixonian attempt to defuse the opposition at home by ending American ground casualties and continuing and accelerating our rain of death and devastation from the air. But this was simply a return to the pre-1965 Johnson policy, a policy that had already failed with Johnson, and which the Pentagon Papers reveal that the astute CIA had long predicted would be a failure.

Ever since World War II, the United States policy-makers have been fascinated with the big bomber. Bombing seemingly allows us to have our cake and eat it too: to punish, devastate, and control nations throughout the globe, while doing it from a safe distance above the ground; we could commit mass murder and not get our hands bloody. But it didn't even work in World War II, even against an industrialized Germany which was far more vulnerable to bombings than the peasant and jungle population of Vietnam or the rest of Southeast Asia. The Strategic Bombing Survey, in Europe after World War II, found to its shock and amazement that mass bombing had had no really crippling effect on the German war machine. Millions of innocent civilians, women and children, had indeed been slaughtered; but the factories continued to produce, and even the torn railroad tracks were quickly rebuilt by the German population. And as for breaking enemy morale, bombings, whether in Germany or

England, only served to cement the population behind their government's policy. But the fascination with mass bombing continues.

Even the Nixon Administration now knows that its hokum about bombing war supplies "at the top of funnel" in North Vietnam is a pack of lies. There is no "funnel." We are bombing in North Vietnam purely out of rage and frustration; out of a vicious vindictiveness; if we can't get to the enemy in the South, if we can't see or touch the NLF or Hanoi troops in the South Vietnamese arena, why we can jolly well kill the civilians up in the North. But the danger is that the pointless murder in the North will be worse than pointless; for part of the American mythology has always been the myth of "outside" control. There is no real problem in South Vietnam, we maintain, and so we have to write off the NLF as purely a puppet of Hanoi; and, proceeding further, we have to write off Hanoi as a puppet of someone else. First it was Peking that was supposed to be pulling the strings; but now, with this myth evidently breaking down, Milhous is yearning for a confrontation with the Soviet Union. We are back to the old discredited myth of Moscow as outside string-puller. The Administration's whining about Russian aid to Hanoi would be ludicrous if it were not so deadly; for Russian aid is less than one/tenth of the massive and enormous aid which the U. S. has been pouring in to shield *our* veritable puppets in Saigon.

The mighty offensive of perhaps the greatest military genious of our age, General Vo Nguyen Giap, has already demonstrated, dramatically and finally, the fraud of "Vietnamization." Is it not crystal clear to everyone, everywhere, that without the massive American air and naval support, as well as military aid, our Saigon puppets would collapse in a matter of days? Where, indeed, is the mythology of the well-armed and heavily primed "million man" Saigon army? Where have they gone? If Saigon really had a million well-trained men, would they have to dangerously deplete their forces around Saigon and in the Mekong Delta and rush them north?

Many Nixonite frauds now lie in shambles. There was the absurd notion that, with "Vietnamization", the NLF would simply "fade away". Some fadeout! There was the totally phony Nixon "peace plan", the sensation of a day and now quietly forgotten. The "peace plan", so widely hailed in the American press, was a humdinger: first a general ceasefire, then the withdrawal and the disarming of NLF and Hanoi troops, and *then* a "free" election in the South, supervised and controlled by the same Saigon crooks who have long made a mockery of all elections in the South (Neutralist opponents of Thieu *still* languish in Saigon jails!) The Paris

(Continued on page 2)

NIXON'S WORLD — *(Continued from page 1)*

peace talks had long been a phony, consistently sabotaged by the Nixon Administration; until they were finally suspended altogether. It was only when Nixon cut off the Paris talks that General Giap finally decided to strike. Now, of course, the Nixon Administration declares that we cannot resume these talks "under fire" and unless we "negotiate from strength," which means no negotiations at all. And then there was the totally fraudulent "prisoner of war" issue, fraudulent because Milhous knows full well that, in every war in history, there is one and only one way to secure return of POW's: by ending the war. If we really want to aid American prisoners of war, the only way to do so is to end the war — to pull out and come home.

There is only one way to end the monstrous horror that is the Vietnam War: and that is for the United States to get out, pronto, lock, stock and barrel. But that is the one thing that Nixon will not do. Only the ouster of Milhous from the White House offers hope that the horror will come to an end.

2. *China.*

The China trip, another sensation of the day, has happily begun to fade from memory. It was a truly repellent spectacle. The idea of normalizing relation with China, of ending the Cold War with that country, is fine, just as all inter-state relations should be so normalized. But this did not mean that Mr. Nixon had to make a total ass of himself, hailing Chinese Communist society, calling for a long march together, engaging in fawning toasts and all the rest. Is the American government, or the American character, really incapable of dignified relations? Must we either condemn every other government as an evil menace about to conquer the world, or *else* picture them as the greatest human invention since the discovery of the wheel? Certainly the TV viewer will long remember the contrast between the dignity and intelligence of Chou En-lai and the silly and insincere fawning of Mr. Nixon. It was not a pretty sight.

Why was it done? Who Knows? But if it was done in the hope that China would put pressure upon Hanoi or the NLF, it was a vain and ludicrous hope. as by now should be evident. The Communist nations are now "polycentric" largely because they had all bowed the knee to Stalin in the past, and had time and again been clobbered and betrayed for their pains. They will never do so again.

3. *Bangladesh.*

We have before denounced Nixon's policy of support of Pakistan and Punjabi imperialism, and its joining China in hostility and near-intervention against the Bengali rebellion. There was, however, method in Mr. Nixon's madness; for Nixon was pursuing the dream of Woodrow Wilson which has guided nearly every Administration in this century: the dream of America intervening to prop up the *status quo* everywhere, to combat "aggression", to put down and stamp out any and all revolutions (whether Communist or not) against all *status quo* States everywhere. It is the evil and imperialist dream of "collective security". The Bengalis were presuming to disturb that *status quo,* and therefore had to be put down. By his policy, and by his lagging in recognition of the new nation, Mr. Nixon has permanently alienated the Indians and the Bengalis.

4. *Ceylon.*

One of the ugliest examples of Wilsonian imperialism in years was the joining together of all the Great Powers — the U. S., Soviet Russia, Great Britain, and China — to send massive aid to the socialist government of Mrs. Bandaranaike in Ceylon, in order to suppress the youthful rebellion by the "Guevarist" JVF in that torn country. All objective observers agree that without that aid, the rebels would have been successful; and we have, again, another bout of mass the account of Richard Nixon.

5. *Cyprus.*

The problem in Cyprus is a complex and knotty one; but suffice it to say that the island is 80% Greek and 20% Turk, and that the Greeks on Cyprus have yearned for decades for unity (*enosis*) with their fellow Greeks on the mainland. The head of the Cypriote government, Archbishop Makarios, though originally pledged to *enosis,* has betrayed the cause. The Greek government has been trying to pressure Makarios to submit. As for the guarantees of autonomy to the Turks on the island, Makarios has been systematically violating them, and one of the reasons for the Greek pressure against him is to preserve the autonomy of the Turks against Greek Cypriote discrimination and possible slaughter. In this situation, *enosis* makes great good sense; wouldn't you know, then, that Mr. Nixon, once again Wilsonian to the core, should, in the recent Cyprus crisis, step in and save the day for Makarios by severely warning the Greek government against any use of violence against the Cyprus regime? Once again, with uncanny accuracy, Milhous intervened where it was none of our business, and on the wrong side.

6. *Northern Ireland.*

As usual, the crisis in Northern Ireland has been grievously misrepresented in the American press. The version we get is: the Catholics and Protestants irrationally "hate" each other, and that Northern Ireland is, after all, largely Protestant and therefore entitled to their own land and autonomy. The hatred is there, of course, but if we only take the trouble to inspect the slogans of the two sides in their marches and clashes, we can begin to see the true situation. For the Catholics call for civil rights, for an end to discrimination and gerrymandering, for an end to internment and torture without trial in British-Northern Irish concentration camps, and for the ouster of the British troops. The Protestants call for crushing the Catholics, for keeping them "in their place", and for hanging the Pope. Get the picture?

More particularly, it is a lie and a myth that Northern Ireland is "largely Protestant." The partition that gave Northern Ireland to the Protestant ascendancy was a phony partition, a typically Wilsonian device imposed by British bayonets. The largest part of the land area of Northern Ireland has a clear majority of Catholics: namely, the counties of Tyrone, Fermanagh, Londonderry (including the torn and bleeding Derry City), southern Armagh, and southern Down. The truly just solution for bleeding Ulster would be a second partition: in which the above areas would join the Irish Republic, leaving to an independent Northern Ireland the city of Belfast and county Antrim, northern Armagh, and northern and eastern Down. The problem would then be reduced to minor dimensions, leaving only the Catholic minority in Belfast in a state of oppression. But, too much blood has flowed for either side to accept such a rational solution. The best that can be hoped for now is unity with the Irish Republic, with strong guarantees of autonomy for the Protestants in the north.

By this time, it is pointless to ask where the Nixon Administration has stood in this crisis; naturally and predictably, it has lent its considerable weight to the British and Northern Irish side, and thereby helped to perpetuate the turmoil.

7. *International Monetary Relations.*

With characteristic vainglory, President Nixon dubbed the Smithsonian agreement of December 18 as the "greatest monetary agreement in this history of the world." It took only a few short months for the "greatest agreement" to show definite signs of crumbling. The soundest — and the most libertarian — international monetary order would be a world gold standard, with each currency indelibly fixed in terms of units of weight of gold; a far distant second best would be a pseudo-world gold standard of the Bretton Woods type; a distant third would be the Friedmanite dream of national fiat moneys and fluctuating exchange rates, a world which emerged on August 15, 1971 and lasted until December 18. But the Nixon Administration has managed to bring us the worst features of both fixed and fluctuating exchange rates: by fashioning a world where exchange

(Continued on page 3)

294

The Party Once More

Mr. David F. Nolan, temporary national chairman of the Libertarian Party, writes in high dudgeon that while it is true that the party had only 52 activist members last November, that it now (March 24) has "nearly 350 members" and six state chairmen. Anyone who thinks that this makes any difference for the viability of a nationwide party is welcome to re-evaluate our position (*Lib. Forum*, March, 1972).

More substantially, Mr. Nolan writes that the primary purpose of the Libertarian Party is not immediate electoral victory but to educate the public in libertarian ideas. We never thought otherwise. But the problem with this approach – a long-standing objective of minor parties – is that the psychology of the mass of the public being educated is overlooked. Let us take, for example, the poor old Socialist Labor Party, which, doggedly, every four years for nearly a century, has been nominating Presidential candidates and getting them on the ballot. What impact on the electorate has the SLP achieved? The problem is that the party has been so small, so flagrantly unviable, that the educational impact for socialism by the SLP has ranged sternly from zero to negative. For what is the reaction of the public? The reaction of the average citizen is that here is a tiny collection of kooks making a mockery of the electoral process (which the average person unfortunately reveres) in presuming to run someone for the Presidency. In short, the SLP is invariably written off as a bunch of crackpots, and their ideology often goes down the drain with them.

Why then does the SLP continue to slog along, decade after decade, even though unheeded by one and all? Because they manage to ingest just enough funds to keep the party bureaucracy going; in short, as so often happens with ideological and social action groups, the ends have been lost sight of, and the means – the preservation of the party bureaucracy – have become the end.

The way to avoid this unhappy dead end is to confine oneself to viable parties, that is to parties whose publicly proclaimed grasp is not absurdly beyond their means. An example are the Liberal and Conservative Parties of New York, which are large enough to have considerable weight within the state. And because of this weight, they *do* have considerable educational impact as well. But note that even they, as powerful as they are, are prudent enough not to extend their reach into any of the other states. ☐

NIXON'S WORLD — *(Continued from page 2)*

rates are fixed but where there is no international money (such as gold) to validate them. Fixed exchange rates with no international money to back them up make no sense whatever, and it would be difficult to find any reputable economist to defend such a system. The pattern of exchange rates fixed on December 18 is already obsolete; the dollar is still overvalued; and the shaky shoring up of the system depends on the continuing willingness of foreign nations to absorb dollars *ad infinitum*, willingness which must soon come to an end. Throughout, Nixon and Secretary Connally stubbornly refuse to consider any restored convertibility of dollars into gold; by this stubborn monetary nationalism they are making inevitable a rapid relapse into the fiat currencies, blocked accounts, exchange controls, and crippling of international trade, of the 1930's.

In short, Mr. Nixon's record in the international monetary field is of a piece with his record in international politics. Both can be summed up as: statism, moral evil, and consequent disaster. ☐

Libertarianism

By John Hospers

(Nash, $10.00, 488 pp.)
—*reviewed by R. A. Childs, Jr.*

Part I

Whenever a new libertarian work appears, we should focus on two aspects of it in evaluating it: what gaps does it fill in the existing body of literature, and what are its flaws? I am assuming that if it is a basically *libertarian* work, that its virtues will be more numerous than its flaws, that it will excel in respects in which it is fundamentally correct than those in which it is not. This is true of the new work by Dr. John Hospers, LIBERTARIANISM. It is a very great contribution to the growing library of libertarian literature, and it has its flaws.

First, the easy question: what are its contributions and strengths? It is, first and foremost, a comprehensive, integrated and systematic statement of the libertarian political philosophy. Those who have been looking for a comprehensive yet not-too-technical work to use in introducing people to the libertarian philosophy need look no longer. In most respects, LIBERTARIANISM is now *the* work to give to people who want to understand what the libertarian political philosophy is all about. It performs an heroic task in integrating most of the libertarian arguments that I have seen on behalf of a social philosophy of freedom. In doing this in terms of essentials, with a very conversational style, it easily replaces more than a half-dozen libertarian works as serving as an overview of our ideology is concerned. One need no longer pile up works by Rand, Rothbard, Hazlitt, Carson, Friedman, Paterson, Mises and the Tannehills for the neophyte to read. LIBERTARIANISM will serve just as well. By thus confronting the most often heard and repeated objections to liberty and *laissez-faire*, Hospers makes it possible for the newcomer to libertarianism to spot those areas and issues which are the greatest problems for *him*, thus enabling him to go on to more specialized study. There is not a great deal here which will be new to someone already acquainted with libertarianism, as Hospers himself is the first to admit. That isn't the purpose of the work — its purpose is to provide for a systematic overview of libertarian arguments for liberals and conservatives alike.

There is a generally excellent discussion of liberty, rights, property, the role of government (Hospers advocates a limited government), rent control, federal housing projects, price fixing, minimum wage laws, social security, tariffs, automation, monopolies, medicine and the state, welfare, public utilities, roads, licensing, inspection, consumer protection, conservation, coinage, education, and so forth. The best part of this type of discussion in the Hospers book is the constant subordination of economic arguments to ethics, though the two are usually integrated. He bases his case strongly on natural rights, which is the greatest virtue of his work *vis a vis* those of Hazlitt, Carson, Mises, and the others who cover some of the same territory.

These, then, are in summary form the greatest virtues of the work: its scope, integration, clarity, and systematic working out of a multitude of arguments for libertarianism.

Its flaws are few, but that doesn't mean that they are insignificant. On the contrary, I think that they are crucially important. To sum up my objections: Hospers errs precisely when and where he follows Rand too closely on three issues — limited government, history, and foreign policy. The limited government dispute isn't that important in the context of the book — Hospers devotes the last chapter to the question "Is Government Necessary?" and presents the anarchist case there, in the form of a dialog

between an anarchist and an archist. Hospers makes one major error here: he takes up the case for the structure of an anarchist society from the Tannehill's book THE MARKET FOR LIBERTY and presents it as though it were something agreed upon by all libertarians of the anarchist variety. But nothing could be further from the truth. Anarchists are alike necessarily only on one issue: they all deny the necessity and legitimacy of a State. For positive alternatives to the State, we have nearly as many proposals as we do anarchists, just as there are as many conceptions of limited government as there are people who take the time to attempt to work out a constitution and define the "proper" functions of government. In a sense, though, while anarchism is fairly well presented, Hospers creates a straw man, by having the anarchist in his dialog state that his "main contention" is that anarchism is a more efficient system. This is not the "main contention" of me, Wollstein, Rothbard, or a host of other anarchists. So the problem with Hospers' treatment of anarchism, as I see it, is that he fails to recognize that *all* anarchism has to do to be validated *as anarchism*, is to refute alleged justifications for the State. Positive theories are a secondary matter. Similarly, all that an atheist has to do to validate *atheism per se* is to refute proofs for the existence of God. Since the burden of proof is on the proponent of any positive theory, "negative" positions such as atheism and anarchism are themselves justified when those positive positions are refuted. What they attempt to put in the place of the positive theory is another matter.

But far more important than anarchism is Hospers' position on matters of history and foreign policy. There is a long chapter on "Liberty and International Relations" which will undoubtedly be second only to the chapter on anarchism in raising controversy. But unlike the anarchism chapter, in his treatment of foreign policy he does not even acknowledge the existence of an opposing libertarian view. His view is, basically, Randian. My view is, basically, Rothbardian. Between these two poles there is a world of difference.

First, on domestic history, Hospers makes absolutely no use of the excellent discoveries and insights of the revisionists. Thus although there is a criticism of business/government partnerships, there is no real critique of the role big businessmen have played in furthering statism. Down deep, Hospers has the view of "big business" as "America's persecuted minority," to use Ayn Rand's phrase. Thus though he is critical of the anti-trust laws, he does not seem aware that the major force in putting them over on America *was* big businessmen and financial leaders, such as J. P. Morgan and Eldridge Gary. Though he is critical of federal housing projects, he does not seem aware that *these* were rammed through largely with the backing of the giants of the construction industry who witnessed falling profits and a "recession" during parts of the 1950's and '60's. Though ostensibly addressed largely to liberals, Hospers overemphasized their role in the growth of American Statism *vis a vis* that of the business and financial community. It was big businessmen and financiers, for instance, who supported the first "liberal" professors in style at the end of the 19th century, who bankrolled the "Progressive Movement," who put up the money for such organizations as the American Historical Association and American Economic Association, and who paid the bills of THE NEW REPUBLIC. Yet none of this is mentioned by Hospers.

Part of my disagreement with this emphasis, or lack of it, by Hospers lies in his distinction between the public and private sector. "In most nations of the world, there is what is called the 'public sector' and the 'private sector.' More accurate labels would be the *coerced* sector and the *uncoerced* sector. In the uncoerced sector — that is, the free market — we have only voluntary exchange. In the coerced

(Continued on page 5)

LIBERTARIANISM — *(Continued from page 4)*

sector, conditions are imposed on the free market by govern-which distorts the market and impedes its efficiency." Now my objection to this is fundamental: the radical distinctions are *not* between the public and private sectors, or public and private ownership and control, but rather between *just* and *unjust* ownership and control. Ultimately, *all* decision making comes down to a few individuals, or one person, over a specific property. It is morally irrelevant whether this be "private" or not. What *is* relevant is whether or not it is *just*. Suppose, for instance, that a thief makes off with someone's watch. Is that watch in his possession now "public" property? Is is "private" property, which, re-member, is *equated* by Hospers (and Rand, apparently) with the uncoerced, free market sector? Or take the case of a government seizing everyone's property and *giving* it to individuals who are not *technically* part of the State apparatus. Is that "private property," or the "free market, uncoerced sector"? Also take the hypothetical case of someone justly owning something and *donating* it to those in the government, such as somebody's donation of a private library to the government. Is this part of the "public sector" which is *equated* with the "coercive sector"?

The point is this: whether public or private, the *real* moral distinction is between property which is justly held, and that which is unjustly held. And a large part of the "private sector" in the world is property which is, by libertarian standards, unjustly held, such as is the case with the land in in the multitude of feudalist countries which still exist. But if this is true in one case, it may also be true in another. Which cases it *is* true in, can only be established by means of detailed research and by the application of libertarian principles. I submit that had Prof. Hospers approached the issue *this* way, he would have been far more harsh on so-called "private" people and institutions than he has been in LIBERTARIANISM. The questions of "ultimate responsibility" and the like are, of course, different issues, and must also be analyzed. But it is Hospers' concern with "public" or governmental actions which has led him to play down the role of practically anyone except liberal intellectuals in the rise of Statism.

There is the same problem in the case of Hospers' critique of student takeovers of university campuses. The argument against this in the case of justly established "private" universities is clear. But what about State universities? And what about the so-called "private" universities which are nearly 90% bankrolled by the state? Or which seize land from its rightful owners by aligning with the State's power of eminent domain? Or those which align with the State to do "research" into ways and means of destroying other people's lives and property? Whatever one's position on these might be, it is surely more complex an issue than Hospers makes it.

Let us take one final, related, issue before zeroing in on foreign policy: the case of the students' reactions to Dow Chemical's presence on campuses across the U. S., at the time when Dow's own napalm was being used to zap Vietnamese peasants at the height of the Vietnam War. Hospers makes it a simple case of free speech. A good case can be made for this position. But if one holds — as I do — that the Vietnam War is a criminal war for which the U. S. is far more responsible than the Communists of North Vietnam, then the issue becomes more complex. In his chapter on international relations, his response to the menace of the Communist criminals is not "having *relations of any kind* with such nations — not diplomatic and, more important, no trade . . ." This is not made clear — does Hospers support U. S. *government* prohibitions of American citizen trading with communist countries? If so, then this is the age-old problem of whether or not one is morally justified in coercively preventing one from trading with a criminal. If one is, and if the U. S. government is *also* criminal (i. e. it initiates force, though

The Liar As Hero

By Walter Block

It is all too easy to be an advocate of free speech when it comes to the rights of free speech of those with whom one is in agreement. It is all too easy to wax eloquent about the free speech rights of people who recite the boy scout pledge or the pledge of allegiance, or who sing the star spangled banner. Or other equally controversial things. The real test of free speech advocacy, is when it comes to controversial speech; better yet, when it comes to vicious, nasty speech that practically *everybody* is against.

There is perhaps nothing nastier or more vicious than libel, especially when it is personal and even false. We must therefore take especial care to defend the free speech rights of the libeler who furnishes us with a most important arena for free speech protection. For if the free speech rights of libelers and slanderers can be protected, the rights of *any* of the rest of us who do not give as much offense will certainly be more secure. If the free speech rights of libelers and slanderers are not protected, they are done a disservice, and the rest of us are that much less secure.

The reason that there has not been much action (to say the least) in behalf of the slanderer and libeler on the part of civil libertarians is that it is widely felt that they (unjustifiably) ruin people's reputations. Grim tales about lost jobs, friends, etc., abound. Far from being concerned with the free speech rights of the libeler and slanderer, civil libertarians have been concerned with protecting what they call the rights of those who have had their reputations destroyed by libelers and slanderers. It should be realized, however, that the *truth* as well as falsity can ruin reputations; so merely stopping false charges from being uttered is no guarantee of maintaining a person's reputation. If we take the view that reputations are all somehow sacrosanct, then we must prohibit all sorts of denigration, even truthful ones. No kind of unfavorable literary criticism, satire, movie, play, music, or book reviews could be allowed. All diminish reputations to some degree.

Although it is interesting that the deniers of free speech to libelers would not be willing to consistently deny free speech to all detractors, this alone will not clearly and unambiguously establish the free speech rights of the libeler. In order to do this, we must realize that a person's reputation is not his private property — as, for instance, is his coat. His reputation is rather what *other* people think of him. His reputation consists *solely* of the thoughts of *other* people. Thus, to prohibit the slanderer from ruining someone's reputation is to prohibit the slanderer from trying to affect the thoughts of other people. A man does not *own* his reputation any more than he owns the thoughts of others — because that is *all* his reputation consists of. A man's reputation cannot be stolen from him any more than can thoughts of *other* people be stolen from *him*. Whether his reputation was "taken from him" by fair means or foul, by truth or falsehood, he did not own it in the first place and hence should have no recourse to the law for damages.

Paradoxically, reputations, owned or not, will probably be more secure without laws prohibiting libelous free speech. Nowadays, with laws prohibiting libelous falsehoods, there is a natural tendency for the public to *believe* any

(Continued on page 6)

perhaps in lesser measure than some other government), then are private citizens justified in preventing other "private" citizens — such as Dow Chemical — from trading with *our* criminal government? This is an extremely complicated issue, and I think that Hospers does it a disservice in discussing it in only a few paragraphs. I myself am opposed to preventing Dow from recruiting on campuses, but the issue is not so simple as Hospers makes it sound. ◼

THE LIAR AS HERO — *(Continued from page 5)*

publicly made libel or slander. "It would not be printed if it were not true," reasons the gullible public. If libel and slander were freely allowed, there would be so much of it, and from every possible slant, that the public would not be so gullible. Scurrilous attacks would have to be checked out or substantiated before they would have much effect. Commercial agencies like Consumers Reports or the Better Business Bureau might arise to meet the demand on the part of the public for more accurate scurrilous information.

Until that great and glorious time when vicious nasty false remarks are accorded their proper free speech protection, we should all, liars and truth tellers alike, give aid and comfort to the libeler and slanderer; failing that, we should at least recognize them for the heroes that they are. For it is the libeler and slanderer who is on the front lines of the battle to protect the freedom of speech of us all. ◼

From The Old Curmudgeon

Psychology and All That.

My strictures against the California Psychology conference gave rise to a few critical letters from the California movement, ranging from the cogent to the frenetic. Roy Childs pointed out, quite correctly, that humanistic psychology is *philosophically* far more akin to libertarians than behaviorism, since both believe in free will. Roy holds that the Conference made no particular commitment to forms of therapy. All this is fine, although the conference literature made far more grandiose claims. But it still leaves the conference as just one recent example of the festering growth, both in the libertarian movement and in the American culture as a whole, of what we might call *psychologism.*

The hallmark of the psychologizer is that the focus of his attitudes undergoes a severe change. Instead of concentrating his activities on grappling with the outside world (including the world of ideas), he turns morbidly inward, and spends his energies worrying about his own psyche and inflicting this worry on all around him. Note that I am not trying to denigrate the almost universal existence of psychological problems, their importance to the individual, or the possible value of therapy. What I am attacking is the person's elevation of his psychic problems into a matter of seemingly cosmic significance, in the course of which the person's effectiveness in dealing with the outside world withers amidst the bog of fuzzy-headed morbidity. A typical psychologizer will say: "I now see that all these political and economic problems are unimportant; the only really important concern is one's inner 'growth', experiencing one's feelings, expanding one's 'openness'."

Not only does all the palaver about inner growth shift the focus from the outside world, thereby often intensifying the person's troubles, but the psychologizing promotes not only chuckleheadedness, but also the very instability, hedonism, and "whim worship" that the world is suffering too much of in the first place. Much of the humanist writings, particularly those of the late Abraham Maslow, contain a great deal of value, emphasizing as they do free individual choice and the importance of individual self-development. But the problem is that even in the best of these writings, whim-worship is encouraged, because they have no moral principles, no ethical guides for choice to offer to their readers and followers. Stressing individual self-development without setting rational moral guides for that development (develop where? in what direction?) leads to caprice, hedonism, instability, and irresponsibility – in short, whim-worship.

I suppose it was bound to happen; much of this is an overreaction against Randianism. Many of these people are former Randians; after spending several years in the cast-iron rigidities of Orthodox Randianism, in which the slightest deviation from the tastes of the cult was condemned as "irrational", many ex-Randians have gone whole hog the other way: in place of a rational ethic they have substituted unstable and hedonic submission to whim and caprice; in place of reason they have set unanalyzed feelings upon the throne.

A large part of the newly burgeoning psychologism in the libertarian movement is due to the intensifying influence of the New Nathaniel Branden, in his post-Randian development. In many ways, the New Branden is Rand-gone-Hollywood, as the old emphasis on reason begins to get lost amidst the hip and the mod, in immersion in all the fashionable, Hollywood-spawned techniques of the day, from hedonism to encounter groups to the Instant Cure. As a veteran battler against Orthodox Randianism, I never thought that I would ever come to say this: but I think that the Movement could benefit from an increased dose of the Old Rand, with her insistence on the primacy of a rational ethnic. Let us not throw out the rational ethical baby along with the Orthodox Randian bathwater. ◼

The Shadow Cabinet

Back in the days when I was a youthful extreme rightist, one of our great party pastimes was to conjure up a "dream cabinet", a cabinet to be installed in the unlikely event that we would "have our druthers". And regardless of the differences of opinion amongst us, there was always one selection we could all agree upon: "For Secretary of Labor . . . Westbrook Pegler." Yes, those were heady days.

But now, lo and behold!, fantasy cabinet-making has come out of the closet. It is now indeed the fashion among those presidential candidates without what used to be called a "Chinaman's chance" for victory. The candidate – be he Dr. Spock or Senator McCarthy – issues a promise of what might have been. Not one to be caught lagging, I hereby present my shadow Cabinet – the men and women whom I would have chosen had I swept to victory on the Libertarian Party ticket this year. Each one of these choices could be trusted to do the appropriate and proper thing by his chosen field of expertise. There are, I'm afraid, many gaps in the Cabinet, but that is because I have not yet been able to find the right man for the vacancy.

And now, heed this, America:

Secretary of State .... Leonard P. Liggio
Head of the Middle Eastern Desk .... Stephen P. Halbrook
Ambassador to the Court of St. James ...... John F. McCarthy
Secretary of Defense .... Robert LeFevre
Secretary of the Treasury .... Jerome Daly
Secretary of Labor .... Sylvester Petro
Secretary of Housing and Urban
            Development .... Edward C. Banfield
Secretary of Transportation, and Head of the
   Obscenity Division of the Dept. of Justice ... Ronald Hamowy
Head, Anti-Trust Division .... Sam Peltzman
Head, Bureau of Indian Affairs .... Rosalie Nichols
Head, National Institute of Mental
                Health ...... Dr. Thomas Szasz
Head, Voice of America .... Karl Hess
Head, NASA and the Patent Office .... Andrew J. Galambos
Administrative Assistant, in Charge of
            Minority Groups ..... Walter Grinder
Administrative Assistant, in Charge of
          Women's Rights .... James D. Davidson
        and last, but certainly not least,
Secretary of Health, Education, and Welfare .... Ayn Rand

"The art of government is the organization of idolatry."
--- George Bernard Shaw.

Recommended Reading

Rothbardiana.

Murray Rothbard continues to proliferate on several fronts. Rothbard's attack on the Value-Added Tax in *Human Events,* "The Value-Added Tax is Not the Answer," (March 11), was inserted into the *Congressional Record* of March 14 by Senator Harry Flood Byrd (Ind., Va.). Byrd states that he is still keeping an "open mind" on the VAT but states that Rothbard "makes some interesting points" on the subject.

Shortly afterward, prominent New Left columnist Nicholas von Hoffman (*Washington Post,* March 17), devoted his column to denouncing Phase II, and quoted at length and approvingly from Rothbard's article on price-wage controls during World War I. The article is from a forthcoming book, edited by Ronald Radosh and Murray Rothbard, *A New History of Leviathan* (Dutton, paperback); von Hoffman clearly absorbed the major lesson of the book, which analyzes American political policy, foreign and particularly domestic, from the Progressive period until the Korean War; that President Nixon is following the Wilsonian doctrine, and that that doctrine involved a close partnership between business and government, for the purpose of cartellizing the American economy. One of the explicit selling points of the *New History of Leviathan* is that New Left and "Old Right" historians here join not in their policy conclusions but in their analyses of the current American political system and how it got that way. The book contains the following articles: Martin J. Sklar on Woodrow Wilson; Murray N. Rothbard on "War Collectivism in World War I"; Rothbard on "Herbert Hoover and the Myth of Laissez-Faire"; Ronald Radosh on "The New Deal"; James Gilbert on James Burnham; David Eakins on "Policy Planning for the Establishment"; and Leonard P. Liggio on National Security Managers from World War I to the present. The book is prefaced by an introduction by the eminent New Left historian William Appleman Williams, in what is probably the most blisteringly anti-State essay that he has ever written.

von Hoffman.

Nicholas von Hoffman, indeed, grows increasingly libertarian. Last year, he published two columns praising the devotion to libertarian principle of libertarian businessman Robert Love of Wichita; now, in his April 10 column in the *Washington Post,* von Hoffman devotes a laudatory essay to the youthful Washington libertarian James Davidson, head of the National Taxpayers Union and a remarkably effective one-man Washington lobby for the cause. Von Hoffman concludes his column by saying that Davidson's "politics are too good to believe in, too good for people to try."

Austrian Economics.

It is always a pleasure to welcome a newcomer to the tiny but rapidly growing world of "Austrian School" economics. Now Miss Sudha R. Shenoy, graduate student in economics at the London School of Economics and daughter of free-market Indian economist B. R. Shenoy, has published an excellent new collection of anti-Keynesian essays by the great Austrian economist F. A. Hayek. The collection is judiciously culled from Hayek's past and current writings, and is preceded by an excellent brief introduction by Miss Shenoy, "The Debate, 1931-1971". The value of the collection, as well as the introduction, is not simply as a critique of Keynesianism, but in setting forth the basic Austrian methodology and point of view, and it is thereby an implicit (and sometimes explicit) critique of Anglo-American macro-economics in general, including the "Classical" and Friedmanite doctrines. This little paperback, published by the free-market English organization, the Institute for Economic Affairs, is must reading for anyone interested in the Austrian point of view. (Sudha R. Shenoy, ed., F. A. Hayek, *A Tiger by the Tail,* London: Institute of Economic Affairs, 1972. Address: 2 Lord North Street, Westmi..ster, London SWIP 3LB, England. Price in England is one pound. IEA publications are often available from Transatlantic Arts, Inc. in New York.)

Miss Shenoy also provides us with the most up-to-date critique of Indian central planning (hitherto provided by B. R. Shenoy) in another IEA pamphlet, *India: Progress or Poverty?* (same price.)

Libertarian Magazines.

Some excellent libertarian periodicals of remarkably high quality have recently been launched. We have already mentioned the new anarcho-objectivist fortnightly tabloid *The New Banner* (35¢ a copy, $7.00 a year, from Box 1972, Columbia, S. C. 29202), but it continues to fulfill the difficult task of putting out a lively and interesting publication, with a nice blend of news and theoretical discussion. Particularly good is the "Market Alternatives" column of Dave Foster, who continues to spin out and defend the concept of private courts and police in the free society against all comers.

One of the best of the new publications is the little-known *Stanford Independent,* issued by the Stanford libertarian movement, whose guiding inspiration is the brilliant Bill Evers. The first, Nov.-Dec. 1971, issue has an excellent article on the theory of justice by Evers, developing the libertarian theory of property rights, citing natural law theory, Locke, Spooner, Rothbard, and Childs. An equally good article by Joe Kalt, "Anarchism Derived," develops the concept of anarchism from natural law and libertarian philosophy. To top it off, Mark Venezia outlines the different strands and factions in the current libertarian movement. The second issue, March, 1972, contains a scholarly legal critique of the law of "statutory rape" by Bob Litterman, a critique of the theory that unions cause inflation by Robin Friedman, and a review by Bill Evers of Andrew Van Melsen's Thomist work on *The Philosophy of Nature.* These are but the highlights of these two issues. *The Stanford Independent* is available free – but all contributions are welcomed – at P. O. Box 2122, Stanford, California 94305.

A mimeographed, but lively, publication is *New Libertarian Notes,* published by the New York University movement and edited by the ebullient Samuel Edward Konkin III. NLN is a 12-pager, comes out ten times a year, and costs $2.50 for the year, 40¢ per issue. Available from Konkin, 235 E. 49th St., New York, N. Y. 10017. The May issue contains, among other things, a continuing series on World War II Revisionism by William Gillespie.

Last but not least there is *Outlook,* a new libertarian monthly emerging out of the old *Abolitionist,* with Jerry Tuccille as its editor-in-chief. *Outlook's* intention is to include material by all wings of the libertarian spectrum, even unto the realms where the libertarianism wears pretty thin. With Tuccille at the helm, we can confidently expect lots of satire, and fun and games. *Outlook* is available for 50¢ an issue, or $5.00 a year, at Box 1027, Newark, N. J. 07101. ◼

Frank S. Meyer, RIP

There are surely few more painful tasks than to write about a very close friend shortly after his death. It was one Frank's remarkable attributes that without giving an inch in argument, he was able to separate the personal from the ideological more clearly than almost anyone I have known: and so he could continue to be close friends with people who differed sharply from him in many areas. Frank indeed was one of the great conversationalists of our day; talking with him was always a profound pleasure, whether in all-night conversations in Woodstock or over late-night phone calls. For Frank's great erudition was matched by a veritable passion for ideas, and so conversation with him meant a fascinating play of ideas and insights over a vast range of human thought, history, events, politics, people, chess (not the least!), and on and on. Frank indeed gave off an intellectual excitement matched by few people in my experience; pacing up and down, a cigarette in one hand and a Scotch in the other, he would convey that excitement to everyone in the room, and enrich all of our lives. He was exciting, stimulating, fun; and with all that, he cared deeply for each and every one of his legion of friends. And so when I think of Frank, I think first not of the towering eminence in the conservative movement that he truly was, but of the wonderful quality of his friendship. The death of Frank Meyer is a great loss in my own life, and I am sure in the lives of all of his friends. Every person is of course unique and irreplaceable, but Frank leaves a gap in our lives that can never come close to being filled.

Frank and I shared a special bond, the bond of dedicated Night People in a world of 9-to-5. One of the tributes to Frank in *National Review* mentioned the joy at always being able to call Frank at 3 in the morning. For a Night Person, this was still more appreciated. Frank was even more steadfast than I in his all-night schedule, and at the times when I would zonk out early, Frank would playfully accuse me of betraying our Night People principles.

One of the great joys of knowing the Meyers' was experiencing the quality of the marriage between Frank and Elsie. Never have I known two people so close, so intimate on every level; in this age of instability, here was a truly rare marriage, a marriage to cherish even for those of us who experienced it as friends.

In the field of ideology, Frank Meyer towered mightily over the rest of the conservative movement. Not only for his erudition and intelligence, but also because among them all he was by far the most dedicated to the liberty of the individual. That I do not believe that his attempt to fuse conservatism and libertarianism can ultimately hold does not detract from the importance and the nobility of the

venture. Among all of his colleagues, Frank Meyer never yielded to the temptation to bend the knee to Power, to join the Establishment, to play patty-cake with President Nixon. He held the banner of his conservative-libertarian principles aloft, and denounced with all the great intelligence at his command all attempts to betray them.

In no area was Frank more dedicated a libertarian than in the field of education. Scorning both the public school system and the miasma of Progressivism that the private schools have become, Frank Meyer, quietly and without fanfare, proceeded on the heroic and enormously difficult task of educating his two sons at home. The energy and devotion that this task consumed can only make the rest of us stand in awe and admiration. The result of this devoted tutoring was two sons who, on the first formal exam of their lives, sailed into Yale and are proceeding to make their mark in the world with brilliance and in steadfast devotion to conservative standards and values. The education of John and Gene Meyer is one of Frank's finest accomplishments.

Frank's quality of taking ideas seriously can be seen from the way in which he handled his defection from the Communist Party, in which he had risen to be one of its leading "cadres." He was not content, along with the bulk of his ex-Communist colleagues, to rush into print with glib explanations and excuses. When he left the Communist Party, Frank Meyer went off to Woodstock and meditated deeply, on his life, his ideas, and values. He took years to do this, but the price was worth it; for when he "returned" to the world of ideas and actions, he had hammered out his new conservative ideology and comprehensive world-view. How many people have had the vision, the fortitude, the dedication, the sheer guts to do this, to take the time and energy to mould their own personal reconstruction?

By the time he had re-emerged, Frank had become a Christian, but various theological doubts had prevented him from joining the Catholic Church. Very shortly before his death on Holy Saturday, however, his doubts resolved, Frank was received into the Church, and a Requiem Mass was held for him the following Wednesday. As soon as he was received into the Church, Frank found peace before the end. One of the writers of tributes in *National Review* said that he was looking forward to the Frank Meyer of old debating Thomas Carlyle in Heaven. Given my own theological views, I can't say that I expect this to happen, but I can hope. And I do.

"Among the natural rights of the colonists are these: first, a right to life; secondly, to liberty; thirdly, to property; together with the right to defend them in the best manner they can."

— Samuel Adams

Subscription is $8.00 per year.

Libertarian Forum Associate subscription $15.00 or more.

THE LIBERTARIAN FORUM
Box 341   Madison Square Station
New York, New York 10010

First Class

Published Every Month. Subscription Rate: $8.00 Per Year

A Monthly Newsletter

THE
Libertarian Forum

Joseph R. Peden, Publisher   Murray N. Rothbard, Editor

VOLUME IV, NOS. 6-7   JUNE-JULY, 1972   75¢

McGOVERN???

At this writing, it is clear that only a miracle will keep George McGovern from the Democratic nomination for President. Perhaps the unions, the centrists, the party bosses, can mobilize a last ditch stand for the "old politics" and stop the crazies — but the chances look slim at best. But even if the McGovern steamroller sweeps to a first ballot victory, the convention will scarcely be a dull one. For the real fun of the convention will be what might be called a "meta-spectacle": the spectacle of contemplating the reactions of the mass of Middle America as they watch the goings-on in Miami over TV.

For what they will be watching is the sudden seizure of power by all the forces whom they hate and fear: the ruthless triumph of the scruffy Left — hippie youth, college kids, blacks, women, Chicanos, welfare mothers — the whole kaboodle. The comfortable old faces and power brokers — the Daleys, the party leaders, the union officials — will be all but gone, swept aside by "grass roots" power fueled by lunatic reforms insisting on quota representation for highly selected "minorities." Along with the visible embodiment of their gut enemies, Middle America will see these forces push through programs and issues which will scare the bejabers out of them: everything from the economic insanity of a $1000 gift for every American to be financed by everyone making more than the gigantic sum of $12,000 a year, to the legalization of homosexual marriages. And even if the more sensible politicos in the McGovern camp are able to tame their power-happy militants and tone down many of these programs, their radical scent will be there, to pervade the convention and the following McGovern campaign with the odor of inevitable and crushing defeat.

Two weeks before the California primary, Hubert Humphrey launched a belated campaign to inform the American public of the real ideas being promulgated by the left kids and their "sincere", slightly cretinous front man. In those two weeks, Humphrey was able to reduce the McGovern lead almost to the vanishing point. But this campaign of education will be as nothing compared to the massive Republican effort, which need only point the finger at the McGovernite programs and at their proponents, to send the South Dakotan down to a defeat more crushing than that of Barry Goldwater. To win the election, McGovern would have to hold the 1968 Humphrey states (essentially the Northeast plus Texas), and pick up a few more key states, such as California, Illinois, and Ohio. The chances of McGovern carrying Texas are surely nil, and he can scarcely carry the other states either, in the face of massive defections of the elderly, Jews, ethnics, WASPS, blue collar workers, etc. — in short, virtually the entire voting population over 30. Furthermore, the humiliated Daley machine will surely sit on its hands, and thus end any chance of carrying Illinois. Even New York is hardly safe for McGovern, considering the likelihood of an ultimate Conservative endorsement for Nixon, and of serious low income Jewish defections from a McGovern ticket.

In the extremely unlikely event of a McGovern triumph in November what would a McGovern administration be like? In the first place, the Left would become totally insufferable once again: any "New Left", anti-statist and anti-Presidential glimmerings would go by the board now that

the Left felt itself in power once again. As New Left columnist Pete Hamill wrote some months ago: "Wouldn't it be wonderful to have a President we could like again?" Decentralization and community control would disappear in a new coalition unpleasantly reminiscent of FDR, and the new push would be on behalf of a compulsory egalitarian variant of collectivism. On the other hand, of course, there would be some compensations: the Conservatives, Bill Buckley, National Review et. al. would suddenly find their anti-statist voice after years of cozying up to Power. In politics, I'm afraid that the vehemence of one's anti-statism depends upon one's own distance from the seats of Power.

More substantively, a McGovern administration would undoubtedly get us out, posthaste, from the horror of the Indo-chinese war. Civil liberties would improve, but whether McGovern could push a repeal of the draft or the promised $30 billion reduction in defense spending through a hostile Congress is doubtful indeed. On the domestic front, the key question is whether McGovern would be able to get his horrendous economic program through the Congress. The one hope for a tolerable McGovern presidency would be to have his economic policies blocked by an extreme right-wing Congress while he is free to "bug out" abroad. Here we have to ponder whether Congress, used to being supine before the President, will really offer determined resistance to McGovernomics. At least, the conservative Republicans, tied inexorably to the statism of Nixonomics, would be able to resume their former resistance, to galloping collectivism.

In the meanwhile, while hoping against hope that a harmless fellow like Muskie will be able to stop McGovern at the pass, there are already a few things to rejoice over in this election year. For a New Yorker, there have been two delights. One was the total collapse of the Lindsay boomlet, to such a degree that we may look forward to a speedy retirement of Big John from public life. A second was the crushing of the monstrous Bella Abzug, that Gorgon blend of Sophie Portnoy laced with Karl Marx. The issue between La Abzug and Bill Ryan on New York's West Side was not so much ideological as aesthetic, and it is pleasant to contemplate the considerable reduction of noise pollution in politics with the departure of "Battlin' Bella" from the public scene. ◙

The Party Emerges

From all sides, I have been bombarded with the question: have I "sold out" to the newly emerged Libertarian Party? Or, to put it less violently, have I shifted my position?

It is true that I have agreed to become an economic adviser to John Hospers, the Libertarian Party candidate for the Presidency, and that I have joined an Academic Advisory Board for the New York party (called "The Free Libertarian Party.") But I have not changed my position in the least. My strictures against the LP were not the result of "anti-party principle"; I never believed that forming a political party itself violates

(Continued On Page 2)

301

The Party Emerges —

(Continued From Page 1)

libertarian principle. My arguments against a national ticket were strategic and prudential; and these arguments still remain. As long as the LP has gone ahead and nominated a national ticket (Hospers-Nathan) I wish it well; but realistically I do not expect much, either by way of votes or of mass conversion, to emerge from the campaign.

I remain, furthermore, more enthusiastic about campaigns on the local level at this stage of the game. The New York FLP is pursuing this kind of strategy by concentrating its energies on two local races in Manhattan (Gary Greenberg for Congress and Forum contributor Walter Block for Assembly), and one on the loosely affiliated "Independent Rights" ticket, with Guy W. Riggs for Assembly from Poughkeepsie. Greenberg and Block, moreover, are happily using the campaign to radicalize the party itself. There are several imaginative ways by which Greenberg and Block are going beyond the rather stodgy laissez-faire platform of the official party. In the first place, Greenberg and Block go beyond the official party call for total amnesty for draft resisters, and advocate "reparations to be paid out of the pockets of the politicians and personnel who maintained the draft." If the draft is slavery and is criminal, then shouldn't the criminals be forced to compensate the victims? Here is "radical" libertarian doctrine not to be found in the orthodox political guidebooks of Objectivism. Greenberg and Block go on from there to another joyously radical demand: "A War Crimes Tribunal should be established to examine whether or not war crimes have been committed during the Kennedy-Johnson-Nixon administrations." Then they pursue the logic to go beyond the mere finger-pointing of, say, the old Bertrand Russell War Crimes Tribunal: "Perpetrators should be prosecuted." Here are planks truly worthy of libertarians who are not afraid to be "radical" — i.e. to pursue the logic of their position to its uttermost.

Greenberg, in his capacity of dealing with taxation at the federal level, has also had the courage to outrage objectivist sensibilities by calling for the raising of income tax exemptions to $12,000, as a concrete first step in the ultimate party objective of abolishing taxation altogether. The objectivists complained that this exemption of lower and middle income groups would increase the degree of progressiveness in the income tax structure. So it would; but the important question is not the degree of progressiveness, but the amount which each group has to shell out in taxes. The wealthy would not suffer by such a program — in fact, they would be slightly better off from the rise in exemptions — and the poor and middle class would benefit enormously by the tax burden being lifted from them. In fact, why stop at $12,000? We need at least a $20,000 tax exemption to liberate the hard-working middle class of this country from income tax slavery.

Contrast, too, the quality of the "populism" exhibited by the tax reform programs of Gary Greenberg and the slightly better-known George McGovern. McGovern's is a completely phony "populism" which would soak to the 'gunnels everyone making over $12,000 a year. Greenberg would completely free the lower and middle income groups from the exploitation and the oppression of income taxation. For real populism, vote Greenberg and Block! ◙

Another Lone Nut?

John F. Kennedy; Malcolm X; Martin Luther King; Robert F. Kennedy; and now George Corley Wallace: the litany of political assassinations and attempts in the last decade rolls on. (And we might add: General Edwin Walker, and George Lincoln Rockwell. In each of these atrocities, we are fed with a line of cant from the liberals and from the Establishment media. In the first place, every one of these assassinations is supposed to have been performed, must have been performed, by "one lone nut" — to which we can add the one lone nut who murdered Lee Harvey Oswald in the prison basement. One loner, a twisted psycho, whose motives are therefore of course puzzling and obscure, and who never, never acted in concert with anyone. (The only exception is the murder of Malcolm, where the evident conspiracy was foisted upon a few lowly members of the Black Muslims.) Even in the case of James Earl Ray, who was mysteriously showered with money, false passports, and double identities, and who vainly tried to claim that he was part of a conspiracy before he was shouted down by the judge and his own lawyer - even there the lone nut theory is stubbornly upheld.

It is not enough that our intelligence is systematically insulted with the lone nut theory; we also have to be bombarded with the inevitable liberal hobby horses: a plea for gun control, Jeremiads about our "sick society"

and our "climate of violence", and, a new gimmick, blaming the war in Vietnam for this climate and therefore for the assault on George Wallace.

Without going into the myriad details of Assassination Revisionism, doesn't anyone see a pattern in our litany of murdered and wounded, a pattern that should leap out at anyone willing to believe his eyes? For all of the victims have had one thing in common: all were, to a greater or lesser extent, important anti-Establishment figures, and, what is more were men with the charismatic capacity to mobilize large sections of the populace against our rulers. All therefore constituted "populist" threats against the ruling elite, especially if we focus on the mainstream "right-center" wing of the ruling classes. Even as Establishment a figure as John F. Kennedy, the first of the victims, had the capacity to mobilize large segments of the public against the center-right Establishment.

And so they were disposed of? We can't prove it, but the chances of this pattern being a mere coincidence are surely negligible. If the only problem is a "sick society", a "climate of violence", and the absence of gun laws, how come that not a single right-centrist, not a single Nixon, Johnson, or Humphrey, has been popped at? ◙

Review of Hospers' Libertarianism

By R. A. Childs, Jr.

Part II

Now on to foreign policy. Perhaps the single most disappointing aspect of Hospers' otherwise excellent book is his lack of a clear, blunt, uncompromising statement of isolationism as an ideal in international relations. This, it would seem, is a crucially important aspect of libertarianism: that the military, and political power of a State should at least be confined to within its borders, and that no State should be allowed to risk war by militarily protecting those who choose to take risks and do business, own property and the like in other nations. In my view — they should be permitted to do such, but at their own risk. They — and the government — should not be allowed to jeopardize the peace and the very lives of other citizens by becoming politically and militarily involved outside the borders of the nation.

This is not the only bad aspect of this chapter. He shares the Randian belief that the Soviet Union is primarily responsible for the Cold War, and an anti-Russian tone permeates this entire chapter, as though that were the primary focus of libertarianism. Indeed, such references to Russia are to be found throughout the book — one instance of Hospers' overly narrow focussing on applications of libertarian principles. Other instances could have been picked from a much wider historical and political scope, and this would have served to differentiate libertarianism from conservatism much more than does Hospers by focussing on the Soviet Union. And there is also the fact that result of the problems caused by the second World War. Suppose, even,

First off, I think Hospers makes several historically inaccurate statements in this chapter. He makes reference to the U. S. grants of food to Russia in 1918, for instance, but curiously omits to mention the 20,000 troops which Wilson sent over to help crush the Bolshevik regime, thus perpetuating the civil war which was not between the forces of Communism and those of freedom, but between Bolsheviks and supporters of the Czar. There is also no mention of the key issue which was responsible for the triumph of Lenin — that he promised to pull Russia out of the first World War, which Kerensky was stubbornly continuing. There is constant reference to the forced labor and other monstrous things adopted in the Bolshevik's reign, but no mention of the sufferings imposed by the Czar, particularly in the war.

But this is really irrelevant. Let us grant that the Soviet Union may well be the most monstrous regime, domestically, that has ever existed. What has this to do with foreign policy? It is the Randian belief that dictatorships are more warlike than "democracies" or "freer countries." But historically this is not true. Besides, the domestic policies of another government should not be considered in considering issues of foreign policy, unless we are to abandon, in principle, the doctrine of isolationism. The most that can be made out, on Randian grounds, is that the American (or another) government can enter a war only in response to another government's having "initiated" military attacks. Barring this, the actions of another government should be, politically and militarily, irrelevant. Morally, it is a different matter entirely.

But the Cold War is a much more complicated matter. Let me approach

(Continued On Page 3)

Libertarianism —

(Continued From Page 2)

the subject this way. Suppose, John Hospers (and all Objectivists), just suppose, that the Cold War was not begun by the Soviet Union. Suppose that the Left in Eastern Europe was quite independently strong as a result of the problems caused by the second World War. Suppose, even that the victory by revolt of the domestic Communist and other Left political groups in Europe during and after the war was not encouraged by Stalin, but perhaps even opposed, on grounds of maintaining stability and not antagonizing the West (remember that the Soviet Union was extemely weak after the war). Suppose that most of the victories of the Left in Europe had little to do with Stalin, and that the same was true in Asia, particularly in China and Vietnam. Suppose that militarily or otherwise, the Soviet Union was no threat to the United States at the close of World War II, and had no aggressive intentions. Suppose that what actions it did take in Eastern Europe were motivated not out of a desire to "conquer the world," but rather from a desire to be surrounded by buffer states, to prevent a recurrence of the three invasions by means of Eastern Europe which had already occurred in the 20th century. Suppose further that U. S. business, financial, intellectual and political leaders mistakenly held that U. S. prosperity depended upon having vast and continually expanding foreign markets for American goods and investments. Suppose that they thought that political stability in most of the world was a necessary condition of this expansion. Suppose that this were threatened by growing nationalistic and revolutionary movements — communist and non-communist alike — across the globe. Suppose that the response of American leaders was to oppose all upsets of this kind not under their control. Suppose that they found it necessary, as one American Senator so eloquently put it at the onslaught of the Cold War, to "scare hell out of the American people" in order to gain widespread support for the policies necessary to accomplish their goals and combat world-wide resistance. Suppose that the myths of the Cold War were in fact founded in this context and for this purpose. Suppose furthermore that the Soviet Union's foreign policy has been largely a response to this and that without this policy of the American government, that they would never have become involved in world politics the way they have, preoccupied as they were with building "socialism in one country." Suppose, finally, that through tortuous routes, it is the U. S. which today is responsible for actively sustaining the Cold War, and not the Soviet Union. What would our attitude as libertarians then be toward the Cold War?

Now it should surprise no one — but unfortunately it will no doubt do just that — to learn that all of these "supposes" have been extensively documented and argued for in a wide variety of sources for the last twenty years or more. Regardless of whether or not these claims are true — the issue is this: should this point of view be carefully and open-mindedly considered? Would one's position on these historical details affect one's appraisal of the Cold War, and the alleged "need" for a large defense establishment? Finally, again, would this affect one's view of U. S. foreign policy, and one's evaluation? I think the answer to all these is a resounding "yes"!

But this is not considered by Hospers. Using mostly right-wing sources for his case here, he maintains that the Allies "gave" Russia "a huge empire constituting almost one-fourth of the world's land mass and a billion people . . . while the U. S. and Britain got nothing out of the war except mountainous debts." All right, let's take a calm look at this. In the first place, no "giving" was involved. In the case of China, as even American military leaders in that country admitted during and after the second World War, Chiang, the ex-communist, was a gangster. Among other things, he heavily inflated the currency of China so that using 1939 as a base year, the price level rose from "1" in that year to about 85,000 seven or eight years later. In an attempt to fight the inflation, Chiang imposed wage and price controls. They were violated left and right. He then completely alienated his supporters by proceeding to murder businessmen and merchants in the public square for violating these monstrous laws. The Communists were the only major force fighting Chiang, and did in fact end the inflation after their victory — which is not to endorse them. The point is that Chiang was a ganster, and that the American government maintained this man in power for years. When they finally reduced their support, Hospers calls this act a "hair-raising horror story" and a "shoddy chapter in American history." It is one thing to oppose the Communists. It is quite another to endorse Chiang-Kai Shek.

Now for another point. Aside from the fact that nothing was "given" to Russia, and that the communist victories in many Eastern European countries were not simultaneously Soviet victories, and aside from the fact that the U. S. had for a long time also supported other gangsters on practically every continent on the globe in the name of "fighting communism," there is much to dispute in his assertion that the U. S. and Britain gained nothing but "mountainous debts."

Let's take up the debts issue. In fact, these debts are mainly to large banking concerns closely aligned with the State who yearly reap literally billions of dollars in interest payments — paid for the loan of money which they just printed up! So someone is benefitting, and we can therefore ask whether or not this, among other things, was what was intended by wracking up such a large debt. Whatever else the debts serve as, it is obviously an excuse for the State to steal people's money to pay off, for the most part, some very influential financiers.

Finally, what else did America get out of the war? Well, let us grant that Britain lost more than it gained by almost any standard. If we use a rational ethic, which alone can define what constitutes a real, objective, "benefit" to someone, then we can say that no one benefitted from World War II, or from any other war. But let's take the issue of "benefit" and "gain" in a narrower, more journalistic sense. Before the war, the U. S. had troops in a handful of foreign countries. Today, it has troops in more than sixty. American foreign investments which pull in handsome profits for a select few of American businesses and investment houses, have grown very rapidly since the war. And with the international monetary scheme patched together at the close of the war, the American government helped to "integrate" other nations into the American monetary system, thus tying them into the complex American state-system. Foreign aid, regularly attacked by rightists as "altruistic," serves the purpose of subsidizing American corporations and of tying foreign nations into the American economic system — all within a basically State-controlled, protectionistic system. The list of this aspect of the fruits of the second World War is virtually endless.

One can also question the validity of Hospers' assertions that the Soviet Union is a military threat — either existentially or even in mere intent — to the U. S. We find Hospers stating this: "It is at least likely, however, that Soviet Russia (perhaps in combination with China) will unleash an aggressive war against the U. S.; its growing missile system is . . . geared less for defense than for an aggressive first strike. As its nuclear weaponry increases and that of the United States decreases relative to it, as is now happening month by month, there is a strong possibility that once the Soviet Union has attained a clear nuclear superiority over the United States, its leaders will issue an ultimatum to the United States government, presenting it with a choice of nuclear annihilation or military takeover and enslavement. There is also a strong possibility that instead of such direct shoot-it-out methods, the Soviet Union may play a waiting game: its leaders, seeing how much of the world has already fallen to them with American help, and seeing how successfully they have mesmerized and deluded American liberals for fifty years, are aware that the United States is becoming gradually collectivized in any case, have only to continue their present policies and the entire world may yet drop into their lap like a ripe plum. With American policy as it has been since World War II, there is considerable likelihood that things will happen exactly in accordance with such anticipations."

I want to make it clear at this point that however much I admire, respect and like John Hospers, I cannot let this passage go by without commenting on it. In my opinion, this attitude is the most dangerous one that a libertarian could take, and is potentially the most destructive for libertarianism as an ideology, and as a movement. Classical liberalism failed largely because of the pitfalls of utilitarianism, evolutionism, and its failure to confront in bold and uncompromising terms the growing militarism of the turn of the century. I think that this is the worst threat to libertarianism as well. This passage is factually inaccurate from beginning to end. It is all backwards. It is the result of failing to keep up with and confront the discoveries of revisionist historians. Moreover, it shows the importance, in a single passage, of something that I have been stressing for two years: of the critical importance of doing intensive research into current and historical world events before passing judgment on them from a libertarian perspective. Unless one confronts the works of Kolko, Williams, Weinstein, Gardner, Horowitz and others, one is making judgments about world affairs with the same justification as a doctor pronouncing on a patient about whom he knows nothing. It is a fact that both theory (which Hospers is generally brilliant in considering) and the minutiae of history are necessary for sound judgments of current world affairs. If one doesn't have theory, then the evaluation is arbitrary and subjective. If one doesn't have the wealth of historical and empirical detail needed, then the evaluation is little more than a guess — and, usually, it is a bad guess.

(Continued On Page 4)

Libertarianism —

(Continued From Page 3)

That is my objection to this and similar passages of Hospers'. By making factual errors regarding the Cold War, he implicitly comes out in favor of increasing the defense budget and of increasing the military capacities of the U. S. government!!! But any libertarian who does that faces a paradox: the defense budget is maintained by robbery, and the military capacity of the U. S. is already great enough to kill everyone on earth several dozen times. What on earth is libertarian about either of these? Is it any wonder that the people of the world often express some anti-American sentiments when they are implicitly threatened by the greatest array of weapons that the world has ever seen? And if the actions of the American State in foreign affairs — which I think are imperialistic, resting on a denial of free trade and on coercive manipulation of other nations — are performed in the name of "free enterprise," is it any wonder that those who would revolt against the blood-stained status quo revolt also against the ideology which cloaks the poison of U. S. foreign policy?

The rest of Hospers' chapter simply misses the points being raised by any major critic of U. S. foreign policy today. He does not understand the mechanisms and anti-free-market nature of colonialism and imperialism. He hasn't studied these crucially important areas enough.

But my disagreements have been emphasized enough. How, after all this, can I still praise the book? Simple — the passages which I am against comprise a maximum of 10% of the book, probably a good deal less. And in other respects, I have merely criticized omissions of issues, such as the role of big business in the rise of Statism. I have dwelt for such a long time on my disagreements because I think they are fundamental and important — especially in view of the fact that these are key issues on which Hospers is most likely to confuse and alienate the Left.

LIBERTARIANISM, thus, is a mixed book. He addressed it largely to intelligent, open-minded liberals, and solved the problems which they raise against laissez-faire. But he left out the potentially strongest part of his case: he didn't make use of any of the left-wing historically revisionist works which in reality bear out the libertarian argument, neither in domestic nor foreign policy. All the major problems faced today, in foreign and domestic policy, are a result of the denial of liberty by the American and other governments. This is the first thing that a libertarian has to show leftists. Furthermore, libertarians need, perhaps more than they are aware, to reject the past of America as well as the rest of the world. There was no garden of laissez-faire in the 19th century, and the aim and purpose of the "founding fathers" was not to establish laissez-faire by means of the constitution. This means that we must look at the 19th century with fresh eyes, praising the men and institutions who deserve it, and damning those who deserve that. This is one of the flaws of LIBERTARIANSIM: it is too defensive, and wants to claim too much of the past, in matter or spirit, as its own ancestor. There is too much of conservatism left in it.

But despite all this, it is really a good book, and is as I said in the beginning: the best book to hand to somebody who has become interested in attaining a comprehensive overview of the libertarian political philosophy. But if we take our ideology and our tiny movement seriously, then we must be careful in our reservations. Ninety per cent of the book is superb. The rest is just plain wrong. ◙

Anationalism and Immortality

By Jerome Tucille

(The following is an excerpt from HERE COMES IMMORTALITY, a new book to be published by Stein & Day later this year. In the preceding chapter, Walt Disney has been thawed out and reanimated on the steps of the Lincoln Memorial, thus becoming the world's first reanimato. The event has been televised around the world and has shaken the very foundations of modern civilization. Now . . .)

The 1990's, under the leadership of the world's first reanimato, marked the beginning of the anationalist age.

Disney was not the first to set up headquarters at sea by any means. In 1975, Burlington Industries became the first corporation to build an island-headquarters in the Atlantic Ocean, two hundred miles east of New York City. There, in international waters, the company was no longer subject to the laws of any nation and was free to trade in the international marketplace without restrictions.

Later in the decade, an offshore complex which included a jetport, nuclear power plant, waste disposal center and deep-water seaport was built off the eastern tip of Long Island. The ostensible reason for this was to relieve air traffic congestion on land, but when the Mayor of New York City moved his administration to the island complex, the true reason was quickly seen by all.

Developers in Cleveland and Chicago followed suit, constructing jetports and power plants supported on caissons in Lake Erie and Lake Michigan. Throughout the 1980's several more companies set up shop off both the east and west coasts of the United States, and six more jetports were established offshore.

But it wasn't until 1991 that the concept of anationalism finally took hold. Disney wasn't interested merely in escaping tax laws by moving out to sea. It wasn't merely freedom from bureaucratic regulation that he was after. The vision Disney had in mind went way beyond these noble, though limited aspirations.

The dream for Disney was the creation of complete and independent parallel societies which, in effect, would compete with governments throughout the world. The concept of multi- or international corporations was already obsolete before it really got started in the mind of the reanimato. Disney would establish a series of island-communities complete with housing, schools, shops, hotels, industry, theaters — everything necessary for comfortable human existence — in international waters all over the globe.

They would not, of course, be subject to the laws of any nation. They would be free to trade among themselves and also with existing nation-states whenever it was possible. These island-societies would, in a sense, be proprietary communities developed and managed by Disney. Enterprises which, in another sense, would become a giant landlord over a new, anationalist, sea-borne world society.

Floating Lefrak Cities on a grand scale, so to speak, with total ocean living for everyone.

When word of exactly what Disney was up to finally got out, sparks began to fly in virtually every country on the planet. The idea of unregulated anational communities was quickly denounced as fascism of the highest order one day, and anarchism of the lowest order the next. Some nations wanted to extend their national limits two thousand miles out to sea thereby rendering the concept unworkable from the start, but in many cases — most notably the newly emerging "Fourth World" nations — the proposed new limit vastly exceeded the size of the countries themselves.

In the United Nations, now situated on the floating jetport off the shores of Long Island, Disney was accused of trying to turn the entire planet into a giant shopping center with himself as universal landlord (earthlord?). The U. S. ambassador to the U. N. maintained that, if Disney were permitted to have his way, the oceans would be filled with gargantua apartment buildings, mile-long department stores, penny arcades, Jerome Mackey judo schools, Fred Astaire dancing schools, high-rise health clubs and sauna baths, psychedelic pizza parlors, and amusement parks the size of Rhode Island.

The earth would eventually start to look like a never-ending Macy's Thanksgiving Day Parade.

At this point the ambassador from the Soviet Union suggested that the idea of One World Government, discussed for decades in government and academic circles, was long overdue. Only by creating a World Presidium with jurisdiction over the entire planet could counterrevolutionary schemers such as Disney be stopped.

The British ambassador politely objected to the world Presidium; he thought the word Parliament sounded much more democratic.

Israel wanted the world governing board to be called a Knesset; the United States held out for Congress; the Chinese delegation remained silent, figuring they would overthrow whatever group came to power anyway; and the Italian delegates fought among themselves, kicking and punching in the aisles, casting aspersions on one another's ancestry.

Meanwhile, as the debate raged inside the towering glass walls of the United Nations, Disney proceeded to build.

His first island-community went up in the Atlantic, sixty miles southeast of Martha's Vineyard off the coast of Massachusettes. His second was built further out to sea, another hundred miles east southeast of the first one. As the third ocean-community was under construction, Disney discovered he was no longer alone in his rush to create an anationalist empire. Competitors were now entering the market, timidly at first, then gradually more boldly, even as the governments of earth debated their fate at the U. N.   (Continued On Page 5)

Anationalism — (Continued From Page 4)

Hughes Industries, Helmsley-Spears, Lefrak, Levittown, Boise-Cascade and other companies were airlifting platforms out into the Atlantic, erecting modular cities in a matter of months. Some had already inaugurated STOL transport services, free of charge to prospective tenants, in a mad race to populate their communities faster than the rest. Within the space of thirty-six months, a veritable man-made archipelago had been built beginning from a point sixty miles off Martha's Vineyard and extending in a wide arc all the way to the Straits of Gibralter. A similar network running from southern California toward Hawaii was also in the works.

On March 8th, 1994, the United Nations passed a resolution calling for the creation of a One World Governing Body with full authority over the entire planet. The World Parlgressidium — a designation finally agreed upon by the various delegates — would consist of two hundred and eleven members, one each from every nation on earth. There would be, in addition, a five-man executive board comprised of the chief executives of the United States, Russia, the European Commonwealth, China and Japan, with veto power over the legislative body. A World Court would also be established which would serve as the final court of appeals in all judicial matters.

Each nation would maintain its traditional methods of selecting officials, whether by majoritarian election, representative democracy, military coup or one-party dictatorship, for the purpose of administering local affairs. Every six years each nation would hold a general election to select its ambassador to the Parlgressidium.

It was a comprehensive plan, thorough in every detail. It was democratic, fair and tough at the same time. Everyone would have a say — to one extent or another at least — in deciding the people who would dictate the fate of the entire planet. It was a bold, daring, adventuresome proposal, highly innovative and imaginative, even revolutionary in all its implications. Disney and the rest of the maverick developers who were attempting to make a mockery of established authority would be given six months to dismantle their sea-borne monstrosities — or else be blasted right out of the water. Enough was enough already. Give a hooligan too much rope, and he tries to hang you with it.

The resolution was read live on global television on April 15th, 1994. The only problem was: no one seemed to be watching. Where the hell was everybody anyway?

As it turned out, Disney had picked that day to throw a monumental bash on Ocean Village number one. There was STOL service from most areas of the globe, and helicopter shuttles from the United States mainland. Who would stay home and watch television when he had a party like this to go to? It was Ringling Brothers, Barnum and Bailey, and all the Worlds Fairs in history rolled up in a single happening.

Disney was a past master at the formula E plus P = PG (Entertainment plus Pizazz = Profits Galore). The mobs flocked in from every nook and cranny on earth, some with their life savings in tow. More lucre changed hands that day than on any other day in memory. Parades? Candy canes? Balloons? Trombones? All the trappings of manufactured gaiety were present in spades. President Rockefeller (elected by a hair in 1992) wanted to send in the Marines to break up the affair; the Secretary-General of the U. N. thought it best to land an international taskforce to avoid the stigma of "U. S. imperialism."

But they discovered too late that Disney had hired the Marines and Green Berets to police his own operation. Cagey entrepreneur — he had anticipated something like this. Most of the military personnel through the world were now working for the anationalist developers who, after all, paid them much more than the current minimum wage. The politicians of the earth were virtually unprotected. They were at the mercy of every thug and rapist who wanted to have at them.

The United Nations sent out an appeal to the masses. We offer you stability, the security of international law and justice, protection from our common enemies. What do they offer? Parades? Gimmicks? A lifelong sideshow? They're turning the whole planet into a great big funhouse.

The consensus was, however, that the people preferred the earth to be a great big funhouse rather than a great big lunatic asylum.

Within a year one of the largest migrations in the history of mankind was well under way. The whole world was going anational — all because of the wacky dream of the world's first reincarnee.

Reanimation and anationalism all before the turn of the century. What, pray tell, could the future hold in store after this? ▣

The Polish Ham Question

By Walter Block

Supposed exponents of free trade, like YAF, conservative clubs, the Birch Society, and other right wing groups have long been actively opposing the importation of Polish hams. We shall prove that whatever principles such actions could be based upon, they are not the principles of the free market, laissez-faire system, which holds supreme the rights of trade, of property, and of voluntary association.

Opposition to the importation of Polish hams has been defended on the grounds that it is immoral to trade with thieves or receivers of stolen merchandise — a description that eminently fits the Polish government. A description, however, which also eminently fits the U. S. government, with its vast taxing system, its monstrous budget deficit, its astronomical national debt! But more destructive of the private property system even than this are the following: it is the U. S. not the Polish government which destroys property more than 10,000 miles from its own shores in the name of defense. It is the U. S. not the Polish government that threatens the destruction of the whole world with a nuclear might capable of doing just that 1,000 times over. It was the U. S. not the Polish government that was the first and only country to destroy human life (the most important private property right) on a scale unmatched before or after by dropping a nuclear bomb on a center of civilian population; and to make matters worse, after the Japanese government had offered to surrender.

Thus if there is anyone who should not be traded with, it is this U. S. government.

Such a course, however noble sounding, is not required by any libertarian principle. The consistent libertarian is no more required to refuse to trade with the U. S. government than he would be required to refuse to hand over his money to a gunman who threatened his life for that purpose. ("Trade" here includes such things as using the self-enforced governmental monopolies in roads, post-office, courts, TVA; it includes trading with government "client" monopolies in such fields as electricity, gas, and state colleges; it includes trading with those who hold a State license in order to trade, like doctors, lawyers, plumbers, barbers and taxi-cab drivers; it includes trading with anyone who deals with State-supported, coercive-restrictive unions; it includes, perhaps most analogously to the gunman, paying taxes). Consistent refusal to deal with government thieves would involve one in committing suicide, since governments control all of the earth's surface. This is anathema to libertarianism, which holds life, not death, as the ideal.

A U. S. citizen's trading with the U. S. but not the Polish government cannot be defended on the ground that "It was the U. S. but not the Polish government that seized the U. S. citizen's property; and therefore it is the U. S. citizen's subsequent trading with only the U. S. government that is an attempt to regain his stolen property. Since trade with Poland would not accomplish this, it is therefore illiegitimate."

There are two weaknesses with this defense. First, the import of this argument does not so much defend trade with the State as it defends re-taking the stolen property from the State. One does not urge trade with the burglar as justified punishment. One can always trade with him.

Second, according to this argument, the U. S. citizen can trade only with governments that have seized his property; he cannot trade with governments (like the Polish government) that have not seized his property. Accordingly, he could not make a trip to Canada, a country that regularly seizes its own citizens property, but one which does not seize the property of U. S. citizens. A U. S. citizen who lives in Maryland, for instance, could not even make a trip to Nevada, for instance, for the state of Nevada, like that of Poland, had not seized any of his property.

The answer to the Polish ham enigma is this: libertarians must realize that we are all faced with overlord States, some more aggressive and some less. The answer is not to single out Communist States for opposition. All are born in aggression and involuntarism. The way to bring the blessings of laissez-faire to the Polish people is first to secure it for ourselves. The enemies of free enterprise and private property rights here in America are immeasurably benefitted when those who favor the free market are too busy worrying about the "tiger-at-the-gate" to wonder at the absence of freedom right here. ▣

305

Arts and Movies

By Mr. First Nighter

Sometimes a Great Nation. dir. by Paul Newman with Newman and Henry Fonda.

A great libertarian and individualist movie, this film predictably bombed out with the left-liberal youth that make up the bulk of the New York movie audience. The picture puzzled them profoundly; it was starkly individualist, fine; but how come that the great enemy of individualism turned out to be unions and their goon squads in the surrounding "community"? And that the heroism of Fonda and his family consisted in the heinous activity of strikebreaking in order to fulfill their business contracts in lumbering? The reviewers set the picture down as glorifying nineteenth-century individualism and its virtues, and that it does. This is a rugged, heroic, explicitly individualist picture; it is one of the great ones, and if the Left and the Women's Libbers don't like it, the appropriate reply is the great gesture of defiance with which Paul Newman, bloody but unbowed, ends this epic.

The Godfather. dir. by Francis Ford Coppola with Marlon Brando and Al Pacino.

The Godfather is one of the great movies of the last several years, and its enormous popularity is eminently well deserved. In the first place, it is a decidedly Old Culture movie, or "movie-movie"; it is gloriously arriere-garde, and there is not a trace of the avant-garde gimmicks and camera trickery that have helped to ruin so many films in recent years. It is a picture with heroes and villains, good guys and bad guys; there is not a trace of the recently fashionable concern with the "alienation" of shnooks and cretins searching endlessly for a purpose in life. The pace is terrific, the suspense and plot and direction and acting all excellent. Many of the lines are memorable, and "we're going to make him an offer he can't refuse" has already burned its way indelibly into American culture.

The key to the movie is the first scene, when an elderly undertaker, having gone to the police and to the courts for justice for his raped and beaten daughter, and failed abysmally to get it, at last turns to the Corleone Family for that precious quality, justice. Brando, as Don Vito Corleone, the "Godfather", berates the undertaker: "Why did you go to the courts for justice? Why didn't you come to me?" And it is further made gloriously evident that the Corleone Family's concept of justice is advanced indeed. When the undertaker asks Don Corleone to kill the assaulters of his daughter, Don Vito is shocked: "But that is not justice. They did not murder your daughter." With a keen sense of the concept of proportionate justice, of punishment fitting the crime, Don Vito agrees to make the rapists "suffer" as the daughter had suffered.

The central theme of the plot is the growth of son Michael Corleone; originally a college lad grown apart from the old Sicilian Family ways, Michael takes his stand with the family when his father is nearly murdered by other, aggressor Families, and toughens into the role of successor to Don Vito. (Actually, the word "godfather" is a weak translation of the Italian word compare, which also has connotations of: friend, best man, patron.)

A crucial political statement in the picture comes when Michael is trying to explain to his disapproving WASP girl friend what the Family is all about: essentially their entrepreneurship of illegal goods and services, their necessity to enforce their own contracts, and (regrettably for the libertarian) their penchant for monopoly in which they are a pale reflection of "respectable" and "legitimate" government. Michael tells his girl that his father is a man of power and influence, and hence the methods he employs, "like the President of the United States." The girl replies: "But the President doesn't order anyone killed", to which Michael rebuts: "Now you're being naive" — a masterpiece of political understatement.

But above all, a movie-movie in the grand tradition: a rugged, magnificent epic. ◘

"Democracy substitutes selection by the incompetent many for appointment by the corrupt few." —George Bernard Shaw.

Garbage in New York

By Joseph R. Peden

High on the list of lasting impressions of New York by the casual visitor is the dirt and trash which litters the public and often private spaces throughout the city. Keeping a city of eight million residents and some two million daytime commuters neat and clean would be a formidable task under the best of circumstances, but longtime residents of New York believe that the situation has worsened greatly in recent years. It is a commonplace of local legend that, following a regional snow storm, roads and streets in suburban communities will be cleared in hours, while city streets remain uncleared for days. In 1968 after a heavy snowfall had stranded residents of many areas of the city for three to four days because local streets were not cleared of snow, the outraged public learned that the city sanitation department had two-thirds of its snow clearing equipment out of service due to faulty maintainance. When citizens organized to complain of failure to pick up garbage regularly, they were likely to be awakened at three or four in the morning by the grinding of mashers and the crash of empty cans being hurled from the trucks by city sanitation men. While sanitation pickup in the slums never could cope with the somewhat cavalier methods of garbage disposal of slum residents — out the nearest window or in the nearest empty lot — service in middle class residential neighborhoods also began to deteriorate noticeably. Meanwhile Mayor Lindsay had paid off his political debt to the powerful Sanitation workers union by granting them wage increases making them the highest paid sanitation men in the nation and guaranteeing them retirement at half pay after twenty years service — a privilege enjoyed previously only by firemen and policemen. The cost of these pensions will burden the city for decades to come — but the Mayor will presumably have retired to another state by the time the bills come due.

The increasing costs of municipal sanitation services prompted the City Administrator to conduct a study of the comparative cost of municipal and private carting services within the city. The private carters are licensed by the city and restricted generally to collecting from commercial and industrial companies whom the municipal sanitation service refuses to serve. Thus while the city maintains a near monopoly over residential collection, and of the sweeping of the streets and collection from litter baskets in public spaces, private carters serve the business community as well as a few large residential estates which find municipal services too untrustworthy, even though free.

The private carters collect about a fourth of all waste in the city, and dispose of it in either the municipal dumps for which they pay a fee, or in private dumps, most of which are located in nearby New Jersey. Maximum rates are set by the municipal agency for private carting which is in the hands of some 450 separate firms.

The City Administrator's report was a blockbuster: it claimed that private cartmen collected refuse at about one-third the cost of the municipal sanitation department — $17.50 per ton compared to $49.00 per ton. A closer study of the report revealed that the municipal costs were $39.71, but using a projected inflationary factor the estimated costs would soon reach the $49 per ton figure. The discrepancy in cost was still so great that the city's sanitation department — newly renamed the Environmental Protection Agency — began in some panic its own study. Two years later, it reported that the private carting costs were only 18% less than the municipal service — $31.43 per ton compared to $38.43 per ton.

The Citizens Budget Commission, a privately funded watchdog agency, non-partisan and a long-time scourge of bureaucratic incompetents decided to make its own survey. Within a month, it issued a report challenging the EPA figures. Its staff concluded that the EPA had excluded 40% of the municipal sanitation routes from its cost estimates, and had used figures from only seven of the 450 private carting firms to estimate private costs. Rather than the $31.43 per ton cost for private carters, the CBC found private costs to range between $20.71 and $25.58, depending on how one computed the weight of waste — by the ton or the cubic yard. It also discovered that the EPA estimate of its cost for collecting waste in districts with one and two-family houses was $47.90 per ton while in two neighboring towns in Nassau County private carters charged $17.50 or less per ton — a figure very close to that for private carting in the city according to the City Administrator's report.

What accounted for the discrepancy between the EPA costs and those of the private carters? The CBC reported that, first of all, the city paid its

(Continued On Page 7)

Garbage In New York —

(Continued From Page 6)

sanitation workers wages 20% higher than those paid by private carters, and the fringe benefits were also somewhat higher. But, the CBC report added, "the most significant difference is in the inherent efficiencies of private as opposed to municipal operations. The incentives of profit and competition act to increase efficiency in a way the Department of Sanitation could never duplicate, even under the most aggressive leadership. The high proportion of owner-supplied labor and direct supervision also acts to increase the relative efficiency of private cartage firms."

The CBC recommended that the "sensible course of action" for the City to follow would be to seek bids from private contractors for selected sanitation districts — beginning with the very high cost areas of one and two family homes. While allowing for time for the private carters to "tool up" for the extra work, a gradual conversion to private cartage might save the fiscally distressed city as much as $59-77 million annually.

Under increasing criticism, the EPA desperately looked for some way to save its bureaucratic empire. Step one was the decision to raise the fee charged to private carters using municipal dumps to dispose of waste. As the private carters soon realized, this was a squeeze play in which the sanitation department reduced its costs per ton while increasing private carters costs per ton — reducing the discrepancy between their respective costs.

Step two was to find a way to delay responding to the recommendations of the CBC and the requests of the private carters association for discussions on future contracting of residential waste collection by private firms. Letters to the EPA went unanswered and the city agency desperately tried to avoid the problem by publicizing other gimmicks. Plans were announced for selling advertising space on municipal litter baskets. Unfortunately, potential advertisers had to accept the fact that about 6000 of the 18,000 baskets disappear from the streets annually — no one knows quite where they go. When private carters offered to empty the public waste baskets in the heavily commercial districts of the city — estimating a cost of 70 cents per basket as against a $2.00 cost to the city — they were met with stony silence. Meanwhile the EPA officials exulted in the fact that an association of real estate managers in mid-town Manhattan announced that they would henceforth undertake the formerly municipal function of keeping the streets in front of their properties clean by daily sweeping. This was not a matter of municipal pride but a commercial necessity if they were to attract tenants to the depressed office space market.

Step three was a political masterpiece in the best New York tradition. The EPA announced in Feb. 1972 that a pilot project to test the comparative efficiency of private waste collection in residential areas would be sponsored by the EPA. The pilot district was to be Bedford-Stuyvesant — the worst black slum in the city if not the nation. And the contract to organize the new garbage collection service would be given, not to experienced, professional commercial carting firms, but to the Bedford-Stuyvesant Restoration Corp., a non-profit social rehabilitation agency established as a pilot project by the late Senator Robert Kennedy for social and economic reconstruction of slum areas through the efforts of their inhabitants. The private carters were stunned by this insanity. An EPA spokesman admitted that it would not be a fair test of private vs. city sanitation services, but it would generate jobs and test whether the slum dwellers could keep the slum cleaner than outsiders. It had two other advantages: it threatened the private carters with involvement in New York's messy racial politics if they opposed the scheme, and it postponed any immediate action on their demands for letting out bids for private garbage collection in other districts by professional, experienced carters. As the EPA explained, further pilot projects were envisioned, but the Bedford-Stuyvesant project had first priority ("Because it is there") and would tie up the limited managerial manpower of the city department for months if not years.

Slightly more than a fourth of America's cities rely entirely on private sanitation services; the rest have either municipal monopoly or semi-monopoly operations like New York. The empirical data produced in New York clearly indicates the superiority of the private over the municipal service. Libertarians might find this a profitable area of political agitation and public education for the hard pressed urban taxpayer. But if we are to turn back the forces of Statism we cannot rely on mere theoretical economic arguments, much less ethical entreaties. What is needed is hard research, using all the techniques of the social sciences, to prove the efficiency, and profitability, of our libertarian approaches to concrete social and economic problems. With the exception of the Chicago economists who have long pioneered in using their economic

analysis to liberate us from Statist solutions, libertarians have tended to rely on pious if true generalities — balm to the convinced but irrelevant to ever-pragmatic Americans. If libertarianism is to make any impact upon American social reality, we must begin to produce the detailed socio-economic research data to support our theoretical economic and philosophical analysis, and use it efficiently in our educational work. A fine example of this kind of work was the excellent study of "Taxis and Jitneys: The Case for Deregulation" (by Sandi Rosenbloom) in the February 1972 issue of Reason(294 Via El Encantador, Santa Barbara, CA 93111, 75 cents). Unfortunately, far more common are articles like that of Clarence Carson on Garbage disposal in The Freeman (October 1969), pp. 622-628. This is essentially a descriptive essay of the problems, and exhortation for a free market solution, and the moralistic charge of "waste not, want not". But not a single word or statistic to ground its argument in the socio-economic realities. Utterly useless to convince the hardheaded businessman, legislator or taxpayer. Mere balm to the faithful. Libertarians need far better factual data if they are to make any impact upon contemporary public opinion. ▣

Academic Freedom?

By Peter Sherman

More phony-white-liberal crocodile tears have been shed over the issue of academic freedom than perhaps over any other. More academics have waxed more eloquent over it than over perhaps any other topic receiving their tender attention. In the eyes of some, it has been equated with the very basis of western civilization. In the eyes of others, judging by their anguish, it has been equated with the Second Coming! There is not a day that goes by that does not see the American Civil Liberties Union in a virtual state of apoplexy over some real or imagined violation of academic freedom. And all this seems pale in comparison with the gnashings of teeth and frothings at the mouth by labor unions of professional academics and teachers in this fair land of ours.

From the name itself, academic freedom would seem to be innocuous enough. All it would seem to mean would be that academics, like anyone else, should have freedom. Freedom of speech, freedom to come and go, freedom to quit a job. The usual freedoms that everyone has. Such is not the case, however. "Academic freedom" has a very special meaning: the freedom to teach the subject matter in whatever way the academic in question wishes the subject taught, despite any wishes to the contrary that his employer may harbour. In other words, the employer may not fire the academic as long as he teaches the subject matter in any manner that the academic, not the employer, wishes. Now this is a very special, not to say spectacular doctrine indeed! This point may easily be proven by applying the doctrine of academic freedom to almost any other occupation. Let us consider "plumbers' freedom" for instance.

What would plumbers' freedom consist of? The right to place pipes and plumbing equipment in the position his experience had taught him was best. But suppose a customer wanted his plumbing in a place that differed with the plumber's professional, artistic, aesthetic, and other judgments as to where the plumbing should be. The plumber is of course free not to take a job if his sensibilities are outraged. (We do not yet have forced labor in this "land of the 'free'", except, of course, when some old men decide to force some young men to fight in a jungle 10,000 miles away and call if a draft). But suppose he demands not simply the right to refuse the job, but the right to take the job and to do it his way. If there were any "plumbers' freedom" analogous to the way "academic freedom" is run, he would have just that right! He would have the right to say that when his professional competence is at odds with the desires of the customer, his views should prevail. The customer is not always right, it would seem.

It will be objected by the academic freedom-lovers that there are great differences between plumbers' freedom and academic freedom and that therefore only the latter is justified. There are several differences. Let us, however, examine them to see if they amount to much.

One alleged difference between plumbers and academics is that plumbers usually rent their services directly to the customer, while the academician rents his services to the customer (students, or parents of students) through an intermediary — the university. But the problem with this objection is that it is by no means or immediately obvious why this should make a difference, or is indeed relevant at all. Secondly, although they are perhaps in a minority, there are many plumbers who do not work directly for the customer, but rather work through an intermediary plumbing firm; and there are likewise many academics

(Continued On Page 8)

Academic Freedom? —

(Continued From Page 7)

who work directly for customers as tutors. In any case, we can consider these two cases and see if "vocational freedom" makes any more sense here than in the usual cases.

Plumbers' freedom makes no more sense in the case of an employed plumber than in the case of a self-employed one. Plumbers' freedom would mean that the employee of a plumbing firm would be free of any job requirements placed upon him by either the owner of the plumbing firm or by the customer. Since the firm serves as an agent of the customer, the employee's plumbing "professionalism" would prevail over the desires of the customers. Any employee could refuse to work on a big construction job if the plumbing specifications were not to his "professional" liking. And of course he could not be fired, for such a firing would violate his "plumbers' freedom".

Likewise, academic freedom makes no more sense in the case of an academic tutor working directly for the customer than it does in the case of an academic serving the consumer indirectly through the intermediation of a university. Such "academic freedom" would mean that the tutor would be entirely in charge of determining the way the lesson would be taught, and that as long as the tutor stuck to the subject matter for which he was hired, **he could not be fired by the student.** This is such an unexpected conclusion that it bears repeating, even though it follows directly from the logic of how academic freedom works in the university context: if a tutor working for a customer-student has what in the university context passes for "academic freedom", he could not be fired from that position for merely exercising his "professionalism" in a way that displeases his student-employer. The only grounds that exist for firing someone with complete rights of "academic freedom" would be gross violations of the law or professional incompetence. He could not be fired by the student over a "mere" disagreement over a substantive issue concerning the subject matter.

Another alleged difference between plumbers and academics, (alleged, let me hasten to add, by academics, not plumbers), is that the academic vocation, but not the non-academic ones require free inquiry, untrammeled rights of expression, the right to pursue their thoughts wherever their intellects shall lead them. What can one say of this arrant nonsense, except that it is probably more indicative of maniacal, religious elitism than anything else? Perhaps the plumbers could reply with the old aphorism that "Those who can, do, while those who cannot, teach." This reply would be just as relevant to the question at hand. For we are not dealing with the question of how onerous or intellectual the various vocational pursuits are. We are dealing with the propriety of "vocational freedom" in protecting the supposed right to a job as long as certain formalistic job requirements are fulfilled **regardless of the wishes and desires** of customers and employers. Even if we accept this elitist allegation on the part of the academics on its own grounds, it still opens up a can of worms for academic freedom-lovers. For if we accept the view that intellectual professions should have the protection of "vocational freedom" we still have to deal with "doctors' freedom", "lawyers' freedom", "chemists freedom", "musicians' freedom", "artists' freedom" and so on, in mind-boggling array. Would "doctors' freedom" give the doctors the "freedom" to prohibit us from smoking

cigarettes, for instance, without giving us the right to fire them for such temerity? Would "artists' or musicians' freedom" give artists and musicians the right to charge us for music and art we did not appreciate? Considering the way "academic freedom" operates, one would be hard pressed to deny these conclusions. One shudders to contemplate what "chemists' and lawyers freedom" would entail. To say nothing of "politicians' freedom".

And if we reject this academic elitism, the panorama is vastly widened. It now would include "taxi-drivers' freedom", where the taxi-drivers go where they want to go and YOU pay for it; "baby-sitters' freedom" where the baby sitter decides when baby goes to sleep. And so on. If we reject intellectual elitism, we find it harder to see just why plumbers, carpenters, tradesmen, etc., should not also have "vocational freedom". Why after all, should "vocational freedom" be reserved to only the teachers of these disciplines? If the vocation is so deserving that the teachers of it must be protected by "freedom", then surely the practitioners must be likewise protected. And if the practitioners are not deserving of the "freedom" not to be fired, then how can the teachers merit such treatment?

What we are dealing with here under the question of "academic freedom" is nothing less than a disguised attack on the very right of individuals to freely contract with one another. It is a denial of the sanctity of contract. It is a denial of the rights of individuals to make contracts with one another that do not include clauses stipulating "rights" of "academic freedom". In its effects it resembles nothing so much as the medieval guild system, in its restrictions, protectionism, and fostering of a caste system.

There is one ground upon which "academic freedom" can be supported, although it is a ground upon which precious few of its adherents would wish to support it. "Academic freedom" may be defended on the ground that it is perhaps the only device by which control over the educational system in this country may be wrested away, at least in part, from the ruling class, or power elite which now controls it. To substantiate this claim would take us too far afield. (The interested reader is referred to "The Higher Circles" by G. William Domhoff.) Supposing it to be true for the sake of argument, however, we can see that it constitutes a defense of "academic freedom". For if the ruling class analysis is true, then it is not the innocent student-consumer who is being defrauded by "academic freedom". It is not the innocent student-consumer who is being forced to maintain in employment an academic whose services he no longer desires. It is the **non-innocent** ruling class which is being so forced. If the ruling class theory is correct, academicians with views favorable to the ruling class have nothing to gain from "academic freedom". They will be retained in any case. It is the academic with views that are not amenable to the ruling class, and he alone, that can benefit from an "acedemic freedom" which prevents **ruling class** employers from firing him on ideological or other non-formalistic grounds.

But this is no reason to continue to obfuscate the issue of academic freedom. Academic freedom, as such, is fraud and theft, because it denies individuals the right of free and voluntary contracts. That it can also be used for good ends should occasion no surprise. Throwing rocks at people is also an illegitimate activity. Yet David could hardly have slain Goliath by eschewing this practice. ◻

The Libertarian Forum
BOX 341
MADISON SQUARE STATION
NEW YORK, NEW YORK 10010

First Class

Published Every Month. Subscription Rate: $8.00 Per Year

A Monthly Newsletter

THE
Libertarian Forum

Joseph R. Peden, Publisher

Murray N. Rothbard, Editor

VOLUME IV, NOS. 8-9   AUGUST, SEPTEMBER, 1972   75¢

Confronting Leviathan

In the very first issue of **Libertarian Forum** (preview issue dated March 1, 1969), the editor expressed our desire "to unite theory and actions", "to see how the current system may be transformed into the ideal" and "to inspire a truly dedicated movement on behalf of liberty". Inspired by these goals, in the same issue, we commended a suggestion by Gerald Gottlieb of the Center for Democratic Institutions that private citizens create an international "Court of Man" to investigate and publicize, and hopefully stop, violations of human rights by sovereign states.

We commented at the time that "perhaps libertarian foundations and scholars could sponsor further study of Gottlieb's proposal — so libertarian in principle and so feasible in practice". In March 1970 we published further comments on the subject in **Lib Forum** and also an account of three privately created international commissions of inquiry which played a significant role in European history between 1920 and 1940. (See J. R. Peden, "Courts against the State", **Libertarian Analysis**, v. 1 Winter 1970). But as far as we know, libertarians have not responded to our suggestions for more research or action along these lines. If our own ideological compatriots have remained idle, others have not. What follows is a brief description of several projects which have been undertaken with great success in limited areas using the technique of privately sponsored citizens' commissions of inquiry.

1. COURT-WATCHING

One of the oldest libertarian associations in the United States is the Society of Friends, better known as Quakers. The Quakers, though few in numbers, have always been formidable enemies of Statists. From their founding in the 17th century in England, they have been frequent victims of persecution by governmental authorities who refuse to respect any limits on their power. The Quakers are generally an intelligent, virtuous, hardworking people, indomitable in their moral certitude and inner self-possession in the face of tyrants. Pacifists and activists with a passion for the works of peace, reconciliation and justice, they have traditionally been the fine cutting edge of libertarian sentiment in America. They were among the first to struggle against the evils of slavery and racism; they fostered prison reform and abolition of capital punishment; they have continuously fought against imperialism and militarism and supported the extension of civil liberties in all areas. The Quakers have not only been courageous, but also remarkably innovative in their work against the injustices of the State. They were active in the peace movement before Wilson's war, helped to care for the refugees that war produced through the American Friends Service Committee, and were influential in founding the American Civil Liberties Union. More recently they have been active in draft and war tax resistance and, most recently, "court-watching".

In January 1970 The Friends' Suburban Project — sponsored by the Philadelphia Yearly Meeting of Friends (Quakers) — began a systematic

---

> The regular editor, Murray Rothbard, is on a well-earned vacation in Europe. Editorial responsibility for this issue is entirely that of the publisher, Joseph Peden.

---

monitoring of the municipal courts of Chester, Pa., a city of some 60,000 people, mostly poor and nearly half Black. The "court-watching" consisted of regular attendance by one or more of the project's members at both arraignments and preliminary hearings in the Chester Police and Court Building.

The Magistrate's court in Chester had long been noted for its corrupt and illegal procedures, and the court-watchers were able over a six-month period to document these irregularities. They discovered (1) that 64% of all defendents had no legal counselor or attorney; (2) that half the occupants of the city jail were being held because they could not post bond while awaiting trial; (3) that 75% of those brought into court were Blacks or Puerto Ricans; that they invariably had more serious charges and a greater percentage of multiple charges placed against them than did whites; (4) that while 33% of all blacks were remanded for trial, only 14.5% of whites were so honored; (5) that 10% of the blacks paid fines of over $100, but no whites did so.

During their court-watching, the monitors did not attempt to disrupt the court, or even intervene in the cases. They were carefully trained to know what legal procedures were required by Pennsylvania statutes and the rights of defendants and spectators in judicial hearings. They prepared and distributed leaflets on the rights of accused persons and sources of legal aid to defendants and notified the magistrates of their presence. They also met with the city solicitor, police chief and others to explain the purpose of their project — to improve the administration of justice in accordance with the federal and state constitutions.

At first the police reacted as expected and on two occasions arrested monitors — only to have the charges dropped when the court found it necessary to recognize the right of citizens to frequent a public building. It soon became apparent that the presence of white, middle-class court-watchers was creating a new atmosphere in the Chester courts. The magistrates were more attentive to each case, tended to set lower bail, and be less abusive and more considerate of the procedural rights of defendants. The police were more cautious in their testimony, more selective in their arrests, and less abusive to the accused.

A number of more important changes have been made. For the first time, court records are now available for public scrutiny; and public defenders are being appointed for all cases involving indictable offenses. Arraignments are no longer held in secret; the time and place of such hearings are posted publicly and the general public is permitted to witness them. Municipal judges are now sending fewer cases to higher courts; charges are lessened or dropped locally to save time and money for both the state and individual. Perhaps most important of all, a bail bond monopoly shared by two friends of the presiding magistrate has been broken; eight bondsmen are now available to defendants and there is a marked tendency to reduce bail or release the accused on his own recognizance.

While the court-watchers were not entirely free of official harassment, the response of the community has been positive, and many state and local officials rallied to the project's support. The sense of professionalism of the legal fraternity was challenged by the court-watchers, and this proved a powerful stimulus in winning their support for reforms. Libertarians — especially those who believe that government is necessary if only to maintain a system of justice — might well

(Continued On Page 2)

Confronting Leviathan —
(Continued From Page 1)

support similar projects in their own towns and cities. Certainly the worst tyranny occurs whenever government officials themselves violate the laws they are committed to uphold. This is especially so when the laws are concerned with civil liberties and judicial procedures. The Court-Watching technique is but one relatively inexpensive way in which a few individuals can expand the realm of liberty in their own community. (Those interested in "court-watching" may write for the "Court Action Handbook" — 50 cents per copy — to Friends Suburban Project, Box 54, Media, Pennsylvania 19063).

2. STORMING THE BASTILLE!

One of the most innovative and successful applications of libertarian principles in recent years has been the creation of an international network of civil libertarians who have undertaken the task of monitoring the fate of unfortunate individuals who have, for reasons of conscience, been arrested and imprisoned for their political beliefs. **Amnesty International** was founded in 1961 in London by a British lawyer, Peter Benenson, to mobilize world public opinion in behalf of all "prisoners of conscience" — **bona fide** victims of some State's violation of their human rights as defined by articles 5, 9, 18 and 19 of the Universal Declaration of Human Rights.

How does Amnesty International work? At its London headquarters a research staff receives information from a variety of sources as to the names of individuals held captive in various countries for "crimes" which stem from the failure of the governmental authorities to recognize basic human rights, as defined by the Declaration. Information about each individual prisoner is obtained, and each case is carefully considered. A crucial standard is that no prisoner will be helped by **Amnesty International** if he has used violence in exercising his human rights. AI supports freedom of thought, conscience, religion, the press and speech; it condemns the use of torture, inhuman or degrading treatment of prisoners; and arbitrary detention, arrest or exile. But it will not support the cause of a prisoner whose resort to violence places him in the status of a common criminal.

Once AI is convinced that the prisoner is eligible for support of the organization, the full case study is sent to one of the hundreds of groups located in 28 countries throughout the world. AI has about 20,000 members organized into local groups or chapters of from 3 to 15 or more members. Each group presently pays annual dues of $129.00 for 8 memberships ($15.00 for each individual member beyond the 8). At any given time the group is assigned three cases — always prisoners of a nationality other than their own, and distributed among the ideological forces of East, West and Third World impartially. Unfortunately, there are oppressive States in all ideological camps so that AI's non-partisanship is secure.

With the information provided by the London staff, the AI chapter prepares a campaign to persuade the respective State to release its prisoner — to grant amnesty. The methods chosen to achieve this vary with the circumstances; letters to the chief officials of the foreign government; visits to the local embassy and consulates; use of private contacts with local business corporations, churches, professional organizations; publicity in the home media of the group; agitation in parliament and press; visits to foreign office officials asking them to intervene. The art of persuasion passes into the need to make a nuisance of the case; to harrass the bureaucrats, embarass the regime, to make such a stink, internationally, that the government will release the prisoner just to quiet the whole affair. The prisoner is kept informed of the work of his friends and his relatives are encouraged by friendly letters and often financial aid. The essential aim is to free the prisoner — and "quiet" diplomacy is preferred to any premature and fatally damaging politicizing of the case.

Amnesty International has tended to be strongest in Northwestern Europe; there are over 300 chapters in West Germany and almost as many in Sweden; these constitute more than half the total number of chapters. In the United States, it has been slower in developing, probably due to preoccupation with the struggle against the Vietnam war. There are now over 2000 individual members and active chapters exist in New York, Los Angeles, San Diego, Denver, Boulder, Columbia, Mo. and Hesston, Kans. Most of the members seem to be college professors and students. It is not necessary to belong to a group; individual members will be assigned a single case to work upon.

The non-partisanship of AI is proven by a sampling of the published lists of recent prisoners which have been helped by the organization:

these include a Roman Catholic bishop held by the Red Chinese; a Taiwanese city councilman imprisoned for circulating a petition asking clemency for a prisoner of the Chiang-Kai-shek regime; a Watusi monarchist imprisoned by the Republic of Rwanda; Huber Matos, imprisoned by Fidel Castro for over 12 years; a Jehovah's Witness whose missionary work was not appreciated by the Soviet Russian government; Captain Howard Levy, the American Army doctor imprisoned because he refused to teach first aid to Green Berets who would use it as a political weapon.

Amnesty International has not limited itself merely to seeking amnesty for prisoners of consciency. In recent years it has caused a sensation in many quarters by sending investigation teams into certain countries to gather evidence of widespread use of torture and abuse of prisoners by certain governments as a matter of deliberate national policy. Their report of the regular use of torture by Israeli officials in interrogating Arab prisoners was bitterly denounced by the Israeli government and other Zionist sympathizers; the British government was similarly enraged when Amnesty teams publicly reported the use of torture by British troops in Aden, and more recently, in the prison camps of Northern Ireland. Their reports on the atrocious treatment of political prisoners in Greece contributed signigicantly to the forced resignation of Greece from the Council of Europe for violating the European declaration of human rights.

Libertarians in search of a meaningful activity which can involve group or individual creative political work might well consider joining **Amnesty International**. How many of us can say that we helped to free a fellow human from a tyrant's bondage? **Amnesty International** has liberated more than 3500 prisoners of conscience in the last decade. Moreover, Rumanian officials admitted privately that the agitation of Amnesty groups compelled the government of that Communist country to review its prisoner problem — resulting in the liberation of some 2000 political prisoners that were unknown to AI and, until then, forgotten by the Rumanian government itself. Write for further information to Amnesty International, 200 West 72nd St. New York, New York 10023.

3. J'ACCUSE

In early November 1971 the People's Coalition for Peace and Justice sponsored a series of anti-war events in Washington that included a rally at the White House during which an eviction notice was delivered to its occupant; meanwhile the direction of the nation's attention was focused on the efforts of thousands of young activists to bring the government machinery to a halt by blocking the bridges and highways leading to the center of the city. The result of that escapade war — the illegal arrest and detention of over ten thousand people at the direction of the Attorney-General of the United States!

While the attention of the media was focused on these dramatic and colorful proceedings — right out of the Late Show Nazi war movies — a possibly more important event was in progress elsewhere in Washington — the special hearings held by a private body known as the People's Grand Jury. A broad spectrum of citizens who have been active in anti-war actions in the last decade sat for nearly 25 hours to hear testimony from experts and eyewitnesses about the actual methods of American warfare in Southeast Asia, the secret war in Laos, prison conditions in South Vietnam, the "Operation Phoenix" assassination teams, chemical and biological weaponry, and domestic political repression. Among the jurors were radical activists like Father James Groppi and Sister Elizabeth McAllister; Rosemary Reuther, a Catholic theologian; Bob Eaton, a Quaker recently freed from prison for draft refusal; and Tom Grace, wounded at Kent State. The testimony itself was more or less an updating of similar testimony presented to the Russell War Crimes Tribunal in 1967.

As expected, the newspapers carried nothing on the contents of the hearings, but they were videotaped and made available for showing through the Peoples Coalition for Peace and Justice, 917 15th St. NW Washington 20005. The publicizing of war crimes and other related criminal activities of the State and its minions is a crucial part of any libertarian movement. It is the most effective method of minimizing these criminal acts and rallying decent public opinion against them. The People's Coalition understands this and is reportedly planning to convene "people's grand juries" in conjunction with the Daniel Ellsberg trial. A similar body met to publicize the harrassment of anti-war activists during the trial of the Harrisburg 8 — Father Philip Berrigan and friends. So far, these "people's grand juries" have attracted only radical support — liberals have been conspicuous in their absence. The reason is, that such private commissions of inquiry implicitly assert that the courts
(Continued On Page 3)

Confronting Leviathan —
(Continued From Page 2)

themselves are not impartial but are in fact agencies of the oppressive state apparatus. In the Harrisburg case the judge confirmed this by refusing to accept the fact that the jury was deadlocked, and three times refused to release them from duty. The result was a compromise verdict in which all were acquitted of the conspiracy charges but two were found guilty of sending messages out of prison — a charge they admitted and which has never before been prosecuted in a federal court.

So far the holding of "people's grand juries" has been useful in focusing public attention on the political character of the prosecutions, or the scope of the government's own criminality. But this tactic is appropriate only in relatively restricted circumstances. What might be more useful would be the establishment of permanent privately sponsored "grand juries" which could regularly hold public hearings to expose governmental corruption, inefficiency, and violations of civil liberties. In other words, a libertarian parallel or alternative to the traditional grand juries of the State. —JRP ▣

Arbitration
A Fundamental
Alternate Institution

By Ralph Fucetola, III

Arbitration is a non-state method of conflict-solving. Historically, arbitration was the professional mediation of disputes within a traditional structure which resulted in a BINDING declaration of rights. This form of adjudication predates the coercive state and generally depended on ostracism and conscience for its binding quality.

With the advent of state-sponsored "justice" several centuries ago, arbitration was neglected and even outlawed. The king would only permit his agents to produce "justice" — and world history tells of the bloody, criminal results, State courts, though, often originated from the nationalization of arbitration institutions. For example, the commercial law aspect of the old English Common Law Courts was taken from the Law Merchant, a type of very successful private arbitration tribunal.

Since the early 1900's, arbitration has undergone a renaissance: governments now permit it — and actively encourage it for international business transactions.

Men have turned to arbitration for one prime reason: arbitrators are usually "persons having special knowledge and experience in foreign trade, commerce, industry, agriculture, transportation, insurance and other related matters as well as law . . ." (Peoples' Republic of China, Arbitration Decree). Expertise separates the arbitrator from the judge; an arbitrator is a person who is trusted for his knowledge and reputation, a judge is a political appointee.

Presently in New York City, arbitration tribunals decide more cases each year than the number of commercial cases decided by the United States District Court there. Besides expertise, three other factors encourage this increasing use of arbitration: (1) arbitration is a private matter, thus privacy may be protected; (2) it can be less time-consuming and less expensive than the government's courts; (3) it is primarily based on the CONTRACT (statutory "law" and procedures are of little importance). Libertarians see two other reasons for engaging in arbitration: firstly, private justice, even its present semi-regulated form, is somewhat removed from the state; secondly, arbitration can make use of libertarian principles of law or even a libertarian law code, thus negating some of the worse features of statutory law.

Arbitration is insulated from the state because the legislation which "legalized" it (which recognized the rebirth of arbitration at the hands of various trade associations around the turn of the century) specifically provides that an arbitration award may be enforced by summary process in the state's courts, and, except for blatant procedural defects, the courts will not look into the reasons for the award. The major failing of modern arbitration is conditioned by its "legality": enforcement is often via the state apparatus, rather than the traditional method of ostracism.

Nonetheless, one may structure an arbitration situation so that the state's mailed fist is as far removed as possible by creating an automatic ostracism which forces the wrongdoer to INITIATE legal action (an action which can be defeated by simply producing the arbitration award.) For example, the original arbitration agreement of the Abolitionist

Association (which publishes "OUTLOOK, the Libertarian Monthly") provided:

> "The parties, expressing a desire to implement libertarian principles of law . . . within the context of the . . . Partnership Agreement . . . (agree) . . . that any party who refuses to cooperate with the arbitration procedure or decision shall be deemed to have withdrawn from the Partnership; and all parties to this Agreement agree to enforce this provision and hereby appoint each other as attorneys-in-fact, separately and irrevocably, for the sole purpose of enforcing this provision . . ."

The agreement further provided an automatic arbitration procedure which resulted in a decision against any party not cooperating, and forced withdrawal under the arbitration clause, resulting in a loss of investment.

Within a condusive social context, totally private arbitration can be more effective than the semi-statist version which the Abolitionist Association was compelled to use. In ancient Ireland, as Joe Peden noted in his article on non-state justice in Ireland (LIBERTARIAN FORUM, April, 1971), a system of family ties and ostracism enforced arbitration for nearly 1,000 years. This was done within the context of a highly decentralized society in which private professional arbitrators developed an island-embracing common law based on the ideas that no man may initiate violence, and all must keep their agreements.

Variations on ostracism are used by various trade associations to give binding effect to their arbitration decisions when the dispute involves members of the association in those fields in which membership-in-good-standing is necessary for economic survival. Other methods of enforcement have been suggested. An example which readily comes to mind is the joint purchase of a bond or insurance conditioned upon performance of the arbitration decree. This requires that potential parties to a dispute prepare the enforcement method in advance of a dispute. In a truly free market situation, arbitration institutions, credit bureaus, trade associations, bonding agencies, insurance firms and banks would all find it in their interest to work together to provide effective economic sanctions (primarily sophisticated versions of ostracism) against those who flaunt arbitration.

Arbitration is a method of conflict-solving without a state. It is not a method of achieving justice — though it may do so; nor does it necessarily apply correct principles of law. It is concerned with the "private law" created by the contract. Even in the most ideal situation, arbitration tribunals are not private, free market courts of law. Arbitration is primarily a devise for private dispute settlement which works best when the opposing parties value their continuing relationships (to each other or to some concerned group) more than they value prevailing in the dispute. Arbitration is an alternative to an institution — the state's courts — and as such deserves our support and our participation. ▣

The Law Of The Sea

One of the earliest European treaties concerning the use of sea territories was negotiated between Rome and Carthage dividing the western Mediterranean into two mutually exclusive commercial monopoly zones. With the expansion of Roman power the whole Mediterranean became a "Roman lake" in which Rome's exclusive control was challenged only by occasional "pirates". During the medieval period, freedom of the seas was the rule, but in practice the merchant-dominated city-states of Italy and the Baltic region tried, with considerable success, to assert regional sea monopolies. In the 15th century Spain and Portugal received a Papal grant of exclusive sovereignty over all the seas and lands west and east, respectively, of a papally drawn line through the Atlantic. Needless to say, these sovereign claims were challenged by the ships of England, Holland and other European powers, and were a constant source of friction among the maritime powers for centuries.

The first theoretical challenge to the concept that the seas could be incorporated within the sovereign territory of a state came, appropriately, from a Dutchman, Hugo Grotius. The Dutch had made a mockery of English, Spanish, Portuguese and Scandinavian claims to sovereignty over the high seas. Dutch merchant adventurers refused to recognize any limitations on their right to sail any sea and trade in any port, and backed up their will by daring military-commercial warfare. Grotius' contribution was to provide an argument on natural law principles denying that property rights can exist over sea territories. He asserted that the seas could not properly be enclosed, or delimited, and are therefore unappropriable as private property. The seas were considered a free good,

(Continued On Page 4)

The Law Of The Sea —

(Continued From Page 3)

open and available to all men, like the air they breathed.

Grotius' argument was not immediately accepted, except by the Dutch, but it entered into the polemics of international law and politics. The United States was one of the first states to officially accept the Grotian doctrine of freedom of the seas, and gradually the other European powers in the 19th century adopted the same position.

Following World War II, a new problem arose due to the advance of technology which permitted drilling for gas and oil in coastal tidewaters. The treasures of the sub-seabed were for the first time becoming open to exploitation and no clear principle of law existed as to the ownership of these resources. In 1942 Venezuela and England negotiated a treaty dividing the sub-seabed mineral resources of the Gulf of Paria between themselves but continuing to recognize the "freedom of the seas" doctrine regarding the sea surface and sea space.

The United States opened a new era in the international law of the sea by the Truman proclamation of Sept. 1945. It asserted that the U. S. considered the "natural resources of the subsoil and seabed of the continental shelf beneath the high seas but contiguous to the coasts of the United States as appertaining to the U. S. subject to its jurisdiction and control". While the "freedom of the seas" was upheld, the U. S. also asserted its right to establish "conservation zones" in those areas of the high seas "contiguous to the United States where fishing activities have been or in future may be developed". The aims of the Truman administration seem to have been twofold: to encourage the negotiation of treaties on conservation of fisheries, and domestically, to assert federal jurisdiction over that of the states over the wealth of the tideland oil deposits. But the effect was otherwise. An international "gold rush" began as every coastal nation hurriedly established claims over contiguous seas before others did so. In doing so these other powers often went beyond the limits of American claims in accordance with their own national interests and the geographical conditions prevailing.

All states had recognized that freedom of the seas had some geographic limits. In the 18th century the three mile limit had become the standard limit of full sovereignty — a distance approximating the range of naval cannon at the time. While the U. S. has steadfastly held to this rule since 1793, other nations have variously held a four, six and even a twelve mile limit. At the Geneva conference on the Law of the Sea in 1958, only 23 of the 86 states represented still held to the 3 mile limit. What was clearly happening was that increasing realization of the potential wealth of the sub-seabed, seabed, sea space resources — minerals, fuels, fisheries — was steadily eroding the previous international legal consensus on the limitation of sovereignty over the seas.

As an editor of the New York Times recently put it, the nations of the world now face the very real prospect of "anarchy at sea". Despite conflicting claims, there is no international consensus — hence no recognized international law — on the sovereignty and governance of the sea surface, sea space, sea bed and sub-seabed. Libertarians would argue that the problem is not a question of "anarchy" — the absence of a monopoly of violence within a given territory — but rather the absence of any recognized law of property covering sea territory and sea resources. Men can live and utilize resources without the sovereign state, but no economic progress or human survival is possible where there is no common consensus as to property rights. The very serious problems of conservation of fisheries, pollution control, mining and drilling, laying of cables, and electronic detectors or other gadgets would be greatly simplified if there were recognized demarcations of property and property rights on, in and under the seas. Ideally, what Murray Rothbard calls the "homestead" principle ought to govern the situation. Effective claim, demarcation and productive utilization of any sea surface, sea space, sea bed or subsoil ought to be recognized as establishing a property right. International law already recognizes these principles in the discovery of new lands; the same principles could as easily be applied to the seas and their resources.

Any move in this direction would have to come from a corporation large enough to make its claims effective. The establishment of the "Republic of Minerva" by promoter Mike Oliver and associates is a model of this libertarian approach. Unfortunately, they have chosen to protect themselves from the existing states of the South Pacific by pretending that Minerva is itself a "state" entitled to recognition as a sovereign entity under existing international law. The limited capitalization of the Minerva project probably precluded a successful operation under their real colors — that of a private real estate development corporation. A real breakthrough would have to have the backing of someone like Howard Hughes whose Hughes Tool Company has already invested over $50 million in undersea dredging machinery to mine for manganese on the sea floor. So far, despite the great power of the multinational oil corporations, none has expressed any desire to "homestead" outside the protective covering of a sovereign state.

If future development of the resources of the seas and seabeds will not take place in a pure libertarian framework, what alternatives seem likely?

There is an extremely strong effort being made to create an Oceanic Regime under whose sovereign control all the surface, space, beds, subsoil and resources of the seas would be placed. This plan has been vigorously advocated by the staff of the Center for Democratic Institutions in Santa Barbara under the leadership of Elizabeth Mann Borgese. In 1968 Mrs. Borgese published a draft of a constitution for an Oceanic Regime. Its chief features were that the regime itself would be sovereign and enjoy a judicial capacity in all land states equal to that enjoyed most fully by any of its citizens; in other words it could sue and be sued, own property and conduct its businesses within the territory of any state in the same capacity as a private citizen or a domestic corporation. The Oceanic regime would be governed by various assemblies and commissions elected by its constituent members — which include all states, inter-governmental and non-governmental associations, private corporations holding licenses from the Oceanic Regime, and the regime's own employees. The regime would have total control over the use of sea territories and their resources, including price and quality controls over goods and services, and competitive factors, control over shipping and cargo, and the movement of armed forces operating on the seabed. This monopolization of all ocean spaces and resources beyond a twelve mile limit, would also render all these great resources common property — res nullius and res communis.

The establishment of the Oceanic regime is just the beginning of a more ambitious project — a universal world state. As Mrs. Borgese puts it: "An ocean-born, landward-spreading world view may be the world view of the 21st century". From a libertarian viewpoint, the Oceanic regime would be an unmitigated disaster — a projection on a universal scale of the corporate state capitalism which is the antithesis of the free market and a voluntarist society. Yet Mrs. B. and the Center staff have been very successful in promoting their scheme. The Center financed an international conference held in Malta in 1970, and another in the same place in 1971. Experts from many fields related to the law and economics of the sea and its riches read papers, exchanged views, and kept their respective governments informed of trends. In addition to publishing their draft constitution, the Center has published a selection of these papers, and articles indicating the progress of discussions. Their efforts were rewarded when the United Nations decided to call an international conference on the Law of the Sea to be held in 1973.

But whether the U. N. conference will take place as scheduled is now uncertain. At a preliminary meeting called to draw up an agenda, the diplomats fell to squabbling about everything. There is a basic division between the supporters of an Oceanic Regime or reasonable facsimile, and those opposed to that approach. Most of the states which lack a coastline realize that only an Oceanic Regime can guarantee them a piece of the action. But coastal states are extremely reluctant to give up control over their contiguous seas.

The major obstacle to adoption of the Oceanic regime is the day-to-day fact that, regardless of international conferences, individual states are acting on their own to assert sovereignty over the seas. The following cases will illustrate the main trends of the situation:

1. Despite continuing opposition from the United States, Ecuador, Peru and Chile have effectively claimed the right to control all fishing within 200 miles of their coastline. Brazil has followed suit and gone further to claim a 200 mile territorial sea. Iceland has been at odds with Britain since 1948 over fishing rights in the North Atlantic. Iceland has progressively expanded the area over which she claims exclusive fishing privileges. Recently she announced that no foreign fishing would be allowed within a zone fifty miles from her coastline. Six governors of the New England states have been unsuccessfully urging Washington to establish a 200 mile fishing zone off the coast of the U. S.

2. Indonesia and Malaysia have provoked a crisis among the maritime nations by asserting a 20 mile limit for their coastal territorial waters. This means that the Straits of Malacca — a vital international waterway through which some 40,000 ships a year now pass — has been effectively annexed by the two neighboring states. While continuing to respect the right of innocent passage, their claim would limit the movement of foreign warships unless 48 hour notice was given. Both U. S. and Soviet fleets ignored this rule during their maneuvering through the Indian Ocean during the Bangla Desh crisis. Also, maritime states realize that

(Continued On Page 5)

The Law Of The Sea —

(Continued From Page 4)

such territorial claims over straits were the cause of the third Arab-Israeli war. The Gulf of Aqaba was closed by Egypt and Arabia as part of their territorial waters. The Israelis claimed this to be a violation of international law and attacked. The unilateral assertion of extensions of territorial waters will increase the number of potential armed clashes over access to narrow waterways.

3. An increasing number of states have cooperated in seizing the seabeds and sub-seabed mineral deposits of their contiguous waters. The North Sea was divided into agreed territorial slices by Germany, Britain, Holland, Denmark, France and Norway. While the immediate purpose of this act was to clear the way for exploitation of gas and oil deposits, it has now been extended to policing the sea for pollution control purposes. Italy and Yugoslavia have divided the Adriatic between them, and the Baltic, Black and Mediterranean Seas are in the process of being similarly treated. Canada has asserted its sovereignty over the territorial seas between the large islands north of its frozen land mass, an action viewed with deep suspicion in Washington.

Given the enormous wealth at stake, it seems to me that the coastal states will not surrender their existing claims to the sea territories and seas resources — some of which are already producing revenues and profits. Also, apart from the United States which loosed this scramble and now is trying desperately to control it, the great powers — Russia, China, France, Britain, Japan as well as many secondary powers like India, South Africa, Brazil and Portugal — all these have extensive coastlines which, if extended 200 miles or more offer great potential wealth. Is it likely that these powers will surrender control of that wealth to some Oceanic Regime? I think not.

Thus the pattern for future ownership and control of the world's sea territories and sea resources seems already to be emerging. Annexation of continental shelves, of sea surfaces and sea beds, of sub-seabed and sea space resources by individual states will become the rule. China has already asserted her support for the 200 mile limit claimed by Peru, Brazil, Chile and Ecuador. The many island-states — large and small — will also find this policy in their interest.

With the claims of sovereignty will come the imposition of national laws regarding property rights. The participation by individuals, private or public corporations in exploiting the seas will be governed by local law. This will not be a libertarian solution; but it at least permits a variety of local practices to prevail. It prevents total monopolization of the world's sea resources by an Oceanic Regime and will allow at least some areas to be developed in a free-market framework. Homesteading on the high seas, even if under the cover of state sovereignty, offers some scope for adventurous free-enterprisers. And international law will once again be created, not by artificial ideological constitution-makers, but by a spontaneous recognition of mutual self-interest signified by contracts (treaties) arrived at by negotiation and consensus among the nations of the world. —JRP ◘

Transnational Relations

I

On June 19, 1972 the International Federation of Airline Pilots' Associations conducted a world-wide strike — the first of its kind in history. The pilots hoped to pressure the United Nations and its member governments into taking stronger measures to prevent international airplane hijacking and to cooperate in the apprehension, extradition and punishment of the hijackers.

We suggest that this strike organized by an international federation or professional associations, directed at the several governments of the world, may be an act of great future significance. The piolots' association is just one of nearly 800 international professional associations that have been developing rapidly over the last several decades at a current rate of some 9 per cent per year. The movement to organize individuals internationally by professions began in the 19th century but really caught on after the second world war under the indirect, and sometimes direct influence of the United Nations, especially through its coordinate organizations like UNESCO, FAO and ILO. Voluntary, privately-financed international professional associations originally were organized to sponsor international congresses where scholars, professional experts and related persons could meet to exchange information and theories of mutual interest. Papers were read, discussed and published; joint research projects undertaken; problems aired; personal friendships

created and sustained. The international "republic of letters and sciences" which had linked the savants of Europe in medieval, renaissance and 18th century Europe, only to be sadly disrupted by the nationalistic disruptions of the 19th and 20th centuries, seemed about to flourish once again. But now to the older professions based on the traditional liberal arts and sciences, there was added the new professions; the ecologists, economists, pilots, financiers, advertising executives, travel agents, journalists, librarians, sportsmen of various specializations. There are now a minimum of 1,515 international, non-governmental organizations which hold between three and four thousand meetings annually, involving at least a million people, and at least half of these are the work of international professional associations.

While many of these associations are relatively free of ideological pressures, other are not. Often they have provided the only neutral forum in which professional persons have been able to meet their fellows from other lands outside the net of international politics and nationalistic restrictions. In many cases these associations have been able to transcend national interests and provide a focus and forum and mechanism by which the policies of nation-states can be effectively challenged. For example, international associations of jurists have been very active in investigating violations of human rights by criminally-minded States; international journalists' and publishers' associations police and publicize attacks upon the freedom of the press; several international sports associations have put effective pressure on the government of South Africa to change its policy of racial segregation which violates, among other things, the professional sportsmen's concept of fair play. Even rather minor groups like the European Union of Ramblers (a federation of hiking clubs) founded in 1969 has, in addition to mapping out international hiking paths throughout Europe, pressured the various European governments to abolish all passport and customs formalities for international hikers and travelers in general.

There is clearly an increasing trend of international professional associations taking action to compel governments to shape their policies and laws in ways which will enhance the work of the professionals, and provide an environment conducive to their respective needs and desires. The strike by the international pilots' association is just the most visible example of the trend. Yet, according to Prof. William M. Evan of the University of Chicago (in an article in International Associations No. 2 (1972) published at 1 rue aux Laines, 1000 Brussels, Belgium), there is little systematic research on the role of these associations as components in the present and future international order. Sooner or later the political scientists will take note of their existence, only to integrate them within the network of a state-structured international system. But would this not be an ideal subject for further study by a libertarian scholar? Here are private, voluntary organizations operating in ways that transcend national boundaries, national ideologies and narrow "political" interests. Might not these associations be models for a libertarian world societal structure of the future?

II

Let us now consider another international phenomenon which is already getting widespread attention — the multi-national corporation (MNC).

It is not the far flung geographic dimensions of the multi-national corporation that is new: the 17th and 18th centuries saw business enterprises, centrally directed from London, Amsterdam and elsewhere in Europe, which owned properties, markets and plantations on several continents. Yet, in addition to their being smaller in the magnitude of their capital resources compared to the larger modern MNC, they usually operated within the framework of a national imperial monopoly system in which most of their products, markets and properties were within the political control of their home country. Efforts to break into foreign markets frequently erupted into international wars, or free marketeering (usually called piracy or smuggling).

But the modern MNC finds its factories, mines, plantations, markets, manpower under the control of a multiplicity of sovereign governments which it must deal with individually to secure its centrally directed ends. Operating often under a dozen flags or more, its entrepreneurial tasks become very complex and its efforts to protect itself from the vagueries of so many governments compel it to maintain a "foreign office" equal to that of many nation states — and better than most if it is to avoid grave diffiuclties. The MNC must have a corps of diplomats and intelligence agents to conduct its corporate relations with the various nation-states. These corporate "State departments" and CIA's are usually discreetly hidden under less traditional political nomenclature, but their existence

(Continued On Page 6)

Transnational Relations —
(Continued From Page 5)

is certain. Occasionally they are exposed to the general public, as in the case of the ITT memos to various Nixon administration officials urging that the U. S. government do something to prevent President Allende of Chile from assuming office after his election. There is some evidence that ITT was prepared to take steps on its own to overthrow the Chilean regime, and more will be revealed in the future. General Motors, with a gross international product surpassed by only three other "corporations" — the United States, West German and Soviet Union governments — set its secret agents to work trying to dig up something with which to blackmail Ralph Nader. Historical literature abounds with well-researched studies of the international policies of United Fruit, Unilever, and the oil companies; and it would be naive to think that corporations with such great economic power as the MNCs are not today using it to manipulate the international political state system for their own ends.

In 1970 Harvard University's Center for International Affairs held a conference on "Transnational Relations". The papers read at the conference are now available (Robert O. Keohane and Joseph Nye, Jr. eds. **Transnational Relations and World Politics**, Harvard University Press, $4.95 paperback). The scholars contributing to this volume challenge the traditional model of international politics in as radical a fashion as the cubists did in the arts, or Galileo and Copernicus once did in astronomy. The message is that multinational corporations, international professional and trade associations are already exercising a controlling influence over the movement of labor, capital, resources and technology across national frontiers; that some 85 MNC have assets greater than some fifty member states of the United Nations; that governments and electorates have little control over the economic destiny of their nations; that nations with the traditional centralized, nationalistic economic structure are doomed when faced with the challenge of transnational corporations which can swiftly move capital, personnel and technology to wherever it will function most efficiently. Special studies on the role of scientists, the transnational role of the Roman Catholic Church, labor unions, and monetary exchange systems are also included.

For libertarians these new international institutions pose new problems. Is the MNC to be feared or cheered from a libertarian perspective? Is the MNC one of the new societal institutions which will replace the state as the norm of large scale socio-economic organization in a libertarian, voluntarist world society? Or is the MNC merely an embryonic form of a new state arising within, and gradually displacing, the older, more familiar but decaying nation-states of our present and recent past? Did not modern Britain, France, Italy, Spain and Germany, and even India, arise from the decadent principalities of the feudal age?

There is no guarantee that a libertarian society would not lapse into statism; and there is no reason to assume that multi-national corporations will retain their present juridical status of private, voluntary corporate societies. Many would go further and say that many nation-states are already merely agents of the large multi-national corporations which are the real sources of political power in society.

Libertarians must give more attention to these problems. We have a decided penchant for regurgitating the problems and analyses of the great libertarian thinkers of the past. But our eyes ought to be equally on the present if we expect to have any impact upon the shaping of the future. It is only a matter of a short time before we will begin to see attempts to engage in international collective bargaining. Multinational corporations are certain to call into being multinational trade unions. The superstructures already exist; the occasion awaits. Where will libertarians stand on this issue? What are the alternatives? Do we expect that American working men will see American corporations shift their capital abroad and close their plants at home and not react? Are we prepared to educate the public on this issue?

Also, how does a person protect himself from the criminal aggressions of large multi-national corporations? We are already deeply involved in the complicated problem of ecological aggressions against the persons and property of individuals who cannot defend themselves against the corporation and its ally — the state.

Clearly we must begin to give greater thought to creating countervailing forces — libertarian in structure and method — to protect individuals from the sheer power exerted by, not only the State, but by any corporate body that begins to act in state-like fashion — coercively in disregard of the natural rights of individuals and the principles of justice. These countervailing forces may take the form of international professional associations, or private commissions of inquiry into the crimes of States and other state-like corporate entities; or it may take

Freedom And The Law

By Bruno Leoni
(Nash Publishing, Los Angeles, 1972)
Reviewed By Gary Greenberg

The Libertarian movement seems to be forever doomed to the tireless debating of Anarcho-capitalism versus Limited Government. After all is said and done, the debate usually snags on the question of objective law and the certainty of knowledge of the laws of the community. Very rarely is any working knowledge of how law developed and how law is practiced ever exhibited.

Those on both sides of the issue who wish to pursue these debates and lack this practical knowledge, ought to call a cease-fire long enough to enable them to read Bruno Leoni's fast reading and informative study FREEDOM AND THE LAW. Written in a manner that is vividly clear for the layman, Leoni examines the major legal systems of Western Civilization, specifically The Common Law and The Code Law.

Common Law is a system of jurisprudence based on a belief in natural law. Common Law holds that there is a set of transcendental values which remain only to be discovered by jurists. The approach of Common Law is to examine disputes on a case by case basis, using the past decisions of jurists as a guide, while applying reason and experience to the facts of the case. A right rule of law exists but it must be found.

Code Law is based on a system that views law as only what is legislated. It is founded on the belief that the source of law is Government. Its proponents assert that the need for certainty and objectivity requires that the rules of law be known in advance and written for all to see. Leoni is clearly in favor of the common law approach to jurisprudence and tries to demonstrate the fallacy of the "certainty" argument offered by the Code advocates as well as the impracticality of the Code compared to the usefulness of the Common Law.

Leonie points out that since the legislature is the source of the written law in Codes, at best Codes offer only a short term certainty. Leoni compares Code advocates to the Keynesians who assert that in the long run we're all dead.

Another intriguing economic argument is made against the code by analogy to the argument against planned economies. Starting from the assumption that Von Mises has proved the impossibility of economic planning in the State-planned economy, Leoni argues that the Code writers try to achieve the same thing as the economic planners, a set of rules to anticipate all the possible interrelations amongst individuals. The author thinks it is more than just a coincidence that those societies that opted for natural law (Rome, England, U. S.) tended to have strong free market-oriented economies, whereas the Code oriented societies (France, Germany, Italy) had weak free market economies.

Both Anarcho-capitalists and Limited Government advocates seem to be heavily involved in a fantasy in which proponents of their side will sit down and write the Libertarian Law Code. This is just an extension of the Code argument. Those who feel that there must be a written law in advance for all situations will profit greatly from reading this book. Hopefully, they will realize that trying to write the Once and Future Libertarian Law is akin to convening a conference of libertarian physicists and writing the One And Only Forever Laws of Libertarian Physics.

Law is a science. One doesn't impose the laws of a science on people. The laws of science find their way into society through the study of the discipline by the scholars in the field and the general agreement among the scholars that the rules work. The same is true of Jurisprudence. Whether or not people's rights will be respected under the law depends upon what the legal philosophers think about the issues and not whether or not the laws are interpreted by Anarchist judges or Limited Government Judges. I think if this point is grasped, much of the debate between the two sides will fade as the proponents of both views realize that there are much more fruitful purposes to which libertarian energies can be applied. Hopefully this Libertarian version of How-Many-Angels-Can-Dance-On-The-Head-Of-A-Pin will become nothing more than a pleasant diversion. ▣

the form of supporting the creation of an expanded international law based on contract with international institutions and procedures for enforcement. Other tactics, structural forms, technological innovations will offer possibilities now unimagined. The important thing is that libertarians turn their attention to these problems which will shape the destiny of the next centuries. —JRP   ▣

Localism And Bureaucracy In The 19th Century China

By Murray Rubinstein

Phillip A. Kuhn in his Harvard East Asian series monograph, **Rebellion and Its Enemies in Late Imperial China**, seems to be describing a society and situations remote and foreign from our own. He examines in both a chronological and cross sectional fashion the development, operation and utilization of organizations created for the purposes of local self-policing and local self-defense in South China during the middle decades of the 19th century. The student and advocate of local control and individualism will find more in Kuhn's study than perhaps Kuhn himself realized or intended. Mr. Kuhn gives us a warning that local autonomy and community control are valid objectives and appropriate systems but may become distorted by either alien or ultra-radical ideology — introduced by means of force — or by operations of the central state and its servants.

The author uses historical, narrative, and sociological analysis to create a picture of a central government in decline and its local branches in a state of flux. He first traces the origins of militia demonstrating that local military units of a voluntary nature were part of the Chinese tradition (though traditionally Chinese intellectuals have tried to create the opposite impression — that Chinese were by nature non-militaristic and that the greatest times are those when the military on all levels is least important). He then examines the origin of the systems designed to halt rebellion during the years 1820 to 1860. The major sections of his book are devoted to examining the varieties of local military-civilian defense structures and the means by which central officials utilized these newly created institutions to defeat the Taipings (the "God Worshipers" — a society following a religion that was an amalgam of Christianity, Confucianism, and local folk belief. The Taipings controlled east central China from 1850 to 1864 and seriously threatened the Central Government) the Nien fei (Nien bandits — a group of guerilla style maurauders who controlled the area just north of Taiping territory in the 1850's and 1860's) and the Moslem rebels (Chinese Moslems of Turkic descent who revolted in the 1860's and 1870's and gained control of large parts of modern Sinkiang province).

The main system created by the officials (in charge of local areas but holding Confucian degrees and appointed by the central government) Kuhn shows, grew out of two existing institutions that were considered mutually exclusive in normal times. The **Pao Chia** system was one in which families, neighborhoods, and towns were organized into units designed to police themselves and root out any people whose behavior differed from the norm. It had originated in the Sung dynasty (900-1200) and had been reintroduced by the ruling dynasty. The **tuan tien** system was created to organize village defense against bandit incursion and local uprising. It was created by local clan leaders and gentry (confucian scholar graduates who had either not accepted or not been given a government post). District officials and gentry returned from government service such as Chiang Chung-Yuan were instrumental in integrating both into an interlocked system of local registration (the Pao-Chia element) and local defense. Villages were organized along family lineage lines into "simples" (single village) and "multiplex" (multiple village) organizations. Out of these surveillance-defense units came the "Braves" — irregular troops of local men, and finally personal and provincial armies that became the common armies which suppressed the rebellions in this period and created the mold for the war lord armies of the twentieth century.

But where the warning and the contemporary relevance? It is this Kuhn is picturing a society in the process of breaking up. Present were many tensions not unfamiliar to us. There was racial and ethnic conflict, rural and urban competition, and finally, the basic tension between the citizen striving for freedom and economic independence and the state trying to control his mind and tax him to his limit of endurance. The local organizations began as independent efforts to solve local problems by local means. The success these efforts had in supressing banditry and in self-policing was seen by the government as a phenomenon that had to be directed or it could easily get out of hand. Thus the officials and the literati came in, creating official structures, introducing confucian precepts and giving the people a feeling they were aiding in an effort beyond the confines of their local area.

Mr. Lindsay proclaims the 51st State. Mr. Rockefeller calls for local government referendums. Mr. Nixon and Senator McGovern say "power to the people". Representatives of the establishment are using the slogans of the masses to create the impression that power will be returned to its rightful place. The Confucian Civil Servants are again at the gate using the people's desire for self-rule to further enslave them. Instead they hope to use populist institutions to preserve and maintain the structure of the state. Kuhn shows us how the state emerged triumphant again in China. Will the new sense of localism, individual consciousness and self-rule be again perverted to the means of the Leviathan? ◘

Bombing The Dikes

The following are direct quotations from testimony given before the International War Crimes Tribunal summoned to meet in Stockholm and later Copenhagen in 1967 by the world-renowned philosopher and mathematician, Lord Bertrand Russell. Five years later, they may prove to be of more than antiquarian interest.

I

"In April 1945 General Eisenhower proposed to send a "very strongly worded message" to the German High Commissioner for Holland, Seyss-Inquart, telling him that

(Continued On Page 8)

Hope In Ireland

Life has conquered, the wind has blown away
Alexander, Caesar and all their power and sway;
Tara and Troy have made no longer stay —
Perhaps the English too will have their day.

—Frank O'Connor

Bombing The Dikes —

(Continued From Page 7)

"the flooding of large areas of Holland with the resulting destitution, starvation and the enormous loss of life to the population will constitute a blot on his military honor . . . He must be told to cease opening the dikes and take immediate steps to assist in every way the distribution of food . . . and that if he fails in this respect to meet his clear obligations and his humanitarian duty, he and each responsible member of his command will be considered by me as violators of the laws of war who must face the certain consequences of their acts". Confronted by such grave warnings, Seyss-Inquart agreed to stop the destruction of the dikes and cooperate in relief measures. Nevertheless, the barbarism of Seyss-Inquart in destroying the dikes and starving the Dutch civilians made him appear in the eyes of the Western officers as "one of the worst war criminals". He was one of the 24 Nazi leaders executed at Nuremberg."

(Testimony of Prof. Gabriel Kolko)

II

"On May 13, 1953, while armistice negotiations in Korea were bogged down, 20 US F-4's attacked and destroyed the Toksan irrigation dam in North Korea. The Americans also bombed the Chasan, Kuwonga, and Toksang dams and scheduled the bulk of the rest for attack — only the armistice prevented their destruction. The flash flood resulting from the destruction of Toksan dam resulted in a deluge of 27 miles of valley farm lands".

(Source: Air University Quarterly VI (1953/54, 40-41.)

III

"Vietnam is a part of the monsoon area, and the rainy season comes in July, August and September. These are the months when the water level is at its highest . . . One who remembers the great disaster which resulted from the breaking of the dike of the Red River in August 1945 which brought death and famine to two million people, and rendered hundreds of thousands of families homeless, can understand just how serious the bombing of dikes during the rainy season can be . . . According to the report of the Vice-President of the Water Conservancy Commission in Hanoi, U. S. bombings of the entire dike network were exceptionally violent and concentrated in the months of July, August and Setpember 1966, when the water level was very high."

(testimony of Tsetsure Tsurishima, member of the Japanese Commission of Inquiry)

IV

"War crimes are the actions of powers whose arrogence leads them to believe that they are above the law. Might, they argue, is right. The world needs to establish and apply certain criteria in considering inhuman actions by great powers. These should not be the criteria convenient to the victor, as at Nuremberg, but those which enable private citizens to make compelling judgements on the injustices committed by any great power. It was my belief, in calling together the International War Crimes Tribunal, that we could do this, and this book is the record of the Tribunal's considerable success. It serves not only as an indictment of the United States by abundant documentation, but establishes the Tribunal as a model for future use."

(Lord Bertrand Russell in his Introduction to the Tribunal's published hearings.)

America's Newest Enemies

"My defense, as far as my fellow Christians are concerned, is something like this. A great world power is grown distracted in mind and gigantic in pretension. The nation is fearful of change, racist, violent, a Nero abroad in the world. It seeks, moreover, to legitimize its crimes. It stifles dissent, co-opts protests, orders its best youth into military camps, where methods of murder exhaust the curriculum. Most Christians accede to the orders. Many do so with sore hearts, most are convinced of the necessity of right reason and patience, and they say "Let us work and wait for better days". But some cannot wait while the plague worsens. They confront Caesar's stronghold, his induction centers, troop trains, supply depots. They declare that some property has no right to existence — files for the draft, nuclear installations, slums and ghettos. They insist, moreover, that these condemned properties are strangely linked one to another — that the military invests in world poverty — that Harlem and Hanoi alike lie under the threat of the occupying and encircling power.

These things being so, some Christians insist that it is in rigorous obedience to their Lord that they stand against Caesar and put his idols to the torch. They say, moreover, that it is not they who are guilty — it is Caesar. It is not they who must answer for crimes against humanity — it is he. It is not they whom the unborn will abominate — it is he."

(Father Daniel Berrigan in No Bars To Manhood)

"The schoolboy whips his taxed top, the beardless youth manages his taxed horse with a taxed bridle, on a taxed road; and the dying Englishman, pouring his medicine, which has paid seven percent, flings himself back on his chintz bed, which has paid twenty-two per cent, and expires in the arms of an apothecary who has paid a license of a hundred pounds for the privilege of putting him to death." —Rev. Sydney Smith.

Subscription is $8.00 per year.

Libertarian Forum Associate subscription $15.00 or more.

THE LIBERTARIAN FORUM
Box 341   Madison Square Station
New York, New York 10010

First Class

Published Every Month. Subscription Rate: $8.00 Per Year

A Monthly Newsletter

THE
Libertarian Forum

Joseph R. Peden, Publisher   Murray N. Rothbard, Editor

VOLUME IV, NO. 8   OCTOBER, 1972   75¢

NOVEMBER??

. Once again we come to our quadrennial extravaganza, and once again libertarians, even hard core libertarians united on basic principles, differ widely on which side, if any, to support in the election. The three contrasting articles in this issue — ranging from anti-McGovern to anti-Nixon to pro-McGovern — attest to this fact, as do the widespread campaigns by the non-voters and by the Libertarian Party. Neither should this broad disagreement cause any distress, for it is inevitable. The important point is that this is **not** a disagreement on basic principle, but on tactical stances in a political world marked by a myriad of confusing "grays". There are, I think we can all agree, elements of truth in all these positions; the problem, as Ludwig von Mises wrote long ago about the task of historians, is to figure out the proper **weights** to be assigned to these arguments, and to make one's final choice accordingly. But there is no ironclad way of wringing a universal agreement on such weighting, even by hard-core libertarians who agree on every single one of the points involved. As the Marxists would say, these disagreements, in contrast to quarrels over basic principle, are "non-antagonistic" rather than "antagonistic" "contradictions".

It is the expectation of total agreement on specific strategy and tactics that could convert a band of colleagues into a totalitarian cult; for since there is no rational way to command full agreement on tactics, such agreement could only be imposed arbitrarily by a Führer or by a party "central committee". This was the trap that the Randian cult fell into, and it is one which I hope we never fall into again. ⬛

No, No McGovern

By Murray N. Rothbard

Having attacked Richard Nixon since the inception of his Administration, having argued early on for a "Dump Nixon" stance by libertarians, I now have to stand up and report that I cannot swallow George McGovern or the McGovernite movement for which he stands as a bumbling front man. I agree with every word of criticism that Joe Peden has for President Nixon; but I come not to praise Richard Nixon but to bury George McGovern.

The argument for dumping Nixon was always for me a presumption rather than an absolute commandment. The presumption was for the pro-peace candidate and for the candidate out of power, and therefore my inclination was to support the Democratic nominee whoever he might be. Other things being equal I would have, but other things are **not** equal, and for me the monstrousness of the McGovernite movement overrides all other considerations in this campaign.

Specifically, I cannot abide McGovernism for two basic reasons. First is his economic program, which would involve a compulsory egalitarianism and a collectivism far beyond anything contemplated by Mr. Nixon. The McGovernite proposal of $1000 grant for every man, woman, and child in America would mean a $210 billion monstrosity that would have to be financed by crippling taxation on the middle class, on all people making over $12,000 a year. The press and the public have been confused in lumping together the "populism" and the "tax reform" measures of McGovern and of George Wallace. Governor Wallace proposes the **lowering** of taxes on the mass of Americans, middle and working class alike; McGovern proposes the drastic **raising** of taxes on these same Americans. George Wallace would lower the exploitation of the average American by the State; George McGovern would enormously increase that exploitation. In short, Wallace is the true populist, while McGovern

(Continued On Page 2)

McGovern For President

By Lyla and Gerald O'Driscoll

It is our contention that libertarians should not sit out the 1972 Presidential election, but should actively support the candidacy of Senator George S. McGovern. This is not to say that McGovern is a libertarian or that all of his policies are sound. Rather, the case to be made is that McGovern's candidacy and tenure in office could serve libertarian causes, and would do so more effectively than that of the incumbent. This, of course, is one of the best reasons for a libertarian to support any candidate.

Consider the neglected issue of statism versus personal liberty. McGovern's opposition to the draft began with his opposition to the Vietnam War and has since then been firm and unequivocal. McGovern favors amnesty for draft resisters — a genuine amnesty, not an opportunity to do alternative service. The McGovern welfare scheme and the planned reduction of military expenditures, whatever their defects, constitute proposals for the beginning of the end of these two overgrown bureaucracies. **Nixon's the one** who would extend the long arm of the state into the living room to restrict the use of drugs and into the operating room to prevent the termination of unwanted pregnancies. **Nixon's the one** who wants more electronic surveillance of citizen activities. **Nixon's the one** who wants the taxpayers to bail out Lockheed and to finance new and ever more expensive playthings for the generals. Is there any question which set of positions on the issue of statism versus personal liberty corresponds more closely to those of the libertarian?

Nixon's the one who brought us 'peace-time' wage and price controls — the most fantastic and costly scheme ever devised as a means of providing employment for sign-makers and printers. McGovern has promised to end the wage and price controls, and to return to a relatively free market, recognizing military expenditures and government waste as

(Continued On Page 3)

317

No, No McGovern —
(Continued From Page 1)
(Continued From Page 1)

proposes a giant leap into oppressive collectivism under the guise of a phony populist rhetoric.

The rebuttal to this charge by my pro-McGovern friends is that Congress would never pass the McGovern program anyway, so why worry? Perhaps; but for me one of the most chilling moments of the Democratic convention was when Speaker Carl Albert arose to pledge his eternal support to McGovern as President. Congress has been supine for decades, and I simply cannot bring myself to trust the cause of the last shreds of economic sanity to the likes of Carl Albert. I don't think we can afford the risk.

My second overriding problem with McGovern is the McGovernite movement itself, particularly as reflected in the lunatic and dangerous quota system which is seeks to impose on American life. No longer is status and advancement to depend on the achievement of each individual; instead, we are to have coerced quotas to bring the "oppressed" groups in the population up to their numerical share of the total population. The groups favored with the "oppressed" label are, of course, highly selective, being confined to women, blacks, youth, and Chicanos, all of whom are to receive their quotal share regardless of individual merit or of the choice of the voters. Already, such McGovern supporters as Jack Newfield and Joe Flaherty have written angrily and bitterly of the discrimination thus imposed on groups not favored by the McGovernites: for where is the quotal representation for blue collar workers, Irish, Italians, Poles, etc.? Furthermore, the imposing of quotas to compel a rise in status of one group means ipso facto that other groups are going to be coercively burdened and discriminated against by the McGovernites. These groups are of course never openly mentioned, but they amount to the most successful groups, largely adult male heterosexual WASPS and Jews.

In its destructive quota thinking, the McGovernite movement is of a piece with its economic program: in both cases, the motivating drive is a compulsory egalitarianism that would tear down the successful on behalf of a highly selective group of the so-called "oppressed". Of course, at bottom, the egalitarianism is as phony as the McGovernite claim to populism and to representing a cross-section of the "peepul". The true reflection of McGovernite "populism" is the statistic that no less than 39% of the delegates to the Democratic convention have attended graduate school! What we are seeing then is a naked grab for power on the part of an eager new elite of graduate students and upper-middle class "reformers" (those who used to be called "parlor pinks.") It is a drive to fasten a new Mandarin class of self-styled intellectuals upon the country, a class that would reach for absolute power and the crushing of other groups and indeed of the bulk of American citizens. Our current ruling classes, as reprehensible as they are, at least allow for a great deal of pluralism, and for relatively secure status for most of the groups in the population. We can see from the ruthlessness of their quota system that the McGovernite elite would be far more totalitarian and hence far more dangerous in their wielding of State power. The sooner and the more completely that the McGovernite movement is crushed to smithereens, the more viable will be the long-run climate of individual freedom in America.

The McGovernite movement is, in short, in its very nature a kick in the gut to Middle America. And yet the libertarian movement, in its program for getting the government off the backs of the individual, aims to be the fulfillment of the aspirations of that same Middle America. When Middle America, therefore inevitably responds in November by its kick in the gut to the McGovernite movement, it behooves libertarians to stand and cheer. The sooner McGovernism is disposed of, the better for us all. Why in the world should libertarians, whose principles are at an opposite pole from McGovernism, agree to tar themselves with the revield McGovernite brush?

It is important, too, for libertarians to drive the lesson home after November that the Nixon victory will be not so much an endorsement of Nixon's Presidency as it will be the absolute repudiation of McGovernite collectivism. The path will then hopefully be cleared for a further expansion of libertarian ideas and activity among the American public.

For me, there was an extra dimension of aesthetic horror at the McGovern convention. For as I watched the convention, I began to have a sense of déja vu, of having seen all this hogwash before; suddenly, I realized the connection: for what I was seeing was an updated version of the Henry Wallace campaign of 1948. There was the same emphasis on left-wing youth, on the "oppressed" minorities; and there was the same emphasis on Old Left folk-songs. Twice in his acceptance speech George McGovern (a former delegate to the Henry Wallace convention) solemnly quoted from left-wing folk songs; and when he ended his speech with

the Woody Guthrie "This land is your land, this land is my land, from the redwood forests to the New York island . . . ", I thought I was living in a rousing comic parody of Old Left baloney. Except that the parody, alas!, was all unconscious; what we were seeing was the worst of the Old Left, from official program to aesthetic values, at last triumphant in the Democratic party. I raise the spectre of Henry Wallace not to red-bait; for the real problem with the Wallace movement was not its Communist associations but its rampant Old Leftism, from its economic program to its aesthetic attitudes.

And while McGovern would clearly be more in favor of peace than Richard Nixon, the peace and the "isolationism" would be strictly limited. For the McGovern foreign policy is unfortunately not "isolationism" at all, but a recredescence of the Wallace and Truman policies before the Korean conflict; in short, McGovern stands for a nuclear deterrent (albeit at lower cost) plus a maintenance of American troops and interventionism in Europe and the Middle East. One of the most shameful aspects of McGovernism at the convention (which went unrecorded by the media) was the way in which McGovern consented to the Jackson platform plank, pledging continued Anerican troops in Europe and the Mediterranean for the support of Israel, and ramming this plank down the throats of the reluctant delegates. In a recent New York Review of Books, McGovern supporter I. F. Stone perceptively termed McGovern's foreign and military policy "left-wing McNamaraism", which means maintaining military intervention in Europe and the Middle East while cutting our losses in Indo-China. While this would be superior to the Nixonite maintenance of the war in Indo-China, it is far from the isolationism and neutrality of libertarian dreams. And on such civil libertarian questions as amnesty and abortion, McGovern has already gone far to undercut his own previously libertarian positions.

On balance, then, McGovernism offers little good and much evil for the libertarian; in the 1972 election I hold that McGovernism is the greater evil and that therefore we should all look forward with equanimity to its pulverization in November.   ◼

Open Letter To The Internal Revenue Service

This is in response to the notice I recently received regarding the non-payment of my taxes.

For your own enlightenment, I would like to refer you to the Internal Revenue Service Code of Ethics which, presumably, you swore to uphold when you accepted your present position. You will note that the first sentence of this Code reads: "The Federal System of taxation is based upon voluntary compliance by the people of the United States."

To the best of my knowledge, the word voluntary has never meant involuntary or mandatory. Voluntary means voluntary, and I have voluntarily chosen not to comply.

Also, for your information, I would like to state that the method you are using to collect taxes is in violation of the Fourth, Fifth, Ninth and Tenth Amendments to the Constitution of the United States. The Constitution specifically protects United States citizens against unreasonable searches and seizures, against incriminating themselves, against doing anything at all which is at variance with their consciences; I'm sure you can see that requiring people to fill out lengthy forms and submit personal papers and documents each year, as well as seizing their property and possessions if they fail to do so, is a clear violation of our Constitutional protections.

It is also illegal. I would like to refer you to the so-called Miranda Decision (I'll be happy to provide you with a copy if you can't dig one up yourself, particularly sections 2, 5, 6, 7, 10, 12, 13, 14, 15, 18, 20, 21, 22, 23, 26, 27, 28, 31, 32, 33, 37, 39, 43, 45, 49, 56, 57, 58, 59, 68, 73 (this one is very important), and 75. In short, you are prohibited by the Miranda decision from forcing people to incriminate themselves, and forcing them to do anything which violates their Constitutional rights.

In view of the fact that the I. R. S. is in violation of established law, I would appreciate your sending me form 843 since I would like to file a claim for taxes which were collected illegally from me over the years.

Thank you for your cooperation, and I look forward to hearing from you at your earliest convenience.

Sincerely,
Jerome Tuccille
Libertarian

McGovern For President —
(Continued From Page 1)

prime causes of inflation. Is there any question which position on this economic issue corresponds more closely to that of the libertarian?

Nixon's the one who bought Teamsters' support by granting a pardon to Hoffa. McGovern owes little to organized labor, and the union bosses know it. That's why, once Hubert Humphrey was our of the running, they were desperate in their attempt to get the Democratic nomination for Nixon's look-alike, talk-alike, the Senator from Boeing. But isn't it great to have a chance to support someone who isn't owned by the unions?

The editor of this journal has protested that while a McGovern administration might be able to end the Indochina War and improve civil liberties, a supine Congress would offer little opposition to the McGovern economic policies; or else the good proposals would be blocked, and the bad ones passed. To this we must reply, in the first place, that at least there are some good proposals in McGovern's platform! In the second place, McGovern has been one of many advocates of a flow of power to the Legislative Branch and away from the Executive. (This used to be a position supported by Conservatives, in recognition of the fact that Congress more closely represents the interests of the people than does a government centralized in the President's office.) Asked by a reporter whether his programs could get through Congress, McGovern replied, roughly, "I want to be a President, not a dictator," and explained the active role he thought Congress should take in policy-making. Libertarians should welcome such talk of decentralization of power. Should McGovern's anti-statist and anti-Presidential 'glimmerings' go by the board (as those of Richard Nixon did) when he is inaugurated, we are probably no worse off than we were before. The past decade has educated many to the dangers of executive power. Those who were angered by the deception and arrogance exhibited in the Cambodian invasion, those who know that they were deliberately misinformed about the facts of the Tonkin Gulf incident, and those who still wonder whether the Marines should have been sent to the Dominican Republic will not roll over and play dead simply because George McGovern is in the White House. Their voices will still be heard. And we might even be better off, for, as the editor points out, McGovern's tenure in office would force conservative Republicans to rediscover their anti-statist voices and sentiments.

McGovern's candidacy can serve the cause of liberty. Now, more than ever, libertarians must find places in the McGovern campaign — registering voters, canvassing precincts, working in campaign offices. Put McGovern in the White House and bring America home again. ◙

Nixon Or McGovern?

By Joseph R. Peden

The readers of **Libertarian Forum** have little doubt as to Murray Rothbard's views on the candidacy and policies of Sen. George McGovern. Clearly McGovern is not the answer to a libertarian's prayer. His economic policies are clearly socialist in intent and method, and his greatest hope is to restore public faith in government! Yet libertarians always face the lesser of two evils when participating in the political processes of contemporary America — and in this case George McGovern is virtually saintly compared to the tyrant of San Clemente.

It was the widespread notion among libertarians that the new Nixon administration was dedicated to reversing the trend towards socialism that induced us to begin the publication of **Libertarian Forum** in March 1969. Murray Rothbard knew that the incoming Nixon team — with Arthur Burns, Dick Cornuelle, Kleindienst and the White House "Objectivists" — with Milton Friedman hovering in the wings — would not be able to cope with the fiscal crisis created by the economic dislocations of the cold war and Vietnam. By July 1969 — less than six months after the Nixon team took over the White House — Rothbard summed up: "After a half year of painful agonizing, of backing and filling, of puttering delays, the pattern of decisions of the Nixon administration is finally becoming clear. In every single case, the Nixon administration has managed to come down on the wrong side, on the side of burgeoning statism" (**Lib. Forum** July 15, 1969).

The intervening years have only confirmed the acumen of that analysis. A year later, **Libertarian Forum's** editor reviewed the "Nixon Mess" (June 15, 1970):

> "Guaranteed income schemes; continuing budget deficits; monetary inflation; and "voluntary" price controls; under the cover of traditional free-enterprise rhetoric the Nixon

administration continues us down the path toward the economy of fascism. But none of this will solve the crises brought on by his and his predecessors policies. He cannot end the war in Southeast Asia by expanding it, and he cannot end price inflation by continuing to inflate the money supply, or by coercive attempts to overrule the laws of supply and demand".

It was precisely fourteen months after this was written that Nixon announced his "New Economic Policy" of price and wage controls, tariff and quota restrictions and devaluation of the dollar. As this is being written, news reports indicate that this year's federal deficit will be about $37 billion. So much for "winning the war" against inflation!

Given Nixon's record on domestic economic and fiscal issues, why would anyone prefer him to George McGovern? If we turn to foreign policy, McGovern is infinitely preferable from a libertarian perspective. McGovern does not merely pledge himself to end the Vietnam War; he pledges to end the "Vietnam thinking" — the paranoia and militaristic mentality which got us into Vietnam and keeps a $14 billion military establishment in Germany nearly 30 years after World War II. Nixon has offered to send troops to Israel during the Jordanian-Syrian crisis, sent aircraft carriers against India, and actively supports military dictatorships in Brazil, Greece, Indonesia, and elsewhere.

Nixon and Laird have made it clear that the detente with Russia and China will not halt the continuing massive spending on military hardware. Plans call for the complete rebuilding of the navy, more ABM missiles to be installed around Washington to match Moscow's defenses; and Indian Ocean task force and bases, and untold varieties of new planes and weapons. Nixon doesn't even pretend that the military budget will be decreased and our military obligations reduced. McGovern has promised to cut the military budget within four years by some $35 billion; to reduce troop commitments in Europe and Asia; to shift our priorities from foreign adventuring to domestic renovation; or as libertarians might put it, to shift from non-productive to productive investments of capital and labor. If McGovern fulfills even part of his promise, he will have shifted national policy significantly in the right direction. Conservative columnist Joseph Alsop has accused the North Dakota senator of being an isolationist in the tradition of Robert Taft. What an endorsement! There is just enough truth in the charge to make this libertarian smile with nostalgic pleasure.

Lastly, can any libertarian deny that McGovern and the Democrat party have consistently been more solicitous of civil liberties than Nixon and the Republicans? Under the Nixon administration, the Justice department has openly claimed the right to wiretap and bug without judicial warrant on the basis of Presidential prerogative. The argument was strengthened by the assertion that neither Congress nor the courts could limit this prerogative by statute or judicial decree. Similarly, Nixon announced that he was not bound by any Congressional restriction on the disposition of troops, ships or planes — by reason of his prerogatives as commander-in-chief. Congressional committees have been denied access to governmental records — including records needed by the General Accounting Office to audit the expenditure of federal funds as required by statutes. Has any libertarian forgotten the prosecutions of the Harrisburg 8, the Chicago 7, innumerable Black Panthers, on the catch-all of charge of conspiracy? That these political trials have resulted in no meaningful convictions is due to the good sense and integrity of the juries -- who were compelled to their findings by the evidential weakness of the federal government's cases. But the prosecutions were meant as much to harass the accused as to convict them — and in this respect were very successful in diverting the defendants from more productive political activities.

If Nixon is re-elected, the Attorney-General for the next four years will be William Kleindienst who publicly asserted that his job as Mitchell's assistant was to prosecute "ideological criminals". Nixon will also continue to nominate jurists of the character and ideology of Burger, Haynesworth, Carswell and Rehnquist. Can any libertarian rest easy with that prospect before him? Does not the fact that the Justice Department actually stopped publication of the Pentagon Papers in the NY Times for ten days, and subsequently has attempted to subpoena Sen. Gravel of Alaska for reading them on the floor of the Senate give sufficient indication of the Nixon administration's valuation on freedom of the press?

If the libertarian movement is to flourish and grow in influence it must have the fullest possible freedom from fear of censorship, harassment, or persecution by government agencies. The whole past history of the Nixon administration indicates that civil liberties hold a low priority and

(Continued On Page 4)

Nixon Or McGovern? —
(Continued From Page 3)

valuation in its thinking, and that another four years in office constitutes an unacceptable risk of further deterioration in our civil liberties. This fact, along with the evident failures to end the war, redirect national priorities along peaceful non-militaristic lines, and halt the gallop of inflationary forces, convinces me that libertarians ought to support and vote for George McGovern in November.

I have voted for Richard Nixon in 1960 and again in 1968. I voted in the hope that he would find a way to end the war in Asia as he promised, and reverse the drift towards socialism. He has not ended the war; he has in fact escalated the level of violence by invading Cambodia and Laos, and unleashing a bombardment of the Vietnamese people greater in magnitude than that of World War II. He publicly admitted his conversion to Keynesian economics, and removed the last political prop of the free market philosophy by his capture of the Republican party. He deserves an ignominious defeat at the polls. I will vote for George McGovern as the lesser of two evils in 1972. ▣

Archy's Last Gasp

Under the hammer-blows of anarcho-capitalism, the intellectual groundwork of the State, including its "limited government" variant, has visibly crumbled in recent years. It is significant, therefore, that in the last days of the State's intellectual respectability, who should rush in to furnish the last defense of the State but the neo-Randian proponents of "limited" government? In the last few months, the neo-Randians, in desperation at seeing the State go down the intellectual drain, have mounted a concerted assault on anarcho-capitalism.

Thus, in its March, 1972 issue, **Reason** magazine contained a "special supplement on anarcho-capitalism", with three articles devoted to attacking anarcho-capitalism and the editor of the **Libertarian Forum**. Mr. James Kuffel, in typical Utopian Randian fashion, feels it to be a smear on government to identify it with coercive taxation — which has in fact always been a hallmark of government. To the Randian mystics, taxation is an "improper" function of government, and therefore a coercive monopoly government abstaining from coercive levies appears to be a realistic alternative. Mr. Kuffel also tries to rescue the Randian smear term "competing governments", which, as far as I know, no anarcho-capitalist has ever used to describe his desired system. Mr. Kuffel believes that conviction in a judicial trial "presupposes the power of prior arrest"; given this fallacy, he finds it easy to attack as unrealistic my own canon that "any sort of force used against a man not yet convicted of a crime is itself an invasive and criminal act . . ." Yet, a trial can and has proceeded **in absentia**; in an anarcho-capitalist society, a defendant accused of crime would be informed of his trial and invited to appear to defend himself; if he refuses, then trial would proceed **in absentia**, and of course the defendant would then opt for considerably reduced chances to avoid conviction. After conviction, seizure and punishment could duly proceed. Also, Mr. Kuffel, ignorant in typically Randian fashion of history, cannot imagine the application of different laws within the same territory. Yet this has happened, and successfully so, in history; in post-Roman Europe, for example, different Germanic tribes (Franks, Visigoths, etc.) lived peacefully side by side, and different laws were applied to the different tribal members. In a legal case, the first question asked was: "What law do you come under?" In the anarcho-capitalist society, of course, the individual would not be stuck in the tribe of his origin, but could subscribe to varying courts or defense agencies. But the point is that in pre-modern Europe and elsewhere, there was no need for a territorial legal monopoly for law to operate successfully.

Mr. Ron Heiner's essay laboriously seeks to show that in any society conflicts will arise that go beyond voluntary arbitration and will necessitate coercive judicial procedures. He also maintains that competing private courts will reduce to warring factions in the absence of general legal rules to which the courts will agree to abide. I do not challenge these contentions, only the **non sequitor** of Mr. Heiner that **therefore** a State is required to lay down these general rules. On the contrary, libertarian legal theory suffices to lay down a general law code — enshrining and developing the implications of the libertarian principle of non-aggression against person and property — which, in my own view of anarcho-capitalism, all the courts would be pledged to follow. Reason, not the State, is the proper agency for laying down this Law Code, and this can be seen in the ways in which judges worked out the principles of the·

best parts of our legal system: the common law, the law merchant, admiralty law. Once again, the Randians reveal themselves abysmally deficient in their knowledge of history. In addition, Mr. Heiner keeps repeating as a talisman that the market can only work in the sphere of voluntary relations, so that any measure of coercion **must** involve non-market principles. But here he is trapped in his own semantics; for the market provides, not merely voluntary relations, but legitimate **services** of all types, including the service of coercive (but legitimate) defense of person and property from violent assault.

Mr. Charles Barr confines his attack to the first chapter of my **Power and Market**, which briefly sets forth the outlines of an anarcho-capitalist defense and judicial system. In a tizzy because I do not mention Ayn Rand in the book (which was largely devoted to other themes), Mr. Barr totally ignores pages 120-23 of **Power and Market**, in which I expose the inconsistencies and fallacies of earlier versions of the Utopian Randian hope for a voluntarily supported government. (As in so many other areas, Miss Rand did not originate this concept.)

Mr. Barr then has some fun with my idea of a "basic legal code", which all anarchistic courts would be pledged to apply. Where does the code come from, he asks in different ways? The answer is simple, and should be particularly simple for a Randian who professes to follow the dictates of rationality: Reason. Reason dictates the basic legal code of non-aggression against person and property, the definitions of property, etc. Will anyone be free to secede from this code, he taunts? But since the code is simply non-aggression, any person who violates it or any court which refuses to abide by it, either commits or sanctions aggression, and thereby becomes an outlaw or an outlaw court. If Jones aggresses against Smith, and a court to which Smith takes his case decides that aggression was justified because it has adopted a different code (e.g. that Smith is a redhead and it is alright to aggress against redheads), then the court has become outlaw and its decisions will not be recognized by the rest of society. What we are dealing with here is not incidental minutiae of legal proceedings, in which there well might be competition (e.g. judges vs. juries), but the basic legal code of nonaggression itself. Mr. Barr professes to find the concept of "social agreement" to this basic code "mysterious"; but of course it should be evident that no social system or legal system from libertarian to theocratic, can endure unless the majority of society agree to it and are willing to abide by it. After all, what are libertarians trying to do except to convince the public to adopt and abide by libertarian principles? What I am simply contending is that a basic libertarian legal code enshrining the principle of non-aggression is a crucial aspect of such agreement. There is nothing mysterious about it. Of course, to Mr. Barr, trapped in apriori and Utopian Randian definitions, "the attempt to set up a legal system in the absence of government" is a "central contradiction." But, again, pace the common law, law merchant, etc.; it was done all the time, Mr. Barr, sometimes by custom, sometimes by reason; or have you forgotten about the latter concept?

Dr. Tibor Machan returns to the assault on anarcho-capitalism in the June 1972 **Individualist**. Dr. Machan professes himself confused about the great archy-anarchy debate, and his confusion is indeed manifest in the article. Like his fellow Randians, he tries to salvage the Utopian Randian vision of government; why **must** government acquire its revenue by the compulsion of taxation, he wants to know? The answer should be clear: once grant to one agency the power to enforce a compulsory monopoly of ultimate defense in a given territorial area, once grant it the right to outlaw competing police and judicial agencies, and its coercive power is already so great that its enforcement of compulsory taxation is a brief further step in its grab for power. This is in theory; in practice, of course, there was never this separation to begin with; the bandit gang that achieved the power to call itself the "State" never had any compunction about exercising as much coercion and extracting as much plunder as it could get away with.

Dr. Machan calls upon anarcho-capitalists to be "complete", to spell out in detail "the precise character of arbitration and defense agencies" in the future society. But this cannot be done, precisely because no one can blueprint the free market in advance; we don't know how many agencies there will be or their precise makeup for the same reason we do not know how many and which companies will be producing iron bars fifty years from now. But we **can** set down certain basic guidelines, and this we have already done. Finally, Dr. Machan falls into the Rand-Barr fallacy by saying that once the anarcho-capitalists commit themselves to "some kind of legal system" they will no longer just be anarcho-capitalists, but presumably also some kind of archists as well. But the

(Continued On Page 5)

Archy's Last Gasp —

(Continued From Page 4)

point about my own view of anarcho-capitalism is that it encompasses the adoption of a libertarian legal code as part of its very core.

Finally, as a kind of comic footnote to the Reason barrage, the Perkinses write in the June-July issue in reply to Reason's anti-anarchist supplement. The Perkinses presume to read me out of the anarchist movement by pointing in horror to my "erroneous concept of a 'basic legal code' without a government." In contrast, the Perkinses repudiate a legal code but call instead for a 'moral code' founded on natural law . . . the moral code of . . . nonaggression and justice." If the Perkinses had given a little thought to the matter, before popping off in all directions, they would have realized that the "basic legal code" of libertarian law that I've been writing about is precisely the natural law code of non-aggression that they are promoting.

We conclude that anarcho-capitalism stands, and that the last desperate attempt by neo-Randian archists to save the State collapses. But let us conclude by hurling a final challenge to the neo-Randians, a challenge which at least two leading Randians have been subjected to in recent years, and which neither could begin to answer. The challenge is as follows (Messrs. Barr, Heiner, Kuffel, Machan et al, please take heed): OK, we know that you are against competing private defense agencies within a given geographical area. But suppose that, heedless of your edicts, two or more such agencies exist already. Each consciously pursues and applies a libertarian law code which all of us would agree to. On which one of these agencies would you bestow your approval, and which would you presume to outlaw? What would be your criteria for choosing one over the others? I await you answer with great interest. ◉

The Slumlord As Hero

By Walter Block

The slumlord, alias the ghetto landlord, alias the rent gouger, alias the tenement landlord, is proof that man can attain to the station of the devil himself while still alive. At least in the view of most people. Recipient of vile curses, pincushion for needle-bearing tenants with a perchant for voodoo, exploiter of the downtrodden, the slumlord is surely one of the most hated figures of the day. And the indictment is truly monumental, as befits so august a villian: he charges unconscionably high rents; he allows the building to fall into disrepair; his buildings have cheap lead paint which poisons the babies who lick it; he never paints; he allows junkies, rapists, and drunks to harass the tenants. The falling plaster, the overflowing garbage, the omnipresent roaches, the leaky plumbing, the roof cave-ins, the fires, are all integral parts of the slumlords domain. Practically the only healthy aspect of the situation is the size of the rats. Or so goes the indictment.

Actually, however, the indictment is spurious. The owner of cheap housing is no different from any other purveyor of low cost merchandise, or for that matter, no different from any other purveyor of any kind of merchandise, cheap or expensive, at least as far as pricing policy is concerned. They all charge as much as they can get.

Consider the purveyors of cheap, low-cost, inferior and second hand merchandise as a class. What they have in common — is that they all buy and sell cheap, low-cost, inferior and second hand merchandise. And one thing stands out about such merchandise above all else: it is cheaply built, inferior, and second hand. Now, a rational person would not expect high quality, exquisite workmanship or superior new merchandise at bargain prices; he would not feel outraged and cheated if bargain merchandise proved to have only bargain qualities. We do not expect from margarine what we expect from butter; from a used car what we expect from a new car; from a rowboat what we expect from a yacht; from the bleachers what we expect from the 50 yard line seat; from the paper dress what we expect from the mink coat. But such is the nature of the human condition, especially in the urban setting, that when it comes to housing, all rationality flies out the window. People expect safe, clean, sound, well kept, well painted, well run housing at prices that do not at all reflect these qualities. They expect mansions at prices proper for hovels.

But what of the claim that the slumlord overcharges for his hovels? That people have a right to expect at least moderately safe, clean, well maintained housing for the high prices they are forced to pay? This claim is completely erroneous. First of all, practically everyone tries to get the highest price obtainable for what he produces (and to pay the lowest

prices for what he buys). Not only landlords. Workers try to obtain the highest wages they can get. Even downtrodden, minority group member workers. Even socialist workers. Even babysitters. Even communal farmers who work with their hands, share and share alike, and eat only "natural" organic foods. Other businessmen beside landlords try to obtain the highest prices possible for their wares. It is not even necessary to list such businessmen. No one has ever heard of a businessman who does not try to obtain the highest prices possible for his wares. Widows and orphans and others who save their money for a rainy day try to get the highest interest rates possible for their savings. We could, with equal reason, namely none, castigate the workers, widows and orphans for trying to exploit the people to whom they are selling or renting their services and capital by trying to obtain the highest return possible. The point is, of course, that the landlords of dilapidated housing are being singled out and blamed for something which is almost a basic part of human nature: the desire to barter and truck, and to get the best bargains possible.

Secondly, the claim fails even implicitly, to distinguish between the desire to charge astronomical prices for one's wares, which practically everyone has, and the ability to do so, which is not quite so widespread. Of course the landlords would like to charge astronomical prices for their real estate; but this is irrelevant. The question that must be answered if any sense is to be made out of the anti-landlord claims is: How is it that the landlords are able to charge such high prices? Now what usually stops anyone from charging an inordinately high price for anything is the competition from others who will begin selling the same product as soon as its price shows any tendency to rise markedly. If the price of frisbees starts to rise, old members of the industry will expand production, new entrepreneurs will enter the industry for the first time, old worn out, used frisbees will start being sold in a second-hand market, etc. All these activities will tend to counter the original rise in price. If landlords are raising the prices of housing because of a sudden housing shortage the same forces will come into play. New housing will be built by both old real estate owners and new ones, entering the industry for the first time;

(Continued On Page 6)

The Slumlord As Hero —
(Continued From Page 5)

old worn-out housing will tend to be renovated; basements and attics will be pressed into use at least until the prices of housing show signs of decreasing again. All these activities will tend to drive the prices of housing back down to where they were before the landlords began raising them in the first place. And they will tend to cure the housing shortage that began the price rise.

If some landlords tried to raise the rents in the absence of a housing shortage, they would discover difficulties in trying to keep their apartments rented. They would suffer from high vacancy rates as the duration of tenancy declined and as they encountered difficulties renting to new tenants; for both the old tenants and the prospective ones would be tempted away by the relatively lower rents of the landlords who had not raised their rents. Even if all landlords somehow banded together to raise rents, so that no tenant could take advantage of the landlords who had not raised their rents, they would not be able to raise rents in the absence of a housing shortage. For one thing, any such attempt would be met by new entrepreneurs who were not party to the cartel agreement rushing in to fill the gap. They could buy up existing housing, or build new housing; this would add to the stock of housing, and tend to drive down rents as tenants began to flock to non-cartel landlords. For another, each landlord who was party to the cartel would begin to feel strong financial pressures to break the agreement. At the new higher prices composed by the cartel, tenants would tend to use less space, whether by doubling up or by just seeking less space than before. As the tenants demanded less space, it would be harder and harder for the cartel landlords to keep their buildings fully rented. Inevitably, the cartel would crack up, as the landlords sought to find and keep tenants in the only way possible: by lowering rents.

In the third place, the argument that the slumlord over-charges for his dwellings is specious because, at bottom, there is really no legitimate, scientific, or even reasonable sense to the concept of overcharging. Overcharging can only be charging more than the buyer would like to pay. But since we would all really like to pay nothing for our dwelling space (or perhaps minus infinity, which would be equivalent to the landlord paying the tenant an infinite amount of money for living in his building), all landlords who charge anything at all, can be said to be overcharging. Everyone who sells anything at any price greater than zero can be said to be overcharging, for that matter, because we would all really like to pay nothing (or minus infinity) for everything we now buy.

On the assumption that the claim that the slumlord overcharges for his dwelling space is spurious, then, we are still faced with the visions of the rats, the garbage, the falling plaster, etc. Is the slumlord responsible here? Although it is fashionable in the extreme to say Yes, I fear that this will not do. For the problem of slum housing is not really a problem of slums or of housing at all! It is either a problem of poverty, or it is no problem at all, but in either case it is not the fault of the slumlord.

To show that slum housing, with all the horrors it contains, need not even be a problem, all we need do is to consider the case of people who could well afford high quality housing, but who instead prefer to live in slum housing, with all the attendant rats, garbage, lead paint, etc., because of the money they can save thereby. Now this might not be to the taste of you or I, but it ill behooves us to class the freely made choices of other poeple which affect themselves only as problems. For which of us, in such a state, would not be in danger of having his most cherished choices, tastes, desires characterized as "problems"? And there might even be conditions under which even you and I would voluntarily choose to live in slum housing, although we could afford better quality. (This, of course, would make it perfectly all right, and not a problem at all.) We could therefore hardly blame the slumlord, in this case, for providing such people with just what they want.

In the most usual case, however, the reason people choose to inhabit slum housing is because they cannot afford better. But this is hardly to say that the fault lies with the slumlord who provides the housing. On the contrary, the slumlord is providing a necessary service, given the poverty of the tenants. If a law were enacted prohibiting the existence of slums, and therefore of slumlords, without doing anything else (like giving these poor people decent housing or a higher income), it would greatly harm not only the slumlords, but the slumdwellers as well. If anything, it would harm the slumdwellers much more, for the slumlords would only lose one of perhaps many sources of income; the slumdwellers would lose their homes, and be forced to rent much more expensive dwelling space, with consequent and very harmful decreases in the amount of money they would have left to spend on food, medicines, and other necessities. So the problem is not the slumlord. It is poverty. The

only way the slumlord can legitimately be blamed for the evils of slum housing would be if he were the cause of poverty in the first place. And this not even the most fervent detractors of slumlords would contend.

Why is it then, if he is no more guilty of underhandedness than other merchants, that the slumlord has been singled out for a vilification perhaps unequaled by any other group of "exploiters". Why all the hue and cry about the slumlord? Although the answer to this can only be speculative, it seems to me that there is a positive and very strong relationship between the amount of governmental interference in an economic arena, and the storm of abuse and invective heaped upon those businessmen responsible for serving that arena. Instead of testing out the implications of this view in all possible areas, let us see if we cannot pinpoint the link between government involvement in the housing market and the sad plight of the slumlord's public relations.

That there is strong and varied government involvement in the housing market cannot be denied. There are scatter site housing projects that create havoc and racial tension. There is public housing in general which has been a cruel hoax on the poor with its rampant crime, poor planning and administration, with its lookalike buildings which in all too many cases are soon reduced to vertical slums. Urban renewal, known by some as "Negro Removal", has destroyed more housing than it has created, destroying neighborhoods on a mass scale in the process. Zoning has served as a thinly disguised veneer for racism. Building codes have led to higher housing costs which get passed on to the poor, graft for the inspectors, but not to the eradication of slums. The list is seemingly endless. In each of these cases, the spillover effects from the bureaucratic red tape and bungling are visited upon the slumlord. The slumlord bears the blame for the overcrowding engendered in many cases by the urban renewal program in the first place. He is blamed for not keeping his buildings up to the standards set forth by the unrealistic building codes, which if met, would radically worsen the status of the slumdweller.

Perhaps the strongest link between the government and the disrepute in which the slumlord is held is the rent control law. This is a very direct link, whereby rent control legislation changes the usual profit incentives that put the entrepreneur in the service of his customers in to those which make him the direct enemy of his tenant-customers.

In the usual case, the way the landlord earns money is by serving the needs of his tenants. If he fails to serve these needs, they will tend to move out more quickly, setting up extra costs for the landlord in terms of greater vacancy rates, extra costs for the greater turnover such as advertising, cleaning up between tenants, greater repairs, the costs of the agent showing the apartment, etc. The landlord who fails to meet the needs of the tenants will also suffer financial losses directly, insofar as tenants will only remain with him and his poor service at lower rents than the apartment would otherwise command. It is like any other business: the customer is always right, and the merchant ignores this dictum only at his own peril.

But in our present rent control system the incentives are all turned around. Here the landlord can earn the greatest return not by serving his tenants well, but by mistreating them, by malingering, by refusing to make repairs, by insulting them, etc. For when the rents are legally controlled at rates far below their market value, the landlord earns the greatest return not by serving his tenants, but by getting rid of them, so that he can replace them with higher paying non rent-controlled tenants.

If the incentive system is all turned around under rent control, so is the self selection process through which entry into the landlord "industry" is determined, for the types of people attracted to an occupation will be strongly influenced by the type of work that must be done in the industry. If the occupation calls (financially) for service to consumers, one type of landlord will be attracted; if the occupation calls (financially) for harassment of consumers then quite a different type of landlord will be attracted. In other words, in many cases the reputation of the slumlord as cunning, avaricious, willing to cut corners, etc., might be well deserved, but it is because of the rent control program in the first place, that the slumlord acts in this way.

We must remember, however, that if the slumlord were prohibited from lording it over slums, and if this prohibition were actively enforced, the welfare of the poor slum dweller would be immeasureably worsened. We must remember too that the basic cause of the problem of the slums is not at all the doing of the slumlord, and that the worst "excesses" of the slumlord are due to governmental programs, especially rent control, and not to the slumlord himself. So the slumlord does make a positive contribution to society. Without him, the economy would be worse off. That he continues in his thankless task, amidst all the abuse and vilification, can only give evidence of his basically heroic nature. ◙

The Schmitz Ticket

I must admit to a sneaking fondness for the Schmitz-Anderson Presidential ticket of the American Independent Party. While Rep. Schmitz lacks the charisma of the party's 1968 candidate, George Wallace, he is infinitely more libertarian and far more intelligent; he brings to the Presidential ticket the perspective of the John Birch Society.

The Birchers have recently been trying, as best they can, to add some realistic analysis to their formerly locked-in and hopped-up anti-Communism. Gary Allen's recent **None Dare Call It Conspiracy**, for example, uses the insights of New Left historian Gabriel Kolko to add opposition to the Big Business ruling class (the Rockefellers, the Kuhn-Loebs, the Council of Foreign Relations, etc.) to the old anti-Communist armamentarium. The Birches have at last begun to realize, in short, that to call Nelson Rockefeller a "Communist" is absurd and misses the whole point; you don't have to be a Communist to yearn for the fruits of State power, and there have of course been statists and totalitarians from time immemorial, long before Karl Marx was born.

Furthermore, as the brilliant New Left journalist Nicholas von Hoffman pointed out in his appreciative reporting of the AIP Convention this summer, Schmitz et al. have been moving from the vague and ambivalent "win it or get out" view on Vietnam to all-out opposition to a frankly labeled imperialist foreign policy of the United States. As part of a consistently anti-war foreign policy, for example, John Schmitz has been trying to form an anti-Establishment alliance in California with the New Left underground paper, the **Los Angeles Free Press**. In an exclusive interview with that paper, Schmitz (September 8, 1972), points out that he is the only Presidential candidate who opposes any American war in the Middle East as well as Vietnam. Thus, Schmitz says:

> "We're the only ones who have taken a stand for neutrality in the Mid-East. I maintain that 'doves' are nothing but 'hawks' for the other side. Some are just mad because they're shooting communists and not Arabs . . . For example, how can McGovern really be anti-war when he's committed to sending troops to the Mid-East . . . Let him explain that to his peace followers."

Schmitz told the L. A. Freep: "If you want a real anti-Establishment, anti-war candidate, I'm your man." Schmitz also denounced Richard Nixon for being "totalitarian," and leading us into a police state in America. When asked about his support base, Schmitz replied that "we appeal basically to those tax-paying Americans carrying the load . . .", and he attacked "welfare at both ends", welfare per se, and "the Lockheed loan, AMtrak, and other types of welfare to big industry." Schmitz concluded that "I maintain with Jefferson 'that government is best which governs least'."

In an interview with **Business Week** (October 14, 1972) John Schmitz explained his economic views, and they are enough to warm the cockles of a libertarian heart. Schmitz denounced the Keynesianism of the Nixon Administration, the swollen national debt, and deficit spending. Likening Nixonism to the "corporate state, as in Nazi Germany", Schmitz again denounced government welfare to business, and called for the federal government to get out of welfare and education altogether. Furthermore, John Schmitz called courageously for a return to the gold standard at a higher, free market price, and denounced the International Monetary Fund for engaging in elitist planning of the international monetary system. When asked by **Business Week** "how else could you coordinate a monetary system involving 124 nations," Schmitz, God and/or Reason bless him, replied:

> "Well, the way economist Ludwig von Mises says, There are certain natural laws and laws of economics that are far better than any man can devise. You just foul things up by intervening."

When **Business Week** asked Schmitz if he gets his economic ideas from von Mises, Schmitz replied:

> "I read his books. Von Mises probably would not go along with our anti-monopoly plank, although he is not as libertarian as some of his disciples."

Schmitz also denounced wage-price controls, and pooh-poohed the idea that a cut in government deficit spending would cause recession: "When you cut spending in the government sector, that money goes into private spending."

Wow! So why not Schmitz for President? Well, I must admit it is with a certain reluctance that I put aside my support. On the theoretical level, however, the Birchers still persist in linking all the conspiracies and

ruling classes together, so that the Rockefellers, et al. wind up secretly controlling the Communists. Why can't there be competing groups of power-seekers? And on the practical political level, the hopped up anti-Communism is still there, leading Schmitz to call for still greater defense and military spending, enabling him to take a seat (though a bit shamefacedly) on the House Internal Security Committee, and leading him to call for prohibiting all trade "with the enemy". And, dammit, to denounce the three released Vietnam POW's as traitors for not immediately checking in with the military on their release.

So I must finally resist the temptation, strong though it is, to support the Schmitz-Anderson ticket. But I must admit that the more votes that Schmitz can roll up the better, for it would provide a base, a groundwork for rallying an opposition to Nixonite despotism in the next four years. ⬚

Unity Or Cadre

Every ideological movement must find a balance between narrow sectarianism and a flabby and diffuse breadth. Both deviations from the correct path must be avoided: a sectarianism which excommunicates everyone who disagrees, however slightly, from the true faith; and a flabby desire for "unity" which ends by embracing everyone at all related to the central position, and thereby eventually forgetting about the basic principles themselves. In short, there are equal dangers in insulating cadre from everyone else, and in dissolving cadre completely into the general population. Both errors tend to liquidate the movement itself: the former by remaining isolated and ineffectual, the latter by dissolving cadre and thereby losing the very point of the whole business: the infusion of the basic core of principles into the body social.

The way around both of these errors is a central position: to emphasize and retain and nourish cadre — the hard core of true-believing militants; and then to use this cadre base to diffuse these principles and influence non-cadre in numerous ways, including the recruitment of some of them

(Continued On Page 8)

Unity Or Cadre — (Continued From Page 7)

into the cadre itself. In the libertarian movement we have not suffered from excessive sectarianism since the breakup of the organized Randian movement in the summer of 1968; indeed, as libertarian ideas have lately been influencing more and more people in all parts of the spectrum, the danger has been far greater of losing cadre and forgetting basic principle in the quest for a phony "unity". Such unity is phony because differences are often so great that "unity" can only be achieved by neglecting vital intellectual issues. As these issues are neglected, the movement itself becomes ever flabbier, and tends to forget about some of its own most basic principles. Keeping the faith on vital issues can only be sustained by polemicizing against error and deviation wherever it rears its head. But "unity" means that we can't spear error for fear of division in the movement.

As in every ideological movement, libertarians have been hearing the cry that "we have only been talking to ourselves." On the contrary, I maintain that we haven't been talking **enough** to ourselves; we have been talking so much to outsiders that we have failed to nourish, reinforce, and advance our own cadre and our own hard-core principles. Thus, in the last few years we have had a host of broad, open conferences designed to attract broad masses of interested people and establish working contacts with partial libertarians. This is all very fine and useful work, and I am not trying to denigrate such conferences. But unfortunately we have at the same time neglected the vital work of organizing, sustaining, and advancing cadre.

Hence, the importance of the highly successful Libertarian Scholars Conference held the weekend of September 23-24 at the Williams Club in New York City. To be a successful cadre conference, the meeting had to be relatively small, and hence the organizers, Professors Block and Grinder, determined that the conference had to be by invitation only. Immediately, of course, the expected howls of rage arose from our "participatory democratic" wing, complaining (a) that any conference by invitation is by itself "elitist", and (b) why wasn't good old Joe Zilch invited? Happily, Block and Grinder stuck by their elitist guns. The proper reply to such griping includes the following: (1) what's wrong with "elitism"?; (2) we've had plenty of open conferences, now we need some small, closed ones; and (3) if you want to organize a conference that is either open or includes good old Joe Zilch then you are free to organize your own.

In any case, the success of the conference raises the hope that this will be the first of many annual such meetings. At last we move toward the nourishment of libertarian cadre. ◙

FREE!!

A few copies of a 4 page Index to Vols. I-II of Libertarian Forum, 1969-70 are available. Please send a stamped, self-addressed business-size envelope.

SUBSCRIBE NOW

Please enter a subscription for:

Name _____

Street _____

City _____ State _____ Zip _____

Subscription is $8.00 per year.

Libertarian Forum Associate subscription $15.00 or more.

THE LIBERTARIAN FORUM
Box 341   Madison Square Station
New York, New York 10010

Recommended Reading

Isolationism and Revisionism.

Justus D. Doenecke, **The Literature of Isolationism: A Guide to Non-Interventionist Scholarship, 1930-1972** (Colorado Springs: Ralph Myles, paper, $1.85, 89 pp. Also available from the Laissez-Faire Book Store, 29A Mercer St., New York, N. Y. 10003.)

A superb work. Professor Doenecke, who has been hard at work for years on a definitive study of World War II isolationists and their attitudes toward the Cold War, here gives us all the benefit of his scholarship, in an appreciative, sprightly, and thorough guide to all the scholarly writings on the area of isolationism. This is not simply a bibliography; all works are discussed and annotated in an ordered context, and each one weighed and evaluated. Doenecke has not only combed published books and journal articles, he has also ferreted out every unpublished doctoral dissertations on the subject (these can all be purchased in bound, Xeroxed copies from University Microfilms, Ann Arbor, Michigan and, while book prices have been rising, Xeroxed book prices have actually fallen in recent years!). Doenecke has not only combed the field with unusual thoroughness, but he is an open-minded scholar in the best sense of that term: he rejects nothing because it might be "unrespectable". This delightful booklet is indispensable for anyone interested in the area of isolationism and revisionist foreign policy. Representative chapter titles: "Theory," "The Interwar Years," "Movements and Leaders", "The Politics of War and Bipartisanship," "Opposition to Consensus Politics", and "The Revival of Isolationism'".

James J. Martin, **Revisionist Viewpoints: Essays in a Dissident Historical Tradition** (Colorado Springs: Ralph Myles, $2.50, paper, 248 pp.)

Dr. James Martin is perhaps our foremost anarcho-revisionist scholar, and this is a sparkling collection of his essays, largely on World War II, but also including the Cold War, most of which once appeared in the now unfortunately defunct **Rampart Journal**. There are some exciting new insights here, including for example Jim Martin's study of the totally neglected Peace Now movement for a negotiated peace during World War II, and the unmerciful smear treatment that the movement received at the hands of the Establishment. Martin also includes both the original German text and his own English translation of a highly revealing foreword that J. M. Keynes wrote to the German edition of his **General Theory**. The edition appeared in Nazi Germany in 1936, and is strangely not at all mentioned in Roy Harrod's "authorized" biography of Keynes. Keynes tells his German readers that "The theory of aggregate production, which is the point of the following book, can be much easier adapted to the conditions of a totalitarian state than the theory of production and distribution of a given production put forth under conditions of free competition . . ." Among other goodies, this book is the only place where Keynes' German preface is available.

The Libertarian Forum
BOX 341
MADISON SQUARE STATION
NEW YORK, NEW YORK 10010

First Class

Published Every Month. Subscription Rate: $8.00 Per Year

A Monthly Newsletter

THE
Libertarian Forum

Joseph R. Peden, Publisher   Murray N. Rothbard, Editor

VOLUME IV, NO. 9   NOVEMBER, 1972   75¢

BEYOND THE SIXTIES

The smashing repudiation of McGovernism (for no one claims to see any great love for Richard Nixon) by the American people is both the symbol and the living embodiment of the death of the 1960's. More specifically, of the final passing from the scene of the second half of the 1960's, the era of the New Left. In a heady rush of excitement during those wild few years, the New Left swiftly escalated their tactics and their goals, from pressure to demonstration to campus takeovers to outright violence. The brief frenzy of violence reached its culmination with the "whiff of grape" at Kent State in 1970; that show of firmness was enough to demoralize and destroy the New Left and to end the flurry of violence. The only thing left was to "work within the system," and the result was the McGovernite movement; now that movement has been smashed to smithereens, and there is nothing now for the Left but to shut up and fade away.

Those were indeed wild and wooly years; but in retrospect we can see far better than at the time that the whole movement was a flash-in-the-pan: a sudden, exuberant, and radical outburst that was destined to disappear as quickly as it arrived. The outburst to be sure, was breathtakingly swift; never before in America had the political, social, and cultural changes — "revolutionary" changes in the broadest sense — been so swift and so seemingly irresistible. It is easy to see now, however, that these changes of attitude and ideology were confined, not simply to youth, but to students and younger faculty in elite Ivy League colleges, people who were well situated by virtue of wealth and articulateness to make far more noise than their numbers or their genuine influence ever deserved. An important recent study by the Hudson Institute only serves to confirm other evidence of how deeply conservative the great bulk of the middle and working classes — including the youth — have continued to be throughout all the hullabaloo. (Frank E. Armbruster, **The Forgotten Americans: A Survey of Values, Beliefs, and Concerns of the Majority**, New Rochelle, N. Y.: Arlington House, 1972, $9.95, 454 pp.)

The academic year 1969-70 (it is fitting to trace this campus-based "movement" in terms of academic years) was the frenzied culmination before the dissolution of the New Left. That was the year when the SDS was captured by the Weathermen, who proceeded to "go underground" after celebrating the Manson Family's torture-murder of Sharon Tate. It was the year of the last giant, violent demonstration in Washington; the year when the Berrigans and their allies talked wildly of "kidnapping Kissinger"; the year that ended when the shock of Kent State brought the movement out of their relatively safe but looney revolutionary posturing and into the harsh light of reality. It was the year, too, when some libertarians lost their perspective and got caught up in the frenzy: from street fighting to drug parties to portentous mutterings about the imminent launching of "urban guerrilla warfare."

In retrospect, too, it is obvious that many of us caught up in the excitement of the moment, far overweighted the libertarian and anti-statist elements of the New Left and underweighted the statism and the dangers of the ongoing "revolution." Of course, that error in perspective was aided by what used to be called a "cultural lag" — by failing to assess the swift changes that always occur in a revolutionary situation, and which

virtually eliminated the libertarian elements in the New Left after a couple of years in the mid-1960's.

It also seems clear that, while its narrow base of support made the passing of the New Left inevitable, the swiftness of its demise may be credited to the brilliant strategic policies of the Nixon administration and its allies in authority throughout the country. The crucial element here was a policy of firmness, a refusal to give in any further to the seemingly irresistible "revolution". The firmness was demonstrated in numerous ways. There was the whiff of grape at Kent State, there were the mass arrests at the Washington traffic-tieup demonstration, and, to a lesser extent, the prosecution of such leading figures of the movement as the Berrigans and the Chicago conspiracy trial. A determined policy of not giving in further to Negro demands, e. g. mobilizing the general public hostility to compulsory bussing, not only defused the black "revolution" but has ended all traces of urban Negro rioting for several years now. In its policy of firmness and determination, the Nixon administration must surely have taken its cue from the public reaction to the police clubbing of demonstrators at the Chicago Democratic convention of 1968. This massive reaction, which surprised many of us at the time but really should not have, was an almost universal condemnation and hostility toward the demonstrators for their provocations, rather than against the police who did the clubbing. That reaction surely told the incoming administration that the public would cheer a policy of firm suppression of the "revolution". And it is certainly instructive to note how little resistance the boastful revolutionaries put up to even the minimal force used by the administration.

Joined together with the firmness of the government was the resistance of the college administrators. Led by S. I. Hayakawa, the administrators found, once again, that a policy of determined resistance to the student rebels was enough to make the rebellion wither away with remarkable rapidity.

In addition to the stick, the carrot. For the Nixon administration again saw, with strategic brilliance, that along with a policy of due firmness and resistance, it must also defuse the major grievances of at least the broad base of followers of the revolution. The major grievances were twofold and interconnected: the draft and the Vietnam War. There was surely no single act that defused the revolution more swiftly than the adoption of the lottery draft. Combined with a steady reduction of draft calls, the lottery quickly ended what had seemed to be, but obviously was not, a principled opposition to the slavery of the draft, and as a consequence the student rebellion itself. Furthermore, the cunning policy of "Vietnamization", while hardly satisfying the true-blue opponents of the war, was enough to defuse the issue, not only for the bulk of the American people but also for most of the campus rebels. For the crucial point was that American troops in Vietnam, and therefore American casualties were swiftly and steadily reduced by the Administration. And that meant, too, that those few young men who were drafted would at least not be sent to the hell of Vietnam. The fact that countless Vietnamese continued to be slaughtered was to become only a remote and abstract concern even for

(Continued On Page 2)

Beyond The Sixties —

(Continued From Page 1)

the erstwhile rebels. The carrot and the stick had done its work with consummate artistry.

There was another important stick, too, that played a large role in eviscerating the New Left and the abortive rebellion. That was the recession of 1969-70, and particularly the **academic** recession for college graduates that hit the following year. Suddenly, a sellers' market for college graduates, the era of the 1960's when every graduate could write his own ticket for jobs, was succeeded by a very tight "buyers' market", with heavy unemployment for educated youths. If the Nixon administration had planned it that way, nothing could be better calculated to end the posturing, the "greening", the phony dropping-out among the youth, than a sharp dose of economic reality in the form of recession and unemployment. It was back to reality, back to studying, to careers, etc. for our former rebels. Suddenly, campus youth wanted, not formless "rapping" and the use of the campus as a base for furthering the "revolution", but course content to prepare them for jobs and careers. The "educational revolution" proved to be as much a flash in the pan as the rest of the hoopla.

What then remains of the New Left, of the heady years of the late sixties? Not very much. There seem to be only three things, none of which can give any comfort to rational libertarians: women's lib, hallucinogenic drugs, and rock. Rock, I am informed, has receded considerably from the noisy cacaphony of the "acid rock" of a few years ago; and not only has rock visibly softened, but there has now arisen a welcome "nostalgia craze" for the Old Culture of the 1950's. And the old "rock-and-roll" of the fifties, while hardly any great shakes as music, was, in its happy innocence, far more the tailend of the great Old Culture popular music of the 1920-1950 era than it was the prefigurement of the irrational "hard rock" of the sixties.

In the monstrously irrational culture of hallucinogenic drugs, marijuana unfortunately remains, but at least there has been a visible recession in the use of LSD and the other powerful "hard drugs", presumably reflecting a drawing back from their ugly Social Darwinist consequences.

Women's lib is still with us, but it is unclear at this point what lasting impact it will have. Beyond a welcome drive for abortion-freedom and beyond a drop in population growth, it seems likely now that the most that will happen will be a greater stimulus for women to fulfill themselves in careers. The man-hating crazies who make up the core and the vanguard of women's lib seem destined to disappear as simply a media shuck; after all, how many more times can the public bear to watch the Robin Morgans and the Kate Millets, or even the Gloria Steinems, cavort on television?

Overall, the rational libertarian can take good cheer from Herman Kahn's shrewd prediction of the cultural trends of the 1970's:"Remember 67 per cent of America is quite square and getting squarer. I call this the counter-reformation, the counter-counterculture. It's the biggest thing going in America today and it will either dominate or heavily influence the next decade or two." (Herman Kahn, "The Squaring of America," **Intellectual Digest,** Sept. 1972, p.18.)

Surely, the massive repudiation of the McGovernite movement is a firm indication that Kahn's prognosis is correct. For one of the elements in that repudiation was Middle America's accurate perception of the McGovernite movement — as exhibited, for example, at the Democratic convention — as the embodiment of the "counter-culture." In smashing McGovernism, Middle America eagerly seized the opportunity to deal a gut blow to the counter-culture it detests: to upper-class kids flaunting drugs, hippies, dirt, rock, open sexual perversion and promiscuity, rejection of the work ethic, and living parasitically off welfare or parental subsidy. Add to this an upper-class embracing poverty as a virtue, and sneering at Middle America's concern about crime in the streets from safe vantage-points in the suburbs.

If, indeed, the seventies loom as a return to the "squaring of America", then what does this imply as the proper strategy for the new and growing libertarian movement? Clearly, it implies that strategy and rational principle meet: that we cast off the trappings of the counter-culture which all too many libertarians adopted in the heady days of the sixties. That we return home, home to our "bourgeois" rational roots, home to the old values which Middle America has miraculously preserved throughout the years when the upper classes and the intellectuals betrayed them. Home to becoming the vanguard of the vast bulk of Middle America, a people whose instincts are sound but who lack the consistent articulation of that philosophy — rational libertarianism — which provides the solution for their irritations and resentments as well as the correct path for achieving their goals of peace and freedom and secure prosperity.

Concretely, what do I mean by a Middle American orientation? What sort of specific work can be done? The sort of thing I mean can be seen by briefly examining four estimable organizations, two scholarly and two activist. In the world of scholarship, the Institute for Humane Studies of Menlo Park, California has done yeoman work over the years in gathering Fellows, in publishing books and pamphlets, and in sponsoring conferences at home and abroad on such vital matters as property rights and human differentiation. There is also the Center for Independent Education of Wichita, Kansas, which has published pamphlets in support of private and full-cost education as contrasted to public schools, and has sponsored a conference on compulsory education, critically examining its legal, historical, economic, and philosophical aspects. On the activist front, there are two admirable organizations, each headed by young libertarians. One is the National Taxpayers Union, where Jim Davidson has done yeoman work, almost singlehanded, in Washington lobbying against taxation and government spending, tipping the balance against the SST and helping to defeat the disastrous Family Assistance Plan. Davidson was also partially responsible for inducing the Republican platform committee to call for the legalization of gold. Earnest Fitzgerald, former high Pentagon official, head of the NTU, and chief exposer of the Lockheed scandal, has recently published a book (**The High Priests of Waste,** Norton), which expands his revelations of waste in government spending.

The other activist organization is the National Committee to Legalize Gold, headed by two youthful New Orleans libertarians, James U. Blanchard III and Evan R. Soulé, Jr. With high professionalism and enthusiastic organization, the NCLG distributes a regular bulletin on gold, and has held a series of press conferences throughout the country calling for legalization of gold, and defying the Treasury Department by holding aloft an illegal bar of gold. And while concentrating on gold legalization as the first step, the NCLG happily makes clear that its ultimate objective is abolition of the Federal Reserve System and the substitution of the gold standard for government fiat paper.

Both the NTU and the NCLG are admirable models of what an activist libertarian organization, oriented to the conerns of Middle America, can accomplish.

Meanwhile, it's a comfort to know that we'll still have Dick Nixon to kick around — for Four More Years. ▣

From The Old Curmudgeon

Watergate, Schmatergate.

Frankly, I've gotten awfully tired of the endless griping about Watergate. Even National Review has expressed its deep concern about the goings-on. All around me I hear left-liberals complaining about the "moral apathy" of the American public on this issue. It is an "apathy" which I confess I share. The public reaction is: "well, that's politics"; politics always consists of dirty tricks by one party on the other. Yes, of course it has. Only pseudo-moralists with little sense of history can claim otherwise. Have we all forgotten the previous elections in which the Democrat prankster Dick Tuck played numerous practical jokes and dirty tricks on the Republicans? Where were the left-liberal moralists then? I'll tell you where they were: right in there enjoying the spectacle of good old Dick Tuck making fools of the Republicans. You don't like the shoe on the other foot, do you fellas? With all the real problems in the world, can we really get so upset about the fumbling capers of the USC clique?

Australopithecus, Where Art Thou?

Australopithecus has been highly touted by the evolutionists as the "missing link", as our ancestor who wandered the earth approximately 2.5 million years ago. But now all this has been knocked into a cocked hat by the finding of a skull by Richard Leakey, about 2.6 million years old, that is closer to modern man than Australopithecus. So now what? It's back to the drawing board, evolutionists! ▣

"The object of the state is always the same: to limit the individual, to tame him, to subordinate him, to subjugate him." —**Max Stirner**

The Senate Rated

One of the pleasant pastimes of ideoligical groups is rating Senators from their own point of view. Not to be outdone, the **Lib. Forum** has taken the rated votes compiled by the **New Republic**, American Conservative Union (published in **Human Events**), and the National Taxpayers Union (published in **Dollars and Sense**), and combined them to rate Senators on libertarian vs. statist votes on various key issues. The numerical ratings after the names of the Senators are the plus-libertarian votes, followed by the statist votes (e. g. 20-22 means 20 libertarian votes and 22 statist votes.) We have also grouped the members of the outgoing Senate into six categories: Very Good, Good, Moderate, Bad, Very Bad, and Excruciatingly Bad. (No Senator rated an Excellent.) We realize that the quantitative vote fails to weigh qualitative matters on the issues, but we feel that enough votes have been recorded to give a pretty good idea of the Senator's ideological drift.

Very Good:

H. Byrd (Ind., Va.) 33-12
Roth (Rep., Del.) 32-13

Good:

Ervin (D., N. C.) 25-18
Proxmire (D., Wisc.) 27-18
Fannin (R., Ariz.) 26-19
Dominick (R., Col.) 24-17
Curtis (R., Neb.) 26-19
Buckley (R., N. Y.) 28-16
Brock (R., Tenn.) 23-15
Hansen (R., Wyo.) 22-16
Jordan (R., Id.) 24-19

Moderate:

Allen (D., Ala.) 23-21
Fullbright (D., Ark.) 20-20
Chiles (D., Fla.) 22-19
Talmadge (D., Ga.) 20-23
Church (D., Id.) 18-22
Stennis (D., Miss.) 21-24
Pastore (D., R. I.) 20-24
Spong (D., Va.) 24-20
Goldwater (R., Ariz.) 20-16
Weicker (R., Conn.) 19-23
Gurney (R., Fla.) 19-25
Griffin (R., Mich.) 21-21
Hruska (R., Neb.) 21-24
Cotton (R., N. H.) 22-23
Hatfield (R., Ore.) 21-17
Bennett (R., Ut.) 21-17
Thurmond (R., S. C.) 20-23

Bad:

Jordan (D., N. C.) 14-22
Bentsen (D., Tex.) 17-26
Stevenson (D., Ill.) 18-27
R. Byrd (D., W. Va.) 17-26
Hartke (D., Ind.) 15-23
Eastland (D., Miss.) 15-22
Symington (D., Mo.) 18-27
Burdick (D., N. D.) 19-26
Pell (D., R. I.) 17-23
McGovern (D., S. D.) 13-21
Dole (R., Kan.) 18-26
Cook (R., Ky.) 19-25
Young (R., N. D.) 18-27
Saxbe (R., Oh.) 16-23
Taft (R., Oh.) 17-26
Bellmon (R., Okla.) 16-23
Tower (R., Tex.) 18-25

Very Bad:

McGee (D., Wyo.) 8-28
Sparkman (D., Ala.) 11-31
Gravel (D., Alaska) 11-27
McClellan (D., Ark.) 11-22
Cranston (D., Calif.) 13-31
Tunney (D., Calif.) 13-31
Ribicoff (D., Conn.) 10-32
Bayh (D., Ind.) 13-30
Hughes (D., Io.) 15-28
Long (D., La.) 13-31
Muskie (D., Me.) 15-27
Kennedy (D., Mass.) 16-28
Hart (D., Mich.) 11-33
Humphrey (D., Minn.) 7-26
Randolph (D., W. Va.) 14-29
Nelson (D., Wisc.) 18-29
Anderson (D., N. M.) 11-27
Hollings (D., S. C.) 15-29
Montoya (D., N. M.) 14-29
Moss (D., Ut.) 10-31
Harris (D., Okla.) 15-25
Magnuson (D., Wash.) 13-32
Bible (D., Nev.) 13-31
Cannon (D., Nev.) 12-31
Mondale (D., Minn.) 15-28
Eagleton (D., Mo.) 14-29
Mansfield (D., Mont.) 12-27
Metcalf (D., Mont.) 7-27
Allott (R., Col.) 14-26
Boggs (R., Del.) 14-31
Fong (R., Haw.) 12-29
Percy (R., Ill.) 15-27
Miller (R., Io.) 14-29
Pearson (R., Kan.) 12-32
Cooper (R., Ky.) 16-29
Smith (R., Me.) 16-29
Beall (R., Md.) 14-30
Mathias (R., Md.) 12-30
Brooke (R., Mass.) 10-33
Case (R., N. J.) 12-32
Javits (R., N. Y.) 16-29
Packwood (R., Ore.) 16-27
Schweiker (R., Pa.) 16-29
Scott (R., Pa.) 11-33
Baker (R., Tenn.) 13-29
Aiken (R., Vt.) 17-27

Excruciatingly Bad:

Inouye (D., Haw.) 7-34
McIntyre (D., N. H.) 7-33
Williams (D., N. J.) 9-34
Jackson (D., Wash.) 6-36
Stevens (R., Alaska) 9-34
Stafford (R., Vt.) 6-33

The Strip Miner As Hero

By Walter Block

There are basically two methods of mining coal: strip mining and deep mining. In deep mining, which is used to mine coal from a great depth, an intricate set of tunnels, shafts, braces must be set deep in the earth at great cost. Apart from this, deep mining has the disadvantage of causing black lung disease, the dread miner's disease caused by breathing in coal particles in deep and enclosed places. Deep mining must also bear the onus of numerous mine entrapments that occur with deathly regularity where hundreds of miners at a time can be trapped far below the surface of the earth due to a cave-in, escaping gas, an explosion, or water seepage.

In strip mining, as the name implies, the earth is stripped, layer by layer, until the coal stream is unearthed. Strip mining is thus very easily utilized for streams of coal which lie close to the earth's surface, and in cases where the surrounding earth is not strong enough to support the braces necessary for deep mining. Although especially well suited for mining coal that lies close to the surface, strip mining has proven feasible at up to moderate depths, competitive therefore with deep mining at some depths. Strip mining is free of the dangers of cave-ins, of black lung disease, and is very much cheaper than deep mining. This makes available to the poor a source of cheap energy, which in many cases may well mean the difference between life and death! In spite of these advantages, strip mining has been roundly condemned by practically all sources of "informed, liberal, and progressive" opinion.

The supposed explanation for this otherwise inexplicable state of affairs centers around two criticisms of strip mining: it causes pollution, and it is a despoiler of the natural beauty of the landscape. But as can be seen from even a cursory examination of the case, these two criticisms of strip mining will hardly suffice as an explanation of the extreme antipathy shown to the strip miners. The vilification and abuse heaped upon the strip miners by the liberals cannot be reconciled with their humanistic principles, which hold human life to be of great value. And life is on the side of strip mining. For there is no black lung disease on the surface of the earth where strip mining takes place; there is no danger of cave-ins and entrapment many miles beneath the surface of the earth for the strip miner. So even on the assumption that the two arguments of despoiling beauty and causing pollution held against the strip miner are correct, it is hard to see how supposedly humanistic people can favor deep mining over strip mining.

It is even more puzzling when we reflect on the fact that the two

(Continued On Page 4)

Grouped by parties, we have Republicans: Very Good — 1, Good — 7, Moderate — 9, Bad — 7, Very Bad — 18, Excruciatingly Bad — 2. If we lump the Goods and Bads together, we get: Republicans: Goodish — 8; Moderate — 9; Baddish — 27.

The Democrats fare considerably worse by libertarian standards, though obviously neither party deserves hosannahs. Very Good — 1, Good — 2, Moderate — 9, Bad — 10, Very Bad — 28, Excruciatingly Bad — 4. Lumping together: Goodish — 3; Moderate — 9; Baddish — 42.

The two best Senators are Roth of Delaware, who is nobly following in the footsteps of his predecessor, John J. Williams; and Harry Byrd of Virginia, following in the footsteps of his economy-minded father. The absolutely worst Senator in a bad lot is none other than the man the Lib. Forum has already called "Mr. State", Scoop Jackson of Washington.

We can now analyze the fortunes of the incumbent Senators on the bases of our classifications. Of the "Good" Senators, 2 (Curtis, Hansen) were re-elected, and 1 (Jordon, Id.) died, and was succeeded by a similarly-inclined conservative, McClure. Make it 3 victories and 0 defeats for the Goods.

Of the Moderates, 3 won (Griffin, Thurmond, Hatfield), and 1 lost (Spong). Of the Bad Guys, 3 won (Eastland, Pell Tower) and none lost. Of 16 Very Bad Guys running for re-election, 10 won (Pearson, Baker, Case, Brooke, Mondale, Metcalf, Percy, Sparkman, McClellan, Randolph), but no fewer than 6 bit the dust (Miller, Smith, Boggs, Allott, Harris — whose conqueror in turn lost to the Republican Bartlett, and Anderson, whose surrogate lost to the Republican, Domenici.) On the other hand, 2 Excruciatingly Bad Guys won (Stevens, McIntyre) and none lost. If we lump the Goods and the Moderates together, we get a record of 5 won and 1 lost; if we lump all the Baddies together, we get 15 won and 6 lost. Dare we then say that in this election, when everything below the Presidential level was ideologically mixed, that the American public was partially hitting out at the worst enemies of liberty?   ▣!

The Strip Miner As Hero —
(Continued From Page 3)

criticisms are by no means correct. First consider pollution. Although it is indubitably true that pollution results from the activity of strip miners, this is hardly a necessary concomitant of strip mining. Rather, it is the result of a failure of the courts of this land to apply the laws of trespass to the strip miners. If the law against trespass were vigorously enforced, there would be no connection between strip mining and pollution at all.

What is presently done during the mining of coal in the stripping method is to take the large amounts of earth that must be peeled away in order to expose the coal, and to pile it up into huge mounds. Now, these mounds are usually piled up near streams of water and substantial amounts of earth are borne away by the stream, contaminating the stream, and the many lakes and other waterways the stream feeds into. Also, the de-nuded land serves as a source of mud slides, with no grass to hold the water. But there is no reason for this! If the strip miners were made to bear the full costs of their activity, and if the people whose downstream property was damaged had the right to obtain preventive injunctions to stop this practice if they were unwilling to be compensated for the damages by the strip miners, then the practice would cease. Strip mining would no longer be linked with pollution.

It is most important to see that the present link between pollution and strip mining is not inherent, but is rather due entirely to the failure to apply the common law of trespass against the strip miners. Imagine if you will, any other industry that was allowed to violate the law in this manner, such as the oil tanker industry. Now, there is no necessary connection between the oil tanker industry and pollution, but if oil spills were allowed, there soon would be a connection between the tanker industry and pollution, at least in the minds of the public. And so it is with the coal mining industry, and with strip mining in particular. There is nothing about the strip mining method of coal mining that is inherently pollutant causing. It is only because the laws of trespass have not been rigidly applied to to the strip miners that the link between stripping and pollution exists. Let these laws be fully adhered to, and this whole argument against strip mining would disappear.

What of the other argument against the strip miner: that stripping spoils the natural beauty of the landscape? The first thing to realize is that when it comes to beauty, there can be no objective standards which ought to be forced upon other people. What is beauty to one person can be ugliness to another; what is ugliness to one person can be beauty to another. It is true that what strip mining does is to remove the vegetation, grass and trees from the landscape. It can turn a lush, fertile landscape into a veritable desert. But some people like the desolation and emptiness of the desert! The painted desert in Arizona, the salt flats of Utah and the Grand Canyon of Colorado are considered by many people to be places whose beauty is without equal.

While hardly an expert on the esthetics of scenery, it seems to me at least that one of the concomitants of natural beauty is contrast. The mountains right next to the ocean along the California coast, the skyscrapers ringing the southern part of Central Park in New York City, as well as the small bits of desolation provided by strip miners among the lush greenery of the Appalachians all benefit from stark contrast and are immeasurably beautified thereby. So, on the grounds of destroying the beauty of the landscape, it does not seem that we can unambiguously and objectively fault the strip miner. If anything, according to at least some tastes, the strip miner beautifies the landscape.

Apart from that, however, this seems to be the wrong way to deal with the objection. For the real question is not whether or not strip mining adds to or detracts from beauty but rather, which people shall be allowed to make the choices on the disposal of land which can affect its beauty? If we take the view of those who criticize the strip miner for despoiling natural beauty, and would forbid him if they had the power, we become enmeshed in unsolvable paradoxes. If the lovers of nature can prevent the strip miner from changing it (perhaps improving it, in his own mind) of then a Pandora's box will be opened. For on the same logical basis, we can prevent all farmers from clearing virgin soil and planting upon it; we can prevent the builder from erecting buildings or bridges, factories, hospitals, etc. And by extending this principle of forbidding everything we decide is ugly, various groups in the population are sure to begin to forbid long hair, dungarees, rock music, beads, pot smoking, or, alternatively crew cuts, tuxedoes, symphonic music, brassiers and whiskey.

Some people argue that striping is unnatural. These liberals would be the first to object if homosexuality or miscegenation were objected to on these grounds. They would point to all the discoveries in medicine which are certainly "unnatural", namely man-made. But when it comes to strip

The Elections

Apart from the smashing repudiation of McGovernism, anticipated by all observers including the **Lib. Forum**, and welcomed by most, the ideological complexion of the rest of the elections was a mixed bag. There are certain results, however, that we can hail with particular and unambiguous joy.

One was the massive roadblock that Governor Arch Moore (Rep., W. Va.) put in the way of the rising young charismatic Rockefeller, John D. (Jay) Rockefeller, IV, for the Governorship of West Virginia. Sweeping in with 55% of the vote, Governor Moore postponed for many years, and perhaps ended indefinitely, the spectre of yet another Rockefeller buying himself a state and vaulting into a national political career. Isn't Nelson enough? One particularly charming aspect of the Moore victory was his use of sophisticated "economic determinist" muckraking to stop young Rocky. Moore asked this pungent question: why has young Rockefeller emigrated from New York, come to West Virginia, and there tried to put an end to the strip coal mining industry in the name of the "environment"? Why if not to confer a monopoly privilege on coal's great competitor, oil, in which the Rockefeller family has a consuming interest? Arch Moore, welcome to the ranks of Revisionism!

Another serendipity was the victory for the Senate in North Carolina of ultra-conservative Jesse Helms over liberal Nick Galifianakis. Helms, a TV commentator, is an advocate of the magnificently libertarian Liberty Amendment, which would abolish the personal income tax and sell all government assets competitive with private enterprise. We expect to hear many great things from Senator Helms.

A third goodie was the victory for the governorship of New Hampshire of Meldrin Thomson, Jr. (Rep.) Thomson; a book publisher, previously ran for the governorship on the American Party ticket, and his major plank was a pledge to keep New Hampshire in its superb role as the only state in the union with neither a sales nor an income tax. Tax rebellion was also responsible for the defeat of high-tax Delaware Governor Russell Peterson (Rep.) by conservative Democrat Sherman Tribbitt, as well as the defeat of high-tax Richard Ogilvie (Rep., Ill.) for the governorship by the charismatic, wealthy young Dan Walker. Ogilvie was heartily punished by the voters of Illinois for daring to put in a state income tax after he had campaigned against the proposal. On the other hand, we must record the defeats of the anti-tax campaigns for the governorship of Ed Smith (Rep., Montana) and Al Rosellini (Dem., Washington.) (Dem., Washington.)

There are a couple of particularly amusing notes in the election. One is the total neglect lavished by the women's libbers on the female candidacies of conservative Republican Louise Leonard for Senator from West Virginia, and of Mary Breeden (who asserted that "taxation is theft") on the American Party ticket for Senator from Kentucky. Another is the total ineptitude of the writing team of conservative Noel Parmentel and liberal George Gilder, who went down to Louisiana to aid the Senatorial campaign of Ben Toledano (Rep.), who was slaughtered with a mere 19% of the votes.

Finally, the election saw the emergence of the Libertarian Party. We still do not know how many votes were recorded for the Hospers-Nathan ticket on the ballots of Colorado and Washington. We have already hailed the New York campaigns of Greenberg and Block in these pages; another Congressional write-in candidacy for the LP was in the 30th Cong. District of California, where the distinguished young libertarian lawyer Manuel Klausner ran on the LP ticket. Klausner, an editor of Reason, followed Greenberg and Block in giving an imaginative individual twist to his campaign literature. He came out, for example, for rational pricing of congested streets and roads, and for a return to the spoils system and an end to the oligarchic tyranny of the civil service system.

Last but not least, we have what seems to be an authentic libertarian in Congress! This is young Steven D. Symms, from the 1st Congressional District of western Idaho. While winning on the Republican ticket, Symms, an apple grower, is also reputed to be a member of the Libertarian Party, the Society for Individual Liberty, and the National Taxpayers Union. Has one of our own actually made it to Congress? Let us scrutinize young Symms' voting record with care, and try to get him to include libertarian literature into the Congressional Record. ▣

mining, all logic flies out the window. To say that a thing either is or is not a result of nature alone or of man alone cannot determine its intrinsic worth. To argue that the desolation caused by strip mining is ugly because it is unnatural or because it perverts nature is to completely ignore the "artificial" contributions to beauty made by such men as Rembrandt or Mozart. ▣

Whither the Democracy?

Where do the Democrats go from here? If they wish to remain a viable national party, with a good shot at the Presidency, their primary task faces them clearly and squarely: the purging from the party of the McGovernite debris. The McGovernites must be blasted loose from their controlling positions in the party structure, and the Democrats must insure against a repeat of the disastrous 1972 convention by getting rid of the McGovernite "reform" rules which imposed the quota system on the delegates. The fight will not be an easy one, since the McGovernites, as ideological fanatics, are determined to hold on at any cost. Already, they are trying to cover themselves by jettisoning the person of McGovern, and claiming that the land slide defeat was merely a problem of his personal "image".

The first step in the required purge is to depose La Westwood from the chairmanship of the National Committee, or to get rid of the person whom the Republican newsletter **Monday** has pungently referred to as "the Democrat National Committee chairthing." The ouster of La Westwood is Consideration No. 1 in the taking back of the Democrat Party from its usurpers. A second task, which will prove more difficult, is to keep the chairmanship out of the hands of someone like the Kennedy stalking-horse Larry O'Brien, whose pro-McGovern rulings at the convention irretrievably compromised his supposedly neutral position in the party.

In the longer run, it is clear to everyone that there is only one man who can unite all factions of the Democrats under his own charismatic, left-liberal banner: obviously Teddy Kennedy. The problem for all sane and sober Americans is: How can we keep from getting Camelot again? How can we nip the Kennedy Dynasty in the bud? How can we keep the choice in '76 from narrowing down to Teddy vs. Agnew? Or Teddy vs. Percy? Isn't it about time for a full-scale investigation of the unclarified anomalies of the Chappaquiddick affair? If Teddy resumes the eternal bellyaching about Watergate, how about a counter-ploy on Chappaquiddick? □

Recommended Reading

Revisionism.
A great book bonanza is now available from Ralph Myles Publisher (Box 1533, Colorado Springs, Colorado 80901). Myles, headed by the eminent revisionist and anarchist historian Dr. James J. Martin, has recently reprinted several classic revisionist works, in hard cover and for the first time in paperback. These are:

Harry Elmer Barnes, **In Quest of Truth and Justice.**
441 pp. Cloth $9.00; paper $2.95.
This is a fascinating and detailed account of Harry Barnes' struggle on behalf of World War I Revisionism, including the text of his debates with detractors and anti-revisionists, and the great muckraking attack on historian-apologists who served as propagandists during the war, by Barnes' student C. Hartley Grattan. Includes a new introduction by the late William L. Neumann. First published in 1928.

Michael H. Cochran, **Germany Not Guilty in 1914.**
268 pp. Cloth $6.95; paper $2.50.
This is a remarkable, unique, and tragically neglected work, first published by Dr. Cochran under Harry Elmer Barnes' aegis in 1931. It is a thoroughgoing, detailed, point-by-point and devastating critique of the outstanding anti-revisionist history of the origins of World War I, Bernadotte E. Schmitt's The Coming of the War 1914. It is a tragic commentary on the historical profession that the Schmitt book continued to win high honors among historians while Cochran's refutation was completely forgotten. With a new introduction by Professor Henry M. Adams.

Arthur A. Ekirch, Jr., **The Civilian and the Military: A History of the American Anti-Militarist Tradition.**
360 pp. Paper $3.00
Originally published in 1956, this book is the finest history ever written of militarism and its opposition in America. By our leading individualist historian. Again, largely neglected since publication, it is all the more welcome in this paperback edition. With a new introduction by Professor Ekirch.

Rothbardiana.
Rothbardiana continues to progress on various fronts. Rothbard has a review article in The Antitrust Bulletin (Summer, 1972) of Robert Heilbroner's edited work in celebration of the socialist Adolph Lowe, R. Heilbroner, ed., Economic Means and Social Ends. Rothbard discusses Lowe's attempt to replace economics by technology and values imposed by an elite, methodology, the entire problem of "prediction" in science and in the world, and the problem of values and economics.
We infiltrate The Nation, with Jerry Tuccille's excellent review of Rothbard's new edition of America's Great Depression! (The Nation, October 16). We understand that there was quite an ideological tussle within the Nation's board of editors before they would print Tuccille's review.

The Weekend edition of The Chicago Daily News (Oct. 28-29) has an article by Dan Miller, "Business Not 'Wild' About Peace", about problems of transition to a peacetime economy should the Vietnam War soon be over. It includes a long paragraph of quotes from Murray Rothbard, including his gloomy prediction that the government, instead of cutting taxes, will undoubtedly shift any cut in war spending to other forms of domestic boondoggles. The article also includes excellent quotes from Northwestern Univ. economic historian Jonathan Hughes, who denounces the effects of government deficits, high taxes, and domestic boondoggles in causing stagnation and inflation. "The people," concludes Professor Hughes, "are already taxed out of their wits." The solution "is for the economy to go back to producing things people want to buy voluntarily. The only way that can be done is with a massive federal tax cut. The government must allow the people to decide how they want to spend their money." Hear, hear!

Revisionism from the Centre

A REVIEW ESSAY

By Chris R. Tame

Exponents of "New Left" historical revisionism will often find their analysis attacked on grounds other than those concerning its objective truth. The obvious political motivations and importance of the work of historians such as William Appleman Williams, Gabriel Kolko, and James Weinstein provides for historians of the "liberal" consensus a convenient excuse for ignoring or denigrating their work. Of course, the even more blatant political motivation and biases in the work of orthodox liberals is rendered culturally invisible (to the majority) by its very dominance. Therefore, the arrival at revisionist conclusions by historians of the "centre", without any strong political motivations (at least, strong radical ones), is doubly welcome — both for its inherent validity and for its utility as "unbiased" verification of radical revisionism. Although we are not, of course, exactly being deluged by such non-radical sources of revisionism, it is nevertheless true that we are increasingly observing the appearance of scattered articles and books which manifest insights and analysis in support of the "New Left" and Libertarian historical case.

Thus, in his essay "The Wisconsin Idea and Business Progressivism" (**Journal of American Studies**, July 1970), Stuart Morris makes his conception of the Progressive Era perfectly clear from the start: "The 'progressive era', 1900-16, can best be interpreted . . . in terms of the 'rationalization' of corporate industrial capitalism . . ." The focus of his essay, however, is on the 1920's a period which for the liberal orthodoxy (e.g. Hofstadter's **Age of Reform**, Schlesinger's **Crisis of the Old Order**) is essentially one of the decline of Progressivism, a "return to normalcy" and the supremacy of optimistic, self-satisfied business forces — in all, "an unfortunate inter-regnum" (H. F. May). Morris demolishes the liberal interpretation. In a close examination of many Progressive (and especially Wisconsin Progressive) intellectuals, he identifies the nature of their thought as essentially elitist and conservative — anti-laissez faire, of course, but anti business most definitely not. For individuals like Charles Van Hise, Herbert Croly, Charles Evans Hughes, F. C. Howe, F. J. Turner, and Richard T. Ely, the core of their approach was the concepts of "efficiency" and "control" — a managerial, elitist ethos. In the words of John R. Commons, "The outstanding fact (is) the importance of Management. Instead of capitalism moving on like a blind force of nature, as Marx thought, here we see it moving on by the will of management." Thus, Morris argues, the movement for business efficiency and rationalization which was manifest in various forms in the 1920's (including, for example, the establishment of university schools of business) was simply a continuation of the same ideological motivation as that of the earlier Progressives. "Business education . . . was not simply a function of economic rationalization", writes Morris, ". . . it was also a product of progressive aims and assumptions". If outright **political** activism declined in the 1920's, this was as much to the nature of Progressivism itself as to other factors. Progressivism had simply shifted its focus to other measures to attain the same ends as before. Thus, F. C. Howe (in **Wisconsin: An Experiment in Democracy**, 1912) saw "scientific efficiency" as "one of Wisconsin's contributions to democracy". Herbert Croly declared that expert administration was the "instrument which society must gradually forge and improve for using social knowledge in the interest of valid social purposes" (**Progressive Democracy**, 1914), and Louis Brandeis became the prophet of **Business, A Profession**, (1914). In Morris' words, "Like the Fabians in England, the progressive intellectuals heralded the arrival of the reformer as **expert** . .

(Continued On Page 7)

Arts And Movies

By Mr. First Nighter

The Ruling Class. dir. by Peter Medak, written by Peter Barnes, with Peter O'Toole.

Here is the umpteenth British film that attacks and satirizes the British upper classes. So what else is new? What is new is the depths of irrationality and absurdity to which the film sinks. Here is the apotheosis of the "non-linear" movie; very little of the film makes any sense at all, either in philosophy, plot, continuity, or camera work. The camera work is mod-absurdist, employing every irritating trick that has unfortunately been learned in the last decade. From the prototype absurdist film that flouts the law of identity, **Morgan**, comes the tactic of people suddenly becoming, and unbecoming, apes, skeletons, or what have you.

Where **The Ruling Class** differs from other irrational films is in three ways: its length, its acting, and its "philosophy". For the film rolls endlessly on; Medak and Barnes are always enchanted with their own supposed brilliance and importance, and every trick of theirs has to be stretched out and beaten over the head. The movie seems like four or five hours long by the end, although I am informed that the excruciating experience lasted for but two hours and a half.

The acting features — and O how does it feature! — Peter O'Toole, who cavorts on the screen for virtually every minute of the picture. Peter O'Toole has been one of the most overrated actors of the last two decades, and given anything like his head, he will twitch, quiver, shake, and generally chew any and all of the available scenery. To save any film what O'Toole needs is a firm directorial boot fastened upon his neck; even in that superb film, **Lawrence of Arabia**, in which O'Toole made his debut, that twitching and quivering augured badly for the future. But in **The Ruling Class**, O'Toole is lovingly given his head, and a veritable shambles ensues.

The "philosophy" with which this pretentious film is encumbered, is a highly jejune one. In the first half of the picture, O'Toole plays a psychotic aristocratic who is convinced that he is Jesus and God, and every once in a while he leaps on to a home-made cross to get back to his roots. O'Toole leaps and quivers, shouting that God is Love and everyone must love one another. Then, after a psychiatrist is sent to cure him. everyone thinks he is cured, since he no longer thinks he is Jesus; but aha! he is secretly convinced that he is Jack the Ripper, and proceeds to systematically murder any girls (and lots of other people) he can get ahold of. While Jack the Ripper, which Medak and Barnes persist in identifying with the Old Testament God of wrath, O'Toole leaps to political leadership of the House of Lords by preaching capital punishment and death to all criminals. You see, the imbecile point of the picture is this: when O'Toole, as a sweet and lovable nut, goes around preaching Love to All, everybody **thinks** he is crazy; but when he shifts to preaching fire and brimstone, he is elevated to leadership of the Tory upper class. Profound? Not really; for let's face it, O'Toole's first incarnation was just as nutty as the second; first, because indiscriminate Love, Love for everybody is as impossible and unnatural a goal as we might conceive; and, second, because O'Toole **was** crazy, after all, and deserved, if not commitment, a wide berth by everyone, especially the long-suffering members of the audience. There is no denying that some scenes in the first part are funny, before the picture turns into a grim welter of random killings, but the humor is completely buried by the deadweight of the picture as a whole.

One of the most unforgivable effects of the New Wave in British movies is that it has managed to destroy a film industry that was once the finest in the world. If you want to see a superb, truly witty, and beautifully acted satire on the British upper class, try to find a rerun of a triumphantly Old Culture film of two decades ago, **Kind Hearts and Coronets** — with Dennis Price and especially Alec Guinness. Back to the Closet, sickies and absurdists, and let us have good movies again! ◙

330

Revisionism from the Centre —
(Continued From Page 6)

. This emphasis on information and practicality served to minimize any distinction between the expert and the reformer and to enlist both in the service of the state''.

However, the most substantial contributions to the revisionist case to derive from non-radical sources have come from two other, more prominent, historians: Robert H. Wiebe and Samuel P. Hays.

Robert Wiebe's Businessmen and Reform: A Study of the Progressive Movement (Quadrangle Books, Chicago, 1968; originally published, 1962) obviously bears immediate comparison to Kolko's The Triumph of Conservatism, but it is only right to say that the latter work is far superior. Both in the arrangement of his material and the depth of his research Wiebe falls far short of Kolko's achievement. He also reveals, in a number of comments, far more elements of a liberal historiographical "hangover". However, this is by no means to denigrate Wiebe's work. Businessmen and Reform is marked by a striking realism in its approach to the issues of government regulation, constantly focusing on the hard actuality of economics ignored by the "liberals". In contrast to the liberal mythology of a monolithic and peculiarly malevolent business community, dogmatically opposed to "government regulation for the public good", Wiebe analyzes the vitally important clash of interests within the ranks of business, making it clear that this economic conflict lay at the root of the demand for government control. Although Kolko's discussion of most of the major areas of conflict (the railroads, anti-trust, banking, etc.) is more detailed and comprehensive, Wiebe's account is far from being worthless or unilluminating. His discussion of anti-trust and the tariff, or his discussion of the triangular conflict between the ambitious city bankers and the small county bankers in the Mid-West and the large established Eastern banking houses, should especially be read in conjunction with Kolko. Overall, then, Wiebe clearly establishes the validity of his fundamental conclusions; " . . . both the idea and impetus for reform," he states, "came from prospering businessmen on the make, men like Edward Bacon, Herbert Miles, and George Perkins . . . the business community was the most important single factor or set of factors — in the development of economic regulation".

Samuel P. Hays is probably known to a segment of Libertarians for his work, Conservation and the Gospel of Efficiency: The Progressive Conservation Movement, 1890-1929 (Harvard Univeristy Press, 1959), in which a number of anti-market myths are dispelled. Specifically, he shows that the range wars of the 1880's were due to the fact that property rights could not be acquired, and that the lumber corporations were not universally engaged in short sighted resource exploitation. However, the importance of the book does not lie merely in these two limited points. For, in fact, in an analysis of this particular aspect of Progressive reform Hays attacks the core of liberal mythology. "The conservation movement", he writes, "did not involve a reaction against large-scale corporate business, but, in fact, shared its view in a mutual revulsion against unrestrained competition and undirected economic development. Both groups (i. e., corporate leaders and Progressive reformers) placed a premium on large-scale capital organization, technology, and industry-wide co-operation and planning to abolish the uncertainties and waste of competitive resource use". This point Hays drives home throughout the book: the demand for conservation regulation came from the large corporations themselves, united with Progressivism in general by a shared elitist and technocratic social ethos. The precise implications of his research, however, are outlined in the essay "The Mythology Of Conservation" (in H. Jarrett, ed., Perspectives on Conservation, Johns Hopkins Press, Baltimore, 1958): "Few can resist the temptation," Hays declares, "to use history to formulate an ideology which will support their own aspirations, rather than look squarely at the hard facts of the past". And the liberal historians, he makes clear, are the most guilty of succumbing to this temptation. Their devotion to the concept of "public control" as the summum bonum of political life has blinded them to the nature of such control in practice. As Hays makes quite clear in the context of his research on Conservation, "Public control is not an end in itself; it is only a means to an end. Conservation means much more than simply public action; and we should be more concerned with the history of its objectives rather than of its techniques. In fact, by dwelling on the struggle for public action historians have obscured the much more basic problem of the fate of conservation objectives". The identification of state intervention as inherently in the "public interest", to be no more questioned than Motherhood or Democracy, distorts historical reality. Holding such concepts the measure of all virtue, it is clear why no examination of the real motives of their proponents — or even of who

those proponents actually were — could emerge from liberal historiography. In Hays' own words: "The widespread use of the concept of the public interest often obscures the importance of political struggle, and substitutes rhetoric for reality. It permits bitter political contests to be far beneath the calm surface of agreed-on language and technical jargon . . . The great danger of the 'public interest' is that it can lull one into complacency by persuading him to accept a mythological instead of a substantive analysis of both historical and contemporary conservation issues".

Professor Hays, moreover, has not merely restricted himself to demolishing this one sphere of liberal mythology. In his essay "The Politics of Reform in Municipal Government in the Progressive Era" (Pacific Northwest Quarterly, October 1964; and reprinted in A. B. Callow Jr., ed., American Urban History Oxford University Press, N. Y., 1969), Hays has performed an analysis as astute and important as Weinstein's work in this field. Once more he demolishes the facade of liberal historiography: "Because the goals of refrom were good its causes were obvious; rather than being the product of particular people and particular ideas in particular situations, they were deeply imbedded in the universal impulses and truths of 'progress'. Consequently, historians have rarely tried to determine precisely who the municipal reformers were or what they did, but instead have relied on reform ideology as an accurate description of reform practice". Liberal historians have thus seen the urban political struggle of the Progressive Era as a conflict between public impulses for "good government" against the corrupt alliance of machine politics and the "special interests" of business. In the modified versions of Mowry, Chandler, and Hofstadter, the role of the middle-class is stressed, but although this interpretation apparently rests upon a slightly more scientific approach, it is equally deficient, in fact, in logic, and depth of research, and is still subject to the same ideological self-delusion. For his definitive analysis of the topic Hays draws from a wide range of research — from the results of his own efforts, from work that has appeared recently, and from work that

(Continued On Page 8)

Revisionism from the Centre —
(Continued From Page 7)

has been available for decades (such as the case studies of the city-manager governments undertaken in the 1930's under Leonard White's direction.) The source of Progressive municipal reform, Hays conclusively demonstrates, lay in the **upper-classes**. The financing of New York's Bureau of Municipal Research, for example, came largely from Carnegie and Rockefeller, and this pattern of corporate financial support for reform organizations is the same in every case. Urban Progressivism derived essentially from the new upper class of corporate leaders and the younger and more advanced members of the professions, individuals who sought to apply "expertise" and "managerial control" to public affairs. A clear examination of Progressive aims reveals that their principal objection to the existing system of local government was to the fact that it gave representation and effective control to the lower and middle classes, rather than to the more suitable elements — **themselves!**

The essence of Progressive municipal reform lay not in such measures as direct primaries, the initiative, referendum and recall, so often emphasized by liberal historians, for these were in fact often irrelevant and ineffective in practice and utilized more for tactical and propagandistic ends. Rather, it constituted the centralization of the system of representation, the shift from ward to city-wide election of councils and school boards and the establishment of the commission and city-manager forms of government. Such centralization destroyed the existing balance of representation and allowed the upper-classes to dominate government. It is no wonder then, that, as the studies carried out under Leonard White's direction revealed, the lower and middle classes overwhelmingly opposed the Progressive reforms. The conclusion of Hays' devastatingly incisive essay is uncompromisingly clear: "The movement for reform in municipal government, therefore, constituted an attempt by upper-class advanced professional, and large business groups to take formal political power from the previously dominant lower-and middle-class elements so that they might advance their own conceptions of desirable public policy".

Hays has thus performed a brilliant analysis of two major aspects of Progressivism and has enunciated clearly the reasons that most liberal historians have been unable either to discover historical actuality or even recognize such actuality when it faces them in the available documentation. Yet he has also attempted to go further, to integrate revisionist perspectives into a general theory of historical causation. His essay "The Social Analysis of American Political History, 1880-1920", (**Policital Science Quarterly**, September, 1965) is thus valuable as a description of this theory as well as for the wealth of bibliographic information it contains (information of which no Libertarian student of history should fail to be aware and to utilize). In fact, the essay is one of the most complete and devastating attacks ever made on liberal historiography. Hays surveys an extensive range of (principally) recent research on a plethora of socio-political topics, all of which, he demonstrates, fail to conform to liberal mythology, and whose significance and importance will go unrecognized as long as this mythology predominates. Thus, in Hays' summary: "The liberal framework, more concerned with the formal and the episodic, has become increasingly restrictive rather than conducive to further social analysis. It has prevented historians giving full attention to

the political role of working people, the influence of ethnocultural factors in politics, the changing characteristics of elites, the role of the business community in reform, the treatment of urban life as a system of social organization, the source of anti-reform impulses, the conflict between local and cosmopolitan cultures, the growth of bureaucracy and administration, the growth of education as a process of cultural transmission and social mobility, the development of ideology and its relationship to practice, and the examination of inter-regional economic relationships. Most important, it has obscured significant shifts in the location and techniques of decision making in a more highly systematized society . . ." And this slashing indictment, it should be emphasized, is thoroughly documented on every point raised. Also of note in this essay, in relation to Stuart Morris' study of the Progressive ethos cited earlier, is Hays' own account of the ideological factors that made possible the cooperation of the new industrial elite, the professional classes, and the intelligentsia: "This new (i.e., corporate) elite", he writes, "was highly attractive to patricians and intellectuals. While many in both groups had rejected the materialism and brashness of the new industrial elite, they found in the tendencies toward rationality and systematization an acceptable outlet for their talents, and thereby became reconciled to the very business community which earlier they had abhorred."

Thus the Libertarian may be well pleased that there has developed a parallel stream of revisionist historical analysis alongside that from the 'New Left', one from, so to speak, the "centre". Yet this "centrist" revisionism does contain implicit dangers, dangers to be found in Hays' general theory of "social analysis" that is offered as an alternative to the "liberal framework". Specifically, this danger lies in economic cum-technological determinism. Thus, the growth of political centralization and the nature of "Progressive" political movements, is seen by Hays as a result of "the systematizing and organizing processes **inherent in industrialism** . . . the dynamic force in social change in modern life . . . Political movements in modern industrial society can be distinguished in terms of the role which they played in this **evolving structure.**" (Emphasis mine). Centralization and the "Progressive" reforms are seen as the "techniques which these systems (i. e., modern industrial ones) require", and the "persistent upward flow of the location of decision-making", as the natural consequence of the "evolution from smaller to larger and larger systems". Of course, there are elements of truth in the view that changing economic structures will involve changing social structures. Yet it is also equally clear that the deterministic tendency in Hays' thought obscures the socio-political alternatives that may have existed. From the point of view of the Libertarian, it is apparent that vital questions of the nature and legitimacy of property rights and of market conditions are overlooked or held of no account. Thus, Hays' social analysis could equally well serve the same function as that presently done by the liberal framework — as an **historical consecration**, a justification for the **status quo** and for that "persistent upward flow of the location of decision making". This tendency is equally apparent in Wiebe's **Businessmen and Reform**, in his statement, ironic now in retrospect, that "With so few signs of domestic upheaval at the beginning of the 1960s (!) any elite would take pride in the record of America's durable business leadership". Revisionism from the centre, therefore, can easily become absorbed once more into the "American Celebration". ◙

The Libertarian Forum
BOX 341
MADISON SQUARE STATION
NEW YORK, NEW YORK 10010

First Class

Published Every Month. Subscription Rate: $8.00 Per Year

A Monthly Newsletter

THE
Libertarian Forum

Joseph R. Peden, Publisher   Murray N. Rothbard, Editor

VOLUME IV, NO. 10   DECEMBER, 1972   75¢

THE MOVEMENT

In a few short years, the libertarian movement has grown rapidly, but not continuously. Essentially, it has grown in two great bursts. The first, which raised it off the ground from a tiny handful of people, centered around the famous libertarian splitoff from YAF in August 1969. It was this split and the self-consciousness gained during it that created the current libertarian movement. The second great burst, which we dubbed "the takeoff", was occasioned by the Lehr-Rossetto article in the New York Sunday Times Magazine, and by the spate of media publicity which followed it in the winter of 1970-71. Since then, we have had numerous new magazines of various and diverse types, continuing publicity, numerous conferences, and a host of Libertarian Parties in various states of the Union.

All this is fine, but one begins to get the distinct feeling that for the last year or so the movement has been stuck on a plateau, that it has in a sense been doing little more than milling around. New magazines have sprouted, but others have fallen by the wayside. In addition to qualitative improvement, to clearer foci of activity, we are in acute need of another "great leap forward", a leap that will bring us sharply out of the "sect" category and begin to make a palpable impact on American life.

For some time, it has been a matter of interest to libertarians to estimate how many of us there really are in the country as a whole. The answers have ranged from the wildly optimistic 100,000 (which would include everyone who has ever purchased an Ayn Rand novel from Academic Associates) to the sober judgment of our old colleague Leonard Liggio, who places the total number of libertarians at somewhere around 300. Your editor, as always a middle-of-the-roader, has estimated the total at 10,000. Of course, much of the difference depends on what level of libertarian activity and consciousness one includes in the definition. In my view, however, one has to be at least a regular reader of a libertarian periodical to be included as an active "member" of the movement. Libertarians who don't bother to read any of their own literature — or, for that matter, to read at all — can hardly be included in any estimate of our total number.

On this basis, however, I am afraid that I must revise sharply downward my estimate of 10,000 libertarians. For there is no libertarian periodical, regardless of promotion, advertising, layout or whatever, that has been able to get its circulation above two to three thousand. Considering organizational membership as well, there seems no real warrant for guaging the movement at more than 3,000.

In the midst of this puzzlement over the size of our active or potential market, Robert D. Kephart, the young genius publisher of **Human Events** who several years ago became a convert to pure libertarianism, had a noble conception. That conception was to found a new periodical, a monthly and eventual bi-weekly, which would be highly professional and geared to the widest possible market, not simply of libertarians but of all those, on the right, left or centre, seriously interested in liberty. Kephart's idea was to found the libertarian counterpart of the spectacularly successful and highly influential **New York Review of Books**. The new periodical was designed to tap the resources, not just of scholarly and knowledgeable libertarians, but of able scholars of all ideologies whose writings or fields of expertise could contribute significantly to libertarian theory and knowledge. To this end, Kephart gathered together a staff of

potential contributors, ranging from objectivist psychologists to New Left historians: all fields of human endeavor, from history to philosophy to the arts and sciences, were to come under the new magazine's purview. Naming the new periodical **The Libertarian Review**, Kephart chose the brilliant young libertarian Roy Childs to serve as the editor. Furthermore, Kephart brought to the new venture all the publishing expertise with which he had managed, in a few short years, to so boost the circulation and efficiency of **Human Events** as to bring it well into the black — a major feat for any ideologically oriented magazine.

The staff was gathered, reviews and articles for the first couple of issues were assigned and secured, and publication of the first issue was scheduled for January 1973. As further essential preparation for the enterprise, Kephart purchased the existing book-selling services of the movement — SIL Book Service, and Libertarian Enterprises —, combining them into Books for Libertarians, and assiduously purchased and gathered together a huge mailing list including everyone remotely associated with the libertarian cause. Then, Bob set about trying to secure enough initial subscribers to L. R. to yield a reasonable prospect of putting the journal on a paying basis.

Kephart estimated that an initial total — or at least the firm prospect of the total — of 10,000 subscribers was needed to make L. R. an economically viable proposition. Yet his best efforts could not boost the prospective number of subscribers above 5,000; and so, as a result, the black news came that **Libertarian Review** had died stillborn; the great conception was not to bear fruit.

The tragedy of the stillbirth of L. R. is that here was the means for our next great leap forward; there is no doubt that this periodical would have served as the great center, the focus of (a) attracting a large number of new libertarians; (b) spreading our ideas rapidly and effectively to the "outside world", and (c) refining and advancing our knowledge of theory and of empirical reality.

Are there really no more than 5,000 libertarians in the entire country who read? Optimistically, Bob still insists that the problem is not so much our total number as the dispersion of the troops — the fact that there is no existing libertarian periodical in which ads for L. R. could tap a high ratio of eager subscribers. In short, any new conservative periodical or organization does not have to rely on costly direct mailing to a scattered and dispersed audience; it can advertise in **Human Events** or **National Review**. We have no such journal that could serve as a similar advertising outlet.

Bob intends to continue running **Books for Libertarians** indefinitely, in wait for the day when a **Libertarian Review** might become feasible. But there is no brooking the fact that we have, all of us, suffered a serious setback. ▣

Whatever fosters militarism makes for barbarism; whatever fosters peace makes for civilization. There are two fundamentally opposed principles on which social life may be organized — compulsory cooperation and voluntary cooperation, the one implying coercive institutions, the other free institutions. Just in proportion as military activity is great does the coercive regime more pervade the whole society.

— Herbert Spencer

Hospers On Crime And The FBI

The Friends of the FBI, Inc., the organized friends of our national secret police, has published an extensive survey of all the presidential candidates and their answers to its questionnarie (Friends of the FBI, Inc., 1660 L St., N. W., Suite 1214, Washington, D. C. 20036, November 3, 1972). It is instructive to compare the libertarian quality of the answers of John Hospers, the Libertarian Party candidate for President, with those of Dr. Benjamin Spock of the People's Party and of Linda Jenness of the Socialist Workers' Party.

1. Q. Do you favor retention of the FBI as it is now constituted?
   A. **Spock:** No. **Jenness:** No. The FBI should be abolished. **Hospers:** I favor the retention of the FBI . . .

2. Q. Do you favor major changes in its area of responsibility? What changes?
   A. **Spock:** It should get out of this business of judging who is politically respectable, spying on protestors, fabricating false evidence (as in my case), interfering with legal demonstrations . . . These latter activities are unconstitutional and harmful to a democracy. **Hospers:** No.

Chalk up a clear libertarian victory for Spock and Jenness.

3. Q. Should overlapping law enforcement responsibilities as now undertaken by the FBI, Bureau of Narcotics and other policing agencies of the federal establishment be consolidated under one command?
   A. **Spock:** Control of narcotics should be made primarily a medical matter. The FBI should be an investigative organization, not a policing or prosecution or publicly accusatory one . . . **Jenness:** The policing of activities such as heroin and other narcotics pushing should be controlled by the Black, Puerto Rican and Chicano communities which are most affected by them. **Hospers:** Yes.

Spock again comes closest to the libertarian position, which is to eliminate narcotics enforcement altogether. Jenness' answer is simply *idiotic*. But Hospers strikes out again.

3. Q. What is your attitude toward court-authorized electronic surveillance?
   A. **Spock:** Dangerous and impermissible in a democracy because it will always be easily abused for political purposes. **Jenness:** Any use of electronic surveillance, whether court authorized or not, is a violation of every person's basic right to privacy. It is furthermore clearly in violation of the Constitution of the United States. **Hospers:** Courts should be very careful as to what surveillance they authorize, so as not to violate the individual's right of privacy.

Again, Hospers' answer is shilly-shallying, less libertarian than Spock's, and far less than Jenness', who gave the answer that the Libertarian Party candidate should have given.

4. Q. (Essentially) For what criminal activities should electronic surveillance be used?
   A. **Spock:** I oppose its utilization for all types of criminal activities. **Hospers:** It should be employed in combatting: espionage; sedition and treason; organized crime; the illicit drug traffic; criminal conspiracy to commit crimes of violence . . .

Spock here joins Jenness in all-out opposition to electronic surveillance, which is clearly an invasion of the individual's right to privacy in his property. Hospers not only endorses such invasion to combat legitimate crimes, but also for "sedition and treason" (What's that? Isn't libertarianism in itself "seditious"?); organized crime (which is largely the sale of legitimate goods and services unfortunately declared illegal); and the drug traffic (ditto.)

5. Q. What program would you favor to streamline the Federal court procedures so that the accused could be given as rapid a trial as possible?
   A. **Spock:** Many more and better lawyers paid for by the government so that all defendants . . . will be assured a fair trial. Many more judges. **Jenness:** The courts should be reformed to insure not only that the accused gets a speedy trial, but also that it is a fair one. This means that Blacks, and members of other oppressed nationalities in this country should have a jury of their peers . . . This also means the end to excessive bail in political cases. **Hospers:** Increase greatly the number of federal and state judges. Also legislation to the effect that if a trial was not conducted within a certain time, the case would be dropped.

All are bad here. Spock wants more government handouts for compulsory egalitarianism and more mulcting of the taxpayers. Jenness is back with the absurd quota system, but at least indicates that there is something wrong with the bail system, which clearly discriminates against poor defendants. Hospers is fine on calling for speedy trials, but is even worse than the others in urging greater mulcting of the taxpayer for still more incompetent and politically-appointed judges. Surely the libertarian answer would include (a) shifting more cases from government judges to private arbitration, and (b) eliminating the bail system so as to free all defendants not actually caught in the act until their conviction has been obtained.

6. Q. What need do you see for prison reform . . .?
   A. **Spock:** Vast and complete prison reform so that prison is for rehabilitation . . . **Jenness:** (A long list of proposed "rights" for prisoners). **Hospers:** No compulsory mental (psychiatric) detention. If many of the present crimes were no longer legal crimes, the prison load would be greatly relieved.

At long last, a clear-cut libertarian victory for Hospers. Spock sinks into the totalitarian liberal miasma of "rehabilitation", which of course would gauge sentences of prisoners on the judgements of physicians or psychiatrists on whether the prisoners have been "rehabilitated." Jenness would hardly distinguish prisoners from anyone else. Hospers' answer is fine, but needs to be supplemented, particularly by a stress on shifting the entire concept of punishment to emphasize restitution by the criminal to his victim, a concept which is now completely forgotten.

7. Q. Do you consider our present penal laws and court interpretation of them to be as fair to victims as to the accused?
   A. **Spock:** Yes, as far as I know. **Jenness:** (A whole string of irrelevancies about taxing the rich, Angela Davis, the Vietnam War, Third World "oppression", etc.) **Hospers:** No. The accused is constantly reminded of his rights, even when it means that testimony necessary for conviction is thereby made impossible. (Hospers then goes on to advocate the restoration of capital punishment, and concludes:) The pendulum should surely swing back to consideration for the rights of victims.

While stiffer sentences for criminals, including restoration of capital punishment for murder, is a fine libertarian position, one stops short at Hospers' attack on "constantly reminding" the accused of his rights. These rights include the right not to be subject in a forced confession, and are basic to any libertarian concept of society. The difference here, and the vital one, is between an accused person and a convicted criminal. Deal harshly with the latter, but be scrupulous about protecting the rights of a man who is, on Anglo-Saxon as well as libertarian canons of justice, innocent until proven guilty. Hospers has tragically forgotten the canon of the great English jurist Blackstone: "It is better that ten guilty persons escape than that one innocent suffer." On balance, Spock wins out again over Hospers.

8. Q. Which of the following areas of criminal activity deserve top federal priority: organized crime; unorganized street crime; illicit drug traffic; sex crimes; other?
   A. **Spock:** Organized crime deserves top federal priority. **Hospers:** Organized crime and unorganized street crime deserve top federal priority as does illicit drug traffic as long as laws prohibit it. Sex crime does not, except for rape.

Note the logical clinkers here. First, the question does **not** ask which laws should be enforced, but which deserve top priority? Surely, then, a libertarian would **not** advocate top priority for enforcing those laws which should not exist on the books at all. Hospers does this for sex crimes; why not for "illicit drug traffic?" If, on the other hand, Hospers insists on taking the blind rightist position that **all** laws should be enforced to the hilt so long as they are on the books, then why exempt sex crimes? In fact, of course, the top priority here should be unorganized street crime, since "organized crime" is largely legitimate entrepreneurship.

9. Q. Should laws against so-called "victimless" crimes be repealed? If so, which ones? Here all three, **Spock, Jenness,** and **Hospers,** came out in favor of repeal of the whole kit and kaboodle, the libertarian position.

For a brief quantitative summary on matters of crime and the FBI, on the eight separable questions above, Dr. Spock gave the best libertarian answer or tied for the best five times, Linda Jenness three times, and John Hospers three times. ▣

The Blackmailer As Hero

By Walter Block

Is blackmail really illegitimate? At first glance it is not hard to answer this question. The only problem it would seem to pose is why it is being asked at all. For do not blackmailers well, . . . **blackmail** people? And what could be worse? Blackmailers prey on your most hidden deep dark secrets, they threaten to publicize them, they bleed you white, they can even drive you to suicide. Blackmail is so evil that even to consider its legitimacy will strike many as an unmitigated evil; even those scholars who would otherwise favor the spirit of free and untrammeled inquiry.

We shall push on in any case. And we shall find that the critique of the blackmailer falls like a house of cards; we shall find that the case against blackmail is based on a tissue of unexamined shibbleths, blown out of all proportion, and on deep philosophical misunderstandings.

What, exactly, is blackmail? Blackmail is the **offer** of a trade; it is the offer to trade something, usually **silence**, for some other good, usually money. If the offer of the blackmail trade is **accepted**, then the blackmailer maintains his silence and the blackmailee pays the agreed amount of money. If the blackmail offer is **rejected**, then the blackmailer may exercise his right of free speech, and perhaps announce and publicize the secret. Notice that there is nothing amiss here. All that is happening is that an **offer** to maintain silence is being made. If the offer is rejected, the blackmailer does no more than exercise his rights of free speech, something he has a complete right to do in the first place, whether or not the offer is made or accepted.

The only difference between a gossip or blabbermouth and the blackmailer is that the blackmailer will refrain from speaking — for a price. In a sense the gossip or the blabbermouth is much worse than the blackmailer, for the blackmailer at least gives you a chance to shut him up. The blabbermouth and gossip just up and spill the beans. A person with a secret he wants kept will be much better off if a blackmailer rather than a gossip or blabbermouth gets hold of it. With the blabbermouth or gossip, as we have said, all is lost. With the blackmailer, one can only gain, or at worst, be no worse off. If the price required by the blackmailer for his silence is worth less than the secret, the secret-holder will pay off, and accept the lesser of the two evils. He will **gain** the difference to him between the value of the secret and the price of the blackmailer. It is only in the case that the blackmailer demands more than the secret is worth that the information gets publicized. But in this case the secret-keeper is no worse off with the blackmailer than with the inveterate gossip. (He may still be better off with the blackmailer, even here, because the typical blackmailer gains **nothing** if he publicizes the secret — except the dubious value of making sure that the secret-keeper knows he is not bluffing — so the secret keeper may well be able to bargain down the blackmailer's price.) It is indeed difficult, then, to account for the vilification suffered by the blackmailer, at least compared to the gossip, who is usually dismissed with merely slight contempt.

Blackmail need not entail the offer of **silence** in return for money. This is only the most well known form. More generally, blackmail may be defined as threatening to do something, anything, (which is otherwise entirely legal) unless unless the blackmailer's demands, financial or otherwise, are met. In its more general form there are several acts which qualify as blackmail but interestingly enough, far from receiving the vilification associated with blackmail, have even attained respectability among certain segments of the population. As an example, let us consider the lettuce boycott, beloved of every radio-lib worth his limousine.

The lettuce boycott is (a form of) blackmail!! What is being done in the lettuce boycott (and every other boycott, for that matter), what the lettuce boycott **consists of**, is making **threats** to various retailers and wholesalers of fruits and vegetables. These threats are that if the retailer or wholesaler handles non-union lettuce, people will be asked not to patronize their establishments. The not inconsiderable energies, time, and money of the lettuce boycott movement will be brought to bear on all handlers of non-union lettuce.

Now, there are plenty of reasons to oppose the boycott of non-union lettuce. But I am here concerned to show that the lettuce boycott is indeed blackmail, and that, as a form of blackmail, it is entirely **legitimate**. We can see that the lettuce boycott conforms perfectly to the more general definition of blackmail as a threat that something otherwise entirely legal will take place unless the blackmailer's demands are met. In this case, the threat is to withhold patronage from establishments unless they refuse to handle non-union lettuce. Although it is not legal to **threaten** this, it is perfectly legal **not to patronize** establishments that one,

for any reason, does not like. So the lettuce boycott is legitimate, and blackmail as well, a pair of strange bedfellows if ever there was one.

Let us consider the question of the **threats** involved in blackmail, because perhaps more than anything else, it is this aspect of blackmail that is most misunderstood and feared. Now threats are usually considered evil, and rightly so. The usual dictum against aggression warns of aggression against non-aggressors **as well as the threat of such aggression.** And the reason is not hard to fathom. If a highwayman were to accost us, it is usually the **threat** of aggression that will get us to do his bidding. It is the **threat** of aggression that will relieve us of our possessions. If the highwayman actually had to use aggression against us, as opposed to the threat thereof, it would be practically an admission of defeat. So the threat of aggression is entirely illegitimate.

But notice that the threat involved in blackmail is entirely different. In aggression, what is being threatened is aggressive violence, something that the aggressor has no right to do. In blackmail, however, what is being "threatened" is something that the blackmailer most certainly **does** have a right to do! To exercise his right of free speech, to gossip about our secrets, or in the case of the lettuce boycott, to threaten not to patronize certain stores. One can hardly call the "threat" in blackmail a real threat. When contrasted to the real threat of the highwayman, the "threat" of the blackmailer can only be characterized as an offer to keep silent, and not as a real threat at all. The blackmailer never threatens bodily violence or any type of violence. If he did, he would no longer be a legitimate blackmailer; he would be an illegitimate aggressor, who uses threats as a means of coercion.

There is one case where blackmail would not be legitimate, but not because it is blackmail. It would rather be illegitimate because it would be in violation of a contract. For instance, if the secret-keeper takes a lawyer or a private investigator into his confidence **on the condition that,** among other things, **the confidence be maintained in secrecy**, then, if the lawyer or private investigator turns around and tries to blackmail him, it would be in violation of the contract, **and therefore** illegitimate. It is only when the blackmail violates an agreement that it is illegitimate. If there is no contract, if it is a perfect stranger who holds the secret, then the blackmail is legitimate because perfect strangers have free speech rights. It is only someone who has sold his right to speak freely (about the secrets of his client) like the lawyer or the private investigator who then has no right to engage in blackmail.

In addition to being a legitimate activity, blackmail has many good effects, the litanies to the contrary notwithstanding. And once we get over the shock that there is anything at all that can be said in favor of blackmail, it is not too surprising that this should be so. For apart from some innocent victims that get caught in the net, who does the blackmailer prey upon? There are two groups. On the one hand we have the murderer, the thief, the swindler, the embezzler, the cheater, the rapist, etc., all criminals and violators of the stricture against aggression upon non-aggressors. On the other hand we have people who engage in activities which are not illegitimate themselves, but go against the mores and habits of the majority of the people. There are the homosexuals, the sado-masochists, the sex perverts, the communists, the adulterers, etc. It is my contention that the institution of blackmail has beneficial, but different, effects on each of these groups, none of which seem to have been realized by writers on the subject. Let us consider them each in turn.

In the case of the criminals, blackmail, the threat of blackmail, and the very existence of the institution of blackmail serves as a hindrance. It makes the payoff to the criminal less certain and less rewarding because if caught, the criminal must now share some of his "hard won" loot with the blackmailer, with the risk that the blackmailer can always turn him in. Even with blackmail illegal, this can have a much greater effect than many people would believe possible. How many of the anonymous "tips" received by the police can be traced, directly or indirectly, to blackmail? And the value of these tips cannot be over estimated. How many criminals are led to pursue crime on their own, eschewing the aid of fellow criminals in "jobs" that call for cooperation — out of fear of possible later blackmail? Since there are always some people on the verge of committing crimes, or at the margin of criminality, as the economist

(Continued On Page 4)

335

The Blackmailer As Hero —
(Continued From Page 2)

would say, where the least factor will propel them one way or another, the additional fear of crime-related blackmail may be enough, in many cases, to dissuade them from crime.

Imagine then how much more effective blackmail would be in curtailing real crime if blackmail itself were legalized! Then the blackmailer would not have to worry about possible legal steps being taken against him because of his public-spirited preying on criminals. This would undoubtedly encourage the quantity and quality of such blackmail efforts, with attendent depredations upon our criminal class.

It is sometimes said that what diminishes crime is not the penalty attached to the crime but the certainty of being caught. Although this controversy rages with great relevance in the debates on capital punishment, we need not enter into it here. For our purposes it will suffice to point out that the institution of blackmail does **both**. It increases the penalty associated with crime, since criminals are forced to share a part of their loot with the blackmailer. It also raises the probability of being caught, as the blackmailers are now added to the police, private citizens, vigilantes and others whose function if not purpose it is to suppress crime. And let it be added that blackmailers who can often be members of the criminal gang in good standing are in an especially good position to foil crimes. Their "inside" position surpasses even that of a spy or infiltrator, who is forced to play a part. The blackmailer can **live** the part of the criminal, for until he turns against the gang as a blackmailer, he really is a criminal. Legalizing blackmail also will at one fell swoop allow us to take advantage of not one but two crime-fighting adages: "divide and conquer," and "take advantage of the lack of honor among thieves." So it is pretty clear that one effect of legalizing blackmail will be to diminish crimes of aggression.

The legalization of blackmail will also have good effects upon actions which may be illegal but are not criminal in the sense that they involve aggression but are at variance with the mores of the majority of the people. Far from suppressing them, the legalization of blackmail will have a liberating effect.

Even now, with blackmail still illegal, we are witnessing some of its beneficial effects. Let us take homosexuality as an example. Homosexuality may be illegal but is not really criminal since it involves no aggression. For **individual** homosexuals, we must admit, blackmail causes untold harm and can hardly be considered beneficial. But for the group as a whole, or rather, **for each individual** as a member of the group, blackmail has helped. Blackmail has helped the gay community as a whole by making homosexuality more widely known, by making the public more accustomed to homosexuality, and by placing the homosexual in a more open light. In so doing, the blackmailer has contributed to forcing the homosexuals to make themselves more known. Let it be repeated. Forcing individual members of a downtrodden group out into the open, or "out of the closet", can by no stretch of the imagination be considered doing them a favor. Forcing anyone to do anything can usually only violate rights; and forcing someone to do something "for his own good" is a particular rung in hell reserved for liberals. But still it must be realized that practically the only way a downtrodden group of people can attain liberation is by being known to each other so that they can cooperate with each other. And it must be realized that one important effect of blackmail is to force people out into the open where they will be able to know each other. In this way blackmail can legitimately claim some small share in the credit for the liberation of groups whose only crime is to deviate from the norm in some non-criminal way.

It is not surprising that this should be so when we reflect upon the old aphorism that "the truth shall make you free". For the only "weapon" at the disposal of the blackmailer is the truth. If it were not for the truth, the blackmailer would be in no position to be able to blackmail. But in using the truth to back up his threats, as upon occasion he must, without any intention on his part he sets the truth free to do whatever good, as well as whatever bad, it is capable of doing. ◙

The law of nature, being co-eval with mankind, and dictated by God himself, is superior in obligation to every other. It is binding all over the globe, in all countries, and at all times; no human laws are of any validity if contrary to this, and such of them as are valid derive their force and all their authority, mediately or immediately, from the original.

—Blackstone

From The Old Curmudgeon

The Flickering Match. Mr. Fred Woodworth is unhappy. That much, at least, is fairly clear. What he is unhappy about is far less clear, but it seems to revolve about the insufficient recognition accorded to the greatness of Mr. Woodworth and his monthly tabloid **The Match.** Having granted to the State the benefit of their hysterical billingsgate for several years, and having failed to accomplish its immediate overthrow, Mr. Woodworth and his colleagues have now turned their baleful attentions to the libertarian movement. Each faction and tendency in the movement, and the movement itself for that matter, has been in its turn excommunicated by Mr. Woodworth for insufficient purity and for failure to acknowledge the primacy and importance of **The Match.** It is quite true that **The Match** has existed for several years, but quantity does not quality make, as witness the turgid and very long-lasting **The Weekly People,** organ of the Socialist Labor Party. Indeed, **The Match** has ranked for clarity and interest scarcely a centimeter ahead of **The Weekly People,** having focussed on repeated and spectacularly unsuccessful calls for immediate overthrow of the State, and lengthy and turgid reprints from the anarcho-communist classics. The general failure of the libertarian movement to pay much attention to **The Match** is the product, not of a conspiracy as Mr. Woodworth seems to believe, but of simple good sense.

Debasement of Language. The latest phase of the assault by the New Barbarians on the English language is at the same time an assault on biological reality: the campaign to purge the word "man" from the language and substitute the unisexual term "person." If the barbarians have their way, we will soon by subjected to such phrases as the following:
"Quick, send for the repairperson."
"A foeperson worthy of his or her steel."
"The sturdy yeopeople of England."
"The rights of huperson beings."
"Friends, Romans, and countrypeople . . ."
"When is the postperson coming?"
"The International Longshorepeople's Union."
"Madpeople in authority . . ."
"God created person in his own image, in the image of God created he him and her . . . The Lord God formed person of the dust of the ground, and breathed into his or her nostrils the breath of life; and person became a living soul."
"Person is the measure of all things."
"The proper study of personkind is person."

The Christmas Spirit. From Pogo:
1st Character: "You mean we're all dedicated to peace an' love for the next month?"
2nd Character: "Yep . . . with goodwill toward all."
3rd Character: "Kind of takes the bloom off'n the bush don't it?" ◙

The International Commission for Inquiry into War Crimes in Vietnam, founded by Lord Russell in 1967, has recently completed its third session in Copenhagen, Denmark. Two earlier meetings were held in Stockholm and Copenhagen in 1967 and 1968. While the American press did its duty by ignoring as much as it could the evidence that emerged from the tribunal's investigations, the press of Europe gave much greater coverage and the resulting horror among the general public did much to dissipate America's image as a defender of liberty and human dignity. What is most surprising about this latest session of the tribunal is that it was officially opened by a speech of the Danish Prime Minister Anker Joergensen who demanded that the U. S. withdraw from Vietnam. This public association with the privately sponsored "war crimes" tribunal by the Danish leader "shocked" the American State Department which sent a note of displeasure to our NATO ally. Among those who signed reports on American War Crimes submitted to the tribunal was Anthony Russo, a co-defendant in the Pentagon Papers trial; Prof. Chandler Morse of Cornell University; Sean MacBride, former Foreign Minister of Ireland; and — Ramsay Clark, former Attorney General in the cabinet of retired war criminal Lyndon B. Johnson! The times they are a-changing!

Ezra Pound, RIP

By James Dale Davidson

Ezra Pound is dead in Venice at the age of 87. He was recognized as a genius. During his long life he helped to shape modern literature, both through his own work and through the immense influence he exerted on others. Pound discovered Robert Frost, Ernest Hemingway and James Joyce. "It is probable," Joyce wrote, "that but for him I would still be the unknown drudge that he discovered." Under Pound's influence, William Butler Yeats abandoned Celtic romanticism for the mature style which made him one of literature's greatest pgets. Ezra Pound edited "The Waste Land," T. S. Eliot's masterwork, cutting it in half. In appreciation, Eliot lauded Pound with the dedication, "il migior fabbro," (the better artisan). Pound authored a prodigious body of poetry. His bitter masterpiece, "Hugh Selwyn Mauberley," expressed the feelings of a generation after the disillusionment of World War I.

There died a myriad,
And of the best, among them,
For an old bitch gone in the teeth,
For a botched civilazation.

. . .

For two gross of broken statues,
For a few thousand battered books.

The Cantos, a huge, rambling poem which occupied Pound for most of his life, has generated divided critical comment. Attacked by some as incoherent, it has been praised by others as the great epic of modern times.

Perhaps one of the great translators in history, Pound published English versions of works written in such diverse tongues as: Chinese, Ancient Egyptian, Anglo-Saxon, Hindi, Italian, Japanese, Latin, Greek, French, and Provencal. He even found time to write an opera, "The Testament of Francois Villon."

Few men have assumed a more dominant role in the literature of their time. Yet Pound died an exile, shunned by the liberal intelligentsia. In an article published in World magazine just two weeks before Pound's death, critic Irving Howe wrote, "The time has not yet come when Ezra Pound should be honored by his fellow writers." That is a rather problematic statement considering that Pound has already been honored by his fellow writers. His great contemporaries, Eliot, Yeats, Joyce, Frost, Hemingway, William Carlos Williams, and others were high in his praise. What Howe really means by the phrase "his fellow writers" is the New York liberal establishment, the self-important moral guardians of the world.

Howe and his associates will be long forgotten when Ezra Pound is still remembered. Yet they should not remain unanswered. Why deny Pound the honor due a great poet? Because he was a bad man? Because he was illiberal? Pound has been considered bad for one reason — he did not support American participation in World War II. In fact, he loudly opposed the war, openly urging an end to the hostilities. His position in regard to World War II was not unlike that of innumerable liberal luminaries toward the unhappy War in Vietnam. Pound spoke out. But in his case he spoke out over Rome Radio and was indicted for treason.

When the U. S. entered the Second World War, Pound was earning a living broadcasting commentary in Italy, where he had been a resident for several decades. Upon hearing that war had been declared, Pound rushed from Rome to his home in Rapallo, sold everything, and planned to leave with the other Americans aboard the last train to Lisbon. But the American consul refused to allow him on the train. Denied the right of refuge, Pound was trapped. Faced with financial ruin, he continued his radio program on the condition he would never be asked to say anything "contrary to his conscience or contrary to his duties as an American citizen — which promise was faithfully observed by the Italian government." Upon the War's end, Pound was arrested by American soldiers and thrown into a prison camp. There he was left exposed to the elements, imprisoned in an open steel cage at the age of 60. Somehow, he survived. When he was returned to the United States he was never able to stand trial. Instead, he was declared "insane" and committed to St. Elizabeth's mental hospital. There he remained for 12 years.

The shoddy treatment which Pound suffered at the hands of the American government was in many ways parallel to the treatment afforded Alexander Solzhenitsyn by the Soviet state. Both were arrested in 1945. Both were arrested for criticizing their respective governments — Solzhenitsyn in a letter and Pound before a microphone. Both confined in conditions of cruelty, Pound in a military prison camp and Solzhenitsyn in Siberia, where he was kept in a cell with frozen walls, protected only by underwear. Both Pound and Solzhenitsyn have been accused of "insanity", primarily because of their political views. The parallel is a strong one. But there it ends.

While Solzhenitsyn is accorded the support he deserves in his struggle with state tyranny, Pound was shunned until the moment of his death. The critics, professors, and cross-word puzzle experts who earn their livings jabbering over the literature Pound helped to create, imagine themselves too moral to extend him their praise.

This is not to say that a writer's values, political and otherwise, are irrelevant to the merit of his work. Far from it. Every writer's reputation should suffer to the extent that his writing extols fallacious and destructive ideas. Most of the poets and novelists of this or any era have been thoroughly mixed up about many facets of life. John Stuart Mill described Samuel Taylor Coleridge as an "arrant driveller," when it came to his abilities as a political economist. From a libertarian perspective, that charge applies to Pound. But that should not blind us to the strengths of Pound's insight. He deserves credit for a valiant effort to penetrate the political and cultural morass in which we still live. As a humane and perceptive man, he sought answers to the sickness of civilization, as it was revealed in the destruction of World War I. Writing in 1918 Pound said he, "began investigation of the causes of war, to oppose same." To his credit, he sought a systematic solution, one which recognized the overwhelming impact of economics. If the solution he achieved was imperfect; tinged with Fascistic implications, Pound more than requited his error by enduring imprisonment for thirteen years.

The fact that Pound admired Fascists is no worse from a libertarian point of view than the fact that Irving Howe and company admire liberal corporatists who are little different from Fascists. In fact, Pound saw some of the evils facing society with a good deal more acuity than his liberal critics. He was almost alone among writers in understanding that inflation is one of the pervasive factors curtailing civilization. Much of his poetry is devoted to attacking the practise of banking as it is known in the modern world — whereby banks create money out of nothing and then charge interest on it. He said:

"and the two largest rackets are the alteration
     Of the value of money
       (Of the unit of money . . .)
and usury   or lending
     that which is made out of nothing."
         (Canto 74)

Even though Pound employed a muddled definition of "usury", this is a valid liberation concern. He simply lacked a sound theoretical base from which to develop a solution.

In studying the causes of World War I, Pound reached much the same conclusion as that achieved by revisionist historians. He felt that the war was brought on by international profiteers. Like the John Birch Society, Pound considered the Federal Reserve to be a private corporation, and agitated for "government" takeover of the money supply. This is why he admired Mussolini. He believed Fascism would end inflation. "Mussolini," Pound wrote, "followed Andrew Jackson in opposing the tyranny of state debt." Too bad he never read What Has Government Done To Our Money?

Pound was off the mark, but not that far off. Although he was accused of Anti-Semitism, he made clear he was not opposed to Jews, only to the Rothschilds, who remain the prototype of scheming bankers. He said, "I am accused of Anti-Semitism. Why then do I respect Spinoza, esteem Montaigne as a writer, and work to re-establish the fame of Alex del Mar, who I believe was a Jew?" Although he erred in believing Fascism could eliminate inflation, Pound had an essentially accurate view of the evils of state control. "Socialism," he said, "is synonymous for imbecility because it wants to govern by multiplying bureaucracies, tyrannicaly controlling all minor activities . . ."

Yes, there is much in Pound to delight a libertarian. What man who said "I have a total contempt for Marx and Freud," could be all bad? His

(Continued On Page 7)

We Make The Electoral College!

On December 18, the august members of the Electoral College met to cast their votes for President and Vice-President of the United States. Constitutionally, the electors can vote for anyone they please, and on that day, to the undoubted consternation of the Establishment, one of the presumed Nixon electors from Virginia cast his vote for John Hospers and Toni Nathan for President and Vice-President.

The publicity value for libertarianism and for the Libertarian Party was enormous, and it surely more than justifies the decision of the LP to wage its campaign. Why, Hospers and Nathan got almost as many electoral votes as McGovern and Shriver!

Who is this intrepid elector, this man who quietly defied the political gods? He does not, in fact, come out of the blue. Middle-aged libertarians remember him well as a leading, if rather moderate, member of the movement: Roger Lea MacBride, grandson and executor of the notable libertarian writer Rose Wilder Lane. Born in 1929, Rober graduated from Princeton, where he was one of the founders of the "Free Enterprise Society", and from which he went on to Harvard Law School, where he managed to keep his strict constructionist outlook. While at Harvard, he wrote a scholarly booklet on The American Electoral College, which Caxton published in 1953. After graduation, Roger settled down in Vermont, and into conservative-libertarian Republican politics; for several years he was a Representative in a State House. In later years, Roger moved to Charlottesville, Virginia, where he rose to prominence in Republican party affairs, in 1972 becoming a Presidential elector. The over-confident Republicans had forgotten the libertarian who lurked beneath the common Republican rhetoric — not knowing that for MacBride the talk of freedom was not just rhetoric but very serious business indeed.

MacBride did not simply cast his maverick vote; he explained his position. He declared his vote to be "an attempt to put party principle ahead of party politics." MacBride added that "in casting my vote for another candidate I am trying to tell (President Nixon) that he has lost his way; that this country should not move to a controlled mercantilistic economy . . ." He explained that he could not vote for Nixon because he has moved the government toward "ever greater control over the lives of us all." (Ronald Taylor, "Electoral College Confirms Nixon Despite Defector," Washington Post, Dec. 19.)

In an appreciative column written on the day of the vote, Nicholas von Hoffman tells us more about Roger and his choice. (von Hoffman, "A First Vote, Maybe a Last," Washington Post, Dec. 18.) Von Hoffman relates that the Republican politicos in Virginia "must have thought he was just another guy after the boodle and not a convinced and deeply strict constructionist." MacBride agonized over the decision ("This is no overly demonstrative Abbie Hoffman of the far right.") He further quotes from Roger his worry about the slide of the country into "Connalyism, the managed controls for corporations . . . the return to mercantilism . . . What I'm really trying to say by this is, 'Break loose from Big Brother.'" Hear, hear!

Von Hoffman also writes appreciatively of the now-forgotten Bricker

Freedom, Pot, And National Review

It is rare indeed that any debate takes place within the august pages of National Review, and few that did not involve the late Frank Meyer, with Frank generally taking the libertarian position. But now the headlines have been made with NR's October 8 issue, over the question of legalizing marijuana. Generally, the libertarian reaction has been chortling or huzzahing over the partial conversion of Bill Buckley to the call for legalization. I submit that this is an unfortunately simplistic response.

In the first place, Richard Cowan's article in favor of legalization was not at all on libertarian grounds. On the contrary, the burden of his article was that pot should be legalized because it is not very harmful, if it be harmful at all. Buckley's conversion is on similar grounds. Even so, he inconsistently advocates not legalization but "decriminalization", which apparently means that the sale of marijuana should be illegal but not its purchase or possession. Buckley apparently feels that it is argument enough to say that "Thus it was, mostly, under prohibition." Is Prohibition to be the model of the free or the good society? In a press conference,

(Continued On Page 7)

Amendment, derided by all right-thinking liberals in the fifties as "isolationist, looney-bin right-wing-ism, and the kind of thinking that martyred Woodrow Wilson and destroyed the League of Nations." He notes that MacBride had written another book in favor of the Bricker Amendment, "a proposed constitutional amendment that would have subjugated to the advice and consent of the Senate the President's powers to make executive agreements with foreign powers." But, as von Hoffman trenchantly concludes, "It got shot down and we marched into Vietnam and now it's Fulbright and the sophisticates (who bitterly opposed the Bricker Amendment at the time) who'd like to get it back."

Welcome, Roger, it's a pleasure to see you strike a powerful and publicity-packed blow for liberty. And the Hospers-Nathan ticket now become, at the very least, immortalized in the record books. ▣

Recommended Reading

Authority vs. Power. Too many libertarians make the mistake of believing that liberty is the polar opposite of "authority". The brilliant conservative sociologist R. A. Nisbet has been demonstrating just the reverse: that genuine authority, the authority of standards, of civilization, of language, above all of reason, is based on voluntary consent. Furthermore, the mistaken revolt against this kind of authority leads to cultural and social chaos, and finally to a turning toward the imposition of social order by force, by the evil of power and coercion, particularly by an adored dictator (Mao, Fidel). For the most recent of his writings on this subject, see Robert A. Nisbet, "The Nemesis of Authority", Intercollegiate Review (Winter-Spring 1972). Should be particularly sobering reading for our left-wing.

Child Labor. Nearly a half century ago, the young English economist William H. Hutt published a remarkable article pointing out that the child labor prevalent in the England of the Industrial Revolution was really a boon to the working children and their families, considered in the context of their previous miserable existence. The article was reprinted in F. A. Hayek's classic volume of collected essays in defense of the Industrial Revolution, Capitalism and the Historians. Last year, the English leftist Brian Inglis attacked the five-decade old article; now Professor Hutt publishes his cogent reply, which serves to update his original contribution. Important for anyone interested in the Industrial Revolution. See W. H. Hutt, "The Poor Who Were With Us," Encounter (November, 1972).

Railroad Regulation. Albro Martin's widely hailed Enterprise Denied is an attempt to criticize American railroad regulation in the twentieth century. But in a devastating review-article, Professor George Hilton, an outstanding authority on railroad history, shows that Martin understands neither the economics of cartels nor the historical contributions of Gabriel Kolko, and thus believes that the railroads have been opposed to federal regulation. Hilton shows that Martin's policy conclusions fit with his analytic mistakes, since he wants only to modify the regulation but leave the crippling cartellizing programs of the ICC. Hilton, in contrast, clearly advocates the ICC's abolition. George W. Hilton, "Albro Martin's Enterprise Denied," The Bell Journal of Economics and Management Science (Autumn, 1972).

Isolationism. Professor Justus Doenecke, our foremost historian of America isolationists, has reworked his study of Lawrence Dennis which originally appeared in Libertarian Analysis. See Justus D. Doenecke, "Lawrence Dennis: Revisionist of the Cold War," Wisconsin Magazine of History (Summer, 1972). ▣

Ezra Pound, RIP —

(Continued From Page 5)

understanding of space exploration seems more to the point than that of some self-processed libertarians. "You cannot live in a Sputnik and you cannot find your food in a Sputnik. What mankind needs is an internal harmony, which may balance the increase of brutality and desperation we are living through." True enough. And in an age when Bleeding-Heart liberalism has permeated everything, with myriad crackpot groups seeking subsidy and "reparations" from the society which has "held them down," it is still refreshing to read Pound. "No one in society," he wrote, "has any right to blame his troubles on anyone else. Liberal thought has been a mess mush because of the tendency to produce this state of mind." He did have a talent for language.

Though the liberals may be silent about Pound, in death as in life, his work contains much to please a discerning reader. With all its obscurity, his poetry sparkles. And it is the record of a man who not only wrote out · his vision of the tragedy of modern life, but suffered for it as well. Remembering his years in prison and the insane asylum it is not hard to hope that "Uncle Ez," as he sometimes called himself, rests in peace.   ▣

Freedom, Pot —

(Continued From Page 6)

Buckley added the sly note that he himself had once smoked the weed, but, as befits a staunch defender of law-and-order, only on a yacht outside the three-mile limit. Are we supposed to applaud Mr. Buckley's fortunate status as yacht-owner?

The libertarian case for legalization of **anything** has nothing whatever to do with whether it is harmful or not. The libertarian maintains that it is up to each individual to run his own life, and that it is his right, as Herbert Spencer once wrote, to go to hell in his own way if he so chooses. The argument against Prohibition had nothing to do with whether or how much alcohol could be harmful; so that medical reports or statistics on drunken driving were totally beside the point. Put on such grounds, it was Professor Jeffrey Hart, an opponent of legalization and an anti-libertarian who had by far the best of the debate. Hart stated at the beginning that he didn't care, in the context of the argument, whether or not marijuana was harmful; for even if it is, "that doesn't mean they (harmful things) should be illegal . . ." Hart seized unerringly upon the note of special pleading in the Cowan article, the implication that Cowan favors legalization because he personally considers it it a good thing. In particular, Hart jumped on this passage of Cowan: "The importance of marijuana to its youthful users is less the pleasure it gives the individual than the tribal value of it. The drug's use in the counterculture is . . . as a social lubricant . . . so fundamental a part of the new social life . . ."

Hart responded to this in a magnificently Old Curmudgeonly manner. Hart replies that "Marijuana is indeed an integral part of the counter-culture of the 1960's", and it is precisely because Professor Hart — along with the bulk of Middle America — would like to smash that counter-culture that he favors maintaining the current status of the law. As Hart writes with relish: "the meaning of those laws in the current historical circumstance is plain enough. They aim to lean on, to penalize the counterculture. They reflect the opinion, surely a majority one, that the counterculture, and its manners and morals, and all its works are bad." He concludes: "as for the 'new social life', écrasez l'infâme."

Mr. Hart has scored some palpable hits. Not only against Mr. Cowan but also against all too many libertarians. For many libertarians address the marijuana issue not simply in the terms: "Everyone has the right to run his own life"; but also with the claim **either** that marijuana is harmless or even that it is a positive good. The underlying note of special pleading on this issue is all too often evident.

It is important for libertarians to set the record straight on this issue. It is important, for one, to make it crystal clear that calling for the **legalization of anything** never implies for the libertarian any sort of advocacy of the thing itself. The libertarian, for example, favors the legalization of gambling, **not** because we advocate gambling as a good thing, but because this is part of every person's right to order his own life in his own way.

There is an excellent way, I submit, to make the libertarian position crystal clear in the case of marijuana; it is a way, furthermore, that will extend the emphasis of the libertarian position itself. And that way is **always** to link marijuana with heroin. For no one says that heroin is harmless; and, what is more no one is running around the country advocating the "philosophy" of taking heroin as a method of "greening" or of "expanding one's consciousness." Every thinking person hates and

A Response To The Challenge

The editor of **The Libertarian Forum** puts the following challenge to those who consider government a morally justifiable, even necessary, part of a free society:

> Suppose that, heedless of your edicts, two or more competing private defense agencies exist already within a given geographical area. Each consciously pursues and applies a libertarian law code which all of us would agree to. On which one of these agencies would you bestow your approval, and which would you presume to outlaw? What would be your criteria for choosing one over the others?

I submit that this is a totally impossible supposition, a contradiction in terms. For the following reasons:

If libertarian law applies within a given area, and that area is inhabited by individuals who own the properties that are part of the area, these individuals could not make a contract with two separate law enforcement agencies pertaining to the protection of the **same** properties. This is because hiring one party to protect my property excludes hiring another to do the same thing in the same respect. So two competing defense agencies cannot exist within the same given geographical area, not under libertarian law. (I am assuming that libertarian law does not violate the laws of identity and non-contradiction.)

The rest of the questions do not apply — no choice need be made between two such agencies in the same area, since two such agencies **could not exist** within the same area. Thus no criteria would have to be established for making such a choice.

The editor of LF posed an interesting challenge. I believe that I have met it. But let me speculate on what he might answer to the response above.

He might say that "given geographical area" does not mean "same given geographical area." It means: "the same general vicinity". But this is something very different. A general vicinity may or may not be suitable for service by different "defense agencies". Thus the general vicinity of Germany is serviced by the government in Bonn, the general vicinity of Spain by the government in Madrid, etc., etc. But the general vicinity of North America is serviced by the governments in Washington and Ottawa, while the general vicinity of South America is serviced by the governments in the various Latin American capitol cities. So what is a general vicinity, a "given geographical area"?

The editor of LF does not say and so his problem is not clearly enough stated for a solution.

The fact is that when we speak of servicing an area with law enforcement, we must specify the criterion of **jurisdiction**. The advocate of **government by the consent of the governed** argues that at any specified period of time, consistent with the type of service involved, etc., only **one** law enforcing agent or agency, under a unified authority, can and ought to be given jurisdiction; this because with more than one agent, conflict of authority, diversity of purpose and method of operations, etc., will develop, such that the goal of law enforcement will suffer. (It is as if one had two "powers of attorneys", two people empowered to act in one's own behalf, each bound separately by the same commitments, each acting separately in one's best interest, each concerned with the same tasks. Impossible.)

Strictly speaking, government by the consent of the governed carries only a minimum of rules or requirements that lead to (contextually) **fixed** provisions. One of them is that two governments cannot service the same geographical area for the same purpose, at the same time, etc. The precise length of service is left open. The condition of disengaging (and engaging) service is left open, also (except for certain moral provisions). And, most importantly, the **size** of the geographical area being serviced by any law enforcer is left open; here the matter hinges primarily on convenience and (contextual) necessity. Just as the markets of bakers, car manufacturers, barbers, and lawyers differ in size, so the markets ser-

(Continued On Page 8)

reviles heroin. So therefore if we always link our advocacy of legalization of the two drugs there will be no possible confusion or implication that we favor pot for its own sake, and, furthermore, the idea of legalizing heroin would also be advanced at the same time. If someone asks us whether we favor legalizing pot, let us therefore always answer: "Yes, and heroin too, and for the same reason." Let the special pleaders wince though they may.   ▣

A Response To The Challenge —

(Continued From Page 7)

viced by a given government would differ, depending on the specific requirements of the service being rendered. (After all, the governments of Lichtenstein and mainland China "service" different size markets — or would, if they were governments by the consent of the governed.)

What the editor of LF and many others do not realize is that in a sense there already exists competition between law enforcement agencies, only their kind of law and enforcement is in need of serious improvement.

Finally, I would like to request of the editor of LF that he refrain from characterizing my view as "Utopian Randian". That is simply a smear and is not called for in the attempt to undertake to solve a difficult set of problems in political theory.

— —Tibor R. Machan

The Editor Replies

Dr. Machan has indeed firmly grasped one horn of the dilemma confronting all advocates of a voluntarily-supported but compulsory monopoly government (whom we may call "Randian" political theorists for short.) But in doing so Dr. Machan has, willy-nilly and apparently unwittingly, fallen headlong into anarcho-capitalism! For by reducing his supposed inner contradiction to the individual ("hiring one party to protect my property excludes hiring another . . .", etc.), he had precisely adopted my position. It is precisely my view that each individual should have the right to subscribe to any police or other defense service he wishes to protect his own property. But if Smith has this right, and Jones, etc. each with his own property, this is what anarcho-capitalism is all about. The Randian position asserts that there must be a single monopoly defense agency over a given territorial area; the area is never specified — which is a basic flaw in the entire position — but whatever it is, whether Canada or Lichtenstein, it must assuredly be larger than the property of one individual. And it is that concept to which I threw down my challenge. For if Dr. Machan is really arguing for the "geographical area" being the property of each individual, then he has indeed adopted anarcho-capitalism, and we must welcome him to our ranks.

Actually, Dr. Machan's alleged inner contradiction is not even correct when dealing with an individual's property. For while it is not very likely empirically, there is certainly no inner contradiction, no impossibility in reality, for an individual to purchase the services of two or more defense agencies in protecting his property. An individual, after all, can and does subscribe to two or more life insurance policies with different companies, or two fire insurance policies over the same property.

To rephrase our challenge to the Randian political theorists: You assert that for any given geographical area (that area being defined as larger than the property of one individual) there must be a compulsory monopoly of defense service. But suppose that two or more such defense agencies, despite your pronouncements, already exist in that area, each consciously pursuing and applying what we would all agree was a libertarian law code of outlawing aggression against the person or property of another. On which one of these agencies would you bestow your approval, and which would you presume to declare an outlaw? And what would be your criteria of choice for one over the others?

Bormann Once More

Every year or so some poor devil in South America is seized by the scruff of the neck, taken to the capital city, and fingerprinted and harassed without mercy, under the claim that he is the Real Martin Bormann, former high official of the Nazi regime. Usually he is an impoverished peasant of German extraction, and usually the legalized kidnapping is done at the behest of the Israeli espionage service, which seems to have the run of the nations of the world. After a couple of weeks, the evidence becomes manifest that the poor lug is not Bormann, sighs of regret go up around the world, and the peasant is kicked back to his home without so much as a by-your-leave. The sighs of regret, it need hardly be added, are not for the injustice done to the peasant, but to the new failure to apprehend Herr Bormann.

Now a new team of writers maintain that they have at last found the True Bormann, and that he is, would you believe, Alive and Well and Living in Argentina. We have no way of knowing at this writing whether he is a true or a pseudo-Bormann, but we would like to advance the heresy that it doesn't really matter very much. And the further heresy that whether he is or not, this new patsy should be left alone, to end his days in peace.

It is now 27 years after the end of World War II, after the liquidation of the Nazi regime. How much longer is that bloody war to go on, to creep onward claiming yet one more victim? We hold no brief for any state official, but Bormann is not being pursued for the rest of his life and perhaps into the grave for any crimes that he or the German state may have committed over its citizens. He and his colleagues are being pursued for the crime of making war, and that is a crime that only the losers in a war ever get punished for. The judgment at Nuremberg, was in the words of the English writer Montgomery Belgion, indeed "victor's justice", and the high war-making crimes of the Allied victors did not so much as come into question, much less enter the dock at Nuremberg. When the war-making rulers of any other country than Germany or Japan begin to receive equivalent justice from war crimes' tribunals, then it will be time enough to pursue the last remnants of the National Socialist regime. In the meantime, how about letting the old guy alone, and turning our attention to currently active war crimes?

While we are on the subject of amnesty for Bormann, we might mention the case of that long-standing "prisoner of peace", Rudolf Hess, who still languishes, 27 years after the war, in solitary confinement in Spandau prison. Hess, defecting from his role as a top official in the Nazi regime, flew alone to Britain during the war in a vain attempt to negotiate peace. Important Communist defectors are invariably given the royal treatment in the West; yet Hess, for his pains, has only received lifetime solitary imprisonment at Spandau. Where are the cries for amnesty in the Hess case? Where are all the leftists who have been howling to "Free Huey", "Free Angela," and "Free All Political Prisoners"? Why are they so silent on the longest-standing political prisoner of them all? Why are there no campus radicals chalking "Free Rudolf" on the walls of ivy?

"In all sorts of government man is made to believe himself free and to be in chains." —King Stanislaus Lesscynski of Poland

340

A Monthly Newsletter

THE
Libertarian Forum

Joseph R. Peden, Pubiisher   Murray N. Rothbard, Editor

VOLUME IV, NO. 11   JANUARY, 1973   75¢

The Apotheosis Of Harry

The American postal authorities used to boast that neither rain nor sleet, etc. shall stay those intrepid couriers on their vital rounds. But as 1972 drew to its end, the mail was suddenly stopped by federal order. In a way, I suppose that this gesture was an appropriate one: a final kick in the teeth of the American public by the shade of Harry S. Truman.

Surely the scale and grandeur of the apotheosis of Harry Truman was unprecedented, even for a media that fawns abjectly upon all Presidents, past and present. When Ike Eisenhower — surely the best President in the past half-century, though this is scarcely a fulsome compliment — died, there was little of the media hysteria lavished upon Truman: at least I do not remember that every network lavished continuing attention for days upon every detail of the President's life as well as his funeral arrangements. And I'm certain that the mail wasn't stopped.

But there is method in the madness. For it was the role of the little "populist" from Kansas City's Pendergast machine to bring this country into the full-scale system that has characterized us since World War II: into our modern role as Corporate State at home and Emperor and Global Crusader abroad. If Franklin D. Roosevelt was the Moses who brought America toward the Promised Land of Corporate Monopoly Empire, with the President as all-powerful Emperor at home and abroad, then Harry Truman was the Joshua who completed the Rooseveltian task. In paying tribute to Harry Truman with the utmost sycophancy, the media are celebrating the present and seemingly permanent **status quo**. It is in this light, too, that we must consider the fulsome tribute paid to Truman by his one-time supposed "enemy", Richard Nixon.

In point of fact, there was scarcely a single act committed by President Truman that was not the quintessence of evil; the Truman administration was an unmitigated disaster for freedom, both at home and abroad. It was Harry Truman who launched and then institutionalized the Cold War; it was Harry Truman who fastened the military-industrial complex and the garrison state upon America. It was Harry Truman who in-stitutionalized government budgets that were gigantic by any peacetime criteria in the history of the country. It was Truman who carved out the policy of permanent counter-revolutionary suppression of radical movements in the Third World: from Greece to Iran to the Middle East. It was Truman who put America permanently in Asia as the world "policeman" by his unconstitutional act of entering the Korean civil con-flict. It was Truman who, in short, first boldly took us into war without so much as requesting a declaration of war from Congress (in Korea), and thereby cemented the absolute despotism of the Chief Executive in foreign affairs in an act far beyond anything which Franklin Roosevelt had ever contemplated. It was Truman who induced the United Nations to seize Arab lands on behalf of the new state of Israel.

It was Truman, furthermore, who took us in a giant leap toward domestic collectivism and bureaucratic socialism, with his Fair Deal program, a program that later bore fruit in federal aid to education, Medicare, and compulsory integration. It was Truman who instituted price and wage controls during the Korean conflict, and whose "state of emergency" has continued ever since, to account for a raft of domestic despotism. It was Truman, moreover, who severely repressed civil liber-ties with his loyalty and security programs; not Joe McCarthy but Harry Truman was the real and effective opponent of civil liberties during the late 1940's and early fifties. Consider the unfortunate hacks whom Truman appointed to the Supreme Court: every one a defender of govern-ment prerogatives in every area as against the liberty of the individual. Look around at the Truman record, and there is scarcely a single area that one can observe without indignation; his administration was truly a cornucopia of horrors.

Last but not least, there was the Truman act of mass murder of inno-cent civilians at Hiroshima, compounded by Nagasaki. His decision to drop the atomic bomb for the first and let us hope the last times, was done for "reasons of State" as a counter in the emerging Cold War. Not only was it totally unnecessary as a measure to defeat Japan, but what is more Truman knew full well that it was unnecessary. In the long and bloody record of shame in American foreign policy, there is no single act of degradation that can compare with this.

In face of the ghastly Truman record, we cannot remain silent in obedience to the polite canon that one must not speak ill of the dead. If we cannot speak ill of the dead, where is the justice that only the historian can bring to the record of the past? The great classical liberal historian Lord Acton once wrote that the muse of the historian must not be Clio, as generally thought, but Rhadamanthus, the legendary avenger of innocent blood. And in the case of Harry S. Truman, there is O so much blood to avenge. ▣

Sex Breaks Up A Cult

Many Americans have gone in for Indian swami cults. In the swami cult, the Swami is the absolute leader whose every word and act is venerated by his adoring followers. One of the most popular and charismatic swamis has been the Swami Satchidananda, who came to the U. S. from Ceylon in the mid-60's, and who amassed, under the aegis of his Integral Yoga Institue: 25 centers, 5000 initiates, and 20,000 serious students. From the revenue from these followers, the Swami has gained a luxurious pad in Connecticut, as well as a jet-set life style and famous show biz luminaries as his disciples.

But then a serpent came to Eden. The Swami had always preached strict celibacy for his cult members, a celibacy which seemed to fit the holiness and wisdom exuded by the Swami's message. But, this summer, it turned out that the Swami may have believed himself to be above the moral law he had preached. For one of his leading disciples broke with the Master and charged in some detail that she and the Swami had been having sexual relations for some time.

Grave crisis struck the cult. As Howard Smith writes in the Village Voice (Dec. 14): "All that inner peace trembled. Coast-to-coast wild rumors and racy stories swirled through the incense smoke. Emergency meetings were held, accusations flew, counter-plots and counter-coups

(Continued On Page 2)

Sex Breaks Up A Cult —

(Continued From Page 1)

were rampant. General confusion led to schisms and disgust. For a while it was like Peyton Place among the Karma Cadre."

Two factions, a pro- and anti-Swami faction, developed. The pros cleverly pointed out that the Swami "had never actually come right out in plain words and said he was celibate. It was they who tricked themselves." The anti-wing left the whole movement in despair, maintaining that "he is a phony therefore it is all phony." The pros were also shaken, but they tried in vain to hush the whole thing up. Finally, even the pros gave the Swami two alternatives: (1) either stay as the Swami but play down the emphasis on celibacy; or (2) get out as the Swami.

After a display of much "righteous anger", the Swami Satchidananda "took a kind of guru-ish Fifth Amendment — I am your master and therefore I shouldn't be questioned." Finally, the Swami wrote a letter to his disciples admitting nothing and telling them it was time for them to take their spiritual enlightenment in their own hands.

Once again, as so many times in history (e.g. the Saint-Simonians, the Comtean movement), Sex had broken up a cult. Do libertarians see any parallels? ◼

The Pimp As Hero

By Walter Block

The honest, hard working, long suffering pimp has been demeaned unjustly long enough. It is time, it is past time, that this ancient wrong be set right. In this day and age, pimps have been singled out for ridicule because of their pinky rings, their flashy custom-made Cadillacs, their fur coats. From time immemorial, pimps have everywhere been treated as parasites who prey upon prostitutes. Even revolutionary groups, who might have been thought to be able to empathize with other downtrodden minority groups, have viciousely turned on pimps.

If we are ever to make a fair assessment of this harassed minority group, we must endeavor to calmly and dispassionately take stock of what in actuality the pimp does. We can no longer depend upon old wives tales or "folk wisdom". But before we begin our analysis, we must clear up one point: the claim that pimps use coercion and the threat of violence (to gather and keep a stable of prostitutes on their payrolls). Of course some pimps do! This, however, in no way contradicts our view of the pimp as an honest and productive workingman. Is there any profession where not one practitioner is guilty of foul play? Of course not. There are bricklayers, plumbers, musicians, priests, doctors, lawyers, Indian chiefs who have gone berserk and violated the rights of their fellow creatures. Are these professions, then, qua professions to be castigated in their entirety? Of course not. And so should it be with the ancient and honorable profession of pimping: the actions of any one, or even of all pimps together, cannot legitimately be used to condemn the profession qua profession, unless the action is a necessary part of the profession. It is in this way that we know, for instance, that the profession of kidnapping small children for ransom is an evil profession, qua profession. The action is evil and is a necessary part of the profession.

In this case, if some of the practitioners perform good deeds like contributing a part of the "take" to charity, or are "good family men", or even if all of them do so, the profession is still an abomination. It is an abomination because by its very nature evil acts are committed in its name. In this article then, we shall try to evaluate the profession of pimping, ignoring the evil acts performed by some pimps which have nothing to do with their profession.

The function the pimping profession serves is that of a broker. Just like brokers of real estate, insurance, stock market shares, investments or commodity futures, the pimp-broker serves the function of bringing two parties to a transaction together at less cost than it would take to bring them together without his good offices. We know that each party to a transaction served by a broker gains from the brokerage. Each party to the transaction is just as free to look for the other party without the aid of the broker, as he (or she) is to make use of the brokerage services for the brokering fee. From the fact that people voluntarily patronize brokers we know that, at least in their own minds, they are benefiting from the existence of the brokers.

And so in the case of the pimps. The customers gain from the use of pimps in that they are spared useless or wasteful waiting and searching time. Many customers would rather phone a pimp whom they trust for an assignation with a prostitute than spend time and effort searching one out. For one thing, the customers can gain the security of knowing that the prostitute comes recommended by the pimp. For another, all the customer need do is pick up the phone; he need not even venture outside to find a prostitute. And on rainy days, this can be of inestimable benefit. As for the prostitute, she (or he) also gains — or else, as we have seen, she would not work through a pimp. The prostitute gains the time that would otherwise be spent in searching for customers. And as every good businessman knows, time is money. The prostitute can also gain the security of knowing that there is some modicum of protection supplied by the pimp; in this profession, the customers that one deals with sometimes leave something to be desired. More important than protection against unruly customers, as important as that may be, is the problem of protection against policemen, whose profession, qua profession, it might be added, consists of harassing prostitutes who are engaged in voluntary trade with consenting adults. The pimp is of inestimable aid to the prostitute in this regard, in that assignations by phone are much less dangerous than streetwalking or bar hopping.

Then there is the problem of wear and tear on sometimes very expensive clothing. The prostitute working without benefit of a pimp must constantly dress and undress between customers. With a pimp setting up appointments one right after the other, there is little or no need for engaging in such costly and uneconomical activity. Thus, far from raising the costs of the service the pimp, like any other broker worth his salt, will actually lower the costs.

The prostitute is no more exploited by the pimp than is the manufacturer exploited by the salesman whom he hires to go out and drum up business for him. The prostitute is no more exploited by the pimp than is the actress who pays an agent a percentage of her earnings to go out and get jobs for her. In all these cases, the prostitute-employer earns more than the cost to her of the employee-pimp, otherwise the employer-employee relationship would not take place. And this is a precise way to look at the relationship that the prostitute bears with respect to the pimp: employer to employee.

We have defended the professional pimp on the grounds that he performs the important and even necessary function of brokering. Actually, however, the pimp's profession is more honorable than many of the other brokering professions because several of them, such as banking, insurance or the stock market in many respects rely on restrictive state laws to discourage their competition. Whatever may be said of pimps, it cannot be said that they have stooped that low. ◼

The High Priests Of Waste

By A. Ernest Fitzgerald
(398 pages. Norton. $8.95.)

Reviewed By Robert Sherrill

(Editor's Note: Robert Sherrill, a distinguished journalist, is Washington editor of The Nation and author of many books and articles. This book is available from Books for Libertarians, 422 First St., S. E., Washington, D. C. 20003).

Ernie Fitzgerald is like a film critic who is smart enough to know that Bob Hope is a wretched peddler of wahoo humor but who is too kind hearted, or something, to hate Paramount for foisting him off on the public. In other words, Fitzgerald is an insider with an insider's shortcomings as well as an insider's strengths. He is inside Arms, which under certain circumstances, can be almost as entertaining an industry as Hollywood; and having been "a part of the arms-buying process for most of twenty years," he says he hopes that the criticisms written into The High Priests of Waste will result in our tidying up the Pentagon — that is to say, "will encourage critics to try to create conditions in which the good guys may thrive rather than damning the whole Pentagonal crew."

If one considers the chronic mismanagement of the military affairs of our government ever since the days of Forrestal (at least), one will conclude quickly enough that Fitzgerald's wish falls far short of our need, which is that Jehovah should rouse himself from his drunkenness long enough to see to it that, in Old Testament style, not one Pentagon stone is left standing upon another and that all its shredded secrets are scattered

(Continued On Page 3)

The High Priests Of Waste —
(Continued From Page 2)

to the four winds. That's the kind of tidying up we need. Then we can build anew.

Meanwhile — a word that in these days signifies preliminary despair — we do at least have Fitzgerald, and despite his kind heartedness, he is quite wonderful.

First of all there is the matter of the Fitzgerald style, the titillating and refreshing effect of which is, like a bubble bath, hard to convey in small doses in this review. Quite a few books in the general category of military-industrial expose have come my way in recent years and without exception I have had to keep reminding myself, as I read them, that life is indeed a grim and unpleasant thing and that these writers were quite justified in their own deadly seriousness. Until Fitzgerald came along, I don't recall ever reading anything on the topic that provoked more than an occasional smile. Fitzgerald, on the contrary, is good for a great many laughs: ". . . for the first principle of the expediting art is to stride purposefully from hide-out to resting place. In addition, of course, the accomplished aerospace expediter never leaves a place of refuge without carrying something — a part, a clipboard, or a sheaf of papers."

And then there is the matter of the Autonetics Division of North American Aviation, from whence (as Adelaide would say) Fitzgerald and his fellow consultants were summarily kicked because they uncovered a melange of costly stupidities, one of which Fitzgerald describes:

"For a number of reasons, it is important that Minutemen missiles point more or less straight up. One of the functions of the airmen manning the missile launching sites was to go to the missile silo periodically and check to make sure the missile was standing straight up. The airmen got cold doing this chore, so Autonetics was commissioned to solve the problem. Autonetics' brilliant engineers correctly concluded that a tent would be a good shelter from the bitter northern wind, confirming the decision of countless generations of Indians who inhabited the region in times past. Unhappily, even though the ignorant savage had solved the problem after a fashion, missile gap technology was not equal to the task. All the Autonetics tents blew away, computers and wind tunnels notwithstanding."

But Fitzgerald's banishment by Autonetics was back in the days when he was a private consultant and could be kicked out by aerospace companies. Later he went to the Pentagon as Deputy for Management Systems in the Air Force, and after that the military-industrialists didn't use their feet on him; they and their allies in the Pentagon used invisible accounting trapdoors and VuGraphs. A VuGraph is a large screen on which Colonels draw intricate charts and from which they deliver interminable lectures to explain why it is absolutely impossible to spend fewer "megabucks" (Pentagonese for one million dollars) on a particular system, and to explain further why waste helps attain the "social goals" of (1) equal employment opportunity, (2) seniority clauses in union agreements, (3) programs for hiring the handicapped, (4) apprentice programs, (5) aid to small business, (6) aid to distressed labor areas, and (7) encouragement of improvements to plant layouts and facilities. That is the summation of an actual lecture which Fitzgerald received.

I won't use the word genius, but it certainly takes a profound talent to explain the complex financial juggling of the Pentagon via both real and simulated case histories in such a way as not to provoke drowsiness in the reader. Fitzgerald is a master of the simulated case history, using Dickensian characters like "General Palmy" and "Colonel Clapsaddle" and "Secretary Crumley Quillpen" to fill out one of the neatest dramas of hokum/fraud — better known as "The Aardvark Missile Case" — that I have read. Aside from being a deft method of instruction, this light comedy is pure subversion. One could read a hundred stories about Pentagon cheating in the Washington Post (that is, if the Post were still reporting such things) and still come away with some middling hope that the Pentagon might yet reform itself. After laughing through the Aardvark Missile Case, all hope is gone — and yet, for the first time one feels that perhaps the billions spent at the Pentagon may be worth it for the sheer diversionary perversiveness fun they provide, something worthy of Nero behind the sofa with a goat. When "Major Buck" succeeds in tricking "Assistant Secretary Doe" into thinking he has caught the key mistake in the Aardvark program — a mistake that was, in fact, planted to give Doe that delusion — and when Major Buck "discovers" that the cost error can be traced back to PIGA, or as he explains to the increasingly baffled Doe, "the pendular integrating gryoscopic accelerometer," then we come to suspect that Samuel Clemens is alive, even if unemployed at the moment, in Washington.

Okay, enough of levity. Back to grimness. As you must already know, Fitzgerald was fired from the Pentagon a few years ago because when he

was called before Senator Proxmire's Joint Economic Committee and asked if the C-5A was going to suffer from a cost overrun, he answered factually: yes, a couple billion dollars worth — an overrun that had been covered up by both Lockheed and the Army in such a way that if the same trick had been pulled in a bank all officials would have wound up in the penitentiary.

That, however, was not the first outburst of honesty that had got Fitzgerald in trouble. He had also been gauche enough to complain when he found that factory labor efficiency on one Minuteman contract ranged from 3.2 percent to 7 percent of what those workers would have been expected to produce if they had been on a civilian, commercial contract. At the same time, their rate of pay was increasing five times faster than commercial contract workers.

Fitzgerald figured that if all the obvious padding were taken out of the contract — and he had itemized the soft areas for his superiors to look over — the Pentagon could save $500,000,000. McNamara's cost-estimating experts refused to even consider Fitzgerald's reform proposals. The reason was that he was defying the principle of "historical costs," the principle that guides the financing of all Pentagon programs. It is such an insane principle that a normal person will inevitably find it hard to follow. It comes to this: The right cost is what the contractor charges.

No, it's not a joke. This is a sacred principle. Costs are not judged by what the weapons could be manufactured for. Costs are judged by what the contractor charges: this, then, becomes history, and thereupon it is elevated to the dogma of Historical Cost, and thereafter all further cost adjustments are built upon it. No looking back is allowed, no turning again to measure the cost of that program by what it would cost if civilians out in the world were doing it.

Contracting between the giant corporations and the Pentagon, explained with precision in this book, makes up in ardor what it lacks in grace; it is experience which Fitzgerald likens to "a track meet with participation limited to middle-aged ladies, each weighing in excess of 300 pounds" and which one of the more candid generals at the Pentagon likened to "contention among bullmoose for the privilege of servicing the government cow."

It is very rewarding love-making, however. General Dynamics, for example, humped the cow so poorly that the milk doubled. It earned twice as much money as originally contracted for by building an F-111 that is not yet safe to fly (at last count, something like 24 had crashed.)

Within the Pentagon and the aerospace industry, serious criticism of such things is not permitted. Revenge is certain and swift. When a small cost control consultant company, Performance Technology Corporation, first broke the code by pointing out how Pratt & Whitney could save federal money and then compounded its sin by showing how the Pentagon could require other economies from other companies, PTC was assassinated by the Air Force. It was done very cleverly. The Air Force hired PTC for a complicated job but kept withholding payment; PTC borrowed heavily to stay in business while it waited for the Air Force payment. After the Air Force owed PTC about 170 percent of the company's net worth, part of the contract was abruptly cancelled retroactively and the company was wiped out.

A Navy contracting officer who tried to affect thrift in the building of the Mark 48 torpedo program was eased out of procurement, then out of the Navy, and — like the end of an Evelyn Waugh story — wound up as an AID buyer in Ghana.

For his heresies, Fitzgerald was in the early days subjected to an endless round of coaching from colonels and GS-15s on the social value of the military-industrial partnership. When that failed to suppress him, he found his mail channeled to other offices where it was opened, and his speeches censured and lost. Finally he was fired.

Knowing the character of the Pentagon from having witnessed previous episodes of revenge, Fitzgerald should not have been surprised when its officials knifed him. I really doubt that he was, though he at least pretends to be.

It took place with unusual flagrancy even for the Pentagon. Fitzgerald went to work at the Pentagon in September 1965. When his three years probation was up in September 1968, he was officially notified that he was being converted to career tenure. This meant that, barring being caught with his hand in the till or dating Christine Jorgenson, he was secure and permanent.

But the official notification had gone out before he had testified to Lockheed's theft of government funds. His snitching on a Georgia defense plant infuriated Senator Richard Russell, who was unfortunately still alive and running the Senate Appropriations Committee. Apparently Russell said something to the Pentagon because shortly thereafter

(Continued On Page 4)

The High Priests Of Waste —
(Continued From Page 3)

Fitzgerald received a note to the effect that the Pentagon bosses were terribly sorry but that the notice of career status had been a computer error and that actually they had meant to tell him he was no longer needed.

What was the excuse? Civil Service records — later grudgingly opened for him to see — showed that officials had compiled a list of his sins which included driving an old Rambler automobile. This, said the bureaucratic gumshoe, indicated Fitzgerald was a "pinchpenny type of person." Lockheed and Autonetics, among others, could have told them that without an investigation.

The C-5A overrun episode is probably recounted here with as many details as most readers would desire. But there are several omissions and several interpretations that I would quarrel with. I feel the officials of Lockheed handled our money in a criminal fashion. I think Fitzgerald should have made the back-alley quality of their thievery a more palpable thing, and I think one way to have done this would have been to point out the stock juggling that was going on behind the scene among Lockheed officials at the same time they were screwing the taxpayer. This was brought out fairly thoroughly in a quiet SEC investigation, but generally ignored by the press at the time. It was also soft-pedaled by the SEC, which said it didn't want to single out Lockheed for rebuke but felt that stock manipulations at all defense corporations should be investigated. It promised to do so. That was how long ago — three years? four years? — and the SEC has not made a move in that direction yet.

I also think Fitzgerald was far, far too easy on the spineless liberals involved in this thing. I mean such fellows as Senator Metcalf of Montana, who has made a career of talking tough about corporations but backs down when he can strike a blow against the crooked ones. Made loquacious and expansive and generous by an overdose of grape, Metcalf came to the Senate floor blowing off about "not wanting to be responsible for unemployment" and cast the deciding vote to bail out Lockheed with a $250 million government-guaranteed loan. I also mean such fellows as Congressman Wright Patman of Texas, who has been posing around here for years as a red hot populist but with increasing frequency opts out in favor of the big corporations, perhaps partly because he is suffering the natural decay of advanced age. Chairman of the House Banking Committee, Patman perhaps could have blocked the loan if he had tried. At least he could have made it much more embarrassing for all the crooks in the deal. But when his fellow Texan, Treasury Secretary John Connally, mastermind of the loan, asked Patman to play along, he did. In fact, he even drafted the loan legislation. Fitzgerald mentions Patman's role only offhandedly and almost sympathetically.

Others may interpret such attitudes in this book in a kindlier way. They may see them as evidence that Fitzgerald came away from his harrowing experiences retaining his balance, without bitterness, slow to excess, etc. I, having none of those qualities where Congress and the Pentagon are concerned, find them a failing in an otherwise invaluable book. ▣

The Other
North American Election

By Samuel Edward Konkin III

While Richard Nixon bored everyone with his landslide on November 7, Canadians were treated to a cliff-hanger a week earlier on October 30. The pollsters confidently predicted a Trudeau return as Maritime provinces' results swung slightly towards the Liberal Party, and Quebec cut the Progressive Conservative seats from four to two (out of 74). True, the Social Credit Rally (Ralliement Creditiste) increased their popular vote substantially, but gained only one seat. Then Ontario came in with the social democratic New Democrat Party and the Progressive Conservatives slashing into the Grit (Liberal) standings. And then the West.

In Alberta, all four Liberal seats were buried under a Tory (PC) avalanche. British Columbia moved the Tories even with the Grits, and brought in the NDP main strength. The Northwest Territories gave the NDP their first "frontier" seat (Grit loss) and the Tories held on to the Yukon to put them one seat up, 109-108.

Canada does not allow absentee balloting, except for one special case. The Social Credit Party's sole gain was at the expense of Jean-Luc Pepin, a Liberal Cabinet Minister involved in what Murray Rothbard called Quebec's "White Terror" suspension of civil rights of a few years ago,

and, since the Creditistes are the federal party which most free market libertarians (especially minarchists) in the U. S. would sympathize with, it seemed like divine justice. Unfortunately, the military votes Grit, and their absentee ballots reversed the 100-vote margin, knocking the Creditistes back to 14 seats. Libertarians can probably read symbolism into that as well.

The final standings of 109 seats each for the Liberals and P. C.'s, 30 for the NDP, 14 for SC, one Independent Conservative and one Independent (speaker of the House Lucien Lamoureux — non-partisan) tell the average American nothing, assuming he even heard of them. For the libertarians wanting to know who to cheer and who to boo — as Dr. Rothbard is wont — even less. I shall undertake here to give you a programme to go with your scorecard.

The Social Credit Party used to be based in the rightist West, Alberta and British Columbia, and was a free market, pro-American party with a funny money policy they could not legislate because they had only controlled provincial governments. They never had more than a minority in the national House of Commons. In 1963, they defeated John Diefenbaker's minority Tory government because he failed to balance the budget. In 1962, Real Caouette led his Quebecers into the House in larger numbers than the Western wing, and the party eventually split. The Western wing withdrew in favor of P. C.'s to stem the Trudeau sweep of 1968, and never recovered. Caouette kept his more orthodix Social Credit position, appealing populistically to the Quebec habitants (peasant farmers) and stayed in the House. Recently he tried to expand westward, but failed to restore the party outside Quebec (although there are still a few Socred diehards lurking in rightist circles in ranch and oil country). The Alberta provincial Socreds were thrown out of office for the first time in 35 years in 1970 by Kennedyesque Tory Peter Lougheed, and their very survival as a party depends on Lougheed's self-destruction. This year in British Columbia, W. A. C. Bennett's 20-year Socred regime was ousted by the NDP in an even greater victory, marking a swing from far Right to far Left in the Canadian four-party spectrum. Although Caouette increased his popular vote markedly, and signs of organization were seen again throughout Canada, the recent net effect for the "good guys" (least worst guys) is down.

The Leftist bad guys, the New Democrat Party, which is labour backed and oriented, like the British Labour Party, now has three provincial governments (B. C., Saskatchewan, and Manitoba) and their largest number of seats ever in the Federal House. American investors are fleeing B. C. right now, and Canadian capitalists are screaming to the federal government to bail them out by preventing nationalization of federal regulated industries. **Plus ça change, plus c'est la même chose.**

The big gains federally were reaped by Robert Stanfield's Progressive Conservative Party, but it cannot take over the government without 25 more seats — and the Creditistes haven't got that many. The Tories are conservative, but in the British/European sense, not (except for a small Ontario faction) in the American quasi-libertarian sense. Hence they love mercantilism and fear gradual socialism much less. Thus NDP support for the right Welfarist concessions is thinkable, and the NDP's and PC's both are anti-American (just as the Liberals and SC's are pro-American). Their foreign policy migh seem more appealing to a libertarian; but it manifests itself in increasing government regulation of corporations (50% of Canadian companies are American controlled) and in little which could be considered objective anti-imperialism. The NDP leader, David Lewis, will "throw his support behind whichever of the old line parties is prepared to deal adequately with unemployment, inflation, old age pensions, and a more equitable tax system."* Coming from a socialist, that seems ominous. I doubt that libertarians could imagine a worse nightmare than a de facto socialist-traditionalist coalition.

Trudeaumania is gone, but Pierre Elliot Trudeau clings on. He has not resigned, and it looks as if he will try to keep governing, daring the Opposition to precipitate an election by defeating him on a non-confidence motion. Here, precedent is murky. There is no reason the figurehead Governor-General can't ask the Tories to try to gain confidence for a majority — but in 1926, Governor General Lord Byng refused Liberal Mackenzie King's request for dissolution of Parliament, and invited Conservative Arthur Meighen to govern. His bungling Progressive supporters blew a "pairing", bringing him down only days later, and William Lyon Mackenzie King rode to victory attacking Byng's interference. Would Roland Michener have the guts of Lord Byng? Ultimately, the Tories may be thwarted by this vestige of royal privilege. Michener was a Conservative, to add to the irony, but was appointed by a Liberal government, following a recent cross-party tradition.

Still, Trudeau has a problem if Michener doesn't give him an issue. The

(Continued On Page 6)

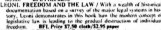

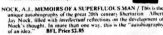

The High Priests Of Waste —
(Continued From Page 4)

electorate might decide to finish the job by giving Stanfield a majority. Diefenbaker ended 22 years of Liberal government in 1957, and dissolved his minority government early in 1958 calling for just such a majority. He won a record 208 out of 265 seats.

On the other hand, Lester Bowles Pearson won two minority governments in a row of 1963 and 1965 after a Tory minority of 1962, failing to get the majority he craved. He limped along in the Centre, depending on Social Credit support.

It is in the Grits' interest to give the Tories the government, so that Stanfield can begin to alienate voters. But it's not in Trudeau's interest, as shown by Diefenbaker's ouster after his election defeat by a particularly brutal purge which caused enough resentment in the West to give Trudeau his 1968 victory in the first place. Trudeau's ouster would not be so regionally oriented, because half of the Liberal seats are in Quebec anyway, and his followers have nowhere to go but the Creditistes, the Tories being unthinkable and the NDP frowned on by the Catholic Church.

The French-English split is being played up by foreign papers, and the Separatists may be bolstered by the defeat of their centralist enemy Trudeau — but that is a Provincial effect, not a Federal one. Furthermore, resentment against compulsory bilingualism/biculturalism is found in the third of the population of non-WASP origin (mostly in the West) such as German, Ukrainian, Galician, Icelander, Dutch, Russian, and others who are just speaking English in the first or second generation. The only real amelioration will be found in reviving the Social Credit and Union Nationale's (a Quebec provincial party, recently defeated by the Grits) demand for greater decentralism and provincial rights. The present trend is the other way, but Canadians are a remarkably non-revolutionary lot, pointing with pride to their "evolution" from Great Britain, as opposed to the Americans' messy violence. Quebec independence will be gained gradually if at all, by the Parti Quebec parliamentarily (with both RIN-socialistic-and RN-Creditiste-wings) and not by the ten to fifteen FLQ**goons.

Revolution in Canada is a bigger joke than in the U. S., and rather than radical change, resulting from elimination of Trudeau's flashy, slightly-leftist liberalism (he flirted with price controls but never implemented them, by the way) one should expect stodginess, anti-communist witch-hunts from Liberal renegade Paul Hellyer, and the ominous economic changes resulting from NDP support. Canadian libertarians and their American allies should be hoping for a new election and a minority government with Creditiste swing vote power. Failing that, how about Parliamentary Chaos?

---

*Page 1, **The Edmonton Journal**, Tuesday, October 31, 1972.
Front de Liberation Quebecois RIN = Reassemblement pour l'Independence Nationale, and RN = Ralliement Nationale. The **Nationale recurring in Quebec party names has the opposite meaning of "nationwide".

SPECIAL NOTE ABOUT THE AUTHOR: Before becoming a well-known libertarian activist and writer, Mr. Konkin was a Socred activist, and Chairman of the University of Alberta Social Credit Party from 1966-68. He became senior participant in the Model Parliaments, and was involved in all Canadian and Alberta elections from 1962 to 1968. He is now a foreign student at New York University, a candidate for a Ph. D. in Theoretical Chemistry.

Arts And Movies

By Mr. First Nighter

This is the time of year for movie critics to roll out their awards and their ten-best lists, and I am forced to take a long, hard look at the cinema from the fact that I cannot come up with a "ten best" list at all. For in the cinema we must wage the same struggle that we should have been fighting in the rest of the culture since the turn of the twentieth century: on behalf of the old, bourgeois values and against the morbidity and unreason of the avant-garde. Unfortunately, the avant-garde has now become "the garde", and so it becomes more important than ever, in the movies as well as in literature, art, and music, to raise the standard of the arriere-garde — a rear-guard struggle against a diseased culture.

The carriers of the disease are of the course the intelligentsia, for the cultural instincts of the middle-class are sound, and generally they put up a lengthy resistance to the irrationalism of the cultural "elite". We then have two cultures: the sound, if often stodgy, "commercial" culture of the bourgeoisie; and the arrogantly morbid, involuted culture of the intellectuals. This unhealthy split between the cultures did not really exist before 1900; before that, when what we might call the "classical culture" held sway, the leaders in art, fiction, music, etc. were of the same cloth, albeit on a far greater and more creative level, as the popular artists; indeed, the greatness of the leaders — of the Rembrandts, Mozarts, Verdis, etc., was cheerfully acknowledged by the mass of the bourgeoisie. "High" culture was profound, to be sure; but it was also understandable on the mass level, as well as repaying long hours of diligent study. Keats, Mozart, Rembrandt, etc. were instantly understandable to the mass as well as being profoundly intellectual leaders of the culture.

But at approximately the turn of the twentieth century, the intelligentsia began to succumb rapidly to morbidity and irrationality; cultural disease swiftly replaced cultural health. The differences between the rationalist, the romantic, etc. variants are not very important here; the vital point is that the glorious "classical" mainstream of art and culture: from the Renaissance to the magnificent Baroque to the 18th century rationalists to the 19th century romantics — that all of these form the noble heritage of Western culture and civilization. And that that heritage began to crumble rapidly into cultural degeneracy: a degeneracy that included the flight from realism, classicism, and rational space in art; from purpose and plot in fiction; from clarity in literature generally; and a flight from melody and harmony in music. It was, in classical terms, a flight from beauty in the fullest sense and the embrace of the ugly; a rush away from optimism, purpose, and life toward morbidity and death; and an escape from reason on behalf of the irrational.

While the bourgeoisie have put up a heroic resistance to this twentieth-century plague, they were bound to lose out when permanently deprived of intellectual and cultural allies. And so in fiction, where have been the great classical writers since Somerset Maugham? In the theater, where are the successors to Shaw and Wilde? In art, the Wyeths, John Koch and a few others have kept the realist tradition beautifully alive, but they have been largely ignored by the chi-chi art world which has rushed to lionize the Picassos, Mondrians, and Pollocks. In music, the barbarities of modern music, from the atonal to the electronic, have fortunately been checked by the customers, who insist on the recording and the concertizing of the classical masters. In popular music, however, both "classical" pop and "classical" jazz have lost out to the barbarities of atonal modern jazz and of acid rock.

For a long time, the movies were the last stronghold of the arriere-garde. There are two good reasons for this: one, that the movies are our newest art form, and two, that since movies are dependent on a mass audience. the basically sound taste of the masses for a long while kept the intelligentsia on a short leash. But now the spread of irrationality has hit the movies in a big way, and the defense of the classical movie — the "movie movie" — must be a bitter struggle against the rising if not dominant tide of "intellectual" degeneracy.

By "degeneracy" I of course do not mean pornography, which serves as a wrong-headed focus for many conservatives. Pornography had always formed a harmonious "left wing" within the Victorian-culture. The problem in the movies is not sex but unreason, an absurdism that infects both the point of view of the film and the techniques of the camera. The Enemy on the movie front is not the California porno king; our war to the metaphorical knife is not with the makers of **Deep Throat** but with the Bergmans. the Bunuels, the Antonionis, the Fellinis, the Godards. The truly obscene is not the happy, fun-loving **School Girl**, but such monstrosities as **Juliet of the Spirits** and **Last Year At Marienbad**.

Neither is "violence" the problem, as so many movie critics are maintaining. Violence is a perfectly proper dramatic tool; the real question is the point of view, is **how** violence is being used in the film. Once again: look to the intellectuals, to the avant-garde, and you will find precisely the wrong point of view. The intelligentsia, for example, loved **A Clockwork Orange**, with its random and meaningless violence, but they hated with a purple passion those films where violence is used as an instrument of justice, of defense against crime. In short, they hate **Dirty Harry** or such great John Wayne films as **Chisum** or **Rio Bravo**, and they have the gall to denounce the supposedly "meaningless" violence of such Sam Peckinpah masterpieces as **The Wild Bunch.** (It is interesting that the intellectuals preferred Peckinpah's inferior **Straw Dogs** to **Wild Bunch**, precisely because the employment of violence, while still defensive, did not have the latter's clarity and point.)

It is of course a standard trick of the intellectuals to take the most banal works of classical culture and to use them as straw men on behalf

(Continued On Page 7)

Arts And Movies —
(Continued From Page 6)

of the avant-garde. But classical culture is certainly not a monolith; there are varying degrees of merit in classical films as anywhere else. Of course, **Mary Poppins**, for example, was banal and boring; but contrast it to such fine musicals as **My Fair Lady** and the magnificent **Gigi!**

The Golden Age of the cinema was the thirties and forties. It was then that we could delight in **Gone With the Wind**, in **Snow White and the Seven Dwarfs**, and **The Lady Vanishes**; it was then that we could enjoy the sophisticated wit of the Cary Grant-Katherine Hepburn movies and the hilarious farce of the Marx Brothers, as well as Mr. Old Curmudgeon himself, W. C. Fields. Indeed, by far the three best movies that I saw in 1972 were revivals from that better age. Two were from GBS: **Major Barbara** and **Pygmalion**. It is instructive to compare **Pygmalion** with the later **My Fair Lady**, the musical based on the former play. While **Pygmalion** lacks the famous music, it has far more of the original Shavian bite: also the acting in **Pygmalion** is far superior: Wendy Hiller is miles ahead of Audrey Hepburn, and even that excellent actor Rex Harrison is eclipsed by the cool austerity and luminous intelligence of Leslie Howard. **Major Barbara**, despite Shaw's socialist beliefs, is one of the great arguments for capitalism in the history of the film, done with high Shavian wit and intelligence; and then there is the magnificent acting of Robert Morley, in addition to Harrison and Hiller.

And finally, the incomparable English film, **The Importance of Being Earnest**, perhaps the greatest motion picture ever made. The marvelously witty Oscar Wilde play never flags for a moment, and the acting is high-style perfection, performed by Michael Redgrave, Michael Dennison, Dorothy Tutin, Joan Greenwood, Margaret Rutherford, and the incomparable Dame Edith Evans. There, my friends, was a movie!

But to return to the cinematic slough of 1972. Certainly the best film of 1972 was **The Godfather**, which we have already hailed in these pages. **The Godfather** is us classicists' candidate in the award sweepstakes. Already, of course, both the masses and the **intelligentsia** have spoken: the masses by perceptively making **The Godfather** the box-office smash of all time; the intellectuals by rejecting it for avant-garde tinsel: the

New York Film Critics choosing the eternally boring and morbid Bergman's latest, **Cries and Whispers**, and the even more pretentious National Society of Film Critics selecting the irrationalist Bunuel's latest offering. (In my view, the only good Bergman was one of his earliest, before he adopted the unbecoming mantle of Profound Thinker: his **Smiles of a Summer Night**, done as a high style Restoration-type farce. Which is just about the one Bergman movie that the critics don't ooh and aah about.) I have faith, however, that the good old bourgeois Academy will spurn the Continental mish-mash and heap its awards on the truly great Godfather.

The other awards? Best director and best picture awards should usually run together, and so **Francis Ford Coppola** gets our accolade. For best actor it's for me a tossup between **Al Pacino** and **Marlon Brando** in our favorite movie. Brando's acting was a mighty and brilliant **tour de force**, by far the best Brando in that actor's checkered career. But, on the other hand, Pacino's was a far longer part, and it was a subtle and splendid performance, in which the character changed gradually but vitally in the course of the picture. For best supporting actor. Robert Duvall will probably get the Academy Award for his **consigliori** in **The Godfather** (even the New York Film Critics selected Duvall), but far superior are two splendid performances by British actors in **Frenzy**: either the subtle acting of **Alec McCowen** as the inspector, or **Barry Foster's** suave and two-faced villain. For best actress, there is simply no one that I can choose; 1972 was a bad year for actresses. Please, Academy, **not** the impossibly awkward and pseudo-elfin Liza Minelli in **Cabaret**! I am afraid, however, that Liza will get the award, purely as a remnant of the still flourishing cult for one of Hollywood's all-time worst singers and actresses: Liza's mom Judy Garland. For supporting actresses, **Vivien Merchant's** gourmet-loving inspector's wife in **Frenzy** towers over an indifferent lot.

As for the "ten best" movies, I cannot find the heart to put nine other movies of 1972 on the list. Certainly one, however, is Alfred Hitchcock's

(Continued On Page 8)

"Work and earn; pay taxes and die." —Old German Proverb.

Recommended Reading

Natural Gas Shortage. Gilbert Burck, "The FPC is Backing Away From the Wellhead", **Fortune** (November, 1972) is a good, up-to-date account of the way in which FPC regulation has created a shortage of natural gas.

World War II Revisionism. In recent years, younger historians of modern Germany, in America and elsewhere, have brought a fresh perspective freed of wartime passions and distortions to their controversial field of study. In a series of brilliant articles, the eminent left-liberal English historian Geoffrey Barraclough, a distinguished historian of Germany who in no sense can be accused of pro-Nazi views, has done a block-buster job of synthesizing the insights of the new literature. Essentially he does for Germany's "domestic" scene what his famous counterpart A. J. P. Taylor did for German foreign policy a decade ago. Particularly important are Geoffrey Barraclough, "The Liberals and German History: Part II, "New York Review of Books (November 2, 1972), and "A New View of German History: Part III," **New York Review of Books** (November 16, 1972). Must reading for revisionists.

Airport Congestion. In recent years, free-market economists have begun to zero in on the cause of airport congestion: the operations of airports, which are invariably government-owned and operated, and which systematically charge a uniform and absurdly low fee for the use of runways. In contrast, the airports grant monopoly privileges to its concessionaires (restaurants, bars, insurance, parking lots) which is turn charge monopoly prices for low-quality service, out of which the airports get a rake-off. The best monograph on the subject has just appeared, a pamphlet by Professor Ross D. Eckert. **Airports and Congestion** (Washington: American Enterprise Institute, 1972, $3.00).

Nisei Revisionism. One of the most barbaric acts in American history was our incarceration of all innocent Japanese-Americans into concentration camps for the duration of World War II. But most revisionist books critical of this action pin all the blame on right-wingers: racist army officers, California business competitors with the productive Japanese, etc. Now, a proper pinpointing of major blame on America's liberals arrives with William Petersen's excellent "The Incarceration of the Japanese-Americans," **National Review** (Dec. 8, 1972).

Guernica Revisionism. For decades, we have been subjected to Left propaganda about Guernica, Fascist planes supposedly deliberately terror-bombing the civilian population of this Basque town. A new book by Luis Bolin, however, reveals that Guernica was not bombed at all, but dynamited by the Red forces themselves in order to launch the propaganda effort. See Jeffrey Hart, "The Great Guernica Fraud," **National Review** (January 5).

Econometric History. An excellent critique of the new econometric history, on general methodological grounds, and particularly as applied to the history of slavery in the U. S., can be found in a lengthy article by Harold D. Woodman, "Economic History and Economic Theory: The New Economic History in America," **Journal of Interdisciplinary History** (Autumn, 1972).

Environmentalism. A good critique of the Club of Rome anti-growth hysteria can be found in Wilfred Beckerman, "The Myth of Environmental Catastrophe," **National Review** (November 24, 1972). **Technology and the Counter-Culture.** A good critique of the anti-technological impetus of the counter-culture, and its similarity to Old European conservatism, can be found in Stephen Tonsor, "Science, Technology and the Cultural Revolution, **The Intercollegiate Review** (Winter, 1972-73).

Arts And Movies —
(Continued From Page 7)

Frenzy in which the Old Master returns to the fine suspense of his early English period — could it be a coincidence that he returned to England to make the film? If not for Coppola's great achievement, I would surely pick Hitchcock as the best director of the year. Another excellent film was the best of the "caper" genre in years, Peter Yates' **The Hot Rock**. A fine blend of humor and suspense, the excellent direction blended sterling acting performances from George Segal and Robert Redford, and featured a marvellously funny Zero Mostel as the crooked lawyer (Zero would place as the best supporting actor on my list below McCowen and Foster.)

When we get past **The Godfather**, **Frenzy**, and **The Hot Rock**, we have to reach a bit. **The Hospital** featured a slashing and witty attack on the large city hospital, highlighted by the typically excellent acting of George C. Scott. I haven't seen **Sleuth**, but the play was splendid and subtly changing suspense; my only a priori reservation is that Sir Laurence Olivier always tends to overact and chew the scenery, especially in productions that he obviously feels are beneath him. As a result, one is supposed to applaud Olivier's acting tricks and to forget the character he is playing. (See, for example, Olivier's performance as the dervish leader in the forgotten **Khartoum**.) Even in classical films, Olivier sometimes ruins the picture by hamming it up, as he did in **Richard III**.

Also on the list, but not with very high marks, is Eric Rohmer's **Chloe in the Afternoon**. Rohmer is one of the few French directors to continue in the classic tradition, and for this he is ostracized by the French film world. As the founder of the famous French journal **Cahiers du Cinema**, Rohmer kept insisting throughout the dark days of the **avant-garde** on the high merits of Hitchcock and even — perhaps going a little too far — of Jerry Lewis! **Chloe** is one of a fascinating set of "moral tales", in which Rohmer single-handedly restores intelligent and subtle dialogue to its rightful place in the cinema. Unfortunately, **Chloe** suffers by comparison with the previous Rohmer tales released here, notably **Claire's Knee** and the superb **My Night at Maud's**. The problem is that in **Chloe** both the hero and the heroine are decidedly unappealing, so that one ends up not really giving a damn whether he succumbs to temptation and sleeps with her or not (the problem of all of the Moral Tales.) Still, **Chloe in the Afternoon** rates as far and away the best foreign picture of the year.

Coming to the bottom of the "eight best" list, we have **Play It Again, Sam** and **They Only Kill Their Masters**. **Play It** is hardly in the same league with Woody Allen's hilarious **Bananas**, but this clumsy movie does center around a warm and affectionate tribute to the great Bogart, and no picture that does that can be all bad. **Masters** is a quiet, gentle detective drama, and would scarcely make any best list in a good movie year; but it is an engaging sleeper, and contains a fine, quietly wry performance from James Garner.

What of my fellow critics? Are there any whom I can generally recommend? Not really; there is unfortunately no one who is really aware of the great classical **avant-garde** struggle, much less wages a consistent battle on behalf of the True, the Good, and the Beautiful. Even the best are a quivering mass of ad hoc sensibility. Perhaps the soundest of the lot is Paul D. Zimmerman of **Newsweek**. Unquestionably the worst is the most famous: Judith Crist of **New York**, who can be depended upon to love the awful movies and hate the good ones. Rex Reed of the **Daily News** always pitches his critiques on a note of scarcely controlled hysteria. On the other hand, Andrew Sarris of the **Village Voice** is better than most: being saved by his being a disciple of Rohmer. John Simon of the **New Leader** is often good, largely because he dislikes almost everything — but not for the right reasons. Stanley Kauffmann of the **New Republic** is often sensible. But all in all, a rum show. ◙

From The Old Curmudgeon

For Closed Marriage. I see that a few libertarians, for some reason, are recommending the jejune best-seller by the O'Neills, **Open Marriage**. In their insipid work, the O'Neills cleverly have it both ways. By being deliberately vague and non-specific, their work can be read on two levels. On one level, it is simply another string of cliches that have come down to us ever since Shakespeare said it far far better: "To thine own self be true." The changes have been rung on this through best-sellers like Dale Carnegie and now the O'Neills. If this is all they mean, that, e.g. each partner in a marriage should fulfill his or her self to its best potential, then the "open marriage" concept is unexceptionable but tediously banal: it would be hard to find anyone to disagree. On the other hand, the book can be read on a second level, and I suspect that it is the titillation of the authors' never-quite-coming out-with-it that is responsible for the mass appeal: i.e. a call for sleeping around by both partners. One can hear the titters: Is that what they mean by all the hoopla about growth by each partner, about seeking independent experiences and then bringing the "new knowledge" to the partner, etc.?

If that is what they mean, then we are simply getting the old seduction shuck: "Come on, it will rejuvenate your marriage"; "you'll bring new experiences to your (husband, wife)." If that is what they mean, then I am foursquare for the "closed marriage", the marriage in which two partners live in trust and fidelity, in which they blend into a lifelong emotional intimacy to the glories of which the promiscuous and the seduction-shuckers are deaf, dumb, and blind. ◙

The only good Indian is . . . (1972-style)

"The real problem confronting the American Indians in the western United States today is that the Bureau of Indian Affairs is carrying out the policy of the Department of Interior . . . and that policy is opposed to the private rights to the use of water of the American Indians. No one is recognizing that in substance and in effect the Indian rights are being communized . . . communized for the use of the non-Indian community."
William H. Veeder, water expert,
in **The Indian Historian**, Summer 1972

A Monthly Newsletter

THE
Libertarian Forum

Joseph R. Peden, Publisher   Murray N. Rothbard, Editor

VOLUME V, NO. 2   FEBRUARY, 1973   75¢

Nixon's Second Term
The Sticks In The Closet

Nixon's second Administration has already taken a fascinating and rather remarkable new turn, a pattern that is consistent in all the major political arenas, foreign and domestic. So far not a single political observer has discerned this important new pattern, and little has been said about the second term except for a few references to personnel changes and some misleading remarks about Nixon's new budget. Yet the new pattern is a vital one, and may well set the political picture of the next four years.

In every major area, foreign and domestic, Mr. Nixon has suddenly and swiftly called a "truce", a major retreat from the overweening statism of his first administration. The truce is not only in Vietnam but everywhere; but, in every case, what we have is a truce rather than a genuine "peace". In the immortal words of Dr. George Shultz and Dr. John Dunlop, the administration is "keeping its stick in the closet", ready to be brandished over the head of recalcitrants. And yet, for the libertarian this is, after all, a major step forward; we would prefer to abolish the stick altogether, but it is far better to have it in the closet than in active and aggressive use.

Let us observe this "armed truce" or retreat in every major arena: among them, Vietnam, the draft, price-wage controls and, more loosely, the new budget.

Vietnam and Indo-China. In Vietnam, of course, we have the official truce or cease-fire. It is not to wash away the blood of millions of innocent Vietnamese victims on the Nixonian and American record to hail the cease-fire that has come at long last. We must credit Mr. Nixon for finally ending the fighting, for stopping the bombing, for pulling out American troops. The truce came far too late, but, Happy Day! it came. The U. S. will be murdering no more people in Vietnam.

What did the war in Vietnam accomplish? Nothing, if we compare, for example, the situation after the truce of 1973 with the truce of 1954. Nineteen years later, the Communists and their allies in the Vietnamese resistance are in far better shape, and control far more population and territory than they did after their misguided adherence to the Geneva Agreements, when they pulled all their troops out of the South. Betrayed after those agreements by the failure of the U. S. to conduct free elections, the resistance forces would of course never agree again to a unilateral disarmament and pullout of troops.

If the war was fought in vain, neither is the current cease-fire in very sturdy shape. Even the Nixon Administration has termed the truce "fragile", which is a hefty understatement. So while we hail the end of the fighting, we must remember that the American stick is very much in the closet; the task of the anti-war forces is to agitate to make sure that we don't pull the stick out once more and begin the tragic and bloody mass murder all over again. The stick is close by: American air power is near at hand, at bases in Thailand and elsewhere, our naval power is off the coast, and those old Kennedy-style "civilian advisers" are still there to support the Thieu dictatorship.

There will undoubtedly be plenty of temptation for the U. S. to use the stick, to send bombers and troops back into that unfortunate country. Thieu has made it crystal clear that he has no intention of arriving at a political settlement with the PRG (Previsional Revolutionary

Government), which means that no true peace in the area has been achieved. The political struggle of the civil war will continue, and could erupt at any moment into military conflict. In order to get the Americans out, the North Vietnamese and the PRG (to the probable unhappiness of the latter) made a remarkable concession: in contrast to every past war, when prisoners **of both sides** were exchanged at the end of the conflict, the North agreed to a **unilateral** release of American prisoners. This means that literally hundreds of thousands of Communists and other resisters will continue to rot in Thieu jails; and their fate remains fuzzy and unclear. The Thieu-Nixon excuse that these prisoners are **not** POW's but civilian dissenters because they didn't wear an official uniform is of course pure sophistry, and deliberately evades the very nature of guerrilla war, in which the civilians are the resistance forces. This truce, then, constitutes a monstrous injustice to the huge mass of prisoners of the Thieu dictatorship; and it is the big reservation that we must have to our joy over the end of the fighting.

The important point now is, that when and if armed civil war erupts again, whether over Thieu's prisoners or over any other issue, that the U. S. keep its hands off: that we at long last allow the Vietnamese to settle their quarrels themselves. We must see to it that Nixon never takes the stick out of the closet again, that he does not re-enter the war; to do that, it would help enormously if he pulled air, naval, and land forces fully and completely out of the entire Asia area.

The same, of course, applies to Laos and Cambodia, where the war continues. At this writing, a similar truce appears likely in Laos, where the Pathet Lao resistance forces are closely allied to Hanoi and may predictably bow to Hanoi's pressure. In Cambodia, however, the situation is different, and here we should call for immediate American withdrawal from propping up the Phnom Penh dictatorship. The point here is that the Cambodian resistance forces, the National United Front, are led, not by Communists but by the deposed ruler, Prince Sihanouk, who is not likely to bow to any Communist desire for a ceasefire. Furthermore, the Sihanouk forces are far closer to total victory than were the opposition in Laos or Vietnam. Only massive American aid is keeping the Lon Nol dictatorship in power in Phnom Penh and a few other outposts; the rest of the country is already in the hands of the Sihanouk forces.

The Draft. Nixon's partial retreat from statism in Vietnam is matched by his decision to end — or sort of end — the draft. This monstrous blot on American life is at last over, and no longer will every American boy and every family be trying to live their lives with the sword of Damocles of enslavement to kill or be killed hanging over their heads. Libertarians must rejoice at the Nixon decision to stop the draft at last — a decision, by the way, brought about largely by the pressure over the years of free-market economists demonstrating that the "shortage" of enlistees in the Army can easily be cured by paying the GI's market wage rates.

But once again, our joy at the Nixon decision must be qualified: the stick is in the closet but it is still alive. We have a "ceasefire" and not a "lasting peace." For the damnable machinery of the draft is still intact, ready to be used at a flip of the Presidential switch; and every American boy will still have to register at the age of 18, endure the dehumanizing in-

(Continued On Page 2)

The Sticks In The Closet —

(Continued From Page 1)

dignities of the pre-induction physical, and receive his number on the roulette-wheel of the national lottery. Furthermore, the draft is not ended at all for the nation's physicians, who are still subject to the special penalties of the doctor draft. Libertarians should get behind the new bill of Senator Mark Hatfield to abolish the entire evil machinery of the draft: the registration, the draft cards, the whole shebang, lock, stock, and barrel. For Senator Hatfield's absolute firmness on the draft question, he can be forgiven much waffling on other issues.

And the stick is there in another sense: for President Nixon remains "hard nosed" on the amnesty question. The idea seems to be that American youth deserve some sort of "punishment" in the form of enslavement: and if they have managed to flee for their lives and avoid enslavement into the army, then at least they should be sent to jail (the conservative solution) or to compulsory bedpan service among the poor (the "Liberal" solution). Amnesty is not a question of whether "we" should mete out deserved punishment to draft evaders or deserters, or whether we should indulge in Christian forgiveness of crime. The draft itself is a supreme crime, and therefore draft evaders and deserters should be regarded not as criminals but as heroes, in precisely the same way as decent men regarded the slaves who ran away via the underground railroad. But the draft evaders and deserters disobeyed the law? Correct, and in precisely the same way as the slaves disobeyed the law; for let us never, never forget that slavery, until the 13th Amendment, was supremely legal.

The most puzzling and distressing aspect of the amnesty affair is the position of many so-called "libertarians" and alleged opponents of the draft who adopt the conservative view of upholding punishment for disobeying the law. Even when the law is enslavement! For some time I have wondered where many of our "libertarians" would have stood on the slavery question if this were 1858 instead of 1973. Would they really have been in favor of immediate and unconditional abolition? One wonders. Or would they have been griping about the salves' "disobedience to law", of the necessity of their abiding by the Constitution and of accepting due punishment? Would they have warned that the slaves must not be freed until the masters were "compensated" for their loss of capital assets? Elementary linguistics would seem to place "liberty" and "slavery" at diametrically opposite poles; but considering the "law über alles" approach of many of our "libertarians", this question becomes a relevant and disturbing one. We have heard, for example, that Ayn Rand is opposed to amnesty, and that our supposed "first libertarian Congressman", Steven Symms, is against amnesty as well. Good Lord, it's enough to make a "LeFevrian" out of us all. Is our First Libertarian Congressman going to be less libertarian on this vital issue than Bella Abzug? Let is be said then loud and clear: THE libertarian position on amnesty is Unconditional Amnesty Now, for draft evaders, resisters, and deserters, with perhaps a parade and a brass band thrown into the bargain. And an apology for the law that forced them to flee.

Price-Wage Controls. On this issue, too, Mr. Nixon has inaugurated Phase 3, with the removal of direct price and wage controls on every area except food, health, and construction (where Nixon has installed permanent price and wage fixing machinery). Again: an action to be hailed; no single act is more destructive of a free economy than price-wage controls, and if we all denounced their imposition on the black day of August 15, 1971 as fascism then we must hail their removal as a major retreat from economic despotism. Once again, the market will be permitted to function.

Of course, the motives for Nixon's action do not seem to be the most noble. Price controls take some time for their flaws and distortions to develop: for the longer they last, the more do their controlled prices diverge from the prices that would be obtaining on the free market. The strains and distortions were beginning to develop by the end of 1972. They were aggravated by the continuing inflation and by the recovery from the 1969-71 recession both of which put on greater pressure for an increase in prices and costs. Furthermore, the potentially disastrous profit restriction on prices was beginning to have its effect. For Phase 2 had mandated that if a business firm were making high profits, it could not raise its price and could even be forced to lower it; whereas a firm making low profits would be allowed to raise prices. While the recession lasted and profits were low, the effective impact of these controls on the economy was negligible. But as profits began to increase upon recovery during

1972, business firms were increasingly feeling the pinch. More and more distortions were piling up, as "black markets" developed in wage controls by phony upgrading of jobs, and as businesses began to create inefficiencies in order to register lower profits. One firm was reported by the pro-control Business Week as deliberately encouraging larger expense accounts among executives, and as scheduling its annual stockholders' meeting for the first time in the Bahamas, because "if we have to be inefficient, we may as well enjoy ourselves." As these distortions piled up, the bulk of American business, which had previously supported controls as a way of keeping down union wage rates, began to shift their allegiance, and began to "rediscover" the merits of the free market.

In switching his position, then, Mr. Nixon knew on which side his bread was buttered. But at least he had the perception to realize what was going on, and to switch out of controls after only a year of Phase 2.

But of course, once again, we have only a truce and not genuine peace. It was for Phase 3 that the Administration coined its phrase about "the stick in the closet." The artificial and arbitrary price and wage "guidelines" are still there, and the Administration can be expected to try to intimidate business, especially large business and large unions, into obeying these "voluntary" yardsticks. Compulsion is available at any time for the Administration to use. So once again, we should not rest content until the entire control machinery is dismantled for good and all.

Mr. Nixon's recent proposal to dismantle the farm price supports is another unexpected and welcome move in the same "ceasefire" pattern. Perhaps the imbecility of using controls to keep prices down while at the same time continuing to keep farm prices up began to impress itself on the Administration. At any rate, Nixon aims to phase out most farm price supports and acreage controls which cut food production — to the horror of the organized farm bloc. Even in Nixon's welcome proposal, however, he does not propose to go all the way, and there would still be provision for maximum acreage control if the government in its wisdom felt that production was likely to be "excessive." However, once again, Mr. Nixon has taken a decisive step to dismantle the farm price-raising program which has plagued this country since the days of Herbert Hoover (not Franklin Roosevelt, by the way.)

The Budget. A lot of nonsense has been written by supposedly astute political observers about the proposed Nixon budget. To talk of a "drastic revolution" in fiscal policy, of "stringent budget cutting", etc. is sheer nonsense. Orwellian "Newspeak" at its worst. In the old days, "cutting the budget" meant just that: reducing government expenditures. Now, Nixon is hailed/accused of being a "budget cutter" because he would increase the federal budget by "only" $18 billion. What kind of a "cut" is that? Despite the "peace dividend" supposed to attend the end of the Vietnam War, military spending is granted a substantial increase. The idea, furthermore, that the government is "committed" to budget items in the future which cannot be removed is again nonsense; no Congress can legally commit a future Congress to anything. The fact that any program, once begun, becomes politically very difficult to remove, is of course true, but this is quite another story. These programs are not natural or divine disasters, like earthquakes not amenable to human interposition. What is required to remove them is political courage, a courage insured and fueled by political pressure from the aggrieved taxpayer.

With all this said, we must still hail the President for daring to call for outright removal of many "welfare" programs, including the racketeering Office of Economic Opportunity and other "anti-poverty" schemes. In this sense, the Nixon budget is a small step forward. It is an even bigger step if it means — which is not yet clear — that Nixon has abandoned his disastrous welfare "reform" plan and his burgeoning scheme for national health insurance. If he has, then his budget, coupled with the retreat on price controls, does constitute a significant partial retreat from domestic statism and a truce against its further advance.

· · · · · · · · ·

All in all, then, the second Nixon Administration has very swiftly developed into a new form which is far more promising for libertarians than anything we might have dared to expect as late as last November. Your editor's judgment in finally landing on Nixon's side seems at this point to have been vindicated. In foreign policy, we are now in curious waters, in some senses in a world which we have not seen since the 1920's.

(Continued On Page 3)

350

Hospers Replies

It was something of a surprise to me that one of several dozen questionnaires which I rather hastily filled out during the recent presidential campaign (and not intended for publication) suddenly appeared in the **Libertarian Forum** (December 1972 issue), and even more that the remarks I made were taken out of context so as to produce a result very different from the one intended. I trust that the motive in doing this was something other than malice; but whatever the motive, I would like to clarify a few points with reference to that questionnaire, without attempting here to discuss the whole of it.

I have profited immensely from reading the **Libertarian Forum** during the last few years, and Dr. Rothbard's articles in particular have been unfailingly incisive, clear and informative, often more so than any other written material on the same subject anywhere. These pieces alone are worth many times the cost of subscription. In general, I agree completely with the articles on economic questions: in fact, many of them have helped to shape my own views on these issues. Virtually my only disagreements have been on one issue, international relations — and then only on some aspects of that. Our differing attitudes toward the police force probably result in large measure from our differing attitudes toward the current international scene.

That a police force of some kind is necessary, given the present state of society, seems obvious; that a private police force (or forces) would be ever so much more efficient than a state or municipal one seems also too plainly true to require much argument (though the questionnaire gave me no opportunity to indicate this: one was given space only to answer the specific questions asked, and no others). And among police forces in this country, my own dealings and those of everyone I know with the F. B. I. have been far more pleasant, or should I say less unpleasant, than with any local or state police force I have ever had dealings with (partly, no doubt, because of the superior training and education of the F. B. I.). Despite the fact that a national police force of any kind is always a great potential danger, I must admit that I would much rather deal with a member of the F. B. I. than with any local policeman I have ever encountered.

Now, unlike (apparently) the editors of this journal, I do believe that international threats to our security do exist — not merely threats to the United States government, but to the safety of individuals in the United States. I do not deny of course that the United States has committed its share of aggressions. (Let me state for the record that I denounced the involvement in Vietnam from its very beginning, though not so much because it constituted aggression by the U. S. when it was entered into as because the U. S. had no business becoming militarily involved in such overseas ventures.) But I also believe that the Soviet Union can hardly be construed as a peaceful and non-aggressive nation (I mean of course its leaders, not its people in general). In the Cuban crisis of 1962, for example, if the Soviet Union had had a 4-1 military lead over the United States instead of the other way round, it seems to me highly probable that Soviet bombs would have dropped on the United States. Except for American military might — which on other grounds is to be deplored, e.g. the advance of statism that usually accompanies militarism — it seems to me

extremely likely that attempts to Sovietize all or part of the world would have been made, and would have been successful. Most people did not believe Hitler when he announced his intentions in **Mein Kampf**, and most people have not believed the writers of the Russian revolution when they say (as the Communist Party theretician Mikhail Suslov said not so long ago) that the present detente with the United States will be only temporary, and will last only until the Soviet Union gains a clearcut military superiority over the United States, at which time there will be "a renewed assault upon the West." And, to quote a historian whom no one who has read his works can call a militarist, an alarmist, or a far right extremist, Professor Carroll Quigley: "We do not know if the Kremlin is insatiable for conquest, as some 'experts' claim, or is only seeking buffer security zones, as other 'experts' believe; but it is clear that Soviet orders to advance were prevented by the American possession of the A-bomb after 1945. It does seem clear that ultimately Soviet forces would have taken all of Germany, much of the Balkens, probably Manchuria, and possibly other fringe areas across central Asia, including Iran. Such an advance of Soviet power to the Rhine, the Adriatic, and the Aegean would have been totally unacceptable to the United States; but, without the atom bomb, we could hardly have stopped it." (Carroll Quigley, **Tragedy and Hope: a History of the World in Our Time**, p. 864. New York: Macmillan, 1966.)

The **Libertarian Forum** apparently does not take such remarks seriously: it seems to be so concerned with fighting statism in this country that it prefers not to believe that there could be unpleasant, if not catastrophic, effects upon Americans of statism overseas; whereas I, while acutely aware of galloping statism in the United States (having spent most of my time in the recent presidential campaign attempting to fight it), am also worried about even more tyrannical statism overseas — not so much as it affects the Russian people (though that too is cause for distress), but as it could well affect the American people in the event that we choose to disarm at this critical juncture in history and thus lay ourselves open to any foreign aggressor that has a yen for Sovietizing the United States by force of arms or by ultimatums based on that force. (See Chapter 10 of my **Libertarianism**.)

It may be, of course, that certain side-effects of military preparedness in the United States — such as destroying American freedom in the very act of trying to preserve it against possible foreign attack — will be so ghastly as to outweigh the effects of preparedness against such aggression. It may also be (not that I necessarily think it is true, but only possible) that if the United States freed its economy by entirely disbanding the Departments of H. E. W., Agriculture, etc., and Defense, the resulting economic prosperity would be so tremendous that it would be worth running the risk of foreign aggression just to see it happen. But I would still be worried lest during the period of transition to a free economy, particularly with the cessation of "loans" of wheat and technological assistance to the Soviet Union, the Soviet Union would interpret this development as being so hostile to its interests that it would take advantage of our disarmament to take military action against us. At least, I do not see how the "disarmament now" libertarians can be so sure of the U. S. S. R.'s peaceful intentions that they would be (as they apparently are) content to risk the lives of millions of Americans by totally, or almost totally, dismantling its present military forces.

It is this difference in the estimate of the intentions of foreign nations that undoubtedly underlies the difference in attitude (between the **Libertarian Forum** and myself) toward the United States military and police apparatus. If military preparedness can deter potential aggressors (and admittedly it can also cause them to arm themselves faster), the result is surely well worth the cost. And if the F. B. I. or any other police organization can prevent the bombing of Grand Central Station by foreign or domestic saboteurs, by discovering the identity of the plotters and apprehending them in time to avert catastrophe, I for one am grateful for it, and consider the money spent on them more than justified by the dividends yielded in protection of life and property. If you and I are safer because these organizations exist, they are to that extent at least worth having around; that after all is what they are for, to protect us. I grant, of course, that they engage in other activities as well which are clearly not protective, and obviously I deplore those activities. The question is whether one should throw the baby out with the bath-water by eliminating at one stroke those organizations which do, at least sometimes, succeed

(Continued On Page 4)

The Sticks In The Closet —
(Continued From Page 2)

For, with the truces in the Cold War which Nixon has in a sense concluded with Russia, China, and now in Vietnam, for the first time in a half-century our government is not holding up before our frightened eyes the spectre of a rampaging Enemy, just about to launch a dreaded attack upon American shores. Of course, the Cold War too is in the closet, ready to be trotted out again at any time that the Administration feels an acute need to conjure up a rampaging "Enemy" once more. But as of this moment, we are more at peace than we have been for a half-century. What will Mr. Nixon do with his all-round truce? Will he turn to something like the Eisenhower posture, and be content to snooze his way through the rest of his reign? Will we really be able to enjoy a relatively passive Administration for the next four years? Or will his restless nature lead Mr. Nixon into some new statist adventure, at home or abroad, to an arena where he can once again exert his potential power and might, where he can launch some new aggression? To paraphrase the old adage, we can hope for — and now even expect — the best, but we must be prepared for the worst. ◘

Hospers Replies — (Continued From Page 3)

in protecting us against threats to our life and liberty from both foreign and domestic sources.

I for one am not prepared to take that risk. At the very least, the proposition that there is no such risk is in no way self-evident, nor is it so obvious as to leave no room for argument. But the attitude of some libertarians appears to be: "I'm so convinced that I'm right (about there being no foreign threats to our safety) that I'm willing to risk not only my life but yours, by disarming, on the assumption that my calculations are correct." Such a person is welcome to risk his own life on that assumption, but I don't want him to risk mine along with it. It is possible, as some libertarians have said, that the chief danger to your and my liberty in 1973 comes not from Brezhnev or Mao but from Richard Nixon; but that no threat arises from these foreign sources at all, in view of their explicitly stated intentions, seems to me so plainly false that only by putting on intellectual blinders and seeing only what one wants to see is one enabled to put forward such an assertion.

My neighbors Smith and Jones may be so anxious to buy a new car that they will spend their money on it rather than on guns or burglar alarms for their homes, rationalizing their action with the consoling thought that the man across the street who has been uttering threats and buying lots of guns will take their example to heart, scrap his guns, and desist from any aggression. But Latvians and Czechs will not be so easily persuaded; they will wisely conclude that it is better to live without the new car than to be in constant danger of being robbed or shot.

□   — John Hospers

The Editor Rebuts

First, I should like to make it clear, to Dr. Hospers and to his many admirers, that I have nothing but the greatest esteem for him, both as a friend and as the outstanding theorist and spokesman for the "limited archy" wing of the libertarian movement. I wrote the article to which he is objecting ("Hospers On Crime and the FBI", Lib. Forum, December 1972) not out of malice — but out of sadness, sadness at the numerous violations of libertarian principle committed by the Presidential candidate of the Libertarian Party in the questionnaire. I am firmly convinced, moreover, that the numerous flaws, fallacies, and inconsistencies in Dr. Hospers' general position stem not from personal eccentricities but from the very essence of his "conservative libertarian" position. Between Conservatism and Libertarianism there are numerous and grave inner contradictions, and the attempt to mix the two will lead inevitably to grave problems and anomalies, as we have all recently seen, for example, in Ayn Rands' attack upon amnesty for draft evaders. But since Dr. Hospers is a man of great rationality, objectivity, and dedication, I have every confidence that he will eventually embrace the truth and jump completely over the conservative wall.

Now as to specifics. Dr. Hospers states that the questionnaire was not intended for publication; yet when a presidential candidate, in the heat of his campaign, answers a questionnaire designed for all the candidates, this is surely and legitimately News, and publication of the results can scarcely be regarded as a breach of confidence. When one runs for the Presidency, and assumes an important role as spokesman for libertarianism, then one's utterances become especially subject to careful scrutiny. Hospers the presidential candidate of the Libertarian Party rather than Hospers the man was the subject of scrutiny in our article.

As for the "context", of course readers can only decide the merits of my summary by obtaining the questionnaire from the Friends of the FBI. But one notable fact is that Dr. Hospers makes not a single rebuttal to any of the points in my article nor an explanation of any of his answers. Instead, virtually his entire reply is devoted to the "Russian Question", a matter irrelevant and out of context if there ever were one. As I recall, there was not a single mention, either in the questionnaire or in Dr. Hospers' answers of the Russian Question, nor of course in my article. Indeed, what in the world the Russian Question has to do with whether or not the FBI should prosecute the drug traffic, or wiretap, or whether the police should remind accused persons of their constitutional rights, passeth understanding. Are we going to be like the typical Conservative, who drags in the Russian Threat like King Charles' Head to justify any and all acts of government tyranny? Once we go that route, once we begin

to justify a loss of liberty now in order to "defend" that liberty later, we are not only abandoning liberty itself: we are justifying every act of statism, from the draft to oil proration laws. Indeed, every such act has been justified by conservatives in the name of the Russian Threat and of national defense." And in these justifications, we can see how the State has for centuries used the "foreign threat" to aggrandize its power over its deluded subjects.

Before getting to the Russian Question itself, I would like to say that I fail to be impressed with the politeness of the FBI. That they are better than many local police is hardly a commendation; do we prefer Attila or Genghis Khan? In fact, on the score of education, intelligence, and suavity, the CIA has the FBI beat hollow; and yet the foul deeds of the CIA have become glaringly known. But the major point is the usual libertarian case for decentralization: that when we confront despotism by the FBI we have no place to go short of leaving the country; whereas to avoid despotism or brutality by, say, the West Waukegan police force all we have to do is to skip to East Waukegan: surely a far more comfortable choice.

But to get to the Russian Question. In the first place, whether or not Russia constitutes a critical military threat is strictly an empirical question, and therefore not a question that can be resolved in a few pages of philosophical or political controversy. For example, it is logically conceivable that Great Britain constitutes an imminent military threat to the U. S., and that Edward Heath is planning a sneak atomic attack on New York in 48 hours. Logically conceivable, but of course empirically laughable — even though we could make out a case of sorts, citing the fact that we were twice in grave military combat with Great Britain, and so on.

Since it is an empirical question, I will have to be a bit high-handed and say flatly that it is my considered view that there is not a single shred of evidence of any Russian aim or plan to launch a military attack upon the United States, either in the past, present, or future. In fact, the evidence is all the other way, even in the time of Lenin, and certainly in the time of Stalin and his successors. Since the time of Lenin and his magnificent (from a libertarian, pro-peace point of view) conclusion of the "appeasement" Treaty of Brest-Litovsk in 1918, the Soviet Union, vis a vis the other Great Powers, has consistently pursued a policy of what they have long termed "peaceful coexistence", in fact often bending over backwards to pursue a peaceful foreign policy almost to the point of national suicide. I am not maintaining that the motivation for this unswerving course was any sort of moral nobility; it is the supremely practical one of preserving the Soviet State at all costs to other aims and objectives, buttressed by the Soviets' firm Marxian conviction that, since capitalist states are doomed anyway, it is foolhardy in the extreme to court or risk war. The Soviet policy has always been the defensive one of hanging on to what they have and waiting for the supposedly inevitable Marxian revolutions in the other countries of the world. Lenin's adherence to that policy was only confirmed by the "socialism in one country" doctrine of Stalin and his successors.

We all too often forget several crucial facts of modern European history; and one is that, from the point of view of ordinary international relations, Russia (any Russia, not just Soviet Russia) was a grievous loser from the settlements imposed by World War I (Brest-Litovisk, Versailles). Any German, Russian, or Austrian regime would have been "revisionist" after the war, i.e. would have sought the restoration of the huge chunk of territory torn from them by the victorious powers. Old Czarist Russia was shorn of Finland, Estonia, Latvia, Lithuania, Western Byelorussia (grabbed by Poland after its war of aggression against Soviet Russia in 1920-21), and Western Ukraine (lopped off by Czechoslovakia and Rumania). Any Russian government would have hankered for its lost and grabbed territories. And yet, the Soviets did very little about this hankering; certainly they made no move whatsoever to make war to get the territories back. The Hitler-Stalin pact, much reviled by the uncomprehending Western press, actually made excellent sense for both major "revisionist" post-Versailles powers, Germany and Russia. For the essence of that pact was the commonality of revisionist interests by both powers: from that pact, Germany got its lost territories back (plus an extra chunk of ethnically Polish Poland), and Russia peacefully re-acquired its old territories, with the exception of Finland. No dire Russian military threat to the West, let alone the United States, can be conjured up out of that.

The next crucial and unfortunately forgotten fact is this: that Hitler

(Continued On Page 5)

The Editor Rebuts —(Continued From Page 4)

turned brutally upon his ally and savagely attacked Soviet Russia on June 22, 1941. In this attack, Hitler was joined by the fascist regimes of Rumania and Hungary (Polish Poland and Czechoslovakia had by this time disappeared, or been swallowed up by Germany.) Why Hitler did this foolhardy act, an act that lost him the war and his head, is still a puzzle to historians. But we can say that his motives were compounded out of two factors: (a) his long-held desire to seize the "breadbasket" of the Ukraine; and (b) his hysterical anti-communism which fully matches the equivalent anti-Communism of the American Conservative movement. In his hysteria, Hitler too, like our conservatives, thought he saw an imminent Russian Threat: and so he decided on what is now called a "preemptive strike." But of course Hitler, like our American Conservatives, was deluded; for the events of the war revealed that Stalin's unwise trust in his ally led him to neglect elementary preparedness and thereby almost lost him the war as a result. Stalin's pacific policy was carried almost to the point of national suicide.

What of Stalin's "expansion" into Eastern Europe? This expansion was scarcely aggression in any rational sense: it was purely the inevitable consequence of Russia's rolling back and defeating the German aggressor and his Hungarian and Rumanian allies. It is only by a grievous "dropping of the context", of forgetting that Russia got into the war as a result of German aggression, that we can possibly point the finger of threat of "aggression" at Russia's military march into the aggressor countries.

As his evidence for alleged Soviet "orders to advance" into Western Europe at the end of the war, Dr. Hospers cites only a paragraph from Professor Carroll Quigley. Yet Professor Quigley is not in any sense a specialist on the history of the Cold War nor does he command any respect whatever in the historical profession. And with good reason. The only place I have ever seen Professor Quigley cited as an authority is in several Birchite tracts, tracts which, whatever their devotion to individual liberty, are scarcely noted for the profundity or the accuracy of their scholarship. If any readers are interested in the best scholarly evidence on Russia and the Cold War, let them turn to the excellent and notable researches of such distinguished historians as Gabriel Kolko, Lloyd Gardner, Walter LaFeber, and Gar Alperovitz, researches which back my interpretation to the hilt. I repeat: there is not a shred of evidence of any Soviet aim or plan, much less "orders", to invade Western Europe at the end of World War II or at any other time. If Dr. Hospers would care to cite some real evidence for his charge, I would be delighted to hear it.

In fact, read correctly, Professor Quigley's citation is simply one more of numerous indications that it was the United States that launched the Cold War, that it was the United States that brutally and immorally brandished its monopoly of atomic weapons in an attempt to cow Soviet Russia into getting out of the conquered territories of Eastern Europe and to open them to American influence and penetration. In fact, historians from such opposite ends of the political and ideological spectrum as Gar Alperovitz (in his great work, **Atomic Diplomacy**) and the late Harry Elmer Barnes, have shown that the very genocidal dropping of the A-bomb on an already vanquished Japan was done largely for the purpose of using atomic diplomacy as a counter in the American-launched Cold War.

As for the Cuban crisis of 1962, there is not a single piece of evidence of any Russian aim to drop missiles on the United States. In fact, the Soviets had plenty of their own missiles; and any idea that Cuba would launch a missile attack on the U. S. seems to me in the Great Britain-as-military threat category. In fact, the Soviet missiles in Cuba were as nothing to the missiles with which the United States had long encircled the Soviet Union. It is evident to me that the only possible purpose of Khrushchev's emplacement of missiles in Cuba was to safeguard Cuba against an American attack: an attack the prospect of which was scarcely ludicrous, considering the 1961 CIA attack on Cuba at the Bay of Pigs. As Richard Walton points out in his excellent recent book on the Cuban crisis, the cause and motive power of the crisis was President Kennedy's aggravated sense of machismo, his dangerous desire to face down the Russians in any sort of confrontation even at the risk of worldwide nuclear devastation. In fact, the Cuban settlement satisfied both parties: Kennedy looked like the macho conqueror, forcing the Russian missiles

out of Cuba; while Khrushchev gained the informal but vital concession from Kennedy that the U. S. would launch no further aggression upon Cuba. Unfortunately for Khrushchev, his Soviet colleagues did not appreciate the loss of macho face, and Khruschchev was deposed for his pains.

Dr. Hospers' only other piece of evidence is unsupported references to various Communist theoreticians, which he likens to Hitler's "announced intentions" in **Mein Kampf**. In the first place, as the eminent left-liberal English historians A. J. P. Taylor and Geoffrey Barraclough have pointed out, far too much has been made of the importance of **Mein Kampf** in assessing Hitler's policies. To say that someone's actions can be fully explained by a tract, written in very different circumstances a decade or more earlier, is highly simplistic as historical method. But more relevantly, Communist "announced intentions" are very different from those of **Mein Kampf**. The announced intentions of all the Marxist-Leninist theoreticians, from Lenin down to the present, are notably different: they call repeatedly and consistently for a policy of peaceful coexistence by Communist countries with the "capitalist" powers. There is never any equivocation about that. However, they do warn (to varying degrees, depending on the wing of Marxism-Leninism) that capitalism inevitably begets imperialism, and that imperialism will tend to launch a war against the Communist powers. Therefore, they call for alert preparedness and oppose any unilateral disarmament by the Communist powers. And given the black record of American aggression in the Cold War and elsewhere, I must say that they have a point: not in the inevitability of capitalism begetting imperialism, but in a wariness over the possibly aggressive intentions of American imperialism. In short, there is infinitely more evidence of an American military threat to Russia than vice versa; and the "announced intentions" of Marxist-Leninism confirm rather than rebut this conclusion.

In fact, after decades of study of Marxist-Leninist writings, I have found only one theorist who has ever advocated a Soviet attack on the United States: and that is the crazed Latin-American Trotskyite, Juan Posadas. But since Senor Posadas has no standing within the world Trotskyite movement, let alone among the Communists in power, I think we can safely assure Dr. Hospers that the Posadas threat is about as critical as our hypothetical threat from the armed might of Prime Minister Edward Heath.

Curiously, Dr. Hospers seems to be most worried about a Russian attack during the period of transition to a free economy, when the U. S. State shall have been abolished. How Russia could see this development as "hostile to its interests" is difficult to see; on the contrary, the Russians would breathe a sigh of relief at being free of the threat of American aggression, a threat which they have felt deeply ever since we intervened with troops and weapons to try to crush the Bolshevik Revolution in 1918-20. The Russians, indeed, have been anxious to conclude a joint disarmament agreement with the U. S., and have ever since they accepted the American proposal to that effect on May 10, 1955: a proposal which the U. S. itself promptly repudiated and has balked at ever since. Contrary to American propaganda, incidentally, the Russian proposal was for general and complete disarmament coupled with unlimited inspection; it was the United States who, while insisting on inspection, balked at any kind of effective disarmament.

To proceed to Dr. Hospers' final point: what of those Americans who are not persuaded by our evidence, and who persist in fearing the Russian Threat? He accuses us anarcho-capitalists who wish to dismantle the American State of "risking not only my life, but yours, by disarming". But the point is that, in an anarchist society, those who fear a foreign threat and wish to arm themselves defensively, are free to go ahead and do so. Dr. Hospers happily concedes that private police forces would be more efficient than the police force of government monopoly; so why not private defense forces or "armies" as well? Contrary to Dr. Hospers, anarchists do not propose to force those who wish to arm defensively to disarm: instead on the contrary it is he and other advocates of archy who are now forcing us to arm against a foreign threat that many of us believe does not exist. It is no more moral to tax someone to pay for one's own defense, whether real or imagined, than it is to draft him for the same purpose. And, besides, if the FBI is really protecting us against the sabotage of Grand Central Station, then why couldn't the owners of that station do a far better job?   ◘

The Old Curmudgeon As Hero

By Walter Block

Imagine, if you will, the problems of the real estate developer trying to supplant a whole city block of moldy decrepit tenements with a modern residential complex replete with gardens, swimming pools, balconies, and all the other accoutrements of fine living. Not so much all the government-made problems such as zoning laws, licensing requirements, bribes, permissions for architectural plans, etc.; to be sure, they are widespread, stultifying, and exasperating. Let us focus instead on the problems posed by the old curmudgeon who happens to live on the block in the most decrepit tenement of all. A building, however, that he is exceedingly fond of. Some might even go so far as to say overly fond of, since he refuses to sell the old homestead to the builder at any price. The builder offers hundreds, then thousands, and then even millions. But the old curmudgeon steadfastly refuses. The builder offers a paid trip to Europe, to Israel, to anywhere but to no avail.

As important as this instance may be, it is only one of the many cases where the old curmudgeon supposedly interferes with the well being of the multitudes. The old curmudgeon, who may be a little old lady, a wizened bitter old man, a great big fat jolly but stubborn person, has long been active, defending the old homestead against the inroads of highway builders, railroad magnates, mining companies, dam and irrigation control projects; indeed, we owe the plots of many of our Western movies to this theme. It is the old curmudgeon, or his spiritual soul mate, who served as the inspiration for the enactment of eminent domain legislation: a staunch human barrier to any and all progress, feet planted firmly at the crossroads, arms stubbornly crossed in front of chest, the motto of the old curmudgeon a strident, defiant "NO!"

So goes the popular view of the holdout. In this paper, however, I shall argue that the popular view is entirely mistaken; that on the contrary, it is the old curmudgeon, seemingly always standing in the way of progress, who actually stands for the greatest hope that progress has ever had; that this attack on the old curmudgeon who refuses to sell his property at the demand of some big builders is really a disguised attack on the concept of private property itself.

It is an attack on the basic concept of private property itself because according to that doctrine, each owner of property shall have the full right to decide its use, as long as this use does not interfere with every other property owner's similar and equal right to the use of his own property. In the case of eminent domain, when the state forces the property owner to give up the rights to his property on terms that he would not voluntarily accept, the rights to private property are abridged.

There are two main arguments for private property: the moral and the practical. According to the moral argument, each man is the complete owner of himself, to begin with. So the primary object of property rights, the person itself, is the foundation of property rights, from whence all other property rights flow. But the ownership and control of each person by himself ineluctably results in certain fruits of that ownership and control. These fruits of man's labor come under the ownership and control of each man in accordance with what he has produced, by the same principle under which he received ownership and control over his own body in the first place. The principle under which each person comes to control and own himself is the principle of homesteading, or of natural control or of natural regulation or of natural governance. That is to say, each person is the natural owner of himself because, in the nature of things, it is he, it is his will, that controls his body. Imagine if nature was different. If everytime I looked, you saw; if everytime I willed an arm to raise and scratch an ear, it was your arm that did so; if everytime you itched, I felt it. And if everytime you looked, I saw; if everytime you willed an arm to raise and scratch an ear, it was my arm that did so; if everytime I itched, you scratched. Then you would no longer own that body, and I would no longer own this one. Rather, you would own this one and I would own that one.

According to this principle of natural homesteading which justifies self ownership, man not only owns his own person, but he also owns the fruits of that person, that which he produces, those parts of nature hitherto unowned with which man mixes his labor and transforms into a more productive existence. The moral way that these non-human properties can change ownership is either through voluntary trade or voluntary gift giving. This is because these are the only ways of changing ownership which are consistent with the original owners natural homesteading

rights: they are the only methods by which the homesteaders maintain control even in giving up ownership rights, for they are the only methods by which ownership is given up on a voluntary basis.

The property now owned by the old curmudgeon was gained for him by just such a process. There was an original homesteader, there were sales of the land, perhaps the land was given in the form of a gift at one time or another. But the final result was that the land passed into the control of the old curmudgeon, if he is indeed the rightful owner, through an unbroken chain of voluntary events, all consistent with the principle of natural homesteading.

Any attempt to wrest it from him without his consent would therefore be in violation of the principle of natural homesteading and hence immoral. It would amount to an act of aggressive force against an entirely innocent party.

Many people realize this when it comes to resisting the demands on the part of a private business for condemnation of the old curmudgeon's property. They realize, perhaps, that one private business has no legitimacy over another. But when it comes to state condemnation, through eminent domain laws, the story is very different. Here, there is very little opposition, even though, in many if not all cases, there are still private interests, using the government's eminent domain powers to their own ends. Much of the urban relocation programs, for instance, are at the behest of private universities, of private hospitals. Much of the condemnation of private property by the government's use of eminent domain laws is done for the special interests of private lobbies and special interest groups. Done to benefit that part of the public that favors the aggrandizement of museums, parks, roads, public theatre, opera, and concert halls. The condemnation of the land now used for Lincoln Center for the Performing Arts in New York City is a case in point. A vast tract of land was condemned to make way for "culture". People were forced to sell at prices the government was willing to pay, involuntarily. Whose culture can be made perfectly clear by reading the list of subscribers to Lincoln Center, which reads like a who's who of the ruling class.

Now let us consider the second argument for private property rights: the practical argument. One practical argument for private property rights is that of stewardship: it is the claim that under the stewardship of private property, the "best" care will be given to the property of the older generation that is handed down to the younger, and that the younger generation will "best" be able to add to its heritage. According to the stewardship view of property, it is not terribly important just precisely who gets control of any given piece of property. What is important is that all property be privately owned, and that precise delineations between the property be clearly marked off.

According to the stewardship view, all property gets given out somehow (equally or unequally, it does not matter), no forced or involuntary transfer of the property is allowed, and each person works his property to the best or worst of his ability (it does not matter which). What does matter though, what is crucially important as a matter of fact, is that a market system be in operation so that those that "mishandle" their property eventually lose some of it and have less and less as time goes on, and that those who nurture and husband it well eventually gain some more and have more and more as time goes on. Thus, as these better able to maintain a good stewardship over property become responsible for more and more, and those unable to maintain a good stewardship have less and less, the general level of stewardship will rise, and better and better carte will be taken of the property.

The way that the laizzez faire market place works this out is simplicity itself. First of all, it defines the "proper maintenence" of property as that kind of maintenence or care-taking that maximizes the money return from or the value of that property. The market then tends to insure that the good caretakers earn more money than the bad ones. This enables the good caretakers, on net balance, to buy out the bad ones. For example, the "good" farmer, the one who maintains his crops and farm animals in good condition, will prosper, earn more money, and in the long run, tend to be able to either buy out the bad farmer, or to be able to bring more and more acres into cultivation. In any case, as time wears on, this stewardship system, in rewarding the good stewards, and penalizing the poor stewards, increases the average level of stewardship. And it does so

(Continued On Page 7)

354

The Old Curmudgeon As Hero —

(Continued From Page 6)

automatically, without political votes every four years, without political purges, without fuss or fanfare.

Of course, this stewardship argument assumes a complete laissez-faire capitalist system. Any government infringements, such as loans and subsidies to prop up failing businesses (bad stewards who mismanage their property) such as the Lockheed loan, vitiate the whole effect. For then the mismanagers will not succumb to the more effective stewardship of the good managers. The government interposes itself between the bad caretaker and in effect, an outraged public, one that did not voluntarily choose to patronize the entrepreneur in question. Other forms such infringements can take are the granting of franchises, licenses and other types of monopoly advantages to one select individual, or group; the granting of tariffs and quotas to protect inefficient domestic "caretakers" against the competition of the more efficient foreign stewards; the awarding of government contracts which pervert the original consumption wishes of the public.

Why, it may be asked, if the goal of this practical argument for property rights is that it tends to promote good stewardship of the scarce resources of the planet, cannot the government help the process along a bit by transferring the control of resources from those who have proved themselves bad managers in the market to those who have proved themselves good managers? In this way, the vagaries of the market system will be suspended, and those who would eventually have been able to prosper in the ordinary course of events will be able to do so much more quickly. The problem with this, of course, is the insurmountable one that the market system works automatically day by day, to determine who are the good and bad managers each day. Past reputation and abilities count for nought. If the government attempts to hasten the process by transferring money from the poor to the rich, it will only succeed in transferring money from those who were poor managers in the past to those who were good managers in the past. (This is true on the assumption of a laissez faire society; of our own society, we can make no such claim. Practically none of the current income transfer from the poor to the rich occurs out of a motivation to encourage good stewardship nor has that effect.) There is no guarantee that the future will resemble the past. That those who were successful entrepreneurs in the past will be successful entrepreneurs in the future. Also, what of the people who are now poor but are destined by their own efforts to be very good managers and in the future become rich? A governmental program whose purpose was to spur on stewardship based on past accomplishments would involve taking money away from these future good managers.

The reason it is important to discuss this question is that it is at the root of the original problem of the old curmudgeon who refuses to sell his property. For what is the old curmudgeon who refuses to sell his property but a "backward", probably poor individual who is by all standards not a good manager? A prime candidate for being relieved of his money by a scheme whose goal is to speed up the market process of creating good stewards. But we have seen why this scheme is bound to fail. When we apply it to the case of the old curmudgeon we can see that not only does the free market have a tendency to reward good managers in the future, but that also, at any given time, there will tend to be a rough proportionality between the amount of private property amassed by an individual and the efficiency with which he cares for it. Of course there will be exceptions. Even assuming a laissez faire economy there will be some good managers with precious little to manage and some bad managers with an embarrassment of riches. But these will be the exceptions, not the rule. On the average in a laissez-faire economy, there will exist at any given time a rough proportionality between stewardship ability and the amount of private property amassed.

Therefore, stripping the old curmudgeon of his rightful possessions because of seemingly poor stewardship, in addition to being immoral, is even impractical from the point of view of the stewardship argument for private property. As small as it is, the old curmudgeon has demonstrated his ability to manage it, if for no other reason than that it is actually in his possession.

There is another practical argument for private property besides the stewardship argument. For want of a better name, we may call this the praxeological argument for private property. One complaint that the praxeologist would have about the stewardship argument would be that

such terms and phrases as "good maintenance", "the greatest good for the greatest number", "efficient stewardship", "proper handling of property", "maintaining property in good order", etc., have no precise definition; that the definition of "proper maintenance" of property in terms of maximizing the money return from or the value of that property begs the question of the perspective from which such evaluations are made. All too often, the praxeologist would charge, the implicit evaluation is made from the perspective of the large builder, and not from the perspective of the old curmudgeon.

The praxeological view focusses on the question of how to evaluate the level of satisfaction inherent in any business transaction or state of affairs. And the answer given is that the only scientific statement that can be made about such occurences is that when a voluntary trade between two people takes place, both gain in the ex ante sense. The ex ante sense is the sense in which both parties to the trade, at the actual time of the trade, each value that which they gain from the .rade at a higher level than that which they must give up in the trade. In the ex ante evaluation of the trade, it is therefore apodictically certain that both parties to the trade gain from it. We know this because the two parties would not have voluntarily agreed to make the trade unless, at the time of the trade, each had valued what he was to receive more than what he was to give up. Thus no one can ever make a mistake on a trade, in the ex ante sense. In the ex post sense of evaluation, which is usually contrasted with the ex ante sense, one can certainly make a mistake in trade. For the ex post sense evaluates the trade from the vantage point of the future. One most certainly can value what one receives in trade more than what one gives up — and then reverse one's evaluation in the future, when it is too late to call off the trade.

Returning to the case of the old curmudgeon who refuses to trade his old homestead even for a million dollars so that the big real estate developer can supplant the whole city block of tenements with a luxury complex. The praxeologist would vehemently reject the contention that

(Continued On Page 8)

Curmudgeon As Hero —

(Continued From Page 7)

there is any loss in welfare, stewardship of property, "proper" usage of property or whatever. For the praxeologist, as we have just seen, the only time that we can make a judgment about welfare, or good stewardship, etc., is when two people make a trade; and the only thing that we can say, as scientists, about the trade, is that both parties to it gain from it in the ex ante sense (or else they would not have voluntarily entered into the trade). But the case of the old curmudgeon refusing to sell his homestead for a million is precisely not a case where two parties enter voluntarily into a trade. It is precisely a case where no trade takes place. We cannot therefore deduce that welfare or good stewardship was thwarted. If anything, the only thing that we can deduce from the failure of the trade to take place is that although perhaps the real estate developer valued the old homestead more than the million dollars he was willing to give up for it, the old curmudgeon decidely did not so value these two properties. On the contrary, from his failure to sell, we can only conclude that he valued the old homestead more than the million dollars. And who is to say him nay? Since no interpersonal comparisons of utility or welfare can have a scientific basis (there is no unit by which such things can even be measured, let alone compared between different people) there is no one who can legitimately say that the refusal of the old curmudgeon to sell his property is "harmful", or causes problems, or is "obstructive". Of course the old curmudgeon's choice is obstructive of the real estate developer's goals. But then, the goals of the real estate developer are just as obstructive of the goals of the old curmudgeon. There is no scientific, let alone moral, reason to regard the curmudgeon's goals and values as inferior to those of the developer. ◻

A Libertarian Poll

Mr. Ferdinand V. Solara, an inveterate chronicler of things libertarian and conservative, has just released the results of a questionnaire polling the intensity of the respondents' devotion to various libertarian individuals, publications, and organizations. It is scarcely Mr. Solara's fault that the representativeness of his sample can be questioned; 155 answers are not a large sample of the movement, and perhaps his Colorado base helps account for the high percentage of objectivists and other "limited archists" among his respondents (approximately ¾ of those answering were limited archists and ¼ anarchists.) Perhaps Colorado also accounts for the fact that 60% of the pollees were Libertarian Party members.

Mr. Solara asked his respondents to rate various magazines and organizations on a scale ranging rom A to E. One interesting result is the picture of the intensity of devotion of members or subscribers, gauged from how many gave an "A" rating to "their" groups or journals. Of

the organizations, there was generally a near 1:1 correlation between members and an "A" rating: that is, the two were roughly equal. One major anomaly is the Liberty Amendment Committee, which had only 4 members but which garnered an "A" rating from 24 respondents; this indicates that many people esteem the Liberty Amendment Committee who wouldn't dream of joining the organization. On the other hand, the other leading anomaly was our old friend YAF, which had 29 members among those polled, but which only got an A from 2 of them. There are presumably a great many disaffected members of YAF, as well there might be.

Of the publications listed, we are happy to announce that a close A/subscriber correlation held true for only three journals: Reason, A is A News, and the Lib. Forum. All the other listed magazines revealed a severe falling off of ratings, presumably reflecting a severe disaffection among their subscribers. There is, however, an anomaly in regard to the Lib. Forum. That is, that while we have developed a high degree of subscriber loyalty, our number of subscribers among the pollees was relatively small, far smaller than several of our colleagues in dire loyalty trouble. In short, folks, we have a great product, but not enough readers imbibing all the goodies we have to offer. Let us remedy that, and round up more subscribers! Why deprive so many people of the blessings conferred by the Libertarian Forum? ◻

Movement Magazines

Manny Klausner, the estimable young editor of Reason, chides us for our gloomy account of the stillbirth of Libertarian Review, (Lib. Forum, December 1972) and wishes to correct the record by pointing out that the monthly Reason now has over 5,000 subscribers and bids fair to rise to over 6,000 in a short time. Well taken, but I doubt whether this happy news is enough to cut the gloom about the current good health of the libertarian movement. For, on the other hand, we must consider that no less than three of our leading libertarian magazines have bit the dust in recent months, and a fourth is at least in serious trouble. The Individualist, formerly a fine monthly magazine issued under the auspices of the Society for Individual Liberty, has apparently expired. Libertarian Analysis, a quarterly journal that tried to be a home for scholarly articles, is dead. And The New Banner, an ambitious tabloid biweekly of high quality produced by the South Carolina movement, has apparently collapsed as well. And now Outlook, an organ of much of the New York movement which had achieved a high quality in recent issues, is, if not expired, at least in the throes of a bitter internecine conflict. It looks as if there is a good chance that we will soon be left with Reason as virtually our only magazine. Despite the many fine qualities of Reason, this means that the fortunes of the movement are in worse shape than we wrote last December, rather than better; apart from Reason, the libertarian publishing world is in a shambles. ◻

The Libertarian Forum
BOX 341
MADISON SQUARE STATION
NEW YORK, NEW YORK 10010

First Class

Published Every Month. Subscription Rate: $8.00 Per Year

A Monthly Newsletter

THE
Libertarian Forum

Joseph R. Peden, Publisher   Murray N. Rothbard, Editor

VOLUME V, NO. 3   MARCH, 1973   75¢

THE MAYORAL CIRCUS

Ever since the open primary was instituted in New York a few years ago, politicians have deeply regretted this extension of democratic choice. And well they might, for the power of the party bosses has been superseded by the fun and games where every man-and-his-brother can, and do, leap in to battle for political office. If they can do so, the politicos will soon wrap up the open primary, but in the meanwhile we can all enjoy the circus spectacle.

The circus has come to full bloom this year, as approximately a dozen "serious" candidates vie for the top prize of the Mayoralty. We hereby present a "reader's guide" to the present status of the New York mayoral race.

The central, overriding fact of the contest is the withdrawal of New York's universally (within the city) despised and reviled incumbent, Big Jawn Lindsay. Lindsay had managed, in a perverse way, to unify the city: for in recent years it has been extremely difficult to find anyone, regardless of race, creed, color, income class, ideology, or national origin, who does not go into a conniption fit at the very mention of the hated Lindsay name. The essential nature of the common hatred of Lindsay is the clue to current New York politics. For Lindsay, in his person and in his policies, embodies the essential program of what has been deliciously dubbed as the "limousine liberals". Limousine Liberalism is the political alliance of arrogant, upper-class, Park Avenue WASPS (richly embodied in Lindsay's person) with the militants of the black and Puerto Rican "ghettoes." Lindsay Liberalism is the aggrandizement of the central municipal bureaucracy and the government, levying ever-higher taxes on the middle and the working classes, for the benefit of the aforesaid bureaucracy, favored big business interests, and the ghetto militants. Lindsay Liberalism is the government sternly telling the middle and working classes of the city: "Let's you and him integrate the schools"; "Let's you and him integrate housing and the neighborhoods"; "Let's you pay more for welfare clients and the housing of drug addicts"; "Let's you sit by while street crime and mugging runs rampant, and let's you 'solve' the crime problem by providing more anti-poverty money and more playgrounds." And while Lindsay and his upper-class colleagues keep issuing such stern injunctions to the average citizen of New York, they themselves are busy sending their own kids to exclusive private schools, and living in Park Avenue apartment houses tightly ringed with security measures to keep out the unwanted.

For the average New Yorker, the nub of the entire problem is crime. He could have continued to put up uncomplainingly with high taxes, galloping welfare, traffic congestion, pollution, and the rest of the urban ills of our society if only crime had been kept under control. And by that he means street crime: the sudden mugging and assault for purpose of robbery, "kicks", or a combination of the two. The New Yorker is no longer impressed with crime statistics that show other cities with a higher rate of crime in forgery, auto theft, embezzlement, or bank robbery. He is of course opposed to these categories of crime, too, but the kind of crime that hits him in the gut, literally and metaphorically, is street mugging, and it is here that New York has come to "excel" — to

the extent that New York has become a nationwide sick joke for television comedians. The New Yorker has lost patience with the age-old liberal "explanations" for crime: economic, historical, and sociological. He wants street crime cracked down on, hard and right now.

Lindsay's first term was difficult enough, but while he quickly lost the support of the Irish, Italian, and Polish middle and working classes — known in New York as "the ethnics" — he still retained the support of the mass of New York Jews, a group which had long been synonymous with the word "liberalism." With Jewish, Negro, and Puerto Rican support, and with his opponents split, Lindsay managed to squeak through to re-election in 1969. But in his second term, the mass of New York Jewry has defected as well; and, indeed, the story of New York politics has been the massive shift "rightward" of the middle and lower-income Jews of Bronx, Brooklyn, and Queens. (There are very few lower-income WASPS in New York City, scarcely enough to constitute a voting bloc.) This rightward shift has been propelled by the hammer-blows of street mugging; as they themselves, their friends and relatives and neighbors, have come under the gun or knife, preservation from street crime has taken first rank in the concerns of New York's Jews as well as the other ethnic groups. The crime question has thus become the central, overriding fact of New York politics, and most of the passion expended on such issues as welfare, public schools, and housing is related to crime at the central core.

The one exception to this loss of Jewish support for Lindsay Liberalism is the West Side of Manhattan, a district rife with middle and upper-class Jewish intellectuals, who continue to cling to their old liberalism, even though even here fissures have begun to surface. The result is that in recent years, New York City politics has seen a dramatic split between Manhattan and the other boroughs: with the other boroughs "conservative" (especially on issues of crime and "law-and-order"), and Manhattan — consisting largely of Negroes, Puerto Ricans, upper-class WASPS, and the aforesaid West Side Jews — remaining stubbornly left-liberal. It is no accident that Manhattan was the only borough that gave McGovern a clear-cut majority in 1972.

After surveying his chances, and despite his evident desire to continue in office, John Lindsay wisely took himself out of the mayoral race. The last straw was when Lindsay's major political supporter, shrewd old Alex Rose, the absolute boss of the Liberal Party of New York, refused to endorse the Mayor's re-election bid. But Lindsay remains as arrogant as ever, and he threatens to run for governor next year, on the theory that he can still command support outside the city. But if he runs, he will undoubtedly be slaughtered at the polls once more.

The field is now wide open for the mayoralty. The June Democratic primary now has about a dozen entries. Let us go down the list, reading approximately from Left to Right.

On the extreme left, there is Assemblyman Jesse Gray, of Harlem. A blend of nine parts crafty street brawler and one part Marxist-Leninist, Jesse is one of the least attractive candidates to come down the pike in

(Continued On Page 2)

The Mayoral Circus —

(Continued From Page 1)

many a year. He is, no doubt, the only black candidate in the field, but even his black support is dubious, for two major reasons: (1) Blacks (and Puerto Ricans) don't vote very heavily in any election in New York — one of the least well-kept secrets of New York politics; and (2) Jesse is not even supported by New York's Black Caucus, headed by Manhattan Borough President Percy Sutton and Brooklyn's Congresswoman Shirley Chisholm; his only major black supporter is Brooklyn's State Senator Waddaba Stewart, who was recently on the losing end of a power struggle in the black Bedford-Stuyvesant area with Shirley Chisholm. Jesse's chances may be set as somewhere close to zero.

Next we come to the major Left candidate, Congressman Herman Badillo of the Bronx. As the only Puerto Rican candidate, Badillo hopes to snag the black and Puerto Rican votes in the June primary. Badillo, however, lost in a ruthless, slam-bang, war-to-the-knife battle at the March convention of the New Democratic Coalition, the umbrella outfit for all the "reform" Democrat clubs in the city. Despite early support, the NDC, consisting largely of left-liberal Jews on the West Side and elsewhere, finally gave its endorsement instead to Albert Blumenthal (see below). The NDC endorsement was coveted largely because it provides the clue to campaign funds from wealthy liberal Jewish contributors. The angry Badillo bitterly charged the NDC with "racism", and the fat is in the fire. Badillo's reliance on black and Puerto Rican votes is probably hopeless because (1) blacks and Puerto Ricans don't vote in large numbers, and (2) the arrogant, grim Badillo is distrusted by many Puerto Ricans in New York. The distrust is personal, religious and ethnic, embodied in: Badillo's cool and arrogant personality, his marriage to a Jewess and his previous courting of NDC and Jewish-liberal support, and to the fact that he is an Evangelical Protestant while the mass of Puerto Ricans are Catholics. Badillo's chances are surely not as negligible as Gray's, but they are now slim indeed.

This brings us to the official NDC candidate, Albert Blumenthal. Blumenthal, the Assemblyman from the West Side, is a cool, tough customer who is proud of his "pragmatic" record in the State Assembly. Now that he has the NDC endorsement, he can be expected to move swiftly to appeal to the crime-fearing masses of New York's outer boroughs. While Blumenthal may well carry Manhattan, the chances of his succeeding in gulling the rest of New York into accepting his more moderate "image" are not very bright.

If Blumenthal is the official candidate of Left-Center Liberalism, there are other dark horse candidates in the same zone who might, but probably will not, catch on. City Councilman-at-Large Robert Postel from Manhattan, has been running on the strength of his fearless exposes of corruption by the young hot-shots in the Lindsay administration. But Postel has garnered little support, political or financial, and can be expected to drop out of the race. Slightly to the right of Blumenthal is former West Side Reform Assemblyman Jerome Kretchmer. While ideologically similar, Kretchmer has a rough-and-ready style that appeals far more to Bronx and Brooklyn ethnics than does the austere Blumenthal. But Kretchmer's credibility is indelibly marred by his having just resigned as Lindsay's garbage commissioner (now called Environmental Protection Administrator), after which he suddenly discovered the corruption of the Lindsay administration. A darker, and more powerful, horse suddenly emerging from the wings is none other than former Mayor Robert Wagner. Wagner was scarcely beloved in his day, and his bid for a comeback was snuffed out four years ago; but eight years of John Lindsay has made Wagner's reign seem like the Golden Age, and the Liberal Party's Alex Rose has been making noises in Wagner's direction. It is possible that Wagner may stay out of the tangled Democrat primary and run only on the Liberal line, where Rose can dictate the candidate.

Moving to the Center, we have Congressman Ed Koch, from the East Side of Manhattan. While one of the original left-liberal Jewish reformers, Koch has moved sharply rightward in recent years, taking up the cudgels against crime and against the Lindsay attempts to place low-income, racially integrated public housing in Forest Hills, Queens (Jewish) and school busing in Brooklyn's Canarsie (Italian and Jewish.) In an increasingly polarized New York, however, Koch has lost the support of the Left, while still not trusted by the conservative masses.

Koch's chances, too, are minimal.

On the surface, one might think that Centrist Sanford Garelik has all the qualifications for success. A "tough cop" most of his life, Garelik has law-and-order appeal; now President of the City Council, Garelik has been conspicuously anti-Lindsay over the last four years. Furthermore, he was supported for his present post by the Liberal Party, and, as a Jew, might be expected to appeal to the now conservative Jewish masses of Brooklyn and the Bronx. Yet Garelik has picked up scant support for the mayoral race. One reason is that Garelik appears to be extraordinarily dumb, even by ordinary political standards. Jokes have been spreading throughout the city about Garelik's supposed inability to find his own office in the morning. The Liberal Party shows no signs of supporting him, and Garelik has been tainted with the corruption issue with a recent disclosure about his accepting Christmas presents while high in the police force. Furthermore, his "tough cop" image among conservatives is greatly dwarfed by that of Mario Biaggi (see below).

One dark horse picking up support, and somewhere in Center or Left-Center, is the Italian lawyer Mario Cuomo. It was Cuomo who engineered the compromise that saved at least some of the homes of a group of beleaguered low-income Italians of Corona, Queens from the Lindsay bulldozer. Cuomo's intelligence and ability has deeply impressed some of the Jewish reformers, and he shows signs of being endorsed by the shrewd, tough leader of the Queens Democracy, Matthew Troy. Troy established himself as leader of the "left-wing" of the Democrat regulars by being the only enthusiast among the regular leadership in the city for the candidacy and the Presidential race of George McGovern. Despite his gloss of liberalism, Troy has connections with his conservative constituency, stemming from his own early conservatism as well as from the far more principled conservatism of his father (Matthew Troy, Sr.) who had long established himself as the loudest advocate of the Catholic cause in Ireland. Cuomo's chances depend, first, on where Troy will go, and much of Troy's actions will be determined by his active personal feud with the Democratic boss of Brooklyn, Meade Esposito.

Moving to the Right of Center, we have the important candidacy of the present Controller of the City of New York, Abraham Beame. As something of a fiscal conservative and well-known budget-cutter, Beame has considerable appeal to the Brooklyn-Bronx mass base, an appeal reinforced by his being Jewish and a long-time member of the Brooklyn Democrat machine. As such he will undoubtedly be backed to the hilt by Brooklyn boss Esposito, and probably by Bronx Democratic leader Patrick Cunningham. Beame is also strongly backed by New York's real estate interests, who probably fell that Beame will not push to re-impose New York's previous and disastrous system of rent control. Beame's support is being spearheaded by the powerful Shubert Theatre chain, headed by one Irving Goldman, and by forces close to the powerful Tammany (Manhattan regular) Surrogate judge, S. Samuel DiFalco. Beame's major drawback is his advanced age; he admits to 67, but the scuttlebutt claims that he is approximately 73. Also, he is a candidate distinctly lacking in charisma, as was revealed in the campaign in which he lost to Robert Wagner. Beame has shrewdly tried to turn the age issue to his advantage, however, by promising to be strictly a one-term mayor, a promise that is a heady one to many New Yorkers surfeited with eight years of Lindsay.

The Right-wing candidate, and the probable favorite at this writing, is Bronx Mario Biaggi. A tough Italian cop for many years, Biaggi is the leading "law and order" candidate, and is thus highly attractive to the now conservative Jewish masses as well as to his own Italian constituency. Biaggi has built an impregnable political base in his home area of conservative, home-owning, middle-class Italian East Bronx, where he was almost unanimously re-elected as Congressman in 1972 with Democrat, Republican, and Conservative support. A moderate on national issues, Biaggi has recently tried a flanker move to the left by calling for the reimposition of rent controls. The political joke in New York is that Biaggi is the "Mafia candidate", but this charge is very often met with the shrug: "Maybe New York needs a Mafioso mayor." In fact, Biaggi's appeal is enhanced by indications that he would be ultra-tough on street crime while at the same time looking the other way on such far less threatening and more entrepreneurial forms of "crime" as gambling. Furthermore, while Biaggi might be strong on the police, he has also shown himself to be anti-militarist, leading the drive to expose and reform brutality in Army camps. As such, Biaggi has been following a long-time tradition among American Italians. Furthermore, Biaggi's

(Continued On Page 3)

The Blackmailer As Villain

By Gary Greenberg

I would like to register a dissent from Water Block's continuing series of articles in which degenerate scum and social vermin are the subject of articles entitled " — As Hero." His article on the blackmailer as hero will serve as an example.

First, no heroic qualities are displayed by the characters depicted, as in the case of the blackmailer article. A hero is someone you admire, respect and would like to emulate due to the excellence of some desirable trait exhibited by the "hero." The blackmailer is certainly not someone who exhibits any admirable traits. The stock and trade of the blackmailer is to withhold information, the release of which is calculated to bring a devastating blow to the existence of a human being. It is the fear of destruction of reputation, life, or freedom that is affected.

Let us concede for the moment (and I don't in fact) that the blackmailer is engaged in legal activity. That certainly doesn't justify him as a hero. Just because a person engages in acts that are rightfully considered vile, although legal by most humane people, doesn't mean we have to admire the scoundrel. The one virtue alleged for the Blackmailer is that the truth shall make us free or some other such cliche. This ignores the fact that a frequent tactic of a blackmailer is to threaten to expose, false, fraudulent, framed or phony information, calculated to result in harm to an individual if released.

One of the problems of the Block series is to slide in his description of the alleged hero from the general conception of the actor to the specific aspects which Block wants to examine. The Blackmailer is not simply thought of as someone who just withholds information for a fee.

To illustrate my point, let's look at some definitions of Blackmail.

Black's Law Dictionary defines Blackmail as "The extortion of money by threats or overtures toward criminal prosecution or the destruction of a man's reputation or social standing." Webster's New World Dictionary (paperback) defines blackmail as "payment extorted to prevent disclosure of information that could bring disgrace." Notice both definitions use the term "extort" which implies the threat of violence or harm for failure to comply.

While some activities of a Blackmailer may be legitimate, much of his usual practice is not. A frequent target of blackmailers is the person who is guilty of victimless crimes. Our "Hero" then threatens to go to the police with the information. This I think is criminal. It is as wrong as taking money at the threat of shooting. The victim of the blackmailer would be justified in killing the blackmailer to prevent the "Hero" from making such disclosures.

One of the legitmate activities of a blackmailer is to withhold information about a person's criminal activities (robbery, murder, stealing) in return for a fee. While there is no obligation to come forward with information of a crime, I certainly hope that no society of civilized people would knowingly extend friendship and society to such an individual. As to the hero, if the crook chooses to off him, or hurt him, I have little sympathy for him and few tears. The Hero knew with whom he was dealing and what kind of person he was. He choose to accept the risk. I choose not to aid him in seeking justice.

The blackmailer may be Walter Block's type of hero, but he is certainly no hero for the Libertarian. I see little value in Libertarian publications holding him out as one. ◻

The Blackmailer As Hero: A Reply

By Walter Block

Were it not for Mr. Greenberg's justly earned and widely known reputation as a careful scholar, meticulous researcher, and courteous gentleman, I would be forced to conclude that he had not read my article at all, and was instead replying merely to its title. Let us review the evidence.

1. "No admirable traits?" In the article, I point out several. Blackmailers help reduce the rewards of crime by forcing the criminals to share with them; by tipping off the police about the criminals; and by reducing the scope of crime on the part of the criminals out of fear of possible blackmail by a member of the larger criminal group. Blackmailers help groups such as homosexuals by bringing this deviation out into the open.

2. "False, phony and fraudulent information?" I cover this case in "The slanderer and libeler as hero". The blackmailer, qua blackmailer, deals only in the truth; if he lies or misrepresents, he is no longer a blackmailer, but a slanderer or libeler.

3. "Extortion? The threat of violence?" Greenberg avoids my definition of blackmail as a threat to do something completely legal and legitimate, such as to exercise one's rights of free speech, or, in the case of the boycott (another form of blackmail) as a threat not to buy from someone. In the paper, I take special pains to point out that what is being threatened is **not** violence, but free speech.

4. "Harm?" It is my view that harming someone should not be proscribed by a libertarian law code since honest competition can harm the loser and this must be allowed. But in the paper I state that if the opponents of blackmail are worried about harm, they should oppose the gossip or blabbermouth even more forcefully, for the blackmailer can at least be bought off, while these others cannot be.

I do not mind that Mr. Greenberg and I do not see eye to eye on this matter; healthy dispute, after all, is good for the libertarian movement, and will hopefully bring us closer and closer to the truth. What I do object to, however, is that Mr. Greenberg chose to avoid practically all of my arguments in support of the blackmailer. Nothing worthwhile can come of a debate where one's arguments are ignored. It is for this reason, as well as out of pique that Mr. Greenberg has stated that he sees "little

value" in my article even being published in a libertarian magazine, that I state: I see little value in the publication of a very poorly written critique which does not even consider the reasons given in the orginial article.

But I hasten to reply to the substantive points raised by Mr. Greenberg, lest I be accused of violating my own strictures.

1. "Degenerate scum and social vermin" is merely name calling and does not deserve a reply.

2. There is nothing illegitimate about "bringing a devastating blow to the existence of a human being" provided that you do not violate his rights! The man who is jilted may be dealt a devastating blow, but since his rights are in no way violated, there is nothing vile going on. After all, the woman, being a free agent, has a perfect right to pick another suitor or none at all. In like manner, there can be nothing illegitimate or vile about the exercise of one's rights of free speech, no matter what harm results.

3. "The stool pigeon." A person who cooperates with the police in their illicit efforts to stamp out victimless crimes such as homosexuality is certainly acting illegitimately himself. But there is something very illogical indeed, in trying to link up this sort of behavior with honest blackmail.

In posing the dilemma for the advocate of the legitimacy of blackmail, Mr. Greenberg is likening the police who try to stamp out victimless crimes to a bunch of hoodlums. He then tries to link the illegitimacy of these hoodlum police to the blackmailer. I would be the first to admit that blackmail in this case is certainly illegitimate, but I must protest that this argument proves entirely too much. It proves that any legitimate activity is illegitimate, provided only that it can be used to aid those involved in aggression, like our police who suppress rights.

For example, the activities of typing, serving food, washing uniforms, cleaning guns, repairing cars, etc., can only be considered legitimate, and non-aggressive. But they are all utilized by coercive police. Are we then to conclude, as the logic of Greenberg's argument would have us conclude for the case of the blackmailer, that all these activities are

(Continued On Page 4)

Heroes And Scapegoats

By Walter Block

Editor's Note: The following is the projected introduction of a book that Professor Block is writing on "Economic Scapegoats", some of the chapters of which have appeared in the pages of the Lib. Forum. In it, Professor Block explains the general purpose of his "hero" series; appended is a comprehensive list of these much-reviled scapegoats, some of whom will receive extended treatment in Professor Block's final manuscript.

In this book you will learn three things about the appended list of economic scapegoats: 1) They are guilty of no wrongdoing whatsoever; 2) in virtually all cases, they are responsible for benefiting the rest of society; 3) that if we prohibit their activities, we do so at our own loss.

As the impetus for this book is firmly based on Libertarianism, it may well help to consider this philosophy in some detail.

The basic premise of libertarianism is that it is illegitimate to engage in aggression against non-aggressors. What is meant here by aggression is not argumentativeness, nor competitiveness, nor adventurousness, dynamism, quarrelsomeness, nor antagonism. What is meant by aggression is the use of violence such as that which takes place in murder, rape, robbery, kidnapping, etc. What the libertarian philosophy prohibits is the **initiation** of such violence upon innocent people or their property; not necessarily pacifists, libertarianism does not forbid the use of violence in defense or in retaliation against the initiation of violence.

Now there is nothing untoward about such a view, nor even anything controversial about it. Most people would give it their whole-hearted support. Indeed, this sentiment is part and parcel of our Western civilization, enshrined in the law, in our Constitution, and in the natural law. There is nothing, then, about this basic premise of libertarianism that stands out in any way.

What is different about libertarianism is the way in which this basic premise is understood. The uniqueness of libertarianism consists of the rigorously consistent, not to say maniacally rigid manner in which this principle is developed. For example, most people do not see a contradiction between this principle (which they presumably support, or at least pay lip service to) and our system of taxation. Libertarians do.

Taxation is contrary to the basic principle and hence anathema to libertarianism because it involves aggression against non-aggressive citizens who refuse to pay (if you don't believe it, try not paying your taxes, and see what happens). It makes not the slightest difference that the government offers goods and services in return for the tax money. What is all important and crucial is that the so called trade (of tax money for government services) is **coerced**. It is not a voluntary trade. The individual is not just as free to accept the offer of the trade as he is to reject it. Nor does it make one whit of difference that a majority of the citizens might be mustered out in support of this coercive taxation. Initiation of aggression is initiation of aggression no matter what are the views of the majority. For the libertarian, no tyranny which violates the basic premise can be acceptable, even if a majority supports it. Righteousness can only be found in consistency with the libertarian premise; it cannot be based on a poll.

Another difference between libertarians and the rest of the society is the obverse of the view that initiatory violence is evil. It is the view that anything **not** involving the initiation of violence **cannot** be evil! It is this

(Continued On Page 5)

Blackmailer As Hero —

(Continued From Page 3)

intrinsically evil? Hardly. We must rather conclude, I think, that otherwise legitimate activities (like typing, cleaning, etc., as well as blackmail) can be undertaken in the service of evil, and thereby become evil themselves, but only in these cases, not in all cases.

4. What are we to make of the contradictory sentiments expressed in the next to last paragraph where Greenberg first encourages the blackmailer **not** to withhold information about real crimes, and then praises the crook for "offering him" for doing that very thing? Either one favors blackmailers exposing real criminals, and then opposes the retaliation, or one opposes the exposed, and favors the retaliation, if one desires to be consistent. It is illogical to favor X, and then to turn around and favor punishing someone for doing X.

Mr. Greenberg calls them "degenerate scum and social vermin", but I think that the accompanying list of scapegoats are rather unsung heroes of the economy, for they insist upon working at their chosen professions under the most adverse conditions. Bad publicity, abuse, name calling, and even physical violence at the hands of the police and "outraged" citizens" are the lot of these economic actors. Yet we have seen that their only function is to benefit their fellow man!

Although seemingly far fetched, one cannot help be reminded of Prometheus, the Greek god who took pity on the misery of mankind and stole fire from heaven for their benefit, and who was then punished for his heroic deed by being chained to a mountain where a vulture devoured his liver each day. Prometheus was reviled by the gods; the economic heroes are reviled by mankind. But both bring inestimable benefits to mankind.

It must be allowed that but for negative public opinion and the opposition of the law, there would be nothing heroic about any of these tasks. They only become heroic when performed under the most trying circumstances. But the same holds true for Prometheus! Surely there is nothing heroic about bringing fire; people strike matches every day, after all. What makes this deed heroic are the great odds which were overcome in the bringing of the fire. It is, then, in accordance with the odds which are overcome in each of the tasks performed by the economic actors, that we can consider them heroic.

It is tempting to say that if there are any "degenerate scum and social vermin" involved in this question, they are the people who cast aspersions on the economic heroes. Tempting, but incorrect. For we must remember that people who maliciously cast false aspersions on others (libelers and slanderers) are heroes themselves, who are merely expressing their rights of free speech.   ◘

The Mayoral Circus —

(Continued From Page 2)

appeal is strengthened by indications that he would gain Conservative Party endorsement, and perhaps even the Republican nomination, since Governor Rockefeller has been looking for a conservative "fusion" candidate that he could back for Mayor. Of course, now that Rockefeller's hated enemy Lindsay is out of the race, the governor's enthusiasm for fusion may well have cooled.

The picture in the other primaries is even cloudier at this writing, though not for the same reasons as the multi-candidate Democracy. Among the Republicans, the previous candidate, the powerful State Senator **John Marchi**, from highly conservative and quasi-rural Staten Island, is anxious to run again. But Marchi's candidacy has many barriers to overcome. One is Rockefeller's desire for fusion, since the chances are nil for Democratic endorsement of the Staten Island Republican. Furthermore, Marchi has lost much of his old Conservative Party support, since he has in recent years endorsed liberal plans for massive low-income housing developments in Staten Island, plans that are bitterly opposed by the conservative masses of that borough. To stop Marchi, Rockefeller might well endorse a patsy candidate, State Senator Roy Goodman, who, as a liberal Jewish Republican from the East Side of Manhattan, has almost no support among liberals, Jews, or Republicans, and therefore could be well calculated to be slaughtered by a Democrat-Conservative Biaggi in November.

And so the New York political stew muddies and thickens. Among the minor parties, the Trotskyite Socialist Workers Party will undoubtedly run a candidate, and the Trotskyite splinter group, the Labor Committee movement, headed by the fanatically pro-"working class" theoretician L. Marcus, has already nominated one **Tony Chaitkin** for the Mayoralty. The Free Libertarian Party of New York is preparing to run a mayoral slate, and will nominate someone at its convention at the end of March. Right now there appear to be two candidates for the FLP nomination, **Paul Streitz** and **Fran Youngstein**, but at this writing we have not been able to determine the ideological differences between the two slates. More on FLP doings at a later date.   ◘

Heroes And Scapegoats —

(Continued From Page 4)

difference that explains the first point mentioned above: that the economic scapegoats are guilty of no wrongdoing whatsoever. They are completely guiltless because they do not initiate violence against non-aggressors, and for the libertarian, such actions are the only criminal or evil acts possible.

It is interesting in this connection to consider the types of people who are **not** included in this seeming greatest all-time list of villains. Made prominent by their absence in such a list of "bad guys" the murderer, the rapist, the arsonist, the thief, the trespasser, and all other criminals who aggress against innocent people and their property. These worthies are left off the list of economic scapegoats because they are pre-eminently not guilty of no wrongdoing whatsoever. On the contrary, they are guilty of the only wrongdoing **possible** (according to the libertarian basic postulate): the use of initiatory aggression.

Notice, also, that the fraudulent is not included on the list of people who are innocent of any wrongdoing, although the blackmailer, the slanderer, libeler, briber, and the liar are. The reason that the fraudulent is not considered innocent (and hence a scapegoat) is that fraud is identically equivalent to theft. In theft, the victim is relieved of his possessions without receiving anything he values as much in return. But the same thing happens in fraud! If a man buys a bag of what is misrepresented as potatoes, but which is actually filled with rocks, he is **also** relieved of his possessions (the money spent for the "potatoes") without receiving anything he values as much.

Once it is realized that no one in this seeming rogues' gallery is guilty of any wrongdoing, it is not so difficult to appreciate the possibility of the second point made above: that they are virtually all responsible for benefiting the rest of society. They **must** benefit the rest of society; for not using aggression, the only other alternative is trade. And voluntary trade must benefit the rest of society, since if it did not, the rest of society would simply refuse to trade with these scapegoats. Both parties must always feel they gain from a voluntary transaction. Given that they are free **not** to enter into the trade, the fact that they **do** decide to trade must prove to be a mutual benefit.

The third premise follows ineluctably from the second: given that trade (the only avenue open to those, such as our scapegoats, who have eschewed violence), must always benefit all parties, then it follows that the prohibition of these trades must **harm** all parties. In actual point of fact, a prohibition of the activities of the scapegoats is even more grave. In addition to harming all potential parties to a trade involving scapegoats, the prohibition can most seriously harm third parties. One blatant example is the prohibition of the activities of the heroin seller. In addition to harming the seller himself, as well as the customer-drug addict, prohibition of the sale of heroin is responsible for a high proportion of the crime committed in our society, for the police graft, and for the general break down of law and order so prevalent in our big city urban jungles.

But the chief point to bear in mind while dealing with these unsung heroes of the economy is the moral difference between the initiation of aggression, on the one hand, and all other displeasing acts, which do not involve such aggression, on the other. It is **only** the act of aggressive violence of a murderer, rapist, thief, kidnapper, etc., that violates man's rights; since there is no economic scapegoat whose function it is to so violate the laws of morality, these unsung heroes, although much reviled by the media, cannot be considered illegitimate by libertarians.

Economic Scapegoats

Contents

I. Labor and Education
scab
rate buster
employer of child labor
truant
child seducer
sweatshop employer
monopsonist (in the labor market)
low wage employer*

II. Free Speech
blackmailer*
slanderer, libeler*
heckler
denier of academic freedom*
pirate radio station
pornographer
person who yells "fire!" (in a crowded theatre)*
advertiser*

III. Financial
pawnbroker, usurer, loanshark*
moneylender*
hoarder, miser*
counterfeiter
inheritor*
person who refuses to contribute to charity
non-tipper

IV. Sexual
pimp*
prostitute
madame
male chauvanist pig*
peeping tom, voyeur
sadist, sado-masochist
fetishist
public fornicator

V. Ecology
noise polluter*
strip miner*
litterbug*
wastemaker* (planned obsolesence)
billboard builder
cosmetician
grafitti writer
breeder

VI. Business and Trade
speculator*
profiteer
middleman
peddler
inventor
undertaker
company town owner
price cutter
honest trillionaire
ghetto merchant
tenement landlord, slumlord, rent-gouger*
reserve clause owner

old curmudgeon holdout*
cigarette manufacturer
monopolist
professional
exploiter
bargainer
importer
mercenary

VII. Medical
drug (heroin) merchant*
quack
unlicensed practitioner of medicine
abortionist
dope addict

VIII. Racism
block buster
discriminator
bigot

IX. Outlaw
fence
black marketeer
vigilante
briber
bootlegger
draft evader
gypsy cab driver*
dishonest cop
numbers racketeer
gun runner, unlicensed gun owner
gold owner
poacher
smuggler
pirate
ticket scalper*
mafia
scofflaw
gambler
tax evader
conspirator

(*already written)

Life vs. Death: The Final Barricade

By Jerome Tucille

It used to be, when you talked about anti-life forces permeating the countryside, you were speaking in a figurative sense. Surely no one was literally anti-life. Anti-life was a calculated exaggeration for anti-reason or anti-freedom. It was an overstatement designed to make a lesser point. The English were the masters of the whimsical understatement which, when properly timed and delivered, exploded in one's psyche with a delayed reaction. We Americans, with our customary immaturity and bulldog aggressiveness, believed in hammering a point home with a sledge hammer to make sure that somebody out there "got it." We have never trusted subtlety.

Now, it seems, we have no choice.

The rapid acceleration of contemporary developments renders all attempts at overstatement a sheer impossibility. Make the claim that Walt Disney will rise from the dead and create Disneyland utopias throughout the globe and, rest assured, the New York Times will publish a story two weeks later informing the world that Disney's heirs — if not the old boy himself — already have that very concept on the drawing board. It is getting more and more difficult to be outrageous. H. L. Mencken and Evelyn Waugh would surely be pacing the floor night after night, denying themselves much-needed sleep, merely to keep their most fantastic satires from becoming grim reality. My own latest offering, Here Comes Immortality, seemed unduly fanciful while it was being written. Scarcely the ink is dry, and my most ironic projections of a year ago are assuming a conserative hue.

What we have finally come to is this: the term anti-life must now be taken in its literal sense.

Out there in this wide, variegated country of ours, a new movement is underway. It has not yet been labeled the Anti-Life Crusade or the Death on Roller Skates Regatta, but surely it ought to be if we are not to further bastardize the English language with cloying euphemisms. But euphemize we will, and consequently this movement I am speaking of has been given the fastidious name, Death With Dignity. The moving light (purple beam of sorrow would be more accurate) behind this latest cultural phenomenon to grip the land is a small, thin, tight-lipped lady doctor in the midwest, a European transplant, named Doctor Kubla-Ross. This lady has written a book (the title of which escapes me for the moment — hopefully, longer that that) claiming that all life is but a mere preparation for death. It is her theory, arrived at after many years in the service of melodramatic emotion, that death is a wondrous and beautiful thing which ought to be faced with resignation, even with yearning. Largely due to her inspiration, courses on death and dying are actually being taught in several colleges and high schools across the country, and Doctor Kubla-Ross will not be fully satisfied until her theories have been institutionalized on the early grammar school level.

(In one high school in the midwest, students are invited to lie down in coffins in the classroom to get the feel of death, so to speak. Dr. Kubla-Ross is all in favor of dragging young children off to wakes and cemeteries to familiarize them with decay and deterioration. She is horrified that Americans shield their youngsters from death, refusing to admit them to hospitals and other morbid institutions. She thinks this is an "unhealthy and selfish" attitude, believe it or not. Since one of my own childhood traumas involved being pushed toward a casket and urged to kiss my "sleeping Uncle Rocco" by some foul-smelling hag dressed in black, I beg to differ with the good doctor.)

More insidious, however, than Doctor Kubla-Ross's attitudes toward death, are her attempts to change the euthanasia laws in the United States. At one time euthanasia had a libertarian basis to it. The idea than an individual should be able to end his own life (or urge someone else like a doctor to end it for him) can be argued from the standpoint of self-ownership. But Doctor K-R is giving us euthanasia with a twist. She wants the doctor or the next-or-kin to decide when to pull the plug, when to decide that a patient has become a vegetable and his or her life is no longer worth preserving. Let it be said loud and clear, Dr. K-R's brand of euthanasia, no matter how she tries to dress it up with humanistic, moralistic sentimentality, is still murder. The taking of someone else's life without his express consent, no matter how vegetative that life may be, is morally reprehensible and should never be legalized in any civilized society. Dr. K-R gives morality a complete, 180-degree twist by

maintaining that a "vegetable on his death bed", who insists on being kept alive, is not really in "his right mind" and, therefore, the doctor is better able to make the proper decision for him.

Used to be that anyone who asked to die was not considered to be in his or her "right mind." Dr. K-R, though she would deny it to the handwringing, tear-streaked end, would have made a great medical experimenter in one of Hitler's laboratories.

As if Dr. K-R were not enough, much more than enough, along comes a disciple of hers, a morbid young science editor named David Hendin, with a book of his own called (choke, gasp, argghh) Death As a Fact of Life. The title gives you a good idea of the "theme" of his book. A week or so prior to this writing, I had the dubious pleasure of debating Hendin, Dr. K-R, and some sleek black-suited undertaker (he would prefer the term mortuary scientist no doubt) on the Kup Show, a TV talk show out of Chicago hosted by columnist, Irv Kupeinet. This was literally a pro-life vs. pro-death lineup, and the forces of life as you see were a 3 to 1 underdog. Gives you some idea of the current cultural climate of this country.

Dr. K-R started off by expounding on her favorite theme: the beauty of death and the dignity of going to one's final resting place with a smile of resignation plastered on his chalky face. Hendin was next, treating the multitudes to a description of his grandmother's funeral that was plainly designed to squeeze the final droplets of tears from a statue and to melt a heart of marble. The scientist of mortuary affairs stared grimly ahead, clearly at home on his own turf.

Then it was time for someone to strike a blow for life, and this I gamely

(Continued On Page 7)

The Rise Of Roy Ash
By Bill Evers

During November and December, the newspapers were full of news of the personnel shuffle being carried out by Nixon in the executive branch of the U. S. government. While many old names are now associated with different posts, a new name is that of Roy L. Ash. Ash was the president of Litton Industries and now is the newly-appointed head of the White House Office of Management and Budget.

Ash's appointment has a special significance. The post he has obtained and the reins of power which he now has gathered in his hands did not even exist four years ago. The Office of Management and Budget was created during an executive branch reorganization planned and designed by Ash himself at the time of Nixon's election to his first term. Now Nixon talks about an "expanded role" for the post. To better understand the what Ash's appointment means, it is necessary to examine the reorganization plans drawn up for Nixon by Ash's task force and also to examine Ash's own background as the accounting and financial expert in Litton, a company whose lifeblood is government contract money.

Realignment

A business leader like Ash has concrete reasons for desiring executive branch realignment. The scope and responsibility of the national govern-

The Final Barricade —

(Continued From Page 6)

did, citing the fact that aging is merely one more disease we will soon know how to overcome, that already we are developing the technology to halt and eventually reverse the aging process with drugs, biofeedback, hibernation, diet and other techniques. Yes, I dared to make the statement that life is fun and pleasurable and something to be valued, that only a lunatic would look forward to death with anything except outrage. I ended by quoting Nietzche:

"The only thing wrong with heaven is that all the interesting people are missing,"

and Dylan Thomas' comments on death:

"Rage, rage against the dying of the light!"

These, in my estimation, are two of the sanest statements ever uttered by man or beast.

When I finished, Dr. K-R was clearly in a snit. How could I be so selfish as to want to hang onto life so tenaciously, and refuse to step aside and make room for future generations? Young Hendin was irked because I apparently didn't give a fiddler's fart about his grandmother's funeral, and our mortician friend glowered at this irreverent character who spoke so slightingly of his own stock in trade.

Irv Kupeinet patted my arm and thanked me for "livening things up a bit." He wanted to know whether I had any youth pills to give away while "there was still time." Sanity was not defeated yet.

"You!" wailed Dr. K-R, her dart-like chin leveled in my direction for a direct frontal assault. "Mr. Selfish over there. Don't you think it's a beautiful thing to face death with dignity after a full, satisfying life? To resign ourselves to nature and retire from this world with a clear mind?"

"A good thing for you, maybe. I go our furious — kicking and screaming all the way."

"This American attitude is a very curious thing," said Dr. K-R, almost to herself. "All this materialism and concentration on pleasure. It's very unhealthy.

Yes, dear reader, something "unhealthy" is afoot in the land, but it is definitely not American "materialism" and the quest for extended youth and pleasure in life. Finally, after a couple hundred years of Puritanism and self-righteous Christian fundamentalism, the American mainstream is beginning to liberate itself. Lifestyles are changing and growing more fluid and open-ended; a morality based in denial, mortification of the flesh, and self-denial is being smashed to smithereens. Dr. K-R and her disciples, along with the Jesus Freak movement, the Hari Krishna mob, and the mind-destroying drug counterculture are representatives of a last-ditch attempt to preserve a death-centered social and political structure. But, like all aberrations in the human condition, they are destined to failure and final extinction.

Life, reason, sanity and liberty will have their day after centuries of darkness and bleak mysticism. Soon humanity will achieve physical life eternal and the divinity of the ancient gods.

Meanwhile we can all stand up and cry with Dylan Thomas: "Rage, rage against the dying of the light!"   □

ment (especially its executive branch) have vastly expanded in the past half-century, beginning during Herbert Hoover's administration. But some feel the structure of government has not kept pace. The existing governmental structure is deemed unsuitable for the activities many influential businessmen and other political decision-makers wish the government would undertake.

In the words of Charles M. Hardin of the Rockefeller Foundation, "Many of the political institutions, organization, and practices as well as much of the political ideology in the United States conspire to elevate local, special, separate, and 'Pluralistic' interests — despite the fact that national survival now depends upon the ability to fix political attention steadily upon national problems and interests." Really, of course, in the name of abolishing special interests, a reorganization plan will allow some special interests to supplant others.

The task force headed by Ash is aimed at diminishing the influence wielded by small, parochial groups and "their" agencies within the governmental structure. Much of the "inefficient" patchwork quilt of boards, agencies, bureaus, etc. found in something like the Department of Agriculture has grown up in response to the desires of localized or functionally narrow interest groups. The present organizational jumble reflects the demands of these petty interests.

Complicated Enterprise

Sen. John McClellan has aptly described the complexity of the government today: "The executive branch is now the largest and most complicated enterprise in the world, with more than 1400 domestic programs distributed among 150 separate departments, agencies, bureaus, and boards."

Under the reorganization plan proposed by Ash, all domestic affairs would be run by a Domestic Council, parallel to the National Security Council in foreign affairs.

Drastic surgery would be performed on the seven domestic departments that are in operation now — Interior; Agriculture; Labor; Commerce; Treasury; Transportation; Housing and Urban Development; and Health, Education, and Welfare. They would be cut up and sewn together again to form a total of four departments — Nautral Resources (to control the nation's physical assets), Human Resources (to retrain the labor force and run the welfare system), Community Development (to build up the nation's infrastructure and rebuild the cities), and Economic Affairs (to handle the currency, labor-management relations, and other business and farm matters).

Key Member

The key member of the Domestic Council would be the Office of Management and Budget, which would be the central fiscal planner for the economy. It would synchronize and coordinate all government domestic action.

Ash's proposed regrouping enables the government in partnership with industry to come to grip with problems in a whole new fashion. If a policy proposal comes up, the budget can be looked at and the program added to it without danger of operating at cross-purposes with another part of the government.

In the Office of Management and Budget will be centralized the measurement of programs' successes and the decisions on which programs work best as a package.

Program Budgeting

The Office of Management and Budget, with the help of the Brookings Institution, has increasingly since its inception been turning to a budgeting procedure known as program budgeting. When budgets are constructed on a program basis, decision-making is centralized and made by visible high-level officals rather than by the invisible subcommittees and lower echelon bureaucrats who tend to formulate budget requests under the item-by-item way of budgeting. Significantly, the lower levels of departments are more likely to reflect petty interests rather than nationally powerful ones like Ash's own Litton Industries.

In fact, the whole idea of program budgeting lends itself to the contracting of government programs to firms (like Litton) outside the government. Program budgeting presents budget requests in terms of the final products, in terms of program packages, rather than in the traditional line-item form which emphasized categories like personnel, overhead, supplies, etc.

Under program budgeting, there is a special plausibility to contracting with a company like Litton to build a large integrated "weapons system" like the McNamara proposal for a worldwide fleet of floating military bases or to operate the War on Poverty's Job Corps Center in Pleasanton, California. In fact, these were actual Litton contracts.

As Karl Hess wrote in the Jan. 15, 1969 issue of Politics newsletter, at

(Continued On Page 8)

Rise Of Roy Ash — (Continued From Page 7)

the time of the initial publicity for Ash's reorganization proposals, "Litton is an industrial conglomerate, one of the new breed of 'capitalist' cats which is created, head to foot, from government contacts and contracts. Lately (Litton) has branched out into what might be called the subcontracting of the business of government."

Litton's contract to run the Job Corps center was hailed by the late Lyle Spencer of IBM as a primary example of the growth and development of what Spencer called the "social-industrial complex," an arrangement parallel to the military-industrial complex, but paying companies tax funds to work the welfare state side of the American system.

Ash's former boss Charles B. Thornton, chairman of the board of Litton, has himself been an advocate of the social-industrial complex approach. Thornton headed an advisory panel to the Kerner Commission on Civil Disorders. His panel, in its recommendations, used the analogy of the space program and defense spending in suggesting that the government's strategy for urban areas be one of granting credits against taxes to business firms.

But Litton has by no means neglected the warfare state side of the American system. In fact, Ash once said about Litton that because "almost all new products have their first application in military uses, we always want at least 25 percent of our business in defense and space."

Ash's statement about the military sector prompted an incisive analysis from David Horowitz and Reese Erlich in **Ramparts.** They wrote, "In the old days, private corporations would develop technological innovations at their own expense, risking the outlay with a view to being rewarded by future returns from the competitive marketplace. This was the very essence of entrepreneurship . . . (But now the corporations) have become accustomed to getting the government to pick up the tab before they move. These corporations have grown economically lazy, in part because they really can live better on the largess of the so-called welfare state."

The **Ramparts** writers added that "if the corporation is spending the government's money, the government is spending the taxpayer's. If he had a very clear idea of it, the taxpayer might frown on this happy arrangement and spoil all the fun . . ."

Now Litton threatens to become a further burden to the taxpayers. According to Sen. William Proxmire, Litton threatens "to become the Navy's Lockheed," Litton has maintained that the Navy should pay it $380 million for cancellation costs and design changes encountered in tis building of five landing helicopter assault ships.

Last June, Proxmire wrote: "I now have reason to believe that because of cash shortages, Litton is confronted with a financial crisis of major proportions. I am informed that in order to extricate itself from its financial problems, the company is attempting to persuade the Navy to pay millions of dollars of worthless and inflated claims. Or, alternatively, to restructure the LHA (landing helicopter assault ship) contract or take other steps to solve Litton's shipbuilding problems, including a Navy takeover of the Litton shipyards at Pascagoula."

The appointment of Ash as head of the Office of Management and Budget indicates the continued importance both of the military-industrial complex and of the rising social-industrial complex and marks a heightened concern of these interests in the fiscal processes of taxation and government expenditure.

Furthermore, those people who do not like governmental aggrandizement, whether by way of subsidization or by way of repression, can only

view negatively the rise of an efficiency expert like Ash. In the name of efficiency power is being transferred from some hands to others. And anyway, what's so wonderful about bad things being done more efficiently? ∎

Denial Of Protection
By Tibor R. Machan

My mail, like that of most of us, is cluttered with literature from all sources — well, perhaps "literature" isn't the right term for it all. Most recently, for instance, I got one of those newsletters in the mail where one of the lesser heroes of the "movement" offered comments about the perennial problem of libertarian political theory — although maybe the problem isn't really with us, after all, only the author has't quite gotten away from it yet.

Those interested in the character of a free society often dispute about the means by which people might best reduce injustice, the violation of human rights, etc., and protect against such violations in the best possible way. That, after all, is the meat of political theory.

The author of the piece I read, however, does not wish to participate in this dispute or discussion or inquiry. Our contributor to mailboxes throughout this land offers, instead, as his version of the solution to this problem that there is no problem at all. Actually, he says, we needn't concern ourselves with the issue since it is evident that whatever one wishes to protect, **he alone** is entitled to protect it. So, our author concludes, that to suggest that some people might volunteer to take on the job of protecting others (who would like to specialize in other aspects of our lives) is out of line and tantamount to entertain "superstitious beliefs". Now there is something odd going on when one who values freedom finds it distasteful that others should choose to operate according to the principle of the division of labor — a rather familiar concomitant of the economic scene which explains the workings of markets in a free society.

To choose to delegate your authority of self-protection is no different from choosing to delegate your authority to tinker with your car, your stomach, your money — delegate it to automechanics, doctors and banks, for instance.

This frequent mailbox visitor maintains that the "Gordian knot" of which means will best serve the purpose of self-defense, or protection of one's goods and investments, has been solved by "libertarian analysis" — his, of course (since "libertarian analysis" solves nothing, **people** do, by offering it at its best). What kind of solution is it when one offers none? Well, no problem here.

I have worked on this matter myself and know that it ain't a simple one to work out. After all, politics deals with one of man's most complex, intricate, delicate and abstract tasks: figuring out what kind of human community suits us best. And none of the suggestions come close to being so weak: for it wipes out the very foundation of man's political goal, namely the attainment of freedom to its maximum within the community of others, so as to enjoy the prospect of achieving their own goals in peaceful cooperation. For by denying the right to seek help in protection, this view denies the right to seek help in any other goal one might have, such as eating well. And that is called "libertarian" analysis? Oh, man we're in trouble. ∎

The Libertarian Forum
BOX 341
MADISON SQUARE STATION
NEW YORK, NEW YORK 10010

First Class

Published Every Month. Subscription Rate: $8.00 Per Year

A Monthly Newsletter

THE Libertarian Forum

Joseph R. Peden, Pubiisher　　　　　　　　　　　　　　　　Murray N. Rothbard, Editor

VOLUME V, NO. 4　　　　　　　　APRIL, 1973　　　　　　　　75¢

FLP Convenes:

PRESENT AT THE CREATION

On the weekend of March 30-April 1, the Free Libertarian Party of New York held its first state convention at the Williams Club in Manhattan, in the process transforming itself from a temporary structure into a permanent. organized political party. Ever since the national Libertarian Party and its state affiliates had been founded a year ago, the editor of the Lib. Forum, while tempted. had held aloof. But to this old political warhorse. the firebell of a Convention proved too much to resist. As the time for the Convention drew near, I made my decision, propitiated the Spirit of Robert LeFevre, and took the plunge: I joined the Party.

As the weekend drew near, I admit to trepidation about what the convention would bring. In the first place, it has been my usual experience that when more than five libertarians (or five anyone-else, for that matter) gather together to meet, it is high time to look for the nearest exit. There is something about any Meeting, or Crowd, that seems either to deaden the spirit or to lead to endless hassles and emotional wrangling. And then there were all the stories one heard about goings-on in various outer reaches of the libertarian movement: ''rational bestiality'', for example. There were the memories of all the Crazies who had flooded into the first 1969 libertarian conference in New York. And, more concretely, there were stories of a severe and lengthy struggle over the FLP Platform, over attempts to ram an archist-Randian platform down the throats of the party, etc. When I opened this door of the libertarian arena on March 30, what joy and/or pain would this new turn bring?

To end the suspense. dear reader. I entered the Williams Club a hopeful skeptic and emerged, exhausted but enthusiastic, forty-eight hours later a celebrant. To my joyful surprise, here was a group of men and women almost all intelligent, dedicated, and knowledgeable about liberty. Here, despite a predictably wide spectrum of temperaments and ideologies, despite occasional emotional hassles, yes despite a twelve (or was it thirteen) hour session on amending the by-laws, here was a group of attractive and intelligent young people who almost literally exuded a spirit of warmth. love, and respect for each other and for the common cause. It was truly a sight to behold. At the risk of being maudlin, I affirm that it was indeed a privilege to be present at the creation of the Free Libertarian Party of New York.

As we shall see further below, the ''instincts'' of this rather large group of people (approximately 95) were remarkably sound: a blend of high libertarian principle and good common sense and mutual respect that is all too rare in or out of the Movement. And these were Real People; gone was the old predominance of hophead kids, stoned out of their minds and mumbling about ''freedom''. These were young people with feet on the ground. who do things. who work in the world: scholars, engineers, television people. advertising men. civil servants. I would say that the typical FLP member is an ex-Objectivist with none of the unfortunate personality traits of the latter. who has been moving rapidly into, or on the edge of. anarcho-capitalism. But both the anarcho-capitalists and the

sizable minority of limited archists (or ''minarchists'', to use the happy phrase of Sam Konkin), showed a happy willingness to work together for the large spectrum of common ends.

And then. wonder of wonders to a veteran of the New York movement, there was actually a sizable number of girls at the Convention, ranging moreover from attractive to ravishing (and if this be Male Chauvinism, then make the most of it!) It was also a standing wry joke in the New York movement that the proportion of females ranged from zero to somewhere around one per cent; surely this new quantum leap is a fine omen for the growth and success of the movement. Furthermore, I had personally met no more than a dozen of the delegates before — and this in a movement whose members for a long while barely spilled over the confines of a small living room!

Skipping over the endless by-law amendments, the first major act of the convention was to adopt a set of by-laws with the following admirable set of principles. principles to which all factions and trends in the party could enthusiastically adhere:

> ''The Free Libertarian Party is a political organization which has as its primary objective the extension of human freedom to its furthest limits.
> ''To that end the Party affirms the following principles:
> 1. That each individual possesses the inalienable right to life and liberty and to justly acquired property.
> 2. That no person or institution. public or private, has the right to initiate the use of physical force against another.
> 3. That all individuals are entitled to choose their own life styles as long as they do not forcibly impose their values on others.
> 4. That the only moral basis of politics is the preservation and protection of human rights.
> 5. That the voluntary exchange of goods and services is fundamental to any socio-economic system which provides for the harmonious integration of divergent value systems.
> ''In recognition of the fact that the initiation of force by government has been the chief instrument for the expropriation of individual rights and freedom, the Free Libertarian Party enters the political arena for the avowed purpose of eliminating the intervention of government in moral. social and economic affairs.''

Bravo!

The first battle. and the first critical decision, of the Convention came on Saturday night. over the adoption of a state platform. By dint of various coincidences and circumstances, the first draft of a platform had been drawn up last summer by one Paul Hodgson, a Randian archist who

(Continued On Page 2)

Tax Rebellion

April is the cruellest month, certainly for the long-suffering taxpayer. As protests against crippling taxation rise and spread throughout the country, we must honor the heroic forces of tax rebellion; the new element in tax rebellion this year is the lead increasingly taken by the nation's libertarians, the most knowledgeable and most dedicated of the tax rebels.

In its March 19 issue, TIME devoted a full page article (p.45), replete with pictures, of one of the most heroic groups of tax rebels, Henry "Hank" Hohenstein and the San Diego Ten. Remarkably, TIME's account was fairly favorable to these libertarian rebels. What happened was that in May, 1972, the IRS presumed, dictatorially and without benefit of court order, to seize the building, trucks and office equipment of the small Heck Transfer and Storage Co. of San Diego, a moving and storage firm owned by John Heck, Jr. The seizure was for payment of some $10,000 in back taxes and penalties which the IRS claimed that Mr. Heck "owed" to the federal government. A few days later, a group of some 80 protestors gathered with Mr. Heck outside his seized office, and Heck, in order to enter, threw a stone through his own door. When a corps of IRS agents tried to interfere, there was some scuffling in the crowd.

The IRS proceeded to bring charges in court against ten of the demonstrators, charging them with "conspiracy to rescue seized property" (Ye Gods! What a "crime"!) and "conspiracy to assault or impede a federal officer." The ten included libertarian real estate investor Hank Hohenstein, who had merely driven down to observe the proceedings.

Needless to say, Hank Hohenstein and the San Diego Ten did not receive the massive international publicity accorded only to Left civil libertarian causes. However, after the jury duly convicted, Judge Nielsen, worried about the murky status of conspiracy law, suspended the jail sentences of the Ten and declared a mistrial for Hohenstein. The latest news is that the government has dropped the charges against Hohenstein.

TIME summarizes the philosophy and outlook of some of the tax rebels; on Hohenstein: "who styles himself a fiscal conservative and strong civil libertarian, he claims to be acting in the tradition of Thoreau and Paine." The freeing of Hohenstein is a welcome victory for liberty.

In the meantime, the Libertarian Tax Rebellion Committee, headed by Kenneth W. Kalcheim, has been doing yeoman work for the tax rebellion cause. The LRTC sells a tax kit for $10, which explains and supports their philosophy of tax rebellion; the LRTC proposal is to file the required April 15 return, but to fill it out, not with the taxpayer's income and expenditure data, but rather with a battery of constitutional arguments against the entire income tax procedure. The tax kit can be obtained from the Libertarian Tax Rebellion Committee, 349 East 65th St., Apt. 5C, New York, N. Y. 10021. ◻

Present At The Creation —

(Continued From Page 1)

presented the early sessions of the platform committee with a full-scale Randian archist platform. It did not quite begin with "Existence exists", but there was definitely around the Hodgson draft the unmistakable aura of the philosophy club rather than the political platform. And in virtually every paragraph the Hodgson draft rubbed the anarchist noses in: "The proper function of government is . . . ." To offset the Hodgson forces, the anarchists on the split platform committee drew up a hastily composed "minority platform". In contrast to Hodgson and his colleagues, there was scarcely a single anarcho-capitalist in the FLP that desired to commit the party to an outright anarchist program, let alone to rule out of court any libertarians who were also Christians, utilitarians, pacifists, or even whim-worshippers. To a man, the anarchists, along with many of the minarchists, wanted an "umbrella" platform that would not drive any of the various tendencies out of the party. But while the Minority Platform was a decided improvement over the Hodgson Platform, it still left much to be desired; and both programs, for example, insisted on taking a stand on the theory of crime and punishment even though this is one of the most disputed and least firmly established aspects of libertarian doctrine.

As the day of the convention neared, then, sentiment in the party grew apace for scrapping the platform altogether. More and more party members began to see that there was no great rush for a state platform: we had the excellent statement of principles, we had, if need be, the national platform adopted last year. But, most interesting of all, sentiment grew, as best expressed by young Tom Avery of the Bronx, for avoiding any platform plank which could not — like the statement of principles — command unanimous consent from each party member. For, otherwise, party members would have to be represented by views and positions which they did not hold. More and more, the "minority" platform writers veered around to a no-platform position, while the few ultra-Randians abandoned the party in disgust.

On Saturday, the Hodgson platform was smashed, gathering only 4 votes (of which only two represented support for the draft in question), and the minority program received no greater shrift. The no-platform position won overwhelmingly. It was agreed, with great good — and libertarian — sense, that the various party candidates could only speak for themselves, for their own individual positions or for the special committees formed on their behalf. There would be no "party literature" as such.

Sunday was the day for choosing party officers and candidates. The elected officers managed to comprise a worthy cross-section of party activists. Chairwoman of the party (or "Chairperson" as they insist on calling it) is the vivacious Andrea Millen, a TV producer and a leader of the FLP from its inception. The two Vice-Chairmen are Howard Rich, another party founder and a leader and candidate in Rockland County; and Raymond Strong, leader of the Brooklyn party and a Ph.D. in mathematics. Secretary is Mike Nichols and Treasurer is the former Chairman, and a leading party founder, Jerry Klasman. After a spirited and very close election for the three posts of State Committeemen-at-large, elected were: Gary Greenberg, attorney, and head of the New York Libertarian Association; the redoubtable Samuel Edward Konkin III, Canadian, graduate student in Theoretical Chemistry at New York University, editor of the ever-improving New Libertarian Notes, and head of the party's Radical Caucus; and Joe Castrovinci, graduate student in history at City College, CUNY, and early member of the Fordham Libertarian Alliance, the first libertarian student group on the Eastern seaboard.

Running for office is a remarkably full slate of determined candidates. For Mayor the party has nominated the lovely and articulate Francine Youngstein, instructor in sales for IBM; for President of the City Council, Bill Lawry of Queens; for Controller, Tom Avery of the Bronx. Also nominated are: Louis Sicilia for Borough President of Manhattan, Paul Streitz (who was given a good going over for his support of the school voucher scheme) for City Councilman-at-Large from Manhattan; Ray Goldfield for City Councilman from the Coney Island region of Brooklyn, and Spencer Pinney for City Councilman from Queens. Also, the dynamic young Sanford Cohen, of the Poughkeepsie region upstate, expressed his determination to begin running now for Rep. Fish's Congressional office in 1974. All candidates were determined to succeed at the very difficult task, in New York, of actually getting on the ballot in November.

The final act of the convention underlined the good sense and even wisdom of the party membership. A proposal was made for the party to endorse legalized abortion. But while a large majority of the Party favors abortion-freedom, it decided by a 2-to-1 majority to respect the deeply held beliefs of those party members who are convinced that abortion is murder — a position which, for any libertarian, is' not self-evidently absurd. In short, the FLP decided not to take a position on the abortion issue.

I submit that the Free Libertarian Party is off to a sparkling start: health, happiness, and long life to the new offspring! ◻

Personal 'Freedom'

Review of Harry Browne's **How I Found Freedom In An Unfree World**
(Macmillan. $7.95)

By R. A. Childs, Jr.

(Editor's Note: I would add only two points to Roy Childs' excellent review of the new Browne book. One is the curious inner contradiction implicit in the book itself and in all the lectures that Harry Browne has been delivering on its major theme. And that is the fact that Browne keeps urging the rest of us **not** to care about the liberty of other persons: in short, that he is investing a considerable amount of personal energy and hence presumably cares deeply that we not care about others.

The second point is that it is considerably easier — if one is so inclined — to drop out of the State if one is, like Browne, a best-selling free lance author than if, like most of us, one must work in some regular and visible capacity.)

This is a very mixed book. In substance, if not in intention, this is Harry Browne's answer to Objectivism, his own personal philosophy of life. Like all books of that sort, it is a mixture of brilliant insights and shallow sophisms. At the outset, it should be stated that Browne is at his best giving certain types of concrete advice concerning what he calls "how you can be free": he is at his worst when he attempts to theorize about things, and to place them in a wide semi-theoretical context.

The book consists of five sections. The Prologue and Epilogue both concern themselves with "freedom in an unfree world," while the remainder of the book discusses "Why You are Not Free," "How You Can Be Free," and "A New Life." There are a number of valuable things in all sections, but the first part, as far as I am concerned, is so monstrously simplistic and wrong-headed that I can barely tolerate it. What Browne does is to discuss thirteen "traps" or reasons why one is not "free." First of all, his concept of freedom is unforgivable: "freedom is the opportunity to live your life as you want to live it." With that one phrase, Browne takes three steps backwards from the semantic advances of the key libertarian philosophers, notably Rand and Rothbard, and obscures a vitally important issue: the distinction between freedom and **ability or power.** By **defining** freedom in terms of "opportunity," Browne semantically enslaves all those who are struggling to get what they want, but who have not yet attained it, for it is precisely the concrete **opportunity** to get what they want that they are lacking. Unhappy? Perhaps. But **unfree?** Not true. Furthermore, are we to call the dictator and tyrant "free" if they have the opportunity to live **their** lives as they wish, i.e. in pursuit of power and control over others? Such a concept of "freedom" makes a free society impossible by definition, for people's whims and impulses will always clash. One person will want to live his life in a way that involves the involuntary participation of another, **ergo** he is not free if that **other** person is free to turn him down and spurn his desires.

But secondly, and more importantly, the thirteen "traps" are an amalgam of truth and absurdity wherein Browne takes two cognitive steps forward, and three back — and then reverses himself. Some of the traps are well put, such as the "Identity Trap" ("1. The belief that you should be someone other than yourself; and 2. the assumption that others will do things the way that you would."), the "Government Traps," "Unselfishness Trap," "Certainty Trap" and many others. Browne analyzes errors which prevent people from getting what they want, and (mostly later on in the book) shows them how to avoid such "traps." But while much of what he says is commonsensical and valid, the rest is completely confused and wrongheaded.

One of his mistakes is an attempt to avoid technical philosophy, even in discussing such issues as those of morality and rights, which obviously require a philosophical perspective. The reader will be interested to learn, for instance, that for Browne both morality and rights are "traps," and that "'free societies' are usually dreams in which the dreamer hopes to escape the simple prices required to live happily in the real world."

His chapter on morality is intellectually disgraceful. Browne sets up three paradigms: (1) absolute morality, (2) universal morality, and (3) personal morality, this last being his own position. "Absolute morality" is roughly equivalent to a deontological morality, which subordinates

happiness to duty. "Universal morality" is a morality based on objective principles which apply to all human beings. "Personal morality" Browne defines as "the attempt to consider all the relevant consequences of your actions," for whatever that is worth qua definition.

Let us dismiss "absolute morality" and concentrate on the other two. What is a "universal morality"? A code based on man's nature, which applies to all men. Browne maintains that there can be no such thing. Why? He isn't clear, but it has something to do with the fact that people are different. Unfortunately, however, no one has ever denied this, and no one advocating a "universal morality" has ever told people to ignore differences. The principles of a "universal morality" do not specify concretes, and are not intended to. The principles constitute a **code** of action, which is **applied** to widely varying concretes. Would Browne claim that mathematics is impossible, since all entities are concrete and different, making a relationship between mathematical principles and concrete quantities impossible? Only if one's approach to "morality" is concrete-bound can one make the claims that Browne does about "universal morality." Furthermore, Browne's position, a variant of subjectivism in ethics, is self-refuting in the context of the book, for what he does constantly is to make the general recommendation for thought and action that there can be no valid general recommendations for thought and action. Browne properly counsels independence in choosing values, but independence cannot entail subjectivism — in fact the value of independence is **derived from man's nature.** Browne also exhorts the reader to take his own feelings and values seriously; a good recommendation — but this too has nothing to do with his conclusions. Browne neither understands the function of morality as a normative integrator of evaluations and actions (performing normatively the same functions that logic and epistemology do cognitively), nor does he understand the relationship between principles and concretes. He almost makes it a principle to ignore principles in favor of concretes.

His view of natural rights is substantially the same as that of positivism. His claim here, in essence and spirit, is that since you cannot eat rights, and cannot use them to physically ward off criminals, that therefore they are useless. "Try forgetting about your rights," he says in the book. "They didn't bring you the good things you've achieved in your life. Why count on them in the future?" Similarly, he counsels political solipsism, claiming that political idealism is not practical, and that political issues and crises should never be dealt with on grounds of principled opposition, but rather on an individual level. His solipsism is even carried further when he claims (ignoring the fact that he earlier said that everything has a specific nature) "It's hard to realize that **you** live in a world of your own — bounded by your own knowledge, your own perception, your own ways of reasoning, your own set of standards." If this is true, then why is Browne bothering to give advice to other people, particularly since they live in a world of **their** own which is obviously not the same as his world?

But the response to all of these claims is the same in principle, and it amounts to a defense of philosophy in general, and of political philosophy and responsibility in particular: the reason why man needs political philosophy, a theory of rights, and political involvement is because men have the same basic natures and live in the same objective reality, the same world. He needs them because his life is not affected, for better or worse, by his own choices and actions alone, but by the society and political system in which he lives. Man needs to associate with other men in order to live and prosper, and he needs to choose and define the proper way of relating to men. Think of what Browne's view of robbery would do if everyone accepted this basic attitude: "To say that I would never steal someone's milk is to acknowledge that I'm different from many of the people in the world — and that I have my own way of trying to achieve happiness. But why should I expect someone else to use my way?" (p. 98) This means, by implication, that dictators and mass murderers merely have a difference of opinion with Browne, and that such a difference is on

(Continued On Page 8)

The I.B.M. Case:
A Comment

By Dr. D. T. Armentano
Associate Professor of Economics   University of Hartford

Recently the IBM pretrial proceedings took a comic turn for the worse. Indeed, the situation was so sadly ludicrous that Ayn Rand might have written the scenario.

It seems that the government had again been the victim of the corporate paper shredder. Only this time instead of some trivial Dita Beard memos, what got vaporized was a valuable index to over 150,000 pages of IBM internal memoranda prepared for IBM's recently concluded antitrust scuffle with the Control Data Corporation. As part of its settlement with IBM, Control Data had agreed to put down all the weapons of war including, apparently, the quiet destruction of that IBM index. Which of course left the government holding the confetti bag, since they had been counting on employing that very index to expedite their own antitrust suit against IBM. Fuming that IBM was not cooperating fully enough in its own corporate destruction, the government attorneys were at last report attempting to obtain a court order to require the computer giant to prepare yet another index! Now that, of course, is Truth, Justice and the American Way.

Actually when the antitrust suit finally goes to court (the case was the final statist shot from the fellows that brought you the Great Society), three important economic issues will be paramount: IBM's market share, reported to be over 70 per cent; IBM's policy of offering substantial price discriminations to some customers; and IBM's attractively "high" rate of return on invested capital. To many economists and trustbusters, these three ingredients spell almost automatic illegal monopolization.

The government will allege — with much academic support, and enough court victories and corporate scalps to fill a substantial trophy case — that "competition" means competitively **structured** markets, that is, markets where no one firm has any significant market share. Indeed, the structure of a market is so overwhelmingly significant in antitrust cases today that a defeat on the market share issue could well doom the entire IBM defense. IBM is apparently aware of this, and is already prepared to demonstrate that the computer market is **larger** than the government contends, and that their share of that market is, accordingly, closer to 40% and declining. This sort of eco-legal strategy was used successfully in the last classic Sherman Act monopoly case, the DuPont Cellophane case of 1956, and IBM doesn't employ 110 lawyers for nothing.

Of course, market share ought to have nothing at all to do with illegal "monopolization". A high market share can just as easily be attributed — in a free market — to buyer acceptance (and, over time, to continued buyer acceptance) as to anything else. And if simple market share is so indicative of "resource misallocation", one wonders why prominent economists such as Samuelson and Friedman — who support antitrust — don't advocate the "busting up" of textbook "monopolies" enjoyed by certain university professors.

Price discrimination means that some users pay lower rates than others for similar services. Without getting into the impossible issue of what services are ever precisely the same — and, therefore, whether real price discrimination ever exists — it might suffice to note that no one ought to get uptight over **lower** prices (no one but the competition that can't match the prices, that is). To observe corporations being prosecuted for "restraint of trade" when they are **lowering** their prices always exposes the antitrust hoax in all its nakedness, though the Ralph Naders among us dare not peek.

No, the lower prices don't come at the expense of the higher ones. And, no again, the lower prices need not necessarily relate directly to costs; costs don't determine prices. Why should a firm have to automatically throw away profits from lower costs by lowering prices? Prices are lowered under certain circumstances because profits can be retained or increased under certain circumstances. Profit-oriented firms will always charge what the traffic will bear, and the traffic will always bear different prices in different situations. Corporations ought not, therefore,

to have to defend price discrimination. It is a normal, natural, and completely beneficial practice for buyers as well as sellers in a free market.

And, finally, what of IBM's "exorbitant" rate of return? Firstly, the concept of normal profits without consideration of **risk** is totally absurd. A 17 per cent rate of return on capital might actually be "low" considering the risks of investing that capital in the computer industry. And, secondly, in the absence of plutocratic restraints on competition, one can simply attribute the return to excellent products, aggressive marketing, and high sustained managerial competence. Does the present culture so abhor individual (corporate) achievement that it must attribute all "success" to everything but individual (corporate) productivity?

Now all this is not to say that there are not any sticky libertarian difficulties with corporations such as IBM; alas, all is not sweetness and light. Patents and government contracts — to name but two issues — will always cloud what might be a super-clean analysis in IBM's favor. Yet, and this is the point, the **antitrust** issues raised are unbridled nonsense, and it is to be hoped that these issues will be thoroughly discredited in open trial. ◻

Contra Psychological "Liberation"

For years now, I have been reading and hearing a mounting and cacaphonous clamor for something called "psychological" or "personal" "liberation." The clamor has been rising from an increasing number of people, libertarians and non-libertarians alike. I confess that even after persistent and faithful reading of much of the Psy Lib literature and listening to a great deal of the caterwauling, I have still not been able to figure out what the shouting is all about. To paraphrase Mencken, even continuing diligence, stopping only for sleep and prayer, has not been enlightened me on what all this fuss is supposed to signify.

At last, however, I think I have it. I think I know at last what all these people are about; and it's not a pretty tale.

Let us take a useful paradigm: the beleaguered Scrabble player. Let us suppose that we have a man, Jim Jones, who is a devoted Scrabble player; but he finds that he is living in a community which hates and reviles Scrabble. If anyone should play Scrabble openly and thereby flaunt his detested desires, his neighbors will then cut him on the street, he won't get invited to the In parties, he might even lose his job. Confronted with this dilemma, what is Mr. Jones to do?

It seems to me that he has four alternatives open to him, each of them reasonable and viable, though some are admittedly more heroic than others.

1) He can be True to his Scrabble-Playing Self and choose to play Scrabble regardless of the consequences. He can say to the rest of the world: To hell with your narrow-minded prejudices, I shall not cater to them even at the price of loss of employment and social obloquy. He then plays Scrabble openly and he takes whatever consequences will follow. If any one may be said to be "psychologically liberated", then Jones (1) surely is.

2) Instead, he can be cool and prudential about the choices that face him. He can say to himself: To hell with it; is Scrabble really that important to me so as to lose my friends, jobs, and generally pleasant relations with the community? Answering No, he abandons Scrabble on behalf of other values that he deems to be far more important.

It seems to me that Jones (2) is, in his own way, also "liberated." Or, at the very least, he has weighed the choices that reality offered him, and made his decision in accordance with his most important values. He, too, has no particular call to belly-ache endlessly about the need for "psychological liberation". He could, after all, have chosen Route (1) but he judged the game not to be worth the candle. He has no grounds for continued caterwauling.

3) He can try to have it both ways: By **pretending** to give up or to abstain from Scrabble, thereby gaining the respect and affection of the community; while at the same time, in the dead of night, In the Closet, he secretly continues to play Scrabble. A Scrabble-Marrano.

What about Jones (3)? Is **he** justified in clamoring for "liberation"? Certainly not; he too could have chosen either the clear-cut paths of Routes (1) and (2); but he too made the conscious choice of trying to have his cake and eat it by paying the possible psychological price of secrecy. He is In the Closet by his own free choice; all he need do to Get Out of the Closet of his own making is to take Routes (1) and (2) (or, for that matter, Route 4). Let him set up no endless griping either; if he is unhappy with the Closet route, let him choose the others and shut up about it.

4) Finally, there is the fourth viable choice open to Jim Jones: to get the blazes out of this community which he finds oppressive, and to flee to some other more congenial community where Scrabble playing openly abounds. He, too, is certainly "liberated": by changing his locale, he manages to play Scrabble openly and to keep the respect and friendship of his neighbors.

The point, then, is that whichever of the four horns of the dilemma Jones chooses to grasp, the very **act** of choice gets him out of the dilemma and ends any need to bleat endlessly for liberation. Whichever route he takes, in accordance with his own temperament and values, he has made his choice and can and should then shut up about the whole business and proceed with the other business of life. It seems to me, then, that the caterwaulers are people who **refuse** to make any of these choices,

who confront the various paths and dither endlessly about adopting any of them. And then they inflict part of the price of that dithering on us by calling upon the rest of us to "liberate" them from their psychic bonds.

What they are trying to do, in short, is to gripe about the fact that reality, harshly and unfairly perhaps, presents them with this dilemma, or indeed with any dilemmas at all. Sure it would be nicer and more pleasant if the community in which Jones lives were more enthusiastic about Scrabble. But the fact is that they are **not**, and instead of haranguing and pestering them to admire and respect Scrabble or **us** to somehow make Jones' neighbors change their attitudes, it behooves our unliberated brethren to confront their four choices clearly and honestly, to make their choice and thereby to **liberate themselves**, and thereby to leave us and everyone else free of the eternal blather about "liberation." Let the unliberated proceed thus to quickly liberate themselves and go on to pursue more constructive concerns.   ◻

Jim Davidson And The Week That Was

On the week of April 2-6, the United States Senate took three notable libertarian actions. In the first place, by a vote of 68 to 23, the Senate, over determined opposition from the U. S. Treasury, voted to legalize the private ownership of gold for the first time in forty years. Since the vote was an amendment to the Administration-requested devaluation of the dollar to one-forty-second of a gold ounce, it is doubtful if the President will veto the entire bill should it pass the House.

Secondly, the Senate voted to prohibit governmental aid to North Vietnam without Congressional authorization. And third, the Senate passed a mandatory across-the-board budget-cut within an overall budget lower than the President's request.

Each of these noteworthy actions is eloquent testimony to the quiet but remarkably effective work done by our one-man libertarian Washington lobbyist, James Davidson of the National Taxpayers Union. At the beginning of 1973, Davidson listed ten modest but important libertarian legislative goals for the year; not only were the above three actions on Davidson's Ten Best list, but all of his other legislative objectives for the year are in good shape and none has been flatly rejected.

How does the young and handsome Davidson, operating with virtually no help and on a shoestring budget, do it? One way is by getting to know and influence key aides to key Senators, who in turn influence the rest of the Senate; and another of his crucial tactics is to do what the Marxists call "exploiting the contradictions within the ruling class." In other words, to push a piece of libertarian legislation or to block a particularly egregious bit of statism, Davidson finds out which interests within the Establishment, not ordinarily libertarian, can be developed as allies on this particular issue. Thus, on the issue of gold legalization, Davidson realized that he could forge a "left-right" alliance on the issue between: conservative gold standard advocates, senators from mining states in the West, and such left-liberal Democrat ideologues as Rep. Reuss (D., Wisc.) who favor the legalizing of gold as a symbol of treating gold as an ordinary non-monetary commodity like any other. Welding this alliance, and working with his eminent NTU colleague and thorn-in-the side of the military-industrial complex, A. Ernest Fitzgerald, Davidson was able to convert the powerful Senator William Proxmire (D., Wisc.) to the cause of gold legalization. This conversion was aided by the fact of Fitzgerald's being an aide to Proxmire's Joint Economic Committee, which gives Congress its major cues on all economic legislation. With Proxmire on the right side, the Senate easily passed the amendment introduced by Senator McClure, conservative Republican from the mining state of

(Continued On Page 7)

From The Halls Of
Montezuma . . .

By Joseph R. Peden

Not too long ago, in the wake of the President's visits to Peking and Moscow, and the winding down of the Vietnam war, political satirist Russell Baker reported a new crisis in the Pentagon — fear that America would soon suffer an "enemy gap". But after extensive research, the strategic master planners discovered a suitable enemy for the '70's — Denmark. While some Army officials were fearful of the morale effect upon the troops who would have to occupy vice-ridden Copenhagen, the missile men considered the challenge of dropping ICBM's on Denmark without splashing any part of Sweden, Norway and Germany to be a useful challenge to their skills. What tipped the scales, however, was the fact that so many Americans had visited Denmark, that the U. S. was filled with people who were "soft on Danes", thus providing the FBI, CIA and innumerable Congressional investigatory committees with years of profitable "work".

But political satire in our age tends to lose its point by being overtaken by reality. National Review also must have been concerned about the enemy gap. While never for a moment supposing that Leviathan (Russia) and Behemoth (China) had been defeated by Richard Nixon, they felt obliged to point to the rise of a new enemy in the field — the Arab republic of Libya — and proposed that the United States should invade, conquer and annex it.

I almost wish this proposal was another one of NR's spoofs, but there is every indication that in this instance they are not joking. In fact, from a certain point of view, it may be quite a reasonable suggestion.

First of all, as NR pointed out, Libya is an excellent base from which any imperial power can dominate the Middle East and Europe. The harbors at Tobruk and Tripoli are among the best along the north African coast; the climate is ideal for maintaining large military airbases; geographically Libya is at the center of the Mediterranean basin, and also has common frontiers with Egypt, Sudan, Algeria, Tunisia, Chad, and Niger. Traditionally, it has had intimate links with the Islamic peoples of west Africa, as well as with Egypt and Sudan to the East. And then, there is all that oil.

But is Libya a threat to the peace of the world? Is it under Communist tyranny? In what way hath it offended?

The Libyans greatest provocation is that they are not under the control of American or European imperialism. Unlike Egypt and Syria which have been forced into dependence upon the Soviet Union for military weapons to defend themselves against Israeli aggression, or Jordan which exists as a client state of the United States and its allies in the Arab world, Libya is geographically more remote from Israel and less subject to danger of invasion, and financially has been able through its enormous oil revenues to buy whatever military equipment it needs for cash. Thus, in its defenses, it is not dependent upon any one of the great powers for its survival. The independence, or arrogance as some would say, that such a situation creates was well illustrated recently when Libyan jet fighters tried to shoot down an American spy plane flying within a hundred miles of Tripoli over the high seas. The Libyans claim a 100 mile restricted zone around their capital city, and challenge any aircraft entering the zone without Libyan permission. When the United States protested this dastardly attack on an — you guessed it — unarmed C-130 transport plane, the Libyans ignored the American note for four days, and then coolly denied the incident had happened.

Nor is Libya ruled by Communists. Would that it were so. As Nixon has proven, you can always do business with Reds if you want to. But Libya is ruled by a small group of fanatic, zealous Moslems who despise infidels and are deeply humiliated by the present disunity in the Arab world, and the shame that has overtaken the Arab people at the hands of Israel and her European allies.

With much of the puritanical zeal of the century-old Senoussi order, a brotherhood dedicated to purifying Islam of all foreign influences and espousing a rigidly orthodox and mystical sense of Arab divine mission, the young military leaders who seized power and overthrew the pro-

western monarchy in 1969 have managed to create a formidable moral as well as political force in the Moslem world. Devoted admirers of Gamal Abdel Nasser, they may yet succeed to his almost mystical power over the Arab masses. They are certainly the most bitter and uncompromising enemies of Israel — and hence of all her friends. This means that they cannot easily be bribed or bought or even scared by the imperialist powers.

But the most disturbing aspect of the Libyan regime is that its power vis-a-vis the Western powers is formidable and growing greater. Libya is the third largest producer of petroleum — only Kuwait and Iran are greater. And her potential reserves have been confirmed at 25 billion and estimated to be possibly 100 billion barrels. Despite the development of fields in the North Sea or the North Alaskan slope, the United States and Europe are becoming more and more dependent upon foreign oil. The first signs of the "energy crisis" — particularly in the heavily populated northeastern United States — have forced Nixon to temporarily suspend some of the import restrictions of fuel oils. But increased imports are unacceptable to the American government for several reasons. The cheaper foreign oil would further undercut the profitableness of domestic oil production, and thus increase dependence on foreign suppliers. But even more serious over the long run is the ever heavier drain on the balance of payments which can be expected as we become more dependent on foreign oil imports. A group of utility companies has recently combined to explore the continental shift off the northeastern United States to locate possible natural gas supplies. Their motive: "Our country faces financial bankruptcy if we have to depend too heavily on imports of natural gas and petroleum."

The unfavorable balance of trade between the western industrial nations and the thinly populated Arab oil exporting states has already endangered the international monetary system. In the most recent monetary crisis, the gnomes of Zurich were replaced by the gnomes of Araby who began to dump billions of dollars into the European money markets — forcing them to close down for more than a week until the United States could be persuaded to devalue the dollar for the second time in six months. It is now clear that already the Arab states control sufficient reserves of European and American currency to create a monetary crisis whenever and whereever they choose. One suggestion has been to encourage the Arab states to invest directly in American industry, thus reducing their quickly convertible monetary reserves. But the vast amounts that are and will be available to the Arabs could produce a situation in which the Arabs would gain a significant control of some sectors of the American economy. Others are urging Washington to coordinate the energy policies of all the western powers to reduce the leverage of the Arab states in negotiating new oil concessions, and pricing and revenue demands. Arab spokesmen have rightly labeled this "common front" approach a "declaration of war". (It is not unreasonable to speculate that Nelson Rockefeller's recent trip to an informal conference of Atlantic statesmen meeting in Holland may have been motivated by these concerns.)

Also alarming to Washington must be the increasing evidence that the Libyans are using their oil revenues to intervene in the affairs of other nations. The Libyans were the chief bankrollers and arms suppliers to the Islamic rebels in French-dominated Chad. De Gaulle had to send in French troops to help the non-Moslem government of Chad to survive a widespread uprising. Reportedly, the Libyans withdrew their support only after France agreed to sell them 100 French Mirage jets. The jets, paid for in cash, created a formidable air power, remote enough from Israel for safety, yet close enough to serve as a strategic reserve for the Egyptians.

The assassination of the American Ambassador to the Sudan and his aide was widely reported as having been financed by Libya which is also a generous supporter of the Palestinian Liberation Movement. The Libyans

(Continued On Page 7)

370

Monthly Index Of Liberty

In an off-the-record briefing for Congressmen, assistant secretary for Far Eastern Affairs, William Sullivan, asked to cite the constitutional authority for the President's continued bombing of Cambodia, replied smilingly, "For now I'd just say the justification is the re-election of President Nixon". Of course. **Vox populi, vox Dei.**

• • •

America's Asian allies — those staunch defenders of freedom and democracy — are at it still. In the Philippines, where the Marcos regime is faced with a full-fledged guerrilla uprising among the Moslems of Mindinao and the Sulu islands, the army has a new "secret weapon" — Mosquitos. The rebel area is ridden by malaria. So the government has stopped spraying. "Sooner or later the rebels will be too weak to fight". And presumably Marcos will have won the hearts and minds of the people. Meanwhile, in Cambodia, Marshal Lon Nol has arrested and jailed 55 of the nation's top astrologers. It seems they were unanimous in predicting that his regime would not survive the end of April. We await the first of May with interest.

Halls Of Montezuma —
(Continued From Page 6)

also showed unseemly, and as it developed unwarranted haste in cheering the aborted assassination of King Hassan of Morocco, and it was assumed that the Libyans may have had something to do with the attempted coup. An unsuccessful coup in the Sudan a year ago may also have been instigated by the Libyans, and the present Sudanese government has failed to participate in the new federal Arab republic engineered by the Libyans and Egyptians.

In Uganda, President Amin was believed to have expelled the Israeli military and civilian advisors from his country, not only because he couldn't pay his debts, but because Libyan political and financial support was promised. The Libyans have been most aggressively establishing financial aid links with black African states who show themselves "loyal" on the Israeli question in the United Nations and elsewhere. Recently, in the midst of a firm refusal of Britain to pay higher rental fees for her naval bases in Malta, the Maltese Prime Minister coolly announced that Libya had offered to make up any financial losses Malta might suffer, if Malta permanently excluded all NATO forces from its soil. Negotiations renewed shortly after, and the Maltese got most of what they wanted. The New York Times has even reported that Philipine army officers are convinced that the Moslem rebels in Mindinao and the Sulu Islands have received arms and money through Libyan sources! One would not be surprised if the federal marshals found a burnoose and water-pipe left behind at Wounded Knee.

What then are the implications of Libya's new found power? Clearly the Libyans can create all sorts of mischief.

With far fewer resources, the Barbary pirates, ancestors of the modern Libyans, held all the states of Europe under tribute to ensure the safe passage of their ships through the Mediterranean Sea during the 16th through early 19th centuries. Even the United States paid almost a million dollars before sending a fleet to punish the pirates of Tripoli. When the Italians invaded the country in 1911 they suffered another of their humiliating military disasters until the collapse of the Turkish empire in 1918, and internal divisions among the Libyans, opened the way for an uneasy Italian occupation. The Libyans have shown themselves to be brave, cunning and formidable enemies, and there is no reason to suppose that they are less so now.

With their immense oil reserves and the revenues that continue to pile up, the less than two million Libyans cast a large shadow in future world affairs. Their trump card is the enormous need for their oil by the western powers — cheap and convenient to the European or American markets. In this kind of situation, Israel might find itself with less sympathy and support in the West: especially if a monetary crisis were added to a cut off of fuel supplies. If there is still another Arab-Israeli war, it would not be surprising to read of a landing and occupation of Tobruk or Benghazi or Sirte by Israeli forces. In fact there might be some people in Washington who would be very pleased with such an operation. It might save them the trouble. ◨

Libertarians have been among the few Americans who have taken a principled stand against the law of eminent domain — that relic of the English common law that views all landed property as belonging ultimately to the Crown. New Yorkers are watching with interest the confiscation of the homes of 90 families, all white working-class ethnics, by the City of New York. The reason? A private manufacturing corporation has threatened to leave the city unless it can expand its present plant facilities. The city government — to save some 500 jobs — has driven 90 families from their homes by confiscation under the law of eminent domain, and plans to turn the property over to the manufacturer.

Nor is this outrage surprising. Two years ago a consultant to the New York City planning commission urged the seizure of the 89 acre Holy Cross Catholic Cemetery in Brooklyn. Why? There is no nearby park facility with "a woodland at least sufficiently deep to camouflage lovers with no other alternatives for privacy". While most citizens gagged on the notion of sexual rumbles on the graves of their loved ones, the ecologists and planners jumped in to urge the necessity of "doing something" about the selfish individuals who preferred to maintain their right to the proverbial plot of landed property which even the poorest American eventually thinks his due. The 4000 or so acres presently owned by New Yorkers as burial plots were depriving 200,000 living persons of decent housing sites, charged an outraged planner. At the very least the "tax-exempt" cemeteries might be put to "multiple uses" — as playgrounds, dog walks, or perhaps even garbage dumps. Of course the government might solve the problem by requiring cremation or dumping at sea instead of inhumation. But that would only arouse the environmental pollution nuts! In India, the Parsees expose the dead on tall stone towers where nature and the vultures harmoniously keep a natural ecological cycle and eliminate all problems of pollution. Come to think of it, do the city fathers realize the amount of space presently wasted, and untaxed, on the thousands of rooftops of New York's skyscrapers?

• • •

Then there is that AP dispatch from London: Police arrested a young man prowling about London's Highgate Cemetery with a flashlight, a cruxifix, and a sharp wooden stake. The culprit told the magistrate that he was hunting vampires. The judge found hunting vampires to be within the law and dismissed the case. It's comforting to know that Englishmen still enjoy **some** liberties. ◨

Jim Davidson —
(Continued From Page 5)

Idaho. Another accomplishment of Davidson's in this battle was to surprise and perturb the Nixon Administration by single-handedly inducing the Republican platform committee to include a call for gold legalization in the 1972 platform.

It is unfortunate in a way that the path of the successful lobbyist in Washington must be a quiet rather than a noisy one, for as a result Jim Davidson's remarkable achievements for the cause have gone unsung within the libertarian movement. It was Davidson, who by converting Senator Harry Byrd (D., Va.) to the cause, managed to tip the scales against the SST. It was Davidson who, more than anyone else and working through Proxmire's aides, managed to convince Senator Long (D., La.) to go all-out to block and thereby defeat the disastrous Family Assistance Plan — a plan which the President has now fortunately abandoned.

It behooves all libertarians to get behind Jim Davidson and the NTU in their lonely battle. Davidson reports, for example, that Congressmen receive remarkably little mail on any given issue, and therefore that a coordinated and well-timed letter-writing campaign by the nation's libertarians could block or promote important pieces of legislation. One way to help Davidson's efforts is to join the National Taxpayers Union and thus to receive his periodical newsletter **Dollars and Sense** (NTU, 319 5th St., S. E., Washington, D. C. 20003). By doing so, you will also be receiving important political information; for example, **Dollars and Sense** last fall predicted a 40% rise in meat prices this winter! The basis for Jim's prediction was the new federal regulations banning the use of hormones in meat. Thus, by joining NTU you will not only be helping the cause but will help yourself find out more of what is really going on at the seat of government. ◨

Recommended Reading

By Mr. First Nighter

Rent Controls.

Despite its importance, rent controls and their consequences have been little studied by economists. Now, the Swedish free-market economist Sven Rydenfelt expands his excellent critique of the unfortunate effects of post-World War II rent controls in Sweden, an early version of which he had published in the Mises Festschrift volume, **Toward Liberty.** See Rydenfelt, "Swedish Housing Policy, 1942-1972: History and Analysis", **Skandinaviska Enskilda Banken Quarterly Review** (1972, No. 3).

Urban Renewal.

Martin Anderson's classic dissection of urban renewal, **The Federal Bulldozer,** had a blockbuster effect in bringing about disillusionment with the program, among Left and Right alike. But Anderson's work is almost ten years old (1964), and there has long been a crying need for bringing it up to date. Now this task has been accomplished by the young Friedmanite economist, Prof. John Weicher, in his new booklet, **Urban Renewal** (Washington: American Enterprise Institute, Dec. 1972, $3.00). A fine contribution to the new "Evaluative Studies" series of the AEI, engaging in critical analysis of various government programs, and edited by Yale Brozen of the University of Chicago.

World War II Revisionism.

While Cold War Revisionism has flourished in recent years, World War II Revisionism has had to make its way against more deeply entrenched opposition. Yet it is growing, and now a leading young political scientist, with impeccable credentials in orthodox academic circles, has written an excellent brief summary of the Revisionist position. In scarcely more than 100 pages, Professor Russett lays both the "Hitler threat" and the "Japanese threat" to American security at rest once and for all. Probably the best brief introduction to World War II Revisionism.

> Bruce M. Russett, **No Clear and Present Danger: A Skeptical View of the U. S. Entry into World War II** (Harper Torchbooks, paper, $1.95).

Those younger libertarians who have not yet broken free of the official mythology in American foreign policy can scarcely do better in beginning their re-education than to read the Russett book. As Russett says: "Participation in the war against Hitler remains almost wholly sacrosanct, nearly in the realm of theology." While Russett's work does not presume to tell the entire story, it succeeds in the necessary task of desanctifying World War II.

Personal 'Freedom' —

(Continued From Page 3)

the same level as other differences between men. Nothing could be further from the truth. But all of this shows the flaws in Browne's approach: man's need of principles in the political realm is greater than in most other areas, for a political system has a lot to do with the choices and options open to one, across the span of a lifetime, and the scope of political error or evil is much greater than in other areas.

No one has ever said that rights are **enough** to make anyone happy; they are rather a necessary but not sufficient condition for individual happiness and well being. And neither is the alternative **either-or** as Browne implies, i.e. **either** we rely on rights **or** we rely on insurance and individual action for protection, for instance. No advocate of natural rights has ever attacked the idea of insurance against theft, and for good reason: the two things are completely different, and have different purposes. Why then does Browne, the symbolic insurance man, have a need to attack natural rights? Obviously they do not defend or help people in the same way, but so what?

Finally, there are an enormous number of concrete suggestions and bits of advice here, some bad, most fairly good-to-excellent. A large part of this has been said before, but it is good to have such a diversity of things under one cover. The distinguishing characteristic of HOW I FOUND FREEDOM is twofold: (a) Browne has more advice about more subjects, and (b) he attempts to put it into a theoretical framework. In the first respect, he is successful, in the latter, he is a dismal failure. I respect Browne's intention, and many will claim that the theoretical aspects of the book are not its primary purpose or function. Fine — but then why aren't they left out all together? Anyone who discusses the theoretical issues which Browne does in this book has certain epistemic obligations: namely, to make sense, to think his position out as far as his intelligence will take him, to resolve contradictions and, finally, to present a position which is **true.** In this respect, Browne's book is a tragic failure. He gives advice while evading the responsibilities of giving such advice, that large-scale consistency and integration which philosophy alone makes possible. Browne has attempted not to **supplement** philosophy with concrete, journalistic advice, but to **replace** it with such advice.

There is nothing wrong with such advice, **except** when it does attempt to substitute itself for philosophy. Then the advice-giver must learn the truth of Thomist philosopher Etienne Gilson's quip: "PHILOSOPHY ALWAYS BURIES ITS UNDERTAKERS." ◻

First Class

Published Every Month. Subscription Rate: $8.00 Per Year

A Monthly Newsletter

THE
Libertarian Forum

Joseph R. Peden, Pubiisher   Murray N. Rothbard, Editor

VOLUME V, NO. 5   MAY, 1973   US-ISSN0047-4517

NOTES ON WATERGATE

No doubt about it: we were dead wrong in pooh-poohing the political significance of Watergate (Nov. 1972). In our defense, however, Watergate remained a minor caper of piddling proportions until James W. McCord, Jr., under the hammer blows of Judge "Maximum John" Sirica, broke and began to implicate the higher-ups.

Sub specie aeternetatis, one set of politicians spying upon and sabotaging another is hardly of cosmic significance. But oh the deliciousness as the whole sleazy, robotic crew, even unto the highest reaches of the White House, gets its comeuppance! Every morning's news brings further revelations, further scandal, as the network of the corruption of power extends upward and outward. One by one they topple, as the President becomes so short-handed that some have to double up on jobs. One thing is certain: it couldn't have happened to a nicer or more deserving bunch of guys, or to a more deserving institution.

• • •

There are many interesting and even neglected facets to Watergate. We see the White House staff as the epitome of the Organization Man: people with one thought and one loyalty — not to truth, or justice, or honor, or even country, but to The President. The President becomes a quasi-divine figure in whose service any and all means may be employed.

And yet what happens when the crust of loyalty is broken, when the pressure is on? Then, The President is forgotten and it's every man for himself, each rushing to try to clear himself and point the finger at his former colleagues. Truly an edifying spectacle of our rulers in action with their well-known devotion to the Public Interest and the Common Good. Come on, have at each other, fellows. Implicate, implicate!

Before the mad rush, of course, there was the Cover-Up. Here we see the inveterate instincts of the Bureaucracy to hush things up, to kick things under the rug, and never never let the long suffering citizen and taxpayer in on what is going on. So much for the "democratic process."

• • •

And then there is all the wailing that Watergate is endangering the credibility, not merely of Mr. Nixon, but of "the office of the Presidency itself." Oh no, surely not that! Here is one of the great consequences of Watergate: the demythologizing, the desanctification of the office of the Presidency that has taken on an increasingly sacral character in recent decades.

In this connection, it is highly instructive that Bill Buckley has finally revealed his cloven hoof. Conservatives are, at the very least, supposed to revere the American Constitution, and if the Constitution says anything it is that the people, and not any branch of government, is sovereign. But let us forever note the reaction of America's leading Conservative to Watergate, and particularly to the increasing talk of impeaching Mr. Nixon. Said Buckley, perfectly seriously:

"In America, the President is the emperor in addition to being the prime minister. He is, no matter that his term as such is limited, the sovereign. When it is contemplated to execute the king, it is necessary to think first about the consequences on the people, rather than on the

judicial poetry of the sentence . . . If Nixon were impeached, the punishment would be visited primarily on the state . . . it is necessary to remind oneself that the sovereign is unique: that the punishment of the whole of the state is never justified." (New York Post, April 28).

There it is, brazen and blatant, from a man who sometimes likes to think of himself as a "libertarian." The President is the king, the sovereign; and the king is the state, and is therefore above retribution. Louis XIV could not have said it better. William F. Buckley has revealed the quintessential nature of the American Conservative movement; it is not Constitutionalist, but monarchist, and absolute-monarchist at that. Bill Buckley is far better suited as a theoretician for George III than he is as an American citizen.

Happily, our publisher, Professor Peden, wrote a letter printed in the Post (May 2) that called Buckley to task. Peden wrote: "When William Buckley baldly states that the President is sovereign, that to punish him for malfeasance of high crimes is to punish 'the whole of the state' . . . Mr. Buckley is guilty of culpable ignorance. He apparently believes that the American Republic is monarchical in its Constitution. As almost any legal authority or political scientist will attest, and even the layman can read in the Constitution's preamble, the American people are the sovereigns in this society . . . Neither the President, nor the Congress nor the Supreme Court are sovereign in any sense of the word. And it is either ignorance or dangerous mischief for Mr. Buckley to claim otherwise."

• • •

"Impeachment"! What a glorious sound the word has! Until a few weeks ago, the very idea of impeaching the President, any President, would have been considered grotesque and absurd. It was only recently that former (another good word) Attorney-General Kleindienst arrogantly informed the Congress that if they didn't like the President's actions they could either vote down the budget or impeach him. Until a few weeks ago, impeachment was thinking the unthinkable; yet now, even such Establishment Congressmen as Rep. Moss, and Goldwater and Thurmond, are seriously contemplating such action. And the general Congressional reaction to current calls for impeachment are not that they are lunatic or absurd, but only that they are "premature." Use of such a word seems to imply that pretty soon the idea of impeachment may indeed mature.

And how many people really believe that Mr. Nixon knew nothing of the vast and extensive bugging-sabotage-espionage operations on the Democrats? When literally millions of dollars were being handed around under the table? And how many believe that he knew nothing of the gigantic and well-coordinated cover-up? Nixon, after all, is no boob like Grant or Harding; he has always been a shrewd and ruthless political operator, and he has always proclaimed the tightness of his political ship. Besides if he really takes "responsibility", isn't that enough to mete out proper punishment?

One of the demurrers on impeachment is that this would bring Spiro Agnew into the Presidency. Apart from the likelihood that Agnew would

(Continued On Page 2)

Notes On Watergate —

(Continued From Page 1)

resign as well. would he really be that much worse then Nixon? Enough worse to give up the magnificent **precedent** that the use of the impeachment power would set? The precedent that would put every future President, and every American as well, on notice that it is possible to topple him. that the President is **not** an absolute dictator for four years. that something can be done, legally and without violence, to remove him forthwith from office.

• • •

And where are all the loud champions of "law and order" in all this? Not, it might be noted, with law and order. The President wistfully refers to the Watergate criminals as good men whose "zeal exceeded their judgement" in the righteous cause of getting him re-elected. Governor Reagan says that these men are not criminals because they were acting in a good cause (I thought it was only the bad old Communists who are always charged with believing that "the ends justify the means").

• • •

One fascinating aspect of the Watergate has not been commented on in the media. It was the breaking of James W. McCord, Jr. that broke open the entire Watergate network. Crucial to McCord's sudden decision to talk, in addition to Judge Sirica's stiff sentencing, was the advice of his new lawyer. Bernard Fensterwald. But who is Mr. Fensterwald, who played such a critical role in the Watergate revelations? Old Kennedy Assassination Revisionists know Fensterwald well: for he is the dedicated head of the Committee to Investigate Assassinations, which for several years has been the major research organization investigating the critical political assassinations of our time: King, the two Kennedys, Malcolm X. etc. Undoubtedly, Fensterwald was intrigued by the Cuban emigre-CIA connections of most of the Watergate burglars, connections which also permeate the Oswald-JFK Assassination case. Perhaps he was hoping that blowing the lid off Watergate might also lead to further revelations on the assassination at Dallas. And who knows? maybe it will.

In this connection. President Nixon promises us that his investigation into Watergate will be "the most thorough investigation since the Warren Commission." To old Kennedy Assassination buffs, this is surely the grisliest joke of the year.

• • •

Everyone. I suppose, has his own particular favorite among the storehouse of goodies unearthed by the Watergate case. My own is the cretinous behavior of the head of the FBI. L. Patrick Gray, Jr., in dumping crucial documents unread into the "burn bag." Another happy result of Watergate. as well as the entire tenure of Gray, is the rapid desanctification of our national secret police. Surely, it will never be the same again.

• • •

While we all chortle at Watergate and its ramifying consequences, we might also keep a wary eye on the future. A seminal article, "The World Behind Watergate", by Kirkpatrick Sale, has recently been published in the **New York Review of Books** (May 3). Here is an article which should be read by everyone interested in the men behind and around Watergate and in the politico-economic roots of the Nixon Administration. Mr. Sale traces the intricate and extensive connections between all the powers in and around the administration. Taking off from Carl Oglesby's trenchant distinction between the "cowboys" and the "yankees" among the power elite. Sale treats the Nixon (as well the Johnson) Administration as the embodiment of the relative accession to power of the **nouveau riche** "Southern rim" elite centered in Southern California, Texas, and Florida — as contrasted to the suaver, more sophisticated "older money" of the Eastern Establishment-corporate liberal elite. The Southern Rim tends to be blunter, more crass, more narrowly focussed and politically conservative. and more prone to short-range crookery; while the Eastern Establishment is smoother, more settled and cosmopolitan, more focussed on wider and long-range concerns, corporate-liberal, and more content to stay within the legal forms.

There is no question about the fact that the Watergate revelations are smashing the political power of the Southern rim clique. and perhaps that of their very own Southern Californian President along with it. But doesn't this forebode a re-accession to power of the Eastern Establishment. which while smoother and less crudely obnoxious is in the long run more dangerous? After all, Rockefeller's personal representative in government, Henry Kissinger, comes out smelling like a rose. as do Rockefeller-connected economic czars George Pratt Shultz and Arthur F. Burns. The suspicious observer may ask: is the Rockefeller-Eastern Establishment pushing the Watergate expose for its own ends? Is it connected with a possible Rockefeller run for the Presidency in 1976? Does the emergence of Boston Brahmin Eliot Richardson and New York liberal Leonard Garment embody a return to power of the Eastern Establishment? And is Texan John Connally riding in to head the Yankees off at the pass?   ◘

For A New Liberty

Reviewed By J. Neil Schulman

The prime axiom of Human Action is that men employ means to gain ends. Mr. Libertarian. Murray N. Rothbard. has just given us one hell of a means toward one of our most treasured ends — the creation of a free society.

No longer must the libertarian point to a succession of formidable-looking tomes on a myriad of complex subjects to initiate the uninitiated to the many joys of his favorite subject. No longer must we suggest books that spend half their space on the subject of Ayn Rand — either praising or demolishing her — or supposedly "libertarian" books that while admittedly comprehensive in scope. are "weak" on this question or that one.

Dr. Rothbard's new book For A New Liberty is a work monumental in both scope of presentation and in the philosophical consistency of its content. It is complete without being verbose. and detailed without unnecessary complexity. Its every claim is based on easily verifiable truths. and it presents its case for human liberty starting with sound theoretical groundwork. proceeding to show concrete applications, and backing it all up with examples of historical precedent.

The book is divided into an introduction and three parts.

In his introduction. Dr. Rothbard gives a simple and beautifully-appealing history of the present libertarian movement — the "New Libertarianism." as he calls it — and introduces the non-aggression doctrine as the defining agreement among all libertarians.

In Part I. the theoretical base of libertarianism is presented with a thorough discussion of how both civil and economic liberties are inseperable because both are based on property rights, and we are treated to frequent examples to back up each point.

The lengthiest portion of the book, Part II. is devoted to a complete picture of the chaos caused by State interventionism, and Dr. Rothbard presents a marvelously rational analysis of how the free market and other purely voluntary institutions could throw oil on troubled waters (and yes: pollution is discussed). There are chapters on involuntary servitude. personal liberty, education, welfare, the public sector, conservation. and war. and throughout Dr. Rothbard is radicalizing us by demonstrating that the draft is slavery. taxation robbery, public schools thinly-disguised compulsory mind control, and war a euphemism for mass murder. To read the injustice done to us daily by the State in such rapid succession is so overpowering that if any of these chapters were ever read to a large audience. it would be enough to have the speaker thrown in jail on charges of "inciting to riot." an absurdity Dr. Rothbard also challenges in his discussion on freedom of speech. And it is also in this section that Dr. Rothbard's chapter on "Police, Law and the Courts" — already famous to readers of **Reason** Magazine — makes its first appearance in book form. It is the most persuasive case for natural law, private defense. and voluntary arbitration ever set to paper, and is

(Continued On Page 3)

Floyd Arthur 'Baldy' Harper, RIP

On the evening of Saturday, April 21, Dr. F. A. "Baldy" Harper died suddenly, of a heart attack, at the age of 68. To say that Baldy's death is an irreparable loss, personally and in every other way, to the libertarian movement, would be a masterpiece of understatement. Ever since he came to the Foundation for Economic Education in 1946 as its chief economist and theoretician, Baldy Harper, in a very real sense, has been the libertarian movement. For all these years, this gentle and lovable man, this wise and Socratic teacher, has been the heart and soul and nerve center of the libertarian cause.

I had the privilege of meeting Baldy in the winter of 1946-47, and from that first meeting, he became my first dear friend and mentor in the libertarian movement. And I was scarcely an isolated example. For years before and ever since, Baldy Harper carried on an enormous and inspiring correspondence, seeking out all promising libertarians, encouraging any signs of their productivity, by his wise teaching and example developing a large and devoted following of friends and students. The thought of never again receiving one of Baldy's famous cryptic and allusive hand-written notes is almost enough to move one to tears. The last letter I had received from him, a brief week or two before his death, was typical: a glowing note about his discovery of a brilliant young mathematics professor who is anxious to move into the field of Austrian economics and to refute the fallacies of orthodox mathematical economics.

It was Baldy's burden, which he bore with his usual uncomplaining grace, that he was a member of a veritable "lost generation" from the libertarian point of view. In the late 1940's, there were some libertarians and free-market economists of the Ludwig von Mises generation or slightly younger: men then in their 60's, such as Mises, Fred Fairchild, Willford I. King. And there were a few of us youngsters coming up. But in

For A New Liberty —

(Continued From Page 2)

perhaps the most important essay — in its own right — since Lysander Spooner's No Treason: The Constitution of No Authority.

In Part III, Dr. Rothbard wraps up with a brief discussion of strategy, how to get from our present coercive society to a free one. He discusses the need for both education and action, and stresses that we must keep our ultimate goal constantly in view even while working for reforms that may fall short of our hopes and expectations. It is a fitting dessert to a magnificently-prepared dinner, and any libertarians who dare disagree with Chef Rothbard's receipe are warned that they are pursuing a hazardous course indeed.

For A New Liberty is unlike Dr. Rothbard's previous major works in that it is not aimed at the scholar already familiar with his subject, but is directed to the casual reader, albeit one in full focus. In its successful attempt at comprehensiveness (I can think of no major topic left undiscussed, or common fallacy about our position left unrefuted), it has made no compromise with either detailed accuracy, or the climate of popular opinion at the present time.

If this view has so far sounded like a sales pitch . . . it is. For A New Liberty is "hard core" and, in my opinion, the single most important book on libertarianism ever published, judging from its potential for converting the general public to our cause. Read it yourself; it will clarify your concepts; and recommend it to anyone with any leanings towards freedom; if he has any intelligence and integrity at all, this book must convince him. If the public gives For A New Liberty even half the attention it so richly deserves, we will be well on our way to a free society.

But then we "New Libertarians" suspected that from the beginning, didn't we?   ◘

his vital "middle generation", there was only Baldy: all of the other intellectuals of his day were leftists and statists. And so Baldy simply set out, in his quiet and gentle way, to create a body of students and followers. In those early days at FEE, for example, almost every staff member had been brought into the movement by Baldy: W. M. Curtiss, Paul Poirot, Ivan Bierly, Ellis Lamborn, all students of Baldy at Cornell. Baldy was indeed a notable inspiration and guide for young people, and his followers are now everywhere in the libertarian world. There were scarcely any of us touched by his special magic who did not come to love Baldy as a mentor and a friend.

Baldy and I came to anarcho-capitalism from laissez-faire at about the same time, driven by inexorable logic, in what for us was the memorable winter of 1949-50. I vividly remember one time I was visiting him at FEE and he quietly pulled out a copy of Tolstoy's anarchist Law of Love and the Law of Violence, which he confided that "some of us are now reading with great interest."

Baldy in those days contributed some vital works to the libertarian literature; perhaps the most memorable was his great anti-war pamphlet, In Search of Peace, and his magnum opus, Liberty: A Path to its Recovery, which brought to libertarian theory an abiding concern for human variety and diversity which reflected Baldy's lifelong interest in the "hard" and the biological sciences. But Baldy's abiding passion was a deep concern for strategy, for the development of a strategic theory and practice for the libertarian cause. It was out of this concern for strategy that Baldy developed his lifelong dream, his vision of the course which libertarians must take for ultimate victory. He saw that the nub and the heart of libertarian strategy must be ideas and scholarship, that activism could never succeed unless informed by a body of ideas and research on the deepest and most advanced levels. Baldy's great vision was to guide and develop a body of libertarian scholarship and research.

In pursuit of this dream, Baldy Harper moved in 1958 to the William Volker Fund, of Burlingame, California, which had been engaged in the vital task of discovering and sponsoring libertarian and allied scholars in all related fields and disciplines, and in aiding and publishing their work as individuals, completely separate from their universities or from such Establishment-agencies as the Social Science Research Council. The Volker Fund concept: of discovering and aiding libertarian scholars, and of bringing them together in meetings and conferences, was an unsung task of enormous importance which developed and held together libertarian scholars during the lonely years of the 1940s and 50s. By the end of the 50s, Baldy saw the importance of establishing the Volker activities on a permanent, funded basis; and he moved to transfer the bulk of the Volker funds to a new Institute for Humane Studies, which would expand the Volker concept and would provide a permanent home for libertarian fellowships, scholarship, conferences, and publications. An endowed IHS would have been of inestimable and incalculable value for the libertarian cause, and the fulfillment of Baldy's lifelong dream. Then, in 1962, just at the point of consummating the new IHS, for various personal and ideological reasons the Volker Fund collapsed, and its funds were forever lost to the cause of libertarian scholarship.

Faced with this shattering blow, Baldy Harper never faltered; with unswerving and inspiring integrity, he determined to build the Institute for Humane Studies even without its promised endowment. Painfully, and at cost of great personal sacrifice, Baldy patiently, step by step, built up the Institute. After nearly a decade of this slow and painfully wrought development, he was able to bring the IHS to the point where it could sponsor conferences, publish books and pamphlets, grant fellowships, and begin to fulfill the Harper dream of a center for libertarian ideas and scholarship.

If, now, despite this grievous blow, we can continue to build the Institute and see that it flourishes, we can build a monument to Baldy which I am sure he would cherish more than any other. It cannot replace this wonderful friend and teacher of us all; but it would be of enormous and indispensable value to the cause of liberty which Baldy held so dear and to which he devoted his life.   ◘

McGovern vs. Rothbard

On November 17, 1972, your editor published a blistering attack on the Quota System, the leftist doctrine that every identifiable group, ethnic, racial, sexual, or whatever, should have its proportionate, pro rata share of all of life's goodies, and that it is the function of the political arm to pressure or coerce that share into being. Our attack was in the form of a letter sent out by the Forum for Contemporary History (P. O. Box 127, Stearns Wharf, Santa Barbara, Calif. 93101), an organization that sends out bi-weekly four-page letters to its vast membership on controversial issues of the day. Recognizing its own built-in liberal leanings, by the way, the Forum is almost desperately eager to publish controversial non-liberal opinions, and libertarians will find a friendly reception from the staff of this new publication. Not only was yours truly invited to join the Forum's Editorial Review Committee, but it has already published letters from libertarians Ernest Fitzgerald and Robert LeFevre. Non-members will be able to read the Rothbard letter in its reprinted form in the February, 1973 issue of Intellectual Digest, there entitled: "The Quota System, In Short, Must Be Repudiated Immediately".

The letter attacked both the theory of the quota system, and its selective leftist application to a few favored and allegedly "oppressed" "minority groups". Part of the attack was levelled against the McGovernite movement, and its insistence on overriding the freely elected choices of Democrats on behalf of imposing a non-elected but quotally pure oligarchy of delegates at the Convention.

Interestingly enough, one of the comments sent to the Forum on the Rothbard letter was by none other than Senator McGovern himself. The most interesting aspect of the McGovern comment is that he explicitly agreed with my strictures — on all aspects of society and the economy except the political party structure! Senator McGovern wrote:

"The central thesis of Professor Rothbard's argument is that the quota system discriminates against people of ability. I accept that as a truism for most purposes . . . In sum, Professor Rothbard raises strong arguments against the quota system in general." (McGovern to the Forum for Contemporary History, December 7, 1972).

The Senator's attempt to exempt political parties from the argument was a specious and tortured one, based on the objective of widening "access to the voting booth." McGovern added:

"Our objective in a democracy is to have leaders who are representative of the population as a whole, not just of those who have superior talent, intelligence, or energy . . . Simple common sense suggests that when we are talking about the electoral process, in which all can and should participate, the relevant arguments differ greatly from those which apply when the subject is upward mobility in the economic system, the right to hold a job, or the practice of a profession."

Libertarian Forum readers might enjoy my reply, which follows in full:

"I am delighted to see that in his comment on my Forum letter, Senator McGovern joins me in repudiating the quota system for the entire economy and for our society, the only apparent exception being the political party structure. I venture to say that if the Senator had made his position explicit or better known to the electorate, he might well have garnered many more votes last November.

"Our only quarrel, then, seems to be over the electoral process. Senator McGovern is concerned about the widest possible participation in the electoral process; but surely, elections in America, both in primaries and in general elections, are now open to all Americans, regardless of race, sex, creed, color, or ethnic origin. In this concern, the Senator is pushing against an open door. But what of the fact that a few people often form slates of candidates? I fail to see anything wrong with that; the point is that any 'few' who wish can form slates and present them to the electorate: why should not Richard Daley have the same privilege in slate-forming as the Rev. Jesse Jackson? And if Mr. Daley had chosen to nominate only one-eyed

Scandinavian-Americans over 6 feet tall, why shouldn't he have had that privilege? The point is that all Democrats of Illinois had the right to participate in the choice of delegates; whom they selected should certainly be up to them. (In point of fact, convention delegates are usually nominated by leaders on the basis of interest and loyalty in party activity, virtues which were scarcely conspicuous in the Jackson delegation.) Overriding the free choice of the electorate by imposing ethnic, etc. guidelines upon them is precisely the anti-democratic quota system which Senator McGovern agrees is bad in every other area of American life.

"One argument of Senator McGovern's is a rather astounding one: that we should 'have leaders who are representative of the population as a whole, not just of those who have superior talent, intelligence or energy.' Does he really mean to endorse Senator Hruska's famous assertion that the mediocre people are entitled to some of their own on the Supreme Court?"

☐

Arts And Movies

By Mr. First Nighter

Deliverance. dir. by John Boorman, written by James Dickey. With Burt Reynolds and Jon Voight.

Several libertarians have touted James Dickey's Deliverance as one of the great libertarian novels of our time, and the recently revived New Banner (Feb. 4-18) has devoted over three full pages to a hagiographical celebration of the movie. I haven't read the novel, but the central fact of the movie, written by Dickey himself, is that it is overwhelmingly boring. It is an attempted adventure movie so poisoned by the search for Significance that the adventure is only a few high spots in a morass of tedium. Boorman has adopted the oldest trick in the business: if you want a movie to seem Profound when you have nothing much to say, then draw out the action, make the camera dwell endlessly on each scene, and focus on the face of each actor as he struggles painfully to emit some inarticulate banality. In other words, if you make the film dull enough, it will trail clouds of Profundity for our gullible moviegoers — especially the gullible critics. Although this time it was not so much the critics but some of our libertarians and other intellectuals who were taken in.

The plot concerns four urban Southerners who set out for a weekend of "conquering nature" by canoeing down a river in the wild mountain country. They are goaded on by their surly macho leader, Burt Reynolds. The central theme of the movie, one that might have been interesting if developed properly, is that Reynolds' much vaunted "nature" is filled with danger and primitive human evil, and that our protagonists are happy to return, half dead, to the arms of urban civilization. And further that the true hero who gets the group through is not the macho Reynolds but the shnooky Voight. But Reynolds conks out with scarcely a struggle, and Voight is simply too shnooky to capture our interest, or to wind up as an authentic hero. Incidentally, none of the four seems to have bothered to chart the river in advance, so that every rapids comes as a shattering surprise. What sort of schlemiehls are these? Furthermore, the brutality is too gratuitous to serve as more than an unintegrated shock to the audience. Perhaps if one of the great classical adventure directors had done the movie, something could have been salvaged from the debris. Certainly it would have been more interesting.

Shamus. dir. by Buzz Kulik. With Burt Reynolds, Giorgio Tozzi, and Dyan Cannon.

Shamus is one of the best and most exciting tough-guy detective movies in some time. The emphasis is as it should be, on fast and vigorous action, sparkling with odd-ball characters and situations. Reynolds does very well in the central role, and Dyan Cannon is her usual sophisticated and sultry self. It is true that the plot tends to be incoherent at times, but in a movie like this, who cares? Giorgio Tozzi leaves the opera boards for an excellent performance as a silky Godfather-type.

The Poseidon Adventure. dir. by Ronald Neame. With Gene Hackman, Ernest Borgnine, and Shelley Winters.

(Continued On Page 5)

Arts And Movies—

(Continued From Page 4)

A gripping adventure tale, propelled along by its sparkling central theme: a mighty ocean-liner's capsizing in mid-sea, and the exciting efforts of a few of the passengers to escape by climbing upward to the bottom of the ship. Each step of the way is fraught with danger, and the movie well deserves its wide popularity at the box-office. The major problem with the film is the phony philosophy and the even more phony theology, all of which is emitted by the hero, the hip young priest Gene Hackman. The "philosophy" rests in undigested globules throughout the picture, capped by the insufferable "Christ-like" demise of Hackman at the end of the film. But the action is compelling enough to allow us to overlook the Message.

The Getaway. dir. by Sam Peckinpah. With Steve McQueen and Ali McGraw.

Sam Peckinpah is one of the most interesting directors functioning today. Most of his work is deeply flawed; one senses that he is trying to direct in the classic tradition of Hollywood adventure movies, but that he cannot arrive at a consistent style or point of view. Hence the erratic, unstable, and flawed nature of his oeuvre. And yet Peckinpah at his worst is still better than most of the directors active today. And his handling of violence is consistently brilliant, as even his worst detractors concede. **The Wild Bunch** was one of the great Westerns of all time; **Straw Dogs** was marred by the slowness of the buildup and the total miscasting of Dustin Hoffman; in a far different vein, **The Ballad of Cable Hogue**, starring Jason Robards, was a beautiful and lyrical evocation of the individualism of the Old West. It is, indeed, Peckinpah's uncompromising individualism, and the readiness of his heroes to use violence to defend themselves against attack, that sticks in the craw of the left-intelligentsia.

The Getaway, unfortunately, is not one of Peckinpah's better efforts. Its central theme — the caper-plus-getaway — is a fine one, and Peckinpah gets down to it well after an unsatisfactory beginning marred by fashionable avant-garde camera jumps in time and space. The scenes of violence are predictably excellent, especially the scene when the cornered McQueen shoots his way out with a shotgun purchased on the spot. But the film is fundamentally flawed by the grievous miscasting of the central protagonists. Once again, Peckinpah has fallen victim to faulty casting. Furthermore, Peckinpah does not have the ability of the great directors to wring superior performances from shoddy and third-rate actors; on the contrary, a poor actor will perform far worse under Peckinpah than he will with most directors. Steve McQueen has always been one of our poorest actors; his expression ranges from surly-and-quizzical to surly-and-quizzical. In Getaway, McQueen is given his head, and he drags down the picture with a stumbling, leaden, inarticulate, surly-quizzical performance.

Ali McGraw completes the acting debacle. Miss McGraw has never been able to act; but her previous directors have been able to enhance her beauty in a rosy glow and to wring at least a passable performance from her. Here, Miss McGraw is a disaster; her acting is abysmal, and she is leaden, chalk white, dead to the core. Peckinpah has never been good with women; his female characters have never been more than dumb and fickle tramps. Faced with the McGraw character as someone closer to heroine status, Peckinpah simply cannot handle the situation; hence her corpse-like quality. Furthermore, McQueen and McGraw are supposed to be in love, and romantic love is the one emotion that Peckinpah is least equipped to portray. Sado-masochistic sex he handles quite well, as in the minor sex interest of Getaway; but the two central "lovers" are stumbling, inarticulate, moribund, and totally unbelievable.

Noel Coward, RIP. The death of the great Noel Coward, almost the living embodiment of the best of the Old Culture, leaves a gap that cannot be filled. Coward's genius as a playwright, composer and actor managed to forge a blend of unabashed and moving romanticism with high and sparkling wit. A difficult feat at best, the great Coward leaves an aching void in a culture and a world from which both romance and wit have virtually disappeared. The only thing those of us left behind can do is to Keep the Faith, to keep the torch of elegant wit and romance burning until a nobler and better time. But this is hardly a difficult task; for shall we ever be able to forget the great play **Private Lives**? (For a moving

theatrical experience, rush out, buy, and listen to the Coward-Gertrude Lawrence recording of this play.) And can we ever forget such marvelously romantic songs as "I'll See You Again"? Bless you, Noel Coward, and rest in peace. We shall not see your like again.

The Jockey Club Stakes. A play by William Douglas Home. With Wilfred Hyde White, Robert Coote, and Geoffrey Sumner. Broadway this season saw what can only characterize as assassination-by-criticism. The **Jockey Club Stakes** came to Broadway, a frothy, delightful, beautifully acted comedy in the wittiest British tradition. The witty spoof on the mores and maneuverings of the British Establishment was acted superbly by a trio of consummate artists who should be familiar to us from British movies, with Mr. Hyde White the central star. And yet this comedy was blasted off the boards by the venomous attacks of such leftists, serioso critics as Julius Novick in the **Village Voice** and John Simon in the New York **Times**; Simon lost his cool so far as to seriously call this play the embodiment of the "loss of the British Empire." What incensed the Left was the obvious fact that the playwright, the brother of the former Tory Prime Minister of England, was delighted with the sly maneuverings of his Tory Establishment characters. All of a sudden, our critics, who hail every exercise in morbidity and degeneracy in the name of separating morality from art, forget all about art-for-art's-sake when their own goose is O so elegantly cooked!

It is, unfortunately, not surprising that the Left was able to insure a brief run for this frothy and delightful comedy. The only humor that seems to succeed in these days of Broadway decay is the heavy-handed, New York-oriented ethnic schlock of Neil Simon. More's the pity.

Fear Is the Key. Directed by Martin Tuchner, with Barry Newman. For years, Alastair MacLean has provided us with an exciting and tingling series of adventure-spy novels, novels more consistently gripping than the delightful James Bond series. The MacLean movies, while certainly to be recommended, have not done full justice to the author: though **The Guns of Navarone** was excellent and **Puppet On A Chain** had chilling and exciting moments. **Fear Is the Key** has the unmistakable stamp of low-budget tawdriness and the plot is often incoherent; but still and all, this is by far the most exciting movie of the season. And Barry Newman is magnificently tough in the central role.

Blaxploitation. One of the most important movie phenomena of the last few years has been what the Left-liberal and Establishment critics bitterly deride as "blaxploitation" movies. These are exciting, often delightful films where black private eyes and black gunmen star in black versions of this familiar white style of motion pictures. Of varying quality, such films as **Shaft, Trouble Man,** and **Cotton Comes to Harlem** almost all convey a sense of drama and a keen appreciation of black argot and ghetto "street smarts." They are all, in short, fun pictures, and it is typical of the insufferably serioso left-critics to get on their neo-Puritan high horse and condemn them as "exploiting" black people by . . . what? By giving them pictures which they intensely enjoy. Anyone who has seen a blaxploitation film will attest to the enjoyment and enthusiasm for these pictures by the virtually all-black audience. The audience identifies with the characters, shouts at the screen, applauds and hisses.

But, you see, according to our left-liberals, blacks must somehow be shielded from the supposedly "degrading" nature of street-private eye-police culture. Black audiences have to be fed "ennobling", if depressing and boring movies such as **Sounder.** How insufferably elitist can one get? (On the humorless Neo-Puritanism of our current Left, see the interesting article by George H. Douglas, "The New Puritanism of the Youth Culture," **Modern Age** (Spring, 1973).

High Plains Drifter. Dir. by and starring Clint Eastwood. Say it ain't so, Clint. Are you being seduced by the avant-garde? Do you, too, yearn to be "significant"? Actually, **High Plains Drifter** is not that bad. Mostly, it is still in the great Eastwood tradition. Clint is magnificently tough, the action is fast, and the bad guys get their comeuppance (and how!) The problem is the pretentious suggestion that The Drifter is somehow the ghost of a town marshal who had been killed by the bad guys, and now comes back to wreak revenge. He is a peculiar kind of ghost, since he apparently does not resemble the martyred marshal, and he quasi-rapes several of the available females in a decidedly non-ghostly manner. But

(Continued On Page 6)

Arts And Movies —

(Continued From Page 5)

there is that annoying "symbolism", with Eastwood painting the houses red, naming the town "Hell", and killing the bad guys while the flames leap upward. The alert viewer can smell a rat at the very first sequence, when Clint rides slowly into town with the lighting so adjusted that we can't see his face. Let's hope that next time Clint drops the mystical symbolism and Comes Home.

John Koch Retrospective. John Koch is unquestionably, and far and away, the greatest painter the twentieth century has produced. A recent Koch retrospective at the New York City Cultural Center was a breathtaking delight. There were a few of the impressionist works from Koch's early period (circa 1940) that fully matched the delightful works of Renoir. But the glory of John Koch was his mature and magnificent classicism, which was fully represented on two floors of the Cultural Center. At the last Koch show, Emily Genauer of the New York Post wrote that Koch was the greatest painter of this century, and the full equal of the old masters. There is no doubt about it. The precision and elegance of Koch's classical realism, the incredible use of light that fully matches Vermeer, the play on perspectives that is the equal of Velasquez, the still lifes, the portraits, the genre scenes, one could go on and on.

Given Koch's evident greatness, why O why has he been systematically ignored by the Art Establishment? Why do the critics patently dislike his work even as they grudgingly concede his "technical perfection"? The ugly explanation is all too clear in their writings. It is because John Koch is not only a realist, he is a painter, not of "ashcan" scenes, not of depressing pessimism, nor of ugliness, but of the elegant life that he clearly loves so well: himself, his friends, his beautifully furnished duplex on Central Park West. Every painting of John Koch rubs his critics' noses in his decidedly unfashionalbe, aristocratic and optimistic view of life and the world. Andrew Wyeth, though a realistic artist far inferior to Koch, can be forgiven for his pessimism and near-despair; Koch's elegant optimism cannot. □

Anti-Tax Demonstration

By Kenneth W. Kalcheim

New York, April 14 — The Libertarian Alliance put on its first successful, major demonstration to exhibit its conviction that the power to tax is the power to destroy. There were about 25 individuals involved in the demonstration. The groups represented were the Free Libertarian Party radical caucus, the Libertarian Tax Rebellion Committee, the Student Libertarian Action Movement, the New York Libertarian Association, and the Free Libertarian Party Liberty Amendment Committee. It was a totally peaceful demonstration as one of the main principles of libertarianism is the non-initiation of force. The highlight of the demonstration took place at noon when Kenneth W. Kalcheim of the Libertarian Tax Rebellion Committee burned his IRS Summons (which he refused to answer or appear on), all his tax records, and his social security card as he also believes that social security is a fraudulent, confiscatory, coercive tax. After the burning, he set up a table with tax rebellion literature inside the front entrance of the building. He was told by a U. S. Treasury Agent to leave the building. He refused as he said he had as much right to be there as anybody else. When the police asked to see his identification, particularly his draft card, he refused to comply.

Meanwhile, outside, the demonstration was still going quite strong. The demonstrators continued to march up and back in front of the entrance to the building. They did not block the entrance or prevent anyone from entering the building. There were no arrests but it was touch and go for awhile. Four individuals were immediately singled by the police as troublemakers. They were Sam Konkin, J. Neil Schulman, John Pachak and Ken Kalcheim. The police advised Kalcheim that he had violated at least three of their laws but they never proceeded any further. Konkin and Schulman were advised that if they continued to "obstruct access to the entrance of the building" they would be arrested. They neither blocked the entrance nor prevented anyone from entering the building.

Subsequently, they were arrested. However due to the intervention of "radical minarchist" Howie Katz they were finally released. Considering that there was a large press turnout representing the major media in New York City, there seemingly was political pressure or censorship to bury the news item as nothing was reported by the press. Only WNEW, a minor, independent TV station, gave us about 15 seconds of reporting. Anything the government considers too radical, they immediately fear. As taxation is a major issue and there is mass dissatisfaction with it around the country, this is the issue the government most fears. This weekend again proves that we are losing more and more of our freedoms day by day. There is very little freedom of the press left, if any at all. The public, media and government might be interested in knowing that there is still a small number of free press left. The demonstration will be covered in many libertarian and leftist publications and newspapers. It will also be reported in these publications that the media has seemingly submitted to government coercion and therefore helped the government destroy our freedoms. □

Hospers On Rothbard's Rebuttal

The trouble with writing a letter responding to an author who is also editor of the same journal is that the editor always has the last word. Nevertheless, I welcome the opportunity to air the exchange of views; so I shall address a few remarks to the Libertarian Forum once again, much more briefly this time. If my last letter was a catalyst for getting Dr. Rothbard's views on foreign policy on paper, it has been worth-while for that reason alone.

1. I admit at the outset that I am not a historian. I have read extensively (and written) in the areas of aesthetics, epistemology and ethics, but not history. And since the issue between us is admittedly an empirical one, about what happened and to whom, I cannot claim to a competence in it based on personal research. The fact is that I am not very happy about writings that give interpretations of historical events: some people find interpretation A more plausible and attack interpretation B; some find B more plausible or utterly convincing and attack A. And whether a person opts for A or for B seems in 99 cases out of 100, to depend on which one he wants to opt for, and which one conforms to his pre-existing prejudices. This leaves me in rather a state of mental paralysis when it comes to making a decision between two specialists who disagree with one another, each of whom has a greater knowledge of the field than I have. For example, I have read not only Quigley but Kolko; as far as my knowledge of the facts is concerned, either of them may be right; and thus far I am no more convinced by the one than by the other.

The historian I am most impressed by, and who has researched some aspects of the issue more than anyone I know, is Professor Anthony Sutton, whose three-volume work American Technology and Soviet Economic Development is a masterpiece of detailed research. Professor Sutton's new book, Our National Suicide, will be published in a few months by Arlington House. Its main thesis is that the United States in the last half century has given, lent, or leased to Soviet Russia the technology which she did not have and would not have had without American help: that this technology, though classified as non-military (e.g., truck factories, ball-bearing plants), has enabled the Soviet Union to achieve the degree of military expertise which it now possesses — e.g., our ball bearings have made their missiles accurate any time they choose to use them on an American city. In other words, the United States as part of its own official policy has caused the Soviet Union to grow into a military giant, and kept that giant alive and in a position to attack us. According to this view, the Soviet Union does represent a military danger to the United States because of the United States' own policy. Dr. Rothbard will be pleased to find data further blackening his least-favorite president. Woodrow Wilson; for it was Wilson who, at the behest of the power-behind-the-throne, Colonel House, attempted to keep all criticism of the Bolshevik regime out of the American press. (I have myself seen a microfilm copy of House's urgent memo to Wilson to this effect, and he did what he could to "win over" the Bolsheviks.) Since that time, the history of United States-Soviet relations has been principally that of the

(Continued On Page 7)

Hospers —

(Continued From Page 6)

self-defeating and perhaps suicidal policy of the nation A raising nation B into a position of strength from which B could threaten A. And yet, Dr. Rothbard says that B is no threat. Possibly; but if so, it is not for lack of attempt on the part of A to make it one. (See Prof. Sutton's article in the Sept. 9, 1972, issue of **Human Events**, pp. 12-13.)

2. But on to non-historical matters. Dr. Rothbard wonders why I would be more worried about a Soviet attack immediately after the depoliticalization of the United States than now. For a plain economic reason: once the United States economy was freed, and it devoted all its efforts to expanding its economy, every nation in the world would be threatened — not militarily, but ideologically. There would be a brain-drain of such dimensions as would dwarf anything that has occurred in the past, with every enterprising person from every country wanting to get to the place where he could now make it on his own without the ball-and-chain of political control over his efforts. This would be such a threat to every statist nation, and particularly to the totally statist Soviet Union, that rather than risk the dramatic demonstration of the absurdity of their socialist ideas, they might well decide to attack the United States (or what was formerly the United States) while they still had the American technology with which to do it, especially now that there was no longer a nuclear defense against them.

3. I do believe that those libertarians who advocate total American disarmament would (if their efforts were successful) be leaving the inhabitants of this country open to any aggressor in any country that cared to throw a few nuclear missiles our way. I believe I would be less safe if these libertarians had their way. But of course, I am aware that those very same libertarians believe that I am advocating policies (preservation of national defense) which are dangerous to them. What is the way out of this impasse? Dr. Rothbard suggests that those who wish

(Continued On Page 8)

Recommended   Reading

Anti-Trust.

The economic literature on anti-trust and industrial organization has long been in sad shape indeed, since all factions have been committed to the evils of anti-trust policy. Now, Professor Armentano has written the first book on anti-trust from an Austrian, and therefore from a pure **laissez-faire**, perspective. Armentano's **The Myths of Antitrust** (Arlington House, $11.95) is a breath of fresh air in the industrial organization quagmire. Armentano concentrates on the major antitrust cases, from the E. C. Knight Case (1895) to the present. Excellent and readable.

The Minerva Caper.

Peter C. Du Bois, "Utopia on the Rocks", **Barrons** (March 26) is a thorough and entertaining history of the ill-fated Minerva venture, the attempt of libertarian and quasi-libertarian retreatists to found their own "republic" on a submerged coral reef in the far Pacific. The Minerva will o' the wisp could be regarded as sheer farce, were it not for the tragic fact that libertarian capitalists sunk hundreds of thousands of dollars into this wild and woolly scheme. This is a tragic waste of precious libertarian resources that we can ill afford. When will our libertarian capitalists invest their resources on behalf of liberty at home, and abandon the kooky quest for a libertarian Shangri-la?

Medical Freedom.

The most recent interview with the scintillating libertarian psychoanalyst, Dr. Thomas Szasz ("Medicine and the State: the First Amendment Violated", **The Humanist**, March-April 1973) is Szasz at his sharp and charismatic best. Szasz here deals not only with his familiar opposition to involuntary commitment, but with the full range of medical despotism in this country. The entire interview is a gem, but here is Szasz, after a blistering attack on monopolistic medical licensing, and after the editor asks: But doesn't the public "need protection from incompetent medical practitioners?" Szasz answers: "Oh, I agree that people **need** protection — but not only from bad, stupid, inept, greedy, evil doctors; they also need protection from bad parents and children, husbands and wives, mothers-in-law, bureaucrats, teachers, politicians — the list is endless. And, then, of course, they'll need protection from the protectors! So the question of how people should be protected from incompetent medical practitioners is really a part of the larger question of how they should be protected from the countless hazards of life . . . The first line of protection for the public lies, I would say, in self-protection. People must grow up and learn to protect themselves — or suffer the conse-

quences. There can be no freedom without risk and responsibility."

Rothbardiana.

Rothbardiana continues apace. In the last couple of months, Rothbard has come out with the following: a Letter on the Quota System, by the Forum for Contemporary History (Nov. 17), reprinted in the **Intellectual Digest** (February, 1973); a two-part Interview in the **Gold and Silver Newsletter** of the Pacific Coast Coin Exchange (Nov. 30 & Dec. 31); a joint interview with Leonard Liggio on "The New Isolationism" in **Reason** (February), which has already drawn considerable blood from the Cold Warriors; a chapter on "Free Market Police, Courts, and Law" in **Reason** (March) taken from his forthcoming "the book" on Liberty; an article on "Libertarianism" for the 1972 edition of the **Encyclopedia Americana**; and the "Introduction" to the Garland Press reprint of Sidney Rogerson's **Propaganda for the Next War**. Also articles for **Outlook**, and book reviews for **Choice**.

And coming very soon: Rothbard's booklet, "The Essential Von Mises" for the revived "minibook" series, published by Oakley Bramble's Constitutional Alliance.

Contra Utilitarianism.

There is nothing like a brutal, genocidal war to lead one to question the validity of the utilitarian approach to ethics, with its cool totting up of "social costs" and "social benefits" from policies imposing various "megadeaths" on society. The Vietnam War has come as a shock to the highest circles of modern philosophy, and is leading to a fundamental re-thinking, and a welcome shift, at long last, away from utilitarian amorality. One important development is the recent, highly-touted book by John Rawls, **A Theory of Justice**, which levels a vigorous critique of the collectivism inherent in the presumption to add and subtract "social costs" and "social benefits". Rawls' positive contribution, however, is an unsatisfactory return to a new form of Hobbesian "contract" theory. Now, the distinguished British philosopher Stuart Hampshire signals his break with utilitarianism in an excellent critique, "Morality and Pessimism", **New York Review of Books** (Jan. 25, 1973). Hampshire charges that utilitarianism can simply **not** defend the individual's overriding right to life, regardless of the alleged social benefits that may ensue from his murder. And, mirabile dictu, Hampshire declares that we must get back to "ancient philosophy," to Aristotle and the theory of natural law, to arrive at an ethic that will be grounded in the right to life. This can be a truly significant breakthrough on the philosophic front, and may make the formidable task of our budding young neo-objectivist philosophers that much easier. ◻

Hospers — (Continued From Page 7)

to defend their lives and property should do so, and those who do not wish to should not. And this is indeed a lovely libertarian precept, and I would accept it in a minute if I thought it would work.

Suppose that I place some machine-guns and even some anti-aircraft weapons in my back yard, and that you, my nextdoor neighbor, fear no foreign enemy and install no defense at all. And suppose that at this point some half-crazed leader of a new Arab or African dictatorship decides to put the fear of God into us by sending some missiles into our midst from an Atlantic submarine. Does anyone think for a moment that the missiles would be so aimed as to strike me rather than you, or vice versa? That's the trouble with modern warfare: just as "the rain falls on the just as on the unjust," so bombs and missiles would fall on those who tried individually to defend themselves as well as on those who did not. Weapons of modern war destroy miles of property and do not distinguish between back yards.

A nuclear offense, or offensive danger, requires a nuclear defense; and there is no way I know of for those who would pay for their own defense against nuclear powers to do so without defending everyone else at the same time (the problem of freeloaders again); and, what is far worse, there is no way for those who would not defend themselves from increasing danger to everyone else by thinning their defense efforts and jeopardizing the success of the defense. If I saw a satisfactory alternative to collective action in the matter of defense against nuclear weapons, I would be enormously grateful. Perhaps such an alternative has been thought of — a practical one, not one conceived in the heads of theorists who care nothing about practical applications — but if so, I would be most indebted to the Editor if he would explain to me what it is and how it works.

— John Hospers

The Editor's Final Rebuttal

I am going to spare the reader in this last of a series of rounds (Dec. 1972-Feb. 1973) by being mercifully brief.

1. I am sorry to see Dr. Hospers adopting the position of historiographical nihilism. If two historians differ, how can the reader come to a judgment? In basically the same way as when two economists differ, or two philosophers differ: by learning and reading more about the discipline of history and about the concrete areas under discussion. On the philosophy of history, in my view the most developed position is that of Ludwig von Mises' grievously neglected **Theory and History**, with the proviso that I would add the moral dimension of the great Lord Acton. On the concretes, space requires me to be simply arbitrary and say here that there are good and sufficient reasons, totally apart from their political conclusions, why Gabriel Kolko is deeply respected as a scholar in the historical profession and Carroll Quigley is not. As for me personally, I did not begin with an emotional preference for the Kolko thesis; I began,

many years ago, by adopting the Cold War historical mythology, and it was by learning more that I some years later changed my position.

2. I have not read Professor Sutton's book, but from the reviews of its admirers I would conclude that his thesis is correct but trivial in importance. Not just the Soviet Union, but all late-developing countries borrow technology from the existing industrialized countries. In the nineteenth century, the United States borrowed technology, often illegally, from Great Britain. So what? The important point for economic development is not technology anyway, but the saving and investment of capital.

3. I'm afraid I cannot be pleased with Dr. Hospers' interpretation of the Wilson policy or of the U. S. policy in general in the past half-century. As Arno J. Mayer has demonstrated in his monumental two-volume work (**Political Origins of the New Diplomacy** and **The Politics and Diplomacy of Peacemaking**), crucial to Wilsonian imperialism was the coercive suppression of Bolshevism in Russia and in Eastern and Central Europe — the latter largely succeeding with the aid of the Social Democrats. As for Russia itself, Woodrow Wilson sent American troops to the Soviet Union and kept them there for several years, along with troops of the Allies, to try to crush Bolshevism in the bud. This is a "suicidal" buildup of Bolshevism?

4. Here I stand on my previous article: that what the Russians are frightened of are our missiles and nuclear weapons as employed by the American Leviathan State; they are not worried about our free-market ideology, because they are Marxist-Leninists and as such they are convinced (wrongly, of course) that their ideological victory is assured by the ineluctable laws of history. They consider us libertarians as harmless reactionary throwbacks to a "pre-imperialist form of capitalism", and far less dangerous to them because we do not endorse or employ State imperialism.

5. I consider it immoral and criminal to force someone else to pay for my own defense. Period. I frankly don't give a damn about the Friedmanite worries about the "free rider" and "external economies". If it costs me more to defend myself because my neighbor is either a pacifist or a blind fool it is just too bad; I should either pay the resulting full cost of my defense or shut up about it.

As for Dr. Hospers' complaint about modern warfare, that is precisely my position, and that is why I oppose any and all use of modern weapons that make it impossible for the rain to fall only on the unjust. As for nuclear weapons, for the present and the foreseeable future there is **no** defense against them: hence the very practical importance of getting rid of them altogether. A practical way of doing this was the American disarmament proposal which we withdrew as soon as the Russians finally accepted it, on May 10, 1955. The essence of the Russian proposal since that date has been for all nations to scrap all of their nuclear weapons, and then to allow any and all groups, private as well as public, to inspect all sites to see that this agreement is being carried out. Right now, of course, the existence of satellites makes the inspection problem an easy one to solve, so that world disarmament of nuclear and other weapons of mass destruction is now more feasible than ever before. (Those interested in the Russians and May 10, 1955 should read the excellent account in Philip Noel-Baker's paperback, **The Arms Race**.)

The Libertarian Forum
BOX 341
MADISON SQUARE STATION
NEW YORK, NEW YORK 10010

Published Every Month. Subscription Rate: $8.00 Per Year

380

A Monthly Newsletter

THE
Libertarian Forum

Joseph R. Peden, Pubiisher　　　　　　　　　　　　　　　　　　　　Murray N. Rothbard, Editor

VOLUME V, NO. 6　　　　　　　　　　　　JUNE, 1973　　　　　　　　　　　　US-ISSN0047-4517

THE MAYORAL CIRCUS, II

At the time of writing, New York's wild and woolly mayoral extravaganza has just lurched to a new stage: the holding of the primary election. It is of no small importance to the meaning and the undercurrents of this election that the voting was held on a Monday, June 3 — for the first time in living memory violating the New York and the American tradition of holding all elections on a Tuesday. It is very possible that the underwhelming size of the vote (only 25% of those eligible in the Democratic primary) was partially due to the strange and disorienting displacement from Tuesday to Monday. In a fighting speech attacking the massive Establishment conspiracy against him (more later), Rep. Mario Biaggi, a conservative Italian-American populist from the East Bronx, referred darkly to the peculiarity of the Monday vote. Why the sudden change? Because Tuesday sundown begins the Jewish holiday of Shevuoth. It is no wonder that many New Yorkers feel outraged that a traditional election day should be changed simply to accommodate a third-rate religious holiday. Where is the much-vaunted separation of Church and State? The Monday vote was simply one more brick in the mounting edifice of ethnic conflict which is increasingly the essence of New York politics. (On the ethnic nature of New York politics see the highly perceptive work of Nathan Glazer and Daniel Moynihan, **Beyond the Melting Pot**, Cambridge, Mass.: MIT Press, 1970, particularly the Introduction to the 2nd Edition.)

In our previous installment of the New York saga (**Lib. Forum**, March, 1973), we saw a mayoral field crowded with a host of candidates. Since then, has come the inevitable shakeout. The weakest Democratic candidates went inevitably to the wall, withdrawing from the race with varying amounts of ill grace. The hopeless Jesse Gray bowed out, snarling at the lack of support by the bulk of the city's black politicians. The left-center proved unviable, ground down by the millstones of Left and Right-Center, and so out went Jerome Kretchmer, Ed Koch, Robert Postel, and Mario Cuomo, whose only hope was support from erratic Queens Democrat leader Matthew Troy, Jr., who opted instead — for a while — for the Biaggi camp. The maverick Postel doggedly dropped down to run for controller, while the other pitiful left-centrist Sanford Garelik settled by trying to run for re-election to his current post as President of the city council. This left the Big 4: Herman Badillo and Albert Blumenthal on the Left, Abraham Beame on the Right-Center, and Mario Biaggi on the Right.

Everyone has complained that the candidates themselves and their public appearances got totally drowned out by the two great dramas of the campaign: both bizarre events brought into being by the Rockefeller-upper class WASP establishment in working control of New York politics. On the other hand, not seeing this crew in daily action was scarcely a loss to the New York citizen. The two dramas, in rapid succession, were the Wagner Caper, and the Biaggi Affair.

The Wagner Caper was generated by the insufferably arrogant decision of Governor Rockefeller to shove down the throats of the citizens of New York the old re-tread, has-been, former Mayor Robert F. Wagner. "Mayah Wagnah" (in his Old New York accent which has now disappeared from all New Yorkers under the age of 60) is scarcely a

charismatic figure. His lengthy reign is remembered with no affection by New Yorkers, and furthermore he was whipped badly in his attempt at a comeback in the Democratic mayoral primary four years ago. The gall of Nelson Rockefeller was compounded by his decision to install this dilapidated Democrat-Liberal not as a Democrat but as a Republican-Liberal — despite his lengthy record of opposition to the Republican Party. The Liberal Party, a one-man fiefdom under the iron control of the powerful, aging Alex Rose, head of the Hatters Union, was delighted to go along with the scheme. After all, with the imminent departure of the universally reviled John Lindsay, Alex was about to lose his accustomed place at the public trough. The dark rumor was that the deal ran as follows: Rockefeller would pull all the stops to force the Republicans to nominate Wagner, in return for which Alex Rose would either endorse Rockefeller for governor next year or put up some patsy who would lose ingloriously and thereby not join with the Democrats in opposing Rocky.

While Wagner waited coyly in the wings, Rockefeller proceeded to try to ram his nomination down the throats of the Republican leaders. According to New York law, a majority of the executive committee of a city party has to give its approval to a non-party member's entering its primary. Except for Vince Albano, the quintessential opportunist hack who runs the Manhattan party, the outraged Republican leaders balked at going along with the deal. Finally, most were persuaded to go along, but they were blocked by the heroic refusal of the Brooklyn party, led by young George Clark who had long been deeply miffed by Rockefeller's long-standing playing footsy with powerful Brooklyn Democrat leader Meade Esposito. The stubborn refusal of the Brooklyn party, combined with the delightfully candid if imprudent expostulation by Bronx leader John Calandra that Wagner is a "moron", greatly angered the former Mayor, who had presumably expected an easy time of it in Republican ranks. Hence, Wagner angrily refused to fight, and walked out of the mayoral race. New York was saved from the Rockefeller-Rose-Wagner threat. The Liberal Party then selected left-liberal Democrat Albert Blumenthal as its mayoral choice.

The favorite for the Democratic nomination was now Mario Biaggi, who was also chosen by the Conservative Party as its mayoral candidate. There next ensued an unprecedentedly savage assault upon Biaggi by the entire New York establishment, an alliance of upper class WASPS and Jews, of "corporate liberalism" at its most strident. The liberal New York press, in alliance with upper class Rockefeller-WASP U. S. Attorney Whitney North Seymour, dug up old grand jury minutes, supposedly sacred in their privacy, which were leaked to the press to embarrass Biaggi. A tragi-comedy ensued in which the emotional lower-class populist Biaggi, who had never gone to school to learn "grace under pressure", was trapped into a series of lies and evasions. The result of this furious tempest in a teapot was a total discrediting of Biaggi, and the end of his chance to win the primary.

The assault on Biaggi was a reflection of the savage hatred and contempt for the Italian-American masses on the part of upper-class liberals. Of all the ethnic groups in New York and indeed in America, the

(Continued On Page 2)

The Mayoral Circus, II —

(Continued From Page 1)

Italians had never Made It in American society. Precious little prestige, wealth, or political or intellectual posts have accrued to the Italians; even within the Catholic Church, they have seen all the power accrue to the Irish who had preceded them. And now that their "turn" as immigrants had come, they had seen themselves elbowed aside and oppressed by an unholy alliance of upper class WASPS and Jews, with black and Puerto Rican "ghetto militants." And yet, in contrast to many other groups that had never been particularly successful, the Italians did not react by destructiveness, violence, or the making of outrageous demands on the rest of society. Instead, they have worked hard, remained relatively poor, and have refused to go on welfare; all they ask of life is to preserve their neighborhoods, to walk safely in the streets, and to keep their taxes low. For this healthy "conservatism" they have only succeeded in being denounced by articulate comfortable upper class intellectuals as petty and "racist."

And then there is the vexed question of "crime." To the lower-class Italian, as to the libertarian, "crime" means assault on person and property: mugging, theft, loot. But to the upper-class WASP (and now Jewish) Establishment Reformer, the really ugly crime, the crime that he tries ever to crack down on, is "organized crime", i.e. the entrepreneurial supplying of such goods and services as drugs, gambling, and prostitution (and formerly, liquor). The Italian sensibly sees nothing wrong with such "crimes" and therefore sees nothing wrong with paying politicians not to crack down upon such legitimate business activities. But the upper-class Reformer has, ever since the Progressive period and before, tried his best to outlaw and suppress these activities. Part of this is the Calvinist heritage of imposing one's own moral principles and customs on everyone else by force. Part of it, too, is aesthetic: the fact that the upper-class can afford to indulge in sex, drugs, gambling, and liquor in more luxurious, decorous, and affluent ways. Thus, among the attempts to outlaw pornography, invariably the government cracks down much more harshly on those activities which are cheaper and therefore more accessible to the working-class. But much of it, too, is political; thus, in the Progressive period, the essence of upper-class-induced Reform was to destroy the political power of the ethnic neighborhood, usually centered in the saloon, and by destroying the saloon to centralize municipal power in their own "efficient", decorous, and "businesslike" hands. (On organized crime and reform, see Mark H. Haller, "Urban Crime and Criminal Justice: The Chicago Case," Journal of American History, December 1970.) In the case of the Italians, the situation is particularly piquant because "organized crime" has provided virtually the only vehicle for Italians to rise and acquire at least a modicum of wealth, prestige, and political influence. And for their pains, they are subjected to a continuing national propaganda assault which they, lacking intellectual savvy or clout, are helpless to answer. And so even this route to success is being taken away from them.

Furthermore, the Italians see that while they are generally reviled by the Establishment and the media as "criminals", that real criminals — muggers, rapists, looters — are continually being coddled and "understood", by this same upper-class liberal elite, and these genuine crimes invariably blamed on the victims: "society." (See Glazer and Moynihan, p. lxvii.)

In the face of this systematic injustice, it is no wonder that the Italian masses of New York City are becoming restive, and moving toward insurgent "right-wing populism." The only wonder is that the awakening has taken so long. The upsurge in recent years of such conservative Italian lower-class populists as Vito Battista, Mario Proccaccino, and now Mario Biaggi is the reflection of this discontent. After he won the Democratic mayoral primary four years ago, the emotional Mario Proccaccino was laughed out of the race by the contemptuous liberal media. But Biaggi could not similarly be dismissed as a clown; he had to be savaged out of the race.

Particularly instructive is the reaction of the Conservative Party to the crucifixion of Biaggi. Since its inception a decade ago, the Conservative Party had been run as a virtual fief by the Buckley family and their political satraps, the brothers-in-law Kieran O'Doherty and Daniel Mahoney. The ideology has been straight National Review-conservatism, which means an upper-crust Establishment pro-statism that frowns on any and all expressions of mass-oriented right-wing populism. Any insurgent populists were promptly isolated and expelled from the party. But with its growth in numbers and power, populism advanced, particularly within the ranks of the New York City party. Very reluctantly, the Conservative leaders were induced by their rank-and-file to go along with the nomination of Biaggi for mayor. But with the grand jury caper, the Buckley clique moved openly to try to withdraw the nomination from Biaggi. They were able to mobilize most of the "stars", the former Conservative candidates for state-wide office: including David Jaquith, Paul Adams, Ed Leonard, and Rosemary Gunning. But the second-rank party leaders stood firm, notably the Bronx leader Thomas F. Cronin (an aide on the Biaggi staff), Brooklyn leader Michael Long, and Manhattan leader Henry Mittendorf, and led by Conservative party vice-chairman Professor Henry Paolucci, political scientist from St. Johns University who once ran for Senate on the Conservative ticket. The Paolucci-led populists were able to resist the Buckleyite domination, and Mario Biaggi will run for mayor on the Conservative ticket in November. Not the least important result of this bizarre mayoral race is the coming of democracy to the Conservative Party of New York.

And so the primary: it was won by right-centrist Abe Beame, supported by his mass base in increasingly conservative lower-income Brooklyn and Queens Jewry, aided by a split-off of disoriented Biaggi supporters. But Beame got only 34% of the small vote, and the new rule is that a vote of less than 40% requires a runoff on June 26 with the runner-up. Biaggi actually came in a respectable third, with 21% of the vote. The surprise is the runner-up, the most left-wing candidate, the Puerto Rican Rep. Herman Badillo of the Bronx (29%), who managed to destroy the picked candidate of the left-liberal reformers of the NDC, Al Blumenthal, who came in last with a measly 16% of the vote. Particularly surprising was Badillo's beating out Blumenthal in the latter's home district of the upper-class left-liberal Jewish West Side of Manhattan. Badillo took leftish Manhattan (upper class WASP and Jewish, and lower-class Negro and Puerto Rican), shrewdly with the help of "ghetto" numbers runners who of all people have a firm base in the community and were able to pull an unprecedented total of blacks and Puerto Ricans to the polls. Badillo was also able to parlay an even split between Beame and Biaggi to add to his Puerto Rican base and win in the Bronx. Beame, as expected, swept lower-class Brooklyn and Queens, but again his margin was diminished by Biaggi support in Italian areas. There is little doubt that Badillo's strength over Blumenthal was due largely to his support by the powerful liberal press: the New York Times and the New York Post. Apparently, Blumenthal, in an attempt to broaden his base, had turned too hard on street crime for Establishment liberalism. There seems little doubt, also, that Beame, despite his advanced age, sobriety, and total lack of charisma, will pick up enough conservative Biaggi votes to defeat Badillo in the run-off.

What of the Republicans? With the Wagner scheme aborted, the Republicans turned to State Sen. John Marchi, of Staten Island, who had run for Mayor on the Republican and Conservative lines four years ago. The Buckley brothers' clique among the Conservatives, reacting against Biaggi, is now openly supporting Marchi for Mayor. But how does their support square with our "Italian populist" analysis, and why didn't the Conservatives back Marchi this year? Therein hangs a fascinating tale in the subtleties of ethnic politics. For Marchi, while thoughtful and intelligent, is not an "Italian" in the American ethnic sense. Whereas virtually all the Italian immigrants came from Southern Italy: Sicily and Calabria (as did, for example, the ancestors of Biaggi and Proccaccino), Marchi is of Northern Italian, Florestine descent. Not only are the Northern Italians anti-populist, it was the despotism of the Northern Italian government (differing culturally, economically, and racially), against which anti-governmental Southern Italian populism arose in the old country. True to his Establishment heritage, Marchi has been openly and bitterly anti-populist; his Conservatism has been statist and National-Reviewish, and hence the support of the Buckley clique is not an accident. The specific issue on which the mass of Conservatives broke with Marchi was his support — alone among Staten Island politicos — of the South Richmond Development Authority, a mammoth public housing project planned for Staten Island that would bulldoze countless homes and destroy the character of the area.

And so the November lineup will be: Beame or Badillo (Dem.), Marchi (Rep.), Blumenthal (Lib.), and Biaggi (Cons.) — almost a replay of the primary with a larger class of voters. And of course Youngstein (Free Libertarian.)   ◼

Blockian Ethics

By Roy Halliday

In an article entitled "Heroes and Scapegoats", in the March 1973 issue of the Libertarian Forum, Professor Walter Block supplied his definition of libertarianism. According to the professor, there are two premises that define libertarianism:

(1) "The basic premise of libertarianism is that it is illegitimate to engage in aggression against non-aggressors."

(2) ". . . anything not involving the initiation of violence cannot be evil."

The first premise is widely accepted and Professor Block's explanation of it is very good. However, the second premise in this definition alienates all people who have any ethical principles beyond prohibition of crime. It estranges people of all religions and excludes non-religious people like Ayn Rand and Murray Rothbard who believes in an objective code of ethics. Can a definition of libertarianism that excludes Murray Rothbard be valid?

Why must libertarians refrain from making personal judgments beyond separating criminals and non-criminals? Couldn't a person accept the libertarian theory of justice and also be a Christian, Muslim, Objectivist, or Rothbardian? Despite what Professor Block may think, libertarianism is not a substitute for all religious and moral values. Libertarianism is not the alpha and the omega of life. It is simply the correct philosophy of justice and its only requirement should be the acceptance of Professor Block's first premise. His second premise defines a certain type of libertarian, a Blockian. We need not all be singleminded Blockians.

Being a libertarian means that we recognize everyone's right to be free from aggression. As individuals, we still may despise and regard as evil what some people do with their freedom. We do not have to approve all nonaggressive activities and pretend that mankind has learned nothing of life in all these centuries. Libertarianism does not mean that we must admire and regard as hero any social outcast who is not an aggressor. Only Blockian libertarians are so compelled.

Why has Professor Block chosen such a restrictive definition of libertarianism? It may be because he has misintrepreted or overextended the subjective theory of value. He has taken the subjective theory of value that explains how voluntary trade operates, and expanded its meaning to include that trade of any kind is morally good and objectively beneficial to society.

"Both parties must **always** feel they gain from a voluntary transaction. Given that they are free **not** to enter into the trade, the fact that they **do** decide to trade must prove to be a mutual benefit."

If trade is objectively good, regardless of what is traded, and regardless of the motives of the traders, then any person who overcomes great obstacles and takes unusual risks in order to complete a trade is automatically a hero. If someone engages in a socially disapproved form of trade (even if it is disapproved for good reasons) that social outcast is a hero. Blockian libertarians always must recognize as heroes precisely those social outcasts who are the most hated and reviled traders in society, even though the public may have good reason for disliking these non-criminals. If libertarians were all Blockians, the libertarian movement would be doomed to be as unpopular as the most despised "professions" in society.

Fortunately, most libertarians reject the premise that all trade is objectively good. Although, at the time of the trade both parties feel that they will benefit, they may be wrong. They may not both benefit from the transaction when it is judged from an objective point of view, or even from their own point of view reconsidered. The subjective theory of value operated smoothly in economic theory because economics is, and should be, a value free science. Professor Block makes the mistake of trying to treat ethics as a value free science instead of as the science of values. He assumes that people do not make mistakes in judgment and that their subjective values are objectively correct. Life is not so uncomplicated. Praxeology cannot take the place of ethics.

Professor Block dismisses charges that in real life his "heroes" actually do commit acts of aggression, by saying that though the charge may be true in any particular case, it is not necessarily true of the social outcasts' profession qua profession. Why, then, does he assume that

Blockian Ethics — A Reply

By Walter Block

The main contention between Mr. Halliday and myself seems to concern the ethical status of certain acts which are disapproved by various segments in our society. Acts such as masturbation, drunkenness, scrabble playing, suicide, heroin addiction, atheism, religious beliefs, homosexuality as well as the acts of my list of scapegoats (see the March issue). We both believe, I think, that such non-aggressive acts, or "victimless crimes" should not be considered illegal, as contrasted with aggressive acts such as murder, rape, theft, trespass, which **should** be considered illegal. We disagree, however, over my contention that ". . . anything **not** involving the initiation of violence (such as these non-aggressive acts) cannot be evil!"

I don't know how to settle this controversy in such a limited space other than for me to say "Yes, yes" and for him to say "No, no." I reserve the word "evil" for acts of violence against other persons, and Mr. Halliday uses the word in a less restrictive way. What I would like to do instead in this reply is to indicate why I think that all the criticisms of my forthcoming book that Mr. Halliday **deduces** from this disagreement simply do not follow.

1. The charge of exclusion. The Blockian Philosophy (heh, heh) does not exclude from libertarianism religious people, atheists like Ayn Rand, nor people like Murray Rothbard who believe in an objective code of ethics. On the contrary, I believe that the two premises quoted by Mr. Halliday **constitute** an objective code of ethics that has my full support. As for restrictiveness, I **include** both the followers of Miss Rand (atheists) as well as religious people as libertarians. (Many in each of these two groups, however, insist upon **excluding** members of the other group from the ranks of libertarianism.)

2. The charge that we must approve of these scapegoat heroes. I do not approve of many of the non-aggressive actions under consideration.

(Continued On Page 4)

anyone who hates and maligns his heroes is **ipso facto** opposed to the nonaggressive nature of the hero's profession, and why does he assume that everyone who criticizes his heroes wants to initiate aggression against them? In short, why does Professor Block assume only the best about pimps, blackmailers, and dope peddlers while he asssumes the worst about their critics? There is nothing intrinsically aggressive about criticizing, disapproving, maligning, not associating with, or even hating someone who is not a criminal.

Professor Block gives the false impression that libertarianism means approval of vice and blindness to all ethical considerations beyond the nonaggression principle. A person does not have to be morally obtuse to be a libertarian. One may be a libertarian not because he believes all values are subjective, but because he believes that objective human values can be achieved best in a free society.

Free trade is not the answer to all of life's problems; instead, it is the framework within which we each can test ourselves against the inexorable forces of nature. If we defend the right of each to pursue peaceful activity, we have done our part. The natural consequences of vice will take their course. We do not have to regard drunkards, for example, as heroes. We must only defend their right to drink. We may still agree with William Graham Sumner that a drunkard lying in the gutter is exactly where he belongs.

In a stateless society, with no coercive means of enforcing mores, customs, propriety, and good taste, the role of social ostracism and other natural, voluntary means of keeping civilized values alive will become of paramount importance. Instead of joining the Blockians in defending the outcasts and dregs of society, the majority would disassociate themselves from despicable characters and, perhaps, even join the maligners of Professor Block's unsung heroes.

By portraying these people as heroes, Professor Block is wasting his talents on unworthy causes. He should be satisfied if he can prove that they are not criminals and that some of them are scapegoats. His book, thus far, does not represent the thinking of most libertarians and, if published in its present form, it will be a disservice to the libertarian cause.   ◻

Blockian Ethics, A Reply —

(Continued From Page 3)

Indeed, I abhor some. (Especially scrabble playing. This is especially distasteful to me. I agree with William Graham Sumner that "a scrabble player lying in the gutter is exactly where he belongs." — there is a slight misquote in Mr. Halliday's version).

But when these acts, however abhorent, are prohibited by law, banned, and universally scorned, and when a practitioner of any of them **insists** upon his rights to do as he pleases without committing aggression against other people, I, for one, cannot help feeling a certain grudging admiration for him. (Although I admit that this is hard to do in the case of the scrabble player.) Even this low level of grudging admiration is not necessary to consider these non-aggressors as heroes, however. All that is necessary, I would contend, for an act to be heroic is that it not be intrinsically in violation of other peoples' rights, **and** that it be undertaken in an atmosphere of repression.

3. *The subjective theory of value.* I do not hold the view that all trade is "good". For example, trade among members of a pillaging band of criminals which enables the hoodlums to pillage at a more efficient rate can by no stretch of the imagination be considered a "good". I agree with Mr. Halliday that the subjective theory of value is beneficial in the sphere of value-free economics but not in the sphere of morality.

There is one thing though to object to in Mr. Halliday's statement concerning the praxeological view of trade: the necessary benefits of trade only occur in the **ex ante** sense, at the time of the trade according to this view. It is therefore an invalid objection to the praxeological view to say that both parties to a trade need not benefit from it "from their own point of view reconsidered". True, they need not. But the contrary was never asserted.

4. Mr. Halliday asserts that "There is nothing intrinsically aggressive about criticizing, disapproving, maligning, not associating with, or even hating someone who is not a criminal" (such as these non-aggressive "heroes") as if this is something that I would not agree with. But in the last issue of LF I stated:

"It is tempting to say that if there are any 'degenerate scum and social vermin' involved in this question, they are *the people who cast aspersions on the economic heroes.* Tempting, but incorrect. For we must remember that

people who maliciously cast false aspersions on others (libelers and slanderers) are heroes themselves, who are merely expressing their rights of free speech."

5. *The stateless society.* Mr. Halliday holds that in a stateless society my support of socially unacceptable behavior would be especially pernicious because without *coercive means of enforcing mores, social* ostracism would be called upon to bear a greater share in maintaining civilized views. Again, I agree with Mr. Halliday.

But in a stateless society there would be no prohibitions on the activities of those Mr. Halliday is pleased to call "dregs" and "despicable". And if there were no prohibitions on their acts, they could no longer be called heroes, according to my criteria! And if they were no longer heroes, and in need of protection from illegitimate prohibitions, there would no longer be any reason to defend them. After all, I have never, ever claimed that these acts are **intrinsically** heroic, or saintly. I have only claimed that these acts violate no **libertarian** codes of behavior, that they are prohibited nevertheless, that these people perservere under great duress, and that therefore they are heroic and ought to be defended.

The reactions of most libertarians to the series of "Scapegoats and Heroes" which have so far appeared in print have been most remarkable. They range from active acceptance to vigorous and sometimes even nasty rejection, with seemingly no middle ground. This is puzzling, to say the least. Also puzzling is that of Mr. Halliday's five criticisms of my paper, I have found myself in agreement with four of them. I agreed with him that 2) we need not approve of all the acts of the heroes; 3) not all trade is "good"; 4) there is nothing wrong with criticizing the heroes; and 5) there would be no need for defense of these scapegoats in a stateless (non-repressive) society. I only disagreed with his first point that I am overly exclusionary. Perhaps the disagreements are not as serious as they appear at first glance.

My usual reaction to criticism from people whose intelligence I admire *which seems to me to be wide of the mark is to assume that there is a severe lack of communication, either on my part or on theirs, or on the* part of both. And this must be my reaction in this case. Perhaps future publication of the articles, with criticism and rebuttal, will clear up the problem. Perhaps Mr. Halliday's reaction to this reply, and my reaction to his, may serve to clarify the situation. I am optimistic about this sort of outcome because, although in my own view all I am doing is tracing out the logical implications of libertarianism, I am fully aware that these deductions are taking some strange and new paths. Maybe all that is needed is time to get used to these new implications. ◘

The Editor Comments

First, I would like to rise to a point of personal privilege and express my conviction that Mr. Halliday need not worry about my being read out of the libertarian movement by Professor Block. On the contrary, Walter Block's "basic premise" is firmly **non-exclusionist**: it encompases as libertarians all people who have arrived at the axiom of non-aggression, regardless of whether they have arrived at it as Christians, objectivists, emotivists, utilitarians, whim-worshippers, or from any other route. I agree with Professor Block's non-exclusionism, although, I believe with Mr. Halliday in a wider system of objective ethics, and believe ultimately that libertarianism cannot be firmly established except as part of that wider ethic. Hence, I reserve the right to try to persuade other libertarians to that wider view.

How about Professor Block's second premise, that evil is only the initiation of violence? Here I think it is possible to partially reconcile the Block and Halliday positions. It is a question of **what context** we are dealing with. I would agree with Block that, **within** the context of libertarian theory, evil must be confined to the initiation of violence. On *the other hand, when we proceed from libertarianism to the question of* wider social and personal ethics, then I would agree with Halliday that there are many other actions which should be considered as evil: lying, for example. or deliberately failing to fulfill one's best potential. But these are not matters about which liberty — the problem of the proper scope of violence — has anything to say. In short, qua libertarian, there is nothing wrong or evil about breaking dates, being gratuitously nasty to one's associates, or generally behaving like a cad: here not only do I join

Professor Block, but I would expect Mr. Halliday and all other libertarians to do the same. On the other hand, **qua general ethicist**, I would join Mr. Halliday in denouncing such behavior, while Professor Block would not.

In general, I join Walter Block in being surprised at the high resistance which has excellent series on "Economic Scapegoats" has been meeting among libertarians. Essentially, what he is doing is sharpening and heightening libertarian consciousness by saying: "Here is activity X; it is voluntary and therefore perfectly permissible for the libertarian, and yet it is scorned and outlawed in our society. And therefore, since a **hero** is defined as any man who proceeds with licit activity even in the face of scorn and coercion, the person doing X is a hero." What Block is simply doing is ringing the changes on this syllogism, applying it to the most shocking and seemingly outrageous cases he can find. And by doing so he drives home the essential libertarian lesson; considering the resistance he has been facing, even among dedicated libertarians, we see all the more the vital importance of Block's projected book.

One important point that Professor Block underlines but apparently needs to be emphasized once more: these scapegoats, by virtue of being outlawed for their licit activity, are heroes but they are not **saints**. Neither they nor their activity possess any intrinsic superior morality: they are only heroic because of the obstacles that government has placed in their path. Those who wish to remove the tag of hero from the pimp, the blackmailer. etc. should advocate the speedy legalizing of these activities. ◘

Harry Browne Replies

To the Editor:

I was pleased to see so much space devoted in your April issue to my new book, **How I Found Freedom in an Unfree World**, through the medium of Roy Childs' review.

Naturally, your reviewer was quite upset with what he considers to be my "wrongheaded" philosophy. The world is full of people like Roy Childs. They come in all philosophical labels — Objectivist, Christian, astrologist, Libertarian, whatever. The one thing they have in common is the unshakeable conviction that each possesses the final, absolute answers to questions of philosophy, morality, and freedom — even if those answers are different from those held a year earlier. What the moralist once accepted as a way of life for himself, he now labels "immoral" and "irrational" when done by someone else.

The point of my book is simple: how to get the Roy Childs' of the world off your back. How to live as you want to — right now — with the knowledge you currently possess, without causing problems you may regret later when you acquire new knowledge. And without having to wait for the millenium in order to be free. I cite techniques for avoiding taxes, staying clear of the moralists, shaking off obligations and responsibilities that other peole think you should have, making more money while working fewer hours, finding good relationships with like-minded people, and other related goals. Naturally, this won't appeal to someone whose future depends upon everyone else conforming to his philosophy.

In the introduction to the review, the editor suggests what he thinks is a contradiction in "the fact that Browne keeps urging the rest of us **not** to care about the liberty of other persons: in short, that he is investing a considerable amount of personal energy and hence presumably cares deeply that we not care about others." It seems strange that I should have to explain to a "libertarian" journal that I trade ideas for money. In three months, the book has sold over 45,000 copies; isn't that a rather self-evident motivation for my interest in the subject?

The editor also suggests that it's easier to avoid the state if one is in my position — that of a best-selling author. One of the points of my book is that you're not likely to make the kind of money I make until you free yourself of taxes, unproductive relationships, and stifling occupations. That certainly has been the case in my own life: I was broke and in debt until I followed my own advice.

Again, thank you for the interest and space devoted to my book.

— Harry Browne

The Editor Rebuts

Mr. Browne's comment is a fascinating revelation of his motivation, his view of the world, and his philosophical ignorance. It is indeed a curious view of the world that finds the important goal in life to "get the Roy Childs' of the world" off our backs. I don't see Roy Childs oppressing anybody; and I feel no need to get him off my back. If I did, all I'd have to do is to stop reading his stuff. It is a strange inversion of reality that finds **the State** no problem at all while worrying about the oppression exerted upon us by Roy Childs.

As to Mr. Browne's philosophical ignorance: when he denounces "moralists", what he is ineluctably and implicitly saying is: "Moralists are bad; avoid them"; but when he says that "moralists are bad" he is trapped in an inner contradiction, because that *itself* is a moral judgment, a moral statement. And so his book lays itself open to Mr. Childs' acute moral analysis.

As for my suggested inner contradictions: that Mr. Browne cares deeply that we not care about the liberty of others, I of course had seen the way out — that Mr. Browne really doesn't give a hoot, and that therefore his motive was purely mercenary — but I was too polite to mention it. ◻

Feds And Rebs

By Kenneth W. Kalcheim

Five days after he led a protest against the Infernal Robbery Service (sic), Karl J. Bray and two of his friends, Francis (Sam) Goeltz and Robert Wrey, all of Salt Lake City, Utah, were arrested and held in the Salt Lake County jail without being charged with any criminal offense.

At about 9:30 P. M. on April 19, 1973, Mr. Bray, owner of The Rocky Mountain Mint, left his office at 1381 South Main Street. As he was approaching his automobile he was confronted with two FBI agents and one IRS special agent. The three agents threw him against his car and searched him. They then handcuffed him, put foot shackles on him and put him in their automobile and proceeded to take him to the county jail. Bray asked several times why he was being arrested and the agents refused to tell him what the charges were. Instead they only told him that he was "being held for the U. S. Attorney". The agents did not have charges for his arrest, nor did they have a warrant. Bray asked repeatedly to know why he was being arrested and the agents failed to inform him of any charges.

The agents transported Bray to the county jail and he was booked. When Bray arrived at the jail he learned that two of his friends, who were at his office earlier that evening, had also been arrested and booked. His friends, Francis (Sam) Goeltz, an airlines flight engineer, and Robert Wrey, an accountant, had been arrested under similar circumstances and were being held without having any charges against them.

Mr. Bray said, "While being booked, the agents, who arrested me, along with about seven other IRS agents, took all of by belongings, including the keys to my office and automobile." After they had taken the keys, one of the agents was overheard saying something to the effect that, "Now we have his keys, let's go get the case." The case he referred to, said Bray "was a briefcase which contained my personal papers and records and also $30,000 in cash."

Bray was allowed to make one phone call and called a friend to handle some matters. One of these matters was to obtain the briefcase and secure the $30,000 in cash. Bray had left the case locked in his car at the time of the arrest. His friend arrived at his office about 11:45 P. M., about fifteen minutes after Bray had called. This was about one hour after the agents had taken the keys. The friend had an extra set of keys and looked in the automobile first for the briefcase but was unable to find it. She then went into the office, which Bray had left locked, and continued to look further for the briefcase. She was still unable to locate it. She then left the office and went to the county jail to see Mr. Bray. About 2:00 A. M., the friend again returned to the office. At this time she found the briefcase in a very conspicuous place. A place she had looked for it earlier. The $30,000 was gone.

The following morning, Mr. Bray's associate, Grey Greggson, went to the office as usual. When he opened the office, he was confronted by three men who identified themselves as IRS special agents. These men were armed with a search warrant from the U.S. District Court and signed by a U. S. Magistrate, Daniel Alsup. They searched the offices for about three hours and were unable to find anything illegal. According to the warrant, they were looking for forms which contained an "illegal Internal Revenue Service insignia". During their search they were unable to find any such forms.

At about 11:00 A. M. on April 20, 1973, Bray, Goeltz, and Wrey were transported to the Federal Building in Salt Lake City for a bail hearing. It was at this hearing that they first heard the charges for which they were being held. They were charged with illegal possession of an Internal Revenue Service insignia. This charge is a misdemeanor. After being charged, they were released on their own recognizance and the leg irons and chains were taken off.

Mr. Bray indicated that it was strange that all this should happen to

(Continued On Page 6)

The Need For A Movement And A Party

(Ed. Note: The following is the gist of an address delivered by the editor of the **Lib. Forum** to the opening session of the first convention of the Free Libertarian Party of New York, March 30.)

I want to deal tonight with three interrelated questions which confront us: (1) Why keep on as libertarians? Isn't the cause of liberty hopeless? (2) Even if the cause of liberty is **not** hopeless, why have a "movement" anyway? Why not simply let libertarian ideas infiltrate and gradually permeate the culture? And (3) Even if a movement **is** necessary, why have a libertarian political party? Why engage in political action? Can't the job be done with informal or formal groups, and **ad hoc** organizations; in other words, can't we continue with the same sort of libertarian movement that we had before the formation of the Libertarian Party in 1972?

I. **Reasons for Optimism.** It would, in my view, be tragic to abandon the libertarian cause **now**, just when, at long last, the movement is beginning to grow apace.

In the first place, the libertarian movement has accelerated greatly in the last four years. Until recently, there **couldn't** have been a libertarian party; there were few libertarians, no magazines, and no **ad hoc** organizations. When I first began as a libertarian, twenty-five years ago, there were scarcely more than one or two libertarians in the entire New York City area. Obviously, the enormous growth of libertarian ideas and of the movement since then should in itself be great cause for optimism for the future.

But may not such growth be a flash in the pan? Is there an objective historical groundwork and basis for the flowering of libertarianism in the current historical epoch? I contend that such sturdy objective grounds for the growth of the movement do indeed exist; and, in fact, what the Marxists call the "objective conditions" for the growth of the movement have developed even faster than the libertarian movement itself.

The current development of these objective conditions for the victory of liberty were discerned and foreseen by Ludwig von Mises, with his usual prescience, in **Human Action** (1949). Mises called such conditions the "exhaustion of the reserve fund", and we would do well to ponder and interpret such "exhaustion" in the broadest possible way. To put it concisely, Mises saw that statism, interventionism, and socialism **cannot** work in the industrial era, that statist measures and policies lead inevitably, in accordance with the ineluctable laws of cause and effect, to bad and disastrous consequences that are increasingly seen as disastrous by the general public. The problem for all these dark decades of statism is that these laws take time, decades, to work themselves out fully; to put it one way, it takes time for the consequences of statist looting and

Feds And Rebs —

(Continued From Page 5)

him so soon after he had led a group of protesters in a peaceful demonstration against the IRS. Bray also had learned that a certain IRS agent who he preferred not to name at this time had been heard to say in a public meeting that he was personally "out to get that Karl Bray." The only thing Bray could figure out about the $30,000 was that someone, who had his keys after his arrest, must have illegally entered his office and automobile between the time he was arrested and the time his friend went to the office, and then must have returned the briefcase before his friend returned at 2:00 A. M. Bray also said that one of the jailers at the county jail had told him that his keys had been taken.

Bray feels that the motive for this type of harassment is that the IRS is just trying to scare the citizens of the United States into submitting to the tyranny of the IRS. He said he "will resist tyrannical government wherever it is."

Bray said he will file criminal charges and civil suits against certain government agents on four charges. He said that he has firm evidence that he was arrested illegally and without a warrant, that his office and automobile were illegally searched and that personal property was taken, and that the IRS has violated a restraining order that was issued by Federal District Judge Willis W. Ritter that ordered the IRS to refrain from harassing Mr. Bray.　▫

repression to wreck the economy and the living standards that relatively free-market capitalism had brought to us in the nineteenth century. What has happened in recent years is that the Effect has increasingly caught up with the cause, and that the consequences of modern liberalism and the corporate state have become increasingly evident to more and more people in our society.

In area after area, modern liberalism and statism has "exhausted its capital", and hence has come increasingly into grave crisis, a crisis recognized at every hand. More and more, the American public, for example, is rebelling against high and crippling taxation, and galloping inflation; more and more we see the breakdown of statism in market dislocations, aggravated inefficiency of government activities and programs, in urban street crime and housing blight, in the crisis of the welfare system and compulsory racial integration. And we have seen the breakdown of liberalism in foreign affairs as well: from the grim failure of collective security liberalism in Vietnam to the growing revulsion against foreign aid and the military-industrial complex. In short, liberalism, the dominant ideology and institution in America during the twentieth century, is in a crisis of aggravated breakdown, and this breakdown is bound to intensify in the months and years ahead.

Outside of the United States, there is a similar exhaustion of the reserve fund. A particularly heartening development has taken place in the Communist countries of Eastern Europe, where, as the economies industrialized, socialist central planning broke down and collapsed; as a result of these increasingly evident failures, Eastern Europe, led by Yugoslavia, has been moving rapidly and inexorably from central planning to an ever freer market economy. And while Yugoslavia has led the process, Hungary, Czechoslovakia, and Poland have been following in its wake. And so the Law of Cause and Effect is catching up with socialism in the Communist countries as well.

But, if the breakdown of statism is inevitable and accelerating as I maintain, why was statism able to endure for thousands of years? Why was it the norm in most ancient civilizations? Couldn't we in fact say that freedom has just been an interlude among centuries of state despotism? No, the reason for optimism here is that a qualitative and virtually irreversible leap occurred in the late eighteenth and nineteenth centuries that changes the entire historical picture: the Industrial Revolution. For statism, while no less evil, can unfortunately last indefinitely in an agricultural, pre-industrial society. For in such a society, the hapless peasants can be exploited by the State, which can expropriate all of their surplus production above the bare subsistence level. But the advent of industrialism changes the story. For, as Mises and other free-market economists have shown since the time of Charles Dunoyer and Charles Comte in the early nineteenth century, statism cannot work, cannot for long operate an industrial system. Virtually all groups and factions in society are now committed to maintaining an industrial economy, and given that commitment, the Law of Cause and Effect and the exhaustion of the reserve fund must do its irrefutable work. It is therefore the irreversible, universal commitment to industrialism that makes the breakdown of statism and hence the victory of liberty "inevitable."

Victory, then, shall be ours. We should therefore adopt a firm policy of **long-run optimism.** Or, let's put it this way: most of us have always believed it naive to hold that we will win simply because **we are right.** Why would truth necessarily win out in the "marketplace of ideas"? I say it will win out because of the Law of Cause and Effect. Because we are in tune with the deep structure, the ontological structure, of reality. And the Effect is now catching up with the Cause.

And finally, even if our cause is not hopeless, even if there are great grounds for optimism, why should we be concerned at all? Why should we **bother?** Why struggle in a long-range cause, even if we can make small short-term gains? Isn't this being naively or wrongly "altruistic"? To get personal for a moment, when I became a "libertarian", approximately twenty-five years ago, the thrill of discovery of this hidden truth, a truth as vital to mankind as the nature of liberty and justice, was so great that it was impossible for me to conceive — and still difficult for me to understand — how anyone, once perceiving this great truth, could possibly defect from or abandon it. There is great joy and satisfaction in committing oneself to such true and vitally important goals and

(Continued On Page 7)

Need For Movement, Party —

(Continued From Page 6)

principles. Being a committed libertarian is **fun**, a great and "happifying" activity.

II. **Reasons for a Movement.** OK, so even if the objective conditions are ripe, even if victory for libertarianism is inevitable, and even if we should bother, why have a **movement**? Why can't libertarianism simply win its way in the world without a libertarian movement to propel it?

The answer is, that, as the Marxists would say, victory requires the fulfillment not only of the "objective" but also of the "subjective" conditions. By subjective conditions, they mean a dedicated self-conscious and aware group of people to carry the ideas forward. No idea, *including liberty, can advance itself, as it were in a vacuum.* To advance libertarian ideas, we need **libertarians** to do the advancing. As Thomas Kuhn has pointed out, in the history of science and scientific ideas, a bad, unworkable theory is **never** abandoned **until** a better one is offered. People have to have some ruling ideology. Or, in the words of the adage, "you can't beat somebody with nobody." Therefore, in order to administer the **coup de grace** to statism, we have to have people, libertarians, offering a better alternative.

All right, assuming that we need libertarians, why must we have an organized movement? Why can't we just write and speak as individuals? The answer is that if we concede the need for people to spread ideas, self-conscious, dedicated, enthusiastic, knowledgeable libertarians to spread the idea of liberty, then we are already implying the need for a movement. For what is a "movement" anyway? A **movement** is libertarians finding each other, talking to and influencing each other, developing theory, checking each other's errors, helping each other, placing each other in positions of influence, helping one another spread the word, etc. In short, a movement is a "cadre" of dedicated, "hard core" libertarians.

No ideas, whether ideological or scientific, in the history of mankind have spread by themselves in a vacuum; they have all needed dedicated "cadre" to spread them and to become influential and apply them in the world. Where would **physics** now be, for example, without **physicists** — not isolated but a dedicated group of interacting persons, communicating with each other, learning from each other, refuting errors, raising ideas, and helping each other's work? Liberty needs a **movement** in the same sense that physics, or chess, or religions, or any ideas need a movement.

III. **Reasons for a Party.** All right, so libertarians must have a movement. But why a **party**? Why can't we continue in the same informal, ad hoc, manner as we did before 1972?

The standard reason for the existence of a "third" party is that the public only listens to political ideas in the context of an electoral campaign, and that therefore a political campaign is a great educational device for the American public. This is true, but is only one among many reasons for the importance of a political party. For it is historically true, certainly for the United States, that a political party is the **only** viable form of organizing adults, certainly adults in the middle-class: in fact the only viable form of organizing anyone off the college campuses. Even the New Left in its heyday in the late 60's, could never, try as it might, organize anyone outside the campuses; it could not even organize recent graduates. Ad hoc, single-issue, or even multi-issue, groups, have never had more than a very limited success. Until the advent of the Libertarian Party the Society for Individual Liberty was the only successful organization, and that remains confined to the college campuses. The rapid growth in the Libertarian Party throughout the country, ever since the Presidential election, is effective testimony to this vital fact of reality.

A Libertarian Party, furthermore, provides a marvellous and indispensable way for libertarians, generally isolated in their own community, to **find** each other, to interact and learn from each other. It provides, moreover, a viable form of **activity** for libertarians. For a long time, innumerable people, once seeing the great truth of libertarianism, have asked me: "OK, I'm converted, what do I **do now**? What can I do to advance liberty?" This has always been a vital problem for libertarians. Only a few people, after all, will write treatises, or engage in libertarian scholarship. Until the Libertarian Party, there has been **nothing, no** activity, for most libertarians to undertake. I am convinced that this has been a major reason for the hopelessness that has led to defections from the libertarian cause. But now, with the Libertarian Party, we have a

Rothbardiana

Rothbard's **For A New Liberty** has now been published (Macmillan), and has garnered favorable reviews from Walter Grinder (**Books for Libertarians**), Roy Childs (BFL, and a forthcoming **Reason**), and Sharon Presley (Laissez-Faire Bookstore). Also favorable reviews in the general press from Richard Wilson (Cowles Pubs.), Victor Wilson (Newhouse Press), and two superb columns by Nicholas von Hoffman (Washington *Post* syndicate). The von *Hoffman* columns are "Back to Basics" (April 13), and "What if they Gave A Revolution and Nobody Came?" (April 16). **Reason** magazine included Rothbard's anarchist chapter on "Free Market Police, Courts, and Law" in its March issue, followed by a debate between Rothbard and Hospers on that chapter ("Will Rothbard's Free-Market Justice Suffice?") in **Reason's** May issue. Also, Rothbard plugged the book on the NBC-TV "Today" show, and on John Wingate's all-night talk show on WOR-Radio in New York. **Penthouse** magazine is planning an article on "The New Libertarians", featuring the libertarian books by

(Continued On Page 8)

viable, continuing form of activity for all libertarians to participate in. Furthermore, as the FLP has shown, a libertarian party can also serve as a center, a nucleus, for special ancillary libertarian activity in specific party clubs.

OK, granted the need for a Libertarian Party, why must it run candidates? The answer is that it has to, because otherwise it would not be a **party**, but would devolve into another ad hoc organization. Losing a major reason for its existence, it would no longer be a political party, and would hence shortly disappear.

A political party, as everyone concedes, can educate a public who will only listen to political ideas during an electoral campaign; and it will be aided in this by the equal time that the media grant to political candidates. But public education is only **one** of the vital functions that a Libertarian Party can perform. It can, eventually, have real political influence, and even elect people to office. Only one or two Congressmen, for example, could have great political influence and leverage by serving as a ginger group, a vanguard for the repeal of oppressive legislation, the whittling down of crippling taxes, and for the general rollback of the State apparatus. We can organize mass public pressure from below against State tyranny.

For we must ask ourselves the vital question: how **else** can we roll back the oppressive State apparatus? How **else** can we repeal despotic laws and crippling taxes? How else than by pressuring the legislature to repeal them, and what better way than by electing persons dedicated to such repeal? To pressure Congress from below, to lobby, is fine, but scarcely enough. What better organizer of State-rollback than people who are part of a functioning, growing, and dedicated Libertarian Party?

The vital point is that our anti-Party libertarians can offer no alternative solution to the problem of repealing and rolling back the State. Libertarian education is great, but scarcely enough; we cannot place any strategic reliance on our rulers reading our books and pamphlets and then saying: "By God, they're right. I resign." Violent revolution, as the New Left demonstrated, is absurd in the American context. Mass civil disobedience, as in the case of Prohibition, is great, but is historically only sporadic and fitful; besides, even repeal of Prohibition required Congressmen willing to vote to end the horrors of Prohibition — a vote that would have been greatly speeded up by some Libertarians in their midst.

The point is that none of us libertarians sought out Politics. Politics has been thrust upon us by the State apparatus, and it is absurd for us not to use the political choices we are allowed to have, to help in the rollback and the eventual abolition of politics and political intervention in our lives.

The final charge of the anti-Party libertarians is that the Libertarian Party may eventually sell out to Power. Of course it may, and so might we all, whether in or out of a political Party. As long as we have free will, *any* of us might choose to sell out. So what? These are the ineluctable risks of life. As the old adage has it, the cure for this problem is eternal vigilance, the inevitable price of liberty. And even if the Party, after many successes, **does** sell out, we will be no worse off, and considerably better off, than we are now. The future, as I have tried to show, is with us. We have nothing to lose but our chains; we have a world to win. And we will win. ◘

Rothbardiana —

(Continued From Page 7)

Macmillan published this season by Rothbard, Harry Browne, and Robert Love on how to set up your own private school. The article will be by veteran libertarian writer Sam Blumenfeld.

Rothbard's mini-book on the contributions of Ludwig von Mises and the Austrian School is now out: **The Essential Von Mises** (available from Oakley Bramble, Box 836, Bansing, Michigan 48904, for $1.00). It is also an intellectual biography and tribute to Mises; Henry Hazlitt will be reviewing it for the **Freeman**.

Rothbard has also published the following this Spring:

A reprint of **What Has Government Done to Our Money?** as an article in a new scholarly journal published by students at The Commerce School of Washington & Lee University, the **Washington & Lee Commerce Review** (Winter, 1973). This publication, and particularly the Rothbard article, has thrown the W&L Commerce Faculty into conniption fits; they don't want the fair name of the school associated with such an "unscholarly" publication. One of Baldy Harper's last deeds on earth was to recommend the piece to the W&L students, and thus to stir up this healthy hornet's nest in "truth-seeking" academe.

"The Future of Capitalism", an article in James Weaver, ed., **Modern Political Economy** (Allyn & Bacon, paper). This was a debate with a rather unintelligent (to put a very kindly face on it) chairman of the economics department at Smith College, Robert Averitt. The rest of this purported text is a slough of leftism, with the exception of a few articles here and there.

Rothbard is a co-author of a new book in the American Forum series, **Herbert Hoover and the Crisis of American Capitalism** (Schenckman, paper). Rothbard's article on "Herbert Hoover and the Myth of Laissez-Faire," is a reprint of his article in **A New History of Leviathan**, but the book is interesting for its four views on Hoover (including the pro-Hoover Robert Himmelberg, the orthodox Liberal Gerald Nash, and the slightly revisionist Liberal Ellis Hawley), and for the rebuttal section where each of the authors gives a critique of the others. The rebuttal section gave Rothbard a chance to expose Hoover's political-Machiavellian use of food in Europe during 1919 — one of the unloveliest aspects of the unfortunate Hoover record.

Rothbard's article, "The Great Society: A Libertarian Critique" is reprinted once again, this time in R. Carson, J. Ingles, and D. McLaud, eds., **Government in the American Economy** (Lex, Mass.: D. C. Heath, paper). The rest of the book, however, is largely a morass of leftism.

"Value Implications of Economic Theory," **The American Economist** (Spring, 1973), is an article by Rothbard attacking various value-loaded pronouncements by economists in the guise of "value-freedom", and maintaining that value-judgments, if made, require an ethical system.

Rothbard enters **Human Events**: a review of Henry Hazlitt's new Conquest of Poverty (May 19), and a movie review of "Billy Jack" (April

28). The dark secret of the identity of "Mr. First Nighter" is thereby implicitly revealed!

Also: the **Journal of the Forum for Contemporary History** (May 7), has Rothbard's reply to Senator McGovern's comment of the former's Forum letter on the Quota System.

"Libertarian Strategy: Reply to Mr. Katz", New Libertarian Notes (May) is a discussion of strategy, left-right, alliances, etc.

On April 28, there was a highly successful testimonial dinner for Rothbard at the Barbizon-Plaza Hotel. About 125 people attended the affair, which was marked by speeches by Leonard Liggio, Walter Block, and Walter Grinder, deft MC-ing by Jim Davidson, a presentation of a surprise gift to Rothbard of the complete reprinted set of Tucker's **Liberty**, the reading of messages from well-wishers, and a speech in reply by Rothbard. The entire proceedings are available on two cassette tapes from Audio-Forum, 422 First St., S.E., Washington, D. C. 20003; and they sell as No. 194 for $13.95. (106 minutes of goodies!)   ◘

The Old Curmudgeon

The Sixties Is Over Dept. John Lennon and Yoko Ono have moved from their Greenwich Village pad to The Dakota, an uptown luxurious and rambling old apartment house much beloved by the Hollywood glamour set. Welcome Home, babes.

Alliance With Left-Wing Anarchists? From time to time, and particularly during the bizarrerie of the late 60s, libertarians have linked themselves with left-wing, or communist anarchists. This has been the guiding principle of the Hunter College Libertarian Conferences of the last two years, as it was with the now defunct magazine Libertarian Analysis. The theory was: if we should ally ourselves with the New Left, why not with Communist Anarchists who are totally opposed to the State? This idea totally misconceives the theory of alliance for libertarians. The idea of alliance, whether with Left or with Right, is on ground of tactics rather than principle. We acquire multiple social leverage by allying ourselves on specific issues with differing groups with whom we agree on those particular issues: with Leftists opposed to the draft, or with Rightists opposed to the income tax, for example. But the danger always is thinking of these as **principled**, permanent linkages. If we look at left-wing anarchists, their absurd ideology and social philosophy, combined with their bizarre and dropout life style, makes their social leverage not only nil but negative. What can we possibly gain, either in theoretical understanding or in social effectiveness, by linking ourselves with the kooky Kropotkinites? No group, in content or in form, is better calculated to turn off middle-class Americans, and with good reason, than the left-wing anarchists. I can think of no group with whom an alliance, at any time, would be less fruitful.   ◘

First Class

Published Every Month. Subscription Rate: $8.00 Per Year

A Monthly Newsletter

THE
Libertarian Forum

Joseph R. Peden, Publisher   Murray N. Rothbard, Editor

VOLUME V, NO. 7   JULY, 1973   US-ISSN0047-4517

ECONOMIC MESS

If Watergate bids fair to bring down the Nixon Administration, Nixonomics is ever more raucously in the background, ready to administer an extra kick in the gut. For in no area has Mr. Nixon looked less like a strong and wise leader, in no area has he done more weaving, stumbling, and bumbling, than in the vital economic arena. Not only that: but Mr. Nixon's economic sins are fast catching up with him; one of the important new facts about the economic world is that evil effects are now taking a lot less time to catch up with evil causes. In previous decades, when there was more "fat" in the capitalist economy, the sins of the fathers could only be visited upon the sons, or even the grandsons; but now chickens sent out by the President take hardly a few years to come home to roost. The sins of each President are now, more and more, visited upon himself.

President Nixon is now in a fearsome economic mess, at home and abroad, and the accelerating number of his gyrations and "phases" are not helping him in the slightest. They only push him wildly from one set of evils to another and back again, while correctly giving the public an image of a confused and bewildered Chief Executive.

Take the accelerating international monetary crisis. On the black day of August 15, 1971, Mr. Nixon scuttled the last of the Bretton Woods System. Under pressure by foreign central banks to redeem some of their huge accumulated stock of nearly $80 billion of dollars in gold which we were pledged to pay on demand but did not have, Nixon simply "shut the gold window" in an act of international bankruptcy and bad faith. By his act, Mr. Nixon replaced a bad system by an intolerable one, by a world without a money, a world of fluctuating fiat currencies each at the mercy of their (more or less inflationary) government, a world which threatened to degenerate into the currency blocs, competing devaluations, exchange control, economic warfare, and the shattering of international trade and investment that marked the 1930s. Struggling to recreate an international order with fixed exchange rates — but **without gold** or any other international money, Mr. Nixon drove into existence a new monetary system in the Smithsonian Agreement of December 18, 1971.

President Nixon has made many absurd statements since assuming office, but surely none was more absurd than his laughable hailing of the Smithsonian as "the greatest monetary agreement in the history of the world." To anyone who knew anything about money, left, right, or center, it was clear that no system will break down faster or more thoroughly than fixed exchange rates **without** an international money. The fact that a wider zone of fluctuations than before was allowed around the exchange rates meant nothing. The "greatest monetary agreement" lasted hardly more than a year, and the great monetary crisis of February-March 1973 sent it smashing to smithereens. For the handwriting was on the wall from the very beginning for the absurdly overvalued dollar and the ditto British pound, overvalued in relation to the West German, Swiss, French, and Japanese currencies and in relation to gold. The loss of confidence in the ever more inflated dollar and other currencies sent the price of gold

on the free market skyrocketing to $125 an ounce — almost a quadrupling of the gold price from the formerly sacred $35 figure. Finally, in February-March 1973, the pressure on the absurdly overvalued dollar and pound broke these currencies, and the Smithsonian along with them. Once again, market forces and economic law had proved far stronger than the will of governments.

Since March, we have been, on the international front, in a Friedmanite heaven. For exchange rates (except within the West European bloc) have been fluctuating, more or less freely. For a short while, bankers and economists spoke with surprise of how "well" the fluctuating system was working. But the rapid plunge of the dollar in early July has brought the American public up short. Good God! This means that the prices of foreign imports are now 50% higher than last year, it means that American tourists have to spend 50% more than even a few months ago, etc.! And not only do we face far higher prices for foreign products; the cheap American exports are now being snapped up by foreign countries, thereby lowering the supply of these goods at home and raising their prices in the U. S. Cheap exports "import inflation" from abroad. We are beginning to wake up to the fact that the Friedmanite Utopia of freely fluctuating exchange rates means in practice a bonanza for American export interests and for inefficient domestic producers, and suffering for everyone else. And since we have already been burdened by a host of policies subsidizing exports and hampering imports — from foreign aid to protective tariffs and import quotas — the shock of an additional push is rather too much to bear. If there is anything America does **not** need now, it is a massive dose of more export subsidies and import restrictions, which is what a depreciating dollar entails.

So now what? Undoubtedly, we will get frantic scrambles back and forth between fixed and fluctuating exchange rates, with neither policy working well as we try to escape one set of evils by embracing another. The frantic plunge of the dollar in early July was only checked by an announcement of more authority by the Federal Reserve to "swap" by borrowing hard currency in order to support the dollar in the exchange market. But this is obviously a temporary stopgap; the market won't long be fooled by this kind of device. And while the world waffles back and forth between fixed and fluctuating rates, the dread spectre of the 1930s remains: in this case of Western Europe refusing to accept — and indeed dumping — their $80 billion stock of more and more useless dollars, the fruits of two decades of deficits in the U. S. balance of payments. At some point, the hard money countries of Western Europe will stop the hated flow of dollars by imposing exchange controls, and we will be back in the economic warfare of the 1930s — with a good chance of a world-wide depression to boot.

And neither Nixon nor any other Administration will get out of this mess until we return to the truly free-market system of the gold standard. It is the United States, above all other countries, that is resisting a return to gold to the uttermost, for the sake of preserving its

(Continued On Page 2)

On Man And Perfection

By Tibor Machan

A great many theories of government and social organization rest on consideration of man's perfection. From the time of Plato, philosophers and political theorists have formulated much of their thinking about political communities in line with some view about the relationship between ideal man and actual people. Invariably actual people were declared to be "imperfect", "flawed", "lowly" and the like. In theological thinking matters were stated in terms of man's original sin, his pride. or his passioned instead of spiritual inclinations.

What is the importance of such thinking for theorizing about the kind of political order mankind ought to institute? And what is the precise meaning of such claims as that man is "flawed" or "imperfect"? To understand what we face in trying to evaluate political alternatives, i.e., different solutions to the basic question of political theory, it is necessary that we become clear on these matters.

References to man's flawed nature, his imperfection and the like, are not simple to understand. Ordinarily when we consider whether something is a flawed or perfect specimen of its kind, we refer to particular items. Thus some particular chair may be ill-designed, some table badly constructed, or some marriage perfect. Even when we consider groups of things. say a line of furniture designed by some firm's team of engineers. we talk about that group's failure to meet standards of excellence appropriate to what is being manufactured. Thus a particular line of furniture may be said to have been badly designed - with reference to certain known purposes chairs - all chairs - have. (Of course it is not easy to offer evaluations even of chairs. A lot depends on what purpose some variety of chair is to serve.) The same is true about, e.g., trees, not just human artifacts. Some, even if few, are perfect for use as christmas trees, others as material for lumber yards, and yet others as models for artists. Still, when we know that some particular purpose someone has is unobjectionable on, say, moral grounds, then we are able to and will freely judge items which are intended to serve it in terms of the standard of how well they will satisfy that purpose. And then, even if rarely, we may judge something perfect.

When we come to evaluating human beings as such - Man - we meet with a number of difficulties. Does Man serve some purpose? Whose? Who is to judge how well He satisfies it? Very often the answer given is that Man serves God's purposes. Yet there is much debate as to whether anyone of us could even know this much, not alone know what God's purposes are. Generally it is wiser to leave religious questions out of political matters. This is because religion rests on human faith, a very personal. incommunicable matter whatever its nature. Politics, on the other hand. reaches out for clear understanding, rational solutions. We would be unwise to expect that matters of personal faith, including what any of us believes about God's purposes and, therefore, man's capacity to satisfy them, are suited for making political judgments. (Consider that for some religious faiths God has no purpose involving man; for others man's existence, just as he does exist at any given time, satisfies God's purpose: for yet others man cannot even fulfill the purpose for which he is created by God except after his life on earth.) With a realm so individual and inaccessible to common understanding as faith, it is wisest not to attempt to introduce it into areas where common understanding is the very cornerstone of reaching solutions.

Outside of a religious context what sense can we make of the idea that man has a purpose? That is, that mankind - the species itself - serves some purpose? Aristotle tried to make sense of this, albeit not with complete success. He believed that the purpose of man as of any other natural being is to fulfill its essence. This. applied to man, means that each of us as rational animals fulfills our purpose if he lives his life in accordance with our human nature, namely as fully rationally as we, with our individual capacities. can.

But Aristotle's idea is not exactly that mankind as such has a purpose. It is that there is a purpose to the life of each member of mankind. This is generally describable as living according to human nature. Yet because each man is at once a member of the class of mankind and also an individual who differs from all others in important ways, that alone could not convey the meaning of "having a purpose for any given individual." Before we can say what a given man's specific purpose is, we must know something about him as an individual. We need to know what living according to his human nature, rationally, must mean for any given individual.

If we consider this approach carefully - and it is the only sensible discussion of purpose closely tied to political theory in all of man's history - an interesting thing emerges. Whether a given individual is or is not perfect cannot be known ahead of time. And whether mankind is perfect is not even an intelligible question. It would be like asking if trees

(Continued On Page 3)

Economic Mess —

(Continued From Page 1)

inflationary system. And now that the free-market gold price is $125 an ounce, it would be easy to return to gold at this — or even a still higher — price. That would give the U. S. and all other currencies three times as much gold to back up their currencies as they have now.

On the domestic economic front, matters are certainly no better. Here we see the Nixon Administration waffling back and forth between innumerable "phases": from tight to loose price-wage controls, to tight to loose again, ad infinitum. And each of these phases is working conspicuously less well than the one preceding. In the February 1973 Lib. Forum we wrote that the second Nixon term seemed to be moving away from controls, but that the "sticks were in the closet." Well, they're out of the closet now, of course, with the Draconian Second Freeze of Phase 3½ succeeding a partly tolerable Phase 3. Phase 3½ idiotically froze all prices, but not wages or unprocessed foods; the result was the very rapid development of food shortages, especially meat and margarine. Phase 4 promises to be Phase 2ish, and so on. But Phases 3½ and 4, as is recognized by virtually all economists, are going to break down much faster than Phases 1 and 2, since the economy is now bursting at the seams in an inflationary boom whereas in 1971 we were in a (less) inflationary recession with lots of slack in the economy. So that while it took over a year for Phases 1-2 to break down, the collapse will be considerably faster for the comparable Phases 3½-4. The point of the whole thing is that the Nixon Administration is now committed to price and wage controls, shifting wildly between tight and loose, while at the same time — and despite the publicity on the "tight money" of high interest rates — it continues to expand the money supply by 8-10% per year. It does not have the guts to stop this policy of inflating (money) while trying to hold down or break the inflation thermometer (prices) even though it knows that its policy is economic lunacy. For it does not have the guts to face the recession that is inevitable once the inflationary process has been stopped.

Even Milton Friedman, who has long held that a recession is not the inevitable consequence of an inflationary boom, now admits that a sharp recession is inevitable should the government stop inflating the money supply. It is curious, by the way, that Friedman reacted with far greater horror to Nixon's second freeze than in his rather mild wrist-slapping of August 1971. Somehow he feels that the second freeze is Nixon's real betrayal of free-market principles; but in our view the basic decision to dump the market for price controls was made in Phase 1: all the rest have been gyrations within that basic decision. But I suppose we should welcome Milton, even if belatedly, to the ranks of the indignant.

The prognosis on the domestic front is scarcely happier than on the foreign. Prices are now accelerating at a rapid rate, far more rapidly than in the previous administrations. But the will to stop inflating is clearly not there. And so we can expect a ratcheting series of price inflations, with the eventual super-catastrophe of runaway inflation and the "crack-up boom" looming ever closer on the horizon. Only an iron will of the Administration to stop inflating could reverse this prognosis, and there is no sign of that will anywhere in the Administration. The poor befuddled public, with its eye on price controls, doesn't even begin to understand the problem, and so can be no help in putting pressure on our rulers. The only comfort for libertarians in this grim picture is that we should be able to convert many people to a libertarian, hard-money, free market position with an impressive catalog of "I-told-you-sos". ◻

On Man And Perfection —

(Continued From Page 2)

or roses or fish or the moon, etc., are perfect. But by what standard? To what must trees measure up to be identified as a perfect? The best we can answer is: to the purpose we have for trees in our own lives. But what of fish, moons and the millions of other kinds of entities in nature? To ask whether these are perfect makes little sense. Perfect by what standard, for what purpose?

With man the issue of perfection is a **moral and personal** issue. It has to do with man's nature as a free and self-responsible being. He is free to cause his actions (although, of course, some people are too impaired either mentally or physically to be thought of this way). And he is responsible to choose those actions that will make his life a success. As Aristotle seems to have believed, and I do too, happiness, the successful state of human life, is each man's **moral** purpose. (Ayn Rand spells this out in detail.) It is with reference to how well each **does** to satisfy this goal that anyone may be evaluated as either perfect, good, mediocre or downright evil. No other sense can be made of the idea of human perfection.

But what of the claims about man's "flawed" and "imperfect" nature? Surely there must be something meant by these remarks. And indeed there appears to be something important to them. That is that no man has a guarantee for success. Moral excellence is not ensured for anyone **ahead of time.** Every person must make the effort to be good on his own - he cannot be **made** to be good.

But the idea that man is "flawed" is often interpreted so that we are given to understand that people cannot be good even if they do their best. Not that man is **fallible** but that he is **necessarily a failure,** flawed by his very nature. Yet this cannot be understood at all. How would anyone be knowledgeable enough to say such a thing? It would seem to be presumptuous to declare of all people, past, present and future, that they cannot live a morally good life, that they cannot achieve the best possible life for themselves, given their capacities and circumstances. This kind of a judgment is best characterized as prejudicial - it disregards the perfectly sensible judicial principle of the presumption of innocence. It confuses "free to do good or ill" with "must do ill".

Believing that man is flawed, Marx, for example, thought that it was the inevitable result of revolutionary social conflicts to make him good. Marx did not believe in free will, so he did not take man's "flawedness"

Harper's Last Article

Baldy Harper's last published writing appeared, a week before his death, in the Santa Ana **Register** for April 13. It is characteristic that Baldy's last writing was in celebration of a powerful tax rebellion movement that has recently appeared in Denmark. (The article is entitled, "Tax Rebel Shows Strong in Dane Poll"). The article writes of the great and rising popularity of Mr. Mogens Gilstrup and his new Progressive Party, the latest poll showing that if an election were now held in Denmark, the Progressives would win 33 out of the 179 seats in the Danish Parliament, making the new party second to the ruling Social Democrats.

Who is Gilstrup, and what is the Progressive Party program? Gilstrup is a tax lawyer and a tax rebel, who two years ago announced on television that had paid no income tax at all on a "very high income," and that he did so through legal tax avoidance. His Progressive Party program is short and sweet: (1) abolish all income taxes over the next six years; (2) reduce the government bureaucracy by 90% (!); and (3) rewrite all the statutes so as to make them short and clear enough for everyone to understand.

Harper, with his keen appreciation of the clear-cut antithesis between the State and private property, concludes as follows:

> "The time may fast be approaching when the tax-bowed citizens of western countries will face up to a clear choice between two views: (1) Taxes are part of the person's income that is confiscated without his consent, or (2) persons are owned by the government, in essence, which means that these incomes were owned by the government before being taken as taxes."

to mean that the possibility of evil, as well as of good, is open to all people. He believed that - by virtue of institutional and similar elusive causes - man is necessarily flawed. Only when man had been made automatically good would the perfect society emerge.

Claiming that some equally elusive problem left man to believe in his own freedom, B. F. Skinner, too, asks us to accept that man can be made good by social control. And when one believes that there is something in human nature itself that makes us flawed, it is not unreasonable to try to wipe the flaw out, to make the necessary reparations. We do this, after all, with faulty chairs, cars, cameras, and even human physical organs. So why not with mankind?

It is often this belief in the flawed nature of man that impels people, especially ambitious and impatient ones, toward social engineering. I believe that a clear grasp of what must be meant when we say that man is not perfect - namely that moral perfection is never guaranteed for anyone but must be earned by the individual himself through hard work - will reduce the inclination toward statism, paternalism and totalitarianism. We could then develop societies that assume neither man's perfectability nor his imperfectability.

Such a system would make sure that those who aim to do well in their lives, who try for moral excellence, would not be disturbed by those who are not willing to try for it. Nor would anyone be **ordered** to live a morally decent life - all he will not be permitted to do is to prevent others from trying. This, I think, is the only nonutopian and yet optimistic approach to man's goal of living in peace with his fellows.

Liberty Or Order: 1970 Domestic Spying Plan

By Bill Evers

William F. Buckley's **National Review** once said of Tom Charles Huston that "he radiates a primal personal integrity and conceals remarkable intellectual and political agility behind a facade of Hoosier folksiness. He is one of the young luminaries of American conservatism."

Huston is the young lawyer and conservative political activist who, in the summer of 1970, as a White House aide drafted an expanded domestic intelligence plan for President Nixon. The plan involved spying, wiretapping, burglaries, and the interception and opening of mail.

How did it happen that Huston, a former national chairman of the Young Americans for **Freedom** student group, came to design a program for the systematic violation of civil liberties?

The answer to this puzzle lies in large part in the ideological concepts of "freedom" and of "order" that are held by men like Huston who are in the leadership of the organized conservative movement in America.

A profile of Huston in the May 24 **New York Times** quoted him as explaining that "repression is an inevitable result of disorder. Forced to choose between order and freedom, people will take order."

The error in Houston's reasoning is twofold. First, there is a philosophical error in not recognizing the difference between a societal "order" that is simply securing to citizens their rights to life, liberty, and the pursuit of happiness and a societal "order" that secures a governmental system, any governmental system in power.

Thus, the American Revolution in the eighteenth century is correctly seen both as a threat to the order of the British Empire and as a defense of the natural order of human liberty. There is always a dichotomy between governmental order per se and liberty. But there is perfect compatibility between total liberty and a natural order securing to all this same liberty.

Secondly, Huston made the practical error of defending not the natural order of full freedom for all, but governmental order. He has subsequently attempted to justify this by contending that at the time the voters were likely to endorse more extensive abrogation of civil liberties, if the Nixon plan was not successful.

But here we see the same opportunistic position that Huston found so distasteful in the Nixon administration's other domestic programs. Borrowing the sort of domestic security program that one might

(Continued On Page 4)

Pareto on the Prospects for Liberty

Editor's Note: One of the important but neglected resources for libertarians is the translation of libertarian works of the past that languish unread because of the great language barrier that afflicts even the most learned Americans. Here, Professor Ralph Raico, of the history department of the State University College at Buffalo, one of the notable translators of the movement who brought us the excellent English translation of Mises' **Liberalismus (The Free and Prosperous Commonwealth)** now gives us, for the first time in English, a beautifully written letter by the great Pareto. Vilfredo Pareto, a great Italian libertarian theorist of the late nineteenth century and the early twentieth, began by the turn of the century to despair of the prospects for liberty. He had good reasons for his pessimism, as he saw libertarianism (or laissez-faire liberalism) ground down between the socialists on the one hand and the right-wing protectionist statists on the other. It was Pareto's despair at the victory of emotional statist appeals that led him later to the sociological view that the persuasive power of reason was helpless in the grip of irrational motivations. The view, especially for that epoch, was understandable though unfortunate, since it neglects the possibility of libertarian appeals blending reason and emotion as contrasted to the merely emotional propaganda of its enemies. Pareto's letter was originally published in **Le monde economique** of April 10, May 8, and June 5, 1897; and was then reprinted in his **Oeuvres Completes, Vol. VI, Mythes et Ideologies** (Geneva, 1956), pp. 113-16.

Letter to M. Brelay
by Vilfredo Pareto

translated by Ralph Raico

My dear colleague,.

You are a stout-hearted fellow, you continue to fight for liberty, your writings and lectures are filled with practical good sense. But even you must have some doubts on the outcome of the battle. For myself, I am tempted to believe that the game is really just about lost, except in England and perhaps in Switzerland. As for the rest of Europe, it may be that the triumph of socialism is only a question of time. Besides, you will notice that by now the fight is already merely between different sects of socialists. In Germany, it is imperial and military socialism that fights it out with the socialism of the masses. In Italy and France, the latter is at grips with protectionist socialism. Do you happen to have any preferences for one or another of these sects? I myself don't; and, in any case, it would not be the socialism of established governments that I would defend.

As for the liberals, I search for them in vain. There are, it is true, a few chiefs left, such as Herbert Spencer and our good friend, M. de Molinari. But as for the common soldiers — where are they? At each election, one sees the number of socialist deputies increase. It is true that the number of liberal deputies does not diminish, but that is for the excellent reason that for a long time now that number has been zero. The majority of young people whom I know in Italy and elsewhere are either opportunists or socialists; it isn't necessary to tell you that I much prefer the latter, who may be deceiving themselves, but who at least have generous and decent intentions.

How does it happen that the liberal party, which, in the time of the Cobdens, the J.-B. Says, the Bastiats, etc., appeared to be assured of a quick victory, now does not even exist anymore in most of the states of the European continent? This fact is due to a great number of causes, which it would take too much time to set forth; but there is one which, though secondary, seems to me rather important, and which I would like to converse with you about a bit.

The great error of the party of economic liberty, in my view, has been and still is today that it is not a political party. When one does pure science, one can and must do analysis; that is, one can and must separate one question from all others and study it apart. No one is more drawn to recognize this principle than myself; I have written a whole treatise on political economy in which I declared that I had no wish to resolve any practical question at all. But when one leaves theory and wishes to lay

down rules for real life, it is necessary to make syntheses. What does it matter to me if free trade permits me gain ten francs, if this same amount is taken away from me again by raising taxes? The loveliest theories are worth nothing if the final result is bad: "I live from good soup, and not from beautiful language." One may hope to make partisans for one's cause by saying: Join us and you will pay thirty or forty centimes for sugar, as the English do, instead of paying one franc ten. But whom does one intend to persuade by saying: Take a lot of trouble, make sacrifices — you will continue, it is true, to pay one franc ten for your sugar, only you will have the satisfaction, the pleasure, the happiness of knowing that it will be because of a fiscal levy and not a protective levy. The point is that in theory this sort of distinction is useful and justified, but in practical politics it is absurd.

Not concerning itself with politics, the party of economic liberty had, it is true, the advantage of recruiting rather promptly a great number of adherents; but it lost in force and intensity of conviction what it gained in

(Continued On Page 5)

Liberty Or Order —

(Continued From Page 3)

anticipate from a George Wallace in order to avert his gaining electoral strength, is hardly acting in accord with any "philosophical view of what government ought to be doing."

Embracing Only Rhetoric

If Huston had recognized that a free society was the proper environment for human activity, he would have held that a net subtraction of freedom is never justified. If Huston had fully belonged to the individualist political tradition, instead of merely partially embracing its rhetoric, liberty would have been his highest political goal, to which all others were subordinated.

However, Huston and the other adherents of the William Buckley circle of conservatives attempt to fuse a devotion to the prevailing traditional order with a devotion to liberty. In times of crisis, they most often come down on the side of the ruling order rather than liberty.

Huston himself is an admirer of the political thought of John C. Calhoun, whose portrait was on his office wall in his White House years. Calhoun's influence no doubt added to Huston's capacity to rationalize setting up the 1970 espionage program.

Calhoun was both a brilliant, original political theorist and an active politician in the period preceding the American Civil War. But Calhoun rejected the Jeffersonian doctrine that all human beings possessed natural and inalienable rights.

Calhoun argued in his **Disquisition on Government** that "it is a great and dangerous error to suppose that all people are equally entitled to liberty."

"It is a reward to be earned, not a blessing to be gratuitously lavished of all alike — a reward reserved for the intelligent, the patriotic, the virtuous and deserving, and not a boon to be bestowed on a people too ignorant, degraded, and vicious to be capable either of appreciating or of enjoying it."

Huston was inclined to believe with Calhoun that when liberty and governmental order came into conflict, liberty must yield to governmental power. Huston was therefore willing to devise a massive plan to control dissenters.

But Huston's and Calhoun's anti-libertarian approach is an attack upon the social conditions that are right for man. Only when it is generally recognized that, in Proudhon's words, "liberty is not the daughter but the mother of order," and when men are ready to defend such a natural order of liberty, will we have a free society, a society in which virtue can prosper.

Reprinted from the **Stanford Daily**, July 6, 1973.   ▢

Prospects for Liberty —

(Continued From Page 4)

extension. It consoles itself agreeably enough by making fun of its enemies, as the Greeks, vanquished by the Romans, consoled themselves by counting up the grammatical mistakes their masters made. When the scandals break that are an inevitable consequence of state socialism, the liberals, far from profiting from the occasion to make the public aware of the advantages of their doctrine, modestly lower their eyes, keep still, hide and seem truly to fear nothing so much as having been too much in the right. In reality, most of the people who call themselves liberal are quite simply the defenders of the interests of the upper social classes. But these are far from rallying to liberal doctrines; they want more than and better than simply to preserve what belongs to them. They intend to enjoy all the benefits of **bourgeois** and protectionist socialism, and hardly concern themselves except with the people who can help them in appropriating the goods of others. They do not absolutely scorn the praises that so-called liberal economists bestow on the luxury of the rich. But frankly that is only meager meat in comparison with the good protective tariffs, the good manufacturing subsidies, with the privileges and monopolies of all kinds that they obtain from the right honorable politicians.

The pseudo-liberals have contributed not a little (aided by the socialists) to create the legend that makes of political economy the enemy of the working classes and reduces it to a kind of casuistry in the service of the rich. One is surprised and pained to see men of talent believing in such nonsense. Thus, an illustrious scholar, of whom I certainly shall only speak with the greatest respect, M. Berthelot,* in a recent speech, pronounced the following words: "Above all, far from us these egoistic doctrines of laissez-faire and laissez-passer, which would suppress any intervention of scientific laws in the direction of societies, as well as the fatal slogan once proclaimed from the height of the tribune as the supreme end of social life: Get rich!"**

What would M. Berthelot say if someone confused the phlogiston theory with modern atomic theory? Well, it is a similar confusion that he commits by mixing up the sometimes illusory speculations of the economists of the optimistic school with economic science.

He probably imagines that "laissez-faire, laissez-passer" is a kind of fetish adored by certain savages. He certainly is unaware that the theorem that proves that free competition leads to the maximum of well-being is quite as well demonstrated as any theorem in theoretical mechanics. He is unaware that the theorem that shows that every indirect transfer of wealth from certain individuals to certain others is accompanied by a destruction of wealth rests on proofs altogether as sure as those which serve to prove the second law of thermodynamics. If we then proceed to apply these theorems to the social aggregate, he cries out that we want to preclude the "scientific direction of societies." It is as if one applied the principles of thermodynamics to steamengines and M. Berthelot complained that "one intends to exclude the science of the construction of these machines." Isn't it profoundly regrettable that a scientist who justifiably enjoys such a great authority talks in this way about such matters, without trying in the least to understand the precise meaning of the theories he condemns?

Then there is the egoism of "laissez-faire, laissez-passer"! Oh, yes, truly — it was through egoism that Bastiat demanded that the people not be plundered by means of tariffs, and it was through egoism that Cobden and his friends delivered the English people from the tribute that they paid the landlords. Hasn't M. Berthelot ever gone to England, hasn't he ever read a book dealing with economic conditions in that country? Is he therefore really unaware that it is because in England one "lets things pass" — wheat, meat, sugar — that the workers of that land enjoy much greater well-being than the workers of the European continent? In what part of the world did one find oneself when, in France, an entry-duty was placed on bread, in order to prevent workers from buying it in Belgium. M. Berthelot has only to read the excellent study of M. G. Francois, **Thirty Years of Free Trade in England**, and he will learn that "laissez-faire, laissez-passer" can, after all, do some good. Let M. Berthelot go to England and he will see the children of workers and farmers eating sweets. Let him then betake himself to Italy, and he will perceive that only the children of the rich may eat candy. Does he know why? Because in England sugar costs forty centimes a kilogram, and in Italy one franc

Public Schools: the Counterattack Begins

By Joseph R. Peden

There is no doubt about the fact that one of the most influential centers of social thought and planning in the United States is the well financed Center for Democratic Institutions in Santa Barbara, California. Under the long time direction of Robert M. Hutchins, former President of the University of Chicago, the Center has become famous for perceiving a crisis before it becomes apparent to others, for setting about the task of creating a "brain trust" to study the various aspects of the crisis-to-be, and then "planning" for its resolution. But unlike so many academic "think-tanks" which send their results in sealed envelopes to appropriate corporate or governmental sponsors, the CDI gives the widest possible publicity to its deliberations and its findings, and often lobbies to get its schemes into being by exerting whatever pressures it can muster.

We have already described the role of the CDI in the creation of an oceanic regime designed to monopolize as much of the territories and

(Continued On Page 6)

eighty. Now, if M. Berthelot is ignorant of the reason for this difference in price I can let him know: it is that in England one "lets sugar pass" at the frontier, while in Italy it is stopped in order to enrich the right honorable manufacturers and refiners of sugar, who, it is true share with the politicians. We laissez-faire liberals prove our egoism because we demand a stop to this sort of plundering of the people. We prove our ignorance because we reject, for the direction of society, this "science" whose real name is the science of plunder, while the dear little saints who grow rich on the benefits of protectionism and state socialism are living examples of the purest love of neighbor!

As for the advice to "get rich," one must distinguish. Does M. Berthelot really believe that an individual cannot become rich except by appropriating the goods of others? That would be going back, in political economy, even further than one would, in chemistry, in adopting the phlogiston theory! But there is another means of getting rich, which does no wrong to anyone and is extremely beneficial to all of society: it is by creating utilities. It is in this way that whole peoples grow rich. How could a people become rich if each individual of which it is composed became poorer? It is solely due to this growth of the wealth of peoples that progress has been possible; otherwise, we would still live like our cannibal ancestors. It is because they lack food that many savage people kill their aged; it is because we are not yet rich enough that we cannot assist all who are weak. Therefore we must still reiterate this advice to "get rich" (by honest means, of course), for if our societies were richer the question of a retirement pension for old people would be immediately solved.

But what is the use of proving to our adversaries that they are wrong? They still go along perpetually repeating propositions that are perpetually refuted. Have you ever seen them come to answer your speeches? Have they ever been able to deny the facts, refute the reasonings by which you expose the evils of protectionism? They are too prudent even to venture to try. They do suspect a little that neither experience nor logic are to be numbered among their allies, and it is to the passions that they appeal, not to reason. In any case, it's probably because of that that they will triumph. Nothing proves that they will not succeed in reducing our societies to some state resembling that of ancient Peru. Our descendants are destined to see some fine things! As for me, I certainly don't begrudge them their bliss.

• • •

* Pierre Eugene Marcelin Berthelot (1827-1907) was a French chemist and politician. His work was particularly notable in the field of thermochemistry. — trans. note

**The phrase "Enrichissez-vous" was supposed to have been spoken by Francois Guizot, French historian and premier under Louis Philippe (1840-48), in response to the query of how non-enfranchised citizens could ever hope to enjoy the right to vote, considering the existence of property qualifications for the franchise. — trans. note

Public Schools —

(Continued From Page 5)

resources of the open seas as it can (**Lib. Forum**, Aug. 1972). Under the direction of old New Deal brain-truster Rexford G. Tugwell, the Center scholars also had the temerity to write a new Constitution for the United States and sponsor dozens of regional conferences throughout the country to "discuss" Tugwell's draft. The reception was so unfavorable in almost all quarters that the scheme seems to have been put in storage for the moment. But if Nixon or his successor ever wishes to formalize his Augustan principate by calling a Constitutional Convention — say in 1976 — the Tugwell draft is there in the dust, like Richard III's crown, waiting to be picked up.

The latest project of Hutchins and his proteges is an open admission that the public education establishment is under seige and in panic; and now is the time for all good men to come to the aid of the "party". Hutchins has announced that the CDI, in conjunction with the Center for Policy Study of the University of Chicago, will undertake an inquiry on public education. Why?

> "The political community should be required to justify the prolonged detention of its citizens in an educational system. We need to enquire into the possibility of such justification. We need to answer the question whether public education is any longer useful. If so, on what terms? If not, what is the alternative?"

The questions raised certainly go to the heart of the issue and are a tribute to radical and libertarian critics of the past decade. The first four questions are almost certainly a plea for some intelligent reply to the criticisms of Ivan Illich (See rev. of Illich's **Deschooling Society** by Len Liggio, **Lib. Forum**, Oct. 1971):

> "Are universal literacy and numericity of sufficient importance in this decade to deserve the substantial share of educational funds and energies? How shall the terminal point of education be determined? How shall assessed national needs and individual aspirations and propensities be reconciled when they are incongruent? Are schools the appropriate institutions for career education? Job training? Shall maximizing the educability of the deprived, least schooled segments of our population be a matter of first priority?"

Other questions reflect the devastating impact on the public educationist establishment of the findings of Christopher Jencks and his associates (**Inequality: A Reassessment of the Effect of Family and Schooling in America**, Basic Books 1972). As Christopher Lasch has so well said:

> "Not only do they (Jencks' findings) undermine the popular belief that schooling is an avenue of economic advancement, they also undermine the progressive version of this national mythology — namely that progressive education policies can be used to promote social justice and a new set of social values: cooperation, spontaneity and creativity. Jencks' evidence strongly suggests that the school does not function in any direct and conscious way as the principal agency of indoctrination, discipline or social control . . .".

This must have been the inspiration for Hutchins' first series of questions:

> "Should the primary concern of education be the creation of a political community? If so, how should the political community be conceived? As primarily economic,

concerned mainly with the livelihoods of its members and the productivity of the whole, or as requiring additional dimensions?" Or elsewhere, "Should schools be concerned with the recast of values and loyalties and reformation of character? If so should the aim be one body of values, loyalties or character traits or should a diversity be sought? If this task is held to be inappropriate to public schools, should it be undertaken at all? If so, by what means?"

And as if in response to the challenge of the libertarian-oriented Center for Independent Education's symposium on compulsory education, (held in Milwaukee in Nov. 1972) Hutchins asks: "What, if any community requirements justify compulsory attendance? To what age?"

For those who have asserted the right to an education determined by diverse ethnic, linguistic or religious preferences, (attacked as long ago as the 1950's by former Harvard President Dr. James Conant as un-American because "divisive"), Hutchins includes the question: "Concerning a common language, history and culture: to what extent and in what form shall these be pursued? What degree and form of patriotism? How shall religion be treated?".

The Hutchins study has rightly recognized the enemies of the public school system and properly is examining its defenses. Of course, it appears from a recent article by Hutchins that he has already reached a conclusion on the main issues (Robert Hutchins, "The Schools Must Stay", **Center Magazine**, Jan./Feb. 1973):

> "The purpose of the public schools is not accomplished by having them free, universal and compulsory. Schools are public because they are dedicated to the **maintenance** and **improvement** of the public thing, the **res publica**; they are the common schools of the commonwealth, the political community. They may do many things for the young; they may amuse them, comfort them, look after their health, keep them off the streets. But they are not public schools unless they start their pupils toward an understanding of what it means to be a self-governing **citizen** of a self-governing **political** community."

Another prominent educationalist, Prof. R. Freeman Butts, Russell Professor of Education at Teachers College, Columbia, and long a leading public education ideological commissar, speaks more bluntly than Hutchins, making the same points. In his article "The Public School: Assault on A Great Idea", (**The Nation**, April 30, 1973) Butts asserts that

> "to achieve a sense of community is the essential purpose of public education. This work cannot be left to the vagaries of individual parents, or small groups of like-minded parents, or particular interest groups, or religious sects, or private enterprisers, or cultural specialties . . . I believe the chief end of American public education is the promotion of a **new civism** appropriate to the principles of a just society in the United States and a just world community . . . We require the renewal of a civic commitment that seeks to reverse and overcome the trend to segmented and disjunctive "alternatives" serving narrow or parochial or racist interests".

Butts' open totalitariansim, which has its intellectual roots in Plato and stretches down to the Papadapoulos regime of modern Greece, cuts through the liberal romanticism of Hutchins and lays bare the root purpose of public education. Yet Hutchins cries that "nobody has a kind word for the public school, the institution that only the other day was looked upon as the foundation of our freedom, the guaranty of our future, the cause of our prosperity and power, the bastion of our security, and the source of our enlightenment".

It's like being ungrateful to God!   ◘

Arts and Movies

By Mr. First Nighter

The Heartbreak Kid. dir. by Elaine May. With Charles Grodin, Cybill Shepherd, Jeannie Berlin, and Eddie Albert.

If, in the old adage, "it takes one to know one," we can perhaps understand some of the brilliance with which the team of Nichols and May hilariously and acidulously satirized the typical conversation and thought-processes of New York-liberal-Jewish intellectuals in their great records of the 1950s and early 60s. Since then, Mike Nichols has gone on to ape the pretentiousness of the people he once satirized, leaving Elaine May to mine the comic vein alone. Her first movie, **A New Leaf**, was simply and happily hilarious, starring the great comedic talent of Walter Matthau, but lacked the old social bite of former days. In **The Heartbreak Kid**, Miss May returns to her old **genre**, and with the notable exception of Philip Roth, no one is as adept in exploring the cultural differences and conflicts between the Jewish and the **goyishe** worlds. **Heartbreak Kid** is a brilliantly crafted, intelligent, and often funny movie, but it lacks the hilarity of, say, Roth's superb **Portnoy's Complaint** (the book, not the abominable movie). Perhaps the main reason is that, in contrast to Portnoy, there is scarcely a character in **Heartbreak** with whom anyone can identify.

The central character, Charles Grodin, is unfortunately so empty, banal, and phony that no one really can care what happens to him (and his fate is left hanging in a highly unsatisfactory "ending"). The obligatory Jewish and WASP wedding scenes are marvellous, but Jeannie Berlin's portrayal of a repellent slob is only countered by the beautiful Cybill Shepherd's portrayal of the WASP girl as a kooky but totally inarticulate dum-dum. As one viewer noted, we are in a heck of a fix when the only admirable character in the picture is the sensible but inarticulate Eddie Albert, playing Cybill's father.

The crucial point is that, to be truly memorable, satire must flow from a firmly held set of values, which the satirist indignantly sees are being violated by the society around him. This was true of such great satirists as Swift, Twain, Chesterton, Waugh, and Mencken. But alas, no positive values are discernible in Elaine May's work and so the satire ultimately sours.

The Day of the Jackal. dir. by Fred Zinnemann. With Edward Fox.

A meticulous and exciting portrayal of the best-selling adventure thriller by Frederick Forsyth, building the step-by-step saga of an unsuccessful, fictional attempt to assassinate Charles deGaulle. The movie is a literal, line-by-line account of the book, which works fine since the novel was virtually written as a screen-play. Unfortunately, Edward Fox is too laconic as the assassin, and therefore his motives and reactions are never touched on, much less explored. The major failure of the movie is the ending, where for some reason Zinnemann unaccountably and for the first time rushes through a situation which requires the continued build-up of suspense. A few more minutes devoted to the ending would have made for a great adventure film.

Sleuth. dir. by Joseph L. Mankiewicz. With Sir Laurence Olivier and Michael Caine.

The great murder-thriller play faithfully transcribed to the screen, probably because author Anthony Shaffer wrote the screenplay. The play-and-movie is an exciting series of gambits and double-crosses which the two principals pull on each other. Olivier does extremely well (fortunately, he does **not** over-act, as he sometimes tends to do); Caine, while certainly adequate, is not up to Keith Baxter's stage version. Still, a must for lovers of intelligent excitement on the screen.

Theater of Blood. With Vincent Price and Diana Rigg.

The horror-movie, when well done, is one of the cinema's great **genres**, though it never receives its due from the **avant-garde** critics. Except when corrupted by camp humor or phony psychology, the horror **genre** consists of an exciting plot with heroes pitted against villains (and **what** villains!) **Theater of Blood** is a virtuoso **tour de force** for the great Price, who here gets his chance to ham it up as an essential part of the plot itself. Scorned by the drama critics, Price, a Shakespearean actor, decides to bump off each of his critics in turn, using appropriate scenes from his Shakespearean repertoire. Price is ably assisted by his

daughter, Diana Rigg, one of England's finest actresses, who always projects a fascinating blend of beauty and high competence.

Live and Let Die. dir. by Guy Hamilton. With Roger Moore and Jane Seymour.

James Bond is back, and all's well with the movie world. The Ian Fleming novels, and for the most part the movies in the Bond series, were the quintessence of the Old Culture: marvellous plot, exciting action, hero vs. villains, spy plots, crisp dialogue and the frank enjoyment of bourgeois luxury and fascinating technological gadgets. Some of the Bond series, notably **From Russia With Love**, were great film classics: can we ever forget the introduction of that excellent actor Robert Shaw to the screen, or the delightful movie menace embodied by GPU agent Lotte Lenya ("Rosa Klebb") and her deadly boot?

For most of us, however, Sean Connery **is** James Bond, a superb blend of toughness and sophistication. But by the last few Bond movies, Connery was visibly aging, and this will not do for Bond. George Lazenby was a weak disaster for one Bond movie, and was quickly dropped. Who to replace the great Connery?

Live and Let Die introduces Roger Moore as the new Bond, fresh from the Saint series on television. Moore is properly suave and silky, but he is too slight and debonair to convey the toughness required for the part; Moore is adequate, but he is no Sean Connery. But, for all that, **Live and Let Die** is a great delight, one of the best of the Bond series: tough, witty, exciting, uncompromising. Guy Hamilton does a superb job of direction as we are vaulted from one danger and chase to another.

Another great thing about **Live and Let Die** is its unflinching integrity, its willingness to bring back the delightful old cliches of the action pictures of the 1930s and 40s, to follow the plot of the Fleming novel regardless of any temptation to soften the blow. For the villains are all Negro, and the plot postulates a giant Negro conspiracy covering taxi drivers in Harlem, funeral marchers in New Orleans, and voodoo priests in the Caribbean. It is particularly delightful that **Live and Let Die** brings back the old voodoo themes, with black natives menacing and torturing white captives and finally, after ritual dances, killing them with cobra bites. At the end of the film, Bond even rescues a white, quasi-virgin, ex-priestess of voodoo, from the dread cobra ritual. And the movie brings back the traditional scene of crocodile-alligator menace. Not only does the movie have the courage to follow the novel's racial theme, it is also of course unabashedly "sexiest", as, once again, James Bond converts female villains to the path of righteousness by the sheer **macho** power of his virility. And yet all this is done with such verve and style that there has not been a single yelp from black or women's lib groups. What a corking good movie!

Shaft in Africa. dir. by John Guillermin. With Richard Roundtree.

The original Shaft was one of the best and toughest of the delightful "blaxploitation" genre. The acting of star Richard Roundtree was such as to make him a most credible tough black private eye despite his lack of the usual physical attributes of the tough hero. Hated by the black intelligentsia for being a rugged **macho** type instead of the embodiment of "noble suffering," Shaft was the delight of black movie audiences. **Shaft in Harlem**, however, was a weak and flimsy sequel; the old black-white confrontation was gone, the movie had little to say, and the protest of black female groups had deprived Shaft of his original penchant for sleeping with white females.

But now, with **Shaft in Africa**, the Shaft series is back on the beam. Adding an international espionage flavor to the Harlem dude, the movie is the equal of the original **Shaft**. The action is swift and exciting, the dialogue is delightfully sassy, and the hero's amatory activities are again inter-as well as intra-racial.

Newport Jazz Festival in New York-1973.

Classic jazz is magnificently Old Culture, an exciting blend of European melody and harmony with African rhythm, developed first in New Orleans at the turn of the twentieth century. As such, it is as far from the mindless cacophony of modern acid rock as it is possible to get.

(Continued On Page 8)

395

Arts and Movies —

(Continued From Page 7)

Classic jazz always featured a small band, with drums, bass, banjo, or piano providing the rhythmic framework (and the latter the melody as well), the cornet or trumpet asserting the lead melody, the clarinet riding high above it and the trombone punching its way below. Classic jazz was creative improvisation around the lead melody, provided by the song being played. In classic jazz, risk, and challenge were high: for the challenge was for the musician to be creative and yet remain always within the framework of the written song, and also to blend in harmoniously with the other players. The danger is either to sink into non-creative banality on the one hand (as Chicago "Dixieland" jazz generally did to its New Orleans model), or, far worse, to abandon the melodic framework altogether and thereby get lost in musical solipsism and absurdity. Big-band **swing** of the late 1930's tended to do both, losing the creativity of improvisation while getting lost in mindless riffs and solo showboating for its own sake (e.g. the endless drum solos of Krupa and Rich.) Finally, at the end of World War II, jazz lost its melody and harmony, and even its rhythm, altogether, and degenerated into "bebop" and ultimately the nihilism of contemporary, or "modern" jazz.

Since great jazz requires great melodic songs at its base, the degeneration of jazz after World War II went hand in hand with the degeneration of the popular song, which finally descended into rock. Without the great melodies, how could jazz remain anchored to a melodic framework and thereby avoid descent into the anti-melodic abyss? Classic jazz, therefore, depended on playing the great tunes, either such marvellous hymns as "Closer Walk to Thee" as with the New Orleans bands, or the superb show tunes of Porter or Rodgers-and-Hart. Hence, the inspired plan of the 1973 Newport-in-New York Jazz Festival to put on "A Jazz Salute to American Song" (July 3) which forced the numerous participants to return, at least in part, to their melodic roots and play classic jazz once more.

The "Jazz Salute" program was, inevitably, a mixed bag. It began with an excellent Dixieland band, headed by the fine cornetist Jimmy McPartland, and ably seconded by Art Hodes on the piano and Vic Dickenson on trombone; playing Irving Berlin tunes, McPartland's band was particularly good in a rousing rendition of "Alexander's Ragtime Band." They were followed by the great jazz pianist, Earl "Fatha" Hines, looking remarkably young as he played notable tunes by Fats Waller, headed by Hines' excellent jazz singing (of which there was alas too little at the concert) of Waller's famous "Honeysuckle Rose." Hines is not my favorite jazz pianist, since he plays not at all lyrically but in great blocks of sound, but he was extremely interesting nevertheless. A special lagniappe was a duet played by Hines and the marvellously breathy tenor saxophonist Illinois Jacquet, of Eubie Blake's "Memories of You." (Blake, by the way, is a magnificent ragtime pianist and composer, still playing at the age of 90, and still far more powerful and forceful a ragtime and jazz pianist than several men one third his age put together.)

Cole Porter was terribly slighted at the concert, first disparaged stupidly by the promoter (who accused Porter of lacking "sentiment" — read cornball banality), and then raced through a few of his lesser tunes by Teddi King, a poor singer, and perfunctory piano by Ellis Larkins. Then came by far the worst set of the concert, in which the great Duke Ellington was butchered by the harsh screeching of R. Roland Kirk, who played the tenor sax, the monzella, and the clarinet simultaneously and badly; and by the tortured bellowing of Al Hibbler.

The evening was quickly set back on course, however, as the superb jazz pianist Barbara Carroll swung her way lightly and lyrically through such marvellous Harold Arlen tunes as "Come Rain or Come Shine," "As Long as I Live", and "Out of this World." She was well assisted by singer Sylvia Sims (but where O where was Lee Wiley, who even now with voice partly gone is far and away the best female jazz singer extant? For heartbreaking and magical jazz singing at its best, go back and listen to Lee Wiley's record, made twenty-odd years ago, singing Rodgers-and-Hart.) Miss Carroll is one of our finest jazz pianists, and it was good to see her return to the musical scene.

The famous jazz pianist Dave Brubeck then led his band through a rousing rendition of great songs by Jimmy Van Heusen, including "Someone in Love", "Rainy Day", and "It Could Happen to You." Except for a tendency to lose the melody at times, there was happily little trace of Brubeck's old modernism.

The Modern Jazz Quartet then played a set of Gershwin melodies. The MJQ was the best and most classical of early "bop" and "modern" jazz, and there they were constrained by the Gershwin melodic structure to play in their best manner of cool and sensuous elegance, a manner insured by the playing of the famous Milt Jackson on the vibes. It's too bad that the MJQ stuck to the corny Porgy and Bess, which is not really vintage Gershwin (where, for example, was the master's magnificent "But Not for Me"?) And they could well scrap their harshly percussive drummer.

A highly interesting set was the playing of the great Rodgers and Hart (in the days before Rodgers was corrupted by the banal, left-liberal sentimentality of Oscar Hammerstein II), particularly two of the greatest pop songs and show tunes ever written, "My Romance" and "It Never Entered My Mind." The band was excellent, headed by the creamy tenor sax of Stan Getz; unfortunately, the singer was Mabel Mercer, who has enjoyed cult status in the fashionable New York supper clubs, but has literally no voice at all, and simply talks her lines. Still, Getz and the band made the playing worthwhile.

The final set was an excellent one, with the delightful Marian McPartland at the piano and Gerry Mulligan playing a sinous and superb baritone sax, as they played Alec Wilder's "It's So Peaceful In the Country", "When We're Young", and "I'll Be Around When He's Gone." All in all, an important reminder that jazz needs great melodies to make it viable.   ◻

Subscription is $8.00 per year.

Libertarian Forum Associate subscription $15.00 or more.

The Libertarian Forum

Box 341   Madison Square Station
New York, New York 10010

Published Every Month. Subscription Rate: $8.00 Per Year

A Monthly Newsletter

THE Libertarian Forum

Joseph R. Peden, Publisher

Murray N. Rothbard, Editor

VOLUME V, NO. 8   AUGUST, 1973   US-ISSN0047-4517

OIL AND AMERICAN FOREIGN POLICY

By John Hagel III

In October 1972 the first Libertarian Scholars Conference was held at the Williams' Club in New York City. The sponsors of the conference planned to present as the main speakers a number of young libertarians who were still completing or had recently completed their doctoral studies. Comment was supplied by the older generation of libertarian scholars. The results were so successful that all present came away with renewed confidence that the libertarian movement was well on the way towards producing a splendid new generation of first-rate intellectual leaders. All agreed that the papers read ought to have a wider audience, but despite the efforts of the sponsors to secure financial support, publication of the excellent papers and discussion was not feasible. Under these circumstances, Libertarian Forum has undertaken to publish those papers which were in publishable form and which we deemed especially significant.

Among the young scholars we are proud to present to our readers is John Hagel III, a graduate of Wesleyan University, Middletown, Ct. and presently a graduate student at Oxford University. He began research on U. S. oil policy while a summer fellow at the Institute for Humane Studies, Menlo Park, Ca. and has continued his studies as a research intern with one of the largest oil corporations in the United States.

"All those who have studied the past from the standpoint of economics, and especially those who have studied economic geography, are aware that, from the material point of view, history is primarily the story of the increasing ability of man to reach and control energy." — Allan Nevins, 1959

"It is even probable that the supremacy of nations may be determined by the possession of available petroleum and its products." — President Calvin Coolidge

The current concern among American policy-makers over the so-called "energy crisis" serves to emphasize a continuing and more far-reaching objective of American foreign policy — the establishment of secure control over foreign sources of essential raw materials. American foreign policy planners have been acutely aware of the importance of guaranteeing reliable and relatively inexpensive supplies of key raw materials for domestic industry and, perhaps more importantly, for the military machine which ensures America's predominance as a world power. One of the most essential raw materials within the context of modern industrial society and the military is crude oil.

American foreign policy planners have perceived control over adequate supplies of foreign crude oil as an indispensable objective of American foreign policy since the early 1920's and, in order to achieve this goal, the government and the major international oil companies have developed a symbiotic relationship which neither now wish to terminate. Historically, the attainment of this objective has necessitated a long term diplomatic strategy designed to challenge the control of British oil interests over the massive crude oil reserves of the Middle East. This essay will cover the basic phases involved in this struggle but, due to limitations of space, this analysis will necessarily constitute only an outline of the subject.

By focusing the analysis on the importance of oil in the formulation of foreign policy, it is possible that this article unintentionally over-emphasizes its role. It must therefore be reiterated that the role of oil can be understood fully only when it is examined within the total context of international economic policy. Second, in the interests of brevity, this article will not fully explore the disagreements which frequently divide the oil industry and which often affect its relationship with the state. The reader must be cautioned against the simplistic view of either the oil industry or the state as monolithic entities but at the same time it should be stressed that the disagreements which do emerge occur within a broadly defined consensus that inherently limits the scope of debate and ultimately provides a basis for minimizing the disruptive impact of the internal divisions.

Perhaps one of the most historically significant events in the development of the oil industry involved the decision by the U. S. Navy to convert its ships to fuel oil. Although initially reluctant to embark upon such a course as a result of uncertainty about available oil supplies in the future, the U. S. Navy Fuel Oil Board issued a report recommending conversion to oil in 1904 and, within ten years, Secretary of the Navy Josephus Daniels had announced that all naval battleships and destroyers were burning fuel. While the Navy remained the largest military consumer of fuel oil, the Army also became increasingly dependent upon oil since much of its new weaponry, tanks and trucks relied on petroleum products.

At a time when the U. S. was aggressively expanding overseas and relying increasingly on the Navy for support in these ventures, policy planners soon expressed concern over the possibility of inadequate domestic crude oil reserves. Thus, even prior to World War I, military planners and government officials were acutely aware of the extent to which the military had become dependent on petroleum products and, in response, sought to develop arrangements which would ensure reliable and inexpensive supplies. Throughout this period, naval planners acted closely with leading civilian conservation spokesmen within the government to oppose the leasing of federal lands containing crude oil reserves. Secretary of the Navy Josephus Daniels and others within the Department of the Navy even went so far as to publicly favor the

(Continued On Page 2)

Oil And American Policy —

(Continued From Page 1)

nationalization of crude oil reserves and facilities to ensure security of supply for the Navy. [1]

British Oil Policies

The U. S. government was not alone in its recognition of the importance of crude oil supplies for military preparedness. Following the conversion of the British Royal Navy to fuel oil-burning ships, Winston Churchill announced in July 1913 that the British government had acquired a majority interest in the Anglo-Persian Oil Company which held highly productive crude oil concessions in the Middle East. In justifying this move to Parliament, Churchill declared that it would permit the government to "draw our supply, so far as possible, from sources under British control or British influence, and along those . . . ocean routes which the Navy can most easily protect." [1] It is not unlikely that American naval planners were carefully following British initiatives in this area and that their proposals for selective nationalization of petroleum reserves and facilities were at least partially inspired by the British model.

If the leading governments of Europe and the United States maintained any illusions regarding the importance of oil, they were quickly dispelled during World War I. France, in particular, experienced a dangerous shortage of petroleum supplies for its mechanized military. Within the U. S., World War I and the vastly greater demand for petroleum products provided a catalyst which transformed the relationship between the oil industry and the government. The government's primary concern became the necessity of maximizing crude oil production and the resolution of unprecedented logistical problems involved in supplying Allied armies, the American military and wartime industry.

Oil and War

To accomplish these tasks, the administration solicited the assistance of A. C. Bedford, chairman of the board of directors of Standard Oil of New Jersey. Throughout the wartime years and into the post-war period, Standard Oil of New Jersey emerged as the primary intermediary between the government and the oil industry. Under its guidance, an extensive institutional framework was established to maximize government-industry cooperation in every phase of petroleum operations and at all levels of management. The network of advisory committees which subsequently evolved was dominated by the large, integrated oil companies and permitted them to stabilize the industry under their control to a degree which had been impossible on the free market. Oil company profits during the immediate post-war period soared to unprecedented levels, often tripling or quadrupling in value.

The business executives who guided the wartime experiment in industry-government cooperation were highly enthusiastic regarding its results and emerged as leaders in the formation of the American Petroleum Institute. At the organizational meeting of the API, three primary objectives were articulated which served as the basis of industry-government cooperation throughout the inter-war years: (1) the rationalization and integration of all phases of domestic oil industry operations; (2) the promotion of greater cooperation within the industry and with the government and (3) development of foreign crude oil sources and markets. [3]

The aggressive search by American oil interests for foreign oil concessions originally became a major factor in American foreign policy during the inter-war period. From the very beginning, the domestic oil industry had been oriented toward the export market. By the end of the Civil War, the value of exported petroleum products had reached $15.7 million and the oil industry ranked sixth in the U. S. export trade. During the latter half of the eighteenth century, net exports of crude oil and petroleum products were equivalent to at least 1/3 of domestic crude production and at times exceeded 3/4 of domestic production. [4] However, the role of the United States as the world's largest crude oil producer during this period had contributed to a complacent attitude within the domestic industry regarding the necessity for exploration and production outside the United States. This attitude ultimately changed as U. S. crude

oil production declined from 98.4% of the world total in 1860 to 42.7% in 1900. [5]

The major petroleum shortages experienced within the U. S. immediately following World War I precipitated the decision by industry leaders and government officials to seek concessions abroad. In 1919, the shortage of crude oil and consequent spiraling of prices prompted the Secretary of the Navy to revive earlier proposals for the nationalization of petroleum resources and to order officers to seize necessary fuel supplies if an acceptable price was not forthcoming. [6] The API denounced the commandeering policies of the Navy and, emphasizing the inadequacy of domestic oil reserves, proposed that the government assist the oil companies in obtaining foreign producing concessions as a long-term solution to the shortage of crude oil.

Once again, Standard Oil of New Jersey emerged in the vanguard of the industry following a major reorganization within the company. None of the members of Nersey's board of directors had been involved in production and most were too old to provide the necessary enthusiasm for a major new venture. However, the badly-needed impetus was provided by a rising young executive, Walter Teagle, who had been placed in charge of the company's foreign operations. One of Teagle's aides summarized the new outlook which guided the company's development during the following years:

> It appears to me that the future of the Standard Oil Company, particularly the New Jersey company, lies outside the United States, rather than in it. This is due primarily to the fact that the New Jersey's company's business is largely outside the United States, its principal refineries are on tidewater, and it is also true that the trust laws of the United States and their present trend seems to preclude continued expansion in this country. [7]

The importance which the American government attached to the overseas ventures of American oil companies is evident in the following memorandum of August 16, 1919 distributed by the State Department to all its personnel abroad:

> The vital importance of securing adequate supplies of mineral oil both for present and future needs of the United States has been forcibly brought to the attention of the Department. The development of proven fields and exploration of new areas is being aggressively conducted in many parts of the world by nationals of various countries, and concessions for mineral oil rights are being actively sought . . .
> You are . . . instructed to lend all legitimate aid to reliable and responsible United States citizens or interests which are seeking mineral oil concessions or rights. [8]

The U. S. entered into the world arena at a relatively late date, discovering that British, French and Dutch oil interests controlled the known reserves overseas and operated in close cooperation with their home governments in their search for exploration concessions. British oil interests, represented primarily by the Anglo-Persian Oil Company (now British Petroleum) and the Royal Dutch-Shell Oil Company, constituted the most formidable rival and their optimism was reflected in a statement by Sir Edward MacKay Edgar, a British petroleum banker, that

> The British position is impregnable. All the known oil fields, all the likely or probable oil fields, outside the United States itself, are in British hands or under British management or control, or financed by British capital. [9]

Seeking to gain entry for U. S. oil companies into areas already dominated by European oil interests, Secretary of State Charles Evans Hughes, the central architect of American foreign oil policy and later counsel for Standard Oil of New Jersey, vigorously championed the Open Door policy. The diplomatic offensive organized by the State Department on behalf of American oil interests focused on three major producing areas abroad — Latin America, the Dutch East Indies and the Middle East. Confronted by strongly entrenched oil interests and more

(Continued On Page 3)

Oil And American Policy —

(Continued From Page 2)

experienced European diplomats, the performance of the State Department left much to be desired, although it did experience some success in promoting the entry of U. S. oil companies in Latin America, particularly Colombia and Venezuela. The complicated diplomatic intrigues accompanying U. S. and British competition for producing concessions in Mexico, however, provide ample evidence regarding the difficulties involved in challenging the predominant British position even directly across the border. [10]

In the Dutch East Indies, the Dutch government steadfastly refused to give American oil interests access to the extremely rich Djambi fields, despite repeated efforts by Secretary of State Hughes to invoke the Open Door policy. In its response to Hughes' protests, the Dutch government cited the difficulties that Royal Dutch-Shell had experienced in obtaining oil leases in the United States as evidence of the double standard underlying the American protests.

The State Department experienced its greatest frustration in its efforts to gain entry into the major oil fields of the Middle East. Within weeks after the cessation of hostilities in this area, the British government denied access to all foreign companies seeking permission to explore and drill in the Palestine and Mesopotamia regions. The British further consolidated their position in this region by negotiating the San Remo Agreement in April 1920 with the French, effectively establishing a detente between the two major European oil interests. Overtly violating the Open Door principle, the Agreement granted the French a 25% share in the British-dominated Turkish Petroleum Company and sought to exclude the nationals from any other countries from engaging in petroleum operations within the Balkans and Near East. The U. S. State Department refused to acknowledge the legality of this arrangement but failed to obtain any concessions from either France or Great Britain.

Although State Department protests over British policies on the Middle East did not produce any immediate results, they did set the stage for an eventual solution to the competition between British and American oil interests. One of the most instrumental personalities in arranging this solution proved to be Calouste Gulbenkian, an Armenian oil magnate with a 5% interest in the Turkish Petroleum Company. Gulbenkian argued vigorously with the British Foreign Office for a more farsighted policy:

> Personally from the inception of the American crisis, I had held the opinion, taking the broader view, that it was sounder and higher policy to admit the Americans into the Turkish Petroleum Company, instead of letting them loose to compete in Iraq for concessions when in reality the company had a very weak grip there. The oil groups are always tempted to seize what they see before them without looking ahead or following broader policies of collaboration. [11]

Gulbenkian's arguments were persuasive and the British companies in the Turkish Petroleum Company initiated discussions with a consortium of American oil companies which culminated in an agreement in 1925 to grant the American consortium a share of the Turkish Petroleum Company. Under the leadership of Walter Teagle of Jersey Standard, the American consortium insisted upon and received an equal share with the three other principal participants (Shell, Anglo-Persian and the French Compagnie Francaise des Petroles).

The agreement effectively integrated the American oil companies into an arrangement for the production of crude oil in the Middle East which preserved British dominance, yet avoided competition for concession agreements between American and British oil interests. It is particularly crucial because it established the model for a series of wide-reaching agreements among the major international oil companies during the late 1920's that represent the first systematic effort to stabilize the oil industry on an international level and to eliminate the rivalry between American and British oil interests. Before considering these agreements, however, it is important to briefly outline the reason for this sudden reversal of previous trends within the international oil industry.

Control of Markets

Within the United States, a fundamental shift in orientation had

occurred within the oil industry and government as a result of discoveries of extensive crude oil reserves both domestically and in foreign producing areas during the mid-1920's. As increasingly large quantities of oil were brought into the market, the price index for petroleum products, which had been steadily rising over the previous decade, began to decline precipitously. The major oil companies sought to limit production through a variety of voluntary arrangements but, when it became evident that these had failed, the companies turned to the state to enforce compulsory pro-rationing schemes designed to stabilize prices by limiting the production of oil.

While this effort succeeded on a national level, the oil industry confronted rapidly expanding production from foreign concessions which seriously weakened the international price structure. In the absence of a world government capable of enforcing a global pro-rationing plan, the major international oil companies, representing both British and American interests, negotiated a system of voluntary agreements in 1928 which would stabilize the market. The Red Line Agreement in 1928 provided a basis for the controlled exploration and development of the massive oil fields believed to exist in the Middle East since it pledged the participants in the Turkish Petroleum Company consortium not to engage in oil exploration or production within the borders of the former Ottoman Empire without first consulting and obtaining the approval of all the other participants. A parallel agreement, known as the Achnacarry or "As Is" Agreement, contained provisions for preserving the existing shares of the international market held by the major oil companies and the pooling of refining and marketing facilities. One oil economist provided a perceptive description of the agreements which were formulated in 1928:

> The international oil companies regarded the stabilization of international markets as an essential auxiliary to the domestic stabilization program they engineered with the help of both state and federal governments during the late 1920's and in the 1930's . . . In 1928, oilmen took steps to translate their common concern about price instability in international oil markets into a program of action . . . in the As Is Agreement we find the first evidence of a conspiratorial arrangement to perpetuate a pricing system that was breaking down under the impact of surplus world production and increasing competition. [12]

These agreements in 1928 provided the framework for the evolution of the international petroleum industry during the period preceding World War II, representing a temporary detente among the leading American, British and European oil interests. However, World War II, the substantial weakening of British imperial hegemony and the systematic challenge launched by American foreign policy planners to replace Britain as the predominant state-capitalist power in the Western world, ultimately doomed the international detente prevailing within the oil industry. On a more immediate level, the advent of World War II once again graphically demonstrated the indispensable role of oil in modern warfare. Its importance in the strategic thinking of the American government is illustrated in the statement by Charles Rayner, the Petroleum Advisor to the Department of State, that "World War II has been and is a war based on oil." [13] While British and American oil interests cooperated closely during the war in supplying Allied war needs, renewed friction became evident in both Saudi Arabia and Iran, two of the major oil producing countries in the Middle East. [14]

American Hegemony

American foreign policy planners anticipated that the war would seriously weaken the British international position and prepared a comprehensive strategy designed to expand and consolidate the American position in the Middle East, believed to contain the highest concentration of crude oil reserves in the world and traditionally a British and French sphere of influence. John D. Lotfus, a prominent State Department official in 1945 prepared a memorandum entitled "Petroleum in International Relations" which outlined the foreign policy objectives of the American government:

> Another major category of problems concerns the support

(Continued On Page 4)

Oil And American Policy —

(Continued From Page 3)

given by the Department on behalf of the United States government to American nationals seeking to obtain or to retain rights to engage in petroleum development, transportation and processing abroad. This is the traditional function of the Department with respect to petroleum. It has continued to be significant, though of temporarily diminished importance, during the war period. As normal conditions return this function will come to be of very great importance . . . . there are . . . areas where after the war there is a genuine possibility of securing an amelioration of the unfavorable discriminatory conditions under which American nationals were able to obtain rights before the war. [15]

By 1947, an interdepartmental committee from the State, Interior, Commerce, Army and Navy Departments had prepared a confidential report outlining the strategy of the American government. The fundamental objective of American policy, according to this report, should be to ''seek the removal or modification of existent barriers (legal, contractual or otherwise) to the expansion of American foreign oil operations and facilitate the entry or re-entry of private foreing capital into countries where the absence of such capital inhibits oil development.'' [16] To implement and coordinate this policy, the State Department designated at least thirteen petroleum officers and attaches to key positions in American embassies around the world. Gabriel Kolko has, with characteristic insight, summarized the strategic importance of the Middle East which

> encompassed all the critical challenges to American goals and power after World War II. There was pre-eminently, the question of Britain's future in the region, and the unmistakable United States intention to circumscribe it in some fundamental fashion to re-allocate Western influence in the area. [17]

The formal end of the detente among oil interests in the Middle East occurred with the announcement of Jersey Standard in January 1946 that it had repudiated the Red Line Agreement of 1928. Standard Oil of New Jersey had sought to join the Arabian-American Oil Company producing consortium in Saudi Arabia and, upon encountering the opposition of its British and French partners in the Red Line Agreement, consulted with, and received the encouragement of, the State Department in its decision to dis-associate from the Agreement. Once again, Standard Oil of New Jersey performed a vital role as an intermediary between the American oil industry and the U. S. government, and other American participants in the Red Line Agreement soon announced their own decision to withdraw from the Agreement.

This agreement had represented the continued hegemony of British and European oil interests within the Middle East and, in the fundamentally new circumstances following the war, American oil interests no longer felt it necessary to accept the secondary role which had been assigned to them. In marked contrast to the diplomatic offensive launched by the U. S. State Department on behalf of American oil interests in the early 1920's, however, this new offensive was not motivated by an urgent search for crude oil supplies to supplement inadequate domestic reserves. Instead, American foreign policy planners recognized the importance of controlling the Middle East oil reserves as one element in their strategy to weaken Britain's international position and, in a more long-range perspective, sought to ensure secure supplies of crude oil and petroleum products for its allies in Western Europe.

The CIA and Iranian Oil

Following the immediate post-war period, the extensive Anglo-Persian concession in Iran, covering some of the most prolific oil fields in the world, represented the one area in the Middle East which remained under the exclusive control of British oil interests. The opportunity for U. S. oil interests to penetrate this last bastion of British supremacy arose when concession negotiations between the Anglo-Persian Oil Company and the Iranian government stalled in 1951 and Iran, under the leadership of

Mohammed Mossadegh, announced the nationalization of all oil operations in the country. Most politically conscious Americans are aware of the role of the CIA in the overthrow of the Mossadegh government and installation of a new government more amenable to the oil companies. Yet the CIA coup proved to be merely the final act of a far more complicated situation, involving extensive preliminary negotiations between American oil interests and the Anglo-Persian Oil Company.

While these negotiations proceeded, the American government adopted a carefully neutral position in the nationalization controversy, advising the British to reconcile themselves to the loss of their assets in Iran. This attitude prompted widespread suspicion within the British Foreign Office that the Americans were maneuvering to replace the British oil interests in Iran. However, once the negotiators had produced an agreement which granted the American oil interests a 40% share in the Iranian producing concession, the CIA dispatched Kermit Roosevelt, a grandson of President Theodore Roosevelt, to Iran to coordinate preparations for the coup. The coup succeeded, replacing Mossadegh with General Fazlollah Zahedi and negotiations were soon announced to establish the consortium of oil companies which would resume producing operations in the country. Several years later, Kermit Roosevelt left the CIA and joined Gulf Oil Company, one of the participants in the Iranian consortium, as government relations director and then, in 1960, as a vice-president. [18]

The Iranian nationalization represented the final step in the consolidation of the position of United States oil interests in the Middle East and, ultimately, in the world. The reversal of roles between American and British oil interests in this area is demonstrated by estimates of the crude oil reserves in the Middle East controlled by each group. In 1940, British interests controlled an estimated 72% of total crude oil reserves in the Middle East while American interests controlled a relatively minor 9.8%. In 1967, on the other hand, Britain's share of the total had declined to 29.3% while American-controlled reserves had risen to 58.6%. [19]

Oil Policies Since 1950

This highly schematic history of the rivalry between British and American interests within the international petroleum industry provides a useful background for understanding the situation within the industry during the past few decades. However, developments in the period since 1950 have had significant implications for the future position of U. S. oil interests abroad and the American government is now in the process of formulating a comprehensive energy policy in response to these developments. To place these changes within the proper context it is necessary first to consider two aspects of the contemporary oil industry: the economic significance of foreign investment in petroleum facilities by U. S. companies and the strategic military significance of foreign crude oil reserves.

Briefly summarized, the international oil companies represent the most important single concentration of economic power in the U. S. The five major American international oil companies possess total combined assets of $40 billion, or 20% of the total assets of the 100 largest U. S. corporations. Overseas investments by American oil companies represent 30% of the total book value of American foreign direct investments and 40% of total U. S. investment in the developing countries. Moreover, this petroleum investment is highly profitable, representing 60% of total U. S. earnings in developing nations.

The profitability of petroleum investment explains its traditionally significant role in cushioning the unfavorable balance of payments experienced by the U. S. Michael Tanzer has estimated that, without the overseas affiliates of American oil companies, the balance of payments deficit of $2.8 billion in 1964 would have been 25% greater. [20] Most importantly, the contribution of the international oil companies to the balance of payments accounts occurs almost exclusively as a consequence of direct investments in producing operations.

Thus, while the U. S. remains the largest producer of oil in the world and, as a consequence, the developed nation least dependent on imports of foreign crude oil, foreign investments by American oil companies in crude oil production have acquired great economic significance, both in terms of profitability and contribution to an unfavorable balance of payments. Nor can the U. S. remain complacent regarding its leadership among oil producers. The geography of oil has shifted dramatically over the past fifteen years and future trends indicate increasing American

(Continued On Page 5)

Oil And American Policy —

(Continued From Page 4)

dependence on foreign imports of crude oil. During the past decade, the U. S. share of world production of crude oil declined from 38% to 24% while the share of Africa and the Middle East rose from 23% to 40% over the same period. Even today, America's production rate can only be sustained as a consequence of an elaborate system of subsidies and tax credits, further enforced by a quota system limiting foreign imports.

Currently, approximately 22% of the petroleum consumed in the United States originates outside the country. Virtually all oil imported into the U. S. is produced either in Venezuela or Canada; the U. S. relies only minimally on Middle Eastern oil. Nevertheless, Western Europe and Japan are almost entirely dependent on the Middle East and North Africa for their supplies of crude oil. In 1968, this area supplied 90% of the oil consumed in Japan, 70% of the oil consumed in Great Britain, 80% in France, 90% in West Germany and 95% in Italy. [21]

A report on foreign economic policy by the Rockefeller Brothers Fund discussed the implications of this situation:

> Europe's economic security today depends on two indispensable factors: (1) her own intellectual and technical vitality and economic enterprise; and (2) an international structure which will enable Europe to have access to foreign markets on fair terms and adequate supplies of materials, if Europe can offer reasonable value in return for them.
>
> Nevertheless, the economic situation of the industrialized nations remains precarious. If Asia, Middle Eastern and African nationalism, exploited by the Soviety bloc, becomes a destructive force, European supplies of oil and other essential raw materials may be jeapordized. [22]

Walt Whitman Rostow, in testimony before the Joint Congressional Committee outlined the broader context:

> The location, natural resources, and populations of the underdeveloped areas are such that, should they become attached to the Communist bloc, the United States would become the second power in the world . . . Indirectly, the evolution of the underdeveloped areas is likely to determine the fate of Western Europe and Japan and, therefore, the effectiveness of those industrialized regions in the free world alliance we are committed to lead. If the underdeveloped areas fall under Communist domination, or if they move to fixed hostility to the West, the economic and military strength of Western Europe and Japan will be diminished, the British Commonwealth as it is now organized will disintegrate, and the Atlantic world will become, at best, an awkward alliance, incapable of exercising effective influence outside a limited orbit, with the balance of the world's power lost to it. In short, our military security and our way of life as well as the fate of Western Europe and Japan are at stake in the evolution of the underdeveloped areas. [23]

One of the basic sources of American influence in the post-1945 period has been its indispensable role in ensuring adequate and reliable supplies of crude oil to its allies. The importance of this role has been most clearly demonstrated during periods of international crisis in which the flow of crude oil from the Middle East has been disrupted, i.e. the Suez Canal crisis of 1956 and the Six Day War in 1967. Thus, the U. S., at least indirectly, has a vital strategic interest in controlling the crude oil reserves located in the Middle East and North Africa.

Moreover, in studying the gross figures of crude oil imports to the U. S., it is possible to seriously underestimate the dependence of the American military on foreign crude oil sources. According to recent estimates, 53.2% of the total bulk fuel purchased by the military in 1968 came from foreign supplies. [24] Even more importantly, however, both NATO and the U. S. military forces in Southeast Asia are almost exclusively dependent on crude oil supplies from the Middle East. [25] These elementary facts are of major concern to American foreign policy planners as indicated by the following observation by Carl Vansant, an energy consultant for the *Department of the Navy*:

> From a military point of view, it is important that the energy supplies for military forces be designed for, and maintained in, a secure posture. It is even more important, however, that national systems for energy supply be built on a secure foundation of political, technical and economic policy; for, in fact, it is the civil structure of energy systems that underlies and braces strategic security. [26]

Foreign crude oil reserves, and specifically those located in the Middle East, have therefore acquired direct strategic importance for American policy-makers in the past decade.

Future Needs

Once the full importance of foreign crude oil reserves for American economic and strategic strength has been recognized, it is possible to appreciate more clearly the implications of a number of current developments in the international oil industry. First, the large international oil companies, for a variety of reasons, have never been able to revive the proto-cartel arrangements which had broken down in the immediate post-World War II period. In fact, the past two decades have produced an unprecedented degree of competition within the international oil industry. This competition has dramatically weakened the position of the companies in their negotiations for concessions and tax agreements from the producing countries. The producing countries have further strengthened their own position by establishing the Organization of Petroleum Exporting Countries (OPEC) which has successfully negotiated significant increases in tax rates and recently initiated a series of negotiations designed to establish government participation in all producing companies operating in OPEC countries. These developments have considerably reduced the profits previously received by the international oil companies from their producing operations and, in the longer run, raise the very likely possibility of total nationalization of producing operations by the OPEC governments.

A number of fundamental changes in the international oil industry can be reasonably projected as a consequence of these recent developments. Most immediately, the international oil companies will seek to raise prices on petroleum products to cushion the impact on their accounts of the higher production taxes. These price rises, and growing evidence of the weakness of the international oil companies in negotiations with OPEC, will further accelerate efforts by the major oil consuming countries in Western Europe and Japan to expand the operations of their own state-owned oil companies and, most importantly, to challenge the control over Middle Eastern crude oil reserves by American oil interests.

This trend must be understood within the broader context of the systematic challenge presented by these countries to America's financial and economic position in the non-Communist world. European state-owned oil companies such as the French Compagnie Francaise des Petroles, the Italian Ente Nazionale Idrocarburi (ENI), the German Deminex and the Spanish Hispanoil have been increasingly aggressive in their competition with the established Anglo-Saxon oil companies for producing concessions in the Middle East. Discussions have also been initiated among the consuming governments of Western Europe and Japan regarding the possible formation of an Organization of Petroleum Importing Countries (OPIC) to by-pass the American and British international oil companies and enter directly into multilateral trade negotiations for crude oil from OPEC.

The short term strategy which the American government and the major oil companies will pursue in response to these recent developments will probably include a variety of elements. It is unlikely, barring a major crisis, that the United States will resort to direct intervention as a means for preserving the position of the American oil interests in the Middle East or other producing areas. Instead, emphasis will be placed on the development of formal partnerships between the oil companies and the host governments in the producing phase of the industry to forestall outright nationalization. Cooperation among the oil companies and coordination with the American government will receive an even higher priority than has been the case previously, as illustrated by the recent suspension of anti-trust laws to enable the oil companies to

(Continued On Page 6)

Oil And American Policy —

(Continued From Page 5)

present a united bargaining team in negotiations with OPEC.

On a more long-term basis, fundamental transformations are envisaged which will result in an even closer relationship between the oil industry and the government in the U. S. An intensive and extensive search for additional crude oil reserves, preferably in politically "safe" areas has already been initiated and, increasingly, the search will focus on subsea exploration and production. While the discovery of crude oil reserves under the jurisdiction of hospitable governments would be optimal, the primary aim is to maximize the number of sources of crude oil to ensure against the disruptive effects which might be produced if one or several of the sources were simultaneously rendered inaccessible to American oil interests. It is only within this context that the significance of the Alaskan North Share discoveries and British North Sea exploration, and even the high level negotiations currently in process to seek American participation in the development of both Russian Siberian and Chinese off-shore oil reserves can be fully appreciated.

On another level, the pressures to minimize American dependence of foreign crude oil reserves are already resulting in the formulation of a comprehensive energy policy by the United States government which will avoid the narrow focus on petroleum as the primary energy source. The most tangible consequence of this new orientation will be the development of extensive, federally subsidized research and development programs by the oil companies to explore the potential of alternative energy sources. The major international oil companies have already quietly diversified into ownership of coal reserves, oil shale reserves and the development of nuclear technology. [27]

One further consequence of recent developments will be the conscious rationalization of energy consumption in the United States to eliminate unnecessary waste. The automobile represents the most inefficient means of surface transportation, in terms of energy consumption, currently in use, and the next few decades will witness the development of systematic, federally subsidized mass transit programs, not because of sudden moral indignation over the ecological damage caused by the automobile, but because of the desire to limit accelerating energy consumption in the U. S.

In summary, therefore, recent developments in the oil industry are likely to result in a much higher degree of sustained interaction between the international oil companies and the American government than the U. S. has ever before experienced. As Michael Tanzer, an oil economist, has pointed out:

> the connection between the government and the international oil companies in the U. S. has generally never been as open nor as close as in Great Britain or France. This is partly because the existence of a large indigenous oil sector has historically made the role of international oil less crucial and also has generated conflicting interests between independent domestic oil companies and the internationals. [28]

While this observation may overlook the assistance received by American oil companies in their effort to challenge British control of the Middle East crude oil reserves, it does focus attention on a crucial advantage historically enjoyed by the United States. However, recent trends demonstrate the increasing dependence of the United States, and particularly the American military, upon crude oil reserves, reserves which have become dangerously concentrated in the politically unstable Middle East. To respond to these developments, the symbiotic relationship which has evolved between the oil industry and the government will become even more pronounced and, more than ever, this relationship will become one of mutual dependence.

Footnotes

[1] Gerald Nash, United States Oil Policy, 1890-1964, University of Pittsburgh Press (Pittsburgh, 1968), pp. 18-19. For further details on naval petroleum policy, see John A. DeNovo, "Petroleum and the U. S. Navy Before World War I", Mississippi Valley Historical Review, Vol. XLI, March 1955.

101 Ways To Promote Libertarian Ideas

1. Be open, friendly and courteous in presenting your ideas. Avoid any taint of fanaticism or infallibility. Just because other people disagree with you, don't put them down as stupid or evil. Libertarian ideas are radical and shocking when first encountered. It takes most people some time to digest them.
2. Is a friend studying a specific subject — political science, economics, psychology? Recommend a book giving a libertarian perspective on

(Continued On Page 7)

[2] Quoted in Richard O'Connor, The Oil Barons, Little, Brown and Company (Boston, 1971), p. 189.

[3] An excellent historical account of this period in the domestic oil industry is available in Gerald Nash, United States Oil Policy, 1890-1964, op. cit., p. 28. Also, Murray Rothbard has written a highly informative article on the close cooperation which evolved between business interests and the government during World War I in Ronald Radosh and Murray Rothbard, eds., A New History of Leviathan, E. P. Dutton & Co. (New York, 1972).

[4] Schurr, Netschert, et. al., Energy in the American Economy, 1850-1975, Johns Hopkins University Press (Baltimore, 1960), p. 100.

[5] Statistics from Petroleum Facts and Figures, 9th edition, 1950.

[6] Gerald Nash, United States Oil Policy, 1890-1964, op. cit., pp. 44-46.

[7] Quoted in Harvey O'Connor, World Crisis in Oil, Monthly Review Press (New York, 1962), p. 66.

[8] Quoted in ibid., pp. 71-72.

[9] Quoted in Ludwell Denny, We Fight for Oil, Alfred A. Knopf (New York, 1928), p. 18.

[10] For details regarding this episode see Ludwell Denny, We Fight for Oil, op. cit., pp. 45-95 and also for general background, see Peter Calvert, The Mexican Revolution, 1910-1914, Cambridge University Press (Cambridge, 1968).

[11] Quoted in Richard O'Connor, The Oil Barons, op. cit., p. 232.

[12] George W. Stocking, Middle East Oil: A Study in Political and Economic Controversy, Vanderbilt University Press (Nashville, 1970), pp. 396-397.

[13] Quoted in Richard J. Barnet, Roots of War, Atheneum (New York, 1972), p. 201.

[14] For further details, see Gabriel Kolko's excellent discussion of the wartime tensions which developed over Middle Eastern oil reserves in The Politics of War, Random House (New York, 1968), pp. 294-313.

[15] Quoted in Richard J. Barnet, Roots of War, op. cit., p. 201.

[16] Quoted in Joyce and Gabriel Kolko, The Limits of Power, Harper and Row (New York, 1972), p. 415.

[17] Ibid., p. 403.

[18] A highly perceptive muck-raking account of this episode is presented in Richard O'Connor, The Oil Barons, op. cit., pp. 366-382.

[19] Statistics presented in Harry Magdoff, The Age of Imperialism, Modern Reader Paperbacks (New York, 1969), p. 43.

[20] These statistics are presented in an excellent analysis of the economic significance of foreign petroleum investments by Michael Tanzer, The Political Economy of International Oil and the Underdeveloped Countries, Beacon Press (Boston, 1969), pp. 41-49.

[21] Business Week, September 26, 1970, p. 24.

[22] Quoted in Harry Magdoff, The Age of Imperialism, op. cit., p. 53.

[23] Quoted in ibid., p. 55.

[24] Carl Vansant, Strategic Energy Supply and National Security, Praeger (New York, 1971), p. 51.

[25] Business Week, September 26, 1970, p. 24.

[26] Carl Vansant, Strategic Energy Supply and National Security, op. cit., p. 83.

[27] Gulf Oil Company has perhaps led in efforts to diversify out of petroleum operations and a recent account of their strategy is available in The Economist, June 10, 1972, pp. 68-69. It is interesting to note that, of the major international oil companies, Gulf Oil is one of the most dependent on Middle Eastern crude oil reserves.

[28] Michael Tanzer, The Political Economy of International Oil and the Underdeveloped Countries, op. cit., p. 50.

Ways To Promote Lib. Ideas —

(Continued From Page 6)

3. If you have read a favorable review of a libertarian book, especially if in a professional journal, have copies xeroxed and distribute them to friends who might be interested in the review professionally.

4. Write a letter a week to some newspaper giving a libertarian viewpoint on some public issue. It will usually be published if short, topical and clearly not "cranky". Keep it practical and to the point.

5. College libraries usually respond to faculty requests for new acquisitions. Regularly request libertarian titles, if you are on the faculty, or ask a friendly faculty member to do so, if you are a student.

6. Have you been assigned a term paper? Choose a topic that will allow you to read in libertarian sources, and develop a libertarian analysis of the topic.

7. Many libertarian books are now available in paperback editions. Give your local bookstore a list of titles and suggest he stock them. To encourage him, give him the publisher's catalogue.

8. Remember Libertarians don't have **all** the answers! You can learn by listening to others.

9. Most colleges have literary societies. If so inclined, join the society. You can then participate in its discussions, play a role in selecting guest speakers, and even contribute poems, short stories and critical reviews to its journal. Literary people are usually very sensitive to the need for true liberty and are a good audience for libertarian ideas.

10. In many colleges, the newspaper is not fully utilized by the student body. Editors are usually short of copy and welcome contributions of material. Send a review of your favorite libertarian book or movie or play. Do an analysis of some local problem from a libertarian perspective. Better yet, join the staff. You are bound to be promoted over a four year period.

11. Have you found a few sympathetic souls who are interested in further study of libertarian ideas? Form a campus study club. Work up a guest speakers' program and apply for student activity funds.

12. Have you ever recommended a book to your teacher? Why not? He doesn't hesitate to recommend them to you! Tell him you would like to discuss it with him after he has read it. Flattery will get you everywhere!

13. The trustees of most colleges usually read the student newspaper. Any strongly worded criticism is likely to catch their attention — and cause questions to be asked. If the economics department excludes free-market texts from its reading lists, ask why? Remember the national furor created in the Fifties by Bill Buckley's **God and Man at Yale?**

14. A libertarian is not a book burner or witch hunter. But he is certainly entitled to know why a political science department ignores individualist anarchism in courses on political theory. Or Austrian economics in courses on economic theory. Or the contributions of Tucker, Warren, Spooner, Nock and Chodorov to American intellectual history. A letter of inquiry to the professor or department involved could change things.

15. Does your student government have a referendum procedure? Make imaginative use of it to spread libertarian ideas. Call for the abolition of the ROTC or compulsory student activity fees.

16. Is your college bookstore a local monopoly with high monopolistic prices? Open up a student cooperative bookstore; or sponsor a free-market used book exchange. And explain why you are doing it!

17. Is your college supposedly a "private institution"? Check it out. The likelihood is that it enjoys some government privilege or subsidy. And what price does it pay for this governmental support? Does it have its books audited by the State? Is it required to submit reports to the HEW on the number of women and ethnic minority members on its faculty? Do its courses and readings have to be submitted for State inspection? Are its records, or your personal records, open to inspection by government agencies? Prepare a report on the parameters of "freedom" at your college or university.

18. Who rules your university? Prepare a detailed report on the trustees and officers of your university. The corporate, governmental and personal relationships are frequently very interesting. At one local center of learning that we know, two trustees were forced to resign when a rather intimate business and personal relationship between

them, the local sheriff and the "Mafia" was revealed as part of a student researched obituary notice in the campus paper. Elsewhere the trustees were involved in conflicts of interest in awarding construction contracts.

19. Do you know what is college policy, and practice, regarding student academic and medical records? Who has access, what is recorded, how long are the records kept? This is especially important if medical or psychological records are kept on students, as rather damaging information may appear in government records at a later time. Some schools in the Sixties kept records of campus political activities also. A civil libertarian might attract support by focusing on this issue.

20. Prepare alternate reading lists for required courses. Distribute them to all "captive" audiences.

21. Student "leaders" are frequently power freaks and even outright grafters. Quietly keep track of their votes, attendance at official meetings, and the number and costs of "official excursions". A voter profile of the "Big Men" on campus might provide some laughs at the next student election.

22. Buy a subscription to your favorite libertarian journal and give a free subscription as a gift to your local library.

23. Buy and display libertarian posters. They are always an excellent way to start a political conversation.

24. Get yourself a libertarian calendar and celebrate libertarian anniversaries. Hold a birthday party for Max Stirner (Oct. 25) or Ludwig von Mises (Sept. 29) and give your guests some literature by the guest of honor. On election eve, Nov. 5, 1973, Britons will be celebrating Guy Fawkes failure to blow up Parliament in 1606. We could at least honor him for trying! Or what about a beer blast on Dec. 5 — the day Prohibition ended in 1933. On Dec. 16, 1973 we ought to celebrate the 200th anniversary of the Boston Tea Party.

25. Does your college have a film society? If so, ask them to show films which would serve as a stimulus for discussion of libertarian viewpoints. If not, why don't you form a film group and use it for libertarian purposes.

26. Many colleges have student-run lecture series, often with large sums to finance guests speakers. Try to get involved with the speakers bureau and promote the invitation of a libertarian guest lecturer.

27. If a guest lecturer is distinctly anti-libertarian, a socialist or behavioralist, for instance, study his published opinions beforehand, and prepare questions for him that will reveal the implications of his errors to the audience.

28. Try to establish a libertarian literature table or reading room on campus or nearby. Even if a student is not immediately receptive to your ideas, you will have made a personal contact that could in time mature into further conversation and thought.

29. Every season there is some issue that seems to arise and receive wide public discussion — the environmental crisis, the crisis of the family, crime, drugs, Watergate. Plan a public debate on the issue, with a libertarian among the speakers, and libertarian pamphlets available for distribution. Have a series of discussions. Many young people were initially attracted to libertarian ideas by a wide distribution of our ideas on the draft.

(To Be Continued)

News Notes

By Joseph R. Peden

In 1972 members of the Jewish Defense League planted a bomb in the New York offices of Sol Hurok, the impresario who has arranged for the performances of the Bolshoi Ballet and other Soviet cultural groups in the U. S. A secretary was killed. Five men were arrested and indicted for the fatal bombing. The Second Circuit of the U. S. Court of Appeals has now dismissed the case against two of the defendants on the ground that Attorney-General Mitchell had unlawfully tapped the telephones of the JDL and later destroyed the tapes. This was in specific violation of federal statutes. Moreover it was revealed that one of the defendants who participated in the bombing was at the time a Government informer. The court in its decision commented: "The problem of crime, particularly the diabolic crimes charged in the indictments here, is of great concern to us. But if we reflect carefully, it becomes abundantly clear that we can never acquiesce in a principle that condones lawlessness by law enforcers in the name of a just end". Then the court quoted Justice Brandeis: "In a government of laws, the existence of the government will be imperiled if it fails to observe the law scrupulously. Our government is the potent, the omnipresent teacher. For good or ill, it teaches the whole people by its example. Crime is contagious. If the government becomes a lawbreaker, it breeds contempt for law; it invites every man to become a law unto himself: it invites ANARCHY."

• • •

In the last-minute rush to complete its work, the New York State Assemblymen voted themselves a pay raise, by a vote of 94 to 59. Unfortunately this was three votes more than there are seats in the assembly. Also, three seats were vacant — two members having died and a third being hospitalized. When a question was raised by reporters, the clerk announced that a mistake had been made — the vote should have been 83 to 60. When the final record was issued it recorded a vote of 78-60. We wonder how many Assemblymen collect pay checks.

• • •

Bunker Hunt Oil Company has announced that Libya's nationalization of its oil concessions has resulted in a loss to the company of 3.85 **billion** dollars, based on the value of its share in the Libyian Oil reserves. It also stated that it had invested $25 million in Libya since 1955. Under U. S. law, companies can claim compensation from the United States Treasury for losses due to nationalization by foreign governments. We wonder what this will cost the taxpayers.

• • •

The Brookings Institution has issued a report on "Economic Aspects of Television Regulation" which deserves attention. Brookings investigators found that in 1969 the profits before taxes of the television industry constituted a 70% return on tangible investment, sharply higher than the 20% average for all manufacturing industries. The reason? The

The Meaning of War

A suggestion from Dr. Benjamin Rush (1745-1813), signer of the Declaration of Independence and pioneer psychiatrist.

Signs of War

"In order more deeply to affect the minds of the citizens of the United States with the blessings of peace, by contrasting them with the evils of war, let the following inscriptions be painted upon the sign, which is placed over the door of the War Office.

1. An office for butchering the human species.
2. A widow and orphan making office.
3. A broken bone making office.
4. A wooden leg making office.
5. An office for creating public and private vices.
6. An office for creating a public debt.
7. An office for creating speculators, stock jobbers, and bankrupts.
8. An office for creating famine.
9. An office for creating pestilential diseases.
10. An office for creating poverty, and the destruction of liberty and national happiness.

In the lobby of this office let there be painted representations of all the common military instruments of death, also human skulls, broken bones, unburied and putrefying dead bodies, hospitals crowded with sick and wounded soldiers, villages on fire, mothers in besieged towns eating the flesh of their children, ships sinking in the ocean, rivers dyed with blood, and extensive plains without a tree or fence, or any other object, but the ruins of deserted farm houses.

Above this group of woeful figures, let the following words be inserted, in red characters to represent human blood: "National Glory."

The above is excerpted from **Selected Writings of Benjamin Rush**, edited by Dagober D. Runes, published in 1947 by the Philosophical Library, Inc., New York, N. Y., with permission.

---

television industry enjoys quasi-monopoly privileges which restricts competitive pricing of advertising allocations. Moreover, 87% of all stations are network affiliates and 85% of prime time is controlled by the three national networks. Brookings recommends that the number of networks could be doubled by the use of UHF channels 2 to 13, that subscription TV be legalized, full development of cable TV, listener-supported outlets, and several technical innovations which could bring cultural events of minority interest to all parts of the country by satellite to home broadcasting or video-cassettes. These would reduce the profits of the present monopoly-owners, but greatly increase competition in pricing, programming and ownership. They also recommend divesting the FCC of any responsibility for content and quality of programming, limiting them to allocation of signal channels and other engineering details.

The Libertarian Forum
BOX 341
MADISON SQUARE STATION
NEW YORK, NEW YORK 10010

First Class

Published Every Month. Subscription Rate: $8.00 Per Year

A Monthly Newsletter

THE
Libertarian Forum

Joseph R. Peden, Pubiisher   Murray N. Rothbard, Editor

VOLUME V, NO. 9   SEPTEMBER, 1973   US-ISSN0047-4517

American Monopoly Statism

By Joseph R. Stromberg

Joseph R. Stromberg is a graduate of Florida Atlantic University in Boca Raton and is presently a doctoreal candidate in American history at the University of Florida. The following paper was read at the Libertarian Scholars Conference in October 1972.

I. Introduction

"The most unprofitable of all commerce is that connected with foreign dominion. To a few individuals it may be beneficial, merely because it is commerce; but to the nation it is a loss. The expense of maintaining dominion more than absorbs the profits of any trade." So wrote the great Anglo-American libertarian Thomas Paine in 1792.[1] Had she heeded such views, America could have avoided the bloodshed and crimes abroad and the bureaucratic tyranny at home which have accompanied the building of her own "informal" empire.

Unhappily, classical liberal ideas never prevailed fully anywhere, not even in England or the United States. Interest-conscious groups, from exporters and manufacturers to missionaries and militarists, utilized the power of the national state as often as fate allowed; their aims included glory, power, land and the engrossing of foreign markets judged essential to national prosperity.

From the inception of the Federal Government in 1789, an American gentry of Northern merchants and Southern planters actively developed an American form of mercantilism symbolized by the "commerce clause" and embracing tariffs, a National Bank and strong central authority. Their program, though not quite reducible to atavistic survivals of feudalism which Joseph Schumpeter saw as the fount of European imperialist expansion, was a conscious continuation of the British mercantilist outlook. James Madison, in particular, fashioned the rationale of the self-consciously imperial American state, reaffirming the basic expansionist axiom of the mercantilist worldview. Even Jefferson with his Physiocratic, laissez faire leanings was at best a left-wing mercantilist when in power.[2]

Despite this early statism, the Jacksonian "revolution" produced significant gains for free trade, including the destruction of the Bank and Taney's decisions overthrowing certain forms of monopoly grant. Jacksonianism was in Hofstadter's words "a phase in the expansion of liberated capitalism."[3] But even in an age of relative liberalism, those interests were many who defined laissez faire as "help without responsibilities."[4] Like the Cobdenites, the radical Jacksonians were unable to sweep away all existing privileges. The liberalism of the period was marred, in addition, by a major violation of Natural Right, chattel slavery, and by the imperialist war with Mexico, a prime instance of "manifestly destined" land-grabbing. Ultimately, sectional conflict over control of the area taken from Mexico brought on the War for Southern Independence.

II. The Decline of Laissez Faire

The Civil War was the occasion of a mammoth resurgence of Hamiltonian statism. First, by forever precluding secession, Northern victory utterly transformed the federal union and dealt a death blow to

real decentralization. The invention out of whole cloth of far-reaching executive "war powers" by President Lincoln paved the way for the 20th-century Presidential Caesarism, just as conscription set a precedent for wartime, and later peacetime, militarization of American society. Civil liberties naturally suffered.[5]

With respect to the political economy, Civil War centralization was equally harmful. While the internationally free-trading South was out of the Union, The Republican Administration secured passage of a "National Bank Act, and unprecedented income tax, and a variety of excise taxes" verging on "a universal sales tax."[6] The tariff, whose lowering had been forced in 1830 by the South, was jacked up to nearly 50 percent, with postwar rates going steadily higher. Wartime greenbacks set a precedent for future inflation.

Aside from protection and American manufactures, perhaps the most flagrant wartime and postwar subsidy consisted of funds loaned and "public" lands given to the railroads by the Federal Government to encourage their growth. In the period from 1862 to 1872, the railroads received from Congress some one hundred million acres of land. (For that matter, the bias in favor of farming written into homestead legislation may have encouraged an uneconomical expansion of agriculture.)[8]

Such was the famed but partly mythical "laissez faire" which one historian, with amusing lack of irony, sees as epitomized in the inflationary-protectionist program of a certain wing of Radical Republicans.[9] In truth, the Gilded Age witnessed a great state-supported "barbecue" rooted in the rampant statism of the war years, whose participants defended themselves with Spencerian rhetoric while grasping subsidies with both hands.[10] The beeves of this "Great" barbecue," as Vernon Louis Parrington called it, were supplied as much by local governments competing for industry as by Washington.

III. Roots — and Rise — of Empire

According to historian William A. Williams, the major political struggles fought out by agrarian and metropolitan interests between 1865 and 1896 concerned providing and regulating a national transportation system; establishing a favorable monetary system; and finding foreign markets for agricultural surpluses. The agricultural businessmen of the West and South sought regulation of the railroads to insure their equitable operation; ultimately, their radical wing, the Populists, proposed nationalization to that end. Another agrarian goal was inflationary coinage of silver to provide easy money, and it was hoped, to enable the penetration of markets in countries on the sterling standard. Great Britain's dominance of world trade could thus be broken.[11]

Above all, the farmers wanted foreign markets for their surplus crops. American farmers had in fact been export-conscious since the founding of the Republic; they continued to look for outlets after the Civil War. The severe depression that began in 1873 gave them added reason to look abroad.[12] But according to Williams, it was an "export bonanza" lasting

(Continued On Page 2)

American Monopoly Statism —

(Continued From Page 1)

from 1877 to 1881 and occasioned by natural disasters which incapacitated European agriculture which really underscored the possibilities of overseas markets held for American prosperity. The recovery of European agriculture and the end of the bonanza only reinforced American convictions about the necessity of overseas expansion.

Although some effort was made as far back as President Grant to open up new markets, on the whole the farmers justifiably felt that their concerns were not fully shared in government circles. Accordingly, their discontent and agitation could only grow.

The turning point came when certain metropolitan Republicans led by the adroit Governor William McKinley of Ohio adopted a significant portion of the agrarian program, thereby winning the crucial support of a good many farmers in 1896. McKinley's advocacy of bimetallism held out the prospect of renewed silver inflation (which Cleveland had recently repudiated). A protectionist, McKinley nonetheless maintained a low profile on the tariff. Most important, McKinley and his colleagues took over completely the agrarians' thesis of "overproduction," generalizing it to the industrial sectors of the economy. Their combined platform of protectionism, bimetallism and reciprocity treaties to open up overseas markets proved very attractive; together with an upturn in wheat exports it carried the election of 1896 for the Republican expansionists.[13]

The expansionist consensus, of which McKinley's policies were the finished expression, had been long developing. It embraced goldbugs and silverites, who agreed more on ends than means. Rooted in a felt need to dominate whole regions for markets, the new policies bespoke a fundamentally imperial conception of America's world role. This conception was reinforced by a "frontier-expansionist" view of history articulated by Frederick Jackson Turner and Brooks Adams which saw the frontier as the source of American democracy and prosperity; with the close of the continental frontier, a "new frontier" must be found if American society was to remain unchanged. Adams and his followers, including Theodore Roosevelt, defined overseas empire as the substitute West for industrial America.[14]

The Panic of 1893 and the economic crisis flowing from it set the stage for the emergence of McKinley as the leader of an expansionist coalition. "From explaining (the Panic) as a consequence of dangerous or out-moded **monetary** theories and policies, (Americans) came to account for it in terms of overproduction and lack of markets"[15] The means to such markets were a modern navy, reciprocity and, when necessary, military intervention to sweep aside obstacles to American expansion. To that traditional American sphere of influence, Latin America, were to be added the markets of Asia — above all China — and the world.

Given the goal of opening up markets, United States policy makers sought to create political conditions favorable to trade and investment in every country regarded as a potential outlet for surpluses. A variety of tactics, from reciprocity treaties to armed intervention, were employed to eliminate or prevent policies adverse to American interests on the part of such countries. This noncolonial strategy of empire, relying on America's preponderant power to achieve "supremacy over the whole region," was remarkably like the British "imperialism of free trade" analyzed by John Gallagher and Ronald Robinson.[16] That as free trade it was somewhat spurious is clear.

The Cuban revolt against Spanish authority presented President McKinley with the necessity of risking war to sustain the imperial program. Aside from protecting American investments and markets in Cuba from the consequences of continued instability, the Administration wished to clear up the mess in Cuba in order to concentrate on the overriding goal of penetrating Asian markets. Impatience led to war in 1898.

By going to war with Spain, America not only pacified Cuba but also gained a foothold in Asia by seizing the Philippines from her. The reluctance of "our little brown brothers" to accept American suzerainty brought on our first Vietnam, the Philippine Insurrection, whose suppression was vigorously opposed by such anti-imperialists as Edward Atkinson.

By asserting the right of Americans to trade as equal competitors in all of China in the Open Door Notes of 1899 and 1900, the United States sought to prevent or reverse the division of China (and the world) into economic spheres of influence by other, less sophisticated imperial powers. To realize the asserted right of Americans to trade as equals everywhere became the key strategy and the sole consistent theme of American foreign policy in the twentieth century. When rival powers staked out empires and when strong nationalist and communist movements arose in the underdeveloped countries, Open Door imperialism began to involve America in intervention and war.[17]

IV. Genteel Fascism at Home

The developments summarized above were not natural out-growths of capitalism proper; rather, they fit the pattern of export monopolism analysed by Joseph Schumpeter and others. Briefly, steep tariffs enabled a great many American firms to price their goods well above world market levels. At these prices the quantities produced could not be sold. But to take full advantage of economics of scale these quantities had to be produced. At this point, the cry went up for foreign markets for the unsold surplus.[18] Before pursuing this other artificial trends toward monopolization bear examination.

Historian Gabriel Kolko has recently shown that vigorous competition was the main drift at the turn of the century; this despite the ample statism we have surveyed. In the Merger Movement of 1897-1901 Big Business failed miserably to gain hegemony over the ecomony. Defeated by competition, Big Business reformers resorted to what Kolko calls "political capitalism." Industry by industry, these corporate "liberals" sought federal legislation to 1) avoid populistic control in the states and 2) "rationalize", i.e., cartelize, their sectors of the economy. Regulation of an industry was typically pioneered by its biggest firms, which controlled the regulatory bureau thus established, to the detriment of smaller competitors.[19]

Concurrently Americans began seeing themselves as members of producers' blocs, not as consumers, and syndicalism (or corporatism) of a sort became the dominant outlook by 1918. The National Civic Federation, a corporate liberal policy group, played a central role in this intellectual transformation. NCF stressed cooperation with nonsocialist unions and opposition to business "anarchists" who took competition seriously.[20]

Not too surprisingly, given the inner unity of "stabilization" at home and abroad, most liberal reformers were expansionists and many expansionists were corporate liberals. As J. W. Burgess wrote in 1915, "the Jingoes and the Social Reformers have gotten together."[21] The combination of paternalistic welfarism and gun-boat imperialism symbolized by Theodore Roosevelt provides a close parallel to British "social imperialism."[22]

Equally important was the "war collectivism" of 1917-18, when Big Business, labor and government happily fixed prices and set quotas for the whole economy thru the War Industries Board. In later years, many corporate liberals agitated for a Peace Industries Board, or its equivalent, to plan the economy for the benefit of monopoly capitalists.[23]

Herbert Hoover was a major architect of peacetime corporatism. As Commerce Secretary he encouraged the cartelistic integration of trade associations with labor unions. As President, he pioneered most of the New Deal measures, which had the unexpected effect of prolonging a depression itself *caused* by governmental monetary policy.[24]

In the election of 1932, important Business liberals shifted their support to FDR when Hoover refused to go over to a fully fascist form of corporatism. By contrast, the Roosevelt Administration pushed through the National Recovery Act, which openly sanctioned the cartelizing activities of trade associations, and the Agricultural Adjustment Act, cartelizing the farm sector.[25] The Wagner Act of 1935 integrated labor into the nascent system.[26] Although the Supreme Court outlawed the openly fascist NRA, the New Dealers nonetheless fastened the shackles of corporate statism on American society by imposing less systematic controls, quotas and virtual cartels.

From the Progressives to the present, the drive to statism could only foster more and more monopoly; and more and more surpluses looking for foreign markets. Further, the brake on innovation and the general inefficiency deriving from the suppression of competition came to seriously limit investment opportunities. Men of power, their pockets bursting with monopoly profits, found yet another surplus — one of capital — crying out for Open Doors abroad. At the same time, intellectuals, reformers, politicians and businessmen increasingly internalized the felt need for overseas expansion.

(Continued On Page 3)

406

American Monopoly Statism —

(Continued From Page 2)

Already under President Wilson

> Tax monies collected from individual citizens came to be used to provide private corporations with loans and other subsidies for overseas expansion, to create the power to protect those activities, and even to create reserve funds with which to make cash guarantees against losses.[27]

Wilson likewise supported the Webb-Pomerene Act of 1918 "permitting cartels in the export trade."[28] Small wonder that after 1937, when the inevitable failure of New Deal reformism became painfully obvious, the New Dealers with sure instinct turned to overseas expansion as the answer to the economic crisis. In the late '30s this meant running up against other expansionist systems. Eventual involvement in another war for the Open Door grew out of "a decision in 1938 to eliminate Axis economic penetration of the (American) hemisphere"[29]

Later, when World War II shaded into Cold War, "defense of the Free World against communism" became the most potent slogan veiling imperial reality. It overlapped reality, since the triumph of revoluntiory nationalists in the undeveloped countries could block the expansion allegedly so crucial to American wellbeing. The permanent garrison state erected after World War II further subsidized the corporate power elite through defense production and research contracts. Finally, foreign aid developed as another subsidy to American exporters paid for by the citizenry.[30]

V. Imperialism, the Highest Stage of Statism

We have seen that neomercantilist inroads on a partly laissez faire economy, gave great impetus to monopoly in the sectors regulated. Originating with agrarians and taken up by industrialists, the cry of "overproduction" was raised to justify an aggressive export policy favorable to various interests. But in general the thesis of overproduction was either a rationalization for entrepreneurial error or an honest, but mistaken explanation of real trends actually rooted in state power.[31] These trends were initiated by protection and subsidies, and aggravated by cartelizing regulatory laws.

The fundamental reason for informal, Open Door Empire was explained in 1899 by Francis B. Thurber, President of the U. S. Export Association: "We must have a place to dump our surplus, which otherwise will constantly depress prices and compel the shutting down of our mills . . . and changing our profits into losses."[32] The English liberal John A. Hobson put it differently:

> The economic root of Imperialism is the desire of strong organized industrial and financial interests to secure and develop at the public expense and by the public force private markets for their surplus goods and their surplus capital. War, militarism, and a "spirited foreign policy" are the necessary means to this end.[33]

Joseph Schumpeter analysed this tendency to "export monopolism" and vividly underscored its precapitalist and anticapitalist character. The tariff made possible domestic monopoly prices well above a free market price; at the same time it created an artificial surplus since the full quantity produced of a good could not be sold at that price. But the full amount was produced in order to enjoy lower unit costs. The ensuing dilemma was resolved by selling or "dumping" the excess abroad "at a lower price, sometimes . . . below cost."

Since existing "cartels successfully impede the founding of new enterprises," foreign investment likewise becomes a necessary outlet. To implement the policy of export monopolism "the idea of military force readily suggests itself." Empire (formal or otherwise) is the outcome.

Imperialism exploits the nation for the benefit of a few; since without it, prices in the home market would be lower. If a given firm could not survive at free market prices in the absence of empire, it was in Schumpeter's words "expanded beyond economically justifiable limits," and its factors of production could be better utilized elsewhere.

Thus, there was nothing inevitable or capitalist about imperialism. In truth, "the rise of trusts and cartels— a phenomenon quite different from the trend to large-scale production . . . can never be explained by the automatism of the competitive system." On the contrary, monopoly is explained as arising from state interference in the ecomony.[34]

Another thorough student of imperialism, E. M. Winslow suggested that in part the monopolistic positions sought by business and labor (and which encouraged imperial expansion) were designed to protect them from the instability of the trade cycle. Understanding the connection between general depressions and credit expansion, Winslow recommended instead of privilege, "social control of the monetary aspects of the economic process."[35] Certainly, the gains for statism occasioned by the 1929 depression indicate that an understandable desire for a minimum of stability can account for part of the drive to corporatism in modern America. Even here, the state must bear primary responsibility inasmuch as state fostered credit expansion is the cause of depressions. There is reason to believe that laissez faire banking would in itself provide the "social control" of the monetary process Winslow proposed.[36]

Murray Rothbard has recently argued powerfully that all government regulation of business promotes monopoly and inhibits innovation. Under the centralized corporate statism of modern America, innovation and the founding of new enterprises is sufficiently discouraged that in Jane Jacob's words "there is nowhere to export the embarrassing superfluity of capital except abroad."[37]

The monopoly structure of the economy by preventing innovation limits domestic investment and promotes aggressive capital export. Simultaneously, monopolistic pricing made possible by tariffs, quotas and all manner of regulations generates surpluses of goods to be sent abroad. Thus, we have traced monopoly and empire to the state and are in a position to see that imperialism is the highest stage of statism, not of capitalism understood as the free market. It is the outcome of the interaction of the permanent state apparatus, whose chief asset is power, with interest groups that wish to utilize that power to exploit those less favored. In Schumpeter's words: "The bourgeoisie seeks to win over the state for itself, and in return serves the state and state interests that are different from its own."[38]

Empire may have wealth as one of its goals and justifications, but it is not a product of capitalism as such. It is not "determined" by purely economic facts as the Marxists would have it. On the contrary, the empire is the extension of the control and influence of a power elite which has already far too much power at home. Its fundamental causes are to be sought in the realm of the will-to-power, state aggrandizement, militarism, aggressive nationalism and other irrational precapitalist and noncapitalist features of the imperial society. In the words of Gustave de Molinari, "The sovereign power of governments over the life and property of the individual is, in fact, the sole fount and spring of militaryism, policy, and protection."[39]

Footnotes

[1] Richard Emery Roberts (ed.), **Selected Writings of Thomas Paine** (New York, 1945), 328.

[2] On the Founding Fathers, see William Appleman Williams, **The Contours of American History** (Chicago, 1966), "The Age of Mercantilism: 1740-1828," esp. 150-162 and 185-192.

[3] Richard Hofstadter, **The American Political Tradition** (New York, 1948), 56, 56-67.

[4] Williams, **Contours**, 212.

[5] Arthur A. Ekirch, Jr., **The Decline of American Liberalism** (New York, 1969), 116-131.

[6] Ibid, 129.

[7] Ibid, 153-4.

[8] Ibid. Murray N. Rothbard, **Power and Market** (Menlo Park, Calif., 1970), 203(57) and 210(54).

[9] Williams, **Contours**, 300-1.

[10] Ekirch, **American Liberalism**, Chapter 10, 147-170. For the radical individualist critique of such Spencerianism, see James J. Martin, **Men Against the State** (Colorado Springs, Colo., 1970), 239-241.

[11] William Appleman Williams, **The Roots of the Modern American Empire** (New York, 1969), 132-404.

[12] For brief but lucid "Austrian" accounts of the depressions of 1837, 1873 and 1893, see Richard W. Grant, **The Incredible Bread Machine** (CR R. Grant, 1966), 27-36.

[13] Williams, **American Empire**, 385-404.

[14] Williams, **Contours**, 364-5, and Walter LaFeber, The New Empire (Ithaca, New York, 1963), 62-101.

[15] William Appleman Williams, "The Acquitting Judge" in David W.

(Continued On Page 4)

American Monopoly Statism —

(Continued From Page 3)
Eakins and James Weinstein (eds), **For A New America: Essays in History and Politics from 'Studies on the Left' 1959-1967** (New York, 1970), 44.

"John Gallagher and Ronald Robinson, "The Imperialism of Free Trade," **The Economic History Review**, 2d Series, VI, 1 (1953), 3, 1-15. For a discussion that concedes much of what the foregoing says but distinguishes this spurious "free trade" from that supported by genuine liberals, see Oliver MacDonagh, "The Anti-Imperialism of Free Trade," **Ibid**, 2d Series, XIV, 3 (April, 1962), 489-501.

"On the Spanish-American War, the Open Door Notes and informal empire, see William Appleman Williams, **The Tragedy of American Diplomacy** (New York, 1962), 16-50. On the war, see in addition, **American Empire**, 408-428.

"Joseph Schumpeter, **Imperialism and Social Classes: Two Essays** (New York, 1955), 79-80, ff.

"Gabriel Kolko, **The Triumph of Conservationism** (Chicago, 1967) and **Railroads and Regulation, 1877-1916** (Princeton, 1965). For a comparative study of liberal and fascist forms of corporatism, see Robert A. Brady, **Business As A System of Power** (New York, 1943).

"James Weinstein, **The Corporate Ideal in the Liberal State, 1900-1918** (Boston, 1968). For broader treatments, see "Part I: American Corporate Liberalism, 1900-1948" in Eakins and Weinstein, **For A New America**, 37-193, and Ronald Radosh and Murray N. Rothbard (eds.), **A New History of Leviathan** (New York, 1972).

"Quoted in F. A. Hayek, **The Consititution of Liberty** (Chicago, 1960), 406.

"Compare Bernard Semmel, **Imperialism and Social Reform** (New York, 1968). on England, with Ekirch, **American Liberalism**, Chapter 11, "The Progressives as Nationalists," 171-194.

"See the pathbreaking new essay by Murray N. Rothbard, "War Collectivism in World War I" in Radosh and Rothbard, **Leviathan**, 66-110. See also Chapter 8, "War As Fulfillment" in Weinstein, **Corporate Ideal**, 214-254, and Ferdinand Lundberg, **America's 60 Families** (New York, 1938), 133-148.

"Murray N. Rothbard, "The Hoover Myth" in Eakins and Weinstein, **For A New America**, 162-179, and "Herbert Hoover and the Myth of Laissez Faire" in Radosh and Rothbard, **Leviathan**, 111-145. On the

monetary causes of the depression, see Murray N. Rothbard, **America's Great Depression** (Princeton, 1963), esp. 16-21. For an almost "Austrian" treatment, see John T. Flynn, **Country Squire in the White House** (Garden City, New York, 1940), 47-53.

"Rothbard, "The Hoover Myth", 176-9. On the reactionary character of the NRA, see Flynn, **Country Squire**, 73-86.

"Williams, **Contours**, 445.

"Williams, **Tragedy**, 76.

"Martin J. Sklar, "Woodrow Wilson and the Political Economy of Modern United States Liberalism" in Eakins and Weinstein, **For A New America**, 80.

"Williams, **Contours**, 449, 452-462.

"Charles E. Nathanson, "The Militarization of the American Economy" in David Horowitz (ed.), **Corporations and the Cold War** (New York, 1969), 205-235; David W. Eakins, "Business Planners and America's Postwar Expansion" in **Ibid**, 143-171.

"On "overproduction" as a rationalization, see Ludwig von Mises, **Planning for Freedom** (S. Holland, Ill., 1962), 64-7.

"Quoted in Williams, **American Empire**, 439. Cf. the views of Andrew Carnegie cited in **Contours**, 326-7.

"J. A. Hobson, **Imperialism: A Study** (Univ. of Michigan Press, 1965), 106. Cf. his remarks on US imperialism in **The Evolution of Modern Capitalism** (London, 1926), 262-3.

"Schumpeter, **Imperialism**, 79-90. On tariffs and related export policy, see Ludwig von Mises, **Human Action** (Chicago, 1966), 365-8, and **Omnipotent Government** (New Haven, Conn., 1944), 66-72. On the impossibility of monopoly on the free market, see Murray N. Rothbard, **Man, Economy and State**, II (Los Angeles, 1970), 560-660.

"E. M. Winslow, **The Pattern of Imperialsim** (New York, 1948), 193.

"On trade cycles, see Rothbard, **Man, Economy and State**, 850-877; on free banking, Rothbard, "What Has Government Done to Our Money?", **Studies in Human Action**, III, 1 (Winter, 1963), 19-26.

"Rothbard, **Power and Market**. Jane Jacobs, **The Economy of Cities** (New York, 1969), 228-9.

"Murray N. Rothbard, "Anatomy of the State," **Rampart Journal of Individualist Thought**, I, 2 (Summer, 1965), 1-24; **Power and Market**. On the ruling elite, see G. William Domhoff, **Who Rules America?** (Englewood Cliffs, New Jersey, 1976). Schumpeter, **Imperialism**, 93.

"Gustave de Molinari, **The Society of To-Morrow** (New York, 1904), 36-7.

□

Libertarianism And Social Transformation

By Steve Halbrook

Libertarianism and Social Transformation

Elsewhere in this issue we pose the question "What must be done?" — what is to be the strategy by which we preserve what liberties we enjoy, and proceed to the ultimate libertarian goal — a stateless society. This was the question discussed by three young libertarian scholar-activists at the first Libertarian Scholars Conference in September 1972. Gary Greenberg, an attorney from New York City, and a candidate for Congress at the time on the Libertarian ticket (subsequently not allowed on the ballot), gave a classical defense of the use of the electoral method for libertarian tactical propagandizing. John Brotschol, a founding editor of Abolitionist/ Outlook, presented a case study of the infiltration of an existing political movement by libertarian activists, and their impact on the organization's policies and work. Dr. Stephen Halbrook of Tuskegee Institute then gave a stirring, intellectually challenging paper that became the focus of most of the later comment and discussion. We are delighted to be able to print Prof. Halbrook's contribution. I have added some remarks of my own made at the time as one of the official commentators, especially as I summarized therein some of the points raised by Messrs. Greenberg and Brotschol whose papers we are not able to print due to space limitations.

(Signed)
J. R. Peden

Libertarianism and Social Transformation

Differing strategies proposed by libertarians tend to reflect differing conceptions of and commitments to libertarianism itself. It is assumed here that libertarianism implies absolute liberty for all groups and

individuals from the use or threat of physical force. Liberty is total in this conception, and thus the goal of the libertarian is to achieve not a few crumbs of liberty thrown down from the table of the ruling class but total revolutionary transformation. The true libertarian is not an intellectual sportsman who merely spends his spare evenings babbling about demunicipalizing garbage collection; rather he is one who devotes the whole of his life to the cause of freedom and who takes seriously Patrick Henry's words that the choice is liberty or death. The immediate concern of the libertarian is the most liberty for the most people, the end of which is complete liberty for all people. This immediate concern necessitates that he seek to abolish those aspects of State oppression which are greatest in quantity and quality. This is why he takes a mass point of view, i.e., is above all concerned with the liberation of the great masses of people of the whole world, and why he zeroes in on the worst oppressions; for instance, why he is concerned more with stopping the napalming of the Vietnamese than with rescuing the postal service from the clutches of the State.

Applying this conception of libertarianism to the concrete situation of today, the implication is that libertarians must acquire precisely what most of them lack: a Third World consciousness. Most libertarians are preoccupied with the problems of a very small minority of the world's population — the people of the United States, especially those who are in the "mainstream" of American life — and are least concerned with the Third World peoples, who are the majority and are the most exploited people today. This First World consciousness is behind the fact that many are concerned with the temporary loss of liberty of the draftee but few

(Continued On Page 5)

Social Transformation —

(Continued From Page 4)

imperialism. The State is identical with aggressive violence, and the major agency of aggressive violence is the US government. The US government holds millions of people in absolute slavery. Each year it kills, maims, tortures. and imprisons tens of thousands of people. Every objection the libertarian has to the State applies above all to the United States. Every week the American Leviathan burns dozens of babies and little children to death everywhere from Vietnam to "portuguese" Guinea. Every day the Special Forces attempt to gun down freedom fighters in Angola, Guatemala, and Bolivia. US agents torture hundreds of men and women in every Third World capital from Saigon to Buenos Aires. Masses of peasants are herded into concentration camps in Cambodia, Laos, and Vietnam while in Brazil and Paraguay Indians are starved or shot, all so that a few US corporations can reap super profits. There is no crime to which the US imperialists will not stoop. The US is the International State, and its lackeys include the Soviet social-imperialists.

It is the revolutionaries of the Third World who are the libertarians in deed. The only massive forces combatting the most Statist institution in human history, US imperialism, are the Third World revolutionary movements. In this sense some of the most important Anarchists of this century include Ho Chi Minh, Che Guevara, and Amilcar Cabral; they are Anarchists without having to declare themselves so, in spite of the fact that they are not as doctrinairely pure in the strictest sense developed by First World "official" libertarian theoreticians. It is the national liberation parties of the underdeveloped countries such as the Viet Cong which are the fiercest enemies of the Modern State, i.e., US imperialism. Libertarians in the First World can have no real strategy without recognizing this and giving total support to the Viet Cong, the Tupamaros and the OPR33, the Bangla Desh Maoists, and the Ceylonese Guevarists. Furthermore, these are principled allies because their positive programs are basically libertarian. General Giap wants to give the land to the peasants; Raul Sendic is for workers' control; Carlos Marighela wanted to smash the bureaucratic State and to replace it with the masses in arms; Cabral is even opposed to having a capital city.

It is a sad fact that the majority of people in the belly of the Monster benefit from the exploitation of the Third World. It is a sad fact that as long as US imperialism gives them more cars and cheaper TVs, those classes which could otherwise be revolutionary — the workers, small businessmen, intellectuals — will remain supporters of Statism. Though oppressed by the State monopoly capitalists, the so-called middle class in this country is bribed by imperialist spoils. Some day these classes may become revolutionary because some day these State privileges will no longer exist due to (1) many Vietnams and the liberation of the colonies from the economic intervention of the US government, or (2) from a crack up boom and depression. In the meantime there are only two classes in the US with which radical libertarians can make common cause. One of these is the student class. A minority of students have been idealistic enough to take the libertarian tradition of 1776 seriously and cast their lot with the oppressed peoples of the world. The other revolutionary class is the black lumpenproletariat. This class has been oppressed by the State more than any other class in US society. In the last century they were directly enslaved; in this century government intervention in the economy insures their unemployment. The anarchist Bakunin and today the neo-Bakuninist Eldridge Cleaver have recognized that the lumpenproletariat is an instrinctively revolutionary class; and indeed the only massive rebellions in the past decades in the US were all carried out in the ghetto. Libertarians must seek to understand the lumpenproletariat and to create an alliance between the lumpenproletariat and the students. If only these two classes are revolutionary before a (possibly far off) economic collapse in the US, then there can be no total revolution in the US — but they can act as a "fifth column" in support of the Third World. To those who deny the possibility of the lumpenproletariat supporting libertarianism, the reply is that this possibility exists due to the fact that libertarianism has more to offer the lumpenproletariat than does any other political program, including that of the orthodox Marxists. The reason is that the lumpenproletariat has lost more in life, liberty, and property than any other class and hence by strict libertarian principles this class should gain the most when stolen property is returned to its rightful owners.

In the coming years libertarians must look forward to the building of a Libertarian Revolutionary Party. No successful revolution has ever occurred without the spontaneous risings of the masses and a Party to insure that the revolution is not diverted from its path. Those who object to a Libertarian Revolutionary Party because they oppose "leadership" are fooling themselves; if there is no libertarian leadership, then there will be non-libertarian leadership, so that indirectly those who oppose organization are supporting the triumph of Statist organizations. "Spontaneity" gives you a Kerensky, a mere change in name and nothing else. Revolutionary organization gives you a Makhno or a Lenin, and that means a true revolution. A Libertarian Revolutionary Party would give a consistently libertarian Leninism, i.e., a well organized, steeled Party which would abolish the State and prevent other parties from "spontaneously" creating a new State. The pitfall of total reliance on spontaneity is that it takes leadership from those who are conscious and committed libertarians and gives it to those who are not, the surest guarantee that libertarianism will not triumph. Those who oppose revolutionary organization in the face of reactionary organizations are objectively agents of the ruling class. This is why resolute struggle must be waged against the present day exponents of Kropotkinite opportunism, the anti-Leninist, utopian "anarcho"-communists.

A Libertarian Revolutionary Party bears no resemblance to a State. The Party may be centralized so as to coordinate action on a wide scale — the centralization of the State necessitates this — but the Party is a voluntary organization, which one joins and quits voluntarily. Lenin often pointed this out about the Bolshevik Party, and if one reflects on the essence of Leninism it is easy to recognize that such figures as Samuel Adams, Bakunin, Sitting Bull, and Durruti were all great Leninists. Leninism merely means organized and coordinated action, action that is well planned. It does entail the acceptance of a general Party line, but there is nothing authoritarian about this; as Lenin pointed out, those who oppose the general line are free to withdraw from the Party. And what could be wrong with a general line which was a libertarian line? If a Libertarian Revolutionary Party existed, should Statists be allowed to join and to represent their views as Party views? Of course not. The Sons of Liberty never allowed the reconcilers to infiltrate and thus to pervert thier party.

The first step toward the creation of a Libertarian Revolutionary Party is bringing together a number of people under a common libertarian ideology. There is strength only in union, which in this context means a libertarian vanguard, a group united under a single strategy for revolution. Some day this will necessitate an all-US Party newspaper which perhaps would initially resemble the old SDS paper New Left Notes. Revolutionary libertarians must also bring together a body of literature which would more explicitly set forth their aims and methods. Libertarianism must be popularized and translated into terms appealing to potential cadre. This necessitates a total revision of Austrian economic theory, which must be purged of its apologia for the old order and shown to be revolutionary. Instead of vindicating imperialism a la Mises, market economics must be applied to Third World development. It must be shown that the "right to property" means that the First World must repay via reparations to the Third World the massive loot it has grabbed over the past century. We must take a broader approach to revisionist history; we must be preoccupied less with the criminal deals of the big powers (especially the US and USSR decision making elites) and more with the revolutionary response. Only this can create a Third World consciousness among libertarians, not to mention the fact that only by stressing the revolutionary and pro-Third World aspects of libertarianism can we recruit old New Left cadre and, someday, appeal to the class demands of the lumpenproletariat.

Libertarians must write more books and do so from a more revolutionary perspective. But that is not all. We must act. We must work with other groups, especially the anti-imperialist movement. What would libertarianism be today had libertarians taken the early initiative to build the anti-war movement? Perhaps we would have a strong national Party and tens of thousands of adherents. Everything now would be fundamentally different. Instead, many "libertarians," especially in the sixties, spent their time condemning Ho's "authoritarianism" and complaining about Viet Cong "terrorism." Only a few libertarians (such as Leonard Liggio) took part in the early anti-war movement and for this were branded "Communist" by other so-called "libertarians." At this point libertarians can at least save face by joining in the anti-imperialist movement, and possibly some day become respectable among radicals. It

(Continued On Page 6)

Social Transformation —

(Continued From Page 5)

is not enough to write an article once a year denouncing the US aggression or to sign a petition; libertarians must act to bring the war home, i.e., to turn the imperialist war into a civil war. Only by becoming action-oriented can libertarianism expect to progress.

The possible alternatives for action to which libertarians may resort involve everything from those as legal as apple pie to those for which our friend the State might heartily scold us. Under the former falls the task of educating the public. The Libertarian Revolutionary Party must be a declasse organization of professional revolutionaries drawn from all parts of the population, and to form this Party as well as to gain fellow travellers and sympathizers there must be some form of education directed to the general public. Thus the need for scholarly books, newspapers, even participation in elections becomes clear. However, such activities as elections must be resorted to only when they may be used as platforms to air libertarian views; participation in elections, as should be learned from the reformist Marxists, may lead to opportunism

and wasteful expenditure of resources, not to mention the fact that elections reinforce the fetishisms surrounding the State. As for wasting time using ballots to dump Nixon, it should be recalled that dumping Johnson only substituted one imperialist for another, whereas the libertarian task is to dump the whole State machine.

In 1902 Lenin wrote: "Give us an organization of revolutionaries, and we will overturn Russia!" Seventy years later, the libertarian watchword can only be: "Give us an organization of revolutionaries, and we will defeat US imperialism!" The truly imperative educational tasks must be directed internally, i.e., for the instructing and steeling of libertarian cadre. Libertarian journals must seriously discuss imperialism and Statism — a joking or humor society we need not — and must deal in depth with revolutionary strategies. "Without revolutionary theory there can be no revolutionary movement," as our friend said. Yet, far from developing a libertarian revolutionary theory, many libertarians have not even done empirical studies on past or present revolutionary movements. A permanent communications network must arise to provoke development of revolutionary theory.

But theory divorced from practice is not enough! "If you want to know the theory and method of revolution, you must take part in revolution," as the modern Chinese proverb says. "All genuine knowledge originates in

(Continued On Page 7)

Use Immunity: Let The Punishment Fit The Crime

Among the multivarious assaults on Constitutional rights perpetrated by the Nixon Administration in the name of law and order and national security was a new law, reputedly designed as a weapon against the Mafia, who are well known to have a deep-seated aversion to police informers or stool-pigeons. The law authorized the courts to grant what has come to be called "use immunity" to witnesses reluctant to cooperate by telling all they know about alleged criminal acts. It was designed to circumvent the Fifth Admendment privilege against being compelled to testify against oneself. It guaranteed to the reluctant witness that nothing which he revealed under threat of contempt of court (and which was not known previously to the prosecutor) could be "used" against him. However, it was expected that the prosecutors would use witness A to tell everything he knew about Mr. B, while Mr. B would be compelled to tell all he knew about Mr. A. In one way or another, A would help convict B, and B incriminate A. If they were uncooperative, they were jailed for contempt of the grand jury or the court. In either case, the Constitution was raped. While reputedly designed to destroy organized crime, the use immunity was (as we predicted in Lib. Forum, Jan. 15, 1970) soon directed against "ideological criminals", as Mr. Kleindienst was wont to put it. Peace activists like the Camden Catholics, witnesses in the Berrigan conspiracy case, the Seattle radicals, and perhaps most infamously, the Ft. Worth 5, were subjected to contempt proceedings and jailed without right to either bail or formal trial. For instance, Ft. Worth 5 were five Irish-born American citizens from New York city, all married, with several children, working men whose only apparent connection with each other was that they had separately involved themselves in raising funds for their fellow Catholics in war-ravaged Northern Ireland. Quite suddenly, each was summoned to appear before a federal grand jury in Ft. Worth, Texas, to tell what they knew about gun-running to Ireland. The five first met each other in the federal court in Ft. Worth, where they were promptly sent to jail for refusing to testify despite the grant of "use immunity." None had ever been anywhere near Texas in his life, no other witnesses were ever summoned, no specific information was ever given them about the gun plot — they were simply imprisoned more than 1000 miles from their homes, wives, children and friends, in a state never notable for its friendliness towards Irish Catholics. They remained there for 14 months — prisoners of John Mitchell and Richard Kleindienst — until recently released by a local judge until the federal attorney takes further steps to pursue or drop the whole "Investigation". The refusal of the five Irishmen to testify under use immunity was perfectly natural. The Irish, living for centuries under foreign oppression, have an utter detestation of "informers" — and no greater shame could befall an Irish family than to have one of its

members "turn informer". And so, instead of frightening off supporters of the IRA, the stupid persecution of the Ft. Worth 5 created new heroes and further swelled their ranks.

Now, with a fine sense of true justice, the fates have decided to savage the Nixon administration with its own weapon — use immunity. While the radicals, peaceniks and Irish have refused consistently to cooperate by submitting to use immunity, John Dean, Jeb Magruder, James McCord, Pat Gray, Howard Hunt and others have embraced it in testifying before the Senate Watergate Committee and the grand jury. Their reason is simple: the more they confess under use immunity, the less there is for which they can be indicted. They have every reason to volunteer information on every conceivable illegal act they perpetrated along with others, since their own voluntary statements on the subject preclude their future indictment for the offense. If the government has already obtained sufficient evidence against them for an act, they can still be prosecuted; if the government has no sufficient evidence, but might get it from other sources in the future, the perpetrator can foreclose future indictment by testifying to his own crime before anyone else "rats" on him. Thus we see the somewhat unedifying "confessions" of Dean, Magruder, Gray and others as soon as they perceived they might become "scapegoats".

The most endangered victim of this "use immunity" truth serum is Spiro Agnew. Federal prosecutor George Beall began his investigation of corrupt practices in Baltimore County in hopes of indicting county executive Dale Anderson, a Democrat and possible candidate for the governorship of Maryland. Beall decided to put pressure on William Fornoff, a non-partisan administrator in the county offices since 1957. Fornoff, in exchange for a promise of leniency and under a grant of use immunity, began to tell the whole story of bribery and extortion in the office of the county executive, involving not only Anderson, but his immediate Republican predecessor — Spiro Agnew. The contractors who had to pay the bribes also took "use immunity" and told everything they knew — further involving the Vice-President. The fact that these contractors were also widely known as personal friends and political supporters of Agnew's rapid rise to state and then national office, made their testimony against him all the more damning.

Thus the Nixon administration has become the principal victim of its own perversion of the Constitution's protection against the abuse of justice that always has been associated with compelling persons to testify against themselves in courts of law.

(J. R. P.)

◻

Social Transformation —

(Continued From Page 6)

are really concerned with the bombing of the workers and peasants of Vietnam. What is so disastrous about this overemphasis on the middle class whites of the advanced industrial countries is that it prevents libertarians from focusing on where the real battle between the State and Anarchism is taking place, namely between US imperialism and Third World revolutionaries.

The highest embodiment of twentieth century Statism is US direct experience." This means that libertarians in deed can only move toward direct action. While this paper refrains from advocating any specific deeds or normative propositions, history teaches us that revolutionary action can be anything from leafleting to urban guerrilla warfare. The point is that the time for phrase-mongering and endless speculation is OVER. Libertarians should begin concrete actions on the local level whenever possible. To those who, like the social democrats, pro-Moscow CPs, and mealey mouthed liberals, parrot infinitely that "conditions are not yet ripe" bla bla bla, one must respond with William Lloyd Garrison that "gradualism in theory is perpetuity in practice." The rebirth of the Sons (and Daughters) of Liberty is long overdue.   ❏

Comment

By Joseph R. Peden

Our three speakers have presented us with essentially three different recommendations as to how we libertarians should engage ourselves in the political process to attain our ends. As each involves the use of a political party structure, I will begin by discussing "third" parties in our political system.

Dissident political viewpoints have traditionally expressed themselves sooner or later through the political process. Usually, after receiving little or no response from the major political parties, the dissidents have undertaken to form third or fourth or fifth parties which then proceed to present their case directly to the electorate.

Third parties have taken one of three forms: (1) they are built around a single clear cut issue; (2) around several issues which express a variety of dissatisfactions; or (3) they offer a total ideological package which, once accepted, offers solution to every question.

The first type has been fairly common in American politics: the one issue party — i.e. the Greenback, Prohibitionist, Women's Suffrage parties. Their aims were limited — they never offered themselves as an alternative government — they merely hoped to persuade the ruling parties to adopt their policies. Though none of our speakers suggests it, libertarians could use this model if an issue of sufficient importance and clarity presented itself. It might even take the form of presenting the electorate with a clear cut choice of policies through the referendum or the recall processes — both much neglected means of political agitation and potential reform.

The second model of a third party structure is the multi-issue reformist party, which presents a broad spectrum of issues and political solutions to the electorate. While willing to take over governmental offices, their main aim is to institute reforms in law and administration, or persuade the major parties to do so by winning a sufficient electoral vote to make them crucial in determining which major party wins control of the government. To achieve their ends they adopt extremely flexible tactics, running their own candidates in some cases, endorsing major party candidates in others; always interested more in gaining acceptance for their political policies than in holding office. In the 19th century the Populist party fit this model and was very successful in having many of its policies implemented by the major parties. In New York we have seen similar success by both the Liberal and Conservative parties, and this was also the rationale of the George Wallace party in 1968. This is the strategy which Mr. Greenberg offers us through the national and local branches of the Libertarian party.

Historically these parties have had a fairly good record of success in getting their policies adopted by other parties, and there is in theory no reason why a Libertarian Party of a multi-issue, reformist character could not be quite successful in this sense also. But let us not kid ourselves. If the LP explicitly espouses anarcho-capitalism, it will no longer fit this second model; it will no longer be merely reformist; it will be explicitly revolutionary — seeking a totally new basis for our society. It will not easily persuade the other two ruling parties to just declare bankruptcy and liquidate the State. My own feeling — which I think Mr. Greenberg shares — is that this should not cause anarcho-capitalists to desert or avoid the LP. Every reform which is libertarian in direction expands the area of our freedom and deserves support from anarcho-capitalists; so long as we understand the reformist nature of the LP and its built-in limitations from an anarcho-capitalist viewpoint and act accordingly.

Prof. Halbrook has offered still a third model for our consideration: the elitist vanguard party, restrictive in membership, purist in dogma, disciplined, and dedicated to a total solution to our present social ills. He calls it Leninist, and indeed it fits the model of Marxist parties of various ideological sects better than that of traditional American party structures. The Socialist Labor party and Progressive Labor parties presently serve as examples of this third type of party. While such parties have been very few in American history, not even the American Communist party fully fits this model (it has frequently supported major party candidates), they have all remained minuscule, unsuccessful at the polls, and especially vulnerable to the vices of sectarianism. Moreover, their influence on other parties has been nil.

At first sight, and given Professor Halbrook's unfortunate use of the term Leninist to describe his concept of a Libertarian Party, the notion of a elitist vanguard cadre, exclusionist in membership, purist or orthodox in doctrine, disciplined ("centralized to coordinate action on a wide scale") "a well organized, steeled Party which would abolish the State and prevent other parties from spontaneously creating a new State" sounds anything but libertarian in spirit or anarchist in conception.

Yet without formally designating themselves as a "party", various libertarians have identified themselves as a "cadre", have held private, invitation-only meetings where they proceeded to plan future movement strategy, have set up organizational structures, and applied ideological criteria by which to establish the orthodoxy of the vanguard cadre, and even extended their exclusionary standards to the audiences which are invited to their "open" functions. I doubt if Professor Halbrook's notion of a Libertarian vanguard elitist party differs much in reality from the notion of an elitist vanguard cadre of certain other libertarian groups. Of course the rhetoric each uses may differ, but a rose by any other name stinks as sweetly.

I remain however very doubtful about the value of such an exclusionist, ideological vanguard party or cadre organization. Given our already high penchant for sectarian exclusionism, and intolerance of any deviation from our own particular vision of truth, such an organization would tend to freeze our intellectual development within the parameters of the initial cadre's ideological framework, and drive dissident viewpoints into outer darkness with appropriate weeping and gnashing of teeth. Also, to continue the Biblical metaphor, we shall hardly win friends and influence people if many are called but few are chosen. Or once chosen, are then expelled.

Prof. Halbrook however understands that a LP of the kind espoused by Mr. Greenberg will never serve the ultimate interests of anarcho-capitalists which are incompatible with a reformist strategy at some as yet undefined point in time. Yet Prof. Halbrook does not rule out the use of the electoral process as a potential platform from which to air libertarian views. But like Mr. Brostshol he fears that electoral politics may lead to waste of resources — and libertarian resources are very scarce.

There is no reason why both party types could not co-exist: for the reform of the present system — the work of expanding liberty wherever opportunity presents itself — through the pragmatic approach of Mr. Greenberg's LP need not preclude Prof. Halbrook's exclusionist ideological party which would concentrate on expounding the pure doctrine and preparing for the apocalypse.

Prof. Halbrook's passionate indignation at the crimes of American imperialism is admirable and greatly to his credit is the fact that he has

(Continued On Page 8)

Comment — (Continued From Page 7)

so often and so ably forced libertarians to confront Leviathan in all the hideousness of its reality. We all know people who work themselves into a frenzy about labor union atrocities and hardly seem conscious of the daily genocidal destruction of Vietnamese society, or even endorse it as necessary to preserve "freedom". But at one point in his analysis, his choice of words does a disservice to his cause by confusing anti-imperialism with libertarianism. Libertarianism is anti-imperialist, but it encompasses a great deal more than that. To call Ho Chi Minh, Che Guevara, etc. anarchists because they are zealous anti-imperialists or espouse the elimination of feudal land systems or decentralization is to misuse the term — at least in so far as we normally understand it in our own circle. There were people who once spoke of Richard Nixon as an anarchist because some of his positive programs were reputedly anarchist. To point out the espousal of anarchist principles and programs within the writings and policies of Chairman Mao or others is useful and valid, but Prof. Halbrook has overstated the case when he writes that, "these are principled allies because their positive programs are basically libertarian." It is a rhetorical overkill; an exaggeration based on a failure to take a wider view of what libertarianism fully encompasses as a theory or ideology or societal model.

Prof. Halbrook has a host of other suggestions which I think deserve our thoughtful attention. He urges more attention be paid to the response of the victims of imperialism in revisionist history which has presently tended to concentrate on the imperialists and their ideas and tactics, and he suggests that this new emphasis would make us more conscious of the problems of third world peoples and in turn create sympathetic attitudes among them towards our wider societal conceptions. Like Mr. Greenberg and Mr. Brotschol, Prof. Halbrook explicitly endorses participation in the work of other groups whose policies are broadly compatible with our own — though based on different philosophic grounding. He mentions rightly the failure of most libertarians to get in on the ground floor of the anti-war movement and its fateful consequences for our movement. Most of all, he rightly places an emphasis on action as the essential ingredient in espousing revolutionary libertarianism. As he says — anything from handing out leaflets to urban guerrilla warfare may be appropriate; concrete actions on the local level whenever possible are needed and he includes the work of the scholar as revolutionary in so far as it contributes to the cause of liberty. Within this context we are urged to do what we can whenever we can; and this I take to be what he refers to elsewhere as becoming a "professional revolutionary" for libertarianism.

I have one other question and that is in reference to Prof. Halbrook's conception of "class", in the context of a revolutionary situation. I don't think of students as a revolutionary class of any significance; they are too temporary in their status. As for Black lumpen-proletariat, or white, pink, red and yellow, my understanding of what makes them lumpen is precisely the fact that they are impervious to any efforts to awaken their class political consciousness. By definition their interest is elsewhere.

While John Brotschol has little confidence in the success of the LP, his grounds for doubt are pragmatic: lack of money and incompetent leadership. He has no theoretical opposition to the idea of using a third party of the reformist, multi-issue variety. But Mr. Brotschol has offered us still another model of the political process — one to which we ought to give very close attention. Here the strategy is to infiltrate existing organizations — organizations that are open to new ideas and new members and which already have some political leverage or power in our society. It is the approach of the Fabian Society, the Free Masons, the Illuminati, the Opus Dei and other small bands who have a common ideology which they quietly implement by being professionally competent, persuasive, working harder than their enemies, and gaining the esteem and friendship and confidence of the powerful. These tightly knit groups create a network of sympathetic contacts within existing institutions and agencies and over a period of time gain dominance over these levers of power in a society.

As I look around the audience here today I am struck by the sociological character of the group — we are predominantly what the Marxists call intellect workers — lawyers, teachers, writers, editors, publishers, artists of various kinds, economists, psychologists, students, physicians. For a movement which extols the virtues of business enterprise, we have surprisingly few honest-to-God entrepreneurs, and fewer blue collar workers, housewives, and farmers. To say nothing of Black lumpen proletarians.

This situation is both our strength and our weakness. It is our weakness because we can only impose our vision of the good society with the consent and understanding of the vast majority of our fellow humans who are never going to read Atlas Shrugged much less Man, Economy and State, and are to a great extent simply beyond our immediate area of contact. It is our strength because the general movement of civilization rests upon the ideas and actions of elites; and in the next century those elites will increasingly be drawn from the intellect workers who dominate the media of communications — press, TV and Radio, education — and are the masters of science and technology. If we can capture the imagination and support of these elites, the rest ought to follow suit. Thus Brotschol's strategy of infiltration of seats of power — the think-tanks of the corporations, political parties or government itself — ought to receive much closer attention, and might even be a suitable theme for a separate panel at a future conference.

Mr. Robert Poole discussed this approach in considerable detail in Reason 3 (June 1971) in a superb article entitled "Leverage Points for Social Change". His basic argument is implicit in each of the 3 papers we have heard today. "The existing coercive political and governmental structure, with its control over lives, is itself the primary problem which must be dealt with.

If coercive restraints began to be removed, the superiority of laissez faire would become increasingly obvious. If this be the case, then the primary task is\ to begin making the right kinds of changes in our institutions, leaving the changes in values and attitudes to follow as a result". Poole quotes Archimedes, "Give me a place to stand and I will move the earth". We are offered here today at least three platforms on which to begin our movement — of the earth.   ◻

The Libertarian Forum
BOX 341
MADISON SQUARE STATION
NEW YORK, NEW YORK 10010

First Class

Published Every Month. Subscription Rate: $8.00 Per Year

A Monthly Newsletter

THE Libertarian Forum

Joseph R. Peden, Pubiisher   Murray N. Rothbard, Editor

VOLUME V, NO. 10   OCTOBER, 1973   US-ISSN0047-4517

Hands Off The Middle East!

As this editorial is being written, the tinder box of the Middle East is threatening to burst into full-scale war. Whether this new scare fizzles or not, another round of warfare is someday inevitable, and another and another, until the fundamental deep-seated conflicts are at last resolved. The fundamental conflict is that the state of Israel has grabbed an enormous amount of Arab land and territory, in the process manufacturing over a million Palestinian refugees who live their lives in the destitution of refugee camps, and creating a subject population of hundreds of thousands of Palestinian Arabs on the west bank of the Jordan. Israel grabbed this land in two aggressive wars, in each case fueled by American arms and money, and backed by the implicit might of the United States in the wings: the UN partition edict and the ensuing war of 1948; and the war of 1967. (The Israeli attack of 1956 was forced back because, for once, Israel lacked American support.)

Whatever the strength of the Arab forces, they have at least one hand tied behind their backs because everyone with eyes to see knows darn well that, should the Israeli forces get into any sizable trouble, American troops, ships, and planes stand ready to bail them out. The reason is startlingly simple: there ain't no Arab votes in the United States, or Arab groups possessed of political or economic power.

Libertarians have, at last, pretty much agreed upon "isolationism" — on the refusal to intervene in foreign wars — as the proper libertarian foreign policy in a world in which nation-States continue to exist. This principle of isolationism, or "non-intervention", has been increasingly accepted in recent years, among liberals and the Left. And perhaps this concept is still not dead among the Old Right, the isolationists of two and three decades ago. With the Vietnamese and Cambodian conflicts still going on, though with less visible American support, the danger now looms that imperial war and foreign intervention is looming for the U.S. once again, with all their attendant evils of mass murder, increased taxes and militarism, and perhaps conscription as well. It is time for the anti-war, anti-intervention forces to have the courage to apply their principles to the Middle East, and not to let their vital principles be overriden by the temptations of ethnic chauvinism. It is time to call upon the United States to get completely out of Middle Eastern politics, to stop sending aid to either side, and to let the contending parties slug it out in any war that may arise without a hint of interference on our part. And not the least of the beneficial results of such rigorous non-intervention will be to avoid any possibility of becoming enmeshed in a disastrous global conflict. Hands off the Middle East!   ◼

Libertarians And Culture: A Challenge

By James D. Davidson

How many libertarians would it take to save America? There is a tricky question. I have no idea what the answer is, but I am sure that it is directly proportional to the quality of person involved. If every individual who now considers himself a "libertarian" were possessed of the brains, dedication, and winning personality of Professor Rothbard, then the task would long since have been complete. On the other hand, if libertarians were mostly an assortment of low-life bums, it would require about 150 million of them. I present this calculation to explain what might otherwise seem to be a gratuitous attack upon some of our friends who are "out of it" culturally.

Why be concerned with aspects of taste? Nothing is more basic to the libertarian credo than the right of any man to live like a slob if he does so peacefully. True enough. But as a question of strategy, even died-in-the-wool-slobs could be asked to forgo their immediate gratification as a short-term sacrifice. For example, if removing the plastic slipcovers from living room furniture would improve the rate of conversion in home meetings, then it might be worthwhile. When freedom is won, the plastic slipcovers could go back on, there to remain, day and night forever. The same is true of gaudy jewelry. No matter how fetching it seems to the

wearer, he might take it off to help the cause. I have personally encountered individuals who showed great potential as libertarians, but who fell away from libertarian circles out of fear their backs were not strong enough to sport the mandatory ten pound gilded dollar sign.

Too many libertarians turn off potential converts by demonstrating retarded cultural awareness. While the veracity of economic arguments is in no way affected by cultural taste, sociology tells us that the rules of assortive mating apply to all voluntary associations. Well educated people, as a rule, do not prefer to associate with folks who applaud between movements of a symphony or drink from a finger bowl. Such behavior has down-home populist appeal. But the down-home populists are not the opinion leaders and intellectuals who must be convinced before freedom is accepted in our present society. If the stereotyped libertarian is a cultural clod, then severe inhibitions against advocating libertarian ideas will slow the progress of the movement.

The noticeable craze for "science fiction" in libertarian circles provides a good case in point. One can hardly hand a copy of a libertarian journal to a sophisticated reader without apologizing for the imitation

(Continued On Page 2)

Libertarians And Culture —

(Continued From Page 1)

Heinlein drivel which too often accompanies sound economic, philosophic and historical analyses. The literature of fantasy has a place somewhere but it need not be incorporated as an integral part of libertarian thought. (It is as if all libertarians were involved fanatically in the sport of metal detection. If jabber about metal detectors and treasure hunts filled libertarian publications the result would be enhanced satisfaction of a few readers, with the permanent alienation of everyone else.) More telling still is the fact that science fiction appeals invariably to individuals who have never studied serious literature. These are emphatically not the opinion molders and influential intellectuals who must be reached.

One can make a case that much of what passes for received culture is ridiculous. And so it may be. But in order to make that case effectively, one must know what received culture is. A passing acquaintance with the major literary figures is essential to any convincing case against them. When libertarians reveal their literary ignorance, as many do, their other opinions are discounted as well.

Much of the blame for identification of libertarianism with schlock culture must be laid upon Ayn Rand, a woman of undoubted intellect who is nevertheless flamboyantly ignorant of many areas of human achievement. As Professor Rothbard has trenchantly noted, Miss Rand's cultural preferences, justified with elaborate mumbo-jumbo, boil down to nothing more than a fondness for the literature and music which were in vogue when she was growing up in Russia after the turn of the century. This is perfectly understandable nostalgia. But Ayn Rand's girlhood memories hardly provide the basis for discerning persons interested in literature and music. Russia, after all, was and is a cultural backwater. The 18th century never happened in Russia. The 17th century, a time of great achievement in English literature, was still the Middle Ages east of Germany.

Libertarians who depend upon Miss Rand's shaky cultural guidance, neglect the more plausible identity between libertarian principles and classical literature for an identification with the wooly excesses of Romanticism. The virtues of a John Milton, for example, a true libertarian, are downplayed on behalf of the sentimentalism of 19th Century French Romantics. This is in spite of the fact that almost all intellectual historians agree that the true significance of Romanticism was to further collectivism. Even conservative Romantics such as Joseph de Maistre, Chateaubriand, and de Bonald were enthusiastic advocates of absolute state authority and subordination of the individual. The irrational content common to all Romantic thinking has been thoroughly identified. Professor Stephen Tonsor, the eminent historian, has made the case that the philosophy of Karl Marx is best explained as an incorporation of typical Romantic attitudes. So why be blindly attached to Romanticism? Its philosophic appeal should be almost nil for a perceptive libertarian. Certainly, one ought not to feel that a consistent friend of freedom is obliged to like Romantic writers in order to keep his self-esteem intact.

A similar case could be made against Ayn Rand's taste in music. She is fond of Romantic music, which has many appealing qualities. But Rand's philosophizing about musicology is even more shaky than that of the Marxist critics who profess to identify bourgeois deviations on the basis of note intervals and sequences. The fact that the music which is popular in Communist Russia today is largely similar to that which Rand advances as ideal for libertarians ought to give one pause. For all but the most perceptive student of philosophy, music, has no literal meaning. Where scholars have attempted to demonstrate an objective content to music, as Deryck Cooke did in The Language of Music, the attempt in no way resembles Miss Rand's arguments. More persuasive than the ideological explanations is the fact that Miss Rand and Russia's present rulers grew up together, listening to more or less the same music. The suggestion that it is any more rational to prefer Tchaikovsky to Bach is ludicrous. It is merely a preference. To dress it in psuedo-philosophic trappings is to invite ridicule. The spectacle of Randians drooling in unison over the same composers turns off disinterested observers. One could easily detest Chopin and admire Claude Gervaise,

Thomas Morely, John Dowland, and William Byrd. This delectation would provide no clue to philosophic understanding. No one who thinks otherwise among libertarians is sufficiently educated to make the case which would be necessary to sustain his position.

There are other idiosyncrasies among libertarians which tend to limit their effectiveness in spreading ideas among the intellectual and opinion-molding class. Many libertarians dress in poor taste. This defies the predisposition of most persons to like others who are most like them. When libertarians who dress like engineers try to persuade an editor of their position, they have two strikes against them at the outset. In order to be acceptable to opinion makers, libertarians should be indistinguishable, by appearance, from the people one would find normally in association with opinion makers. The suggestion here is not that one ape fashion trends, but merely be aware of the dress of those he intends to influence. Chances are that dressing sensitively is more important than a half a dozen syllogisms.

Many similar complaints about bad taste among libertarians could be extended. But it would be futile to elaborate the argument further. Most persons do not value freedom, and have never thought about anything. When someone is an exception to those unhappy generalizations it is probably too much to hope that he will also have a sense for public relations. Even more futile is the hope that the average libertarian, in addition to having a winning personality, will have the dedication and brains to elaborate libertarian theory on his own. Few persons will ever be philosophers. In spite of the pretensions of Randians that man is a rational animal, even most Randians have never had an original thought in their lives. Their rationality in solving proximate problems does not contradict this. It can be likened to the actions of a cat avoiding a car in the street. The fact that they act and act rationally promises nothing about their capacity for philosophy. The vast majority of men, libertarians no less than others, enjoy a free ride because of the mental efforts of a few individuals.

It is useless to develop arguments in epistemology for persons of normal intelligence, regardless of their dedication to freedom. All they will ever understand is the fleeting highlights; the conclusions which are enough. Let those who are not philosophers leave philosophy alone. Observation of the proven principle of the division of labor would suggest that good thinkers do the thinking and those who are not, but interested in promoting freedom, provide whatever their skills and disposition allow. If that means hustling for converts, it could also include casting off the cheap, schlock dollar sign jewelry, buying some new clothes, burying the plastic slip covers; turning from Mickey Spilane to John Milton, listening to Bach, and otherwise conducting oneself as fittingly as one can to strike up contacts among persons it would be important to convert.

Hopefully (from the point of view of hastening the day of ultimate success) many of the libertarians scattered through America, even those with the worst of taste, are persons of genuine intellectual potential. For those who can understand a philosophic argument well enough to make something of it, I have a suggestion whereby they could stick with the element of fantasy which they love in science fiction, while reaching an important and neglected group of intellectuals. Throw away the science fiction magazines and subscribe to The Journal of Theological Studies (c/o the Clarendon Press, Oxford) and The Harvard Theological Review. This is absolutely the best way of purging residual Randism. Reading these two journals, both of which boast works of superb scholarship, you will notice an amazing thing. There is just as much libertarian content in some religions fantasy as there is in Heinlein. But it is far better for you. The arguments of the theologians are still drawn out with Thomistic rigor, and scholarly skill. Since it is common knowledge that most theologians don't believe in God, few of the arguments will be offensive to other than militant atheists. But even better than the fantasies of the science fiction writers, is the earnest and profound concern of the theologians for great issues: the well-being of the individual man in his ultimate geopolitical environment. This high moral concern is exactly what one needs to be a libertarian. The a priori mode of argument is a familiar one to those who have studied libertarian economics. The disposition, then, among theologians is not more unkind to the progress of libertarian thought than is the case among science fiction fans.

If more libertarians would fall in among theologians, the result could be a progress of pro-freedom arguments among that group with a still-considerable influence. And the theologians might do us the favor of introducing the narrowly educated libertarians to the broad outlines of Western culture. They might even hook a few Randians on Bach. ◻

Send Money!

In the five years of existence of the **Lib. Forum**, we have not made a pitch for money for any cause or group, even for ourselves. But we now urge all libertarians or even quasi-libertarians to send as much money as they can spare, and right away, to the Youngstein for Mayor cause in New York City. For, by dint of heroic efforts and operating on a shoestring, the intrepid workers of the Free Libertarian Party managed to amass over 20,000 signatures (!!) to put the entire mayoral slate on the ballot, including the Manhattan candidates headed by Gary Greenberg as the only opponent of the aging Frank Hogan for District Attorney.

This is it; this is what makes party activity worthwhile — the couple of months before Election Day when the party and its candidates can spread its message to an often willing electorate. An intelligent and lovely candidate, Fran Youngstein, has been waging a remarkably active campaign, and has won recognition and publicity on television, radio, in the press, and in public forums. Fran and the FLP already have earned at least recognition among broad masses of the public; so that many men-in-the-street have heard the name and are at least vaguely familiar with our principles. There is no better time for a libertarian dollar to be contributed with more explosive effect. Furthermore, several outstanding advertising and other media people have joined the campaign, and they have already drafted a potential full-page ad in the prestigious New York **Times** which will be a knockout — if the campaign can raise the money, fast, to pay for the ad. We need $11,600 to put this sockeroo of an ad in the **Times**. How about it, libertarians; how about investing some money in your ideals and your lives and liberties?

Send your contributions, please, to the:

Youngstein for Mayor Committee,
Free Libertarian Party,
Suite 201,
15 West 38th St.
New York, N. Y. 10018.   ◘

'The Libertarian': The Gospel According To LeFevre

Robert LeFevre has been silent — at least in print — for quite a while, and now he is back with a minibook, **The Libertarian**, which has been billed as a convenient and presumably objective introduction to libertarianism and the current libertarian movement. It is not; it is LeFevre riding his familiar hobby horses, with some further errors of fact thrown into the pot. Also added is the irritating habit of referring to his own views as "the moralist" position, so that he is the moralist and all the rest of us are, by implication, amoral pragmatists and sinners. Presumably, LeFevre has yet to learn that positions differing from his own may not only be within the dissident's right to hold, but may be perfectly moral as well.

LeFevre's peculiar variant of the libertarian position is that he holds **defensive** violence — the use of violence to defend one's person or property against violent attack — to be **just as immoral** as aggressive violence itself. Defense against force is, for LeFevre, equally as immoral as the initiation of force against another. In short, to LeFevre, it is violence **per se** that is immoral (indeed, virtually the **only** immorality), and not the use that is made of it. The entire LeFevrian political philosophy is a logical derivation from this basic moral axiom. But I submit that this axiom is simply balderdash, derivable from nothing in the nature of man or the universe, an **ad hoc** precept imported from God knows where. It is not an accident that most people, libertarians and non-libertarians alike, regard this ultra-pacifist axiom as balderdash as well.

It is not that LeFevre is opposed to the rights of private property. On the contrary, he upholds them and denounces aggression against them. Fine; **except** that he equally denounces the use of force to repel such aggression. To be more precise, he divides up the defense function into several parts: "protection", defense (in hot-encounters), retaliation, and punishment. The last three are all condemned by LeFevre as the immoral use of violence, which allows one only "protection", a most attenuated concept which boils down to installing "a good bolt lock" on one's door. For the rest, we are abjured to confine ourselves to attempting to reason with and persuade the aggressor as he is moving in on us. LeFevre on hot-encounters, e.g. being mugged on the street, reasons as follows:

> "The pacifists and moralists (i.e. LeFevre), while admitting that they, too, might do anything at all under the pressure of expedience, contend that they should not violate the boundaries of an aggressor, and if they do in the excitement of the occasion, they would be in error and performing a wrongful act." (LeFevre, p. 42).

LeFebre's seeming concession about the pressure of the moment is, of course, irrelevant; the point is that he is condemning as evil and wrongful the "violation of the boundaries of an aggressor." As far as I am concerned — and presumably this also holds for most other libertarians — I don't give a damn about violating an aggressor's "boundaries." In fact, the speedier and more effective such "violation" the better, in order to stop the aggression.

Conservatives often worry, and for good reason, about the "coddling of criminals" that goes on in our current society. But Robert LeFevre would elevate such coddling to the status of a high-flown axiom: beyond a stout lock and gentle persuasion, nothing can morally be done to stop a criminal in his aggression, to compel restitution or retribution for his crime, or to see to it that he doesn't commit aggression again.

If I were addicted to **ad hominem** arguments, I could point out that a stout lock might do well in the peaceful climes of Orange County, California, but that it would hardly suffice against the predatory muggers of New York City or Washington, D. C. And in a hot encounter with a mugger, LeFevre may be content to try to "remotivate the aggressor by peaceful means" on the spot, but most of us are scarcely willing to rely on what will be, in that situation, a flimsy reed indeed.

But what about the stout lock? I submit that LeFevre, so enamoured of "boundary" arguments, cannot sustain the boundaries of his definition of "protection" with any proper precision. If a stout lock is OK for LeFevre, I presume that a fence would be too. But what about an electrified fence? Our precious criminal, trying to get over such a fence, is going to have his "boundaries" very much violated. Or, if a **mildly** electrified fence is OK with LeFevre, how about a **severely** electrified fence, which might well send our criminal to Kingdom Come? Or, how about a fence which, if violated automatically discharges a bullet into the offender? Or, going the other way, if LeFevre would condemn an electrified fence as immoral, how about a simple barbed wire fence? After all, the barbed wire might tear at our criminal's bodily boundary. And even without the barbed wire, the poor criminal might hurt himself trying to climb the fence, or even in trying to pry open the lock.

The alternative, then, to LeFevre's curious moral axiom is to hold, not that **all** violence is immoral, but that only aggressive violence deserves the label, and that defensive violence is perfectly moral, proper, and legitimate. Those of us, then, who are not absolute pacifists are **not** amoral pragmatists or believers in "situational ethics", as LeFevre believes; it is simply that we hold a very different moral axiom for the libertarian creed.

In his anxiety to attack all defensive violence from whatever source, LeFevre goes so far as to make common cause with the statists in denying the workability of anarcho-capitalism, with its belief in private, competing defense agencies on the free market. Here he repeats the old statist canards about what would happen if A belongs to one agency and B another, and if A accuses B of a crime. Here his scenario, as usual,

(Continued On Page 4)

415

Gospel According To LeFevre —

(Continued From Page 3)

assumes that market defense agencies would be total fools ignorant of how arbitration and judicial service could be provided on the market or of how beneficial such agreed-upon services would be for their own profits. Here I would simply refer LeFevre to various accounts of how anarcho-capitalism could work that have been published in recent years: including my own, Wollstein, Perkins, and Friedman. Unfortunately, LeFevre writes as if none of this has been written or thought about.

Pressing on to attack the Libertarian Party or any political activity whatever among libertarians, LeFevre claims that the **consistent** libertarian must be "a-political". Why? Because, the politically active libertarian is demanding a society "closed" to any but libertarian concepts." In contrast, the "a-political" libertarian wants an "open" society in which anyone can believe anything he wishes. This is a curious position, since the "political" libertarian wants the same thing; but, asserts LeFevre, the "political" libertarian seeks to "impose his views (in support of liberty) upon others." (p. 56).

This of course is a distortion of the "political" libertarian position. What we want is not to impose any "views" on anyone, but to combat and repress aggression against person and property. But there we have it, because that, too, according to LeFevrian axioms, is just as immoral as aggression itself. The "politics" turns out to be simply trying to use force to prevent forcible aggression, and we are back philosophically to what we do with the mugger in the hot-encounter. But the implications of the LeFevrean position are even more bizarre. For what he is saying is that any use of the political process (i.e. force) is as immoral as **any other**, and that **therefore**, for example, while voting for the draft is admittedly evil and immoral, voting to **repeal** the draft is equally immoral. For, then, you see, the proponents of the criminal draft are being deprived of what they would like to be doing; in a basic sense, they are being **forced** to leave the rest of us alone.

The important point here is that LeFevre's dogmatic hostility to libertarian political action has really nothing to do with the qualms that all of us have in associating with the State apparatus. It really has nothing to do with widespread worries about capitulating to a lust for power. It stems clearly and single-mindedly from LeFevre's basic axiom that defensive and aggressive force are equally evil and equally to be condemned. One can admire LeFevre for his consistency, but that cannot prevent us from a hard and critical look at the basic absurdity of his central axiom, an absurdity which makes the rest of his structure fall to the ground.

Given his political philosophy, there is little point in dwelling on the fact that LeFevre has no real strategy for the recovery of liberty and for the liquidation or even the whittling away of statism. Violent revolution, political action, **anything** that smacks of defensive force in any sense is equally condemned. All that leaves us with is to persuade the mugger, to persuade the State to resign and liquidate itself **en masse**. The rest of us can only wish LeFevre luck in this task, while also however employing other means (such as Libertarian Party activity) which we deem to be perfectly moral.

This brings me to LeFevre's errors of fact about myself in this booklet. Describing me, he writes: "Rothbard has not always been predictable. He began with conservative economic leanings, then moved into the establishment of the left, attracting followers as he went. Disenchanted with this flirtation, he backed away and returned to a relatively pure libertarian position as an economist." (p. 12) Sternly eschewing the temptation to delve into LeFevre's own past peccadilloes and lapses from "predictability", I must again state that this description of my activities is pure balderdash. My "conservative" or libertarian economic leanings — indeed my libertarian position as a whole, — have remained fixed and unchanging for approximately twenty-five years. My "flirtation" with some of the New Left in the 1960's was simply a recognition of many libertarian elements that then existed in that movement. Indeed, a little later on, LeFevre himself engages in such "flirtation" by commending the libertarian contributions of former New Left leader Carl Oglesby (p. 19). Apparently what is sauce for the LeFevrian goose is not sauce for the gander.

Furthermore, fruitful collaboration with the sensible and quasi-libertarian elements and remnants of the New Left continues to the present-day. And not only with Carl Oglesby. Myself and many other

Revolution In Chile

It looked like the theorists of the Left had it all worked about Revolutions. Revolutions were admirable events in which the People rose up, in a series of strikes against the oppressive bourgeois State, building pressure from below until the final moment when armed struggle was used to deliver the **coup de grace** to the State apparatus. After the victory, retribution was to be meted out to the remnants of the old ruling class enemy; and the retributive process, while admittedly stern, was treated as either (a) giving the old ruling class its just deserts as well as guarding against the threat of a counter-revolution; and/or (b) the regrettable but insignificant excesses attendant on any required historical change. You can't make an omelet, we were told long ago, without breaking some eggs. Furthermore, in a genuine revolution, organized women rise to the fore, rebelling thereby also against the super-exploitation meted out to their gender.

So then Revolution came to Chile. Acting against the oppression of Allende's attempt to impose Marxian socialism, against intensified nationalization, against an inflation that tripled the price level over the last year, against a price control structure that caused widespread shortages of food and other commodities, against armed hordes of Marxist workers who seized factories with Allendist consent, the people rose up. For make no mistake, Chile was not just another Latin-American military coup by the armed forces. The Chilean armed forces had a long tradition of not interfering in national politics, however distasteful. What they faced was a genuine revolutionary process rising spontaneously from below — rising, not from "outside agitators" as counter-revolutionaries always charge, but from the deeply felt grievances against the regime suffered by the people themselves. The spark was set off by the nation's self-employed truckers, the heart of Chile's entire transportation system; the truckers went out on strike in protest against impending Allendist nationalization. After weeks of heroic strike activity by the truckers, the rest of the oppressed middle class also went on strike: the professionals, the small shopkeepers, etc. And the super-exploited women rose up too; organized anti-socialist women played a large part in the revolutionary pressure and demonstrations. Then, as in the Left Revolutionary script, armed force was used as the final smashing blow to the Allendist state apparatus, after which a process of revolutionary retribution has ensued.

So fine; did, then, our Leftist theorists hail the Chilean Revolution as a shining new example of revolutionary success? You can bet your sweet life they did **not**. Not in a long while have we seen such a mass orgy of

(Continued On Page 5)

libertarian scholars continue to have fruitful collaboration, for example, with such New Left historians and revisionists as Ronald Radosh, Lloyd Gardner, and Barton Bernstein, and New Left historian Gabriel Kolko's great works have been used to good effect by Gary Allen and other Birch Society writers. Also I and other libertarians interested in combatting public schooling and compulsory education continue to collaborate fruitfully with such New Left educational theorists as John Holt, Joel Spring, and Ivan Illich. Ron Radosh and myself recently co-edited a book, **A New History of Leviathan**, which contained articles critical of twentieth-century American statism by both libertarian and New Left historians.

As for the rest of the New Left, it disappeared in an orgy of Leninist sects and frenzied bomb-throwing, and few of us will mourn its demise.

But of course I **do** believe in the propriety (if not always the expediency) of defensive force against aggression, and therefore I seek always, as a "political activist", to find ways and means to whittle down State power in any given historical period, and to form whatever alliances are called for in particular historical circumstances to carry forth this task (e.g. alliance with the Left against conscription in one period, with the Right against income taxes in the same or another period, etc.) Hence, what LeFevre chooses to see as "unpredictability" is really the employment of strategy in attempting to whittle down State power and to expand the area of human liberty. So be it; but let it be noted that for LeFevre, any libertarian believing in defensive force and wishing to do something to improve the prospects for liberty will reap a similar complaint. Through it all, of course, Bob LeFevre remains all too predictable, hurling his anathemas at anyone who does not share his peculiar moral axioms.   ▫

Revolution In Chile —

(Continued From Page 4)

blubbering and hand-wringing as we have over the fallen Allendist collectivists. But fellows, how about the Inevitable Excesses of the Revolution? How about the necessity to prevent a counter-revolution? I guess it depends on whose ox is being gored. Because one vital lesson that the Left theorists of Revolution have failed to learn is that genuine grievances can and do occur under any State, including a Marxian State, and that therefore revolutions **against** Marxism can be just as genuine as revolutions on its behalf.

But what about all the weeping and wailing about the abolition of "Chilean democracy?" Well, in the first place, we all learned from the Revolutionaries about the use of the democratic form to camouflage the realities of State despotism. And we learned from Marcuse about the "repressive tolerance" in which democratic forms are used to fool the masses into accepting the State. And, furthermore, Allendism wasn't all that democratic. Allende was elected by one third of the electorate, and his voting support never rose above 40%. And so The People, restricted by the formalistic trappings of the legal structure, brushed aside petty legalism to cast aside Allendist oppression. (And besides, Allende, scion of a wealthy family, looked and acted like a "bourgeois", didn't he?)

But weren't the workers and peasants solidly behind Allende? Not really. The peasants had soured on the Allende regime when its land reform failed to grant the promised land to the individual peasants, and instead tried to force the peasants onto State farms: a fate even worse then feudal landlordism. Also, food prices were kept far below the free market levels by severe price control, and this led to widespread distress on the farms as well as food shortages in the cities. It is true that the urban workers, coddled by subsidies and by compulsory makework imposed by the regine, supported Allende, but that was scarcely enough.

So it turns out that the Left is narrowly selective in its support of People's Revolutions; only Marxist People's Revolutions will do. There is no question about the fact that the Allendist Marxists had brought Chile to the brink of economic and social disaster; in addition to the ruinous inflation, price controls, and shortages, the nationalized industries could produce very little under Marxian management. The Chilean economy was grinding to a halt, and the Revolution has now lanced the boil; the Revolutionaries have a glorious opportunity to set Chile on the road to freedom.

What will they do with this opportunity? The issue is still in doubt. Apparently, most of the nationalized industries have been returned to their private owners, and the State farms have been granted to the peasants. Foreign investment is being welcomed once again. And the regime has hired a team of bright young U.S.-trained economists who advise a return to a free market and open competition. This would mean not only elimination of price controls and of the special measures artificially holding down the price of food, but the eradication of the high protective tariffs behind which inefficient domestic manufactures have long sprouted. If the economists' free market recommendations are heeded, that would be great, and prospects look favorable. But on the other hand, it looks certain that the Chilean State will hang on to its nationalized copper mines, with their drastic drop in output under State rule; and as long as they do that, how can the new regime claim to be pursuing a policy of free markets? And not only that, but the price controls still in effect are being upheld by the new regime's shooting of people who sell goods at "black market" prices. The new revolutionary Chile claims to be dedicated to the "extermination of Marxism" and to the "extirpation of the Marxist cancer." (What grand rhetoric! You don't get to hardly hear any of that no more!) But how can a regime "extirpate the Marxist cancer" when it shoots black marketeers and hangs on to its nationalized copper mines?

One interesting side effect of the Chilean Revolution: We have heard for years the Social Democrat myth that there's nothing wrong with Communism except the suppression of free elections, and that therefore no one would really object to a Communist regime if the Communists only eschewed violent revolution and stuck to "peaceful," democratic forms. A corollary Social Democratic myth is that Communists or Marxist-Leninists have never risen to power via free elections. But first there was tiny San Marino, which freely elected a Communist government, after which Italy, which totally surrounds San Marino, blockaded the little country until the Communist regime was deposed.

Friedman's Value-Free Value: Human Liberty

By Tibor R. Machan

In his exciting book **The Machinery of Freedom** — which deserves thorough study from those interested in how well a market system can solve problems most of us acknowledge require solution — David Friedman makes some by now familiar disclaimers about the usefulness of morality in political discourse and action. He tells us that "I have said almost nothing about rights, ethics, good and bad, right and wrong, although these are matters central to the ideas of most libertarians." He goes on to explain that he has "couched (the) argument throughout in terms of practicality."

Friedman expands on the decision to avoid moral questions by telling us that "I have found that it is much easier to persuade people with practical arguments than with ethical arguments." And he ends the section which contains these disclaimers — a single page long, entitled "Postscript for perfectionists" — with the observation: "I have never met a socialist who wanted the kind of society that I think socialism would produce." (p. 223)

For succinctness David Friedman must especially be commended. Of all the "value-free" defenses of human liberty — an odd notion right off — Friedman's is the least cumbersome as well as the most revealing. I will not attend to anything but these remarks of his, mainly because they pertain most directly to the kind of work I consider valuable in the protection and preservation of liberty. Indeed the sorts of matters Friedman would consider less likely to succeed in efforts to establish greater liberty are considered by me "central." Moreover, maybe due to my personal experiences that have been very different from Friedman's, I venture to say there are socialists who want the kind of society socialism produces. I lived in such a society and indeed many around me wanted it badly enough to wipe out those who preferred otherwise. But these matters may be the result of Friedman's not having met enough socialists.

To turn to this discussion by Friedman, let me say first that he does indeed say a lot about rights — he speaks of property rights throughout the book. And he says a great deal about good and bad, right and wrong — as when he tells us that "I have described what should be done, but not who should organize and control it." (p. 220) The "should" is here surely something like the "should" of morality — Friedman then is describing the right sort of actions to be taken by us. What he does not tell us is, indeed — and to some deficiency of his thesis — why these are the right things to do. Perhaps he would answer: Because they will produce liberty. But it still needs to be learned why that is good. And here Friedman says he has only "practical arguments" to offer. Such arguments usually take the form of "If one's purpose or goal is X, then, by reason of our familiarity with the better and worse ways to achieve X, one should do such and such." Thus to become free, we should give up government or the state. Since the argument is conditional, one who does not have as his purpose to become free has the logical right to reject the advice offered.

Friedman may be right, to think that most people want to be free but just don't know how to do it. So not a political treatise but a manual for liberty will achieve enough to establish the required case. But then the case serves only those who already want freedom. The case for freedom is assumed, the audience is taken to have bought it prior to coming to Friedman's advisory bureau.

That is why Friedman must spend some time persuading the reader that there are no socialists who really (deep in their hearts) want what

(Continued On Page 6)

And then there was the freely elected Popular Front government of Guatemala, overthrown by an armed invasion fueled by the CIA. But now we have the clincher: a freely elected Marxist-Leninist government overthrown by popular armed struggle. The strategic possibility of a peaceful, democratic road to Marxism turns out to be virtually nil. And the real menace of Marxism is clearly not the kind of route it adopts to try to gain power, whether violent or democratic: the real manace is the kind of State it imposes once it gets there. ◻

Friedman's Value-Free Value —

(Continued From Page 5)

socialism amounts to, lack of freedom, or slavery. But his efforts here are indeed meager to the task. They seem, although perhaps only facetiously to rest on Friedman's having met a select class of socialists — those who don't want socialism.

But this may not be fair. Don't all people want freedom? In a sense most, at least, do — for themselves (although you will find hosts of them defending taxation, laws prohibiting hundreds of sorts of activities on their part). Taking it that most people want freedom, this usually amounts to wanting others off one's back in areas of activities one wants to perform. But not in those one cares little about. So most people want a type of freedom that does not quite amount to the political liberty Friedman and other libertarians want: the freedom to do what they consider the right things, the freedom to act as one should act. But not the freedom to do what one should not do — never mind that these doings may have nothing to do with hurting others, enslaving them or the like. The kind of liberty, then, that most people want (implicitly — for few of them expound on it fully rationally) is what Professor John O. Nelson has called the continental conception (Hegelian or neo-Hegelian/Marxist type) of freedom. (Two sources should suffice to get one clear on this matter: Nelson's own essay in my forthcoming anthology The Libertarian Alternative: Essays in Social and Political Philosophy, to be out from Nelson-Hall Co., Chicago, in November 1973, and Andrew McLaughlin's essay "Freedom versus Capitalism" in Dorothy James Outside Looking In, out from Harper and Row Publishers in Spring 1972.) Its basic feature is that freedom is the power to do the right thing, while slavery is the weakness or impotence that leads to doing wrong.

Surely Friedman does not have this sort of liberty in mind. Yet this is what most people want — judging by their actions and acquiescence concerning political and legal practices today. The unproven but assumed premise Friedman's practical arguments require is not the one Friedman has succeeded in finding even among those socialists he has met. Their meaning of the concept "freedom" is totally alien to what I take to be Friedman's.

None of this shows that the practical arguments have no value, only that they do not do the work Friedman asks of them — to show how we should get where "almost everyone" wants to get, to a free society. Nor does Friedman fail to give support to liberty with his able delineation of how its absence has produced all sorts of misery for people. What he hasn't shown is why it is wrong to produce such misery. And do not say — well that is obvious. The lover of freedom is not hostile to the misery of those who would obstruct it. After all, thieves and murderers should be miserable in consequences of what they have done. A clear identification of why misery, through the absence of liberty in the lives of those who have not murdered and stolen, should not obtain is, then, not provided by Friedman.

Let me now touch on a very practical problem that arises by "couching arguments in terms of practicality." Ralph Nader and David Friedman both agree that the Fed's regulatory agents have done more harm than good for us all. But Nader advises that therefore we should make them more efficient, install better people, expand the powers of these people, etc., while David Friedman — as well as Milton Friedman and the entire Chicago crew — counsels that therefore we should get rid of these people, fire them, and leave people free to run their business in voluntary cooperation.

The source of the discrepancy in the face of such clear agreement should interest the value-free folks. Ralph Nader has values! Oh, he may be unable to demonstrate their validity, to justify them. But we might say that "these values are widely held by people." They include a safe toy, harmless drug, lack of soot in the air, low prices, protection from nasty businessmen, the reduction of racial prejudice, etc., etc. These are the values Nader has in mind securing by way of improving the quality of regulation, by electing and appointing virtuous statists. These are the goods that he accepts, the ethical purposes for which he asks for the statist measures we all know well.

Without benefit of ethics Friedman can respond to Nader only by citing cost/efficiency data. But Nader says: wait until I get the right folks in the driver's seat, see if we cannot have the service for the cost and the efficiency of the performance to attain our goals. But, says Friedman, history speaks against that. Nader can then say: history hasn't heard of

Technology Forever *

By Jerome Tuccille

Technology and revolution. At first glance the words do not sit well together, and yet our "dehumanizing" technology may transform the dream of an open-ended, mass-market, "people's" paradise into a living reality. Technology may well be the factor that brings the revolution to a close.

This is ironic, in a way, since the people with the greatest vested interest in revolutionary change have been the most vocal opponents of the new technology. The "professional" revolutionists among us have been strutting around the countryside wailing against our "love affair with machines," our "obsession with growth and progress," conjuring apocalyptic visions of a Doomsday Society over-peopled, over-polluted, over-mechanized, visions of a gutless humanity with the heart and

(Continued On Page 7)

*A Chapter from Tuccille's forthcoming book, Paradise Found: A Nonfiction Romance.

me — and anyway, is there nothing new under the sun? Might it not happen this time? As a good empiricist, Friedman cannot resort to his kind of logic here. For indeed, as the high prince of empiricism, Hume, has told us, anything might happen so far as reason is concerned.

Yet this again might sound unfair. So, OK. Strict deductive logic does not prove the impossibility of Nader's success. Surely good common sense militates against it, and that should be enough.

Unfortunately here Friedmanesque arguments cannot match the ethical ones. The plain fact is that where moral matters are involved we often do and should ignore cost and efficiency. Bad swimmers in expensive suits will jump to save drowning friends — the goal is so important that risk of failure and ultimate injury to self simply have no significance. Nader, then, would simply admit that, granted it isn't likely that the Feds will do much to solve our problems, to achieve our values, our morally respectable — even commendable — goals, these are too important to give up in the face of minor matters such as cost and impending failure. So the drowning person may not be saved — it looks very unlikely from here that we can do much for the chap. But, dammit, trying itself is better than nothing, even at great risks. (You think up your own examples — there are lots.)

In short, in the face of values that have even the appearance of moral validity, efficiency, practicality and the host of so called value-free considerations are impotent. Yes, in the practical task of persuading people, just what Friedman is after!

To fight the argument that Nader and Co. offer one has to produce a moral argument that shows that doing what the Feds do — even cheaply and efficiently, not as they have done it thus far — is wrong. We need not even bother to show that what Nader wants to achieve is itself wrong — quite the contrary, we may have to accept that unsafe toys are bad, that dangerous drugs and vicious businessmen are all bad. The issue is whether it is good to deprive others of their liberty to prevent the occurence of these bad things; not whether we at times — even most of the time — fail to achieve the goals Nader has in mind without incredible cost and inefficiency. That is to be expected when great things are at stake. No, we are concerned with whether Nader's suggested cures, even when perfectly administered, at low cost, are not in fact worse for us than what he aims to avert with them.

Thus: imprisoning people because they might engage in "monopolistic" practices — is that not a violation of their human rights; does it not violate the principle "innocent until proven guilty" (not: proven capable of guilt); does forcing toymakers to produce this instead of that kind of toy because the latter might harm some child presume guilt before proof? Should people be deprived of honest earnings and acquisitions just so others' safety and pleasure be achieved? In short, should force be used to achieve some admittedly admirable goals? And unless a moral argument can be produced, one that can stand the test of scrutiny, the Naders of our land have the better side of the argument — morality versus value-free liberty. (Just consider: valued purposes and goals versus value-free purposes and goals — how can they miss?)

But enough. Friedman's moral advice against offering moral advice lacks what much of his competent book lacks — moral justification. Yet the machinery of freedom needs just that. ◻

Technology Forever —

(Continued From Page 6)

brains bred out of it, capable only of stumbling trance-like into the future, hurtling mindlessly toward certain oblivion. By and large, our Doomsayers have been clamoring for a return to an idyllic past which never existed in reality, a green, halcyon, agricultural fairyland where everyone can play flutes under the trees, swim in rivers of May wine strewn with strawberries, and grab each other's buttocks as they roll naked among the wildflowers. Strangely enough, these seventeenth-century wonderlands are always devoid of such tacky annoyances as red ants, poison ivy, snapping turtles, and coldspells. Nature is always kind, the month is always May, and the weather is always balmy in Dreamland. Somehow feudalism, poverty, disease, and hunger — all of which were rampant in the pre-industrial economy — have vanished into the Ether.

Well all this is very pretty, very romantic, and very unrealistic. If we are going to have our paradise on earth it will only be by harnessing our technology, by controlling it totally and making it subservient to our own desires — not by abandoning it to the Wasteland of history. For it is only technology which can tidy up the mess we have already made, provide us with the clean environment we all want, free us of the tyrannies of hunger, poverty, disease, and death, and deliver a genuine paradise on earth. Also, it is only technology that can remove one of the final barriers between us and the anarchic or democratic ideal: the tyranny of isolation, alienation, and provincialism.

Perhaps the greatest enemy of a universal utopia is the distrust and intolerance of our fellow man bred by provincialism. Throughout history the human race has been sectioned off in hamlets, villages, towns, and nation-states. We have lived in little pockets of ignorance, each one surrounded by an iron wall of stupidity, suspicion, and superstition. Human ostriches, we buried our heads in the sterile sands of fear and security, and regarded everything different as a threat to our existence. Foreigners, communists, atheists, easterners, dwarfs, and one-eyed lepers were all prime candidates for the gas chamber. Better dead than red — or queer, or short, or swarthy — has been the warcry of every narrow-minded hick from the olive fields of ancient Greece to the flat and dreary cornfields of middle America.

And yes, nationalism is nothing more than provincialism run amuck.

My flag is brighter than yours, my skin lighter than yours, my God stronger than yours, my President nobler than yours, my town cleaner than yours, my tribe more sacred than yours, my country/town/village/tribe right or wrong. God, of course, is always on my side. The Old Fool is on everyone's side — the Germans, Italians, Americans, Japanese, Outer Mongolians, and Tanzanians — even as they hack each other's arms off and bomb an industrious citizenry somewhere back to the Stone Age.

(While behind the scenes of history the Billy Grahams of the world give the whole fiasco their blessings, tossing fuel onto an already raging inferno. How nice to snuggle warmly in the White House praying for the safety of one American emperor after another. It is much more sensible to prance about in double-knit suits and diamond pinky rings than to share a jailcell with a claque of unwashed subversives.)

("So it goes," said Kurt Vonnegut when he saw what was happening.)

Provincialism (nationalism on a smaller scale) is synonomous with ignorance, and the most dangerous thing about ignorance is that the damned condition is contagious. It breeds more fear, suspicion, petty (if not cowardly) heroics, and all this inevitably results in violence. Get them — hippies, commies, freaks, and un-Americans — before they get us. Before they sneak in our homes at night and rape our daughters, poison our sons with drugs and loud music, chop us up in our beds, and desecrate the American flag. Before they piss on the American dream. Hunter Thompson, Ken Kesey, and Fidel Castro all belong on the torture rack. Crucifixion is too good for them.

As long as this infectious condition exists (and it is a global disease; the American strain is only a bit more pronounced because of a certain native flamboyance), paradise will remain at best a distant dream; at worst we will usher in the Apocalypse instead, replete with man-made volcanos, faster-than-light warships, and a race of human gargoyles manufactured on demand in genetic engineering laboratories throughout the solar system.

But how to fight provincialism, isolation, and ignorance? Certainly not with guru chants, May wine, and love beads. And not by turning the earth into a global village, notwithstanding the worthy exhortations of Messers. McLuhan, Fuller, and Company. Herman Kahn is more on target when he speaks in terms of a global metropolis. In the past it has been in the cities where the civilized life has flourished, where the pristine hillbilly has been miraculously transformed into a tolerant, urbane, sophisticated, and cosmopolitan World Citizen. It is in the cities where provincialism (and ignorance) are beaten down and drummed out of existence. It is in the cities where music, literature, art, civility — all the worthwhile things of life — have found their voice, come into their own, and been rendered into magic.

How to end provincialism? By destroying the provinces and, with them, the provincial mentality. By making the earth a global city, a world metropolis, a universal seedbed of the civilized life, a paradise, a region of supreme felicity and delight.

A city is a state of consciousness, a condition of life. No proclamation or political act can make a village into a city — except on paper. A city is a state of mind, and this is where technology comes in.

The cement that holds the city together, that gives it its status and identity, is the technology of communications. As this technology evolved from hand-scrawled, hand-delivered letters to the printing press, the telephone, the telegraph, radio and television, and now to global satellites, the cities also grew up, grew more efficient and sophisticated, and finally reached a point where they are ready to burst through their boundaries, explode and self-destruct with uncontrollable energy.

They can no longer be contained but, rather, need room to expand and flesh out the universe.

For the first time in human history we have the technology at hand to create our global metropolis, obliterate the provinces, and deliver paradise to the entire world. For something like six dollars and seventy-five cents on weekends and after eight o'clock in the evening, the most isolated rube in South Dakota can pick up his telephone and contact his counterpart in Samoa, Mozambique, and the Australian outback. There is still a language barrier, to be sure, and there will be for quite some time to come, but at least the physical barriers isolating one community from another (the westside of Manhattan from Ringoes, New Jersey for that matter) have been overcome.

These relatively inexpensive round-the-world telephone calls are possible only if the telephones are working in the first place. Vandalism has transmogrified most of our public telephone booths — especially in the larger cities — into little more than urban outhouses, but Mother Bell is reportedly working on a system to change all that. In the near future we will be carrying portable telephones around with us. The phones will be activated when we step inside circular electromagnetic fields created by the telephone company, and the calls will be billed to credit cards or our home telephone numbers.

Hopefully the electromagnetic "phone booths" will continue to function no matter how many times they are urinated on.

Fantastic as this concept sounds, it is only the next step in a long string of advances Bell has in store for us. Also in the planning stage are cassette telephones for sending messages to many people simultaneously; self-dialing telephones that respond to a voice command; wristwatch telephones which will bring us another step beyond the Dick Tracy two-way wrist radio; home sentinel telephones which will inform us of fires, burglaries, and other extraordinary occurrences while we are away; picture phones, already being used commercially, for the home (the more advanced models will supply printed pictures of the screen image); credit phones allowing the caller to order merchandise and pay bills without leaving bed; and the list grows longer and longer even as we pause a moment to catch our breath. What all this translates into is the fact that instantaneous global communication grows more and more commonplace as time goes on; provincial barriers (and, hopefully, attitudes) are broken down as the world becomes a single, dynamic, interrelating community. Words such as foreign, alien, strange, different, and enemy lose their meaning when we are all citizens of the same global society.

Notwithstanding the dire predictions of Marshall McLuhan, the printed word is destined to play an even more important role in the Electronic Society than it does today. The book publishing industry will be modernized and wrenched out of the nineteenth century where it has been wallowing for the past one hundred and seventy-plus years. Through microfiching, more than a hundred books can be imposed on a four-by-six

(Continued On Page 8)

Technology Forever —

(Continued From Page 7)

inch plastic card. Instead of visiting mammoth bookstores with sturdy volumes toppling off the shelves — bookstores incapable of storing the forty-thousand books published in the United States alone each year — we will go to microfiching libraries capable of storing any number of printed words in a comparatively small area. If you want a certain book you simply visit the nearest library or "bookstore," and computerized machines will print it out and bind it for you in minutes. This will save the publisher a boodle in production costs since he will no longer have to manufacture and distribute thousands of books beforehand (and worry about remainders afterward), and it relieves the bookseller of the guesswork regarding which book should be ordered and kept in stock.

(The only casualties under this system will be the authors, themselves, who glory at the sight of their own books prominently displayed near the cash register when they walk into Brentano's. Perhaps advertising posters will provide the same balm for ruptured egos.)

Super phones and instant books. What else will our global cosmopolitan paradise have to offer? Well electronic newspapers are also on the horizon. Gone forever is (or will be soon) the sweaty romanticism of the Runyonesque reporter, his filthy fedora jauntily angled on the back of his head, the constant cigarette working in the corner of his mouth as he taps out an "exclusive" on a typewriter built during the early years of the Middle Ages. Yes, Jimmy Breslin could be the last of a dying breed while the Tom Wolfes of the profession neatly make the transition into the razzle-dazzle kaleidoscopic future. Video typewriters transmitting news stories directly to production via computerized phototypesetting equipment. Features written and edited electronically and transformed into newsprint without once having been tainted by human hands. The whole industry streamlined beyond recognition as newsrooms lose their cluttered hustle-bustle atmosphere and assume the aspects of a tile and chrome-plated, self-service cafeteria.

(Ah, nostalgia! You prick the psyche with guilt-inducing memories. You fill the dismal past with romanticized fantasy. You distort reality. To hell with nostalgia! We are determined to plunge guiltlessly and ruthlessly into the future.)

Our paradise of instantaneous universal communications (hence, of the constant Here and Now; of the ubiquitous unifying Media) will also offer copier equipment, courtesy of Xerox, 3M, Hitachi, et al, designed to transcend even the time zones. Yes, Time the Tyrant may soon be emasculated and disemboweled as the newest telecopiers enable us to send printed matter, including photographs, around the earth by telephone in a matter of seconds. In **living color** yet!

The boob tube also promises to make communications easier with juke box or cable cassette TV bringing dozens — eventually hundreds — of programs into the home simply by dialing a number. Or, if you can't wait until you get home, you will be able to tune in Lawrence Welk on a wrist TV set, now technologically feasible with the development of tiny silicone circuit "picture tubes."

(A nightmare filled with legions of lobotomized robots parading through the streets, their eyes forever glued to the image of the Beverly Hillbillies sparkling on their wrists? Or a paradise of peace, erudition, and urbanity through the magic of universal communication? A tricky dilemma. And a copout for this author who hypocritically lampoons the herd even as he urges it on toward the plastic, silicone, kandy-colored, tangerine-flake future.)

Yes I, too, will benefit in a paradise of talking textbooks. How comfortable to do one's research from home by dialing the local library and having a computer read selected pages of books and magazines, and to store all sorts of irrelevant material in lithium niobate "filing cabinets" the size of a sugar cube. No more overflowing metal cabinets which threaten to drive the researcher from his apartment.

And so we humble ourselves before the altar of technology. Almighty Technology, deliver us from our sins and bring us to the Promised Land. Hallowed be thy name. Thy kingdom come. On earth. Live and reign among us, in paradise on earth, forever and ever, amen. ▫

Arts And Movies

By Mr. First Nighter

Badge 373, dir. by Howard W. Koch, with Robert Duvall; written by Pete Hamill.

Badge 373 is a rough, exciting touch-cop picture, which could easily be named **Son of French Connection**. It is far inferior to its brilliantly directed, suspenseful ancestor, and is simply a minor sequel in the saga of touch narco cop Eddie Egan. The picture is chiefly remarkable for the attemps at censorship which have come down on its head, including picketing by the Puerto Rican Action Council because the villains happen to be part of a Puerto Rican political **cum** criminal gang. The Egan character is no more of an "ethnicist" than he was in **French Connection**, which called forth no protests from professional defenders of the clans. But for some reason **Badge 373** has done it, as the world gets increasingly **less** tolerant about allowing any depiction whatever of sins committed by various ethnic groups. The whole hullaballoo is absurd and even dangerous; are we to arrive at a day when gangsters will have to have only WASP names in order to remain safe from the would-be censors? And if organized WASPS also start getting into the act, the criminals and villains in our movies won't be allowed to have any names at all! The important thing is that the movie producers and exhibitors have the guts to say a quick and firm NO to the ethnic pests and pressure groups who are trying to keep us from seeing movies which they don't like. Television is of course plagued with similar problems, as organized Jewish groups managed to help eliminate the harmless **Bridget Loves Bernie** series (does anyone remember the very similar play, **Abie's Irish Rose**, which ran for years on Broadway with no protest whatever?), and organized Catholics tried to suppress two **Maude** episodes in which the leading actress decided to have an abortion. Again, guts are required in an increasingly gutless media. ▫

First Class

Published Every Month. Subscription Rate: $8.00 Per Year

A Monthly Newsletter

THE
Libertarian Forum

Joseph R. Peden, Publisher

Murray N. Rothbard, Editor

VOLUME V, NO. 11   NOVEMBER, 1973   US-ISSN0047-4517

Ludwig von Mises, RIP*

And he is gathered to the kings of thought
Who waged contention with their time's decay,
And of the past are all that cannot pass away.

— Shelley, **Adonais**

On October 10, Ludwig von Mises, well designated by the New York Times obituary as "one of the foremost economists of this century", died in New York City, shortly after his 92nd birthday.

For those of us who have loved as well as revered this great and noble man, words cannot express our sense of loss: of this gracious, brilliant, and wonderful man; this man of unblemished integrity; this courageous and lifelong fighter for human freedom; this all-encompassing scholar; this noble inspiration to us all. And above all, this gentle and charming friend, this man who brought to the rest of us the living embodiment of the culture and the charm of pre-World War I Vienna. For Mises' death takes away from us not only a deeply revered friend and mentor, but it tolls the bell for the end of an era: the last living mark of that more gracious, freer and far more civilized era of pre-1914 Europe.

Mises' friends and students will know instinctively what I mean: for when I think of Ludwig von Mises I think first of all of those landmark occasions when I had the privilege of afternoon tea at the Mises': in a small apartment that virtually breathed the atmosphere of a long lost and far more civilized era. The graciousness of Mises' devoted wife Margit; the precious volumes that were the remains of a superb home library destroyed by the Nazis; but above all, Mises himself, spinning in his inimitable way anecdotes of Old Vienna, tales of scholars past and present, brilliant insights into economics, politics, and social theory, and astute comments on the current scene.

Readers of Mises' majestic, formidable and uncompromising works must have often been surprised to meet him in person. Perhaps they had formed the image of Ludwig Mises as cold, severe, austere, the logical scholar repelled by lesser mortals, bitter at the follies around him and at the long trail of wrongs and insults that he had suffered.

They couldn't have been more wrong; for what they met was a mind of genius harmoniously blended with a personality of great sweetness and benevolence. Not once has any of us heard a harsh or bitter word escape from Mises' lips. Unfailingly gentle and courteous, Ludwig Mises was always there to encourage even the slightest signs of productivity or intelligence in his friends and students; always there for warmth as well as for the mastery of logic and reason that his works have long proclaimed him.

And always there as an inspiration and as a constant star. For what a life this man lived! Until near the end Ludwig Mises led his life very much in the world, pouring forth a mighty stream of great and immortal works, a fountainhead of energy and productivity as he taught continually at a university until the age of 87, as he flew tirelessly around the world to give papers and lectures on behalf of the free market and of sound economic science — a mighty structure of coherence and logic to which

he contributed so much of his own creation.

I am strongly reminded of perhaps the finest obituary in the history of economic thought — Joseph Schumpeter's tribute to his and Mises' great mentor of the Austrian School, Eugen von Bohm-Bawerk. (J. A. Schumpeter, "Eugen von Bohm-Bawerk, 1851-1914," **Ten Great Economists**, Oxford University Press, 1951, pp. 143-90.) Much of Schumpeter's eulogy applies to Mises as well:

"And now this great master has left us. No one who has been close to him both personally and scientifically would be able to describe the feeling that lies heavy on all of us. No words can express what he has been to us, and few of us if any will have yet resigned ourselves to the realization that from now on there is to be an impenetrable wall separating us from him, from his advice, his encouragement, his critical guidance — and that the road ahead will have to be traversed without him . . . .

"He was not only a creative mind but also a fighter — and to his last moments a live, effective force in our science. His work belongs not to one generation, not to one nation, but to mankind . . . .

"The silhouette of the man is everywhere the same — in all the fields comprehended by the wide orbit of his life, the intensive beat of his pulse left its mark. In all these fields we are met by the same brilliant personality, the same large and strong features — the statue appears cast of one metal at one pouring, no matter from what point we view it . . . .

"And in politics and scientific work the same character proved its mettle: the same self-control and intensiveness, the same high standard of duty which impressed itself on subordinates as well as on disciples, the same ability to see through men and things without the cold detachment of the pessimist, to fight without bitterness, to deny himself without weakness — to hold to a plan of life at once simple and grand. Thus his life was a completed whole, the expression of a personality at one with itself, never losing itself, everywhere proving its superiority by its own weight and without affectation — a work of art, its severe lines gilded by an infinite, tender, reserved, and highly personal charm.

"Bohm-Bawerk's (Mises') scientific lifework forms a uniform whole. As in a good play each line furthers the plot, so with Bohm-Bawerk (Mises) every sentence is a cell in a living organism, written with a clearly outlined goal in mind. There is no waste of effort, no hesitation, no deviation, but a calm renunciation of secondary and merely momentary successes . . . . The full superiority of the man,

(Continued On Page 2)

421

Libertarian Party

The elections of 1973 have come and gone, and the major result from our point of view has been the establishment of the Libertarian Party, and the Free Libertarian Party of New York in particular, as the central organizational force in the libertarian movement. And not only that: the fledgling FLP has now become a force to reckon with in New York politics.

The FLP campaign of Fran Youngstein for mayor provided a central focus for libertarians throughout the country. Libertarians all across the nation, even those with grave philosophical qualms about political activity, poured contributions into the Youngstein campaign, and enabled Fran and the FLP to gain an enormous amount of publicity and favorable recognition, and even endorsements from TV, radio, the press, columnists, and the public at large. Fran received approximately 9,000 votes for Mayor, far more than any minor party has received in New York City in many years, and FLP's Gary Greenberg, as the only candidate running for District Attorney of Manhattan against the gravely ailing Frank Hogan, polled over 8,200 votes, approximately 4% of the total vote. Not only that: the FLP campaign has gained libertarianism a powerful recognition factor among New York City voters, so that a remarkable number of men-in-the-street, while scarcely converted, knew instantly who we were and roughly what we stood for. The publicity, the TV spots (a first for a minor party candidate in New York!) were done remarkably well, aided immeasurably by expert advertising and media people who joined the party and aided the campaign.

One exciting development highlighted by the campaign was the fulfilling of the strategic vision that many of us once had in the abstract: namely, that it theoretically should be just as easy to attract libertarian converts from the liberal Left as it is from the conservative Right. When this notion was first put forward, it appeared in a context in which the then existing libertarian population had come exclusively from the Right. But in the last couple of years, events have caught up with theory, and many of our most active libertarians had formerly been liberals, including Fran Youngstein herself. Indeed, the FLP message stressed our kinship with liberals on victimless crimes and civil liberties on the one hand, as well as with conservatives on property rights and the free market on the other. In fact, of course, only libertarianism can consistently fulfill both of these promised liberties, on which liberals and conservatives themselves fall down and lapse into inner contradictions. It is precisely this consistent fulfillment offered by libertarianism that draws liberals and conservatives alike into our ranks. Politically, this across-the-spectrum strength was embodied in the fact that Fran was quietly supported by various candidates and clubs in both the Conservative and Liberal parties in New York. The Youngstein campaign has vividly demonstrated the cross-spectrum pull that can make libertarians a vital political and ideological force in American life.

A word should be said here about the remarkable personal qualities which enabled Fran Youngstein, a political neophyte, to hold down a highly responsible and demanding job at IBM while still waging a notably vigorous and energetic campaign. Such intelligent and tireless dedication to the cause deserves the heartfelt gratitude of every libertarian.

The FLP has high hopes: presumably it plans now to take advantage of the momentum achieved by its electric burst into New York City politics, by running a full-scale ticket for Governor and Senator in 1974. For this it will need more manpower and more support by libertarians throughout the country. The point is this: if the FLP can win 50,000 votes for

(Continued On Page 3)

Ludwig von Mises, RIP —
(Continued From Page 1)

motivated by a great task and full of living creative power, is here revealed to us: the superiority of the clear, self-possessed mind which from a feeling of intellectual duty renounced many a passing distraction. And this integrated plan was carried out in full. Completed and perfect, his lifework lies before us. There cannot be any doubt about the nature of his message.

"He knew as few did what he wanted to do, and this is why it is so easy to formulate. He was a theorist, born to see — and to explain — large relationships; to seize instinctively, but with a firm hand, on the threads of logical necessities; to experience the most intimate joy of analytical work. At the same time he was a creator, an architect of thought, to whom even the most varied series of small tasks, such as the course of scientific life offers to any man, could never give satisfaction . . . .

"To say that his work is immortal is to express a triviality. For a long time to come, the memory of the great fighter will be colored by the contending parties' hates and favors. But among the achievements of which our science can be proud his was one of the greatest. Whatever the future will do to it or make of it, the traces of his work will never perish."

And yet, in contrast to his celebrated teacher Bohm-Bawerk, Ludwig Mises was made to suffer grievous neglect in the last four decades of his life. Mises' steadfastness and courage in the face of treatment that would have shattered lesser men, was a never-ending wonder to us all. Once the literal toast of both the economics profession and of the world's leaders, Mises was to find, at the very height of his powers, his world shattered and betrayed. For as the world rushed headlong into the fallacies and evils of Keynesianism and statism, Mises' great insights and contributions were neglected and scorned, and the large majority of his eminent and formerly devoted students chose to bend with the new breeze.

But shamefully neglected though he was, coming to America to a second-rate post and deprived of the opportunity to gather the best students, Ludwig Mises never once complained or wavered. He simply hewed to his great purpose, to carve out and elaborate the mighty structure of economics and social science that he alone had had the genius to see as a coherent whole, and to stand four-square for the individualism and the freedom that he realized was required if the human race was to survive and prosper. He was indeed a constant star that could not be deflected one iota from the body of truth which he was the first to see and to present to those who would only listen.

And despite the odds, slowly but surely some of us began to gather around him, to learn and listen and derive sustenance from the glow of his person and his work. And in the last few years, as the ideas of liberty and the free market have begun to revive with increasing swiftness in America, his name and his ideas began to strike chords in us all and his greatness to become known to a new generation.

Optimistic as he always was, I am confident that Mises was heartened by these signs of a new awakening of freedom and of the sound economics which he had carved out and which was for so long forgotten. We could not, alas, recapture the spirit and the breadth and the erudition, the ineffable grace of Old Vienna. But I fervently hope that we were able to sweeten his days by at least a little.

Of all the marvelous anecdotes that Mises used to tell I remember this one the most clearly, and perhaps it will convey a little of the wit and the spirit of Ludwig Mises. Walking down the streets of Vienna with his friend, the great German philosopher Max Scheler, Scheler turned to Mises and asked, with some exasperation: "What is there in the climate of Vienna that breeds all these logical positivists (the dominant school of modern philosophy that Mises combatted all his life)?" With his characteristic shrug, Mises gently replied: "Well, after all, there are several million people living in Vienna, and among these there are only about a dozen logical positivists."

But oh Mises, now you are gone, and we have lost our guide, our Nestor, our friend. How will we carry on without you? But we have to carry on, because anything less would be a shameful betrayal of all that you have taught us, by the example of your noble life as much as by your immortal works. Bless you, Ludwig von Mises, and our deepest love goes with you.

* A briefer version of this article appeared in **Human Events**, October 20, 1973.

From The Old Curmudgeon

Psy Lib Once More. Our friends at Rampart College are apparently intending to push heavily on the Psy Lib front, attempting to integrate "humanist psychology" with libertarian politics, ethics, and economics. On the face of it, the Psy Libbers have a formidable task on their hands. Not only do they have to demonstrate that psychology is a scientific discipline somewhere significantly above the level of mumbo-jumbo and witch-doctory — a tough task in itself. But they also have to answer what might be called the "Davidson challenge" to science fiction and metal detection ("Libertarians and Culture," Lib. Forum, October, 1973); namely, the relevance to libertarianism. One is reminded of the **Libertarian Connection's** recent fascination with vitamin pills — an admirable devotion, no doubt, but rather difficult to link up with libertarian concerns. Or, to put it another way, even if it were true, should libertarian journals allocate some of their preciously scarce space to the latest news on the technique of filling cavities?

From what I can gather, the Rampart answer to this challenge on relevance goes somewhat as follows: we have all had the experience of beaming our libertarian views at people and not seeing them converted. Since our ideas are correct, why do people not accept them? On this view, the answer **must** be "psychological hangups", a failure to be humanistic, an uptightness about other people, an authoritarian personality or whatever. In short, people must be converted to the precepts and life-styles of humanistic psychology before they can be ripe for conversion to the libertarian creed.

This argument strikes me as a mass of **non sequiturs.** In the first place, it is simply empirically wrong. I know lots of people with "hangups", "authoritarian personalities," etc. who are excellent libertarians.

Similarly, there is no logical connection whatever. For example, let us postulate a typical Authoritarian Libertarian, worried about the loss of traditional morality, "uptight" about drugs, promiscuity, and bestiality; he may firmly believe that many people around him are doomed to Hell, either on earth and/or in the nether regions, but he may also firmly believe that they have the right to do so, that everyone has the right to go to Hell in his own way, and that they and everyone else should be left alone. There is surely no contradiction here, and empirically such people have abounded in our great libertarian past, and even, **mirabile dictu,** are still around in our permissive present. Perhaps even our Rampart friends, as psy liberated as they are, may have a few qualms about heroin addiction, and yet this does not stop them or any other libertarian from advocating heroin freedom. In short, and this is surely an elementary libertarian lesson, one does not at all have to approve of something to advocate a person's right to do it.

There is another consideration here: our liberated brethren are not so free of "hangups" or moral judgments themselves. What happens is that the moral and social pressure simply cuts the other way. What happens, for example, to the guy in a "non-judgmental", "humanistic" encounter group who doesn't **want** to be touched, who values his personal and emotional privacy, who wants to be "closed" rather than "open", who wants to preserve his own principles rather than "flow with it"? In the old expression, what happens to him shouldn't happen to a dog. Similarly, the inevitable thrust of a "libertarian-humanist" approach would be to cast into outer darkness all of those libertarians who are not and emphatically don't want to be "liberated", who are, in short (name one:

(Continued On Page 4)

Libertarian Party —

(Continued From Page 2)

Governor next year, then it achieves a permanent line on the New York ballot, with none of the time-consuming hassle required to gain petitions to get on the ballot for each year's election. If we can achieve a permanent line on the ballot, stepping up to the status of the current four major parties, then the political clout and influence of the FLP throughout the state will accelerate enormously. This will enable us to achieve the balance of power, and even the victories, which the Liberal and Conservative parties have managed to achieve after gaining their permanent lines. The 1974 campaign will therefore be vital to the continued growth of the FLP.

As for the mayoralty election, apart from Fran and the FLP, it turned out to be dull as dishwater, by all agreement the dullest mayoralty campaign in decades. Only slightly over 40% of the eligible voters bothered to turn out to the polls. The reason was the universally-anticipated landslide victory of Democrat Abe Beame, a colorless but "safe" right-centrist, whose major asset was to offer a refreshing contrast to John Lindsay's leftish charisma. Of his three major opponents, John Marchi's Republican candidacy was undercut from the start by the almost savagely open support given to Beame by Governor Nelson Rockefeller, already tooling his forces for his (hopefully) final try at the Presidency in 1976. West Side liberal reformer Al Blumenthal's Liberal campaign was made still more hopeless by the unseemly haste of his fellow Democrat reformers to leap on the Beame bandwagon, jostling each other for future patronage. As for poor old Biaggi, in addition to the desertion to the Marchi camp by the Buckley family and their powerful crew of Establishment Conservatives, Biaggi himself, savaged by the revelation of his lying about taking the Fifth Amendment before a grand jury, was rumored to have made a deal with the Democratic leaders to run a very, very quiet campaign. Having made no waves, the right-centrist Democratic leaders will welcome Biaggi back into the fold. All in all, a campaign for snoozing, which increased the willingness of possible Biaggi and Blumenthal voters to vote their conscience and cast their ballots for Youngstein. With the outcome a dead certainty, the "lesser evil" argument cut no ice in any political camp.

It is appropriate at this point to take stock of the libertarian movement itself. Not only the Youngstein campaign, but also such successful activities as the Ohio party's hosting of the Libertarian Party's national conference this summer, as well as the forthcoming libertarian-feminist conference organized by the Kentucky party, make clear that the LP is currently the only flourishing vehicle for libertarian organizing. The LP is organized at last count in 34 states, and in each state the party is forming the nucleus for the ingathering of new converts, as well as the return to vigorous libertarian activity by those who had formerly become torpid or disenchanted, or who simply could not see any activist outlet for their libertarian impulses. No other libertarian organization is making a comparable record, which makes anti-party sentiment among libertarians look all the more sectarian and futile.

Looking at other libertarian activities, there has been a mixed record of retrogression in some areas and advances in others. On the East Coast, three important journals have folded. The monthly **Outlook,** founded in the high hopes of forming a vehicle and a locus of activity for the New York movement, has collapsed, partly due to personal feuds; the Outlook activists have either shifted their focus to the FLP or have dropped out altogether. The highly ambitious attempt to organize a biweekly tabloid, **The New Banner,** by the South Carolina movement has toppled in the midst of schisms and a police bust. The monthly **Individualist,** a Maryland publication of the Society for Individual Liberty, has also folded. SIL itself, however, now exclusively Philadelphia based, and headed by Don Ernsberger and Dave Walters, continues to be active as our only national campus organization. On November 17, SIL conducted a successful libertarian conference at Philadelphia. Energetic political lobbying continues to be conducted by the National Taxpayers Union, in Washington, and the National Committee to Legalize Gold, headquartered in New Orleans.

The collapse of several journals, however, has left the movement weak on the publication front. We are left with our one major "professional" magazine, the monthly **Reason,** published in southern California; a few newsletters; the mimeographed **Libertarian Connection** (also southern California); and the monthly **New Libertarian Notes,** published in New York by Sam Konkin and centering around his "radical caucus". A particularly hopeful sign, however, is the growing prosperity of Bob Kephart's monthly review **Books for Libertarians,** which has now absorbed the defunct Brandenian **Academic Associates News,** and may soon expand to a regular tabloid format. Furthermore, we are improving in book dissemination, the major sources now being **Books for Libertarians,** and New York's Laissez-Faire Bookstore. Chuck Hamilton, of New York, is now launching a new publishing venture, which will begin by reprinting several libertarian classics, including: Nock's **Our Enemy the State,** Flynn's **As We Go Marching,** and Oppenheimer's **The State.** All in all, a time of excitement, ferment, and the emergence of the Libertarian Party as our major organizational vehicle.   ◻

The Middle East

Let it not be thought that the current cease-fire in the Middle East is anything more than another interlude of uneasy peace in what is bound to be a protracted decades-long struggle, a struggle which will continue so long as the grievances of the Palestinian Arabs remain unsatisfied. The press does everyone a disservice by concentrating on the superficial maneuverings of the Sadat regime in Egypt, the Syrian government, most of the other Arab states, and even the "orthodox" Palestinian guerrilla movement headed by Al Fatah, whose basic objective of a rollback of Israel to the pre-1967 borders would leave the Palestinian Arab question still unresolved.

In this chronic and permanent crisis, the major task of American libertarians is to call for the elimination of American intervention in the Middle East. President Nixon's frenetic world-wide alert is only one alarming indication of the lengths to which an unstable President with zero credibility at home is willing to go to recoup his political fortunes. The call for American "isolationism", for non-intervention in the Middle East, is more than simply an application of libertarian political theory to one more foreign crisis; it is essential for American survival in a world suffering under the ever-present threat of nuclear destruction.

All this highlights the importance of the advertising campaign launched by the National Taxpayers Union in the midst of the recent crisis. The NTU placed a full-page ad in the Washington Star-News and other newspapers throughout the country, signed by Congressman Steven Symms (R., Id.), chairman of the newly-founded Taxpayers for Peace, and by the Executive Committee of the NTU (James D. Davidson, A. Ernest Fitzgerald, Robert D. Kephart, and Murray N. Rothbard.) The ad (e.g., Washington Star-News, October 21) began with the headline: "Do We Need Another War?" It continued with a marvellous quote from the grand old isolationist and conservative-libertarian Congressman H. R.

Gross (R., Iowa). Gross, speaking on the floor of the House on October 17, asserted: "I do not know who is going to win the war in the Middle East, but I do know one thing for dead sure and certain — that I can name the loser. That will be the common, garden-variety citizen and taxpayer of the United States of America. He and she will be the losers, and mark this well. It is time this government tended to its own business and that is the welfare of the American people. It is time we stopped intervening in the affairs of others all over the world."

The ad continued by calling for demands that Congress "deny funds which the Pentagon is seeking to pay for still greater involvement in the Mideast." It also urged a demand for "an immediate end to foreign aid," in the Middle East and elsewhere. Attacking U. S. aid to Israel as well as to the Soviet Union, the ad continued: "You should insist that your representatives in Congress repudiate all 'sweetheart' deals with foreign dictators. Suspension of all taxpaper sponsored foreign credits and loan guarantees would also help prevent your money from financing wars." Hitting hard at special interests using the government apparatus, the ad then urged that "this prohibition should extend to the operations of mischief-making international banks — which finance arms acquisitions with your money and credit. Remember that we have nothing to gain from this war no matter who wins. Remember also that powerful special interests are eager to use this war as an excuse to seize even more of your hard-earned money. When these special interests have had their way in the past, many Americans have died in foreign wars. This will happen again if we let it." Revisionism reborn! The ad concludes by urging readers to join the Taxpayers for Peace. All interested parties should get in touch with the National Taxpayers Union, 325 Pennsylvania Ave., S. E., Washington, D. C. 20003.   ◻

From The Old Curmudgeon —

(Continued From Page 3)

closed, private, authoritarian, uptight, morally principled).

Let us take even the extreme case of an Authoritarian Person who has what might be called a bureaucratic or a sado-masochistic personality, in short, someone who either feels a great need to obey orders and commands, and or feels a great need to hand out orders and commands and have them obeyed. Is such a person, at least, an inveterate enemy of libertarianism? Certainly not, for he might very well hold that all s-m activities must be strictly voluntary; in a free, libertarian society, then, he can voluntarily join private s-m clubs, or voluntarily abase himself before a guru, a Perfect Master, or some other Authority, or gather around him willing subjects to whom his every wish will be their command. Certainly not a very healthy picture, but perfectly compatible with the freedom that libertarians are looking for, the freedom to form whatever interactions one wishes so long as they are voluntary.

We conclude, then, that if the drive for liberty has to be more or less suspended until everybody's psyche is "liberated", we will have to wait forever. Happily for our cause, liberty does not have to wait for everyone's psyche to shape up in some way that we want; we don't have to wait for a world of "humanists" or rationalists or traditional moralists. Libertarianism, the free society, is compatible with any psyche that holds firmly to the rights of person and property, whether for humanistic, traditionalist, or totally non-psychological reasons.

But what of the broader question? Why don't we libertarians enjoy the instant conversion of everyone who hears our message? Here, the strategists of Marxism, who have cogitated on these matters for over a hundred years, have a lot more to say to us than the murky purveyors of psychological nostrums. We do not, as do the liberators and the Randians, have to hurl psychological anathemas at the unconverted. The basic problem is simply that most people are not really interested; every person is busy about his or her personal and everyday affairs, and certainly this kind of preoccupation with one's daily life is not self-evidently irrational. The demands on their attention, on their thought, in

their free time are enormous, and they are bombarded from every direction, from all manner of cults, groups, interest groups, activities, etc. On most of these matters, they simply cannot give thought or attention, and so they tend to absorb their views on matters of marginal concern from the world around them: parents, teachers, friends, the media. And since, in ideological matters, most of these influences tend to favor whatever status quo exists, their tendency is to go along with the current system. The fact that a few of us — happily growing in number — are fascinated by ideological concerns and devote a great deal of thought and care to them is splendid, but is not by itself enough to convince the busy and harassed citizen that he must go and do likewise.

So what does stir these people up, command their attention, cause them to devote themselves to political and ideological problems? As the Marxists point out, it is the occurrence of crisis situations, situations which call their attention to the evident fact of a breakdown in the existing system. Such breakdowns could be of many sorts: a losing war, a depression, a runaway inflation, a sudden "energy shortage." Whatever they are, we libertarians know that statism will inevitably bring them about, and furthermore that they will come about with accelerating frequency in the months and years ahead. As these crises occur, more and more people will be induced to give attention and thought to these matters, and more and more of them will inevitably become libertarians. But they can't do so if they don't hear the message, or if they haven't heard the message in the past, predicting the crises upon them. The task of dedicated, self-conscious libertarians (the "cadre", in Marxist terminology) is to spread this message, to stand ready to do so, until, in crisis situations, our ranks are significantly swelled. As a matter of fact, it seems very plausible that the enormous increase in the number of libertarian cadre in the last few years is not unrelated to the accelerating number of such crisis, in domestic and foreign affairs.

Let us, then, not become so frustrated by the failure of instant mass conversion, by the failure to heed our message, that we start reaching for psychological smears with which to bombard the unconverted (either that they are "uptight" or that they are "loose-lipped evaders", depending on one's psychological theories). Let us treat the unconverted with the same respect with which we ourselves would like to be treated. Sometimes the Golden Rule is the best as well as the simplest guide ◻

Music: The Art No One Thinks About

By Kenneth LaFave

There is a classic and semi-humorous response to the question, "What do you know about art?" "What do I know?" comes the reply, "Well, I know what I like!" The exchange usually concerns the visual arts, but will here serve our purpose as the signpost to a discussion of music: for music is the art everyone "feels", writes poetry about, and uses as a catalyst to magnificent fantasies. Music is the art no one thinks about.

"No one" is admittedly an overstatement, but only a small one. Musicians and the musically knowledgeable are always a little confused by otherwise scholarly folk who, when listening to music, invariably engage in reveries about their childhood or their first romance. To these people, music means nothing more than "association." The "goodness" or "badness" of a piece of music depends on the place, time, or event associated with it. If you associate Bach with church, your attitude toward his work may well depend on what kind of experiences you've had with churches and religion. One way or the other, Bach loses, and so do you. Associating certain music with fond memories, of course, can be quite pleasurable, and I'm not entirely dismissing the purely associational value of my favorite art form. Yet most people go no further than to accept such patterns as criteria for "knowing what they like", which is my thesis exactly.

Two questions should be raised here: 1) what is meant by "thinking about music", and 2) what is the purpose of doing so. I shall begin by stating what I do not mean by "thinking about music."

By "thinking about music" I do not mean reading and contemplating the lives of famous composers. This is strictly public school "music appreciation" stuff. One is presumably able to "hear" the composer's life in his work: we "hear" Beethoven rage against his deafness in the Ninth Symphony; we "hear" Tchaikovsky's loneliness and desolation in the "Pathetique" Symphony. This kind of nonsense is related to another elementary school trick — "painting" mental pictures to music. In other words, not thinking about the music, but about what the music reminds you of. Whether concerned with the composer's emotions or your own visual imagination, these games are just two more forms of association, and give additional credence to my claim that people will do almost anything to keep from truly intellectualizing what they consider a mere emotional indulgence.

By "thinking about music" I also do not mean analyzing the emotional effects of music. To find out why people react in such-and-such a way to music is fine, but such is psychology, not aesthetics. Emotions are a product of music, not a part of it. Emotions may even be the purpose of music, but they are not music itself.

Music is sound organized along certain principles of acoustics. To "think about" it means to identify what a composer (the "organizer") is doing in a certain piece — i.e., how he is structuring some harmonic progression, what form he is using, how he varies some melodic passage. It is also interesting to consider the nature of a given performance: how a performer interprets the music, how brilliant is John Doe's technique, etc. But this is not the intellectual core of music, it's not what music is about. The understanding of music does not consist of emoting over a Rachmaninoff prelude, or even playing one well. It consists of identifying how Rachmaninoff organized sound in terms of musical language.

That may sound simple, and even obvious, but we are immediately faced with a seemingly insurmountable barricade — for the key word in my last sentence is "language." Music is not a language in the way that English, Chinese, or Dutch are languages. All of the latter have the power to denote; they all contain sounds and symbols which have reference to something in the "real" world. "Bird", for instance, refers to a particular kind of thing that exists. But we cannot sing the pitch, "la" for a specific duration and mean the same thing as the word "bird". (No doubt such a system could be devised, but it would not bear much if any relation to what we know as music.)

This classic and oft-noted point has several important ramifications. Primarily, it places music in a unique position among the major art forms. Both literature and the visual arts have the power of reference: the poet can write of a bird and the painter can paint his image on a canvas, but the composer cannot "compose" a bird, without the aid of words in the form of a title or program. Take away the title, and the programmatic "meaning" of Stravinsky's "Song of the Nightingale" is up for grabs. It could be "Song of the Sea", if you wanted it to be that.

So music has no content, as such, and is more akin to architecture or chess than to poetry or painting. It is all style, and that will make our analysis of that Rachmaninoff a little more difficult. We will have to understand musical form, structure, counterpoint, harmony, etc. In short, we will have to learn the musical language. By this I do not mean a subset of English comprised of the above words, but the things to which those words refer. By "musical language" I mean the concepts and applications of counterpoint, harmony, etc. Perhaps the closest analogy to "musical language" is another "language" which defies translation into denotative words: the language of mathematics.

Ask a mathematician to explain a higher equation to you without understanding the concepts expressed in that equation and you'll only walk away frustrated. And so it is with trying to understand a Bach fugue or even our Rachmaninoff prelude without knowing much about music. Again, this places music in a unique position among the arts. It is not necessary to have knowledge of meter or perspective in order to enjoy poetry or painting, though such knowledge does no doubt enhance one's enjoyment, but it is impossible to really enjoy music beyond the merely associational or "cultural" (associational on a societal scale) level, without "speaking the language."

Music, far from being the most subjective of the arts, is the most rigorously logical. Its objective basis is acoustics, the science of sound, and all good composers take that into account. Were I to make a case for the evaluation of music, I would base it on the degree of musical (contrapuntal, harmonic, etc.) interest a piece generates. Just as a difficult equation is of more interest than a simple arithmetical problem, so the Bach fugue is of more interest, objectively, than the Rachmaninoff prelude. But that is another essay, and a harder one.

Now it is time to consider the second question: why should we, why should anyone, "think about music." What does the objective analysis of organized sound have to offer us that mathematics doesn't? In order to sufficiently answer this, I hope the reader will excuse what may seem like a digression.

We are at an all-Beethoven concert of symphonic music. We have never heard Beethoven before, nor have we heard "live" symphonic music: it is a totally new experience for us. The major work on the program is the famous Fifth Symphony, and as we witness the performance, our first impression is a physical one — the sheer strength of the music, the massive power of the sound. We do not like the second movement much, as it doesn't have the mere volume that was so physically exciting to experience in the first movement. The last movement proves to be our favorite: the physical sensation of sound waves striking our ear drums and our bodies is exhilirating.

We go home, forget about the concert for a few days, until, quite by accident, we hear Beethoven's Fifth on the radio. We remember with delight our evening at the concert: the sensations we experienced come back like a welcome dream. But over the radio, much of this physical dimension is lost, and as we listen a second time, we are struck with a vague sense of "something important is going on here". It is not just a physical sensation anymore, it is a real intellectual observation, based on our ability to discern variations in amplitude, pitch, duration, etc. in same way as we might look at a building and say, "I don't know a thing about architecture, but something about that building seems to deserve my investigation." So we read a few books on music — Bernstein's THE JOY OF MUSIC is great for beginners; buy a pocket dictionary of music (THE HARVARD BRIEF DICTIONARY OF MUSIC); and even learn to

(Continued On Page 6)

Arts And Movies

By Mr. First Nighter

A Touch of Class. dir. by Melvin Frank, with George Segal and Glenda Jackson.

One of the great movie **genres** was the sophisticated comedy of the 1930's, usually starring Cary Grant, Katherine Hepburn, or Carole Lombard. The scintillating wit, the high style, the sophisticated intelligence of both hero and heroine were a joy to behold. In these days, when intelligence and wit have been virtually expunged from the cinema, the "Cary Grant-type" comedies of the 1930's seem as remote as a Golden Age of long, long ago. Not since such isolated and wondrous bursts of late glory as the Hepburn-Tracy movies of the 1950's ("Pat and Mike", "Adam's Rib") have we seen anything to compare with the classics of the thirties.

A Touch of Class is an interesting attempt to harken back to the great tradition. For most of the picture, the dialogue crackles, and the wit sparkles, until Frank felt that he had to end on a note of leaden moralism. Glenda Jackson is particularly good: there is even a trace of the great Hepburn in her intelligence and in her command of every situation. In her previous pictures furthermore, Miss Jackson had been generally cast in somehow decadent roles; here she hits her stride as a "classical" comedienne.

The major problem here is George Segal. Certainly a funny actor, Segal is far from the classic mould of intelligence and wit; instead, his is the humor of the self-deprecating **schnook**; the style might be called New York-Jewish. There is certainly a place for this brand of humor in movies: Segal himself was brilliantly cast in that hilarious movie about third-rate New York Jewish intellectuals, **Bye, Bye Braverman** (from the equally hilarious Wallace Markfield novel, **To An Early Grave**). But for attempting classical comedy, Segal, for all his amusing moments, is a fish out of water. Such is the dearth of wit in the movies, however, that it is difficult to suggest a replacement, barring the magic ability to make Cary Grant thirty-five years younger.

Music —

(Continued From Page 5)

read music (it is not difficult for an intelligent adult) well enough to make sense out of the reader's score of the Beethoven Fifth. All this takes some time and a little money. We could spend less time and a lot more money if we decided instead to build ourselves the greatest stereo in the world, but we're intelligent and know that it's much more important to **understand** what comes out of a pair of speakers than to worry about "marvelous tone". That would be like pronouncing Chinese perfectly and not understanding a single word.

So, after some weeks of study, we buy a recording of the Fifth and give it a listen, following it, perhaps, with a copy of the score. What happens is amazing. The physical and associational aspects are there still, but they take a back seat to an entirely new dimension: **understand**. "Meaningless" notes now have meaning as part of the structural whole. And we are overwhelmed with a great sense of — **emotion!** Not physical "feeling", not association, but emotion over the logic of the music. For music is like mathematics with a physical dimension: **music is logic incarnate.**

We have for the first time experienced emotion over the music itself, not over something we associate with it, not physical "feeling" devoid of understanding, but emotion. The experience of music, then, is on three levels: physical, "feeling", association (good or bad) with extra-musical places or events, and emotion. The first two happen quite naturally, the last can only occur via knowledge of the art. Almost everyone stops on the second level.

I am not suggesting that everyone go out and buy books, take lessons, and spend the time necessary for the further enjoyment of music. Nor am I denying the validity of using music for purposes of association, relaxation, dancing or any one of a thousand other conceivable uses. My purpose is simply to make people aware of deeper musical dimensions

Paper Moon. dir. by Peter Bogdanovich. With Ryan O'Neal, Tatum O'Neal, and Madeline Kahn.

Peter Bogdanovich is perhaps the most interesting of our younger film directors. Bogdanovich is a brilliant neo-classicist, consciously moulding his movies in the classical, Old Culture form. His typical mode is to return to the classical cinema by casting his pictures in the period of the old movies, and then to make them in a similar manner. **The Last Picture Show** was Bogdanovich's remarkable tribute to the culture and the world of the 1950's, as well as the classical kind of movie of the pre-60's era which he remakes in the current world. **The Last Picture Show**, however, was marred by a deeply pessimistic outlook, so that the movie was an elegy to a dying small town in the Southwest. But now, with **Paper Moon**, Bogdanovich has gone further back — to the world and to the movies of the 1930's — to make a delightful, heartwarming movie free of any taint of the bleak pessimism of his earlier work.

Paper Moon marvellously recreates the world of the 1930's, its way of life, its pop culture. Like all great directors, Bogdanovich has always wrung superb performances from all of his actors, and he does it again here. Ryan O'Neal is plucked out of pretty-boy roles to turn in an excellent performance as a lovable, roving conman; little Tatum O'Neal steals the picture as a tough little kid with a heart of gold (or at least, silver.) Madeline Kahn is superb as a floozy with airs.

A lot of nonsense has been written about Tatum O'Neal being a conscious contrast to the simperingly sweet kid acting of such thirties' stars as Shirley Temple. These critics forget that the thirties also had a lot of tough little urchins in the movies, including Jane Withers and the Dead End Kids; Tatum O'Neal is simply another jewel in a re-created tradition. With each movie of loving recreation of an older day, Peter Bogdanovich is raising a standard against the irrationality and morbidity of today's avant-garde. ▢

available to them. It may also serve to make a few people aware of the appallingly low level of music criticism in this country, with the exceptions of a few major newspapers and here and there a journal. Music criticism in "popular" magazines and most newspapers is incredibly trashy, dwelling, as most of it does, on the "feeling" (a mere physical sensation) of the music.

A major mistake made by many well-meaning individuals, and particularly rampant among Rock musicians and critics, is the equation of "good music" with that which is technically performed well. But the **playing** of music is not music's essence. Music is sound organized according to certain principles of ascoustics. The essence of music is **composition**, not performance. But, thanks largely to this mistake, we have the spectacle of an entire musical culture (Rock) pretending to be "intellectual" because its members know a lot about amplifiers and different kinds of guitars. That's like claiming knowledge of literature because you know how to bind books.

There is no space within the confines of this or any other single essay to begin an adaquate discussion of musical theory. There are books on that subject. I only know there is more than coincidence to the poet's analogy of romantic love to music; both sublimely combine the physical and the intellectual, and few people ever attain the real understanding of either. ▢

Roman History In A Paragraph

The Romans had many gifts, but statesmanship was not one of them. No major reform was ever carried out without civil war; the achievement of the Republic was to fill Rome with a pauperized rabble, to ruin Italy and provoke slave revolts, and to govern the Empire — or at least the richer parts — with a personal rapacity that an Oriental monarch would not have tolerated; while the achievement of the Principate was to accept the fact that political life was impossible, and to create, in its place, a machine.

H. D. F. Kitto in **The Greeks** (Penguin 1951).

The Fall Of The Republic

One of the inevitable effects of the Watergate affair has been to compel a wide spectrum of public men to take cognizance of the transformation of our political institutions and practices during the last century. The claims of the Presidency in the last decade have established the legal setting for virtually unrestricted exercise of power by one man — the President. His claims have included the right to make war without effective congressional control or authorization; to wiretap, bug, and even burglarize any person or place without the due process of judicial warrant; to impound legislatively mandated expenditures at his will; to withhold information from the Congress and the courts, even when it clearly involves obstruction of justice; to deny that either the Congress or the courts have any power to restrict the President's actions except through impeachment. In effect, as many now realize, the Presidency is changing before our eyes into a monarchical office of the type known to historians as an Augustan principate. While the tenure of the officeholder still remains limited in time, the powers of the office are monarchical in character.

Benjamin Franklin is reputed to have remarked when asked what kind of government he had helped to create, "A republic, sir, if you can keep it!". He was not the only observer to be skeptical about the viability of the republican form of government. A century later, one of the most able and respected juriconsults of the age, Charles O'Conor of New York, a man considered by Benjamin Tucker to be one of those unterrified Jeffersonian Democrats who followed their premises logically into anarchism, held that the first American revolution had attempted to abolish both monarchy and aristocracy and create a democracy in which all citizens enjoyed equal rights under law. But it had failed to do so. The founding Fathers recognized the "necessity of repressing in the newly conceived system the most conspicuous abuses; standing armies were denounced as dangerous to liberty; wars for the extension of territory were regarded as unjust and foreign alliances as inexpedient; and public debt as mischievous; but strangely enough, no barriers were instituted against any of these practices . . . On the contrary, powers to introduce and foster the most dangerous of them were expressly delegated, in the name of the people, to their public agents . . . We have seen, accordingly, that whilst ostracizing monarchy, the founders of the American Union invested it with most of the powers by which the few had oppressed the many in all previous times" (Charles O'Conor, Democracy, N. Y. 1876.)

O'Conor identified two principal bulwarks of increasingly despotic governmental power: indirect taxation (excise and sales taxes, and all other taxes which are obscured from the immediate awareness of the taxpayer) and public debt. O'Conor believed that, if all taxes were collected directly from the pocket of each taxpayer, this experience would create a vigilant and frugally-minded citizenry who would in their own interest deny the government all but the most obvious and needed expenditures.

As for public debt, he saw it as one of the principal means by which the State gratifies its penchant for war, waste and the creation of privilege. Moreover, public debt created a new aristocracy — the bond holders — whose personal financial interest it now became to encourage the state to further warfare, waste and increasing indebtedness. O'Conor called for constitutional barriers to the creation of any public indebtedness for any reason whatever. Also, he argued that the government should be prohibited from exercising any authority over coinage, and commerical paper, or from issuing its own paper for circulation as money. No revenue should be derived from lands in the public domain, and no gifts made therefrom to any but actual settlers.

We are now almost a century beyond Charles O'Conor's analysis of what had happened. O'Conor frequently spoke of the need for a second American Revolution — a revolution that would fulfill the promise of 1776 and abolish all trace of monarchy and aristocracy forever, creating a democratic system by securing to all citizens the utmost measure of freedom. The task of reformers was, he believed, "to break the sceptre of the trading politician and thus, at last, to establish liberty on the only reliable basis — a popular censorship on democratic principles, perpetually stimulated to its duty by the simple operation of intelligent

Mr. First Nighter, Soft on the Enemy?

By H. Primae Noctis

Is "Mr. First Nighter" soft on avant-garde culture? Could it be that the apostle of rearguard is secretly soft on the enemy? Surely it isn't so. But yet here is evidence. Along with an excellent series of capsulated reviews, Mr. First Nighter praises "Shamus," starring Burt Reynolds. "Shamus?" Booh Mr. First Nighter! You're giving in to the enemy. The incoherent plot of this movie betrays it for what it is — imitation arriere-garde. Hollywood should never be able to get away with it. We know they are watching, waiting for the good word. I say hold out. Don't give your critical blessing to a flick that only has some of the trimmings of a good movie. Sure "Shamus" has some old-fashioned hard-hitting action. But it lacks old-fashioned coherence which made the movie upon which "Shamus" was modeled so much more interesting. "The Big Sleep," starring Humphrey Bogart, did make sense. The meaning was there for the true detective fan to piece together. "Shamus," on the other hand, doesn't make it. Let's demand that movie makers produce arriere-garde flicks, not just imitations which capture some of the trappings — but lack the essence of the old-fashioned action movie.

To this end, I suggest a more precise rating form in the future. Mr. First Nighter should use a scale of from 0 to 4 squares for each movie reviewed. Each square could stand for a favorable attribute. For example, if a film used sane camera techniques, but lacked any other redeeming virtue, it would be only a one square movie. If it had both good cinemagraphic technique and portrayed sane, real people, it would merit two squares. Three squares would be reserved for movies, which added to the aforementioned virtues, the element of a coherent plot. The final accolade. the fourth square, should be reserved for movies which toe the party line. Thus Mr. First Nighter's fans could be sure of getting the straight scoop on cinema. The ratings could even be extended to other areas of cultural endeavor. Which brings me to my last point: the r.i.p. for Noel Coward may have gone too far. He was a delightful and talented man. But inspite of his fetching qualities he was only a three square playwright . . . a bit too weird to merit that last square.

• • •

MFN replies: It is always a pleasure to be attacked from a more extreme position than my own. And so I welcome Mr. Primae Noctis' contribution: for. to paraphrase the old adage. "the price of a rational, classical aesthetic is eternal vigilance."

---

self-interest."

The task set down by O'Conor was not accomplished. Today the forces of monarchy and aristocracy are infinitely stronger, more secure, and more prone to violence than a century ago. O'Conor witnessed the transformation of the Jeffersonian republic into the post-Civil War triumph of Hamiltonian mercantilism. We now have witnessed the further transformation through monopoly capitalism to corporate state capitalism exercising a world-wide imperium, and the institutional change from the republican simplicity of Washington and Jefferson as chief magistrates to the Caesarian principate of R. Milhous Nixon, Imperator Augustus.

Time is running out O'Conor and the Radical Democrats of the late 19th century fought bravely and resourcefully to retard the growth of Leviathan; Tucker and his circle did their best to clarify the issues even more plainly. Yet we must face the fact that they failed. We know who won; we know who won; we know what was lost, is being lost still. At the very least we must examine more carefully the failures of the libertarian forces of the past, and learn from their mistakes. We cannot combat the array of power which crushes and robs the bulk of the productive people of America unless we develop a grand strategy that will involve more than the few thousand readers of Lib. Forum, Reason and the few other publications espousing a libertarian ethic and political philosophy. Every day's headlines press us more and more to answer Lenin's famous question: What is to be done?

(J. R. P.) ◘

For Conspiracy Theorists Only!

1. Air America Inc. is the well known CIA-owned air transport company operating chiefly in Indo-China. Its books are audited by Coopers and Lybrand Inc. The Southern Air Transport Co., whose most profitable asset has been a federal contract to fly charter freight to SE Asia, Africa and Latin America, has just been revealed to have been founded and owned by the CIA. It shared Washington offices with Air America, and had the firm of Coopers and Lybrand as its auditors. President Nixon has now published an accounting of his financial relations with Bebe Rebozo and Robert Abplanalp in the purchase of the Western White House at San Clemente. The auditors of this public accounting — Coopers and Lybrand!

2. New York's muckraking weekly, **The Village Voice**, is running a series of articles detailing the friendship and business partnership of Richard Nixon and Bebe Rebozo, especially concentrating on the history of the Biscayne Bay land properties which are part of the Florida White House complex. It is a tale involving the alliance of Meyer Lansky and his ''business'' associates with Fulgencio Batista, late dictator of Cuba. and his friends, and the process by which money was ''laundered'' by passing through Cuba back into Florida where it was invested in real estate, banks and other enterprises in a series of complex sales, re-sales, mortgages, loans, and other gimmicks that would confuse and hide the real sources and ownership of the wealth. While Nixon claims his friendship with Rebozo dates from 1951, the Voice suspects otherwise. Nixon is known to have visited Cuba to investigate business opportunities in 1940 shortly after completing law studies at Duke University. By 1942 Bebe Rebozo was in the tire-recapping business in Florida — a business he financed through Frank Smathers, father of George Smathers, later Senator from Florida and close personal friend of Nixon. Nixon during this year was in Washington working in the Office for Price Administration. His particular unit was responsible for supervising the tire industry. George Smathers was at that same time an attorney for the tire interests of Standard Oil of Kansas which was allegedly routing American-made tires through Cuba to avoid American rationing controls. And Rebozo is reputed locally to have made the ''seed money'' of his fortune in the ''grey market'' of tire-rationed wartime Florida. Of course, this is possibly just a coincidental parallel of time, of men and interests. But clearly biographers (to say nothing of prosecutors) ought to examine the career of young Mr. Nixon more closely.

— J.R.P.

The 'Final Solution' To The Arab Problem

Freedom, the English anarchist weekly published a brief report entitled Israel: a Nazi State? (23 June, 1973) which contained several quotations of prominent Israeli generals made at a symposium on the problem of the occupied territories. General Yitzhak Rabin, recent Israeli ambassador to Washington, urged the view that ''conditions should be brought about now, which, in the future years, would, quite naturally cause a drift of (Arab) population towards the east bank of the Jordan''. This would be accomplished ''without resorting to force''. It is now reported in the New York Times that the ruling Labor party in Israel will undertake to sponsor and encourage the ''purchase'' of Arab-owned private land in the conquered Gaza strip, west bank of Jordan and Golan Heights. All purchases must be authorized by the Israeli government and priority will go to developers of new towns, factories and kibbutzim. In this way the most valuable properties will be transfered from Arab to Israeli ownership — encouraging the Arab property-owning class to liquidate its assets in Israeli-held territories, and migrate abroad.

Defense Minister Moshe Dayan summarized the Israeli government's viewpoint thusly:

> We have settled in this region essentially to create a Jewish State, and we will simply not allow the Arabs to control its frontiers. Had we wished to show any respect for the supremacy of the Arabs and their desires when they had occupied the country so extensively and for so long a period, it would have been impossible to create a Jewish State. They (the Arabs) no doubt believe themselves to be in the right, but if our aim is to fashion our own State, I do not see how we can avoid stepping on their toes. It is certain that Jews will come and establish themselves in the very areas which were formerly inhabited by the Arabs. The moment we accept the principle that we must ask permission of the Arabs in order to settle in regions where they themselves live, then we can say goodbye to our notion of a Jewish State.

Perish vilely all that delight in monarchy or oligarchy in the State; for the name of liberty is worth all the world, and even if one have but little, he is deemed to have great possessions.

— Euripides

The Libertarian Forum

BOX 341
MADISON SQUARE STATION
NEW YORK, NEW YORK 10010

First Class

Published Every Month. Subscription Rate: $8.00 Per Year

A Monthly Newsletter

THE Libertarian Forum

Joseph R. Peden, Publisher   Murray N. Rothbard, Editor

VOLUME V, NO. 12   DECEMBER, 1973   US-ISSN0047-4517

CONGRESS '73

Mr. Eric Scott Royce has gone to the trouble of compiling the voting records of every Senator and Congressman for 1973, listing their votes on 25 key measures in each House, and judging and rating them from a libertarian point of view. Every libertarian interested in politics will want a copy (available for $1.50 from Libertarian Information Service, Box 31638, Aurora, Colo. 80011.) My major quarrel with Mr. Royce is that in his rating system based on the data he treats an absent vote as equivalent to a wrong vote from the libertarian point of view. My own rating system simply ignores absences and lists the number of favorable as against unfavorable votes. Mr. Royce's methodology treats indifference or illness as equivalent to aggressive evil, which I can't quite bring myself to do. (The only exception he makes is with poor old mugging victim Senator Stennis, who would otherwise have acquired a close to zero libertarian rating for being on a sickbed. But if Stennis is exempt, why not others?)

In my own rating system for Senators (leaving the House members to Mr. Royce), I have taken Royce's 25 votes, and added to them a listing and judgment on an additional 13 votes. Seven were omitted from Mr. Royce's tabulation (continuing the Rural Electrification loan program — libertarian vote is No; allowing the cities to use existing highway funds for mass transit — Yes; the rural environment assistance program —

No; river and flood control program — No; airport development — No; allowing the Alaskan pipeline to be built — Yes; and lowering the minimum wage rate for teenagers — Yes); and five more came later than Mr. Royce's July 31 cutoff date (the Trident program — No; overseas troop cuts — Yes; overriding Nixon's veto of the war powers curtailment bill — Yes; the Emergency Energy Control Act — No; and government financing for Presidential campaigns — No). A special addition was a "negative vote" which I added for each of the ten benighted and addle-pated Senators who went to the White House to bend the knee to their liege lord and to swear eternal fealty to Richard Nixon on Watergate (the Tomfool Ten: Curtis, Cotton, Fannin, Helms, Young, Bartlett, Thurmond, Tower, Bennett, and Hansen, all Republicans.) My own 13 votes added to Royce's 25, make a total of 38 votes for the Senate.

Instead of percentages, I have, in this Royce-Rothbard Report, grouped the Senators into categories, with their libertarian and anti-libertarian votes listed after each name. As compared to our ratings of the Senators in 1971-72 (Lib. Forum, Nov. 1972), we have, after poring over the voting charts, decided to add two categories to the list: "Fairly Good", between "Good" and "Moderate"; and, for those whose evil is too great to be contained within the category "Excruciatingly Bad", we have added the category "Super Bad." Our list follows:

Very Good:
Scott (R., Va.) 24-10
Bartlett (R., Okla.) 26-12

Good:
Roth (R., Del.) 23-14
Byrd (D., Va.) 23-14
McClellan (D., Ark.) 21-13
Packwood (R., Ore.) 21-14
Hatfield (R., Ore.) 21-14

Fairly Good:
Fannin (R., Ariz.) 21-15
Bellmon (R., Okla.) 21-15
Buckley (R., N. Y.) 18-12
McClure (R., Id.) 21-16
Helms (R., N. C.) 21-16
Brock (R., Tenn.) 20-16
Ervin (D., N. C.) 20-17

Moderate:
Hansen (R., Wyo.) 20-18
Bennett (R., Ut.) 16-14
Nunn (D., Ga.) 19-17
Talmadge (D., Ga.) 19-18
Cranston (D., Calif.) 16-15
Goldwater (R., Ariz.) 11-11

Weicker (R., Conn.) 18-18
Curtis (R., Neb.) 19-19
Cotton (R., N. H.) 13-14
Hart (D., Mich.) 16-17
Hollings (D., S. C.) 18-19
Abourezk (D., S. D.) 16-17
Hruska (R., Neb.) 18-19
Bentsen (D., Tex.) 18-19
Hughes (D., Io.) 16-18
Proxmire (D., Wisc.) 18-20
Church (D., Id.) 17-19
Johnston (D., La.) 16-18

Bad:
Dominick (R., Col.) 16-19
Stennis (D., Miss.) 3-6
Domenici (R., N. M.) 17-20
Eastland (D., Miss.) 14-18
Gurney (R., Fla.) 16-20
Thurmond (R., S. C.) 17-21
Clark (D., Io.) 16-21
Chiles (D., Fla.) 16-21
Nelson (D., Wisc.) 16-21
Haskell (D., Col.) 16-21
Taft (R., Oh.) 14-19
Griffin (R., Mich.) 16-20

Very Bad:
Mathias (R., Md.) 14-20
Saxbe (R., Oh.) 10-16
Mondale (D., Minn.) 13-20
Tunney (D., Calif.) 15-22
Case (R., N. J.) 15-22
Eagleton (D., Mo.) 13-20
Young (R., N. D.) 16-23
Bible (D., Nev.) 15-22
Beall (R., Md.) 15-22
Hathaway (D., Me.) 15-23
Stafford (R., Vt.) 13-21
Stevenson (D., Ill.) 15-23
Gravel (D., Alaska) 14-22
Bayh (D., Ind.) 13-21
Schweiker (R., Pa.) 15-23
Tower (R., Tex.) 14-22
Metcalf (D., Mont.) 15-24
Mansfield (D., Mont.) 13-22
Moss (D., Ut.) 15-24
Percy (R., Ill.) 14-23
Pell (D., R. I.) 15-24
Byrd (D., W. Va.) 15-24
Ribicoff (D., Conn.) 15-24
Kennedy (D., Mass.) 14-23
Aiken (R., Vt.) 14-23

Excruciatingly Bad:
Fulbright (D., Ark.) 9-19
Cannon (D., Nev.) 13-23
Dole (R., Kan.) 14-24
Symington (D., Mo.) 13-23
Huddleston (D., Ky.) 13-23
Burdick (D., N. D.) 13-24
Stevens (R., Alaska) 11-22
Randolph (D., W. Va.) 13-24
Fong (R., Haw.) 13-24
Inouye (D., Haw.) 13-24
Muskie (D., Me.) 11-22
Brooke (R., Mass.) 13-24
McGovern (D., S. D.) 13-24
Baker (R., Tenn.) 11-22
Biden (D., Del.) 10-22
Montoya (D., N. M.) 13-25
Williams (D., N. J.) 11-23
Javits (R., N. Y.) 12-24
Scott (R., Pa.) 12-24
Allen (D., Ala.) 12-25
Hartke (D., Ind.) 11-24
Magnuson (D., Wash.) 11-24
Sparkman (D., Ala.) 9-23

(Continued On Page 2)

Congress '73 —

(Continued From Page 1)

Pearson (R., Kan.) 10-24	Jackson (D., Wash.) 6-31
Cook (R., Ky.) 9-26	Long (D., La.) 11-25
	Pastore (D., R. I.) 10-24
Super Bad:	Humphrey (D., Minn.) 11-26
McGee (D., Wyo.) 4-25	McIntyre (D., N. H.) 9-25

Grouping the parties and categories together, we have, for the Republicans: Very Good — 2; Good — 3; Fairly Good — 6; Moderate — 7; Bad — 6; Very Bad — 10; Excruciatingly Bad — 9; Super Bad — 0. Travelling from the Good to the Bad end of the spectrum, the Republicans start low and gradually increase to reach a peak of 10 Senators at Very Bad, and 9 at Excruciatingly Bad. This record is bad enough, but is topped a long way by the Democrats, whose score is as follows: Very Good — 0; Good — 2; Fairly Good — 1; Moderate — 11; Bad — 6; Very Bad — 15; Excruciatingly Bad — 20; Super Bad — 2. The Democrats begin very low at the Good end of the spectrum, reach a minor peak at Moderate, and then soar up to 20 at Excruciatingly Bad. We can get a further idea by lumping the Goods and the Bads together, which give us: Republicans: 11 Goodish, 7 Moderate, 25 Baddish; while the Democrats weigh in at: 3 Goodish, 11 Moderate, and no less than 43 Baddish. Lumping still further, we see the parlous state of the Senate by finding 14 Goodish Senators, 18 Moderates, and a whopping 68 Baddish.

How did the Senators fare as compared to the 1971-72 record? As a group, the Democrats scored about the same, and the Republicans did a bit better, raising their Goodish ranks from 8 to 11. Individually, the top spots changed hands, as our former heroes (?) Roth and Byrd (Va.) fell from the Very Good to the Good category, to be replaced by two freshmen: Bartlett and Scott (Va.) Of our current Goods, Hatfield raised himself from Moderate, while the two others in the Good ranks (Packwood and McClellan) managed to vault spectaculraly up from the Very Bad. None of our former Goods fell that far, all dropping a bit into the ranks of the Fairly Good and the Moderate.

A particularly chilling note is the huge expansion of the very bottom end of the spectrum. In the last Congress, there were only 6 Excruciatingly Bad Senators; now there are 29 Excruciatingly Bad and 2 Super Bad, a truly appalling increase in the ranks of evil. Once again, of course, as last time, the absolutely worst Senator of all is Mr. State, Scoop Jackson.

Mr. Royce's report is particularly useful in giving us the tools to analyze the voting record of our avowedly libertarian freshman Congressman, Steve Symms (R., Id.) Symms did not run on the Libertarian Party line, but he was endorsed by the Libertarian Party of Idaho, is perhaps himself a party member, and at the very least is anxious to be considered as a libertarian purist. We owe it, both to the cause and to the individual himself, to scrutinize the record of any libertarian who achieves public office with the utmost vigilance. If we are to remain enthusiastic about Libertarian Party activity, we must meet the challenge of the LeFevrians and the other critics of political party efforts by treating our successful candidates with a microscopic scrutiny to see to it that they indeed remain pure. Any deviations from purity must be denounced with the utmost vigor. For if we elect a Libertarian who proceeds to deviate from libertarian principle, he thereby gives the cause a black eye from which it will be difficult to recover. If a Libertarian "leaks" away from principle, how will our principles ever be taken seriously again? To safeguard principle, then, we must be alert to such sins and heresies and be prepared to denounce them without fear or favor.

Let us then examine Steve Symms' voting record on the Royce Report's 25 votes. We find, to our stunned horror, that Steve voted libertarian on only 18 measures, and voted anti-libertarian on no less than 7! What gives here? If we analyze the Seven Sins, we find that many of them fall into the broad category of the military-foreign policy-patriotic. The military-foreign-patriotic sphere is of course a grave and vital issue, here revealing that on the most important issue-area of our time, Steve is not a libertarian at all but an anti-libertarian Conservative. Let us list his deviant votes point by point:

1) Steve voted to continue appropriations for the bumbling, outrageously anti-civil libertarian House Internal Security Committee.

Are We Another Rome?

By Joseph R. Peden

Recently, the New York Times' house conservative, columnist William Safire, one time speech writer for Richard Nixon, who recently learned that his boss was tapping his telephone, wrote a marvelous Shakespearean parody. In it General Al Haig gave a funeral oration over the corpse of his dead leader, crying out: "Friends, liberals, civilians, lend me your ears! I come to bury Nixon, not to praise him. The good that Presidents do lives after them; the evil can be interred with their tapes". And so on.

Safire is not the first commentator to turn his mind to the history of ancient Rome in a moment of great national stress and fear. Tom Wicker, his liberal counterpart on the Times opinion page, had earlier openly called attention to the new Caesarism that seemed to animate the Nixon White House. Arthur Schlesinger, after a lifetime of exalting the Executive has now published a new book on the "Imperial Presidency", and prescient Senators in Washington have long since realized the emasculation of their body to be analgous to the fate of its Roman prototype. Perhaps then, it was not an accident that when General Haig called the deputy Attorney General with the Presidential order to fire Archibald Cox, he reminded the reluctant Mr. Ruckelshaus that this order came from his Commander-in-Chief. This incident suggests that the American Presidency is now operating on the basis of its military rather than civil authority — a characteristic feature of the Roman emperorship.

But is the use of Roman history in political rhetoric or for political

(Continued On Page 3)

For shame!

2) Steve voted to establish an American Revolutionary Bicentennial Administration. Steve, are you really willing to force the taxpayers to pay for this boondoggle? Do you expect historical truth to emerge from the federal government? Has a misguided patriotism distorted your vision?

3) Steve voted to oppose the Gross proposal to cut off all federal funds for research and development into urban mass transportation. What gives here? What big cities are there in Idaho that require federal aid to mass transit; what votes would Symms have lost to oppose this piece of statism?

4) Steve voted for a federal research subsidy to the National Science Foundation. Steve, didn't Baldy Harper send you literature against government subsidized and controlled science? What mighty science complex in Idaho requires bending principle here?

5) Steve voted against the bill to prohibit any further federal expenditure of funds for U. S. combat operations in Laos or Cambodia. Here is a crucial point; when the State sounds its blood-stained war trumpet, do we pack up libertarian principle for the "duration"?

6) Steve voted against a bill to place a maximum limit on federal farm subsidies to each farmer. Farm voters in Idaho are not enough to justify abandonment of principle.

7) Steve voted against placing a ceiling on American troops overseas. Once again, a vote for militarism and interventionist foreign policy over liberty and isolationism.

The example of Steven Symms should be a lesson to all Libertarian Party activists: namely, that tactical maneuvering that doesn't violate principle is one thing, but betrayal of principle is quite another. Any betrayal of principle destroys the cause, for if we don't uphold libertarian principle who will? The Symms case demonstrates the acute need for eternal vigilance over our own representatives in public office, as well as instant repudiation for any of their backsliding. If we don't pledge ourselves to this, we may as well pack up political party activity right away, and go back to cheering for or against Republicans or Democrats who at least don't claim to be libertarians.

Ironically, Steve Symms cannot even sustain the relativistic claim that at least he had the most libertarian record in the House in 1973. The following Congressmen, none of them official Libertarians, did as well or better than Symms' 18-7 voting record: Blackburn (R., Ga.) 16-4; Crane (R., Ill.) 18-5; Gross (R., Io.) 21-3; Rarick (D., La.) 17-5; Huber (R., Mich.) 18-7; Camp (R., Okla.) 17-6; and Shuster (R., Pa.) 18-7. It is pleasant, in contrast, to take this opportunity to hail the Grand Old Man of the Old Right, libertarian-conservative-isolationist H. R. Gross of Iowa, a marvellous and flinty character almost out of the storybooks □

Are We Another Rome? —

(Continued From Page 2)

analysis really useful or even justifiable?

The "grandeur that was Rome" has captivated the imagination of thoughtful men from the very days of the collapse of the Roman empire in the West during the fifth century. The very men who conquered Rome, the Germanic kings of the Franks and Ostrogoths and Vandals, etc. eagerly sought Roman titles and symbols of imperial dignity from the Roman emperors in Constantinople. Countless German kings, following the example of Charlemagne, sought the title of Emperor of the Romans, and wasted their lives and treasure, and those of their subjects, trying to give reality to the revered but illusory Roman empire of the middle ages. With the revival of the study of Roman law in the medieval universities in the 12th century, the kings and princes of Europe dreamt of the absolute power of Roman emperors, and insinuated whenever they could the principles and practices of Roman despotism into the laws and constitutions of their own feudalistic states.

But absolute monarchy in medieval times met three sources of vigorous resistance: first, from the Christian Church, especially under the vigorous leadership of such popes as Gregory VII, Innocent III and Boniface VIII. Ironically, it was the Papacy which resurrected the Roman imperial tradition when Pope Leo III crowned Charlemagne emperor in A. D. 800. But subsequent experience caused the Papacy to reverse its original support, and tenaciously to oppose all further tendencies towards monarchical despotism, seeing clearly that the liberty of the Church would not withstand such concentration of power. Secondly, the cumulative resistance of the forces of feudal society, based on a contractual and customary notion of rights and liberty, rather than rule by the arbitrary will of the prince, successfully prevented the development of absolute monarchy. The familiar story of the struggle between the evil king John and the barons and bishops of England climaxing with the publication of the **Magna Carta** has parallels throughout medieval Europe, and the later absolute monarchies which we associate with Louis XIV of France were possible only after the Christian Church had been rent asunder by the Protestant Reform, and kings were no longer dependent upon the feudal nobles for income and military services.

Thirdly, absolute monarchy and the Roman imperial tradition faced opposition from the newly emerging urban commercial class who established in Italy and elsewhere communal republics as an alternative to imperial and kingly dominion. These bourgeoisie looked to the traditions of Republican Rome, rather than to the Rome of the Caesars. This viewpoint began among the Florentines of the fifteenth century, quickly found a welcome response from the Venetians and other Italians living in communal republics, and spread throughout Europe wherever similar political institutions were developing. Tentative criticism of the Roman Caesarian tradition had first come from Petrarch. His **Africa** extolled the Carthaginians, and in a dream sequence, he mourned that Caesar had turned his "ever victorious hands against the flesh and blood of his own commonwealth, and stained his triumph over foreign enemies with the blood of citizens". Yet in a biography of Caesar, Petrarch is openly in awe of the bloody dictator. But by 1440 a more common opinion among the Italian humanists is that of the Venetian Pieto del Monte who expressed his "frank detestation of Caesar, the infamous parricide, destroyer of Roman liberty and bitter enemy of his patria". Hans Baron has brilliantly demonstrated the great significance of this Roman republican tradition in his masterpiece, **The Crisis of the Early Italian Renaissance** (Princeton, 1966). But by the year 1599, a humanist attached to the court of the Grand Duke of Tuscany would argue that "Rome was never as free as at the time when she lost her liberty" by which he sought to soothe the feelings of the liberty-loving Florentines now subjects of Medici princes.

It is especially important for us to note that there is not just one Roman tradition to which one can appeal for a usable past. In fact there are at least three Roman themes which have attracted the attention of orators and political pundits: first, the grandeur and achievement of the Roman empire — a multi-national political entity stretching at its zenith from the Irish Sea to the Tigris and Euphrates; from the Rhine and Danube to the Sahara and Sudan. This empire is traditionally justified as an agency for civilizing barbaric and unruly peoples, imposing upon them order and law — of world wide scope — the famous **Pax Romana**.

This tradition plays a continuing role in the consciousness of American leaders. In August 1965 the editors of **Fortune** — the house journal of America's ruling elite — openly acknowledged that, while no one had planned it that way, America had indeed acquired a world empire. And that our characteristic idealism made us willing to bear the great sacrifices which our world mission would entail. Among these sacrifices was the need to bear any burden to ensure peace and order in Asia, (and Europe and everywhere else one assumes). With the ruling elites thus fortified for the great mission of empire, **Fortune's** fellow editors at **Life** soon created a multi-issue illustrated history of the greatness of Imperial Rome — civilatrix of the ungrateful barbarian nations. The clear message of this popularly directed propaganda was that the American people were privileged to take up the burden of perpetual war for perpetual peace, as had the ancient Romans.

political rhetoric. the **Pax Americana** (Ronald Steel adopted this as a title of his excellent study of contemporary American foreign policy.)

How appropriate is this rhetoric in contemporary political propaganda? First of all, many recent historians of Rome have little sympathy for those who boast of Rome's civilizing mission. H.D.F. Kitto puts it very succinctly:

> "The Romans had many gifts, but statesmanship was not one of them. No major reform was ever carried out by them without a civil war; the achievement of the Republic was to fill Rome with a pauperized rabble, to ruin Italy and provoke slave revolts, and to govern the empire with an open personal rapacity that an Oriental monarch would not have tolerated; the achievement of the Empire was to accept that political life was impossible, and to create, in its place, a machine." (H.D.F. Kitto, **The Greeks**, (Penguin Books) p. 97)

As historians become more familiar through archaeological research with the remains of Roman ruins in the provinces, the sterility and sameness of Roman material culture stands out in marked contrast to the aborted but vigorous remains of pre-conquest local cultures. What is seldom considered is the tremendous loss that may have occurred through the cultural genocide perpetrated by Roman imperial conquests. Only an occasional voice has filtered through to speak of the feelings of the conquered races. Tacitus records one such voice, that of a Briton whose people are about to be vanquished by Roman arms:

> "Brigands of the world, they (the Romans) have exhausted the land by their indiscriminate plunder, and now they ransack the sea. The wealth of an enemy excites their cupidity, his poverty their lust of power. East and West have failed to glut their maw. They are unique in being as violently tempted to attack the poor as the wealthy. Robbery, butchery, rapine, the liars call Empire; they create a desert and call it peace." Tacitus, **Agricola**

Prof. Oscar Halecki, in his **The Millenium of Europe** (Notre Dame, 1963) rightly points out that the "Roman Peace" was an illusion, a myth.

> "In addition to the permanent hostility with Persia, a source of endless conflicts, there was an equally permanent tension along the whole long European border. Even the reign of Augustus, which started with the closing of the temple of Janus and the dedication of the **ara pacis** in 9 B. C., was troubled in 9 A. D. by the disastrous defeat in the German war. . . . As conditions of life in subsequent centuries became much worse, and almost all parts of the once powerful empire suffered from uninterrupted warfare and destruction as a consequence of invasions and penetrations. (And I would add — uprisings and civil conflicts between armies of the empire) the bygone age of the Pax Romana seemed almost an ideal situation to which men would look back in times of even more troubles".

Halecki goes on to point out that

> "following Roman precedent, all conquerors of future ages who had established their dictatorial rule at home and tried to force it upon one foreign country after another, were to justify their imperialistic policies by pretending that they would create a new and better order, putting an end to the

(Continued On Page 4)

Are We Another Rome? —

(Continued From Page 3)

rivalries among the troublesome smaller states and unifying large areas to the economic advantage of the populations. That fallacy reached its climax in the days of Hitler. whose Third Reich wanted to continue for the next millenium the imperial tradition which the first German empire had inherited from Rome".

As Halecki concludes:

Rome's "unquestionable greatness and her amazing achievements in the first one or two centuries of the Christian era must not make us overlook the fact that the imperial tradition is the most questionable part of our Greco-Roman heritage. different from its highest, truly humanistic ideals, and that it is at the same time the part which is most difficult to reconcile with our Christian heritage."

Halecki's warning was echoed by the late Frank Meyer, one of the most thoughtful conservatives of our time. Meyer wrote an article in National Review in 1957 (Sept. 9) commenting upon Amaury de Riencourt's widely discussed analysis of postwar Europe and America entitled The Coming Caesars. De Riencourt, as a European, saw America as the New Rome whose Caesars with their atomic armed legions would create a new world order ushering in universal peace and progress but at the expense of liberty. Americans were, like the Romans, "iron, soulless administrators" who had arisen in the late summer of a culture to preserve order and the civilized forms when the creative heart has gone out of the society.

Significantly. Meyer rejected the analogy between Rome and America. First of all, he identified America's true political ideals more closely with the individualism and love of personal freedom of the Greeks rather than the collectivist penchant for order of the Romans. And he found one overwhelming defect in the Roman analogy: Western civilization is unlike that of Rome; it is essentially different since "it is based on the Christian vision of the innate value of the human person and of his freedom under God". As Meyer concluded, "If the Caesars come, borne on the wave of mediocrity. it will not be because America imposed them on Europe, but because in neither continent have there been enough men dedicated to truth and freedom to resist them".

It is disturbing to note that two of the most notable liberal critics of American foreign policy, Senators Fulbright and McCarthy, have failed to base their critiques on the firm basis suggested by Halecki or Meyer — the moral defect in any imperialist tradition. McCarthy's book, The Limits of Power, and Fulbright's collection of essays entitled The Arrogance of Power, center their argument on the pragmatic questioning of whether we have tried to exercise an imperial sway beyond the capacity of our resources. This argument is essentially a reflection of the great 18th century historian of Rome's decline and fall, Edward Gibbon, who wrote:

"The decline of Rome was the natural and inevitable effect of immoderate greatness; the causes of destruction multiplied with the extent of conquest; Prosperity ripened the principle of decay and as soon as time or accident had removed the articicial supports, the stupendous fabric yielded to the pressure of its own weight."

Rome then was at the end reduced to "a pitiful helpless giant" — to borrow a current phrase.

Clearly this liberal critique of empire is doomed to failure. Who can say with assurance what the "limits of American power" are? Or how much greatness is immoderate? Does anyone publicly suggest that America become anything less than the greatest power on earth? Not if he wants to get elected to political office. An appeal to the fate of the fall of the Roman empire must fail also on the most obvious pragmatic ground. The Roman empire lasted for five centuries or so. And there is not a politician. soldier. stockholder. corporate executive or banker in the military-industrial complex that rules this society who wouldn't settle for a fraction of that timespan for America's empire.

A second tradition frequently used by those who look to Rome for their rhetorical analogies is that Rome "fell" because of moral decay brought on by luxury and vice. Here again Gibbon may be consulted for his view that "prosperity hastened the principle of decay". This was also a favorite ploy of classical historians. It can be used in a variety of interesting ways according to the occasion. Puritans use it to denounce those who spend money in ways they disapprove; socialists denounce the maldistribution of wealth; conservatives complain about the Roman policy of "bread and circuses" for the masses as the very root of Rome's destruction. All this is such nonsense that it was inevitable that it would capture the fervid imagination of Richard Nixon. Speaking to a group of 130 newspapermen in Kansas City in July 1971, our beloved Leader said that when he looks at the pseudo-classical architecture of Washington, "I think of seeing them in Greece and Rome and I think of what happened to the great civilizations of the past. As they became wealthy, as they lost their will to live. to improve, they became subject to the decadence that destroys a civilization. The United States is reaching that period." It makes you wonder if Nixon isn't trying to destroy the prosperity of the economy deliberately in order to save us from ourselves!

The third theme derived from Roman experience is the tradition of the Roman republic. It has been seen as a self-governing and liberty loving society. The Florentine humanists of the 15th century were the first to exploit the fully republican aristocratic tradition of Rome exemplified in the works of Cicero. Livy and Tacitus, much of whose work was unknown to previous generations. This republican tradition thrived on libertarian aspects of the Republican regime and compared its virtues and liberal values to the sterility and despotism of the later Roman imperial regime. To these Florentines, trying to preserve their communal republic from the tyranny of Renaissance despots, Brutus was the great hero of the last age of the Republic, and the Caesars were the villains. It was this tradition that animated some of the American revolutionaries like Patrick Henry who reminded his audience in the House of Burgesses that Caesar had his Brutus, and Charles I his Cromwell, and that George III might profit by their example.

The founding fathers of the American Republic were well educated men, and in that age that meant well educated in classical literature. A reading of the Federalist papers reveals the ease with which Hamilton, Jay and Madison summoned the events and personalities of ancient Greece and Rome to argue their case for the new constitution.

Madison, for instance, found that "the liberties of Rome were the final victims of her military triumphs" and warned that a standing army was as dangerous as it was possibly necessary. "On the smallest scale it has its inconveniences, on an extensive scale, its consequences may be fatal" as in the case of Rome's Republic.

At first sight. the Republican tradition of Rome might appear to be a useful device against the trend towards Caesarism — which is a fourth Roman tradition which has beguiled all men who lusted for power over their fellow humans. But the republican tradition has its own inherent limitations for us. Sir Ronald Syme points out that

"In all ages, whatever the form and name of government, be it monarchy. republic or democracy, an oligarchy lurks behind the façade; and Roman history, republican or imperial. is the history of a governing class . . . Liberty and the laws are high sounding words. They will often be rendered. on a cool estimate, as privilege and vested interests." (Sir Ronald Syme in The Roman Revolution (Oxford 1939))

And it should be remembered that the civil wars which brought the downfall of the Roman republic were essentially a struggle for power and offices within the aristocracy. If the victors happened to be rhetorical champions of the "people", they did not radically reorder the structure of Roman society. Human slavery remained a basic institution in society; the masses of citizens remained politically disenfranchised; the lower classes remained subject to the aritrary will of the ruling aristocracy — occasionally renewed by fresh blood and hungry for the privileges that the rulers of Rome always enjoyed. After the fall of the Republic, the new senatorial aristocracy, lacking the pride and tradition of liberty of the old, kept their mouths shut and enjoyed the profits of their new-won power under the dictatorship of the Emperors.

I remain skeptical of the value of using any of the major themes of Roman history as political propaganda in. our contemporary situation. First. there is little in the history of the Roman empire's long rule to convince any one that we should abandon our own imperial destiny.

(Continued On Page 5)

The Machinery Of Friedman

By Joseph Salerno

In **The Machinery of Freedom**, David Friedman bases his apologia for anarcho-capitalism on solely "practical" considerations. In so doing, he eschews the bedrock foundation of the natural rights ethic and rests his theoretical structure on the dangerously shifting sands of utilitarianism. All this, we are told, to avert the popular disapprobation that attends ethical vis a vis practical concerns. Consequently, we find Mr. Friedman in chapter 34 equably discussing the production and utilization of retaliatory nuclear weapons in a free society, without recognition of the moral problem entailed in the very existence of weapons of indiscriminate mass annihilation. But this particular shortcoming bears an integral relation to an overriding general flaw in Friedman's exposition.

In essaying to banish ethics from the purview of his analysis, Friedman has effected a monstrous bifurcation between anarcho-capitalism and libertarianism. He posits an anarcho-capitalist society in a political and ethical vacuum, and then goes on to analyze law "production" in economic terms, blithely unaware of his transgression against the most elemental dictates of common sense. For it is absurd to assume the existence of the economic institutions of anarcho-capitalism outside the politico-ethical framework of libertarianism. An objective, libertarian legal code, predicated on the Spencer-Rothbard axiom of nonaggression, and its acceptance by a large proportion of the populace, is the sine qua non of the establishment of anarcho-capitalism. Viewed in this light, Friedman's attempt in chapter 31 to adduce proof that anarcho-capitalism would be libertarian is at best supererogatory.

Friedman also commits a grave strategic error in refusing to argue his case on an ethical level. The enemies of the free society are conceded the eminently defensible ethical position by default, while libertarians myopically scurry about seeking evanescent victories in disjointed small scale skirmishes. This strategy will doom libertarians to long run failure as surely as it did their classical liberal kinsmen a century ago. Issue must also be taken with Friedman's asseveration that the masses are impervious to argumentation along ethical lines. This leaves unexplained the tremendous popular appeal of socialism in its multitude of variations and transmogrifications, a doctrine with explicitly normative underpinnings. No doubt Friedman would even have us believe that the intense conflagration enveloping the abortion issue was ignited by arsonists bereft of moral convictions. So let us not decapitate the beauteous corpus of libertarian doctrine, but rather strengthen and purify her that she may better show up the hag of statism.

Let us now proceed to an examination of the substance of Friedman's analysis. Here his errors are dishearteningly numerous and grievous. The first of three sections of the book is given over to a utilitarian defense of private property. In chapter 1 Friedman badly misconceives the true nature of "public property." Unbelievably he does not controvert the proposition that the "public" in fact exercises control and disposition over such euphemistically denominated property. The government in his view acts as a surrogate for the public will in controlling and disposing of public properties, though it performs the task more inefficiently and with less regard to the wishes of the minority than the free market. But nowhere does Friedman admit the possibility that the government is employing public property as a means to achieve its own ends, and is not the benign though bumbling executor of the public will depicted in democratic mythology.

In chapter 3 Friedman misleadingly employs the term "power" in reference to a private property regime. An individual who owns the whole food supply, he asserts, is more "powerful" than one who exercises ownership over a smaller proportion of the food supply. But this example removes the discussion of power from its proper context of freedom vs coercion. Power implies the existence of coercive relationships among men. It is the ability of some individuals to effect the infringement or denial of the property rights of other individuals. Thus it is befuddling and unfelicitous at best to describe a person owning the total supply of a given good as "powerful".

In two pages entitled "interlude," Friedman entreats us to look to historical quasi-capitalist experiments in order to substantiate the viability of a free society. It is here that his nonethical apologia becomes subtly an antiethical one. He informs us that "human societies are far too complicated for us to have confidence in a priori predictions about how institutions that have never been tried would work." Presumably if historical retrospection yielded us adverse evidence regarding the efficacy of capitalist institutions, the coup de grace will have been delivered to the case for liberty. But if workability is to be the sole criterion by which human societies are judged more or less desirable, all ethical concerns in the matter are rendered stiose.

In the second section, Friedman proffers us his pet solutions to the myriad of problems besetting a statist social order. Many are more than faintly redolent of the palliatives prescribed by the Chicago School of Economics for various social maladies. The presentation is unsystematic, one might say haphazard, as Friedman deftly avoids the confines of a comprehensive schema of reform. Not unpredictably, many of the solutions he propounds are a. halting steps in the direction of liberty which, if not augmented by longer, more forceful strides, will strand us far from our goal in a barren compromise and b. downright illibertarian.

In chapter 10, as a solution to the egregious problem of schooling in a politicized society, Friedman advocates the "voucher plan." Under this plan the parents receive a certain sum of money, a voucher, from the government for the education of each school-aged child with the stipulation that it must be redeemed at a "qualified" school. Curiously, Friedman opposes the much more libertarian scheme of tax rebates, which calls for the return of a certain sum of tax monies to parents of school-aged children without the corresponding stipulation of expenditure enforced by state compulsion. This would signal an end to compulsory education laws. A system of tax rebates also averts the pernicious increase in the state's power to control private schools, which occurs under the voucher system in the guise of the necessity to qualify the

(Continued On Page 6)

Are We Another Rome? —

(Continued From Page 4)

Pragmatically, from the point of view of the rulers of Rome, their empire was a success, not a failure. And most Americans would agree that it was a success — on a practical level. Rather than suggesting that America in the 20th century is a new Rome, we should do everything possible to destroy the notion that the two are in any way analogous in character, structure or circumstances. Frank Meyer is correct on this point. The existence of atomic weapons alone ought to make that perfectly clear. Moreover, as Halecki and Meyer both point out, the legacy of Christendom stands between us and the Romans. The concept of the personal dignity of man, his personal responsibility for his acts, the concept of natural rights, the dignity of labor, the Christian concepts of justice, love and mercy, ethics — all these make any analogy with Rome meaningless — unless one believes that ideas have no consequences. Our world is permeated with the ideology of liberty and the idea of the dignity of man — the product of two thousand years of historical development in the West. And its brightest achievements were most often made in the struggle to defeat the recurrent revival of Roman traditions of order and empire. Let us then concentrate on promoting these positive moral perceptions and ideals, for they are the only real alternatives to the abyss of a modern Pax Romana and of Caesarism.

As James Madison pointed out, many institutions and events in Roman history used as models in political debate are unfit for imitation or use as they are repugnant to "the genius of America". Allowing due weight for the consideration that "there are many points of similarity which render these Roman examples not unworthy of our attention." he urged "extreme circumspection" in reasoning from one case (Rome's) to another (America's).

That advice is even better today than when it was first uttered. ◻

433

The Machinery Of Friedman —

(Continued From Page 5)

legitimate recipients of vouchers.

It is on this last point that Friedman overtly abandons libertarian doctrine. He contends that it is necessary for the state to obtrude into the educational system via the enforcement of standards of qualification, in order "to prevent parents from setting up fake schools in order to transfer the voucher money to their own pockets." But why David shouldn't parents set up fake schools and transfer money to their own pockets? Is it not simply reclaiming stolen money from a thief? Why should parents be compelled to send their offspring even to a gloriously competitive school system? Why not clamor for the state to cease forthwith and in toto its interventions in the educational process, surely a cause more worthy of libertarian time and effort than the implementation of the voucher plan? And why, David, is it necessary to confront you, a self-proclaimed libertarian, with such queries?

As for Friedman's contention that the voucher system is preferable to a system of tax rebates because it provides the poor with greater benefits, one can only point out that it is based on egalitarian, and not libertarian considerations. One might also refer Mr. Friedman to the treatment that the question of the provision of goods and services to the poor in a competitive free economy has received in the works of various libertarian theorists e.g. Rothbard, Hospers, etc.

In chapter 12 and 13 Friedman argues that the present hierarchically-structured university will give way to radically decentralized, "free market" institutions and tutors in a free society. First of all, one must question whether it is proper to attempt to prognosticate the exact configuration of a given market i.e. the market for higher education. After all it depends to a great extent on the configuration of consumer demand, a scientifically unpredictable variable. If market participants desire a university where the board of trustees, alumni and faculty to varying degrees set policy and formulate the curriculum without student participation, institutions of this type will preponderate on the free market. The libertarian qua libertarian can say no more about it. This raises the question of the propriety of Friedman's designation of the particular type of institution he favors as "free market." This leaves us with the ridiculous inference that the presently constituted university, which as we saw above could subsist on a purely free market, is something other than a free market institution.

Chapter 14 is a rather mawkish entreaty for the abolition of immigration laws. What is astounding is Friedman's solution to the potentially distorted influx of immigrants which could be caused by the relatively munificent welfare benefits provided by the American State. Instead of rectifying the problem by calling for an end to the whole kit and kaboodle, he suggests incorporating a fifteen year national residency requirement into the present welfare system. He also succeeds in obscuring the distinction between the libertarian position regarding government interdiction of immigration, and immigration itself. Libertarianism makes no judgement as to whether immigration per se is a good thing. In a free society it is conceivable that immigration would be restricted by private property owners e.g. road owners, stockholders or residents of private communities, ship companies etc.

In chapter 17 Friedman again deviates from libertarian principles by formulating a plan to decentralize local government and thereby ameliorate the inefficiency that has been plaguing it. Understandably, libertarians are in sympathy with any reduction in the size of a governmental unit, provided it is attended by a **reduction in government power and control over the individual.** Needless to say this does not imply that libertarians should favor the streamlining of government as an end in itself, especially if it results in a. a greater efficiency in government coercion e.g. tax reforms that provide the state with greater revenues and b. decreasing popular discontent with government. Thus it is disconcerting to find a libertarian outlining a blueprint for the more efficient functioning of local government, complete with a proposal for the most efficient method of setting tax rates and collecting revenues. This is repellent enough, but must he partake in the bureaucratic assault on linguistic integrity and aesthetics and serve us up the likes of "subcities" and "mini-mayors"?

In chapter 23 we encounter a cavalier dismissal of the 1968 Paris revolt as socialistic and comparable in motivation to the occupation of Prague by Soviet armor. Friedman exhibits a total lack of cognition of the issues involved. He ignores the gruesomely meticulous regulation of all aspects of economic and social life by the fascistic French government, and the stratified caste structure of French society, as well as the incipient anarchism of many of the student rebels. Further on in the chapter, Friedman's egalitarian predilections again surface when he asserts that the greater the dispension of wealth in a given society, the better would its economy approximate a free enterprise economy. This is a fallacious proposition. Two societies, possessing widely differing distributions of wealth and income, could both theoretically qualify as purely free societies. The determining characteristic is the presence or absence of coercive relations among men. The fact that empirically societies with relatively free economies tend to possess a greater equality in the distribution of wealth and income does not comfute the theoretical conclusion.

The third section of the book is for the most part an exposition of the nature, form and viability of anarcho-capitalist institutions. The general lines of the analysis, which assumes the existence of anarcho-capitalist institutions outside a politico-ethical framework, have been criticized above. It remains for us to evaluate particular aspects of the positive analysis.

Friedman grounds his discussion of the problem of national defense on the spurious concept of a collective or public good. Here one can do no more than recommend Professor Rothbard's brilliant and definitive demolition and interment of the collective good, and the closely related, external benefits fallacies in **Man Economy and State.** Constraints of space do not permit that his argument be reconstructed here. Suffice it to say that crippled in its inception, Friedman's analysis cannot but lead to lame conclusions. Our expectations are borne out when we are apprised that: 1. Neither government nor market can provide us with a "perfect" solution to the national defense problem. 2. As a matter of fact, there is a good chance that the market may perform more imperfectly than government, and lo and behold "by a freak of fate" a vestigial state may be "temporarily useful." 3. Anyway he (David) would rather pay taxes to Washington than Moscow. And so the closet archist emerges.

On the subject of revolution, Friedman remonstrates libertarians to abjure the tactic of civil disruption. This is a fine position for a libertarian to take, but one must remember that it is a function of strategic and not moral considerations. The absolute moral right to defend oneself against aggression, whoever the perpetrators, is freely ceded to the individual by libertarian ethics. The decision to exercise this right, however, depends on many considerations, such as the available weapons, the enormity of the aggression, the strength of the aggressor, the long run prospects of success etc. These considerations apply to state as well as private aggression. Thus it is today that any defensive violence brought to bear against the American State without popular support, would surely be premature and result in a catastrophic setback to the movement and its goals. This is not to say that revolution may never be warranted on strategic grounds. Indeed the time may come when a great proportion of the populace has been imbued with libertarian ideas. Then it may be strategically and morally proper for libertarians to rise up and violently dislodge the proprietors of the state, for it is folly to assume that they can be induced to capitulate by nonviolent means. But to oppose revolution on moral grounds, as Friedman does, is to repudiate libertarian ethics. To counsel libertarians, again on moral grounds, to "(C)limb into a hole . . . and come out when people stop shooting each other," is to advocate moral idiocy. What if, David, the people shooting each other were a Jewish shopowner and Nazi thugs? What if, David, the people shooting each other were the future heroes of a libertarian resistance and statist henchmen?

The bibliography would be comprehensive were it not for the glaring omission of the works of Murray Rothbard. It is inexcusable to exclude the contributions of a thinker of Rothbard's stature from a general compendium of libertarian works, whether the author happens to enjoy intellectual solidarity with him or not.   ◻

Royal power is by nature the mother of injustice.
— Dionysius (432-367 B. C.)

The virtuous need but few laws; for it is not the law which determines their actions, but their actions which determine the law.
— Theophrastus (370-286 B. C.)

Maddox Attacks Revisionism

By Bill Evers

Robert James Maddox. The New Left and the Origins of the Cold War (Princeton, N. J.: Princeton University Press, 1973), 169 pages, $7.95.

Beginning earlier, but achieving increased recognition in the mid-1960's, new "revisionist" interpretations of the origins of the Cold War have upset what had been the accepted account.

The essence of historical revisionism, whether on the First World War or Vietnam, and the source of its political impact is to be found in its close and critical examination of official accounts and official propaganda. Because all history situates us at the end of a chain of events, it provides us with a concrete, empirical basis on which to act in accord with our values. Thus new historical evidence and explanations which are in important disagreement with the official statements of decision-makers have direct political consequences.

After the Second World War the Rockefeller Foundation and the Council on Foreign Relations instituted a program of subsidized scholarship in order to head off the development of revisionism in the writings of the war's history.

Knowing their record of interest in such matters, it is no surprise that similar influential groups are applauding and promoting this new anti-revisionist book by Robert James Maddox.

In appraising Maddox's book as a piece of scholarship, two difficulties become immediately apparent. First, the book is not a full scale anti-revisionist account of the period like John Lewis Gaddis' new and unsatisfactory United States and the Origins of the Cold War. Second, Maddox is not providing a critique of the casual theories of revisionists, as Robert W. Tucker does in his often excellent Radical Left and American Foreign Policy.

Footnotes

Instead, what Maddox provides is an examination of a few of the footnotes found on a few pages and covering the short time between the Yalta and Potsdam conferences in 1945 in seven books by revisionist historians (William Appleman Williams, D.F. Fleming, Gar Alperovitz, David Horowitz, Gabriel Kolko, Diane Shaver Clemens, and Lloyd C. Gardner).

The conclusion which Maddox draws after checking these footnotes is "that these books **without exception** are based upon pervasive misusages of the source materials."

To determine whether Maddox is right we can turn to published government documents and then compare Maddox's description of them with the revisionists'. We can also read Alperovitz's reply to Maddox in the March 1973 **Journal of American History**, the replies of the seven revisionists published in the June 17 **New York Times Book Review**, and the lengthy mimeographed replies obtainable on request from Kolko, Horowitz, and Gardner.

Not Pro-Moscow

The first type of error that Maddox makes is implying that Horowitz and Kolko are pro-Moscow. On the contrary, Horowitz has long been influenced by Issac Deutscher's Trotskyist views, and Kolko considers the Soviet Union like Britian and the U.S. to be an imperial power "less concerned with democratic politics than friendly nations."

In fact, the remarkable thing about Kolko's chapter on Yalta is not what Maddox thinks he finds in it. It is rather, as Robert D. Schulzinger has noted, that Kolko's description of the great powers' cynical disregard of Yalta for the rights of the peoples of small nations is similar to the contemporary complaints of Robert Taft, John Bricker, and Westbrook Pegler about Yalta's secret diplomacy.

A second sort of error that Maddox makes is in dropping the overall political context of American diplomacy. For example, in his treatment of Horowitz and Kolko on the Polish question, Maddox fails to weigh correctly the extent to which American decision-makers saw Poland in terms of U.S.-Soviet relations.

Finally, Maddox simply makes factual errors. He misconstrues the question of admitting Argentina to the United Nations in criticizing Horowitz. He distorts, in attacking Williams, Alperovitz, Kolko and Garder, the attitude of American policy-makers toward the conditions for

Rand On The Middle East

The neo-Randian weekly newspaper **Ergo** has given us a detailed account of Miss Rand's answers during a question period following her annual Ford Hall Forum speech in Boston (**Ergo**, Oct. 31) Rand's remarks on the Middle East are a chilling revelation of her lack of knowledge of the concrete facts of reality, as well as a grievous betrayal of her own oft-proclaimed libertarian moral principles.

Asked what the American people and the government should do about the Middle East war, Rand answered unhesitatingly: "Give every help possible to Israel." Not American soldiers, she conceded; but military weapons. We need not stress here the assault on liberty involved when the U.S. government taxes Americans in order to send arms abroad; surely, this is as statist and immoral, though not to the same degree, as sending American soldiers to the Middle East. As for the American people, Miss Rand sounds for all the world like the United Jewish Appeal: "Give everything you can" (Give till it hurts?). Reaffirming her supposed and longtime opposition to altruism, Rand added that "this is the first time I have contributed" to public causes, but now apparently we have a vital exception.

Why? What is the overriding cause for which we must set aside libertarian principle, isolationist principle, and opposition to altruism; why is Israel's "emergency" to be a claim on our hearts and pockets? Given Miss Rand's militant atheism, it surely could not be the necessity for the reestablishment of the Temple, or the fulfillment of the old prayer, "next year in Jerusalem"; given her professed individualism, it surely could not be (one hopes) the Zionist call to blood, race, and soil. So what is it? Russia is of course dragged in, but even Miss Rand concedes that the Russian Threat is not the real issue here.

The real issue? Because "civilized men" are "fighting against savages", and when that happens, says Rand, "then you have to be on the side of that civilized man no matter what he is." The fact that Israel is

(Continued On Page 8)

foreign aid to Russia after World War II. He misrepresents the **de facto** situation on Poland's western border in attacking Kolko.

But these are not new errors on Maddox's part. They can be found in an exchange of letters in the May 18, 1972 **New York Review of Books**, in which Ronald Steel corrected Maddox's mistakes.

Most important of all in assessing Maddox's work is the question of whether he zeroes in on footnotes that materially damage the thesis of any book he is criticizing.

The first problem is that Maddox often misunderstands or distorts the thesis of a book when he is attacking it. He certainly does not accurately convey the central contention of William Appleman Williams about the Open Door ideology.

Maddox describes Horowitz as finding a radical dichotomy between the foreign policies of Roosevelt and Truman, whereas Horowitz's considered such changes only stylistic. Horowitz's real point was that the postwar power distribution left most important decisions in U.S. hands.

Key Point Not Faced

The second problem is that Maddox does not confront the revisionists by picking footnotes essential to their thesis. In the case of Alperovitz, for example, Maddox does not face Alperovitz's key argument that the possession of the atomic bomb by the U.S. was the major reason for a policy shift toward Russia in the middle months of 1945.

Useful critiques of Alperovitz's view can really only be found in the work of other revisionists like Kolko and Athan Theoharis.

Despite the obvious weakness of Maddox's work, it has been promoted by historians like the late Herbert Feis (one-time State Department economic policy-maker), George Kennan (another State Department official and original formulator of the containment doctrine), Arthur Schlesinger, Jr. (adviser to President Kennedy), and Eugene V. Rostow (Under Secretary of State under Kennedy).

I think, however, that the only objective evaluation that one can make of Maddox's book is that it is a poor job. Under close scrutiny, the book falls apart. Reconsidering the origins of the Cold War after having had the dubious benefit of Maddox's contribution, one can only conclude that the revisionists have made an important and probably lasting contribution to our understanding of what really happened.

Reprinted from the **Stanford Daily**.   ◻

Rand On The Middle East —

(Continued From Page 7)

socialistic. she adds. pales into insignificance before this great imperative.

There are two grave problems here: of the facts of reality, and of moral principle. Factually. what does Miss Rand mean by "savages"? Once work through the emotional connotations of the term, and the concept becomes a vague one. She explains that the Arabs are "primitive" and "nomads." Here she betrays total ignorance of Palestine and its history. The only "nomads" in the region are not the Palestinian Arabs, who were driven out of their lands and homes by the Zionists. but the Jordanian Bedouins. who as hirelings of King Hussein are in effect anti-Palestinian and pro-Israel. Palestinian Arabs were not nomads but agriculturists; long before Israel. they "made the desert bloom." The "nomad" theory was convenient Zionist propaganda. and nothing more. Perhaps the Palestinian Arabs are "savages" because they live miserable lives in hovels on the desert; but they do so because — one and a half million of them — they were driven out of their homes and properties by the Zionists. and they remain in dire poverty as refugees. Miss Rand's strictures are chillingly reminiscent of the English who drove the Irish out of their farms and lands by force, in the sixteenth and seventeenth centuries. and then looked down their noses at the "wild, savage" Irishmen who unaccountably spent their lives wandering around the forests.

Miss Rand asks herself the question: why are the Arabs against Israel? Unbelievably. she answers that they resent Israel because they are "savages" who "just do not want to use their minds"; deliberately choosing not to use their minds. they resent the superior technology and civilization of the Zionists. Surely this is the oddest explanation for Arab resentment ever penned. For what Miss Rand omits from the discussion is the one-and-half million Palestinian Arabs driven out of their homes and lands by force. to which were latter added another half-million ruled by Zionist conquerors. A crucial omission indeed! Where is the Palestinian refugee problem in Miss Rand's attempt at explanation? Blankout!

This brings us to the even more important moral question: namely, assuming that one can really define "savagery", what's wrong with being a "savage"? Isn't a nomad or a savage, a person? Doesn't he therefore possess inslianable rights? Isn't he to be allowed to own his own person and his property? What happened to the great libertarian principle. to which Miss Rand presumably adheres, of no initiation of force against another person? If savages are people, what is the justification for initiating force against them? Or are we to amend the great libertarian axiom to read: No one is allowed to initiate force against the person or property of another, except if he be civilized and the other a savage? But then we are on murky and dangerous ground. What if Group A is a bit more "civilized", and Group B a bit more "savage"; is it therefore legitimate and moral for A to attack and rob B? I am sorry to say that this is fascist ethical theory, and that therefore in this respect

the many charges about Randianism being "fascist" seems to have a certain core of truth.

And yet Miss Rand says it; without going into the rights or wrongs of the case. of the aggression or the property rights or the liberty involved, she states flatly: "When you have civilized man fighting against savages, then you have to be on the side of that civilized man no matter what he is." But surely, on any of her own apparent criteria, Soviet Russia, highly technically developed, is then far more "civilized" than, say, Mongolia. Does that mean that if Russia were to attack and sweep into Mongolia that we would all be honor bound to cheer for the Russians, and even to kick in our dollars for the great cause? And if not, why not?　□

The Libertarian Forum
BOX 341
MADISON SQUARE STATION
NEW YORK, NEW YORK 10010

First Class

Published Every Month. Subscription Rate: $8.00 Per Year

A Monthly Newsletter

THE
Libertarian Forum

Joseph R. Peden, Pubiisher   Murray N. Rothbard, Edito

VOLUME VI, NO. 1   JANUARY, 1974   US-ISSN0047-451

ENERGY FASCISM

Two years ago, in response to the first freeze of Phase I of Nixon's new economic policy, I wrote that "on August 15, 1971, fascism came to America." Some critics felt that the label was overblown; but here we are, two years later, well into the next "phase" of the fascist logic upon which the Nixon Administration has embarked: totalitarian controls such as allocations and rationing. He who says A must say B, and the logic of price and wage controls is marching us straight into a totalitarian, collectivist state: in short, fascism.

The crucial point on the energy crisis is that the crisis is **not**, as the Administration and the Establishment would have us believe, a visitation from on high, the result of the actions of the Arab sheiks, or a consequence of "excessive greed" on the part of the American consumer or of the oil companies. The crisis is, pure and simple, the creature of the American government itself and its statist interventions into the economic system. And while the rest of us are placed into increasing subjection by the government, in the name of aiding or curing the energy crisis, the **cause** — government policy — continues on its merry way unchecked.

The major evil stems from the government's policy of price controls below the free market level. There is one and only one possible cause of the phenomenon of a shortage, and that is government price control below the market. There are myriad actions of the government which have made energy fuels artificially **scarce**: but a **shortage** can only be caused by price control.

Economists define a "shortage" as a condition where consumers are not able to **find** the product. Regardless of how scarce the supply of a product may be, there is never any need for a shortage, for a disappearance of the product from the shelves. For on the free market, if a product becomes more scarce, the price rises until the market is "cleared", i.e. until there is sufficient supply available for those who wish to purchase the product at the market price. And so, if the free price system is permitted to operate, increased scarcity will cause a higher price, but not an outright disappearance, or "shortage", of the product. Take Rembrandt paintings, for example. Here is a product that is mighty scarce indeed, in fact it is difficult to think of another product in shorter supply; furthermore, barring a perfect and undetectable forger, there is no prospect of the supply of Rembrandts ever increasing. And yet, there are no complaints or lamentations about a "Rembrandt shortage". The reason is because there are no price controls on Rembrandts. As a result, if you have a couple of million dollars to spend, you will be able to find a Rembrandt to buy.

Shortages are solely the product of price controls, of not permitting the free market mechanism to function. The bigger the discrepancy between the government controlled price and the free market price, the bigger the shortage. Suppose, for example, that the government in its wisdom suddenly decreed that Wheaties may not be sold for more than a nickel a box. What would happen? After a brief flurry during which every kid and mother in the land would rush to the grocer to buy their bargain

Wheaties, the Wheaties would disappear from the shelves never to return. We would be in the throes of a nationwide Wheaties "shortage". Faced with the prospect of a swift revenue of a nickel a box, the Wheaties manufacturer would shift to corn flakes or go into some other line of business. Black marketeers would be beckoning consumers to buy "hot Wheaties" at a price far **above** the free market level (due to the cut in production, the inability to advertise an illegal transaction, the risk of being caught and arrested, and the cost of paying off the police to look the other way.) There is no need to conjure up Arab sheiks, "greedy profiteers", or anyone else as the culprits for the shortage. We can have as much of a shortage of **anything** as we want; all we need is to push the control price far enough below the market price.

When the black day of August 15, 1971 arrived, we free-market economists predicted that shortages of all sorts of products would result from the price control, and that the shortages would develop increasingly after a period of time. On the day of the freeze, everything seems to be functioning smoothly, and so the general mood is one of euphoric success. What is generally overlooked is that, since prices on August 15 corresponded to free-market levels, the frozen prices the next day would naturally correspond to these levels in much the same way. Free-market prices don't change that much in one day. But it was predictable that as weeks and months wore on, and as the government continued to inflate the money supply and hence free-market price levels, the gap would grow steadily worse and eventually lead to aggravated shortages of product after product.

The rise in free-market price levels was aggravated by the accelerating expansion of the money supply by the government and by the fact that the lingering recession of 1971 was soon succeeded by a boom, thus removing any slack in the economy. When Tricky Dick imposed Phase I in August, 1971, price inflation was proceeding at something like a rate of 4% per year. Now, after 4½ "phases" of varying degrees of price dictation, and continued monetary inflation by the government, we are suffering a price inflation rate of something like 10% per year; and prices rose in December, 1973 at an annual rate of approximately 26%. The rate of inflation is accelerating, and, apart from other evil consequences of this condition, the gap between the free and controlled prices of many goods continues to widen, and the shortages to emerge and grow steadily worse. It is not only natural gas and petroleum that have suffered aggravated shortages due to price control; it is also and increasingly such crucial commodities as paper, steel, and plastics.

Since we were probably due for a "normal" recession this year anyway, the shutdowns and layoffs that may flow from a disappearance of these crucial raw materials may well plunge the American economy into a severe depression. The same may more swiftly happen in Western Europe, where inflation and price controls are in some areas more severe than they are here. As price controls cause products and raw materials to disappear, plant shutdowns and layoffs could ensue, causing widespread

(Continued On Page 2)

Energy Fascism —

(Continued From Page 1)

drops in production and employment, i.e. a depression. We have already had a taste of this when the federal government, in its wisdom drastically cut its mandatory allocations of fuel oil from factories making private airplanes; after all, the bureaucrats reasoned, private planes are a luxury, so let's slash their allocations. Since private airplane factories happen to be concentrated in Wichita, Kansas (Cessna, Lear), the nearly 50% cut decreed by the government caused immediate large-scale unemployment in that city, and only massive protest by the Wichita citizens succeeded in getting the ruling reversed. This is only a foretaste of things to come.

And so price controls, as was predicted, have led to shortages in industry after industry. If the price system is allowed to function, then the free market quickly wipes out any shortage as the price rises to "clear" supply and demand on the market. Shortages under price controls persist and get worse, there being no market mechanism to remove them. If prices are allowed to rise, then the price increase performs two important economic functions: (1) the "rationing" function, as buyers voluntarily restrict their purchases, in accordance with each individual buyer's needs and abilities; and (2) the incentive function, the higher price stimulating increased production and supply over a period of time. Price control prevents both of these crucial functions from being performed, smoothly and voluntarily; instead, shortages persist and intensify.

In such a shortage situation, there must be some way of "rationing" the short supply. With prices not allowed to perform this task, other, arbitrary methods come into play: e.g. lining up for gas for several hours, or selling to favored purchasers. The next step, which has already occurred, is for the government to step in to ration by coercion, to allocate supplies in ways that it sees fit — ways that are always uneconomic and irrational as well as coercive and despotic. We already have gasoline rationing at earlier than retail levels: pace the government's arbitrary shutting off of fuel to the private airplane industry. And even at the costlier and more complex retail level, gasoline, for example, is already being "rationed" by arbitrary restrictions, and by official rationing in several states (at this writing Hawaii, Oregon, New York, and New Jersey).

There are two major problems with all these rationing schemes: (a) they are arbitrary, irrational, and totalitarian, and (b) they freeze the shortage, since they fail to allow prices to rise to induce greater supplies of the product.

Take, for example, the arbitrary shutdown of filling stations on Sundays. All that this accomplishes is to cause a rush on gasoline on Saturdays, as well as levying great hardship on drivers who have to travel somewhere, say in a sudden emergency, on a Sunday. How many potential hospital patients have already been injured or even killed by the blunderbuss orders to shut down on Sundays? The next step taken by our all-wise rulers was to impose maximum limits on each individual purchase of gasoline. The result, as could have been foreseen, was an uneconomical inducement to stop at a whole slew of filling stations until the desired amount is purchased. Since Christmas, the New Jersey Turnpike has imposed lunatic maximum limits on each car's purchase of gas: such that it is impossible to drive over more than a small fraction of the Turnpike. Each Turnpike ticket is stamped so that no more gas can be purchased. The result, of course, was that cars have been getting off and on the Turnpike repeatedly, picking up a new ticket along the way and getting the allotted amount at each turn. This absurd harassment is typical of the consequences of government intervention.

Furthermore, the gasoline scare — the fear that no filling stations may be open or available further down the road — has led everyone to keep their gas tanks as filled as possible, thus increasing the total purchase of gasoline as the average "inventory" of gas in the tank has risen. Now, the governments have reacted to this development by beginning to impose minimum limits on the amount (in gallons or dollars) of gasoline purchased, so that no one may keep his gasoline inventory high. But minimum limits, by their very existence, seem destined to lead, in their own right, to a higher consumption of gasoline. Moreover, to have both minimum and maximum limits on purchases begins to approach Alice-in-Wonderland; perhaps one day some clown in the bureaucracy will

inadvertently set the minimum limits higher than the maximum: and then all of us gas consumers will go bughouse in response to this new and devilish form of "Catch-22".

In contrast to these irrational and meat-axe measures, formal gasoline rationing would at least have the merit of allocating to each consumer his 30 or 40 gallons a month, and then allowing him to consume them in any pattern he wishes: on Sundays, on the Turnpikes, or whatever. A rationing system, however, would be highly costly, would require an army of unproductive bureaucrats to administer and enforce, and would be even more comprehensively totalitarian. It would also freeze the scarce supply and the shortage permanently.

The government is already confused about what sort of rationing system it is going to impose. There is the old and much reviled (justly so) World War II rationing system, in which no one was allowed to give away or sell his surplus ration tickets to anyone else. This prohibition made no sense at all. If the number of ration tickets matched the scarce supply (as it was supposed to), then if I (for example) sold my surplus anchovy tickets (as a non-anchovy eater) for someone else's candy tickets (the other person being a dieter), then both of us would be better off. Why shouldn't trading in ration tickets be allowed? Indeed, this was the entering wedge, in Henry Hazlitt's excellent novel **Time Will Run Back**, to move from a Communist economy of the future to a free market; the first step was: why not allow people to exchange their ration tickets?

Since Nixon's economic advisers claim that they favor the "free market", they have been reportedly toying with various "freeish market" versions of rationing. One is to allow a "white market", with people being allowed to buy and sell ration coupons; if I don't use my car much or at all, I can sell my surplus coupons to those who wish to use more than their allotted 40 gallons. OK, this plan (apparently the brainchild of Secretary Shultz), is certainly an improvement on the "traditional" World War II system. But the very improvement points up the imbecility of the whole rationing scheme. Suppose, for example, that the current controlled price of gasoline is 50¢ a gallon. No one knows what the free market price would be (indeed it is impossible to know without letting the free market rip), but estimates have ranged from 58¢ to 80¢ or $1.00 a gallon. Suppose that the free market price is 80¢. Then the result of this curious white market will be that the demands of the over-40 gallon buyers will drive the price up to approximately the 80¢ level. In other words, we would all be paying the 80¢ a gallon, and therefore there would be no further shortage; but the hitch is that the oil industry would be getting only 50¢ a gallon, while us under-users would be reaping the remaining 30¢. The moral issue is: why should I receive 30¢ a gallon for gasoline, I a non-producer? The economic issue is that the oil companies would still have no incentive to expand production and sales to the consumer market, so that we would be paying the higher free-market price without the benefit of inducing an increased supply. The idiocy of such a "solution" to the problem would be crystal-clear.

To complete the picture of rationing schemes, the above "extremist free market" proposal is countered by another variant, a "middle of the road" scheme in between World War II and Shultz. In this scheme, no one would be allowed to buy and sell ration tickets on their own and to each other; instead, the federal government would "nationalize" the ration ticket market. Everyone would have to sell their surplus stamps to the government, which in turn would resell them. In addition to getting its own unnecessary and uneconomic "cut" for these dubious monopoly services, the government would be making the fumbling attempt to find the market clearing price. This plan has all of the defects of the Shultz scheme plus many more; the government would clearly do a terrible job at trying to find the market price, a discovery job for which only the market itself is equipped.

Let us not despair completely, however; at least a partial salvation from this iniquity is already under way. It is an open secret that the heroic Mafiosi, always zealous at supplying goods and services that the State has declared to be illicit and illegal, have already revved up to print counterfeit ration tickets on a massive scale. Presumably, the Mafia is using sources of information inside the government to find out exactly what the tickets will look like. It has been estimated that fully 15% of the gasoline sold for ration coupons in World War II was sold for black-market, counterfeit coupons. And that was in the midst of a war supported with enthusiasm by most of the populace. If counterfeiting and black markets were so extensive in the midst of that patriotic fervor, what will it be now, when there is no popular war and the government is

(Continued On Page 6)

Mises And History

By Leonard P. Liggio

The death of Ludwig von Mises has brought forth numerous essays on his contribution to economics. It is equally in order to discuss his work in the historical sciences, as he called them. Having had the honor and pleasure of attending Mises' graduate seminar during the years in which he wrote Theory and History and devoted his seminar to that subject, I had the rare opportunity of participating in the final formulation of his long-considered concepts of the historical sciences. But, before discussing that part of his contribution in another article, I shall indicate some of the substantive historical analyses which Mises made.

Faced with the rise of classical liberalism in the 19th century and its collapse since the first world war, Mises had very special motives for examining contemporary history. Mises emphasized that ideas are the base on which all social activity takes place. It is in the realm of ideas that the battle for civilization and progress takes place. Mises emphasized the fact and the necessity that classical liberalism had to be obstinate and uncompromising. Success of liberal ideas required the enlightenment of people who studied ideas who would convince the citizenry of their correctness. Mises advocated a revolution in ideas as the necessary step to the revolution of the practice of freedom. However, the advocates of classical liberalism in the 19th century were not obstinate and uncompromising. The English utilitarians, especially Ricardo, had incomplete and compromised notions leading succeeding liberals not to correct and complete them but to turn away to more compromises as in the case of John Stuart Mill.

One of the important causes of the decline of liberalism, Mises believed, was the illusion that society would necessarily continue to accept and perfect its ideas. Mises believed that as classical liberalism came closer to realization, it was necessary for its advocates not to rest, but to increase their activity and perfect the theoretical base of classical liberalism. Instead, liberalism was swept away by the emergence of parties speaking to special interests. For Mises liberalism meant the abolition of special privileges. In discussing class conflict, Mises emphasized: "Conflicts of interests can occur only in so far as restrictions on the owners' free disposal of the means of production are imposed by the interventionist policy of the government or by interference on the part of other social forces armed with coercive power." Coervice power, government intervention are the sole causes of war between interests. For Mises, the supporters of feudalism, privilege and status were clearly defeated by classical liberalism. The rise of the new challenge to classical liberalism came from within itself, from the failures of utilitarian economists. Mises said:

> But in Ricardo's system of catallactics one may find the point of departure for a new theory of the conflict of interests within the capitalist system. Ricardo believe that he could show how, in the course of progressive economic development, a shift takes place in the relations among the three forms of income in his system, viz., profit, rent, and wages. It was this that impelled a few English writers in the third and fourth decades of the nineteenth century to speak of the three classes of capitalists, landowners, and wage-laborers and to maintain that an irreconcilable antagonism exists among these groups. This line of thought was later taken up by Marx.
> "In the Communist Manifesto, Marx still did not distinguish between caste and class. Only later, when he became acquainted in London with the writings of the forgotten pamphleteers of the twenties and thirties and, under their influence, began the study of Ricardo's system, did he realize that the problem in this case was to show that even in a society without caste distinctions and privileges irreconcilable conflicts still exist. This antagonism of interests he deduced from Ricardo's system by distinguishing among the three classes of capitalists, landowners, and workers . . . At no time, however, did Marx or any one of his many followers attempt in any way to define the concept and nature of classes. It is significant

that the chapter entitled "The Classes" in the third volume of Capital breaks off after a few sentences. More than a generation elapsed from the appearance of the Communist Manifesto, in which Marx first makes class antagonism and class war the keystone of his entire doctrine, to the time of his death. During this entire period Marx wrote volume after volume, but he never came to the point of explaining what is to be understood by a "class."
> (Mises, The Free and Prosperous Commonwealth (trans. by Ralph Raico; ed. by Arthur Goddard), Princeton, Van Nostrand Series in the Humane Studies, 1962, pp. 163-64.)

However, the wedge of Ricardian concepts of disharmony of interests in a perfect capitalist society, and the existence of special interest political parties in societies claiming to be capitalist, permitted th' socialists to appear the champions of the abolition of privilege, of classless society resulting from the withering away of the state. Mise emphasized that in the absence of an uncompromisingly presentec liberalism, socialism appeals to people who think more clearly and seek a serious solution to government by special interests. Through the dominant position socialism gained at the Universities, it was able, in Mises' view, to gain the sincere, honest, and best minds among the youth. In many ways, the success of socialism was due to its ability to appear to be what liberalism actually is. Mises described the many ways that the parties of the special interest state have prevented the presentation and success of liberal ideas and. thus permitted the success of socialism. Mises insisted that liberals must emphasize the fact that since liberalism serves no special interest there is "no class that could champion liberalism for its own selfish interests." For Mises liberalism could not be the special party of capitalists. Historical reality has demonstrated that the wealthy tend to support any other party except the liberals. Indeed, for capitalists to support liberalism, it is necessary for them to rise above their self-interest to the level of general principles. Mises noted:

> The "have's" do not have any more reason to support the institution of private ownership of the means of production than do the "have-not's." If their immediate special interests come into question, they are scarcely liberal. The notion that, if only capitalism is preserved, the propertied classes could remain forever in possession of their wealth stems from a misunderstanding of the nature of the capitalist economy, in which property is continually being shifted from the less efficient to the more efficient businessman. In a capitalist society one can hold on to one's fortune only if one perpetually acquires it anew by investing it wisely. The rich, who are already in possession of wealth, have no special reason to desire the preservation of a system of unhampered competition open to all. . . . They do have a special interest in interventionism, which always has a tendency to preserve the existing division of wealth among those in possession of it. But they cannot hope for any special treatment from liberalism, a system in which no heed is paid to the time-honored claims of tradition advanced by the vested interests of established wealth.
> (Ibid., p. 186)

Mises deduced from history that all governments inherently recognize no limitations on power. Complete domination over property is the goal of all governments, and if they accept limitations it is merely tactical since the admission of any government control over property implies total control. Mises concluded:

> "Thus, there has never been a political power that voluntarily desisted from impeding the free development and operation of the institution of private property of the means of production. Governments tolerate private

(Continued On Page 4)

Mises And History —

(Continued From Page 3)

property when they are compelled to do so, but they do not acknowledge it voluntarily in recognition of its necessity. Even liberal politicians, on gaining power, have usually relegated their principles more or less to the background... . A liberal government is a **contradictio in adjecto**. (**Ibid.**, p. 68)"

Mises insisted that the concept of self-determination was the most logical derivation from liberalism. Self-determination made sense not as a collective concept, but as an individualist concept. "If it were in any way possible to grant this right of self-determination to every individual person, it would have to be done." But, Mises considered individual self-determination to be technically impractical; however, as a matter of principle it was irrefutable that the individual must have the right to individual self-determination. In foreign policy, Mises applied this concept to self-determination consistently.

The right of individual self-determination was clearly applicable in the area of education. For Mises, compulsory education in any circumstances was a violation of this right. Compulsory education is a clearly political act. "There is, in fact, only one solution: the state, the government, the laws must not in any way concern themselves with schooling or education. Public funds must not be used for such purposes. The rearing and instruction of youth must be left entirely to parents and to private associations and institutions."

Mises made an important, if often unrecognized, analysis of imperialism, which is another aspect of the negation of the right self-determination. Mises indicated that the origins of imperialism can be found in the desire of states to create protected export "markets." A desire to avoid the effects of competition, Mises said, led states

to the adoption of the policy of using import duties to protect domestic production operating under less favorable conditions against the superior competition of foreign industry, in the hope of thereby making the emigration of workers unnecessary. Indeed, in order to expand the protected market as far as possible, efforts are made to acquire even more territories that are not regarded as suitable for European settlement. We may date the beginning of modern imperialism from the late seventies of the last century, when the industrial countries of Europe started to abandon the policy of free trade and to engage in the race for colonial "markets" in Africa and Asia . . .

"The basic idea of colonial policy was to take advantage of the military superiority of the white race over the members of other races. The Europeans set out, equipped with all the weapons and contrivances that their civilization placed at their disposal, to subjugate weaker peoples, to rob them of their property, and to enslave them. Attempts have been made to extenuate and gloss over the true motive of colonial policy with the excuse that its sole object was to make it possible for primitive peoples to share in the blessings of European civilization . . . . If, as we believe, European civilization really is superior to that of the primitive tribes of Africa or to the civilizations of Asia — estimable though the later may be in their own way — it should be able to prove its superiority by inspiring these peoples to adopt it of their own accord. Could there be a more doleful proof of the sterility of European civilization than that it can be spread by no other means than fire and sword? (**Ibid.**, 123-25)."

Mises countered the argument that the liberal solution — immediate withdrawal of governement (European colonial) and leaving the inhabitants alone — might lead to chaos or oppression. Since Europe exported the worst of its civilization under imperialism, it is not the fault of the natives that they may adopt all the evils taught them by the Europeans. Since imperialism is the negation of liberalism, there was no possibility for non-Europeans to come into contact with liberal concepts and practices. Imperialism itself was one of the means by which European politicians sought to escape from the logical necessity of completing the liberal revolution in Europe. Just as mercantilism was

Danish Delight

It takes a lot for the august and stately New York Times to lose its cool; sometimes one gets the impression that if Canada were suddenly to launch an atomic attack on the U. S. tomorrow, the Times would comment in low and measured tones. But the Times has lost its cool, and it has taken the sudden and magnificent emergence of libertarianism on the international scene to do it. And for the second coolest newspaper, the Washington Post, to suffer the same trauma.

The occasion was the Danish elections of December 5, when the ruling Social Democrats were decimated in the Parliament, while the old-style opposition suffered just as badly. Instead, leaping on to the scene was a brand new party, the Progress party, formed only recently, and corralling no less than 28 seats to make it the second largest party in the country.

The Progressives are led by their charismatic founder, Mogens Glistrup, a wealthy tax lawyer who has been stumping Denmark championing an all-out libertarian program. Boasting that he has managed to legally avoid payment of income tax for years, Glistrup promised a grievously tax-ridden public that he would abolish the income tax, beginning with all incomes less than $10,000 a year. He also called for drastic cuts in the government bureaucracy and in the welfare system, and magnificently called for changing the name of Prime Minister to Minister in Charge of Abolishing Government Activities. One of the problems with previous libertarian-style parties in Europe, from the nineteenth century to the present, has been the temptation to be patriotic: to abandon libertarian principle on behalf of militarism and war. But not Glistrup; instead he and the Progressives call for abolition of the Danish military. His foreign policy? An automated tape recorder on a hot line to Russia, saying "We surrender."

The Washington Post so lost its vaunted "objectivity" that in its news headline it said "Clowns Win in Denmark". The New York Times editorial (Dec. 6), succumbed to scarcely concealed hysteria. It noted in the Danish elections (and indeed in Norway and Sweden as well) "a

(Continued On Page 5)

the overseas extension of feudalism, so imperialism was the overseas extension of neo-mercantilism.

For Mises none of the arguments in support of imperialism could have any basis in liberalism. Abolition of all forms of imperialism was alone consistent with liberalism. Mises felt that the evil consequences of imperialism would become evident only after the withdrawal of European troops and bureaucrats because only then would the full extent of the impact of European illiberalism flower. The longer the Europeans remained the more poisonous the blossoms. Thus, the immediate end of imperialism would reduce the effects, and its prolongation "in the interests of the natives" would intensify it. Mises added:

"If all that can be adduced in favor of the maintenance of European rule in the colonies is the supposed interest of the natives, then one must say that it would be better if this rule were brought to an end completely. No one has a right to thrust himself into the affairs of others in order to further their interest, and no one ought, when he has his own interests in view, to pretend that he is acting selflessly only in the interest of others. (**Ibid.**, p. 127)."

Mises total commitment to classical liberalism, pure and uncompromised, made him an heir in history to the great 19th century classical liberals who dealt with history generally, such as Acton, or with contemporary history, such as Cobden and Bright. Mises was fearless, as were Acton, Cobden and Bright, in attacking the state in all its aspects, not the least in its more recent manifestation, imperialism. The Individual and the State are irreconcilable. History confirms what reason teaches us, that the State is the negation of the individual and his extension, private property, just as where the Individual and his property rightfully exist, that the State be abolished. It was because of the failure to pursue and achieve that freedom by 19th century liberals, that the current struggle is necessary. Mises has emphasized that it is by study of that failure that the lessons will be learned to achieve liberty. Those who dare not study history will be bound to repeat it.   ❐

440

Arts And Movies

By Mr. First Nighter

The Tough Cop. The tough cop genre is definitely coming into its own. On TV, the new **Kojak** series, starring the tough and cynical Telly Savales, has become one of the best shows on television. In the movies, it is particularly significant that two of the great Western heroes have recently shifted to the tough cop role. As urban crime has become the concern of ever greater numbers of Americans, the tough crime fighter — in this case John Wayne and Clint Eastwood — has doffed his horse and ten gallon hat for the Magnum and the police badge.

John Wayne moves into the role of tough cop hero in **McQ**, dir. by John Sturges. There is no such thing as a bad John Wayne picture, and it is good to have Big John, or Lt. McQ, on hand to carry on a one-man struggle against the rackets and against crooked colleagues. And yet, the picture is no better than workmanlike. It is surprisingly slow, for one thing, and the creaky action only highlights the age of Wayne and Eddie Albert. Also, the standard behavior of the females in falling all over the hero lacks a certain amount of credibility in the case of the aging Wayne. Al Lettieri makes a promising, shambling villain, but the female leads lend no help: Diana Muldaur seems to have only one expression: hangdog, while Colleen Dewhurst — billed on all sides as one of the great actresses of our epoch — croaks her way through a terrible performance. Warning to Warner Brothers: if McQ is going to stick around, you'd better come up with faster action and a better director.

The tough cop picture has done far better by Clint Eastwood. His first effort, in **Dirty Harry**, was one of the great films of the last several years. The leftist intellectuals virtually sputtered with fury over **Dirty Harry**, for here was Eastwood as Inspector Harry Callahan of San Francisco stalking a mad dog killer while being subverted and hobbled at every hand by liberals, politicians, and bleeding hearts. **Dirty Harry**, apart from being fast and exciting, was an explicitly right-wing, anti-criminal-coddling, movie, and thus drove the liberal critics to inchoate rage. But it was not only the movie and its theme that aggravated them; it was also Eastwood himself. For of all the heroes in movies, Eastwood is the most ruthless, the most implacable, in his battle for the right and against criminal aggression. The critics who scorn Eastwood for his "lack of acting ability" don't understand the character that he is creating. For Eastwood's implacable calm is the result of his decisiveness, his ability to make instant — and correct — decisions in the midst of drama and danger, to make what he **knows** are the right decisions without moping or agonizing. Hence, Clint Eastwood is the polar opposite of the whining modern anti-hero beloved by the avant-garde. In a sense, the left, intelligentsia were quite right in identifying Eastwood — or rather the Eastwood figure — as their deadly enemy. Hence their vituperation.

Now dirty Harry is back, in **Magnum Force**, dir. by Ted Post. Like its predecessor, it is fast, tough, and exciting, beginning with a dramatic shot of Harry Callahan's Magnum revolver, and continuing to the final reel. If it is a bit less rightwing or less exciting than its predecessor, it remains one of the best movies of recent months.

The plot is particularly interesting in the light of the previous picture. At the end of **Dirty Harry**, Harry had tossed his badge into the river, the symbol of his disgust with the liberal, criminal-coddling System. At the beginning of **Magnum Force**, Harry is inexplicably back in the police force; early into the picture, he finds that the killers he seeks are a group of young police rookies organized into a paramilitary squad to wreak vengeance upon criminals whom the courts let loose. Harry rejects what seem to be youthful disciples of his own creed, and defends law and order against them. Why does he do so? Unfortunately, Harry doesn't seem to be able to articulate his own position, confining himself to: "You guys misunderstood me", and "I hate the System too, but you've got to stay within it until a better one comes along." Has Harry gone liberal? I think we can reassure Harry fans that it ain't so. If Harry could spell out his own position, perhaps he would say that he exacted vengeance on his own against a mad-dog monster, and not against mere racketeers; also his was an individual response, and not an organized gang — a gang, by the way, that committed unforgivable excesses, including the murder of fellow policemen. No, Harry has not gone liberal; his is the optimum degree of "dirt", neither bleeding-heart nor fascist. Long may he prosper.

The Sting, dir. by George Roy Hill, with Paul Newman and Robert Redford. **The Sting** is a truly superior picture, a charming blend of 1930's nostalgia, raffish con-men (a la **Paper Moon**), the caper picture, and the excellent acting of Newman and Redford, building on their success as a team in **Butch Cassidy and the Sundance Kid**. Hill has directed the film with a deft, light, but exciting touch, as humor is neatly blended with a series of twists and surprises in the plot. Cons and super-cons are piled on each other in marvellous abandon, and the movie is filled with a richness of texture that marks the truly first-rate film. Certainly one of the best pictures of the year.

Sleeper. dir. and with Woody Allen.

Woody Allen is surely the outstanding comic in the films today, and **Sleeper** is one of his best efforts. Put simply, **Sleeper** is hilarious. One interesting facet of the movie is that it represents a partial shift from Allen's previous emphasis on witty dialogue and on his **persona** as a New York **shnook**, that is not simply a loser, but a loser "in" psycholanalysis.

(Continued On Page 6)

Danish Delight —

(Continued From Page 4)

disturbing tendency by voters to endorse the quack doctrines once hawked in France by Pierre Poujade." (The editorial was entitled "Poujadism in Denmark"). It then weeped about "fragmentation" in Parliament, which "will make effective government exceedingly difficult" (Tsk! Tsk!). The **Times** went on:

"As the Norwegians and Swedes had done in September elections, the Danes rebelled in great numbers against the high taxes required by one of the most pervasive social security and welfare systems in the world. They rebelled so mindlessly as to elect 28 candidates of the Progress party, led by the cynical Copenhagen lawyer, Mogens Glistrup, a millionaire who boasts that he pays no income tax and advocates its abolition."

The **Times** added that the word Progressives is "a misnomer if ever there was one", and that the new party has "enormous scope for mischief and obstruction".

So? Clowns; cynics; quacks; mindless; mischief and obstruction. Things look good when the noble **Times** so rants. Clearly what is happening is that the Third Way, the welfare state-quasi socialist Scandinavian experiment so beloved by our left-liberals, is falling apart, smashing on the rock of crippling taxation and topheavy bureaucracy. The fact that libertarianism is now politically strongest in one of the most socialistic countries in the West gives us hope, and supports our analysis of the case for optimism: that as statism continues to accelerate, it can no longer live off the fat of previous capitalism, and that therefore statist measures will increasingly create problems that will destroy it. The fact that the cutting edge of the revolt against statism is now in Scandinavia shows that even generations of statist culture and society cannot destroy the human love of freedom. Liberty lives!

Who was this Poujade that the New York **Times** enigmatically equates with the face of evil? Two decades ago, Poujade and his organized movement and party arose and achieved a great deal of support in France, particularly among peasants and small shopkeepers. Its aim: to slash and dismantle the taxing system that was crippling the French economy and society. Poujadism bid fair to achieve power, when it ran aground on the very issue mentioned above, the issue that has split so many classical liberal movements: militarism and foreign policy. Poujade himself was a hawk on the Algerian question, and it soon became clear that Poujadists who wished to exert maximum force against the Algerians could scarcely call for slashing taxes at home. And so Poujadism, sundered and deprived of its great purpose, dissolved and disappeared. A particularly cheering point about Glistrup and the Progressives is their irreverent and libertarian attitude toward the Danish military and their determinedly peaceful foreign policy.

All this bodes beautifully for the Progress party's future. When will we form the first Libertarian International? ◻

Energy Fascism —

(Continued From Page 2)

looked upon with healthy suspicion and hostility by the bulk of the American citizenry?

At first, of course, the Nixon Administration tried its best to rekindle the old wartime fervor. Establishment intellectuals, ever ready to call for sacrifice and scourging (of other people) wrote solemn if idiotic thinkpieces hailing the energy crisis as really, down-deep, a good thing. Why? Because we, the American public, have gotten too soft, too affluent, too personal in our concerns. But now, whoopee!, the energy crisis will rekindle that good old wartime (!) spirit of self-sacrifice, of hardship, of rallying behind our beloved President to fight another "war", this time against the energy shortage. For a brief while, this hogwash seemed to work, as people always respond initially to calls for belt-tightening, self-sacrifice, national unity, etc. But, praise the Lord, it didn't take very long for the good old spirit of American individualism and "selfishness" to surface once again. The lack of "credibility" of our government surely helped speed this process of public awakening. For when the shortage actually began to bite, when gasoline lines developed and filling stations closed, reason and individualism came bounding back. The public has been getting good and mad, and fist fights have been dotting the gasoline queues. The striking truckers, as wrong-headed as they were, were at least lashing out in an attitude of rebellion and pugnacity at the government-imposed system.

There are other hopeful signs. The Chamber of Commerce of the United States, the National Association of Manufacturers, and the AFL-CIO, each of whom hailed Nixon's Phase I with joyous hosannahs, are now each and all committed to an all-out fight against price-wage controls. Unfortunately, they do not have the guts and/or the insight to oppose the rationing and other despotic energy edicts, but at least they now oppose the control system which leads to the rationing schemes. It is particularly refreshing to see the NAM return home to an anti-control stand. The NAM was born, at the turn of this century, as a free-market, small business-oriented, opponent of the emerging corporate state system, for which they were lambasted by the corporate liberal National Civic Federation as "anarchists." During the 1930's and 40's, the NAM played a vigorous free-market role. Then, during the 1960's, the NAM changed its structure from rotating annual presidents to a full-time permanent president, W. P. Gullander, hailing from a corporation which would scarcely last a week without government contracts and subventions — General Dynamics. Under Gullander's aegis, the NAM enthusiastically embraced the idea of "partnership between government and industry", taking its place happily in the Welfare-Warfare Corporate State. But last year a revolution occurred within NAM, Gullander was sent packing, and the rotating presidency restored. Since then, the NAM has returned to a vigorous free-market position.

Other important anti-control sentiment has arisen. C. Jackson Grayson, head of the Cost of Living Council and boss of Phase II, and now back in private life, has recently delivered a blistering speech denouncing all price and wage controls. Perhaps in response to all this growing opposition, the Nixon Administration has announced the end of controls by April 30, thereby inaugurating Phase V. But there are several important clinkers in the scheme. One is that energy controls will be tighter than ever; another is that direct controls will be replaced by long-term "voluntary" agreements by industry not to raise prices and wages beyond a certain amount, these pledges to be monitored by the government on threat of reimposing direct enforcement. And so direct controls will continue past May, but in another and phonier guise.

Meanwhile, on the energy front, the threat of government dictation looms ever larger. Economic insanity is running rampant in the Congress, with plans emerging to: impose a federal tax on gasoline, and/or a "rollback" of prices, and/or an excess profit tax on the oil industry, and/or anti-trust prosecution, and/or a new federal oil corporation to produce and sell oil, and/or outright nationalization of some or all of the oil corporations.

A federal excise tax on gasoline to raise prices to market-clearing levels, would have effects similar to the "white market" scheme (provided that the government in its wisdom can find the market-clearing price!) Except instead of myself and other "under-users" reaping the hypothetical 30¢ a gallon, the government would get it, increasing its tax revenues. Not only would there still be no incentive to increase oil production, but the government would increase its already crippling

siphoning of resources from private to its own hands, aggravating the growing burden of parasitic statism on the private sector and on private production.

A "rollback" of prices — something never achieved even during World War II — would disastrously increase the gasoline and oil shortage. Anti-trust prosecution would help to destroy a vitally essential industry, and would intensify the shortage instead of alleviating it. Nationalization or a federal corporation means a massive leap toward socialism, with all the inefficiencies, shortages, parasitism, and totalitarianism that such a leap entails.

An excess profits tax is a particularly bizarre form of government intervention. A shattering event occurs — the event may be a war, or an energy shortage. Imposing an excess profits tax necessarily requires defining what "excess" means, and invariably "excess" is defined as any profits greater than the base year before the event occurred. But since profits are earned in proportion to the speed and efficiency by which the business firms adapts to the new event, this means that corporations are penalized precisely in proportion to their success in adapting to the new conditions. A firm that meets the new conditions successfully earns profits and would be penalized by a severe tax; while the firm that sluggishly fails to adapt or to produce the newly-demanded product, suffers no penalizing tax at all. If the new event is an energy shortage, this means that firms successfully producing energy are penalized, while firms that inefficiently produce energy or don't shift to the energy field are not penalized at all. No better way can be found to cripple the efficiency and flexibility of the free enterprise system than an excess profits tax.

Profits on the market are a measure of the efficiency and rapidity by which business firms meet the changing needs of the consumers. To denounce an oil company for making "windfall" profits from an energy shortage makes as much moral and economic sense as denouncing physicians for making extra incomes during an epidemic. We should all rejoice when a corporation or other business firm makes high profits, for that is an indicator of great usefulness to the consumers; we should reserve our scorn for the firms that make losses and thereby display their inept management and lack of entrepreneurial ability.

Even apart from the great social merit of high profits, the hysteria about high oil profits is a piece of statistical charlatanry. The United Stated suffered a recession in 1969-71, and so corporate profits in those years were abnormally low; price controls based on profit margins in these recession years imposed further burdens on corporations, even past late 1971. In the oil industry, for example, left liberals point the finger of hysterical alarm at "swollen" oil profits in 1973, and point to the huge percentage increase of those profits over 1972. But any increase of profits over an abnormally low base will yield a high and seemingly "excessive" percentage increase. Thus, if Oil Company A had a net profit of $1000 in 1972, and $1,000,000 in 1973, leftist critics can screech about a huge 1000% increase in profits; still better, if the company made zero profits in 1972, they could bleat about an infinite increase in profits. The point here is that the years 1969-72 were years of abnormally low profits for much of the oil industry, and that the higher profits in 1973 were bounce back to pre-1969 levels. Change the base year and you can make any set of figures seem excessive and unwarranted.

Thus, Business Week (Feb. 2) prints the profit statistics for the past decade of the 10 leading oil companies in the country. For four of these companies, the estimated 1973 profits are not yet available, but we have these estimated figures for the other six, which includes the top three (Exxon, Mobil, Texaco), and the fifth through the seventh ranking firms (Standard Oil of California, Standard Oil (Indiana), and Shell). Taking

(Continued On Page 7)

Arts And Movies —

(Continued From Page 5)

The persona and the dialogue are still there, but in Sleeper they share the spotlight with a cinematic comic timing and action that hearken back to the great days of the silent film comedians of the 1920's: especially Harold Lloyd and Buster Keaton. It is a pleasure to see that great and now dead tradition of visual and cinematic humor recreated, although it is still heresy to mention Woody Allen in the same bracket with the incomparable Keaton. But at least the attempt is there, even if at times the New York shnook and the Keatonesque figure don't quite mesh. The point is that the ever-inventive Allen is moving in the right direction◻

Energy Fascism —
(Continued From Page 6)

these figures, we have made the following calculations: the average rate of profit on invested capital of these six leading oil companies, for the average of the five pre-recession years, 1964-68, was 11.1%. Profits then dipped from 1969-72, and rose again in 1973. The average rate of profit for these firms in 1973 was 11.2%. In short, profit rates are now what they were in the pre-recession years. And so even ignoring the beneficial nature of profits and considering the issue solely on left-liberal terms, we find that the bleating about swollen and excessive oil profits is totally unwarranted, a piece of statistical legerdemain moulded to suit the ideological purposes of the critics. In the words of the old adage: "There's three kinds of liars: liars, damned liars, and statistics."

Western Europe, as everyone knows, is in the throes of an energy shortage even more severe than ours. The reason, however, is not as well known: because the inflation and price controls are even more severe there than here. There is one exception to the European energy shortage, however: West Germany. How come, since an economy as industrialized as West Germany is highly dependent on oil? How come there have been no electric blackouts and no rationing there? A New York Times article provides the clear-cut answer: no price controls on petroleum products. (Craig R. Whitney, "West Germans, At a Price, Avoid Oil Crisis," New York Times, Jan. 24). The article points out that West Germany has no price controls on gasoline, heating oil or other oil products — in contrast to Britain, Italy, Sweden, and the Netherlands, which are suffering from an oil shortage. The article quotes oil company officials as stating that, as a result, "it was always in their interest to keep supplying West Germany while it was sometimes not in their interest to keep supplying the other markets." And West Germany has been far more dependent on Arab oil imports than the U. S.; yet the free market allowed a plentiful supply of oil to be imported and sold. The cost to the German car owner of keeping an ample supply of gasoline was a mere 10% increase in price.

Gerhard Hess, trade director of the German firm, Geisenberg Oil, noted that in contrast to West Germany, "in Italy there was a price limit of $30 a ton for heavy industrial oil. But now, Libyan crude oil costs $76 a ton at the port in Libya. For the companies, it just doesn't make sense at those prices to deliver to Italy." Hess trenchantly summed up the West German experience this winter: "The free-price system has proved itself so well, that only an idiot would say we should impose another system. Because we were not cut off from the free market, we got through this crisis."

There is another great advantage to be reaped from allowing the free market to set the prices of oil. We hear a great deal about alternative potential sources of energy, from shale oil to solar energy to tropical oceans; whatever their technological status, they have not been tapped till now because they have been uneconomic — too expensive in relation to the more orthodox sources of energy. A rise in the price of oil on the market will induce greater production and technological innovation into alternative energy sources, which will become increasingly competitive with existing fuel. And even within existing energy sources, a rise in the price of oil will, say, stimulate increased production of coal, of which there is enough under ground in America to provide all of our heating requirements for many generations to come.

There are, in addition to the controls-created shortage, numerous ways in which the U. S. government has artificially restricted the supply of energy, thus making energy more scarce and artificially raising the free-market price. Indeed, it almost seems as if every step of the way in the energy industries, government has been there to restrict supply and hence to raise price. The abolition of these myriad interventions would allow a greatly increased production and supply of energy to the American consumer, at a lower market price. Some of these restrictions have been partially or wholly relaxed in recent months, but this easing has scarcely been enough as yet to overcome years, and sometimes decades of crippling restrictions on energy production. Here we can do little more than list some of the most glaring and important of these restrictions.

1) Most notorious have been the severe maximum price controls on natural gas, which have been imposed by the Federal Power Commission for two decades. As time went on, the gap between the low controlled price and the rising free market price became greater and greater, drying up the search for natural gas reserves, and leading to the current crippling shortage. Whatever natural gas remains is either sold intrastate, where the dead hand of the FPC cannot make itself felt, or else exported abroad. The latter is scarcely surprising, if we consider that the regulated price is approximately 25¢/1000 cu. ft., while natural gas can be sold for $1.00/1000 cu. ft. abroad.

Furthermore, when natural gas was made artificially cheap, it helped to put much of the coal industry out of business. In recent years, the shortage of natural gas has led to artificially increased demand for fuel oil, thus raising its market price.

Another consideration is that natural gas and crude oil are often found together. When the artificially low price of natural gas dried up exploration for new reserves, it also cut the supply of newly found reserves of crude oil, thereby lowering supply from what it would have been and raising the price.

Who was responsible for the economic insanity of the coerced low price for natural gas? As in so many other areas of government intervention, what we had was an Unholy Alliance of political pressure groups: left-liberal ideologues who generally favor government control and artificial rollbacks; along with public utility companies who wished to feast for a number of years on artificially cheap fuel. It is the all-too-common alliance of statist ideology and vested privilege.

2) The federal government is itself sitting on vast and virtually unused crude oil reserves of trillions of barrels, enough to last for many generations to come. It has been doing this sitting — and withholding of oil from the market, for many decades, thereby restricting oil supply and raising the price. These reserves are in the control of the U. S. Navy, and include the Elk Hills reserve in California, Teapot Dome in Wyoming, the North Slope in Alaska, and others. What is the Navy waiting for? Must we keep trillions of barrels unused, wasted forever, while the Navy waits until some battleship needs the oil in some unknown war of the future?

3) Similarly, the federal government, which owns outright the vast majority of all land in the Western states, owns almost all of the land in the Mountain States where enough shale oil exists to meet oil needs for the indefinite future. And yet the government has been holding this shale off the market, refusing to lease its land for purposes of developing the shale oil resource and producing the oil for the market.

4) For over forty years, the state governments, led by the Texas Railroad Commission, and with the blessing and coordination of the federal government, have levied maximum quotas on the drilling of crude oil. In this "prorationing" system, each state is assigned a maximum production of crude for the following month, and then each oil well receives its fractional quota of that maximum. The result has been to restrict production and raise price of crude and of all petroleum products.

5) As a corollary to the domestic cartellization of the above point, the federal government has levied, for two decades, oil import quotas, placing maximum limits, and quotas for each firm as a fraction of such limits, on the importation of foreign crude. The resulting price increases have ratified and made possible the price rises due to prorationing.

6) There have been a great many complaints about the "failure" of the oil companies to produce new refineries in recent years, especially on the Eastern seaboard. But since, on the market, need and demand will create profitable opportunities for investment, further inquiry should have been: why have such refineries been unprofitable? The recession and low profits from 1969 helped; but another factor was the oil import quotas, which restricted and made uncertain a steady supply of crude oil, especially on the East Coast. Another recent problem, for refineries and for many other areas of energy, has been the harassment and restrictions on building any new plants imposed by the government under pressure from the environmentalists. The environmentalists have two major gripes: air pollution, which may or may not be valid in particular cases, and "defacing the environment", which imposes the environmentalists' own particular and peculiar aesthetic values by force on the rest of the public. If the environmentalists feel that a new factory or refinery "defaces" the landscape, then let them buy the landscape and keep it undefiled, or forever hold their peace. Certainly it is unconscionable for them to force the rest of us to adhere to their esthetics, and to coercively prevent property owners from using their own property as they see fit.

7) The development of nuclear energy for peaceful uses has been held up for many years by the environmentalists.

8) The environmentalists have managed to delay the construction of the Alaskan pipeline for five years, including the importing from the north of Alaska of several million barrels of oil per day. The environmentalists were worried about two problems: (a) defacing the tundra (to these

(Continued On Page 8)

Energy Fascism —

(Continued From Page 7)

people, any man-made change in the environment, any alteration from pristine nature, is ipso facto "defacement.") It is instructive to note that the Alaskans themselves, up there close to the tundra, have no wish whatever to preserve it forever undefiled. Their fondest wish is to reshape the tundra and achieve some jobs, income, and economic development. It is affluent, comfortable New York intellectuals, for example, who are busiest at trying to preserve someone else's tundra. And (b) they worried about the migratory patterns of the caribou, who would not be able to walk across the pipeline. Even when the pipeline company, at considerable expense, agreed to build bridges over the pipeline so that the caribou could walk over them, the environmentalists continued to gripe about the fact that the caribou might still be reluctant to walk over a surface to which they were not accustomed. All right, it is about time that we take our choice Americans: who should win out, humans or the caribou? Whereas the noisy minority of environmentalists will choose the caribou (or any other species, for that matter) over man, we trust that enough sanity still prevails among the bulk of the population so that a resounding choice will be made for the human species. And if this be "human-chauvinism", so be it!

9) There is lots of crude oil off our coasts. But off-shore drilling has been restricted and crippled by the self-same busybody environmentalists working as usual through government. Yes, you guessed it, the oil once in a while spills into the ocean, thus injuring the fish and other sea life. Choose America: humans or plankton!

10) The U. S. has an abundant supply of coal, as we have noted. But coal has suffered most from the dictates of government-environmentalism. Coal heating causes air pollution; but one might think that after centuries of such pollution we could struggle along for a few years more until anti-pollution devices were invented and installed on the chimneys. Instead, the meat-axe approach has bankrupted a lot of coal mines, disemployed many coal miners, and restricted our supply of heating fuel. Furthermore, the relatively new technology of **strip** mining is less polluting, less expensive, and avoids such classic problems of old-fashioned pit mining as black lung and mine caviens. There is lots of strip coal available in the Mountain States that remains untapped. But, once again, the environmentalists have come down especially hard on strip mining. Why? You guessed it: "defacing the environment." If the incubus of the environmentalists is removed, and if the federal government unloads it strip coal resources into private hands, we could produce a great deal of fuel. Another boon is that the United Mine Workers, which have crippled the coal industry through pushing up wage rates, is weak in the Mountain States and could not succeed in blighting the coal industry there.

Thus, the federal government, and it alone, has created the energy mess in two sets of ways: (1) by a series of restrictions on production it has created artificial **scarcities** and thereby raised the free market price

of energy sources; and (2) it has then greatly compounded the mess by imposing price controls below the free market price and creating the current shortages. The immediate cure for the shortage is simple: to abolish the price controls. The longer-range solution for the scarcities is to abolish all of its varied restrictions.

It is incumbent upon libertarians to take the lead in combatting the energy fascism being fastened upon this country. We must call for resistance to the totalitarian edicts telling us how much, what, and when we can use or purchase energy. We predicted the consequences of price controls: that controls would lead to shortages and then in turn to rationing and other acts of despotism. We must point out that government is not the cure for the energy shortage but the cause of the disease; and the disease can only be abolished by getting government completely out of the energy field, and especially out of price-wage controls. One distrubing point is that, even among conservatives and libertarians who have written and spoken soundly and correctly on the energy crisis, there has been a certain torpor, a certain measured sobriety of tone, that ill befits our proper reaction to the latest acceleration of tyranny. As citizens, even more as people with a passion for liberty and justice, we must respond with passion to the new crisis. So far no conservative or libertarian has matched the fiery and passionate instincts of left-liberal New York **Post** columnist Pete Hamill in his gut reaction to energy fascism. Totally lacking any understanding of the market economy and hence of the true causes of the current crisis, Hamill yet saw unerringly the evil of government dictation that lay at the heart of the issue. In his **Post** column of Nov. 12 ("The Phony Crisis"), Hamill searingly wrote:

"Now they've even taken away our skyline. It had been ours since that day in 1945 when we all raced to the rooftops of Brooklyn to see those million lights blink on again, dazzling, joyous, triumphant and unbelievably beautiful, signalling to us that the war was over. I remember a woman crying on the rooftop that time, knowing that the long night of the Second World War was finished, that New York was blazing again with its electric beauty, that blackouts and dimouts were behind us, that the troopships would soon be home. The New York skyline: ours forever.

'And now it's gone again. Moving along the city's highways, there is a joyless sense of defeat and loss in the town. It's as if the malignant hand of Richard Nixon had reached out from the bunker in Camp David and pulled the lightswitch on all of us, spreading his personal darkness. The Empire State Building is a blinking red light in the dark. The great pile of downtown buildings, Turman Capote's 'diamond iceberg', is a hole in the night sky . . . .

"It's time to call their bluff. They might be able to fool a lot of farmers, but they shouldn't get away with this hokey fraud in Our Town. We are overdue for a rebellion against the corrupt, criminal government in Washington, and now we have one opportunity to make that rebellion overt. Turn on all your lights. Drive 65 miles an hour (will Rockefeller order air strikes on the Thruway to stop us?) Refuse to turn down thermostats. Let Washington know we've made them again for liars. And lets get back our skyline."

Published Every Month. Subscription Rate: $8.00 Per Year

A Monthly Newsletter

THE
Libertarian Forum

Joseph R. Peden, Publisher

Murray N. Rothbard, Editor

VOLUME VI, NO. 2 FEBRUARY, 1974 US-ISSN0047-4517

Two Tiers Crumble

In March, 1968, the august authorities of the international monetary Establishment undertook a reform that would copper-rivet their rule and banish gold forevermore. Since World War II, the basis of the international monetary order had been the Bretton Woods system, in which every national currency was fixed in terms of the almighty dollar, and the dollar in turn was fixed in price at $35 an ounce of gold. The capstone of the system was the $35 an ounce gold system, which all the leading economists and bankers and bureaucrats assured us was written in tablets of stone. Never, never would an alteration of the magical $35 figure take place. The problem was that as American inflation continued and grew, the free markets of the world evaluated the dollar as ever less and less valuable in relation to the hard money, gold. Hence, the free gold markets of the world — notably London and Zurich — felt enormous pressure upward on the gold price from $35 an ounce. In order to maintain the price at $35, the United States Treasury kept dumping gold on the free market. But inflation and the subsequent acceleration of upward pressure, meant that the U. S. Treasury lost even more gold than continued to flow abroad from the ever-weakening dollar. Finally, a dollar panic on the free gold market in the spring of 1968 led the world Establishment to reconstitute the international monetary system: to end the pesky gold problem and eject it from the monetary order.

The countries decided to ignore the free gold market by sundering the gold market in two: from March, 1968 on, the monetary authorities would simply ignore the free gold market, would have nothing further, ever to do with it. Let it go to blazes! Instead, the Federal Reserve System would continue to redeem the dollar at the rate of $35 per ounce in gold, to any Central Banks that wished such redemption; and the Central Banks would continue to evaluate gold at this ordained price. There would now be "two-tiers" in the gold market, or rather, two "markets"; and the world Central Banks would simply go about their business, insulated from the free market. Gold would be cut off from the real business of the monetary authorities, and would remain as only an accounting device between governmental central banks. To maintain this, all the Central Banks pledged themselves never, ever to buy or sell gold again in the free market, or in any way outside their own cozy cabal.

It is instructive to remember how the whole raft of anti-gold economists, from Milton Friedman and Fritz Machlup on the right to the Samuelsons on the left, greeted this development. They all solemnly assured us that it was not gold that propped up, or gave backing to, the dollar. The truth was the other way round! Now cut off from its dollar moorings, they opined, gold would soon fall to its "proper", non-monetary price on the free gold markets: in short, to somewhere around $10 an ounce. The wicked gold speculators and the evil South Africans (the largest suppliers of new gold) would at last get their comeuppance.

The rest is history. In the years since, not once did the free-market gold price fall below $35 an ounce; on the contrary, it has generally been considerably above that, and as accelerating inflation has weakened public confidence in the dollar and other fiat currencies (a process intensified by the U. S. abandoning all gold redemption in August, 1971),

the price of gold has risen ever more sharply. Proposals of pro-gold economists to double the price of gold to $70 an ounce were, until very recently, greeted with ridicule by the anti-gold economic Establishment. A price of $70 was considered absurdly high and out of the question by almost all of the "experts." And yet, at last reading, the price of gold on the free market had risen to no less than $150 an ounce, and the end is scarcely in sight. Once again, it is us "gold bugs" who have had the last laugh; gold has once again buried its would-be undertakers.

Now, at last, in November, 1973, in a little-heralded move, the U. S. and its allies in the monetary Establishment have thrown in the towel. The two-tier gold system, the lofty isolation of the Central Banks from the free gold market, is no more. The U. S. and the other nations announced that no longer would there be the two-tier isolation; from now on, any Central Bank would be free to buy or sell its gold at will.

Incredibly, the United States was able to save face on making the announcement by conning the media into claiming that here, once more, was the coup de grace to gold and to all the wicked speculators and "gold hoarders." Fed Chairman Arthur Burns loftily announced that now Central Banks would be able to sell gold on the free market and thereby bring the price down. What Dr. Burns neglected to mention, of course, is that Central Banks would also be free to buy gold and dump some of their supply of excess and unwanted dollars. Whether gold was to be the winner or the loser from the liquidation of the two-tier system became obvious when no Central Bank was observed rushing to sell any of its precious stock of gold. And, indeed, they would have to be unusually dim-witted to do so. If you were a central banker, would you sell gold at $150 an ounce when all indications were that gold would keep rising in the future?

Another result of the crumbling of the two tiers is to render obviously and strikingly idiotic the "official" U. S. definition of the dollar as weighing 1/42 of a gold ounce (i.e. the official U. S. gold price of $42 an ounce). So long as the two tier system remained, we could preserve the fiction of $42 (embodying two tiny devaluations over the last few years from $35), because the Central Bank "market" was to be kept insulated from the unclean doings on the free gold market. But now that Central Bank isolation has been ended, the $42 an ounce price becomes so much hot air. In fact, every Central Bank, including even the fanatically anti-gold Federal Reserve Bank, will be increasingly and irresistibly tempted to upvalue their gold stocks from the phony $42 to the realistic free gold price. Any country that does so will find that, as if by magic, it will have nearly four times as much precious gold as it did before (i.e. their stock of gold ounces will be worth four times as much.) Why should the U. S., for example, struggle along with a dwindling and puny gold stock of $11 billion when, by simply recognizing the facts of reality, it could jump instantaneously to something like $40 billion?

No, gold is alive and flourishing throughout the world. Its health, and its role, is better than it has been in decades, and its prognosis is terrific. Natural law is once again winning the fight against the schemes of economic dictators. ◻

Relevance?

The strictures of your editor and of James Davidson against irrelevance among libertarians (October and November issues of the Lib. Forum) have drawn more and louder comment than any articles in years. To the many readers who commented favorably, I can only say "God and/or Reason bless you", and thank you for your sentiments. But particularly interesting here are the host of unfavorable critics, whose comments have ranged from dignified restraint to scarcely controlled hysteria, on behalf of their respective "irrelevant" causes, from science fiction to "humanistic" psychology to vitamin pills. Basically their arguments are twofold. First, that their hobby-horses are "really" relevant (science fiction often presents models of a free or unfree society, vitamin pills "extend life" and libertarians surely favor the extension of life, etc.) And after all, liberty narrowly defined is certainly not the only concern of a libertarian! Second, is the tu quoque argument that even we ourselves are "inconsistent" with our own position by publishing movie reviews and occasional cultural articles.

Of course, if one is anxious to stretch the point, almost everything can be dragged in as in some remote way "relevant" to libertarian concerns. All truth, after all, is one and interconnected. Columns on chess could be justified as "training the mind", and libertarians must use their minds, etc. A defense of Old Culture movies and a rational esthetic is part of the general theory of rational individualism of which libertarianism is a subset. But in a profound sense, it is the very vehemence of the reaction against our articles that most proves our point: i.e. the increasing emphasis away from liberty and in favor of all the other special hobby horses that pervade the movement. Clearly, it is scarcely a matter of high principle — comparable to the Non-Aggression Axiom — that no space whatever be accorded to these peripheral issues. The problem is one of proportion, of balance. Our argument is directed against the growing amount of energy and space that have been devoted to these peripheral matters, in contrast to the central issues and principles of libertarianism. What has been happening in all too many cases is that various groups and journals of libertarianism begin to stress not just liberty but liberty-cum-science fiction or liberty-cum-"humanism" or whatever. Then, in a short while, like a creeping cancer, the science fiction or the "humanistic psychology" begins to take over, as the groups involved begin to feel that it is these special matters that are really important, while liberty itself becomes relegated to the edge of their concerns. New Libertarian Notes is now increasingly infected with the science-fiction bacillus. In its current, January 1974 issue, of the 20 pages of text, 14 are devoted to science fiction, 3 to neo-Tolkien fiction, 1 to a poem, and 2 to an attack on us for criticizing science fiction. A perfect score! And on the West Coast, "humanist psychology", from "open relationships" to "touchie-feelie" encounter groups, is increasingly the major focus of many groups of libertarians. It's as if the Lib. Forum were to devote its entire space to a defense of John Wayne over Antonioni (a far more relevant cause!)

In the current Libertarian Connection (Jan. 24), Miss Natalee Hall, Mr. Skye D'Aureous, and Mr. Ron Chusid make the point that, after all, liberty is not all of life, that libertarians must surely favor the extension of their lives, and that therefore information on vitamin pills, or, indeed, the filling of cavities, is a legitimate concern for a libertarian publication. The problem is that the last term of the syllogism does not really follow from the first two. What we have in this kind of argument is a flouting of the vital concept of the division of labor. There are, after all, an enormous number of available sources of information about vitamin pills, cavities, medicine, or, for that matter, science fiction or humanistic psychology. There are incomparably more sources of information about these topics than there are about libertarianism Unless we are to assume — God forbid — that our readers get all of their information about life and reality from our little magazines, it becomes a tragic waste of space to allocate so much of it to these tangential or irrelevant matters.

So, won't you come home, Libertarians?   ▫

What Kind Of 'Purity'?

Now that the Libertarian Party has grown more successful and has become the major organizational form for libertarians throughout the country, internal discussions have inevitably emerged about the Party's future course.

At one extreme, the "pragmatists" argue that when, as, and if we elect anyone to public office, that official should be prepared to make the compromises required by his august position. A Libertarian Congressman, for example, should be able to logroll, and vote statist on some issues in return for cadging the votes of his colleagues on more vital concerns. I am not aware of any Libertarian who actually defends the Symms voting record in Congress, but it is clearly the "Symms model", in a modified form, that attracts the pragmatist camp. If a Congressman comes for example, from a potato growing area, then the claim is that he should be allowed or encouraged to vote for potato subsidies for his constituents so that he can remain in office and fight for liberty on grander issues.

The pragmatist view, however, not only violates libertarian principle; it defeats the whole purpose of a Libertarian Party in the first place. The purpose of the Party is to advance the libertarian cause in the political and public arena; and any votes for statism whatsoever undercuts the pushing of the libertarian cause. Libertarianism is a seamless web; and pragmatic voting destroys that web and permanently prevents the voting public from grasping the theory and its ineluctable applications. If, moreover, our object is to get "from here to there" from the current mixed system to a world of pure liberty, then any violation by a libertarian of his own credo undercuts the goal itself, and virtually destroys any prospect of ever achieving it. The purpose of libertarians in general, and the Libertarian Party in particular, is, in the old motto, to uphold a standard to which the wise and honest will repair. Flouting our own principles destroys the standard itself. If the Libertarian Party is to be pragmatic in this sense, then it would be far better for the cause to scrap the Party altogether and confine our political activity to pressuring Republicans and Democrats; let these infidels do the logrolling and potato-mongering. Praise the Lord, then, that Steve Symms is a Republican and not a Libertarian Party Congressman. As a Republican he is tolerable; as a Libertarian he would be an unmitigated disaster.

Fortunately, there is no present prospect of the pragmatists being strong enough to take over, or even have much influence within, the Libertarian Party; and let us hope and make sure that the Party will remain that way.

At the other extreme, there are some Libertarians, now roughly confined within and around the "radical caucus" of the Free Libertarian Party of New York, who maintain that anarchist purity requires the virtual absence of any structure within the Party. Any move toward centralization of funds, toward any sort of efficient structure, indeed any move away from pure participatory democracy, is attacked by this faction as a violation of anarchist purity. It is necessary to remind this group that there is nothing whatever in anarchism or libertarianism that denies the value of organization, or structure, or even (voluntary!) centralization. There is no need whatever to conjoin liberty with any sort of "democracy", participatory or otherwise.

Presumably (one hopes!) the "decentralist" faction does not oppose the existence of corporations or of the wage system. Yet corporations, or indeed any sort of employer-employee relationship, are ipso facto "hierarchical" and exclude participatory democracy. In return for a wage payment, the employer tells the employee the tasks he is expected to perform, and the employee agrees to these tasks in return for

(Continued On Page 3)

An Open Letter To Irving Kristol

Ed. Note: In September, 1972, at the biennial meeting of the Mont Pelerin Society at Montreux, Switzerland, Professor Irving Kristol of the City University of New York delivered a thoughtful and hard-hitting critique of the free-market, libertarian position. Since Professor Kristol delivered his sally at a meeting of an international group of allegedly free-market economists, I have been awaiting some response from a member of this august group in defense of their supposed position. But I have waited in vain. As their next biennial conference approaches, not only have there been no criticisms of Professor Kristol, but instead, his speech was universally hailed by the members as brilliant, seminal, and definitive, and was similarly greeted with hosannahs by conservative-"libertarian" John Chamberlain. As the conservative co-editor of **The Public Interest,** and as a powerful leader of the "New York intellectuals" who in a sense determine public consciousness, Professor Kristol had won what is by now the dubious distinction of being Richard Nixon's favorite intellectual. Since no one has replied to Professor Kristol's challenge, your editor has leaped into the breach. The following is slightly modified from an unanswered letter to Mr. Kristol (Kristol's speech later appeared in his **Public Interest.**)

Dear Irving:

Your speech was the best presentation of the conservative, anti-libertarian case I have seen in a long time. Since no libertarian seems to have replied, I thought that I might enter the lists.

I agree that, in their presentation of the case for the libertarian, free society, free-market economists have generally been gravely deficient in ignoring the entire sphere of the moral order. But where I disagree with you is in your view that this defect is inherent in the libertarian position. Unfortunately what happened is that economics grew up at the same time, and conjoined with, utilitarianism. Hence economists — whether free-market oriented or not — have generally been utilitarians. Hence the idea that in order to be happy, all one has to do is to be free to pursue one's own utility schedules — an idea that ignores the existence of an objective moral order and what the Thomists call the existence of a "science of happiness."

But there is another tradition in economics, even in free-market economics. As we have learned in the last two decades, the scholastic philosophers were largely free-market oriented (Karl Marx was **not,** contra Tawney, the "last of the Schoolmen"), and Aristotelian philosophy always heavily influenced French and Italian economics, and later even the Austrian School, as Emil Kauder has demonstrated. In the present-day, Wilhelm Ropke has cleaved (roughly) to the free market and to objective moral principles. Outside the realm of professional economics, some conservative-libertarian thinkers have integrated a libertarian position **with** a firm belief in an objective moral order which is disobeyed at one's peril. In the nineteenth century, I might cite Herbert Spencer, and in the present day, the late Frank Meyer.

Let me put it this way: I agree with you that utilitarians are wrong in believing that every person knows automatically what will make him happy. I have two basic comments on this — one as an economist and another as a Libertarian. As an economist, I don't agree that economics assumes this (only the utilitarian excrescence on economics.) The free-market economist, as **economist,** only assumes that utility scales have been adopted in **some** way by each individual; all he need assume to pursue the science of economics is that every person has a set of utility scales. **How** he has arrived at them or whether or not they are morally valid is not the concern of the economist. It **should,** however, be the concern of the social philosopher, or the economist-as-social philosopher, and unfortunately economists-as-social philosophers have not recognized this. Also, as an economist I emphatically don't agree that ascetic or quasi-ascetic or deeply religious communities can dispense with economics. There is nothing flouting of economics to contemplate a world that does not pursue material gain. As Mises and Hayek have shown, furthermore, an elite, including a religious elite, cannot calculate economically to rationally produce those goods they

(Continued On Page 4)

Political Kidnapping

It would seem to be belaboring the obvious to denounce the monstrous and unconscionable kidnapping of Miss Patricia Hearst; that is not only the libertarian position, it is the position of every decent human being. But denunciation is necessary, since many elements of the Left seem to be taking a position that is at least ambivalent, and even friendly, toward the kidnapping.

Thus, in a New York **Post** interview with leading leftists in California (Feb. 13), one leading Berkeley radical described the rationale of the "Symbionese Libertarian Army" for the kidnapping as "very beautiful"; another stated that "you've got to admire them. They made some brilliant maneuvers." Even leftists who opposed the move did so, not on the grounds of criminal immorality, but of strategy and tactics. One left-wing physician commented that: "personally, I don't agree with what they did, since there was no mass base. But this is the most attention the movement has gotten in a long time." The clear implication, of course, is that if the SLA had a "mass base", then kidnapping of innocent people would be justifiable. As for "attention", let us hope that the SLA will get the kind of "attention" it won't like very much, such as being pulverized by the police. Less ambivalent but still amoral in their criticisms were Angela Davis of the Communist Party and Huey Newton of the Black Panthers, who attacked the SLA action as "adventuristic" and "delusionary". True enough, but hardly addressed to the critical moral issue involved.

Even apart from the Left, there seems to be an unfortunate tendency to excuse or mitigate this crime by citing its political or ideological rationale. Even Miss Hearst — although she is clearly under coercion and hardly responsible for her statements — stated that "these people have been very honest with me. . . . They are perfectly willing to die for what they do." It should be affirmed, loud and clear, that the motives for a crime in no way mitigate the crime itself; kidnapping is kidnapping and evil, whatever the motivation. It makes no difference whether the kidnappers are bandits out for money, psychos out for "kicks", or ideologues pushing some political cause, whether left, right, or center. They are monsters, and should be treated accordingly.   ◘

What Kind Of 'Purity'? —

(Continued From Page 2)

payment. There is no room here for "democracy" or, indeed, any sort of voting. If, as presumably even the decentralists and the "radical caucus" would agree, there is nothing inimical to liberty in corporations or wage contracts, then why the hysterical denunciations of any sort of structure — or division of labor — within the Libertarian Party itself?

In a sense, this entire issue has been obscured by the fact that the Party has so far been a strictly volunteer (i.e. unpaid) organization. But if the Party is to grow and expand, it will have to begin hiring professional, full-time organizers. And when that happens, it will be clear that there will be no room for "voting" by the paid organizers, let alone a need for "participatory democracy" by the paid staff. But once that reality principle occurs, once the necessarily hierarchical and "undemocratic" nature of this relationship becomes clear, then one hopes that the strident calls for participatory democracy within the Party as a whole will begin to wither away.

As the Marxists have long since informed us, what any ideological group or movement needs is rigidity in principle, but flexibility in tactics. How one votes in Congress, or what the **content** of Party platforms or resolutions may be, is a matter of high principle where no violations may be tolerated. What the **form** or structure of our organizations may be, however, is purely a matter of tactics, and hence of efficiency and practicality. In short, the proper realm of "pragmatism" is that realm where principle does not apply. Since there is nothing in libertarian principle which prescribes "democracy" or prohibits structure or hierarchy, it is precisely here where considerations of efficiency must prevail. Let us not cry "wolf" where no wolf does or can exist.   ◘

447

Rothbardiana

We have not been able to report on Rothbardiana since our June, 1973 issue, but since then, matters have proceeded apace. **For A New Liberty** was the recipient of two thoughtful, though wrong-headed critiques: in **The Civil Liberties Review** (Fall, 1973) by the eminent, quasi-Marxist political philosopher Christian Bay; and in **The Christian Century** (Nov. 7, 1973), by Professor James W. Woelfel of the University of Kansas. As might be expected, Professor Bay attacked FNL as too "bourgeois", while Professor Woelfel attacked it as ignoring original sin (!). **Plus ca change** . . . . . or, as the saying goes, so what else is new?

Rampart College has just published (January, 1974), a second, revised, and updated edition of the long-selling **What Has Government Done to our Money?** (Available from Rampart College, Box 11407, Santa Ana, Calif. 92711, for $2.00). The new edition adds a twelve-page chapter on "The Monetary Breakdown of the West", summarizing the breakdown of the international monetary system over the last century, and updating the advance of this decay until mid-1973.

Rothbard returns to praxeology! in a lengthy article summarizing the praxeological method in economics and outlining the embryonic use of this method by various classical economists of the nineteenth century. In "Praxeology as the Method of Economics", in M. Natanson, ed., **Phenomenology and the Social Sciences** (Northwestern University Press, 1973), Volume II.

Rothbard reviews Samuelson! In a review-article of the ninth Edition (Ye Gods!) of Samuelson's infamous text. In the **Wall Street Review of Books** (December, 1973).

Also the following articles have appeared by Rothbard: "Interview: Rothbard Discusses Libertarianism," **Stanford Daily**, June 5; "The Original Machine-Haters: Review of M. I. Thomis' The Luddites," **Business and Society Review** (Spring, 1973); Letter on the "Deschooling of Society," **Journal of Forum for Contemporary History**, June 4; "Foreword to W. Block's Economic Scapegoats," **New Libertarian Notes** (October, 1973); "Revisionism and Libertarianism," NLN (December, 1973); two columns in **Reason**: "Watergate, and the Argument from Knowledge," (October, 1973), and "Privacy or the 'Right to Know'?" (January, 1974). The following book reviews have appeared in **Books for Libertarians**: of Benjamin Tucker's magazine Liberty (October, 1973); Days of H. L. Mencken (November, 1973); P. T. Bauer's Dissent on Development (December, 1973); W. H. Hutt's The Strike-Threat System (January, 1974); and the Collected Works of Lysander Spooner (February, 1974).

Finally, a slashing attack on egalitarianism, "Egalitarianism as a Revolt Against Nature," originally delivered at a Conference on Human Differentiation in Gstaad, Switzerland, held by the Institute for Humane Studies, appeared in **Modern Age** (Fall, 1973). And, hot news!, this will be the leadoff essay in a collection of Rothbard essays now in press in book form, some unpublished and others appearing in obscure and now defunct periodicals. The title will be **Egalitarianism as a Revolt Against Nature, and Other Essays**, forthcoming soon from Books for Libertarians Press. Rothbard will have a new introduction to the essays, with a foreword by R. A. Childs.   ◘

Open Letter To Irving Kristol —

(Continued From Page 3)

must have to survive; even the fiddlers on the roof need a price system to know what to produce and how to do so with any sort of efficiency. Otherwise, how are their fiddles going to be produced?

As a libertarian, I agree, as I've said, that we cannot assume that every individual knows a priori what will make him happy. I also agree that he must learn these principles from a set of elite "ethicists", be they ministers or whatever, and then must apply these principles. But my position is that every individual has the **right** to be free to try to find his happiness, or even, as I think Spencer once wrote, to go to hell in his own way. (Of course, empirically I think you would agree that very often the elite know only the broad principles, and that each individual is a better expert over the specifics of his concrete circumstances, but my position does not rest on this.)

I would agree that the world is in dire need of moral instruction. But there are at least two grave flaws, it seems to me, in what I take to be your reliance on the State to provide such moral guardianship. One is the anomaly of relying on the organized coercion-wielders for such service. Sorokin once perceptively wrote of the high percentage of criminality (even as defined by non-libertarians) among State rulers (Sorokin and Lunden, **Power and Morality**), and this is readily explained in one of Hayek's great chapters in the **Road to Serfdom**, "Why the Worst Get to the Top." Placing the State in charge of moral principles is equivalent to putting the proverbial fox in charge of the chicken coop.

Secondly, by coercing the moral act, which I take it you wish to do, you are paradoxically depriving the person of the chance of **being** moral. It seems to me that moral choices make no sense in the absence of freedom to choose, a freedom which is precisely the glory of the species man. If an individual is faced with alternatives A, B and C; and if we can agree that A is the moral alternative, then the individual is deprived of the chance to choose morally if alternatives B and C are made illegal.

I maintain, then, that every person has the right to be free to choose his moral principles, whether they be from the Church, his own whim, or, the Lord forbid, Marcuse or Charles Reich. But what, you ask, if he uses his freedom, as he has been doing increasingly, to choose "hippie nihilism", which I agree contravenes the workings of any modern society, free or not?

In the first place, I would maintain — in contrast to many other libertarians — that every family has not only the right but the moral duty

to instruct its children in the proper bourgeois virtues and the "Protestant ethic." It is the failure of such instruction, under a misapplication of libertarian theory, that is responsible for much of the current madness. (For magnificently "conservative" educational pronouncements by libertarian thinkers, see the writings of Isabel Paterson and Albert Jay Nock.) But, in any case, what are we to do with the increasing number of nihilists that we suffer from?

There are two libertarian answers to this. One is that it is precisely when we have Big Government that the danger from hippie nihilists is the greatest; for once nihilists gain control of the governmental machinery, we have all had it. But, if government were minimal or non-existent, there would no channel of destructiveness open to nihilistic takeover. Secondly, in a free society, the objective moral order would be free to do its work, and the hippie nihilists would swiftly learn the law of cause and effect. This basic knowledge — what used to be called "Social Darwinism" — has unfortunately been forgotten by many current libertarians, but we find it beautifully spelled out in the writings of Spencer and Sumner. Let me put it this way: we know that hippie nihilism is dysfunctional for the individual and for society; in a free, libertarian society, without State and welfare palliatives, the hippie nihilists would find this out soon enough. Some years ago, when hippie communes were first sprouting and I was worried about them, one of my libertarian colleagues cheerfully set me straight: "Don't worry, one hard winter will take care of them." And he was right. Without the patina and cushion of welfare statism, one hard winter would work its constructive lessons. Already, the hippie phenomenon has receded considerably since its flood tide in the late 60's, as the need for jobs and careers has become increasingly evident among the youth. Furthermore, even amidst the horrors of the drug culture, I understand that "Social Darwinism" has caused a considerable dropoff in the use of LSD — its destructiveness became all too clear and evident, even for the hippies.

In the free society, finally, where neighborhoods would be privately owned, the "straight" bourgeois residents could simply exclude hippies and other undesirables by not allowing them onto their privately-owned streets. It is because, I might point out, the streets are all State-owned that we of the West Side of Manhattan have to put up with the monsters that infest us. In a free, privately owned society, the hippie nihilists would have to go into their own self-isolated areas, where they would not bother or wreak their ill effects on the rest of us, and where Social Darwinism would work all the more rapidly and correctively.

Libertarianism, in short, does not have to be morally mushy. It can be the hardest of hard-nosed.   ◘

Arts And Movies

By Mr. First Nighter

Mel Brooks: An Appreciation

The appearance of what is unquestionably the funniest movie of the last several years (**Blazing Saddles**, dir. by and with Mel Brooks, and with Gene Wilder, Cleavon Little and Madeline Kahn), offers a welcome occasion for an appreciation of a man of prodigious and exhilirating comedic talent. Beginning — as did so many other leading humorists — as a writer for Sid Caesar's "Your Show of Shows" in the 1950's, Brooks burst on the entertainment scene with his justly famous hit record which he wrote and narrated, "The Two Thousand Year Old Man". In that record, Brooks presented the trivial side of world history (In Yiddish accent, as nearly as I can remember: "Napoleon? Sure I remember him. Short fella, bad stomach.")

Since then, Brooks has made all too few movies, but they have been outstanding. One, **The Producers**, made in 1968, still stands as the funniest movie of the last two decades. In that picture, the fabulous Zero Mostel, playing a sleazy, down-on-his luck New York Jewish theatrical producer, decides to fleece a group of backers by drastically over-selling shares in a new production: if it is a sure flop, then Mostel and Gene Wilder, a young accountant whom he inducts into the swindle, could skip town with the proceeds and no questions asked. Trying to insure a flop, Mostel and Wilder put on a pro-Nazi musical, "Springtime for Hitler", written by an ex-Nazi soldier, marvellously played by Kenneth Mars. An inspired and hilarious movie, from first moment to last.

Blazing Saddles, while no **Producers**, also provides an occasion for a contrast and comparison of Brooks with Woody Allen, whose hilarious **Sleeper** also opened recently, and was reviewed in these pages. For both Brooks and Allen embody the best of two variants of what might be called "New York Jewish humor." Allen's has essentially been Jewish humor of the 1950's: cerebral, quasi-intellectual, left-liberal, the Allen **persona** a worried, bumbling shnook obviously "in" and around psychoanalysis. The fact that **Sleeper** blends these long-standing features of Allen's humor with the marvellously visual, cinematic Keaton-Lloyd tradition of 1920's movie comedy doesn't change Allen's essential stance as a Man of the Fifties. Brooks, on the other hand, hearkens back to an older, healthier, and — as far as I am concerned — a far funnier tradition: Jewish humor of the 1930's. The humor is absurdist, linguistic-cultural rather than political, emphasizing — particularly in **Blazing Saddles** — a series of dazzling and explosive "one-line" situations and gags rather than plot continuity. The Brooks persona, which appears far less often than Allen but of course shines through the material at all times — is far different from Allen's: it is brash, self-confident, constantly on top of the situation rather than buffeted by life. In a profound sense, Brooks harks back to the great, superb tradition of the Marx Brothers pictures of the 1930's: with the possible exceptions of the W. C. Fields canon, the funniest pictures ever made. With the Marx Brothers, too and even more so, not a moment was wasted: every millimeter of film was one of a series of dazzling and absurdist gags and situations. Of course, **Blazing Saddles** doesn't compare to such great Marx Brothers' epics as **Duck Soup** and **Night at the Opera** — but after all, what can? The Marx Brothers provided a harmonious and wondrous blend of visual and dialogue comedy, with Harpo basically providing the former and Groucho the latter. It is no accident that these great comedies were written by perhaps the finest humorist of the twentieth century, S. J. Perelman, whose essays provide us with a truly remarkable erudition in language and culture in the service of hilarious comedy. But it is not a small boon to have a film which at least harks back noticeably to the great Marx Brothers tradition.

Blazing Saddles, as did the **Producers**, also delights the viewer by bringing back one of the finest traditions of American comedy: ethnic and racial humor. Under the repressive hammer blows of serioso left-liberalism, ethnic humor has virtually died out in America in this generation (pace the driving of **Amos and Andy** off the air). But Brooks realizes that, precisely because of this suppression, and now that hard-core pornography can be seen everywhere, ethnic humor has become the last taboo in our culture, and therefore the best subject for comedic genius. **Blazing Saddles** brings ethnic humor back with a bang.

This movie is the definitive spoof of the movie Western; every cliche scene and set is taken and put through the wringer of the inimitable Brooksian humor. Seeing **Blazing Saddles** is enough to reveal the inadequacy and feebleness of previous attempts at spoofing the Western (e.g. **Cat Ballou** or the older **Buttons and Bows**.) The movie opens with a typical scene of the Old West: workin' on the railroad, the workers this time being Chinese (wearing coolie hats) and blacks. The white foremen ride up and demand that the Negroes "sing your nigger folk-songs . . . you know, your nigger work-songs." The blacks look at each other in confusion ("nigger folk songs?"), and finally break into a rendition of Cole Porter's "I Get A Kick Out of You". The white cowboys are confused in their turn, and say: "No, No; you know, songs like 'Camptown Races' ", after which, to illustrate, they break into a rendition of "Camptown Races" strongly reminiscent of the exaggerated writhing of the singing in the Marx Brothers' films.

The movie continues in this vein of hilarity. There is, for example, a remarkable spoof of Marlene Dietrich Westerns (e.g. **Destry Rides Again**) as dumpy Madeline Kahn sings her way with a Germanic lisp, in a Western bar and dance hall, through a takeoff of "Falling in Love Again" ("Tired"), as the songstress "Lilli Von Shtupp". To defeat the bad guys and save the town, the black sheriff, the protagonist of the film, builds an exact replica of the town overnight in order to confuse the bad guys and induce them to shoot up the replica instead of the town itself. Mel Brooks himself plays the brash, dopey looking, and crooked governor of the state.

Probably the funniest moment of the film comes as the black (and Ivy League-type) sheriff reminisces about his family's move to the West. As they were bringing up the rear of a long and racially segregated wagon train, we see the train set upon and massacred by the mighty forces of the Sioux nation. The Sioux then gather round the wagon with the black family, and gaze at it in puzzlement. After a moment (and bearing in mind that there had been no Yiddish humor yet in the film), the Indian chief, Mel Brooks, dressed in Indian costume and looking solemn, bewildered, and even dopier than as the governor, exclaims: (in thick Yiddish accent): "Schwartzes!!" And then: "luz em geh ("let them go"), they're darker then we are."

Mel Brooks is possibly the funniest man around, and long may he wave. That he is personally hilarious was demonstrated a few years ago, when David Susskind put on a panel of six or eight Jewish comedians to discuss The Jewish Mother. In this impromptu program, Brooks, a constant stream of hilarious wit, simply walked off with the show. But he virtually Said It All when, early in the program, Susskind asked Brooks to describe his own Jewish Mother: "Fierce she was. Fierce . . . and short."

The Paper Chase. dir. and written by James Bridges. With Timothy Bottoms, Lindsay Wagner, and John Houseman.

An interesting picture, with a new twist on academe; instead of hippies or rebels in college, this movie deals with the joys and terrors of law school (Harvard, to be precise.) The pressures of school, the love of learning, the problems of discipleship to a martinet teacher, the pure terror at exam time, all these are caught and portrayed well and sensitively. Unfortunately, the entire picture suffers from diffusion, meandering, lack of organization. Tight editing and the imposition of a firm directorial hand are almost desperately needed. As a consequence, the ending is weak and confused, as the movie, like so many other films these days, just dribbles to a halt, instead of having its problems or themes satisfactorily resolved. Particularly weak is the love interest, as Lindsay Wagner, the female lead, is given virtually no lines and leads a shadowy and unmotivated existence.

The picture is not helped by Timothy Bottoms, as the central character, who wanders through the film with his gentle hippie air and distracting mannerisms belying his supposed sense of purpose. A shining light in the picture is the superb performance of John Houseman as the professor whose silky surface hardly conceals his iron and subtly sadistic character.

(Continued On Page 7)

449

Background Of Middle East Conflict*

By Bill Evers

Suppose a war breaks out between Ruritania and Walldavia, two hypothetical states which we shall use for purposes of analysis. In determining war guilt, it is not enough to know merely who fired the first shot or who crossed what line first.

Instead an in-depth historical inquiry is necessary. If the Ruritanians have in the past conquered and subdued or dispossessed half of the Walldavian people, that does make a difference when one is trying to determine war guilt.

The political roots of the present-day conflict in the Middle East go back to the World War I era. At that time, officials of the British Empire promised in somewhat vague terms a homeland in Palestine for organized Zionism and promised national independence in the Middle East to Arab nationalist leaders.

Without in any way acknowledging the rightfulness of British imperialist meddling, we can distinguish between these promises by noting that the Arabs were struggling to throw off the foreign rule of the Ottoman Turks and to achieve national self-determination, whereas the Zionists were foreigners laying claim to the land the Arabs were living on.

Promises Never Kept

In any case, the British never fulfilled either promise. Britain and her allies divided up the land of the old Ottoman Empire, and Britain took control of Palestine.

Several surveys covering land tenure in British Palestine in the late 1940s just before the formation of the State of Israel show that Arabs owned 49 percent of the land in Palestine; Jews, six percent; government land and land owned in common by Arab and Jewish villages, six percent. The rest was desert, some of which was the regular pasturage of Bedouin tribes. Included in the category of government land by these surveys was territory claimed by Ottoman sultans and their successors, but occupied for generations by thousands of Arab peasants who claimed the equivalent of freehold tenure.

Of further importance is the fact that the Zionist Jews bought most of their land from feudal landlords, whose claims to the land originated in conquest, not in cultivation.

Large Landowners

A. Granott, an Israeli land expert whose writings are quoted by both Palestinians and Zionists, notes that "no less than 90.6 percent of all (Jewish) acquisitions were of land which formerly belonged to large landowners, while from fellaheen (Arab farmers) only 9.4 percent was purchased."

The study "Land Ownership in Palestine, 1880-1948," published by the Office of the Premier of the State of Israel, also states that "most of the Jewish land purchases involved large tracts belonging to absentee-owners."

Thus, an additional question of justice arises because of the feudal system in early twentieth-century Palestine. According to the libertarian theory of justice, a feudal landlord is not the legitimate owner of land; instead, the land belongs to his bondsman who has been homesteading it. Thus the Zionist settlers obtained a clear and just title only in cases in which previously unowned land was homesteaded or in which land was bought from native Palestinians.

Justifications

One of the justifications often given for Israeli seizure of Arab houses and farmlands after the formation of the State of Israel is that the Arabs fled after having been ordered to leave by the radio broadcasts of the Arab political leadership.

However, subsequent scholarly examination of the monitoring transcripts kept by the British Broadcasting Corporation and the U. S.

Central Intelligence Agency shows no evidence that orders to leave were broadcast and shows that some exhortations not to evacuate were broadcast.

Apparently the confusion of battle and fear of the terrorism of some Zionist military organizations like the Irgun group prompted departures. Nonetheless, even if it could be shown beyond a shadow of a doubt that the Arab people of Palestine had been ordered to leave, this does not alter the legitimacy of their title to the land.

There is now some increased consciousness among Israeli intellectuals of the fact that they live on stolen land. During the summer of 1972, members of the literary intelligentsia argued that the Israeli government should permit the Arab inhabitants of the villages of Ikrit and Berem to return to the homes from which 25 years before they had been expelled, in a supposedly temporary evacuation.

Israeli Premier Golda Meir told these intellectuals that restoring the rights of these pro-Israeli Arabs would set a dangerous precedent. The New York Times said the Israeli press reported her fearing that all sorts of claims might be put forward, by hundreds of thousands of refugees of the 1948 war.

Although the territory controlled by the Israeli government has expanded considerably over the years, Israel's might does not make her right. One can only hope that eventually justice will prevail and that the Palestinian Arab refugees will once again be masters in their own homes.

*Reprinted From The Stanford Daily, Oct. 10, 1973.   ☐

Save The Oil Industry!

Not even at the height of the left-wing climate of the 1930's has there been such a savage anti-business assault by politicians and by the media as is now being levelled at the oil industry. An economically insane proposal to rollback crude oil prices, "excess" profits taxes on the oil industry, destructive compulsory allocations by the Federal Energy Office, a proposal for a "yardstick" oil company owned and operated by the federal government, and even the AFL-CIO proposal for nationalization of the oil industry. Two men for some curious reason beloved by the nation's "conservatives" are at the center of this furore: George Meany, and Mr. State himself, Scoop Jackson. Energy fascism proceeds on the path of its grisly logic, pushing from one frenetic piece of government botch to another, with the government frantically attempting to add new interventions to rectify the miseries brought about by its previous aggressions. Full collectivism is around the corner unless these proposals are fought and fought hard. The fact that some of the oil majors have courted government subsidy and privilege in the past does not excuse the current social-fascist drive by one iota. Unless we all rally round to save the oil industry now we will go the path of Britain and, eventually, Russia.   ☐

New Associates

We wish to acknowledge with gratitude the advent of three new Libertarian Forum Associates. They are:

Dr. Walter Block
Mr. Hal Jindrich
Mr. Donald McKowen

The Home Front

Geoffrey Perrett, Days of Sadness, Years of Triumph: The American People, 1939-1945 (New York: Coard, McCann, and Geoghegan). $10.00. 512 pp.

Reviewed By Justus D. Doenecke

Good social history is always difficult to write. Few efforts by non-professionals have been successful. Most soon become "source books," from which the trained scholar can find the telling example or the revealing anecdote which supposedly "illuminates" an entire period. To what degree, for example, does our picture of the "lost generation" derive from Frederick Lewis Allen's Only Yesterday (1931) or our image of Harding's leadership come from Mark Sullivan's Our Times (5 vols.; 1926-1935)?

The author, himself born during World War II, combines graduate work in law with a varied career as a journalist, laborer, and even paratrooper. Readers who lived through the period will relish Perrett's treatment of "Mairzy Doats," Forever Amber, zoot suits, the Sinatra craze, the Jane Russell movie The Outlaw, Dr. Friedrich Hayek, Victory Girls, the Tanaka Memorial, Professor Sorokin, and the Curtiss-Wright scandal. One learns of the uncertainty of the 1940 defense boom, the panic among Americans after the fall of France, popular hostility towards European refugees, and the patronizing treatment offered American blacks. Telling points are made — sometimes almost in passing — concerning Roosevelt's exploitation of the Kearny incident, increasing callousness towards the bombing of civilians, the strident nationalism behind supposedly "internationalist" rhetoric, and the wartime turn to the political right.

Amid this potpourri of wartime fads and foibles, some important demythologizing takes place. Perrett correctly takes the American Civil Liberties Union to task for boasting in 1943 that America possessed an almost flawless civil liberties record. He refuses to see the Nesei internments as an isolated case; rather it was characteristic of a hysteria that claimed over ten times as many victims as World War I and gave the United States the worst civil liberties record among English-speaking democracies. It should be an eye-opener to learn that conscientious objectors were often beaten; that the top pay for Japanese-American physicians was $19 a month; that black newspapers were harassed by the FBI; that bloody racial clashes at military bases were almost a daily occurence; and that the arrests of such "subversives" as aviatrix Laura Ingalls and German-American propagandist George Sylvester Viereck were clearly ex post facto prosecutions.

American liberals were far more Jeffersonian in theory than in practice. Columnist Dorothy Thompson said that freedom of speech and assembly had doomed the Weimar Republic. Professor Carl Friedrich wanted people to monitor the political beliefs of their neighbors. Lewis Mumford called for compulsory labor service for all children. Walter Lippmann endorsed Roosevelt's "concentration camps" (a word FDR liked to use) both for Japanese-Americans and for the Dies Committee. The very journals so self-consciously militant in propounding the ideology of democracy — such as The New Republic — fired isolationist columnists, called for the drafting of striking miners, and wanted the America First Committee investigated. Essayist Clifton Fadiman remarked, "The only way to make a German understand is to kill him," while Senator J. William Fulbright boasted that the American way of life was "the only way worthy of a free man." Even Hollywood got into the act, reviling actor Lew Ayres for registering as a conscientious objector. Roosevelt's Supreme Court turned persecutor of the Jehovah's Witnesses, declaring that local government could curb religious freedom.

This book has many of the flaws of popular history. Footnoting is treated in a cavalier fashion. The bibliography lacks crucial items. Like the Civil War history of Bruce Catton, it is far better at capturing a mood than asking significant questions. Loaded and emotive language becloud many an issue (e.g. "From beginning to end (isolationism) was clogged by stodginess, silliness and faintheartedness"). Some writing is hackneyed (e.g. "Pepper enthused"), some is meaningless (e.g. "America triumphed over itself and its history"). Much of Perrett's material is better covered elsewhere.

Yet, despite such obvious limitations, the book deserves a wide reading and a paperback edition. Despite columnist John Roche's references to "the good war," World War II can never again be seen through Star Spangled glasses. ◻

Arts And Movies —

Continued From Page 5

The Incomparable Perelman. Writing about Mel Brooks gives me the opportunity to celebrate the work of the incomparable S. J. Perelman, unquestionably the master wit and humorist of our time. Perelman as screen writer for the classic Marx Bros. movies is but an example of his output. In a sense, Perelman is the thinking man's Groucho or Mel Brooks. An unequalled master of the English language, Perelman is the past-master of the inverted cliche; with dazzling virtuousity, he twists and bends one cliche after another into an amalgam of continuous hilarity.

The best work of Perelman was published in what we might call his "Middle Period", in the 1930's and 40's. (His brief earlier period was simply feeling his oats). Since then, Perelman's dazzling performance and consistent hilarity has unfortunately declined, beginning with his nostalgia series "Cloudland Revisited"; the cultural and linguistic erudition is still there, but a certain flat sobriety has taken over. But now, in paperback, Dell has emerged with the best of Perelman's Middle Period, Crazy Like a Fox (published in 1947 Modern Library hardcover as The Best of S. J. Perelman).

Perelman was particularly master of the parody, and in this collection he combines his triumph over the cliche with a series of stunning literary parodies. The temptation to quote the whole book is almost irresistible. Particularly outstanding are his parodies of: science fiction ("Captain Future, Block that Kick!"); tough-guy detectives ("Somewhere a Roscoe" and "Farewell My Lovely Appetizer"); Maugham on Gauguin ("Beat Me, Post-Impressionist Daddy"); stream-of-consciousness ("Pale Hands I Loathe"); Dostoievsky ("A Farewell to Omsk"); Dunsany ("The Idol's Eye"); and Odets ("Waiting for Santy"); also his profiles of Arthur Kober and Vincente Minelli; and his own marvellous introduction under the name of "Sidney Namlerep."

Take, for example, Perelman's parody of the left-wing New Yorkese blather of Clifford Odets. The scene of the playlet is the workshop of Santa Claus, an evil capitalist sweatshop employer, who exploits his seven gnomes "Rankin, Panken, Rivkin, Riskin, Ruskin, Briskin, and Praskin." Rivkin, a young gnome, is in love with Stella Claus, Santa's daughter.

Rivkin (to Stella): "I can't sleep, I can't eat, that's how I love you. You're a double malted with two scoops of whipped cream; you're the moon rising over Moshulu Parkway; you're a two weeks' vacation at Camp Nitgedaiget! I'd pull down the Chrysler Building to make a bobby pin for your hair!

Stella: I've got a stomach full of anguish. Oh, Rivvy, what'll we do?

Panken (sympathetically): Here, try a piece fruit.

Rivkin (fiercely): Wax fruit — that's been my whole life! Imitations! Substitutes!"

One almost incredibly dazzling example of Perelmanian wit and I must reluctantly conclude. The following is the first paragraph, in its entirety, of Perelman's profile of the playwright Arthur Kober:

"Picture to yourself a ruddy-cheeked, stocky sort of chap, dressed in loose but smelly tweeds, a stubby briar between his teeth (it has resisted the efforts of the best surgeons to extract it), with a firm yet humorous mouth, generous to a fault, ever-ready for a flagon of nut-brown ale with his cronies, possessing the courage of a lion, the tenderness of a florence Nightingale, and the conceit of a diva, an intellectual vagabond, a connoisseur of first editions, fine vintages, and beautiful women, well above six feet in height and distinguished for his pallor, a dweller in the world of books, his gray eye belying the sensual lip beneath, equally at

(Continued On Page 8)

451

Arts And Movies —

(Continued From Page 7)

home browsing through the bookstalls along Fourth Avenue and rubbing elbows (his own elbows) in the smart literary salons of 57th Street, a rigid abstainer and non-smoker who lives entirely on dehydrated fruits, cereals, and nuts, rarely leaving his monastic cell nowadays except to dine at the Salmagundi; an intimate of Cocteau, Picasso, Joyce and Lincoln Kerstein, a dead shot, a past master of the foils and the International Woodmen of the World, dictating his novels, plays, poems, short stories, **commedias dell'arte**, aphorisms and ripostes at lighting speed to a staff of underpaid secretaries, an expert judge of horseflesh, the owner of a model farm equipped with the most slovenly dairy devices — a man as sharp as a razor, as dull as a hoe, as clean as a whistle, as tough as nails, as white as snow, as black as the raven's wing, as poor as Job, a man up with the lark, down on your toes, and gone with the wind. A man kind and captious, sweet and sour, fat and thin, tall and short, racked with fever, plagued by the locust, beset by witches, hagridden, cross-grained, fancy-free, a funloving, addle-pated dreamer, visionary, and slippered pantaloon. Picture to yourself such a man, I say, and you won't have the faintest conception of Arthur Kober.''

The Way We Were. Dir. by Sydney Pollack from screenplay and novel by Arthur Laurents. With Barbra Streisand and Robert Redford.

This has been touted as an old-fashioned and romantic "movie movie", and to a certain extent it is. With this and nostalgia too, how could they go wrong? But the trouble is that old-fashioned is not always good, and what we have here is a throwback to the left-wing "message" movies of the 1940's. That kind of old-fashioned we could do without. Furthermore, the potentially rich background drops away, often to the point of being incomprehensible, in order to focus on the banally overstated and repetitious confrontation of character and attitudes between the two leads.

As to the confrontation, the cards are outrageously stacked for the left-wing message. Barbra Streisand is a loud, pushy, aggressive, serious-about-her-values, caring, socially conscious, Communist New York Jewess — and **therefore**, so Messrs. Pollack and Laurents insist, lovable and great. The stereotypes proliferate. Robert Redford is a handsome, talented, socially unconscious, opportunistic, easygoing, smiling, and therefore at bottom unlovable wealthy WASP. Treated particularly outrageously by the film are the WASP girls: every one dumb, inarticulate, shallow, uncaring. The WASPS spend all their time telling silly jokes while **serioso** Barbra tells them off and fights for world peace, world war, civil liberties, you name it. If there were a WASP Anti-Defamation League, they would be justified in making an angry, caring, articulate, socially conscious protest. The entire picture is a blatant piece of ethnic chauvinism. As for the Communist Party, it is treated as

101 Ways To Promote Libertarian Ideas

30. Hold a Libertarian Festival — a "teach-in on libertarian views on a dozen subjects.

31. Is your university giving an honorary degree to a prominent politician, soldier, or corporation executive? Prepare a research profile on his career from a libertarian perspective. To what extent has he contributed to the preservation and extension of liberty? Or has he used politicial power to restrict, destroy or subvert freedom? Has he plundered the taxpayers to enhance the profits of his corporation? Has he used state-power to avoid the risks of the free market? Has he supported violations of international laws on human rights? Publish your report. Petition for an alternate to be honored with a degree.

32. Libertarianism is not a cult in which one person or book has all the answers to one's personal or the world's problems. It is essentially a philosophic committment to the ideas that voluntarism is the only legitimate ethical basis for human action. Beyond that, libertarians hold a variety of viewpoints on almost every subject. Some are atheists, others Christians; some are pacifists, others will defend their liberty to the death; some are Austrians, others Friedmanites; some anarchists, others liberal limited government advocates; some uphold natural law theory, others deny its validity. Libertarianism is a house with "many mansions" and this should always be made clear to those unfamiliar with the variety of libertarian thought.

33. Interested in radio? Use the college radio station for libertarian propaganda. Start an interview show, a telephone listener response program. Or offer to broadcast one of the taped series of lectures by Murray Rothbard and others available from **Books for Libertarians**, 422 First St., Washington, D. C. 20003.

34. Do you want some professional help in organizing a campus group? Contact **The Society for Individual Liberty**, RM 304 Empire Building, 13th and Chestnut Sts., Philadelphia, Pa. 19107.

35. Having trouble finding libertarian books in your local bookstore? Send for the catalogues of either **Books for Libertarians**, 422 First Street SE, Washington, D. C. 20003 or to **The Laissez-faire Bookstore**, 208A Mercer Street, New York, NY 10012. ◻

---

basically right as rain, though perhaps a wee bit strident. Twists and turns of the party line? Mass murders by Stalin? You won't find any of them in **The Way We Were**.

Redford does well as usual; as for Streisand, she is, as usual, Streisand. The next person who insists that "you know, she's really beautiful", deserves a punch in the nose. Fortunately, we were spared her caterwauling of the great pop songs. Let us count our blessings. ◻

The Libertarian Forum

BOX 341
MADISON SQUARE STATION
NEW YORK, NEW YORK 10010

Published Every Month. Subscription Rate: $8.00 Per Year

A Monthly Newsletter

THE
Libertarian Forum

Joseph R. Peden, Publisher   Murray N. Rothbard, Editor

VOLUME VI, NO. 3   MARCH, 1974   US-ISSN0047-4517

SEVEN DAYS IN MAY??

Day by day, piece by piece, the Truth in all its majesty and inexorability is closing in on the Tricky One. Piece by piece, the high crimes, low crimes, and misdemeanors of Richard Nixon are becoming increasingly evident, even to the blindest Nixonite loyalist. The Nixon strategy — highlighted by the absurdities of the short-lived (and revealingly named) "Operation Candor" — is clearly shown to be a series of lies, evasions, and retreats to hastily prepared fallback positions. The only purpose is to cling to the power and perquisites of office as long as he possibly can.

Impeachment per se is beginning to look too good for the Monster Milhous. Somehow, even the courageous Leon Jaworski has discovered somewhere in the Constitution (?) that a sitting President cannot be indicted for any crime whatever. Why must the President be exempt from the common criminal law? Vice-President Agnew was not, and he was only able to escape the hoosegow by plea-bargaining for a simple resignation and reprimand. But at any rate, this means that Nixon must be impeached before he can be indicted, convicted, and punished for his numerous crimes, high and low. It is not only being booted out of office that now looms for Mr. Nixon, but beyond that, the spectre of the jailhouse door — a spectre which more imminently faces his former chief henchmen in the Administration. Perhaps that is why Mr. Nixon is fighting with such desperation.

But that very desperation, coupled with certain hints in his defense against impeachment, gives rise to some very scary possibilities for America's future. If these Unthinkable Thoughts seem paranoid, remember that almost every seemingly crazy piece of Left-wing paranoia about Richard Nixon over the years has turned out to be all too true. What possibly may loom ahead is a blend of the Philip Roth scenario (in a hilarious but chilling parody of Nixon's "speech on the day of his impeachment" published a year ago in the New York Review of Books) with Fletcher Knebel's exciting portrayal of a military takeover in Seven Days in May.

Let us first consider one of Mr. Nixon's major defenses against the impeachment proceedings: that the charges are too broad, that to be impeached he has to have committed (been convicted of?) actual crimes, major crimes at that, and furthermore crimes ancillary to his high office. (Presumably, income tax fraud is not enough ancillary to the office, misprision of a felony in not reporting the hush money plot to the Attorney-General is too "low" a crime, etc.) Historically, as an interpretation of the Constitution, Mr. Nixon's argument is palpable

(Continued On Page 8)

European Politics

By Leonard P. Liggio

Just before the recent English elections took place, there was a radio program on the voters' attitudes. It started with a man saying that it was necessary to end all the government controls and to allow the free play of economic forces. Later, when his interview was presented in full, it turned out he was not one of our English libertarians but was a Labourite attacking the Conservative government. Since the Conservatives, and not only in England, have become the leading advocates of strong state economic authority, including controls, it should not be surprising to find that other parties take up some kind of critique of controls. The recent elections gave the Conservatives a well deserved defeat without giving the Labour Party any mandate that it could turn into a push for more socialism. One commentator said: "Mr. Heath went to the country on the issue of who governs and the answer he got was nobody." The New York Times declared that that had been "the worst possible result." Who were the gainers? The Nationalists from the Celtic areas of Scotland, Wales, western England and Northern Ireland made important victories. Building on their first victory in 1970, the Scottish Nationalists won

several by-elections last fall, and won seven seats in the early March general elections. The Welsh Plaid Cymru won two seats. The ultra Ulster Unionists, who call for a separate Protestant-controlled Northern Ireland, won eleven seats. The Liberals, who won fourteen seats, also reflect a nationalist feeling, especially in the Celtic western English counties. The large Liberal vote — six million — represented about twenty per cent of the total vote, and denied either major party its victory. Voting Liberal was a sound way of punishing the Conservatives without giving the Labourites a mandate. With that number of votes, the Liberals should have had ten times the number of seats they actually received in Parliament. Heath tried to get them into a coalition with the Conservatives but the Liberals (supported by the Manchester Guardian) rejected Heath's continuing in power. The Liberals demand a reform of the election system as well as a separate Parliament for Scotland and something similar for Wales. The Liberals have attracted the youth vote on a program of support for capitalism against regulations or controls

(Continued On Page 2)

453

European Politics —

(Continued From Page 1).

over economic or private life, support for the Common Market and the 'radition of free trade, and for decentralization or "'community politics." The Liberals' image is that of radical capitalism and decentralization. On Wilson's new cabinet, the Liberals bitterly attacked it as "an old-fashioned Socialist government of the type which failed the country ›efore."

There is a possibility that the Labour government may be less inflationary than the Conservatives. The chancellor of the exchequer, Denis Healy, favors floating exchange rates rather than controls. Harold Lever, chancellor of the Duchy of Lancaster, and key economic advisor to Wilson, strongly opposes increased taxes. But should the battle against inflation fail it has been suggested that Enoch Powell will benefit. Powell refused to run for Parliament in the election due to his opposition to wage and price controls and to the inflationary monetary policies of the Conservatives. This action places him once more in a serious political position instead of the dead end of opposition to the free movement of people and goods that he had been emphasizing. Powell called on his supporters to vote Labour to save the country from the Conservatives' price-wage controls and inflation. The New Statesman declared: "Who would be the beneficiary? It could be Enoch Powell, who in my view has — so far from committing political suicide — played his cards adroitly by placing himself outside the party arena. To rise above the enmities of Right and Left, to 'unite the nation', is a well-tried but always potentially effective technique." To whom has Powell been appealing? Powell has represented Birmingham which, according to Jane Jacobs, was the center of the flexibility and quick responses to the market which are the flower of capitalism. The Manchester Guardian commented on Powell's new influence from concentrating on issues of controls and inflation (Powell had earlier contributed to England's abandonment of imperialist positions around the world and to the reduction of defense spending): "The West Midlands is the home of independent capitalism. The typical voter is not a frightened bank clerk of Carshalton but a small businessman with three men working for him somewhere in Cradley Heath. He doesn't like an incomes and prices policy."

The developments in England reflect some changes that have been occurring in other parts of the Commonwealth. The Labour parties of Australia and New Zealand were victorious after long periods of opposition, mainly in response to Conservative inflations. Since coming to power, these Labour governments have had the courage to break with U. S. domination of their foreign policies and defense programs. In Canada, the Liberals have been ruling as a minority party from the increase a year and a half ago of the New Democratic party and the decline of the Social Creditists who also lost their strongholds as the provincial governments in Alberta and British Columbia. The only unifying element in Canadian politics appears to be a desire to stem the influence of American investments. That theme has been carried further in Quebec, where the French population would like to limit the role of English-speaking Canadians. Last fall in provincial elections the separatist Parti Quebecois, led by Rene Levesque, received 29% of the vote against 55% for the Liberals, with the rest going to the National Union and to the Creditistes.

In Holland and Scandinavia there have been important electoral developments. In Holland, a year and a half ago, the electorate polarized. The religious parties — a Catholic one and several Protestant ones, headed by the Anti-Revolutionary party (aimed against the classical liberalism and freedom of religion of the French Revolution) — lost their joint control of national politics. The Dutch voted against the traditionalist parties and their no-issues campaign and favored parties taking strong stands. The Dutch Liberals, with the Young Liberals in the vanguard, made strong gains among the youth vote opposed to inflation and to the repression of new culture. The Radical People's Party similarly made gains as people have left the old religion-oriented culture for the new culture.

In Sweden last September the long dominant Social Democrats lost heavily, and now rule in a Parliament in which their coalition has only half the seats. The biggest Swedish gainer was the Center party which appealed to a "desire among many for the simple life that preceded industrial society." The Center party seemed to represent the Sweden of

the past before the shifts of population from country to city — "a nostalgia for the day when the people didn't have to move to cities and work in factories." At the same time in Norway the thirty years of Labor rule was maintained only barely. The growth of the opposition is somewhat similar to Sweden. Five per cent of the vote went to the "Anders Lange party for the sharp reduction of taxes, levies and public interference." Anders Lange does not like taxes. A lot of people don't include a lot of Danes. Last December Berkeley-trained Mogens Glistrup and his Progress party won 28 seats in Denmark's Parliament. Glistrup seeks abolition of the income tax and burning of the papers of the revenue office, and wants to start budget cuts with defense. Glistrup declared: "I'm also against spending money on defense . . . If we had our own defense, we could last five hours, without it, five minutes. So who needs it?" This view represents the result of serious study by Europeans of defense problems and the economic advantage of peace and peace policy rather than defense spending. The New York Times went out of its mind when Glistrup received so many votes. The Times editorial was entitled: "Poujadism in Denmark." Poujadism in mid-1950s France sought to organize tax resistance. At the time it attracted the attention of libertarians in America as a significant contribution to serious politics rather than to verbal exercises. However, both the National Review and Human Events rejected articles expounding the role of tax resistance in France and indicating its value for organizing a popular libertarian movement in America. No taxes, no warfare state!

In Germany the Free Democrats continue to make gains at the expense of the Socialists and Christian Democrats. The Free Democrats' leader, Walter Scheel, the present foreign minister, seems likely to be elected the next president of Germany. When formed after the second world war, the Free Democrats united those opposed to the socialism of the Socialists and the dominance of religion in society of the Christian Democrats. They opposed high taxes, government interference with private lives and the pro-American foreign policy which they felt did not reflect a nationalist position between America and Russia. As radical capitalists the Free Democrats are to the left of the Socialists on many issues. This radicalism was reflected in their breaking with Ludwig Erhard in 1966 when he violated a pledge not to increase taxes as he bowed to U. S. demands that he increase contributions to defense. Under Scheel Germany has been engaged in a massive investment program in the Soviet Union, most recently a plan to build an over 1 billion dollar steel plant. Germany and the Soviet Union have agreed to set up joint companies to operate in third countries with mixed Soviet-German capital, management and production. The Free Democratic resurgence has been explained as the result of changes in German society away from traditionalist attitudes. Time has noted: "discipline is giving way to what sociologist Ralf Dahrendorf, who also happens to be the Free Democrats' leading thinker, calls the individual search for happiness by people freed of the fetters of tradition and thrown into the affluent society." Writes Dahrendorf in Society and Democracy in Germany: "Discipline, orderliness, subservience, cleanliness, industriousness, precision, and all the other virtues ascribed by many to the Germans as an echo of past splendor have already given way to a much less rigid set of values, among which economic success, a high income, the holiday trip, and the new car play a much larger part than the virtues of the past. Younger people especially display little of the much praised and much scorned respect for authority, and less of the disciplined virtues that for their fathers were allegedly sacred. A world of highly individual values has emerged, which puts the experienced happiness of the individual in first place and increasingly lets the so-called whole slip from sight."

Scheel and the German government have been major targets during this March of Nixon and Kissinger. Nixon wants the Europeans to continue to underwrite the costs of American inflation; they refuse. Likewise, they do not wish to have America dominate Europe's defenses. But, especially, they wish to have the freedom to operate in the world market to purchase raw materials, mainly oil, without the intrusions of American political demands. Kissinger has attacked Michel Jobert, French foreign minister, for seeking since last July to block U. S.-European defense arrangements under NATO, as well as for opposing U. S. claims that there was a Soviet threat during the Middle East crisis.

However, the big blow-up came during the February Washington meeting that Kissinger had determined would present a solid, hard-line toward the Arab countries. Jobert presented a blistering critique of American policy and affirmed France's independent policy toward the

(Continued On Page 3)

454

The British Elections

Given the unspeakable state of British politics and the economy, the results of the recent elections were the best that could be hoped for. The Labor Party is now gung ho socialist, and so a victory for Labor in the elections would have been an unmitigated disaster: Labor was pledged, for example, to the nationalization of a host of vital industries, as well as to the monstrous despotism of compulsory abolition of the private schools of Great Britain. Under former Prime Minister Edward Heath, however, the Conservatives were proceeding to wreck the British economy by the familiar combination of large-scale inflation of the money supply coupled with severe price and wage controls (Is Britain ten years further down the American road?) While we cannot condone the stranglehold of union monopoly in Britain, the immediate cause of the breakdown of the British economy and the miners' strike was Mr. Heath's stubborn insistence on keeping wage controls far below the free market level. Heath's policy was particularly repellent for its Nixonian quality: masking collectivist policy in a cloak of free-enterprise rhetoric. A clear-cut victory for Heath, then, would simply have endorsed his disastrous economic policies.

Through the closeness of the vote, and still more by the large increase of votes for the minor parties, the British electorate has made sure that neither incubus of a major party could command a majority in Parliament. Furthermore, in the short run, Prime Minister Wilson was able to solve the economic crisis by in effect removing wage controls on the coal miners and thereby ending the strike. Labor's minority status insures that Mr. Wilson will not be able to push through the gallopping collectivism of the full Labor program. Since both major parties are horrendous, a stalemate government blocking both party programs was the best that could be extracted from the situation.

But there are even more goodies in the British election. For the striking increase in the votes for the Liberals and for the Nationalists can only be beneficial in themselves. The Liberal Party is, alas!, very far from its libertarian Cobdenite origins. But while it is a confused, middle-of-the-road party, the Liberals are not prepared to go along with the pet collectivist extremes of either the Laborites or the Tories. At least the Liberals will throw some sand in the collectivist machinery of either major party. Even healthier is the rise of the Scottish and Welsh Nationalists, the former increasing their number of seats phenomenally from 2 to 7, amassing over one-fifth of the Scottish vote; while the latter, the Plaid Cymru, gained 2 seats in Parliament over their previous zero. Americans tend to think of all the inhabitants of the British Isles as "English". Nothing could be further from the truth. For centuries, the Scottish and the Welsh, each with a totally separate language and culture, have been the victims of English imperialism and English oppression, and the rise of the Plaid Cymru and the "Scot Nats" presages a dramatic shift toward home rule for these minority nations. Furthermore, while the Scot Nats are hardly champions of the free market, they are at least staunchly opposed to the Labor program for the nationalization of the large new oilfields that have recently been discovered off the North Sea coast of Scotland.

It is characteristic of the growing adherence to the Establishment of Bill Buckley that he gave Heath and the Tories an all-out endorsement before the election. Or else it was a breakdown of his much-vaulted "strategic intelligence." For Buckley explicitly rejected the only political strategy that carries hope for Britain in the foreseeable future: that of the dissident stormy petrel of British politics, Enoch Powell. For Powell, head of the "right wing" of the Tories, refused to stand for reelection to Parliament, and urged his supporters to break the Heath administration by voting Labor. Only in that way, only by turning the Tories out, was there hope for overturning Heath and thereby paving the way for a later ride of Enoch Powell to power. In fact, Powell's defection was responsible for the loss of at least six Tory seats in the West Midlands, the major base of Powell's political support.

Decades of horrific British policies have created a rigid, stratified, and cartellized economy, a set of frozen power blocs integrated with Big Government: namely, Big Business and Big Labor. Even the most cautious and gradualist of English libertarians now admit that only a radical political change can save England. Enoch Powell is the only man on the horizon who could be the sparkplug for such a change. It is true, of course, that for libertarians Enoch Powell has many deficiencies. For

one thing he is an admitted High Tory who believes in the divine right of kings; for another, his immigration policy is the reverse of libertarian. But on the critical issues in these parlous times: on checking the inflationary rise in the money supply, and on scuttling the disastrous price and wage controls, Powell is by far the soundest politician in Britain. A sweep of Enoch Powell into power would hardly be ideal, but it offers the best existing hope for British freedom and survival.   ◘

European Politics —

(Continued From Page 2)

Arab world. Jobert's standing in French public opinion has skyrocketed and he has become a leading contender to succeed to the French presidency. Even the very influential Le Monde, almost never having praised Gaullist attitudes, strongly attacked the American leaders and defended the French position of independence. President Nixon has given dire warnings to the Europeans and threatens to unleash his secret weapon — i.e., he may not visit them this year. The Europeans may emerge from this situation stronger and more independent, which would be a plus for world peace as well as a check on the Nixon administration's taste for super-run-away inflation.   ◘

Libertarianism And Humanist Psychology

By Martin Andrews
Department of Psychology
St. John's University, Minnesota

In the last few years a new movement has grown up in psychology. This movement is variously designated as humanistic psychology, the "human potential" movement, existential psychology, or, perhaps most commonly, the "third force". The phrase "third force" is used to distinguish this brand of psychology from the first two forces, psychoanalysis and behaviorism. This loosely organized group has its own professional society, the Association for Humanistic Psychology, and has, more or less, been given the official seal of approval with the formation of Division 32 of the American Psychological Association, the Division for Humanistic Psychology. There are many different points of view among the various members of the movement, and some of these differences are quite significant, but there do seem to be large areas of agreement among them, in addition to their common opposition to behaviorism and psychoanalysis. Some of the characteristics of this new psychology can be seen in the following partial listing:

1. A belief in man's free will and responsibility
2. An emphasis on experience as the basic datum of psychology
3. The idea that the person is or should be the main concern of psychologists
4. A commitment to the investigation of more meaningful problems than psychology has traditionally dealt with, even if this means a considerable loss of rigor
5. A belief in the moral necessity for the full development of human potential
6. A belief that man has considerable freedom from his past, and that much of his behaviour is determined by his plans and goals for the future
7. A belief in the natural goodness of man
8. The view that man is pre-eminently a social being, and can find fulfillment only through relatedness to others
9. The idea that values should be of great importance to psychologists

I take it as more or less axiomatic that libertarians have a valid interest in the views of psychologists. Since one's views about the proper kind of society are presumably based on one's view of human nature, and human nature is perhaps the chief professional interest of psychologists, it would be remarkable if libertarians, as social philosophers, did not have this interest. In any case, it would seem that libertarians have generally taken a positive view of the third force. A number of California libertarians, report has it, have become involved in the human potential movement. As another evidence of this, I note that the Laissez-faire Books catalog prominently features in its listings works on transactional analysis and gestalt therapy, both typical third force therapies, as well as the major works of Abraham Maslow, the father of the "third force." In light of this interest, and in view of the importance of arriving at a reasonable psychology for any sort of social philosophy, it would perhaps be useful to offer some critical commentary on the humanistic movement.

A real grasp of the meaning of the third force can probably best be gained by a consideration of its historical genesis. As indicated above, this movement arose largely as a reaction against behaviorism and psychoanalysis, and this reaction is intimately related to both its good and its bad points. Since the humanists' objections to behaviorism and psychoanalysis are rather different, it would probably be wise to examine these criticisms separately.

The criticisms directed against the behaviorists by the humanists seem to reduce to two. The first such objection is that behaviorism has trivialized psychology. By its rejection of such "mentalistic" categories as mind, reason, purpose, value, consciousness, and feeling, in the name of a spurious scientific objectivity, the humanists argue, the behaviorists have made impossible the study of any but trivial problems. The malign influence of behaviorism, they say, has forced psychologists to investigate only such phenomena as can be treated objectively, namely such things as what influences the rate at which rats press a bar in a Skinner box. The study of more significant problems, they urge, is greatly needed. The second charge is that behaviorism views man as purely "reactive". That is, behaviorists view all behavior as having its cause in either past or present stimulation. The recognition of man's freedom and spontaneity, the humanists think, is needed in order to get a proper picture of the human person.

It is clear that one could hardly accuse psychoanalysis of being trivial, whatever its other sins may be. The charges against this doctrine, then, assume a somewhat different form. The psychoanalysts, the humanists say, paint a needlessly gloomy picture of human nature and its possibilities. If one might be permitted to caricature the psychoanalytic view of man, one might say that the analysts tend to see man as powerfully driven by anti-social sexual and aggressive needs kept in check only by the forces of repression and the necessities of social life, as a prisoner of his past, doomed to endlessly repeat the same neurotic script throughout his life, and that fundamentally there is very little that can be expected by way of alleviation of this unhappy situation. The humanists' response to this is twofold. First, they assert, this view fails to recognize the potentiality for goodness possessed by mankind. Second, they say, the psychoanalysts make the same mistake the behaviorists do, when they argue that man is a prisoner of his past. This is to fail to realize that man is free and can change himself.

The basic question, of course, is what we are to make of this series of assertions put forth by the humanists. It is clear, I think, that much of what the humanists hold is justified. It seems to me to be unquestionably true that the behaviorists' ruling out of "mentalistic" terms was a great mistake. The reasons for this, though, contrary to what many humanists seem to think, are for the most part scientific, rather than metaphysical or ethical. It is also true, I believe, that the study of values, and the explication of the concept of purpose are essential to any reasonable account of human behavior, just as the humanists assert. It is true, again, that the psychoanalysts' world-view is deeply depressing, at least to anyone who takes it seriously. This, of course, tells us nothing about the truth or falsity of the doctrine. Fortunately, though this is not the place to go into the subject, there is a great deal of evidence that the psychoanalysts were wrong about many things.

It seems to be the case, then, that the humanists have made a number of valid points at the expense of their opponents. Unfortunately, however, there are a number of places where the views of the humanists are open to severe criticism. I will here concentrate on four of them. These are: 1) the humanists' idea of freedom; 2) their influence on psychological thinking; 3) the political implications of some of their doctrines; 4) their utter disregard for the value of privacy.

Turning first to the question of freedom, it would seem to the writer that it is important to make a distinction between political and economic freedom, in the sense of freedom from coercion, and metaphysical freedom, in the sense of freedom of the will. The two concepts are logically independent, and to confuse them, as I believe the humanists frequently do (so do some libertarians), is to risk getting mired in some

(Continued On Page 5)

Humanist Psychology —

(Continued From Page 4)

philosophical quagmires. It is often felt, for example, that it is only on the premise of free will that it makes any sense to speak of responsibility. This would seem to be the reverse of the truth. If an act is truly free, it would seem to imply that it is uncaused or random. It is difficult to see in what sense it is reasonable to assign blame for a random act. It is peculiar to express moral outrage at the outcome of the toss of dice, and illogical to expect censure to affect the next toss. Responsibility, then, is more compatible with determinism than with free will, in the writer's view.

A second, and in many ways more serious, difficulty with the doctrine of free will is that such a doctrine is ultimately inconsistent with any concept of human nature. If human beings operate under no constraints, save those of physical nature, then it is clear that they can make themselves into anything they want, and there is no obvious reason why one such choice should be better than another. Some of the existentially oriented writers seem to have seen this difficulty and more or less faced up to it. Sartre, for example, explicitly states that there is no such thing as human nature, and that we are free to make of ourselves what we will. The concept of the gratuitous, random act occurs in the writings of Gide, for another example. The concept of free will, I believe, is ultimately nihilistic, and therefore incompatible with any vision of social life, libertarian or otherwise. The point to be made here is that the "third force" has a considerable intellectual indebtedness to the existentialists, and are infected, to that extent, with the existentialists' nihilism.

The second point of criticism of the third force is that their influence on psychological thinking has, in many ways, been bad. Because of their objections to the peculiar kind of rigor practiced by the behaviorists, they have all too often thrown out the concept of rigor altogether, and placed the highest value on subjectivity. Subjectivity, to be sure, has its place in science as in all other endeavors, but when one rejects the possibility of some kind of objectivity, there is clearly no way of settling disputes, and truth comes to be measured by intensity of conviction, the dangerousness of which, I assume, needs no elaboration. A related point is that the humanistic psychologists have tended to discourage the kind of analytic thinking that has been characteristic of experimental psychology at its best, in favor of what, for want of a better term, could be called synthetic intuitions. The chief point here is that analytical and rigorous thinking is, when all is said and done, a necessity for the life of the mind.

The humanists, as noted above, tend to believe in the natural goodness of man, his great potential for better things, and his freedom to achieve them. This aspect of humanism seems to be taken largely from the philosophy of Rousseau (as do several other aspects of humanism). The difficulty with a point of view of this type is that it tends to lead to utopian expectations and extreme dissatisfaction with present institutions. Dissatisfaction with present institutions, especially the government, the libertarian would be sure to add, is wholly justified in this age, as in any other that we are aware of, but if all human unhappiness is to be attributed to social institutions, then the justification for violent revolution becomes clear, and the way is opened for all the suffering that this would entail. It is often said that utopianism is a vital part of the human spirit. I can only say that as science fiction or fantasy it is unobjectionable, but as thought, it stinks. Most libertarians, including this one, would favor revolution under some circumstances. However, it is clear to me that I would not support any of the revolutionary movements that seem to have any chance of success today. Ultimately I think the view of Nock and Mencken is a humane one, namely that when men are convinced of the need for liberty, it will be forthcoming with a minimum of bloodshed. This concludes our third point of criticism of humanistic psychology, its encouragement of utopian thinking.

The last point, that of the humanists' lack of regard for privacy, can perhaps best be made by an extract from an article in **Psychology Today** (September, 1969), written by a prominent philosophical psychologist, Sigmund Koch, and entitled, "Psychology cannot be a coherent science." (I would add that I agree with Koch's sentiments on humanistic psychology, but not necessarily with the major point of the article). In this article he discusses attending a symposium conducted by a humanistic psychologist, Paul Bindrim, the originator of "nude marathon group therapy". The extract is as follows:

Bindrim's methods, for the most part, are the standard devices of group therapy. He was enthusiastic at the symposium, however, about a therapeutic intervention of his own inspired coinage that he calls "crotch eyeballing". The crotch, he notes, is the focus of many hang-ups. In particular, three classes: (1) aftermath difficulties of toilet training; (2) masturbation guilts; (3) stresses of adult sexuality. Why not blast all this pathology at once! Thus two group members aid in (as Bindrim says) the "spread-eagling" of a third member and the entire company is instructed to stare unrelentingly and for a good long interval at the offending target area. Each group member is given an opportunity to benefit from this refreshing psychic boost. Scientist that he is, Bindrim is unwilling to make a decisive assessment of the benefits until more data are in. But he is encouraged.

Admittedly, Bindrim's is only one of many approaches in group therapy. But all these methods are based on one fundamental assumption: that total psychic transparency — total self-exposure — has therapeutic and growth-releasing potential . . . Every technique, manipulative gimmick, cherished and wielded by the lovable, shaggy workers in this field is selected for its efficacy to such an end . . .

The human potentialists . . . are saying in effect that a world of private stimulations is unhealthy . . . In no time at all (they) have achieved a conception of human nature so gross as to make behaviorism seem a form of Victorian sentimentality.

Koch, I believe, has made the point about as well as it can be made. It is certainly true that the humanists have concentrated most of their efforts on the development of methods of group therapy, and that the idea of the private person often appears repugnant to them, perhaps even immoral. While I like to look at crotches as well as the next man — indeed my taste for this sort of thing may even exceed the average man's — it seems ridiculous to me to think that a viewing of "Deep Throat", for example, is a powerful therapeutic experience. One thing that can be said about nudity is that it is a great equalizer. As the dean of a great university once said about his faculty, "In their underpants you can't tell them from the students". If you are a great believer in equality, then, perhaps nudity is the proper form of dress for psychotherapy. A related point is that this need to submerge oneself in the mass that seems to be so characteristic of group therapies would seem to be inconsistent with the kind of differentiation among individuals that libertarians presumably regard as a good thing. Again, the view of human nature that seems to be typical of the "third force" can probably be traced back to Rousseau.

At this point a brief summary would seem to be in order. It appears that much of the inspiration for humanistic psychology can be traced to Existentialism and to Rousseau. Thus, the representatives of the "third force" get into trouble when they discuss the nature of freedom. Their influence on psychology has probably been more bad than good. Their belief in the natural goodness of man is surely untenable, and their emphasis on group therapy and total self-disclosure often seems to disguise a desire to get into situations where no social distinctions are made and one can lose one's identity in the mass. I would conclude, then, that Sartre and Rousseau are poor models for the libertarian, and that while the third force has made some valid points, the libertarian would be well advised to shop elsewhere for a psychology.

Ed. Note:
Professor Andrews' welcome article needs, in my view, an important philosophical corrective — one, however, which does not injure the main thrust of his position. The random concept of freedom of the will which he is criticizing is faulty post-Cartesian version. What we need to return to is the classical Aristotelian-Thomist concept of free will as self-determination, and emphasizing the freedom to reason. Particularly welcome is Andrews' critique of the fashionable and massive invasion of individual privacy in the name of "openness" and "humanism." ◻

The laws were most numerous when the State was in a condition of decay.

— Tacitus

Why No Oil Refineries?

One of the most severe indictments of the oil companies in the current crisis is that they have failed to build any new refineries on the East Coast in the last several years. Hence, the oil and gas shortage. On the face of it, this charge is economically ignorant. If there was indeed such a great social demand for new oil refineries, then this demand would have been reflected in high expected profits, and in response the oil companies would have leaped at the chance. The fact that no such onrush took place indicates to the economist that (a) either there was no such demand, or, in this case more likely (b) that the government was right in their doing something to discourage such building.

In early March an event took place which highlights the reasons for the dearth of new refineries. Aristotle Onassis and his Olympic Refineries have been planning to build a new giant $600,000,000 oil refinery on the coast of New Hampshire. Terrific, you say? Surely the good citizens of New Hampshire have welcomed this contribution to aid the energy crisis with open arms and hosannahs? You bet your sweet life they have not. On the contrary, the citizens of New Hampshire have been moving heaven and earth—or rather various levels of government — to prohibit the new refinery. And this month various local town governments have voted to ban a new refinery; furthermore, despite the support for the refinery of conservative Governor Meldrin Thomson, the state legislature has voted to endorse the actions of the localities. And so, a giant and productive new refinery on the East Coast will not be built.

What were the objections? The usual environmentalist crazies were at work. Refineries by definition "deface" the unspoiled earth, mar the governmental beaches, and maybe even injure a few plankton while they're about it. How much longer are we all going to continue to suffer hardship so that the environmentalists can impose their peculiar esthetics on the rest of us by governmental coercion?

And while we're on the subject of the oil industry, we must alert ourselves to a new, horrendous bill introduced into the Senate by Adlai Stevenson (D., Ill.), and Warren Magnuson (D., Wash.) The Stevenson-Magnuson proposed "Consumer Energy Act of 1974", reports **Human Events** (March 16), would do the following:

1) Instead of deregulating natural gas from the clutches of the FPC and thereby end the natural gas shortage in interstate commerce, the bill would extend FPC regulation to cover **intrastate** commerce as well — thereby effectively killing off the natural gas industry.

2) It would extend the same degree of federal regulation to petroleum as it has to natural gas.

3) It would create a socialistic Federal Oil and Gas Corporation, owned by the federal government, which would locate and develop oil and natural gas.

4) It would give power to the FPC to demand any information it wanted from any oil or gas company, and to make it public at its own discretion. But — and here is the zinger — should any owner, agent, or official of such a company "neglect or refuse" to answer any request made to him by the FPC or any of its agents, he would be liable to criminal penalties of a stiff fine and one to two years of imprisonment!

Hey, Liberals, what happened to the Fifth Amendment? What happened to the constitutional prohibition of self-incrimination? And what happened to the usual mushy-headed Liberal attitude toward punishment of crime? What the Liberal attitude apparently boils down to is this: for murderers, rapists, kidnappers, muggers, and bank robbers, a light slap on the wrist and heaps of "understanding" of their psyches and their environments; for productive citizens who sell above controlled prices or who neglect to answer questions directed at them by meddling bureaucrats, not one whit of "understanding", and instead escalation of punishment. How about going all the way and restoring the death penalty only for businessmen who fail to answer questions or who sell above controlled prices? For those who think this question purely a facetious **reductio ad absurdum**, there is all too ample precedent, at least for the punishment meted out to businessmen: Roman Emperor Diocletian, the French Revolution, Chiang kai-Shek, Marshal Ky, and Soviety Russia, which only a few weeks ago executed a dozen people for the "economic crime" of selling in the black market.

How To Deal With Kidnapping

It looks very much as if we are in for a rash of "political" kidnappings, inspired by the evident success of the Symbionese Liberation Army's kidnapping of Patricia Hearst. If we are not to suffer a reign of terror in this country from groups of thugs, we must nip this "movement" in the bud. Basically, there is only one way to do it, as rigorous and even "hard-hearted" as it may seem. And that is for everyone to make up his mind, and to shout it loud and clear well in advance of any such crimes, that no one will collaborate in any way with the kidnappers' demands: no money, no food to the starving masses, no free publicity, no "negotiations", no nothing. If potential kidnappers are put on clear warning from the very start that no demands they make will be satisfied by one iota, then kidnappings will cease before they begin, and the lives of their victims and family will not be shattered. In the long-run, this is the least "hard-hearted" position to take, in addition to clearly being the only one consonant with justice. Evil and crime must never be rewarded.

But isn't this too morally rigorous a position to expect parents to take? Isn't Randolph Hearst's grovelling before the SLA monsters to be expected? Perhaps. But there is surely no need for anyone else besides the parents involved to follow their lead. If Mr. and Mrs. Hearst were not strong enough to avoid succumbing to the SLA outrage, then all the other collaborators involved should have been. In short, none of the friends, relatives, or business associates of Mr. Hearst should have collaborated one inch in providing the ransom money or food; if they had not done so, then the kidnappers would have learned clearly and emphatically that the failure to achieve their demands was not the fault of the Hearst parents. And certainly all future kidnappers would have gotten the message all the more clearly. Even more morally repellent has been the collaboration of

the leftish welfare agencies in supplying the free food, as well as the media in treating the SLA with dignity and respect as some sort of legitimate ideological organization worthy of ever continuing dialogue. What the SLA kidnappers deserve is not dialogue but the business end of a machine gun.

This brings us to the punishment to be meted out to apprehended kidnappers. The U.S. Senate has been sensible and statesmanlike in voting to restore the death penalty for kidnappers who kill their victims. The idea that the death penalty never deters murder is almost self-evident hogwash. The abolition of the death penalty was philosophic left-sentimentality, as well as juridical nonsense. Philosophically, a person who murders another forfeits his own right to life, on the principle that he who deprives others of rights deserves to lose his in proportion. Juridically, to say that the Constitutional prohibition of "cruel and unusual punishment" prohibits the death penalty flies in the face of the common use of that penalty at the time the Constitution was written, and after it was established. No Founding Father issued a protest of alleged unconstitutionality. The Supreme Court argument that the death penalty is now "unusual" is purely a product of the success of left-wing jurists in recent years in stalling and blocking the use of capital punishment. Allow the death penalty to flow freely in cases of murder and the punishment would soon no longer be "unusual."

On the other hand, the Senate acted well in not restoring the previous death penalty for kidnapping per se. Not only does such punishment go beyond the rule of proportionality; it also fails to deter the murder of a victim after he or she has been kidnapped. If passed, the present bill will

(Continued On Page 7)

458

Libertarian Songs — I

No ideological movement has ever gotten anywhere without songs: songs to express their ideology, their joy in the struggle, their hopes and expectations for ultimate victory. And yet the libertarian movement has been singularly unproductive in forging songs of freedom. (Of course, there are precious few songs in general, anymore, and this may have a lot to do with the dearth of songs in the libertarian movement.) At any rate, we hereby begin a series of songs that were composed by members of the old "Circle Bastiat", the tiny group that virtually constituted the entire New York movement during the dark days of the 1950's. In the old ideological tradition set by the IWW at the turn of the century, we took standard songs and composed new words to fit the new mood and ideology.

Note A: the hint of megalomania that permeates most of these songs was deliberate. It was of course on one level amusing and ironic for a literal handful of people, in a seemingly hopeless minority, to talk so confidently of imminent victory. On another level, however, it expressed our fond hopes for the future.

Note B: The "Circle" in these songs refers to our little group; in the present context, "movement" would supply the analogous meaning.

The Battle Hymn of Freedom
(sung to the tune of the "Battle Hymn of the Republic")

O'er these murky, troubled waters shines the Circle's beacon light,
That brilliant guiding beam that draws men daily to the Right,
Oh, its glory is a refuge from the State's inhuman might,
For Anarchy we fight.
Freedom, freedom, blessed freedom (repeat twice)
For Anarchy we fight.
In that free world of tomorrow which now rushes to the fore;
Man shall bow his noble head to neither gods nor caesars more;
And this shall end forever all the State's communal lore,
For all shall know the truth.
Upward, upward go black banners (repeat twice)
For all shall know the truth.
Look up there, Circle brothers, see the black banners unfurled;
How they wave in expectation of a new and better world.
The lines are drawn, the ranks are firm, the challenge has been hurled,
The Circle marches on.
Vict'ry, vict'ry lies before us (repeat twice)
The Circle marches on.
All of freedom's blessed martyrs are here marching by our side,
Ours the spirit, ours the cause for which they smiling bled and died.
With us now they cut the fetters which man's mind and body tied,
Man will at last be free.
Nothing now will ever stop us (repeat twice)
Man will at last be free.
One by one the States are dying, see the age old monsters fall,
As the world resounds in answer to the Circle's trumpet call.
We'll not rest until all States are gone and men are freemen all,
And that day lies at hand.
Onward, onward Circle brothers (repeat twice)
For that day lies at hand.

Libertarian Songs — II

The State
(sung to the tune of "America the Beautiful")

It's yours to right the great wrong done
Ten thousand years ago,
The State, conceived in blood and hate,
Remains our only foe.
Oh, Circle brothers, Circle brothers,
Victory is nigh,
Come, meet your fate, destroy the State,
and raise your banners high.

Libertarian Dinner Club

Back in the winter of 1969, in retrospect the origins of the current movement, our publisher helped to organize a series of libertarian dinners in New York, featuring a speaker and social get-together. The dinners were so successful that we moved on to a libertarian conference in the fall, about which the veil of History may be mercifully draped. At any rate, the dinner club idea fell into the discard. Now, inspired by the growth of the New York movement and the successful, continuing Libertarian Supper Club in Los Angeles, young J. Neil Schulman has organized The Libertarian Circle to revive the old dinner series in New York, in a series which will hopefully gather regularly every month.

The first two dinners have already been scheduled, at the Roast Beef and Brew restaurant, Madison Ave. and 79th St., Manhattan. The first dinner will be on Tuesday evening, April 23rd, with Murray Rothbard speaking on the "Next Economic Crisis"; the second dinner will be on Tuesday, May 21st, with Jerome Tuccille speaking on "Libertarianism and the Future". Price per dinner is $9.95. For information on reservations, write to The Libertarian Circle, 208A Mercer St., New York, N.Y. 10012. ◻

Kidnapping —

(Continued From Page 7)

help greatly in bringing the kidnapping era to a close before it gets underway. But more important is a determination by every person and group in society to give no quarter, and to yield to no demand, of any kidnappers.

On this topic, the farcical nature of the "right-wing" kidnapping is an apt commentary on the current political scene. For a short while it looked as if there were a right-wing terrorist group, the "American Revolutionary Army." dedicated to kidnapping prominent liberals as part of a campaign for a right-wing coup. Yet, in this case, the authorities acted swiftly; the victim was speedily returned to his home and family; the ransom money was promptly recovered; and the existence of the ARA turned out to be a hoax. When will the day arrive when the leftist SLA, which is surely **not** a hoax, is treated with the same efficiency and dispatch? When will the media treat left-wing bandits with the same revulsion and contempt as they treat their real or alleged right-wing counterparts? ◻

"Our purpose is the abolition, not only of all existing States, but of the State itself . . . And what is the State? It is not a thing that can be especially defined by Russia, Germany, Great Britain, or Massachusetts. The State is a principle, a philosophical error in social existence. The State is chaos, rioting under the guise of law, order, and morality. The State is a mob, posited on unscientific premises. We propose to supplant the mob by that true social order which is pivoted on the *sovereignty of individualities* associated for mutual well-being under the law of natural attraction and selection — Liberty."

— Benjamin R. Tucker

"O Freedom, thou queen of Perfection,
   Sweet nurse of the brave and the free,
The choice of our heart's deep election,
   We tender devotion to thee!
With Reason thy consort forever,
   And Justice the law of thy realm,
Thy kingdom shall perish, O never,
   No tyrant thy power shall o'erwhelm!"

— J. William Lloyd

Civil Liberties, Selective Style

How many millions of words have been poured out on behalf of the plight of Soviet Jewry? Surely, countless numbers, especially if we add in the deluge on behalf of Solzhenitsyn and other political prisoners in the Soviet Union. Countless intellectuals, right, left, and center, intellectuals devoted to civil liberties in general as well as those whose devotion seems confined either to Jews or to the inhabitants of the territory east of Leningrad and west of Vladivostok — all these have written, signed full page ads, poured forth their zeal without stint. As well they might.

But it looks very much as if this outpouring and this zeal for civil liberties is curiously selective, even among such staunch civil libertarians as Village Voice columnist Nat Hentoff. For there is one State of all, one State alone whose violations of civil liberties — even of the civil liberties of Jews, if that detail should matter — never call forth any mass deluge of protest. No full page ads attacking its practices appear in the august pages of the New York Times or the Village Voice. The voices of civil libertarians with regard to this State are strangely stilled. We refer, of course, to that "little bastion of democracy" in the Middle East.

Thus, how many words have you read in the Establishment press, the Left press, or the Right press, about two flagrant cases of oppression and political imprisonment recently committed by the State of Israel? Both were against Jewish citizens. One was the case of Uri Davis, well-known Israeli writer and pacifist of long standing. Davis was forced to spend five months in an Israeli prison for the high crime of entering a "military zone" without a government permit. This "military zone" consisted of land which had been expropriated from its Arab owners and then converted by the State of Israel into an all-Jewish settlement from which all Arabs are excluded by law.

And then there is the case of another Jewish citizen of Israel, Rami Linveh. A few months ago Mr. Linveh was sentenced to ten years in prison for the crime of failing to report to the Israeli authorities meeting a Palestinian Arab alleged by the prosecution to be a "foreign agent."

So: Nat Hentoff, Irving Kristol, Max Lerner, et al., where are those protests?   ◘

There is most wrongdoing where there are most laws.
— Arcesilaus (4th century B. C.)

Seven Days In May?? —

(Continued From Page 1)

nonsense, as any competent historian will attest. But is this just historical balderdash born out of delaying tactics? Or is something more sinister involved?

Suppose, as seems more and more likely, the House votes to impeach Mr. Nixon, and the great impeachment trial is launched in the U. S. Senate. At this point, there does not seem to be the two-thirds majority needed to convict in the Senate, but who knows what will happen when the facts pour out at the impeachment trial? Already, Senator James Buckley, in an eloquent speech calling for Nixon's resignation, has virtually pinned the responsibility, and hence the blame, on Nixon for the admitted actions of his top subordinates; does this presage at long, long last, abandonment of Nixon's cause by the Conservatives? Or are they really willing to walk the last mile and go down the tubes politically with Mr. Nixon? Suppose, then, that the Senate does vote Nixon guilty, by a vote just above two-thirds. The chilling speculation is: what happens then?

The general assumption is that Mr. Nixon would at that point, and at last, step down, though of course kicking and snarling as he went. But can we count on that? Suppose that the following happens: Mr. Nixon goes on the air, praises the Congress for performing its task as best it can, but then says that, according to his view of the Constitution, the impeachment vote is unconstitutional because his crimes were not sufficient to warrant the action. Suppose, then, that he refuses to leave the Presidential office. What happens next? Can we really be sure that this will not happen? If we couple the Nixonian claim about the charges being too broad with what Anthony Lewis has called his "L'Etat c'est Moi" attitude and with what we know of his character, then this scenario begins to appear all too realistic.

So: what happens then? Will they, in the marvellous metaphor of Martha Mitchell, "have to drag him out of the White House in chains?" And who will do it? Already, a Village Voice reporter went to several top Pentagon officials and posed for them this hypothetical situation. What would they do? To a man, they gave the now famous "Eichmann answer", that their job in life is to obey all orders of their Commander-in-Chief without question; and they left no doubt that in that situation they would still consider Mr. Nixon as their Commander-in-Chief. So what happens then? Civil War? Backtracking by the Congress? Dragging out in chains? Will we ever be able to rid ourselves of Richard Nixon by constitutional means? Will the American Republic last long enough to be able to celebrate its Bicentennial? If Senator Buckley is worried about a "crisis of the regime", to use his curiously Petainist phrase, there my countrymen would be a crisis indeed.   ◘

First Class

Published Every Month. Subscription Rate: $8.00 Per Year

A Monthly Newsletter

THE
Libertarian Forum

Joseph R. Peden, Publisher

Murray N. Rothbard, Editor

VOLUME VI, NO. 4   APRIL, 1974   US-ISSN0047-4517

FIVE YEARS OLD!

Yes, dear reader, with this issue the **Libertarian Forum** celebrates its fifth anniversary. Anniversaries are traditionally a time for nostalgia and self-congratulations, but I believe that the latter is more justified here than is usually the case.

In the first place, we are spectacularly long-lived for a libertarian publication. Unlike all too many sister publications which have begun with pomp and fireworks and then have quickly gone kerplooey, we began with modest aims, and perhaps for that reason are still around and thriving more than ever. We did not aspire, for example, to become the counter-TIME or counter-**National Review** of the movement, or to provide staff positions for half of the movement.

Secondly, there are few if any ideological magazines — left, right, or center — that do not run on deficits, some of them spectacular. It is a source of pride that the **Libertarian Forum** has never in its history suffered a deficit. We have always either broken even or earned a modest profit, and we have grown steadily over the years to over double the original circulation. Not only that: for such was the rush of advance subscriptions after we announced our coming birth that we have never had to put a nickel of our own money into the magazine.

Thirdly, we have never suffered either from the financial debility or the faction fights that come with over-staffing. We have adhered strictly to individual responsibility and the division of labor, with yours truly in charge of the content and Joe Peden in charge of the business management of the magazine. As a result, we have enjoyed five years of smooth and felicitous harmony. Because of this strictly defined division of labor, the only instance of friction on the **Forum** had no effect on the content of the magazine as a whole. That was when Karl Hess, our original Washington editor, left us after a year because, in his rapid ideological course leftward, he could not remain on a journal which sharply criticized the Black Panthers. But since Karl, was only responsible for his own Washington column, this disagreement could have no effect on the rest of the contents of the **Forum**. Apart from Karl Hess our staff has consisted of two people, period.

Fourth and most important, we have been able to succeed in our aims when founding the magazine. What indeed were those aims? They of course included establishing a continuing libertarian periodical, which was virtually non-existent in early 1969. They included the hope — successful beyond our imaginings — of helping to launch a nationwide libertarian movement, then only a gleam in our and others' eyes. And so we have celebrated and disseminated news and critiques of the movement. But above all we have wanted to provide an outlet for a continuing application of libertarian theory to the social and political events of the day. It is this function that was not only non-existent in 1969, but is still — after the great expansion of the libertarian movement in intervening years — virtually unique to the pages of the **Libertarian Forum**. There have been quite a number of periodicals willing to discourse at great length on "John Galt as Hero", on whether A is or is not always A, or on "Concept and Percept in the Theory of Rational

Bisexuality". But where O where are the journals eager to discuss the energy crisis or Richard Nixon or the latest events in France or the Middle East from the point of view of libertarian analysis? Where else are the applications of libertarian doctrine to current events? I still don't understand why we have no sister publications in this area, but we continue as we started as virtually the only periodical to perform this vital function.

Let us quote at some length from our first editorial in the preview issue of five years ago; apart from the fact that the movement has now become much larger and better organized, the statement of aim is as valid now as it was then:

"The need is acute for far more cohesion and inter-communication in the libertarian movement; in fact, it must become a movement and cease being merely an inchoate collection of diffuse and haphazard personal contacts . . .

"We believe that one of the greatest needs of the movement at this time is for a frequently appearing magazine that could act as a nucleus and communications center for libertarians across the country. We also believe that while many libertarians have thought long and hard about their ideal system, few of them have been able to rise above the merely sectarian exposition of the pure system to engage in a critique of the present state of affairs armed with the libertarian world-view. This kind of 'critique' is not merely 'negative', as many libertarian sectarians believe. For it is the kind of work that it is indispensable if we are ever to achieve victory, if we are ever to get our ideal system off the drawing board and applied to the real world. In order to change the present system we must be able to analyze and explore it, and to see in the concrete how our libertarian view can be applied to such analysis and to the prospects for social change.

"One would think that such a need would be obvious. No movement that has been successful has ever been **without** organs for carrying out this kind of analysis and critique. The key word here is 'successful': for a magazine like **The Libertarian (Forum)** is desperately needed only if we wish to unite theory and action, if we wish not only to elaborate an ideal system but to see how the current system may be transformed into the idea. In short, it is needed **only** if our aim is victory; those who conceive of liberty as only an intellectual parlor game, or as a method for generating investment tips, will, alas, find little here to interest them. But let us hope that **The Libertarian (Forum)** will be able to play a part in inspiring a truly dedicated movement on behalf of liberty."

• • • • • •

To be specific, the **Lib. Forum** had its origin on a rainy automobile trip to Virginia undertaken in January, 1969 by your editor, his wife, and Joe Peden. It was on one of the boring turnpike stretches that Joe Peden first conceived — or at least launched — the idea of the **Lib. Forum**. It didn't take much persuasion to talk me into it. Yours — and my — favorite

(Continued On Page 2)

Five Years Old —

(Continued From Page 1)

magazine was born.

The background was particularly propitious for the new venture. In the first place, Joe and I, without as yet much concrete evidence, had sensed that the libertarian movement was beginning to grow rapidly in New York and throughout the country. In New York, it seemed that — for the first time in over twenty years — the movement was growing beyond the confines of one small living-room. How right we were was demonstrated far beyond our expectations when, on return from the trip, Joe and Jerry Woloz founded the Libertarian Forum dinners, a series of dinners and after-dinner talks among New York libertarians. It was at the first such dinner that the forthcoming launching of the **Lib. Forum** was first publicly announced. Sending out notices to a restricted mailing-list, we all expected about twenty-five guests to show up. When over sixty persons attended this initial dinner, some coming from as far away as Buffalo, Delaware, and South Carolina to attend the affair, it was clear that the movement was growing far more rapidly than we had believed.

At the same time that the movement was beginning to grow, there was a particular dearth of libertarian journalism. In 1965, at a time when the libertarian movement had dwindled almost to nothing from being trapped in a conservative movement that had virtually swallowed it up, Leonard Liggio and myself, as a desperation measure, had founded the three-times yearly journal **Left and Right**. The purpose was to find and mobilize the lingering libertarian elements that had been all but absorbed into the Conservative movement — a movement that had changed spectacularly from the quasi-libertarian movement that it has been from the late 1930's to the mid-1950's (the "Old Right"), to a Bill Buckley-dominated "New Right" that was driving in the profoundly statist and anti-libertarian direction of global war, repression of civil liberties and militarism at home, and a theocratic social philosophy. Leonard and I felt it vital to try to retrieve libertarians from the embrace of the New Right, to differentiate them and split them away from the Right-wing, to try to form a separated and self-conscious movement of our own. Secondly, and as a corollary to the process of weaning away the libertarian movement from the Right-wing, we sought to discover the libertarian elements of the then just emerging New Left and to make common cause with them against the Vietnam War, the draft, and military-industrial bureaucracy. Or, to put it briefly, we wanted to put an end to a situation where the only journal I could find to publish a critique of the deterioration from Old Right to New Right (in 1964) was an obscure Catholic theological quarterly.

Having founded **Left and Right** in 1965, and achieved considerable success in our aims, continuing deficits finally forced us to close its doors in 1968. Besides, we now felt that a periodical more directly oriented to the growing libertarian movement was more sharply necessary. The vacuum in libertarian journalism was accentuated by the collapse, around the same time, of the laissez-faire quarterly published at the University of Chicago, **New Individualist Review**, and of Rampart College's **Rampart Journal**.

But there was also another concrete objective and reason for launching the **Forum** at that particular time. For the Nixon Administration was just beginning, and we could already see the onrush of Conservatives to worship at the new idol of Power. We didn't want libertarians to be caught up once again in the Eisenhower-coddling that had helped to wreck the Old Right in the 1950's. And so we conceived it to be one of our vital functions to expose and attack the new Nixon Administration: how important such a task was even we did not know at the time.

And so, ever since April 1969, first twice and then once every month — though sometimes late — we have proceeded on our allotted tasks. Even in our preview issue, we began our ceaseless criticisms of the then new Nixon Administration:

"Changeovers in Administration are always a disheartening time for any thoughtful observer of the political scene. The volume of treacle and pap rises to the heavens, as the wit and wisdom and the high statesmanship of both the outgoing and incoming rascals are trumpeted across the land. But this year things are even worse than ever. First we had to suffer the apotheosis of Lyndon Baines Johnson, before last November the most universally reviled President of modern times; but after November, suddenly lovable and wise. And now Richard Nixon has had his sharp edges dissolved and his whole Person made diffuse and mellow; he too has become uniquely lovable to all. How much longer must we suffer this tripe? It is bad enough that we have to live under a despotic government; must we also have our intelligence systematically defiled?"

In our first, April 1, 1969 issue, we warned of the ascendancy in the new Administration of Dr. Arthur F. Burns, "The Scientific Imperial Counsellor". We noted that, despite his powerful government post, Burns still thought of himself as simply a scientific technician, in the service of society: "I'm not interested in power and influence, I'm interested in doing a job." "Thus," we commented, "Burns has become almost the caricature of modern American social science: a group of disciplines swarming with supposedly value-free technicians, self-proclaimed non-ideological workmen simply 'doing a job' in service to their masters of the State apparatus: that is, to their military-political-industrial overlords. For their 'scientific' and 'value-free' outlook turns out to be simply marginal wheeling and maneuvering within the broad frames of reference set by the American status quo . . ."

We then noted that — with high irony in the light of our present hindsight — Arthur Burns disclosed to **Business Week** that he felt his major task to be something spectacularly non-value-free: "For, Burns opines, the really important problem is that 'a great many of our citizens have lost faith in our basic institutions . . . They have lost faith in the processes of the government itself.' 'The President keeps scratching his head,' Burns goes on, 'and I as his adviser keep scratching my head — trying to know how to build new institutions . . . to restore faith in government.' "

To "restore faith in government!" We then concluded our editorial:

"So that is what our new imperial Counsellor is up to. The aggressively 'scientific' statistician has become our purported faith-healer, our evangelical Witch Doctor, who has come to restore our faith in that monster Idol, the State. Let us hereby resolve, everyone, one and all, that Arthur is not going to get away with it.

"But soft, we must guard our flank, for there is a host of so-called 'libertarians' and free-market advocates who swear up and down that Arthur Burns is God's gift to a free-market economy. Which says a great deal about the quality of their devotion to liberty, as compared to their evident devotion to Power."

No sooner had we been fairly launched, then we were able to play a major role in what is now the almost legendary beginning of the organized libertarian movement of today: the libertarian split from YAF in August 1969 at St. Louis. In our August 15 issue we wrote "Listen, YAF", urging the strong libertarian minority within YAF to break away from antithetical conservatism and to break free into a new, separated, and self-conscious libertarian movement. Our small group of "radical libertarians" took thousands of extra copies of the "Listen, YAF" statement and bombarded the YAF delegates with the message. That, plus Karl Hess's personal speech-making, and the hysterical overreaction of the YAF trads at one of our anarcho-capitalists burning (a facsimile of) his draft card on the floor of the convention, effected the great split which formed the modern movement. Jerry Tuccille's exultant report on the YAF split, "Report from St. Louis: The Revolution Comes to YAF", in our Sept. 15 issue, later reprinted in the first book of the new libertarian movement, Tuccille's **Radical Libertarianism**, was to become the cherished and almost mythic account of the birth of the new movement.

The movement having grown spectacularly during the year, we in New York figured that the times were ripe for a Libertarian Conference, and issued a call for one over the Columbus Day weekend. The disasters as well as the triumphs of that conference were duly recorded in our November 1 issue, in what I must say was a strikingly honest piece of reporting in a world where ideological movements generally feel constrained to report their advances and to hide their setbacks. It was at that point that I realized that the necessary attacks on "right-wing deviationism" within the movement (devotion to YAF, an interventionist foreign policy, U. S. militarism) had left a weakness on our left flank, with the result that many of our people, especially in the New York-Washington area, had gone over to "ultra-left adventurism" in tactics and even communism in basic social philosophy. This Left tendency was fed by the final burst of left-adventurism during that winter of the expiring of the New Left in random violence. Consequently, we devoted much of the following year to a continuing attack on the Left tendency, finally succeeding, I believe, in isolating that tendency and separating it

(Continued On Page 3)

FLP Convention: One Step Forward, One Step Back

They tell me that the **other** Libertarian Parties across the country, including the overall national party, work more or less like clockwork, that they are smoothly functioning and sensible organizations, that factions are at a minimum and that the Real People are firmly in control, with the lunatic fringe confined strictly to the fringe. Oh happy day! So what have **they** done right, and where has New York gone wrong? What we in New York badly need is a spiritual CARE package of advice from our sister parties.

It is a measure of the state of the Free Libertarian Party of New York that our marathon annual convention (March 29-31) was scarcely enough to finish the Party business. This despite a preceding Special Convention at which we wrangled over the party logo and chose delegates to the National Convention in Dallas in June, and despite the fact that the Convention began every morning promptly at 10:00 A. M. and lasted through special caucuses and post-mortems until after the bars closed at 3:00 A. M. Yet we concluded with no resolutions on issues and no platform, these being put back to yet **another** mini-convention at the end of April. Three conventions in two months begins to resemble the unfortunate and frenetic Peace and Freedom Party of 1968, which reached a crescendo of almost continuous conventioneering before its rapid demise.

The FLP had emerged the previous April from its founding convention with a superb statement of principles and with a remarkably intelligent and dedicated set of leaders over the embryonic internal Party structure. The accomplishment of the FLP under this leadership in 1973 was staggering: founding the party, maintaining and advancing it as a vital force with limited resources, and running a remarkably successful mayoralty campaign in New York City. For this dazzling success the best elements of this leadership were rewarded with repudiation at the 1974 convention. Internally, the FLP structure is now a shambles. Yet, the convention cannot be set down as an unmitigated disaster, because almost miraculously out of the rubble came an excellent slate of candidates for the 1974 elections in New York State. Whether the FLP can long continue with an internal party mess joined to fine prospects for "external" campaigning is problematic: but right now, all is not lost. Prospects for the future are a mixed bag.

• • • • • • • •

"The mob is easily led and may be moved by the smallest force, so that its agitations have a wonderful resemblance to those of the sea." — Polybius.

"Every one that was in distress, and every one that was in debt, and every one that was discontented, gathered themselves unto him; and he became a captain over them." — I Samuel XXII, 2.

"Calumniate! Calumniate! Some of it will always stick." — Beaumarchais.

"No one ever went broke underestimating the intelligence of the American people." — H. L. Mencken.

What went wrong? Why was virtue rewarded with defeat? Such questions can never receive exact answers, but the best estimate may be encapsulated in the above four quotations. Part of the answer is wrapped up, also, in the question of time and energy available. The FLP leadership were almost all Real People, i.e. people who work in the world, who have jobs, whose grip on reality is of a high order. (In another sense, the question: "What or who are the Real People?" may be answered in Louis Armstrong's famous reply to the question: "what is jazz?": "If you have to ask, you won't know the answer.") Being busy and productive, the leadership had its hands full in running campaigns, and in keeping party affairs going; it did not have the time to engage in inner party squabbles, to hold the hands of those craving for attention, or to answer personal calumny that seemed to be ridiculous on its face — and which, so they thought, would fall of its own lack of weight. In short, it did not have the time to organize a "power" base or structure within the party. Looked at another way, the leadership put its trust in the innate intelligence and good sense of the FLP rank-and-file. There was its fatal error.

While it was thus busy attending brilliantly to important matters, the leadership of the FLP left a "power vacuum" within the party that others hastened to begin to fill. Malcontents, **Luftmenschen**, "people of the air and wind", people with nothing better to do, began to gather together, to plan to seize power within the party. Malcontents — even of widely disparate views — found each other in a common cause to repudiate those in power and to substitute themselves. And certainly a vital part of this coalescing of forces was envy: envy of the manifest competence and intelligence of the leadership. It was, of course, ever thus: in the words of Thomas Middleton (our fifth quote),

"If on the sudden he begins to rise:
No man that lives can count his enemies."

Three major groups came together in what the Marxists would call this "unprincipled coalition." One was the Radical Caucus, which pushed the manifestly anti-libertarian and egalitarian idea that all party structure is evil, that all leadership is coercive and un-libertarian, and that true anarchism requires an abandonment of leadership and the division of labor within the Party on behalf of a participatory democracy in which everyone votes on virtually every decision. The Radical Caucus raised the cry of "decentralization", forgetting that decentralization is only a sound policy in the area of government, precisely because we want government to be as ineffective, as limited and as powerless as possible. If we want any sort of effective libertarian organization, including a Libertarian Party, on the other hand, pushing for decentralization as a supposedly moral issue is simply madness. The only RC member who saw this clearly was its charismatic founder, Samuel Konkin, who explicitly avowed that he was pushing decentralization precisely in order to destroy the Libertarian Party. Yet, even though he made no bones about his objective, the other RC members somehow overlooked Konkin's stated

(Continued On Page 4)

Five Years Old —

(Continued From Page 2)

from the mainstream of the libertarian movement.

That separation was compounded by the wave of publicity, and the resulting accelerated growth, given to the libertarian movement in January and February of 1971. For if the August 1969 YAF convention was the birth of the modern movement, it was the events of early 1971 that catapulted it into nationwide publicity and thereby fed its accelerated growth. If, in short, 1969 was the beginning, early 1971 was the "takeoff", a launching and an acceleration that continues unto the present day. (This launching was celebrated in the **Lib. Forum** in "Takeoff", Feb. 1971 and "Takeoff II", March 1971 issues.) The continuing nationwide publicity began with the article by Stan Lehr and Lou Rossetto, "The New Right Credo — Libertarianism", in the New York **Sunday Times Magazine** section of January 10: Lehr and Rossetto had been discovered by the **Times** the previous fall as heads of a Columbia University group that had been called "libertarian" supporters of Buckley for Senate. After that came articles in the highly influential New York **Times** Op-Ed page by Jerry Tuccille and myself, with an attack by Bill Buckley; and the movement was off to the races.

• • • • • • • •

We stand today at the threshhold of great new growth for the libertarian movement, and for the spread of the ideas of liberty throughout the country and indeed across the seas as well (**pace** the recent spectacular growth of libertarian-type parties in Norway and Denmark.) That growth will be further fueled by the accelerated inflation and the rest of the economic and social messes that statism will be getting us into. As in the past, the **Lib.** Forum stands ready to record and analyze these developments, and to be, as before, the shield of the valiant and the scourge of the evildoer. And so, to our long-suffering readers: Happy Fifth Anniversary!   ◘

FLP Convention —

(Continued From Page 3)

goals and adopted decentralism as a moral imperative for the party.

Why was Konkin out to wreck the FLP from within? Because he believed, along with LeFevrians and many other anarchists, that any political party whatever is per se aggressive and part of the State apparatus. Where Konkin differed from his colleagues, of course, is that they believed that the moral course was to have nothing to do with the LP, or to attack it from the outside. Employing demagogy from within was not their style. Day after day, then, in meetings and in the pages of his New Libertarian Notes, Konkin hammered away at the FLP leadership, denouncing them as the "Partyarchy", and as crypto-archists. Since the "Partyarchy" treated these charges as manifestly absurd, they went unanswered, and the charges, however absurd, began to stick.

The second bloc in the upsurge of the nihilist coalition was the Constitutional Coalition, formed by Howard S. Katz, who had previously abandoned a career as investment counselor to be a "professional libertarian writer." In the FLP, probably alone among the state parties, the believers in limited government (the "minarchists") are in a minority, since both the RC and the Partyarchy were largely anarchists. Katz was thereby able to appeal to the disaffected minarchists in the party. Remarkably, the supposed polar extremes — the Katz clique, and the Radical Caucus — found themselves in close emotional and organizational affinity in their joint malcontent. Katz, too, was a radical decentralist, at least when others were doing the centralizing; thereby the Katz clique took on the certainly unique posture of being at one and the same time pro-statist in content and anti-party-structure in form. Of the four possible permutations: pro-structure anarchist, anti-structure anarchist, pro-structure archist, and anti-structure archist, the latter Katzite position is certainly, whatever else one may say about it, the most bizarre.

Katz's style was to bombard FLP members, day in and day out, with lengthy letters attacking his enemies and setting forth his own position. Presumably he had nothing better to do with his time. Katz employed two major tactics. One was to find a Demon-figure and to hammer away, day after day, with personal attacks upon him. He found that figure in Gary Greenberg, manager of the Youngstein campaign, and who was also the major theoretician and strategist of the "centralist" or pro-structure wing of the leadership. Greenberg, for example, had concluded that the FLP was hamstrung by its excessively decentralized structure; not having any platform or resolutions, no one in the FLP leadership was empowered to make statements for the party, to issue press releases on vital issues of the day on its behalf, or to commit party funds to those ends. Greenberg therefore called for remedying this lack, for making the FLP effective by changing the by-laws to permit the State Chairman to make public statements on behalf of the party if they met with the approval of 2/3 of the State Committee. This sensible proposal, coupled with Greenberg's being an easy visible target of attacks as a dedicated and highly effective campaign manager and as a person who does not suffer fools gladly, led to an unremitting campaign of personal calumny waged against him by Katz and by others in the party.

If one of Katz's major tactics was to denounce Greenberg personally as morally evil and as a luster after power, his other tactic was to strike a pose as the moral conscience of the FLP. Greenberg and the rest of the Partyarchy were immoral pragmatists; the Radical Caucus, while lovable and moral, were sectarian and ineffective; only Katz stood aloft, a fuser of "soul" and body, an integrator of morality and practical effectiveness. Again, treating this pose as manifest nonsense, the leadership spent little time in rebutting the endless sermons sent through the mails by the Rev. Katz. Clearly, another big mistake.

The third group of malcontents were various members from outlying districts who felt that not enough attention was paid to their particular campaigns. Manhattan, in short, was tyrannizing over neglected Poughkeepsie where the real action lay. The Poughkeepsie bloc was led by Sanford Cohen, running for Congress from the area, who was euphemistically described by his campaign manager as "hard driving."

The combustible ingredients were there, and they came together at the 1974 convention. Even so, however, the nihilist coalition might not have won were it not for a basic split within the leadership itself. For the leadership too was divided on the vexed "centralism" question. In the

"hard nosed" camp were: Gary Greenberg; Fran Youngstein, the superb mayoralty candidate; Howard Rich, a young businessman who served as a Vice Chairman of the party and as indefatigable leader of fund-raising and petition drives in the campaign; Leland Schubert; and the editor of the Lib. Forum. The "soft", middle-of-the road, quasi-decentralist camp was led by Andrea Millen, the highly effective State Chairwoman of the FLP; and it included Raymond Strong, mathematician and the other Vice Chairman of the party, and Secretary Michael Nichols. A unified opposition and a divided leadership had to spell defeat.

The convention itself was wild, woolly, and often bizarre. Two hours were consumed in wrangling over the party logo. Finally, the "open hand" won out over the "Libersign." The "furthest-out" point of the convention came when young Michael Maslow, leader of the small "ultra" wing of the Radical Caucus, exuberantly and seriously proposed that the party logo consist of the Jewish Star of David with a swastika inside, thus presumably integrating the great Nazi and Jewish traditions. It was a measure of the convention that it was surprising that enough good sense remained to shout down the Maslow proposal. The high point came when, at the very end of the convention, the endorsement of candidates was nearing its close. One delegate then moved to rescind all previous endorsements in order to provide sexual and ethnic balance to the ticket. To which another exasperated delegate replied: "What this party needs is not ethnic balance but mental balance!"

The chairman-as-spokesman proposal went down to resounding defeat, by something like 35 to 12, backed as it was by only the hard-nosed wing of the party. Considering the mood of the convention, the vote was scarcely surprising. The big fight came the next day, Sunday, over the elections for party officers and the State Committee at Large. Gary Greenberg, as the focal target of the nihilist coalition, prudently decided not to run for any office whatever; a wise decision, but it meant that Katz and the RC had accomplished their purpose in driving him out of any leadership in the party. Howie Rich also decided not to run for party office. The Partyarchy, including both the "moderate" and what we must unfortunately, for labelling purposes, call the "right wing", agreed on a joint slate: for Chairman, Raymond Strong, a Millen disciple; for Vice-Chairmen, Fran Youngstein (right) and Mike Nichols (moderate); for secretary, Lee Schubert (right); for treasurer, Dolores Grande (moderate). The "left" (again, for want of a better term), ran Bill Lawry against Strong. With Sam Konkin, his work accomplished, on the way toward leaving the FLP altogether, Lawry had become head of the Radical Caucus. The united Right and Center managed to win a handy victory for Strong by a vote of 33 to 20, but Lawry was a harbinger of later events in accumulating the votes of the entire Nihilist Coalition: the Radical Caucus, the Katz clique, and the Cohen-Poughkeepsie forces.

The crucial vote then came on the two slots for Vice-Chairmen. The Left again ran Bill Lawry as well as Howie Katz; since there was general agreement on the moderate Nichols, the real fight was between Lawry and Youngstein. Incredibly, Youngstein was defeated — a substantive and symbolic victory for the nihilists of major proportions. Since Fran Youngstein almost manifestly deserved the post, and since the vote also amounted to a repudiation of the great mayoralty campaign, this vote amounted to a veritable Night of the Long Knives. The insult to Fran Youngstein was further compounded and made even more unbelievable by the fact that Katz tied Youngstein for third and fourth place in the voting. The long and persistent campaign of absurdities and defamations was, mirabile dictu, paying off. The votes were: Nichols 29, Lawry 28, Youngstein, 25, and Katz 25.

But more was yet to come. Next came elections for the posts of 5 State Committeemen at Large (Schubert and Grande ran unopposed.) Twelve entries began the complex voting procedure. Again, the result was a smashing victory for the Left, which won three of the five seats; the others went to Andrea Millen (the leader in the voting), and, yes, Fran Youngstein, who rejected the advice of some of her militant supporters to withdraw her sanction from the proceedings by not running for a State Committee post. The important point here, however, is that despite impassioned pleas by Millen and Strong to put at least one "rightist" on the State Committee and thus lend a bit of balance to that body, Fran picked up only three more votes in the State Committee balloting. As a symbolic and moral gesture to express our intense disapproval of the rebuff to Youngstein, some of us (Rich, Greenberg, and myself) organized a bullet vote for Youngstein with four abstentions. The bullet-vote movement, in a bit of fresh air at the convention, managed to

(Continued On Page 5)

The Mysterious World Of The CLA

We have just received a press release from Miss Elizabeth Keathley, who describes herself as an "Anarchist Feminist Writer", and as a "spokesperson for the California Libertarian Alliance", announcing her candidacy for the nomination for governor of California on the Peace and Freedom Party ticket. This is to be a primary race against one or more of what she concedes to be "socialist" candidates.

We must say that we are bemused. The California Libertarian Alliance, along with the Society for Individual Liberty, emerged as the result of the famous August 1969 split of libertarians from YAF. The "Libertarian Alliance" concept has always pushed the following: direct action of some sort as opposed to political action, an alliance of all wings of libertarians in such action, and (implicitly) a counter-culture lifestyle. In practice, the latter two motifs have led to stress on unity only with left-wing anarchists. Apparently, unity with such middle-class minarchists as John

Hospers doesn't carry the emotional satisfaction sought by the Alliance movement.

In the 1960's, alliance with the Left on such issues as Vietnam and the draft made a lot of sense; in the 1970's, alliance with conservatives on the crucial free-market economic issues makes an equal amount of sense. But in neither epoch does an alliance with left-wing anarchists make any sense at all. Left-wing anarchists (a) are befuddled of intellect to the point of mindlessness; (b) are emotionally and ideologically opposed more to private property and the free market than they are to coercion; and (c) their counter-culture lifestyle and emotional hostility to jobs and careers turn off not only the middle class but almost everyone else as well. Hence, the left-wing anarchists have no social leverage whatever; in fact, their social leverage is negative. One left-wing anarchist at

(Continued On Page 6)

FLP Convention —

(Continued From Page 4)

accumulate eight votes in only a few minutes of politicking.

Of the ten members of the new State Committee, the ideological breakdown may be set forth as follows:

Left-Nihilists: Lawry (Radical Caucus), Katz (Katz clique), Charles Blood (Katz clique), Ellen Davis (Cohen-Poughkeepsie) — 4 votes.

Moderate-Millenites: Millen, Nichols, Grande, Strong — 4 votes.

Rightists: Youngstein, Schubert — 2 votes.

There is a strong possibility that the new County organizations will later be allowed representatives on the State Committee. In that case, the Left may well take over full control, what with prospective representatives from Poughkeepsie, Queens, Brooklyn, and Suffolk.

Meanwhile, while all this was going on, the other, quieter drama was in trying to run a full slate of candidates in the 1974 elections. Particularly important was running a strong candidate for governor, since the FLP, to win a permanent spot on the ballot, must gain 50,000 votes in the gubernatorial race. Fortunately, our old **Forum** contributor Jerome Tuccille was induced to shift from the Senate to the Governor race; Tuccille's campaign manager will be the sound thinker and strategist Lee Schubert, who is also running for Attorney-General. For U. S. Senate, the Party endorsed Percy L. Greaves, Jr., veteran Republican politician and a distinguished free-market follower of Ludwig von Mises; the endorsement was a heroic act of rising above petty sectarianism to choose a man who will stress the vital economic issues of this era, and who is also a sound libertarian on civil liberties issues and a veteran isolationist in foreign policy. The heroic good sense came in endorsing a man who is not an anarchist, but who is a libertarian on all the crucial political issues of our time. How come such good sense from delegates who had, only hours before, shown a disposition to be petty, sectarian, and to tear up the pea patch in almost professional acts of troublemaking? Even the Radical Caucus and the Katz clique (with the exception, of course, of Katz himself) voted to endorse Percy Greaves. How come? Who knows? Perhaps it was good sense surfacing at last; perhaps it was a desire not to alienate the right-wing permanently and irrevocably. Furthermore, the Greaves race will be fortunate in having the veteran Republican politician and libertarian Gerry Cullen of Buffalo as campaign manager.

The other candidates on the state ticket also come from the sensible wing of the party: Louis Sicilia of Manhattan for Lieutenant Governor; Dr. Robert Flanzer of Brooklyn for Comptroller; and the aforesaid Lee Schubert for Attorney-General.

Not only were Tuccille, Greaves and the others endorsed virtually unanimously, but the convention was stirred to great enthusiasm by the rousing acceptance speeches of Greaves and Tuccille. Running a largely "middle-class" oriented campaign, furthermore, the ticket has a good chance of picking up disaffected Conservative Party votes in New York, disaffected from the Conservative endorsement of Republican hack Malcolm Wilson for Governor, and its apparent decision to put up an unknown patsy against the hated Jacob Javits. We may well have a good chance for the 50,000 votes!

In reciting the good points of the convention, we should not overlook the beautiful keynote address of Roger MacBride, our electoral voter from Virginia in 1972. MacBride linked libertarians with the radical wing — the Sam Adamses, the Tom Paines — of the American Revolution, which he properly called the "first libertarian revolution." It was up to us, he declared, to make the second such "revolution". Just as Patrick Henry exclaimed, upon the signing of the Declaration of Independence, that "we are no longer Virginians but Americans", so, Roger declared, the result of the "second libertarian revolution" will be to declare that "we are no longer Americans, or Britons, but libertarians." MacBride for President in '76?!

The lesson for the sensible folk in the FLP emerges clearly from the mixed results of the Convention: the internal structure of the party, already weak, is now, and at least for the coming year, hopeless. The only hope there lies in long-range, patient organization and internal re-education within the party, the neglect of which led directly to the present shambles. But even last year, the party structure, hobbled as it was, was unimportant: the **real** action, the chance at educating the "outside world" which is, after all, our real purpose, lies with the candidates in a campaign. And we have, once again — as in previous years — an excellent slate of candidates to concentrate on.

All this leads, also, to some basic philosophical reflections on membership organizations **per se**. The market works, and works beautifully. And so do business firms within the market, where individual employers and employees contract for pay for the performance of certain tasks. There is no nonsense there about voting; there is a minimum faction fighting or waste of energy in trying to win majority consensus for every decision. Membership organizations with voting power are inherently wasteful and ineffective, especially since the assets of the organization are communally owned, with each member having one vote over the communal assets. Similarly, it is no accident that producers' cooperatives, business firms with each worker having one vote over communally owned assets, have always and without exception been outcompeted in the free market by individually owned or corporate-owned firms. (In the latter, the only voting is **per share** voting by the stockholders in proportion to their ownership of assets.) Individually owned firms; partnerships; corporations, all work; voting cooperatives do not. Legally, there is no way to form a political party on a non-communal structure, on a structure that would not be subject to upheavals against the mighty principles of individual responsibility and the division of labor. The best that can be done with political parties is to try to inject as much individual responsibility and division of labor, as little participatory democracy, as possible and as necessary for efficiency.

But while the basic structure of political parties cannot be changed, non-party organizations can. It is possible to establish activist libertarian organizations that don't mess with participatory egalitarianism. (Sam Konkin, for example, has now established his own New Libertarian Alliance which is totally subject to his personal control. No nonsense about "decentralization" there!) May it not be possible for a libertarian organization to be formed, nationwide, with no nonsense about voting, with professional, fulltime paid organizers that can create a mighty, mass activist organization of libertarians? We can only hope.   ◻

Phillip H. Willkie, RIP

I see by the papers that Phil Willkie is dead, at the age of 54, in his home town of Rushville, Indiana. I knew Phil in the years just after World War II, when he was going to Columbia Law School and I was a graduate student there.

Phil was a leader in the Social Democratic wing of the American Veterans Committee, a short-lived leftish veterans group formed to offset the "reactionary" American Legion and Veterans of Foreign Wars. He and others in that wing were locked in struggle with the Communists and their allies, who formed the left-wing of the AVC. About that particular struggle I couldn't care less, then or now. But Phil Willkie was an interesting character. Here he was, beginning a law career as the only son of a man who had been catapulted to the Republican Presidential nomination only half a dozen years or so earlier — in as bizarre a nomination as we might ever hope to see in America. Wendell Willkie had been a literal public unknown a few short months before the nomination, an obscure utility magnate with no political experience whatsoever and even a Democratic party registration. Yet the powerful Eastern Establishment bankers and industrialists who financed the Republican party and who were intensely eager to enter World War II, were then bereft of a Presidential nominee: for the leading candidates, Robert A. Taft and Thomas E. Dewey, were at that time both isolationists and opponents of American entry into the war (Dewey was later, under the aegis of the Rockefeller-controlled Chase National Bank, to see the light.) And so the Eastern Establishment, using every dirty trick in the book and coining some new ones of their own, put across this unknown on the Republican convention. But one thing they did know about Willkie: he could be trusted to support the Roosevelt drive toward war. Which he did not only then but during the war, when he wrote an idiotic if highly touted little book called **One World**. But there is no question about the fact that Wendell Willkie looked like a President, with his leonine head and rugged good looks; also he was, indeed, an authentic Hoosier and could therefore be put across as a good Middle American.

And so here was Phil Willkie, much paler but otherwise looking remarkably like his old man, large head and all. Never have I met a man who was more purely a political animal, his every waking thought the staking out of a political career which he hoped, hoped, hoped would bring him to the Presidency. His leadership in the AVC was to be the opening gun of a campaign to inherit his father's presumed leadership of the liberal internationalist wing of the Republican party. Phil even had, tagging along with him at all times, a self-appointed campaign manager and political adviser, a skinny kid eager to rise to the top along with his charge. And so the two of them would sit, hour after hour, plotting the measured drive to the brass ring. There was a lot of pathos about the whole business, even in those days. Wendell had never had any true base of support in the party, and so there was only the father's name to inherit, and that name was bound to grow more shadowy over the years. Who knows of Wendell Willkie now? And then there was the fearful fate of the young Roosevelts, uppermost in Phil's mind at the time: how to avoid their laughable role as jackanapes? I remember that at one point the kid adviser solemnly advised Phil to cultivate support among the conservative stalwarts of the Republican party by telling dirty jokes — in private, of course — about Eleanor Roosevelt. I don't remember Phil's response, but I think he viewed it as a good idea.

I never saw Phil Willkie since those Columbia days, but once in a while I would see a little squib about Phil's being a state legislator in Indiana. And now I will never know whether his remarkably restless and driven soul was able to make peace with the fact that he would clearly never catch that brass ring: not even State Senator much less President of the United States. I am sorry for Phil, though I must admit not for the rest of the country, that he never made it in politics; whether or not he found contentment in his life in Rushville, I hope that his soul will rest in peace.

Mysterious World Of CLA —

(Continued From Page 5)

libertarian gatherings will alienate two or more regular people from the libertarian ranks. Alliance with left-wing anarchists is therefore at all times pointless; if we want to read rousing anti-State passages from Bakunin, we don't need these people to show us the way. Furthermore, to top it off, the sort of rootless **Luftmenschen** who enjoy close quarters with left-wing anarchists are also the sort of people for whom left egalitarianism seems to exert a fatal attraction. The complete leftward drift of the Hunter College libertarian "festivals" in New York is only the most recent example of the inherent failure of the Alliance concept.

A leading feature of the Alliance idea was always direct rather than political action. Which makes particularly puzzling the entry in force of the California Libertarian Alliance (CLA) into the Peace and Freedom Party. Why in blazes the Peace and Freedom Party (PFP) rather than the Libertarian Party, which is particularly strong in California? Does the CLA feel closer to the admitted socialists in control of the PFP than they do to the LP? If so, then why? Those numerous libertarians who denounce all political action as sanctioning the State have a cogent, if in our view an erroneous, position. But if one **does** believe in political action, then why for heaven's sake the Peace and Freedom Party? Even the idea of penetrating a **major** party in force, Democrat or Republican, makes a certain amount of sense. But the Peace and Freedom Party? The actions of the CLA passeth understanding. Could it be the emotional attraction of a counter-culture haven? Let us hope not.

Joining the PFP was a cogent position in 1968, when Vietnam and the draft were the critical issues, and when no Libertarian Party was in existence. But now? For us in New York, mention of the PFP is like an unwelcome voice from the past. The PFP, though a small party in New York (it had considerably fewer members than the Free Libertarian Party has today), was faction-ridden to the point of rapid demise. When launched in early 1968, it had no platform or socialist guidelines; it had only a two-point statement of principles to which every party member had to subscribe: the first was an innocuous plank about every individual and group controlling their own lives, to which even Richard Nixon could have adhered; the second was a call for immediate withdrawal from Vietnam. It soon became apparent that the PFP, both in New York, and in California and in points in between, was under the total working control of the Draperite wing of the Trotskyite movement, that wing owing allegiance to one Hal Draper, a librarian at Berkeley. Although there were only a few hundred Draperites throughout the country, organized into the Independent Socialist League (now grandiosely called the International Socialists), every Draperite had been sent into the PFP and had early won all the positions of power, including all the paid organizing posts within and between each state. The Draperite straw boss of the New York party was one Sy Landy, and the Draperites, anxious for "minorities" within the party, had acquired Chicano cachet by booming the mysterious, charismatic figure of one Carlos Aponte as national organizer. In New York, the Draperites were able to keep control by securing the support of left-wing anarchists and assorted hippies and "artists". Before the year was out, the New York party had died a mercifully swift death.

Right now, the Peace and Freedom Party is confined to its original California base. Whether the Draperites are still in control we know not, though it appears from Miss Keathley's statement that socialists of one sort or another are still running the show. On the national scene, the PFP certainly has no future; it is an unwanted relic of the past, even on the Left. Why should libertarians get themselves tied to a dead end, and a socialist dead end to boot?

In all ages, whatever the form and name of government, be it monarchy, republic or democracy, an oligarchy lurks behind the facade.

Sir Ronald Syme in **The Roman Revolution**

Arts And Movies

By Mr. First Nighter

The Oscars. Most of the comment on the Oscars has been devoted to the always boring, bumbling, but somehow lovable Academy Awards dinner that ran an hour over on nationwide television. Far more important, however, was the content of the awards themselves, and in particular the titanic struggle that was waged between **The Sting** and **The Exorcist** for Academy honors.

The Sting, directed by George Roy Hill, was a charming, brilliantly directed, suspenseful, richly textured comedy about two lovable con-men and the con they pulled during the 1930's on a leading gangster. It embodied the best of Old Culture film-making. **The Exorcist,** on the other hand, was the embodiment of all that is sick and degenerate in modern culture, pandering to the fashionable cult of the occult, to morbidity and irrationality, and to Pop religion at its most decayed. Particularly sickening, furthermore, was the central point of the film: the swinish degradation of a young girl. Where were the protests of the women's libbers? The roping in of a spate of Jesuits as technical advisers secured the mass audience, defused the otherwise expected opposition of church groups, and gained a family rating when Triple X would have been a more cogent label. The thumping repudiation of this Friedkin-Blatty swill by the Academy members was a welcome sign that health still exists in American culture and in the film industry. This year's Oscar award therefore had a special, and an exhilirating, significance.

Unfortunately, Blatty did win the award for the Exorcist screenplay. But Hill happily won as Best Director. The acting awards, too, displayed good sense by the membership. The only clinker was Jack Lemmon, hopelessly miscast in **Save The Tiger** as a depressed Jewish garment manufacturer; this award reflected the usual Academy sentimentality for comic actors who turn, once in a while, to a "serious" performance. But, happy day, Glenda Jackson won for her superior acting performance in **A Touch of Class,** beating out the impossible Streisand playing Streisand in **The Way We Were.** John Houseman certainly deserved the best supporting actor award for his brilliant performance as an arrogant law professor in **The Paper Chase,** as did the marvellous Tatum O'Neal for her tough, lovable urchin role in **Paper Moon.** (Though Tatum was scarcely a **supporting** actress, and should have been entered for the lead actress award.) Of the defeated nominees, we would like to see more of Marsha Mason, whose off-beat acting lent a special magic to a tawdry nothing called **Cinderalla Liberty** and to its standard whore-with-heart of gold role.

Women in Movies. The cynical degradation of Linda Blair in **The Exorcist** lends point to the growing feminist charge that women have been treated badly in movies in recent years. No question about it, and the problem is not simply degradation, but the fact that women have been reduced to generally nothing roles. Actors rather than actresses are now the box-office draws, and get the juicy parts. Typical of female roles was the treatment of the leading girl in **Paper Chase.** The lead actress led a shadowy, unmotivated and peripheral existence, and the love interest in the film had about the same stature. Whatever the reason, it is **not** a centuries-old male conspiracy. For if we contrast the Golden Age of the 1930's and 40's, we see a rich and vital role for female actresses, ranging from intelligent, independent and sophisticated roles for the Katherine Hepburns, Carole Lombards, and Rosalind Russells, to the "sex object" roles, ranging from Sophia Loren to the Jean Harlows and Ann Sheridans. And even the Harlows and Sheridans were often sassy rather than purely passive types. I don't know the full explanation for the decay of the female role in films, but I submit that one likely reason is the decay from Old to New Culture, from Hero to Anti-Hero in films. The Old Culture heros, the Gables and Tracys and Grants, were so strong and — yes, let's say it — manly that they could afford to play opposite independent heroines, and both the film and the audience benefited thereby. But now, in the age of the weak, purposeless, and snivelling anti-hero, the female lead has to be reduced to a virtual zero to lend the anti-hero any substance at all. So, while the New Culture seems to be more egalitarian, and lends rhetorical support to women's lib, the upshot of the whole shebang is that women are given a raw deal. Which may have relevance not just for movies but for society as a whole. ◻

Apologies!

Apologies are due our readers for delays in the last couple of issues. Much of the delay has been due to our printer's problems with equipment, which are now hopefully remedied. Also, by an unfortunate juxtaposition in our March issue, it looked as if the poem by J. William Lloyd, follower of Benjamin Tucker in the late nineteenth century, was part of our "Libertarian Songs — II". Actually, the two are unrelated, even though — to confuse the matter — Lloyd's lyrics are obviously set to the tune of "Columbia, the Gem of the Ocean". ◻

Review Of John T. Flynn, 'As We Go Marching'

By William Stewart

Review of John T. Flynn's As We Go Marching, Free Life Editions, 1973.

Modern day social science classes, when they bother to discuss fascism at all, take one of two highly questionable approaches. Either they view fascism as something peculiar to the German and Italian experiences (perhaps arising out of some flaw in the German and Italian cultures) and hence something that could never happen in America; or they tell us that America will definitely become fascist, unless we wise up and adopt the entire spectrum of socialist politics and culture. Now, with the reprinting of John T. Flynn's As We Go Marching, there is a highly readable and marvelously informative work of the third general approach to fascism.

Unlike socio-cultural approaches, Flynn sees fascism as primarily arising out of economic phenomena. Unlike the Marxists and other socialists, these economic forces are not borne out of dialectical forces of history, but from the nature of the market economy and systematic intervention in the market. By attempting to regulate and manage the economy, the government sets in motion forces with which it cannot cope - except with further intervention. The internal logic of the development of a totally planned economy is remarkably similar to the analysis put forth by economist Ludwig von Mises in his famous article, "Middle-of-the-Road Policy Leads to Socialism." Like the Marxists, Flynn offers two alternatives: either continue down the road to fascism, or return to the more traditional American system of freedom and free enterprise.

To discover the nature of fascism, Flynn spends the first two-thirds of the book looking for the essential features of fascism in an historical analysis of Germany and Italy (the book is worth reading just for this historical analysis). He finds eight essential and defining features of fascism: (1) no restraint upon government powers, i.e., totalitarianism, (2) management of the government by a dictator — the leadership principle, (3) the government is organized to manage the capitalist economy under the leadership of an immense bureaucracy, (4) the economy is organized on the syndicalist model, i.e., producing groups are formed into craft and professional categories under the supervision of the state, (5) the society operates on the planned, autarchial principle, (6) the government holds itself responsible to provide the nation with adequate purchasing power by public spending and borrowing, (7) militarism is used as a conscious mechanism of government spending,

and (8) imperialism is included as a policy flowing from militarism and other elements of fascism. Other elements found in fascist societies, such as racism, are mere window dressing and not necessary to the fascist system. If we find a nation using all of these devices, Flynn states, we will know that it is a fascist nation.

In comparing these elements with America (this book was first published in 1943) Flynn finds all the necessary elements save dictatorship and full totalitarianism. In applying his framework to modern America, we find that most of these elements, especially in the management of the economy, more prevelent than ever. With 'conservative' Richard Nixon announcing that he is a Keynesian and the abortive attempt at full wage and price controls, control of the economy and a spiraling public debt indicate that Flynn may indeed be correct: we are being drawn down the road to fascism. Moreover, the popularity of 'energy self-sufficiency' and neo-mercantalist economic theorizing, the autarchial principle is in full bloom.

Militarism is probably only temporarily kept under the table (a sudden revival of it after the post-Vietnam disallusionment dies down would not be surprising) and as for dictatorship — well, we have the John Birch Society warning of powerful executive orders which spell out the mechanism for a full takeover of the American society.

At the very least, As We Go Marching should be food for thought and an impetus to further scholarship into the nature of fascism and the forces operating behind the American political scene. The only shortcoming of this edition is that it lacks an updated bibliography to serve as a starting point for further reading by those not familiar with Flynn's point of view. Flynn's 1943 bibliography does not include Hayek's The Road to Serfdom and more recent analysis by authors such as Murray Rothbard, Ayn Rand and James Martin would serve as a good starting point for anyone concerned with the erosion of individual and economic freedom in America.

A brief introduction by New Left historian Ronald Radosh places Flynn in his proper historical perspective. Flynn is probably best known for his anti-communist works in the McCarthyite era, but As We Go Marching is more representative of his consistent anti-militarist and anti-imperialist (indeed, his pro-individualist) point of view. As We Go Marching is an indispensable work for anyone concerned with economic freedom and the contemporary American Scene. ◘

Published Every Month. Subscription Rate: $8.00 Per Year

A Monthly Newsletter

THE
Libertarian Forum

Joseph R. Peden, Publisher   Murray N. Rothbard, Editor

VOLUME VI, NO. 5   MAY, 1974   US-ISSN0047-4517

IMPEACH THE . . .
(EXPLETIVE DELETED)

The net is closing in inexorably on the Tricky one, and it couldn't happen to a more deserving guy. The now famous transcripts released by Tricky Dick with an astonishing flourish of triumph, is the final straw that will do him in. Bowdlerized, deleted, meretricious as they are, they present a face of the President and his top aides calculated to send the most fawning Nixonite loyalist running desperately for cover. For one thing, they desanctify the Oval Office and the State itself far better and with greater punch than a thousand libertarian broadsides. Here is the Face of the State, and of its most illustrious representative, the President, revealed to the world in all its ugly nakedness.

It is almost amusing to read the horror and disgust on the part of the readers of these transcripts. Where, for heaven's sake, they ask, is any concern whatever, among all these conversations of the top rulers of the land, for moral principle, for right and wrong, for the "public interest" or the "general welfare"? Where are all the pious platitudes habitually emitted by politicians about their deep concern for the public weal? Take, for example, the eloquent editorial of William Randolph Hearst, Jr., who, until the day of the transcripts, was a down-the-line Nixon loyalist. In his evidently sincere anguish, Hearst writes that "I have never heard anything as ruthless, deplorable and ethically indefensible as the talk on those White House tapes." Hearst calls the transcripts "incredible and sickening." Even Senator Hugh Scott (R., Pa.) who all his life has been the leading toady for the national Republican machine (first for Dewey, and then for Nixon), lashed out at the "deplorable, disgusting, shabby, immoral performances" by all the participants in the taped conversations. And when Scott goes, who will soon be left, except General Haig?

One very common social science myth has been totally exploded by the tapes: the myth cherished by economists and political scientists that, while ordinary citizens are wrapped up in their petty, short-run concerns, our wise, far-seeing government officials, and particularly the President and his aides, are able to take the long, far-sighted, view of events. While the rest of us grub from day-to-day the State rulers are free to plan for the next several generations, and even centuries. Bah! Humbug! Nixon and his cronies are clearly concerned, not just with the short-run, but with hour-by-hour gains, with the very next 6 o'clock news broadcast. The momentary concerns of the Tricky One and his crew make the rest of us seem like people devoted only to the 21st century. Speak of "high time-preference", Nixon's and his pals is almost infinite, which perhaps accounts for his monumental blunder in thinking only about his 24-hour propaganda coup from the fact of releasing the transcripts. "But, Mr. President, what happens when people start reading these transcripts", we can see someone asking; "Bah, who cares about that? That's far-off speculation about the future" — except that Tricky hardly seems able to

formulate such a coherent sentence.

And then there is Bill Buckley, still in his off-beat way a defender of the President. Buckley, for example, deplores the invasion of Nixon's privacy involved in the tapes and transcripts. Somehow Buckley seems to have forgotten the major point: that these tapes were played at the behest of Tricky Dick, and that no one else — except — Haldeman — knew of their existence. It seems to us that it is not Tricky's privacy that has been invaded by the tapes, but that of the other poor suckers who thought that what they were saying was said in confidence.

Even the august New York Times has been moved, among other observers, to call Richard Nixon a "Godfather" on the evidence of the transcripts. That's getting close, especially when we consider Nixon's wistful wish at one point that he had the skills of the Mafia. But the smile really smears the Mafia, because no Godfather worth his salt could be as ruthlessly disloyal to his own aides, to the loyalists who, in the immortal words of Chuck Colson, would "walk over their grandmother for Richard Nixon". Whatever else they are, Godfathers are always loyal to their Families. Milhous wouldn't have lasted a year among the Mafiosi.

In the final analysis, William Randolph Hearst, in his agonized editorial, said it all: "The voices on the tapes, even the censored parental guidance version, comes through like a gang of racketeers talking over strategy as they realize that the cops are closing in on them." Precisely. A "gang of racketeers." Let us cling to this powerful and illuminating glimpse that we have all had into the nature of the State apparatus and of our leading rulers. For once, we have seen the face of the State plain, stripped of all hogwash, phony rhetoric, and grandiloquent propaganda. We have for once been permitted to view the Emperor without his clothes. Let us ever hold to this knowledge in our hearts. ◻

BFL Expands

With its April, 1974 issue, the monthly periodical **Books for Libertarians** has taken a giant leap forward on the way to becoming the outstanding libertarian magazine in the country. Its new expansion from eight to twelve pages per issue reflects a burgeoning prosperity and a great growth in its circulation. Twelve pages means that it can and does have longer book reviews, letters of comment to the editor, and longer "essay reviews" by scholars of interest to libertarians.

Among many other goodies, for example, the April issue of BFL has two contrasting reviews of two "anti-women's lib" books by George Gilder and Steven Goldberg: one by yours truly and the other by Mrs.

(Continued On Page 3)

Uncle Miltie Rides Again

Economists used to have an instructive term for the man who comes up habitually with a single technocratic gimmick to solve deep and complex economic problems. Such a man used to be called a "crank." If Professor Milton Friedman were not the august holder of a chair at the University f Chicago, the undisputed head of the powerful and influential Chicago School of Economics, the unofficial adviser to Presidents, and the commander of a comparatively astronomical income, that is precisely what he would have been called long before now. Yes, under cover of the free enterprise rhetoric, Uncle Miltie is a crank. Invariably, when the State has really been fouling things up, when its own created messes have brought insuperable problems that have threatened to bring much of the State system tumbling down, Milton Friedman has ridden to the State's rescue with some crank scheme that has managed to befuddle the issue and to save the State's bacon, at least for a good while. With friends and champions like that, the free market economy hardly needs any enemies.

Consider: when the State needed a huge increase in income tax to pay for World War II, but clearly could not collect the required lump sum on the Ides of March, it was Milton that came up with the withholding tax scheme — a "wartime emergency" measure that is now the linchpin of the entire monstrous income tax structure. More recently, when the clamor rose from Left, Right, and Center against the accelerating breakdown of the public school system, it was Milton that deflected discussion from dismantling that system into the crank "voucher scheme" for formidable government control of private schooling, a scheme that both Left and Right were able to latch onto and call their own. And then, when the welfare system threatened to break down and was attacked by Left and Right alike, and it looked as if we might be able to dismantle the entire welfare mess, it was Milton Friedman who came up with the disastrous crank scheme for the "negative income tax", which might well wreck the economy in not too many years from now. Again, both Left and Right have rushed to embrace the negative income tax or its numerous variants as a way to save the essence of the welfare system.

And now, just when the State's continuing and accelerating monetary expansion has brought us to the threshhold of runaway inflation, and it looked as if public pressure might truly build up to force the government to stop its inflating, Milton has once again come to the rescue with an egregious gimmick that might well have the effect of taking the steam out of any public effort to stop the inflation. Milton has always been at his weakest in the area of money — and has typically spent most of his time and energy in this particular field. In the first place, he has always been soft on inflation, taking the position that: who cares about inflation so long as there are no price or wage controls to distort the allocation of resources? He has long sneered at gold as money, and has advocated the total control of the money supply by the central government, in the form of fiat paper. Then, after having ceded total control of money to the central government, he implores it to keep hands off exchange rates and to inflate the money supply by a fixed percentage (varying, depending on which Friedman article you read, from 3 to 5 percent per year,) thereby supposedly keeping a stable price level. A believer in the spurious positivist methodology that "science is prediction", and that it doesn't matter how false the assumptions of one's theory so long as one can predict accurately, his predictions have been often grossly off the mark, e.g., his forecast that if gold were ever to be cut loose from the dollar, its price would fall to its "proper", non-monetary level of something like $10 an ounce. The fact that, since gold was cut loose from the dollar in the spring of 1968 its free price has always been above the official rate (then $35 an ounce, now $42 an ounce), and has now risen to something like $170 an ounce, has not dented Milton's air of infallibility in the slightest. He still denounces gold as an "overpriced", speculative commodity.

And now the new Friedman gimmick to make inflation endurable and even harmless: everyone will have his monetary assets and income continually revaluated by some index of general prices; everyone will benefit by a floating "escalator clause", and so inflation will have no terrors: we can all relax and enjoy it. If the price index doubles, then the worker making $10,000 a year will find his wages doubled; the creditor will find his return doubled, and so on.

While the Friedmanites have long held that the sting could be taken out

of inflation — even runaway inflation — by a universal escalator clause, Friedman did not begin pushing his scheme until he visited Brazil for a few weeks earlier this year. Milton returned from Brazil starry-eyed about the "economic miracle" enjoyed under that dictatorial regime; perhaps the Brazilian bureaucrats fed him too much tequila. Adopting universal "escalator clause" or "monetary correction", Friedman opines, Brazil has been able to bring down the annual rate of general price inflation from 30% to 15% since 1967. Hedging his bets a tiny bit, Friedman concedes that "The monetary correction is an accounting nuisance and it cannot be truly universal. A world of zero inflation would obviously be better." But — and here comes the technocratic crank — "given the inevitable, if temporary, costs of reducing inflation rapidly without such a measure, the Brazilians have been extremely wise to adopt it. I believe that their miracle would have been impossible without the monetary correction", and he even adds that "they may be able to succeed in gradually bringing inflation down to near zero . . . It is past time that the U. S. applied the lesson." (Newsweek, Jan. 21.)

Unfortunately for Milton's acumen, at the very time that someone in Brazil was handing him a snow job, the Brazilian "miracle" was in the process of turning sour. By early April, the London Economist was noting that price inflation for the first three months of this year in Brazil was running at an annual rate of 28% (the bad old pre-"miracle" rate!) (Economist, April 6). Furthermore, in contrast to Friedman's assertion that Brazil had abolished price and wage controls, the economy was suffering from tight price controls, with all the attendant shortages and dislocations. Thus, as the New York Times reported (April 7): "As they face endless lines for milk and vegetable oils, shortages of rice and sugar and inaccessible prices for meat, many Brazilians have begun to ask, 'what became of their miracle.' "

One of the numerous and insuperable problems with Friedman's Index Scheme is: what "index", and who produces it? If he knew anything about "Austrian" economic theory, for example, Friedman would know that there is no such thing as a single, scientific index of the movement of general prices. All such indexes are strictly arbitrary, and there are a huge number of possible indexes, all of which create insuperable economic distortions. The official U. S. government statistics, for example, denote at least three such indexes: the wholesale price index, the consumer cost of living index, and the broad-based "GNP deflator", each of which differs widely from the others. Which one should be used? There is no non-arbitrary answer. Even if we confine ourselves to the cost-of-living index, the obstacles are insurmountable; whose cost-of-living, for example, do we measure: that of the classic Dayton, Ohio blue-collar housewife with two kids, or that of a bachelor professor in California? Every individual and group in the country experiences different cost-of-living "indexes" (the price of books, for example, will loom much larger in the cost of living of the professor), and any one overall index will fit none of the actual, living individuals concerned. And then there is the question of the timing of the adjustments: will they be annual? In that case, the person will suffer for eleven months, before he earns his "correction". Daily? But then the practical difficulties of arriving at the index are again insurmountable. No, the entire scheme is an absurd chimera.

Neither have the index problems been conspicuously solved in Friedman's beloved Brazil. Barron's (April 15) reports that the index which, as everywhere, is under total control of government statisticians, is in Brazil based only on prices prevailing in the state of Guanabara (Rio de Janeiro), which notoriously lag behind the inflation in the rest of the country. Furthermore, the index includes fictitious government-controlled prices in many instances. Also, the government has juggled the Index to make it look good; thus, "when the cost of milk and meat continued to surge, both products were abruptly stricken from the index."

Furthermore, the escalator system has not worked with universal and harmonious smoothness in Brazil. On the contrary, the average worker has consistently lagged behind his "monetary correction", so that the real wages (in terms of purchasing-power over goods and services) have in recent years been cut by over 30 per cent. Brazil has been able to get

(Continued On Page 3)

470

Purity And The Libertarian Party

The vexed and troubled question of purity has again raised its head in the Libertarian Party. Such questions are inherent in the nature of a Party, precisely because a Party has to be something more than simply a philosophy club. If it were only such a club, with a purely educational function for ourselves and for the greater public, then keeping the message pure would be relatively simple. Even then, of course, neo-Randians and anarcho-capitalists, Christians and atheists, natural lawyers and Stirnerites, could well be at each other's throats. But then there would always be a simple remedy — not really available to a political party — of splitting off, and having separate organizations for each of the doctrinal factions.

But for the Libertarian Party we want something else, something **more** than just a philosophical and educational instrument; we want to exert **influence** in the political arena, to take the lead in the vital and necessary process of rolling back and dismantling State power. To do so, we must begin by unity among the various factions, at least to the extent of remaining and working within the same overall Libertarian Party umbrella. Hence the strategic futility, among other problems, with the earlier LP tendency (happily, now presumably defunct) of beginning its platforms with every sectarian Objectivist clause from "A is A" down. We want all libertarian factions — from neo-Randian to Christian to feminist — in the Party, and therefore we must stress what unites us rather than alienate and divide our ranks with sectarian pronunciamentos. (This holds for **official** Party pronouncements; this does **not** mean that the various factions should not continue to polemicize other factions within our common ranks, and try to win them over. **That** is surely fair game.) Hence, statements of principles, resolutions, and platforms must be unexceptionably libertarian, and here, in the urgent quest for both purity and commonality, a lot of what outsiders might consider "nit-picking" is fully justified.

So far so good; but here we come to a much thornier and more difficult problem: **how broad** should our "libertarian" umbrella become? Even though I am a dedicated anarchist, I submit that this umbrella should include our cousins the **laissez-faire** liberals: the Mises-Read types who believe in a minimal government strictly limited to police and judicial protection of the rights of person and property. I submit that we are, in the first place, the heirs of these "classical liberals"; we are, to paraphrase the great Benjamin Tucker, "unterrified **laissez-faire** liberals" who believe in pushing **laissez-faire**, the free market, to its logical and moral conclusion in the service of protection and defense. But not only are we their heirs; we are the natural allies of the **laissez-faire** liberals. We would not be totally happy if Ludwig von Mises or Leonard Read were able to "push the button" and achieve their ideal world tomorrow; but surely we would be 95% happy. In this world of galloping statism, of economic and social crisis at every hand, is **now** the time to get the knives out and repudiate the **laissez-fairists** forevermore? Sure, **within** the Libertarian Party umbrella, we should polemicize, show them the error of their ways, etc., but we still must regard them as allies as against the rest of the world. My contention is that we must, to use the Marxist terminology, form a "united front" with the **laissez-faire** liberals. Otherwise, we may as well call it the "Anarchist Party" outright and resign ourselves permanently to sectarian impotence in the real world. The very term "libertarian" has grown up as a concept that includes anarcho-capitalists, neo-Randians, and Mises-Read **laissez-faire** liberals; are we really ready to repudiate this very sensible concept?

The problem of purity has now arisen on two different fronts within the Libertarian Party; on the FLP's nomination of Percy L. Greaves, Jr. for U. S. Senate from New York State; and on the battle between Edward H. Crane III and Eric Scott Royce for national chairman of the Libertarian

(Continued On Page 7)

Uncle Miltie Rides Again —

(Continued From Page 2)

away with this expropriation of the working class because, under its dictatorial regime, labor unions are government-controlled and the press is strictly censored. In short, the escalator system has been used to mask an inflation that has redistributed wealth from the poorer to the wealthier classes; as Senor Bezerra de Mello, president of the Othon Hotels Corp. of Brazil, has conceded: "the Brazilian model has been good for businessmen, but labor has been punished." (New York Times, April 14). Hence the wisdom of the warning of Chairman of U. S. Council of Economic Advisers Herbert Stein — not usually the most astute of observers — that "Unless you have the economy perfectly indexed, somebody is bound to get stuck." (Washington Post, April 11.)

Precisely — and if this monstrous scheme were to be instituted in the United States, we know darn well who is going to "get stuck", whose escalator will fall behind in the mad scramble for the "monetary correction." I can assure Milton, for example, that professors at the Polytechnic Institute of New York aren't going to get any escalator clauses, nor will the local cleaning lady; but, on the other hand, we can rest assured that the Teamsters Union and Nelson Rockefeller's multifarious enterprises and activities will be very early at the escalator trough.

One might ask Milton **how** in blazes his Universal Escalator is going to get instituted in the United States. If it is supposed to be voluntary, with all contracts, existing pensions, savings, etc. voluntarily adopting the "correction", then the lags and the injustices will be simply enormous: pace, for example, the Polytechnic Institute of New York. Any idea that all assets and contracts will be simultaneously and universally corrected by voluntary action is to contemplate the fantasies of a Never-Never Land. How, then, make it universal and simultaneous? Obviously, the only way would be by totalitarian dictation of the entire economy by the government, with the government compulsorily dictating every minute area of correction. Such a system would make a total mockery of Friedmanite pretensions to advocacy of a "free market" economy. And, of course, even such a monstrous totalitarianism would not work, since

the various indexes and corrections would be eternally subject to political pressures upon the bureaucracy.

Furthermore, Friedman's notion that the universal escalator would make governmental tight money easier because politically less painfull is clearly bizarre; instead, the scheme would help to lull people into accepting the evils of inflation by sowing the illusion that it can be made painless. The anti-inflationary ardor of the American public, just getting under way in earnest, would be gravely weakened. Inflation would be virtually institutionalized.

The left-liberal New York Post writes (April 15) that Friedman "is usually labelled a 'conservative', but in fact he is an unorthodox thinker (read "crank") with a record of winning acceptance for his ideas." It then quotes Friedman's friend, former Treasury Secretary George Pratt Shultz that "Milton Friedman is always worth listening to". Even Barron's, in its otherwise trenchant critique of Friedman's latest concoction, repeats the "always worth listening to" line. I submit that there is no surer way of generating an economic breakdown than listening to Milton a bit more often. A few more "positive proposals" from Friedman's fertile imagination and we will all have to head for the caves.

BFL Expands —

(Continued From Page 1)

Riqui Leon. It also has its first essay-review of Brand Blanshard's great anti-positivist work **Reason and Analysis** by the leading Aristotelian philosopher Henry Veatch, chairman of the philosophy department at Georgetown University. The excellent Veatch article is alone worth the price of admission.

Again among other fine reviews, the May issue of BFL has an excellent review of F. A. Hayek's great work, **Monetary Theory and the Trade Cycle** by Walter Block, and an essay-review of James J. Martin's monumental anti-interventionist two-volume work, **American Liberalism and World Politics** by the libertarian historian Arthur Ekirch.

Books for Libertarians is must reading for libertarians or for anyone else interested in the libertarian scene. Furthermore, it is available for the measly price of $6 a year from 422 First St., S.E., Washington, D. C. 20003.   ◻

The Growth Of Revisionism From The Centre: A Review Essay

By Chris R. Tame

In an earlier essay in **Libertarian Forum** (November 1972), I dealt with the phenomenon of what I termed "revisionism from the centre" — that is, the increasingly common appearance of works by historians who, while still remaining within the bounds of the "liberal" (i.e., statist) paradigm, were arriving at insights and analyses which confirm the historical interpretations of New Left and Libertarian scholars. The importance of this liberal or "centrist" revisionism, I argued, was a two-fold one, arising not only from its inherent value and validity but also from its utility as an "unbiased" verification of an interpretation previously characterised by its obviously political motivations and implications.

In my original essay I reviewed the works of three particular expositors of revisionism from the centre, those of Stuart Morris, Robert Weibe, and Samuel P. Hays (1). However, there have been a number of other equally important contributions which I did not touch upon but which also deserve to be brought to the attention of those Libertarians who realize the importance of historical revisionism in the formation of a relevant and fully radical Libertarian ideology.

Perhaps one of the most notable works to appear in the wake, so to speak, of Gabriel Kolko's seminal studies in economic and political history is K. Austin Kerr's **American Railroad Politics, 1914-1920: Rates Wages, Efficiency** (Pittsburgh University Press, 1968). Especially interesting in the context of this essay is the fact that Kerr's study was conducted with an awareness of the work of both New Left and liberal revisionists. His research was first begun in a seminar conducted by Samuel P. Hays at Iowa University in 1959, and continued at Pittsburgh University as a doctoral dissertation under Hays' direction, while at the same time Kerr also received assistance from Kolko himself. While praising the latter's work, however, Kerr does make the qualification that "because he (i.e., Kolko) analyzes railroad affairs primarily from the point of view of only one group, the railroads themselves, Kolko misses many of the complexities of railroad politics" (p. 236). This is indeed a valid point. Although Kolko was undoubtedly aware of the role of the clash of divergent business interests in the movement for regulation (2), his focus in **Railroads and Regulation** was certainly upon the views and actions of the railroads themselves. A broader approach can surely supply us with a lot more equally valuable material, and in this respect **American Railroad Politics** constitutes a valuable adjunct to Kolko's volume. This should not be taken as any detraction from the latter's achievement, however. Kolko was not only dealing with a more extensive period of time (the years 1877 to 1916, as compared with Kerr's analysis of the years 1914 to 1920), but could hardly be expected to pursue in one volume every aspect of his basic subject. Kerr's work, then, builds on that of Kolko but extends it to draw a more detailed portrait of the complexity of affairs in the business community. It consequently provides a useful corrective against seeing 'business' in terms of a monolithic entity and conspiracy, with Kerr's view of the Progressive Era" (interpreting its) system of decision-making as one which satisfied the business community's general desire for regulation but failed to grant consistently the ends sought by any one group" (p. 4). Kolko's interpretation of the period as one of the rise of "political capitalism" finds ample confirmation by Kerr, however. As he puts it himself:

"Railroad regulation developed historically as a system of resolving differences among competing economic groups that had a common concern with transportation. At issue were freight rates, wages, profits, and operating efficiency . . . past studies have failed to analyze systematically the origins within American industrial society of arguments over railroad issues. There has been no explicit awareness of the contrasting, competing interests among the economic groups involved with transportation, and no cognizance of the changing bargaining relationships among them" (pp. 2, 3).

Kerr also launches into a heartwarming attack on liberal historiography, rejecting the orthodox liberal vision of the Progressive Era as a period of conflict between the "public" and the "interests" and of the post-World War I period as one of conservative reaction and "return to 'normalcy". The purveyors of this mythology, as Kerr so incisively puts it,

"have for the most part overlooked the essentially pro-business nature of federal regulation in the Progressive Era. The rhetoric of railroad regulation during the pre-war period, to be sure, advocated public control of private interests. However, this rhetoric, if taken alone, seems only to obscure the significant practice. We must understand it in relation to the ends sought in the argumentation of issues. Primarily, these ends involved the desire of business groups to use governmental, public means to control — if not to solve — private economic problems. Although important transitory changes occurred during the war, both the rhetorical assumptions and the general goals of the business groups concerned with railraod policy remained strikingly similar throughout the period leading up to the Transportation Act of 1920. The war experience reinforced the prevailing prewar commitment to federal regulation as the most desirable way of resolving economic differences. This reinforcement of the basic assumptions underlying federal regulation stands out in retrospect as a bold continuity in American political history" (pp. 4-5).

And thus Kerr concludes,

"If we view the ideological rhetoric of these years as an expression of particular perceptions instead of adopting it as interpretive verity, we can observe a continuous political force functioning within American industrial society, wherein business was able to exploit governmental power in order to make capitalism a more viable system. This political force was a complex phenomenon involving a high degree of competitive rivalry between groupings within the business community" (p. 229)

Not surprisingly, the area in which the revisionism of Kolko and Weinstein has perhaps been hardest to disregard is that of economic and business history. The pages of the **Business History Review**, for example, have thus attested to the growing impact and influence of the revisionist perspective. Robert Asher's "Business and Workers' Welfare in the Progressive Era: Workmen's Compensation Reform in Massachusetts, 1880-1911." (**Business History Review**, Vol. XLIII, No. 4, Winter 1969) is a case in point. Citing the work of both New Leftists like Kolko and Weinstein and liberals like Weibe and Hays, Asher focuses on the less extensively analysed subject of the attitudes and role of business in reform at the **state** level. In the case of workmen's compensation reform in Massachusetts in the period examined Asher confirms the basic revisionist account: reform, he states, "was supported by economic groups usually, and justifiably, considered conservative" (p. 453). Similarly, his description of the motivation of these businessmen also provides further detailed evidence of that vein of thought so aptly termed by the New Left as "corporate liberalism".

"Workmen's compensation legislation promised to rationalize the wasteful and pernicious defects employers observed in the existing liability-litigation system. Many employers thought workmen's compensation reform would conserve the stability of established social institutions by removing a major source of friction and antagonism between workers and employers. Workmen's compensation reform also would help conserve the welfare of an important national resource: human labor. Thus . . . (it) appealed to enlightened, class-conscious employers . . . and to conservative, efficiency and cost-minded employers" (pp. 453-454).

However, Asher does make some critical comments on Weinstein's seminal essay, "Big Business and the Origins of Workmen's Compensation", stating that his own research "in New York, Minnesota, and Massachusetts has shown that the model workmen's compensation

(Continued On Page 5)

Growth Of Revisionism —
Rhodesia —

(Continued From Page 4)

bill circulated by the National Civic Federation did not exert any impact on the course and final result of workmen's compensation legislation" (p. 474). Moreover, he argues that not only does Weinstein overrate the role of the NCF in the movement for this particular reform, but that he "does not sufficiently emphasize the negative effects that the cost-conscious conservative employers had on compensation legislation. Unlike the work of the liberal employers of the Boston Chamber of Commerce's Committee on Industrial Relations, the activities of conservative employers within the (NCF), in Massachusetts and elsewhere, delayed the implementation of pioneering workmen's compensation systems and reduced the quantity and quality of assistance extended to injured workers" (p. 474) In reply to these criticisms, it should be stressed that Weinstein never portrayed business as a monolithic entity and was fully cognizant of the complexities of motivation, the clashes of interest and ideas among businessmen. Whether he **sufficiently** emphasized the point Asher raises seems to me a rather nebulous matter, related more to the specific and subjective interest of the historian than to any question of substance. While Asher's study does, then, provide material of interest regarding what occurred in one state, it does not, in my view even here constitute the final view. He does not really draw an adequate picture of the roots and development of corporate liberal ideology among the business elite nor perceive its central importance for our understanding of the period.

However, a rather more valuable contribution to the body of revisionist analysis is Mansel Griffiths Blackford's essay "Businessmen and the Regulation of Railroads and Public Utilities in California during the Progressive Era" (**Business History Review**, Vol. XLIV, No. 3, Autumn 1970). Similarly citing the work of both Kolko and Weibe regarding the reform movement at the national level, Blackford focuses on the specific situation in California and provides a useful confirmation of the revisionist case. Regarding railroad and utilities regulation there he demonstrates that "(g)roups of businessmen were in the vanguard of both reforms" (p. 307). Like Kerr — and in contrast to Kolko — Blackford deals mainly not with the railroads themselves but with the other business interests which sought state regulation. These interests were primarily concerned with reducing competition between themselves and "stabilizing" business conditions — as in the case of the competition between Los Angeles and San Francisco for the trade of the San Joaquin Valley. While not emphasizing the views and activities of the railroads themselves, however, Blackford does observe that by 1911 the railroads offered no opposition at the public hearings over (Governor) Hiram Johnson's regulatory bill. The cost of rebating to the railroads was indeed considerable, he notes, and undoubtedly disliked by them. In the case of the movement that resulted in the Public Utilities Act of 1912, however, it was the utilities themselves that sought regulation.

"The public utility companies, especially the larger ones, were in the vanguard of those clamoring for its (i.e., the 1912 Act) passage. They hoped that by the enactment of a law giving a state commission power over rates they could escape constant hassling with the often corrupt municipal and county authorities. Some also expected to use the commission to end competition among themselves. In addition, regulation was also favored as a means of enhancing the character and improving the market for public utility stock and bond issues" (p. 313). And the expectations of the utilities were in fact fulfilled. The railroad commission, in which was also vested the task of utility regulation, acted in both its areas of concern to prevent rate wars and restrict competition, arguing on the specious grounds that both railroads and utilities were "natural monopolies", that "duplication of facilities" was a "wasteful inefficiency", and that unregulated competition was self-destructive and led ultimately to monopoly and higher rates.

Like New Left revisionism, the focus of revisionism from the centre has generally been upon economic and political history. The examination of ideas and ideology in their own right, the perspective of the historian of ideas, has tended to take a back seat. Nevertheless, a number of works have appeared which add substantially to our understanding of the nature of American progressive, 'liberal', and reform thought — and whose observations fit nicely into the revisionist framework. Putting aside such questions as to what extent "purely" intellectual factors — beliefs

and moral values — are a major causative factor independent of direct economic interest and motive, what we are concerned with here are those works which, in demonstrating the fundamentally conservative, authoritarian, and elitist character of most of the Left and "liberal" mainstream, render clear how the nefarious aims of the corporate power elite were able to find sanctification by the intellectuals — what the liberals really had in mind behind their grandiloquent rhetoric. Orthodox liberal historiography has, of course, always recognized the elements of conservatism and "moderation" within the tradition of liberal and progressive thought, but it has generally passed over their true significance and nature in a rather glib manner and preferred not to probe too deeply. Fortunately, however, a few have gone further. For example, William E. Leuchtenburg's "Progressivism and Imperialism: The Progressive Movement and American Foreign Policy, 1898-1916" (**Mississippi Valley Historical Review**, Vol. XXXIX) stressed the commitment of the major Progressive politicians, publicists, and intellectuals to imperialism and nationalism, and argued that "this explains much about the basic character of the Progressive movement" (p. 507). Despite its frequently evangelical tone, Leuchtenburg characterized Progressivism as reformist rather than revolutionary, accepting traditional American values and ideals — including racist and authoritarian ones — and ultimately suffering from an inner tension "between humanistic values and nationalist aspirations" (p. 503). Similarly, John P. Diggins in his essay "Flirtation With Fascism: American Pragmatic Liberals and Mussolini's Italy" (**American Historical Review**, Vol. LXXI, No. 2, Jan. 1966) and his longer study **Mussolini and Fascism: The View From America** (Princeton University Press, 1972) demonstrated how a large and important segment of liberals were attracted to European fascism and the corporate state. For such thinkers fascist corporatism seemed to embody the core of their ideals, those of "social engineering" and the creation of a scientifically and consciously ordered social system in which all class and group interests were represented and harmonized in the service of the higher national interest. Ironically, however, one of the most interesting re-examinations of liberal thought, Sidney Kaplan's "Social Engineers as Saviors: Effects of World War I on Some American Liberals" (**Journal of the History of Ideas**, Vol. XVII, No. 3, June 1956) received little attention at the time of its publication, Kaplan dealt primarily with the work of such major liberal thinkers as Dewey, Croly and Lippmann showing their commitment to a **scientistic** vision of the Good Society, one in which "organized social intelligence" was embodied in a "vanguard" elite of administrators. Class conflict was thus to be eradicated in a system characterized by efficiency, science and a competent, paternalistically humanitarian elite of scientists, "the new kind of businessman", experts, and social administrators. World War I, while leading to disillusionment in some cases — most notably that of Randolph Bourne — had no such effect on others or even led to an **enhancement** of their conservative, anti-democratic temper (as in the case of Lippmann) or to the adoption of an equally conservative element of mystic religiosity (as in the case of Croly).

The process of critical re-examination of the liberal heritage by a contemporary liberal scholar has been taken furthest, however, by Charles Forcey in his **The Crossroads of Liberalism: Croly, Weyl, Lippmann and the Progressive Era, 1900-1925** (Oxford University Press, N. Y., 1961) Forcey's study indeed starts on an auspicious and critical note. In his Preface he expresses some doubts about liberalism, recounting that, as an undergraduate, liberalism "was, of course, a good thing. But that only made it more difficult to explain the fearsome tragedies that had overtaken America and the world when liberals were in power" (p. iii). The less than totally satisfactory record of liberalism led Forcey, therefore, to ask "(w)ere there fatal flaws in liberalism itself?" (p. iii). It is to answer this question, then, that Forcey selected The New Republic and its founders as his subject, as a "convenient medium for exploring some of the dilemmas of liberalism" (p. iv).

The Crossroads of Liberalism in fact constitutes an excellent account of the ideas of Croly, Weyl and Lippmann, certainly three of the most influential exponents of statist liberalism. Forcey traces the development of their ideas (including some often most interesting doubts and dilemmas in their later years) against the background of political events, and those ideas emerge quite clearly in the garb of elitism, authoritarianism and nationalism. Unfortunately, however, while undoubtedly a useful intellectual portrait, Forcey's book is grievously

(Continued On Page 6)

Growth Of Revisionism —

(Continued From Page 5)

deficient in its evaluation. Although perceptively stressing "how dangerously ambiguous a focus nationalism was for the new liberalism" (p. 260) Forcey reveals again and again how irrevocably wedded he is to the dogmas of orthodox "liberalism". His conception of "creative social change" is still nothing but "social democracy" and the extension of state power. While not totally blind to the dangers of executive power he still parrots such old saws as "(n)o one can deny the need for strong executives in a country where reformers are often hamstrung by constitutional restrictions and political anachronisms" (p. 311) ! (Those who do maintain the presumptuous desire not to be 'socially engineered' by such enlightened and humanitarian liberals are well and truly consigned to a state of non-existence !) Moreover, apparently still adhering to the Hofstadter/status revolution interpretation of the Progressive movement, Forcey totally fails to realize that the business elite was immersed in the movement for reform, both politically and intellectually, and that the formulas of state regulation were quite to their taste. Taken in by the facile rhetoric of "social democracy", he fails to see how the statist panaceas common to "scientific socialism" and "liberalism" have **objectively** served the interests of the corporate power elite. In all, he fails to grasp the significance of his **own** description of the liberalism of Croly and co., how their elitist and authoritarian ethos reflects so well the **reality** of "social democracy" in practice — how it constitutes in every sense of the term a **corporate liberalism!**

Yet if none of these re-examinations of the liberal heritage which we have described have gone far enough in their analysis, there are some signs that a truly radical revisionism is beginning to gain some academic ground. The most notable example of this is E. K. Hunt's essay "A Neglected Aspect of the Economic Ideology of the Early New Deal" (**Review of Social Economy**, Vol. XXIX, No. 2, Sept. 1971). Rejecting the orthodox liberal historiography in which a "progressive" government intervened in the economy to curb the power of big business, Hunt cites the revisionist analysis of both New Left **and** Libertarian scholars: "a smaller group of economists and historians", he states, "with points of view as far apart as Gabriel Kolko and Murray Rothbard have shown that the twentieth century evolution of the interventionist state was accomplished only because it had the support of big business. In fact big businessmen have been the driving force in this evolution" (p. 180). Hunt, however, concentrates in this essay on the **intellectual background** of the rise of the corporate state and indeed provides a most useful (although by no means definitive) analysis of that background. Specifically, he makes the perceptive point that "(t)he active intervention of the government to create cartels and to promote industrial cooperation rather than competition seems to have paralleled closely the German experience of the late nineteenth century" (p. 180) and thus takes as his major theme the demonstration that "the apparent similarity between the philosophy underlying the New Deal and the philosophy underlying German cartelization in the late nineteenth century was not entirely accidental" (p. 180).

Hunt in fact selects as a key figure Simon N. Patten, whom he correctly describes as "one of the most influential teachers of economics in the United States in the late nineteenth and early twentieth centuries" (p. 182). What was significant was that Patten in fact studied for a period in Germany, in the intellectual atmosphere of the "Socialists of the Chair" of the **Verein fur Sozialpolitik.** Indeed, Patten studied directly under many of the members of the **Verein** and became the portege of one of its founders, Professor Johannes Conrad. And thus Patten became thoroughly — nay, religiously, as he himself said — imbued with a world view which, while "anti-socialist", was equally and militantly anti-laissez faire, urging a programme of vigorous interventionism, coercive cartelization, and welfare-statism. It was this creed that Patten embodied in his subsequent and voluminous works: an all-out attack on the "waste", "inefficiency", and "immorality" of the free-market. In the place of the market he advocated a new order of "corporate collectivism", in which competition was eradicated and the "socialized capitalist" — united with a consevative labour unionism — administered an economy of abundance in the 'public interest'.

It should be immediately pointed out that Hunt sees the rise of the corporate state by no means simply as the consequence of the nefarious

influence of intellectuals like Patten. The enthusiasm of big business itself for corporate collectivism, especially after their experience of the War Industries Board, had not a little to do with the matter, as Hunt readily indicates! Nevertheless, the contribution of Patten and his disciples to the ideology and the creation of the present system is certainly significant. Indeed, it is especially worth noting that such New Dealers and architects of the NIRA as Frances Perkins and Rexford Tugwell were proteges and disciples of Patten. The case of Tugwell is also illuminating since, as Hunt points out, he "has been considered by many historians to represent the radical or left-wing element of Roosevelt's brain trust" and since "the common assumption that New Deal reforms had a leftist orientation is often based on the belief that Tugwell was a spokesman for the left" (p. 186).

Hunt, then, vigorously indicts liberal historiography for its "myopic historical misinterpretation of the economic, social and political significance of the New Deal and post World War II American Corporate Liberalism" (p. 187) and for its failure to grasp the thoroughly conservative nature of "liberalism" and welfare-statism.

"While the dominant economic ideas and policies of 'welfare-statism' of late nineteenth century Germany are almost unanimously regarded as profoundly conservative, highly similar ideas and policies in the United States which were directly influenced by those from Germany are often treated as progressive or even radical" (p. 187). Hunt's conclusion is both ringing and radical in its revisionism — and especially refreshing in its recognition of the singular inappropriateness of the appellation "conservative" when applied to libertarian and individualist critics of the status quo.

"The post World War II American 'Corporate State' appears to this writer to be based upon a profoundly conservative coalition of government, big business, conservative labor leaders and 'liberal' intellectuals. Kaiser Wilhelm I and Bismark would certainly smile approvingly on contemporary American capitalism. And yet most American economists insist on reserving the label 'conservative' for advocates of individualist liberalism many of whom are among the most thoroughgoing critics of contemporary American capitalism" (pp. 190-191).

The growth of revisionism from the centre is clearly a development to be welcomed by the Libertarian. Yet one major qualification must be especially stressed, and that is that there is nothing **inherently** radical in its revelations. As I showed in my earlier essay in **Libertarian Forum**, such liberal revisionists as Robert Weibe, for example, portrayed the role of business in the attainment of "reform" in no critical light but rather as a **praiseworthy** achievement! Similarly, Samuel P. Hays offered an interpretation of American history, a "social analysis", which portrayed the growth of political and economic centralization as an inevitable consequence of industrialization, technology, and the "evolution from smaller to larger and larger systems". In other words, while certainly describing the rise of our present corporate state in a more realistic manner, such liberal revisionist works also act simultaneously as its intellectual consecration, as a historiographical justification of the **status quo.** This apologetic role is also played by many of the works we have reviewed in this essay. Robert Asher, for example, in his essay on workmen's conpensation, describes the various corporatist and interventionist policies as "great positive contributions to the rationalization and elimination of iniquitious social and economic practices and institutions" (**Op. cit.,** p. 452) And Mansel Griffiths Blackford also completely embraces the specious anti-market arguments of the architects of corporate collectivism:

"(I)t is probably wrong to see too sharp a dichotomy between the best interests of business groups and the general public . . . all profited from the (railroad and utilities) commission's policy on competition. By protecting public service corporations within their fields of operation, the commission both strengthened the financial positions of the utilities and prevented rate wars and the duplication of facilities, the costs of which, as the commissioners frequently pointed out, were ultimately borne by the public" (**Op. cit.,** p. 319)

In fact, another recent essay in the **Business History Review** underlines our point regarding the ideological ambiguity of revisionism from the centre very well. In "The Emerging Organizational Synthesis in Modern American History" (Vol. XLIV, No. 3, Autumn, 1970), Professor Louis Galambos offers an interpretation of recent historiography in which the works of both New Left and liberal scholars are subsumed in a tendency

(Continued On Page 7)

Purity And Libertarian Party —
(Continued From Page 3)

Party, the issue to be resolved at the national conference in Dallas this June.

The nomination of Percy Greaves has occasioned a great deal of grumbling in LP ranks throughout the country, the most extreme being the resignation in high dudgeon from the Ohio LP of its Maximum Leader, Kay Harroff. The charge is basically twofold: that Percy believes in taxation, and that he favors the draft. On the tax question, yes of course he believes in taxation, since he is a laissez-faire liberal, and classical liberals have of course always believed in taxation. We come square against the question of whether we wish to include laissez-fairists in our ranks. I have already answered this question in general. But to be more specific: Percy Greaves is the living embodiment, in his politico-economic philosophy, of the late Ludwig von Mises. Does any LP member have the temerity to say that Mises, if he had wished it, should have been denied the nomination for U. S. Senate? Even to ask such a question is to see its grotesquerie. But then to gripe about Percy's nomination is equally grotesque. Percy Greaves is a distinguished Misesian economist who will hit hard at the economic statism and crises of our time. It is true, yes, that he favors taxation; but the level of taxes that he would impose in a "Greavesian world" in which government is strictly limited to police and judicial protection, and to an isolationist foreign policy, would be so very much lower than what we have now that we would all heave a sigh of relief before we gird our loins to press on for full tax abolition. Is tax abolition such an immediately pressing issue that we cannot afford to endorse someone who merely calls for a drastic reduction of taxation?

In addition to his economic libertarianism, Percy Greaves, consistent with his laissez-faire stand, is in favor of civil liberties and against coerced morality and "victimless crime" laws. The fact that he refused the proferred Courage Party nomination for U. S. Senate because the party had an outlaw-abortion plank in its platform should be evidence enough of Percy's principled libertarianism across-the-board. As for the draft, Percy only favors the draft specifically for defense against foreign invasion. Since foreign invasion of the U. S. is about as likely as immediate abolition of taxation, the draft problem with him is only a moot one for libertarians.

So much for our defense of the "impure" Percy Greaves, who, as a laissez-faire liberal, is pure on everything except anarchism. Having said this, we come now to the Crane-Royce fight, where we must come down on the side of the "pure" position. Is this inconsistent? Let us see.

Edward Crane, a bright young California lawyer, is running for national chairman. In the current issue of Reason, Crane has a letter in which he soberly but trenchantly criticizes Congressman Steve Symms (Rep., Idaho) for his substantial deviations from libertarian purity, both in his voting record and in his previous interview in Reason. 22-year-old Royce has decided to campaign for national chairman as a critic of the Crane letter, attacking Crane for sectarian purity and for injuring libertarian effectiveness with a Congressman as sympathetic to the cause as Symms. Why do we strongly side with Crane in this dispute?

For one thing, as far as I can determine, Ed Crane is not an anarchist, his "purity" therefore taking on the broader laissez-faire connotations which I have been calling for. His critique of Symms (as well as my own forays in the Lib. Forum) is not based on Steve's deviations from anarchism, but from laissez-faire. Crane's and my own criticisms of Symms are not necessarily related to anarchism; they would have been the same had I, for example, been a laissez-faire liberal. In my view, and presumably in Crane's, it would be disastrous to apply the term "libertarian" or the Libertarian Party label to someone who is simply a conservative (or for that matter a New Left) sympathizer with much of the libertarian position. I would be happy to "work with" Symms in the sense of trying to influence him further in the direction of the libertarian position; but to call him a "libertarian Congressman", or to refrain from criticizing his deviations from purity, is a very different story. For that is the point at which we begin to betray our libertarian principles which is the whole raison d'etre, the very purpose of the existence of a Libertarian Party. It is perhaps a fine line to draw, but it is a vital one nevertheless.

To his credit, Rep. Symms has never pretended to be a libertarian purist; a great fellow personally, he has instead been eager to learn and to apply the libertarian position as much as he can. The attack on Symms has not been so much directed at him as against elements in the Libertarian Party who are willing to abandon principle in order to cozy up to someone in political power. In the ticket of Ed Crane for national chairman and Andrea Millen of New York for vice-chairman, we have a slate of party officers dedicated to an uncompromising adherence to basic libertarian principle. The lines are clearly drawn. A Royce victory would be a long step toward the dissolution of the most promising vehicle for libertarian organizing and influence in the history of our fledgling movement.

There is another vital point to be made here; in applying standards of purity, it is far more important to be strict and unyielding toward Libertarians in political office than it is toward candidates for such office. For a candidate in office has not yet sipped of the poisonous potion of public office. But a Libertarian in office has already become — from an anarchist viewpoint steeped in "sin", while from a laissez-faire viewpoint he is at least surrounded by "occasions for sin." To achieve ultimate libertarian victory, it will undoubtedly become necessary for Libertarians to attain political office, but they and we should be always and ever aware of the ever-present peril to their — if not lives and fortunes — at least to their sacred honor. In the old motto, "eternal vigilance is the price of liberty", and so unsparing criticism of any "deviations" by Libertarians in public office will not only be vitally necessary for the libertarian cause, but for their own souls as well. □

Growth Of Revisionism —
(Continued From Page 6)

which he terms the "organizational school of history" (p. 280). In essence, the common denominator of the works in this "organizational" category, as Galambos sees it, is their focus on the "important changes which have taken place in modern America (and which) have centered about a shift from small-scale, informal, locally or regionally oriented groups to large-scale, national, formal organizations. The new organizations are characterized by a bureaucratic structure of authority" (p. 280). Interestingly, Galambos himself perceives the ambiguous ideological implications of liberal organizational approaches. On the one hand, "(o)rganizational analysis could blend with New Left ideology to produce a synthesis which would appeal to those scholars who demand that history be 'relevant' in some precise and immediate way", while on the other "some historians may find it impossible not to surrender their own judgment to the pragmatic and self-serving viewpoints expressed by their organizational subjects" (p. 289). Precisely! And we might justifiably add that Galambos' own interpretation of the "emerging organizational synthesis" is actually insidiously conservative, due to its implicitly and explicitly economic and 'organizational' determinism. Such deterministic interpretations are indeed extremely convenient for the beneficiaries of the existing corporate collectivist system.

Whatever our satisfaction at the development of revisionism from the centre, and for that matter, New Left revisionism, our reading of both, however, surely underlines the importance of radical libertarians participating actively in such historical endeavours. For only such direct involvement can prevent the value of the revisionist perspective from being vitiated by either the conservative apologetics of the liberals or the barren and disastrous socialist dogmas of the New Left.

Notes

(1) The works I dealt with were, specifically: Stuart Morris, "The Wisconsin Idea and Business Progressivism", Journal of American Studies, July 1970; Robert Weibe, Businessmen and Reform: A Study of the Progressive Movement (1962; Quadrangle Books, Chicago, 1968); Samuel P. Hays, Conservation and the Gospel of Efficiency: The Progressive Conservation Movement, 1890-1929 (Harvard University Press, 1959); "The Mythology of Conservation", in H. Jarrett, ed., Perspectives on Conservation (Johns Hopkins Press, 1958); "The Politics of Reform in Municipal Government in the Progressive Era", Pacific Northwest Quarterly, October 1964; "The Social Analysis of American Political History, 1880-1920", Political Science Quarterly, Sept. 1965.

(2) See his comments regarding the conflict between the independent oil producers of the Petroleum Producers Union and Standard Oil, or the rivalry between the New York merchants and those of Boston, Philadelphia and Baltimore. Railroads and Regulation, 1877-1916 (1965; W. W. Norton, N. Y., 1970) pp. 22-26. ◻

Rhodesia — Unjust Land Seizure

By Bill Evers

"Reprinted from the Stanford Daily, April 11, 1974."

The history of European conquest of and rule over African Rhodesians is a history of continual theft by Europeans of land belonging to Africans.

In addition to this massive land seizure, during the last 40 years there has been a fully developed system of racial segregation in land ownership, in which sections of the country are designated as for whites or for blacks.

In recent years, this policy of land assignment led to a dramatic confrontation between the Rhodesian government and African peasants who refused to leave the land they and their forefathers had occupied and cultivated.

Forcible Uprooting

In the late 1960s, the Rhodesian government had to use troops and police to expropriate the land of the Tangwena people in the Inyanga area. The Rhodesian government uprooted forcibly approximately 300 families (approximately 3000 people) in this removal operation.

The roots of this problem lie in the activities of some of the early European colonists in Rhodesia. Dr. Jim Jameson was an administrator for the British South Africa Company, a mercantilist entity created by Cecil Rhodes. Under Jameson's rule in Rhodesia, large tracts and vast estates were granted to aristocratic young blades in England. These tracts became the holdings of absentee-landowning companies.

Jameson not only parcelled out these tracts in the manner of a feudal chieftain, he also paid no attention to whether such land was occupied by Africans, and happily shared in the looting of Ndebele cattle.

Injustices Recognized

By the turn of the century, some sentiment had developed in England that recognized that grave injustices were being done to the Africans in Rhodesia. But the attitude was one of paternalistically regarding the Africans as wards, rather than one of defending the African's full rights and liberties. Some areas were provisionally set aside to cushion the effects of change on tribal life.

Dr. Robin Palmer notes that "by 1914 the Colonial Office (in London) was resigned to the fact that it could do little to prevent the eviction of Africans from European farms." From this time on, one finds the informal policy of racial segregation of land areas. What had originally been an area temporarily designated as a tribal backwater, now became an area which was viewed as the only place Africans were to be given any privileges at all.

Although constitutionally an African in Rhodesia at this time was supposed to be able to "acquire, hold, encumber, and dispose of land on the same conditions" as a European, in fact the British South Africa Company refused to allow Africans to buy land.

European Rhodesian Fear

By the late 1920s, the self-governing European Rhodesians became afraid that middle-class African farmers interested in cash-crop agriculture would press to exercise their constitutional right to own land outside of the segregated tribal areas.

In response to these white attitudes, a Land Apportionment Act was passed in 1930 formally segregating land ownership in the country.

The Tangwena people and their chief Rekayi were among the last victims of this Land Apportionment Act.

In 1969, the Rhodesian government revised and revamped the system of possessory segregation. The parliament of Ian Smith's government scrapped the old law and passed a Land Tenure Act and the Tribal Trust Land Development Act.

Intensive Development

Under the latter act a Tribal Trust Lands Development Corporation is authorized by the government to undertake intensive development of the Tribal Trust Land.

An August, 1973, publication of the African nationalist, Zimbabwe African Peoples' Union points out that "at no stage of the corporation's future is it envisaged that freehold title will pass" to individual African peasants or to a group of African peasants.

An information booklet put out by the Rhodesian government emphasizes correctly the intensity of feeling about land: "Both here and abroad there is a tendency . . . to believe that Africans have had a raw deal over land. There is no doubt that this is one of their most deeply emotional grievances and agitators have used it to stir up opposition against the government."

The trouble is not the agitators, but that the Rhodesian government has absolutely no intention of rectifying what the Africans rightly perceive as injustices.

Published Every Month. Subscription Rate: $8.00 Per Year

A Monthly Newsletter

THE
Libertarian Forum

Joseph R. Peden, Publisher   Murray N. Rothbard, Editor

VOLUME VI, NO. 6   JUNE, 1974   US-ISSN0047-4517

REFLECTIONS ON
THE MIDDLE EAST

1. And so we are to be subjected to a long round of rodomontade on the Kissinger "miracle" in the Middle East. President Tricky, a desperate man clutching at straws, is trying to save his neck by taking credit for Achieving a Lasting Peace in the Middle East. The Establishment press, which has always had a soft spot for Kissinger and is at any rate incapable of rising above superficiality in its foreign coverage, goes along with the hoopla. Besides, as inveterate pro-statists, they would love to say something good about the American government these days, and this is it. Politicians everywhere, their eyes fixed inveterately on the present and immediate future, shout hosannahs; and Arabs and Zionists alike kiss (literally!) and cosset Kissinger while lining up at the American trough. There hasn't been such a lavish and repellent display of international adoration since Nixon's trip to Peking.

2. And make no mistake about the lining up at the trough; for whatever short-run benefits Kissinger has achieved by the cease-fire agreements have been gained strictly at the expense of Uncle Sap, the American taxpayer. Already we hear of literally hundreds of millions of dollars of American aid that will be poured into the coffers of every state in the Middle East, Arabs and Israel alike. The most lucrative occupation in the world right now is to get yourself a sheikhdom somewhere in the Middle East and to get on line for American handouts. More ominous is Kissinger's "secret" commitment to Israel (reported in the New York Times) to back her in any reprisals directed against Palestinian guerrilla activity.

3. The current political situation in the Middle East should put the quietus once and for all to the right-wing and Establishment line that the Arab governments are mere puppets of "Soviet expansionism." In particular, Egypt and Syria have long been supposed to be Soviet puppets, so that the silly season is again here for the American press, which has actually been talking about the "miraculous" changeover of Egypt and Syria from Soviet puppetry to a "pro-American" stance. Yet the press doesn't draw the obvious lesson that the notion of Egypt or Syria or any other Arab country as a "tool of Moscow" was always Cold War hogwash.

4. In fact, Soviet foreign policy, once again as for so many decades, has shown itself to be dedicated to one overriding goal: peace, or detente, with the United States at virtually any price; ever since the days of Stalin, the Soviets have been willing to sell any and every one of their allies down the river at the drop of a hat. They have done it to a roster of allies too long to cite: Yugoslavia and the Chinese Communists (the origin of their respective breaks with Moscow); the Greek Communists, the French and Italian Communists, and on and on. Reliable reports indicate that the reason for the final capitulation of Syrian president Hafez el-Assad to the cease-fire was that Soviet Foreign Minister Andrei

Gromyko, anxious to avoid endangering the detente by angering Kissinger, flatly told Syria that it would withdraw Russia's support to the Syrian forces in any further conflict. And so Russia became a supine collaborator in its own replacement by the United States as the leading force in the Arab world.

5. To unravel the complex tangle of Middle East politics, and to understand what is going on, one must keep one's eye on the central and leading issue: the rights of the dispossessed Palestinians. A brief history of the situation is in order to untangle the web. After Israel displaced and ejected the Palestinians in the 1948 war, the demoralized Palestinians relied upon the contiguous Arab states to accomplish their goal of recapturing their homes, lands, and properties. That reliance was aided by the characteristic braggadoccio of the Arab states, whose rulers talked frequently and grandiloquently about "driving the Zionists into the sea." After a generation of nothing happening, the proof of the pudding was the 1967 war, in which Israel easily seized an enormous amount of Arab territory, including Arab Jerusalem and the West Bank of Palestine which had been grabbed by Jordan in 1948, the Gaza Strip of Palestine which had similarly been appropriated by Egypt, and the Sinai Peninsula and the Golan Heights, belonging to Egypt and Syria respectively. There thus emerged two sets of grievances: that of the Palestinians, including their original dispossession plus the further expulsions and military occupation by Israel; and the new grievances of Egypt, Syria and Jordan, which wanted back their pre-1967 territories.

The Palestinians now began to see that they could no longer rely on the other Arab states to advance their interests; and so there developed a variety of fedayeen, or Palestine guerrilla groups, devoted to final victory by carrying the war to Israel and the occupied zones. Since the Arab States now had grievances of their own, and since the fedayeen were highly popular throughout the Arab world, the Arab States formed a tentative and uneasy alliance with the Palestinians.

The goal of the Arab States was to get their pre-1967 land back. What was the political goal of the Palestinians? The political goal, as implied by the goal of allowing the displaced Palestinians to get their homes and lands back, was, to be sure, the liquidation of the state of Israel and its replacement by a state of Palestine, in which, all the Palestinian groups agree, all Jewish, Moslem, and Christian citizens would enjoy equal civil and religious liberty. Contrary to Zionist claims, the "destruction of the state of Israel" in the minds of the Palestinians does not imply the destruction of the individual Jews living in Israel. While the Palestinians all agree on the principle of equal civil rights, there is a split among these groups, for some of the militants advocate a transition period of

(Continued On Page 2)

Reflections On Middle East —

(Continued From Page 1)

"deZionizing" Palestine, which might imply placing the Jews of Palestine into a period of second-class tutelage. At any rate, even if the Jews were to attain immediate full citizenship in a new Palestine, the necessity of their giving up the seized lands would put them back into that tiny percentage of pre-1947 Palestinian territory which was purchased by the Zionists on a truly voluntary basis, and from the Arab peasants themselves and not their Turkish or other feudal overseers.

Unfortunately, as in the case of Northern Ireland, no group on either the Arab or Zionist side seems to have advocated a new partition, in which the state of Israel would be confined to its truly and voluntarily purchased land area. Certainly, at least at this point, there is no sign whatever of any group in Israel accepting such an arrangement.

At any rate, the Palestinian guerrilla groups grew into a formidable force until those fateful weeks in September, 1970, known from then on among the Arabs as "Black September", when King Hussein of Jordan turned upon the fedayeen, who were mainly based in Jordanian territory, and massacred them wholesale. The fedayeen almost did not recover from the blow.

Here we must understand the unique role of Jordan in the Arab world. Ever since its creation after World War I, Jordan has been ruled by the Hashemite monarchy (first by King Abdullah, now by King Hussein), which was virtually a creature of British imperialism. The formidable Jordanian army, consisting of Bedouin nomads from eastern Jordan, was staffed, trained, and commanded by British officers. The majority of Jordanians are now urban and agricultural Palestinians, who, however, have no voice in the Hashemite dictatorship, whose army still consists of Bedouins from the Eastern desert. One of the earliest grounds for the splits among the fedayeen was the relationship of the Palestinian movement, first to Jordan and the Hashemite monarchy, and ultimately to the other Arab States. The leading guerrilla group, Al Fatah, headed by Yasir Arafat, took the seemingly sensible line that the only real fight was with Israel, and therefore that it was senseless to take on the Arab states as well. But while seemingly sensible, this ignored the major differences of goals and structures between the Arab States and especially Jordan on the one hand, and the Palestinians on the other. One would have thought that Black September would have taught Al Fatah a lesson, but it really did not; the only lesson was narrowly confined to total hostility to Jordan, which even Al Fatah agrees to. But Al Fatah continues to put its trust in "princes", now especially Egypt and, to a lesser extent, the Soviet Union.

6. Why did Egypt launch the October War (which it did, by the way, without notifying Syria), and why did it gain great early victories, only to fumble and begin to lose? From his and Egypt's point of view, Anwar el-Sadat's launching of the war was a brilliant tactical masterstroke. The fedayeen, almost miraculously, had recovered from Black September and had begun to draw attention to its cause through dramatic incursions and "terror" tactics. But that cause could only win, at best, after a very long and protracted struggle. Meanwhile, nothing was happening on the Egyptian front. Israel was sitting on its 1967 conquests and showed no signs of budging. Indeed, why should it? So when was Egypt going to get its territory back, and when was it going to be able to reopen the Suez Canal? The UN was a hopeless debating club. Something dramatic had to be done to get the Middle East off dead center. Hence the launching of the war, which did indeed get the Middle East off dead center, gained foreign aid and the forthcoming Geneva conference, and pushed Israel a bit back from the Suez Canal. The gain in Arab morale, after a generation of unbroken and disastrous defeats, was of course enormous.

The surprise attack, and the massive weaponry, accounted for the early Egyptian victories; but why the later setbacks? The setback can be traced to the Egyptian decision to stop after the early gains and consolidate, instead of taking advantage of the early demoralization of the Israeli army by launching mobile and lightning thrusts deep into the Sinai. By stopping and holding, Egypt granted precious time to Israel to allow her to regroup, bring up reinforcements, and to engage in her own flexible and lightning tank tactics which had become famous in the 1967 war. Thus Israel could cross the Suez Canal, and surround large chuncks of the Egyptian Army on the east bank of the Suez.

So we come then to the critical military puzzle: why did Egypt stop at the point of a massive victory, and allow Israel to recoup? There seem to be two answers. One is that Sadat was not interested in a massive

victory; all he wanted was short-run gains, which could be used to force Israel into a peace conference. Second is the sort of strategy and tactics employed by Sadat throughout. We know that the massive Soviet air and military aid was almost all in defensive rather than offensive weapons, thus effectively preventing Egypt from undertaking an all-out offensive. But even more important is the fact, that under Soviet military advice, Sadat adopted the sort of military strategy and tactics that the Soviets had learned on the Eastern front in World War II: namely, massive and slow advance, covering territory and then consolidating that territory. It is the sort of strategy suitable for massive, ground-churning inter-State warfare. But to win militarily in the Middle Eastern situation, Sadat would have had to engage in very different strategy and tactics: i.e., in guerrilla warfare, which would have meant a kind of war suitable to insurrections by native populations against a State. Guerrilla warfare means (a) arming the native Arab population, so that the Arab populace could engage in massive aid to the soldiers, could have been — in the famous phrase of Che Guevara — the "water" in which the "fish" of the soldiery would have swum; (b) heavy reliance on Palestinian fedayeen to be that "fish" instead of on Egyptian State troops; and (c) emphasis on the tactics of mobility, flexibility, tank thrusts, and lightning-fast encirclement behind the Israeli lines. This strategy would have meant pressing on and encircling the demoralized Israeli troops in the early stages of the October war.

But to fight such a war, Sadat would have had to be prepared to fight a guerrilla war, for Palestinian aims. But Sadat's attitude toward the Palestinians and their aims has always been one of wary distrust, for what he is interested in is not a Palestinian insurrection but the advance of the territorial aims of the Egyptian State. It is safe to conclude that Sadat would rather lose, or at least stalemate, an orthodox inter-State war, than win a Palestinian guerrilla war against Israel.

An orthodox military rebuttal to the idea of guerrilla tactics in the Sinai peninsula is that, in that uninhabited desert, there is no native Arab population to form the water for the soldierly fish. But what this rebuttal neglects are the great military lessons of the Montgomery-Rommel tank warfare in the North African desert in World War IV. For, in such a case, the desert itself can be the friendly "water", and can be used as the base and medium for lightning fast tank raids and encirclements. Certainly there is no unfriendly population there to tip off the opposing army.

This guerrilla vs. inter-State theme is confirmed when we look at the Syrian theater of war. For how do we explain the fact that while Egypt fell into dire straits fairly soon, and hence was happy to conclude a cease-fire rather quickly, that Syria was never really defeated, and that while it lost some territory in the Mt. Hermon salient, it continued to fight on stubbornly until the June cease-fire? I think we can conclude that the basic reason was, that in contrast to the Egyptians having nothing militarily to do with the fedayeen, Syria rather heavily used and supported its own favored wing of the Palestinian guerrillas, the As Saiqa. Syria's partial devotion to guerrilla warfare may well account for the military differences in the Syrian and Egyptian outcomes.

7. So what now? Syria, deserted by all the other Arab States (except for Libya, which is far from the scene, and Iraq, also not contiguous to Israel and which has its hands full in its massive counter-revolutionary war to suppress the Kurds), and pressured finally by Russia, at last agreed to a cease-fire. In doing so, el-Assad gained a short-run tactical victory, since Syria regained the Mt. Hermon salient, plus a wafer-thin slice of the Golan Heights, including (an empty gesture) the ghost town of El Quneitra. But for those gains, Syria, in another "secret" agreement undertook to suppress any Palestinian guerrilla activity emanating from Syrian territory. Once again, Palestinian interests were sacrificed for the territorial goals of the Syrian state.

All this has thrown the Palestinian movement into a mighty dither, and indeed their choices now are extremely difficult. The majority of the Palestinians, headed by the leading guerrilla group Al Fatah, but also including the Syrian-oriented As Saiqa and the Maoist Popular Democratic Front for the Liberation of Palestine (PDFLP), headed by Nayef Hawatmeh, appear ready to accept a "mini"-Palestinian state in the pre-1967 areas of the West Bank of the Jordan and the Gaza Strip — and, in effect, to accept in return the legitimacy of the state of Israel within its pre-1967 borders. The minority of Palestinian militants, including only the Popular Front for the Liberation of Palestine (PFLP), headed by Dr. George Habesh, and the tiny Iraq-oriented Arab Liberation Front, is opposed to any mini-Palestinian state as either implicitly or explicitly recognizing, for the first time, the legitimacy of the post-1947

(Continued On Page 7)

European Politics

By Leonard P. Liggio

There has been a single theme in the foreign policy philosophy of the Nixon Administration; it was re-emphasized in a recent headline datelined Key Biscayne, Fla., May 27: NIXON FEARS NEW ISOLATIONISM. The immediate task of the president was to gain support for the most massive military budget yet put forward. The long-term aspect concerned America's domination over Europe. This had been undermined by French president De Gaulle, and was not repaired during the term of Georges Pompidou. Pompidou had taken the lead in insisting that European unity could be based only upon opposition to United States domination of Europe. He expressed this strongly last December at the Common Market summit meeting in Copenhagen. It was restated by French foreign minister Michel Jobert in his strong exchange last February in Washington with Henry Kissinger. It was reexpressed that month when French finance minister Valery Giscard d'Estaing abruptly decided to float the franc — always a threat to American monetary policies — rather than borrow money from international sources in order to artificially maintain the franc. These policies had led Kissinger on March 21 to repeat Nixon's constant warnings about the growth of neo-isolationism in America.

Thus, the recent presidential elections in France were of considerable importance to the Nixon administration. If there was a basic aspect to the election it might be said to have been the issue of principle. Giscard has a non-political image. He has been an economic expert, no more and no less. Mitterand, on the other hand, had a particularly political image. He became head of the Socialist party even though he had not been a member of that party, in order to run for president against De Gaulle in 1965 (he did better than expected with 45% of the vote). Mitterand had been the disciple in the 1950s, of Rene Pleven, a center politician and member of almost every cabinet, who always seemed to want what the U.S. wanted in military and foreign policy. Pleven and Mitterand fought against the program of the French right-wing which was for reconciliation with Russia. Mitterand served in many French cabinets of the Fourth Republic and his major disagreement with the Fifth Republic of De Gaulle was that he never again was called into the cabinet. Like so many of the center politicians, against who Gaullist politics was based, Mitterand has slept in more than one political bed. But, in politics as elsewhere, there is a large body of support for monogamy. Giscard benefited from not having been involved in the swapping of French parliamentary politics.

Giscard's economic policies are not great. He invented the value-added tax; he has used price controls; he thinks in Keynesian terms; there is a bias in his politics toward inflation to aid business undertakings rather than toward the deflation favored by the saving population. Giscard was supported by the planners and reformers. Giscard appointed several of them to his new cabinet. In addition to the technocrats, he appointed four center party leaders to the cabinet, including Jean Lecanuet and Jean-Jacques Servan-Schreiber. One of Giscard's objectives in appointing the centrists, in addition to their support for him in the election, is to try to create a more middle-of-the-road image. The election was one of the closest — Giscard, 50 plus percent; Mitterand, 49 plus. If Mitterand relied only on Socialist and Communist support, there would have been no contest. The Fourth Republic had a six-sided politics — Communists, Socialists, Radicals, Catholics, Gaullists and the Independents (which was led by Giscard's mentor, Antoine Pinay, a no-nonsense hard money advocate who initiated the sound financial base of the Gaullist period on which Giscard could play with his newer economic policies). De Gaulle's majorities were based on the latter three groups plus many of the former voters for the Radicals. In the meantime, a lot of older voters had died and a lot of the newer voters without any memory of Mitterand's earlier role as politician viewed him as the non-political candidate against those who have been in office for the past decade and a half, like Giscard.

Thus, in addition to the Socialist and Communist votes, Mitterand was supported by a lot of centrists. If he had been elected, Mitterand would have appointed the extreme centrist and pro-American mayor of Marseilles, Gaston Defferre, as prime minister. In fact, there might have been a lot of old politician faces of the pro-American heyday back in the

cabinet had Mitterand won. Even the few possible Communist cabinet members might have fitted in by not being pro-Soviet. During the election, the Soviet ambassador made a public call on Giscard — no doubt to discuss some pressing aspect of French investment in the Soviet Union that could not wait the few days until the election was over. Doubtless it never crossed the Soviet ambassador's mind that this highlighted the image of Giscard as a strong advocate of detente with the Soviet Union. However, the French Communist press denounced the action and protested the Soviet Union's interference in French domestic politics. Once more, a local Communist movement was sacrificed to broader Soviet foreign policy objectives.

Giscard's foreign policy is likely to be less publicly anti-American than Pompidou's but more directed to building up France's relations with Europe and Russia. The new foreign minister, Jean Sauvagnargues, was the recent ambassador to Germany, who in the nineteen thirties studied German culture "when there was a surge in French interest in German romanticism and a fascination with the rise of Hitler." He entered the diplomatic service during the Vichy regime of Marshal Petain. He has had long experience in the Arab and African worlds. The new prime minister, Jacques Chirac, was a brain truster for Pompidou and then chief aide to Giscard at finance, and more recently, agriculture and interior minister; his father-in-law is the director general of the foreign ministry and major contributor to De Gaulle's foreign policy. Chirac was a new Gaullist of the Pompidou variety rather than an old Gaullist. He will take a leading role in trying to split the new from the old Gaullists to form a new coalition around Giscard. The new finance minister, Jean-Pierre Fourcade had been an aide to Giscard at the finance ministry. The most important member of the cabinet will be the minister of state and interior minister (in charge of police), Michel Poniatowski, a leader of Giscard's Independents and a cousin of Giscard's wife. Poniatowski is a descendent of the family of the last king of Poland; one nephew of that king became a French marshal, dying at the Battle of the Nations near Leipzig in 1813, and another nephew, the grand treasurer of Lithuania, was the father of a senator of France under Napoleon III and was the ancestor of the present Michel.

Pompidou before his death was attempting to create a new political alignment of Giscard's Independents, the younger Gaullists such as Chirac, and the reform center. Pompidou had removed Jacques Chaban-Delmas as prime minister so that he would not be the heir of Pompidou. Chaban-Delmas had led the Gaullists in the nineteen fifties during De Gaulle's retirement and had been Gaullist speaker of the national assembly under De Gaulle. Chaban-Delmas has been mayor of Bordeaux for twenty-five years and was allied with the Gaullist party bosses led by Alexandre Sanguinetti. In the recent election, Chaban-Delmas received only about fifteen per cent of the vote. It was not surprising that Sanguinetti not only warned Chirac against causing defections in parliament from Gaullism, but pressed the new cabinet to push the Gaullist concept of worker participation in industrial management which was a major policy since De Gaulle issued his 1947 call. Sanguinetti said that the Gaullists would pay more attention to the workers and cause workers to press the unions toward Gaullist "corporatist" notions rather than socialist ones. The Gaullists did have voting support among the industrial workers, but in this election that disappeared. The Catholic labor federation supported Mitterand and joined the Socialist and Communist federations in the Cartel des Gauches. The industrial north-east, a stronghold of Gaullist worker votes, went over to Mitterand as early as the May 5 vote.

Pierre Gaxotte, in Le Figaro (May 11), recalled May 5 as the two hundredth anniversary of the death of Louis XV — the Well-Beloved (in many ways) — which ushered in the short-lived finance ministry of Turgot. However, May 5's election (first round) represented the loss of the Gaullist strongholds — Paris and the north-east. The other old Gaullist centers — the East and the West — went for Giscard. Gaullist and general right-wing strength has been centered in the northern half of France; the agricultural south has tended to be left-wing-Socialist and

(Continued On Page 4)

For Tuccille

By Roger Lea MacBride

I hear
That in New York this year
The Democrats will select Reid, Samuels or Carey
None of whom to us is the least bit scary.

> Libertarians think them the absurdest.

I hear
That in New York this year
The Republicans will choose incumbent Malcolm Wilson
Who if re-elected promises the state to tilt some.

> Libertarians' greeting: a cold blast.

I hear
That in New York this year
The Conservative choice is a surprise: Wilson, Malcolm
Who to a majority may prove less than walcome.

> Libertarians need a fistful of aspirin.

I hear
That in New York this year
The Marxist parties will struggle to get on the ballot
Some strange exemplar — maybe this time a shallot?

> Libertarians would rather run up Mt. Everest.

When we put it all together, what have we got?
I submit to you a hell of a lot.

> The absurdest: Too silly.
> A cold blast: Too chilly.
> A fistful of aspirin: Too pilly.
> A run up Mt. Everest: Too hilly.

All four points agree, you see.
In 1974 it's Jerome Tuccille!!

Note by Roger Lea MacBride:
The common law copyright in the above has been hastily assigned to Joey Rothbard. While of course I hope that large sums will flow into her coffers as a result of requests to reprint, candor prompts me to admit that the major motive was to protect myself from potentially damaging law suits.

Reply from Joey Rothbard:
Since my taste in poetry is as low as my taste in music, I am tickled to have the copyright, and am eagerly awaiting the large sums.

European Politics —

(Continued From Page 3)

Communist (the Communists have massive peasant support in France). Northern France was the old center of feudal law and administrative government; while southern France was the center of civil law and representative institutions. These divisions seemed to have continued in the present political situation.

Chaban-Delmas thus gained strength in the formerly non-Gaullist center, the south-west, around Chaban's center of power, Bordeaux. But, in the second round election on May 19, this area shifted to the left again. Similarly, the votes of former cabinet member, Jean Royer, the mayor of Tours, shifted to Mitterand in the second round, even though Royer ran as an anti-inflation but even more as an anti-pornographic candidate representing the puritan wing of Catholicism. The poor showing of this campaign paralleled the events surrounding the vote to repeal the new law in Italy permitting divorce. The voters approved the new divorce law by a 3-2 vote. The new law was opposed by the Catholic hierarchy led by the Pope himself (including removal of Catholic spokesmen favoring non-church interference in civil matters such as the abbot of the historic monastery of St-Paul's Outside the Walls). The Communists and Socialists were joined by the right-wing Italian Liberals and the center Republican's in supporting the law while the Christian Democrats were allied with the new Fascist party. Italian senate president and former prime minister Fanfani led the Christian Democratic faction that wanted to repeal the law as a step to his returning to power. As he is left-wing on domestic matters and pro-American on foreign affairs his defeat is a major step to an improvement in Italy's politics — strong anti-inflationary monetary policy which will reduce reliance on the U.S. economically and a more neutralist foreign policy. Italy's long-standing favorable relations with the Arab oil countries and its mergence as a refining, storage and petro-chemical center increased Italy's independence from the United States.

Portugal, which has been a keystone of American military power, experienced a total overturn in its politics which should cause it to end its special military ties with the United States and become part of the widening European bloc which Kissinger sees as defining itself in opposition to the United States. The revolution resulted directly from the desire of major elements of Portugal to direct its attentions to concentrating upon Europe, and to experience a modernization of the economy in a capitalist direction. Until now, Portugal has been a strong support for U.S. policy regarding NATO; Portugal's main interest has been its wars to maintain colonialism in Africa and its alliance with South Africa. Like South Africa, Portuguese colonies had large numbers of European settlers who prefer to be bureaucrats ruling over millions of Africans rather than establishing themselves as a European state in the portions of Africa which they settled and which were not settled by African peoples. Instead of being satisfied with settlement of a small area which was totally European, they preferred rule over a huge native population. The colonialism and monopoly enterprises of the previous regime are being dismantled by the revolution which was led by General Antonio de Spinola, the new president, who was removed from the army in February for publishing, "Portugal and the Future," in which he called for a Lusitanian Community of Portugal and its former colonies, similar to the British Commonwealth. The African revolts had started in December 1960 in Angola (inspired by the revolt and independence in the Congo in that summer in which the BaKongo people of the lower Congo and northern Angola had taken the lead), and in Guinea-Bissau in West Africa. The guerilla war in Guinea was led by the late Amilcar Cabral who was assassinated last fall. The war was based on the stateless Balante people against the pro-Portuguese feudal Fula emirs. Cabral had advocated a future government which would be without a capital and without bureaucratic departments attempting to run people's lives from a central government. Cabral in his book, **Revolution in Guinea,** challenged the established Marxist notions of revolution and of society in liberated Guinea. The Portuguese government is composed of liberals, socialists and Communists (a Communist party totally controlled by Moscow and thus extremely moderate; the Communist cabinet members' role is to maintain low wage rates among the workers on the model of the Soviet Union.)

Outside of Europe, the revolution of the Kurds of northern Iraq is worthy of note. The revolt has been going on for about two decades, and at times was well covered by the New York **Times** Middle East correspondent who periodically would take a couple of months to cross through the Turkish mountains to reach Kurdistan. There are about two and a half million Kurds in Iraq and about six million in eastern Turkey

(Continued On Page 5)

Arts And Movies

By Mr. First Nighter

Thunderbolt and Lightfoot. dir. by Michael Cimino. With Clint Eastwood.

First, I have to report, as a dyed-in-the-wool Clint Eastwood fan, that this picture is a total disaster. It is not Clint Eastwood's fault; he struggles manfully through the role. The fault is strictly Cimino's, may he retire for the rest of his life to television. Eastwood is cast as the hero of a crime caper to recover buried loot, for which both another set of crooks and the police are chasing him. It sounds interesting, but it isn't, largely because action disappears into the twin killers of any good action-suspense movie: a lot of witless horseplay, interspersed with much moping and "tragedy."

Walking Tall. dir. by Phil Karlson, with Joe Don Baker.

Walking Tall, on the other hand, is an authentic hero picture, and a smashing success. For weeks, I was put off by news of its "underground" success, and ad comparisons to one of the turkeys of all time, **Billy Jack.** But the two, rest assured, are as different as day and night. **Walking Tall** is not only expertly directed and acted, but the plot is truly heroic, and is, as most everyone knows, the true story of Buford Pusser, first as citizen-farmer and then as sheriff, battling a passel of bad guys in rural Tennessee. Left-liberals who complain about Pusser's "puritanism" ignore the fact that the bad guys' gambling was crooked and that the hero and friend were nearly killed when they tried to get their money back; and that the moonshine was poisonous enough to kill a dozen customers. Joe Don Baker makes a great hero, in the classic tradition of an innocent who is victimized, and then fights back to conquer the victimizers. It's great to see Phil Karlson back after many years, and let's hope that he makes many more films.

Chosen Survivors. dir. by Sutton Roley. With Jackie Cooper.

A pleasant, though scarcely a great, politico-science fiction film, with — let us strongly note — an explicit libertarian content. The villain of the piece is the U. S. government, its computers, and its **verdamte** "behavioral scientist"; the government shanghais and drugs a group of people chosen by its computer to serve as unwilling guinea pigs in a behavioral science experiment. Shipped far underground to a "totally controlled environment", the poor experimentees are told that nuclear war has just wiped out virtually everyone on earth, and that they are among the few chosen survivors, who would have to remain underground for years until radiation on the surface had disappeared. It's all, however, a trick, for the good of "research."

Interestingly enough, the capitalist in the group, well played by Jackie Cooper, is the only one to smell a rat and to keep agitating for the group to escape. Treated by everyone as a greed-filled and selfish pariah, it turns out that the pesty capitalist was right all along. For this we can forgive Roley some of the crudities derived from his TV background.

Daisy Miller. dir. by Peter Bogdanovich. With Cybill Shepherd.

Written by Frederic Raphael, from the novel by Henry James.

Dare I say it? Dare I think the unthinkable? Namely, that I have always found Henry James b-o-r-i-n-g; is there anything quite so excruciatingly boring as the old gentleman's endless, quibbling, and plotless stories? I have said before that Peter Bogdanovich is one of our best young directors, but here he is trapped by his own major **leitmotif** — his reverence and love for "classical" literature and cinema, his rejection of the **avant-garde.** For Bogdanovich is here trapped by his neo-classicism — usually a virtue of his — into a faithful translation of the original vapidity to the screen. For James, the most uncinematic of writers, such a faithful rendition may be of interest to antiquarians, but it is a film disaster. If one wants to translate James to the screen, he must be made cinematic; a literal rendition is a disaster, in this case **Daisy Miller.**

For one point, for those who like that sort of thing the charm of James is his endless filagree and subtlety of language; since all that has to drop out in any movie version, what we are left with is a plotless plot, and endless shots of the passive protagonist of the film standing around moping as he observes Daisy's pointless antics. Another problem here is that Bogdanovich and Raphael, as sophisticated Americans of the 1970's, seem incapable of understanding that James' viewpoint of a century ago, in his endless novels and stories about crude Americans visiting aristocratic Europe, was pro-Europe and anti-American. In pitching the movie in precisely the opposite direction, Bogdanovich and Raphael have

made hash of whatever point James was laboring to make.

To top off the whole stew, Bogdanovich fell into another trap, one that has been mentioned by most of the critics. Usually, he is a master at getting sterling performances from his actors; but here he cast the crucial role of Daisy with his current **amour,** Cybill Shepherd, who either can't act at all or can't do so under Bogdanovich's direction. I suppose it's something like the old motto that a lawyer should never argue his own case. At any rate, Miss Shepherd, who is supposed to be a charming flirt, rattles on in a machine-gun delivery, and with such an evident lack of even feigned, much less genuine, interest in any of her suitors, that the center of the film never has a chance to hold. ◘

European Politics —

(Continued From Page 4)

and north-western Iran. The leader of the Kurds is Mullah Mustafa Barzani. The Kurds were promised independence by the Treaty of Sevres in 1920, one of the post-World War I peace treaties. This treaty gave public recognition to the secret Anglo-French Skyes-Picot Agreement of 1916 whereby France was to receive Syria and England Iraq, from the Ottoman Empire. The Agreement had to do with hoped for petroleum resources which had been feared would fall to German possession in 1914 through the Berlin to Bagdad concession. The important area, the vilayet of Mosul, was a known petroleum reserve and England wanted it. Although the war in Mesopotamia had ended in November 1918 with English forces (Indian troops) sixty miles south of Mosul, English forces gradually moved to and beyond the city. In 1923 as one of the seventeen agreements signed at Lausanne, Turkey agreed to what amounted to English control over Mosul while nothing was said about carrying out the treaty of Sevres' provision for an independent Kurdistan (which would have included Mosul). Under the English imposed Hashemite family the Kurds' struggle continued. After the establishment of the Iraq Ba'athist regime in the nineteen sixties, recognition of Kurdish autonomy seemed possible. The Ba'ath, which also rules in Syria, is a complex political philosophy founded by a Syrian Christian on the basis of French Catholic social theory. But, the Iraq Ba'ath did not live up to their agreements and the conflict continues in and around the petroleum center of Mosul. (For a really valuable explanation of Middle East politics and American policy in that area, read Miles Copeland, **The Game of Nations;** Copeland, a pr man in Cairo for decades, was involved in more crucial diplomatic activities than a thousand ordinary overseas ad men; it is a first-hand deep-cover overview).

Meanwhile, India has exploded an atomic weapon. A very strong criticism was issued by the Gandhi Peace Foundation secretary, Radha Krishna: "The economic costs of this program are unimaginable. There is also the likelihood of it adding to our monstrous inflation. When the country's economic situation is one of great stress, on account of gross underutilization of industrial capacity and available resources including human resources, the search for a new source of energy of doubtful immediate use, does not exactly square up with our national priorities . . . Is prestige not synonymous with the assertion of our national ideals — no begging for food, our entire people sweating it out in the task of national reconstruction and very friendly relations between the countries in the subcontinent?" Asher Brynes, author of **We Give To Conquer,** dealing with foreign aid, noted in **The Nation** (June 8, 1974) that Nobel Peace Prize winner and Rockefeller Foundation spokesman, Dr. Norman Borlaug, had chewed out Indian bureaucrats. Echoing what Milton Friedman had said about foreign aid in India in the 1950's, Borlaug demonstrated the complete failure of bureaucracy. Since foreign grain is either given by the U.S. to the Indian government when it behaves or is purchased by government agencies, there is no room for private enterprise. The government officials did not buy wheat for reserve stocks, and then flooded the American commodity markets on a panic basis driving up the price two or three times. No oil reserves were undertaken by the government monopolies so the grain regions of India will not be able to produce full yields due to absence of oil for the massive irrigation pump system and of synthetic fertilizers. ◘

481

For Kurdistan

Why is it next to impossible for people to approach foreign affairs from the point of view of justice? This chronic difficulty has been fatally aggravated in the last thirty years by the exigencies of the Cold War. National liberation movements are evaluated, by the Establishment and by the Left alike, solely on the basis of their Cold War orientation (are they "pro" or "anti" — "West"?) rather than on the actual merits or the concrete history or facts that are involved. The result is not only moral blindness, but a positive distortion, on both Right and Left, of what is actually going on in a large portion of the world.

Take, for example, the Kurds, a distinct nation of several million strong who, for literally several millennia, have been striving for independence from an endless series of imperial conquerors and occupiers. In contrast to the Leninist view that imperialism is a product of "finance capitalism", this phenomenon has been around since one tribe or nation began to conquer and rule over another: in short, imperialism has been almost co-terminous with the existence of the State itself.

The Kurds are still striving for national independence, and they are still as far from ever from attaining it. "Kurdistan", the once and future goal of the Kurdish people, is a distinct area encompassing northeastern Iraq, northwestern Iran, and southeastern Turkey, with a tiny area in the southern tip of the Soviet Caucasus and another tiny area in the northeastern tip of Syria. In short, Kurdistan is wholly occupied under the heel of three States, as well as two other minor carvers of the Kurdish pie. After World War I, the major thrust of Kurdish nationalism was against Turkish rule, and Kurdish leader Sherif Pasha vainly presented the case for Kurdish independence from Turkey at the Versailles conference. Since World War II, the major thrust of Kurdish aspirations has been in Iraq, and the great leader of the Kurdish movement in Iraq for the entire time has been General Mustafa Barzani.

But while the Kurdish national movement in Iraq under Barzani has been a constant force in the Middle East for thirty years, the interpretation and the attitudes toward Barzani and the Kurds have changed drastically with the winds of the Cold War and of the general conflicts in the Middle East. In the post-World War II years, the American Establishment press, headed by the New York Times, treated Barzani as a virtual Communist, and as a pawn of Russian imperial interests. In those days, the U. S. was allied with the Iraqi government, and so any disruption of the status quo was blindly considered subversive and an instrument of the Soviet Union. Actually, Barzani was in no sense a Communist; as a national liberation leader, he took the usual approach of accepting any aid from any quarter that wishes to give it — in much the same way as the American Revolutionaries gladly accepted aid from France, Spain, and other enemies of the British empire. In neither case were the revolutionaries "tools" of anyone; it was simply that they were willing to accept aid without dominance from any quarter in opposition to their imperial masters.

Three decades have passed; and General Barzani and the Kurds are still fighting the Iraqi government on behalf of national independence. In fact, they have been willing to settle for autonomy within Iraq, and have concluded several agreements over the years with the Iraqis. But in each and every case, the Iraq government has betrayed its agreement as soon as it has felt strong enough to resume the fighting against the Kurdish guerrillas. The latest agreement was made in 1970, and the latest betrayal was the refusal to grant the full autonomy to the Kurds that Iraq had pledged itself to grant by March of 1974. Hence, since this March, fighting between the Kurds and Iraq has again broken out on a large scale.

But this time the shoe is on the other foot. The Iraq government is solidly anti-Israel and a staunch defender of the rights of the dispossessed Palestinian Arabs to return to their homes and lands. Hence, the Soviets are now, at least for the moment, pro-Iraq, and it is now the Left that regards the Kurds and poor Barzani as a "tool" of Western imperialism and of the American allies in Turkey and Iran. True to his policy of accepting aid from any quarter against Iraqi rule, Barzani has indeed been accepting Western aid. Which makes him no more of a "tool of the West" now than he was a "Commie" thirty years ago. Where anyone stands vis a vis Israel or the Soviet Union is irrelevant to the Kurdish issue; that issue is simply the battle of the Kurdish people against age-old

and continuing aggression by the imperial rule of the Iraqi State.

The two million Kurds of Iraq are now engaged in a classic national liberation-guerrilla confrontation with the Iraqi government. Once again, as in the armed Kurdish rebellion of the 1960's, the 40,000-strong Kurdish guerrilla army does very well against Iraqi troops in the mountainous terrain of Kurdistan despite Iraqi use of napalm and once again, the major Iraqi weapon is the barbaric use of air raids and bombs against the civilian Kurdish population. Aid is coming across the Turkish and Iranian frontiers because the Iraq government has imposed a savage blockade on the movement of food into the Kurdish areas. Meanwhile, Iraq has executed nearly 100 leaders of the Kurdistan Democratic Party in Bagdad.

A complicating factor in the war is the fact that the great Iraqi oil center of Kirkuk is in Kurdish territory, and that is one area that the Iraqis are particularly reluctant to yield to Kurdish autonomy. So oil politics adds to the intensity of the conflict.

But an ever-constant factor in the shifting power struggles in the Middle East is the unfulfilled and legitimate aspirations of the Kurdish people. Some day, the Kurds will achieve their Kurdistan; and the sooner, Left, Right, and Center adjust to that fact, the better for all concerned; certainly the better for the cause of justice. ◼

The Hiss Case Revisited

It was on the famed perjury conviction of Alger Hiss that Richard Nixon built the formidable reputation that finally gained him the Presidency of the United States. Not only that: the Hiss Case provided the major bulwark of the Red-hunting crusade within the United States, the spy-hunt, the general fears of the "international Communist conspiracy", and even much of the Cold War mythology itself.

The clinching evidence against Hiss arose from the allegation that the American government documents found in admitted Communist spy Whittaker Chambers' famous pumpkin had been typed on Alger Hiss' own typewriter, and that the Hiss defense itself had introduced into evidence the very typewriter that was then determined by experts to have typed these crucial Pumpkin Papers. Since the defense itself had introduced the typewriter as Hiss' own, Hiss was then inevitably hoist on his own petard. The case was clinched.

Hiss could only feebly maintain that the FBI had committed "forgery by typewriter", in short, had constructed a new typewriter to fit the typing on the documents, and then had led him to discover it in a Washington junk shop, masquearding as his own. Who could believe such a wild story? Who could believe that the then sainted FBI could do such a devious and foul deed of frameup?

In the light of the Watergate, we are all wiser now about what the U. S. government and the FBI are capable of doing. The first crack in the formidable government case came in the first edition of Richard Nixon's famous book of self-congratulation, "My Six Crises". In that work, Nixon stated that the FBI had "found" the typewriter. But since Alger Hiss himself had presumably discovered it in the junk shop, the implication was startling: for if the FBI had really "found" it, then it must have planted the typewriter in the shop as a decoy, and led Hiss to find it later; and, furthermore, what had the FBI done to the typewriter in the meantime? In the second edition of the Nixon book, the telling statement was changed to the opposite: that the FBI had not been able to find the typewriter. As the New York Times writes (May 3, 1974), "Mr. Nixon explained the change at the time by saying that it was an error by his researcher."

Indeed! We are now all too familiar with Mr. Nixon's "errors" and "explanations." But now, in the already infamous Nixon transcripts, we find another cryptic and illuminating reference to the Hiss typewriter. In a conversation of Feb. 28, 1973, Nixon advises John Dean to study the Hiss case as a good example of how to have to get things done. Said the Tricky One: "We got the typewriter; we got the pumpkin papers." So; "we" got the typewriter, eh? For almost twenty-five years, since his conviction in 1950, Alger Hiss has been trying to obtain the FBI files on his case; it is high time that these documents be released, and that the whole Hiss Case be re-examined. ◼

Reflections On Middle East —

(Continued From Page 2)

State of Israel. At the June meeting of the Palestinian National Council, the overall Congress of the Palestinian movement, the majority view was ratified. This, of course, places the Palestinian majority in line with the interest of the Arab states, who also want restoration of the **status quo ante** 1967. The only exception is Jordan, which would lose the West Bank, but the other Arab States are prepared to jettison Jordanian territorial interests; no wing of the Palestinians would accept a return to Jordanian rule over the West Bank.

The road to a long-range peace agreement in the Middle East, however, is scarcely clear-cut, to say the least. For Israel has shown no signs of accepting the idea of a mini-State; in fact, it has not yet even recognized the existence of the Palestinians. The Geneva peace conference, originally intended for this summer, will not be convened before the end of this year, if then.

8. And yet, having said that, we must also note that Israel has just experienced its first significant political change since its inception in 1947. Since its founding, Israel has been governed by a coalition headed by the Labor (Mapai) Party, led first by David Ben-Gurion, then by Levi Eshkol, and lately by Golda Meir. The actual leadership of the Mapai, and hence of the Israeli government, however, has been for all these years in the hands of the Gush clique, headed by Finance Minister Pinhas Sapir, and including the aforementioned premiers. Old-line and European-born, the Gush have always taken the position that the Palestinian Arabs do not exist, that they are either "South Syrians" or "West Jordanians" or just plain non-people. If we adopt the Israeli practice of considering the "left"-"right" spectrum of Israeli politics as signifying "dove"-"hawk" on the Arab question, then the Gush has always been strongly to the right of center, hard-line opponents of negotiations with the Arabs, and apt to adopt military solutions to political problems.

Over a decade ago, the Mapai, to maintain its rule, was forced to merge with several other parties, including the Mapam and the Achdut Avodah, forming the Labor Alignment Party which still governs Israel. But the old parties still exist as recognizable factions within the greater Labor Alignment. Both the Mapam and the Achdut Avodah were considerably more "dovish", hence to the "left" of, the Mapai and the Gush. The Mapam, the erstwhile pro-Soviet party, however, and originally the major representative of the (voluntary) communist **kibbutzim**, has largely faded away, probably in accordance with the dwindling importance of the **kibbutzim** in Israeli life. This left the Achdut Avodah, headed by Vice-Premier Yigal Allon, as the major "left-wing" force within the Labor Alignment. Meanwhile, there grew up on the right-wing of the latter party the Rafi faction, a highly hawkish group led by the charismatic leader of the 1967 conquest, General Moshe Dayan. Also included in the Meir coalition along with the Labor Alignment, was the National Religious Party, the major party of Orthodox Jewry, which, because of its crucial balance-of-power role in the Parliament (Knesset) has been able to impose a rigid Orthodox theocracy on a largely non-Orthodox, if not atheist, country. In foreign affairs, the NRP advocates the maximum territorial extent of Biblical Judaism.

The seemingly eternal role of the Gush was shaken irretrievably by the enormous shock of the October war. For the first time, the Israeli military suffered severe losses, and the much vaunted Israeli intelligence services were taken completely by surprise. The Israeli arrogance and illusion of invincibility was shattered beyond repair by the initial losses. As Minister of Defense, Moshe Dayan's political goose was completely cooked, and Golda Meir, after hanging on desperately to power, was finally forced to retire and thereby to accept the responsibility for the quasi-defeat at the hands of the Arabs.

The crucial question of Israeli politics then became: who would succeed Mrs. Meir? There ensued a fierce and highly important struggle for succession between Shimon Peres, the Interior Minister under Meir, and the leader of the Rafi faction after Dayan; and General Yitzhak Rabin, a member of the Achdut Avodah faction. The fight was close and dirty, but Rabin finally won, helped by the fact that, as a late-comer to politics, he had not been an actual member of the Achdut Avodah party before the merger of the 1960's. The result was the final defeat of the

From The Old Curmudgeon

What Price "Purity"? Sam Konkin's New **Libertarian Notes**, which specializes in wrapping itself in the "purity" mantle and judging other libertarians thereby, has, in its May issue, an attack on the FLP for nominating the "impure" Percy Greaves for the U. S. Senate. And yet, in the very same "Christian Libertarian" issue, NLN contains an article by the Rev. Edmund Opitz, who is not only at least as impure as Greaves (to employ some Christian charity), but has spent a large part of his energy and output in the last couple of decades in attacking anarchism. So what price "purity" now? To mix our metaphors, I guess it all depends on whose "purity" is being gored. How did the Good Book say it: "Let him who is without impurity cast the first stone." ◻

Gush, with not only Mrs. Meir, but also General Dayan , Pinhas Sapir, and Foreign Minister Abba Eban, leaving the Cabinet and retiring to the back benches. Israel is now under the control of the Rabin-Allon (still Deputy Premier and now Foreign Minister Achdut Avodah action.

On the "dove-hawk" spectrum, the Achdut Avodah faction may be termed "slightly to the left of center." Mr. Rabin, Israel's first native-born (sabra) Premier, at least recognizes the existence of the Palestinians, and his "dovish" hand is strengthened by the fact that the NRP is no longer in the governing coalition, being replaced by the much more dovish Civil Rights Party, headed by Mrs. Shulamit Aloni, who is anathema to the Gush and to the groups further right in Israel. But, in the traditional center-izing role of party politics, Mr. Rabin, with a wafer-thin majority in the Knesset, has been at least initially forced to take a line on the Arabs almost as hawkish as Mrs. Meir's, in order to block any major right-wing defections from the Labor Alignment. Indeed, within the mainstream of Israeli politics, only Mrs. Aloni's CRP calls clearly for the return of Israel to the 1967 borders — i.e. only the CRP takes a position which could lead to a general peace agreement. The only more dovish groups than the CRP in Israel are a few tiny anti-Zionist groupings, the major one being the Marxist party, the Matzpen.

Any dovishness within Israel would be further stifled by the fact that the major opposition to the Labor Alignment is the far more hawkish grouping, the Likud, headed by the fiery ultra-hawk, Menachem Beigin, long-time leader of the "extreme rightist" Herut party. The Herut, the dominant faction within the Likud, is the child of the long-time World Zionist-Revisionist movement, dedicated above all things to military conquest of the maximal territory of Biblical Jewry, "on both sides of the Jordan". On domestic matters, Herut is state corporatist, in contrast to the laborite socialism of the Labor Alignment; thus, the predecessor of Beigin, Vladimir Jabotinsky, the founder of Zionist-Revisionism, expressed admiration for the corporate state of Mussolini. The other major faction within the Likud is the Liberal Party, oriented to the General Zionist movement within the United States, which is devoted to some form of free enterprise on domestic matters, but which is almost as anti-Arab as the Herut. There is unfortunately no faction within Israel that is both dovish and pro-free enterprise.

8. Finally, even in the unlikely event that Israel should come to accept the idea of a mini-Palestinian state, there would still be almost insuperable problems to solve. For the Palestinians would accept nothing less than a fully independent mini-Palestine State, whereas Israel would accept nothing more than a demilitarized Palestinian state (while Israel, of course, remained armed to the teeth) with UN supervision and Israeli right of inspection. And so, despite the hoopla, the confusion, and the considerable and significant political changes throughout the Middle East, the long-run prospect is still for protracted conflict with no end in sight. ◻

Obit Note

The police have now disclosed that Phillip Willkie, subject of an RIP in our April issue, committed suicide.

Contra Federal Campaign Funding

By Bill Evers

Various proposals to limit campaign spending and to substitute in whole or in part money taken from the taxpayers are at present being debated in the halls of Congress and in the news media. These proposals are all direct attacks on the First Amendment rights of free speech and a free press.

Any limitation on an individual's right to contribute infringes upon his right of free expression. The essence of freedom of speech is the prohibition of governmental interference with a man's hiring a hall to say whatever he wants.

Similarly, the essence of freedom of the press is the prohibition of governmental interference with publishing.

If a person is prohibited from spending money to express his support for a political candidate, then that person's liberties have been severely undermined. An election commission with tyrannical powers would be presiding over political expression.

Citizen's Rights?

The proposal to have tax-supported election campaigns not only takes a citizen's earnings, but puts that money in the pockets of men the citizen may very well oppose.

Michael Killian of the Chicago **Tribune** zeroed in on the issue involved: "Picture yourself as a South Side Chicago black who has just turned over a substantial portion of his income to the IRS and then turns on his television set to watch part of it being spent on a TV spot for George Wallace. Or a Vermont conservative watching a federally financed George McGovern talking about how this country needs more taxes."

To add some parallel examples to Killian's, imagine a New Leftist looking at a Nixon plug he has paid for, a feminist paying for an ad for an anti-abortion candidate, or an anarchist who doesn't like any of the candidates he is paying to promote.

Anyone who has paid his federal income tax recently knows that the new "checkoff" program of federal financing pays only for the Presidential campaigns of the Establishment's Republican and Democratic parties.

Choices Limited

When this program was launched, it was stated that those who participated could designate to which party they wished to have the tax money go. But the tax form does not allow this.

Supporters of the Peace & Freedom Party, the American Independent Party, the Libertarian Party, the Socialist Workers Party, and other groups are forced to pay for Republican and Democratic campaigns.

Most of the various campaign spending bills now in Congress require a government - sanctioned classification of groups into major parties and minor parties.

The groups designed as minor are effectively frozen into a situation in which uncertain prospects, little money, and stringent requirements paralyze them.

Status Quo Maintained

At a time when the public is dissatisfied with the large political parties, they are about to ensure their own wealthy and perpetual existence. In September 1973, a Gallup poll showed that one-third of the American public identifies with neither the Republicans nor the Democrats.

At a time when respect for politicians and trust in the government itself is at a low ebb, the established politicians are engineering a successful new raid on the taxpayers' pocketbook.

At the same time, corporate liberal business figures (Miles Rubin, Daniel Noyes, Stanley Steinbaum, and Max Palevsky) are rallying behind the idea of tax-funded elections because they hope to re-stabilize a system shaken by the Watergate revelations.

In the November 10, 1973 issue of **National Journal Reports**, Mrs. Susan B. King, who runs the Center for Public Financing of Elections, is quoted on the large support the idea has received from the wealthy.

Big-Business Support

Business Week for September 15, 1973 reported that many business executives are strongly in favor of limiting campaign contributions and says that "many are willing to consider some government subsidy."

These corporate liberal leaders feel uncomfortable with the local interests who gain a voice through present-day election spending. Instead these corporate liberals, whose own activities are national in scope, feel comfortable with the politicking of government-business planning groups like Nelson Rockefeller's Critical Issues Commission or the Committee for Economic Development.

Reforms' Loopholes

Under the proposed campaign reforms, we can expect simply that payments from large business and labor groups will no longer be in money form. Personnel will be donated, equipment will be loaned, meeting sites will be made available at no cost.

Campaigns for programs that are linked in the public's mind with a specific candidate will be promoted by "public interest" groupings of the candidate's followers.

In sum, the proposed campaign financing laws are an assault on free political expression. As Yale professor Ralph Winter says, "A law forbidding someone from spending a certain amount cannot be distinguished from a law forbidding speeches of over 10 minutes in public parks." In addition, the law favors the incumbent politicians and those who like the American system as it is.

*Reprinted from The Stanford Daily, April 4, 1974.

The Libertarian Forum

BOX 341
MADISON SQUARE STATION
NEW YORK, NEW YORK 10010

Published Every Month. Subscription Rate: $8.00 Per Year

A Monthly Newsletter

THE
Libertarian Forum

Joseph R. Peden, Publisher

Murray N. Rothbard, Editor

VOLUME VI, NO. 7   JULY, 1974   US-ISSN0047-4517

WORLD-WIDE INFLATION

It is no secret that virtually the entire world is now suffering from a severe "double-digit" inflation, and that we have all moved to a scary new plateau of inflationary acceleration. It is no comfort to us "Austrian" economists that we have predicted the current mess; it is still less comfort that very few people have taken the Austrian lessons to heart. It is true that the free gold market has finally begun to price gold realistically in relation to the depreciating currencies of the world; but the monetary authorities show no real disposition to do anything to halt the looming takeoff to worldwide currency destruction. Do the monetary authorities, the politicians, and the Establishment economists understand that the cause of the mess is a continuing expansion of the money supply in the various nations? Yes and no; many of them don't know, while those who do understand, mumble about the "political realities" and go along with the accelerating destruction. The much-vaunted "tight money" policy of the Federal Reserve System is simply a grisly joke; money is not "tight" when the Fed **still** continues to increase the money supply at a rate of approximately 10% per annum. Really tight money doesn't mean high and rising interest rates, which are inevitable in the later stages of an inflationary boom and reflect "inflation premiums" on the price of credit. Tight money means **ceasing** to inflate the money supply, period; or even decreasing it. That such truly tight money is scarcely in the offing was seen by the response of the Fed in pouring in $1 billion of new money to save the Franklin National Bank from the consequences of its own misdeeds.

The public is solidly opposed to inflation, as it increasingly hits their savings and their cost of living, and as they increasingly find that rising interest rates make stocks an extraordinarily bad hedge against inflation. Unfortunately, the public cannot be expected to understand the arcane processes by which the Fed and other central banks keep increasing the money supply and thereby bring about continuing and accelerating inflation. One thing the public knows — at least for the time being, while its memory is fresh: price and wage controls don't work, in fact only aggravate the inflationary problem, and cause distortions, severe lags in real income, and shortages throughout the economy. One heartening sign of this public knowledge was the recent Canadian election, which was fought largely on the question of price and wage control for the severe Canadian inflation: the Progressive Conservatives called for price and wage control, while Trudeau and the Liberals countered by pointing to the acknowledged failure of such controls in the U. S. The result was a sweeping victory for the Liberals.

Unfortunately, the public is still ignorant of the cause of inflation: the expansion of the money supply by the Fed and the other central banks. Even some of the nation's "gold bugs", who oppose printing press paper money and call for a restoration of gold as money, are so ignorant of the processes of monetary expansion that they hold that the Fed cannot expand the money supply any further; hence, they are predicting a deflation — a fall in prices and the cost of living — at the very time when the inflation is accelerating dangerously. Unfortunately, now that the last vestiges of the gold standard are gone, the Fed has the power to create more money indefinitely; and so long as we continue to allow them to retain such power, they will continue to use it, with disastrous results.

The important point to realize is that the banking system, and particularly the Federal Reserve Banks, create money out of thin air. They are, in short, legalized counterfeiters. The Fed does this in two ways: one is simply printing cash, or Federal Reserve Notes, which are legal tender money. But more insidious, and more significant a way in the modern world, is the Fed's creation out of thin air of "checkbook money", or "demand deposits", which are redeemable at any time in cash, and which serve as "high powered money", as reserves for a six-fold pyramiding of "checkbook money" by the tightly controlled commercial banking system. The Fed creates this "high-powered money" by buying any asset on the "open market", i.e. by buying an asset from some member of the public. In practice, these assets are always U. S. government securities, but they don't have to be; buying them is simply a greater convenience for the Fed and for government as a whole. It is these "open market purchases" that the Fed is still, at this very moment, indulging in, week after week, to pump inflationary new money into the economy.

Thus, suppose that the Fed purchases a U. S. government bond now held by John Jones for $1000. It gets the bond and adds it to the asset column on its books. Where does the Fed "get" the $1000 with which to buy the bond? It gets it by creating a new $1000, in the form of a check on itself. John Jones can only use the check by depositing it in whatever bank he has an account. This adds to his money supply to the tune of $1000. But the important point is that his bank takes that check and deposits it with the Fed, with which each commercial bank has a checking account. This adds $1000 to the reserves of the banking system at the Fed, and the banks then can and do create new checkbook money of their own at a multiple of 6:1, so that $6000 of new checkbook money, or "demand deposits", are quickly added to the economy. And so when the Fed buys $1 billion of government bonds from the public, it quickly causes the creation of $6 billion of new

(Continued On Page 2)

Destutt de Tracy: Early French Classical Liberal

By Leonard P. Liggio
Department of History, City College, CUNY

July 20 is the 220th anniversary of the birth of Destutt de Tracy (1754-1836), a founder of the Ideologue school and a leading laissez-faire economist. He was raised by his mother and his grandmother, who was the grand-niece of the leader of Jansenism, Arnauld. He was a disciple of the Encyclopedists, and especially of Voltaire whom he visited at Ferney. He read and re-read the works of his hero of reason. He was elected in 1789 a deputy to the Nobles in the Estates-General, and with the Marquis de Lafayette, he led the assault on feudalism and government privileges which marked the French Revolution. He later retired to the suburb of Auteuil to the house of Mme. Helvetius, which served as a center for the last of the eighteenth century philosophes, Condorcet and Cabanis. Condorcet died in prison during the Terror and Destutt de Tracy barely escaped execution. He returned to Mme. Helvetius' home and worked with the physician Cabanis who married Charlotte de Grouchy, the sister of Mme. Sophie de Condoreet, widow of the philosopher, and translator of Adam Smith's **Theory of Moral Sentiments**. Mme. de Condorcet married the Irish general, O'Conor, and with Cabanis and Dominique Joseph Garat published the complete works of Condorcet, which became an intellectual support for the opposition to Napoleon. Along with the historians Constantin Volney and Pierre Claude Daunou, and the editor, J.-B. Say, the Ideologues exercised a major intellectual influence during the period of the Directory (1795-99) and the Consulate (1799-1804). But, when Napoleon crowned himself emperor, he denounced the Ideologues as his most dangerous opponents.

Destutt de Tracy's major work, **Elements of Ideology**, included in its section on will his analysis of political economy. The major influences on his psychological thought were Locke and Condillac. Destutt de Tracy and Dupont de Nemours were the two Frenchmen who had the longest association and influence on Thomas Jefferson. Jefferson translated and published (in 1811) Destutt de Tracy's **Commentary on Montesquieu's Spirit of the Laws** (written in 1806 but not published in France until 1817). One of the few works on his thought is Jean Cruet, **La Philosophie Morale & Sociale de Destutt de Tracy** (1909), from whom the following quotations are taken:

"The social philosophy of Destutt de Tracy included a political part and an economic part. Such are very much in effect the two essential elements of the revolutionary ideal. The Revolution had been at the same time a political crisis and an economic crisis; it had been the protestation of the public conscience against the despotic regime; but it did on the other hand profoundly modify the economic regime of France. We find in the works of Destutt de Tracy the expression of this double tendency.

"One has often said that the great merit of the Revolution was to have founded its political ideal on a perfect knowledge of human nature. It had taken men as they are and not as they ought to be. It allowed a free field to human egoism. In giving as a foundation to his social philosophy a psychological study of men, Destutt de Tracy rested in the revolutionary tradition." (pp. 40-41)

"Finally the political philosophy of Destutt de Tracy is an individualist philosophy. For the French Revolution had been — one cannot doubt it — unreservedly individualist. Destutt de Tracy had defended individual property, condemned the intervention of the State in the affairs of individuals, and declared on several occasions that communism was a "utopia" or an "aberration." The economic system of competition, of freedom of labor, of wages, and of heredity, appeared to him the strong support of the political ideal of the Revolution . . . The socialists and the republicans (liberals) have, to our conception, the same political ideal founded on different economic principles. Is that not the secret of their conflicts, and also of their union against the parties of the Old Regime (conservatives)?" (pp. 165-66).

"The economic theories of Destutt de Tracy are today still those of the republican liberal party. Destutt de Tracy rejected, as equally contrary to the intimate nature of man, the Christian concept and the Communist concept of society. Destutt de Tracy is a utilitarian and an individualist: with that double title he is the type of republican without epithet. After having read the **Elements of Ideology**, one understands better the "Declaration of the Rights of Man and of the Citizen" (1789), at once in its political part and in its economic part." (p. 100)

"From the faculty of feeling and the faculty of willing is born the idea of personality; from the idea of personality is born in its turn the idea of property. Property has its origin in a natural and necessary fact. Property was a fact, it does not depend on us to make it that or not to make it that . . . There is a fundamental property, anterior and superior to all institutions. In other terms, for Destutt de Tracy, the foundation of property is the psychological order. Man is born property-owner." (pp. 52-53)

Destutt de Tracy considered government to be sterile at best, but generally a source of exploitation. He organized the deposition of Napoleon in 1814 (as he had sought to do for ten years) and was a source of support for public and secret opposition to the succeeding governments. ◻

New Forum Policy

1. Bargain!

As the American and world-wide inflation sweeps along, the **Lib. Forum** hereby makes its contribution to the fight against inflation by lowering its price! Where else can you find such a policy? Specifically, we are now offering our readers the following bargain: if you subscribe to the **Forum** for two years, you pay only $15.00! The one-year price remains the same.

2. Computerizing.

Keeping in swing with the modern world, we have just computerized our mailings. This means that we will hopefully be more efficient in the future. However, all things have their price, and, if past history is a guide, we will probably be less efficient for a brief transition period, while the bugs are being ironed out. If you suddenly find that you have been unaccountably dropped from the list, please let us know.

One important point: in keeping with our sister major magazines, we will no longer be able to cope rapidly with changes of address. It will take us from 6 to 8 weeks to put a change of address into effect. Also, it will help a great deal when you send in a change of address, to send in also the address label from your current copy of the **Forum**; the label contains your subscription number, and will help us in processing the change. Thanks a lot. ◻

World-Wide Inflation —

(Continued From Page 1)

checkbook money in the economy, which adds fuel to the inflation.

The first necessary step to stopping the inflation is, then, simplicity itself, once we penetrate to the arcane processes of how the money supply expands: a command to the Fed to stop, forevermore, any purchases of assets; better yet, would be to gain credibility by forcing the Fed to sell some of its assets and thereby contract the swollen supply of checkbook money. Of course, longer-run measures would also be vital: including the separation of money and banking from the State by a return to the gold standard at a realistic gold "price", and the abolition of the Federal Reserve System. But the first step would be a permanent command to the Fed to stop! its inflationary process. And the Fed will, of course, never do this unless it is compelled by mass public pressure from below. And to do that we need a massive public education in the cause of the inflationary disaster. Furthermore, similar public pressure on the other central banks of the world is also vitally necessary. ◻

Conservative Myths In History

LEFTISM: FROM DE SADE AND MARX TO HITLER AND MARCUSE,
by Erik von Kuehnelt-Leddihn (New Rochelle, N. Y.: Arlington House,
1974), 653 pp., $12.95.

reviewed by Ralph Raico
Department of History
State University College at Buffalo

An important part of the process of transforming the American right
into an imitation of old-line European conservatism (a transformation
which Murray Rothbard in particular has described very well in a
number of places) has been the seeping into American rightist thinking of
the philosophy of history that sees the germs of modern "decay" and
"chaos" in the various critical movements of the past few centuries,
especially the Enlightenment, but going back even to the Reformation
and, beyond that, to certain medieval "heresies." All modern ideologies
are seen as anti-theologies, and God forbid that any significant historical
change should be interpreted as the result of earthly, economic interests.
The incorporation of elements of this **Weltanschauung** has given current
American conservatism an air of profundity, old-world wisdom and
downright "class" which is the main product retailed, for instance, by
the "Intercollegiate Studies Institute" and by **Modern Age**, as well as by
National Review in its more "philosophical" moments. When carried
through by a genuine scholar like Eric Voegelin, this approach has a
certain interest. The present work is an example of the approach at its
very worst. So, with an eye to the possible impact of **Leftism** in
reinforcing a fundamentally reactionary and anti-libertarian
interpretation of the course of modern history among American rightists,
I beg the reader's indulgence to venture a lengthy and what could be
termed **spirited** attempt at nipping that impact in the bud.

A comment is in order concerning Kuehnelt-Leddihn's scholarliness:
there is no doubt in my mind that the greater part of his reknown within
the American right is due to the circumstance that (as he says of himself
in the Preface) he reads twenty languages and speaks eight. This, and the
fact that he travels to interesting places, rather than his mediocre and
derivative books or his remarkably uninformative column in **National
Review** on continental affairs, account, I think, for what reputation he
has in this country. Now, **Leftism** is filled with close to two hundred pages
of back-of-the-book notes, demonstrating his knowledge of languages and
his wide reading, and these are evident also in the text. (Some of the
apercus that are supposed to be the fruit of this rich learning, though, I
find ridiculous: to the **pensee**, for instance, that "socialism and the
Jewish mind do not easily mix," my reaction would be: Someone ought to
tell them about it!) But the quality of K-L's thought is so low, his power of
reasoning so dim, that the rest just does not matter very much. Take a
look at this try at linguistic fireworks, at the beginning of the chapter on
"Right and Left":

> Right and left have been used in Western civilization from
> times immemorial with certain meanings: right (German
> **rechts**) had a positive, left a negative connotation. In all
> European languages (including the Slavic idioms and
> Hungarian) right is connected with "right" (ius), rightly,
> rightful, in German **gerecht** (just), the Russian **pravo**
> (law), **pravda** (truth), whereas in French **gauche** also
> means "awkward, clumsy," (in Bulgar: **levitsharstvo**). The
> Italian **sinistro** can mean left, unfortunate or calamitous.
> The English **sinister** can mean left or dark. The Hungarian
> word for "right" is **jobb** which also means "better," while
> **bal** (left) is used in composite nouns in a negative sense:
> **balsors** is misfortune.

How this stuff is conceivably connected with the **political** terms "left"
and "right" — which stem from the accident that radicals were seated to
the left in the French National Assembly of 1789 and reactionaries to the
right — will perhaps be made clear to us in the hereafter, when we no
longer see as through a glass darkly. Meanwhile, I submit that we have
here to do with an author whose sense of judgment is fundamentally
spoiled and who is not above trying to show off (as another example of his
corrupt judgment, there is the fact that he mentions Tom Paine four

times in the book, never discussing his political ideas, but twice
mentioning that he was the hero of a play by a certain Nazi playwright
named Hanns Johst). All in all, I cannot recall ever coming across a case
such as K-L's, where a scholarly apparatus of similar magnitude was put
to the service of such a low-grade intellectual effort. A few preliminary
examples: the author is discussing the criminal code of the Soviet Union;
he suggests that the very existence of punishment there contradicts the
regime's official philosophy: "since materialism rejects the notion of
free will, why should there be punishment for anything?" This is all he
says on the subject, so we are left to wonder: What does it profit a writer
on social questions to read twenty languages and yet never to have heard
of the deterrentist theory of punishment? In another place, K-L advances
the claims of the neo-liberals, like Roepke, as against older liberals such
as Mises, stating that the former "admitted curbs on mammothism and
colossalism to preserve competition. They thought that the state had a
right and then a duty to correct possible abuses of economic freedom —
just as we give a mature person a driving license and the right to travel
wherever he wants but still make him submit to traffic laws." With
grade-school stuff like this, just whom does K-L think he is writing for?
Moreover, there are little gaps in his reading which tend to disqualify him
from writing on the subjects he does: note fifty-two on page 482 shows
that he probably has not even heard of the Clapham-Ashton-Hartwell
view on the effects of the Industrial Revolution on the British working-
class or at least certainly has no idea of its significance.

K-L's languages and life of reading allow him to make disdainful
comments (justifiable, I suppose) about all kinds of ignorant, man-in-the-
street Americans (it's part of his indictment of democracy, you see); but,
judged by the standards of the better sort of academic thinking prevalent
here, he doesn't begin to qualify as a serious intellectual.

In coming to grips with **Leftism**, we can leave aside the completely
superficial discussions of key concepts in social thought, such as
"liberty," "equality," "democracy," etc., contained in the first few
sections; the book is clearly no treatise on political philosophy. We ought
to note, however, K-L's petty sniping at such "leftist" concepts as
equality before the law — as well as his sneaky rationalizations, sprinkled
through the book, of such oppressive institutions as European serfdom
and even Negro slavery ("In many cases the blacks could have been
grateful to have ended as house slaves in Virginia rather than as human
sacrifices in bloodcurdling ceremonies such as the **Zenanyana**, the 'Evil
Night' in Dahomey"). And in his continuing attack on democracy,
childish touches are not lacking: rape is referred to as "sexual
democracy" and cannibalism as "nutritional democracy" (why not
"aristocracy"?). On this level of analysis of concepts, however, his
definitions of "right" and "left" deserve some examination, since they
help determine the structure of the book. It is here that the mishmash
begins in earnest.

How, the reader might wonder, does Hitler wind up on the left? The
answer is simple: **everything evil is identified with the left** in K-L's mind,
just as everything good is identified with the right. Get these as unbiased
definitions, meant to help us organize modern political ideas and
developments: "The right stands for liberty, a free, unprejudiced form of
thinking, a readiness to preserve traditional values (provided they are
true values), a balanced view of the nature of man . . . but the left is the
advocate of the opposite principles." So that Hitler — even if he hadn't
been a believer in democracy (K-L's interpretation) was necessarily a
leftist. All methods of political repression are leftist, according to our
author — for instance, censorship (hasn't K-L ever heard of the Index of
Probited Books? — or was this a "leftist" element in the Church of the
Counter-Reformation?). For this reason, he claims that even

(Continued On Page 4)

487

Conservative Myths —

(Continued From Page 3)

Metternich's system was partially leftist: "it assumed authoritarian features and aspects which must be called leftist, as for instance the elaborate police system based on espionage, informers, censorship and controls in every direction." My own scholarship is, alas, quite modest; but even I have come across the fact that, among the penalties imposed on the Arians at the Council of Nicaea (325 A.D.) was that all copies of Arius's books had to be surrendered under pain of death; so that the history of the thin hand of the Church guiding the strong arm of the State in smashing heretics and intellectual deviants goes back at least as far as that. Informers were used by the various Inquisitions, of course, and part of the instrument of recantation which Galileo was forced to sign under threat of torture compelled him to inform on other Copernicans. (Naturally, the ecclesiastical powers have not been able to do much along these lines in more recent centuries, but then it has been a long while since the world belonged to them.) Guess for yourself the value and integrity of a work that starts with this fundamental distinction: "If we identify, in a rough way, the right with freedom, personality, and variety, and the left with slavery, collectivism, and uniformity, we are employing semantics that make sense." Thus, the implication is that a sensible terminology would classify the Romanovs as leftists; and Jefferson and Paine, who are termed "mild leftists," would have to be moderate supporters of collectivism.

The heart (and bulk) of this much too long book is constituted of a history — a history of "leftist" ideas in the modern period and of their working out in political developments. K-L's presentation of key episodes in this continuing story is completely tendentious and largely worthless. To take one example in connection with early modern history: he cites the Anabaptist excesses at Muenster, but not the preceding attempts by both Lutherans and Catholics to annihilate, by the most brutal methods imaginable, peaceful Anabaptists who asked only for the right to ignore the State. His chapter on the French Revolution is a joke. He finds himself able to discuss the taking of the Bastille (and to conclude that the Marquis de Sade inspired the whole incident, as well as the brutality that accompanied it), without any reference to the fact that the activity in Paris was a response to a military coup put afoot by the Court. He describes in absurd detail various horrors committed during the Reign of Terror, but does not even mention the war going on at the time against most of Europe, nor does he inform the reader that the French perhaps had cause for panic in the circumstance that the King and Queen had betrayed them to an enemy who had publicly threatened to give the city of Paris over to military execution. Very significant is that K-L scrupulously ignores the rather well-known thesis of Tocqueville, that the Revolution (and Napoleon) basically simply continued the statist and centralizing tendencies of the monarchy: this is an interpretation which he, with his uncritical adulation of European monarchism and his hatred of the great Revolution of 1789 (a hatred which is nothing but Taine shorn of every shred of intelligence, or, better, Gaxotte shorn of all esprit and style), could not afford to consider.

The lengthy descriptions of leftist atrocities is a favorite pastime of K-L's in this book. Meanwhile, massacres committed under the auspices of monarchy, imperialism, rightist regimes or especially his own Church are either sloughed off with an adjective such as "harsh" or consigned to utter oblivion. Thus, we look in vain for gory details when it is a question of the expulsion of the Spanish Jews in 1492, the activities of Franco's Moorish troops during the Civil War, or the atrocities of Leopold II's agents in the Congo (K-L foolishly talks about the Congo's brutal exploitation by "private companies" — trying slyly to shift the debit from the side of imperialism and monarchy to the side of capitalism, by passing over the fact that these "private companies" were set up and largely owned by the King of the Belgians). As for any number of rivers of blood shed by the political and religious powers legitimized through tradition or by regimes defending the status quo there is not a word: not a word, for example, of what the Crusaders did when they captured Jerusalem in 1099, of what those who responded to Innocent III's call did to the Albigensians, of what French Catholics did to the Huguenots on St. Bartholomew's Day, of what the Versailles soldiers did to the Communards in 1871 (they killed about twice as many people as were killed during the Reign of Terror). Since K-L is into dwelling on the interesting little physiological facets of political killings, he might have

shared with his readers an example or two of how the kings of Europe for centuries put to death those they judged to be felons. A very good example would be Damiens, executed in 1759 for attempting to assassinate Louis XV. (The description is in Iwan Bloch's biography of de Sade, which K-L cites.) It is possible that no other human being in the history of our race ever suffered as much in one day as did Damiens.

The snide remarks K-L permits himself in regard to leftists are totally inexcusable and shameful. "Demolition," he asserts, "delights all leftists, fills them with diabolic glee" (including Kautsky, Bernstein and Jean Jaures? — or were these perhaps men of the right?). He refers to "the great leftist delight, i.e., the defiling of cemeteries" (look — I personally know two or three leftists who, I am morally certain, do not delight in defiling cemeteries!). This garbage is repeated again and again: "One should never forget: Sadism is the outstanding characteristic of the entire left." He terms FDR "nearly insane" and says that "he could not be held morally responsible for many of his utterances and actions" (but the most he says about Hitler along these silly psychiatric lines is that he was "neurotic"). He piggishly calls American student demonstrators "screaming and shouting bearded spooks." For the following, the reader (unless he or she has a copy of the book handy) must take my word that it appears in Leftism: "Nicolas Calas exhorted leftists with the words, 'Comrades, be cruel!' Hitler followed the call. Not in vain have we been told by Charles Fourier, grandfather of socialism, in his Theorie de l'unite universelle: 'The office of the butcher is held in high esteem in Harmony.' " Just take in for a moment this thoroughly dishonest juxtaposition of statements! K-L is obviously making a desperate gamble on the ignorance of his readers, on their not being aware of what is probably the single best known of Fourier's ideas: namely, that he wanted to make all socially-necessary work enjoyable; one method was through raising the social esteem of indispensable but dirty jobs, such as the butcher's. To use this concept of Fourier's in order to associate him somehow with political atrocities and Hitler is really as simple and direct a case of intellectual knavery as I have ever seen in print in my lifetime.

The section on Marx is filled with all sorts of personal nonsense about the great socialist. K-L writes of Marx's "mad ambitions" as a young man, i.e., to make a name for himself as a poet (surely, every young man who had ideas of that kind must be mentally unbalanced!), and states that: "The non-fulfillment of his (artistic) dreams made him a revolutionary, and here we have a strong analogy with Hitler." (Really, instead of irrelevantly footnoting articles in Hungarian in Munich reviews on the non-existence of serfdom in medieval Hungary, such an assertion as this one might be thought to require some substantiation — but none is furnished.) We have petty shots: "There is no doubt that Marx, initially at least, loved his wife and daughters dearly . . ." (emphasis added), as well as large-scale silliness: "the dominant characteristic of Marx: self-hatred" (actually, his dominant characteristic was rebellion). K-L's plain lack of intelligence comes out in his comment on Engels in his relationship to Marx: "This wealthy manufacturer from the Ruhr Valley also had sufficient funds to support the penurious cofounder of international socialism and communism. Lenin's 'useful idiots' thus existed long before Lenin." Just what is this supposed to mean? The words say that Engels was a dupe, a kind of 1940's Hollywood-type, maybe like Edward G. Robinson or John Garfield — but such an interpretation of Friedrich Engels' role in the history of socialism would be . . . incorrect.

What to say about K-L's treatment of classical liberalism? Well, first of all, there are incomprehensible stupidities: he thinks that the Manchester School was contemporaneous with Adam Smith, and he lists Bismarck (and Mazzini) as an "Old Liberal" along with Gladstone, Cobden (who evidently did not belong to the Manchester School) and Mises! Then, to smear German liberalism, he takes the National Liberals to be representative of it, never mentioning the truly liberal Freisinnige Partei and its great leader, Eugen Richter: the difference is that, where the former supported the laws against the socialists and Catholics, and protectionism, imperialism and militarism, the latter opposed these. Whatever K-L's forte is, it is not analytical thought, so that it would not be worth our while to enter into an examination of his ideas as to the evolution of liberalism through various phases. As an anti-totalitarian Christian conservative, what he is trying to prove, of course (so what else is new?), is that classical liberalism somehow set the stage for totalitarianism and statism, in Germany and elsewhere. But, to prove

(Continued On Page 5)

Comment On The CLA

By Lynn Kinsky

I was just reading the April 1974 Forum and would like to take issue with your critique of the CLA. It would appear to me that you are falling into the same factionalist "bag" that Konkin and others are into, by insisting that there is one route to social change and one party line and we can't have a movement unless we're all doing the same thing. (For what it's worth I think such insistence on conformity is a major cause of the FLP's problems.)

In fact, American society is not a unity — it is composed of numerous sub-cultures, even within the middle class, which is hardly the only class (if one can define classes with any precision in the first place). As I see it one of the real strengths of the Southern California libertarian movement is that it implicitly realizes or takes into account this cultural pluralism. The question is not should we ally with the straights or with the freaks this year (which often seems to be the way you New Yorkers operate) but rather who feels most competent and comfortable working with which sector. People who are science fiction fans can work at bringing libertarianism to science fiction types (who have already been softened up by writers such as Heinlein and Anderson). Libertarians who are nudists can work with local free-beach groups to expand that area of civil liberties. Other libertarians can work with nuclear power plant opponents to work for the repeal of the very evil Price-Anderson Act; others can work for the repeal of laws discriminating against women, blacks, gays. People who are into conventional political action can do that, and can work with one or several parties depending on their evaluation of the situation. Meanwhile, people who are down on political action can get involved in the League of Non-Voters or some other group — I doubt if they ever change anyone's mind about voting or not (most elections are doing good if 30% of the eligible citizens vote) but they do provide a rationale for people's not voting that delegitimizes government in those

people's minds. People who are into changing society by creating alternative institutions should try their hand at that. What it comes down to is that each person's interests and talents are different and it makes sense for them to advance libertarianism the best way they can — I think in business it's called division of labor and diversified marketing.

(All of this is not to say that I think every method is equally effective — I've got my favorites and am doing graduate work in sociology specifically to expand my knowledge of social reality and the means of affecting it.)

On the specific issue of the CLA — I really don't see where it's a case of that or the Lib Party (in fact the CLA doesn't even see it that way — they support LP candidates Susel, Taylor, Bergland, (and Jindrich) for PFP write-ins on the primary). The election coming up is a primary — with Keathley trying to get the Peace and Freedom nomination. It isn't a case of supporting her or Hospers — the Libertarian Party, since it isn't on the ballot (but PFP is) isn't involved in the June 4 election at all except for Jindrich in a non-partisan race. If by some chance Keathley gets the nomination then we're in the position of having a libertarian on the ballot (Keathley) and another as a write-in (Hospers) in November. Sure, then there's a problem of who to push for and vote for but to my mind it isn't insurmountable — I expect I would push Keathley among my friends over at school (who are mainly young Marxists and who would find Hospers hopelessly bourgeois) and Hospers among the rest of the people I know (who would consider Keathley too radical). As to my vote (and that of other movement libertarians) I would probably advocate writing in Hospers on the grounds that neither of them will win and so the votes should be used for the purpose of trying to get the LP qualified to be on the ballot in future elections.

(Continued On Page 6)

Conservative Myths —

(Continued From Page 4)

anything, one must deal with coherent propositions. Now, K-L says that: "it is not surprising that old liberalism became illiberal. If one is solemnly convinced that all strong stands, all firm affirmations, all orthodoxy, all absolutes in thought are evil . . ." etc., etc. But he himself lists Mises and Gladstone (and one would suppose he would include writers like Spencer and de Molinari) as Old Liberals. Did these men not take strong stands, not make firm affirmations? What value as historical interpretation could we expect to find contained in such a collection of absurdities, distortions and self-contradictions as this?

The prime example of the bitter fruits of liberalism and "leftism" is, naturally, Nazism. It came into being because the Germans "divorced themselves from religion and willfully turned their backs on great traditions." The old conservative song-and-dance. Yet what evidence is there that the majority of Germans who voted for the Nazis were not sincere Christians? K-L correctly points out that part of the Nazi vote came from voters who had previously supported the "liberal" parties (such as they were in Germany by then); but why not mention that the Enabling Act of March, 1933, the basis for the Nazi consolidation of power, was supported by the Catholic Center Party in the Reichstag? At times, Catholicism did offer some resistance to the Nazis, and deserves credit for it. On the other hand, there were instances such as the proclamation issued by Cardinal Innitzer of Vienna, speaking for the bishops of Austria, which celebrated the "extraordinary accomplishments of National Socialism in the sphere of voelkisch and economic reconstruction as well as social policy." This was in 1938. Naturally, the complexity of this cluster of problems is not something that K-L could be expected to do justice to. More generally, as a brief response to this line of conservative interpretation, we would have to say: the maintenance of Christian faith cannot be the key to solving the problem of how to have a humane world, since Christian faith has historically been compatible with every manner of swinishness

perpetrated on human beings, especially before humanism came to temper religious fanaticism and liberalism to limit its possibilities for doing harm. In any case, it is not for a member of that Church to lay the blame for massive diabolical mistreatment of human beings at the door of "leftism," agnosticism and liberalism.

Although they do nothing to redress the balance, there are a few good points to be noted in Leftism: K-L has an attractive curiosity about and love of certain kinds of facts — facts about persons, places, tribes and nations and their traditions, and so on. Many of his judgments and values are commendable: he is a strong revisionist on the Paris Settlement of 1919; dislikes Wilson, Roosevelt and Churchill heartily; hates Eleanor (although he overestimates her importance); has contempt for American left-liberals and fellow-travellers; realizes that the war criminals of World War II included those who caused the ovens to be lit not only at Auschwitz and Dachau, but also in downtown Hamburg and Tokyo, in Dresden and Hiroshima. The author passes some friendly comments on anarchism and admits that he would not be reluctant to call himself a "Christian Conservative Anarchist" (but what could this amount to if he is, for example, a lover of the Franco regime? Probably not much more than a relish in "variety"). Occasionally, the quality of his thinking passes muster: Chapter 20, for instance, on some of the dilemmas historically faced by European conservative thought, is decent enough. But this is all in all as bad a book as has come to my notice in many years; and I believe I have given adequate grounds for this judgment. If the reader thinks I have been too "harsh" on K-L, let him or her recall his slanders, explicit and implied, on hundreds of thousands of socialist men and women, the class of people for whose intelligence and good intentions Hayek had enough respect to dedicate to them his Road to Serfdom.

In the minds of many of those who keep up with Buckley's magazine and with the American conservative movement, there is, I think, the sense that writers like Russell Kirk and Kuehnelt-Leddihn are being presented as the conservative counterparts of libertarians like Mises and Hayek; the former are their big guns and deep scholars, some attempt at an answer to the obvious excellence of the latter. Actually, as symbolizing the relative intellectual power behind the two movements, this notion seems to me entirely correct. ◻

The Prophetic Vision Of Hilaire Belloc

by John P. McCarthy—Department of History, Fordham University

Late 18th, 19th, and early 20th century European thinkers are generally categorized as rightist or leftist; conservative or liberal. The left stressed human reason which formulated universal principles applicable to all men. The foremost of these was the value and priority of the individual. Social organizations, whether states, businesses, guilds, or fraternal groups, existed to serve the individual. The right, on the other hand, in reaction to the revolutions that grew from the application of leftist principles, deemphasized human rationality. In its place they stressed custom and tradition, which naturally varied greatly from place to place; hence, an abandonment of universality. The exaltation of localism prompted a subordination of the individual to the group, which was both the source and the product of custom. The individual was seen as being able to attain his full humanity only as part of the group. The extremes to which leftist and rightist thought could run were obviously anarchism on one side and nationalist totalitarianism on the other.

However, in the greater part of the 20th century, the prevailing pattern of politics in the West has not fitted either category. Instead, the left has accepted rightist social organicism as a rationale for social welfare programs and a controlled economy, while the established right has accepted leftist socio-economic reforms in return for the maintenance of power. Two successful 20th century political figures who personified this right-left amalgam were David Lloyd George, a one-time radical, Welsh nationalist, and anti-imperialist, who helped introduce the social welfare state to Britain and then went on to preside over a predominantly Tory-Imperialist cabinet during World War One; and the American patrician, Franklin Delano Roosevelt, who also fostered the social welfare state and commanded the nation in a global war. These modern Caesars came from opposite sides of the tracks socially, yet their programs-social welfare, controlled economy, and mass total war — completed the congealing of the modern state without revolution or the usurpation of an incumbent establishment. Significantly, both men transformed their own political parties away from their old liberal or individualist heritage (that is Gladstone Liberalism in Britain and Jeffersonian Democracy in the United States).

A perceptive and prophetic observer of the pattern of Western political

development in the 20th century was the English Catholic publicist, Hilaire Belloc (1870-1953). Today, unfortunately, he is either forgotten, appreciated only as a poet, or inaccurately dismissed as a rightist, neo-medievalist romantic. This has been a consequence either of antipathy to some of his attitudes, such as his anti-Semitism and his Catholic apologetics, or a failure to understand, or more likely, to read his political and social writings. Actually, going by the right-left categories we mentioned, Belloc, because of his rationalism, his commitment to universal principles, and his individualism, would very definitely belong with the left.

His ancestry, especially on his mother's side, would almost by itself give him radical credentials. A great, great, grandfather was Joseph Priestly, the philosopher-scientist whose library was burned by a Tory mob in Birmmingham because of his support for the French Revolution. His grandfather was Joseph Parkes, the radical political agent and associate of James Mill and Francis Place who in 1832 sought to further the chances for the Reform Bill by threatening to format a revolution if it would not be passed. His mother, Bessie Rayner Parkes, was a feminist and a Unitarian-turned-Catholic. His French father's family were republicans, and a great grandfather was an Irish Protestant exile who had served as a colonel in the Napoleonic armies.

Politically Belloc was a radical-liberal of the Bright-Cobden variety who regarded the key villain in British society to be the landed establishment — the beneficiary of state protection, perpetuation, and privilege. That class had ruled England since its triumph over the monarchy in the 17th century Civil War and the Glorious Revolution. The standard "Whig History" of England saw this gentry and their climb to power as the key to British liberty because it meant parliamentarianism and the rule of law. But a radical like Belloc saw instead a privileged oligarchy ruling at the expense of the masses. Belloc's Catholic historiography reinforced his radical hostility for the landed establishment when it is recalled that the landed class got its great leap forward by purchasing at bargain rates the monastic lands seized by Henry VIII in the 16th century as part of the break with the Church of Rome.

Belloc sought to specify the central principles of his radicalism in one of his first published works, a contribution to a collection entitled Essays in Liberalism. He claimed that the central aim in the liberal tradition had and ought to be "the representation of individuals rather than corporate bodies, ranks, or interests."[1] Therefore, radical liberalism sought to tear down privilege and to create an open society. Victories in this cause had been the abolition of rotten boroughs, religious disestablishment, free trade, expansion of the franchise, a meritorious rather than elitist public service, and freedom of press and political association.

In the 1890's, however, when Belloc was a student at Balliol College, Oxford, a "New Liberalism" was becoming fashionable. The new liberalism, which Belloc opposed, derided the "negativism" of the older liberalism — especially its preoccupation with government retrenchment and free trade. The new attitude drew inspiration from the neo-Hegelianism of the Oxford philosopher, T. H. Green, which radically departed from the empirical and individualist spirit of English philosophy by idealizing the state as man's educator and guardian, as well as being the agency for human fulfillment. As a result many liberal political

(Continued On Page 7)

Comment On The CLA —

(Continued From Page 5)

And as to whether Keathley, Timko, etc should be in PFP in the first place — I expect it's the one political party they can feel comfortable in, as long as they can feel they're at all effective (and Timko has gotten coverage for libertarianism in media that the LP could never penetrate), since the other parties (including the LP) are made up of people with pretty conventional life-styles. I realize you see this as an indictment against Keathley et. al. — but I don't see where the moral superiority of alcohol over pot, stockings and heels vs. blue jeans, bras vs. no-bra, selling hareware vs. selling incense, etc. has been established. To me it's simply a matter of personal preference and goals, and I don't think I'm alone — freak vs. straight just doesn't seem to be an issue among SoCal libertarians.

The Editor Replies:

I, too, am all in favor of diversity. If there are, for example, any libertarians involved in the flourishing "backgammon movement", let them by all means agitate among their backgammon colleagues, perhaps also showing (if true) that taxes and tariffs raise the price of backgammon boards. My quarrel with the Keathley forces is not so much their counter-cultural life-style, but, as Ms. Kinsky seems to concede, the fact that they make their political choices on the basis of which cultural political party "they can feel comfortable in". It seems to me that choosing lifestyles over ideology is a damaging indictment of the CLA forces.

It is true that, since Ms. Kinsky wrote her letter, the Keathley ticket swept to victory in the June PFP primary, and is therefore on the ballot in November. On the national scene, however, the PFP remains at a hopeless dead end, and therefore this applies to the state level as well. ◻

Hilaire Belloc —

(Continued From Page 6)

figures, like the Earl of Rosebery, H. H. Asquith, and Edward Grey called for the party to champion bold new state programs designed to improve the quality of life and civilization. Significantly, the same figures were calling for Liberals to take up the imperialist banner being so successfully exploited by the Conservatives and to drop the anti-imperialism or Little England which had been a central radical attitude.

At the same time the Conservatives, in keeping with their traditional paternalistic rhetoric, could easily endorse a more active state that could be pictured as a domestic version of the civilizing mission undertaken in the overseas empire. To complete the circle, the Fabian Socialists, at heart elitists, were convinced that their hopes of reorganizing society and eliminating human idiosyncrasies and ignorance, could best be attained, not by mass political action, but by working through the existing establishments of both parties, Conservatives and Liberals. Significantly, many Fabians, like G. B. Shaw, endorsed the Boer War because the expansion of the more advanced British Empire over the primitively conservative Boers was seen as a civilizing step similar to the promotion of universal education. Consequently, there was developing a national consensus for strong imperialist policies abroad and extensive state control and regulation at home. Some called the consensus "National Efficiency," others labeled it "Social Imperialism." Many in both parties endorsed it as a means of putting aside the "dated" struggles over franchise extension, free trade, removal of privileges, and religious disestablishment. A fictional blueprint for the consensus was the political novel of the sometime Fabian and perennial utopian, H. G. Wells, entitled **The New Machiavelli.** Significantly, the science of politics seemed to be prevailing over political principle.

Belloc has to be understood as an opponent of this spirit. After finishing at Oxford, he soon made a name for himself as a satirical poet and novelist (in addition to writing laudatory biographies of Robespierre and Danton). Examples of his literary efforts include **Lambkin's Remains,** a satirical assault on the academic neo-Hegelians that is a tribute to an imaginary don whose philosophical theories were considered valid because they were "admitted by all European philosphers in Germany"[2]; "The Modern Traveller," a mock Kiplingesque poetical account of imperialist exploits by a journalist from "The Daily Menace," accompanied by "Commander Henry Sin," a mercenary adventurer, and "William Blood," a swindler[3]; and **Emmanuel Burden,** a novel in which the hero is an honest radical entrepreneur who made his fortune by production, not speculation nor state subsidization, and who combats a fraudulent imperialist commercial venture undertaken by bankrupt aristocrats, Jewish speculators, bankers, and journalist glorifiers of Empire.[4]

Belloc was especially annoyed at the Germanophilia that was strong in certain quarters in late Victorian England. The Germans were pictured as the pace setters for that type of modern efficient administrative state that ought to be emulated by inefficient and laissez-faire English society. It was argued that unless England did so and abandoned her "doctrinaire" anti-statism, she would fall behind in the international race (for what?). Are there not certain parallels in the fashionable attitudes in post-Sputnik America vis a vis the Soviet Union?

In 1906 Belloc was elected to parliament in a freakish overwhelming Liberal victory that was partly caused by a split in Conservative ranks following Joseph Chamberlain's protectionist proposals. Entering parliament with a radical democratic naivete, he expected such an electoral mandate to be followed by the implementation of radical liberal programs. However, it was asking a little too much to expect a radical, anti-imperialist, government-retrenchment program from a ministry which included such Liberal Imperialists as Asquith, Grey, and Haldane, not to mention the political wizard (if not moralist) Lloyd George and the temporarily former Tory, Winston Churchill.

Belloc became so disillusioned that he left parliament in 1910. He had become convinced that the party struggle in parliament was really a sham battle between the two front benches who were the two teams into whom "the governing group is divided arbitrarily . . ., each of which is, by mutual understanding, entitled to its turn of office and emolument." They raise periodically "a number of unreal issues, defined neither by the people nor by the Parliament, . . . to give a semblance of reality to their empty competition." In reality, the front benches were identical in

outlook and interest, and were beholden to pretty much the same financial backers. The rank and file MP's, supposedly the spokesman of the electorate, were in reality only pawns in the game.[5]

Perhaps the thesis presented by Belloc and Cecil Chesterton in their book, **The Party System,** as well as in the weekly journal they edited, **The Eye-Witness,** was a bit overdrawn. Yet there is no doubt that Britain and the rest of the Western World was moving into the age of highly disciplined political parties and dominance of the executive over legislatures. The expanded activities of the state also weakened legislatures. For one thing the enabling legislation for the new programs gave great arbitrary power to the executives. Furthermore, that legislation was usually drafted by administrative experts and, because there was so much of it, there was little time for the calm and deliberate discussion of its value (or for supervision of its administration) by legislatures. Paradoxically, the independent MP of the type Belloc idealized, who would be responsible only to his constituents, seemed to have disappeared with the commencement of democary. Democratic electorates tend to think primarily in terms of parties or leaders rather than local representatives. Hence, the latter are subordinated to the former, especially in matters of financing national campaigns and determining political platforms.

In 1911, a year after he left parliament, Belloc hit on an issue which seemed a classic example of party collusion (or what the establishme: would call consensus). It was Britain's original social insurance legislation which appealed to both the paternalism of the Tories and the active statism of the New Liberals. To Belloc, it was a fraud benefitting only the more highly skilled workers well able to provide their own insurance, and was offensive because it was compulsory. It was a cornerstone in a development that he would prophetically label the Servile State.

The Servile State was that society where individualism and the right of contract disappeared and were replaced by a situation "in which the mass of men shall be constrained by law to labour to the profit of a minority, but as a price of such constraint, shall enjoy a security which the old Capitalism did not give them."[6] The various reforms then being proposed for the alleviation of the industrial proletariat, such as minimum wage laws, compulsory arbitration, compulsory social insurance, and nationalization or muncipalization of industry, would really work to protect the wealthy from the consequences of the market and competition. The masses, on the other hand, under the cover of comfortable amenities, would become bound to a servile status.

Belloc emphasized that the projected society would not be socialism, that is the public ownership of the means of production (which he equally deplored), because the capitalist class would still really possess their wealth. However, it would satisfy many idealistic socialists because the laboring classes would be spared "the special evils of insecurity and insufficiency," although at the price of "the destruction of freedom." Also satisfied would be that type of socialist reformer like the Fabian for whom "the occupation most congenial . . . is the 'running' of men: as a machine is run."[7] The working class would not oppose compulsory amenities which provide security and comfort, such as social insurance, minimum wage laws, and compulsory arbitration, even though they would ultimately lead to the elimination of their freedom of contract. The workers' acceptance of this inevitability is because their bargaining position was not great to begin with, but also because they had "lost the tradition of property and freedom," and were "most powerfully inclined" to accept the loss of freedom because of the positive benefits of security.[8] The resultant situation would be that

> Society is recognized as no longer consisting of free men bargaining freely for their labour or any other commodity in their possession, but of two contrasting status. owners and non.owners.[9]

The ownership class would be delighted with the prospective developments also, for "Capitalism has seen to it that it shall be a winner not a loser by this form of sham socialism,"[10] as it also would be guaranteed a security non-existent in the free market. The explanation is that nationalization or municipalization would not be simple acts of confiscation nor would they be compensated by taxation. Rather they would be financed by loans made from the same original ownership class that would now be guaranteed both compensatory annuities usually exceeding the rate of profit when the enterprise had been in private

(Continued On Page 8)

New Rothbard Book

This year's new Rothbard book is out! It is an **inexpensive**, handsomely bound paperback, published by the new Libertarian Review Press, a spinoff of **Books for Libertarians**, with a picture of the famous Deanne Hollinger poster of Rothbard on the front cover. The price is only $2.50!! Where can you get a book for that price nowadays?

The new book, **Egalitarianism As A Revolt Against Nature, and Other Essays**, is a collection of some of the best Rothbard essays, all of which have been either unpublished, or only published in obscure and now defunct journals. Now they are for the first time, not only in print but easily accessible. Rothbard has a spirited new introduction to the collection, which begins with the sentence: "Probably the most common question that has been hurled at me — in some exasperation — over the years is: 'Why don't you stick to economics?' " The remainder of the introduction answers that question and summarizes the contribution of each essay. A Foreword by R. A. Childs, Jr. asserts that Rothbard is the Karl Marx of the libertarian movement.

The following are the essays included in the new book:

"Egalitarianism as a Revolt against Nature". (From **Modern Age**). Individual diversity vs. egalitarianism.

"Left and Right: the Prospects for Liberty" (From the famous first issue of **Left and Right**). A libertarian manifesto and world-view.

"The Anatomy of the State" (from **Rampart Journal**). The State as the enemy: how it arises and perpetuates itself.

"Justice and Property Rights" (unpublished; from Symposium on Origin and Development of Property Rights, University of San Francisco). A philosophic theory of justice in property rights.

"War, Peace, and the State" (from **The Standard**). A libertarian theory of foreign policy.

"The Fallacy of the Public Sector" (from **New Individualist Review**). The fallacy of economists' arguments for the legitimacy of the public sector.

"Kid Lib" (from **Outlook**). The theory of self-ownership and property rights as applied to children.

"The Great Women's Lib Issue: Setting it Straight" (from the **Individualist**). Rothbard's first writing on this currently explosive issue.

"Conservation and the Free Market" (from the **Individualist**). Application of free-market economics and libertarian property rights theory to the issues of conservation and ecology.

"The Meaning of Revolution" (from **Libertarian Forum**). What is "revolution", and to what extent are libertarians "revolutionaries"?

"National Liberation" (from **Libertarian Forum**). The application of libertarianism to the concept of "national liberation".

"Anarcho-Communism" (from **Libertarian Forum**). A critique of the communist wing of anarchism.

"The Spooner-Tucker Doctrine: an Economist's View" (from **A Way Out**). A critique of nineteenth century individualist anarchism from the free-market point of view.

"Ludwig von Mises and the Paradigm for Our Age" (from **Modern Age**). A tribute to von Mises' contribution, and a philosophico-sociological explanation for his neglect in the current age.

"Why Be Libertarian?" (from **Left and Right**). A plea to adopt libertarianism on the basis of a passion for justice.

All this: 15 sparkling essays, plus an introduction, plus a foreword, for only $2.50. There are discounts for larger amounts purchased. Write to: Libertarian Review Press, 422 First St. S. E., Washington, D. C. 20003.

Hilaire Belloc —
(Continued From Page 7)

directorates would be rehired by the public companies, but now at enlarged and guaranteed salaries. Furthermore, massive public works, ostensibly of a socially benevolent nature, whether schools, hospitals, or slum clearances, would tend to be financed not by taxation but by loans and would provide to the wealthy classes further forms of guaranteed income.[11]

In short, the capitalists would welcome and indeed promote most of the massive programs for state intervention and control of the economy. These reformist projects would serve to guarantee and enlarge their wealth and power and minimize their having to face the market.

Are not Belloc's prophecies validated by the recent experiences in our country, where national price and wage controls have been implemented by a "pro-business," Republican administration, and in our state (New York) where "pro-business," Republican legislators proclaim the necessity for the state to guarantee with public monies (no doubt to be raised by bonds) the dividends of the monopoly utility, Con Edison? Furthermore, do not the Watergate revelations, with all the elements of business-political collaboration to guarantee prices and profits, cause one to give greater credence to Belloc's insistence on the extensiveness of corruption in the politics of his time?

1., Hilaire Belloc, "The Liberal Tradition," **Essays in Liberalism** (London: Cassell, 1897), p.7.
2., Hilaire Belloc, **Lambkin's Remains** (London: Duckworth, 1920; 1st ed. 1900), p. 214.
3., Hilaire Belloc, "The Modern Traveler" (1st ed 1898), **The Verse of Hilaire Belloc** (Holland: The Nonesuch Press, 1954)
4., Hilaire Belloc, **Emmanuel Burden** (New York: Scribner's, 1904).
5., Hilaire Belloc and Cecil Chesterton, **The Party System** (London: Stephen Swift, 1911), pp 33-34.
6., Hilaire Belloc, **The Servile State** (London: Constable, 1912) p. 146.
7., Ibid., p. 127. 8., Ibid, p.144. 9., Ibid., p. 168. 10., Ibid., p. 182.
11., Ibid., pp. 145-152, 179-182.

The Libertarian Forum
BOX 341
MADISON SQUARE STATION
NEW YORK, NEW YORK

Published Every Month. Subscription Rate: $8.00 Per Year

A Monthly Newsletter

THE
Libertarian Forum

Joseph R. Peden, Publisher   Murray N. Rothbard, Editor

VOLUME VI, NO. 8   AUGUST, 1974   US-ISSN0047-4517

WHOOPEE!!

Away with all the solemn and hypocritical nonsense about the "anguish", the infinite "sadness", the terrible "tragedy" of this great event. Let joy be unconfined; let jubilation reign. We have brought down the Monster Milhous; never again will we have to watch his repellent visage or listen to his pious blather. We have brought down the tyrant, and dusted off the ancient and honorable weapon of impeachment, fallen almost into disuse, to check the spectre of unconfined Executive dictatorship.

Who would have thought it? Who would have thought that our country was still so unfrozen, still with so many options available, that Justice could so swiftly bring into the dock all the highest reaches of the White House, from the Vice President, two Attorneys-General, all of the President's top aides, his personal lawyer, his two most powerful assistants, and even unto Him in the dread Oval Office itself? Who could have thought, when Agnew resigned in guilty disgrace not many months ago, that those of us who said, wistfully, "One down, and one to go", would turn out to be right? Wow!!

Watergate was not simply "chicken thief" stuff, to use the disparaging Buckley phrase (and shouldn't chicken thieves **also** be prosecuted to the full extent of the law?) With the admitted adoption of the monstrous Huston plan, of which the famous "plumbers" were only a spinoff, we came closer than ever before to a full-fledged police state. Much too close for comfort. The Huston plan for systematic bugging, wiretapping, and espionage upon critics of the Administration, was too much even for J. Edgar Hoover, and no record of its alleged "rescinding" has ever been found.

There are some minor, but still heartwarming corollaries to the fall of the Big Tyrant. No more will we have to suffer the lies of Ronald Ziegler, who, one hopes, will return to the Disneyland from whence he came. And no more will we have to suffer the hogwash of Nixon's two favorite clerics: the egregious Rabbi Korff, who will presumably sink back into the obscurity from which he was plucked; and his kept Jesuit, Father McLaughlin (is he still intoning somewhere the claim that Nixon is "the greatest man of this third of the twentieth century"?) — will his order do the right thing and put him on bread and water for a few years of penance?

It is important to resist the prevailing **motif** that we must have "compassion" for the man, that he has "suffered enough" by losing his job, that "forgiveness" is noble, etc. This idea violates the very essence of the Christian concept of forgiveness. That concept rests ineluctably on genuine repentance, on full confession of moral wrongdoing, and on throwing oneself on the mercy of one's previous victims. Milhous has confessed nothing, repented nothing. A vague and unspecified reference to a few "errors of judgment" means nothing, especially when self-righteously coupled with the unctuous claim that even they were all committed "in the national interest."

The idea that he has "suffered enough" by losing his job is also sheer hogwash. Since when do criminals, in America or anywhere else, suffer only loss of employment? What are prisons for? Why should thousands of criminals go to jail and Milhous go scot free? Are we to send to jail only unemployed criminals, while everyone else gets off with loss of status and employment? Also, the point of the impeachment and attendant proceedings is that no man, from the king to the pauper, can be above the law; by granting immunity to Nixon we absolve the President and only the President from paying for his crimes. And when did Nixon show compassion for any criminal, except for the mass murderer Calley? How about his stern stand against all amnesty for "draft dodgers", men whose only "crime" was to defend their liberty against the long arm of the State? For the arch-criminal Nixon there must be no special immunity, and no amnesty.

The final line of defense of the Nixon loyalists was that all politicians, all Presidents, do similar misdeeds. Why pick on Nixon? But that sort of defense of criminality is it to say that "everybody's doing it?" Even if true, the proper response is not to condone and do nothing about the whole mess, but to begin somewhere, to begin to clean the Augean stables wherever one can. And what better place to begin than with Richard Nixon? Hopefully, we can never return to the naive innocence about the Presidency and about government of the pre-Watergate era; once the Pandora's Box of true knowledge about the workings of government and of the Executive branch has been opened it can never be closed again. And once the dread unknown weapon of impeachment has been used, and we have not all been struck dead by lightning, we will all be far more ready to turn to the impeachment process again. All future successors of President Nixon are now eternally on notice; they will never rest easy again, secure in the belief that once the November elections are over they can get away with anything they like. Even a President, henceforth, can feel the strong arm of Justice.   □

Kennedy Marriage
Revisionism

If, among the primal passions of Man, the Achilles Heel of Richard Nixon has been Money and Knowledge (of other people: tapes, bugging, breaking-in to psychiatrists' offices), then surely the Achilles Heel of the Kennedy clan has been that ole debbil Sex. There is of course Chappaquiddick, and now veteran columnist Earl Wilson has detailed the torrid affairs of both Jack and Bobby Kennedy with Marilyn Monroe. It is intriguing that, among all the host of Camelotomanes, no one has disputed the accuracy of the Wilson account, which has either been studiously ignored or accused of "bad taste". (As if politicians themselves are not bad taste!) That Jack had a plethora of extra-marital

(Continued On Page 2)

Libertarian Advance

As nearly every libertarian knows, the current libertarian movement was created in two great breakthroughs: the split from YAF in September 1969, and the media publicity of early 1971. Our antennae here at the Forum sense that the movement is now going through a third Great Leap Forward, a great advance in libertarianism and libertarian influence. The signs are everywhere: in the growing influence, for example, of libertarian ideas in the media, among investment advisers (a beleaguered group nowadays!), politicians, graduate students, and the general public. Libertarian publications are expanding in readership and influence. Thus, the monthly **Reason**, the leading general magazine in the field, has expanded to a phenomenal circulation of over 12,000.

Everywhere there is ferment. The current generation of YAF is — once again — bubbling with libertarian ideas; and the recent national convention of YAF in San Francisco crackled with libertarian enthusiasm. California YAF is reportedly led by libertarians, and the libertarian "hospitality suite" at the San Francisco convention was the major center of interest, as outside libertarian experts worked hard to push delegates and observers toward liberty. Libertarians in out of the California LP are working furiously on State Senator H. F. "Bill" Richardson, the Republican nominee for the U. S. Senate, to widen his libertarian perspective from narrowly economic to civil libertarian

concerns. In Los Angeles, the Libertarian Alternative has gained wide interest and respect from the media in its task of answering statist editorials on radio and TV.

But perhaps the most spectacular growth in the movement lies in two distinct directions: in the solid expansion of the Libertarian Party, and in the enormous and rapid growth in free-market, or "Austrian" economics.

The battle within the Libertarian Party, detailed in these pages, is now over, with the result a smashing victory for the forces of soundness and sanity in the party. We can all now rejoice and go forward with high hopes. At the national convention in Dallas in June, the sound, pure, and responsible ticket headed by the bright and able young investment counselor Edward H. Crane III, won a shattering victory over the disruptive Royce-Konkin coalition. Crane triumphed over Royce by a smashing 4-1 majority. With the excellent slate of Ed Crane and Andrea Millen in firm control of the national party, we can expect great things from the national party, which will now have its headquarters in San Francisco. The stage is now set for energetic expansion of the party with no compromise of principle. Furthermore, reliable reports have it that the national platform is greatly improved from its 1972 concessions to the

(Continued On Page 3)

Kennedy Marriage —

(Continued From Page 1)

affairs while in the White House is now generally conceded. But amidst this spate of Kennedy Revisionism — which includes Richard J. Walton's excellent reminders of Kennedy's bellicose foreign policy which almost got us into the Last Nuclear War — one question, a sensation of the moment, has not yet been reevaluated: what we might call the First Kennedy Marriage Caper.

To understand the impact, we must hark back to the days of Camelot, when the media was having a universal and unrestricted love affair with the Kennedy Administration. JFK was the shining prince, leading us toward the New Frontier. It was in the midst of this atmosphere during 1961, that a friend of mine who was high up in conservative circles first told me about a fascinating entry in an obscure book published a few years earlier, "The Blauvelt Family Genealogy." The entry in this family genealogy on one Durie Malcolm referred to Durie's "third marriage" to "John F. Kennedy, son of Joseph P. Kennedy, one time Ambassador to England." If true, this was indeed a bombshell, as it would have made the Jack-Jackie marriage illegal according to Catholic doctrine.

Paul Krassner published the item in his iconoclastic magazine The Realist, for March 1962. Kennedy Administration pressure kept the item out of the news media until the fall, when publication in Europe broke the voluntary censorship logjam in the American press. Durie Malcolm, admittedly a former girl friend of Kennedy, denied all and refused to see the press, the White House issued a curt denial, the compiler of the book, Louis Blauvelt, was dead, and the alleged supplier of the item, one Howard Durie, denied the whole thing. For lack of further confirmation, the story died down.

Now, however, Ron Rosenbaum, an intrepid "politician Revisionist" for the Village Voice, has revived the tale (July 4). What intrigued Rosenbaum was a cryptic passage between John Dean and Nixon in a Feb. 28 conversation on the famous Nixon transcripts. The passage was as follows:

"P. Did your friends tell you what Bobby did . . . Bobby was a (characterization deleted.) But the FBI does blatantly tell you that — or Sullivan told you about the New Jersey thing. He did use a bug up there for intelligence work (inaudible).
D. Intelligence workers all over the property."

There then follows some cryptic references to the FBI trying to talk a

doctor into asserting that some "poor old gent" had a brain tumor.

Rosenbaum was intrigued by the "New Jersey thing" and mentioned it in a Voice story in late May. In response to the note, Rosenbaum was put into contact with an employee for a federal law enforcement agency, who claimed that he knew who the "old gentleman in New Jersey" was. Since he insisted on remaining anonymous, and in honor of the famous Bernstein-Woodward top informant on Watergate known as "Deep Throat", Rosenbaum dubbed the informant, "Strep Throat." Strep Throat claimed that "They went bananas over that thing at the White House. He hit the tree like this was an Ellsberg thing. He just put the FBI right onto that thing."

Strep Throat went on to claim that the "old gent" in question was Howard Ira Durie, of Hillsdale, New Jersey, the alleged supplier of the Durie Malcolm marriage item. According to Strep Throat, the FBI put "a full court press" on Howard Durie, including a 24-hour surveillance, and seized all the records in the Durie home. Strep Throat asserted that when he himself called Durie at the time, Durie told him that "I can't talk, I can't talk, I've already discussed the matter with the FBI." Strep Throat added that "I've never heard a man so scared in my life." Rosenbaum adds, however, that his informant had no information on the "brain tumor" part of the story.

On doing further checking, Rosenbaum found that some of the Blauvelt family were convinced of the truth of the Durie Malcolm item. A New York Times story during the 1962 flurry reported that "an aide of the President" had gone up to the home of Louis Blauvelt's son-in-law in New Jersey where the Blauvelt genealogical files were stored, and that he had found no supporting evidence in the Durie Malcolm file. But a Blauvelt from Saddle River, New Jersey, told Rosenbaum that incriminating evidence was removed from the file, because the genealogical card for the Malcolm file mentioned material that was missing from the files themselves, and also mentioned that the material had been supplied by Howard Durie. A call from Rosenbaum to Durie himself drew fervent denials of any further or supporting evidence on the marriage story. However, while Durie denied any visits from the FBI, he did assert that the FBI had gone through the files of Blauvelt's son-in-law, Mr. Smith, and that Smith "had been bothered by the FBI." A call to Smith, however, elicited the response that the FBI had never bothered him, or gone through the files, and Smith also hotly denied the existence of any missing information.

There, so far, the story rests. Not a saga of vital importance, but an intriguing bit of Americana. As Rosenbaum concludes, "secret wedding or no secret wedding, something funny seems to have been going on between the Kennedys and the Blauvelts (and, he might add, the FBI) back in 1962." ◾

Libertarian Advance —

(Continued From Page 2)

State, with all references to "the proper function of government is . . . " at last expunged, and the platform confined to stating what the government should not be doing.

In California, Hal Jinkrich, LP member running for the non-partisan post of State Superintendent of Instruction, gained the phenomenal total of 200,000 votes in the election. Now it is true that our California friends caution us that the votes are not meaningful, that Mickey Mouse would have gotten a similar number of votes just for being on the ballot. Still and all, it cannot be gainsaid that Jindrich, with virtually no money at his command, ran a pure race, calling for the absolute separation of education from the State, including abolition of compulsory attendance laws and of the public school system. And with this number of votes amassed, can't we realistically estimate that a bang-up Presidential campaign in 1976 could pile up 1 million votes?

Central to our goal of 1 million LP votes in '76 is getting on the permanent ballot in New York State. To achieve that goal, the New York gubernatorial candidate this year must earn 50,000 votes. 50,000 votes will make the FLP the fifth major party in New York State, and earn us major-party status and influence comparable to the Liberal and Conservative parties. 50,000 votes will make an enormous impact on the media, and let us never forget that New York City is the media capital of the world. If we achieve major party status in New York, the media will come a-courting and the influence of libertarian ideas in the country as a whole will expand beyond our wildest dreams.

Hence the central importance of our old friends and Forum contributor Jerry Tuccille's campaign for governor of New York. Jerry is devoting all of his considerable energies and talents to the campaign. Furthermore, Jerry is too bright and realistic to mouth the usual campaign nonsense that he expects to win this year; what he is aiming for and expects to achieve this year is 50,000 votes. To help Jerry in this effort, New York libertarians have mounted a campaign of superb skill and professionalism, comprising men and women of great talent in media, publicity, and campaigning. Laura Wertheimer, a young conservative-libertarian professional campaign manager who has served in F. Clifton White's notable campaigns, has taken on the task of being Jerry's campaign manager, and is doing so with great professional skill. The enormously talented multi-media people of Ad Lib Communications, headed by John Doswell, are running the advertising and publicity of the Tuccille campaign. Ad Lib's multi-media show on behalf of the Tuccille race was the undoubted and spectacular hit of the Dallas LP convention. The enthusiasm is high. Already, Roger MacBride, the libertarian Virginia lawyer who cast his electoral vote in 1972 for the Hospers-Nathan ticket, flew Tuccille in his private plane all over New York State, gaining widespread media coverage throughout the state, and sparking FLP and Tuccille campaign organization everywhere en route.

The able Tuccille strategists estimate that getting 50,000 votes for governor requires the raising of $165,000 in campaign contributions. To aid in this effort, Roger MacBride and myself have mailed a joint letter to libertarians throughout the country asking for contributions and explaining the unique importance of the Tuccille effort. It is important that we all set aside grousing and nit-picking to aid in this mighty effort, an effort which can succeed. Send your contributions to The Committee for 50,000 Votes, Suite 918, 225 West 34th St., New York, N. Y. 10001.

The Tuccille campaign will stress the appeal of libertarianism to the great middle class of this country, crippled and hag-ridden as they are by taxes, inflation, and government spending; Tuccille will also hammer away at rule by "idiocracy", the idiocracy of countless schemes of government spending. Thus, a recent Tuccille handbill reads:

Free Libertarian Party
A message they can't ignore
I'm fed up with seeing the taxpayer's hard-earned dollars go to politicians who splurge it on headline-grabbing projects and countless welfare schemes.
Only the Free Libertarian Party is dedicated to reducing the size and budget of government, and 50,000 votes for me will put our party on the New York State ballot permanently.
If I can get 50,000 votes in November, they'll listen.
50,000 votes can't be ignored.

The Tuccille and other FLP campaigns are drawing considerable support from conservatives who are fed up with the Establishment power plays of the Conservative Party. New York YAF has invited Tuccille to address its convention, and Mary Jo Wanzer, running for Assembly on the FLP ticket, has received Conservative Party endorsement, with no watering down of her devotion to personal liberty.

The 50,000 vote goal is realistically grounded in the 9,000 votes that Fran Youngstein received in her race for Mayor of New York City last year. The Youngstein campaign organization has now published a beautifully mounted Yearbook of the campaign, including articles by Youngstein, Rothbard, Tuccille, Dave Nolan, Gary Greenberg and others, and replete with press clips and pictures of Fran. Available for only $3.50 from Ad Lib Communications, Hotel Empire, Bway. & 63rd, N. Y., N. Y.

Meanwhile, we can add another country to our list of organized libertarians. The fledgling Australian movement is now meeting to form a Libertarian Party in Australia. Good luck to Liberty in the Antipodes!

The other especially heartening development in the world of libertarianism is the extremely rapid growth of free-market, or "Austrian", economics. Even though Austrianism has had to make its way painfully without a single graduate department to nurture and train young Austrians, and with zero, if not negative, prestige in the profession, the number of serious and able young Austrian professors and graduate students is multiplying by leaps and bounds. No doubt the total inability of the other, more orthodox (or even heterodox) schools of economic thought to explain or offer any solutions for the increasingly runaway inflation or for the inflationary recession has had a great deal to do with the increasing interest in the Austrians.

Business Week, August 3, has an excellent, and not really unfavorable article on the Austrian revival, entitled: "The Austrian School's Advice: 'Hands Off!' " Subtitle of the article is "Government interference as the source of all economic ills". The article includes pictures of three leading "Austrians": Profs. Israel Kirzner of New York University, Walter Grinder of Rutgers, and the Lib. Forum editor.

Business Week also mentions a Symposium on Austrian Economics that was held at Royalton College, Vermont, at the end of June. The week-long conference, sponsored by the Institute for Humane Studies of Menlo Park, California, featured lectures by Kirzner, Rothbard, and Professor Ludwig M. Lachmann of the University of Witwatersrand, South Africa, and brought together over fifty bright young Austrians and quasi-Austrians from all over the country, including participants from England and Australia. Discussion was at a very high level, the science of Austrian economics was further developed, and, above all, everyone was immensely heartened to discover like-minded and knowledgeable colleagues whom they scarcely knew existed. The Royalton conference should mark a great takeoff point for the development and spread of the Austrian cause. Plans are now afoot for publishing not only the major lectures at the conference, but also some of the brilliant papers delivered by the younger participants. Look out, world of economics: the Austrians Are Coming!

As I write, the Wall St. Journal is scheduled to come out with an article of its own on Austrianism and the Royalton conference. Watch the Forum for a further report.

One heartening point about the rapid discovery of bright young Austrian School economists is the contrast with the situation of the libertarian movement five years ago. Five years ago, we were getting an influx of bright new kids into the movement, but they were all college kids, and a dishearteningly large proportion of them were soon to drop out into drugs, instability, caprice, or general decay. But now we are getting an influx of graduate students who are sober, able, hard-working and dedicated to both scholarship and freedom. We are emphatically building from a new and higher plateau. In the libertarian movement, as in the culture generally, the irrational nonsense and degeneracy of the late 60's looks more and more like a flash in the pan fading away into the bad old past. What with recent advances and developments in the Libertarian Party, in Austrian economics, and elsewhere, the future has never looked brighter for the libertarian cause. ◻

School Or Jail?

The Twelve Year Sentence: Radical Views of Compulsory Schooling,
edited by William Rickenbacker, Open Court Publishing, La Salle, Illinois
1974. $6.95.

Reviewed by Joseph R. Peden

The title of this collection of essays succinctly summarizes its theme
and point of view: that compulsory attendance in America's public
schools is equivalent to a 12 year sentence in "prison". It is rather odd
that in a society with such concern for liberating pornographers, sexual
deviants, abortionists, mass murderers, convicted felons, bored
housewives; and whatever other individuals who have run afoul of some
oppressive law or contract, few have taken up the plight of the oppressed
child, except such pioneer libertarians as Paul Goodman, Ivan Illich and
our own good editor, Murray Rothbard. Goodman spoke out eloquently on
the need for total freedom in the learning process throughout the sixties;
Illich shook the educational establishment with his demand for
"deschooling" society in the early seventies; and Murray Rothbard
finally found a publisher for his Education Free and Compulsory (Center
for Independent Education, 197) a work written in the early fifties but
considered unmarketable earlier. This delay underlines the great
importance of the media breakthrough of left anarchists like Goodman
and Illich in opening the way for wider public acceptance of individualist
anarchist social critiques.

It was in this favorable climate that the Institute for Humane Studies
and the Center for Independent Education co-sponsored a scholarly
conference on compulsory schooling in Milwaukee in November 1972. The
Twelve Year Sentence is a collection of the papers read at this Milwaukee
conference.

The lead article by Murray Rothbard presents an historical analysis of
the origins of compulsory schooling under the aegis of the great
reformers, Martin Luther and John Calvin, who sought control of
conscience through compulsory schooling of impressionable youth.
Passive obedience to Church and State through schooling came to
America with the Puritans, and in the 19th century became the hoped for
means of Americanizing (and Protestantizing) the new non-Anglo-Saxon
immigrants who poured into an America distrustful and distainful of the
manners and morals of all foreigners. The Federalists had entered the
field of battle in the early 19th century hoping to suppress Jacobin-
Jeffersonian tendencies among the untutored masses by compelling their
children to submit to their propaganda as to true morals and the duties of
citizenship. In his usual brisk, pungent style, Rothbard traces the
political and social context in which compulsory schooling became the
great unchallenged good in American society.

The second essay by George Resch of the Institute for Humane Studies
is a brilliant philosophic analysis of the most tenacious myth in American
education — that the public school system and compulsory schooling are
vital to the achievement of every American's right to equality of
opportunity. Resch traces much mischief to Thomas Jefferson's ill
chosen phrase, "all men are created equal". Whether it was just a "noble
lie" or a typical obscure phrasing of some more subtle 18th century
philosophic idea, Resch pinpoints it as the origin and justification for a
host of anti-libertarian policies, including the notion of compulsory
schooling as the basis for assuring each citizen equality of opportunity.
Like one holding and slowly turning a flashing prism, Resch calls forth an
impressive variety of authorities who, each in his own words and with his
special expertise, present their own flash of insight into human variation
and individuality. The geneticist, biologist, psychologist, anatomist,
neurosurgeon, biochemist, economist, historian and philosopher testify to
the absurdity of egalitarianism, each illuminating the question from his
own scientific perspective until Resch brings it all together in a
compelling affirmation that "so long as individuals vary as they do, there
can be no such thing as equality of opportunity. An unequal performance
is exactly what we would expect from unequal individuals." And so the
case for compulsory schooling to ensure a mythic equality of opportunity
is shattered.

The third essay by Joel Spring, author of the superb study of the role of
the State in the schooling of the citizenry, Education and the Rise of the
Corporate State (Beacon Press, paperback, Boston 1972) is by far the
most controversial. The early part is a survey of the role of the state in
shaping the education of the masses through compulsory schooling to
serve the ends of the ruling elites. It is well done, if not here very
elaborately documented, but is substantially documented in his other
published works. He points to the dubious wisdom of the demand for
government-subsidized day care centers, rightly fearing these would
become a new instrument for social control of the lower classes. Yet he
sees a complication here because day care centers are held to be a
necessary factor in the further emancipation of women from the
supposed slavery of family and household obligations. He also sees the
end of compulsory education as helping to liberate women, weakening the
power of the family, and even possibly eliminating marriage — all
desirable in his view. He thinks that compulsory schooling has
strengthened family power over children by prolonging their dependence
upon parents for economic support. While Spring seems plausible in the
latter specific instance, I am not certain that he is correct in his general
linking of the end of compulsory schooling with women's liberation or the
disintegration of the family as now constituted in American society.
These views are not elaborated upon; no authorities are cited, and
perhaps their remarks are no more than "ruminations" as the title of the
essay would suggest. But they do underline the fact that the end of
compulsory schooling is inextricably linked with other institutional
problems which may demand equally radical change. For instance,
though Spring does not mention it, the child labor and minimum wage
laws will almost certainly have to be modified if compulsory schooling
ends. The welfare laws also presently discourage youths from seeking
employment, and will have to be changed.

Spring is not, of course, a libertarian. But the extent of his
conservatism on the question of ending compulsory schooling was a
surprise. In fact, citing Jefferson's view that every child in the republic
should know how to read, write and calculate, Spring wants to reduce the
"12 year sentence" to three! Why anyone should be compelled to learn
the three R's at all if he chooses otherwise, is left unexamined. While I do
not advocate the fostering of illiteracy, though encountering it all too
frequently among graduates of our contemporary public schools, I think a
case can be made that such illiteracy does not do so much harm today as
it may have in Jefferson's day. Between pocket calculators, and the aural
and visual sources of extensive information through radio, tapes, TV and
film, even illiterates are probably better "educated" today than the
literate but isolated farmers of the 18th century.

Even more distressing is the final paragraph of Spring's ruminations
where, considering the fundamental changes in all aspects of our society
which the end of compulsory schooling might induce or require, Spring
opines that "there may be little we can do" to achieve it until a total
transformation of society occurs. And he leaves the implication that for
the present all we can do is study the phenomenon as a physician studies
cancer, without the immediate prospect of achieving any cure. This
pessimism is unfortunate in a scholar who has already in so many ways
contributed mightily to making the nature of compulsory schooling
known to a wide audience, and thus setting the stage, for the first time in
a century, for reversing public opinion on the issue.

The remaining three essays are all impressive and very informative.
Libertarian lawyer Robert Baker reviews the issue of compulsory
schooling as it is reflected in the statutes and court decisions of the
several states: detailing in the concrete terms the oppressive, vindictive
and vicious character of the compulsory school laws as they are enforced
on isolated individuals. Attorney Gerrit Wormhoudt does the same for the
decisions of the U.S. Supreme Court. Both provide an excellent
background for those interested in using law suits to extend diversity,
freedom and the sovereignty of the family in the education of children.
George Resch has added an extensive and superbly annotated
bibliography which is not the least valuable part of this most valuable
book. The last essay is an historical survey of the economic factors
involved in the growth of compulsory schooling in the 19th century,
especially in England, in which E. G. West concludes that the economic
costs of universal compulsory schooling were "so severe as to outweigh
the benefits", while "selective compulsion can be a constructive, proper

(Continued On Page 5)

496

From The Old Curmudgeon

Psychodrama. The other night I flipped on the **Tomorrow** show, and there was this young psychologist from L.A. (where else?) who had taken over the program for the occasion, conducting a massive group "psychodrama" on the "inter-generational problems of human sexuality" (presumably, the viewers weren't ready for animals yet.) The young psychologist (to whom I naturally took an instant dislike) explained that various younger and older people would play the roles of children and parents, and that he would not try to lead the process in any way, but would let everybody flow with the occasion. He also swore up and down that he was not going to be judgmental, that everyone would make his or her own decisions, etc. Well, it took only a few minutes to find out how **that** was going to turn out. For this pest soon took a very active leading role, stepping in always to hype up the conversation, yelling as "parent" and as "child" when the action flagged. At one point, our non-judgmental leader yelled at the assemblage: "Come on, this is too much of a head trip, let's get our **feelings** into it." Off flipped the tube. So there we have it; no moral judgments are going to be made by the psychodramatist, **except** that "head trips" are **verboten**, and "feelings", goddamit, are going to be expressed, even if the pyschodramatist does most of the prodding and feeling.

Illiterate Principals. How does one do parody if the world is becoming in itself a massive parody? It has just been discovered in New York City that half a dozen public school principals are **illiterate**, and the term is meant not metaphorically but literally (excuse the pun.) In short, they can scarcely read or write English. The literate principals are kind of concerned about this situation, as I hope are some of the parents and children; the critics, however, have been attacked as "racists" — the principals in question being either black or Puerto Rican. How does one comment on this idiocy? One point: can you imagine a **private** school appealing to parents by saying: "Hey, send your kids to our school and learn how **not** to read and write"? Anyone want to send in a paean to the glories of the public school system?

Men's Lib. For years I've wanted to enjoy the benefits of being a member of an "oppressed minority group", but being a white, English-speaking male, have not had much opportunity in recent years. But now I find out that I'm a member of an oppressed "minority" after all . . . men! We find in the New York Times (June 11) that men's lib is a rapidly growing, if still small, movement. Who are men supposed to be liberated **from**, you might ask? Betty Friedan, Blondie, Gloria Steinem? No such thing, for men's lib is a movement organized by the leading **women's** lib organization, the National Organization for Women. So what's going on here? Who we're supposed to be liberated from remains unclear, but **what** we're supposed to be liberated from is highly explicit in the article: namely, **not** having feelings, and — particularly — careers.

On the former, according to the men's lib leaders, it turns out that men don't have any feelings, and don't talk to anybody, as one participant in the recent men's lib conference plaintively put it, he came there because "I needed some men to talk to." Now I don't know what universe these guys come from, but I've never met any men who don't talk and feel, and I bet they haven't either.

The careers gambit is far more interesting. The idea is that men should be liberated **from** careers, in which they have become mere "success images". From careers **to what**, one might ask? Here are some men's lib suggestions: young men to drop out "into a journey of self-exploration" (What if they "journey" for years and find nothing there?); executives to drop out and "go back to school to start all over"; husbands to shift into housework; fathers to leave their jobs to raise their children; and — my own special favorite — "middle-aged men (to) chuck well-paying positions to go off and raise organic potatoes".

The ploy on the part of NOW is almost blatantly obvious: at the same time that **women** are instructed in the joys of careers and the stultifying boredom of housework and raising children, the male enemy is instructed on "the boredom and dehumanization of their jobs", and advised to drop out, change places, **in short,** to leave their careers to make room for the female aspirants. It is, I suppose, a shrewd strategy; if the men are really boobs enough to fall for it, they deserve their fate. Somehow I

doubt it; while it is always hazardous to estimate highly the intelligence of the American public, I still can't believe that men's lib is going to advance beyond the few hundred asses who showed up for the conference.

My message to the Men's libbers: hey, guys, where's your militancy? How can I believe that you're serious until you demand a 50% male quota in the top leadership positions of NOW and MS. magazine? And another thing: one of the most bizarre aspects of the women's lib movement is that it is considered somehow treasonous to criticize in any way any fellow female, any "sister". Do you remember the long dispute about whether or not, for example, Jackie Kennedy Onassis is equally as "oppressed" as _____ (fill in the blank?) (**You** should be so "oppressed".) But one thing I can assure you; regardless of what social pressure you put upon me, I'm **not** going to start considering Richard Nixon as one of my "brothers", who can't be criticized in public. And one final promise: It will be a cold, cold day in Hell before I go off and grow organic potatoes. And if that's Uncle Tomming my "male brothers", you know (expletive deleted) well what you can do about it. ◻

Recommended Reading

AEI Studies.

The American Enterprise Institute, which had long been marked by factual studies of the American economy with a mildly free-enterprise leaning, has in recent months taken a giant leap forward. Led by a series of excellent empirical "evaluation" studies edited by Professor Yale Brozen, of the University of Chicago, the AEI has now become the center of empirical economic studies from a largely free-market point of view. The following are some of the best of the recent AEI booklets (all obtainable from the American Enterprise Institute for Public Policy Research, 1150 Seventeenth St., N. W., Washington, D. C. 20036). All are $3.00 each.

Edward J. Mitchell, **U. S. Energy Policy: A primer**
John Haldi, **Postal Monopoly**
D. Gale Johnson, **The Sugar Program**
Thomas Gale Moore, **Freight Transportation Regulation**
Sam Peltzman, **Regulation of Pharmaceutical Innovation**
Alvin Rabushka, **The Changing Face of Hong Kong.**

Professor Johnson's study of the Sugar Program was apparently influential in the Congress' almost miraculous decision to scrap the cartellizing Sugar Act, with which we have been saddled since the early days of the New Deal. ◻

School Or Jail —

(Continued From Page 4)

and humane provision in society". Not being an economist, this reviewer will not attempt a critique of Prof. West's argument on the economic utility of "selective compulsion" but further study of this aspect of his findings might yield other conclusions.

The participating scholars, the sponsors of the conference, the editor, the publisher and designers of this book deserve great praise for a singularly fascinating achievement, a book that will be wanted by every libertarian, and is needed by everyone interested in the future of American education.

J. R. Peden   ◻

In Search Of The
Old Curmudgeon

By James D. Davidson

Or the Importance of Laughing Down the Left

Readers of LIBERTARIAN FORUM used to be able to depend upon the Old Curmudgeon. He would sally forth with a certain indignation and much good humor to deflate the socio-political buncombe which is so widespread in America today. The Old Curmudgeon had good sense. And he understood the devastating power of the laugh, a power which he used to enforce Jacques Barzun's point that intellect deteriorates with each surrender to folly. The Old Curmudgeon did his best to see that folly did not pass into us, but rather passed by us. In this respect, that irascible gentleman did us a favor. But whatever happened to him? Time passes; culture deteriorates, and we haven't heard a peep from our stalwart. In his place we have Murray Rothbard, that all-too respectable voice of moderation and scholarly detachment.

When Professor Rothbard wrote about the current kidnapping binge, for example, he made some valuable points in his own way. But he fell well short of what we might have expected from the Old Curmudgeon. My comments cannot fill the gap. My nature is too gentle and I am hardly old. Yet someone must speak out to put a little starch into the positions that Professor Rothbard has been ironing over with his scholarly detachment — hence this critique and plea that the Old Curmedgeon be brought out of retirement.

In the case of the Hearst Kidnapping, to which Professor Rothbard addressed a few passing comments, we have further proof that Albert J. Nock's dictum that the worst sort of people read the papers. Patricia Hearst's kidnappers and Patricia herself grew up on a steady diet of newspaper philosophy. If researchers in the Hearst case discover that all the principals read Hearst papers, that alone would explain the profound moral and ethical confusion which motivated their acts. It is little wonder, then, that Patricia apparently has nestled in with the preposterous world view of her captors. One can suppose that the morality that Patricia derived from her parents as a girl was of no more substance than the editorial policy of their newspaper. In that instance it probably boiled down, in addition to the perfunctory religion and welfare state civics, to something like "Don't be late for dinner."

Patricia was evidently ripe for the comic opera doctrines of the "Symbionese Liberation Army" precisely because she had never had anything sufficiently potent to believe. Bob Love says that no one of fair intelligence, who is taught both the socialist and free market philosophy in childhood could possibly become a socialist. Even if that is a bit of an exaggeration, can anyone imagine how a properly reared individual could be impressed with the SLA philosophy? Could anyone with walking-around sense, let alone an acquaintance with the classics of Western thought, believe that marriage and monogamy could be outlawed, as is proposed in the SLA platform?

Such preposterous positions and more abound in the canon of the SLA. If this represented no more than the rantings of a few psychotics it would be distressing enough. Yet we find, not surprisingly, that the young leftish terrorists are not alone in their opposition to all forms of "racism, sexism, ageism, capitalism, individualism, possessiveness, (and) competitiveness." The SLA merely takes up and exaggerates attitudes which are fast becoming cliches of contemporary culture. Distressingly, even persons who otherwise lay claims to libertarian disposition have proven weak marks when it comes to resisting some of the current assault upon human nature.

What is at stake is the understanding which T. S. Eliot aptly said is on the "pre-political" level. That is, "the stratum down to which any sound political thinking much push its roots, and from which it must derive its nourishment." Somewhere along the line, the great mass of persons, including, unfortunately, many advocates of free market economics, has

lost sight of the fundamental fact that man has a nature; that he is not merely silly putty to be re-shaped according to passing fad. So-called "racism, sexism, ageism, etc." exist because, no matter how imperfectly, they incorporate certain truths about the human condition. It may well be, for instance, that there is a fundamental difference between male and female which explains the observable phenomena of all human cultures — that the male — as a rule — predominates. This does not mean, and no sensible person would claim otherwise — that all males will dominate and out-perform all females. Yet acknowledging that, how silly is it for women to be constantly badgering radio stations to give equal time to female composers? A station with a great library might then muster enough programming to stay on the air for an afternoon.

The same might well be said, although it is a lapse of taste, about the so-called "racist" issue. In a free society, knowledge that members of one race might tend to be less nimble mentally than members of another would be almost totally useless information. It would tell nothing about any given individual, just as it would be virtually useless to know that most short persons are of lower intelligence than those six feet tall or greater. Since there are always geniuses who are midgets as well as tall idiots, knowing that an individual was tall or short would tell you nothing. It is only in a statist society where recognition of such tendencies of nature becomes meaningful — precisely because a hue and cry is raised deploring "racism" or "shortism", "ageism" or the like, whenever statistical analysis does not reveal a proportional representation among all groups in the higher income levels of society. When the issue is forced, it then becomes crucial to know, as many scholarly studies have suggested, that members of one race may indeed tend to be in certain ways less capable.

This line of reasoning could be elaborated to fine detail. But the point is clear. Anyone with insight should know that biological reality, and not "brainwashing" or environmental control, is the prime factor informing man's existence. What must always be borne in mind, as Eliot said, is that no political philosophy can escape the right answer to this question: "What is Man? what is his misery and what his greatness? and what, finally, his destiny?" (See George A. Panichas, "T. S. Eliot and the Critique of Liberalism," MODERN AGE, Spring, 1974)

The strength of the libertarian position is precisely that it is a philosophy which harmonizes with understanding of man's basic nature. To work, it awaits no wonderful transformations. Man need be no stronger, wiser, finer than he is at present for free market economics to succeed, because the principles of the free market are deduced from axiomatic truths about reality. This is not to say, that man might not be at least wiser, if not finer and stronger, if a free market did exist. The masses could then see clearly evident the truth of libertarian positions, such as there is no reason to have a state monopoly post office and that public education is not the essential cornerstone of civilization. Man would become wiser in that he would simply be privy to revealed economic truths rather than being forced upon his own meagre logical resources to dope out the form of an economic system. The only other sense in which the free market might elevate man is that since it is more productive, it would afford greater leisure for contemplation. This might redound to the benefit of civilization.

Many libertarians, however, fail to understand this. They reason, erroneously, that since the masses have been indoctrinated to believe that the free market will not work, that any and all other opinions or values of the masses can be equally wrong. Thus, women's liberationists do battle with "sexism" on the assumption that male/female sex roles are not essential components of the human experience, but rather

(Continued On Page 7)

Search Of Old Curmudgeon —

(Continued From Page 6)

cultural whimsy, of the same order as an opinion about agricultural price supports or foreign policy. Of course, sex roles are not opinions, nor are they matters of indoctrination. They are matters of hormonal chemistry. Because this is so emphatically the case, there is no grave danger of the women's liberationists succeeding. The only mischief that they can do is bureaucratic. They can agitate for quotas and regulation of jobs and promotion by fiat. They may generate a bit of short term inequity by displacing more qualified persons (of either sex) from positions they might otherwise have held. They may cause confusion and unhappiness by causing young children to feel guilt over inclinations to follow normal sexual roles. But in the long run, so-called women's liberation is bound to come to nothing because it is based on a profound misunderstanding of human nature. Short of wholesale chemical manipulation of the populace men will ever be men and women will be women.

The attack upon sexual stereotypes, of course, is valid to the extent that those stereotypes are false. But any individual, woman or man, who wished to defy the so-called sex roles could do so at any time. A man could always stay home to mind the kids. The woman could always work, except where legal impediments (which all libertarians oppose) bar the way. But the real thrust of women's lib has not been an opposition to discriminatory laws, but rather a gripe against nature. What especially galls the women's libbers is that being a woman has some decisive meaning which is distinct from being a man. In this sense, the women's liberation movement is an extension of the tendency of modern life noted by Soren Kierkegaard, to "level" humankind to a mathematical equality in which no one would be afforded any individuality or access to novel pleasures. As the mere existence of distinct sexes stands in the path of such a philosophy, an assault has been aimed with particular relish at the main expression of human sexual nature — heterosexual love. The mounting militancy of homosexuals, especially in the women's movement, testifies to this effort to reduce mankind to an indifferent, amorphous mass. The SLA membership, studed with dykes, has merely seized upon the essential content of women's liberation by seeking to do away with all forms of individuality.

It is hardly likely that this or any like-minded revolutionary movement should succeed. Nature stands in the way of that. But the revolutionaries can and will make a botch out of society and culture if they are not treated to the widespread derision which is their rich desert. The SLA and its ilk should be despised for what they are — a congregation of lowlife ruffians, aided and abetted by some bored and humorless middle class brats. It should be the task of everyone concerned about the quality of life to laugh them back into the shadows rather than afford them the limelight and dignity which the media and liberal commentators extend to their "thought." And not only should the terrorists and kidnappers be punished with the shame that their preposterous criminality deserves, but they should be dispatched to quick justice.

The underlying elements in the culture which nourish and give rise to left wing terrorism and destructive violence should also be singled out for attack. Thus libertarians should use the harshest rigors of logic to understand the ultimate consequences of such apparently harmless fads as "women's lib" and other egalitarian movements. Aspects of those movements which have merit from a strictly libertarian position, such as opposition to political restrictions, should be supported. But never should libertarians join in the agitation against nature which is at the heart of most current "reform" movements. For if women's lib, and its inevitable successor movements, such as "ageism", "pansism," "shortism" and the like prosper, the chief casualty will be culture. The turgid and graceless propaganda of the leftish groups gives fair warning of what their version of civilized living would be if they came to dominate society. There would be precious little humor. The dreadful seriousness needed to sustain the effort to change man would see to that. Instead of accepting human nature as it ultimately is, with literature and art directed toward elucidating man's limitations and foibles, we'd have only such "truth" as would make the Russian version of "socialist realism" as flippant as Mother Goose. No one could laugh at anything.

Before we slip so low, there is still time to allow the power of laughter to save us. Let's hear, then, from the Old Curmudgeon, while we still

have the discretion to laugh out loud at the assault upon human differences. In its way, that could contribute as much as scholarly detachment to the evolution of "a more civilized world of dignity, reason and order" which we hopefully can find, without riding as Virgil's hero did, in a rowboat through hell.

The Old Curmudgeon replies:

I'm still around, Jim; the Old Curmudgeon lives! But what a pleasure to see a young lad like Jim Davidson even more curmudgeonly than the Old Master; you can't get hardly any of that from the Younger Generation these days. God bless ye, Jimmy; it's a pleasure for this grizzled old-timer to know that after he hangs up his six-shooter for the last time, Jim Davidson will be around to ride point on behalf of the ontological order.   ☐

About Quotas

It is baffling to hear quotas still advocated as a serious remedy to the injustice caused by discrimination, since the philosophical case against them is straight-forward and definitive. There are, of course, no such things as "group" rights, for rights, and the related concept, justice, pertain only to single persons. It follows that injustice can be redressed only for the individual who suffered it, and retribution can justly be exacted only from those who caused it. Discrimination, in particular, is perpetrated by individuals upon individuals, not by groups upon groups. Hence this cannot be rectified by penalizing the offending group qua group, nor by giving preference to the offended group qua group, without imposing new injuries upon innocent persons.

It is most instructive to recall the precise nature of discrimination: that one person receives less favorable treatment than do others with the same assessable merit, because of extraneous factors such as race or sex. The right thereby transgressed is not one's special "group" right as a woman or a black, but rather the individual right, common to us all, to be judged by the same standard of value as anyone else. The unfairness resides wholly in the departure from a uniform merit standard in the first place — in fact, it is fair to say that a quota already was in use. It should be stressed that the standard used to determine that discrimination has occurred is the merit standard itself; without the prior existence of ascertainable merit, the judgment of unfairness is without meaning.

It follows that only one way exists to counteract this unfairness, namely, to adhere strictly to merit. And what is meant by a merit standard is simply a performance requirement of credential, publicly announced in advance, which is equally applicable to all — the same attributes that a good law ought to have. The futility of quotas should be obvious, since, rather than eliminating inequity, they aim purely at changing its target. A notable advance. We can state this quantitatively: the degree to which a quota policy actually succeeds in admitting different persons than would enter under a merit standard accurately measures the extent to which it continues the old policy of unfairness to individuals. Hence, to talk of goals, timetables and good faith efforts as distinctly different from quotas is merely to miss the force of this criticism, which is against the use of numerical ratios of any sort that are not firmly grounded in measurable ability. And to consider it an improvement, as many do, if a previously sheltered group now has to bear a little of the discriminatory burden, is likewise a mistake: the individual nature of rights and of justice means that any departure from a policy of elevating persons according to a common performance yardstick necessarily results in the visitation of new injustices rather than the rectifying of old ones.

The use of quotas has often been advocated not as an ultimate end but merely as a temporary measure intended to "fade away" when no longer needed. But they will never simply fade away, for there are real factors, other than discrimination, that contribute to group differences. For example, most women have the option, closed to most men, of being financially supported in exchange for homemaking services. At any given level, let us say, that of awarded Ph.D.'s, a smaller proportion of women than of men would probably elect to advance to the next rung, simply

(Continued On Page 8)

About Quotas —

(Continued From Page 7)

(Continued From Page 7)

because they have an additional alternative. In this instance, quotas to maintain "equal" representation would never disappear, since they would be in opposition to the natural, i.e., free choice, result. A second example is the "disproportionate" representation of Jews in the professions. When seen properly, that is, at the level of individuals, this representation is unquestionably a reflection of the true occurrence of talent among them: hence, a quota to "correct" this likewise would never end. Finally, even if proportionate numbers of the respective groups were hired, but for whatever reason (pregnancy, sickle cell anemia, etc.) one group intended to turn over more rapidly than another, than an employment survey at any given time would indeed reveal, Ecce, a disproportion; yet this would in no way result from discriminatory hiring or promotion. Once again, the temporary quota would become a permanent fixture. There are doubtless many other nondiscriminatory influences preferentially affecting a given group (e.g., its recency of immigration to this country) which deserve proper attention by sociologists. But these examples suffice to illuminate the Procrustean nature of quotas.

A seldom recognized feature of the sociology of small group differences is the peculiar statistical behaviour of distributions about a mean, to wit; that a pair of such curves, differing only moderately in the position of their means, will differ dramatically at their extremes. In particular, a determinant shifting just slightly the mean of the employment profile of a given group will result in a whopping "disproportion" in the very worst and very best jobs. Hence, to assert that the surprisingly low numbers of women that are full professors at the best universities, or at the tippy top of any other professional ladder, "prove" pervasive discrimination, is eyewash; a substantial part of this, perhaps most, might well result from nondiscriminatory factors having rather slight overall effects. This leads us inescapably to the view that the usual tactic, of offering an employment breakdown displaying disproportionate group representation as prima facie proof of discrimination, is, unless qualified by an estimation of the magnitudes of the other contributing influences, a downright hornswoggle. That such influences are operative is suggested by the otherwise puzzling circumstance of why market forces have not functioned to break the monopoly of "white males" in good jobs; specifically, why have not second string institutions made use of the allegedly large pool of underutilized and bargain priced but top rate and eager talent in order to gain an advantage over competitors? A white male conspiracy, which is, in effect, the answer usually offered (the "old-boy" network) seems less than an adequate explanation of the observed group differences.

These considerations make clear that the proper focus of anti-discriminatory efforts must necessarily be the implementation of efficacious merit policies. Conversely, the idea of quotas can manifestly be seen to be antithetical to the true goal of a liberal society, namely, to maximize freedom of choice, such that a person electing any given occupation would not find that being a woman or a black had any independent bearing on his or her chances. This proper goal is entirely compatible with there being wide variations in the group averages resulting from the exercise of free choice. While the rhetoric of quotas might at first sound plausible, given the mental inertia of an unfocused mind, a little critical effort shows the concept to be entirely nugatory in achieving the goal of fairness to all. ◻

Arts And Movies

Death Wish. with Charles Bronson. dir. by Michael Winner.

Death Wish is a superb movie, the best hero-and-vengeance picture since Dirty Harry. Bronson, an architect whose young family has been destroyed by muggers, drops his namby-pamby left-liberalism, and begins to pack a gun, defending himself brilliantly and uncompromisingly against a series of muggers who infest New York City. Yet he never kills the innocent, or commits excesses. Naturally, even though he is only defending himself against assault, the police, who have failed to go after the muggers and who acknowledge the fall in the crime rate due to Bronson's activities, devote their resources to pursuing him instead of the criminals who terrorize New York. It is a great and heroic picture, a picture demonstrating one man's successful fight for justice.

As might be expected, Death Wish has been subjected to hysterical attacks by the left-liberal critics who acknowledge the power and technical qualities of the picture, which they proceed to denounce for its "fascist ideology" (self-defense by victims against crime) and its "pornography of violence" (in a just cause.) Bronson is attacked for his "wooden acting", although this is by far his best acting performance in years, far better than in The Mechanic, where the violence was hailed by the critics precisely because it was meaningless and not in defense against aggression. Don't miss Death Wish; it says more about "the urban problem" than a dozen "message" documentaries, and it helps bring back heroism to the movies.

The Tamarind Seed. with Julie Andrews and Omar Sharif. dir. by Blake Edwards.

Tamarind Seed is a welcome breath of fresh air in the cinema, an unabashedly romantic movie, a "movie-movie" in the classical tradition. It combines suspense and espionage with a romantic theme, and integrates both love and espionage into the plot. Direction and acting are excellent. A delightful movie on every level. Once again, the left-liberal critics are generally hostile, largely because it flouts current convention to such an extent that Miss Andrews and Sharif do not hop into bed at the first opportunity. Love ripens first, and what could be more "reactionary" than that? Hooray for Reaction. ◻

A Monthly Newsletter

THE Libertarian Forum

Joseph R. Peden, Publisher

Murray N. Rothbard, Editor

VOLUME VI, NO. 9   SEPTEMBER, 1974   US-ISSN0047-4517

Natural Law, Or The Science Of Justice

By Lysander Spooner

Lysander Spooner has many great distinctions in the history of political thought. For one thing, he was undoubtedly the only constitutional lawyer in history to evolve into an individualist anarchist; for another, he became steadily and inexorably more radical as he grew older. From the time that Benjamin R. Tucker founded the scintillating periodical, **Liberty,** in 1881, Spooner and Tucker were the two great theoreticians of the flourishing individualist anarchist movement, and this continued until Spooner's death in 1887, at the age of 79.

Spooner and the younger Tucker differed on one crucial point, though on that point alone: Tucker was strictly and defiantly a utilitarian, whereas Spooner grounded his belief in liberty on a philosophy of natural rights and natural law. Unfortunately, Spooner's death left Tucker as the major influence on the movement, which quickly adopted the utilitarian creed while Spooner's natural rights-anarchism faded into the background. The present-day followers of Spooner and Tucker, in the United States and England, have also forgotten the fundamental natural-rights grounding in Spooner and have rested on the far more shaky and tenuous Tuckerian base of egoistic utilitarianism.

Lysander Spooner published **Natural Law, or the Science of Justice** as a pamphlet in 1882; the publisher was A. Williams & Co. of Boston. The pamphlet had considerable influence among American and European anarchists of the day, and was reprinted in three editions in the three years following publication. Spooner meant the pamphlet to be the introduction to a comprehensive masterwork on the natural law of liberty, and it is a great tragedy of the history of political thought that Spooner never lived to complete the projected treatise. But what we have retains enduring value from the fact that, of all the host of Lockean natural rights theorists, Lysander Spooner was the only one to push the theory to its logical — and infinitely radical — conclusion: individualist anarchism.

Those who are interested in delving further into Spooner's exhilirating writings will be greatly rewarded by reading his **No Treason** and his **Letter to Thomas F. Bayard,** published together under the title **No Treason** by the Pine Tree Press, Box 158, Larkspur, Colorado, and available for $1.50.

The following is the complete and unabridged pamphlet by Spooner; his characteristic subtitle to the pamphlet was: **A Treatise on Natural Law, Natural Justice, Natural Rights, Natural Liberty, and Natural Society; Showing That All Legislation Whatsoever is an Absurdity, a Usurpation, and a Crime.** Spooner also appended another characteristic note that: "The Author reserves his copyright in this pamphlet, believing that, on principles of natural law, authors and inventors have a right of perpetual property in their ideas."

The Science Of Justice

I.

The science of mine and thine — the science of justice — is the science of all human rights; of all a man's rights of person and property; of all his rights to life, liberty, and the pursuit of happiness.

It is the science which alone can tell any man what he can, and cannot, do; what he can, and cannot have; what he can, and cannot, say, without infringing the rights of any other person.

It is the science of peace; and the only science of peace; since it is the science which alone can tell us on what conditions mankind can live in peace, or ought to live in peace, with each other.

These conditions are simply these: viz., first, that each man shall do, towards every other, all that justice requires him to do; as, for example, that he shall pay his debts, that he shall return borrowed or stolen property to its owner, and that he shall make reparation for any injury he may have done to the person or property of another.

The second condition is, that each man shall abstain from doing to another, anything which justice forbids him to do; as, for example, that he shall abstain from committing theft, robbery, arson, murder, or any other crime against the person or property of another.

So long as these conditions are fulfilled, men are at peace, and ought to remain at peace, with each other. But when either of these conditions is violated, men are at war. And they must necessarily remain at war until justice is re-established.

Through all time, so far as history informs us, wherever mankind have attempted to live in peace with each other, both the natural instincts, and the collective wisdom of the human race, have acknowledged and prescribed, as an indispensable condition, obedience to this one only universal obligation: viz., **that each should live honestly towards every other.**

The ancient maxim makes the sum of a man's legal duty to his fellow men to be simply this: **"To live honestly, to hurt no one, to give to every one his due."**

This entire maxim is really expressed in the single words, to live honestly; since to live honestly is to hurt no one, and give to every one his due.

II.

Man, no doubt, owes many other moral duties to his fellow men; such as to feed the hungry, clothe the naked, shelter the homeless, care for the

(Continued On Page 2)

501

Natural Law — (Continued From Page 1)

sick, protect the defenseless, assist the weak, and enlighten the ignorant. But these are simply moral duties, of which each man must be his own judge, in each particular case, as to whether, and how, and how far, he can, or will, perform them. But of his legal duty — that is, of his duty to live honestly towards his fellow men — his fellow men not only may judge, but, for their own protection, must judge. And, if need be, they may rightfully compel him to perform it. They may do this, acting singly, or in concert. They may do it on the instant, as the necessity arises, or deliberately and systematically, if they prefer to do so, and the exigency will admit of it.

III.

Although it is the right of anybody and everybody — of any one man, or set of men, no less than another — to repel injustice, and compel justice, for themselves, and for all who may be wronged, yet to avoid the errors that are liable to result from haste and passion, and that everybody, who desires it, may rest secure in the assurance of protection, without a resort to force, it is evidently desirable that men should associate, so far as they freely and voluntarily can do so, for the maintenance of justice among themselves, and for mutual protection against other wrongdoers. It is also in the highest degree desirable that they should agree upon some plan or system of judicial proceedings, which, in the trial of causes, should secure caution, deliberation, thorough investigation, and, as far as possible, freedom from every influence but the simple desire to do justice.

Yet such associations can be rightful and desirable only in so far as they are purely voluntary. No man can rightfully be coerced into joining one, or supporting one, against his will. His own interest, his own judgement, and his own conscience alone must determine whether he will join this association, or that; or whether he will join any. If he chooses to depend, for the protection of his own rights, solely upon himself, and upon such voluntary assistance as other persons may freely offer to him when the necessity for it arises, he has a perfect right to do so. And this course would be a reasonably safe one for him to follow, so long as he himself should mainfest the ordinary readiness of mankind, in like cases, to go to the assistance and defense of injured persons; and should also himself "live honestly, hurt no one, and give to every one his due." For such a man is reasonably sure of always having friends and defenders enough in case of need, whether he shall have joined any association, or not.

Certainly no man can rightfully be required to join, or support, an association whose protection he does not desire. Nor can any man be reasonably or rightfully expected to join, or support, any association whose plans, or method of proceeding, he does not approve, as likely to accomplish its professed purpose of maintaining justice, and at the same time itself avoid doing injustice. To join, or support, one that would, in his opinion, be inefficient, would be absurd. To join or support one that, in his opinion, would itself do injustice, would be criminal. He must, therefore, be left at the same liberty to join, or not to join, an association for this purpose, as for any other, according as his own interest, discretion, or conscience shall dictate.

An association for mutual protection against injustice is like an association for mutual protection against fire or shipwreck. And there is no more right or reason in compelling any man to join or support one of these associations, against his will, his judgment, or his conscience, than there is in compelling him to join or support any other, whose benefits (if it offer any) he does not want, or whose purposes or methods he does not approve.

IV.

No objection can be made to these voluntary associations upon the ground that they would lack that knowledge of justice, as a science, which would be necessary to enable them to maintain justice, and themselves avoid doing injustice. Honesty, justice, natural law, is usually a very plain and simple matter, easily understood by common minds. Those who desire to know what it is, in any particular case, seldom have to go far to find it. It is true, it must be learned, like any other science. But it is also true that it is very easily learned. Although as illimitable in its applications as the infinite relations and dealings of men with each other,

it is, nevertheless, made up of a few simple elementary principles, of the truth and justice of which every ordinary mind has an almost intuitive perception. And almost all men have the same perceptions of what constitutes justice, or of what justice requires, when they understand alike the facts from which their inferences are to be drawn.

Men living in contact with each other, and having intercourse together, cannot avoid learning natural law, to a very great extent, even if they would. The dealing of men with men, their separate possessions and their individual wants, and the disposition of every man to demand, and insist upon, whatever he believes to be his due, and to resent and resist all invasions of what he believes to be his rights, are continually forcing upon their minds the questions, Is this act just? or is it unjust? Is this thing mine? or is it his? And these are questions of natural law; questions which, in regard to the great mass of cases, are answered alike by the human mind everywhere.*

Children learn the fundamental principles of natural law at a very early age. Thus they every early understand that one child must not, without just cause, strike, or otherwise hurt, another; that one child must not assume any artitrary control or domination over another; that one child must not, either by force, deceit, or stealth, obtain possession of anything that belongs to another; that if one child commits any of these wrongs against another, it is not only the right of the injured child to resist, and, if need be, punish the wrongdoer, and compel him to make reparation, but that it is also the right, and the moral duty, of all other children, and all other persons, to assist the injured party in defending his rights, and redressing his wrongs. These are fundamental principles of natural law, which govern the most important transactions of man with man. Yet children learn them earlier than they learn that three and three are six, or five and five ten. Their childish plays, even, could not be carried on without a constant regard to them; and it is equally impossible for persons of any age to live together in peace on any other conditions.

It would be no extravagance to say that, in most cases, if not in all, mankind at large, young and old, learn this natural law long before they have learned the meanings of the words by which we describe it. In truth, it would be impossible to make them understand the real meanings of the words, if they did not first understand the nature of the thing itself. To make them understand the meanings of the words justice and injustice, before knowing the nature of the things themselves, would be to make them understand the meanings of the words heat and cold, wet and dry, light and darkness, white and black, one and two, before knowing the nature of the things themselves. Men necessarily must know sentiments and ideas, no less than material things, before they can know the meanings of the words by which we describe them.

V.

If justice be not a natural principle, it is no principle at all. If it be not a natural principle, there is no such thing as justice. If it be not a natural principle, all that men have ever said or written about it, from time immemorial, has been said and written about that which had no existence. If it be not a natural principle, all the appeals for justice that have ever been heard, and all the struggles for justice that have ever been witnessed, have been appeals and struggles for a mere fantasy, a vagary of the imagination, and not for a reality.

If justice be not a natural principle, then there is no such thing as injustice; and all the crimes of which the world has been the scene, have been no crimes at all; but only simple events, like the falling of the rain, or the setting of the sun; events of which the victims had no more reason to complain than they had to complain of the running of the streams, or the growth of vegetation.

---

* Sir William Jones, an English judge in India, and one of the most learned judges that ever lived, learned in Asiatic as well as European law, says: "It is pleasing to remark the similarity, or rather, the identity, of those conclusions which pure, unbiassed reason, in all ages and nations, seldom fails to draw, in such juridical inquiries as are not fettered and imanacled by positive institutions." — **Jones on Bailments, 133**

He means here to say that, when no law has been made in violation of justice, judicial tribunals, "in all ages and nations," have "seldom" failed to agree as to what justice is.

(Continued On Page 3)

Natural Law — (Continued From Page 2)

If justice be not a natural principle, governments (so-called) have no more right or reason to take cognizance of it, or to pretend or profess to take cognizance of it, than they have to take cognizance, or to pretend or profess to take cognizance, of any other nonentity; and all their professions of establishing justice, or of maintaining justice, or of regarding justice, are simply the mere gibberish of fools, or the frauds of imposters.

But if justice be a natural principle, then it is necessarily an immutable one; and can no more be changed — by any power inferior to that which established it — than can the law of gravitation, the laws of light, the principles of mathematics, or any other natural law or principle whatever; and all attempts or assumptions, on the part of any man or body of men — whether calling themselves governments, or by any other name — to set up their own commands, wills, pleasure, or discretion, in the place of justice, as a rule of conduct for any human being, are as much an absurdity, an usurpation, and a tyranny, as would be their attempts to set up their own commands, wills, pleasure, or discretion in place of any and all the physical, mental, and moral laws of the universe.

VI.

If there be any such principle as justice, it is, of necessity, a natural principle; and, as such, it is a matter of science, to be learned and applied like any other science. And to talk of either adding to, or taking from, it, by legislation, is just as false, absurd, and ridiculous as it would be to talk of adding to, or taking from, mathematics, chemistry, or any other science, by legislation.

VII.

If there be in nature such a principle as justice, nothing can be added to, or taken from, its supreme authority by all the legislation of which the entire human race united are capable. And all the attempts of the human race, or of any portion of it, to add to, or take from, the supreme authority of justice, in any case whatever, is of no more obligation upon any single human being than is the idle wind.

VIII.

If there be such a principle as justice, or natural law, it is the principle, or law, that tells us what rights were given to every human being at his birth; what rights are, therefore, inherent in him as a human being, necessarily remain with him during life; and, however capable of being trampled upon, are incapable of being blotted out, extinguished, annihilated, or separated or eliminated from his nature as a human being, or deprived of their inherent authority or obligation.

On the other hand, if there be no such principle as justice, or natural law, then every human being came into the world utterly destitute of rights; and coming into the world destitute of rights, he must necessarily forever remain so. For if no one brings any rights with him into the world, clearly no one can ever have any rights of his own, or give any to another. And the consequence would be that mankind could never have any rights; and for them to talk of any such things as their rights, would be to talk of things that never had, never will have, and never can have existence.

IX.

If there be such a natural principle as justice, it is necessarily the highest, and consequently the only and universal, law for all those matters to which it is naturally applicable. And, of consequently, all human legislation is simply and always an assumption of authority and dominion, where no right of authority or dominion exists. It is, therefore, simply and always an intrusion, an absurdity, an usurpation, and a crime.

On the other hand, if there be no such natural principle as justice, there can be no such thing as injustice. If there be no such natural principle as honesty, there can be no such thing as dishonesty; and no possible act of either force or fraud, committed by one man against the person or property of another, can be said to be unjust or dishonest; or be complained of, or prohibited, or punished as such. In short, if there be no such principle as justice, there can be no such acts as crimes; and all the professions of governments, so called, that they exist, either in whole or in part, for the punishment or prevention of crimes, are professions that they exist for the punishment or prevention of what never existed, nor ever can exist. Such professions are therefore confessions that, so far as crimes are concerned, governments have no occasion to exist; that there is nothing for them to do, and that there is nothing that they can do. They are confessions that the governments exist for the punishment and prevention of acts that are, in their nature, simple impossibilities.

X.

If there be in nature such a principle as justice, such a principle as honesty, such principles as we describe by the words mine and thine, such principles as men's natural rights of person and property, then we have an immutable and universal law; a law that we can learn, as we learn any other science; a law that is paramount to, and excludes, every thing that conflicts with it; a law that tells us what is just and what is unjust, what is honest and what is dishonest, what things are mine and what things are thine, what are my rights of person and property and what are your rights of person and property, and where is the boundary between each and all of my rights of person and property. And this law is the paramount law, and the same law, over all the world, at all times, and for all peoples: and will be the same paramount and only law, at all times, and for all peoples, so long as man shall live upon the earth.

But if, on the other hand, there be in nature no such principle as justice, no such principle as honesty, no such principle as men's natural rights of person and property, then all such words as justice and injustice, honesty and dishonesty, all such words as mine and thine, all words that signify that one thing is one man's property and that another thing is another man's property, all words that are used to describe men's natural rights of person or property, all such words as are used to describe injuries and crimes, should be struck out of all human languages as having no meanings; and it should be declared, at once and forever, that the greatest force and the greatest frauds, for the time being, are the supreme and only laws for governing the relations of men with each other; and that, from henceforth, all persons and combinations of persons — those that call themselves governments, as well as all others — are to be left free to practice upon each other all the force, and all the fraud, of which they are capable.

XI.

If there be no such science as justice, there can be no science of government; and all the rapacity and violence, by which, in all ages and nations, a few confederated villains have obtained the mastery over the rest of mankind, reduced them to poverty and slavery, and established what they called governments to keep them in subjection, have been as legitimate examples of government as any that the world is ever to see.

XII.

If there be in nature such a principle as justice, it is necessarily the only **political** principle there ever was, or ever will be. All the other so-called political principles, which men are in the habit of inventing, are not principles at all. They are either the mere conceits of simpletons, who imagine they have discovered something better than truth, and justice, and universal law; or they are mere devices and pretenses, to which selfish and knavish men resort as means to get fame, and power, and money.

XIII.

If there be, in nature, no such principle as justice, there is no moral standard, and never can be any moral standard, by which any controversy whatever, between two or more human beings, can be settled in a manner to be obligatory upon either; and the inevitable doom of the human race must consequently be to be forever at war; forever striving to plunder, enslave, and murder each other; with no instrumentalities but fraud and force to end the conflict.

XIV

If there be no such obligation as justice, there can certainly be no other moral obligation — truth, mercy, nor any other — resting upon mankind To deny the obligation of justice is, therefore, to deny the existence of any moral obligation whatever among men, in their relations to each other.

(Continued On Page 4)

Natural Law — (Continued From Page 3)

XV.

If there be no such principle as justice, the world is a mere abyss of moral darkness; with no sun, no light, no rule of duty, to guide men in their conduct towards each other. In short, if there be, in nature, no such principle as justice, man has no moral nature; and, consequently, can have no moral duty whatever.

Natural Law Contrasted With Legislation

I.

Natural law, natural justice, being a principle that is naturally applicable and adequate to the rightful settlement of every possible controversy that can arise among men; being, too, the only standard by which any controversy whatever, between man and man, can be rightfully settled; being a principle whose protection every man demands for himself, whether he is willing to accord it to others, or not; being also an immutable principle, one that is always and everywhere the same, in all ages and nations; being self-evidently necessary in all times and places; being so entirely impartial and equitable towards all; so indispensable to the peace of mankind everywhere; so vital to the safety and welfare of every human being; being, too, so easily learned, so generally known, and so easily maintained by such voluntary associations as all honest men can readily and rightfully form for that purpose — being such a principle as this, these questions arise, viz.: Why is it that it does not universally, or well nigh universally, prevail? Why is it that it has not, ages ago, been established throughout the world as the one only law that any man, or all men, could rightfully be compelled to obey? Why is it that any human being ever conceived that anything so self-evidently superfluous, false, absurd, and atrocious as all legislation necessarily must be, could be of any use to mankind, or have any place in human affairs?

II.

The answer is, that through all historic times, wherever any people have advanced beyond the savage state, and have learned to increase their means of subsistence by the cultivation of the soil, a greater or less number of them have associated and organized themselves as robbers, to plunder and enslave all others, who had either accumulated any property that could be seized, or had shown, by their labor, that they could be made to contribute to the support or pleasure of those who should enslave them.

These bands of robbers, small in number at first, have increased their power by uniting with each other, inventing warlike weapons, disciplining themselves, and perfecting their organizations as military forces, and dividing their plunder (including their captives) among themselves, either in such proportions as have been previously agreed on, or in such as their leaders (always desirous to increase the number of their followers) should prescribe.

The success of these bands of robbers was an easy thing, for the reason that those whom they plundered and enslaved were comparatively defenseless; being scattered thinly over the country; engaged wholly in trying, by rude implements and heavy labor, to extort a subsistence from the soil; having no weapons of war, other than sticks and stones; having no military discipline or organization, and no means of concentrating their forces, or acting in concert, when suddenly attacked. Under these circumstances, the only alternative left them for saving even their lives, or the lives of their families, was to yield up not only the crops they had gathered, and the lands they had cultivated, but themselves and their families also as slaves.

Thenceforth their fate was, as slaves, to cultivate for others the lands they had before cultivated for themselves. Being driven constantly to their labor, wealth slowly increased; but all went into the hands of their tyrants.

These tyrants, living solely on plunder, and on the labor of their slaves, and applying all their energies to the seizure of still more plunder, and the enslavement of still other defenseless persons; increasing, too, their numbers, perfecting their organizations, and multiplying their weapons of war, they extend their conquests until, in order to hold what they have already got, it becomes necessary for them to act systematically, and co-operate with each other in holding their slaves in subjection.

But all this they can do only by establishing what they call a government, and making what they call laws.

All the great governments of the world — those now existing, as well as those that have passed away — have been of this character. They have been mere bands of robbers, who have associated for purposes of plunder, conquest, and the enslavement of their fellow men. And their laws, as they have called them, have been only such agreements as they have found it necessary to enter into, in order to maintain their organizations, and act together in plundering and enslaving others, and in securing to each his agreed share of the spoils.

All these laws have had no more real obligation than have the agreements which brigands, bandits, and pirates find it necessary to enter into with each other, for the more successful accomplishment of their crimes, and the more peaceable division of their spoils.

Thus substantially all the legislation of the world has had its origin in the desires of one class of persons to plunder and enslave others, **and hold them as property.**

III.

In process of time, the robber, or slave-holding, class — who had seized all the lands, and held all the means of creating wealth — began to discover that the easiest mode of managing their slaves, and making them profitable, was not for each slaveholder to hold his specified number of slaves, as he had done before, and as he would hold so many cattle, but to give them so much liberty as would throw upon themselves (the slaves) the responsibility of their own subsistence, and yet compel them to sell their labor to the land-holding class — their former owners — for just what the latter might choose to give them.

Of course, these liberated slaves, as some have erroneously called them, having no lands, or other property, and no means of obtaining an independent subsistence, had no alternative — to save themselves from starvation — but to sell their labor to the landholders, in exchange only for the coarsest necessaries of life; not always for so much even as that.

These liberated slaves, as they were called, were now scarcely less slaves than they were before. Their means of subsistence were perhaps even more precarious than when each had his own owner, who had an interest to preserve his life. They were liable, at the caprice or interest of the land-holders, to be thrown out of home, employment, and the opportunity of even earning a subsistence by their labor. They were, therefore, in large numbers, driven to the necessity of begging, stealing, or starving; and became, of course, dangerous to the property and quiet of their late masters.

The consequence was, that these late owners found it necessary, for their own safety and the safety of their property, to organize themselves more perfectly as a government, **and make laws for keeping these dangerous people in subjection:** that is, laws fixing the prices at which they should be compelled to labor, and also prescribing fearful punishments, even death itself, for such thefts and trespasses as they were driven to commit, as their only means of saving themselves from starvation.

These laws have continued in force for hundreds, and, in some countries, for thousands of years; and are in force today, in greater or less severity, in nearly all the countries on the globe.

The purpose and effect of these laws have been to maintain, in the hands of the robber, or slave-holding class, a monopoly of all lands, and, as far as possible, of all other means of creating wealth; and thus to keep the great body of laborers in such a state of poverty and dependence, as would compel them to sell their labor to their tyrants for the lowest prices at which life could be sustained.

The result of all this is, that the little wealth there is in the world is all in the hands of a few — that is, in the hands of the law-making, slave-holding class; who are now as much slave-holders in spirit as they ever were, but who accomplish their purposes by means of the laws they make for keeping the laborers in subjection and dependence, instead of each one's owning his individual slaves as so many chattels.

Thus the whole business of legislation, which has now grown to such gigantic proportions, had its origin in the conspiracies, which have always existed among the few, for the purpose of holding the many in subjection, and extorting from them their labor, and all the profits of their labor.

And the real motives and spirit which lie at the foundation of all

(Continued On Page 5)

Only One
Heartbeat Away

As the Watergate revelations poured out in the last years, our esteemed publisher, Joe Peden, began to say, in some awe: "all the most flagrant 'paranoia' of the New Left turns out to be correct analysis!" Of course, he could have substituted or added the Birchers for the New Left. "Paranoia" lives! and after the Pentagon Papers and the Watergate revelations the fashionable sneering at the "conspiracy theory of history" will never sit quite so smugly again. The "conspiracy theory of history" — which is really only praxeology applied to human history, in assuming that men have motives on which they act — has never looked so good or so rational.

Being away in Europe at the time of the amazing, cataclysmic appointment of Nelson Rockefeller to the Vice-Presidency, I did not have a chance to observe the reactions of American opinion. But as far as I know, no one has pointed to the most important aspect of the appointment: that it provides a remarkable empirical confirmation of the leading "conspiracy thesis" about the Watergate Affair: the Oglesby-Sale, "Cowboy vs. Yankee" hypothesis. The appointment of the man who embodies the Big Business Corporate State, the living representative of the corporate statism that has grown like a cancer since the Progressive Period in America (after about 1900), to be the heir apparent, and a heartbeat away from the most powerful post in the world, is enough to give any American, let alone any libertarian, the heebie-jeebies. The accession of Nelson Rockefeller to total power would mean the final fusion of the most colossal aggregation of political and economic power that the world has ever seen. And the only groups that have warned us of this coming event have been the major groups totally outside the American power structure: the extreme left and the "extreme", or Birchite, right, who in their different yet complementary ways have been writing unheeded about the menace of the "Rockefeller World Empire" and its drive for total dominion.

* * * * *

When Nelson Rockefeller first appeared on the electoral scene in his

Natural Law— (Continued From Page 4)

legislation — notwithstanding all the pretenses and disguises by which they attempt to hide themselves — are the same today as they always have been. The whole purpose of this legislation is simply to keep one class of men in subordination and servitude to another.

IV.

What, then, is legislation? It is an assumption by one man, or body of men, of absolute, irresponsible dominion over all other men whom they can subject to their power. It is the assumption by one man, or body of men, of a right to subject all other men to their will and their service. It is the assumption by one man, or body of men, of a right to abolish outright all the natural rights, all the natural liberty of all other men; to make all other men their slaves; to arbitrarily dictate to all other men what they may, and may not, do; what they may, and may not, have; what they may, and may not, be. It is, in short, the assumption of a right to banish the principle of human rights, the principle of justice itself, from off the earth, and set up their own personal will, pleasure, and interest in its place. All this, and nothing less, is involved in the very idea that there can be any such thing as human legislation that is obligatory upon those upon whom it is imposed. ◻

successful race for the New York governorship in 1958, Frank S. Meyer, the valiant leader of the quasi-libertarian wing of the National Review clique, denounced Rockefeller as "Caesar Augustus", the destroyer of the American Republic. The feeble and perfunctory opposition that NR has put up to Rockefeller now (combined with its kept Conservative Party's endorsement of Rocky's stooge Malcolm Wilson) only indicates how far National Review has gone in its urge to join the ruling Establishment. In addition to Meyer, there emerged also an eccentric (to use a charitable term) eye doctor in New York named Dr. Emanuel M. Josephson, a conspiracy theorist to end all conspiracy theories, a "paranoid" among the paranoids. But while the good doctor's historiographic methodology left a great deal to be desired (e.g. his idea that the Rockefellers run world Communism, plus many other aberrations), he was and probably still is the world's outstanding "Rockefeller-batter", an enthusiastic collector of any and all facts about the Rockefeller family. At any rate, Josephson sprang into action, declaring that the Rockefellers felt so secure of their political control of the country that they were now ready to reach for open (in contrast to their previously hidden) political power, in the shape of Nelson as President. Not only that: six years earlier, in 1952, Dr. Josephson had written, in his magnum opus, Rockefeller "Internationalist": The Man Who Misrules the World, the following paragraph, which now seems remarkably prophetic:

> "The pattern of his activities indicates that it is the objective of the Rockefellers to place Nelson Rockefeller in the White House by some means, whether direct, indirect or cataclysmic. Direct election as President is now possible with the sham 'philanthropic', 'benevolent' and 'public-spirited' build up he has had; but it is improbable. More probable would be his nomination as Vice-Presidential candidate on one of their 'bipartisan' or 'omnipartisan' tickets at the side of a Presidential candidate whom they know to be tottering at the edge of the grave, or who could be disposed of by some other of the methods of purging that have become so commonplace during the New and Fair Deals." (p. 49)

* * * * *

Before proceeding to the Nelson appointment and its background, a brief but vitally important sketch is in order of what I believe to be a sound "conspiracy" analysis of the essence of twentieth century political and politico-economic history. By the late nineteenth century, the Democratic Party was largely in the control of the Morgan financial empire, and of its financial and industrial allies. Augustus Belmont, a Morgan ally, was the secretary of the national Democratic Party for decades, and an analysis of the Cleveland Administrations (the only Democratic regimes from the Civil War to Woodrow Wilson) shows Morgan partners and lawyers dominant in the key Cabinet positions. By the latter years of the century, on the other hand, the Republican Party became more loosely under the control of the Rockefellers, through Rockefeller domination of the Ohio Republican Party (old John D.'s original home and economic base was in Cleveland). Note that Ohio Republicans formed every Republican Administration since and including Benjamin Harrison (e.g. William McKinley, William Howard Taft, and Warren G. Harding). While both the Morgans and the Rockefellers used their political power for subsidies and contracts, and for imperial expansion abroad, the roughly laissez-faire system meant that the evil effects on the country and the economy of these power plays

(Continued On Page 6)

One Heartbeat Away —

(Continued From Page 5)

were relatively limited. Then, around 1900, the Big Business interests, especially those grouped around Morgan, having failed dismally to achieve monopolies in each industry on the free market, decided to change the American system into a corporate state, into a neo-mercantilist Big Government which would cartellize the economy for their benefit. While Rockefeller did not fight this trend, the Morgans were far more assiduous in pushing the new system and the new theory.

The delicate political balance of power was broken with the assassination of Rockefeller's man William McKinley, for, as a gesture to appease the Morgans, who had fought the McKinley nomination, the Republicans had chosen the young Morgan man, Theodore Roosevelt, for the seemingly harmless post of Vice-President. (The Morgans were forced to shift, at least temporarily, to the Republicans because of the capture of the Democratic machinery by the leftish populist William Jennings Bryan). As soon as Teddy Roosevelt became President by the accident of (Yes, another!) "lone nut", he began to wield the Sherman Anti-Trust Act, which had been a literal dead letter until then, as a political club. The club was used savagely to batter — guess who? — the Rockefellers, leading to the coerced dissolution of the Standard Oil combine by the federal government. It was at this point, Dr. Josephson speculates — probably correctly — that old John D. decided to beat his enemies at their own game, to become even more statist than they, to use every political and public relations weapon at his and his allies' command. Roosevelt's successor, William Howard Taft, an Ohio — and therefore Rockefeller — Republican, also wielded the anti-trust weapon, to try to dissolve some other "bad" trusts. And what were these trusts? Again, you guessed it: key flagships in the Morgan empire: U. S. Steel, and International Harvester. The war of the titans was on, masked as high devotion to the anti-trust ideal.

In retaliation for the Taft-Rockefeller policies, the Morgans and their numerous allies engineered the creation of the Progressive Party, which nominated Teddy Roosevelt for President for the successful purpose of destroying Taft. The Progressives, who not coincidentally had as their national chairman Morgan partner George W. Perkins, also served the ancillary goal of ideologically fostering the proto-New Deal system of the corporate state in America. The breaking of Taft swept into office Woodrow Wilson, who was also an ally of the Morgans, and who served to institute corporate state and Big Government policies in America, in both domestic institutions and in an interventionist and globalist foreign policy. By this time, the Morgans were losing ground in the competitive financial race to Kuhn-Loeb and the Jewish investment banking firms; but the Morgans were able to recoup by pushing the Wilson Administration into war with Germany, a war necessary to the Morgans because the latter were the financial agents of the British and French governments, and had loaned heavily to Britain and France. Furthermore, the Morgans and their allies were heavily invested in the American export industries which received a great shot in the arm from Allied purchases and government war contracts. Among big businessmen, only Rockefeller was hostile to the American entry into the war.

During the interwar years, with both financial groups converted to statism, the Morgans, still heavily invested in Britain and France, began to drive toward American war with Germany, which, with its bilateral economic agreements, remained stubbornly outside the Morgan financial ambit. On the other hand, the Rockefellers, with financial ties to I. G. Farben in Germany, were isolationists in Europe, with top Rockefeller ideologist (we'll see why a bit later) John Foster Dulles — later the chief spokesman for pietistic global war — writing a realistic book, War, Peace, and Change, calling for peaceful revision of the Versailles Treaty to meet legitimate German territorial demands in Europe. On the other hand, the Rockefellers, with heavy investments and financial ties with China, were pushing for war with Japan, while the European-centered Morgans were in favor of peaceful coexistence in Asia (thus, virtually the only high State Department official opposing war with Japan was Ambassador to Japan, Joseph C. Grew, a Morgan partner.)

World War II, which ended any sort of neo-populist phase the New Deal may have had, and cemented the corporatist Big Business alliance with the Welfare-Warfare State, may be considered to be a deal between the Rockefellers and Morgans, with both getting a piece of the pie: the Morgans their war in Europe, and the Rockefellers their war in Asia.

Since World War II, American political history can no longer be analyzed in terms of a stark Morgan-Rockefeller conflict; instead, with of course shifting marginal influence, both groups have settled down into a happy joint "Eastern Establishment" rule over the United States, an "East" which more and more has included Chicago and the Old Middle West. In domestic affairs, this meant running an increasingly mighty Leviathan Corporate State; in foreign affairs, it meant global imperialism and the waging of counter-revolution and the Cold War throughout the globe. The final victory of this Eastern team was the literal stealing of the 1952 Republican nomination from Senator Taft (no longer a Rockefeller ally), by means of savage Wall St. banker pressure on the delegates who had been committed to the isolationist Taft.

One stark example of Rockefeller influence on American politics — particularly in the higher administrative positions — was the makeup of the Eisenhower Administration. The powerful Secretary of State and virtual maker of foreign policy was John Foster Dulles. Who was Dulles? A partner, in the first place, of the Rockefeller Wall St. law firm of Sullivan and Cromwell; but, in addition to that, and a little known fact, Dulles was married to Janet Pomeroy Avery, first cousin of John D. Rockefeller, Jr. Thomas E. Dewey's political mentor was Rockefeller kinsman, Winthrop W. Aldrich, head of the extremely powerful Chase National Bank (its successor, Chase Manhattan, is now of course openly headed by David Rockefeller.) Head of the extraordinarily powerful and secret CIA was Dulles' brother Allen, and their sister Eleanor was at the Asian desk of the State Department. To top it all off, Under Secretary of State was Christian Herter, whose wife was a member of the Pratt family, which has been intimately associated with the Rockefellers since old John D. got his start a century ago.

Even the New York Times cottoned to the egregious nature of Nelson's claim that his personal stockholdings give him no major control over large corporations. First, we must realize that the Rockefeller Family votes and acts together through their family corporation; when we add Nelson's, David's, Laurence's, and John's holdings, plus their family trusts, plus the enormous stock held by the numerous Rockefeller Foundations, plus their extremely powerful Chase Manhattan Bank, with its loans, holdings, and trust department, plus their long-time allied families (the Pratts, Flaglers, Whitneys, Bedfords, et al), plus their looser allies, plus the fact that working control of modern corporations does not need 51% of the stock, we get an idea of the enormous Rockefeller power. From a free-market point of view, of course, there is nothing wrong with economic "power" per se; but when we realize the intimate connection between the Rockefellers and the corporate State of the U. S. government, our view changes. This is not free market money but intimate government-business partnership and control. (For the most recent scholarly study of current Rockefeller financial control, see James C. Knowles, "The Rockefeller Financial Group," in R. Andreano, ed., Superconcentration Supercorporation (Andover, Mass.: Warner Modular Publications, 1973).

* * * * *

This brings us to the great Nixon Caper. One of the glories of the market is that, even when greatly hobbled, competition and new wealth can break through. During the 1960's, a loosely allied variety of new wealth and new industrial firms arose to challenge the dominance of the old Rockefeller-Morgan Eastern Establishment. The new money was centered in such new industries as plastics, computers, and electronics, defense firms such as aircraft, in real estate, and in Texas oil (hide-bound Standard Oil, originally centered in Cleveland and western Pennsylvania oilfields, had been slow to realize the potential of the newly discovered Texas and Oklahoma oil fields.) Geographically, the new wealth was centered in what Kirkpatrick Sale has called "the Southern Rim": Texas, southern California, and Florida. Much of this new wealth was Texas-centered, and the political rise of Lyndon Johnson and John Connally was both fostered by and encouraged the economic rise of the new wealth.

Carl Oglesby's happy term for the two new conflicting groups was the "Yankees" and the "Cowboys". The fact of old vs. new wealth also engendered a difference in ideology, attitudes, and lifestyles between the two groups. The Eastern Establishment Yankees, entrenched for generations, was and is aristocratic, smooth, cosmopolitan, well-educated, and highly sophisticated, able to mask their power and

(Continued On Page 7

The Non-Dismal Science

By Leonard P. Liggio

Percy L. Greaves, Jr., UNDERSTANDING THE DOLLAR CRISIS, with a foreword by Ludwig von Mises, Boston, Western Islands, 1973, 302 pp., $7.00.

Gottfried Haberler, ECONOMIC GROWTH & STABILITY, Los Angeles, Nash Publishing, 1974 (Principles of Freedom Series), 291 pp. $10.00.

"Economics is not a dry subject. It is not a dismal subject. It is not about statistics. It is about human life. It is about the ideas that motivate human beings. It is about how men act from birth to death. It is about the most important and interesting drama of all — human action." Thus, Percy Greaves launched his very readable book concerned with explaining to the general reader economics in general and monetary matters in particular. The book is based on the lectures which Greaves presented to the Centro de Estudios sobre la Libertad in Buenos Aires at the invitation of Alberto Benegas Lynch. Greaves' experience as an economic author began as a financial editor for the United States News. During World War II he was Research Director of the Republican National Committee until he resigned over the party's shift to support for Federal aid to education, public housing, etc. During 1945-46 he was Chief of the Minority (Republican) Staff of the Joint Congressional Committee on the Investigation of the Pearl Harbor Attack, and in 1947 was a congressional expert in drafting the Taft-Hartley Law. For the past quarter century, Greaves has been a noted economic columnist and lecturer (Freedom School and Foundation for Economic Education), and Armstrong Professor of Economics at the University of Plano in association with Professor von Mises.

The first part of the work, concerned with general economics, presents a clear analysis of the misunderstanding of value by the classical economists, and the rectification by the Austrian School. Greaves' fine

(Continued On Page 8)

Only One Heartbeat Away

(Continued From Page 7)

government loot behind a facade of intellectual apologetics, set forth by kept intellectuals, experts, and university professors. Being less hungry and more far-sighted, furthermore, the Yankees are typically willing to allow more dissent, civil liberties, and adherence to democratic forms, so long as their power remains essentially undamaged. The Southern Rim "Cowboys", on the other hand, symbolized again by Johnson and Connally, take on the typical characteristics of the nouveau riche: hungrier, less sophisticated, more immediately grasping, and more willing to scuttle civil liberties in their thirst for power.

After Yankee Jack Kennedy was deposed by a "lone nut", Cowboy Johnson was catapulted to power. What of the Nixon Administration? While Nixon himself was personally Cowboy (Southern California), his administration was clearly a Cowboy-Yankee coalition, with foreign policy wrapped up by the Rockefellers (Henry Kissinger was for years Nelson Rockefeller's personal foreign policy adviser.) Economic policy was also basically Rockefeller, Arthur Burns having long been in the Dewey-Rockefeller ambit, and George Shultz being a member of the Pratt family (his middle name is Pratt). But the rest of the Administration was Cowboy, a designation that clearly applies to the West Coast and USC White House power boys, as well as Connally, and to Bebe Rebozo (Florida and Cuba: how Southern Rimmy can one get?)

The interesting focal question about the great media revelations on Watergate is: how come the powerful Establishment press (the New York Times, Washington Post, CBS, NBC) suddenly got honest? How come, that after years of supinely accepting federal government press handouts, they suddenly became demon investigative reporters in the great old, but forgotten, tradition? The point is not that the press was wrong and Nixon victimized about Watergate, but that how come the press suddenly got right? A conspiracy analysis provides the only plausible explanation: namely, that the press expose was the spearhead of a massive Eastern Establishment-Yankee counterrevolution to smash the Nixonite cowboys: almost all of whom are now banished, under indictment, or in jail. Why the Yankees concluded that they must take such drastic measures, even unto impeachment, is not completely clear: part of it was certainly the naked grab for power, the burgling and the espionage, on the part of the Nixon Cowboys. But another part centers on the still mysterious role of the CIA, which was strongly if muddily concerned with Watergate. The catalyst seems to have been Nixon's appointment of James Schlesinger to head the CIA, after which Schlesinger began to purge the "Old Guard" of the CIA, which had always been thoroughly Yankee-Eastern Establishment. It is certainly possible that James McCord, who finally blew the whistle on the plot, was a double agent of his beloved Yankee-controlled CIA, in bringing down Nixon and his Plumbers.

At any rate, we come down to the great empirical test of the Yankee-Cowboy conspiracy analysis of the Watergate Struggle: if true, if the fight over Watergate was a massive counter-revolution engineered by the Rockefeller-Morgan Yankees, then who would be appointed Vice-President by the cipher Jerry Ford (who himself was a political disciple of Yankee-controlled Arthur Vandenberg?) If the conspiracy thesis were correct, then either Yankee Brahmin Eliot Richardson, or, even more blatantly, Nelson himself, would be appointed. And the rest is history. With Rockefeller receiving general hosannahs as heir-apparent, with Donald Rumsfeld now in and Kissinger still around, the Yankees have now taken over completely. Dr. Josephson's seemingly paranoid analysis of twenty-two years ago has virtually come true; the man who could not have been nominated, let alone elected, on his own, is only a heartbeat away from total power, and is the front-runner for 1976.

As a corollary of this mammoth fusion of political and economic power, it is not surprising that Nelson Rockefeller, as much as Scoop Jackson, is Mr. State: in every policy field, Rockefeller opts for statism and Big Government. High taxes, high government spending, fiat paper over gold, jail for drug addicts, compulsory racial integration, military-industrial complex, Cold War and global intervention, you name it, Nelson Rockefeller is in the forefront of the drive for Leviathan State power. The monstrous choice of Nelson Rockefeller, and the confirming of the conspiracy thesis, does not of course mean that we libertarians should retract our hosannahs over the bringing down of the corrupt and tyrannical Nixon gang. No group of men have more richly deserved such a fate. But the State of course rolls on, albeit under rather different management. The Yankees may be smoother and more civil libertarian, but they are in the long run more dangerous, and this especially applies to Nelson. Now that we have used the once rusty impeachment weapon so successfully, let us keep it revved up and at the ready. Boy are we going to need it.

The Non-Dismal Science —

(Continued From Page 7)

summary of the position of mathematics in economics deserves quotation:

> Mathematics in the field of economics is always statistics, and statistics are always history. Mathematics cannot and does not enter into measuring the ideas or values that determine human action. There are no constants in these. There is no equality in market transactions. Therefore, mathematics does not apply. The use of mathematics requires constants. Mathematics cannot be used in economic theory.

He notes a debate between Walter Heller and Milton Friedman which was described as "a readable exchange between two of the nation's best-known economists who take contrasting views of **government's role in managing the national economy.**" (Emphasis added by Greaves.) A fine critique is presented of the fallacies of Friedman's monetary thought. As Greaves notes, Friedman is a good economist in areas such as labor economics, or foreign aid, but unfortunately he does not stick to matters that he understands, but dabbles in monetary theory. One may judge the correctness of one's monetary theory by the distance of the economist from the President's ear.

Basing himself on Boehm Bawerk and Mises, Greaves undertakes a thorough historical analysis of modern American monetary problems. He calls to mind the anti-inflation writings of Pelatiah Webster (1726-1795). The center of his attention is the monetary and banking policies of the 1910's and 1920's, and the special relationship of the New York Federal Reserve Bank and the Bank of England. Of special importance was Churchill's 1925 blunder of overvaluing the English pound; it ranks along side his 1940 foreign policy as the Alpha and Omega of England's total decline. Greaves details the role of foreign policy and war as the steps used by the New Deal to escape the consequences of its economic programs. War production and Lend-Lease to the Aillies was financed by increases in the money supply ($46.5 billion at the end of 1938, $64.5 billion at the end of 1941). Greaves also shows the very important relationship between inflation of the money supply after World War II and the Marshall Plan and foreign aid programs; this analysis is must reading.

Especially good is Greaves' discussion of the "Effect of Wage Rate Intervention," and his critique of publicly financed education.

> Anyone who understands the benefits of competition must hold that the system that is best for producing what people

want most through the market forces is also the best system for producing the best education.

The most valuable part of Gottfried Haberler's book is the current analysis of the energy crisis, and the correct, market mechanisms for dealing with the energy crisis. His treatment of that topic alone makes the book worth reading. But, his discussion of business cycle, inflation, and the international monetary situation are valuable for the general reader and expert alike. He devotes much attention to the conflicts over monetary policies, for example, creeping inflation:

> On these questions the line-up of different economists is curiously mixed. Some laissez-faire liberals like Milton Friedman and good Keynesians like Paul Samuelson and Robert Solow take a relaxed view of creeping inflation while others, such as F. A. Hayek and some adherents of the "New Economics" (in the 1967 controversy over the tax increase) take it much more seriously. . . . I made it clear earlier that I do not question that creeping inflation per se is by far a lesser evil than severe depressions. But this does not tell us how high the cost of creeping inflation actually is. Is it possible that creeping inflation, if allowed to continue for a long time, brings with it some delayed dangers? Furthermore, it is necessary to pay any price at all in the form of inflation for the kind of growth we had during the postwar period? In other words, is growth without inflation altogether impossible.?

Haberler offers in his discussions of each major topic the Keynesian and non-Keynesian explanations for the developments. His postscripts ending many chapters concern the immediate events of the crises of the winter of 1973-74, and underscore the earlier controversies on policies. □

The Libertarian Forum
BOX 341
MADISON SQUARE STATION
NEW YORK, NEW YORK 10010

**Published Every Month. Subscription Rates:
$8.00 Per Year; $15.00 Two Years**

A Monthly Newsletter

THE
Libertarian Forum

Joseph R. Peden, Publisher   Murray N. Rothbard, Editor

VOLUME VI, NO. 10   OCTOBER, 1974   US-ISSN0047-4517

The Ford In Our Present,
Or Can Greenspan Save Us?

For the libertarian there is no period more nerveracking than the inevitable "honeymoon" that attends each new President's inception in office. Of course one knows that each of these honeymoons is doomed, but in the meantime one has to grit one's teeth and sweat it out: endure all the sickening adulation heaped on the Leader from left, right, center and all points of the political compass. Happily, in the case of President Ford the universal honeymoon was the shortest-lived in history, so much so that I was able to sail right through it while cut off from political news in Europe. Hardly had I a chance to suffer the "honeymoon" than the brief "nightmare" (to use a term wrongly applied to Watergate) was happily over. The egregious blanket pardon granted to our disgraced ex-President was enough to liquidate the honeymoon and bring us back to a healthy distrust of government and the Executive. Surely the best comment on the pardon was the hilarious headline in the English **Guardian**: "Ford Absolves Nixon of All His Sins".

Fortunately, I was also able to escape most of the blather about the much-ballyhooed "economic summits", properly dubbed by the New Left economists as a "charade" (though not for the right reasons.) In all the thousands of words of hogwash about the summits, by far the best was the excellent article by the increasingly libertarian columnist Nicholas von Hoffman (**Washington Post**, September 16). In his typically scintillating fashion, von Hoffman wrote that "the front page of the New York Times says the (summit) conference will represent almost the 'entire spectrum' of American economic thought, but it's not so. The difference between John Kenneth Galbraith and Milton Friedman isn't from A to Z but from A to B and that's as wide a gap as will be turning up in Washington." Von Hoffman goes on to pose the truly radical, "Austrian"-free-market alternative to the summitteers. As von Hoffman adds, "The Secretary of the Treasury will be able to slink off, as he recently did, to secret meetings with the heads of foreign central banking systems to enter into who knows what kind of horrendous agreements, while we are given Jerry Ford on television playing 20 questions with 20 professors rounded up by Nelson Rockefeller's talent scouts from the softest centers of American erudition."

But how about Greenspan? When I left for Europe in mid-August, Alan Greenspan, an Objectivist, had been chosen as head of the Council of Economic Advisors, to the hosannahs of many libertarians who felt that Greenspan would save us all from economic perdition. (My own early extreme skepticism about this prospect can be found in the October **Reason**.) At any rate, the first time I flipped on the TV after returning in early October, who did I see but Greenspan testifying before the Senate. Despite Ayn Rand's having bestowed her avowed disciple with the accolade of "heroic", Greenspan looked like anything **but** a Galtian hero. Not only was there no clear-eyed self-esteem, no 100-page speeches on epistemology or A is A or even natural rights, but there was only

mumbled confusion, failure to answer questions, and the assertion that a tax cut had to be opposed unless it were made up by higher taxes somewhere else!

So this is our John Galt come to save us from statism, and his sole contribution is to oppose a tax cut!? What we have here is not simply the abject failure of the Randian Movement to come up with a Hero to come within a thousand miles of the Galtian model. What we have is the logical conclusion of the Randian theory of strategy, which, in contrast to the fine rhetoric about liberty, voluntarism, and the non-initiation of force as a matter of **remote** ideals, is in practice the servant of cautiously pragmatic gradualism. The great insight of William Lloyd Garrison that "gradualism in theory is perpetuity in practice" is once again shown to be all too chillingly true. Alan Greenspan's role as an apologist for our crippling level of taxation supplies the answer as to why the Establishment — and all of its economists, from left to right — were perfectly happy with the Greenspan appointment. The Establishment cares not a farthing about an official's ultimate ideals — be they Buddhist or Randian — **provided** that those ideals do not affect or show up in the person's concrete day-to-day proposals. Following the disastrous Randian strategic theory of gradualism, the result is that Greenspan — in practice — sounds no different from all of his failed predecessors: all the "free-market" servitors of Power from McCracken to Shultz to Stein.

None of these gentry seems to realize that to advocate high taxes in order to stop inflation is like advocating the guillotine as a cure for cancer. Regardless of how bad a high price is, say, for a loaf of bread, it is **still** better than a tax, for at least one can eat the bread, whereas a tax provides no service to the consumer whatsoever. In fact, of course, the situation is still worse, because a tax is only used to build up the coercive machinery of the Leviathan State. It is incumbent, then, on any libertarian or free-market economist worthy of the name, to advocate any tax cut anywhere, and thereby a cut in coercion and parasitic burdens on the economy. Greenspan's advocacy of high taxes is eloquent testimony to the severe split between ideals and practice, or what Randians would call a "mind-body split", that permeates Randian strategic theory.

Moreover, Greenspan's **gaffe** is still further evidence of what had been clear from his public interviews earlier this summer: that he does not understand the cause of inflation in the government's expansion of the supply of money. Instead, Greenspan is what might be called a "right-wing Keynesian", placing the blame for inflation on budget deficits, which leads him to put first priority on balancing the budget — a priority even higher than reducing the burden of tax coercion and theft. In short, Greenspan does not understand the point agreed upon by both the Friedmanites and the Austrians: that the government and its central

(Continued On Page 2)

LP Platform

The official platform of the national Libertarian Party, as adopted in its June convention this year in Dallas, is an enormous improvement over the first, 1972 platform. The basic problem with the old platform is that it was neo-Randian, and therefore studded with such phrases as "the proper function of government is . . ." For those of us who believe that the only proper function of government is to disappear, such phrases were like red flags to a bull. They were a standing affront to the substantial body of anarchists in the Party. The new platform has happily expunged these provocative phrases and reworded its principles and planks to say: "the government may not do" X, Y, and Z. In that way, without explicitly calling for anarchism, the new platform provides a commodious home which both anarcho-capitalists and laissez-faire limited statists can live with. For the new platform neither calls for abolition of the State nor does it explicitly endorse government; by confining itself to the negative function of attacking the depredations of government, it can be endorsed by all anarchists and laissez-faire liberals who do not wish to drive the members of the other camp out of the party.

As an example, instead of the old formulation: "We . . . hold that the sole function of government is the protection of the rights of each individual", the new platform says, "We . . . hold that where governments exist, they must not violate the rights of any individual". The anarchist insight that all governments necessarily violate the rights of the individual is left in abeyance, neither affirmed nor denied.

In addition to this heartening and basic change, the first section, on Individual Rights and Civil Order, has been greatly strengthened. Added is a clause stressing that the major purpose of criminal punishment is to force the criminal to make restitution to his victim. Furthermore, an excellent section has been added opposing any form of involuntary mental commitment. Added, too, is a clause attacking any discrimination violating equality of rights by the government, while also opposing any governmental attempts to regulate private discrimination. The "protection of privacy" clause has been notably strengthened as well. The old platform unaccountably waffled by saying that "electronic and other covert government surveillance of citizens should be restricted to activity which can be shown beforehand, under high, clearly defined standards of probable cause, to be criminal . . ." Shown to whom? And what "showing" can justify such clear invasion of the rights of person and property? The new platform clearly states that "the government should not use electronic or other covert surveillance of an individual's actions on private property without the consent of that property owner." Also, the previous very weak clause on the right of secession, which limited that right to one "supported by a majority within the political unit" (what "unit"?) and other qualifications, has been replaced by a clear "We support recognition of the right to political secession. Exercise of this right, like the exercise of all other rights, does not remove legal and moral obligations not to violate the rights of others."

The only weak clause remaining in this section is the one on the "Volunteer Army", which unfortunately goes beyond a simple call for abolition of the draft to positively hailing "a well paid volunteer army" as a "more effective means of national defense". "Well paid", of course, means at the expense of the taxpayers, especially since the clause does not call for a voluntarily financed army. Furthermore, there is still no recognition of the serfdom involved even in a "voluntary" army structure that does not allow voluntary resignation which all other jobs, including police, do allow. Furthermore, the call for unconditional amnesty is still limited to draftees and does not yet include non-draftee deserters.

The "Trade and the Economy" section is also strengthened by calling, as "immediate reforms", for "drastic reduction" of taxes and government spending instead of the old, weak "reduction". Furthermore, the old, weak-kneed "Those who have entered into . . . activities with promises of government subsidy will be forewarned by being given a cutoff date . . ." has fortunately been excised. The party of principle must stick to principle and not concede the immorality of "cutoff dates" for theft. The clause calling for "eventual repeal of all taxation" has been strengthened by support for constitutional challenges to taxation, and by opposition to the withholding and other compulsory tax collections as involuntary servitude. A timely clause has also been added opposing all government control of energy pricing and subsidies to energy research, as well immediate repeal of the egregious 55 m.p.h. speed limit. The major

weakness here is still the failure to call for return to the gold standard, i.e. for return of the people's gold confiscated by the federal government in 1933.

The "Domestic Ills" section has also been greatly strengthened. Naderite regulations are now specifically opposed, as well as compulsory "self-protection laws", and drug regulations or prohibitions. There is a clear-cut call for the abolition of the Food and Drug Administration. The "Population" clause has been strengthened by attacking special tax burdens on single people or on the childless. Also, welcome clauses have been added: opposing all compulsory or tax-supported health insurance, attacking medical licensing and other interference with free medical choice, opposing all government control of land use, and demanding the repeal of the crippling OSHA.

The "Foreign Policy" section has also been greatly improved by eliminating the Wilsonian call for diplomatic recognition of only "legitimate" governments in the old platform, and substituting the genuine isolationist policy of non-intervention and de facto recognition to all other governments. However, the "currency exchange rates" clause is still unfortunately Friedmanite, in calling for freely floating exchange rates rather than currencies tied to a non-governmental, market commodity such as gold. But another excellent change is the elimination of the old platform's call for U.S. military alliances with non-"despotic governments", including even a "nuclear umbrella". Instead, the new platform clearly states that "American foreign military policy must be directed toward avoiding involvement of the United States in war." It also includes an eloquent attack on the horrors of aggressive war, with the mass murder and economic statism that such wars inevitably breed. Also, the previous call for "sufficient nuclear capacity" as a deterrent is eliminated, and replaced by a simple "we shall support the maintenance of a sufficient military force to defend the United States against aggression." More needs to be done in calling for disarmament of nuclear and other weapons of mass slaughter, as well as a questioning of whether such threats of aggression against the United States actually exist. However, the condemnation of war and the call for its avoidance is a

(Continued On Page 3)

Ford In Our Present —

(Continued From Page 1)

bank's continuing expansion of the money supply — its legalized counterfeiting, to be blunt about it — is the only cause of inflation. Higher taxes, even in balancing the budget, will only redistribute money and income from private to governmental hands, and will not solve the cancerous problem of governmental money growth.

All of this also highlights another crucial strategic point which neither the Randians nor the Friedmanites understand: you cannot roll back or whittle away statism — whether it be the government's inflation, its budget, or its numerous depredations and controls on the economy — by getting a few "good guys" in there to speak Truth to Mr. President. Elitist conversations behind closed doors will only provide conservative and "libertarian" blessings to the evil march of the Leviathan State. The government is going to keep expanding and legalized counterfeiting because it is in the economic interests of the government and its "ruling class" allies to do so. He who is given the power to counterfeit will do so unless stopped by counter-pressure. In the case of the State, the only thing that will roll back State power in any and all areas is the growth of a mass movement from below, i.e. among the public outside of and subjected to State power. Only a mass movement from below and outside: either by individual or organized actions, by ad hoc organizations, or by a Libertarian Party, or by all together, can hope to exert the pressure necessary to roll back the State. The sooner we all realize this, the sooner we will stop playing cozy games with Power and the sooner we will start to channel the increasing sentiment among all strata of the population for greater liberty into an effective force to reverse the statist tide. But to do so, we must have no more Greenspans or other collaborators in the seats of Power. ◻

Austrian Economics On The Rise

By Richard M. Ebeling

During the week of June 15-22, 1974, the quaint and rustic Vermont village of South Royalton came alive in a way that it probably hasn't since the Revolutionary War. Under the auspices of the Institute for Humane Studies, fifty professors and students from the United States, Australia and England, gathered for a Conference on Austrian Economics.

Slightly over 100 years ago the Austrian School of Economics was founded by Carl Menger. One of the pathfinders to break asunder the myth of the Labor Theory of Value that had dominated Economics from the time of Adam Smith, Menger developed the Subjective Theory of Value. The value of a good, Menger explained, was not determined by the input of labor into the product, but rather the labor was **given** value by the intensity felt for the product by the individual who would finally consume it. And since individuals valued things differently and by different scales, there was no way to objectively determine value other than relating it back to the individual valuer.

Menger was soon followed by two disciples who refined Austrian theory to such a point that it became a major force in the world of ideas. First, Friedrich von Wieser, who explained the Theory of Imputation and Opportunity Cost, by which is meant that supply is, in reality, indirect demand, for we value the resources necessary for making a product in relation to the forgone uses (demands) that cannot now be carried out with them. And second, Eugen von Bohm-Bawerk, who expounded on the Theory of Subjective Value and related them to the problems of Capital and Interest.

In this century, the Austrian approach was extended by Ludwig von Mises. Mises applied Subjective Value Theory to the area of money and out of this developed the Austrian (or Circulation Credit) Theory of the Trade Cycle. Government manipulation of bank credit and the money supply disturbed the rate of interest (which acts as the allocator of goods between those produced in the present and those in the future), thus, creating shifts in the ratio of consumer goods vs. capital goods and, therefore, causing the business cycle. Mises also showed that under Socialism, the elimination of money and private ownership of the means of production, would put insurmountable barriers in the way of rational economic calculation. And, finally, Mises developed the methodology of Praxeology, e.g., the science of human action. Praxeology declares that men carry out rational action to achieve ends through chosen means. Thus, unlike the natural sciences, the social sciences have as their subject matter the purposeful action of reasoning individuals.

Further developments in Austrian theory were the product of the versatile mind of Friedrich von Hayek. Besides adding his own contributions to Business Cycle Theory, Methodology and Capital Theory, Hayek presented a radically different Theory of Competition. Market activity was seen, not as a disturbance to equilibrium, but, rather as a never ending discovery process for knowledge as men pursue their ends.

The Institute for Humane Studies brought to Vermont three of the leading Austrian theorists living today. Professor Murray Rothbard of the Polytechnic Institute of Brooklyn, author of **Man, Economy and State**, **America's Great Depression** and **Power and Market**. Professor Israel Kirzner of New York University, author of **The Economic Point of View**, **Market Theory and Price System** and most recently **Competition and Entrepreneurship**. And, Professor Ludwig M. Lachmann, of the University of Witwaterstrand, South Africa, author of **Capital and its Structure** and **Macro-economic Thinking and the Market Economy**. Also among the Conference attendants were such notables as, Henry Hazlitt, W. H. Hutt, D. T. Armentano, Sudha R. Shenoy, Walter Block, Gary North and William Peterson.

The first day was highlighted by an opening evening banquet. In the late afternoon, Milton Friedman, who resides in Vermont, arrived at the South Royalton Inn, the site of the Conference. Surrounded by a multitude of people, he declared that the optimum government policy would be one to insure zero inflation. When someone asked if it wouldn't be mere optimal for the money supply to be kept constant and allow prices to gently fall with greater productivity, Friedman grudgingly conceded that it probably would be the more optimal choice. Soon afterwards, Friedman led the group out to the hotel porch where he proceeded to wax eloquent over the merits of "indexing." (For a critque of indexing, see

"Uncle Miltie Rides Again," **Libertarian Forum**, May, 1974). After listing economists from 1702 to the present who have supported an index program, someone asked if we can now see a pure application of the program in the military dictatorship of Brazil? To which Friedman conceded, yes. He was then asked if this verified what his son, David, said at a meeting of the Philadelphia Society, that he (Milton) had latent Fascist tendencies? Friedman muttered that he felt that David had been unfair.

At the dinner that evening, Henry Hazlitt reminisced about how he first met Ludwig von Mises in the 1940's. W. H. Hutt talked about the contributions that Mises made to economics and Murray Rothbard related some of the anecdotes Mises told during his graduate seminars at NYU. When Milton Friedman was asked to make a few comments, he admitted that Mises had made a few contributions, but that he was much too "extreme." And, besides which, Friedman added, there was no such thing as "Austrian Economics," only good economics and bad economics. (A rather unusual statement, because just a few weeks before he had been on public television and spent several minutes explaining the special characteristics of "Chicago Economics.")

Starting the next day, a week of rigorous and incisive lectures began dealing with every facet of "Austrian" theory. Professors Rothbard and Kirzner laid the foundation by explaining the implications of Praxeology. The study, Rothbard pointed out, begins with the fundamental axiom that man acts, that conscious action is taken to achieve chosen goals. This also implies that all action is purposeful and rational from the point of view of the actor. All action, besides which, occurs through time. Action is taken now with the expected attainment of some result in the future. It also means that man acts without omniscience, for if an individual knew what the future would be, then his action to replace one state of affairs with another would be pointless. With a guaranteed and certain future, action becomes worthless, because nothing can be changed in that future.

The fact that action is purposeful, chosen and subjective, also means that any statistical or historical studies that attempt to measure or predict human activity must be seen as worthless. Professor Kirzner used the example of a man from Mars looking down at the earth through a telescope. The Martian observes that out of a box every day comes an object that enters another rectangular box that then moves away through a maze of canals and intersections. The Martian notices that on certain days the object that comes from the first box moves rapidly to catch up to the second, rectangular box. He then draws up a statistical study showing that 1 out of 10 times the object will move rapidly to reach the rectangular box and uses this for predictions of "earthly" activities. What has been totally overlooked by this method is that the first box happens to be an apartment building out of which comes an individual who goes to the street corner to catch the morning bus to work. The fact that on occasion the individual in question oversleeps and has to rapidly chase after the bus, so as not to miss it, does in no way guarantee that he may not get a better alarm clock, go to sleep earlier, or in the future, oversleep even more often. Nor does one individual's actions determine how another individual will act in the same circumstances. Thus, to base ones understanding of Man on statistics and historical studies is to ignore that human action is volitional, purposeful and changeable, dependent on

(Continued On Page 4)

LP Platform — (Continued From Page 2)

giant step forward in the new platform. Unfortunately, specific isolationist and anti-war clauses passed by the Platform Committee, including: withdrawal of foreign-based U. S. troops, the ending of U.S. alliances and foreign military aid, and strict neutrality in the Middle East, were stricken by the Hospers-Nathan neo-Randian forces on the floor of the convention.

All in all, however, the national LP platform, despite room for improvement, is now one which both anarchists and laissez-faire liberals should be able to accept and work with. ◻

Austrian Economics —

(Continued From Page 3)

the goals and means of the acting individual.

The inability of the economics profession to grasp the mainsprings of human action has resulted from the adoption of economic models totally outside of reality. In the "models" put forth as an explanation of market phenomena, equilibrium, that point at which all market activities come to rest and all market participants possess perfect knowledge with unchanging tastes and preferences, has become the cornerstone of most economic theory.

Professor Lachmann, in an illuminating lecture, explained that the market is not a series of equilibrium points on a curve, but rather, it's a constant process kept moving because the underlying currents of human action never rest. Men, lacking omniscience, integrate within their plans the information provided by a constant stream of knowledge, about changes in resource availabilities, the relevant action of other man and unexpected occurrences. But because each man's perspective and interpretation of this stream of knowledge will be different, what seems relevant to one individual will be discarded as insignificant by another. The unknowableness of the future means that individuals draw conclusions based upon expectations of what will happen over time. Divergent expectations and unexpected change, therefore, results in potential inconsistency of interpersonal plans. And when errors become visible to individuals, each market participant will learn different lessons from the revised, available information. And, thus, we are again faced with the possibility of inconsistency of different market plans.

But, if the plans of market participants can never be expected to smoothly and automatically mesh, what forces in the market tend towards an equilibrating, or dovetailing of human action? At this point, Professor Kirzner's follow-up lecture offered the clue. Acting man is not merely a blind "taker" of prices and resource offerings; rather, because of the fact that unexpected change occurs in an uncertain future, man is also "watchful." Alertness to previously unseen opportunities serves as the key to the equilibrating market force. This human capacity for alertness, said Kirzner, is the entrepreneurial role. It is not merely the difficult task of knowing when to hire and where to place the worker. It's a much more subtle and rarified knowledge; it's the ability of knowing where to get knowledge, of picking up bits of information that others around you have passed up and seeing the value of it for bringing into consistency a human plan or plans that otherwise would have remained in disequilibrium. The chance to profit from information about market opportunities that others have failed to see acts as the incentive for people to keep their eyes open for inconsistencies in human plans.

This train of thought was continued the following day with lectures by Professors Lachmann and Kirzner on the Austrian Theory of Capital. Capital is the intermediate product used to produce a goods for consumption. Yet, the many attempts to measure and quantify "society's" capital stock falls apart when we once again emphasize the nature of purposeful action. For a goods is seen as a production good only within the context of the human plan. That which is seen as a capital good in one instance may become totally worthless or shift to a consumer good dependent upon the subjective valuation of the actor. The elusiveness of market equilibrium often means, as well, that, as Lachmann pointed out, a tendency of structural integration of interpersonal plans may exist, but some combinations that are found not to fit within re-evaluated plans may result in a scrapping of certain goods and, therefore, are "not really capital," in the eyes of the valuer. Kirzner continued the discussion with an excellent critique of John Hicks' recent attempt to place all theorists either in the category of "materialists," e.g., those who measure the quantity of physical "capital" objects, or as "fundists," e.g., those who attempt to sum up market values to measure capital goods. Rather, pointed out Kirzner, capital is the complex of "half-baked cakes," the interim form the resource takes in the process of a human plan.

Professor Rothbard delivered an interesting and comprehensive lecture on the Austrian Theory of Money. It was Ludwig von Mises, Rothbard pointed out, who first applied the principles of marginal utility to money, showing how money originated and how exchange values were established on the market. Professor Rothbard suggested three areas for possible future research: 1) How to separate the State from money; 2) The question of free banking vs. 100% gold dollars; and 3) The defining of the supply of money.

He followed up with a lecture on "New Light on the Pre-History of the

Austrian School," and showed the development of marginal utility theories through the Middle Ages in Spain and Italy.

Professor Lachmann finished his series of lectures with critiques of Macro-economics and the recent Neo-Ricardian Counter-Revolution. One of the errors, Lachmann suggested, was that macro-economics too often assumes a Walras-Paretian long-run equilibrium price structure. But, the basis of national income statistics is not long-run market outcomes but the output flows of "market-day equilibrium" prices. Prices that are affected by changing streams of knowledge and data that result in constantly shifting patterns of prices and equilibriums. The attempt to find consistent aggregate macro-variables is impossible.

The inability to successfully explain the workings of the economy from a macro foundation has resulted in a counter-revolution of "Ricardian" economists. A redevelopment of cost of production theories, a "methodological egalitarianism" which overlooks the entrepreneural contribution and an ignoring of the nature of diversity and expectations are their main contributions. But, says Lachmann, the neo-classical establishment (e.g., Samuelson, Hicks, Halm, etc.) are unable to give a satisfactory response within the macro framework. Here is where the Austrians must step forward and present the micro-economic solution. The methodological individualism that will enable an understanding of how the economic process unfolds through human action. Lachmann offered the Conference participants the slogan of calling ourselves "Radical Subjectivists."

On the last day of the Conference, Professors Kirzner and Rothbard summed up the Austrian approach within a consideration of the "Philosophical and Ethical Implications of Austrian Economic Theory." Kirzner restated the principle of Wertfrei, value-free, economic analysis. As an economist, the Austrian theorist does not make judgements on ends chosen. Rather, following the lead of Mises, he says, suppose someone wishes to enhance the economic welfare of the community. The economist need take no stand on the end chosen, but he can say whether the means chosen for that end will be successful. And, thus, he can make a judgement of "good" or "bad" within the context of the goal chosen by the valuer.

While admitting this, Professor Rothbard wondered if the economist could be totally value-free in all instances. What if a politician has as his end the economic impoverishment of the nation so as to use demagognery for gaining political power? Are we to tell him that this is a "good" means to achieve his end? Thus, Rothbard concluded, it may often be necessary to have certain value-laden principles to judge ends as well as means.

Some extremely interesting papers were delivered in informal sessions during the week by other conference participants as well. Edwin Dolan, S. Pejovich and E. Clayton discussed the changes from central planning to quasi-markets in socialist countries. Roger Garrison delivered an interesting paper on "Technique Reswitching and Capital Reversing." In a very well received paper, Gerald O'Driscoll analyzed Austrian Theories of Competition and Business Cycles in a lecture on "F. A. Hayek and the Neo-Classical Synthesis." Other topics included, "Empirical Testing of Austrian Models" by Art Carol, "Subjectivism, Marginal Utility and the Marginal Revolution," by M. Rizzo and H. Young and a talk on the success of free trade in Hong Kong by Sudha R. Shenoy.

In 1892, Friedrich von Wieser stated that, "The actual calculation of the economic world constitutes an unsurpassable work of art in which nothing is isolated or unconnected, and it is not completely grasped by theory so long as anything in it seems to be without connection with other portions of the system."

It is perhaps because Austrian theorists have always taken Wieser's words to heart, that while other economists were gaining notoriety with "tracts for the times," they were studiously building an edifice of economic theory to explain all human action.

While other economists were trying to find the origin of economic crises in sunspots and statistical comparisons, Austrian thinkers listened to Bohm-Bawerk that, "A theory of crises can never be an inquiry into just one single phase of economic phenomena. If it is to be more than an amateurish absurdity, such an inquiry must be the last, or the next to last, chapter of a written or unwritten economic system. In other words, it is the final fruit of knowledge of all economic events and their interconnected relationships." The result was the building of a theory of money and credit on the foundation of subjective marginal utility by Ludwig von Mises.

In the United States, the Austrians have been in a theoretical

(Continued On Page 5)

Davidson And 'Women's Lib'

By Linda V. Seawright

I would like to comment on James Davidson's article titled **In Search of the Old Curmudgeon** (August issue) with reference to his comments on women's liberation.

I am not sure what Mr. Davidson's motives are for taking the attitude that he does towards women's liberation but there is nothing very unique in this approach as it has been going on for centuries.

He says that it may well be that there is a fundamental difference between male and female which explains the observable phenomena of all human cultures — that the males as a rule — predominate. As he does not go on to explain further here, he creates an impression that the more "privileged" role of the male is justified somehow or other.

Of course there is a difference and it is not so mysterious either. Until recently women have had little option but to be the child bearers. To-day the situation is still not what it might be, as this responsibility is not a shared one and methods of contraception fall short of the ideal. In addition, social attitudes lag behind the times and conditioning and social pressures play their part in sending women down this path. Maybe the child-bearing capacity is not necessarily inherently unfortunate but throughout history its practice has imposed obvious restrictions on freedom and has taken its toll in terms of life, health, energy and time. While paying rather hypocritical tribute to women as mother, society has not compensated for the drawbacks of this role but has in reality aggravated the drawbacks. Also it is a fact that on average men are stronger in terms of muscular strength. This has probably been a factor favouring the role they have traditionally played and gave them the edge in any situation that may have bordered on confrontation. Furthermore, I suspect that men are inherently somewhat more aggressive (the sex hormone testosterone increases aggression) but I think that this difference is magnified many times by a society that makes a virtue out of male aggression.

Mr. Davidson refers throughout his article to mysterious hormonal differences and attributes a great deal of weight to this, while dismissing the power of indoctrination. The only hormonal difference between the sexes that may have any significant effect on behaviour is the one I mentioned above, and while I do not dismiss this difference and think it may help explain the **origins** of sex-roles, I consider it much less important than indoctrination. Unfortunately most people are quite susceptible to the cultural indoctrination that is so prevalent, but they are often unaware of this. As much of this goes on in childhood and young adolescence, much of the information is absorbed in the subconscious and the individual is not aware of how much he has absorbed. I have known men who believe that they are enlightened about women and yet in their personal (and sometimes public) lives act out oppressive behaviour without dealing with the contradiction.

Mr. Davidson says that what especially galls the "women's libbers" (a rather belittling term by the way) is that being a woman has some decisive meaning which is distinct from being a man. I think that if all cultural indoctrination and role-playing were removed the decisive meaning would evaporate into something less significant — but not completely. Gender difference is but one of many differences that may exist between individuals. It is possible that two suitably matched individuals of the opposite sex may, on occasion, have more in common from a hormonal point of view than with an unsuitably matched person of their own sex as sex hormones are only part of the hormonal picture (there may even be an overlap there on occasion).

I would also like to take issue with Mr. Davidson's point that sex-roles help safeguard individuality in society. Indeed, I have always seen matters in the opposite light. It appears to me that sex roles **interfere** with individuality because they emphasize the sex difference over individuality and shape the members of the one group into one mold and the members of the other group into another mold. This helps to create difference, but not an individual one. This happens to men (who may be less aware of it) but even more so to many women. I consider one of the most unfortunate aspects of sex roles to be the confinements they attempt to place on a woman's individuality. The less of an individual she is, the less she suffers under this system. While gender may be a part of

identity, I consider that the most individualistic of all people are those whose identity is not formed and seen primarily in **relation to the** "opposite sex" but as a person — a human being. It is much more difficult to be a real person, with the courage that implies (especially in this society) than to take refuge under the umbrella of one's sex-role.

It is rather distressing to see Mr. Davidson use principles of individuality to support a system which is opposed to those goals. I would have thought that libertarian philosophy would be compatible with the goal of the freedom to be human which is what the more enlightened women in this world are looking for.

I offer these comments in a spirit of goodwill and hope that they receive fair consideration and are not treated with derision.   ◼

Austrian Economics —

(Continued From Page 4)

underworld in an environment dominated by Keynesianism. But as the structure of Establishment economics has fallen more and more into disrepute, individuals have discovered an alternative approach that explains more clearly the workings of reality. Building up momentum slowly, the Austrian School has silently been finding adherents around the country, as well as the world.

Sensing the rightness of the times, the Conference on Austrian Economics was planned as a catalyst for expanding interest in the Praxeological approach. To this end, the Conference must be declared a resounding success. It opened up lines of communication among individuals who were developing ideas along similar lines but did not know of each other's existence, let alone the work being done. It probably can safely be said that every participant, whether totally convinced of the Austrian method or not, went away desiring to give careful thought to this theoretical framework.

The Keynesian macro model has lost its credibility. Socialist economics has long ago proven itself defunct. Only the market economy can offer solutions to the economic problems the world faces. But its acceptance will be dependent on the case offered for its adoption. The Austrian framework offers such a case. Starting from the foundation of economic activity, the subjective choices of acting individuals, all economic phenomena cannot only be explained but easily comprehended. For all men act, all men choose, all men plan. It is a theoretical construction self evident to all thinking men.

As a further step in developing interest and understanding of Austrian theory, Percy L. Greaves has put together a comprehensive glossary of Ludwig von Mises' **Human Action**, entitled **Mises Made Easier**. As an added treat, an appendix has been included with a never-before-in-English critique by Mises of Bohm-Bawerk's Time-Preference Theory. The volume is scheduled to be in print this fall.

Also, Bettina Bien Greaves, a senior staff member of the Foundation For Economic Education, has recently translated three works by Mises never before available in English.

The first of these translations, entitled **Stabilization of the Monetary Unit-Considered from the Point of View of Theory**, was published in 1923, shortly before the total collapse of the German currency. In this essay, Mises explains the redistributing effects of inflation to those who first receive the new money at the expense of the others who face higher prices before their incomes rise. Also, the fact that as the depreciation progresses, a "flight" from money becomes so general that "The monetary units available at the moment are not sufficient to pay the prices which correspond to the anticipated future demand for, and supply of, monetary units . . ." This "phenomena of advanced inflation . . . is the other side of the 'crack-up boom'." Mises dissects the "Balance of Payments" Doctrine and the "Inflationist Argument" that it is more painless to depreciate the currency than raise taxes. Finally, Mises declares that the "first condition of any monetary reform is to halt the

(Continued On Page 6)

513

Science And Human Liberty

By Tibor R. Machan
Department Of Philosophy, State University College, Fredonia, N. Y.

Many people who are thinking about political matters today assert that science has demonstrated the need for the planned society. Among these people we find economists, psychologists, sociologists and other members of the community of social scientists. Is there truth in this belief about the scientific displacement of freedom in favor of a planned, centrally organized, fully regimented political system?

From what I have said above it may seem that advocacy of the planned society has only recently begun to be based on so called scientific discoveries. Actually there have been many advocates of centralized political systems in past centuries equally enamoured of science. Such well known philosophers as Thomas Hobbes, August Comte, and, yes, Karl Marx defended their case for the collectivization of human affairs on what they believed were scientific grounds. But only recently did this case gain popular support — mainly because many people acknowledge the tremendous benefits of science and technology. Thus, for instance, Professor B. F. Skinner of Harvard University starts his most recent book, **Beyond Freedom and Dignity**, with the following statements:

> In trying to solve the terrifying problems that face us in the world today, we naturally turn to the things we do best. We play from strength, and our strength is science and technology.

From this observation Dr. Skinner develops his case for a society governed by behavioral technologists. In the process of building the case for the centrally planned and governed society, Dr. Skinner, whose book was on the **New York Times'** best seller list for several months, rejects human rights, the literature of freedom and dignity, and a host of other ideas that are central to the free society.

The question is, does a scientific approach to human affairs really contradict the values of freedom, dignity, human self-responsibility, and individualism in general? Before I answer this question I should mention that not everyone who respects science believes that it must lead to the abolition of human liberty. The philosopher Michael Polanyi, who acknowledges the enormous value of science and technology, is a staunch defender of the free society. Drs. Milton Friedman, Yale Brozen, Harold Demsetz, James Buchanan and others have been some of the most fervent advocates of liberty. Nevertheless, in other circles and in the population as a whole there lingers a strong belief about the basic antagonism between science and human liberty. So it would be worthwhile to explore the issue of whether such an antagonism is real or imaginary.

What is science? Such a question does not rest easy with many thinkers — no more than does the question "What is art?" or "What is philosophy?" Yet, based on what mankind has learned about these matters, and with the realization that developments in human knowledge may require the revision of our ideas, it is possible to answer such questions with a high degree of accuracy. Science is the systematic, rational, conscientious activity of investigating the nature and character of distinct and identifiable realms of reality. There are many sciences because there are many discernible realms of reality. Not all of these realms of reality have come under successful and mature scientific scrutiny, but many have. The question we are concerned with is whether the activity of science contradicts the ideas and ideals of a free human community. To answer, we must first find out what makes it appear that science opposes these ideas and ideals. If these appearances turn out to be correct, then we must assent to a rejection of beliefs in support of human freedom. But are they correct?

During the 17th and 18th centuries science and the physical sciences in particular began to grow at a tremendous rate. Physics, chemistry, astronomy and biology developed more rapidly than ever before. What produced this is not generally agreed upon, although ironically enough these were the times of human history when the ideas and ideals of human liberty captured the attention and imagination of mankind. So it is not unlikely that science developed in part, because of the greater freedom of investigation that was made possible by the lessening of state and church authority over the activities of people in general, and those curious about nature in particular.

With the rise of science a great many thinkers — not always scientists themselves — began to extrapolate from certain scientific findings to

(Continued On Page 7)

Austrian Economics —

(Continued From Page 5)

printing presses" and "refrain from financing government deficits by issuing notes, directly or indirectly." Inflation, Mises concludes, is always the "product of human action and man-made policy." It is a part of the total politico-economic and socio-philosophical ideas or our time. A sound monetary system must firmly be "grounded on a full and complete divorce of ideology from all imperialist, militarist, protectionist, statist and socialist ideas."

The second essay is his 1928 work **Monetary Stabilization and Cyclical Policy.** Mises states the problem of the day as the attempt to stabilize the value of money, the attempt to preserve the "price level." Mises explains at length that any goods that are the products of human action, like money, cannot have their value "fixed." "There is no such thing as a stable purchasing power, and never can be . . . only an economy in the final state of rest, where all prices remained unchanged, could have a money with fixed purchasing power." It also shows, says Mises, that measuring changes in purchasing power is impossible as well. Exchange ratios on the market are constantly subject to change and for a measurement ". . . we must imagine an unchanging man with never-changing values." Mises then offers a critique of Fisher's index number proposal for adjusting changes in purchasing power. Everything Mises says about Fisher's idea can equally be said about Friedman's Indexation plan. Since purchasing power cannot be scientifically measured, points out Mises, any index program would become a political issue. Governments would be pressured to index purchasing power favorable to some groups at the expense of others. Also, changes in money prices don't affect all commodities at the same time and to the same extent. Only gradually does the change in purchasing power work its way through the economy. And because the price changes will bring shifts in income distribution, the exchange ratios will be different from what they started. Even if the indexing attempts to be "precise" by measuring on a narrow month to month basis, "the step-by-step emergence of changes in purchasing power" are accruing during the month. Thus, the "adjustment calculated at that time is based on the index number of the **previous** month when the full extent of that month's monetary depreciation had not been felt because all prices had not yet been affected."

Mises, in the second half of this essay, develops in **complete detail** his famous Trade Cycle Theory. He explains why price stabilization results in a "destabilizing" of price-ratios and brings about the imbalance of capital goods and consumer goods by credit expansion artifically lowering the rate of interest. And how the end result of such policies must be an eventual readjustment of the structure of production, representing the actual savings and consumption of market participants.

The third essay, entitled **Causes of the Economic Crisis: an Address,** was delivered by Mises in 1931 and represents his analysis of the causes and prolonging of the depression. He gives an incisive critique of the mass unemployment problem, "easy money" policies, price supports and tax policy. Mises concludes that the only lasting solution is to give ". . . up the pursuit of policies which seek to establish interest rates, wage rates and commodity prices, different from those the market indicates."

The essays have been organized under the title **Money, Inflation and the Trade Cycle: Three Theoretical Studies** by Ludwig von Mises. Besides being translated by Bettina Bien Greaves, they have been edited by Percy L. Greaves and a special introduction to the volume is planned by him. Present plans are for the book to be published some time next year.

With a Conference on Austrian Economics and newly translated works by Ludwig von Mises soon to be available to the public, a turning point in the economics profession may be just before us. ◘

Hayek And The Nobel Prize

The grant of a 1974 Nobel Prize in Economic Science to the great Austrian free-market economist Dr. Friedrich A. von Hayek comes as a welcome and blockbuster surprise to his free-market admirers in this country and throughout the world. For, since the death last year of Hayek's distinguished mentor, Ludwig von Mises, the 75-year-old Hayek ranks as the world's most eminent free-market economist and advocate of the free society. The Nobel award comes as a surprise on two counts. Not only because all the previous Nobel prizes in economics have gone to left-liberals and opponents of the free market, but also because they have gone uniformly to economists who have transformed the discipline into a supposed "science" filled with mathematical jargon and unrealistic "models" which are then used to criticize the free enterprise system and to attempt to plan the economy by the central government. F. A. Hayek is not only the leading free-market economist; he has also led the way in attacking the mathematical models and the planning pretensions of the would be "scientists", and in integrating economics into a wider libertarian social philosophy. Both concepts have so far been anathema to the Nobel Establishment.

We can only speculate on the motivations of the Nobel committee in this welcome, if overdue, tribute to Friedrich von Hayek. Perhaps one reason is the evident and galloping breakdown of orthodox Keynesian "macroeconomics", which leads even the most hidebound economists to at least consider alternative theories and solutions. Perhaps another reason was a desire to grant a co-Nobel Prize to the notorious left-wing socialist Dr. Gunnar Myrdal, and granting one to Hayek out of a recognized need for political "balance". Thus, in granting prizes to these two polar opposites, the Royal Swedish Academy of Sciences cited both Hayek and Myrdal "for their pioneering work in the theory of money and economic fluctutations and for their pioneering analysis of the interdependence of economic, social and institutional pheonemona."

At any rate, regardless of the motivations of the Nobel committee, we can only hail their richly deserved tribute to the towering contributions and achievements of Friedrich von Hayek. Hayek's first monumental contribution to economics was his development of the "Austrian" theory of the business cycle, based on the pioneering outline of von Mises. Appearing in the late 1920's, on the basis of which Mises and Hayek were among the very few economists in the world to predict the 1929 depression, Hayek's two great works on the business cycle appeared in English as **Monetary Theory and the Trade Cycle** (1933) and the more technical **Prices and Production** (1931). During the early 1930's, when Hayek had immigrated from Austria to teach at the London School of Economics, the Mises-Hayek theory of the business cycle began to be adopted widely in England and even in the United States as an explanation of the Great Depression; unfortunately, this Austrian Theory was swept aside in the jubilation of the Keynesian Revolution (1936)

(Continued On Page 8)

Science And Human Liberty —
(Continued From Page 6)

other areas of human interest. This meant that laws and principles discovered about some areas of nature, were extended to explain things and events in other, not yet fully investigated areas. Many people who were justifiably impressed by Sir Isaac Newton's laws (that explained the behavior of physical objects) lifted these laws from the realm where they actually applied and imported them into other realms, making it appear that not just the behavior of physical objects but everything in nature conformed to these laws. In fact, even today many people believe that the laws of mechanics, although no longer fully adequate to explain the behavior of all of physical reality, suffice to explain everything that happens in all of reality.

Having achieved great success in the attempt to understand and explain the things and events of physical reality, many people believed that the same scientific principles that yielded this result should be used to understand and explain — even control — human affairs. Thus there were influential thinkers, among them the "father of sociology," August Comte, who advocated that human action and the affairs of society be subjected to a scientific analysis. But at this point the term "scientific" changed its meaning considerably. Instead of taking a fresh and inquisitive look at human affairs, many believed that it would be enough simply to accept the laws of physics, astronomy, and chemistry, and impose them on a conception of human affairs.

The important idea here is that in imposing these principles and laws on a conception of human affairs, a crucial feature of the scientific approach to nature is violated. No longer is it accepted that scientists should discover principles and use them only to explain things within the realm in which the discoveries were made. Many thinkers have advocated the imposition of these principles on yet unexplored areas, including on human affairs. But this in fact was very unscientific. Lest the idea of science be taken to be virtually meaningless — as it would be if mere control, regulation, and organization of something were to be construed as sufficient to be scientific — it is important to realize that a scientific approach must be based on discovery, first and foremost. Yet today virtually anything that has a semblance of organization, control or the like seems to acquire the understandably honorific term "science." We have "sciences" such as transcendental meditation, scientology, psychiatry, and many more, all of which are highly controversial, lack precision and common standards of method, and admit members with extremely divergent views on what their fields imply, what their findings are, and what is included within their scope.

Underlying the proposal that science contradicts the ideals and ideas of human liberty we find the belief that science requires that everything in nature is made of physical matter and contain nothing different from what stones, rocks, metals and other physical materials contain. But this is not really a requirement of science as such. Despite what many thought, this belief has more to do with what some philosophers have assumed about the implications of science than about what science in fact has discovered. As mentioned before, following the successes in physics (and other sciences which studied the physical aspects of reality), many hopeful and ambitious thinkers advocated that these successes be utilized in human affairs. By exporting the principles of Newton and others into meagerly examined realms of reality, they also exported some of the contrete findings of these special sciences. Since the laws of physics apply to physical reality, exporting these laws into human affairs without qualification leads to the view that human beings are no more than complicated constructions composed of physical materials. Thus by way of the imperialism of the special sciences, the general philosophy of materialism gained considerable prominence. Many began to think that everything in nature conformed only to laws that material objects conformed to.

By now it is clear what the answer to our question will be. Only if we allow mistaken ideas of science to flourish do we commit ourselves to the belief that science contradicts the idea of human liberty, of the freedom of the individual to choose, and of his moral responsibility to choose right over wrong. Science, as such, says nothing that contradicts the view that human beings can choose what they will do. Not unless one assumes, quite unscientifically, that human beings must conform in all respects to the laws that we have discovered about physical objects.

I have not tried here to develop a justification for human liberty. There is no room for that in a short comment. It is important, however, to dispel the widely held dogma that science stands in opposition to the ideas and ideals of the free society — especially its basic thesis that human beings are free and can be responsible. But it is worth noting that there are those in various sciences who have given support for the case of human liberty on scientific grounds. Several scientists in the fields of psychophysics, neurophsiology, psychobiology and biochemistry, have made discoveries that support the view that human beings, unlike inanimate objects or even plants and most animals, have capacities that justify the belief that man is a creative, active being, an agent of his conduct, and responsible, in the main, for what he does. What with the powerful philosophical defense of the idea of free will — including the idea that without the capacity to choose we could not tell the difference between truth and falsehood even in the sciences — it appears to be entirely consistent with science to advocate the free society. And so with the corresponding ideas and ideals of the freedom of the individual to govern his own life and be responsibile for how well he brings off this task.　　　　　　　　　　　　　　　　　　　　　　　　　□

515

Nobel Prize — (Continued From Page 7)

(Continued From Page 7)

without being even considered, much less refuted by the statist Keynesians. Now that Keynesianism is crumbling both theoretically and empirically, the world of economics should be ripe to consider the Austrian theory seriously again, for the first time in forty years.

Briefly, the importance of the Hayek theory of the business cycle is that it puts the blame for the boom-bust cycle squarely on the shoulders of the government and its controlled banking system, and, for the first time since the classical economists of the nineteenth century, completely absolves the free-enterprise economy from the blame. When the government and its central bank encourages the expansion of bank credit, it not only causes price inflation, but it also causes increasing malinvestments, specifically unsound investments in capital goods and underproduction of consumer goods. Hence, the government-induced inflationary boom not only injures consumers by raising prices and the cost of living, but also distorts production, and creates unsound investments. The government is then faced repeatedly with two basic choices: either stop its monetary and bank credit inflation, which then will necessarily be followed by a recession which serves to liquidate the unsound investments and return to a genuinely free-market structure of investment and production; or continue inflating until a runaway inflation totally destroys the currency and brings about social and economic chaos. The relevance of the Hayek theory to the present-day should be glaringly obvious, as any hint of recession causes the government to panic and turn on the inflationary taps once again. The point is that, given any inflationary boom, a recession is painful but necessary, in order to return the economy to a sound state.

The political prescription that flows from the Hayekian theory is, of course, the diametric opposite of the Keynesian: stop the artificial inflationary boom, and allow the recession to proceed as fast as possible with its work of readjustment. Postponement and government attempts to stop or interfere with the recession process will only drag out and intensify the agony, and lead to our current and probably future turmoil of inflation combined with lengthy recession and depression. The Mises-Hayek analysis is not only the only cogent theory of the business cycle; it is the only comprehensive free-market answer to the Keynesian morass of government planning and "fine tuning" that we are suffering from today.

But F.A. Hayek did not stop with this monumental contribution to economics. In the 1940's he widened his approach to the entire area of political economy. In his best-selling Road to Serfdom (1944) he challenged the pro-socialist and pro-Communist intellectual climate of the day, showing how socialist planning must inevitably lead to totalitarianism, and demonstrating examples in the way in which the socialistic Weimar Republic paved the way for Hitler. He also showed how the "Worst Always Get to the Top" in a statist society. In his brilliant series of essays in Individualism and the Economic Order (1948), Hayek pioneered in demonstrating how socialism cannot rationally calculate because it lacks a free market pricing system, particularly

since the free market is uniquely equipped to transmit information from every individual to all other individuals. Lacking a genuine price system, socialism is necessarily devoid of such crucial information. Furthermore, in the same work, Hayek brilliantly dissected the unrealistic orthodox model of "perfect competition", demonstrating that the real world of free competition is far superior to the absurd call for "perfection" by trust-busting lawyers and economics. As a corollary, Hayek in this work began a devastating series of attacks on the mathematical economists' model of "general equilibrium", showing how absurd and unrealistic such a criterion was with which to beat free enterprise over the head.

In 1952, Hayek published his superb Counter-Revolution of Science, which remains the best attack on the pretensions of would-be planners to run all of our lives in the name of "reason" and "science." Two years later, in the very readable Capitalism and the Historians, Hayek contributed to and edited a series of essays which showed conclusively that the Industrial Revolution in England, spurred by a roughly free-market economy, enormously improved rather than crippled the standard of living of the average consumer and worker in England. In this way, Hayek led the way in shattering one of the most widespread socialist myths about the Industrial Revolution. Finally, in his Constitution of Liberty (1960), Studies in Philosophy, Politics and Economics (1967), and Law, Legislation and Liberty (1973), Hayek, among other notable contributions, upheld the forgotten ideal of the rule of law rather than men, and emphasized the unique value of the free market and the free society in creating a "spontaneous order" which can only emerge from freedom. As merely one of his achievements, his much anthologized article, "The Non-Sequitur of the 'Dependence Effect' ", demolished J. K. Galbraith's The Affluent Society in pointing out that there is nothing wrong with individuals learning and absorbing values and consumer desires from one another. And in his scintillating essay, "The Intellectuals and Socialism", F. A. Hayek set forth the proper strategy for libertarians to follow: the importance of having the courage to follow the socialists in being consistent, in refusing to surrender to the short-run dictates of compromise and expediency; only in that way will we be able to roll back and defeat the collectivist tide.

We could go on and on. But enough has been said here to point to the great scope, erudition, and richness of F. A. Hayek's contributions to economics and to political philosophy. Like his great mentor Ludwig von Mises, F. A. Hayek has persisted with high courage in opposing the socialism and statism of our time. But not only has he unswervingly opposed the current fashions of Keynesianism, inflation, and socialism; he has, with nobility, courtesy, and great erudition, pursued his researches to provide us with the alternative concepts of the free economy and the free society. F. A. Hayek richly deserves, not only the Nobel Prize, but any honors which we can bestow upon him. But the greatest tribute we can make, to Hayek and to Mises, is to dedicate ourselves to rolling back the statist tide and proceeding onward to a society of freedom.

*This essay is reprinted from Human Events.   ◻

The Libertarian Forum
BOX 341
MADISON SQUARE STATION
NEW YORK, NEW YORK 10010

First Class

Published Every Month. Subscription Rates: $8.00 Per Year; $15.00 Two Years

A Monthly Newsletter

THE
Libertarian Forum

Joseph R. Peden, Publisher   Murray N. Rothbard, Editor

VOLUME VI, NO. 11   NOVEMBER, 1974   US-ISSN0047-4517

THE ELECTIONS

1. The most important fact of the election was the evisceration of the Republican Party. The unrecognized great truth of American politics is that the Republican Party has been moribund for many years; it has been twenty years since the Republicans have controlled Congress, and there is no sign of resumed control in even the far distant future. Nixon's landslide in 1972 was less important than the remarkable fact that the Democrats continued in total control of both houses of Congress, and have done so throughout the Nixon-Ford administrations. We have had a one-party system for twenty years, and there can be no healthy evolution in American politics until we all become aware of that fact. The massive repudiation of the Republican Party in 1974 should begin the healthy process of officially burying its moribund carcass.

2. The happily low participation in the vote (about 38% of eligible voters) is a clear sign that what the public was doing was not so much endorsing the Democrats as registering their disgusted repudiation of the Republicans. Indeed, the disgust with both parties was evident throughout the country. And why should the party of Watergate, of tyranny and corruption, of me-tooing the left-liberal big spending and statist policies of the Democrats, not have been repudiated? The Republicans stand for nothing except personal power, and the era of Watergate has made this stance crystal clear. As for the conservative wing of the Republican party, they discredited themselves forevermore by supinely forming the last loyalist bastion of the insufferable Nixon. One of the happy results of the election was the repudiation of the most visible Nixon loyalists: the thuggish Sandman, the numskull Maraziti, the obfuscating Dennis, the egregious Landgrebe who vowed to stay loyal to Nixon "if they have to take both of us out to be shot."

3. One of the most interesting aftermaths of the election has been the continuing call by the conservative weekly **Human Events** for repudiating, at long last, the Republican Party, and for the formation of a Reagan third-party ticket in 1976. It has finally become clear to **Human Events** that whether or not there is "an emerging conservative majority among the public, there sure won't be any "emerging Republican majority" (to quote the famous phrase of conservative strategist Kevin Phillips.)

A conservative third-party would have the healthy consequence of possibly completing the destruction of the discredited Republican party, and thereby forcing an ideological re-alignment of American politics comparable to the destruction of the Whigs and their replacement by the Republicans in the 1850's.

A truly "Old Right" party, a renascent party of small government, drastic tax and budget cuts, and a free economy would be a truly pleasant development. Not only would its emergence be a healthy development in itself, but it would also form the "water" for a Libertarian Party to "swim in", for the LP could continually point to the inevitable gap between the Old Right party's libertarian rhetoric and its compromised reality, and thereby serve to push such a party in an ever more

libertarian direction. Libertarian ideas could only advance in such a climate.

But the chances of such a genuinely limited government party emerging are small indeed. For the right-wing has suffered for two decades now under the thrall of the cunning and articulate statists of **National Review**, and it shows no signs of casting off this domination. In an age that evidently suffers from a swollen and aggrandized Executive, **National Review** now calls once more for an even **stronger** Presidency, a call implicitly supported by the actions of the moronic loyalists of the Nixon regime. Furthermore, under the **National Review** aegis, the right-wing continues to be the party of global war and intervention abroad, and of state big-business corporatism, the military-industrial complex, and coerced "morality" at home. A new "Old Right" party, to be credible to the American public, would have to be consistent: it would have to oppose, for example, government spending on warfare as well as on welfare. It would have to adopt a frankly "isolationist" policy of peace and non-intervention abroad, thereby appealing to a public sick of war scares and foreign giveaways. But to do so, it would have to engage in a true ideological "revolution" against the **National Review** and allied leadership, and this it shows no real signs of doing. Certainly, such a revolutionary change **could** be effected; but it would require both an intelligence and a will that shows no signs of forthcoming on the right-wing. Neither does Ronald Reagan evidence any desire to lead **that** sort of third-party movement.

4. There are, however, some encouraging results of the November election, of thrusts in a libertarian direction. Apart from the Libertarian Party (detailed further below), the most notable was the surprise victory of independent James B. Longley as governor of Maine, for the first time in decades a genuine independent beat both of the far-better known and organized Democrat and Republican candidates. Equally important was the reason for Longley's candidacy and presumably his victory. Longley, a wealthy 50-year-old insurance executive who rose from the ranks of poverty, had been the head of a Maine Management and Cost Survey, which recommended a cut in the Maine budget of $24 million per year. When the politicians ignored the commission's recommendations, Longley dropped out of the Democratic Party to run for governor on the cost-saving platform. In short, Longley ran and won purely on the crucial issue of cutting government taxation and spending.

Uncompromising and independent, Longley noted, after his victory, that "credibility of politicians was definitely an issue in this campaign. Too many politicians follow the strategy of going where the fish are and saying what the fish want to hear. I just refused to do that." Also notable was the Longley campaign's attraction for a large number of volunteer college students throughout the state. Furthermore, Longley sees the national significance of his victory: "This election is shining like that beacon off the coast of Maine. I can see other candidates all over the

(Continued On Page 2)

Voting And Politics

On the night before election, and again on the **Today** show on election morn. I appeared on nationwide NBC-TV, denouncing politics and declaring that I never vote. Despite the fact that the interview was a pure fluke, taken while minding my own business on a New Haven bus, that it was severely edited and truncated on TV to fit the anti-politics theme of mass sentiment as picked up by the reporters, I was immediately besieged by phone calls from libertarians throughout the country. Some LP people attacked me for not mentioning Tuccille and the LP, while the anti-politics forces hailed me for — at last — denouncing all politics and voting. Since I have been accused of inconsistency in being one of the few libertarians who favor **both** the Libertarian Party **and** Sy Leon's League of Non-Voters, perhaps I can seize this occasion to make my views on the politics-voting question — I hope — crystal clear:

1. I am indeed opposed to the State and therefore to politics. If the State-and-politics disappeared tomorrow no one would be happier than myself.

2. The fewer people that vote in any election, therefore, the better. The fewer the votes, the greater the evident anti-politics sentiment throughout the country, and the greater the implicit repudiation of the entire political system. The fact that only 38% of the eligible voters cast their ballots in the 1974 election — the lowest voting percentage in three decades — is one of the most heartening results of the election. It is no coincidence that all politicians from President Ford on down begged the electorate to endorse the American Way by voting, voting for either party ("We don't care who you vote for, but for God's sake VOTE!") Think of how glorious it would be if the next President were elected by a popular vote of five, to four for his opponent. The smaller the vote, the more ridiculous the claim for a "popular mandate" for the victor.

Unfortunately, politicians tend to interpret low voting as "apathy" instead of hostility to the political system (although that concept is now changing, **pace** the findings of NBC-TV that throughout the country people are disgusted with all politicians.) Hence the importance of the League of Non-Voters' campaign to transform the alleged "apathy" of non-voters into an explicit repudiation of the political system.

3. I don't vote, and haven't done so in two decades, **not** because I believe voting itself to be immoral (as do the anti-LP libertarians), but because of the reasons in point No. **2, and** because one person's vote is of marginal importance, approaching zero. And for another and for me overriding reason: that the roll for compulsory jury slavery is taken from the voting lists. Compulsory jury duty differs only in degree, not in kind, from the slavery of conscription.

4. However, and unfortunately, neither politics nor voting are going to disappear overnight. Confronted with the fact that tens of millions of Americans are going to continue voting, what party should we support? Whom should we hope wins the elections? Does it make any difference who wins? I contend that it usually makes a great deal of difference. Jefferson **was** better than Hamilton, Jackson than Adams, Gladstone than Disraeli, Judge Parker than Teddy Roosevelt, etc. **A fortiori,** the Libertarian Party is infinitely better than any of the other contenders, for many important reasons: as an educational vehicle of unequalled force in influencing the public and the media; as a method of putting pressure on the other parties and on the government to curb their statist policies; and as an eventual conduit for rolling back the State. Of course, there are risks in the LP becoming corrupted if it becomes a major political force, but there are risks in any course of action or inaction. Life itself is a risk. The gripers who sit on the sidelines and carp about the LP have a responsibility, it seems to me, to come up with a course of action that will be at least as, if not more, effective than the LP in spreading the ideas and the influence of libertarianism. So far, the non-party **ad hoc** organizations have had only a minimal impact. The more impact that any tactical roads may have — be they the LP or any form of non-party organization — the better. This, the area of tactics, is one of the few cases where the pragmatic attitude is the proper one. Let a hundred libertarian flowers bloom. As far as I know, no one in the LP spends any time criticizing the various non-party individuals or organizations; why do the latter expend so much of their time criticizing the LP? Is it because the LP has been so successful? ◻

The Elections — (Continued From Page 1)

country doing what I did." (On Longley, see Robert W. Merry, "Pols Scratch Heads Over Upset in Maine," **National Observer**, Nov. 16; and the New York Times, Nov. 7.)

5. Which brings us to the campaigns of the Libertarian Party for this was the first election in which the fledgling LP fielded candidates in many parts of the country. In California, the California Libertarian Alliance, with the help of some LP members, accomplished the seemingly impossible by not only triumphing over the socialists in the Peace and Freedom Party primary, but also by winning control at the state party convention, and proceeding to adopt a platform that is, from all reports, even more libertarian than the LP platform. The new PFP platform calls for the abolition of taxation, and for the immediate withdrawal of all American troops and armed installations outside the territory of the U.S. Bravo! It also advances the principle of secession and decentralization by calling for the secession of California from the U.S. In the competition for purity of libertarian principle, can the LP remain behind?

In fact, the libertarians of California had a true embarasse de richesse this November, with two sets of state-wide slates, the Hospers ticket on the LP, and the Elizabeth Keathley ticket on the PFP. Unfortunately, the LP was not on the ballot, and from all accounts the Hospers write-in campaign did not garner very many votes. On the other hand, the Keathley slate obtained somewhere in the neighborhood of 100,000 votes; and one of its state-wide candidates managed to obtain the 2% of the total vote needed for the PFP to remain on the California ballot for the next four years. Huzzahs are in order, although I understand that the one candidate who accomplished this was one of the non-libertarians on the slate. The question remains: granting the splendid nature of the Keathley victory in the primary and at the state convention, and the success of the PFP in remaining on the ballot, will the libertarian forces be able to retain control in the face of an expected attempt at counter-revolution by

the socialists? At any rate, the Keathley campaign garnered a great deal of media publicity, and, if the libertarians keep control, they may grant the Presidential ticket of the LP in 1976 a line on the ballot in a state that has more organized libertarians than any other.

In Ohio, Kathleen Harroff, formerly chairman of the Ohio LP, ran a determined and energetic campaign as an independent for the U.S. Senate (the nature of Ohio election laws precluded an LP race for the Senate.) She obtained the remarkable total of 79,000 votes, approximately 2.7% of the total vote.

In New York, Jerry Tuccille's campaign for governor mustered the energy and enthusiasm of a large number of bright and able libertarians. It gained the quiet support of numerous important Conservatives disgruntled with the statist Buckleyite rule of the Conservative Party, and Free Libertarian Party candidates for state Assembly Mary Jo Wanzer and Virginia Lee Walker gained Conservative Party endorsement, the latter by defeating the C.P. designee in the party primary. Mrs. Walker, by the way, garnered about 6.5% of the total vote for Assembly on the Conservative line (FLP votes have still not been reported by the laggard state officialdom.)

Perhaps the most important fruits of the Tuccille campaign were the attention and publicity it gained for libertarianism in the media. At least four favorable articles about the campaign were published in the New York Times, as well as in other newspapers in New York City and throughout the state. The Tuccille campaign, operating on a veritable shoestring, managed to buy TV-space with a splendid ad — a first for a minor party in the history of New York State. Furthermore, favorable national media attention was gained for the Tuccille campaign. George F. Will, syndicated columnist for the Washington Post, endorsed Tuccille — an interesting defection from the Conservative ranks by National Review's Washington editor. Furthermore, the increasingly libertarian Washington Post columnist Nicholas von Hoffman — in addition to several splendid articles on the national economy — endorsed the

(Continued On Page 3)

After Rabat, What?

The inter-Arab conference at Rabat, Morocco, held at the end of October, was not just another conference: it was one of the most significant events in the modern history of the Middle East. Rabat changes the scene in the Middle East and will be affecting world history for many years to come. The significance of Rabat was that, for the first time, the Arab nations have forged an impressive unity on the vexed question of Palestine. Inspired by the Arab successes in the Yom Kippur War of last year, and by the substantial Arab unity in the world-wide oil crisis of last winter, Rabat has placed the endorsement of the entire Arab world on the Palestinian movement.

The most vital aspect of this endorsement was the demolition of the Jordanian roadblock. Ever since its artificial creation after World War I, the Hashemite kingdom of Jordan has been an obsequious ally of Western imperialism; and ever since its grab of the West Bank of Palestine after the 1948 conflict, it has been the major and determined Arab enemy of the national aspirations of the displaced and dispossessed Palestinian Arabs. Jordanian King Hussein's sudden massacre of the Palestinian guerrillas in the "black September" of 1970 almost wrote finis to Palestinian aspirations. But now all that is ended; and King Hussein at Rabat once and for all liquidated all his claims to the West Bank on behalf of the Palestinians and their representatives in the Palestine Liberation Organization. Hussein and Jordan will no longer form a major implicit support for the continued aggrandizement of the State of Israel. Even Egypt, which Hussein had counted on for support, joined the other Arab nations in support of Palestine, as did the conservative King Faisal of Saudi Arabia, motivated to a large extent by a desire to end the Zionist-Israeli occupation of Jerusalem, a city dear to the religions of Moslems as well as Christians and Jews. Hussein's capitulation, indeed, was purchased by an annual subsidy of $300,000,000, contributed by the Arab states, and largely by King Faisal.

It was because of Rabat that the United Nations received Yasir Arafat, head of the PLO, as a conquering hero, with full honors of statehood. The recognition of the PLO has irrevocably shifted attention from the humanitarian problem of the Palestinian refugees to the political question of the national as well as the property rights of the Palestinians. Rabat made particularly absurd the reply to Arafat by Israeli UN delegate Yosef Tekoah, who reiterated the old Jordanian canard that the Palestinians do not need a state because they already have one in Jordan; Tekoah doggedly repeated the old Jordanian slogan that "Jordan is Palestine and Palestine is Jordan." Since Jordan had itself finally abandoned this absurdity at Rabat, Israel's desperate attempt to resurrect this notion was grounded in air. As Jordanian UN delegate Abdul Hamid Sharaf rebutted to Tekoah, the Israeli position had "closed itself to right, to reality and to truth and had made itself a captive of its own dogmatism."

Arafat's appearance was treated with the usual incomprehension by the American media. On the lower levels, the media expressed surprise that the PLO delegates were cultured individuals and not inchoate "barbarians." On the higher levels, the media expressed disappointment that Arafat had not been moderated by world politics to become "responsible" and "realistic." Here, the American press showed itself unable to comprehend the politics of ideology, assuming as always that all nations' politics are cast in the opportunistic, unprincipled mould of the contemporary United States. Arafat and the PLO are revolutionaries, and no revolutionaries are going to sound like Eric Sevareid or Evans and Novak, regardless of the hopes and dreams of American "moderation." Reciting the history of Zionism and its conquest of Palestine, Arafat reaffirmed before a world audience the oft-expressed Palestinian ideal of a new, secular democratic state in Palestine, a land of full religious freedom "where Christian, Jew, and Muslim live in justice, equality, fraternity, and progress."

What next, then, in the Middle East? First, it is all too clear that the Kissinger "miracle", ballyhooed only a few months ago, lies in complete shambles, as the Lib. Forum predicted ("Reflections on the Middle East", June. 1974). If Israel persists in its refusal to recognize or negotiate with the PLO, then the only sensible forecast is for another war in the Middle East. If such a "fifth round" develops, then the vital consideration for Americans, and even for the peace of the world, is that the United States stay the hell out, that it cease being the supplier of

arms, aid and comfort for the State of Israel. Unfortunately, the chances of the U. S. remaining neutral are not very bright. In fact, they are made even dimmer by the disquieting saber-rattling going on in Washington, the muttering threats of a U. S. invasion of one or more Arab countries in order to grab their oil. It is indeed bizarre that American leaders should virtually ratify the Leninist theory of imperialism by asserting that we must go to war in order to seize natural resources. There is, of course, another way to obtain Arab oil — a method hallowed in American and Western tradition — by buying it. If the price is "too high" (whatever that may mean), then the Arabs will have to lower their price in order to sell their oil, or else we can proceed to develop oil or other energy sources elsewhere.

Already, in fact, market forces are beginning to lower the price of oil and oil products. Gasoline price wars are happily beginning to appear once again throughout the United States. Business Week (November 9) recently reports that the hysteria heard last year about an American oil refinery "shortage" has already disappeared, to be replaced, mirabile

(Continued On Page 4)

The Elections — (Continued From Page 2)

Tuccille campaign in a ringing column (Oct. 25). Noting that the Free Libertarians "have that peculiar buoyancy which comes from believing in what you're doing and contrasts so strongly with the mainline politicians," von Hoffman added that the FLP are the spiritual descendants of Locke and Mill. He hailed the FLP slogan, "Legalize Freedom", which the Libertarians apply to gold as well as heroin, as well as to "dumping the Lockheeds, the Franklin National Banks and the Penn Central Railroads". Von Hoffman also pointed out that the FLP has cast off the "status quo aroma" of former times, and attracts former liberals fully as well as former conservatives. Cheering rather than apologizing for libertarianism as a "middle-class movement", von Hoffman pointed out that "that's hardly surprising since our concepts of individual liberty were born with the middle class and have never thrived in societies which don't have a large one." Von Hoffman ringingly concluded that "for the overtaxed, overregulated, overburdened and underpowered millions of the American middle class", the Libertarians "are the only people worth voting for."

But the publicity coup of the campaign was a favorable article about libertarianism, centered around the Tuccille race, in Newsweek (Nov. 11). Considering the quickie nature of its research, the Newsweek writers did a fine job in summing up the ideas and the movement of libertarianism, summed up in Jerry Tuccille's statement that "A libertarian is a conservative who believes in letting people have fun."

National LP chairman Ed Crane, who has been doing a bang-up job since being installed this summer, promptly issued a Xeroxed flyer of the Newsweek and von Hoffman articles. In timely press releases, Crane has also denounced the Rockefeller nomination and called for attention to the neglected Austrian School of economics in handling the nation's economic crisis.

Due to the sloth of our "public servants," we still do not know at this writing whether or not Tuccille garnered the 50,000 votes needed to put the FLP permanently on the New York ballot. Rumors since that election have varied from optimistic to pessimistic, with the most recent rumors being rather gloomy. Early estimates by the campaign managers were that the FLP would have to raise $150,000 from contributions by libertarians across the country to amass the 50,000 votes. Considering that the most diligent efforts were only able to raise something like $60,000, it would not be surprising if the 50,000 vote goal was not attained. The fault for falling short of the goal, if this indeed happened, certainly does not lie with the FLP members or with the campaign staff, who have every reason to be proud of the enthusiasm, the dedication, and the ability with which the Tuccille campaign was conducted. Certainly, it is difficult to find another group of people who achieved a more widespread influence for the libertarian cause per dollar or per man-hour of energy expended. A heartfelt salute to all the dedicated men and women of the Tuccille campaign, from Jerry on down, should be accorded by everyone dedicated to the cause of liberty. ☐

Economic Determinism, Ideology, And The American Revolution*

It is part of the inescapable condition of the historian that he must make estimates and judgments about human motivation even though he cannot ground his judgments in absolute and apodictic certainty. If, for example, we find that Nelson Rockefeller made a secret gift of $650,000 to Dr. William J. Ronan, we can choose to interpret Rockefeller's motivation in one of at least two ways: we can conclude, as did that eminent student of contemporary politics Malcolm Wilson, that Nelson made this and similar gifts purely as "an act of love"; or we can conclude that some sort of political **quid pro quo** was involved in the transaction. In my view, the good historian (1) cannot escape making a judgment of motivation, and (2) will opt for the latter political judgment. Those historians who have made the realistic and what I hold to be the correct judgment have often been condemned as "materialists", "economic determinists", or even "Marxists", but I contend that what they have simply done was to use their common sense, their correct apprehension of reality.

In some matters, where the causal chain of economic interest to action is simple and direct, almost no one denies the overriding motive of economic interest. Thus, when the steel industry lobbies for a tariff or an import quota, and despite the fact that their **stated** motivations will include every bit of blather about the "public interest" or the "national security" that they can think of (even "an act of love" if they thought they could get away with it), it would be a rash historian indeed who did **not** conclude that the prime motivation of the steel industry was to gain higher profits and restrict foreign competition. Similarly with Nelson's "loving" largesse. There will be few charges of "Marxism" hurled in these situations. The problem comes when the actions involve longer and more complex causal chains: when, for example, we contemplate the reasons for the adoption of the American Constitution, or the Marshall Plan, or entry into World War I. It is in these matters that the focus on economic motives becomes somehow unpatriotic and disreputable.

And yet, the methodology in both sets of cases is the same. In each case, the actor himself tries his best to hide his economic motive and to trumpet his more abstract and ideological concerns. And, in each case, it is precisely because of the attempted cover-up (which, of course, is more successful in the longer causal chains) that the responsibility of the historian is to unearth the hidden motivations. There is no problem, for example, for the historian of the Marshall Plan to discover such ideological motivations as aid to the starving people of Europe or defense against Communism; these were trumpeted everywhere. But the goal of subsidizing American export industries was kept under wraps, and therefore requires more work by the historian in digging it up and spreading it on the record.

Neither is the Mises point that men are guided not by their economic interests but by ideas very helpful in discussing this problem: for the real question is what ideas are guiding them — ideas about their economic interests or ideas about religion, morality, or whatever? Ideas need not be a highly abstract level; it did not take profound familiarity with philosophy, for example, for the export manufacturers to realize that foreign aid would provide them a fat subsidy out of the pockets of the American taxpayer.

No "economic determinist" worth his salt, however, has ever held that economic motives are the sole or even always the dominant wellsprings of human action. Thus, no one who has ever studied the early Calvinists could ever deny that fiery devotion to their new religious creed was the overriding motivation for their conversion and even for their secular activities. Although even in the case of the Reformation, we cannot overlook the economic motivation, for example, for the German princes in siding with Luther or for Henry VIII's confiscation of the wealth of the Roman Catholic monasteries. The point is in each case to give the economic motivation its due.

Can we, however, provide ourselves with a criterion, with a guide with which we can equip ourselves in at least our preliminary hypotheses about the weights of motivation? In short, can we formulate a theoretical guide which will indicate in advance whether or not an historical action will be predominantly for economic, or for ideological, motives? I think we can, although as far as I know we will be breaking new and untried ground.

Some years ago, an article in the **Journal of the History of Ideas**, in an attempt to score some points against the great "economic determinist" historian Charles A. Beard, charged that for Beard it was only his historical "bad guys" who were economically determined, whereas his "good guys" were governed largely by ideology. To the author, Beard's supposed "inconsistency" in this matter was enough to demolish the Beardian method. But my contention here is that in a sense, Beard wasn't so far wrong; and that, in fact, from the libertarian if not from the Beardian perspective, it is indeed true in a profound sense that the "bad guys" in history are largely economically motivated, and the "good guys" ideologically motivated. Note that the operative term here, of course, is "largely" rather than "exclusively".

Let us see why this should be so. The essence of the State through history is that a minority of the population, who constitute a "ruling class", govern, live off of, and exploit the majority, or the "ruled." Since a majority cannot live parasitically off a minority without the economy

(Continued On Page 5)

After Rabat, What? —

(Continued From Page 3)

dictu, by a "surplus of capacity". The "shortage" was removed by additions to refinery capacity, and especially by the American government's removal, in the spring of 1973, of its disastrous 14-year program of restricting oil imports.

Furthermore, the much-touted theory that the increase in Arab oil prices is "responsible" for inflation is economic balderdash. An increase in one price does not "cause inflation". On the contrary, the paying of higher prices for one product would ordinarily leave consumers with only one option: to cut their demand for other products, and thereby to lower other prices. The rise of prices in general cannot be caused by occurrences in one industry; they can only result from increases in consumer demand, which in turn can only come about from governmental increases in the supply of money — of dollars and of other world currencies. To blame the Arabs for American and Western accelerating inflation is but one more example of the age-old device of governments to find scapegoats for their own counterfeiting, their own continuing creation of new supplies of money. Throughout history, scapegoats for inflation have been found by governments among numerous unpopular groups: speculators, black marketeers, big businessmen, unions, greedy consumers, aliens, Jews . . . and now the Arabs. Meanwhile, government's own inflationary activities go merrily on, as President Ford, in his "anti-inflation" speech, while abjuring us to clean our plates and sporting a numskull WIN button, hastens to assure us that the Federal Reserve Board will continue to pour out "adequate" amounts of new money.

Meanwhile, there is only one hope for Israel in the short run to avoid another round of war: to abandon its post-1967 conquests and to allow a "mini-Palestine" state organized by the PLO in the West Bank and the Gaza Strip. In the likely event that Israel refuses to do so, it guarantees substantive unity between the PLO and the militant Palestinian forces that reject the entire idea of a transitional mini-state and insist on nothing less than an immediate establishment of the full "maxi" Palestine. Refusal to deal with Arafat and the PLO will force a confrontation with the ideas, if not the personnel, of Dr. George Habash and his "rejection front", which may make Israel long for the days of Arafat just as it now longs for the days of King Hussein.∎

Economic Determinism —
(Continued From Page 4)

and the system breaking down very quickly, and since the majority can never act permanently by itself but must always be governed by an oligarchy, every State will persist by plundering the majority on behalf of a ruling minority. A further or corollary reason for the inevitability of minority rule is the pervasive fact of the division of labor; the majority of the public must spend most of its time about the business of making a daily living. Hence the actual rule of the State must be left to full-time professionals who are necessarily a minority of the society.

Throughout history, then, the State has consisted of a minority plundering and tyrannizing over a majority. This brings us to the great question, the great mystery if you will, of political philosophy: the mystery of civil obedience. From Etienne de La Boetie to David Hume to Ludwig von Mises, political philosophers have shown that no State — no minority — can continue long in power unless supported, even if passively, by the majority. Why then do the majority continue to accept or support the State when they are clearly acquiescing in their own exploitation and subjection? Why do the majority continue to obey the minority?

Here we arrive at the age-old role of the intellectuals, the opinion-moulding groups in society. The ruling class — be they warlords, nobles, feudal landlords, or monopoly merchants, or a coalition of several of these groups — must employ intellectuals to convince the majority of the public that their rule is beneficent, inevitable, necessary, and even divine. The dominant role of the intellectual through history is that of the Court Intellectual, who in return for a share, a junior partnership, in the power and pelf offered by the rest of the ruling class, spins the apologias for State rule with which to convince a deluded public. This is the age-old alliance of Church and State, of Throne and Altar, with the Church in modern times being largely replaced by "scientific" technocrats.

When the "bad guys" act, then, when they form a State or a centralizing Constitution, when they go to war or create a Marshall Plan or use and increase State power in any way, their **primary** motivation is economic: to increase their plunder at the expense of the subject and taxpayer. The ideology that they profess and that is formulated and spread through society by the Court Intellectuals is merely an elaborate rationalization for their venal economic interests. The ideology is the smokescreen for their loot, the fictitious clothes spun by the intellectuals to hide the naked plunder of the Emperor. The task of the historian, then, is to penetrate to the essence of the transaction, to strip the ideological garb from the Emperor State and to reveal the economic motive at the heart of the issue.

What then of the actions of the "good guys", i.e., those unfortunately infrequent but vital situations in history when the subjects rise up to diminish, or whittle away, or abolish State power? What, in short, of such historical events as the American Revolution or the classical liberal movements of the eighteenth and nineteenth centuries? It goes without saying, of course, that the economic motive for diminishing or throwing off State power is a "good" one from the libertarian point of view, in contrast to the "bad" economic motives of the statists. Thus, a move by the ruling class on behalf of higher taxation is a bad economic motive, a motive to increase their confiscation of the property of the producers, whereas the economic motive against taxation is the good one of defending private property against such unjust depredations. That is true, but that is not the major point I am trying to make here. My contention is that, in the nature of the case, the **major** motive of the opposition, or the revolutionaries, will be ideological rather than economic.

The basic reason is that the ruling class, being small and largely specialized, is motivated to think about its economic interests twenty-four hours a day. The steel manufacturers seeking a tariff, the bankers seeking taxes to repay their government bonds, the rulers seeking a strong state from which to obtain subsidies, the bureaucrats wishing to expand their empire, are all professionals in statism. They are constantly at work trying to preserve and expand their privileges. Hence the primacy of the economic motive in their pernicious actions. But the majority has allowed itself to be deluded largely because its immediate interests are diffuse and hard to observe, and because they are **not** professional "anti-statists" but people going about their business of daily living. What can the average person know of the arcane processes of subsidy or taxation or bond issue? Generally he is too wrapped up in his

daily life, too habituated to his lot after centuries of State-guided propaganda, to give any thought to his unfortunate fate. Hence, an opposition or revolutionary movement, or indeed any mass movement from below, cannot be primarily guided by ordinary economic motives. For such a mass movement to form, the masses must be fired up, must be aroused to a rare and uncommon pitch of fervor against the existing system. But the only way for that to happen is for the masses to be fired up by ideology. It is only ideology, guided either by a new religious conversion, or by a passion for justice, that can arouse the interest of the masses (in the current jargon to "raise their consciousness") and lead them out of their morass of daily habit into an uncommon and militant activity in opposition to the State. This is not to say that an economic motive, a defense for example of their property, does not play an important role. But to form a mass movement in opposition means that they must shake off the habits, the daily mundane concerns of several lifetimes, and become politically aroused and determined as never before in their lives. Only a common and passionately believed in ideology can perfrom that role. Hence our strong hypothesis that such a mass movement as the American Revolution (or even in its sphere the Calvinist movement) must have been centrally motivated by a newly adopted and commonly shared ideology.

The turn now to the insight of such disparate political theorists as Marx and Mises, how do the masses of subjects **acquire** this guiding and determining ideology? By the very nature of the masses, it is impossible for them to arrive at such a revolutionary or opposition ideology on their own. Habituated as they are to their narrow and daily rounds, uninterested in ideology as they normally are, concerned with daily living, it is impossible for the masses to lift themselves up by their own bootstraps to hammer out an ideological movement in opposition to the existing State. Here we arrive at the vital role of the intellectuals. It is only intellectuals, the full-time professionals in ideas, who can have either the time, the ability, or the inclination to formulate the opposition ideology and then to spread the word to the mass of the subjects. In contrast to the statist Court Intellectual, whose role is a junior partner in rationalizing the economic interests of the ruling class, the radical or opposition intellectual's role is the centrally guiding one of formulating the opposition or revolutionary ideology and then to spread the ideology to the masses, thereby welding them into a revolutionary movement.

An important corollary point: in weighing the motivations of the intellectuals themselves or even of the masses, it is generally true that setting oneself up in opposition to an existing State is a lonely, thorny, and often dangerous road. It would usually be to the direct economic interests of the radical intellectuals to allow themselves to "sell out", to be coopted by the ruling State apparatus. Those intellectuals who choose the radical opposition path, then, can scarcely be dominated by economic motives; on the contrary, only a fiercely held ideology, centering on a passion for justice, can keep the intellectual to the rigorous path of truth. Hence, again, the inevitability of a dominant role for ideology in an opposition movement.

Thus, though perhaps not for Beardian reasons, it turns out to be true that the "bad guys", the statists, are governed by economic motivation with ideology serving as a smokescreen for such motives, whereas the "good guys", the libertarians or anti-statists, are ruled principally and centrally by ideology, with economic defense playing a subordinate role. Through this dichotomy we can at last resolve the age-old historiographical dispute over whether ideology or economic interests play the dominant role in historical motivation.

If it is the shame of the intellectuals that the Court Intellectual has been their dominant role over the course of world history, it is also the glory of the intellectuals that they played the central role in forming and guiding the mass movements of the modern world in opposition to the State: from the Calvinist upsurge of the Reformation to the classical liberal and radical movements of the seventeenth, eighteenth, and nineteenth centuries.

* * * * * * * * *

Let us now apply our framework to an analysis of the historiography of the American Revolution. In the long-standing controversy over the Beard-Becker economic determinist school of American history dominant in the 1920's and 30's, it has generally been assumed that one must either accept or reject this basic outlook wholesale, for each and every period of American history. Yet our framework explains why the Beard-Becker approach, so fruitful and penetrating when applied to the

(Continued On Page 6)

Economic Determinism —

(Continued From Page 5)

statist drive for power which brought about the U. S. Constitution, fails signally when applied to the great anti-statist events of the American Revolution.

The Beard-Becker approach sought to apply an economic determinist framework to the American Revolution, and specifically a framework of inherent conflict between various major economic classes. The vital flaws in the Beard-Becker model were twofold. First, they did not understand the primary role of ideas in guiding any revolutionary or opposition movement. Second, and this is an issue we have not had time to deal with, they did not understand that there are no inherent economic conflicts on the free market; without government intrusion, there is no reason for merchants, farmers, landlords, et al. to be at loggerheads. Conflict is only created between those classes which rule the State as against those which are exploited by the State. Not understanding this crucial point, the Beard-Becker historians framed their analysis in terms of the allegedly conflicting class interests of, in particular, merchants and farmers. Since the merchants clearly led the way in revolutionary agitation, the Beard-Becker approach was bound to conclude that the merchants, in agitating for revolution, were aggressively pushing their class interests at the expense of the deluded farmers.

But now the economic determinists were confronted with a basic problem: if indeed the revolution was against the class interests of the mass of the farmers, how come that the latter supported the revolutionary movement? To this key question, the determinists had two answers. One was the common view — based on a misreading of a letter by John Adams — that the Revolution was indeed supported by only a minority of the population; in the famous formulation, one-third of the populace was supposed to have supported the revolution, one-third opposed, and one-third were neutral. This view flies in the face of our analysis of opposition movements; for, it should be clear that any revolution, battling as it does the professional vested interest of the State, and needing to lift the mass of the people out of their accustomed inertia, must have the active support of a large majority of the population in order to succeed. As confirmation, it was one of the positive contributions of the later "consensus" school of American history of such scholars as John Alden and Edmund Morgan, to demonstrate conclusively that the Revolution had the active support of a large majority of the American public.

The Beard-Becker school had another answer to the puzzle of majority support of the Revolution: namely that the farmers were deluded into such support by the "propaganda" beamed at them by the upper classes. In effect, these historians transferred the analysis of the role of ideology as a rationalization of class interests from its proper use to explain State action to a fallacious use in trying to understand mass movements. In this approach, they relied on the jejune theory of "propaganda" common in the 1920's and 1930's under the inspiration of Harold Lasswell: namely, that no one sincerely holds any ideas or ideology, and that therefore no ideological statements whatever can be taken at face value, but must be considered only as insincere rhetoric for the purposes of "propaganda." Again, the Beard-Becker school was trapped by its failure to give any primary role to ideas in history.

The economic determinists were succeeded by the "consensus" school of American history, as part of the general "American celebration" among intellectuals after World War II. At its best, the consensus historians, notably Edmund Morgan and Bernhard Knollenberg, were able to show that the American Revolution was a genuine multi-class movement supported by the great majority of the American public. Furthermore, the economic determinists, in their eagerness to show the upper merchant class as duping the farmers into supporting the Revolution, emerged — in a curious kind of left-right alliance with the pro-British "Imperial" historians — as hostile to the American Revolution. The consensus historians restored the older view that the colonists were rebelling against genuine invasions of their liberties and property by the British Empire: that their grievances were real and compelling, and not simply a figment of upper class propaganda.

At its worst, however, and under the aegis of such major consensus theoreticians as the "neo-conservatives" Daniel Boorstin and Clinton Rossiter, the consensus school was moved to the truly absurd conclusion that the American Revolution, in contrast to all other revolutions in history, was not really a revolution at all, but a purely measured and conservative reflex against the restrictive measures of the Crown. Under the spell of the American celebration and of a Cold-War generated hostility to all modern revolutions, the consensus historians were constrained to deny any and all conflicts in American history, whether economic or ideological, and to absolve the American republic from the original sin of having been born via a revolution. Thus, the consensus historians were fully as hostile to ideology as a prime motive force in history as their enemies, the economic determinists. The difference is that where the determinists saw class conflict, the consensus school maintained that the genius of Americans has always been to be unfettered by abstract ideology, and that instead they have met every issue as ad hoc problem-solving pragmatists.

Thus, the consensus school, in its eagerness to deny the revolutionary nature of the American Revolution, failed to see that all revolutions against State power are necessarily radical and hence "revolutionary" acts, and further that they must be genuine mass movements guided by an informed and radical ideology. Furthermore, as Robert A. Nisbet has recently pointed out in his scintillating pamphlet, The Social Impact of the Revolution, the consensus view overlooks the truly revolutionary and libertarian consequences of the American Revolution in diminishing the role of government, in dismantling church establishments and winning religious freedom, in bringing about bills of rights for the individual's liberty and property, and in dismantling feudal land tenure in the colonies.

Nisbet's stress on the revolutionary and libertarian nature and consequences of the American Revolution brings us to the most recent and now dominant school of historiography on the Revolution: that of Professor Bernard Bailyn. Against the hostility of both of the older schools of historians, Bailyn has managed, in scarcely a decade, to win his way through to become the leading interpretation of the Revolution. Bailyn's great contribution was to discover for the first time the truly dominant role of ideology among the revolutionaries, and to stress that not only was the Revolution a genuine revolutionary and multi-class mass movement among the colonists, but that it was guided and impelled above all by the ideology of radical libertarianism; hence what Bailyn happily calls "the transforming libertarian radicalism of the Revolution." In a sense, Bailyn was harking back to an older generation of historians at the turn of the twentieth century, the so-called "Constitutionalists", who had also stressed the dominant role of ideas in the revolutionary movement. But Bailyn correctly saw that the mistake of the Constitutionalists was in ascribing the central and guiding role to sober and measured legalistic arguments about the British Constitution, and, secondarily, to John Locke's philosophy of natural rights and the right of revolution. Bailyn saw that the problem with this interpretation was to miss the major motive power of the Revolutionaries; Constitutional legalisms, as later critics pointed out, were dry-as-dust arguments that hardly stimulated the requisite revolutionary passions, and furthermore they neglected the important problem of economic depredations by Great Britain; while Locke's philosophy, though ultimately important, was too abstract to generate the passions or to stimulate widespread reading by the bulk of the colonists. Something, Bailyn rightly felt, was missing: the intermediate-level ideology that could stimulate revolutionary passions.

Guided by the extensive research into English libertarian writers by Caroline Robbins, Bailyn found the missing and vital ingredient: in the transforming of Lockean natural rights theory into a radical and passionate, and explicitly political and libertarian framework. This task was accomplished by radical English journalists who, in contrast to Locke, were read very widely in the colonies: notably, the newspaper essays of Trenchard and Gordon written during the 1720's. Trenchard and Gordon clearly and passionately set forth the libertarian theory of natural rights, went on to point out that government in general, and the British government specifically, was the great violator of such rights, and warned also that Power — government — stood ever ready to conspire to violate the liberties of the individual. To stop this crippling and destructive invasion of Liberty by Power, the people must be ever wary, ever vigilant, ever alert to the conspiracies by the rulers to expand their power and aggress against their subjects. It was this spirit that the American colonists eagerly imbibed, and which accounted for their "conspiracy view" of the English government. And while Bailyn himself, by concentrating solely on the ideology of the colonists, is ambivalent about whether such English conspiracies against liberty actually existed, the work of such historians as Bernhard Knollenberg has shown

(Continued On Page 7)

Report From Europe

The two parts of your editor's European trip this summer of interest to libertarians were: the biennial meeting of the Mont Pelerin Society at Brussels, and sizing up the state of the libertarian movement and of the general political situation in Great Britain.

Mont Pelerin.

The Mont Pelerin Society is an international organization of several hundred people ostensibly devoted to the free market economy. Begun just after World War II by several distinguished economists, led by F. A. Hayek, the Society rapidly expanded during the fifties and sixties, at the same time substantially losing its character as a free-market organization. Many of the hundreds of economists, businessmen, and writers among the members are no closer to libertarian or free-market principles than a simple opposition to Communism. Many of the industrialist members are in intimate partnership with their respective governments, and must be set down as State Monopoly Capitalists rather than advocates of the free market. At any rate, fortunately for all of us, the Society is not empowered to pass any resolutions or to make any statements; its sole function is to hold pleasant annual (regional) and biennial (international) meetings, which serve as a center for social contacts. The formal sessions have become dull as dishwater, with endless repetition of the same arguments hashed over to no conclusion over the last twenty years: e.g. Are Unions or the Money Supply Responsible for Inflation? What Form Should Anti-Monopoly Policy Take? Mired down in what have become ritualistic discussions, the Society has not displayed the will either to move on to broader philosophical topics or even to apply free-market principles to newly discovered problems (e.g. ecology, or the cultivation of the oceans).

The social structure of the Mont Pelerin Society is now approximately as follows: there are a host of elderly members from Western Europe, often statist in outlook. Yet the Western Europeans do not seem to have been able to generate new, younger members. Of the younger members, most are from the United States, which is therefore bound to serve in the future as the center of gravity of the organization. Of the younger American members, there is now competition among three groups to seed members into the Society: the Friedmanites, the anarcho-capitalists, and the Buckleyite young conservatives.

Perhaps as a result of rising pressure by younger members, a new and restive spirit was evident at this year's Brussels meeting. More and more, discontent with the fusty old topics have pressured the organizers into allowing meetings from below that had not been part of the official schedule. Thus, pressure from admirers of Ludwig von Mises induced the organizers to add an affecting memorial session in tribute to Mises.

An early sign of rising libertarian sentiment occurred midway during the week-long sessions. One of the organizers of the meeting asked me why I had not spoken more at the sessions. The answer, of course, was that I had scarcely attended any, since the informal conversations in the corridors and at the bar were a lot more enjoyable and instructive than the same old stuff at the formal sessions. "Oh no, Murray, you should talk. Five, ten years ago everyone regarded you as a nut, but now there's increasing interest in your position." Taking that as a cue, I and a few others decided to organize, as one of the now allowed, informal sessions, a meeting on "Anarchism and Capitalism", with myself as official chairman and Roger MacBride as moderator. The response was fantastic, for at the meeting over 130 members and guests appeared, and the response at the meeting was interested and generally favorable. At the session — the first, of course, in the history of Mont Pelerin, on anarcho-capitalism — I first gave a brief, overall sketch of the philosophy, showing how it is the logical extension of free-market principles. Then, we had Reports from the Movements in various countries, most of which we hadn't known existed until finding each other at Brussels. These reports not only served to inform each group of the existence of the others, but also to impress the newcomers with the rising tide of the libertarian movement in the various countries.

Thus, we heard from Michiel van Notten, dynamic young Dutch businessman who is forming an anarcho-capitalist group in Holland, consisting of about nine persons. We found out that a thriving movement of lawyers, economists, and businessmen has developed in Madrid,

consisting of a Misesian circle of about 40 people who meet regularly, of whom from five to nine are anarcho-capitalists known as the "Rothbardaneros." The Spanish group regularly translates Austrian economics and libertarian works into Spanish. The attorney Luis Reig reported from this group. From England we heard from the dynamic and indefatigable Pauline Russell, who has sparked a rapid growth of anarchist and quasi-anarchist libertarians in that country. Pauline as well as most of the English movement may be best described as teetering somewhere between limited government and anarcho-capitalism, with national defense and an emotional attachment to the monarchy still posing some problems. Then Roger MacBride wound up the reportage

(Continued On Page 8)

Economic Determinism —

(Continued From Page 6)

conclusively that the conspiracy was all too real, and that what some historians have derided as the "paranoia" of the colonists turned out to be an insightful apprehension of reality, an insight that was of course fueled by the colonists' understanding of the very nature and essence of State power itself.

While Bernard Bailyn has not continued his studies beyond the Revolution, his students Gordon Wood and Pauline Maier have done so, with unfortunate results. For how can one apply the concept of a "transforming libertarian radicalism", of a mass ideological hatred of the State and of the executive, to the movement for a Constitution which was the very antithesis of the libertarian and radical ideal? By trying to do so, Wood and Maier lose the idea of radical libertarianism altogether, and wind up in yet another form of consensus view of the Constitution. Yet the battle over the adoption of the Constitution was a fierce ideological and economic conflict; and in understanding that movement and that conflict we must turn to the neo-Beardian approach of such historians as Jackson Turner Main, E. James Ferguson, and Alfred Young, which stresses the economic and class interests behind this aggrandizement of a powerful central government. Furthermore, the Anti-Federalist resistance to the Constitution was fueled, not only by resistance to these economic depredations, but also and above all by the very ideology of Liberty versus Power that had sparked and guided the American Revolution. A glance at the eloquent speeches against the Constitution by Patrick Henry is enough to highlight the libertarian leitmotif of the anti-statist Revolution as well as the anti-statist resistance to the Constitution. Hence, the original insight of the Beardians was correct: that the Constitution was a reaction against the Revolution rather than its fulfillment.

The idea of economic motivation as the prime mover of **statist** actions through history, as contrasted to ideology as the major guide of **anti-**statist movements, is thus confirmed by analyzing the historiography of the American Revolution. Perhaps adoption of this basic framework will prove fruitful in the analysis of other important events and movements in human history. ◘

* A paper delivered at the Libertarian Scholars Conference, Oct. 28, in New York City.

"All the extravagance and incompetence of our present Government is due, in the main, to lawyers, and, in part at least, to good ones. They are responsible for nine-tenths of the useless and vicious laws that now clutter the statute-books, and for all the evils that go with the vain attempt to enforce them. Every Federal judge is a lawyer. So are most Congressmen. Every invasion of the plain rights of the citizen has a lawyer behind it. If all lawyers were hanged tomorrow, and their bones sold to a mah jong factory, we'd all be freer and safer, and our taxes would be reduced by almost a half."

— H. L. Mencken

523

Report From Europe —
(Continued From Page 7)

with a description of the growth of the Libertarian Party in the U.S. and Canada. All in all, it was a great breakthrough for anarcho-capitalism in a setting that no one would have predicted a few years ago could ever be in the slightest degree hospitable. Will we have our own Libertarian International in a few years?

The British Situation.

Great Britain is clearly in a total economic mess, ten (twenty?) years ahead of the United States down the road to galloping inflation, crippling controls, and stifling taxation. Controls are causing the usual haphazard succession of shortages, and, when we were in England, sugar and bottles were disappearing from the market. No one, but no one, invests in the English stock market, which makes ours seem a picture of health and prosperity. While many politicians understand the monetary cause of inflation, there is no will to stop the process because of the phobia about recession and unemployment (sound familiar?) At any rate, British society seems to be polarizing very rapidly, what with the ever-present threat of general strikes by powerful left-wing unions, countered by the emergence of two sets of private armies dedicated to keeping industry going: a right-wing group under General Walker and a centrist, "non-political" one under Colonel Stirling. It is scarey to watch the BBC and see impeccable Englishmen with bland understatement quietly discussing whether or not civil war will break out in the not too distant future.

Amidst this turmoil, the most heartening sign is the rapid growth of libertarians and anarcho-capitalists in a country that only a few years ago had virtually no one even as "extreme" as Milton Friedman. The major libertarian group is centered around Pauline Russell, and includes businessmen, journalists, economists, and others ranging from anarcho-capitalists to neo-Randians to the Selsdon Group, the free-market ginger group within the Conservative Party. Most of this group is friendly with the notable Enoch Powell, who of all the politicians in England is the only one with both the knowledge and the will to stop the monetary inflation and to put through a free market program and an end to wage and price controls. Powell, himself, despite his Tory devotion to the monarchy (which is seconded even by many of the English anarcho-capitalists), has grown increasingly libertarian. The Powell forces were working on a gusty strategy for the then forthcoming October elections: voting Labour in order to smash the statist leadership of Edward Heath. This strategy has already helped bring about the recent Labour victory, and it looks very much as if Ted Heath will happily be sent to the showers. Whether or not the third step in the strategy — the accession of Enoch Powell to the

Note To Our Readers

From time to time, we hear from subscribers who have mysteriously stopped receiving the **Lib. Forum.** Since any minority movement is bound to suffer from incipient paranoia, many feel that they may have been "purged" from the rolls for some sort of "deviationism." (A practice that certain other movement magazines have practiced in the past.) However, we hasten to assure all of our readers that no one has or will ever be purged from our subscription list. We welcome any and all subscribers, left, right, or center, and even our once and perhaps present CIA readers. If you haven't received issues of the **Lib. Forum** and you are a subscriber, there are two possible reasons: (a) our own error, either manually or by our computer; or (b) because you failed to report your change of address. In a highly mobile movement, the latter is often the problem. So, in either case, **please** notify us promptly if you haven't been receiving issues, or when you change your address. At any rate, we can assure you of one thing: you haven't been "purged."

Tory leadership — will follow is certainly problematical, at least for the short run. Of the Tories now in the running to succeed Heath, the most free-market oriented is Sir Keith Joseph, who however suffers from the familiar syndrome of politicians in being far more libertarian out of power than he is in power. At any rate, Powell has cleverly found a new political base among the Ulster Unionists and is now back in Parliament after refusing to run on the Tory platform in the previous election.

In some ways, the small but growing English movement is a microcosm of the American. Split off from the Pauline Russell group is a smaller group of "hard core anarcho-capitalist purists", who scorn any form of political action, or indeed any truck with non-purists, as a sellout of libertarian principle. This youthful group is led by Mark Brady and Chris Tame. The Russell wing, in the meanwhile, took the first tentative steps in the October election toward the formation of a Libertarian Party of Great Britain (in Britain, it is relatively easy and inexpensive for a new party to get on the ballot.) The libertarian businesswoman Mrs. Theresa Moore Gorman ran for Parliament as an "Independent Freedom" candidate from her home constituency of Streatham, an outlying suburb of London. We have not yet been able to find out how Teresa fared at the balloting.

Finally, just before leaving for Europe, we found out that the small but growing libertarian movement in Australia has decided to form the Libertarian Party of Australia. For the first time, libertarianism is bidding fair to become a genuine international movement.

Published Every Month. Subscription Rates: $8.00 Per Year; $15.00 Two Years

524

A Monthly Newsletter

THE
Libertarian Forum

Joseph R. Peden, Publisher   Murray N. Rothbard, Editor

VOLUME VI, NO. 12   DECEMBER, 1974   US-ISSN0047-4517

THE EMERGING CRISIS

The United States is now entering a period of what might well be the greatest crisis in its history. While all the lineaments of the crisis are as yet unclear, it very much looks as if we will be plunged into the Greatest Leap Forward into collectivism since the New Deal — in fact, that we may soon be looking back upon the New Deal as a relative haven of freedom and free enterprise. The signs are ominous and everywhere. And while this means that the failures of statism are rapidly multiplying the "objective conditions" for a libertarian victory, they might be pulling swiftly ahead of the "subjective conditions" — the rapid expansion of libertarian numbers and influence. If this prognosis is correct, we are in for dire times indeed.

The core of the crisis is economic: rooted in the abject failure of the Keynesian Establishment to foresee or to solve the accelerating inflation combined with the deepening recession/depression. 1974 saw the recession spreading and deepening to such an extent that even our economic and political Pollyannas have been forced to concede the gloomy picture. The Keynesian chickens have come home to roost — as forty years of expanding money supply, federal deficits, and government spending have finally brought us to our accelerating inflationary recession. The nation's economists, after helping to foist this Keynesian mixed economy upon the country, are rapidly despairing of being able to understand or prescribe for what is going on. Briefly, the Keynesian nostrum of government budget surpluses to combat inflation, with deficits to offset a recession, have totally run aground in the face of an economy where both are happening at the same time. Even the Friedmanite quasi-Establishment has been discredited in also not being able to predict or explain the inflationary recession.

The economic Establishment, in short, is in despair. But does that mean that they are at least having the grace to keep quiet? Anyone who knows economists knows also the futility of such a hope. No indeed: ignorant and/or totally hostile to the Austrian School, laissez-faire, hard money alternative to the present system, and of its great record in both prediction and explanation of the current mess, the Establishment economists are rapidly turning to full-fledged collectivism as the way out. Some weeks ago, for example, the New York **Times** published an article noting that most economists, as well as businessmen and politicians, are again turning to comprehensive wage-price controls as the remedy for the inflationary recession. How can they do this, asked the writer, when the various Phases of price-wage control were scrapped less than a year ago as a total failure (controls that rang all the changes on freezes, stiff controls, and loose controls)? How? Because, the **Times** writer admitted, they don't know what else to do. Clearly, the simple maxim of doing nothing if one doesn't know what to do is unacceptable to all of these "enlightened" groups. And so, and even though wage-price controls have always failed and have only caused widespread hardship and shortages, and even though collectivism itself has had a black economic record in this century, it looks as if we are going to get it, full blast. When the Keynesians led the way to the inflationary mixed

economy in the 1930's, they proclaimed that they were thereby "saving American capitalism". Only a few free-market voices warned that they were, instead, digging capitalism's grave. And now that this "salvation" hasn't been working, they are ready to scrap the free-market economy altogether. Thus, as Soma Golden writes in a year-end economic survey in the New York **Times** (Dec. 29, 1974), "1975 shapes up as a critical year, one that could usher in a fundamental transformation of the American economy towards increased government planning and controls. For if the economy fails to show a marked improvement by the end of the year, in terms of both prices and unemployment, traditional economic policies will seem to have failed." Golden quotes the prominent moderate Keynesian economist, Otto Eckstein of Harvard, as stating that "we either work our way out of this mess in 1975, or we are in real trouble. If policy does not meet the challenge next year, we'll have to examine how to change the economic system." Golden goes on: "Some economists think that frustration with inflation and recession could lead to the nationalization of major industries or the placement of government officials on private boards of directors. Others point out that this is already happening as the Government — without any prior plan — has stepped into emergency situations to bail out such enterprises as the Franklin National Bank and passenger railroads in financial trouble. A few economists, including Harvard's Nobel Prize winner (and long-time left-Socialist) Wassily Leontief, say some form of national commitment to planning will be the ultimate solution." Golden concludes the **Times** article, "If the convergence of painful economic events continues, the United States eventually might be forced into some form of planned economy. According to Professor Leontief of Harvard — who at 68 is still some years ahead of his profession — 'It's only a matter of time.'"

This horrendous but possibly accurate prognosis is bolstered by the significant changes that have been at the same time occurring in both major political parties. In both parties, the moderate statists centers of gravity have been drastically shifted in a leftward and collectivist direction. In the Democratic party, the mid-term national party conference in Kansas City this December was marked by a complete takeover of the national party by extreme-leftist McGovernite forces. The centrist, old New Deal faction headed by the AFL-CIO and its political operative Alexander Barkan, was virtually driven out of the party as the Left triumphed in both form and content. In the form of internal party machinery, the left-wing quota system for "oppressed minorities" was permanently enshrined. This institutionalizing of the quota system for delegates received so much publicity that the monstrous content of the mid-term conference economic platform was overlooked in the media. What was overlooked was the fact that the national Democratic party is now committed to a comprehensive leap into collectivism. For this economic platform features the following: (1) "an across-the-board system of economic controls, including prices, wages,

(Continued On Page 2)

The Emerging Crisis —

(Continued From Page 1)

executive compensation, profits and rents", by the federal government. Also included is a provision for compulsory "wage catch-ups" and "price rollbacks". The Nixon control program was criticized for ineffective enforcement, so we can look to a vast bureaucracy to administer, and a Gestapo to police, the program. (New York Times, Dec. 8, 1974). (2) a new Reconstruction Finance Corporation, to bail out inefficient and bankrupt businesses; (3) stepped-up trust-busting to penalize "monopolistic" and efficient businesses; (4) comprehensive national health insurance, i.e. socialized medicine; (5) compulsory energy "conservation", energy self-sufficiency, and, "as a last resort," rationing of gasoline and fuel oil; (6) expanded "public service employment" and unemployment compensation — i.e. socializing the job market in a new WPA. and subsidizing the creation and maintenance of unemployment in the private market.

How is this monstrosity being greeted by the Republican party, and by the Ford Administration? The Republican Establishment is reacting by trailing the Democrats by a few months or years. After the idiocy of the "voluntary" WIN program and other absurd attempts to "fight inflation" and to "conserve energy", the Ford Administration is moving rapidly toward the same collectivist programs. The same forces which only a year ago kept the price of gasoline and fuel oil below the free market price, thereby generating an artificial "shortage", and which then reluctantly allowed the market to work, leading to a consequent and seemingly miraculous disappearance of the "shortage", are now taking the reverse tack. Where as last year they claimed that oil and gasoline prices could not be allowed to rise because the "poor" would be hurt, they now call stridently for a whopping gasoline tax in order to compel an artificial reduction of energy consumption, to create an artificial scarcity and an artificially high price. Oil is being cartellized further by government. as oil import restrictions are being imposed again, and the talk is of further controls and allocations, as well as possible rationing. The excuse for this price-raising policy of artificial scarcity, for this cartellizing and protectionism, is that if we don't impose such "sacrifices" and achieve energy "self-sufficiency" now, then the evil Arabs might do the same thing at some time in the future. In short: to avoid the possibility that the Arabs might cut our throats in the future, let us do so now! National health insurance and a guaranteed minimum income are being revived by the Ford Administration, as is the threat of wage-price controls in 1975.

Or, shall we say, the Rockefeller Administration? For the essence of the dramatic change in the Republican party is the post-Watergate crushing of the Cowboys (opportunistic, despotic, more pro-war, more economically conservative) by the Rockefeller wing of the Yankee Establishment. Almost the entire Cowboy political leadership, from the Nixon-Agnew administration leaders to John Connally, are either banished, in jail, or under indictment. After long-time Rockefeller man George Beall (of Maryland) pulled the plug in the Justice Department of ex-Rockefeller man Agnew (of Maryland), the scene was set for the creation of two vacancies in the Presidency, and for the assumption of Rockefeller to total power. The dismal spectacle of both liberals and conservatives rolling over and playing dead for Nelson, despite the revelations of vast monetary payments by Rocky and of his massive politico-economic power, simply reveals the extent of Rockefeller power and policial influence. Rockefeller has been openly named domestic czar, and with long-time Rockefeller flunky Henry Kissinger in total charge of foreign policy, the administration now belongs to Rockefeller root and branch, while Ford bumbles along the ski slopes. In contrast to the nitwit Ford, Rockefeller is smart and tough, and a corporate statist to the very core: the emerging cartellizing policy on gasoline and oil is but one reflection of the total Rocky takeover in the works. The tiny list of Republican conservatives in Congress that dared to rise up and oppose Nelson's appointment is a list of men of courage who refused to be bought.

The victory of Rockefeller has been followed closely by a purging of the remaining Cowboys in positions of power. Once again, the key is the mysterious and dangerous Central Intelligence Agency, where the remaining Cowboy war-mongers and repressors of domestic dissent, in particular the Angleton clique, have been purged from the CIA. A leading member of the Cowboy set in the CIA, of course, is E. Howard Hunt, who

is headed for jail. Barry Goldwater's outlandish expostulation that domestic break-ins and spying by the CIA are necessary to keep tabs on the Ellsbergs is the last gasp of the Cowboy mentality in Washington. Replacing it will be the Yankee policy of "repressive tolerance", with free speach and cultural liberty being allowed so long as they do not endanger the seats of power. Furthermore, the sudden rash of Assassination Revisionism (in the Bobby Kennedy and Martin Luther King cases) is an indication that the victorious Yankees are about to pull the plug openly on the possible assassination activities of the previously ruling Cowboy forces.

The chances of a conservative third party to give voice to the right-wing populism of the large mass of all effectively disenfranchised populace remain dim — although this seems like the only short-run hope of putting some breaks on either the Rockefeller-corporate state or the left-Democrat forms of collectivism. While the conservative **Human Events** has been calling loudly for a third party, the veteran Judas Goats of National Review are split: with Bill Buckley clearly willing to accept the Rockefeller dispensation, and Senator Jim Buckley voting for the Nelson appointment; while Bill Rusher and George Will intensify their opposition to the new regime. In the meanwhile, the long-time National Review theoretician, statist James Burnham, has called for a $1.00 a gallon tax on gasoline to push for energy self-sufficiency, while "traditionalist" conservative Jeffrey Hart demands that all conservatives rally around the concept of a strong and mighty Presidency. While Ronald Reagan showed some signs of interest in leading a third party drive in '76, this has been effectively undercut by his conservative financial backers in California, who are moving toward rapprochement with the Ford-Rockefeller team.

And, speaking of Judas Goats, what has been the role of "libertarian", top Randian Alan Greenspan in all of this? Unfortunately, Greenspan's performance has more than confirmed the gloomy forecasts of the Lib. Forum editor. Two recent reports on Greenspan's role: the New York Times noted that Greenspan has been active in trying to push a reluctant Jerry Ford into adopting a stiff gasoline tax; and now the authoritative Evans and Novak report that Greenspan **opposed** the heroic fight of Secretary of the Treasury William Simon against a huge expansion of government spending! In the fight of Simon against Roy Ash to limit the expansion of the federal budget, "Alan Greenspan, the President's supposedly arch-conservative chief economic adviser, was considerably less ardent an economizer than Simon." (Evans and Novak, Jan. 2, 1975). In consequence, the latest forecast is for a whopping $40 billion federal deficit. So much for our "Galtian" hero! And so much for Randian strategic theory and for the idea of Rand as a "libertarian".

And so we libertarians are on our own. We cannot depend upon conservatives as allies, and we certainly cannot depend upon "divine" intervention from above: from "libertarians" enscouced in the cozy seats of Power. But in this gloomy picture there are a few rays of light; one of them being the truly revolutionary sentiment welling up among the masses in this country in opposition to the current public school system. In the mountain country of Kanawha County, West Virginia, a massive revolution from below is shaping up against liberal educationists trying to use the public school system to "lift up" the Fundamentalist, working class masses into the general American culture, to use the textbooks and public school teacher as a conscious "agent of social change." In an article surprisingly sympathetic to the Fundamentalist revolutionaries, the left-liberal Paul Cowan ("A Fight Over America's Future," **Village Voice**, Dec. 9. 1974) points out that the fight against upper class liberals is in many respects a highly articulate and intelligent one. Cowan quotes the daughter of one Fundamentalist minister as saying: "We're not asking that they teach Christianity in the schools. We're just asking that they don't insult our faith." Where are the libertarians here? Why are there none to aid in the battle and to point out the larger libertarian implications?

This lack, however, has been happily remedied in the other fierce struggle over the schools now raging in this country: in the fight of the Irish of South Boston against compulsory bussing. For one of the heroes of the South Bostonians in this battle has been the young libertarian (non-Irish) radio commentator Avi Nelson, whose radio program is alone in the media to support the people of South Boston in their opposition to bussing. Mass meetings in South Boston are ringing to the call of "Avi! Avi, Avi!" Indeed, it is possible that polarization around the public school system may become as explosive an issue throughout the country as the

(Continued On Page 3)

Libertarian Scholarship Advances

The year 1974 saw a notable acceleration of libertarian scholarship, with the burgeoning of high-level scholarly conferences and papers, and the finding and developing of a remarkable number of new young scholars in various libertarian fields. In June, the Institute for Humane Studies sponsored what was undoubtedly the first Austrian School economics conference since the days of old Austria, at Royalton College in Vermont. The conference brought together over fifty Austrians, most of them brilliant graduate students and younger professors, and the proceedings will probably be published in book form. (For a report on the conference, see Richard M. Ebeling, "Austrian Economics On the Rise", **Lib. Forum**, October, 1974). A second Austrian School conference is now planned for the University of Hartford, for June, 1975, featuring papers by some of the best of the younger attendees at Royalton. One of these attendees, Dr. Gerald P. O'Driscoll, Jr., recently completed his doctoral dissertation at UCLA, on "Economics as a Coordination Problem: the Contribution of Friedrich A. Hayek."

Libertarianism has also been "invading" the regular scholarly associations, hitherto almost impervious to such incursions. The annual November 1974 meeting of the Southern Economic Association at Atlanta, Georgia included an excellent session of papers devoted to "The Contribution of Ludwig von Mises." Organized by Dr. Laurence Moss, of the University of Virginia, the session, chaired by Mises' old student Fritz Machlup of Princeton and New York Universities, included papers by: Moss on the monetary theory of Ludwig von Mises, Murray Rothbard on "Mises and Economic Calculation Under Socialism", Professor Israel Kirzner of New York University on "Mises' Theory of Capital and Interest", Professor William P. Baumgarth of Wake Forest University on "Ludwig von Mises and the Theory of the Liberal Order," and a commentary weaving together these varied themes by Professor Karen I. Vaughn of the University of Tennessee. It was truly a day to remember, and the session was one of the best attended at the meeting, even by several distinguished Friedmanites. The papers at the Mises session will hopefully be published in a separate volume. Also on the economics front in 1974, Murray Rothbard's review of Israel Kirzner's distinguished Misesian book, **Competition and Entrepreneurship** (University of Chicago Press) was published in the leading book review medium in the economics profession, **The Journal of Economic Literature.**

That libertarianism is truly in the scholarly air on a broad front is also shown by the fact that the prestigious American Society for Political and Legal Philosophy decided to devote its annual December meeting in Washington to the theme of "Anarchism." Organized by Professor Robert Paul Wolff of the University of Massachusetts, whose book **In Defense of Anarchism** a few years ago made the topic respectable in the philosophy profession for the first time, the meeting was launched with a paper delivered by Murray Rothbard on "Society Without a State". The session, organized in conjunction with the larger meeting of the American Philosophical Association, was filled to overflowing, as Rothbard defused some common anti-anarchist arguments, and went on to adumbrate how arbitration and the courts might work in an anarcho-capitalist society; comments on the paper were made by Christopher Stone, professor of law at the University of Southern California, and by David Wieck, of the philosophy department of Rensselaer Polytechnic Institute. Wieck, a left-wing anarchist, burst into tears at the "hardheartedness" displayed by Rothbard in merely discussing the problem of murder in an anarchist society. The proceedings are scheduled to be published, in more elaborate form, by the ASPLP.

Interest among the philosophers present in the topic was keen, and the meeting and party afterward also brought together a host of brilliant young libertarians in the philosophy profession, ranging from limited-government to outright anarchist. Among the libertarian philosophers present were Professors John Hospers (USC) and Robert Nozick (Harvard) in the senior ranks, and, among the younger scholars (with dissertation topics, completed or pending, in parentheses), were: Professor Paul Sagal (Boston University), Dr. Eric Mack (Harvard University, natural rights), Dr. Jeffrey Paul (Univ. of Cincinnati, methodological individualism), Miss Bee Fletcher (USC, property

rights), Roger Pilon (University of Chicago, negative freedom), and John T. Sanders (Boston University, anarcho-capitalism and the critique of arguments for government.)

Last but not least, the weekend of October 26-28 saw the convening of the Second Libertarian Scholars Conference in New York City. Organized by Professor Walter Grinder of the economics department of Rutgers University and Dr. Walter Block of **Business Week,** the conference drew several dozen invited scholars to hear a glittering array of papers in various fields of the libertarian discipline. Featured in particular was the first magnificent fruits of the researches of Professor Leonard Liggio, of the history department of City College, CUNY, into the origins of libertarian thought in nineteenth-century France, in particular the thought of J. B. Say, Charles Comte and Charles Dunoyer. Commenting were Murray Rothbard and a particular welcome and incisive paper by Professor Ralph Raico, of the history department of the State University College at Buffalo. Another highlight of the conference was the first fruits of the research of our publisher, Professor Joseph Peden of the history department of Baruch College, CUNY, into the life and thought of an important but neglected 19th century American libertarian, Charles O'Conor of the New York City bar.

Another session of the LSC was devoted to a fascinating debate on "Value-Freedom in Economics," with contrasting papers put forth by Roy A. Childs, Jr. and Professor Israel Kirzner of NYU. Another highlight of the conference was the presentation of two chapters from a work in process by Walter Grinder and John Hagel III of Harvard Law School, applying Austrian economics and libertarian ruling class theory in a new and illuminating way to an analysis of the social reality of modern America. Bill Baumgarth of Wake Forest University department political science, delivered a paper on virtue, power and order, the historian Dr. R. Dale Grinder analyzed the role of the intellectuals in installing and perpetuating the hegemony of Power, and Murray Rothbard applied a theory of historical determination to the American Revolution (see Rothbard, "Economic Determinism, Ideology, and the American Revolution," **Lib. Forum**, November, 1974).

With these inquiries into history of libertarian thought, political philosophy, philosophy of economics, history and sociology, a great time was had by all, and libertarian scholarship was greatly enriched by the papers and the meeting. ◘

The Emerging Crisis —

(Continued From Page 2)

economic crisis; and in this set of issues, it is only the libertarians who have the answer that can cut through and resolve the numerous conflicts around bussing, textbooks, religion, sex, etc. that are rife in the public schools. And that answer, of course, is to abolish the public school system root and branch, and thereby to allow any groups of parents and students to have the schools, integrated or segregated, Fundamentalist or atheist, disciplined or permissive, that they respectively and individually prefer.

At any rate, the prospects ahead are grim, and it behooves all libertarians to rise up and redouble their efforts on behalf of their cause, their country, and their own liberties. For make no mistake: there is no place to hide. Your gold coins, your caves in the woods stocked with canned goods, your retreats to new islands, your Swiss bank accounts, are not going to be worth a tinker's dam when the U.S.A. goes collectivist. If we stand up and oppose the trend, we might succeed in avoiding the holocaust; at the very least, we will be able to tell ourselves and our grandchildren that we did our best. If we do nothing but run to the cave, literally or metaphorically, we will deserve the scorn of present and future generations. ◘

Women's Lib: Goldberg Replies To Kinsky

By Steven Goldberg

Department of Sociology
City College, CUNY

(Editor's Note: Unfortunately, the most heated controversies in the libertarian movement in the last few years have been generated by issues perhaps fascinating in themselves but only tangential to libertarianism: science fiction and women's "liberation." Let us hope that this does **not** mean that all too many libertarians are more interested in such peripheral matters than in liberty itself. At any rate, the current brouhaha began in April, 1974, when the **Lib. Forum** editor published a favorable review of a brilliant work by the young sociologist Steven Goldberg. **The Inevitability of Patriarchy**, in Books for Libertarians (now Libertarian Review.) Even though the BFL review was balanced by a negative review by Mrs. Riqui Leon in the same issue, a raft of hysterical letters bombarded the magazine, which then published the best of them, by Miss Julia White, along with my reply, in its June, 1974 issue. **BFL** then saw fit to publish two critical letters on my review and on the Goldberg book by Miss Lynn Kinsky, executive editor of **Reason** magazine. The first was in the same June issue, and the next, longer critique of my reply and of the book itself was in **BFL's** August, 1974 issue. Since I felt I had had my say on the subject and could only repeat my rather lengthy June letter, I turned over the second Kinsky letter to Professor Goldberg, who is far more qualified than I on the subject, and deserves his chance to reply. Professor Goldberg's reply was too long for Lib. Review's space requirements, and so we are privileged to be able to publish it, in its entirety, below. I have just received a letter from a distinguished libertarian sociologist hailing the Goldberg book as a "sterling" work, and particularly admiring the "air of cold authority" with which he writes. That air is also a hallmark of the present article. I would also like to call our readers' attention to the new paperback version of Goldberg's **The Inevitability of Patriarchy** (William Morrow, 1974, $2.95), which includes over 60 additional pages, further explaining his theory and replying to the various critics of the hardcover original. David Gutmann, in his review of the original book in **Commentary**, hailed Goldberg as "at all times icily logical", and there is no field of current controversy in which icy logic is more badly needed.)

* * * * * * * * * * * * * *

To the editor of **BFL**:

I have just come across Lynn Kinsky's letter concerning my **The Inevitability of Patriarchy** (BFL, August). While Miss Kinsky's criticisms are based on a most simplistic view of physiological dimorphism, it is a view that is held by many sociologists and I would be most grateful for the opportunity to respond.

At its most basic, **Patriarchy** argues that:

A. In all societies that exist or have existed males attain the overwhelming number of upper hierarchical positions (patriarchy), males perform those non-maternal roles and tasks — whichever they are in any given society — that are given highest status (male attainment), and dominance in male-female relationships — as evidenced in the emotions of males and females, the values and customs that reflect these emotional expectations, and the authority system in which nearly every woman comes under the authority of either her husband or brother — is associated with the male (male dominance).

B. The only explanation of this universality that is internally logical, concordant with the anthropological evidence, plausible, and inclusive of the physiological evidence is an explanation positing a physiological dimorphism that is such that males are more strongly **motivated**, by the environmental presence of a hierarchy or member of the other sex, to manifest whatever behavior is necessary in any given environmental setting to attain dominance in hierarchies and male-female relationships. It is irrelevant for our theoretical purposes whether one conceptualizes this emotional-behavioral differentiation in terms of a greater male "drive", a lower male threshold for the release of dominance behavior, a greater male "need" of dominance, or even a weaker male ego that needs shoring up by attainment and dominance (just as it is unimportant whether one conceptualizes the physiologically-rooted motivating factors we loosely refer to as the "sex drive" as a "drive" or as a "need").

C. We need not merely postulate the relevance of physiological dimorphism to emotional and behavioral differentiation (though the anthropological evidence and the requirements of parsimony would force us to do so even if there were no direct physiological evidence). The direct endocrinological study of humans and hundreds of controlled experiments on the effects of hormonal masculinization of female subjects of other mammalian species demonstrates beyond reasonable challenge that the testicularly-generated fetal hormonalization of the male central nervous system promotes early maturation of the brain structures that mediate between male hormones and outward behavior, thereby rendering the male hypersensitive to the later presence of the hormones that energize dominance behavior ("aggression", as I use the term). Most of **Patriarchy** is concerned with the way in which socialization and institutions conform to, and exaggerate, the reality of the differentiated behavior that is rooted in dimorphism and that is observed by the population, but Miss Kinsky does not address this and I need not summarize that material here.

> Miss Kinsky writes: "I am surprised at (Murray Rothbard) being so gullible as to believe Goldberg when he says there is such a thing as 'status drive' or 'initiative' able to be defined precisely and measured in such a way that a sociologist can say that this person has more of it than that person does or that this group has more of it than that group does — and that it can be shown to correlate with one and only one physical attribute. (And a nondichotomous one at that: both sexes produce both estrogen and testosterone with levels being roughly equal until puberty, and most men only draw slightly ahead of most women in testosterone production after age 18 or so!).

There is so much confusion and irrelevance in Miss Kinsky's paragraph that it is impossible to straighten it out in just a few words. But I might make these points:

A. I do not use the term "status drive", though I think that this term is satisfactory as a shorthand for the behavior that satisfies the "need" for attainment and dominance that is greater in the male and that is precondition for attainment and dominance. The important correlation is between testosterone and attainment (for the group of males as opposed to the group of females) and no one denies that this correlation is very high (i.e. upper hierarchical positions are attained almost exclusively by males in every society and in every society males have higher testosterone levels than females). The point at issue is not whether there is such a correlation, but whether there is the causal relationship I describe. (Incidentally, males have adult testosterone levels roughly twelve times those of females, not just "slightly" higher; a young adult woman with a testosterone level that would be normal for a male is in big medical trouble.)

B. More importantly, it is grossly simplistic to speak only of "hormone levels". It is not merely the level of hormones, but the sensitivity of the CNS to the effects of testosterone — a sensitivity that is greater in males as a result of the fetal preparation of the male CNS by the testicularly-generated testosterone — that is relevant to dominance behavior.

C. Thus the fact that male and female testosterone levels are roughly equal before puberty does not demonstrate that the pre-pubertal male's greater dominance behavior is owing only to socialization. (Moreover, even if dominance behavior were a function of only testosterone levels, this would still not indicate the irrelevance of dimorphism to children.

(Continued On Page 5)

528

Goldberg Replies To Kinsky —

(Continued From Page 4)

Socialization reflects observation of adults and is preparation for adulthood. Adult males would be more "aggressive" even if only testosterone levels were relevant.)

D. It is quite true that both males and females have both testosterone and estrogen, but this no more demonstrates the irrelevance of hormones to dominance behavior than it demonstrates that women can grow beards (a male "ability" that derives from the male's higher testosterone level). It is the ratio of testosterone and estrogen, and the sensitivity of the CNS, that is crucial.

E. Miss Kinsky makes the common, but fallacious, argument that it behooves me — if I am to argue for the determinativeness of physiological dimorphism to dominance behavior and to socialization relevant to dominance behavior — to demonstrate that hormone differences account for differing **individuals'** dominance behavior. If Miss Kinsky means that it is incumbent upon me to show that males in upper hierarchical positions have higher testosterone levels than other males and that the physiological factor precedes the attainment, I would say that I think it not at all unlikely that males do vary in their physiologically-engendered propensity for dominance behavior, but that it is irrelevant to the theory advanced in **Patriarchy** whether they do or not. An analogy may make this clear: one can demonstrate the determinativeness of the male's greater physical strength to the fact that all boxing champions are male (and to socialization of little girls away from boxing) without assuming that strength is determinative within the group of males. Indeed, boxing champions are not the strongest males; once the strength precondition is met, then other factors become relevant. Likewise, the emotional-behavioral differentiation of men and women that is observed by every population and that is reflected by, and exaggerated by, every social system, is sufficient to explain why every society is partriarchal. (Such a "sufficient" explanation is the purpose of Patriarchy.) Once the physiological precondition is met, as it is met by all hormonally-normal males, then other factors become determinative to dominance behavior. If Miss Kinsky is arguing that I must show a perfect correlation between maleness and dominance, then her argument is just silly. Obviously there are many exceptions (i.e. many women who manifest dominance behavior more strongly or more readily than many men). There are many exceptions even when we are considering characteristics that are almost purely physiologically-engendered (i.e. there are many women who are taller than many men). We should hardly be surprised to find exceptions when we consider a factor (dominance behavior) that is a result not only of physiological factors, but psychological, familial, and social factors as well. The theory presented in Patriarchy does not argue that every male is more aggressive than every female, but that, as a result of dimorphism and the emotional-behavioral differentiation it engenders, **most** males more strongly manifest dominance behavior and that this is observed by the population and is manifested in the socialization system and the society's institutions.

Miss Kinsky does make an interesting point when she takes a behaviorist approach, but I do not find her arguments much more telling than her analyses of physiology. I have addressed the behaviorist criticisms at length in the paperback edition of **Patriarchy** and can here make only a few points:

Miss Kinsky argues that: (A) biologists consider dominance behavior only in terms of attack behavior, (B) we cannot invoke the presence of emotion in an explanation of animal behavior (because animals cannot report their feelings verbally), and (C) terms such as "male dominance" are operationally meaningless. (A) is simply incorrect. In the experimental studies hierarchy and dominance are the primary objects of study. Attack behavior is sometimes — but by no means always — the mode by which hierarchical position and dominance in male-female encounters is attained. (B) is the sort of argument that is invoked only when one dislikes the conclusions arrived at by an experiment. If the experimental animals were of a low order, then one might reasonably argue that the physiological factor is an instinct to fight and that emotion is an irrelevant consideration. But with non-human mammals — as with people — attack behavior (or other behavior leading to attainment or dominance) is not merely instinctive reaction, but action in the service of emotional predisposition (i.e. the "drive" or "need" discussed above). This predisposition is greater in males for the physiological reasons

discussed above. Note that no one, least of all the feminist sociologist, denies the relevance of the emotional predisposition to dominance in human beings. Feminists describe at length the emotional and behavioral differentiation of males and females and then **incorrectly**, ascribe the causation of the emotional-behavioral differentiation primarily to social factors and socialization. This feminist "explanation" is no explanation at all, but merely a begging of the question: **why** does every society's men and women associate dominance behavior with males, **why** does no society socialize its **women** towards dominance behavior, and **why** are the male and female emotions relevant to dominance not reversed in even one society? (C) is incorrect "Patriarchy" is defined in terms that would satisfy the most rigid behaviorist; one need merely count the numbers of men and women in hierarchies. "Male dominance" is identified by both the expressed expectations of men and women and by its manifestation in the authority system (relevant to male-female relationships); there is no society in which individuals' emotions (as expressed in verbal accounts, proverbs, songs, legal expectations, etc.) fail to associate dominance with males and no society in which women do not come under the authority of a husband or brother (usually by law, always by social expectation). It is quite true that it is difficult to specify on a general level the **actions** that will lead to attainment and dominance in particular societies because — while willingness to sacrifice time, health, longevity, affection, familial life, and other sources of satisfaction will nearly always be relevant — the specific actions will be determined by the culture of the particular society. It is the underlying physiologically-generated need that is the motivational factor. This need finds its mode of satisfaction within the limits imposed by the particular culture. When fighting behavior leads to attainment, males will be more motivated to fight; when sacrificing one's family to the corporation leads to attainment, then those individuals willing to make this sacrifice will mostly be men. Again: no feminist denies that such emotional differentiation exists; the feminist identifies such expectations and then attributes to them an etiology that ignores the one factor capable of explaining the universality of the emotional differentiation and the institutions that reflect them. (Miss Kinsky is incorrect in her implication that this analysis is tautological; it is falsifiable by the development or discovery of a single society in which the emotions of male dominance, and their manifestation in socialization and institution, are not present.)

Much of Miss Kinsky's letter is an attack on sociological epistomology. I suspect that Miss Kinsky has not read **Patriarchy** and therefore believes that, because I am in a department of sociology, this attack somehow casts doubt on the book. In fact, **Patriarchy** is not "sociological" in any sense for which her epistemological criticisms would be relevant and I need not consider them here.   ◻

Boston Libertarian Dinners!

Two libertarian students at Harvard Law School have decided to organize a monthly dinner series to provide an opportunity for libertarians of all persuasions in the Boston area to meet on a regular basis. Following each dinner, a prominent libertarian will speak informally to the group, and field questions from the assembled guests.

The first dinner in the series has already been scheduled: on February 19 at 7:30 P. M. at the Hong Kong Restaurant, 1236 Massachusetts Ave. in Cambridge. Dr. Robert Nozick, professor of philosophy at Harvard University and author of the recently published work, **Anarchy, State, and Utopia**, will be the featured speaker.

To attend, mail $2 per person cover charge to the Center for the Study of Social Systems, P. O. Box 920, Boston, Mass. 02103. Guests who show up at the door without reservations will be required to pay a $3.00 cover charge. Each guest will order dinner and pay for it individually on an a la carte basis. This is a non-profit venture, and the cover charge will be used to pay for organizing expenses in arranging the dinner series, and to help pay transportation expenses for out-of-town libertarian speakers.

Libertarians who are unable to attend this first dinner but who want to be placed on the mailing list for invitations to subsequent dinners, are urged to contact the Center at the above address. Also, please feel free to suggest additional names and addresses of people who might be interested in receiving future mailings on these dinners.   ◻

Henry Hazlitt
Celebrates 80th Birthday

It is indeed a pleasure to have the opportunity to honor Henry Hazlitt on his 80th birthday (November 28). One of the most distinguished and productive economists, writers and intellectuals in this country, Hazlitt at 80 looks and acts a full 20 years younger. A remarkable combination of a brilliant and incisive mind, an unusually clear and lucid style, and an unfailingly cheerful, generous, and gentle soul, Henry Hazlitt continues to be a veritable fount of energy and productivity.

No one, moreover, can match Henry Hazlitt in blending great and broad erudition with a clarity and simplicity of style that makes him a joy to read. The great stylist H. L. Mencken's tribute to Hazlitt 40 years ago *that he was the only economist that could be understood by the general public* remains true to this day.

Why, then, does Henry Hazlitt remain grievously neglected by the nation's intelligentsia, by the self-proclaimed intellectual elite that moulds so much of "educated" public opinion? Why does Hazlitt, for example, never appear, either as writer or reviewed author, in the highly influential **New York Review of Books**?

There are several factors that contribute to this shameful neglect of one of the country's outstanding writers and thinkers. They all add up to his being totally out of the intellectual fashion of our day.

In the first place, he lacks either a Ph.D. or an academic post — those twin passports to intellectual and academic respectability. For a scholar to discuss or footnote a book by Hazlitt — no matter how important or scholarly — would be to lose caste and Brownie points in the status-anxious-world of academe.

Secondly, in an age of hyper-specialization, when the fashion is to aspire to be the world's foremost expert on some extremely narrow and trivial topic, Henry Hazlitt simply knows too darn much about an enormous range and variety of subjects. Surely, then, he *must* be unsound.

Thirdly, Hazlitt writes too clearly; surely, someone who writes so that he can be generally understood lacks the "profundity" that only obscurantist jargon can provide. One of the main reasons for the popularity of Karl Marx and John Maynard Keynes among intellectuals was precisely the staggering obscurity of their prose; only when a writer *is obscure can a cult of followers gather around to serve as the semi-official interpreters and exegetes of the Master.* Henry Hazlitt has always lacked that fog of incomprehensibility necessary to become celebrated as a Profound Thinker.

Fourthly, as an economist, Hazlitt has always been too honest to don the robes of soothsayer and prophet, to tell us precisely what the GNP or the unemployment rate is going to be in six or nine months.

Last but certainly not least, Henry Hazlitt has been totally outside the modern fashion in battling for many years as an uncompromising adherent of laissez-faire and the free market economy. If only Hazlitt had been a statist or Socialist, perhaps he would have been forgiven for his other intellectual sins. But not the greatest sin of all — of arguing, year in and out, for free-market capitalism.

In the course of his remarkably productive career, Henry Hazlitt has been distinguished as a journalist, editor, literary critic, philosopher, political scientist and, above all, economist. His major base has been in journalism.

Born in Philadelphia in 1894, young Hazlitt left college early to be a financial writer, successively for the **Wall Street Journal**, the New York **Evening Post**, and the Mechanics and Metals National Bank of New York. In 1921 he became financial editor for the New York **Evening Mail**. Then, during the 1920s, he expanded his horizons into the general editorial and literary fields, first as editorial writer for the New York **Herald** and the New York **Sun**, and then as literary editor for the **Sun** in the late 1920s, from which he went to the **Nation** as literary editor from 1930 to 1933. When H. L. Mencken left the editorship of the **American Mercury** in 1933, he was happy to select Hazlitt as his successor to that distinguished post.

After leaving the Mercury the following year, Hazlitt became an editorial writer for — *mirabile dictu* — the New York **Times** for the next

dozen years. It was Hazlitt who largely accounted for whatever conservative tone the **Times** adopted during that era.

It was shortly after he joined the **Times** that an event occurred which would change and shape Hazlitt's life *from that point on*. Reviewing the first English translation of Ludwig von Mises' great work **Socialism** in 1936, Hazlitt was converted to a position of uncompromising adherence to free-market capitalism, and hostility to statism and socialism that would mark all of his work from that time forward.

Hazlitt became a leading follower of the great Austrian, free-market economist, and was to become one of Mises' closest friends and co-workers from the time that Mises emigrated to the United States during World War II.

It was as a leading "Misesian" that Hazlitt was to write the bulk of his more than a dozen books and countless journal and newspaper articles.

As the New York **Times** moved inexorably leftward, Henry Hazlitt *departed to become weekly economic columnist for* **Newsweek** magazine. There, for 20 years, from 1946-1966, Hazlitt, week in and week out, penned lucid and incisive defenses of the free market, private property rights, and the gold standard, as well as trenchant critiques of the evils of government intervention in the economy.

In countless radio and television debates, and on the lecture platform, Hazlitt carried on the battle against the growth of Big Government. Furthermore, he was co-editor-in-chief of the **Freeman** in its early years, 1950-53, when that magazine was a noble attempt to serve as a weekly periodical on behalf of the conservative-libertarian cause.

But it is his host of published books that will serve as an enduring monument to this great and much neglected man. The scope and merit are enormous: ranging from his first work on clear thinking, **Thinking As a Science** (1916, reissued in 1969), to literary criticism, **The Anatomy of Criticism** (1933).

Particularly important, both in quantity and quality, is his post-1936 or "Misesian" output. His first work in this period was a notable contribution to political science, **A New Constitution Now** (1942, and soon to be reissued; see HUMAN EVENTS, Nov. 16, 1974, page 10). This work, in which Hazlitt argued for the scrapping of the American Constitution on behalf of a European Parliamentary government, was not calculated to please Constitutionalist conservatives.

But whether or not one agrees fully with Hazlitt, he made an extremely important point which has taken on far more importance in these days of unbridled executive and presidential power. For he argued that the great defect of the American Constitution is that it permits runaway executive power, unchecked by Congress or the public.

A *Parliamentary* system could at least make the executive far more responsive to Congress, and serve as a check on executive tyranny. In the era of Watergate, there would have been no need for the clumsy impeachment process, since the President could have been removed far more easily and swiftly.

In 1946, Hazlitt published his most popular book, **Economics in One Lesson**, which remains to this day the best introductory primer to economic science. With his usual lucidity, Hazlitt set forth the merits of the free market, and the unfortunate consequences of all the major forms of government intervention, all of which continue to plague us today.

There is still no better introduction to free market economics than Economics in One Lesson. The "lesson" derives from the 19th Century libertarian French economist Frederic Bastiat, who was also distinguished for the clarity of his style: the difference between "what is seen" as a result of government intervention and "what is not seen."

For example, if the government taxes the public to build housing, what is seen is the new housing, which may seem on the surface to be a net advance; what is not seen is what the public would have done if they had been allowed to keep their own money.

The following year, Hazlitt came out with his booklet, **Will Dollars Save the World?**, his dissection of the Marshall Plan and one of the first

(Continued On Page 7)

Arts And Movies
By Mr. First Nighter

Musicals: the Nostalgia Boom.

Two of my most delightful experiences in the arts this year were exercises in musical nostalgia: watching a revival of Cole Porter's "Anything Goes", with the 40's singing and dancing star Ann Miller; and seeing the revival of the once-famous Andrews Sisters in their highly successful new Broadway hit, "Over Here!" Nostalgia was certainly a great part in the delight: How great Miss Miller looked! Not a day older than in her successful movie musicals of twenty and thirty years ago! And to see the cheerful Andrews Sisters once more (minus LaVerne, who died some years ago), to hear their infectious and swinging renditions, was, indeed, to return to a past that was at least culturally happier than today. Indeed, after the curtain fell on a remarkably good throwback by Richard and Robert Sherman, to 1930's musicals, the wildly enthusiastic audience ,prompted Patty and Maxine Andrews to spend twenty minutes on the stage, singing the renditions of their fabulous hits of the past: each number punctuated by the cheers and "Bravos!" of the audience. In their famous "I'll Be With You in Apple Blossom Time", the audience could not refrain from singing along, and the stage-wise Andrews Sisters promptly brought the entire audience into the act: "What a WON-derful wedding it will be", everyone belted out, knowing the renditions down to the last phrase.

But my main point here is that far more than simple nostalgia was involved. After all, there were a large number of kids and young people in the audience, to add their chorus of approval to the nostalgia of the middle-aged. Why did the young people love the show?

I submit that the reason is that the old musicals were far better than today, and that this fact is sensed by young and old alike. The good old days were better, at least in music and the popular arts. No better clue can be found to the cause than to read the brilliant critique of modern music, written two decades ago, by the eminent music critic Henry Pleasants. The Agony of Modern Music (Simon and Schuster, 1955). Pleasants' work was a critique of modern "serious" music, and a demonstration of why that music has been in a state of decline and collapse since Wagner (and, in many respects, since Beethoven.) Briefly, in contrast to the heyday of classical music (roughly from Monteverdi and the beginning of the seventeenth century to the mid-nineteenth), modern music had been marked by the destruction of melody, rhythm, and tonality. In the classical period, music had been marked by tuneful melody, and by a strong, regular rhythmic beat, to which a strictly tonal harmony had been subordinate. In contrast, modern music had destroyed melody by making it thematic and harmonic, and had wrecked the rhythmic beat by substituting vertical harmonies and varying rhythms. Melody and rhythm had been destroyed on behalf of harmony, which in turn had lost its strong tonality. One of the hallmarks of the classical symphony, for example, is that it was pianistic; and could readily be transcribed for the piano. In later, modern music, orchestration had taken command, and a conductor became needed to impose order on the players.

More relevant to our topic is what modern music did to the opera. Classical opera had been marked by the dominance of the singer and the song, the melodic song as delivered in arias, duets, etc. Modern music destroyed the opera by eliminating the melodic song, by subordinating the singer to the orchestra and by confining the singer to talky recitative; while pure music was transformed into the "tone poem." The "integration" of music and the song into the orchestra and the dramatic text had succeeded only in destroying the opera form.

Mr. Pleasants went on to point out that twentieth century American jazz and popular music constituted a renaissance of the classical musical form, and therefore carried on the best traditions of "serious" music. Jazz and popular music restored the dominance of melody and rhythm,

(Continued On Page 8)

Henry Hazlitt — (Continued From Page 6)

important critiques of the postwar foreign aid program. This was followed by his Illusions of Point Four (1950), on Truman's boondoggle program of aid to what is now known as the "Third World."

In 1951, Hazlitt turned to the novel form, publishing what is one of my own favorite parts of the Hazlitt canon, The Great Idea (1951, later reissued as Time Will Run Back, 1966). The Great Idea was roasted by critics as a novel, but I confess I enjoyed it thoroughly, and it has long been one of my favorite works of fiction. This despite (or perhaps because of) the fact that it frankly cloaks sound economic theory in a readable, novelistic form.

For one thing, it is one of the best and most thorough discussions of the economic fallacies of socialism to be found anywhere. The plot is fascinating: by happenstance, an intelligent political innocent inherits the post of dictator of a future World Communist State.

> Beginning simply as a search for ways of making the disastrous Communist economy work better, the dictator alters the economy, step by inexorable logical step, in the direction of freedom until he changes the world into a purely free market economy and free society.

Beginning with allowing citizens to exchange their ration tickets, the dictator comes to rediscover the forgotten free market, gold money, and the rights of private property. If the aesthetes are worried about the lack of avant-garde symbolism or of morbid psychologizing in The Great Idea, then so much the worse for them!

A few years later came a veritable labor of love, The Free Man's Library (1956). Hazlitt's annotated bibliography of libertarian and conservative books. It still serves as the only work of its kind, and an updating of this book would be one of the most useful projects to inspire and instruct a new generation of libertarians.

In 1959, Hazlitt published his greatest contribution to economic science, the massive, thorough The Failure of the New Economics, a step-by-step and page-by-page evisceration of Lord Keynes' mischievous and enormously influential General Theory. Employing Misesian, "Austrian" economics in a masterful fashion, Hazlitt left not a shred standing of Keynes' famous system. It was a superb exercise in economic demolition.

The massive neglect of Fallacies by the economics profession, which, when it deigned to consider the book at all, dismissed it as mere "pamphleteering," is a shameful blot on the state of the economics profession. As a one-two punch to Keynesianism, Hazlitt followed up this work by collecting the best anti-Keynesian critiques by economists in his The Critics of Keynesian Economics (1960).

In the same year, Hazlitt wrote his searching critique of the inflationary policies of our time, warning of accelerating inflation and calling for a return to the gold standard in his What You Should Know About Inflation (1960, revised editions in 1965 and 1968). Happily, Hazlitt is now busily at work on a new book on this all too timely topic.

Not content with economics, political science, journalism and literary criticism, Hazlitt next turned to an important work on political and ethical philosophy, The Foundations of Morality (1964). In a work fully as neglected by the academic philosophers as his economic writings were ignored by the nation's economists, Hazlitt argued for a utilitarian ethic and for the morality of free-market capitalism.

In his latest two books, Henry Hazlitt dealt with the vital problems of poverty and the welfare state: Man vs. the Welfare State (1970) and The Conquest of Poverty (1973). In these works, Hazlitt showed that only capitalism can conquer poverty and provide genuine welfare, and he demolished the fallacies of the welfare state. Also included is the best available refutation of the potentially disastrous Milton Friedman proposal for a "negative income tax."

Thus, throughout his remarkably productive life, Henry Hazlitt has fought for freedom and a free-market economy with a unique combination of the erudition of a scholar and the lucidity and popular appeal of a lifelong writer and journalist. In a healthier cultural and intellectual climate, he would have honors heaped upon him by scholars and by the general public. As it is, we can only do our part by greeting this vibrant and gracious gentleman, this distinguished scholar and libertarian, and by looking forward to the many important books and articles which will doubtless flow from his pen in the years to come.

Reprinted from Human Events, Nov. 20, 1974.

531

Arts And Movies—(Continued From Page 7)

harmony was once again tonal and subordinate to the other elements. Even the seemingly new motifs of vocal and instrumental improvisation was a return to pre-nineteenth century vocalising and to such forms as the concerto grosso.

It struck me that the same kind of development that happened to opera had also happened within the popular musical, although not in nearly as destructive a way. Pleasants seemed to recognize this when he pointed out in passing that George Gershwin's highly touted excursions into the semi-classical or quasi-symphonic or operatic form, such as **Rhapsody in Blue** or **Porgy and Bess**, were far inferior to his marvellous show tunes, such as "Embraceable You" or "But Not for Me." Unfortunately, Gershwin, one of our great pop song composers, suffered from an inferiority complex vis a vis "serious" music, and so was ever trying to blend into what our intelligentsia persisted in defining as "legitimate" music. If such critics as Pleasants had been writing in the 1920's and 30's, the course of Gershwin's career might have been very different.

The heyday of the popular song was the 1920's and 30's, led by such masters of the blending of sentiment and sophistication as Gershwin, Porter, Rodgers and Hart, Berlin, and Arlen. Their songs were built around the show tune, and the vehicle of the show tune was the Broadway musical — or what can now be described as the "old-fashioned" or pre-1940's musical. One of the great delights, then, of seeing "Anything Goes" or the reminiscent "Over Here!" was being able to re-experience the true Broadway musical. Much derided now, the old-fashioned musical, like Pleasants' criteria for the classical opera, strictly subordinated the drama and the plot to the song and the melodic tune. Yes, the plot of the old musical was a thin clothes-line on which to hang the lovely and melodic tunes, but so what? Nobody wanted any more; if people wanted plots, they could go to plays or motion pictures.

The destruction of the Broadway musical can be dated as precisely as the advent of the late Wagnerian operas, and indeed the course of their decline unconsciously recapitulated the post-Wagnerian decay of the opera. Specifically, the precipitous decline and fall began with Rodgers and Hammerstein's famous 1940 musical "Oklahoma!" "Oklahoma!" was unfortunately hailed by the critics and the intellectuals for precisely the wrong reasons because it subordinated the song and the tune to the dramatic text, and integrated the songs into the drama. Starting with Rodgers and Hammerstein, furthermore, the musical composers (in a sense recapitulating Wagner) began to freight their drama with pretentious pseudo-"philosophical" messages, as exemplified by the fuzzy "brotherhood" themes in **South Pacific** and **West Side Story**. The older musical now looked hopelessly "old-fashioned", and it took only a few years for the tunes to disappear altogether; how many years has it been since a truly memorable Broadway musical? Again, as in the classical symphony or opera, a hallmark of the decay has been the disappearance of the hummable or singable tune — the analog of the collapse of the aria or the pianistic symphony. Deprived of their major vehicle, the show tune, the great song composers — the Porters and Harts

and Cowards — died out and there were none to take their place. By the 1950's, the popular song had decayed to such an extent that rock-and-roll was able to rush in and fill the vacuum, and we must now be content with such second-rate song composers as Bert Bacharach.

The entering wedge to the decline and fall of the show tune and the musical, then, was the weakness of Richard Rodgers as a composer. For, in contrast to many other composers, the great Rodgers has always been dominated musically by his lyricist. In the 1920's and 1930's, Rodgers and the magnificent Lorenz Hart collaborated on some of the greatest songs in the history of popular music, a blend of melody and sophistication unmatched by anyone but the superb Cole Porter. Listen, for example, to one of the most affecting and magnificent of the female pop singers, Lee Wiley (in her heyday, twenty-odd years ago) singing such stunning songs as "Glad to Be Unhappy" and "It Never Entered My Mind", for a recording of popular song-and singing-at its best. Unfortunately, after the death of Larry Hart, Rodgers began to collaborate with Oscar Hammerstein II, who promptly proceeded to impose a gushy and cornball over-sentimentality on Rodgers' creative output, a sentimentality combined with vaguely leftish "messages", that was to lead to the music-drama and the destruction of the genuine Broadway musical. Compare, for example, the Rodgers-Hammerstein "I'm as Corny as Kansas in August" to the earlier Rodgers-Hart tunes. Like the post-Wagnerians in relation to Wagner, Rodgers' successors were devoid of his melodic genius and thereby swiftly brought about the destruction of the musical. In the post-Hammerstein music drama, only the great song writer Frank Loesser was able to preserve the first-rate melody, in his "Guys and Dolls." The rest is Old Night.

The very same decline and fall, incidentally, also occurred in pop music's cousin, jazz. Jazz had reached its summit in its earliest, or "classical", period: New Orleans, from approximately 1900-1920. It was in New Orleans jazz, in its funeral marching bands, dance bands, and whorehouse pianists, that the classical period of "serious" music was most fully restored, and jazz reached its most inspired form of melodic improvisation within the rhythmic beat of the drum, the banjo, and the slap double-bass. As jazz moved north to Chicago in the "Dixieland" of the 1920's, the power and inspiration cooled, and the music became lighter and more routinized. But the classic jazz form was still there. Jazz became further corrupted in the lush, monotonous "swing" of the big band era of the late 1930's (Mahler, Bruckner?), but it was still at least dimly recognizable in the classical jazz tradition. The destruction of jazz came with the "bebop" and post-bebop eras after World War II (Schoenberg?), as jazz, too, lost its melody and rhythm, and turned to the dominance of harmonic variety that has marked modern "serious" music. Like modern music, jazz became "cerebral" and cut off from its emotive roots and popular audience. Indeed, it is often difficult to distinguish between modern jazz and modern serious music, if one in fact cares enough about either to bother searching for the distinction. Both serious music and jazz have reached a dead end, although there are still enough viable elements left, in jazz and popular music at least, to permit a future renaissance. ◼

The Libertarian Forum
BOX 341
MADISON SQUARE STATION
NEW YORK, NEW YORK 10010

First Class

Published Every Month. Subscription Rates: $8.00 Per Year; $15.00 Two Years

A Monthly Newsletter

THE
Libertarian Forum

Joseph R. Peden, Publisher

Murray N. Rothbard, Editor

VOLUME VII, NO. 1   JANUARY, 1975   US-ISSN0047-4517

GOVERNMENT AND
THE ECONOMY

The Tax Cut.

The Ford Administration has clearly abandoned its feeble attempts to restrict its own inflationary policies, and has gone for broke — literally as well as metaphorically — in expansionist Keynesian policies to try to combat the deepening recession. The money supply is being inflated rapidly once again, to try to stay one step ahead of the "liquidity crunch" that is in the process of driving to the wall inefficient businesses which had overexpanded during the boom. But the major new policy is the Keynesian one of enormous government deficits, now estimated (probably conservatively) at $40 billion. Part of the deficit is to emerge from a substantial cut in income taxes. Immediately, however, the Ford Administration will find itself in a cleft stick; for the very severe nature of the liquidity crunch means that businesses are scrambling for capital in a tight market, and the pouring of $40 billion worth of government bonds onto such a market is going to clobber the private capital market, and greatly intensify the depression. The only way out of that bind will be for the Federal Reserve authorities to **create** approximately $40 billion of new money with which the banks will be able to buy the new bonds; and that will mean an enormous increase in the inflationary process.

The liberals are supporting an income tax for the wrong, inflationary reasons: the Keynesian theory that consumers will then spend more money, and help lift us out of the recession by their increased spending. In reality, if the deficit is financed through the Federal Reserve, it will, as we've just pointed out, accelerate the inflation. Because of their opposition to inflation, conservatives and many libertarians are opposing the income tax cut, the latter if the cut is not accompanied by an equivalent cut in government spending.

I submit that for libertarians to oppose the income tax cut is disastrous, both on principle and for strategic reasons. Strategically, we would then be supporting a high tax regime which the bulk of Americans hates and clamors against, and would be allowing the ordinarily high-tax liberals to run away with what is a libertarian issue **par excellence**. On principle, taxation is theft, and **any** reduction in taxation whatsoever must be welcomed as allowing producers and individuals to keep more of their own money. Furthermore, in the long run, this can only help the economy by shifting production toward the desires of private consumers. Even on the current recession, furthermore, an income tax cut will help by shifting funds from wasteful government hands into the hands of private savers and investors, whose increased saving will help to ease and speed up the recession-adjustment process. To help the recession, the more the tax cut is geared to increasing saving and investment rather than consumption the better, but the point is that **any** tax cut will have a

beneficial effect, morally and economically, in both the long and the short run.

Of course it would be still better if an X billion dollar tax cut were matched by an X billion dollar cut in government spending, but getting the government to cut its spending is politically, at this juncture, a Utopian dream. When was the last year that government spending was actually reduced? The answer is lost in antiquity. The point is that given the choices before us, we must take and welcome **any** reduction of government that we can get, anywhere down the line. If the liberals are proposing a large income tax cut, even for the wrong reasons, we should happily make use of this agitation for our own libertarian purposes. After we get the tax cut, we can then agitate for government either to cut its spending, or, at least, to finance its deficit in a non-inflationary manner. Furthermore, looking at the situation strategically, the only way that we might possibly get the government to cut its spending is to reduce taxes first, and then force it to trim its sails on the strength of the general horror at the mammoth size of the deficit. Let us remember Parkinson's Law: expenditures rise to meet income. Then only hope, at this time, of getting government to cut or restrict its expenditures is to cut off its income. An income tax is a giant step in that direction. Libertarians must realize that we are in no position to **plan** an orderly retreat for government, even if that were desirable; government is the enemy, and therefore we must take whatever chunks out of that enemy that circumstances might permit. Hence: hooray for any tax cuts, anywhere, in any area!

Oil Policy.

In the meantime, the Ford Administration, seconded by the almost universal clamor of the media, is preparing to aggravate both the inflation and the recession by restricting the supply, and raising the price, of oil and oil products. Restricting the supply of oil will raise prices, and also depress the economy by cutting demand and investment in non-petroleum sectors of the economy. Furthermore, since the Administration proposes to effect the restriction by a massive tax on the import and domestic production of oil, this means that the increased tax revenue from oil will partially offset the good effects of the tax cut, and deepen the recession still further.

The current plan of the Administration is to impose a $3 per barrel tax on the importation of oil, which is supposed to fulfill the Kissinger-Ford goal of a compulsory cut of 1 million barrels per day in the importation of crude oil, a figure which Kissinger admits he chose purely for its "dramatic effect." In this way, the protectionist forces in the oil industry

(Continued On Page 2)

Government And Economy —

(Continued From Page 1)

are able to return to their cherished policy, ended a couple of years ago by Nixon during the dramatic and short-lived oil "shortage", of restricting imports in order to raise oil prices. In short, while only a year ago we heard that gasoline prices must be kept below free-market levels by the government because "the poor" would be hurt by a price rise, we now hear that the government must artificially **raise** the price of gasoline (by something like 10¢ a gallon), and the poor are heard of no more.

One of the stated aims of oil protectionism is to assure the United States "self-sufficiency" in energy. Such an aim is simply economic insanity. Why not a prohibitory tax on bananas to stimulate hot-house growth of bananas in Florida, and make the U.S. "self-sufficient in bananas"? It is best for all of us, in all countries of the world, to have each country and territorial area, and each of the individuals and firms within such areas, specialize in the production of what each is relatively most efficient at producing, and then selling those products in exchange for the most efficient products of other firms and countries. In short, it is best for all of us to allow the free market, and the international division of labor, to operate across international boundaries ("freedom of trade"). Furthermore, economics shows us that even if another country places artificial barriers on trade, it is still better for us as consumers to allow free trade; any sort of retaliatory tariffs, quotas, or enforced cartels only cut off our noses to spite our faces. Or rather, cut off the noses of American **consumers** in order to confer special privileges to various American businesses. A protective tariff on "widgets" **not only** injures foreign "widget" producers and foreign consumers; it **also** injures American consumers by preventing them from purchasing cheaper widgets, in short, from using their income and resources most efficiently. Furthermore, productive resources in the U.S. are kept by U.S. government coercion from leaving the industry at which they are inefficient (widgets) and moving to other industries where they are more competitive with foreign producers.

This analysis, of course, applies to oil as well as anything else. An import tax on oil (e.g. tariff), as well as import quotas, injures American consumers and the productivity and health of the American economy for the benefit of American oil producers who cannot compete with imported crude.

The Establishment asserts over and over again that the OPEC countries have artificially and sharply raised the price of crude oil, through a government created and enforced cartel. Granted, but so what? The Establishment concludes that the U.S. must restrict oil imports, thereby raising the price of oil and petroleum products **still further**. Does that make any sense; is the way to combat an artificially raised oil price, for the U.S. to increase oil prices **still further**? Of course, it **does** make sense, from one point of view: from the viewpoint of protectionist American oil interests who want to get in on the cartellizing and restrictionist gravy train.

It is also said that we must tighten our belts and cartelize, because if we don't, the evil Arabs of OPEC **might** eventually place another embargo on oil. But does it make any sense to place our own "embargo" on oil permanently, for fear that the Arabs might temporarily do so some time in the future? Furthermore, if it's really the Arabs we're worried about, why are we going to place an equivalent $2 a barrel tax on domestic crude oil production? Clearly, the reason is for purposes of over-all cartellization, of government-coerced price-raising in the oil industry. What is more, the entire Arab scare is an Establishment-created bogeyman. For the U.S. does not import a very large amount of its oil from the Arab countries. It is, on the contrary, the countries of Western Europe that are almost totally dependent on Arab oil imports, and yet it is the U.S. and Henry Kissinger that are trying to induce the reluctant Europeans to go along with the tough anti-Arab oil policy. As Dr. Hollis Chenery correctly points out in the January issue of **Foreign Affairs**, Western Europe can better afford to pay the high price of Arab crude oil, than to "depress their economies by squeezing it out" and by following the Kissinger-Ford policy of anti-Arab-oil protectionism.

The Establishment also has the gall to assert that the higher tax on oil is a "market" policy, since the tax works by restricting supply, and raising price, on the market! It claims that the policy is necessary in order to "conserve" oil, and to stimulate the search for new energy sources in America. In the first place, the high-flown claim of

"conservation" is the standard excuse for all monopolizing and cartellization. The free, tax-less market does precisely enough "conserving" of oil on its own; when the Arabs raised the price of crude oil to $10 a barrel, this automatically induced each oil user to cut his purchases, to "conserve" oil, in whatever way was best suited for him. The free price system stimulates precisely as much or as little "conservation" of any resource as is necessary. On the basis of the Establishment reasoning, why not slap a $100 per barrel tax on crude oil, and thereby drive up oil and gasoline prices astronomically? If it wants to, the U.S. government can "conserve" oil forever by making sure that none of it is ever bought and sold; what then would we be conserving the oil for? And as for new energy sources, once again the free market price calls forth the optimum amount of such research. The higher price of $10 a barrel will stimulate as much research as will be economically optimal; once again, how about a $100 a barrel tax which would really and wildly stimulate a search for new energy sources?

To search for an explanation for a seemingly loony policy, we can therefore forget about the argument that we must combat restricted oil supplies and a higher price, precisely by restricting and raising the price still further! A more cogent clue is a report in the New York Times to the effect that, far from the much-heralded oil "shortage", we now have a welcome (to us consumers) oil **surplus**! Thus, the **Times** (Dec. 19) notes: "A slowdown in world economic activity and continued conservation efforts — whether voluntary or induced by higher priced petroleum products — have combined to create a worldwide oil surplus. Stocks on hand of all three major petroleum products . . . are all considered by industry experts to be more than adequate in the United States and other

(Continued On Page 3)

Society Without A State*

By Murray N. Rothbard

I

In attempting to outline how a "society without a State" — i.e. an anarchist society — might function successfully, I would first like to defuse two common but mistaken criticisms of this approach. First, is the argument that in providing for such defense or protection services as courts, police, or even law itself, I am simply smuggling the State back into society in another form, and that therefore the system I am both analyzing and advocating is not "really" anarchism. This sort of criticism can only involve us in an endless and arid dispute over semantics. Let me say from the beginning that I define the State as that institution which possesses one or both (almost always both) of the following properties: (1) it acquires its income by the physical coercion known as "taxation"; and (2) it asserts and usually obtains a coerced monopoly of the provision of defense service (police and courts) over a given territorial area. Any institution, not possessing either of these properties is not and cannot be, in accordance with my definition, a "State". On the other hand, I define anarchist society as one where there is no legal possibility for coercive aggression against the person or property of any individual. Anarchists oppose the State because it has its very being in such aggression, namely, the expropriation of private property through taxation, the coercive exclusion of other providers of defense service from its territory, and all of the other depredations and coercions that are built upon these twin foci of invasions of individual rights.

Nor is our definition of the State arbitrary, for these two characteristics have been possessed by what is generally acknowledged to be "States" throughout recorded history. The State, by its use of physical coercion, has arrogated to itself a compulsory monopoly of defense services over its territorial jurisdiction. But it is certainly conceptually possible for such services to be supplied by private, non-State institutions, and indeed such services have historically been supplied by other organizations than the State. To be opposed to the State is then not necessarily to be opposed to services that have often been linked with it; to be opposed to the State does not necessarily imply that we must be opposed to police protection, courts, arbitration, the minting of money, postal service, or roads and highways. Some anarchists have indeed been opposed to police and to all physical coercion in defense of person and property, but this is not inherent in and is fundamentally irrelevant to the anarchist position, which is precisely marked by opposition to all physical coercion invasive of, or aggressing against, person and property.

The crucial role of taxation may be seen in the fact that the State is the only institution or organization in society which regularly and systematically acquires its income through the use of physical coercion. All other individuals or organizations acquire their income voluntarily, either (a) through the voluntary sale of goods and services to consumers on the market, or (b) through voluntary gifts or donations by members or other donors. If I cease or refrain from purchasing Wheaties on the market, the Wheaties producers do not come after me with a gun or prison to force me to purchase; if I fail to join the American Philosophical Association, the association may not force me to join or prevent me from giving up my membership. Only the State can do so; only the State can confiscate my property or put me in jail if I do not pay its tax-tribute. Therefore, only the State regularly exists and has its very being by means of coercive depredations on private property.

Neither is it legitimate to challenge this sort of analysis by claiming that in some other sense, the purchase of Wheaties or membership in the A.P.A. is in some way "coercive"; there again, we can only be trapped in an endless semantic dispute. Apart from other rebuttals which cannot be considered here, I would simply say that anarchists are interested in the abolition of this type of action: e.g. aggressive physical violence against person and property, and that this is how we define "coercion". Anyone who is still unhappy with this use of the term "coercion" can simply eliminate the word from this discussion, and substitute for it "physical violence or the threat thereof", with the only loss being in literary style

rather than in the substance of the argument. What anarchism proposes to do, then, is to abolish the State, i.e. to abolish the regularized institution of aggressive coercion.

It need hardly be added that the State habitually builds upon its coercive source of income by adding a host of other aggressions upon society: ranging from economic controls to the prohibition of pornography to the compelling of religious observance to the mass

(Continued On Page 4)

Government And Economy —

(Continued From Page 2)

industrial countries to meet the needs of this winter . . . Europe and Japan are virtually awash in supplies." So here we have a vital clue: the new restrictions and cartellizing of the U.S. are an attempt to combat — not high oil prices — but the threat that market forces will break the OPEC cartel and bring about a sharp drop in oil prices. Once again, we are being conned by the Establishment, and both the Democratic and Republican parties are collaborating in the swindle.

Back to Gold.

Inexorably, and in the teeth of extreme reluctance and hostility by the U.S. authorities, gold is forcing its way, step by step, back into the central monetary role that it deserves. After cutting loose from the private gold market (in the "two-tier" system) in 1968, and after cutting the dollar completely from the gold standard in 1971, the Establishment was confident that gold was on the way to being banished forever, to be replaced by the dollar or by a new paper fiat unit, completely controllable by governments. Instead, gold has been forcing its way back, and at each step of the way the Administration has tried to "cover up" by claiming that gold was now one step further out of playing an important monetary role. More important even than the Treasury's finally and grudgingly allowing the will of Congress to prevail and allowing the U.S. citizens to buy and own gold, was the December, 1974 agreement at Martinique between the U.S. and France. For decades, the U.S. has been trying to push gold out of the picture by forcing other nations to evaluate it at an absurdly and artificially low price, first $35 an ounce, and lately $42 an ounce. But the enormous rise in the free gold market price in the last few years, in response to the continuing depreciation of paper currencies, put irresistible pressure on all countries to re-evaluate their gold stock at the market price, and thereby to stave off impending financial bankruptcy. Finally, at Martinique, the U.S. made the crucial concession, that "It would be appropriate for any government which wished to do so to adopt current market prices as the basis for valuation of its gold holdings." Typically, the U.S. covered its surrender by asserting, once again, that this was another step toward ending the monetary role of gold. Actually, of course, the step was quite the reverse: for now, as country after country upgrades its gold stock to evaluate it at the market price, the monetary role and importance of gold will enormously increase. Not only that: the re-valuation could pave the way for an eventual return to a full-fledged gold standard, i.e. the redeemability of dollars and other currencies in gold, which would not have been possible at the artificially low price. This possible return to gold is precisely what the inflationist U.S. authorities were desperately anxious to prevent.

Following up the Martinique agreement, the French fulfilled the promise of the agreement on January 9 by officially revaluing their gold stock at the roughly market price of $170 an ounce. Can other countries be far behind?

"Libertarian" Economist Note.

Professor Milton Friedman, alleged "libertarian" economist, was asked to comment in a radio interview on President Ford's address on January 13. Friedman endorsed the proposed tax on imported oil in order to put pressure on the OPEC countries. What happened to Friedman's proclaimed belief in unilateral free trade? Devotion to what cause has led to Friedman's abandonment of free trade-free market principles this time?   ◘

Society Without State —

(Continued From Page 3)

murder of civilians in organized warfare. In short, that the State, in the words of Albert Jay Nock, "claims and exercises a monopoly of crime" over its territorial area.

The second criticism I would like to defuse before beginning the main body of the paper is the common charge that anarchists "assume that all people are good", and that without the State no crime would be committed. In short, that anarchism assumes that with the abolition of the State a New Anarchist Man will emerge, cooperative, humane, and benevolent, so that no problem of crime will then plague the society. I confess that I do not understand the basis for this charge. Whatever other schools of anarchism profess — and I do not believe that they are open to this charge — I certainly do not adopt this view. I assume with most observers that mankind is a mixture of good and evil, of cooperative and criminal tendencies. In my view, the anarchist society is one which maximizes the tendencies for the good and the cooperative, while it minimizes both the opportunity and the moral legitimacy of the evil and the criminal. If the anarchist view is correct, and the State is indeed the great legalized and socially legitimated channel for all manner of anti-social crime — theft, oppression, mass murder — on a massive scale, then surely the abolition of such an engine of crime can do nothing but favor the good in man and discourage the bad.

A further point: in a profound sense, no social system, whether anarchist or statist, can work at all unless most people are "good" in the sense that they are not all hell-bent upon assaulting and robbing their neighbors. If everyone were so disposed, no amount of protection, whether State or private, could succeed in staving off chaos. Furthermore, the more that people are disposed to be peaceful and not aggress against their neighbors, the more successfully any social system will work, and the fewer resources will need to be devoted to police protection. The anarchist view holds that, given the "nature of man", given the degree of goodness or badness at any point of time, anarchism will maximize the opportunities for good and minimize the channels for the bad. The rest depends on the values held by the individual members of society. The only further point that need be made is that by eliminating the living example and the social legitimacy of the massive legalized crime of the State, anarchism will to a large extent promote peaceful values in the minds of the public.

We cannot of course deal here with the numerous arguments in favor of anarchism or against the State, moral, political, and economic. Nor can we take up the various goods and services now provided by the State, and show how private individuals and groups will be able to supply them far more efficiently on the free market. Here we can only deal with perhaps the most difficult area, the area where it is almost universally assumed that the State must exist and act, even if it is only a "necessary evil" instead of a positive good: the vital realm of defense or protection of person and property against aggression. Surely, it is universally asserted, the State is at least vitally necessary to provide police protection, the judicial resolution of disputes and enforcement of contracts, and the creation of the law itself that is to be enforced. My contention is that all of these admittedly necessary services of protection can be satisfactorily and efficiently supplied by private persons and institutions on the free market.

One important caveat before we begin the body of this paper: new proposals such as anarchism are almost always gauged against the implicit assumption that the present, or statist, system works to perfection. Any lacunae or difficulties with the picture of the anarchist society are considered net liabilities, and enough to dismiss anarchism out of hand. It is, in short, implicitly assumed that the State is doing its self-assumed job of protecting person and property to perfection. We cannot here go into the reasons why the State is bound to suffer inherently from grave flaws and inefficiencies in such a task. All we need do now is to point to the black and unprecedented record of the State through history: no combination of private marauders can possibly begin to match the State's unremitting record of theft, confiscation, oppression, and mass murder. No collection of Mafia or private bank robbers can begin to compare with all the Hiroshimas, Dresdens, and Lidices and their analogs through the history of mankind.

This point can be made more philosophically: it is illegitimate to compare the merits of anarchism and statism by starting with the present system as the implicit given and then critically examining only the anarchist alternative. What we must do is to begin at the zero point and then critically examine both suggested alternatives. Suppose, for example, that we were all suddenly dropped down on the earth de novo, and that we were all then confronted with the question of what societal arrangements to adopt. And suppose then that someone suggested: "We are all bound to suffer from those of us who wish to aggress against their fellow men. Let us than solve this problem of crime by handing all of our weapons to the Jones family, over there, by giving all of our ultimate power to settle disputes to that family. It that way, with their monopoly of coercion and of ultimate decision making, the Jones family will be able to protect each of us from each other." I submit that this proposal would get very short shrift, except perhaps from the Jones family themselves. And yet this is precisely the common argument for the existence of the State. When we start from those zero point, as in the case of the Jones family, the question of "who will guard the guardians?" becomes not simply an abiding lacuna in the theory of the State but an overwhelming barrier to its existence.

A final caveat: the anarchist is always at a disadvantage in attempting to forecast the shape of the future anarchist society. For it is impossible for observers to predict voluntary social arrangements, including the provision of goods and services, on the free market. Suppose, for example, that this were the year 1874, and someone predicted that eventually there would be a radio manufacturing industry. To be able to make such a forecast successfully, does he have to be challenged to state immediately how many radio manufacturers there would be a century hence, how big they would be, where they would be located, what technology and marketing techniques they would use, etc.? Obviously, such a challenge would make no sense, and in a profound sense the same is true of those who demand a precise portrayal of the pattern of protection activities on the market. Anarchism advocates the dissolution of the State into social and market arrangements, and these arrangements are far more flexible and less predictable than political institutions. The most that we can do, then, is to offer broad guidelines and perspectives on the shape of a projected anarchist society.

One important point to make here is that the advance of modern technology makes anarchistic arrangements increasingly feasible. Take, for example, the case of lighthouses, where it is often charged that it is unfeasible for private lighthouse operators to row out to each ship to charge it for use of the light. Apart from the fact that this argument ignores the successful existence of private lighthouses in earlier days, e.g. in England in the eighteenth century, another vital consideration is that modern electronic technology makes charging each ship for the light far more feasible. Thus, the ship would have to have paid for an electronically controlled beam which could then be automatically turned on for those ships which had paid for the service.

II

Let us now turn to the problem of how disputes — in particular, disputes over alleged violations of person and property, — would be resolved in an anarchist society. First, it should be noted that all disputes involve two parties: the plaintiff, the alleged victim of the crime or tort, and the defendant, the alleged aggressor. In many cases of broken contract, of course, each of the two parties alleging that the other is the culprit is at the same time a plaintiff and a defendant.

An important point to remember is that any society, be it statist or anarchist, has to have some way of resolving disputes that will gain a majority consensus in society. There would be no need for courts or arbitrators if everyone were omniscient, and knew instantaneously which persons were guilty of any given crime or violation of contract. Since none of us are omniscient, there has to be some method of deciding who is the criminal or lawbreaker which will gain legitimacy, in short whose decision will be accepted by the great majority of the public.

In the first place, a dispute may be resolved voluntarily between the two parties themselves, either unaided or with the help of a third mediator. This poses no problem, and will automatically be accepted by society at large. It is so accepted even now, much less in a society imbued with the anarchistic values of peaceful cooperation and agreement. Secondly and similarly, the two parties, unable to reach agreement, may decide to submit voluntarily to the decision of an arbitrator. This agreement may arise either after a dispute has arisen, or be provided for in advance in the original contract. Again, there is no problem in such an

(Continued On Page 5)

Society Without State —

(Continued From Page 4)

arrangement gaining legitimacy. Even in the present statist era, the notorious inefficiency and coercive and cumbersome procedures of the politically run government courts has led increasing numbers of citizens to turn to voluntary and expert arbitration for a speedy and harmonious settling of disputes.

Thus, William C. Wooldridge has written that

> "arbitration has grown to proportions that make the courts a secondary recourse in many areas and completely superfluous in others. The ancient fear of the courts that arbitration would 'oust' them of their jurisdiction has been fulfilled with a vengeance the common-law judges probably never anticipated. Insurance companies adjust over fifty thousand claims a year among themselves through arbitration, and the American Arbitration Association (AAA), with headquarters in New York and twenty-five regional offices across the country, last year conducted over twenty-two thousand arbitrations. Its twenty-three thousand associates available to serve as arbitrators may outnumber the total number of judicial personnel . . . in the United States . . . Add to this the unknown number of individuals who arbitrate disputes within particular industries or in particular localities, without formal AAA affiliation, and the quantitatively secondary role of official courts begins to be apparent." *

Wooldridge adds the important point that, in addition to the speed of arbitration procedures vis a vis the courts, the arbitrators can proceed as experts in disregard of the official government law; in a profound sense, then, they serve to create a voluntary body of private law. "In other words," states Wooldridge, "the system of extralegal, voluntary courts has progressed hand in hand with a body of private law; the rules of the state are circumvented by the same process that circumvents the forums established for the settlement of disputes over those rules . . . In short, a private agreement between two people, a bilateral "law", has supplanted the official law. The writ of the sovereign has ceased to run, and for it is substituted a rule tacitly or explicitly agreed to by the parties." Wooldridge concludes that "if an arbitrator can choose to ignore a penal damage rule or the statute of limitations applicable to the claim before him (and it is generally conceded that he has that power), arbitration can be viewed as a practically revolutionary instrument for self-liberation from the law . . ." *

It may be objected that arbitration only works successfully because the courts enforce the award of the arbitrator. Wooldridge points out, however, that arbitration was unenforceable in the American courts before 1920, but that this did not prevent voluntary arbitration from being successful and expanding in the United States and in England. He points, furthermore, to the successful operations of merchant courts since the Middle Ages, those courts which successfully developed the entire body of the law merchant. None of those courts possessed the power of enforcement. He might have added the private courts of shippers which developed the body of admiralty law in a similar way.

How then did these private, "anarchistic", and voluntary courts insure the acceptance of their decisions? By the method of social ostracism, and the refusal to deal any further with the offending merchant. This method of voluntary "enforcement", indeed, proved highly successful. Wooldridge writes that "the merchants' courts were voluntary, and if a man ignored their judgment, he could not be sent to jail . . . Nevertheless, it is apparent that . . . (their) decisions were generally respected even by the losers; otherwise people would never have used them in the first place . . . Merchants made their courts work simply by agreeing to abide by the results. The merchant who broke the understanding would not be sent to jail, to be sure, but neither would he long continue to be a merchant, for the compliance exacted by his fellows . . . proved if anything more effective than physical coercion." * Nor did this voluntary method fail to work in modern times. Wooldridge writes that it was precisely in the years before 1920, when arbitration awards could not be enforced in the courts,

> "that arbitration caught on and developed a following in the American mercantile community. Its popularity, gained at

a time when abiding by an agreement to arbitrate had to be as voluntary as the agreement itself, casts doubt on whether legal coercion was an essential adjunct to the settlement of most disputes. Cases of refusal to abide by an arbitrator's award were rare; one founder of the American Arbitration Association could not recall a single example. Like their medieval forerunners, merchants in the Americas did not have to rely on any sanctions other than those they could collectively impose on each other. One who refused to pay up might find access to his association's tribunal cut off in the future, or his name released to the membership of his trade association; these penalties were far more fearsome than the cost of the award with which he disagreed. Voluntary and private adjudications were voluntarily and privately adhered to, if not out of honor, out of the self-interest of businessmen who knew that the arbitral mode of dispute settlement would cease to be available to them very quickly if they ignored an award." *

It should also be pointed out that modern technology makes even more feasible the collection and dissemination of information about people's credit ratings and records of keeping or violating their contracts or arbitration agreements. Presumably, an anarchist society would see the expansion of this sort of dissemination of data and thereby facilitate the ostracism or boycotting of contract and arbitration violators.

How would arbitrators be selected in an anarchist society? In the same way as they are chosen now, and as they were chosen in the days of strictly voluntary arbitration: the arbitrators with the best reputation for efficiency and probity would be chosen by the various parties on the market. As in other processes of the market, the arbitrators with the best record in settling disputes will come to gain an increasing amount of business, and those with poor records will no longer enjoy clients, and have to shift to another line of endeavor. Here it must be emphasized that parties in dispute will seek out those arbitrators with the best reputation for both expertise and impartiality, and that inefficient or biased arbitrators will rapidly have to find another occupation.

Thus, the Tannehills emphasize:

> "the advocates of government see initiated force (the legal force of government) as the only solution to social disputes. According to them, if everyone in society were not forced to use the same court system . . . disputes would be insoluble. Apparently it doesn't occur to them that disputing parties are capable of freely choosing their own arbiters . . . They have not realized that disputants would, in fact, be far better off if they could choose among competing arbitration agencies so that they could reap the benefits of competition and specialization. It should be obvious that a court system which has a monopoly guaranteed by the force of statutory law will not give as good quality service as will free-market arbitration agencies which must compete for their customers . . .
>
> Perhaps the least tenable argument for government arbitration of disputes is the one which holds that governmental judges are more impartial because they operate outside the market and so have no vested interests .
>
> owing political allegiance to government is certainly no guarantee of impartiality! A governmental judge is always impelled to be partial — in favor of the government, from whom he gets his pay and his power! On the other hand, an arbiter who sells his services in a free market knows that he must be as scrupulously honest, fair, and impartial as possible or no pair of disputants will buy his services to arbitrate their dispute. A free-market arbiter depends on his livelihood on his skill and fairness at settling disputes. A governmental judge depends on political pull." *

If desired, furthermore, the contracting parties could provide in advance for a series of arbitrators:

> "It would be more economical and in most cases quite sufficient to have only one arbitration agency to hear the case. But if the parties felt that a further appeal might be necessary and were willing to risk the extra expense, they

(Continued On Page 6)

Society Without State

(Continued From Page 5)

could provide for a succession of two or even more arbitration agencies. The names of these agencies would be written into the contract in order from the 'first court of appeal' to the 'last court of appeal'. It would be neither necessary nor desirable to have one single, final court of appeal for every person in the society, as we have today in the United States Supreme Court." [5]

Arbitration, then poses little difficulty for a portrayal of the free society. But what of torts or crimes of aggression where there has been no contract? Or suppose that the breaker of a contract defies the arbitration award? Is ostracism enough? In short, how can courts develop in the free-market, anarchist society which will have the power to enforce judgments against criminals or contract-breakers?

In the wide sense, defense service consists of guards or police who use force in defending person and property against attack, and judges or courts whose role is to use socially accepted procedures to determine who the criminals or tortfeasors are, as well as to enforce judicial awards, such as damages or the keeping of contracts. On the free market, many scenarios are possible on the relationship between the private courts and the police; they may be "vertically integrated", for example, or their services may be supplied by separate firms. Furthermore, it seems likely that police service will be supplied by insurance companies who will provide crime-insurance to their clients. In that case, insurance companies will pay off the victims of crime or the breaking of contracts or arbitration awards, and then pursue the aggressors in court to recoup their losses. There is a natural market connection between insurance companies and defense service, since they need pay out less benefits in proportion as they are able to keep down the rate of crime.

Courts might either charge fees for their services, with the losers of cases obliged to pay court costs, or else they may subsist on monthly or yearly premiums by their clients, who may be either individuals or the police or insurance agencies. Suppose, for example, that Smith is an aggrieved party, either because he has been assaulted or robbed, or because an arbitration award in his favor has not been honored. Smith believes that Jones is the party guilty of the crime. Smith then goes to a court, Court A, of which he is a client, and brings charges against Jones as a defendant. In my view, the hallmark of an anarchist society is one where no man may legally compel someone who is not a convicted criminal to do anything, since that would be aggression against an innocent man's person or property. Therefore, Court A can only invite rather than subpoena Jones to attend his trial. Of course, if Jones refuses to appear or send a representative, his side of the case will not be heard. The trial of Jones proceeds. Suppose that Court A finds Jones innocent. In my view, part of the generally accepted Law Code of the anarchist society (on which see further below), is that this must end the matter, unless Smith can prove charges of gross incompetence or bias on the part of the court.

Suppose, next, that Court A finds Jones guilty. Jones might accept the verdict, either because he too is a client of the same court, because he knows he is guilty, or for some other reason. In that case, Court A proceeds to exercise judgment against Jones. Neither of these instances pose very difficult problems for our picture of the anarchist society. But suppose, instead, that Jones contests the decision; he, then, goes to his court, Court B, and the case is retried there. Suppose that Court B, too, finds Jones guilty. Again, it seems to me that the accepted Law Code of the anarchist society will assert that this ends the matter; both parties have had their say in courts which each has selected, and the decision for guilt is unanimous.

Suppose, however, the most difficult case: That Court B finds Jones innocent. The two courts, each subscribed to by one of the two parties, have split their verdicts. In that case, the two courts will submit the case to an appeals court, or arbitrator, which the two courts agree upon. There seems to be no real difficulty about the concept of an appeals court. As in the case of arbitration contracts, it seems very likely that the various private courts in the society will have prior agreements to submit their disputes to a particular appeals court. How will the appeals judges be chosen? Again, as in the case of arbitrators or of the first judges on the free market, they will be chosen for their expertise and reputation for efficiency, honesty and integrity. Obviously, appeals judges who are

inefficient or biased will scarcely be chosen by courts who will have a dispute. The point here is that there is no need for a legally-established or institutionalized single, monopoly appeals court system, as States now provide. There is no reason why there cannot arise a multitude of efficient and honest appeals judges who will be selected by the disputant courts, just as there are numerous private arbitrators on the market today. The appeals court renders its decision, and the courts proceed to enforce it if, in our example, Jones is considered guilty — unless, of course, Jones can prove bias in some other court proceedings.

No society can have unlimited judicial appeals, for in that case there would be no point to having judges or courts at all. Therefore, every society, whether statist or anarchist, will have to have some socially accepted cut-off point for trials and appeals. My suggestion is the rule that the agreement of any two courts be decisive. "Two" is not an arbitrary figure, for it reflects the fact that there are two parties, the plaintiff and the defendant, to any alleged crime or contract dispute.

If the courts are to be empowered to enforce decisions against guilty parties, does this not bring back the State in another form and thereby negate anarchism? No, for at the beginning of this paper I explicitly defined anarchism in such a way as not to rule out the use of defensive force — force in defense of person and property — by privately supported agencies. In the same way, it is not bringing back the State to allow persons to use force to defend themselves against aggression, or to hire guards or police agencies to defend them.

It should be noted, however, that in the anarchist society there will be no "district attorney" to press charges on behalf of "society". Only the victims will press charges as the plaintiffs. If, then, these victims should happen to be absolute pacifists who are opposed even to defensive force, then they will simply not press charges in the courts or otherwise retaliate against those who have aggressed against them. In a free society that would be their right. If the victim should suffer from murder, then his heir would have the right to press the charges.

What of the Hatfield-and-McCoy problem? Suppose that a Hatfield kills a McCoy, and that McCoy's heir does not belong to a private insurance, police agency, or court, and decides to retaliate himself? Since, under anarchism there can be no coercion of the non-criminal, McCoy would have the perfect right to do so. No one may be compelled to bring his case to a court. Indeed, since the right to hire police or courts flows from the right of self-defense against aggression, it would be inconsistent and in contradiction to the very basis of the free society to institute such compulsion. Suppose, then, that the surviving McCoy finds what he believes to be the guilty Hatfield and kills him in turn? What then? This is fine, except that McCoy may have to worry about charges being brought against him by a surviving Hatfield. Here it must be emphasized that in the law of the anarchist society based on defense against aggression, the courts would not be able to proceed against McCoy if in fact he killed the right Hatfield. His problem would arise if the courts should find that he made a grievous mistake, and killed the wrong man; in that case, he in turn would be found guilty of murder. Surely, in most instances, individuals will wish to obviate such problems by taking their case to a court and thereby gain social acceptability for their defensive retaliation — not for the act of retaliation but for the correctness of deciding who the criminal in any given case might be. The purpose of the judicial process, indeed, is to find a way of general agreement on who might be the criminal or contract-breaker in any given case. The judicial process is not a good in itself; thus, in the case of an assassination, such as Jack Ruby's murder of Oswald, on public television, there is no need for a complex judicial process since the name of the murderer is evident to all.

Will not the possibility exist of a private court that may turn venal and dishonest, or of a private police force that turns criminal and extorts money by coercion? Of course such an event may occur, given the propensities of human nature. Anarchism is not a moral cure-all. But the important point is that market forces exist to place severe checks on such possibilities, especially in contrast to a society where a State exists. For, in the first place, judges, like arbitrators, will prosper on the market in proportion to their reputation for efficiency and impartiality. Secondly, on the free market important checks and balances exist against venal courts or criminal police forces. Namely, that there are competing courts and police agencies to whom the victims may turn for redress. If the "Prudential Police Agency" should turn outlaw and extract revenue from victims by coercion, the latter would have the option of turning to the "Mutual" or "Equitable" Police Agency for defense and for pressing

(Continued On Page 7)

Society Without State —

(Continued From Page 6)

charges against Prudential. These are the **genuine** "checks and balances" of the free market, genuine in contrast to the phony checks and balances of a State system, where all the alleged "balancing" agencies are in the hands of one monopoly government. Indeed, given the monopoly "protection service" of a State, what is there to prevent a State from using its monopoly channels of coercion to extort money from the public? What are the checks and limits of the State? None, except for the extremely difficult course of revolution against a Power with all of the guns in its hands. In fact, the State provides an easy, legitimated channel for crime and aggression, since it has its very being in the crime of tax-theft, and the coerced monopoly of "protection." It is the State, indeed, that functions as a mighty "protection racket" on a giant and massive scale. It is the State that says: "Pay us for your 'protection' or else." In the light of the massive and inherent activities of the State, the danger of a "protection racket" emerging from one or more private police agencies is relatively small indeed.

Moreover, it must be emphasized that a crucial element in the power of the State is its legitimacy in the eyes of the majority of the public, the fact that after centuries of propaganda, the depredations of the State are looked upon rather as benevolent services. Taxation is generally not seen as theft, nor war as mass murder, nor conscription as slavery. Should a private police agency turn outlaw, should "Prudential" become a protection racket, it would then lack the social legitimacy which the State has managed to accrue to itself over the centuries. "Prudential" would be seen by all as bandits, rather than as legitimate or divinely appointed "sovereigns", bent on promoting the "common good" or the "general welfare". And lacking such legitimacy, Prudential would have to face the wrath of the public and the defense and retaliation of the other private defense agencies, the police and courts, on the free market. Given these inherent checks and limits, a successful transformation from a free society to bandit rule becomes most unlikely. Indeed, historically, it has been very difficult for a State to arise to supplant a stateless society; usually, it has come about through external conquest rather than by evolution from within a society.

Within the anarchist camp, there has been much dispute on whether the private courts would have to be bound by a basic, common Law Code. Ingenious attempts have been made to work out a system where the laws or standards of decision-making by the courts would differ completely from one to another. [5] But in my view all would have to abide by the basic Law Code, in particular, prohibition of aggression against person and property, in order to fulfill our definition of anarchism as a system which provides no legal sanction for such aggression. Suppose, for example, that one group of people in society hold that all redheads are demons who deserve to be shot on sight. Suppose that Jones, one of this group, shoots Smith, a redhead. Suppose that Smith or his heir presses charges in a court, but that Jones' court, in philosophic agreement with Jones, finds him innocent therefore. It seems to me that in order to be considered legitimate, any court would have to follow the basic libertarian law code of the inviolate right of person and property. For otherwise, courts might legally subscribe to a code which sanctions such aggression in various cases, and which to that extent would violate the definition of anarchism and introduce, if not the State, then a strong element of statishness or legalized aggression into the society.

But again I see no insuperable difficulties here. For in that case, anarchists, in agitating for their creed, will simply include in their agitation the idea of a general libertarian Law Code as part and parcel of the anarchist creed of abolition of legalized aggression against person or property in the society.

In contrast to the general law code, other aspects of court decisions could legitimately vary in accordance with the market or the wishes of the clients e.g., the language the cases will be conducted in, the number of judges to be involved, etc.

There are other problems of the basic Law Code which there is no time to go into here: for example, the definition of just property titles or the question of legitimate punishment of convicted offenders — though the latter problem of course exists in statist legal systems as well. [6] The basic point, however, is that the State is not needed to arrive at legal principles or their elaboration: indeed, much of the common law, the law

New Rothbard Books!

January 17 is the publication date of the first volume of Murray Rothbard's projected multi-volume history of colonial America, **Conceived in Liberty.** Published by Arlington House and over 500 pages in length, Volume I covers the American colonies during the 17th century. Note: this is **not** an economic history, but a general history dealing with all aspects of the new American colonies: ideological, religious, social, and political, as well as economic. The general focus of the book is — surprise! — on liberty and voluntary social arrangements ("social power") vs. the State. Price is $15.00

Why the need for so many pages on the colonial era? Despite the fact that American history textbooks dismiss the colonial era in 20 or so pages, this period covers almost 170 years, and more if we include the pre-colonial explorations. An enormous number of exciting and important events occurred during these years, and **Conceived in Liberty** brings us the full narrative flavor of the period, the actual events that occurred in their historical cause-and-effect sequence. Furthermore, while many standard textbook "heroes" are debunked and shown to have feet of clay, other, totally forgotten libertarian heroes are rediscovered.

****

Also, the Libertarian Review Press (422 First St. S.E., Washington, D.C. 20003) has just reprinted, in booklet form, Murray Rothbard's 1962 essay, "The Case for a 100 Percent Gold Dollar", which had appeared in a totally neglected book by L. Yeager, ed., **In Search of a Monetary Constitution** (Harvard University Press). Needless to say, the topic is far more timely now than it was 13 years ago. Copies of **The Case for a 100 Percent Gold Dollar** may be obtained for $2.00 from the Libertarian Review Press. ◻

"Herein, indeed, lies the chief merit of democracy, when all is said and done: it may be clumsy, it may be swinish, it may be unutterably incompetent and dishonest, but it is never dismal — its processes, even when they irritate, never actually bore."

— H. L. Mencken

merchant, admiralty law, and private law in general, grew up apart from the State, by judges not making the law but finding it on the basis of agreed upon principles derived either from custom or reason. [7] The idea that the State is needed to **make** law is as much a myth as that the State is needed to supply postal or police service.

Enough has been said here, I believe, to indicate that an anarchist system for settling disputes would be both viable and self-subsistent: that once adopted, it could work and continue indefinitely. **How to arrive at** that system is of course a very different problem, but certainly at the very least it will not likely come about unless people are convinced of its workability, are convinced, in short, that the State is not a **necessary** evil.

*A paper delivered before the American Society for Political and Legal Philosophy, Washington, D. C., on Dec. 28, 1974.

*William C. Wooldridge, **Uncle Sam, the Monopoly Man** (New Rochelle, N.Y.: Arlington House, 1970), p. 101.

[2] **Ibid.**, pp. 103-04.

[3] **Ibid.**, pp. 95-96.

[4] **Ibid.**, pp. 100-101.

[5] Morris and Linda Tannehill, **The Market for Liberty** (Lansing, Michigan: privately printed, 1970), pp. 65-67.

[6] **Ibid.**, p. 68.

[7] E.g. David Friedman, **The Machinery of Freedom** (New York: Harper & Row, 1973).

[8] For an elaboration of these points, see Murray N. Rothbard, **For A New Liberty** (New York: Macmillan, 1973).

[9] Thus, see Bruno Leoni, **Freedom and the Law** (Princeton, N.J.: D. Van Nostrand Co., 1961). ◻

The Demise Of Fractional Reserve Banking?

By Karl E. Peterjohn

Fractional reserve banking is in trouble. Last year two major banks, Franklin National and I.D. Herstatt, collapsed. They left behind a trail of liabilities across the international banking system which are still being felt. The cause of these bank failures is likely to repeat itself, while banks taking action to correct their currently weak financial reserve positions may become the targets of scurrilous politicians.

When the Federal Reserve System (hereafter the Fed) expands credit (also known as counterfeiting), this expansion of the money stock takes place through the banking structure. New funds are now available for loans to firms and individuals from the banks. Interest rates decline due to increased funds being available. The banks, anxious to make a profit with these new funds, and following the government's expansion-oriented economic policy, loan the funds to borrowers. Through the fractional reserve structure, an increase in bank deposits of $100 can be multiplied into loans worth many times that value.

Naturally when the credit expansion creates inflation, government policy changes. The Fed stops expanding credit to fight inflation. Since the increase in the supply of loanable funds came from the Fed's money creation, rather than from market action, the supply of loanable funds contracts. Interest rates rise and a credit crunch occurs.

As interest rates rise, investors try to maximize the returns on their savings. Since the banks have loaned out funds for 10 or 20 years at the low interest rates created by the Fed's credit expansion, the credit crunch would force the banks to raise interest rates to attract more savings or liquidate loans. The banks could be forced to pay higher interest rates for savings than the interest bank is receiving on outstanding loans. To prevent this from happening, and to restrict competition, the banks convinced the Fed to enact Regulation "Q", which limits the maximum interest rate savers can receive from banks.

As interest rates rise, savings flow from banks with their low interest rates to bonds, credit unions, loan companies, and other financial devices which offer higher interest rates for savers. Economists call this process disintermediation. To make sure that the banks can cover loans made at the low interest rate, the government has created a number of agencies, besides the Fed, which will prevent disintermediation from causing bank runs. The Federal Home Loan Bank Board, the Veterans Administration, and the Department of Housing and Urban Development all provide funds to banks to protect low interest loans. In this manner any test of the financial soundness of the Financial Deposit Insurance Corporation is avoided.

As 1975 begins, we have been through the credit expansion-boom-inflation-credit crunch cycle four times in the last fifteen years. The U.S.

fractional banking system can't take much more of it. Inflation is consuming capital and the real value of savings at a tremendous pace. Since the returns on stocks are being clobbered by inflation and taxes, the only ready sources of investment funds for most firms are bank loans. However, the Fed's credit expansion is the only new source of loanable funds for the banks. Since the banks are the only ready source of investment funds, the banks are increasingly involved with the firms they make loans to. For this reason a number of superficial economists are pointing out how the banks are "taking over" control of a wide variety of non-financial corporations through loan arrangements. In Great Britain this government loan process has reached the point where the government is making loans outright to industry. Here the government has created the Fed, which uses the banks to make and oversee the loans to firms.

Since so many banks came close to collapse (even the ones not involved in foreign currency transactions) during the last credit expansion-boom-inflation-credit crunch cycle, the Fed issued orders that banks are supposed to increase their reserves. Banks will be less likely to flounder in our next credit cycle if substantial reserve assets are available to protect against the next credit crunch.

The Fed has in the last few weeks been expanding credit rapidly in a belated effort to stem our recession. As the new credit cycle begins with the renewed credit expansion, the banks will be faced with a difficult decision. If the banks go along with the Fed and lower their prime interest rate, lending out all available funds, the spectre of bank failure arises as soon as the Fed decides to switch gears and fight inflation by stopping the flow of new dollars. The resultant credit crunch, where interest rates rise to 15 to 20%, could bring down many banks that are overextended. If this happens, the banks will be blamed for overextending themselves and not following Fed policy.

However, if the banks try to protect themselves by not expanding credit and do keep substantial reserves, the banks are now going against government policy. Many firms unable to get loans, or to get loans at a "fair" interest rate, as well as irate consumers unable to purchase 8% home mortgages, will cry bank conspiracy. Politicians will be able to claim that the banks are thwarting the government's economic policy and preventing economic recovery. The politicians will then have the perfect whipping boy. To prevent being crucified by the politicians, and unwilling to forego interest on loans, most banks will make loans and hope that the Fed will be able to protect them when the credit crunch arrives. It is, for the economy and for the banks a forlorn hope.   ◻

The Libertarian Forum
BOX 341
MADISON SQUARE STATION
NEW YORK, NEW YORK 10010

First Class

A Monthly Newsletter

THE
Libertarian Forum

Joseph R. Peden, Publisher

Murray N. Rothbard, Editor

VOLUME VII, NO. 2   FEBRUARY, 1975   US-ISSN0047-4517

OIL WAR AND OIL IMPERIALISM

1. Revving Up For Oil War in the Middle East

It all began two years ago, when Bill Buckley's **National Review** called for the American invasion of Libya. It was our esteemed publisher, Joe Peden, who first spotted this call as a harbinger of things to come, as the discovery of a brand new post-Vietnam "enemy", rather than the aberrant saber-rattling with which most analysts dismissed the Buckley war-cry. (See Joseph R. Peden, "From the Halls of Montezuma . . . ", **Lib. Forum**, April 1973).

Now, of course, Kissinger and Ford are leading the well-orchestrated call for U.S. invasion of the Middle East. This phase began with a note circulated at a meeting of Ford's energy advisers in mid-December 1974 at Camp David. The note read: "Let's try the low-cost option — war". (**International Bulletin**, Jan. 17, 1975.) This is typical economists' jargon, that of course deliberately avoids the question: "low-cost" for **whom**? For the American boys who will fight and die? For the American taxpayer who will be forced to pay the bill? For the Arabs who get killed (or don't they count?) For people of all countries who might get incinerated in a new world war? Or for the American oil companies who want to extract some of the cartel profits from the Arabs?

The call for invasion also provides an excellent and unwitting support for the Leninist theory of imperialism, and for those of us who (cynically? realistically?) attribute economic motives to American foreign policy in the past decades and generations. For the Leninists, Williamsites, and "economic determinists" have attributed U.S. wars and interventions to desires to grab economic loot, ranging from war contracts to the seizure of raw materials. But what is the Kissinger-Ford war threat in the Middle East but a blatant and outright economic imperialist grab, namely that certain American oil companies are trying to use force to grab oil rather than have to pay the current price asked by the Arab countries? This is in contrast to orthodox historians, who attribute wars to motives of national honor or military strategy. And yet, in the current crisis, it is the Pentagon that is reluctant to pursue the war-mongering course. As Drew Middleton reported in the New York **Times** (Jan. 10), "Senior American and Western European military officers consider the seizure of selected Middle East oil fields militarily feasible but politically disastrous." In contrast, as Jack Anderson reports in his column of Jan. 6, it is the civilian policymakers of the Ford Administration who "are calling for a showdown with the oil-producing countries before it is too late. They want President Ford to serve notice upon the oil potentates that present oil prices . . . constitute hostile action . . .

While Drew Middleton reports that the Pentagon's preferred site for a U.S. oil invasion is Libya, (shades of Buckley-Peden!), the most comprehensive plan for U.S. oil invasion was presented, as Joe

Stromberg writes below, by "isolationist" Prof. Robert W. Tucker in **Commentary** ("Oil: The Issue of American Intervention," **Commentary**, Jan. 1975). Tucker advocates American invasion of a "mostly shallow coastal strip" some 400 miles long on the Arabian peninsula fronting on the Persian Gulf. Seizure of such a strip, from Kuwait down Saudi Arabia to Qatar, would give the U.S. control of 40 percent of OPEC production and 50 percent of OPEC reserves. (**This** is "isolationism"?!) Tucker opines that "since it (the strip) has no substantial centers of population, and is without trees, its effective control does not bear even remote comparison with the experience of Vietnam."

As I. F. Stone demonstrates in his brilliant critique of Tucker in the **New York Review of Books** (I. F. Stone, "War for Oil?", **New York Review of Books**, Feb. 6, 1975), Tucker's thesis, apart from its gross immorality, displays a buffoonish ignorance of the nature and the history of guerrilla warfare. Trees are not necessary; the very name "guerrilla" originated in the successful Spanish struggle against Napoleon by guerrilla bands in the arid and treeless mountains of northern Spain. And has Prof. Tucker never heard of T. E. Lawrence and his scintillating success in Arab guerrilla warfare against the Turks in the treeless deserts of the Middle East during World War I? Perhaps this is yet another indication that "political scientists" are ignorant of history. "Trees" indeed!

Tucker ignores the fact that Saudi Arabia has plenty of people and plenty of weapons — largely supplied by the U.S. itself. In the last two years, the U.S. and other Western countries have supplied $3 billion of military equipment to Saudi Arabia and the other Persian Gulf states, including the F-14 fighter, the harpoon anti-ship missile, and various SAM systems. It is, in fact, highly ironic that in precisely these states there are no Commies around for the U.S. to wax hysterical about — these states have been among the most reliable American allies. And, while the Pentagon in Middleton's account worries about "political difficulties" in the U.S. and Western Europe, it ignores the important difficulties in the Arabian peninsula itself. For just as there are no Commies in these countries, so there are no reliable American puppets such as Thieu, Chiang, or Rhee. If we overthrow King Feisal or the Persian Gulf emirs, we will have no allies whatsoever in the population, whether among the ruling class or among the populace. Every man's hand will be against us — a perfect requisite for successful guerrilla war.

As Stone points out, "The population is ample and trained enough for a fierce desert guerrilla campaign. The idea that you can slice away a coastal strip of a country's territory, containing most of its wealth, and just sit there, happily enjoying the fruits of occupation and shipping out the oil spurting from its wells, belongs in an anthology of military-

(Continued On Page 2)

Oil War — (Continued From Page 1)

political delusions.'' Thus, after we take over the coastal strip, what will we do with Saudi Arabia's capital city of Riyadh? It is only 200 miles from the coast. As Stone writes, ''Do we seize it, or leave it as a center of resistance? What about a new capital further inland, or across the Peninsula in Mecca or Medina? How subdue the country without destroying its government and occupying the whole of it? This desert area is bigger than a dozen South Vietnams combined. And how do you protect American lives and property in the rest of the Arab world?''

And what of our client states, Japan and Western Europe? ''How do we supply Western Europe and Japan with oil while we repair the blown-up Arabian wells, try to repel guerrilla attacks, and somehow placate the anger in the other oil-producing states? Can this be done quickly enough to prevent the gravest kind of social disorder and economic breakdown in the two areas we are presumed to be defending — Japan and Western Europe . . .?

And what of the Soviet Union? Even Tucker acknowledges that the Russians would probably move armed forces into Iraq to protect its leading Arab oil ally. His answer to this? That we should establish ''a substantial American military presence in Kuwait'' to confront the Russians in Iraq. Tucker and his colleagues are not ''realists'' but dangerous fanatics, playing with matches in a tinder-box that could set off World War III. They are ''crackpot realists.'' For what if the Russians misread the Kuwait occupation as an ''offensive'' instead of a ''defensive'' signal? As Stone points out, ''No more need be said to suggest the dangers of an American invasion in an area so close to the Soviet Union. A comparable event geographically would be a Russian invasion of Venezuela or seizure of the oil refineries in the Dutch West Indies.

And even if World War III is avoided, what in the world would be the ''costs'' of such an invasion? As Stone concludes, ''And while we are thus supposedly trying to save ourselves and our allies from high oil prices, what will be the cost of all these military measures? Vietnam has cost well over $100 billion and the end still is not in sight. This new episode in militarism might easily cost several times as much as the new price of oil.'' But, of course, its cost will be to the hapless American soldiers and taxpayers, and not to the oil companies.

In the following articles, Joseph Stromberg presents an ''Old Right'' critique of the Tucker-Ford oil threats, and the great libertarian and isolationist Rep. Howard H. Buffett (R.-Neb.) is represented by a speech he delivered in Congress on March 2, 1944, attacking Harold Ickes' imperialist proposal for an Arabian oil pipe line to be built by the U.S. government. Howard Buffett's hard-hitting analysis is, of course, all too relevant today.

2. Oil on the Brain: An Old Right Critique

By Joseph R. Stromberg

As if to prove the adage that consistency is the hobgoblin of little minds, Professor Robert Tucker of Johns Hopkins University, who obviously thinks big where possible waste of human life is concerned, has emerged in recent weeks in the vanguard of the ''kill a wog for petrol'' school of foreign policy. He has stolen a march on all but the most ardent Zionists by providing a rationale for US Middle East intervention in an essay published, appropriately enough, in Commentary (Jan., 1975). The National Observer has reprinted part of the Tucker piece (Jan. 25, 1975), presumably on the ground that such an inflammatory argument deserves wider readership. Most recently, Tucker appeared on William F. Buckley, Jr.'s Firing Line, where he and the archinterventionist Buckley deplored the ''pacifism'' of ''post-Vietnam'' public opinion,* particularly among the young, and struck a blow for getting ''force'' back on center stage. To avoid being ''asphyxiated'' by the Arab nations, we have to be able to think the old unthinkable, even unto the sacred mushroom, putting aside the petty considerations of international law and mere humanity.

This would not seem nearly so bad but for the fact that until now many of us sincerely believed Prof. Tucker to be a true comrade in the cause of peaceful coexistence and isolationism. On the basis of his The Radical Left and American Foreign Policy (Baltimore, 1971), which provided a useful and sympathetic corrective to New Left revisionist history, and The New Isolationism (New York, 1972), which ably refuted standard arguments for an American role as world gestapo, it was easy to regard

Prof. Tucker as a near relation of libertarian and peace forces. Like the Rational Lady who backed the Crook, Tucker has found The Big ''Emergency.'' This emergency is supposed ''strangulation'' of the West by the great unbreakable oil cartel, which threatens to raise the price of fuel by a few cents. But as Tucker and Buckley explicitly agree, the real crime of the Arabs is that they wish to modify American foreign policy — using oil as a weapon (unlike Sen. Jackson, who would use trade as a weapon to influence another nation's domestic policy). They unreasonably want America to cease being the main supply depot of their enemies. Briefly, they want America to abandon a policy she shouldn't have in the first place. If Tucker can defect so quickly, one shudders to think who will be next: William Appleman Williams? Staughton Lynd? Murray Rothbard? Presumably not, but the present warlike climate leaves one a little shaky.

The anti-economic reasoning of the ''strangulationists'' has its obvious attractions. The authors of America's new depression would like nothing better than to pawn their creation off on some unpopular foreign devils. The idea that increased petroleum prices can cause general price inflation is, of course, on a par with the conservative myth that trade unions cause general price inflation, and deserves no respect. Among recent commentators the respected socialist historian Geoffrey Barraclough has stated the case most clearly. Writing in The New York Review of Books (Jan. 23, 1975), he scorns the New York Times line of Arab guilt for the world economic crisis and revises the eco-freak hysteria about the impending shortage of everything. (So don't rush out and buy The Last Whole Ramparts!) The crisis we are in is the logical outcome of advanced state monopoly capitalism. (Of course, Barraclough would abolish the market as the great cure.) Likewise the food crisis: Barraclough shows that there is simply no shortage of arable land in the famine-ridden Third World. Hence the food crisis has purely institutional causes: feudal land monopoly in those countries, and American dumping of agricultural surpluses on their markets (foreign aid — i.e., export subsidies paid by our taxes). The indicated solution, he says, is radical land reform — an eminently libertarian position.

Ironically, Tucker, who is a great critic of Gabriel Kolko, now behaves as if he subjectively believes in Kolko's much disputed ''raw materials'' thesis, i.e., Kolko's view that US foreign policy is largely determined by a felt need to control the sources of strategic raw materials. Having argued that US policy is not so determined, Tucker now argues that it should be! There is more irony in the fact that the impending ''scarcity'' of petroleum has been ballyhooed before, about as convincingly. In 1943-44 Secretary of the Interior Harold Ickes began prophesying a disastrous shortage — only a few years away — if Congress failed to appropriate funds for an Arabian oil pipeline. This would have been a whopping subsidy to the American oil companies involved, and a real soporific for uneasy rear admirals wondering where their fuel was to come from.

The place of oil in the bitter subsurface Anglo-American imperial rivalry has been brought out in lavish detail by Kolko in The Politics of War (New York, 1968), esp. pp. 294-313. Kolko shows how American oil firms and the American state sought to reduce the British to a subordinate role in Middle East economic imperialism. Fortunately, Secretary Ickes' pipeline scheme, at least, was defeated. The libertarians of the day vigorously assailed the scheme. The Old Right anti-imperialist newsletter Human Events was quite vehement in its opposition. Writing in the Feb. 23, 1944 issue, Felix Morley commented that the proposal was symptomatic of a ''strongly imperialistic'' post-war policy. Such involvement in the Middle East would drag America into the middle of Russo-British rivalries in the region (Iran especially) as well as into potential conflict between Arab nationalism and Zionism in Palestine. It was no accident, Morley asserted, that permanent conscription was being urged upon the Congress simultaneously. He summarized a number of reasons advanced for the pipeline, including ''the alleged exhaustion of our oil reserves.'' Ickes was predicting total depletion of known reserves within fourteen years. (Sound familiar?) Another argument possible lack of fuel for the next major war. Morley wrote that he expected that possible ''drastic gas rationing'' would be advanced as another reason for the pipeline. Morley asked what the Secretary of the Interior was doing anyway, booming a project ''as remote from the interior'' of the US as geographically possible? He warned against becoming ''permanently involved in the perils of this Middle East entanglement,'' calling for Congressional determination of policy.

Congressman Howard Buffett, Republican of Omaha, likewise

(Continued On Page 3)

Tax Rebellion In Willimantic

One of the most hopeful events on the current scene was the heroic tax rebellion in the city of Willimantic, Connecticut. Willimantic still has the old New England town meeting system in which any citizen can come and vote on the city budget. Last December 2, an unexpected and wondrous event occurred: the town meeting rejected the submitted budget of $2.6 million. The citizens insisted that the budget and the tax level was much too high. Twice more, last month, the citizens of Willimantic rejected a submitted budget, first a 3% tax cut, and next a cut of 7%. Then, at the end of December, they refused to grant the city permission to borrow money while trying to work out an acceptable budget. The officials of Willimantic were desperate; good God, the bureaucrats were in danger of remaining unpaid! Unfortunately, the city attorney found an obscure statute allowing for emergency borrowing even though permission had been refused by the public. But the sword of Damocles remained, to hang over the bureaucracy.

Finally, on January 15, the citizens of Willimantic approved a further reduced budget, this time with taxes cut by 9%. It was at least a partial victory for the rebels. Unfortunately, however, the citizens became scared to pursue the rebellion further; when one of the leaders, Richard M. Jackson, proposed a 50% budget cut, it was rejected overwhelmingly. But still, it was a healthy "message" beamed to the bureaucracy. As Mayor David Calchera stated, "there were people here who wanted more than a 50 per cent tax cut, they were so mad."

What were they mad about? As far as we can tell, there were no libertarians in Willimantic to focus the dissatisfaction and to take leadership and intensify the rebellion. But even without that, the citizens were mad: suffering as they were from a high rate of unemployment (the major employer is the American Threat Company, which had to cut employment severely due to the recession), the lowest per capita income in the state, combined with a massively high tax rate, aggravated by the fact that the 17,000 residents of the city of Willimantic have to pay taxes twice: once to Willimantic and once to the town of Windham, in which the former is included. As a result, the harassed citizens of Willimantic had to pay a property tax rate of $81 for every $1,000 of assessed valuation, which compares to $73.50 paid by the residents of New York City. On top of all that, last fall the city's inefficient and debt-ridden water company raised its water rates by 60%. Then came the great December budget revolt, which arrived even though the proposed budget called for no increase over 1973 levels.

A further prod to anger among the citizens was the fiasco of urban renewal in Willimantic. In 1967, the city began a massive urban renewal project which gutted over 13 acres of downtown land, and since then, has done nothing to replace the destroyed buildings. The downtown has of course since become a disaster area.

And so, the conditions in Willimantic were ripe for the spark of tax revolt. Surely, similar conditions exist throughout the country. Libertarians should be alert for such situations and take the lead wherever the opportunity appears.

(On the Willimantic case see the New York Times, Jan. 17, p. 35)◻

Oil War — (Continued From Page 3)

denounced both the specific pipeline proposal and Middle East intervention. Buffett was a fiery and uncompromising Old Right "isolationist," and his remarks are reprinted here in full. Their timeliness speaks for itself.

(from the Appendix to the **Congressional Record**, Vol. 90, Part 8. 78th Congress, 2nd Session, p. A1036.)

3. The People Should Choose Between Empire and Freedom

By Rep. Howard H. Buffett

(March 2, 1944)

Mr. Speaker, Secretary Ickes plans that the American government shall spend $165,000,000 or more on an Arabian pipe line. The objective is to provide substantial oil supplies to supplement America's diminishing oil reserves.

This proposal presents squarely to the American people the issue of empire versus freedom. No, I am mistaken; the proposal does not present to the American people the issue of empire versus freedom. The people are having nothing to say about this gigantic long-distance venture into imperialism. Not even the representatives of the people, the Congress of the United States, are given the opportunity of passing on this issue of empire versus freedom. No, the people or their elected Congress are not consulted on this venture. Why not?

A few short years from now, the sovereign Government of the United States may conscript your boy and mine and send them to fight, bleed, and die on the trackless sands of Arabia to defend this pipe line. Why? Because then it will be the patriotic duty of that boy to defend the honor and the possessions of the United States, as represented by this investment. The fighting and the dying is always done by the people. Why, then, should not the fundamental decision on this fundamental issue be made by the people or their elected representatives?

I use the phrase, "empire versus freedom." What does the term "freedom" have to do with empire? Simply this: That to defend this far-away imperialistic economic venture a volunteer army large enough could not be raised. This war has demonstrated that no modern government commands sufficient confidence of its people to depend on a volunteer army.

It is difficult to appraise properly the evil consequences of this scheme. Perhaps first a comparison would be helpful. Suppose that Russia made a deal with Mexico to finance and develop tremendous oil or other resources in Mexico? How would America regard such a scheme? The probabilities are fairly clear. It would arouse violent opposition in this country, sooner or later, and probably sooner. Similar results can be expected from a United States Government venture in Arabia.

This proposal is advocated on the basis of barrels of crude petroleum it will add to our own diminishing reserves. Against this hazardous addition to our oil reserves must be measured the many-sided effects of this imperialistic adventure on both America and the rest of the world.

The Arabian pipe line would mark a clear-cut change in American policy abroad. It is, of course, a violation of the spirit, if not the letter, of the Atlantic Charter.

It would terminate the inspiring period of America's history as a great nation not resorting to intercontinental imperialism. This venture would end the influence exercised by the United States as a government not participating in the exploitation of small lands and countries.

These traditions are America's greatest asset in international affairs. This venture will destroy them within and without. It would mark the elimination of the fundamentals of genuine morality in our foreign policy.

I am no expert on the economic or military value of this proposed venture. However, it is safe to say that militarily it would be at least as indefensible as the Philippines. From an economic standpoint there is no practical way to judge it because it would probably mean war sooner or later — and no one can measure by any finite standards the monetary and material costs of twentieth-century warfare.

This proposal either should be dropped or should be presented fairly and squarely to the American people or their Congress. Let the people decide.

It may be that the American people would rather forego the use of a questionable amount of gasoline at some time in the remote future rather than follow a foreign policy practically guaranteed to send many of their sons, if not their daughters, to die in faraway places in defense of the trade of Standard Oil or the international dreams of our one-world planners.

*akin, no doubt, to the "post-Watergate morality"!   ◻

Foreign Affairs

By Leonard P. Liggio

Last May, the Danish Progress Party, the anti-tax party which was second largest in the parliament, averted a government crisis by supporting a sales tax. In January, 1975 the governing Liberal party called elections, and jumped from 22 seats to 42 seats. The largest party, the Social Democrats, gained seven seats to total 53. The Liberal premier, a former pastor, called the elections when he could not get support in parliament for wage and price freezes. His gains in the elections came at the expense of his supporters and was considered cannibalism by political commentators. The conservatives lost six seats, the Radical Liberals lost seven, and the Progress party lost four of the 28 seats gained in the December 1973 elections. Led by Mogens Glistrup, the Progress party can be the balance of power between the Socialist and the Liberal coalitions. But, can one be surprised that despite the good showing of 14 per cent the Progress party's vote for increased taxes rather than abolition of taxes cast it some credibility? A few weeks after the election, the Liberal premier resigned after losing a vote of confidence by one vote.

Taxes and the economy have been the basis of the crisis which continues to befall Italy. The short-lived government of Mariano Rumor, composed of Christian Democrats, Republicans, Socialists and Social Democrats, had fallen over the need to reduce government spending. Last fall, the president of the Senate, former premier Amintore Fanfani, was called upon to form a government. Fanfani was a leading Catholic intellectual whose social ideas parallelled those of corporatism. He has been a strong supporter of NATO and the US, and follows the usual path of being very socialistic domestically and anti-communist internationally. He headed the first "Opening to the Left" government, and as foreign minister served as UN General Assembly president during the beginning of the US aggression in Vietnam and undercut efforts in the UN to end the aggression. Returning to Italy, he became secretary general of the increasingly failing Christian Democratic party. Fanfani led the attempt to end the newly passed divorce law; but despite the support of the Vatican, including the silencing of bishops and abbots opposed to changing the new divorce law, Fanfani's efforts were defeated. This led to his inability to form a government last fall, and the calling on foreign minister Aldo Moro. Moro, in a previous stint as premier, had attempted to include the Communist party as part of the coalition, but was blocked by Fanfani. Moro is in favor of rigid economy in government, and balanced budgets, but is viewed as leader of the left-wing of the Christian Democrats because he is not a tool of the U. S. Moro, as foreign minister, greatly improved Italian-Soviet relations and created much good will among Middle Eastern nations. Moro succeeded in forming a new cabinet, which left out the socialists and the social democrats since he could not also include the communists. The Republican party is strongly opposed to increased taxes and to inflation, as well as committed to civil liberties. Its leader, Emilio Columbo, is Treasury minister.

Its earlier strong ties with Middle Eastern countries, based on its long-standing oil policy independent of US interests, is gaining the Moro regime investments from Iran and Saudi Arabia. Led by the Governor of the Bank of Italy, Guido Carli, a leading monetary expert, Italy is undertaking a severe criticism of US economic policies. Carli has been attacking the US for exporting its own inflation; the US's exporting of its own Vietnam War-based inflation has generated anti-American feelings in Italy. Carli is able to build on a national reaction to increasing US interference in Italian domestic affairs. Carlo Donat-Cattin, a leader of the Christian Democratic party, quoted US ambassador John Volpe as pushing for an early election to create a coalition including the NATO-loving Liberals and excluding the Socialists who are united with the Communists in the trade union movement (the Catholic unions are also united with the Communist unions). Donat-Cattin detailed this in an interview in the Genoa daily, Secolo XIX Nuovo.

The New York Times has noted that Carli "is now opposing proposals by Secretary of State Kissinger on how to avoid further damage to the industrialized nations from the energy crisis on the grounds that they are inflationary. Mr. Carli also says that the situation and interests of the United States and Western Europe in the oil crisis are basically different and that interdependence between the two should be reduced rather than increased . . . Mr. Carli said that the Kissinger project was aimed at blocking all possible financial outlets so as to force oil producers to purchase United States Treasury bills with their dollar surpluses. If they did that, Mr. Carli observed, the oil-producing nations would pile up, 'though in the form of dollars, pieces of scrap paper that they wouldn't know how to spend whose future conversion into real resources is endangered by continuing inflation.' "

Similarly, in France, there has been increasing reaction to President Giscard d'Estaing's apparent bowing to American pressure and abandoning of the independent foreign policy of the late Charles de Gaulle and the late Georges Pompidou. Furthermore, Premier Jacques Chirao surprisingly gained the post of secretary general of the Gaullist party. This is likely to modify that party's healthy anti-Americanism. However, Michel Jobert, Pompidou's foreign minister, is striving to set up an alternative for the supporters of an independent foreign policy. Jobert had engaged in the famous clash with Kissinger a year ago in Washington. Jobert's Movement of Democrats has gained national support and is planning to run candidates in the next national elections.

Similarly, the US faces increased independence from Japan as a result of the election of Takeo Miki as prime minister. Miki has been a member of parliament since 1937, holding posts of foreign minister, minister of international trade and secretary general of the Liberal-Democratic party. The party was formed under the pressure of the United States out of a conservative party and a laissez-faire party, and the election of Miki prevented the break-up of the party. Miki had outspokenly broken with the past four prime ministers. Miki had demanded less reliance on the US and the recognition of China. He is an advocate of peaceful coexistence with the Soviet Union, an opponent of large Japanese military forces, an opponent of sending Japanese armed forces abroad (as urged by the US during the Vietnam War), and a defender of the "no war" clause of the Japanese constitution. In addition to a strong suppoerter of diplomatic and trade relations with China, Miki is the Japanese leader closest to the Arab nations. In late 1973, he toured the Middle East to emphasize Japan's friendliness to the Arab states upon whom Japan is totally reliant for oil.

The recent Kissinger outburst threatening US invasion of the Middle East sounds like the death rattle of a dying Empire. The very ability of the US to carry out the purely physical aspects of such an invasion is open to question. There are no allies between Long Island and the Suez (except Israel) where US planes carrying paratroops could land and re-fuel. Germany, France and Italy drew the line in October 1973; Greece and Turkey have done so since the Cyprus crisis. Spain and Portugal have said no. The only hope for US geopoliticians is the Soviet Union. Would it allow US use of its Black Sea airfields for an invasion of Araby? Despite the dependence of the Soviet Union on the US, it is unlikely to do that, but one can never rule out the willingness of the Soviet Union to serve the US. (US-Soviet relations might have been close even had the Soviets permitted Nixon and his cohorts a place of exile in Yalta!)

Drew Middleton, in the New York Times of January 10, presented the Pentagon's assessment of Kissinger's threats. The Arabs would have warning — from the Soviets — of impending US invasions, and could destroy the oil fields. But, the real problem for the military officers is maintaining intervention once it had begun. The US does not have forces trained for desert warfare, and would face a Lawrence of Arabia guerrilla war. Western military leaders in NATO indicated that NATO would be destroyed by any American military action against Arab oil. The reaction of Iran and Saudi Arabia, the two largest oil suppliers, would be violently anti-American. The US has been giving and selling billions of dollars of high efficiency hardware to these two countries as the most conservative in the Middle East. Yet, the threats of US aggression have caused Iran to move to an anti-US position. Iran is now giving financial and military aid to the Arab states. Although a Moslem country, Iran follows a different form of Islam. However, it has allied with Saudi Arabia's desire to gain the independence of Moslem holy places in Jerusalem.

Until October 1973 Saudi Arabia had found a powerful Israel a barrier to

(Continued On Page 5)

Foreign Affairs — (Continued From Page 4)

radical Arab Nationalism. Saudi Arabia aided Syria and Egypt in October 1973 only after they had made unexpected gains. After the Six Day War of 1967. US Secretary of State William Rogers sought to implement UN Resolution 242 calling for immediate return to pre-1967 borders. But, with Black September 1970 and King Hussein's massacre of the Palestinian guerrillas, and the elimination of Jordan as a major sector of their conflict with the Israeli regime, Rogers' plan was dropped and Kissinger moved into the dominant position with a plan to recognize the 1967 conquests. Jewish settlements were introduced in the conquered lands and according to Abba Eban (New Republic, March 23, 1974), General Ari Sharon spoke of Israel conquering everything between Khartoum and Algeria, and Teheran and the Persian Gulf. After the Arab success in October 1973, Kissinger shifted to the Rogers plan, which is no longer operable, as indicated by the total recognition of the Palestinian cause at the Rabat conference.

Yet, the kind of "stability" that Kissinger is aiming for in the Middle East — one which gets the administration off the hook through the 1976 election — is likely to ensure the continuity of the conflict and more US dollars poured into the area. (There is almost no doubt that the Soviet Union was pleased to turn over the Egyptian situation to US funding as it would bankrupt the Soviet Union to try to supply arms and domestic development funds to Egypt; but the US taxpayer gladly takes on the task!). The mere creation of a Palestinian state on the basis of UN resolutions would only continue the path of conflict and confrontation. What we must do is go outside the current state of the question, which permits no solution. As the present state of the matter is illegal in international law as a violation of the initial UN trusteeship plans, it would be useful to go to the original plans as a starting point. This was the concept of a single Palestinian state, composed of two commonwealths or cantons based respectively on the European Jewish and Arab Jewish populations, and on the Christian Arab and Islamic Arab populations. Within the original concept of a single political entity, the growth of the Jewish homeland and of the Palestinian nation could follow the original expectations of the trusteeship and of the leaders of the respective communities.

Noam Chomsky, the MIT professor and moderate analyst of the Middle East problem, explained some of the basic issues in an article in the October, 1974 University Review:

> If short-run stability is imposed, the most that the Palestinians can hope for is a mini-state subject to Israeli and Jordanian control. Israel will remain a Jewish state, that is, a state based on the principle of legal and institutional discrimination against non-Jews. . . Thus, more than ninety percent of the pre-1967 territory of Israel is, by law, owned in perpetuity by the Jewish people. Non-Jewish citizens may not lease, rent, or work on these lands. The Law of Return grants automatic citizenship to Jews, and excludes Palestinians who fled or were driven from their homes. All-Jewish settlement areas are developed, with no protest from liberal opinion; imagine the reaction if all-White settlement areas were designated by law in New York City . . . Internally, Israel can hardly avoid religious domination of social life, regardless of popular feelings about the matter, since some principled basis must be established for distinguishing the privileged majority from other citizens or from stateless Arabs in Israel — a growing category, since statelessness is inherited, contrary to standard practice in the Western democracies.

A relevant recent development regarding Palestine was the recognition of the Palestine Liberation Organization and the establishment of an official representative by India. Although African, Asian and some European nations had PLO offices, the Indian government was the first non-Arab and non-Communist government to grant diplomatic status. The PLO emphasized the long tradition of Indian nationalist support for the rights of the Palestinians. The founder of Modern India, Mohandas Gandhi, published a famous dialogue on the insistence of Zionist organizations on establishing a Jewish state in Palestine, though already inhabited by another people. They did so rather than choose an uninhabited part of the world where they would neither be aggressors nor unwelcome, especially as several such offers had been made to Jewish

organizations. Gandhi was anxious to avoid the great problem faced by India due to two different religious groups. For this he was criticized by Moslem extremists and assassinated by a Hindu extremist.

Gandhi's point was well taken, as the attempts to set up a separate Moslem state of Indian Moslems have not succeeded. A hundred million Moslems have lived in India for a quarter-century; among those that selected to set up a Moslem state — Pakistan — the majority revolted, to set up their own state independent of the north-west Moslems. Bengal is a Moslem state closely allied to India, while Pakistan remains the tool of western imperialism for which it was created, first, by the British as they left India and now by the US. The PLO representative to India noted that Pakistan, as a religious, Moslem state, "will not solve the problems of Moslems," and that "to establish a state on the basis of religion will not solve communal problems planted by other forces." The PLO representative declared: "India can do a great deal for us in convincing Jews and world Jewry that a secular, democratic state in Palestine is the only solution. India has its own experience in creating this kind of state." Regarding the Palestinian cause, he added: "This is not a struggle against Jews. It is a struggle against Israel." However, the PLO delegate indicated that the PLO had not asked India to end the Israeli consulate in Bombay as demanded by members of Parliament and by the popular weekly Blitz. Indians are struck particularly by the refusal of Israel to accord the rights of Jews to many Indian Jews on the grounds that they can never be Jews according to the racial concepts of the Orthodox rabbis (who also exclude Conservative and Reform Judaism from Israel).

The partitions of India and Palestine by the British colonialists have had the same effects — conflict, division, continuity of political influence — that occurred in Ireland. Just as the Jordanian monarchy and its English-officered Arab Legion and the Pakistanian army were a means of maintenance of English imperial influence, so the partition of Ireland following the Irish Revolution attempted to use the different populations for English political purposes.

When the Republic of Ireland was created in 1922, it was composed of three of the four provinces of Ireland, plus three counties of the fourth province, Ulster. The remaining six counties of Ulster were included in a new entity — Northern Ireland. The Republic of Ireland contained a population which was 95% Catholic and five percent Church of Ireland (Episcopal or Anglican). The Church of Ireland was not only respected and supported, but members of it were given a majority on the Supreme Court and large representation in the Senate of the Irish Republic, in order to give a sense of security to the Anglican population. Recently, an Anglican, son of an IRA martyr, was elected president of the Irish Republic. Most of the counties of Fermanagh, Tyrone and Derry — west of the Bann River — have Catholic majorities with Church of Ireland minorities. Similarly, south Armagh and south Down, adjacent to the Irish Republic, have Catholic majorities. It would have been possible to have included these in the Irish Republic in 1922, leaving an overwhelming Presbyterian majority in Antrim (and Belfast), northern Armagh-Down, and northest Derry (around Coleraine). But, the English army demanded the western and southern areas as a defense in depth sector in case of invasion from the Irish Republic, so that the war could be fought in the Catholic areas of Northern Ireland. As Northern Ireland is divided by population into thirds — Catholic, Church of Ireland and Presbyterian — the Catholic demands for equal rights gained support among the Anglicans although opposed by the hard-core Calvinists. The introduction of the British army — for whatever motives — gave a boost to the Irish Republican Army faction led by the Provisional Sinn Fein Party (the Official Sinn Fein Party and its IRA have developed a non-violent, political program of civil disobedience and political struggle) because the IRA alone defended Catholic urban neighborhoods against British army invasions. This defense by the IRA gave them a huge popular support which they otherwise would not have had.

However, this popular support for the IRA (Provisionals) was on the verge of being undercut last spring by the formation of a coalition government composed of the moderate Catholics and the Anglicans. It was made up of the Alliance party which combines Catholics and Anglicans, the Social Democratic Party of Northern Ireland which is the main Catholic political party, and the Anglicans in the Unionist Party (which used to be the dominant party under the system reducing the Catholic electorate). This coalition had every chance of gaining complete support from the Catholics and totally eliminating the IRA from popular support. It would have given the Catholics equality of rights in education,

(Continued On Page 6)

Foreign Affairs — (Continued From Page 5)

housing, employment, health, etc., within the Ulster entity. A paper formal conference system between the prime ministers of the Republic and of Ulster would provide for conferences between the two parts of Ireland. The extreme Presbyterians opposed this (moderate Protestant leaders in Belfast have been assassinated for supporting the coalition concept). However, the coalition found its real enemy in the officer corps of the British army in Ulster, and, through threats of mutiny among the officers, the coalition government in Ulster was overthrown in mid-1974. The most hopeful attempt to solve the Irish problem had failed. The result was to give popular strength to the Provisional IRA, so that, after the Christmas truce, the British representatives in Ulster, through the intermediary role of Irish Protestant clergy in both parts of Ireland, have had to recognize the political role of the IRA. During the Christmas ceasefire, the English leaders missed a major chance to end the violence by releasing a large number of the illegally jailed Catholics, but it freed only a few. In addition to freeing large numbers of jailed Catholics, Prime Minister Harold Wilson seems about to agree to further talks with the IRA for the gradual withdrawal of the almost 15,000 British occupation troops from Ulster.

The question of communal divisions continues to plague Yugoslavia. The Kingdom of Yugoslavia was created by the Western Allies after World War I under the dominance of Serbia. The Serbian dynasty had come to the throne only after 1900, after assassinating the whole of the previous royal family, and then had expanded in the Balkans, under the auspices of Tsarist Russia, incorporating Macedonia before World War I. Then, it desired to expand to the sea by incorporating the non-Serbian Croatians and Slovenians who were Catholics and Latin cultured rather than Orthodox and Greek cultured like the Serbians. For this purpose, the Serbians assassinated the heir of the Austro-Hungarian Monarchy and started World War I. The events leading up to this are well detailed in the work of the revisionist historians: Sidney B. Fay, **Origins of the World War** (2 vols.) and Harry Elmer Barnes, **Genesis of the World War.**

The dissident Yugoslav writer, Mihajlo Mihajlov, has an article in the February 3 issue of the Welfare-Warfare, socialist-militarist journal, **The New Leader,** entitled: **Disentangling History — The Mihajlovich Tragedy.** Mihajlov starts off on a bad foot to disentangle history by stating that the Kingdom of Montenegro, which was aggressively annexed by Serbia after World War I, had "fought on the Axis side during World War I." Not only was there no Axis during World War I, since the Axis only came into existence in the late 1930's, but Montenegro was an ally of Serbia, fighting on the side of Russia against Austria-Hungary. The royal family of Montenegro, which went back many centuries, was deposed in favor of the upstart Serbian dynasty.

But, the major area of opposition to incorporation into the Allied-created Yugoslavia was Croatia. Croatia was the historic kingdom on the Afriatic Sea with a long and glorious cultural tradition tied to Italy, Austria and Western Europe. Although most Croatians were Catholics, many of those living in Bosnia were Islamic, as a result of conversion during the Turkish rule. Thus, in Bosnia a third of the people were Moslem while a quarter were Catholics and about forty-percent were Orthodox. Yugoslavia has a large Moslem population (about 15%), which facilitates relations with the Moslem world and gives Yugoslavia a leadership role of the non-aligned powers. In the total population, Orthodox account for about forty percent and Catholics about thirty-five percent. But, religion and nationality overlap — Catholic equalling Croatian and Slovenian and Orthodox equalling Serbian, Montenegrian, Macedonian and Albanian.

Mihajlov harkens back to the beginning of World War II. The Yugoslavian government was split between supporters of an alliance with Germany and its Balkan allies, and an alliance with England and its power in the Mediterranian. The pro-German group allied with the Germans and attempted to settle the deep nationalities crisis by setting up a Serbian and a Croatian state. The extreme Serbian royalists, led by Draja Mihajlovich, carried out a guerrilla war against the Serbian and Croatian governments allied with Germany. Mihajlovich's Chetniks were lionized in the literature and movies of England and America. But, although strongly supported by England, the Chetniks were more interested in preparing for England's victory and restoration of the Serbian domination; they carried out campaigns to destroy the Croatian nationalist movements. Josef Broz Tito, having fought in the

The Day-Care 'Shortage'

A few years ago, the new feminist movement began to raise the cry of a nationwide "shortage" of day-care centers, with a corollary clamor for government to sponsor, subsidize, or operate a fleet of such centers so that mothers could work in jobs and careers. To economists, the outcry was a peculiar one; the free market never suffers from shortages, as supply always rises to meet demand. The answer clearly was: **either** the demand for day-care centers was far less than the feminists claimed, **or** — more likely — that somewhere government was deliberately restricting the supply and thereby itself creating the shortage.

That the latter hunch is correct is made clear by a recent hysterical campaign by the New York City Health Department. The Health Department has now issued a frenzied statement that "illegal" private day-care centers are "spreading like a cancer throughout the city" (New York **Sunday News,** Jan. 26, 1975). Aha! Literally "hundreds" of such centers have appeared through the city, **unlicensed,** dedicated (horrors!) to the making of a profit. But never fear, the Health Department is in the process of cracking down on this rash of illegality.

In short: the numerous requirements imposed by the New York city government are so onerous and costly that the supply of day-care centers is severely restricted, and so black-market, illegal centers have had to appear in response to consumer demand. Some of these requirements are: licenses from the Health Department; certificates of occupancy from the Buildings Department; and passing inspection by the Fire Department. The paternal city authorities are worried both because the fees charged by the private centers are "too high" (the fees "can go sky high") and also too low: they can make money "even if they only charge $25 a week." (Tsk! Tsk!)

It is OK, for some reason, for mothers to hire private baby-sitters, or even to use a local neighbor as a personal day-care center. These, too, are of course unlicensed, and yet the authorities do not seem to worry here about licensing, health, safety, building codes, or the proper educational facilities. Yet, for private day-care centers, defined as an outfit that takes in more than five young children and meets more than 5 hours a

(Continued On Page 7)

International Brigades of the Spanish Civil War, organized the Croatian resistance — the Partisans — under communist leadership. But, having an "internationalist" perspective, the communists also included anti-monarchical Serbs, Montenegrans and Macedonians. Since the Chetniks were tools of the English foreign office, the US gave its support to the Partisans and by December 1943 forced Churchill to support Tito too. Mihajlov correctly notes that this was not desired by Stalin, who distrusted Tito's militant nationalism and who preferred his agreement with England. Stalin urged Tito to join with the English aligned forces led by King Peter and Mihajlovich. After the war, Tito continued his clearly anti-Soviet policies, and eventually established close ties with the US while formally calling himself non-aligned. In 1946, Mihajlovich was captured, tried and shot. Tito defeated him because he offered a modernizing, non-unitary approach to solve Yugoslavia's nationality crisis in place of Mihajlovich's Orthodox religious approach, his Serbian domination over the other nationalities, his massacres of Croatians and Moslems. Although there are many problems remaining in regard to the nationalities question in Yugoslavia, Tito eliminated the most serious and dangerous ones, as Mihajlov emphasized. Although Yugoslavia has made great strides toward a market economy, in the last few years brakes have been put on that development. Advocates of increased personal freedom in economic and cultural areas have been labelled "anarcho-liberals," and "anarcho-liberalism" has been the major target of attack by the official press. The one hopeful development is the re-emergence of Edvard Kardelj, 64, as the heir apparent to Tito. Kardelj initiated the struggle against Soviet influences and the introduction of market approaches to economic problems, as well as general concepts of freedom in Yugoslavian politics. But, in recent years, it was thought he was losing influence as chief theoretician of the League of Yugoslav Communists. But, Kardelj has become the authoritative spokesman recently, and was elected the representative of the Republic of Slovenia to the collective presidency comprised of one member from each of the national republics. In place of Tito, he would be the natural leader of Yugoslavia. ◻

Sense On Oil — At Last!

Those of us who have combed the media for some sign of sense on the oil program have been prey to an aura of unreality. For, in the thousands of words on the subject, everyone has blithely assumed that we must cut oil imports into the U.S. by 1 million barrels per day. The bizarre problem is not simply that all the media are espousing some form of statist program; the really grotesque point is that no one has bothered even to defend the seemingly self-evident assumption that oil imports must be cut. Whatever dispute there is, has occurred only within that matrix: as the Ford administration takes the "market" view (ye gods!) that a high tariff and tax must be placed on oil imports and production, while the Democrats counter with the even more socialistic view that oil and gasoline use should be cut by a totalitarian scheme of rationing. As a result, the only alternatives placed before us are one or another form of statism.

In this blighted atmosphere, good sense has now come from a wholly unexpected quarter — from columnist Joseph Kraft, who has never been distinguished for clarity of thought or for libertarian acumen. And yet, Kraft's column for February 3 (New York Post) is a searching and brilliant critique of the unexamined axiom of the million barrel a day cut in oil imports. Kraft begins his column by posing what he calls "the million-barrel question": what do we gain, and what do we lose by trying to force a million-barrel cut in oil imports? Kraft answers that "the loss turns out to be staggering, both in its impact on this country and its allies." On the other hand, the "gain", which Kraft correctly sees as "totally foggy", "seems to rest on some obscure foreign policy point bootlegged past the White House by Henry Kissinger."

Kraft goes on to note that both Ford and the Democrats accept the million barrel axiom, Ford trying to attain the goal by oil tariffs and taxes, and the Democrats by rationing and a tax on gasoline. He then points out that Ford's proposals involve a double burden: adding to inflation by raising prices of petroleum and petroleum products, and intensifying recession and unemployment by cutting production and demand for oil and for other products. To counterbalance these tangible losses of the Ford program, he then asks, what are supposed to be the gains? Kraft notes that "that question has not been systematically posed by the President's domestic economic advisers." In fact, "John Sawhill, the former Energy Administrator, testified the other day that he did not even know the basis of the million-barrel-per-day target." Kraft then notes that the State Department has come up with a kind of rationale for the import cut: that this will spur oil independence in the United States, and especially in Western Europe and Japan. "But," Kraft comments, "both of these points are subject to serious questions." For one thing, "oil at present seems to be plentiful" — so why the hassle about the oil "shortage"?

We noted, in the January Lib. Forum, that oil has been rapidly becoming a "surplus" commodity. More evidence on this has been piling up. Reports in the oil press note that several countries — Kuwait, Saskatchewan, and Ecuador — have recently reduced oil production because of a paucity of demand at the current price. The oil tanker trade is also in the doldrums for the same reason. A recent Oil Daily reported that "with less oil being demanded and with more tankers around to carry it, the market has collapsed, pushing charter rates through the floor and leaving dozens of ships totally without work." The article goes on to say that there are now four and a half million tons of tankers now awaiting oil cargo in the Persian Gulf. Furthermore, in recent months, new and large scale oil finds have been made: a huge strike in the North Sea off Norway; an important find off the coast of Brazil; discoveries in Mexico and off the China coast. All this highlights a speech last year by J. K. Jamieson, chairman of the board of Exxon Corporation. Jamieson predicted that oil consumption would decline by 2% over 1973, and that the decline would continue this year. This speech highlights the memorandum in the files of Standard Oil of California, discovered by Senate investigators in the late 1960's. The memorandum warned of an "excess supply" of oil in the early 1970s unless something were done to curtail production. And, just the other day, a report was issued by the OECD (advanced Western countries), predicting a reduction of oil consumption in these countries by 1980.

And so we begin to see the true nature of the oil "crisis" and the new axioms of oil policy. We are suffering not from an oil "shortage", which exists only in the fevered imagination of the media, but from an oil "surplus", i.e. that the current OPEC cartel price of $10-$11 per barrel is too high. The Ford program is a program to intensify the cartel, to restrict the supply of oil further and to raise the price: short, to protect the oil cartellists from the powerful forces of market competition, to prevent any fall in oil prices, and to raise those prices still further by U. S. government coercion. And, of course, to cut the American oil companies into a larger share of the world cartel pie. All at the expense of the consumers, here and abroad. One important tipoff on this policy was President Ford's bald-faced proposal to place a compulsory minimum floor on the price of oil. How stark a cartellizing program can we have?

The excuse, of course, is to protect alternative sources of energy from the competition of oil, when its prices will decline. In short, use government coercion to protect the oil cartel, and then include the alternative sources in on the cartel as well! The point should be clear: despite all the hoopla about alternative sources of energy, be they nuclear, solar, or hot water, they are still inefficient and uneconomic, even at the current high price of oil. Oil and coal are still the best sources

(Continued On Page 8)

Day-Care 'Shortage' —

(Continued From Page 6)

week, somehow these often absurd and restrictive requirements become absolutely mandatory for the alleged safety and educational nurture of the children. As Edith Clute, of the Health Department, puts it, "Parents must look for the license in any center. If there is none, they should try to think of an alternative like family day care, or a grandmother to take care of the youngsters or a babysitter. Adequate care is more than health and safety. Qualified staff members who have expertise and understanding are very important." Licenses, furthermore, are granted only after careful scrutiny by "department experts who are certified by the state as early childhood education consultants."

So then, how come that babysitters, grandma, or Mrs. Jones down the block don't have to be "qualified staff members"? Why is the consumer trusted to look out for her children in the former case, but not in the larger day-care centers? The answer should be clear: because the former do not compete directly with the licensed private centers. The licensed centers have been granted a monopolistic privilege by the city, and no direct competition is to be brooked from cheaper, and unlicensed competitors. The high prices and restricted supply granted to the monopolistic centers have to be protected by the coercive arm of government.

This "cynical" or realistic hypothesis may be checked by investigating the source of the current furore. It stemmed from a "rash of complaints" — some from grumbling parents, to be sure (who, however, could easily exercise their option of removing their children) but others from what a News reporter describes as "legitimate" centers. So here we have, in microcosm, the essence of the "welfare state": privileged monopolists find their privileged income being reduced by free competition, and they call upon the friendly government authorities to use their coercive powers to outlaw the competition. The "welfare state" is the monopoly state. And it is a state that produces "shortages" wherever it goes. ∎

"The artificial creation of expenses by those who deem a public debt a public blessing will easily suggest plausible pretenses for taxation, until every class is burdened to the utmost stretch of forbearance, and the great body of the people reduced to penury and slavery."

— Mercy Warren, 1805

Sense On Oil —

(Continued From Page 7)

of energy, and they will continue to be for a long time to come. Our policy should be a pro-consumer and pro-freedom policy: to encourage oil imports by eliminating all tariffs and quotas, and to encourage domestic oil production by abolishing proration laws and oil price controls, and by opening up the vast oil reserves on the government-owned public domain to private homesteading and private property rights — and therefore to private production. All the U.S. government has to do is to cease forthwith its various measures crippling the importation and production of oil, coal, and natural gas.

But back to Joe Kraft. Kraft goes on to cite a recent series of studies, by the World Bank, the U.S. Treasury, and Morgan Guaranty Bank, debunking the widespread hysteria about the "recycling" of dollar assets accumulated by the oil producing countries. What will the Arabs do with all those dollars? Well, what can they do except buy American products or invest in American assets; so much for the "missing dollars". Kraft notes that all these recent reports show "that the vast dollar assets accumulated in the past year by the petroleum producers are being distributed in normal and manageable ways on investment, consumption and foreign aid." Therefore, he notes, "the danger of what Kissinger calls strangulation by the oil exporters seems very, very remote." And what about Western Europe and Japan, whom we are supposedly "saving" from the Arabs? Kraft asks: Are they "hooked on the idea of an American lead in cutting oil consumption? Or wouldn't they much prefer a healthy American economy where they can buy and sell with ease?" Absolutely! Kraft concludes on an excellent and challenging note:

"In any case, the basic question wants to be examined in a systematic way. It is not enough just to take it on Kissinger's authority that the country ought to curtail consumption of oil by a million barrels a day in the next year. Given the weak state of the American economy and the dependence of foreign countries on U.S. prosperity and the current surplus of oil and the apparent manageability of the petrodollar problem, the burden of proof on the million-barrel question lies upon Kissinger and his men at the State Dept."

The Morgan Guaranty Trust report, mentioned by Kraft and appearing in the January issue of its World Financial Markets, stresses the recent (1) reduction in the demand for oil from the OPEC countries, and (2) heavy buying of products by these oil producing countries from the industrial nations. While oil consumption has been declining, imports into the OPEC countries rose by 70-75% in 1974. Already, Algeria is heading for a balance of trade deficit, and Venezuela and Iran are heading rapidly in the same direction. So much for the "missing petrodollars"!

Of course, our strictures on the absurdity of the media do not apply to our favorite libertarian-ish columnist, Nicholas von Hoffman. In his January 28 column (New York Post), von Hoffman points out that the word "crisis" has been semantically redefined; once, it used to mean "an acutely painful or dangerous situation demanding immediate action." In that ordinary language sense, "there is no energy crisis, although the White House proclaims it, the Congress debates it and the press accepts it. If we continue to buy foreign oil as we have been no catastrophe will befall us. There is no emergency." Von Hoffman goes on to make the trenchant and crucial point that, for the first time in the history of the world, there is a great agitation for the rationing of a product (gasoline) which is in sense in short supply. As von Hoffman puts it, "if Senate majority leader Mansfield (D-Mont) and his liberal Republican allies get their gas rationing law passed, it will be the first time since the days of the royal salt monopolies that the state will have attempted to ration a universally needed commodity available in abundance. For not only is there presently no oil shortage, but the large oversupply is bursting the rivets of the world's storage tanks." Von Hoffman concludes that "imperialist fantasies such as energy or raw material 'independence' aside, no reason exists either for the President's oil import taxes or his opponents' rationing schemes. The problem isn't economic, but psychological." Hooray!

—————————

"Let the history of the federal government instruct mankind that the mask of patriotism may be worn to conceal the foulest designs against the liberties of the people."

— Benjamin Bache.

—————————

"The one bright moment in the Taft Administration, in fact, came when Dr. Taft was given his drubbing in November, 1912. Turning out such gross incompetents, to be sure, does very little practical good, for they are commonly followed by successors almost as bad, but it at least gives the voters a chance to register their disgust, and so it keeps them reasonably contented, and turns their thoughts away from the barricade and the bomb. Democracy, of course, does not work, but it is a capital anaesthetic."

— H. L. Mencken

A Monthly Newsletter

THE
Libertarian Forum

Joseph R. Peden, Publisher   Murray N. Rothbard, Editor

VOLUME VII, NO. 3   MARCH, 1975   US-ISSN0047-4517

Inflationary Depression

When does a "recession" become a "depression"? Basically, the question is a matter of degree and therefore of semantics, and so the answer is in large part subjective. However, we are in an economy where industrial production has declined a whopping 10% from last September to this January, and where the unemployment rate heads inexorably up to 10%, and indeed has hit 10% in key industrial areas. In the face of these figures, as rough as they may be, it is absurd not to call the current situation a "depression."

The only counter to this description by the optimists seems to be that the situation is not as bad as in the Great Depression of the 1930's. (Thus, see Philip Shabecoff, in the New York Times, March 7): Happily true, but irrelevant, since the Great Depression was the worst depression in American history, and hardly the standard by which to gauge all other depressions. Indeed, before the 1930's, all business cycle contractions were called depressions — some of which were mild, and some severe — and it was only after World War II that the word "depression", now considered politically intolerable, was abolished and the milder sounding "recession" put in its place. But even considering that change, a 10% fall in production in six months, and 9-10% unemployment, is a "depression" in anybody's book.

The liberals and Keynesians, anxious for a vast reviving up operation for monetary and fiscal expansion, are claiming that inflation is no longer a problem, and that only heartless reactionaries still worry about it. But while it is happily true that basic commodity and industrial raw material prices have fallen sharply since mid-1974 (the index of industrial raw material prices having fallen from about 240 in the spring of 1974 to about 180 in February, 1975), and while it is also true that the index of wholesale prices has declined slightly in the last couple of months, it is also and more importantly true that the cost of living index was still increasing at an annual rate of 8.5% at the end of the year. And it is consumer prices, the cost of living, that is the only gauge of whether or not we are still suffering from price inflation. 8.5% is of course better than 14% — our previous rate — and may bring us into the magic world of "single digit" rather than "double digit" inflation, but it is still a very large and ominous rate of inflation. We are, in short, in an inflationary depression.

As the Federal Reserve gears up for a massive injection of new money, and as it prepares to finance a big chunk of the huge prospective federal deficit for the next two years (now estimated in many quarters as well over $100 billion), the rate of inflation is bound to accelerate dangerously in the next two years.

What we have to realize, hard as it may be for liberals to swallow, is that the recession-depression has been the healthiest thing that has happened to the American economy in a decade. For once inflationary credit expansion has proceeded and accelerated as it has in the last decade, the distortions of investment and production make a depression healthy and necessary — necessary to liquidate unsound capital goods investments, and to bring about a healthy-free market structure of production, with less investment and resources going into capital goods and more into consumer goods production. As the "Austrian School" of

economics teaches us, the faster the depression is allowed to do its work and the less government interferes with that work, the sooner it will be over, and the stage set for a healthy free-market recovery in the structure of investment and production.

Furthermore, only the Austrian School — and neither the Keynesians nor the Friedmanites — can explain the puzzling phenomenon which has hit us squarely and clearly in the current depression: how it is that industrial commodity prices can fall sharply, while wholesale prices remain stable, and yet consumer prices continue to rise rapidly. Contrary to the Left, the cause is not some sort of diabolical conspiracy of businesses or retailers. It is the fact that it is precisely through such diverse price movements that the market process of depression does its work, shifting resources from capital goods to consumer goods. In fact, recessions and depressions of the past have always lowered capital prices and raised consumer prices relative to each other. Thus, in the Great Depression of the 1930's, industrial and commodity prices fell very sharply, while the cost of living fell considerably, but much less so than industrial prices. And so, after 1929, consumer prices, as in the case of the current economy, rose relatively to other prices. The big difference between then and now is that all prices fell sharply because of a healthy fall in the money supply ("deflation"). Since all prices fell, the consumers did not complain about the cost of living falling less than other prices. But, now, because of our far more inflationary money and banking system, the government has been able to keep inflating the money supply and thereby to prevent an overall deflation. Hence, the Keynesian policies of the federal government have stopped neither inflation nor depression, as the arrogant economic Establishment had promised for forty years; the only thing they succeeded in doing was to prevent deflation and hence to prevent consumers from enjoying the one thing that made past depressions palatable: a fall in the cost of living. Government tinkering with the economy has not cured business cycles; it has only brought us the new phenomenon of inflationary depression, of the worst of both worlds at the same time.

If the government doesn't interfere too much in the depression process (a big "if" of course) the depression should be over in a year, just in time to receive a giant inflationary stimulus from the Fed financing of the gigantic federal deficits. In this situation, the most important single consideration is to stop the Fed from inflating the money supply. At this critical point, where do the Friedmanites stand? Long-time readers of the Lib. Forum should be able to guess: the Friedmanites are now attacking Burns and the Federal Reserve for not inflating enough, for not meeting Friedman's arbitrary crystal-ball target of "optimum monetary growth" (i.e. optimum amount of inflationary counterfeiting) for the economy.

Libertarian apologists for Friedman who claim that the Friedmanites and the Austrians really have the same views on economic policy (e.g. the egregious Alan Reynolds of National Review) cite an esoteric journal article by Milton Friedman to the effect that the real, down-deep optimal

(Continued On Page 2)

Arts And Movies

By Mr. First Nighter

The Godfather — Part II. dir. by Francis Ford Coppola, with Al Pacino and Robert DeNiro.

Sequels, of course, are never quite touched with the glory of the originals, and Godfather II does not enjoy the tightly wrought magnificence of the first Godfather, one of the great films of our time. Still and all, Godfather II deserves this year's Academy Award. It gets a bit draggy at times, as the camera lingers for long stretches on Al Pacino's face, in an attempt to lend "psychological depth" to the story. Great as that face is, the tautness of the action suffers. Apparently, Coppola was stung by moralistic and left-liberal criticisms of the allegedly pro-Mafia stance of the original (actually, it was only in favor of the Corleone family within the Mafia); hence the phony "psychology", and the depiction of more Corleone excesses than in the original. But these are only warts on a masterpiece. I still walked out at the end of the three-hour Godfather II hoping against hope for a Part III of equal length. The basic drama and the superb acting are still there.

Part II goes back and forth between the later story of Michael Corleone (Pacino), and his continuing triumph against enemies from within and without the family; and the early story of the original Brando-Godfather, played with equal brilliance by Robert DeNiro as he rises from a poor Sicilian boy on the run from the Mafia there to the establishment of his own family in New York (c. 1900-1920). I came to the movie prepared to resent the cutting back and forth between the two stories, but they are done very well, and there is no sense of discontinuity. There is still room for a Part III covering the middle years of Brando-DeNiro.

There is still plenty of exciting action in Part II, and Pacino remains triumphant. The inner logic of Part I prepares us for the betrayal of the weak brother Fredo, and for the punking out of Pacino's wife Diane Keeton, who simply cannot stand the gaff. (Is the moral that Sicilians should beware in marrying WASPS?) Lee Strasberg, the notorious founder of the "method" acting of the Actor's Studio, lends an excellent dimension to the story in his portrayal of a Meyer Lansky-type (Lansky is the famous Jewish Mafia leader). The Lansky type comes across as a steely and arresting figure, cloaking his post as leader of the rackets with the homilies of a Jewish patriarch ("the important thing, my son, is to have your health," as he prepares to wipe the "son" out.)

There are, once more, some superb and striking scenes: the vengeance wreaked by DeNiro on the Sicilian Mafia leader who slaughtered his family; the Kefauver-type hearing when the Corleones bring the Valachi-type informer's brother from Sicily to shame him out of being a stoolpigeon; the Batista-Mafia feast in Havana just before the Castro takeover.

On to Part III!

Young Frankenstein, dir. by Mel Brooks, with Gene Wilder, Madeline Kahn, and Cloris Leachman.

I am delighted to see that the media have now discovered Mel Brooks, pace the lengthy and hilarious interviews with our prime film humorist in Newsweek and Playboy. The problem is that the media, as usual, suffer from a cultural time lag, so that the attention that should have been showered on the zany and magnificent Blazing Saddles — Brooks' previous film — has instead been directed at Young Frankenstein. The problem is that the public is being deluded into believing that Young Frankenstein is a film similar to Blazing Saddles. It is not. Despite Brooks' stated creed of going always for the belly laugh, of aiming at leaving the audience helplessly on the floor with laughter (as Saddles did), Young Frankenstein is not that kind of film at all. In addition to being controlled rather than anarchic, Frankenstein is a film for chuckles rather than belly laughs. It is a sweet, affectionate tribute to the horror film, in particular of course the Frankenstein genre. It is, in essence, a revision and reconstruction of the Frankenstein story so as to bring about a happy ending, with the monster sweetly taking his place in human existence. The acting, as is usual for the Brooks repertory company, is excellent, with Wilder playing Dr. Frankenstein's grandson who reluctantly finds himself sucked into following in his illustrious grandfather's footsteps.

A fine picture, provided one remembers that it does not provide anywhere near the inspired hilarity of Saddles or of the phenomenal Brooks film, The Producers.

Murder on the Orient Express, dir. by Sidney Lumet, with Albert Finney and a host of others.

It was a fine idea to film the Agatha Christie mystery classic, which takes place on the exciting and luxurious Orient Express, the site of so many interwar espionage and mystery thrillers. Unfortunately, Sidney Lumet was the director, and Lumet's pretentious and plodding direction virtually provided the kiss of death. Since there is not much action in this Hercule Poirot mystery, the film needed a director who is a master at building suspense out of small details — where O where was the great Hitchcock? Instead, Lumet drags it out — for example, there were what seemed like five minutes of external shots of the Orient Express leaving the station at Istanbul. The host of stars did well, but were gravely hampered by the Lumet framework. Finney is particularly good as the fussy Belgian detective, although all Poirot fans know that the great detective is supposed to be bald, rather than have slicked down straight hair. ◻

Inflationary Depression —

(Continued From Page 1)

(Continued From Page 1)

growth of the money supply in the U. S. is not Friedman's magic 3-5% per year, but zero, which would indeed make Friedman as hard-money oriented as the Austrians. But the vital point is that this article has had no influence whatever on concrete Friedmanite policy positions, which, for example, are now bitterly attacking the Fed for its "over-restrictive policy" in not inflating the money supply sufficiently.

For example: in the March 10 issue of Newsweek, Friedman attacks the Federal Reserve for not inflating the money supply enough since July 1974. It appears that from June 1974 to January 1975, the Fed has "only" increased M-1 (currency plus demand deposits) by the annual rate of 1%, while M-2 (M-1 plus time deposits at commercial banks) has "only" increased by 5%. Friedman attacks this as "over-restrictive" and "undesirably low." As far as I and the Austrian School are concerned, this monetary growth is at least 5% too much. Where is the alleged Friedmanite goal of zero monetary growth now? Nowhere, as usual.

The fact must be faced once and for all, especially by libertarians, that the Friedmanites, for all their free-market rhetoric, are simply moderate statists and moderate inflationists, and that none of this moderation does the cause of the free market or of sound money any good whatsoever. The Friedmanites, especially on the money question, are Pied Pipers down the path of inflation and Big Government.

While we are at it, another article in Newsweek on Alan Greenspan (Feb. 24) illuminates the question of how Greenspan can square his high-sounding libertarian and Objectivist rhetoric, with his concrete role as statist compromiser and equivalent Pied Piper. At one point, Newsweek sees the problem: "Like Rand, Greenspan believes that government has no business meddling with free enterprise — yet here he is helping to make policy for an American government that intervenes in nearly every aspect of the economy." The answer: "Greenspan rationalizes the seeming contradiction by arguing that since he cannot 'prove beyond a doubt' that his laissez-faire principles are right, it is possible for him to compromise."

So there we have it. As our alleged "libertarian" moves among the heady and corrupting atmosphere of Power, he asks himself, "What the hell? How do I know I'm really right . . . ?" That's John Galt? Never has Lord Acton's great dictum about the corruption of Power been demonstrated more elegantly. Let all libertarians engrave this lesson on their hearts. And to Tibor Machan, who wrote an apologia for Greenspan recently in Reason magazine, are you listening? ◻

Profits Regulation And Inflation

By Hartwell C. Herring III, Ph.D., CPA
And
Fred A. Jacobs, Ph.D., CPA
Dept. Of Accounting
The University Of Tennessee

The presence of persistent inflation that is showing signs of maintaining or increasing its momentum has given rise to a multitude of proposed solutions from almost every sector of society. Many popular proposals would encourage the use of governmental intervention in the private sector to control the activities of business and labor. These proposals have a significant political appeal, which has already resulted in the temporary establishment of wage and price controls accompanied by a regulatory board. Although by no means universally accepted, such controls do remain an alternative with considerable support among some economic interests. Furthermore, some rather influential labor leaders have flatly stated that they will not support any future wage and price control program without similar controls on corporate profits.[1]

We believe that there are some significant dysfunctional aspects of profits regulation which make such a policy ill-advised from a technical standpoint. The purpose of this article is to state these limitations and to draw conclusions regarding their implications for economic policy.

History of Profits Regulation

The history of profits regulation has been primarily that of imposing taxes on corporate income. Such taxes have been levied continuously in the United States since 1913.[2] The corporate income tax legislation required many years and much debate to formulate, primarily because of the traditional fear that the incentive to increase production would be reduced or eliminated. The income tax was, in fact, a compromise between proposals that would eliminate incentive and those that would reduce incentive.

Currently, the corporate income tax rate approaches fifty percent (twenty-two percent of the first $25,000 of profits and forty-eight percent for all profits over that amount.)[3] Literally, the corporation is allowed to keep about one-half of each additional dollar earned without limit. Therefore, it is apparent that the incentive to produce more goods and services is reduced, but it is not eliminated. In other words, the corporation can earn unlimited profits because the regulation is directed toward each additional dollar earned, i.e., the profits ceiling refers to a percentage rather than to an absolute dollar amount. Because of this characteristic, income taxes do not constitute profits-regulation in the strictest sense.

Profits-Regulation — Contemporary Proposals

Quantity-Limits

The simplest form of profits regulation is the placing of an absolute limit on the amount of annual profit that could be earned by a given corporation. Such a policy would require that individual consideration be given to the amount of profit allowed each single company being regulated.

There are four significant limitations to the quantity-limit approach. First, someone or some group must decide how much profit, in absolute dollars, a company is permitted to earn annually. This decision process is susceptible to various political influences through special interest lobbying that may not be in the best interest of the country. Second, a complex and costly administrative problem is created by the need to consider each corporation on an individual basis. Thirdly, disincentives to produce, to increase efficiency, and to increase employment would result if a company were not allowed to increase profits as its business expanded or as efficiencies were attained. Finally, successful companies may be encouraged to operate inefficiently and to "live-it-up" in order to increase expenses and thereby avoid excess profits when that company anticipates a good year. The result of these disadvantages is that each additional dollar of profits earned by a firm, as it approaches the maximum limit, acts as an albatross around the neck of the earner and

becomes something undesirable, something to contend with, and a potentially serious liability.

Rate-Factor Limits

A somewhat more feasible alternative to quantity-limits is the imposition of a maximum permitted rate-of-return on invested capital. Such methods are now used to regulate the rates charged to customers of public utility companies, which are government-sanctioned monopolies. This method has some conceptual merit in that it relates maximum allowed profits to the total amount of invested capital. The maximum profit allowed, then, is determined by multiplying the quantity of invested capital by a selected percentage. Regulatory difficulties have historically involved implementation controversies concerning the measurement of invested capital and the selection of an appropriate return factor. In view of the fact that this method has some theoretical appeal and that it has been used for many years in some industries, it is intuitively attractive as a viable policy. Therefore, it is relevant to examine the extent to which this method overcomes the disadvantages of the quantity-limits approach.

First, even though the rate-factor limits approach allows the maximum profits permitted a corporation to vary with the level of invested capital, a ceiling is effectively placed on profits since the amount of invested capital is relatively fixed in the short run. A commission or agency would be required, as with the quantity-limits approach, to determine that ceiling by selecting an acceptable rate of permitted profit. Lobbying effort directed toward influencing this commission would likely be primarily from industry groups, because of the rate-factor limits would tend to be industry-wide. The concentration of lobbying effort at industry level would indicate that considerable funds might be available to support this activity. We conclude that the use of rate-factor limits would create an even more undesirable situation regarding political pressure than would quantity-limits regulation of individual firms.

Second, rate-factor approaches to profits control would not appear to materially reduce the administrative problems associated with quantity-limit methods. The continuing need for public utility regulatory bodies provides ample evidence of this fact.

Finally, rate-factor methods create a ceiling profit in much the same manner as do quantity-limit approaches. Consequently, similar disincentives for efficiency and increased production exist for both alternatives.

In summary, the differences between rate-factor methods and quantity-limit methods of profit control appear to be more cosmetic than substantive. Additionally, the disadvantages of the above methods are made much more significant due to the lack of consensus in the financial community concerning the definition and computation of profit.

The Problem of Profit Definition

Contrary to popular belief, the determination of profit is an imperfect process. Many people, inside as well as outside government, believe that profit can be determined as exactly as one measures the height or weight of a child. This popular misconception has been caused, in part, by the fact that profit is easy to understand conceptually and easy to communicate at an abstract level. For instance, there is much agreement among economists that profit can be defined as:

> "Pure surplus or excess of total receipts over all costs of production incurred by the firm."[4]

The problem and disagreements result from attempts to apply the concept to a real-life situation. These pragmatic problems have been the

(Continued On Page 4)

The Aliens Are Among Us

By J. Neil Schulman

They are here: invisible, silent, and fearsome. They drain away the lifeblood of hard-working Americans. They infiltrate our borders by several millions per year. They take jobs away from honest American workers. They are a curse, a plague, an invasion. They are the bane of our failing economy: to be hunted down, to be stopped at all costs.

And they don't even pay income tax.

Clearly, aliens are a national pestilence and have been so for a number of years. Americans, however, are not insensitive to this grave national menace: in 1938 an Orson Welles radio drama about an alien invasion was enough to send thousands of patriotic Americans into the streets ready to do battle. (Curiously, that radio drama was broadcast also during one of this nation's periodic, economic downturns.) Three years later fiction became fact as the United States went to war against aliens, and actually found a large number of them masquerading as native-born American citizens. Naturally, the alien imposters were immediately locked into prison camps for the duration of the war.

(Few Americans were thinking about the economy at that point. The aliens were a much more serious problem.)

It is most important to realize that oftentimes there is little or no difference in physical appearance between an alien and an American — "Star Trek" propaganda to the contrary. (Indeed, that television has been dominated by alien interests from its inception is virtually axiomatic; have you ever encountered a television receiver not linked to the telltale antennae?) Aliens do not necessarily have green skin — though other shades are quite fashionable — or antennae, or even pointed ears, for that matter. As an example, one alien, Clark Kent, was smuggled into the United States as a child, maintaining his cover throughout World War Two by serving with distinction. He was later deported because the immigration quota for Krypton was filled the year he entered.

Nevertheless, inasmuch as aliens precipitate panics, depressions, and wars, Americans have had good cause to feel alienated. We find ourselves again in another of our periodic, economic downturns, and there is sufficient evidence to once more place the blame where it belongs: squarely on the shoulders of the aliens.

It can be clearly demonstrated that aliens have infiltrated our economy, taking welfare and jobs away from deserving American citizens. It is now more important than ever that we understand how these aliens have wormed their way into decent American society, and take drastic measures to dig them out.

To begin with, aliens are naturally lazy, untrained, unfamiliar with our business practices, sickly, and able to speak English only with great difficulty. These qualifications are used by aliens to obtain free medical and welfare benefits. As a stopgap measure, it is strongly advisable that patriotic Americans stage a slowdown, "call in sick," and muddle their English. These are surefire tactics to win back our hard-earned benefits for ourselves.

Next, the aliens seduce jobs from greedy American employers by agreeing to work "off the books." Inasmuch as the employer no longer must withhold income or social security taxes from that employee's paycheck, the alien is able to walk away with the same pay as a citizen, while saving his employer a good deal of money. (These traitorous employers can be easily identified by their uncanny ability to undersell their competitors at a profit.) Here, particulary, is where immediate action is called for: until these aliens can be dealt with directly, it is the patriotic duty of every American to cease paying these taxes, to restore the competitive edge to those loyal employers who have stuck with American labor. It is unusual, of course, but it's a matter of saving American jobs for American workers.

Most importantly, the aliens must not be allowed to reproduce. They must be stopped now before it's too late. Several hundred years ago a relatively small group of aliens landed on this continent and systematically multiplied. For the results, ask any Indian. If you can find one. ◼

Profits Regulation —

(Continued From Page 3)

source of much controversy in the financial community for many decades, resulting in numerous and continuing attempts by the accounting profession to establish generally accepted measurement standards. For example, the economists' definition of profit requires capital appreciation to be recognized as income when the appreciation occurs. Tax law and accounting rules permit recognition of capital appreciation only when property is sold because a market transaction is required to precisely measure the profit. Nevertheless, failure to include capital appreciation in the income measurement process distorts it as a measure of economic reality. Similarly, the cost of a factor of production is considered by economists to be the equivalent of the benefits foregone from the most profitable alternative use of the factor.[3] As a practical matter, accounting rules and tax law define cost as the actual purchase price of the factor. In reality, the differences between the two measures may be significant. The latter approach has been adopted by the business community and by taxing authorities because it can be precisely computed in spite of the fact that it may constitute a significant distortion of economic reality.

Because of attributes such as capital appreciation and alternative use benefit cannot be precisely measured in many instances, the economists' theoretical concept of profit cannot be practically implemented. Conversely, it is apparent that the approximations used in tax law and accounting have no substantive theoretical support — a factor which prevents either government or business from reaching a consensus about how profit should be measured.

One need only examine the Internal Revenue Code and the rather voluminous regulations and cases which interpret it to determine that the government has never resolved the problem of what constitutes taxable profit. Reference to Securities and Exchange Commission regulations (Accounting Series Releases) leads one to reach the same conclusion. The accounting profession has not been successful in establishing a uniform set of generally accepted accounting principles governing income measurement in spite of continuing efforts to do so for more than thirty years.[6]

Conclusion

It is, therefore, apparent that attempts to regulate profit as a tool for combating inflation is ill-advised simply because there is no generally accepted definition of how profit can be measured. This problem should certainly be resolved before one risks creating massive production and efficiency disincentives in the economic system that could result in economic chaos and increasing inflationary pressures due to curtailment of supply.

[1] Business Week (March 10, 1973), p. 40.

[2] Chatfield, Michael. A History of Accounting Thought (Hinsdale, Ill.: The Dryden Press, 1974), p. 207.

[3] Internal Revenue Code, Sec. 11.

[4] Leftwich, Richard. The Price System and Resource Allocation (New York: Hold, Rinehart, and Winston, Inc., 1966), p. 168.

[5] Ibid., pp. 126-127.

[6] An analytical explanation of these issues is extremely technical and beyond the scope of this paper. ◼

Spooner Vs. Liberty

By Carl Watner

Recently our Editor has published an essay entitled "Justice and Property Rights." The main theme of his article is first, to demonstrate that libertarians must have a means, independent of the State, to determine the rightness or wrongness of property holdings, and secondly, to furnish us with such a theory of proprietary justice. His program is based on two fundamental premises: "(a) the absolute property right of each individual in his own person, his own body; this may be called the **right of self-ownership**; and (b) the absolute right in material property of the person who first finds an unused material resource and then in some way occupies or transforms that resource by the use of his personal energy. This might be called the **homestead principle** . . ."¹ These same premises, in one form or another, were bandied about by the 19th Century native American individualist anarchists. Since today's libertarians are more or less their direct descendants, it will be enlightening to examine their disputes about the homesteading and self-ownership axioms.

Probably the two most famous of the American anarchists of the last half of the 19th Century were Benjamin Tucker and Lysander Spooner. Fortunately for us, Spooner's writings have been preserved and reprinted. Although Tucker was not a book writer, his thought has been carried down to us through his writings in his periodical LIBERTY (1881-1908). As we will see, some of their ideas are yet in accord with our contemporary libertarian thought. Although Murray Rothbard has seen fit to criticize Spooner and Tucker in his essay, "The Spooner-Tucker Doctrine from the Point of View of an Economist," in fact, much of Spooner's thinking on land titles was actually in accord with the program Dr. Rothbard advocates.²

Spooner defended unlimited private land ownership and grounded his support of this theory on the homesteading axiom: "The right of property in material wealth is acquired, . . . in one of these two ways, viz.: first, by simply taking possession of natural wealth, or the productions of nature; and, secondly by the artificial production of other wealth . . . The **natural wealth** of the world belongs to those who **first** take possession of it . . . There is no limit, fixed by the law of nature, to the amount of property one may acquire simply by taking possession of natural wealth, not already possessed, except the limit fixed by (a person's) power or ability to take such possession, without doing violence to the person or property of others."³ Spooner would have definitely agreed with Rothbard, that ". . . once a piece of land passes justly into Mr. A's ownership, he cannot be said to truly own that land unless he can convey or sell the title to Mr. B, and to prevent B from exercising his title simply because he doesn't choose to use it himself but rather rents it out voluntarily to Mr. C, is an invasion of B's freedom of contract and of his right to his justly-acquired private property."⁴

Spooner had expressed his ideas on land ownership in his LAW OF INTELLECTUAL PROPERTY (1855) and in his pamphlet, REVOLUTION: A REPLY TO 'DUNRAVEN' (1880). Tucker took him to task in LIBERTY: "I call Spooner's work on 'Intellectual Property' positively foolish because it is fundamentally foolish, — because, that is to say, its discussion of the acquisition of property starts with a basic proposition that must be looked upon by all consistent Anarchists as obvious nonsense. I quote this basic proposition. 'The natural wealth of the world belongs to those who first take possession of it . . . So much natural wealth, remaining unpossessed, as anyone can take possession of first, becomes absolutely his property.' "⁵ Tucker charged Spooner with being a defender of unlimited land ownership since Spooner's proposition would allow that ". . . a man may go to a piece of vacant land and fence it off; that he may then go to a second piece and fence that off; then to a third, and fence that off; then to a fourth, a fifth, a hundredth, a thousandth, fencing them all off; that, unable to fence off himself as many as he wishes, he may hire other men to do fencing for him; and that then he may stand back and bar all other men from using these lands, or admit them as tenants at such rental as he may choose to exact."⁶ In these circumstances, Tucker asked: "What becomes of the Anarchistic doctrine of occupancy and use as the basis and limit of land ownership?"⁷

Tucker was a great critic of the land ownership system existing in the 19th Century. Absentee land ownership presented a serious problem in Ireland. Due to the agitation of the "No-Rent Movement" and the Irish Land League and the publicity of the ideas of Henry George, the subject of land ownership was very much a topic of public concern. Tucker believed that the occupancy and use theory of land holding solved the problem of justice in land ownership. The essence of the theory was that only actual users or possessors of the land (i.e., the Irish tenants) could be considered its owners. Occupancy and use as the basis for land ownership would free for use all land not actually being occupied by its owners. Thus landlords would cease to exist, as would all renting or leasing of real property, since the absentee landlord could claim no title or control over his unoccupied property. Spooner was quite critical of this doctrine: in fact he labelled it communism. The premise of any argument denying property rights in any form is communism. ". . . There is, therefore, no middle ground between absolute communism, on the one hand, which holds that a man has a right to lay his hands on any thing, which has no other man's hands upon it, no matter who may have been the producer; and the principle of individual property, on the other hand, which says that each man has an absolute dominion, as against all other men, over the products and acquisitions of his own labor, whether he retains them in his actual possession or not."⁸

Tucker believed that "a man cannot be allowed, merely by putting labor, to the limit of his capacity and beyond the limit of his personal use, into material of which there is a limited supply and the use of which is essential to the existence of other men, to withhold that material from other men's uses; and any contract based upon or involving such

(Continued On Page 6)

'Under'-Population?

It was bound to happen. We can almost formulate a sociological law: that social "problems", real or alleged, get discovered and complained about only when they are beginning to fade away, and that, furthermore, the peak of belly-aching about them is reached after they have disappeared. Note, for example, the widespread wailing, largely unjustified, about the level of population. In the 1920's and 1930's, the falling birth rate led to sharply falling population growth. The cry went up then that the world was getting gravely underpopulated, and that we were on the way to "racial suicide." Governments gave bounties for large families, and heavy propaganda was beamed at the public about the great and good virtues of large numbers of babies, the more the better. The major reason was a desire of the governments for more cannon fodder for future wars.

After World War II, the large-family movement paid off, aided and abetted by the desire of returning war veterans to put down roots and to produce new lives after their personal and international confrontation with death. The result was an unusual — and clearly temporary — reversal in the long-run secular pattern of declining population growth throughout the Western world. The post-war "baby boon" had arrived.

In the last half-dozen years, as we all know, hysteria about "over-population" has mounted to a fierce crescendo, replete with anti-baby propaganda, a strident call for Zero Population Growth and even no-child families. During and after World War II, the three great constants of general social sanctity in America were the flag, motherhood, and "Mom's apple pie." The flag has certainly received a severe — and long overdue — social setback. I don't know how the country now feels about apple pie, but "motherhood" has certainly fallen from its recent high pedestal. The irony, however, is that the ZPG hysteria reached its peak precisely at a time when the rate of population growth in America had resumed its sharp pre-war downward trend, so that the goal of ZPG has now been nearly achieved as a result of natural social forces. The census of 1970 soon revealed the sharply declining birth rate, along with the rapid declines in absolute levels of population throughout the South and Middle West, as well as the slow declines in population levels in most of the inner cities of the country. (Only the suburbs experienced a sharp rise in population.)

A year or so ago, realistic social analysts began to realize that it was only a matter of time when the old hysteria about "under" population would rapidly begin to replace the worry about "over" population. The one constant **motif** in all the clamor, whichever contradictory form it may take, is that the natural, free market levels of population are undesirable, and that government control of some sort must supply a corrective. Sure enough, the cry of underpopulation has already begun to appear. It began as a cloud no bigger than a man's hand with the results of the 1970 census. Since cities throughout the country receive federal subsidies per head of population, mayors and governors across the land began to have fits, shouting that the Census had underestimated their population, and desperately calling for recounts to beat the bushes to find more people, the more the better.

That clamor was so blatantly self-serving that few took it seriously. But it was a beginning. Now, Owen Moritz reports in alarm that the New York City metropolitan area is (Woe, O Woe!) "running out of people," (?) (Owen Moritz, "Sub-Zero Population Growth," New York Sunday News, January 26, 1975).

In the late 1930's, Professor Alvin Hansen, the leading Keynesian economist in the United States, wailed that declining population growth was one of the major factors prolonging the Great Depression. (Presumably because not enough bassinets, etc. were being purchased.) Now, we hear the same theme again, as Moritz reports that the Mayor and Governor of New York are worried about "fewer babies, empty classrooms, more old people, a loss of middle-class whites, a falloff in black migration and a shrinking of the work force," in the suburbs as well as in "the graying cities." So — now we hear about the grave evils of a "shrinking work force" and the increased ratio of old people to kids, which everyone might have predicted would flow from declining population growth. Yet, these consequences seem to hit the Establishment as a bolt from the blue. The young people, wails the News reporter, are "disappearing" from New York. Doesn't this at least help

"overcrowding" and welfare breakdowns which had previously been held to be grave problems? No answer.

In suburban Nassau County, County Executive Ralph Caso delivered a county message complaining bitterly about the decline in the number of school kids, "raising the spector of empty classrooms." The exuberant News writer even refers to school kids as an "endangered species" — killed off by fascistic macho hunters, no doubt. The Regional Plan Association has also raised the grave warning that the New York City region has "stopped growing" (Tsk! Tsk! Truly a ghost area!) The formerly much desired but apparently now dreaded ZPG has hit throughout the New York area, and young people are heading out to rural areas. The RPA concluded "sorrowfully", that "benefits of no-growth are eluding us. Instead of reducing the need to control land-use, no-growth makes it even more urgent." Of course; clearly, whatever happens, whether population rises, falls, or remains the same, the **conclusion** is always the same: more government control of population and land use. Clearly, the RPA and other Establishment planners would like to fix, not only the total level of population, but also the population, by age strata, in each particular land area. Freeze everybody where they are! They will never be happy until a form of serfdom has been re-instituted, with everyone tied to his or her geographic area, and other and even more sinister forms of population control established in each of the areas. Or, as the News puts it, "The aged population grows. What it means is that the tax-paying force is shrinking and threatens to shrivel more — and this . . . is the ominous thing."

Yes, it looks as if hysteria about under-population will soon be with us, with a concern for more warm taxpaying bodies replacing the older concern for more cannon fodder. The logical implication of all this is fascist totalitarianism and a new serfdom. It is high time that we call for the size and shape of the population, urban, rural, or total, to be left alone, to be the result of voluntary action by all individuals in the society. It is high time, in short, that we forget about population and concentrate our worries on the numerous ways in which the government and its minions are seeking to place us all in a totalitarian prison-society. □

Spooner — (Continued From Page 5)

withholding is as lacking in sanctity or legitimacy as a contract to deliver stolen goods.'" Under Tucker's theory, if "a man exerts himself by erecting a building on land which afterward, by the principle of occupancy and use, rightfully becomes another's, he must, upon demand of the subsequent occupant, remove from this land, the results of his self-exertion, or, failing to do so, sacrifice his property rights therein. The man who persists in storing his property on another's premises is an invader and it is his crime that alienates control of this property. He is 'fined one house,' not for 'building a house and then letting another man live in it,' but for invading the premises of another.'" Thus Tucker admitted that homesteading, in the form of original possession or self-exertion furnished no basis for a continuing claim to land ownership, after the homesteader left the land. To further illustrate his differences with Spooner, Tucker related a conversation that he had with Spooner concerning the rightfulness of the Irish rebellion against absentee landlords: "Mr. Spooner bases his opposition to Irish and English landlords on the **sole** ground that they or their ancestors took their lands **by the sword** from the original holders. This he plainly stated, — so plainly that I took issue with Mr. Spooner on this point when he asked me to read the manuscript (REVOLUTION) before its publication. I then asked him whether if Dunraven (the absentee landlord) or his ancestors had found unoccupied the very lands that he now holds, and had fenced them off, he would have any objection to raise against Dunraven's title and to leasing of these lands. He declared emphatically that he would not. Whereupon I protested that his pamphlet, powerful as it was within its scope, did not go to the bottom of the land question.'"

Much of Tucker's concern with the land problem was based on his apprehension of the monopoly problem. He is well known for his four-

(Continued On Page 7)

Spooner — (Continued From Page 6)

pronged attack on monopolies: land, banking, tariff, and copyright and patent. Tucker feared that the right of contract would be carried to an illogical extreme: ". . . It would be possible (under a regime of unfettered freedom of contract in land) for an individual to acquire, and hold simultaneously, virtual titles to innumerable parcels of land, by the merest show of labor performed thereon; . . . (and) . . . we should be forced to consider . . . the virtual ownership of nearly the entire earth by a small fraction of its inhabitants . . ."[12] Analogous to his position on land ownership, Tucker also attacked the literary monopolization of ideas based on copyright. Spooner was a consistent defender of property in all forms and claimed for inventors and authors a perpetual copyright in their work. It is plain that neither could agree until their theories of ownership were harmonized, and both either adopted or rejected the homesteading principle.

The question over land ownership and the homesteading principle was not the only controversy carried on in the pages of LIBERTY. Equally interesting is the letter and editorial writing concerning the self-ownership axiom which took place under the guise of discussing the rights of parents and children. Originally the question began as whether parents should be legally responsible for abuse and neglect of their children. Tucker's initial conclusion was that we must not interfere to prevent neglect of the child, but only to repress positive invasion.

However, Tucker, having reconsidered his opinion, resolved that ". . . the change then which my opinion has undergone consists simply in the substitution of certainty for doubt as to the non-invasive character of parental cruelty, — a substitution which involves the conclusion that parental cruelty is not to be prohibited . . ."[13] Tucker's opinion is grounded on the fact that he views the child as the property of the mother. Children, in Tucker's estimation, belong in the category of things to be owned, rather than as being owners of themselves. However he does note that the "child differs from all other parts of that category (of things to be owned) in the fact that there is steadily developing within him the power of self-emancipation, which at a certain point enables him to become an owner instead of remaining part of the owned."[14] Tucker saw ". . . no clearer property title in the world than that of the mother to the fruit of her womb, unless she has otherwise disposed of it by contract. Certainly the mother's title to the child while it remains in her womb will not be denied by any Anarchist. To deny this would be to deny the right of the mother to commit suicide during pregnancy, and I never knew an Anarchist to deny the right of suicide. If, then, the child is the mother's while in the womb, by what consideration does title to it become vested in another than the mother on its emergence from the womb pending the day of its emancipation?"[15]

Tucker clearly refused to invoke the self-ownership axiom towards children, at least until they had reached the age of being able to contract and provide for themselves. In the meantime, he recognized the right of the mother to throw her property into the fire. "I answer that it is highly probable that I would interfere in such a case (as a mother throwing her infant into the flames). My interference no more invalidates the mother's property right in the child than if I prevent the owner of a Titian painting from destroying it. If I interfere in either case, it is only as an invader and I would have to be prepared to suffer the consequences."[16] According to his logic "the outsider who uses force upon the child invades, not the child, but its mother, and may be rightfully punished for doing so. The mother who uses force upon her child invades nobody . . . To be consistent, I must convict a man of murder in the first degree who kills a father in the act of killing his child."[17]

One of Tucker's critics realized that Tucker could not be attacked until the concept of contract as the ethical basis of anarchism was overthrown. Said this critic, "I do not accept contract as the ethical basis of Anarchism in the first place, and, in the second, do not regard children as the property of anybody . . . I base my anarchism on Natural Right . . . Perhaps no Anarchist will deny the right of the mother to commit suicide during pregnancy, but I do deny it after the embryo becomes a human being. The mother has a right to kill herself, but no one else."[18] "In my category of the owners and the owned I state it thus: Each being owns himself = No human being owns another."[19] Of course, we recognize this as a reformulation of the self-ownership axiom.

For Tucker, rights only begin as a social convention. Rights are liberties created by mutual agreement and contract. He defended his concept of self-emancipation by stating that "any child capable of

declaring to the association's (an anarchistic enforcement agency) officers its desire for release from its owner that it may thereafter either care for itself or entrust itself to the care of persons more agreeable to it thereby proves the presence in its mind of the idea of contract . . . From the moment that a child makes a deliberate declaration of this character it should cease to be property and should pass into the category of owners."[20] Tucker refused to see any alternative to his own position. "If we take the other course and admitting, that the child has the possibilities of the man, declare that therefore it cannot be property, then we must also for the same reason, say that the ovum in the woman's body is not her property, . . ." and thus being made to conceive when she is raped, she thereby loses her right to commit suicide.[21] Tucker failed to realize that no human "being has a right to live, unbidden, as a parasite within or upon some person's body."[22] He refused to view the fetus as a possible invader of the mother's body, since it was already her property to do with as she pleased. Consequently any invasive treatment of the child was not wrong since it was the mother's property.

The foregoing narrative of these two disputes, between Spooner and Tucker over land ownership, and between Tucker and his critics concerning property rights in children, should hold our strong interest. Here is one reason why a theory of justice in all forms of property is necessary. If libertarians cannot settle on such a theory of justice, a libertarian society will be disrupted by such disputes. Similarly, if no such theory of justice is arrived at, it will be impossible for libertarians to consistently attack our present governmental system.   ◘

Footnotes

[1] Murray N. Rothbard, EGALITARIANISM AS A REVOLT AGAINST NATURE AND OTHER ESSAYS, p. 58.
[2] Ibid., p. 128.
[3] Lysander Spooner, THE LAW OF INTELLECTUAL PROPERTY, pp. 21-22.
[4] Rothbard, op. cit., p. 128.
[5] LIBERTY (March 21, 1891) Whole No. 180, p. 4.
[6] Ibid.
[7] Ibid.
[8] Spooner, op. cit., p. 88.
[9] LIBERTY (January 25, 1896) Whole No. 331, p. 4.
[10] Ibid.
[11] LIBERTY (April 18, 1891) Whole No. 182, p. 6.
[12] LIBERTY (February 1897) Whole No. 350, p. 4.
[13] LIBERTY (August 24, 1895) Whole No. 320, p. 4.
[14] LIBERTY (June 29, 1895) Whole No. 316, p. 3.
[15] LIBERTY (August 24, 1895) Whole No. 320, p. 4.
[16] LIBERTY (September 7, 1895) Whole No. 321, p. 1.
[17] LIBERTY (September 21, 1895) Whole No. 322, pp. 5, 8.
[18] J. Wm. Lloyd, LIBERTY (September 21, 1895) Whole No. 322, p. 6.
[19] LIBERTY (November 2, 1895) Whole No. 325, p. 7.
[20] LIBERTY (November 2, 1895) Whole No. 325, p. 5.
[21] LIBERTY (December 14, 1895) Whole No. 328, p. 5.
[22] Murray N. Rothbard, FOR A NEW LIBERTY, p. 121.

"The state . . . in all kinds of countries, and in all kinds of forms, . . . is setting up shop as a universal savior. Its qualifications for that office, at first glance, look very impressive. It has power of an extremely papable and overt variety, flowing from the end of the policeman's espantoon. It penetrates to every nook and fissure of the national life, and so takes on an appearance of omniscience. It is staffed by men who are, by definition, eminent, and in that character are heard politely, even when they talk nonsense. Most of all, there is something mystical about it, something transcendental and even supernatural, so that simple people, thinking of it, slip naturally into the moony ways of thought that they employ in thinking about the awful enigmas of Heaven and Hell.

Its real nature thus tends to be concealed, and, in the long run, forgotten. That real nature may be described briefly. The state . . . consists of a gang of men exactly like you and me. They have, taking one with another, no special talent for the business of government; they have only a talent for getting and holding office. Their principal device to that end is to search out groups who pant and pine for something they can't get, and to promise to give it to them. Nine times out of ten that promise is worth nothing. The tenth time it is made good by looting A to satisfy B. In other words, government is a broker in pillage, and every election is a sort of advance auction sale of stolen goods."
                                                                — H. L. Mencken

Forthcoming Spring Books

We cannot, of course, recommend the following books (except for paperback reprints), since they have not yet appeared, but the following is a list of books to be published this spring which give promise of being of interest to libertarian readers.

Dr. Walter Block's long-awaited "Hero" series, some of which have been published in the Lib. Forum, will be brought out in book form by Fleet Publishers. Walter Block, **Defending the Undefendables: The Pimp, Prostitute, Scab, Slumlord, Libeler, Usurer, and Other Scapegoats in the Rogue's Gallery of American Society**, will be published on May 10. Walter Block is distinguished for being a fearless logician, and his "Hero" series has long served as the **pons asinorum** of one's devotion to libertarianism. It is easy enough — and correct, too — to present libertarianism in the vaguely humanist form of the voluntary way, and of one's right to control one's own life. Fine enough; but how many of us are ready to defend, with equal relish, the pimp, the scab, the libeler, the slumlord, et al? In their notice on the book, Fleet asks: "Should deviant but non-aggressive behavior be permitted in a just society? Yes, says Dr. Walter Block in his rogue's gallery depicting the life of 'objects of universal revulsion' . . ." A challenging work for all but the hardest of the hard core.

Long-time Lib. Forum contributor and noted author Jerome Tuccille's next book, **Who's Afraid of 1984?** will be published by Arlington House in May. It will present the fruit of his researches into the New Deal origins of the present system, as well as a critique, grounded on his profound social optimism, of leftish doomsayers.

Ex-rightwinger, ex-neo-Randian, ex-libertarian, ex-Lib. Forum contributor, Karl Hess, presents his odyssey from right to left in **Dear America** (William Morrow, May 7), which Morrow is slating for major publicity and distribution. It will presumably present his current left-syndicalist views, and whatever else we may say about it, will undoubtedly be very well-written.

We have not yet had a satisfactory political history of the origins of the American Revolution (Bernard Bailyn's work is brilliant and indispensable, but it is an intellectual and not a political history.) By far the best work has been the superb volume by Bernhard Knollenberg, **The Origin of the American Revolution, 1759-65**. But we have not had the story for the crucial years between 1765 and the outbreak of the Revolution at Lexington and Concord. Now, the Free Press is publishing the final volume — unfortunately posthumous — of Knollenberg's history: **The Growth of the American Revolution, 1766-75** (April). Warning: judging from all of Knollenberg's previous work, the book will not be stirringly or sparklingly written; but it will be definitive.

In contrast to the other books, John P. Diggins, **Mussolini and Fascism: the View from America** is a known quantity, since it has been out for some time in hard cover. Now, Professor Diggins' excellent revisionist work is being published in paper this spring by Princeton University Press. Diggins shows the lure that Italian Fascism held, throughout the 1920's and 30's for both liberal intellectuals and businessmen in America, since it seemed to provide a harmonious, nationalistic "third way" between Communism and laissez-faire. Highly recommended.

Finis Farr's **Fair Enough** (Arlington House, April) is a prominent conservative writer's biography of the courageous right-wing muckraking journalist, Westbrook Pegler. The only extant biography of "Peg" is by the rather hysterical liberal Oliver Pilat, and Farr's work is certain to do far more justice to this late, controversial figure.

Ronald Radosh's **Prophets on the Right** (Simon & Schuster) — which promises to be a scintillating study of "right-wing" isolationists and opponents of both World War II and the Cold War, is already driving Radosh's Marxist colleagues up the wall. A co-editor with Murray Rothbard of **A New History of Leviathan**, Prof. Radosh presents what should be an important revisionist study of: Charles A. Beard, John T. Flynn, Robert A. Taft, Lawrence Dennis and Oswald Garrison Villard. Radosh has already contributed a notable and laudatory review of Wayne Cole's revisionist study of Lindbergh, **Charles A. Lindbergh and the Battle Against American Intervention in World War II**, to the New York Sunday Times Book Review.   ◻

"Dr. (John W.) Davis is a lawyer whose life has been devoted to protecting the great enterprises of Big Business. He used to work for J. Pierpont Morgan, and he has himself said that he is proud of the fact. Mr. Morgan is an international banker . . . (whose) operations are safeguarded for him by the manpower of the United States. He was one of the principal beneficiaries of the late war, and made millions out of it. The Government hospitals are now full of one-legged soldiers who gallantly protected his investments then, and the public schools are full of boys who will protect his investments tomorrow."

— H. L. Mencken

A Monthly Newsletter

THE
Libertarian Forum

Joseph R. Peden, Publisher   Murray N. Rothbard, Editor

VOLUME VII, NO. 4   APRIL, 1975   US-ISSN0047-4517

The Death Of A State

What we are seeing these last weeks in Indochina is, for libertarians, a *particularly exhilirating experience: the death of a State, or rather two* States: Cambodia and South Vietnam. The exhiliration stems from the fact that here is not just another **coup d'etat**, in which the State apparatus remains virtually intact and only a few oligarchs are shuffled at the top. Here is the total and sudden collapse — the smashing — of an entire State apparatus, its accelerating and rapid disintegration. Of course, the process does not now usher in any sort of libertarian **Nirvana**, since another bloody State is in the process of taking over. But the disintegration remains, and offers us many instructive lessons.

One lesson is an illustration of the profound truth set forth by David Hume and Ludwig von Mises: that no matter how bloody or despotic any State may be, it rests for its existence in the long-run (and not-so-long run) on the consent of the majority of its subjects, on the "voluntary servitude" (as La Boetie first phrased it) of the bulk of its victims. This mass acceptance need not be active enthusiasm; it can be passive resignation; *but the important thing is that it rests on the willingness of* the masses to obey the orders and commands of the State apparatus — to accept the dictates of the oligarchy, to pay its taxes, to fight in its wars. What happened in South Vietnam, in particular, was what often happens after a long harrowing period of losing war: a sudden and infectious decision of the masses to say: Enough! We've had it; we quit. The supposedly mighty million-man South Vietnamese (ARVN) army, trained for decades by American commanders, armed to the teeth by the United States, praised as "little tigers" by the U. S. military, just quit and ran, leaving behind over $1 billion in U. S. taxpayer-financed arms.

The best description of this momentous event has been portrayed, not by one of our famous heavy-thinking pundits, but by the supposedly "light" San Francisco columnist Arthur Hoppe. (Arthur Hoppe, "The Land That Never Was," **San Francisco Chronicle**, April 7, 1975). Hoppe's column is worth quoting at length:

"All last week we watched the Republic of South Vietnam fall apart. One day The Republic of South Vietnam was a sovereign nation. It had an army of a million men. It had an air force, tanks, artillery and tons of ammunition. It had a president and a vast bureaucracy of tax collectors, prosecutors and policemen. It had its own diplomats, its own currency, its own flag.

It had a population of 20 million people who, whether they favored it or not, believed that there was such a thing as The Republic of South Vietnam. It had, then, all that is required for an area delineated on a map to be termed a sovereign nation.

And yet, virtually overnight, this sovereign nation all but ceased to exist.

What happened? . . . Why didn't the soldiers of this sovereign nation fight? Yet no rational soldier fights because he wants to fight. He fights because he is told by his sergeant who is told by his captain who is told by his general

who is told by his president, who is the embodiment of the sovereign nation, to fight.

He and his fellow soldiers fight because they believe in the power of their sovereign nation to require them to fight. And they flee when they no longer believe in that power. So the soldiers fled because they lost faith in their officers and the power of the sovereign nation they represented. And the people and the bureaucrats fled in bloodshed and terror because they lost faith in the army and the power of the sovereign nation to defend them.

So this loss of faith spread in an ever-expanding chain reaction until the sovereign nation of The Republic of South Vietnam all but ceased to exist . . . .

In the way it rapidly fell apart in horror last week, it seemed to demonstrate that sovereign nations exist on faith alone. They are created in the minds of men. They exist only in the minds of men. They have power over their citizens solely because their citizens believe they have power. . . . And once that mystical, ephemeral faith that binds together the citizens of any sovereign nation is all but lost, that sovereign nation inevitably all but ceases to exist."

Precisely! And whatever we may say of the myriad supporters of the PRG and of the North Vietnamese regime, they certainly have the faith. *An essential reason for the loss of faith by the South Vietnamese soldiery and population is that the government had no real roots in popular support.* The Saigon regime has for generations been a puppet of some outside imperialist power: first of the French, and then of the United States. Hence its supporters were mainly only that relative handful that either worked for the Americans or were the recipients of American **largesse.** If it were not for the might of France, all of Vietnam would have — almost did — gone Communist in 1945, and if not for the increasingly massive intervention of the U. S., would have done so in 1954 or any of the years since.

A corollary lesson of the collapse, then, is the long-run impossibility for an imperialist-dominated regime to survive, when opposed by guerilla warfare backed by the great majority of the population. And this despite the enormous advantage in firepower and in modern weaponry that the imperialist power, and then its puppets, initially enjoy. **Where** did the guerrillas manage to get their arms from? Not mainly, as U. S. mythology so long proclaimed, from the Russians, or down the so-called "Ho Chi Minh Trail." Where they got it was from losing and defecting puppet forces themselves, who served as a conduit for American arms. The ARVN's leaving behind of over $1 billion of American arms for the benefit of the PRG and North Vietnam is only the most dramatic *manifestation of this vital fact.*

Imperialism, then, cannot win; and we have now learned this lesson

(Continued On Page 2)

Death Of A State —

(Continued From Page 1)

after the Johnson-Nixon regimes managed to murder a million or more Vietnamese, North and South, along with over 50,000 American soldiers. All that blood and treasure just to postpone the inevitable!

But while the American public has apparently learned this cruel lesson, the egregious and absurd Ford Administration obviously has not. There they go, down with the ship, to the bitter end, mouthing the same tired old hooey: about "one more chance", about the need for the U. S. to spend yet another $700 million to buy a few months' time, about the old discredited "domino theory", about the necessity of the U. S. taxpayer to "fight for freedom throughout the world" as Ford once again put it. For "freedom" read a bloody fascist dictatorship (of the Thieu clique in Vietnam, the Lon Nol-Long Baret clique in Cambodia); for "one more chance" read another billion dollars to be poured down the same old rathole in which we've already poured countless billions. And then, the final slice of baloney: the need to send in American troops once more, this time to "evacuate" those South Vietnamese to whom we have a commitment" and who will suffer a "bloodbath" if we don't rush in. Fortunately, praise the Lord!, Congress and the American people have apparently had enough themselves. Maybe they could be tricked into massive aid and another war somewhere else; but in Vietnam? Again? The left-liberal Democrats are militantly opposed, and even the Republicans seem, at long last, to be sick of the whole affair and eager to stay out. Fortunately, the 1973 Congressional prohibition against military intervention by the U. S. stands like a bulwark against the Ford-Kissinger itch to get into the fray once more. If they want to fight, let Ford, Kissinger and company outfit a boat or plane themselves with their own money, and set sail. Let us see how far they get without the American soldiers and the American taxpayers as suckers to pay the price. And good riddance! As for the wailing about the "bloodbath", it comes with ill grace indeed from the very U. S. government which has caused rivers, oceans of innocent blood to be shed in Indochina. Enough!

And of course, through it all, the eternal leitmotif of U. S. imperialism is sounded once more by Ford and his crew: the attack on "isolationism." Well, after several decades of bloody intervention everywhere, with nothing to show for it except murder, waste, militarism, and the continuing growth of indigenous Communist regimes, the collapse of interventionist imperialism should be evident to everyone. It is dawning increasingly on the American public, and even on the deluded liberals, that isolationism is precisely the only sane — much less libertarian — foreign policy for the United States. To paraphrase the late Harry Elmer Barnes, the chickens of the interventionists have come home to roost, and we are all absorbing the lesson. At the least the liberals are, and all that the conservatives need to get interred with the dodo bird is to continue their post-World War II enthusiasm for American global intervention. Knowing the mind-set of conservatives, that, of course, is probably exactly what they will do.

Fortunately, too, there has been in recent days a healthy backlash in the United States against the "baby hysteria", which looks very much like a desperate, last-ditch ploy by the administration to get us involved in Vietnam by appealing to our humanitarian and sentimentalist instincts. Many knowledgeable Vietnamese-Americans have been pointing out that (a) the Communists are scarcely about to go around butchering babies, whatever their other faults; and (b) that there is grave grounds for suspicion that the American welfare agencies have been literally kidnapping many of the babies from the Vietnamese orphanages. Many of these babies are not really orphans at all, but parked there by parents for temporary safe-keeping, until the fighting is over. Apparently, the agencies have been deliberately stripping the babies of all papers and markings, and then spiriting them to the United States, so that their Vietnamese parents will never be able to recover them.

One of the abject failures now starkly revealed is the once-famous Nixon policy of "Vietnamization". Remember that one? The Nixon theory was that we could withdraw American troops and planes, and leave a heavily armed and well-trained ARVN force to carry on; and we were assured of the success of this plan by the Pentagon until recent weeks. The howls about the North Vietnam and PRG "violation of the Paris agreements" come with peculiarly ill grace from an American-Saigon team which violated those agreements from the very beginning; egging the ARVN on to seize a large chunk of PRG territory at the

LP Convention — Come One, Come All!

The Libertarian Party is beginning to gear up for its greatest extravaganza to date: a mighty national convention in New York City this Labor Day weekend, August 28-31. At the convention, approximately 300 delegates will meet to choose a Presidential ticket for 1976, to give the LP plenty of time to get on as many state ballots as possible. But there will be place for 1,000 people in the auditorium, and so any and all interested observers are welcome to attend, at minimal cost. The party actively welcomes friends, sympathizers, and interested citizens to attend and see Libertarian Party people in action. Presumably, there will also be discussions or attempts to change the party platform. Further concrete details of time and place will be listed in the Lib. Forum. But think of it: the massed distillate of the leading LP members throughout the country will be gathering for the big event. Who can pass up such an opportunity?

Already, we have our first announced candidate for the Presidential nomination: Roger Lea MacBride, lawyer and author, who provided the LP ticket in 1972 with an electoral vote from Virginia. MacBride has formidable qualifications for the post. Bright, articulate, aristocratic, a purist libertarian who yet has a strong sense of reality, MacBride would furnish the LP ticket with a sparkling, full-time, extremely active and energetic campaign. Already, MacBride has been flying around the country (often in his own private plane) addressing LP groups and other meetings and organizations interested in the libertarian cause. In a MacBride race, we would have a candidate capable of mounting a newsmaking campaign that would yet remain sound in principle. MacBride would be shooting for a seemingly wildly remote goal: one million votes in '76. But considering the candidate, and considering the breakdown of the major party system, of the economy, and of the old misplaced American faith in government, MacBride might just be able to do it. Surely here would be a campaign and a goal for which to work with enthusiasm.

Meanwhile, New York's Free Libertarian Party has had its annual spring convention. Your editor is living in California for the spring, and so was not able to attend, but from all reports the convention was almost remarkably smooth and harmonious, free of the factionalism and of the barely suppressed hysteria of the year before. In a personal triumph, the able but formerly widely attacked Gary Greenberg has been elected state chairman. The National Office continues to be ably and dynamically run by national chairman Ed Crane; unfortunately, Ned Hutchinson, former Reagan appointments secretary and highly experienced political pro, died suddenly and tragically after joining the LP and becoming its full-time national director. He has been replaced by Robert Meier of Illinois, and by Toni Nathan, vice-presidential candidate in 1972.

All in all, the Libertarian Party continues to improve, both organizationally and in devotion to principle, year after year. Exciting times loom ahead.   ◻

precise time the cease-fire went into effect; refusing to carry out the agreement to allow Communist political parties to participate in free elections; leaving "civilian" advisers in Vietnam to carry on covert American intervention. The chickens of Vietnamization, too, are coming home to roost. As is the Nixionian intervention into Cambodia, which only prolonged and intensified the agony of the Phnom Penh regime, as the Cambodian ambassador has recently charged. And now, at the last minute, the pitiful goal of the U. S. to buy time so that the Communists will negotiate with Saigon and Phnom Penh. Why, after so many rebuffs, should the Communists negotiate now when they are at the point of victory? What boobs would they have to be to do so? And the even more pitiful covert requests by Washington to bring back Prince Norodom Sihanouk to try to cheat the Khmer Rouge out of their victory in Cambodia; and this after the U. S. engineered the right-wing coup against Sihanouk in the first place! What gall, and what stupidity!

And finally, the pitiful and egregious Ford is preparing yet another "stab in the back" myth for his 1976 campaign. All would have been well, supposedly, if only Congress had agreed to one more intervention, one more dose of massive aid, one more military adventure. Does he think

(Continued On Page 3)

The AIB Conference

From Scholarship To Political Activism
In Assassination Revisionism

By Alan Fairgate*

Libertarians who were active in the anti-draft and anti-war movements of the late 1960's and who despaired over the wave of political apathy that accompanied the collapse of the New Left at the end of the decade, will undoubtedly be encouraged to learn that a new, and potentially very promising, effort is being made to organize a mass-based political movement. The first tentative steps in this direction were made at a three-day "Politics of Conspiracy" conference sponsored by the Assassination Information Bureau in Boston on January 31-February 2, 1975. Carl Oglesby, the former president of SDS and author of the eloquent book **Containment and Change** which called for an alliance between the New Left and the libertarian Right, has emerged as a leading organizer in this new movement and it has been largely his vision that has shaped its initial organizing efforts. The focus of this new movement is a broad-based campaign to challenge the credibility of the "official" theories which have been advanced to explain the constellation of political assassinations beginning with John F. Kennedy's death in Dallas on November 22, 1963.

The "Politics of Conspiracy" conference marked a major shift in strategy among the informal network of assassination researchers which has coalesced on a national level during the past five years. The earlier attitude among assassination researchers was typified by the activities of the Washington-based Committee to Investigate Assassinations, organized by James Earl Ray's attorney, Bernard Fensterwald. During this early period, assassination research showed dangerous signs of degenerating into an intensely incestuous activity among a small "elite" of researchers who would periodically gather and exchange reports about the latest progress in the detailed probing of events and personalities surrounding the assassinations. While much of the work accomplished during this period, particularly in the form of legal suits to compel disclosure of government documents, proved extremely valuable, relatively little attention was devoted to the equally important task of publicizing the results of the research which had already been performed. The Assassination Information Bureau, which was formally established last September, emerged as the rallying point for those researchers who felt the time had come to consider the political implications of assassination research, and to develop a strategy for focusing public attention on the issues raised by the research already done.

As the position paper of the AIB makes clear: "the purpose of the AIB is to politicize the issue of the presidential assassinations." The position paper, which was written by Carl Oglesby and distributed at the conference, argues that the question "Who Killed JFK?" serves as "the root political question of the current disorder" since the answer to that question necessarily requires considerable insight into the meaning, and shifting distribution, of power in contemporary American society. While stressing the critical importance of this question, the paper cautions that it will not be settled outside the courts and that any effort to formulate a preliminary answer must be carefully labelled as mere speculation. Even more cautiously, the paper suggests that there may be an underlying interconnection uniting the various assassinations of the past decade:

> ". . . a sharp convergence of political and physical circumstances supports the view that to expose one of these conspiracies is to expose them all. We will abandon this hypothesis as coming evidence may dictate and certainly do not propose it as dogma. But on the face of the larger facts as they are currently discernible, the linked-conspiracy hypothesis illuminates better than rival theories the primary observable features of the situation three presidential assassinations and an attempted fourth (Wallace) have brought about."

In a section devoted to political strategy, the paper proceeds to outline a broad platform which can serve as an "appeal for a movement beyond the customary political lines of left and right and opening up the possibility of new configurations." Scrupulously avoiding refuge in Marxist categories or rhetoric, Oglesby appeals to the "three main ideological traditions in American politics": democracy, republicanism and nonpartisanship. On the basis of these elementary values, Oglesby argues that all principled Americans will be able to unite in a movement dedicated to exposing the truth of Dallas. Such a movement, the paper proposes, will capitalize on the mass disillusionment precipitated by the Watergate revelations and the growing awareness of the need for "a new framework of political thought, a framework that coherently situates the seemingly random concatenation of murders in an overall perspective on the evolution of American politics during the Cold War." In addition, the fortuitous coicidence of the Bicentennial Celebration and the 1976 presidential elections provides an opportunity for a two-pronged strategy emphasizing a return to the original constitutional values, and exposing the role of Gerald Ford as "one of the most aggressive members of the Warren Commission in 'selling' the lone-assassin theory".

In a "tentative and experimental sketch" of the specific programs which might be launched to implement such a political strategy, the paper suggests: (1) structured discussions of organizing strategy, (2) inauguration of a newsletter service, (3) establishment of an information office in Washington to coordinate lobbying efforts, (4) the promotion of local organizing and educational programs, including the possibility of establishing week-long summer institutes to train educational cadre, and (5) continuation of national speaking tours and other programs for the systematic distribution of information in the form of books and tapes.

The conference itself was designed to gather the leading assassination researchers and political activists from around the country and to focus

(Continued On Page 4)

Nozick Award

We extend our warm congratulations to Harvard philosophy professor Robert Nozick for winning the prestigious National Book Award in Religion and Philosophy for his quasi-libertarian inquiry into political philosophy, **Anarchy, State, and Utopia**. The book has performed the seemingly impossible feat of making the topic of libertarianism respectable in philosophic circles, and in making the doctrine something that philosophers have to study and conjure with. The book has therefore made it enormously easier for graduate students in philosophy to write dissertations on libertarian themes. Hence, it paves the way for libertarians to make great gains in the philosophy profession in the future. Professor Nozick has recently joined the Massachusetts Libertarian Party.

Death Of A State —

(Continued From Page 2)

that the American public is **that** dumb?

More and more, the Ford administration is shaping up as the true legatee of the Nixon administration. Aside from personal style, and — an important difference — the abandonment of the budding Cowboy police state at home, it's Nixon-Ford or Ford-Nixon all the way. The interventionist-imperialist foreign policy is the same, a Kissinger-Rockefeller policy; the wild-spending, interventionist economic policy under the cloak of free-market rhetoric is the same as well. Retiring Ford-Kissinger-Rockefeller to the showers begins to loom as one of the happy events to anticipate in 1976. ◻

AIB Conference —

(Continued From Page 3)

discussion on strategies for politicizing the assassination investigation issue as a basis for a mass-based political movement. Following a keynote speech by Mark Lane on Friday evening, Saturday was devoted to numerous workshops designed to introduce the participants to the latest developments in various areas of assassination research. These workshops covered the JFK, Martin Luther King and RFK assassinations; the Wallace shooting; the Chappaquidick incident; "organized crime and the economics of conspiracy"; domestic intelligence operations; and a presentation of Carl Oglesby's Yankee/Cowboy model. Saturday evening was devoted to a panel discussion on the theme "Who Done It?", which sought to summarize the results of a decade of research, and then a general session on Sunday afternoon focused on an open discussion of organizing strategy.

The participants in the conference represented a broad spectrum of researchers and included many of the leading people in the field. Mark Lane, an attorney and author of **Rush to Judgment** (the first book effectively to break the "blackout" imposed by the mass media on assassination research), emerged as the leading representative of the "moderate" faction, arguing for caution and restraint in presenting the evidence of the assassination researchers to the public. On the other hand, Sherman Skolnick joined with Mae Brussel in throwing caution to the wind and thereby straining the credulity of even many of the conference participants.

Skolnick is chairman of the Citizen's Committee to Clean Up the Courts, a Chicago organization which has acquired considerable prestige for its investigative work resulting in the indictment and conviction of numerous prominent public officials on bribery and corruption charges. Largely by coincidence, involving another investigation on which he was working, Skolnick became interested in the crash of the United Airlines flight carrying E. Howard Hunt's wife, Dorothy. Skolnick believes the plane was deliberately sabotaged as a means of frustrating an attempt by the Hunts to blackmail Nixon. While many researchers agree that Skolnick has uncovered presuasive evidence of sabotage in the airline crash, his credibility has been damaged by other allegations such as the charge that Rennie Davis and Tom Hayden were government agents planted in SDS as "agents provocateurs".

Mae Brussel produces a nationally syndicated radio show entitled "Dialogue Conspiracy" and has written for the **Realist** magazine. She periodically boasts that she has read and cross-indexed all 26 volumes of the Warren Commission report and, relying on the research she has accumulated, Brussel is willing to list by name everyone who was involved in the JFK assassination. Brussel rivals anyone in her ability to detect an all-pervasive conspiracy, involving such diverse elements as systematic climate control and an obscure global network of Croat terrorists known as the Eustasi which are based in Australia, Spain and California.

In contrast, Carl Oglesby emerged as the leading proponent of the need for a more systematic, and radical, analysis of the political system which spawned the assassinations. Several other conference participants approached the discussions from a radical perspective, including Peter Dale Scott who has undertaken a detailed study of the configurations of financial and political power in Texas and has attempted to integrate this research within the context of a national power structure. Tim Butz, a former Army Intelligence officer, represented the Fifth Estate, a Washington-based organization dedicated to researching the structure and activities of the domestic and military intelligence communities. Donald Freed, co-author of the book **Executive Action** and head of the Citizen's Research and Investigation Committee in California, diligently sought throughout the weekend to foster unity among the conference participants and to minimize the disruptive impact of conflicting ideological positions and personal rivalries.

Finally, the conference participants included an extremely heterogeneous group of researchers which defied classification. Theodore Charach, a broadcast journalist and producer of the documentary "The Second Gun", has been perhaps the most active investigator involved in the Robert F. Kennedy assassination. The Martin Luther King assassination has been the major focus of the work of Wayne Chastain, a Memphis newspaper reporter who will soon publish his book **Who Really Killed Dr. King?** Penn Jones, former editor of the **Midlothian Mirror** in Texas, has attracted considerable attention among

assassination researchers for his work documenting the growing number of witnesses and investigators into the JFK assassination who have met sudden deaths, often under mysterious circumstances.

Robert Cutler, a Massachusetts architect, typifies the large number of researchers who have devoted their free time to this work in addition to pursuing their own careers in other fields. Cutler has privately published two studies of the Dallas assassination, and his latest work has focused on the unanswered questions surrounding the Chappaquidick incident. Some researchers have become highly specialized — Robert Groden, for example, is a professional photographer who has concentrated almost exclusively on an analysis of the photographic evidence of the JFK assassination, and his work on a "bootleg" copy of the Zapruder film has proved particularly important.

With such a diverse group of participants, it is a tribute to the organizers at the AIB that the conference proved highly successful in managing to avoid much of the factionalism that had hampered previous gatherings in this field. The weekend began on an auspicious note: an overflowing audience estimated at between 800-1,000 crowded into the Boston University auditorium where the opening session was held. Bob Katz of the AIB opened the session with a brief presentation outlining the history of the organization and the objectives of the conference in politicizing the assassination issue.

Katz then introduced Mark Lane, who provided the audience with a moving account of the difficulties confronting the early researchers into the JFK assassination. When the audience broke out into laughter following Lane's description of the unbelievable path which the Warren Commission solemnly insisted one of the bullets allegedly fired by Oswald had followed, Lane reminded the audience: "the difference between then and now is that no one laughed then." Lane particularly emphasized the role of Jerry Ford as a member of the Warren Commission and he charged that "Ford is guilty as an accessory after the fact in the murder of John F. Kennedy."

Lane also described the harrassment experienced by Jim Garrison, the New Orleans District Attorney who had undertaken the first attempt to submit to a jury the evidence suggesting that a conspiracy had been responsible for Kennedy's assassination. He reminded the audience that the jury had found beyond a reasonable doubt that Oswald had not acted alone and was involved in a conspiracy, but that Garrison had been unable to convince the jury that Clay Shaw was involved in the conspiracy. The fatal flaw in Garrison's case had been his inability to prove that Shaw was a member of the CIA as he had charged. Now, almost six years after Shaw's original indictment and less than a year after Shaw's death (under mysterious circumstances), Victor Marchetti, a former official of the CIA and co-author of the bestselling **The CIA and the Cult of Intelligence**, has revealed that Clay Shaw was a high-level CIA operative in New Orleans and had been involved along with David W. Ferrie, E. Howard Hunt, Frank Sturgis, and Bernard Barker in preparations for the CIA's Bay of Pigs venture.

After summarizing the growing body of evidence which had accumulated to undermine the credibility of the conclusions of the Warren Commission report, Lane interrupted his talk for a showing of a collage of films that had been assembled to provide a comprehensive photographic record of the events of Dealey Plaza. Using slow motion and blow-ups of particular frames and pinpointing specific details in the film, the narrator methodically challenged the underlying contention of the Warren Commission report: that all the bullets were fired in a period of 5.6 seconds from the sixth floor of the Book Depository above and behind President Kennedy. The audience was visibly affected by the graphic detail of a segment of the Zapruder film which showed the impact of a bullet hitting the right half of the top of Kennedy's head and clearly hurling him backward into the seat, strongly suggesting that the bullet was fired from the front rather than from behind.

Even more fascinating were the segments of another film which had been enlarged and which revealed the blurred figure of a man who seemed to be crouched in a classic military sniping position behind a barricade on the grassy knoll in front of the motorcade. Shortly after the shots were fired, another filmed view of this area reveals that this man had disappeared. The most dramatic moment in the film, however, involved the presentation of several computer-assisted blow-ups of frame No. 413 of the Zapruder film. During the enlargement process, the figures necessarily tend to become blurred, but these blow-ups reveal with sufficient detail the figure of a man hidden in a clump of bushes on the

(Continued On Page 5)

AIB Conference —

(Continued From Page 4)

grassy knoll and pointing a rifle in the direction of the presidential limousine. This frame in the film occurs shortly after the fatal shots had been fired and it therefore had not been subjected to a detailed scrutiny until a few months ago. The photographic evidence of the presence of additional assassins provides strong corroboration to ballistics evidence and to the reports of a large number of witnesses who were convinced that they had heard shots from the grassy knoll area in front of the presidential limousine.

Following the film presentation, Lane shifted from a review of the progress of assassination research in recent years to focus on several themes which were to underlie many of the discussions during the following two days. First, he stressed the political importance of the assassination issue, since it involved not only an unsolved crime but also because it suggested the existence of a well-coordinated campaign to suppress the evidence of a conspiracy to assassinate Kennedy — a campaign which involved both Kennedy's successor as president and the Chief Justice of the Supreme Court. Also, the assassination signalled the first stage of a virtual coup d'etat within the top levels of the executive branch, one which immediately preceded the sustained escalation of the war in Southeast Asia.

Secondly, Mark Lane argued that research into the Kennedy assassination had reached an impasse marking the culmination of an initial stage. Researchers had systematically probed the available evidence and demonstrated the inadequacy of the "lone assassin" theory. While speculative theories could be fashioned from the existing evidence to suggest the possible dimensions of the conspiracy responsible for the assassination, the ultimate truth would not be available without unrestricted access to government documents which have thus far remained confidential. Thus, efforts to uncover the conspiracy would have to shift from independent research work to a second stage of political organizing around the demand to re-open the official investigation of the Kennedy assassination and to de-classify all relevant government documents.

Lane pointed out that the Watergate episode had served an invaluable function in increasing the "credibility gap" between the government and the public and that, in a growing atmosphere of distrust, people were now far more willing to question "official" explanations of events than they had been a decade ago. Particularly now that there is a much more sophisticated awareness of the extent of the CIA's role, both domestically and abroad, the public should prove more receptive to the suggestion of CIA involvement in a conspiracy to assassinate Kennedy. While characterizing the challenge to the Warren Commission report as "an idea whose time has come," Lane warned the audience that it would not prevail by itself.

Lambasting the liberals for their failure of political will in challenging the Warren Commission whitewash, Lane called for mass organizing efforts which would be necessary to mobilize public opinion behind a demand for a new investigation. Without a sustained and broad-based movement to back up such a demand, politicans in Congress could not be relied upon to act on such a demand. Lane received a standing ovation as he finished his presentation with the exhortation that "they must hear from us, and hear from us until finally they act for us."

Following the dramatic opening of the conference on Friday evening, the conference participants settled down on Saturday to attend the various workshops devoted to a more detailed examination of the status of current research efforts. However, the most interesting workshop, and certainly one of the highlights of the entire conference, was devoted to Carl Oglesby's presentation of his Yankee/Cowboy model. Speaking to a standing room only crowd of 300, Oglesby devoted more than two hours to an eloquent extemporaneous presentation of his model, tracing the historical evolution of an underlying tension within the American political elite from the transformation of the traditional North-South rivalries subsequent to the Civil War to the emergence of a well-defined Yankee-Cowboy split in the second half of the twentieth century. As he proceeded to set forth the outline of this evolution, Oglesby occassionally expressed the fear that perhaps he shouldn't linger on such areas which were only tangentially related to the Kennedy assassination and, each time, he was met with cries from the appreciative audience: "Linger! Linger!"

While it is impossible to summarize adequately the elaborate detail

supporting Oglesby's model, it essentially contends that, within the political consensus that unites the members of the American political elite and that establishes the parameters of political decision-making, there is also a continuing tension stemming from two distinct and competing world-views which have deep economic and cultural roots. On the one hand, there are the Yankee members of the political and economic elite who are primarily concentrated in the old, established families of the Northeast and whose power is derived from their control of Wall Street financial firms and vast, multinational corporations. These are the people who direct the affairs of the vast network of interlocking institutions that comprise the "Eastern establishment". Strongly Anglophile, the Yankees perceive the North Atlantic industrial community as the focus of their economic, political and cultural interests. The Rockefellers, Morgans, Harrimans and Dillons are some examples of Yankee families.

The Yankees captured control for the first time over the national executive in the struggle culminating in the Civil War and the Reconstruction period. In the following century, the traditional Southern planter aristocracy which had provided the core of Southern leadership prior to 1860, rapidly receded in importance as a consequence of the country's westward expansion. In its place, a new political and economic configuration began to emerge along the entire "Southern rim" of the U. S., encompassing Miami, New Orleans, Dallas, Houston, Phoenix, Las Vegas and Los Angeles.

Originally based in independent oil companies, textile enterprises and the growth of agri-business, this constellation of Cowboy economic interests was decisively strengthened by the consolidation of a vast military-industrial complex throughout the South and West. Another, often overlooked, factor in the rise of the Cowboy faction was the cartellization of organized crime during the Prohibition era as individual "families" were progressively integrated into an institutional framework, and as the massive financial revenues generated through the production and distribution of illegal liquor were channeled into "legitimate" business. The result is a complex intertwining of "legitimate" and syndicate interests within the Cowboy axis. The Cowboy members of the political elite share a common cultural heritage, which is largely derived from the frontier heritage of the West and sharply distinguishes them from their Yankee associates. Unlike the Yankees, the Cowboys perceive the Pacific basin as the focus for their essential interests and tend to be far more doctrinairely anti-Communist.

Within this framework, Oglesby argues that the Kennedy assassination in 1963 represented a **coup d'etat** within the political elite, transferring leadership from the Yankee elements to the Cowboy elements represented by Johnson and Nixon. However, as the Yankee elements in the political elite became increasingly concerned over the profound domestic economic and political instability precipitated by American involvement in Southeast Asia and the growing domestic repression, they moved to reassert their control within the political elite. The Watergate investigation, carefully orchestrated by Yankee representatives to remove Nixon without revealing the full extent of covert activities by government agencies, is characterized by Oglesby as a second coup d'etat which neutralized three leading Cowboy challengers (Nixon, Agnew and Connally) while placing Nelson Rockefeller and his protege, Henry Kissinger, in virtual control of the executive branch. Oglesby finished his **tour de force** by quoting from Bernard Bailyn's **Ideological Origins of the American Revolution** and urging the audience to perceive power as our revolutionary forefathers did, as an "act of trespassing", "grasping and tenacious, like a cancer."

The Sunday session, featuring an open discussion of organizing strategy, unfortunately proved to be the most disappointing part of the conference. The AIB sponsors had decided that the creation of a national membership organization at this point would be premature, and they had scheduled the Sunday session simply to provide an opportunity to generate ideas for programs that the participants might begin to implement on a local level. The participants, on the other hand, seemed to have anticipated that a more detailed program of action would be presented, and several members of the audience expressed frustration over the lack of focus in the discussion. In fact, all the contradictions and tensions which characterize the assassination field seemed to surface during the "open mike" session.

Perhaps the most fundamental, and unresolved, tension which pervaded the entire conference involved the differing perspectives of the

(Continued On Page 6)

Assassination Revisionism Once More

Alan Fairgate's article in this issue points up the growing importance of the Kennedy Assassination question in American politics. Indeed, since the AIB conference in early February, indeed in the last two weeks, assassination revisionism has finally burst through on television, for the first time in many years. Photographer Robert Groden's careful analysis of the famous Zapruder film has hit the public consciousness; remarkably, the Warren Commission never even bothered viewing the film itself, contenting itself with viewing slides of fuzzy third-generation copies.

Assassination revisionism had been a tough row to hoe for a long time. It began immediately after the JFK assassination with Mark Lane's penetrating questions to the authorities in the **Guardian**; over the years, it has developed a devoted cadre of semi-professional buffs, who have tracked down innumerable leads, and have battered at the government to release documents and evidence, much of which still remains under lock and key. And if Oswald was only a lone nut, why the sequestering of evidence?

Actually, there is not just one mysterious political assassination or attempted assassination since JFK, but a whole raft of them: of JFK, of Officer J. D. Tippit, of Lee Harvey Oswald himself, of RFK, of George Wallace, of Martin Luther King, of Malcolm X, and possibly of Mary Jo Kopechne at Chappaquiddick. In each case, the culprit was immediately dismissed as a lone nut (in Jack Ruby's case, one lone nut killing another), except for the Malcolm assassination which could not be treated that way, and so was blamed rather conveniently on the Black Muslims — even though the one non-Muslim assassin swears up and down that the Muslims had nothing to do with the slaying. In each case, impressive evidence contradicting the lone nut theory has been almost fiercely swept under the rug by the authorities. Since last year, in addition to the Groden film analysis, ex-Congressman Al Lowenstein has managed to reopen the Bobby Kennedy case (the contention being that other assassins than Sirhan Sirhan fired the fatal shots), and James Earl Ray's attempt to reopen the King case — charging that his first lawyer flummoxed him into a guilty plea — has been denied by the courts.

But the major change in climate for revisionism comes from the post-Watergate climate. It is not simply that we now know that the FBI and the CIA are capable of vile deeds, including assassinations and association with Mafia gangsters — thereby lending credence to strong evidence of their involvement in at least the JFK murder. It is also that we now understand clearly the relationship between deed and "coverup". For one of the anti-revisionist contentions ever since Dallas was the question: what? Are you saying that they're **all** in on the assassination: Johnson, Warren, Gerry Ford, etc.? We now see that the bigshots in on the coverup don't have to have been parties to the original assassination. It is now easy to visualize an immediate command decision: it's **got** to be a lone nut, otherwise the public will . . . be panicked, will ask too many embarrassing questions about our secret police, will "endanger national security", etc. And then, **that** line is fed to all the Establishment patriots, who go along with their seemingly patriotic obligations.

Now that the Congress is launching an investigation of our intelligence arms of government, a demand for opening the books, for unleashing the archives, for asking hard questions — at long last! — of everyone concerned, becomes a politically viable position for the first time in twelve years. The pressure in the media and of the AIB might well accomplish its purpose. There is no need, as Mr. Fairgate points out, for this agitation to be an exclusively leftish affair. Indeed, of all the old New Left, only the relatively libertarian Carl Oglesby is involved in the new drive, both organizationally and with his sparkling concept of the Cowboy-Yankee split among the power elite. Actually, the Marxists have long been hostile to this sort of power-elite muckraking, since they contend that such pinpointing of specific individuals and groups distracts the attention of the public from the "capitalist system" allegedly at fault. (It's also a lot of work). But there is no such thing as an abstract "ruling class", capitalist or otherwise: it does exist, but only as embodied in **specific people**, and an understanding of who they are, what alliances or splits they may be undergoing, is vital for anyone's, and especially any libertarian's, understanding of existent political reality. It is not enough to say simply that the State is shafting us: who are they? Which groups? Who's on top now? are also vital questions.

Two excellent articles, presenting the most up-to-date material on JFK Assassination Revisionism, appear in the April 24, 1975 issue of **Rolling Stone**. One is a thorough and careful article by the aforesaid Robert Groden, "A New Look at the Zapruder Film", a detailed analysis of the film, along with supporting pictures, which are impressive even though printed on the fuzzy paper of **Rolling Stone**. In summary, Groden demonstrates that there must have been at least **four** assassins, firing a total of six shots, plus one or two others firing a blank signal shot just before the assassination, and possibly two or three more (none being Oswald, by the way) at or near the famous window on the sixth floor of the Textbook Depository Building — but that **none** of the six shots were fired from this officially designated spot. Instead, Groden contends that one person fired two shots from the **second** floor of the TDB, another fired two shots from the **western** corner (rather than the official eastern end) of the sixth floor of the TDB, one fired a shot from in front on the grassy knoll, and that the fatal shot was fired by a fourth person from in front of JFK and behind a wall on the grassy knoll.

In the same issue of the magazine, Robert Blair Kaiser, in "The JFK Assassination: Why Congress Should Reopen the Investigation", provides

(Continued On Page 7)

AIB Conference —
(Continued From Page 5)

liberal and radical participants. Among a broad range of participants, an important motivating factor seems to have been a deep nostalgia for the liberal idealism which they believed Kennedy epitomized, and a sense of anger over the assassination. The natural response of this group tended to focus on traditional liberal reformist solutions: lobbying in Washington and seeking media coverage. There seemed to be relatively few hard-core radical veterans of the New Left present, but those who were there, and most notably Oglesby himself, persistently sought to discuss the assassination issue in terms of its role in radical social analysis, and viewed strategy in terms of mass-based organizing efforts to create the basis for a new radical movement. Even Oglesby, however, seemed at times to demonstrate a pronounced favoritism towards the Kennedy administration and the "liberal wing" of the Yankees generally.

This vague ambivalence among the participants assumed a more explicit form in the periodic debates addressing the relative role of facts and theory within the assassination research movement. While the more radical participants expressed profound appreciation for the patient investigative work of the assassination researchers, they criticized the tendency of many researchers to adopt the role of "sleuths", focusing exclusively on the collection and collating of facts without engaging in the equally important task of synthesizing and integrating these facts within a systematic framework of social analysis.

Another division which threatened at times to disrupt the fragile unity among the conference participants paradoxically joined both liberals and radicals in an effort to keep the "crazies" under control. Both Lane and Oglesby stressed the need to distinguish carefully between hard forensic evidence of a conspiracy, and speculative, educated guesses which might be made on the basis of such evidence. In a blistering attack on the "ludicrous statements" and "irresponsible charges" of Mae Brussel and Sherman Skolnick, Lane cautioned that "to make statements which most reasonable Americans cannot accept will set back the movement so many years that it will be the twenty-first century before we find out the truth" and warned that "it must be (the Warren Commission's) credibility that is in question, not ours."

The AIB sponsors of the conference are aware of the unresolved

(Continued On Page 8)

Arts And Movies

By Mr. First Nighter

The Oscars. From the beginning, it was clear that the Oscar race for best picture of 1974 was between two films: "Godfather, Part II" and "Chinatown." As pointed out in these pages, (**Lib. Forum**, March, 1975), "Godfather", a marvellous film, clearly deserved the award. In contrast, the morbid, cynical "Chinatown" (neatly skewered in **Libertarian Review** by Barbara Branden) was the darling of the **avant-garde** intellectuals, serving as it did as an "anti-hero" reversal of the great detective films of the 1940's.

Part of the excitement of Oscar night is to watch the race between the top pictures build up as the minor awards are allocated. From the beginning of the night, it became clear that "Chinatown" was losing out, as it was defeated in one minor award after another. Unfortunately, this meant that the cool, subtle, and nuanced performance of the beautiful Faye Dunaway in "Chinatown" lost out to Ellen Burstyn's hammy, tearful performance in "Alice Doesn't Live Here Anymore" as Best Actress, but the consolation was the clear meaning that "Chinatown" had had it. Sure enough, "Godfather, Part II" swept the boards, gaining its deserved triumph as Best Picture, and the directorial award for Francis Ford Coppola.

While justice triumphed splendidly in the Best Picture and Best Director awards, the splendid Al Pacino unfortunately lost out in the race for Best Actor; so too did the intellectuals, who were rooting for Jack Nicholson's anti-hero detective in "Chinatown". Instead, the old Hollywood **penchant** for boozy sentimentality won out, with old favorite Art Carney winning the award for the piece of fluff, **Harry and Tonto**. Fortunately, however, the expected sentimentality did **not** triumph for the Best Supporting Actor award. Fred Astaire, who has **always** been a poor actor, was particularly weak and even grotesque in a minor role in **The Towering Inferno**; but the scuttlebutt had it that he would win anyway, in an orgy of collective Hollywood guilt for **not** having given him an Oscar in the 1930's for his glorious dancing in the famous Astaire movies of that era. However, justice again triumphed, as the award went to one of the finest young actors in recent years, Robert DeNiro's "proto-Brando" young godfather in "Godfather, Part II." Sentimentality **did** triumph in the award to Ingrid Bergman for Best Supporting Actress in "Murder on the Orient Express", in expiation of Hollywood's collective guilt for casting Miss Bergman into outer darkness thirty years ago for an act of personal "immorality" which would **now** be considered positively square and old-fashioned. However, in Miss Bergman's case, there was no harm done, since hers was probably the best performance out of a rather poor lot.

And so, the classical aesthetic has won out over its **avant-garde** enemies for the third straight year: in the awards to "Godfather" in 1973, in "The Sting" exorcising "The Exorcist" last year, and now in the victory of "Part II." With luck, maybe we can enter the lists with a "Part III" for 1977.

Shampoo, dir. by Harold Ashby, produced and co-written by Warren Beatty. With Warren Beatty, Julie Christie, Goldie Hawn, and Jack Warden. This picture has been absurdly over-praised by the critics. It is in no sense a "profound" statement about our time. It is, instead, a modern (or "mod") version of the old bedroom farce (Restoration-Moliere), with predatory males and females, and people hopping in and out of bed and closets (here replaced by bathrooms).

Since it is almost impossible to ruin a bedroom farce **completely**, on one level it is possible to flow with the action and get some enjoyment out of Shampoo. But oh the differences from the old farces! In the first place, of course, Shampoo is far more explicit than the Restoration playwrights, in keeping with our 1970's culture. There is, I suppose, some shock value in the glorious Julie Christie bellowing out four-letter words on film. But there are much more profound differences as well. For one thing, the wit is gone; the dialogue generally gravitates between the banal and the inchoate. For another — and on a deeper level — the characters in Moliere and the other dramatists may have been caught in bewildering situations; but they at all times knew what they were doing. They were real people, with understandable purposes and motivations, even if they were busy juggling incompatible goals. The Beatty-Ashby characters are nothing if not machines out of a B.F. Skinner dream (or nightmare): they

are mere stimulus-response mechanisms, with hardly a thought or a motive lasting more than fifteen minutes. They are scarcely **people** at all, but only flotsam and jetsam tossed around by the circumstance of the moment. Why does Warren Beatty pine for Goldie Hawn at one moment, and ten minutes later — and, apparently, with equal sincerity — propose to Julie Christie, whom he had only re-connected with the night before? Why does Jack Warden, with some justice, dismiss Miss Christie as a "whore", only to marry her the next day? Who knows? And, more important, who cares? For it is impossible for the viewer to empathize with, or care about, any of these cretins. Who can give a darn about a stimulus-response machine?

The major interest is in Miss Christie, but for reasons that have little to do with the movie itself. It is not simply that she is a marvellous actress, and worth seeing even in a turkey. For the movie, because of Miss Christie, cannot help but evoke that outstanding herald of the mod age, **Darling**. That film of the early 60's was both a portrayal of the new phenomenon of "swinging London", and a harbinger of the new Western culture then being born. While its values were decadent, **Darling** was a superb evocation of what the mod world was coming to be, and Julie Christie was both its new star and its quintessence. In a sense, **Shampoo** is Miss Christie a decade later; older, coarser, jaded, dissipated, the swinging London chick has now landed in a millionaire's pad in Hollywood. It is, indeed, a logical progression. I hope that some young director of the 1980's doesn't decide to show us the next step.

Jack Warden and Lee Grant are excellent as the older predators (Lee Grant, I am happy to say, is growing old quite disgracefully). I hope to see no more of Miss Hawn; **Shampoo** confirms my conviction that Miss Hawn comes over as a nitwit even when she is not trying (pace **Cactus Flower**). Young Carrie Fisher (offspring of the famous Fisher-Debbie Reynolds match) makes her debut in this film, and I hope it is also her farewell appearance. Warren Beatty is Warren Beatty.   ◻

Assassination Revisionism —

(Continued From Page 6)

an excellent overall summary of the latest findings and lacunae, focussing among other points on newly discovered peccadilloes of the Warren Commission. Kaiser also reveals that a former staff member of the Warren Commission has now called for reopening the case — Burt W. Griffin, now a state judge in Cleveland. Judge Griffin states: "I don't think some agencies were candid with us. I never thought the Dallas Police were telling us the entire truth. Neither was the FBI . . . We accepted the (FBI) answers we got, even though they were inadequate and didn't carry the battle any further. To do so, we'd have had to challenge the integrity of the FBI and the CIA. Back in 1964, that was something we didn't do."

In the search for the truth, and for credibility in that search, it is important to be careful and scholarly. Hence, the importance, as Mr. Fairgate indicates, of repudiating the "crazies", such as Mae Brussel and Sherman Skolnick, whose confidently asserted theories have run light years ahead of the facts. In his article, Robert Kaiser, for example, performs a service by shooting down Dick Gregory's photo hypothesis of two members of the Watergate conspiracy team — E. Howard Hunt and Frank Sturgis — being the same as the famous "tramps" who were mysteriously arrested by the Dallas police just after the assassination, and released supposedly without finding out who they were. It remains true, however, that a lot of people happened, by odd coincidence, to be in Dallas on November 22, 1963. Frank Sturgis was one; so was James W. McCord; and so too was private citizen Richard M. Nixon, addressing a business group.

At any rate, libertarians do not have to commit themselves to any assassination theory to raise the cry of the importance of the public finding out the facts, of the closed archives and evidence being opened, and of hard and persistent questioning being directed to the government authorities.   ◻

AIB Conference —

(Continued From Page 6)

contradictions which shaped much of the discussion at the conference, but they express the hope that a basic consensus is evolving which will prove strong enough to overcome any tendencies toward factionalism which might threaten the movement. For the moment, the AIB perceives its role as facilitating discussion within the movement to strengthen the existing consensus and to precipitate a sustained debate over the organizational forms which might be appropriate or necessary for the movement. There seems to be a pronounced reluctance to impose a formal organizational structure on the movement at this point, and instead the AIB prefers to serve as a "foco" for local organizing efforts.

This movement offers enormous potential for libertarian involvement. It has remained remarkably free from the rigid Marxist rhetoric and categories of analysis that marked the decline of the New Left, and the issues which it raises are naturally compatible with a libertarian perspective. It pinpoints a series of criminal conspiracies spawned within specific agencies of the state apparatus, conspiracies which have utilized murder as an instrument of political competition beneath the democratic facade of elections and which have been protected from exposure by the veil of secrecy which shrouds government operations. The exposure of these conspiracies would prove extremely valuable in de-legitimizing the state and focusing public attention on its underlying criminal character.

Furthermore, as several conference participants noted, the widespread public disillusionment with the government which has emerged as a consequence of the publicity surrounding the Watergate investigations, has created a particularly ripe opportunity for focusing attention once again on the Kennedy assassination. People who were once hostile to the anti-war and anti-draft movements and who scoffed at charges of domestic repression are now proving increasingly receptive to conspiracy theories and to attacks on the credibility of the government. A demand for re-opening the investigation into the Kennedy assassination that avoids Marxist rhetoric would also provide a potentially valuable organizing tool for reaching an increasingly alienated middle class constituency.

One of the greatest dangers confronting the movement that is beginning to emerge around this issue, is that it may repeat the old error of the New Left anti-war movement by becoming isolated within traditional liberal and youth strongholds and failing to establish an authentic grass-roots base. By formulating the options in terms of an either/or choice between two factions of the political elite, Oglesby's Yankee/Cowboy model reveals an uncomfortable bias in favor of Yankee political interests and tends to reinforce the latent liberal sympathies of many participants in the movement. While the Yankee/Cowboy model provides an invaluable

analytical tool in analyzing the dynamics of American political decision-making, this bias within the model must be corrected if the movement ever hopes to transcend the limitations of the earlier New Left organizing strategy. Perhaps an important step in this direction would be to integrate Oglesby's Yankee/Cowboy model, which is largely restricted to a description of the tensions within the political elite, with Leonard Liggio's highly perceptive analysis of the Redskin/Paleface conflict (originally published in **Left and Right**), which more broadly focuses on inter-class relations in the historical evolution of the U.S.

The essential problem that must be overcome in the development of a successful mass-based organizing strategy, is that the vast majority of the American population has been coopted into the Cowboy camp: their political champions are the Cowboy politicians, their heroes are Cowboy heroes and their culture is the Cowboy culture. These people have an instinctive hatred and suspicion of traditional Yankee power centers and politicians, and they will prove hostile to any movement which appears to threaten their Cowboy symbols while reinforcing Yankee hegemony.

Thus, the assassination investigation movement will have to be careful to avoid liberal reformist tendencies. Instead, it should concentrate on mobilizing an initial cadre with the analysis and understanding to perceive that both the Yankee and Cowboy factions are integral components of a national ruling class, a ruling class that must be dismantled, and then concentrate on an elaboration of grass-roots organizing strategies designed to appeal explicitly to the vast middle classes by de-mythologizing Cowboy symbols of authority and stressing that the Cowboy interests, like their Yankee rivals, parasitically rely on the political means to enrich themselves while impoverishing the American population.

The assassination investigation movement is still in its formative stages and, as a result, there is great potential for libertarians to become involved in the movement and to influence its development. Whether or not libertarians prove able to rise to this challenge and to respond constructively to one of the most promising movements to have emerged in recent years will provide a revealing indication of the level of their political consciousness.

(Libertarians who are interested in local organizing activities in this field should contact the AIB directly for information. The AIB address is: Assassination Information Bureau, 63 Inman Street, Cambridge, Massachusetts 02139. The AIB is currently preparing material to assist in organizing local teach-ins and conferences, and it also has teams of speakers available with copies of the Zapruder film to address local groups.)

*Mr. Fairgate is a graduate student in business administration and law at a prominent American university.

A Monthly Newsletter

THE
Libertarian Forum

Joseph R. Peden, Publisher

Murray N. Rothbard, Editor

VOLUME VII, NO. 5   MAY, 1975   US-ISSN0047-4517

MAYAGUEZ, BY JINGO

And so President Ford has seized his heaven-sent opportunity to flex the muscles of U. S. imperialism and his own **macho** muscles as Commander-in-Chief. Boy, we showed teeny Cambodia, didn't we? After losing a disastrous and chronic war in Southeast Asia, we showed that we've got the Marines, by jingo, and the bombs, by God, and we can blast them! We dropped more bombs than ever before in history in Vietnam, and it didn't do us any good, but give us a specific target, like one ship, and wow!

Or **was** the opportunity really heaven-sent, or was there a more sinister, man-made force involved? Was this, perhaps, another fraud like the **Pueblo** and Gulf-of-Tonkin capers, provoked or engineered by the U. S. to give imperialism a show of strength, and to unify the country — even the half-hearted peaceniks in Congress — behind a policy of bluster, jingoism, and violence? "Senior American officials" have already been reported as saying that the administration saw the Mayaguez incident as "an opportunity for the United States to demonstrate it will remain in Asia following the Indochina deoacles." Of course, Ford and his stooge Ron Nessen deny this, but who in his right mind believes **them**?

In the course of his hysterical response to the Mayaguez incident, Ford managed to violate a host of treaties and agreements, and to commit multiple aggression — as well as to bring about the deaths of a hundred American Marines and numbers of Cambodians. In his haste to jump the gun and not wait for ordinary diplomacy to run its course, our "commander-in-chief" (a) took off from Okinawa without asking Japanese permission, thereby violating our agreement with Japan; (b) landed 1,100 Marines in Thailand against the express desire of the Thais, thereby violating our agreement with them and aggressing against Thai territory; (c) invaded a Cambodian island, bombed a few ships and perhaps sunk them, and killed an unknown number of Cambodians, and (d) after the deed was done, gratuitously flexed some more muscles by bombing the Cambodian mainland, for good measure so to speak. All this was done, moreover, **after** the Cambodians had agreed to release the ship and its crew, **and** in direct violation of several American laws absolutely prohibiting the use of American military force in Southeast Asia. Ford deserves impeachment on the latter ground alone, but of course there is no chance of that, with even the supposed peace forces in Congress rushing to hail the our newly "decisive" President. The violations of law are supposedly made to be superseded by the much-trumpeted "constitutional" powers of the Commander-in-Chief, which have been interpreted to provide a virtual blank check for Presidential commitments and actions in military affairs.

In addition to the numerous violations of law, treaty, and right committed by the Ford adventure in gunboat diplomacy, another vital point has been generally overlooked: namely that, according to well-accepted principles of international law, the Cambodians were right! The American contention that the Malaguez was sailing on the high seas, in "international waters", is an outright lie; even the Ford administration concedes that the Mayaguez was captured only eight miles from the Cambodian island of Poulo Wai; the Cambodians themselves say three

miles, but no matter. Eight miles is enough to destroy the American case. For Cambodia has, for many years, claimed 12 miles as its territorial limit from its shores. The 12-mile limit was maintained, not only by the Sihanouk regime, but also be the American-supported Lon Nol clique. Furthermore, the 1975 Geneva conference on the Law of the Sea reached a general, tentative agreement on 12 miles as the territorial limit of each State, and the United States has openly supported this 12-mile agreement. And so, by the standards of the U. S. itself as well as by the Geneva agreements, the Mayaguez was invading Cambodian waters, and Cambodia had every right, under international law, to seize the ship and its crew for invading its territory. Far from Cambodia's action being that of "piracy", as the Ford administration charged, it was Ford and his Marines and bombers who were the pirates.

Furthermore, the Cambodians were certainly justified in being suspicious of the Mayaguez. The ship was reported in the U. S. press to be an "unarmed" merchantman; actually, it was under charter to the U. S. military. The Cambodian charge that "this ship came to violate our waters, conduct espionage and provoke incidents to create pretexts or mislead the opinion of the world people . . ." certainly has the ring of plausibility, and deserves careful investigation.

A clinching argument against the Ford adventure is the very different treatment that the Nixon-Ford administration has been handing out to the Ecuadorians. Ecuador has been claiming a territorial limit of, not 12 but 200 miles, out to sea, and has been seizing private fishing vessels and arresting their crew; and in the case of Ecuador, there seems to be no possibility of the ships being covers for CIA military or espionage operations. And yet, we have heard no hysterical denunciations of Ecuador, there have been no midnight bombings of Ecuador, nor commando landings by Marines to free the crews of the fishing vessels. When it came to Ecuador, the patient processes of diplomacy were allowed to work. Why the double standard, if all Ford was interested in was protection of American persons and property?

The general reaction in America was as disheartening as one might expect. The evil Kissinger boasted that "the President's stroke demonstrated that a great power leads not so much by its words as by its actions, that initiative creates its own consensus." In short, the old trick of conning the public to rally behind a war-making President. Unfortunately, it worked once more. The Conservatives were as bloodthirsty as one might expect. Senator Buckley called immediately for massive bombing of Cambodia and he got most of what he wanted; Senator Jesse Helms burbled that "I am proud of him (Ford) today". The chicken-hearted liberals, with a few honorable exceptions such as Senator Nelson (D., Wisc.) tagged along in the new, but hopefully short-lived, "consensus". Perhaps the most egregious statement was that of the always insufferable Arthur Schlesinger, Jr., who exulted that Ford's action "represents a much needed and timely affirmation of the freedom of the seas." It is high time, indeed, to re-evaluate the hoary "freedom of the seas" doctrine. For centuries it was used by the English imperialists

(Continued On Page 2)

565

Peasants And Revolution:
A Review Essay

By Joseph R. Stromberg•

Reviewing Carroll Quigley's **Tragedy and Hope** in the June 1974 issue of **Books for Libertarians**, John Hospers remarked on Quigley's view that income redistribution would solve nothing in Latin America unless people there learn to use excess incomes "constructively." This attitude, which surely reflects some obtuseness, is quite widespread. One finds libertarians, e.g. the able economist Henry Hazlitt, who write of land reform as if it were communism. All we need, it seems, is "a good business climate" in Free World Despotism X, Y or Z, and, drip, drip, drip, prosperity will trickle down to the masses — someday.

At a time when libertarians need reminding of the radicalism of their **Weltanschauung,**• it is heartening to find a book on the agrarian question which thoroughly discredits the **status quo** and confirms one's fondest prejudices in favor of change. Ernest Feder's **The Rape of the Peasantry: Latin America's Landholding System** (Garden City, NY, 1971) is such a book. Granting that mere "income inequality is not **per se** unjust," Professor Feder delineates the unnatural concentration of land in the Americas and the corresponding destitution of the peasantry. Since the data is incomplete in this area, Feder deliberately errs on the conservative side throughout the book. Hence, the actual Latin American situation is probably much worse than the book indicates.

According to Feder, poverty, unemployment and productivity so low that agricultural countries import food are all rooted in "latifundismo," or feudal land monopoly, dating from the Spanish conquest. The landed elite and their political henchmen exploit the peasants and maintain an agrarian reserve army of cheap and docile labor by means of one-sided sharecropping contracts, punitive evictions, feudal labor dues, fraud,

inflation (which devours small savings), and ultimately armed violence by "vigilantes"• or the national army. (See Chapters 9-15.)

Small wonder, then, that the peasants display self-hatred and unambitious behavior which supposedly proves their stupidity. As Feder puts it, "they are forcefully shut off from the market mechanism." The problem is hardly one of "scarce" land or even technological backwardness. Feder argues persuasively that the monopoly of **good land** creates gross inefficiency, waste, mismanagement and low productivity on the latifundia. A cluster of built-in disincentives discourage the peasants, who gain nothing from harder work. The large estates resemble islands of socialist "calculational chaos" (though Feder does not use this term), except that collective farmers probably eat better — provided they love Brezhnev. Far from reflecting economies of scale, the politically based latifundia are so overexpanded that often as much as one third of the work force is required to boss the other demoralized two thirds.

By contrast, poor people are actually capable of great economic rationality and capital accumulation. Feder finds that the small sector of family farms is much more land-intensive and productive than the better capitalized estate sector. Given the irrationalities of the feudal sector and the destitution of people who could be productive, Feder argues for land reform on grounds of simple justice. Against the charge that reform violates property, he properly replies that it actually "aim(s) at an expansion of private property." For libertarians, both Lockean natural

(Continued On Page 3)

Mayaguez — (Continued From Page 1)

in the way that Ford-Schlesinger are using it now: to justify any and all encroachments by U. S. (English) vessels anywhere on the liquid surface of the globe. In the deeper philosophical sense, "freedom of the seas" really means "ocean communism", i.e. a state of no-property in the ocean. While the ocean used to be a super-abundant resource, it is no longer so, particularly in the North Atlantic and along the continental shelves; the ocean is in these places a scarce resource, and it has been substantially kept out of productive use because "ocean communism" has been able to prevent private property in parts of the ocean. As a result, the ocean is under-utilized in the same way that land was in the centuries before private property was allowed in land. Only hunting and gathering (of fish, minerals) is allowed in the oceans now, just as only hunting and gathering was feasible in the days before private landed property. It was only private property in land that made agriculture (the transformation of the land by human energy) possible, thereby enormously increasing land productivity; and only private property in parts of the ocean will eventually make "aquaculture" feasible, and lead to a vast and mighty boom of resources and production in the vast ocean storehouse.

To return to the Mayaguez adventure, it points up several important lessons. One is a need to press forward with an isolationist and anti-imperialist foreign policy; it is clear that even the supposedly "anti-war" liberals, let alone everyone else, have not learned the real lessons of our debacle in Southeast Asia. Second is the need to press on with a call for the U. S. to get out of Asia; specifically, to get our troops completely out of their remaining bases in South Korea, Thailand, Japan, and Okinawa. At the very least, that would force Ford to take more time before his next plunge into war and violence. Moreover, it would keep us out of the next possible tinder-spot, South Korea, where the dictatorship of President Park Chung Hee has managed to alienate severely the bulk of the South Korean population. Third, it would be helpful to have a constitutional amendment stripping the President of his beloved "commander-in-chief" status. During the pre-Articles of Confederation days of the Revolutionary war (which we did, after all, manage to win), the

Commander-in-Chief, George Washington, was strictly under the control of Congress, which appointed and could have fired him at will. Why not return to this sort of status, where at least Congress would have to deliberate a bit before plunging into war? It would scarcely be a panacea in itself, but it would at least strip the President of his principal excuse and weapon in his personal making of war.

FLASH! As we go to press, we find that the U. S. Coast Guard has just seized an unarmed Polish fishing ship, the Kalmar, charged with "violating U. S. territorial waters" off Monterey, California. (The San Francisco Examiner, May 18). The ship was hauled into San Francisco and its captain and crew arrested. The only high crime of the Kalmar was to fish at a point slightly over 10 miles from U. S. shores. The Coast Guard explained that, while the U. S. formally maintains a 3-mile limit as its territorial waters, it has international agreements that have established a 12-mile limit as its "contiguous fishing zone".

Coming so soon after the Mayaguez incident, the Coast Guard was "concerned" that the parallels would be inevitable: how does the seizure of the Kalmar differ from that of the Mayaguez? The Coast Guard's attempt to find a difference was both pathetic and revealing: "This was simply a violation of the U. S. contiguous fishing zone . . . It is a recognized international situation (recognized by the Soviets and us) . . . The Mayaguez was just a happensiance of Cambodia." In short, the Soviets (and Poles?) recognize our 12-mile limit and usually don't interfere with it, but we don't give a hang about the Cambodian's 12-mile limit. There is the much-vaunted U. S. "respect for international law" and "freedom of the seas."

In truth, there is only **one** difference between the Kalmar and Mayaguez incidents: that the Kalmar was an innocent, productive fishing vessel, while the Mayaguez might well have been an espionage ship and a deliberate provocation to the Cambodians. The hypocrisy of U. S. foreign policy has never been more clearly exposed. Alright, President Ford, Senator Buckley, Senator Helms, and Arthur Schlesinger, Jr.: **should** Poland now bomb California and land commandoes in San Francisco to free the kidnapped Poles? And if not, why not?   ◘

Peasants And Revolution —

(Continued From Page 2)

law arguments and utilitarian considerations make land reform imperative.

Feder sees spontaneous peasant "land invasions" (usually suppressed) as a hopeful sign. He exposes token official "reform," financed in part by the Alliance for Progress, as marginal and deliberately irrelevant. (Bureaucratic rakeoff ran up to 50% of the funds.) A final chapter is devoted to the danger of "technocratic reform" from above. Feder hopes real "reformers" prevail. Knowing what we know about liberal reformism, libertarians should put their hopes on armed peasants and wish them good theory to guide their practice.

Parasitism and Subversion: The Case of Latin America (New York, 1966) is a broadly focused work by Stanislav Andreski, an unorthodox sociologist who deals with the land question and much more. The author sets out to account for the chief structural uniformities of Latin American societies. Where generalization fails for the whole continent, the book becomes classificatory as well. But informities abound, and Andreski presents a convincing survey of them.

Andreski believes that most of Latin America's troubles stem from an inherited pattern of parasitism, or what we might call statist exploitation. Interestingly, he derives his conception of parasitism from the **Traite de Legislation** (1826), the major work of the French sociologist Charles Comte, whose importance as libertarian theorist has been discovered by Leonard Liggio. Parasitism, which severs work from reward, is a necessarily strong barrier to social progress.

An important form of parasitism is land monopoly, which restricts production and impoverishes the masses. (On this subject Andreski differs little from Feder.) Direct political appropriation of wealth by Latin American police, customs inspectors and the like is "enormous" according to Andreski. Although conditions vary from country to country, high tariffs, state loans, the license-and-bribery syndrome, government contracts, and even tax-farming (in Peru) contribute to the popular view that all governments are "merely bands of thieves." (Hear, hear!) In Mexico, where state intervention is most extensive, pay-offs are naturally highest. Everywhere taxation falls mainly on the poorer classes. Militarism also wastes needed resources. Conscription exists in Latin America mainly to justify the bloated officer corps. Since Latin armies are too large for internal policing and too small for war, they are really huge bureaucracies which often intervene directly in politics. Their normal care, plus what they rake off when running a country, make their upkeep "the most important form of parasitism in Latin America."

Latin America is thus cursed with "parasitic involution of capitalism," which Andreski defines as "the tendency to seek profits and alter market conditions by political means in the widest sense." Accordingly, the continent suffers from "hypertrophy of bureaucracy." The middle classes mainly consist of bureaucrats and frustrated holders of diplomas who want state jobs. Many of them are drawn to state socialism and nationalization of foreign firms because of the Mandarin employment that would be created thereby. Parasitic appropriation of wealth, constricted markets (given peasant poverty), uneconomic welfare legislation to buy off the urban poor, and rapid inflation make for permanent economic stagnation. This condition in turn fosters permanent political instability. In general, the superimposing of democratic constitutions on seignorial, feudal economies has led to "constitutional oligarchy" or outright repression. Mexico is unique in having a stable bureaucratic regime.

A few more of Andreski's conclusions are worth mentioning. In a region of high infant mortality the richer classes outbreed the poor. This has "whitened" the population. Although darker features correspond to poorer status, Andreski finds that racism is not the problem. A poor, defenseless person will be exploited regardless of color! In the realm of Latin values, disdain for work, a legacy of slavery, promotes parasitism, just as capricious and authoritarian child-rearing fosters machismo and irresponsible aggression in males. Further, economic parasitism reinforces the anticommercial bias of the culture, aiding communist movements. Andreski believes US imperialism has played a somewhat minor role in Latin difficulties — chiefly one of propping up local dictators. (Unhappily, he accepts the Pollyanna theory of JFK, the brush-fire-war imperialist.) On the other hand, he is mildly revisionist on the Cuban Revolution: Cuba is no more totalitarian than many a Free World despotism and Castro is personally honest — unlike most Latin leaders. (He does foresee bureaucratic degeneration in Cuba, however.) All in all, **Parasitism and Subversion** is an excellent place to begin the study of statist culture in its extreme form.

David Mitrany's **Marx Against the Peasant: A Study in Social Dogmatism** (Chapel Hill, 1951) is a unique study of the great political paradox of the twentieth century. All successful modern-day revolutions have been made by peasant masses and have been opposed by orthodox Marxists. Leninists, including Maoists, have coopted, led, and in varying degrees betrayed these peasant revolutions. Mitrany treats both Marxian dogma on agriculture and the practical response of the peasant to their plight, showing how communist practice based on dogma clashed head-on with peasant practice (and emergent theory) based on experience.

Marx's agrarian dogma derived from his belief in large-scale production. Small peasant proprietors were doomed to succumb to historical laws of accumulation. Peasants were dull and reactionary and the proletarian revolution would properly put them into huge farm brigades and curb their petty-bourgeois "property-owner fanaticism." So ran Marx's theory. As an urban Westerner, Marx generalized from western European experience; but even there, after 1895, statistics revealed the unexpected persistence of small farms. As Mitrany notes, the large estates in the West, partly destroyed wherever the antifeudal French Revolution reached, had never been the result of free competition but were political creations. Marx's inferences were therefore quite unwarranted.

In preindustrial eastern Europe, including Russia, the role of politics was clear. There the politically powerful landed elite created enormous latifundia "in recent times." To capitalize on new markets for cereals in the West, the lords dispossessed the peasants, retaining them as cheap labor. When World War I broke the power of the landed ruling class, the peasant masses rose up everywhere (with the exception of Hungary) and divided the great estates. Unable to do much else, the "liberal" semiparliamentary successor regimes in these countries "gave" the peasants the land. This revolutionary breakthrough, Mitrany states, finished the emancipatory process begun in France. The difference was that where peasants made the revolution they took all the land, whereas in the earlier western reforms urban liberals tended to preserve large estates and only freed the serfs to become landless workers.

In Russia, the Bolsheviks "led" the revolution, conceding land to the peasantry. After the failure of agricultural levies, Lenin "retreated" to the New Economic Policy, "a reversion to individualism." Mitrany believes the NEP was solely a tactic and curiously ignores Bukharin's role as a defender of the NEP free market and the "worker-peasant" alliance. In any event, after 1928, forced-draft industrialization proceeded under Stalin with all the murder and violence necessary to make the state the new landlord.

Outside Russia, peasant revolutionaries created peasant parties to protect their gains, and "peasantist" ideology flourished. It was too late, however, for their enemies regrouped everywhere under a program of neomercantilism or state capitalism. Like Preobrazhensky, Trotsky, and Stalin, the bourgeois "liberal" industrialists and politicians believed in building heavy industry on the backs of the masses. Indirect taxes, high tariffs, and subsidies put the burden on the people. The peasant parties responded with a relatively libertarian program for development which looked to the parallel evolution of agriculture and light industry.

I cannot summarize here Mitrany's interesting discussion of peasantist ideology. He does call attention to the similar views of Proudhon. He cites evidence that family farms can survive or even outcompete large enterprises in a free market. Hence, there was nothing utopian about the peasantist program. In addition, peasantism, reflecting real love of the land, was a force for peace, since such love and murderous nationalism have nothing in common.

Unfortunately, the peasants' organization and ideology lagged behind their seizure of the land. Their political opponents, generally including the socialists, crushed the peasant movement, overriding liberal constitutional forms. After World War II, with Communist parties thrust into power, development followed Stalinist lines. Everywhere, however, peasant resistance forced compromise. In Yugoslavia collectivization was virtually abandoned. A Yugoslav politician (quoted by Mitrany) asks what can you do with people who regarded five centuries of Turkish rule as "a stop-gap?"

(Continued On Page 4)

Hobbes And Liberalism

By Bill Evers*

Hobbes is often counted by modern political theorists as a liberal, and often as a liberal whose views reflect the needs of an entrepreneurial, market-oriented capitalism.[1]

This argument has two prongs. One is the contention that Hobbes's society had already become bourgeois and that his theory was meant to provide stable ground rules for existing capitalist competition. The second is that Hobbes's theory provides an ideological basis for liberal society — the society of property, individual rights, and the market.

The first contention is an empirical claim about the character of the society in which Hobbes lived. Recent studies have shown, however, that the institutions of liberal society were not dominant in Hobbes's time (and are not dominant in the society that he describes in his books), and so it is not fruitful to pursue this prong of the argument here.[2]

Instead, we will take up the second prong of the argument, which contends that Hobbes's theory was designed to sustain and was plausibly capable of sustaining a liberal society. We will scrutinize the claim that Hobbes's theory was a doctrine of political individualism.[3]

Some problems of method come immediately to the fore. For example, "the market" itself is an abstract term that we use to designate the exchange by individuals of property titles. Because of the interdependence of the concepts involved, before one can adequately discuss whether the market is a prevalent institution in a society, one must first consider the nature and extent of individual self-ownership, of individual rights to property, and of governmental power.

Such inquiry into the character of rights and of governmental power is necessary because these matters are inextricably wrapped up in what we mean by a "liberal society." It is not enough to know that in some society children are permitted to trade baseball cards, to call this trading "the market", and then to call the whole society "liberal." When we talk about a liberal society, therefore, we are very much concerned with the structure of rights.

Hobbes's Doctrine

Hobbes viewed property as a useful violence-reducing mechanism that only existed because it was defined and authorized by the absolute sovereign.[4] There has been some scholarly discussion which questions this sort of summary of Hobbes's property theory. This discussion has explored the possibility that Hobbes, like the Levellers and Locke, might have believed in property rights that antedate the institution of government.[5]

In several versions of his political thought, Hobbes contended that patriarchs and slaveholders would have control over some persons and possessions in the state of nature.[6] These patriarchs and slaveholders would be small-scale sovereigns in their own little kingdoms, all within the overall insecurity of the state of nature. In early versions of his theory, Hobbes also speaks of incorporating, as is, these successful patriarchal and servile holdings into the new social compact that establishes the state. For example, an unused draft of his Elements of Law included: "Men entering in peace, retain what they have acquired."[7]

Hobbes decreases the possible strength that such a state-of-nature, family-sized unit might have from one version of his theory to the next. By the writing of Leviathan, the family group, when it confronts the sovereign power, is like a small band of soldiers that when surprised by an army must lay down its arms and beg to be spared.[8]

These patriarchal and servile holdings in the state of nature were property in the sense that they were effectively controlled by their owners. But they were not property in the sense of being derived from some principle of just original acquisition (as found in the writings of the Levellers and later in Locke). Nor were they property in the sense of being rights integrated into a non-contradictory network of rights and capable of being protected by legitimate force. Nor were they property in the sense of being rights that others outside the family were morally obliged to observe. Even as he is still talking about possessions and the transfer of possessions within the state of nature, Hobbes is saying that the laws of this state of nature oblige only in the court of conscience.[9]

Because this theory of property in the state of nature is radically different from the liberal view of the Levellers and Locke, it seems extravagant to say, as Lopata does, that Hobbes's early property doctrine contained the "seeds of a right of revolution," and that Hobbes's experience in the Civil War caused him to alter his doctrine.[10] There does not seem to be any radical break in Hobbes's property theory. Even in his late work, the Dialogue on the Common Laws of England, Hobbes speaks of possession in the state of nature when he describes how landlords obtain their holdings.[11]

We may safely say that Hobbes in all his writings believes that the sovereign (or a small-scale sovereign, the head of the family) determines all property relations. He also believes in all his writings, even those written before the Civil War, that the claim of an absolute right to property is subversive of orderly society.[12] The radical-liberal Levellers, in contrast, maintained that an absolute right to property was the only secure foundation of an orderly and just society.

In sum, we may say that Hobbes has a consistently legal positivist view of property rights, emphasizing the command of the sovereign.[13] Indeed, some of Hobbes's contemporary liberal critics like George Lawson and John Whitehall attacked him on precisely this point.[14]

Whitehall, for example, says that Hobbes's assignment of the property of the people to the sovereign will lead the people to rise up against the Hobbesian state and try to overthrow it, "that they may have something to be called their own."[15] Furthermore, Whitehall asserts, according to Hobbes's view it would have been perfectly all right for Cromwell's New Model Army to have seized "all the property of the people of England" in 1651, when — depending on your point of view — either England had collapsed into a state of nature or the Army had become sovereign.[16]

Locke himself, though less radical a liberal than others, notes that giving the sovereign absolute power, leaves the sovereign in a state of war vis a vis his subjects. Now the individual subject, whenever his property in his person or goods is invaded at the command of the sovereign, is defenseless in the face of a ruler who wields the only armed might in the society. Men in a non-governmental condition would be idiots to turn over absolute authority and all weapons to some Jones family. "This is to think that men are so foolish that they take care to avoid what mischiefs may be done them by polecats, or foxes, but are content, nay think it safety, to be devoured by lions."[17]

Further examination of Hobbes's arguments will give us additional reasons to believe that Hobbes's contemporary liberal critics had a more accurate view of the character of his proposals than do present-day political theorists who call Hobbes a liberal. Additional insight can be gained by looking at Hobbes's discussion of conquest, servitude, and the somewhat related matter of contracts agreed to under duress.

During the Civil War period, the radical-liberal Levellers denied that a conqueror or his heirs (either the recent conqueror Cromwell or the Stuarts as heirs of the Normans) had any claim upon the obedience of the people.[18] The liberal Levellers argued that only a government which secured man's natural rights in his own person and in his goods was legitimate. In contrast, Hobbes, an absolute monarchist and a defender of the Stuart cause, taught that a subject is obliged to obey a conqueror.[19]

(Continued On Page 5)

Peasants And Revolution —

(Continued From Page 3)

You can do what peasants everywhere have asked for a very long time: Clear the ways and let them alone . . . but clear the ways!

*Now that numerous trendy conservatives are swiping our hard-won label.

•Mr. Stromberg is a doctoral candidate in history at the University of Florida, and assistant editor of News of the Nation.

*We might say "local bullies and bad gentry."   ◻

Hobbes And Liberalism —

(Continued From Page 4)

Indeed, he basically equates the situation of someone who is enslaved in a state of nature by a stronger person, with the situation of a subject who adheres to a sovereign in international war, or via the social compact institution of a government, or in any other way.

As an example of a compact, Hobbes points to the situation of a captured man who is not kept constantly in chains. This privilege granted by his master that the slave not always be in chains, according to Hobbes, sets up a voluntary compact under which the slave is obliged to obey the absolute will of his master (who is here very like the governmental sovereign.) The slave is said by Hobbes to be enjoying a condition of liberty because he is not always in shackles and thus has some liberty of motion.[20]

The historian David Brion Davis zeroes in on the relationship of Hobbes's doctrine on slavery to his doctrine on the state when he writes:

> "There is no inherent reason that slavery should be incompatible with the ideal of a functional or utilitarian state. Indeed, for later champions of individual liberty, like William Lloyd Garrison and Mikhail Bakunin, all states were founded on the principle of slavery. For Thomas Hobbes, slavery was an inevitable part of the logic of power; the bondsman had no cause for complaint when he was provided with sustenance and security in exchange for being governed . . ."[21]
> This model of slave-making resembled in many respects Hobbes's concept of the social compact. Hobbes stated quite explicitly that the only difference between the free subject and the 'servant' was that one served the city and the other served a fellow subject."[22]

Hobbes makes the claim that the social compact and acquiesence in slavery are voluntary because he rejects the liberal doctrine that contracts made under duress are null and void.[23] Hobbes argues that a promise to pay ransom to a kidnapper or highwayman is a binding contract. This allows validity for the formation of governments by way of or in the face of threats against the people. It should be noted, however, that most moralists among Hobbes's contemporaries, as well as Locke later on, rejected the validity of contracts made under duress.[24]

In addition, Hobbes's equivocal and confusing usage of such terms as "voluntary" and "liberty" facilitates the cloaking of illiberal acts in the rhetoric of liberalism.[25] Since volition for Hobbes simply refers to a morally inconsequential part of the process of deliberation, and since all human acts have costs and inconveniences, situations which involve the coercion of some persons by others can be designated as voluntary relationships by Hobbes. In utilitarian fashion, he sees no radical dichotomy between coerced and uncoerced human activity. Similarly, since liberty for Hobbes refers to the absence of chains, if the kidnapper or the sovereign does not put you in chains or try to kill you, you are still free.

Considering Hobbes's concepts of property, individual rights, contract, and sovereignty, it is difficult to term him an ideological liberal. Looking at his views on economic policy, we find additional confirmation that he is not a liberal. Hobbes favored sumptuary laws,[16] import licenses,[17] military conscription in emergencies,[18] compulsory poor relief,[19] and laws to encourage and subsidize fishing, farming, navigation skills, and education.[30] He believed in the unlimited right of the sovereign to tax the people.[31] He bitterly opposed wage labor in manufacturing industries.[32] While hardly the economic program of an advanced state socialist, neither is it a liberal program like that of the Levellers or that of Herbert Spencer.

In conclusion, it seems untenable to claim that Hobbes is a liberal. He differs drastically with the liberal political tradition on essential doctrinal matters, and for this reason was opposed to and opposed by the liberals of his own time.

Notes

1. For example, Laurence Berns writes: "To the extent that modern liberalism teaches that all social and political obligations are derived from and in the service of the individual rights of man, Hobbes may be regarded as the founder of modern liberalism." Laurence Berns,

"Thomas Hobbes," in Leo Strauss and Joseph Cropsey, eds., History of Political Philosophy (Chicago: Rand McNally, 1972), p. 375. See also Leo Strauss, Natural Right and History (Chicago: University of Chicago Press, 1953), pp.181-82; C. B. Macpherson, "Hobbes: The Political Obligation of the Market," in The Political Theory of Possessive Individualism (London: Oxford University Press, 1962), pp.9-106; and C.B. Macpherson, "Natural Rights in Hobbes and Locke," and "Hobbes's Bourgeois Man," in Democratic Theory (London: Oxford University Press, 1973), pp.224-37 and 238-50.

2. Peter Laslett, "Market Society and Political Theory," Historical Journal, vol.7, no.1 (1964), pp.150-82; William Letwin, "The Economic Foundations of Hobbes's Politics," in Maurice Cranston and Richard S. Peters, eds., Hobbes and Rousseau (Garden City, L.I.: Doubleday, 1972), pp.143-64; and Keith Thomas, "The Social Origins of Hobbes's Political Thought," in Keith Brown, ed., Hobbes Studies (Cambridge, Mass.: Harvard University Press, 1965), pp.185-236.

3. Hobbes makes the individual the basic unit of political analysis throughout his writings, but this is not sufficient ground for calling him a proponent of political individualism. Hobbes was also an early adherent of a version of the subjective theory of value in political economy. See Elements of Law, in Richard S. Peters, ed., Body, Man, and Citizen (New York: Collier, 1962), p.291; De Cive, chap.3, art.6, in English Works (1841; Scientia Verlag Aalen, 1966), vol.2, p.34; Leviathan (Oxford: Basil Blackwell, n.d.), chap.10, p.57. Again, this view in economic science does not make Hobbes an individualist in his assessment of proper political institutions. Cf. Macpherson, Possessive Individualism, pp.37-39, 63; "Hobbes's Bourgeois Man," p.242.

4. On property as a violence-reducing mechanism, see De Cive, pp.vi-vii. For a modern restatement of the Hobbesian position, see James M. Buchanan, "Before Public Choice," in Gordon Tullock, ed., Explorations in the Theory of Anarchy (Blacksburg, Va.: Center for the Study of Public Choice, 1973).
On the role of the sovereign in defining property rights, see Elements, p.342; De Cive, chap.6, art.15, p.84; Lev., chap.24, pp.161-62; Dialogue on the Common Law of England, in E.W., vol.6, pp.29-30.

5. M. M. Goldsmith, Hobbes's Science of Politics (New York: Columbia University Press, 1966), p.199;
Benjamin B. Lopata, "Property Theory in Hobbes," Political Theory, vol.1, no.2 (May 1973), pp.203-18.

6. Elements, pp.295-97; De Cive, chap.6, art.15, p.84n; chap.8, art.1, p.109; art.8, p.112; Lev., chap.17, p.109; chap.20, pp.129-36.

7. Goldsmith, p.199n.

8. Lev., pp.133-34.

9. De Cive, chap.3, art.18, p.41; art.27, pp.45-46; chap.5, art.1, pp.63-64.

10. Lopata, p.211.

11. Dialogue, p.147.

12. Elements, p.371; De Cive, chap.12, art.7, p.157; Lev., chap.29, p.213; chap.30, p.224; Behemoth, in E.W., vol.6, pp.168-69. Hobbes considered natural rights liberalism a major cause of the Civil War.

13. Compare Hobbes's property theory to the similar legal positivist view of Cromwell's son-in-law, Henry Ireton, See G.P. Gooch, English Democratic Ideas in the Seventeenth Century (New York: Harper, 1959), p.138; H.N. Brailsford, The Levellers and the English Revolution (Stanford, Calif.: Stanford University Press, 1961), p.281; Macpherson, Possessive Individualism, p.139.

14. On the property theory of Locke's precursor Lawson, see John Bowle, Hobbes and His Critics (London: Jonathan Cape, 1951), p.99.

15. Bowle, p.177.

16. Bowle, pp.178.

17. John Locke, Two Treatises of Government, rev. ed. (New York: Mentor, 1965), Second Treatise, pars. 91-93, pp.370-72. The lions and foxes quotation is on p.372. Laslett contends that Locke is criticizing not Hobbes but Filmer in these passages. For Hobbes's reply to Locke's sort of argument, see Dialogue, pp.10-11, 20-21. For Locke's contention that tyranny is worse than the state of nature, see Second Treatise, par.225, pp.463-64.

18. Christopher Hill, Puritanism and Revolution (New York, Schocken, 1964) pg.75-82.

19. On the property rights acquired by conquerors, see Lev., chap.24, p.163; Dialogue, p.149. On the parallels between Hobbes's doctrine of conquest and the obligation of the Cromwellian de facto theorists, see the writings of Quentin Skinner.

(Continued On Page 6)

Say's Law Revisited

By Richard M. Ebeling*

Following the 1936 publication of John Maynard Keynes' **The General Theory of Employment, Interest and Money**, an intellectual deluge occurred that silenced almost all critical opinion. The movements of Macro-economic aggregates and the forces determining the nature of "effective demand" became the focal points of academic concern among economists.

Courageous was the individual who chose to move against the tide and question the "laws" of the New Economics. Professor W. H. Hutt, following John Stuart Mill's dictum that "No one can be a great thinker who does not recognize that as a thinker it is his first duty to follow his intellect to whatever conclusions it may lead," has been one of those courageous souls.

For fifty years, he has not only defended the much disparaged "orthodox" Micro-economic approach, but added clarity and depth in his expositions, as well. Whether it be his critical analysis of compulsory unionism in the free society, **The Theory of Collective Bargaining** (1931) and **The Strike-Threat System** (1973) or his devastating critique of Keynesian economics, **The Theory of Idle Resources** (1939) and **Keynesianism-Retrospect and Prospect** (1963), his pen has always searched out the "inner contradictions" of incorrect theory that passes as the foundation of contemporary economic thought.

Now, in his latest book, **A Rehabilitation of Say's Law** (Ohio University Press: Athens, 1974) $8.00, Professor Hutt has again returned to the attack. He postulates that, correctly understood, Say's Law "is indispensable for an understanding of the true genesis of depression and of prosperity without inflation; that attempts at dynamic treatment of the economic system which ignore it are worthless . . ."

The present definition of Say's Law, that "supply creates its own demand," was coined by Keynes in **The General Theory** and is a distortion of the true meaning of the Law. Rather, what Say was attempting to formulate was the most obvious fact that "the source of demand for any particular input or output produced is the flow of inputs and outputs of all the things which do not compete with it; for some part of that flow is destined to be exchanged for it." Thus, what we exchange are goods and services for goods and services. And that which we choose not to keep for ourselves out of our own production will be traded away for what we value more highly.

When the Keynesian theorist refers to excess aggregate supply and the weakness of "effective demand" to purchase that supply, he is looking through the wrong end of the telescope. There could not be an "aggregate" excess of supply unless there was a super-abundance of all inputs and outputs such that they had no value (and, thus, would not be an economic good); what this does mean is that certain goods may be in relatively greater abundance than other goods that are in shorter supply. What is preventing their purchase is not "ineffective demand" on the part of purchasers, but ineffective pricing on the part of suppliers for the market to be "cleared." For, in Hutt's words, "no one can purchase unless someone else sells . . . every act of selling and buying requires that the would-be seller price his product to permit the sale and that the would-be buyer offer a price which the seller accepts." If saving-preferences rise, demand for consumer goods will decrease and demand for capital goods will increase. Price relationships will shift, with the consumer offering a smaller supply of goods and services for consumer goods and a greater supply of goods and services for capital goods.

Indeed, it is in the unwillingness of resource owners to price their products or services at levels commensurate with consumer demand that Professor Hutt finds the cause of prolonged depressions. "Disco-ordination in one sector of the economy will, if there are price rigidities in other sectors, bring about these successively aggravating reactions, one decline in the flow of services inducing another." Whenever "inappropriate pricing" results in the withholding of supplies, this will limit the demand for other goods and services the would-be supplier would have purchased.

Interestingly, Hutt develops an alternative to the accepted Keynesian theory of the Multiplier. In fact, it proves that, contrary to what Keynes believed, his theory depends on the validity of Say's Law. Since the problem is disequilibrium pricing, the lowering of any price to its market-clearing level "will tend to initiate a positive 'real multiplier' effect — a cumulative rise in activity and real income . . ." The Keynesian notion of government-induced expenditures is really only a means of getting the release of withheld supplies (at prices acceptable to the supplier), so they, in turn, can generate demand at price levels high enough to entice the release of other withheld supplies. Thus, whether it is monetarists talking about an "adequate money supply" or Keynesians referring to an "adequate rate of spending," they are "really envisioning the process under which 'supplies' (and hence 'demands') withheld through pricing can be restored" by unanticipated inflation.

In a series of important chapters, Professor Hutt dissects some of the most prominent post-Keynesians such as Harry Johnson, Leland Yeager, Robert Clower and Axel Leijonhufvud. All, in one form or another, fall under a veil of "money illusion." For them, the use of money somehow changes the nature of the market experience. For instance, an increase in the demand for money held may place a dampener on the "effective demand" for finished output, thus, acting as a depressant on the economy. But this, says Hutt, is failing to see that money like any asset or commodity has a value in being held as well as traded. "An increase in the relative demand for money simply means that the aggregate real value of money rises relatively to the aggregate real value of non-money." Adjustments in the price relationships would still enable the market to "clear." We "do not say that some portion of the demand for rye is 'ineffective' because some former purchasers of it demand wheat instead."

But some critics contend that even if the money wage-rate was the "correct" one, that the "excess" supply of labor still wouldn't be absorbed. This is part of Leijonhufvud's argument. In a case of barter where an over-seeing auctioneer could view the marginal values of different factors, supply would equal demand. But the contention is that because of faulty communications and market signals, business firms will fail to hire labor even if only labor's marginal product is being asked for. In who's eyes, asks Hutt, is that value of the marginal product? To an

(Continued On Page 8)

Hobbes And Liberalism —
(Continued From Page 5)

20. De Cive, chap.8, art.1-9, pp.108-13; Lev., chap.20, pp.132-34.
21. David Brion Davis, **The Problem of Slavery in the Age of Revolution, 1770-1823** (Ithaca, N.Y.: Cornell University Press, 1975), p.263.
22. David Brion Davis, **The Problem of Slavery in Western Culture** (Ithaca, N.Y.: Cornell University Press, 1966), p.117.
23. Elements, p.286; De Cive, chap.2, art.16, pp.23-24; Lev., chap.14, p.91.
24. Thomas, p.233.
25. On Hobbes's equivocal concept of liberty, see J. Roland Pennock, "Hobbes's Confusing 'Clarity' — The Case of 'Liberty' ", in Brown, pp.101-16, esp. p.105; John Plamenatz, **Man and Society** (New York: McGraw-Hill, 1963), vol.1, p.139.
26. Elements, p.381; De Cive, chap.13, art.14, p.178; Lev., chap.24, p.163; chap.30, p.226; Thomas, p.228.
27. Lev., chap.24, pp.163-64.
28. Lev., chap.21, p.143.
29. Lev., chap.30, p.227.
30. De Cive, chap.13, art.14, p.177.
31. Elements, p.342; Lev., chap.30, pp.162-63; Behemoth, pp.168-69; Dialogue, pp.29-30, 154.
32. Behemoth, pp.320-21.

*Mr. Evers is a doctoral candidate in political science at Stanford University.

Libertarian Ripoff
Of The Month Dept.

A couple of years ago a friend of mine was visiting California for a scholarly conference. There he ran into a fellow who had in his possession a rare copy of an unpublished manuscript of someone on whom my friend was engaged in writing a doctoral dissertation. The fellow told my friend that if he gave him $30 he would soon ship him a xerox of the manuscript. My friend was highly skeptical, but the call of dissertation — it is always heady and so my friend forked over the $30, fully expecting that this would be the last he would ever hear of either the $30 or the manuscript. Much was his astonishment when, a few weeks later, the promised xerox arrived in the mail. My friend was agog. "Jesus," he told me, "that was the first time I ever had business dealings with a libertarian that I wasn't ripped off."

An exaggerated estimate, perhaps; but certainly an understandable one. There used to be a highly naive view widespread in the libertarian movement, that because someone was a libertarian, and therefore respected property rights, that one could always rely on libertarians to be honest and rational in their business dealings. Hah! I daresay that there are few ideological movements in recent times that have been beset by more frauds, shysters, and bunco artists than the libertarian movement. Why this should be so we will try to explore below.

The latest libertarian ripoff is on a massive scale and one that has, furthermore, hit the public headlines. Last fall I began to hear breathless comments about a new "libertarian car" (what the hell, one might have asked, is a **libertarian** car?) that a formidable, neo-Randian lady was in the process of building in California. The lady was going to set Detroit on its ear. The car was going to be made of some kind of new "Rearden metal", it would be a three-wheeler that would go 70 miles on a gallon of gas, and would sell for less than $2,000. Wow! And, what's more (nudge, nudge) the lady's company was called "Twentieth Century Motors" (get it?).

The lady — Mrs. G. Elizabeth Carmichael — was indeed a heroine straight out of a Randian novel (albeit a bit earthier.) She gave interviews in which she proclaimed that she gave all the orders and made all the decisions in her company, and that her subordinate executives were simply yes-men carrying out her orders. She held forth with a parody of a Commodore Vanderbilt-Rand speech, announcing that she didn't "give a s - - t about the public", that all she cared about was Liz Carmichael, and for that reason she was going to produce a car, the Dale, that would "knock the hell" out of Detroit. As a **Newsweek** story reported afterwards, "A visitor to her Encino (Calif.) office recalls her as a big, stocky woman, at least 6 feet tall, thrusting out a large, beefy hand with pink nails and saying in a low, husky voice: 'I am a genius.' " (Newsweek, Mar. 3, 1975). Plenty of "self-esteem" there! Scorning her subordinate executives, she declared that she had "more b - - - s than all of them put together." Yes, truly a tough tycoon in the heroic mould.

Liz Carmichael's financial methods were, to say the least, unorthodox, as she sold shares in her company to "countless" numbers of people. One gimmick that she used: she would take out Situation Wanted ads in the newspapers, and when the applicant applied for a job in Twentieth Century Motors, he wouldn't get the job, but she would manage to sell him shares of stock. (Unorthodox, slightly shady financing, but unorthodox means "heroic" and innovative, right?)

The lady was flying high. Liz Carmichael claimed to have raised $30 million and swore that she would be producing 88,000 Dales by the end of 1975. But by early 1975, the shades of night began to close in. The highly respected **Road and Track** magazine analyzed the proclaimed car, and subjected it to a withering critique, pointing out, for example, that its supposed 40 h.p. engine was considerably smaller than that of many motorcycles. No wonder it would get 70 miles per gallon! But would it get any speed on the road? More formidably, various arms of the law began to zero in on Twentieth Century Motors. In late January, the firm's P.R. man, an ex-convict, was shot to death by another ex-con employee in the company's offices. Investigations ensued. In eary February, top officers of the firm were arrested, charged with conspiring to commit theft by selling dealerships and options based on false claims. Shortly afterward,

a judge placed the company in receivership, and the sheriff of Dallas (where Liz Carmichael had moved the company) went looking for our entrepreneur. Liz skipped town, and there is now a warrant out for her arrest. And no one seems to know how much money was taken in, or where the money is (presumably with Liz Carmichael.) And presumably there isn't any workable car either.

It soon turned out that nobody knew who Liz Carmichael was. The town where she claimed she was born never heard of her, and there was no record of her in the colleges she claimed to have attended. Her social-security number and driver's license turned out to be fakes, and the earliest record anyone had of her was in 1971, when she was wanted for passing a bad check. There also seemed to be no record of the five children that had been living with her.

An even more bizarre note appeared when the police searched Mrs. Carmichael's home, and found a substantial amount of curious clothing: including wigs, a waist cincher, and a crotch suppressor — standard transvestite fare. As a reporter for the **San Francisco Chronicle** wittily concluded: it might turn out that Liz Carmichael's boast that she had more b- - - s than all of her male executives put together was the only true statement "she" ever made.

The latest chapter in the Liz Carmichael saga are A.P. dispatches for April 8 and 14. The authorities have now identified and captured "Liz Carmichael" as one Jerry Dean Michael, 47, a federal fugitive since 1962 when he jumped bail on a counterfeiting charge. The Dallas D.A.'s office, furthermore, has charged that no plans ever existed to produce the Dale car.

And so there we have it: the latest "libertarian" ripoff, and a transvestite one at that. I have no idea how many wealthy and not-so-wealthy libertarians invested in this con-game, but knowing the movement and the record of its brief history, I have a strong hunch that the number of libertarian suckers is formidable.

We return to our original question: what is there in the libertarian makeup that makes us patsies for bunco artists (the motivation of the bunco artist himself is, of course, all too clear)? I have an answer that can only be speculative, but it seems to have a good deal of persuasive power. There is in all too many libertarians the Randian-Great Man theory of history, a mind-set that holds that history is constantly being turned upside down by heroic innovators who arrive on the scene out of left field, and proceed to make millions and affect the course of the world. They arrive out of the blue, they invent some sort of "Rearden metal," and presto! the world is changed. Of course, once in a great while such innovators do arrive on the scene. But, in the first place, their inventions and innovations generally take a long while to make their way to fame and fortune. More importantly, for every Thomas Edison there are thousands of crackpot "innovators" whose new inventions don't amount to a hill of beans, or who are frauds, con-men, and ripoff artists. Reciting a list of the Great Men who Made It is terribly misleading if we forget the far more numerous list of the cranks and screwballs who **didn't** make it. And so, to the general gullibility of the public (best expressed in the immortal P. T. Barnum phrase, "there's a sucker born every minute") we add the Great Man mind-set of libertarians influenced by the Randian world-view.

What we desperately need, therefore, is a healthy skepticism about new and dramatic announcements of great new entrepreneurs that have just arrived on the scene. Particularly should we be skeptical of the **luftmenschen** with no visible credentials, who suddenly appear out of the blue to announce their great new thing. For there is a profound sense in which the mass of skeptics who grudgingly greet the news of all allegedly great innovations are right; for if it's really going to be a new "Rearden metal", it will eventually make its way in the marketplace. There is no need for libertarians to rush into the field with hooplas everytime somebody announces the greatness of their new invention or discovery. Otherwise, all we accomplish is a tragic waste of all-too-scarce libertarian resources.   ◼

Say's Law Revisited —
(Continued From Page 6)

over-seeing auctioneer, maybe; but with imperfect knowledge it is the "prospective yield" from labor investment, from the standpoint of the entrepreneur, that will result in hiring. The wage-rates have not been lowered enough to represent the "marginal value" within the pessimistic perspective of the business firm. And "when wage offers have been sufficiently adjusted for entrepreneurs generally to accept them, each output expansion is contributing to a state of affairs in which, through dynamic reactions set going, higher marginal prospective labor products will generally emerge and higher money wage-rates will be forced by the market."

Finally, Professor Hutt discusses the claim that the pre-Keynesian "orthodoxy" had no explanation of situations of less than full employment and what cures were necessary for alleviating the depression. Hutt quotes from Lavington's 1922 book, **The Trade Cycle**, that "No entrepreneur can fully expand his output until others expand their output." And Edwin Cannan's 1933 words that "General unemployment appears when asking too much is a general phenomena." Thus, showing the validity of Say's Law that just as much as is supplied will generate an equivalent demand for non-competing resources. And in his earlier work **Politically Impossible . . .?** (Institute of Economic Affairs, London, 1971), Hutt quoted such "leftist" spokesmen as welfare economist A. C. Pigou, who told a government committee in 1931 that lower wage-rates "would employ more people,'"and the Fabian socialists Sidney and Beatrice Webb, who called the Trade Union leaders "pigs" for sabotaging British employment levels by asking for excessive wage-rates.

Though Hutt doesn't mention them, of all the economists and schools of thought who would be least guilty of this Keynesian accusation, the "Austrians" would have the best record. Starting in the 1920's, they were not bedazzled by the promises of Irving Fisher's Stabilized Price Level movement. For, as Schumpeter astutely observed " . . . the Austrian way of emphasizing the behavior and decision of individuals and of defining exchange value of money with respect to individual commodities rather than with respect to a price level of one kind or another has its merits, particularly in the analysis of an inflationary process." Ludwig von Mises pointed out in 1928 that, "Exchange ratios on the market are constantly subject to change," because they are the result of the subjective valuations of market participants; and "the idea of a general state of prices, a price level, which is raised or lowered uniformly is . . . fictitious . . ." In the same year Gottfried Haberler observed that businesses are influenced by prices relevant to its particular line of production, rather

than a "price level." So, "a general index rather conceals and submerges than reveals and explains those price movements which characterize and signify the movement of the (business) cycle." Based on this type of analysis, Friedrich von Hayek predicted the coming depression in the February, 1929 **Monthly Report of the** Austrian Institute for Business Cycle Research.

When the depression struck and employment figures remained at a low level, Mises pointed out, in 1931, "that unemployment, as a long-term phenomenon, is the consequence of the policy adopted by the unions of driving wage rates up." Hayek, in the same year, stated that "absorption of the unemployed resources" could be achieved only "by the slow process of adapting the structure of production to the means available for capital purposes." Which meant flexibility in money wages and prices. And, finally, as Fritz Machlup observed in 1935, "no interest policy can succeed in stimulating production when the maladjustment in cost-price relations persists; in other words, if the costs of labor and material fail to adjust themselves, low interest rates cannot do anything for creating investment."

What Keynes was really criticizing, then, was not that the "orthodox" economists didn't have an answer to the depression problem. Rather, it was that the reigning orthodoxy offered no solution that was acceptable to trade union monopolies that did not want to cut back from the money wages of the "prosperous" 1920's. The Keynesian solution is inflation. For as Keynes explicitly admits in **The General Theory**, "a movement by employers to revise money-wage bargains downwards will be much more strongly resisted than a gradual and automatic lowering of real wages as a result of rising prices." The whole New Economics becomes summed up as a particular case of Say's Law. A case in which government monetary expansion and expenditure attempts to seduce the release of withheld supplies, at prices and wages desired by the privileged groups, so they, in turn, can demand the withheld supplies of others at higher prices.

Professor Hutt concisely and brilliantly explained the problem in the introduction to his **Theory of Idle Resources**: "Competition and capitalism are hated to-day because of their tendency to destroy poverty and privilege more rapidly than custom and the expectations established by protections can allow. We accordingly find private interests combining to curb this process and calling on the State to step in and do the same; and unless the resistance is expressed through monetary policy, the curbing takes the form of restrictions on production."

Mr. Ebeling is a student of economics at California State University at Sacramento.

Published Every Month. Subscription Rates: $8.00 Per Year; $15.00 Two Years

A Monthly Newsletter

THE
Libertarian Forum

Joseph R. Peden, Publisher   Murray N. Rothbard, Editor

VOLUME VII, NO. 6   JUNE, 1975   US-ISSN0047-4517

THE CASE FOR OPTIMISM

Looking at the state of the country today, it is all too easy for the libertarian to fall prey to a profound pessimism. The crises which libertarians and Austrian economists have been predicting for years are now coming true, in area after area of government activity. A severe inflation combined with the biggest depression since the 1930's; huge and ever-increasing federal deficits; virtual bankruptcy in New York City; the total collapse of American foreign policy; near-bankruptcy in New York City; violence over forced bussing; the crises brought about by Big and growing government are multiplying at every hand. It is easy, then, to despair and to look forward gloomily to a march into total collectivism. In some libertarians, the tendency is therefore to look for a personal cop-out, into one's cave or onto one's lonely island.

But this despair is the result of a linear, mechanistic view of the historical process; it is tragically one-sided, for it leaves out the essential dialectic — the action and reaction — of the historical process, an action-and-reaction that comes to a head in times of pervasive and systemic crisis such as the United States has now entered. By "dialectic", I hasten to add, I am not referring to the Marxian "dialectical materialism", but simply to the vital but complex action-and-reaction, cause-and-effect linkages in human affairs. It is precisely **because** we have entered a mighty systemic crisis, a crisis of the entire U.S. polity and political economy, that the outlook for the future of liberty in the United States has, in my view, never been brighter — at least for well over a century.

For the pervasive American crisis is precisely a crisis of the **breakdown** of statism. We libertarians have been preaching for years that statism, in addition to its gross immorality, **doesn't work**, particularly in an industrial economy such as we have had for over a century. Until the last few years, our pronouncements have been whistling in the wind. No matter how sound or even persuasive our theory, the American economy and polity has **seemed** to be working, and working splendidly. In particular, the great post-World War II boom that only collapsed in 1973-74 seemed to be splendid and unending. In that sort of euphoric atmosphere, very few people were disposed to listen to us or to the libertarian message. Who cared about the growth of the State when, domestically, living standards were increasing, unemployment was low, and, in foreign affairs, America was seemingly the mightiest nation on earth? Unfortunately, especially in a pragmatic world, morality cuts very little ice so long as the system seems to be successful. We knew that the prosperity and the seeming world strength were false and hollow, but no one is disposed to listen to Jeremiah or Cassandra while apparent success has been achieved.

But, in the last few years, and especially since 1973, statism has reached its permanent, systemic crisis; statism is collapsing on every hand, breaking down from its own inherent and grave inner contradictions. We have at last reached what Ludwig von Mises foresaw twenty-five years ago: in his terms, "the exhaustion of the reserve fund." When the modern march toward statism and away from approximate laissez-faire began at the turn of the twentieth century, there was an enormous amount of "fat" in the economy, a fat created by a century of roughly laissez-faire capitalism. So great was the fat, or cushion, that government intervention and regulation **seemed** to have no ill effect. The ill effects, libertarians and **laissez-faire** liberals knew full well, were there all right, but they were hidden by the general prosperity created by the previous free economy, and by the remaining preponderance of the free market. And so the general public, intellectuals, businessmen, the media, could blithely hack away at the foundations of our prosperity and our freedom with total disregard or ignorance of the eventual unfortunate consequences.

Furthermore, the two major forms of twentieth-century statism were, at least in form, brand-new. One form was Marxian socialism, which claimed to be able to bring about the classical liberal **ideals** (peace, freedom, prosperity for the mass of the population) through old-style despotic and collectivistic means. Proletarian socialism was, indeed, a brand-new idea and system in world history, it presented what to many people were attractive features, and the Marxist call for their seemingly noble "social experiment" proved to be a seductive one in an age that had abandoned principle for a mindless pragmatism. Why not give it a chance? That chance has now manifestly failed. The other new system was the corporate state, essentially the present system, which began in the Progressive period, and flowered in many forms here and abroad: the Keynesian mixed economy, fascism, corporatism. While we knew that this was only the old discredited mercantilism in a new form, the rest of the world failed to see this; for the new mercantilists were able to cloak their system in the rhetoric of a Tory democracy, a welfare-warfare State seemingly tailored to the requirements of the new industrial era. In short, the neo-mercantilist conservatives, too, abandoned their devotion to old-style monarchy and the established Church, and refurbished their authoritarian statism to mould a new system of corporate industrialism cloaked in a democratic, demagogic form. **This** was the system that soon came to triumph in the United States and in the Western world, and **this** is the system that is now rapidly coming apart at the seams in the U.S. and in Western Europe, riven at long last on the ineluctable but heretofore hidden rock of its momentous inner contradictiosns.

And the great thing is that all over the country, people in all walks of life, among former liberals, intellectuals, the media, the general public, and **even** among confused and bewildered politicians, are realizing that it is precisely **statism** that is breaking down. In the Great Depression of the 1930's, it was easy for socialists and corporatists to pin the blame for that breakdown on "laissez-faire". Again, we knew that the cause was the inflationist interventionism of the Federal Reserve System and other central banks during the 1920's; but it proved impossible to get this message across to intellectuals and to the general public; for **they** had all been under the impression that we had had a **laissez-faire** system during the 1920's. Hence, laissez-faire got tagged with the blame for the Great Depression, and corporatist statism and collectivism could take an

(Continued On Page 2)

Case For Optimism —

(Continued From Page 1)

enormous leap forward into our present system.

But now, except for a few fringe Marxists who persist in blaming "capitalism", it is more and more generally realized that it is the State and statism that are breaking down. Everyone knows, for example, that we have had an enormous amount of statism and government intervention, foreign and domestic, for forty years now; and so it is clear to virtually everyone that laissez-faire cannot take the blame this time. Furthermore, it is increasingly clear that the major locus of failure is precisely in government, in the spheres of uniquely or preponderantly government activity or influence; government is now so clearly and manifestly to blame that more and more people, even former advocates of government and the Welfare-Warfare State, are jumping ship and are adopting libertarian or quasi-libertarian ideals.

In short, the "objective" conditions for the ending of statism and the triumph of liberty are now at hand in the overall, systemic crisis of the State; and the "subjective" conditions for victory are now rapidly arriving, in that more and more people, in all walks of life, are seeing and understanding that breakdown and hence shifting rapidly to libertarian positions. The "exhaustion of the reserve fund" means that every time government acts it creates an "instantaneous negative feedback" — so that the evil consequences of government, heretofore masked, are now glaringly evident to all. Statism is breaking down, people are more and more realizing that fact, and hence the triumph of liberty comes ever closer. Instead of being pessimistic, libertarians should rejoice, because the march of history is now ineluctably ours. We have turned the corner. We always knew that, in the long run, we would triumph because truth was on our side and because statism could not work in the industrial era; but now that long-run is at hand. We are at last entering the "long-run".

And so it was perfectly legitimate for our libertarian forefathers at the turn of the twentieth century, and in the thirties and forties of this century, to despair. They knew, most of them, that in the long run we would probably triumph. But all they had to look forward to was decades, maybe generations, of the closing in of the dark night of statism and collectivism. They could only look back nostalgically to the nineteenth century as a Golden Age, and gird themselves to face mounting statism and despair. They had every right to despair, our forebears who suffered through the tragic growth of statism and collectivism on every hand, and who saw the devotees of liberty and the free market shrink to a tiny band who could only keep the flame for future generations. They were, as the great Albert Jay Nock despairingly wrote, only "the remnant", though a glorious remnant they were. And so let us hail them and emphathize with their suffering and their courage in holding out against the world: Spencer, Pareto, Tucker, Ortega, Mencken, Nock, and all the others, who each in their way tried to fight a battle that seemed increasingly lost. But let us not become so mired in the despair of the past that we fail to recognize that we have turned the corner, and that the prognosis for liberty is now onward and upward into the glorious light of a new dawn. We have indeed reached the light at the end of our tunnel.

It is our good fortune that the breakdown of the American State is systemic and pervasive in every part: not just in economic policy, but in social and foreign policy as well. And in all these areas, more and more people are increasingly pinning the blame right where it belongs: on government itself, not just on "bad" leaders, but on the very system of government intervention. There is, for example, the pervasive and magnificent distrust of government per se, the healthy "post-Watergate" climate. Not in generations have the press and the media, and formerly liberal intellectuals, been so cynical about government per se. Never again will we have the blind pre-Watergate trust in our secret police: the FBI, CIA, etc. Never again will we regard the once sacred President as a quasi-divine monarch who is fated to lead the world and who can do no wrong. In the wake of Vietnam, never again will we have blind faith in the Wilson-FDR-etc. foreign policy of "collective security" and global meddling. Never again will we have blind faith in any politician.

On the economic front, there is of course the inflationary depression, which has put the boots to the arrogant pretensions of Establishment economists, to our faith in the Keynesian way. But not only that: the near bankruptcy of such a revered institution as the Social Security system has now led to a widespread disenchantment with that system. It is increasingly reported that to remain solvent in the future, social security

taxes alone will have to rise to 40%, an intolerable level for the average American. The near-bankruptcy of New York City government is a glorious blessing; because it has brought home to everyone the truth that local and state governments cannot keep spending and borrowing indefinitely; that the day of reckoning is at hand, and that, since the public will not tolerate higher tax burdens, government budgets will have to be cut and cut sharply in the years ahead. The public is finally learning that you can't have your cake and eat it, now that the "fat" on the cake (to mix our metaphors) is no longer there. Who would have thought ten, even five years ago that the day would ever come in our lifetime when the good, grey New York Times would spend a quarter-page debating the merits and demerits of New York City government defaulting on its bonds? And the very opposition to default highlights its libertarian merits: for once New York City defaults, not only will no one buy its bonds in the future, but all municipal bonds will be discredited hereafter, and all governments will have to cut back.

Furthermore, the breakdown of regulated industries — notably railroads and increasingly the airlines — is bringing home even to liberals that government regulation itself is the cause of the problem. More and more, in surprisingly high circles, the reasoned call is coming for the abolition of government regulatory agencies altogether. No less a high personage than Federal Trade Commission chairman Lewis Engman has called repeatedly for the abolition of the ICC, CAB, and other regulatory agencies. Even Senator Kennedy, of all people, is increasingly receptive to the idea of such abolition.

Another hopeful straw in the wind is the fact that Senator Edward Brooke (R., Mass.), heretofore a standard left-liberal, has just adopted the full Austrian theory of our current inflation, blaming our economic crisis on the "malinvestments" (Brooke even uses this uniquely Austrian term) brought about by the boom in inflationary bank credit. Brooke concludes that we should (a) stop monetizing government debt, (b) cut the government budget, and (c) lower taxes on private saving and investment. When someone like Senator Brooke becomes an Austrian economist surely our victory is at hand. (See the May 20 release from Senator Brooke, "Brooke Urges New Economic Policy").

There are also hopeful developments in the sphere of concrete political action. New York State has just repealed its pernicious structure of "fair trade" laws, which for forty years has crippled retail competition and raised prices to consumers. The Federal Trade Commission is moving to abolish all state laws that, at the behest of the organized pharmacists, have prohibited pharmacies from advertising prescription drug prices, and have thereby kept drug prices unconscionably high and crippled competition among retail pharmacies. On the civil liberties front, California has just abolished laws prohibiting various sexual activities among consenting adults, at least in private.

Particularly heart-warming is the article by Larry Martz, "Say-Nay Politics", in Newsweek, June 9. Martz writes soberly about the new, pervasive mood in America of distrust of government, and of moving to reduce the role of government in American life. Martz writes of a "current stirring in America", a "new mood . . . running strong in the city halls, the statehouses and the talk of both major parties." The mood he identifies as a "mistrust of government itself and a doubt approaching despair that the nation's problems can be solved at all (by government)". Martz estimates that the result "could be a change in American politics as basic as the upheaval of the Depression years . . . forcing both parties to campaign on a new set of issues."

The most prominent embodiment of this new mood is the startling record of the new California governor, Jerry Brown. In his brief term in office, Brown, seemingly a standard left-liberal in the past, has "out-Reaganed Reagan" to embark on a systematic campaign of reducing government activity on every front. Brown has been preaching government austerity, has pared the budget, fired bureaucrats, and has denounced conservatives for inconsistently favoring Big Government in the military sphere, and civil libertarians for advocating Big Government in economics. Brown states that "people feel that things are being done to them, not for them. Sometimes non-action is better. Sometimes we need fewer programs, less planning, more space to live our lives." Martz writes that, "since taking office in January, Brown has taken a 7 per cent cut in his own salary and asked his Cabinet to follow suit. His social attitudes are even tougher; as one example, he declares flatly that prisons are for punishment, not rehabilitation." (The Szasz line?) On the other hand, Brown took the lead in pushing through the sexual victimless

(Continued On Page 3)

From Crank-Up To Crack-Up

By Ludwig von Mises

(Ed. Note: The **Libertarian Forum** is proud to present, for the first time anywhere, an English translation of an article written by the great economist Ludwig von Mises in the depths of the great world depression, in 1933. In his essay, Mises warned against the popular attempts to "reflate" prices back up to 1929 levels, by means of inflationary credit expansion propelled by governments and their controlled banking system. His warning against supposedly "moderate" inflationism to combat depression is, of course, particularly relevant in today's world. Mises' article was entitled, "Der Stand und nachste Zukunft der Konjunkturforschung," ("The Current State and Immediate Future of Trade Cycle Research"), and it appeared in the **Festschrift fur Arthur Spiethoff** (Munchen, Duncker & Kumblot, 1933). The translation is by Joseph R. Stromberg, doctoral candidate in history, University of Florida.)

People now and then have defended the view that an understanding of the causes which induce the trade cycle will lead to a smoothing out of these waves by means of economic measures designed to prevent crises. They would choke the boom off early, in order to mitigate the bust which must inevitably succeed it. Thus greater symmetry would appear in the course of economic life. Phenomena accompanying the boom, regarded by many as unwelcome, would disappear entirely in the future, or at least for the most part. Above all, we could severely limit or entirely avoid the sacrifices, which crisis and crackup exact, and which hardly anyone sees as other than negative.

Many have received this prospect with little joy, believing that the beneficent workings of the boom are worth the price of the losses of the depression. Not everything produced in the boom is the result of error, they say, nor must everything be sacrificed in the crises; there are also permanent fruits of the benign cycle, and economic progress cannot do without them. By contrast, the majority of economic policy advocates have termed the elimination of cyclical fluctuations desirable and necessary. Some have arrived at this position because they believe it will contribute to preserving the capitalist system, of which they approve, if the economy is spared the shudders of crises that recur every couple of years; still others have welcomed the coming age of no crises precisely because they believe that in an economy not endangered by cyclical variations no difficulties would arise from elimination of the entrepreneur, who in their eyes is the dispensable beneficiary of an odd sort of diligence.

All these writers, whether they looked with favor or disfavor on the smoothing out of cyclical waves, were of the opinion that deeper insight into the causes of the changing circumstances would bring us nearer to an age of smaller fluctuations. Were they correct?

Economic theory cannot answer this question. Here is a problem not of theory, but much more of economic policy, or more properly, economic history. In the future, will we again adopt measures which must lead from boom to crackup, even though the circles which give economic policy its direction are today better informed on the effects of the expansion of circulation credit — however mischievous their economic training may otherwise be — than was the case at least on the Continent of Europe, in other centuries?

Today we can consider the circulation credit theory (monetary theory) of the trade cycle as almost the reigning outlook. Even those who advance other doctrines feel constrained to make decisive concessions to the circulation credit theory. All proposals advanced for combatting the present economic crisis follow chains of reasoning which presuppose the circulation credit theory. Some wish to "crank up" the cycle through expansion of the quantity of fiduciary media because they demand a way out of monetary difficulties at any price — even that of a new crisis following the upswing; others forego these stimuli because they want to avoid the false idyll of a prosperity created by credit expansion and the inevitably succeeding crisis. Even the promoters of the "crank up" and pump-priming programs recognize, insofar as they do not belong to the class of completely hopeless dilettantes and ignoramuses, the certainty

(Continued On Page 4)

Case For Optimism —

(Continued From Page 2)

crime repeal. Martz also writes that Brown, "taking a populist leaf from Alabama Gov. George Wallace's book, . . . governs as the gadfly of his own bureaucrats, deriding their attache cases, deploring their jargon and very nearly calling them pointy-headed."

Furthermore, one of our leading libertarians recently had a three-hour conference with Gary Davis, Brown's executive secretary and the leading theoretician of Brown's administration, and was dumfounded to find Davis, on his own and without prompting, going on and on to propound fully libertarian positions and sentiments. Davis's denunciation of government per se was startling to our libertarian friend, well-versed and skeptical as he is in the ways of politicians.

In Illinois, as Martz points out, Governor Daniel Walker has been pursuing a similar course for the last three years. Firing bureaucrats, calling for lower taxes, cutting the state budget, Walker has managed to anger all the politicians and vested interests in state government, but has solidified his popularity among the voters. Walker has managed, over intense opposition by the entrenched Illinois bureaucracy, to cut the number of state employees by 10 per cent, and to stop any increase in taxes.

Martz points to the following highly-placed politicians who are adopting variants of this new budget-cutting line: Governors Carey of New York, Apodaca of New Mexico, Longley of Maine, Boren of Oklahoma, and Lamm of Colorado, as well as mayors Bradley of Los Angeles and Young of Detroit. Furthermore, he notes that prominent Atlanta lawyer David Gambrell is now promoting a "Wait-a Damn Minute" movement, "aimed at fending off nearly all government action, with a nostalgic motif from Will Rogers: "There is good news from Washington today. The Congress is deadlocked and can't act."

Martz notes that the new anti-government mood is pervasive, particularly among the broad bulk of the nation's middle class. But, he adds, "the disaffected stretch across the social spectrum, showing increasing resentment not only at the inadequacies of government but at its intrusion into their lives — whether in heavy-handed regulation of business, intervention in a community's choice of school textbooks, forced busing to achieve integration or the maddening imposition of auto seat-belt interlocks (now happily repealed.)". Moreover, he recognizes the solid roots of this new mood in economic reality, particularly the inflationary erosion of the real incomes of the masses, as well as the growing whipsaw burden of the progressive income tax. Martz concludes that "Inflation and the growing burden of the Federal debt are finally breaking up the coalition of interests that has supported most government programs ever since the New Deal. 'As long as the pie was expanding,' said Atlanta educator (Dr. Lisle) Carter, 'the deal was that you could have yours as long as I got mine. But that was very expensive, and the problem is you can't keep expanding the pie indefinitely.' 'We've reached the limit of the national debt,' said June Degnan, a Democratic contributor and fund raiser in San Francisco. 'That's what the liberals have learned. For every new dollar of spending, something is going to have to be cut. It's exactly like dealing with a case of cancer — either amputate or die." Precisely; the recognition of the exhaustion of the reserve fund!

And so, fellow libertarians, we stand at the threshhold of the rollback of statism and the victory of liberty; the forces of statism are in rout at every hand, and libertarianism is popping up everywhere, even in the most surprising and unexpected places. The time for optimism is now; how can we fail to lift up our hearts and plunge with joyous enthusiasm into the ever-growing success of the libertarian cause? ◻

The Bankruptcy Of Liberalism

The monthly magazine **Commentary**, published by the American Jewish Committee, is a distinguished journal of middle-of-the road liberalism. In recent years, **Commentary** has published many trenchant attacks on left-egalitarianism. In its June, 1975 issue, contributing editor Milton Himmelfarb (brother of the eminent historian, the neo-conservative and anti-libertarian Gertrude Himmelfarb), turns his attention to a critique of Libertarianism ("Liberals & Libertarians"). Focussing on Robert Nozick's recent book and mentioning your **Lib. Forum** editor in passing, Himmelfarb, in attempting to combat our "hypertrophy of the principle of liberty", first flounders around a bit in confusion and flagrant disregard for logic. Thus, he quotes Nozick's blistering attack on the typical/centrist defense of outlawing acts of consenting adults committed on public streets: "If the majority may determine the limits on detestable behavior in public (e.g., nudity or fornication or inter-racial handholding), may they, in addition to requiring that no one appear in public without clothing, also require that no one appear in public without wearing a badge certifying that he has contributed n per cent of his income to the needy during the year, on the grounds that they find it offensive to look at someone not wearing the badge? . . ." To this keen exercise in logic, Himmelfarb can only throw up his hands in horror and say that "this is the debater speaking, who wants to razzle-dazzle us into believing there is no ethical difference. . . .," etc.

After a few pages of this sort of twaddle, Himmelfarb falls back on his ultimate — and really only — refusation of libertarianism, on which he expounds for the remainder of the article. His final defense is: no less than the religion of Orthodox Judaism. Chiding Nozick and (without naming him, Boston radio commentator Avi Nelson) for being untrue to the Orthodox Jewish tradition (Nelson is even a "rabbi's son" — tsk, tsk!). Himmelfarb goes on to lengthy quotes from the Old Testament and other elements of the Orthodox rite. Himmelfarb, furthermore, thinks he has caught Nozick in a deep contradiction because Nozick repeatedly quotes Jews such as Martin Buber and I. B. Singer. He adds that he expects libertarianism to appeal more to "non-Jewish Jews" because libertarianism "seeks to break the chains of tradition and traditional community."

There is no doubt about it; Himmelfarb is right; the God of Israel, the god responsible (according to his own acolytes) for countless mass murder, injustice, and theocratic despotism, is not a libertarian. Not hardly. But so what? Is the last defense of liberalism really to fall back upon a religion of theocracy, of tribalism, of rank superstition? So much the worse for liberalism; never has the bankruptcy of liberalism been more starkly revealed. Surely few people in the modern world are ready to abandon reason and enlightenment for the swamp of tribal superstition. Yes, Himmelfarb is right that libertarianism "seeks to break the chains of tradition and traditional community" when those chains, as in Orthodox Judaism, clamp fetters of theocracy and tribalism upon the reason and the freedom of the individual person. Yes, Himmelfarb, libertarian radicalism promises that "no more tradition's chains shall bind us"; the dead hand of Orthodox Judaism disappeared with the emancipation of the Jews of the western world after the French Revolution, and no Humpty-Dumptys — even the last remnants of intellectual liberalism — can put it together again. □

Crank-Up To Crack-Up —

(Continued From Page 3)

of the chain of reasoning of the circulation credit theory. They seek to parry the objections from the standpoint of this theory not at all by disputing its validity, but by hinting that they propose merely a "moderate" or "measured" credit expansion or "creation of money," solely to arrest or weaken the further decline of prices. Even in the expression "re-deflation," eagerly used in this connection of late, there is an admission of the circulation credit theory; that significant errors accompany this admission is of course indisputable.

The credit expansion which begins the boom is always undertaken in the belief that we must overcome stagnation through "easy" money. Some (of us) have fruitlessly sought to characterize this position as invalid. Only unfamiliarity with economic history and the political economic literature of the last generation can lead people to dispute that a permanently lower interest rate has appeared as the ideal of economic policy, just as hardly anyone ever has dared to defend the creditor's view in which the formerly higher interest rate necessarily appears desirable.[1] The desire for easier credit has fostered creation by banks of fiduciary media and has required the continued lowering of the interest rate by them. All measures taken to prevent the "screwing up of bank rates" had as their root the notion that creation of credit for the economy must be made easier. As a rule no one noticed that the lowering of the interest rate through credit expansion must lead to higher prices. For if that had been realized, no one would have sought the policy of easy money.

In the area of price formation public opinion is not as firm as on the question of the interest rate. On this there have always been two opinions: on the one hand, the demand of producers for higher prices, and on the other hand, that of consumers for lower prices. Governments and political parties have declared both demands just — if not exactly at the same time — and have written now one, now the other slogan* on their banners — depending on their voting blocs, for whose favor they strive,** and depending on short-run movements of prices. As prices have risen, they have preached a crusade against the increasingly high cost of living. When prices have fallen, they have declared themselves ready to do everything to assure producers "reasonable" prices again. As a rule, they have acquiesced in measures to reduce prices which could not

possibly have obtained the desired result; they have not adopted the only effective measure, the reduction of circulation credit, because they have not wished to drive interest rates back up.[2] On the other hand, in times of falling prices they have found it that much easier to adopt measures of credit expansion, since this expansion could only be realized through an already desired reduction of the interest rate.

Likewise, it is nothing new if today they seek to weaken scruples against circulation credit expansion by claiming that they only wish to reverse the price fall of the last few years or at least to hinder a further decline of prices. Similar arguments were used in the days of the bimetallist movement.

The knowledge that the economic consequences of altering the value of money (leaving aside the effects on the content of liabilities expressed in money terms) can only be ascribed to the fact that the changing value of money does not express itself simultaneously and equally in terms of all goods and services, i. e., that not all prices rise at the same time or to the same degree — this knowledge is hardly still disputed today. People misconstrue, although not as commonly as was still the case a few years ago, the fact that the great length of the present crisis is above all attributable to the way that wages, by means of trade union policy, and some prices, by various supports, have been held constant so that they conform to the downward movement of the prices of most goods, not at all or only with excessive delay. They grant, leaving aside all countervailing political checks, that continuing mass unemployment is a necessary consequence of the attempt, by intervention, to hold wages above the level they would reach on the unhampered market. Even so, they do not draw quite the correct conclusions for economic policy.

Nearly all proposals for "cranking up" through credit expansion take it as self-evident that wages will not follow the rising movement of prices until their relative over-valuation has disappeared. People approve all manner of inflationary projects precisely because they do not dare to openly combat the wage policy of the trade unions, favored by public opinion, and its promotion by governments. But as long as the views prevalent today on the formation of wage rates and their implementation through interventionist measures persist, it is not justifiable to assume that in a period of rising prices, money wages can be held constant.

People misunderstand the causal relationships even more when they attach special expectations to proposals for limited credit expansion.

(Continued On Page 5)

Recommended Reading: Hayek Interview

Hayek Interview. In the course of his current tour of the United States, Nobel Laureate in economics, and dean of the Austrian School, F. A. Hayek, has given an excellent and hard-hitting interview to the **Gold & Silver Newsletter** (June, 1975). In the interview, Hayek sets forth an uncompromising Austrian explanation of the length of the Great Depression of the 1930's. The significance of this is that Hayek, in the past, had sometimes given hostage to the Keynesian view that at least the **length**, though not the **onset**, of the Depression was caused by a non-Austrian "secondary deflation", to be combatted by Keynesian methods. But in this interview, Hayek is firmly Austrian all the way. Thus, in explaining the length of the Depression of the 1930's, Hayek states:

> "Instead of allowing the market to correct the misdirections of labor and resources that occurred

during the inflationary boom, the government believed they could cure the depression by keeping up wages. Hoover began the policy, but Roosevelt greatly expanded it. . . . Policies of government intervention in the economy led internationally to exchange controls, restrictions on foreign trade and other policies that only made matters worse.

The absence of a sound international monetary system was another factor that was responsible for the length of the depression. One of the single most important mistakes that unnecessarily prolonged the depression was Roosevelt's decision to go off the gold standard." (So much for Milton Friedman!)

The **Gold & Silver Newsletter** is available from Monex International, Ltd., 4910 Birch St., Newport Beach, Calif. 92660◨

Crank-Up To Crack-Up —

(Continued From Page 4)

Entrepreneurs are seduced by the plentiful and easier credit available, into busying themselves with ventures which did not appear profitable at the higher interest rate corresponding to the unhampered money market, provided they believe that the lower interest rates will persist indefinitely so that they can base their calculations on them. If it becomes widely known that the creation of extra credit is going to end, people will in due course become concerned and the expected effect will be lacking. No one will undertake new ventures when he knows in advance that they cannot be carried out profitably. The failure of the pump-priming attempts of recent times shows that people, with a view to the pronouncements of the authorities responsible for the policies of the banks of fiduciary media, must have realized that the period of easy money would soon come to an end. One cannot "crank-up" through credit expansion without speaking already of future contraction. That every credit expansion must finally end through suspension of further extra credit issue, and that this suspension must cause a change in the state of business, was known long ago to the economists, and a glance at the daily and weekly press during boom years since the middle of the last century shows that this realization was not limited to a small circle. But speculators, averse to all theory, did not know it and undertook new ventures. When, however, governments proclaim that the expansion of credit can only continue a short while, then (the truth) can escape no one.

People are quite prepared to overrate what has been accomplished in recent years towards understanding the trade cycle, and greatly to underrate the achievements of the Currency School. For practical cyclical policy we have not yet exhausted what can be learned from the doctrines of the old Currency theorists. Up to now, practice has hardly been able to learn anything from modern cycle theory that it could not have already learned from the Currency doctrine. Unfortunately, theory always leaves practice in the lurch just where advice is most urgent: in the understanding of declining prices. The general price decline was considered at all times unwelcome: today the downward rigidity of wages and many other cost factors upset any impartial treatment of the problem, more than previously. It is high time fundamentally to examine

the effects of declining money prices and to consider the widespread viewpoint that declining prices and gradual enlargement of the social product, and also of wellbeing, are incompatible. This raises the question of whether it now follows that only inflationary processes make possible progressive capital formation and the shaping of the productive mechanism. As long as naive inflationary theories of progress are held, proposals to induce the boom through credit expansion will always be adopted. The Currency theory has already demonstrated the necessary connection between credit expansion and the course of fluctuations — if only in a chain of reasoning which merely considered credit expansion limited to a single nation and did not know how to judge correctly the case of uniform actions in all states, which, in an age of efforts toward cooperation between the (central) banks issuing fiduciary media are especially important. That, nonetheless, the banks of fiduciary media have always set out on the path of credit expansion is traceable to the view of the benefits of rising prices and their indispensability for "progress," and to the belief that expansion of circulation credit is an appropriate means to keep the interest rate low. The relationship between the issue of fiduciary media and the formation of interest rates is today sufficiently clear, at least adequate to the immediate requirements of economic policy. The problem of falling prices remains to be resolved.

1. It was always so. Public opinion has always sided with debtors. (Cf. Bentham, **Defence of Usury**. Second Edition, London, 1790, p. 102 ff.) The idea has not been given up that the creditor is a rich, idle exploiter, hardheartedly insisting on his paper rights, while the debtor is a poor unfortunate victim of usury — even in this age of stocks and bonds and bank and savings deposits.

*Losung, which we translate here as "slogan", has the same spelling as another German word which translates as "droppings."

**Buhlen, which we translate as "strive", has a secondary meaning of "have illicit intercourse." Since Mises could have used a number of other German words for "strive" one concludes perforce that he is subtly smiting the enemy hip and thigh. This, of course, is the Cervantean method of attack. Translator's Note.

2. A gross example: the discount policy of the German Reichsbank during the period of inflation. Cf. Graham, **Exchange, Prices and Production in Hyper-Inflation: Germany, 1920-1923** (Princeton, 1930), pp. 65f.　　　　◨

On Income Differences

By William R. Havender
Dept. of Genetics
University of California, Berkeley

Recent articles in **Commentary** and other publications that have reviewed Christopher Jencks' new book, "Inequality," have debated what should be done to reduce income disparity. But at least two essential issues have largely been ignored in these discussions. The first is the means by which income inequalities arise. These come about differently in different social systems, and the moral case for their elimination, rather than being self-evident, depends critically upon the social context. In an aristocracy, the wealth of the elite is extracted by force from the common people in a sort of zero sum game, where the income of some must be lost by others. An egalitarian policy in this setting would undoubtedly serve the interests of morality, since the income distribution initially results from compulsion. This is not true of a market economy, where one's income is set by the value placed upon the services one offers to others. Market-determined income is a **return** for rendered benefits, whose magnitude is specified in voluntary negotiation with one's clients. Differences in income reflect different market valuations of these services, and great incomes are generated by supplying others with resources of great value or rarity. Felix Wankel, for example, will probably well be able to keep himself supplied with fine wines, if the extra value of his engine to each of millions of users turns out to be as much as one dollar. Since no one loses, income inequality in this case cannot so routinely be identified with inequity.

But such mutual benefit is on principle a property of every voluntary exchange. Income disparity arising in this context comes about solely from the specialization of labor, and from the fact that certain services are more desired, or are scarcer, than others. That is why it is not clear what is meant by the concept of a "just" distribution of income, as somehow distinct from that which results from the plebiscite of the market; the market's verdict already is very just, in the sense that one's income, and hence, one's claim upon the limited resources of society, is proportional to the value of one's services to others. Similarly off the mark is the assertion that "the people" object to and demand redress of income inequality, when, in fact, income differences originate in the first instance through the people's casting of dollar votes in the marketplace; these differences, therefore, are the manifestation, over time, of the expressed will of all the people in this regard. It is obvious, then, that those who oppose this do not speak for the majority.

Because of the voluntary nature of market exchanges, it is exceedingly difficult to justify the intrusion of third parties — such as sociologists, or politicians — into two party transactions, as for example when they attack the income profile which thereby results. Does one have an unconditional right to negotiate the terms under which one will exchange one's services, or not? To argue that third parties do have standing to interfere simply diminishes the extent to which one's work serves one's own purposes, a view more usually associated with fasc'~m than with actual income distribution in America reflects the impact of involuntary or nonmarket forces such as discrimination, fraud or government indulgences. And so it does. But these influences should be vigorously opposed precisely because they do cause a departure from the income allocation which otherwise would correspond to the people's market wishes, and so cannot be used to buttress the much greater departure which the goal of income equality itself represents.

The second curiously omitted yet surpassingly important issue is this: immanent in any proposal to eliminate income inequality is the necessity of creating a much greater inequality of political power. In simple words, the right to determine the disposal of earned income will be transferred from a large number of moderately or very wealthy individuals to the small number of archons momentarily regnant in the offices of government. Whilst the money may well be passed to the poor, the power will remain with "them above" — the State. No matter what public purpose might superficially be served by this transfer, the essence of the political change will be a vast increase in the centralization of social control. And the ensuing inequality of political power — that between rulers and subjects — could not be rendered innocuous by the democratic process, since transitory majorities are as capable as monarchs of arbitrary tyranny against politically weak groups. More than likely, the grand increase in the stakes brought about by this increment in state authority would greatly intensify and embitter the political struggle for power, as has already occurred in those areas where the government has sought to control private economic power through regulatory agencies. This prospect is much more sinister than what, by contrast, appears to be the mild and **diffuse** inequality of power now accompanying existing income differences.

Since this aggrandizement of political inequality manifestly would be the paramount result of a policy of equalizing income, it is baffling that Christopher Jencks would offer, as one of the grounds for his income-flattening proposals a desire to ensure "that everyone exercise the same amount of political power." Exactly the opposite is the likely consequence, should this intellectual frolic ever be adopted. Moreover, this authority must of necessity be used for more than mere redistribution. For, if a person will have the same level of living whatever he does, what will make him work? "If there is no carrot to encourage effort, there will have to be a stick. Enforced egalitarianism also means a slave state. It is a horrible, not an inspiring, vision." (Milton Friedman, Newsweek, 2/28/72).

Income differences, then, are inescapable and unobjectionable in a society grounded in personal liberty. Here, as always, the attenuation of our political freedom has been gussied up with an obscuring veil of lofty but illusive objectives. Hence, one must scrutinize this bride, egalitarianism, with assiduous care before closing the purchase. ◻

The Ethics Gap

The scientific revolution of the last decade in the fields of genetics and the life sciences has been more an affirmation of the imagination of science fiction novelists than of the expectations of the average citizen. In less than a decade, the transplanting of vital organs — heart, kidney, lungs, eyes — have become normal medical procedures; genetic engineering, gene therapy, cloning and in vitro fertilization open the way to human control of population and procreation almost beyond our psychic toleration; the breakdown in the traditional Judaeo-Christian reverence for life which prohibited abortion, sterilization, suicide and euthanasia is now manifest in our society, and ethical limitations on future scientific manipulation of our biological, neurological and behavioral systems are weak or non-existent. The scientific revolution has created the need for extensive ethical research to provide some moral framework for the scientists themselves, for physicians, law makers, and individual citizens faced with technological possibilities unknown to previous generations. Just the prolongation of ordinary life span threatens vast economic dislocations in a society unprepared for a population in which those over sixty may come to outnumber those under twenty; the social security system, the insurance industry, the public and private school systems and the various industries that have developed around the high birth rates of post-1945 America face severe economic crisis in the next quarter century. To what extent will the productive work force subsidize the non-productive: the aged, the sick, the incompetent, the insane, the early pensioner? If nothing else interposed itself, inflation alone would create an increasing proportion of the aged population who will be unable financially to support themselves until normal termination of life. Thus, the revolution in the life sciences is

(Continued On Page 8)

Burton K. Wheeler, Montana Isolationist, RIP

By Leonard P. Liggio

Several years ago the Merv Griffin Show featured Burton K. Wheeler, former Senator from Montana, and Earl Browder, former general secretary of the Communist Party USA. Both ancients had suffered purges by their respective parties, essentially for the same reason — their commitment to Americanism. Browder, Kansas-born, was in the tradition of native American radicalism, and had joined the CP as the heir to that tradition. His slogan that "communists were as American as apple-pie" brought perhaps millions to join the CP as the partner of Roosevelt's New Deal. However, his pragmatism brought him into conflict with the Marxist ideologues who probably could not stand being associated with the masses that Browder recruited. The hard-line Hegelians came to the fore and Browder was purged for taking the capitalist road. (Philosophically, many American Marxists have come out of the Pragmatic tradition, typified by Dewey's pupil, Sidney Hook, whose amalgm of Pragmatism and Hegelianism, made his positions the most diabolic in modern American philosophy.) Browder noted the anguish of the CP leadership at having to shift the line after the June, 1941 German invasion of the Soviet Union, for before that the Communists were a major force in the American isolationist movement. Wheeler centered his attention on that period because before June, 1941 his opposition to US entry into war was called Communists, while immediately afterwards his opposition was called Fascist; such has been the clear thinking in American politics.

Wheeler had been the leader of the investigation of the Teapot Dome oil grants and of the successful fight of the Senate to block FDR's Supreme Court packing plan in 1937. Thus, he was approached in May 1940 by those military officers who opposed FDR's plans to involve the US in war, to lead the opposition to those plans. In FDR's May 16, 1940 defense message to Congress, he had warned that if Germany was victorious in Europe, it might gain control of Dakar in West Africa and the Cape Verde Islands, which would place it 1500 miles from Brazil from which vital American zones would be attacked and American cities bombed. The military pointed out to Wheeler that German did not have bombers with a range more than 500 miles and that Brazil was further from America than Berlin. FDR's geopolitics was later demolished by Hanson Baldwin, in United We Stand (1941).

Wheeler immediately agreed to speak to a mass rally in Washington on June 7, 1940 attacking FDR's geopolitics. On July 1, he addressed the Keep America Out of War Congress in Chicago, and was approached by students from several universities who wanted to organize a national anti-war movement. He sent them to General Robert Wood, chairman of Sears Roebuck, and the America First Committee was formed. However, at the Democratic National Convention which nominated FDR to a Third Term, Wheeler encountered a run around end by FDR. FDR wanted the convention platform to call for forcing everyone in America into a government designated role during the emergency. Heroic Senator David I. Walsh of Mass. denounced it as totalitarianism, and Wheeler led the fight to throw it out. But, the interventionist forces were given direct access to the platform writing through the work of FDR's agent Senator Jimmy Byrnes. Chicago Mayor Edward J. Kelly, one of the heroic but died-out breed of anti-war Chicago mayors, noted that none of his wards would vote for a president running on a war platform. Jimmy Byrnes cornered Kelly in the men's room to pressure him; Wheeler went in and declared he would belt the convention if a war platform were adopted, and Kelly returned to continue his battle against the defense plank. Given the choice between FDR and Willkie, Wheeler voted the Socialist ticket, since Norman Thomas was opposed to war and was to justify Wheeler's faith in the Socialist's anti-war commitment by appearing with Wheeler at America First rallies despite the charge of sentimentalists and liberals that he was sharing the platform with capitalists and businessmen.

Wheeler realized that Secretary of State Hull was anxious to get the US involved in a war against Japan, and fought FDR's scheme for Lend-lease. On "American Forum of the Air" (which along with "Town Meeting of the Air" were important lost parts of American politics; they were dropped because it would no longer be permitted to have two sides to any issues, there was only the official, Liberal Establishment side), Wheeler declared: "The lend-lease program is the New Deal's triple-A foreign policy; it will plow under every fourth American boy." FDR went out of his mind, and Wheeler became the leading speaker, along with Lindbergh, at America First rallies. Joseph P. Kennedy, on returning from the ambassadorship to England, warned Wheeler that Neville Chamberlain had betrayed his Revisionist foreign policy and allowed England to go to war over the Polish boundary dispute with Germany

(Continued On Page 8)

The Ethics Gap —

(Continued From Page 6)

going to create within a few short years enormous strains upon the economy as it is now structured, and create problems of a social, political, legal and especially ethical dimension almost beyond our imagination.

In 1969 a research center was established in Hastings-on-Hudson, New York, to study the ethical and socio-legal implications of the rapidly developing technologies of the biological, neurological and behavioral life sciences. Under the direction of Daniel Callahan, a distinguished theologian and philosopher, the Institute for Society, Ethics and the Life Sciences began publication of an annual **Bibliography of Society, Ethics and the Life Sciences**, an invaluable tool for anyone interested professionally in the problems raised in the field defined by the title; it also has published a series of special studies, and a 16-page **Hastings Center Report** (six issues annually) which contains specialized bibliographies, brief reports on special issues of concern, and a number of "case studies" followed by debate on the ethical or legal implications. Among the recent topics were: a study on the right to privacy ("The Psychiatrist as a Double Agent"); the use of behavioral modification techniques in prisons; use of the methodone treatment as an alternative to other methods; various incidents involving definitions of medical ethics, fetal research, abuses in sterilization practices; genetic screening; and the social implications of technology.

The Institute does not appear to have any particular ethical bias: it chiefly seeks to stimulate an awareness of the frequently ignored ethical implications of scientific and technological innovation. Thus, while not committed to a systematic libertarian analysis, by placing a stress on ethics and its relationship to the life sciences, the Institute encourages its contributors and audience to confront the human rights of individuals and the full dimensions and demands of the concept of human dignity.

The work of the Institute should be of great interest to all libertarians, and I would highly recommend use of their publications, especially by those interested in legal, medical, ethical or scientific problems. Membership privileges include receipt of all publications. (Students, $10; others $15, Institutions, $25.) Write to: Institute of Society, Ethics, and the Life Sciences, 623 Warburton Avenue, Hastings-on-Hudson, New York 10706.   ▢

Burton K. Wheeler —

(Continued From Page 7)

because of "pressure from the United States."

As Charles Tansill has shown in **Back Door to War** (Regnery), Roosevelt and Hull played a prominent role in bringing about the conflict in Europe in 1939. Wheeler noted that Roosevelt refused to act as mediator to bring an end to hostilities, as he was interested only in English victory at whatever cost to England and America. He criticized Hull for not seriously negotiating with Japan and recognizing its claims for markets and raw materials; Hull increased the pressure on Japan until Japan finally reacted, which satisfied Hull since he felt it was better to fight the Japanese earlier than later.

Wheeler was at the center of a major furor in the fall of 1941. Military friends gave Wheeler the top secret plan for American military intervention in Europe and Africa in order to save England from defeat. Wheeler gave it to that great journalist of the Chicago Tribune, Chesly Manly, who published the original expose of the August 1941 Atlantic Charter meeting of Churchill and FDR. This December 4, 1941 story was an immediate blockbuster, "the greatest scoop in the history of journalism", according to Col. Robert R. McCormick, in whose Washington Times-Herald the article appeared. As the tide of public opposition to the plan rose, the anti-interventionist movement was silenced by the beginning of war on December 7, 1941. Much of the Chesly Manly scoop remains unknown.   ▢

"Dr. (John W.) Davis is a lawyer whose life has been devoted to protecting the great enterprises of Big Business. He used to work for J. Pierpont Morgan, and he has himself said that he is proud of the fact. Mr. Morgan is an international banker . . . (whose) operations are safeguarded for him by the manpower of the United States. He was one of the principal beneficiaries of the late war, and made millions out of it. The Government hospitals are now full of one-legged soldiers who gallantly protected his investments then, and the public schools are full of boys who will protect his investments tomorrow."

H. L. Mencken

The Libertarian Forum
BOX 341
MADISON SQUARE STATION
NEW YORK, NEW YORK 10010

First Class

Published Every Month. Subscription Rates: $8.00 Per Year; $15.00 Two Years

A Monthly Newsletter

THE
Libertarian Forum

Joseph R. Peden, Publisher   Murray N. Rothbard, Editor

VOLUME VII. NO. 7   JULY. 1975   US-ISSN0047-4517

DICTATORSHIPS

For sixty years, American foreign policy has been set on a course of global intervention, ostensibly on behalf of "making the world safe for democracy", and of securing and expanding the "free world." Now, sixty years later, the world — and the United States — manifestly far less free than when we began to launch our global Crusades; and dictatorships abound everywhere. Surely, at the very least, we must have been doing something wrong. Indeed, that wrong is the very policy of global intervention itself.

Three burgeoning dictatorships have been much in the news recently, and they provide instructive lessons for libertarians and for Americans generally. The most dramatic, of course, is the brutal takeover of India by Mrs. Indira Gandhi, jailing thousands of political opponents and imposing a drastic censorship on the press. Ever since World War II, the New York Times and the rest of the Establishment press have trumpeted the glories and virtues of India as the "world's largest democracy"; massive amounts of foreign aid have been pumped into India by the U.S. on the strength of this rosy view of the Indian subcontinent. At the very least, the Establishment press, standing there with egg on its face, will have to mute its paeans to Indian "democracy" in the future. Predictably, American press reaction has been far more in sorrow than in anger, and replete with pitiful hopes that Mrs. Gandhi will revert to democracy soon.

But Indian "democracy", let alone Indian liberty, has been a sham and a mockery from the beginning. Even in political form, India has suffered from its inception under the one-party rule of the Congress party, with other opposing political groupings shunted to the periphery to preserve democratic camouflage. More important, the Indian polity is one of the most thoroughly rotten in the world: a collectivist mass of statist activities, controls, subsidies, taxes, and monopolies, all superimposed upon a frozen caste system that governs in the rural villages in which most Indians continue to live. Considering this unholy mess, the savaging of the opposition by Mrs. Gandhi comes, not as a sudden and inexplicable act, as Americans tend to see it, but as merely the last link in a chain of statist despotism fastened upon that blighted land. When we discard the myths propagated by the American Establishment, we see that, rather than a source of wonder, Mrs. Gandhi's takeover becomes all too explicable.

Portugal is another country in the news — as a land sliping rapidly into a military-Communist dictatorship, or rather, into a military despotism employing Communist ideology and the Communist Party as its only political ally. Once again, the American press has reacted to the dramatic events without asking the crucial question: How come? For here was Portugal, governed for fifty years by the fascist military dictatorship of Salazar (and, then, his successors.) So seemingly efficient was Salazar in suppressing dissent that the Birch Society, in its annual "scoreboard" of nations, regularly adjudged Portugal as somewhere around zero percent "Communist". Much American aid had been poured

into the Salazarean regime. And yet, scarcely more than a year after the bloodless Spinola "revolution of the roses", here in **Portugal**, of all places, going Communist!

But it is precisely here that an important lesson lies. Far from being a "bulwark" against each other, we should realize that fascist and communist dictatorships are not only similar but easily transformed one into the other. Right-wing and left-wing military dictatorships are readily convertible; for each of them build up the collectivist institutions of statist rule, of big government domination of the economy and of society, of militarist and police repression of their subjects. And so, Salazarean fascist corporatism, with its network of monopolies, restrictions, and controls, its military rule, its apparatus of police terror, can be easily transformed into Communist military rule. The institutions of statism are there; and all that is needed is a reshuffling of the power elites and ruling groups at the top. In this way, the centrist collectivism of the Weimar Republic smoothly paved the way for Hitler's National Socialism; and the Nazi occupation of Europe, in turn, paved the way for the near takeover by Communist-led Resistance forces after World War II. The important lesson is that it doesn't really matter who controls the statist and collectivist institutions of Big Government; the important point is the existence of these institutions themselves.

Another crucial, and corollary, point is the non-existence, in these countries, of any classical liberal (let alone libertarian) tradition of ideology or of activist political movements. Classical liberal thought and opinion has been non-existent in India; and the same is true for Portugal. Whatever such movement might have arisen was stamped out in advance by a half-century of Salazarean repression. Portugal, too, is an anomaly within Western Europe. A Backward and still semi-feudal land, Portugal has never really joined the Industrial Revolution, nor has it has any tradition of classical liberal thought or activism. Joined to this was a special Portuguese problem: already dominant in a backward land, the Portuguese military had been swollen and overblown in order to fight an endless and losing colonial war to keep its possessions in Africa. The Portuguese army suffered from an aggravated and triple source of resentment: the losing counter-guerrilla war in Africa; the spectre of obsolescence and unemployment as Portugal liquidates its colonies in Africa and brings the troops back home; and relative loss of income and status to the emerging middle class who had begun to develope in the last decade or so with the beginnings of economic development. In France, the resentful army in Africa turned rightward after its losing war in Algeria; but the Portuguese army scarcely had that option, since it was impossible to become more rightist than Salazar. Furthermore, the imposition of a fully military-Communist regime promised a hefty increase in jobs and status for the now obsolescent and over-expanded army; in short, the Portuguese army could now turn its "imperial" power inward, upon its own economy and society. And as usual under fascist repression, only the disciplined Communist party managed to

(Continued on page 2)

DICTATORSHIPS— (Continued from page 1)

retain its underground cadres, and so could function as civilian allies. And so the Portuguese army went Left.

Whether military-Communism will succeed in ruling Portugal is still open to question. For the Portuguese Communist Party, headed by the hard-line fanatic Alvaro Cunhal, rests within the rather broad spectrum of world Communist opinion somewhere on the near-lunatic fringe. Cunhal almost makes Stalin look like Tolstoyan pacifist. And so, they might just blow it. But, at any rate, the crucial point is to see the interpenetrability of despotism, right and left, and the hopelessness of liberty in a land where no movement exists on behalf of even classical liberalism, let alone libertarianism.

In seeming contrast to Portugal's left-wing military dictatorship, Chile's right-wing military despotism was born, in the fall of 1973, in a revolutionary' coup against Allende's Marxist regime. Part of that overthrow was a genuine popular revolution — especially, the revolt of the self-employed truckers and other middle-class groups against the statism and runaway inflation suffered under Allende. But the major faction that engineered the coup — the armed forces, with the help, it now turns out. of the CIA — simply proceeded to continue all the worst features of the old regime, and to add to it a systematic use of massive torture against dissidents and political prisoners. After nearly two years in office. Chile still suffers from nationalization and controls — and from a staggering runaway inflation rate of nearly 400% per year. Unemployment ranges from 13 to over 26%, the armed forces enjoy nearly half the national budget. and foreign investments have not really materialized. Moreover, military officers are in charge of all high schools and colleges, the teaching of all "conflictive subjects" is prohibited. and a compulsory nightly curfew is still in effect.

As Professor Petras writes, even the New York bankers (especially the First National City Bank), the leading backers of the Chilean junta, have become disgusted and are unwilling to pour more good money after bad. As Petras writes, for the New York bankers, "the problem is the disintegrating state of the Chilean economy and the frightening spectacle of a 400 per cent inflation rate." Chilean Finance Minister Jorge Cauas discovered at his meeting on May 8th with the bankers, that the latter are no longer satisfied with the new regime's shifting of all the blame on Allende for the present crisis. For "U.S. bankers want to know how promises of cutbacks in public spending, credits and public employment can take place when the junta promises at the same time to reduce unemployment by financing massive public works programs." (James Petras. "The Chilean Junta Besieged," The Nation, June 28, 1975, pp. 784ff.)

The final irony is that Cauas is an avowed disciple of Milton Friedman and the Chicago School, and has been busy using Friedmanite rhetoric as a cloak for the galloping statism and inflationism of the dictatorial regime. Thus. once again (as in Friedman's misguided endorsement of the indexing policy of the Brazilian dictatorship), Friedmanism is being used as a free-market cloak for state despotism. Such is the tragedy that must result when "free-market" economists attempt to influence the State from above, and to become efficiency experts for despotism. (See Frank Maurovich, in the San Francisco Sunday Examiner & Chronicle, July 13, 1975).

Again, the major lesson of the Chilean tragedy should be clear. Once again. a right-wing dictatorship has simply taken over the pernicious institutions created by a previous left-wing dictatorship. Right and left are brothers under the skin. Once again, massive U.S. foreign aid (supplemented this time by CIA) has only succeeded in strengthening the yoke of despotism upon a foreign land. And, finally, once again we see the absurdity of expecting victories for liberty in a land where no libertarians _or classical liberals exist.

The lessons of India, Portugal, and Chile, in short, are the same lessons as those offered by the debacle of American policy in Southeast Asia. The United States must cease its interventions and meddling in foreign lands; interventionism is not only immoral and aggressive; it doesn't work. We must regain liberty at home, end all interventions in other countries, and return to the historic, forgotten "foreign policy" of serving as an example and a beacon-light of liberty to the rest of the suffering and stife-torn world.

□

The Division of Labor And The Libertarian Movement

By Tom Palmer*

The Libertarian movement has grown to the point where there must either be a division of labor or a slow disintegration. That division is between the libertarian theorist, and what I choose to call the libertarian technician. Many libertarians fail to realize this basic truth, leaving them in the disastrous position of not practicing what they preach. There seems to be a constant striving on the part of these scholastic "purists" for the ideal "well rounded" libertarian who knows everything about anything. while at the same time scolding those who don't fit their notion of the ubermensch.

We libertarians have a sound intellectual background and foundation we have the cause of truth, liberty and justice. But these do us no good unless they are promoted professionally. Don Ernsberger, writing in the SIL News. has made an especially unrealistic remark reflecting this dysfunctional strategy. Commenting on the small number of cadre members who attended the last Libertarian Scholars Conference, he petulantly asked "Where are the envelope stuffers now?" (referring to the Tuccille campaign). "Where are the petition circulators and literature distributors?" Obviously, they were elsewhere, pursuing their own utility . . . . doing what they enjoyed. With all due respect to the notable scholarship of Professor Liggio, not all libertarians are interested in the history of French anarchism. While a greater turnout would certainly have been cause of rejoicing, it is ridiculous to chide those who have no interest for not showing up. The envelope stuffers have shown their dedication to liberty, and should be thanked for their useful contribution. rather than the recipients of a backhanded attack.

Our movement has reached the point where we bid fair to become a mass movement against the state. Obviously, not every convert to the cause of liberty will be interested in reading Human Action or The Theory of Money and Credit. As pleasant as the thought of Professor Von Mises' works standing among the top ten best sellers is, I'm not holding my breath.

We must learn to market our ideas, and to do so professionally. The Libertarian Party is a good vehicle, and an excellent training ground. There is no better way to learn how to market a product than actually to do so.

A little boning up beforehand helps, however. Several excellent books are available, and I suggest that the present or potential promoter of freedom check them out. They include How to be Heard: Making the Media Work For You by Ted Klein and Fred Danzig, You Can Make The Difference by Lee and Ann Edwards, and How To Win An Election by Steven Shadegg. Of these, the first is by far the best and most professional.

Classes at colleges and universities are often offered in public relations. and are generally worth taking. That, plus a good deal of common sense and experience are the ingredients of professionalism and success.

Don't get the wrong idea, now. I'm not advocating that anyone halt the glorious and rewarding scholarship that marks our movement. Rather, I'm arguing that not to apply the principle of division of labor to ourselves is fatal. It ignores a basic fact of reality and tenet of libertarian individualism. that people are different.

*Mr. Palmer is a youth organizer for the Libertarian Party.   □

Fanfani's Fall

By Leonard P. Liggio

Amintore Fanfani's leadership of the Italian Christian Democratic Party abruptly but at long last has come to an end. Fanfani's career began in the 1930's when he wrote a book on Christian and socialist corporatism which paralleled the New Deal. American New Dealers saw him as one of the hopes of the post-New Order Italy, and with the defeat of Italy in World War II, Americans pushed Fanfani's career. At the end of the Fascist regime in Italy, it was feared that the only successors would be the Communist party and its Socialist party ally. But, this was forestalled when the general secretary of the Communist Party of the Soviet Union ordered Gian Carlo Paccetta, leading Italian Communist advocate of armed struggle who has seized control of the administration of Milan and Lombardy, to turn power over to General Mark Clark. The Soviet Communist Party wished to respect the war-time agreements that western Europe would be the Anglo-American sphere and Eastern Europe the Soviet's sphere. For over thirty years, the Italian Communist Party has been a strong minority in Italian politics, and with its alliance with the Italian Socialist party almost has a majority. In fact, in the recent provincial elections which contributed to Fanfani's final fall, the Communist party gained control over half a dozen regional administrations in central and northern Italy — expanding the Red Belt that it dominates under the recently instituted Italian decentralization. In cities like Bologna, where the Communists had control for thirty year, the climate for business-expansion is very favorable. Not only is there not any corruption, but the Communists pride themselves on creating an atmosphere for business investment. In fact, many of the leading businessmen have become important members of the Communist party, enjoying the added dividend of no-strike pledges from the Communist-dominated unions (Christian unions tend to have a policy of refusing no-strike pledges, which is inconvenient for business planning). The Communist party has many kinds of organizations for various sectors of the economy-cooperatives for farmers and small businessmen and shopkeepers, etc.

Fifteen years ago the continued strength of the Communist party in the midst of the Italian economic miracle caused the Kennedy administration to suggest a new approach to Italian politics. The "Opening to the Left" was the answer: To detach the Socialist party from the Communist party and to make the former a partner in the government. Fanfani was the Christian Democratic leader chosen for that role over the other major candidate Aldo Moro. Moro was more moderate than Fanfani on domestic issues, but was less committed to NATO and America policy ·Communist participation in the coalition. Fanfani's strong commitment to socialist philosophy, plus his support for NATO and America policy generally caused him to get the nod. His leadership as premier or foreign minister, however, did not bring the desired results. Instead, his policies led to inflation and a temporary setback to Italy's economic miracle. Inflation meant increased support for the Communist party. The recent crisis of energy resources increased the pressure on Italy's economy.

Energy resources have been an important determinant on Italy's policies in the twentieth century. Italy entered World War I against its allies Germany and Austria, and on the side of England and France, on the promise of participation in the Allies' control of energy resources. (The entry into the war caused the creation of the Italian Communist Party in protest.) The failure of the Allies to live up to their promises led to the rise of Fascism. In the 1930's Britain attempted to gain Italy's support by allowing Italy to seek development of oil resources in East Africa. But, when Britain reneged, and formed an opposition to Italy in the League of Nations, Italy was forced to ally itself with Germany, creating the foundations for World War II. The irony of the situation was that Italy already possessed a colony — Libya — under which was a reservoir of oil, yet unknown. In the 1950's, under Enrico Mattei, Italy was able to develop access to oil resources outside of the market-dominating Seven Sisters of the international oil industry. Italy gained an independent position and very good relations with the Islamic world before the mysterious death of Mattei who, as a power in the Christian Democratic Party, favored a coalition with the Communist party. Italy's tradition and increasing good relations with the Islamic world are the most likely barrier to Italy's continued role in NATO.

Naples is the headquarters for the U.S. Sixth fleet, with its transports filled with thousands of American marines ready to repeat the assault on Tripoli. as well as the Southern command of NATO. Naples gives that command control of the western Mediterranean (west of Sicily) and easy access to the larger eastern Mediterranean. But, since the major objective of any American military operation in the Mediterranean is the Islamic world: Turkish; Arab or Iranian, Italy's access to oil and its economic miracle will require a government willing to wish the Sixth fleet farwell and send it back to its rightful location — Norfolk, Virginia. It is most unlikely that Italy will withdraw from NATO. Although there are strong forces in the Christian Democratic, Republican and Socialist parties favoring Italy's withdrawing from NATO, there is one party which, whatever its public statements, will not push for withdrawal: the Italian Communist party. The Italian Communist party, like its sister, the French Communist party, is the heir to the nationalism created by the French Revolution (Italy was second to France in the effect of the French Revolution and the emergence of a heroic, middle-class Jacobin tradition against church and state). In Italy, the Communists are the Italian nationalists which the Christian Democrats are the admitted agents of two internationalisms — the Vatican and the U.S. States Department. Millions vote Communist as the only viable and committed alternative to Vatican-State Department dominance of Italy. One of the issues on which the Communist Party of Italy, and the Vatican and State Department, differ is relations with the Soviet Union. The Italian Communist party is much less pro-Soviet than the current Vatican and State Department lines. The Italian Communist party in its domestic policy, such as pro-business and pro-consumer attitudes and its organizational policy of more democratic and less hierarchical approaches, differs greatly with the Soviet Union. But, since the vicious Soviet invasion of Czechoslovakia, which received the blessing of the United States, the Italian Communist party (like the Chinese Communist party which opened a dialogue with the United States to protect itself from a similar fate) is anxious to have diplomatic space in which to move. The Italian Communist party, if it entered into a coalition government, would not push for withdrawal from NATO. Unlike the right-wing French regimes of De Gaulle, Pompidou and Giscard, which have received unbroken foreign policy support by the Communists against the US-backed centrist parties, which have de facto thrown out NATO, the Italian Communists would prefer a NATO prescence in Naples to remind Soviet hardliners not to interfere with the bourgeois Communists of Italy. (The alternative explanation that the Italian Communist party is taking these positions due to the large secret funds paid to it by American oil companies seems as likely as explaining current American culture on the basis of the large non-secret funds paid to the Public Broadcasting System in America.)

Fanfani's recent removal by the national committee of the Italian Christian Democratic Party was due to his own steadfastness in his guiding concepts which permitted the Communists to make larger gains. Fanfani insisted on committing the Christian Democrats to repeal of the recently enacted liberal divorce law. The majority of voters supported the parties, led energetically by the Communists, who championed liberal divorce laws. At the same time, Italy was faced with an inflation caused by the economic policies which Fanfani had advocated. While the so-called free enterprise Liberal party spent all its energies supporting United States foreign policy, the small, Republican party demanded an end to inflation and forced the Christian Democrats to throw out their inflationary wing and appoint last year a new cabinet devoted to fighting inflation, headed by Aldo Moro. In ousting Fanfani, the factions now dominate in the Christian Democratic party gave a vote of confidence to Aldo Moro's premiership, encouraging his policies of fighting inflation, increasing good will with the Islamic world, and working to gain a coalition with the Communists on the basis of sound money and anti-inflation. As the president of the Bank of Italy, Guido Carli, has emphasized, Italy's anti-inflation battle is a battle against the United States' exporting its inflation to the rest of the free world and making countries like Italy bear the burden of the effects of America's unsound monetary policies, deficit spending and Keynesianism. Fanfani's downfall is another defeat for the overseas agents of American Keynesian imperialism. ◻

The Second Austrian Conference

By Richard Ebeling*

The world economic crisis has brought a parallel crisis in economic theory. The "noble experiment" of socialist central planning has failed. Having rediscovered the Miracle of Market, eastern European economists are writing tracts on the efficiency of the Price System. The Keynesian Revolution that promised an end to the "vicious" boom-bust cycle has produced the worst of both worlds: simultaneous inflation and recession.

In the midst of the long-range consequences of short-range policies, economists have begun groping for a new theoretical paradigm to explain the facts. The "groping process" has resulted in renewed interest in the Austrian School of Economics. Founded by Carl Menger and Bohm-Bawerk in the latter nineteenth century, it has been developed in the twentieth by Ludwig von Mises and Friedrich von Hayek. It has emphasized micro-economic analysis within a dynamic framework.

To feed this interest the Institute for Humane Studies (Menlo Park, Calif.) sponsored a Conference on Austrian Economics in June, 1974 at South Royalton, Vermont. The lectures, on the foundations and implications on Austrian analysis, were given by Professors Rothbard, Kirzner, and Ludwig M. Lachmann, with informal presentations given by other Conference participants (see Richard M. Ebeling, "Austrian Economics of the Rise," Libertarian Forum, Oct., 1974).

Because of the enthusiastic response following the Vermont Conference, the Institute for Humane Studies, in conjunction with the University of Hartford, Connecticut, sponsored a Symposium on Austrian Economics during the week of June 22-28, 1975. Rather than having a series of lectures by the "senior" Austrian theorists again, the format was one of papers by "young" Austrians. The informal lectures at Vermont were so impressive that it was decided to ask some of the up and coming "Austrians" to deliver what came to a total of fifteen papers during the week at Hartford. Commentators on the papers included

From The Old Curmudgeon

Parody is difficult in the modern world, for it is hard to reduce to absurdity ideas and movements which are continually skirting the edge of absurdity in the first place. So it is with "women's liberation" and the quota system. In many cases, all we can do is to report the facts, and that is enough.

Thus: a committee of generals reported recently (New York Times, July 14) that women are discriminated against in the Army, and that this practice must stop forthwith. In what way? Because, "looks, figure and personality are considered when female personnel are nominated for assignment to high level staff." The committee, the General Officers' Steering Committee on Equal Opportunity, pontificated that this practice "discriminates against the individual who is not as physically attractive as others. Physical attributes are less important than proficiency."

OK, so what is supposed to be done about this vile practice? How are we going to stamp out the natural tendency of army officers to select attractive instead of ugly females? Are we to set up a board to judge the physical attractiveness of each female, and are we to set up a quota system to insure that ugly females are promoted in proportion to their number in the . . . army? the population as a whole? Fixed numbers for various selected categories: beautiful, pretty, plain, and ugly, or what? And how are the standards going to be selected? And who is going to apply them? Are we going to have official representatives of the uglies, the plains, etc.? How about righting past wrongs by deliberately hiring only ugly females until the balance is redressed? The possibilities stagger the imagination. Are we to raise the cry, at long last, that "Ugly is Beautiful"? Or, shall we, once and for all, adopt the "solution" to this terrible discrimination envisioned by L. P. Hartley decades ago in his penetrating and prophetic(?) novel, Facial Justice: namely, to have compulsory plastic surgery on all females so as to make both ugly and beautiful girls uniformly plain, so that pro-beautyism will be stamped out forevermore?

□

Professors Friedrich von Hayek, Murray Rothbard, Israel M. Kirzner, Emil Kauder, Leland Yeager, Percy Greaves, W. H. Hutt, D. T. Armentano and Lawrence Moss.

The week began with an opening evening banquet with a keynote address by Friedrich von Hayek. Professor Hayek gave his reflections and memories of the Austrian School. The founding of the School by Menger and the intellectual atmosphere of Vienna in the late nineteenth century; what it was like to study in the seminar of Friedrich von Wieser; and the turbulent years of the inter-war period. He recalled that 40 years ago he would have hesitated to label himself an Austrian Economist. He and his fellow Viennese theorists took pride in the fact that what had been an "Austrian" tradition was swiftly becoming part of the standard economic orthodoxy.

But the Austrians, looking out from Vienna, were so thrilled by the seemingly "Austrian" twist that theory was taking in general, failed to notice that other trends were starting to develop, as well. In fact, Hayek confessed that "though I was publicly involved in the controversies of the day with Keynes, for a very long time I did not realize that the main difference between Keynes and myself was not over particular points of theory, but very really and ultimately over different approaches. Keynes had marked, in effect, as far as the public was concerned, a transition from microeconomics, with its methodological individualistic roots, to a macroeconomics which looks for the forces behind events among observed causal connections between statistical magnitudes. It was just this development, very much to my regret and against all my wishes, which has justified that we now again revive the name of Austrian Economics . . . I'm sure . . . that it will prosper and succeed."

The papers at the Symposium covered topics as far ranging as methodology, the history of Austrian Economics, the theory of competition, international economics, problems concerning the trade cycle and Austrian analysis applied to contemporary problems. Space, obviously, does not permit discussion of all the papers or the commentaries and debates that followed their presentation. Instead, the present writer will offer an overview using some of the papers that seemed to catch the flavor and relevance of the contemporary Austrian revival.

John Blundell, a student at the London School of Economics, discussed some interpretations of "Carl Menger and the Founding of the Austrian School of Economics." What is most striking, suggested Blundell, was the wide discrepencies in views over why and how the Austrian School came about. Some, such as Schumpeter, have seen Menger as an original thinker groping for "new principles of knowledge" to refute the already half discarded carcass of Classical Economic Thought. While Spiegel, on the other hand, sees the influence of Kant. His conclusion was that the Kantian notion of the human mind "creating" the forms of the external world made the environment ripe for a subjective theory of value. And, further, Spiegel wondered about the political motivations. The possibility of Menger developing a universal theory of human action so as to offer an intellectual foundation that would "fortify the multinational empire of the Hapsburgs." Perhaps the most interesting charge that Mr. Blundell discussed was the accusation that Austrianism was meant to be a counter weight to a rising Socialism. For as Blundell pointed out, Menger was a Reformist Liberal who was often concerned about the "poor girl" who "has often only the choice between becoming a prostitute or a seamstress." While Wieser believed that "In view of the helplessness of the individual, the slogan of the liberal school, 'laissez faire', becomes almost a mockery," and that protective legislation was needed for workers and securing the public inteests. While Philippovich was a socialist who founded the "Vienna Fabians." And Emil Sax presented the first argument for progressive income tax based on marginal utility theory.

In the twentieth century, the Austrian tradition had been carried forward by Ludwig von Mises and Friedrich von Hayek. Indeed, Hayek, during his 19 year stay at the London School of Economics beginning in

(Continued on page 5)

Austrian Conference—

(Continued from page 4)

1931, not only saw the "great drama" of economic theory unfold, but was a central figure.

Gerald O'Driscoll, in his excellent paper, "Hayek and Keynes: A Retrospective Assessment," discussed and contrasted the differences between the two main center stage actors of the years of high theory. The central error in Keynes' approach was the attempt to analyze dynamic economic problems in a static equilibrium framework that implied the existence of stable macroeconomic relationships. The emphasis and search for aggregate relationships between such magnitudes as investment and consumption, investment and income, and consumption and income resulted in the total neglect of the microeconomic foundations of economic activity and, in particular, microeconomic relationships involving production decisions. The difficulty of Keynes' analysis was multiplied by the ambiguity and contradictions in his use of concepts and his inability to distinguish between changes on the firm level as opposed to the economy as a whole.

The differences between Keynes and Hayek, are crystalized in their theories of investment. For Keynes, the effect of a lowering of the money rate of interest is to change the rate at which the prospective yield of fixed capital is capitalized. The result being that capital goods, seen merely as substitutes for each other, will have succeedingly small marginal yields because they merely repeat the work of existing capital.

But for Hayek, the investment process is not such a simple matter. Rather, as O'Driscoll observes, the rate of interest and capitalization are not cause and effect, but are, instead, both the result of the relative scarcity of "means" for investment. And that the scarce means are not an aggregate sum that can be represented as a simplistic downward sloping Marginal Efficiency of Capital curve.

Instead, investment goods are seen as a complementary pattern of interrelated stages of production involved in a dynamic process over time. Thus, changes in the rate of interest (which is supposed to be a reflection of consumer preference for consumption and savings, i.e., consumption in the future) will effect not only the value of new capital, but existing capital as well. Thus, the profitability for investment arising from changes in the interest rate will effect the choice of utilizing different forms of investment structures. The stages of production will become longer and more roundabout and will form a completed tapestry of a capital structure only if the resources needed to complete and sustain the more complex capital patterns are avilable. In Hayek's words, from his 'Reflections on the Pure Theory of Money of Mr. J. M. Keynes,' "Economica, Feb., 1932, "It seems never to have occurred to him (Keynes) that the artificial stimulus to investment, which makes it exceed current savings, may cause a dis-equilibrium in the real structure of production which, sooner or later, must lead to a reaction."

The general theme of errors from investment decisions was discussed further by John B. Egger in his paper, "Information and Unemployment in the Trade Cycle." In a state of equilibrium the idea of unemployment becomes meaningless, for it represents a state of affairs in which human plans have been made compatible through a meshing of the "means" chosen by a multitude of individual actors in the economy as a whole. The ex post situation is identical with the ex ante expectations in a state of equilibrium.

In the Austrian framework, however, the market process is seen not as a movement from one equilibrium state to another, but instead, as an on going discovery procedure. Individuals, having decided on ends to pursue, decide on what appear as appropriate means. But since in the market economy one's own goals depend on the actions and intentions of others, the entire process is a "fluid" system where adjustments must be constantly made. The adjustments are in response to both the changing plans of one's own shifting value scale and in response to information about the actions of others that. The acquisition of knowledge requires revision in one's own plans and expectations where the activities of others effect the achieving of one's own goals. The fact that information about incorrect expectations will be learned by market participants and that this will almost always result in modification of plans means that the system will always have some amount of "slack," or unemployment, that represents the adjusting for erroneous past decisions.

The unemployment experienced during the trade cycle, Mr. Egger emphasized. is a symptom of a cluster or multiplication of errors and wrong expectations caused by faulty information in earlier periods of the cycle. Credit expansion through the banking system transmits market information signals that result in entrepreneurs rearranging production plans around capital intensive investments; labor invests in "human capital" skills which are found to be misdirected once the malinvestments of the "boom" become visible in the readjustment period brought about by the Ricardo Effect. The artificial stimulus of investment has brought about a series of "false prices" throughout the system. Expectations and plans have been drawn up by market actors that cannot be fulfilled. The period of unemployment and idleness of resources is the time when the errors are sorted out and plans begin realigning around the "real" economic facts.

In the theory of investment, as well as all other market activities, the Austrians, beginning with Menger, emphasized the importance of the concept of time. This was taken up by Rogar W. Garrison in his paper "Reflections on Misesian Time Preference." The essence of the Misesian theory is that time preference permeates all choices and actions of individuals. Every action implies a preferring of satisfaction of "felt uneasiness" in the nearer future than in the more distant future. But this preference should be seen in a slightly different light than the choosing of goods and services. While with goods, the act of choice implies a preference for more units of goods over less units of a goods, the choice of action in time is an either-or proposition. In Mises' words, action "can never be affected at the same instant; they can only follow one another in more or less rapid succession." Thus, each action is not one of a "marginal" preference for now over later, but one of the present over the future as such.

Mr. Garrison, after considering some of the earlier time preference theorists. contrasted Mises' conception with that of Frank Knight. In the Knightian framework, a uniform or "base line" of consumption is postulated with this starting point referred to as zero time preference. If an individual consumes below this level, this shows negative time preference and consumption above this level demonstrates positive time preference. But as Garrison observes, this is a meaningless concept for it arbitrarily establishes a level of "uniform" consumption which is somehow viewed as 'normal;' deviations from this norm then determines whether time preference is high or low.

Garrison draws the analogy of measuring temperature. Under the Kelvin scale, a relationship is established between temperature and molecular motion. When molecular motion is non-existant, the point is defined as zero. Likewise, in the Misesian presentation of time preference the choice of non-action demonstrates zero time preference and all action by the individual shows a positive time preference for achieving a goal now rather than waiting for some future date. While under the Fahrenheit standard, an arbitrary point was chosen to designate zero and to measure changes in temperature. In Knight's system, a "uniform pattern of consumption" is likewise arbitrarily chosen to measure changes in time preference. Thus, while Mises' method of basing time preference on the actions of men is grounded on the nature of human beings in the real world, Knight devises an artificial standard that bears little relationship to actual economic phenomena, and human action in general.

In an extremely interesting paper Joseph T. Salerno presented "The International Adjustment Process: An Austrian View." Mr. Salerno first discussed the development of currency and exchange theories of the Classical economist and the different methods by which the older economists tried to explain the movement of money across borders and the "natural" tendencies that existed for self-correction; also the movement of the world economy toward equalization of the value of money internationally and the equilibrating of prices for all commodities that are the "same."

The Austrian contributions to the theory of international exchange not only clarified the many correct conclusions in Classical analysis, but integrated the problem into the subjective theory of value. Mr. Salerno elaborated on the Misesian theory of the purchasing power of money. There is no single market for money, and, therefore, no single price. Rather, money exists in a "state of barter" with every other goods and service, with a "unique set of exchange rates existing between money and all other commodities" at any moment in time. There tends to be an

(Continued on page 6,

Austrian Conference —

(Continued from page 5)

equality of purchasing power in the sense that relative prices adjust to reflect the particular value of different goods in relation to changes in the amount of the money commodity. There does not exist an aggregate purchasing power represented by a price level. When it is said that the standard of living is higher or lower in one country than another it is a failure to see the value of goods in the subjective sense. Coffee in Brazil is not "cheaper" than in New York. Because of the spatial component, they are not the same goods. Brazilian coffee is a production good that needs to be combined with the complementary transportation factors before it become the "same" consumer good in a New York supermarket.

For Mises, the movement of money is the cause, not the effect, of trade imbalances. Each individual determines the marginal utility of money on his value scale and appropriately adjusts his cash balances, either increasing or decreasing it, in relation to other goods; the same applies to any increases in the quantity of money. Individuals first getting the new money either hold or spend it, based on the marginal value of the units to them. If this process passes over borders, then the international adjustment process "is nothing more nor less than the market process which effects the distribution of money among market participants in a accordance with its marginal utility."

If we realize that what is causing changes in trade balances is not a mere shifting of goods and services from country "A" to country "B", but a dynamic microeconomic process our insight becomes that much clearer in comprehending catallactic phenomena. Mr. Salerno, using Hayek's **Monetary Nationalism and International Stability** as a starting point, brilliantly emphasized that the process begins with individuals in country "A" changing the level of their cash balances. An array of **particular** prices decline. Individuals in country "B", facing lower imported goods prices, in turn, adjust their cash balances in relation to the marginal value of money units. Money flows to country "A" which is received by particular individuals as income and which, again, results in changes in purchasing power and cash balances. This then tends, eventually, to reverse the process. But as individual incomes are effected, the process may work back and forth innumerable times. Also, while it may seem that the country getting the initial amount of additional goods because of lower import prices is the one better off, it may in fact be the one that suffers the most loss of income during the process.

Perhaps the most original, as well as path-breaking, work in the Austrian framework was offered in two papers by John Hagel, "From Laissez Faire to Zwangswirtschaft: The Dynamics of Intervention," and Walter E. Grinder, "The Austrian Theory of the Business Cycle: Reflections on Some Socio-Economic Effects."

Mr. Hagel presented a clear and closely reasoned analysis of the steps by which the economic system moves from a relatively free spontaneous Catallaxy (market order) to the overall planning of Single Economy (state control). Once the market order has been tampered with, the destablizing effects of interventionist programs move the system further towards a regressive collectivist program. The first part of the process sees the change from a "pure market system" to "political capitalism". Political capitalism has three substages: the first stage being sporadic interventions represented by subsidies, state contracts and local monopolies; the second stage develops into a program for "rationalization" and "stabilization" of the economy and takes the form of regulatory agencies and government-assisted cartellization; in the third sub-stage of political capitalism, there emerges a "cohesive ruling class capable of defining its own interests within the context of a broader system of political intervention." Finally, the stage of all-round planning, Zwangswirtschaft (compulsory economy), is reached. All the problems discussed by Mises and Hayek in reference to central planning and economic calculation now come to the fore.

The mainspring of the growing intervention, Mr. Hagel pointed out, was war and inflation. War acts as a "pump priming" device to stimulate "effective demand" in times of recession brought on by previous interventions. The banking system becomes a vital link in the interventionist program since it facilitates the expenditure activities of the government.

It is the banking link in the interventionist program that Mr. Grinder discussed in his paper. Since Austrian monetary theory emphasizes the fact that increases of the medium of exchange do not effect all individuals and all places at the same time, but rather changes the economic position of some people before others, we can see the method by which class stratification is developed.

When the Federal Reserve System finances the government deficits, the State, itself, becomes the first gainer because it is able to obtain access to resources that previously had been beyond its reach. The Banking System is the second major gainer because of the profit opportunities from additional loans from expansion of fiduciary media. The third group of gainers are the contracters of government projects. Further "gainers" from monetary expansion become hard to pinpoint without study of the particular cases in point, but obviously those firms who are able to borrow funds at the artificially lower interest rates obtain, at least temporarily, "forced savings." The Banking System is the focal point for control of all major economic activities, both during the "crank-up" and "crack-up" phases of the trade cycle process. This segment of the economy, whose destiny is bound up with the perpetuation of interventionism, becomes the nucleus of the Statist class structure. And their position as one of the biggest net gainers from monetary manipulation means their interest and future becomes more and more tightly bound up with the maintenance and growth of political capitalism, right into the eventual establishment of Fascism and Zwangswirtschaft.

The other papers at the Symposium included Professor Armentano's presentation of "Competition and Monopoly Theory: Some Austrian Perspectives," Gary North's "Three Critiques of Bureaucracy: Mises, Weber and the Counter Culture," and J. Huston McCullough's interpretation of "The Austrian Theory of the Marginal Use." An additional problem was discussed in Sudha R. Shenoy's paper, "The English Disease: An Austrian Analysis," about the distortion in the capital structure caused by government interventionist programs in Great Britain since the Second World War.

During the evenings, a series of informal lectures were given by three of the senior commentators. Professor Kirzner shared "Some Thoughts on Austrianism in Contemporary Economics." He discussed the recent revival of interest in the Austrian tradition, particularly in the works of Sir John Hicks and Erich Streissler (professor of economics at the University of Vienna). While seeing this as a favorable sign, Kirzner was not sure that the implications of Austrian analysis had been completely grasped in much of this recent work.

Professor Leland Yeager, who in conversation said that the greatest influence on his own thinking about monetary theory had been from reading Ludwig von Mises' **The Theory of Money and Credit**, lectured on the disastrous consequences of government intervention in the economy. Using a Hayekian framework, he contrasted the spontaneous market order that utilized the millions of small bits of knowledge belonging to all market participants with the attempt by the government, through regulation and intervention, to organize market activities with the few minds (and, therefore, limited knowledge) of State planners.

The most interesting and controversial of the talks was the one given by Professor Murray Rothbard, "In Defense of Deflation." Rothbard explained that the Chicago School notion of a stable price level was a spurious concept and not an acceptable subsitute for the present policy of perpetual inflation. Instead, the inflation should be stopped and a deflationary process be allowed to run its course. Deflation would bring about the necessary "smashing" of downwardly rigid wages and prices, so the appropriate resource allocations could occur to help bring about sound long-term economic activity. Also, the consumer would benefit from falling prices as productivity and purchasing power increased.

A lively debate ensued between Rothbard and Hayek about the establishment of a Gold Standard to guarantee that government did not manipulate the money supply. While agreeing that the Gold Standard was the long term solution, Hayek said that he thought it would soon collapse again if established at the present time, because no government would be willing to see the falling of prices within its boundaries that adherence to the Standard would probably require. Rothbard insisted that the Gold Standard was necessary now to "smash" the Central Bank System which is the engine of world inflation. Hayek replied that if Professor Rothbard was talking about an international Gold Standard that involved

(Continued on page 7)

Austrian Conference —

(Continued from page 6)

the elimination of the fractional reserve system, then he (Hayek) was for it completely. This was followed by a round of thunderous applause.

On the closing evening of the Symposium another banquet dinner was held. The sentiments of all participants were summed up in the dinner remarks of Sudha Shenoy, who has been nicknamed the Joan Robinson of the Vienna School. Addressing herself to Professor Hayek, she said that the new generation of Austrians "shall do all that is in our power to ensure that the economic mind of the age does move with relentless logic, with consistent consistency to the priori conclusions of the Austrian system . . . we shall always return to the charge against the forces of macro-darkness now threatening to overwhelm the world . . . I give you two toasts: to victory in the future, and to the last best legacy of Vienna to the world, Professor Hayek."

The momentum that has been built up from these two Austrian Conferences is picking up even more. Regional Austrian Conferences are being planned for New York, Virginia, southern California and London, England, by the end of 1975. Plus, another annual Austrian Conference is already in the works for either June or July, 1976.

The Institute for Humane Studies is also sponsoring a new series of Austrian Economic works. The volumes, which start appearing this summer, will include reprints of Rothbard's **America's Great Depression**, Kirzner's **The Economic Point of View, an Essay in the History of Economic Thought** and Menger's **Principles of Economics**. Also among the volumes will be the lectures by Rothbarb, Kirzner and Lachmann given at the Vermont Austrian Conference and the papers delivered at a symposium in honor of Ludwig von Mises, held at the Southern Economics Association Convention in 1974, which was chaired by Fritz Machlup. Also, a number of new works including Gerald O'Driscoll's dissertation on **Economics as a Coordination Problem: The Contributions of Friedrich von Hayek**. Plus, translations of never-before-in-English works by Austrian economists. The series is being published by Sheed and Ward (Kansas City and New York) in both hardcover and paperback editions.

On the last day of the Symposium, the present writer interviewed Professors Hayek and Kirzner. Excerpts are printed here:

Ebeling: Professor Hayek, let me begin by congratulating you on receiving your Nobel Prize for economics. The new interest in the Austrian approach seems to have developed more or less as a result of human action rather than human design. Individuals have come to the Austrian tradition because of the unsatisfactory state of present economic activity. Do you think the time is right for successful presentation of the Misesian-Hayekian framework to the profession?

Hayek: Well, it looks like it, although I have really no explanation except the evident failure of what has been the predominant view of the past twenty-five years, but even this isn't an adequate explanation at the moment. Everybody seems to recognize that the Keynesian view has been wrong, because we have now got both inflation and unemployment. But the revival of interest in the Austrian tradition did start a little earlier than there was any evident external cause. It has been growing slowly, but with accelerating speed of the past three or four years.

E: In your banquet comments last Sunday night, you said that thirty years ago you would have resisted the use of the label "Austrianism" because the contributions of the school were basically being accepted but that with the rise of macro-economics it was now necessary to respond with a micro-economic counter-attack. If the term "Austrian Economics" is used to designate it, you have no objections. But there are those who work within the Austrian framework who feel that the orthodox micro-approach with its emphasis on perfect competion and comparative static models must be opposed as much as macro models. Do you agree?

H: I think you are right in this although this approach with emphasis on perfect competition is really in a sense through the influence of, at least, mathematical models which always tend a little toward macro-economics. Not necessarily through logical necessity but I think a great temptation for people who think in mathematical terms.

E: From the papers delivered and symposium discussions and personal conversations with the attendents here at the conference, do you feel that this Austrian revival is a sound one?

H: Yes, it's certainly sound; it's very promising — maybe very important. You ask me why — I mean — you never know why the truth is ultimately recognized, but to me it seems that's what happened.

E: What do you see as the reason for the almost dogmatic refusal of the economics profession to even take under consideration different methodological approaches that might more successfully explain social phenomena?

H: Oh, very largely prejudices about what is "scientific", which have been spread, which are essentially the same which I described thirty years ago in **The Counter-Revolution of Science** which is still very much operative, but I do't think my description fits in exactly, but still is that belief that in order to be scientific, you have to measure.

E: Based on that answer, what do you think would be the most successful avenues for Austrians to explore and to try to influence the economics profession into different, more fruitful, directions?

H: To provide more plausible explanations for what is happening.

E: In America, the Chicago School of economic has received much attention and often presents the image of being a counterforce to Keynesianism; but a good number of Austrian School theorists feel that the Chicago economists use a methodological approach and a quantity theory of money that often fails to perceive the nature of the social sciences and the effects of monetary expansion on the economy. Would you please comment on how you see the differences between the Chicagoans and the Austrians on these two issues?

H: Well, you see, we are fighting on the same front, but the quantity theory which the Chicago School has revised is a very crude statement of an elementary truth; but which is helpful for gross problems like stopping inflation but can become misleading in detail. Forty years ago, in **Prices and Production** you'll find this statement that while I think that the pure quantity theory to be oversimplified and often misleading, I pray that the public at large should never cease to believe in it, because only a simple explanation can persuade them that you must stop increasing the quantity of money. I rather regret that highly intelligent people like the Chicago School people do not use it merely as a means of proper explanation but are sometimes misled by it by taking it too literally.

E: And how do you view the difference — the methodological difference — between the Austrians and the Chicagoans, over such a thing as aggregate statistical studies?

H: Oh, it's the same point we discussed before, that you have of course there, by scientific prejudices, a commitment to quantitative methods and the belief that unless you have statistical confirmation, the thing can not be adopted. It's what I explained in my Nobel lecture, that sometimes the better theory's been rejected and the inferior theory adopted because the better theory cannot be demonstrated statistically and the inferior theory has some, if very inadequate, statistical confirmation.

E: It's well known that you are somewhat pessimistic about the economic and social future of Western Civilization. Do you see any optimism for thinking that the Austrians can be successful in changing the direction of the economics profession?

H: Well, this takes a long time, yes, I think if you think in terms of twenty or thirty years, certainly. When you say I'm pessimistic, I'm pessimistic of the next five or ten.

E: How do you feel about the renewed interest in your own earlier monetary and business cycle works?

H: Well, it's pleasant but surprising in a way — oh — why it should have become so completely forgotten after the first period of intense discussion is still a puzzle to me as I have been watching it; but particularly what puzzles me most is that so long as Keynes was alive there was still the realization there were two views. The moment he died his views became the only ones which were recognized, the others forgotten. Perhaps it was that his pupils were much more dogmatic than he.

E: Thank you very much, Professor Hayek.

* * * *   (Continued on page 8

Austrian Conference —

(Continued from page 7)

Ebeling: Professor Kirzner, there have now been two conferences on Austrian Economics. In fact, these have been the first Austrian conferences since the Mises circle in Vienna. Is this a serious attempt to revive the Austrian approach?

Kirzner: Yes. I think these represent two very promising steps toward reviving the Austrian approach. These two conferences were called in response to a wide-spread interest that has evidenced itself among many young scholars, graduate students, young professors, in the works of the recent Austrians, in particular those of von Mises and Hayek and Rothbard; in fact the latest conference as I understand it was forced to turn away many interested participants. All this augurs very well indeed for the future growth of interest in Austrian economics.

E: There seem to be two developing Austrian schools in the world today. Are the people who've attended the conferences in Vermont and Connecticut here and the "European" variant developing with such people as Sir John Hicks and Eric Streissler of the University of Vienna — are they incompatible. and on what points do they differ?

K: It is certainly true that there is a very sharp difference between those of us who've been coming to the Vermont and Hartford conferences on the one hand and others who have in one way or another associated themselves with Austrian or neo-Austrian positions. I think, to put the matter very simplistically, that the American version — if one wishes to call it that — of the Austrian school stems, primarily, from the influence of Mises; while others who to one extent or another call themselves Austrians do so for a variety of reasons . . . For example, Sir John Hicks' Austrianism is based rather narrowly on the time structure of production introduced by Bohm-Bawerk. Streissler's view of Austrianism, again, is rather different from most other views of Austrianism. In Streissler's view any disaggregated work is essentially Austrian in character . . . I do not quite think that Hicks and Streissler constitute in any sense a well-knit group such as I think we see developing here in this country.

E: If this Austrian revival is a serious one, the important point then comes up as to what we can do to successfully get the methodology and theory across to the profession. What basically is the most strategic technique?

K: I think there's no secret here, there's no mysterious technique that has to be discovered. Straightforward intellectual steps are of course available to us. We have to show the profession that the Austrian approach is a fruitful, meaningful one. We can do this by pursuing the Austrian method to attack various economic problems. to elucidate difficult theoretical questions in economics, and by publishing our work, by having our work critized, and having others see what we are doing. This is

the time-honored a_l I think a perfectly sufficient method of spreading our position.

E: You've now written four books and your latest one, COMPETITION AND ENTREPRENEURSHIP, was published by the University of Chicago Press. What feedback have you had, if any, about the interest this has sort of engendered in the Austrian approach?

K: I've been encouraged by the number of kind of reviews that have indicated interest and at least partial acceptance of the Austrian approach. I've been encouraged by the interest of individuals, undergraduates, graduates, and young professors who have written to me about the book and lead me to believe that it does fill a felt need in current theory. To the extent that this represents — is recognized as representing — an Austrian view, I think this can perhaps give some help in engendering a more receptive climate for Austrian views generally.

E: Now some have suggested that if the Austrians are to grow as a school of thought, and to be listened to and respected in the profession, it's necessary to have a graduate department and thus to have a focal point for training people in the Austrian approach similar to the way the monetarists have used the University of Chicago. Will this be a future requirement, and if so, how can it be done?

K: I myself have some reservations about the advisability of establishing a specific graduate school. I recognize that years ago there was in fact nowhere where a graduate student interested in Austrian economics could receive a decent hearing and was able to have his work listened to and appreciated on its merits. I think the atmosphere has changed and there are a number of graduate schools where even non-Austrians recognize the worth of the Austrian tradition and are prepared to encourage students to proceed. Of course wherever an opportunity exists for an Austrian economist to gain a position in a graduate school where graduate students can be exposed to Austrian views, this would be a desirable intellectual development. I'm not sure that the advantages of specifically Austrian department might not be offset significantly by a sort of narrow, sectarian image that such a graduate school might generate.

E: Finally, Professor Kirzner, are you optimistic over the future of the Austrian School?

K: Yes, I certainly am. New recent developments in the past five years have been enormously encouraging. Ten or fifteen years ago, the number of people who would give Mises a respectful hearing in the academic community was very very small. We have seen drastic changes in this regard and I have no question in my mind that this trend will continue and expand in a very healthy intellectual and academic fashion.

E: Thank you, Professor Kirzner.   ◻

*Mr. Ebeling is a student of economics at Saramento State University.

The Libertarian Forum
BOX 341
MADISON SQUARE STATION
NEW YORK, NEW YORK 10010

First Class

Published Every Month. Subscription Rates: $8.00 Per Year; $15.00 Two Years

A Monthly Newsletter

THE
Libertarian Forum

Joseph R. Peden, Publisher   Murray N. Rothbard, Editor

VOLUME VIII, NO. 8   AUGUST, 1975   US-ISSN0047-4517

WINSTON CHURCHILL:
AN APPRECIATION
BY RALPH RAICO

(Ed. Note: We do not ordinarily publish articles of this length in the Lib. Forum. But Professor Raico's scintillating article is of such importance that we are waiving that rule in order to publish it in one piece. Winston Churchill's reputation—fueled by massive propaganda machines in the West—is generally one of uncritical adulation, especially in conservative and even in libertarian circles. We venture to predict that, after Professor Raico's article, that reputation will never be the same again.

We are also proud to announce that Dr. Raico plans to write a bi-monthly column for us, "The Tory Watch", which will keep a sharp and criticial eye on the conservative movement in the United States. Dr. Raico is a professor of history at State University College at Buffalo.)

> The Prime Minister . . . considered that we should wait till we had got Russia against Japan. We should then establish air bases near Vladivostok from which Japan could be bombed, and, according to him, we should then sing the "Ladybird Song" to the Japs: "Ladybird, ladybird, fly away home, your house is on fire, and children at home."
>
> —from the Diary of Field Marshall Lord Alanbrook, April 22, 1943

> Marching ever further on the way of interventionism, first Germany, then Great Britain and many other European countries have adopted central planning, the Hindenburg pattern of socialism. It is noteworthy that in Germany the deciding measures were not resorted to by the Nazis, but some time before Hitler seized power by Bruening . . . and in Great Britain not by the Labor Party but by the Tory Prime Minister, Mr. Churchill.
>
> —Ludwig von Mises, Human Action, p. 855

I

Winston Churchill, whose centennial occurred last year, is considered by many to be the Great Man of the Twentieth Century. He was, for instance, the first and so far only person to be made an honorary citizen of the United States (in the course of this . . . appreciation, we shall have occasion to examine the precise nature of the blood link between Churchill and the American people). Of all his idolators, American neo-conservatives have been the most frenzied. James J. Martin, the revisionist authority, is probably correct in suggesting that this is due to "their urgent necessity to retain at least one towering figure in which they can vest their faith and verbal reflexes" (so inner-directed are they!). The "duel" between Churchill and Hitler fascinates them, as it does others, and is the foundation of Churchill's "greatness" (This may well turn out to be the most enduring injury Hitler inflicted on humanity; that, besides causing the slaughter of so many, he permanently lowered the standards by which political conduct is judged, so that, compared to him, virtually any other mass-murderer—except maybe Stalin—is seen to

be as white as the driven snow.) The facts about the forced repatriation of hundreds of thousands of anti-Communist Soviet subjects to the USSR, to almost certain imprisonment or death, are just now becoming public knowledge; and Churchill's cruial role in this process is probably causing many conservatives some uneasy moments. But those who had to await this to begin to suspect that all was not well with their hero simply know nothing of Churchill's career. In fact, as I will try to show, he was, at best, a not particularly good specimen of his class and type, and, on the critical occasions when he held history-shaping power, by every rational definition and many times over a war criminal who badly wanted hanging.

Before we examine his political record in some detail, a few comments are in order regarding the general cast of Churchill's character and mind. The word most often connected with his name, before 1940 at least, was "opportunist," and with reason. He had, after all, changed party affiliation twice, from Conservative to Liberial and back again. As protege of Lloyd George, he opposed the call for increased armaments in 1909; after becoming First Lord of the Admiralty in 1911, he pushed for larger and larger budgets, spreading wild rumors of the strength of the German Navy (as, in the 1930s, he was to do in regard to the German Air Force). Just before the First World War he spoke out as a Cobdenite Free Trader, and was sympathetic even to the ideas of Henry George; during the War he promoted war socialism in Britain, calling for nationalization of the railroads, and saying, in a speech at Dundee: "Our whole nation must be organized, must be socialized if you like the word." He went in for faddish issues; for a number of years, for instance, he regularly attacked "the horrid liquor traffic" (an amusing bit of hypocrisy from someone who all his life was a controlled alcoholic).

Churchill's opportunism continued throughout his career: after 1945, his speeches against the policies of the Labour Government echo The Road to Serfdom, while it had been Churchill himself who, in December, 1942, had accepted the Beveridge Plan as the basis for the postwar welfare state. Small wonder that Francis neilson writes of him: "I cannot find in his own works or in the memoirs of his colleagues a single economic or political principle that he held steadfastly." Churchill's career spanned over fifty years—and yet, there is not the slightest reason to dissent from the judgment passed on him already by 1914 by John Morley, the last of the great Manchester liberals, who knew him in the Asquith cabinet: "Winston has no principles."

One might have thought that the one cause to which he would have remained true was anti-Bolshevism (he had called the Bolshevik leaders, quite rightly, "bloody baboons" and "the foul murderers of Moscow"). But then there is his record during World War II of instant and unconditional support of Stalin. This may be symbolized by the incident Fuller reports: "On 29th November (1943) at Teheran , Mr. Churchill, to the stains of the Internationale, presented Marshall Stalin with a Crusader's sword." (Conservatives concerned to define "obscenity" ought to meditate on the nature of that act.) Well, yes, there was one

589

cause which claimed his loyalty throughout: the British Empire—that
meaningless flash-in-the-pan (what price "Empress of India" now?) for
which over the centuries so much human blood was shed. Better
Englishmen than he have undestood that Empire for the Aztec altar it
was. The Empire is what Richard Cobden had in mind when he said: "We
have been the most combative and aggressive community that has
existed since the days of the Roman dominion," and which led Lord Acton
to state: "No Christian annals are as sanguinary as ours." Imagine to
yourself a person whose one true love was a world-wide military-
bureaucratic despotism! With Churchill it was a case, as with Disraeli, of
a self-intoxication and revelling in fantasies and empty symbols on the
part of an alienated man who happened to have, on a vulgar level, a way
with words.

This brings us to what one suspects has impressed American
conservatives, Life magazine readers, Book of the Month Club members,
etc., more than anything else about Churchill: his literary style. At times
it could be close to charming (in describing his own early life and war
experiences, for example), and he was always good at depicting battles
and the rush of war. But whenever it came to writing about the larger
issues involved in politics, whenever he had to try to cope with what
might be enduring and really significant in human conflict, what he has to
offer is something quite different: Whig rubbish, bombast at every
remotely plausible point, a constant grabbing for the would-be spine-
tingling symbol or metaphor, the product of a very poor man's Macaulay,
as "fine old British stuff" as, say, the Wilkinson Swordblade commerical
(with its Churchillian "Balaclava, Omdurman . . ."). One tires of the
Churchill style after the first couple of hundred pages—and there are
many thousands more to come.

II.

Churchill was born into the ruling class of Britain in an age when it was
also the ruling class of a quarter of the globe. The family name and
fortune had been made by John Churchill, first Duke of Marlborough, the
famous general in the wars against Louis XIV (he "humbled six marshals
of France," Macaulay wrote, in his corny way). After the wars had come
to an end, Marlborough was censured by the House of Commons for
corruption on a vast scale, and the Crown proceeded against him to try
and recover some of the funds he had gained through graft from war
contracts. Besides this sort of corruption—admitted to be such even by
other members of the privileged orders of the time—he and Duchess held
offices and pensions to the annual value of over 60,000 pounds.
Marlborough and his descendants, in other words, belonged to the caste of
aristocratic parasites who have, through most of human history, lived on
the tribute exacted from working men and women. (After 1789, the
French people opened the eyes of some of these parasites—rather
forcefully—to certain important truths about social reality.) Later,
Winston composed a four volume work in praise of his ancestor; even if
he had not owed everything he had and was to Marlborough, he would
most likely have found him a man completely to his taste anyway, for, as
he says: "With all his faults, right or wrong, (Marlborough) was always
for fighting: which is something." More than anything else, Churchill
inherited from his family the old aristocratic hereditary taint: the view
that mankind is divided into two species, and that it is good that some are
little, so that others may be great. Throughout his life, this was the way
Churchill looked out on the world. Combine this with his love of war, and
endow the combination with Power, and it was easy to foresee that the
product would be no blessing to the human race.

In what follows, we shall be speaking practically incessantly of wars, of
the plotting of them and of their conduct. The reader may come to find
this tedious, but there is no help for it. We are dealing with a man whose
life and career were intertwined with the wars waged by the British State
since 1899. War, one may say, was the life of Winston Churchill. He
himself traces his orientation back to his childhood, when he had an
immense collection of toy soldiers (nearly 1500 of them) and played with
them for years after most boys turn to other things. They were "all
British," he tells us, "and organized as an infantry division with a cavalry
brigade." He fought battles with his younger brother Jack, who "was only
allowed to have coloured troops; and they were not allowed to have
artillery." His early fascination with the military led his father to choose
Sandhurst, the British military academy, for his higher education (there
was in any case no alternative, since Winston had no Greek at all and used
to crib his Latin translations from a fellow student at Harrow). Churchill
later described his state of mind as a young man:

If it had only been 100 years earlier, what splendid times we should
have had! Fancy being nineteen in 1793 with more than twenty
years of war against Napoleon in front of one! Luckily, however,
there were still savages and barbarous peoples. There were Zulus
and Afghans, also the Dervishes of the Soudan . . . There might
even be a mutiny or a revolt in India.

So lustful for war was Churchill at one and twenty that, there temporarily
being none in which Britain itself was involved, in 1895 he volunteered for
the Spanish Army to fight the Cuban rebels, and it was at Las Villas that
he first came under fire. H. G. Wells later insightfully compared him to
D'Annunzio (adding dryly that "he is a great amateur and collector of
texts upon Napoleon"). The comparison is apt. With both there is the
view that life is worthless if not filled with great deeds in battle; a
burning thirst for glory, together with a cruel lack of genius; and an
almost effeminate habit of self-glorification.

During the next few years, England was "lucky" enough to become
involved in a number of colonial wars, and Churchill was able to serve
under his own flag. He saw action on the North West frontier and with
Kitchener in the Sudan, and was captured by the Boers in South Africa;
each of these times he acted also as a correspondent, sending back
chauvinistic accounts of the engagements to the London press. His
background and contacts helped get him into the House of Commons as a
Tory, but in 1904, Churchill crossed the floor to the Liberal side on the
issue of Free Trade.

After the Liberals returned to power in 1906, Churchill began to climb
the conventional ladder of political success. As Home Secretary in 1910-
11, his most famous exploit involved the police "battle" with a group of
anarchists who had barricaded themselves in a house on Sidney Street, in
London. Churchill showed up at the scene for no apparant reason, and
"when the building caught fire and the fire brigade arrived he gave
instructions to the fire-brigade officer on his authority as Home
Secretary that he was to allow the building to burn." (Emrys Hughes,
Winston Churchill: British Bulldog, the best revisionist work on the
subject.) Among the charred bodies that were recovered, however, there
was missing that of the alleged leader, Peter the Painter. This evidently
galled Churchill, for he continued the fight against this "wild beast" (his
words), years afterwards writing that "rumor" had it that Peter the
Painter had later turned up in Russia and become one of the Bolshevik
leaders insanely bent on decimating that wretched country. That this was
highly improbable on the face of it, since, historically, there have
existed—shall we say—problems between anarchists and Marxists, was
not something Churchill could be expected to know. For him, all the
enemies of the established order of inherited privilege and Anglo-Saxon
world hegemony were, and would always be, "wild beasts." (Compare
his exultant cry at the news of the murder of Mussolini: "Ah, the bloody
beast is dead!") There was no particular reason to make fine distinctions
among the animals.

The position Churchill developed for himself around this time was that
of "social imperialist," perhaps the dominant political philosophy in
most Western countries by the outbreak of the First World War.
Masquerading as a form of radicalism, social imperialism essentially
signified the paying out, inch by inch, of the system of competitive
capitalism and private property—through social welfare legislation,
occasional nationalizations, promotion of "responsible" trade unionism,
subsidies of all kinds, etc.—in order to marshal the masses behind the
imperialist policies of their respective rulers. It adored the national
collective, and was fond of thinking with fictitious concepts such as
"national energy" and "national resources" (intended to include the
mental and physical abilities of the people). Its pose as the wave of the
future was the most contemptible thing about it. Churchill at the time had
no qualms about cashing in on that pose, however. He said, in a speech to
his constituents: "I am on the side of those who think that a greater
collective element should be introduced into the State and
municipalities. I should like to see the State undertaking new functions,
stepping into new shpheres of activity. . ." A sample of Churchill as
conservative philosopher: "No man can be a collectivist alone or an
individualist alone. He must be both an individualist and a collectivist.
The nature of man is a dual nature. The character of the organization of
human society is dual. Man is at once a unique being and a gregarious
animal. For some purposes he must be a collectivist, for others he is, and
he will for all time remain, an individualist." Deep, deep. Actually, on the

590

fundamental issues, Churchill never progressed beyond such stuff. It could not, obviously, stem the socialist tide. In any case, that wasn't the point. As long as the masses could be persuaded that their government was "socially conscious," and so kept in line for the next war, things might after all work out. The height of Churchill's willingness to trade off what remained of an economically free society against his foreign policy aims came during World War II. Then, in order to calm socialist discontent and help unify the nation even more firmly behind the one important goal—the total destruction of Germany—Churchill announced his adherence to the welfare state: "You must rank me and my colleagues as strong partisans of national compulsory insurance for all classes for all purposes from the cradle to the grave."

In 1911 Churchill abandoned the field of domestic concerns, for which he never had the slightest ability and very little interest, and became First Lord of the Admiralty. Now, as head of one of the great branches of the British world-imperial machine, helping to make die grosse Politik along with all the other masters of men, he was in his element. Naturally, he quickly allied himself with the war party in the British government. At the time of the Second Moroccan Crisis (1911) he fanned the fires of war by sending a memorandum to Foreign Secretary Edward Grey suggesting that England prepare itself to ship an army to Belgium and be ready to put "extreme pressure" on the Dutch (the first example, I believe, of a continuing trait of Churchill's: the propensity to bully small neutrals). The crisis passed, but by the next year, he, along with other key figures in the Asquith cabinet, were talking privately of the inevitable coming war with Germany and the preparations it would require. When the final crisis came, in July, 1914 (who can read about the accelerating plunge into war of those days without a sickening feeling? From that crisis was to come, directly, the deaths of some ten or twelve million men, and, indirectly, Bolshevism and Nazism, the age of perpetual war, and the slide towards a totally collectivist world; **and all those responsible for that war died in their beds!**—no, at least the Tsar received a just reward)—when the great crisis came, Churchill must have felt like a sadist with a dawning appreciation that he is about to be put in charge of a concentration camp. Of course, he frantically pushed for war. His own Prime Minister later wrote of him: "Nothing would do him but immediate mobilisation. . .Winston, who has got all his war paint on, is longing for a sea fight in the early hours of the morning to result in the sinking of the Goeben." The mobilization of the British fleet (or, rather, the order not to disperse, since it had already been concentrated for "war games") was given on July 26, two days before the first Russian general mobilization orders, and it encouraged the warmongers in Petersburg. On the afternoon of July 28, three days before the invasion of Belgium, Churchill ordered the British fleet—the greatest naval force ever assembled in the history of the world to that time—"to proceed during the night at high speed and without lights through the Straits of Dover from Portland to its fighting base at Scapa Flow" (Sidney Fay, **The Origins of the World War**). "Fearing to bring this order before the Cabinet, lest it should be considered a provocative action likely to damage the chances of peace (sic!), Mr. Churchill had only informed Mr. Asquith, who at once gave his approval." Now, what Churchill could do to insure that England would not be left out of the Great War, he had done. There is no reason for surprise that, according to the other, relatively reluctant members of the British war party, was visibly thrilled and all smiles when the ultimatum to Germany expired without a satisfactory reply, and England was in the war.

III.

In regard to Churchill's role during World War I, we will omit any discussion of his plan for a naval attack on the Dardanelles, which led to the fiasco of the Gallipoli campaign (a disaster which clung to Churchill's name for many years to come). Instead, much more important for an understanding of Churchill is the story of a ship called the **Lusitania**.

The indispensable work on this subject is Colin Simpson's recent intelligent and highly praised book, **The Lusitania.** The facts (uncontested) which Simpson presents have to appear incredible to anyone raised on the Churchill legend. Basically, as First Lord of the Admiralty, Churchill, from the first days of the war, pursued a policy deliberately conceived and designed to destroy all rules of warfare in the North Atlantic, with the aim of involving the United States in war with Germany. (Ultimately he was sucessful.) For example, masters of British merchant ships were instructed to attack surfaced U-boats; as Churchill himself wrote: "The first British countermove, made on my responsibility . . . was to deter the Germans from surface attack. The

submerged U-boat had to rely increasingly on underwater attack and thus ran the greater risk of mistaking neutral for British shipping and of drowning neutral crews and thus embroiling Germany with other Great Powers." Other orders included flying neutral flags on all British ships, killing captured U-boat survivors, and the startling: "In all action, white flags should be fired upon with promptitude."

The reader interested in a truly fascinating account both of high and sinister politics and of war at sea should by all means read Simpson's book, where he or she will be able to follow in detail the story of how the United States was "embroiled" with Germany from 1914-1917, and thus launched on the road to global responsibility. Here we can only focus on the strange doings in London in the first days of May, 1915, as the Lusitania, on its way to Liverpool and loaded with munitions of war, was nearing submarine-infested waters off the southern coast of Ireland. Colonel House was having the eerie experience, on two different occasions, of being asked suddenly and unaccountably, by Edward Grey and then by George V, what would happen if the Lusitania were sunk? To both he responded that that would certainly bring the United States into the war. Now the scene shifts to the Admiralty. In Simpson's words: "Admiral Oliver drew Churchill's attention to the fact that the Juno (originally intended to convoy the Lusitania) was unsuitable for exposure to submarine attack without escort, and suggested that elements of the destroyer flotilla from Milford Haven should be sent forthwith to her assistance. At this juncture, the Admiralty War Diary stops short, perhaps understandably, as it was here the decision was made that was to be the direct cause of the disaster. No one alive knows who made it, but Churchill and Fisher must share responsibility. Shortly after noon on May 5 the Admiralty signaled to the Juno to abandon her escort mission and return to Queenstown . . . The Lusitania was not informed that she was now alone, and closing every minute to the U-20 . . . . It was an incredible decision by any standards and can only be explained on two grounds: that both Churchill and Fisher were so pre-occupied with the Dardanelles and their personal problems that they failed to appreciate it (but the Lusitania was the most famous ship in the world, known by them to be in imminent danger of being sunk—rr); or that it was the pinnacle of Churchill's higher strategy of embroiling the U-boats with a neutral power."

For the student of the Pearl Harbor attack there are numerous ironic pre-echoes in the Lusitania affair: the fact that the German code had been broken by the British, so that they were aware of the position of the submarines in the path of the Lusitania (as the American goverment was aware of many facets of the "surprise" attack of December 7, likewise because of having broken the Japanese code); the mystifying overruling of a subordinate naval officer who proposes what, under the circumstances, is Standard Operating Procedure (as Admiral Stark overruled the officer who urged, on the morning of December 7, that the commanders at Pearl Harbor be informed of the imminence of war); the attempt to set up the Lusitania's captain, William Turner, as the fall guy (much as Kimmel and Short were set up for the role); Churchill's abruptly leaving, after the decision had been make not to send an escort, for Paris and making himself incommunicado (as General Marshall was incommunicado the moring of the Pearl Harbor attack); and, of course, the official horror and wringing of hands at the unheard of atrocity by the enemy—in reality, the fruit of tireless planning on the part of Churchill and Roosevelt respectively, and the fulfillment of their heart's desire.

Later in 1915, when the Cabinet was reorganized, Churchill was removed from the Admiralty as a condition of the Tories joining the government. The excitement of battle being temporarily withdrawn, he was utterly despondent ("the black dog" was his private name for the periodic fits of depression to which he was subject). To one visitor, Churchill said, pointing to the war maps which covered his office wall: "This is what I live for . . . Yes, I am finished in respect of all I care for—the waging of war, the defeat of the Germans." (For the critic looking to condemn Churchill out of his own mouth, there is truly an embarrassment of riches.)

Two items regarding Churchill in the immediate post-World War I period, when he was Minister of War and then Colonial Secretary, must be mentioned (many others, for instance his nearly involving England in another war with Turkey over the "Chanak incident" in 1922, and his "little wars" against colonial peoples, in Mesopotamia and elsewhere, simply cannot be dealt with here: Churchill's life was just too "action-packed" for every warmongering action and initiative to be listed): the

591

continuation of the British blockade of Germany for months after the Armistice. and the armed intervention against the Bolshevik Revolution.

In his capacity as Minister of War (incidentally, one can say of Churchill in this office what Tansill said of Stimson as Secretary of War—No one ever deserved the name more), he ceaselessly promoted a crusade against the new regime in Russia (in 1942, in Moscow, he asked Stalin—literally—whether he "forgave" him for this policy). Lloyd George said of him at this time: "The most formidable and irresponsible protagonist of an anti-Bolshevist war was Mr. Winston Churchill," and added. with a shrewd guess as to part of the motivation: "His ducal blood revolted against the wholesale elimination of Grand Dukes in Russia." The cost of armed British intervention was officially estimated at 100,000,000 pounds. and the attempt to strangle Cummunism "in its cradle" earned. naturally enough, the lasting enmity and suspicion of the Russian leaders. It is also possible, as Emrys Hughes suggests, that it helped consolidate nationalist-minded support behind them, and thus aided Lenin and Trotsky in winning the Civil War; in which case, one would have to add to the debit side of Churchill's career a small item having to do with some fifty years of Red Terror in the Soviet Union.

The point of continuing the blockade was to increase the misery and privation of the Germans so that they would have no alternative to accepting the Carthaginian terms of the Paris Settlement. No one was in the dark as to what the blockade meant. Churchill himself told the House of Commons in March, 1919: "We are enforcing the blockade with rigour, and Germany is very near starvation. All the evidence I have received from officers sent by the War Office all over Germany show: firstly, the great privation which the German people are suffering; and, secondly, the danger of a collapse of the entire structure of German social and national life under the pressure of hunger and malnutrition."

Historians often write as if Hitler's concept of "zoological warfare," of war as aiming at the systematic weakening of an enemy people in the most basic physiological sense, came to him from reading a few murky, nutty Social Darwinist tracts in Vienna cafes. These are supposed to have sparked in his "sick" mind what a victorious Germany might feel justified in doing to a defeated Poland or Russia. I would suggest a different interpretation as a possibility: his experience of the actual behavior of the triumphant Entente after the First World War (especially the blockade and the French invasion of the Ruhr in 1923). More generally. it seems to me that Hitler's goals for Europe and the methods he was prepared to achieve them, and his well-known admiration for the British Empire are two elements in his makeup that deserve to considered together. As evidence for this interpretation, there is his famous conversation with his military officers in 1940, reported by General Blumentritt: "He then astonished us by speaking with admiration of the British Empire . . . He remarked with a shrug of the shoulders, that the creation of its Empire had been achieved by means that were often harsh, but 'where there is planning, there are shavings flying.' " Hitler. in other words, did not come out of a political vacuum, nor are the "roots" of National Socialism to be found in a few 19th century scribblers. Rather, the actual practice of Western imperialism, particularly by Britain, is a main source. After all, what did British imperialism mean but the "Master Race" idea applied to the colored races? The scandal came when Hitler made it clear that he intended to abolish the artificial distinction which Western imperialists had drawn between the white and colored races; that he meant to treat the Slavs, for instance. much as the Congolese and the Javanese had been treated. (This enables us to understand the Nazi ideological nonsese about the non-contribution to "world civilization" of the non-civilized and thus, according to the rules accepted by all Western imperialists, making them fit objects of exploitation.) That in the end England and its Empire were to suffer greatly at the hands of a Hitler motivated by such notions, may suggest to some that there is an ironic justice in the moral economy of the world.

IV.

In 1924 Churchill rejoined the Conservative Party and was made Chancellor of the Exchequer, a position his father had held (Lord Randolph was noted, when he held the position, for having been puzzled by the decimals—what were those "damned dots"?). Although just the year before, as a Liberal, Churchill was still supporting Free Trade, he now included in his 1925 budget the protective McKenna duties, assisting Britain along the road to protectionism that it was to complete in 1932. Doubtless his most famous act as head of the Exchequer was to return

England to the gold standards, but at the unrealistic pre-war parity, thus seriously harming the export trade and the economy at large, and ruining the good name of gold in the public's mind. There would be scarcely anyone today who would argue with A. J. P. Taylor's evaluation of Churchill's action here: he "did not grasp the economic arguments one way or the other. What determined him was again a devotion to British greatness. The pound would once more 'look the dollar in the face'; the days of Queen Victoria would be restored." Lord Esher had said of him in 1917: "He handles great subjects in rhytmical language, and becomes quickly enslaved by his own phrases," and whatever issue he put his mind to. in foreign or domestic affairs, this was the level on which his mind operated.

After the fall of the Baldwin government in 1929, Churchill was out of office. The question of India having become prominent, he soon distinguished himself as the head of the reactionary Tory clique in the House of Commons which insisted on a hard-line towards Gandhi and the Indian National Congress. Churchill's ideas on this subject were pure Tory guff, and a good example of what Esher was referring to, e. g.: "The loss of India would mark and consummate the downfall of the British Empire. That great organism would pass at a stroke out of Life into History. From such a catastrophe there could be no recovery." Contrast to the alienated Churchill, who lived by a system of lovingly self-wrought pictures in his head—whose mind was constituted of such pictures—an Englishman with his feet on the ground, Richard Cobden, who in 1836 wrote: "It is customary . . . to hear our standing army and navy defended as necessary for the protection of our colonies, as though some other nation might otherwise seize them. Where is the enemy(?) that would be so good as to steal such property? We should consider it to be quite as necessary to arm in defence of our national debt!"

To the end. Churchill was virtually the stereotype of the Tory imperialist. In 1942, he had Gandhi and other Congress leaders arrested, and the government which less than a year before had signed the Atlantic Charter announced from Bombay an Emergency Whipping Order, permitting as many as "thirty strokes with a cane in the presence of a doctor." Finally, of course, it was Churchill's very policy of war with Germany to the bitter end that so weakened Britain economically and militarily as to make the loss of the Empire, including India, inevitable.

As the totalitarian States began to emerge from the 20s on, Churchill, the century's great hero of liberal democracy, praised their leaders one after the other. The prime example of this is Mussolini; for whom Churchill expressed unstinting admiration right up until he became Hitler's ally; as late as 1935 he referred to Mussolini as "so great a man and so wise a ruler." But even Hitler did not escape Churchill's verbal caresses: late in 1937, he stated: "One may dislike Hitler's system and yet admire his patriotic achievement. If our country were defeated I hope we should find a champion as indomitable to restore our courage and lead us back to our place among the nations." Here is a perfect example of Churchill's value system in operation. Consider: by 1937 Hitler had imprisoned or executed some thousands of political opponents, legislated against the Jews, entirely dismantled the system of civil liberties, and was clearly set on erecting a totalitarian State with the annihilation of the individual which that implies. And yet, because he played the old game of nationalist politics—and played it very, very well—he could still command Churchill's respect! The bother only came when Hitler was perceived as threatening England's world position.

Similarly with the Russian Communist leaders. Lenin and Trotsky, with their concept of world revolution, were "bloody baboons"; Stalin, on the other hand, who appeared to be more concerned with socialism in one country, and was, in any case, an ally against Hitler, was an excellent candidate for the role of "great man." Churchill's comments after June, 1941, on Stalin and Stalinism are priceless: here's an example, from May, 1944, which it would be hard to better from the lips of any fey fellow-traveller of the time: "Profound changes have taken place in Soviet Russia. The Trotskyite form of communish has been completely wiped out (on oblique, favorable reference to the purges of the late 30s, which claimed some 700,000 lives!—rr). The victory of the Russian armies has been attended by a great rise in the strength of the Russian state and a remarkable broadening of its views. The religious side of Russian life has had a wonderful rebirth," etc., etc. To my mind, what we have in these almost unbelievable eulogies by Churchill is a case of that terrible freemasonry of spirt among the high governing class, whereby each can empathize with and sympathetically understand the "problems" the other faces—Hitler's shrug at the "shavings flying" in the wake of British imperialism—and which makes the much closer to one another in their outlook on life than to those on whose necks their feet are respectively planted.

From 1929 to the outbreak of war in 1939, Churchill was out of office, ostracized by the leaders of his own party, an unprecedented occurrence for someone who had filled the high positions which he had. A major reason is that he was known as a fomentor of wars (Herbert Morrison could casually call him a "fire-eater and a militarist" without raising eyebrows—this was simply the common view), and there was a strong pacifist tide running in Britain. After Hitler came to power, however, Churchill began to attract attention once more, as the head of the faction that favored a "firm" policy towards Germany. As he put it to General Robert E. Wood when they lunched together in November, 1936: "Germany is getting too strong and we must smash her."

Churchill has covered his name with glory in the eyes of many for thus having been the leader of the war party in the middle and late 30s, and pushing for British "rearmament" (actually, Britain, like France and the French allies in East Central Europe, had never disarmed—they were, in fact, all armed to the teeth—and it had rejected every plan, put forward by successive German governments and even by Litvinov, for a general European disarmament). This he may be conceded. But what was his peace plan? In 1933 he had denounced Mussolini's proposal for a Four-Power Pact to revise the Paris Settlement peacefully, as in 1938 he was to denounce the Munich Agreement. He never once, however, suggested an alternative course—except to increase British armaments even further and grimly resolve to defend Versailles by force. In this spirit he applauded Chamberlain's lunatic unconditional guarantee to Poland in March, 1939 (pledging England to war if anything occurred that "clearly threatened Polish independence, and which the Polish Government accordingly considered it vital to resist with their national forces"). Afterwards Churchill himself criticized the guarantee in these terms: "Here was decision at last, taken on the worst possible grounds, which surely lead to the slaughter of tens of millions of people."

The policy Churchill urged and which was ultimately adopted by the British Government, is understandable only on the basis of the establishment's line: namely, that Hitler wanted to "conqure the world." (Funny how easily that goal is imputed to those who happen to find themselves at odds with the British or American States: as if "conquering the world"—that is, defeating the various powers of Europe and Asia and garrisoning their territories, occupying Africa, sending armadas to attack and occupy North and South America, and so on—and all this without encountering any disheartening difficulties—were something that would quite naturally occur to the head of a country, like Germany, with some 25 million adult males, or the leaders of a country, like Japan, with 15% of the GNP of the United States—but then there is their well-known "insanity" to explain the astonishing lack of realism. Meanwhile, the fact that Britain had already conquered and was in possession of one-fourth of the world is accepted as a datum of the Cosmos.) A. J. P. Taylor has shown, though, that Hitler's plans can much more adequately be explained as centering on a restoration of Brest-Litovsk—the settlement of 1918 between Germany and Russia which established German hegemony in Eastern Europe. Why anyone should feel that such a state of affairs threatened vital British interests is a mystery. In any case, it would surely be difficult to maintain that the final outcome of the Second Crusade—the hegemony over the eastern half of the Continent by a more formidable power—was vastly and obviously to be preferred.

At all events, in September, 1939, war came once more between the Western allies and Germany (the fixedness of the past gives the illusion that this was inevitable, but that is far from being the case). Churchill was immediately recalled to his old job as head of the Amiralty, and, in May, 1940, his life's ambition was realized. He became Prime Minister.

V.

In directing the British war effort from 1940 to 1945, Churchill, the "great strategist," was wrong much more often than he was right. (His overall expertise can be gathered from the fact that, in 1938, he referred to the French Army as "the most perfectly trained and faithful mobile force in Europe.") The decision to send troops to North Africa was a wise one; the decision to send them to Greece, from which they were forced to withdraw in a second Dunkirk, was the opposite, and prevented finishing off the Italian North African forces before Rommel could arrive. His philosophy of the offensive in warfare helped hasten the fall of France (it would have been more sensible, according to Fuller, to try to hold the river-lines). Later, disastrously underestimatng Japanese air power, Churchill sent the two great battleships Prince of Wales and Repulse to Singapore, to deter a Japanese attack. They were sunk by land-based bombers in the first days of the Pacific War, swinging the balance of naval power to Japan and destroying the morale of the forces at Singapore. Britain was saved from defeat in the Second World War not by Chruchill's military genius (he had none), but by Hitler's invasion of the Soviet Union and by the circumstance that the White House was occupied by a man as boyishly eager as Churchill himself to bring war to his people.

More than any other of his acts in this war, Churchill's plan (while he was was still at the Amiralty) to take over neutral Norway was a fiasco. Hitler, in early 1940, had declared himself satisfied with a genuinely neutral position for Norway, but on February 6, 1940, the British War Council approved the plan to seize Narvik and occupy northern Norway and Sweden by force, as well as the Swedish port of Lulea on the Baltic. As a preliminary to the attack, the British violated and then began mining Norwegian territorial waters, leading the Germans to forestall the British occupation by their own invasion of Norway (Denmark was taken on the way). What the Norwegians and Danes suffered in World War II, they owe to Winston Churchill.

A very important sidelight of this affair is that Churchill's plan included sending an expeditonary force to help Finland against the Red Army (this was also to provide a pretext for the invasion of the neutral countries). Thus, in 1940, England came perilously close to war with both Russia and Germany. That Churchill was prepared to risk that shows that the man lived in a dangerous fantasy-world much of the time. If England had faced what Germany did by 1945, there is little doubt that historians would now be recording much the same breakdown of mind and personality in Churchill's case that the world knows so well in Hitler's.

A famous incident in the early stages of the war, now mostly forgotten, was the treacherous attack ordered by Churchill on the French Mediterranean fleet, following the fall of France. Not trusting in his ally's promise never to allow the fleet to come into German hands, Churchill ordered British commanders in the Mediteranean to demand the instantaneous surrender of French naval units, and in case of their ultimatum immediately to open fire. According to Liddel Hart, "all three admirals concerned—Cunningham, Somerville, and North at Gibralter—were horrified by Churchill's orders." At Alexandria, Cunningham disregarded the fantic urgings of this ruthless man, and gained the end through patient negotiations. At Mers-el-Kebir (Oran), however, French ships were fired on, resulting in the deaths of hundreds of French sailors (just as, in the course of the liberation of France, there were to be nearly as many deaths of French civilians from British and American bombers as Britons killed by German bombers). What was left of the French fleet retired to Toulon, where, in 1942, when the Germans threatened to seize it, the French honored their word and scuttled their ships.

That Churchill could be a dangerous ally may well have been learned the hard way by the Poles also, although here the full facts will most probably never be known. What is certain is that General Wladyslaw Sikoriski, Prime Minister of the Polish Government in Exile in London, was seriously endangering Churchill's policy of cooperation and accomodation with Stalin, by demanding that the truth about the Katyn Forest massacre be made public, and by insisting on Poland's pre-1939 eastern frontier (he did not want most of the German territories which Churchill tried to palm off on him). Sikoriski was killed, along with his entourage, in an airplane crash shortly after take-off from Gibralter (the Czech pilot who had been provided him survived). This was the third "accident" in a row for Sikorski in a British aircraft; considering that he was the Head of State of an allied power, a bit sloppy. MacFarlane, the Governor of Gibralter, afterwards said: "The Russians could not have done it," and told Madame Sikorska: "It cannot have been an accident." Still, it is possible that Sikorski's death was due to mechanical failure of the airplane. The Polish exile community in London at the time, however, was convinced that he had been killed pursuant to Churchill's orders.

Concerning another, and much more significant plot, there was at one time a good deal of controversy, but would now be difficult in the extreme to dispute the main lines of the revisionist interpretation: that Churchill conspired with Roosevelt to involve the United States in war with Germany. There is no need to delve into details here; the interested reader may find the case summarized in Chapters Vand VI of William Henry Chamberlin's America's Second Crusade, and elaborated in the works of Beard. Tansill and others. Here let us simply quote from The New York Times of January 2, 1972: "WAR-ENTRY PLANS LAID TO ROOSEVELT. Britain Releases Her Data on Talks with Churchill. London. Jan. 1 (AP)—Formerly top secret British Government papers made public today said that President Franklin D. Roosevelt told Prime Minister Winston Churchill in August, 1941, that he was looking for an incident to justify opening hostilities against Nazi Germany . . . . On Aug. 19. Churchill reported to the War Cabinet in London on other aspects of the Newfoundland (Atlantic Charter) meeting that were not made public . . . . 'He (Roosevelt) obviously was determined that they should come in. If he were to put the issue of peace and war to Congress, they would debate it for months,' the Cabinet minutes added. 'The President had said he would wage war but not declare it and that he would become more and more provocative. If the Germans did not like it, they could attack American forces . . . Everything was to be done to force an incident." By the end of the year, Churchill's "higher strategy" had once again culminated in American involvement in a European war. He duly took credit for it. as well he might from his point of view; after the United States came into the war, Chruchill said in a radio broadcast: "This is what I have dreamed of, animed at, worked for, and now it has come to pass."

We are entering now on to the darkest passage in a life that could boast many: Churchill's policy of the calculated terror bombing of the cities of Germany. First. let us note that, militarily, the policy was a foolish one: up until the end, it had nothing like the crushing effect on German morale that had been expected (the American bombing policy that was in operation through most of the war against Germany, of concentrating on certain industrial targets, especially oil refineries, was much more successful); and what A. J. P. Taylor calls "the British obsession with heavy bombers" led naturally, to scarcities in other areas—for instance, of fighter planes at Singapore and landing craft at Normandy.

But besides creating technical problems for the war effort of the Allied leaders. the program also had what could be called "a human angle." About 800,000 German civilians were massacred from the air, according to the estimate of the West German government (other estimates are somewhat lower). and great cities, famous in the annals of science and art, turned into heaps of smouldering runs. Nothing is more certain than that air war far from the front lines, with the enemy's civilians as the deliberate target. was begun after 1939 by the British, whose plans for this went back many years. In fact, high British Air Ministry officials after the war boasted of the boldness and originality of their government in pioneering this ingenious innovation. The story can be found set forth lucidly and in detail in F. J. P. Veal's extremely important book, Advance to Barbarism.

The whole business is one of unremitting horror, but even within it there are high-points. Thus, in March, 1942, the British Cabinet accepted the plan proposed to it by Churchill's friend and scientific advisor Professor Lindemann, whereby "top priority" in bombings was to go, not to middle-class areas, which tended to be somewhat spread out, but to working-class quarters, which were more compact and densely-populated. (Lindemann's character is superbly captured in Rolf Hochhuth's play about Churchill, Soldiers; here he is shown to be a repulsive ascetic. impassioned by little besides death, a brother to SS Dr. Mengele—he of the advanced medical experiments—and to Professors Frost and Wither of C. S. Lewis's That Hideous Strength: all devils incarnate.) Another nice twist is Anthony Eden's whining complaint that his colleagues were ignoring the "claims" of the smaller German cities to be bombed. A famous milestone in the story is the attack, on July 27-28. 1943, on residential Hamburg. The bombing and the resulting firestorm killed 42,600 people and seriously injured 37,000 others. And so we come to Dresden.

Here the reader should consult David Irving's definitive work, The Destruction of Dresden (Irving is by no means a thorough-going revisionist, but the facts speak for them selves). Towards the end of 1944, the British, under prodding from the Americans, had been shifting their air attacks to industrial targets. In Janurary, 1945, however, Churchill sharply criticized his air commanders for having been unresponsive to his inquires as to "whether Berlin, and no doubt other large cities in East Germany should not now be considered especially attractive targets."

"The immediate result of this hard reply," Irving writes, "was to stampede the Air Staff . . . into issuring an instruction to Sir Arthur Harris which would make it inevitable that the Eastern population centres, including Dresden" would now be subjected to saturation bombing. (Space is limited, I reluctantly admit, but still the reader has the right to know who Harris was: through most of the massacring of German civilians from the air, he was in charge of Bomber Command; he continually pushed for the killing of civilians, when others preferred more directly military targets; and his viewpoint on the ethics of the matter may be summed in Irving's words: "the only international restriction which he considered to be binding on him and his Command. . . was an agreement dating back to the Franco-Prussian War, which prohibited the release of explosive objects from gas-filled dirigibles; this restriction, as he pointed out, was rigidly complied with throughout the Second World War by Bomber Command"—here a whiff of the macabre humor about killing that marks the authentic sadist-murderer, reminiscent of Jacobin jokes about the guillotine. By the end of the war, Harris's name so stank that he was the only Air Commander not made a peer by the "victory"-intoxicated British Government.)

Irving points out that, as with the inhabitants of Hiroshima, the people of Dresden were pawns in a larger game. "Clearly (Churchill) had secured his immediate aim: soon after the 4th February, at the climax of the Crimea conference (Yalta), he would be able to produce a dramatic strike on an Eastern city which could hardly fail to impress the Soviet delegation" (if Dresden, why not Kiev?). As it happened, the attack had to be postponed because of weather conditions; but the Soviets doubtless got the message as the lesson of Hiroshima was also not lost on them. Americans simply have no conception of what a looming terror the Anglo-Saxon air forces have been to the poeples of the world.

To be brief: by February, 1945, Dresden contained well over one million inhabitants, including refugees. It was virtually defenseless, there being no flak batteries remaining in the city and the Luftwaffe fighter planes being largely grounded for lack of fuel. It most likely came within the definition of an open city according to the Hague Convention of 1907. What minor industrial targets Dresden contained were not marked for attack by the RAF. The blow was aimed, rather, at the residential areas. It succeeded. Probably about 135,000 persons were killed. The city's authorities has to give up hope of burying the dead and resorted to mass cremation. When the vultures escaped from the Dresden Zoo, there were some fine scenes to behold.

As the shock of horror spread in the neutral countries with access to the news (if not in New York and Washington, at least in Zurich and Stockholm, one had heard of a city named Dresden), Churchill started to panic. Cute is how he tried to get the air commanders to accept a memo implying that they had been solely responsible for the bombing (Irving, pp. 250-253: he refers there to the need to review the standing policy of "bombing German cities solely for the sake of increasing terror, though under other pretexts"—thus giving the whole game away). The memo was indignantly returned, the officers in question realizing that Churchill was using them in an attempt to clear his own name with history.

That attempt seems hopeless. The destruction of Dresden was, directly, the result of Churchill's specific request to his air commanders, and, indirectly, the outcome of his whole attitude towards the war. He had, for example, told the House of Commons, in 1943: "To achieve the extirpation of the Nazi tyranny there are no lengths of violence to which we will not go." And at the start of the war he had said of the Germans: "We will break their hearts." Well, so he did. But we may hope that in partial recompense for his great triumph, the names of Churchill and Dresden will be licked in an embrace for so long as men remember, from time to time, what States have done to human beings.

Schlafen Sie wohl, Englaender. Schlafen Sie wohl.

VI.

There are other great massacres—realized, or only projected—for which Churchill must share responsibility, as he must for the catastrophic political decisions of World War II. Let us deal with the latter first.

Churchill's admirers seem to assume that it is in the regular course of nature, a thing calling for no particular explanation, that a nation like Britain should gain its most complete military victory and simultaneously find itself in the most dangerous position in its history. But there exists by now a large body of evidence and expert opinion to the effect that the practical defeat of England in the Second World War is largely traceable to Churchill's decisions. The root of the fateful error was Churchill's famous "single-mindedness," a not especially valuable trait in those dealing with complex issues, and certainly not in someone underaking to shape world history. When his secretary questioned him, in June, 1941, on the decision to give all-out aid to Stalin, Churchill replied: "I have only one aim in life, the defeat of Hitler, and this makes things very simple for me." In February, 1943, Franco transmitted to Churchill a memorandum warning of the dangerous spread of Russian power on the Continent. Churchill responded by ridiculing Franco's fears, adding: "I venture to prophesy that, after the war, England will be the greatest military Power in Europe. I am sure that England's influence will be stonger in Europe than it has ever been since the days of the fall of Napoleon." This fantasy of perpetual and overweening British power, then, was the foundation of of Churchill's wartime policies. As Liddell Hart has said: "Britains's leader was too excited by the battle to look ahead, and see the inevitable consequence of the smashing victory for which he thirsted. It makes no sense."

The most direct expression of the demand for total, smashing victory was Roosevelt's policy, from early 1943 on, of exacting unconditonal surrender from Germany, Italy and Japan (the demand was afterwards dropped in Italy's case). When Roosevelt made the announcement at Casablanca, Churchill's sycophantic reaction was to look thoughtful, grin and then say: "Perfect! And I can just see how Goebbels and the rest of 'em'll squeal!" (In fact, Goebbels considered the slogan a godsend, since it identified the German State with the Nazi regime.) The doctrine of unconditional surrender necessarily led to Communist control of East Central Europe and the Balkans, and of Manchuria and North Korea. After it had begun to work its inevitable effects, Churchill desperately tried to block them—this, ironically, is another cause for his high repute among conservatives—by pushing for invasion by Anglo-American forces of the Balkins and the Danube basin (the famous "soft underbelly of Europe"—the Italian campaign showed that concept up for the idiocy it was). Really—through all the torrent of his self-serving rhetoric, and after all his glamorizing at the hands of Luce and the rest of the establishment press is done—just what value are we to place on the political sense of someone who simply did not comprehend that the extinction of Germany and Japan as powers entailed . . . certain consequences. Is it a Metternich or a Bismarck we are dealing with here? Or is this rather a case of a Woodrow Wilson redivivus, of another Prince of Fools?

To pose a fairly basic question: what actually did Churchill believe he was fighting against in the Second World War? Was it a crusade against the diabolical Hitler of the death-camps and the medical experiments? This later, more sophisticated view of what World War II was about played no role at all in Churchill's thinking. Instead, it was a question in his mind of a "gangster" regime threatening the "liberties of Europe" (that is, the right to rule of the various parasitic regimes in the individual countries), and, equally, of—Prussian militarism! "The core of Germany is Prussia. There is the source of the pestilence . . . . Nazi tyranny and Prussian militarism are the two main elements in German life which must be absolutely destroyed," he proclaimed. /The Allies were battling the same mad Junker dream of world conquest, he went on to say, which had "twice within our lifetime, and three times counting that of our fathers . . . plunged the world into their wars of expansion and aggression."

This is a serious man? If his words are to be believed, Churchill's interpretation of the great epic of World War II was the one ground out by some bored French press secretarty in the Washington Embassy. Forget about a tyrant and "blood-stained usurper" (as John Stuart Mill called him) named Napoleon III, who was, equally with Bismarck, responsible for the Franco-Prussian War. Forget about the Tsarist Russian imperialists and their French allies who, more than anyone else, brought about World War I. Wars are caused by Prussians, and this war is no different from any other. Thus, according to Churchill, the Second World War was no singular confrontation with the hair-raisingly demonic, as we have so often been told since, but—one can hardly grasp it—simply the third act of the old battle against the monsters of monocled arrogance who have all along been planning for the Day when Berlioz will be replaced by Brahms and we will all be forced to eat sauerkraut at the point of a bayonet! Even the old Third Republic politician, Paul Reynaud, had a less obsolete interpretation of what the war meant when he told his

ministers in 1940: You think you have to do with Wilhelm II, but I tell you that you have to do with Ghenghis Khan. Churchill believed that fundamentally he had to do with Wilhelm II (or even Wilhelm I!), and total war, the exhaustion and eclipse of England, the plot to deceive the American people into entering the war, and all the rest—these were all justified by the burning need to—stop the Junkers!

Naturally, with this prespective, Churchill could have no sympathy with or appreciation for the heroes of the German opposition to Hitler. Even the Tory publicist, Constantine FitzGibbon, is compleased to say that, after the officers' plot of July 20, 1944, "Churchill in the House of Commons exactly echoed Goebbels's speech about the conspirators, describing them as a small clique of officers and expressing a certain satisfaction that 'dog eat dog.' " Churchill's fanatical—really, brainless—anti-Germanism blinded him to the possibility that a Germany run by Beck and Goerdeler might conceivably be more desirable from a Western point of view than one controlled either by Hitler or Stalin. And as for Prussianism, let this be said: the Prussina officer class (those mad dogs, infinitely worse, of course, than the products of Sandhurst, St. Cyr and West Point) no longer exists, and Prussia—which, after all, was Humboldt as well as Hegel—now is not even a name on a map. But Prussianism's final act was the attempt to kill Hitler and to salvage something of the honor of Germany—a not unworthy way to leave, for the last time, the stage of history. If we contrast these officers with others who were in a similar position, is it the Prussians who suffer from the comparison? It is by no means certain that Tukhachevsky and the other Red Army Marshals actually were contemplating killing Stalin; and as for Roosevelt, Truman and Churchill, there is no evidence at all that the idea ever entered the heads of their respective military subordinates.

The projected mass-murder in which Churchill had a hand was, of course, the Morgenthau Plan to demolish German industry and mining after the war, in order to turn the Germans into a peaceable agricultrual and pastoral people. At the Quebec Conference of 1944, Churchill, at first reluctant to agree to the Plan, was converted when "Morgenthau pointed out that the destruction of German productive capacity would free German overseas market areas for British trade, and . . . offered England postwar credit of $6.5 billion. The President agreed that the United States would impose no restrictions on the use of this credit" (Anne Armstrong, Unconditional Surrender, p. 75). Now, the millions of deaths from starvation and cold (the Plan called for flooding the coal mines of the Ruhr!) which would have resulted from its implementation surely merit placing it in the same category with certain Nazi plans for the treatment of Russia after the war (one sign of how truly staggering the concept was, is that even Stimson was horrified by it). The diplomacy of the Second World War offers few scenes as fascinating for their quality of perfectly distilled evil as the US Secretary of the Treasury, in his choking hate, trying to bribe the Prime Minister of Great Britain to consent to the genocide of the German people—and the British Prime Minister, in his frenzied greed, accepting the bribe!

While the Morgenthau Plan was never carried out (although it indirectly guided Allied policy in Germany for a couple of years), Churchill's agreement to the mass transfer of German populations westward from Pomerania, East Prussia, Silesia and Sudetenland—all German territories for many centuries—was, and it caused the deaths of some two or three millions. And we must record also that Churchill was an accomplice in Truman's decision to begin the atom bombing of the cities of Japan, and to continue putting them out, one by one, until either Japan surrendered unconditionally or there were no more Japanese, whichever came first.

Let's stop for a moment. Action said that we should judge the great actors in history by the final maxim that govern our own lives. On that basis, what do you think of someone who lived a life such that, in describing it, the fact that he was an accomplice in Hiroshima and Nagasaki is a throw-away line?

In nailing Churchill with these crimes, we are not, the reader should note, judging from any novel or arcane standard of morality spun out of the brain of a ressentiment-filled Jacobin or "crazy" Russian anarchist. Nor is it the tithe of the tithe of moral rectitude that we are insisting upon, and compared to which we just happen to find Churchill wanting. We are dealing, rather, with decisions and acts that led to the deaths of millions or would have led to the deaths of other millions. It appears to us self-evident that the least of these decisions and acts would—if justice ruled *this world*—in itself be enough to cause its perpetrator to be torn to pieces by a crowd.

In the midst of the Potsdam Conference, in 1945, Churchill was thrown out as Prime Minister by the British voters (he had never been popular in his own country except during the brief period of the Battle of Britain). While leader of the Opposition, his most celebrated act was helping to declare the Cold War with his famous "Iron Curtain" speech in Fulton, Missouri, in March, 1946. Europe having been left a political shambles by his very own policies, he called upon the New World to redress the balance of the Old. Naturally, the interventionists in the United States made great capital out of his warnings; Churchill by this time was looked on as practically a professional sighter of attemps-to-conquer-the-world. Not coincidentally, his own England profited from the resulting anti-Russian hysteria: a $6 billion-plus loan in 1946, then more billions from the Marshall Plan, finally additional billions in military aid when NATO was established.

In 1951 Churchill became Prime Minister once more, with a small majority. And now the world saw what no one would have believed it could ever see: Churchill as peacemaker, Churchill warning against the dangers of another war and proposing a summit conference to work towards reconciliation between the Western powers and Russia! The key to what would otherwise be a maddening riddle lies in the fact that, shortly before, the American monopoly of nuclear weapons had been broken by the Soviet Union, and it was estimated by experts that it would require only eight hydrogen bombs to write finis to those Sceptered Isles; by the summer of 1954 Russia was thought to have more than that number. Future great wars, alas, would not be fought over the lands of Africans and Asians, nor by visiting death from the air on the peoples of the European continent. Russia thechnological advances made it inevitable that from now on any great war would result not in limited casualties for England (such as the 380 deaths that followed the German attack on Coventry), but in the virtual annihilation of the British race. Thus, the New Churchill. But many thought they could detect at least a touch of hypocrisy in his suggestion that the nuclear powers solemnly agree to use their weapons only against enemy troops in the field. . .and not against cities.

We will conclude this survey by observing that, in October, 1953, Churchill received the Nobel Prize for Literature, thus joining the Immortals such as Haldor K. Laxness and Juan Ramon Jimenez, other Nobel Laureates in Literature, and Pearl S. Buck (whose Prize for the pro-Chinese The Good Earth, had been as politically-motivated as Churchill's own). Churchill was especially commended by the Nobel Committee for having "mobilized" the English language in time of war. It was reported, though, that he had had his heart set on the Nobel Prize for Peace. Well, why not? It had, after all, been awarded to Theodore Roosevelt (of whom Charles Beard said that he was probably the only high politician in American history who believed that war was good in

itself), and afterwards it was to be bestowed on George Marshall and on Henry Kissinger. There is a school of modern literature, the Theatre of the Absurd, which would maintain—with more than a grain of truth, I think — that the world we are doomed to live in is precisely the sort of place where a Winston Churchill could receive the Nobel Price for Peace.

VII.

Finally, a word to the reader: if this essay has seemed to you one long tirade; if you have grown weary — as I must confess I at last have — of the endless recital of wars and bloodshed; if your mind is by now dazed from the simple repetition of the words massacre, murder, slaughter and kill — what can I tell you? It isn't my fault; it's not my life I've been relating. Did you really think that the British Empire was the kind of campy joke American conservatives have implied it was? "No Christian annals are as sanguinary as ours," Acton said, in his cool and collected, deep-Christian way. After all, one acquires and maintains the most formidable Empire of any State in history in no other manner than by breaking human bodies and hearts. And our subject has been the Great Man who felt honored to be the humble servitor of the British State in the age of total war.

Let us try to sum up the career of this enormously influential man.

In Winston Churchill we have, above anything else, a militarist, one who yearned for even more wars than actually occurred, a jaundiced personality whose nose only began to twitch when there was bloody conflict afoot, a decadent who could refer to the years without war as "the bland skies of peace and platitude." We have a schemer clever enough to have embroiled America in two world wars in defense of the British Empire (he used our people in his plans as he might have the Greeks and the Turks), and the great master of stomach-turning Anglo-Saxon cant, the apotheosis of the tradition of Palmerston and Edward Grey, of Wilson, Stimson and Roosevelt — but nontheless a foolish and futile politician (even from his own standpoint), one of the main destroyers of the balance of power in Europe and East Asia, and the grave-digger of the Empire of the State he served. We have a Man of Blood, whose most characteristic acts were to arrange that the Lusitania would be sunk, and to send the planes winging to set Hamburg and Dresden on fire — perhaps the main architect of the system of total war which yet put an end to the human race. And we have, when all is said and done as far as his beloved country is concerned, a mere social imperialist and politico without principle, in the tacky line of those who have made the England of Gladstone's time into what it is today.

Yes, truly, the Man of the Century.

For a fitting epitaph, there's a choice: either the one that seems demanded: If you seek his monument, look around. Or the one I prefer: —

He was better than Hitler.

A Monthly Newsletter

THE
Libertarian Forum

Joseph R. Peden, Publisher   Murray N. Rothbard, Editor

VOLUME VIII, NO. 9   SEPTEMBER, 1975   US-ISSN0047-4517

THE LP CONVENTION

It was an exciting, gigantic, rip-roaring extravaganza — the greatest nationwide gathering of libertarians in modern times: the "Presidential Convention" on Labor Day week, at the Statler-Hilton Hotel, New York City. Fueled by the showmanship of the New York party and by the public relations knowhow of David Grant and Laura Wertheimer, the Libertarian Party came on like a real nationwide party, gaining unprecedently extensive (and favorable) media coverage, highlighted by several minutes on national CBS television. It was the best of times; it was the worst of times; it was week of highs and lows, a cauldron of love and hate; but out of that cauldron emerged, at last, a great Presidential ticket (Roger MacBride of Charlottesville, Va. and David Bergland of Los Angeles, for President and Vice-President), a superb platform, and an excellent set of national officers dedicated to making an indelible Libertarian mark on American political life.

As I see it, the vision animating the new L.P. leadership is a noble and exciting one: the expansion of the L.P. into a major force and influence on American life and on the American political scene. The point is that the L.P. motto, "The Party of Principle", involves two vital and interrelated parts: refining and cleaving to pure libertarian principle, and the spreading of those principles through a competent, professional political party structure. The idea is to expand from local kaffeeklatsches and discussion clubs to a cohesive and coherent party structure that will be as competent and as professional as possible. Only if we expand from a small sect to a cohesive and nationwide political party can we expand our political and public influence and have a decisive impact on public policy. To be taken seriously we must begin to amass votes; increased votes will of course mean increased publicity and expanded impact on the political arena. This does not mean of course that discussions of philosophy and theory are not important; but simply that the main emphasis of a political party must be on running candidates and gaining votes and influence for those libertarian principles.

It is the correct perception of the MacBride team that such a mighty effort is not in the least quixotic: that, on the contrary, the time is ripe for such a great libertarian political effort as never before in this century. As we have repeatedly been asserting in the pages of the Lib. Forum, America is now mired in a multiple, systemic crisis of statism — a crisis, furthermore, which more and more people, from all ideologies and walks of life, are perceiving as the consequence of statism and Big Government. The crisis is systemic: in economics, civil liberties, foreign policy, and the moral attitudes (post-Watergate) toward government itself. Only libertarianism stands ready to provide a consistent, "radical" alternative to the system of policies that has brought us to this unfortunate pass. Already, all of us have seen the attraction that the libertarian ideology and alternative holds for the media, and for citizens in all walks of life. There are a large number of Americans who are yearning for a way out, for a plausible alternative to the present system, and who would flock to our standard if they were only able to learn of our

existence. But to do so they must hear about us, and that can only be done in the context of a dedicated, extensive, professional kind of Presidential campaign, which the MacBride-Bergland ticket is prepared to undertake.

It is, furthermore, the perception of the MacBride team that libertarian ideology is a highly "radical" one — far outside the present political matrix. There are, of course, elements of libertarianism which will appeal to all parts of the ideological and occupational spectrum. But, since our political principles and program are radical, it would be folly indeed to couch those programs in a needlessly radical form. In short, it would needlessly alienate the voters and the public if the L.P. candidates came on like a bunch of "kooks". There is nothing inherently "kooky" or nutty about the content of the libertarian position, radical though it may be; but the mass of the voters will not give us a considered hearing, will not give our ideology a fair chance, if it is needlessly clothed in a bizarre and kooky image. Hence, the great importance, for the libertarian cause, of running Real People as candidates, and of coming on like a real, seagoing political party. This twin policy may be encapsulated in the slogan: "radical in content, 'conservative' in form." This is the only way to lift the L. P. out of the sect status and to make it a major force in American life.

It was a dim perception of, and fierce resistance to, this projected great leap forward of the L. P. that animated the mergence of what might be called—for want of a better term—a Left Opposition at the convention, an Opposition that provided an undercurrent of hostility to the MacBride candidacy, and then erupted in ferocity and hysteria shortly afterward, in opposition to MacBride's endorsed running-mate, Manuel Klausner, publisher of Reason magazine. Whereas MacBride, clearly the superior candidate, won handily over two opponents on the first ballot (by 142 out of 244 votes cast), the Left Opposition arose to limit Klausner to 86 votes and to deadlock the convention. It was an emotional roller-coaster indeed! After the enthusiasm accorded to MacBride's acceptance speech at noon on Saturday, August 30, hysteria and paranoia ran rampant for the remainder of that afternoon and all Saturday night, threatening to split the Party until Dave Bergland flew in from California at the last minute to become the overwhelmingly elected dark horse candidate for Vice-President.

As the Left Opposition arose and created the "firestorm" that Saturday, it animating principles and attitudes became all too clear, attitudes which echoed and expanded the outlook of the Left at the stormy FLP convention in New York, in the Spring of 1974. (For an account of that convention, see "FLP Convention: One Step Forward, One Step Back, " Lib. Forum, April, 1974). Let us examine some of these elements.

First, there was an undercurrent of opposition to MacBride, and later more vocally to Klausner, precisely because they are Real People. MacBride was opposed because he is wealthy—a peculiar position to take

(Continued On Page 2)

597

The LP Convention —

(Continued From Page 1)

for supposed believers in laissez-faire capitalism! Both were reviled because of their obvious competence, articulateness, professionalism, and conservative life-style: the fact that they wear suits and ties. Clearly "un-libertarian" from the point of view of the Left Opposition! What this syndrome starkly reveals is a pervasive egalitarianism, an envy-soaked hatred and distrust of wealth, competence, and ability to function successfully in the real world. In short, what we see in the Left Opposition is some of the ugliest aspects of modern values and attitudes: envy and revulsion against the able and the successful.

Second, and allied to the first, is a bizarre notion of what "libertarian principle" is all about. This is the view that leadership, and exercising the functions of leadership—even in a voluntary organization—is somehow "anti-libertarian" and a "violation of libertarian principle." Only among such a bizarre group would an endorsement of a Vice-Presidential candidate by the selected Presidential candidate of the party prove counter-productive, amidst hysterical charges of "dictatorship" and "rule by a Partyarchy." Once again, this is rampant egalitarianism in action, and a failure to realize that no organization can function except by a division of labor, by selecting competent leaders who are allowed to exercise their leadership function. No organization can function along the lines of egalitarian "participatory democracy" so beloved by the Left Opposition. Such people do not belong in any organization, much less a political party.

Third, and again allied to the other two strands, is a rampant sectarianism that sniffs "abandonment of principle" in every use of strategic intelligence, in any attempt to put forward principle in application to the real world. As the Marxists have long ago discovered, all radical ideological or political movements are apt to suffer from two separate and contrasting grave strategic "deviations": "right opportunism" and "left sectarianism." The right opportunist is ever willing to surrender ideological principle on behalf of coalition with other and larger forces; there are, happily, very few such in the L.P., confined to a tiny handful who wished to coalesce with either the Republican party or with some new conservative third party. Our problem at this convention was with left sectarianism — the view that any use of strategy, any attempt to go beyond mere reiteration of principle among small groups of the already-converted, is somehow a "sellout" of basic principle. It is this group for example, which is incapable of grasping the concept of "radical in content, conservative in form."

Fourth, and closely allied with the third, is another bizarre view by the Left Opposition of what "libertarian principle" is all about. Apart from hostility to the very function of leadership or the division of labor, the Left Opposition is vitally concerned with what it calls "living liberty", or with picking candidates who "exemplify liberty." Now I personally fail to understand what "living" or "exemplifying" liverty is supposed to mean; what it should mean is not being a murderer or a bank-robber, in short, not being an aggressor. Obviously, none of the proposed candidates were in that category. But, to the Left Opposition, "exemplifying liberty" means something else, from not wearing suits and ties to openly engaging in activities deemed illegal (unjustly) by the State. The idea that it is somehow the moral duty of the L.P. to select candidates who engage in such activities can only be considered absurd and bizarre—as is the idea that it somehow "violates libertarian principle" not to select candidates who would distract from libertarian ideology by alienating the public right off the bat. To push the Left Opposition thesis to its absurd — but logically consistent — conclusion, it is as if we say that, in order to prove our sincerity in advocating freedom to sell or ingest heroin, we must therefore nominate for President a junkie who shoots up on television!

Finally, the famous minarchist vs. anarcho-capitalist controversy is only dimy related to the struggle over the Left Opposition. Basically that controversy was happily settled at the Dallas convention in 1974 when it was decided that the L.P. platform should be purely and consistently libertarian, but that no stand should be taken one way or another on archy vs. anarchy, thus fostering a coalition which both sides can live with. Most of the anarchists in the party were not in the Left Opposition. On the other hand, it is true that most of the Left were anarchists with an

ALL FOUNDED

One of the important spinoffs of the L.P. convention was that it provided the occasion for the launching of a new and promising organization: the Association of Libertarian Lawyers. Organized by its President, Don Feder, ALL's founding meeting included 30 attorneys and law students, and offers of support have already been received from 84 attorneys and law students in twenty states and Canada, with student contacts at 17 law schools. Law and politics are intimately related, and the opportunities for important work by libertarian lawyers are almost endless — from trial work to defense of libertarians to scholarly research to formulating a libertarian law code.

Officers of ALL are President Don Feder, an attorney in upstate New York; Vice-President Linda Abrams, a Los Angeles lawyer specializing in civil liberties cases; Secretary Dennis Schuman, a negligence lawyer in New York City; and Treasurer Dolores Grande, legal librarian at John Jay College, New York City.

ALL has decided to have two classes of members: voting members, which includes attorneys, law students, law graduates and legal professionals; and non-voting, associate member. ALL has already

(Continued On Page 3)

important minority of minarchists.

The sort of confusion that cropped up on this issue was exemplified by two accusations hurled at me in the course of the convention. In the midst of pressing (successful) for expanding and radicalizing the L.P. platform (but consistent with both anarchism and laissez-faire) one of the conservative leaders accused me of using "salami tactics" (an old World War II-Cold War slogan) on behalf of committing the Party to anarchism. I replied: "Yes, I'm using salami tactics—to go to laissez-faire!" On the other hand, a day or so later, a Left Opposition delegate accused me of betraying the anarchist cause by nominating for the Executive Committee someone who didn't know what the black flag represented! I tried to reply that the point of the Party was an anarchist-laissez-faire coalition toward our vast range of common goals.

However, I do not mean to dwell excessively on the headaches and heartaches of the convention. The overwhelmingly important point is that the Left Opposition was roundly defeated, and that we have a superb team of national candidates and party officials who have the proper vision of an effective expanded Libertarian Party, and have the professionalism and the competence to achieve these great goals. We have a real Libertarian Party of and for Real People. The kooks, the sectarians, the egalitarians, are destined to fade into the background which they so richly deserve. It is their dim perception of just such a looming fate that undoubtedly accounts for the ferocity of what will turn out to be their Last Hurrah.

A final word about the Platform, which was improved and radicalized simply by applying common libertarian principles to specific and important political issues of the day. Notably, civil liberties provisions were greatly strengthened by an explicit section on repeal of victimless crimes, and by a call for abolition of the FBI and CIA. Isolationist principles were strengthened by urging withdrawal from NATO and all other military alliances, cessation of governmental intervention in the Middle East, and independence for America's colonial possessions. The call for amnesty was expanded to deserters who had volunteered for the armed forces — with a slight weakening due to an erroneous theory of contracts which holds that voluntary slave contracts should be enforced, if only by paying damages (even to the State!)A mild but important plank calling for negotiations toward mutual and general nuclear disarmament was passed after a great deal of opposition. The right of taxpayers to learn about government activities was upheld, with an exception added from the floor for secrets defending the country against invasion. The right of victims to reclaim stolen property was — if rather vaguely —upheld. And Friedmanite elements were eliminated from the platform on behalf of the Austrian, free-market, gold standard position. And a call was added for repeal of the parasitic civil service system, which entrenches a permanent bureaucracy upon the public. All in all, a magnificent platform on which to take our stand. ◻

DEPRESSION AND INFLATION

by
Richard M. Ebeling*

For decades the economics profession has craved recognition as a "true" science. It has desired to cast off the labels of being a "moral science" or a subject concerned with mere theory. Economists have striven to live up to the standard that Science is Measurement. Thus, all theories become only hypotheses that must be empirically tested; and even then they still remain suspect.

The error in this approach is the inability to understand the nature of the subject matter under study. The social sciences deal with complex phenomena involving the purposeful action of conscious entities. Only by gasping and comprehending the meaning of human action and human purpose can the regularity of social phenomena finally be put in a satisfactory paradigm. But this requires that a theory be developed and spun out from the axioms of human action and purpose before the "facts" of the social sciences can be made intelligible. Indeed, this was succinctly summed up by Goethe when he said, "It would be best of all to realize that all that is factual is already theory."

Almost all twentieth century attempts to explain business cycles have used the "empirical" approach. Economists have believed that by gathering data on the movement of prices, outputs and employment levels in different sectors of the economy, as well as the economy as a whole, a pattern will miraculously appear and a theory will "pop out" from the facts.

In the 1920's, one of these "theories" to emerge from the "facts" was the belief in a stable price level. If only the overall aggregate of all prices were not allowed to either rise or fall, then neither inflation nor depression would occur. The death toll of business cycles would finally be sounded. But the beautiful dream turned into a nightmare, when after a decade of monetary manipulation to keep the aggregate level of prices stable, the Great Depression struck in 1929.

Only a handful of economists had questioned the validity of this theory in the 1920's. They were the economists of the Austrian School, in particular Ludwig von Mises and Friedrich von Hayek. An exposition of this theory and its application to explain the phenomena of the 1920's and its aftermath is now once again available with the reprinting of Murray N. Rothbard's definitive work on **America's Great Depression** (Sheed and Ward, Kansas City and New York, 1975), $4.95 (paper) or $12.00 hard cover. The volume is the first in a series on Austrian Economics being sponsored by the Institute for Humane Studies (Menlo Park, Ca.).

Monetary manipulation by central bank authorities is the key to an understanding of Austrian Theory of the Business Cycle. On the free market, a banking system acts as the equilibrator of the desires of savers and investors. The consumer decides how much of his income he wishes to spend on present consumption and how much he wishes to save for future consumption. That part which is saved is lent out to businessmen by bankers and "invested in a mighty structure of capital, in various orders of production." This "mighty structure" is either longer or shorter depending on how much resources (i. e. how much savings) are available to build more and more complex investment projects able to produce larger quantities of consumer goods at some point in the future.

If, however, the banking system is able to expand credit without an equivalent amount of savings, then "Bunsinessmen . . . are misled by the bank inflation into believing that the supply of saved funds is greater than it really is." The availability of larger amounts of credit at a lower interest rate will induce producers to carry out new investment projects. They will use the money to bid for resources and labor. But as the new money is received as income, the recipients will most likely spend it in their "old consumption/investment proportions" and demand will shift back to consumer goods, thus raising their value and price in relation to capital goods industries. With the resources now bid away from them, businessmen will not be able to complete investment projects they have begun.

As Professor Rothbard concludes, "businessmen were misled by bank credit inflation to invest too much in . . . capital goods" and these investments "are seen to have been wasteful." Thus, the "boom" "is. . .a period of wasteful investment . . . The 'crisis' arrives when the consumers . . . restablish their desired consumption-savings patterns." And "The 'depression' is . . . the process by which the economy adjusts to the wastes and errors of the boom."

This, in fact, was the exact path the boom of the twenties took. In July, 1921, the money supply was $45.3 billion. By July, 1929 it had increased by $28.0 billion, or 61.8% over the eight year period. Since at the beginning of the period currency in circulation totalled $3.68 billion and at the end of the period totatalled $3.64 billion, "The entire monetary expansion took place in money substitutes, which are products of credit expansion." Between 1921 and 1925 alone the Federal Reserve allowed total bank reserves to expand by 35.6%. "Thus the prime factor in generating the inflation of the 1920's was the increase in total bank reserves." The mechanisms used by the Fed for this expansion were primarily the rediscount rate (the rate of interest at which member banks may borrow from the Fed) which was constantly kept below the goint market interest rate during the period; Bills Bought (banker acceptances) through open-market operations; and, to a lesser extent, U. S. government securities, which were also manipulated through open-market purchases.

This was a relative inflation rather than an absolute one, for the price level, as measured by several prominent indexes of the day, remained relatively constant. As Professor Rothbard points out, "Federal Reserve credit expansion . . . managed to keep the price level stable in the face of an increasing productivity that would, in a free and unhampered market, have led to falling prices and spread of increased living standards for everyone . . .".

And, as expected from the Austrian Theory of the Business Cycle, the inflation induced a disporportionate increase in the capital goods industries. Rothbard shows that both wages and prices of the capital goods industries were bid up significantly in relation to other sectors of the economy during the boom. Once the bust set in, they were the prices to fall, not only absolutely, but relatively as well, in comparison with consumer goods industries. Thus, the Austrian analysis of boom-induced

(Continued On Page 4)

All Founded —

(Continued From Page 2)

established several important standing committees.

Ralph Fucetola, a New Jersey lawyer and long-standing libertarian, heads the Consitution and By-Laws Committee, which will also formulate a statement of principles for the Association, setting forth its support of economic freedom and its opposition to victimless crime laws and to state monopolies in the practice of law. Linda Abrams is chairing a Litigation Committee, which plans to file amicus curiae brief in important cases, and to explore the use of the judicial system to expand individual liberty. Manuel Klausner, Los Angeles attorney and publisher of **Reason** magazine, heads the Law Review Committee, which hopes to begin publishing a libertarian law journal. Randy E. Barnett, a second year student at Harvard Law School, is chairman of the Law School Organizing Committee, which will organize law students. And Stanton Towne, a student at Columbia Law School, heads a Committee on Educational Conferences and Seminars. And last but not least, ALL is planning to publish a bi-monthly newsletter, to be edited by Dennis Schuman, to keep members informed about the Association's activities.

The **Lib. Forum** extends heartiest best wishes to the new organization, and wishes it a long and successful life. All those interested in information or membership in the Association of Libertarian Lawyers should contact:

Don Feder, 102 W. 1st Avenue, Johnstown, N.Y. 12095.   ◨

ROTHBARDIANA

Several books and contributions to books by Murray N. Rothbard have recently been published. One is **Conceived in Liberty, Volume II**, subtitled "Salutary Neglect: The American Colonies in the First Half of the Eighteenth Century." (Arlington House, $12.95). This book brings the saga of American colonial history from approximately 1710 to the end of the French and Indian War in 1763. One of the highlights of the book is the beginning of Benjamin Franklin Revisionism, Rothbard regarding Franklin as one of the major monsters of the American colonial period.

Also, the 3rd Edition of **America's Great Depression** has just been published by Sheed & Ward, including a new introduction by Rothbard — in hard cover ($12) and paperback editions ($4.95). (See the review by Richard Ebeling in this issue of the **Lib. Forum**.)

Moreover, Free Life Editions of New York City has done a great service to libertarian scholarship by reprinting the first libertarian essay in modern political thought: Etienne de La Boetie's **Discourse on Voluntary Servitude.** (The title of this edition: **The Politics of Obedience: The Discourse of Voluntary Servitude**). The book is paperback at a price of $2.95. There is a lengthy introduction essay by Murray Rothbard, "The Political Thought of Etienne de La Boetie."

Other recent contributions to published books are: "Gold vs. Fluctuating Fiat Exchange Rates", in H. Sennholz, ed., **Gold is Money** (West port, Conn.: Greenwood Press), a critique of the Friedmanite policy of fluctuating fiat exchange rates. "Devotion to Truth", **Tribute to Mises** (Kent, Eng.: Mont Pelerin Society), in a group of memorial tributes to Mises delivered at the Mont Pelerin meeting in Brussels, summer 1974.

Depression And Inflation —
(Continued From Page 3)

capital malinvestment was clearly shown.

Having stimulated a misdirection of resources that differed from actual demand, Austrian Theory would have the policy implication of allowing labor and capital to readjust as best it could, so a healthy recovery could begin. Instead, as Rothbard chronicles, the Hoover Administration immediately began sponsoring government-led programs to keep all wages and prices from falling to preserve purchasing power. Between 1929 to 1933, the index of durable (capital goods) manufactures fell 77%, while nondurable (consumer goods) manufactures fell only 30%. But between 1929-1933, wages fell only 23%. "Therefore, real wage rates, for the workers still remaining employed, actually increased." And this at a time when unemployment reached 25% in 1932-1933 and up to 47% in selected manufacturing industries. Professor Rothbard also relates the infusion of giant public works projects, state and Federal, and the notorious Reconstruction Finance Corporation used to prop up inefficient, bankrupt businesses that should have been liquidated following the boom. As Rothbard points out, "if we define 'New Deal' as an anti-depression program marked by extensive governmental economic planning and intervention . . . Hoover must be considered the founder of the New Deal in America."

In a new introduction for the volume, Rothbard analyzes the present economic milieu and concludes, "The current inflationary depression has revealed to the nation's economists that their cherished theories — adopted and applied since the 1930's — are tragically and fundamentally incorrect."

These "cherished theories" were developed by John Maynard Keynes and his followers during the Great Depression. The errors in the Keynesian-Macro approach are given a devastating critique by the leading Austrian Economist and 1974 Nobel Laureate Friedrich von Hayek in a new three-essay booklet entitled **Full Employment at Any Price?** (Institute of Economic Affairs, London, July 1975), L1.00.

Two of the essays discuss "Inflation, the Misdirection of Labour, and Unemployment" and "No Escape: Unemployment Must Follow Inflation." Professor Hayek explains that modern theories of what causes unemployment are totally wrong. That, the "true . . . explanation of extensive unemployment . . . (is) . . . a discrepancy between the distribution of labor (and the other factors of production) between industries (and localities) and the distribution of demand among their products." Thus, if demand shifts for different goods and services and the relative prices and wages do not, in turn, adjust to reflect the new market conditions, then those resources (including labor) which attempt to demand prices and wages above their market value will become unemployed.

But rather than admit the true cause of the problem, the Keynesians have developed the theory "that unemployment is predominantly due to an insufficiency of aggregate demand compared with the total of wages which would have to be paid if all workers were to be employed at current rates." But this is nothing but the businessman's "age-old belief" that prosperity is dependent on keeping consumer demand high," against which economic theory had been arguing for generations."

The mistaken idea in this concept, made by both Keynesians **and** Monetarists, is to look only upon how monetary expansion affects the general price level for goods and services "and not to the effects on the structure of relative prices." The expansion of money and credit leads to changes in the **relative** strength of demand for different goods and services and "these changes in relative demand must lead to further changes in relative prices and consequent changes in the direction of production and the allocation of the factors of production, including labor." Once having been drawn into particular productive activities by this artificially created demand any "slowing down or cessation of the inflation" will result in the unemployment of these resources and labor. The choice is then not inflation or unemployment, but the realization that once inflation has misdirected economic factors of production, some of them will have to be temporarily unemployed when the inflation is ended. Professor Hayek pointed out that, "As had happened at the beginning of the period of modern finance we have again been seduced by another silver-tongued persuader into trying another inflationary bubble." Now that the bubble has burst and the disastrous consequences of macro-oriented policy have become visible, the Keynesians, having "thoroughly discredited themselves . . . ought to do penance in sackcloth and ashes."

The third essay is Professor Hayek's Nobel Lecture on "The Pretence of Knowledge," in which he elaborates further his now famous critique of "Scientism," the misuse of certain scientific methods in the social sciences. In the natural sciences, Hayek points out, we deal with events which are "directly observable and measurable." Our concern is centered around observed pheneomena involving "comparatively few variables — either particular events or relative frequencies of events." But in the social sciences, we attempt to formulate a "theory of complex phenomena" referring to "to a large number of particular facts," all of which would have to be ascertained before predictions could be made. But social phenomena, being so complex and being concerned with purposive human action, can never be measured and quantitatively determined like natural phenomena. Hayek critizes macro-economic theory for its attempt to guide policy based on the statistical relationship between monetary expenditure and employment. The Keynesians, always looking for measurable empirical relationships, fail to understand the micro-level misallocation of resources their policy brings about.

The "superiority of the market order" is precisely its ability to use "more of the knowledge of particular facts which exists only dispersed among uncounted persons, than any one person can possess." And, Hayek concludes, if the "scientistic" approach is applied for social planning and policy, man "may well . . . destroy a civilization which no brain has designed, but which has grown from the free efforts of millions of individuals."

ON THE WOMEN'S LIBERATION
OR
The Male Chauvinist Pig As Hero

by
Walter Block*

The women's liberation movement is an amalgam of different types of programs; it is composed of very different kinds of people, many with very different purposes. It should occasion no surprise, therefore, that the discriminating intellect may accept only some of the aims, purposes, motivations, and programs of women's liberation, and reject others. It can only be folly to treat as equivalent a whole host of different values and attitudes, merely because they have been packaged together. An enemy of women's liberation in one area need not necessarily reject the contentions of the women's movement in all areas. In this paper, I shall divide the views of the women's liberation movement into three broad categories, each of which will be treated quite differently.

I. Coercive actions taken against women

Perhaps the most coercive action taken against women apart from murder is rape. Yet in this male dominated society of ours, rape is not even always illegal. For instance rape is not illegal when perpetrated upon a woman by her husband! Although rape is illegal outside of the "sanctity" of mariage, the way in which it is punished leaves much to be desired. For one thing, if there was any previous acquaintance between the rapist and his victim, the presumption of the court is that there was no rape. For another, it is necessary, in order to prove rape, that there have been a witness to the proceedings. Also, if the rapist can get several of his friends to swear that they have had sexual intercourse with the victim, so that the woman can be characterized as "immoral", it is virtually impossible to obtain punishment. If the victim is a prostitute, it is just as impossible to obtain a conviction for rape. The reasoning behind the legal inability to rape a prostitute seems to be the ludicrous one that it is impossible to compel a person to do that which she (or he) does willingly (at other times). As if no one had ever forced a doctor or any other service professional to do that which he does willingly at other times!

The prevention of prostitution by the civil powers is another case of coercive action taken against women. It is a case of prohibiting trade between mutually consenting adult business partners. It is harmful to women in that it prevents them from earning an honest living. It is spiteful and discriminatory in that although prostitution is just as illegal for the customer as for the seller, it is a rare case indeed in which the male customer is also arrested, in addition to the female seller, for the "crime" of engaging in prostitution.

Abortion is another case in point. Although in this modern day and age inroads are finally being made on this age-long prohibition, abortion is still ringed in by compulsory rules. Outright prohibition of abortion and the present looser controls both deny the great moral principle of self-ownership. They are both a throwback to the old days of slavery, where barriers were put up between people and ther complete and utter right of self ownership. If a woman fully owns her body (and what else is a complete denial of slavery?) then she owns her womb. This follows directly from the laws of logic once it is admitted that the womb is part of the body. But if she owns her womb, then she has the complete and full right to determine what shall live in it and what shall not. She has the complete right to decide which parasitical growths she shall allow to live there and which she shall not. And only she has this right. Since infringements upon abortion are a denial of this right, they amount to (partial) slavery.

Until very recently women did not have the same rights as men to own property or to engage in contracts; there are still laws on the books, however, that prevent married women, but not married men, from selling property or engaging in business without the permission of their spouses. Women must pass stiffer entrances requirements than men for some state universities. Then there is the infamous tracking system

engendered by our public school system which shunts young boys into "male" activities like sports and shop and shunts young girls into the "female" roles of cooking and sewing. Perhaps the most embarrassing type of aggressive activity which women have to put up with is the pinches they meet with on the streets of our cities.

It is important to realize that the problems listed above all have two things in common; they are all instances of aggressive force being used against women; and they are all inextricably bound up with the apparatus of the state. Let us dwell on this point a bit, since except for the case of rape, it is by no means obvious to most people that this claim is true. This is easy to show in the case of prostitution. For it is the state that declares prostitution illegal and then proceeds to use force against those who peacefully go about the legitimate business of prostitution. And it is the state that uses the compulsion of the jail sentence in order to enforce its will. What does it mean to say that women do not have the right to abort, or to own property, or to set up businesses? It means no more and no less than that if women were to persist in their attempts to abort, own property, or set up businesses, then the state will step in with compulsions, fines, or jail sentences.

In order to see why discrimination by the state amounts to compulsion (as in higher entrance requirements for the state university, the tracking system in the public schools, etc.) we may compare this to private discrimination, which does not amount to compulsion. When a private individual discriminates, he (or she) does so with his (or her) own resources, in his (or her) own name. When the state discriminates, it does so with resources taken from all of us. It does so in the name of all of us. In the name and with the resources of those discriminated in favor of as well as those discriminated against. Now surely here is a crucial difference. It is one thing to discriminate against someone with your own resources, but it is quite another thing to discriminate against people with their own money. Moreover, if a private enterprise such as a school discriminates, it runs the real risk of losing money and going bankrupt. At least all people who oppose discrimination have the chance to withhold funds, and to not patronize the discriminating enterprise. When the state discriminates, it is altogether different. The state enterprise that discriminates runs no real risk of going bankrupt. If people who oppose its discrimination withhold their funds from it, i.e. do not patronize it as students as in the case of a state university, this will not force an end to the discrimination. The state enterprise can make up for the short-fall in voluntary funds with funds from tax revenues; and these must be paid under threat of compulsion.

Even the pinches that women must put up with are inextricably bound up with the state apparatus. We may see this point by contrasting two different cases of pinching: one that takes place within the confines of a private place like Macy's Department Store and one that takes place outside — for instance, on the street, a block away from Macy's. When a pinch takes place within the confines of a private place, the whole force of the profit-and-loss free enterprise system comes to bear to solve the problem. For it is always in some entrepreneur's self interest to apprehend and discourage the pinching (on the assumption that women do not want to get pinched; for the case of masochistic women who enjoy being pinched, this program of protection against pinching will not be in the self interest of the entrepreneur). The reason that it is in the self interest of the entrepreneur to initiate a program to stop the pinching is that if he does not, and the pinching continues, he will lose customers to competitors. There will be a competition, as it were, on the part of all department stores, to provide this anti-pinching service. The ones that

(Continued On Page 6)

601

Woman's Liberation Movement —

(Continued From Page 5)

succeed in ridding their stores of this scourge to the greatest degree will tend to reap the greatest profits. The ones who fail, whether because they ignore the problem entirely, or are unsuccessful in implementing their programs, will tend to make the greatest losses. This is not guaranteed to end pinching once and for all time. There will always be some as long as people remain imperfectly moral. All this system will do is to encourage, by profits and losses, those who are most able to end pinching. While it is not a perfect system, (what human system can ever be perfect?), it would be folly to underestimate its effects, especially as time goes on.

Contrasted with what occurs in the public domain, however, this private system begins to look like perfection itself. For in the public domain, there is almost the complete absence of any incentive whatsoever to end the pinching. There is no one who automatically loses any paying customers whenever there is an outbreak of pinching. The city police are supposedly charged with ending this epidemic of pinching. But they must function without benefit of the automatic profit and loss incentive system. Their salaries, coming from taxation, are not tied to their performance. They suffer no financial loss from every pinch. Is it any wonder, then, that most of this type of harassment occurs on the streets and sidewalks of a city, and not within its shops and stores?

II. Non-coercive actions taken against women

Another type of pinching or sexual harassment is that between a secretary and her boss. Although to many people, and especially to many people in the women's liberation movement, there is no real difference between this pinching and the pinching that occurs on the street, the fact is that the pinching that takes place between a secretary and her boss, while objectionable to many women, is not a coercive action. It is not a coercive action like the pinching that takes place in the public sphere because it is part of a package deal: the secretary agrees to all aspects of the job when she agrees to accept the job and especially when she agrees to keep the job. A woman walking along a public sidewalk, on the other hand, can by no means be considered to have given her permission, or tacitly agreed to begin pinched. The street is not the complete private property of the pincher, as is the office. On the contrary, if the myths of democracy are to be given any credence at all, the streets belong to the people. All the people. Even including women.

There is a serious problem with considering pinching or sexual molestation in a privately owned office or store to be coercive. If an action is really and truly coercive, it ought to be outlawed. But if pinching and sexual molestation are outlawed in private places, this violates the rights of those who voluntarily wish to engage in such practices. And there is certainly nothing coercive about any voluntary sex practices between consenting adults. The proof of the voluntary nature of an act in a private place is that the person endangered (the woman, in the cases we have been considering) has no claim whatsoever to the private place in question, the office or the store. If she continues to patronize or work at a place where she is molested, it can only be voluntary. But in a public place, no such presumption exists. As we have seen, according to accepted theory at least, the public domain is owned by all, women included. It would be just as illegitimate to assume that a woman gave tacit agreement to being molested on the public street because she was walking there as it would be to assume that she gave tacit agreement to an assult in her own house, because she happened to be there.

There are many other cases of actions taken against women that are not strictly speaking, coercive. Or more exactly, there are many other instances where many women feel put upon, but where there is no coercion at all involved: such as referring to women with sex organ-linked expletives; the sexual double standard mores; many rules of etiquette, such as the ones concern who proceeds whom out of the elevator; the encouragement of the mental capacity of boys and discouragement of girls; the societal opprobrium of women participating in "men's" athletic activities; the pedestals that women are placed upon. There are two important points to be made with regard to these insults and other exacerbations which do not constitute coercion. 1) Although considered reprehensible by many, none of these actions actually constitute coercion; therefore it would be illegitimate to outlaw them. Any attempt to outlaw them would involve the mass violation of rights of other individuals in the society. After all, it is the right of free speech that gives us the right not to utter things that everyone agrees with — which do not need free speech protection in any case, but the right to utter reprehensible things, things in poor taste, boorish things. 2) To a much greater degree than realized by many, certainly to a much greater degree than realized by many who consider themselves advocates of women's liberation, these reprehensible but non-coercive actions are engendered by reprehensible coercive activities. Were these coercive activites to cease, the free market would tend to rid us of many of these reprehensible but non-coercive acts.

Let us consider the case of bosses pinching secretaries and see how the market would tend to eliminate such unwanted activity, were the coercive and reprehensible activity of taxation to support government bureaucracy eliminated. In order to see this, we must first understand what the labor economist calls "compensating differentials". A compensating differential is an amount of money just necessary to compensate an employee for the psychic losses that go with a job. For instance, consider two job opportunities. One is in an air-conditioned office, with a good view, with pleasant surroundings and pleasant companions: The other is in a damp, dank basement, surrounded by evil-smelling fellow workers. Now there is some wage differential large enough to attract most people into accepting the less pleasant job. This will vary for different people, depending upon their relative tastes for the working conditions in the two places. There might even be a negative compensating differential for those who prefer the basement job. They would be willing to take a salary cut rather than move to the office job.

The same analysis can be applied to the case of the office pincher. On the assumption that all women would prefer not to be pinched, and that bosses vary in their desires to so indulge, there will be a whole range of wage rates paid to otherwise equally productive secretaries, depending on the proclivity of their bosses to engage in sexual harassment. There will be a positive relationship between the amount of sexual harassment and the wage rate that the bosses find thay must pay. But now contrast the boss of a private business with the boss in a government bureaucracy. Even on the assumption that both bosses on the average have the same proclivity to engage in sexual harassment, it is clear that the private boss will have to pay for his little gambols, while the public one will not. The secretaries of both private and public pinchers will have to earn more than the secretaries of the non-pinchers. The compensating differential. The main difference between the private and the public pincher is that the extra money comes out of tax monies for the latter and out of his own money for the former. Even in the case of a private boss-pincher who is not the ultimate owner of the business, the same applies, only now slightly more indirectly. The ultimate owner of the business, in addition to losing money if he himself is a pincher, also loses money if any of his executives are pinchers. So in addition to having a monetary incentive to cut down on his own pinching, he also has a monetary incentive to try to stop all the bosses in his company from so doing.

This might not seem like much of an incentive to stop pinching. But it is an improvement over the public case where these disincentives are completely lacking. This way of looking at the problem, however, has more merit than might be readily apparent. One reason pinching does not come to an abrupt end even in the private market is because many women are by no means unalterably opposed to being pinched, as we have been assuming. But the analysis can be applied to the more realistic cases where women are being harassed and mistreated and do object.

III. The male chauvinist pig as hero
In this section I wish to consider in some detail, several grievous errors committed by the adherents of women's liberation. It is for his good sense in opposing these programs tha the male chauvinist pig can be considered a hero.

1. Laws compelling "equal wages for equal work". The klinker in this program, of course, is, How shall "equal work" be defined? If equal work means equal work in all senses, relative to the productivity that an employer can get out of an employee, in the short run as well as in the long run, taking account of psychic differentials, the discrimination of customers and other workers, of the ability of the worker to mesh in with the likes and dislikes, the foibles and the idiosyncrasies of the entrepreneur, in short, if equal work is exactly the same thing as equal profitability for the entrepreneur, then in the free market workers with

(Continued On Page 7)

Woman's Liberation Movement —
(Continued From Page 6)

such equal abilities will tend to earn equal wages. If equal workers in this sense were not paid equally, for instance, if women were paid less than men even though they were equally good workers in this sense, this would set up incentives on the part of entrepreneurs which, when carried to their conclusion, would ensure equal pay. How would this work? The entrepreneur would be able to make extra money by replacing male workers with female workers. By hypothesis, the employer will be able to pay the woman less than the man and yet earn just as much from her work as from the man's work. The conclusion is inescapable. The employer will have a great incentive to fire men and hire women in their places.

Even supposing that there were employers who under no circumstances would hire women to do "men's" work, and still other employers who would only do so if the wage differential rose to a certain amount (thus only ensuring that the wage differential between men and women could not rise above a certain figure) there will still be great forces pushing the free market toward equality between men's and women's wage rates. Even if there were only a very small percentage of entrepreneurs willing to supplant men with women, this would be the case. We must realize that every employer who substituted a woman for a man would have a competive advantage over the ones who refused to do so. The profit maximizing employers would continually earn greater profits than would the discriminatory employers. The profit maximizers would be able to undersell the discriminators, take away their businesses, and, other things being equal, eventually drive them into bankruptcy.

We can have no guarantee that the wages of men and and women will ever acutally come to exact equality. This process only guarantees that there will be enormous pressure exerted, day in and day out, pushing the economy toward this end. On the assumption, that is, of identically equal productivity.

In actual point of fact, however, the proponents of equal wages for equal work have no such strict equality in mind. What they seem to have in mind in their definition of equality is equal years of schooling equivalent college degrees, and perhaps similar scores on qualification tests. But people with vastly differing abilities to earn profits for employers can be virtually identical with respect to such criteria. For example, consider two workers, one male, one female, identical as far as test scores and college degrees are concerned. It is an indisputable fact that in the event of a pregnancy, it is far more likely for the woman to stay home and raise the child. Now we are not considering whether this is fair or not. Only whether it is factual or not. But if the woman stays at home, interrupting a career in midstream, she will be worth less to the employer's likelihood of profitability. In this case, at any one moment in time, the workers might well be identical as far as profit criteria are concerned. But in the long run view, which counts very heavily in present wage considerations, it is the man who is more productive than the woman.

Paradoxically, many pieces of evidence supporting the view that supposedly equally productive men and women are not at all equal come from the womens lib movement itself. Several studies have shown that while it might be true that samples of women had higher innate abilities than given samples of men when the two groups were tested in isolation from each other, when the two groups were tested together or in competition with each other, the men invariably did relatively better than the woman, and in many cases did absolutely better than the women. Again, let it be emphasized that we are not here concerned with the fairness of such occurrences; but with the effects of such situations when coupled with laws compelling equal pay for "equal work". The point is that in the world of work women will often find themselves in competition with men. If they constantly defer to the men, and cannot do their best in competition with men, they may well be of less help in procuring profits for the entrepreneur than men. And if women otherwise equal to men in test scores and such are really inferior to them when it comes to strict profit maximizing, then the equal pay for equal work law will prove disastrous for women.

It will prove disastrous to women because now the profit maximizing incentives will be all turned around. Instead of the market exerting a strong steady push toward firing men and hiring women in their place,

which tends to drive the wages of women toward equality with men, the market will give incentives to employers to fire women and hire men in their place. This will have exactly the opposite effect on wage equality. The employer, required to pay men and women the same wages, will be able to increase profits to the degree that he can supplant the highly productive men (from who he can make a profit) for the lesser productive women (from whom he now cannot make a profit or as much of a profit). Just as in the other case, employers who refuse to go along with this, perhaps out of a desire not to pay women less than men for "equal work", will tend to make lower profits and to be undersold and sent into bankruptcy by the other firms who stick to their profit maximimizing behavior. The end result will be that instead of unleashing forces toward the equalization of wages, the "equal pay for equal work" doctrine will cause instead the unemployment of women. To the extent that the male-chauvinist pig resists such a trend, he can only be counted a hero.

2. Laws compelling non-discrimination. McSorleys is a bar in New York City that used to cater exclusively to men. Until it was "liberated", that is. Under the banner of the new anti-discrimination law in New York State, hordes of presumably thirsty women trooped in to be served for the first time in the history of the establishment. This event was hailed as a great progressive step forward by our liberal, progressive, and womens liberation factions. The basic philosophy behind the law and the attendant liberation of McSorleys seems to be that it shall be illegitimate to discriminate on a sexual basis when choosing customers or people to deal with.

If the problems with this philosophy are not readily apparent, they can be made so by considering several reductions ad absurdum. A strict application of the philosophy, for instance, would not allow separate bathrooms for men at "public" places; it would not allow men's residence halls. More shockingly, at least to the "progressive"

(Continued On Page 8)

Woman's Liberation Movement—
(Continued From Page 7)

community, it would not even allow exclusive homosexuality. For in all these cases, there is discrimination with respect to women. Women are discriminated against. By not allowing women in men's bathrooms. By not allowing women in men's residence halls. By the male homosexual choosing only other males instead of females. This philosophy would not allow women to marry men, moreover. For, women who only consider marrying men discriminate just as assuredly as do homosexuals: they discriminate against other women whom they could have married, had they not been so hung up on men, and discriminatory. The philosophy thus also leads to compulsory lesbianism.

Of course all of these cases are "ridiculous". Ridiculous in the sense that hardly any of the proponents of the liberation of McSorleys would go along with them. But for all that, these cases are fully consistent with the philosophy they are based on is ridiculous.

It is important to realize that all of human action implies discrimination in the only sensible definition of that much abused term: picking and choosing, out of all the alternatives available, that one which, in the chooser's own opinion, best serves his interests. There is no action taken by human beings which fails to accord with this dictum. We discriminate when we choose a tooth paste, when we decide upon a means of transportation, when we decide to marry; the discrimination practiced by the gourmet or wine taster is and can only be the discrimination practiced by all human beings, although carried to a degree not attainable without much hard labor. Any attack upon discrimination, therefore, can only be interpreted as an attack upon the choice inherent in human action; as an attempt to restrict the options open to human beings.

But what of the choice on the part of women to drink at McSorleys that is closed off by discrimination? This is identical to the choice closed off to the man by the woman who rejects his sexual favors. The woman who refuses to date a man is no more guilty of violating his rights than is a group of men who wish to drink in the company of members of their own sex guilty of violating women's rights. In neither case do these rights exist, because they are the rights of other people. It is only in a slave society that this is not so. It is only in a slave society that the master can compel the slave to do his bidding without closing off any of the options of the slave, because, by definition, the slave has no options. To the extent, then, that the antidiscriminatory forces succeed in foisting their philosophy upon the general public, they also succeed in foisting upon the general public the cloven hoof of slavery. And to the extent that the male chauvinist pig succeeds in holding back these forces of barbarism, he must again be counted as a hero.

*Walter Block is associate professor of economics at Rutgers University.

"No chapter of history is steeped further in blood than the history of colonialism. Blood was shed uselessly and senselessly. Flourishing lands were laid waste; whole peoples destroyed and exterminated. All this can in no way be extenuated or justified. The dominion of Europeans in Africa and in important parts of Asia is absolute. It stands in the sharpest contrast to all the principles of liberalism and democracy, and there can be no doubt that we must strive for its abolition." — Ludwig von Mises, **The Free and Prosperous Commonwealth**.

Published Every Month. Subscription Rates: $8.00 Per Year; $15.00 Two Years

A Monthly Newsletter

THE
Libertarian Forum

Joseph R. Peden, Publisher   Murray N. Rothbard, Editor

VOLUME VIII, NO. 10   OCTOBER, 1975   US-ISSN0047-4517

THE SINAI TRAP

Super-K is back, and the Sinai Pact has received all the adulation that the Establishment, from President Ford on down, can bestow. We are once again being told that "peace" has been virtually achieved in the Middle East. For a small chunk of Sinai territory given back by Israel to Egypt, the United States has surrendered a great deal. How much precisely is not known, amid the raft of "secret" and quasisecret assurances being given by the U.S. to Israel. One certain loss is $3 billion of U.S. taxpayer aid in one year, most of it to Israel, along with some non-military aid to Egypt. According to Jack Anderson, however, secret agreements push up the bill to the staggering sum of $15 billion!

The risk of war in the Middle East is further accelerated by the multi-billion dollar American-financed buildup of the Israeli war machine. But even more ominous is the famous agreement by the U.S. to supply 200 "technicians" on the front line to monitor an attack from either side. The admitted fact that the "technicians" will be CIA and other U.S. intelligence agents — and the ominous parallel with our CIA "technicians" in Vietnam is laughed off as of no consequence. On the contrary, it means that U.S. government agents will be front-line hostages to any war that breaks out, thus insuring American entry into the next conflict, and the menace of a new World III. All this for a small chunk of the Sinai desert!

The only hopeful sign in the expected Congressional endorsement of the Pact is the strong and cogent opposition that developed to the measure; for once, Congress was not totally supine to the combined lobbying of the Administration and organized Zionism. In fact, a new and hopeful left-right coalition came together in the Senate against the Pact, including such liberal Democrats as Joseph Binden of Delaware and Dick Clark, majority leader Mike Mansfield of Montana, and old Rightists Carl Curtis and Roman Hruska of Nebraska. A new isolationist coalition seems to be in the making. Thus, liberal Democrat Senator James Abourezk of South Dakota warned that "the days should be over when the Secretary of State and the President can be allowed to shoot dice under a blanket, where they are the only ones allowed to see the dice. That kind of policy has cost us far too much in the past."

The most effective opposition in Washington against the Sinai Pact came from former Undersecretary of State George Ball, never known for any isolationist or pro-Arab proclivities. Ball warned that, far from a step toward Mid-East peace, the Pact would be interpreted by the other Arab countries (let alone the Palestinians) as a sell-out, would bring war on the part of Syria and the others closer, and would make Israel more intrasigent, relieved as it is from pressure from its strongest Arab opponent. Ball concluded that the Pact has frozen "a situation that is inherently unstable and explosive, while engaging America more deeply as a guarantor." At least there is a possibility that the organized opposition will slow down further American involvement in the Middle East. (See, for example, the articles by Leslie Gelb and by Bernard Gwertzman in the New York Times for Sept. 21 and October 7.)

One part of George Ball's forecast has already come true: the Arab unity forged at Rabat in October, 1974 has already been shattered by the Sinai Pact. Syria has already taken the unprecedented step of openly denouncing Egypt on the floor of the United Nations. And Egypt has silenced the Voice of Palestine radio station in Cairo, operated by the PLO. and substituted its own pro-Kissinger propaganda for the Palestinian attacks on the Sinai agreement.

In retrospect, in fact, it is clear that the Sinai Pact was only the final step in the shattering of the Spirit of Rabat, in which all the Arab countries united behind the Palestine Liberation Organization. The support for the PLO by its old enemy King Hussein of Jordan, had been literally purchased by King Faisal of Saudi Arabia; Faisal, a conservative and no particular friend of the Palestinians, was moved by his long-standing and ever-increasing desire to recover Jerusalem for the Moslem religion. The critical change came with the assassination last winter of King Faisal, by yet another "lone nut". (See the excellent article by Russell Stetler, "Whatever Happened to Arab Unity?" International Bulletin, Oct. 10, 1975). In the name of continuing Faisal's policies, his successors have dropped the old cry of "Liberate Jerusalem" and have put up hundreds of millions to up-grade Hussein's war machine, including jets and missiles. In a three-cornered deal, the Ford Administration drove through Congress a $350 million supply of 14 anti-aircraft missle systems to Jordan, to be paid for by Saudi Arabia. When some of the pro-Israeli bloc in Congress objected, the Ford Administration let it be known that Jordan was going to be on the American-Israeli side. Indeed, Hussein, in his tour of the United States last August, repeatedly assured reporters that the Palestinian guerrillas "will never be allowed to enter this country again."

What's next in the Middle East? The next sticking-point is Syria, far harder-nosed than Egypt, and co-belligerent in the October War of 1973. Israel is still sitting on a large chunk of the strategic Syrian Golan Heights, where Israeli artillery is within range of the Syrian capital of Damascus. Kissinger's next task is to try to pressure Syria into negotiations with Israel and to concluding its own agreement with Israel — thereby isolating the Palestinians. Syria, feeling isolated by the Egyptian separate peace, has refused to negotiate on Golan, and has rejected all "partial" solutions to the Middle East. For its part, Israel has declared that it will not surrender Golan, and Kissinger has had the brass to hint at a meaningless three-kilometer withdrawal of Israel from the Golan front (less than two miles!) Syria's President Hafez Assad bluntly told the New York Times, Sept. 28, that "If I held a referendum for my people on a three-kilometer withdrawal, it wouldn't get ten votes. We can do without the three kilometers till the time Israel withdraws from all of Golan." Furthermore, Assad declared once again on October 6 that he would not enter into negotiations on Golan unless there were simultaneous negotiations between Israel and the PLO — which Israel has shown no signs whatever of doing.

The UN peacekeeping force on the Golan expires on November 30, which may well prove a danger date in the Middle East. A key question is: will Syria, now again at odds with Egypt, Jordan, and Saudi Arabia, agree to abandon the PLO in exchange for a possible Kissinger-induced Israeli agreement to withdraw from the Golan? It will be a test of Syria's mettle. If such an agreement does take place, there will be short-run peace on both military fronts in the Middle East, but a continuing festering of the most important problem in the area: the problem of the Palestinians.   ◻

IS THE GRASS ANY GREENER . . . ?

Review of **The Australian Alternative**; by Laura and Odie B. Faulk, Arlington House,
New Rochelle, N. Y. 1975. $7.95.

In both liberatarian and conservative circles, it is not uncommon to hear people express their frustration with the political and social ills of America by threatening to escape to some other more congenial land — a favorite being Australia. Few Americans have actually been there, its distance and the cost of reaching it being a great barrier to tourism. But we have become familiar with it through novels and films; the sheep ranches, rough and tumble mining towns, incomparable beaches and surf, strange flora and fauna, mysterious aborigines, and the colorfully different yet familiarly Anglo-Saxon language and cultural heritage.

Prof. Odie Faulk of the Oklahoma State University and his wife and children decided to spend three months of his sabbatical leave touring the various provinces of Australia with the particular goal in mind of assessing whether emigration to the "Land Down Under" was a solution to any American's unhappiness with his own society. Faulk is a conservative politically, and to some extent culturally as well. He is smugly happy to hear that an Australian politician advocating a modification of Australia's policy of racial exclusion of Asian immigrants has been defeated for re-election, and he ominously warns that the Japanese seem to be increasingly active in economic penetration of the Australian market. At the same time he seems unaware that the high prices of all household appliances and automobiles, of which he complains, could be materially reduced by allowing even greater importation of such goods from Japan, or that Japan is probably destined to be the principal market for Australia's food and mineral exports which complement so well the needs of Japan.

Written in the form of a travel diary, Faulk's book contains a great deal of trivial comment — Australian restaurants don't serve water with meals — alongside quick descriptions of the towns, scenery and more obvious mores of the natives (an uncommon amount of heavy drinking, says this near teetotaling Oklahoman). He also complains of the penetration of "plastic" American culture in the form of omnipresent American TV shows and movies, Col. Sanders and MacDonalds, Coke (perth vintage), and many other products, as well as of certain American service industries like the Mafia. At the same time he complains about the poor quality of Australian hotels, central heating and coffee. In other words, he is a rather typical tourist.

The value of this book may lie in the fact that the Faulks attempted to find out why Americans emigrated to Australia by interviewing informally as many as they could find. They discovered that most wished to escape from the normal ills of American urban society — racial tensions, crime, drug cultures, pollution, and the economic "rat race". Most came from large urban cities — and most settled in Sydney, Melbourne or Adelaide where all the problems they sought to escape — except racial conflict — are also to be found. They have had to take a considerable drop in standard of living, capital accumulation is very difficult due to heavy taxation, and rampant inflation is above American levels. And racism is not entirely absent as both aborigines and other non-Caucasians are discriminated against in Australian society by either law or social custom. The Faulks found the little differences in Australian customs to be the most irritating: despite rumor to the contrary, Australians do not speak the same language as do most American. Faulk found that he was understood (the influence of TV) but could not always understand the local dialect. Despite the same nomenclature, Australian beef, milk, coffee, sausage, bologna and even water do not tast like their American namesakes; though he found Australian wines very palatable, he was stunned by the custom of serving spaghetti on toast for breakfast along with fried tomatoes.

The few liberal American emigrants that Faulk found fled from the growing fascism of America, only to drop out of politics completely in their new homeland. Faulk makes no analysis of the Australian political scene other than to complain of lazy bureaucrats, high taxes, politicians' antics, and the ominous presence of "bleeding heart liberals" who express concern over the government's willingness to remove the aborigines from whatever lands suddenly attract the lust of business

interests. But he is particularly bitter about the Australian's lack of enthusiasm for hard work (farmers are excepted) and the evil power of unions in Australian society, a situation far worse than in the United States, and one which leads Faulk to predict that Australia will get more and more like England rather than like America in the future. Why an American college professor enjoying a sabbatical year off, in addition to the usual long vacation and short hours of that profession, should wax

(Continued on page 3)

Arab Wars

While attention in the Middle East continues to focus on Israel versus the Arabs, two little known inter-Arab conflicts are beginning to escalate into full-scale wars. At the western end of the Arab world, King Hassan II of Morocco has whipped up a bizarre "March of Conquest", in which no less than 350,000 of his subjects are being mobilized to march southwestard into the Spanish Saharra, backed up by the Moroccan army. The Establishment press unsurprisingly misinterprets the Moroccan march as a nationalist grab for mere teritory; as a **New York Times** correspondent puts it, the Moroccan "hearts appreared to be moved by a nationalist claim to a piece of territory, however barren and unpeopled." (New York Times, Oct. 28, 1975).

The Sanish Sahara is not unpeopled (it has a population of 80,000), and it is certainly not "barren"; on the contrary, it has an enormous reserve of 1.7 billion tons of phosphates, so essential to the production of chemical fertilizers. If Morocco succeeds in grabbing the Spanish Sahara, it will then control over 80% of the world's phosphates supply. The reason for Hassan's haste at this time is that Spain has promised to leave its colony this year, and to hold a referendum among the populace. Most observers believe that three-quarters of the Spanish Saharans would vote for the territory's independence movement, POLISARIO, a leftist movement whose guerrilla war has now forced Spain to abandon its colony. POLISARIO is allied to the Algerian government, a leftist regime, which, under Saharan independence, would be able to ship its iron ore directly from far western Algeria through the Spanish Sahara to the sea. This October, the World Court rejected Morocco's dubious claim to the Spanish Sahara — hence the March. A war between Morocco on the one hand, and POLISARIO and Algeria on the other, is a distinct possiblity.

In the meanwhile, at the other end of the Arab world, on the Arabian peninsula, Oman and neighboring South Yemen are virtually at war. Oman, a depsotic monarchy under the one-man rule of Sultan Qabus bin Said, has been unsuccessfully trying to crush a leftist guerilla rebellion in its western province of Dhofar. The counter-guerilla war has been directed by a British general, with an officer corps of 200 members of Britain's Green Beret-ish Special Air Services, and a few thousand Iranian "advisers". Unable to stamp out the guerillas, Oman has begun to extend the war to the neighboring territory of leftist South Yemen, including an air stricke on October 17. Particularly important is that Oman used TOW missiles against South Yemeni gun emplacments, the misslas having been delivered to Oman last February by good old Uncle Sam. Not only that: but the American squeeze against South Yemen has been increased by continuing negotiations with North Yemen to supply up to $100 million in arms, to be paid for by Saudi Arabia, in return for the termination of Soviet military contracts to the North Yemenis.

Favorable U.S. interest in Oman is due to its strategic location in control of the narrow strait of Hormuz, through which passes nearly half of the world's oil; its hostile view of South Yemen, to its command of the Bab el-Mandeb straits entering the Red Sea.

(For information on the Spanish Sahara and Oman, see International Bulletin, Oct. 24, 1975. This excellent biweekly newsletter on foreign affairs can be obtained for only $8 a year, at P.O. Box 4400, Berkeley, Calif. 94704.)

Arts And Movies

By Mr. First Nighter

Encyclopedia of Pop Music and Jazz. At last — an encyclopedia has been published that offers a storehouse of delight for a lifetime! It is Roger D. Kinkle, **The Complete Encyclopedia of Popular Music and Jazz, 1900-1950** (4 volume set, Arlington House, 2644 pp., $75.00). Aided by the *enthusiasm and vast knowledge of the subject of Arlington House* publisher Neal McCaffrey, Kinkle's encyclopedia is the result of a vast amount of knowledge and research. As Kinkle admits, the title is in a sense a misnomer, since Kinkle's work follows the careers of the composers and musicians and jazz and pop down to 1974, provided that their careers were launched before 1950. Because of the time framework, Kinkle covers the Golden Age of pop and jazz, and happily omits the disintegration after the 1940's into trivia and then into rock and roll.

Volume I is a year-by-year chronology, listing the major songs, Hollywood and Broadway musicals, and records, each year. It is clear from the chronology that popular songs reached its apogee during the 1920's and 30's, and then began their precipitate decline during and after World War II, fueled by the death of the great composers the victory on radio recordings of BMI over the superior composers of ASCAP, and the muscians' strike during the war which, combined with a tax on dance halls, that killed the big bands. Volumes II and III are a marvellously comprehensive biography, arranged alphabetically, including composers, musicians, and vocalists, Volume II covering A through K, and Volume III, L through Z. The leading songs and records of each performer or composer are listed in the individual biography. Volume IV is a set of indexes and appendices, including the complete list of jazz poll and Academy Award winners; a list of all the principal record labels, by consecutive number; and complete alphabetical indexes by name, by song, and by musical, for the previous three volumes.

One of the things that struck me about the encyclopedia is how high a proportion of the great popular songs were written by a relative handful of songwriters. We all know about the top-ranking ones: Porter, Rogers and Hart, Gershwin, Berlin, Arlen, and Kern. But a surprisingly large proportion of great songs were written by composers now relatively forgotten: the Tilzer brothers, Albert and Harry; J. Fred Coots, Harry Woods, Harry Warren, Ralph Rainger, and others.

There are undoubtedly errors in this work, as Kinkle concedes, since there must be such in a mammoth tome of this type; but I must report that a diligent search over many happy hours of reading failed to find any. Once, I thought that the book had omitted the song "Treasure Island" (Joe Burke and Edgar Leslie, 1935). But then I found that I was wrong, since the title was "On Treasure Island." The old song "Winter Time" is omitted, but, who knows?, it may have been composed before 1900.

And so, rush out and buy this book—a fitting monument to a great and vanished era in popular music. Sure, the price is steep, but consider this: (a) all encyclopedias are expensive, (b) the price is cheap when we consider that it can be amortized over a lifetime of delighted reference and reading; and (c) best of all, that the price of the four-volume work is only $15 (yes, that's right, fifteen) if one joins the Nostalgia Book Club. For information, write the Nostaligia Book Club, 525 Main St., New Rochelle, N. Y. 10801

Jaws. dir. by Steven Spielberg, with Robert Shaw, Richard Dreyfus, and Roy Scheider.

Jaws is a good, scary movie, no doubt about that. But it is hardly the best movie of all time, or even the scariest. And so that film hardly warrants its runaway best-seller status, the long lines at movie theaters throughout the country, and its rapid climb to the biggest box-office draw of all time. It is what used to be called "good hot weather fare", and no more than that.

In the recent disaster genre, Jaws is better than "The Towering Inferno", and far better than the turkey "Earthquake", and is happily free of the phony moralism of the earlier pictures. The highly touted shark scenes are indeed terrific (whether they overrate the shark menace or not I leave to the shark specialists.) One problem is that there are several important clinkers in the movie, including especially its idiotic ending, which violates both the letter and the spirit of the Peter Benchley novel. More important is the uniformly poor quality of the

acting, a flaw which we can lay straight at the door of young Spielberg. Roy Scheider is patently miscast in the important role of the sheriff; what kind of credible sheriff walks around with a perpetually gentle, hangdog expression? Richard Dreyfuss is not as obnoxious as in his central role in "The Apprenticeship of Duddy Kravitz", but neither does he begin to come across as a young New England aristocrat. Another example of grievous miscasting by Spielberg.

But particularly unfortunate is what happended to Robert Shaw, one of the finest actors in motion pictures. The central role of the fanatical shark-killer Quint, as should have been clear from the novel, should be played with quietly controlled force, punctuated by bursts of passion. Instead, Shaw hams it up from the very beginning, destroying much of the point by making Quint a garrulous old fool instead of the best sharkhunter in the business. Again, such a misconception *of the role is at least* as much the director's fault as Shaw's, especially since Shaw is not usually given to chewing the proverbial carpet.

Tom Wolfe Rides Again. Several years ago, the brilliant and scintillating social critic Tom Wolfe demonstrated the power of the pen by single-handedly demolishing the now famous (as dubbed by Wolfe himself) phenomenon of "radical chic". Now, in a book that essentially reprints his lengthy article in the April Harper's, **The Painted Word**, Wolfe. with equal hilarity and wit, does a superb domolition job on *modern art. In the course of his book*, Wolfe gives us a history and sociology of the development of modern art, and exposes the fact that the Modern Art Emperor has no clothes. Can he single-handedly destroy modern art as he did radical chic? It is not likely, but at least we can hope. Surely, the pretentious pomposities and absurdities of modern art will never quite be the same again.

The War Between the Tates. We usually do not discuss fiction in this column, but we must break the mold to sing the praises of Alison Lurie's

(Continued on page 4)

Is The Grass Any Greener ? —

(Continued from page 2)

indignant over a common workingman's desire for an annual month off and a forty hour week is something of a puzzle. But such attitudes are common among conservatives.

Prof. Faulk's conclusion on Australia is that it may be a nice place to visit, but he wouldn't want to live there. I think his conclusion is sound: that those wishing to escape the urban problems of America can *do as* well by simply moving into some smaller American city or more rural area. If they don't like what they hear on TV each morning, shut it off. If they wish to escape the "rat race", they can do so in greater comfort in many parts of the United States, and without the trauma of living in a foreign land and quite foreign culture. All the problems of America already exist in Australia; if their magnitude seems smaller, it is merely because they exist among 13 million rather than 220 million people. Many of the new emigrants from America found no real solutions in Australia; many found only new problems; many carry problems around in their head. Though the Faulks were unaware of it, Australia has *proven its* right to be considered a society in the American pattern, not some provincial backwater. It has witnessed in the last year the founding of its first liberatarian political party, The Workers' Party, dedicated to the free mind, the free market and the free life — but not the free lunch. Any country needing a libertarian party, and spontaneously creating it, is not likely to be any better than our own, and may even be worse from a libertarian viewpoint. At least we Americans don't pledge allegiance to a parasitical monarch, yet.

Any potential expatriates, or tourists will find this easy to read travelogue useful. But they should be warned that Prof. Faulk absolutely hated Hawaii, and therefore may just be extraordinarily hard to please.

J. R. P.

607

From The Old Curmudgeon

Psychobabble.

One good thing about being an older, as opposed to a younger, curmudgeon is that one has the privilege of seeing cultural fads go as well as arrive. The "psychobabble" of my younger days was pop-Freudianism, and one had to suffer through cocktail conversation about "Oedipus Complexes", "repression", and "transference." Happily, Freudianism, once so triumphant, has seen better days, only to be replaced by the modern, more mindless, but more pervasive psychobabble derived from the so-called "human potential" movement. (For a scintillating dissection of the current mode, as well as older trends, and for the name of the syndrome, see R. D. Rosen, "Psychobabble," New York Times, Oct. 31, 1975.)

The new psychobabble seems to be a blend of compulsive pshycho-confessionalism, "philosophical" hogwash, Eastern mysticism, pop psychojargon, and the reconstruction of one's personality by an untrained but self-confident guru. It is particularly distressing to find so many libertarians, as well as the rest of society, falling for this irrational cretinism. In his humorous and astute article, Mr. Rosen indicates the difference from the older, Freudian pop-jargon: "The old Psychobabble, however, was really just the wholesale use of Freudian terms, less banter than a sort of intellectual one-upmanship. In post-World War II America, Freudian terminology was embraced by liberal magazines, novelists and enough of the middle class so that the growing demand for psychoanalysis easily outdistanced the supply of doctors." In the new version, however, even the dubious intellectual content of Freudianism has disappeared, to be replaced by vague and ritualistic phrase-mongering. Rosen tells the typical story of phychoanalyst confronting a patient engaged in the New Psychobabble. To every interpretation offered by the analyst, the patient responded "I hear you. I hear you." The following dialogue ensued:

"'I'm sorry,' said the doctor. 'I didn't know you were a little deaf.'

'I'm not. I hear you. It means I comprehend.'

'Well, what do you comprehend?'

The patient paused. 'Jesus,' he replied. 'I don't know.'"

The psychobabble, as Rosen concludes, is a "set of repetitive verbal formalities" that "seem to free-float in some linguistic atmosphere." They are also, one might add, close to gibberish. It is impossible, for example, to make any sense of most of the lucubrations of the latest super-guru, Werner Erhard, founder of Est, which has been lately sweeping the country and the liberatarian movement. (See, for example, the expository and only mildly critical new book on all this by Adam Smith, and the refreshingly critical reporting of Esalen and Est by Annette Duffy in one of this summer's issues of The Village Voice.) It is clear that amidst all the mindless concentration on one's psyche — as filtered through the pseudo-philosophical jargon — the world of reality is left far behind. We are informed, for example, that "Werner hasn't read anything in ten year"; apparently, facts, reality, knowledge of the world, only clutter up the psyche, which must be left free for the psychobabble.

Adam Smith tells us that Werner Erhard received the revelation for Est when it suddenly hit him one day that "Whatever is, is, and whatever isn't, isn't." As Smith comments, "deep, deep." One would think, indeed, that libertarians and ex-Randians have heard it all before: "Existence exists, A is A." Indeed, in many ways Est and the other cults are a sort of village Randianism, that is, Randianism without its best apsect: systematic thought. What is left is the cult and the proferred panacea for all personal ills.

Hopefully, a reaction is setting in, as the Rosen and other articles attest. Particularly important is a devastating report on Est by an intrepid reporter who went through the entire Est training, including "graduate seminars": Mark Brewer, "'We're Gonna Tear You Down and Put You Back Together'", Psychology Today (August, 1975). Mr. Brewer details the horrendous brainwashing techniques, accompanied, as usual, by severe sensory deprivation and authoritarian harrassment, which results in "happy", robotized subjects, ready to go spout "philosophical" hogwash and to go out and gather more, unpaid volunteer-recruits for Est. The essence of the new message is that: "whatever you

do is perfect, since you're doing it". Anything else is a "belief system" and therefore wrong. To "learn" this nonsense one has to be robotized and "ested"?! As Brewer concludes: "The use of brainwashing techniques, ostensibly to enhance people's lives, becomes bizarre when the outcome is to create unpaid salesman. Smiling, they march out each week to share their brainwashed joys with friends, neighbors and co-workers, and they know that many will want to be sold. A friend of mine, an enthusiastic est graduate . . . until it all began to seem insidious, wistfully recalled the power of the training. 'They could've told me anything!'"

The horror is that so many libertarians could sit still long enough to be bulldozed in this manner, that they could submit themselves as fodder for authoritarian and brutal gurus.

Another important recent reaction to the psychobabble is a subtle, friendly but nonetheless devastating demolition of the quasi-Freudianism of Erik Erikson (the founder of the "identity crisis") by Professor Frederick Crews ("American Propet," New York Review of Books, Oct. 16.) The backlash can come none too soon. More and more, it is becoming clear that these cults and fads can only sweep the country because most people lack a built-in b.s. detector or repellent (to paraphrase Hemingway.) A sufficient if not a necessary condition for such a repellent is a sense of humor, which is even more rare. Oh, H. L. Mencken, where are you now that we really need you? Can you imagine Mencken's reaction, for example, to a new book by some cretinous adherent of the new movement, entitled, revealingly, It's Me and I'm Here! Surely the proper response is something like: Who the hell cares?

Probably the screwiest of the new psycho-cults is "rolfing" — also used as an allied technique by many of the other cults — founded by one Ida Rolfe, in which the "therapist" punches, pummels, and generally hurts the patient, whose "life (but of course!) is changed" by "working through the pain." Reminiscent, of course, of nothing so much as the old joke about a guy, when asked why he was hitting his head against a wall,

(Continued on page 5)

Arts and Movies—

(Continued from page 3)

witty, perceptive, and extremely well-written novel, now out in paperback. From her inside perch as a professor at Cornell, Mrs. Lurie offers us a brilliant dissection of the academic world, its attitudes, pomposities, and values — as set in the era of conflicting values and standards of the late 1960's and early 70's. It is a comedy of manners in the classic sense. Particularly perceptive and hilarious is Mrs. Lurie's description of a faculty department meeting, in political science; in a few pages, she manages to Say it All about an institution (faculty meetings) in which an enormous amount of pretentious blather is habitually expended on petty and bureaucratic issues. A must!

Randian estheticians will doubtless balk at the admittedly antiromantic motif of the novel. There is no question about the fact that there are no heroes or heroines in the novel; everyone is an ass. But there is an important role in fiction for the realistic novel. At its best, the novel can capture an age or a way of life far more accurately than can the most thorough and sober historian. Randians deride the realistic novel as "journalistic", but the journalist, trapped in mountains of mere fact, cannot step outside of the given historical concretes to capture the essence of the way people feel, think, or act in any given historical setting. The novelist can, however; Galsworthy's Forsythe Saga, for example, so superbly captured on television a few years ago, gives us a far better idea of the way people felt and acted in Edwardian England than any historian can hope to do. Mrs. Lurie's novel is the subset of the realistic novel known as the "comedy of manners", in which nothing very tragic occurs, and the characters are treated amusedly but gently (in contrast to the savage modern genre of "black" or absurdist comedy.) All in all, a penetrating and delightful book. ◻

Class Analysis And Economic Systems
By David Osterfeld*

It is usually assumed that capitalism and socialism are diametrically opposed. This assumption is both true and false, for there are two mutually exclusive definitions of capitalism found in Marxist literature. On the one hand the term is used to denote production according to the dictates of the market, or in Marxist terminology, "commodity production."[1] On the other, capitalism is defined in terms of class relations, i.e., ownership of the means of production by the "bourgeoisie" or ruling class. The former may be termed the economic definition and the latter the sociological definition. Marx apparently thought that the two were compatible and slides back and forth between the two without warning. However, if the economic definition is used, it follows that the less government control and manipulation of the market, the more capitalistic the society. This means that price controls, subsidies, licensing restrictions, etc., must be classified as anti-capitalistic since they constitute modifications or restrictions of the market. Since the state does not sell its services on the market, it is incompatible with the economic definition of capitalism. Not only is "state capitalism" a contradiction in terms, but it can readily be seen that taken to its logical extreme capitalism leads inexorably to anarchism.

But if the sociological definition is used, the state becomes perfectly compatible with capitalism, for whatever serves to entrency the bourgeois class, the owners of the means of production, in power is, ipso facto, "capitalistic." Since Marx argued — however wrongly — that market competition would force the "rate of profit" to fall and ultimately to disappear altogether, the two definitions lead to mutually exclusive conclusions. Since the economic definition entails pure laissez faire, any government intervention to protect the interests of the bourgeoisie is anthema. But this is precisely the essential element when the sociological definition is used. Even though his economics may have been faulty, Marx saw that for the dominant economic class to entrench itself in power it must first be able to institutionalize its position, and this it can do only by obtaining control of the state. With the state behind them the bourgeoisie are then able to protect their positions from the threat of competition by establishing tariff barriers, licensing restrictions, and other statist measures. For Marx, the state is the principal instrument by which the dominant economic class is able to exploit the rest of society. Thus he writes that "the executive of the modern state is but a committee for managing the common affairs of the whole bourgeoisie." Political power is defined as "the organized power of one class for oppressing another." And even more clearly: "every class struggle is a political struggle."[2] In short, while the state is incapatible with the economic definition, it is absolutely essential for the sociological one.

The inapplicability to the market of class analysis.

The utility of class analysis depends not only on a rigid social structure but, just as important, on whether the dominant class has obtained and/or is maintaining its position at the expense of, i.e., exploits, the other class(es) in the society. One conceivable socialist argument is that the two definitions may in fact be consistent if it can be shown that the operations of the market result in a stratified social structure where one class benefits itself at the expense of the other(s). Marx's own economic analysis, however, precludes such an interpretation. Marx of course knew that for the capitalist to remain in business he must earn profit, or surplus value as he called it. But since all capitalists, he reasoned, are faced with the same task, they are forced by the laws of the market to compete against each other by lowering their prices and even, at times, by raising wages. The least efficient, usually the small-scale producers, are driven out of business. As Marx puts it, "one capitalist always kill many." Capital becomes ever more centralized. The ranks of the proletariate swell from the increasing numbers of former bourgeoisie. Such is the process until finally, "this integument is burst asunder. The knell of capitalist private property sounds. The expropriators are expropriated."[3]

Such is Marx's analysis according to market criteria. The first thing to notice is that even according to Marx there is movement between classes, if only downward from the borgeoisie to the proletariat. While this in itself would be enough to question the rigidity of the class structure under the market, Marx ignored the fact that just as there is movement

downward, so there is movement upward, as the Fords, Rockefellers and numerous others less famous indicates. In short, far from a socially stratified society, the market is characterized by the perpetual movement between classes.

Further, far from benefitting themselves at the expense of others, the bourgeoisie can only maintain its position in a market society by serving others better than can anyone else. This, in fact, is implicit in Marx's analysis: those who are able to stay in business can only do so on the market by offering higher wages to get better workers and by lowering their prices to attract more consumers. This is exactly why Marx felt the "rate of profit" would have to fall. While this would seem to demonstrate the irrelevance of class analysis for the market, one final argument might be that two or more capitalists could band together to form a monopoly, thereby both institutionalizing their position and benefitting themselves at the expense of others. The fallacy in this charge lies in the failure to realize that the elimination of the external market thereby precludes economic calculation within the firm. Since the monopoly would no longer be in a position to rationally allocate its specific factors, it would suffer severe losses and break apart.[4]

From the above it can be seen that there is no overlap whatsoever between the economic and sociological definitions: the former is incompatible with the state, the latter requires it; the former is characterized by movement between classes, the latter by social stratification; the former is premised on exchange for mutual benefit, the latter on exploitation. While it is fruitless to engage in arid debates over which definition is the "correct" one, it should be pointed out that the sociological definition is practically identical to what libertarians refer to as mercantilism. It should therefore not be surprising to find that, while running directly counter to Marxian economics on the one hand, there are on the other significant parallels between Marxism and libertarianism in the areas of class analysis and its correlary, imperialism.

Class Analysis.

While there is disagreement between libertarians and Marxists concerning the origins of the state, and while Marx's class analysis is partially vitiated by his ideological tendency to equate the "whole bourgeoisie" with the ruling class,[5] there is still much of value for libertarians — with the caveat that one is careful to distinguish between the two definitions of capitalism. What then emerges from the Marxian class analysis is an insightful dissection of traditional laissez-faire theory. Classical liberals had refrained from extending market analysis to its anarchist extreme and urged a "night watchman" state to maintain order and protect private property. But despite the shortcomings of Marxian economics, Marx realized that the position of the capitalist on the free market was always insecure. He also understood that since the first concern of the capitalist was to make money, he did not have any great attachment to the market as such. After all, freedom of competition meant that he could never relax. No sooner would he triumph over one competitor than he would be met by others intent upon cutting

(Continued on page 6)

From The Old Curmudgeon—
(Continued from page 4)

replying: "because it feels so good when I stop." What can anyone say about this lunacy except that it is better to be a rolfer than a rolfee? I can think, in fact, of a few people I would happily agree to "rolfe" for a very small fee.

In the meanwhile, lacking Mencken himself, we will have to peg along in his spirit, and hope that all this, too, shall pass. Mr. Rosen ends his article by pointing to the example of a friend of his, as a method of dealing with the new psychobabble. When a girl asked him directly, "Are you getting your head together?", the friend replied: "Yes. I can feel it congealing." ◻

Class Analysis— (Continued from page 5)

into his share of the market. Since this would force prices down, the capitalist could only preserve his profits by introducing new methods that would lower costs. But, argued Marx, this would only temporarily preserve profits since all other competitors would soon follow suit. Hence, "this extra surplus-value vanishes so soon as the new method of production has become general . . . ."⁵ Marx completely misunderstood the nature of both interest and profit, and therefore erroneously believed that they could (and would) eventually disappear. But what he did clearly understand, however, was that while the capitalist desired to realize a profit, the rigors of the market meant that this was a difficult and perpetual struggle for an ever elusive object. Hence Marx noted that it was only natural for the capitalist to turn to the state which, with its monopoly on the use of force, could institutionalize his profits by implementing various statist measures to keep out competition and hold down wage rates.⁶ It is not surprising that the capitalists, as Marx notes, "all employ the powers of the State," ranging from "brute force" to the granting of "exclusive monopolies," for it is only by this means that they can "fix prices and plunder at will." It is also quite understandable why Marx terms political power as "itself an economic power."⁸

From this it can be seen that Marx did not succeed in demonstrating that wealth by itself confers power but the much different idea that wealth greatly facilitates the acquisition of power. The wealthy are able to use their wealth to obtain control of the state. Once in control, they are in a position to use the state to perpetuate their own position in the social hierarchy. Since he believed that the market would eliminate profit, it is the state, and not the market as assumed by most commentators, that is the principal vehicle for exploitation according to the logic of the Marxian system. Marx, in fact, is very clear on this point. In **The German Ideology** Marx and Engels define the state as "nothing more than the form of organization which the bourgeois necessarily adopt both for internal and external purposes, for the mutual gurantee of their property and interest." And in his **Critique of Hegel's Philosophy of Right**, Marx is severely critical of Hegel's view of the bureaucracy as a universal class. For Marx the bureaucracy is, as Shlomo Avineri puts it, "an institutional license for sectional interests." And in the **18th Brumaire** Marx argues that the success of all previous revolutions depended on the acquisition of state power: "The parties that contended . . . for domination regarded the possession of this huge state ediface as the principal spoils of the victors."⁹ In short, while Marx's analysis is often muddled due in large part to his failure to recognize the incompatibility of his two definitions of capitalism, what emerges from a close reading of Marx is rather surprising: while wealth on the free market confers no power, the alliance of wealth with the state does divide society into antagonistic classes and enables the wealthy strata to maintain its position via the exploitation of others.

In pointing out the natural affinity between wealth and political power Marx demonstrated the naivete of the classical liberal ideal of limited-government capitalism. Since the state is the only vehicle for the institutionalization of profits, the night-watchman state, even if attained, would soon transform itself into the mercantilist state, and Lenin's "personal link-up" between the bankers and the government officials marks precisely this transition. The realization that wealth does not confer power but does facilitate its acquisition has significant import for libertarians, for it means that the problem of power in society can only be handled by striking at its source: the state. There is, in other words, no half-way point between anarchism and mercantilism. Either the state is eliminated altogether or it will grow.

Imperialism.

While libertarians might benefit from a careful and selective reading of Marx, socialists might just as well profit from a study of the libertarian analysis of imperialism. The elements of the Hilferding-Lenin-Bukharin theory of capitalism imperialism are well know. Since the role of the state in the securing and policing of the colonial system is central, it is the sociological, and not the economic, definition of capitalism that is used. It is not too surprising therefore that the communist theory of "capitalist" imperialism bears a striking similarity to the capitalist theory of mercantilist imperialism, for in actuality the two are referring to the same thing. In fact, there is probably no severer indictment of imperialism than that found in Adam Smith's **Wealth of Nations**. Smith argues that under mercantilism, monopolistic privileges were granted to

a few favored firms, permitting them to sell at exorbitant prices, while tariffs were enacted to keep out foreign competition. But if a nation were to eliminate imports it would have to have its own exclusive colonies in order to obtain raw materials. The power of the state, of course, was ideally suited to carve out and police the resulting colonial system.

Smith charged that the mercantilist system not only hurt those in the colonies but the workers in the mother country as well. Its only beneficiaries were "the rich and powerful." Permitting the colonists to trade only with the mother-country enabled merchants to sell at monopoly prices in the colonies. The colonists, therefore, were unable to pay for the administration of colonial government as well, so the workers in the home-country were taxed to defray this cost, thereby perpetuating the profits of the merchants. Furthermore wages, said Smith, were kept low and prices high in the mother-country through the use of selective subsidies. The effect of mercantilism, said Smith was that "the interest of one little order of men in one country" was promoted at the expense of "the interest of all other orders of men in that country, and of all other orders of men in all other countries."¹⁰

What Smith urged was the replacement of mercantilism by free trade. This, of course, would logically entail the abandonment of the entire colonial system and Smith doesn't shrink from drawing that conclusion. One also finds similar statements in the writings of other proponents of the market such as Richard Cobden and John Bright as well as Herbert Spencer, Frederic Bastiat and others.¹¹

While the leninist and libertarian solutions for imperialism are manifestly dissimilar there are, however, marked similarities between their respective critiques of imperialism. By being careful to distinguish between the two definitions of capitalism not only can libertarians find much of value in such works as Lenin's **Imperialism**, Bukharin's **Imperialism and World Economy**, and Magdoff's **Age of Imperialism**, but

(Continued on page 7)

610

"Libertarian" SCI FI

A Review of Commune 2000 A.D., by Mack Reynolds. Bantam 1974. (A novel.)

"Robert Owen lives!". This is the code phrase identifying members of conspiratorial group trying to overthrow the well-ordered and prosperous utopia of United America in 2000 A.D. The new utopia began with the establishment of the Guranteed Annual Income for all citizens. The bulk of the population being technologically unemployable, work is done by those who are chosen annually by computer analysis which decides who shall work, where and at what, based on the Ability Quotient of each citizen. The rest are free to pursue their hobbies and obsessions, drawing money as needed from their GAI. Automated cars, roads and food service, books on home screens by tapping a central data bank, legal use of soft drugs (hard drugs are suppressed), disposable clothing, home delivery of new household goods or clothing by pneumatic chute, and sexual freedom, sex of all kinds, casual, guiltless, loveless, all are the bread and circuses of the masses.

The heart of the new utopia is a data bank which has absorbed all the census, social welfare, police, medical and other governmental information, and the data contained in the libraries of Congress and the British Museum. All this is available at the touch of a button, and by adding school and work records, the managers of the economy can pinpoint any citizen's Ability Quotient and command his talents for the benefit of the whole society. But while most accept this conscription as a reasonable and even desirable burden, rumors of increasingly widespread work-evasion lead the managerial elites, who are more or less permanently tenured (because they have tampered with the computer selector-evaluator), to send aspiring academics into the communes to find out what is happening. The hero is an unemployed ethnologist who is suddenly told that he is to write his dissertation on life in the communes, reporting back to his mentors (police agents) what he finds. He discovers that the communes — each set up by affinity groups

such as lesbians, Amish, nudists, Hellenophilic athletes, etc. — are harboring work-dropouts who live on the surplus GAI of their fellow communards, and that they also fail to file accurate data annually into the central computer bank. As historian William Marina would put it, they are living in the interstices of the computer society. In fact, the hero is horrified to learn that a conspiratorial core within the communal societies have espoused some antisocial philosophy called "Anarchism" or "Libertarianism". Yes! Robert Owen lives!

The resolution of the novel suggests further adventures ahead for the hero. As is so often the case with novels of this kind, the plot is mechanistic, the characterization one dimensional at best, and the motivation is not quite convincing. But equally disturbing are the ideological inadequacies of this allegedly "libertarian" novel. Isaac Asimov, insists that in reviewing science fiction, one criterian which must be applied is that the science be at the very least accurate, within the realm of the possible. If we apply the same standard to this novel we find that it is premised upon the belief that, within 25 years, the problem of scarcity will have been all but eliminated, and massive unemployment will be tolerable due to the surplus of capital or goods produced through automation. Such a situation within 25 years, if ever, is simply not credible, and since it is the major premise of the novel, it weakens it fatally. The author has probably been reading Murray Bookchin's writings on post-scarcity anarchism and has failed to recognize the fictional quality of his utopian projections. Ayn Rand has proven the tremendous power of fiction in the promotion of libertarian philosophical principles; but we must retain some sense of responsibility in accepting allegedly libertarian fiction. Is it credible on its premises? Is it accurate in its principles? Is it compelling as literature? Does it enlighten the mind or move the heart? For Commune 2000 A.D., the verdict is "Not guilty"!

Arthur McRory*

*Mr. McRory is a long-time observer of the fiction scene.   ◻

Class Analysis— (Continued from page 6)

socialists can just as well benefit from a reading of such libertarian works on the subject as Mises' Omnipotent Government or Robbins' The Economic Causes of War.

Conclusion.

Marx had two mutually exclusive definitions of capitalism: an economic and a sociological. The failure to realize that Marx's sociological definition was tantamount to what libertarians refer to as mercantilism meant that the two groups often talked past each other when, in fact, they were in basic agreement. While I do not want to exaggerate the similarities between libertarianism and Marxism and believe that on balance the areas of disagreement far outweigh those of agreement, I do feel that a re-reading of Marx, untangling the economic from the sociological definitions, can prove worthwhile for libertarians. After all, it is pointless to throw out the wheat with the chaff.

Footnotes

¹On the role of "commodity production" in Marxist literature see P. C. Roberts and M. Stephenson, Marx's Theory of Exchange, Alienation and Crisis (Standord, 1973).

²Karl Marx and Friedrich Engels, The Communist Manifesto (New York, 1969), pp. 61, 73 and 95.

³Karl Marx, Capital, Vol. I (New York, 1906), pp. 836-7.

⁴Murray Rothbard, Man, Economy, and State (Los Angeles, 1970), p. 585. For supporting empirical evidence see D. T. Armentano, The Myths of Antitrust (New Rochell, 1972), and A. S. Dewing, "A Statistical Test of the Success of Consolidation," The Quarterly Journal of Economics (1921), pp. 84-94.

⁵ The "whole bourgeoisie" does not constitute the ruling class, but only that portion of it in a position to obtain economic benefits from the state. An obvious example is that while a tariff might benefit those in a business facing foreign competition, it would hurt those in the import-export businesses.

⁶Marx, Capital, p. 350.

⁷Note the similarity to A. J. Nock's and F. Chodorov's "law of parsimony."

⁸Marx, Capital, pp. 823-5.

⁹First quote in Ralph Miliband, "Marx and the State," Karl Marx Ed.: Tom Bottomore (Englewood Cliffs, 1973), p. 134, emphasis supplied; second quote from Shlomo Avineri, The Social and Political Thought of Karl Marx (Cambridge, 1972), p. 23; third quote in Miliband, p. 145.

¹⁰Adam Smith, The wealth of Nations, Vol. II (New Rochelle, n.d.), pp. 207-62.

¹¹Richard Cobden wrote in 1958 that "I am opposed to any armed intervention in the affairs of other countries. I am against any interference by the Government of one country in the affairs of another nation, even if it be confined to moral suasion. Nay, I go even further, and disapprove of the formation of a society or organization of any kind in England for the purpose of interfering in the internal affairs of other countries." William Dawson, Richard Cobden and Foreign Policy, (New York, 1927), p. 108. Dawson himself summarizes Cobden's position by saying that "Had he had his way England would not have had so much as a back garden of a colony . . . ."; p. 203. In 1867 John Bright, in a speech on the British colonies, remarked: "For my share, I want the population of these Provinces to do that which they believe to be the best for their own interests — remain in this country if they like . . . or become independent States if they like." In James Sturgis, John Bright and the Empire (London, 1969), p. 101. Herbert Spence wrote that "great as are the evils entailed by government colonization upon both parent State and settlers, they look insignificant when compared with those it inflicts on the aborignes of the conquered countries." Herbert Spencer, Social Statics (New York, 1892), p. 196. And Fredeiic Bastiat wrote: "We see government everywhere greatly preoccupied either in giving exchange special favors or with restricting it. To carry it beyond its natural limits, they seek after new outlets and colonies . . . This intervention of force in human affiars is always accompanied by countless evils." Frederic Bastiat, Economic Harmonies (Princeton, 1964), p. 80.

*Mr. Osterfeld is a doctoral candidate in Political Theory at the University of Cincinnati. He plans to write a dissertation on "The Antecedents of Anarcho-Capitalism."   ◻

Friedman And The Liberals

By Tibor R. Machan*

In his October 6, 1975, Newsweek column Milton Friedman delivered a view point on politics that should be of considerable interest to all who have concluded that liberty is the prime political value in a human community. In this column Friedman addresses the problem of busing. After a brief introduction he poses the question: "What is wrong?" He answers as follows:

> . . . I submit that the answer is intolerance — not intolerance of whites for blacks, which surely exists, but intolerance of liberal reformers who "know" what is good for other people are prepared to force it on them, intolerance of liberal reformers who can and mostly do exercise choice among schools for their own children — by living in affluent suburbs or sending them to private schools — but refuse to grant a similar freedom of choice to the less fortunate parents who at present have no alternative to the public school . . . .

Friedman then goes on to emphasize his opposition to intolerance in the following passage:

> No boubt, the violent reaction of whites to compulsory integration via forced busing partly reflects racial intolerance. However, true tolerance requires tolerance of what we regard as intolerance. It requires us to persuade, not force, to set an example, not retire to our cozy segregated (by income) existence while sending out the police, the National Guard and Federal marshals to force on others not the values we actually live by but values we believe others should live by . . . .

It is not my intention to comment on the above ideas. What I wish to do is to provide a contrasting view, offered by the late professor Leo Strauss, a view that will, I think, provide food for thought concerning the problems advocates of liberty face when they select the arguments by which they will give support to liberty.

In his book **Natural Right and History** (1953), Strauss offers the following reflections:

> . . . (G)enerous liberals view the abandonment of natural right not only with placidity but with relief. They appear to believe that our inability to acquire any genuine knowledge of what is intrinsically good or right compels us to be tolerant of every opinion about good or right or to recognize all preferences or all "civilizations" as equally respectable. Only unlimited tolerance is in accordance with reason. But this leads to the admission of a rational or natural right of every preference that is tolerant of other preferences or, negatively expressed, of a rational or natural right to reject or condemn all intolerant or all "absolutist" positions. The latter must be condemned because they are based on a demonstrably false premise, namely, that men can know what is good. At the bottom of the passionate rejection of all "absolutes," we discern the recognition of a natural right or, more precisely, of that particular interpretation of natural right according to which the only thing needful is respect for diversity or individuality. But there is a tension between the respect for diversity or individuality and the recognition of natural right. When liberals became impatient of the absolute limits to diversity or individuality, they had to make a choice between natural right and the unihibited cultivation individuality. They chose the latter. Once this step was taken, tolerance appeared as a value or ideal among many, and not intrinsically superior to its opposite. In other words, intolerance appeared as a value equal in dignity to tolerance. But it is pratically impossible to leave it at the equality of all preferences or choices. If the unequal rank of choices cannot be traced to the unequal rank of their objectives, it must be traced to the unequal rank of the acts of choosing; and this means eventually that genuine choice, as distinguished from spurious or despicable choice, is nothing but resolute or deadly serious decision. Such a decision, however, is akin to intolerance rather than to tolerance. Liberal relativism has its roots in the natural right tradition of tolerance or in the notion that everyone has a natural right to the pursuit of happiness as he understands happiness; but in itself it is a seminary of intolerance. (pp. 5-6)

I believe that Strauss shows in this passage that Milton Friedman and the modern liberals Friedman condemns start from a very similar point of view, namely skepticism about ethics (and values in general). Friedman happens to be a (clasical) liberal and his preference lies with tolerance even of the intolerant. The supporters of busing, modern liberals, prefer other values. They are more intense, they focus on particular wrongs that are very difficult to deny, even while one is a skeptic on broader issues. So their choice is a "deadly serious" one, while Friedman's is but a choice in support of abstract principle whose pratical effects takes lengthy chains of reasoning to appreciate. The classical liberal confronted with the modern liberal ends condemned by the modern brother as callous. And if the classical liberal really has no better ground for his defense of liberty than his preference for tolerance, the intensity of the opposition from his brother will surely win within the realpolitik of a human community.

Intellectually, then, timidity in the defense of liberty is no virtue however much the practice of political tolerance requires support. That support is simply inadequate without a clear, unabashed affirmation of other, more basic values that can give such tolerance deadly serious backing.

*Dr. Machan teaches philosophy at State University College, Fredonia, N.Y., and is now a fellow at the Hoover Institution, Stanford, Cal.

The Libertarian Forum
BOX 341
MADISON SQUARE STATION
NEW YORK, NEW YORK 10010

First Class

Published Every Month. Subscription Rates: $8.00 Per Year; $15.00 Two Years

A Monthly Newsletter

THE
Libertarian Forum

Joseph R. Peden, Publisher   Murray N. Rothbard, Editor

VOLUME VIII, NO. 11   NOVEMBER, 1975   US-ISSN0047-4517

POLITICS: NOVEMBER '75

During the first week in November, two important political events in the United States hit the front pages: the 1975 elections, and President Ford's "Halloween Massacre." Amidst the spate of press interpretations of these two events, no one has presented what I believe to be the correct analysis: that both of these were significant victories for libertarianism.

1. Bond Issues.

The most heartening aspect of the election was the resounding and smashing defeat delivered by voters, across the country, to massive proposals for issues of government bonds. The voting was a great public protest against swollen government spending, as well as heavy taxation for taxation would eventually have been needed to pay for the principal and interest on the bonds. It was a resounding defeat to Big Government, made even more spectacular by the fact that, in most cases, all organized groups were ardent advocates of the bond issues: the politicians, the AFL-CIO, business groups, religious and "good government" groups, etc. In New Jersey, as one observer noted, "everyone was in favor of the bond issues except the people." An upsurge in libertarian attitudes among the public is becoming manifest; how much more will come to life when the Libertarian Party becomes organized to give these strong but often inchoate public feelings a clear, organized, and institutional voice?.

Across the country, $6.3 billion in bond issues were put before the public this month; of these $5.9 billion, or 93 percent, were rejected at the polls! The biggest rejection was directed against the mammoth $4.5 billion bond issues proposed by the Ohio state government, of which nearly $3 billion were to go to capital improvement projects, and nearly $2 billion to transportation. The capital improvement bond issue was rejected by no less than 82% of the Ohio voters, and the transportation issue by 84%. All this despite Republican Governor Rhodes' ardent support as a "blueprint for Ohio", which would have been financed by increased sales and gasoline taxes. Ohio Democratic leaders were astute enough to oppose the bond issue, Lieutenant Governor Richard Celeste perceptively calling it a "blueprint for bankruptcy."

The second largest state bond package was in New Jersey, where Democrat Governor Byrne, supported by most Republicans and all other organized groups in the state, submitted four bond issues, totalling $922 million, which were to go to water development, transportation ($600 million, to be split, half going to to mass transit lobby and half to the highway lobby), housing, and other institutions. All were turned down by substantial majorities, transportation, for example, losing by 960,000 to 580,000 votes.

The protest in New Jersey was also directed against Governor Byrne's pet project of a state income tax, which he has not been able to ram through the state legislature (partly due to the noble opposition efforts of the New Jersey Federation of Taxpayers, which includes many libertarian members and activists.) As one New Jersey Assemblyman observed, "It means you can kiss goodbye any thought of an income tax and you have to start thinking about cuts, and more cuts after that." The libertarian emphasis of the New Jersey voters was also shown by their discriminating selectivity on the state proposals; for they approved, by two to one, a proposition for tax deductions for elderly citizens. And so

the public is willing to consider tax cuts, but not increases.

In New York State, the voters rejected by 700,000 votes a proposed $250 million bond issue that would have subsidized housing for the ederly. In the state of Washington, voters, by a margin of 2 to 1, turned down a proposed 12% tax on corporate profits to finance $200 million for the state's schools.

All observers noted the chilling effect of New York City's financial disaster. As well it might; for New York City should stand as a permanent warning bell against runaway government and profligate spending. Akron State Senator Oliver Ocasek's plea against the bond issue: "We can't afford to have Ohio become another New York City" should, and undoubtedly will, reflect sentiments in every state and municipality in the country.

2. Defeat for the ERA.

The voters of New York and New Jersey roundly defeated the Equal Rights Amendment for their respective states. Once again, organization, financing, and access to the media were heavily on the side of the fashionable ERA: politicians, business, labor, newspapers, religious and civic groups and of course the omnipresent NOW. In contrast, the opposition was haphazard and ad hoc, consisting largely of local housewives' groups organized for the occasion. The smashing defeat of the ERA in New York, classic home of the Left, was particularly shattering to the ERA forces: the vote was 1.8 million to 1.4 million. And this despite an overwhelming 3-to-1 triumph of the ERA in the very home of Left-liberalism, New York County (Manhattan) where the vote was 131 to 41 thousand in favor. Particularly important was the embittered admission of the ERA forces that the defeat was brought about, not by the male chauvinist enemy, but by women themselves.

The blow to the national ERA also stems from the fact that this was the first time that ERA was put to an actual major test among the voters themselves. It is one thing to push the federal amendment through a complaisant state legislature, propelled by the propagandists of NOW. Then the feminists could plausibly claim to represent all of American womanhood. But now, in the vote to defeat ERA in New York and New Jersey, the "silent majority" of American women have at last spoken out. Presumably this writes finis to the ERA movement.

Libertarians have differed on ERA, but for me a stand in opposition to the amendment seems crystal-clear. In the first place, such vague terms as "equality of rights under the law" can be interpreted in almost any way by the courts. And, considering the way that the courts have been interpreting the laws in the last few decades, and considering also that almost all private activities have been ruled to be in some way "governmental", an equal rights clause applying supposedly to government, or, even more vaguely to "the law", will inevitably be held to apply to private firms and organizations as well. ERA would most probably be used to fasten a permanent, egalitarian and "anti-discrimination" tyranny upon private employers, clubs, and organizations.

The supposedly sophisticated proponents derided the grassroots

(Continued on Page 2)

Politics: November '75 —

(Continued from Page 1)

opposition for "lies and misrepresentations" in holding that ERA might well mean the imposition of such things as compulsory unisex toilets. But why not? The opposition women had the good sense to realize that if government is given power, the power will be used and abused, and that given the rampant egalitarianism of our age, such rulings might well occur in the future. The fact that existing states with ERA have not so ruled, as the proponents kept rebutting, does not mean that such rulings would not be imposed in the future.

So that ERA should be opposed because it would mean aggravated government interference with private activity. But it should even be opposed if strictly confined to government itself. But shouldn't government, at least, be prohibited from sex discrimination? Not necessarily. For, suppose that government oppresses Group A in some manner that does not apply to Group B. To order government not to discriminate between the two could mean one of two things: either that the special oppression is removed from Group A, or that equivalent oppression is now imposed on Group B. To libertarians the difference is crucial. For it is better to impose oppression on A only, than to extend that oppression to both A and B.

An anology may be drawn to the case of runaway slaves. Suppose that a portion of slaves are able to run away. If we react by insisting that all slaves be treated "equally before the law", we could be saying that all should go free; but more likely we would be saying that the runaway slaves must be dragged back because it is "unfair" for them to be free while their brothers and sisters are in chains. But surely the latter course is worse than "discrimination." Equality might well mean equality of all in slavery. Hence the very concept of "equality" is dangerous to liberty, and should be opposed.

If this is held to be a far-fetched example, then let us take the slavery of the draft. In our society, only males are drafted, and women are exempt. The national ERA would undoubtedly mean that women, too, would be subject to the draft — equality and non-discrimination in slavery! But surely it is monstrous, from the point of view of liberty, to correct the horrors of the draft by extending those horrors to the female sex. No, we should rejoice that women are exempt, and strive to extend that exemption to men as well.

And so libertarians should oppose ERA right down the line. Are the instincts of the masses more libertarian on this issue than the organized libertarian movement itself?

3. The "Halloween Massacre."

If the election results should be the liking of libertarians, what about the much-reviled "Halloween Massacre" indulged in by President Ford? The "massacre" has had a very bad press, which has been ranting and raving about "dictatorship", "weakness", et al.

a. The Form of the "Massacre."

The press has complained at length about the suddenness, the dictatorial nature of the "Massacre", the bloodletting of our best and brightest, etc. ad nauseam. Dark comparisons have been made to Nixon's infamous "Saturday Night Massacre" of Cox and Richardson. But this totally misses the point. The horror of the firing of Cox was that Cox was on special assignment to investigate despotism, corruption, and illegality within the White House itself, with Nixon himself under grave suspicion. Surely this does not apply to the firing of Schlesinger and Rockefeller. And surely, too, the President has the right to select his Cabinet. Every President has done so and has fired cabinet officers in mid-stream. Why the big fuss over this one?

b. Exit Schlesinger.

One reason for the fuss was the unceremonious dumping of Secretary of Defense Schlesinger. Well, should he have been dumped? Pipe-smoking, intelligent, and professorial he was, but what was the content of his beliefs? Surely that is more important than his IQ or his demeanor. Put bluntly, James Schlesinger was the single most dangerous man in the Administration. For it was Schlesinger who represented all the hawks, all the ultras in the Pentagon and in society at large. It was Schlesinger who fought bitterly against detente, against any cuts in military budgets, against any slight approach to nuclear disarmament, toward alleviating

New Associates

The Libertarian Forum wishes to welcome to the ranks of Libertarian Forum Associates three new members:

Frederick Cox of Decatur, Ga.

Ronald S. Hertz of New York City

Charles Jefferson of Arlington, Va.

Their support is greatly appreciated.

---

the terrible threat of the nuclear destruction of the human race. I am no fan of the balance-of-power politics of Henry Kissinger, but compared to Schlesinger, Super-K was the embodiment of peace and isolationism. Better balance-of-power maneuvering than hawkish drive toward nuclear war. Every friend of liberty and peace must rejoice at the speedy retirement of James Schlesinger to the private life that he so richly deserves.

By their friends ye may know them. Who, characteristically, was the very first politico to leap in with a denunciation of the Schlesinger ouster, to hint darkly that this was a sellout to the Russians? Why none other than Mr. State himself, Scoop Jackson, old friend of Schlesinger. And second and third were the ultra-hawks, Senator Jim Buckley and Ronald Regan.

Along with the departure of Schlesinger, came a cleanout of the intelligence "community", notably William Colby as head of the CIA and General Graham, hawk Schlesingerite, as head of the powerful, little-known, Defense Intelligence Agency (DIA).

c. Exit Rocky.

The press couldn't understand it: the ouster of Schlesinger angered the Republican Right, while the (virtual) ouster of Rockefeller angered the "moderates". How interpret this puzzling phenomenon? To do so, one must go beyond the "left" and "right" categories to the realities of foreign and domestic policy. The ouster of Schlesinger was a blow against the right-wing hawks; the ouster of Rockefeller was a blow against statist fiscal policy, particularly against the powerful forces lobbying for Federal aid to New York City to prevent default, a fate that New York richly deserves. After showing a few signs of buckling under intense pressure by the New York bankers, media, and politicians (including Nelson), Ford, in a manly and noble speech, told New York off, exposed its profligate spending policies, and threatened a veto of any bail-out speech (a stand reportedly stiffened by gutsy Secretary of the Treasury William Simon.) It is true that Ford caved in a bit: promising Federal aid to "essential services" after a default, allowing new debt certificates after default that would take precedence over older bonds (but who would buy them?), and implying (through Arthur Burns) various forms of aid to New York City banks overloaded with near-worthless New York City debt. But at least Ford held firm on default.

By holding on default, President Ford was listening to the libertarian instincts of the mass of Americans, angry at the very idea of Federal aid to prevent a wild-spending New York City government from meeting at least a bit of its just desserts (Actually, as many critics have pointed out, if Beame, Lindsay, Rockefeller et al. had been running a private corporation instead of a government, they would all be in jail by now for doctoring the books.)

And so, by firing Schlesinger and Rockefeller, Ford was moving toward peace on the foreign front, and fiscal conservatism on the domestic front — both steps toward liberty.

And there is another point: the firing of Rockefeller itself is an important step, for it moves against a man who embodies the corporate-state, with its dangerous fusion of political and economic "power", of government and business. Moving Rockefeller away from the Presidency is highly desirable in itself, apart from the New York problem. If Ford can manage to overcome his accident-prone nature until the end of 1976, and continue to avoid such people as Squeaky Fromme and FBI-informant Sara Moore, perhaps America will be free of the menace of a Rockefeller Presidency. ◼

Foreign Affairs Review

By Leonard P. Liggo*

"More Polish Workers Going Into Private Enterprise," was the headline of an article by Malcolm Browne (New York Times, October 17). Capitalism has not only held on in Poland but it is continuing its renaissance in the non-agricultural sector. While there was strong collectivization in other East European countries, which had had more of a feudal tradition, Poland, with a recent period of de-feudalization, stopped collectivization after the 1956 revolt. About eighty percent of Polish agriculture is privately owned and a successful base for the Polish economy. Browne attributed the maintenance of capitalist attitudes to the strength of Catholic thought in Poland.

"The Government has tacitly acknowledged that many products and services can be provided better and more efficiently by private organizations than by Communist state enterprises. Under the present policy of putting a high priority on improving the quality of life for all Poles, the Government is encouraging private enterprise.

"By the end of last year, about 400,000 Poles were working for private organizations, with 62,000 others as apprentices. In 1960, there were 251,000.

"Meanwhile, artisans working in small private workshops have been steadily increasing the value of their output, adapting themselves to the general limits imposed by the system. Last year, the artisan sector did 15 percent more business than in 1973. Scores of interviews with Polish artisans disclosed wide agreement that really good craftsmanship resulted only from private enterprise, not from state factory product.

"There is also a general belief that craftsmanship now is threatened not only by the Communist economic system but by the changes in worker psychology it has brought about.

It is a simple, easily provable fact that Communism makes people lazy, a middle-aged machinist said.

"Most people don't like to think about their work and under Communism they don't have to. That's why relatively few Poles want to be private artisans anymore, even though we are better paid than socialist-sector workers, even though we work shorter weeks and even though we get real pleasure out of our work. We have to think and put our hearts into what we do, and that is what most young people reject these days."

England

Meanwhile, the English Conservative party has moved to economic liberalism or radical liberalism. Sir Keith Joseph, who has replaced Enoch Powell (gone off the deep end in support of Ulster oppression of Catholics) as chief spokesman for sound monetary policy and fighting inflation, was roundly applauded at the recent annual party conference for defending radicalism. Daphne Preston, chairman of the Conservative Political Center's advisory committee, declared: "We must get the Government off our back." Former cabinet minister Michael Heseltine said: "We are now the sole and embattled guardians of the rights of individuals and the family against the claims of a collectivist state. So let us state the position of our party in moral terms, and bring to the fight against sterile restrictions of Socialism the fervor and enthusiasm of a moral crusade." Under Churchill, Eden, Macmillan, Douglas-Home and Heath, the Conservative party held to traditional Tory opposition to the free market. After losing the election in February 1974, Heath was defeated for leadership by Mrs. Margaret Thatcher.

Mrs. Thatcher's victory in the party was due to the work of libertarian-oriented young conservatives who are referred to as the Selsden Group, after an important program on which Heath was able to win his election to the prime ministership in 1970. Heath then abandoned the Selsden free market program for the "middle road." Sir Keith Joseph, chief policy-maker for Mrs. Thatcher, attacked middle of the roadism. "The trouble with the middle ground is that we do not choose it or shape it. It is shaped for us by the extremists. The more extreme to the left, the more to the left is the middle ground. It is a will-of-the-wisp which we follow at our peril." Part of this development can be attributed to Hayek's receiving the Nobel Prize in Economics and the speeches and articles he has given in the last year in England. This fall, Hayek had two articles in the Daily Telegraph as well as a four page interview in its supplement. The only cloud on the horizon for the liberal revival in England is the traditional Tory imperialism. The Celtic peoples of the British Isles in Cornwall, Wales, Scotland and Northern Ireland find Tory governments oppressive and unresponsive to their needs, while the Labour party's strength is in the Celtic regions of western and northern British. If the Conservatives can disassociate themselves from Unionism in Ulster, and come out for decentralization in Wales and Scotland, there is a fair chance for classical liberalism to have a renaissance in England.

Norway

Like Scotland, Norway is becoming a major oil producer in its North Sea fields. It is on the verge of becoming one of the richest industrial nations in the world. "Norway is no longer a country of lumberjacks and fishermen," said Per Ravne, a former ambassador to China and now special adviser for oil and energy in the Foreign Ministry. "We are highly industrialized. We are a nation of importance." Norway has seen a re-birth of nationalism. It rejected membership in the Common Market in 1972.

The present policy is to limit oil production to 90 million tons, which will yield a revenue of 1 billion dollars. Radicals to the left of the dominant Labor party made substantial gains in the 1973 elections because of their strong nationalism. However, the conservatives are gaining strength due to their support for decentralization and preservation of small communities and limitation on industrial growth. The conservatives had emphasized development of industrial plants among the farmers and fisherman of the north; shipbuilding, chemicals, aluminum industries were built. But, oil production will draw workers to the south and upset the traditional balance of the northern communities and southern cities. A major policy, which contributed to the defeat of the Common Market, is to limit immigration. Common Market countries provide free immigration for citizens of former colonial areas. Other racial groups would bring their own social and cultural traditions, and the problems of immigrants of non-European background. All parties seem committed to limiting industrial growth due to new oil production to the limits of available Norwegian population growth. Could King Olav V's visit to the United States have been a subtle attempt to lure the millions of descendants of Norwegian immigrants from Brooklyn, St. Paul, Fargo and San Francisco back to Norway?

Germany

Germany's Social Democrats and Christian Democrats both fared badly in recent elections in the city-state of Bremen. The big winners were the Free Democratic party, winning 13 per cent of the vote (up from 7 per cent). They ran on an economy platform and demanded a fight against inflation. The New York Times in a lead editorial, "Bremen's World Message," declared that the rebuff to Chancellor Helmut Schmidt contained an important message for President Ford. The Times emphasized that the Free Democrats were the big winners in the protest vote due to their deeply anti-inflationary position.

German Chancellor Helmut Schmidt has been busy supporting the Socialists in Portugal. Germany, supported by the Low Countries' and Scandinavian Socialists, poured money into the Socialist party (major rumors claim that the German Socialists have been conduits for CIA funds into Portugal; one must read the late Westbrook Pegler's famous reports of U. S. union representatives overseas carrying CIA funds to support left-wing groups in Europe, to place the whole thing in perspective). France, Italy and England have not given support to the Socialists in Portugal because they would not be unhappy to see a Communist party victory in Portugal. A Communist victory would cause their electorates to support their middle-to-right wing governments against continental coalitions of socialists and communists who are on the verge of gaining electoral victory in Italy and France.

(Continued on Page 4)

Foreign Affairs Review —

(Continued from Page 3)

Portugal

The April, 1974 revolution in Portugal overthrew a fascist government of forty-eight years standing. In 1962 a strong call to the US was made by liberal opponents of the regime to support the overthrow of the dictatorship. Kennedy and Johnson opted for support of the fascist government over the unpredictability of liberalism. The consequences are a socialist rather than a liberal revolution, and an anti-capitialist, anti-feudal and anti-mercantilist revolution. For the last two decades the Portuguese army was involved in fighting anti-liberation wars in its African colonies and in Timor in the East Indies. India seized Goa in 1962 and China has been pleased to have the Portugese possess Macao as a port of entry for prohibited western goods. In fighting the colonial wars, the army officers spent year after year studying Marx, Lenin and Mao in an attempt to understand and counter the successes of the anti-colonial liberation movements.

Thus, the army officers spent all their time studying socialist economics and the problems of underdeveloped, imperialist, mercantilist economies in Africa. They did not study market economics, the economic problems of the industrial Common Market, or of industrial countries. The legacy of the imperialist era is an elite which is trained to administer other countries with other kinds of economies than Portugal. After decades of administering African colonies, military administrators are trying to apply the same procedures to administering a European country.

Portugal emerged along the Atlantic Coast of the Iberian peninsula during the push in the eleventh century of the small Christian refugee states in the northern mountains to re-conquer central Iberia from Islam. While Castile and Leon pushed down the center and Aragon and Catalonia pushed down the Mediteranean coast, the Portugese conquered as far as the Tagus River where Lisbon is located. As in Spain, the reconquest stopped for many centuries, with Islamic emirates controlling the southern territories. Thus, as in Spain, the northern provinces contain the private farms of individual peasants with a long tradition of autonomy. Such areas tend to be the strongholds of Catholicism. In Portugal, the area from Lisbon north is the area of rural homesteads, high population density, illiteracy and clericalism. Along the coast, Oporto, Coimbra, Lisbon, the large cities have become industrial centers, and the strongholds of the Portuguese Socialists. The south, the Alentejo and Algarve, were only conquered from Islam in the fifteenth century shortly before the voyages of discovery, which were continuations of these southward conquests by Portugal and Castile. The lands seized from the Moslems were granted to high nobles who established huge estates to support them at the court in Lisbon. Moslem serfs, and later landless migrant laborers were the basic populations. The voyages of discovery were seeking African slaves to work these huge estates, but with the seizure of Brazil it was more profitable to trade in slaves with the sugar plantations than with the wheat and olive estates of Portugal. Need it be said that the serf, tenant and day laborer population of the feudal south of Portugal are the mass base of the Communist party. Thus, the difference among the revolutionary movements in Portugal are rooted in whether the land system was private as in the north or socialist-fuedal as in the south. The state socialism of fedualism has created the massive crisis of Portugal. No party that does not recognized that all laws must be designed with double application can long retain leadership. For the north, there must be recognition of private property; in the south, there must be abolition of feudalism. If uniformity is tried, then the northerners will revolt in the name of liberty or the southerners will revolt in the name of liberty. Either one would be justified.

Spain

In Spain, a revolutionary situation is developing. The revolution goes back to the time of the French Revolution when the royalists, the liberals, and the supporters of a pro-French regime fought among themselves. The royalists defeated the liberals and Francophiles. The royalists' strength were the Armies of the Faith composed of northern Spanish peasants. In the 1930's, Spain again was divided: in the extreme north, the Basques of the industrial coastal region were radicals. Led by their revolutionary clergy, the Basques demanded autonomy as an independent, pre-Indo-European race. Today the Basques are the major force in the revolutionary movement against Franco. Still led by their bishops and priests, the Basques' program is radicalism and self-determination. The rest of the north is the center of clerical, conservative politics, with the Kingdom of Christ as the objective of these soldiers of the Cross. The Carlists of Navarre represent that tradition.

The industrial east of Spain, along the Mediterranean, Catalonia and Aragon, were the centers of the anarchist movements and the life-force of the revolution until crushed by the Communist-allied central army. The central army officers preferred working with the disciplined, pragmatic Communists than with the decentralist, principled anarchists. In addition to the army officers, the Communists had a mass base among the tenants and agrarian workers of southern Spain, where again the lands conquered from the Moslem emirates were distributed to the great nobles rather than created into private property. Feudalism is the seedbed for Communism. The Socialists were supported by the white collar middle class of the cities and towns. Since the Catholic Church was treated like a great noble it received many large estates and was part of the fedual system. Thus, the conflict between the left, which wished to end feudalism including the economic base of the Church hierarchy, and the right which wished to maintain feudalism. The Catholic Church supported Franco in the Civil War. But, after the war Franco kept power rather than turning it over to Catholic-oriented politicals like Gil Robles. The result has been a unity of all the opposition from the Basques and Communists to the Catholics. The contradictions of the Church supporting war to maintain its fedual privileges weighed heavily on the younger clergy of that day. They are now bishops and cardinals and support radicalism among the clergy. The Francoists call the archbishop of Madrid the Red Cardinal. A bishop of Madrid was recently exiled to Rome to protect him from attack by Francoists. Things are likely to get worse if the radicals are led by a Red Cardinal, which means that in American Catholic terms he is the right of American bishops.

The Basque, and the Catalan (which, of course, is led by the Benedictine monks of the Abbey of Montserrat near Barcelona) self-determination movements are paralled by similar movements in France and Italy. The traditional independence movement in France is that of Celtic Brittany, which has increased in recent years. But, there was a blossoming of nationalism in southern France, Langue d'Oc, which had been conquered in the middle ages by the Franks of the north, and culturally ravished by educational centralization for the last two hundred years. The people of the Midi are not Franks, French, and they want everyone to know it. The Midi is now applied to the area bordering the Mediteranian while the Atlantic area of ancient Acquitaine is called Octian. But, the major center of self-determination activity is the island of Corsica. One problem is that when France ended its colonial empire it decided to plant its Foreign Legion in Corsica; this has led to much hostility to the French government. The militants are called the Action for the Renaissance of Corsica, and they claim that Corsica is treated as a colony. Policemen sent to Corsica are given an extra year's seniority for each year served in Corsica. The French invasion by police has caused a hardening of support, since the gun battles involving hundreds of youths created solidarity against government repression by the close-knit clans. Recently there was a European-wide conference of colonized European peoples including the Basques, Catalonians, Scots, Welsh, Cornish, Irish, Bretons, Octians, Corsicans, Sardinians and Sicilians.

Italy

The analysis of Italian political developments and American government attitudes about them which was presented this summer in the Libertarian Forum seems confirmed by recent events. The Council on Foreign Relations had invited Sergio Segre, director of the foreign section of the Italian Communist party, to confer with the Council's members about US-Italian relations when the Communists have to be included in a future government coalition. This reflected the recognition by leading groups in the US that the Italian Communist party could be an ally of the US in foreign affairs — since the Italian Communists would not fight to get Italy out of NATO — as it is an ally of large Italian business. However, the Administration in Washington denied a visitors visa on the ground that it would publicly demonstrate US recognition of the Christian Democratic party's weakness. In the US, the denial caused controversy because the US had just signed the Helsinki accords with the Soviet Union

(Continued On Page 5)

Foreign Affairs Review —

(Continued From Page 4)

putting pressure on the Russians to permit freedom of travel while the US was denying freedom of travel. In Italy, the issue further strengthened the Communist party because the US embassy in Italy and the US state department had aided the visit recently of Giorgio Almirante, leader of Italian Fascism. He not only was greeted by members of Congress but met with two members of the National Security Council. This caused further fears in all parties in Italy that the Communists must be included in a coalition of all parties to preserve constitutionalism. The State Department's control over visas is a violation of traditional American concepts.

Tom Wicker, in a recent article in the New York Times outlined the Italian Communist party's program to "reprivatize" the economy. Forty-five per cent of Italian gross national product is produced by state-owned or state-partner industries. Wicker says: "The ironic fact is that the Communists are saying that their economic program might **reduce** the nationalization of private industry in Italy and even "reprivatize" some concerns that haven't worked will under state control." The Italian Communists do not see any possibility of maintaining a democratic regime and a socialist economy; since the elimination of the market prevents calculation and shortages are constant in the Eastern Bloc countries with socialist economies, the Italian Communists wish to maintain the market and private industry and to use the state budget to influence the economy. Since that is exactly what the US economy has been, and the results of such state capitalism are now clearly evident, the Italian Communists clearly have been trapped between admitting the validity of market economics or accepting the last vestige of socialism, the contemporary American economy. The Italian Communist economists, such as Lucinao Barca, are in a dilemma. "This approach is also influenced by what Mr. Barca sees as the failure of Keynesian economics to produce in any society a stable relationship between employment, the rate of inflation and the balance of payments. Italy, for example, has sharply improved its balance of payments — but only at the cost of a drastic cut in demand, brought on by declines in employment and production, now down to about 70 per cent of capacity."

"The idea, Mr. Barca says, is to avoid development of "bureaucratic socialism," with everything run by the state, but to influence entrepreneurs to choose the right options for the public good." The Italian Communists point to state ownership of food industries as examples of the need for "reprivatizing." Instead of farm subsidies which create corp surpluses in certain crops while others are constantly imported, food firms would develop long-term contracts with farmers to assure stable prices and purchases. The state-owned firms seem to the Communists to be drained by large excess bureaucracies which private firms would not have. Italian Communists appeal to those who wish to emphasize research and application of technology. Wicker adds: "All of this seems carefully designed to avoid any hint of the kind of heavy-handed socialization of most aspects of the economy that is to be found in Eastern Europe and the Soviet Union. . . The Communists may be able to 'get results' even without power because businessmen and industrialists as well as workers are looking for new approaches to Italy's problems; and because the regional and provincial governments are becoming more important in Italy, just as the Communists have greatly extended their power in those governments."

Turkey

Recent elections in Turkey maintained the equal balance between the two major parties while weakening the smaller conservative parties. The conservative parties wish a return to strict Moslem observance enforced by law. The present government, run by the Justice party, lost seats in the voting although it increased its popular vote at the expense of the more conservative parties. The Justice party supports an Islamic point of view but does not want state support of Islam. It does try to maintain the traditional village culture and agrarian system rather than encourgae industrial development, with the result that large numbers of Turks unable to find either agricultural or industrial work in Turkey must migrate to Germany to work in industrial firms there. The Justice party is more pro-American bases and less inclined to embarrass the US over the Cyprus dispute.

Against these conservative parties stands the Republican party, which has the largest popular support in Turkey, about forty-five percent of the voters. The Republican party was established by the founder of modern Turkey, Kemal Attaturk. It is a secular party which wishes to eliminate the influence of religious thought in society and emphasizes science, industry and technology. As the modernizing party in Turkey, it wishes to encourage a climate of industrial expansion and investment and is critical of the taxing and spending policies of the present government. It opposes the present currency losses and large budget deficits. It is strongly supported in the cities and by educated and non-religious Turks. It is a nationalist party, strongly supported by the military officers who have been educated in modern concepts and is opposed to the control of Turkish foreign policy by US needs. It opposes US bases in Turkey and it carried out the Turkish occupation of the Turkish northern sectors of Cyprus when a pro-American right- wing Greek group attempted to oust Cyprus president, Archbishop Makarios, and attach Cyprus to the then military regime in Athans. The Turkish occupation led to the fall of the pro-American Greek dictatorship. Cyprus, Greece and Turkey have been the center of American interest in the eastern Mediterranean as bases for US influence in the oil regions of the Middle East. That was the reason the Sixth Fleet was stationed in the Mediterranean after World War II and why the Truman Doctrine launched the anti-communist crusade in March, 1947.

Israel

An interesting discussion of the Middle East appeared in the Social Democratic, pro-Zionist quarterly, **Dissent**. Henry Pachter's "Who are the Palestinians?" raised very important questions for such a source as **Dissent**. Pachter described the Arab liberation of Syaria (including Palestine and Jordan) and Iraq from Turkish control in return for a British promise of sovereignty and self-determination.

The British foreign secretary issued a declaration of support for a Jewish immigration to a home in Palestine (the foreign secretary in his Memoirs "wondered how anybody could have been misled into thinking that they meant anything." On the eve of World War II, there were 1.1 million Moslems, 450,000 Jews and 150,000 Christians in Palestine. After World War II, the US refused to lift the immigration restrictions imposed after World War I mainly to keep Jews out of the US. Large numbers of Jews who wished to leave Europe and to go any place but Palestine could not find any place that would take them; once the traditional refuge for immigrants, the US, was closed, they had to go to Palestine. A UN Security Council resolution stated the terms on which a Jewish and an Arab state would each be created in Palestine. Three noncontinuous territories containing all Jews and an equal number of Arabs were created as a Jewish commonwealth, while the other half of the Moslem and Christain Palestinians were placed in the areas of an Arab commonwealth. The assumption was that the two commonwealths would form a single economic and social unit, while political and cultural life would be separate in each commonwealth. Arabs opposed being included in the Jewish sectors. The Zionist leadership sought to create a Contiguous Jewish state and to expel the Arabs from their lands in those territories. The UN resolution is the only legitimate basis in law for the solution or the Palestine question; a restoration of the status quo to the terms of the UN resolution would stabilize the situation in Palestine.

Pachter explains: "Much has been made of the Histradruth's (Jewish labor organization requiring high-wage Jewish labor instead of low-wage Arab labor) job policy. Obviously, in terms of Lenin's theory of imperialism, Jewish business has not been guilty of exploiting cheap Arab labor; rather, Jewish colonists have been guilty of making Arabs jobless and driving them from their lands. I have to explain here a subtle-ty of feudal law: fellahim can be sold along with the land jobless and driving them from their lands. I have to explain here a subtle-ty of feudal law: fellahim can be sold along with the land on which they have been sitting; but the land cannot be sold without them, pulling it away from under them. When the Jewish Agency, aware only of capitalist law, bought land from the callous effendis, it may honestly have thought that thereby it had acquired the right to expel the fellahim. settlers, who had naively begun to cultivate this ground (including kibbutzniks who did so in the name of "socialism"), wondered why the former owners or tenants of those grounds were firing at them from afar or staging surprise attacks on their innocent children: from the vantage of expelled Palestinians, the settlers were usurpers, colonizers,

(Continued On Page 6)

Recommended Reading

Compiled by Bill Evers

(Mr. Evers is a doctoral candidate in political science, Stanford University.)

Henry W. Berger, "Bipartisanship, Senator Taft, and the Truman Administration," **Political Science Quarterly**, Summer 1975. Discussion of Truman's creation and manipulation of the notion of bipartisanship. Taft's belief in foreign policy debate and his opposition to intervention abroad and to executive branch aggrandizement of foreign policy decision-making.

Barton J. Bernstein, "Roosevelt, Truman, and the Atomic Bomb: A Reinterpretation," **Political Science Quarterly**, Spring 1975. Now the definitive revisionist account of the decision to drop the atom bomb. Supersedes Alperovitz and Kolko.

Leon G. Campbell, "Black Power in Colonial Peru: The 1779 Tax Rebellion in Lambayeque," **Black Academy Review**, Spring-Summer 1972. (Issue sold for $4 by Black Academy Press, 135 University Ave., Buffalo, N.Y. 14214).

Walter Cohen, "Herbert Hoover: Some Food for Thought," **Pacific Research**, November-December 1971. The politics of food aid at the conclusion of World War I.

Walter Cohen, "U.S. Foreign Policy — A Radical Study Guide," **Pacific Research**, March-May 1972. Includes a thorough reader's guide to "right-wing" and "left-wing" revisionist material on foreign policy. (May be obtained from Pacific Studies Center, 1963 University Ave., East Palo Alto, Calif. 94303, $.60 per back issue.)

Sime Djodan, "The Evolution of the Economic System of Yugoslavia and the Economic Position of Croatia," **Journal of Croatian Studies**, 1972. Yugoslavian liberal Marxist economist criticizes bureaucratic socialism and the exploitation of Croatia. (Available for $8.00 from the Croatian Academy of America, P.O. Box 1767, Grand Central Sta., New York, N.Y. 10017.)

G. William Domhoff, ed., "New Directions in Power Structure Research," **Insurgent Sociologist**, Spring 1975. Special issue of scholarly work on the Council on Foreign Relations, Advertising Council, the Industry Advisory Council to the Department of Defense, and other phenomena. (Issue available for $3.00 from **Insurgent Sociologist**, Dept. of Sociology, University of Oregon, Eugene, Ore., 97403.)

Dan Feshbach and Less Shipnuck, "Corporate Regionalism in the United States," **Kapitalistate**, May 1973. Study of regional government in the U.S.

"From Wall Street to Watergate: The Money Behind Nixon," **Latin America and Empire Report** (North American Congress on Latin America), November 1973. A financial interest group interpretation of Watergate.

David M. Hunter, "Ohio's Usury Laws and Their Effect upon the Home Mortgage Market," **Akron Law Review**, Fall 1974.

Sabri Jiryis, "The Legal Structure for the Expropriation and Absorption of Arab Lands in Israel," **Journal of Palestine Studies**, Summer 1973. (Available for $3.00 from P.O. Box 329-A, R.D. No. 1, Oxford, Pennsylvania 19363).

Clark S. Knowlton, "Land-Grant Problems among the State's Spanish-Americans," **New Mexico Business**, June 1967. Detailed historical review that provides the background for the New Mexico landgrant struggles of 1967 led by Reies Lopez Tijerina. Published by the Bureau of Business Research, University of New Mexico, 1821 Roma Avenue, N.E., Albuquerque, New Mexico 87106.

Stephan Leibfried, "U.S. Central Government Reform of the Administrative Structure During the Ash Period (1968-1971)," **Kapitalistate**, Dec. 1973-Jan. 1974.

Michael Levin, "Marxism and Romanticism: Marx's Debt to German Conservatism," **Political Studies**, December, 1974 Shows that Marxism derives some of its important ideological views from the German conservative political tradition.

Jonathan Marshall, "Review of D. Borg and S. Okanoto, eds., **Pearl Harbor as History**," **Pacific Research**, March-April 1974.

Jonathan Marshall, "Southeast Asia and U.S.-Japan Relations, 1940-1941," **Pacific Research**, March-April 1973. Marshall's articles, based on new archival research, stress the desire of the American power elite to control access to S. E. Asian raw materials.

Charles W. McCurdy, "Justice Field and the Jurisprudence of Government-Business Relations: Some Parameters of Laissez-Faire Constitutionalism, 1863-1897," **Journal of American History**, March 1975.

(Continued On Page 7)

Foreign Affairs Review —

(Continued From Page 5)

imperialists in person, not the tools of mysterious powers across the sea."

Since the Arab peasants were the Lockean owners of the lands on which the effendis levied taxes and claimed to "own" under the Turkish regime, it is debatable that the Jewish Agency was operating under capitalist concepts of law. Pachter quotes George Antonius, **The Arab Awakening** (New York, Capricorn Books, 1965): "The revolt is largely manned by the peasantry, that is to say by the people whose life and livelihood are on the soil but who have no say whatever in its disposal; and their anger and violence are as much directed against the Arab landowners and brokers who have facilitated the sales as against the policy of the mandatory Power under whose aegis the transactions have taken place." Pachter adds: "The Jewish leaders — except for the Communists, Martin Buber, and some Chalutzim — never thought of allying themselves with these victims of colonization." Pachter also suggests that the Jewish armed groups initiated the terrorist approach to politics in Palestine. He adds: "But the Isrealis who justify their claim to the land by their tribal memory of 2,000 years obviously have no argument against people whose claim is based on tribal memories reaching back only 30 years. More than the expellees' actual misery, the bitterness of the sacrifice that was imposed on them intensifies the hate that defines the Palestinians as a nation distinct from other Arabs." Pachter recommends that the Palestinian Arabs be given a choice of

compensation for lost land, residence or job, or returning to Palestine. Pachter does not say whether or not they should, if they return, be given their rightful land, residence or job, but obviously that is the only just solution. Of course, that would have to occur in the context of legal equality and the ending of special legal positions for Jews. Since the implementation of the 1947 UN security council resolution is the only international legal basis for ending the problem of Israel, these suggestions could be important contributions to the overall settlement. Pachter discusses the necessity to recognize the Arab commonwealth in Palestine as the basis for peace. He says: "There can be no settlement, no truce and no confidence between Arabs and Jews as long as their status is not determined equitably and as long as there is not international machinery to ascertain the will of the Palestinians themselves." He adds: "Both these peoples are too primitive in their tribal instincts or too immature as nations to be reasonable on such questions where self-respect is at stake." He thinks that the great powers have to impose solutions on the parties concerned. "In the beginning, a Palestinian state would probably make obstreperous noises at international gatherings, nor might it in other ways be the most desirable neighbor one would wish to have. Nevertheless, I believe that the nonsatisfied demand for a Palestinian state is now a major source of posturing, gesturing, and confrontation." (For a discussion of groups in Israel thinking about peaceful answers to Arab-Jewish relations, see Arthur Waskow's article in **Link**, Sept., 1975, published by the Institute for Policy Studies, 1901 Q Street, Northwest Washington, D. C. 20009.)

*Mr. Liggio teaches history at SUNY, Old Westbury.   ◘

Is Dayan Just Another Rommel?

By Joseph R. Stromberg*

Review of The Other Israel: The Radical Case Against Zionism ed. Arie Bober (Garden City, N.Y., Doubleday, 1972).

This important and comprehensive work is a collection of historical and political essays written by members of the Israeli Socialist Organization. ISO is the only genuine anti-Zionist organization on the Israeli political spectrum; and it is a group which accepts Arabs as full members. Despite denunciation as "Fatah agents" and police harassment, ISO maintains a consistent line of national liberation and self-determination for all Middle Eastern peoples.

By recognizing and espousing the rights of the Palestinians to their homeland, as well as the rights of the new Israeli people to areas which individual Jews legitimately pioneered and peacefully settled before 1948, ISO directly attacks the foundations of the Zionist state. On the basis of uncompromising Marxist humanism ISO has arrived at essentially the same overall position on the Palestinian question that a libertarian would come to on the basis of his own natural law (or other) premises.[1]

The essays properly compare the Zionist establishment to the settler regime of the Boers in South Africa. Israel is thus a modern example of the original conquest-states described by the German sociologist Franz Oppenheimer in his numerous works. Sir Ronald Storrs, first civil governor of Palestine under the British mandate, welcomed the Zionists as "a little loyal Jewish Ulster" in the midst of dangerous Arab nationalists. Like Ulster, which is a tool of British imperialism in Ireland, Israel continues to function as a tool of Western imperialism in the Middle East. Unlike many conquest states, however, "Zionist colonialism displaces and expells" instead of retaining the bulk of the former owners of the soil as cheap labor. The early colonizers bought huge tracts of land "owned" by reactionary Arab effendis and threw off the Arab tenants. The slogan of "Jewish labor only", consistently followed since the beginnings of the Zionist enterprise, has even undercut the rational market option of hiring the cheapest labor; this "narrow" bourgeois alternative has always been largely defeated by the forces of Zionist nationalism and the Jewish labor bureaucracies.

A number of essays brings out Israeli expansionism, the repression of the darker Jews, native to the area, and the mistreatment of native populations. A reading of the evidence forever discredits the myth of the beleaguered little "democracy" fighting for its life. The "emergency regulations," for example, a carry-over of British measures of 1936-39, allow instantaneous martial law, including arbitrary arrest, restrictions on freedom of movement, and confiscation and destruction of property, such as the punitive dynamiting of homes. Even worse, whole areas can be sealed off from the outside, leaving the inhabitants with a choice: get out or starve. No wonder the Palestinians "voluntarily" depart. Much land has been taken over since 1948 by selective application of these regulations. No Hayekian "rule of law" here! Indeed, for repression and tyranny Israeli officialdom can compete with just about any state in existence today.

An interesting chapter discusses the class structure of Israel. Israel emerges as a society in which European Jews lord over native Jews and Arabs, and which only survives because of massive outside infusions of capital from the United Jewish Appeal, the Bonn government (which accepts Israel as the institutional expression of the victims of Nazism and pays reparations to Israel), and, of course, the United States government. But this mass of capital does not go to the national bourgeoisie, but to the Israeli state, the quasi-state Jewish Agency and the labor party bureaucracies — especially the Histadrut, a national labor monopoly which must make George Meany grind his teeth in envy. Even the much touted glorious kibbutzim are completely subsidized by the state, private firms, and banks, and are living on stolen land.

Chapters on the Israeli Left and Borochovism reveal the built-in limitations of all factions which work within the Zionist framework. Even Uri Avnery, supposed left-wing statesman, appears to accept the Zionist status quo and attempts to evade the self-created problems of Zionism by speaking of "post-Zionist" politics and proposing a binational federation with the Palestinians. ISO regards the latter proposal as the equivalent of an Arab Bantustan.

Such left-wing Zionism, including Borochovism which claims to derive Zionism from Marxism, ignores the central contradiction within Zionism. Zionism as European Jewish nationalism had to oppress and displace the Palestinians, once it was determined that only Palestine would be considered for Zionist colonization. A number of essays, especially, "Zionism and Universal Ethics," attack Zionism for rejecting traditional Jewish universalism and humanism. Taking anti-Semitism as a special Jewish problem, Zionism proposed a special solution and even cooperated with anti-Semites in bringing it about. Ethnocentric history and European Jewish chauvinism, which assumed that all non-Jews were the potential enemy, were central to Zionism.[2] Understandably, Hitler's crimes made Zionism seem perfectly plausible.

While these ISO essays only hint at such an interpretation, they point directly at the deeply rooted fascist philosophical trend in Zionism. Zionist repudiation of universalism, humanism and transcendent values in favor of the politicized tribal community defined as the highest good, brings Zionism well within the philosophical definition of fasicism offered by Ernst Nolte, a contemporary German historian.[3] Thus "When Zionism

(Continued On Page 8)

Recommended Reading —

(Continued From Page 6)

A fair-minded exposition of the legal thought of a famous classical-liberal Supreme Court judge.

James O'Connor, "Political Economy of State Expenditures and Revenues: A Bibliography," Kapitalistate, May 1973. Valuable bibliography on public finance.

Marc Pilisuk, International Conflict and Social Policy (Englewood Cliffs, N.J.: Prentice-Hall, 1972.) A power-elite analysis of foreign policymaking based on thorough knowledge of the social science literature. Includes as a chapter the famous 1965 article on the military-industrial complex which Pilisuk co-authored with Tom Hayden.

"Regionalism and the Bay Area," Pacific Research, November-December 1972. An in-depth case study of metropolitan government.

D. I. Roussopoulos, ed., The Political Economy of the State (Montreal: Black Rose Books, 1973.) A radical examination of who benefits from the government budget in Canada. (Available for $3.00 from Black Rose Books, 3934 rue St. Urbain, Montreal 131, Quebec, Canada.)

Larry Sawers and Howard M. Wachtel, "The Distributional Impact of Federal Government Subsidies in the United States," Kapitalistate, Spring 1975. (Issues available for $2.50 from James O'Connor, Dept. of Economics, California State University, San Jose, Calif. 95114).

Harry N. Scheiber, "Property Law, Expropriation, and Resource Allocation by Government: the United States, 1789-1910," Journal of Ecnomic History, March 1973. Includes important information on how businesses took land from private owners via the eminent domain process.

Harry N. Scheiber, "The Road to Munn: Eminent Domain and the Concept of Public Purpose in the State Courts," Perspectives in American History, 1971. Extensive and detailed discussion of land confiscation via eminent domain.

"Southern Militarism," Southern Exposure, 1973. (Published by the Institute for Southern Studies, 88 Walton St., N.W., Atlanta, Georgia 30303.) The military-industrial complex in the American South.

David Vogel, "Corporations and the Left," Socialist Revolution, No. 20, April-June 1974. Examination of the doctrine of corporate responsibility. (Issue available from Agenda Publishing Co., 396 Sanchez St., San Francisco, Calif. 94114. for $2.00).

Steve Weissman, ed., Big Brother and the Holding Company: The World Behind Watergate (Palo Alto, Calif.: Ramparts Press, 1974). $3.45. Significant New Left interpretations of the Watergate affair.   ◻

Dayan Another Rommel? —

(Continued from Page 7)

had to choose between the Jews and the Jewish state, it unhesitantingly preferred the latter."⁴ Statis to the core, such antitranscendence parallels the positions developed by Charles Maurras, the Italian socialist Mussolini, and — Adolf Hitler. It is clear from ISO's evidence that Israeli ideology justifies all criminal (from the standpoint of universal ethics) acts of the "sovereign, martial, inwardly antagonistic racial community" (Nolte's phrase for the fascist society). According to ISO, even such characteristically fascist rhetoric as "the eternity of war and the sanctity of blood" enjoys growing popularity within Israel³ — a veritable revival of blood-and-soil nonsense.

The chapter on the background of the 1967 preemptive war brings out the importance of the "eternal enemy" theme in Israeli thought. Israel is a society completely militarized for the eternal struggle for illusory security — just one more crusade and we will be safe.⁴ But, as Nolte demonstrates, a paranoiac conception of eternal wars for "self-defense" is at the heart of genuine fascism.⁷ The fascist sincerely believes that his crimes are necessary to preserve the fragile, surrounded racial community and its incomparable culture. The interesting question of how far official statist Cold War nationalism has pushed American society down the fascist path of course deserves treatment at another time.⁸

ISO sees the solution in a revolutionary transformation of the Middle East in which the new Israeli people will become an autonomous community somehow linked to the regional socialist system. Despite its tying of constructive change to socialism and a certain weakness on the peasant issue, ISO's Marxist universalism allows it to break out of Zionism and propose self-determination of all peoples — a position strikingly similar to that which Ludwig von Mises took in The Free and Prosperous Commonwealth on the basis of liberal universalism.

For ISO, socialism is necessary to eliminate all "alienation," including all market relations. Yet the fact that socialist states behave as badly as other states ought to tell them something. Stalin is of course the classic case of a distinctly fascist leader utilizing an amalgam of Marxist and nationalist rhetoric, although his Bolshevik mind-set perhaps prevented him from deviating as far in words as that other nationalized Marxist, Benito Mussolini. ISO even terms nationalism a form of alienation. A libertarian would add that nationalism is part of the real problem itself: the state. In Bakunin's words the state is "the negation of humanity." Fascism in Israel or anywhere else is merely the most thorough affirmation of this alienating machine based on the atavistic fears it promotes among its subjects; fascism is the ideological affirmation of statist crime in the face of all transcendent values and institutions such as humanist ethics, natural law, universal religion, and the world marketplace.

Despite these criticisms, The Other Israel is a valuable and significant study, especially at a time when Henry Kissinger and Jerry Ford are committing American treasure and probably lives to the long-range defense of its miniature Leviathan state, founded on the repudiation of the best in the Judaic heritage.⁹

FOOTNOTES

¹For a libertarian exploration of the issue, see the brief essay by Imad-a-Din Ahmad, "The Right to Rule in the Middle East," Abolitionist, I, 8, p. 8 and I, 9, pp. 3-4.

²Two radical analyses which touch on Jewish chauvinism (from a Jewish perspective) are Norman Fruchter, "Arendt's Eichmann and Jewish Identity" reprinted in James Weinstein and David W. Eakins (eds.), For A New America: Essays in History and Politics from Studies on the Left, 1959-1967 (New York, 1970), pp. 423-454; and David Horowitz, "The Passion of the Jews," Ramparts, XIII, 3 (October, 1974), pp. 21-8 and 56-60. The latter essay is especially perceptive and compassionate.

³Ernst Nolte, Three Faces of Fascism: Action Francaise, Italian Fascism, National Socialism (New York, 1969). Nolte's thought-provoking study deserves to be read in full.

⁴The Other Israel, p. 171.

⁵Ibid., p. 235.

⁶Garry Willis, whose National Review traditionalism and current Berrigan-style leftism appear to be products of a medieval Catholic outlook, actually defends Israel as a chivalric crusader kingdom in a recent issue of Esquire (July, 1975).

⁷Nolte, pp. 507-515.

⁸An interesting beginning of such an analysis is the editorial, "The Ultra-Right and Cold War Liberalism," Studies on the Left, II, 1 (1962), pp. 3-8. For libertarians it would be especially important to investigate how far right-wing Objectivism, by internalizing Cold War American nationalism, has gone down the fascist path — a point to which I hope to return in a future essay. For an "economic determinist" approach to Zionism by a Bakuninist libertarian, see Stephen Halbrook, "The Philosophy of Zionism: A Materialist Interpretation", in Ibrahim Abu-Lughod and Baha Abu-Laban (eds.), Settler Regimes in Africa and the Arab World: The Illusion of Permanence (Wilmette, Ill., 1974), pp.20-30.

⁹For an early critique of Israel by a libertarian's libertarian who stressed the opposition between Judaism and Zionism, see Frank Chodorov, "Some Blunt Truths About Israel," American Mercury, LXXXIII, 390 (July, 1956), 55-9. This appeared, incidentally, long before the Mercury's degeneration into a neo-Nazi organ.

*Mr. Stromberg is a doctoral candidate in history at the University of Florida, Gainesville.

The Libertarian Forum
BOX 341
MADISON SQUARE STATION
NEW YORK, NEW YORK 10010

First Class

Published Every Month. Subscription Rates: $8.00 Per Year; $15.00 Two Years

A Monthly Newsletter

THE
Libertarian Forum

Joseph R. Peden, Publisher   Murray N. Rothbard, Editor

VOLUME VIII, NO. 12   DECEMBER, 1975   US-ISSN0047-4517

STOP REAGAN!

The newly burgeoning candidacy for President of Ronald Reagan is a grave danger and a menace to individual liberty, and libertarians should hope that he is knocked out of the box as quickly as possible. The Reagan candidacy is a menace on three levels: (a) the content of a future Reagan presidency; (b) the direction in which the Reagan movement will push the weak-kneed and centrist Ford administration in the coming months; and (c) the illusions that Reaganism will sow among libertarians and among instinctively libertarian voters throughout the country. The fact that this statement will shock and aggravate many libertarians is itself a sign of the gravity and the depth of the illusions that Reaganism has already sown among libertarians across the country.

What is Reagan and why is he a looming menace? In brief, because Reagan is, purely and simply, a **conservative**, with all that that label implies. Being a conservative, Reagan has consistently been an ultra-hawk on foreign policy, constantly pushing toward a war position across the globe; has shown himself to be weak — at the very best — on civil liberties; and has pledged a devotion to domestic and economic free-market policy which is all rhetoric and no action. The fact that Reagan likes to quote from Bastiat means little when ranged alongside his war-mongering foreign policy and his lack of concrete action to roll back the State at home.

How long will it take libertarians to realize that, on the scale of important issues, war and foreign policy are far more important than domestic consideration? What benefit would come to liberty from a President who would cut welfare expenditures, but embroil us into a series of wars, or even into the holocaust of World War III? The biggest single enemy of liberty, the biggest threat to the life, liberty and property of Americans and of the entire human race is modern nuclear warfare. We need above all a President who would act to remove the menace of such world destruction from over our heads, and not one who would act to bring such devastation to pass. Yet Reagan is and has long been an ultra-hawk. Furthermore, in addition to the danger of war and military intervention abroad, Reagan, as a good conservative, consistently pushes for greater militarism at home: for increasing military expenditures, and for the grave threat to domestic liberty and to distortions of production and the American economy which such militarism entails.

Every significant leap away from liberty and into statism in the past century has come about as a result of American (and other countries') entry into war, aggression, militarism, and empire. War has been the great killer of human liberty as well as human lives. Yet Reagan would not only bring war far closer but would rivet much further the yoke of militarism upon the lives, liberty, and property of all of us.

It should also be remembered that the power of the President in domestic affairs is strictly limited, limited by a Congress which will remain solidly in Democratic hands. Where the President's power is frighteningly unlimited is in foreign affairs, and that is precisely where Reagan is at his most dangerous — this would-be "Wyatt Earp at the O.K. Corral", as the British delegate to the U.N. spoke of the new conservative-Social Democratic hero, Pat Moynihan. Think: do you want

Ronald Reagan's finger on the nuclear button?

Reagan has been fully consistent with his hawk-conservative image. His was one of the first voices to protest at the alleged surrender to the Russians when the hawk Schlesinger was fortunately booted out of the Secretaryship of Defense. Reagan has opposed even the picayune SALT agreement to limit the arms race, and has consistently pressed for increases in the swollen boondoggle of military spending. On foreign affairs he has attacked detente — which at least has defused some of the most hazardous aspects of the Cold War — and has fought the idea of at least normalizing relations with Cuba and of abandoning our collectivist imperialism in the Panama Canal Zone (collectivist in that all the Americans there are employees of the U.S. Army occupation force.)

Neither has Reagan been a stalwart of civil liberties. Can we really trust Reagan to abolish victimless crimes to refrain from bugging and spying on American citizens? Reagan's record in going down the pike with the tyrant Nixon until the very end is scarcely reassuring on his civil libertarian aims. Recently, Reagan has flatly refused to criticize the shameful actions of the FBI in harassing, spying upon, and blackmailing Martin Luther King.

So if Reagan is bad on foreign policy and bad on civil liberties, what's he good on? The budget? But in California, during his eight years as governor Reagan doubled the size of the state budget, and strove to cement the current neo-mercantilist "partnership" between government and business. His free-market rhetoric is fine, but rhetoric divorced from action is not simply unfortunate; it is worse than useless, for it misleads everyone, supporters and opponents of the free economy alike, into believing that Reagan is really an economic libertarian. Four years of Reaganite statism will simply convince both sides that a truly substantial rollback of Big Government is impossible; for "even Reagan came out for . ." will be the universal cry. By spouting libertarian rhetoric that he has no intention to put into reality, Reagan does grave disservice to the libertarian cause, not the least because he has duped many libertarians and quasi-libertarians into following his star.

Finally, even Reagan as contender, let alone as President, is a threat to peace and liberty, for the stronger the showing he makes, the more likely his candidacy will be to push the weak centrist Ford into more and more hawkish positions on foreign policy. What happens in 1975-76 is particularly important because the Ford administration has been stalling on implementing the SALT II "pre-agreement" that Ford and Brezhnev concluded at Vladivostok last year. For the major problem in an arms ceiling accord is the insistence of the U.S. in continuing work on a new "cruise" missile, tipped with nuclear warheads. The problem of the cruise missile is simply this: Russia's greatest fear is that America may proceed to develop a "first strike capability", enabling the U.S. to launch a nuclear war while fending off Soviet retaliatory missiles. Nothing is better calculated to drive the Russians into panicky military actions and arms escalations. Secondly, the best thing about the current nuclear "balance of terror" is that both sides are now able to inspect and verify

(Continued on Page 2)

621

On Nozick's Anarchy, State, And Utopia — I

(Editor's Note: Last Year, Robert Nozick's **Anarchy, State and Utopia** was published, gaining the prestigious National Book Award in 1975. This book, by a Harvard professor of philosophy, defends the minimal, laissez-faire state and attempts to rebut the case for free-market anarchism. A complex work, it is fitting that the book be treated complexly, for the book has two kinds of importance, external and internal to the libertarian movement. Externally, the fame of the work has had great importance in making the topic of libertarianism and anarchism respectable for the first time in philosophy courses and facilities, and paving the way for libertarians to write term papers and dissertations in a previously verboten area. The book has also caused considerable shock and bewilderment in left-liberal intellectual circles. Precisely because the book is by a Harvard professor, it cannot be ignored, as it undoubtedly would had Nozick been a professor at Little Rock State Teachers. It was precisely the anguish at a **Harvard** man writing such a book that forms a central theme in the disgusting review of the book in the journal **Political Theory** by the eminent political philosopher Brian Barry.

While Nozick's book has aided the libertarian cause externally, it plays no such role **within** the movement; for here Nozick's main thrust has been to attack the anarchist position. Nozick's anti-anarchism deserves a considered critique, which has already begun in a **Reason** (November, 1975) review by Professor Eric Mack. The **Libertarian Forum** plans to aid in this task by printing, one at a time (because of space considerations) the brilliant critiques of Nozick presented at the Third Libertarian Scholars Conference on October 25 at New York City.

This first essay in the series is by Mr. Randy E. Barnett, a student at Harvard Law School. Mr. Barnett wrote his bachelor's honors thesis at Northwestern University on the philosophy of anarchism.)

Whither Anarchy?
Has Robert Nozick Justified The State?

By Randy Barnett

One can appreciate **Anarchy, State & Utopia** on many levels. Its emphasis on individual freedom is a refreshing change of pace. It questions assumptions that have long been sacrosanct. It puts forth a theory of entitlement which is nothing short of remarkable in this day and age. And most importantly, it is being taken seriously by the press and, hopefully, the establishment philosophers as well.

But Professor Nozick has attempted more than this. He has attempted to refute the anarchist position. This is a rare endeavor. Few have taken the anarchist position seriously enough to refute it. Few understand it well enough to do it justice. Dr. Nozick displays an intimate knowledge of the anarchist position and yet he rejects it. His refutation is novel, intricate and many faceted. But does it succeed? In this paper I shall try to outline a few reasons why I think it does not.

Nozick begins by asserting that "Individuals have rights..." (ix).* The purpose of the first part of his book (the only part which we shall treat here) is to see if it is possible to evolve a state or "state-like entity" (118) without any violation of individual rights. He concludes that such a thing is possible and likely as well. I shall confine my examination to the possibility that a state might exist which does not violate individual rights ab inito.

"In a state of nature an individual may himself enforce his rights, defend himself, exact compensation, and punish." (12) But an individual may also delegate this right to friends, relatives, or hirelings. A company which specialized in defense of its customers Nozick would call a protective association. (12) The protective association has no rights of action other than the sum of the rights delegated to it by its subscribers. (89) To this point the anarchist has no problem. At least he thinks he has no problem. He has yet to hear what Professor Nozick believes is the content of these individual rights.

Nozick analogizes rights to a sort of boundary which "circumscribes an area in moral space around an individual." (57) What happens if one person does something which risks crossing the boundary of another? Nozick answers that you may prohibit the risky activity provided that "those who are disadvantaged by being forbidden to do actions that only might harm others must be compensated for these disadvantages foisted upon them in order to provide security for the others." (83) This he calls the "principle of compensation." It "requires that people be compensated for having certain risky activities prohibited to them." (83)

It follows from this principle that an individual may be prohibited from using a procedure of enforcing his rights which is risky or unreliable, provided that the principle applies to this type of activity. Nozick gives two parallel justifications for applying the principle to dispute settlement.

Since he maintains that a protective association has no rights of action other than the sum of the rights delegated to it by its subscribers (89), Nozick first seeks to ground his justification on some right held by every individual. He turns hopefully to the notion of "procedural rights." "Each person has a right to have his guilt determined by the least dangerous of the known procedures for ascertaining guilt, that is, by the one having the lowest probability of finding an innocent person guilty." (96) The association's right to prohibit risky procedures, therefore, derives directly from the individual's procedural rights.

Secondly, Nozick insists that the prohibition of "unreliable" procedures is valid even if there were no procedural rights. He contends that epistemic considerations govern the use of retaliatory force. That is, you must know that an aggressor has violated someone's rights before you may retaliate. Use of force on an aggressor without knowing that he is guilty is itself aggression. "If someone knows that doing act A would

(Continued on Page 3)

*All parenthetical numbers are from **Anarchy, State & Utopia**, Basic Books, 1974, Robert Nozick.

Stop Reagan! — (Continued from Page 1)

arms agreements, and to find out what the other side is doing with its missiles. They are able to do this because both sides have satellites which can spot the deployment of all nuclear and other missiles and strategic bombers. The cruise missiles threaten to destroy that balance because they can be fired with great accuracy from ordinary planes and ordinary submarine torpedo tubes. A U.S. cruise missile would mean that the Soviets would have no way of knowing how many such missiles we had, how they were deployed, or whether we were readying them for a surprise first strike attack against Russia. One of the dangers of Schlesinger is that he was a firm supporter of cruise missile development, which might be ready for actual testing next year. Kissinger is less firmly committed to the cruise missile. The greater the Reagan strength in the primaries, the more the Ford administration will be pushed to proceeding on this meancing course for world peace and for any hope of limiting or eventually reversing the arms race.

And so, while some of the nation's media persist in thinking of libertarians as some sort of ultra-wing of the Reaganite movement (and some libertarians unfortunately agree), libertarians should hope instead for a smashing defeat of Reagan as soon as possible, and his ouster from the Presidential race.

Whither Anarchy? —

(Continued from Page 2)

violate Q's rights unless condition C obtained, he may not do A if he has not ascertained that C obtains through being in the best feasible position for ascertaining this." (106)

On this analysis, a protective association may prohibit others from using procedures which fail to meet some standard of certainty since failure to meet this standard means that the enforcer lacks the requisite knowledge of guilt.

Once you swallow the principle of compensation and its applicability to dispute settlement, the introduction of the minimal state-like entity is all downhill. Nozick envisions one association coming to dominate the market. By his principles, this association would have the right to prohibit all competitors who in its opinion employed risky procedures (provided, of course, "compensation" was paid). Voila! We have a state-like entity which arises without violating anyone's rights, right?

Everything hinges on whether Nozick has successfully outlined an "invisible hand" explanation of the state where no rights are violated in the process. Consequently, Nozick's conception of rights and their basis becomes crucial here. Yet early in the book he apologizes for not presenting a theory of the moral basis of rights. (xiv) Still it is possible to discern a notion of rights being used here.

A right is a freedom to do something, that is, to use property which includes one's body in a certain way unimpinged by external constraints (force or threat of force). The right of self-defense is contained within the concept of right itself. It is simply a means of exercising your right when someone is trying to prevent you from doing so. The fact you have a right of action means you may act in that way even if another attempts to prevent this. Self-defense, then, is implicit in the notion of rights.

Where do rights come from? How are they grounded? Nozick doesn't say and I will not pretend to offer a final answer to this question. But it seems that since the concept of right carries within it the freedom to use property, rights are created along with property ownership. To my way of thinking this is what ownership means. Rights (to use property in a certain way), then, can be homesteaded, exchanged, or bestowed to employ the Lockean trichotomy.

Has Nozick's minimal state violated individual rights? You remember that the reason the dominant protective association has a right to prohibit risky, unreliable enforcement methods is that its members, indeed all people have procedural rights. "Each person has the right to have his guilt determined by the least dangerous of the known procedures for ascertaining guilt, that is, by the one having the lowest probability of finding an innocent man guilty." (96) "The principle is that a person may resist, in self-defense, if others try to apply to him an unreliable or unfair procedure of justice." (102)

But where would such a right come from? Was it homesteaded, exchanged or received as a gift? And does this right of self-defense bear any resemblance to the right of self-defense I discussed earlier? Nozick deals with none of these questions. He simply assumes the existence of procedural rights and then proceeds to speculate on what form they should take. This does not mean that Nozick is wrong. It means only that we have no reason to believe he's right.

At the same time Nozick chides the natural-rights tradition which, he says, "offers little guidance on precisely what one's procedural rights are in a state of nature, on how principles specifying how one is to act have knowledge built into their various clauses, and so on. Yet," he continues, "persons within this tradition do not hold that one may not defend oneself against being handled by unreliable or unfair procedures." (101)

I maintain that this is precisely what the natural rights tradition does hold or, at least, should hold: That there are no natural procedural rights. Let me briefly defend this claim.

In the state of nature one has the right to defend oneself against the wrongful use of force against person or property. But if you commit an aggressive act, the use of force by the victim to regain what was taken from him is not wrongful. If you have stolen a T.V., the rightful owner may come and take it back. You may rightfully resist only if you are innocent or have some legitimate defense. What are we then to make of procedural rights?

Though only the innocent party may rightfully use self-defense, it is often unclear to neutral observers and the parties involved just who is innocent. As a result there exists the practical problem of determining the facts of the case and then the respective rights of the disputants. But I must stress here that this is a practical question of epistemology not a moral question. The rights of the parties are governed by the objective fact situation. The problem is to discern what the objective facts are, or, in other words, to make our subjective understanding of the facts conform to the objective facts themselves.

The crucial issue is that rights are ontologically grounded, that is grounded in the objective situation. Any subjective mistake we make and enforce is a violation of the individual's rights whether or not a reliable procedure was employed! The actual rights of the parties, then, are unaffected by the type of procedure, whether reliable or unreliable. They are only affected by the outcome of the procedure in that enforcement of an incorrect judgment violates the actual rights of the parties however reliable the procedure might be.

The point is that you have a right of self-defense if you are innocent but not if you are guilty. Only if a procedure finds an innocent man guilty and someone enforces that finding has anyone's rights been violated. You have the right to defend yourself against all procedures if you are innocent, against no procedures if you are guilty. The reliability of the procedures is irrelevant. Unless an innocent person agrees to be bound by the outcome of a judicial proceedings, he retains his right of self defense even after a "reliable" procedure has erred against him.

The purpose of any procedure then, is to induce adherence to the decisions of the arbitrators. The parties and the community must be convinced that there is a good chance of a just decision before they will be willing to bind themselves to any possible outcome. In a culture which held that rights are based on the facts of the case, disputants would demand procedures suited to discover those facts. The better it worked, the more acceptable it would be. Thus procedures would and should be judged on the basis of utility.

Procedures, then, for discovering the fact situation are not to be confused with rights themselves. You only have a right to a procedure, like any other service, if someone, e.g. your protective association has contracted to provide you with it.

What then of Nozick's second line of attack — the epistemic justification. "On this view, what a person may do is not limited by the rights of others. An unreliable punisher violates no right of the guilty person; but he still may not punish him." (107) It is not enough that the guilty party is guilty. The punisher must know he is guilty. One is tempted to label this the 'what you don't know can hurt you' approach.

This approach neatly avoids an assertion of procedural rights and, in addition, is a conscious effort to answer the objection that a guilty person may not defend himself against unreliable procedures and may not punish someone else for using them upon him. (103) Our attention is now shifted from the rights of guilty persons to the "morality" of protective associations. From the question of whether a guilty person can defend himself against his victim we now move to consider whether a third party can protect the guilty person if that third party isn't sure of the client's guilt. "But," as Nozick asks, "does this difference in knowledge make the requisite difference?" (108)

He believes the epistemic problem at least allows the protective association to delay the imposition of penalties on its client until it can determine his guilt. This is provided they pay compensation for the delay if it turns out that his client is guilty. While I am unsure about the rightfulness of this delay, it does not appear to present a major difficulty. Nozick, however, goes on to assert that a person using an unreliable procedure "is in no position to know that the other deserves punishment; hence he has no right to punish him." (106) It is one thing to assert that if a protective association delays sanctions against its guilty client it must compensate the victim for the delay. To claim that the association may rightfully prevent any punishment by an enforcer it deems unreliable is quite another matter.

I leave aside the question of whether anyone has the right to "punish" if by punish we mean something other than "make restitution to victims." If punishment were limited to restitution, this might minimize Nozick's

(Continued on Page 4)

Whither Anarchy? —

(Continued from Page 3)

visceral reaction against the actions of third parties. For clearly he fears the prospect of persons stealing from or hurting someone and then trying to dig up some past indiscretion by the victim in order to "justify" their aggression.

A restitutional standard would justify the actions of thieves who stole from someone who turned out himself to be a criminal only if the thieves had given their booty to the original victim. If the thieves kept the loot, the fact that the victim was himself a criminal would in no way justify their acts. This is hardly a carte blanche for indiscriminate "punishing."

But Nozick's epistemic justification is more than a gut reaction against loopholes for criminals. It sets forth a principle of morality. Unfortunately he doesn't justify this principle beyond its deterrence value on enforcers using unreliable procedures. (105) And even on this point he concedes that "not anything that would aid in such deterrence may be inflicted;" but the true question is the (moral) legitimacy of "punishing after the fact the unreliable punisher of someone who turned out to be guilty." (106)

But while this epistemic consideration may be relevant as a practical problem or even a moral problem, I question its relevance to issues of rights. (And I'm sure Dr. Nozick shares my contention that rights and morals are not co-extensive.) If the nature and moral foundation of rights are what I alluded to earlier — a freedom to use property, created along with property ownership — then epistemic considerations cannot create or alter rights. The right of self-defense we contend is a direct result of an infringement on a property right. Its purpose is to protect and restore what is rightfully owned. Since it is ontologically grounded this right exists against an aggressor independently of whether we know who the aggressor is. Consequently we are entitled to take compensation from the actual aggressor whether or not we are sure of his guilt. That is, the actual guilt or innocence of the suspect as opposed to our subjective knowledge of his guilt determines if taking restitition from him is justified.

Nozick's epistemic considerations are relevant to whether one who indiscriminately takes restitution from people he's not sure are aggressors (but happens by chance to be right) is a good man. This is a question of morality, not rights. Epistemic considerations are also relevant when we realize that we are likely to aggress against innocent people and be responsible to them if we aren't careful about whom we "punish." This is a practical question, not one of rights.

This analysis, like the anlysis of procedural rights, highlights the crucial need for a theory of rights and the difficulties we face in political philosophy without such a theory. The fact is that in laying down my argu-ment, I too fail to provide a detailed theory of the moral basis and nature of rights. The purpose of this treatment, however, is merely to show how essential such a theory is and how starkly divergent conclusions flow from even a slightly different conception of rights.

How then are we to properly view the relationship between procedural safeguards, epistemic considerations for enforcers and the right of self-defense? Perhaps Dr. Nozick's intriguing distinction between moral constraints and moral goals would be of service here. "The side constraints view forbids you to violate these moral constraints in the pursuit of your goals; whereas the view whose objective is to minimize the violation of these rights allows you to violate the rights (the constraints) in order to lessen their total violation in the society." (29) Let me briefly clarify this.

We may take as our moral goal or end a certain state of affairs. Anything which enhances this state of affairs we may do provided we don't violate certain moral side constraints on our actions. Nozick correctly argues that the protection of rights is not a moral goal since this would allow us to violate the rights of a few in order to generally enhance the rights of the many. For example, one may not torture the innocent person to gain information which will prevent the explosion of a bomb even though this would generally enhance the goal of protecting people's rights (in this case the rights of the potential victims). Rights of in-dividuals are moral side-constraints. We may strive to achieve our goals in any way which does not violate an individual's rights.

I would adapt this view to our discussion here. For practical and moral reasons, procedural fairness and knowledge by enforcers of the guilt of their suspects are moral goals to be striven for. Our efforts to achieve them, however, cannot violate the rights of any individual. To punish a victim for taking restitution from his actual aggressor just because he wasn't sure it really was his aggressor is a violation of that victim's right of self-defense and, therefore, a violation of our moral side-constrain. The right of self-defense, then, dictates that procedural fairness and epistemic certainty are goals, not constraints.

In this discussion, I've tried to show how Professor Nozick has failed to apply his "principle of compensation" to dispute-settlement situations, the lynch-pin of his justification of the ultra-minimal state. But what of this principle of compensation itself? I think Professor Nozick will agree that if it fails there can be no doubt that that the ultra-minimal state is unjustified.

"The principle of compensation requires that people be compensated for having certain risky activities prohibited to them." (83) In other words it is okay for you to forcibly forbid another from engaging in a risky activity provided you compensate him for it. Nozick anticipates our response by pointing out that "it might be objected that either you have the right to forbid these people's risky activities or you don't. If you do, you needn't compensate the people for doing to them what you have a right to do; and if you don't, then rather than formulating a policy of compensating people for your unrightful forbidding, you ought to simply to stop it." (83)

Nozick claims this dilemma is "too short" (83); that there is the middle ground of "prohibit so long as you compensate." This middle ground, he says, is based on a distinction between "productive" exchange which you have a right to engage in and "non-productive" exchange which you do not. Since you have no right to non-productive exchange in the first place, the prohibition of such an exchange isn't a violation of your rights.

In a productive exchange each party is better off than if the other party's acitvity wasn't done or the other party didn't exist at all. (84) "Whereas if I pay you for not harming me, I gain nothing from you that I wouldn't possess if either you didn't exist at all or existed without having anything to do with me." (84) The principle of compensation merely says that if the prohibition of a non-productive exchange causes you to forego some benefit (other than what you might have charged in the exchange) you are entitled to compensation.

Our concern in this discussion is not so much whether such a distinction exists, but whether such a distinction is relevant to political philosophy or, more particularly, to rights. What seems to have occurred here is an unfortunate mixing of economic explanation with moral imperatives. The concept of an ex ante increase in individual psychic utility as a result of exchanges was developed as an axiomatic explanation of why voluntary exchange occurs. It was never intended to serve as a moral or political justification of that exchange. Its use as such disregards the whole notion of title.

If something belongs to me what I own is the title to that object. I may do with it what I wish and that includes exchanging my title for other titles. The reason I exchange is to maximize my psychic utility but this says nothing about my right to make the exchange. In Nozick's example of a blackmailer it is true that the black mailed party would be better off if the blackmailer didn't exist (as opposed to an auto purchaser who would not be better off if G.M. did not exist). But the reason why this is true is because the blackmailer is a free man who has the right to tell what he knows as we all do. Wouldn't a businessman be better off without competition? If a rival company offered to leave the market for a price would the remaining company have the right to prohibit any further competition by the rival simply because the rival was offering a non-productive exchange? I think not.

Nozick admits that even under his principle of compensation, the blackmailer may charge for what he foregoes which Nozick incorrectly assumes to be little or nothing. What the blackmailer foregoes is his right to use his body in any way which he sees fit, i.e. speech. This introduces the fallacy of a "just price." There is no just price for this right or, more precisely, his title to use some property — the body — in a certain way. It

(Continued on Page 5)

From The Old Curmudgeon

My New Year's Wish For The Movement

I know it's a hopeless fantasy, but I can dream, can't I? My devout wish for the libertarian movement, and for the state of my own blood pressure, is for a whole year's moratorium on the following:

On Survival. I am sick and tired of reading about how we should all *stock up on a year's supply of dried beans, and back-pack it to the hills.* Fellas, I've got news for you: I ain't eating any dried beans, and I ain't back-packing it to the hills. I will stick to the market, crippled though it may be, and continue to dine in plush urban comfort on Pepsis, vodka martinis, and veal parmigiana. I have often wondered why our bean-eating back-packers don't really head for the hills and leave the rest of us alone and blissfully outside of their consciousness. The horrible thing is that I have a dark suspicion that our tub-thumping survivalists are themselves spending their time in urban comfort guzzling martinis and wolfing down the aforesaid parmigiana.

On the New Libertarian Country. For over a decade now I have heard the drums beat for the new Eden, an island, natural or man-made, that would live in either anarchistic or Randian bliss. One would think that if man can really learn from experience, then the total and abject failure of each and every one of these cockamamie stunts should have sent all of their supporters a "message"; namely, to come back to the real world and fight for liberty at home. Come to think of it, I don't see very many of the New Countryites shlepping out to Minerva, Abaco, Atlantis, and ocean platform, or a moon of Jupiter. Once again, I would love at least a year of these brethren removing themselves from the consciousness of the rest of us: either by remaining silent and returning to concerns nearer home, or, preferably, really hieing themselves posthaste to the New Atlantis and Randspeed to them.

On Psychobabble. Wouldn't it be great? A whole year of **nothing**, not a word, not a peep, about "open relationships", "growing as a person", "getting in touch with your feelings", "opening up a space", "non-authoritarian relations", "living free", and all the rest of the malarkey. But, then, what in the world would all our psycholibertarians have to talk about? Well yes, that would be an interesting experiment indeed. Either they would have to painfully make their way to developing an interest in history, current affairs, economics, political philosophy — in short, the real world, or else they would have to descend into a blissful silence (blissful, that is, for the rest of us.)

On Griping from the Sidelines. It is easier, I suppose, to sit around and pick holes in the 85th word of the eighteenth paragraph of the fourth press release by Roger MacBride or of someone else who actually writes or does something to advance the cause of liberty, than actually to work for liberty yourself. That way, you have the luxury of hugging the mantle of "purity" tightly around your shoulders without having to do anything to move toward a libertarian society. But how about a year of concentrating on one's own constructive action? Again, it would be interesting to see whether a year of abstinence from griping would really clear the decks for constructive work (And, come to think of it, the gripers and the psychobabblers are often one and the same.)

On Reading Science Fiction. There is nothing wrong with science fiction per se, but is has become all too clear that for many libertarians science fiction has taken on a cultic status. A year's abstinence from sci-fi would clear the decks, and clear a lot of minds as well. But for what? What in the world is there to read if you are deprived of science fiction? Well, look around, and maybe a new world of other things to read will be revealed.

An impossible dream, this magnificent moratorium? Perhaps. But maybe if we wait till next year . . . .   ◘

Whither Anarchy —

(Continued from Page 4)

has no intrinsic, objectively measurable value. Its only fair price is the freely bargained one. Anything less would mean a right of title has been taken by force from its owner. By definition this is a violation of the blackmailer's rights.

This just price fallacy permeates the whole of Nozick's discussion of "compensation". It confuses the morally permissable exchange with the penalty for violating a right which is compensation. If someone violates another's rights, the victim is entitled to compensation to make up for the transgression. This simply means he is entitled to what was taken from him. We don't pretend that money is the equivelant or even "fair price" for the loss of life or limb. We say only that some attempt must be made to restore to that victim what was taken from him as far as humanly possible.

The crucial distinction here is while voluntarily paying a purchase price makes an exchange permissible, compensation does not make an aggression permissible or justified. It is not permissible to deprive you of free speech provided I "compensate" you. You would have the right to defend yourself. If you were unsuccessful, unable or unwilling to defend yourself, you would then, in addition, have a right to compensation. Put in more analytic terms, voluntariness is a necessary condition for a morally permissible exchange of values. Compensation is not a sufficient condition for justifying or permitting a violation of rights.

Contrary to Nozick's principle of compensation, all violations of rights should be prohibited. That's what right means. The only way rights are abdicated is by consent of the right holder. Nozick rejects this on the grounds that "some factor may prevent obtaining this prior consent or make it impossible to do so. (Some factor other than the victim's refusing to agree)". (71) To this one must reply, "so what?" Practical problems of obtaining consent sometimes can't be avoided it's true, but this doesn't mean that consent is not required. Nor will an argument from utility suffice since utility we saw can only be applied to moral goals and not to rights which are moral side-constraints (to employ the Nozickian distinction). Nozick is too quick to reject the principle that rights violations are always prohibited.

Whither Anarchy?

Political reality dictates that the practical burden of proof falls on those who wish to make a radical change in society. Anarchists must face this burden. But it is those who seek to impose a state, those who wish to justify their use of force against the individual who face the moral burden of proof.

As I tried to emphasize at the beginning of this paper, there are many reasons why we should be grateful to Robert Nozick for writing this book. Not the least is that he has properly perceived the moral burden of proof. More than this, he has tried to meet that burden. I have tried to determine whether he has succeeded. Has Robert Nozick justified the state? I conclude that he has not, though not for want of an intricate and ingenious effort.

It is essential to his endeavor that he show that the rise of the state violates no individual rights. He has attempted to show this by implicitly redefining rights. The crucial step in this process is the principle of compensation and its application to dispute settlement. I believe that the application of the principle to dispute-settlement via procedural rights and epistemic considerations fails. The principle itself, I contend is grounded on a misguided economic-type explanation rather than a moral argument. Lastly I feel that Nozick's own concepts of moral constraints and moral goals helps us to see where he falls short.

Nozick's book neither claims to be nor succeeds in being the last word on the anarchist-minimal state controversy. For that matter, neither does this paper. I conclude simply that Nozick fails to meet his burden of proof. The state remains unjustified.   ◘

Recommended Reading

Machan On The Kantian"Purists." It was a pleasure to read Professor Tibor Machan's essay in the December **Reason**, "Libertarianism: Has Its Time Really Arrived?" It is an excellent, lucid, and well-written defense of Roger MacBride and an attack on the arguments of the Left Opposition, whom Machan properly identifies as Kantian moralists: namely, people who "hold onto certain 'intuitive', purely formal moral principles and ask everyone to stick by them, come hell or high water", regardless of consequences, in short the "deontological" view that "virtues could have nothing to do with the consequences of one's conduct, only with the **pure** basis of its motivation." Machan also correctly points out that these Kantians confuse **moral** principles with **political** theory. As Machan writes: "there is no a **priori** moral principle in terms of which no one with a record of tax avoidance should be denied a place on the (Libertarian) party's ticket. Libertarianism is not an **ethical** system; it is a **political** theory . . . Libertarianism includes principles that should govern the administration of political or legal justice, not principles that should govern all private conduct."

Machan further points out that representing the Libertarian Party in a campaign is itself not a **political** act but a private action, a private "business position." "And for purposes of running a campaign so as to bring libertarian political philosophy to the attention of people, the proper and improper moves cannot be evaluated by reference to libertarian political principles. To attempt to do so is to commit an error some philosophers call the category mistake. Imposing the ethics of government on the conduct of private individuals is to confuse the issue very seriously indeed."

More broadly, we might add that grave ethical errors are bound to set in when people divorce themselves from natural law ethics and natural rights political philosophy. Natural law ethics is an integrated system which combines attention to the essence of an act, to its grounding in the nature of man and the universe, and **therefore** to its natural law **consequences**. The tragedy of post-classical ethics has been to sunder ethical philosophy into two, equally fallacious and unsatisfactory parts: either utilitarianism, which abandons concern for the moral essence and nature of action to focus only on a "cost-benefit" analysis of its consequences; **or** into Kantianism or other forms of intuitive ethics, which plucks "absolute" moral principles out of the thin air and without grounding in natural law or regard to consequence. Free-market economists have been, almost entirely, utilitarians, and therefore all **too** willing to abandon libertarian principles at the drop of an **ad hoc** hat; and now we have our "purist" Kantians who see "moral principles" under every conceivable bed, and sniff "sellout of principle" at any attempt to set strategic priorities, and to act in the real world to bring about the libertarian ideal. In both cases, with both sets of fallacies, victory of liberty in the real world becomes impossible.

Hamill On The Counter-Culture. It is not often one finds something to recommend in the New York **Sunday Times Book Review**, so how much the more delightful to find Pete Hamill's superb, trenchant, and hardhitting attack on two new books lauding the counter-culture (November 30)! (Books by Jim Hougan and Theodore Roszak.) Hamill laces into the mysticism, irrationality, solipsism, and flight from technology and reality of the counter-culture.

Attacking both books as examples of "Doomsday Chic", Hamill points out that Hougan calls for "decadence" and Roszak for mystical religion as their "solutions" for current world problems. Hamill writes: "Theodore Roszak walks the street with the sandwich board that reads, 'religious revival'; Jim Hougan offers 'decadence'; both advocate a form of staring at the bellybutton. In their vision of the world someone else will have to pick up the garbage."

What does Hougan mean by the "decadence" he wants to take over? Quoting from Hougan, "Its edges are defined by a preoccupation with the senses. an affection for the moment, and an insistence upon the supremacy or inconsequentiality of an individual's existence or acts. Decadence takes place at the extremity of self-indulgence, but it is seldom. if ever, marred by self-importance." Hamill's gem of a comment: "Wonderful. Feel like raping a baby? How about driving a knife into the thoat of a school teacher? Okay, as long as you have an 'affection for the moment' and your act isn't 'marred by self-

importance.'" Hamill adds: "The counter-culture was really a supermarket, with counters labeled drugs, Marx, rock, Zen and love; the children of the middle class sampled them all frenetically, and now the ruined. demoralized remanants of the guitar army have headed for the woods, to play Nero (a Hougan hero) while the industrial Rome burns."

Roszak sees and hails the advent of a "new", "evolutionary" "shift of consciousness", a "transformation of human personality". As Hamill writes: "Roszak bases these fantastic claims on the revived interest in the occult, in Oriental religions, in disciplines such as Yoga . . . and all the other faddish examples of quackery, from the Reverend Moon to the Esalen Institute, that exist on the fringe of American Life . . . . In flight from the hard, tedious, boring work of truly changing the injustices of the real world, Roszak embraces the antirational with a fervent, hyperbolic, all-forgiving bear hug." In particular, Roszak embraces "the Few", gurus, shamans, "spiritual masters", who, in Hamill's terms "oppose history. technology and reason with myth, magic and mystery". Roszak calls. in his own terms, for "an insurrection of the clowns and gurus, in behalf of their strange, beautiful, and transcendent sanity (sic) . . . ."

Hamill's accurate and penetrating conclusion: "But if Hougan's 'Decadence' is a smarmy rationalization for quitting, Roszak's religious revival is infinitely more dangerous. Religion has led to an incredible history of slaughter and destruction; mysticism, with its insistence on passivity, has led millions down the road that ends on the diseased streets of Calcutta. Glib retreat, either to Nero's balcony or the shaman's mountaintop, is just another escape. These books are only additional items for the middle-class supermarket, placed somewhere between acid and zoroastry . . ." Hooray! ▫

LP Literature

The national staff, surely one of the jewels of the Libertarian Party, has now published the first three of a projected series of very brief position papers in leaflet form. All are excellent in boiling down the libertarian position into a lucid and succinct form. The first position papers are Professor Ralph Raico's Civil Liberties; Murray Rothbard's Inflation: Its Cause and Cure; and R. A. Childs, Jr., Libertarianism. Roy Childs' scintillating leaflet is particularly important in providng the best brief overall summary of the libertarian position to be found anywhere; all, and especially the Childs piece, are excellent for handing out to friends and acquaintances who are interested in finding out what libertarianism is all about. Single copies of each leaflet are avilable free, and 100 for $5, from Libertarian Party, National Headquarters, 1516 P Street, N. W., Washington D. C. 20005.

The superb 1975 L. P. Platform is now also available at the same address for 25¢, and lower prices for bulk quantities.

The national headquarters also publishes the periodical L. P. News, brilliantly edited by Bill Evers, which is undoubtedly the best libertarian news magazine. The September-October issue has the best and most judicious reportage available on the L. P. convention. In addition, the issue contains an excellent article by National Chairman Ed Crane pointing to and attacking conservative Kevin Phillips' denunciation of libertarianism, and shows that Phillips, in the course of his polemic, nakedly reveals the cloven hoof beneath conservatism's usual libertarian-sounding rhetoric: Phillips calls explicitly for "Caesarism", for "order. authority and restraint", and maintains that the answer to the world's problems "lies in the power of sword and state." Also: effective tips by LP youth leader Tom Palmer on how to organize Young Libertarian Alliance and Students for MacBride/Bergland chapters on campuses: the Childs' position paper on libertarianism; news of the various state parties; Rothbard's stirring banquet address to the L. P. convention: a summary of changes in the party platform; news on the media coverage of the convention; recommended reading for party activists: and an edited text of MacBride's acceptance speech at the convention. ▫

The Polish Question In Roosevelt-Churchill-Stalin Diplomacy

By Leonard P. Liggio*

Ralph Raico's masterful "Winston Churchill: An Appreciation," (Libertarian Forum, August 1975) makes some telling points regarding Britain's relations with Poland. Recently released secret diplomatic papers have revealed that Ralph Raico's suspicions about Churchillian foul-play in the death of General Wladyslaw Sikorski, prime minister of the exiled Polish regime in London, were on-target. Britain had broken the German secret codes, and knew of a number of successful German sabotagings of aircraft carrying important Allied officials. In order not to allow the Germans to know that the codes were broken, these people, including Sikorski, died in plane crashes.

What was to be gained by this death? What was the state of Allied relations with Polish officials in July, 1943? Ralph Raico has noted that, after numerous calls by European leaders for a revision of the criminal provisions of the Versailles Treaty of 1919, the British government began at Munich in September 1938 to take the first step toward revision. However, the British government during 1939 drew back from this realistic diplomacy, and, probably at the behest of the American president, gave a blank check to the Polish colonels who ruled the state created by the defeat of Germany and Russia in World War I. As Ralph Raico notes: "Afterwards Churchill himself criticized the guarantee in these terms: "Here was decision at last, taken on the worst possible grounds, which surely lead to the slaughter of tens of millions of people." The British blank-check caused all the deaths of World War II, and without any ability to provide military support for the Poles. The British condemned the Poles to endless years of occupation. Having refused German requests for boundary rectification and extra-territorial railroad passage between Germany proper and East Prussia (divided by West Prussia which had been given to Poland by the World War I Allies), Poland found itself at war without any British aid, except fine words. Meanwhile, the Soviet Union had chosen to re-establish the historic German-Russian entente which had maintained peace in Europe during the 19th century. The Russians took control of the non-Polish White Russian and Ukrainian provinces taken by Poland at the treaty of Riga (1921), by means of the German-Russian protocol of August 23, 1939 and the German-Russian treaty of September 28, 1939. This restoration of traditional diplomacy was broken by the irrational German attack on Russia on June 25, 1941.

Immediately, Russia became an ally of Britain (and its secret ally, the United States, which provided lend-lease to Russia). In Polish-Russian negotiations in July, 1941 between Sikorski, Polish foreign minister August Zaleski, and Soviet ambassador to London, Maisky, the Soviets renounced the treaty with Germany, and agreed to aid Poland's re-establishment of its national frontiers, i.e., frontiers inhabited by Poles, but not areas inhabited by White Russians and Ukrainians formerly under Polish control.

When the U.S. formally entered the war on December 7, 1941, British foreign secretary Eden was in Moscow. U.S. secretary of state Hull wrote to U.S. ambassador to Britain, Winant, that Eden could not make commitments for a post-war settlement. Since that was on December 5, two days before U.S. entry into the war, one might wonder why Hull thought that a non-belligerent, like the U.S., could act as though it was a belligerent? Did Hull know something? In Moscow, Stalin told Eden that Russia hoped to keep the Ukrainian and White Russian areas, while Poland should receive East Prussia. (Eden reported this to Winant who reported to Hull who told Roosevelt by February 4, 1942.) Eden felt that Russia was stronger than the U.S. or Britain had thought, and telegraphed Churchill, who was in Washington, to accept the Russian plan.

Churchill rejected Eden's proposal and said that after the war the U.S. and Britain would be powerful economically and militarily while Russia would be exhausted. Thus, Russia would have to accept peace plans drawn by Roosevelt and Churchill. Was this view something that Churchill picked up at the White House? It seemed to be the keystone to American wartime diplomacy. In May, 1942 Molotov negotiated in London with Eden and again asked recognition of the new borders. Hull

wired his refusal, and the British declined. Molotov then flew to Washington where he dropped his border requests in return for an American promise that the U.S. and Britain would establish a second front in 1942, which would draw away at least forty German divisions from the eastern front. This did not take place and the Russians, after their victory at Stalingrad, felt that the U.S. and Britain would not invade Europe early enough to have any say in Eastern Europe. A "Union of Polish Patriots" was established in Russia in March, 1943, as the Polish army raised in Russia by General Anders had departed to Iran on its way to join the British in the Mediterranean. In April, 1943 the German government, retreating from Russia, announced that it had discovered a mass grave of thousands of Polish soldiers in the Katyn forest, apparently the work of retreating Soviet officials following the German invasion of June, 1941. The Polish government in exile demanded an international investigation, for which the Soviet Union broke off relations with the London Poles. The Russians then set up a Kosciuszko Division of Poles to fight alongside the Russian army. It was at this low point of relations with the London Poles that Sikorski was allowed to die by the Churchill government.

The new Polish exile prime minister, Mikolajczyk, the leader of the militant anti-feudal Peasant Party, held the view that the war would end with U.S. and Britain occupying Germany with 300-400 fresh divisions and a victorious air force, while an exhausted Soviet Union would be dependent on the U.S. for food and reconstruction, and would have to recognize Allied power in Europe. The U.S. at one time had plans for an army of that size, but had long since dropped them as disruptive of domestic support of the war effort, which was why there was no second front in 1942 or 1943. But, Mikolajczyk's view seemed to have been shared by some segments of American policy-making up to that point, especially in the State Department. But, the State Department views were being replaced by those of the White House-Pentagon.

At the Teheran conference in November, 1943 it was agreed not to turn over the White Russian and Ukrainian areas to Poland, and to compensate Poland with German territories. If no Polish exile government would agree, then a Polish government in Poland would be created with a strong Communist component as an assurance of friendly relations with the Soviet Union. On January 2, 1944 Churchill told Mikolajczyk what Chamberlain had wisely told Czech president Benes and which Chamberlain should have told Polish foreign minister, Colonel Beck (which would have saved ten million lives): that the U.S. and Britain would not go to war over the borders of an eastern European country. Mikolajczyk was told that the Allies recognized the changed borders of Poland and was urged to make an agreement with the Soviet Union while he still had a chance. Instead, the Polish government in exile refused to reconstitute itself to exclude fascist elements whom the Allies opposed. The Russians responded by establishing in Lublin a Polish government to which was added Poles from the United States — Professor Oscar Lange, Fr. Orlemanski, and close contact with Leo Krzycki, of the American Clothing Workers' Union and head of the American Slav Congress.

Roosevelt's evasion of the implications of his low manpower military strategy, creating the dominant position of the Soviet Union in Eastern Europe due to the geography of its military strength, caused ambiguities in American diplomacy toward Eastern European countries, especially Poland. Roosevelt's promise to Molotov of a second front in Europe in 1942 meant that he was promising a second front manned by British troops, since American forces were not ready. Since the whole point of Britain's wishing U.S. entry into the war was to spare British troops, the plan for a 1942 second front in Europe was dropped. As the late William L. Neumann, ("Roosevelt's Foreign Policy Decisions, 1940-1945," Modern Age, Summer, 1975) shows, U.S. inability to create a full military force due to domestic considerations, created many of the complexities of the wartime and postwar worlds. The original projection of a 400 division

(Continued on Page 8)

Polish Question—

(Continued from Page 7)

army had to be cut to 200 divisions, and finally to less than 100 divisions in the last year of the war.

Roosevelt delayed informing the Poles in London of his acceptance of boundary changes between Russia and Poland. Roosevelt's attitude of evasion caused the London Poles to believe that the United States supported their resistence to serious negotiations with the Soviet Union. In the end, the Soviet Union concluded that the London Poles opposed any attempt to find a basis for good Soviet-Polish relations. Finally, Roosevelt and Churchill became exasperated by the refusal of the London Poles to negotiate with Russia. They concluded that it was necessary for the Russians to form a Polish government friendly to the Soviet Union and willing to negotiate with it.

When Mikolajczyk visited Roosevelt on June 7, 1944, he was told that Poland might receive Silesia, East Prussia, Lvov and Tarnapol, if the London Poles negotiated with the Russians. Stalin wrote Roosevelt on June 24, 1944 that he would meet with Mikolajczyk if the Polish government in exile were reconstructed. At the end of July, the Soviet armies neared Warsaw. The commander of Polish forces in exile, General Kazimierz Sosnkowski, opposed any Polish uprising against the Germans as a waste of Polish forces. But General Bor, commander of the Home Army, started an uprising on August 1, 1944. Mikolajczyk met with leaders of the Lublin government on August 6, with inconclusive results.

During the Churchill-Stalin talks of October, 1944, Churchill had Mikolajczyk return to Moscow. Churchill and Stalin demanded that the Polish London government accept the eastern border changes and called for a coalition of half London and half Lublin governments. Mikolajczyk refused, and was told by Churchill these words — which he should have said in 1939 when Chamberlain gave Poland a blank-check: "Because of quarrels between Poles we are not going to wreck the peace of Europe. In your obstinacy you do not see what is at stake. It is not in friendship that we shall part. We shall tell the world how unreasonable you are. You will start another war in which 25 million lives will be lost. But you don't care." In mid-November, 1944 Roosevelt wrote Mikolajczyk that U.S. accepted compensation for Poland in the west, and Mikolajczyk accepted the American decision about the borders. But he was outvoted by the London Polish government and he resigned.

Having been engaged in a vast miscalculation due to the duplicity of Churchill and Roosevelt, the London Poles refused to accept an accomodation with the Soviet Union, and were criticized as inflexible by Churchill and Roosevelt who made other arrangements during the Yalta Conference of February, 1945. The Lublin government became the dominant element because they accepted the Roosevelt-Churchill-Stalin

Right-Center Chic

The Village Voice (December 1) contains a hilarious and penetrating article by Alexander Cockburn and Jack Newfield, "Know Your Military-Intellectual Complex", which lists the leading figures in the new intellectual fashion of "right-center chic." The lists include the leaders of each of various departments of life and thought. The new right-center alliance is united on several basic political tenets: including admiration for the "new" Nixon of the mid-1960's; opposition to detente and a peaceful foreign policy; anti-Communism; opposition to quota systems; and adherence to Zionism. Some members of the coalition, as the authors point out, "trace their ancestry back to the CIA-funded Congress for Cultural Freedom."

The hero of the group, who appears on almost every one of the lists, is the notorious hawk and "Left-Nixonian", Patrick Moynihan. The right-center journalists include: (along with Moynihan) Robert Bartley (Wall St. Journal), Robert Bleiberg (Barron's), Hobart Rowen (Wash. Post), Harry Schwartz (N.Y. Times),Martin Mayer, Dorthy Rabinowitz, Walter Goodman, Howard K. Smith, Hedley Donovan (Time), and William Safire, among others. "Hitmen" include Moynihan, John Lofton, Pat Buchanan, Kevin Phillips, Evans & Novak, Ralph de Toledano, Ben Wattenberg, Nancy Kissinger, and Albert Shanker. "Institutions" include Commentary, Public Interest, Wall St. Journal, National Review, and parts of the New York Times. And so on. I particularly liked the Cockburn-Newfield lists of "Bores" (Teddy White, Allan Drury, Norman Podhoretz, and Saturday Review); "Theoreticians" (Irving Kristol, Daniel Bell, Sidney Hook, Nathan Glazer, Peter Drucker, Moynihan, and George Meany); "Economists" (Friedman, Greenspan, and Gary Becker); "Academics" (Edward Shils, Robert Tucker, S.I. Hayakawa, Robert Nisbet, S.M. Lipset, Richard Scammon, Ernest van den Haag, Buchanan & Tullock, and Moynihan); "Rabble" (Roy Cohn, Richard Nixon, Martin Abend, and Norman Podhoretz), and "Martyrs", which include James Angleton (CIA), James Schlesinger, and Max Schachtman (former right-wing Trotskyite who later moved to the pro-Cold War wing of the Socialist Party.) "Phobias" of the right-centrists include: Noam Chomsky, Daniel Ellsberg, detente, Philip Roth, and I.F. Stone, while its "Blind Spots" consist (in full) of the CIA, racism, anti-Communist dictatorships, and Elliot Richardson.

There is more, but everyone should see for themselves. ▢

---

requirement of friendship toward the Soviet Union.

*Mr. Liggio, teaches history at SUNY, Old Westbury, and was assistant author of Volumes I and II of M. Rothbard's Conceived in Liberty. ▢

Published Every Month. Subscription Rates: $8.00 Per Year; $15.00 Two Years